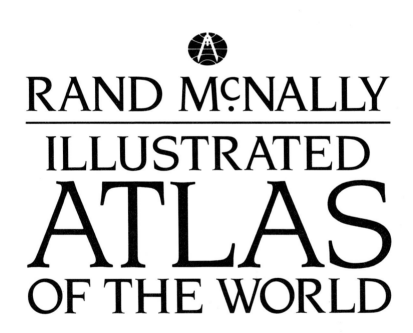

RAND McNALLY

ILLUSTRATED
ATLAS
OF THE WORLD

ILLUSTRATED
ATLAS
OF THE WORLD

 RAND McNALLY & COMPANY

CHICAGO • NEW YORK • SAN FRANCISCO

CONTENTS

ILLUSTRATED ATLAS OF THE WORLD
Rand McNally & Company
Third printing, 1986

Our Planet Earth Section
Copyright © 1982
Rand McNally & Company and
Mitchell Beazley Publishers

International Map Section
Copyright © 1982
Istituto Geografico De Agostini

Pages 1 through 240 and
A·1 through A·144 from
The Great Geographical Atlas
Copyright © 1982
Rand McNally & Company,
Mitchell Beazley Publishers,
Istituto Geografico De Agostini

SBN: 528-83190-9

Library of Congress
Catalog Card Number: 85-42651

Printed in the
United States of America by
Rand McNally & Company
P.O. Box 7600
Chicago, IL 60680

Jacket and title page photos by Ray Atkeson

Our Planet Earth Section

International Map Section

Geographical Information & International Map Index

Maps

MAP 1

WORLD, PHYSICAL

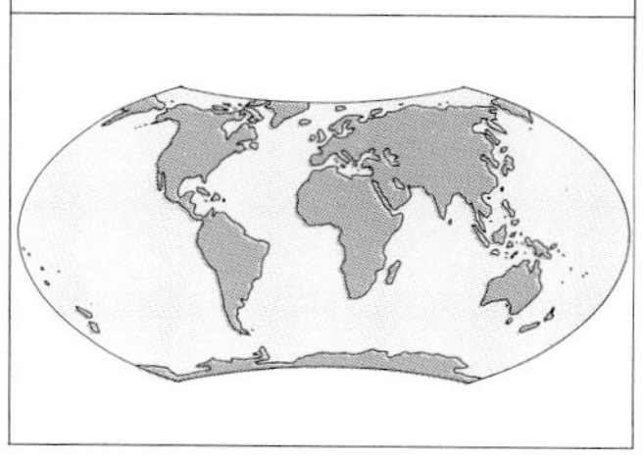

Pages 118–119

Scale 70 000 000

MAP 2

WORLD, POLITICAL

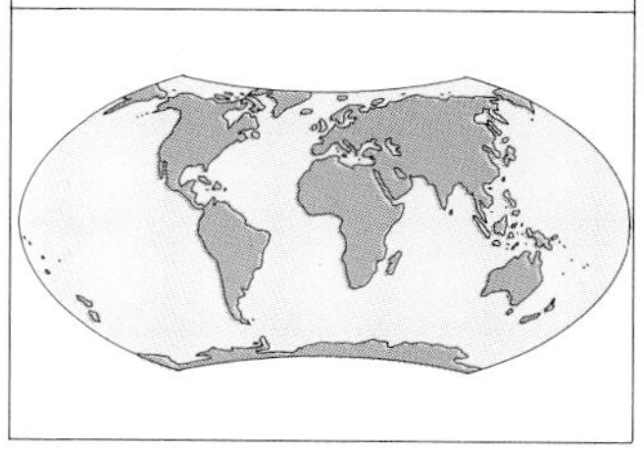

Pages 120–121

Scale 70 000 000

MAP 3

THE OCEANS

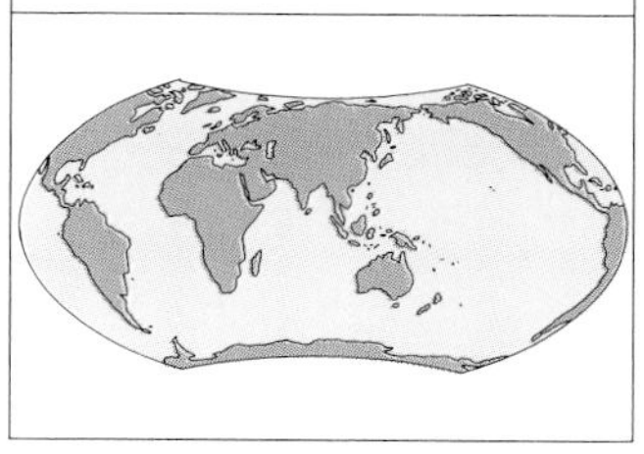

Pages 122–123

Scale 70 000 000

MAP 4

WORLD TRANSPORTATION AND TIME ZONES

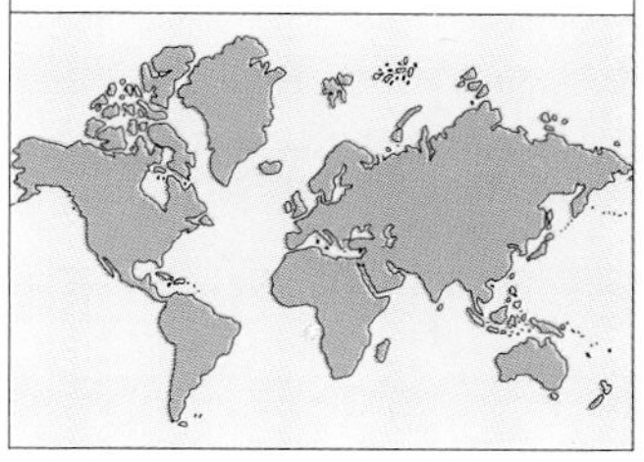

Pages 124–125

Scale 1 : 90 000 000

MAP 5

EUROPE, PHYSICAL

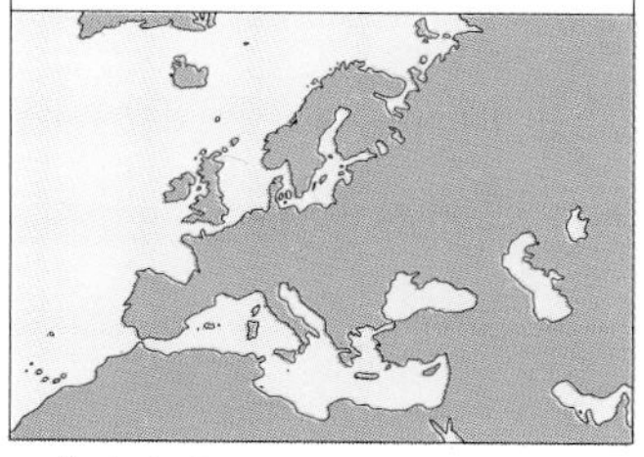

Pages 126–127

Scale 1 : 15 000 000

MAP 6

EUROPE, POLITICAL

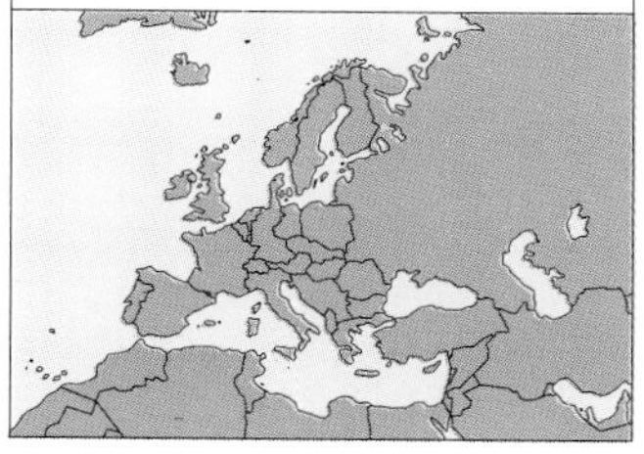

Pages 128–129

Scale 1 : 15 000 000

MAP 7

NORTHERN EUROPE

Denmark, Finland, Iceland, Norway, (Soviet Union), Sweden

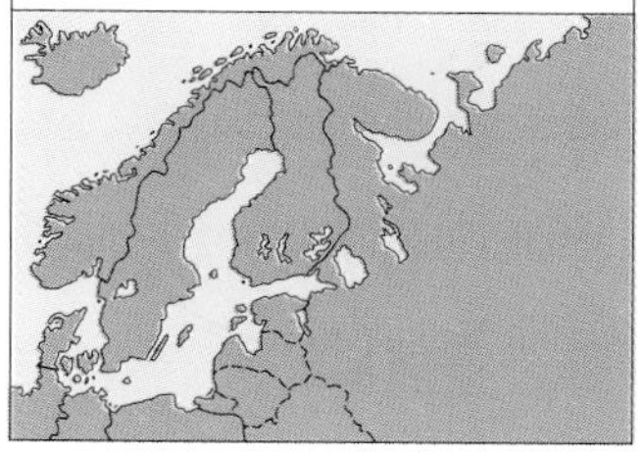

Pages 130–131

Scale 1 : 6 000 000

MAP 8

BALTIC REGION

Denmark, (Finland), (Norway), (Soviet Union), (Sweden)

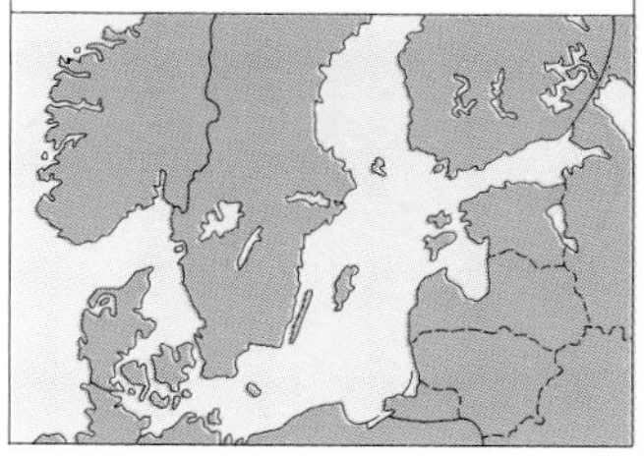

Pages 132–133

Scale 1 : 3 000 000

MAP 9

BRITISH ISLES

Ireland, United Kingdom

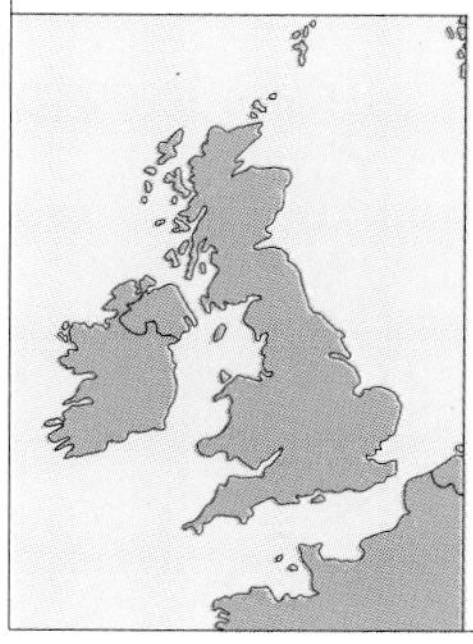

Pages 134–135

Scale 1 : 3 000 000

MAP 10

CENTRAL EUROPE

Austria, Czechoslovakia, German Democratic Republic, Germany, Federal Republic of, Hungary, Liechtenstein, Luxembourg, Poland, (Soviet Union), Switzerland, (Yugoslavia)

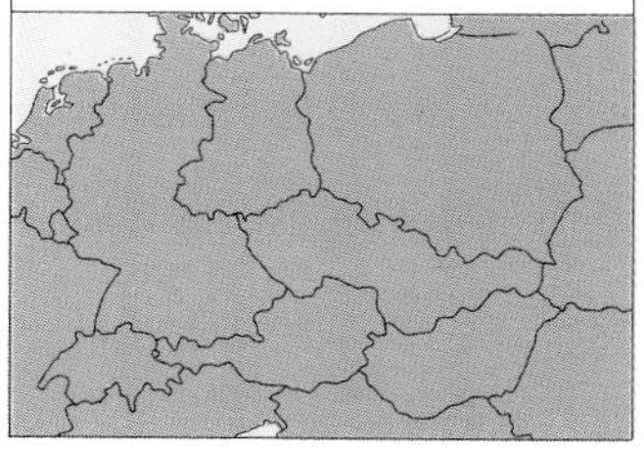

Pages 136–137

Scale 1 : 3 000 000

MAP 11

FRANCE AND BENELUX

Andorra, Belgium, France, Luxembourg, Monaco, Netherlands, (Spain), (United Kingdom)

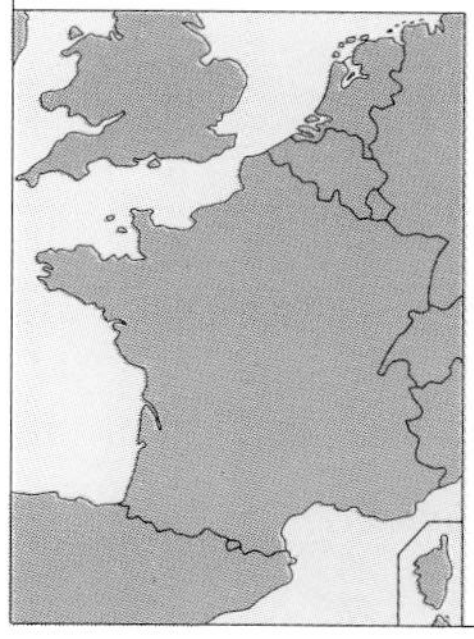

Pages 138–139

Scale 1 : 3 000 000

MAP 12

BELGIUM, NETHERLANDS AND LUXEMBOURG

Belgium, (France), (Germany, Federal Republic of), Luxembourg, Netherlands, (United Kingdom)

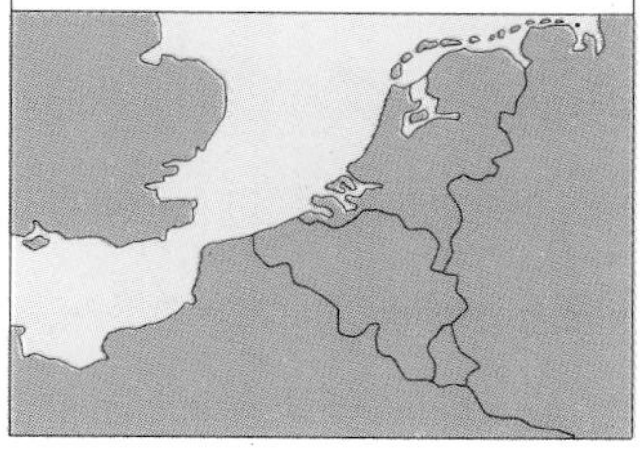

Pages 140–141

Scale 1 : 1 500 000

MAP 13

SPAIN AND PORTUGAL

(Algeria), Andorra, Gibraltar, (Morocco), Portugal, Spain

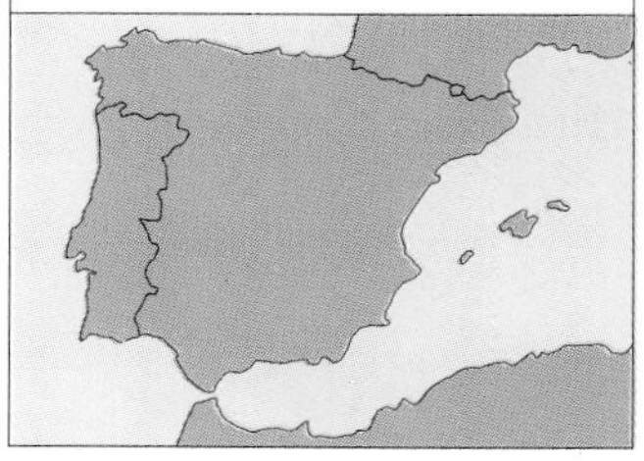

Pages 142–143

Scale 1 : 3 000 000

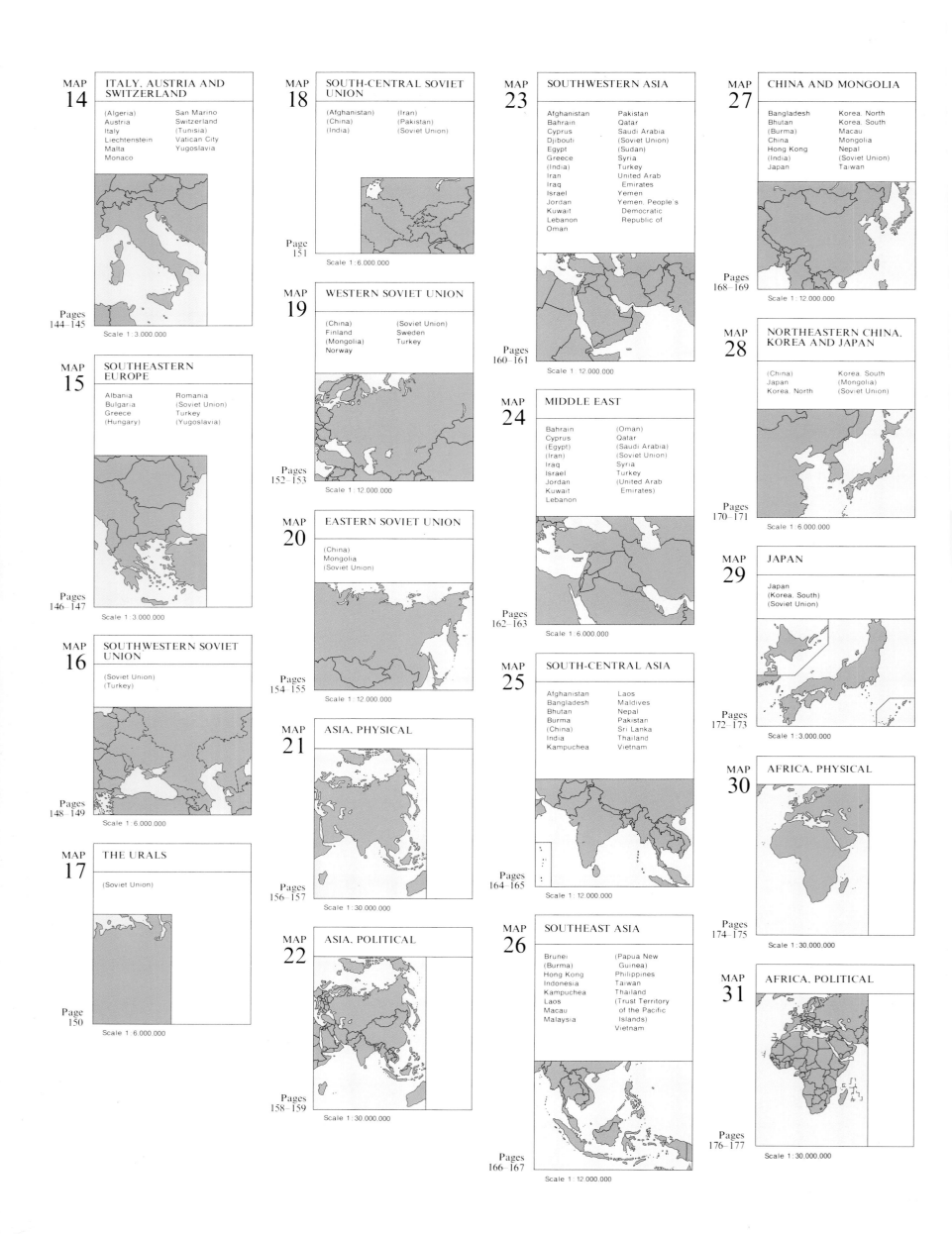
MAP 14
ITALY, AUSTRIA AND SWITZERLAND
(Algeria)
Austria
Italy
Liechtenstein
Malta
Monaco
San Marino
Switzerland
(Tunisia)
Vatican City
Yugoslavia
Pages 144–145
Scale 1:3.000.000
MAP 15
SOUTHEASTERN EUROPE
Albania
Bulgaria
Greece
(Hungary)
Romania
(Soviet Union)
Turkey
(Yugoslavia)
Pages 146–147
Scale 1:3.000.000
MAP 16
SOUTHWESTERN SOVIET UNION
(Soviet Union)
(Turkey)
Pages 148–149
Scale 1:6.000.000
MAP 17
THE URALS
(Soviet Union)
Page 150
Scale 1:6.000.000
MAP 18
SOUTH-CENTRAL SOVIET UNION
(Afghanistan)
(China)
(India)
(Iran)
(Pakistan)
(Soviet Union)
Page 151
Scale 1:6.000.000
MAP 19
WESTERN SOVIET UNION
(China)
Finland
(Mongolia)
Norway
(Soviet Union)
Sweden
Turkey
Pages 152–153
Scale 1:12.000.000
MAP 20
EASTERN SOVIET UNION
(China)
Mongolia
(Soviet Union)
Pages 154–155
Scale 1:12.000.000
MAP 21
ASIA, PHYSICAL
Pages 156–157
Scale 1:30.000.000
MAP 22
ASIA, POLITICAL
Pages 158–159
Scale 1:30.000.000
MAP 23
SOUTHWESTERN ASIA
Afghanistan
Bahrain
Cyprus
Djibouti
Egypt
Greece
(India)
Iran
Iraq
Israel
Jordan
Kuwait
Lebanon
Oman
Pakistan
Qatar
Saudi Arabia
(Soviet Union)
(Sudan)
Syria
Turkey
United Arab Emirates
Yemen
Yemen, People's Democratic Republic of
Pages 160–161
Scale 1:12.000.000
MAP 24
MIDDLE EAST
Bahrain
Cyprus
(Egypt)
(Iran)
Iraq
Israel
Jordan
Kuwait
Lebanon
(Oman)
Qatar
(Saudi Arabia)
(Soviet Union)
Syria
Turkey
(United Arab Emirates)
Pages 162–163
Scale 1:6.000.000
MAP 25
SOUTH-CENTRAL ASIA
Afghanistan
Bangladesh
Bhutan
Burma
(China)
India
Kampuchea
Laos
Maldives
Nepal
Pakistan
Sri Lanka
Thailand
Vietnam
Pages 164–165
Scale 1:12.000.000
MAP 26
SOUTHEAST ASIA
Brunei
(Burma)
Hong Kong
Indonesia
Kampuchea
Laos
Macau
Malaysia
(Papua New Guinea)
Philippines
Taiwan
Thailand
(Trust Territory of the Pacific Islands)
Vietnam
Pages 166–167
Scale 1:12.000.000
MAP 27
CHINA AND MONGOLIA
Bangladesh
Bhutan
(Burma)
China
Hong Kong
(India)
Japan
Korea, North
Korea, South
Macau
Mongolia
Nepal
(Soviet Union)
Taiwan
Pages 168–169
Scale 1:12.000.000
MAP 28
NORTHEASTERN CHINA, KOREA AND JAPAN
(China)
Japan
Korea, North
Korea, South
(Mongolia)
(Soviet Union)
Pages 170–171
Scale 1:6.000.000
MAP 29
JAPAN
Japan
(Korea, South)
(Soviet Union)
Pages 172–173
Scale 1:3.000.000
MAP 30
AFRICA, PHYSICAL
Pages 174–175
Scale 1:30.000.000
MAP 31
AFRICA, POLITICAL
Pages 176–177
Scale 1:30.000.000

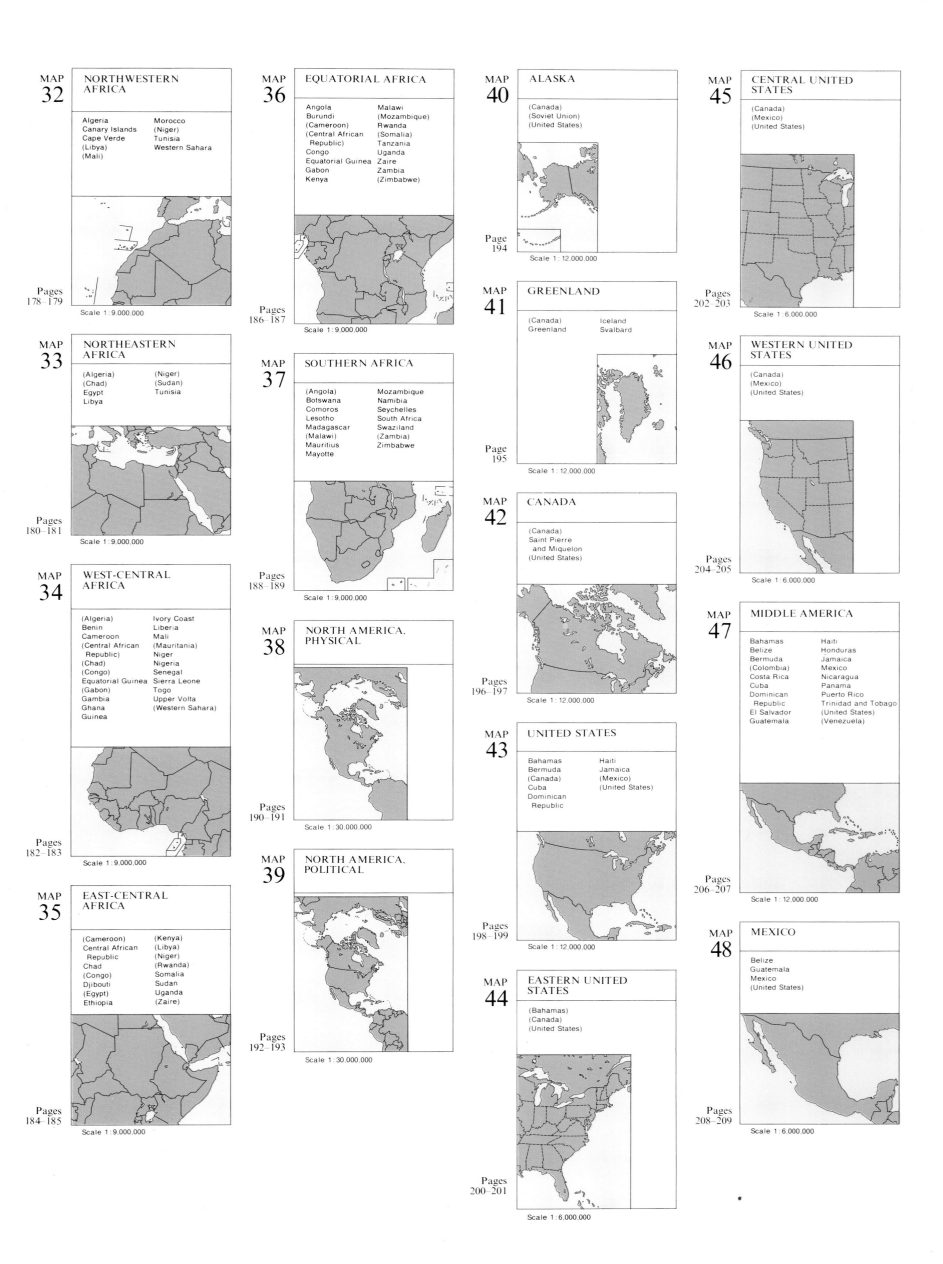

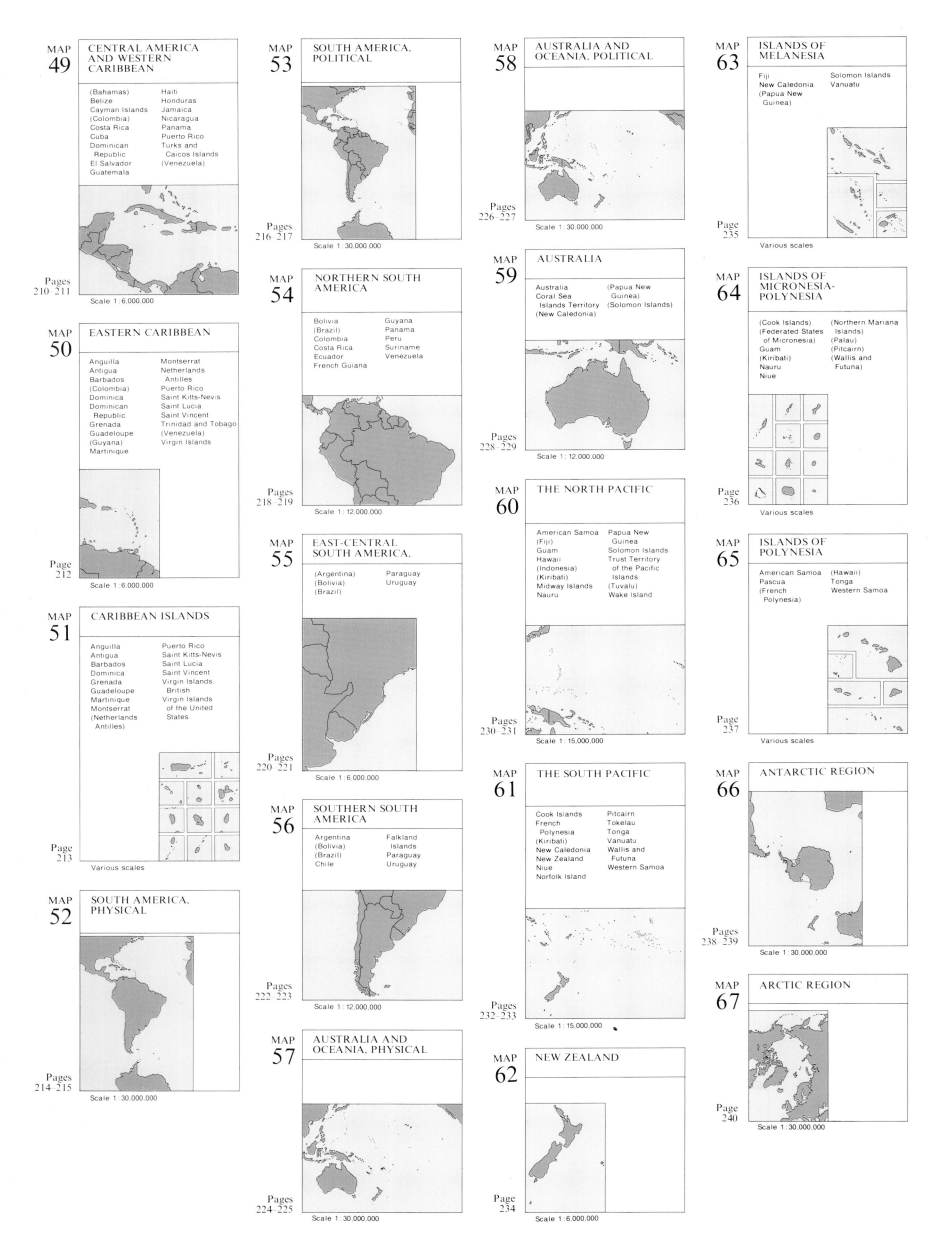

OUR PLANET EARTH SECTION

Part 1

THE EARTH AND THE UNIVERSE

How the universe began · Earth's place in the Solar System
How the Earth became fit for life
Man looks at Earth from outer space

CREATION AND DESTRUCTION

Violent activity pervades our universe and has done so ever since the primordial fireball of creation. Evidence of violence comes from radio telescopes scanning the farthest reaches: entire galaxies may be exploding, torn apart by gravitational forces of unimaginable power. Some very large stars may burst apart in supernovas, spraying interstellar space with cosmic debris. From this violence new stars and new planets are constantly being formed throughout the universe.

The Big Bang theory (left) of the origin of the universe envisages all matter originating from one point in time and space—a point of infinite density. In the intensely hot Big Bang all the material that goes to make up the planets, stars and galaxies that we see now began to expand outward in all directions. This expansion has been likened to someone blowing up a balloon on which spots have been painted. As the air fills and expands the balloon, the spots get farther away from each other. Likewise, clusters of galaxies that formed from the original superdense matter began, and continue to move away from neighboring clusters. The Big Bang generated enormous temperatures and the remnants of the event still linger throughout space. A leftover, background radiation provides a uniform and measurable temperature of 3°C. It is generally believed that the universe will continue to expand into complete nothingness.

Stars vary enormously in size, temperature and luminosity. The largest, so-called red giants like Antares (1)—the biggest yet known—or Aldebaran (2), are nearing the end of their lives: diminishing nuclear "fuel" causes their thinning envelopes to expand. Rigel (3) is many times brighter than our Sun (4)—a middle-aged star—but both are so-called main-sequence stars. Epsilon Eridani (5) is rather like the Sun. Wolf 359 (6) is a red dwarf.

Our Solar System was formed from a collapsing cloud of gas and dust (A). Collapse made the center hotter and denser (B) until nuclear reactions started. Heat blew matter from the heart of the now flattened, spinning disc (C). Heavier materials condensed closest to the young Sun, now a hot star, eventually forming the inner ring of planets; the lighter ones accumulated farther out, making up the atmosphere and composition of the giant outer planets (D).

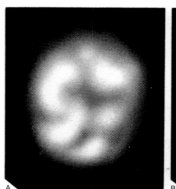

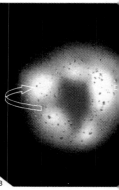

Billions of galaxies exist outside our own Milky Way, each thousands of light-years across and filled with millions of stars. Found in clusters, they are either elliptical or spiral in form. The clusters recede from each other following the space-time geometry, as established by Hubble in 1929, proving that the universe is expanding.

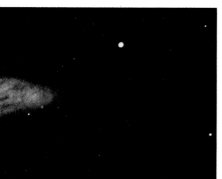

The "exploding" galaxy M82 may be an example of the violence of our universe. Clouds of hydrogen gas, equivalent in mass to 5,000,000 suns, have been ejected from the nucleus at 160 km (100 miles) per second. Black holes may cause the explosions, when gravity sucks in all matter, so that even light cannot escape.

Our own cluster of galaxies (below), the Local Group (A), consists of about 30 members, weakly linked by the force of gravity. Earth lies in the second-largest galaxy, the Milky Way (B)—here shown edge-on and at an angle—which is a spiral galaxy of about 100,000 million stars. Its rotating "arms" are great masses of clouds, dust and stars that sweep around a dense nucleus. In the course of this new stars are regularly created from dust and gas. Our Sun (S) lies 33,000 light-years from the nucleus and takes 225 million years to complete an orbit. The Andromeda Galaxy (C), known to astronomers as M31, is the largest of our Local Group. It too is a spiral, and lies about two million light-years away. Roughly 130,000 light-years in diameter, it appears as a flattened disc, and indicates how our galaxy would look if viewed from outside. Two smaller elliptical galaxies, M32 and NGC 205, can also be seen.

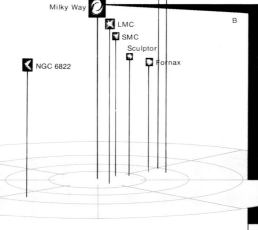

Milky Way
Leo II
Leo I
LMC
SMC
Sculptor
Fornax
NGC 147
NGC 185
NGC 6822
M31
M33
M32
NGC 205
1613
B

Nucleus (N)　　Sun (S)
100,000 light-years

Stars are being born (left) in the Great Nebula of Orion, visible from Earth. The brilliant light comes from a cluster of very hot young stars, the Trapezium, surrounded by a glowing aura of hydrogen gas. Behind the visible nebula there is known to be a dense cloud where radio astronomers have detected emissions from interstellar molecules, and have identified high-density globules. These probably indicate that stars are starting to form.

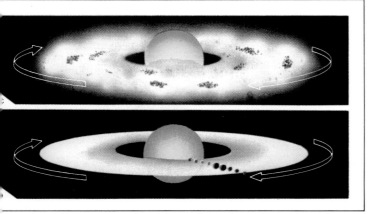

The Making of the Universe

Most astronomers believe that the universe began in a great explosion of matter and energy – the "Big Bang" – about 15,000 million years ago. This event was implied by Einstein's theory of general relativity, as well as by more recent astronomical observations and calculations. But the clinching evidence came in 1965, when two American radio astronomers discovered a faint, uniform, background radiation which permeated all space. This they identified as the remnants of the primordial Big Bang.

The generally accepted explanation for the so-called "cosmic microwave" background, detected by American astronomers Arno Penzias and Robert Wilson, is indeed that it is the echo of the Big Bang itself, the radio noise left over from the fireball of creation. In recognition of their discovery, Penzias and Wilson shared a Nobel Prize in 1978.

The Big Bang has also been identified by astronomers in other ways. All the evidence shows that the universe is expanding, and its constituent parts—clusters of galaxies, each containing thousands of millions of stars like our Sun—are moving away from each other at great speeds. From this and other evidence scientists deduce that long ago the galaxies must have been closer together, in a superdense phase, and that at some time in the remote past all the material in the universe must have started spreading out from a single point. But this "single point" includes not only all three-dimensional matter and space but also the dimension of time, as envisioned in Einstein's revolutionary concept of space-time. Einstein's theory of relativity describes the phenomenon, not in terms of galaxies moving through space in the expansion, but as being carried apart by the expansion of space-time itself. Space-time may be imagined as a rubber sheet speckled with paint blobs (galaxies), which move apart as the rubber sheet expands.

Galaxies consist of star systems, dust clouds and gases formed from the hot material exploding outward from the original cosmic fireball. Our own Milky Way system, the band of light that stretches across the night sky, is typical of many galaxies, containing millions of stars slowly rotating around a central nucleus.

Exploding space

The original material of the universe was hydrogen, the simplest of all elements. Nuclear reactions that occurred during the superdense phase of the Big Bang converted about 20 percent of the original hydrogen into helium, the next simplest element. So the first stars were formed from a mixture of about 80 percent hydrogen and 20 percent helium. All other matter in the universe, including the atoms of heavier elements such as carbon and oxygen—which help to make up the human body or the pages of this book—has been processed in further nuclear reactions. The explosion of a star—a relatively rare event called a supernova—scatters material across space, briefly radiating more energy than a trillion suns and ejecting matter into the cosmic reservoir of interstellar space. This is then reused to form new stars and planets.

Thus, from the debris of such explosions new stars can form to repeat the creative cycle, and at each stage more of the heavy elements are produced. Today's heavenly bodies are very much the products of stellar violence in the universe, and indeed the universe itself is now seen to be an area of violent activity. During the past two decades the old idea of the universe as a place of quiet stability has been increasingly superseded by evidence of intense activity on all scales. Astronomers have identified what appear to be vast explosions involving whole galaxies, as well as those of individual stars.

Black holes

The evidence of just why these huge explosions occur is often hard to obtain, because the exploding galaxies may be so far away that light from them takes millions of years to reach telescopes on Earth. But it is becoming increasingly accepted by astronomers that such violent events may be associated with the presence of black holes at the centers of some galaxies.

These black holes are regions in which matter has become so concentrated that the force of gravity makes it impossible for anything—even light itself—to escape. As stars are pulled into super-massive black holes they are torn apart by gravitational forces, and their material forms into a swirling maelstrom from which huge explosions can occur. Collapse into black holes, accompanied by violent outbursts from the maelstrom, may be the ultimate fate of all matter in the universe. For our own Solar System, however, such a fate is far in the future: the Sun in its present form is believed to have enough "fuel" to keep it going for at least another 5,000 million years.

A star is born

The origins of the Earth and the Solar System are intimately connected with the structure of our own galaxy, the Milky Way. There are two main types of galaxies: flattened, disc-shaped spiral galaxies (like the Milky Way), and the more rounded elliptical galaxies, which range in form from near spheres to cigar shapes. The most important feature of a spiral galaxy is that it is rotating, a great mass of stars sweeping around a common center. In our galaxy the Sun, located some way out from the galaxy's center, takes about 225 million years to complete one circuit, called a cosmic year.

New stars are born out of the twisting arms of a spiral galaxy, with each arm marking a region of debris left over from previous stellar explosions. These arms are in fact clouds of dust and gas, including nitrogen and oxygen. As the spiral galaxy rotates over a period of millions of years, the twisting arms are squeezed by a high-density pressure wave as they pass through the cycle of the cosmic year. With two main spiral arms twining around a galaxy such as our own, large, diffuse clouds get squeezed twice during each orbit around the center of the galaxy.

Even if one orbit takes as long as hundreds of millions of years, a score or more squeezes have probably occurred since the Milky Way was first formed thousands of millions of years ago. At a critical point, such repeated squeezing increases the density of a gas cloud so much that it begins to collapse rapidly under the inward pull of its own gravity. A typical cloud of this kind contains enough material to make many stars. As it breaks up it collapses into smaller clouds—which are also collapsing—and these become stars in their own right.

Our own Solar System may have been formed in this way from such a collapsing gas cloud, which went on to evolve into the system of planets that we know today.

3

Earth in the Solar System

The Sun is an ordinary, medium-sized star located some two-thirds of the way from the center of our galaxy, the Milky Way. Yet it comprises more than 99 percent of the Solar System's total mass and provides all the light and heat that make life possible on Earth. This energy comes from nuclear reactions that take place in the Sun's hot, dense interior. The reactions convert hydrogen into helium, with the release of vast amounts of energy – the energy that keeps the Sun shining.

Nuclear reactions in the Sun's core maintain a temperature of some 15,000,000°C and this heat prevents the star from shrinking. The surface temperature is comparatively much lower —a mere 6,000°C. Thermonuclear energy-generating processes cause the Sun to "lose" mass from the center at the rate of four million tonnes of hydrogen every second. This mass is turned into energy (heat), and each gram of matter "burnt" produces the heat equivalent of 100 trillion electric fires. The Sun's total mass is so great, however, that it contains enough matter to continue radiating at its present rate for several thousand million years before it runs out of "fuel."

The Sun's retinue
The Solar System emerged from a collapsing gas cloud. In addition to the Sun there are at least nine planets, their satellites, thousands of minor planets (asteroids), comets and meteors. Most stars occur in pairs, triplets or in even more complicated systems, and the Sun is among a minority of stars in being alone except for its planetary companions. It does seem, however, that a single star with a planetary system offers the greatest potential for the development of life. When there are two or more stars in the same system, any planets are likely to have unstable orbits and to suffer from wide extremes of temperature.

The Solar System's structure is thought to be typical of a star that formed in isolation. As the hot young Sun threw material outward, inner planets (Mercury, Venus, Earth and Mars) were left as small rocky bodies, whereas outer planets (Jupiter, Saturn, Uranus and Neptune) kept their lighter gases and became huge "gas giants." Jupiter has two and a half times the mass of all the other planets put together. Pluto, a small object with a strange orbit, which sometimes carries it within the orbit of Neptune, is usually regarded as a ninth planet, but some astronomers consider it to be an escaped moon of Neptune or a large asteroid.

Planetary relations
Several planets are accompanied by smaller bodies called moons or satellites. Jupiter and Saturn have at least 17 and 22 respectively, whereas Earth has its solitary Moon. Sizes vary enormously, from Ganymede, one of Jupiter's large, so-called Galilean satellites, which has a diameter of 5,000 km (3,100 miles), to Mars' tiny Deimos, which is only 8 km (5 miles) across.

The Earth's Moon is at an average distance of 384,000 km (239,000 miles) and has a diameter of 3,476 km (2,160 miles). Its mass is $\frac{1}{81}$ of the Earth's. Although it is referred to as the Earth's satellite, the Moon is large for a secondary body. Some astronomers have suggested that the Earth/Moon system is a double planet. Certain theories of the origins of the Moon propose that it was formed from the solar nebula in the same way as the Earth was and very close to it. The Moon takes 27.3 days to orbit the Earth—exactly the same time that it takes to rotate once on its axis. As a result, it presents the same face to the Earth all the time.

Our planet's orbit around the Sun is not a perfect circle but an ellipse and so its distance from the Sun varies slightly. More importantly, the Earth is tilted, so that at different times of the year one pole or another "leans" toward the Sun. Without this tilt there would be no seasons. The angle of tilt is not constant: over tens of thousands of years the axis of the Earth "wobbles" like a slowly spinning top, so that the pattern of the seasons varies over the ages. These changes have been linked to recent ice ages, which seem to occur when the northern hemisphere has relatively cool summers.

Patterns of time
The Earth's movements on its axis and around the Sun give us our basic measurements of time—the day and the year—as well as setting the rhythm of the seasons and the ice ages. One rotation of the Earth on its axis—the time from one sunrise to the next—originally defined the day, and the time taken for one complete orbit around the Sun defined the year. Today, however, scientists define both the day and the year in terms of time units "counted" by precision instruments called atomic clocks.

A third basic rhythm is set not by the Sun but by the Moon, which runs through a cycle of phases $29\frac{1}{2}$ days long. This is the basis of the calendar month. But just as the modern calendar cannot cope with months $29\frac{1}{2}$ days long, so too it would have trouble with the precise year, which is, inconveniently, just less than $365\frac{1}{4}$ days long. This is the reason for leap years, by means of which an extra day is added to the month of February every fourth year.

Even this system does not keep the calendar exactly in step with the Sun. Accordingly, the leap year is left out in the years which complete centuries, such as 1900, but retained when they divide exactly by 400. The year 2000 will, therefore, be a leap year. With all these corrections, the average length of the calendar year is within 26 seconds of the year defined by the Earth's movements around the Sun. Thus the calendar will be one day out of step with the heavens in the year 4906.

Cosmic rubble
The other planets are too small and too far away to produce noticeable effects on the Earth, but the smallest members of the Sun's family, the asteroids, can affect us directly. Some of them have orbits that cross the orbit of the Earth around the Sun. From time to time they penetrate the Earth's atmosphere: small fragments burn up high in the atmosphere as meteors, whereas larger pieces may survive to strike the ground as meteorites. These in fact provide an echo of times gone by. All the planets, as the battered face of the Moon shows, suffered collisions from many smaller bodies in the course of their evolution from the collapsing pre-solar gas cloud.

Eclipses occur because the Moon, smaller than the Sun, is closer to Earth and looks just as big. This means that when all three are lined up the Moon can blot out the Sun, causing a solar eclipse. When the Earth passes through the main shadow cone, or umbra, the eclipse is total; in the area of partial shadow, or penumbra, a partial eclipse is seen. A similar effect is produced when Earth passes between the Moon and the Sun, causing a lunar eclipse. At most full moons, eclipses do not occur; the Moon passes either above or below the Earth's shadow, because the Moon's orbit is inclined at an angle of 5° to the orbit of the Earth.

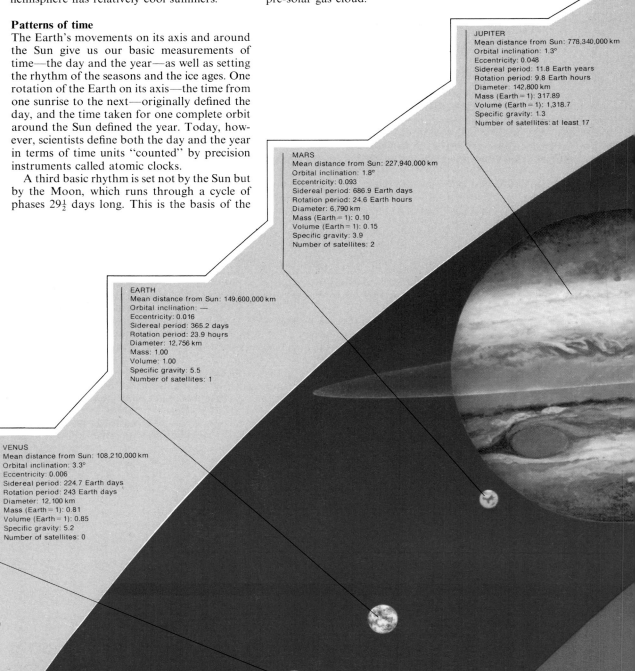

JUPITER
Mean distance from Sun: 778,340,000 km
Orbital inclination: 1.3°
Eccentricity: 0.048
Sidereal period: 11.8 Earth years
Rotation period: 9.8 Earth hours
Diameter: 142,800 km
Mass (Earth = 1): 317.89
Volume (Earth = 1): 1,318.7
Specific gravity: 1.3
Number of satellites: at least 17

MARS
Mean distance from Sun: 227,940,000 km
Orbital inclination: 1.8°
Eccentricity: 0.093
Sidereal period: 686.9 Earth days
Rotation period: 24.6 Earth hours
Diameter: 6,790 km
Mass (Earth = 1): 0.10
Volume (Earth = 1): 0.15
Specific gravity: 3.9
Number of satellites: 2

EARTH
Mean distance from Sun: 149,600,000 km
Orbital inclination: —
Eccentricity: 0.016
Sidereal period: 365.2 days
Rotation period: 23.9 hours
Diameter: 12,756 km
Mass: 1.00
Volume: 1.00
Specific gravity: 5.5
Number of satellites: 1

VENUS
Mean distance from Sun: 108,210,000 km
Orbital inclination: 3.3°
Eccentricity: 0.006
Sidereal period: 224.7 Earth days
Rotation period: 243 Earth days
Diameter: 12,100 km
Mass (Earth = 1): 0.81
Volume (Earth = 1): 0.85
Specific gravity: 5.2
Number of satellites: 0

MEMBERS OF THE SOLAR SYSTEM
The Sun has nine planetary attendants. They are best compared in terms of orbital data (distance from the Sun, inclination of orbit to the Earth's orbit, and eccentricity, which means the departure of a planet's orbit from circularity); planetary periods (the time for a planet to go around the Sun—sidereal periods, and the time it takes for one axial revolution—the rotation period); and physical data (equatorial diameter, mass, volume and density or specific gravity—the weight of a substance compared with the weight of an equal volume of water).

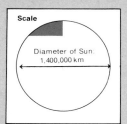

Scale
Diameter of Sun:
1,400,000 km

MERCURY
Mean distance from Sun: 57,910,000 km
Orbital inclination: 7°
Eccentricity: 0.205
Sidereal period: 87.9 Earth days
Rotation period: 58.7 Earth days
Diameter: 4,870 km
Mass (Earth = 1): 0.05
Volume (Earth = 1): 0.05
Specific gravity: 5.5
Number of satellites: 0

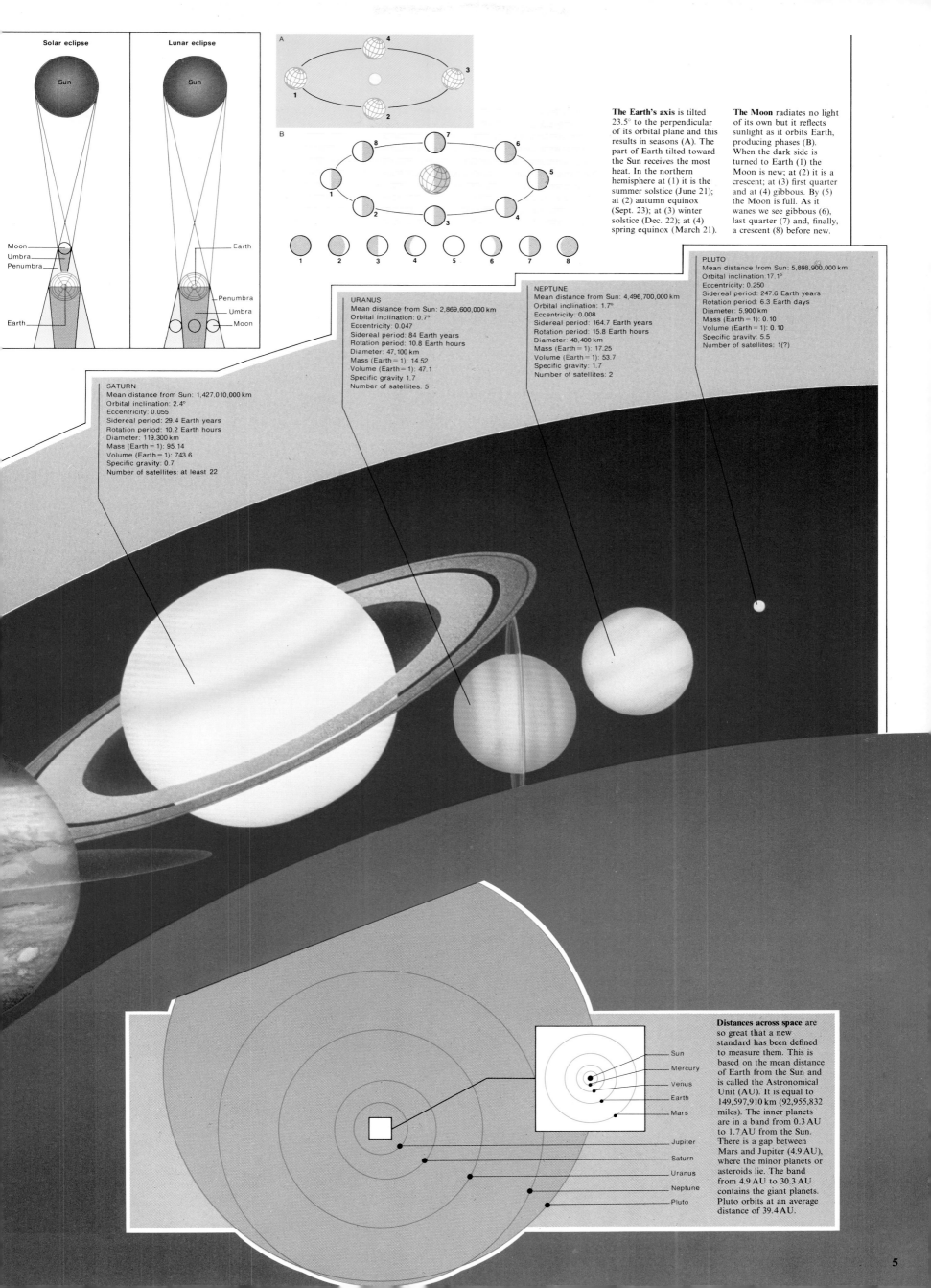

Solar eclipse

Lunar eclipse

Sun

Sun

Moon
Umbra
Penumbra

Earth

Earth

Penumbra
Umbra
Moon

A

B

The Earth's axis is tilted 23.5° to the perpendicular of its orbital plane and this results in seasons (A). The part of Earth tilted toward the Sun receives the most heat. In the northern hemisphere at (1) it is the summer solstice (June 21); at (2) autumn equinox (Sept. 23); at (3) winter solstice (Dec. 22); at (4) spring equinox (March 21).

The Moon radiates no light of its own but it reflects sunlight as it orbits Earth, producing phases (B). When the dark side is turned to Earth (1) the Moon is new; at (2) it is a crescent; at (3) first quarter and at (4) gibbous. By (5) the Moon is full. As it wanes we see gibbous (6), last quarter (7) and, finally, a crescent (8) before new.

SATURN
Mean distance from Sun: 1,427,010,000 km
Orbital inclination: 2.4°
Eccentricity: 0.055
Sidereal period: 29.4 Earth years
Rotation period: 10.2 Earth hours
Diameter: 119,300 km
Mass (Earth = 1): 95.14
Volume (Earth = 1): 743.6
Specific gravity: 0.7
Number of satellites: at least 22

URANUS
Mean distance from Sun: 2,869,600,000 km
Orbital inclination: 0.7°
Eccentricity: 0.047
Sidereal period: 84 Earth years
Rotation period: 10.8 Earth hours
Diameter: 47,100 km
Mass (Earth = 1): 14.52
Volume (Earth = 1): 47.1
Specific gravity 1.7
Number of satellites: 5

NEPTUNE
Mean distance from Sun: 4,496,700,000 km
Orbital inclination: 1.7°
Eccentricity: 0.008
Sidereal period: 164.7 Earth years
Rotation period: 15.8 Earth hours
Diameter: 48,400 km
Mass (Earth = 1): 17.25
Volume (Earth = 1): 53.7
Specific gravity: 1.7
Number of satellites: 2

PLUTO
Mean distance from Sun: 5,898,900,000 km
Orbital inclination: 17.1°
Eccentricity: 0.250
Sidereal period: 247.6 Earth years
Rotation period: 6.3 Earth days
Diameter: 5,900 km
Mass (Earth = 1): 0.10
Volume (Earth = 1): 0.10
Specific gravity: 5.5
Number of satellites: 1(?)

Sun
Mercury
Venus
Earth
Mars
Jupiter
Saturn
Uranus
Neptune
Pluto

Distances across space are so great that a new standard has been defined to measure them. This is based on the mean distance of Earth from the Sun and is called the Astronomical Unit (AU). It is equal to 149,597,910 km (92,955,832 miles). The inner planets are in a band from 0.3 AU to 1.7 AU from the Sun. There is a gap between Mars and Jupiter (4.9 AU), where the minor planets or asteroids lie. The band from 4.9 AU to 30.3 AU contains the giant planets. Pluto orbits at an average distance of 39.4 AU.

5

Earth as a Planet

Viewed from space, the Earth appears to be an ordinary member of the group of inner planets orbiting the Sun. But the Earth is unique in the Solar System because it has an atmosphere that contains oxygen. It is the nature of this surrounding blanket of air that has allowed higher life forms to evolve on Earth and provides their life-support system. At the same time the atmosphere acts as a shield to protect living things from the damaging effects of radiation from the Sun.

Any traces of gas that may have clung to the newly formed Earth were soon swept away into space by the heat of the Sun before it attained a stable state powered by nuclear fusion. Farther out in the Solar System, the Sun's heat was never strong enough to blow these gases away into space, so that even today the giant planets retain atmospheres composed of these primordial gases—mostly methane and ammonia.

The evolution of air
Until the Sun "settled down," Earth was a hot, airless ball of rock. The atmosphere and oceans—like the atmospheres of Venus and Mars—were produced by the "outgassing" of material from the hot interior of the planet as the crust cooled. Volcanoes erupted constantly and produced millions of tonnes of ash and lava. They also probably yielded, as they do today, great quantities of gas, chiefly carbon dioxide, and water vapor. A little nitrogen and various sulphur compounds were also released. Other things being equal, we would expect rocky planets, like the young Earth, to have atmospheres rich in carbon dioxide and water vapor. Venus and Mars do indeed have carbon dioxide atmospheres today, but the Earth now has a nitrogen/oxygen atmosphere. This results from the fact that life evolved on Earth, converting the carbon dioxide to oxygen and storing carbon in organic remains such as coal. Some carbon dioxide was also dissolved in the oceans. The Earth's oxygen atmosphere is a clear sign of life; the carbon dioxide atmospheres of Venus and Mars suggest the absence of life. Why did the Earth begin to evolve in a different way from the other inner planets?

When the Sun stabilized, Earth, Venus and Mars started off down the same evolutionary road, and carbon dioxide and water vapor were the chief constituents of the original atmospheres. On Venus the temperature was hot enough for the water to remain in a gaseous form, and both the water vapor and carbon dioxide in the Venusian atmosphere trapped heat by means of the so-called "greenhouse effect." In this process, radiant energy from the Sun passes through the atmospheric gases and warms the ground. The warmed ground re-radiates heat energy, but at infrared wavelengths, with the result that carbon dioxide and water molecules absorb it and stop it escaping from the planet. Instead of acting like a window, the atmosphere acts like a mirror for outgoing energy. As a result, the surface of Venus became hotter still. Today the surface temperature has stabilized at more than 500°C.

Mars, farther out from the Sun than Earth, was never hot enough for the greenhouse effect to dominate. The red planet once had a much thicker atmosphere than it does today, but, being smaller than the Earth, its gravity is too weak to retain a thick atmosphere. As a result, the planet cooled into a frozen desert as atmospheric gases escaped into space. Mars then, in fact, suffered a climatic change. At one time—hundreds of millions of years ago—there must have been running water because traces of old riverbeds still scar the Martian surface. Today, however, Mars has a thin atmosphere of carbon dioxide and surface temperatures below zero.

Earth—the ideal home
On Earth conditions were just right. Water stayed as a liquid and formed the oceans, while some carbon dioxide from outgassing went into the atmosphere, and some dissolved in the oceans. The resulting modest greenhouse effect

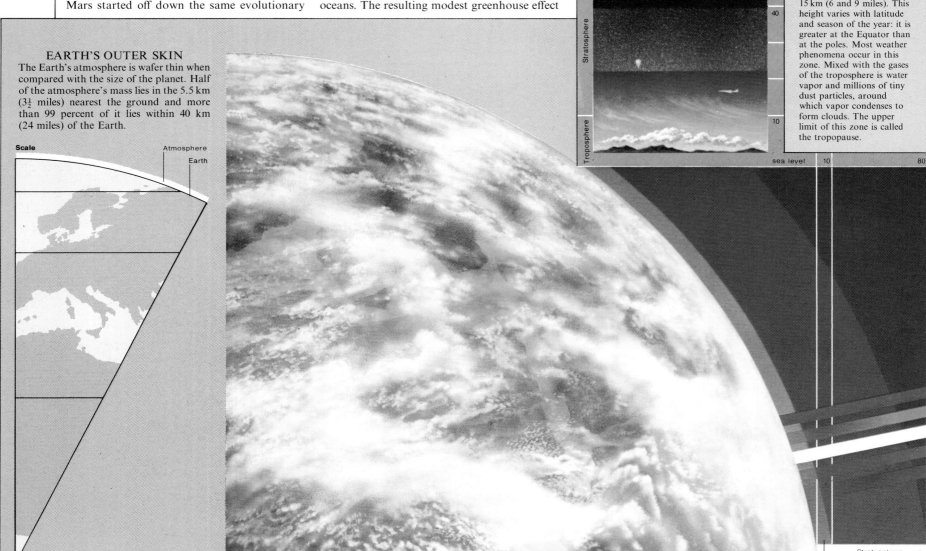

The thermosphere extends from 80 km (50 miles) up to 400 km (250 miles). Within this zone temperatures rise steadily with height to as much as 1,650°C (3,000°F), but the air is so thin that temperature is not a meaningful concept. At this height the air is mostly composed of nitrogen molecules to a height of 200 km (125 miles), when oxygen molecules become the dominant constituent.

The mesosphere is between 50 and 80 km (30 and 50 miles) above ground level. The stratopause is its lower limit and the mesopause its upper. This zone of the atmosphere is mainly distinguished by its ever decreasing temperatures and, unlike the stratosphere, it does not absorb solar energy.

The stratosphere is the level above the troposphere and extends as far as 50 km (30 miles). The chemical composition of the air up to this height is nearly constant and, in terms of volume, it is composed of nitrogen (78%) and oxygen (20%). The rest is mostly argon and other trace elements. The percentage of carbon dioxide (0.003) is small but crucial because this gas absorbs heat. There is virtually no water vapor or dust in this region of the atmosphere, but it does include the ozone layer, which is strongest between 20 km (12 miles) and 40 km (24 miles) high.

The troposphere extends from ground level to a height of between 10 and 15 km (6 and 9 miles). This height varies with latitude and season of the year: it is greater at the Equator than at the poles. Most weather phenomena occur in this zone. Mixed with the gases of the troposphere is water vapor and millions of tiny dust particles, around which vapor condenses to form clouds. The upper limit of this zone is called the tropopause.

EARTH'S OUTER SKIN
The Earth's atmosphere is wafer thin when compared with the size of the planet. Half of the atmosphere's mass lies in the 5.5 km (3½ miles) nearest the ground and more than 99 percent of it lies within 40 km (24 miles) of the Earth.

Scale

Atmosphere
Earth

Earth's radius: 6,378 km

Stratosphere and Mesosphere
Troposphere

Earth reduced by 90% in proportion to this scale

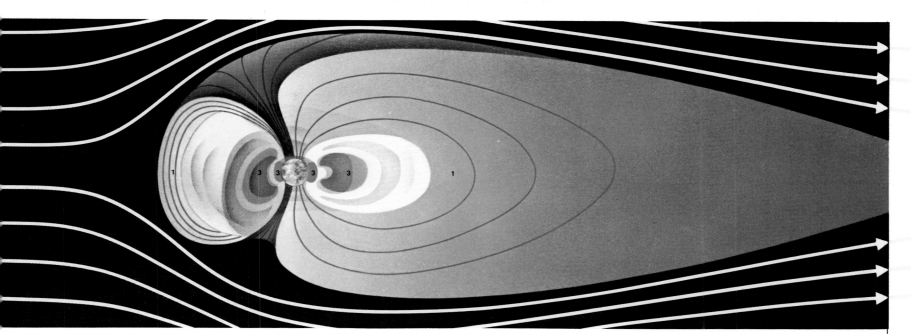

was compensated for by the formation of shiny white clouds of water droplets which reflected some of the Sun's radiation back into space. Our planet stabilized with an average temperature of 15°C. This proved ideal for the emergence of life, which evolved first in the seas and then moved onto land, converting carbon dioxde into oxygen as it did so.

In any view from space, planet Earth is dominated by water—in blue oceans and white clouds—and water is the key to life as we know it. Animal life—oxygen-breathing life—could only evolve after earlier forms of life had converted the atmosphere to an oxygen-rich state. The nature of the air today is a product of life as well as being vital to its existence.

An atmospheric layer cake

Starting at ground level, the first zone of the atmosphere is the troposphere, kept warm near the ground by the greenhouse effect but cooling to a chilly −60°C at an altitude of 15 km (9 miles). Above the troposphere is a warming layer, the stratosphere, in which energy from the Sun is absorbed and temperatures increase to reach 0°C at an altitude of 50 km (30 miles). The energy—in the form of ultraviolet radiation—is absorbed by molecules of ozone, a form of oxygen. Without the ozone layer in the atmosphere, ultraviolet rays would penetrate the

The Earth's magnetic field behaves as if there were a huge bar magnet placed inside the globe, with its magnetic axis tilted at a slight angle to the geographical north–south axis. The speed of rotation of the liquid core differs from that of the mantle, producing an effect like a dynamo (below). The region in which the magnetic field extends beyond the Earth is the magnetosphere (1). Streams of charged particles (2) from the Sun distort its shape into that of a teardrop. Zones of the magnetosphere include the Van Allen Belts (3), which are regions of intense radioactivity where magnetic particles are "trapped."

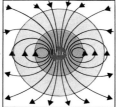

ground and sterilize the land surface: without life, there would be no oxygen from which an ozone layer could form.

Above the stratosphere, another cooling layer, the mesosphere, extends up to 80 km (50 miles), at which point the temperature has fallen to about −100°C. Above this level the gases of the atmosphere are so thin that the standard concept of temperature is no real guide to their behavior, and from the mesosphere outwards the atmosphere is best described in terms of its electrical properties.

In the outer layers of the atmosphere, the Sun's energy is absorbed by individual atoms in such a way that it strips electrons off them, leaving behind positively charged ions, which give the region its name—the ionosphere. A few hundred kilometers above the Earth's surface, gravity is so feeble that electromagnetic forces begin to determine the behavior of the charged particles, which are shepherded along the lines of force in the Earth's magnetic field. Above 500 km (300 miles), the magnetic field is so dominant that yet another region, the magnetosphere, is distinguished. This is the true boundary between Earth and interplanetary space.

The magnetosphere has been likened to the hull of "spaceship Earth." Charged particles (the solar wind) streaming out from the Sun are deflected around Earth by the magnetosphere

like water around a moving ship, while the region of the Earth's magnetic influence in space trails "downstream" away from the Sun like the wake of a ship. The Van Allen Belts, at altitudes of 3,000 and 15,000 km (1,850 and 9,300 miles) are regions of space high above the Equator where particles are trapped by the magnetic field. Particles spilling out of the belts spiral towards the polar regions of Earth, producing the spectacle of the auroras—the northern and southern lights. The Earth and Mercury are the only inner planets with magnetospheres such as this. The cause of the Earth's magnetism is almost certainly the planet's heavy molten core, which is composed of magnetic materials.

The Earth's atmosphere exhibits a great variety of characteristics on a vertical scale. As well as variations of temperature and the electrical properties of the air, there are differences in chemical composition—in the mixture of gases and water vapor—according to altitude. The Earth's gravitational pull means that air density and pressure decrease with altitude. Pressure of about 1,000 millibars at sea level falls to virtually nothing (10^{-42} millibars) by a height of 700 km (435 miles) above the Earth. All these factors, and their interrelationships, help to maintain the Earth's atmosphere as a protective outer covering or radiation shield and an essential life-support system.

The ionosphere is another name for the atmospheric layer beyond 80 km (50 miles). The region is best described in terms of the electrical properties of its constituents rather than by temperature. It is here that ionization occurs. Gamma and X-rays from the Sun are absorbed by atoms and molecules of nitrogen and oxygen and, as a result, each molecule or atom gives up one or more of its electrons, thus becoming a positively charged ion. These ions reflect radio waves and are used to bounce back radio waves transmitted from the surface of the Earth.

The exosphere is the layer above the thermosphere and it extends from 400 km (250 miles) up to about 700 km (435 miles), the point at which, it may be said, space begins. It is almost a complete vacuum because most of its atoms and molecules of oxygen escape the Earth's gravity.

The magnetosphere includes the exosphere, but it extends far beyond the atmosphere—to a distance of between 64,000 and 130,000 km (40,000 and 80,000 miles) above the Earth. It represents the Earth's external magnetic field and its outer limit is called the magnetopause.

The atmosphere protects the Earth from harmful solar radiation and also from bombardment by small particles from space. Most meteors (particles orbiting the Sun) burn up in the atmosphere, but meteorites (debris of minor planets) reach the ground. Of all incoming solar radiation, only visible light, radio waves and infrared rays reach the surface of Earth. X-rays are removed in the ionosphere, and ultraviolet and some infrared radiations are filtered out in the stratosphere. Studies of such radiations have, therefore, to be made from observatories in space.

| 160 | 240 | 320 | 400 | 480 | 560 | 640 | 720 kilometers |

Thermosphere/Ionosphere   Exosphere/Magnetosphere   Space

Man Looks at the Earth

Orbiting satellites keep a detailed watch on the Earth's land surface, oceans and atmosphere, feeding streams of data to meteorologists, geologists, oceanographers, farmers, fishermen and many others. Some information would be unobtainable by any other means. Surveys from orbit are quicker and less expensive than from aircraft, for example, because a satellite can scan a much larger area. And, surprisingly enough, certain features on the ground are easier to see from space.

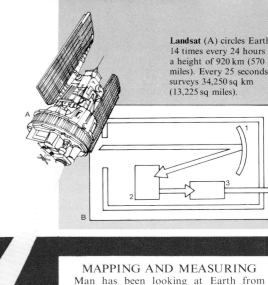

Landsat (A) circles Earth 14 times every 24 hours at a height of 920 km (570 miles). Every 25 seconds it surveys 34,250 sq km (13,225 sq miles).

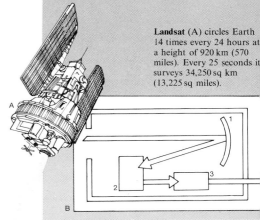

MAPPING AND MEASURING

Man has been looking at Earth from satellites since the beginning of the 1960s, and has firmly established the value of surveys from space to those engaged in a variety of earthly pursuits. Chief of these activities are resource management, ranging from monitoring the spread of deserts and river silting to locating likely mineral deposits; environmental protection, which includes observing delicate ecosystems and natural disasters; and a whole range of mapping and land-use planning.

Satellites give us a greater overview of numerous aspects of life on Earth than any earthbound eye could see.

Of all the information gleaned from satellites, accurate weather forecasts are of particular social and economic value. The first weather satellite was Tiros 1 (Television and Infrared Observation Satellite), launched by the United States in 1960. By the time Tiros 10 ceased operations in 1967, the series had sent back more than half a million photographs, firmly establishing the value of satellite imagery.

Tiros was superseded by the ESSA (Environmental Science Services Administration) and the NOAA (National Oceanic and Atmospheric Administration) satellites. These orbited the Earth from pole to pole, and they covered the entire globe during the course of a day. Other weather satellites, such as the European Meteosat, are placed in geostationary orbit over the Equator, which means they stay in one place and continually monitor a single large region.

Watching the weather

In addition to photographing clouds, weather satellites monitor the extent of snow and ice cover, and they measure the temperature of the oceans and the composition of the atmosphere. Information about the overall heat balance of our planet gives clues to long-term climatic change, and includes the effects on climate of human activities such as the burning of fossil fuels and deforestation.

Infrared sensors allow pictures to be taken at night as well as during the day. The temperature of cloud tops, measured by infrared devices, is a guide to the height of the clouds. In a typical infrared image, high clouds appear white because they are the coldest, lower clouds and land areas appear gray, and oceans and lakes are black. Information on humidity in the atmosphere is provided by sensors tuned to wavelengths between 5.5 and 7 micrometers, at which water vapor strongly absorbs the radiation.

To "see" inside clouds, where infrared and visible light cannot penetrate, satellites use sensors tuned to short-wavelength radio waves (microwaves) around the 1.5 centimeter wavelength. These sensors can reveal whether or not clouds will give rise to heavy rainfall, snow or hail. Microwave sensors are also useful for locating ice floes in polar regions, making use of the different microwave reflections from land ice, sea ice and open water.

Satellites that send out such pictures are in relatively low orbits, at a height of about 1,000 km (620 miles), and they pass over each part of the Earth once every 12 hours. But to build up a global model of the Earth's weather and climate, meteorologists need continual information on wind speed and direction at various levels in the atmosphere, together with temperature and humidity profiles. This data is provided by geostationary satellites. Cloud photographs taken every half-hour give information on winds, and computers combine this with temperature and humidity soundings to give as complete a model as is possible of the Earth's atmosphere.

Increasing attention is also being paid to the Earth's surface, notably by means of a series of satellites called Landsat (originally ERTS or Earth Resource Technology Satellites), the first of which was launched by the United States in 1972. The third and current Landsat is in a similar pole-to-pole orbit as the weather satellites, but its cameras are more powerful and they make more detailed surveys of the Earth. Landsat rephotographs each part of the Earth's surface every 18 days.

How to map resources

The satellite has two sensor systems: a television camera, which takes pictures of the Earth using visible light; and a device called a multispectral scanner, which scans the Earth at several distinct wavelengths, including visible light and infrared. Data from the various channels of the multispectral scanner can be combined to produce so-called false-color images, in which each wavelength band is assigned a color (not necessarily its real one) to emphasize features of interest.

An important use of Landsat photographs is for making maps, particularly of large countries with remote areas that have never been adequately surveyed from the ground. Several countries, including Brazil, Canada and China, have set up ground stations to receive Landsat data directly. Features previously unknown or incorrectly mapped, including rivers, lakes and glaciers, show up readily on Landsat images. Urban mapping and hence planning are aided by satellite pictures that can distinguish areas of industry, housing and open parkland.

Landsat photographs have also proved invaluable for agricultural land-use planning.

They are used for estimates of soil types and for determining land-use patterns. Areas of crop disease or dying vegetation are detectable by their different colors. Yields of certain crops such as wheat can now be accurately predicted from satellite imagery, so that at last it is becoming possible to keep track of the worldwide production of vital food crops. Fresh water, too, is one of our most valuable resources, and knowing its sources and seasonal variation is vital to irrigation projects.

Finally, the geologist and mineral prospector have benefited from remote sensing. Features such as fault lines and different types of sediments and rocks show up clearly on Landsat pictures. This allows geologists to select promising areas in which the prospector can look for mineral deposits.

Another way to study the Earth is by bouncing radar beams off it. Radar sensing indicates the nature of soil or rock on land and movement of water at sea, for example. This was not done by Landsat, but by equipment aboard the United States' Skylab and by a short-lived American satellite called Seasat. The Soviet Union has included Earth surveying in its Salyut program, and resource mapping is also a feature of the spacelab aboard the American space shuttle. All these activities help man to manage the limited resources on our planet and to preserve the environment.

A multispectral scanner (B) has an oscillating mirror (1) that focuses visible and near infrared radiation on to a detector (2). This converts the intensity of the radiation into a voltage. An electronics unit (3) turns the voltage pattern into a series of digitized numbers that can be fed into a computer.

The numbers (C) are then transmitted back to a receiving station (D) as a radio frequency at the rate of 15 million units a second. The numbers are translated back into the digital voltage pattern and converted by computer (E) into the equivalent binary numbers, each of which represents a color.

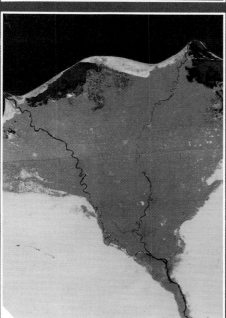

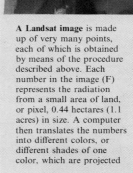

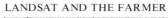

A Landsat image is made up of very many points, each of which is obtained by means of the procedure described above. Each number in the image (F) represents the radiation from a small area of land, or pixel, 0.44 hectares (1.1 acres) in size. A computer then translates the numbers into different colors, or different shades of one color, which are projected on to a TV screen (G) and the image is seen for the first time. Finally, photographs of this false-color image are produced (H). This picture, showing a forest fire in the Upper Peninsula, Michigan, is of use to those engaged in forest management. Other satellite data of use in forestry include types of trees, patterns of growth and the spread of disease.

Observation of waterways and coastal areas (above) shows pollution and deposition of sediments. This is of importance to the fishing industry. Fish congregate in areas where upwelling brings nutrients to the surface, for example. The large yellow-orange halo around Akimiski Island in James Bay (A)— a southern extension of Hudson Bay in Canada— is fine sediment resulting from wave action on a silty shore. Seeing the sediment in this way helps to determine current patterns in the Bay. In a predominantly desert area, the Nile delta (B) stands out dramatically. The red is an intensively cultivated area: cotton is the main crop. The larger irrigation canals can be seen on the photograph. Thermal imagery, or heat capacity mapping, is used to identify rocks, to study the effects of urban "heat islands," to estimate soil moisture and snow melt,

and to map shallow ground water. In this photograph of the northeast coast of North America (C) purple represents the coldest temperatures—in Lakes Erie and Ontario. The coldest parts of the Atlantic Ocean are deep blue, whereas warmer waters near the coast are light blue. Green is the warmer land, but also the Gulf Stream in the lower right part of the image. Brown, yellow and orange represent successively warmer land surface areas. Red is hot regions around cities and coal-mining regions found in eastern Pennsylvania (to the upper left of center in the picture); and, finally, gray and white are the very hottest areas—the urban heat islands of Baltimore, Philadelphia and New York City. Black areas in the upper left are cold clouds. The temperature range of the image is about 30°C (55°F).

The Earth seen from space shows phases just like the Moon, Mercury and Venus do to us. These dramatic photographs were taken from a satellite moving at

35,885 km (22,300 miles) above South America at 7.30 am (1), 10.30 am (2), noon (3), 3.30 pm (4) and at 10.30 pm (5), and clearly show the Earth in phase.

Weather satellite imagery can save lives and property by giving advance warning of bad weather conditions, as well as providing day-to-day forecasts. This Tiros image (left) shows a cold

front moving west of Ireland with low-level wave clouds over southern and central England. There are low-pressure systems over northern France and to the northwest of Ireland.

LANDSAT AND THE FARMER

sown	grows	dormant	grows	ripe	harvest

Sep	Oct	Nov	Dec	Jan	Feb	Mar	Apr	May	Jun	Jul	Aug

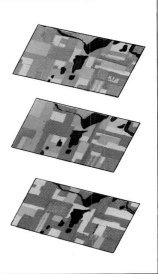

Agriculturists benefit from "multitemporal analysis" by satellites (left). This is the comparison of data from the same field recorded on two or more dates. It is also able to differentiate crops, which may have an identical appearance, or signature, on one day, but on another occasion exhibit different rates of growth. The pattern of growth is different for small grains than most other crops. A "biowindow" is the period of time in which vegetation is observed. These three biowindows (right) show the emergence and ripening (light blue to red to dark blue) of wheat in May, July and August.

Part 2

MAKING AND SHAPING THE EARTH

The structure and substance of the Earth
Forces that move continents · Forces that fashion Earth's landscapes
How man has changed the face of the Earth

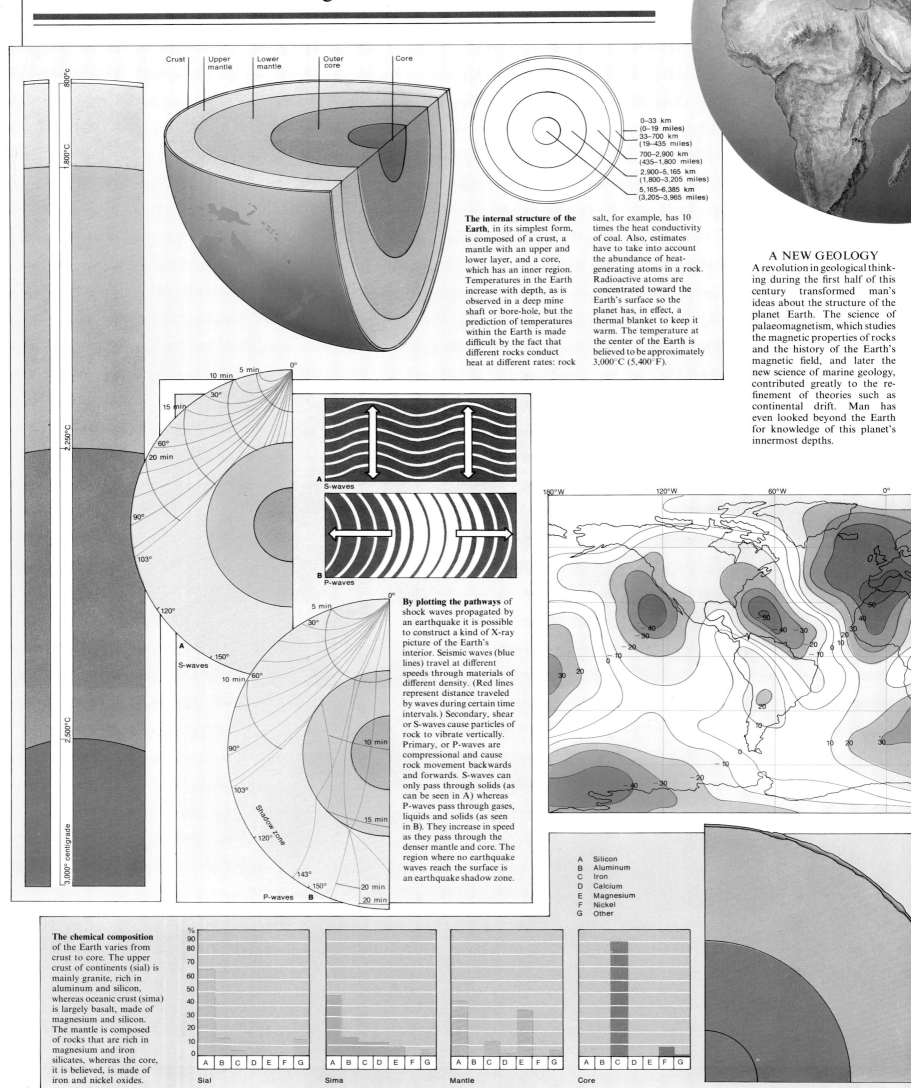

Crust | Upper mantle | Lower mantle | Outer core | Core

0–33 km
(0–19 miles)
33–700 km
(19–435 miles)
700–2,900 km
(435–1,800 miles)
2,900–5,165 km
(1,800–3,205 miles)
5,165–6,385 km
(3,205–3,965 miles)

The internal structure of the Earth, in its simplest form, is composed of a crust, a mantle with an upper and lower layer, and a core, which has an inner region. Temperatures in the Earth increase with depth, as is observed in a deep mine shaft or bore-hole, but the prediction of temperatures within the Earth is made difficult by the fact that different rocks conduct heat at different rates: rock salt, for example, has 10 times the heat conductivity of coal. Also, estimates have to take into account the abundance of heat-generating atoms in a rock. Radioactive atoms are concentrated toward the Earth's surface so the planet has, in effect, a thermal blanket to keep it warm. The temperature at the center of the Earth is believed to be approximately 3,000°C (5,400°F).

A NEW GEOLOGY

A revolution in geological thinking during the first half of this century transformed man's ideas about the structure of the planet Earth. The science of palaeomagnetism, which studies the magnetic properties of rocks and the history of the Earth's magnetic field, and later the new science of marine geology, contributed greatly to the refinement of theories such as continental drift. Man has even looked beyond the Earth for knowledge of this planet's innermost depths.

A — S-waves
B — P-waves

By plotting the pathways of shock waves propagated by an earthquake it is possible to construct a kind of X-ray picture of the Earth's interior. Seismic waves (blue lines) travel at different speeds through materials of different density. (Red lines represent distance traveled by waves during certain time intervals.) Secondary, shear or S-waves cause particles of rock to vibrate vertically. Primary, or P-waves are compressional and cause rock movement backwards and forwards. S-waves can only pass through solids (as can be seen in A) whereas P-waves pass through gases, liquids and solids (as seen in B). They increase in speed as they pass through the denser mantle and core. The region where no earthquake waves reach the surface is an earthquake shadow zone.

Shadow zone

A S-waves
B P-waves

A Silicon
B Aluminum
C Iron
D Calcium
E Magnesium
F Nickel
G Other

The chemical composition of the Earth varies from crust to core. The upper crust of continents (sial) is mainly granite, rich in aluminum and silicon, whereas oceanic crust (sima) is largely basalt, made of magnesium and silicon. The mantle is composed of rocks that are rich in magnesium and iron silicates, whereas the core, it is believed, is made of iron and nickel oxides.

Sial | Sima | Mantle | Core

Earth's Structure

The Earth is made up of concentric shells of different kinds of material. Immediately beneath us is the crust; below that is the mantle; and at the center of the globe is the core. Knowledge of the internal structure of Earth is the key to an understanding of the substances of Earth and an appreciation of the forces at work, not only deep in the center of the planet but also affecting the formation of surface features and large-scale landscapes. The workings of all these elements are inextricably linked.

A 17th-century diagram of the Earth shows an internal structure of fire and subterranean rivers.

Our knowledge of the Earth is largely restricted to the outer crust. The deepest hole that man has drilled reaches only 10 km (6 miles)—less than 1/600th of the planet's radius—and so our knowledge about the rest of the Earth has had to come via indirect means: by the study of earthquake waves, and a comparison between rocks on Earth and those that make up meteorites—small fragments of asteroids and other minor planetary bodies that originated from similar materials to the Earth.

The Earth's crust
The outermost layer of the Earth is called the crust. The crust beneath the oceans is different from the material that makes up continental crust. Ocean crust is formed at mid-ocean ridges where melted rocks (magma) from the mantle rise up in great quantities and solidify to form a layer a few kilometers thick over the mantle. As this ocean crust spreads out from the ridge it becomes covered with deep-ocean sediments. The ocean crust was initially called "sima," a word made up from the first two letters of the characteristic elements—silicon and magnesium. Sima has a density of 2.9 gm/cc (1 gm/cc is the density of water).

Continental crust was named "sial"—from silicon and aluminum, the most abundant elements. Sial is lighter than sima with a density of 2.7 gm/cc. The continental crust is like a series of giant rafts, 17 to 70 km (9–43 miles) thick. As a result of numerous collisions and breakages, these continental rafts have been bulldozed into their present shape, but they have been forming for at least 4,000 million years. The oldest known rocks, in Greenland, are 3,750 million years old, which is only about 800 million years younger than the Earth itself. The complex history of the continents' evolution over this vast time span makes construction of an ideal cross section difficult, but the rocks of the lower two-thirds of the crust appear to be denser (2.9 gm/cc) than the upper levels.

The Moho, or Mohorovičić discontinuity, discovered in 1909, marks the base of the crust and the beginning of the mantle rocks, where the density increases from 2.9 to 3.3 gm/cc. The Moho is at an average depth of 10 km (6 miles) under the sea and 35 km (20 miles) below land.

The mantle
Our knowledge of the mantle comes from mantle rocks that are sometimes brought to the surface. These are even more enriched in magnesium oxides than the sima, with lesser amounts of iron and calcium oxides. The uppermost mantle to a depth of between 60 and 100 km (40–60 miles), together with the overlying crust, forms the rigid lithosphere, which is divided into plates. Below this is a pasty

layer, or asthenosphere, extending to a depth of 700 km (435 miles). The upper mantle is separated from the lower mantle by another discontinuity where the density of the rock increases from 3.3 to 4.3 gm/cc.

Scientists now believe that the mantle is the planetary motor force behind the movements of the continents. By studying in detail the chemistry of the volcanic rocks that have come directly from the mantle, they have gathered much information about this mantle motor. The rocks that come up along oceanic ridges and form new oceanic crust reveal by their chemical composition that they have formed from mantle that has undergone previous melting. By contrast, islands such as Hawaii and Iceland have formed from mantle material that, for the most part, has never been melted before. One explanation for these chemical observations is that, while the top 700 km (435 miles) of the mantle region is moving in accordance with movement of the plates, the mantle beneath it is moving independently and sending occasional rivers of unaltered material through the surface to form islands like volcanic Hawaii.

The core
Structurally, the most important boundary in the Earth lies at a depth of 2,900 km (1,800 miles) below the surface, where the rock density almost doubles from about 5.5 to 9.9 gm/cc. This is known as the Gutenberg discontinuity and was discovered in 1914. Below this level the material must have the properties of a liquid since certain earthquake waves cannot penetrate it. Scientists infer from the composition of meteorites, some of which are composed of iron and nickel, that this deep core material is composed largely of iron, with some nickel and perhaps lighter elements such as silicon. The processes involved in the formation of a planet have been compared to the separation of the metals (the core) from the slag (the mantle and crust) in a blast furnace.

The core has a radius of 3,485 km (2,165 miles) and makes up only one-sixth of the Earth's volume, yet it has one-third of its mass. In the middle of the liquid outer core there is an even denser ball with a radius of 1,220 km (760 miles)—two-thirds the size of the Moon—where, under intense pressure, the metals have solidified. The inner core is believed to be solid iron and nickel and is 20 percent denser (12–13 gm/cc) than the surrounding liquid.

Electric currents in the core are the only possible source of the Earth's magnetic field. This drifts and alters in a way which could arise only from some deeply buried fluid movement. At the top of the core, the pattern of the field moves about 100 m (330 ft) west each day. Every million years or so during the Earth's history, the north–south magnetic poles have switched so that compasses pointed south, not north.

The dynamo that generates magnetism and its strange variations is still not fully understood. Motion in the core may be powered by giant slabs of metal that crystallize out from the liquid and sink to join the inner core. Our knowledge of the Earth's structure has increased greatly over the last 50 years, but many intriguing questions remain to be answered.

The Earth is not a sphere but an ellipsoid (below) that is flattened at the poles, where the radius is 6,378 km (3,960 miles), and bulging at the Equator, where the radius is 6,536 km (4,060 miles). This results from the Earth's rapid rotation. But, rather than a perfect ellipsoid, the true shape is a "geoid"—the actual shape of sea level—which is lumpy, with variations away from ellipsoid of up to 80 m (260 ft) (left). This reflects major variations in density in Earth's outer layers.

The Earth as a Geoid

60°E   120°E   180°E

The Earth's magnetic field is strongest at the poles and weakest in equatorial regions. If the field were simply like a bar magnet inside the globe, lines of intensity would mirror lines of latitude; but the field is inclined at an angle of 11° to the Earth's axis. The geomagnetic poles are similarly inclined and they

do not coincide with the geographic poles. In reality, the field is much more complex than that of a bar magnet. In addition, over long periods of time, the magnetic poles and the north–south orientation of the field change slowly. The strength of the Earth's magnetic field is measured in units called oersteds.

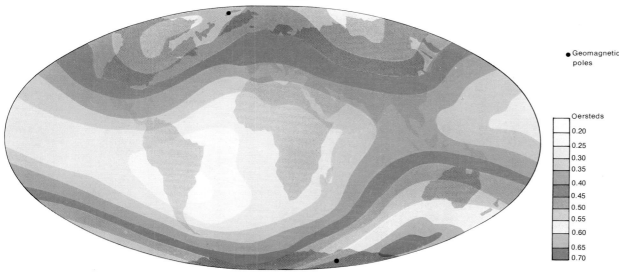

• Geomagnetic poles

Oersteds
0.20
0.25
0.30
0.35
0.40
0.45
0.50
0.55
0.60
0.65
0.70

Earth's Moving Crust

The top layer of the Earth is known as the lithosphere and is composed of the crust and the uppermost mantle. It is divided into six major rigid plates and several smaller platelets that move relative to each other, driven by movements that lie deep in the Earth's liquid mantle. The plate boundaries correspond to the zones of earthquakes and the sites of active volcanoes. The concept of plate tectonics – that the Earth's crust is mobile despite being rigid – emerged in the 1960s and helped to confirm the early twentieth-century theory of continental drift proposed by Alfred Wegener.

THE DYNAMIC EARTH

As early as the 17th century, the English philosopher Francis Bacon noted that the coasts on either side of the Atlantic were similar and could be fitted together like pieces of a jigsaw puzzle. Three hundred years later Alfred Wegener proposed the theory of continental drift, but no one would believe the Earth's rigid crust could move. Today, geological evidence has provided the basis for the theory of plate tectonics, which demonstrates that the Earth's crust is slowly but continually moving.

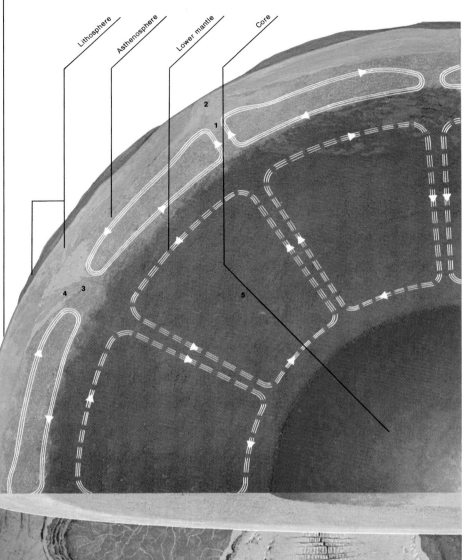

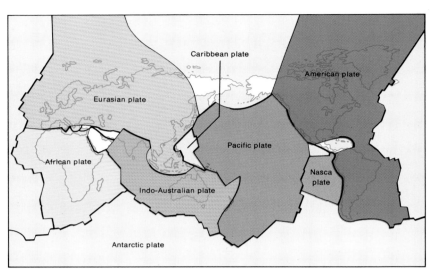

Earth's lithosphere—the rocky shell, or crust—is made up of six major plates and several smaller platelets, each separated from each other by ridges, subduction zones or transcurrent faults. The plates grow bigger by accretion along the mid-ocean ridges, are destroyed at subduction zones beneath the trenches, and slide beside each other along the transcurrent faults. The African and Antarctic plates have no trenches along their borders to destroy any of their crust, so they are growing bigger. This growth is compensated by the subduction zone that is developing to the north of the Tonga Islands and subduction zones in the Pacific. Conversely, the Pacific and Indo-Australian plates are shrinking. Along the plate boundaries magma wells up from the mantle to form volcanoes. Here, too, are the origins of earthquakes as the plates collide or slide slowly past each other.

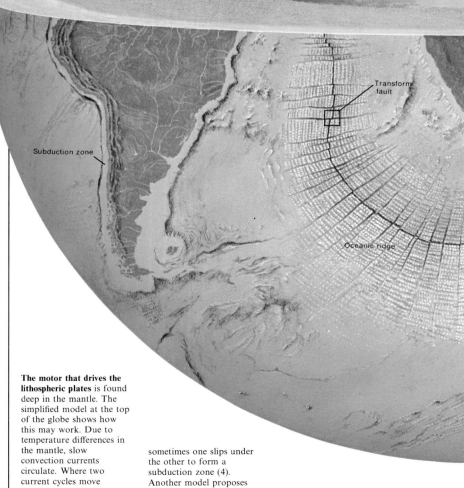

Subduction zones are the sites of destruction of the ocean crust. As one plate passes beneath another down into the mantle, the ocean floor is pulled downward and a deep ocean trench is formed. The movement taking place along the length of the subduction zone causes earthquakes, while melting of the rock at depth produces magma that rises to create the volcanoes that form island arcs.

An oceanic ridge is formed when two plates move away from each other. As they move, molten magma from the mantle forces its way to the surface. This magma cools and is in turn injected with new magma. Thus the oceanic ridge is gradually forming the newest part of Earth's crust.

The motor that drives the lithospheric plates is found deep in the mantle. The simplified model at the top of the globe shows how this may work. Due to temperature differences in the mantle, slow convection currents circulate. Where two current cycles move upwards together and separate (1), the plates bulge and move apart along mid-ocean ridges (2). Where there is a downward moving current (3), the plates move together and sometimes one slips under the other to form a subduction zone (4). Another model proposes that the convection currents are found deep in the mantle (5). Only time and more research, however, will reveal the true mechanism of plate movement.

Transform, or transcurrent, faults are found where two plates slide past each other. They may, for example, link two parts of a ridge (A, B). A study of the magnetic properties of the seabed may suggest a motion shown by the white arrows, but the true movements of the plates are shown by the red arrows. The transform fault is active between points (2) and (3). Between points (1) and (2) and between (3) and (4) the scar of the fault is healed and the line of the fault is no longer a plate boundary.

The early evidence for continental drift was gathered by Alfred Wegener, a German meteorologist. He noticed that the coastlines on each side of the Atlantic Ocean could be made to fit together, and that much of the geological history of the flanking continents—shown by fossils, structures and past climates—also seemed to match. Wegener compared the two sides of the Atlantic with a sheet of torn newspaper and reasoned that if not just one line of print but 10 lines match then there is a good case for arguing that the two sides were once joined. Yet for 50 years continental drift was generally considered to be a fanciful dream.

Seafloor spreading
In the 1950s the first geological surveys of the oceans began, and a 60,000 km (37,200 mile) long chain of mountains was discovered running down the center of the Atlantic Ocean, all round the Antarctic, up to the Indian Ocean, into the Red Sea and up the Eastern Pacific Ocean into Alaska. Along the axis of this mid-ocean ridge system there was often a narrow, deep rift valley. In places this ridge was offset along sharp fractures in the ocean floor.

The breakthrough in developing the global plate tectonic theory came with the first large-scale survey of the ocean floor. Magnetometers, which were developed during World War II for tracking submarines, showed the ocean floor to be magnetically striped. The ocean floor reveals magnetic characteristics because the ocean crust basalts are full of tiny crystals of the magnetic mineral magnetite. As the basalt cooled, the magnetic field of these crystals aligned itself with the Earth's magnetic field. This would be insignificant if it were not for the fact that the magnetic pole of the Earth has switched from north to south at different times in the past. Half the magnetite compasses of the ocean floor point south rather than north.

In the middle 1960s, two Cambridge geophysicists, Drummond Matthews and Fred Vine, noticed that the pattern of stripes was symmetrical around the mid-ocean ridge. Such an extraordinary and unlikely symmetry could mean only one thing—any two matching stripes must originally have been formed together at the mid-ocean ridge and then moved away from each other as newer crust formed between them to create new stripes. It was soon calculated that the North Atlantic Ocean was growing wider by about 2 cm ($\frac{3}{4}$ in) a year. At last, drifting continents was accepted.

Consumption of the seafloor
Seafloor spreading soon became included in an even more sensational model—plate tectonics. If the oceans are growing wider, then either the whole planet is expanding or the spreading ocean floor is consumed elsewhere. In the late 1950s a global network of seismic stations had been set up to monitor nuclear explosions and earthquakes. For the first time the positions of all earthquakes could be accurately defined.

It was found that the zones of earthquake activity were predominantly narrow, following the mid-ocean ridges and extending along the rim of the Pacific, beneath the island arcs of the

West Pacific and beneath the continental margins in the East Pacific as well as underlying the Alpine-Himalayan Mountain Belt. The seismic zones around the Pacific dipped away from the ocean and continued to depths as great as 700 km (430 miles). They intercepted the surface at the curious arc-shaped deep-ocean trenches. It had been known for 20 years that the pull of gravity over these trenches is strangely reduced, so to survive they must continually be dragged downwards. Here was the site of ocean-floor consumption—now known as a subduction zone. Subduction zones must be efficient at consuming ocean crust because no known ocean crust is older than 200 million years—less than five percent of Earth's lifetime.

The oceanic lithosphere (the Earth's rocky crust) is extraordinarily rigid. Even where the oceanic lithosphere becomes consumed within subduction zones it still maintains its rigidity. As it bends down into the Earth it tends to corrugate, forming very long folds. These corrugations give rise to the pattern of chains of deep-ocean trenches and chains of volcanic islands formed above the subduction zone.

As oceanic lithosphere grows older it cools, contracts and sinks. From the depth of the ocean floor it is possible to make an accurate estimate of the age of the crust beneath. Even the steepness of the subduction zone is a function of the age, and therefore the density, of the lithosphere. The oldest crust provides the strongest downward pull and hence the steepest angle of dip of the subduction zone.

As well as the spreading ridges (constructive margins) and the subduction zones (destructive margins) there is another kind of plate boundary (conservative margins), where the plates slip past one another along a major fault such as the San Andreas Fault of California.

The past positions of the continents
Continental drift is thus the result of the creation and destruction of oceanic lithosphere, but only the continents can record the oceanic plate motions taking place more than 200 million years ago. The discovery of ancient lines of subduction zone volcanoes can testify to the destruction of long-gone oceans. One particularly important technique for finding the positions of the continents is to study the magnetism of certain rocks, particularly lavas, that record the position of the north–south magnetic poles at the time when the rock cooled. If the rock "compass" points, for example, west, then the continent must have rotated by 90°. The vertical dip of the rock compass can reveal the approximate latitude of the rock at its formation (the dip increases from horizontal at the Equator to vertical at the magnetic poles).

As longitude is entirely arbitrary (defined on the position of Greenwich) one can only hope to gain the relative positions of the continents with regard to one another. The best additional information is provided by studies of fossils—if the remains of shallow-water marine organisms are very different they must have been separated by an ocean. The full impact of continental drift on the development of land animals and plants is only beginning to be realized.

THE DRIFTING CONTINENTS
It is now accepted that the continents have changed their positions during the past millions of years, and by studying the magnetism preserved in the rocks the configuration of the continents has been plotted for various geological times. The sequence of continental drifting, illustrated below, begins with one single landmass—the so-called supercontinent Pangaea—and

the ancestral Pacific Ocean, called the Panthalassa Ocean. Pangaea first split into a northern landmass called Laurasia and a southern block called Gondwanaland, and subsequently into the continents we see today. The maps illustrate the positions of the continents in the past, where they are now and their predicted positions in 50 million years' time.

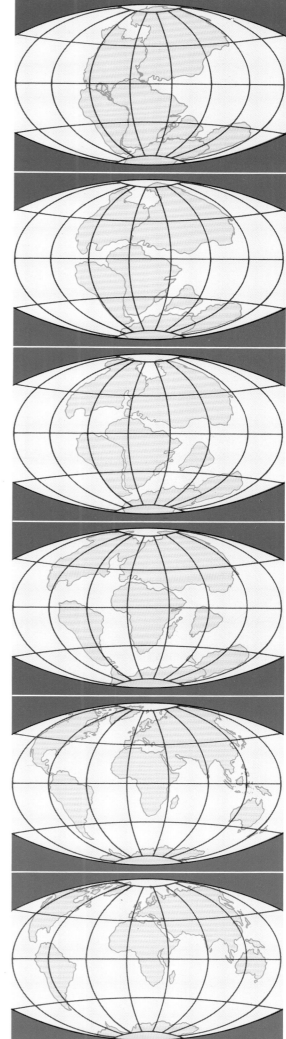

225 million years ago one large landmass, the supercontinent Pangaea, exists and Panthalassa forms the ancestral Pacific Ocean. The Tethys Sea separates Eurasia and Africa and forms an ancestor of the Mediterranean Sea.

180 million years ago Pangaea splits up, the northern block of continents, Laurasia, drifts northwards and the southern block, Gondwanaland, begins to break up. India separates and the South American–African block divides from Australia–Antarctica. New ocean floor is created between the continents.

135 million years ago the Indian plate continues its northward drift and Eurasia rotates to begin to close the eastern end of the Tethys Sea. The North Atlantic and the Indian Ocean have opened up and the South Atlantic is just beginning to form.

65 million years ago Madagascar has split from Africa and the Tethys Sea has closed, with the Mediterranean Sea opening behind it. The South Atlantic Ocean has opened up considerably, but Australia is still joined to the Antarctic and India is about to collide with Asia.

The present day: India has completed its northward migration and collided with Asia, Australia has set itself free from Antarctica, and North America has freed itself from Eurasia to leave Greenland between them. During the past 65 million years (a relatively short geological span of time) nearly half of the present-day ocean floor has been created.

50 million years in the future, Australia may continue its northward drift, part of East Africa will separate from the mainland, and California west of the San Andreas Fault will separate from North America and move northwards. The Pacific Ocean will become smaller, compensating for the increase in size of both the Atlantic and Indian oceans. The Mediterranean Sea will disappear as Africa moves to the north.

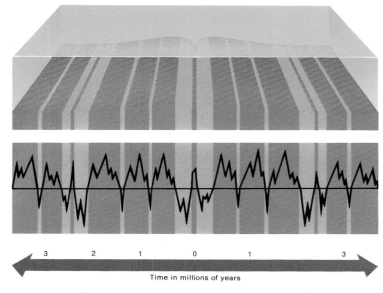

Magnetic surveys of the seabed helped build the plate tectonics theory. Research vessels equipped with magnetometers sailed back and forth over a mid-ocean ridge and recorded the varying magnetism of the seabed. The Earth's magnetic pole has switched from north to south at different times in the past, and this mapping revealed a striped magnetic pattern on the seabed. It was noticed that the stripes on either side of the ridge were symmetrical. The explanation was that the matching stripes must have formed together and moved apart as more crust was injected between them—a notion that was subsequently supported by dating of the seafloor.

3   2   1   0   1   3

Time in millions of years

Folds, Faults and Mountain Chains

The continents are great rafts of lighter rock that float in the mantle of the Earth. When drifting continents collide, great mountain chains are thrown up as the continental crust is forced to thicken to absorb the impact of the collision. The highest mountains are formed out of thick piles of sediment that are built up from the debris of erosion constantly washed off the land and deposited on the continental margins. Through the massive deformations of rock faults and folds these remains of old mountains become recycled, thus building new mountains from the remains of old ones.

For the formation of mountain ranges such as the Appalachians or the Himalayas, or the Caledonian mountain chain of Norway, Scotland and Newfoundland, the pattern of development is very much the same. First, a widening ocean with passive margins is located between two continents.

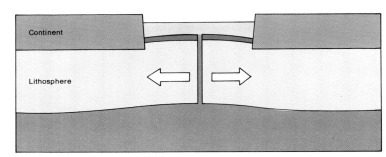

As more ocean floor is created the continents move farther apart, and at the edge of each continent sediment accumulates from the debris of erosion. These piles of thick sediment are known as sedimentary basins.

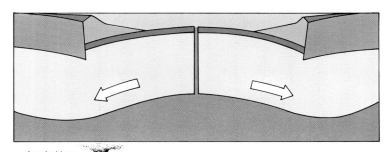

For the formation of the Appalachians, the ancestral Atlantic Ocean began to close, a subduction zone was formed at the ocean–continent boundary, and the oceanic lithosphere began to be absorbed into the mantle. Magma intruded to form granite "plutons" and volcanoes, and much of the sedimentary basin was metamorphosed.

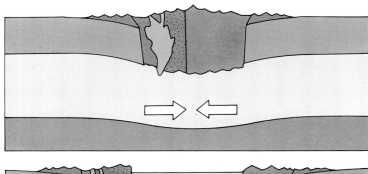

The ocean continued to close until North America and Africa were joined together, further compressing the sediments in the sedimentary basin at the passive ocean margin. The two continents were joined like this between 350 and 225 million years ago.

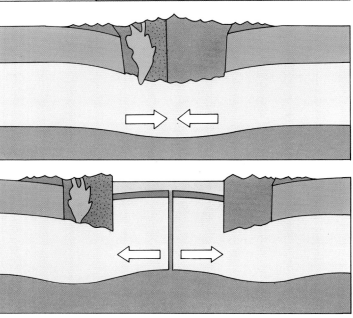

About 180 million years ago, after the original Appalachians had been worn down in size, the present Atlantic Ocean opened along a new break in the continental crust, offset from the line of the original mountains. As the continents split, so the crust became stretched along great curved faults.

Parts of the ancient Appalachian mountains have been eroded to sea level, leaving the Appalachians, that formed on the edge of the old continent, inland.

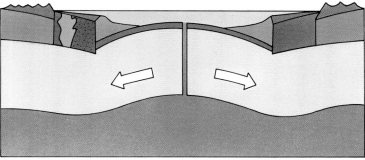

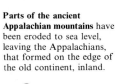

○ Continental shelf
○ Granite
○ Metamorphic rock
○ Sediment
○ Ocean crust

BIRTH AND DEATH OF A MOUNTAIN

Mountains are thrust upward by the pressure exerted by the moving plates of the Earth's crust, and are formed out of the sediments that have been eroded from the continental masses. Young mountains are lofty and much folded, but the agents of erosion and weathering soon begin to reduce their height, and over many millions of years the mountain range is eroded to sea level. This eroded material accumulates in the sea at the edge of the continents and becomes the building material for another phase of mountain building.

ISOSTASY

The continents float in the Earth's mantle, and because they are only slightly less dense (2.67 g/cc compared to 3.27 g/cc), 85% of their bulk lies below sea level. Thus the higher the mountain the deeper the mountain root. And as the crust can exist only to a maximum depth of about 70 km (43 miles) before it is liquefied in the mantle, mountains can never rise above a maximum of 10 km (6 miles) above sea level.

Folds are generally related to underlying faults. The commonest simple folds are monoclines, formed when a single fault exhibits underlying movement. With continued movement a simple symmetrical anticline (1) may fold unevenly to form an asymmetric anticline (2). More movement bends the strata further into a recumbent fold (3) and eventually the strata break to form an overthrust fold (4). Over a long period an overthrust fold may be pushed many kilometers from its original position to form a nappe (5). Faults are generally of three kinds: faults of tension known as normal faults, when one block drops down (6); faults of horizontal shear (7), known as strike-slip faults; and faults of compression (8), known as thrust faults.

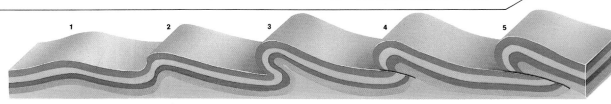

Continents float in the Earth's mantle like icebergs in the sea—more than four-fifths of their bulk lies beneath the surface. The continental crust is 28 km (17 miles) thick at sea level, and where mountains rise above this level there is a corresponding thickening in the crust beneath. The maximum thickness of crust is 70 km (43 miles), so mountains can only ever rise to a maximum height of approximately 10 km (6 miles) above sea level. This relation between upper and underlying crust is known as isostasy, or state of equal pressure.

As mountains become eroded, the process of isostatic rebound allows them to recover about 85 cm (34 in) for every 1 meter (40 in) removed. When, after about 100 million years, a major mountain range has been eroded down to sea level, the rocks exposed at the surface are those that were 15–25 km (9–15 miles) underground when the mountains were at their highest. Such rocks are coarsely crystalline, and make up the fabric of the old, tough continental crust.

Sedimentary basins
As early as the nineteenth century it was noticed that the biggest mountains formed where there had previously been the thickest pile of sediments. According to the principle of isostasy, a thick pile of sediments can form only where the Earth's crust is thin and sinking. The Aegean Sea in the eastern Mediterranean, for example, is at present being pulled apart, and therefore becoming thinner. Over the next few million years, as the Aegean crust sinks, a thick pile of sediments—a sedimentary basin—will accumulate. Most sedimentary basins are at present shallow seas, and form the continental shelves. The depth of water over these shelf seas has been determined by the erosion that accompanied the lowest sea levels of the past 100 million years—about 140 m (460 ft) below the present sea level.

Mountain building
When continents collide, it is the regions of stretched crust that are the first to absorb some of the impact. Such a former sedimentary basin is being turned into the Zagros Mountains in southwestern Iran as Arabia advances northeastward into Asia. The individual blocks of continental crust appear to be sliding back along curved faults, and the sediments that have built up over the thinned crust are now being forced into folds.

Early in the life of such a sedimentary basin sea water may become cut off from the ocean and evaporate to form extensive deposits of salt. Such salt deposits reduce friction and allow the folded pile of sediments overlying the continental blocks to become disconnected and to slide up to 100 km (62 miles) away from the collision zone. In the Zagros Mountains this process has only just begun, but in older mountain ranges, such as the Canadian Rockies or the European Alps, the formation of nappes—disconnected sediment piles forced ahead of the main compression zone—has been widespread.

As mountain ranges often form out of the sedimentary basins along the boundaries between a continent and the ocean, new mountains tend to add on to the fringes of the continents. In North America, for example, the oldest remnants of ranges that make up large tracts of the Canadian shield are found in the center of the continent, while the process of mountain building is continuing in the west.

Other continents show a more complex pattern of mountain ranges through subsequent phases of splitting and amalgamation, and the Himalayas and the Urals have formed where smaller continents have come together to make up the continent of Asia.

The boundary between the continent and the ocean along the western coast of the Atlantic Ocean is not a plate boundary and is therefore termed passive, in contrast to active boundaries such as the eastern coast of the Pacific Ocean, where the ocean plate is moving down into the mantle at a subduction zone beneath the Andean mountain chain. The highest Andean mountains are tall volcanoes of andesite (formed from magmas pouring off the underlying subduction zone). The bulk of the mountain range consists of enormous underground batholiths, in which the magma has solidified before being able to erupt, and compressed and uplifted sedimentary basins formed along the continental margin.

The crustal region immediately beyond the volcanoes that form above subduction zones, however, is very often in tension and in the process of being pulled apart. This appears to be caused by mantle material being dragged down with the oceanic lithosphere. Small ocean basins, such as the Sea of Japan, may open up under such conditions.

Folds and faults
When movement of the Earth's crust has taken place along a planar fracture through sedimentary rocks, it can be easily identified by the breaks in the layers, and such planes of movement are known as faults. Folds form where rock layers bend rather than break. Generally, faults form when rocks are brittle, and folds are found when rocks are plastic.

Sediments close to the surface are often so soft that they behave plastically, as do rocks at depths greater than 15–20 km (9–12 miles), where the continental crust is of sufficiently high temperature and pressure for slow rock flow to take place. Thus most continental faults are found between these levels. All major folds found in soft sediments apparently have a fault of some kind beneath them, and it is the failure of the fault to pass right through to the surface that creates the fold.

Folds are often extremely complicated and some geologists have tended to describe them in extraordinary detail, but in fact they are little more than brush strokes in the overall picture. Pre-existing faults beneath the folds tend to determine the folds' orientation. Once a continental fault has formed, it provides a plane of weakness wherever the continental crust is subject to stress. Many faults around the Mediterranean Sea came into existence during a period of tension, and these are now being reactivated and produce the large earthquakes associated with the continuing collision of Africa with Europe.

At the end of all the complications and intricacies of continental collision, the final phase of mountain building—that involving uplift—remains perhaps the least understood. In the last two million years, for example, while man has been increasingly active on Earth, 2,500,000 sq km (almost 1,000,000 sq miles) of Tibet has risen 4,000 m (2 miles). But the origin of such gigantic and rapid movement lies within the Earth's mantle.

The highest mountains are the product of continental collisions. As the rocks are squeezed, folded and faulted, the original continental crust becomes shortened and thickened. Although the overall extent and height of mountain chains is controlled by mountain building, the whole range can only be viewed from a spacecraft. For the earthbound mountain visitor the familiar shapes of peaks and valleys are those formed by mountain destruction (1). Snow at high altitudes consolidates to form ice that moves slowly downhill in the form of glaciers. To wear away a mountain range at an average of 5 km (3 miles) above sea level requires the removal of more than 20 km (12 miles) of rock, as the thick continental crust that floats in the underlying mantle rises to compensate for the loss of surface mass. Half-eroded mountains (2), such as the Appalachians, pictured above, may linger on for tens of millions of years until, like large regions of the Canadian interior, the mountains are all eroded away and only the hard crystalline surface rocks that were once buried 20 km (12 miles) underground remain (3).

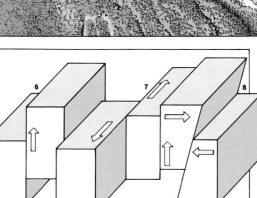

Rock Formation and History

All the rocks on Earth are interrelated through the rock cycle – a never-ending chain of processes that forms and modifies rocks and minerals on the Earth's surface, in its crust and in the mantle. These events are powered both by energy from the Sun and the heat of the Earth itself, and the processes include the forces of nature – from wind and water to the movements of the continents. This geological cycle of creation and destruction is one of the most distinctive features of our planet. Each feature of geological activity, each agent of landscape-making is but a stage of the continuing rock cycle.

CONSTANT CHANGE
The processes of formation and destruction of the three basic rock types—igneous, sedimentary and metamorphic—are linked in an interminable cycle of change. Igneous rocks are thrown up from inside the Earth, are eroded and eventually laid down as sediments. As accumulated sediments sink into the Earth, they are changed by heat and pressure—metamorphosed—before surfacing again in the processes of mountain building.

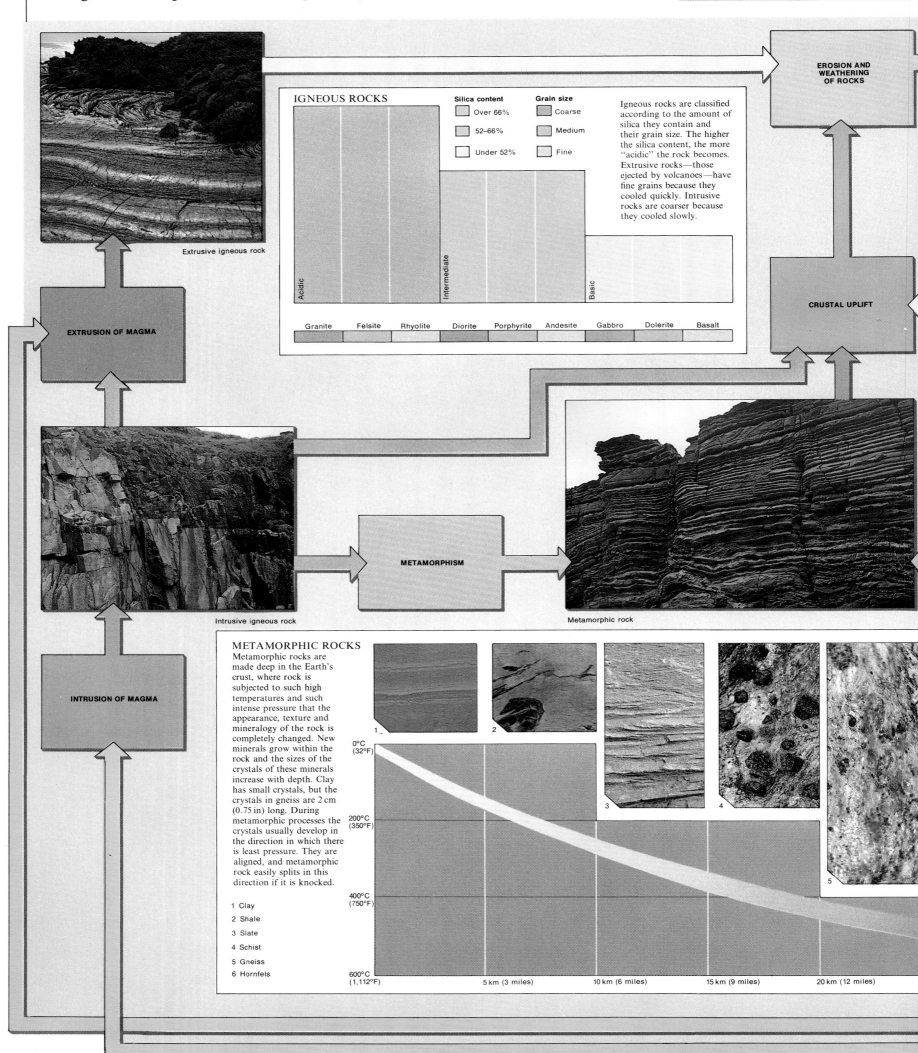

Extrusive igneous rock

EROSION AND WEATHERING OF ROCKS

IGNEOUS ROCKS

Silica content
- Over 66%
- 52–66%
- Under 52%

Grain size
- Coarse
- Medium
- Fine

Igneous rocks are classified according to the amount of silica they contain and their grain size. The higher the silica content, the more "acidic" the rock becomes. Extrusive rocks—those ejected by volcanoes—have fine grains because they cooled quickly. Intrusive rocks are coarser because they cooled slowly.

Acidic — Intermediate — Basic

Granite | Felsite | Rhyolite | Diorite | Porphyrite | Andesite | Gabbro | Dolerite | Basalt

CRUSTAL UPLIFT

EXTRUSION OF MAGMA

INTRUSION OF MAGMA

METAMORPHISM

Intrusive igneous rock

Metamorphic rock

METAMORPHIC ROCKS
Metamorphic rocks are made deep in the Earth's crust, where rock is subjected to such high temperatures and such intense pressure that the appearance, texture and mineralogy of the rock is completely changed. New minerals grow within the rock and the sizes of the crystals of these minerals increase with depth. Clay has small crystals, but the crystals in gneiss are 2 cm (0.75 in) long. During metamorphic processes the crystals usually develop in the direction in which there is least pressure. They are aligned, and metamorphic rock easily splits in this direction if it is knocked.

1 Clay
2 Shale
3 Slate
4 Schist
5 Gneiss
6 Hornfels

0°C (32°F)
200°C (350°F)
400°C (750°F)
600°C (1,112°F)

5 km (3 miles) | 10 km (6 miles) | 15 km (9 miles) | 20 km (12 miles)

SEDIMENTARY ROCKS

Sediments can be turned into rock by means of three main processes. Cementation is the term used when water percolates between grains of sand. As it does so, any iron oxide, silica or calcium carbonate that were in solution are deposited in thin layers around the grains, thus cementing them into a hard sandstone (1). As more sediment is laid down, the increasing weight of the sediments on top exerts pressure on the underlying layers. Water is squeezed out and a dense rock is formed (2) by the process of compaction. This is the way clay becomes mudstone. Finally, during mountain-building processes forces are exerted on rock minerals that cause them to recrystallize into a solid mass of rock (3) that has no spaces between its mineral constituents.

TRANSPORTATION AND DEPOSITION OF SEDIMENTS

BURIAL AND FORMATION OF ROCK FROM SEDIMENTS (LITHIFICATION)

Sedimentary rock

METAMORPHISM

MELTING

5 km (15 miles)   30 km (18 miles)

All the rocks on Earth are formed at one stage or another in what is known as the rock cycle. All high ground on the continents suffers erosion; the eroded material is transported and deposited on lower ground; in time, these sediments may be elevated by mountain-building processes and so, in turn, become eroded. If, between their formation and destruction, sediments pass deep into the Earth's crust, they may be transformed by heat or pressure into metamorphic rock; or, at even greater depths, they may melt to form yet another kind of rock—igneous rock.

Materials at the bottom of a thick pile of sediments may be heated enough to melt. If this material then cools and solidifies underground, it is called plutonic rock. Sometimes, however, it escapes to the surface by means of a short cut—a volcano—to become part of the rock cycle. On the other hand, some sediments are lost off the edge of the continents on to the deep ocean floor, and they disappear into the mantle of the Earth by means of the downward movements of the oceanic crust. A measure of the difference between the input and the output of the continental rock cycle is a measure of how fast the continental crust is increasing or decreasing. Scientists believe it is increasing—at a rate of between 0.1 and 1.0 cu km a year.

Types of rock
The range of rock types found on the continents has been classified under three headings: sedimentary, igneous and metamorphic. Sedimentary rocks include all those formed at low temperatures on the Earth's surface; igneous rocks have all solidified from molten rock, or magma; and metamorphic rocks are sedimentary or igneous rocks that have changed their nature under conditions of high temperature and pressure.

There is a certain amount of difficulty in defining the boundaries between the different types. Ash formed from solidified magma falling out of the air after a volcanic eruption is igneous, but what if it should move downhill in a mudslide? If a metamorphic rock is deeply buried it may start to melt and form a "migmatite," which is part liquid and part solid. Is this igneous? And where does the boundary lie between a deeply buried sediment and a metamorphic rock? Coal seams that have been thoroughly metamorphosed from their original peat deposits are found as layers in unaltered sandstones. This classification does, however, provide a useful preliminary guide to understanding the nature of different types of rock.

Rock types are defined by studying their texture, the way they were formed, and their composition. There are interesting textural similarities between evaporites—salt deposits formed as an inland sea dries up—and some plutonic igneous rocks. Both have crystallized directly from a liquid. There are similarities between sandstones and plutonic "cumulates," which form at the base of enormous magma reservoirs where strong magma currents deposit thick layers of crystals. So rock types must be defined in terms of more than just texture.

Rock formation
The simplest sedimentary rocks are those made up of whole fragments of eroded material. "Scree" deposits that accumulate at the base of a cliff or a steep valley side from angular rock fragments that have broken off the rock face above can make a sedimentary "breccia." A rock made from rounded stream pebbles is a "conglomerate." Further erosion reduces the rock into three components: dissolved ions (atoms with an electrical charge) such as those of calcium or magnesium; mineral grains (sand) that cannot be broken down chemically, such as quartz; and a variety of minerals containing sheet-like layers of silicate and alumina (silicon and aluminum oxides)—the minerals that are often the main constituents of clays.

A river carrying these minerals first deposits the sand, and then the clay, while the dissolved ions pass out into the sea, where some are absorbed by living organisms and used to construct protective shells and rigid skeletons. When the creatures die, the shells and bones again become part of the rock cycle, building up great thicknesses of limestone.

Igneous rocks are chemically far more complex than are sedimentary rocks, but are texturally simpler. The slower the magma cools, the larger are the crystals that form within it. If it cools too quickly it may not crystallize at all, forming instead a super-cooled liquid, or glass. A plutonic igneous rock—one cooled deep underground—is coarse grained; a volcanic rock is fine grained. A rock can, however, have both large and small crystals, testifying to a more complex history.

The most striking feature of Earth magmas is their uniformity. With few exceptions, they are all rich in silica. The greater the silica content, the higher their viscosity (resistance to flowing). Those rich in silica tend to solidify underground. The complex chemistry of magmas comes from the melting of the variety of minerals making up the mantle.

The chemistry of metamorphic rocks is like that of their igneous or sedimentary starting materials. As these become more deeply buried and heated, the constituent minerals grow larger. A mudstone metamorphoses to a slate, then to a schist and finally a gneiss. The "slatiness" or "schistosity" of these rocks is provided by micas and other sheet-shaped mineral grains. Such minerals require abundant alumina to form. If this is not present in the starting rock, it will be metamorphosed into more granular material.

A record in the rocks
Rocks contain an unwritten history of the Earth. Sedimentary rocks hold information about climates of the past and fossil relics of organisms that lived when the sediments were laid down. Igneous rocks record periods of crustal activity that relate to the movements of the continents; and metamorphic rocks indicate periods of uplift that exposed previously buried rock. From such information it is possible to construct a geological time scale. Although fossils are a useful means of correlating one pile of sediment with another, good fossils go back only 600 million years. Earlier organisms are believed to have been soft bodied and were not easily fossilized.

The only complete time scale comes from the radioactive "clocks" in many igneous and metamorphic rocks. Certain forms of natural elements, or isotopes, are unstable and emit energy. By measuring the amount of "daughter" atoms that have been formed by the radioactive decay of a larger "parent" atom, it is possible to determine the age of a rock and events in the history of its formation. The dating of rocks from radioactive decay has thus enabled a true time scale for the history of the Earth to be constructed.

Earth's Minerals

Minerals are the basic ingredients of the Earth, from crust to core. They make up not only the ores on which man has based much of his technology, and the gemstones which he values for their beauty or rarity, but also the components of rocks, pebbles and sands. Two million years ago minerals – in the form of stones – provided early man with his first tools. Today, man's use of minerals, such as uranium for nuclear power or silicon for microcomputers, is revolutionizing our lives.

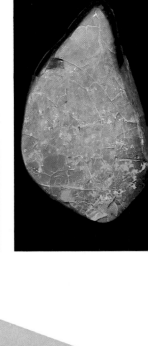

SUBSTANCES OF THE EARTH
Minerals are made up of chemical elements, arranged according to various crystal structures. Man's chief interest in minerals has been as precious stones and, increasingly, as a resource in the form of useful metal ores. But of the 2,500 minerals so far identified, the majority are rock-forming substances—the material components of the Earth. Relatively infrequent geological processes over vast time spans are responsible for concentrating minerals dispersed through rocks into richer deposits, and it is these economically important ores that have provided man with his supply of workable mineral resources through the ages.

Minerals, and the metals derived from them, have always had an inherent fascination for man, as well as providing the basis for his technology. Gold in particular, which was worked in Egypt as early as 5000 BC, still retains its mysterious attraction. Because of its chemical inactivity it is imperishable, immutable and nontarnishing, and has served as the basis of world trade for almost 2,000 years. Copper has been smelted since the early part of the third millennium BC, to be replaced eventually by harder alloys. Arsenical bronze, for instance, bridged the gap between the Copper and Bronze ages (bronze is an alloy of copper and tin). More complex technology was needed for the working of iron, which began c.1100 BC, whereas brass (an alloy of copper and zinc) did not appear until Roman times.

Although the steel-making process had its roots in antiquity, it was not until the nineteenth century that new techniques changed man's attitude to minerals. Before the modern age of plastics, the capacity to produce steel was the hallmark of industrial development, and together with coal it formed the linchpin of western industrial progress. Today minerals have come to assume their greatest importance as exploitable—but nonrenewable—resources.

Components of the Earth
The terms "mineral," "rock" and "stone" are often used interchangeably, but in fact all rocks are made up of minerals, which are natural and usually inorganic substances with a particular chemical makeup and crystal structure.

Certain stones have properties that satisfy basic human needs for beauty and color. Some possess a flashing sparkle, others have special optical characteristics such as refraction and dispersion ("fire"), or contain inclusions that give rise to phenomena like the "asterism" found in opals and sapphires. About 100 such minerals are classified as gemstones and valued for their beauty, durability or rarity.

Most minerals occur as either pure (ore) deposits or mixed with other minerals in rocks—an economically important difference. Their exploitation has been vastly extended in recent decades through our greater understanding of the mineral-forming processes that take place in the Earth's crust. All mineral ores result from a separation process in which a mineral-rich solution separates into its various components according to the temperature, pressure and composition of the original mixture. Precipitation is the simplest kind of separation, as when calcium salts separate from circulating groundwater to yield stalactites and stalagmites in caves, in the form of calcite crystals.

Mineral formation
Most deposits of metallic ores originate in the intense physicochemical activity that takes place at the boundaries between the Earth's huge crustal plates. Very high concentrations of minerals occur in association with warm solutions coming from springs in the seabed, notably along the spreading zones in the southeastern Pacific Ocean, the Red Sea, the African Rift Valley and the Gulf of Aden. This process also occurs in shallow-water volcanic areas, as near the Mediterranean island of Thira and the submarine volcano of Bahu Wuhu, Indonesia. Cold seawater penetrates the crust and leaches out minerals from the basalts of these "hot spots," returning to the surface of the seabed as hot springs. The minerals then precipitate in the cold, oxygen-rich seawater.

Mineral separation may also occur when part of the deep-seated magma forces its way into the upper layers of the Earth's crust and begins to cool. The great plugs of magma that form the

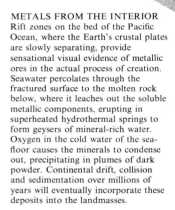

rock kimberlite, in which diamonds are found, must have come from a depth of at least 100 km (62 miles). If the magma reaches the surface through fissures as extrusive rocks, the pattern of minerals in the surrounding rocks is also changed by a process called contact metamorphism, with various bands or zones of minerals occurring at various distances from the contact boundary.

As rocks become weathered, mineral concentrations that resist weathering may be left. Alternatively, all the weathered materials may be transported by running water, becoming concentrated as they are sorted out according to their different densities. Gold is the best-known example of this alluvial type of mineral deposit—known as a placer deposit. If the minerals are washed into the sea, they may be distributed over deltas or over the seafloor, but when this happens the concentrations of minerals are usually very low.

Mineral energy
Fossil fuels such as coal and petroleum are major mineral sources of energy. But with the twentieth-century discovery of nuclear fission, uranium also became an important energy resource. The richest deposits occur, as with other minerals, as veins deposited in fractures by hot-water movements. These deposits, consisting of a uranium oxide called pitchblende, were the first to be mined, for example at Joachimstal (Czechoslovakia), Great Bear Lake (Canada) and Katanga (Zaire). Weathered products of such rocks, redeposited as sandstones, also contain uranium, as in Wyoming (USA) and in the Niger basin. In many respects uranium is similar to silver: both occur with similar geological abundance, their ores are enriched about 2,000 times during processing, and the metals are recovered by using chemicals to dissolve the metal selectively and then by "stripping" the metal from the solution.

MINERALS FROM THE OCEAN
Ocean sediments that originally came from land contain organic matter that absorbs the oxygen in the sediments. As a result, solutions of minerals such as manganese and iron are released, seeping upwards through the debris. When they come in contact with the oxygen in seawater they are precipitated, condensing into so-called "manganese" nodules in amounts that may eventually prove to be a valuable source of mineral wealth. Metallic elements also accumulate very slowly from the seawater itself.

METAL-RICH BRINES
Scientists have recently discovered deep hollows on the floor of the Red Sea and other similar enclosed basins connected with rift valleys. These prevent normal circulation of water and form undersea pools of hot, high-density brines. The brines contain sulphur and other minerals in very high concentrations, and overlie sediments rich in metals such as zinc, copper, lead, silver and gold. Hot springs in fissures below the pools escape into them, carrying up solutions of the metallic minerals which combine with sulphur to create a concentrated broth rich in metals.

METALS FROM THE INTERIOR
Rift zones on the bed of the Pacific Ocean, where the Earth's crustal plates are slowly separating, provide sensational visual evidence of metallic ores in the actual process of creation. Seawater percolates through the fractured surface to the molten rock below, where it leaches out the soluble metallic components, erupting in superheated hydrothermal springs to form geysers of mineral-rich water. Oxygen in the cold water of the seafloor causes the minerals to condense out, precipitating in plumes of dark powder. Continental drift, collision and sedimentation over millions of years will eventually incorporate these deposits into the landmasses.

Uranium, chromium and many other minerals are widely distributed through the Earth's crust, but they are valuable as a resource only if the technology exists to extract them economically. In mineral development, the high-grade ores are worked out first, followed by the poorer deposits if demand remains or increases. With uranium, the low-grade deposits contain far more of the total quantity of the mineral, but these are worth exploiting because of uranium's importance and because the technology exists. Chromium, on the other hand, is currently extracted only from high-grade ores. Large deposits of low-grade ores do exist, but technology for exploiting them economically has not yet been developed.

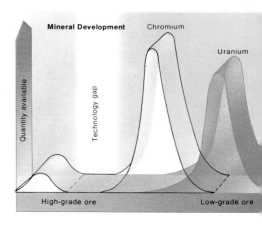

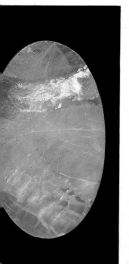

Opal (above), a silica mineral, often contains impurities which give it a range of colors. These flash and change according to the angle of vision, a result of the interference of light along minute internal cracks in the stone.

Sapphire gemstone (left), a form of the dull gray mineral carborundum (below), owes its color to inclusions of titanium and iron. If cut with a rounded top it gives a starry effect known as asterism.

MINERALS IN THE SERVICE OF MAN

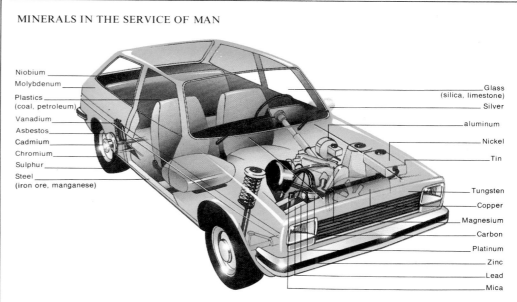

Niobium
Molybdenum
Plastics (coal, petroleum)
Vanadium
Asbestos
Cadmium
Chromium
Sulphur
Steel (iron ore, manganese)

Glass (silica, limestone)
Silver
aluminum
Nickel
Tin
Tungsten
Copper
Magnesium
Carbon
Platinum
Zinc
Lead
Mica

The modern automobile makes use of a whole alphabet of minerals in its composition, from aluminum to zinc. The importance of plastics, made from petroleum and coal, is constantly increasing, but the need for specialist metals is as great as ever. Cadmium, for example, is used in electroplating; carbon goes into making electrodes and graphite seals; transistors and electric contact points require platinum; sulphur is present in vulcanizing rubber and lubricants; lamp filaments contain tungsten. Of basic metals, iron and steel still account for almost three-quarters of the total quantity of the metals used; lead for 1.19 percent and copper for only 0.94 percent. But the amount of useful metal is often a small fraction of the rock that has to be mined and processed. A copper ore, for instance, only yields about 0.7 percent of metal, so to equip a single car's radiator with copper well over one and a half tonnes of rock will have to be excavated, of which 99.3 percent will simply be discarded.

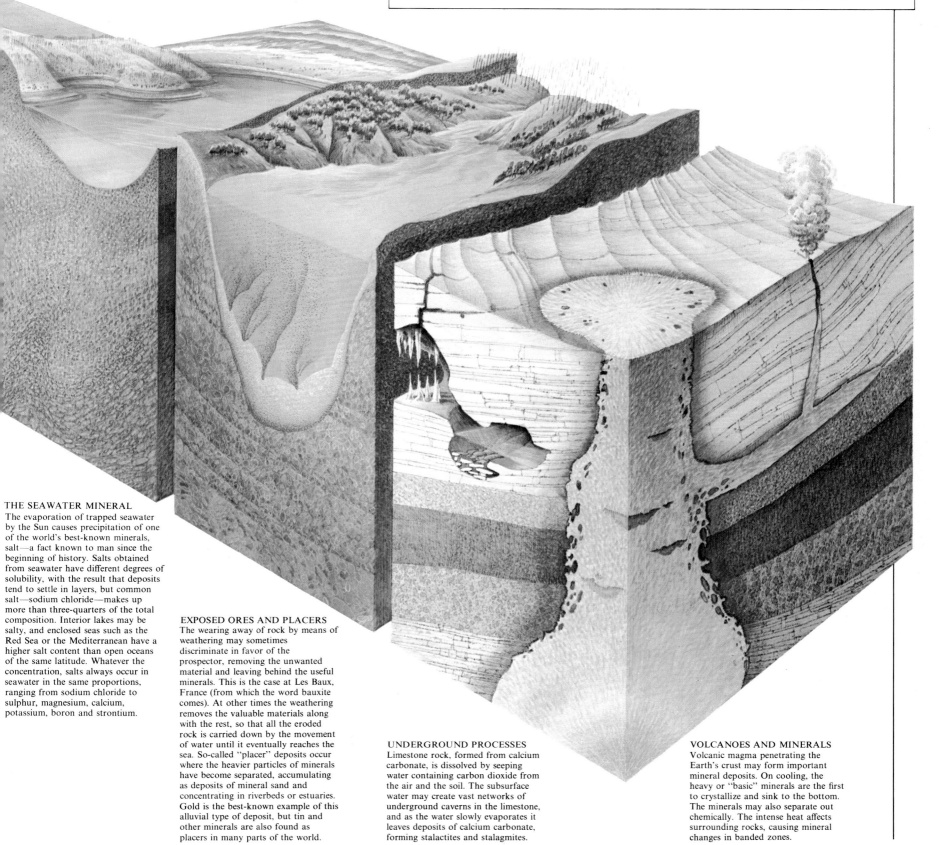

THE SEAWATER MINERAL
The evaporation of trapped seawater by the Sun causes precipitation of one of the world's best-known minerals, salt—a fact known to man since the beginning of history. Salts obtained from seawater have different degrees of solubility, with the result that deposits tend to settle in layers, but common salt—sodium chloride—makes up more than three-quarters of the total composition. Interior lakes may be salty, and enclosed seas such as the Red Sea or the Mediterranean have a higher salt content than open oceans of the same latitude. Whatever the concentration, salts always occur in seawater in the same proportions, ranging from sodium chloride to sulphur, magnesium, calcium, potassium, boron and strontium.

EXPOSED ORES AND PLACERS
The wearing away of rock by means of weathering may sometimes discriminate in favor of the prospector, removing the unwanted material and leaving behind the useful minerals. This is the case at Les Baux, France (from which the word bauxite comes). At other times the weathering removes the valuable materials along with the rest, so that all the eroded rock is carried down by the movement of water until it eventually reaches the sea. So-called "placer" deposits occur where the heavier particles of minerals have become separated, accumulating as deposits of mineral sand and concentrating in riverbeds or estuaries. Gold is the best-known example of this alluvial type of deposit, but tin and other minerals are also found as placers in many parts of the world.

UNDERGROUND PROCESSES
Limestone rock, formed from calcium carbonate, is dissolved by seeping water containing carbon dioxide from the air and the soil. The subsurface water may create vast networks of underground caverns in the limestone, and as the water slowly evaporates it leaves deposits of calcium carbonate, forming stalactites and stalagmites.

VOLCANOES AND MINERALS
Volcanic magma penetrating the Earth's crust may form important mineral deposits. On cooling, the heavy or "basic" minerals are the first to crystallize and sink to the bottom. The minerals may also separate out chemically. The intense heat affects surrounding rocks, causing mineral changes in banded zones.

Earthquakes and Volcanoes

Earthquakes and volcanic eruptions challenge man's faith in the stability of the world, but these violent releases of energy testify to our planet's ever-dynamic activity. Earthquakes are caused when the rigid crust is driven past or over itself by underlying movements that extend deep into the Earth's mantle. Stress builds up until it exceeds the strength of the rocks, when there follows a sudden movement. Volcanoes occur where molten rock, or magma, from the mantle forces its way to the surface through lines of weakness in the crust, often at the lithospheric plate boundaries.

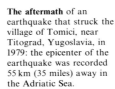

Earthquakes occur when slabs of the Earth's crust move in relation to each other. The focus of the earthquake is the point where movement occurs (1), and the epicenter is the point on the surface directly above it (2). Blue lines represent zones of surface damage as measured on the Modified Mercalli scale.

MODIFIED MERCALLI SCALE

I Earthquake not felt, except by a few.

II Felt on upper floors by few at rest. Swinging of suspended objects.

III Quite noticeable indoors, especially on upper floors. Standing cars may sway.

IV Felt indoors. Dishes and windows rattle, standing cars rock. Like a heavy truck hitting a building.

V Felt by nearly all, many wakened. Fragile objects broken, plaster cracked, trees and poles disturbed.

VI Felt by all, many run outdoors. Slight damage, heavy furniture moved, some fallen plaster.

VII People run outdoors. Average homes slightly damaged, substandard ones badly damaged. Noticed by car drivers.

VIII Well-built structures slightly damaged, others badly damaged. Chimneys and monuments collapse. Car drivers disturbed.

IX Well-designed buildings badly damaged, substantial ones greatly damaged, shifted off foundations. Conspicuous ground cracks open up.

X Well-built wood-structures destroyed, masonry structures destroyed. Rails bent, ground cracked, landslides. Rivers overflow.

XI Few masonry structures left standing. Bridges and underground pipes destroyed. Broad cracks in ground. Earth slumps.

XII Damage total. Ground waves seem like sea waves. Line of sight disturbed, objects thrown into the air.

The Earth's crust generally breaks along pre-existing planes of weakness, or faults. Such breakages give rise to an "explosive" release of stress that is familiar to surface dwellers as the vibrations of an earthquake.

Not all earthquakes, however, take place along pre-existing faults, otherwise no new faults would be generated. Many recent large earthquakes have been located immediately north of the Tonga Islands because a giant rent is developing through previously unbroken ocean crust. The crust to the south is being swallowed down into the mantle and that to the north continues at the surface to be subducted farther to the west. Once a fault has formed, however, it remains a plane of weakness even though the two sides tend to become partly resealed, so that when movement does occur there is a considerable release of energy.

Measuring earthquakes

Earthquakes are quantified in two ways. The actual energy release (magnitude) at the source of the earthquake (the focus) is measured on the Richter scale, a log scale where every unit of increase represents approximately 24 times the energy release. A magnitude 7 earthquake is roughly equivalent to the explosion of a one megaton nuclear bomb (one million tonnes of TNT). The strongest earthquake recorded this century was a magnitude 8.5 event in Alaska in 1964. Earthquakes as they are perceived are measured on the Modified Mercalli scale by their impact in terms of the amount of surface destruction. A medium-size earthquake under a town, such as that beneath Tangshan, China, in 1976 which killed more than a quarter of a million people, might record higher on the Mercalli scale than the Alaska event, which affected a large but sparsely populated region.

The magnitude of the earthquake depends on the frictional resistance that has to be overcome before movement can take place. This total frictional resistance, therefore, increases with the area of the fault plane. So the bigger the fault plane that moves, the bigger the earthquake. The largest earthquakes occur on wide fault planes that dip at a very shallow angle and can pass through a great deal of relatively shallow crust that will not deform plastically.

Earthquakes are unlikely to occur where rocks are plastic and can flow to accommodate the buildup of stress. Some faults, such as the San Andreas Fault in the western United States, pass from brittle rocks into a plastic zone at depths of only a few kilometers. Therefore, the next San Francisco earthquake cannot be as great as the 1964 Alaskan one, although this may be of little comfort to the potential victims. Along some sections of the San Andreas Fault the plastic zone comes directly to the surface, and motion occurs without large earthquakes.

Earthquake prediction is still in its infancy, although it is recognized that a number of phenomena may occur before a major earthquake—the ground may swell, the electrical conductivity of groundwater may change, and the water height of wells may rapidly alter.

How volcanoes are formed

Volcanoes, although spectacular, are safer than earthquakes. While an average of 20,000 people are killed each year in earthquakes, only about 400 are killed by volcanoes; and many of the victims die from starvation due to crop failure after heavy ash falls.

Volcanoes are formed when molten rock (magma) escapes through the Earth's crust to the Earth's surface. Most of this magma forms within the upper mantle between 30 and 100 km (20–60 miles) underground. The temperature increases with depth between 20° and 50°C per

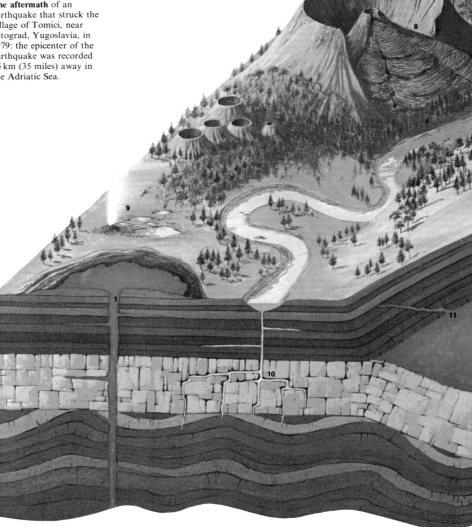

The aftermath of an earthquake that struck the village of Tomici, near Titograd, Yugoslavia, in 1979: the epicenter of the earthquake was recorded 55 km (35 miles) away in the Adriatic Sea.

km (35°–90°F per 3,250 ft) from the crust to the mantle, but even so the rocks are normally not hot enough to melt.

Basaltic magmas, found along mid-ocean spreading ridges and oceanic islands, are formed when hot, deep mantle rises and, on reduction of pressure, begins to melt. Such "basic" magmas generally have low silica and water content, a high temperature and flow easily—often, as in Hawaii, "quietly erupting" to form volcanoes with very gentle gradients known as shield volcanoes. Silica-rich magma forms under continental crust. Ocean crust sucks up water after it has formed at the oceanic spreading ridges and much of this water later becomes taken with the crust down a subduction zone, where it helps to lower the melting point of both mantle and ocean-crust rocks.

By the time these magmas reach the surface they are cooler and have a higher water content than basalts. These "intermediate" or andesite magmas are also more viscous (less willing to

flow) because they contain more silica. The eruptions are more explosive as the water and other gases dissolve out of the magma as it approaches the surface, and the lava remains close to the volcanic vent, building up the archetypal steep-sided conical stratified volcano, such as Mount Fujiyama in Japan. Sometimes the conical form may be destroyed in catastrophic eruptions, as has happened at Mount St Helens in the United States.

The most violent of all eruptions are found where magmas from the mantle have penetrated and melted a great thickness of continental rocks, so as to create highly viscous silica- and water-rich "acid" magmas. As such magmas approach the surface they may turn into a red-hot froth that blasts out from fissures to cover enormous areas in a volcanic material known as ignimbrite. The most extensive eruption known to have occurred in the past 2,000 years was probably on Mount Taupo, on North Island, New Zealand. In AD 150 it discharged some

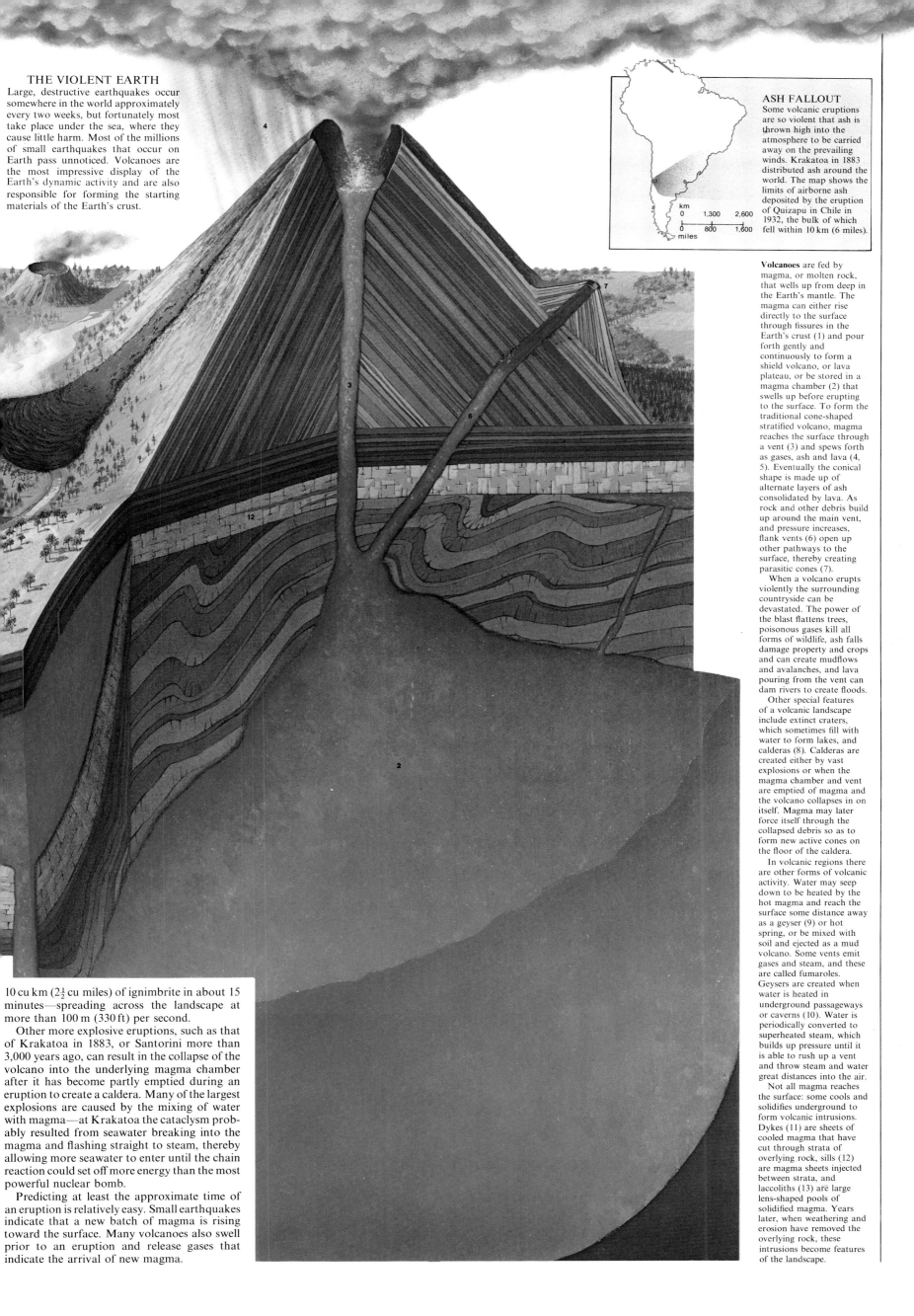

THE VIOLENT EARTH

Large, destructive earthquakes occur somewhere in the world approximately every two weeks, but fortunately most take place under the sea, where they cause little harm. Most of the millions of small earthquakes that occur on Earth pass unnoticed. Volcanoes are the most impressive display of the Earth's dynamic activity and are also responsible for forming the starting materials of the Earth's crust.

Volcanoes are fed by magma, or molten rock, that wells up from deep in the Earth's mantle. The magma can either rise directly to the surface through fissures in the Earth's crust (1) and pour forth gently and continuously to form a shield volcano, or lava plateau, or be stored in a magma chamber (2) that swells up before erupting to the surface. To form the traditional cone-shaped stratified volcano, magma reaches the surface through a vent (3) and spews forth as gases, ash and lava (4, 5). Eventually the conical shape is made up of alternate layers of ash consolidated by lava. As rock and other debris build up around the main vent, and pressure increases, flank vents (6) open up other pathways to the surface, thereby creating parasitic cones (7).

When a volcano erupts violently the surrounding countryside can be devastated. The power of the blast flattens trees, poisonous gases kill all forms of wildlife, ash falls damage property and crops and can create mudflows and avalanches, and lava pouring from the vent can dam rivers to create floods.

Other special features of a volcanic landscape include extinct craters, which sometimes fill with water to form lakes, and calderas (8). Calderas are created either by vast explosions or when the magma chamber and vent are emptied of magma and the volcano collapses in on itself. Magma may later force itself through the collapsed debris so as to form new active cones on the floor of the caldera.

In volcanic regions there are other forms of volcanic activity. Water may seep down to be heated by the hot magma and reach the surface some distance away as a geyser (9) or hot spring, or be mixed with soil and ejected as a mud volcano. Some vents emit gases and steam, and these are called fumaroles. Geysers are created when water is heated in underground passageways or caverns (10). Water is periodically converted to superheated steam, which builds up pressure until it is able to rush up a vent and throw steam and water great distances into the air.

Not all magma reaches the surface: some cools and solidifies underground to form volcanic intrusions. Dykes (11) are sheets of cooled magma that have cut through strata of overlying rock, sills (12) are magma sheets injected between strata, and laccoliths (13) are large lens-shaped pools of solidified magma. Years later, when weathering and erosion have removed the overlying rock, these intrusions become features of the landscape.

10 cu km (2¼ cu miles) of ignimbrite in about 15 minutes—spreading across the landscape at more than 100 m (330 ft) per second.

Other more explosive eruptions, such as that of Krakatoa in 1883, or Santorini more than 3,000 years ago, can result in the collapse of the volcano into the underlying magma chamber after it has become partly emptied during an eruption to create a caldera. Many of the largest explosions are caused by the mixing of water with magma—at Krakatoa the cataclysm probably resulted from seawater breaking into the magma and flashing straight to steam, thereby allowing more seawater to enter until the chain reaction could set off more energy than the most powerful nuclear bomb.

Predicting at least the approximate time of an eruption is relatively easy. Small earthquakes indicate that a new batch of magma is rising toward the surface. Many volcanoes also swell prior to an eruption and release gases that indicate the arrival of new magma.

The Oceans

Earth is the water planet. Of all the planets of the solar system only the Earth has abundant liquid water, and 97 percent of this surface water is found in the seas and oceans. The water of the oceans appears to be passive and unchanging, whereas the rain and rivers seem active, but this is far from true. In reality the oceans are a turmoil of giant sluggish rivers – far larger than any of the land rivers – and of circulating surface currents that are driven by the prevailing winds.

No topographic map of the Earth can be drawn unless there is some kind of base line from which to measure depths and heights. This base line has always been taken as the level of the sea, yet the sea is perpetually changing level. One can choose some kind of average to call "sea level," but even today different countries have defined that base line in different ways. The currents found within the sea itself can also give the water surface a slope—the calm Sargasso Sea off the northern coast of South America is, for example, about 1.5 m (5 ft) higher than the water to the west adjacent to the Gulf Stream.

Waves

The changes in the level of the sea, at its surface, provide the most familiar image of motion within the waters. Various changes take place over many different time periods, but the most rapid are those that we call waves.

Waves are produced by the wind moving over the water and catching on the surface. They can move at between 15 and 100 km/hr (10–60 mph) and wave crests may be separated by up to 300 m (1,000 ft) in the open ocean. In general, the greater the wavelength, the faster the wave's speed and the farther the distance traveled by the wave. Waves that have traveled a long way from the winds that created them are known as swell. Without the wind continually pushing them they become symmetrical and smooth. Wind waves produce spilling breakers more like the rapids of a mountain torrent, whereas swell produces giant plunging breakers.

A combination of strong winds and low atmospheric pressure associated with storms can cause yet another kind of wave, known as a storm surge. A storm surge is formed by the water being driven ahead of the wind, and rising as the atmospheric pressure weighing down on the water decreases. Where storms drive water into funnel-shaped coasts, the water can rise more than 10 m (33 ft) above normal sea level, flooding large areas of low-lying land at the head of the bay. Venice, the Netherlands and Bangladesh have been particularly subject to destructive storm surges. Other catastrophic changes in sea level have their origins in the seabed. These are tsunamis (Japanese for "high-water in the harbor") and are generally triggered by underwater earthquakes that suddenly raise or lower large areas of the seafloor.

Tides

As the Earth orbits around the Sun the water in the oceans experiences a changing pull of gravity from both the Moon and the Sun. The Sun is overhead once a day, and because the Moon is itself orbiting the Earth, it is overhead once every 24 hours 50 minutes. The pull of gravity from the Sun is less than half that from the Moon, and so it is the Moon that sets the rhythm of the water movements we call tides. The variation in gravitational pull from the Moon is extremely small, however, and even if the whole of the Earth were covered with deep water a tide of only about 30 cm (12 in) would be produced, rushing around the world keeping

pace with the circling Moon. Yet the tides in shallow coastal regions are often very much higher than this—for example, up to 18 m (60 ft) in the Bay of Fundy, Canada. The seas and bays with the highest tides are located where the whole mass of water is resonating—rebounding backwards and forwards like water in a bath, as the smaller tides in the outlying oceans push it twice each day.

The Bay of Fundy experiences a particularly high tidal range because it happens to have a resonant frequency—a range of movement—very close to the 12½-hour frequency between tides. Large enclosed seas such as the Mediterranean have very small tides because there is no outside push from an ocean to set them resonating. In contrast, where water movement associated with the tides passes through a narrow channel it can produce tidal currents of up to 30 km/hr (19 mph), such as the famous maelstrom of northern Norway.

After these relatively short-lived disturbances the sea returns to its normal, or at least to its average, level again. When the total volume of free water at the Earth's surface alters, or when the shapes of the ocean basins vary, the sea level itself may start to wander.

How does the volume of water vary? It can be buried in rocks—but the steam clouds above volcanoes return such water so it is normally recycled rather than lost. Some vapor can be broken down through radiation in the upper atmosphere and the hydrogen lost to outer space, but this is relatively insignificant. Or it can be frozen and stacked up on land in the form of ice—this is significant as we are still living in an ice age. The lowest ice-age sea levels produced beaches at about 130 m (430 ft) below present sea level, and the low-lying coastal regions of that period have now become flooded to form the continental shelves.

The salt content of the oceans

Average ocean water contains about 35 parts per 1,000 of salts which include 14 elements in concentrations greater than 1 part per million—the most abundant being sodium and chlorine. Where there is considerable surface evaporation, for example in enclosed seas such as the Dead Sea, the salt concentration builds up and the water becomes denser. Where the sea-surface is turning to ice the salt also becomes concentrated in the water.

The coldest, saltiest ocean water comes from the Antarctic. As it is also the densest it hugs the ocean bottom as it flows northwards, reaching as far as the latitudes of Spain. A similar current from the Arctic is slightly lighter and therefore rides above it—but traveling southwards, as far as the southern Atlantic. A second slightly lighter body of Antarctic water rides above the Arctic water—again traveling northwards. Where these water movements meet each other they rise up, bringing to the surface oxygenated water that can support a profusion of life in oceans that have been compared to a desert because of their lack of biological activity. Unlikely as it seems, it is the icy, stormy, polar waters that provide the lungs of the oceans.

Both the Sun and the Moon exert gravitational pull on the water in the oceans, but the pull of the Sun is less than half that of the Moon. It is the Moon, therefore, that sets the rhythm of the tides. Because the Moon orbits the Earth every 24 hours and 50 minutes, the time of high or low tide advances approximately an hour each day. When the Moon is in its first and last quarters (1, 3) it forms a right angle with the Earth and the Sun and the gravitational fields are opposed, thus causing only a small difference between high and low tide. These are called neap tides. When the Sun, Moon and Earth lie in a straight line (2, 4), at the full and the new Moon, then the high tides become higher and the low tides lower. These are the spring tides. The graph illustrates tidal range over a period of a month.

1 Continent
2 Continental shelf
3 Continental slope
4 Continental rise
5 Submarine canyon
6 Abyssal plain
7 Abyssal hills
8 Mid-ocean ridge
9 Oceanic trench
10 Island arc
11 Continental sea

Depth in meters
0 1 2 3 4 5 6 7 8

Depth in meters

Depth in meters

Sun   Earth   Moon
1
Neap tide

Sun   Earth   Moon
2
Spring tide

Sun   Earth   Moon
3
Neap tide

Sun   Earth   Moon
4
Spring tide

Depth in meters
0
1,000
2,000
3,000
4,000
5,000
6,000

7,000

8,000

THE CHANGING OCEANS

Nearly two-thirds of the Earth's surface is covered by the seas and oceans and this great expanse of water is continually in movement. The most familiar movements are waves formed by the wind and the rising and falling tides that respond to the position of the Moon. But even greater movements take place. Currents driven by prevailing winds form whirlpools an ocean in width, and below the surface flow great rivers of colder water. Sea level is also rising as ice melts from the polar caps.

Cl	55.0%
Na	30.6%
SO₄	7.7%
Mg	3.7%
Ca	1.5%
K	1.5%

Seawater is about 96% pure water and the rest is made up of dissolved salts. Many elements are present in minute quantities, but only chlorine (Cl), sodium (Na), sulphate (SO$_4$), magnesium (Mg), calcium (Ca) and potassium (K) appear in concentrations of more than 1% of the total dissolved salts.

The surface currents of the world's oceans (A) are driven by the prevailing winds (B). The winds and the spinning motion of the Earth drive the currents into gyres—massive whirlpools the width of an ocean. These gyres draw warm water away from the Equator and pull cold polar waters towards it. The centers of gyres are characterized by areas of high pressure, around which winds circulate. Because the Earth is spinning, gyres formed in the northern hemisphere rotate in a clockwise direction, whereas those of the southern hemisphere turn anticlockwise. In all, there are five major gyres, made up of the 38 major named currents. The formation of warm (red) and cold (blue) surface currents is not difficult to understand, given the regions from which they flow. However, even in temperate and subtropical regions, the warm waters of the oceans' surfaces have a permanent layer of cold water beneath them. This cold layer has been formed in the polar regions, where, as the ocean waters have been chilled, they have sunk and then spread out into all the other major ocean basins of the world. The warm subtropical and temperate waters float like an oil slick, from 10 m to 550 m (33–1,900 ft) thick, on top of this cold layer. There is very little mixing between the two layers because the warm water is lighter than the cold water.

Much of the Earth's water is locked up as ice and stacked on the land. As the ice melts the sea level rises. Only 20,000 years ago the sea level was a full 100 m (330 ft) lower than it is today, and the continental shelves were dry land. About 10,000 years ago the sea level was rising as fast as 3 cm (1 in) each year. Today the melting ice is causing the sea level to rise about 1 mm (0.04 in) each year: only a small increment, but if all the ice melted, the sea level would rise by about 60 m (197 ft) and would flood many of the world's major cities.

- ⦿ < 60 m
- ⦿ > 60 m
- • Major cities

The seabed, more uniform than the land surface, also contains a landscape of underwater features that resemble the plains, valleys and mountains of the continents. Off the edge of continents lie the flat, shallow continental shelves, which are bounded by the steeper incline of the continental slope, which meets the true ocean floor at the continental rise. Here deep submarine canyons may be found. These seem to be in a process of continual erosion from turbidity currents. River water pouring into major estuaries and carrying sediment can also scour out the slope—especially during periods of low sea level. The abyssal plain is rarely interrupted by volcanic hills and mountains. The largest chains are at the mid-ocean ridge, where two crustal plates are moving apart and new ocean floor is being created. At some ocean margins deep trough-shaped valleys or trenches are the sites of ocean floor consumption at a subduction zone. The volcanic island arcs that form behind it sometimes isolate a continental sea.

TSUNAMIS

Tsunamis are generated by massive underwater earthquakes (A) and are common around the Pacific. They can travel at more than 700 km/hr (435 mph) and individual waves may occur at intervals of 15 minutes, or 200 km (125 miles). Low-lying atolls of the Pacific have extremely steep sides underwater, and are generally unharmed, but the gently shelving islands such as Hawaii slow down the tsunami and build it into a giant wave 30 m (100 ft) or more in height. This map plots the hourly position of a tsunami that originated south of Alaska.

Polar easterlies
Southwesterlies
Northeast trades
Southeast trades
Northwesterlies
Polar easterlies

60° N
30° N
0°
30° S
60°S

Landscape-makers: Water

Of all the natural agents of erosion at work on the Earth's surface, water is probably the most powerful. Many of the finer details of the landscape, from the contouring of hills and valleys to the broad spread of plains, are the work of water. In recent years we have come to understand more fully the subtle factors at work in a river, for example, as it deepens mountain gorges or builds up sedimentary layers in its approach to the sea. The full force of a waterfall, the instability of a meandering stream, the multiple layering of river terraces – all are features of this most versatile landscape-maker.

Ninety-seven percent of the world's water is in the oceans, another two percent is locked up in the ice caps of Greenland and Antarctica, which leaves one percent only on the surface of Earth, under the ground and in the air. The importance of this one percent is, however, inestimable: most life forms could not exist without it, and yet at the same time many are threatened by it, in the form of flood and storm.

The Sun's energy "powers" the evaporation of water from the oceans. Water vapor then circulates in the atmosphere and is precipitated as rain or snow over land, from which it eventually drains back to the oceans. This is the vast, never-ending water cycle. Water in the air that falls as, for example, rain is replaced on average every 12 days. The total water supply remains constant and is believed to be exactly the same as it was 3,000 million years ago.

From raindrops to rivers

Rain falling on to the surface of the land has a great deal of energy: large drops may hit the ground with a terminal velocity of about 35 km/hr (20 mph). If the rain falls on bare soil, it splashes upwards, breaking off and transporting tiny fragments of soil, which come to rest downhill. Vegetation-covered soil breaks the impact and some of the rain may evaporate without ever reaching the ground.

Soil is rather like a sponge. If the holes or pores are very small, rain finds it difficult to penetrate and water runs over the surface of the soil. If the pores are large, rain infiltrates, filling up the pore spaces. Soils that are thin, have low infiltration rates, or already have a lot of water in them, are very susceptible to overland flow. The water may then concentrate into a channel called a gully, and this can have a dramatic effect upon the landscape. The creation of gullies, together with the splash effect, leads to soil erosion. The problem is particularly severe in semiarid regions, where rainfall is sporadic but intense, vegetation is sparse and overgrazing is common. In extreme cases, badlands are formed and by this time recuperation of the land is impossible or is prohibitively expensive.

Where the infiltration rate is high, water percolates through the soil and eventually into the bedrock. There are two well-defined regions, the saturated and the unsaturated. The upper limit of the saturated zone is the water table. Beneath this, water moves at a rate of a few meters a day, but in rocks such as limestone it can move much more quickly along cracks and joints. In most rock types there are some soluble components which are removed as water continually flows through. In limestone regions, the dissolution of calcium salts results in spectacular cave formations.

Groundwater often provides a vital source for domestic consumption. In porous materials, especially chalk, water is stored in large quantities. Such strata are called aquifers and in some areas, notably North Africa, it is believed that water being pumped up now resulted from rainfall when the climate was wetter tens of thousands of years ago.

Water from a number of sources—from overland flow, soil seepage and springs draining aquifers—produces the flow in rivers. Groundwater appears days or even weeks after a heavy rainfall, but overland flow reaches the channel in hours, producing the sudden peak in flow that may cause flooding and occasionally great damage farther downstream. Flood waves usually rise quickly in mountain areas and the wave moves downstream as the river collects more and more water from its tributaries. Eventually, although the volume continues to increase downstream, the flood wave becomes broader and flatter, so it moves more slowly and causes less damage. The most serious floods occur after intense rainfall on already saturated soils where upland rivers issue on to plains.

Rivers at work

The work of a river from its source to its mouth involves three processes, the first of which is erosion. This includes corrasion, or abrasion—the grinding of rocks and stones against the river's banks and bed—which produces both

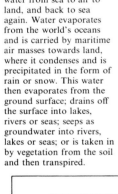

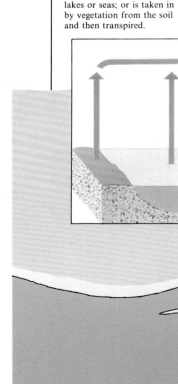

The hydrological cycle involves a vast transfer of water from sea to air to land, and back to sea again. Water evaporates from the world's oceans and is carried by maritime air masses towards land, where it condenses and is precipitated in the form of rain or snow. This water then evaporates from the ground off the surface into lakes, rivers or seas; seeps as groundwater into rivers, lakes or seas; or is taken in by vegetation from the soil and then transpired.

When a river reaches the sea, providing the coast is sheltered and the sea is shallow with no strong currents, its speed is checked and material is deposited (1). The river then forms distributaries (2) in order to continue its flow to the sea. A delta forms its characteristic fan shape (3) as it grows sideways and seawards. A river needs active erosion in its upper course in order to form a delta.

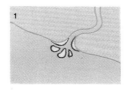

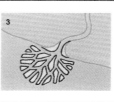

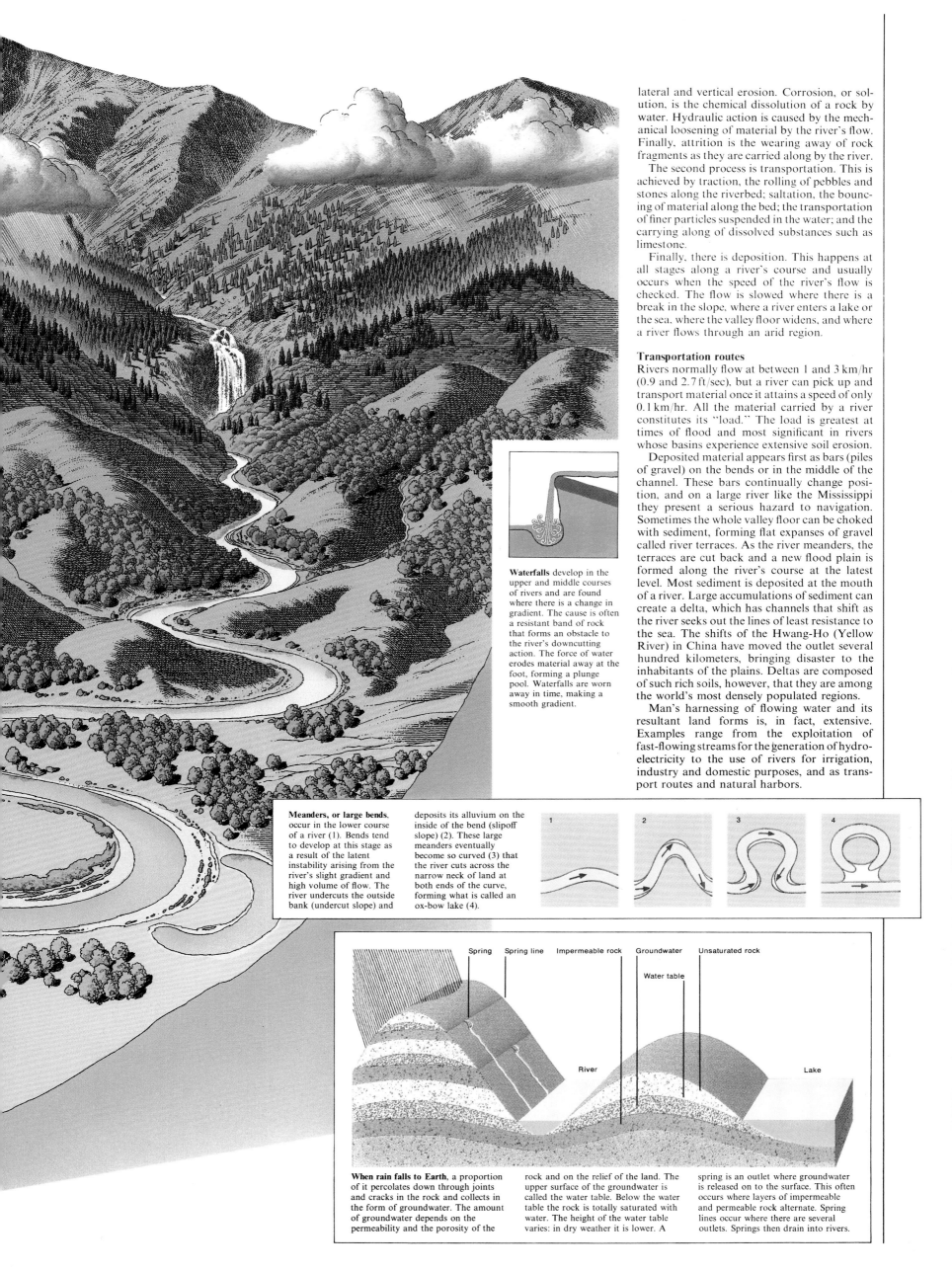

lateral and vertical erosion. Corrosion, or solution, is the chemical dissolution of a rock by water. Hydraulic action is caused by the mechanical loosening of material by the river's flow. Finally, attrition is the wearing away of rock fragments as they are carried along by the river.

The second process is transportation. This is achieved by traction, the rolling of pebbles and stones along the riverbed; saltation, the bouncing of material along the bed; the transportation of finer particles suspended in the water; and the carrying along of dissolved substances such as limestone.

Finally, there is deposition. This happens at all stages along a river's course and usually occurs when the speed of the river's flow is checked. The flow is slowed where there is a break in the slope, where a river enters a lake or the sea, where the valley floor widens, and where a river flows through an arid region.

Transportation routes
Rivers normally flow at between 1 and 3 km/hr (0.9 and 2.7 ft/sec), but a river can pick up and transport material once it attains a speed of only 0.1 km/hr. All the material carried by a river constitutes its "load." The load is greatest at times of flood and most significant in rivers whose basins experience extensive soil erosion.

Deposited material appears first as bars (piles of gravel) on the bends or in the middle of the channel. These bars continually change position, and on a large river like the Mississippi they present a serious hazard to navigation. Sometimes the whole valley floor can be choked with sediment, forming flat expanses of gravel called river terraces. As the river meanders, the terraces are cut back and a new flood plain is formed along the river's course at the latest level. Most sediment is deposited at the mouth of a river. Large accumulations of sediment can create a delta, which has channels that shift as the river seeks out the lines of least resistance to the sea. The shifts of the Hwang-Ho (Yellow River) in China have moved the outlet several hundred kilometers, bringing disaster to the inhabitants of the plains. Deltas are composed of such rich soils, however, that they are among the world's most densely populated regions.

Man's harnessing of flowing water and its resultant land forms is, in fact, extensive. Examples range from the exploitation of fast-flowing streams for the generation of hydro-electricity to the use of rivers for irrigation, industry and domestic purposes, and as transport routes and natural harbors.

Waterfalls develop in the upper and middle courses of rivers and are found where there is a change in gradient. The cause is often a resistant band of rock that forms an obstacle to the river's downcutting action. The force of water erodes material away at the foot, forming a plunge pool. Waterfalls are worn away in time, making a smooth gradient.

Meanders, or large bends, occur in the lower course of a river (1). Bends tend to develop at this stage as a result of the latent instability arising from the river's slight gradient and high volume of flow. The river undercuts the outside bank (undercut slope) and deposits its alluvium on the inside of the bend (slipoff slope) (2). These large meanders eventually become so curved (3) that the river cuts across the narrow neck of land at both ends of the curve, forming what is called an ox-bow lake (4).

When rain falls to Earth, a proportion of it percolates down through joints and cracks in the rock and collects in the form of groundwater. The amount of groundwater depends on the permeability and the porosity of the rock and on the relief of the land. The upper surface of the groundwater is called the water table. Below the water table the rock is totally saturated with water. The height of the water table varies: in dry weather it is lower. A spring is an outlet where groundwater is released on to the surface. This often occurs where layers of impermeable and permeable rock alternate. Spring lines occur where there are several outlets. Springs then drain into rivers.

Landscape-makers: Ice and Snow

A series of glacial periods has punctuated the Earth's history for the last two million years. During the last glacial, the ice covered an area nearly three times larger than that covered by ice sheets and glaciers today. Its remnants are still found in the ice caps of the world: most present-day glacial ice is in Antarctica and Greenland in two great ice sheets which together contain about 97 percent of all the Earth's ice. The rest is in glaciers in Iceland, the Alps and other high mountain chains.

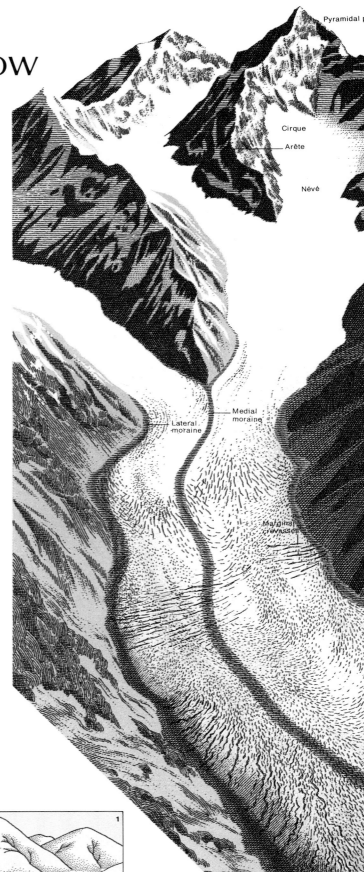

During the Earth's major glacial periods, ice sheets almost as big as that of present-day Antarctica spread over the northern part of North America, reaching as far south as the Ohio River, and over northern Europe as far south as southern England, the Netherlands and southern Poland. Today glacial activity is more restricted, but the mechanisms by which it carves dramatic features of the Earth's landscape remain the same.

Types of glacier
There are six main types of ice mass: cirque glaciers, which occupy basin-shaped depressions in mountain areas; valley glaciers; piedmont glaciers, in which the ice spreads in a lobe over a lowland; floating ice tongues and ice shelves; mountain ice caps; and ice sheets. Climate and relief are responsible for these differences, but glaciers can also be classified according to their internal temperatures.

Cold glaciers are those in which the ice temperature is below freezing point and they are frozen to the rock beneath. This condition, which hinders the movement of glaciers, exists in many parts of Antarctica and Greenland, where air temperatures are low, as well as at high altitudes in some lower-latitude mountain regions. Temperate glaciers, on the other hand, show internal temperatures at or close to the melting point of ice. Unlike cold glaciers, they are not frozen to the rock beneath and can therefore slide over it. Ice melts on the surface of the glacier when the weather is warm, and underneath the glacier as it is warmed by geothermal heat from inside the Earth. Streams collecting meltwater may flow over, through or under the ice and emerge at the ice edge. In other glaciers, cold ice may overlie temperate ice.

Glaciers are formed from snow that, as it accumulates year after year, becomes compacted, turning first into "névé" or "firn" and eventually, after several years or even decades, into glacial ice. This process of accumulation is offset by ablation, through which ice is lost by

melting, evaporation or, in glaciers that end in the sea or in lakes, by calving. If accumulation exceeds ablation, the glacier increases in size; conversely, if ablation is higher, the glacier shrinks and eventually disappears.

Glaciers move because of the force of gravity. The fastest-moving glaciers, for example those of coastal Greenland which descend steeply from areas of great accumulation, move at speeds of more than 20 m (65 ft) a day. A few meters a day is more common, however. Some glaciers move exceptionally quickly in surges, which usually last for a few weeks; rates of more than 100 m (330 ft) a day have been recorded. At the other extreme, some glaciers or parts of glaciers—the central zones of ice sheets and ice caps for example—are virtually motionless. When the ice in a glacier is subject to pressure or tension—as it flows down a valley, for example—it behaves rather like a plastic substance and changes its shape to fit the contours of the valley. Part or all of the movement of a glacier is accomplished by means of this internal deformation. In temperate glaciers, or glaciers whose lower layers are temperate, there is also basal sliding. Movement of a glacier produces cracks or crevasses in areas where stress exceeds the strength of the ice.

The work of glaciers
Glaciers and ice sheets can profoundly modify the landscape by both erosion and deposition. Measured rates of erosion of bedrock may be as much as several millimeters a year. Rock surfaces are scratched, or striated, and worn down by the constant grinding action (abrasion) of rock fragments embedded in the base of the ice. The extreme pressure of thick glacial ice on a basal boulder has been known to rupture solid bedrock beneath it.

The products of bedrock erosion range from fine clays and silts produced by abrasion, to large boulders picked up and transported by the ice. Some rocks have been carried hundreds of kilometers, from southern Scandinavia to

A U-shaped valley, such as Langdale (below) in the English Lake District, is a clear indication of a glaciated past. The floor is quite flat and the valley sides rise steeply from it.

A crevasse (below left) is created by stress within a glacier. Internally, the ice is rather like plastic but its surface is rigid and brittle. This causes tension and cracking on the surface.

This erratic (below right) is made of Silurian grit, yet it sits on a limestone perch. Ice left Yorkshire 20,000 years ago, since when the limestone surface has been lowered by solution.

Before the onset of glaciation a mountain region is often sculpted largely by the work of rivers and the processes of weathering. The hills are rounded and the valleys are V-shaped (1). During a period of glacial activity, valleys become filled with snow and eventually glaciers and, after thousands of years, the region shows a typically glaciated landscape (2). When the ice has finally disappeared there remains a glacial trough (3) with hanging valleys, truncated spurs, waterfalls and all the landforms associated with deposition of material.

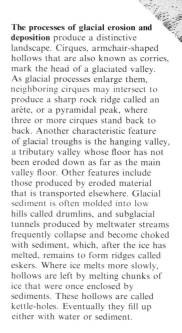

The processes of glacial erosion and deposition produce a distinctive landscape. Cirques, armchair-shaped hollows that are also known as corries, mark the head of a glaciated valley. As glacial processes enlarge them, neighboring cirques may intersect to produce a sharp rock ridge called an arête, or a pyramidal peak, where three or more cirques stand back to back. Another characteristic feature of glacial troughs is the hanging valley, a tributary valley whose floor has not been eroded down as far as the main valley floor. Other features include those produced by eroded material that is transported elsewhere. Glacial sediment is often molded into low hills called drumlins, and subglacial tunnels produced by meltwater streams frequently collapse and become choked with sediment, which, after the ice has melted, remains to form ridges called eskers. Where ice melts more slowly, hollows are left by melting chunks of ice that were once enclosed by sediments. These hollows are called kettle-holes. Eventually they fill up either with water or sediment.

THE SNOW LINE

Glaciation is still evident today in regions that are above the snow line—the lowest limit of perpetual snow cover. The height of the snow line varies with latitude: from about 5,200 m (17,000 ft) at the Equator, to 2,700 m (9,000 ft) in the Alps, to 1,200 m (4,000 ft) in Scandinavia and sea level nearer the north and south polar regions.

A glaciated valley exhibits a distinctive shape and profile. A cross section shows a U-shape, while longitudinally the valley floor is marked by a series of rocky steps and basins. The zone of accumulation is characterized by a cirque, in which snow collects to produce a firn field. A bergschrund is a type of crevasse that opens up near the top of the firn field where the head of the glacier is pulled away from the cirque walls. A rock step is where the gradient becomes much steeper. The speed of the ice flow is accelerated and consequent tension within the ice creates a number of deep crevasses called an ice fall. The zone of ablation has large accumulations of various kinds of rock debris.

Glacial erosion of rock surfaces is typified by a roche moutonnée, a resistant rock hummock that lies in the path of the ice. The upstream side is smooth as a result of abrasion by rock debris that is frozen into the base of the glacier. This debris scratches and scrapes rock, producing striations. The downstream side is rough as a result of ice plucking. Meltwater removes the small blocks of rock.

A great variety of material arrives at the terminus or snout of a glacier—ranging from large blocks of rock and boulders to very finely ground rock "flour." All the material is dropped in a haphazard way as the ice melts. The mixture of clay and boulders is termed glacial till. If the ice margin remains stationary, till accumulates to form a terminal moraine. If the snout recedes continuously, no ridge forms.

eastern England, for example, and such far-traveled rocks are termed erratics. The finer sediments, compacted at the base of the glacier by the weight of the overlying ice, form till or boulder clay.

The surface of a glacier is often strewn with rock debris, which either rests on the ice or is within the glacier and revealed as the ice melts. Lateral moraines consist of rock debris that has accumulated along the sides of the glacier as a result of rockfall from, and erosion of, the valley sides. Where two glaciers join, the inner lateral moraines merge to form a medial moraine. In the ablation zone, the surface of the glacier becomes increasingly laden with debris "melting out" so that the ice may become completely buried. At the end of the glacier all rock debris is dumped, forming a terminal moraine.

Meltwater streams pouring out from glaciers or flowing in tunnels beneath them can be powerful agents of erosion and can transport large quantities of sediment. Bedrock surfaces become potholed and carved by channels that are eroded with great speed. As the streams emerge from the edge of the ice, they carry with them and deposit vast quantities of sand and gravel which form flood plains (outwash plains). Alternatively, meltwater streams may deposit sediment between the edge of the glacier and valley side, leaving a "kame terrace" when the ice finally melts. Meltwater streams feeding glacial lakes that are dammed by a glacier or moraine, for example, construct deltas of sand and gravel and lay down finer sediments (varved clays) on the lake floor.

Snow processes

Snow plays a smaller part than glacial ice in landform sculpture. Its most important role is in avalanches, which, in mountain regions, regularly bring down thousands of tonnes of rock debris. The mixture of snow, rock and other debris forms avalanche boulder tongues on the flat ground where the avalanche comes to rest and the snow melts. Gullies (avalanche chutes) on mountain slopes are swept clean of loose debris several times a year and they are gradually enlarged. Snow patches that remain stationary on more gentle slopes or in hollows encourage rock weathering under and around them. Such a process, termed nivation, may lead to deepening and enlargement of hollows and further snow accumulation. This is one way in which new glaciers are formed.

Landscape-makers: The Seas

The coastline is both the birthplace and the graveyard of the land. Over tens of thousands of years, geological uplift of a continent, or a fall in sea level, may create an emerging fringe of new land, whereas a period of submergence drowns the coasts and floods the adjacent river valleys, destroying land but producing some of the most attractive coastal landscapes. More rapid are the changes brought about by the sea itself. Erosion of coastal rocks or beaches can cut back the coastline at a rate of several meters a year, whereas other coastlines are built up at a comparable rate from marine sediments.

Changing coastlines are apparent on a human time scale. In temperate latitudes, beaches tend to be combed down and narrowed by winter waves, only to be restored during the calmer weather of summer. They may be lost one week and replenished the next, demonstrating an invaluable ability to recover from the wounds of all but the most devastating storms. Cliffs are generally much less dynamic, particularly if composed of resistant rock, but any loss that they suffer is permanent because there is no process that is capable of rebuilding them.

Coasts vary greatly around the world. Tropical areas often have wide beaches made up of fine material which in many cases forms broad mangrove swamps that collect sediment and build up the coast. In more exposed tropical zones coral reefs are common, either fringing the shore or (particularly where the sea level is rising) separated from the shore by a lagoon to give a barrier reef. Continued submergence of a small island surrounded by such a reef may produce an atoll. In contrast, Arctic beaches are narrow and coarse, and may be icebound for up to 10 months each year. Recession of soft rock cliffs results more from melting of ice in the ground than from wave erosion.

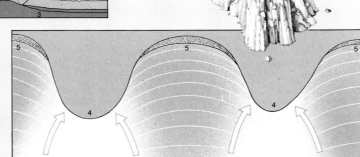

Cliffs are attacked by waves at the zone that lies between high tide (HT) and low tide (LT). The rate of erosion depends on the strength and jointing pattern of the rock and the angle at which the strata are presented to the sea. Erosion begins when water and rocks are hurled at the cliff and new fragments are broken off. The pressure of the water also compresses air in joints and cracks to shatter the rock face. As the base of the cliff is attacked, a notch (1) may be cut, and as this is made deeper the cliff above collapses. Eventually a wave-cut platform (2) is created, the top of which is exposed at low tide. The debris from the cliff is carried along the coast or deposited offshore (3). The shallow seabed now slows down incoming waves: they attack the cliff (4), but their energy is reduced. In calm water, for example at the head of a bay (5), wave energy is diffused and light material such as sand is deposited as beaches.

Waves at work

Across great expanses of open ocean energy is transferred from the wind to the sea surface to produce waves, thus fueling the machine that ultimately creates the coast. Originating as waves with heights of up to 20 or even 30 m (65–100 ft), they lose part of their energy quite rapidly as they travel, and once they have been reduced in height to the lower but more widely spaced ocean swell, they continue to travel across enormous distances.

The coasts of western Europe receive waves produced almost 10,000 km (6,200 miles) away off Cape Horn, and swell reaching California has sometimes crossed more than 11,000 km

THE SEA COAST

The coastline is continually changing, whether day by day as the tides sift and sort the sand and shingle on the beaches, or over tens of thousands of years as the erosive power of waves carves out headlands and bays. And over millions of years the coastline is subjected to major changes of sea level, whether it is the land uplifting or sinking, or the sea itself rising or receding. Today, interference by man can damage the coast. Dam building and river-channel engineering drastically reduce the amount of sediment reaching the coast; and sea walls built to protect the coast and groynes constructed to retard sand removal both pose a long-term threat to adjacent coasts, which become starved of the sediment that previously supplied their beaches.

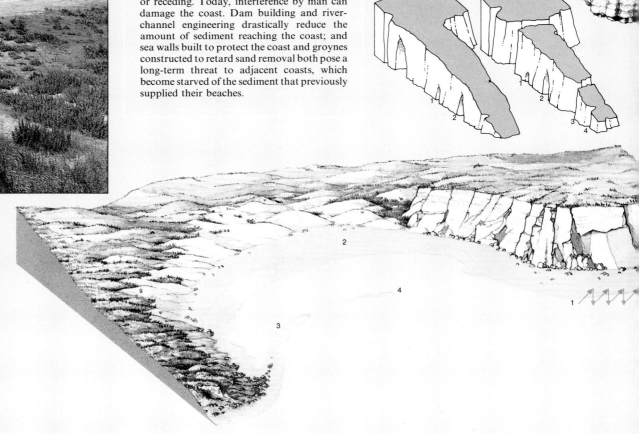

When a headland has been created (below), wave erosion continues on both sides and a cave (1) may be formed. After many years of wave action the cave will break through to the other side and an arch (2) may be created.

Light material such as mud, sand and shingle is carried by the sea. Waves tend to push the particles obliquely up a beach (right), but the backwash moves the material down again at right-angles to the shore. Thus the materials move in a zigzag fashion along the beach (1). This is known as longshore drift. When the load-carrying capacity of the waves is reduced for any reason, the material is deposited and forms a variety of features. The largest beaches (2) are found in the calmest waters such as in bays or at river mouths, with the finest grains sorted out nearest to the sea and larger pebbles stranded higher up. Spits (3) and bars (4) are sand ridges deposited across a bay or river mouth. When one end of the ridge is attached to the land it is called a spit. Spits are very often shaped like a hook as waves are refracted around the tip of land. Bars are formed where sand is deposited in shallow water offshore across the entrances to bays and run parallel to the coastline. Dunes, pictured above, are formed when sand on the beach is driven inland by onshore winds. Very often they isolate flooded land behind them to form coastal features such as salt marshes and mud flats.

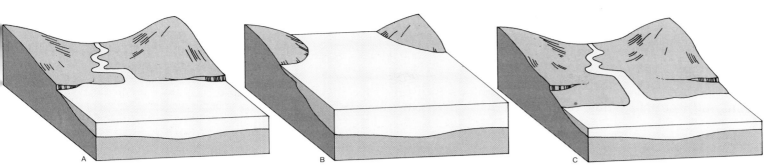

There are two major kinds of coastline—coastlines of submergence and coastlines of emergence. They are created by either a sinking or an uplift of the land, or by a change in sea level. A coastline with wave-cut cliffs and a river valley (A), for example, that experiences a rise in sea level will produce a new coastline (B) with a drowned estuary, coastal uplands isolated as islands, and a submerged coastal plain. The same coastline subjected to a drop in sea level (C) results in an extended river, abandoned cliffs far inland, and a raised beach that forms a new coastal plain.

(6,800 miles) of the Pacific from the storm belt south of New Zealand. The waves thus act as a giant conveyor for the energy that is finally used up in a few seconds of intense activity. Few other natural systems gather their energy so widely and then concentrate it so effectively.

A ball floating on the sea surface shows that, although a passing wave form moves forward, the water (and ball) follow a near-circular path and end up almost where they started. Beneath the surface the water follows similar orbits, but the amount of movement becomes progressively less with depth, until it dies out altogether. The greater the wavelength (the distance between crests) the greater is the depth of disturbance.

Long-swell waves approaching a gentle shore start disturbing the seabed far from the coast and these waves slow up, pack closer together and increase in height until they become unstable, thus producing the spilling white surf that carries much sediment to build up wide sandy beaches. Shorter local storm waves disturb the water to less depth, and thus reach much closer inshore before they interact with the seabed. Such waves do not therefore break until they plunge directly down on to the beach, leading to severe erosion, which results in the production of steep pebble beaches.

Waves slow up in shallow water, and so an undulating seabed causes their crests to bend and change their direction of approach. As a result, waves converge toward headlands (where their erosional attack is concentrated),

but they diverge as they enter bays, spreading out their energy and encouraging the deposition of the sediment they carry across the seabed close inshore. The high-energy waves at the headlands remove any rock fragments that become detached and transport them to the beaches that form at the bayheads.

Erosional coasts

Much of the local variability of coastal scenery results from differing rates of erosion on different types of rock. Bays are cut back rapidly into soft rocks such as clay, sand or gravel. Headlands are evidence that the sea takes longer to remove higher areas of harder rock such as granite or limestone. Despite the enormous power of storm waves, erosion of resistant rocks is slow and relies on any weakness that the sea can exploit.

Joints, faults and bedding planes are etched out by the water and by rock fragments hurled against them by breaking waves. Air compressed into such crevices by water pressure widens and deepens them into cracks and then into caves. In this way a solid cliff face can be eroded to form the great variety of features.

Resistant rocks can form steep, simple cliffs of great height—more than 600 m (2,000 ft) in some places—and the sea may have to undercut them to produce collapse and retreat. Cliffs of weaker rocks rarely reach 100 m (330 ft) in height and are more rapidly eroded by atmospheric processes, by running water and by

landslips. There the role of the sea is largely confined to removing the rock debris from the foot of the cliff. Soft rock cliffs are gently sloping but complex in form.

Coasts of deposition

Although waves bend as they approach the shore, they rarely become completely parallel to the coastline. Wave crests drive sediment obliquely toward the beach, whereas the troughs carry it back directly offshore down the beach slope. In this way, sand and pebbles are transported in a zigzag motion, called longshore drift, away from the areas where they are produced. One such source of material is cliff erosion, but on average about 95 percent of the material moving on to beaches was originally carried to the coast by rivers.

Beaches are built up wherever longshore drift is impeded (for example, by a headland) or where wave and current energy is reduced (as at the head of a bay). An abundant supply of sediment may build a sandbar across the mouth of a bay or in shallow water offshore. Where the coast changes direction, longshore drift may continue in its original direction and build a spit out from the land. Depositional features may become strengthened by vegetation. Plants may take root and bind together newly deposited sediments, but they constitute relatively delicate coasts that are vulnerable to erosion if for any reason they are not continually supplied with fresh deposits of sediment.

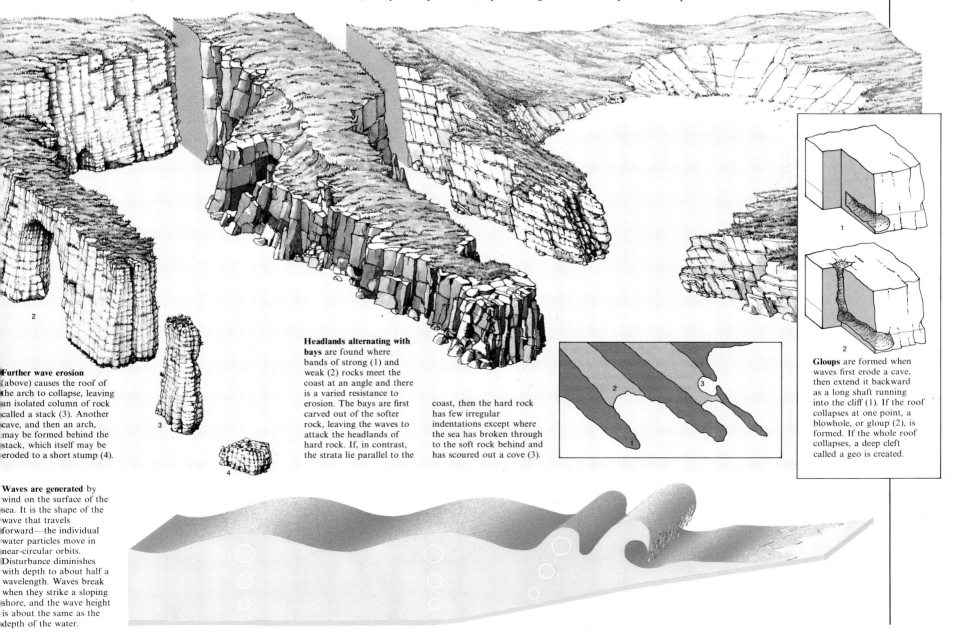

Further wave erosion (above) causes the roof of the arch to collapse, leaving an isolated column of rock called a stack (3). Another cave, and then an arch, may be formed behind the stack, which itself may be eroded to a short stump (4).

Waves are generated by wind on the surface of the sea. It is the shape of the wave that travels forward—the individual water particles move in near-circular orbits. Disturbance diminishes with depth to about half a wavelength. Waves break when they strike a sloping shore, and the wave height is about the same as the depth of the water.

Headlands alternating with bays are found where bands of strong (1) and weak (2) rocks meet the coast at an angle and there is a varied resistance to erosion. The bays are first carved out of the softer rock, leaving the waves to attack the headlands of hard rock. If, in contrast, the strata lie parallel to the coast, then the hard rock has few irregular indentations except where the sea has broken through to the soft rock behind and has scoured out a cove (3).

Gloups are formed when waves first erode a cave, then extend it backward as a long shaft running into the cliff (1). If the roof collapses at one point, a blowhole, or gloup (2), is formed. If the whole roof collapses, a deep cleft called a geo is created.

Landscape-makers: Wind and Weathering

Winds are part of the global circulation of air and they can affect landforms wherever surface material is loose and unprotected by vegetation. The effects of a strong wind are a familiar sight—whether in the dust clouds that rise from a plowed field after a dry spell, or in the sand swept along the beach on a windy day. Weathering is the disintegration and decomposition of rocks through their exposure to the atmosphere. It includes the changes that destroy the original structure of rocks, and few on the Earth's surface have not been weathered at one time or another in the history of our evolving landscape.

Active and fixed dunes in Africa and western Asia

Sand dunes cover only 20 percent of the world's deserts, and tend to be concentrated in a small number of sand seas, or ergs, such as the Erg Bourharet in Algeria (above).

Longitudinal, or seif, dunes (below) are long, narrow ridges that lie parallel to the direction of prevailing winds. Surface heating and wind flow produce vertical spiraling motions of air.

Direction of wind

Most sand seas today are being actively molded by winds. The landscape has long been shaped by wind, and some dune fields produced in dry climates in the distant past may be "fossilized" now by soils and vegetation cover. Desertification often occurs where this vegetation is disturbed by man.

Fixed sand dunes

Active sand dunes

EROSION AND WEATHERING

Winds result from the differential heating of regions of the globe. They act indirectly as agents of erosion through water or waves, but they also directly affect the surface of the Earth, molding landforms either by erosion or deposition. The nature of weathering processes and the rate at which they operate depend upon climate, the properties of the rock and the conditions of the biosphere. Both wind erosion and the various weathering processes are significant landscape-makers.

Many rocks are formed deep in the Earth, where they are in equilibrium with the forces that created them. If they become exposed at the surface, they are in disequilibrium with atmospheric forces. This brings about the changes —adjustments to atmospheric and organic agents—that we call weathering. Products of weathering are moved by agents of erosion, one of which is the wind. Where the surface is protected, for example by vegetation, the wind has little effect, but where strong winds attack loose surface material that is unprotected, erosion, abrasion and deposition may occur, producing characteristic landforms.

How wind shapes the surface

Strong winds occur in many places, but nowhere are they more effective in forming the surface of the land than in deserts, where their work is largely unhindered by vegetation. There the wind can pick up material and then, charged with sand particles, blast away at the ground, carrying away the debris and depositing it. Many notorious desert winds are associated with sand movement and dust storms—the harmattan of West Africa and the sirocco of the Middle East, for example.

Wind erosion occurs where winds charged with sand attack soils or rock. Dry soils may be broken up and the resulting debris, which includes soil nutrients, is carried away as dust. This poses a serious problem, especially when arid and semiarid lands experience drought. Wind erosion involving the lifting and blowing away of loose material from the ground surface is called deflation.

Erosion by sand and rock fragments carried by winds is called abrasion. In this way winds erode individual surface pebbles into distinctive shapes known as ventifacts. They can also mold larger rock masses into aerodynamic shapes known as yardangs—features that often look rather like upturned rowing boats. Some of these features are so large that they have been identified only since satellite photographs have become available. Finally, winds erode by attrition, which involves the mutual wearing down of particles as they are carried along.

Winds can transport material in three different ways. They can lift loose, sand-sized particles into the air and carry them downwind along trajectories that resemble those of ballistic missiles: the particles rise steeply and descend along gentle flight paths. This produces a bouncing movement known as saltation in a layer extending approximately 1 m (3 ft) above the

in · Direction of wind · cm

Grain path · Rebound

Sand cloud

Surface creep

Loose sand surface

Sand particles move in a series of long jumps—a process called saltation. Particles describe a curved path (above), the height and length of which depends upon the mass of the grain, the wind velocity and the number of other particles moving around. Saltation only occurs in a layer extending up to approximately 1 m (3 ft) above the ground surface. Sand grains moving in this way are also responsible for the abraded base of features such as pedestal rocks (right). These landforms are weathered first—for example by the crystallization of salts—and are then eroded by the sand-laden winds.

Chemical and mechanical weathering occurs in the soil zone. Jointed bedrock assists both processes. The roots of trees help to break up rock, and rainwater gives rise to chemical weathering. Organic acids produced by bacteria in the soil living off decaying organisms also cause decomposition. All these processes contribute toward soil formation.

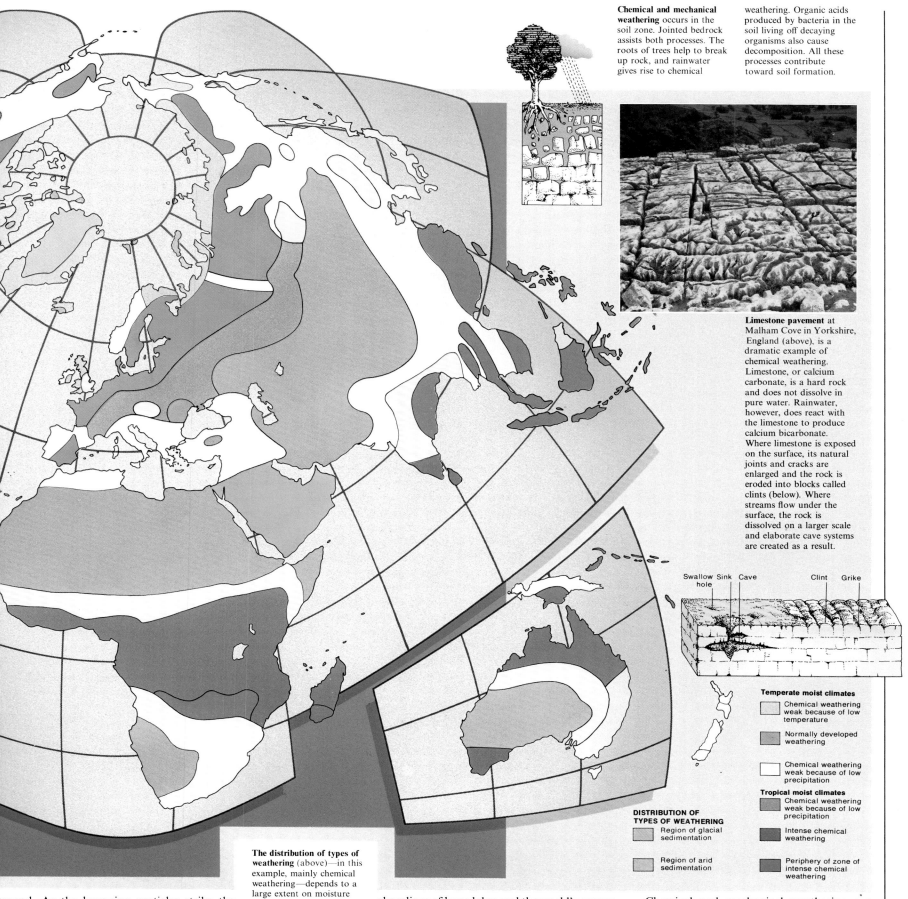

Limestone pavement at Malham Cove in Yorkshire, England (above), is a dramatic example of chemical weathering. Limestone, or calcium carbonate, is a hard rock and does not dissolve in pure water. Rainwater, however, does react with the limestone to produce calcium bicarbonate. Where limestone is exposed on the surface, its natural joints and cracks are enlarged and the rock is eroded into blocks called clints (below). Where streams flow under the surface, the rock is dissolved on a larger scale and elaborate cave systems are created as a result.

Swallow hole | Sink | Cave | Clint | Grike

DISTRIBUTION OF TYPES OF WEATHERING

- Region of glacial sedimentation
- Region of arid sedimentation

Temperate moist climates
- Chemical weathering weak because of low temperature
- Normally developed weathering
- Chemical weathering weak because of low precipitation

Tropical moist climates
- Chemical weathering weak because of low precipitation
- Intense chemical weathering
- Periphery of zone of intense chemical weathering

The distribution of types of weathering (above)—in this example, mainly chemical weathering—depends to a large extent on moisture and temperature. When classifying regions with different rates of chemical weathering in terms of climatic zones, many areas of the world can be placed into one of two principal categories: tropical moist climates and temperate moist climates. The white areas on the map are mountain ranges or regions of tectonic activity where there is no appreciable weathering mantle.

ground. As the bouncing particles strike the surface, they push other particles along the ground (creep or drift). Fine particles that are disturbed by saltation rise up into the airflow and are carried away as dust (suspension).

The materials eroded and transported by winds must eventually come to rest in features of deposition, the most extensive of which are sand dunes. Sand seas at first sight appear to be random and complex, rather like a choppy ocean, but their features generally fall into three size groups: small ripples, which have a wavelength of up to 3 m (10 ft) and a height of 20 cm (8 in); dunes, with a wavelength of 20–300 m (65–1,000 ft) and a height of up to 30 m (68 ft); and sand mountains or "draa," which have a wavelength of 1–3 km (0.6–1.5 miles) and rise to a height of up to 200 m (650 ft). Within each size group various forms can be explained in terms of the nature of the sand and the kinds of winds that blow over it. Where winds blow consistently from one direction, long linear dunes form parallel or transverse to the wind direction. Where sand supply is limited, horned "barchan" dunes may form. If winds blow from several directions during a year, then star-shaped dunes and other complex patterns appear. Sand dunes are also common along the

shorelines of large lakes and the world's oceans, where onshore winds can pile quite extensive areas of loose drifting sand.

Agents of weathering

Weathering takes two forms: mechanical weathering breaks up rock without altering its mineral constituents, whereas chemical weathering changes in some way the nature of mineral crystals. One agent of mechanical weathering is temperature change. It used to be thought that rocks disintegrated as a result of a huge daily range of temperature (thermal weathering). Despite travelers' tales of rocks splitting in the desert night with cracks like pistol shots, there is little evidence to support this view. In the presence of water, however, alternate heating and cooling of rocks does result in fracture. Frost is also an effective rock breaker. The freezing of water and expansion of ice in the cracks and pores of rocks create disruptive pressures; alternate freezing and thawing eventually causes pieces of rock to break off in angular fragments. Finally, the roots of plants and trees grow into the joints of rock and widen them, thus loosening the structure of the rock. Animals burrowing through the soil can have a similar effect on rocks.

Chemical and mechanical weathering can work hand in hand. In arid regions, for example, the crystallization of salts results in the weathering of rock. As water evaporates from the rock surface, salt crystals grow (from minerals dissolved in the water) in small openings in the rock. In time these crystals bring to bear enough pressure to break off rock fragments from the parent block.

Chemical weathering is most effective in humid tropical climates, however, and it usually involves the decomposition of rocks as a result of their exposure to air and rainwater, which contains dissolved chemicals. Carbon dioxide from the air, for example, becomes dissolved in rainwater, making it into weak carbonic acid. This reacts with minerals such as calcite, which is found in many rocks. Similarly, rocks can be oxidized by oxygen in the air. This happens to rocks that contain iron, for example, if they are exposed on the surface: a reddish iron oxide is produced which causes the rocks to crumble.

Over many thousands, even millions, of years, the processes of mechanical and chemical weathering have affected many of the rocks on the Earth's surface. When rocks are weakened in such a way, they then fall prey to the agents of erosion—water, ice, winds and waves.

Landscape-makers: Man

Man has done much to reshape the face of the planet since his first appearance on Earth more than two million years ago. Early man did little to harm the environment but, with the rise of agriculture, the landscape began to change. An increasing population and the growth of urban settlements gradually created greater demands for agricultural land and living space. But industrialization during the last 200 years has had the biggest impact. Man's search for and exploitation of the Earth's resources has to a large extent transformed the natural landscape and at the same time created totally artificial man-made environments.

MAN THE GEOLOGICAL AGENT
In 1864 a conservationist named George Perkins Marsh introduced the thesis that "man in fact made the Earth" rather than the converse. The idea of man as a geological agent was further developed in the 1920s. Man modifies the landscape in many ways; sometimes he transforms the Earth completely—he even creates land where no land was before.

Man's major impact on the landscape has been through forest clearance. He made the first attack on natural forests about 8,000 years ago in Neolithic times in northern and western Europe, as revealed by the changing composition of tree pollen deposited in bogs. After Roman times, especially in the Mediterranean region, there was another spate of forest clearance, so that by the Middle Ages little original forest survived in the Old World. As population and emigration increased, it was the turn of trees in the New World and Africa to fall before the axe and plow. Man's present voracious appetite for timber and its products could, if unchecked, clear most of the Earth's great forests by the end of this century.

Forest clearance not only changes the appearance of the landscape but can alter the balance of nature within a region. The hydrological cycle may be affected, and soil erosion may be increased, which in turn chokes rivers with sediment and leads to the silting up of harbors and estuaries. The coastal area of Valencia in Spain, for example, has widened by nearly 4 km (2.5 miles) since Roman times, much of which can be accounted for by forest clearance, and subsequent soil erosion and the deposition of the material by rivers as they near the sea. Reafforestation of an area can reduce soil erosion and the threat of flooding. Landscape management can reduce wind speeds: for example, shelter belts in the Russian steppes have been planted over distances of more than 100 km (62 miles).

Water management
The second great impact of man has been on the waterways of the world. The most spectacular changes are caused by the construction of dams to make vast new lakes. Such projects have frequently had effects far beyond those originally anticipated. The Aswan High Dam on the River Nile was completed in 1970, creating Lake Nasser and making possible the irrigation of an additional 550,000 hectares (1,358,000 acres) in upper Egypt. But some would argue that the dam holds back silt from the rivers and stores it in the lake, a fact that has seriously reduced the rate of silting in the Nile delta. This has resulted in increased salinity and some loss of fertility of the soil, as well as changes to the delta's coastline. The storage of silt in Lake Nasser has caused increased erosion of the riverbed downstream and the undermining of the foundations of bridges and barrages.

Other man-made changes to rivers include straightening and canalization, usually for

Massive power plants (left) symbolize man's modifications to the landscape in modern, industrialized society. Demand for energy and mineral resources has led to the creation of huge holes in the ground like this borax mine (below left) in the Mojave desert in California. The open pit is 100 m (330 ft) deep, 1,460 m (4,800 ft) long and 915 m (3,000 ft) wide. In opening up resource areas in Brazil, the Trans-Amazonian highway has disturbed the forest (below).

ong Kong's bustling aterfront (below) captures e true essence of urban an. If space is in short pply, he expands his orld vertically and aximizes his use of every uare meter. Central siness districts in the orld's major cities reflect s concern with space.

flood protection, but also to prevent the channel from shifting. As long ago as the third millennium BC, during the reign of Emperor Yao, a hydraulic engineer was apparently appointed to control the wandering course of the Hwang-Ho (Yellow River), and the system he devised survived for at least 1,500 years. Even so, over the centuries, the river has changed course radically, and today measures are still being taken to control the fine sediment that the river carries and the flooding caused by its deposition. The Missouri River in the United States is estimated to erode material from an area of about 3,680 hectares (9,000 acres) annually over a length of 1,220 km (758 miles). It is little wonder that engineers attempt to control rivers by means of realignment or try to "train" a river's flow by using concrete stays.

New land from old

The continuing pressure of population on food resources and the need to create new agricultural land illustrate still further the impact of man as a landscape shaper. As part of irrigation projects land is often leveled and new waterways are created in the form of canals. Pakistan has one of the most extensive man-made irrigation systems in the world. It controls almost completely the flow of the Indus, Sutlej and Punjab rivers through some 640 km (400 miles) of linking canals.

A huge demand for rice in many parts of southeastern Asia has led to farmers terracing steep slopes on many mountainous islands. In the Netherlands, about one-third of the entire cultivated area of the country is land that has been reclaimed from the sea. In the future more grandiose schemes are likely. Any large-scale expansion of agricultural land in the Soviet Union will be mainly dependent on water supply. There have been plans since the 1930s to divert northward-flowing rivers to irrigated areas in the south and west. This idea, and it is believed that it might become a reality by the turn of the century, could have serious implications for the waters of the Arctic Ocean. If the amount of fresh water flowing into the ocean is reduced, salinity will increase, thus affecting the melting of ice floes and, consequently, sea level.

Man has also made his mark along the coastlines, from small-scale measures, such as

the construction of groynes—wooden piles that reduce the amount of sand that is transported along the beach by wave action—to large-scale man-made harbors.

Modern man, the urban dweller of the machine age, has brought great changes to the face of the landscape. The need for materials for the construction of the urban fabric has led to the creation of huge quarries, in which building stone and road-building materials are extracted from the ground. Demand for energy and minerals leads to extensive modification of the landscape, especially where mineral deposits are near the surface and can be extracted by open-cast mining. The largest holes on Earth (excluding ocean basins) are those that result from the extraction of fuel (coal) and minerals.

The side effects of mining can be detrimental to the environment. Land may subside and despoliation of the landscape by slag heaps, for example, is considerable. Escaping coal dust can suffocate vegetation in a mining area, and gases given off during some mining operations can also damage plant and animal life.

Reclamation of spoiled areas is obligatory in many countries. Old open-cast workings are often filled with water to be used for recreational facilities, and slag heaps are treated and planted with vegetation: research has produced certain strains of plants that will grow even in the most acidic soils.

The true impact of man

During the last hundred years or so man has become much more aware of his role as an agent of landscape creation and destruction. The significance of man the landscape-maker, in comparison with slow, natural changes, is the speed with which he effects transformation, the sheer amount of energy which he can apply to a relatively small area, and the selectiveness and determination with which he applies that energy. Man's increased impact has not been a smooth and continuous process: it has occurred at different rates in different places and at different times. While it can be argued that some landscapes have been constructed which themselves conserve and often beautify the natural environment, man's active role has primarily been destructive: he has transformed the Earth's surface, perhaps irreversibly.

THE DUTCH POLDERS

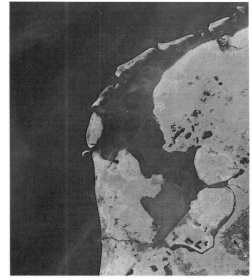

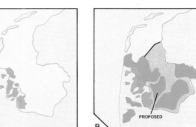

Reclamation of the Dutch polders from the North Sea is an example of man creating land. Many centuries ago a large part of what is now the western Netherlands was beneath the sea. From the 15th to the 17th centuries (A) dykes were constructed to enclose land and protect it against inundation from the sea, and enable it to be farmed. Later, windmills were used to drain away sea water. Further reclamation in the 19th and 20th centuries (B) has brought the total area to

165,000 hectares (408,000 acres). In 1932 a 40 km (25 mile) dam was completed, enclosing the Zuider Zee—which is now a freshwater lake that was renamed the IJsselmeer—and reducing Holland's vulnerable coastline by 320 km (200 miles). To create a polder, a dyke is built and the water pumped out. Reeds are grown to help dry out the soil. After a few years drains are put in to remove water remaining. Newly created polders (light blue) show up well on this satellite image (top).

Man-made environments have become increasingly complex and large scale. Highway construction—this vast interchange (left) is in Chicago—is typical of the extensive use of land for modern transport systems alone. The acreage of land use classified as urban continues to increase. Man's endeavors to make still more land available for his many purposes have extended to cultivating previously inhospitable desert lands (above). More than half the land in Israel is naturally unproductive because of its aridity. By means of elaborate water carriage and storage schemes and scientifically researched irrigation projects, the desert has been totally transformed from a barren wasteland into intensively cultivated fields. Output from agriculture can also be increased by terracing. In densely populated areas, or mountainous regions, as in Luzon in the Philippines (right), man's skillful landscaping has completely reshaped the topography.

Part 3

THE EMERGENCE OF LIFE

How life on Earth began and developed
How life has evolved and spread over the planet
How man came to inherit the Earth

THE STAGES OF LIFE
Simple organic molecules, the precursors of life, could certainly have evolved in Earth's primitive atmosphere. Energy from the Sun, volcanoes and electric storms had the power to combine the basic chemicals into the amino acids and other molecules that are the constituents of living matter, forming droplets of "pre-life" in pools and on shorelines. Concentrations of droplets collected around some minerals, coagulating in a "soup" of long-chain polymers—proteins and nucleic acids which together form the living cell. Thus far have scientists re-created life's origins, but the combining of proteins and nucleic acids into a living unit remains to be achieved.

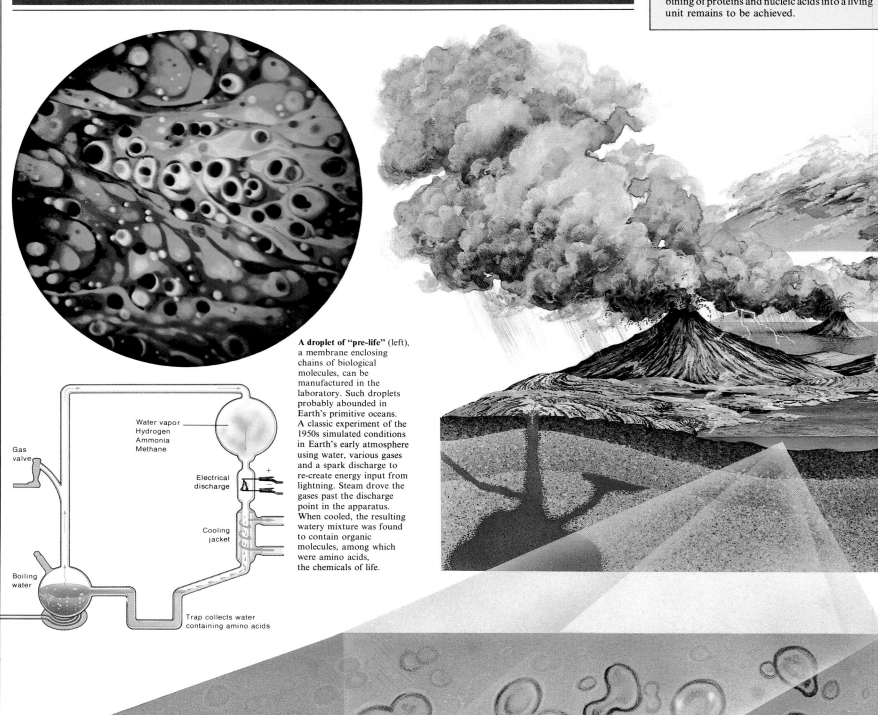

A droplet of "pre-life" (left), a membrane enclosing chains of biological molecules, can be manufactured in the laboratory. Such droplets probably abounded in Earth's primitive oceans. A classic experiment of the 1950s simulated conditions in Earth's early atmosphere using water, various gases and a spark discharge to re-create energy input from lightning. Steam drove the gases past the discharge point in the apparatus. When cooled, the resulting watery mixture was found to contain organic molecules, among which were amino acids, the chemicals of life.

Water vapor
Hydrogen
Ammonia
Methane

Gas valve

Electrical discharge

Cooling jacket

Boiling water

Trap collects water containing amino acids

LIFE BEGINS
A "primordial soup" of organic molecules, each separated from the water by a membrane, formed thick concentrations in Earth's shallow pools. From these evolved the long-chain polymers that form proteins and nucleic acids in every living cell.

34

The Source of Life

Life may have come to Earth from outer space – some meteorites contain life-like organic molecules – but the basic constituents of life, the biochemical structures called proteins and nucleic acids, could just as well have formed on Earth itself. By simulating possible primitive conditions on Earth, and applying a likely energy source, American scientists of the 1950s manufactured, from inorganic substances, the amino acids that form the subunits of all living things.

Water played a key part in the creation of life on Earth. At first the temperature of the newly formed planet was far too high for water to exist in a liquid state. Instead, it formed a dense atmosphere of steam, which, as the Earth cooled, condensed into droplets of rain that poured down for perhaps thousands of years. This torrential, thundery rain eroded the land and dissolved the minerals, which collected in pools on the surface.

Earth's original atmosphere was also very different from today's. Most importantly, it contained no free oxygen, the gas which makes air-breathing possible; the primitive atmosphere was composed of carbon monoxide, carbon dioxide, hydrogen and nitrogen. But the absence of oxygen created two conditions that are essential if life is to evolve. First, without oxygen the atmosphere could have no layer of ozone (an oxygen compound), which now acts as a barrier to most of the Sun's high-energy radiation (mainly ultraviolet light). Second, the absence of free oxygen meant that any complex chemicals that might be formed would not immediately break down again. Thus the molecules of life could form.

The chemistry of life
Life may be distinguished from nonlife in three ways: living organisms are able to increase the complexity of their parts through synthetic, self-building reactions; they obtain and use energy by breaking down chemical compounds; and they can make new copies of themselves.

It is the combined properties of the chemicals of life that make them so special, not just the chemicals themselves. Experiments in the last few decades have given us a very good idea of how life could have arisen from the simple, non-living chemicals which compose it. In the early 1950s, Harold Urey and Stanley Miller simulated the atmosphere of a primitive world by filling a flask with water, ammonia, methane and hydrogen. They supplied it with energy in the form of heat and an electric spark—to simulate lightning—and the experiment was left to run for a week.

Analyzing the mixture formed, they found it contained many chemicals that are associated with living things, particularly nitrogen compounds called amino acids—the really important chemicals of life. Further experiments brought together other gas mixtures, including the one that is now thought to have covered the young Earth, and these gave similar results, as long as there was no free oxygen present. The resulting mixture of organic compounds in water came to be known as the "primordial

soup," and it is from this "soup" that life may have emerged.

Miller and Urey had shown that the basic substances of life can be derived from a primitive atmosphere. But there are still large gaps in our understanding of how these substances became more organized and self-regulating: in other words, how they became alive. More complex molecular structures somehow developed through the linking up of the basic units to form long, chain-like sequences of larger units, called polymers. But how this happened is still not fully understood.

The two most important classes of biological molecules are proteins and nucleic acids, both of which are polymers. Proteins are the building materials of living matter, the chief components of muscles, skin and hair. They also form enzymes—the chemicals that control biochemical reaction in living cells. Nucleic acids— DNA (deoxyribonucleic acid) and RNA (ribonucleic acid)—are so called because they are found in the central nuclei of cells. They are the cell's genetic material, the raw stuff of heredity. They act as the memories and the messengers of life, storing information in units called genes, and releasing that information to the cells when it is needed. Nucleic acids can reproduce themselves and, without this ability, life would not exist or continue.

The basic units that link together to form proteins are amino acids, and all proteins in living organisms are made up of just 20 different amino acids. In chemical terms, a protein molecule is a polymer consisting of a long chain of amino acid units joined together in a particular sequence, and the code to this sequence is held by DNA.

How living chemicals joined
Experiments with simulated primordial conditions have produced many amino acids other than the 20 commonly found in proteins. All amino acids (and other types of chemicals) tend to "stick" onto the surface of clay, but those 20 found in proteins stick particularly well to clays rich in the metal nickel. This suggests that the first proteins may have been formed in pools or on the fringes of seas, where the primordial soup was in contact with nickel-rich clays. There heat from the Sun or a volcano could have combined the amino acids to form a primitive protein.

The four classes of chemicals that form the basic components of nucleic acids have also, like the amino acids, been "cooked up" in a primordial soup, and they too will stick to clay to form long-chain polymers. And, just as nickel-rich clays are best at absorbing the amino acid constituents of protein, so clays rich in zinc absorb the building blocks of nucleic acids. This suggests that such clays could have been the birthplace of genes, which are the "messengers" of inheritance.

However, the coupling of proteins and nucleic acids, which together form the living cell, has yet to be explained, and it is improbable that proteins or nucleic acids alone could have provided the basis for life.

The Russian biochemist I. A. Oparin has shown that, in water, solutions of polymers (such as proteins) have a tendency to form droplets surrounded by an outer membrane very like that which encloses living cells. As these droplets grow by absorbing more polymers, some split in two when they become too large for stability. If such a droplet had protein enzymes to harness energy and make more polymers, and if it had nucleic acids with instructions for making those proteins, and if each new droplet received a complete copy of the nucleic acid instructions, the droplet would be alive—it would be a living cell.

THE RADIANT SUN
A dense atmosphere of water vapor and various gases—but not oxygen— formed round the cooling planet Earth after its creation 4,600 million years ago. Oxygen in the atmosphere would have prevented the evolution of life from nonliving organic matter by blocking the Sun's ultraviolet radiation (which may have provided energy for the forming of organic compounds), and free oxygen would also have destroyed such compounds as they began to accumulate.

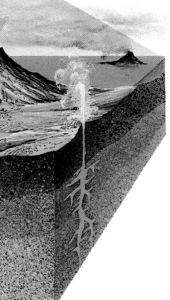

THE PRIMITIVE ATMOSPHERE
Volcanic eruptions drove water vapor and gases into the atmosphere of the young Earth; lightning and other discharges of atmospheric electricity accompanied the torrential rain; dissolved minerals collected in the pools. These were some of the preconditions for life on Earth, whereby mixtures of organic compounds in water may have combined to form more complex units essential for life.

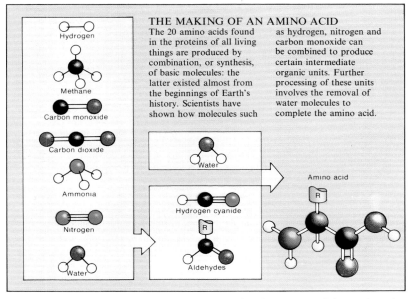

THE MAKING OF AN AMINO ACID
The 20 amino acids found in the proteins of all living things are produced by combination, or synthesis, of basic molecules: the latter existed almost from the beginnings of Earth's history. Scientists have shown how molecules such as hydrogen, nitrogen and carbon monoxide can be combined to produce certain intermediate organic units. Further processing of these units involves the removal of water molecules to complete the amino acid.

Hydrogen

Methane

Carbon monoxide

Carbon dioxide

Ammonia

Nitrogen

Water

Water

Hydrogen cyanide

Aldehydes

Amino acid

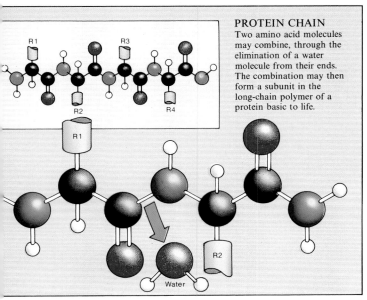

PROTEIN CHAIN
Two amino acid molecules may combine, through the elimination of a water molecule from their ends. The combination may then form a subunit in the long-chain polymer of a protein basic to life.

Water

The Structure of Life

All life forms stem from a single cell, and every cell contains in its nucleus instructions for the re-creation of the organism of which it forms a part. These are encoded in chromosomes, which contain the miraculous molecular substance of DNA, sectioned into units of heredity called genes. The genetic code determines in detail the physical characteristics of an individual creature, so that variations in DNA cause variations in the individual. Scientists believe that it is the interaction of the individual variation with the environment that ultimately leads to the evolution of the similar, interbreeding groups of creatures that are known as species.

THE HIDDEN SECRET
Dramatic discoveries in recent decades have revolutionized biology, the primary life science. Scientists can now trace parts of the genetic blueprint that lays down the pattern for every form of life, linking the large-scale unfolding of species that we know as evolution with the ultramicroscopic activity of the molecules within the nucleus of every cell. This may be the secret behind the rich diversity of life on Earth.

Deoxyribonucleic acid (DNA) consists of a "backbone" of alternating sugar and phosphate molecules, and to each sugar is attached one of four nitrogenous bases (adenine, guanine, thymine and cytostine, or A, G, T, C). A single gene might contain 2,000 of these bases, and in the body cell of a human being the 46 chromosomes (thread-like bodies of DNA and protein) run to 3,000 million bases. The sequence of these bases stores the information for making amino acids into proteins, just as the sequence of letters in this sentence stores the information for making a particular verbal structure. But the DNA alphabet has only four letters (A, G, T, C).

The thread of life

DNA is a double molecule, resembling a twisted ladder, its two main strands twining around each other to form the famous double helix. The strands are linked by pairs of bases—A and T, or G and C—whose shape is such that each pair fits together neatly, like pieces of a jigsaw, to form the rungs of the DNA ladder. As a result, the information on the strands can be duplicated by "unzipping" the double helix and making new strands by using the old ones as templates. DNA stores, duplicates and passes on the information that makes life alive.

Cells multiply by splitting in two, and each newly made cell thus gets instructions for its existence by the mechanism of heredity, the gene. But heredity is a word more often applied to the passing on of DNA from an organism to its offspring. In sexual reproduction the offspring gets some of the DNA (usually half) from one parent, and the rest from the other, ending up with a unique mix all of its own.

The laws of heredity

Man has long known that characteristics can be passed on from one generation to the next, for he has been selectively breeding crops and animals for thousands of years. However, it was not until the mid-nineteenth century that an obscure Austrian monk, Gregor Mendel (1822–84), discovered the laws that govern inheritance, and his work was ignored until the beginning of the twentieth century, when more powerful microscopes made possible the direct observation of the cell.

Mendel experimented with pea plants because they had easily recognizable traits, and because, although normally self-fertilizing, they could be cross-fertilized with pollen from a different plant. Mendel made many crosses between different pure-bred plants and found that in the offspring, or hybrids, some characters always prevailed over others: red flowers over white, tall plants over short, and so on. He called the prevailing characters dominant, and the nonprevailing characters recessive. He then let the first-generation hybrids self-fertilize, and found not only that the recessive traits reappeared in the hybrids' offspring, but also that they reappeared in a constant proportion of three dominant to one recessive; the second generation contained three times as many red-flowered peas as white-flowered peas.

To explain his results, Mendel proposed that each plant had two hereditary "factors"— today called alleles—for each character, and that the dominant factor suppressed the recessive factor. If a plant inherited both a dominant and a recessive factor, the dominant one would prevail. Only if both factors were recessive would the recessive character be apparent. Mendel found many other pairs of traits where one form was dominant and the other recessive. He established that permutations arising from the crossing of the two first-generation hybrids allows the dominant gene to be present in three out of four crosses in the second generation; but

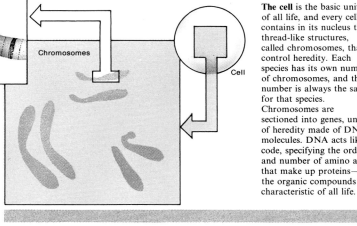

Genes

Chromosomes

Cell

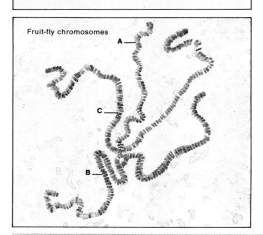

Protein (myoglobin)   Amino acids

Fruit-fly chromosomes

A

C

B

The cell is the basic unit of all life, and every cell contains in its nucleus the thread-like structures, called chromosomes, that control heredity. Each species has its own number of chromosomes, and the number is always the same for that species. Chromosomes are sectioned into genes, units of heredity made of DNA molecules. DNA acts like code, specifying the order and number of amino acid that make up proteins— the organic compounds characteristic of all life.

Chromosomes (below left) of the fruit fly, much magnified, show bands of DNA arranged in sections that correspond exactly with specific genes, the chemical units of heredity. The proof of this correspondence came when the American geneticist Hermann Muller introduced the use of ionizing radiation to damage the fruit flies' chromosomes at ultra-microscopic points, causing precise point mutations in offspring of parents whose DNA had been damaged at the places indicated. Random mutations may occur in any organism, and not only as a result of radiation. A gradual accumulation of minor mutations may lead to evolutionary change.

Fruit fly
Drosophila melanogaster

A   Curly wings

B   Dark body

C   No wings

in the fourth cross, only the two recessive alleles of the genes are present. So there is always a three-to-one ratio of dominant to recessive.

Theories of evolution

Mendel's work was of course unknown to his contemporaries, Charles Darwin and Alfred Russel Wallace, who even then were providing solutions to the major mystery of biology—the way that species evolve, change and develop over time. Evolution was not a new idea in Darwin's day. In 1809 the French naturalist Jean-Baptiste Lamarck had proposed a theory of the inheritance of acquired characteristics, suggesting that new habits learned by an organism in response to environmental change may become physically incorporated in the animal's descendants. For instance, the fact that the ancestral giraffe had to stretch its neck to reach food might give its offspring long necks to enable them to reach food more easily. Less satisfactory than the "natural selection" theory of Darwin and Wallace (who independently reached the same conclusion), Lamarckism founders on the fact that there is no genetic mechanism enabling acquired characters to pass on in this way.

Darwin's theory of natural selection has three key elements: all individuals vary, and some variations are passed on to the next generation; the gap between the potential and the actual number of offspring reproduced by organisms is very wide and implies that not all will survive; organisms best adapted to the environment will survive, their offspring will have been selected, and the favorable variation

will spread through the population, perhaps eventually changing it.

Genetic variation, the mainspring of natural selection, is reflected in variations of DNA, the material substance of heredity. Changes in the order of DNA's nitrogenous bases—called mutations—produce changes in the proteins which are usually, but not always, harmful. More important than these is the effect of genes recombining in sexually reproduced offspring.

Sexual reproduction provides the offspring with two sets of DNA, one from each parent. The processes that give rise to a half-set of chromosomes in a sperm or egg shuffle and recombine the genes on each chromosome to provide new combinations. Then, when sperm and egg fuse together at fertilization, the half-sets come together and even more combinations are produced. The world's enormous diversity of life can be explained in terms of a struggle that favors certain genetic combinations.

Iiwi
Vestiaria coccinea

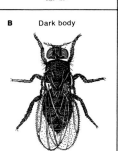

Apapane
Himatione sanguinea

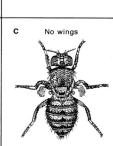

Laysan finch
Psittiros cantans

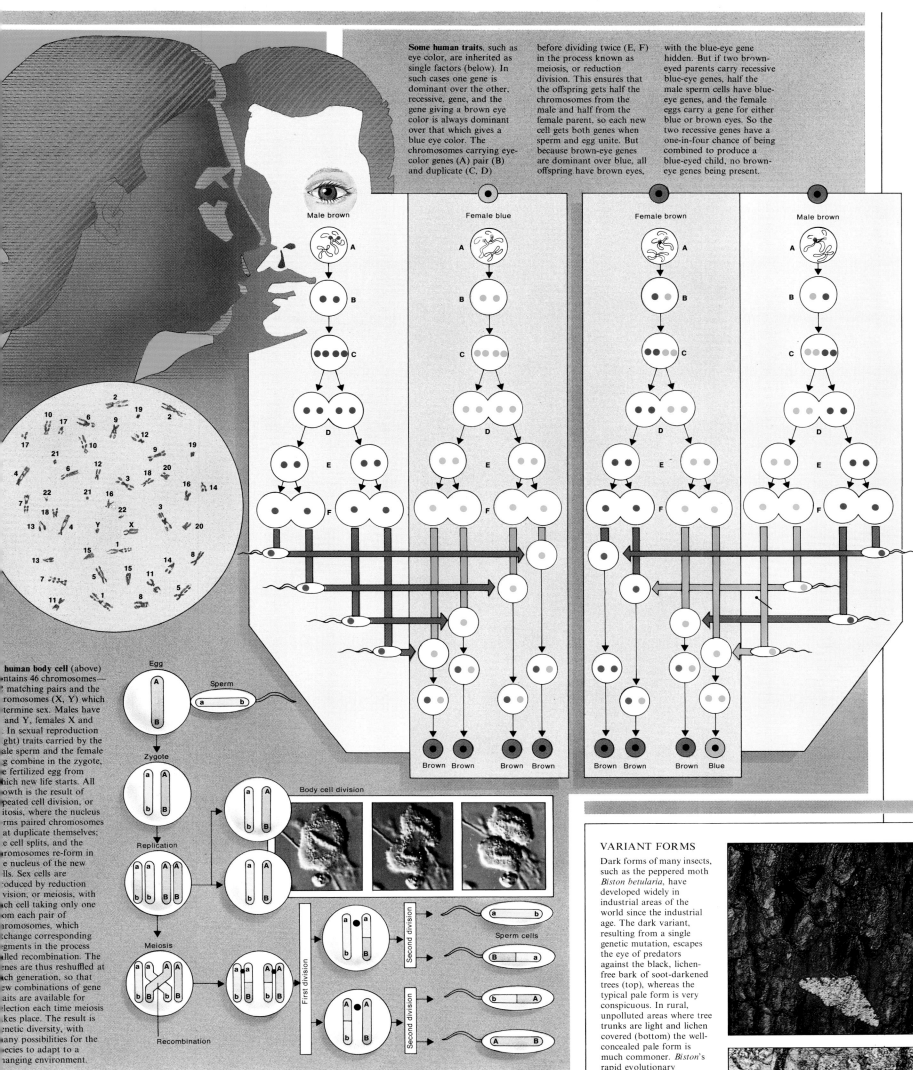

Some human traits, such as eye color, are inherited as single factors (below). In such cases one gene is dominant over the other, recessive, gene, and the gene giving a brown eye color is always dominant over that which gives a blue eye color. The chromosomes carrying eye-color genes (A) pair (B) and duplicate (C, D)

before dividing twice (E, F) in the process known as meiosis, or reduction division. This ensures that the offspring gets half the chromosomes from the male and half from the female parent, so each new cell gets both genes when sperm and egg unite. But because brown-eye genes are dominant over blue, all offspring have brown eyes,

with the blue-eye gene hidden. But if two brown-eyed parents carry recessive blue-eye genes, half the male sperm cells have blue-eye genes, and the female eggs carry a gene for either blue or brown eyes. So the two recessive genes have a one-in-four chance of being combined to produce a blue-eyed child, no brown-eye genes being present.

Male brown   Female blue   Female brown   Male brown

A   B   C   D   E   F

Brown Brown   Brown Brown   Brown Brown   Brown Blue

human body cell (above) ...ntains 46 chromosomes— ...matching pairs and the ...romosomes (X, Y) which ...termine sex. Males have ...and Y, females X and ...In sexual reproduction (right) traits carried by the ...ale sperm and the female ...g combine in the zygote, ...e fertilized egg from ...hich new life starts. All ...owth is the result of ...peated cell division, or ...itosis, where the nucleus ...rms paired chromosomes ...at duplicate themselves; ...e cell splits, and the ...romosomes re-form in ...e nucleus of the new ...lls. Sex cells are ...oduced by reduction ...vision, or meiosis, with ...ch cell taking only one ...om each pair of ...romosomes, which ...tchange corresponding ...gments in the process ...lled recombination. The ...nes are thus reshuffled at ...ch generation, so that ...ew combinations of gene ...aits are available for ...lection each time meiosis ...kes place. The result is ...enetic diversity, with ...any possibilities for the ...ecies to adapt to a ...anging environment.

Egg   Sperm   Zygote   Replication   Meiosis   Recombination   Body cell division   First division   Second division   Sperm cells

diversity of forms (left) ...as stemmed from a single ...ncestor of the Hawaiian ...oneycreeper, which now ...umbers 14 species. These ...ave adapted in their mid-...acific isolation to fill ...iches usually taken by ...ther birds, ranging from ...e nectar-feeding iiwi to ...e Laysan finch with its ...ick beak for cracking ...eeds, and the short-billed ...apane, which includes

insects in its diet. But the honeycreepers' success in divergence may have led to overspecialization, with at least eight species now extinct. The Australian marsupial mouse and the Indian spiny mouse (right) look very similar, due to the fact that they fill similar ecological niches, but they belong to groups evolving separately for almost 100 million years.

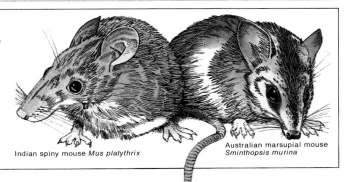

Indian spiny mouse *Mus platythrix*   Australian marsupial mouse *Sminthopsis murina*

VARIANT FORMS

Dark forms of many insects, such as the peppered moth *Biston betularia*, have developed widely in industrial areas of the world since the industrial age. The dark variant, resulting from a single genetic mutation, escapes the eye of predators against the black, lichen-free bark of soot-darkened trees (top), whereas the typical pale form is very conspicuous. In rural, unpolluted areas where tree trunks are light and lichen covered (bottom) the well-concealed pale form is much commoner. *Biston*'s rapid evolutionary response is remarkable: in 1849 only one dark example was recorded at Manchester, England, but by 1900 98% of the moths caught in the area were of the dark type. A similar change occurred in other industrial areas, during the period when the most coal was being burned and the population was most rapidly expanding. But with today's clean-air laws the number of pale moths in these areas is once again on the increase.

Earliest Life Forms

Earth's original atmosphere lacked oxygen, without which there could be no survival for air-breathing creatures. This vital gas was supplied by life itself, in the form of microscopic organisms that flourished in the atmosphere of the time and emitted oxygen as "waste." In this way a breathable atmosphere built up; increasingly complex life forms were able to develop in the seas; early plants and insects gained a foothold on the shores; and, finally, larger animals could survive on land.

The Solar System forms
5,000 million years
Earth forms
4,000
Oldest micro-fossils
Oxygen-creating bacteria
Stromatolites, blue-green algae
3,000
Ozone shield forms
Oxygen in atmosphere
2,000
Breathable atmosphere
Many oxygen-using animals
Sexual reproduction
1,000
Multi-cellular life
900
800
700
Soft-bodied animals

A BREATHABLE ATMOSPHERE

Without oxygen, life as we know it could not exist; yet Earth's original atmosphere contained practically none. The oxygenation of the atmosphere was the work of the planet's first life—primeval bacteria and algae. Of these, some released oxygen as waste while consuming carbon dioxide or nitrogen in photosynthesis. Colonies of algae forming stromatolites ("stony carpets") generated even more oxygen, but this was first taken up by ocean rocks, visible today as "banded iron formations." Once all the ocean rocks were oxidized, an oxygen-rich atmosphere could develop, with an ozone layer to filter out harmful radiation from the Sun.

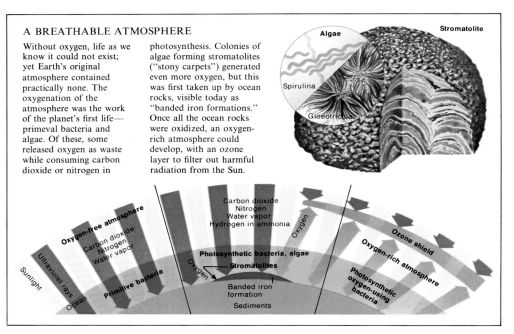

Scientists have identified bacteria-like microfossils in the rocks that were formed more than 3,500 million years ago. Some of these organisms appear to have been capable of photosynthesis—the process of utilizing sunlight, water and carbon dioxide for "food," with release of oxygen as the vitally important by-product. As a result, surplus oxygen very gradually accumulated in the Earth's atmosphere, forming an upper-atmosphere shield of ozone (which kept out damaging ultraviolet radiation from the Sun) and providing an oxygen-rich atmosphere in which breathing life could develop.

At least five types of microfossil have been found in ancient sediments of Western Australia, aged about 3,560 million years, and these provide the earliest evidence of life so far discovered. Other early proof of life comes from the so-called "stromatolites," some of which may date back as far as 3,400 million years. These curious columns, growing in warm, shallow waters, are formed of blue-green algae which have entrapped chalky sediments, bacteria and other microfossils. Their study is made easier by the fact that similar structures have developed at later geological times, and some are even being formed at the present day.

Living below the surface of the water and not initially reliant on oxygen for life, such bacteria and algae were shielded from the Sun's ultraviolet rays as they imperceptibly altered the Earth's atmosphere. For hundreds of millions of years life of this kind persisted, with few obvious developments or changes.

Breathing life
About 1,800 million years ago, the effects of these microscopic photosynthesizers became dramatically apparent in the "rusting" of the ocean sediments, when the red color of the rocks being formed at that time indicates that there was enough free oxygen on Earth to bring about the process known as oxidation. Once the ocean rocks capable of absorbing oxygen had done so, forming the red "banded iron formations" known to geologists, oxygen could enter the atmosphere in ever greater quantities.

It has been estimated that a breathable atmosphere existed on Earth about 1,700 million years ago, and aerobic (oxygen-using) organisms first became abundant not very long afterwards. These organisms were single celled, and it may have been almost 1,000 million years before multicellular animals evolved. The fossilized remains of animals alive 800 million years ago have been found in many parts of the world, but it is not yet known whether multicellular animals had a long history before these earliest known forms, or whether they had developed and radiated rapidly from a creature capable of feeding as well as photosynthesizing.

One of the earliest collections of animals of this type was discovered in the Ediacara Sandstones of the Flinders Range in Australia, where some 650 million years ago the rocks once formed part of an ancient beach. Here a spectacular collection of soft-bodied animals, similar to today's coelenterates (such as jellyfish) and worms, was washed ashore and preserved in silt from the nearby shallow sea. Comparable, mainly floating forms have been found in other parts of the world in rocks dating from between 650 and 580 million years ago.

The first vertebrates
One of the most important changes in animal life seems to have occurred about 580 million years ago. At that date many creatures evolved hard, protective shells, which also acted as areas of muscle attachment and as support for their bodies—in other words, as external skeletons. Hard shells were more easily preserved as fossils than the soft bodies of earlier animals, so rich collections have been recovered from rocks of the Cambrian Period, beginning 580 million years ago, as well as from later strata.

The first fish-like animals—the earliest true vertebrates—are found in rocks of the Ordovician Period, from about 500 million years ago, and these were in many ways very similar to the lampreys and hagfishes of today. But unlike them, these ancient creatures were heavily armored with external bone. They must have been poor swimmers, living mainly on the seabed and filtering edible particles from the sediments, which they sucked into their jawless mouths. From them arose true fishes, with backbones, jaws and teeth, and they came to replace the less efficient earlier forms.

During the Devonian Period, about 400 million years ago, the fishes diversified greatly, adapting to fit all kinds of aquatic environments. Some grew to a huge size, such as *Dunkleosteus*, which achieved a length of up to 9 m (29 ft 7 in), although it belonged to a group of fishes that retained heavy armor. Some of these curious creatures probably used their stilt-like pectoral fins to hitch themselves across the beds of the pools in which they lived.

From water to land
The fishes that teemed in the seas and fresh waters of the Devonian world found their way into difficult environments such as swamps and oasis pools, where there was a danger of drying out in the warmer weather. Many of these fishes had rudimentary lungs, and one group developed powerful jointed fins.

Such marginal habitats were not ideal for fishes, but they were nevertheless rich in species, and it is from them that the first land vertebrates developed. When the water dried up they survived, for their strong fins held them up so that they did not flop over helplessly.

They found themselves in a new, dry world, but one which was already inhabited, at least round the water's edges, with plants related to modern liverworts, mosses and club mosses. There were also numerous invertebrate animals such as millipedes, spiders and wingless insects. These plants and animals provided shelter and food, so that the environment was not wholly hostile to larger animals.

The first steps on land probably took the form of strong flexions of the body—desperate swimming movements which swung the fins forward, pegging the animal's position in the drying mud. But in a very short time geologically, animals had evolved in which the rays of the lobe fins had vanished, leaving stubby legs with which the animals—no longer fishes but amphibians—could haul themselves over land. But they still had to return to water to breed and lay eggs.

THE FIRST SHELLED CREATURES
These evolved (right) in the seas when conditions allowed soft-bodied life to form protective casings. In the fossil record of 550 million years ago, soft and shelled forms are found. The trilobites (1, 2, 3)—a now extinct order of woodlouse-like animals—dominated the scene, but other early arthropods (4) included a possible insect ancestor (5), and there may even have been an ancestor to fish (6). Sponges (7), crinoids (8), early moluscs (9), bristleworms (10) and lampshells (11) were plentiful, but other creatures (12) are bewilderingly strange.

THE FIRST AMPHIBIANS
Amphibians (1) emerged some 345 million years ag (right), inhabiting swamp environments with luxuria vegetation—club mosses and ferns (2, 3) that made up the early coal forests. Lungfish (4) were well adapted to life in oxygen-poor waters, but the mov to land was probably mad by related fish with a passage linking nostrils to throat—*Eusthenopteron* (5 Land offered food (6, 7, 8 and suitably damp conditions for a possibly stranded aquatic animal.

Palaeozoic				Mesozoic			Cenozoic	
500	400		300		200	100		0

Millions of years ago

A timescale of life on Earth emerges from the record of fossils embedded in rock strata. Major breaks in faunas (animal assemblages) separate eras coinciding roughly with periods of intense mountain-building activity. These eras are broken down into geological periods, which are separated by lesser faunal breaks and which are generally named from the area where rocks of that age were first discovered. The geological eras and periods do not imply particular rock types.

600 | Shelled/skeletal animals | CAMBRIAN | 550 | First fishes | ORDOVICIAN

THE AGE OF
JELLYFISH
ellyfish (left) and other soft-
odied animals flourished
n the pre-Cambrian seas,
nore than 600 million
ears ago. The forms of
ne group, imprinted on
and, have been preserved
s fossils in the Australian
diacara Sandstones. They
nclude varieties similar to
nodern jellyfish (1, 2);
orm-like crawlers (3); sea
ens (4) very like modern
pes; segmented worms
5); "three-legged"
reatures like no known
nimal (6); and sand casts
f burrowing worms (7).

LIFE ON SEA AND LAND

For more than half the Earth's existence, its atmosphere has been hostile to air-breathing life. Then, about 1,600 million years ago, the photosynthesizing action of minute organisms built up enough free oxygen in the atmosphere for more complex oxygen-dependent forms to develop. The first multicellular life led to the soft-bodied animals of the pre-Cambrian time—worms, jellyfish and sea pens. About 580 million years ago many animals developed hard parts, including shells. Over 1,200 new marine species date from this period, and the evolutionary explosion came to fill the Earth's seas with fishes. Some of these had powerful jointed fins and rudimentary lungs, and lived in swamps where primitive plants and insects had already made the move to land. As the pools dwindled the stranded animals could survive by breathing air.

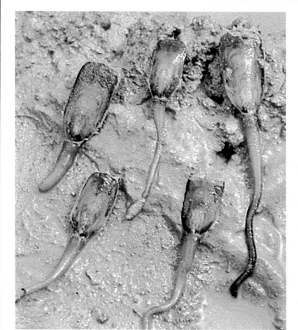

LIVING FOSSILS

Some life forms that emerged 570 million years ago have survived virtually unchanged to the present day. These "living fossils" include *Lingula* (left), today found in warm, brackish coastal waters, poor in oxygen and unsuited to most life, off the Pacific and Indian oceans. *Neopilina* (below), a primitive marine mollusc first found alive in 1952, has features unlike other molluscs but suggesting much closer affinities with the annelids (worms) and arthropods (insects, crabs, etc.).

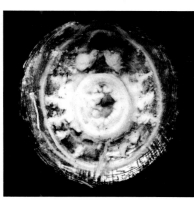

THE AGE OF JELLYFISH
1 Jellyfish (*Ediacaria*)
2 Jellyfish (*Medusina*)
3 Flatworm (*Dickinsonia costata*)
4 Sea pens (*Rangea, Charnia*)
5 Segmented worms (*Spriggina floundersi*)
6 Unknown animal (*Tribrachidium*)
7 Burrowing worm (fossil casts)
8 Sponges and algae (hypothetical)

THE FIRST SHELLED CREATURES
1 Trilobites (*Waptia*)
2 Trilobites (*Marella splendens*)
3 Trilobite (*Olenoides serratus*)
4 Primitive arthropod (*Perspicaris dictynna*)
5 Primitive arthropod (*Aysheaia pedunculata*)
6 Ancestral lancelet fish (*Branchiostoma*)
7 Sponge (*Vauxia*)
8 Crinoids (*Echmatocrinus*)
9 Mollusc (*Wiwaxia*)
10 Bristleworm (*Nereis*)
11 Brachiopod (*Lingulella*)
12 Unknown animal (*Hallucigenia sparsa*)

THE AGE OF FISHES
1 Primitive plant (*Nematophyton*)
2 Psilophite plant (*Asteroxylon*)
3 Psilophite plant (*Rhynia*)
4 Primitive insect (*Rhyniella*)
5 Placoderm fish (*Bothriolepis*)
6 Placoderm fish (*Phyllolepis*)
7 Placoderm fish (*Dunkleosteus*)
8 Early shark (*Cladoselache*)
9 Lungfish (*Dipterus*)
10 Lobe-fin fish (*Osteolepis*)
11 Crustacean (*Montecaris*)

THE FIRST AMPHIBIANS
1 Amphibian (*Ichthyostega*)
2 Club moss (*Cyclostigma*)
3 Fern (*Pseudosporochnus*)
4 Lungfish (*Scaumenacia*)
5 Rhipidistian fish (*Eusthenopteron*)
6 Millipede (*Acantherpestes ornatus*)
7 Early scorpion (*Palaeophonus*)
8 Spider-like creature (*Palaeocharinoides*)
9 Small plant (*Sciadophyton*)

THE AGE OF FISHES

Fishes (left) filled the brackish Devonian waters, about 350 million years ago, while primitive plants and insects had pioneered the land. Giant weeds (1) grew above muddy waters, and vascular plants (2, 3) colonized the shores, sheltering early insects (4). Primitive fishes (5, 6, 7) remained, but ray-finned types (8)—ancestors of modern fish—were dominant. However, it was from the lobe-finned fishes (9, 10) that the first land vertebrates emerged.

The Age of Reptiles

When the Carboniferous Period began, the world was already populated with animals and plants of many kinds. The oceans were full of fishes, invertebrates and aquatic plants. The land, meanwhile, was producing dramatic new species: giant mosses and ferns, spiders and insects and, most important of all, the rapidly evolving amphibians. These creatures were taking the first evolutionary steps on a path that would lead to some of the most remarkable creatures ever to live – the dinosaurs.

The broad, low-lying, swampy plains of the late Carboniferous provided ideal conditions for the world's early plants. They spread and diversified, and some of them grew to enormous size. Giant club mosses, huge horsetails and luxuriant tree ferns took on the proportions of modern-day trees and formed the world's first forests. These new forests were full of animal life: primitive spiders and scorpions hunting their prey, giant dragonflies hovering over the marshy waters and other insects scavenging or hunting on the mossy forest floor or in the branches of the "trees." In the huge coal-forest swamps, the most advanced of all animals, the amphibians, were rapidly evolving. Some of these would ultimately return to life in the water. But others were developing stronger legs and were becoming better able to cope with an existence on dry land.

It was from this second group that the reptiles evolved—the first animals to be equipped with waterproof skins. Unlike their amphibian ancestors, they could stay out of the water indefinitely without losing their body fluids through their skins. They were no longer tied to the water's edge and the pattern of life was revolutionized. The world was soon inhabited by the first wave of land vertebrates—reptiles, which then rapidly diversified.

Included among these first reptiles were creatures known as sailbacks. They had a row of long, bony spines that supported a great fin running down from the back of their heads to the base of their tails. This whole apparatus functioned as a heat-exchange organ: the fin absorbed heat from the atmosphere in the early, cooler parts of the day, when the animal was cold, and blushed off warmth later, when it became overheated. Unlike the cold-blooded reptiles, sailbacked reptiles could, to a certain extent, regulate their body temperatures.

Mammal-like reptiles

It was only about 50 million years later, however, that animals skeletally identical to mammals were found throughout the world. Almost certainly these creatures had a degree of warm-bloodedness. But they were all rather small—the biggest was no larger than a domestic cat—and this may account for their decline. They were destined to be overshadowed for many millions of years by the dinosaurs.

The late Triassic Period, about 200 million years ago, is marked by a sudden decline in the

THE RULING REPTILES
Seymouria and other advanced amphibians evolved to form the first reptiles, such as *Scutosaurus*. From these a multitude of adaptations evolved. Some herbivores, such as *Corythosaurus*, developed 2,000 or more teeth, to help them consume tough, fibrous food plants. Another herbivorous group attained enormous size—*Brachiosaurus* weighed as much as 80 tonnes—and this may have been an adaptation to regulate body temperature (large objects lose and gain heat more slowly than small objects). Another adaptation, but one that developed mainly in the carnivores, was that of offensive weaponry: *Deinonychus* had a huge sickle-shaped claw on each hind foot and the later *Tyrannosaurus* combined a massive body with a jagged mouth of 60 teeth. Armor plating was a defensive adaptation, produced by herbivores such as *Triceratops*, where speed of movement was developed both by some herbivores and by small carnivores such as *Struthiomimus*.

Corythosaurus

Seymouria

Scutosaurus

Deinonychus

Lystrosaurus

Dimetrodon

THE MAMMAL LINE
Sailbacks such as *Dimetrodon* mark the beginning of mammal history. These reptiles had developed the first method of regulating body temperature—each was equipped with a large fin on its back which acted as a heat-exchange organ, a living solar panel. From these strange creatures, para-mammals such as *Lystrosaurus* evolved, animals with many mammal-like features. Some of the later members of this group, such as *Thrinaxodon*, probably even had fur on their bodies. Then, about 200 million years ago, the first true warm-blooded mammals, such as *Morganucodon*, developed. But by this time the group as a whole was declining in response to reptilian competition. Mammals would have to wait 140 million years before becoming successful again.

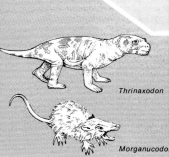

Thrinaxodon

Morganucodon

COAL FORMATION
Coal consists of carbon from plant remains and most of it was formed in the swamp-forests from which reptiles emerged. First, peat formed from rotted vegetation. Sea levels rose, ocean covered the peat bogs and marine sediments were laid down. The resulting pressure converted peat to coal. The cycle recurred and the deepest coal seams were compressed and hardened.

Coal-forming forest swamp
Peat layer
Lignite seam
Bituminous seam
Anthracite seam

Palaeozoic | Mesozoic | Cenozoic
500 400 300 200 100 0
Millions of years ago

Three geological eras mark the evolution of life on Earth. It was the Mesozoic era, beginning 230 million years ago, that spanned the age of reptiles. Until then, throughout the Palaeozoic era, life had been slowly evolving from the primitive organisms that appeared 400 million years earlier.

By the Mesozoic, the earliest reptiles had developed. Among their descendants were dinosaurs and early representatives of the mammalian line. Mammals, however, would have to wait another 165 million years, until the Cenozoic, before they achieved dominance.

The plant communities underwent as many developments in the course of the Mesozoic era as did the reptiles. The end of the Palaeozoic saw changes in climate—the Permian Period was much drier than the Carboniferous. Giant horsetails, ferns and club mosses that had formed the world's first forests gave way to other types of plant: early conifers and their relatives

(the gymnosperms) came the fore. These new species such as the Cycadales, had evolved a new, improved method of reproduction—using seeds not spores. By Jurassic times, the climate had changed again and the moist conditions supported dense forests of ferns and of conifers. The final major Mesozoic development took place in Cretaceous times, when the flowering plants evolved.

Cycadale

Gingko biloba

mammal-like reptiles and by the extraordinary evolutionary radiation of the so-called Archosaurs ("ruling reptiles"). These began to fill every available ecological niche. They evolved into carnivores, herbivores and omnivores. They included the Crocodilians, which adapted to a life in the water; the flying pterosaurs, which were the first vertebrates to fly, and, most important of all, the dinosaurs, whose evolutionary reign over the land was to endure for the next 140 million years.

Dinosaurs adapted well to life on the land. They developed "fully erect" limbs (not unlike those of the later higher mammals) rather than the splayed legs found in most other reptiles. The new position of their limbs, which gave them the necessary mobility on dry land, was also accompanied by a general increase in size. But the dinosaurs were not the only land reptiles of the time; many other forms, including tortoises, snakes and lizards, were also carving their niches during the Mesozoic era.

Similarly, the pterosaurs did not remain the only creatures of the sky. By 170 million years ago, birds in the form of claw-winged *Archaeopteryx* had evolved, and these were to prove a serious challenge to the primitive winged reptiles which had poor flying abilities.

Aquatic reptiles
Just as the land and the air were rapidly inhabited by newly evolving forms, so the water produced many new developments. Several of the Mesozoic reptiles began to adapt to aquatic life in ways often parallel to present-day mammals: the long-necked, fish-eating plesiosaurs led a life much like that of seals; the larger

pliosaurs had a streamlined shape similar to that of certain whales; some mollusc-eating placodonts could be likened to the walrus; and the elegant icthyosaurs were in many ways like dolphins. Large invertebrates were also found in the seas. The most dramatic of these were the ammonites—shelled relatives of the octopus—some of which grew to more than 2 m (6 ft) in size. Among fishes a new type emerged, the Teleosts, and these were destined to become the dominant fishes of the modern world.

Wholesale extinction
At the end of the Cretaceous Period, the reptiles were flourishing. Then suddenly, 65 million years ago, a catastrophe occurred. Virtually every species, including all the large animals, were wiped out. Throughout the Mesozoic, a series of dinosaurs and other reptiles had been evolving and slowly becoming extinct, but they were always replaced by other species. This wholesale extinction was unprecedented.

The cause of the catastrophe is unknown, but since the nature of the Earth itself was unchanged, it seems likely that some outside phenomenon was responsible. One theory suggests that a large meteorite collided with the Earth, throwing enough dust into the atmosphere to blot out the sun for several years—long enough to kill almost all the green plants on land and in the sea. If this was the case, only small animals that fed on carrion, decaying vegetation, seeds or nuts could hope to survive. Whatever the cause, the reign of the reptiles was at an end, leaving the small, adaptable mammals and birds to recolonize the virtually empty planet during the Cenozoic era.

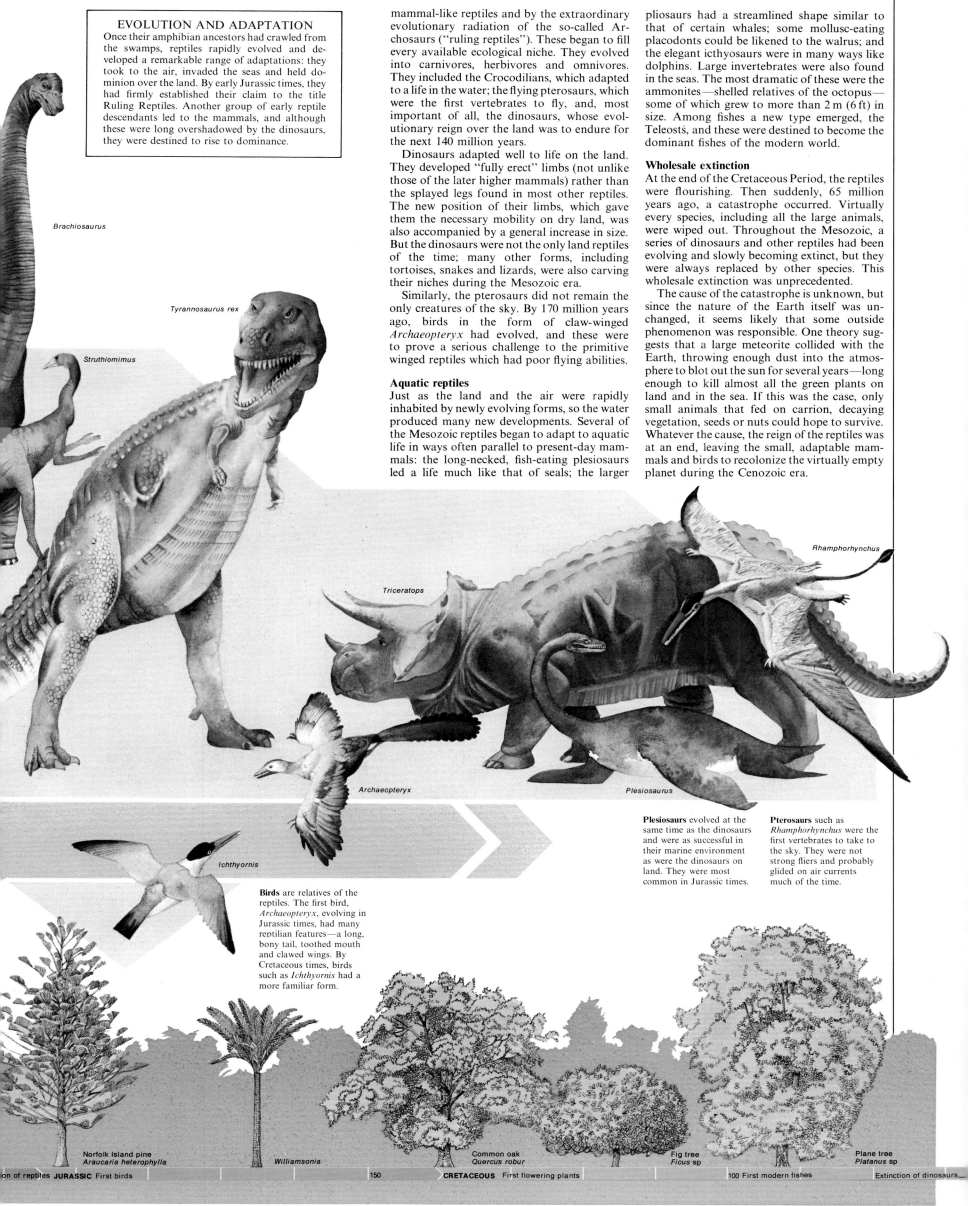

Brachiosaurus

Tyrannosaurus rex

Struthiomimus

Triceratops

Rhamphorhynchus

Archaeopteryx

Plesiosaurus

Ichthyornis

Plesiosaurs evolved at the same time as the dinosaurs and were as successful in their marine environment as were the dinosaurs on land. They were most common in Jurassic times.

Pterosaurs such as *Rhamphorhynchus* were the first vertebrates to take to the sky. They were not strong fliers and probably glided on air currents much of the time.

Birds are relatives of the reptiles. The first bird, *Archaeopteryx*, evolving in Jurassic times, had many reptilian features—a long, bony tail, toothed mouth and clawed wings. By Cretaceous times, birds such as *Ichthyornis* had a more familiar form.

Norfolk Island pine
Araucaria heterophylla

Williamsonia

Common oak
Quercus robur

Fig tree
Ficus sp

Plane tree
Platanus sp

on of reptiles **JURASSIC** First birds | 150 | **CRETACEOUS** First flowering plants | 100 First modern fishes | Extinction of dinosaurs

The Age of Mammals

After the time of the great dying, 65 million years ago, reptiles never regained the importance they had achieved during the Mesozoic era. A new era, the Cenozoic, had begun. On the continental landmasses, mammals and birds, newly released from 160 million years of reptilian domination, began to occupy their niches in the rich, empty habitats. They flourished and diversified, and the cold-blooded reptiles became second-class citizens in a world of warm-blooded animals.

While reptiles still dominated the world, during the late Mesozoic, a new group of mammals had arisen. These were the first creatures on Earth to give birth to fully formed, live young. Until this time, the most advanced of the mammals had been marsupials whose young were still virtually embryos at birth and had to develop in the mother's pouch, or marsupium. The new mammals had evolved a more sophisticated system—the mother retained the fetus safely inside her body until it was fully formed, nourishing it during this time through a special organ, the placenta, developed during pregnancy. These mammals, the placentals, were destined to become the major mammalian group.

Although all the Mesozoic placentals were small, they had already evolved into a number of different forms that existed alongside the dinosaurs. Besides the insectivores, which were the ancestral type, they included early representatives of the Primates (precursors of modern monkeys and apes), the Carnivores, and the now extinct Condylarthrans (primitive hoofed mammals). When suddenly, 65 million years ago, there was no longer competition from the large land reptiles, these early groups rapidly evolved and extravagant forms developed.

But just as the first reptiles had passed through an early evolution, largely to be replaced by a second evolutionary wave, so the first large mammals were, in many cases, superseded by other, more successful lines. In the earliest part of the Cenozoic era, the different groups of placentals, although not closely related, all tended to be heavy limbed and heavy tailed and to walk on the whole length of their feet (as do modern bears) or on thick, stubby toes. These ungainly, thickset mammals soon died out. Some became extinct because their descendants, more efficiently adapted to their environment, overtook and replaced them. Others, such as the powerful taeniodonts and the large rodent-like tillodonts, seem to have been evolutionary blind alleys.

Spectacular developments

It was the Oligocene Period, 36 million years ago, that saw the end of most of these early essays in mammalian gigantism, but, in many parts of the world, they were replaced by others just as spectacular. In South America, the giant sloths and glyptodonts (massive relatives of the armadillos) survived until comparatively recently. The ground sloths, at least, were contemporaries of the first men on the continent.

As each group of early mammals evolved, during the early and middle part of the Cenozoic era, many of their developments closely reflected changes taking place in their environment. The first horse-like creature, for example,

was *Hyracotherium*, also called *Eohippus* or "dawn horse." It lived 54 million years ago and was a small, multi-toed creature, well adapted to its densely forested habitat. The teeth of its descendants gradually changed in size and complexity, but it was not until the Miocene Period, nearly 20 million years later, that any radical alterations took place. This was the time when grasses (the Gramineae), until then a rare family of plants, came to the fore. The world's plains suddenly became clothed in a food plant very suitable for the attention of grazing creatures such as the early horses.

Animals of the grasslands

Horses and many other animals moved from the forests to make use of this new and abundant food supply. Once on the plains, different adaptations for survival were required: high-crowned teeth to deal with tough grasses; limbs enabling the animal to run tirelessly without extra, unwanted weight from supporting side toes (which were lost); large eyes capable of seeing for long distances and placed far back on the head for detecting predators approaching from any direction (as a result of which, however, the ability to judge distances ahead had to be sacrificed). Thus, the modern horses are plains-dwelling animals, perfectly adapted to their present way of life.

Mammals reached the climax of diversity during the Pliocene Period, 10 million years ago. But in the following period, the Pleistocene, ice sheets swept down from the polar regions and from the high mountains of the north, bringing massive and sudden changes to the ecology of virtually every region in the world. This dramatic disturbance to the environment brought extinction to an enormous number of species.

The survivors consisted mainly of the smaller species. Unfortunately for many of them, however, they included *Homo sapiens*. Man rose to success at the end of the Pleistocene and has, in the last 10,000 years, taken dominion over virtually every part of the world. During this time, he has proved far more destructive to other animal species than any natural force has ever been. More than 5,000 years ago, the giant sloths may have been a dying species, but there is no doubt that early human hunters hurried on their extinction. Since then, the list of species eliminated by man has grown ever longer. Today the human race is causing the extinction of both animals and plants at a rate comparable to that of 65 million years ago, when some dramatic natural catastrophe swept the dinosaurs from the face of the world. Unless man, the super-efficient species, can curb his numbers and his destructive activities, a new age of dying may soon be upon the world.

By early Cenozoic times, many forms had evolved from the insectivorous mammals of the Mesozoic Period. *Miacis*, *Hyaenodon* and *Oxyaena* were flesh eaters. Plant-eating mammals, such as Taeniodonts, *Arsinoitherium* and *Phenacodus* (one of the first hoofed mammals), had also evolved, while other early forms, such as *Andrewsarchus*, were omnivorous. The early Primates, however, remained insect eaters for millions of years.

EARLY STAGES

Miacis

Andrewsarchus

Hyaenodon

Diatryma

Euryapteryx

CENOZOIC BIRDS

Giant flightless birds came to the fore more than once during the Cenozoic era. *Diatryma*, a massive, flesh-eating bird, ruled the North American grasslands in early Cenozoic times, while mammals were still small, fairly primitive and easily dominated. *Euryapteryx* and its relatives (the moas) evolved in New Zealand, where, because there were no mammals, they filled an empty ecological niche.

The Carnivores diversified into two major types—the cats and their kin (Aeluroidea), and the dogs and their relatives (Arctoidea). During the Oligocene Period, about 36 million years ago, Aeluroidea gave rise not only to early relatives of modern cats, such as sabre-toothed *Hoplophoneus*, but also to two other families, the civets and the hyenas. At the same time, Arctoidea also diversified and produced the dogs, weasels, bears and racoons. It was a complex group, with many forms that were later to become extinct—such as the massive bear-dogs, such as *Daphoenus*, for example, which lived during the Miocene Period. Cats and dogs evolved to exploit different habitats. The cats adapted to life in forests, and learned to hide and then stalk and ambush their prey. Dogs evolved as plains animals, and used pack-hunting techniques to catch fleet-footed, grassland animals.

Perissodactyls and Artiodactyls were two important groups that evolved from the primitive hoofed mammals; Perissodactyls had an odd number of toes on each foot, Artiodactyls had an even number. These two groups suffered very different fortunes. Artiodactyls are still at the height of their success; the early stock produced the modern pig, camel, deer, giraffe, hippopotamus, antelope, sheep, goat and cow. Perissodactyls, however, are in decline and the only survivors are the horse, rhinoceros and tapir. But they were once important and many, now-extinct, kinds such as *Moropus* and *Brontotherium* existed alongside more familiar types such as *Hyracotherium*. Few remained after the Pliocene Period, however. This was when the Artiodactyls came to the fore. They, too, had had casualties—the pig-like *Archaeotherium* was by the extinct—but many other Artiodactyls, such as the early giraffe, *Palaeotragus*, were evolving. Most important, however, was small *Archaeomeryx*, for it had developed the key to Artiodactyl success. Most important, however, was small *Archaeomeryx*, for it had developed the key to Artiodactyl success—it was a ruminant and this enabled it to make the best possible use of the world's new grasslands.

Palaeozoic			Mesozoic		Cenozoic
500	400	300	200	100	0

Millions of years ago

Three geological eras mark the slow evolution of life on Earth. The Palaeozoic era, 570 million years ago, saw the appearance of the first primitive life forms. By the end of the era, 340 million years later, the reptiles had evolved and the following Mesozoic era was the age of reptilian domination. This reign over the land ended 65 million years ago as the Cenozoic era began. Then mammals came to the fore and the age of mammalian dominance of the world had dawned.

EARLY GRASSES

Grasses first appeared in the densely forested lands of 60 million years ago. Probably similar to the sedges (right) found in wet woodland areas today, they offered an attractive meal to many mammals. But it was not until the Miocene Period, when a change in climate reduced forest cover, that grasses became widespread. Then many forest creatures migrated to grassland areas.

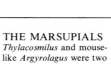

Wood sedge
Carex sylvatica

THE MARSUPIALS

Thylacosmilus and mouse-like *Argyrolagus* were two of the many forms of marsupial mammal that evolved in Cenozoic times in South America. Almost everywhere else, the marsupials, unable to compete with their more efficient placental cousins, met with an early extinction. But in two remote regions—South America (then separate from North America) and Australia—there was no competition from placentals, and there the marsupials flourished.

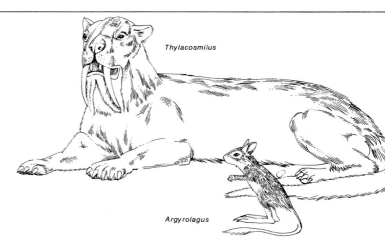

Thylacosmilus

Argyrolagus

TERTIARY	First radiation of mammals and birds		Forest horses		Second radiation of mam
Palaeocene	60	Eocene	50	40	Oligocene

42

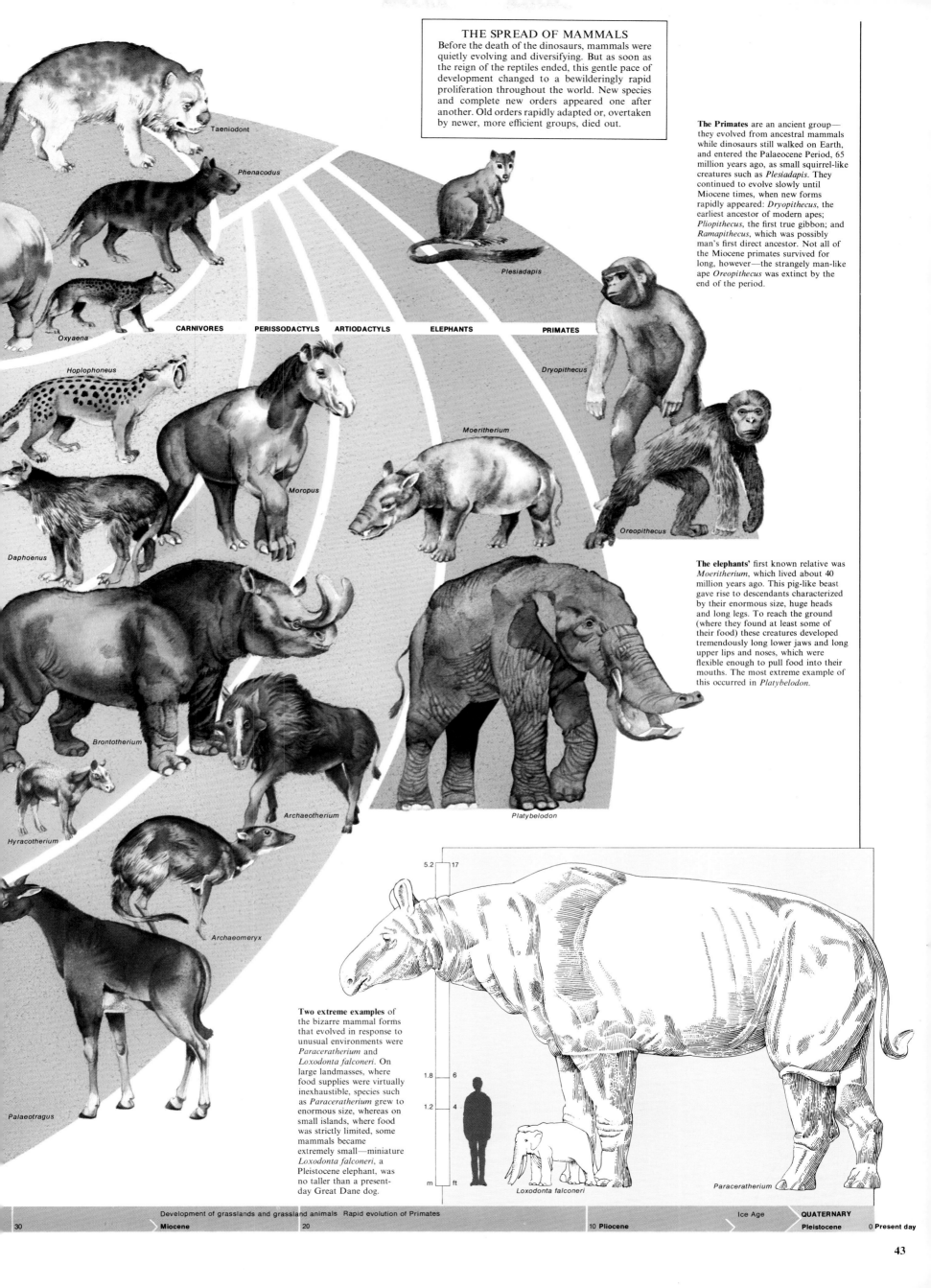

Before the death of the dinosaurs, mammals were quietly evolving and diversifying. But as soon as the reign of the reptiles ended, this gentle pace of development changed to a bewilderingly rapid proliferation throughout the world. New species and complete new orders appeared one after another. Old orders rapidly adapted or, overtaken by newer, more efficient groups, died out.

The Primates are an ancient group—they evolved from ancestral mammals while dinosaurs still walked on Earth, and entered the Palaeocene Period, 65 million years ago, as small squirrel-like creatures such as *Plesiadapis*. They continued to evolve slowly until Miocene times, when new forms rapidly appeared: *Dryopithecus*, the earliest ancestor of modern apes; *Pliopithecus*, the first true gibbon; and *Ramapithecus*, which was possibly man's first direct ancestor. Not all of the Miocene primates survived for long, however—the strangely man-like ape *Oreopithecus* was extinct by the end of the period.

Taeniodont

Phenacodus

Plesiadapis

Oxyaena

CARNIVORES   **PERISSODACTYLS**   **ARTIODACTYLS**   **ELEPHANTS**   **PRIMATES**

Hoplophoneus

Dryopithecus

Moeritherium

Moropus

Daphoenus

Oreopithecus

The elephants' first known relative was *Moeritherium*, which lived about 40 million years ago. This pig-like beast gave rise to descendants characterized by their enormous size, huge heads and long legs. To reach the ground (where they found at least some of their food) these creatures developed tremendously long lower jaws and long upper lips and noses, which were flexible enough to pull food into their mouths. The most extreme example of this occurred in *Platybelodon*.

Brontotherium

Hyracotherium

Archaeotherium

Platybelodon

Archaeomeryx

5.2   17

1.8   6

1.2   4

Two extreme examples of the bizarre mammal forms that evolved in response to unusual environments were *Paraceratherium* and *Loxodonta falconeri*. On large landmasses, where food supplies were virtually inexhaustible, species such as *Paraceratherium* grew to enormous size, whereas on small islands, where food was strictly limited, some mammals became extremely small—miniature *Loxodonta falconeri*, a Pleistocene elephant, was no taller than a present-day Great Dane dog.

Palaeotragus

m   ft

Loxodonta falconeri

Paraceratherium

Development of grasslands and grassland animals   Rapid evolution of Primates   Ice Age   **QUATERNARY**

30   **Miocene**   20   10 **Pliocene**   **Pleistocene**   0 **Present day**

Spread of Life

Different parts of the Earth have their own characteristic groups of animals, and this pattern of distribution caused nineteenth-century zoologists to divide the world into zoogeographical regions. Charles Darwin suggested how these assemblages of animals may have come about by the process of evolution. But we now know that movements of the Earth's land surfaces are also responsible for the present-day distribution of many of the world's animal species and groups.

The evolution of a major group of animals, such as the reptiles or the mammals, tends to follow a set pattern in five stages. First the original ancestral group spreads out, with each subgroup adapting to its environment. This process, called adaptive radiation, results in a variety of different kinds of animals, each suited to life in a particular niche or habitat—determined largely by food supply and environmental conditions. The different kinds then move into all of the areas they can reach in which the environment is right, producing the second stage of widespread distribution.

Competition for food or living space, or changes in climate may then cause some forms to decline and disappear from parts of the range, resulting in a third stage of discontinuous distribution. Any further reduction leads to isolated relict populations—the fourth stage—in which the animal exists only in one or two limited areas. The final stage is extinction.

In all distribution patterns, however, there is not only an ecological element but also a historical one, with past events determining where animals are and where they are not. There are thus two basic types of distribution: continuous, where the area is not interrupted by an insurmountable barrier (such as a mountain range), and discontinuous, where the area of distribution is subdivided and there is no way that members of one group can interchange with members of another.

One of these factors—the earliest and most important—is the (continuing) movement of the Earth's tectonic plates. This caused the supercontinent Pangaea to break up, probably in the Triassic Period (225–180 million years ago), and the continental masses to drift apart to their present positions. New oceans developed, separating the Americas from the Euro-African block and splitting both from Antarctica. Madagascar and Australia became islands, India moved north from Africa to join the Asian block, and mountain ranges such as the Alps, Andes, Rockies and Himalayas were thrown up. As a result, animal types that had already evolved on Pangaea or its fragments before they had significantly separated (i.e. all the major invertebrate groups and most of the earlier vertebrates) can be expected to exist on all the present-day continents.

Bridging the continents

Independently of these activities, ice ages occurred from time to time, resulting in the vast accumulations of ice at the poles and a consequent general lowering of the sea level by as much as 100 m (330 ft). This temporarily exposed the previously submerged continental shelves, providing additional land for colonization, and new corridors that linked existing areas, such as the land bridge that appeared between Alaska and Siberia.

Groups that had evolved after the breakup of Pangaea, e.g. the hare, squirrel and dog families, made use of land bridges as the climate allowed, and came to occupy more than one continent. Flying animals—birds and bats—also made intercontinental crossings and established themselves on both sides of oceans, although a surprising number of these have remained very restricted in distribution. But most animals have to stay where they are because of special dietary or environmental requirements, or because they are "trapped" on islands, such as Madagascar and Australia, and cannot get off. These areas have the most distinctive faunas in the world.

Barriers and corridors

The extent to which an expanding group can spread from its original area depends on whether there are barriers, such as mountain ranges, deserts or seas, or corridors that link major areas in which the animals can live. Different animals have different environmental requirements, and so a topographical feature that is a barrier for one may be a corridor for another.

The dispersal of many animals is achieved by "hopping" from lake to lake across a continent, or from island to island across a sea. Some, such as insects, are good at this, whereas others, such as land mammals, are bad. Thus a considerable range of weevils (Curculionidae) are found on islands from New Caledonia to the Marquesas, some 6,500 km (4,000 miles) across the southern Pacific Ocean, whereas the marsupials of the region are concentrated in Australia, Papua New Guinea and a few adjacent islands, with only one genus reaching the Celebes and none crossing Wallace's Line into Borneo.

An example of colonization by "hopping" is seen on the volcanic island of Krakatoa near Java, which exploded in 1883 destroying all life. Within 25 years there were 263 species of animals on the island. Most were insects, but there were three species of land snails, two species of reptiles and 16 of birds. In another 22 years, 46 species of vertebrates had arrived, including two species of rats.

The effect of man

Animal distribution cannot be considered merely as a natural phenomenon, because it has been greatly and increasingly modified by man's impact on the environment. Agricultural practice has made large sections of the land area unsuitable for many of the animals that originally lived there, notably through the clearing of forests and the draining of marshes.

Man has also introduced animals, either deliberately or accidentally, to regions where they were not endemic. The rabbit in Australia and the deer in New Zealand were both deliberately introduced, but rats, cockroaches and many other animals have been accidentally transported throughout the world on ships and aircraft. The enormous growth in human population has driven many animals from their natural homes and into more remote environments, such as mountains. Indeed, in the past century human interference has altered the pattern of animal distribution more drastically than any topographic or climatic change.

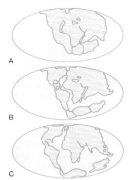

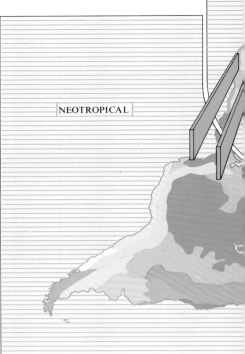

NEOTROPICAL

Earth's original single landmass, Pangaea (A), probably began to break up more than 200 million years ago. Species that had already evolved diversified on the Noah's Arks of the drifting supercontinents (B), called Laurasia and Gondwanaland. As the process continued (C), related animals flourished in the separated continents of the southern hemisphere.

PATTERNS OF ANIMALS
Over the ages the shape of the Earth has changed. Whole continents have moved; mountains and deserts have grown; land bridges between continents have opened and closed. These events, together with food supply, climate and other animals, account for the present natural pattern of life in the six zoogeographical regions, each containing a unique mix of animals. But man's activities have drastically affected this natural distribution in all parts of the world.

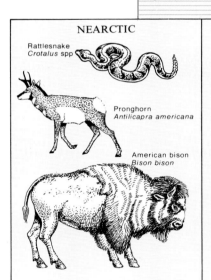

NEARCTIC

Rattlesnake
Crotalus spp

Pronghorn
Antilicapra americana

American bison
Bison bison

The Nearctic or "New North" region covers all of North America, from the highlands of Mexico in the south to Greenland and the Aleutian Islands in the north. Its climate and vegetation resemble that of the Palearctic region, and many of its mammals crossed over from the Palearctic via the Bering land bridge, which linked Siberia and Alaska when the sea level was lower. Animals unique to the Nearctic group include the pronghorn, an antelope-like mammal that inhabits the grasslands and plains of western and central America, and the bison, another large mammal that inhabits the prairies. Several species of rattlesnake also belong to the Nearctic group, although they are not exclusive to this region.

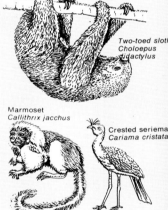

NEOTROPICAL

Two-toed sloth
Choloepus didactylus

Marmoset
Callithrix jacchus

Crested seriema
Cariama cristata

The Neotropical or "New Tropical" region consists of South America, the West Indies and most of Mexico. The climate and vegetation are mostly tropical—only the southern tip is in the temperate zone—and it is linked to the Nearctic by the Central American corridor. The Neotropical region has more distinctive families than any other. These include, among mammals, the sloth, which inhabits the tropical forests and has adapted to an upside-down existence. Among birds, the long-legged crested seriema is also unique to the region. Neotropical monkeys, such as the marmoset, have lateral-facing nostrils, which distinguish them from their downward-nosed relatives found in the Old World.

Land routes around the world have altered with the ages, sometimes allowing invaders to penetrate new lands, or closing to form natural sanctuaries for less efficient animals. The Central American isthmus (A) opened South America to placental mammals from the north. The Sahara desert closed most of Africa (B) to Eurasian species. Asia and Australia (C) share "island hoppers" in the transitional zones, but sea barriers have kept the regions separate.

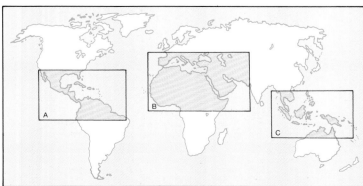

A land bridge between the Americas emerged about three million years ago, breaking the long isolation of the south. The primitive pouched mammals which had developed there were now threatened by more advanced mammals from the north, and many extinctions followed. Northern invaders included peccaries, raccoons and a llama-like camelid. But members of the armadillo and opossum families were successful in making their way to the northern region.

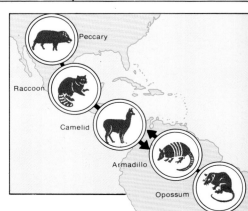

Peccary

Raccoon

Camelid

Armadillo

Opossum

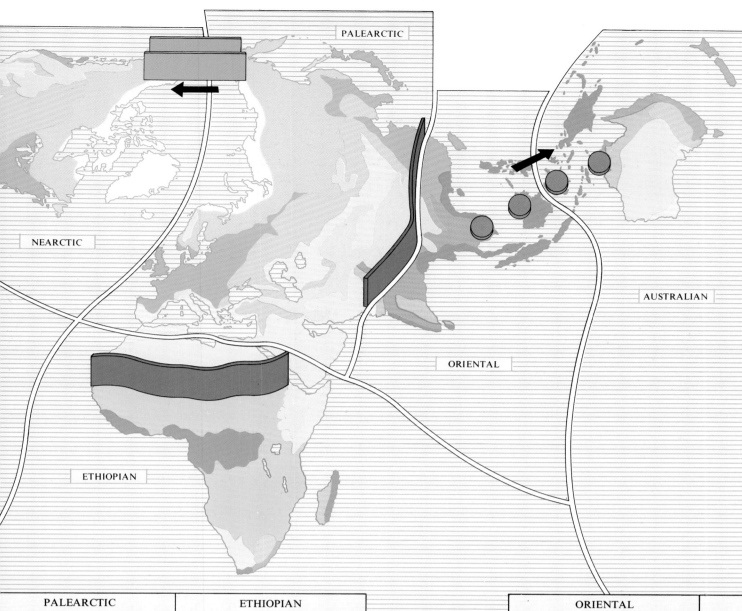

PALEARCTIC

NEARCTIC

ETHIOPIAN

ORIENTAL

AUSTRALIAN

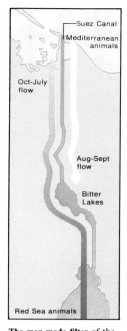

Suez Canal
Mediterranean
animals

Oct-July
flow

Aug-Sept
flow

Bitter
Lakes

Red Sea animals

The man-made filter of the Suez Canal, cut in 1869, is an animal corridor between the Mediterranean and Red Sea. But movement is mainly from the latter, for the channel passes through the hot, salty Bitter Lakes, favoring animals adapted to these conditions, and the current flows northwards for 10 months of the year. However, not all the 130 invading species are likely to survive Mediterranean conditions.

PALEARCTIC

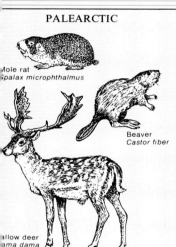

Mole rat
Spalax microphthalmus

Beaver
Castor fiber

Fallow deer
Dama dama

The Palearctic or "Old North" region covers the entire northerly part of the Old World, with seas to the north, east and west. To the south, the Sahara desert and the Himalaya mountains form barriers that separate the Palearctic from the Ethiopian and Oriental regions, although these regions are all part of the same landmass. One of the few species of mammals unique to the Palearctic is the Mediterranean mole rat, a thick-furred rodent. Another Palearctic rodent, the beaver, is shared with the Nearctic region. Fallow deer occur throughout Europe. They have been introduced by man into many other parts of the world, but their origin is almost certainly Mediterranean.

ETHIOPIAN

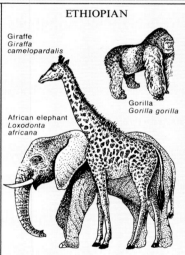

Giraffe
Giraffa camelopardalis

Gorilla
Gorilla gorilla

African elephant
Loxodonta africana

The Ethiopian region includes southern Arabia as well as all Africa south of the Sahara. It resembles in many ways the Neotropical region and is almost as rich in unique families. Its fauna also has much in common with the Oriental region. Unique mammals include the giraffe, at 5.5 m (18 ft) the tallest of living land animals, which inhabits the savanna. The region also supports two of the world's four great apes, the gorilla and the chimpanzee, which are found in the forests of western and central Africa. (The other great apes, the orangutan and the gibbon, are Oriental.) The African elephant is distinguished from its Indian relative by its greater size and by its huge ears and massive tusks.

Polar

Tundra

Taiga

Mountain

Temperate forest

Temperate grassland

Mediterranean

Savanna

Tropical rainforest

Monsoon

Desert

Barrier

Corridor

Stepping stone

Prevailing movement

ORIENTAL

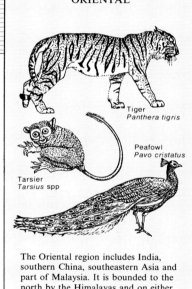

Tiger
Panthera tigris

Peafowl
Pavo cristatus

Tarsier
Tarsius spp

The Oriental region includes India, southern China, southeastern Asia and part of Malaysia. It is bounded to the north by the Himalayas and on either side by ocean, and is separated from the Australian region by a line known as Wallace's Line. It shares a quarter of its mammal families with Africa, but has more primates than any other region. The tarsier, a small relative of the monkey, is unique to southeastern Asia and represents an important early stage of primate evolution. The tiger was once widespread, but its natural habitats are steadily diminishing and the tiger itself is in danger of extinction by man. The peacock is one of the region's many brilliantly colored birds.

AUSTRALIAN

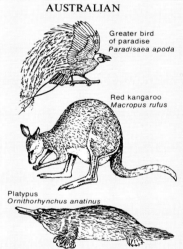

Greater bird of paradise
Paradisaea apoda

Red kangaroo
Macropus rufus

Platypus
Ornithorhynchus anatinus

The Australian region is unique in having no land connection with any other region. Its native fauna has developed in isolation from the rest of the world for at least 50 million years. Most of the mammals are marsupial—animals such as the kangaroo that carry their young in a pouch. Even more of a biological curiosity than the marsupials is the duckbilled platypus, a monotreme or egg-laying mammal. It lives along the banks of streams in Australia and Tasmania, and lays small, leathery eggs like those of snakes and turtles, but it is a true mammal and nurses its young with milk. Some 13 bird families are unique to the region, including the magnificent bird of paradise.

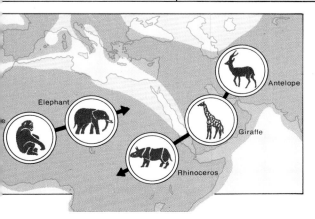

Elephant

Antelope

Giraffe

Rhinoceros

A desert barrier gradually began to form in northern Africa about nine million years ago, replacing the forest corridor between the Ethiopian and Palearctic regions. During the change, many animals typical of the African plains moved in from the north, including ancestors of today's antelopes, giraffes and rhinoceroses. But African animals also moved up north: early elephants and, much later, apes, which may have been precursors of modern man.

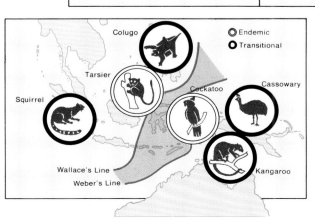

Colugo

Tarsier

Squirrel

Cockatoo

Cassowary

Kangaroo

Wallace's Line

Weber's Line

Endemic

Transitional

The transitional area of "Wallacea" contains animals from both the Oriental and Australian regions, bounded by Wallace's and Weber's Lines, but few have crossed to the other region. Some Oriental mammals, such as tarsiers, are found in Wallacea, but the gliding colugo and varieties of squirrel are not. The Australian cockatoo has reached the transition area, but the flightless cassowary and the tree kangaroo have not.

Spread of Man

Modern Man, *Homo sapiens sapiens*, has proved a highly successful animal since his emergence some 50,000 years ago: today more than 4,000 million members of this subspecies of the *Homo* (Man) group occupy the Earth, living in even the most inhospitable regions. But the fossil record shows that man's lineage goes back millions of years, with different stages of development leading to a greater control of the environment, and with climate itself helping man's ultimate domination of Earth.

Man's lineage may go back at least 14 million years to a small woodland creature known as *Ramapithecus* (Rama's ape). Since the first discoveries of *Ramapithecus* in the Indian subcontinent, its fossils have come to light in many parts of the world, including China, eastern Europe, Turkey and eastern Africa. Fossil remains show that it survived for several million years until, about eight million years ago, there is a tantalizing gap in the fossil record. Then, about four and a half million years later (according to recent discoveries in eastern Africa), we have solid evidence of an upright hominid—a member of man's zoological family. This is "Lucy," a fossil skeleton found in 1973 by Donald Johanson and Tom Gray, and subsequently classified with many other finds as *Australopithecus afarensis*.

This may be man's ancestral "rootstock," but a little later there existed two kinds of "ape-man" (*Australopithecus*), and our own direct ancestor Handy Man (*Homo habilis*). Datable volcanic ash found with the fossils provides a time scale and indicates that, about two million years ago, ape-man and "true" man lived side by side in the lush grassland that then covered the eastern African plains.

One and a half million years ago, according to the fossil evidence, there was again only one hominid species. The varieties of australopithecines had died out, and Handy Man (*Homo habilis*) had apparently evolved into Upright Man (*Homo erectus*). Remains of Upright Man have been found in many regions of the world, from various parts of Africa and Europe to China and Indonesia, although not in the Americas. But there is reason to believe that it was in Africa, well over one million years ago, that he evolved from his ancestor, and began a very gradual expansion out of the continent.

Upright Man had about one million years to spread across the Old World, adapting as he did so to local conditions, just as people of today are adapted in their various ways. He was a nomadic hunter gatherer, socially organized in groups. His skills included the use of fire and cooking, as well as the making of quite large structures out of wood. Recent discoveries suggest that, during the million years of his existence, *Homo erectus* gradually evolved into the next stage of man – *Homo sapiens*.

The next step is revealed most clearly in fossils from more than 100,000 to less than 50,000 years ago. Called Neanderthal Man in Europe, Solo Man in Indonesia, and Rhodesian Man in southern Africa, these types of human being were all descendants of *Homo erectus*.

Variable in brain size, but with prominent eyebrow ridges and receding jaws, they may have been dead ends on the evolutionary road; or some may have led to, or been incorporated in, Modern Man (*Homo sapiens sapiens*).

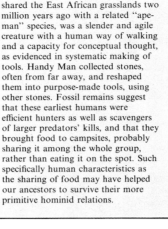

THE AFRICAN CRADLE
Handy Man (*Homo habilis*), who shared the East African grasslands two million years ago with a related "ape-man" species, was a slender and agile creature with a human way of walking and a capacity for conceptual thought, as evidenced in systematic making of tools. Handy Man collected stones, often from far away, and reshaped them into purpose-made tools, using other stones. Fossil remains suggest that these earliest humans were efficient hunters as well as scavengers of larger predators' kills, and that they brought food to campsites, probably sharing it among the whole group, rather than eating it on the spot. Such specifically human characteristics as the sharing of food may have helped our ancestors to survive their more primitive hominid relations.

MAN THE FIRE-BRINGER
Upright Man (*Homo erectus*) emerged about 1.5 million years ago, evolving from his predecessor, Handy Man. For one million years these people developed and adapted, spreading over most of the Old World and following a nomadic hunter-gatherer life-style, assisted by a more sophisticated tool technology. The cooler climates of northern Asia and Europe may have encouraged their most impressive innovation—the use of fire for warmth, cooking and hunting game—and also their ability to construct quite elaborate shelters. It seems likely that they possessed language; and traces of ocher lumps at a campsite perhaps 400,000 years old suggest the possibility of ritual adornment or some kind of body painting.

THE HUMANIZING OF MAN
Modern man's predecessor, although called Wise Man (*Homo sapiens*), was long regarded as more brutish than human. But widespread finds have now changed this image, as can be seen in an old and an updated reconstruction of the same Neanderthal skull (right). Many scientists believe that these people showed a human concern for each other, burying their dead with ceremonial reverence, and looking after disabled members of the group. In their Neanderthal form they inhabited Europe and the Middle East from about 100,000 to 40,000 years ago, and were perhaps adapted to ice-age conditions. *Homo sapiens* counterparts of Neanderthal Man also occur in Africa and southeastern Asia.

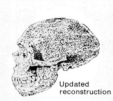

Updated reconstruction

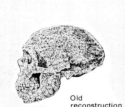

Old reconstruction

The burial of a Neanderthal man took place 60,000 years ago at Shanidar in the Iraq highlands. Fossil traces suggest that the body was laid on a bed of branches, and that flowers were brought to the grave and placed deliberately around the body. The flowers included many varieties still known locally for their medicinal properties. Ritual burials occur at many Neanderthal sites, from the Pyrenees to Soviet Asia, and indicate a sensitivity that contradicts Neanderthal Man's traditional image.

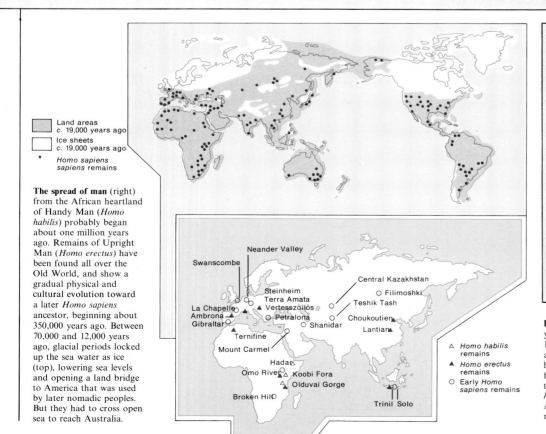

Land areas
c. 19,000 years ago

Ice sheets
c. 19,000 years ago

• Homo sapiens sapiens remains

The spread of man (right) from the African heartland of Handy Man (*Homo habilis*) probably began about one million years ago. Remains of Upright Man (*Homo erectus*) have been found all over the Old World, and show a gradual physical and cultural evolution toward a later *Homo sapiens* ancestor, beginning about 350,000 years ago. Between 70,000 and 12,000 years ago, glacial periods locked up the sea water as ice (top), lowering sea levels and opening a land bridge to America that was used by later nomadic peoples. But they had to cross open sea to reach Australia.

Neander Valley
Swanscombe
Steinheim
Terra Amata
Vertesszöllös
La Chapelle
Ambrona
Gibraltar
Petralona
Ternifine
Mount Carmel
Hadar
Omo River
Koobi Fora
Olduvai Gorge
Broken Hill
Central Kazakhstan
Filimoshki
Teshik Tash
Choukoutien
Shanidar
Lantian
Trinil Solo

△ Homo habilis remains
▲ Homo erectus remains
○ Early Homo sapiens remains

THE AGE OF ART
Toward the end of the last Ice Age, from about 35,000 years ago, truly modern humans began to depict their world in wonderfully vivid terms. The age of art may have reached its peak at Lascaux, France, some 15,000 years ago, but less well-preserved cave paintings from Africa show that the artistic impulse was equally present elsewhere. Called Cro-Magnon Man in Europe, these people spread to all parts of the world, crossing to the Americas by way of the Bering land bridge (when ice locked up the water of the straits), and even venturing over the seas to Australia. Physically these people were just like present-day humans. They led a nomadic, hunter-gathering life, living in large, organized groups, hunting such animals as mammoths, reindeer, bison and horses, and using a technology, as well as an artistry, far in advance of anything previously developed.

Fossils almost four million years old, found since 1973, may mark the ancestral "rootstock" of humanity, but the earliest form of true man is thought to be *Homo habilis*, who shared his African habitat with "ape-man" relatives some two million years ago. His successor, *Homo erectus*, spread over Asia and Europe, evolving gradually into modern man's predecessors, creatures whose large brow ridges belie many typically human characteristics. These were replaced by Modern Man.

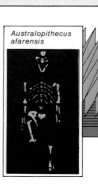

Australopithecus afarensis

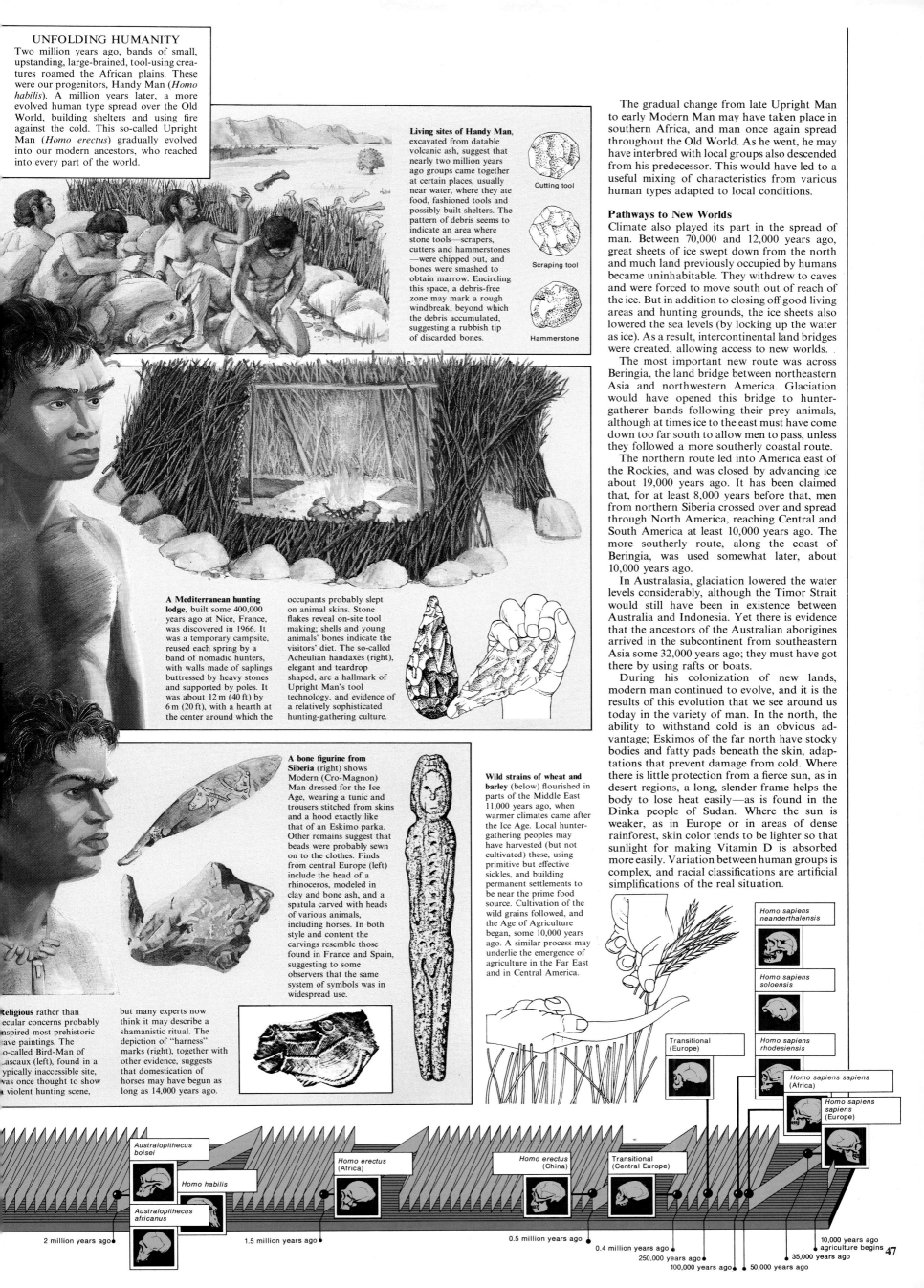

UNFOLDING HUMANITY

Two million years ago, bands of small, upstanding, large-brained, tool-using creatures roamed the African plains. These were our progenitors, Handy Man (*Homo habilis*). A million years later, a more evolved human type spread over the Old World, building shelters and using fire against the cold. This so-called Upright Man (*Homo erectus*) gradually evolved into our modern ancestors, who reached into every part of the world.

Living sites of Handy Man, excavated from datable volcanic ash, suggest that nearly two million years ago groups came together at certain places, usually near water, where they ate food, fashioned tools and possibly built shelters. The pattern of debris seems to indicate an area where stone tools—scrapers, cutters and hammerstones—were chipped out, and bones were smashed to obtain marrow. Encircling this space, a debris-free zone may mark a rough windbreak, beyond which the debris accumulated, suggesting a rubbish tip of discarded bones.

Cutting tool

Scraping tool

Hammerstone

A Mediterranean hunting lodge, built some 400,000 years ago at Nice, France, was discovered in 1966. It was a temporary campsite, reused each spring by a band of nomadic hunters, with walls made of saplings buttressed by heavy stones and supported by poles. It was about 12 m (40 ft) by 6 m (20 ft), with a hearth at the center around which the occupants probably slept on animal skins. Stone flakes reveal on-site tool making; shells and young animals' bones indicate the visitors' diet. The so-called Acheulian handaxes (right), elegant and teardrop shaped, are a hallmark of Upright Man's tool technology, and evidence of a relatively sophisticated hunting-gathering culture.

A bone figurine from Siberia (right) shows Modern (Cro-Magnon) Man dressed for the Ice Age, wearing a tunic and trousers stitched from skins and a hood exactly like that of an Eskimo parka. Other remains suggest that beads were probably sewn on to the clothes. Finds from central Europe (left) include the head of a rhinoceros, modeled in clay and bone ash, and a spatula carved with heads of various animals, including horses. In both style and content the carvings resemble those found in France and Spain, suggesting to some observers that the same system of symbols was in widespread use.

Wild strains of wheat and barley (below) flourished in parts of the Middle East 11,000 years ago, when warmer climates came after the Ice Age. Local hunter-gathering peoples may have harvested (but not cultivated) these, using primitive but effective sickles, and building permanent settlements to be near the prime food source. Cultivation of the wild grains followed, and the Age of Agriculture began, some 10,000 years ago. A similar process may underlie the emergence of agriculture in the Far East and in Central America.

Religious rather than secular concerns probably inspired most prehistoric cave paintings. The so-called Bird-Man of Lascaux (left), found in a typically inaccessible site, was once thought to show a violent hunting scene, but many experts now think it may describe a shamanistic ritual. The depiction of "harness" marks (right), together with other evidence, suggests that domestication of horses may have begun as long as 14,000 years ago.

The gradual change from late Upright Man to early Modern Man may have taken place in southern Africa, and man once again spread throughout the Old World. As he went, he may have interbred with local groups also descended from his predecessor. This would have led to a useful mixing of characteristics from various human types adapted to local conditions.

Pathways to New Worlds

Climate also played its part in the spread of man. Between 70,000 and 12,000 years ago, great sheets of ice swept down from the north and much land previously occupied by humans became uninhabitable. They withdrew to caves and were forced to move south out of reach of the ice. But in addition to closing off good living areas and hunting grounds, the ice sheets also lowered the sea levels (by locking up the water as ice). As a result, intercontinental land bridges were created, allowing access to new worlds.

The most important new route was across Beringia, the land bridge between northeastern Asia and northwestern America. Glaciation would have opened this bridge to hunter-gatherer bands following their prey animals, although at times ice to the east must have come down too far south to allow men to pass, unless they followed a more southerly coastal route.

The northern route led into America east of the Rockies, and was closed by advancing ice about 19,000 years ago. It has been claimed that, for at least 8,000 years before that, men from northern Siberia crossed over and spread through North America, reaching Central and South America at least 10,000 years ago. The more southerly route, along the coast of Beringia, was used somewhat later, about 10,000 years ago.

In Australasia, glaciation lowered the water levels considerably, although the Timor Strait would still have been in existence between Australia and Indonesia. Yet there is evidence that the ancestors of the Australian aborigines arrived in the subcontinent from southeastern Asia some 32,000 years ago; they must have got there by using rafts or boats.

During his colonization of new lands, modern man continued to evolve, and it is the results of this evolution that we see around us today in the variety of man. In the north, the ability to withstand cold is an obvious advantage; Eskimos of the far north have stocky bodies and fatty pads beneath the skin, adaptations that prevent damage from cold. Where there is little protection from a fierce sun, as in desert regions, a long, slender frame helps the body to lose heat easily—as is found in the Dinka people of Sudan. Where the sun is weaker, as in Europe or in areas of dense rainforest, skin color tends to be lighter so that sunlight for making Vitamin D is absorbed more easily. Variation between human groups is complex, and racial classifications are artificial simplifications of the real situation.

Homo sapiens neanderthalensis

Homo sapiens soloensis

Transitional (Europe)

Homo sapiens rhodesiensis

Homo sapiens sapiens (Africa)

Homo sapiens sapiens (Europe)

Australopithecus boisei

Homo habilis

Australopithecus africanus

Homo erectus (Africa)

Homo erectus (China)

Transitional (Central Europe)

2 million years ago   1.5 million years ago   0.5 million years ago   0.4 million years ago   10,000 years ago
                                                                                                          agriculture begins   47
                                                                                  250,000 years ago   35,000 years ago
                                                                               100,000 years ago 50,000 years ago

Part 4

THE DIVERSITY OF LIFE

Earth's habitats from the Poles to the Equator
Plants and animals of the Earth's natural regions
Man the preserver and man the destroyer

WEATHER STATIONS

1 MASSAWA (Ethiopia)
°C TEMPERATURE °F
40 100
30 80
20 60
10 40
0
J F M A M J J A S O N D
cmRAINFALL in
20 8
10 4
0 0
Very hot and dry all
year round, rain
infrequent, nights cool

2 ALLAHABAD (India)
°C TEMPERATURE
40
30
20
10
0
J F M A M J J A S O N
cmRAINFALL
20
10
0
Heavy summer rain,
mild and dry winter,
three seasons

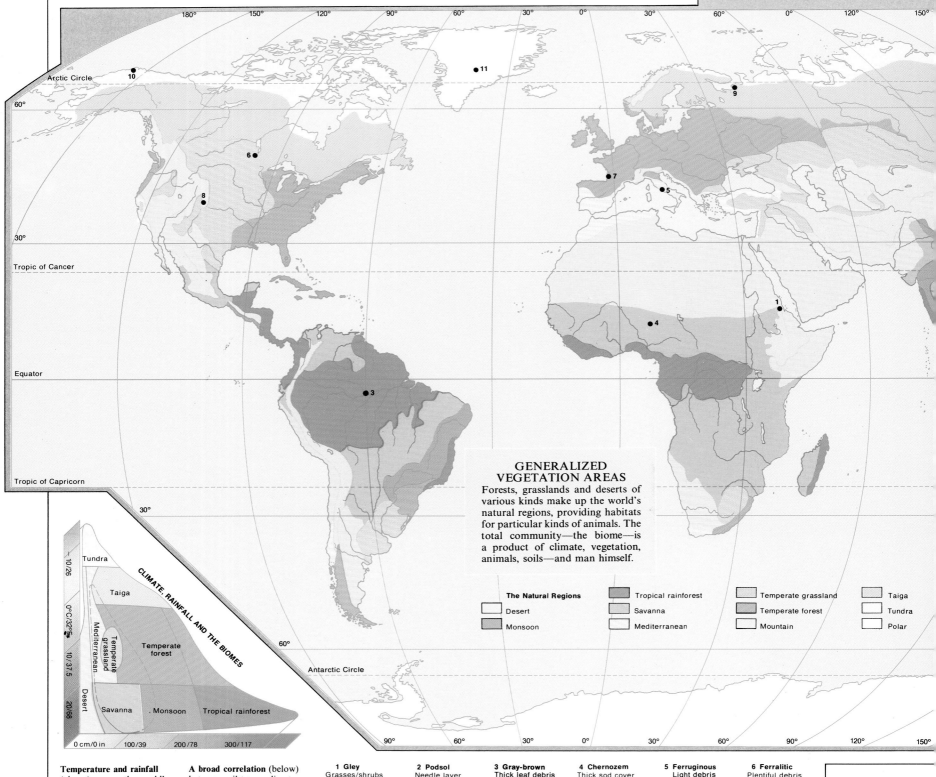

GENERALIZED VEGETATION AREAS

Forests, grasslands and deserts of various kinds make up the world's natural regions, providing habitats for particular kinds of animals. The total community—the biome—is a product of climate, vegetation, animals, soils—and man himself.

The Natural Regions
- Desert
- Monsoon
- Tropical rainforest
- Savanna
- Mediterranean
- Temperate grassland
- Temperate forest
- Mountain
- Taiga
- Tundra
- Polar

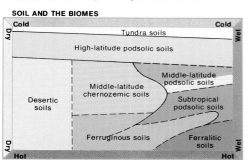

Temperature and rainfall (above) govern the world's zones of plant and animal life. Dryness prevents tree growth both in icy tundra and in hot deserts. Wetter conditions cause savannas and grasslands to yield to forest biomes, tropical or temperate (the dotted line indicates zones within which variations occur).

A broad correlation (below) between soil types, climate and vegetation areas shows the interconnections that define the biomes. The soil of the biome is related to climatic conditions and is also modified by plant and animal activity, but soil types are not necessarily confined to any one particular biome.

SOIL AND THE BIOMES

1 Gley Grasses/shrubs
- Waterlogged soil
- Clay silt, Sand, rock fragments
- Permafrost
- Bedrock

2 Podsol Needle layer
- Acid humus
- Rapid leaching of oxides
- Iron pan
- Oxides deposited
- Bedrock

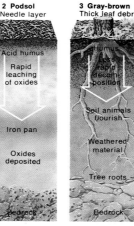

3 Gray-brown Thick leaf debris
- Humus
- Rapid decomposition
- Soil animals flourish
- Weathered material
- Tree roots
- Bedrock

4 Chernozem Thick sod cover
- Soil animals nourish
- Upward movement of soil solution
- Nodules of calcium carbonate
- Calcium carbonate

5 Ferruginous Light debris
- Wet season / Dry season
- Soil solution rises
- Silica removed
- Kaolinitic material over igneous rocks
- Some silica

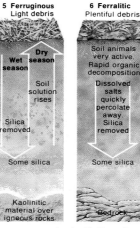

6 Ferralitic Plentiful debris
- Soil animals very active. Rapid organic decomposition
- Dissolved salts quickly percolate away Silica removed
- Some silica
- Bedrock

Soil profiles (above) from surface to bedrock reflect the influence of climate and vegetation on the rock. Depths vary from 1 m in the tundra to 30–40 m at the Equator. Waterlogged gley (1) may form above tundra permafrost. Podsol (2) is typical of taiga forests, where spring snow-melt is heavily leached through a needle layer, sometimes forming an iron "pan." Gray-brown forest soil (3) has rich, organic humus, as has chernozem (4), the typical temperate grassland soil. Ferruginous soils (5) occur in dry-season tropical climates (monsoon, savanna), and ferralitic soils (6) where there is constant rainfall.

ECOSYSTEM DYNAMICS

An ecosystem consists group of organisms a physical environment. marshland ecosystem North America (right) shows the dynamic interactions between p and animal communiti and their habitats, whi include climate, soil an water. The energy and food in the system init derive from the Sun— main energy source fo living things, notably plants. Plants are food for herbivores, on land and in water; herbivor are food for carnivore decomposers (bacteria fungi) nourish plants,

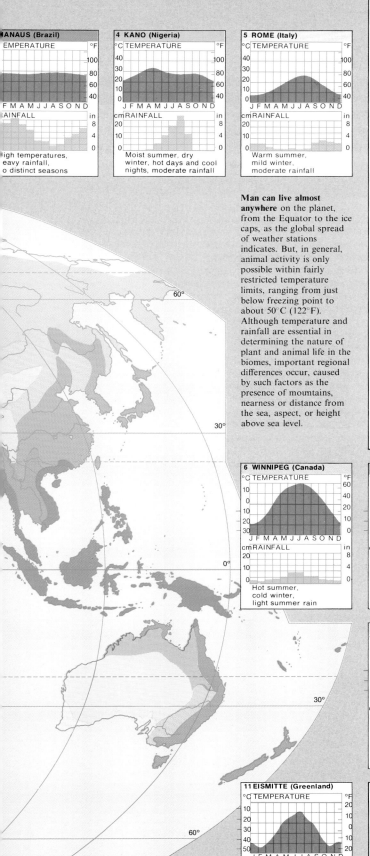

ANAUS (Brazil)
°C EMPERATURE °F
100
80
60
40
F M A M J J A S O N D
RAINFALL in
8
4
0
igh temperatures,
eavy rainfall,
o distinct seasons

4 KANO (Nigeria)
°C TEMPERATURE °F
40 100
30 80
20 60
10 40
0
J F M A M J J A S O N D
cm RAINFALL in
20 8
10 4
0 0
Moist summer, dry
winter, hot days and cool
nights, moderate rainfall

5 ROME (Italy)
°C TEMPERATURE °F
40 100
30 80
20 60
10 40
0
J F M A M J J A S O N D
cm RAINFALL in
20 8
10 4
0 0
Warm summer,
mild winter,
moderate rainfall

**Man can live almost
anywhere** on the planet,
from the Equator to the ice
caps, as the global spread
of weather stations
indicates. But, in general,
animal activity is only
possible within fairly
restricted temperature
limits, ranging from just
below freezing point to
about 50°C (122°F).
Although temperature and
rainfall are essential in
determining the nature of
plant and animal life in the
biomes, important regional
differences occur, caused
by such factors as the
presence of mountains,
nearness or distance from
the sea, aspect, or height
above sea level.

6 WINNIPEG (Canada)
°C TEMPERATURE °F
60
10 40
0 20
10
20 10
30 0
J F M A M J J A S O N D
cm RAINFALL in
20 8
10 4
0 0
Hot summer,
cold winter,
light summer rain

7 BORDEAUX (France)
°C TEMPERATURE °F
60
10 40
0 20
10
20 10
30 0
J F M A M J J A S O N D
cm RAINFALL in
20 8
10 4
0 0
Warm summer,
mild winter,
four distinct seasons

8 PIKE'S PEAK (USA)
°C TEMPERATURE °F
60
10 40
0 20
10
20 10
30 0
J F M A M J J A S O N D
cm RAINFALL in
20 8
10 4
0 0
4,300 m (14,111ft)
Temperature decreases
with increasing altitude

9 ARKHANGELSK (USSR)
°C TEMPERATURE °F
60
10 40
0 20
10
20 10
30 0
J F M A M J J A S O N D
cm RAINFALL in
20 8
10 4
0 0
Short summer, long
and cold winter,
light summer rain

10 BARROW (Alaska)
°C TEMPERATURE °F
60
10 40
0 20
10
20 10
30 0
J F M A M J J A S O N D
cm RAINFALL in
20 8
10 4
0 0
Brief summer, very
long and cold winter,
very light rainfall

11 EISMITTE (Greenland)
°C TEMPERATURE °F
10 20
20 10
30 0
40 10
50 20
J F M A M J J A S O N D
RAINFALL
No data
Very light precipitation,
annual temperature
variation 15.3°C/27.5°F

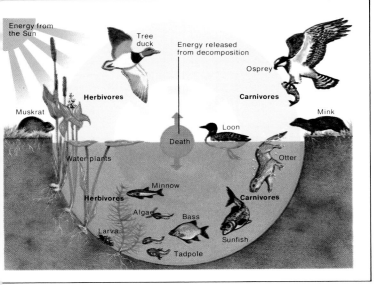

Energy from
the Sun
Tree
duck
Energy released
from decomposition
Osprey
Herbivores
Carnivores
Muskrat
Mink
Loon
Death
Water plants
Otter
Herbivores
Minnow
Carnivores
Algae
Bass
Larva
Sunfish
Tadpole

Earth's Natural Regions

Geographers have long looked for ways of classifying conditions such as climate, soil and vegetation to describe the general similarities and differences from area to area throughout the world. By identifying distinctive patterns of climate and vegetation they have provided a convenient global division into natural regions or biomes. And recent developments in ecology – the study of plants and animals in relation to their environments – have given such divisions a greater depth.

Divisions according to climate were first suggested by the Greek philosopher Aristotle, and his ideas were still in use until about 100 years ago. Aristotle posited a number of climatic zones—called torrid, temperate and frigid —defined by latitude. But with time it became increasingly apparent that the complex distribution of atmospheric pressure, winds, rainfall and temperature could not be related to such a simple frame. Nineteenth-century scientists divided the world into 35 climatic provinces. Then in 1900 the German meteorologist Wladimir Köppen produced a more sophisticated climatic classification based on temperature and moisture conditions related to the needs of plants. At about the same time other scientists studied the distribution of vegetation types throughout the world. These studies together provided the basis for much of the later work on climatic regions.

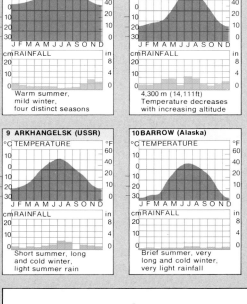

An important step forward was made in 1904 by the British geographer A. J. Herbertson. He argued that subdivision of physical environments should take into account the distribution of the various phenomena as they related to each other. He conceived the idea of *natural regions*, each with "a certain unity of configuration (relief), climate and vegetation." His final classification contained four groups or regions: Polar Types, Cool Temperate Types, Warm Temperate Types and Tropical Hot Lands. Herbertson's scheme, controversial at first, was later much used for teaching geography.

Ecology

Meanwhile the study of environmental problems had been advanced by the idea of *ecology*, the relationship of living things between each other and their surroundings. The term was first used in 1868 by Ernst Haeckel, the German biologist, but it was not until the end of the nineteenth century that scientists really began to study life forms in relation to their habitat. In addition to the central ideas of interdependence between the members of plant and animal communities and between the community and the physical environment, there now came the suggestion that communities develop in a sequence that leads to a "climax"—a final step of equilibrium or balance. Their climax stage depends on conditions of climate or soil.

Later the British botanist A. G. Tansley, a leading exponent of ecological thinking, introduced the term *ecosystem* to describe a group of living organisms and its effective environment. Tansley's definition of 1935 referred to the whole system, including "not only the organism complex, but also the whole complex of physical factors forming what we call the environment of the biome." The idea became very influential and has been used in the social sciences as well as in the natural ones. But it is difficult to apply in practice, partly because of the highly complex and often diverse interactions that take place in different parts of the ecosystem.

Ecologists have developed special methods and have given particular attention to the ways in which energy is transferred within the system. The term *biome* refers to the whole complex of organisms, both animals and plants, that live together naturally as a society. By *environment* is meant all the external conditions that affect the life and development of an organism.

Biomes

The biomes shown on the map are broadly drawn generalizations. They should be regarded as idealized regions, within which many local variations may exist—for example, of climate or soil conditions. On a larger scale such features as mountain ranges may cause variations at a regional level. Scientists have tried to work out "hierarchies" that include many levels or orders of scale leading to the major climatic-vegetation realms or biomes. These realms give a broad picture that is useful at the world level of scale, and which forms a starting point for further analysis. Any map of the biomes has to have lines to indicate the boundaries of each region, but these too are generalizations. Although climate and vegetation do sometimes change abruptly from place to place, more often there are transitional zones, and the boundaries on the maps give the broad locations of these.

Herbertson's concept of natural regions attempted also to take account of the influence of man as an important factor in the environment. But he was not totally successful in including man in his analysis, no doubt because of the complexity of the problems involved and because of the immense influence that man has had upon the natural vegetation of the world. The cutting of forests, the drainage and reclamation of land, the introduction, use and spread of cultivated plants, the domestication of animals, the development of sophisticated systems of agriculture and many other actions all create, over large areas of the biomes, landscapes that are more man-made than natural.

Resource systems

An idea that clarifies the study of the interrelations of societies and environments, and the ways in which these change with the passage of time, is that of the *resource system*. This is a model of a population of human beings and their social and economic characteristics, including their technical skills and resources, together with those aspects of the natural environment that affect them and which they influence. The model includes the sequences by which natural materials are obtained, transformed and used. It tries to show how societies are organized according to their natural resources, the effects of that use, and the ways in which natural conditions limit or expand the life and work of the society. But it is easier to apply such a model to societies that have direct relations with natural conditions, through farming, fishing or forestry, than to great urban–industrial complexes.

The sections that follow present a picture of the diversity of habitats from ice caps to equatorial forests, the principal ways man has modified the environment and the problems of maintaining healthy resource systems.

Climate and Weather

The pattern of world climates depends largely on great circulations of air in the atmosphere. These movements of air are driven by energy from the Sun, and they transfer surplus heat from the tropics to the polar regions. Over a long period of time – such as months, seasons or years – they create the climate. Over a short period – day by day, or week by week – they form the weather. Together, climate and weather are among the most significant natural components of the world's diverse environments.

The world's tropical zones receive more heat from the Sun than they re-emit into space, and so their land and sea surfaces become warm. The polar regions, on the other hand, emit more radiation than they receive, and so they become cold. Warm air is less dense than cold air, and this means that atmospheric pressure becomes low at the Equator and high at the poles. As a result, a circulation of air—both vertical and horizontal—is set up. But because of the Earth's rotation and the distribution of land and sea there is not a simple air circulation pattern in each hemisphere; winds are deflected to the right in the northern hemisphere and to the left in the southern hemisphere, a phenomenon known as the Coriolis effect.

A climatic patchwork
When warm air rises it expands and cools and the water vapor it is carrying condenses to form clouds. For this reason heavy, showery rain is frequent in the belt of rising air near the Equator. In the subtropical zones (where the air is sinking), clouds evaporate and the weather is fine. Air moves out of the subtropical high-pressure belts in the lower atmosphere. Some of it flows towards the poles and meets colder air, flowing out of the polar high-pressure region, in a narrow zone called the polar front. This convergence of air is concentrated around low-pressure systems known as depressions.

The pattern of climates does not remain constant throughout the year because of seasonal changes in the amount of radiation from the Sun—the "fuel" of the atmospheric engine. In June, when the northern hemisphere is tilted towards the Sun, the radiation is at a maximum at latitude 23°N and all the climatic belts shift northwards. In December it is summer in the southern hemisphere and all the belts move southwards.

Climate is also affected by the distribution of land and sea across the globe. The temperature of the land changes more quickly than that of

POLAR WEATHER
Weather in high latitudes is marked by consistently low temperatures—on the ice caps temperatures are nearly always below freezing. At the poles the sun never rises for six months of the year and for the remaining six months it never sets. Even in summer it stays low on the horizon and its rays are so slanted that they bring very little warmth. On the tundra the temperature rises above freezing for a few months in summer, but severe frosts are likely to occur at any time. As well as being bitterly cold, polar weather is predominantly dry. The lower the temperature the less moisture the air can contain. Clouds, when they form, are high, thin sheets of cirrostratus. Composed of ice crystals, they often produce a halo effect around the sun. Snow, when it falls, is usually dry and powdery.

DEPRESSIONS
Low-pressure weather systems, or depressions, form when polar and subtropical air masses converge. Cloud and rain usually occur at the boundary, or front, of the different air masses. Seen in cross section, a fully developed depression shows both warm (A) and cold (B) fronts. As the wave of warm air rises over the cold, its moisture condenses into the "layered" clouds that usually precede a warm front. Behind the warm front, cold air forces under the warm air, producing the wedge-shaped cold front.

FOG
Fogs form as a result of the condensation of water vapor in the air; they may occur when warm, moist air is cooled by its passage over a cold surface. Off the coast of California, for example, air near the surface of the sea is cooled by the cold California current and sea fog is frequent. The air at higher levels is still warm and acts like a lid over the fog, and mountains prevent the fog from dispersing in an easterly direction. Fumes and smoke are trapped by this temperature inversion, creating the notorious Los Angeles smog.

THUNDERSTORMS
These develop when air is unstable to a great height. Particularly violent storms occur when cold, dry air masses meet warm, moist air, causing the latter to rise rapidly. As the warm air surges upwards it cools and its moisture condenses into cumulonimbus, or thunder, clouds. Flat cloud tops mark the level where stable air occurs again. Quickly moving raindrops and hail in the clouds become electrically charged and cause lightning, and the explosion of heated air along the path of the flash creates the sound wave that is heard as thunder.

HURRICANES
These are tropical storms on a vast scale that build up over warm oceans. Their core is an area of low pressure around which large quantities of warm, moist air are carried to the high atmosphere at great speed. The Earth's rotation is responsible for the huge swirling movement: in the northern hemisphere the movement is anticlockwise, in the southern hemisphere it is clockwise. Towering bands of clouds produce torrential rain. The central region, or "eye," of a hurricane, however, has light winds, clear skies and no rainfall.

THE WORLD'S CLIMATIC REGIONS
Climate is the characteristic weather of a region over a long period of time. It is often described in terms of average monthly and yearly temperatures and rainfall. These in turn depend largely on latitude, which determines whether a region is basically hot or cold and whether it has pronounced seasonal changes. Climate is also influenced by prevailing winds, by ocean currents and by geographical features such as the distribution of land and water. Highland climates are influenced by altitude and are always cooler than those of nearby lowland regions. Tropical climates are always warm. Near the Equator rain falls for most of the year, but towards the subtropics the wet and dry seasons are more marked. Temperate climates reflect the conflict between warm and cold air masses. They range from the Mediterranean type with hot, dry summers and mild, moist winters to the cooler, wetter climates of higher latitudes. The subarctic is mainly cold and humid; polar climates are always cold and mainly dry.

Types of Climate

- Polar
- Subarctic
- Cool temperate
- Warm temperate
- Dry
- Tropical
- Highland

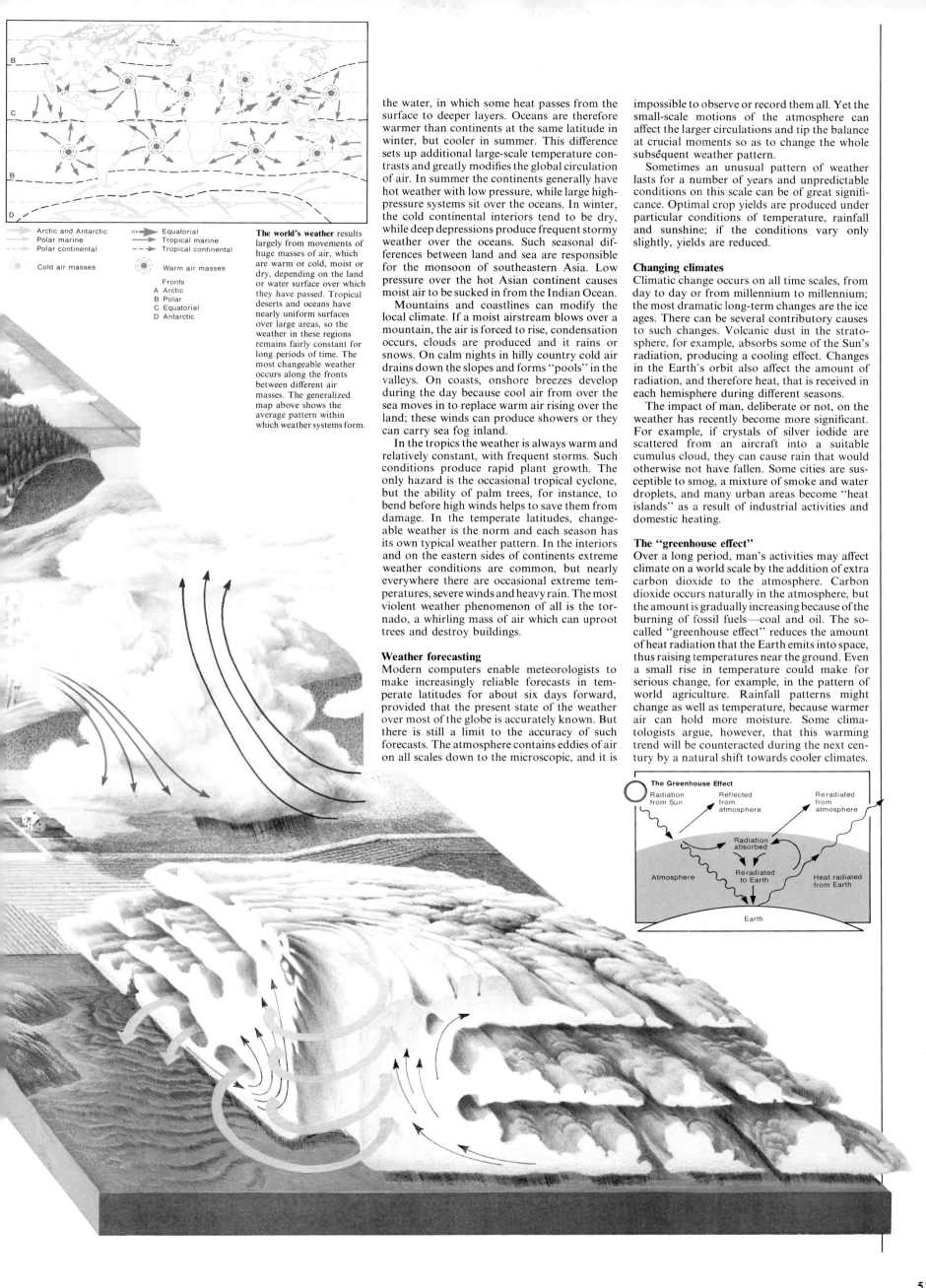

the water, in which some heat passes from the surface to deeper layers. Oceans are therefore warmer than continents at the same latitude in winter, but cooler in summer. This difference sets up additional large-scale temperature contrasts and greatly modifies the global circulation of air. In summer the continents generally have hot weather with low pressure, while large high-pressure systems sit over the oceans. In winter, the cold continental interiors tend to be dry, while deep depressions produce frequent stormy weather over the oceans. Such seasonal differences between land and sea are responsible for the monsoon of southeastern Asia. Low pressure over the hot Asian continent causes moist air to be sucked in from the Indian Ocean.

Mountains and coastlines can modify the local climate. If a moist airstream blows over a mountain, the air is forced to rise, condensation occurs, clouds are produced and it rains or snows. On calm nights in hilly country cold air drains down the slopes and forms "pools" in the valleys. On coasts, onshore breezes develop during the day because cool air from over the sea moves in to replace warm air rising over the land; these winds can produce showers or they can carry sea fog inland.

In the tropics the weather is always warm and relatively constant, with frequent storms. Such conditions produce rapid plant growth. The only hazard is the occasional tropical cyclone, but the ability of palm trees, for instance, to bend before high winds helps to save them from damage. In the temperate latitudes, changeable weather is the norm and each season has its own typical weather pattern. In the interiors and on the eastern sides of continents extreme weather conditions are common, but nearly everywhere there are occasional extreme temperatures, severe winds and heavy rain. The most violent weather phenomenon of all is the tornado, a whirling mass of air which can uproot trees and destroy buildings.

Weather forecasting

Modern computers enable meteorologists to make increasingly reliable forecasts in temperate latitudes for about six days forward, provided that the present state of the weather over most of the globe is accurately known. But there is still a limit to the accuracy of such forecasts. The atmosphere contains eddies of air on all scales down to the microscopic, and it is impossible to observe or record them all. Yet the small-scale motions of the atmosphere can affect the larger circulations and tip the balance at crucial moments so as to change the whole subsequent weather pattern.

Sometimes an unusual pattern of weather lasts for a number of years and unpredictable conditions on this scale can be of great significance. Optimal crop yields are produced under particular conditions of temperature, rainfall and sunshine; if the conditions vary only slightly, yields are reduced.

Changing climates

Climatic change occurs on all time scales, from day to day or from millennium to millennium; the most dramatic long-term changes are the ice ages. There can be several contributory causes to such changes. Volcanic dust in the stratosphere, for example, absorbs some of the Sun's radiation, producing a cooling effect. Changes in the Earth's orbit also affect the amount of radiation, and therefore heat, that is received in each hemisphere during different seasons.

The impact of man, deliberate or not, on the weather has recently become more significant. For example, if crystals of silver iodide are scattered from an aircraft into a suitable cumulus cloud, they can cause rain that would otherwise not have fallen. Some cities are susceptible to smog, a mixture of smoke and water droplets, and many urban areas become "heat islands" as a result of industrial activities and domestic heating.

The "greenhouse effect"

Over a long period, man's activities may affect climate on a world scale by the addition of extra carbon dioxide to the atmosphere. Carbon dioxide occurs naturally in the atmosphere, but the amount is gradually increasing because of the burning of fossil fuels—coal and oil. The so-called "greenhouse effect" reduces the amount of heat radiation that the Earth emits into space, thus raising temperatures near the ground. Even a small rise in temperature could make for serious change, for example, in the pattern of world agriculture. Rainfall patterns might change as well as temperature, because warmer air can hold more moisture. Some climatologists argue, however, that this warming trend will be counteracted during the next century by a natural shift towards cooler climates.

Arctic and Antarctic
Polar marine
Polar continental
Cold air masses
Equatorial
Tropical marine
Tropical continental
Warm air masses

Fronts
A Arctic
B Polar
C Equatorial
D Antarctic

The world's weather results largely from movements of huge masses of air, which are warm or cold, moist or dry, depending on the land or water surface over which they have passed. Tropical deserts and oceans have nearly uniform surfaces over large areas, so the weather in these regions remains fairly constant for long periods of time. The most changeable weather occurs along the fronts between different air masses. The generalized map above shows the average pattern within which weather systems form.

The Greenhouse Effect
Radiation from Sun
Reflected from atmosphere
Reradiated from atmosphere
Radiation absorbed
Atmosphere
Reradiated to Earth
Heat radiated from Earth
Earth

Resources and Energy

Resources, it has been said, comprise mankind's varying needs from generation to generation and are valued because of the uses societies can make of them. They represent human appraisals and are the products of man's ingenuity and experience. While natural resources remain vitally important in themselves, they must always be regarded as the rewards of human skill in locating, extracting and exploiting them. The development of resources depends on many factors, including the existence of a demand, adequate transport facilities, the availability of capital and the accessibility, quality and quantity of the resource itself.

The world's extraction of its resources highlights the inequality of their distribution. Each resource shown on the map is attributed to the three countries with the largest production percentages of that commodity. So, in 1976, the three leading bauxite producers were Australia (26.69%), Jamaica (14.19%) and Rep. of Guinea (13.9%). Usually, the larger and more wealthy a state the greater its monopoly of resources—although the tiny Pacific island of New Caledonia produces more than 14% of the world's nickel. China is reputed to mine 75% of the world's tungsten and to be increasing its oil supply rapidly. Energy consumption figures are for the year 1976, since when there have been some outstanding changes to patterns of availability, perhaps most noticeably in Britain's new-found oil and gas surplus. Bahrain and Tobago, too small to be shown on this map, also have surpluses of energy production.

A dictionary defines the term "resource" as "a means of aid or support," implying anything that lends support to life or activity. Man has always assessed nature with an eye to his own needs, and it is these varying needs that endow resources with their usefulness. Fossil fuels such as oil have lain long in the Earth, but it was not until about 1900 that the large-scale needs fostered by the rising demands of motor vehicles led to the development of new techniques for locating and extracting this raw material. Today oil has also become precious in the manufacture of a wide variety of industrial products, which themselves are resources that are much used by other industries.

The nature of resources

Resources can be most usefully classified in two groups: "renewable" and "nonrenewable." The latter is composed of materials found at or near the Earth's surface, which are sometimes known as "physical" resources. They include such essential minerals as uranium, iron, copper, nickel, bauxite, gold, silver, lead, mercury and tungsten. Oil, coal and natural gas are the principal nonrenewable fuel and energy resources, but after they have been used for producing heat or power their utility is lost and part of the geological capital of 325 million years of history is gone for ever. Some minerals such as iron and its product, steel, can be recycled and renewed, however. "Renewable" resources are basically biological, being the food and other vegetable matter which life needs to sustain human needs. Provided soil quality is maintained, their productivity may even be increased as better strains of plants and breeds of animals are developed.

Work has long been in progress to improve renewable resources, and has moved forward to manufacturing vegetable-flavored protein (VFP) from soybeans as a meat substitute and to viable experiments to extract protein from leaves. In Brazil, many cars have been converted to run successfully on alcohol extracted from sugar. One renewable resource—the tree—can be closely related to other resources: some conservationists are alarmed at the overuse of firewood as a source of fuel and energy in the semiarid areas of Africa. This may be an important factor in increasing the tendency for the deserts to spread in that continent, and in such a situation there is a new realization of the concept of closely managing resources such as soil, timber and fisheries. This is partly because we have a clearer understanding of the ecology of vegetation and the important interdependence of climate, soil, plants and animal life. Much, however, remains to be done.

The politics of nonrenewable resources

Today we are naturally troubled about the availability of natural resources. Oil is a prime cause for concern. Although many believe that production will grow until the mid-2020s and that new oil reserves will be discovered, oil's scarcity, based on a growing rate of demand and increasingly wasteful use, is now widely accepted. Because, like many resources, it is unevenly distributed, those countries with large and accessible supplies—such as the members of OPEC—have used their political power on a number of occasions to raise oil's price, with adverse effects on the economies of most importers. Ironically, these substantial price rises have had the effect of stimulating exploration and development in many new areas; there are already signs of increased production in China.

Other nonrenewable resources are also distributed unevenly, but have not been mined on any scale comparable with their availability; vast reserves of coal in the USSR and China have not been worked on any scale resembling their known extent.

New energy sources

As resources such as oil become less available and more expensive, the renewable resources of power such as water, wind, waves and solar energy, all of which are currently under study or development, will receive new injections of capital. Attention will also have to be paid to more widespread nuclear energy production. Energy has been called "the ultimate resource," and it is imperative that we make wise provisions for its future availability.

Future resources

It has been calculated that within four years of the launch of Sputnik I, more than 3,000 products resulting from space research were put into commercial production. These included new alloys, ceramics, plastics, fabrics and chemical compounds. Satellite developments have meant that land use can now be measured quickly and potential mineral sources closely identified. A satellite capable of converting solar power to electricity and contributing to the Earth's energy deficit has been widely discussed, while the Moon and planets have been mooted as future possible sources of minerals.

Conclusions

Resources are, in the main, the products of man's skill, ingenuity and expertise, and their widespread use, as in the case of timber and iron for shipbuilding, became apparent only as man's needs for them became clear. Our forebears were once concerned about the availability of flint, seaweed, charcoal and natural rubber; countries even went to war over supplies of spices. Today our requirements are slightly different—we no longer depend only on local sites for resources, and improved transport facilities and appropriate technologies have lowered the costs of obtaining materials for manufacture.

Nevertheless, the principles remain the same. A continual search for new resources capable of exploitation and wide application must be maintained, together with a close regard for the value of the renewable resources such as animal and vegetable products required to support man in his search for new resources. Perhaps the most vital consideration is the need for wise policies of conservation relating to the proven reserves of nonrenewable resources still in the ground, and the careful future use of such valuable deposits known or thought to exist.

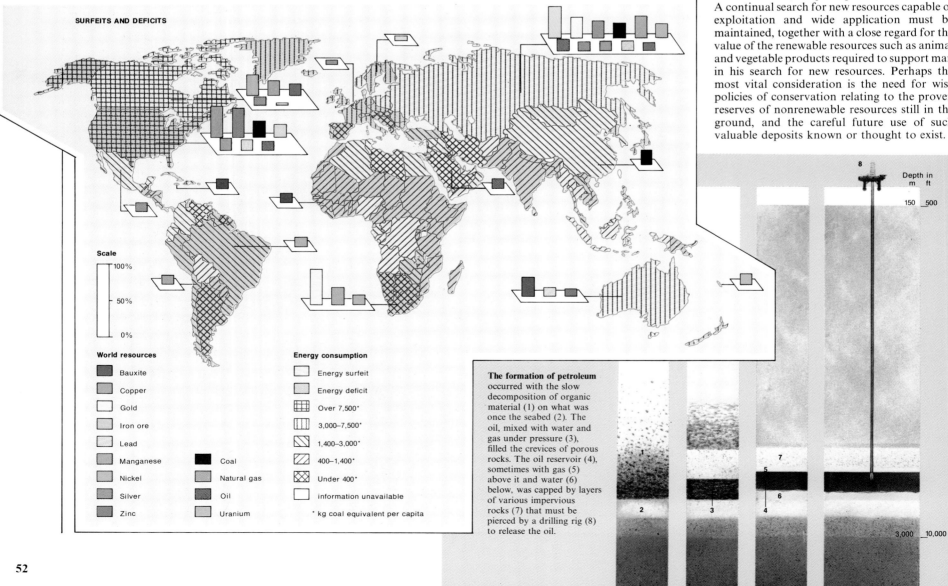

SURFEITS AND DEFICITS

Scale
100%
50%
0%

World resources
- Bauxite
- Copper
- Gold
- Iron ore
- Lead
- Manganese
- Nickel
- Silver
- Zinc
- Coal
- Natural gas
- Oil
- Uranium

Energy consumption
- Energy surfeit
- Energy deficit
- Over 7,500*
- 3,000–7,500*
- 1,400–3,000*
- 400–1,400*
- Under 400*
- information unavailable

* kg coal equivalent per capita

The formation of petroleum occurred with the slow decomposition of organic material (1) on what was once the seabed (2). The oil, mixed with water and gas under pressure (3), filled the crevices of porous rocks. The oil reservoir (4), sometimes with gas (5) above it and water (6) below, was capped by layers of various impervious rocks (7) that must be pierced by a drilling rig (8) to release the oil.

Depth in
m   ft
150   500

3,000   10,000

MAN'S ENDURING INGENUITY
A continuing search for new energy supplies has led man to explore potential oil sources in the offshore waters of the main continental land-masses. A firmly anchored production platform exemplifies the many new sites from which oil is being extracted, in an attempt to reduce reliance on the monopoly of reserves held by powerful organizations such as OPEC.

Natural gas   Hydroelectric power   Oil   Coal   Nuclear power

■ Japan
■ USSR/Eastern Europe
  Western Europe
  North America
■ World

Primary energy consumption (above), globally totalling nearly 7,000 million tonnes of coal equivalent (mtce) in 1979, is dominated by a reliance on the fossil fuels coal and oil (nearly 75%), with little contribution from nuclear energy. However, the use of nuclear fission to generate electricity has increased rapidly in recent years (right). While areas such as North America and Western Europe have kept their early leads, their proportional contributions to consumption are falling as more power stations in Japan and Eastern Europe are brought into use.

mtce
160
150
140
130
120
110
100
90
80
70
60
50
40
30
20
10
0

1969 1970 1971 1972 1973 1974 1975 1976 1977 1978 1979

The refining of oil into many valuable components (or fractions) is an involved process that makes fullest use of the resource. Crude oil is distilled into a wide range of products including the three main constituents of gasoline, kerosene (for jet fuel) and diesel fuel, of which part is further separated into gas. Other fractions are treated to give fuel oil and lubricating oil, from which wax as paraffin is removed. Chemical feedstock and bitumen are also important by-products.

Crude oil → Separation Conversion Treatment →

Gasoline Kerosene Diesel fuel
Gas
Fuel oil
Lubricating oil
Wax
Chemical feedstock
Bitumen

An oil drilling platform is firmly anchored on foundation piles driven 45 m (150 ft) into the sea bed to protect the structure from the 150 m (500 ft) deep waters of the rough North Sea. At its peak rate, a well can produce about 2,000 barrels (320,000 liters) per day and the platform may have an economic life of some 20 years. Such platforms come into use three or four years after oil is struck and annual operating costs can be expected to be in the area of $100 million. Of the world's total oil output, about 20% currently originates beneath the sea.

NEW ENERGY SOURCES
An orbiting collector, shown here, would transform solar radiation to direct-current electric power by the powerful photocells and mirrors positioned on its surface. The electrical energy would be converted into microwaves and beamed to Earth, where they would be converted back to electricity. Because such a geostationary satellite would be independent of clear skies or any seasonal variations, its potential is being quite heavily promoted. A space shuttle would probably be used in its construction. But earnest research continues into many other spheres of energy production, such as Earth-based solar panels, wind power and the extraction of heat from deep in the Earth. Tidal power, hydroelectric power and Ocean Thermal Energy Conversion (OTEC) are receiving much current attention. They are each *renewable* sources, so will relieve the pressure on our reserves of nonrenewable fuels.

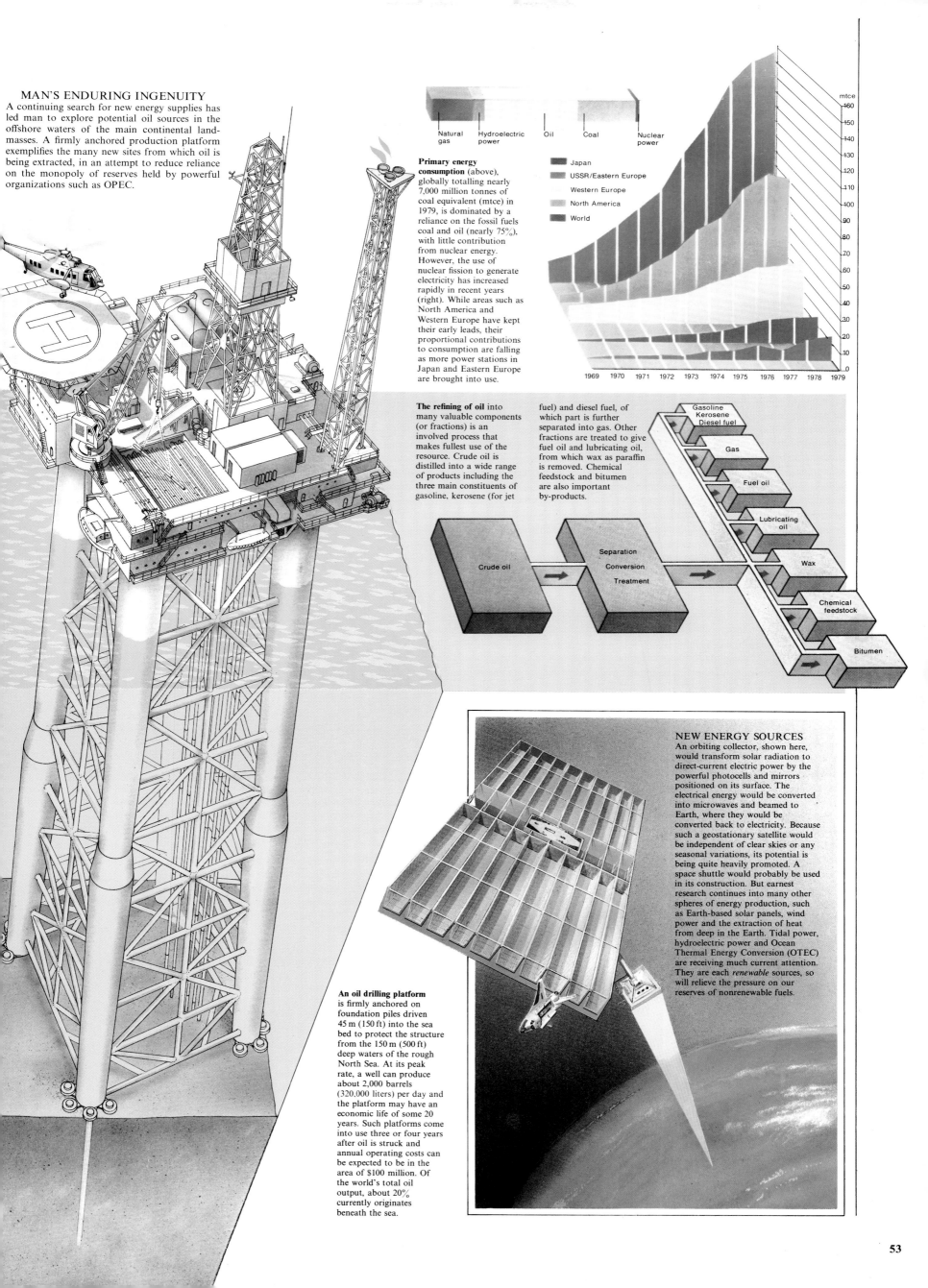

Population Growth

Every minute of every day, more than 250 children are born into the world. The Earth's population now stands at about 4,300 million and is continuing to grow extremely rapidly. The problems associated with such growth are enormous – already, about two-thirds of the world's people are underfed, according to United Nations' recommended standards of nutrition. And an even greater number live in very poor housing conditions, have inadequate access to medical facilities, receive little or no education and, at present, have no hope of improving their lot. As yet, there are no simple or immediate solutions.

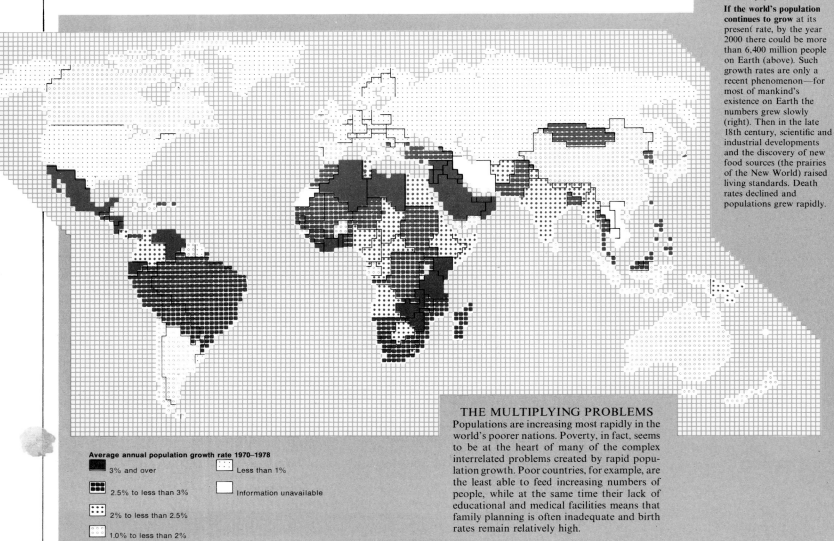

Average annual population growth rate 1970–1978

- 3% and over
- 2.5% to less than 3%
- 2% to less than 2.5%
- 1.0% to less than 2%
- Less than 1%
- Information unavailable

World population (millions)

■ World population
▨ Projected world population

If the world's population continues to grow at its present rate, by the year 2000 there could be more than 6,400 million people on Earth (above). Such growth rates are only a recent phenomenon—for most of mankind's existence on Earth the numbers grew slowly (right). Then in the late 18th century, scientific and industrial developments and the discovery of new food sources (the prairies of the New World) raised living standards. Death rates declined and populations grew rapidly.

THE MULTIPLYING PROBLEMS
Populations are increasing most rapidly in the world's poorer nations. Poverty, in fact, seems to be at the heart of many of the complex interrelated problems created by rapid population growth. Poor countries, for example, are the least able to feed increasing numbers of people, while at the same time their lack of educational and medical facilities means that family planning is often inadequate and birth rates remain relatively high.

In 1830, there were only about 1,000 million people on Earth. By 1930, this figure had doubled. And by 1975, it had doubled again. If the present rate of increase continues, it will have doubled again by the year 2020.

This may not happen—it is extremely difficult to predict how world population will behave. What is certain is that it will continue to increase and, moreover, that this increase will not be evenly distributed. Since more than 50 percent of the human race lives in Asia, it is inevitable that the largest population increases will take place there. In fact, by the year 2000, the population of Asia may well have grown from about 2,000 million to more than 3,600 million. Substantial increases, of 400 million or more, will probably also occur in Africa, and Latin America is growing equally quickly.

In more prosperous North America and Europe, however, population growth seems to be stabilizing as women have fewer children and families become smaller—several countries, such as West Germany, now record a zero population growth rate. The poorer countries, the so-called Third World, are therefore gaining, and will probably continue to gain, an increasing share of the world's people. In 1930, about 64 percent of the human race lived in the poor countries of Asia, Africa and Latin America. By 1980, this proportion had increased to more than 75 percent. Population growth in these regions is creating enormous problems. It is estimated that there are now

more than 800 million people living in absolute poverty in the developing world, and these numbers can but increase as populations swell.

An obvious solution is to reduce birth rates, but this cannot be achieved quickly. In much of Africa and Asia, a very high proportion of the population is made up of young people who are, or soon will be, of childbearing age. Population increases are therefore inevitable. This will probably change as family planning becomes more widespread and women have fewer children, but such relief lies in the future and is likely to affect the poorest countries last. The most pressing problem for the growing numbers of impoverished people today is that of hunger.

Food – the fundamental problem
In theory, no food supply problem should exist—already enough food is produced in the world to feed a population of 5,500 million people. In fact, however, two-thirds of this food is consumed by the rich industrialized nations, and supplies are not reaching many of those in need. The developed nations dominate world food markets because developing nations, and people within those nations, are too poor to buy food, and are themselves unable to produce sufficient quantities to feed their growing populations. The answer to undernutrition and malnutrition lies largely in raising the incomes of poor peoples and improving distribution of supplies of food.

At a local level, food produced or imported

by developing countries must reach those in need at a price they can afford. One way of doing this is to encourage the rural poor to produce their own food. Small-scale, intensively farmed plots often prove to be the most efficient form of agriculture in areas where labor is plentiful. At present, many of the rural poor are either without land, or hold plots on extremely unfavorable terms of tenancy. By providing land, appropriate technology (small-scale, inexpensive farming equipment such as windpumps to draw water for irrigation), financial aid and information and education, small farmers could be helped to farm their land as effectively and efficiently as possible.

At a national level, too, developing countries must become more self-sufficient in food. This has already been achieved in some countries. India, although at one time heavily dependent upon imports of one of its staple foodstuffs—rice—has now increased production on such a scale that imports are no longer necessary. Unfortunately, for many developing countries this is not the case. Zaire, for example, was once an exporter of food. Today the country can no longer produce enough to keep pace with the demands of its own expanding population. At a world level, food production must be maintained as well, for unless production is kept high, prices are unstable and at times of bad harvests the poorer nations cannot afford to import essential supplies.

Food alone, however, is not enough to solve

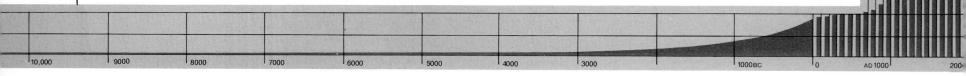

10,000   9000   8000   7000   6000   5000   4000   3000   1000BC   0   AD 1000   200

FEEDING THE WORLD

How are the growing numbers of people on Earth to be fed when millions are already undernourished? In the short term, the food problem could be solved by improving distribution of supplies that are already available. But the world can also be made to produce more food. Fertilizers and pest control can make land more productive and genetic engineering could produce higher-yielding and more nutritious crops.

The world will have to produce more food than it does today (below) if future populations are to be fed. At present, large areas of the Earth's land surface cannot be farmed—they are either too cold, dry, marshy, mountainous or forested. Cultivatable areas could be extended, given the necessary investment.

THE HEALTH OF NATIONS

Many developing nations are severely short of medical and welfare facilities for their growing populations. Yet these are the very countries with high incidences of disease—mainly because of malnutrition, lack of clean water supplies, and inadequate and overcrowded housing. Furthermore, without health services family planning facilities are not widely available, and expanding populations continue to strain existing resources.

Birth and Death Rates
- High birth rate/ High death rate
- High birth rate/ Moderate or low death rate
- Low birth rate/ Low death rate
- Information unavailable

THE NONPRODUCTIVE LANDS

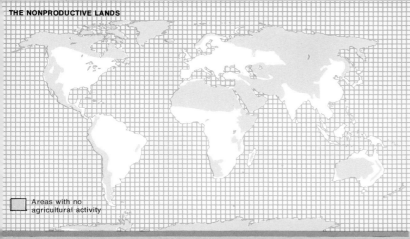

Areas with no agricultural activity

PATTERNS OF POPULATION GROWTH

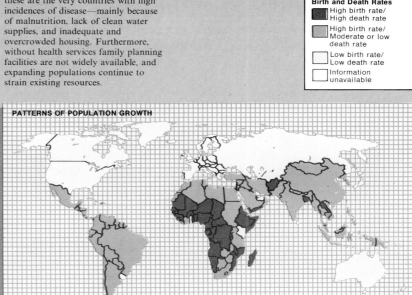

FOOD CONSUMPTION

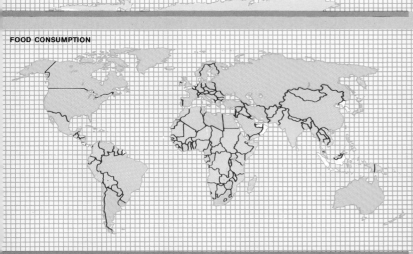

As a country's health facilities improve, its mortality rates decline. Birth rates, however, do not immediately fall (above). Thus, ironically, an improvement in facilities at first exacerbates the problem of rapid growth in population. A country with a declining death rate and a high birth rate gains an increasing percentage of young people who are, or will be, of child-bearing age. Population pyramids (right) plot the percentage balance between age and youth in a nation.

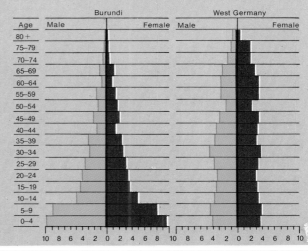

Calories per capita
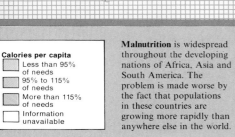
- Less than 95% of needs
- 95% to 115% of needs
- More than 115% of needs
- Information unavailable

Malnutrition is widespread throughout the developing nations of Africa, Asia and South America. The problem is made worse by the fact that populations in these countries are growing more rapidly than anywhere else in the world.

the problems created by population growth. Broadly based economic development, such as in manufacturing and industry, is essential if developing countries are to have the income and other resources to enable them to cope with their evergrowing numbers of people.

Economic growth

To achieve economic development, certain obstacles must be overcome. First, the Third World needs energy supplies at a price it can afford, for, with the exception of Nigeria and the now-rich Middle East, most developing regions are woefully short of the energy resources needed to fuel growth. Second, for sustained economic development a skilled labor force is required, as are educational facilities to provide the necessary skills from within the nations themselves. Third, investment is required to enable developing nations to exploit the resources they do have—minerals, for example. And this investment must be on terms that are as beneficial to the developing nations as they are to powerful multinational organizations that frequently fund such projects. Finally, and most important, more enlightened social and political outlooks are needed within many countries if their growing populations of impoverished people are to benefit from any economic development and consequent increase in national wealth.

It has been said that wealth is the best method of contraception and, judging by the history of population growth in the rich industrialized nations, this seems to be the case. If it is, economic development of the Third World may well alleviate many of the problems created by population growth.

INCOME

When the income level of a population is raised sufficiently, it seems that birth rates ultimately decline. This has been the pattern that has emerged in the Western world. If this is the case, then economic development of the Third World countries could eventually help to stabilize world population growth, as well as provide nations with the means to cope. It could also help provide for their growing numbers.

POVERTY AND WEALTH

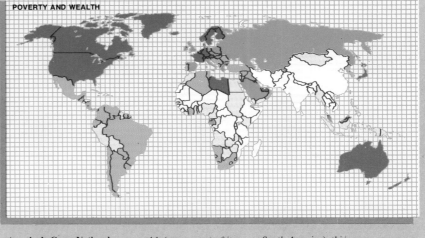

Gross National Product per capita 1978 ($US)

- Less than $300
- $300 to $699
- $700 to $2,999
- $3,000 to $6,999
- $7,000 and over
- Information unavailable

A nation's Gross National Product (GNP), when divided by the number of its population, gives some indication of the relative wealth (or poverty) of its people. But because national wealth is not evenly distributed in many countries (particularly in South America), this figure can conceal the extreme poverty of very large numbers of a nation's people.

EDUCATIONAL RESOURCES

Education is essential if the people of the developing world are to be equipped to improve their lot. Basic education on health and hygiene could dramatically reduce the incidence of disease; education about birth control would help lower birth rates; agricultural advice could help the rural poor to produce more food. Finally, general schooling is required to provide skilled labor.

ILLITERACY

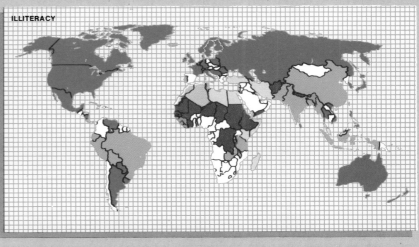

Illiteracy rate

- 80% and over
- 60% to less than 80%
- 40% to less than 60%
- 20% to less than 40%
- Less than 20%
- Information unavailable

Literacy rates are in fact improving in developing countries and national expenditure on schools is growing more quickly than is population. Two major problems are, first, the social traditions that severely restrict the number of girls attending school and, second, the reluctance of many rural poor to send to school children who provide valuable manual labor on the land.

Human Settlement

Man is naturally a gregarious animal. As an agriculturist he first settled in small communities, but it was not long before the emergence of towns and cities. Now nearly half the world's people live in these larger settlements, and by the year 2000, for the first time in history, more people will live in cities than in the countryside. Cities have grown up for various reasons, and are unevenly distributed across the world; but it is in the developing countries that the most rapid rates of urban growth are today taking place.

City life has a long and varied history going back to the early population centers of the Tigris–Euphrates, Indus and Nile valleys. Administrative and political needs led to the development of capital cities. Some, like London and Paris, evolved on conveniently located river crossings; others, such as Canberra, Islamabad and Brasilia, have locations that were deliberately planned.

Types of towns and cities
Market towns were established to exchange produce and, as trade expanded, hierarchies of service centers became established. These ranged from small "central places" that supplied rural areas with simple goods and services from elsewhere, to large cities that provided highly specialized services. Through such centrally placed systems, rural areas became connected with major industrialized areas. Mining towns such as Johannesburg, South Africa, and Broken Hill, Australia, sprang up as man began to exploit the Earth's mineral resources, their locations determined by the presence of rich ore deposits. Fishing ports and settlements dependent on forestry fall into the same group.

Increasing specialization, exemplified by the Black Country, England, and the Ruhr, West Germany, was a feature of European industrial development in the eighteenth and nineteenth centuries, and was based on the availability of capital investment and the presence of sources of fuel and power, especially water and steam power. Such industrialized cities relied on newly developed forms of transport to bring in new materials and to carry away manufactured products. Chicago is a good example of the relationship between the development of rail and water routes and the growth of a city as a market, agricultural processing and manufacturing center. As transport developed, further specialized centers concentrated on locomotive, ship or aircraft construction.

Uneven settlement patterns
Across the world, density and distribution of population are uneven. The land surface of the Earth as a whole has a density of 28 people per sq km (73 per sq mile) although Manhattan, for example, has 26,000 per sq km (63,340 per sq mile) and Australia has only 1.5 per sq km (4 per sq mile). In Brazil, towns and cities are mostly sited in the rich southeast, in contrast to a sparseness of settlement in its interior. Contrasts also occur between Mediterranean North Africa and the deserted Sahara to the south; or Canada of the St. Lawrence and the Canadian Shield to the north. Here the causes are not hard to find: extremes of climate, terrain and vegetation form effective barriers to settlement. Geographers estimate that two-thirds of the world's population lives within 500 km (310 miles) of the sea.

Any true consideration of human settlements must, however, be placed within the context of the economic, political and social systems in which they have evolved. Physical considerations alone cannot fully explain the urban concentrations of Western Europe, Japan or the northeastern USA, or the comparative absence of cities elsewhere. Only 5 percent of Malawi's and 4.7 percent of New Guinea's populations live in towns; in Belgium the percentage is 87, in Australia 86, in the UK 78 and in the USA 73.5. The figure for Norway is only 42 percent. Urbanization is a varied phenomenon and cities grow for many reasons.

The attractions of the city
Cities have always acted as magnets to poor or unemployed rural populations, and migrations from the countryside have assisted high rates of

THE DISTRIBUTION OF POPULATION
Human settlement is highly uneven because it is related to many social and topographical factors. At first, man was tied to the sites of his crops and the grazing land of his cattle; life in nonrural centers only became a typical feature of population development as specialized services came into demand and towns and cities arose to support these needs. But during the 20th century there has been a vast increase in urban populations, particularly in Third World countries.

Oil and gas deposits
Iron ore railroads
Farming
• **Towns**
⊙ **Hydroelectric projects**
+++ **Iron ore railroads**
═══ **Current oil and gas pipelines**

Boston
New York City
Philadelphia
Baltimore
Washington DC
Richmond

Ciudad Guayana
Ciudad Bolivar
VENEZUELA
GUYANA

Expanding settlements (above) and new lines of communication are being developed in the poorly populated eastern lowlands of Venezuela in order fully to exploit the resources being discovered there. Huge deposits of iron ore and large supplies of oil and gas have been located, and Ciudad Bolivar and Ciudad Guayana have become steel-making and service centers. To feed the people of these new settlements, agriculture has been greatly expanded.

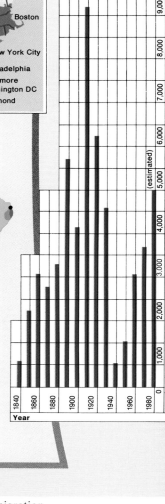

Immigration to the United States (below) from Europe was partly responsible for the growth of the vast Washington–Boston urban mass known as "Megalopolis." Since World War II, more immigrants have come from Puerto Rico and Mexico.

city growth. Very large cities—Tokyo, New York and Los Angeles—are still found in the northern world, but many cities with far faster growth rates are sited in the Third World, especially in Asia. There the total number of inhabitants living in towns and cities is still much lower than in Europe, but centers such as Shanghai, Karachi, Bandung, New Delhi, Seoul, Jakarta and Manila are among the world's most rapidly expanding urban centers. Perhaps as many as a third of these city dwellers in Asia, Africa and Latin America put up with makeshift housing in shanty towns that present enormous problems of health, sanitation, education and unemployment: city growth in the developing world is a daunting prospect.

People on the move
In the past, one solution to population pressure on the land could be found in the migrations which occurred on a large scale from Asia into Europe, from Europe to the Americas and Australasia, and from China into southeastern Asia. But as claims are being made on almost every habitable area of the Earth, mass migrations have largely declined in importance. Many nations restrict movement to or from

their countries. Australia has strict immigration quotas; Vietnam and the USSR restrict emigration for largely ideological reasons. Large movements of labor still take place, however, from the poorer regions of the Mediterranean to the industrial cities of France and Germany. Migrant workers from neighboring countries in Africa also play an essential part in the mining economy of South Africa.

New trends in urbanization
In many industrialized countries, a strong process of decentralization is leading to reductions in the populations of cities and corresponding increases in those of the suburbs and beyond. In 1951 the geographer Jean Gottman showed how groups of city regions tend to form chains of functionally linked cities, to which he gave the term "megalopolis." His prime example was Megalopolis, USA, stretching from north of Boston to south of Washington DC. Similar settlements occur in the Tokyo–Yokohama–Osaka area of Japan and the Ruhr megalopolis of northwestern Europe. Ultimately, equally drastic and large-scale patterns are likely to emerge in the already overcrowded human settlements of the Third World.

Migrating refugees, the world total of which increases on average by 2,000–3,000 every day, can affect settlement patterns. The Ugandan children (below) fled to the northern province of Karamoja in the wake of the 1979 war with Tanzania and the resultant famine that occurred in much of Uganda.

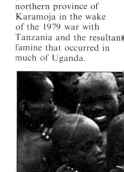

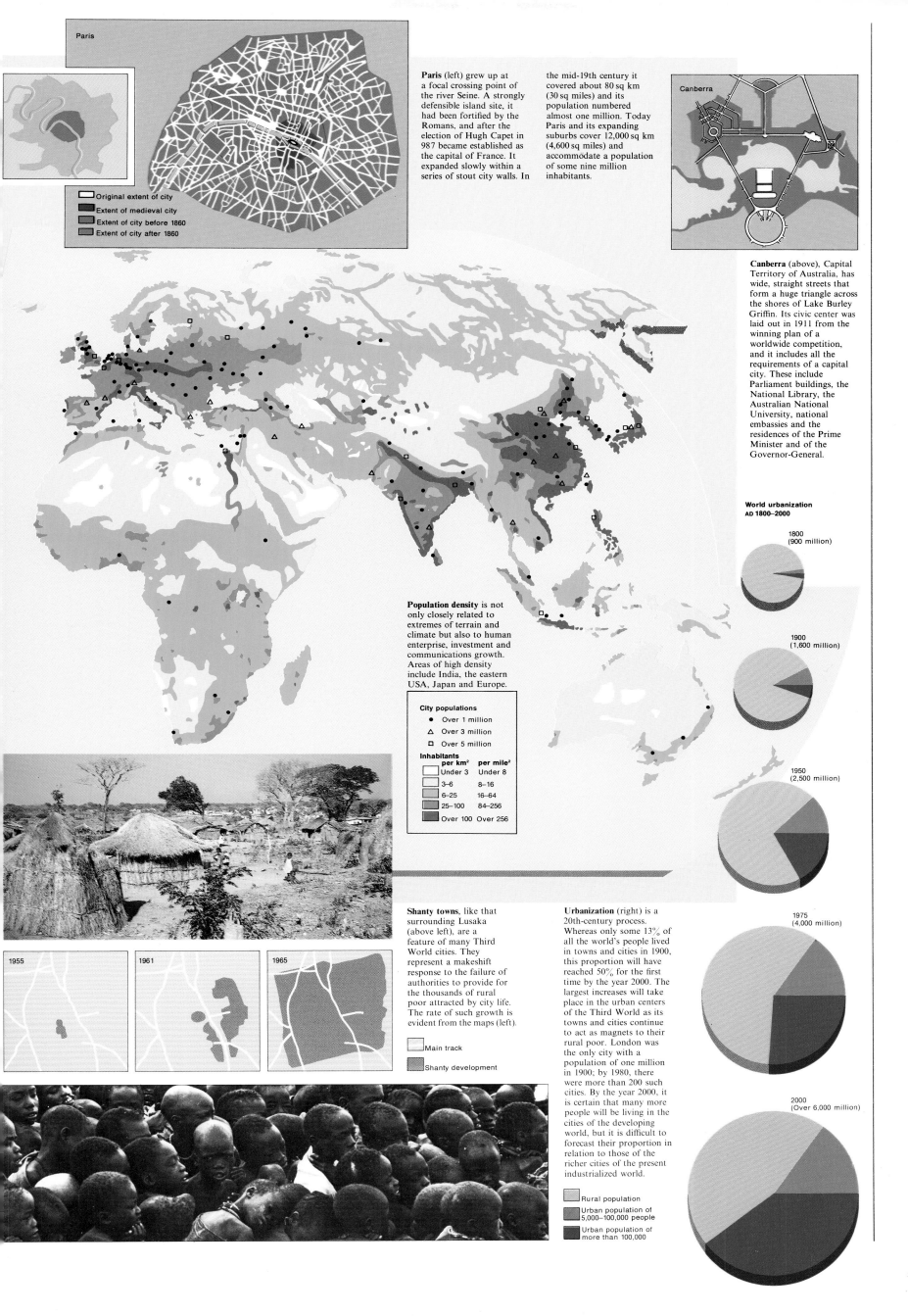

Paris

Original extent of city
Extent of medieval city
Extent of city before 1860
Extent of city after 1860

Paris (left) grew up at a focal crossing point of the river Seine. A strongly defensible island site, it had been fortified by the Romans, and after the election of Hugh Capet in 987 became established as the capital of France. It expanded slowly within a series of stout city walls. In the mid-19th century it covered about 80 sq km (30 sq miles) and its population numbered almost one million. Today Paris and its expanding suburbs cover 12,000 sq km (4,600 sq miles) and accommodate a population of some nine million inhabitants.

Canberra

Canberra (above), Capital Territory of Australia, has wide, straight streets that form a huge triangle across the shores of Lake Burley Griffin. Its civic center was laid out in 1911 from the winning plan of a worldwide competition, and it includes all the requirements of a capital city. These include Parliament buildings, the National Library, the Australian National University, national embassies and the residences of the Prime Minister and of the Governor-General.

Population density is not only closely related to extremes of terrain and climate but also to human enterprise, investment and communications growth. Areas of high density include India, the eastern USA, Japan and Europe.

City populations
● Over 1 million
△ Over 3 million
□ Over 5 million

Inhabitants
	per km²	per mile²
	Under 3	Under 8
	3–6	8–16
	6–25	16–64
	25–100	84–256
	Over 100	Over 256

World urbanization
AD 1800–2000

1800
(900 million)

1900
(1,600 million)

1950
(2,500 million)

1975
(4,000 million)

2000
(Over 6,000 million)

1955

1961

1965

Shanty towns, like that surrounding Lusaka (above left), are a feature of many Third World cities. They represent a makeshift response to the failure of authorities to provide for the thousands of rural poor attracted by city life. The rate of such growth is evident from the maps (left).

Main track

Shanty development

Urbanization (right) is a 20th-century process. Whereas only some 13% of all the world's people lived in towns and cities in 1900, this proportion will have reached 50% for the first time by the year 2000. The largest increases will take place in the urban centers of the Third World as its towns and cities continue to act as magnets to their rural poor. London was the only city with a population of one million in 1900; by 1980, there were more than 200 such cities. By the year 2000, it is certain that many more people will be living in the cities of the developing world, but it is difficult to forecast their proportion in relation to those of the richer cities of the present industrialized world.

Rural population
Urban population of 5,000–100,000 people
Urban population of more than 100,000

57

Trade and Transport

It is a commonplace that we live in a "shrinking" world. During the last century the development of communications has been so rapid that man appears almost to have conquered the challenge of distance; but such a concept depends on the kind of area to be covered and the cost of transporting goods in relation to their value, bulk and perishability. People, goods and services become accessible by trade. Transport makes trade possible: trade's demands lead to improvements in transport.

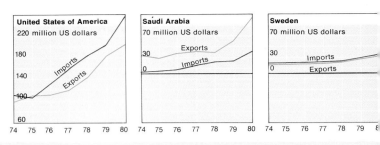

Exports in millions of US dollars (A)

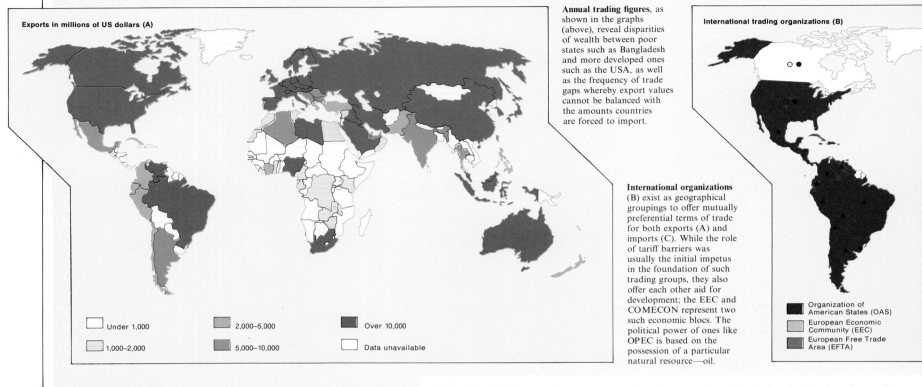

Under 1,000
1,000–2,000
2,000–5,000
5,000–10,000
Over 10,000
Data unavailable

Annual trading figures, as shown in the graphs (above), reveal disparities of wealth between poor states such as Bangladesh and more developed ones such as the USA, as well as the frequency of trade gaps whereby export values cannot be balanced with the amounts countries are forced to import.

International trading organizations (B)

International organizations (B) exist as geographical groupings to offer mutually preferential terms of trade for both exports (A) and imports (C). While the role of tariff barriers was usually the initial impetus in the foundation of such trading groups, they also offer each other aid for development; the EEC and COMECON represent two such economic blocs. The political power of ones like OPEC is based on the possession of a particular natural resource—oil.

Organization of American States (OAS)
European Economic Community (EEC)
European Free Trade Area (EFTA)

Japanese export of electronic products (1979)

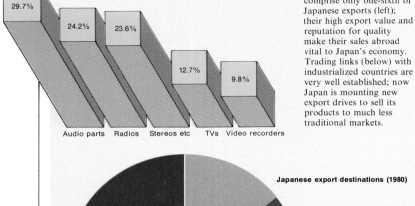

29.7% — Audio parts
24.2% — Radios
23.6% — Stereos etc
12.7% — TVs
9.8% — Video recorders

Electronic products comprise only one-sixth of Japanese exports (left); their high export value and reputation for quality make their sales abroad vital to Japan's economy. Trading links (below) with industrialized countries are very well established; now Japan is mounting new export drives to sell its products to much less traditional markets.

Japanese export destinations (1980)

Industrialized countries
North America
Australasia
Europe

Developing countries
Oil exporters
Asia (inc. China)
Others

Soviet bloc (including
Mongolia & N. Korea)

It is only a little more than two centuries since navigators completed the mapping of the world's major landmasses and much less since the mapping of the continental interiors was completed—even today some gaps still remain. Canals like the Suez (1869) and Panama (1915) reduced the extent of long sea voyages—the Suez Canal shortened the distance from northwestern Europe to India by 15,000 km (9,300 miles)—so that in transport terms, the various parts of the world became more accessible, especially as steamships and motor vessels replaced sailing ships, and time distances were reduced still further by the airplane.

Locational advantages
Inland waterways, roads and railroads opened up new areas for mining or specialized agriculture, and created opportunities for the manufacture of goods and for the distribution of the finished products. The contrast, however, between locations such as London, Tokyo or Chicago (which are accessible to all forms of transport) and parts of South America where modern transport hardly penetrates, has become much more marked over the years. New transport developments tend to connect major centers first of all, and thus increase their already high locational status.

Such developments must nevertheless be seen in the light of the demand for communications and trade between different points, the nature of the goods being carried and the actual cost of transport. Transport improvements have allowed different parts of the world to share ideas

and products; ironically, they have also made such places more dissimilar, since each area of the Earth has had the chance to specialize in the services it can provide most efficiently.

Specialization of area
Before the widespread development of canals and railroads, road transport was expensive and towns and villages tended to be more self sufficient. Railroads played a vital role in reducing transport costs in relation to distance and in providing an opportunity for different areas to specialize. After the emergence of railroad networks in North America, specialized areas of agricultural production quickly developed because they were well adjusted to the climatic conditions needed for growing maize (corn), cotton, fruit and fresh vegetables for the new urban markets. In the southern hemisphere steamships and the introduction of refrigeration enabled meat, butter and cheese to be kept fresh on their journeys to the north.

This concept of specialization of area is basic to world trading patterns, since regions tend to concentrate on commodities and services that they can exchange for other specialized goods and products from other regional or world markets. Countries and areas do best when they concentrate on products for which they have comparative cost advantages in terms of the presence of natural resources, the availability of the skills to develop them, and a demand for the products. Enterprise in adapting natural conditions for the production of goods at competitive price levels is also important. Settlers in New

Man's expanding world

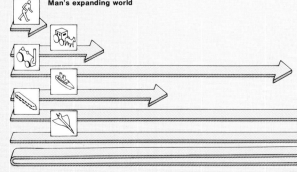

Technological change in transport has resulted in important reductions in the cost of trade. A man trading on foot might travel half the area a

draft horse could cover in a 12-hour day, but it was the acceptance of steam after *The Rocket* (1829) that made trade more reliable and greatly

expanded the potential for international commerce. Modern jet airliners can easily fly thousands of kilometers in half a day, and while they are being

used more and more for freight, most bulk freight is still carried by train or by specialized cargo vessel. The graph below plots changing transport technology.

0   120   240   360   480   600   720   840   960   1,080   1,200   1,320   1,440   1,560
Kilometers traveled in 12 hours

THE WEALTH OF NATIONS

Economists measure a country's richness in terms of Gross National Product (GNP), the value of the goods and services available for consumption and for adding to its wealth. The difference in value between its exported and imported goods is often an important aspect of a nation's economy, and effective systems to transport such goods must play a major role in overseas trade. The 1980 Brandt Report highlighted the huge gap between the income of the rich world and the poverty of many developing states, but solutions to such problems of inequality will be difficult to obtain.

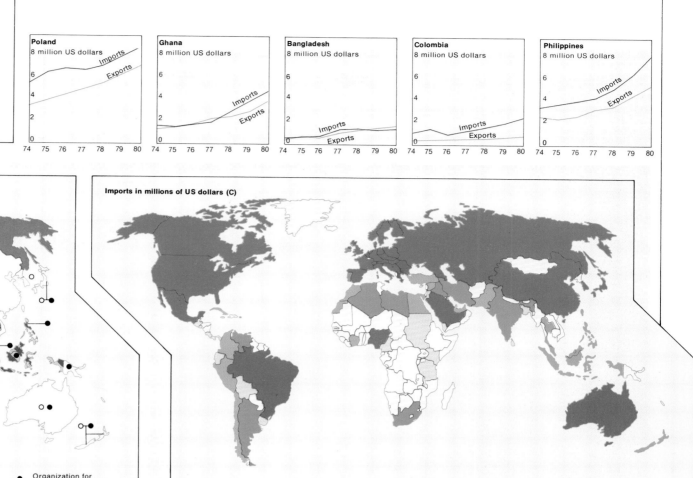

Poland — 8 million US dollars — Imports / Exports — 74 75 76 77 78 79 80

Ghana — 8 million US dollars — Imports / Exports — 74 75 76 77 78 79 80

Bangladesh — 8 million US dollars — Imports / Exports — 74 75 76 77 78 79 80

Colombia — 8 million US dollars — Imports / Exports — 74 75 76 77 78 79 80

Philippines — 8 million US dollars — Imports / Exports — 74 75 76 77 78 79 80

Imports in millions of US dollars (C)

- Council for Mutual Economic Aid (COMECON)
- Organization of Petroleum Exporting Countries (OPEC)
- Association of South-East Asian Nations (ASEAN)
- Organization for African Unity (OAU)
- ▲ Latin American Free Trade Association (LAFTA)
- ■ Arab League (AL)
- ○ Colombo Plan
- ● Organization for Economic Cooperation and Development (OECD)

Under 1,000 | 1,000–2,000 | 2,000–5,000 | 5,000–10,000 | Over 10,000 | Data unavailable

Zealand, for example, had little hesitation in clearing the prevailing tussock grass to create a new pastoral environment for their large-scale production of sheep and dairy products.

In the real world, however, there are many impediments to the operation of a free market system, and it is unwise for states like New Zealand to assume that they will always dominate Commonwealth dairy trade.

Impediments to free markets

Countries erect protectionist tariff barriers to assist their home industries and/or to obtain extra revenue. Import or export quotas may be imposed, and trade agreements with other countries give special preference to certain commodities. Problems arise from the exchange of currencies and their fluctuations in value. Tariff barriers may be erected for political, welfare or defense reasons. Sometimes special measures may be adopted to encourage the internal production of certain goods rather than obtaining them more cheaply from abroad, and such methods may be economically important to a new country that has always relied on the export of raw materials for its income but now wishes domestically to manufacture previously imported goods.

Political ties are vital to the groupings of certain countries. For reasons of international politics, countries such as those of the Soviet bloc trade with each other rather than with the outside world; and historical links, as between the UK and the Commonwealth, France and her ex-colonies, and Spain and Portugal with

Latin America, are also influential. The European Economic Community (EEC) is composed of countries that have formed a strong bloc among the developed countries.

Rich man, poor man

The developed countries of "the North" have more than 80 percent of the world's manufacturing income but only a quarter of its population, whereas the poorer peoples of "the South" number 3,000 million and receive only a fifth of world income. Attempts have been made to obtain a better economic balance. The 1948 General Agreement on Tariffs and Trade (GATT) and the United Nations Conference on Trade and Development (UNCTAD) provided mechanisms for multinational trade negotiations, and the World Bank and the International Monetary Fund (IMF) together with the 1960 International Development Association (IDA) have all provided easier loans for less developed states.

The widening gap between rich and poor countries has led to understandable demands for a new international order calling for basic changes in the structure of world production, aid and trade, and the transfer of resources. The 1980 Independent Commission on International Development Issues (The Brandt Commission) advocated just such a transfer to the Third World. But during a major world recession there seems little sign of any international political will strong enough to take action on the scale needed to solve the problems that contrasts in wealth and poverty involve.

- Land over 1,000 meters
- Trans-African highways
- Major railroads
- Copper belt

The weakness of African communications (above) results from the severe obstacles presented by its terrain and also from its very short period of economic development. Northern Zambia (below right) has copper which comprises some 90% of its exports and is much sought after by the industrialized world. But recent history has severely hampered its economic routes out of Africa; even though Zimbabwe and Mozambique no longer present export barriers, Zambia badly needs to invest in new track and rolling stock.

Zaïre / Tanzania / Angola / Mozambique / Zambia / Zimbabwe

1,800 1,920 2,040 2,160 2,280 2,400 2,520 2,640 2,760 2,880 3,000 3,120 3,240 3,360

Polar Regions

Sunless in winter, and capped with permanent land ice and shifting sea ice, the world's polar regions present an image of intense and everlasting cold. But permanent ice caps have been the exception rather than the rule in the 4,600 million years of Earth's history. The most recent intensification of the present ice age (which began at least two million years ago) reached its maximum about 20,000 years ago and still continues to fluctuate. Polar conditions preclude all but the toughest life forms on land, but the plankton-rich waters attract many animals, and man is beginning to exploit the polar regions' potential.

There have been about a dozen ice ages since the world began. During the intervening periods there was still a zonal pattern of world temperatures, with hot equatorial regions and cooler poles. But the ice caps, which are both chilling and self-sustaining, were absent altogether—the poles being cold temperate rather than icebound. The shiny ice surfaces of today's poles reflect more than 90 percent of the solar radiation which reaches them from the low-angled summer sun, while in winter the sun never rises at all. Thus the regions are now permanently ice capped.

Antarctica, the great southern polar continent, lies under an ice mantle 14 million sq km (5.4 million sq miles) in area, and sometimes more than 4,000 m (13,000 ft) thick. Many of its neighboring islands also carry permanent ice. In the Arctic, the three islands of Greenland lie under a pall of ice of subcontinental size, more than 1.8 million sq km (700,000 sq miles) in area and up to 3,000 m (9,800 ft) thick.

The ice cover of polar seas varies. The central core of the Arctic Ocean carries a mass of permanent pack ice, slowly circulating within the polar basin, which is added to each winter by a belt of ice forming over the open sea. Currents and winds break this up to form pack ice that also circulates, gradually melting in summer or drifting south. Antarctica too is surrounded by fast ice, which breaks up in spring to form a broad belt of persistent pack ice. Circulating slowly about the continent, the pack ice forms huge gyres spreading far to the north, dotted with tabular bergs that have broken away from the continental ice sheet.

The frozen land

In the present glacial phase, the ice caps reached their farthest spread about 20,000 years ago, and then began the retreat which brought them, some 10,000 to 12,000 years ago, to their current position and size. Since then the climate of the polar regions has been both warmer and colder than it is at the present time.

The coldness of the poles is caused by the tilt of the Earth's axis, which prevents sunlight from reaching them at all in the winter. Even in summer, little heat is received from the sun because of the low angle at which its rays reach the surface; much even of this is reflected away by the ice.

The fluctuating nature of the polar climates creates very difficult conditions for plants and animals. Very little will grow on the terrestrial ice caps, but water scarcity rather than cold is the most important factor inhibiting plant growth: the small patches of lichens, algae and mosses that occur on rock faces and nunataks (points of rock jutting above the land ice) are usually in the path of a snowmelt runnel. Vegetation patches sometimes contain tiny populations of insects and mites, which may be active for only a few days each year when the sun warms them from a state of dormancy.

However, these tiny scattered plant communities appear all over Antarctica wherever rock surfaces break through the ice cap, and have been seen less than 300 km (190 miles) from the South Pole, and on peaks 2,000 m (6,600 ft) above sea level. Insects and mites occur within 600 km (380 miles) of the Pole itself. In specially favored positions on the Antarctic Peninsula and the offshore islands, carpets of moss and grasses may be seen. Conditions around the northern terrestrial ice cap are similar, with aridity, strong winds and cold discouraging all but the hardiest plants and the smallest, toughest animal colonies.

The frozen seas

The marine ice caps, by contrast, are relatively lively places, especially during summer, when days are long and the sea ice is patchy. Water-lanes between floes are often rich in microscopic algae and the minute zooplanktonic animals that feed on them. These animals in turn attract fish, sea birds and seals in their thousands, as well as whales—including the largest baleen species. Some of the richest patches of sea are close to islands where strong currents stir the water and bring nutrients to the surface, and these attract semipermanent populations of seals and birds. The birds breed on the island cliffs and feed in the sheltered waters among the ice; the seals may breed on the ice itself, producing their pups on a floating nursery where food is close at hand.

Different species of seals are found on inshore and offshore ice environments. In the Arctic bearded and ringed seals, which produce their young in spring as the inshore ice begins to break up, are often preyed upon by floe-riding polar bears; Eskimos too prize both species for their meat, blubber and skins. Farther out on the offshore pack ice live hooded and harp seals, where their pups are safe from all but the ship-borne commercial hunters. In the Antarctic, Weddell seals are the inshore species, whereas crabeater and Ross seals prefer the distant pack ice. Crabeaters, which feed largely on planktonic krill (once thought to be crab larvae), are probably the most numerous of all seal species with a population estimated at 10 to 15 million.

Sea ice in the north provides a precarious platform on which coastal human populations of the Arctic, such as Eskimos, can extend their winter hunting range. When the land is snowbound and animals are scarce, the sea may still provide food for hunters skilled in fishing, and in stalking seals to their breathing holes.

Nonindigenous inhabitants of the ice cap have greatly increased in recent years, following the discovery and exploitation of oil in the north, as well as other valuable minerals in both the regions. Scientists and technicians today occupy bases and weather stations which in some cases, such as the Amundsen-Scott at the South Pole, are several decades old and have to be maintained by means of aircraft.

EARTH'S FROZEN LIMITS
The permanent ice around Earth's poles covers whole oceans, as well as landmasses of immense size. These ice sheets fluctuate, and on land may be thousands of meters thick, sometimes covering all but the highest mountains, and allowing hardly any life. In the circumpolar seas, however, conditions encourage a very rich growth of plankton, and this supports a plentiful and varied range of wildlife. Man, too, is active in the Arctic, where there are indigenous populations. But in the far south the presence of man is confined to scientists and their support groups. The Antarctic Treaty of 1959 has reserved the continent for nonpolitical scientific use.

THE FAR SOUTH

ATLANTIC OCEAN

PACIFIC OCEAN

INDIAN OCEAN

Antarctic convergence

Arctic summer

Arctic spring

Arctic winter

Arctic autumn

A crushing weight of ice (above) permanently covers the continent and seas of Antarctica, forcing much of the land below sea level. The Antarctic convergence (right), the line at which northern and southern water masses meet, marks a sharp change in temperature and marine life. Especially in areas of upwelling, nutrients make these waters rich in plankton. This feeds a multitude of shrimp-like krill that provide food for a huge number of other animals—fish, penguins, flying birds, seals and whales. The Antarctic landmass allows little natural life, but since the 1959 Antarctic Treaty it has proved to be an area of international scientific cooperation.

- Whales
- Emperor penguin rookeries
- Adélie penguins
- Antarctic terns and petrels
- Ross and crabeater seals
- Leopard seals

Scientific research stations
- United Kingdom
- USSR
- Japan
- Australia
- USA
- Chile
- France
- New Zealand
- Argentina

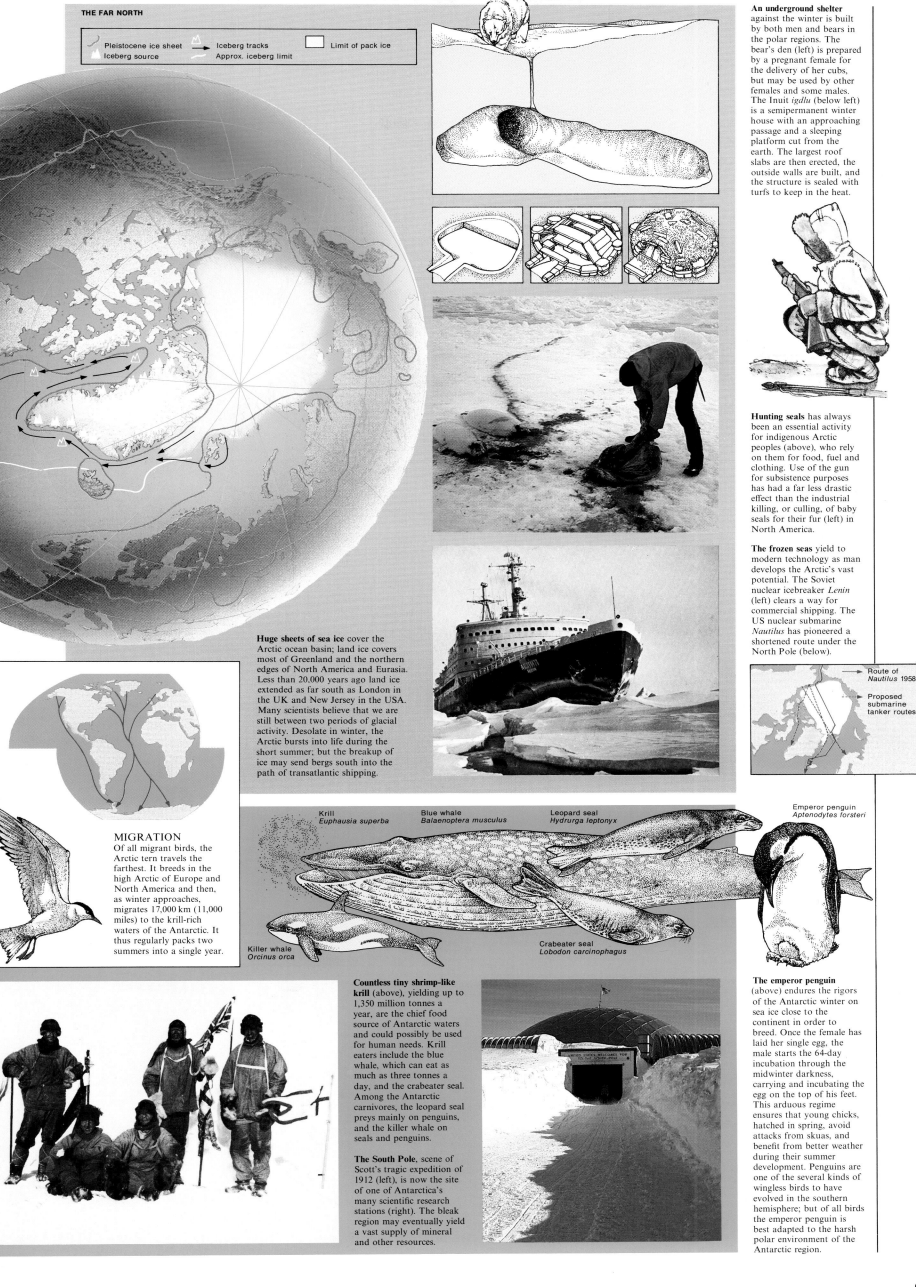

THE FAR NORTH

- Pleistocene ice sheet
- Iceberg source
- Iceberg tracks
- Approx. iceberg limit
- Limit of pack ice

An underground shelter against the winter is built by both men and bears in the polar regions. The bear's den (left) is prepared by a pregnant female for the delivery of her cubs, but may be used by other females and some males. The Inuit *igdlu* (below left) is a semipermanent winter house with an approaching passage and a sleeping platform cut from the earth. The largest roof slabs are then erected, the outside walls are built, and the structure is sealed with turfs to keep in the heat.

Hunting seals has always been an essential activity for indigenous Arctic peoples (above), who rely on them for food, fuel and clothing. Use of the gun for subsistence purposes has had a far less drastic effect than the industrial killing, or culling, of baby seals for their fur (left) in North America.

The frozen seas yield to modern technology as man develops the Arctic's vast potential. The Soviet nuclear icebreaker *Lenin* (left) clears a way for commercial shipping. The US nuclear submarine *Nautilus* has pioneered a shortened route under the North Pole (below).

Route of *Nautilus* 1958

Proposed submarine tanker routes

Huge sheets of sea ice cover the Arctic ocean basin; land ice covers most of Greenland and the northern edges of North America and Eurasia. Less than 20,000 years ago land ice extended as far south as London in the UK and New Jersey in the USA. Many scientists believe that we are still between two periods of glacial activity. Desolate in winter, the Arctic bursts into life during the short summer; but the breakup of ice may send bergs south into the path of transatlantic shipping.

MIGRATION
Of all migrant birds, the Arctic tern travels the farthest. It breeds in the high Arctic of Europe and North America and then, as winter approaches, migrates 17,000 km (11,000 miles) to the krill-rich waters of the Antarctic. It thus regularly packs two summers into a single year.

Krill
Euphausia superba

Blue whale
Balaenoptera musculus

Leopard seal
Hydrurga leptonyx

Emperor penguin
Aptenodytes forsteri

Killer whale
Orcinus orca

Crabeater seal
Lobodon carcinophagus

Countless tiny shrimp-like krill (above), yielding up to 1,350 million tonnes a year, are the chief food source of Antarctic waters and could possibly be used for human needs. Krill eaters include the blue whale, which can eat as much as three tonnes a day, and the crabeater seal. Among the Antarctic carnivores, the leopard seal preys mainly on penguins, and the killer whale on seals and penguins.

The South Pole, scene of Scott's tragic expedition of 1912 (left), is now the site of one of Antarctica's many scientific research stations (right). The bleak region may eventually yield a vast supply of mineral and other resources.

The emperor penguin (above) endures the rigors of the Antarctic winter on sea ice close to the continent in order to breed. Once the female has laid her single egg, the male starts the 64-day incubation through the midwinter darkness, carrying and incubating the egg on the top of his feet. This arduous regime ensures that young chicks, hatched in spring, avoid attacks from skuas, and benefit from better weather during their summer development. Penguins are one of the several kinds of wingless birds to have evolved in the southern hemisphere; but of all birds the emperor penguin is best adapted to the harsh polar environment of the Antarctic region.

Tundra and Taiga

Tundra is land that has been exposed for only about 8,000 years, since the retreat of the ice caps, and only relatively recently occupied by plants. In consequence, few plants and animals have yet had time to adapt to the virtually soilless and treeless environment. The less rigorous conditions of neighboring taiga forest allow a longer growing season and a somewhat wider range of species. The delicately balanced ecology of both areas is being increasingly threatened, however, by the activities of man.

"Tundra," from a Lapp word meaning "rolling, treeless plain," defines the narrow band of open, low ground that surrounds the Arctic Ocean. It lies north of the line beyond which the temperature of the warmest month usually fails to reach 10°C (50°F). North of this trees do not generally grow well, so the line forms a natural frontier between tundra and the broad band of coniferous forest that circles the northern hemisphere to its south between about 60°N and 48°N. This forest, forming the world's largest and most uninterrupted area of vegetation, is usually referred to by its Russian name of "taiga."

Cheerless landscapes

The tundra presents a desolate and restrictive environment for most of the year: in winter there are several months of semidarkness. While there is considerable variation in the climates of places at the same latitude, temperatures average only −5°C (23°F) and are well below freezing for many months of the year. Frost-free days are restricted to a few weeks in midsummer and even then, although days are warmer, the sun is never high in the sky. Nearly all tundra has been free from ice for only a few thousand years. As a result, it either has no soil at all or has developed only a thin covering of

sandy, muddy or peaty soil, successfully colonized by only a few types of plants.

Trimmed by such grazing animals as hares, musk oxen and reindeer or caribou, and by strong winds carrying abrasive rock dust and ice particles, typical tundra vegetation forms a low, patchy mat a few centimeters deep. Much of it grows on permafrost — ground that thaws superficially in summer but remains perennially frozen beneath the surface. Here drainage is poor, shallow ponds are frequent and the scanty soils tend to be waterlogged and acidic. Nevertheless, a small number of grasses, sedges, mosses and marsh plants may grow well and the summer tundra in flower can be an impressive sight. Knee-high forests of dwarf birch, willow and alder grow in valleys sheltered from the strong and biting wind.

The taiga also is a dark and monotonous habitat. Again, while there is a good deal of variation in climatic conditions, on average the region has somewhat milder summers than the tundra with mean average temperatures of 2–6°C (34–42°F), less wind and a slightly longer growing season. The taiga is mostly older than the tundra, and its soils have had longer to mature. They support a small number of tree species, with coniferous spruce, pine, fir and

larch predominating. Short-season broadleaves such as willows, alders, birches and poplars tend to occur on the better soils of river valleys and the edges of forest lakes.

Animals of the far north

The number of animal species supported throughout the year by tundra and taiga is also comparatively small, with interdependent populations that may fluctuate wildly from season to season. In winter both tundra and taiga are silent, although far from deserted. Mice, voles and lemmings remain active, living in tunnels under the snow, which keeps them well insulated from the wind and subzero temperatures. Above the snow Arctic hares forage; they tend to gather in snow-free areas where food can still be found. Arctic foxes are mainly tundra animals and the musk oxen, too, winter on high, exposed tundra where their dense, shaggy coats protect them from the worst

The circumpolar north tha surrounds the permanentl frozen ice cap is dominate by tundra—open plain th remains snowfree for only several months in the summer—and taiga, the vast coniferous forest stretching right round the northern hemisphere. The Siberian taiga, for examp is one-third larger than th entire United States.

Producers

■ USSR

■ USA

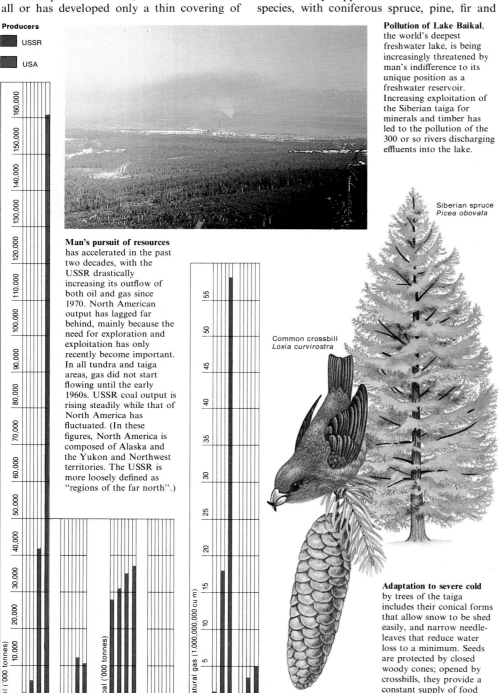

Man's pursuit of resources has accelerated in the past two decades, with the USSR drastically increasing its outflow of both oil and gas since 1970. North American output has lagged far behind, mainly because the need for exploration and exploitation has only recently become important. In all tundra and taiga areas, gas did not start flowing until the early 1960s. USSR coal output is rising steadily while that of North America has fluctuated. (In these figures, North America is composed of Alaska and the Yukon and Northwest territories. The USSR is more loosely defined as "regions of the far north".)

Oil ('000 tonnes) / Coal ('000 tonnes) / Natural gas (1,000,000,000 cu m)

1960 1965 1970 1975

Pollution of Lake Baikal, the world's deepest freshwater lake, is being increasingly threatened by man's indifference to its unique position as a freshwater reservoir. Increasing exploitation of the Siberian taiga for minerals and timber has led to the pollution of the 300 or so rivers discharging effluents into the lake.

Siberian spruce
Picea obovata

Common crossbill
Loxia curvirostra

Adaptation to severe cold by trees of the taiga includes their conical forms that allow snow to be shed easily, and narrow needle-leaves that reduce water loss to a minimum. Seeds are protected by closed woody cones; opened by crossbills, they provide a constant supply of food during winter.

Reindeer or caribou
Rangifer tarandus

Raven
Corvus corax

Arctic fox
Alopex lagopus

Capercaillie
Tetrao urogallus

Snowy owl
Nyctea scandiaca

Brown lemming
Lemmus lemmus

Arctic skua
Stercorarius parasiticus

January
February
March
April
May

Movement in these regions takes many directions. The capercaillie spends all winter in the taiga, where it thrives on the abundant conifer needles, buds and shoots. Some move southward into deciduous woods during the summer months. The Arctic skua breeds on the tundra but moves to the warmer oceans in winter, while the tundra movements of the all-scavenging raven and the snowy owl are governed by those of their

prey. The raven picks clea the carcasses left by other predators; the snowy owl feeds on small rodents suc as mice and lemmings, as does the Arctic fox. Lemmings remain static and inconspicuous in normal years but some populations expand rapid every third or fourth year, leading to mass local migration in every direction, possibly caused by an abundance of vegetation that encourage more frequent breeding.

□ Tundra   □ Taiga

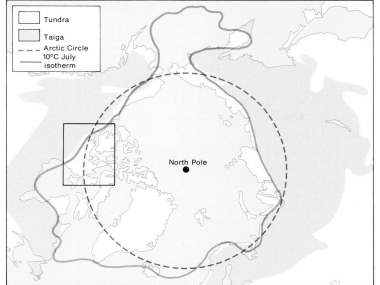

Tundra
Taiga
Arctic Circle
10°C July isotherm

The rough boundary between the tundra and taiga—the tree line—approximates to the 10°C July isotherm, the climatic point north of which trees fail to grow successfully. Seasonal caribou migration in the Canadian barren grounds (boxed) is shown in the main diagram (below). Such migration is also undertaken by reindeer in northern Eurasia.

North Pole

weather. Bears, badgers, beavers and squirrels are common taiga mammals. Elk and reindeer (in North America, moose and caribou) winter in the shelter of the taiga; wolves are mostly woodland animals in winter, following their prey to the open tundra in spring. Red foxes, coyotes, mink and wolverines also move to the tundra in summer.

Snow buntings, ptarmigans and snowy owls live on the tundra throughout the coldest months and are fully adapted to life there. Crossbills and capercaillies are among taiga residents, equipped to live on its abundant conifer buds, seeds and needles. Enormous populations of migrant birds, especially water birds and waders, fly north to both tundra and taiga with the spring thaw. Waxwings, bramblings, siskins and redpolls leave their temperate latitudes to feed on the lush and fast-growing vegetation and the profusion of insects that appear as soon as the snows begin to melt.

Man in the northlands

These circumpolar regions act as a strategic buffer between the USA and the USSR. Situated between the world's greatest centers of population, they are now crisscrossed with air routes. A total population of about nine million people currently inhabits the tundra and taiga. Numbers have been increased by the immigration of technicians and administrators during the last few decades; oil prospecting and mining, forest exploitation and other activities of these newcomers is altering the seminomadic lives of the million or so aboriginal peoples such as the Khanty (Ostyaks) and Nentsy (Samoyeds) of the USSR, the Samer (Lapps) of Scandinavia and the Soviet Union, and the Inuit (formerly Eskimos) of North America. New roads, exploitation of minerals and forests, and pipeline construction have disrupted the migration of their reindeer (caribou) and their land has been appropriated for hydroelectric schemes.

In the taiga, the Soviets are constructing railroads and towns and extracting huge amounts of timber; they have prospected widely and successfully for gold, nickel, iron, tin, mica, diamonds and tungsten, and have discovered vast reserves of oil and natural gas in western Siberia. Alaskan oil, discovered in 1968, now flows across the state at 54–62°C (130–145°F), and to protect the permafrost from this heat the pipeline has had to be elevated for half its 1,300 km (800 mile) length. The pipe's route to the ice-free port of Valdez has interfered with the migration of caribou; hunting and other pressures have led to a drop in their population from three million to some 200,000 in about 30 years. Only official protection has saved the musk ox from a similar fate. These bleak areas are so vast and inhospitable that living space there will never be threatened. However, if only on a local scale, their ecologies are under increasing pressure from man.

The summer tundra—seen here in Swedish Lapland—provides a wide cover of low plants including "reindeer mosses" and other lichens. Grazing reindeer return minerals to the soil. Shallow ponds form as the frozen ground above the permafrost thaws for a few months in summer. Mountains stay partly snow covered in the warmest weather and are a prominent physical feature of the tundra.

Many Norwegian Lapps (or Samer) derive their income from reindeer, which they domesticated many centuries ago to provide meat, milk and skins. Now they follow them through the seasons along well-worn and familiar routes. Such nomadic life styles are becoming rarer as Samer settle down.

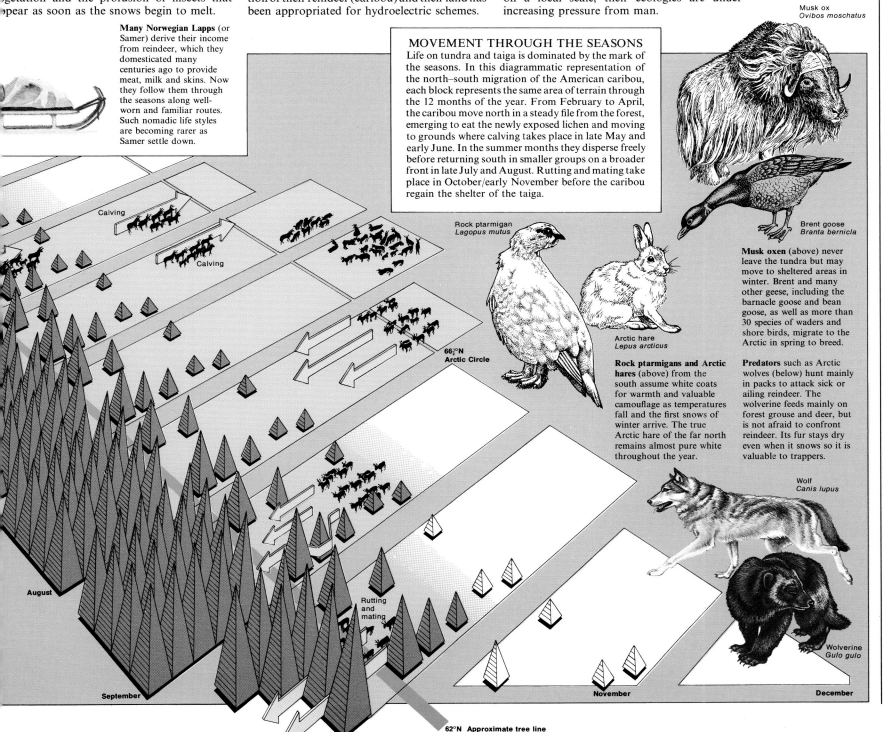

MOVEMENT THROUGH THE SEASONS

Life on tundra and taiga is dominated by the mark of the seasons. In this diagrammatic representation of the north–south migration of the American caribou, each block represents the same area of terrain through the 12 months of the year. From February to April, the caribou move north in a steady file from the forest, emerging to eat the newly exposed lichen and moving to grounds where calving takes place in late May and early June. In the summer months they disperse freely before returning south in smaller groups on a broader front in late July and August. Rutting and mating take place in October/early November before the caribou regain the shelter of the taiga.

Calving

Calving

66½°N
Arctic Circle

August

September

Rutting and mating

62°N Approximate tree line

October

November

December

Musk ox
Ovibos moschatus

Rock ptarmigan
Lagopus mutus

Brent goose
Branta bernicla

Arctic hare
Lepus arcticus

Musk oxen (above) never leave the tundra but may move to sheltered areas in winter. Brent and many other geese, including the barnacle goose and bean goose, as well as more than 30 species of waders and shore birds, migrate to the Arctic in spring to breed.

Rock ptarmigans and Arctic hares (above) from the south assume white coats for warmth and valuable camouflage as temperatures fall and the first snows of winter arrive. The true Arctic hare of the far north remains almost pure white throughout the year.

Predators such as Arctic wolves (below) hunt mainly in packs to attack sick or ailing reindeer. The wolverine feeds mainly on forest grouse and deer, but is not afraid to confront reindeer. Its fur stays dry even when it snows so it is valuable to trappers.

Wolf
Canis lupus

Wolverine
Gulo gulo

Temperate Forests

At one time, dense, primeval forests blanketed large areas of North America, Europe and eastern Asia. Almost all of the trees that flourished in these temperate regions were deciduous – they shed their leaves in autumn, stood bare branched through winter and produced new foliage every spring. Little of this forest now exists. The few remaining pockets, however, still provide habitats for a large range of shade-loving plants: lichens and fungi, tree-hugging mosses, scrambling creepers and shrubs. And this vegetation in turn provides sanctuary for a surprisingly wide variety of forest creatures.

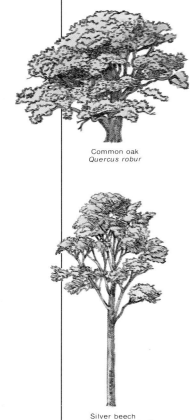

Common oak
Quercus robur

Silver beech
Nothofagus menziesii

Deciduous trees such as the oak (top) make up the temperate forests in cooler temperate regions. In milder, wetter climates, where the seasons are less distinct, evergreens such as southern beech (above) are typical temperate species.

The greater part of the temperate forest zone lies in the northern hemisphere, where winter soil temperatures reduce the ability of plants to absorb water. Hence the trees tend to shed their leaves, which use up moisture through evaporation. In the southern hemisphere, however, the temperate latitudes encourage a type of rainforest in such areas as southern Chile, Tasmania, New Zealand and parts of southeastern Australia. Here the climate is maritime, often with high rainfall and frequent fogs, and evergreen rather than deciduous types of trees grow. Temperate rainforests also occur in the northern hemisphere, in China and in northwestern and northeastern North America.

Deciduous forest consists of a mixture of trees, sometimes with one variety predominant. In central Europe, beech is the leading—and sometimes the only—tree species, whereas oaks mixed with other species made up the forest farther west and east. In North America, beech and maple were once extensive.

The climate in temperate forest zones varies sharply according to seasons—summers tend to be warm, winters moderately cold, and rainfall fairly regular. In fact, the seasonal rhythm is a central feature of temperate forests, and it affects the entire ecosystem—the whole community of plants and animals found there. Soils are generally of the fertile "brown earth" type: the leaf litter of deciduous forests in particular breaks down easily, and is quickly worked into the soil by burrowing animals such as earthworms. In wetter or rockier regions, the soil is more "podsolic"—bleached, sandy and less fertile than the true brown earths.

After the ice

Two million years ago, a series of ice sheets began to extend into the temperate latitudes. In Europe, species moving south before the advancing cold were cut off from the warmer climates by the east–west run of mountains. As a result, many varieties of plants and animals

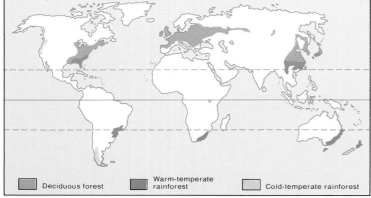

Natural distribution: in the northern hemisphere's temperate zone deciduous forests occur in the cooler areas—in eastern USA, northeastern China, Korea, the northern parts of Japan's Honshu island and western Europe. These forests only give way to evergreens in the warmer and wetter parts of the zone. In the southern hemisphere, the climate is generally much milder throughout the temperate zone and so there are virtually no deciduous forests. Evergreen forests, however, can be found in southeastern South Africa, Chile, New Zealand, Australia and Tasmania.

Deciduous forest	Warm-temperate rainforest	Cold-temperate rainforest

were killed off. Species were reduced still further in islands such as Britain, where the newly formed barriers of the English Channel, Irish Sea and North Sea made recolonization even more difficult after the ice had retreated.

Eastern Asia was one of the few areas in the world that escaped the extreme climatic changes of the ice ages and therefore its temperate forests, unlike those of Europe, still contain an enormous variety of tree species. North America also fared better than Europe, for although glaciers at one time extended deep into the continent, the north–south direction of the mountain ranges allowed relatively easy migration of trees southwards as the climate worsened. Hence most species survived and were able to reoccupy their former territories when the ice retreated. As a result, some 40 species of deciduous trees occur in the North American forests, and contribute to the spectacular display of color during the autumn, notably in

the eastern USA. But a combination of climatic change and, more recently and importantly, of intense human activity, has meant that the remnants of temperate forest seen today differ greatly from the original forest in both composition and form. Only in remote regions such as the southern Appalachian Mountains do substantial areas of the original forest survive. Elsewhere, regrowth has occurred, but much of this is essentially scrub woodland.

The forest structure

Mature temperate deciduous forest is made up of distinct horizontal layers, particularly where the dominant tree is the oak, which allows enough light for a rich shrub layer to grow beneath it. The largest trees, such as oak, maple or ash, may be 25–50 m (80–160 ft) tall, and beneath them grows a prominent layer of smaller trees such as hazel, hornbeam or yew. Lower down again, a varied ground cover of perennial herbs, ferns, lichens and mosses flourishes in the comparative dampness of the forest floor. Because the trees are bare of leaves in winter, many of the plants growing on the forest floor take advantage of the warmth and light of spring to flower early in the year before the main trees come into full leaf and prevent the sun from reaching them. Various woody climbers, such as ivy and honeysuckle, are also present, growing over the trees and shrubs.

Much of the food supply in temperate forests is locked up in the trees themselves, but the annual fall of leaves in the deciduous forests produces a soil rich in nourishment. This supports a vast quantity of life, ranging in size from earthworms and insects to microscopic bacteria of the soil. The death of individual trees and branches also releases the food supply back to the earth. In shady, damp locations, insects, fungi, bacteria and other decomposing agents break down the leaves and other plant and animal debris more quickly, returning them to the soil as food for new plants.

Creatures of the forest

Temperate forests once contained many varieties of animal life, including several species of large animals. Herbivores such as wild oxen, wood bison, elk and moose ate grass and leaves; scavengers such as wild pigs rooted in the forest floor; predators such as wolves preyed on the other animals. Most of these have now been hunted to extinction by man or are extremely rare. Smaller animals still survive in comparatively large numbers, and include squirrels, chipmunks and raccoons, hedgehogs, wood mice, badgers and foxes.

The bird life of temperate forests is very diverse. Some species are insect eaters, exploring the bark and crevices for insects and grubs. Others, such as the wood pigeon, concentrate on seeds. Yet others, like the tawny owl, are predators. Complex interactions between predators and prey have developed at all levels of the forest, from the high canopy to the rotting ground litter, with each group evolving more efficient techniques of capture or escape in a kind of evolutionary race for survival.

The invertebrate insect life is also extremely varied and numerous, and forms a key component of the ecosystem. Oaks are particularly rich in insect life, and more than 100 species of moths feed on their leaves.

The plant and animal life of the temperate forest is remarkably rich and plentiful. And yet it is only a fraction of what once existed. Ever since man has occupied these regions he has found them so suited to his needs that he has long since cleared most of the original tree cover, replaced it with "civilization" and, in the process, destroyed innumerable species of forest wildlife.

THE SEASONAL CYCLE

It is the cycle of the four seasons that gives the temperate deciduous forest its distinctive character. All animals and plants have adapted their ways of life to cope with the seasonal changes in heat, light, moisture and food. The yearly shedding and regrowth of the forest's leaves is one of the most striking and important of adaptations to the seasonal cycle and one that affects all other life in the forest. In summer the leafy canopy of the trees blocks out the sunlight from the forest floor and creates unsuitable conditions for many other plants to flourish. When the leaves fall they form a layer over the soil and provide winter protection for the plant roots and hibernating animals beneath the ground. Finally, once the dead leaves have been broken down, they give fertility to the soil and provide food for future generations of plants.

SPRING

Between February and April, the low spring sun climbs steadily higher in the sky, streaming through the still leafless branches of the trees, falls more directly on the forest floor, warming the soil and melting the last frosts. As soon as the days become warmer the sluggish sap in the trees begins to flow more quickly, carrying nutrients to the branches, where leaf buds start to form.

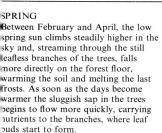

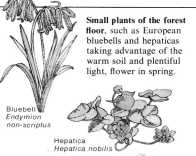

Bluebell
Endymion non-scriptus

Hepatica
Hepatica nobilis

Small plants of the forest floor, such as European bluebells and hepaticas taking advantage of the warm soil and plentiful light, flower in spring.

Forest insects emerge in spring, some, such as the emperor moth, from their winter cocoons, some from hibernation and some newly hatched from eggs.

Small emperor moth
Saturnia pavonia

European blackbird *Turdus merula*

Birds building nests in early spring make use of the forest's winter litter— broken twigs, dead leaves and dried grasses all serve as construction materials.

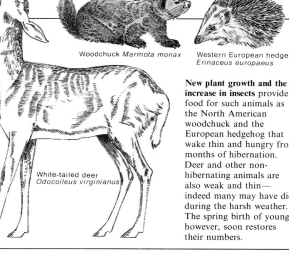

Woodchuck *Marmota monax*

Western European hedgehog
Erinaceus europaeus

White-tailed deer
Odocoileus virginianus

New plant growth and the increase in insects provide food for such animals as the North American woodchuck and the European hedgehog that wake thin and hungry from months of hibernation. Deer and other non-hibernating animals are also weak and thin— indeed many may have died during the harsh weather. The spring birth of young, however, soon restores their numbers.

SUMMER

By early summer the leaves of the trees are fully grown. They form a dense canopy, blocking out the sun and cooling the soil of the forest floor. Most of the small ground plants have long since finished flowering, but their leaves remain green and they continue actively storing food in their roots ready for their rapid spring growth.

Cranberry *Vaccinium oxycoccus*

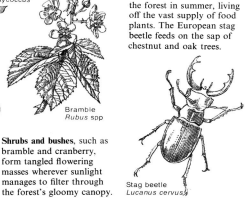

Bramble
Rubus spp

Shrubs and bushes, such as bramble and cranberry, form tangled flowering masses wherever sunlight manages to filter through the forest's gloomy canopy.

Stag beetle
Lucanus cervus

Hordes of insects inhabit the forest in summer, living off the vast supply of food plants. The European stag beetle feeds on the sap of chestnut and oak trees.

Willow warbler
Phylloscopus trochilus

The North American pewee and the willow warbler are two of the forest's many summer visitors that feed on the insect population. Some seed-eating birds, finches for example, also take advantage of this summer food supply.

Eastern wood pewee
Contopus virens

Hazel mouse
Muscardinus avellanarius

The hazel mouse protects its young by raising them in a summer nest, which it builds in a tree: almost every creature in the forest is viewed as a source of food by some other animal and the young litters are particularly at risk.

AUTUMN

As the autumn days grow shorter and cooler the forest foliage begins to turn color; the trees are responding to the drop in temperature and are cutting off the food supply to their leaves, which lose their green color and fall to the ground, forming a thick carpet on the forest's floor. Rain, frost, insects, earthworms and fungi then break down the leaves, making them part of the fertile forest soil.

Ripe fruits and seeds of the forest trees—acorns, beech nuts and hazel nuts—drop to the ground, where a few are buried in the layers of dead leaves and remain protected until they sprout in the early spring.

Common hazel
Corylus avellana

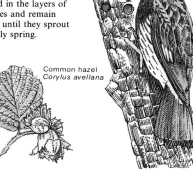

Preparing for winter, the acorn woodpecker stores seeds in holes that it drills in tree trunks. Chipmunks hide supplies of nuts in their winter nests.

Acorn woodpecker
Melanerpes formicivorus

American black bear
Ursus americanus

Oak
Quercus spp

Eastern chipmunk
Tamias striatus

The black bear of North America, like other winter hibernators, consumes vast quantities of food during autumn to build up its winter stores of food in the form of body fat.

WINTER

By winter, only evergreen shrubs and a few small hardy plants remain green. Many of the plants of the forest floor lose their green leaves during the first deep frost. The leaves of the trees still lie rotting on the bare ground, but within the soil, beneath the protective layers of leaf litter, plants are growing and spring flowers are developing buds.

Late-fruiting plants, such as holly, mistletoe and dog rose, provide food for winter residents of the temperate forest such as the European hawfinch.

Hawfinch
Coccothraustes coccothraustes

Holly
Ilex spp

European woodcock
Scolopax rusticola

North American screech owl
Otus asio

Woodcocks are insect-eaters. They can survive winter by prizing insects from the soil with their long beaks, providing that the ground is not too deeply frozen.

Owls and foxes remain fairly active in winter, regularly leaving their nests or lairs to catch small animals or birds that are also in search of food.

Red fox
Vulpes vulpes

European badger
Meles meles

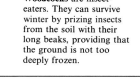

European badgers, like racoons, opossums, bears and skunks, are "shallow" hibernators. On mild winter days they wake and go to search for food.

THE EVERGREEN TEMPERATE RAINFORESTS

There are two main kinds of temperate rainforest, the warm temperate, such as can still be found on North Island, New Zealand (left), and the cold temperate, such as that of the Chilean coast. Both of these kinds of forest have one major feature in common: they have enough water for even the most moisture-greedy plants, such as mosses and ferns, to grow throughout the year. The animal life of the forest is also affected by the abundance of rain, so that snails, slugs, frogs and other water-loving creatures flourish. Most temperate rainforest is of the warm-temperate kind, normally found on the edges of subtropical regions, and the vegetation, with palms, lianas, bamboos, as well as ferns and mosses, is similar to, although less rich than, the tropical rainforest's vegetation. The cold-temperate rainforests grow in cooler regions but their coastal position means that the climate is milder and wetter than inland (where deciduous trees dominate). Their vegetation is less lush and less varied than the warm-temperate forests, but mosses and ferns grow in abundance. Broad-leaved evergreens, such as New Zealand's southern beech, are the most common trees of these forests, although on the northwestern coast of North America Douglas firs and other conifers outnumber the broad-leaved evergreen species.

Man and the Temperate Forests

Temperate forests have suffered enormously at the hands of man. For the great civilizations of China, Europe and, later, North America the forests not only yielded cropland for expanding populations but also contributed materials and fuel for early technologies. More recently the demands of industry have reduced the forests still further. But today, scientists believe that this depleted resource could again play an important role in providing energy, food and materials for future generations.

PERMANENT SETTLEMENT
The Bronze Age and, later, the Iron Age laid the foundations of Chinese and Western civilizations. The forest shrank as permanent settlements grew (3) and, with the use of metals and improved technology, agricultural land was extended (4). But the forest was recognized as an important resource and areas were protected. Management techniques were introduced that, especially in medieval Europe, changed dense forest to coppice woods (5).

EARLY INDUSTRIAL TIMES
Sources of cropland and timber had been discovered in the New World, but in the Far East and Europe forests were drastically reduced. Virtually no Chinese forest remained, and in Europe nations began importing timber to serve growing industrial needs (6). To help solve shortages, plantations were established on country estates (7), which were often landscaped into parkland and planted with introduced species of trees (8).

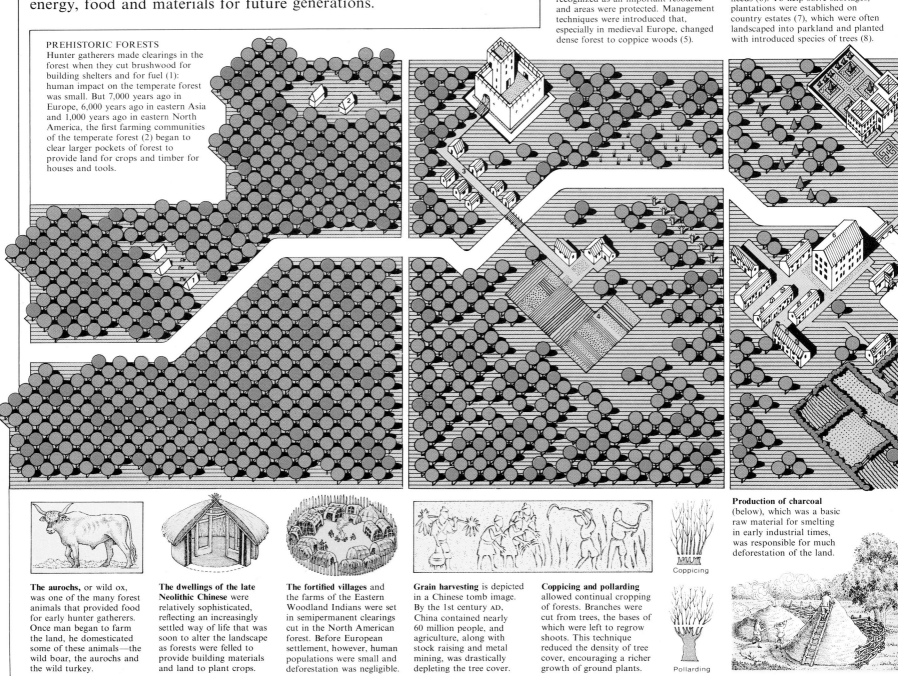

PREHISTORIC FORESTS
Hunter gatherers made clearings in the forest when they cut brushwood for building shelters and for fuel (1): human impact on the temperate forest was small. But 7,000 years ago in Europe, 6,000 years ago in eastern Asia and 1,000 years ago in eastern North America, the first farming communities of the temperate forest (2) began to clear larger pockets of forest to provide land for crops and timber for houses and tools.

The aurochs, or wild ox, was one of the many forest animals that provided food for early hunter gatherers. Once man began to farm the land, he domesticated some of these animals—the wild boar, the aurochs and the wild turkey.

The dwellings of the late Neolithic Chinese were relatively sophisticated, reflecting an increasingly settled way of life that was soon to alter the landscape as forests were felled to provide building materials and land to plant crops.

The fortified villages and the farms of the Eastern Woodland Indians were set in semipermanent clearings cut in the North American forest. Before European settlement, however, human populations were small and deforestation was negligible.

Grain harvesting is depicted in a Chinese tomb image. By the 1st century AD, China contained nearly 60 million people, and agriculture, along with stock raising and metal mining, was drastically depleting the tree cover.

Coppicing and pollarding allowed continual cropping of forests. Branches were cut from trees, the bases of which were left to regrow shoots. This technique reduced the density of tree cover, encouraging a richer growth of ground plants.

Coppicing

Pollarding

Production of charcoal (below), which was a basic raw material for smelting in early industrial times, was responsible for much deforestation of the land.

Human interference with the forests goes back deep into prehistory. There is evidence that fire was used to stampede hunted animals in southern Europe as long as 400,000 years ago. Human populations, while they remained small, had only a slight effect on the vast stretches of primeval forest. Even so, hunting practices and the use of fire to clear land reduced some of the forests of Europe and Asia even before the invention of agriculture. In the New World, too, Eastern Woodland Indians had already affected the North American forests, and early Maori hunters had burned much of the tree cover of New Zealand by the time Europeans arrived.

Nevertheless it was the development of agriculture in Neolithic (New Stone Age) times that had the first really destructive effect on the temperate forests. Clearings were made for crops and the felled trees provided fuel and building material for the new communities. Large forest animals suffered as well, some (such as deer) being hunted for food and others (such as wolves) because they threatened grazing animals. But it was the population increase resulting from the new, settled way of life that caused the extension of man-made cropland deep into former forests.

With man's development of metals, more forests were destroyed: wood and charcoal were used for smelting and the new iron tools made tree clearance easier and more thorough. Firing of forests was also a familiar military ploy, used by such warriors as the Romans.

Medieval woodlands

By medieval times, large tracts of forest had been cleared in Europe and in the Far East, although in the former area there remained extensive royal hunting forest reserves. Local woodlands were carefully managed to serve the needs of the community; the techniques used included pollarding and coppicing.

Pollarding involved the cropping of main branches at a certain height above ground. In coppicing, the "coppice with standards" method was used to harvest the smaller species, such as hazel and hornbeam, whereas the standards (such as oaks) were cut on a longer rotation of 100 years or so. Alternatively, the oak itself could be part of the coppice crop, its stems being cut near ground level so that shoots arose from the stump, to be cut 10 to 20 years later. For local communities, industries and cities, forests provided a variety of materials for building, tanning and fencing, as well as dyestuffs, charcoal and domestic fuel.

The growth of the iron and shipbuilding industries in the sixteenth century devastated so much woodland and forest that in many regions good timber became scarce and had to be imported from considerable distances. The pressure on woodland continued until the production of coke and cheap coal brought some relaxation, but by the early twentieth century the coppice system had broken down and management of Europe's woodlands had largely been abandoned. In Europe the poor state of the deciduous forests was further worsened by two world wars. Many countries have since set up organizations with the specific task of building reserves of timber. Economic pressures, however, have led to the planting mainly of quick-growing conifers, rather than typical trees of the temperate deciduous forest.

New World forests

The migrants who settled in the New World were the descendants of the people who had largely destroyed the forests of Europe. Confronted by the temperate deciduous forests of eastern North America, they virtually continued where they had left off. Tracts were cleared to create arable and range land and to provide the massive amounts of timber needed for the colonization, industrialization and urbanization of North America. With the opening of the prairie lands for agriculture, however,

Disturbance to the natural vegetation has occurred throughout the temperate forest zone. Exploitation of this biome's greatest resource, its agricultural potential, has been one of the major causes of deforestation. The only forests that have escaped major disturbance are in remote areas, too rocky or too steep for cultivation. Today, intensive farming is still a major economic activity of the temperate forest regions. But farmland is not the only important resource to have disturbed the forests. Mining for key minerals such as copper, iron and coal, all of which made possible the development of Western and Chinese civilization, has also contributed to destruction of the forest cover. For centuries the forests provided man with food, fuel and materials, but, ironically, it has been the removal of the forest that has enabled man to exploit the most important of these regions' resources.

THE CHANGING LANDSCAPE
Mankind has been occupying the temperate forest regions for many thousands of years, at first with little effect on the natural forest ecology. But during the last 2,000 years human activity has destroyed the original tree cover at an accelerating pace. As populations increased and economies developed —at different rates in the three major regions— forests disappeared to be replaced by farms, cities, industries and communications networks. Today, scarcely any of the original forest cover remains.

THE 19TH CENTURY
The Industrial Revolution developed in Europe and the New World, large towns and cities sprang up (9), pushing back the woodlands and forests still farther. This process was aided by the spreading network of railroads (10). Coke, iron and other minerals were replacing timber products as raw materials for growing industries (11), but demands were still made on the forests to provide, for example, railway sleepers and mine pit props.

FORESTS TODAY
The 20th century has seen an increasing trend towards urbanization in areas that were once temperate forest. Housing complexes (12) and new factory sites (13) cover large areas, while roadbuilding (14), industrial agriculture (15) and open-cast mining (16) destroy remaining woodland. Leisure areas (17) and nature reserves protect some woods, but plantations of exotic conifers (18) do not always provide suitable wildlife habitats.

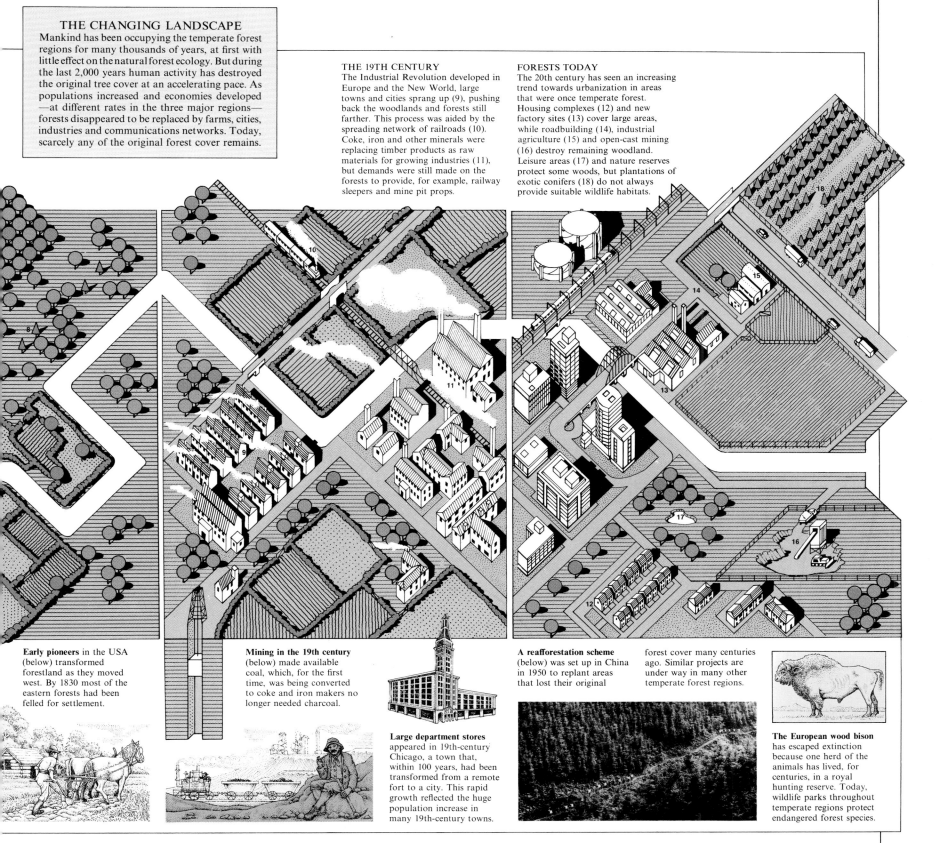

Early pioneers in the USA (below) transformed forestland as they moved west. By 1830 most of the eastern forests had been felled for settlement.

Mining in the 19th century (below) made available coal, which, for the first time, was being converted to coke and iron makers no longer needed charcoal.

Large department stores appeared in 19th-century Chicago, a town that, within 100 years, had been transformed from a remote fort to a city. This rapid growth reflected the huge population increase in many 19th-century towns.

A reafforestation scheme (below) was set up in China in 1950 to replant areas that lost their original forest cover many centuries ago. Similar projects are under way in many other temperate forest regions.

The European wood bison has escaped extinction because one herd of the animals has lived, for centuries, in a royal hunting reserve. Today, wildlife parks throughout temperate regions protect endangered forest species.

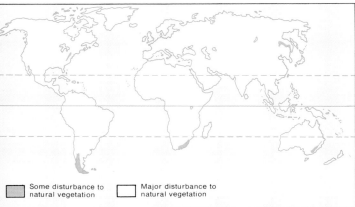

Some disturbance to natural vegetation

Major disturbance to natural vegetation

the pressures shifted, some of the east coast deciduous forest grew up again, and it is possible that parts of the eastern USA may have nearly as much forest cover now as when the settlers first arrived. Nevertheless, other areas of forestland have been destroyed in recent decades by strip mining and the creation of a vast road and rail network. In the southern hemisphere, especially in the last 200 years, the temperate rainforests of Australia and New Zealand have been subjected to much the same pattern of events, although on a smaller and somewhat less devastating scale.

Conservation
Today the general need to preserve and extend the woodlands is clearly recognized, but great uncertainty exists about their future. The demand for hardwoods for veneers, quality papermaking and furniture still exceeds supply. Oak is still the preferred material for some types of boat building and, especially in Europe, for joinery work. But one of the major difficulties with forestry as a land use is forecasting future trends within the industry, largely as a result of the long-term nature of the crop—hardwood trees planted today will not yield their timber until well into the next century. Government tax policies can be all important in deciding whether the majority of woodlands are, or will

continue to be, sound economic investments.
Temperate forests and woodlands still exist in sizeable quantities in central Europe and the USA, but many of today's plots, particularly in western Europe, are far too small for efficient conservation of plant and animal life, and are isolated from other woods. As a result, successful breeding and exchange of genetic material is very difficult, especially when modern agriculture is rapidly destroying the linking corridors of hedgerows. The use of woodlands for recreation is also presenting considerable problems. Controlling agencies have been formed to cope with leisure demands, and a start has been made in the multiple use of forests for recreation, conservation and timber felling, but progress still needs to be made in harmonizing these potentially conflicting interests. Meanwhile, natural expanses of woodland and forest are still being lost to agricultural and urban expansion and to plantations of nonnative conifers.
Temperate forests are a biologically efficient form of land use. In terms of biomass—the amount of living material (animal and plant) in any one area—they could still play an important role in the provision of food, materials and even renewable energy. Thus on scientific, economic and aesthetic grounds a strong case can be made for immediate conservation measures.

Mediterranean Regions

Forests of evergreen trees once covered much of the Mediterranean regions. They flourished in spite of the hot, rainless summer months – as the original plant life, they had evolved to survive such harsh conditions. Man, however, has proved to be a greater threat than the climate. He introduced domestic animals and cleared the land to grow crops; the natural vegetation was burned, browsed and plowed into nonexistence. Man's activities left behind tracts of impoverished soil which rapidly became scrubland. Today, scrub is the most typical vegetation in all the Mediterranean climate zones throughout the world.

CONVERGENCE
Isolated from each other by enormous areas of land and ocean, regions with a Mediterranean type of climate rarely have any plant species in common. But, by a process known as "convergent evolution," the plant communities in each of these areas have produced remarkably similar responses to their similar environments. This can be seen in the conifer communities, the broad-leaved evergreen trees, and in the various hardy shrubs and ground plants typical of each of the regions.

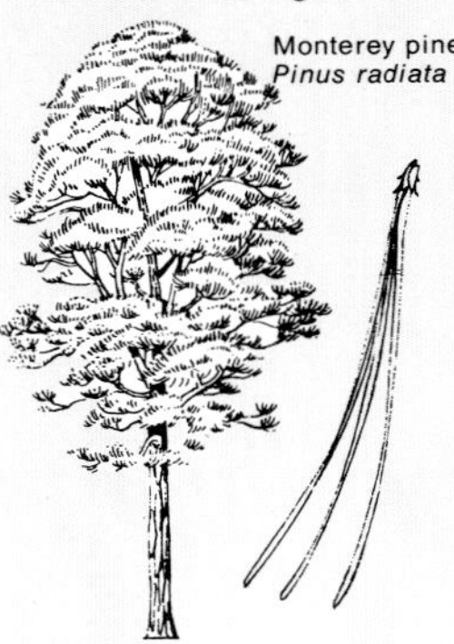
Monterey pine
Pinus radiata

California's Monterey pine and other Mediterranean conifers—South African podocarps and Chile pines, for example—have needle-shaped leaves that prevent rapid loss of water from such trees during drought.

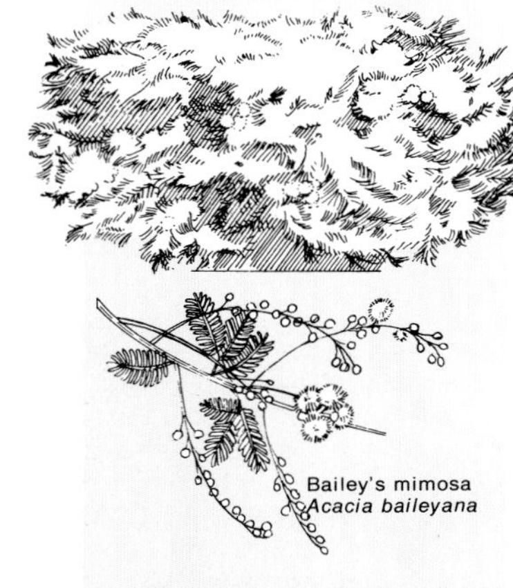
Bailey's mimosa
Acacia baileyana

Nonconiferous evergreens such as Australia's acacias and eucalypts, Chile's *quillajas* and California's evergreen oaks are typical Mediterranean trees. Their leathery leaves limit summer moisture loss.

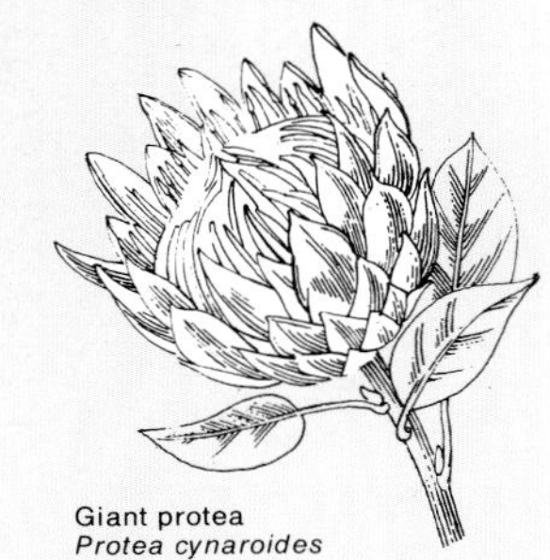
Giant protea
Protea cynaroides

Shrubs and ground plants show various adaptations to drought. South African proteas and Europe's laurel have thick evergreen leaves. Narrow leaves and water-storing roots are other common adaptations.

Long, hot, dry summers and warm, moist winters form the seasonal rhythm of the "Mediterranean" year. This climatic pattern can be found in small areas of nearly every continent in the world, typically on the western side of landmasses and in the mild, temperate latitudes. North America's "Mediterranean" is in California, South America's occurs in Chile and Africa's lies at the southern tip of Cape Province. Australia has two small "Mediterranean" areas, one on the southern coast and one on the western. Europe's Mediterranean region, which has given its name to this climate, covers much of the southern part of the continent and extends into northern Africa.

Wherever Mediterranean conditions prevail, the native plant life has adapted to survive the scanty annual rainfall and the long summer droughts. Some species have developed deep root systems that can tap low summer water tables, and many of the ground plants—such as bulbs and aromatic herbs—grow vigorously only in early summer while rain still moistens the soil. But it is the broad-leaved evergreens with their drought-resistant leaves that are the most typical of the Mediterranean areas.

This natural pattern of vegetation has been drastically altered by man. In southern Europe in particular, almost all the original evergreen forests have long since been destroyed and thickets of fast-growing, tough scrub plants have grown up in their place. This scrub, which once probably covered only small areas, is now so widespread that it is considered the most typically Mediterranean of all kinds of vegetation. It is the *maquis* of France, the *macchia* of Italy and the *mattoral* of Spain. A similar type of vegetation (although containing different species) can also be found in South Africa's fynbos, in California's chapparal, and in Australia's tracts of natural mallee scrub.

Classical land use

Southern Europe, with its long history of human settlement, farming and pastoralism, is the most altered of all the Mediterranean regions. Over the centuries vast tracts of original vegetation have been removed, either by farmers (for crop growing) or by grazing animals. And, particularly on the steep slopes and rocky outcrops, this has resulted in extensive deterioration and erosion of the soil. Agriculture generally has less serious effects upon the vegetation than has animal grazing. Mankind has learned, over many hundreds of years, which are the most suitable crops for the various soils, terrain and climatic conditions of the region. The Mediterranean "triad" of wheat on the lowlands and olives and vines on the hills has been a successful combination since Classical times.

Pastoral plundering of the land, however, has more serious consequences. The virtually omnivorous goat is particularly damaging and can strip a whole forest of its foliage, bark, shrubs, ground plants and grass. After such an assault the vegetation rarely returns to its former condition; normally, a scrubby growth of kermes oak and shrubs springs up to form a typical maquis-type vegetation.

The rise and fall of each great Mediterranean civilization has seen forests destroyed in one area after another. The Greek colonization of southern Italy was provoked by deforestation and soil erosion in Attica. The Romans extended clearance north to the Po valley and into eastern Tunisia. From the seventh century onwards, Muslims made great inroads into the forests of North Africa as well as southern and eastern Spain; and in the north of Spain and southern France, medieval monks cleared forested valleys. During the seventeenth and eighteenth centuries large areas of Provence and Italy were cleared to plant vines and this process continued in the 1800s, when the great wine-producing areas of Languedoc and Algeria were established. During this time the iron industries of Spain and northern Italy, with their growing need for charcoal, were adding to the destruction. Recent reafforestation efforts have been puny compared to past degradation.

Protected species

But throughout this history of forest removal some tree species have been protected. These have been the natural tree crops that have, at times, supported complete peasant economies. The chestnut forests of Corsica, for example, sustained a large rural population until this century; the chestnuts provided flour for bread and fodder for pigs. In Portugal and Sardinia the cork-oak forests are still important today.

It is the olive, however, symbol of peace and of New Testament landscapes, that is the Mediterranean's most characteristic tree crop. Of all the Mediterranean plants, it is the most perfectly adapted to its environment, with its deep roots to search out scarce water and its hard, shiny leaves to conserve what it finds. In fact, the summer drought is essential to olive growers for it encourages the build-up of oil in the fruit. Paradoxically, however, the olive—like the vine, the fig and many other "Mediterranean" crops—did not originate in the Mediterranean but was introduced from Asia Minor.

In spite of massive destruction of the natural landscape, mankind has learned many valuable lessons during his occupation of this region. Ideas that were to become important in laying the foundations of sound land management policy were developed in the Mediterranean area. Hillside terracing, irrigation, crop rotation and manuring were all, from necessity, practiced from early times. The flourishing agricultural industries of the world's other Mediterranean regions—the wine industry of California, the vast soft-fruit plantations of Australia and the citrus industry of South Africa—all owe a considerable debt to the generations of farmers who learned to exploit the red soils of the Mediterranean basin.

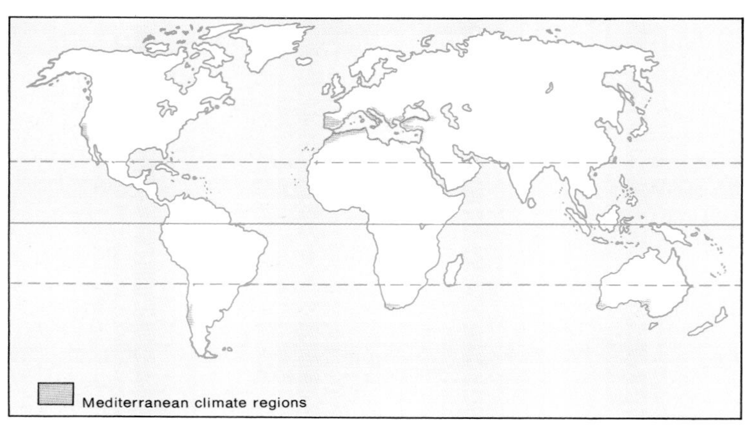
Mediterranean climate regions

The Mediterranean regions occur between the latitudes 30° and 40°, on the western and southwestern sides of the continents. These areas are affected in summer by the high-pressure systems of nearby desert regions, and in winter by wet, low-pressure systems brought in from the oceans and over the land by the prevailing Westerlies. This distinct seasonal shifting of major influences on the climate produces the hot, waterless summers and warm, moist, sometimes stormy winters typical of the Mediterranean climate.

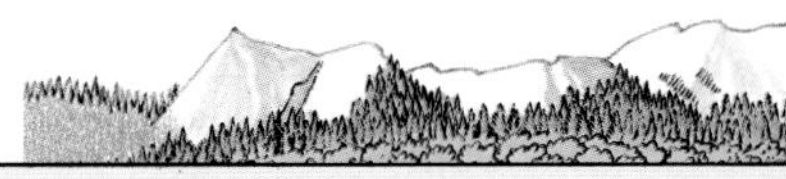

MAN AND THE MEDITERRANEAN
Even by Classical times, the once-forested lands fringing the Mediterranean Sea were suffering from massive deforestation and soil erosion. In the 5th century BC, Plato described the bare, dry hills of Attica, recently stripped of their woodlands. "What now remains," he wrote, "is like the skeleton of a sick man, all the fat and soft earth having been wasted away." By the end of the Classical period, irreparable damage had been done. At the same time, however, mankind was gradually learning through the mistakes he had already made. Suitable patterns of land use, better farming practices and improved land management techniques were slowly being adopted and were enabling man to make better use of the much-altered Mediterranean landscape.

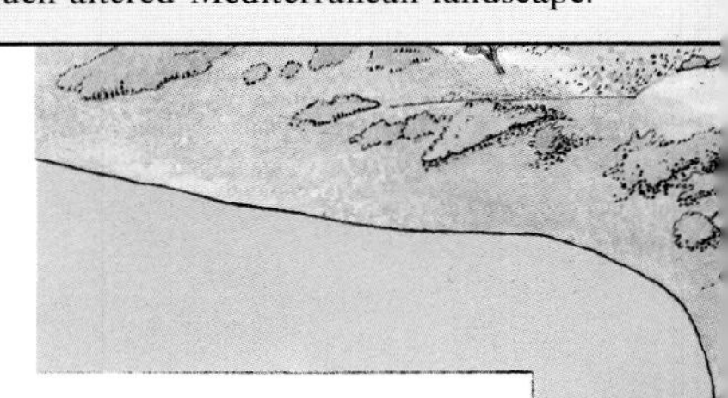

THE ORIGINAL LANDSCAPE
The landscape, unaltered by man, held a rich variety of vegetation. On high mountains, conifers such as black pine and cedar grew. On the lower slopes, these gave way to warmth-tolerant deciduous trees such as Turkey oak. In the foothills and valleys, forests of holm oaks, strawberry trees and other broad-leaved evergreens flourished. Limestone outcrops, common in the area, supported a poorer vegetation. Here, stunted Aleppo pines mixed with herbs such as lavender. Over sandstone, scrubby olives and cork oaks grew and by the sea stood isolated, wind-bent maritime pines.

THE CLASSICAL AGE
Civilizations followed one after another, each taking its toll of the environment. In the mountains, forests were felled, the tall, straight conifers sought after by shipbuilders such as the Phoenicians, and deciduous hardwood timber in demand for charcoal to fuel growing industries. Some replanting did take place, especially as groves of crop trees such as chestnuts. Below in the foothills, agriculture and the grazing of animals had destroyed vast areas of natural forest. Terracing techniques, however, helped to stop soil erosion, and irrigation reached the height of its Classical art with Roman aqueducts and canals. Tree crops, such as olives, were found best suited to the thin hill soils. On the plains, especially where alluvial soils had been deposited, cereals were grown. Meanwhile, towns sprang up and the coastline became densely populated as ships and ports were built and sea trade grew. Exotic food plants, such as pomegranate trees, citron trees and vines, were brought into the region by merchant seamen.

THE MEDITERRANEAN TODAY
The region today bears the scars of many centuries of human activity. The once-forested mountains will never return to their former state, although some regrowth and some replanting (mostly with introduced tree species) has occurred. As in Classical times, hillsides are terraced and planted with vines and fruit trees. But with modern irrigation and fertilizing, land is less readily exhausted and abandoned now. On the plains, native shrubs, such as lavender, are commercially cultivated and grain is widely grown, particularly durum wheat used for making pasta. Cork oaks are planted, especially over dry sandstone areas, but indigenous vegetation has not suffered by this—scrubby woodland is more widespread than ever and can be found throughout the landscape. Perhaps the single most important part of the Mediterranean basin today is the coastline, for this has produced the region's major modern industry—tourism.

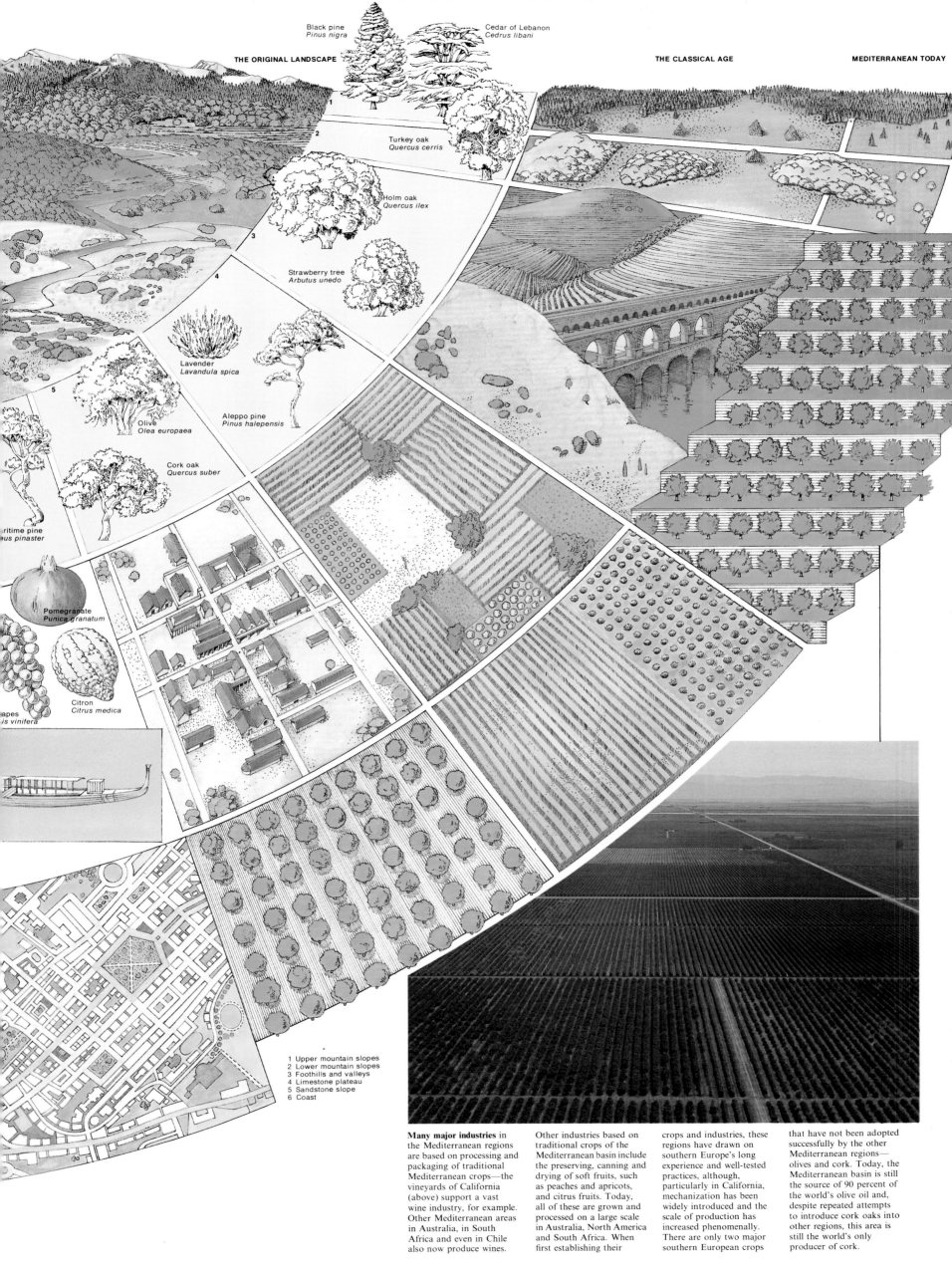

Black pine
Pinus nigra

Cedar of Lebanon
Cedrus libani

Turkey oak
Quercus cerris

Holm oak
Quercus ilex

Strawberry tree
Arbutus unedo

Lavender
Lavandula spica

Aleppo pine
Pinus halepensis

Olive
Olea europaea

Cork oak
Quercus suber

laritime pine
us pinaster

Pomegranate
Punica granatum

Citron
Citrus medica

apes
is vinifera

1 Upper mountain slopes
2 Lower mountain slopes
3 Foothills and valleys
4 Limestone plateau
5 Sandstone slope
6 Coast

Many major industries in the Mediterranean regions are based on processing and packaging of traditional Mediterranean crops—the vineyards of California (above) support a vast wine industry, for example. Other Mediterranean areas in Australia, in South Africa and even in Chile also now produce wines.

Other industries based on traditional crops of the Mediterranean basin include the preserving, canning and drying of soft fruits, such as peaches and apricots, and citrus fruits. Today, all of these are grown and processed on a large scale in Australia, North America and South Africa. When first establishing their

crops and industries, these regions have drawn on southern Europe's long experience and well-tested practices, although, particularly in California, mechanization has been widely introduced and the scale of production has increased phenomenally. There are only two major southern European crops

that have not been adopted successfully by the other Mediterranean regions—olives and cork. Today, the Mediterranean basin is still the source of 90 percent of the world's olive oil and, despite repeated attempts to introduce cork oaks into other regions, this area is still the world's only producer of cork.

Temperate Grasslands

Compared with other flowering plants, grasses are newcomers to the Earth. They appeared only 60 million years ago, but since then they have proved to be an extremely successful family of plants. Today, the grasses dominate large areas of the world's natural vegetation and play a vital part in the intricate balance of plant and animal life in these regions. In spite of the inroads made by man, vast stretches of original grassland still cover the interiors of the North American and Eurasian landmasses.

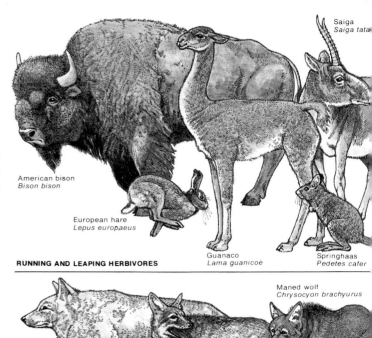

American bison
Bison bison

European hare
Lepus europaeus

Saiga
Saiga tatari

Guanaco
Lama guanicoe

Springhaas
Pedetes cafer

RUNNING AND LEAPING HERBIVORES

The prairies of North America and the steppes of Eurasia extend far into the interiors of the northern continents. These are the best known and the most extensive of the world's temperate grasslands. The southern hemisphere, however, has examples in the veld of South Africa and the pampas of South America. Extensive grasslands also occur in southern Australia, although these are sometimes described as semiarid scrub because of the high average temperatures and the prolonged droughts in the region.

Temperate grasslands probably developed wherever the rainfall was too low to support forest and too high to result in semiarid regions, conditions found typically in the interiors of large continents. Continental interiors tend to be somewhat drier than coastal regions, but they are also characterized by extreme changes in temperature from one season to the next. In the North American grasslands, for example, winter temperatures may fall well below freezing whereas summer temperatures of 38°C (100°F) are not unusual. And these sharp fluctuations in seasonal temperature greatly influence how much of the rainfall is made available to plants. In summer particularly, when most of the rain falls, high temperatures, strong winds and lack of protective tree cover cause much of the moisture to evaporate before it can be absorbed into the soil.

Climatic conditions are not the only factor responsible for the distribution and form of the temperate grasslands. There are many pointers that indicate the importance of fire in determining their continuing existence and their extent. Natural fires, caused by lightning and fueled by the dry summer grasses, have always been a feature of these regions, but more recently, man-made fires have been crucial in fixing the boundary between forest and grassland.

Trees and shrubs frequently invade the margins of grasslands, but whenever there is a fire few of them survive. Grasses, however, have certain characteristics that enable them to withstand the potentially destructive impact of fire. The growing point of grasses is at the base of the leaves, close to the ground, and so destruction of the leaves above this point does not interrupt growth—in fact it may stimulate it. These same characteristics also serve to protect grasses from destruction by grazing animals. The large animals of these lands, such as the North American bison and the Eurasian horse, are able to crop the grasses without permanently damaging their food supply.

Grazers and predators

Large migrating herbivores with a strong herd instinct characterize one of the major types of temperate grassland animal. In the North American grasslands the bison (which may have numbered 60 million before being virtually exterminated by settlers) and the antelope-like pronghorn were the major examples of large herbivores. In Eurasia large herds of saiga antelopes, wild horses and asses at one time roamed the steppes, although they too have suffered from human activities, as has South America's largest grassland herd animal, the pampas deer. As these herds of grazing animals have been reduced, so have the carnivorous animals of the grasslands that preyed upon them. At one time, however, these predators played an important part in protecting the grasslands by continually keeping the numbers of grazing herd animals in check.

Plains wolf
Canis lupus nubilus

Coyote
Canis latrans

Maned wolf
Chrysocyon brachyurus

RUNNING CARNIVORES

European souslik
Citellus citellus

Marsupial mole
Notoryctes typhlops

Prairie dog
Cynomys ludovicianus

Viscacha
Lagostomus maximus

SMALL BURROWING ANIMALS

Black-footed ferret
Mustela nigripes

Marbled polecat
Vormela peregusna

Pampas cat
Lynchailurus pajeros

Gopher snake
Pituophis melanoleucus

SMALL CARNIVORES

The dominant native species of grass varies from area to area. In the undisturbed prairies, for example, tall bluestem and Indian grass grow in the east and in wet central lowlands and mix with switch grass in drier parts. Farther west and on high land in the east, little bluestem and also western wheatgrass grow. June grass grows in the north, and buffalo grass and blue grama grow farthest west.

Many flowering herbs grow in the grasslands and have developed resistance to summer droughts: Russian tarragon has narrow leaves to help prevent moisture evaporation; rhizomes and bulbs, such as Eurasia's iris and anemone, store water in their specialized "root" systems.

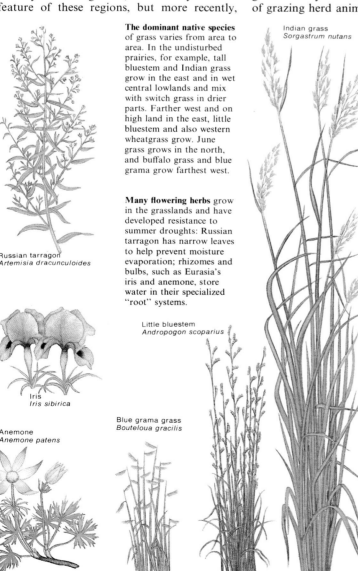

Russian tarragon
Artemisia dracunculoides

Iris
Iris sibirica

Anemone
Anemone patens

Blue grama grass
Bouteloua gracilis

Little bluestem
Andropogon scoparius

Indian grass
Sorgastrum nutans

The natural distribution of the temperate grasslands is dictated mainly by rainfall: most occur in continental interiors where there is too little rain for forest but enough to prevent desert from forming. Between these limits the large range in rainfall allows three main types of grassland: tall grass in wetter areas, mid-grass, and short grass in drier parts. The largest grasslands exist in North America, Eurasia, South America, in Australia's Murray–Darling river basin and on the South African plateau.

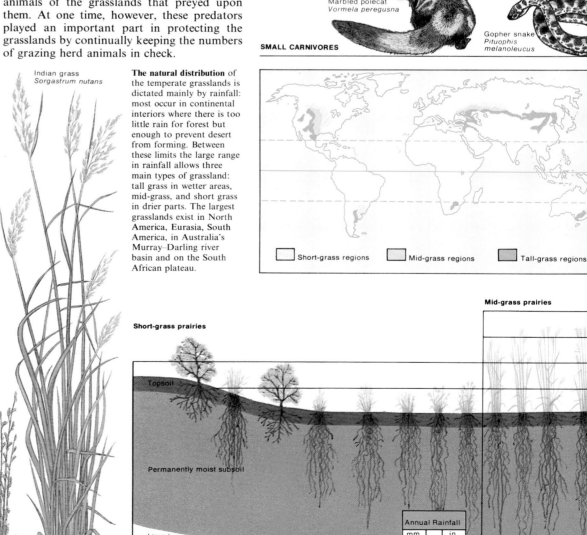

Short-grass regions   Mid-grass regions   Tall-grass regions

Short-grass prairies

Mid-grass prairies

Topsoil

Permanently moist subsoil

Lime layer

Permanently dry subsoil

Annual Rainfall	
mm	in
1,250	50
1,000	40
750	30
500	20
250	10

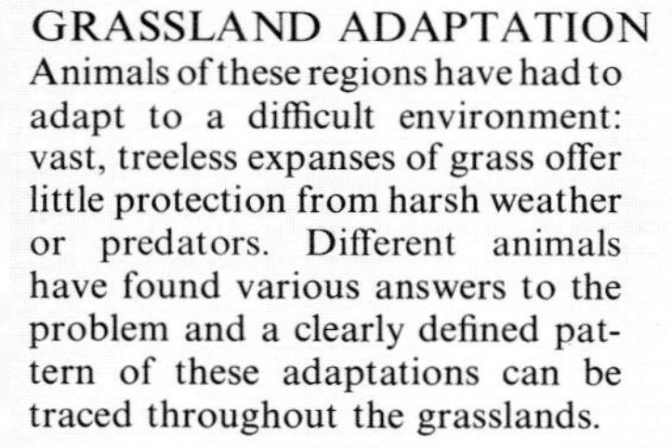

GRASSLAND ADAPTATION

Animals of these regions have had to adapt to a difficult environment: vast, treeless expanses of grass offer little protection from harsh weather or predators. Different animals have found various answers to the problem and a clearly defined pattern of these adaptations can be traced throughout the grasslands.

Running and leaping herbivores survive because of their ability to move faster than a pursuer. The larger animals such as the Eurasian saiga, North America's bison and pronghorn and the guanaco of South America are runners. The leaping herbivores are usually smaller creatures that escape danger by bounding away to bolt-holes. They include the European hare and the African springhaas.

Running carnivores follow, and prey on, running and leaping herbivores. These animals, such as the coyote and the now extinct plains wolf of North America, and South America's maned wolf, also depend on speed—to enable them to catch their prey.

Small burrowing animals hide from predators by digging under the ground. Some, such as Australia's marsupial mole, spend most of their lives below ground. Others, such as the European souslik, South America's viscacha and North America's prairie dog, live and sleep under the ground but come to the surface to find food.

Small carnivores concentrate on the burrowers as their main source of food. They either, like the pampas cat, rely on surprise attack of their prey, or, like Eurasia's marbled polecat and the grasslands' many kinds of snake, depend on their long, lithe shape to follow creatures into their burrows.

Two distinctive types of grassland bird can be distinguished: the sky birds, which spend long periods of time on the wing, and the ground birds.

Birds of the sky include songbirds such as the skylark which, having no perch from which to proclaim its territory, sings in the sky, and birds of prey such as Eurasia's tawny eagle and North America's red-tailed hawk and prairie falcon, which ride the thermals scanning the ground for their prey.

Ground birds rarely take to the wing, although none has actually lost the ability to fly when necessary. They include birds such as the New World sage grouse and burrowing owl (which lives below ground in abandoned prairie dog burrows), the black grouse of Eurasia and songbirds such as North America's meadowlark.

Insects and other invertebrates have developed many different survival techniques. Some use camouflage: the praying mantis resembles a leaf bud and the tumble bug is the color of the dark grassland soil. Grasshoppers are miniature leaping herbivores and earthworms are small-scale versions of the grassland burrowers.

Skylark
Alauda arvensis

Red-tailed hawk
Buteo jamaicensis

Tawny eagle
Aquila rapax

Prairie falcon
Falco mexicanus

BIRDS OF THE SKY

Western meadowlark
Sturnella neglecta

Burrowing owl
Speotyto cunicularia

Sage grouse
Centrocercus urophasianus

Black grouse
Lyurus tetrix

GROUND BIRDS

Lubber grasshopper
Romalea microptera

Tumble bug
Canthonlaevis drury

Common earthworm
Lumbricus terrestris

Praying mantis
Mantis religiosa

INSECTS AND OTHER INVERTEBRATES

A typical cross section, based on the North American prairies, shows temperate grasslands in relation to rainfall. Annual rainfall determines the depth of the permanently moist subsoil, which in turn dictates the length to which grass roots can grow. Tall grasses have deep root systems and need a considerable depth of moist subsoil. As the rainfall decreases, they gradually give way to shorter grass species. Short grasses require less water and their shallower roots are well suited to drier regions. On dry margins, desert plants start to dominate, and on the wet margins, trees appear.

Another major type of animal found in the temperate grasslands, and one that is better adapted to survive man's activities, is the small, burrowing animal, for example the prairie dog and the gopher of North America, the viscacha of South America and the little ground squirrel known as the souslik in Eurasia.

Unlike the large herd animals, these creatures tend not to migrate. Many of them live together in complex, permanent, underground communities. The colonial "townships" of the prairie dog, for example, may house more than one million individuals, which each year excavate vast quantities of the grassland soil. This has considerable effect upon the structure of the soil. By bringing up earth from lower layers to the surface, these animals are responsible for changing the mineral content of certain areas of topsoil. This then encourages isolated pockets of different plant species to flourish.

A third group of grassland animals, consisting of insects and other invertebrates such as earthworms, has an even more important effect upon the soil. They live in or on the soil and play a vital role in maintaining grassland fertility. These creatures may be herbivores, carnivores or primary (first stage) decomposers (which break down such material as dead grass and animal remains). These three types of activity allow a complete range of organic matter to be processed and incorporated into the earth, where it is further broken down by the second-stage decomposers, the countless millions of soil bacteria. In this way nutrients continuously flow back to the earth and restore its fertility.

Fertile black earths

The topsoil of temperate grassland regions, therefore, contains large amounts of organic material, which is produced every year and is quickly incorporated into the soil. The low and intermittent rainfall and the protective cover of grasses mean that the topsoil undergoes little chemical leaching, a process in which minerals are removed and carried down to lower layers by rainfall percolating through the earth. The soils are thus dark in color, generally fertile and of the "black earth" type ("chernozem" in Russian) which is, at least at first, capable of producing high yields of crops.

The most suitable and most widely grown crops are, predictably, the cultivated grasses, and it is these grasses that provide more food for mankind (either directly as grain or indirectly as animal fodder) than any other source. The temperate grassland biome is therefore an important agricultural resource. Undisturbed natural grasslands, however, are also valuable resources. They need to be preserved both for the information that they can provide about how complex communities of wildlife function efficiently, and because, as a rich source of genetic material, they hold many of the answers to the major agricultural problems that probably lie ahead for the human race.

Tall-grass prairies

cm	ft
215	7
180	6
150	5
120	4
90	3
60	2
30	1
0	0

Annual Rainfall

mm	in
1,250	50
1,000	40
750	30
500	20
250	10

Annual Rainfall

mm	in
1,250	50
1,000	40
750	30
500	20
250	10

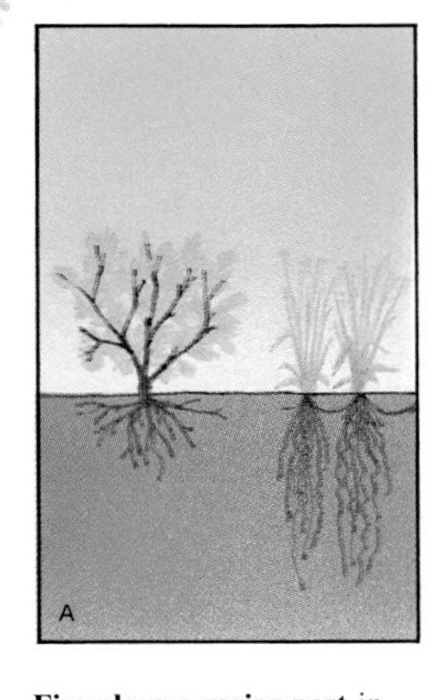

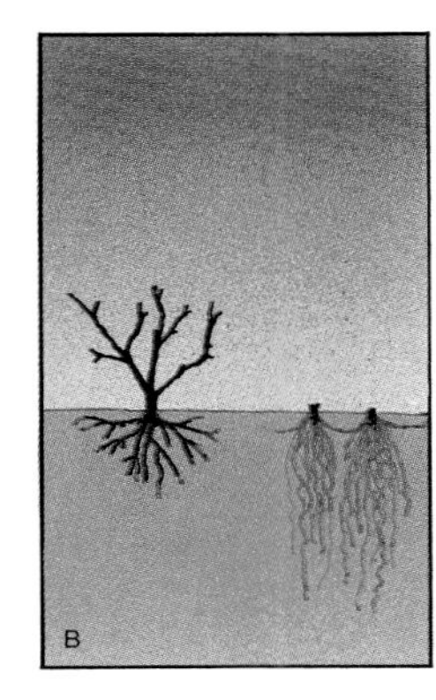

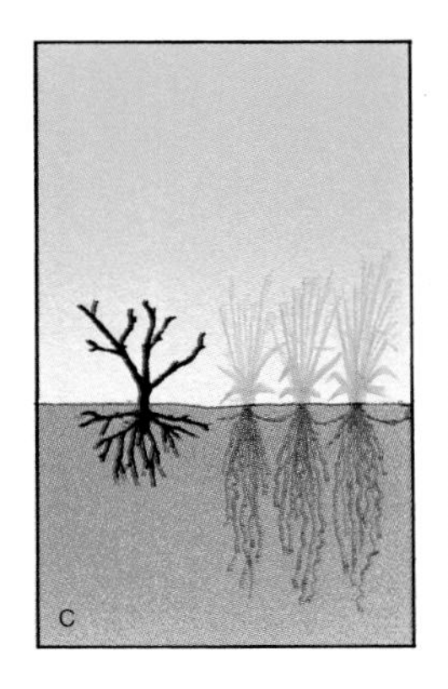

Fire plays a major part in fixing and maintaining the natural boundaries of the temperate grasslands, where tree saplings and shrubs are continually attempting to invade (A). Man-made fires are recent phenomena, natural fires have always occurred. In summer, low-pressure systems build up in continental interiors, causing violent electrical storms. The dry sward of summer grass is easily ignited by lightning and fire is quickly spread by wind. Shrubs and saplings are killed or badly damaged by fire, but grasses, with their growing points close to the soil, remain unharmed (B). They may even benefit from this "pruning" and grow more quickly. Some species grow new buds from their underground shoots. Removal of the main shoot may encourage growth of "tillers" (shoots growing out sideways), which then increase the spread of the grasses as they begin to invade the area left vacant by the dead, or slowly recuperating, shrubs (C).

71

Man and the Temperate Grasslands

The vast areas of temperate grassland lay virtually empty until the end of the eighteenth century. Over the next 125 years they were occupied by millions of people, most of them migrants from overcrowded Europe. By 1914, the grasslands had become the granaries and the stockyards of the world. Today, they are still the most important food-producing regions on Earth and their riches, properly distributed, are the world's first reserve against the possibility of a hungry future for the human race.

The great nineteenth-century migration to the grasslands proved of immense significance to the human race. It meant that, within a single century, the area of productive land available was suddenly enlarged by thousands of millions of hectares. In all of mankind's history, such a thing had never happened before.

But before the grasslands could be occupied a number of major problems had to be solved. First, in order to reach these regions it was almost always necessary to travel deep into the continental interiors, and there were few navigable rivers and no mechanized forms of transportation for early pioneers. Second, with virtually no indigenous population, newcomers had to learn by their mistakes how best to exploit the new and unfamiliar environment. Third, even if settlers succeeded in using the land, they still had to find markets for their produce.

A number of technological developments, however, that took place in the nineteenth century provided the right combination of circumstances for the opening up of the grasslands. The Industrial Revolution in Europe produced the steamship and the railway locomotive, which created both a means of travel to and from these distant parts and an internal transport system for moving produce to ports and markets. It also produced the kind of machinery needed to plow and farm the great new open spaces; it made it possible for one family to cultivate an area 50 times as large as that which most farmers had known in Europe. Industrialization also threw thousands of Europeans out of work, and therefore provided a large supply of eager migrants. And it crowded further thousands into cities, thus creating vast markets for the settlers' produce.

It was the coming together of these various circumstances that acted as the catalyst and converted, for example, the Russian penetration of the Eurasian steppes in the late eighteenth

THE CRADLE OF AGRICULTURE
Stands of wild einkorn (A), emmer wheat (B) and wild barleys can be seen today in the grassy foothills that flank the Taurus and the Zagros mountains, and the uplands of northern Israel. It was in this region 10,000 years ago that the world's earliest farmers gathered seeds from these species and sowed the first crops. Wild einkorn is probably the oldest of all wheats and the parent of every modern variety—including the most important and most widely grown kind of grain in the world today, common bread wheat (C).

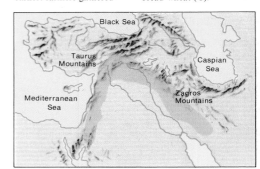

GRASSLAND EXPLOITATION
Today, temperate grasslands provide mankind with a superabundance of food. But the vast potential of these regions was not exploited until the mid-19th century, when mass migration by Europeans, combined with new technology, allowed full-scale development and settlement.

BEFORE EUROPEAN SETTLEMENT
The grasslands were sparsely populated. Most of the indigenous tribespeoples were nomadic hunters and gatherers. They wandered widely over the regions, making temporary camps (1) as they followed the movement of their quarry—the plentiful herds of grazing animals (2). These peoples made little impact on the natural grasslands.

GRASSLAND SETTLERS
Early pioneers relied on animal-drawn transport (3), primitive farm tools (4) and unpredictable free-range livestock grazing (5). During the 19th century, farming became more productive: better equipment cultivated larger areas (6); barbed wire made stock raising efficient (7); railways and the telegraph improved communication (8).

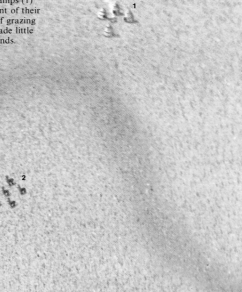

Tehuelche Indians (above) adopted horses for hunting from early Spanish settlers to the pampas. In South Africa and North America, too, the introduced horse became a valued asset for grassland hunters. For people of the Eurasian steppes, for example the Mongols (right), native horses have always been culturally important.

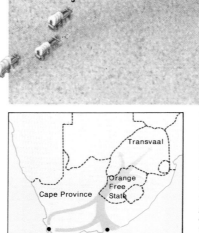

The South African veld was first settled by Europeans after 1836 (left). Dutch farmers (Boers), rejecting British rule of the Cape Colony, trekked north in search of new land. Moving into the Transvaal they discovered rich grassland, recently emptied of its original inhabitants, who had fled to escape the aggressive attentions of neighboring Zulus.

Vaqueros were the original cowboys (left). Tending herds of cattle for the missionaries in 18th-century California, they developed techniques and traditions that served hundreds of later cowboys working the prairie ranges. In other grassland regions, as free-range stock raising became important, similar "cowboy" professions evolved—the Australian stockman and the gaucho of South America.

century into the explosive movement of hundreds of thousands of settlers a few years later. In the USA, too, by the year 1850, settlement had reached and then rapidly crossed the Mississippi. In the Argentine, genuine colonization of the pampas had begun, in South Africa, the Boers had reached the high veld, and in Australia pioneer settlers were moving outwards from the various areas of coastal settlement into the scrub grasslands of the interior.

Farmers or ranchers?

The fundamental question posed for these settlers was whether their newly found land should be used for crops or for livestock. Most grasslands have a dry edge and a wet edge, and it was therefore sensible to use the drier parts for stock raising and the wetter parts for cultivation. But the question was complicated by the fact that most of the newcomers were cultivators, and also that the line dividing dry from wet was vague—worse, it shifted from year to year.

Early attempts to define the dividing line tended to be ignored by the settlers themselves, and they pushed the limit of cultivation into areas where plowing the soil led to its destruction. Several generations of farmers had to learn this bitter lesson, and they learned only slowly: the worst disasters on the American grasslands occurred in the 1930s and created the infamous

Dust Bowl region in the dry grasslands of the Midwest. Similarly, the Soviet Virgin Lands Program for growing cereal crops on the dry steppes was established in 1954 and is still experiencing difficulties.

Special methods are required both for farming and for ranching the grasslands successfully. Farming has to take account of the open, treeless surface, the scanty and variable rainfall and the comparatively shallow topsoil. To minimize the risk of soil erosion, farmers plant windbreaks, plow fields along the contour, and protect the soil with a covering of the previous year's stubble and by planting cover crops in rotation with cereals. Ranchers, too, have learned to live with variable rainfall. They build stock ponds, irrigate areas of fodder crops to be used as a reserve in dry years and avoid overstocking and consequent overgrazing, which destroys the quality of the grass.

Food for the world

Today, the world's principal trading supplies of cereals and meat flow from these lands, over the networks of railway which link the grasslands to mill towns, slaughter yards and ports of shipment such as Adelaide in Australia, Buenos Aires in Argentina and Montreal in Canada. Without these links to large towns, the grasslands would be of little value, for even

today their populations are sparse and the local markets are relatively insignificant.

Throughout most of the world, however, the human population continues to soar and it remains to be seen whether the grasslands can continue to supply these growing numbers with food. Undoubtedly, the output of cereals and meat can be increased, although at considerable cost in fertilizers, new crop strains, more irrigation and more machines. On the other hand, the problem at present is not mainly one of production, nor will it be in the near future. The land can produce more, but there is no point in doing so unless the yields can be made available where they are most needed.

The world's hungry people live in other regions, many of them in countries that are unable to afford imported food supplies, particularly during those years when prices are high. The major importers of temperate grassland produce are the rich industrialized nations, such as those of western Europe. Furthermore, much of the grain imported by these countries is not consumed by humans but used to feed stalled, beef-producing cattle—a highly inefficient way of using these supplies. Consequently, unless producer nations and wealthy importing nations can create a system for produce to reach those in need of it, extra output from the grasslands will be irrelevant.

9

MODERN-DAY FARMING
Livestock feed on carefully selected grasses, which are sown and fertilized by aircraft (9). Fodder crops are grown as reserve animal feed (10), and stock ponds ensure against drought (11). Feedlots (12) fatten stock on grain (13). Cereal farms (14) are highly mechanized, and road and rail serve even the remotest regions (15).

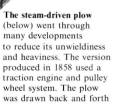

The steam-driven plow (below) went through many developments to reduce its unwieldiness and heaviness. The version produced in 1858 used a traction engine and pulley wheel system. The plow was drawn back and forth between these by a power-driven cable. This design was, however, superseded by the steam tractor, which, although unsuited to small European fields, was ideal for drawing multifurrow plows across the grasslands.

Sand-smothered farms in the heart of the Dust Bowl were rapidly abandoned during the 1930s and 40s (above). This was one costly lesson that man had to learn in the process of developing the grasslands. Traditionally grazing land, the western part of the prairies was first plowed this century. Years of drought arrived, crops died and the desert encroached.

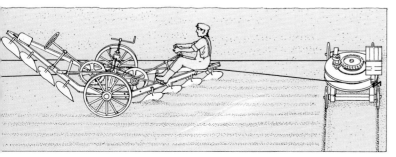

World cereal supplies flow from temperate grasslands (right). North America is the most important producing region, for although almost all nations produce grain, few can grow enough to feed their populations and even fewer have any surplus to export or hold in reserve against poor harvests. But North America, with its prairie cornfields and its small population, exports many millions of tonnes.

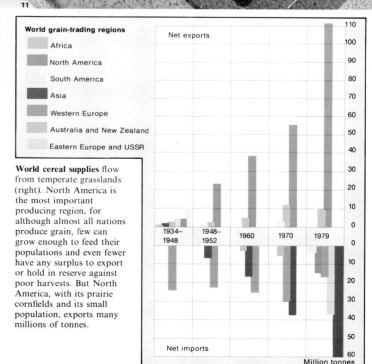

World grain-trading regions
- Africa
- North America
- South America
- Asia
- Western Europe
- Australia and New Zealand
- Eastern Europe and USSR

Net exports

1934–1948 1948–1952 1960 1970 1979

Net imports

Million tonnes

Deserts

Much of the Earth's land surface is so short of water that it is defined as desert. Not all deserts are hot, sandy wastelands; some are cold, some are rocky, but all lack moisture for most of the year. Even so, a surprising variety of plants and animals have adapted to these hostile environments. Plants have developed ingenious ways of surviving long periods of drought, and many desert animals shelter during the intense heat of the day, emerging only at night to feed.

LIFE IN THE DESERT

The overriding need to obtain and conserve water dictates the pattern of desert life. Many plants close their pores during the day and most daytime creatures limit their activity to early morning and late afternoon. At night the temperature drops sharply and dew provides welcome moisture. Some plants bloom at night, and the desert is alive with insects, night-hunting birds, reptiles and small mammals.

DESERTS BY DAY

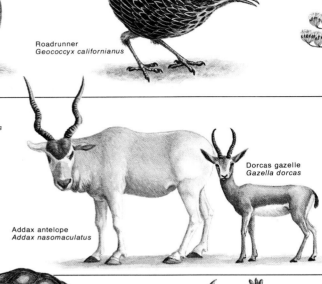

Many birds are at home in the desert. The lanner falcon of Africa and Asia gets all the moisture it needs from its diet of small birds and rodents. Sandgrouse live in the open deserts of Eurasia and North Africa; mainly seed eaters, they must make long flights each day to find water. Roadrunners, in American deserts, hunt insects, lizards and small rattlesnakes.

Lanner falcon
Falco biarmicus

Pallas's sandgrouse
Syrrhaptes paradoxus

Roadrunner
Geococcyx californianus

Large mammals are nomadic and obtain most of the moisture they need from plants. Camels can go for long periods without food or water because their humped back stores fat which can be drawn on when food is scarce, and water stored in their body tissues prevents dehydration. Addax antelopes survive entirely on plants. They roam remote parts of the Sahara, their broad hooves enabling them to travel easily over soft sand. Gazelles rely on speed. Small and fleet footed, they are able to disperse quickly over great distances to find food and water.

Arabian camel
Camelus dromedarius

Asian camel
Camelus bactrianus

Dorcas gazelle
Gazella dorcas

Addax antelope
Addax nasomaculatus

Insects and reptiles are well adapted to desert life. Desert locusts, when overpopulation threatens their food supply, change from a solitary to a swarming migratory form. Harvester ants store seeds against times of drought; desert tortoises withstand drought by becoming torpid. Lizards are cold blooded and need the sun to warm them, but must shelter from the intense heat of midday. The thorny devil, a small Australian ant-eating lizard, is protected from potential predators by its prickly scales.

Desert locust
Schistocerca gregaria

swarming adult

solitary hopper

Harvester ants
Pogonomyrmex sp

Desert tortoise
Gopherus polyphemus

Gridiron-tailed lizard
Callisaurus draconoides

Thorny devil
Moloch horridus

Desert plants have evolved various ways of coping successfully with drought. The ocotillo of southwestern America sheds its leaves, reducing its need for water. Euphorbias, and cacti such as the prickly pear, store water in their stems. Blue kleinia, a South African succulent, has a waxy coating that limits water loss. Agaves mature very slowly, building up reserves of food and water in their leaves before they flower. Esparto, a needlegrass, is typical of many desert grasses.

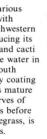
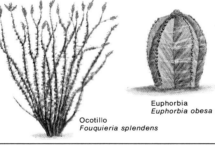

Ocotillo
Fouquieria splendens

Euphorbia
Euphorbia obesa

Prickly pear
Opuntia ficus-indica

Blue kleinia
Senecio articulatus

Agave
Agave americana

Esparto grass
Stipa tenacissima

Deserts occur where rainfall is low and infrequent and where any moisture quickly evaporates or disappears instantly into the parched ground. In the driest deserts, rainfall rarely exceeds 100 mm (4 in) a year, and is so unreliable that some places may have no rain for 10 years or more. These are deserts in the truest sense of the word: harsh wildernesses that are almost totally without life. Regions with less than 255 mm (10 in) of rain a year are generally classified as arid and those with less than 380 mm (15 in) as semiarid.

Hot deserts have very high daytime temperatures in summer, although they drop sharply at night, and the winters are relatively mild. In the so-called cold deserts the summers are hot but the winters are so cold that temperatures may fall as low as $-30°C$ ($-22°F$).

Desert climates and landscapes

In the subtropical latitudes, swept by hot, drying winds, high-pressure weather systems prevent rain clouds from forming. In these regions, rain comes only from local storms or follows low-pressure weather systems (often seasonal) when they move in across the desert. Large areas of central Asia have become desert because they are so far from the sea that clouds have shed all their rain before they reach them. Other deserts occur because mountains cut them

off from moisture-bearing winds. The Andes, for example, shelter the drylands of Argentina, and a high sierra stops rain from reaching the Mojave and Great Basin deserts of North America. Rain is also rare on the western sides of continents where cold ocean currents flow from the polar regions towards the Equator.

Desert climates vary not only from place to place but also with time. Over short periods rainfall is much less predictable than it is in temperate regions and droughts are frequent. Some droughts, such as those that occur along the southern fringe of the Sahara, are so severe that it may seem that the climate has changed permanently. But most droughts are short-lived and are followed by years of normal (although sparse) rainfall. Over longer periods of time, however, desert climates do change. Prehistoric cave drawings in the Saharan highlands, for example, show that elephants, rhinoceroses and even hippopotamuses—animals that are at home in wetter climates—lived in these now dry, barren uplands in a more moist period between 7,000 and 4,000 years ago.

Desert landscapes also vary enormously. They are as contrasted as the Colorado canyon country of the United States and the sandy wastes of the Middle East, but most include one or more of several basic features: steep, rocky mountain slopes, broad plains, basin floors

dominated by dry lake beds or sand seas, and canyon-like valleys. In low-lying areas, evaporation sometimes leaves a glistening residue of salt. Where there is soil, it is often sandy or consists of little more than fragmented rock, and because plant life is usually sparse there is little or no humus to enrich the ground.

Where water is life

Plant growth depends on water, and desert plants are usually widely spaced to reduce competition for what little moisture is available. Many plants rely on short, sharp rainstorms; others make use of dew and grow in locations, such as crevices in rocks, where water can accumulate. Some complete their life cycle in a single wet season, producing seeds that lie dormant during the following drought and germinate only when enough moisture is available for them to grow. These are the ephemerals that carpet the desert with a brief but brilliant display of flowers shortly after rain has fallen.

Most desert plants, however, are able to tolerate or resist drought. These are the xerophytes ("dry plants") and phreatophytes ("deep-water plants"). Xerophytic trees and shrubs have a wide-spreading network of shallow roots that take in water from a large area of ground. Many xerophytes also limit the amount of water

Adaptations to desert life: kangaroo rats, jerboas and gerbils (A) make prodigious leaps with their long back legs to escape predators, and some desert lizards (B) run at high speed on their hind legs when pursued, using their tail for balance. Spadefoot toads have scoop-like hind feet with which they dig burrows to avoid the intense heat of day. Skinks use flattened toes fringed with scales to "swim" through the sand. Fan-toed geckos have toes that spread into fans at the tips, enabling them to walk easily on sand dunes, and the Namib palmate gecko has webbed feet that support it on loose sand.

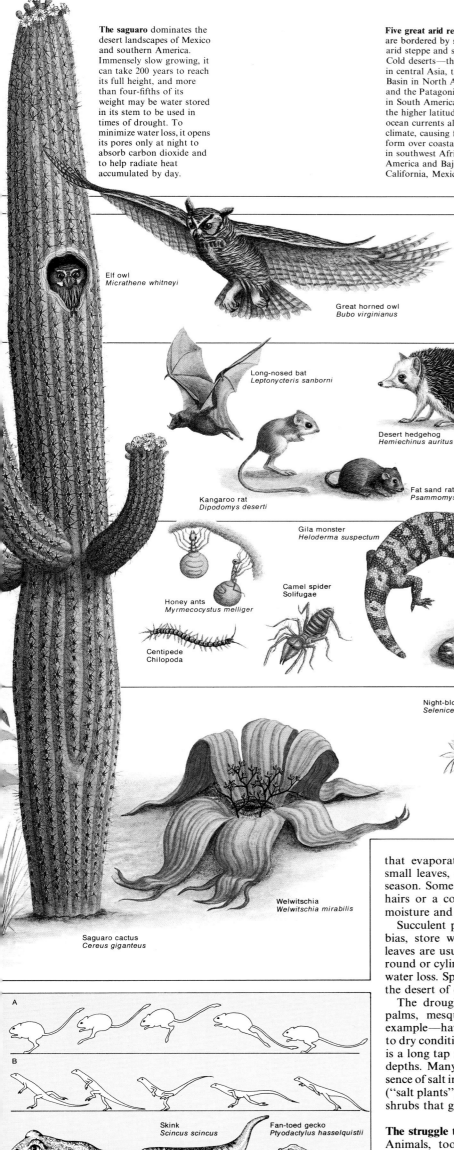

The saguaro dominates the desert landscapes of Mexico and southern America. Immensely slow growing, it can take 200 years to reach its full height, and more than four-fifths of its weight may be water stored in its stem to be used in times of drought. To minimize water loss, it opens its pores only at night to absorb carbon dioxide and to help radiate heat accumulated by day.

Five great arid regions are bordered by semi-arid steppe and scrub. Cold deserts—the Gobi in central Asia, the Great Basin in North America and the Patagonian Desert in South America—lie in the higher latitudes. Cold ocean currents also affect climate, causing fogs to form over coastal deserts in southwest Africa, South America and Baja California, Mexico.

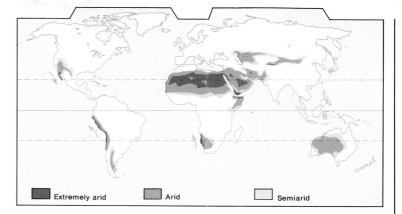

Extremely arid · Arid · Semiarid

Elf owl
Micrathene whitneyi

Great horned owl
Bubo virginianus

White-throated poorwill
Phalaenoptilus nuttallii

Owls and nightjars hunt under cover of darkness. Elf owls shelter by day, emerging at dusk to catch insects, and great horned owls often come into the desert at night to hunt. The poorwill, a small desert nightjar, is known to American Indians as "the sleeper." An insect eater, it sometimes survives the rigors of winter, when food is scarce, by hibernating.

Long-nosed bat
Leptonycteris sanborni

Desert hedgehog
Hemiechinus auritus

Kangaroo rat
Dipodomys deserti

Fat sand rat
Psammomys obesus

Fennec fox
Fennecus zerda

Most small animals are active at night. Nectar-eating bats visit plants that blossom at night, pollinating the flowers while they feed. American kangaroo rats obtain water from a dry diet of seeds and conserve moisture by producing very concentrated urine. The sand rat of North Africa feeds on salty succulents and excretes great quantities of extremely salty urine. Hedgehogs are mainly insect eaters; the long ears of desert species help to disperse body heat. The Saharan fennec, the smallest type of desert fox, hunts lizards, rodents and locusts.

Gila monster
Heloderma suspectum

Scorpion
Buthus occitanus

Camel spider
Solifugae

Honey ants
Myrmecocystus melliger

Centipede
Chilopoda

Sidewinder rattlesnake
Crotalus cerastes

Darkling beetle
Tenebrionidae

Among insects and other invertebrates the hunt for food intensifies at night. Honey ants gather nectar; centipedes and camel spiders hunt insects. The gila monster, a poisonous American lizard, eats centipedes, eggs and sometimes other lizards, and uses its tail to store fat. The sidewinder, a small rattlesnake, is active mainly at night, leaving its distinctive parallel tracks in the sand. Scorpions emerge from their burrows to stalk insects and spiders, and darkling beetles feed on dry, decomposing vegetation.

Night-blooming cereus
Selenicereus spp

Some desert plants are nocturnal, in the sense that they bloom only at night or make use of the dew that forms when the temperature falls. The welwitschia, unique to the Namib Desert in southwest Africa, has broad, sprawling leaves on which moisture condenses at night. The night-blooming cereus of the American deserts flowers for a single night in summer. Like other nocturnal plants, its flowers are luminously pale and strongly scented to attract pollinating night insects.

Welwitschia
Welwitschia mirabilis

Saguaro cactus
Cereus giganteus

Skink
Scincus scincus

Fan-toed gecko
Ptyodactylus hasselquistii

Palmate gecko
Palmatogecko rangei

Spadefoot toad
Scaphiopus couchi

that evaporates from their leaves by having small leaves, or by shedding them in the dry season. Some produce a protective covering of hairs or a coating of wax to prevent loss of moisture and to help to withstand heat.

Succulent plants, such as cacti and euphorbias, store water in their thick stems. Their leaves are usually reduced to spines, and their round or cylindrical shape also helps to reduce water loss. Spines have the added advantage in the desert of discouraging foraging animals.

The drought-resisting phreatophytes—date palms, mesquite and cottonwood trees, for example—have a similar variety of adaptations to dry conditions, but their most typical feature is a long tap root that draws water from great depths. Many plants can also tolerate the presence of salt in the soil. These are the halophytes ("salt plants") such as saltbush and other small shrubs that grow in and around salt pans.

The struggle to survive

Animals, too, need to obtain and conserve water at all costs and to be able to adjust to extremes of temperature. Most are small enough to shelter under stones or in burrows during the intense heat of day; others survive adverse conditions by becoming dormant or by migrating. For most desert creatures it is also an advantage to be inconspicuous, and many are

pale in color so that they are hard to see against their light background of sand or stones.

Many animals, especially those that are active by day, show adaptations that are strikingly similar to those of desert plants. Frogs and toads are activated by rain, emerging from dormancy to feed and mate in temporary pools and then quickly burying themselves until the next rain falls. Mammals have hairy coats that reduce water loss and also help to keep their body temperature at a tolerable level. Most desert insects have a waxy coating that serves much the same purpose.

Some geckos and other lizards store food, in the form of fat, in their tails, and camels store fat in their humped backs to sustain them when food is scarce. Honey ants force-feed nectar to some members of the colony, creating living "honey pots" for the rest of the community to feed from in times of drought. Many creatures are able to survive on the moisture contained in their food, and rarely need to drink. Most desert dwellers also have extremely efficient kidneys that produce very concentrated urine, so that little or no moisture is lost in the process.

Man enjoys no such advantages. Nevertheless, he still seeks to live in deserts, as he has for thousands of years, and the pressures he exerts on the environment may well have irrevocably changed much of the world's desert landscapes.

Man and the Deserts

Water is the key to man's survival in deserts: where water has been available, great civilizations have flourished, and man's dream of making the desert bloom has become a reality. More recently, discoveries of great mineral wealth have spurred the opening up of some of Earth's most inhospitable regions. But while man's ingenuity has made many deserts both habitable and productive, the human tendency to increase the extent of deserts has become a problem of international proportions.

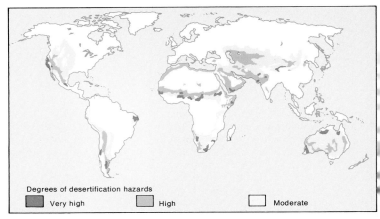

Degrees of desertification hazards

☐ Very high   ☐ High   ☐ Moderate

Given water, much is possible, and not surprisingly man has tended to settle where water is most readily available: along the courses of rivers (such as the Nile) that rise outside the desert, and around oases fed by springs or by wells that tap groundwater supplies. But desert rainfall is so unreliable that often runoff and spring flow are uncertain in quantity and timing. Much groundwater is either also unreliable or it is fossil water that has accumulated in the geological past and is not being replenished by today's rainfall. Thus in areas such as southern Libya and some of the oasis settlements of the Arabian Gulf, and in America's arid west, groundwater is a nonrenewable resource that is being rapidly depleted.

Making water go farther

Man has also used great ingenuity to secure water supplies and to transport them to where they are needed. Runoff from flash floods that follow rare desert storms may be collected in channels and distributed to crops in nearby fields, and terracing slopes to trap runoff is a traditional way of obtaining the maximum benefit from limited rainfall. Reservoirs, ranging from the small night tanks of the southern Atacama desert in Chile to the massive artificial lakes along the Colorado river in the United States, store seasonally or perennially unreliable runoff. Also, surface runoff may be increased by reducing the permeability of runoff surfaces, a

solution engineered by the Nabataeans in the Negev desert more than 2,000 years ago and being reemployed by the Israelis today.

The transport of water is a fundamental desert activity. Open canals are typical, usually carrying water to irrigated fields—a practice used throughout the fertile crescent of Mesopotamia more than 8,000 years ago and still widespread today. A striking alternative are the ancient qanats, which limit the evaporation of water while it is in transit. Qanats are still found in the Middle East, although today pipelines are increasingly used.

Ultimately the conversion of salt water to fresh water may ensure plentiful supplies for many desert regions. The process is expensive, but large-scale desalination has already become a reality in some affluent communities such as oil-rich Saudi Arabia and Kuwait. Increasing emphasis is also being placed on more efficient use of existing freshwater supplies: in Egypt and Israel, waste water from towns is being purified and recycled for use in agriculture.

Cultivating the desert

The successful control of water has enabled large areas of otherwise arid and semiarid land to be made productive. The Egyptian civilization along the Nile depended, and still depends, on the management of seasonal floodwaters. In North America, the large-scale, long-distance piping of water has made central

Desertification—the advance of desert areas across the Earth—now affects more than 30 million sq km (12 million sq miles) and deserts are continuing to expand at an alarming rate. In recent years, on the southern edge of the Sahara alone, as much as 650,000 sq km (250,900 sq miles) of land that was once productive have been lost, and in places there is little left to show where the Sahara ends and the Sahel-Sudan region begins. Intense and often inappropriate human pressures are major causes, frequently aggravated by drought: overcultivating vulnerable land, chopping down trees for fuelwood and grazing too many livestock, especially on the margins of arid lands.

THE SHIFTING SANDS

Recent decades have seen unprecedented changes in the world's deserts. Increasing pressure on the environment, especially from pastoralists and farmers, has caused extensive damage and a rapid expansion of barren land. In many desert regions, nomadism has long been the only way in which man could survive, except in oases. Today, even these traditional ways of life are changing as the exploitation of oil and other mineral resources, and the introduction of new agricultural techniques, are drawing many of the deserts into a spectacular new age of development.

The traditional pastoral response to limited water supplies and forage in desert regions is nomadic livestock herding, still practiced by the Tuareg of the northern Sahara (right) and by tribal groupings in Mongolia (left). The nomadic way of life has, however, become severely restricted in recent years. Long-distance migrations are often incompatible with the requirements of the modern state, and the poor rewards no longer match the incentives to settle in towns and cities.

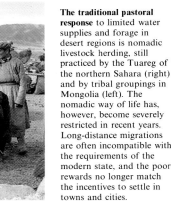

Oases have provided welcome refuges in deserts since ancient times. Secure water supplies from wells or springs make settled life possible in the midst of the most arid landscapes. Many oases are intensively cultivated with three tiers of vegetation: tall date palms shade orchards of citrus fruits, apricots, peaches, pomegranates and figs, and both palms and orchard trees shade the ground crops of vegetables and cereals. Irrigation channels distribute water to the desert soils, which are frequently rich in plant foods although they lack humus. Windbreaks help to protect cultivated land from erosion and from migrating dunes, although many oases are losing the battle with encroaching sands and the oasis people are leaving to find work in the oil fields.

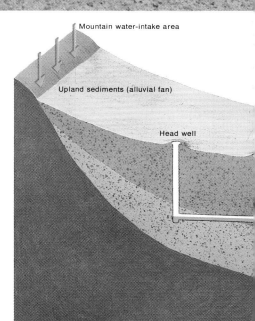

Mountain water-intake area

Upland sediments (alluvial fan)

Head well

lifornia the most productive agricultural
ion in the world. But while irrigation can
ng enormous benefits, it can also create
oblems. Too much water causes waterlogging
the land, and where water evaporates in the
desert air, concentrations of dissolved salts
ild up in the soil.

Farming without irrigation is possible only
ere rainfall, although meager, is sufficient to
stain crops with a short growing season. Soil
isture is conserved by using dry surface
ulches, by fallowing and crop rotation, by
anting seeds sparsely and by controlling
eds. Geneticists are also producing new
rieties of cereal crops that can survive for
eks without water. Dry farming, however, is
ecarious. Especially at times of drought it can
use serious problems of soil erosion, chiefly by
e action of wind.

an the desert maker

e extension of dry farming into unsuitable
gions, and waterlogging and the accumu-
ion of salts in irrigated areas, are major
uses of desertification—the spread of deserts
o formerly habitable land. Other major
uses are the overgrazing of livestock on land
h too little forage and the removal of trees
d shrubs for firewood by communities that
ve no alternative fuel supply. A sequence of
er than normal years does the rest.

Many scientists believe that desertification
n be reversed, provided the pressures on the
id are reduced sufficiently to allow vegetation
recover. But desertification affects such
ge areas, often crossing national frontiers,
t broad-scale, international cooperation is
eded to coordinate reductions in population
d livestock pressures and to improve under-
nding of drought.

n some countries the battle against desertifi-
ion has already begun. In China, extensive

planting of drought-tolerant trees has created
windbreaks to control sand movement and to
protect farmland. In Algeria, a broad belt of
trees has been planted to keep the Sahara at bay,
and in Iran, advancing dunes have been halted
by spraying them with petroleum residue: when
the spray dries it forms a mulch that retains
moisture and allows vegetation to grow, and
much desert land has been reclaimed.

The deserts' riches

The exploitation of resources has also led to an
"opening up" of many deserts. The rushes for
precious metals in Arizona, Australia and
South Africa started man's development of
these regions in the nineteenth century. Some
minerals, such as the evaporite deposits of
Searles Basin in California and the nitrates of
the Atacama desert in Chile, are actually products of the arid environment.

A resource that deserts also possess in abundance is solar power, and in many hot, dry
regions the heat of the sun is used to evaporate
mineral-rich solutions of salts, as well as being
harnessed as a source of energy. Sunshine and
the dry, clear air are also drawing ever-
increasing numbers of tourists to the "sun
cities" of the western United States and to
Saharan oases, which were, until recently, only
remote desert outposts.

No resource, however, has created as much
attention or wealth as has oil. Oil has transformed the fortunes of several desert nations
and provided an economic boom that has led to
rapid industrialization and spectacular urban
growth. The benefits of such growth in terms of
affluence are substantial. The problems—the
weakening of traditional desert societies, the
submerging of traditional cities in the concrete
labyrinths of modern complexes, and the pre-
cariousness of prosperity that is based on finite
resources—are also clear.

Mineral wealth provides a
powerful incentive for
man's development of arid
lands, and today the flow
of oil rather than water is
often a measure of a desert
nation's prosperity. In
some of the world's most
desolate regions, flares
signal the presence of

modern "oases" where
fossil fuels are being
extracted—products, like
the fossil waters that are
sometimes trapped in the
same sedimentary rocks, of
the desert's geological past.
Uranium, another mineral
"fuel," also often lies
beneath desert sands. Arid

environments may also
provide a rich harvest of
other minerals: potash,
phosphates and nitrates,
valuable sources of
commercial fertilizers;
gypsum, manganese and
salt; and borax, source of
the element boron, used in
nuclear reactors.

A "plastic" revolution has
helped transform much of
Israel's desert hinterland
into productive farmland.
Plastic cloches, plastic
mulches and greenhouses
trap moisture and reduce

evaporation, and water
trickled through thin
plastic tubes irrigates the
plants' roots with a
minimum of wastage. Such
innovative agricultural
techniques enable Israel to

produce most of its own
food requirements, and
fruit and vegetables grown
in the relatively mild desert
winters are also exported
to Europe, where they
command high prices.

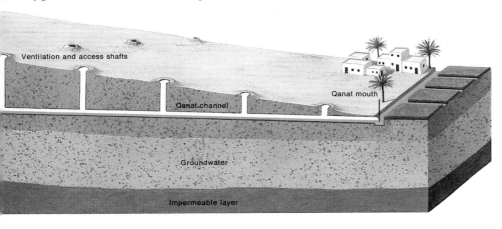

**ne of the most ingenious
ays** man has devised of
ringing water to desert
egions is by the ancient
nderground system
nown as the qanat.
vented by the Persians in
e first millennium BC,
anats tap groundwater in

upland sediments and carry
it by gravity to the surface
on lower land. The head
well is dug first, sometimes
to a depth of 100 m
(330 ft), until water is
reached. A line of shafts is
then sunk to provide
ventilation and to give

access to the channel being
tunneled below. Work
begins at the mouth end,
and a typical channel is
10–20 km (6–12 miles) long
when completed, depending
on the depth of the head
well and the slope of the
land. Its slight gradient

ensures that water flows
freely but gently down to
ground level. Surface
canals then divert the
water to where it is needed.
Thousands of such qanats
are still in use, their routes
marked by mounds of
excavated debris.

Ventilation and access shafts

Qanat mouth

Qanat channel

Groundwater

Impermeable layer

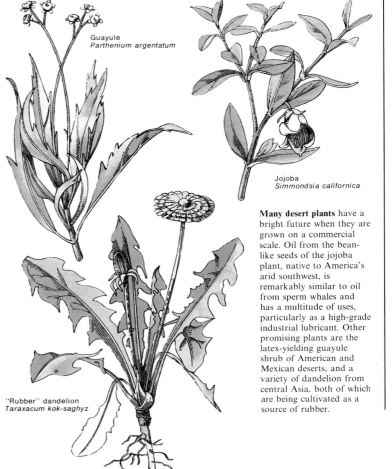

Guayule
Parthenium argentatum

Jojoba
Simmondsia californica

"Rubber" dandelion
Taraxacum kok-saghyz

Many desert plants have a
bright future when they are
grown on a commercial
scale. Oil from the bean-
like seeds of the jojoba
plant, native to America's
arid southwest, is
remarkably similar to oil
from sperm whales and
has a multitude of uses,
particularly as a high-grade
industrial lubricant. Other
promising plants are the
latex-yielding guayule
shrub of American and
Mexican deserts, and a
variety of dandelion from
central Asia, both of which
are being cultivated as a
source of rubber.

Savannas

Between the tropical rainforest and desert regions lie large stretches of savanna, which are characterized by seasonal rainfall and long periods of drought. Those nearest to the forests usually take the form of open woodland, whereas those nearest to the deserts consist of widely scattered thorn scrub or tufts of grass. Unlike temperate grasslands, where the summers are hot but the winters are cold, savanna regions are always warm and in the wet season rain falls in heavy tropical downpours.

The most extensive areas of savanna are in Africa, north and south of the rainforest, and in South America, where the two main regions are the *llanos* of Venezuela, north of the Amazon rainforest, and the *campos* of Brazil in the south. Smaller areas of savanna also occur in Australia, India and southeastern Asia.

Savannas range from thickly wooded grasslands to almost treeless plains. Some are the result of man's destruction of the forest, and most are maintained in their present state by the high incidence of fire, both natural and manmade. The grasses tend to be taller and coarser than their temperate counterparts and they grow in tufts rather than as a uniform ground cover. In areas of high rainfall some grasses grow up to 4.5 m (15 ft) tall. Trees and bushes are usually widely spaced so that they do not compete with each other for water in the dry season. Humid, or moist, savannas experience 3 to 5 dry months a year, dry savannas 6 to 7 months, and thornbush savannas 8 to 10 months. Rainfall also varies widely, from more than 1,200 mm (47 in) a year in humid savannas to as little as 200 mm (8 in) where the savanna merges into desert.

Types of savannas

Humid woodland savanna presents an abrupt contrast to the rainforest. Trees tend to be scattered and some are so low growing that they are dwarfed by the tall grass that springs up during the summer rains. In the dry season the grass fuels fierce fires, which destroy all except thick-barked, large-leaved deciduous trees. Consequently, the proportion of fire-resistant trees and shrubs is large, and the grass quickly regenerates with the coming of the next rains.

In Africa this type of savanna is known as Guinea savanna north of the rainforest and as miombo savanna south of the rainforest. In South America it is known as *campo cerrado*, from the Portuguese words meaning field (*campo*) and dense. (*Campos sujos* are *campos* in which stretches of open grassland predominate and *campos limpos* are grasslands from which trees are entirely absent.) The *llanos*, or plains, of northern South America are grasslands interspersed with forests and swamps.

North of the Guinea savanna in Africa lies a belt known as Sudan savanna. The annual rainfall is in the range 500 to 1,000 mm (20–40 in) and the dry season lasts from October to April. This is typical dry savanna. Tall grasses between 1 and 1.5 m (3–5 ft) form an almost continuous ground cover and acacias and other thorny trees dot the landscape, together with branching dôm palms and massive water-storing baobab trees. Because of the interrupted tree cover the old name given to many savannas of this type was orchard steppe, and this description gives a good idea of the countryside. Like the humid woodland savannas it is maintained by regular burning of the grass in the dry season, and there is a delicate balance and interaction between climate, soil, vegetation, animals and fire. On the desert margins the grasses grow in short tufts and the scattered acacias are seldom more than 3 m (10 ft) tall. The scrub and grasses are too widely dispersed for fires to spread, and this type of savanna is modified not by fire but by aridity and blistering heat.

Thorn-scrub and thorn-forest savannas frequently form transitional zones between tropical forests and grasslands. The *caatinga*, or "light forest," of northeastern Brazil is a typical thorn-forest savanna. Long, hot, dry seasons alternate with erratic downpours of rain, and the rate of evaporation is high. Drought-resisting trees and thorny shrubs mix with bromeliads, cacti and palm trees.

Abundance of life

No other environment supports animals so spectacular in size and so immense in numbers as do the African savannas. In spite of the concentration of animal life, however, competition for food is not severe. Each species has its own preferences and feeds from different levels of the vegetation. Giraffes and elephants can easily reach the upper branches of trees, antelopes feed on bushes at different heights from the ground, zebras and impalas eat the grasses and warthogs root for the underground parts of plants. With the onset of the dry season, massed herds assemble for the great migrations that are a major part of savanna life, moving to areas where rain has recently fallen and new grass is plentiful.

Following the grazing animals are the large predators: the lions, leopards and cheetahs. Wild dogs hunt in packs, and the scavengers—jackals, hyenas and vultures—move in to dispose of the remains of the kill.

The savannas of South America and Australia are much poorer in animal species. The only mammal of any size on the South American savanna is the elusive, nocturnal maned wolf, which eats almost anything from small animals to wild fruit. On the Australian savanna the largest inhabitant is the kangaroo, and the prime predator—apart from man—is the dingo, or native dog.

Many of the resident savanna birds are ground-living species such as the ostrich in Africa and its counterparts, the rhea in South America and the emu in Australia. The warm African climate attracts large numbers of visiting birds, which migrate each year across the Sahara to escape from the severe winter of the northern hemisphere.

For many thousands of years man has lived in harmony with the savanna. Within the last century, however, and in recent decades in particular, the savanna has come under increasing pressure. Inevitably, there is competition between the needs of the environment and those of the human population, and the future of the savanna is very much in the balance.

On each side of the Equator are broad tracts of tropical grassland known as savannas. In these regions there are distinct wet and dry seasons and temperatures are high all the year round, seldom falling below 21°C (70°F). Rain falls mainly in the hottest months, whereas the cooler months are generally dry. Thorn-scrub and thorn-forest savannas occur where the rainfall is more erratic; they have relatively little grass cover, and trees and bushes can tolerate long periods of drought.

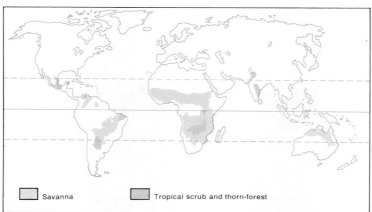

Savanna · Tropical scrub and thorn-forest

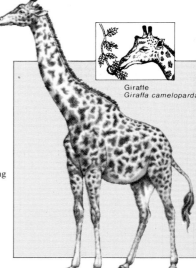

Giraffe
Giraffa camelopardalis

THE PLANT EATERS
Most plant eaters have adapted to feeding at a particular level of the vegetation. Giraffes browse on acacia tips that other animals cannot reach and elephants use their trunks to tear down succulent branches and leaves, although both feed on low-growing vegetation when it is easily available. Elephants will also uproot trees to gather leaves that are otherwise out of reach. The black rhinoceros plucks low-growing twigs and leaves by grasping them with its upper lip (the white rhinoceros has a broad, square mouth for grazing on grass). Eland often use their horns to collect twigs by twisting and breaking them. Zebra, wildebeest, topi and gazelle all graze on the same grasses, but at different stages of the plants' growth.

Lion
Panthera leo

HUNTERS OF THE PLAINS
The plant eaters provide rich hunting for the carnivores. Lions kill the largest prey and hunt in family groups; the lioness usually makes the kill but the male is the first to eat. The leopard is a solitary hunter. It lies in ambush or stalks its prey, mainly at night, in brush country where it has ground cover. Cheetahs are the swiftest of all the hunters. They usually hunt in pairs in open grassland, stalking their prey and then charging in a lightning-fast sprint. Hunting dogs travel in well-organized packs. They exhaust their quarry by chasing it to a standstill and attacking as a team. Whereas lions, leopards and cheetahs usually kill by leaping for the neck or throat, packs of hunting dogs characteristically attack from the rear.

Jackal
Canis aureus

THE SCAVENGERS
When the hunters have eaten, the scavengers move in. Jackals, small and quick, make darting runs to snatch titbits while packs of hyenas use their powerful bone-crushing jaws to demolish the bulk of the carcass. Hyenas are the most voracious of the carnivores, often driving the primary predator from its kill. Vultures are frequently the first to see a kill as they circle high in the sky, but must await their turn to feed on the skin and scraps because their descent attracts the more aggressive scavengers. Carrion beetles, carrion flies and the larvae of the horn-boring moth dispose of what is left. Most of the large scavengers, particularly the hyenas, also do their own hunting, singling out prey that is small, weak or sickly.

Plants in the savanna are remarkably well adapted to withstand drought, fire and the onslaughts of the animals that eat them. Acacias tolerate both drought and fire, and are armed with sharp thorns—although many animals do feed on them, thorns and all. Red oat grass survives fire because its seeds twist deep into the ground. Bermuda, or sawtooth, grass is a favorite food of many grazers, but it recovers quickly from close cropping because its growing point lies too flat against the ground to be eaten.

Acacia
Acacia sp

Red oat grass
Themeda triandra

Bermuda grass
Cynodon dactylon

Zebras

Wildebeest and topi

Gazelles

SAVANNA SWAMPS, LAKES AND MARSHES

Swamps, lakes and marshes are especially characteristic of the African savanna. Many are fringed with papyrus, the paper reed, *Cyperus papyrus* (1) which grows to a height of 3.5 m (12 ft) or more, and most are rich in microscopic organisms that play the same role in the water as grass does on the plains, supporting large numbers of birds and animals. Swamps and marshes also act as natural reservoirs, which collect and hold excess water during the rainy season, and provide welcome dry-season grazing for plains animals when other savanna productivity is at its lowest. The lakes of the Great Rift Valley, which form a chain down the northeastern side of the continent, are also rich with life. Many provide a refuge for crocodiles, their numbers seriously depleted by systematic hunting, and for multitudes of birds, including huge flocks of flamingos.

Many birds and animals have adapted to a semiaquatic way of life. The shoebill stork *Balaeniceps rex* (2) uses its feet and the hooked tip of its beak to stir up mud and dislodge the frogs, fish and soft-shelled turtles that form the bulk of its diet. The goliath heron *Ardea goliath* (3) is a shallow-water fisher. The sitatunga *Tragelaphus speki* (4) has long, splayed hooves that support its weight on soft mud. It hides by day among reeds on the edge of the swamp and moves to dry ground at night to feed. The jacana, or lily trotter, *Actophilornis africana* (5) relies on long toes and constant motion to walk on floating plants. The hippopotamus *Hippopotamus amphibius* (6) wallows in the water for most of the day and leaves the swamp at dusk to graze. It helps to fertilize the swamp with the enormous amounts of waste matter it excretes.

Elephant
Loxodonta africana

Black rhinoceros
Diceros bicornis

Eland
Taurotragus oryx

Wildebeest
Connochaetes taurinus

Grant's zebra
Equus quagga boehmi

Topi
Damaliscus lunatus topi

Thomson's gazelle
Gazella thomsoni

Cheetah
Acinonyx jubatus

Leopard
Panthera pardus

Cape hunting dog
Lycaon pictus

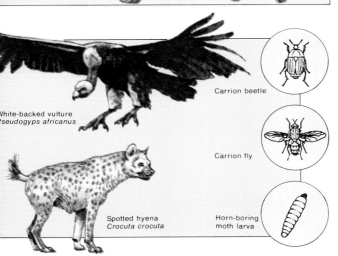

White-backed vulture
Pseudogyps africanus

Carrion beetle

Carrion fly

Horn-boring moth larva

Spotted hyena
Crocuta crocuta

Ostrich
Struthio camelus

Secretary bird
Sagittarius serpentarius

LONG-LEGGED BIRDS

The ostrich, up to 2.4 m (8 ft) tall, can see for great distances across the plains and can outrun most of its enemies. Its territory is often shared with grazing animals, such as wildebeest, which take advantage of the ostrich's keen sight to alert them to danger. The secretary bird (so-called because of its quill-like crest) strides through the grass hunting small mammals, insects and snakes; it kills snakes by battering them with its powerful, long-clawed feet.

Large termite mounds are a distinctive feature of many savanna landscapes. The mounds, or termitaria, are made of soil excavated by the termites and bound with their saliva. Thick walls help to keep the interior at a constant temperature, and some species of termite cultivate fungus "gardens" as a source of food. The royal chamber deep inside the mound is occupied by the colony's queen, grossly distended with eggs, and her consort. Predators include the aardwolf and the aardvark. The aardwolf is related to the hyena but is smaller and has weak jaws; it digs the termites out of their mound and scoops them up with its long sticky tongue. The aardvark, distantly related to the elephant, uses its powerful hoof-like claws to break into termite nests.

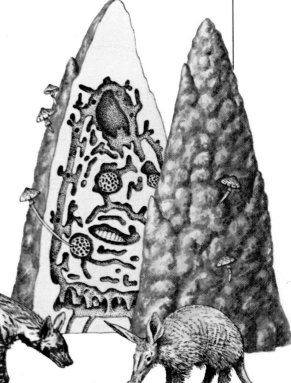

Aardwolf
Proteles cristatus

Aardvark
Orycteropus afer

Man and the Savannas

In their natural state, savannas are among the most strikingly productive of all Earth's regions. Before the coming of man they supported a wealth of animal life that has seldom been surpassed. As yet they are relatively undeveloped, but many of them lie in areas where the pressures of population growth are becoming increasingly acute. Wisely used, they offer great hope for the future, both as cattle lands and for the cultivation of food crops. But without proper management savannas can rapidly turn into wasteland, and man will be the poorer for the loss of such a great natural resource.

Throughout much of the savannas the climate is semiarid and the soils tend to be poor: stripped of their plant cover, they bake hard and crack during the long months of hot sunshine, and during the wet season they often become waterlogged or are washed away by the rains. Man's indiscriminate use of fire, unwise agricultural methods and the unrestricted grazing of domestic animals have already led to much soil loss, and erosion is widespread in tropical Africa, Asia, South America and Australia.

Systematic burning has long been practiced by the people of the savannas. Large areas are burned each year to clear land for agriculture or to remove dead grass and encourage a fresh growth to feed livestock. The resulting ash provides much-needed nutrients for crops, and the grasses rapidly produce new green shoots that provide a rich pasture for domestic herds. But although the short-term effects may be beneficial, repeated burning is harmful to the vegetation, the animals and the soil.

Trees are always more or less damaged by fire. Their trunks become twisted and gnarled, fresh shoots are killed and young trees are prevented from growing. Constant burning can destroy some species altogether, and when they disappear so too does the wildlife that depends on them for food and shelter.

Grasses, on the other hand, may be encouraged by burning, and the lush new growth that springs up when the first rains break the long dry season provides welcome nourishment for domestic herds and game animals alike. But whereas game animals move freely over the range, cropping grasses at various stages of growth, cattle tend to feed on grass only in the neighborhood of wells and other sources of drinking water. They may trample the soil and continue to graze the same area until the grass is completely suppressed.

The hazards of large projects

Cultivation in marginal areas that are unsuited to intensive agriculture also contributes to the impoverishment of the savanna. The Sahel and Sudan savannas on the fringes of the Sahara are particularly vulnerable to large-scale development projects that fail to take account of local climate and soil. Mechanized agriculture in fragile areas bordering the desert may well lead to soil erosion and dustbowl conditions, and large-scale irrigation schemes often result in waterlogging and an accumulation of salts in the soil. Cultivation in the savannas requires understanding and care. Many smaller schemes are safer—and usually more productive—than a few large ones, but not all planners yet realize that agricultural methods that are effective in temperate regions seldom come up to expectations in tropical climates.

Man first inhabited the savannas, as he did many other regions of the world, as a hunter and gatherer. He took from the land only what he needed from day to day, and although he used fire as a hunting tool, his impact was little more than that of any other savanna inhabitant. In East Africa, groups of nomadic Hadza (left) still hunt game and collect roots, fruit and the honey of wild bees, building grass huts as temporary shelters.

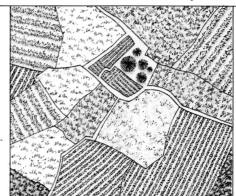

Small farms are scattered over much of the savannas. Plots close to houses are farmed continuously; beyond them lie the main fields, where periods of cultivation are usually followed by periods of fallow. Maize, millet and peanuts are the main food crops, and early and late crops are sometimes sown on the same plot to extend the growing season. Most of the work is done by hand, and any surplus to a family's needs is sold.

THE VULNERABLE WILDERNESS

Nowhere has man's impact on the tropical grasslands been felt more keenly than in Africa, although much of what is happening in Africa is happening also in savannas elsewhere. The majority of the people still live on the land, where the determining factor is the length and severity of the annual dry season. In the moister savannas the people are primarily cultivators, while in savannas that are too dry to sustain agriculture the main occupation is raising livestock. Most of the savannas are as yet sparsely settled, but competition is inevitably growing between man and wildlife, particularly in Africa, for the remaining tracts of relatively untouched wilderness.

The development of mineral resources and industries has led to an increasing movement of people—mainly young adults—from rural areas to towns and mining centers, attracted by opportunities for work—often at the expense of agriculture, since the heavy work of farming is left to the women, old people and children. Mining enterprises such as those in the Zambian Copper Belt (above), may recruit large labor forces from the surrounding countryside. Mining also dramatically alters the landscape, especially where the bedrock containing the ore reaches the surface and is quarried in huge terraces. The need for electricity to power mining and other industries leads, in turn, to the development of hydro-electric schemes, many of which entail resettling people whose villages are flooded by the creation of large artificial lakes.

Large areas of savanna have been set aside in East and Central Africa, and to a lesser extent in South America and Australia, as national parks and reserves where the landscape is kept intact and animals can be studied in their natural habitats. In Africa, observation platforms are frequently built close to waterholes where animals congregate to drink, and wardens use light aircraft to patrol the vast areas involved. Camel units are also used to patrol near-desert regions where much of the wildlife flourishes. Animals, such as elephants, whose numbers can grow out of control in the protected environment of the reserves are culled by licensed hunters to prevent the vegetation being destroyed. Culling maintains the health of the community as a whole and is also an economic source of meat in many countries where the people are short of protein foods.

Similarly, the introduction of European breeds of cattle into the savannas has not been an unqualified success. Not only are these breeds more susceptible to tropical pests and diseases than are the local varieties, but they are also adversely affected by the hot climate and their productivity is greatly reduced. In Africa and Brazil, native breeds are replacing more recent importations, and their productivity is being enhanced by selective breeding. In Australia, where most of the cattle are of British stock, tropical zebu, or humped cattle, are being introduced into the herds.

In the future, much more of the savanna may be developed as ranch lands, because the temperate grasslands will become less able to support enough animals to satisfy the world demand for meat. The *llanos* of Venezuela, the *campos* of Brazil and the tropical grasslands of Argentina and Australia already carry large herds of beef cattle. Throughout the savannas, however, ranching is still hampered by lack of water, poor natural pasture and remoteness from markets. In Africa, where herding is mainly nomadic, the sinking of wells by government organizations is changing the traditional ways of life, and cattle raising on a commercial scale is likely to become increasingly important. In Africa, too, the conservation and controlled cropping of game animals could become one of the most productive—and constructive—forms of land use.

Game as a resource
The value of game animals as a source of food is considerable. Buffaloes, for example, and kangaroos in Australia, can thrive on natural grasses that will not even maintain the weight of domestic stock, and they show greater gains in weight than African and European cattle on most forms of vegetation, while several species of antelopes can survive on a water ration that is wholly inadequate for cattle.

In recent years attention has been directed toward the economics of controlled cropping of wild game, and of ranching animals such as eland, which can be kept as if they were domesticated stock and can convert poor pasture into excellent meat. Game animals are also more resistant than cattle to the tsetse fly, which infests large areas of Africa and transmits the disease trypanosomiasis (known as nagana in cattle and as sleeping sickness in man).

But for the most part game animals are still considered to be a nuisance by man, and it is perhaps fortunate that by denying much of the savanna to domestic animals—and to man—the tsetse fly has preserved these regions from exploitation at the expense of the game. Many countries have also set aside large tracts of savanna as national parks and game reserves, where the natural environment is preserved and the wildlife can thrive.

Safeguarding the savanna
At a time when the pressure of the expanding human population calls for the development of areas hitherto uninhabited or only sparsely populated, it may seem paradoxical to maintain that the development of national parks and nature reserves is essential to the welfare of mankind. The aim of game conservation, however, is not simply to preserve rare or unusual animals for the enjoyment of posterity, or even for their scientific interest. It is to ensure that the land is put to its most economic and efficient use. The next few decades will show whether the savannas of the world will be developed into major sources of food and revenue for the countries that own them, or whether they will be misused and degraded into desert.

Commercial agriculture is important to the economies of many savanna countries. Cotton and coffee are major cash crops in Africa and Brazil, together with maize, tobacco, sisal and peanuts—crops that need a cycle of wet and dry seasons and year-round warmth. But large-scale cultivation of one crop tends to attract pests and diseases, and dependence on a single crop makes the economy vulnerable to fluctuating world prices.

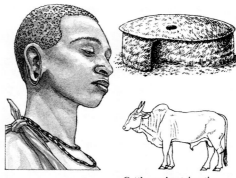

Cattle rearing takes the place of cultivation in areas that are too dry to be cropped successfully. In Africa, people such as the Masai are nomadic herders, moving their cattle long distances in search of pasture. Wealth is counted in terms of the numbers rather than the quality of the cattle they own, but improved management of their herds and better control of animal diseases are now making their cattle much more productive.

SAVANNA FIRES
Fires have been sweeping the savannas for thousands of years. Hunters set fires to flush game from cover, farmers use fire to clear land for crops, and cattle owners burn off parched, unpalatable grasses to make way for a fresh new growth for their stock. At the end of the dry season, when fires are particularly fierce, large areas of savanna lie under a thin haze of smoke.

Poaching, together with the takeover of wildlife ranges by farms and livestock, has led many animals to near-extinction in areas where they were once plentiful. Poisoned arrows are capable of killing even the biggest African game: sometimes they are set as traps and are triggered by the animal itself walking into a trip line. More sophisticated poachers use machine-guns and high-powered assault rifles, and airlift their illicit cargos of skins, ivory and rhinoceros horn. Illegal hunting for meat, which is dried and sold, has also become a large, highly organized and very profitable business in many areas.

Game animals also provide the spectacular displays that attract tourists and make tourism an important source of income for many developing nations. Today, most tourists pursue game with cameras instead of guns. The hunting that led to the wholesale slaughter of wildlife in previous years is banned, and so is the traffic in trophies, although even in the sanctuary provided by parks and reserves animals still fall prey to poachers.

Animals are frequently transferred from areas where they are at risk to safer areas such as game parks and reserves. In Kenya, helicopters came to the rescue of a herd of rare antelopes when their range was threatened by a proposed irrigation scheme and moved them to Tsavo National Park. Animals are also moved to introduce new blood to small, isolated herds or to restock areas from which they have been lost.

Tropical Rainforests

Tropical rainforests, extremely rich in both plant and animal life, consist of a series of layered or stratified habitats. These range from the dark and humid forest floor through a layer of shrubs to the emerging tops of the scattered giant trees towering above the dense main canopy of the forest. Each layer of vegetation is a miniature life zone containing a wide selection of animal species. These can be divided into a number of ecological groups according to their various ways of life, and many have evolved special adaptations to enable them to make maximum use of the plentiful food supply surrounding them.

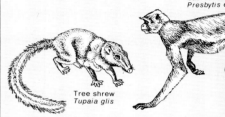

Crested tree swift
Hemiprocne longipennis

Crowned eagle
Stephanoaetus coronatus

Tropical rainforests occur only in the regions close to the Equator; they have a heavy rainfall and a uniformly hot and moist climate. There are slightly more of these forests in the northern half of the world than in the southern half and they occur at altitudes of up to 1,500 m (5,000 ft). Temperatures are normally between 24°C and 30°C (77°–86°F) and rarely fall below 21°C (70°F) or rise above 32°C (90°F). The skies are often cloudy and the rain falls more or less evenly throughout the year. Rainfall is usually more than 2,000 mm (78 in) a year and is never less than 1,500 mm (59 in). A distinctive feature of this tropical, humid climate is that the average daily temperature range is much greater than the range between the hottest and coolest months.

A stratified habitat
There are usually three to five overlapping layers in the mature tropical rainforest. The tallest trees (called "emergents") rise above a closed, dense canopy formed by the crowns of less tall trees, which nevertheless can reach more than 40 m (130 ft) tall. Below this canopy is a third or middle layer of trees—the understory; their crowns do not meet but they still form a dense layer of growth about 5–20 m (16–65 ft) tall. The fourth layer consists of woody shrubs of varying heights between 1–5 m (3–16 ft). The bottom layer comprises decomposers (fungi) that rarely reach 50 cm (20 in) in height.

Although the trees are so tall, few of them have really thick trunks. Nearly all are evergreens, shedding their dark, leathery leaves and growing new ones continuously. Many of the larger species grow buttresses—thin, triangular slabs of hardwood that spread out from the bases of their trunks. These support the trees, so removing the need for a heavy outlay of energy and resources on deep root systems. Hanging lianas (vines), thin and strong as rope, vanish like cables into the mass of foliage. They are especially abundant on riverbanks, where the canopy of trees is thinner; their leaves and flowers appear only among the treetops.

Epiphytes—plants that grow on other plants but do not take their nourishment from them—festoon the trunks and branches of trees, and up to 80 may grow on a single tree. They include many kinds of orchid and bromeliad. Their aerial roots make use of a humus substitute derived from the remains of other plants, often

Moth orchid
Phalaenopsis sanderana

Flowering plants of the forest include epiphytes such as bromeliads and orchids like the species of *Phalaenopsis* illustrated here. Epiphytes grow on other plants such as trees where they can receive sunlight and are nourished by humus in the bark. Many epiphytic orchids have swellings in their roots or at the bases of their leaves where water can be stored. Seventy species of *Phalaenopsis* grow in southeast Asian forests and *P. sanderana*, one of the most beautiful, was first discovered in the Philippines in 1882.

Tropical rainforests are located in the hot and wet equatorial lands of Latin America, West Africa, Madagascar and Asia. These areas have consistently high temperatures throughout the year and receive high rainfall from the moist and unstable winds blowing in from the oceans.

Tropical rainforests

The hummingbird numbers about 300 species, most of which are confined to the forests of South America. It is renowned for its ability to hover while gathering nectar, a feat achieved by the almost 180° rotations of its wings, which beat rapidly more than 80 times per second.

brought together by ants. The bases of their leaves may be broad and bowl shaped and collect and hold water; they also provide homes for a variety of insects and reptiles.

Rainforest soils are not as fertile as might be supposed by the luxuriance of their vegetation. On the contrary, the silicates and compounds necessary for plant growth are leached away by the rain to leave red or yellow soils of poor quality. This process, known as laterization, is widespread in the humid tropics. Humus is rapidly broken down by bacteria, fungi and termites, while earthworms, which in more temperate regions normally contribute to the mixing of humus with mineral particles, are usually absent.

In rainforests there are often up to 25 different tree species on a single hectare of land (60 species to the acre). Most temperate forests have only a fifth of this number, with nothing like the abundance of plants that grow in the tropics. This incredible variety supports—directly or indirectly—a corresponding variety of animal species which has an abundant food supply because the forest never ceases to be productive. This is why most mammals do not move far; they stay where their food grows.

Life in the canopy
The dense leaves and branches of the canopy provide the most food and so support the greatest number of species. Macaws and toucans (from the American tropics) and parrots and trogons (which live in forests throughout the tropics) eat the fruit growing in the

THE LAYERS OF THE FOREST
Stratification—the existence of distinct layers forest vegetation—is especially pronounced in the tropics, where there are usually five main storys These can overlap greatly and may vary in height from area to area. The large differences between the layer present many varied habitats and ecological niches for a very wide range of animals.

CANOPY LAYER
This dense story exerts a powerful influence on the levels below since its trees, which grow between 20 m (65 ft) and 40 m (130 ft) tall, form such a thick layer of vegetation that they cut off sunlight from the forest below. The canopy is noted for the diversity of its fauna. Many birds and animals are adapted to running along branches to get the flowers, fruits or nuts that form their diets. The pointed tips of canopy leaves encourage rapid drainage.

Sacred lang
Presbytis er

Tree shrew
Tupaia glis

MIDDLE LAYER
This understory comprises trees from 5 m (16 ft) to 20 m (65 ft) tall whose long, narrow crowns do not become quite so dense as those of the canopy. There is very often no clear distinction, however, between this level and the canopy. Middle-layer trees are strong enough to bear large animals such as leopards that spend part of their lives on the ground. Epiphytes are plentiful in this layer.

Leopard
Panthera pa

Pouched tree frog
Gastrotheca ovifera

Orang-utan
Pongo pygmaeus

SHRUB LAYER
The vegetation of this level is sparse in comparison with that above it and consists of treelets and woody shrubs that rarely reach 5 m (16 ft). These grow up in any available space between the abundant boles of large trees. Life in this story exists equally well at ground level.

Four-striped squirrel
Funisciurus lemniscatus

Oriental civet
Viverra tangalunga

Tree pango
Manis tricus

GROUND LAYER
Shade-tolerant herbs, ferns and tree seedlings represent the only flora at ground level; there is no grass here. Light is less than one percent of full daylight so that many mammals are well camouflaged in the gloom, whereas others have compact bodies to facilitate movement through the undergrowth. Ants and termites are well adapted to the high humidity and darkness of the forest floor. Fungi and a host of invertebrates quickly break down the litter of rotting leaves, fruit and fallen branches to provide vital nutrients for the fast-growing trees of the tropical rainforest.

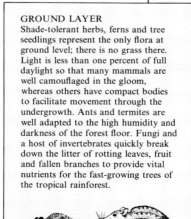

Okapi
Okapia johnstoni

Forest buffalo
Syncerus caffer nanus

Indian tiger
Panthera tigris tigris

Malayan tapir
Tapirus indicus

Congo forest mouse
Deomys ferrugineus

Short-eared elephant shrew
Macroscelides proboscideus

Orange-rumped agouti
Dasyprocta aguti

Mandrill
Mandrillus sphinx

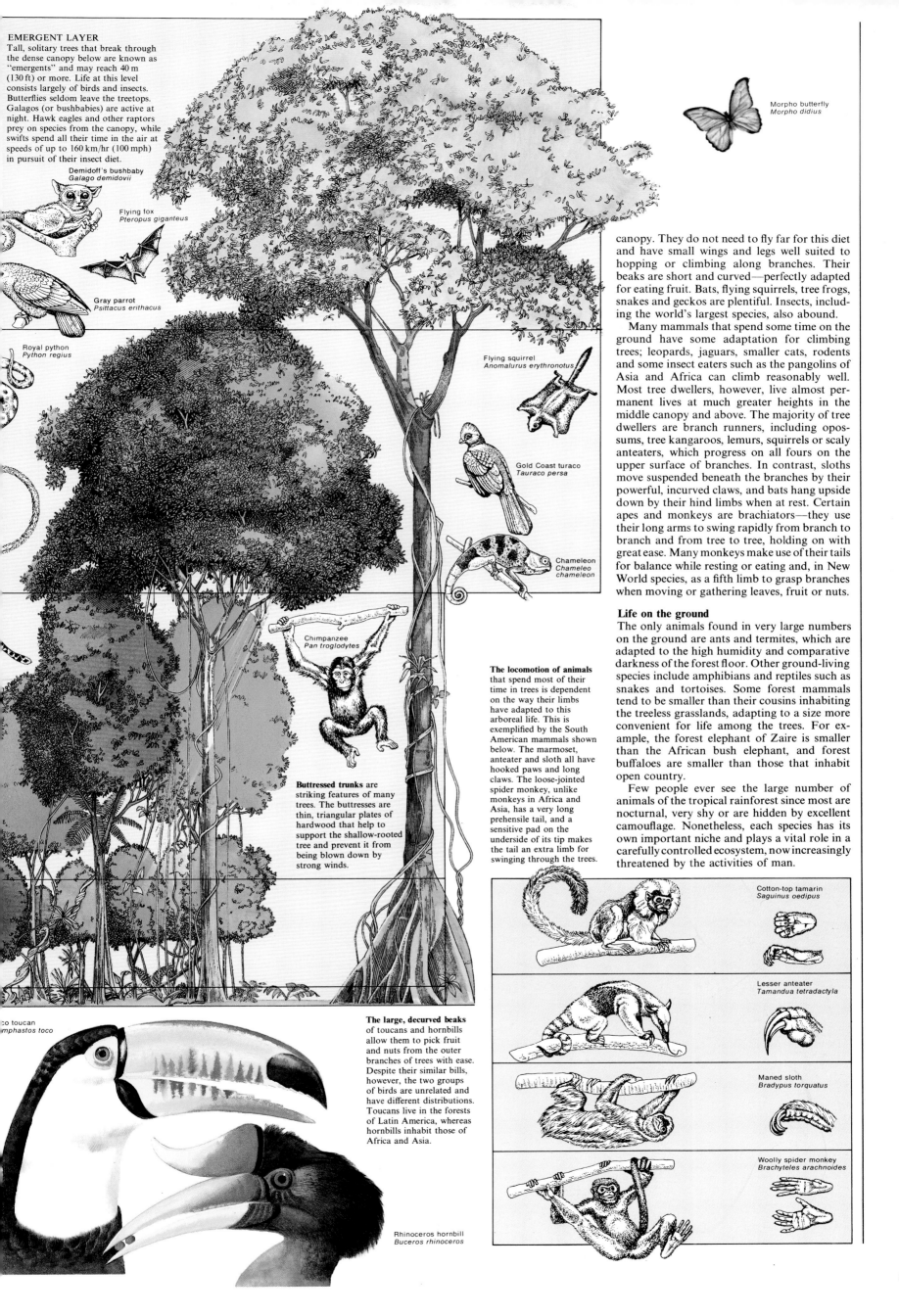

Tall, solitary trees that break through the dense canopy below are known as "emergents" and may reach 40 m (130 ft) or more. Life at this level consists largely of birds and insects. Butterflies seldom leave the treetops. Galagos (or bushbabies) are active at night. Hawk eagles and other raptors prey on species from the canopy, while swifts spend all their time in the air at speeds of up to 160 km/hr (100 mph) in pursuit of their insect diet.

Demidoff's bushbaby
Galago demidovii

Flying fox
Pteropus giganteus

Gray parrot
Psittacus erithacus

Royal python
Python regius

Flying squirrel
Anomalurus erythronotus

Gold Coast turaco
Tauraco persa

Chameleon
Chameleo chameleon

Morpho butterfly
Morpho didius

Chimpanzee
Pan troglodytes

Buttressed trunks are striking features of many trees. The buttresses are thin, triangular plates of hardwood that help to support the shallow-rooted tree and prevent it from being blown down by strong winds.

The locomotion of animals that spend most of their time in trees is dependent on the way their limbs have adapted to this arboreal life. This is exemplified by the South American mammals shown below. The marmoset, anteater and sloth all have hooked paws and long claws. The loose-jointed spider monkey, unlike monkeys in Africa and Asia, has a very long prehensile tail, and a sensitive pad on the underside of its tip makes the tail an extra limb for swinging through the trees.

The large, decurved beaks of toucans and hornbills allow them to pick fruit and nuts from the outer branches of trees with ease. Despite their similar bills, however, the two groups of birds are unrelated and have different distributions. Toucans live in the forests of Latin America, whereas hornbills inhabit those of Africa and Asia.

co toucan
mphastos toco

Rhinoceros hornbill
Buceros rhinoceros

canopy. They do not need to fly far for this diet and have small wings and legs well suited to hopping or climbing along branches. Their beaks are short and curved—perfectly adapted for eating fruit. Bats, flying squirrels, tree frogs, snakes and geckos are plentiful. Insects, including the world's largest species, also abound.

Many mammals that spend some time on the ground have some adaptation for climbing trees; leopards, jaguars, smaller cats, rodents and some insect eaters such as the pangolins of Asia and Africa can climb reasonably well. Most tree dwellers, however, live almost permanent lives at much greater heights in the middle canopy and above. The majority of tree dwellers are branch runners, including opossums, tree kangaroos, lemurs, squirrels or scaly anteaters, which progress on all fours on the upper surface of branches. In contrast, sloths move suspended beneath the branches by their powerful, incurved claws, and bats hang upside down by their hind limbs when at rest. Certain apes and monkeys are brachiators—they use their long arms to swing rapidly from branch to branch and from tree to tree, holding on with great ease. Many monkeys make use of their tails for balance while resting or eating and, in New World species, as a fifth limb to grasp branches when moving or gathering leaves, fruit or nuts.

Life on the ground

The only animals found in very large numbers on the ground are ants and termites, which are adapted to the high humidity and comparative darkness of the forest floor. Other ground-living species include amphibians and reptiles such as snakes and tortoises. Some forest mammals tend to be smaller than their cousins inhabiting the treeless grasslands, adapting to a size more convenient for life among the trees. For example, the forest elephant of Zaire is smaller than the African bush elephant, and forest buffaloes are smaller than those that inhabit open country.

Few people ever see the large number of animals of the tropical rainforest since most are nocturnal, very shy or are hidden by excellent camouflage. Nonetheless, each species has its own important niche and plays a vital role in a carefully controlled ecosystem, now increasingly threatened by the activities of man.

Cotton-top tamarin
Saguinus oedipus

Lesser anteater
Tamandua tetradactyla

Maned sloth
Bradypus torquatus

Woolly spider monkey
Brachyteles arachnoides

Man and the Tropical Rainforests

Every three seconds a portion of original rainforest the size of a football field disappears as man fells the trees and extends his cultivation. Although tropical conditions allow rapid regrowth of secondary forest, the loss of primary forest is destroying thousands of plant and animal species that will never again be seen on Earth. Even by conservative estimates, it is likely that all the world's primary tropical forest will have disappeared within 85 years unless the trend is reversed.

The activities of man have only recently begun to threaten the tropical rainforest. Since prehistoric times, forests have offered shelter to people who, lacking any knowledge of agriculture, have existed as hunters and gatherers. They used only stone and wooden weapons such as bows and arrows to kill their animal prey, and collected berries, fruit and honey from their surroundings. Their influence on the forest environment was minimal and today a few races such as African pygmies and the Punans of Borneo still live in such a simple state of balance with nature. The Punans, for example, have no permanent homes, but use leaves and branches to construct temporary shelters that are used for only a few weeks before being abandoned. The pygmies build similar homes.

Shifting agriculture

Most forest dwellers, however, live in more permanent settlements and grow most of their food in forest clearings they have made. Such people are expert at chopping down trees in order to set fire to them, and this "slash-and-burn" farming results in small areas littered with charred logs and stumps whose ashes enrich the ground. Crops such as wild tapioca (cassava or manioc) are widely grown, but after a year or two the soil loses the little fertility it once had so that a new tract of forest has to be cleared and burned. Such shifting agriculture provides food for more than 200 million inhabitants of the Third World. As a farming system it has been used throughout the world for more than 2,000 years. When there were few farmers per kilometer the land was allowed to lie fallow for at least 10 years so that the soil could recover. Today, however, population pressures are so great that fallow periods have been drastically reduced and a swift repetition of slash-and-burn degrades and removes nutrients from the soil.

Effects on world climate

Tropical forest floors seldom have deep layers of humus so that, once trees are removed, the shallow topsoil is exposed and soon becomes eroded. In turn, this reduces the capacity of the ground to retain moisture, and without this sponge-like effect runoff can become very erratic and lead to floods, such as those that frequently occur in India and Bangladesh. Estuary sedimentation is often greatly increased

A DIMINISHING RESOURCE
This idealized tract of rainforest includes many of the activities of man that are daily endangering the survival of the forest. Shifting "slash-and-burn" cultivation and excessive logging present the greatest threats. Antidotes such as reafforestation have so far made very little headway.

Living in harmony with the forest are small groups of hunter gatherers who mainly live on a flesh diet, killing their prey with bows and arrows. Nuts and berries supplement this diet, and leaves gathered from the immediate jungle cover their temporary dome-shaped shelters. These are abandoned as an area becomes exhausted and the tribe moves on. Twenty or so pygmies need about 500 sq km (200 sq miles) to support themselves.

Selective logging by gangs of men seeking out the straightest and most valuable hardwood species has been the most common form of tree extraction, even though 75 percent of the canopy might have to be destroyed to remove just a few important trees. Today heavy axes are being replaced by power saws that have no difficulty in cutting down the large buttresses that were once left behind.

Plantation forestry has made increasing inroads into the forests over the decades. The commercial advantage of products that can be cropped several times during the hardwoods' maturation period is becoming increasingly apparent to farmers in the regions. Many rubber plantations in southeastern Asia consist of small holdings that have tended to encroach upon the forest, and intercropping now takes place between the long-established trees.

Shifting cultivation converts thousands of square kilometers of primary forest to substandard cultivation every year. Forest is cleared by slash-and-burn, the resulting fertile clearing is cropped with staples such as manioc, and then left to degrade to secondary forest once the ash-strewn ground has lost its poor fertility. Inevitably, the ground becomes permanently degraded. One encouraging antidote to the futility of such shifting agriculture is the recent strategy of agroforestry (as used by countries such as Nigeria and Thailand), which encourages the planting of fast-growing trees at the same time as the farmer's normal crops. Such intercropping offers considerable financial incentives to the small itinerant farmer.

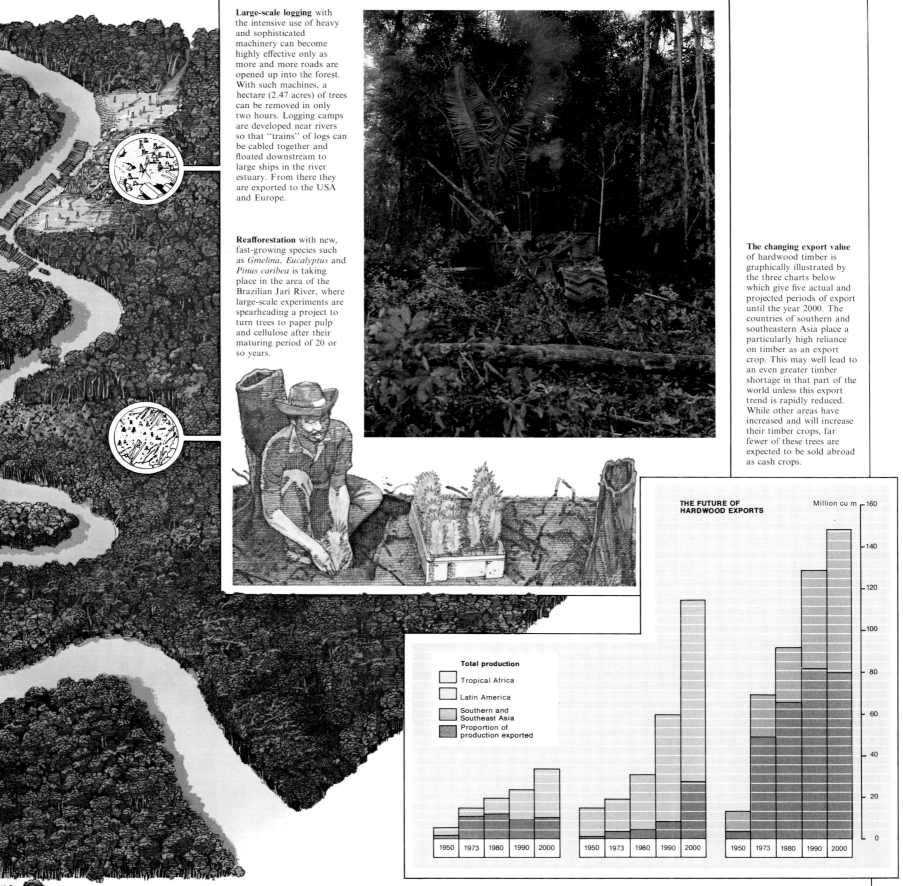

Large-scale logging with the intensive use of heavy and sophisticated machinery can become highly effective only as more and more roads are opened up into the forest. With such machines, a hectare (2.47 acres) of trees can be removed in only two hours. Logging camps are developed near rivers so that "trains" of logs can be cabled together and floated downstream to large ships in the river estuary. From there they are exported to the USA and Europe.

Reafforestation with new, fast-growing species such as *Gmelina*, *Eucalyptus* and *Pinus caribea* is taking place in the area of the Brazilian Jari River, where large-scale experiments are spearheading a project to turn trees to paper pulp and cellulose after their maturing period of 20 or so years.

The changing export value of hardwood timber is graphically illustrated by the three charts below which give five actual and projected periods of export until the year 2000. The countries of southern and southeastern Asia place a particularly high reliance on timber as an export crop. This may well lead to an even greater timber shortage in that part of the world unless this export trend is rapidly reduced. While other areas have increased and will increase their timber crops, far fewer of these trees are expected to be sold abroad as cash crops.

THE FUTURE OF HARDWOOD EXPORTS   Million cu m

Total production
- Tropical Africa
- Latin America
- Southern and Southeast Asia
- Proportion of production exported

1950 1973 1980 1990 2000   1950 1973 1980 1990 2000   1950 1973 1980 1990 2000

as the forest topsoil is simply washed away by torrential rain. In parts of Asia, deforestation has caused changes in water flow that have interfered with the production of new high-yield rice crops.

Tropical forests contain an enormous store of carbon, and some authorities believe that its release into the air (as carbon dioxide) when the forest is burned down may be as great in volume as that released by the rest of the world's fossil fuels. The higher proportion of carbon dioxide in the atmosphere may lead to an increase in global temperatures, especially at the poles. Trees also release oxygen into the air through photosynthesis, and some scientists have estimated that half of the world's oxygen is derived from this source. Others estimate that half of the rainfall of the Amazon basin is generated by the forest itself, so that any great reduction in tree cover would turn Amazonia into a much drier region.

Threats to Amazonia
Much attention has been paid to the situation of Amazonia, covering as it does some 6.5 million sq km (2½ million sq miles). In an attempt to give better access to timber and mineral reserves, the Brazilian government's

building of the TransAmazonian Highway (3,000 km or 1,860 miles long) has opened the way to deforestation, and settlers have been encouraged to make small holdings on the cleared forest beside the road. Between 1966 and 1978, the government calculated that farmers and big business interests had turned 80,000 sq km (31,000 sq miles) of forest into grazing land for 6 million cattle intended for hamburgers. However, like the wholesale extraction of timber, this has proved to be of doubtful economic value. Because costs rise steeply as less accessible areas are tapped, expenses tend to eliminate logging profits.

Threats in Africa
Even greater threats to tropical forest land have come from less cautious and realistic governments, such as that of Ivory Coast. There neither shifting agriculture nor excessive logging for valuable export sales appear to be under any sort of control. Accordingly, between 1966 and 1974, the area of forest declined from 156,000 sq km (60,000 sq miles) to 54,000 sq km (20,000 sq miles), much of the latter being secondary forest that can never be returned to its original status. Like many other developing countries, Ivory Coast has been more keen to

cut down and export its profitable timbers than to think about protecting its invaluable forest environment. Inevitably, forest farmers move into cleared areas and often establish plantation cash crops such as coffee, cocoa and rubber, while the establishment of national parks to curtail depletion has often had very little profitable effect. The Malaysian rainforest is also disappearing rapidly, through widescale logging and open-cast mining for bauxite (aluminum ore).

A large proportion of the world's rainforest occurs in tropical countries faced with severe problems of population control. It is therefore inevitable that the pressures on such forests will be great. Human interference does more than merely destroy the primary forest, to be replaced in time by secondary growth; more importantly, the wholesale removal of trees also drastically reduces the vast genetic reservoir contained in the number of plant and animal species the forests harbor. This in itself is a sound ecological argument for preserving forests and for reversing current trends towards monoculture in the tropics. All the warnings about forest depletion appear to be clear, yet there seems little hope that man will heed them until it is too late.

Monsoon Regions

The word monsoon often conjures up the image of torrential rain and steaming tropical jungles. Yet such a view is misleading, for very great contrasts occur in the regions of the tropical world with a monsoon climate. What distinguishes monsoon regions is not so much the amount of rainfall or the permanently high temperatures, but the dramatic contrast between seasons, with an extended dry season as an essential feature. And in fact the word monsoon derives from the Arabic word for season.

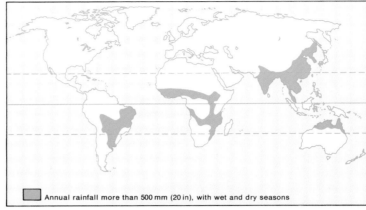

THE SEASON OF RAIN
Life in the monsoon regions balances on the expectation of seasonal heavy rain. In much of India, for instance, 85 percent of the annual rainfall occurs during the limited monsoon periods, and humans as well as plants and animals depend on it wholly. About half the world's people live in these regions, in communities whose rhythm of life necessarily reflects the rains' seasonal nature.

This contrast between wet and dry seasons reflects the reversals of winds over sea and land, which in the northern hemisphere blow from the northeast in the dry winter season, and from the southwest in the wet summer periods.

The monsoon regions occur most widely in southern, southeastern and eastern Asia to the south of latitude 25°N, and in western and central Africa north of the Equator, but there are also smaller regions with a characteristically monsoon climate in eastern Africa, northern Australia and central America. Despite the similar overall climatic pattern, however, the monsoon regions are otherwise very diverse.

Before human settlement the original vegetation of the monsoon regions reflected the dominance of an extended dry season followed by a period of violent rainfall. Typical forest cover was provided by the sal (*Shorea robusta*) deciduous forest, which adjusts to extended periods of moisture deficiency by shedding its leaves. However, within the monsoon region rainfall varies from 200 mm (8 in) a year to more than 20,000 mm (800 in), and the rainy periods may vary between three and nine months.

The range of vegetation found in the monsoon regions reflects this diversity. Where tropical rainforest alters to monsoon forest, as in eastern Java, there is a sharp fall in the total number of plant and animal species, and species adapted to endure seasonal drought begin to be seen. At the other extreme of rainfall the forest thins and shades into semidesert vegetation in India's northwest. But if there is a "type" of monsoon vegetation it is tropical deciduous forest, with sal as the dominant species.

As well as contrasts in climate, the monsoon regions also exhibit pronounced changes in temperature and vegetation as a result of variations in altitude. The Western Ghats of India and the foothills of the Himalayas in Assam both rise to more than 2,500 m (8,200 ft). Temperatures decrease sharply at such altitudes with corresponding changes in vegetation. In southern India on the Nilgiri Hills a wet temperate forest is characteristic, with an intermingling of temperate and tropical species. Magnolias, planes and elms all grow there.

Agriculture in monsoon regions
Despite its extensive area there is no part of the monsoon world that is untouched by man and by man's activities. In southern Asia, agricultural activity can be traced back at least 5,000 years, and there have been agricultural settlements throughout the monsoon regions for at least 1,500 years. Man's activity and the grazing of domesticated animals have interfered with, and progressively modified, the natural vegetation. The range of species indicates that, in the whole of the monsoon biome, there is now virtually no primary forest left. The pace of man's interference has speeded up considerably over the last 100 years. As a result, less than 10 percent of the land in southern Asia is now forested, and other parts of the monsoon

Many parts of the world experience "monsoon" winds, blowing from sea to land in summer, and from land to sea in winter; but typical monsoon vegetation is most clearly seen in the regions of southeastern Asia and the Indian subcontinent. In climatic terms, however, the monsoon circulation of seasonal wind reversals, with wetter summers and dry winters, also affects considerable areas of Africa, South America and northern Australia.

☐ Annual rainfall more than 500 mm (20 in), with wet and dry seasons

regions are similarly losing their forest cover.

Many of today's farming methods incorporate traditional cultivation practices, but there have also been very significant changes in recent decades. Traditional agriculture in the monsoon regions has been developed to take into account the seasonal nature of its rainfall pattern and the total rainfall received. The fundamental role of water throughout the region and the absence of low temperatures have placed great importance on either cultivating crops that can tolerate the seasonal rainfall pattern, or on providing irrigation.

Through most of southern Asia, overwhelmingly the most populous of the monsoon regions, the most important single crop is rice, which covers about one-third of the total cultivated area. Rice needs a great deal of water and for this reason is grown mainly in areas of high irrigation, such as the delta lands of the southern and eastern coasts of India, and in areas where rainfall is more than 1,500 mm (59 in) a year. Its cultivation creates a very distinctive landscape as a result of the fact that rice must spend much of its growing period with a few centimeters of water over the soil.

Rice cultivation gives the monsoon regions their characteristic pattern of paddy fields, but other cereal crops such as wheat, the millets and sorghum are also very important. These can tolerate far drier conditions than can rice and occur in areas such as central India or upland Thailand, where uncertain and less abundant rainfall puts a premium on drought tolerance.

Even with traditional crops, man has often interfered extensively with the environment in order to increase yields and attempt to guarantee successful cropping. Traditional irrigation schemes range from diverting rivers at times of flood, in order to lead water to dry land, to digging wells and building small reservoirs. But recent technological developments have brought a new dimension to agricultural activity in the monsoon regions. Large-scale dam and irrigation canal schemes have become important in Africa as well as in monsoon Asia. The introduction and speed of electric or diesel "pumpsets" have transformed well irrigation in regions with extensive groundwater. The

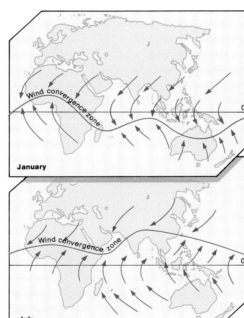

January

July

Heat differences in the atmosphere cause the seasonal wind reversals (left) characteristic of monsoon circulation. In January the northern hemisphere is tilted away from the sun, and cold, d winds blow from the central Asian landmass toward the Equator. Here they change direction (an effect of the Earth's rotation), converge with other winds, and drop the rain. In July the situation is reversed when the heate Asian landmass attracts a flow of cooler air from th equatorial oceans, which moves northward with the sun. The moist air condenses on reaching land, and the monsoon rains descend.

reliable water supply that irrigation can give has brought in its train the opportunity for farmers to adopt a wide range of new farming practices. Chemical fertilizers and new strains of seed have made possible great increases in the productivity of the land in many parts of the monsoon regions, but their use is generally restricted to areas of reliable water supply.

Subsistence cultivation over thousands of years has been by far the most important element in the transformation of the landscape and vegetation of the monsoon world, but the introduction of plantation cultivation during the last centuries has also had a major effect. Tea plantations, for instance, have led to the almost total replacement of natural vegetation in the hills of southern India and Sri Lanka.

Populations in all the countries of the monsoon regions are rapidly increasing, and demands for economic development are constantly growing, placing increasing pressures on the environment, pressures which to date have seemed almost irresistible.

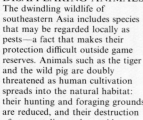

DISAPPEARING ANIMALS
The dwindling wildlife of southeastern Asia includes species that may be regarded locally as pests—a fact that makes their protection difficult outside game reserves. Animals such as the tiger and the wild pig are doubly threatened as human cultivation spreads into the natural habitat: their hunting and foraging grounds are reduced, and their destruction of crops or livestock provides villagers with an obvious incentive for killing them in order to protect their own livelihoods.

Wild pig
Sus scrofa

Tiger
Panthera tigris

SELF-SUFFICIENCY IN CHINA
Local materials are turned into saleable products at a ratan factory in southern China. This factory is not owned by the state but by the village-sized brigade responsible for the manufacturing. The brigade functions as a smaller economic unit within the Ting Chow people's commune of 20 to 30 villages, but is encouraged to act independently, owning what it creates. The commune takes care of such matters as waterways—it contains 82 km (51 miles) of canals.

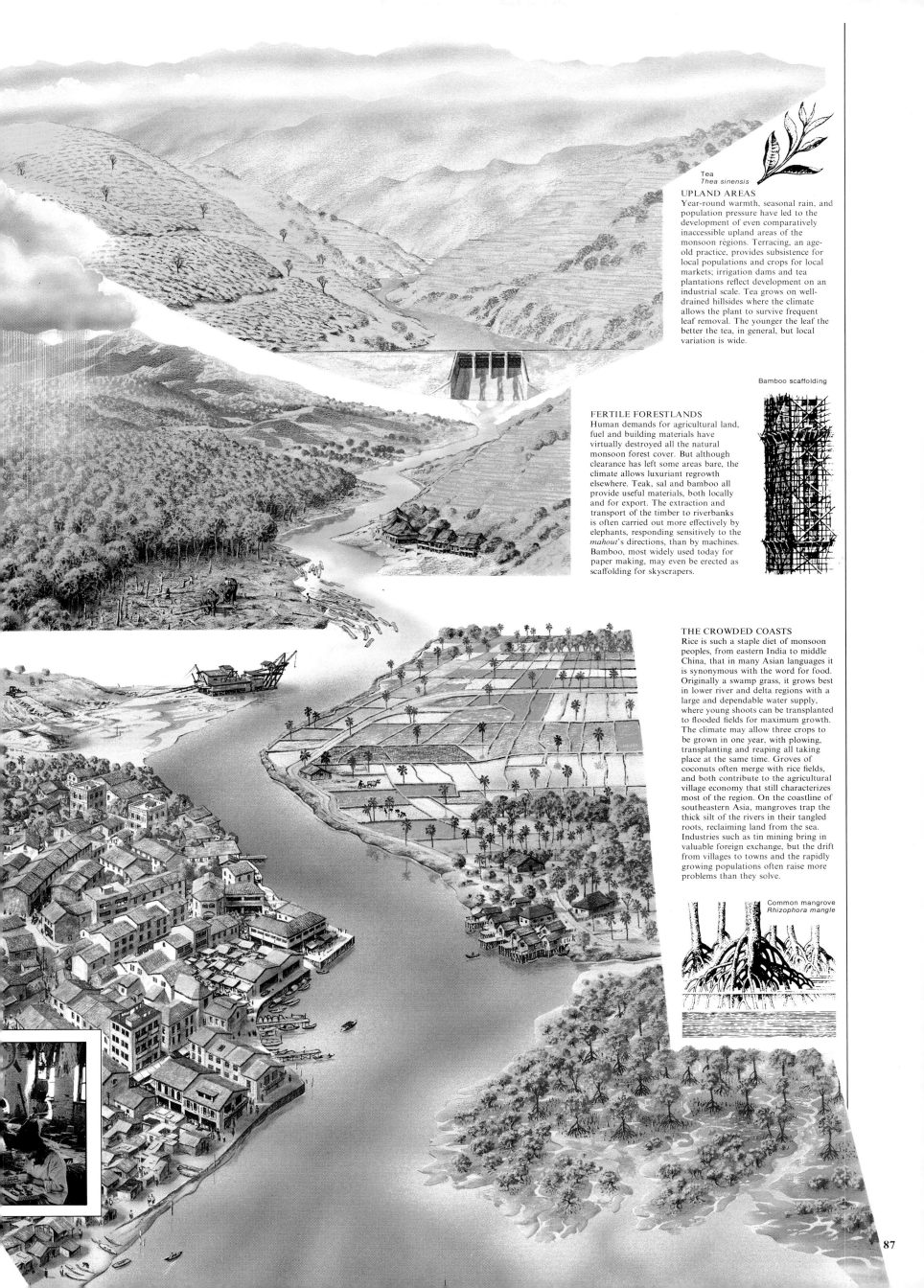

UPLAND AREAS

Year-round warmth, seasonal rain, and population pressure have led to the development of even comparatively inaccessible upland areas of the monsoon regions. Terracing, an age-old practice, provides subsistence for local populations and crops for local markets; irrigation dams and tea plantations reflect development on an industrial scale. Tea grows on well-drained hillsides where the climate allows the plant to survive frequent leaf removal. The younger the leaf the better the tea, in general, but local variation is wide.

Tea
Thea sinensis

Bamboo scaffolding

FERTILE FORESTLANDS

Human demands for agricultural land, fuel and building materials have virtually destroyed all the natural monsoon forest cover. But although clearance has left some areas bare, the climate allows luxuriant regrowth elsewhere. Teak, sal and bamboo all provide useful materials, both locally and for export. The extraction and transport of the timber to riverbanks is often carried out more effectively by elephants, responding sensitively to the *mahout*'s directions, than by machines. Bamboo, most widely used today for paper making, may even be erected as scaffolding for skyscrapers.

THE CROWDED COASTS

Rice is such a staple diet of monsoon peoples, from eastern India to middle China, that in many Asian languages it is synonymous with the word for food. Originally a swamp grass, it grows best in lower river and delta regions with a large and dependable water supply, where young shoots can be transplanted to flooded fields for maximum growth. The climate may allow three crops to be grown in one year, with plowing, transplanting and reaping all taking place at the same time. Groves of coconuts often merge with rice fields, and both contribute to the agricultural village economy that still characterizes most of the region. On the coastline of southeastern Asia, mangroves trap the thick silt of the rivers in their tangled roots, reclaiming land from the sea. Industries such as tin mining bring in valuable foreign exchange, but the drift from villages to towns and the rapidly growing populations often raise more problems than they solve.

Common mangrove
Rhizophora mangle

Mountain Regions

A quarter of Earth's land surface lies at heights of 1,000 m (3,300 ft) or more above sea level. But the highland regions are thinly populated by man, who is, generally speaking, a lowland dweller (most major population centers are less than 100 m (330 ft) above sea level). Some formerly lowland animals have fled from man to the harsh refuge of the mountains, joining with specially adapted plants and wildlife, but today man himself is finding the highland regions increasingly useful and desirable.

The world's highest mountain peaks rise to almost 9.6 km (6 miles) above sea level, but these heights are small compared to the total diameter of the Earth. The rough surface of an orange would have mountains higher than the Himalayas if scaled up to world size. But mountain environments, although they vary enormously from system to system, all tend to demand remarkable endurance and adaptability from the plants and animals that inhabit them.

Altitude rather than geological variation determines conditions of life on mountains. The temperature falls by 2°C with every 300 m (3.4°F every 1,000 ft)—hence the snowcapped beauty of the heights—and life forms must be adapted to increasingly harsh conditions as height increases. As a result, zones of different life occur at different levels, from tropical forests (at the base of low-latitude mountains) to arctic-type life in the zone of ice and snow at the summit. The latitude of the mountain affects the heights to which these zones extend: trees occur at 2,300 m (7,500 ft) in the southern Alps, whereas farther north, in central Sweden, trees cannot survive above 1,000 m (3,300 ft).

Life at the top

The specially adapted plant and animal life of the mountains occurs above the tree line, for here the variations in living conditions reach their greatest extremes. A plant that has found a foothold on a bare rock face may have to endure intense heat, even where the average temperature is low, when the summer sun blazing through the clear air warms the slabs to tropical temperatures. But when that part of the mountain falls into shadow, the temperature decreases very rapidly, often assisted by the high winds that blow almost constantly throughout the year in many mountain areas.

Soil necessary for plant life develops with the breakdown of the rock through the agency of water, frost and ice. Lichens, whose acids may aid in this destruction, can survive at very high levels, and as they die may add some humus to the newly forming soil. This may first accumulate in sheltered places where plants requiring high humidity, such as mosses and filmy ferns, are found. Flowering plants follow where a greater depth of soil has formed, although some grow in cracks between rocks.

Flowering plants of the mountains all tend to be small (to avoid harsh, drying winds), deep rooted (to anchor the plant firmly), and abundantly flowering (to benefit from the short growing season). Many unrelated species have independently developed a similar cushion form. This enables them to shed excess rainwater easily and to retain heat better in a tight tangle of stems and leaves, where the temperature may be more than 10°C (18°F) higher than that of the outside air. Insects sheltering there are well placed to perform the vital task of pollination. But pollinating insects are relatively rare at high altitudes, and some mountain plants are wind pollinated. The brilliant color of many others may be to increase their attractiveness for the insects. Nearly all upland plants are very slow-growing perennials, and many are evergreen, with leaves that exploit all available light.

Some large animals, such as the ibex or the Rocky Mountain goat, are adapted to spend their lives among the rocks and slopes. These stocky creatures, with hooves that act rather like suction cups, produce their summer young in the security of the heights, although in winter they descend to the shelter of the upper forests. Among smaller mammals, most of which are rodents, some dig burrows in which they hibernate through the winter. Others have very thick insulating coats, and may stay awake through the coldest weather in burrows under the snow.

Refugees from the lowlands

Some mountain animals, particularly carnivorous mammals and birds, have been driven by human persecution into remote mountain fastnesses. Many birds of prey, which could otherwise survive well in lowland areas, have their last strongholds among the mountains. They survive by feeding on small rodents, many of which are extremely wary. Some upland birds feed on insects or on seeds, but their number is comparatively small. The Alpine chough is one of the most interesting of mountain birds, for it has learned to find food among the scraps provided by climbers and skiers, whom it often follows to very high altitudes.

Insects and other small invertebrates, like their Arctic counterparts, may take several years to mature. Some are wingless, and many tend to fly low in order not to be blown away from their home range. Jumping spiders have been seen at heights of 6,700 m (22,000 ft) on the slopes of Mount Everest, where they exist on small flies and springtails, but even above this level springtails and glacier "fleas" occur where there are no plants, apparently surviving on wind-blown insects and pollen grains.

Man and the mountains

The remote beauty of the mountains has led many peoples to identify them as the abode of the gods, but man himself prefers to live in the more convenient lowlands. The rarefied atmosphere of the heights makes physical work difficult, although some mountain-dwelling peoples have developed adaptations of the blood system to enable them to carry scarce oxygen more efficiently. The short growing season prevents cultivation of all but the hardiest cereal crops, and most uplanders rely on their livestock—cattle, sheep, llamas or yaks—for their existence. The animals are often driven to high pasture during the summer, descending to the valleys in the winter.

Modern, urbanized man finds the beauty and freshness of mountains increasingly attractive. Climbers have invaded most of the world's mountain regions, and in winter hosts of skiers flock to the resorts. Many important wildlife sanctuaries and national parks, particularly in the United States, are in mountain areas.

Lowland populations often rely on the pure mountain streams for both water and energy. Whole upland valleys are sometimes flooded to store water for distant conurbations. And the forceful flow of the water as it descends from the snow-fed heights is frequently harnessed to produce electricity for entire regions hundreds of kilometers away. The clear mountain air also offers the best conditions for astronomical observation, and most observatories today are built in dry, cloudless mountain areas.

LIFE ON THE HEIGHTS
Mountain climates become colder the higher one goes. This change in conditions creates distinctive horizontal zones of plant and animal life, although the pattern may vary according to the latitude and aspect of a mountain. Some life forms manage to eke out a precarious existence even on the roof of the world. Lower down, the brief growing season encourages a short burst of plant and animal activity above the timber line, conspicuous for the brightly colored summer flowers. Man mainly inhabits the lower slopes and valleys. He exploits mountain resources but rarely lives on the inhospitable heights.

Many peoples have believed that the gods have their abodes in the high places of the world. Tibet (above), one of the highest and most mountainous of all countries, has a large number of religious sites. Modern man also finds the clear, dry air suitable for the study of heavenly bodies: most modern observatories, such as Kitt Peak, USA (right), are built on mountain sites far from cities.

Activity in Earth's crust has produced mountains in every continent (left). Some thrust up sharply, while older mountains have been eroded to rounded shapes. The Scottish Highlands were made by mountain-building forces 400 million years ago (170 million years before the Appalachians and the Urals). The Rockies are 70 million years old and the Alps 15 million years old.

- Ancient mountains (Caledonian orogenesis)
- Intermediate mountains (Hercynian orogenesis)
- Recent mountains (Alpine orogenesis)

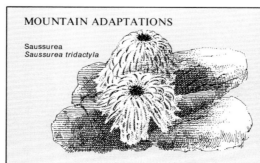

MOUNTAIN ADAPTATIONS

Saussurea
Saussurea tridactyla

Ingenious adaptations to harsh mountain conditions have been evolved by many plants, most of which have tiny cells with thick sap that does not freeze easily. Saussurea masks itself with white hair to reduce evaporation from the leaf surface. Alpine soldanellas are active even under snow, pushing up their flowers before the thaw.

Alpine soldanella
Soldanella alpina

SNOWBOUND PEAKS

Perpetual snow, violent winds and atmospheric dryness impose harsh conditions on life in the high Himalayas. But wind-blown organic debris from the plains does support some life forms—springtails, flies and jumping spiders—where the air is too dry to allow even lichens to survive. Lower down, a cushion plant may take root in a rock-base niche, but there is little other vegetation. Among birds, the Alpine chough is a scavenger that has followed Everest expeditions to heights of 7,900 m (26,000 ft).

Jumping spider
Salticus scenicus

Alpine chough
Pyrrhocorax graculus

Cushion pink
Parrya lanuginosa

Fly
Diptera sp

Primula
Primula rosea

Blue sheep
Pseudois nayaur

Royle's pika
Ochotona roylei

Himalayan blue poppy
Meconopsis horridula

Domestic yak
Bos grunniens

Snow leopard
Panthera uncia

MOUNTAIN MEADOWS

Between the snow line and the zone of coniferous trees, the Himalayan slopes exhibit a glorious variety of flowering plants during summer. Small and slow growing, these often have bright flowers which attract pollinating insects such as fly-like *Diptera*. The pika and other small, thick-furred rodents are the most common animals, although larger creatures, such as blue (bharal) sheep and yaks, also find summer pasturage at these heights. Snow leopards tend to inhabit the coniferous forests, but they travel up to higher parts to prey on the grazing herds. Few people live within the zone, but some Sherpas take their yak herds as high as 4,600 m (15,000 ft) for summer grazing, and even grow crops of potatoes at this height. Their permanent villages, however, are on the lower alpine slopes.

FORESTED SLOPES

Isolated birches mark the tree line— the transition from meadow to coniferous and rhododendron forest. In the upper parts of the forest, trees are dwarfed by cold and lack of moisture, and are twisted and bent from the wind. These low and tangled masses provide shelter for animals such as the Asian black bear and the red panda. Below the conifers lies a zone of broad-leaved evergreens, and in the foothills these in turn give way to tropical monsoon forests of sal trees (*Shorea robusta*) and thickets of bamboo. The raucous flocks of hill mynahs represent just one of the many kinds of birds found in this zone, which has the widest range of wildlife of all the kinds of mountain vegetation. Unfortunately, many species are in danger of extinction, for here man has settled, cut down forests and terraced hillsides to grow crops.

Rhododendron
Rhododendron sp

Asiatic black bear
Selenarctos thibetanus

Red panda
Ailurus fulgens

Hill mynah bird
Gracula religiosa

7,600 m
25,000 ft

4,900 m
16,000 ft

4,300 m
14,000 ft

3,700 m
12,000 ft

3,000 m
10,000 ft

2,400 m
8,000 ft

1,800 m
6,000 ft

1,200 m
4,000 ft

Permanent snow

Alpine meadows

Isolated birches

Coniferous forest

Rhododendron groves

Broadleaved evergreen forest

Bamboo

Tropical monsoon forest

Rocky Mountain goat
Oreamnos americanus

Animals and humans adapt to mountain conditions in many ways. The Rocky Mountain goat (left) has evolved a fleecy undercoat and hooves with concave pads to grip on any surface. Comparison of the blood counts (right) of a lowlander (A) and an Andean (B) shows how the latter has a higher total content and more red cells.

liters pints

The golden eagle *Aquila chrysaetos* (left) epitomizes the grandeur of the heights. Although it lives and nests in remote regions, it could equally well find its food in the lowlands were it not for human competition. An eagle's territory may cover 130 sq km (50 sq miles): it preys on small mammals and even (it is believed) on young deer and lambs. It mates for life and returns each year to the same nest.

Freshwater Environments

Broad, muddy rivers, fast-running streams, miniature ponds and deep, ancient lakes all provide their own distinctive environments for populations of animals and colonies of aquatic plants. And in spite of the fact that these, the world's freshwater systems, contain only a minute proportion of the Earth's total supplies of water, the remarkable variety and richness of the wildlife they support make them among the most valuable and significant of all the world's natural habitats.

Fresh water is never really pure for, like sea water, and indeed like all other natural waters, it contains various dissolved minerals. Fresh water differs from seawater only in the relatively low concentrations of the minerals it contains. But these mineral traces are extremely important; they provide essential nutrients without which freshwater plants could not exist. And without plant life, there would be virtually no animal life either.

Not all parts of every freshwater system are rich in both plants and animals. Large, deep lakes are very similar to oceans—no light can penetrate their gloomy depths, and few plants can live in these conditions. The surface waters, on the other hand, where light is plentiful, teem with microscopic floating plants, mainly single-celled algae such as desmids and diatoms. The edges of lakes provide a different set of conditions again, for here the water is shallow and light can penetrate right through it. Plants can take root in the silt on the bottom, grow up through the water and thrust their leaves out into the light and air. Edges of lakes and, for the same reasons, the waters of small ponds are usually full of such plant life, which in turn supports many freshwater animals.

Running waters
Just as the still waters of lakes and ponds offer a variety of habitats, so the running waters of rivers support many different forms of life, each adapted to the particular conditions of its environment. In the upper reaches, where rivers are scarcely more than upland streams, water is fast flowing and clear of silt. Few plants, except close-clinging mosses, can gain a hold on the bare stony bottom and most of the fish are well muscled and strong bodied to enable them to withstand the constant tug of the current. As a river swells to form a mature lowland water course, however, it becomes slower moving and the water is warmer and richer in nutrients. Plants grow readily in these lower reaches and provide a supply of food for aquatic animals.

With such a wide range of conditions, freshwater environments support an enormous variety of animal life—insects, fishes, amphibians, reptiles, mammals and birds. In some ways insects are the most important of all these creatures: freshwater systems contain more insects and other invertebrates, representing a greater variety of species, than any other kind of animal. Furthermore, these, the smallest representatives of the freshwater animal world, provide one of the most important links in the complex freshwater food chain.

Insects may be the most numerous, but fishes are probably the most familiar of all freshwater creatures, and they certainly show some of the greatest varieties of adaptations to the many different habitats. Their sizes vary from the tiny, 14 mm ($\frac{1}{2}$ in) of the virtually transparent dwarf goby fish found in small streams and lakes in the Philippines to the 4 m (14 ft) of the arapaima found in deep rivers in tropical South America. Their feeding habits vary from those of the ferocious carnivorous piranha of South America to those of the North American paddle fish which, although more than three times the size of the largest piranha, feed solely on microscopic organisms which they filter from the water with their specially adapted throats.

The breeding habits of freshwater fish also vary widely, from the carefully maternal instincts of the African mouthbreeding cichlids—these retain the developing eggs safely in their mouths until the offspring hatch—to the rather more common ejection of eggs into the water, where their fertilization and survival is simply left to chance. Other adaptations include the ability to breathe air (as does the African lungfish), to leap waterfalls (a common practice among migrating salmon) and to emit an electric shock of up to 600 volts (an adaptation of the South American electric eel).

Creatures of the water's edge
Of all the other major groups of animals, amphibians (such as frogs and toads) are probably the most reliant on freshwater systems. Because their skins must not dry out and they have to lay their eggs in water, few amphibians can venture far from the water's edge. And because they cannot tolerate the salt in seawater (it causes them to lose their body fluids through their skins) they are totally dependent upon fresh water for their existence. Reptiles, rather less typical of freshwater environments, range in size from miniature North American terrapins to the giant crocodiles that live along the banks of the Nile. Freshwater mammals, on the other hand, with the considerable exception of the hippopotamus, all tend to be rather small creatures such as otters, beavers, coypus, aquatic moles and water shrews.

Birds are another important group of freshwater creatures. Although few birds are truly aquatic an enormous number of species live in or near freshwater systems and take advantage of the various food supplies: the plants and fish within the waters; the bankside vegetation and small animal life; and the many forms of freshwater insects. Marshes and swamps, for example, provide some of the richest bird habitats in the world.

Also numbered among the species dependent on Earth's freshwater systems is man. And although strictly a nonaquatic, land-living animal, man uses more fresh water than any other creature. His needs seem to be inexhaustible as he harnesses, channels, diverts and often pollutes freshwater systems throughout the world. Unfortunately, the vast requirements of the human race are not always compatible with the rather more humble needs of all other species that depend upon fresh water.

Volume of Lakes in cu km (cu miles)	Discharge of Rivers in cu m (cu ft) per second

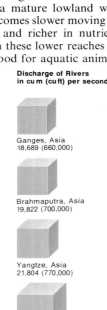

Huron, North America
3,447 (827)

Ganges, Asia
18,689 (660,000)

Nyasa, Africa
8,373 (2,009)

Brahmaputra, Asia
19,822 (700,000)

Superior, North America
12,153 (2,916)

Yangtze, Asia
21,804 (770,000)

Congo, Africa
39,644 (1,400,000)

Tanganyika, Africa
19,418 (4,659)

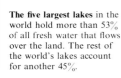

Baikal, Asia
23,260 (5,581)

Amazon, South America
212,376 (7,500,000)

The five largest lakes in the world hold more than 53% of all fresh water that flows over the land. The rest of the world's lakes account for another 45%.

The world's largest river, the Amazon, discharges more than one-fifth of all fresh water that flows from the mouths of the world's rivers into the oceans.

THE UPPER REACHES
Here, water flows rapidly. Tumbling over bare rocks and stones, it is chilly, oxygen-rich and free of silt. Bird life attracted to these reaches includes the sure-footed dipper, which walks the stream bed hunting for caddis larvae. Slightly farther downstream, but where the river is still narrow and easily dammed, beavers are found. Few plants can live within the water, but river crowfoot has feathery underwater leaves that remain intact where most other plants would be shredded by the current. Many fish, such as trout, have streamlined bodies to offer the least resistance to the stream's pull, while others survive on the bottom by bracing against the rocks—the bullhead, for example. Insects have various means of anchoring themselves to the stream bed—blackfly larvae have hooks to fix themselves to pebbles.

Dipper
Cinclus cinclus

Beaver
Castor fiber

River crowfoot
Ranunculus fluitans

Brown trout
Salmo trutta

Blackfly larvae
Simulium spp

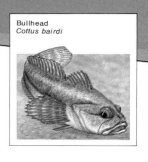

Bullhead
Cottus bairdi

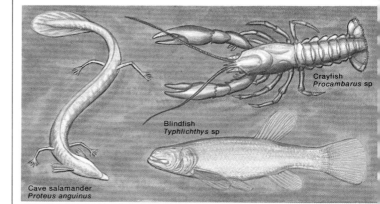

Crayfish
Procambarus sp

Blindfish
Typhlichthys sp

Cave salamander
Proteus anguinus

THE LIFE OF A RIVER

As a river makes its way from its upland source to the sea, it gradually changes its character. And at every stage in its progress, the animals and plants that inhabit the riverbanks and the waters reflect these changes by their adaptations to their environments. Most distinctive and dramatic are those adaptations produced in the wildlife of the upper and lower river reaches.

THE LOWER REACHES

The slowly flowing river and its muddy banks are rich in animals and plants. Many birds live along the water's edge; spoonbills wade in the shallows, filtering food from the water with their beaks. The banks, fringed with reedmaces and other plants, provide habitats for many reptiles, such as the American painted turtle, and mammals, such as the platypus. Plants also grow on the water—they range from large waterlilies to tiny algae that are food for river fishes: Africa's upside-down-feeding catfish, for example. In these waters, mammals as well as fish are to be found—Amazonian manatees live entirely aquatic lives. The plentiful river plants, such as curled pondweed, provide food for water snails and other herbivores, and cover for predators such as pike. Crustacea and insects living in the silt of the riverbed are food for bottom-feeding fish such as the strange-looking North American paddle fish.

LAKES: CHANGE AND EVOLUTION

No two lakes are alike: each is virtually a self-contained world for its population of aquatic animals and plants. Furthermore, no individual lake remains the same for long: in every lake, slow, inexorable changes in conditions are gradually but constantly changing the balance of species inhabiting the lake bed, the bankside and the water.

Changing conditions may be caused by one of several processes. Accumulating sediments, one of the most common of these processes, may eliminate a lake altogether. The water becomes shallower as sediments thicken (1) and these sediments are then added to and consolidated by water plants taking root. Ultimately, land plants (2) invade the area.

Lakes develop their own peculiar species when the aquatic wildlife that evolves within them has no means of migrating to other freshwater systems to interbreed. The world's only existing species of freshwater seal, for example, is found in just one lake—isolated Lake Baikal in Asia.

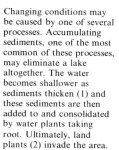

Baikal seal
Phoca sibirica

frican spoonbill
latalea alba

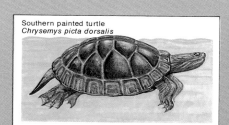

Southern painted turtle
Chrysemys picta dorsalis

Reedmace
Typha sp

Platypus
Ornithorhynchus anatinus

Waterlily
Nymphaea sp

African catfish
Synodontis batensoda

Amazonian manatee
Trichechus inunguis

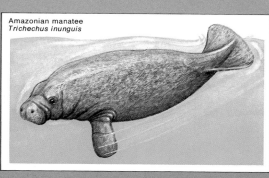

Curled pondweed
Potamogeton crispus

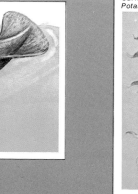

White ramshorn snail
Planorbis albus

Pike
Esox lucius

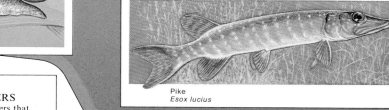

DARK WATERS

Underground rivers that flow through many of the world's cave systems support surprising numbers of creatures that have adapted to the permanent darkness. Many of these, such as the American cave crayfish, have lost the coloration of their surface-living kin. Some, such as Kentucky blind fishes, no longer possess eyes. Some salamanders are sighted and black when born, but become blind and colorless by adulthood.

Paddle fish
Polydon spathula

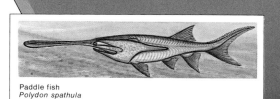

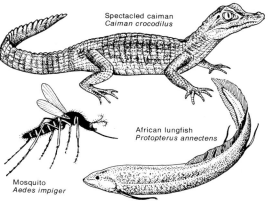

Spectacled caiman
Caiman crocodilus

African lungfish
Protopterus annectens

Mosquito
Aedes impiger

WETLANDS

Marshes and swamps are the richest of freshwater habitats. Wading birds, such as Asia's painted stork *Ibis leucocephalus* (above), are particularly common. Reptiles include caimans, which lay their eggs in swamps' warm, rotting vegetation. Of the many insects, mosquitoes are probably the most numerous, and of the many fishes, African lungfish are perhaps best adapted to life in wetlands. They survive drought, when marshes dry up, by their ability to breathe air.

Man and the Freshwater Environments

From earliest times, man has been finding new uses for and making new demands upon the world's freshwater resources. Today, the whole of modern society depends upon a vast supply to serve its agricultural, industrial, domestic and other needs. To meet the ever-growing demand for water, man has performed remarkable engineering feats: altering the courses of rivers, creating and destroying lakes, drowning valleys and tapping water sources that lie deep within the Earth.

Water is essential to human life. Simply to remain alive, an active adult living in a temperate climate needs a liquid intake of about two liters ($3\frac{1}{2}$ pints) every day. In warmer climates, the body's fluid requirements are even greater. Consequently, man has always been tied to reliable sources of drinking water—rivers, springs, lakes and ponds—and the availability of these, until very recently, has dictated the routes of all his wanderings and determined the sites of all his settlements.

From the time of the earliest human settlements, however, man has looked upon freshwater systems not simply as a source of drinking water but also as an increasingly useful resource for a multitude of other purposes. Today, water enters into virtually every aspect of modern life, and enormous quantities are used in agriculture, in industry, in the home, in the production of energy, for transport and for recreation.

The farmer's resource

Of all the major activities that rely on fresh water, agriculture is by far the world's largest consumer. In much of Europe and North America, rainfall is usually plentiful and lack of sufficient water for crops is rarely a problem. But in other parts of the world the climate simply does not produce enough rainfall and water shortages are a perennial problem. There, irrigation is not just a sophisticated technique to improve the yields and increase the varieties of crops grown; it is, and always has been, an essential element of agriculture.

Methods of irrigation range from small-scale devices—such as miniature windpumps—used in many developing countries simply to lift water from rivers for bankside crops, to vast dams, reservoirs and canal systems such as the Indus River project in Pakistan, which irrigates 10 million hectares (25 million acres) of land.

Traditional irrigation techniques usually involve using open channels or furrows for conducting water to fields. But one of the major problems with these, particularly in hot climates, is that much of the water evaporates and is lost before it can be used. Several new techniques, such as sprinklers and drip-feed systems, have recently been developed, however, to help make more efficient use of available supplies.

Although the most severe water deficiencies are experienced in the dry subtropical and tropical regions of the world, the temperate regions of North America and Europe, in spite of their relatively wet climates, do suffer shortages. Large towns and cities rarely have enough locally available rainfall or river flow to satisfy both domestic demand and the insatiable needs of industry. In the developed nations, industry consumes more water than any other activity.

Industrial demands

Fresh water is not only an integral part of almost every manufacturing process, it has other important industrial uses. As a source of power, it has been used since the early days of civilization—water wheels were one of man's first industrial inventions. Today, these simple devices are rarely seen in industrial societies, but water power is more important than ever before. Giant dams allow enormous volumes of water to be controlled and the power harnessed to drive turbines and generate electricity.

Freshwater systems have also, for centuries, provided industry with an important means of transporting its goods, and canal systems are still an essential part of industrial infrastructure in many countries of the world: the Europa Canal, when completed, will link three of Europe's major rivers, the Rhine, Main and Danube, and so form a continuous waterway running east–west across the breadth of Europe.

Already, the finished sections of the canal are carrying oil, chemicals, fertilizers, coal, coke and building materials to and from some of Europe's major industrial regions.

Many of Europe's waterways date back to the great canal-building days of the Industrial Revolution. Although a few of these are still used for commerce, many are today considered too narrow to transport economical quantities of goods. Some, however, are now finding a role to play in one of the world's fastest-growing new industries—the leisure market. Today, canals provide a wide range of aquatic activities for holiday makers, tourists and sportsmen.

Recreation and sport

Freshwater systems throughout the world, in fact, are rapidly being recognized and developed as major recreational resources. Lakes and reservoirs are stocked with fish for anglers, silted waterways are dredged to provide sailing and swimming facilities, and old quarries and open-cast workings are landscaped and flooded to provide entirely new freshwater systems purely for leisure pursuits. The projects not only help to rejuvenate previously misused land, they also provide significant incomes to otherwise underdeveloped areas, especially highland regions that are too remote to attract other industries, and are unsuitable for farming.

Unfortunately, however, few of the world's freshwater systems can continue indefinitely to absorb the ever-growing demands that are being made upon them. Overuse of water resources is already a problem and has led to the pollution and destruction of many water systems—in some places overtapping has lowered water tables so drastically that rivers and lakes have been permanently destroyed. Although steps have been taken to protect certain waterways, legislation to guard against misuse and overuse is costly, time consuming and, inevitably, comes up against vested interests. Nevertheless, stringent conservation measures are becoming increasingly necessary if society is to maintain one of its most precious resources.

Man obtains fresh water by trapping it as it passes through one of the stages in the hydrological cycle—the never-ending circulation of Earth's waters from the ocean, to the atmosphere, to land. This cycle can be traced from the point at which water evaporates from the sea. The water vapor is blown across the land and falls as rain, hail or snow. Some then evaporates, but the rest completes the cycle by flowing over the land or through the soil or rocks back to the sea. It is at this point in its journey that man obtains his water supplies—from lakes (1), boreholes and wells (2) and dammed rivers (3). These supplies are then either used locally, or are transported by pipe or canal (4) to reservoirs (5) where they are stored ready for distribution.

→ Movement of water in the hydrological cycle

▨ Water-bearing rock

RESERVOIRS

About 70 trillion liters (15 trillion gallons) of fresh water are held in storage during any one year. Reservoirs ensure a continuous supply of water in spite of the inevitable seasonal fluctuations in demand and in the natural supply from rivers and rainfall. And where reservoirs are formed by damming rivers, there are additional benefits—the vast quantities of water held can be controlled and the power used to generate electricity. The Kariba Dam in Zimbabwe (right) has the potential for producing 8,500 million kilowatt hours of electrical power every year.

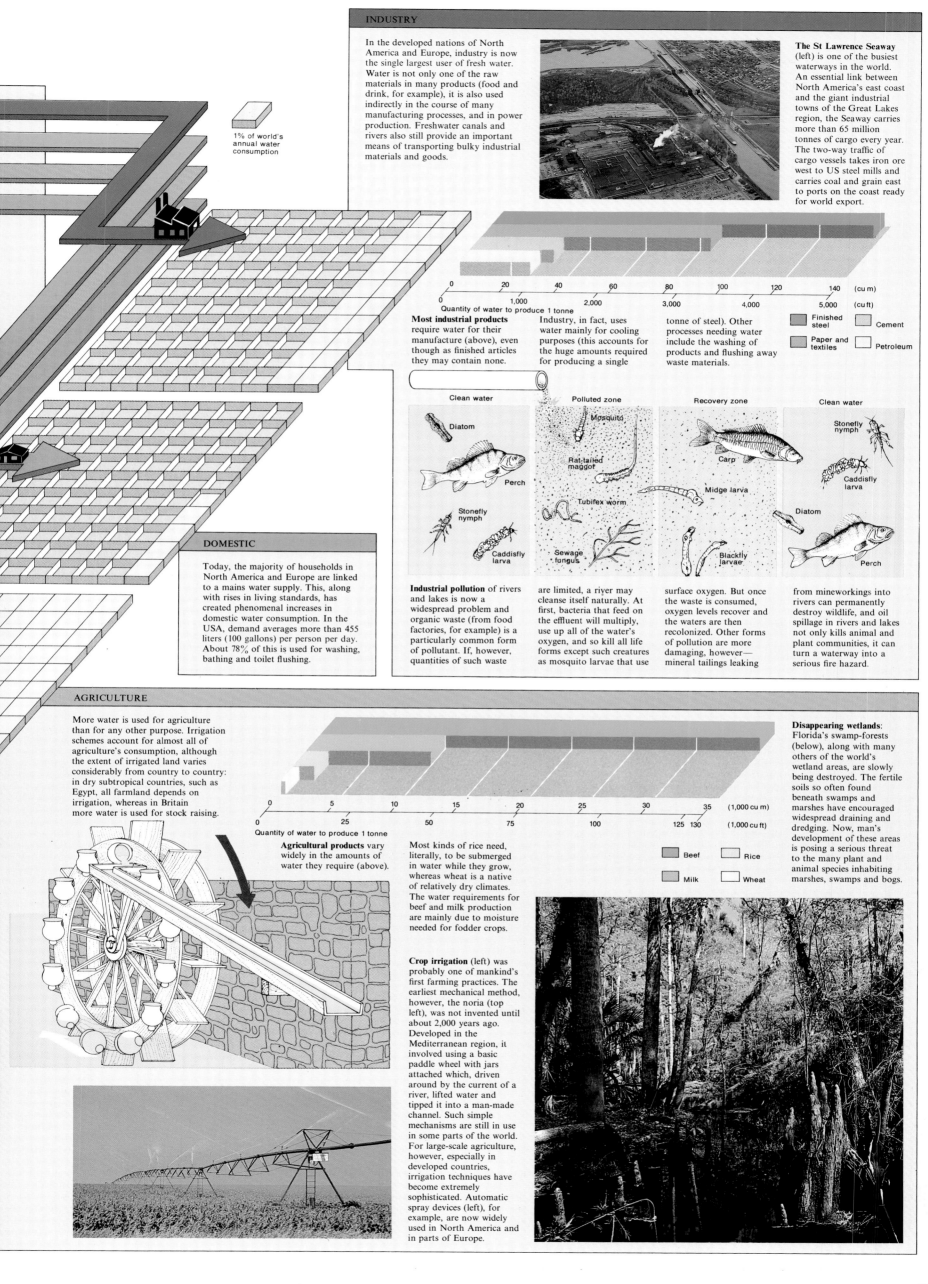

INDUSTRY

In the developed nations of North America and Europe, industry is now the single largest user of fresh water. Water is not only one of the raw materials in many products (food and drink, for example), it is also used indirectly in the course of many manufacturing processes, and in power production. Freshwater canals and rivers also still provide an important means of transporting bulky industrial materials and goods.

The St Lawrence Seaway (left) is one of the busiest waterways in the world. An essential link between North America's east coast and the giant industrial towns of the Great Lakes region, the Seaway carries more than 65 million tonnes of cargo every year. The two-way traffic of cargo vessels takes iron ore west to US steel mills and carries coal and grain east to ports on the coast ready for world export.

1% of world's annual water consumption

| 0 | | 20 | | 40 | | 60 | | 80 | | 100 | | 120 | | 140 | (cu m) |
| 0 | 1,000 | | 2,000 | | 3,000 | | 4,000 | | 5,000 | (cu ft) |

Quantity of water to produce 1 tonne

Finished steel · Cement · Paper and textiles · Petroleum

Most industrial products require water for their manufacture (above), even though as finished articles they may contain none.

Industry, in fact, uses water mainly for cooling purposes (this accounts for the huge amounts required for producing a single tonne of steel). Other processes needing water include the washing of products and flushing away waste materials.

Clean water — Diatom, Perch, Stonefly nymph, Caddisfly larva

Polluted zone — Mosquito, Rat-tailed maggot, Tubifex worm, Sewage fungus

Recovery zone — Carp, Midge larva, Blackfly larvae

Clean water — Stonefly nymph, Caddisfly larva, Diatom, Perch

Industrial pollution of rivers and lakes is now a widespread problem and organic waste (from food factories, for example) is a particularly common form of pollutant. If, however, quantities of such waste are limited, a river may cleanse itself naturally. At first, bacteria that feed on the effluent will multiply, use up all of the water's oxygen, and so kill all life forms except such creatures as mosquito larvae that use surface oxygen. But once the waste is consumed, oxygen levels recover and the waters are then recolonized. Other forms of pollution are more damaging, however— mineral tailings leaking from mineworkings into rivers can permanently destroy wildlife, and oil spillage in rivers and lakes not only kills animal and plant communities, it can turn a waterway into a serious fire hazard.

DOMESTIC

Today, the majority of households in North America and Europe are linked to a mains water supply. This, along with rises in living standards, has created phenomenal increases in domestic water consumption. In the USA, demand averages more than 455 liters (100 gallons) per person per day. About 78% of this is used for washing, bathing and toilet flushing.

AGRICULTURE

More water is used for agriculture than for any other purpose. Irrigation schemes account for almost all of agriculture's consumption, although the extent of irrigated land varies considerably from country to country: in dry subtropical countries, such as Egypt, all farmland depends on irrigation, whereas in Britain more water is used for stock raising.

| 0 | | 5 | | 10 | | 15 | | 20 | | 25 | | 30 | | 35 | (1,000 cu m) |
| 0 | 25 | | 50 | | 75 | | 100 | | 125 | 130 | (1,000 cu ft) |

Quantity of water to produce 1 tonne

Agricultural products vary widely in the amounts of water they require (above).

Most kinds of rice need, literally, to be submerged in water while they grow, whereas wheat is a native of relatively dry climates. The water requirements for beef and milk production are mainly due to moisture needed for fodder crops.

Beef · Rice · Milk · Wheat

Disappearing wetlands: Florida's swamp-forests (below), along with many others of the world's wetland areas, are slowly being destroyed. The fertile soils so often found beneath swamps and marshes have encouraged widespread draining and dredging. Now, man's development of these areas is posing a serious threat to the many plant and animal species inhabiting marshes, swamps and bogs.

Crop irrigation (left) was probably one of mankind's first farming practices. The earliest mechanical method, however, the noria (top left), was not invented until about 2,000 years ago. Developed in the Mediterranean region, it involved using a basic paddle wheel with jars attached which, driven around by the current of a river, lifted water and tipped it into a man-made channel. Such simple mechanisms are still in use in some parts of the world. For large-scale agriculture, however, especially in developed countries, irrigation techniques have become extremely sophisticated. Automatic spray devices (left), for example, are now widely used in North America and in parts of Europe.

Seawater Environments

The oceans form by far the largest of the world's habitable environments, covering almost three-quarters of the Earth's surface at an average depth of more than 3,500 m (11,500 ft). Little more than a century ago, scientists believed that the deep sea's low temperatures, perpetual darkness and immense pressures made life in these regions completely untenable. But we now know that animals live at all depths in the ocean, even at the bottom of trenches more than 11,000 m (36,000 ft) deep.

THE PATTERN OF MARINE LIFE

The distribution of life in the seas is like an inverted pyramid whose broad base is formed by billions of minute single-celled plants—the phytoplankton. Plants need sunlight and nutrient salts, so phytoplankton occurs only in the upper, sunlit layers and where salts are present. Elsewhere, the distribution of marine life thins out rapidly.

Shore life belongs to both land and sea, and thus has to cope with a wide range of conditions. Seaweeds get all their food from the sea and are quite unlike land plants. Many animals take refuge below the surface: tellin shell molluscs sift food particles through special "lips"; lugworms swallow sand, digesting any organic matter; cockles take in food and eject waste through two siphons. Some birds have bills adapted for opening bivalve molluscs.

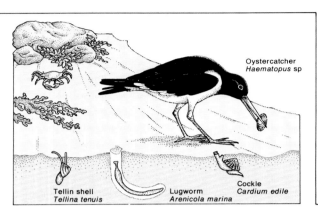

Oystercatcher
Haematopus sp

Tellin shell
Tellina tenuis

Lugworm
Arenicola marina

Cockle
Cardium edile

Marine plant life consists largely of diatoms—minute single-celled specks, each enclosed in a lidded box of silicon. Dinoflagellates, classed as plants but able to swim, dominate warmer waters. Both are food for copepods, the flea-sized grazers whose total weight, in the North Sea alone, is some seven million tonnes.

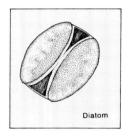

Diatom

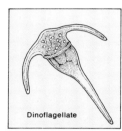

Dinoflagellate

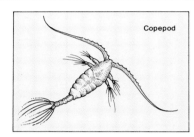

Copepod

A coral atoll, forming in warm shallow water round an extinct volcano, makes up a living aquarium for thousands of tropical marine life forms. Countless billions of tiny polyps, each secreting a hard, calcareous skeleton, form the first layer of the reef, but die as the volcano gradually sinks. Their skeletons provide a base for further layers of corals, which enclose the sinking island to create a shallow, salt water lagoon. Different coral species in the same reef provide homes for a great variety of life.

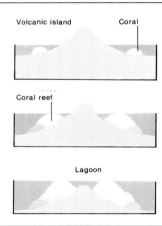

Volcanic island   Coral

Coral reef

Lagoon

Life is by no means evenly distributed throughout the oceans, either vertically or horizontally. The great majority of marine creatures are concentrated in the upper few hundred meters, for the biological organization of life in the seas, as on land, depends on photosynthesis (the process by which plants use the Sun's energy to combine carbon dioxide and water to produce more complex compounds). This near-surface layer is the euphotic ("well-lighted") zone.

Some of the Sun's rays are reflected from the surface of the sea, and those that penetrate are scattered and absorbed as they pass through the water, so that even in the clearest oceanic water there is insufficient light to support photosynthesis at depths greater than about 100 m (330 ft). In turbid inshore regions, where the water is less clear, this near-surface layer may be reduced to a very few meters. So the large seaweeds that anchor themselves to the seabed are restricted to the small areas of the sea where the water is sufficiently shallow to allow them to photosynthesize. Of much greater importance over most of the oceans are the tiny floating plants of the phytoplankton, which live suspended in the sunlit surface layers.

Pastures of the sea
Phytoplankton, like all plant life, requires not only sunlight for survival but also adequate supplies of nutrient salts and chemical trace elements. River waters carry down considerable quantities of dissolved mineral salts and other matter, so that high levels of phytoplankton production may occur locally around major estuaries. But a far more important source of nutrient supply to the euphotic zone is the recycling of salts that have sunk into the deeper layers, locked up in the bodies of plants and animals or in their fecal pellets.

In those areas of the oceans that overlie the continental shelves (about six percent of the total), the depth is nowhere more than about 200 m (650 ft), and the nutrient-rich bottom water is fairly readily brought back to the surface by currents and the stirring effect of storms. This stirring can reach much greater depths in near-polar latitudes, where the "water column" is not layered by temperature but remains more or less uniformly cold from top to bottom. In the Antarctic, cold (and therefore heavy) surface water sinks and is replaced by nutrient-rich water that may surface from depths of 1,000 m (3,300 ft).

In subtropical and tropical regions of the open ocean, where the warm surface layer is only a few tens of meters deep, the temperature falls rapidly with depth. There is little exchange between deep and shallow layers, and the euphotic zone receives an adequate supply of nutrient salts only in certain areas. These occur between westward-flowing and eastward-flowing currents in each of the major oceans. The Earth's rotation causes these currents to diverge so as to create an upwelling of nutrient-rich water along their common boundaries.

Finally, in restricted coastal regions of the tropics and subtropics the local climatic conditions cause an offshore movement of surface water, which is again replaced by upwelling nutrient-rich deep water. The central oceanic regions, including the deep blue subtropical waters, are in effect the deserts of the sea.

Sea grazers and carnivores
The abundance of animals in the oceans closely follows that of the plants. But very few of the larger marine animals can feed directly on the phytoplankton because the individual plants are so small—often only a fraction of a millimeter across. Instead, the phytoplankton supports an amazingly diverse community of planktonic animals, which also spend their lives in mid-water and are swept along by the ocean currents. This community, the zooplankton, includes many different protozoans (single-celled animals), crustaceans, worms and molluscs, and also the juvenile stages of fishes and of many invertebrate animals that live as adults on the seabed. Most members of the zooplankton are very small and many of them graze on the phytoplankton. But some planktonic animals, particularly among the jellyfish and salps, may be a meter or more across and are voracious carnivores feeding on their planktonic neighbors. In turn, the zooplankton provides food for many of the active swimmers such as the fishes and baleen whales, while at the top of the food chain are larger carnivores including

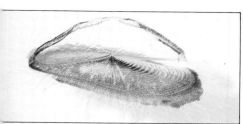

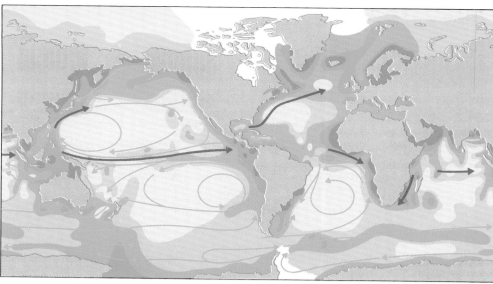

The by-the-wind sailor, *Velella,* is a so-called colonial animal, consisting of a whole collection of animals that function as a single individual. The gas-filled float of its body carries a vertical sail to catch the wind, and below dangle a group of modified polyps specialized for particular roles such as deterrence, reproduction, feeding and digesting.

Phytoplanktonic cells need not only sunlight but also nutrient salts, and so they are restricted to areas where these are available: coastal regions, high latitudes (particularly the Antarctic), narrow tongues extending across the tropical regions of the main ocean basins, and a number of subtropical upwelling regions.

Zones of life (below) extend from the teeming euphotic ("well-lighted") layer to the sparsely populated bathypelagic ("deep-sea") depths, while benthic ("bottom") life occurs at all seabed levels. Phytoplankton (plant life) (1) dictates the pattern of the rest, flourishing where surface conditions allow nutrient salts to well up from lower depths. Herbivores such as minute zooplankton (2) provide food for a host of surface-layer life, which in turn feeds larger predators. Dead animals and fecal pellets fall to lower levels, where they sustain life, but in far smaller quantity.

1 Phytoplankton
2 Zooplankton
3 Blue whale *Balaenoptera musculus*
4 Herring *Clupea harengus*
5 Gray seal *Halichoerus grypus*
6 Bluefin tuna *Thunnus thynnus*
7 Bottlenosed dolphin *Tursiops truncatus*
8 Mackerel *Scomber scomber*
9 Common squid *Loligo* spp
10 White shark *Carcharadon carcharias*
11 Hatchet fish *Argyropelecus hemigymnus*
12 Giant squid *Architeuthis* spp
13 Sea anemone *Cerianthus orientalis*
14 Tripod fish *Benthosaurus grallator*
15 Scarlet shrimp *Notostomus longirostris*
16 Angler fish *Linophryne bicornis*
17 Brittle star *Ophiothrix fragilis*
18 Sea cucumber class Holothuroidea

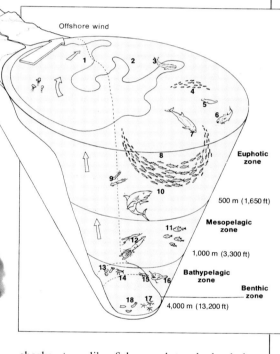

Bizarre life forms new to science live in the sunless depths, where plumes of hot mineral-rich water gush through deep-sea vents in the Earth's crust. These oases of life support huge, gutless tubeworms more than 1.5 m (5 ft) long, which appear to take food particles from the hot vents through blood-red tentacles. Other creatures include blind crabs and large white clams.

sharks, tuna-like fishes and toothed whales.

Beneath the euphotic zone, of course, there can be no herbivores at all, although some animals that spend the daylight hours in the deeper layers move upwards at night to feed in the plankton-rich surface waters. All of the permanent members of the deep-living communities are dependent for food upon material that sinks or is carried downwards from the euphotic zone. Many of them feed on dead animal remains and fecal material as it sinks through the water column or after it reaches the seabed. These detritus eaters in turn support the predatory carnivores that feed upon the detritivores or upon each other.

In shallow areas the food material that reaches the bottom supports complex communities, notably the rich and varied groups of invertebrates and fishes associated with coral reefs. In the deep sea, however, where the euphotic zone is separated from the seabed by several kilometers of water, much of the sinking material is recycled within the water column and relatively little reaches the bottom. Life on the deep-sea floor therefore becomes more and more sparse with increasing depth, but in recent years scientists have discovered that this community includes a surprising number of fishes, some many meters in length. So far man's knowledge of these deep-sea communities is relatively meager, but with our increasing use of the deep oceans we may need to know much more about the life in this environment.

Man and the Seawater Environments

For thousands of years man has used the oceans as a source of food and other materials, and as a repository for wastes. But only in the last 100 years have technological advances and fast-growing human populations had a significant effect, to a point where overfishing and pollution are becoming a cause for concern. Harvesting of krill and seaweeds may ease the pressure on traditional seafoods, but legal restrictions on dumping of wastes or on overfishing are notoriously hard to enforce.

Until about the middle of the nineteenth century the seas had always seemed to be a boundless source of food and of income for fishermen who were brave enough to face the elements with their relatively small sailing ships and primitive gear. But once fishing vessels began to be fitted with steam engines in the 1880s they became relatively independent of the weather, while improvements in the fishing gear itself, such as steam-powered winches in trawling and harpoon guns in whaling, made the whole business of fishing much more efficient.

At first these advances resulted in enormous increases in catches, but in many fisheries this was rapidly followed by a distressing fall in the catch per unit of effort—that is, it was becoming more and more difficult in successive years to catch the same amount of fish as before. In most fisheries the initial response to this situation was to increase the size and number of fishing vessels and to search for new fishing grounds. But as the fishing pressure on the stocks increased, with smaller fish being captured, often before they were able to reproduce, the catch per unit of effort frequently continued to fall.

In many cases attempts were made to counter the effects of overfishing by introducing regulations to control the mesh size of the nets, so allowing the small fish to escape; by establishing closed seasons or quotas of fish which might legitimately be taken from a particular fishing ground in any one year; or even, as in the case of the British herring fishery in the late 1970s, by imposing a complete ban on fishing. Moral questions also sometimes intervene, as in whaling operations, which, many conservationists believe, have driven some species close to extinction despite attempts to rationalize the fisheries.

Fisheries in decline

The North Sea trawl fishery, the first to be affected by the new technology in the nineteenth century, has been declining in terms of catch per unit of effort since the early decades of this century. Dramatic but short-lived improvements after the "closed seasons" of the two world wars proved that fishing pressure had a serious effect on stocks, but by the 1970s many North Sea fishing ports had become almost deserted. This decline put pressure on more distant fishing grounds used by European fishermen, and recent decades have been marked by a series of fishing disputes, with nations fighting for the continued existence of their fisheries despite clear evidence that there are not enough catchable fish to satisfy everyone.

A similar story of declining catches during the present century could be told of many of the old-established fisheries around the world, but at the same time the demand for fish in a protein-hungry world has increased. To satisfy this demand the total annual world catch increased by about seven percent from the end of World War II until the early 1970s, by this time reaching a figure of around 60–70 million tonnes. But this increase was achieved only by exploiting previously unfished stocks or new geographical areas. Such an increase cannot go on indefinitely, for we are rapidly running out of "new" areas and some of the new fisheries have already shown the same symptoms of overfishing as the older ones—and sometimes even more dramatically.

New foods from the sea

The indications are that the present total catch is close to the maximum that can be obtained from relatively conventional fisheries even with careful management, and that, to increase the total, or even to sustain it, we must look to completely new sources such as krill, the shrimp-like food of the whalebone whales.

Estimates of the sustainable annual catch of krill in the Antarctic range from about 50 to 500 million tonnes, that is up to about seven times as much as the current total from all other fisheries put together. Of course, the use of such an enormous quantity of small crustaceans would present considerable problems. Part of it might be converted into a protein-rich paste for human consumption, but much would be used indirectly as a feed for farm animals.

Many larger seaweeds are already cropped in several parts of the world, particularly in Japan, and are used not only for human food but also for animal food and in many industrial processes. About one million tonnes of seaweed are taken each year, but because seaweeds grow naturally only in relatively shallow areas of the oceans this figure could probably not be significantly increased using natural populations. However, seaweeds can be grown artificially on frames floating over deep water. Experiments suggest that, by enriching the surface layers through artificial upwelling of nutrient-rich deep water, each square kilometer of such a floating seaweed farm could produce enough food to feed 1,000–2,000 people, and enough energy and other products to satisfy the needs of a further 1,000. With an estimated 260 million sq km (100 million sq miles) of "arable" surface, the seas might thus support up to 10 times the present world population.

Polluted waters

Of course, the present century has seen an increase not only in what man takes out of the sea but also in the harmful substances that he throws into it. Not only oil but many other substances are dumped into the seas accidentally or intentionally, usually either in the discharged effluent from industrial plant or as a result of agricultural chemicals being leached into rivers and thence into the ocean. In many cases the amounts are very small compared with the amounts present in the oceans as a whole; the problem is that they are usually released, and accumulate, in restricted inshore areas near which we live and from which we obtain most of our sea-caught food.

Since the 1930s there have been both national and international attempts to control pollution by legislation, and since 1958 a series of United Nations conferences has sought agreement on many aspects of international maritime law, including pollution. Despite many prophecies of imminent doom, it does not seem that marine pollution yet poses any general threat to humanity. Nevertheless, with ever-increasing industrialization and the production of more and more toxic materials, including radioactive wastes, it is essential that we monitor the effects of man's activities on the ocean.

Drilling derrick

The ocean is home to the Bajau (above), the "sea gypsies" of southeastern Asia, who inhabit a tract of sea and islands stretching more than 6,500 km (4,000 miles).

Each group has its own clan pattern, blazoned on the sails of their *praus*. The Bajau may live on the open sea in clusters of boats, or in stilt-house villages built over estuaries.

Hydrophones

THE MARINE RESOURCES
Modern technology has enabled man to expand his age-old exploitation of the seas to the limit in some areas, and a need for the careful management of our marine resource is imperative. But in some fields, such as energy and the extraction of fresh water, the seas may yield inexhaustible riches.

Sonar beacons

Core sample tube

Drilling head

The deep-sea drilling ship *Glomar Challenger* (above) plays an important role in surveying and prospecting the oceans. It can drill in water depths of 7,000 m (23,000 ft) and obtain core samples 1,200 m (4,000 ft) below the ocean bed. The ship is positioned over the drill hole through signals from a sonar beacon to hydrophones in the hull.

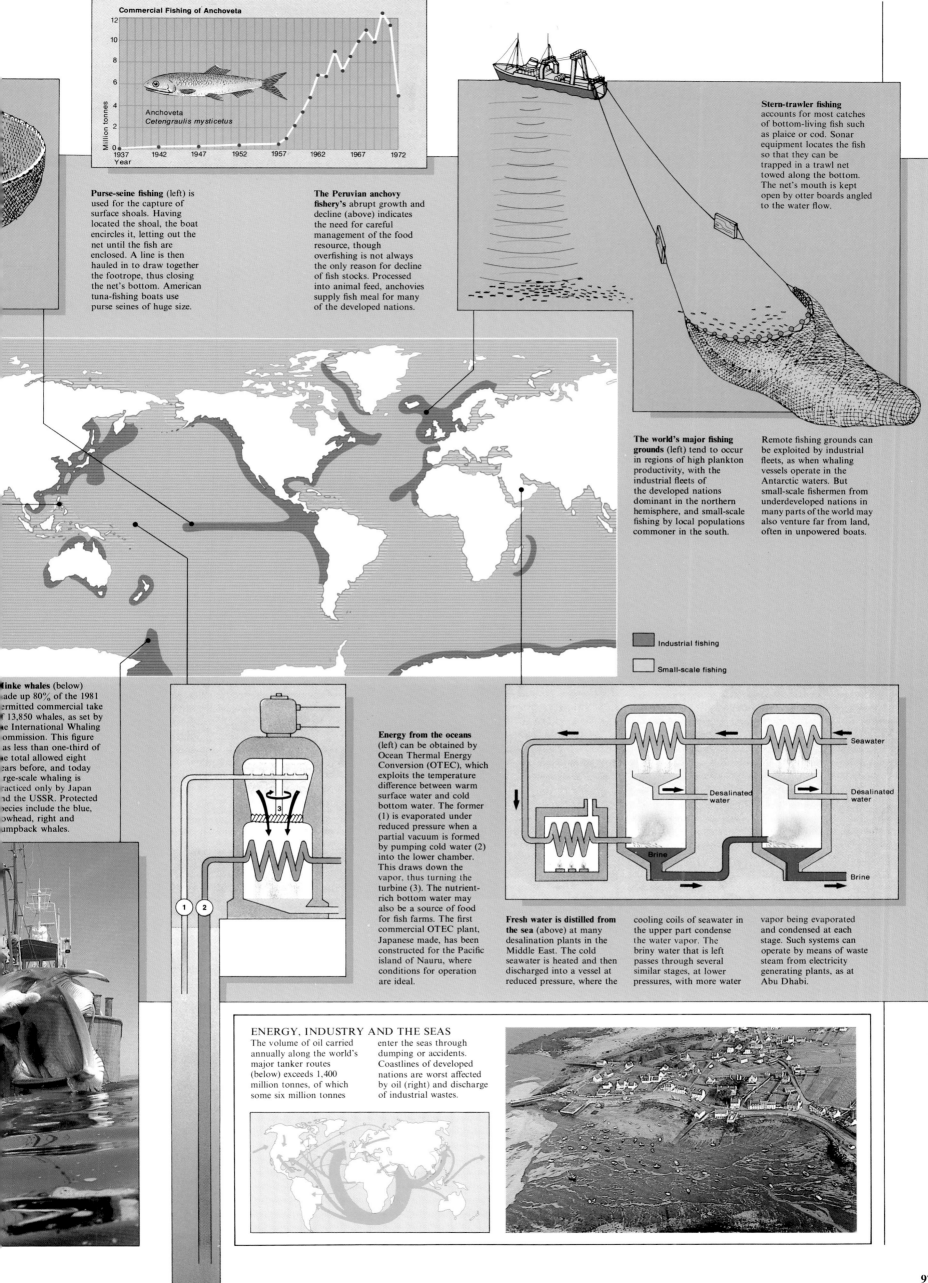

Commercial Fishing of Anchoveta

Anchoveta
Cetengraulis mysticetus

Million tonnes — Year: 1937, 1942, 1947, 1952, 1957, 1962, 1967, 1972

Purse-seine fishing (left) is used for the capture of surface shoals. Having located the shoal, the boat encircles it, letting out the net until the fish are enclosed. A line is then hauled in to draw together the footrope, thus closing the net's bottom. American tuna-fishing boats use purse seines of huge size.

The Peruvian anchovy fishery's abrupt growth and decline (above) indicates the need for careful management of the food resource, though overfishing is not always the only reason for decline of fish stocks. Processed into animal feed, anchovies supply fish meal for many of the developed nations.

Stern-trawler fishing accounts for most catches of bottom-living fish such as plaice or cod. Sonar equipment locates the fish so that they can be trapped in a trawl net towed along the bottom. The net's mouth is kept open by otter boards angled to the water flow.

The world's major fishing grounds (left) tend to occur in regions of high plankton productivity, with the industrial fleets of the developed nations dominant in the northern hemisphere, and small-scale fishing by local populations commoner in the south.

Remote fishing grounds can be exploited by industrial fleets, as when whaling vessels operate in the Antarctic waters. But small-scale fishermen from underdeveloped nations in many parts of the world may also venture far from land, often in unpowered boats.

Industrial fishing
Small-scale fishing

Minke whales (below) made up 80% of the 1981 permitted commercial take of 13,850 whales, as set by the International Whaling Commission. This figure was less than one-third of the total allowed eight years before, and today large-scale whaling is practiced only by Japan and the USSR. Protected species include the blue, bowhead, right and humpback whales.

Energy from the oceans (left) can be obtained by Ocean Thermal Energy Conversion (OTEC), which exploits the temperature difference between warm surface water and cold bottom water. The former (1) is evaporated under reduced pressure when a partial vacuum is formed by pumping cold water (2) into the lower chamber. This draws down the vapor, thus turning the turbine (3). The nutrient-rich bottom water may also be a source of food for fish farms. The first commercial OTEC plant, Japanese made, has been constructed for the Pacific island of Nauru, where conditions for operation are ideal.

Seawater
Desalinated water
Desalinated water
Brine
Brine
Seawater

Fresh water is distilled from the sea (above) at many desalination plants in the Middle East. The cold seawater is heated and then discharged into a vessel at reduced pressure, where the cooling coils of seawater in the upper part condense the water vapor. The briny water that is left passes through several similar stages, at lower pressures, with more water vapor being evaporated and condensed at each stage. Such systems can operate by means of waste steam from electricity generating plants, as at Abu Dhabi.

ENERGY, INDUSTRY AND THE SEAS
The volume of oil carried annually along the world's major tanker routes (below) exceeds 1,400 million tonnes, of which some six million tonnes enter the seas through dumping or accidents. Coastlines of developed nations are worst affected by oil (right) and discharge of industrial wastes.

Part 5

UNDERSTANDING MAPS

What maps are and how they are made
New horizons and latest developments in maps and mapmaking
How to read the language of maps

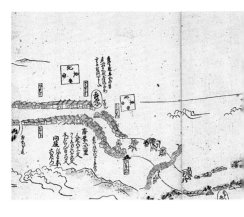

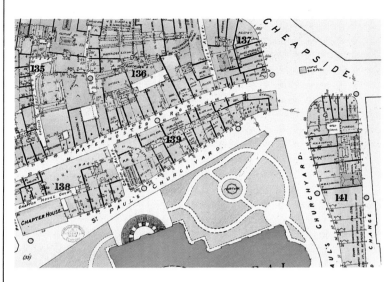

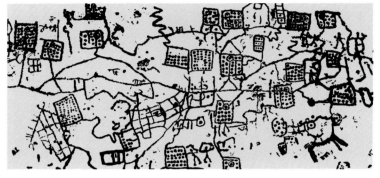

Maps defining territory and ownership are almost as old as the human territorial instinct itself. The rock-carving maps of the Val Camonica, Italy (above), dating from the second and first millennia BC, show stippled square fields, paths, river lines, houses, and even humans and animals. It is uncertain whether their purpose was legal, but the need to establish ownership is a basic function of many maps, as seen in a detail from Goad's 19th-century insurance map of London (left), where every occupation is recorded.

Elegant road maps with pictorial and geographical features have been produced by many different cultures. The woodcut map of the Tōkaidō (detail above), the great Japanese highway, 555 km (345 miles) long, between Edo (Tokyo) and Kyoto, was drawn as a panorama by the famous artist Moronobu in 1690. Its pictorial details do not prevent it being an accurate representation of the road's track. A Mexican map of the Tepetlaoztoc valley (right) drawn in 1583 marks roads with footprints between parallel lines, and hill ranges with wavy lines. Symbols in panels represent place-names.

America first appears as a separate continent (below) in an inset to Martin Waldseemüller's world map of 1507, with the two hemispheres facing each other. Presiding over the Old World is Claudius Ptolemy, the 2nd-century geographer whose remarkably scientific maps, copied and recopied over a thousand years, were revised and emended by Waldseemüller to show some of the results of Portuguese exploration. His New World counterpart is the Italian Amerigo Vespucci, one of the early explorers of the continent, after whom it was named. This is the first map to show the Pacific (not yet named) as an ocean between America and Asia. The west coast of South America, still to be explored by Europeans, seems to be inspired guesswork. The island between the landmasses is Cipango (Japan) known from Marco Polo.

The earliest surviving Chinese globe (above) was made in 1623 by two Jesuit missionaries, probably for the emperor of China. The long legend in Chinese expresses terms and ideas derived from early Chinese cosmology. It describes the Earth as "floating in the Heavens like the yolk of an egg . . . with all objects having mass tending toward its center"—one of the first known references to gravity.

High-altitude photography (left) allows accurate updating of topographic maps (right), while data gathering by satellites (above) expands the range. Landsat satellites carry electronic remote-sensing equipment that detects the energy emitted by surface materials and translates it into images. Healthy plants may show as bright red, sparse vegetation as pink, barren lands as light gray, and urban areas as green or dark gray. The folded shape of the Appalachians (1) is clearly seen; the Canada–US border (2) is revealed by land-use patterns; silt from the Mississippi (3) builds up the delta. Sudan irrigation (4) shows up as brilliant red.

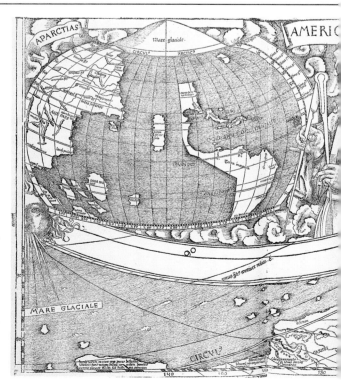

Mapping, Old and New

Mapmaking must have its origins in the earliest ages of human history, since people of preliterate as well as literate cultures possess an innate skill in map drawing. This innate capacity is further indicated by the ease with which almost anyone can sketch in the sand or on paper simple directions for showing the way. But maps may also define territory and express man's idea of the world in graphic representation. Today, modern technology has vastly extended the scope of cartography.

3 4

Many non-European cultures developed ingenious route-map techniques: the North American Indians, for example, made sketch maps of routes on birch bark. These were diagrammatic maps in which directions and distances were not accurate but relationships were true, as in New York Subway or London Underground maps. The people of the Marshall Islands in the western Pacific made route maps over the seas, depicting the direction of the main seasonal wave swells in relation to the islands.

Although maps of routes are the simplest type of map in concept, they developed complex forms as cartography progressed. A road map of the whole Roman Empire, drawn about AD 280, survives today in a thirteenth-century copy known as the Peutinger Table. Hernando Cortes, the Spanish conqueror, made his way across Mexico in the 1520s with the help of pre-conquest Mexican maps painted on cloth. These showed roads with double lines or colored bands marked with footprints. Another type of map is the strip map depicting a single road along its entire length. Pictorial maps of the Tōkaidō highway from Edo to Kyoto in Japan, made from a survey of 1651, were popular in the Edo period of Japanese history.

Nautical charts evolved as a special type of direction-finding map to meet the needs of seamen. Those of the late Middle Ages came to be known as "portolan" charts, from the word "portolani," or sailing directions. They showed the sea and adjacent coasts superimposed on a network of radiating compass lines.

Territorial maps

Another basic type of map derives from man's sense of territorial possession. The earliest example of a "cadastral" plan (a map showing land parcels and property boundaries) appears to be that preserved as rock carvings at Bedolina in Val Camonica in northern Italy. However, in the ancient civilizations of Mesopotamia and Egypt, land surveying had become an established profession by 2000 BC. An idea of what Egyptian surveyors' plans of 1000 BC were like can be seen from the "Fields of the Dead" representing the Egyptians' idea of life after death. These show plots of land surrounded by water and intersected by canals. The Romans used cadastral surveys to determine land ownership and assess tax liability.

Another form of map showing territorial demarcations is the map of administrative units. The Chinese in the thirteenth century AD were making official district maps to help in the organization of grain supplies and the collection of taxes. Many of their gazetteers (*fang chih*), written in the form of local geographies and

histories from the eleventh century onward, were illustrated with maps. Political maps showing the boundaries of states were increasingly significant in European cartography from the sixteenth century onward.

A third major class of map is the general or topographical map expressing man's perception of the world, its regions and its place in the universe. A Babylonian world map of the seventh century BC is drawn on a clay tablet and shows the Earth as a circular disc surrounded by the Earthly Ocean. With the ancient Greeks, geography developed on scientific principles. The treatise on mapmaking by Claudius Ptolemy (AD 87–150), later known as the *Geographia*, was the most famous cartographic text of the period. It influenced the Arabic geographers of the Middle Ages, notably Muhammad Ibn Muhammad, Al-Idrisi (1099–1164), and with the revival of Ptolemy in fifteenth-century Europe became one of the major works of the Renaissance. Published, with engraved maps, at Bologna in 1477, the *Geographia* ranks as the first printed atlas in the western world. The invention of techniques of engraving in wood and copper facilitated a wide diffusion of geographical knowledge through the map-publishing trade. The first atlas made up of modern maps to a uniform design was Abraham Ortelius's *Theatrum Orbis Terrarum* published at Antwerp in 1570. From 1492, when Martin Behaim made his "Erdapfel" at Nürnberg, globes also became popular, and globemakers vied with each other to make larger and more elaborate ones to keep pace with the growth of knowledge about the world.

Over the last two hundred years cartography has made rapid and remarkable advances. Observatories built in Paris in 1671 and at Greenwich in 1675 enabled the location of places to be established more exactly with the use of astronomical tables. Improvements in surveying instruments facilitated more accurate and rapid land survey. France was the pioneer in establishing (from 1679 onward) a national survey on a geometrical basis of triangulation. By the end of the eighteenth century national surveys on small and medium scales had been begun by most European countries. In the United States the Geological Survey was set up in 1879 to undertake the topographical and geological mapping of the country.

Mapping today

Since World War II cartographic techniques have undergone a revolution. The use of air survey and photogrammetry has made it possible to map most of the Earth's surface. Electronic distance measurement by laser or light beams in surveying, and digital computers in mapping, are among the most recent advances in methods. Mosaics or air photography are used to produce orthophoto maps which can supplement or substitute for the conventional topographic map. Artificial satellites and manned space craft make it possible to provide a world-wide framework of geodetic networks.

Earth Resource Technology Satellites (ERTS) imagery has made it possible to map mountain ranges in Africa and features on the surface of Antarctica that were hitherto unknown. The imagery is made available by means of remote-sensing instruments, carried by the satellites, that are sensitive to invisible portions of the electromagnetic spectrum—longer and shorter wavelengths than can be sensed by the human eye. Remote-sensing instruments usually work in the infrared bands. They can also pick up the energy emitted by all types of surface material—rocks, soils, vegetation, water and man-made structures—and produce photographs or images from it.

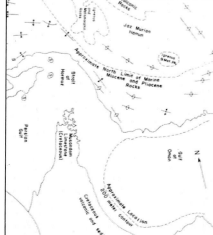

Space technology helps cartographers to map even interior details of the planet: its geology and mineral wealth. A photo (below) taken from Gemini 12 at an altitude of 272 km (168 miles) forms the basis of a geologic sketch map of SW Asia (below right), showing the oil-rich area around the region between the Persian Gulf and the Gulf of Oman. The symbol S on the map indicates salt plugs; diamonds show fold trends; double-headed arrows anticlines.

The Language of Maps

Mapmakers for more than 4,000 years have tried to find the best way to represent the shape and features of the three-dimensional Earth on two-dimensional paper, parchment and cloth. The measurement of distance and direction is a basic requirement for accurate surveys, but until about 1800 theoretical understanding of the method was well in advance of the technical equipment available. Today the use of lasers and light beams sometimes takes the place of direct measurement on the ground.

A reference system must be used to show distance and direction correctly in the construction of maps. The simplest type is the rectangular or square grid. The Chinese mapmaker Pei Xin made a map with a grid in about AD 270, and this system remained in continuous use in China until modern times. The Roman system of centuriation, a form of division of public lands on a square or rectangular basis, was also a "coordinate" system starting from a point of origin at the intersection of two perpendicular axes. Roman surveyors' maps, dating from the first century AD, are the earliest known European maps based on a grid system.

Latitude and longitude

Makers of small-scale regional maps and of world maps in early times also had to take account of the fact that the Earth is a sphere. The Greeks derived from the Babylonians the idea of dividing a circle into 360 degrees. In the second century BC the Greek geographer Eratosthenes (c. 276–194 BC) was the first to calculate the circumference of the globe and was reported to have made a world map based on the concept of the Earth's sphericity. From this the Greeks went on to develop the system of spherical coordinates which remains in use today. The poles at each end of the Earth's axis provide reference points for the Earth in its rotation in relation to the celestial sphere. Parallel circles around the Earth are degrees of latitude and express the idea of distance north or south of the Equator. Lines of longitude running north and south through the poles express east–west distances. One meridian is chosen as the meridian of origin, known as the prime meridian.

Whereas latitude from early times could be observed from the height of the Sun or (in the northern hemisphere) from the position of the Pole Star at night, accurate observations of longitude were not possible until the middle of the eighteenth century, when the chronometer was invented and more accurate astronomical tables were provided. In 1884 most countries agreed, at an international conference in Washington DC, to adopt the prime meridian through the Royal Greenwich Observatory in England and to calculate longitude to 180 degrees east and west of Greenwich.

Projection and distortion

The mathematical system by which the spherical surface of the Earth is transferred to the plane surface of a map is called a map projection. The Greek geographer Ptolemy gave instructions in his geographical treatise of AD 150 for the construction of two projections. When the *Geographia* was revised in Europe in the fifteenth century, and navigators began sailing across the oceans, mapmakers devised new projections more appropriate to the expanding geographical knowledge of the world. The Dutch geographer Gerard Mercator invented the projection named after him, applying it to his world chart of 1569. This cylindrical projection, in which all points are at true compass courses from each other, was of great benefit to navigators and is still one of the most commonly

used projections. Another advance was made when Johann Heinrich Lambert of Alsace (1728–1777) invented the azimuthal equal-area projection, in which the sizes of all areas are represented on the projection in correct proportion to one another, and the conformal projection, in which at any point on the map the scale is constant in all directions.

Since all projections involve deformation of the geometry of the globe, the cartographer has to choose the one that best suits the purpose of his map. "Conformal" or "orthomorphic" projections, in which angular relations (or shape) are preserved, are widely used for the construction of topographical maps. "Equivalent" or "equal-area" projections retain relative sizes and are particularly useful for general reference maps displaying economic, historical, political and other geographical phenomena.

Since the mid-fifteenth century, European mapmakers have generally arranged their maps with north at the top of the sheet. Earlier maps, however, were not standardized in this way. The circular world maps of the Middle Ages were orientated with east at the top, because this was where the terrestrial paradise was traditionally sited. Indeed, the word "orientation" originally meant the arrangement of something so as to face east.

Map scale

Scale is another basic property of a map. The scale of a map is the ratio of the distance on the map to the actual distance represented. Whereas the Babylonians, Egyptians, Greeks and Romans drew surveys to scale, in medieval Europe mapmakers used customary methods of estimating. The earliest known local map since Roman times which is drawn to scale (it displays a scale bar) is a plan of Vienna, 1422.

Projection, grid, orientation and scale form the framework of a map. The language of maps in concept and content is much more complex. To represent the surface of the Earth on a map, the cartographer must select and generalize from a vast quantity of material, using symbols and conventional signs as codes.

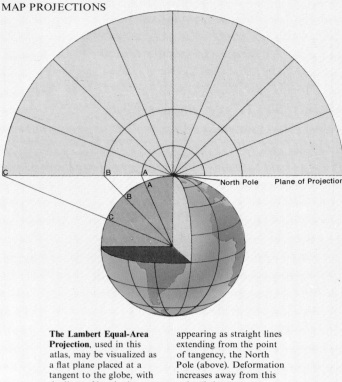

MAP PROJECTIONS

North Pole — Plane of Projection

The Lambert Equal-Area Projection, used in this atlas, may be visualized as a flat plane placed at a tangent to the globe, with the lines of longitude appearing as straight lines extending from the point of tangency, the North Pole (above). Deformation increases away from this point (below).

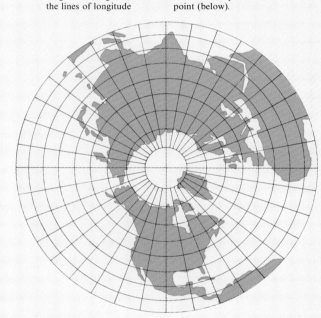

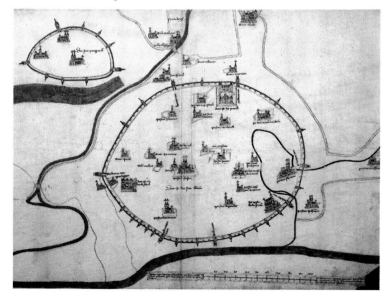

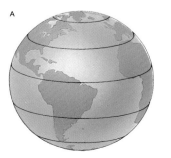

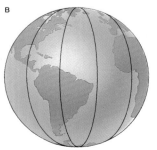

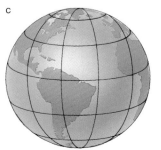

Map scales express the relationship between a distance measured on the map and the true distance on the ground. A plan of Vienna (left), originally made in 1422, is drawn in the bird's-eye-view style typical of early medieval town plans. But the scale bar at its foot shows that it has been explicitly drawn to scale, indicating that the concept of a uniform scale had been grasped in medieval Europe.

Direction and distance are concepts used in the relative location of two or more points (below). These concepts are organized according to a general frame of reference with direction following the grid system of coordinates. Thus places shown in (A) can be precisely located in terms of longitude and of latitude (B), with the degrees further subdivided into one-sixtieths of minutes.

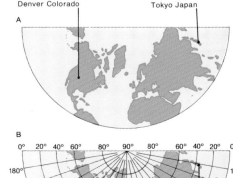

Denver Colorado   Tokyo Japan
A

Superimposed on the globe (left), lines of latitude (A) and longitude (B) allow every place to be exactly located in terms of a coordinate system (C). The parallels of latitude measure distance from 0° to 90° north and south of the Equator. The meridians of longitude measure distance from 0° to 180° east and west of a "prime meridian" at Greenwich.

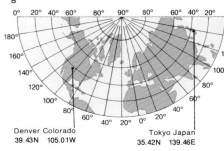

B

0° 20° 40° 60° 80° 90° 80° 60° 40° 20° 0°

180°
160°
140°
120°
100°
80°   60° 40° 20° 0° 20° 40° 60° 80° 100° 120° 140°

Denver Colorado   Tokyo Japan
39.43N 105.01W   35.42N 139.46E

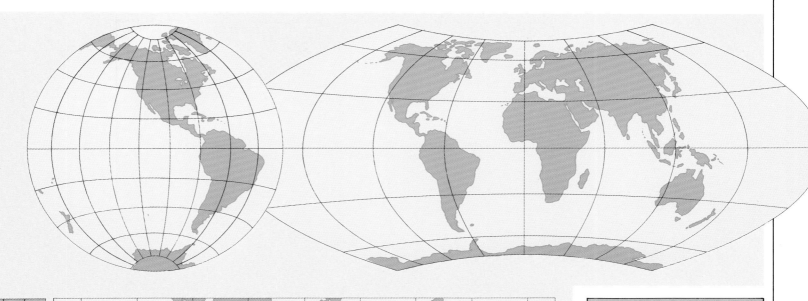

The Hammer Projection (far right), developed from the Lambert Projection of the hemisphere (right), is designed to show the whole world in a single view, and is used in this atlas in a version modified by Wagner and known as the Hammer-Wagner projection. The Earth appears as an ellipse because the lines of longitude are plotted at twice their horizontal distance from the center line, and numbered at twice their previous values. The central meridian is half the length of the equator.

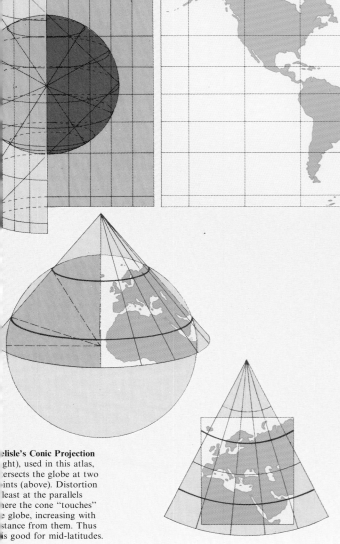

Delisle's Conic Projection (right), used in this atlas, intersects the globe at two points (above). Distortion is least at the parallels where the cone "touches" the globe, increasing with distance from them. Thus is good for mid-latitudes.

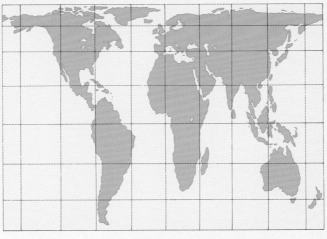

In a cylindrical projection like Gall's (above left), the sphere is "unwrapped" on to a cylinder, making a complete transformation to a flat surface. Mercator's Projection (above), devised in 1569, is a cylindrical projection that aids navigation by showing all compass directions as straight lines. A projection (below), based on Peters', distorts shape to show land surface area ratios, emphasizing the Third World.

Photogrammetric plotting instruments (above) are now used in the preparation of large-scale accurate topographic maps. These are sophisticated machines that provide very precise measurements, plotting the map data in orthogonal projection.

The theodolite (above), a basic surveying instrument dating back to the 16th century, can measure angles and directions horizontally and vertically. A swivel telescope with cross-hairs inside it permits accurate alignment, and it may be used in the field.

EARTH MEASUREMENT THROUGH THE AGES

Surveying—the technique of making accurate measurements of the Earth's surface—is as old as civilization and has been an essential element in mankind's development of his environment. The need to establish land boundaries arose at least 3,500 years ago in the fertile valleys of the Nile, Tigris and Euphrates rivers. Man's urge to explore and to describe the world also led to the development of instruments determining position, distance and direction. The astrolabe, sometimes called the world's oldest scientific instrument, may date to the 2nd century BC. Today's techniques make increasing use of computers.

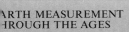

An Egyptian wall painting (left) from the middle of the second millennium BC shows what appears to be the measurement of a grain field by means of a rope with knots at regular intervals on its length.

The astrolabe (right), used in classical times to observe the positions of celestial bodies, became a navigational instrument in the Middle Ages, when it was developed to permit establishment of latitude.

How to Use Maps

Today maps play a role more important than ever before in increasing our knowledge of the Earth, its regions and peoples. How maps communicate knowledge is now a subject of scientific study. The process comprises the collection and mapping of the data and the reading of the map. In this final stage the map user is all important. Through him the map is transformed into an image in the mind, and the effectiveness of the map depends on the reader being able to understand it.

The cartographer's map has to convey an objective picture of reality. To compile the map the cartographer selects and generalizes information, taking into account the purpose of his map. If he is making a topographical reference map, he has to reduce the three-dimensional landforms of the Earth on to the flat surface of the map. He adds cultural detail such as towns, roads and railroads, and features not apparent to the eye, such as administrative boundaries. On the topographical base map he adds appropriate place-names, using typefaces which reflect their class and significance. All this requires the classification of phenomena, with emphasis to direct the reader's attention.

Themes and symbolization

The cartographer who seeks not merely to represent visible features but to convey geographical ideas about specific phenomena uses the techniques of thematic cartography, where the emphasis is on one or two elements, or themes. Maps today provide one of the most effective means of communicating many kinds of data and ideas relating to the world and its peoples. Their extensive use makes them an important force in education, planning, recreation and in many other human affairs.

The map is designed in code, with symbols to represent features, and a legend, or key, to explain them. There are three types of symbol: point, line and area. Point symbols usually denote places, which may be distinguished into classes by the shape, color and size of the symbol. Line symbols express connections, such as roads or traffic flow, and they may also define and distinguish areas. Area symbols in which variations of color are often combined with patterns of lines or dots are used to depict spatial phenomena, such as types of soil, vegetation and density of population.

How much detail can be shown on a map will depend on its scale, which controls the process of generalization. Scale expresses the relationship of the distance on the map to the distance on the Earth, with the distance on the map always given as the unit 1. It is denoted in various ways: as a representative fraction such as 1:1,000,000; as a written statement; or by means of a graph or bar. Some map scales have become widely used and are generally familiar to map users. The scale 1:25,000 is ideal for walkers and relief can be shown in detail. That of 1:50,000 is a typical medium scale for national surveys. The publication of an international map of the world on a scale of one to

one million (1:1,000,000) has been in progress since 1909. On this scale 1 mm represents 1 km on the ground. The regional maps of countries in this atlas are drawn on scales of 1:6,000,000, 1:3,000,000 and 1:1,500,000; those of the continents are at 1:30,000,000 and 1:15,000,000. The Map Section index maps show the arrangement.

Terrain depiction

Since the early days of map making in ancient Chinese and classical Greek and Roman civilizations, map makers have been concerned to show the configuration of the land. For many centuries they symbolized mountains and hills by pictorial features often looking like caterpillars or sugar loaves. As topographical mapping developed in Europe from the seventeenth century onward, new techniques were devised to improve the visual impression of the features and to depict them accurately in terms of height and location. The system of hachuring (shading with fine parallel or crossed lines), first used in 1674, gives a good idea of relief but not of height. The use of contours, which became general from the nineteenth century onward, is more exact in representing actual elevation, but for many regions, especially those of irregular relief, the appearance of the land is lost.

The addition of hypsometric tints (tints between contours which show elevation) helps clarify the elevation. Applying shadows to the form of the land through the process called hill shading or relief shading creates a visual impression of the configuration of the land surface. Hypsometric tints combined with hill shading gives both elevation information and surface form of the area being depicted, leading to an almost three-dimensional effect.

Maps are classed (right) as either general (A) or thematic (B,C). The purpose of a general reference map is to provide locational information, showing how the positions of various geographical phenomena relate to each other. Thematic maps concentrate on a particular type of information, or theme, such as the distribution of people (B) or rainfall (C), and are generally based on statistical data.

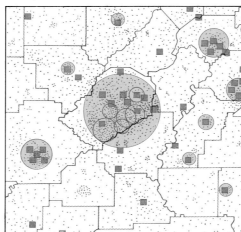

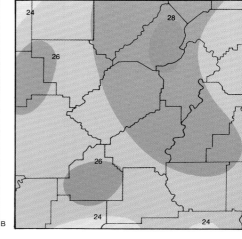

The ratio between a map's dimensions and those of the physical world is defined by the map scale (left and below), with the map distance always given as the unit 1. The larger the reduction, the smaller the scale, so that a scale of 1:6,000,000—1 mm (.04 in) to 6 km (3.74 miles)—is twice that of 1:12,000,000 (.04 in to 7.5 miles). The size of the scale reflects the amount of detail that needs to be shown. The projections are the Lambert Azimuthal Equal-Area (left) and Delisle Conic Equidistant (below).

A simplified version (right) of the map of California on the opposite page shows how a flat map image on the atlas page can easily be translated into a three-dimensional image in the mind. A low-lying central valley, green on the original map, is enclosed by mountains (brown), their steepness shown by the hill shading. The major urban centers are located by interpreting the large, bold typeface, and the nature of the coastline can be visualized from the rapidity with which the coastal ranges descend to the sea. By these means, the map reader can summon up mental pictures of utterly unfamiliar lands.

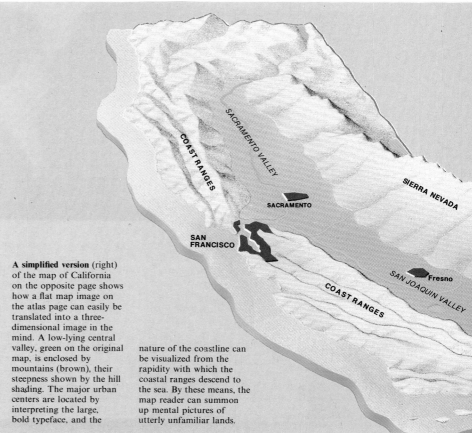

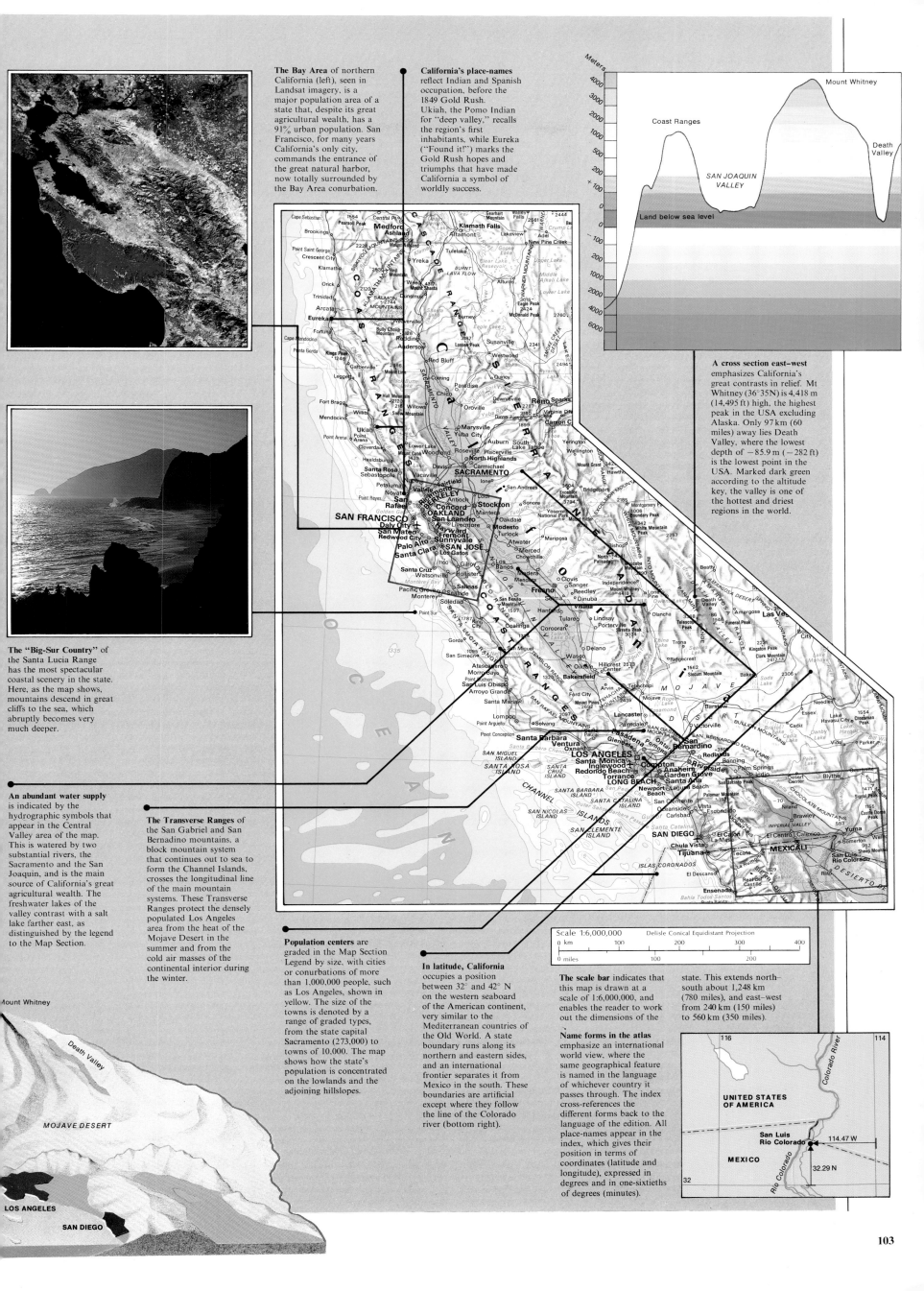

The Bay Area of northern California (left), seen in Landsat imagery, is a major population area of a state that, despite its great agricultural wealth, has a 91% urban population. San Francisco, for many years California's only city, commands the entrance of the great natural harbor, now totally surrounded by the Bay Area conurbation.

California's place-names reflect Indian and Spanish occupation, before the 1849 Gold Rush. Ukiah, the Pomo Indian for "deep valley," recalls the region's first inhabitants, while Eureka ("Found it!") marks the Gold Rush hopes and triumphs that have made California a symbol of worldly success.

A cross section east–west emphasizes California's great contrasts in relief. Mt Whitney (36°35N) is 4,418 m (14,495 ft) high, the highest peak in the USA excluding Alaska. Only 97 km (60 miles) away lies Death Valley, where the lowest depth of −85.9 m (−282 ft) is the lowest point in the USA. Marked dark green according to the altitude key, the valley is one of the hottest and driest regions in the world.

The "Big-Sur Country" of the Santa Lucia Range has the most spectacular coastal scenery in the state. Here, as the map shows, mountains descend in great cliffs to the sea, which abruptly becomes very much deeper.

An abundant water supply is indicated by the hydrographic symbols that appear in the Central Valley area of the map. This is watered by two substantial rivers, the Sacramento and the San Joaquin, and is the main source of California's great agricultural wealth. The freshwater lakes of the valley contrast with a salt lake farther east, as distinguished by the legend to the Map Section.

The Transverse Ranges of the San Gabriel and San Bernadino mountains, a block mountain system that continues out to sea to form the Channel Islands, crosses the longitudinal line of the main mountain systems. These Transverse Ranges protect the densely populated Los Angeles area from the heat of the Mojave Desert in the summer and from the cold air masses of the continental interior during the winter.

Population centers are graded in the Map Section Legend by size, with cities or conurbations of more than 1,000,000 people, such as Los Angeles, shown in yellow. The size of the towns is denoted by a range of graded types, from the state capital Sacramento (273,000) to towns of 10,000. The map shows how the state's population is concentrated on the lowlands and the adjoining hillslopes.

In latitude, California occupies a position between 32° and 42° N on the western seaboard of the American continent, very similar to the Mediterranean countries of the Old World. A state boundary runs along its northern and eastern sides, and an international frontier separates it from Mexico in the south. These boundaries are artificial except where they follow the line of the Colorado river (bottom right).

The scale bar indicates that this map is drawn at a scale of 1:6,000,000, and enables the reader to work out the dimensions of the state. This extends north–south about 1,248 km (780 miles), and east–west from 240 km (150 miles) to 560 km (350 miles).

Name forms in the atlas emphasize an international world view, where the same geographical feature is named in the language of whichever country it passes through. The index cross-references the different forms back to the language of the edition. All place-names appear in the index, which gives their position in terms of coordinates (latitude and longitude), expressed in degrees and in one-sixtieths of degrees (minutes).

Scale 1:6,000,000   Delisle Conical Equidistant Projection

ACKNOWLEDGMENTS

Senior Executive Art Editor
Michael McGuinness

Executive Editor
James Hughes

Coordinating Editor
Dian Taylor

Editors
Lesley Ellis
Judy Garlick
Ken Hewis

Art Editor
Mike Brown

Designers
Sue Rawkins
Lisa Tai

Picture Researcher
Flavia Howard

Researchers
Nicholas Law
Nigel Morrison
Alicia Smith

Editorial Assistant
Barbara Gish

Proofreader
Kathie Gill

Indexers
Hilary and Richard Bird

Production Controller
Barry Baker

Typesetting by Servis Filmsetting
Limited, Manchester, England

Reproduction by Gilchrist
Brothers Limited, Leeds, England

CONTRIBUTORS AND CONSULTANTS

GENERAL CONSULTANT
Professor Michael Wise, CBE, MC, BA, PhD, D.Univ, Professor of
Geography, London School of Economics and Political Science

EDITORIAL CONSULTANT
John Clark

Frances Atkinson, BSc

British Museum (Natural History), Botany Library

Robert W. Bradnock, MA, PhD, Lecturer in Geography with special
reference to South Asia at the School of Oriental and African
Studies, University of London

Michael J. Bradshaw, MA, Principal Lecturer in Geography, College
of St Mark and St John, Plymouth

Dr J. M. Chapman, BSc, ARCS, PhD, MIBiol, Lecturer in Biology,
Queen Elizabeth College, University of London

Dr Jeremy Cherfas, Departmental Demonstrator in Zoology, Oxford
University

Dr M. J. Clark, Senior Lecturer in Geomorphology, Geography
Department, Southampton University

J. L. Cloudsley-Thompson, MA, PhD(Cantab), DSc(Lond),
Hon DSc(Khartoum), Professor of Zoology, Birkbeck College,
University of London

Professor R. U. Cooke, Department of Geography, University
College, London

Professor Clifford Embleton, MA, PhD, Department of Geography,
King's College, University of London

Dr John Gribbin, Physics Consultant to *New Scientist* magazine

Dr John M. Hellawell, BSc, PhD, FIBiol, MIWES, Principal,
Environmental Aspects, Severn Trent Water Authority, Birmingham

Dr Garry E. Hunt, BSc, PhD, DSc, FRAS, FRMetS, FIMA, MBCS,
Head of Atmospheric Physics, Imperial College, London

David K. C. Jones, Lecturer in Geography, London School of
Economics and Political Science

Dr Russell King, Department of Geography, University of Leicester

Dr D. McNally, Assistant Director, University of London
Observatory

Meteorological Office, Berkshire

Dr Robert Muir Wood, PhD

Dr B. O'Connor, Department of Geography, University of London

J. H. Paterson, MA, Professor of Geography in the University of
Leicester

Dr Nigel Pears, Department of Geography, University of Leicester

Joyce Pope, BA

Dr A. L. Rice, Institute of Oceanographic Sciences, Wormley, Surrey

Ian Ridpath, science writer and broadcaster

Royal Geographical Society

Helen Scoging, BSc, Department of Geography, London School of
Economics and Political Science

Bernard Stonehouse, DPhil, MA, BSc, Chairman, Post-Graduate
School of Environmental Science, University of Bradford

Dr Christopher B. Stringer, PhD, Senior Scientific Officer,
Palaeontology Department, British Museum (Natural History)

J. B. Thornes, Professor of Physical Geography and Head of
Department, Bedford College, University of London

UN Information Office and Library

Professor J. E. Webb, DSc, *Emeritus,* Department of Zoology,
Westfield College, University of London

Peter B. Wright, BSc, MPhil

UNDERSTANDING MAPS
Helen Wallis, MA, DPhil, FSA, The Map Librarian, British Library

A great many other individuals, organizations, and institutions have
given invaluable advice and assistance during the preparation of this
Our Planet Earth Section and the publishers wish to extend their
thanks to them all.

ILLUSTRATION CREDITS

Maps in the Our Planet Earth Section by Creative Cartography Limited
unless otherwise specified. Map of the world's climatic regions, page 50,
adapted from *An Introduction to Climate* 4th edition by Trewartha/
Elements of Geography by G. T. Trewartha, A. H. Robinson and
E. H. Hammond © McGraw-Hill Book Co., N.Y., 1967. Used with
permission of McGraw-Hill Book Co. Map diagram page 101 (bottom)
courtesy Doctor Arno Peters.

2–3 *Exploding universe* Product Support (Graphics); *others* Quill.
4–5 Bob Chapman. 6–7 Bob Chapman. 8–9 Mick Saunders;
Landsat diagrams Gary Marsh; *biowindows* Chris Forsey. 10–11
Mick Saunders. 12–13 Bob Chapman. 14–15 *Diagrams* Chris Forsey;
mountain sequence Donald Myall. 16–17 Colin Salmon. 18–19 Peter
Morter; *graph* Mick Saunders; *car* Peter Owen. 20–21 Bob
Chapman; *diagram* Chris Forsey; *map* Colin Salmon. 22–23 Chris
Forsey (*including maps*). 24–25 Brian Delf. 26–27 Brian Delf.
28–29 Dave Etchell/John Ridyard. 30–31 Creative Cartography Ltd.
32–33 Mick Saunders. 34–35 Chris Forsey; *experiment* Gary Hincks;
others Mick Saunders. 36–37 Chris Forsey; *fruit flies, birds and mice*
Donald Myall. 38–39 Chris Forsey; *time scale* Mick Saunders;
stromatolite and diagram Garry Hincks. 40–41 Donald Myall;
time scale Mick Saunders. 42–43 Donald Myall; *time scale* Mick
Saunders. 44–45 Creative Cartography Ltd. 46–47 Donald Myall;
diagram Kai Choi; *skulls* Jim Robins. 48–49 Creative Cartography
Ltd. 50–51 Peter Morter; *diagram* Marilyn Clark. 52–53 Kai Choi.
54–55 Creative Cartography Ltd. 56–57 Creative Cartography Ltd.
58–59 Creative Cartography Ltd. 60–61 Creative Cartography Ltd;
illustrations Jim Robins. 62–63 *Migration diagram and graph* Kai
Choi; *illustrations* Coral Mula. 64–65 Donald Myall. 66–67
Landscape diagram Bill le Fever; *illustrations* Russell Barnett. 68–69
Donald Myall. 70–71 Jim Robins; *plants, bottom left* Andrew
Macdonald. 72–73 Rory Kee; *bottom left* Russell Barnett; *plow*
Kai Choi; *grains and graph* Creative Cartography Ltd. 74–75 Bob
Bampton/The Garden Studio; *animal adaptations* Russell Barnett.
76–77 Donald Myall; *qanat* Bob Chapman. 78–79 David Ashby.
80–81 David Ashby. 82–83 Coral Mula; *trees, orchid, toucan and
hornbill* Donald Myall. 84–85 Jim Robins. 86–87 Creative
Cartography Ltd. 88–89 Brian Delf; *blood counts diagram* Colin
Salmon. 90–91 Bob Chapman; *hydrological cycle* Bob Chapman. 94–95 Andy
Farmer; *shore and plant life* Russell Barnett; *coral atoll* Colin
Salmon. 96–97 Creative Cartography Ltd. 98–99 *Topographic maps*
Rand McNally; *sketch map* Space Frontiers Ltd. 100–101 *Diagrams*
Creative Cartography Ltd. 102–103 *Maps* Istituto Geografico De
Agostini; Rand McNally; *diagrams* Creative Cartography Ltd.

PICTURE CREDITS

Credits read from top to bottom and from left to right on each page. Images that extend over two pages are credited to the left-hand page only.

2 US Naval Observatory; California Institute of Technology and Carnegie Institution of Washington. **3** Both pictures from Royal Observatory, Edinburgh. **8** All pictures from NASA. **9** All pictures from NASA except top and top right, courtesy of Garry Hunt, Laboratory of Planetary Atmospheres, University College, London. **14–15** Maurice and Sally Landre/Colorific! **16–17** All pictures courtesy of Dr Basil Booth, Geoscience Features. **18** Institute of Geological Sciences. **19** Paul Brierley; Institute of Geological Sciences. **20** Camera Press, London. **26** Barnaby's Picture Library; Barnaby's Picture Library; Institute of Geological Sciences. **28** Dr Alan Beaumont. **30** Tom Sheppard/Robert Harding Picture Library; Professor Ronald Cooke. **31** Institute of Geological Sciences. **32** Stuart Windsor; Sefton Photo Library, Manchester; Rio Tinto Zinc; Douglas Botting; Aspect Picture Library. **33** NASA; Mireille Vautier; Explorer/Vision International. **34** Paul Brierley. **37** Paediatric Research Unit, Guy's Hospital Medical School; Dr Laurence Cook, Zoology Department, University of Manchester. **39** Both pictures from British Museum (Natural History). **46** Colophoto Hans Hinz. **47** Dr P. G. Bahn, School of Archaeology and Oriental Studies, University of Liverpool/Musée des Antiquités Nationales, St. Germain-en-Laye. **56** UNICEF (Photo no. 8675 by H. Dalrymple). **57** Dr A. M. O'Connor, Department of Geography, University College, London. **61** International Fund for Animal Welfare; K. Kunov/Novosti Press Agency; Popperfoto; Charles Swithinbank. **62** Alan Robson. **63** Gösta Hakansson/Frank Lane Agency. **65** G. R. Roberts. **67** Anglo-Chinese Educational Trust; Aerofilms. **69** Ted Streshinsky. **72** Engraving from *At Home with the Patagonians.* **73** The Mansell Collection. **76** J. Bitsch/Zefa; Penny Tweedie/Colorific! **77** Alan Hutchison Library; Bill Holden/Zefa. **80** Syndication International; Gerald Cubitt/Bruce Coleman Ltd; Bruce Coleman Ltd. **81** Alan Hutchison Library; R. and M. Borland/Bruce Coleman Ltd; M. P. Kahl/Bruce Coleman Ltd; Jan and Des Bartlett/Bruce Coleman Ltd. **84** J. von Puttkamer/Alan Hutchison Library. **85** Marion Morrison. **86–87** Richard and Sally Greenhill. **88** Alan Hutchison Library; The Association of Universities for Research in Astronomy, Inc. **89** Gunter Ziesler/Bruce Coleman Ltd. **91** Mike Price/Bruce Coleman Ltd. **92** Ian Murphy. **93** Paolo Koch/Vision International; J. Allan Cash; M. Timothy O'Keefe/Bruce Coleman Ltd. **94** Heather Angel. **95** Institute of Oceanographic Sciences. **96** Fritz Prenzel/Bruce Coleman Ltd; Gordon Williamson/Bruce Coleman Ltd. **97** Martin Rogers/Susan Griggs Agency. **98** British Library; British Museum; Centro Camuno di Studi Preistorici; British Library; NASA; NASA; Rand McNally; British Museum. **99** British Museum; NASA; NASA; Rand McNally; Space Frontiers Ltd; Paul G. Lowman/NASA Goddard SFC/Space Frontiers Ltd. **100** Historisches Museum, Vienna. **101** Hunting Surveys Ltd; Michael Holford/Science Museum, London; Michael Holford; Michael Holford/Science Museum, London. **103** Space Frontiers Ltd; F. Damm/Zefa.

**Cartographic and
Geographic Director**
Giuseppe Motta

**Geographic
Research**
G. Baselli
M. Colombo

**Toponymy and
Translation**
C. Carpine
M. Colombo
H. R. Fischer
R. Nuñez de las Cuevas
Rand McNally
Cartographic Research Staff
I. Straube

**Computerized
Data Organization**
C. Bardesono
E. Ciano
G. Comoglio
E. Di Costanzo

Index
S. Osnaghi
T. Tomasini

**Cartographic
Editor**
V. Castelli

**Cartographic
Compilation**
G. Albera
L. Cairo
C. Camera
G. Conti
G. Fizzotti
G. Gambaro
M. Mochetti
O. Passarelli
M. Peretti
G. Rassiga
A. Saino
F. Valsecchi

**Terrain
Illustration**
S. Andenna
E. Ferrari

**Cartographic
Production**
F. Tosi
G. Capitini
A. Carnero

Filmsetting
S. Fiorini
P. L. Gatta
E. Geranio
G. Ghezzi
L. Lorena
R. Martelli
E. Morchio
M. Morganti
C. Pezzana
P. Uglietti
D. Varalli

**Photographic
Processing**
G. Fracassina
G. Klaus
L. Mella

Coordination
S. Binda
L. Pasquali
G. Zanetta

The editors wish to thank the many organizations, institutions and individuals who have given their valuable help and advice during the preparation of this International Map Section. Special thanks are extended to the following:

Agenzia Novosti, Rome, Italy
D. Arnold, Acting Chief of Documentation and Terminology Section, United Nations, New York, USA
Australian Bureau of Statistics, Brisbane, Australia
J. Breu, United Nations Group of Experts on Geographical Names, Vienna, Austria
Bureau Hydrographique International, Monaco, Principality of Monaco
Canada Map Office, Ottawa, Canada
Cartactual, Budapest, Hungary
Census and Statistical Department, Tripoli, Libya
Central Bureau of Statistics, Accra, Ghana
Central Bureau of Statistics, Jerusalem, Israel
Central Bureau of Statistics, Ministry of Economic Planning and Development, Nairobi, Kenya
Central Department of Statistics, Riyadh, Saudi Arabia
Central Statistical Board of the USSR, Moscow, USSR
Central Statistical Office, London, UK
Centro de Informaçao e Documentaçao Estadística, Rio de Janeiro, Brazil
Committee for the Reform of Chinese Written Language, Peking, China
Danmark Statistik, Copenhagen, Denmark
Defense Mapping Agency, Distribution Office for Latin America, Miami, USA
Defense Mapping Agency, Washington DC, USA
Department of National Development and Energy, Division of National Mapping, Belconnen ACT, Australia
Department of State Coordinator for Maps and Publications, Washington DC, USA
Department of State Map Division, Sofia, Bulgaria
Department of Statistics, Wellington, New Zealand
Direcçao Nacional de Estadística, Maputo, Mozambique
Dirección de Cartografia Naciónal, Caracas, Venezuela
Dirección de Estadística y Censo de la Repubblica de Panamá, Panama
Dirección General de Estadística, Mexico City, Mexico
Dirección General de Estadística y Censos, San Salvador, El Salvador
Direcţia Centrala de Statistică, Bucharest, Romania
Directorate of National Mapping, Kuala Lumpur, Malaysia
Directorate of Overseas Surveys, London, UK
Elaborazione Dati e Disegno Automatico, Torino, Italy
Federal Office of Statistics, Lagos, Nigeria
Federal Office of Statistics, Prague, Czechoslovakia
Geographical Research Institute, Hungarian Academy of Sciences, Budapest, Hungary
Geological Map Service, New York, USA
G. Gomez de Silva, Chief Conference Services Section, United Nations Environment Programme, New York, USA
Government of the People's Republic of Bangladesh, Statistics Division, Ministry of Planning, Dacca, Bangladesh
High Commissioner for Trinidad and Tobago, London, UK
L. Iarotski, World Health Organization, Geneva, Switzerland Information Division, Valletta, Malta
Institut für Angewandte Geodäsie, Frankfurt, West Germany
Institut Géographique, Abidjan, Ivory Coast
Institut Géographique du Zaïre, Kinshasa, Zaïre
Institut Géographique National, Brussels, Belgium
Institut Géographique National, Paris, France
Institut Haïtien de Statistique, Port-au-Prince, Haiti
Institut National de Géodésie et Cartographie, Antananarivo, Madagascar
Institut National de la Statistique, Tunis, Tunisia
Institute of Geography, Polish Academy of Sciences, Warsaw, Poland
Instituto Geográfico Militar, Buenos Aires, Argentina
Instituto Nacional de Estadística, La Paz, Bolivia
Instituto Nacional de Estadística, Madrid, Spain
Istituto Centrale di Statistica, Rome, Italy
Istituto Geografico Militare, Florence, Italy
Istituto Idrografico della Marina, Genoa, Italy
Landesverwaltung des Fürstentums, Vaduz, Liechtenstein
Ministère des Affaires Economiques, Brussels, Belgium
Ministère des Ressources Naturelles, des Mines et des Carrières, Kigali, Rwanda
Ministère des Travaux Publics, des Transports et de l'Urbanisme, Ouagadougou, Upper Volta
Ministry of Finance, Department of Statistics and Research, Nicosia, Cyprus

Ministry of Lands, Housing and Urban Development, Surveys and Mapping Division, Dar es Salaam, Tanzania
Ministry of the Interior, Jerusalem, Israel
National Census and Statistics Office, Manila, Philippines
National Central Bureau of Statistics, Stockholm, Sweden
National Geographic Society, Washington DC, USA
National Institute of Polar Research, Tokyo, Japan
National Ocean Survey, Riverdale, Maryland, USA
National Statistical Institute, Lisbon, Portugal
National Statistical Office, Zomba, Malawi
National Statistical Service of Greece, Athens, Greece
J. Novotny, Prague, Czechoslovakia
Office Nationale de la Recherche Scientifique et Technique, Yaoundé, Cameroon
Officina Comercial del Gobierno de Colombia, Rome, Italy
Ordnance Survey of Ireland, Dublin, Ireland
Österreichisches Statistisches Zentralamt, Vienna, Austria
Państwowe Przedsiebiorstwo Wydawnictw Kartograficznych, Warsaw, Poland
Scott Polar Research Institute, University of Cambridge, Cambridge, UK
Secrétariat d'Etat au Plan, Algiers, Algeria
Servicio Geografico Militar, Montevideo, Uruguay
Z. Shiying, Research Institute of Surveying and Mapping, Peking, China
Statistisches Bundesamt, Wiesbaden, West Germany
Statistisk Sentralbyrå, Oslo, Norway
Survey and National Mapping Department, Kuala Lumpur, Malaysia
Ufficio Turismo e Informazioni della Turchia, Rome, Italy
United States Board on Geographic Names, Washington DC, USA
M. C. Wu, Chinese Translation Service, United Nations, New York, USA
Z. Youguang, Committee for the Reform of Chinese Written Language, Peking, China

The editors are also grateful for the assistance provided by the following embassies, consulates and official state representatives:

Angolan Embassy, Rome
Australian Embassy, Rome
Austrian Embassy, Rome
Embassy of Bangladesh, Rome
Embassy of Botswana, Brussels
Brazilian Embassy, Rome
British Embassy, Rome
Burmese Embassy, Rome
Embassy of Cameroon, Rome
Embassy of Cape Verde, Lisbon
Consulate of Chad, Rome
Chilean Embassy, Rome
Embassy of the People's Republic of China in Italy, Rome
Danish Embassy, Rome
Embassy of El Salvador, Rome
Ethiopian Embassy, Rome
Finnish Embassy, Rome
Embassy of the German Democratic Republic, Rome
Greek Embassy, Rome
Honduras Republic Embassy, Rome
Hungarian Embassy, Rome
Consulate General of Iceland, Rome
Embassy of India, Rome
Embassy of the Republic of Indonesia, Rome
Embassy of the Islamic Republic of Iran, Rome
Irish Embassy, Rome
Embassy of Israel, Rome
Japanese Embassy, Rome
Korean Embassy, Rome
Luxembourg Embassy, Rome
Embassy of Malta, Rome
Mexican Embassy, Rome
Moroccan Embassy, Rome
Netherlands Embassy, Rome
Embassy of New Zealand, Rome
Embassy of Niger, Rome
Embassy of Pakistan, Rome
Peruvian Embassy, Rome
Philippine Embassy, Rome
Romanian Embassy, Rome
Somali Embassy, Rome
South African Embassy, Rome
Spanish Embassy, Rome
Consulate General of Switzerland, Milan
Royal Thai Embassy, Rome
Consulate of Upper Volta, Rome
Uruguay Embassy, Rome
Embassy of the Socialist Republic of Vietnam in Italy, Rome
Permanent Mission of Yemen to United Nations Educational, Scientific and Cultural Organization, Paris

INTERNATIONAL MAP SECTION

Hydrographic and Topographic Features
Symboles hydrographiques et morphologiques
Gewässer- und Geländeformen
Idrografia, Morfologia
Hidrografía y morfología

 River, Stream
Cours d'eau permanent
Ständig wasserführender Fluß
Corso d'acqua perenne
Corriente de agua de régimen permanente

 Lake
Lac d'eau douce
Süßwassersee
Lago d'acqua dolce
Lago de agua dulce

 Rocks
Ecueils, Roches
Klippen, Felsriffe
Scogli, Rocce
Escollos, Rocas

 Summer Limit of Pack Ice
Limite du pack en été
Packeisgrenze im Sommer
Limite estivo del pack ghiacciato
Límite estival de banco de hielo

 Intermittent Stream
Cours d'eau intermittent
Zeitweilig wasserführender Fluß
Corso d'acqua periodico
Corriente de agua intermitente

 Intermittent Lake
Lac d'eau douce temporaire
Zeitweiliger Süßwassersee
Lago d'acqua dolce periodico
Lago de agua dulce intermitente

 Reef, Atoll
Barrière, Atoll
Riff, Atoll
Barriera, Atollo
Barrera de arrecifes

 Winter Limit of Pack Ice
Limite du pack en hiver
Packeisgrenze im Winter
Limite invernale del pack ghiacciato
Límite invernal de banco de hielo

 Disappearing Stream
Perte de cours d'eau
Versickernder Fluß
Corso d'acqua che si inabissa
Corriente de agua que desaparece

 Salt Lake
Lac d'eau salée
Salzsee
Lago d'acqua salata
Lago de agua salada

 Mangrove
Mangrove
Mangrove
Mangrovie
Manglar

 Limit of Icebergs
Limite des glaces flottantes
Treibeisgrenze
Limite dei ghiacci alla deriva
Limite de hielo a la deriva

 Undefined or Fluctuating River Course
Cours d'eau incertain
Fluß mit veränderlichem Lauf
Fiume dal corso incerto
Corriente de agua incerta

 Intermittent Salt Lake
Lac d'eau salée temporaire
Zeitweiliger Salzsee
Lago d'acqua salata periodico
Lago de agua salada intermitente

Continental Ice-cap
Glacier continental
Inlandeis, Gletscher
Ghiacciaio continentale
Glaciar continental

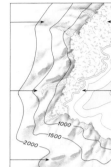 **Ice Shelf**
Banquise
Schelfeis oder Eisschelf
Banchisa polare (Ice-shelf)
Banquisa

 Waterfall, Rapids, Cataract
Chute, Rapide, Cataracte
Wasserfall, Stromschnelle, Katarakt
Cascata, Rapida, Cateratta
Cascada, Rapido, Catarata

Dry Lake Bed
Lac asséché
Trockener Seeboden
Alveo di lago asciutto
Lecho de lago seco

Glacial Tongue
Langue glaciaire
Gletscherzunge
Lingua di ghiaccio
Lengua de glaciar

Limit of Ice Shelf
Limite de la banquise
Schelfeisgrenze
Limite della banchisa
Límite de la banquisa

 Canal
Canal
Kanal
Canale
Canal

 Lake Surface Elevation
Cote du lac au-dessus du niveau de la mer
Höhe des Seespiegels
Altitudine del lago
Elevación de lago sobre el nivel del mar

Rocky Areas (Antarctica)
Région de roches (Antarctique)
Eisfreie Gebiete, Gebirge (Antarktika)
Aree rocciose (Antartide)
Area rocosa (Antártida)

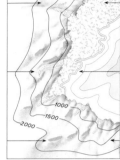 **Contour Lines in Continental Ice**
Courbes de niveau dans les régions glaciaires
Höhenlinien auf vergletschertem Gebiet
Curve altimetriche nelle aree ghiacciate
Curvas de nivel en áreas heladas

 Navigable Canal
Canal navigable
Schiffbarer Kanal
Canale navigabile
Canal navegable

 Lake Depth
Profondeur du lac
Seetiefe
Profondità del lago
Profundidad del lago

Defined Shoreline
Trait de côte définie
Küsten- oder Uferlinie
Linea di costa definita
Línea de costa definida

 **Bathymetric Contour**
Courbe bathymétrique
Tiefenlinie
Curva batimetrica
Curva batimétrica

 Swamp
Marais
Sumpf
Palude d'acqua dolce
Pantano

 Sand Area
Région de sable, Désert
Sandgebiet, Sandwüste
Area sabbiosa, Deserto
Zona arenosa, desierto

Undefined or Fluctuating Shoreline
Trait de côte indéfinie
Unbestimmte oder veränderliche Uferlinie
Linea di costa indefinita
Línea de costa indefinida

 Depth of Water
Valeur de sonde
Tiefenzahl
Quota batimetrica
Cota batimétrica

 Salt Marsh
Marais d'eau salée
Salzsumpf
Palude d'acqua salata
Pantano de agua salada

 Sandbank, Sandbar
Banc de sable
Sandbank
Bassofondo sabbioso
Banco submarino de arena

Mountain Range
Chaine de montagnes
Bergkette
Catena di monti
Cadena montañosa

 **Mountain**
Mont
Berg, Bergmassiv
Monte
Monte

Salt Pan
Marais salant
Salzpfanne
Salina
Salina

Port Facilities
Installations portuaires
Hafenanlagen
Impianti portuali
Instalaciones portuarias

Elevation
Cote, Altitude
Höhenzahl
Quota altimetrica
Cota altimétrica

Mountain Pass, Gap
Passage, Col, Port
Paß, Joch, Sattel
Passo, Colle, Valico
Paso, Collado, Puerto de montaña

Key to Elevation and Depth Tints
Hypsométrie, Bathymétrie
Höhenstufen, Tiefenstufen
Altimetria, Batimetria
Altimetría, Batimetría

Scales in Metric and English Measures
Échelle des teintes hypsométriques et bathymétriques
Farbskala der Höhen- und Tiefenstufen
Scala delle tinte Altimetriche e Batimetriche
Escala de tintas hypsométricas y batimétricas

 Land Elevation Below Sea Level
Dépression et cote au-dessous du niveau de la mer
Senke mit Tiefenzahl unter dem Meeresspiegel
Depressione e quota sotto il livello del mare
Depresión y elevación bajo el nivel del mar

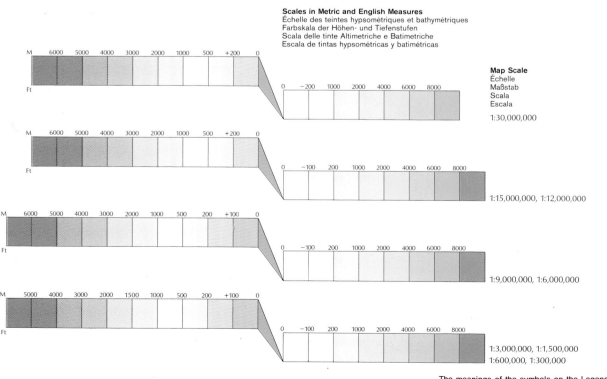

Map Scale
Échelle
Maßstab
Scala
Escala

1:30,000,000

1:15,000,000, 1:12,000,000

1:9,000,000, 1:6,000,000

1:3,000,000, 1:1,500,000
1:600,000, 1:300,000

Map Projections
Projections cartographiques
Kartennetzentwürfe
Proiezioni cartografiche
Proyecciones cartográficas

The projections appearing in this atlas have been plotted by computer

Les réseaux des projections ont été obtenus par élaboration automatique à partir de formules mathématiques

Die Kartennetze aller im Atlas vorkommenden Abbildungen wurden mit Hilfe der Datenverarbeitung (EDV) völlig neu errechnet

I disegni delle proiezioni presenti in quest'opera sono stati realizzati interamente ex-novo con l'uso del computer e del plotter a partire dalle formule matematiche

El reticulado de las proyecciones (redes geográficas) incluidas en esta obra han sido obtenidas por proceso automático a partir de las formulas matemáticas

The meanings of the symbols on the Legend pages are in English, French, German, Italian, and Spanish languages to permit the interpretation of the maps by a broad readership.

Boundaries, Capitals
Frontières, Soulignements — Confini, Sottolineature
Grenzen, Unterstreichungen — Límites, Subrayados

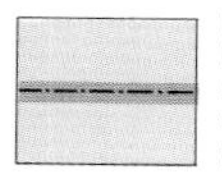

Defined International Boundary
Frontière internationale définie
Staatsgrenze
Confine di Stato definito
Límite de Nación definido

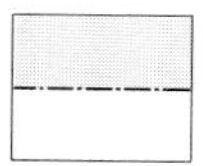

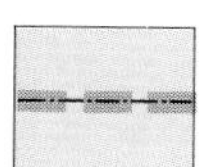

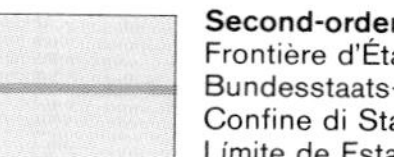

Second-order Political Boundary
Frontière d'État fédéré, Région
Bundesstaats-, Regionsgrenze
Confine di Stato federato, Regione
Límite de Estado federado, Región

International Boundary (Continent Maps)
Frontière internationale (Continents)
Staatsgrenze (Erdteilkarten)
Confine di Stato (Carte dei Continenti)
Límite de Nación (Continentes)

Third-order Political Boundary
Frontière de Province, Comté, Bezirk
Provinz-, Grafschafts-, Bezirksgrenze
Confine di Provincia, Contea, Bezirk
Límite de Provincia, Condado, Bezirk

Undefined International Boundary
Frontière internationale indéfinie
Nicht genau festgelegte Staatsgrenze
Confine di Stato indefinito
Límite de Nación indefinido

Administrative District Boundary (U.S.S.R.)
Frontière de Circonscription
Kreisgrenze
Confine di Circondario
Límite de Circunscripción administrativa

International Ocean Floor Boundary Defined by Treaty or Bilateral Agreement
Frontière d'état en mer définie par traités et conventions bilatéraux
Durch Verträge festgelegte Staatsgrenze im Meeresgebiet
Confine di Stato nel mare definito da trattati e convenzioni bilaterali
Límite de Nación en el Mar definido por los tratados bilaterales

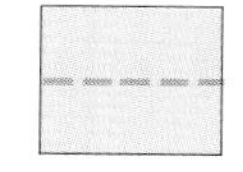

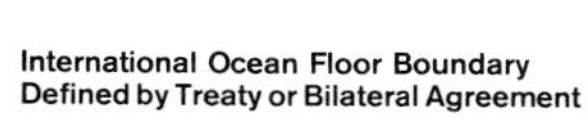

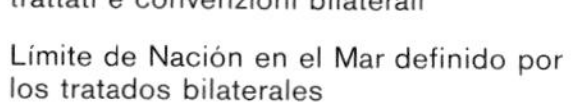

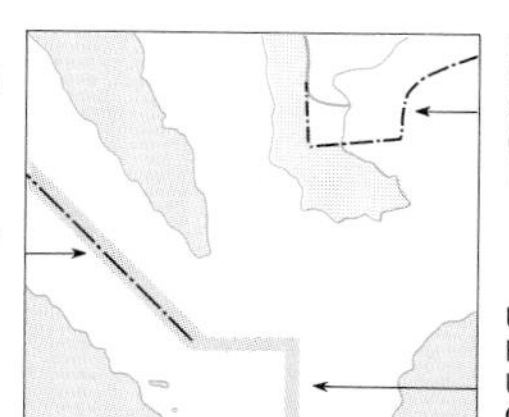

International Ocean Floor Boundary
Frontière d'état en mer
Staatsgrenze im Meeresgebiet
Confine di Stato nel mare
Límite de Nación en el mar

Undefined Ocean Floor Boundary
Frontière indéfinie d'état tracée en mer
Unbstimmte Staatsgrenze im Meeresgebiet
Confine di Stato indefinito nel mare
Límite indefinido de Nación en el mar

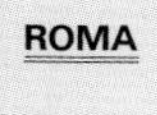

National Capital
Capitale d'État
Hauptstadt eines unabhängigen Staates
Capitale di Stato
Capital de Nación

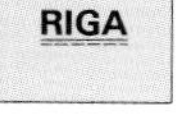

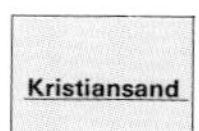

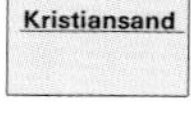

Third-order Capital
Capitale de Province, Comté, Bezirk
Provinz-, Grafschafts-, Bezirkshauptstadt
Capoluogo di Provincia, Contea, Bezirk
Capital de Provincia, Condado, Bezirk

Dependency or Second-order Capital
Capitale d'État fédéré, Région
Bundesstaats-, Regionshauptstadt
Capitale di Stato federato, Regione
Capital de Estado federado, Región

Administrative District Capital (U.S.S.R.)
Capitale de Circonscription
Kreishauptstadt
Capoluogo di Circondario
Capital de Circunscripción administrativa

Populated Places
Population — Popolazione
Bevölkerung — Población

Continent Maps
Cartes des Continents — Carte dei Continenti
Erdteilkarten — Mapas de Continentes

- < 25 000
- 25 000-100 000
- 100 000-250 000
- 250 000-1 000 000
- > 1 000 000

Regional Maps
Cartes à plus grande échelle — Carte di sviluppo
Karten größeren Maßstabs — Mapas a gran escala

- < 10 000
- 10 000-25 000
- 25 000-100 000
- 100 000-250 000
- 250 000-1 000 000
- > 1 000 000

Symbols represent population of inhabited localities
Les symboles représentent le nombre d'habitants des localités
Die Signaturen entsprechen der Einwohnerzahl des Ortes
I simboli sono relativi al valore demografico dei centri abitati
Los símbolos son proporcionales a la población del lugar

Town area symbol represents the shape of the urban area
Le petit plan de la ville reproduit la configuration de l'aire urbaine
Die Plansignatur stellt die Gestalt des Stadtgebietes dar
La piantina della città rappresenta la configurazione dell'area urbana
El pequeño plano de la ciudad representa la forma del área urbana

Other Symbols
Symboles divers — Simboli vari
Sonstige Zeichen — Signos varios

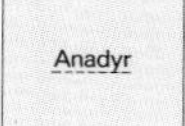

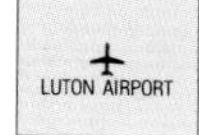

International Airport
Aéroport international
Internationaler Flughafen
Aeroporto internazionale
Aeropuerto internacional

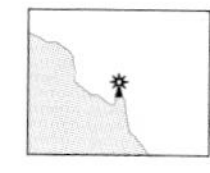

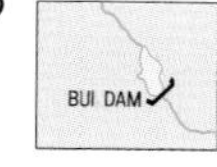

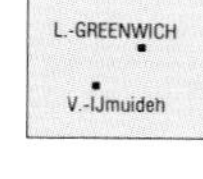

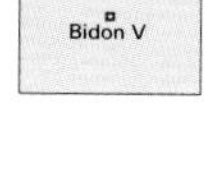

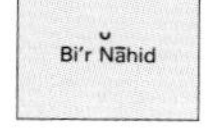

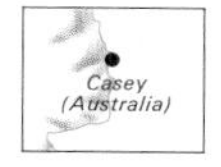

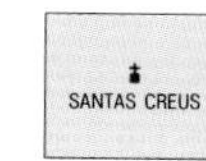

Church, Monastery, Abbey
Monastère, Eglise, Abbaye
Kloster, Kirche, Abtei
Monastero, Chiesa, Abbazia
Monasterio, Iglesia, Abadía

Lighthouse
Phare
Leuchtturm
Faro
Faro

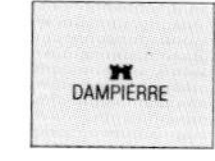

Castle
Château
Burg, Schloß
Castello
Castillo

Dam
Barrage
Staudamm, Staumauer
Diga artificiale, Sbarramento
Presa

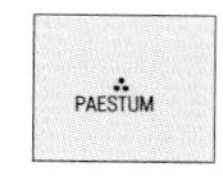

Ruin, Archeological Site
Ruine, Centre archéologique
Ruine, Archäologisches Zentrum
Rovina, Zona archeologica
Ruina, Zona arqueológica

Section of a City
Faubourg
Stadt- oder Ortsteil
Sobborgo urbano
Suburbio

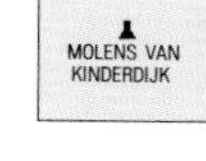

Monument, Historic Site, etc.
Monument
Denkmal
Monumento
Monumento

Uninhabited Locality, Hamlet
Ville inhabitée, Ferme, Hameau
Unbewohnte Stadt, Gehöft, Weiler
Città disabitata, Fattoria, Nucleo di case
Ciudad despoblada, Granja, Casar

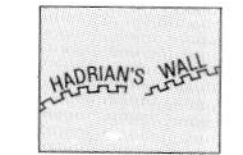

Wall
Muraille
Wall, Mauer
Vallo, Muraglia
Muralla

Periodically Inhabited Oasis
Oasis habitées périodiquement
Zeitweilig bewohnte Oase
Oasi periodicamente abitate
Oasis periodicamente habitados

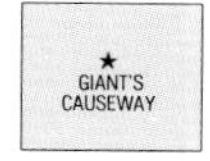

Point of Interest
Curiosité
Sehenswürdigkeit
Curiosità
Curiosidad

Scientific Station
Base géophysique
Geophysikalische Beobachtungsstation
Base geofisica
Base geofísica

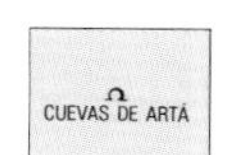

Cave
Grotte, Caverne
Höhle
Grotta, Caverna
Cueva, Gruta

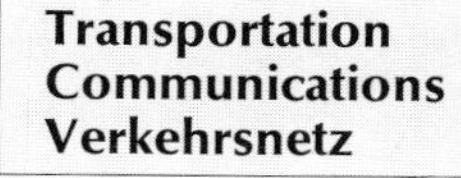

Transportation
Communications — Comunicazioni
Verkehrsnetz — Comunicaciones

Primary Railway
Chemin de fer principal
Hauptbahn
Ferrovia principale
Ferrocarril principal

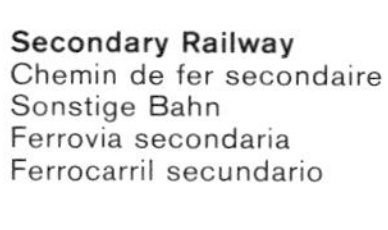

Secondary Railway
Chemin de fer secondaire
Sonstige Bahn
Ferrovia secondaria
Ferrocarril secundario

Motorway, Expressway
Autoroute
Autobahn
Autostrada
Autopista

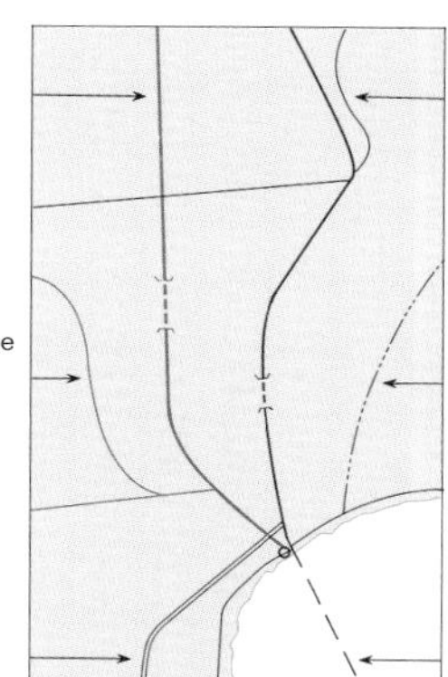

Road
Route de grande communication, Autres Routes
Fernverkehrsstraße, andere Straßen
Strada principale, Altre Strade
Carretera principal, Otras Carreteras

Trail, Caravan Route
Piste, Voie caravanière
Wüstenpiste, Karawanenweg
Pista nel deserto, Carovaniera
Pista en el desierto, Vía de Carabanas

Ferry, Shipping Lane
Bac, Ligne maritime
Fähre, Schiffahrtslinie
Traghetto, Linea di navigazione
Transbordador (Ferry), Línea de navegación

Type Styles
Caractères utilisés pour la toponymie — Caratteri usati per la toponomastica
Zur Namenschreibung verwendete Schriftarten — Caracteres utilizados para la toponimia

ITALY
Hessen RIBE

Political Units
Etat, Dépendance, Division administrative
Staat, abhängiges Gebiet, Verwaltungsgliederung
Stato, Dipendenza, Divisione amministrativa
Nación, Dependencia, División administrativa

Ankaratra — Monte Bianco
Tsiafajavena — Ngorongoro Crater
Nevado del Tolima — Kings Peak

Small Mountain Range, Mountain, Peak
Petit massif, Mont, Cime
Bergmassiv, Berg, Gipfel
Piccolo gruppo montuoso, Monte, Vetta
Macizo pequeño, Monte, Cima

LABRADOR SEA
Gulf of Alaska Hudson Bay
Estrecho de Magallanes

Sea, Gulf, Bay, Strait
Mer, Golfe, Baie, Détroit
Meer, Golf, Bucht, Meeresstraße
Mare, Golfo, Baia, Stretto
Mar, Golfo, Bahía, Estrecho

SAXONY
THRACE SUSSEX

Historical or Cultural Region
Région historique ou culturelle
Historische oder Kulturlandschaft
Regione storico - culturale
Región histórica y cultural

Cabo de São Vicente — Land's End
Mizen Head — Point Conception
Col de la Perche — Passo della Cisa

Cape, Point, Pass
Cap, Pointe, Passe
Kap, Landspitze, Paß
Capo, Punta, Passo
Cabo, Punta, Paso

West Mariana Basin
Galapagos Fracture Zone
Mid-Atlantic Ridge

Undersea Features
Formes du relief sous-marin
Formen des Meeresbodens
Forme del rilievo sottomarino
Formas del relieve submarino

PATAGONIA
BASSIN DE RENNES
PENÍNSULA DE YUCATÁN

Physical Region (plain, peninsula)
Région physique (plaine, péninsule)
Landschaft (Ebene, Halbinsel)
Regione fisica (pianura, penisola)
Región natural (llanura, península)

MAHÉ ALDABRA ISLANDS
CORSE CHANNEL ISLANDS
SULU ARCHIPELAGO

Island, Archipelago
Ile, Archipel
Insel, Archipel
Isola, Arcipelago
Isla, Archipiélago

Tarfaya
Tombouctou
Agadir
Nouakchott
BRAZZAVILLE
CASABLANCA

Size of type indicates relative importance of inhabited localities
La dimension des caractères indique l'importance d'une localité
Die Schriftgröße entspricht der Gesamtbedeutung des Ortes
La grandezza del carattere è proporzionale all'importanza della località
La dimensión de los caracteres de imprenta indica la importancia de la localidad

PYRENEES
CUMBRIAN MOUNTAINS
SIERRA DE GÁDOR LA SILA

Mountain Range
Chaîne de montagnes
Bergkette, Gebirge
Catena di monti
Cadena montañosa

Thames Po Victoria Falls
Lotagipi Swamp Gota kanal
Lago Maggiore

River, Waterfall, Cataract, Canal, Lake
Fleuve, Chute d'eau, Cataracte, Canal, Lac
Fluß, Wasserfall, Katarakt, Kanal, See
Fiume, Cascata, Cateratta, Canale, Lago
Río, Cascada, Catarata, Canal, Lago

INDEX MAPS

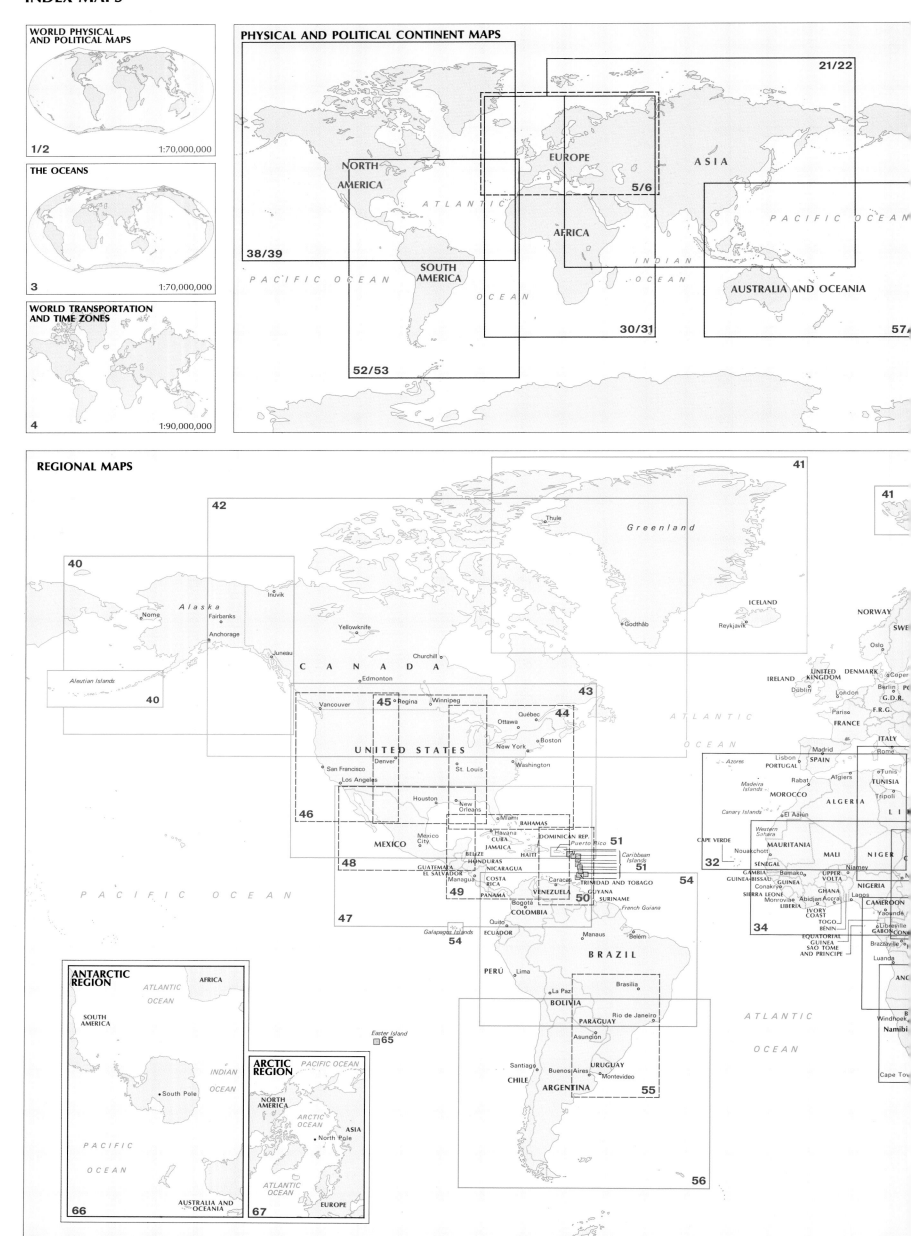

WORLD PHYSICAL AND POLITICAL MAPS

1/2   1:70,000,000

THE OCEANS

3   1:70,000,000

WORLD TRANSPORTATION AND TIME ZONES

4   1:90,000,000

PHYSICAL AND POLITICAL CONTINENT MAPS

NORTH AMERICA

EUROPE   5/6

ASIA   21/22

AFRICA

SOUTH AMERICA

AUSTRALIA AND OCEANIA

ATLANTIC OCEAN   PACIFIC OCEAN   INDIAN OCEAN   PACIFIC OCEAN

38/39   52/53   30/31   57

REGIONAL MAPS

40   42   41   43   44   45   46   47   48   49   50   51   54   55   56   32   34

Alaska   Nome   Fairbanks   Anchorage   Juneau   Aleutian Islands

CANADA   Inuvik   Yellowknife   Churchill   Edmonton

Greenland   Thule   Godthåb   ICELAND   Reykjavik

UNITED STATES   Vancouver   Regina   Winnipeg   Québec   Ottawa   Boston   New York   Washington   San Francisco   Denver   St. Louis   Los Angeles   Houston   New Orleans   Miami

MEXICO   Mexico City   BAHAMAS   Havana   CUBA   JAMAICA   HAITI   DOMINICAN REP.   Puerto Rico   Caribbean Islands

BELIZE   HONDURAS   GUATEMALA   EL SALVADOR   NICARAGUA   Managua   COSTA RICA   PANAMA   VENEZUELA   Caracas   TRINIDAD AND TOBAGO   GUYANA   SURINAME   French Guiana

COLOMBIA   Bogotá   Quito   ECUADOR   Galapagos Islands   Manaus   Belém

PERÚ   Lima   BRAZIL   La Paz   BOLIVIA   Brasilia   Rio de Janeiro   PARAGUAY   Asunción   Easter Island   65

Santiago   CHILE   Buenos Aires   Montevideo   URUGUAY   ARGENTINA

NORWAY   SWE   Oslo   IRELAND   UNITED KINGDOM   DENMARK   Dublin   London   Berlin   G.D.R.   Paris   F.R.G.   FRANCE   ITALY   Rome   Madrid   SPAIN   Lisbon   PORTUGAL   Azores   Rabat   Algiers   Tunis   TUNISIA   Tripoli   Madeira Islands   MOROCCO   ALGERIA   LI

Canary Islands   El Aaiun   Western Sahara   CAPE VERDE   Nouakchott   MAURITANIA   MALI   NIGER   SENEGAL   Bamako   Niamey   GAMBIA   GUINEA-BISSAU   GUINEA   UPPER VOLTA   NIGERIA   Conakry   SIERRA LEONE   GHANA   CAMEROON   Monrovia   Abidjan   Accra   Lagos   LIBERIA   IVORY COAST   TOGO   BENIN   Yaoundé   Libreville   GABON   CON   EQUATORIAL GUINEA   SAO TOME AND PRINCIPE   Brazzaville   Luanda   ANG

ATLANTIC OCEAN   Windhoek   Namibi   Cape Tow

ANTARCTIC REGION

AFRICA   ATLANTIC OCEAN   SOUTH AMERICA   INDIAN OCEAN   South Pole   PACIFIC OCEAN   AUSTRALIA AND OCEANIA   66

ARCTIC REGION

PACIFIC OCEAN   NORTH AMERICA   ARCTIC OCEAN   ASIA   North Pole   ATLANTIC OCEAN   EUROPE   67

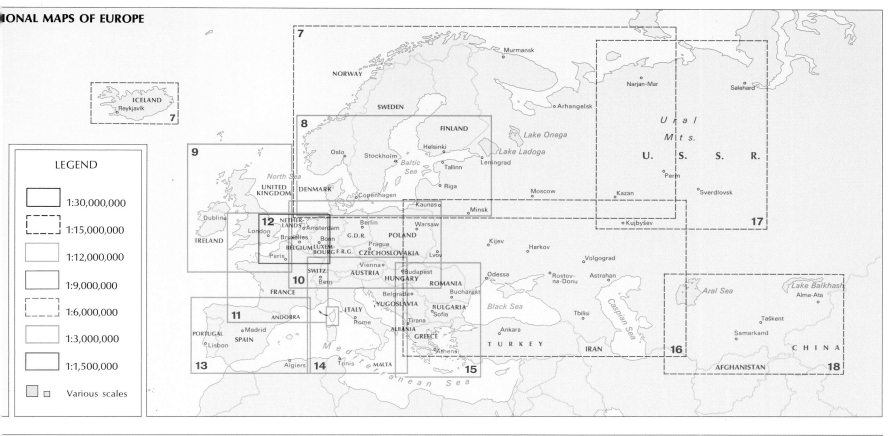

IONAL MAPS OF EUROPE

LEGEND

☐	1:30,000,000
☐	1:15,000,000
☐	1:12,000,000
☐	1:9,000,000
☐	1:6,000,000
☐	1:3,000,000
☐	1:1,500,000
☐ ☐	Various scales

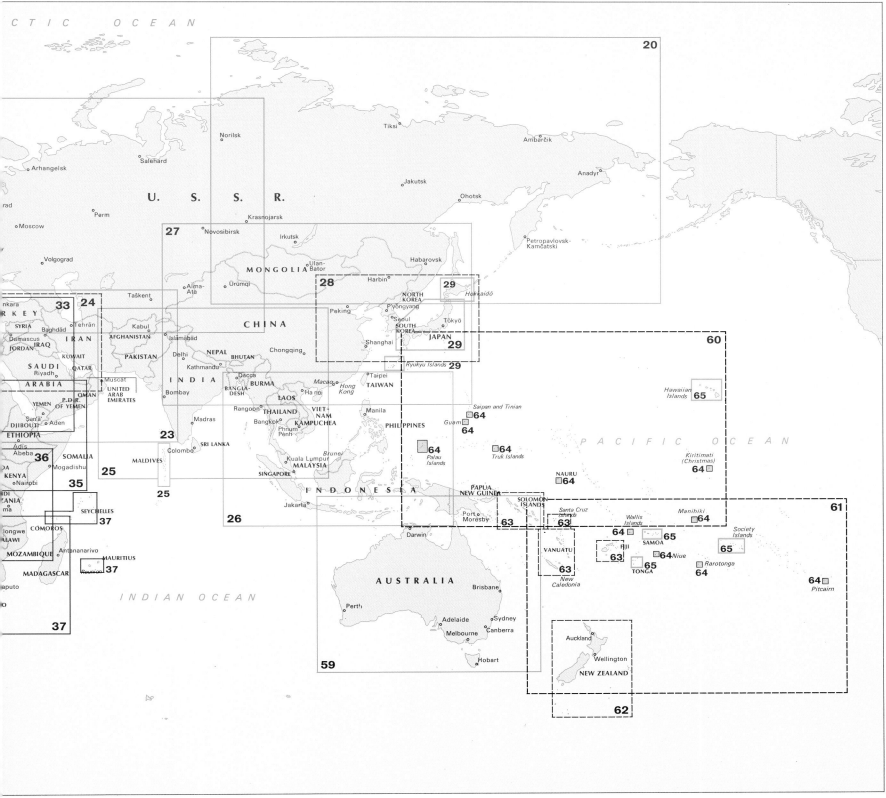

Map 1 **WORLD, PHYSICAL**

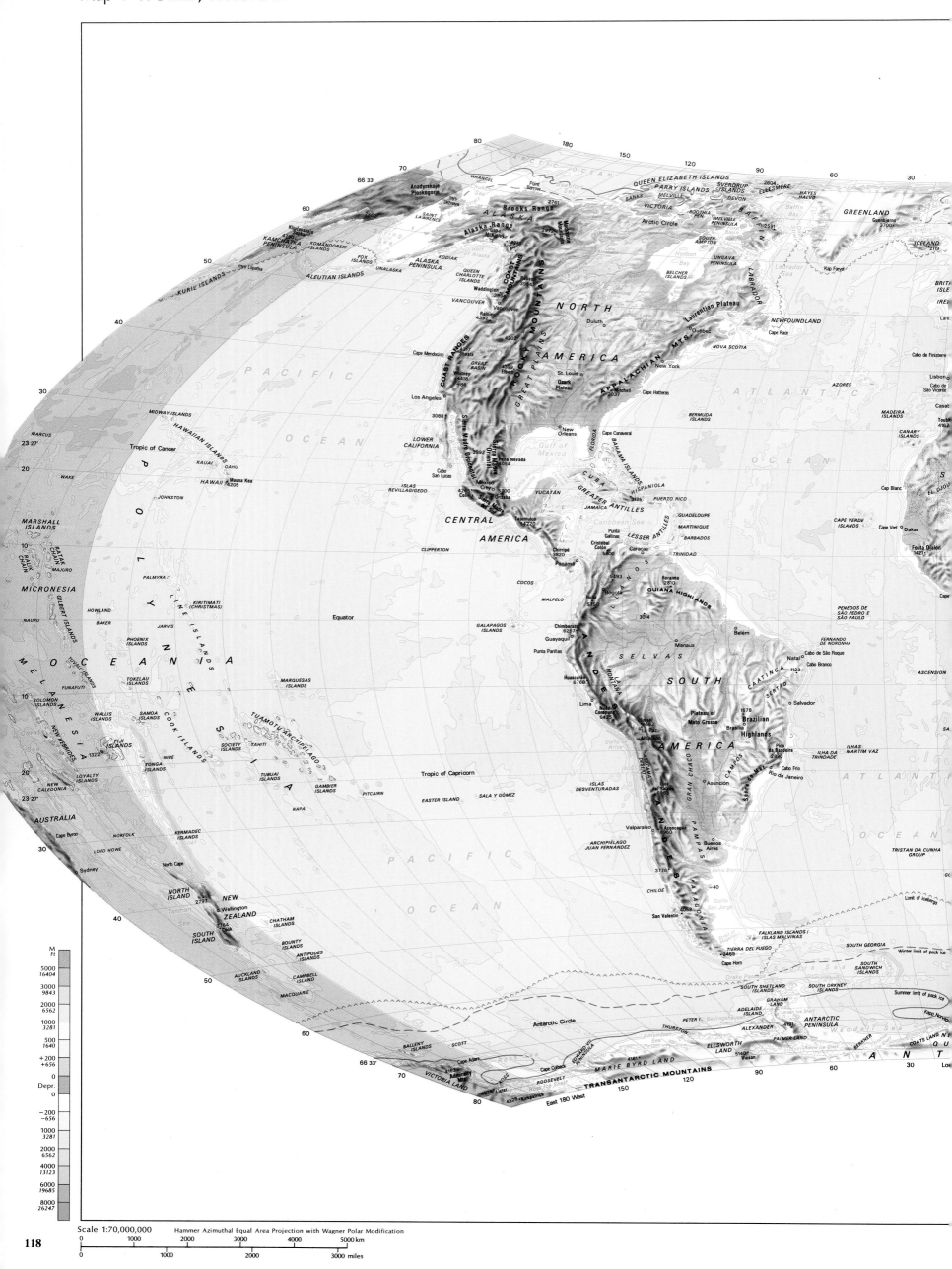

Scale 1:70,000,000
Hammer Azimuthal Equal Area Projection with Wagner Polar Modification
0   1000   2000   3000   4000   5000 km
0   1000   2000   3000 miles

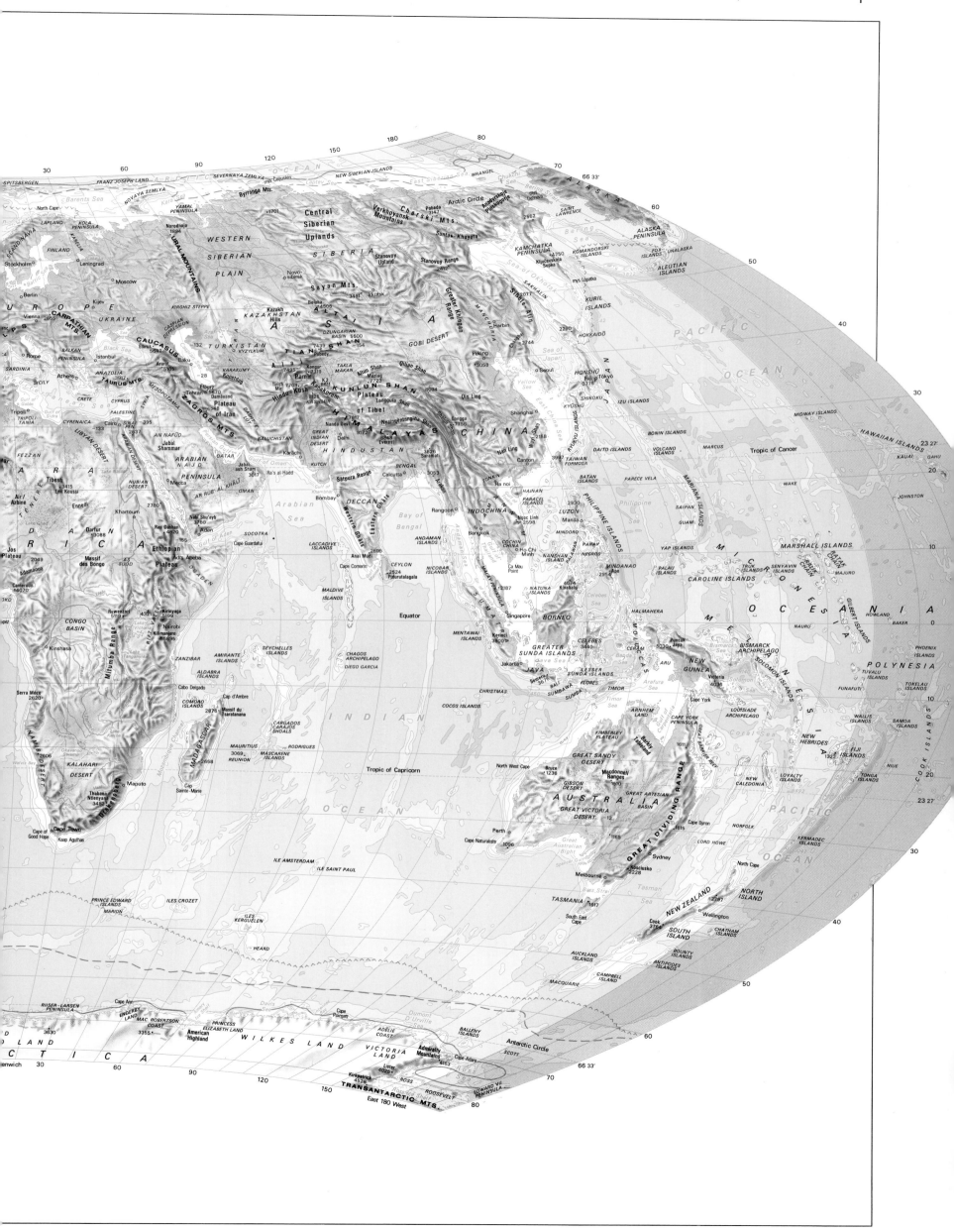

SPITSBERGEN
FRANZ JOSEPH LAND
SEVERNAYA ZEMLYA
NEW SIBERIAN ISLANDS
WRANGEL
Barents Sea
NOVAYA ZEMLYA
Byrranga Mts.
YAMAL PENINSULA
Central Siberian Uplands
Verkhoyansk Mountains
Cherski Mts.
Arctic Circle
Anadyrskoje Ploskogorje
ALASKA
SAINT LAWRENCE
North Cape
LAPLAND
KOLA PENINSULA
FINLAND
KARELIA
SCANDINAVIA
Stockholm
Leningrad
Moscow
Berlin
WESTERN SIBERIAN PLAIN
URAL MOUNTAINS
SIBERIA
Stanovoy Upland
Stanovoy Range
Suntar-Khayata
KAMCHATKA PENINSULA
KOMANDORSKI ISLANDS
ALASKA PENINSULA
FOX ISLANDS
UNALASKA
ALEUTIAN ISLANDS
Sea of Okhotsk
SAKHALIN
mys Lopatka
KURIL ISLANDS
Sayan Mts.
Irkutsk
Novosibirsk
Kijev
EUROPE
UKRAINE
CARPATHIAN MTS.
Vienna
KIRGHIZ STEPPE
Kazakh Hills
KAZAKHSTAN
ALTAI
ASIA
Greater Khingan Range
MANCHURIA
Sikhote Alin
Harbin
HOKKAIDO
PACIFIC
OCEAN
CASPIAN DEPRESSION
CAUCASUS
Elbrus 5642
BALKAN PENINSULA
Black Sea
Rome
Istanbul
SARDINIA
SICILY
Athens
TURKISTAN
KYZYLKUM
DZUNGARIAN BASIN
TIAN SHAN
GOBI DESERT
Peking
Seoul
Sea of Japan
HONSHU
Tokyo
JAPAN
ANATOLIA
TAURUS MTS.
Ararat 5165
Baku
KARAKUMY
Kopetdag
Pamir
Kongur
TAKLA MAKAN
Altun Shan
Qilian Shan
Elburz
Tehran
Damavand
Hindu Kush
Karakoram
K2 8611
KUNLUN SHAN
Plateau of Tibet
Tanggula Shan
Qin Ling
Yellow Sea
East China Sea
SHIKOKU
KYUSHU
IZU ISLANDS
CRETE
CYPRUS
MESOPOTAMIA
ZAGROS MTS.
Plateau of Iran
SYRIA
PALESTINE
Tripoli
TRIPOLITANIA
CYRENAICA
Gulf of Sidra
Cairo
SINAI PEN.
HIMALAYAS
Nanda Devi 7817
Everest 8848
Nyainqentanglha Shan
Gongga 7556
Shanghai
MIDWAY ISLANDS
LIBYAN DESERT
AN NAFUD
Jabal Shammar
BALUCHISTAN
GREAT INDIAN DESERT
Delhi
HINDUSTAN
CHINA
Nan Ling
RYUKYU ISLANDS
BONIN ISLANDS
HAWAIIAN ISLANDS
23 27'
FEZZAN
ARABIAN
NAJD
QATAR
Persian Gulf
Gulf of Oman
Karachi
KUTCH
BENGAL
Saramati
Canton
TAIWAN FORMOSA
DAITO ISLANDS
VOLCANO ISLANDS
MARCUS
Tropic of Cancer
KAUAI
OAHU
Tibesti
Emi Koussi
PENINSULA
Mecca
Jabal ash Sham 3017
Ra's al Hadd
Satpura Range
Calcutta
TONKIN
Ha noi
HAINAN
BATAN ISLANDS
PARECE VELA
MARIANA ISLANDS
WAKE
Aïr
Azbine
TENERE
Ennedi
NUBIAN DESERT
AR RUB' AL KHALI
OMAN
Bombay
DECCAN
Arabian Sea
Bay of Bengal
PARACEL ISLANDS
LUZON
Manila
PHILIPPINE ISLANDS
Philippine Sea
SAIPAN
GUAM
JOHNSTON
Khartoum
Nabi Shu'ayb 3760
Aden
Gulf of Aden
SOCOTRA
Cape Guardafui
Rangoon
INDOCHINA
Ngoc Linh 2598
MINDORO
Darfur
Ras Dashan 4620
Ethiopian Plateau
Addis Abeba
OGADEN
Western Ghats
Eastern Ghats
LACCADIVE ISLANDS
ANDAMAN ISLANDS
Bangkok
COCHIN CHINA
Ho Chi Minh
PALAWAN
PANAY
NEGROS
YAP ISLANDS
MICRONESIA
MARSHALL ISLANDS
RATAK CHAIN
RALIK CHAIN
Jos Plateau
Massif des Bongo
Adamaoua
Cameroon 4070
Anai Mudi
Cape Comorin
CEYLON
Pidurutalagala
NICOBAR ISLANDS
Ca Mau Point
NANSHAN ISLAND
Sulu Sea
MINDANAO
Apo
PALAU ISLANDS
TRUK ISLANDS
SENYAVIN ISLANDS
CAROLINE ISLANDS
MAJURO
MALDIVE ISLANDS
MALAY PENINSULA
NATUNA ISLANDS
Kinabalu 4074
Celebes Sea
HALMAHERA
GILBERT ISLANDS
HOWLAND
BAKER
CONGO BASIN
Ruwenzori 5119
Kirinyaga 5199
Nairobi
Kilimanjaro 5895
RIFT VALLEY
Lake Victoria
Equator
SUMATRA
Singapore
BORNEO
MOLUCCAS
OCEANIA
MELANESIA
NAURU
Kinshasa
Mitumba Range
SEYCHELLES ISLANDS
MENTAWAI ISLANDS
Kerinci 3800
CELEBES
Puncak Jaya 5030
CERAM
GREATER SUNDA ISLANDS
BISMARCK ARCHIPELAGO
PHOENIX ISLANDS
ZANZIBAR
AMIRANTE ISLANDS
CHAGOS ARCHIPELAGO
DIEGO GARCIA
Jakarta
Java Sea
JAVA
Banda Sea
ARU
NEW GUINEA
SOLOMON ISLANDS
POLYNESIA
TUVALU ISLANDS
ALDABRA ISLANDS
Cabo Delgado
Semeru 3676
BALI
LESSER SUNDA ISLANDS
FLORES
Arafura Sea
Victoria 4036
TOKELAU ISLANDS
Serra Môco 2620
Cap d'Ambre
COMORO ISLANDS
Massif du Tsaratanana
CHRISTMAS
SUMBAWA
SUMBA
TIMOR
Timor Sea
Cape York
FUNAFUTI
COCOS ISLANDS
INDIAN
ARNHEM LAND
CAPE YORK PENINSULA
LOUISIADE ARCHIPELAGO
WALLIS ISLANDS
SAMOA ISLANDS
MADAGASCAR
CARGADOS CARAJOS SHOALS
KIMBERLEY PLATEAU
Barkly Tableland
GREAT BARRIER REEF
Coral Sea
NEW HEBRIDES
FIJI ISLANDS
COOK ISLANDS
NAMIB DESERT
KALAHARI DESERT
MAURITIUS
RODRIGUES
REUNION
MASCARENE ISLANDS
GREAT SANDY DESERT
Macdonnell Ranges
NIUE
Tropic of Capricorn
North West Cape
Bruce 1236
GIBSON DESERT
NEW CALEDONIA
LOYALTY ISLANDS
TONGA ISLANDS
Maputo
Drakensberg
Thabana Ntlenyana 3482
Cap Sainte-Marie
AUSTRALIA
GREAT ARTESIAN BASIN
GREAT DIVIDING RANGE
GREAT VICTORIA DESERT
OCEAN
Cape of Good Hope
Cape Town
Kaap Agulhas
Perth
Cape Naturaliste
Great Australian Bight
Cape Byron
NORFOLK
LORD HOWE
KERMADEC ISLANDS
Sydney
ILE AMSTERDAM
ILE SAINT PAUL
Melbourne
Kosciusko 2228
North Cape
NORTH ISLAND
Bass Strait
Tasman Sea
PRINCE EDWARD ISLANDS
MARION
ILES CROZET
TASMANIA
South East Cape
NEW ZEALAND
Wellington
ILES KERGUELEN
Cook 3764
SOUTH ISLAND
CHATHAM ISLANDS
HEARD
AUCKLAND ISLANDS
BOUNTY ISLANDS
ANTIPODES ISLANDS
CAMPBELL ISLAND
MACQUARIE
RIISER-LARSEN PENINSULA
Cape Ann
ENDERBY LAND
MAC. ROBERTSON COAST
PRINCESS ELIZABETH LAND
American Highland
Cape Poinsett
ADELIE COAST
Dumont d'Urville Sea
BALLENY ISLANDS
WILKES LAND
VICTORIA LAND
Admiralty Mountains
Cape Adare
Antarctic Circle
SCOTT
Lister 4025
Kirkpatrick 4528
ROSS
ROOSEVELT
EDWARD VII PENINSULA
TRANSANTARCTIC MTS.
East 180 West
66 33'

Map 2 **WORLD, POLITICAL**

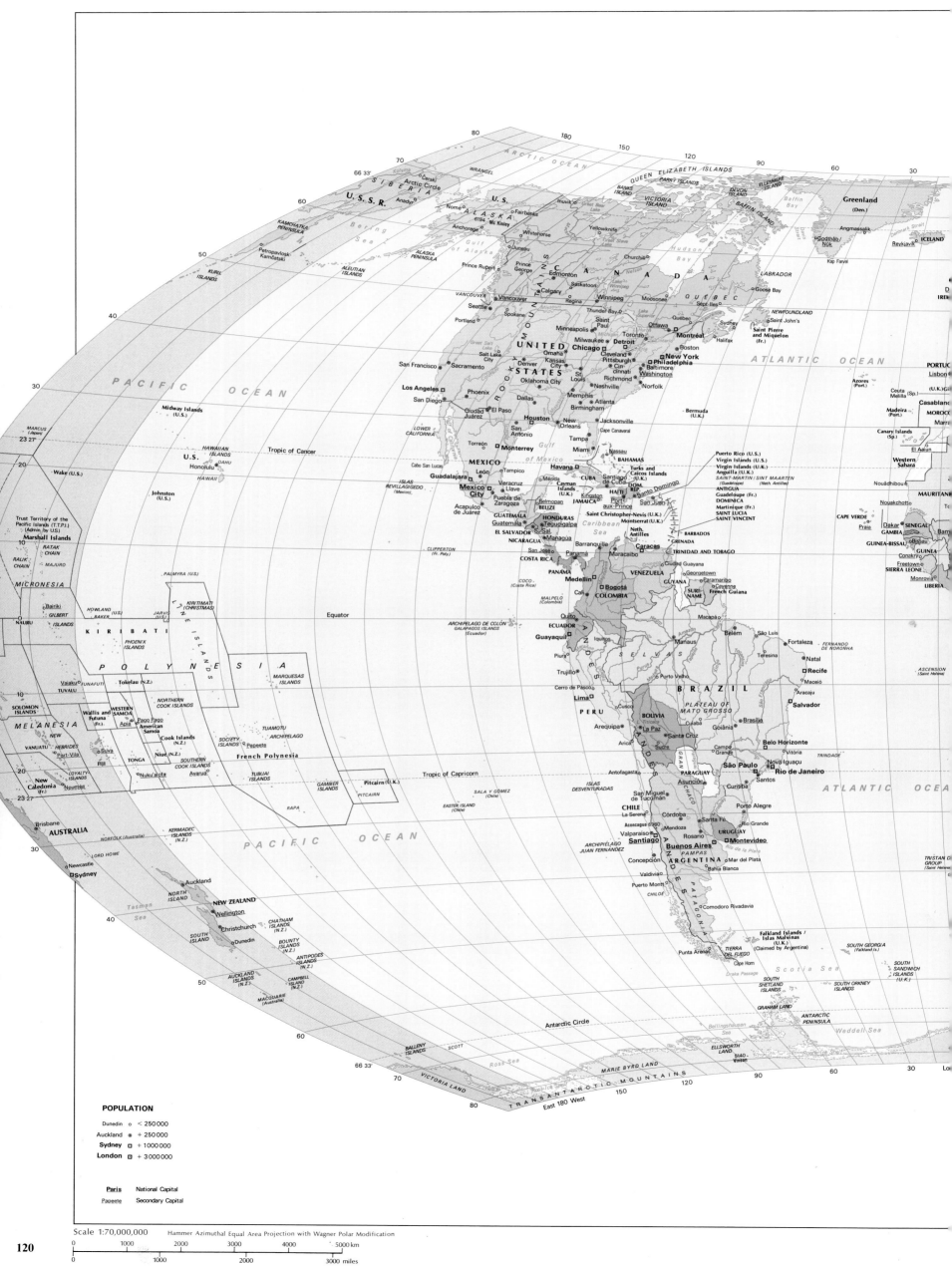

POPULATION

Dunedin	○ < 250 000
Auckland	◉ + 250 000
Sydney	◻ + 1 000 000
London	▣ + 3 000 000

Paris   National Capital

Papeete   Secondary Capital

Scale 1:70,000,000   Hammer Azimuthal Equal Area Projection with Wagner Polar Modification

0	1000	2000	3000	4000	5000 km

0	1000	2000	3000 miles

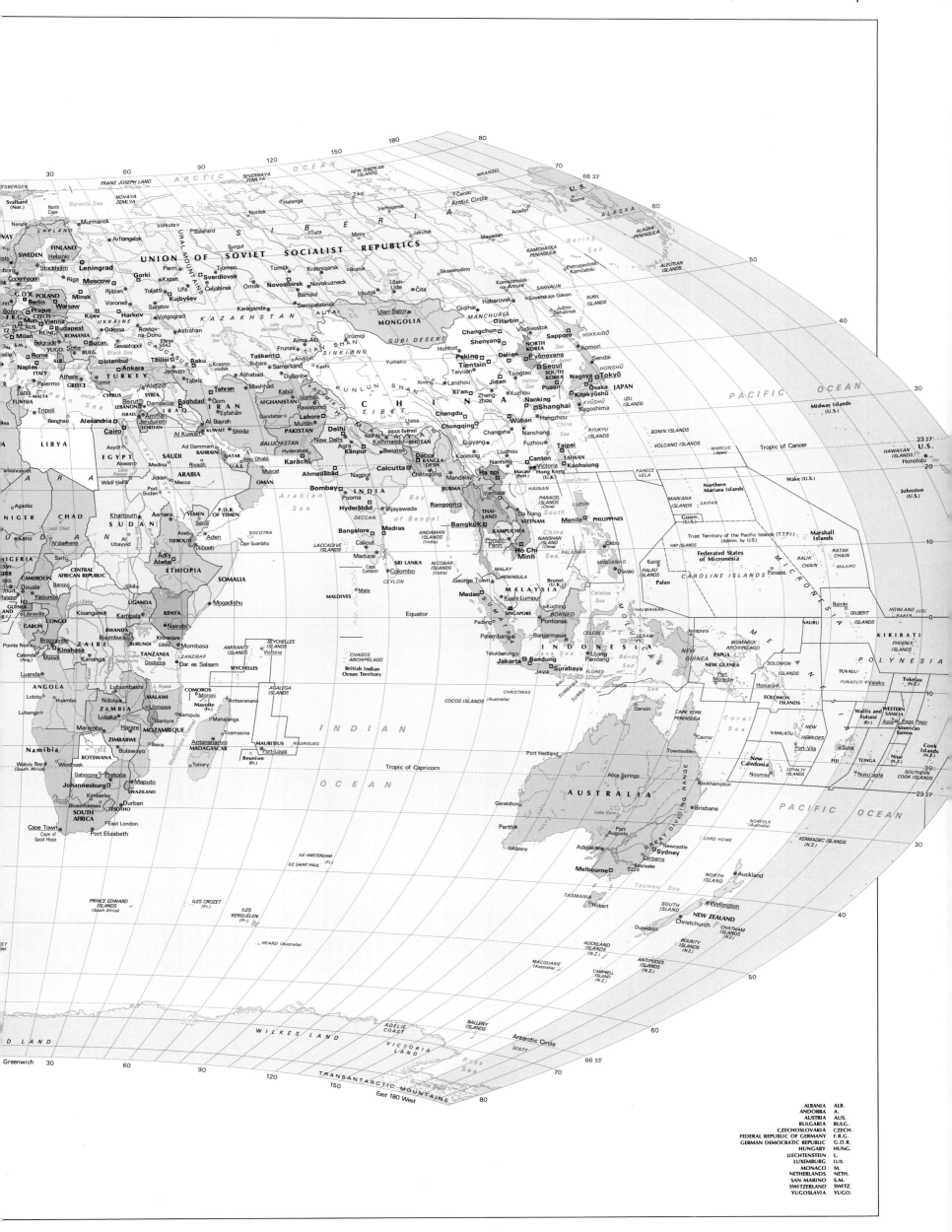

ARCTIC OCEAN
SEVERNAYA ZEMLYA
FRANZ JOSEPH LAND
NOVAYA ZEMLYA
NEW SIBERIAN ISLANDS
WRANGEL
Svalbard (Nor.)
Barents Sea
North Cape
Murmansk
LAPLAND
FINLAND
Helsinki
SWEDEN
Stockholm
Copenhagen
Leningrad
Riga
Moscow
Minsk
G.D.R.
POLAND
Berlin
Warsaw
Prague
CZECH.
Vienna
Budapest
HUNG.
ROMANIA
Bucar.
Belgrade
YUGO.
Sofia
BULG.
Rome
Naples
ITALY
Milan
Bonn
F.R.G.
Kijev
UKRAINE
Odessa
Sevastopol
Harkov
Voronež
Rjazan
Gorki
Kazan
Perm
Toljatti
Ufa
Kujbyšev
Saratov
Volgograd
Rostov-na-Donu
Astrahan
Elbrus 5642
Tbilisi
Baku
Krasnovodsk
Jerevan
Tabriz
Istanbul
Ankara
TURKEY
Izmir
Athens
GREECE
Palermo
Tunis
MALTA
TUNISIA
Tripoli
Benghazi
LIBYA
Alexandria
Cairo
EGYPT
Asyût
Aswan
Wâdi Halfa
CYPRUS
Beirut
LEBANON
ISRAEL
Jerusalem
Amman
JORDAN
SYRIA
Aleppo
Damascus
Baghdad
IRAQ
Qom
Tehran
IRAN
Esfahān
Mashhad
Ashabad
Al Basrah
KUWAIT
Al Kuwait
Shīrāz
SAUDI ARABIA
Ad Dammam
BAHRAIN
QATAR
Abu Dhabi
U.A.E.
Riyadh
Medina
Jiddah
Mecca
Muscat
OMAN
Port Sudan
Khartoum
SUDAN
Asmera
YEMEN
Sana
P.D.R. OF YEMEN
Aden
SOCOTRA
Cape Guardafui
Aseb
DJIBOUTI
Djibouti
Addis Abeba
ETHIOPIA
SOMALIA
Mogadishu
CHAD
N'djamena
NIGER
Kano
NIGERIA
CAMEROON
Douala
Yaoundé
CENTRAL AFRICAN REPUBLIC
Bangui
EQ. GUINEA
Libreville
GABON
CONGO
Brazzaville
Pointe Noire
Kinshasa
ZAIRE
Kisangani
Kananga
Cabinda (Ang.)
Matadi
Luanda
ANGOLA
Lobito
Huambo
Lubango
UGANDA
Kampala
KENYA
Nairobi
RWANDA
BURUNDI
Bujumbura
Kilimanjaro 5895
Mombasa
TANZANIA
Dodoma
Dar es Salaam
ZANZIBAR
Lubumbashi
Ndola
ZAMBIA
Lusaka
MALAWI
Lilongwe
Blantyre
Harare
ZIMBABWE
Bulawayo
Maramba
MOZAMBIQUE
Beira
Nampula
Maputo
SWAZILAND
Namibia
Walvis Bay (South Africa)
Windhoek
BOTSWANA
Gaborone
Pretoria
Johannesburg
Kimberley
LESOTHO
Bloemfontein
Durban
SOUTH AFRICA
East London
Cape Town
Cape of Good Hope
Port Elizabeth
COMOROS
Moroni
Mayotte (Fr.)
Antseranana
Mahajanga
Toamasina
Antananarivo
MADAGASCAR
Toliary
MAURITIUS
Port-Louis
RODRIGUES
Reunion (Fr.)
AMIRANTE ISLANDS
SEYCHELLES ISLANDS
Victoria
SEYCHELLES
AGALEGA ISLANDS
CHAGOS ARCHIPELAGO
British Indian Ocean Territory
INDIAN OCEAN
Tropic of Capricorn
Equator
UNION OF SOVIET SOCIALIST REPUBLICS
SIBERIA
URAL MOUNTAINS
Vorkuta
Salehard
Norilsk
Hatanga
Tiksi
Verhojansk
Tura
Mirny
Jakutsk
Magadan
Anadyr
Čerski
Arctic Circle
Surgut
Tjumen
Sverdlovsk
Čeljabinsk
Omsk
Tomsk
Novosibirsk
Novokuzneck
Barnaul
Krasnojarsk
Bratsk
Irkutsk
Ulan-Ude
Čita
Skovorodino
Komsomolsk-na-Amure
Habarovsk
Sovetskaja-Gavan
SAKHALIN
Južno-Sahalinsk
KURIL ISLANDS
KAMCHATKA PENINSULA
Petropavlovsk-Kamčatski
Bering Sea
Semipalatinsk
Karaganda
KAZAKHSTAN
Alma-Ata
Frunze
Taškent
Bukhara
Samarkand
Dušanbe
Andižan
Kashi
TIAN SHAN
SINKIANG
Ürümqi
ALTAI
Ulan-Bator
MONGOLIA
GOBI DESERT
Yumeno
Hohhot
KUNLUN SHAN
CHINA
TIBET
Lhasa
Xining
Lanzhou
Xi'an
Chengdu
Chongqing
Guiyang
Kunming
Nanning
Liuzhou
Changsha
Wuhan
Nanchang
Fuzhou
Canton
Hong Kong (U.K.)
Macao (Port.)
Victoria
Zhengzhou
Xuzhou
Nanking
Shanghai
Hangzhou
Jinan
Taiyuan
Peking
Tientsin
Tsingtao
Dalian
Shenyang
Changchun
Harbin
Qiqihar
MANCHURIA
Vladivostok
NORTH KOREA
P'yongyang
SOUTH KOREA
Seoul
Pusan
Sapporo
HOKKAIDŌ
Aomori
Sendai
HONSHŪ
Tokyō
Nagoya
Ōsaka
JAPAN
Kitakyūshū
KYŪSHŪ
Kagoshima
IZU ISLANDS
RYUKYU ISLANDS
BONIN ISLANDS
VOLCANO ISLANDS
MARCUS (Japan)
Taipei
TAIWAN
Kaohsiung
East China Sea
Yellow Sea
South China Sea
Sea of Japan
Sea of Okhotsk
HAINAN
PARACEL ISLANDS (China)
AFGHANISTAN
Kabul
Gandahar
Islamabad
Rawalpindi
Lahore
Multan
PAKISTAN
BALUCHISTAN
Hyderabad
Karāchi
KASHMIR
HIMALAYA
8848 Everest
NEPAL
Kathmandu
BHUTAN
Delhi
New Delhi
Agra
Kānpur
Benares
INDIA
Ahmadābād
Nagpur
Bombay
Poona
DECCAN
Hyderābād
Vijayawada
Bangalore
Madras
Calicut
Madurai
Cape Comorin
SRI LANKA
Colombo
CEYLON
LACCADIVE ISLANDS
MALDIVES
Male
Arabian Sea
Bay of Bengal
ANDAMAN ISLANDS (India)
NICOBAR ISLANDS (India)
Calcutta
Dacca
BANGLADESH
Chittagong
BURMA
Mandalay
Rangoon
THAILAND
Bangkok
Vientiane
Ha noi
Da Nang
VIETNAM
KAMPUCHEA
Phnum-Penh
Ho Chi Minh
NANSHAN ISLAND (China)
PALAWAN
LUZON
Manila
PHILIPPINES
Cebu
MINDANAO
Davao
MALAY PENINSULA
George Town
Medan
MALAYSIA
Kuala Lumpur
SINGAPORE
SUMATRA
Padang
Palembang
Brunei (U.K.)
Kuching
BORNEO
Pontianak
Banjarmasin
CELEBES
Celebes Sea
HALMAHERA
MOLUCCAS
CERAM
INDONESIA
Java Sea
Telukbetung
Jakarta
Bandung
JAVA
Surabaya
Ujung Pandang
BALI
SUMBAWA
FLORES
SUMBA
TIMOR
Banda Sea
Arafura Sea
CHRISTMAS
COCOS ISLANDS (Australia)
Jayapura
NEW GUINEA
PAPUA NEW GUINEA
Port Moresby
BISMARCK ARCHIPELAGO
SOLOMON ISLANDS
Honiara
CAPE YORK PENINSULA
Darwin
Coral Sea
Cairns
Townsville
AUSTRALIA
Port Hedland
Alice Springs
Rockhampton
GREAT DIVIDING RANGE
Brisbane
Geraldton
Perth
Albany
Lake Eyre
Port Augusta
Adelaide
Newcastle
Sydney
Canberra
Kosciusko 2228
Melbourne
TASMANIA
Hobart
Tasman Sea
LORD HOWE
NORFOLK (Australia)
KERMADEC ISLANDS (N.Z.)
NORTH ISLAND
Auckland
Wellington
SOUTH ISLAND
NEW ZEALAND
Christchurch
Dunedin
CHATHAM ISLANDS (N.Z.)
BOUNTY ISLANDS (N.Z.)
ANTIPODES ISLANDS (N.Z.)
AUCKLAND ISLANDS (N.Z.)
CAMPBELL ISLAND (N.Z.)
MACQUARIE (Australia)
ILE AMSTERDAM
ILE SAINT PAUL (Fr.)
PRINCE EDWARD ISLANDS (South Africa)
ILES CROZET (Fr.)
ILES KERGUELEN (Fr.)
HEARD (Australia)
WILKES LAND
ADELIE COAST
VICTORIA LAND
BALLENY ISLANDS
Antarctic Circle
SCOTT
Ross Sea
TRANSANTARCTIC MOUNTAINS
East 180 West
Greenwich
U.S.
ALASKA
Nome
ALASKA PENINSULA
ALEUTIAN ISLANDS
PACIFIC OCEAN
Midway Islands (U.S.)
Tropic of Cancer
HAWAIIAN ISLANDS
U.S.
Honolulu
Johnston (U.S.)
Wake (U.S.)
PARECE VELA
Northern Mariana Islands
MARIANA ISLANDS
SAIPAN
Guam (U.S.)
Trust Territory of the Pacific Islands (T.T.P.I.) (Admin. by U.S.)
YAP ISLANDS
Federated States of Micronesia
Koror
PALAU ISLANDS
Palau
CAROLINE ISLANDS
Ponape
MICRONESIA
Marshall Islands
RATAK CHAIN
RALIK CHAIN
MAJURO
Bairiki
GILBERT ISLANDS
HOWLAND (U.S.)
BAKER
NAURU
KIRIBATI
PHOENIX ISLANDS
MELANESIA
POLYNESIA
TUVALU
FUNAFUTI
Vaiaku
Tokelau (N.Z.)
Wallis and Futuna (Fr.)
WESTERN SAMOA
Apia
Pago Pago
American Samoa
VANUATU
NEW HEBRIDES
Port-Vila
FIJI
Suva
TONGA
Nuku'alofa
Niue (N.Z.)
Cook Islands (N.Z.)
SOUTHERN COOK ISLANDS
New Caledonia
Nouméa
LOYALTY ISLANDS
30
60
90
120
150
180
80
70
66 33'
60
50
40
30
23 27'
20
10
0
10
20
23 27'
30
40
50
60
66 33'
70
80
ALBANIA ALB.
ANDORRA A.
AUSTRIA AUS.
BULGARIA BULG.
CZECHOSLOVAKIA CZECH.
FEDERAL REPUBLIC OF GERMANY F.R.G.
GERMAN DEMOCRATIC REPUBLIC G.D.R.
HUNGARY HUNG.
LIECHTENSTEIN L.
LUXEMBURG LUX.
MONACO M.
NETHERLANDS NETH.
SAN MARINO S.M.
SWITZERLAND SWITZ.
YUGOSLAVIA YUGO.

Map 3 **THE OCEANS**

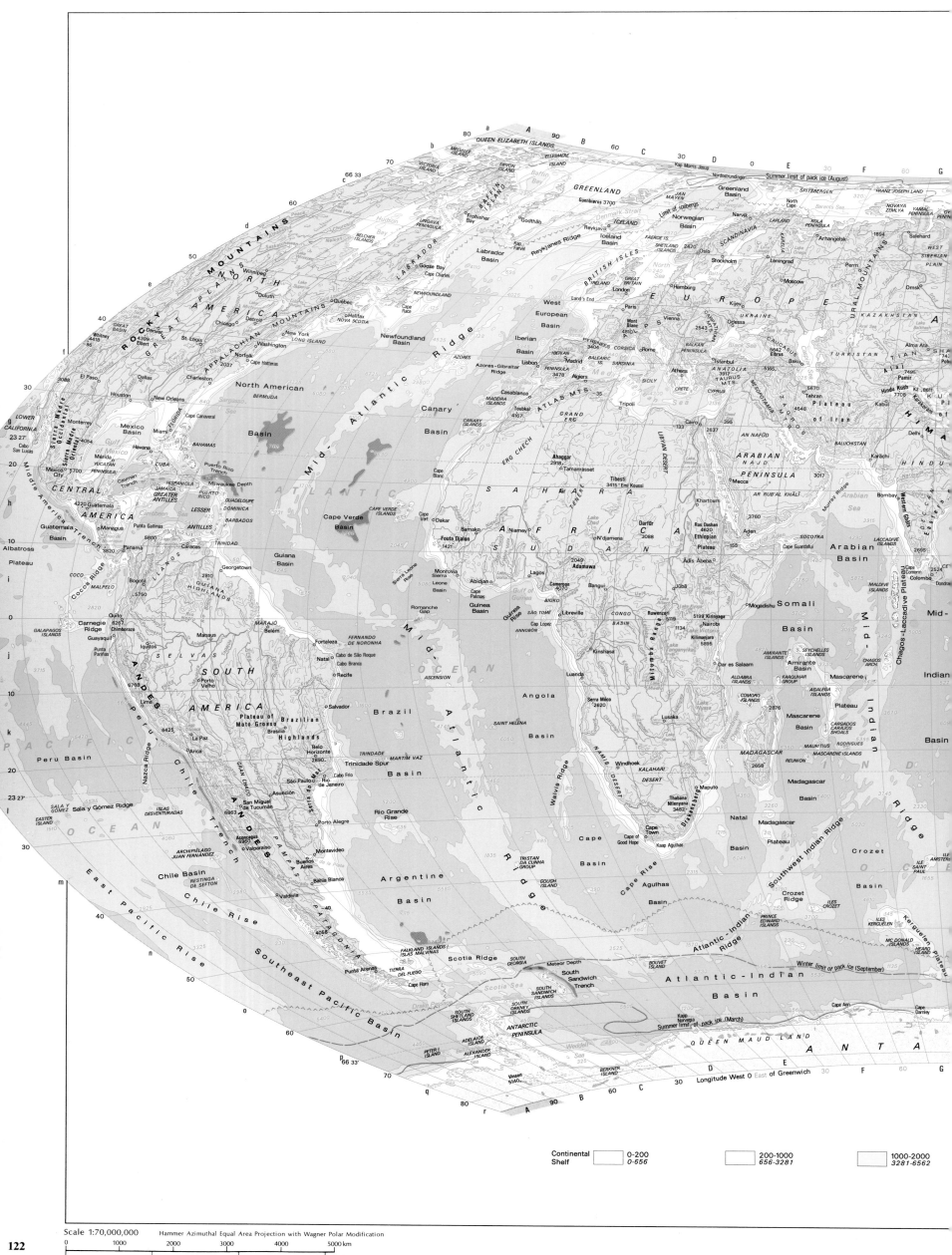

Continental Shelf		0-200		200-1000		1000-2000
		0-656		656-3281		3281-6562

Scale 1:70,000,000   Hammer Azimuthal Equal Area Projection with Wagner Polar Modification

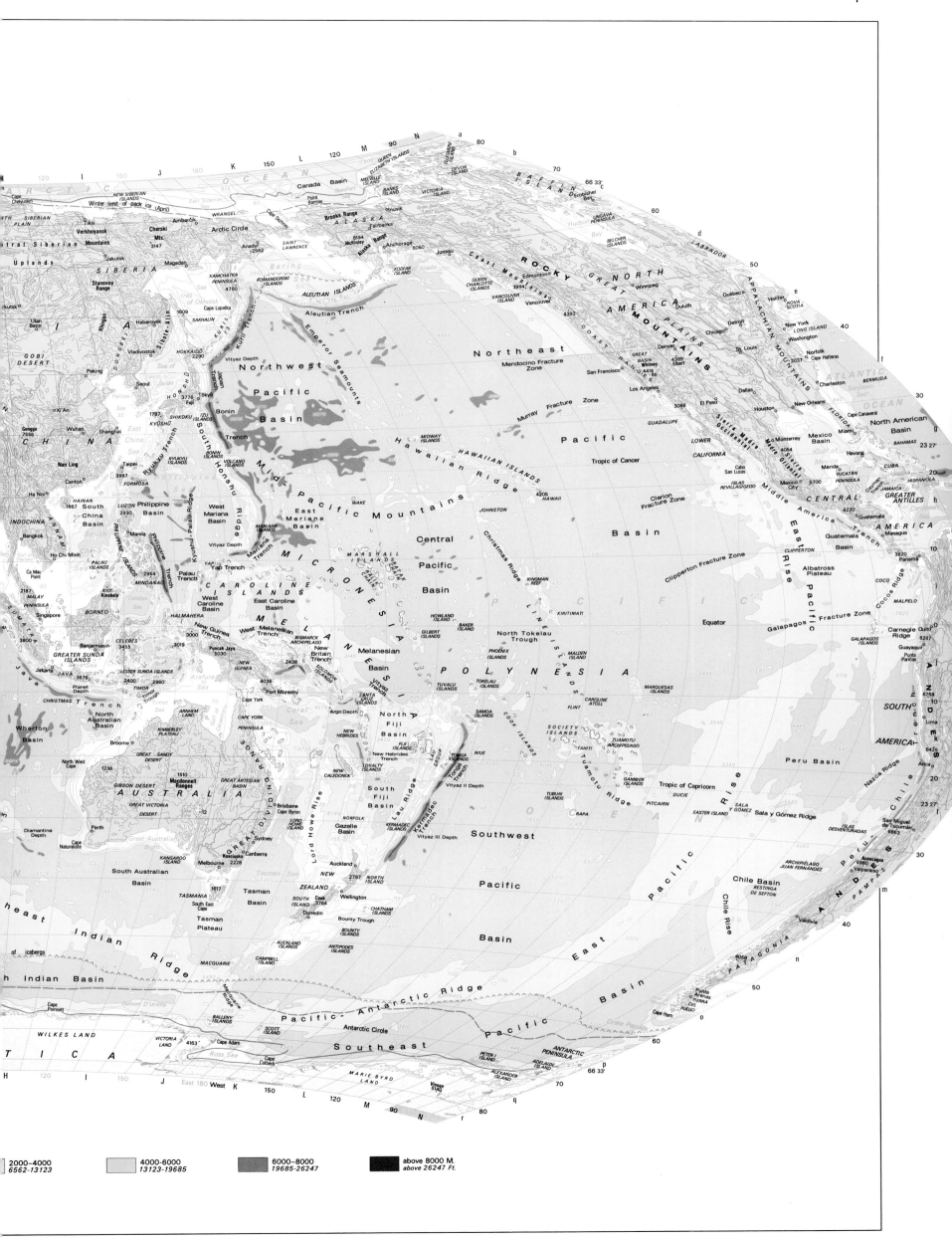

2000–4000 6562-13123	4000–6000 13123-19685	6000–8000 19685-26247	above 8000 M. above 26247 Ft.	

Map 4 **WORLD TRANSPORTATION AND TIME ZONES**

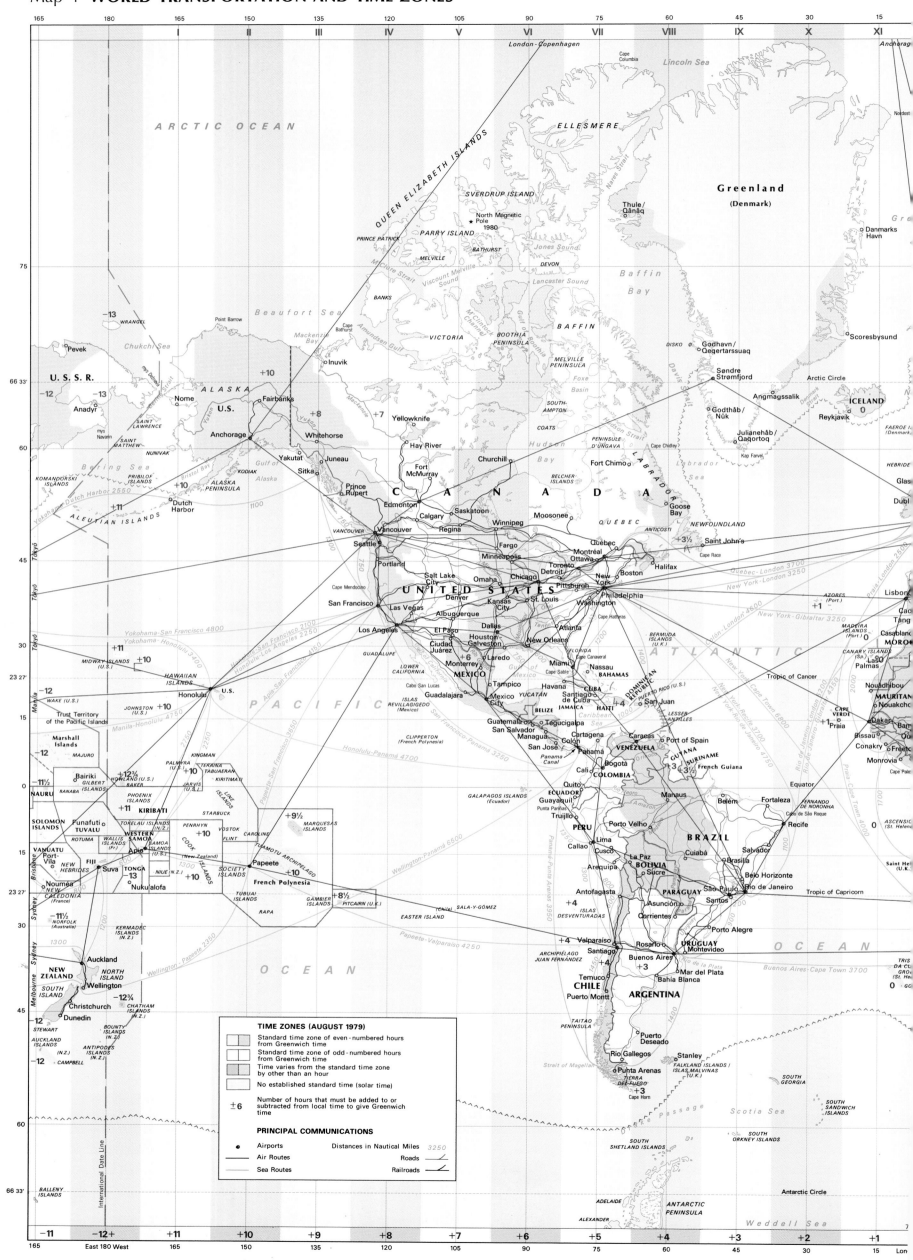

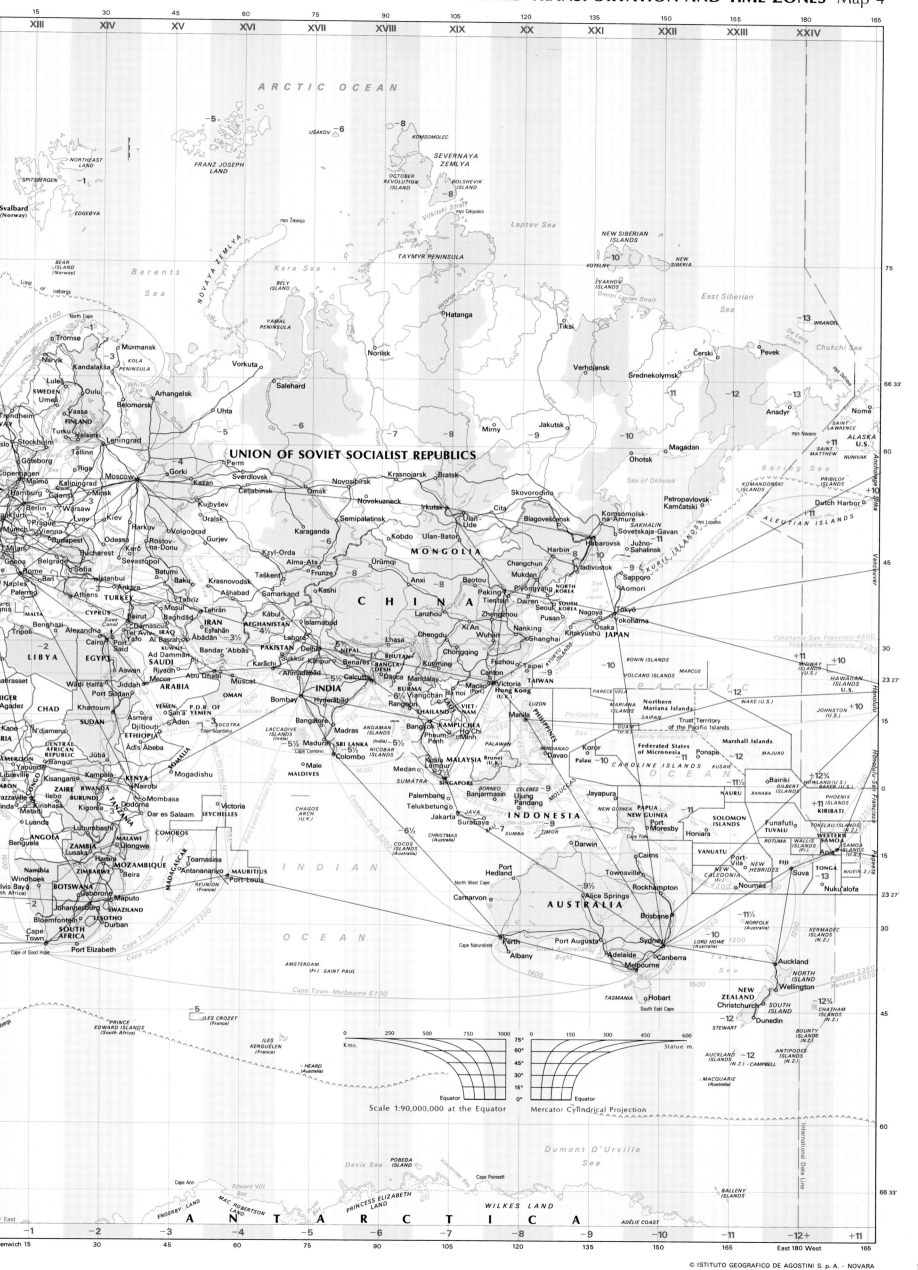
ARCTIC OCEAN
FRANZ JOSEPH LAND
SEVERNAYA ZEMLYA
OCTOBER REVOLUTION ISLAND
BOLSHEVIK ISLAND
KOMSOMOLEC
NORTHEAST LAND
SPITSBERGEN
Svalbard (Norway)
EDGEØYA
BEAR ISLAND (Norway)
Barents Sea
Kara Sea
NOVAYA ZEMLYA
TAYMYR PENINSULA
Laptev Sea
NEW SIBERIAN ISLANDS
NEW SIBERIA
East Siberian Sea
WRANGEL
Chukchi Sea
Bering Sea
UNION OF SOVIET SOCIALIST REPUBLICS
Murmansk
Arhangelsk
Vorkuta
Salehard
Norilsk
Hatanga
Tiksi
Verhojansk
Srednekolymsk
Čerski
Pevek
Anadyr
Nome
Jakutsk
Mirny
Magadan
Ohotsk
Sea of Okhotsk
Petropavlovsk-Kamčatski
KOMANDORSKI ISLANDS
ALEUTIAN ISLANDS
Dutch Harbor
ALASKA U.S.
Leningrad
Moscow
Gorki
Perm
Sverdlovsk
Kazan
Čeljabinsk
Omsk
Novosibirsk
Novokuzneck
Krasnojarsk
Bratsk
Irkutsk
Ulan-Ude
Cita
Skovorodino
Blagoveščensk
Komsomolsk-na-Amure
Habarovsk
Sovetskaja-Gavan
SAKHALIN
Južno-Sahalinsk
KURIL ISLANDS
Vladivostok
Harbin
Changchun
Mukden
Kujbyšev
Uralsk
Volgograd
Rostov-na-Donu
Gurjev
Karaganda
Semipalatinsk
Kzyl-Orda
Alma-Ata
Frunze
Taškent
Samarkand
Ašhabad
Krasnovodsk
Baku
Batumi
Kiev
Harkov
Odessa
Sevastopol
Minsk
Kaliningrad
Riga
Tallinn
Helsinki
FINLAND
SWEDEN
Stockholm
Göteborg
Copenhagen
Malmö
Gdańsk
Berlin
Warsaw
Lvov
Prague
Munich
Vienna
Budapest
Bucharest
Belgrade
Sofia
Istanbul
Ankara
Athens
TURKEY
Rome
Naples
Bari
Genoa
Milan
Palermo
MALTA
CYPRUS
Beirut
Damascus
Tel Aviv-Yafo
Baghdad
IRAQ
IRAN
Tehrān
Esfahān
Ābādān
Al Başrah
KUWAIT
Bandar 'Abbās
Ad Dammām
SAUDI ARABIA
Riyadh
Mecca
Jiddah
Abu Dhabi
Muscat
OMAN
YEMEN
P.D.R. OF YEMEN
Aden
SOCOTRA
AFGHANISTAN
Kābul
Islamabad
Lahore
PAKISTAN
Karāchi
Sukkur
Delhi
Kanpur
Ahmadabad
Bombay
Hyderabad
Bangalore
Madras
Madurai
INDIA
NEPAL
BHUTAN
BANGLADESH
Dacca
Calcutta
Benares
Lhasa
SRI LANKA
Colombo
MALDIVES
Male
LACCADIVE ISLANDS (India)
ANDAMAN ISLANDS (India)
NICOBAR ISLANDS
CHINA
MONGOLIA
Ulan-Bator
Kobdo
Ürümqi
Kashi
Anxi
Lanzhou
Baotou
Peking
Tientsin
Dairen
Xi'An
Zhengzhou
Nanking
Shanghai
Wuhan
Chengdu
Chongqing
Kunming
Fuzhou
Canton
Victoria
Hong Kong (U.K.)
Macao (Port.)
Taipei
TAIWAN
Pyŏngyang
NORTH KOREA
Seoul
SOUTH KOREA
Pusan
JAPAN
Tōkyō
Yokohama
Nagoya
Osaka
Kitakyūshū
Sapporo
Aomori
BURMA
Mandalay
Rangoon
Viangchan
LAOS
Ha noi
VIET-NAM
THAILAND
Bangkok
KAMPUCHEA
Phnum-Pénh
Ho Chi Minh
MALAYSIA
Kuala Lumpur
SINGAPORE
Brunei (U.K.)
Medan
SUMATRA
Palembang
Telukbetung
Jakarta
JAVA
Surabaya
BALI
BORNEO
Banjarmasin
CELEBES
Ujung Pandang
INDONESIA
MOLUCCAS
SUMBA
TIMOR
PHILIPPINES
LUZON
Manila
MINDANAO
Davao
NEW GUINEA
Jayapura
PAPUA NEW GUINEA
Port Moresby
SOLOMON ISLANDS
Honiara
Koror
Palau
Federated States of Micronesia
CAROLINE ISLANDS
Ponape
KUSAIE
Marshall Islands
MAJURO
NAURU
BANABA
GILBERT ISLANDS
Bairiki
KIRIBATI
PHOENIX ISLANDS
HOWLAND (U.S.)
BAKER (U.S.)
TUVALU
Funafuti
TOKELAU ISLANDS (N.Z.)
WESTERN SAMOA
Apia
SAMOA ISLANDS (U.S.)
WALLIS ISLANDS (Fr.)
ROTUMA
FIJI
Suva
TONGA
Nuku'alofa
NIUE (N.Z.)
VANUATU
Port-Vila
NEW HEBRIDES
NEW CALEDONIA (Fr.)
Nouméa
Northern Mariana Islands
MARIANA ISLANDS
SAIPAN
GUAM (U.S.)
Trust Territory of the Pacific Islands
WAKE (U.S.)
JOHNSTON (U.S.)
MIDWAY ISLANDS (U.S.)
HAWAIIAN ISLANDS U.S.
BONIN ISLANDS
VOLCANO ISLANDS
MARCUS
RYUKYU ISLANDS
PACIFIC OCEAN
AUSTRALIA
Darwin
Cairns
Townsville
Rockhampton
Brisbane
Sydney
Canberra
Melbourne
Adelaide
Port Augusta
Perth
Albany
Port Hedland
Carnarvon
Alice Springs
Cape York
Great Australian Bight
TASMANIA
Hobart
South East Cape
NORFOLK (Australia)
LORD HOWE (Australia)
Tasman Sea
NEW ZEALAND
NORTH ISLAND
SOUTH ISLAND
Auckland
Wellington
Christchurch
Dunedin
STEWART
CHATHAM ISLANDS (N.Z.)
KERMADEC ISLANDS (N.Z.)
BOUNTY ISLANDS (N.Z.)
ANTIPODES ISLANDS (N.Z.)
AUCKLAND ISLANDS (N.Z.)
CAMPBELL
MACQUARIE (Australia)
LIBYA
Tripoli
Benghazi
Alexandria
Cairo
Port Said
Suez Canal
EGYPT
Aswan
Wadi Halfa
Port Sudan
Khartoum
SUDAN
CHAD
N'djamena
NIGER
Agadez
ETHIOPIA
Asmera
Djibouti
Ādis Ābeba
SOMALIA
Mogadishu
KENYA
Nairobi
Mombasa
Kampala
TANZANIA
Dodoma
Dar es Salaam
Kigoma
RWANDA
BURUNDI
ZAIRE
Kisangani
Kinshasa
Matadi
CENTRAL AFRICAN REPUBLIC
Bangui
Libreville
Yaoundé
Luanda
ANGOLA
Benguela
Lubumbashi
ZAMBIA
Lusaka
MALAWI
Lilongwe
ZIMBABWE
Harare
MOZAMBIQUE
Beira
Maputo
SWAZILAND
LESOTHO
Durban
BOTSWANA
Gaborone
Namibia
Windhoek
Johannesburg
Bloemfontein
SOUTH AFRICA
Cape Town
Port Elizabeth
Cape of Good Hope
MADAGASCAR
Antananarivo
Toamasina
MAURITIUS
Port-Louis
REUNION (France)
SEYCHELLES
Victoria
COMOROS
CHAGOS ARCH. (U.K.)
COCOS ISLANDS (Australia)
CHRISTMAS (Australia)
INDIAN OCEAN
AMSTERDAM (Fr.)
SAINT PAUL
PRINCE EDWARD ISLANDS (South Africa)
ILES CROZET (France)
ILES KERGUELEN (France)
HEARD (Australia)
Scale 1:90,000,000 at the Equator
Mercator Cylindrical Projection
Kms.
Statue m.
Equator
Dumont D'Urville Sea
Davis Sea
POBEDA ISLAND
Cape Poinsett
Cape Ann
ENDERBY LAND
MAC ROBERTSON LAND
PRINCESS ELIZABETH LAND
WILKES LAND
ADÉLIE COAST
BALLENY ISLANDS
ANTARCTICA
International Date Line
East 180 West
Cape Town-Melbourne 6100
Colombo-Perth 3250
Yokohama-San Francisco 4800
Yokohama-Honolulu 3400
Manila-Honolulu 4750
Honolulu-San Francisco
Anchorage-Sitka
Papeete
Honolulu
Vancouver

Map 5 **EUROPE, PHYSICAL**

GREENLAND

KING FREDERIK VI COAST

KING CHRISTIAN IX LAND

GREENLAND SEA

JAN MAYEN

Mohns Ridge

Denmark Strait

Limit of icebergs

Limit of pack ice (April)

ICELAND

Reykjavík

VATNAJÖKULL

Reykjanes Ridge

Iceland Basin

Iceland-Faeroe Ridge

FAEROE ISLANDS

Arctic Circle

NORWEGIAN SEA

Norwegian Basin

LOFOTEN

VESTERÅLEN

Trondheimsfjord

Trondheim

Ålesund

Dovrefjell

Jotunheimen Glittertind

Bergen

Oslo

Kristiansand

NORWAY

SVEALAND

GÖTALAND

Göteborg

Norwegian Trench

Skagerrak

Kattegat

Ålborg

København Copenhagen

SKÅNE

Malmö

BORNHOLM

MID-ATLANTIC RIDGE

ATLANTIC OCEAN

WEST EUROPEAN BASIN

SHETLAND ISLANDS

ORKNEY ISLANDS

Rockall Rise

Rockall

Porcupine Bank

BRITISH ISLES

HEBRIDES

LEWIS

SKYE

MULL

ISLAY

GRAMPIAN MTS.

Glasgow

Edinburgh

Southern Uplands

Moray Firth

Aberdeen

NORTH SEA

IRELAND

Ireland Trough

Galway Bay

Dublin

Belfast

Cork

MAN

ANGLESEY

PENNINES

Liverpool

Snowdon

WALES

Birmingham

Cambrian Mts.

Bristol

London

GREAT BRITAIN

ENGLAND

CELTIC SEA

Saint George's Channel

Land's End

ISLES OF SCILLY

CORNWALL

ENGLISH CHANNEL

Dover Strait

Calais

WIGHT

FRISIAN ISLANDS

FRIESLAND

Amsterdam

Rotterdam

Hamburg

Kiel

RÜGEN

POMERANIA

GERMAN PLAIN

Berlin

Poznań

NORTH EUROPEAN PLAIN

SILESIA

Wrocław Breslau

Leipzig

HARZ

SUDETEN

ARDENNES

Bruxelles Bruxelles

Köln

Bonn

RHENISH SLATE MOUNTAINS

Frankfurt

Luxembourg

Le Havre

NORMANDY

BRITTANY

Armorican Massif

Brittany Hills

Brest

Pointe de Saint-Mathieu

BELLE ILE

ÎLE DE RÉ

ÎLE D'OLÉRON

Nantes

PARIS BASIN

Paris

Orléans

CHAMPAGNE

VOSGES

BLACK FOREST

THURINGIA

Ore Mountains

Praha Prague

BOHEMIA

MORAVIA

BOHEMIAN FOREST

SWABIAN JURA

München Munich

BAVARIA

BAVARIAN PLATEAU

Wien Vienna

AZORES

GRACIOSA

SÃO JORGE

TERCEIRA

PICO

FAIAL

SÃO MIGUEL

Ponta Delgada

SANTA MARIA

Iberian Basin

Azores-Gibraltar Ridge

Faraday Seamounts

Josephine Seamount

Ampère Seamount

Seine Seamount

PORTO SANTO

MADEIRA ISLANDS

Funchal

ILHAS DESERTAS

Dacia Seamount

CANARY ISLANDS

LA PALMA

GOMERA

HIERRO

TENERIFE

Santa Cruz de Tenerife

Las Palmas de Gran Canaria

GRAN CANARIA

LANZAROTE

FUERTEVENTURA

ILHAS SELVAGENS

Bay of Biscay

La Coruña

Cabo de Finisterre

Estaca de Bares

Picos de Europa

GALICIA

CANTABRIAN MTS.

Bilbao

AQUITAINE BASIN

Bordeaux

Toulouse

MASSIF CENTRAL

Cévennes

LANGUEDOC

PROVENCE

Marseille

Gulf of Lions

CÔTE D'AZUR

JURA

Bern

Mont Blanc

ALPS

Genève Geneva

Milano Milan

PO VALLEY

Torino Turin

Venezia Venice

Gulf of Venice

ISTRIA

SLOVENIA

CROATIA

CARPATHIANS

DINARIC ALPS

ADRIATIC SEA

DALMATIA

BOSNIA

HERZEGOVINA

CORSICA

Monte Cinto

Ajaccio

SARDINIA

Cagliari

ASINARA

TUSCAN ARCHIPELAGO

ELBA

Gran Sasso d'Italia

APENNINES

Roma Rome

Bologna

Ancona

Napoli Naples

Vesuvius

TYRRHENIAN SEA

Tyrrhenian Basin

ARCIPELAGO CAMPANO

LIPARI ISLANDS

USTICA

EGADI ISLANDS

Palermo

Messina

Etna

SICILY

Capo Spartivento

GOZO

MALTA

PANTELLERIA

PELAGIE ISLANDS

KERKENNAH ISLANDS

DJERBA

Gulf of Gabès

TRIPOLITANIA

Tripoli

Tarābulus

GEFARA

JABAL NAFŪSAH

AL HAMĀDAH AL HAMRĀ

PORTUGAL

Porto

Douro

SERRA DA ESTRELA

Cabo da Roca

Lisboa Lisbon

ALGARVE

Cabo de São Vicente

IBERIAN PENINSULA

SUBMESETA NORTE

SUBMESETA SUR

SISTEMA CENTRAL

Madrid

IBERIAN MOUNTAINS

ARAGON

Serranía de Cuenca

LA MANCHA

CATALONIA

Catalan Coastal Range

Barcelona

Cabo de Creus

Valencia

Gulf of Valencia

BALEARIC ISLANDS

MINORCA

MAJORCA

IBIZA

FORMENTERA

Palma

Cabo de la Nao

SIERRA MORENA

Guadalquivir

Sevilla Seville

ANDALUSIA

SISTEMAS BÉTICOS

SIERRA NEVADA

Mulhacén

Murcia

Cabo de Palos

Cádiz

Málaga

Cabo de Gata

Cabo Spartel

Tangier

Ceuta

ISLA DE ALBORÁN

MEDITERRANEAN

Gibraltar

Oran

ALGERIAN BASIN

Algiers

Al Jazā'ir

Cap Bon

Tunis

Constantine

MONTS DE LA MEDJERDA

MASSIF DE L'AURÈS

TELL ATLAS

ATLAS MOUNTAINS

SAHARAN ATLAS

HAUTS PLATEAUX

RIF

Meknès

Rabat

Casablanca

Safi

Marrakech

MIDDLE ATLAS

HIGH ATLAS

ANTI ATLAS

JBEL BANI

JBEL OUARKZIZ

HAMADA DU DRAA

Agadir

El Aaiún

Cabo Bojador

Dakhla

GRAND ERG OCCIDENTAL

GRAND ERG ORIENTAL

Touggourt

El Goléa

Béchar

Scale 1:15,000,000

Lambert Azimuthal Equal Area Projection

0   200   400   600   800   1000 km

0   250   500 miles

Longitude East 0 of Greenwich

BARENTS SEA
KARA SEA
NOVAYA ZEMLYA
YAMAL PENINSULA
KOLA PENINSULA
KANIN PENINSULA
WHITE SEA
LAPLAND
KARELIA
SUOMENSELKÄ
SALPAUSSELKÄ
ESTONIA
LIVONIA
INGERMANLAND
TIMAN RIDGE
URAL MOUNTAINS
POLAR URALS
SUBPOLAR URALS
NORTHERN URALS
CENTRAL URALS
SOUTHERN URALS
NORTHERN UVALS
WEST SIBERIAN PLAIN
ISHIM STEPPE
VALDAI HILLS
MOSCOW UPLAND
MOSCOW BASIN
SMOLENSK MOSCOW UPLAND
CENTRAL RUSSIAN UPLAND
VOLGA HILLS
OBŠČI SYRT
MUGODŽARY
TURGAI UPLAND
TURGAI GATES
KAZAKH HILLS
KAZAKHSTAN
BETPAK-DALA
KIRGHIZ STEPPE
CASPIAN DEPRESSION
POLESYE
PRIPET MARSHES
VOHYNIA
UKRAINE
DNEPR UPLAND
DON UPLAND
DONEC RIDGE
JERGENI
VOLGA DELTA
BUZACHI PENINSULA
MANGISTAU
USTJURT PLATO
WESTERN TURKISTAN
KYZYLKUM
KARAKUMY
CARPATHIAN MOUNTAINS
TRANSYLVANIAN ALPS
WALACHIA
CRIMEA
SEA OF AZOV
CISCAUCASIA
CAUCASUS
TRANSCAUCASIA
LESSER CAUCASUS
GEORGIA
CASPIAN SEA
APSHERON PENINSULA
KRASNOVODSKIJ PENINSULA
KOPETDAG
ELBURZ MOUNTAINS
BLACK SEA
BALKAN MTS.
RHODOPE MTS.
THRACE
ANATOLIA
ARMENIA
KURDISTAN
AZERBAIJAN
TAURUS MOUNTAINS
MESOPOTAMIA
AL JAZĪRAH
PLATEAU OF IRAN
DASHT-E KAVĪR
DASHT-E LŪT
KHORASAN
ZAGROS MTS.
LORESTĀN
KHŪZESTĀN
FARS
LĀRESTĀN
SYRIAN DESERT
AL WIDYĀN
AL HAMĀD
AN NAFŪD
PERSIAN GULF
AL HASA
QATAR
BAHRAIN
CYPRUS
CRETE
RHODES
KARPATHOS
KYTHERA
LEBANON
PALESTINE
SINAI PENINSULA
EL TIH DESERT
NILE DELTA
MARMARICA
QATTARA DEPRESSION
JARABUB OASIS

M	Ft
5000	16404
4000	13123
3000	9843
2000	6562
1000	3281
500	1640
+200	+656
0 Depr. 0	
-100	-328
200	656
1000	3281
2000	6562
4000	13123

Map 6 EUROPE, POLITICAL

Greenland (Den.)

ICELAND

NORWAY

SWEDEN

DENMARK

IRELAND

UNITED KINGDOM

NETHERLANDS

BELGIUM

LUXEMBOURG

GERMAN FED. REP. OF GERMANY

GERMAN DEM. REP.

CZECHOSLOVAKIA

FRANCE

SWITZERLAND

LIECHTENSTEIN

AUSTRIA

PORTUGAL

SPAIN

ANDORRA

ITALY

VATICAN CITY

SAN MARINO

MONACO

YUGOSLAVIA

MOROCCO

WESTERN SAHARA

ALGERIA

TUNISIA

TRIPOLITANIA

LIBYA

ATLANTIC OCEAN

Azores (Portugal)

Madeira (Portugal)

Canary Islands (Spain)

ATLAS MOUNTAINS

MEDITERRANEAN SEA

Scale 1:15,000,000   Lambert Azimuthal Equal Area Projection

0 200 400 600 800 1000 km

0 250 500 miles

Longitude East 10 of Greenwich

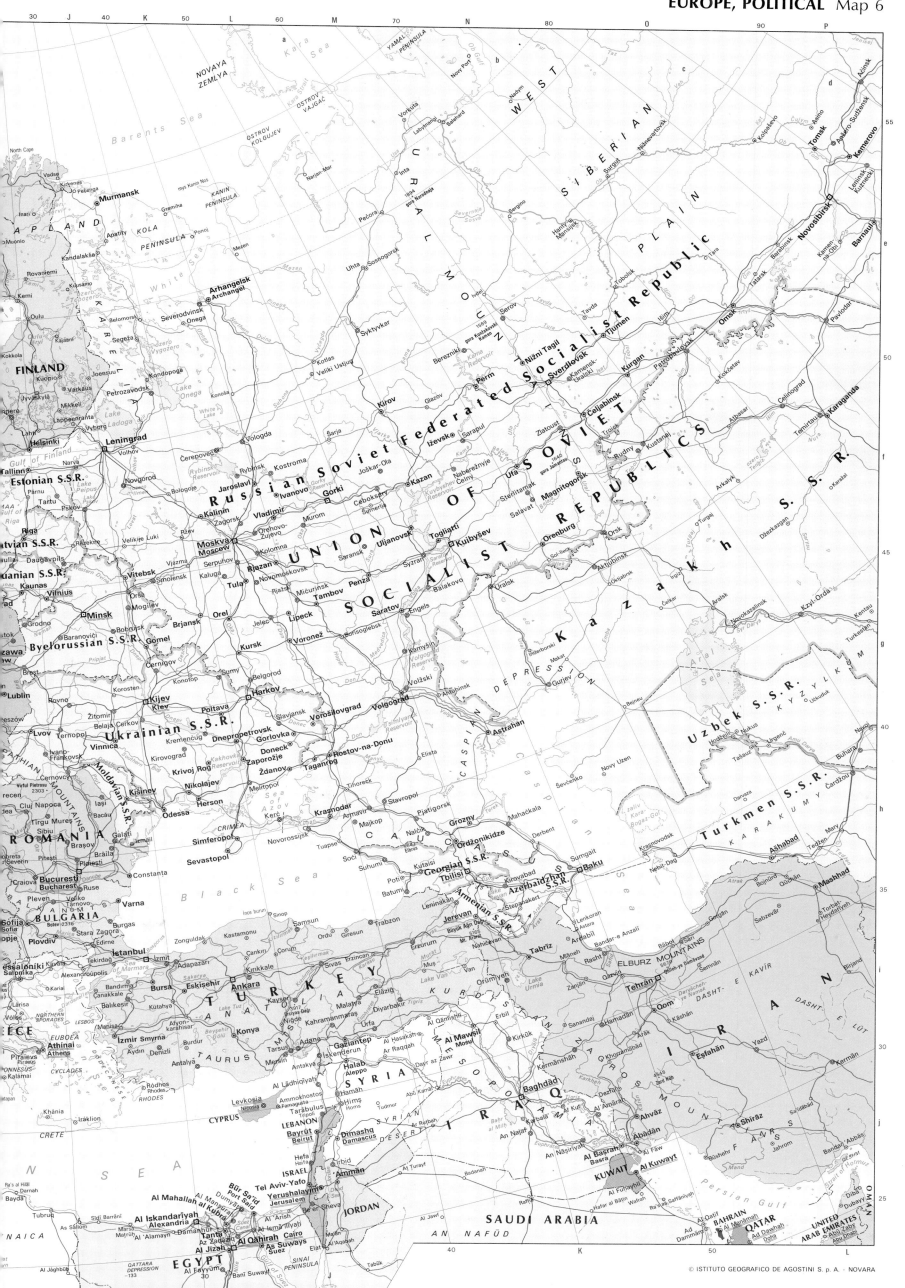
Barents Sea
Kara Sea
NOVAYA ZEMLYA
WEST SIBERIAN PLAIN
URAL MOUNTAINS
Russian Soviet Federated Socialist Republic
UNION OF SOVIET SOCIALIST REPUBLICS
Kazakh S.S.R.
Uzbek S.S.R.
Turkmen S.S.R.
Ukrainian S.S.R.
Byelorussian S.S.R.
Estonian S.S.R.
Moldavian S.S.R.
Georgian S.S.R.
Armenian S.S.R.
Azerbaidzhan S.S.R.
FINLAND
ROMANIA
BULGARIA
TURKEY
SYRIA
IRAQ
IRAN
CYPRUS
LEBANON
ISRAEL
JORDAN
EGYPT
KUWAIT
SAUDI ARABIA
BAHRAIN
QATAR
UNITED ARAB EMIRATES
Black Sea
Caspian Sea
Aral Sea
White Sea
Persian Gulf
CAUCASUS
CASPIAN DEPRESSION
ELBURZ MOUNTAINS
ZAGROS MOUNTAINS
TAURUS
ANATOLIA
KURDISTAN
MESOPOTAMIA
SYRIAN DESERT
AN NAFŪD
KYZYLKUM
KARAKUMY
DASHT-E KAVĪR
DASHT-E LŪT
Moskva Moscow
Leningrad
Kijev Kiev
Helsinki
Tallinn
Riga
Vilnius
Minsk
Kišinev
Bucureşti Bucharest
Sofija Sofia
Istanbul
Ankara
Tbilisi
Jerevan
Baku
Tehrān
Baghdād
Dimashq Damascus
Bayrūt Beirut
'Ammān
Al Qāhirah Cairo
Al Kuwayt
Murmansk
Arhangelsk Archangel
Volgograd
Sverdlovsk
Novosibirsk
Omsk
Gorki
Kazan
Kuibyšev
Harkov
Odessa
Rostov-na-Donu
Astrahan
Mashhad
Esfahān
Shīrāz
Tabrīz
Ashabad
Karaganda
Tomsk
Kemerovo
Barnaul

Map 7 **NORTHERN EUROPE**

ÍSLAND ICELAND

ATLANTSHAF
ATLANTIC OCEAN

Long. West 20 of Greenwich

West 0 East

**NORGE
NORWAY**

**SVERIGE
SWEDEN**

SUOM

FINLA

**DANMARK
DENMARK**

**BUNDESREPUBLIK
DEUTSCHLAND
FEDERAL REPUBLIC OF GERMANY**

HAMBURG

BREMEN

HANNOVER

BERLIN

**DEUTSCHE
DEMOKRATISCHE
REPUBLIK
GERMAN DEMOCRATIC REPUBLIC**

**POLSKA
POLAND**

SZCZECIN STETTIN

BYDGOSZCZ

**KØBENHAVN
COPENHAGEN**

**GDAŃSK
DANZIG**

KALININGRAD

KAUNAS

VILNIUS

MINSK

**Lietuvos TSR
Lithuanian SSR**

**Latvijas PSR
Latvian SSR**

RĪGA

TALLINN

**Eesti NSV
Estonian SSR**

Tartu

**HELSINKI/
HELSINGFORS**

STOCKHOLM

OSLO

GÖTEBORG

Scale 1:6,000,000

Delisle Conic Equidistant Projection

M Ft
2000 6562
1000 3281
500 1640
200 656
+100 +328
Depr. 0
−100 −328
200 656
1000 3281
2000 6562

0   100   200   300   400 km

0   100   200 miles

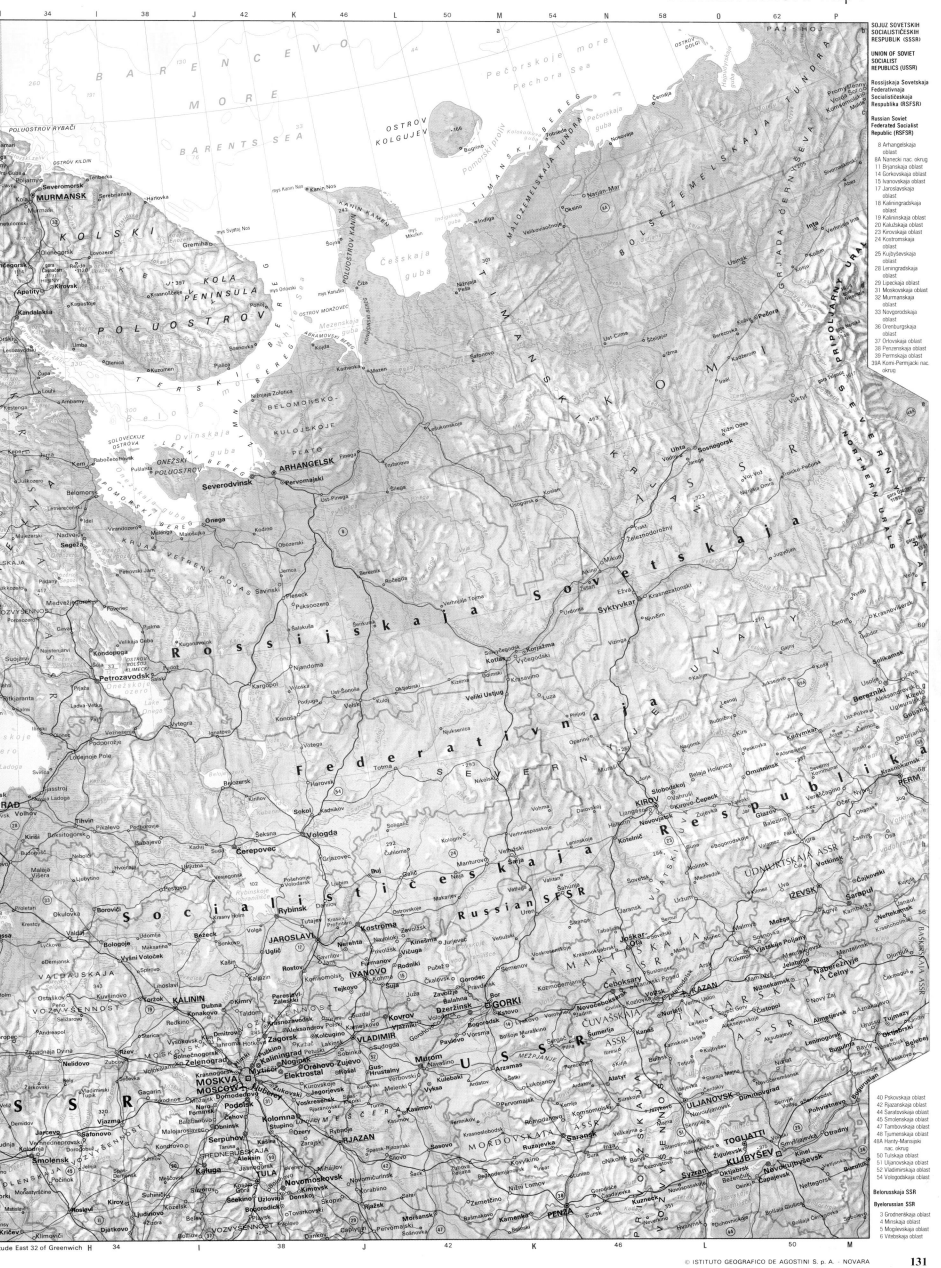

SOJUZ SOVETSKIH
SOCIALISTIČESKIH
RESPUBLIK (SSSR)

UNION OF SOVIET
SOCIALIST
REPUBLICS (USSR)

Rossijskaja Sovetskaja
Federativnaja
Socialističeskaja
Respublika (RSFSR)

Russian Soviet
Federated Socialist
Republic (RSFSR)

8 Arhangelskaja
  oblast
8A Naneckei nac. okrug
11 Brjanskaja oblast
14 Gorkovskaja oblast
15 Ivanovskaja oblast
17 Jaroslavskaja
  oblast
18 Kaliningradskaja
  oblast
19 Kalininskaja oblast
20 Kalužskaja oblast
23 Kirovskaja oblast
24 Kostromskaja oblast
25 Kujbyševskaja
  oblast
26 Leningradskaja
  oblast
29 Lipeckaja oblast
30 Moskovskaja oblast
31 Murmanskaja
  oblast
33 Novgorodskaja
  oblast
36 Orenburgskaja
  oblast
37 Orlovskaja oblast
38 Penzenskaja oblast
39 Permskaja oblast
39A Komi-Permjacki nac.
  okrug

40 Pskovskaja oblast
42 Rjazanskaja oblast
44 Saratovskaja oblast
45 Smolenskaja oblast
47 Tambovskaja oblast
48 Tjumenskaja oblast
48A Hanty-Mansijski
  nac. okrug
50 Tulskaja oblast
51 Uljanovskaja oblast
52 Vladimirskaja oblast
54 Vologodskaja oblast

Belorusskaja SSR

Byelorussian SSR

3 Grodnenskaja oblast
4 Minskaja oblast
5 Mogilevskaja oblast
6 Vitebskaja oblast

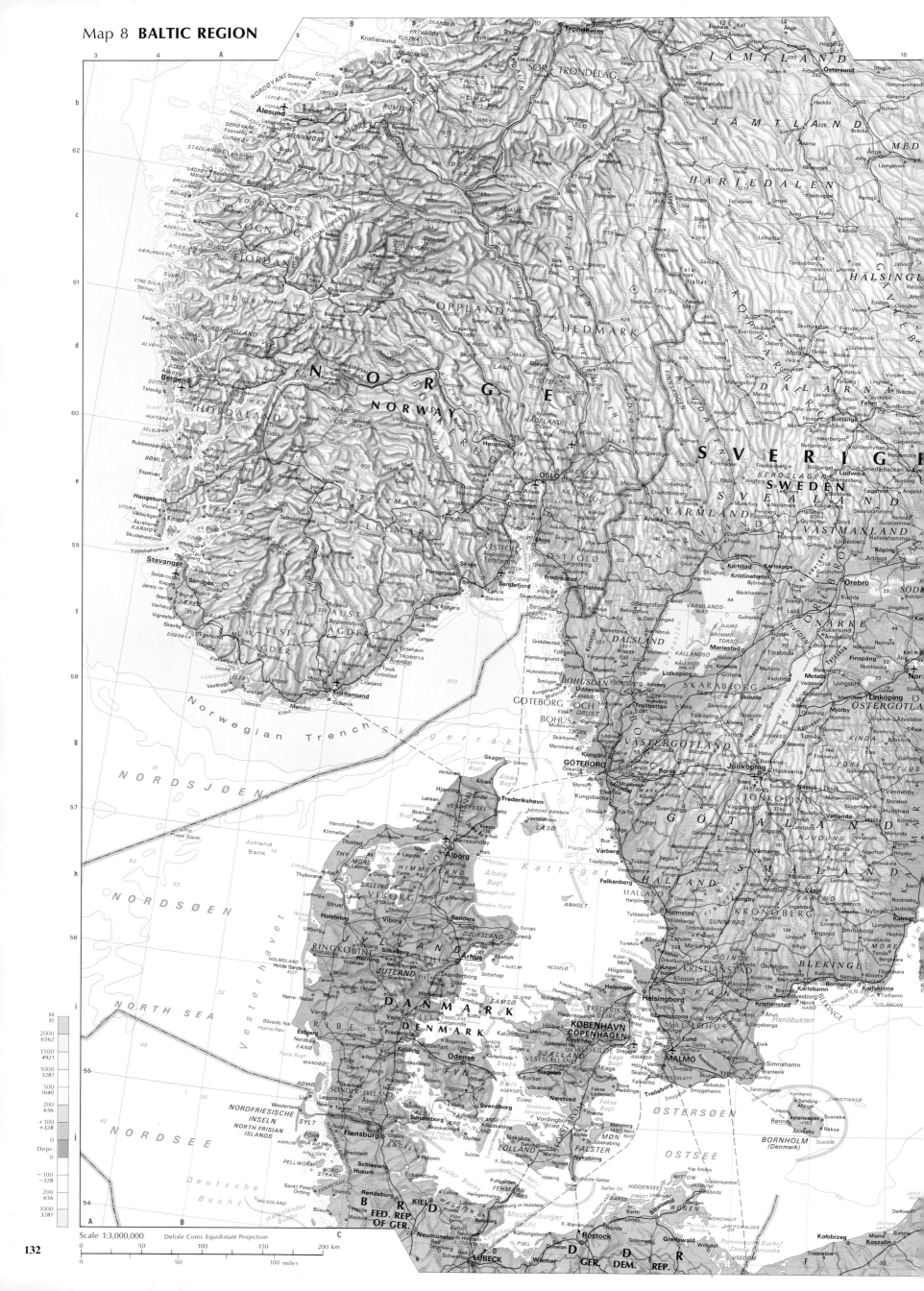

Map 8 **BALTIC REGION**

Scale 1:3,000,000

Delisle Conic Equidistant Projection

0   50   100   150   200 km
0   50   100 miles

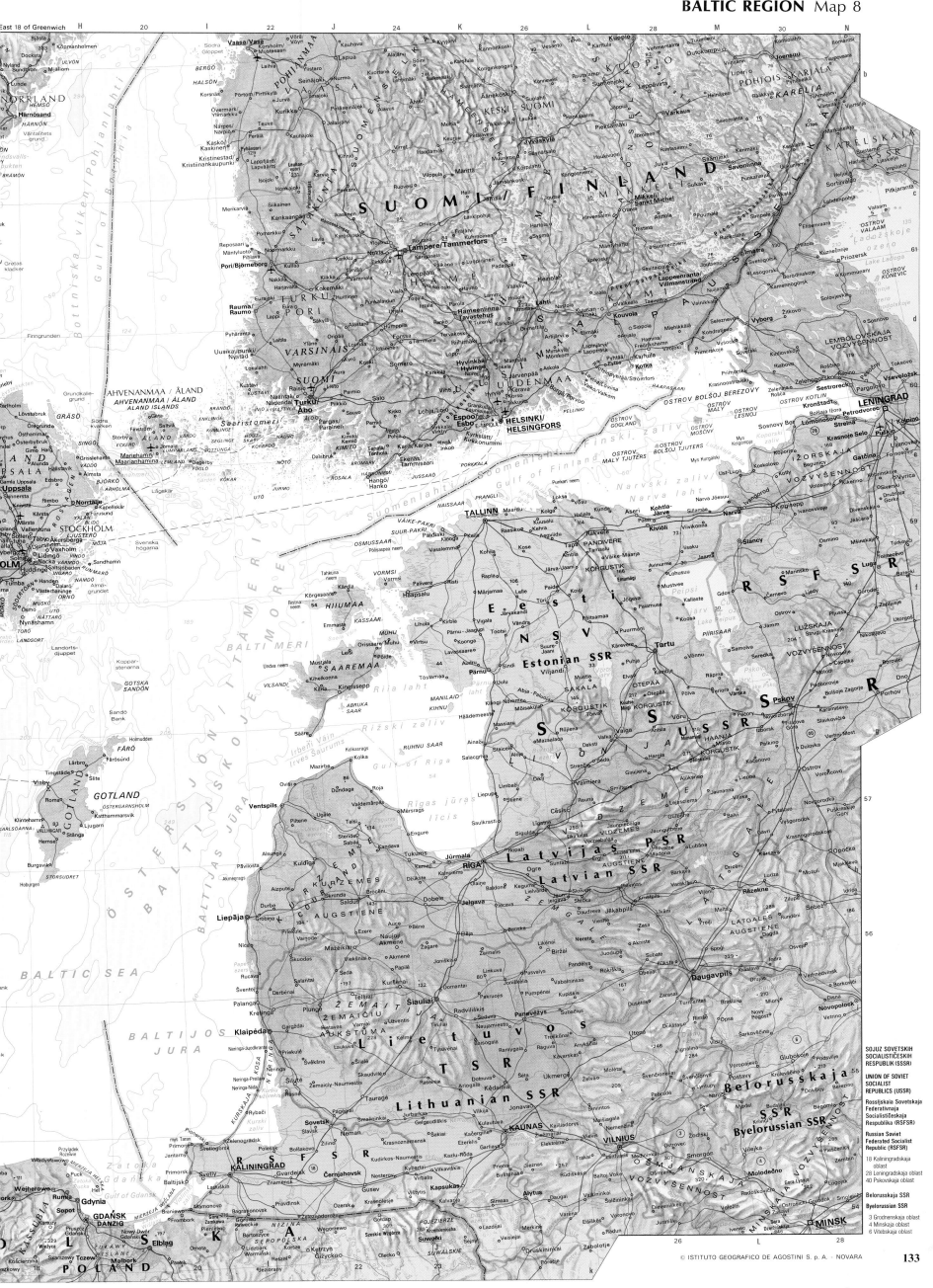
East 18 of Greenwich
SUOMI / FINLAND
Helsinki / Helsingfors
Tampere / Tammerfors
Turku / Åbo
Tallinn
Eesti NSV
Estonian SSR
Latvijas PSR
Latvian SSR
Rīga
Lietuvos TSR
Lithuanian SSR
Vilnius
Kaunas
Kaliningrad
Leningrad
Pskov
Minsk
Belorusskaja SSR
Byelorussian SSR
RSFSR
Gdańsk / Danzig
Gdynia
Stockholm
Gotland
Saaremaa
Hiiumaa
Ahvenanmaa / Åland
Suomenlahti / Finska viken / Gulf of Finland
Rižskij zaliv / Gulf of Riga
Baltic Sea
Östersjön
Baltijskoje More
Bottniska viken / Pohjanlahti
Ladožskoje ozero / Lake Ladoga
Peipsi
Poland
SOJUZ SOVETSKIH SOCIALISTIČESKIH RESPUBLIK (SSSR)
UNION OF SOVIET SOCIALIST REPUBLICS (USSR)
Rossijskaja Sovetskaja Federativnaja Socialističeskaja Respublika (RSFSR)
Russian Soviet Federated Socialist Republic (RSFSR)
18 Kaliningradskaja oblast
28 Leningradskaja oblast
40 Pskovskaja oblast
Belorusskaja SSR
Byelorussian SSR
3 Grodnenskaja oblast
4 Minskaja oblast
6 Vitebskaja oblast

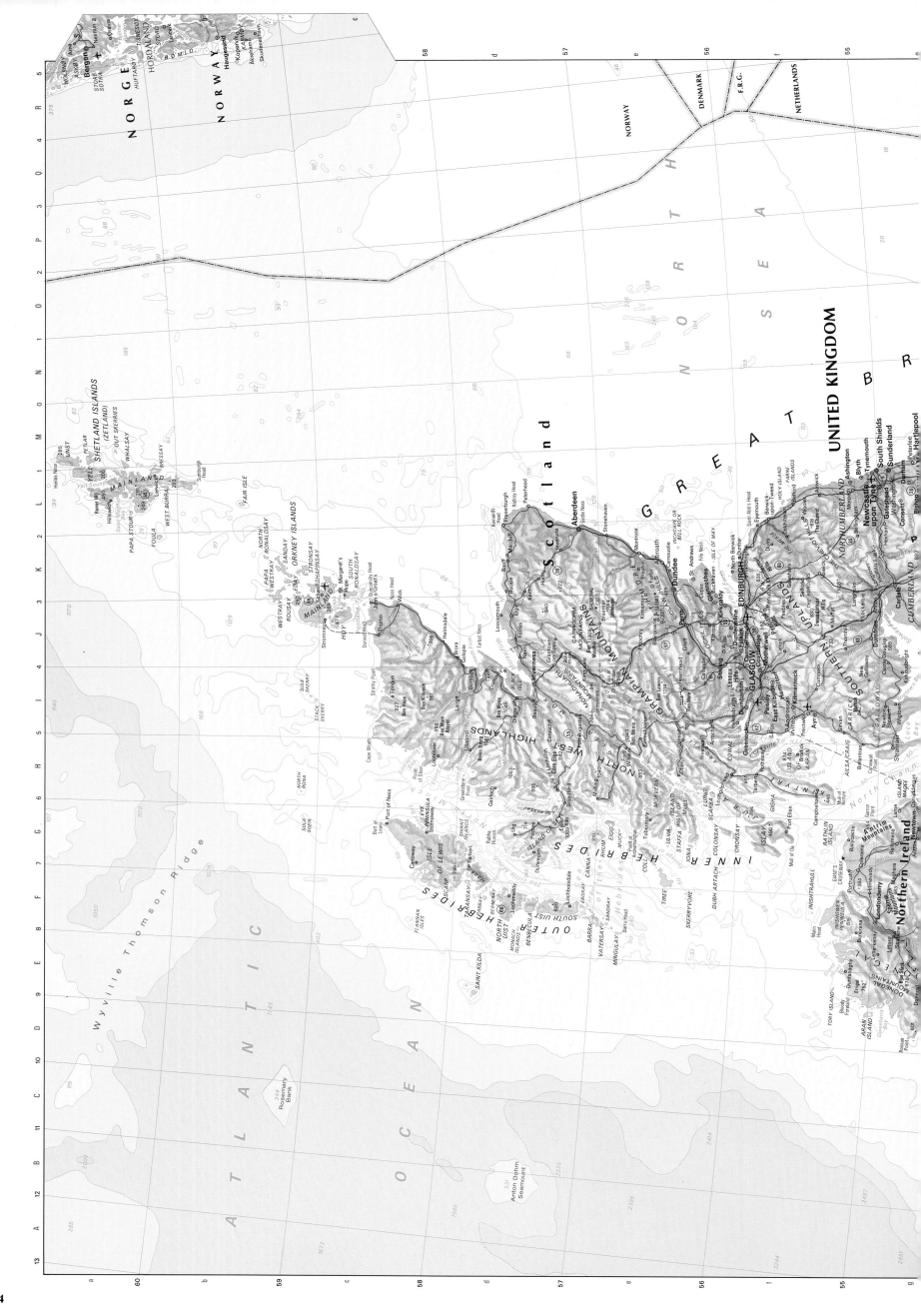

NORGE
NORWAY
Bergen
Haugesund
HORDALAND
DENMARK
F.R.G.
NETHERLANDS
NORTH SEA
UNITED KINGDOM
GREAT BRITAIN
Scotland
Northern Ireland
SHETLAND ISLANDS (ZETLAND)
ORKNEY ISLANDS
FAIR ISLE
FOULA
Aberdeen
Dundee
EDINBURGH
GLASGOW
Inverness
Perth
Stirling
Paisley
Motherwell
Kilmarnock
Ayr
Dumfries
Carlisle
Newcastle upon Tyne
Sunderland
South Shields
Hartlepool
Ashington
Blyth
Tynemouth
Londonderry
GRAMPIAN MOUNTAINS
CAIRNGORM MOUNTAINS
NORTH WEST HIGHLANDS
SOUTHERN UPLANDS
CHEVIOT HILLS
INNER HEBRIDES
OUTER HEBRIDES
ISLE OF LEWIS
HARRIS
NORTH UIST
SOUTH UIST
MULL
ISLAY
ARRAN
KINTYRE
SAINT KILDA
Stornoway
Ben Nevis
Wick
Thurso
Cape Wrath
Butt of Lewis
Wyville Thomson Ridge
Rosemary Bank
Anton Dohrn Seamount
ATLANTIC
OCEAN

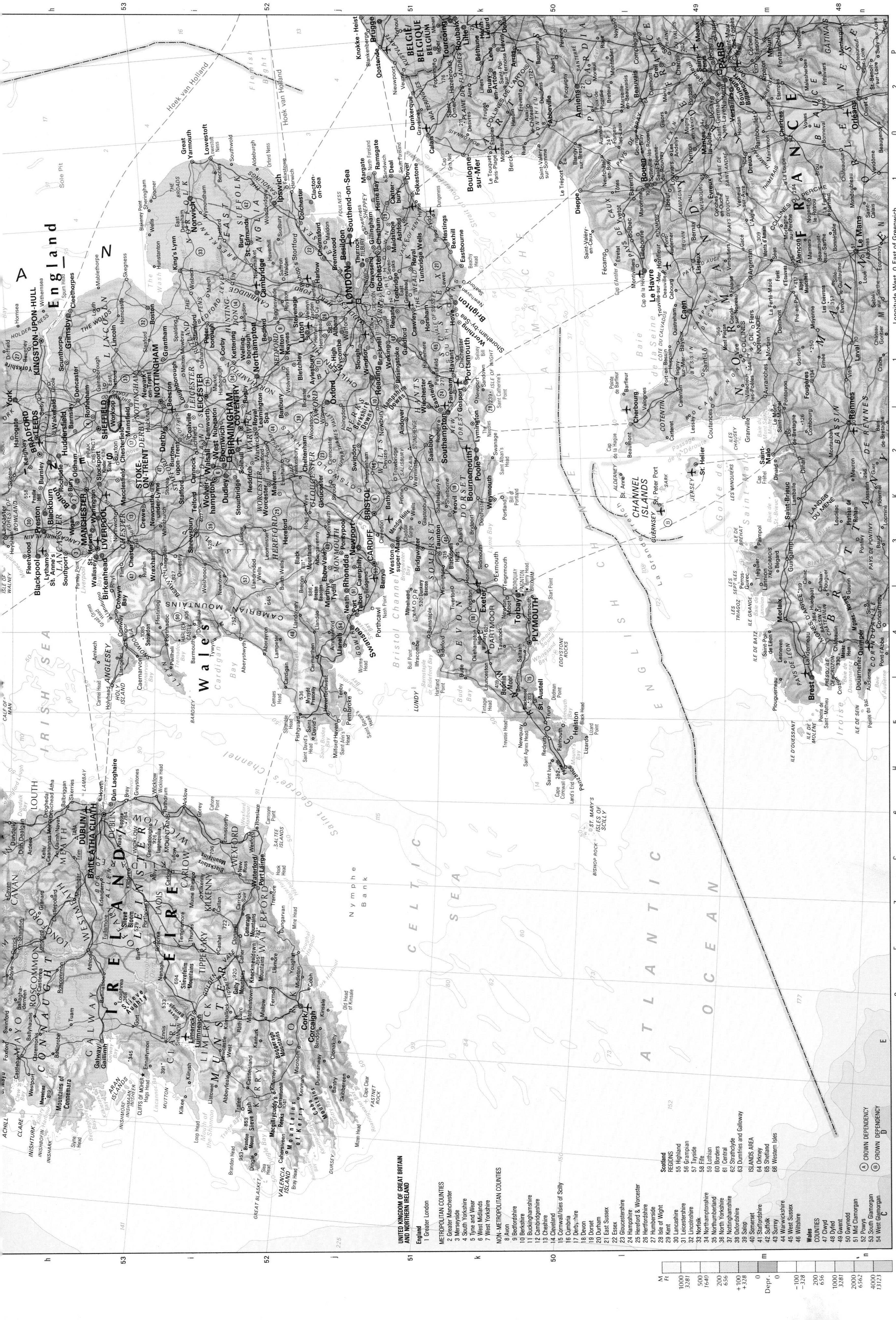
IRISH SEA
CELTIC SEA
ATLANTIC OCEAN
England
Wales
IRELAND
EIRE
FRANCE
CHANNEL ISLANDS
LONDON
DUBLIN
PARIS
BIRMINGHAM
MANCHESTER
LIVERPOOL
BRISTOL
CARDIFF
PLYMOUTH
UNITED KINGDOM OF GREAT BRITAIN AND NORTHERN IRELAND
England
1 Greater London
METROPOLITAN COUNTIES
2 Greater Manchester
3 Merseyside
4 South Yorkshire
5 Tyne and Wear
6 West Midlands
7 West Yorkshire
NON-METROPOLITAN COUNTIES
8 Avon
9 Bedfordshire
10 Berkshire
11 Buckinghamshire
12 Cambridgeshire
13 Cheshire
14 Cleveland
15 Cornwall/Isles of Scilly
16 Cumbria
17 Derbyshire
18 Devon
19 Dorset
20 Durham
21 East Sussex
22 Essex
23 Gloucestershire
24 Hampshire
25 Hereford & Worcester
26 Hertfordshire
27 Humberside
28 Isle of Wight
29 Kent
30 Lancashire
31 Leicestershire
32 Lincolnshire
33 Norfolk
34 Northamptonshire
35 Northumberland
36 North Yorkshire
37 Nottinghamshire
38 Oxfordshire
39 Salop
40 Somerset
41 Staffordshire
42 Suffolk
43 Surrey
44 Warwickshire
45 West Sussex
46 Wiltshire
Wales
COUNTIES
47 Clwyd
48 Dyfed
49 Gwent
50 Gwynedd
51 Mid Glamorgan
52 Powys
53 South Glamorgan
54 West Glamorgan
Scotland
REGIONS
55 Highland
56 Grampian
57 Tayside
58 Fife
59 Lothian
60 Borders
61 Central
62 Strathclyde
63 Dumfries and Galloway
ISLANDS AREA
64 Orkney
65 Shetland
66 Western Isles
A CROWN DEPENDENCY
B CROWN DEPENDENCY
Scale 1:3,000,000
Delisle Conic Equidistant Projection
200 km
100 miles
Longitude West 0 East of Greenwich
© ISTITUTO GEOGRAFICO DE AGOSTINI S. p. A. - NOVARA
M
Ft
1000 3281
500 1640
200 656
+100 +328
0
Depr.
0
-100 -328
200 656
1000 3281
2000 6562
4000 13123

Map 10 CENTRAL EUROPE

DEUTSCHE
DEMOKRATISCHE
REPUBLIK

GERMAN
DEMOCRATIC
REPUBLIC

BEZIRKE
1 Berlin (Ost)
2 Cottbus
3 Dresden
4 Erfurt
5 Frankfurt
6 Gera
7 Halle
8 Karl-Marx-Stadt
9 Leipzig
10 Magdeburg
11 Neubrandenburg
12 Potsdam
13 Rostock
14 Schwerin
15 Suhl

Scale 1:3,000,000

Delisle Conic Equidistant Projection

J Longitude East 14 of Greenwich K

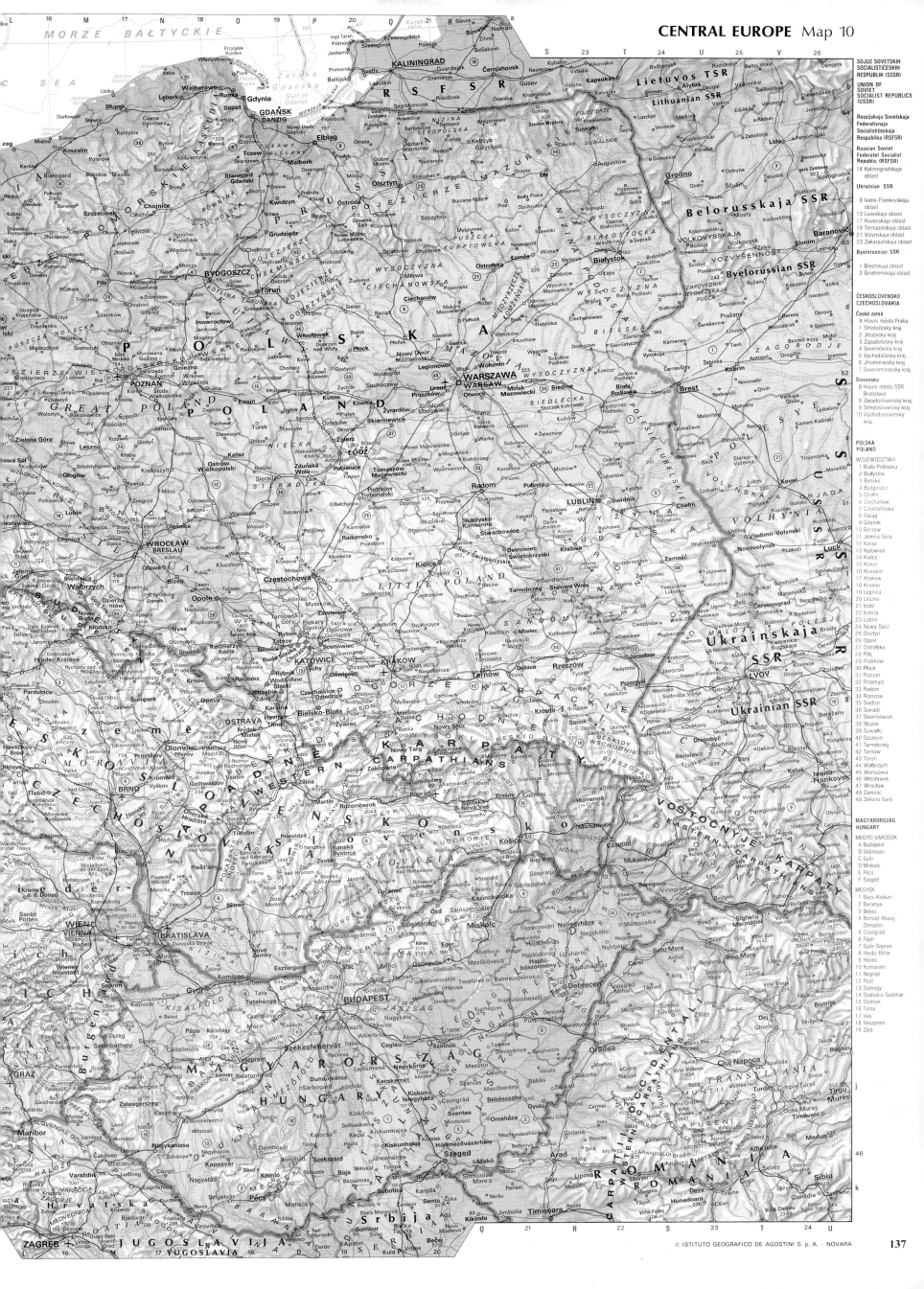

SOJUZ SOVETSKIH SOCIALISTIČESKIH RESPUBLIK (SSSR)

UNION OF SOVIET SOCIALIST REPUBLICS (USSR)

Rossijskaja Sovetskaja Federativnaja Socialističeskaja Respublika (RSFSR)

Russian Soviet Federatet Socialist Republic (RSFSR)

18 Kaliningradskaja oblast

Ukrainian SSR

9 Ivano-Frankovskaja oblast
13 Lvovskaja oblast
17 Rovenskaja oblast
19 Ternopolskaja oblast
21 Volynskaja oblast
23 Zakarpatskaja oblast

Byelorussian SSR

1 Brestskaja oblast
3 Grodnenskaja oblast

ČESKOSLOVENSKO
CZECHOSLOVAKIA

České země
A Hlavní město Praha
1 Středočeský kraj
2 Jihočeský kraj
3 Západočeský kraj
4 Severočeský kraj
5 Východočeský kraj
6 Jihomoravský kraj
7 Severomoravský kraj

Slovensko
B Hlavní město SSR Bratislava
8 Západoslovenský kraj
9 Stredoslovenský kraj
10 Východoslovenský kraj

POLSKA
POLAND

WOJEWÓDZTWA
1 Biała Podlaska
2 Białystok
3 Bielsko
4 Bydgoszcz
5 Chełm
6 Ciechanow
7 Częstochowa
8 Elblag
9 Gdansk
10 Gorzów
11 Jelenia Góra
12 Kalisz
13 Katowice
14 Kielce
15 Konin
16 Koszalin
17 Kraków
18 Krosno
19 Legnica
20 Leszno
21 Łódz
22 Łomża
23 Lublin
24 Nowy Sącz
25 Olsztyn
26 Opole
27 Ostrołęka
28 Piła
29 Piotrków
30 Płock
31 Poznań
32 Przemyśl
33 Radom
34 Rzeszów
35 Siedlce
36 Sieradz
37 Skierniewice
38 Słupsk
39 Suwałki
40 Szczecin
41 Tarnobrzeg
42 Tarnów
43 Toruń
44 Wałbrzych
45 Warszawa
46 Włocławek
47 Wrocław
48 Zamość
49 Zielona Góra

MAGYARORSZÁG
HUNGARY

MEGYEI VÁROSOK
A Budapest
B Debrecen
C Győr
D Miskolc
E Pécs
F Szeged

MEGYÉK
1 Bács-Kiskun
2 Baranya
3 Békés
4 Borsod-Abaúj-Zemplén
5 Csongrád
6 Fejér
7 Győr-Sopron
8 Haidú-Bihar
9 Heves
10 Komaróm
11 Nógrád
12 Pest
13 Somogy
14 Szabolcs-Szatmár
15 Szolnok
16 Tolna
17 Vas
18 Veszprém
19 Zala

Map 11 **FRANCE AND BENELUX**

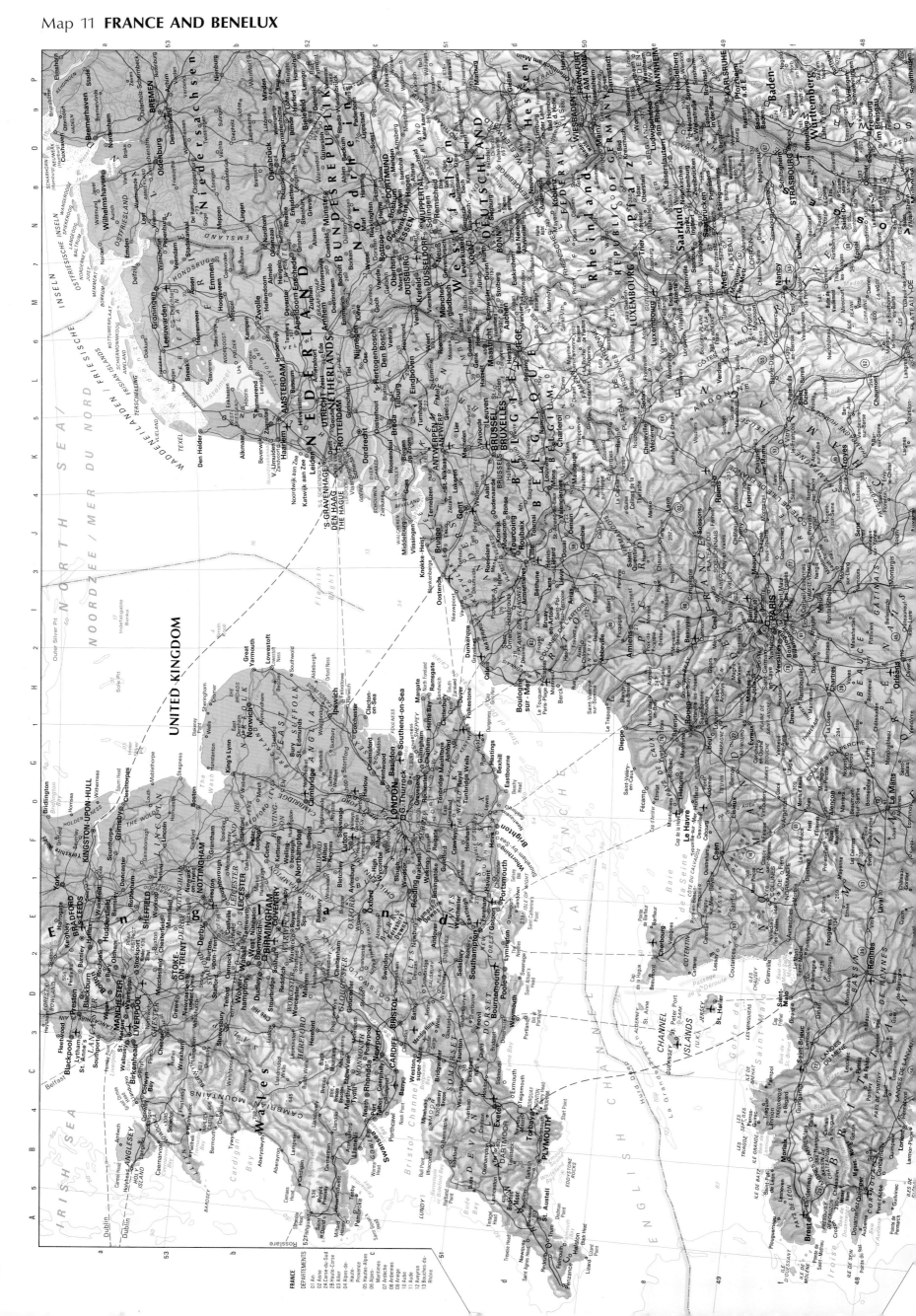

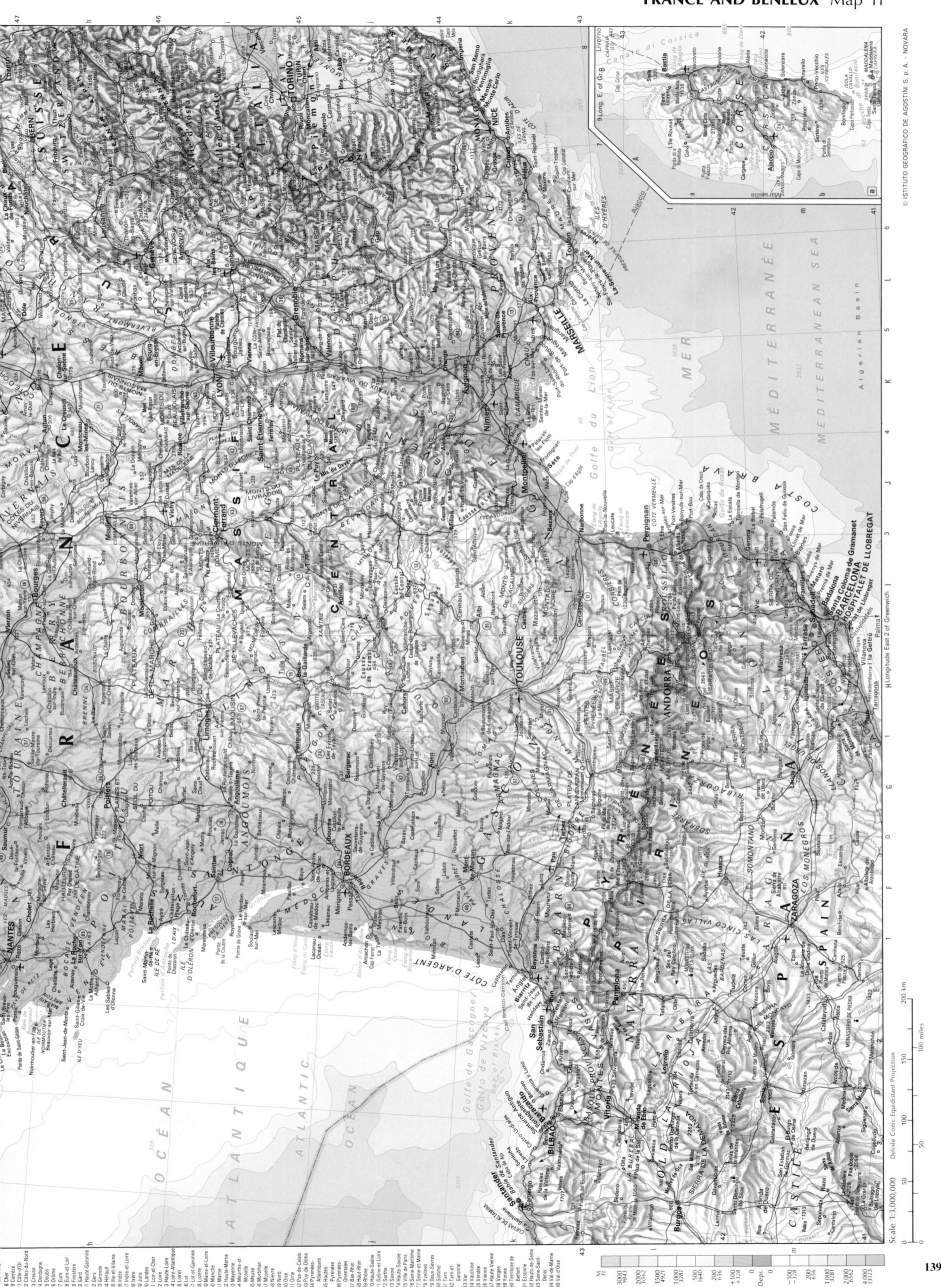
FRANCE
SPAIN
SWITZERLAND
ITALY
ANDORRA
MONACO
MASSIF CENTRAL
PYRÉNÉES
MER MÉDITERRANÉE
MEDITERRANEAN SEA
OCÉAN ATLANTIQUE
ATLANTIC OCEAN
Golfe de Gascogne
Bay of Biscay
Golfe du Lion
Longitude East 2 of Greenwich
Scale 1:3,000,000
Delisle Conic Equidistant Projection
© ISTITUTO GEOGRAFICO DE AGOSTINI S. p. A. - NOVARA
18 Cher
19 Corrèze
21 Côte-d'Or
22 Côtes-du-Nord
23 Creuse
24 Dordogne
25 Doubs
26 Drôme
27 Eure
28 Eure-et-Loir
29 Finistère
30 Gard
31 Haute-Garonne
32 Gers
33 Gironde
34 Hérault
35 Ille-et-Vilaine
36 Indre
37 Indre-et-Loire
38 Isère
39 Jura
40 Landes
41 Loir-et-Cher
42 Loire
43 Haute-Loire
44 Loire-Atlantique
45 Loiret
46 Lot
47 Lot-et-Garonne
48 Lozère
49 Maine-et-Loire
50 Manche
51 Marne
52 Haute-Marne
53 Mayenne
54 Meurthe-et-Moselle
55 Meuse
56 Morbihan
57 Moselle
58 Nièvre
59 Nord
60 Oise
61 Orne
62 Pas-de-Calais
63 Puy-de-Dôme
64 Pyrénées-Atlantiques
65 Hautes-Pyrénées
66 Pyrénées-Orientales
67 Bas-Rhin
68 Haut-Rhin
69 Rhône
70 Haute-Saône
71 Saône-et-Loire
72 Sarthe
73 Savoie
74 Haute-Savoie
75 Ville de Paris
76 Seine-Maritime
77 Seine-et-Marne
78 Yvelines
79 Deux-Sèvres
80 Somme
81 Tarn
82 Tarn-et-Garonne
83 Var
84 Vaucluse
85 Vendée
86 Vienne
87 Haute-Vienne
88 Vosges
89 Yonne
90 Territoire de Belfort
91 Essonne
92 Hauts-de-Seine
93 Seine-Saint-Denis
94 Val-de-Marne
95 Val-d'Oise

Map 12 **BELGIUM, NETHERLANDS AND LUXEMBOURG**

UNITED KINGDOM

England

LINCOLNSHIRE
NORFOLK
SUFFOLK
EAST ANGLIA
CAMBRIDGESHIRE
HUNTINGDON
BEDFORDSHIRE
HERTFORDSHIRE
NORTHAMPTONSHIRE
LEICESTERSHIRE
RUTLAND
WARWICKSHIRE
BUCKINGHAMSHIRE
OXFORDSHIRE
BERKSHIRE
HAMPSHIRE
HANTS
SURREY
KENT
WEST SUSSEX
SUSSEX
SOUTH DOWNS
NORTH DOWNS
THE WEALD
ESSEX
ISLE OF WIGHT

NOTTINGHAM
Derby
LEICESTER
NORWICH
Great Yarmouth
Lowestoft
Ipswich
Cambridge
Northampton
Luton
Oxford
LONDON
GREATER LONDON
Reading
Southampton
Portsmouth
Brighton
Hastings
Eastbourne
Dover
Folkestone
Margate
Ramsgate
Canterbury
Maidstone
Chatham

NORTH SEA / NOORDZEE / MER DU NORD

Flemish Bight
Brown Bank

'S-GRAV...
NE
NI
ZEELAND
WALCHEREN
Middelburg
Vlissingen
Knokke-Heist
Oostende
Brugge
De Panne
Dunkerque
Calais
Boulogne-sur-Mer

WEST-VLAANDEREN
VLAAMS
Ieper
Kortrijk
Roeselare
GENT / GHENT
Lille
Roubaix
Tournai
NORD
PAS-DE-CALAIS
ARTOIS
Arras
Béthune
Lens
Douai
Valenciennes
Cambrai
CAMBRÉSIS
PICARDIE
Amiens
SOMME
Abbeville
Saint-Quentin
AISNE
OISE
Beauvais
Compiègne
Soissons

ENGLISH CHANNEL / LA MANCHE
Strait of Dover / Pas de Calais

Baie de la Seine
Bay of the Seine
Le Havre
Rouen
Dieppe
Caen
Lisieux
Évreux

SEINE-MARITIME
NORMANDIE
CALVADOS
MANCHE
EURE
PAYS DE CAUX
FRANCE
VEXIN
PAYS D'OUCHE

PARIS
VELINES
SEINE-ET-MARNE
EURE-ET-LOIR
Versailles
Dreux

M Ft
500 1640
200 656
100 328
0
Depr. 0

Scale 1:1,500,000   Delisle Conic Equidistant Projection

0   25   50   75   100 km
0   25   50 miles

140

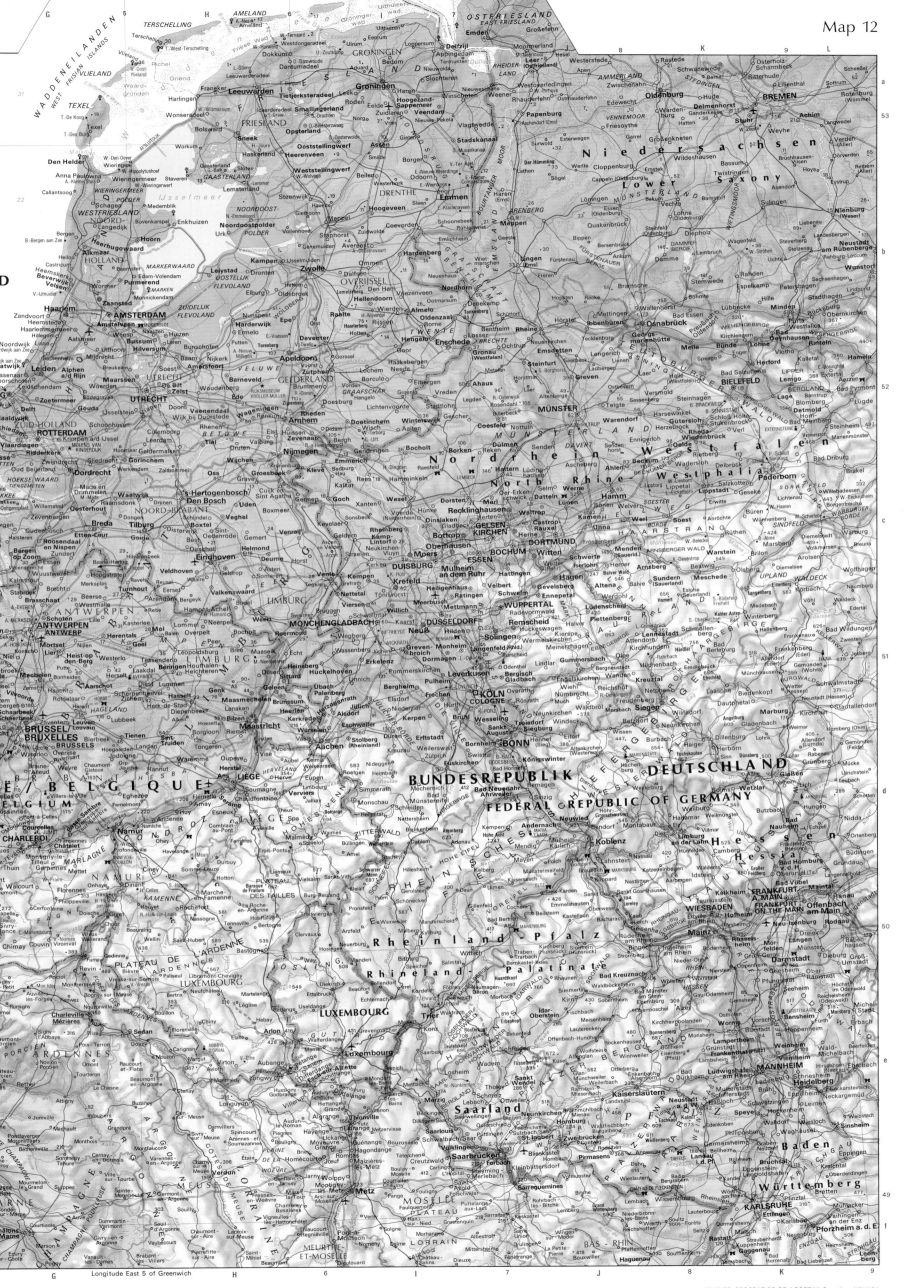
BUNDESREPUBLIK DEUTSCHLAND
FEDERAL REPUBLIC OF GERMANY
Niedersachsen
Lower Saxony
Nordrhein-Westfalen
North Rhine-Westphalia
Rheinland-Pfalz
Rhineland-Palatinate
Hessen
Hessia
Saarland
Baden
Württemberg
BELGIQUE
LUXEMBOURG
WADDENEILANDEN
WEST FRISIAN ISLANDS
OSTFRIESLAND
EAST FRIESLAND
AMSTERDAM
ROTTERDAM
UTRECHT
BRUSSEL/BRUXELLES
BRUSSELS
ANTWERPEN
ANTWERP
LIÈGE
Luxembourg
KÖLN
COLOGNE
BONN
DÜSSELDORF
ESSEN
DORTMUND
BREMEN
Osnabrück
MÜNSTER
BIELEFELD
WUPPERTAL
FRANKFURT A.MAIN
FRANKFURT ON THE MAIN
WIESBADEN
Mainz
MANNHEIM
Heidelberg
KARLSRUHE
Saarbrücken
Metz
Koblenz
Trier
Aachen
Maastricht
Groningen
Leeuwarden
Zwolle
Arnhem
Nijmegen
Eindhoven
IJsselmeer
Longitude East 5 of Greenwich

Map 13 **SPAIN AND PORTUGAL**

Longitude West 5 of Greenwich

PORTUGAL

SPAIN

MOROCCO

AL MAGHRIB

Scale 1:3,000,000   Delisle Conic Equidistant Projection

FRANCE
LANGUEDOC
PROVENCE
CAMARGUE
TOULOUSE
Montpellier
Nîmes
Avignon
Marseille
Toulon
Narbonne
Perpignan
Béziers
Sète
Golfe du Lion
Gulf of Lion
ÎLES D'HYÈRES
CÔTE D'ARGENT
LANDES
Bayonne
Biarritz
Pau
Tarbes
Lourdes
PYRÉNÉES
ANDORRA
ROUSSILLON
CÔTE VERMEILLE
Port-Bou
Genova
Ajaccio
NAVARRA
Pamplona
HUESCA
Huesca
ARAGÓN
ZARAGOZA SARAGOSSA
ZARAGOZA
LOS MONEGROS
LÉRIDA
Lérida
CATALUÑA
GERONA
Gerona
COSTA BRAVA
BARCELONA
Barcelona
HOSPITALET DE LLOBREGAT
Badalona
Santa Coloma de Gramanet
Sabadell
Tarrasa
Manresa
Mataró
Granollers
COSTA DORADA
TARRAGONA
Tarragona
Reus
Tortosa
Delta del Ebro
TERUEL
Teruel
CASTELLÓN
Castellón de la Plana
COSTA DEL AZAHAR
ISLAS COLUMBRETES
VALENCIA
Valencia
Golfo de Valencia
Sagunto
Gandía
Alcoy
ALICANTE
Alicante
Elche
Benidorm
Denia
MURCIA
Murcia
Cartagena
Lorca
Mar Menor
COSTA BLANCA
Albacete
Cuenca
ISLAS BALEARES
BALEARIC ISLANDS
BALEARES
MENORCA
MINORCA
Mahón
Ciudadela
ISLA DEL AIRE
MALLORCA
MAJORCA
PALMA
ISLA DRAGONERA
ISLA CABRERA
ISLA CONEJERA
IBIZA IVIZA
Ibiza
FORMENTERA
San Antonio Abad
Algerian Basin
MEDITERRANEAN SEA
BAHR MUTAWASSIT
AL BAHR AL ABYAD AL MUTAWASSIT
AL JAZA'IR
ALGIERS
ALGERIA
TIZI OUZOU
GRANDE KABYLIE
PETITE KABYLIE
BOUIRA
Béjaïa
Sétif
Blida
Médéa
MÉDÉA
ATLAS TELLIEN
OUARSENIS
ORAN
Oran
MOSTAGANEM
Mostaganem
MASCARA
Tiaret
SIDI BEL ABBES
Sidi Bel Abbes
TLEMCEN
Ain Témouchent
M'SILA
PLAINE DU HODNA
DJELFA
BATNA
Bou Saâda
Chott el Hodna

Map 14 **ITALY, AUSTRIA AND SWITZERLAND**

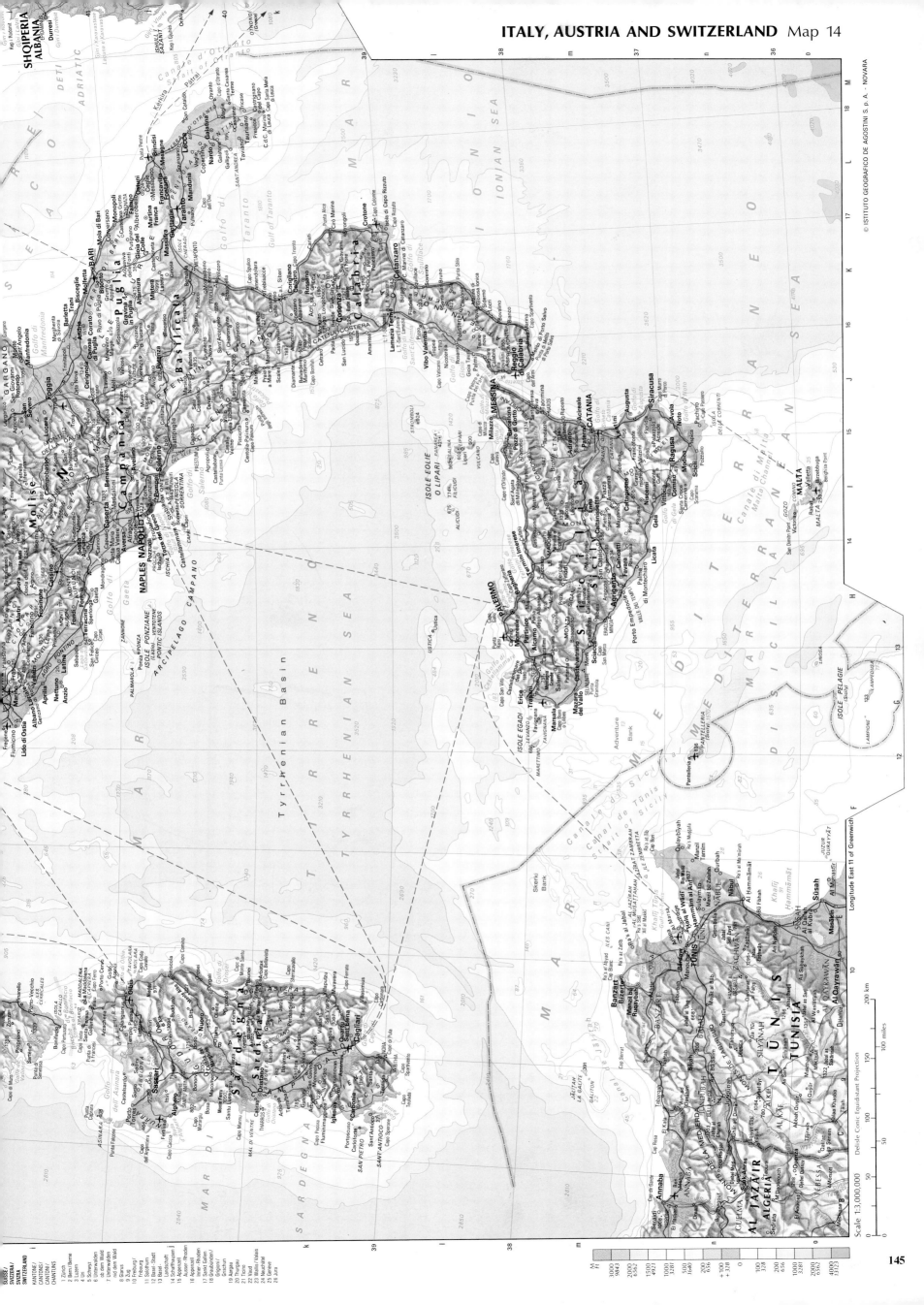

© ISTITUTO GEOGRAFICO DE AGOSTINI S. p. A. - NOVARA

Scale 1:3,000,000

Delisle Conic Equidistant Projection

Longitude East 11 of Greenwich

Map 15 **SOUTHEASTERN EUROPE**

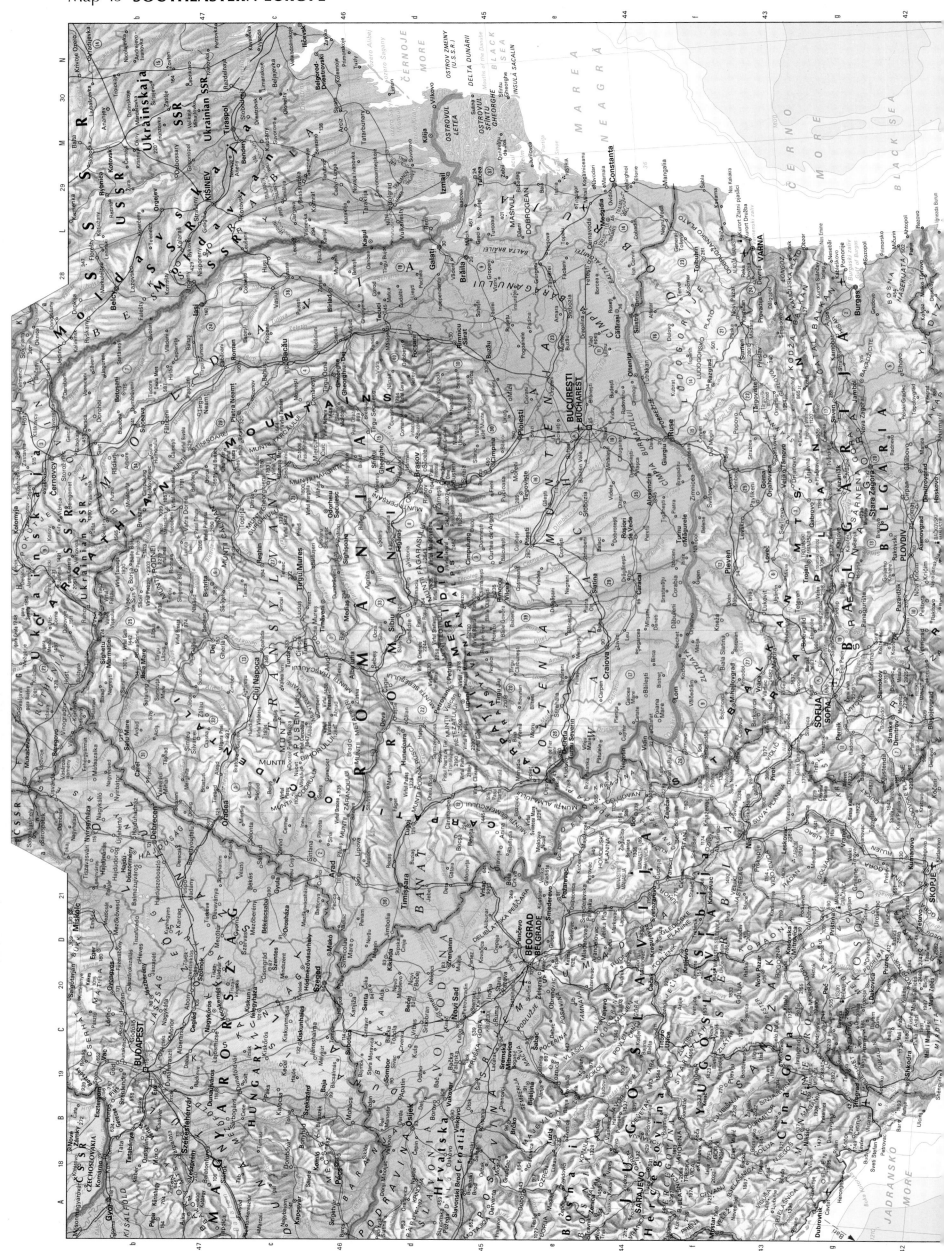

Map 15
ELLÁS
GREECE
TÜRKIYE
TURKEY
SHQIPËRIA
ALBANIA
ITALIA
ITALY
Makedhonía
Thessalía
Ípiros
Pelopónnisos
Stereá Ellás kai Évvoia
Nísoi Aiyaíou
Kríti
Crete
Iónioi Nísoi
IONIAN ISLANDS
IONIAN SEA
MESOYÉIOS THÁLASSA
MEDITERRANEAN SEA
AKDENIZ
ATHÍNAI
ATHENS
THESSALONÍKI
SALONIKA
İZMİR
SMYRNA
İSTANBUL
BURSA
KIKLÁDHES
CYCLADES
Scale 1:3,000,000
Delisle Conic Equidistant Projection
Longitude East 25 of Greenwich
© ISTITUTO GEOGRAFICO DE AGOSTINI S. p. A. - NOVARA

Map 16 **SOUTHWESTERN SOVIET UNION**

Scale 1:6,000,000   Delisle Conic Equidistant Projection

SOJUZ SOVETSKIH
SOCIALISTIČESKIH
RESPUBLIK (SSSR)

UNION OF
SOVIET
SOCIALIST
REPUBLICS (USSR)

Rossijskaja Sovetskaja
Federativnaja
Socialističeskaja
Respublika (RSFSR)

Russian Soviet
Federated Socialist
Republic (RSFSR)

3 Krasnodarski kraj
3A Adygejskaja
avtonomnaja oblast
6 Stavropolski kraj
6A Karačajevo-
Čerkesskaja
avtonomnaja oblast
9 Astrahanskaja oblast
10 Belgorodskaja oblast
11 Brjanskaja oblast
12 Čeljabinskaja oblast
14 Gorkovskaja oblast
15 Ivanovskaja oblast
17 Jaroslavskaja oblast
19 Kaliningradskaja
oblast
19 Kalininskaja oblast
20 Kalužskaja oblast
23 Kirovskaja oblast
24 Kostromskaja oblast
25 Kujbyševskaja oblast
26 Kurganskaja oblast
27 Kurskaja oblast
29 Lipeckaja oblast
31 Moskovskaja oblast
33 Novgorodskaja oblast
36 Orenburgskaja oblast
37 Orlovskaja oblast
39 Penzenskaja oblast
40 Pskovskaja oblast
41 Rostovskaja oblast
42 Rjazanskaja oblast
44 Saratovskaja oblast
45 Smolenskaja oblast
47 Tambovskaja oblast
50 Tulskaja oblast
51 Uljanovskaja oblast
52 Vladimirskaja oblast
53 Volgogradskaja oblast
55 Voronežskaja oblast

Ukrainskaja SSR
Ukrainian SSR

1 Čerkasskaja oblast
2 Černigovskaja oblast
3 Černovickaja oblast
4 Dnepropetrovskaja
oblast
5 Doneckaja oblast
6 Harkovskaja oblast
7 Hersonskaja oblast
8 Hmelnickaja oblast
9 Ivano-Frankovskaja
oblast
10 Kijevskaja oblast
11 Kirovogradskaja oblast
12 Krymskaja oblast
13 Lvovskaja oblast
14 Nikolajevskaja oblast
15 Odesskaja oblast
16 Poltavskaja oblast
17 Rovenskaja oblast
18 Sumskaja oblast
19 Ternopolskaja oblast
20 Vinnickaja oblast
21 Volynskaja oblast
22 Vorošilovgradskaja
oblast
23 Zakarpatskaja oblast
24 Zaporožskaja oblast
25 Žitomirskaja oblast

Belorusskaja SSR
Byelorussian SSR

1 Brestskaja oblast
2 Gomelskaja oblast
3 Grodnenskaja oblast
4 Minskaja oblast
5 Mogilevskaja oblast
6 Vitebskaja oblast

Kazahskaja SSR
Kazakh SSR

1 Aktjubinskaja oblast
7 Gurjevskaja oblast
9 Kzyl-Ordinskaja oblast
11 Kustanajskaja oblast
12 Mangyšlakskaja
oblast
18 Uralskaja oblast

Uzbekskaja SSR
Uzbek SSR

Gruzinskaja SSR
Georgian SSR

1 Jugo-Osetinskaja
avtonomnaja oblast

Azerbajdžanskaja SSR
Azerbaidžan SSR

1 Nagorno-Karabahskaja
avtonomnaja oblast

Turkmenskaja SSR
Turkmen SSR

1 Ašhabadskaja oblast
3 Krasnovodskaja oblast
4 Tašauzskaja oblast

Map 17 THE URALS

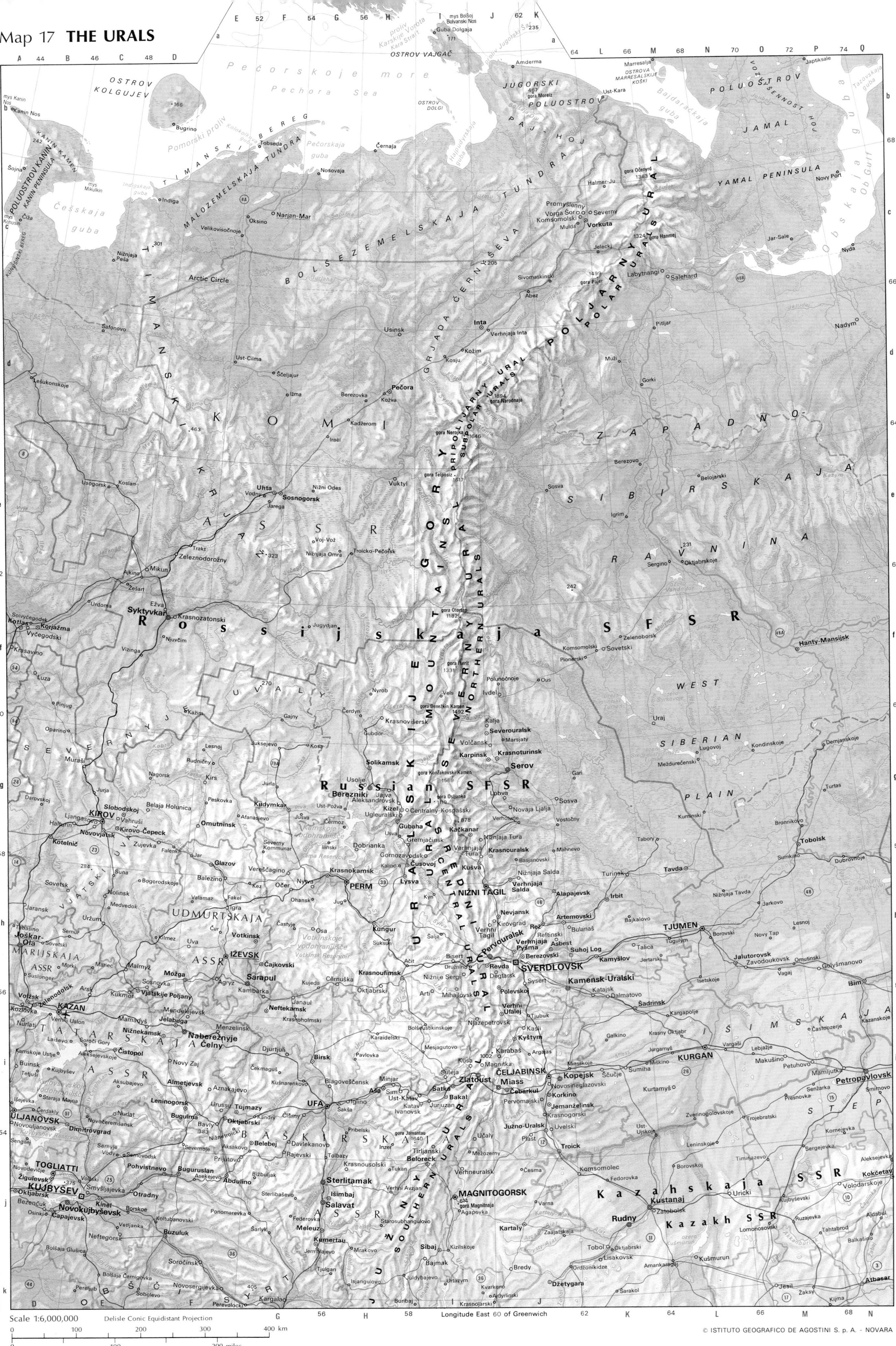

SOJUZ SOVETSKICH
SOCIALISTIČESKICH
RESPUBLIK (SSSR)

UNION OF
SOVIET
SOCIALIST
REPUBLICS

Rossijskaja Sovetskaja
Federativnaja
Socialističeskaja
Respublika (RSFSR)

Russian Soviet
Federated Socialist
Republic

8 Arhangelskaja oblast
8A Neneckí nac. okrug
12 Čeljabinskaja oblast
14 Gorkovskaja oblast
23 Kirovskaja oblast
24 Kostromskaja oblast
25 Kujbyševskaja
   oblast
26 Kurganskaja oblast
35 Omskaja oblast
36 Orenburgskaja oblast
39 Permskaja oblast
39A Komi-Permjacki
    nac. okrug
44 Saratovskaja oblast
46 Sverdlovskaja
   oblast
48 Tjumenskaja oblast
48A Hanty-Mansijski
    nac. okrug
48B Jamalo-Neneckí
    nac. okrug
51 Uljanovskaja oblast
54 Vologodskaja oblast

Kazahskaja SSR

Kazakh SSR

3 Celinogradskaja
  oblast
10 Kokčetavskaja
   oblast
11 Kustanajskaja
   oblast
15 Severo-
   Kazahstanskaja
   oblast
17 Turgajskaja oblast

Scale 1:6,000,000   Delisle Conic Equidistant Projection

Longitude East 60 of Greenwich

0   100   200   300   400 km
0   100   200 miles

150

© ISTITUTO GEOGRAFICO DE AGOSTINI S. p A. - NOVARA

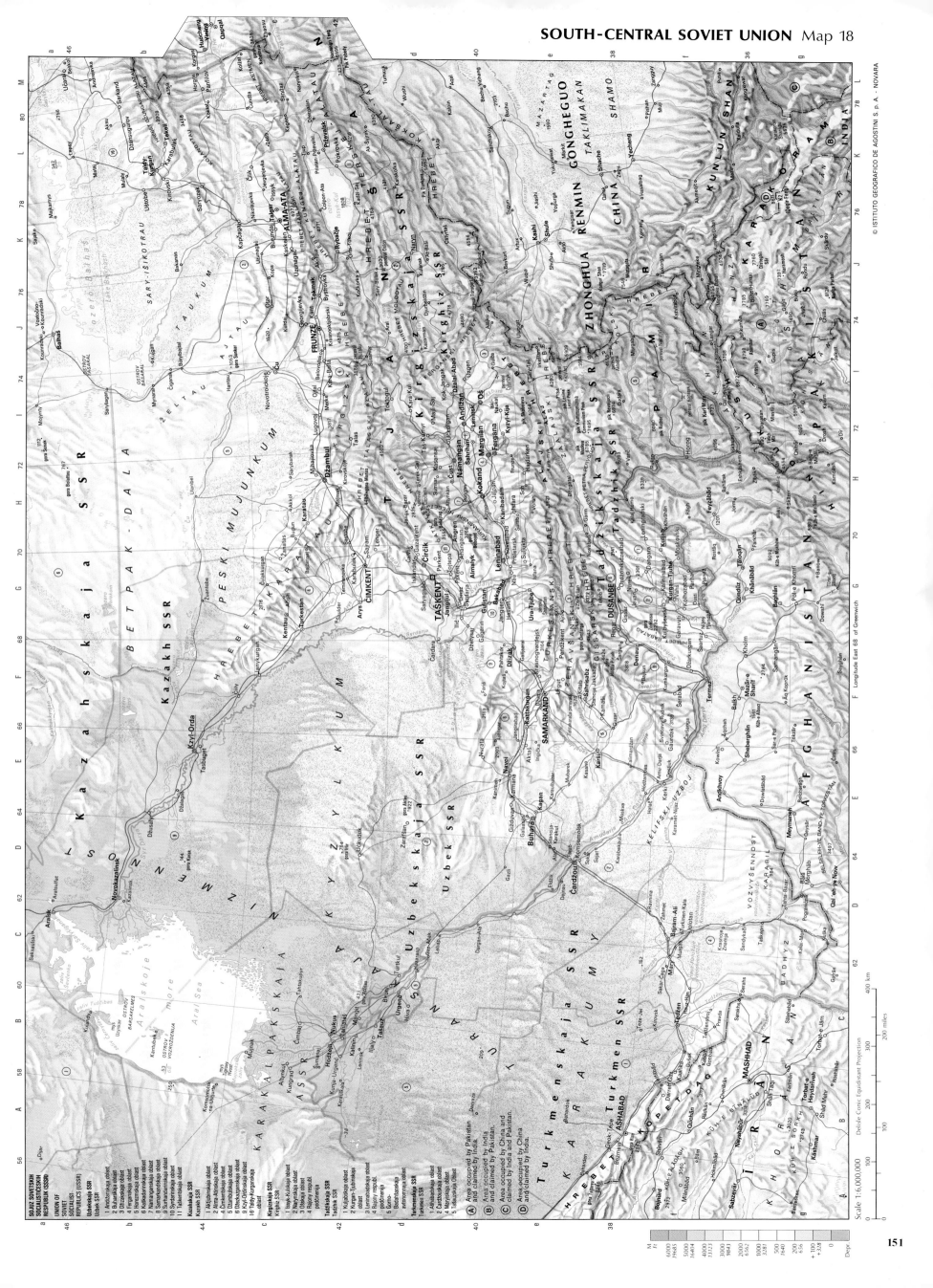

© ISTITUTO GEOGRAFICO DE AGOSTINI S. p. A. - NOVARA

Scale 1:6,000,000

Delisle Conic Equidistant Projection

SOJUZ SOVETSKIH
SOCIALISTIČESKIH
RESPUBLIK (SSSR)

UNION OF
SOVIET
SOCIALIST
REPUBLICS (USSR)

Uzbek SSR Uzbekskaja (USSR)
1 Andižanskaja oblast
2 Buharskaja oblast
3 Džizakskaja oblast
4 Ferganskaja oblast
5 Horezmskaja oblast
6 Kaškadarinskaja oblast
7 Namanganskaja oblast
8 Samarkandskaja oblast
9 Surhandarinskaja oblast
10 Syrdarinskaja oblast
11 Taškentskaja oblast

Kirgiz SSR Kirgiz SSR
1 Issyk-kulskaja oblast
2 Narynskaja oblast
3 Oškaja oblast
4 Kirgiz republic
5 podčinenija

Tadžikskaja SSR Tadžik SSR
Gorno-Badahšanskaja
avtonomnaja oblast

Turkmenskaja SSR Turkmen SSR
1 Ašhabadskaja oblast
2 Čardžouskaja oblast
3 Krasnovodskaja oblast
4 Marysskaja oblast
5 Taškauzskaja Oblast

Kazakh SSR Kazak SSR
1 Aktjubinskaja oblast
2 Alma-Atinskaja oblast
3 Džambulskaja oblast
4 Čimkentskaja oblast
5 Kzyl-Ordinskaja oblast
6 oblast

(A) Area occupied by Pakistan and claimed by India.
(B) Area occupied by India and claimed by Pakistan.
(C) Area occupied by China and claimed by China and Pakistan.
(D) Area occupied by China and claimed by India.

151

m Ft
6000 19685
5000 16404
4000 13123
3000 9843
2000 6562
1000 3281
500 1640
200 656
+ 100 +328
0
Depr.

400 km
300
200
100
0

200 miles
100
0

Map 19
SOJUZ SOVETSKIH SOCIALISTIČESKIH RESPUBLIK (SSSR)
UNION OF SOVIET SOCIALIST REPUBLICS (USSR)
Rossijskaja Sovetskaja Federativnaja Socialističeskaja Respublika (RSFSR)
Russian Soviet Federated Socialist Republic (RFSFR)
3 Krasnodarski kraj
3A Adygejskaja avt. oblast
6 Stavropolski kraj
6A Karačajevo-Čerkessakaja avt. oblast
8 Arhangelskaja oblast
8A Nenecki nac. okr.
9 Astrahanskaja oblast
10 Belgorodskaja oblast
11 Brjanskaja obl.
12 Čeljabinskaja obl.
14 Gorkovskaja obl.
15 Ivanovskaja obl.
17 Jaroslavskaja obl.
18 Kaliningradskaja oblast
19 Kalininskaja obl.
20 Kalužskaja obl.
23 Kirovskaja obl.
24 Kostromskaja obl.
25 Kujbyševskaja oblast
26 Kurganskaja obl.
27 Kurskaja obl.
28 Leningradskaja oblast
29 Lipeckaja obl.
31 Moskovskaja obl.
32 Murmanskaja obl.
33 Novgorodskaja oblast
35 Omskaja obl.
36 Orenburgskaja oblast
37 Orlovskaja obl.
38 Penzenskaja obl.
39 Permskaja obl.
39A Komi-Permjacki nac. okr.
40 Pskovskaja obl.
41 Rostovskaja obl.
42 Rjazanskaja obl.
44 Saratovskaja obl.
45 Smolenskaja obl.
46 Sverdlovskaja obl.
47 Tambovskaja obl.
48 Tjumenskaja obl.
48A Hanty-Mansijski nac. okr.
50 Tulskaja obl.
51 Uljanovskaja obl.
52 Vladimirskaja obl.
53 Volgogradskaja oblast
54 Vologodskaja obl.
55 Voronežskaja obl.
Ukrainskaja SSR
Ukrainian SSR
1 Čerkasskaja obl.
2 Černigovskaja obl.
3 Černovickaja obl.
4 Dnepropetrovskaja oblast
5 Doneckaja obl.
6 Harkovskaja obl.
7 Hersonskaja obl.
8 Hmelnickaja obl.
9 Ivano-Frankovskaja oblast
10 Kijevskaja obl.
NORGE
NORWAY
SVERIGE
SWEDEN
SUOMI FINLAND
SCANDINAVIA
LAPLAND
BARENCEVO MORE
BARENTS SEA
NOVAJA ZEMLJA
KOLSKI POLUOSTROV
KOLA PENINSULA
Beloje more
White Sea
MURMANSK
ARHANGELSK
KARELSKAJA ASSR
KARELIAN ASSR
HELSINKI
STOCKHOLM
OSLO
KØBENHAVN
GÖTEBORG
MALMÖ
TALLINN
LENINGRAD
RIGA
VILNIUS
KAUNAS
MINSK
Belorusskaja SSR
Byelorussian SSR
MOSKVA
MOSCOW
GORKI
KAZAN
KUJBYŠEV
PERM
ORENBURG
SARATOV
VOLGOGRAD
ROSTOV-NA-DONU
KIJEV
Ukrainskaja SSR
Ukrainian SSR
HARKOV
ODESSA
SIMFEROPOL
SEVASTOPOL
KIŠINEV
POLSKA
POLAND
WARSZAWA
ROMÂNIA
BUCUREŞTI
BǍLGARIJA
BULGARIA
ČERNOJE MORE
BLACK SEA
TÜRKIYE
TURKEY
İSTANBUL
ANKARA
TBILISI
JEREVAN
BAKU
ASTRAHAN
CASPIAN DEPRESSION
KASPIJSKOJE MORE
CASPIAN SEA
Turkmenskaja SSR
Turkmen SSR
ASHABAD
ĪRĀN
TABRĪZ
AL 'IRĀQ
IRAQ
SŪRĪYAH
SYRIA
LUBNĀN
LEBANON
BAYRŪT
DIMASHQ
YISRA'EL
ISRAEL
KYPROS/KIBRIS
CYPRUS
MEDITERRANEAN SEA
MASHHAD
Scale 1:12,000,000
Delisle Conic Equidistant Projection
0
200
400
600
800 km
0
200
400 miles
Longitude East 55 of Greenwich

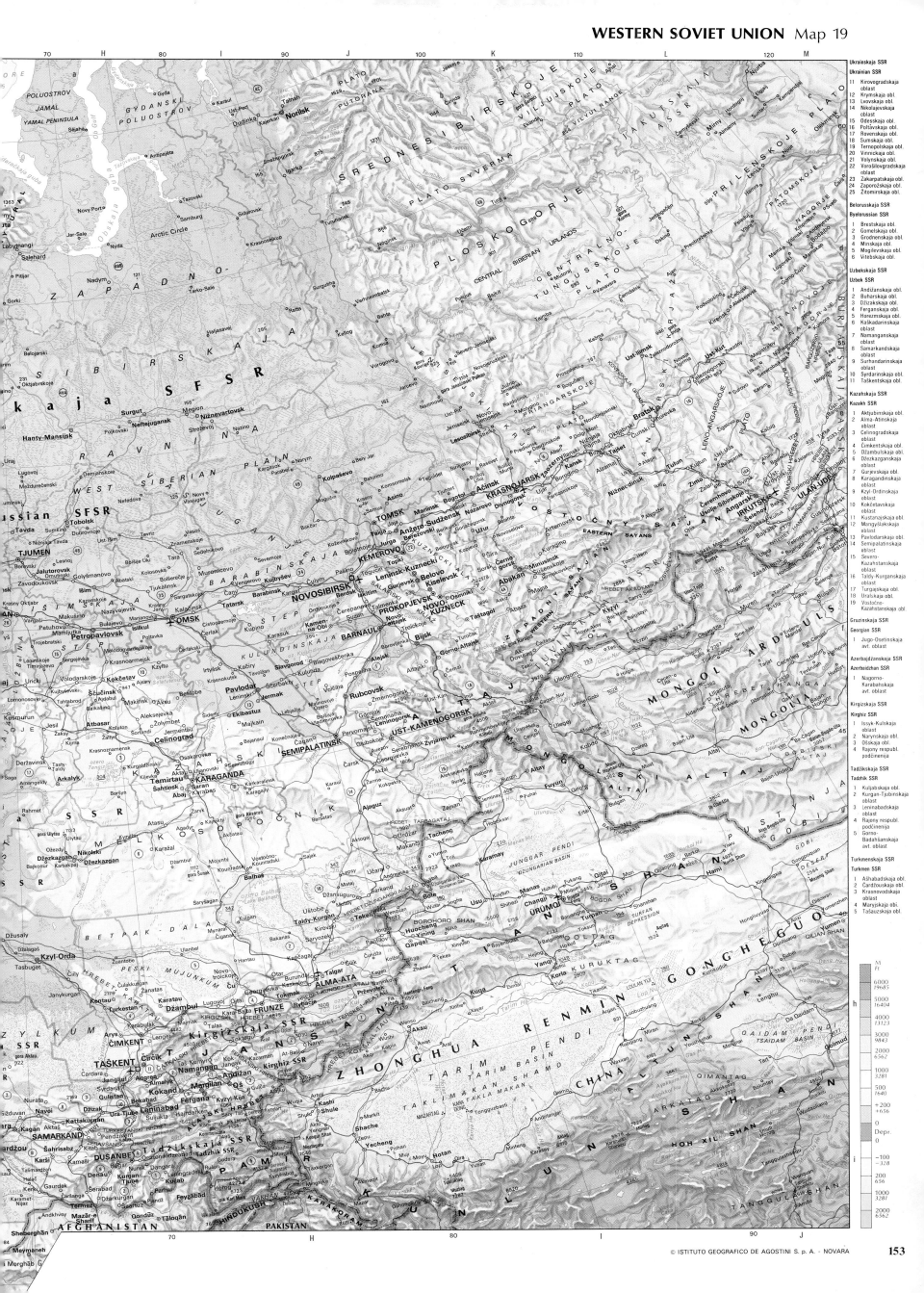

Ukrainskaja SSR
Ukrainian SSR
11 Kirovogradskaja obl.
12 Krymskaja obl.
13 Lvovskaja obl.
14 Nikolajevskaja oblast
15 Odesskaja obl.
16 Poltavskaja obl.
17 Rovenskaja obl.
18 Sumskaja obl.
19 Ternopolskaja obl.
20 Vinnickaja obl.
21 Volynskaja obl.
22 Vorošilovgradskaja oblast
23 Zakarpatskaja obl.
24 Zaporožskaja obl.
25 Žitomirskaja obl.

Belorusskaja SSR
Byelorussian SSR
1 Brestskaja obl.
2 Gomelskaja obl.
3 Grodnenskaja obl.
4 Minskaja obl.
5 Mogilevskaja obl.
6 Vitebskaja obl.

Uzbekskaja SSR
Uzbek SSR
1 Andižanskaja obl.
2 Buharskaja obl.
3 Džizakskaja obl.
4 Ferganskaja obl.
5 Horezmskaja obl.
6 Kaškadarinskaja oblast
7 Namanganskaja oblast
8 Samarkandskaja oblast
9 Surhandarinskaja oblast
10 Syrdarinskaja obl.
11 Taškentskaja obl.

Kazahskaja SSR
Kazakh SSR
1 Aktjubinskaja obl.
2 Alma-Atinskaja oblast
3 Celinogradskaja obl.
4 Čimkentskaja obl.
5 Džambulskaja obl.
6 Džezkazganskaja oblast
7 Gurjevskaja obl.
8 Karagandinskaja oblast
9 Kzyl-Ordinskaja oblast
10 Kokčetavskaja obl.
11 Kustanajskaja obl.
12 Mangyšlakskaja oblast
13 Pavlodarskaja obl.
14 Semipalatinskaja oblast
15 Severo-Kazahstanskaja oblast
16 Taldy-Kurganskaja obl.
17 Turgajskaja obl.
18 Uralskaja obl.
19 Vostočno-Kazahstanskaja obl.

Gruzinskaja SSR
Georgian SSR
J Jugo-Osetinskaja avt. oblast

Azerbajdžanskaja SSR
Azerbaidžan SSR
N Nagorno-Karabahskaja avt. oblast

Kirgizskaja SSR
Kirghiz SSR
1 Issyk-Kulskaja oblast
2 Narynskaja obl.
3 Oškskaja obl.
4 Rajony respubl. podčinenija

Tadžikskaja SSR
Tadzhik SSR
1 Kuljabskaja obl.
2 Kurgan-Tjubinskaja oblast
3 Leninabadskaja oblast
4 Rajony respubl. podčinenija
5 Gorno-Badahšanskaja avt. oblast

Turkmenskaja SSR
Turkmen SSR
1 Ašhabadskaja obl.
2 Čardžouskaja obl.
3 Krasnovodskaja obl.
4 Maryjskaja obl.
5 Tašauzskaja obl.

M	Ft
6000	19685
5000	16404
4000	13123
3000	9843
2000	6562
1000	3281
200	656
0	0
Depr.	
-100	-328
200	656
1000	3281
2000	6562

Map 20
KARSKOJE MORE
KARA SEA
NOVAJA ZEMLJA
OSTROV VAJGAČ
SEVERNAJA ZEMLJA
OSTROV OKTJABRSKOJ REVOLJUCII
OSTROV BOLŠEVIK
OSTROV BELY
OSTROV SIBIRJAKOVA
OSTROVA ARKTIČESKOGO INSTITUTA
OSTROVA IZVESTI CIK
OSTROVA SERGEJA KIROVA
OSTROVA NORDENSKJOLDA
POLUOSTROV JAMAL
YAMAL PENINSULA
GYDANSKI POLUOSTROV
POLUOSTROV TAJMYR
TAYMYR PENINSULA
GORY BYRRANGA
BYRRANGA MTS
SEVERO-SIBIRSKAJA NIZMENNOST
Ob Gulf
Obskaja guba
Arctic Circle
BOLŠEZEMELSKAJA TUNDRA
KOMI A.S.S.R.
PRIPOLJARNY URAL
POLJARNY URAL
SEVERNY URAL
PAJ-HOJ
ZAPADNO-SIBIRSKAJA RAVNINA
WEST SIBERIAN PLAIN
VASJUGANJE
BARABINSKAJA STEP
KULUNDINSKAJA STEP
PLATO PUTORANA
ANABARSKOJE PLOSKOGORJE
SREDNESIBIRSKOJE PLOSKOGORJE
CENTRAL SIBERIAN UPLANDS
PLATO SYVERMA
VILJUJSKOJE PLATO
VILYUI RANGE
CENTRALNO TUNGUSSKOJE PLATO
ROSSIJSKAJA
PRIANGARSKOJE PLATO
LENO-ANGARSKOJE PLATO
PATOMSKOJE NAGORJE
STANOVOJE NAGORJE
Russia
ALTAJ
ZAPADNY SAJAN
WESTERN SAYANS
VOSTOČNY SAJAN
EASTERN SAYANS
TUVINSKAJA A.S.S.R.
TANNU-OLA
Kazahskaja SSR
Kazakh SSR
Ozero Bajkal
HAMAR-DABAN
BURJATSKAJA A.S.S.R.
JABLONOVY HREBET
YABLONOVY RANGE
ČITA
MONGOL ALTAJ
MONGOL ARDULS
MONGOLIA
GOBI DESERT
JUNGGAR PENDI
DZUNGARIAN BASIN
TIAN SHAN
BOGDA SHAN
TURFAN DEPRESSION
KURUKTAG
ALTUN SHAN
GREATER KHINGAN
ZHONGHUA RENMIN GONGHEGUO
Norilsk
Vorkuta
Salehard
Surgut
Nižnevartovsk
Tobolsk
Tomsk
Omsk
Novosibirsk
Barnaul
Kemerovo
Novokuzneck
Prokopjevsk
Bijsk
Semipalatinsk
Ust-Kamenogorsk
Pavlodar
Krasnojarsk
Abakan
Kyzyl
Bratsk
Irkutsk
Ulan-Ude
Čita
Ulan-Bator
Ürümqi
Hami
Igarka
Dudinka
Dikson
Hatanga
Mirny
Ust-Kut
Scale 1:12,000,000
Delisle Conic Equidistant Projection
0 200 400 600 800 km
0 200 400 miles
M
Ft
5000 16404
4000 13123
3000 9843
2000 6562
1000 3281
500 1640
+200 +656
0
Depr
0
-100 -328
200 656
1000 3281
2000 6562
4000 13123
6000 19685
8000 26247

SOJUZ SOVETSKIH SOCIALISTIČESKIH RESPUBLIK (SSSR)
UNION OF SOVIET SOCIALIST REPUBLICS (USSR)
Rossijskaja Sovetskaja Federativnaja Socialističeskaja Respublika (RSFSR)
Russian Soviet Federated Socialist Republic (RSFSR)
1 Altajski kraj
1A Gorno-Altajskaja avtonomnaja oblast
2 Habarovski kraj
2A Jevrejskaja avtonomnaja oblast
4 Krasnojarski kraj
4A Hakasskaja avtonomnaja oblast
4B Evenkijski nac. okrug
4C Tajmyrski (Dolgano-Nenecki) nac. okrug
5 Primorski kraj
7 Amurskaja oblast
8A Nenecki nac. okrug
13 Čitinskaja oblast
13A Aginski Burjatski nac. okrug
16 Irkutskaja oblast
16A Ust-Ordynski Burjatski nac. okrug
21 Kamčatskaja oblast
21A Korjakski nac. okrug
22 Kemerovskaja oblast
30 Magadanskaja oblast
30A Čukotski nac. okrug
34 Novosibirskaja oblast
35 Omskaja oblast
43 Sahalinskaja oblast
48 Tjumenskaja oblast
48A Hanty-Mansijski nac. okrug
48B Jamalo-Nenecki nac. okrug
49 Tomskaja oblast
Kazahskaja SSR
Kazakh SSR
13 Pavlodarskaja oblast
14 Semipalatinskaja oblast
19 Vostočno-Kazahstanskaja oblast
NOVOSIBIRSKIJE OSTROVA
NEW SIBERIAN ISLANDS
OSTROVA ANŽU
ANJOU ISLANDS
OSTROVA DE-LONGA
DE LONG ISLANDS
LJAHOVSKIJE OSTROVA
LYAKHOV ISLANDS
OSTROV WRANGEL
ČUKOTSKOJE MORE
CHUKCHI SEA
VOSTOČNO-SIBIRSKOJE MORE
EAST SIBERIAN SEA
ČUKOTSKI POLUOSTROV
CHUKCHI PENINSULA
ANADYRSKOJE PLOSKOGORJE
KOLYMSKAJA NIZMENNOST
JUKAGIRSKOJE PLOSKOGORJE
KORJAKSKOJE NAGORJE
KOLYMSKOJE NAGORJE
HREBET ČERSKOGO
VERHOJANSKI HREBET
POLUOSTROV KAMČATKA
KAMCHATKA PENINSULA
SREDINNYJ HREBET
OHOTSKOJE MORE
SEA OF OKHOTSK
BERINGOVO MORE
BERING SEA
KOMANDORSKIJE OSTROVA
KOMANDORSKIYE ISLANDS
Aleutian Trench
Obruchev Rise
KURILSKIJE OSTROVA
KURIL ISLANDS
Kuril Trench
Kuril Basin
TIHI OKEAN
PACIFIC OCEAN
OSTROV SAHALIN
SAKHALIN
JAPONSKOJE MORE
SEA OF JAPAN
HOKKAIDŌ
NIPPON
JAPAN
HONSHŪ
Jakutsk
Magadan
Petropavlovsk-Kamčatski
HABAROVSK
Komsomolsk-na-Amure
Južno-Sahalinsk
VLADIVOSTOK
Nahodka
Blagoveščensk
SAPPORO
HAKODATE
HARBIN
QIQIHAR
MUDANJIANG
ALDANSKOJE NAGORJE
ALDAN PLATEAU
STANOVOJ HREBET
STANOVOY RANGE
HREBET DŽUGDŽUR
DZHUGDZHUR RANGE
SIHOTE-ALIN
Arctic Circle
Longitude East 150 of Greenwich

Map 21 **ASIA, PHYSICAL**

© ISTITUTO GEOGRAFICO DE AGOSTINI S. p. A. · NOVARA

Scale 1:30,000,000

Lambert Azimuthal Equal Area Projection

Map 22 **ASIA, POLITICAL**

INDIAN OCEAN
CHINA
TIBET
INDIA
PAKISTAN
BURMA
THAILAND
LAOS
VIETNAM
KAMPUCHEA
MALAYSIA
INDONESIA
PHILIPPINES
AUSTRALIA
SAUDI ARABIA
OMAN
P.D.R. OF YEMEN
YEMEN
SOMALIA
ETHIOPIA
MADAGASCAR
SRI LANKA
BANGLADESH
BHUTAN
MALDIVES
SEYCHELLES
MAURITIUS
COMOROS
Arabian Sea
Bay of Bengal
Andaman Sea
South China Sea
Java Sea
Timor Sea
Banda Sea
Gulf of Aden
Gulf of Thailand
Equator
Tropic of Capricorn
Longitude East 80 of Greenwich
Scale 1:30,000,000
Lambert Azimuthal Equal Area Projection
© ISTITUTO GEOGRAFICO DE AGOSTINI S. p. A. - NOVARA

Map 23 **SOUTHWESTERN ASIA**

Scale 1:12,000,000

Delisle Conic Equidistant Projection

0   200   400   600   800 km

0   200   400 miles

AFGHANISTAN

VELĀYAT

1 Badakhshān
2 Bādghīsāt
3 Baghlān
4 Balkh
5 Bāmiān
6 Farāh
7 Fāryāb
8 Ghazni
9 Ghowr
10 Helmand
11 Herāt
12 Jowzjān
13 Kābul
14 Kāpisā
15 Konarha
16 Laghmān
17 Lowgar
18 Nangarhār
19 Nīmrūz
20 Orūzgān
21 Paktiā
22 Parvān
23 Qandahār
24 Qondūz
25 Samangān
26 Takhār
27 Vardak
28 Zābol

ĪRĀN

OSTĀN

1 Āzarbāijān-e Gharbī
2 Āzarbāijān-e Sharqī
3 Bakhtīārī va Chahār Mahāll
4 Balūchestān va Sīstān
5 Boyer Ahmadī-ye Sardsīr va Kohkīlūyeh
6 Būshehr
7 Esfahān
8 Fārs
9 Gīlān
10 Hamadān
11 Īlām va Poshtkūh
12 Jazāyer va Banāder-e Khalīj-e Fārs va Daryā-ye 'Omān
13 Kermān
14 Kermānshāhān
15 Khorāsān
16 Khūzestān
17 Kordestān
18 Lorestān
19 Māzandarān
20 Semnān
21 Tehrān
22 Yazd
23 Zanjān

A Area occupied by Pakistan and claimed by India.
B Area occupied by India and claimed by Pakistan.
C Area occupied by China and claimed by India and Pakistan.
D Area occupied by China and claimed by India.

Scale 1:6,000,000
Delisle Conic Equidistant Projection

Longitude East 40 of Greenwich

0   100   200   300   400 km
0   100   200 miles

Legend (elevation):

M	Ft
5000	16404
4000	13123
3000	9843
2000	6562
1000	3281
200	656
+ 0	+ 328
0	
Depr.	
− 100	− 328
200	656
1000	3281
2000	6562
4000	13123

Administrative index (left margin):

AL URDUN
JORDAN
MUḤĀFAẒAT
1 Al Balqā'
2 Al Karak
3 Al Khalīl
4 Al Quds
5 'Ammān
6 Irbid
7 Ma'ān
8 Nābulus
West Bank:
Occupied by Israel

YISRA'EL
ISRAEL
MEḤOZ
1 HaDarom
2 HaMerkaz
3 HaZafon
4 Ḥefa
5 Tel Aviv
6 Yerushalayim

SŪRIYAH
SYRIA
MINṬAQAT
A Dimashq
MUḤĀFAẒAT
1 Al Ḥasakah
2 Al Lādhiqīyah
3 Al Qunayṭirah
4 Ar Raqqah
5 As Suwaydā'
6 Dar'ā
7 Dayr Az Zawr
8 Dimashq
9 Ḥalab
10 Ḥamāh
11 Ḥimṣ
12 Idlib
13 Ṭarṭūs
Golan Heights:
Occupied by Israel

Major labels (selection):

KARADENIZ / BLACK SEA
TÜRKİYE / TURKEY
ELLAS / GREECE
KYPROS / KIBRIS / CYPRUS
AKDENIZ / AL BAḤR AL-MUTAWASSIṬ / YAM KHATIKHON / MEDITERRANEAN SEA
SŪRIYAH / SYRIA
LUBNĀN / LEBANON
YISRA'EL / ISRAEL
PALESTINI / PALESTINE
AL URDUN / JORDAN
MIṢR / EGYPT
AL 'ARABĪYAH AS SA'ŪDĪYAH / SAUDI
BĀLGARIJA / BULGARIJA
ISTANBUL
ANKARA
İZMIR / SMYRNA
KONYA
ADANA
GAZİANTEP
HALAB / ALEPPO
DIMASHQ / DAMASCUS
BEIRUT / BAYRŪT
TEL AVIV-YAFO
YERUSHALAYIM / JERUSALEM
'AMMĀN
AL ISKANDARĪYAH / ALEXANDRIA
AL QĀHIRAH / CAIRO
ASWĀN
AL MADĪNAH / MEDINA
BĀDIYAT ASH SHĀM / SYRIAN DESERT
SINAI PENINSULA / SĪNĀ'
NILE DELTA
QATTARA DEPRESSION / MUNKHAFAD AL QATTĀRAH
RHODOS / RHODES
KRITI / CRETE

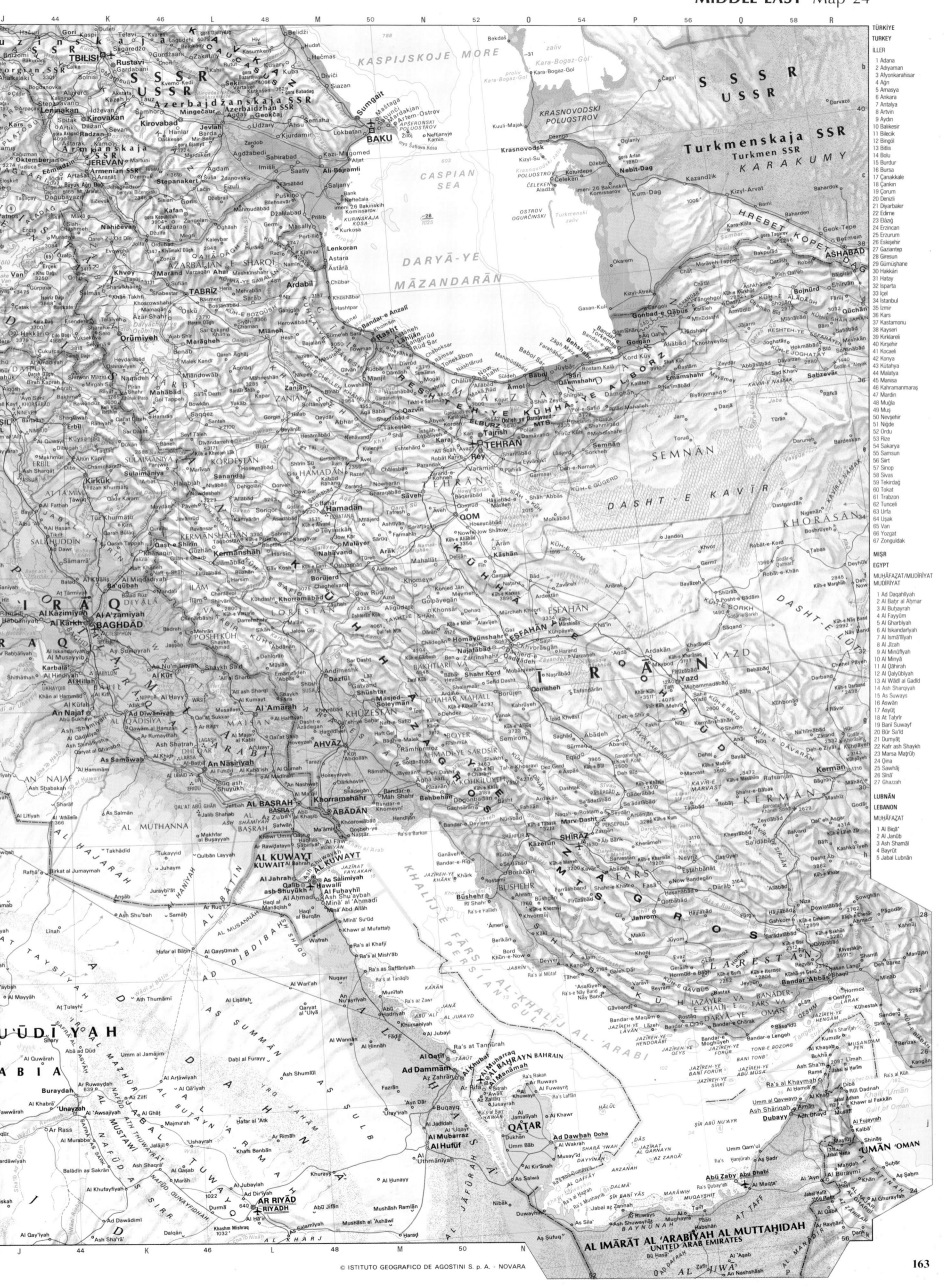

TÜRKİYE
TURKEY
İLLER

1 Adana
2 Adıyaman
3 Afyonkarahisar
4 Ağrı
5 Amasya
6 Ankara
7 Antalya
8 Artvin
9 Aydın
10 Balıkesir
11 Bilecik
12 Bingöl
13 Bitlis
14 Bolu
15 Burdur
16 Bursa
17 Çanakkale
18 Çankırı
19 Çorum
20 Denizli
21 Diyarbakır
22 Edirne
23 Elâzığ
24 Erzincan
25 Erzurum
26 Eskişehir
27 Gaziantep
28 Giresun
29 Gümüşhane
30 Hakkâri
31 Hatay
32 Isparta
33 İçel
34 İstanbul
35 İzmir
36 Kars
37 Kastamonu
38 Kayseri
39 Kırklareli
40 Kırşehir
41 Kocaeli
42 Konya
43 Kütahya
44 Malatya
45 Manisa
46 Kahramanmaraş
47 Mardin
48 Muğla
49 Muş
50 Nevşehir
51 Niğde
52 Ordu
53 Rize
54 Sakarya
55 Samsun
56 Siirt
57 Sinop
58 Sivas
59 Tekirdağ
60 Tokat
61 Trabzon
62 Tunceli
63 Urfa
64 Uşak
65 Van
66 Yozgat
67 Zonguldak

MISIR
EGYPT
MUHĀFAZAT/MUDĪRĪYAT
MUDĪRĪYAT

1 Ad Daqahlīyah
2 Al Baḥr al Aḥmar
3 Al Buḥayrah
4 Al Fayyūm
5 Al Gharbīyah
6 Al Iskandarīyah
7 Al Ismā'īlīyah
8 Al Jīzah
9 Al Minyā
10 Al Minūfīyah
11 Al Qalyūbīyah
12 Al Wādī al Gadīd
13 Ash Sharqīyah
14 As Suways
15 Aswān
16 Asyūţ
17 At Taḥrīr
18 Banī Suwayf
19 Būr Sa'īd
20 Dumyāţ
21 Kafr ash Shaykh
22 Marsa Maţrūḥ
23 Qinā
24 Sawhāj
25 Sīnā'
27 Ghazzah

LUBNĀN
LEBANON
MUHĀFAZAT

1 Al Biqā'
2 Al Janūb
3 Ash Shamāl
4 Bayrūt
5 Jabal Lubnān

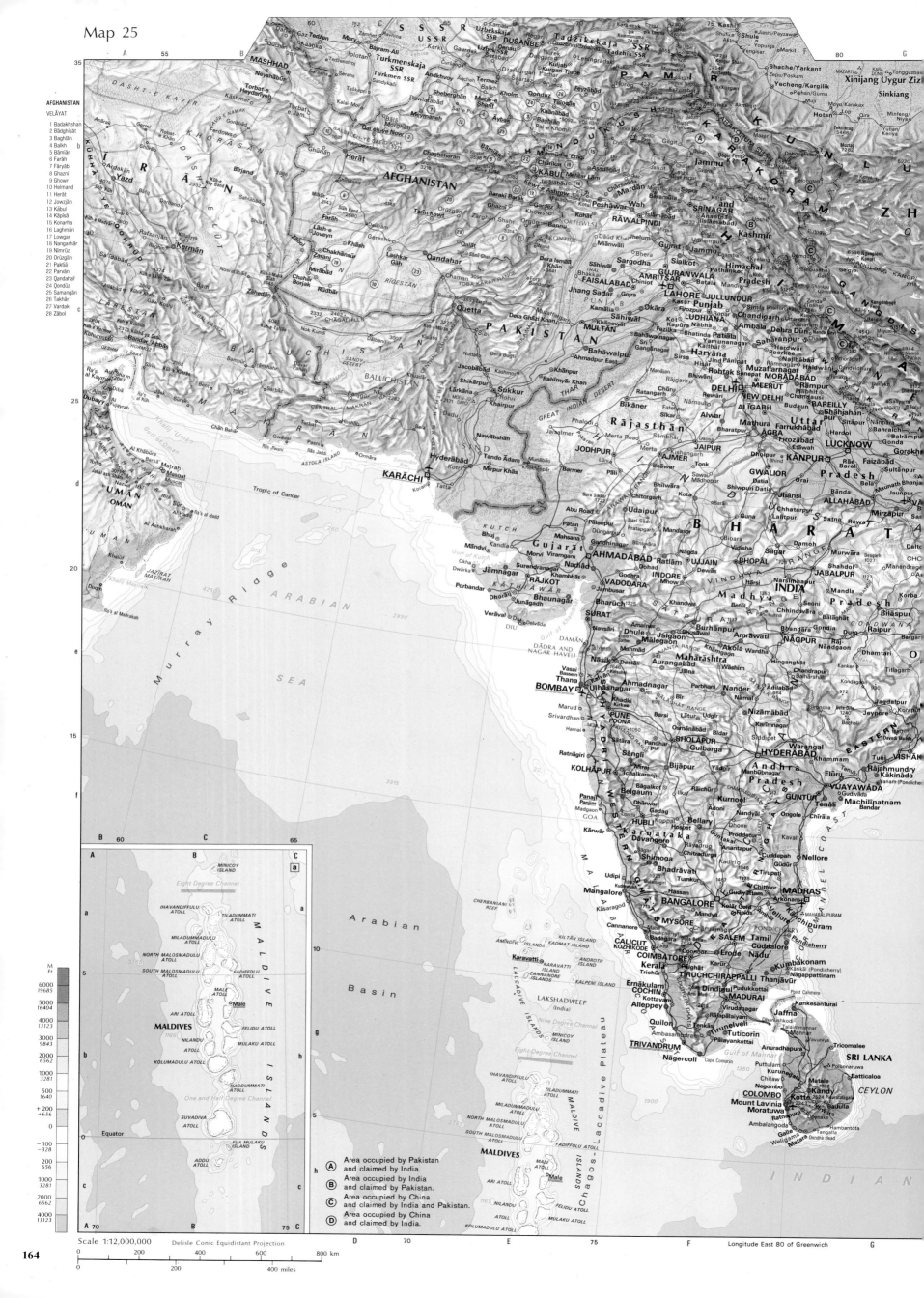

Map 25

AFGHANISTAN
VELĀYAT
1 Badakhshān
2 Bādghisāt
3 Baghlān
4 Balkh
5 Bāmiān
6 Farāh
7 Fāryāb
8 Ghazni
9 Ghowr
10 Helmand
11 Herāt
12 Jowzjān
13 Kābul
14 Kāpisā
15 Konarha
16 Laghmān
17 Lowgar
18 Nangarhār
19 Nīmrūz
20 Orūzgān
21 Paktiā
22 Parvān
23 Qandahār
24 Qondūz
25 Samangān
26 Takhār
27 Vardak
28 Zābol

Ⓐ Area occupied by Pakistan
and claimed by India.
Ⓑ Area occupied by India
and claimed by Pakistan.
Ⓒ Area occupied by China
and claimed by India and Pakistan.
Ⓓ Area occupied by China
and claimed by India.

Scale 1:12,000,000   Delisle Conic Equidistant Projection

Longitude East 80 of Greenwich

ZHONGHUA RENMIN GONGHEGUO
CHINA
QAIDAM PENDI
TSAIDAM BASIN
QIMANTAG
ARKATAG
BAYAN HAR SHAN
ANYEMAQEN SHAN
QINGZANG GAOYUAN
PLATEAU OF TIBET
TANGGULA (DANGLA) SHAN
NYAINQENTANGLHA SHAN
Xizang Zizhiqu
Tibet
NINGJING SHAN
DAXUE SHAN
HENGDUAN SHAN
QIN LING
DABA SHAN
SICHUAN PENDI
YUNNAN GAOYUAN
NANLING
Guangxi Zhuangzu Zizhiqu
Kwangsi
Ningxia Huizu Zizhiqu
LANZHOU
Xining
Golmud
CHENGDU
CHONGQING (YUZHOU)
XI'AN
LUOYANG
ZHENGZHOU
KAIFENG
XUZHOU
WUHAN
CHANGSHA
XIANGTAN
HENGYANG
GUIYANG
KUNMING
NANNING
GUANGZHOU
CANTON
MACAU
Zhanjiang
Haikou
HAINAN DAO
Lhasa
Xigaze
Arunachal Pradesh
Assam
Meghalaya
Nagaland
Manipur
Tripura
Sikkim
DRUK BHUTAN
BANGLADESH
DACCA
NARAYANGANJ
KHULNA
CHITTAGONG
CALCUTTA
HOWRAH
West Bengal
Bay of Bengal
Mouths of the Ganges
Kachin
Sagaing
Chin
Shan
Arakan
Kayah
Mon
BURMA
MANDALAY
RANGOON
PEGU
Moulmein
Bassein
Sittwe (Akyab)
IRRAWADDY
Mouths of the Irrawaddy
Gulf of Martaban
PREPARIS ISLAND
COCO ISLANDS
NORTH ANDAMAN
MIDDLE ANDAMAN
SOUTH ANDAMAN
Port Blair
LITTLE ANDAMAN
ANDAMAN ISLANDS
Ten Degree Channel
ANDAMAN AND NICOBAR (India)
CAR NICOBAR
NICOBAR ISLANDS
GREAT NICOBAR
Andaman Basin
ANDAMAN SEA
MERGUI ARCHIPELAGO
Mergui
Tavoy
TENASSERIM
MUANG THAI
THAILAND
KRUNG THEP BANGKOK
Chiang Mai
Nakhon Ratchasima
KHORAT PLATEAU
Gulf of Thailand
ISTHMUS OF KRA
Phuket
Songkhla
Hat Yai
LAOS
Viangchan
Vientiane
Louangphrabang
Savannakhet
KAMPUCHEA
PHNUM PENH
Tonle Sap
VIET-NAM
HA NOI
HAI PHONG
Gulf of Tonkin
Vinh Bac Phan
Hue
DA NANG
Qui Nhon
Nha Trang
HO CHI MINH
SAIGON
MEKONG DELTA
SOUTH CHINA SEA
BIEN DONG
XISHA QUNDAO PARACEL ISLANDS (China)
CON SON
LAUT CINA SELATAN
MALAY PENINSULA
MALAYSIA
KUALA LUMPUR
GEORGE TOWN
Ipoh
Kuala Terengganu
Kuantan
Johor Baharu
SINGAPURA SINGAPORE
SUMATERA
SUMATRA
MEDAN
Banda Aceh
INDONESIA
KEPULAUAN NATUNA
ANAMBAS
KEPULAUAN BATU
Equator
NIAS
SIMEULUE
OCEAN

Map 26 SOUTHEAST ASIA

Scale 1:12,000,000 at the Equator

Mercator Cylindrical Projection

Longitude East 110 of Greenwich

TAIWAN
KEELUNG
TAIPEI
Hsinchu
TAICHUNG
Changhua
Chiayi
TAINAN
KAOHSIUNG
Pingtung
Xiamen Amoy
Quanzhou
Zhangzhou
SHANTOU
Tropic of Cancer
NIPPON JAPAN
NANSEI-SHOTŌ
RYUKYU ISLANDS
OKINO-TORI-SHIMA
PARECE VELA
(Japan)
Kyushu - Palau Ridge
P H I L I P P I N E   S E A
Philippine Basin
West Mariana Basin
P A C I F I C   O C E A N
LUZON
BATAN ISLANDS
BABUYAN ISLANDS
Laoag
Vigan
San Fernando
Baguio
Dagupan
Tarlac
Cabanatuan
Angeles
Olongapo
QUEZON CITY
MANILA
PILIPINAS
PHILIPPINES
CATANDUANES
Batangas
Lucena
Legazpi
Naga
MINDORO
MASBATE
SAMAR
Calbayog
Catbalogan
Tacloban
LEYTE
PANAY
Iloilo
Bacolod
NEGROS
CEBU
BOHOL
Surigao
Butuan
Cagayan de Oro
Iligan
Dumaguete
Dipolog
ZAMBOANGA
Cotabato
DAVAO
MINDANAO
General Santos
Basilan City
Isabela
Jolo
SULU ARCHIPELAGO
PALAWAN
Puerto Princesa
Sulu Basin
SULU SEA
Philippine Trench
Sandakan
Sabah
Tawau
Tarakan
CAROLINE ISLANDS
Trust Territory of the Pacific Islands
(Administered by the United States)
PALAU ISLANDS
Koror
YAP ISLANDS
Colonia
Yap Trench
ULITHI ATOLL
West Caroline Basin
KEPULAUAN TALAUD
LAUT SULAWESI
Celebes Basin
CELEBES SEA
SULAWESI UTARA
Manado
MINAHASSA
Gorontalo
HALMAHERA
PULAU MOROTAI
Ternate
Tidore
Equator
PULAU WAIGEO
Sorong
Manokwari
PULAU BIAK
PULAU YAPEN
JAZIRAH DOBERAI
KEPULAUAN SULA
KEPULAUAN OBI
PULAU MISOOL
SERAM
SERAM CERAM
PULAU BURU
Ambon
MALUKU
MOLUCCA SEA
LAUT MALUKU
LAUT SERAM
LAUT BANDA
BANDA SEA
Palu
SULAWESI TENGAH
SULAWESI
CELEBES
SULAWESI SELATAN
SULAWESI TENGGARA
Kendari
UJUNG PANDANG
MAKASAR
PULAU BUTUNG
Baubau
LAUT FLORES
PULAU FLORES
Ende
PULAU SUMBAWA
NUSA TENGGARA BARAT
PULAU SUMBA
Waingapu
NUSA TENGGARA TIMUR
TIMOR
PULAU TIMOR
Kupang
Dili
PULAU WETAR
PULAU ALOR
KEPULAUAN TANIMBAR
KEPULAUAN KAI
Tual
KEPULAUAN ARU
Aru Basin
IRIAN JAYA
PEGUNUNGAN SUDIRMAN
Puncak Jaya 5030
Jayapura
New Guinea Trench
PULAU IRIAN
NEW GUINEA
PAPUA NEW GUINEA
PULAU DOLAK
Merauke
LAUT ARAFURA
ARAFURA SEA
LAUT TIMOR
TIMOR SEA
Timor Trough
AUSTRALIA
Darwin
BATHURST ISLAND
MELVILLE ISLAND
Cape Wessel
Nhulunbuy
Cape Arnhem
Torres Strait

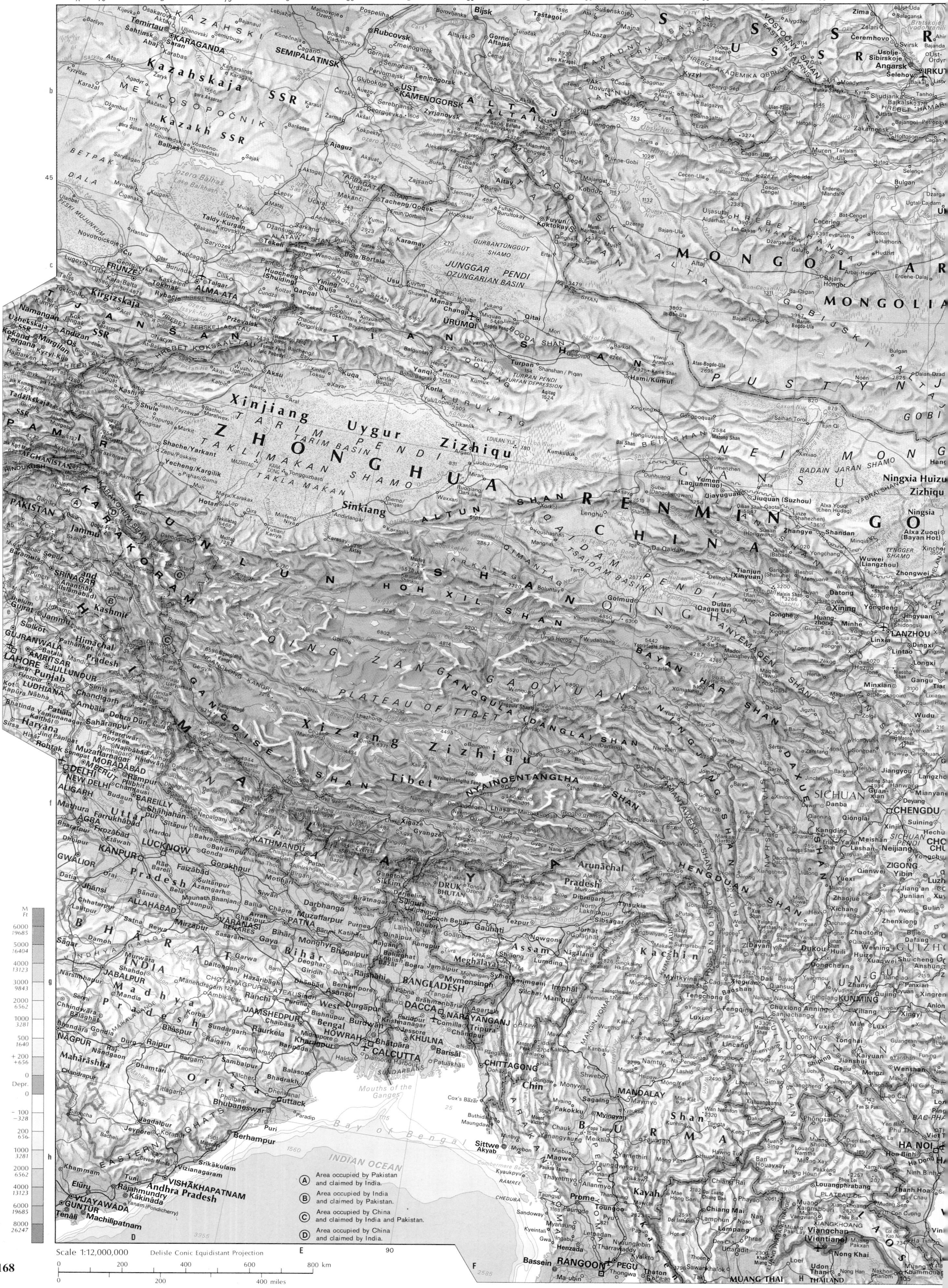

Map 27 **CHINA AND MONGOLIA**

Scale 1:12,000,000   Delisle Conic Equidistant Projection

| 0 | 200 | 400 | 600 | 800 km |
| 0 | 200 | | 400 miles | |

M
Ft
6000 19685
5000 16404
4000 13123
3000 9843
2000 6562
1000 3281
500 1640
+ 200 +656
Depr.
- 100 −328
200 656
1000 3281
2000 6562
4000 13123
6000 19685
8000 26247

Ⓐ Area occupied by Pakistan
    and claimed by India.

Ⓑ Area occupied by India
    and claimed by Pakistan.

Ⓒ Area occupied by China
    and claimed by India and Pakistan.

Ⓓ Area occupied by China
    and claimed by India.

ZHONGHUA
RENMIN
GONGHEGUO
CHINA
1 Beijing Shi
2 Shanghai Shi
3 Tianjin Shi
Longitude East 120 of Greenwich
BEIJING PEKING
SHANGHAI
TIANJIN
TIENTSIN
SHENYANG
HARBIN
CHANGCHUN
DALIAN (LÜDA) DAIREN
QINGDAO TSINGTAO
NANJING NANKING
HANGZHOU
WUHAN
GUANGZHOU CANTON
NEW KOWLOON
VICTORIA
Hong Kong (U.K.)
MACAU
Macao (Port.)
TAIPEI
KAOHSIUNG
TAIWAN
FORMOSA
P'YONGYANG
CHOSŎN M.I.K.
NORTH KOREA
SEOUL SŎUL
TAEHAN-MIN'GUK
SOUTH KOREA
PUSAN
NIPPON
JAPAN
TŌKYŌ
YOKOHAMA
ŌSAKA
KYŌTO
NAGOYA
SAPPORO
HOKKAIDŌ
HONSHŪ
SHIKOKU
KYŪSHŪ
Russian SFSR
Rossijskaja SFSR
HABAROVSK
Vladivostok
OSTROV SAHALIN
SAKHALIN
Nei Mongol Zizhiqu
Inner Mongolia
GOBI
DA HINGGAN LING
GREATER KHINGAN RANGE
XIAO HINGGAN LING
LESSER KHINGAN RANGE
Japan Basin
JAPONSKOJE MORE
TONG-HAE / NIPPON-KAI
SEA OF JAPAN
HUANG HAI / HWANG-HAE
YELLOW SEA
DONG HAI / HIGASHI-SHINA-KAI
EAST CHINA SEA
Shikoku Basin
Philippine Basin
PHILIPPINE SEA
PACIFIC OCEAN
TAIHEIYŌ
Tropic of Cancer
RYUKYU ISLANDS
NANSEI-SHOTŌ
NAN HAI
SOUTH CHINA SEA
South China Basin
HAINAN DAO
Haikou
LUZON
PHILIPPINES
PILIPINAS
BATAN ISLANDS
BABUYAN ISLANDS
Luzon Strait
Bashi Haixia
Balintang Channel
DONGSHA QUNDAO
Kyushu-Palau Ridge
Nankai Trough
Bonin Trench

Map 28 **NORTHEASTERN CHINA, KOREA AND JAPAN**

Scale 1:6,000,000   Delisle Conic Equidistant Projection

0   100   200   300   400 km

0   100   200 miles

NIPPON
JAPAN
1 Hokkaidō Ken
2 Aomori Ken
3 Iwate Ken
4 Miyagi Ken
5 Akita Ken
6 Yamagata Ken
7 Fukushima Ken
8 Ibaraki Ken
9 Tochigi Ken
10 Gunma Ken
11 Saitama Ken
12 Chiba Ken
13 Tōkyō To
14 Kanagawa Ken
15 Niigata Ken
16 Toyama Ken
17 Ishikawa Ken
18 Fukui Ken
19 Yamanashi Ken
20 Nagano Ken
21 Gifu Ken
22 Shizuoka Ken
23 Aichi Ken
24 Mie Ken
25 Shiga Ken
26 Kyōto Fu
27 Ōsaka Fu
28 Hyōgo Ken
29 Nara Ken
30 Wakayama Ken
31 Tottori Ken
32 Shimane Ken
33 Okayama Ken
34 Hiroshima Ken
35 Yamaguchi Ken
36 Tokushima Ken
37 Kagawa Ken
38 Ehime Ken
39 Kōchi Ken
40 Fukuoka Ken
41 Saga Ken
42 Nagasaki Ken
43 Kumamoto Ken
44 Ōita Ken
45 Miyazaki Ken
46 Kagoshima Ken

CHOSŎN M.I.K.
NORTH KOREA
1 Chagang-Do
2 Ch'ŏngjin Si
3 Hamgyong-Namdo
4 Hamgyong-Pukto
5 Hwanghae-Namdo
6 Hwanghae-Pukto
7 Kaesŏng Si
8 Kangwŏn-Do
9 P'yŏngan-Namdo
10 P'yŏngan-Pukto
11 P'yŏngyang Si
12 Yanggang-Do

TAEHAN-MIN'GUK
SOUTH KOREA
1 Cheju-Do
2 Chŏlla-Namdo
3 Chŏlla-Pukto
4 Ch'ungch'ŏng-Namdo
5 Ch'ungch'ŏng-Pukto
6 Kangwŏn-Do
7 Kyŏnggi-Do
8 Kyŏngsang-Namdo
9 Kyŏngsang-Pukto
10 Pusan Si
11 Sŏul Si

ZHONGHUA RENMIN
GONGHEGUO
CHINA
1 Beijing Shi
2 Shanghai Shi
3 Tianjin Shi

Ⓐ Ostrov Kunašir, ostrov Iturup and
Malaja Kurilskaja Grjada, occupied by
the U.S.S.R. since 1945, are claimed by
Japan pending a final peace treaty.

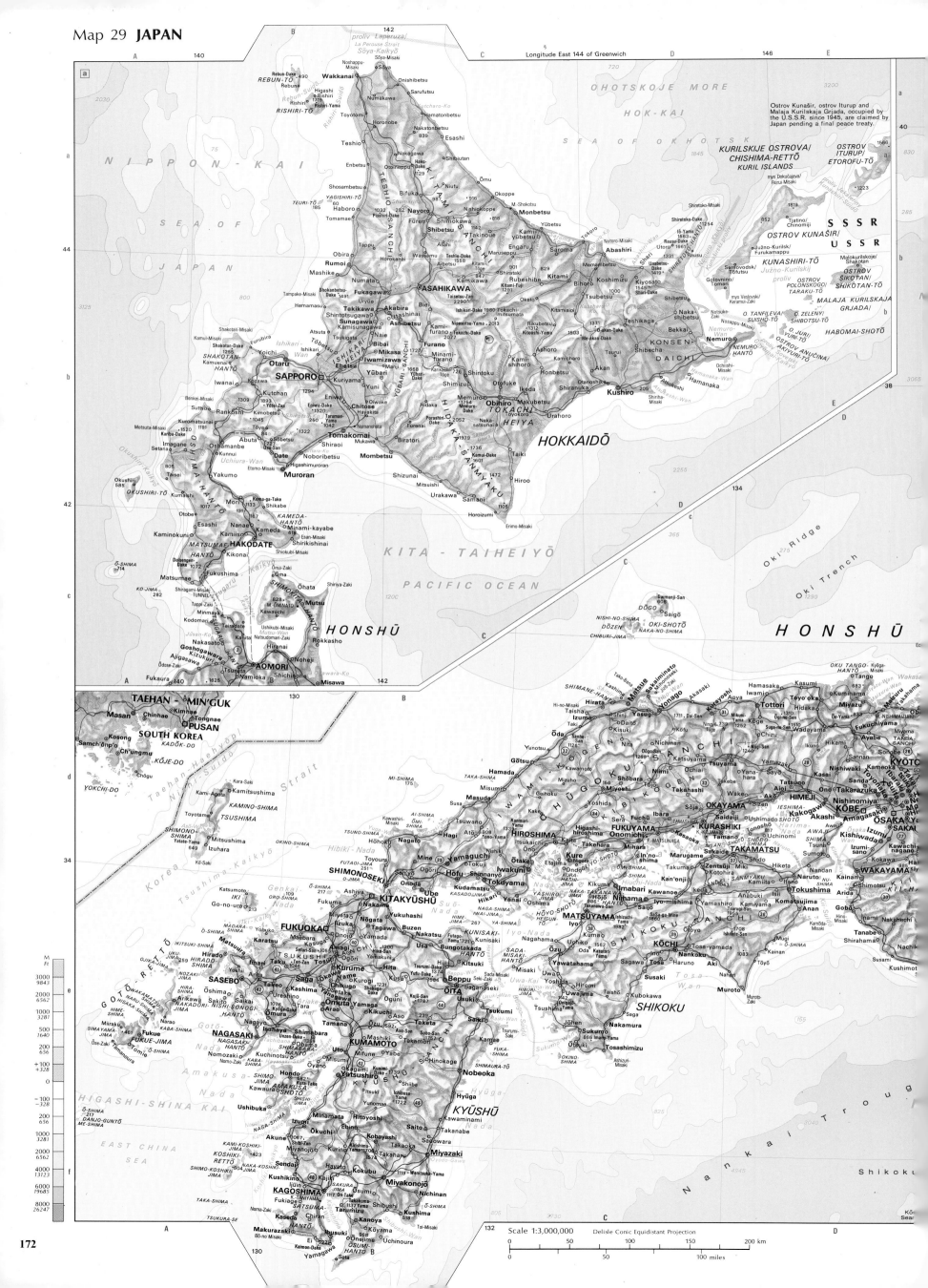
Longitude East 144 of Greenwich
proliv Laperuza/
La Perouse Strait
Sōya-Kaikyō
OHOTSKOJE MORE
HOK-KAI
SEA OF OKHOTSK
Ostrov Kunašir, ostrov Iturup and Malaja Kurilskaja Grjada, occupied by the U.S.S.R. since 1945, are claimed by Japan pending a final peace treaty.
KURILSKIJE OSTROVA/
CHISHIMA-RETTŌ
KURIL ISLANDS
OSTROV ITURUP/
ETOROFU-TŌ
SSSR
USSR
OSTROV KUNAŠIR/
KUNASHIRI-TŌ
OSTROV SIKOTAN/
SHIKOTAN-TŌ
MALAJA KURILSKAJA GRJADA/
HABOMAI-SHOTŌ
NIPPON-KAI
SEA OF JAPAN
REBUN-TŌ
RISHIRI-TŌ
TEURI-TŌ
YAGISHIRI-TŌ
Wakkanai
Sōya
Esashi
Teshio
Haboro
Rumoi
Nayoro
Shibetsu
Monbetsu
Abashiri
Kitami
ASAHIKAWA
Takikawa
Sunagawa
Otaru
SAPPORO
Iwamizawa
Ebetsu
Yūbari
Chitose
Tomakomai
Muroran
Date
Obihiro
Kushiro
Nemuro
Shibetsu
Akan
Taiki
Hiroo
Urakawa
Erimo-Misaki
TOKACHI-HEIYA
HOKKAIDŌ
KONSEN DAICHI
HIDAKA-SANMYAKU
KITAMI-SANCHI
TESHIO-SANCHI
ISHIKARI-HEIYA
Uchiura-Wan
OSHIMA-HANTŌ
OKUSHIRI-TŌ
Okushiri
Esashi
Hakodate
Matsumae
Fukushima
Ō-SHIMA
Tsugaru-Kaikyō
SHIMOKITA-HANTŌ
Mutsu
Ōma
Rokkasho
Noheji
AOMORI
Misawa
Fukaura
HONSHŪ
KITA-TAIHEIYŌ
PACIFIC OCEAN
Oki Ridge
Oki Trench
OKI-SHOTŌ
DŌGO
DŌZEN
Saigō
HONSHŪ
TAEHAN-MIN'GUK
SOUTH KOREA
PUSAN
Masan
Chinhae
Kimhae
KŌJE-DO
TSUSHIMA
Izuhara
Korea Strait
Tsushima-Kaikyō
IKI
Genkai-Nada
Matsue
Yonago
Tottori
Hamada
Masuda
Hagi
Yamaguchi
SHIMONOSEKI
KITAKYŪSHŪ
FUKUOKA
Kurume
Saga
SASEBO
NAGASAKI
Shimabara
KUMAMOTO
Ōita
Beppu
Nobeoka
Miyazaki
Miyakonojō
KAGOSHIMA
Sendai
Minamata
Yatsushiro
Hitoyoshi
KYŪSHŪ
GOTŌ-RETTŌ
Fukue
AMAKUSA-SHOTŌ
KOSHIKI-RETTŌ
SATSUMA-HANTŌ
ŌSUMI-HANTŌ
HIROSHIMA
Kure
Iwakuni
Tokuyama
Hōfu
Ube
Onomichi
FUKUYAMA
OKAYAMA
KURASHIKI
HIMEJI
KŌBE
ŌSAKA
KYŌTO
WAKAYAMA
TAKAMATSU
Tokushima
MATSUYAMA
Imabari
Niihama
KŌCHI
Uwajima
SHIKOKU
CHŪGOKU-SANCHI
SHIKOKU-SANCHI
Iyo-Nada
Suō-Nada
Hibiki-Nada
Tosa-Wan
Hyūga-Nada
HIGASHI-SHINA KAI
EAST CHINA SEA
Amakusa-Nada
Nankai Trough
Scale 1:3,000,000
Delisle Conic Equidistant Projection
0 50 100 150 200 km
0 50 100 miles

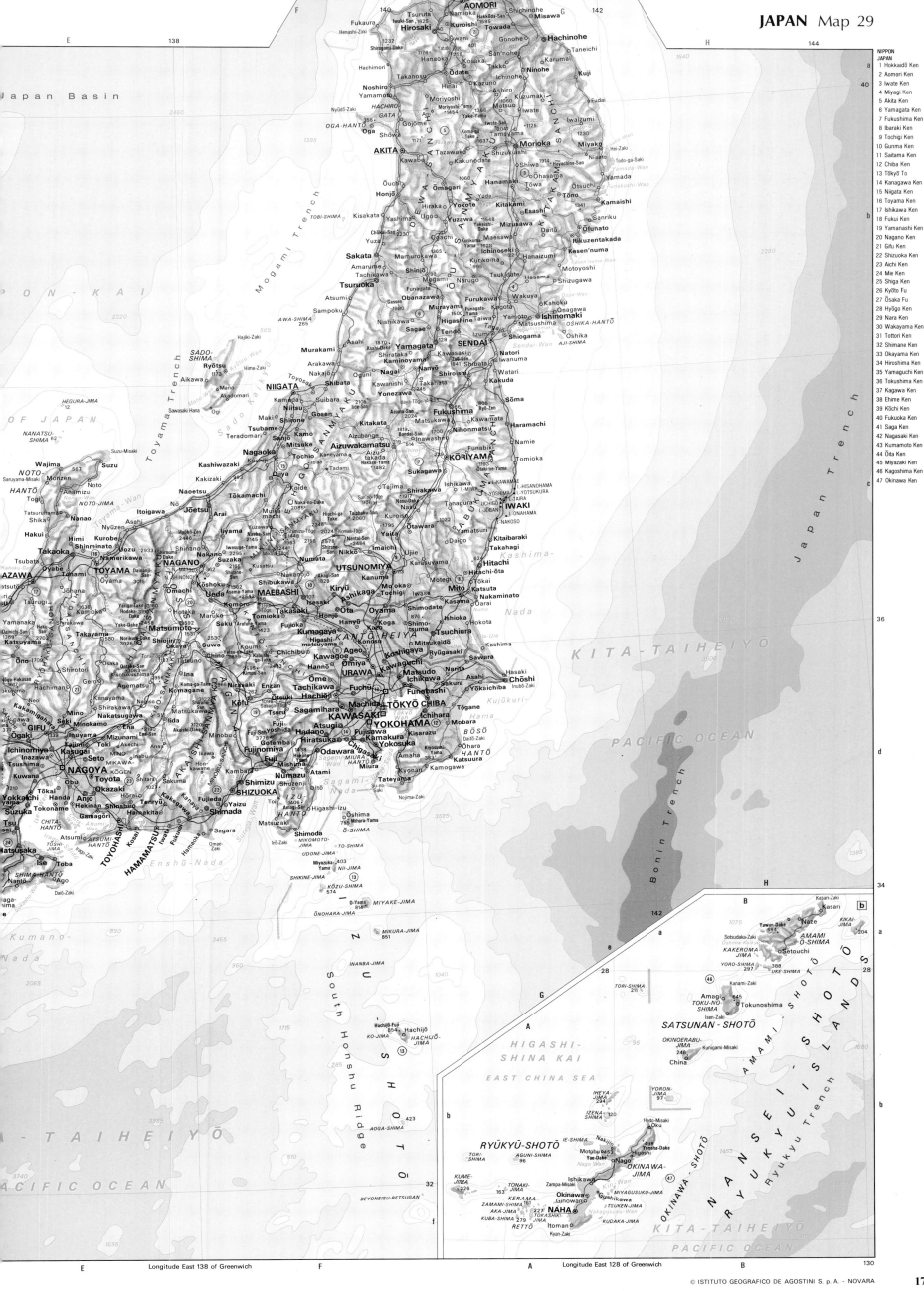

NIPPON
JAPAN
a 1 Hokkaidō Ken
   2 Aomori Ken
   3 Iwate Ken
   4 Miyagi Ken
   5 Akita Ken
   6 Yamagata Ken
   7 Fukushima Ken
   8 Ibaraki Ken
   9 Tochigi Ken
  10 Gunma Ken
  11 Saitama Ken
  12 Chiba Ken
  13 Tōkyō To
  14 Kanagawa Ken
  15 Niigata Ken
b 16 Toyama Ken
  17 Ishikawa Ken
  18 Fukui Ken
  19 Yamanashi Ken
  20 Nagano Ken
  21 Gifu Ken
  22 Shizuoka Ken
  23 Aichi Ken
  24 Mie Ken
  25 Shiga Ken
  26 Kyōto Fu
  27 Ōsaka Fu
  28 Hyōgo Ken
  29 Nara Ken
  30 Wakayama Ken
  31 Tottori Ken
  32 Shimane Ken
  33 Okayama Ken
  34 Hiroshima Ken
  35 Yamaguchi Ken
  36 Tokushima Ken
  37 Kagawa Ken
  38 Ehime Ken
  39 Kōchi Ken
  40 Fukuoka Ken
  41 Saga Ken
  42 Nagasaki Ken
  43 Kumamoto Ken
  44 Ōita Ken
  45 Miyazaki Ken
  46 Kagoshima Ken
  47 Okinawa Ken

Map 30 **AFRICA, PHYSICAL**

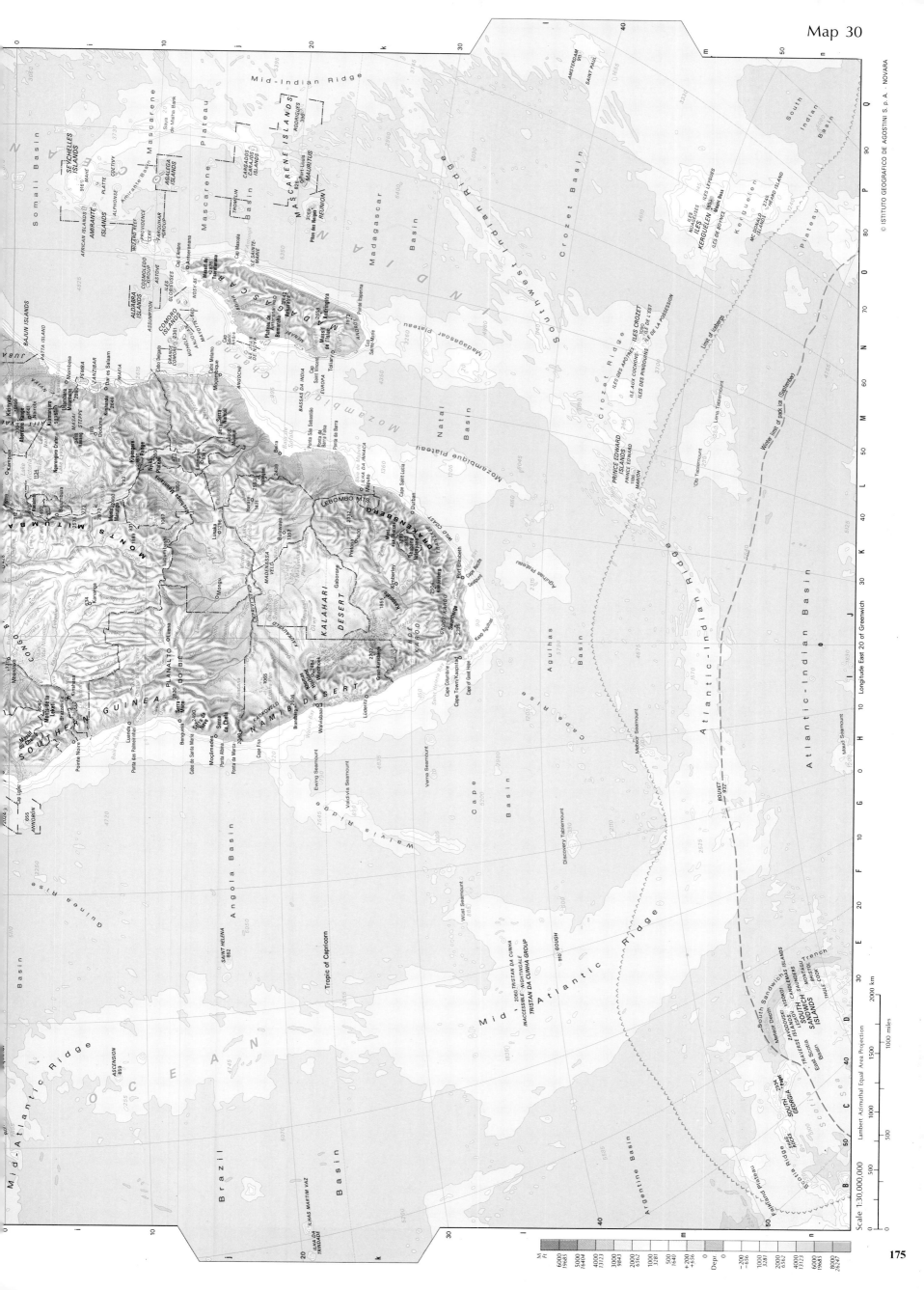

Mid-Atlantic Ridge
Guinea Rise
Brazil Basin
Angola Basin
Tropic of Capricorn
Walvis Ridge
Cape Basin
Cape Rise
Agulhas Basin
Agulhas Plateau
Argentine Basin
Atlantic-Indian Ridge
Atlantic-Indian Basin
Falkland Plateau
Scotia Ridge
Scotia Sea
East Scotia Basin
South Sandwich Trench
Meteor Depth
Somali Basin
Mascarene Plateau
Mascarene Basin
Mid-Indian Ridge
Madagascar Basin
Mozambique Channel
Mozambique Plateau
Madagascar Plateau
Natal Basin
Southwest Indian Ridge
Crozet Basin
Crozet Ridge
Kerguelen Plateau
South Indian Basin
OCEAN
INDIAN
ASCENSION
859
SAINT HELENA
862
ILHA DA TRINDADE
ILHAS MARTIM VAZ
TRISTAN DA CUNHA
INACCESSIBLE
NIGHTINGALE
TRISTAN DA CUNHA GROUP
GOUGH
Ewing Seamount
Valdivia Seamount
Verna Seamount
Wüst Seamount
Discovery Tablemount
Meteor Seamount
Maud Seamount
BOUVET
932
SOUTH GEORGIA
SHAG ROCKS
SOUTH SANDWICH ISLANDS
ZAVODOVSKI
VISOKOI
CANDLEMAS ISLANDS
TRAVERSE ISLANDS
LESKOV
SAUNDERS
MONTAGU
BRISTOL
THULE
COOK
PRINCE EDWARD ISLANDS
MARION
ILES CROZET
ILES DES APOTRES
ILE AUX COCHONS
ILES DES PINGOUINS
ILE DE L'EST
ILE DE LA POSSESSION
Ob Tablemount
Lena Tablemount
ILES KERGUELEN
Mount Ross
ILES DE BOYNES
MC DONALD ISLANDS
HEARD ISLAND
AMSTERDAM
SAINT PAUL
Limit of icebergs
Winter limit of pack ice (September)
SEYCHELLES ISLANDS
MAHÉ
AFRICAN ISLANDS
AMIRANTE ISLANDS
PLATTE
ALPHONSE
COETIVY
ALDABRA ISLANDS
COSMOLEDO GROUP
ASSUMPTION
ASTOVE
WIZARD REEF
PROVIDENCE
FARQUHAR GROUP
AGALEGA ISLANDS
Saya de Malha Bank
COMORO ISLANDS
GRANDE COMORE
MOHÉLI
ANJOUAN
MAYOTTE
ILES GLORIEUSES
NOSY-BE
TROMELIN
CARGADOS CARAJOS ISLANDS
MASCARENE ISLANDS
RODRIGUES
MAURITIUS
Port-Louis
RÉUNION
Piton des Neiges
BASSAS DA INDIA
EUROPA
ILE JUAN DE NOVA
ILE SAINTE-MARIE
MADAGASCAR
Antseranana
Toliary
Cap Sainte-Marie
Pointe Itaperina
Massif de l'Isalo
Andringitra
Plateau de Antananarivo
Ankaratra
Massif du Tsaratanana
BAJUN ISLANDS
PATTA ISLAND
PEMBA
ZANZIBAR
MAFIA
ANNOBÓN
Cap Lopez
SOUTHERN GUINEA
CONGO
MONTS MITUMBA
PLANALTO DO BIÉ
NAMIB DESERT
KALAHARI DESERT
KAOKOVELD
CAPRIVI STRIP
MADENASSA VELD
KAUKAUVELD
DRAKENSBERG
LEBOMBO MTS
HOË KAROO
GROOT KAROO
TRANSKEI
WILD COAST
MASAI STEPPE
Muchinga Mountains
Nyika Plateau
Kipengere Range
Aberdare Range
Usambara Mountains
Ngorongoro Crater
Kilimanjaro
Kirinyaga
Serra Moco
Serra da Neve
Serra da Chela
Khomas Hochland
Mont aux Sources
Thabana Ntlenyana
Swartberge
Kompasberg
Kaapplato
Groot-Karasberge
Pointe Noire
Brazzaville
Kinshasa
Mbandaka
Luanda
Benguela
Moçâmedes
Lobito
Cape Fria
Walvisbaai
Windhoek
Lüderitz
Cape Columbine
Cape Town/Kaapstad
Cape of Good Hope
Kaap Agulhas
Port Elizabeth
Cape Recife
Durban
Cape Saint Lucia
Maputo
ILHA DA INHACA
Gaborone
Pretoria
Kimberley
Bulawayo
Harare
Lusaka
Mongu
Lubumbashi
Lilongwe
Beira
Moçambique
Cabo Delgado
Dar es Salaam
Mombasa
Dodoma
Nairobi
Kampala
Bujumbura
Kananga
Longitude East 20 of Greenwich
Scale 1:30,000,000
Lambert Azimuthal Equal Area Projection
0 500 1000 1500 2000 km
0 500 1000 miles
M / Ft: 6000 19685; 5000 16404; 4000 13123; 3000 9843; 2000 6562; 1000 3281; 500 1640; +200 +656; 0; Depr.; 0; −200 −656; 1000 3281; 2000 6562; 4000 13123; 6000 19685; 8000 26247
© ISTITUTO GEOGRAFICO DE AGOSTINI S. p. A. · NOVARA

Map 31 **AFRICA, POLITICAL**

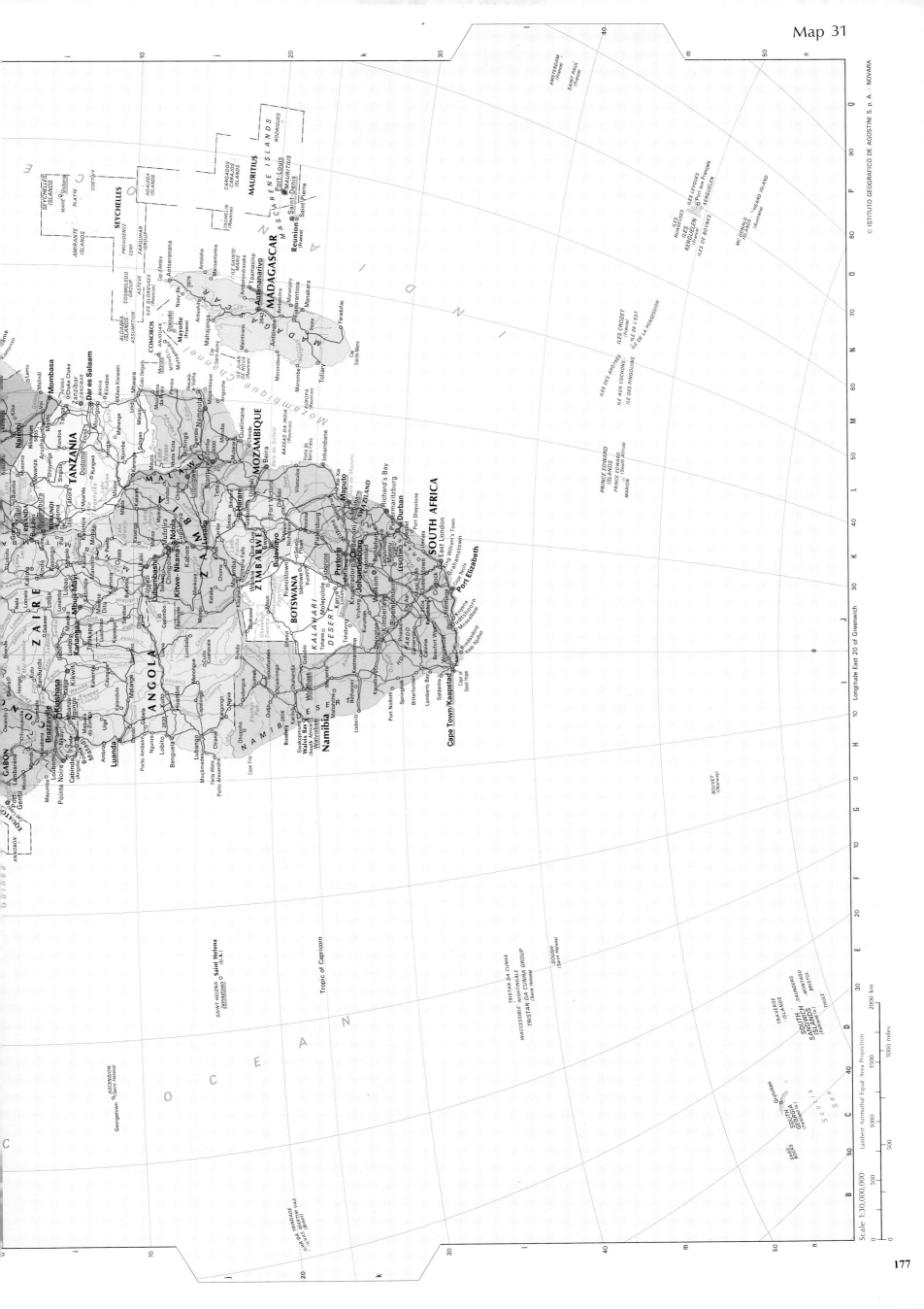

Map 31

© ISTITUTO GEOGRAFICO DE AGOSTINI S. p. A. - NOVARA

Scale 1:30,000,000   Lambert Azimuthal Equal Area Projection

Map 32

AL JAZÄ'IR
ALGERIA

WILÄYATE
1 Adrar
2 Al Jazä'ir
3 Annaba
4 Batna
5 Bèchar
6 Bejaia
7 Biskra
8 Blida
9 Bouira
10 Chelif
11 Constantine
12 Djelfa
13 Guelma
14 Jijel
15 Laghouat
16 Mascara
17 Médéa
18 Mostaganem
19 M'Sila
20 Oran
21 Ouargla
22 Oum el Bouaghi
23 Saïda
24 Sétif
25 Sidi Bel Abbes
26 Skikda
27 Tamanrasset
28 Tebessa
29 Tiaret
30 Tizi Ouzou
31 Tlemcen

AL MAGHRIB
MOROCCO

PRÉFECTURES
A Casablanca
B Rabat-Salé

PROVINCES
1 Agadir
2 Al Hoceima
3 Ar Rachidiya
4 Azilal
5 Beni Mellal
6 Boulemane
7 Chechaouene
8 El Jadida
9 El Kelaa des Srarhna
10 Essaouira
11 Fès
12 Figuig
13 Kenitra
14 Khemisset
15 Khenifra
16 Khouribga
17 Marrakech
18 Meknès
19 Nador
20 Ouarzazate
21 Oujda
22 Safi
23 Settat
24 Tanger
25 Tan Tan
26 Taounate
27 Tata
28 Taza
29 Tétouan
30 Tiznit

TÜNIS
TUNISIA

WILÄYATE
1 Al Käf
2 Al Mahdiyah
3 Al Munastir
4 Al Qaṣrayn
5 Al Qayrawän
6 Bäjah
7 Banzart
8 Jundubah
9 Madaniyïn
10 Näbul
11 Qäbis
12 Qafṣah
13 Qamüdah
14 Ṣafäqis
15 Silyänah
16 Süsah
17 Tünis
18 Zaghwän

Ⓐ Western Sahara is occupied by Morocco.

Scale 1:9,000,000   Lambert Azimuthal Equal Area Projection

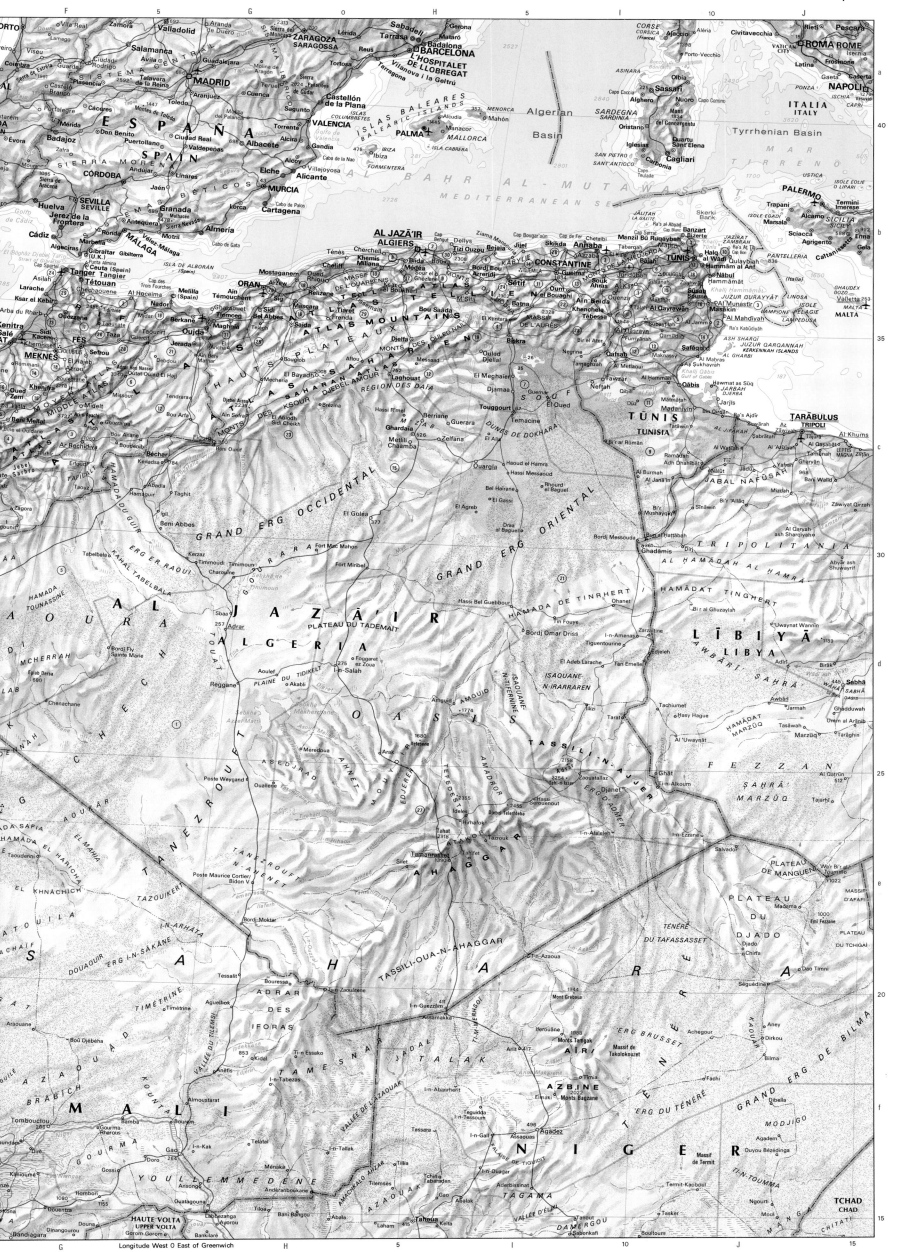
ESPAÑA
SPAIN
MADRID
AL JAZĀ'IR
ALGIERS
AL JAZĀ'IR
ALGERIA
TŪNIS
TUNISIA
LĪBIYĀ
LIBYA
MALI
NIGER
ITALIA
ITALY
Algerian Basin
Tyrrhenian Basin
GRAND ERG OCCIDENTAL
GRAND ERG ORIENTAL
AHAGGAR
TASSILI-N-AJJER
TANEZROUFT
ATLAS MOUNTAINS
FEZZAN
TRIPOLITANIA
TARĀBULUS
TRIPOLI
TŪNIS
Longitude West 0 East of Greenwich

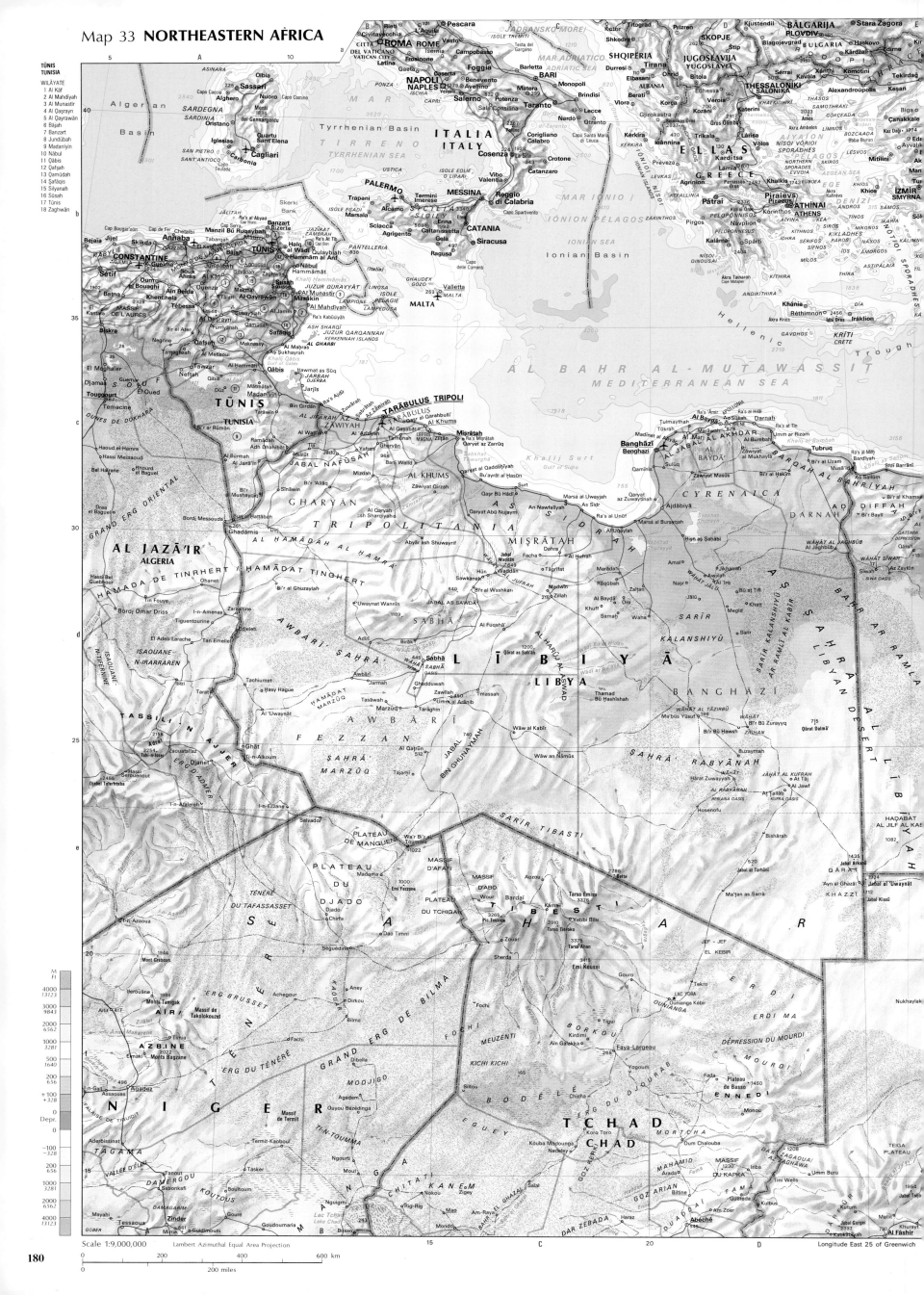

Map 33 NORTHEASTERN AFRICA
TŪNIS
TUNISIA
WILĀYATE
1 Al Kāf
2 Al Mahdīyah
3 Al Munastīr
4 Al Qaşrayn
5 Al Qayrawān
6 Bājah
7 Banzart
8 Jundūbah
9 Madanīyīn
10 Nābul
11 Qābis
12 Qafşah
13 Qamūdah
14 Şafāqis
15 Silyānah
16 Sūsah
17 Tūnis
18 Zaghwān
AL BAHR AL-MUTAWASSIT
MEDITERRANEAN SEA
LĪBIYĀ
LIBYA
AL JAZĀ'IR
ALGERIA
TŪNIS
TUNISIA
TCHAD
CHAD
NIGER
ITALIA
ITALY
ELLAS
GREECE
MALTA
TARĀBULUS TRIPOLI
Banghāzī
Benghazi
TRIPOLITANIA
CYRENAICA
FEZZAN
TIBESTI
M
Ft
4000
13123
3000
9843
2000
6562
1000
3281
500
1640
200
656
+100
+328
0
Depr.
0
−100
−328
200
656
1000
3281
2000
6562
4000
13123
Scale 1:9,000,000
Lambert Azimuthal Equal Area Projection
0 200 400 600 km
0 200 miles
Longitude East 25 of Greenwich

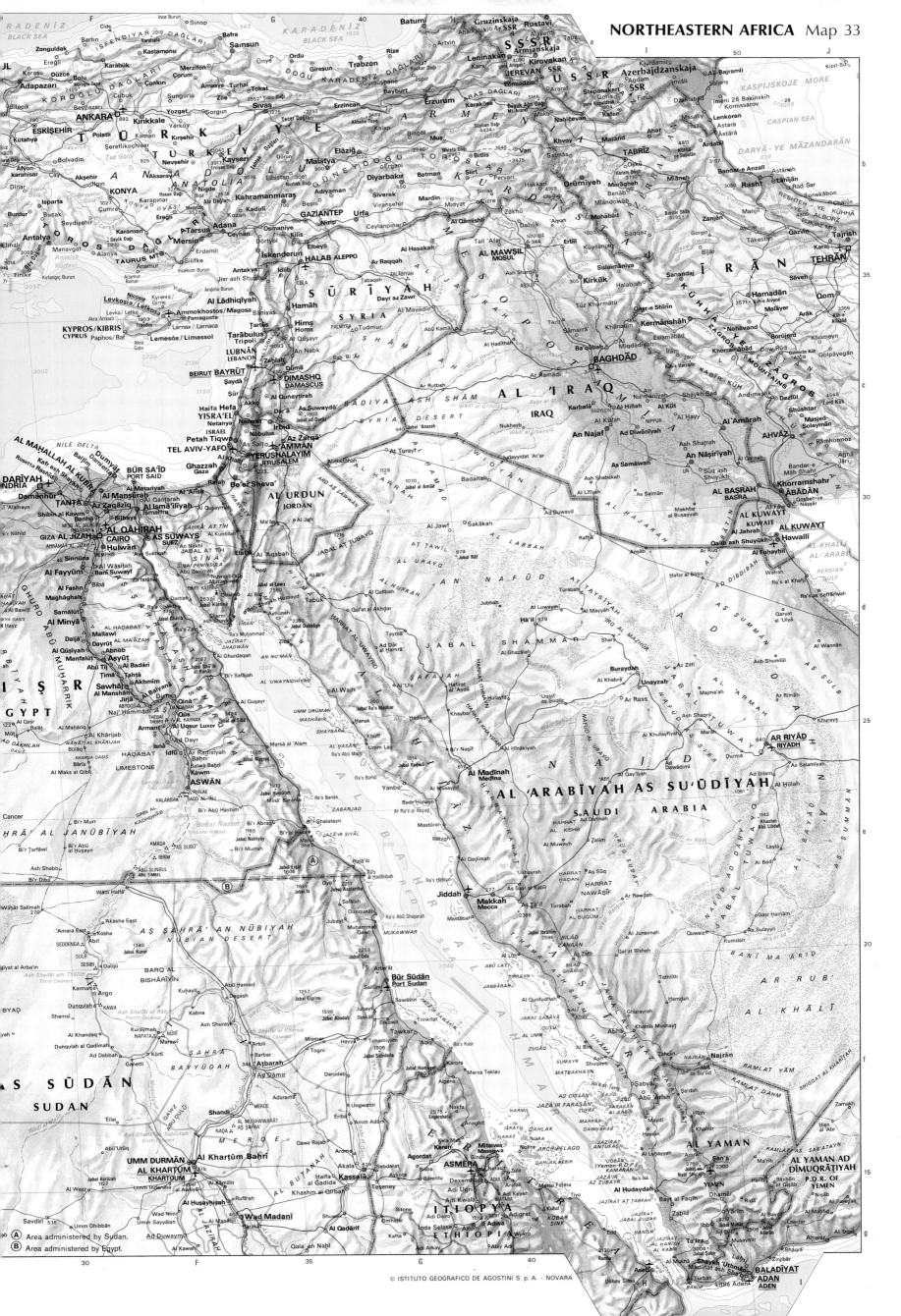

A Area administered by Sudan.
B Area administered by Egypt.

© ISTITUTO GEOGRAFICO DE AGOSTINI S.p.A. - NOVARA

181

Map 34 **WEST-CENTRAL AFRICA**

LIBERIA
COUNTIES
1 Bong
2 Cape Mount
3 Grand Bassa
4 Grand Gedeh
5 Lofa
6 Maryland
7 Montserrado
8 Nimba
9 Sinoe

CÔTE D'IVOIRE
IVORY COAST
DÉPARTEMENTS
1 Abengourou
2 Abidjan
3 Aboisso
4 Adzopé
5 Agboville
6 Biankouma
7 Bondoukou
8 Bongouanou
9 Bouaflé
10 Bouaké
11 Bouna
12 Boundiali
13 Dabakala
14 Daloa
15 Danané
16 Dimbokro
17 Divo
18 Ferkessédougou
19 Gagnoa
20 Guiglo
21 Issia
22 Katiola
23 Korhogo
24 Lakota
25 Man
26 Mankono
27 Odienné
28 Oumé
29 Sassandra
30 Séguéla
31 Soubré
32 Tengrela
33 Touba
34 Zuenoula

HAUTE-VOLTA
UPPER VOLTA
DÉPARTEMENTS
1 Centre
2 Centre-Est
3 Centre-Nord
4 Centre-Ouest
5 Est
6 Hauts-Bassins
7 Komoé
8 Nord
9 Sahel
10 Sud-Ouest
11 Volta Noire

TOGO
RÉGIONS
1 Centre
2 Kara
3 Maritime
4 Plateaux
5 Savanes

BÉNIN
PROVINCES
1 Atakora
2 Atlantique
3 Borgou
4 Mono
5 Ouémé
6 Zou

Ⓐ Abuja is the future federal capital of Nigeria.

Ⓑ The political subdivisions shown for Guinea represent statistical areas and are not recognized for administrative purposes.

M
ft
3000 / 9843
2000 / 6562
1000 / 3281
500 / 1640
200 / 656
+100 / +328
0
−100 / −328
200 / 656
1000 / 3281
2000 / 6562
4000 / 13123
6000 / 19685

Scale 1:9,000,000
Lambert Azimuthal Equal Area Projection
0   200   400   600 km
0   200 miles

Longitude West 5 of Greenwich

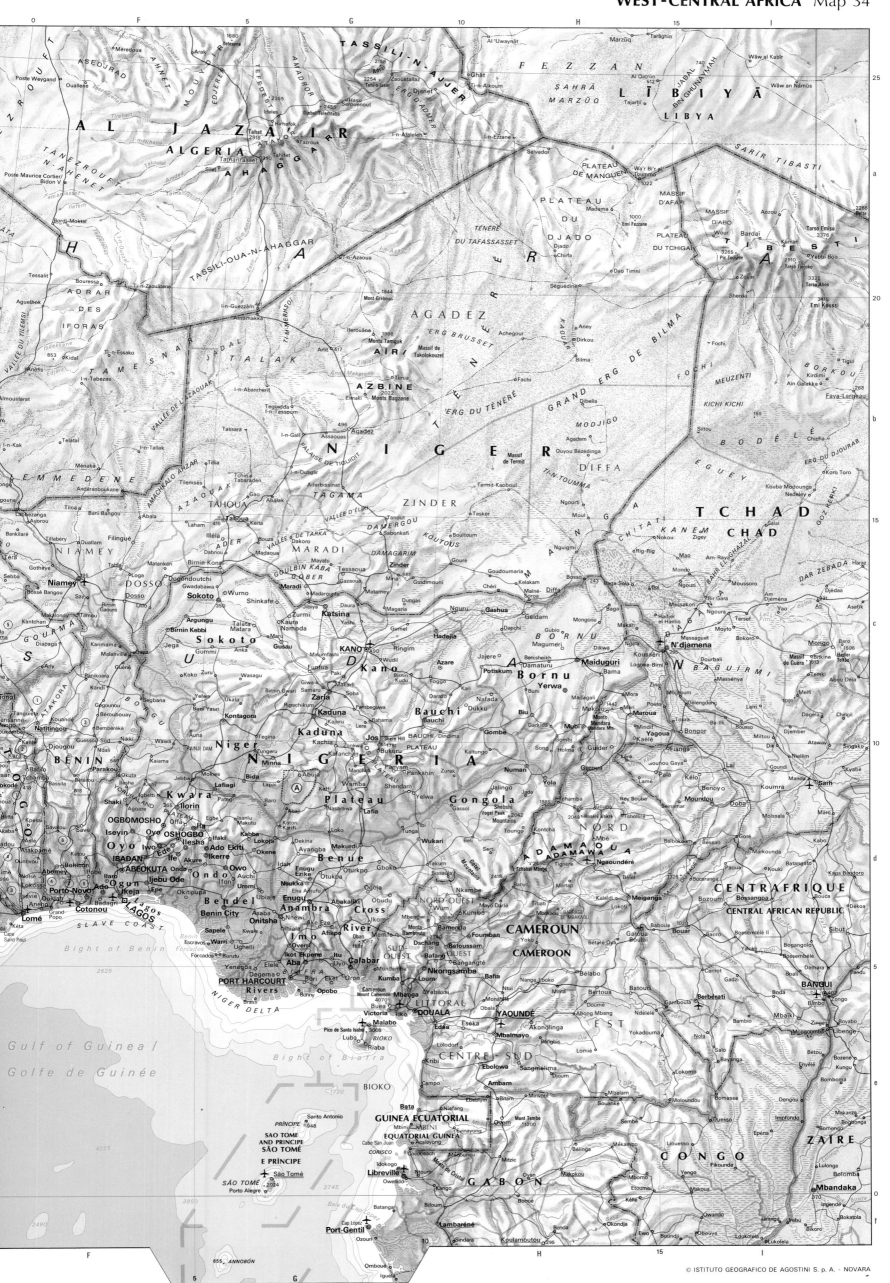
AL JAZĀ'IR
ALGERIA
TASSILI-N-AJJER
AHAGGAR
TASSILI-OUA-N-AHAGGAR
TANEZROUFT
FEZZAN
ṢAḤRĀ MARZŪQ
LĪBIYĀ
LIBYA
SARĪR TIBASTĪ
PLATEAU DE MANGUENI
PLATEAU DU DJADO
TÉNÉRÉ DU TAFASSASSET
TIBESTI
Emi Koussi
AGADEZ
AÏR
ERG DU TÉNÉRÉ
GRAND ERG DE BILMA
TÉNÉRÉ
NIGER
ZINDER
MARADI
NIAMEY
DOSSO
TAHOUA
DIFFA
TCHAD
CHAD
KANEM
BORKOU
BODÉLÉ
Niamey
Agadez
Zinder
Sokoto
Katsina
Kano
Kaduna
Zaria
Bauchi
Maiduguri
N'djamena
NIGERIA
BÉNIN
TOGO
Lomé
Cotonou
Porto-Novo
Lagos
Ibadan
Abeokuta
Ilorin
Kwara
Oyo
Ogun
Ondo
Bendel
Benin City
Anambra
Imo
Cross River
Rivers
Port Harcourt
Calabar
Plateau
Benue
Gongola
Bornu
Yola
Jos
Minna
Abuja
Niger
SLAVE COAST
Bight of Benin
NIGER DELTA
Gulf of Guinea
Golfe de Guinée
Bight of Biafra
BIOKO
Malabo
CAMEROUN
CAMEROON
Douala
Yaoundé
LITTORAL
CENTRE-SUD
ADAMAOUA
NORD
EST
Ngaoundéré
Garoua
CENTRAFRIQUE
CENTRAL AFRICAN REPUBLIC
BANGUI
GUINEA ECUATORIAL
EQUATORIAL GUINEA
MBINI
Bata
SAO TOME AND PRINCIPE
SÃO TOMÉ E PRÍNCIPE
São Tomé
PRÍNCIPE
ANNOBÓN
GABON
Libreville
Port-Gentil
Lambaréné
CONGO
ZAÏRE
Mbandaka

Map 35 **EAST-CENTRAL AFRICA**

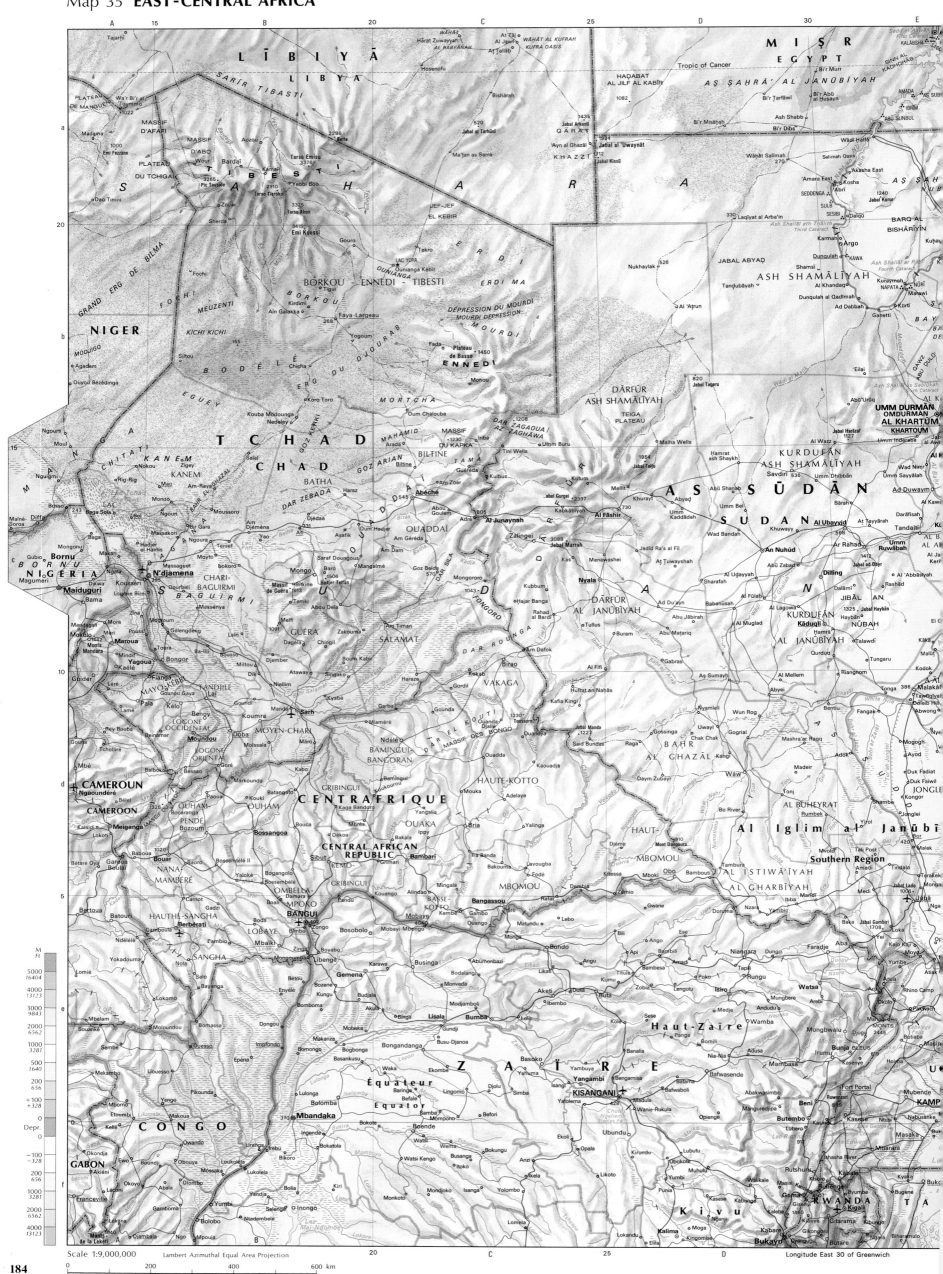

Scale 1:9,000,000
Lambert Azimuthal Equal Area Projection

0   200   400   600 km

0   200 miles

184

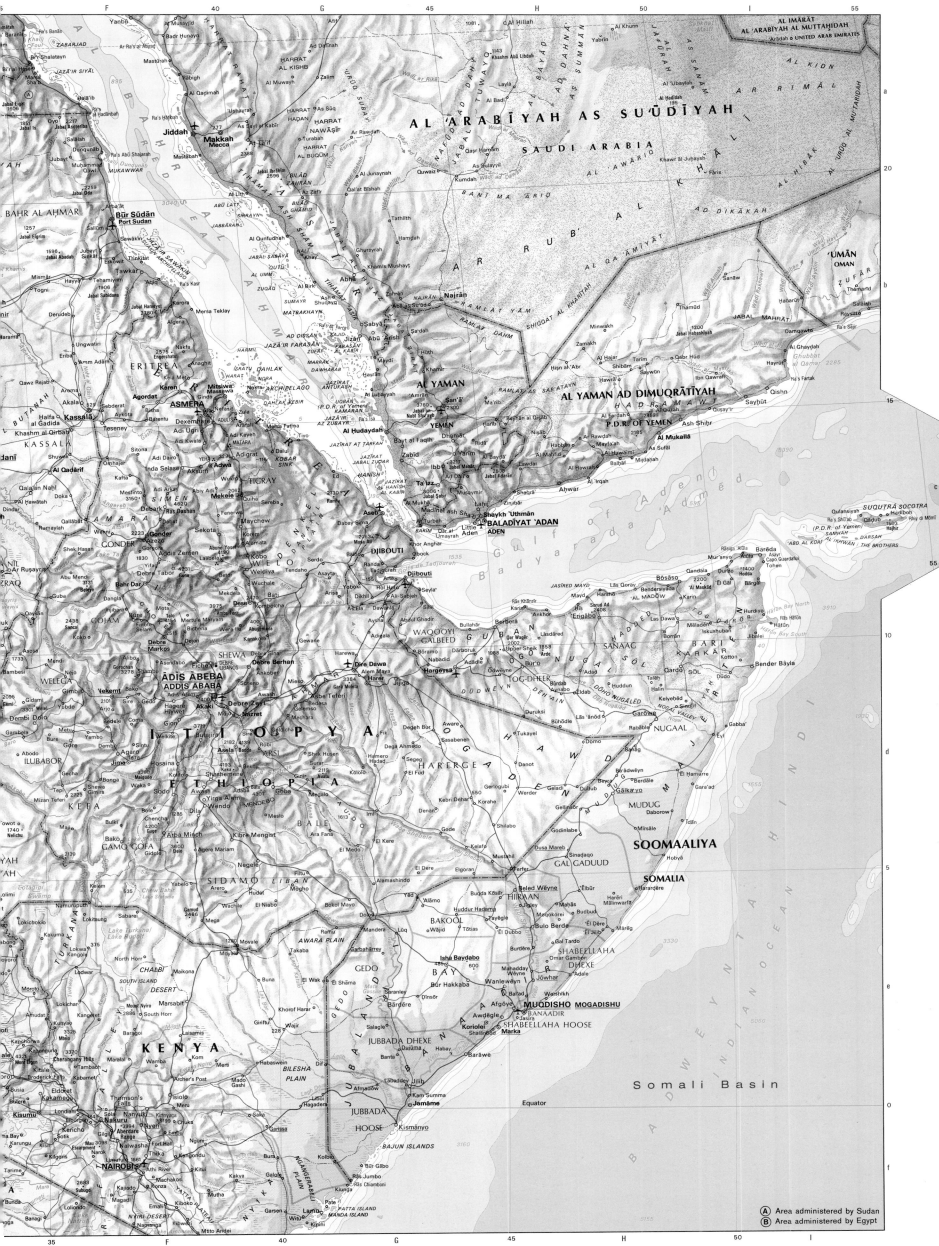
AL 'ARABĪYAH AS SU'ŪDĪYAH
SAUDI ARABIA
AL YAMAN
AL YAMAN AD DIMUQRĀTĪYAH
P.D.R. OF YEMEN
AL IMĀRĀT AL 'ARABĪYAH AL MUTTAḤIDAH
UNITED ARAB EMIRATES
'UMĀN
OMAN
AR RUB' AL KHĀLĪ
ITIOPYA
ETHIOPIA
ERITREA
DJIBOUTI
SOOMAALIYA
SOMALIA
KENYA
Jiddah
Makkah
Mecca
Būr Sūdān
Port Sudan
Kassalā
Asmera
Ṣan'ā'
Al Ḥudaydah
Ta'izz
BALADĪYAT 'ADAN
ADEN
Al Mukallā
Djibouti
Hargeysa
Berbera
Dire Dawa
Harer
ĀDĪS ĀBEBA
ADDIS ABABA
MUQDISHO
MOGADISHU
Kismānyo
NAIROBI
Kisumu
Nakuru
Gulf of Aden
Badyarada 'Admed
SUQUTRĀ SOCOTRA
Somali Basin
INDIAN OCEAN
BADWEYNTA HINDI
Equator
Ⓐ Area administered by Sudan
Ⓑ Area administered by Egypt

Map 36 **EQUATORIAL AFRICA**

Scale 1:9,000,000   Lambert Azimuthal Equal Area Projection

AS SŪDĀN
SUDAN
ITIOPYA
ETHIOPIA
UGANDA
KENYA
SOOMAALIYA
SOMALIA
RWANDA
BURUNDI
TANZANIA
Tanganyika
MALAWI
MOÇAMBIQUE
MOZAMBIQUE
ZIMBABWE
MADAGASIKARA
MADAGASCAR
COMORES / COMOROS
SEYCHELLES
INDIAN OCEAN
KAMPALA
NAIROBI
MOMBASA
MUQDISHO
MOGADISHU
DAR ES SALAAM
Zanzibar
Kigali
Bujumbura
Lilongwe
Blantyre
HARARE
Moroni
Mayotte (France)
ANTANANARIVO
Lake Victoria
Lake Tanganyika
Lake Turkana / Lake Rudolf
Canal de Moçambique
Mozambique channel
Longitude East 30 of Greenwich

Map 37 **SOUTHERN AFRICA**

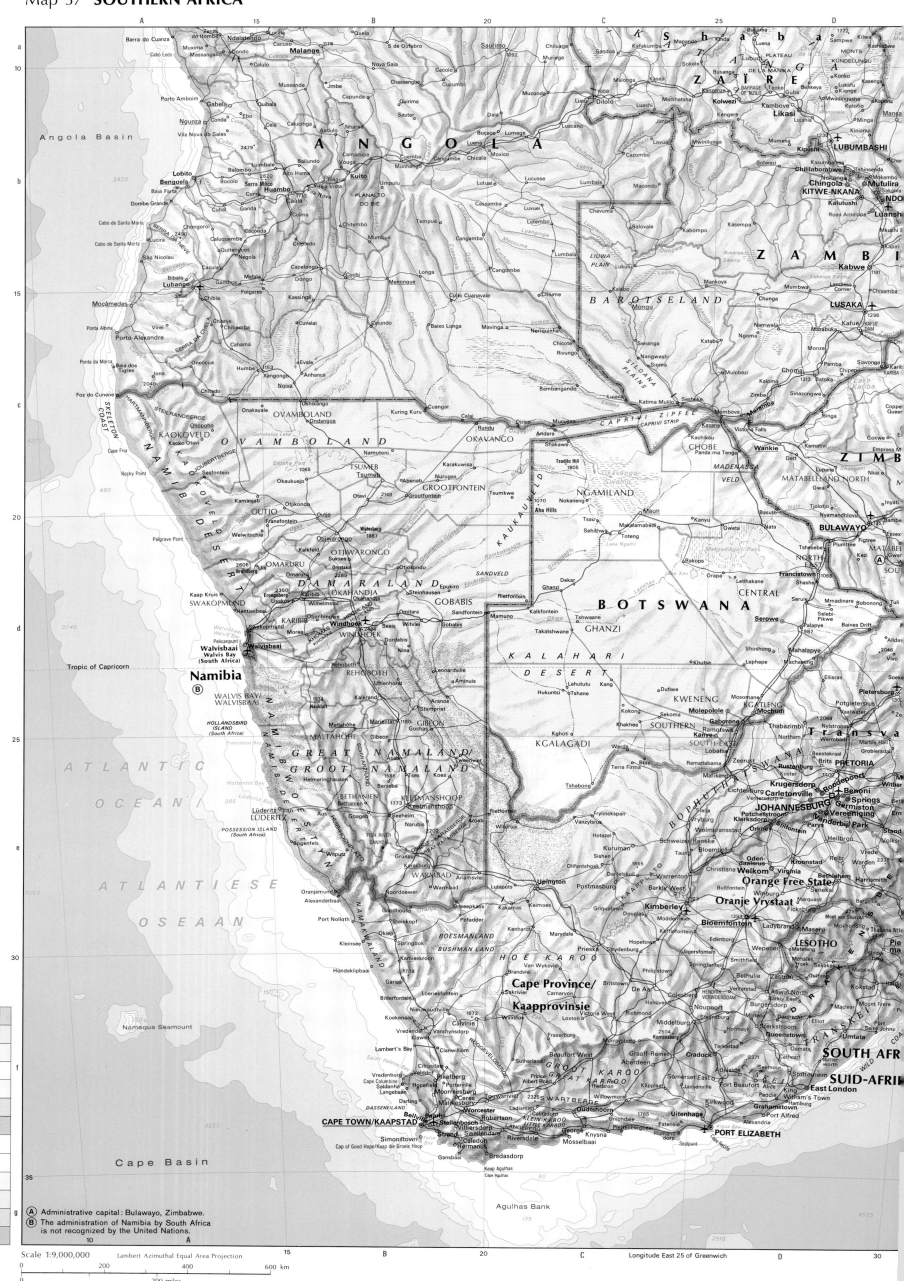

Scale 1:9,000,000

Lambert Azimuthal Equal Area Projection

Longitude East 25 of Greenwich

0   200   400   600 km

0   200 miles

Ⓐ Administrative capital: Bulawayo, Zimbabwe.

Ⓑ The administration of Namibia by South Africa
is not recognized by the United Nations.

MOÇAMBIQUE
MOZAMBIQUE
MADAGASIKARA
MADAGASCAR
COMORES / COMOROS
Mayotte (France)
SEYCHELLES
MAURITIUS
Réunion (France)
MALAWI
Lilongwe
Blantyre
Nampula
Quelimane
Beira
Inhambane
MAPUTO
Richard's Bay
Mahajanga
ANTANANARIVO
Toamasina
Fianarantsoa
Toliary
Antseranana
Moroni
Port-Louis
Saint-Denis
Victoria
OCEANO ÍNDICO / OCÉAN INDIEN
INDIAN OCEAN / INDIESE OSEAAN
Natal Basin
Mozambique Plateau
Madagascar Plateau
Canal de Moçambique
Mozambique Channel
ILES MASCAREIGNES/ MASCARENE ISLANDS
ALDABRA GROUP
AMIRANTE ISLANDS
Amirante Basin
Amirante Trench
Longitude East 50 of Greenwich

Map 38 **NORTH AMERICA, PHYSICAL**

© ISTITUTO GEOGRAFICO DE AGOSTINI S. p. A. - NOVARA

GUIANA HIGHLANDS

Mid-Atlantic Ridge

North American Basin

Sargasso Sea

Bermuda Islands

Blake Ridge

Blake Plateau

BAHAMAS

GRAND BAHAMA
ABACO ISLAND
ANDROS
ELEUTHERA
CAT ISLAND
SAN SALVADOR
GREAT EXUMA
LONG ISLAND
CROOKED ISLAND
ACKLINS
CAICOS ISLANDS
GREAT INAGUA

CUBA
La Habana
Havana
ISLA DE LA JUVENTUD

HISPANIOLA
JAMAICA
Kingston
CAYMAN ISLANDS

GREATER ANTILLES

LESSER ANTILLES

WINDWARD ISLANDS
LEEWARD ISLANDS
VIRGIN ISLANDS
PUERTO RICO
Puerto Rico Trench
GUADELOUPE
DOMINICA
MARTINIQUE
SAINT LUCIA
SAINT VINCENT
BARBADOS
GRENADA
TOBAGO
TRINIDAD
Port of Spain

Caribbean Sea

Venezuelan Basin

Colombian Basin

PENÍNSULA DE LA GUAJIRA

CORDILLERA DE LA COSTA

PENÍNSULA DE PARAGUANÁ
Caracas
Sierra Nevada de Santa Marta
Barranquilla
Cartagena

Golfo de Maracaibo

ISTMO DE PANAMÁ

Gulf of Panama

ISLA DE MALPELO
ISLA DEL COCO

Cocos Ridge

COSTA DE MOSQUITOS

YUCATAN PENINSULA
Mérida
Belize City

Bahía de Campeche

Gulf of Mexico

Mexico Basin

FLORIDA
Cape Canaveral
Jacksonville
Tampa
Miami

Cape Hatteras
New York
Philadelphia
Washington
Norfolk
Charleston

APPALACHIAN MOUNTAINS
PIEDMONT
Cumberland Plateau
Cleveland
Cincinnati
Chicago
St. Louis
Memphis
New Orleans
Houston
Kansas City
Omaha
Oklahoma City

PLAINS

GREAT PLAINS

Ozark Plateau
Ouachita Mountains
Edwards Plateau
LLANO ESTACADO

Pikes Peak
Denver
FRONT RANGE

Sangre de Cristo Mountains
Sacramento Mountains
El Paso
BOLSÓN DE MAPIMÍ
MESETA CENTRAL
PLATEAU OF MEXICO
SIERRA MADRE ORIENTAL
SIERRA MADRE OCCIDENTAL
SIERRA MADRE DEL SUR
ISTMO DE TEHUANTEPEC
Monterrey
Tampico
Matamoros
Veracruz

DESIERTO DE ALTAR
LOWER CALIFORNIA
Gulf of California
La Paz
Cabo San Lucas

GREAT BASIN
SIERRA NEVADA
DEATH VALLEY
MOJAVE DESERT
SAN JOAQUIN VALLEY
RANGES
WASATCH RANGE
Wheeler Peak
Mount Whitney
San Francisco
Los Angeles
San Diego
Cape Mendocino

ISLAS REVILLAGIGEDO
ISLAS MARÍAS
CABO CORRIENTES
ISLA DE GUADALUPE

CLIPPERTON

Clarion Fracture Zone
Clipperton Fracture Zone
Galapagos Fracture Zone

Carnegie Ridge

ARCHIPIÉLAGO DE COLÓN
GALAPAGOS ISLANDS
ISABELA
FERNANDINA
SANTA CRUZ
SAN CRISTOBAL
SAN SALVADOR

ANDES
CORDILLERA OCCIDENTAL
CORDILLERA CENTRAL
CORDILLERA ORIENTAL
ALTIPLANO
YUNGAS
MONTAÑA

Quito
Guayaquil
Lima
Trujillo

Peru-Chile Trench
Peru Basin
East Pacific Rise

VENEZUELA

LLANOS

CHAPADA DOS PARECIS
MATO GROSSO
PLATEAU
PANTANAL
SERRA DOS PARECIS
LLANOS DE MOJOS
CHACO BOREAL
CHACO CENTRAL
CHACO AUSTRAL
GRAN CHACO

Manaus

Tropic of Cancer
Tropic of Capricorn
Equator

Middle America Trench
Guatemala Basin
Albatross Plateau

PACIFIC OCEAN

Longitude West 100 of Greenwich

PITCAIRN
HENDERSON
DUCIE
OENO
PUKARUHA
REAO
MARIA
MORANE
MANGAREVA
TEMOE

Scale 1:30,000,000
Lambert Azimuthal Equal Area Projection

2000 km
1500
1000 miles
1000
500

M
Ft
5000 16404
4000 13123
3000 9843
2000 6562
1000 3281
500 1640
+200 +656
Depr. 0
-200 -656
1000 3281
2000 6562
4000 13123
6000 19685
8000 26247

Map 39 **NORTH AMERICA, POLITICAL**

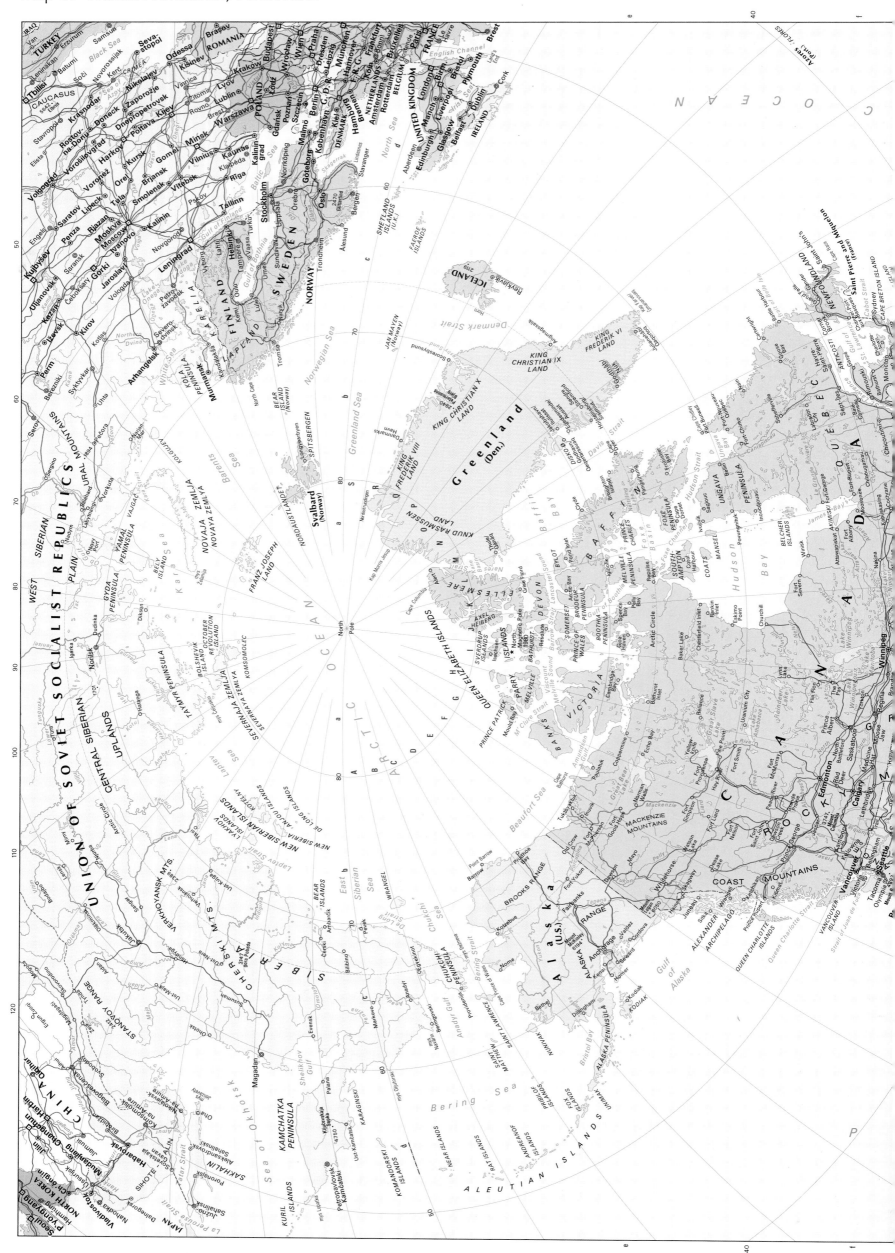

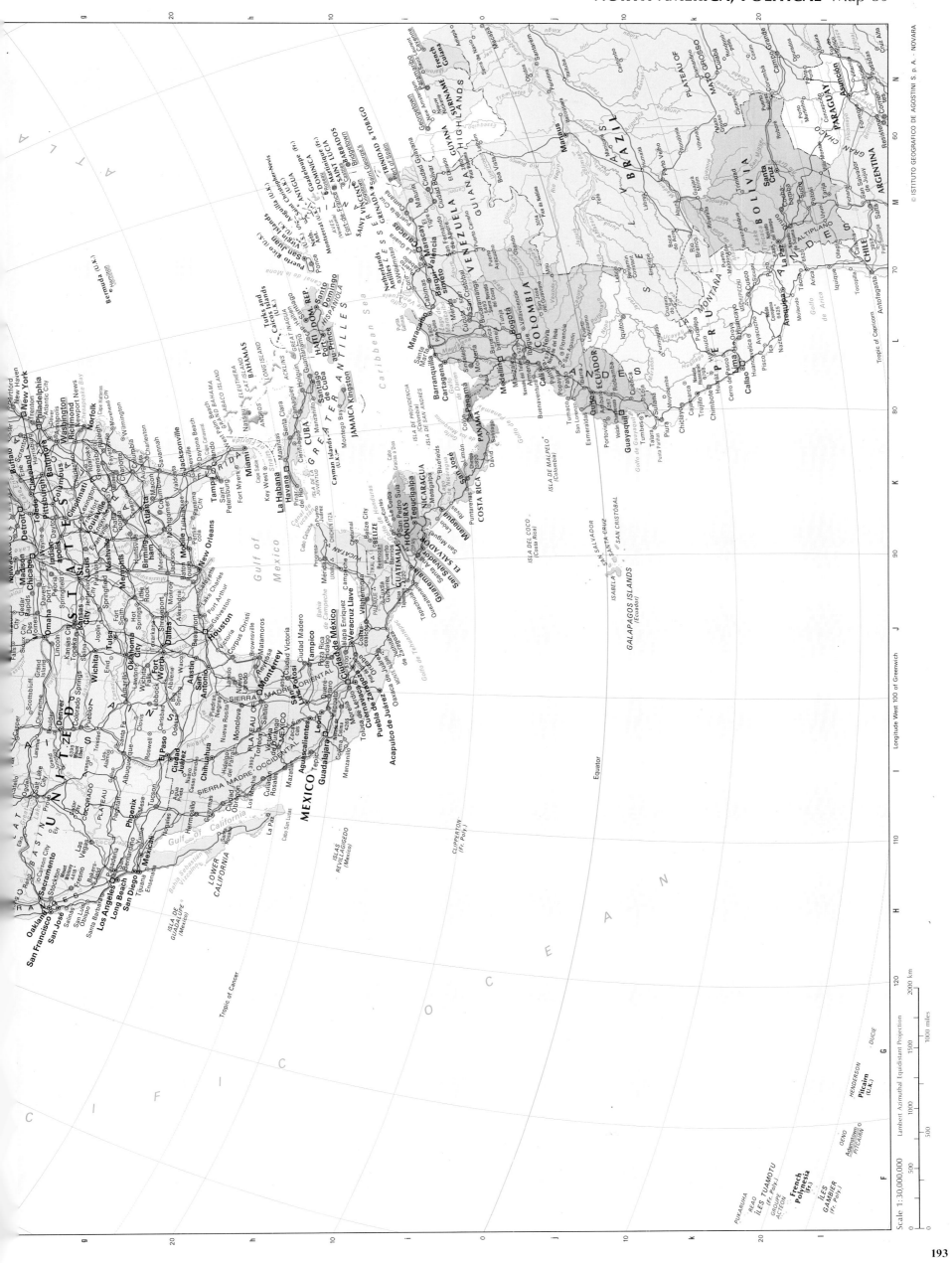
UNITED STATES
MEXICO
Gulf of Mexico
Caribbean Sea
BAHAMAS
CUBA
La Habana
JAMAICA Kingston
HAITI
DOM. REP.
Santo Domingo
GREATER ANTILLES
LESSER ANTILLES
Puerto Rico (U.S.)
Bermuda (U.K.)
GUATEMALA
BELIZE
HONDURAS
EL SALVADOR
NICARAGUA
COSTA RICA
PANAMA
COLOMBIA
VENEZUELA
GUYANA
SURINAME
French Guiana
ECUADOR
PERU
BRAZIL
BOLIVIA
PARAGUAY
CHILE
ARGENTINA
GALAPAGOS ISLANDS (Ecuador)
New York
Washington
Chicago
Houston
Dallas
New Orleans
Miami
Los Angeles
San Francisco
Ciudad de México
Guadalajara
Monterrey
Bogotá
Caracas
Quito
Lima
La Paz
Asunción
Manaus
Pitcairn (U.K.)
French Polynesia (Fr.)
Tropic of Cancer
Tropic of Capricorn
Equator
Longitude West 100 of Greenwich
Scale 1:30,000,000
Lambert Azimuthal Equidistant Projection
© ISTITUTO GEOGRAFICO DE AGOSTINI S. p. A. - NOVARA

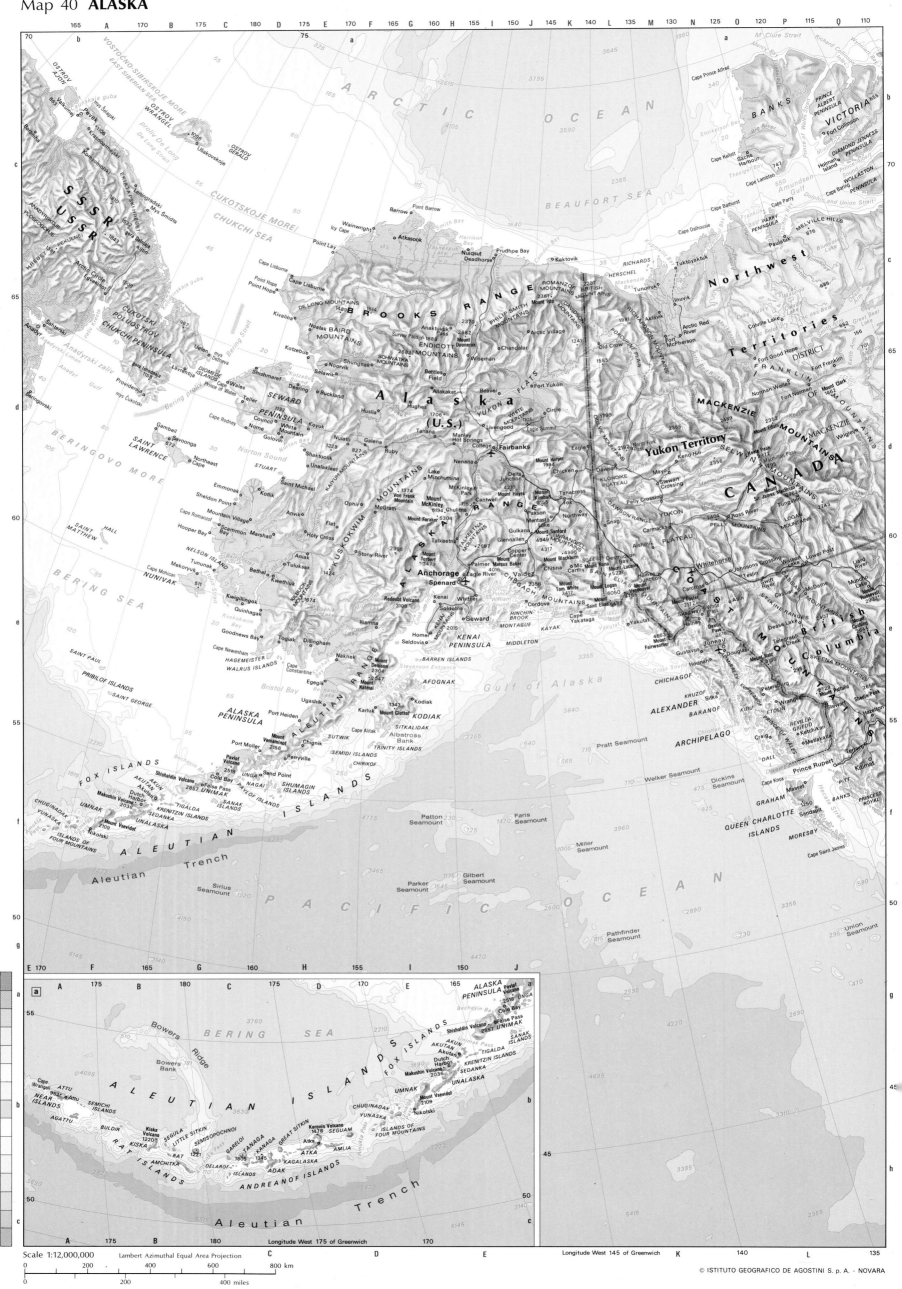

Map 40 **ALASKA**

A 165 B 170 C 175 D 180 E 175 F 170 G 165 H 160 I 155 J 150 K 145 L 140 M 135 N 130 O 125 P 120 Q 115 110

ARCTIC OCEAN

BEAUFORT SEA

CHUKCHI SEA

SSSR
USSR

CUKOTSKI
POLUOSTROV
CHUKCHI PENINSULA

BROOKS RANGE

DE LONG MOUNTAINS
BAIRD MOUNTAINS
ENDICOTT MOUNTAINS
SCHWATKA MOUNTAINS

Northwest Territories

BANKS

VICTORIA

MACKENZIE
MACKENZIE MOUNTAINS

CANADA

Alaska (U.S.)

YUKON FLATS

Yukon Territory

KLONDIKE PLATEAU

YUKON

Fairbanks

SEWARD PENINSULA

Nome

Mount McKinley
6194

ALASKA RANGE

BERINGOVO MORE
BERING SEA

SAINT LAWRENCE

SAINT MATTHEW

NUNIVAK

NELSON ISLAND

KUSKOKWIM MOUNTAINS

Anchorage
Spenard

Valdez

Gulf of Alaska

CHUGACH MOUNTAINS

WRANGELL MOUNTAINS

BRITISH COLUMBIA

COAST MOUNTAINS

Whitehorse

Juneau

KENAI PENINSULA

KODIAK

ALASKA PENINSULA

ALEXANDER ARCHIPELAGO

PRIBILOF ISLANDS

Bristol Bay

AFOGNAK

QUEEN CHARLOTTE ISLANDS

FOX ISLANDS

UNIMAK

ALEUTIAN ISLANDS

Aleutian Trench

PACIFIC OCEAN

a A 175 B 180 C 175 D 170 E 165

BERING SEA

Bowers Ridge
Bowers Bank

ALASKA PENINSULA

ALEUTIAN ISLANDS

ATTU
NEAR ISLANDS
SEMICHI ISLANDS
AGATTU

RAT ISLANDS
Kiska Volcano 1220
KISKA
AMCHITKA

ANDREANOF ISLANDS

ADAK
KAGALASKA
ATKA
AMLIA
SEGUAM

FOX ISLANDS

Shishaldin Volcano
Akutan
UNIMAK
SANAK ISLANDS
KRENITZIN ISLANDS
SEDANKA
UNALASKA
Makushin Volcano 2036
CHUGINADAK
UMNAK
Mount Vsevidof 2109
Nikolski
ISLANDS OF FOUR MOUNTAINS
YUNASKA

Aleutian Trench

M Ft
5000 16404
4000 13123
3000 9843
2000 6562
1000 3281
500 1640
200 656
100 328
0
200 656
1000 3281
2000 6562
4000 13123
6000 19685

Scale 1:12,000,000   Lambert Azimuthal Equal Area Projection
0   200   400   600   800 km
0   200   400 miles

Longitude West 175 of Greenwich   Longitude West 145 of Greenwich

© ISTITUTO GEOGRAFICO DE AGOSTINI S. p. A. - NOVARA

Grønland
Kalaallit Nunaat
Greenland
(Denmark)

ARCTIC OCEAN

QUEEN ELIZABETH ISLANDS

SVERDRUP ISLANDS

ELLESMERE

DEVON

BYLOT

Northwest Territories

CANADA

CUMBERLAND PENINSULA

Baffin Bay

Davis Strait

Labrador Sea

Newfoundland

LABRADOR

NORDGRØNLAND

PEARY LAND

KNUD RASMUSSEN LAND

KONG FREDERIK VIII LAND

KRONPRINS CHRISTIAN LAND

DRONNING LOUISE LAND

KONG CHRISTIAN X LAND

KONG FREDERIK VI KYST

KONG CHRISTIAN IX LAND

KRONPRINS FREDERIKS BJERGE

Mont Forel

Gunnbjørns Fjeld

Godthåb / Nûk

Reykjavík

ISLAND / ICELAND

Svalbard (Norway)

SPITSBERGEN

BARENTS SEA / BARENTSHAVET

Greenland Basin

GREENLAND SEA / GRØNLANDSHAVET

Mohs Ridge

Jan Mayen (Norway)

South Jan Mayen Ridge

Arctic Circle

Reykjanes Ridge

Iceland Basin

ATLANTIC OCEAN / ATLANTERHAVET

Labrador Basin

Mid-Atlantic Ridge

Denmark Strait / Danmarksstraedet

Longitude West 40 of Greenwich

Scale 1:12,000,000   Lambert Azimuthal Equal Area Projection

0   200   400   600   800 km
0   200   400 miles

© ISTITUTO GEOGRAFICO DE AGOSTINI S. p. A. - NOVARA

195

M Ft
3000 / 9843
2000 / 6562
1000 / 3281
500 / 1640
200 / 656
0
100 / 328
200 / 656
1000 / 3281
2000 / 6562
4000 / 13123

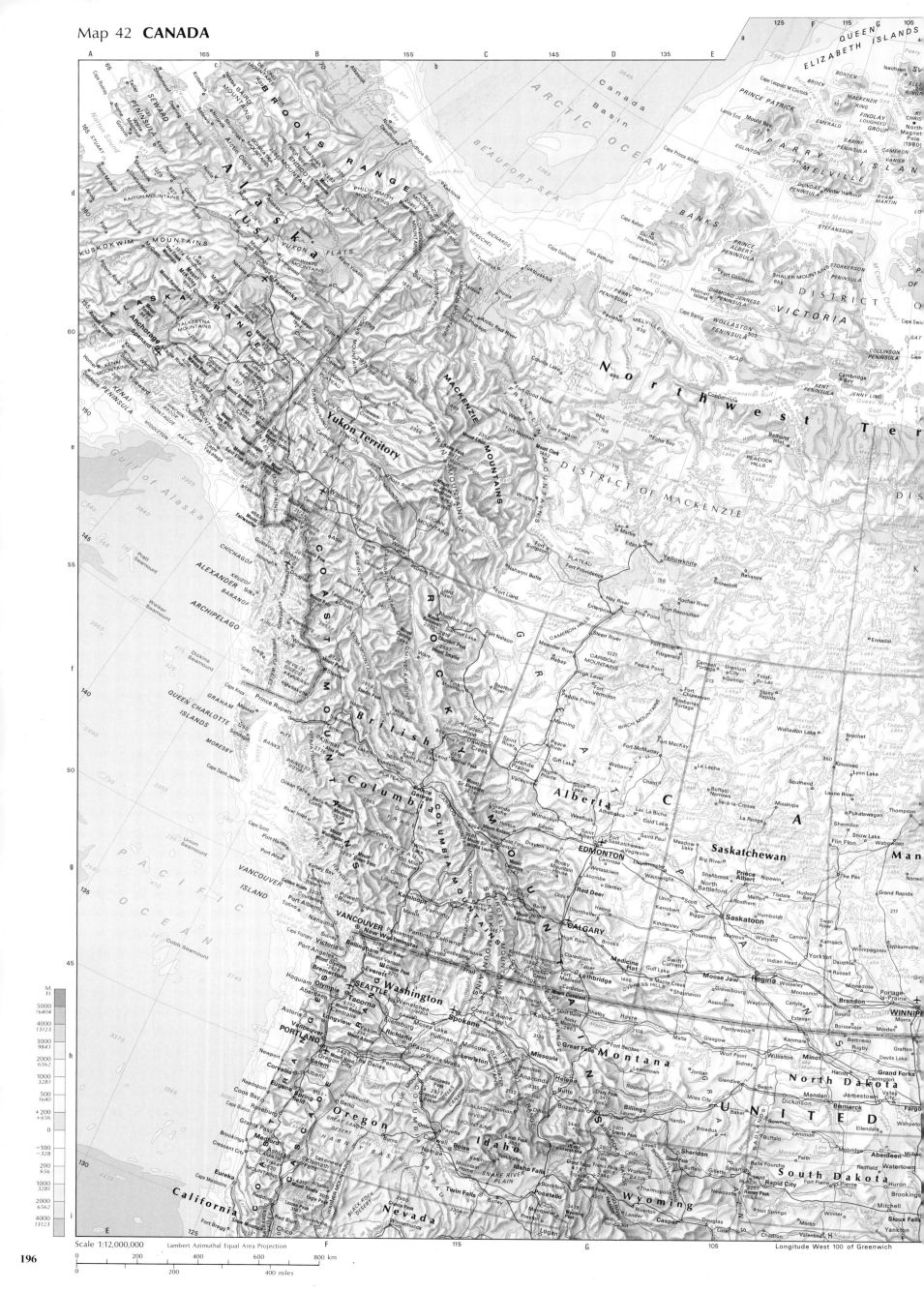

Map 42 CANADA

Scale 1:12,000,000

Lambert Azimuthal Equal Area Projection

Longitude West 100 of Greenwich

Grønland
Kalaallit Nunaat
Greenland
(Denmark)
VESTGRØNLAND
ØSTGRØNLAND
Baffin Bay
Davis Strait
BAFFIN
Foxe Basin
Hudson Strait
Ungava Bay
Hudson Bay
James Bay
LABRADOR SEA
ATLANTIC OCEAN
Labrador Basin
Newfoundland
NEWFOUNDLAND
LABRADOR
COAST OF LABRADOR
PÉNINSULE D'UNGAVA
Québec
Ontario
CLAY BELT
LAURENTIDES
PLATEAU DU LABRADOR
Gulf of Saint Lawrence
ÎLE D'ANTICOSTI
Prince Edward Island
New Brunswick
Nova Scotia
Saint-Pierre et Miquelon
Grand Banks of Newfoundland
Gulf of Maine
Maine
Wisconsin
New York
Pennsylvania
DEVON
BYLOT
SOUTHAMPTON
MELVILLE PENINSULA
FOXE PENINSULA
CUMBERLAND PENINSULA
HALL PENINSULA
ISLAND ICELAND
Thule Air Base
Upernavik
Godthåb
Nuuk
Fort Chimo
Nain
Schefferville
Sept-Îles
Saint John's
Corner Brook
Halifax
Fredericton
Moncton
Saint John
Sydney
QUÉBEC
MONTRÉAL
OTTAWA
TORONTO
HAMILTON
BUFFALO
DETROIT
CHICAGO
MILWAUKEE
SAINT PAUL
CLEVELAND
BOSTON
NEW YORK
Thunder Bay
Sudbury
Timmins
Chicoutimi
Sherbrooke

Map 43 **UNITED STATES**

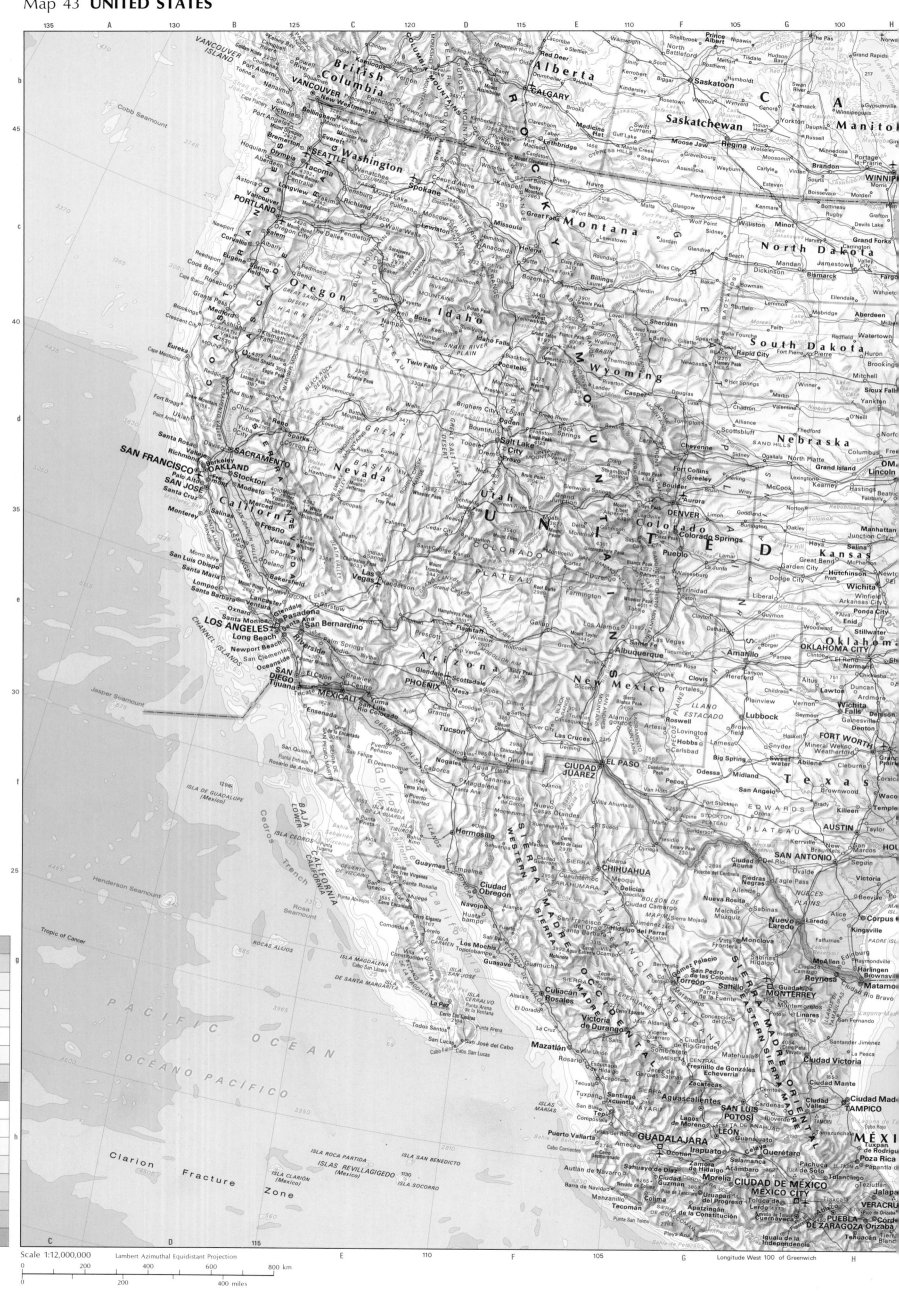

Scale 1:12,000,000

Lambert Azimuthal Equidistant Projection

Longitude West 100 of Greenwich

0   200   400   600   800 km

0   200   400 miles

Ontario
Québec
New Brunswick
Prince Edward Island
Nova Scotia
Saint-Pierre et Miquelon St. Pierre and Miquelon (France)
NEWFOUNDLAND
Thunder Bay
Sudbury
MONTRÉAL
OTTAWA
QUÉBEC
TORONTO
HAMILTON
Halifax
Saint John
Fredericton
Moncton
Sydney
Maine
BOSTON
Providence
NEW YORK
PHILADELPHIA
BALTIMORE
WASHINGTON
Pennsylvania
New York
Ohio
Indiana
Illinois
Wisconsin
Michigan
Kentucky
Tennessee
Virginia
West Virginia
North Carolina
South Carolina
Georgia
Alabama
Mississippi
Louisiana
Florida
Delaware
CHICAGO
DETROIT
MILWAUKEE
CLEVELAND
PITTSBURGH
BUFFALO
TOLEDO
COLUMBUS
CINCINNATI
INDIANAPOLIS
LOUISVILLE
ST. LOUIS
NASHVILLE
MEMPHIS
ATLANTA
BIRMINGHAM
NEW ORLEANS
JACKSONVILLE
TAMPA
MIAMI
RICHMOND
NORFOLK
SAINT PAUL
ATLANTIC OCEAN
Sargasso Sea
Blake Plateau
Blake Ridge
Blake Basin
New England Seamounts
Kelvin Seamount
Bermuda (U.K.)
Gulf of Mexico / Golfo de México
Mexico Basin
BAHAMAS
Nassau
LA HABANA HAVANA
CUBA
Santiago de Cuba
Guantánamo
JAMAICA
KINGSTON
Cayman Islands (U.K.)
HAITI
PORT-AU-PRINCE
REPÚBLICA DOMINICANA DOMINICAN REPUBLIC
SANTO DOMINGO
Turks and Caicos Islands (U.K.)
WEST INDIES
INDIAS OCCIDENTALES
ANTILLAS MAYORES
GREATER ANTILLES
Yucatan Basin
Cayman Trench
MÉRIDA
PENÍNSULA DE YUCATÁN YUCATAN PENINSULA
BELIZE

CANADA
Québec
Ontario
New Brunswick
Nova Scotia
Maine
New Hampshire
Massachusetts
Connecticut
Rhode Island
New York
New Jersey
Pennsylvania
Ohio
Indiana
Illinois
Wisconsin
Michigan
Minnesota
Iowa
West Virginia
Maryland
Delaware
Georges Bank
Hudson Canyon
Gulf of Maine
MONTRÉAL
OTTAWA
TORONTO
BOSTON
NEW YORK
PHILADELPHIA
BALTIMORE
WASHINGTON
PITTSBURGH
CLEVELAND
DETROIT
CHICAGO
MILWAUKEE
INDIANAPOLIS
CINCINNATI
COLUMBUS
ST. LOUIS
LOUISVILLE
BUFFALO
ROCHESTER

© ISTITUTO GEOGRAFICO DE AGOSTINI S. p. A. · NOVARA

Scale 1:6,000,000

Delisle Conic Equidistant Projection

200 miles

400 km

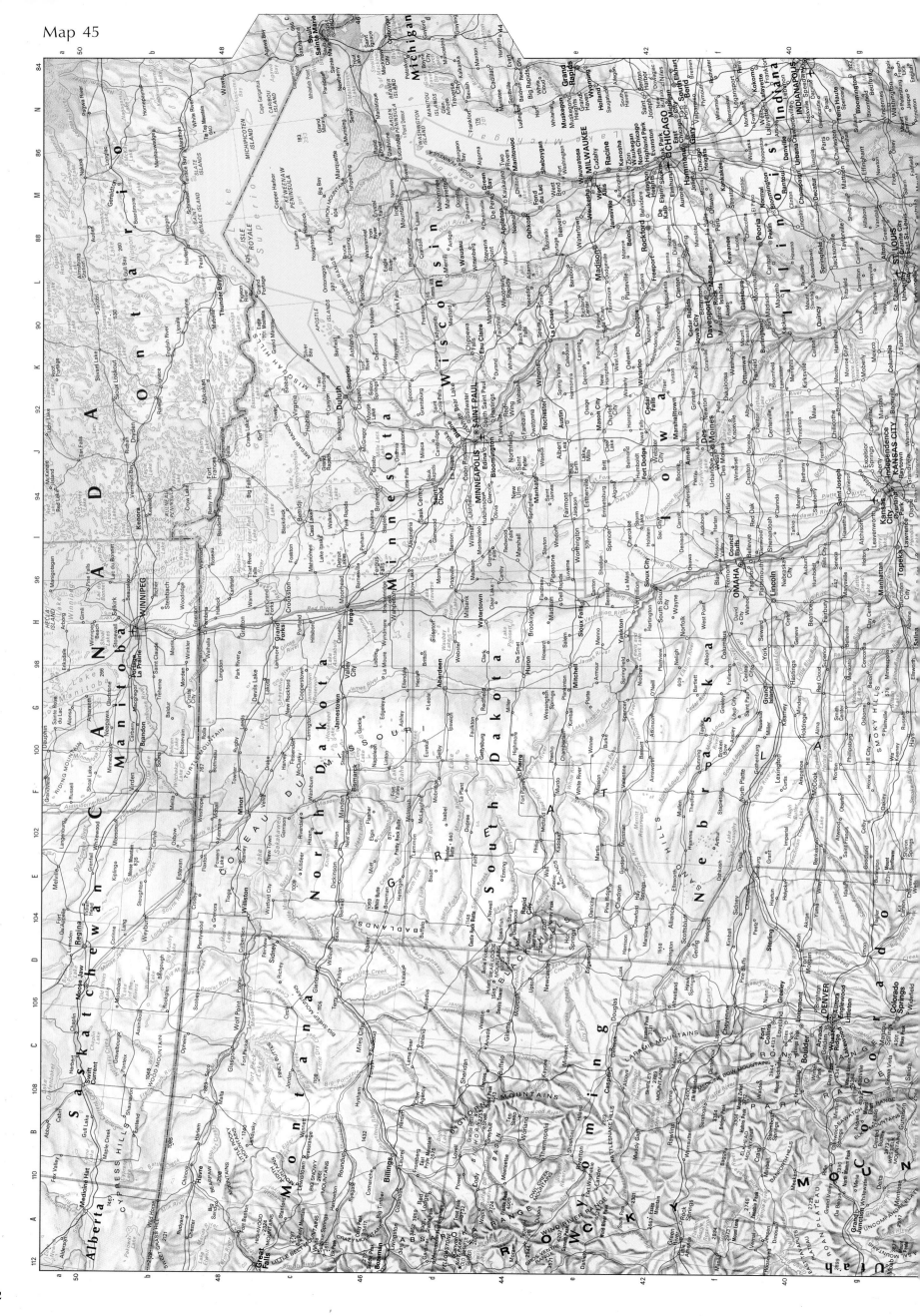
CANADA
Alberta
Saskatchewan
Manitoba
Ontario
Montana
North Dakota
South Dakota
Minnesota
Wisconsin
Michigan
Iowa
Illinois
Indiana
Nebraska
Wyoming
Colorado
Lake Superior
WINNIPEG
MINNEAPOLIS
SAINT PAUL
MILWAUKEE
CHICAGO
OMAHA
DENVER
KANSAS CITY
ST. LOUIS
INDIANAPOLIS

© ISTITUTO GEOGRAFICO DE AGOSTINI S. p. A. - NOVARA

Scale 16,000,000

Delisle Conic Equidistant Projection

Longitude West 98 of Greenwich

Map 46 **WESTERN UNITED STATES**

© ISTITUTO GEOGRAFICO DE AGOSTINI S.p.A. - NOVARA

SANGRE DE CRISTO MOUNTAINS

COLORADO PLATEAU

New Mexico

Arizona

California

NEVADA

SIERRA NEVADA

COAST RANGES

SAN JOAQUIN VALLEY

MOJAVE DESERT

COLORADO DESERT

AMARGOSA DESERT

DEATH VALLEY

PAINTED DESERT

GRAND CANYON

KAIBAB PLATEAU

KAIPAROWITS PLATEAU

Chihuahua

Sonora

SIERRA MADRE OCCIDENTAL

Sinaloa

Baja California Norte

Baja California Sur

LOWER CALIFORNIA

Gulf of California

Golfo de California

SIERRA DE JUAREZ

DESIERTO DE ALTAR

DESIERTO DE VIZCAINO

SIERRA DE SAN PEDRO MARTIR

Cedros Trench

Cities and places

SACRAMENTO
SAN FRANCISCO
Oakland
Berkeley
San Jose
Stockton
Modesto
Fresno
Bakersfield
LOS ANGELES
Long Beach
Santa Monica
Pasadena
Glendale
Inglewood
Compton
Anaheim
Garden Grove
Santa Ana
Riverside
San Bernardino
Redlands
Ontario
Pomona
Palm Springs
Santa Barbara
Ventura
Oxnard
San Diego
Chula Vista
Oceanside
Carlsbad
Laguna Beach
Newport Beach
San Clemente

Santa Rosa
Napa
Vacaville
Fairfield
Vallejo
San Rafael
Daly City
San Mateo
Redwood City
Palo Alto
Santa Clara
Los Gatos
Santa Cruz
Watsonville
Salinas
Monterey
Pacific Grove
San Luis Obispo
Morro Bay
Arroyo Grande
Lompoc

Las Vegas
North Las Vegas
Henderson
Boulder City
Kingman
Needles
Lake Havasu City
Parker
Blythe
Yuma
El Centro
Calexico
Brawley

PHOENIX
Scottsdale
Tempe
Mesa
Glendale
Chandler
Gilbert
Casa Grande
Eloy
Coolidge
Superior
Globe
Miami
Safford
Tucson
Nogales
Bisbee
Douglas
Benson

Albuquerque
Santa Fe
Las Vegas
Farmington
Gallup
Zuni
Grants
Socorro
Truth or Consequences
Las Cruces
Deming
Lordsburg
Silver City
Alamogordo

EL PASO
CIUDAD JUAREZ
Agua Prieta
Cananea
Nogales
Magdalena
HERMOSILLO
Guaymas
Ciudad Obregón
Navojoa
Huatabampo

Ensenada
Tijuana
Mexicali
San Felipe
Santo Tomás
San Quintín

ISLA CEDROS
ISLA GUADALUPE
ISLA TIBURON
ISLA ANGEL DE LA GUARDA
SANTA CATALINA ISLAND
SAN CLEMENTE ISLAND
SANTA CRUZ ISLAND
SANTA ROSA ISLAND
SAN MIGUEL ISLAND
SAN NICOLAS ISLAND
SANTA BARBARA ISLAND
CHANNEL ISLANDS

Jasper Seamount

PACIFIC OCEAN

Longitude West 116 of Greenwich

Delisle Conic Equidistant Projection

Scale 1:6,000,000

0   100   200   300   400 km

0   100   200 miles

Map 47 **MIDDLE AMERICA**

Grid columns: A 115 B 110 C 105 D 100 E 95 F 90

MÉXICO

ESTADOS

D.F. Distrito Federal
1 Aguascalientes
2 Baja California Norte
3 Baja California Sur
4 Campeche
5 Coahuila
6 Colima
7 Chiapas
8 Chihuahua
9 Durango
10 Guanajuato
11 Guerrero
12 Hidalgo
13 Jalisco
14 México
15 Michoacán
16 Morelos
17 Nayarit
18 Nuevo León
19 Oaxaca
20 Puebla
21 Querétaro
22 Quintana Roo
23 San Luis Potosí
24 Sinaloa
25 Sonora
26 Tabasco
27 Tamaulipas
28 Tlaxcala
29 Veracruz
30 Yucatán
31 Zacatecas

Elevation legend (M / Ft):
5000 / 16404
4000 / 13123
3000 / 9843
2000 / 6562
1000 / 3281
500 / 1640
+ 200 / +656
0 Depr. 0
− 100 / −328
200 / 656
1000 / 3281
2000 / 6562
4000 / 13123
6000 / 19685
8000 / 26247

Equator

OCÉANO PACÍFICO

PACIFIC OCEAN

Middle America Trench

Albatross Plateau

Guatemala Basin

Gulf of Mexico / Golf

Major labels include: LOS ANGELES, San Diego, Tijuana, MEXICALI, PHOENIX, Tucson, El Paso, CIUDAD JUÁREZ, CHIHUAHUA, Hermosillo, Ciudad Obregón, Los Mochis, La Paz, Mazatlán, Culiacán, Durango, ALBUQUERQUE, Santa Fe, Roswell, Lubbock, Amarillo, OKLAHOMA CITY, TULSA, FORT WORTH, DALLAS, AUSTIN, SAN ANTONIO, HOUSTON, Corpus Christi, MONTERREY, Saltillo, Torreón, Matamoros, Reynosa, Ciudad Victoria, TAMPICO, Ciudad Madero, SAN LUIS POTOSÍ, GUADALAJARA, LEÓN, Morelia, Querétaro, CIUDAD DE MÉXICO / MEXICO CITY, PUEBLA DE ZARAGOZA, VERACRUZ LLAVE, Orizaba, Acapulco de Juárez, Oaxaca de Juárez, MÉRIDA, Campeche, Villahermosa, Tuxtla Gutiérrez, GUATEMALA, SAN SALVADOR, Nueva San Salvador, NEW ORLEANS, Baton Rouge, Shreveport, Little Rock, Jackson

Scale 1:12,000,000
Lambert Azimuthal Equal Area Projection

0 200 400 600 800 km
0 200 400 miles

Longitude West 90 of Greenwich

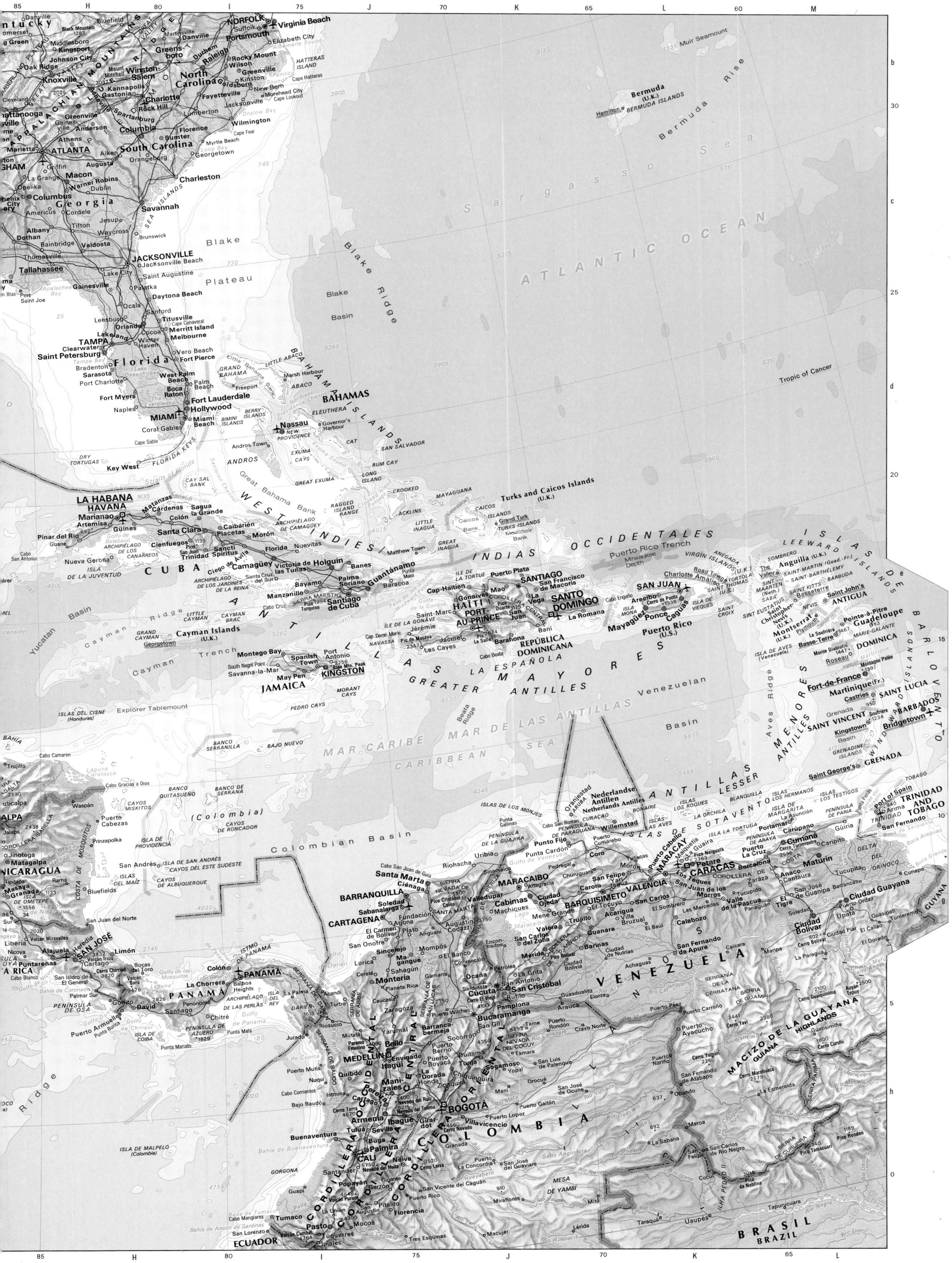

ATLANTIC OCEAN

Sargasso Sea

Bermuda (U.K.)
BERMUDA ISLANDS
Hamilton

Tropic of Cancer

BAHAMAS
BAHAMA ISLANDS
GRAND BAHAMA
ABACO
ELEUTHERA ISLAND
Nassau
NEW PROVIDENCE
ANDROS
SAN SALVADOR
CAT
RUM CAY
LONG ISLAND
GREAT EXUMA
CROOKED
ACKLINS
MAYAGUANA
LITTLE INAGUA
GREAT INAGUA

Turks and Caicos Islands (U.K.)
Grand Turk
TURKS ISLANDS

Puerto Rico Trench
VIRGIN ISLANDS
LEEWARD ISLANDS
ISLAS DE SOTAVENTO

Anguilla (U.K.)
SAINT-MARTIN (Guad.-Fr.)
SAINT-BARTHÉLEMY
SAINT KITTS
ANTIGUA
Saint John's
NEVIS
Montserrat (U.K.)
Guadeloupe
Basse-Terre
MARIE-GALANTE
DOMINICA
Roseau
Fort-de-France
Martinique (Fr.)
Castries SAINT LUCIA
SAINT VINCENT
GRENADINES ISLANDS
Kingstown BARBADOS
Bridgetown
GRENADA
Saint George's
TOBAGO
TRINIDAD AND TOBAGO
Port of Spain
San Fernando

CUBA
LA HABANA / HAVANA
Marianao
Matanzas
Cárdenas
Sagua la Grande
Colón
Pinar del Río
Güines
Santa Clara
Cienfuegos
Sancti Spíritus
Florida
Nuevitas
Ciego de Ávila
Camagüey
Victoria de las Tunas
Holguín
Banes
Manzanillo
Bayamo
Palma Soriano
Santiago de Cuba
Guantánamo
Baracoa

ISLA DE LA JUVENTUD

Cayman Islands (U.K.)
GRAND CAYMAN
Georgetown
LITTLE CAYMAN
CAYMAN BRAC

JAMAICA
Montego Bay
Spanish Town
Savanna-la-Mar
May Pen
KINGSTON
Port Antonio
Blue Mtn. Peak

HAITI
Cap-Haïtien
Gonaïves
PORT-AU-PRINCE
Saint-Marc
Jérémie
Les Cayes
ÎLE DE LA GONÂVE
ÎLE DE LA TORTUE

REPÚBLICA DOMINICANA
Puerto Plata
SANTIAGO
San Francisco de Macorís
Mao
La Vega
SANTO DOMINGO
La Romana
Barahona
Bani
Pico Duarte
LA ESPAÑOLA

Puerto Rico (U.S.)
SAN JUAN
Arecibo
Mayagüez
Ponce
Caguas
ISLA MONA
ISLA DE VIEQUES
SAINT CROIX
Charlotte Amalie SAINT THOMAS

GREATER ANTILLES
GRANDES ANTILLAS MAYORES
INDIAS OCCIDENTALES
WEST INDIES
ANTILLES
ANTILLAS

MAR CARIBE
CARIBBEAN SEA

Venezuelan Basin
Colombian Basin
Aves Ridge

Netherlands Antilles
Nederlandse Antillen
ARUBA
Oranjestad
CURAÇAO
Willemstad
BONAIRE
ISLAS LOS ROQUES
LA ORCHILA
ISLA LA TORTUGA
LA BLANQUILLA
ISLA MARGARITA
La Asunción
ISLAS LOS HERMANOS
ISLAS LOS TESTIGOS

ISLAS DEL CISNE (Honduras)
ISLAS DEL MAÍZ
CAYOS MISKITOS
ISLA DE PROVIDENCIA
ISLA DE SAN ANDRÉS
CAYOS DEL ESTE SUDESTE
CAYOS DE ALBUQUERQUE
San Andrés (Colombia)
BANCO SERRANILLA
BAJO NUEVO
BANCO QUITASUEÑO
BANCO DE SERRANA

NICARAGUA
Managua
Masaya
Granada
Matagalpa
Jinotega
Bluefields
Puerto Cabezas
Prinzapolka
Rama
Cabo Gracias a Dios

COSTA RICA
SAN JOSÉ
Alajuela
Cartago
Puntarenas
Limón
Liberia
Nicoya
PENÍNSULA DE OSA

PANAMÁ
PANAMA
Colón
La Chorrera
Balboa Heights
David
Santiago
Chitré
Penonomé
ARCHIPIÉLAGO DE LAS PERLAS
ISLA DEL REY
PENÍNSULA DE AZUERO
ISLA DE COIBA
GOLFO DE PANAMÁ
Puerto Armuelles

COLOMBIA
BOGOTÁ
MEDELLÍN
CALI
BARRANQUILLA
CARTAGENA
Cúcuta
Bucaramanga
Santa Marta
Riohacha
Valledupar
Montería
Sincelejo
Pasto
Popayán
Buenaventura
Armenia
Ibagué
Manizales
Pereira
Tunja
Neiva
Florencia
Quibdó
PENÍNSULA DE LA GUAJIRA
CORDILLERA OCCIDENTAL
CORDILLERA CENTRAL
CORDILLERA ORIENTAL
SIERRA NEVADA DE SANTA MARTA
Golfo de Venezuela

VENEZUELA
CARACAS
MARACAIBO
VALENCIA
BARQUISIMETO
MARACAY
Cumaná
Barcelona
Puerto La Cruz
Maturín
Ciudad Bolívar
Ciudad Guayana
Coro
Punto Fijo
Barinas
San Cristóbal
San Fernando de Apure
Calabozo
El Tigre
MACIZO DE LA GUAYANA
GUIANA HIGHLANDS
PENÍNSULA DE PARAGUANÁ
PENÍNSULA DE PARIA

GUYANA

BRASIL / BRAZIL

ECUADOR

California
Arizona
New Mexico
UNITED
Sonora
Chihuahua
Coah
Durango
Zacatecas
Nayarit
Jalisco
Colima
Baja California Norte
Baja California Sur
SAN DIEGO
Tijuana
Mexicali
Yuma
Tucson
El Paso
Ciudad Juárez
Nogales
Hermosillo
Guaymas
Ciudad Obregón
Chihuahua
Culiacán Rosales
Mazatlán
Victoria de Durango
Tepic
Guadalajara
La Paz
Colima
Torreón
Golfo de California
Gulf of California
SIERRA MADRE OCCIDENTAL
WESTERN SIERRA MADRE
ALTIPLANICIE MEXICANA
PLATEAU OF ME
BOLSÓN DE MAPIMI
Tropic of Cancer
OCÉANO PACÍFICO
PACIFIC OCEAN
ISLAS REVILLAGIGEDO
(Mexico)
ISLA SOCORRO
ISLA CLARIÓN
ISLA SAN BENEDICTO
ISLA ROCA PARTIDA
ISLAS MARÍAS
ISLA CEDROS
ISLA TIBURÓN
ISLA ÁNGEL DE LA GUARDA
ISLA MAGDALENA
ISLA DE SANTA MARGARITA
Cedros Trench
Middle
Rosa Seamount
Mathematicians Seamount
Scale 1:6,000,000
Delisle Conic Equidistant Projection
0 100 200 300 400 km
0 100 200 miles
Longitude West 104 of Greenwich

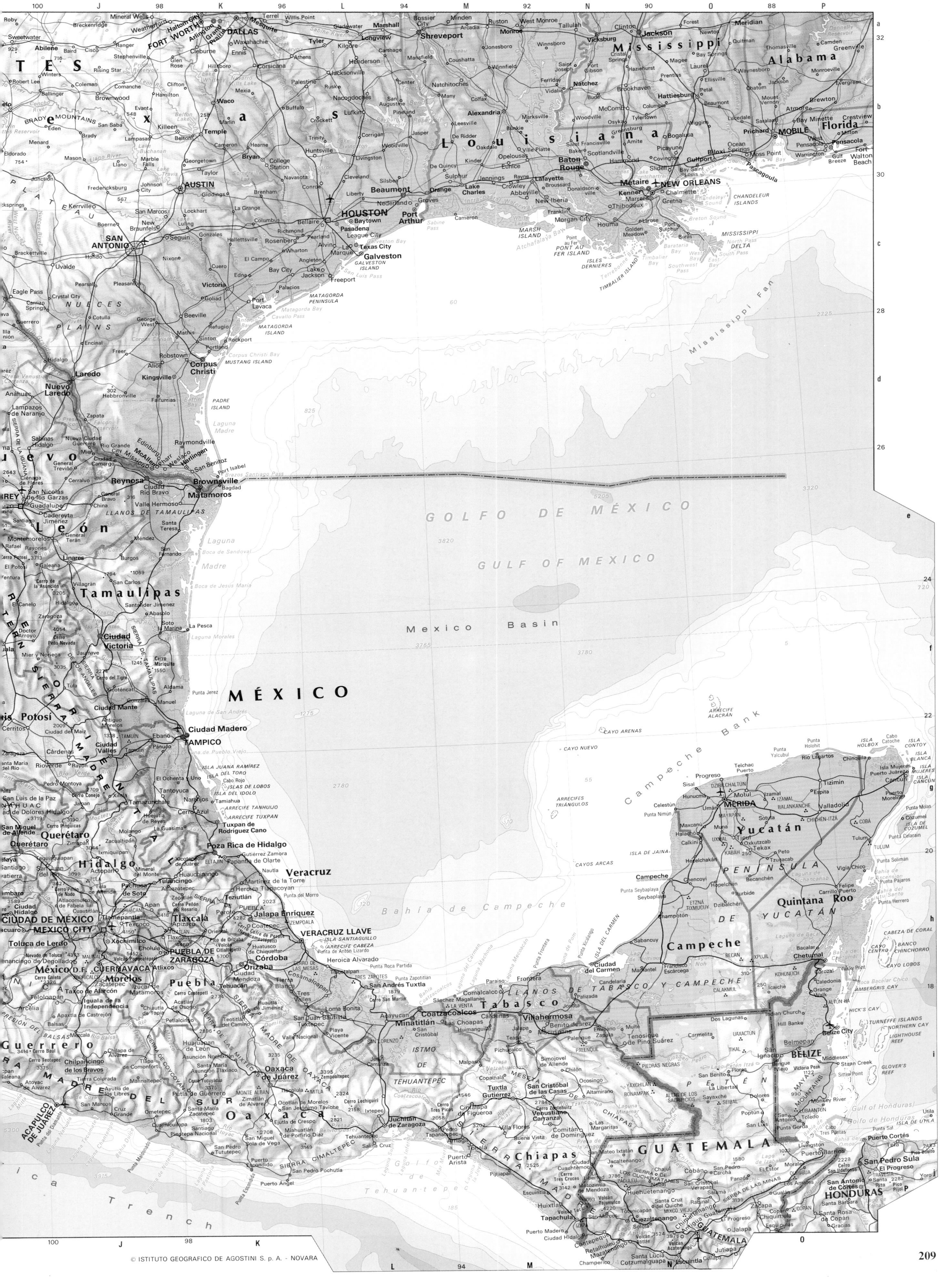

MEXICO

GOLFO DE MÉXICO

GULF OF MEXICO

Mexico Basin

Bahía de Campeche

Golfo de Tehuantepec

TEXAS
Louisiana
Mississippi
Alabama
Florida

Tamaulipas
Nuevo León
Veracruz
Hidalgo
Querétaro
Guerrero
Oaxaca
Puebla
Morelos
Chiapas
Tabasco
Campeche
Yucatán
Quintana Roo
PENÍNSULA DE YUCATÁN

GUATEMALA
HONDURAS
BELIZE

FORT WORTH
DALLAS
Waco
AUSTIN
SAN ANTONIO
HOUSTON
Corpus Christi
Laredo
Nuevo Laredo
Reynosa
Matamoros
Brownsville
Ciudad Victoria
TAMPICO
Ciudad Madero
Veracruz
Jalapa Enríquez
VERACRUZ LLAVE
Poza Rica de Hidalgo
MÉXICO CITY
CIUDAD DE MÉXICO
PUEBLA DE ZARAGOZA
Orizaba
Córdoba
CUERNAVACA
Oaxaca de Juárez
ACAPULCO DE JUÁREZ
Chilpancingo de los Bravos
Coatzacoalcos
Minatitlán
Villahermosa
MÉRIDA
Campeche
Ciudad del Carmen
Chetumal
Cancún
Tapachula
Tuxtla Gutiérrez
San Cristóbal de las Casas
New Orleans
Baton Rouge
Shreveport
Lafayette
Mobile
Pensacola

SIERRA MADRE ORIENTAL
SIERRA MADRE DEL SUR
ISTMO DE TEHUANTEPEC
LLANOS DE TABASCO Y CAMPECHE

Map 49 **CENTRAL AMERICA AND WESTERN CARIBBEAN**

Scale 1:6,000,000   Delisle Conic Equidistant Projection

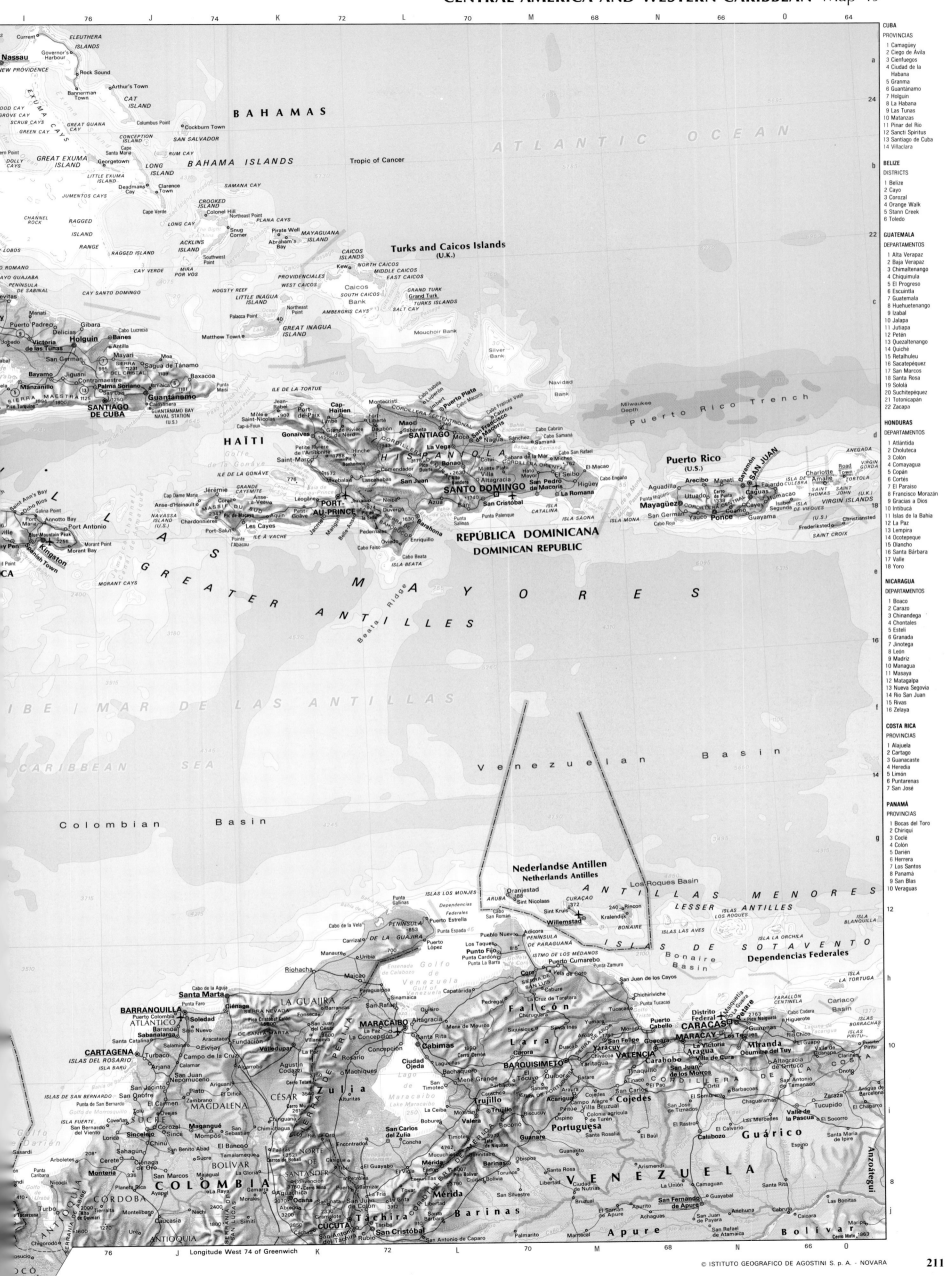

Longitude West 74 of Greenwich

CUBA
PROVINCIAS
1 Camagüey
2 Ciego de Ávila
3 Cienfuegos
4 Ciudad de la Habana
5 Granma
6 Guantánamo
7 Holguín
8 La Habana
9 Las Tunas
10 Matanzas
11 Pinar del Río
12 Sancti Spíritus
13 Santiago de Cuba
14 Villaclara

BELIZE
DISTRICTS
1 Belize
2 Cayo
3 Corozal
4 Orange Walk
5 Stann Creek
6 Toledo

GUATEMALA
DEPARTAMENTOS
1 Alta Verapaz
2 Baja Verapaz
3 Chimaltenango
4 Chiquimula
5 El Progreso
6 Escuintla
7 Guatemala
8 Huehuetenango
9 Izabal
10 Jalapa
11 Jutiapa
12 Petén
13 Quezaltenango
14 Quiché
15 Retalhuleu
16 Sacatepéquez
17 San Marcos
18 Santa Rosa
19 Sololá
20 Suchitepéquez
21 Totonicapán
22 Zacapa

HONDURAS
DEPARTAMENTOS
1 Atlántida
2 Choluteca
3 Colón
4 Comayagua
5 Copán
6 Cortés
7 El Paraíso
8 Francisco Morazán
9 Gracias a Dios
10 Intibucá
11 Islas de la Bahía
12 La Paz
13 Lempira
14 Ocotepeque
15 Olancho
16 Santa Bárbara
17 Valle
18 Yoro

NICARAGUA
DEPARTAMENTOS
1 Boaco
2 Carazo
3 Chinandega
4 Chontales
5 Estelí
6 Granada
7 Jinotega
8 León
9 Madriz
10 Managua
11 Masaya
12 Matagalpa
13 Nueva Segovia
14 Río San Juan
15 Rivas
16 Zelaya

COSTA RICA
PROVINCIAS
1 Alajuela
2 Cartago
3 Guanacaste
4 Heredia
5 Limón
6 Puntarenas
7 San José

PANAMÁ
PROVINCIAS
1 Bocas del Toro
2 Chiriquí
3 Coclé
4 Colón
5 Darién
6 Herrera
7 Los Santos
8 Panamá
9 San Blas
10 Veraguas

Map 50 **EASTERN CARIBBEAN**

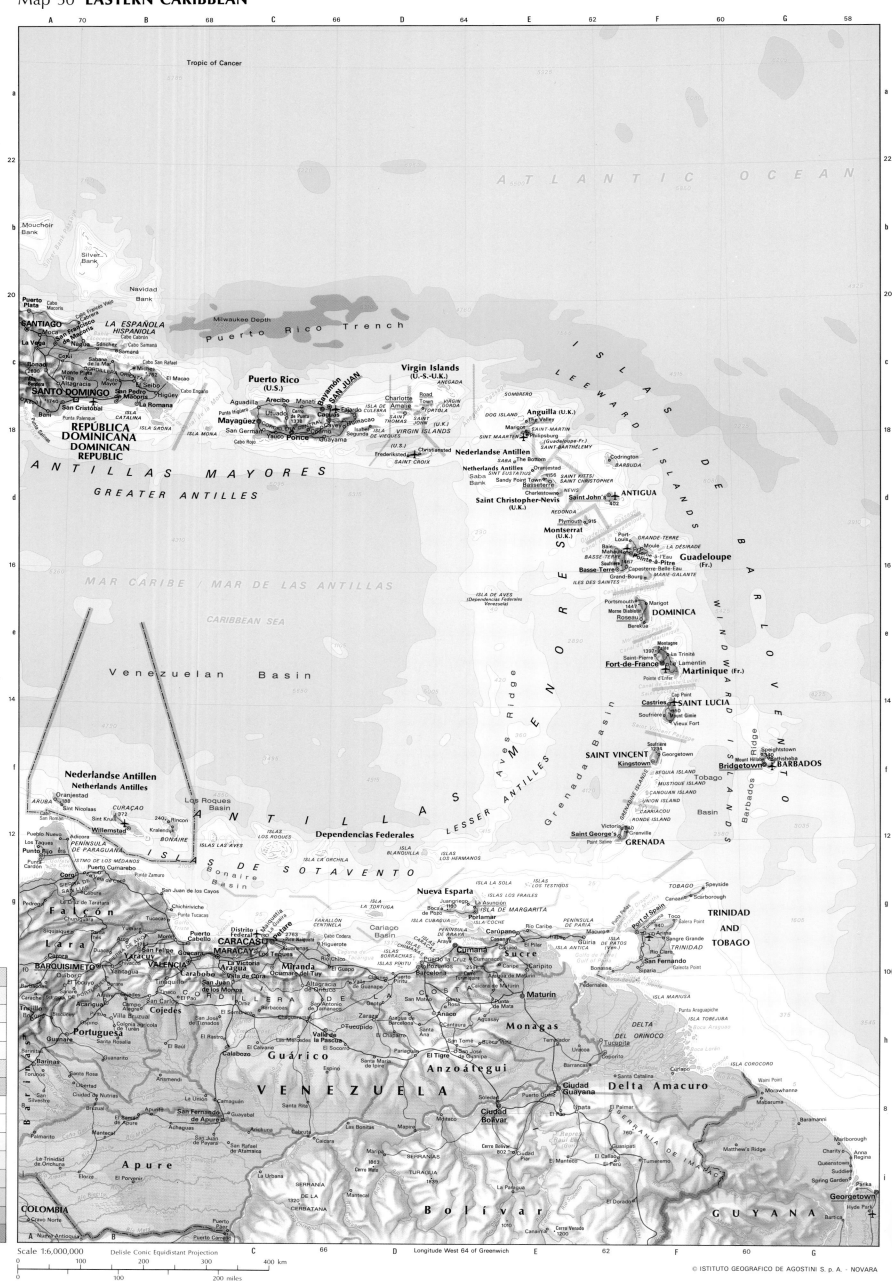

Scale 1:6,000,000   Delisle Conic Equidistant Projection

0   100   200   300   400 km

0   100   200 miles

Longitude West 64 of Greenwich

© ISTITUTO GEOGRAFICO DE AGOSTINI S.p.A. - NOVARA

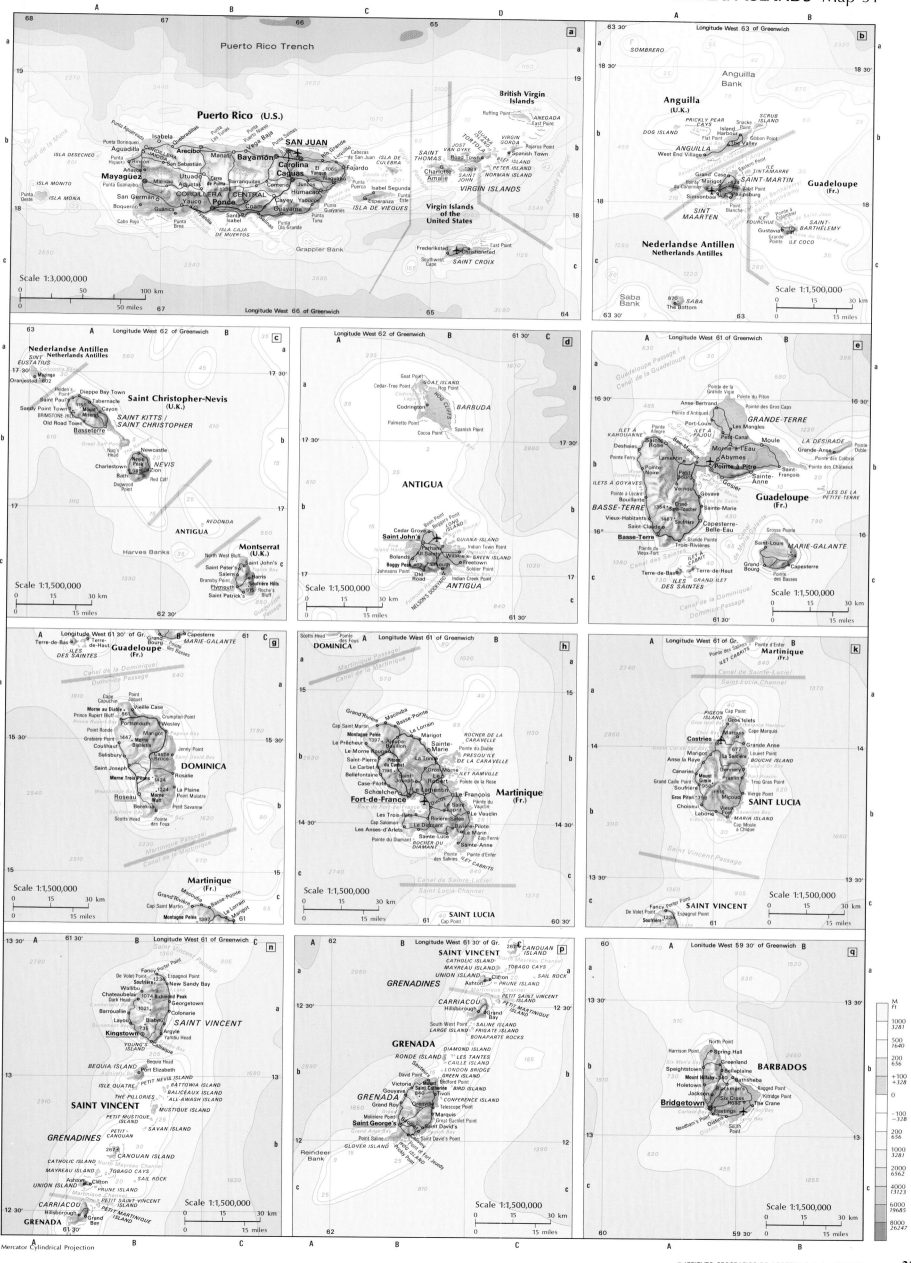
Puerto Rico Trench
Puerto Rico (U.S.)
SAN JUAN
Bayamón
Carolina
Caguas
Mayagüez
Ponce
Arecibo
Aguadilla
CORDILLERA CENTRAL
Grappler Bank
British Virgin Islands
VIRGIN ISLANDS
Virgin Islands of the United States
SAINT THOMAS
SAINT CROIX
ISLA DE VIEQUES
ISLA DE CULEBRA
ISLA MONA
Scale 1:3,000,000
Longitude West 66 of Greenwich
Anguilla (U.K.)
Anguilla Bank
SAINT-MARTIN
SINT MAARTEN
SAINT-BARTHÉLEMY
Guadeloupe (Fr.)
Nederlandse Antillen
Netherlands Antilles
Saba Bank
SABA
Scale 1:1,500,000
Longitude West 63 of Greenwich
Saint Christopher-Nevis (U.K.)
SAINT KITTS / SAINT CHRISTOPHER
Basseterre
NEVIS
Montserrat (U.K.)
Plymouth
REDONDA
Harves Banks
Longitude West 62 of Greenwich
BARBUDA
Codrington
ANTIGUA
Saint John's
Guadeloupe (Fr.)
GRANDE-TERRE
BASSE-TERRE
Pointe-à-Pitre
Basse-Terre
MARIE-GALANTE
LA DÉSIRADE
ILES DES SAINTES
Longitude West 61 of Greenwich
DOMINICA
Roseau
Portsmouth
Canal de la Dominique / Dominica Passage
Martinique Passage / Canal de la Martinique
Martinique (Fr.)
Fort-de-France
Canal de Sainte-Lucie / Saint Lucia Channel
SAINT LUCIA
Castries
SAINT VINCENT
Kingstown
Saint Vincent Passage
GRENADINES
BEQUIA ISLAND
MUSTIQUE ISLAND
CANOUAN ISLAND
UNION ISLAND
CARRIACOU
GRENADA
Saint George's
BARBADOS
Bridgetown
Longitude West 59 30' of Greenwich
Mercator Cylindrical Projection

Map 52

SOUTH AMERICA, PHYSICAL

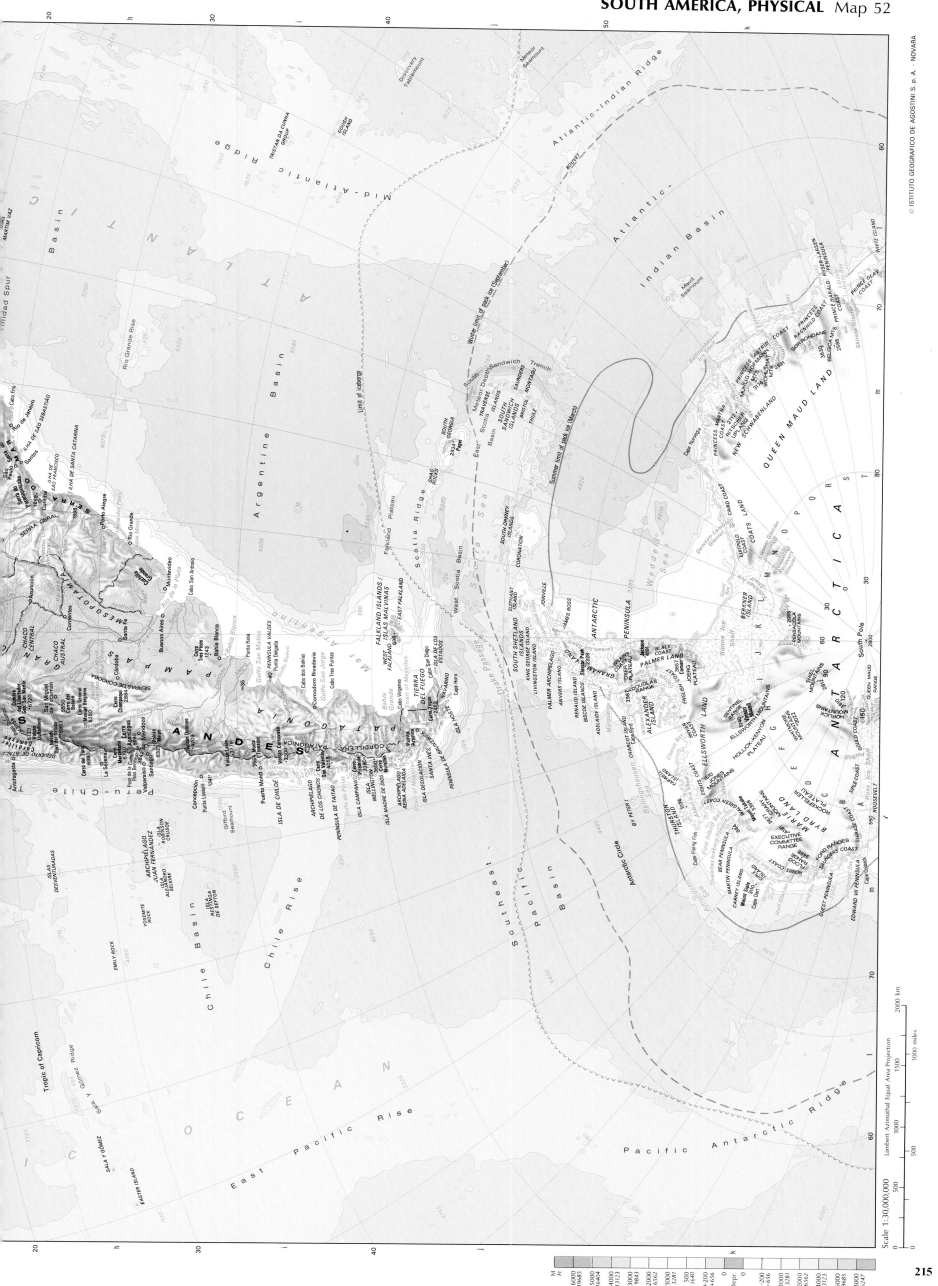

© ISTITUTO GEOGRAFICO DE AGOSTINI S. p. A. - NOVARA

Scale 1:30,000,000

Lambert Azimuthal Equal Area Projection

Map 53

SOUTH AMERICA, POLITICAL

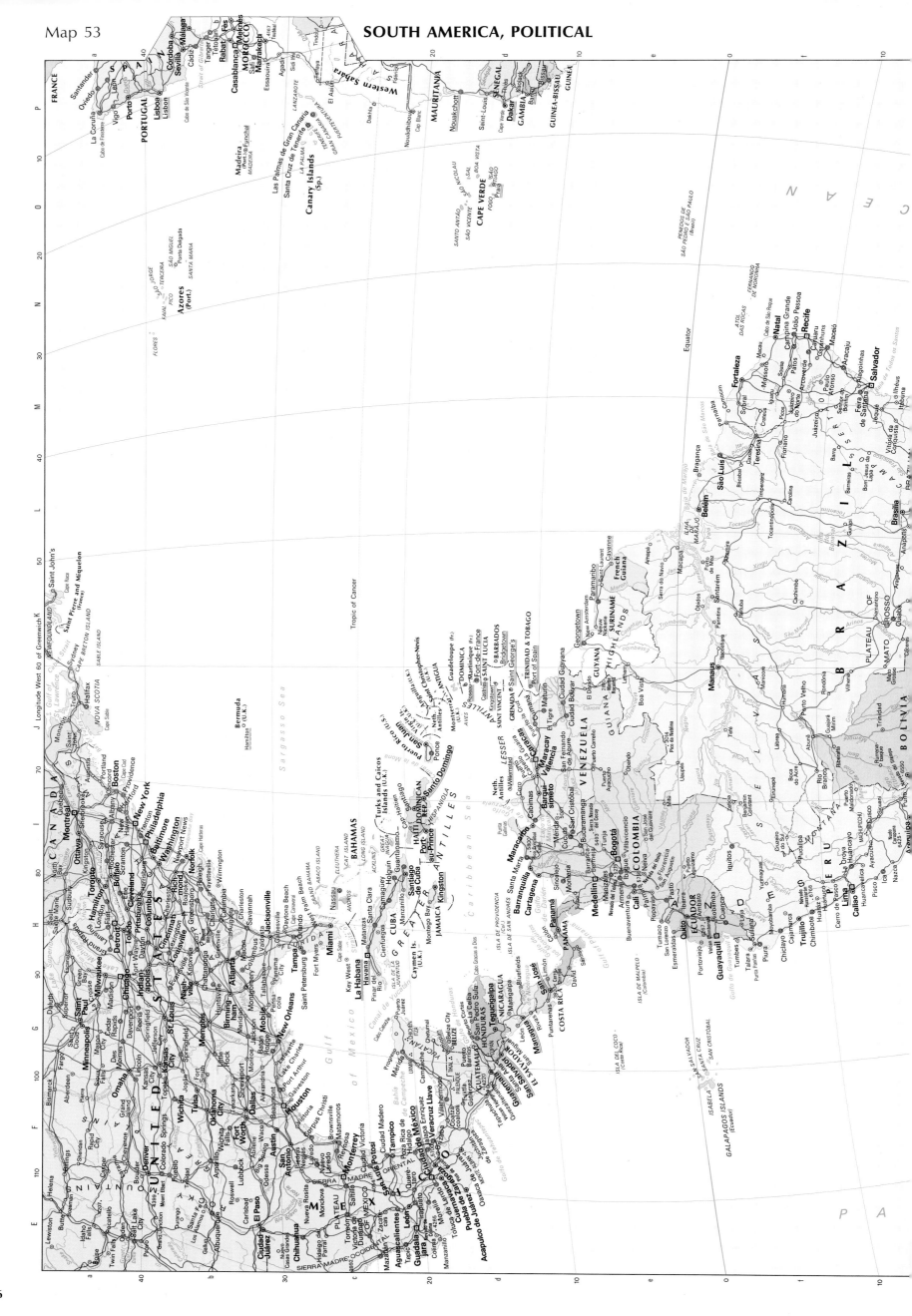

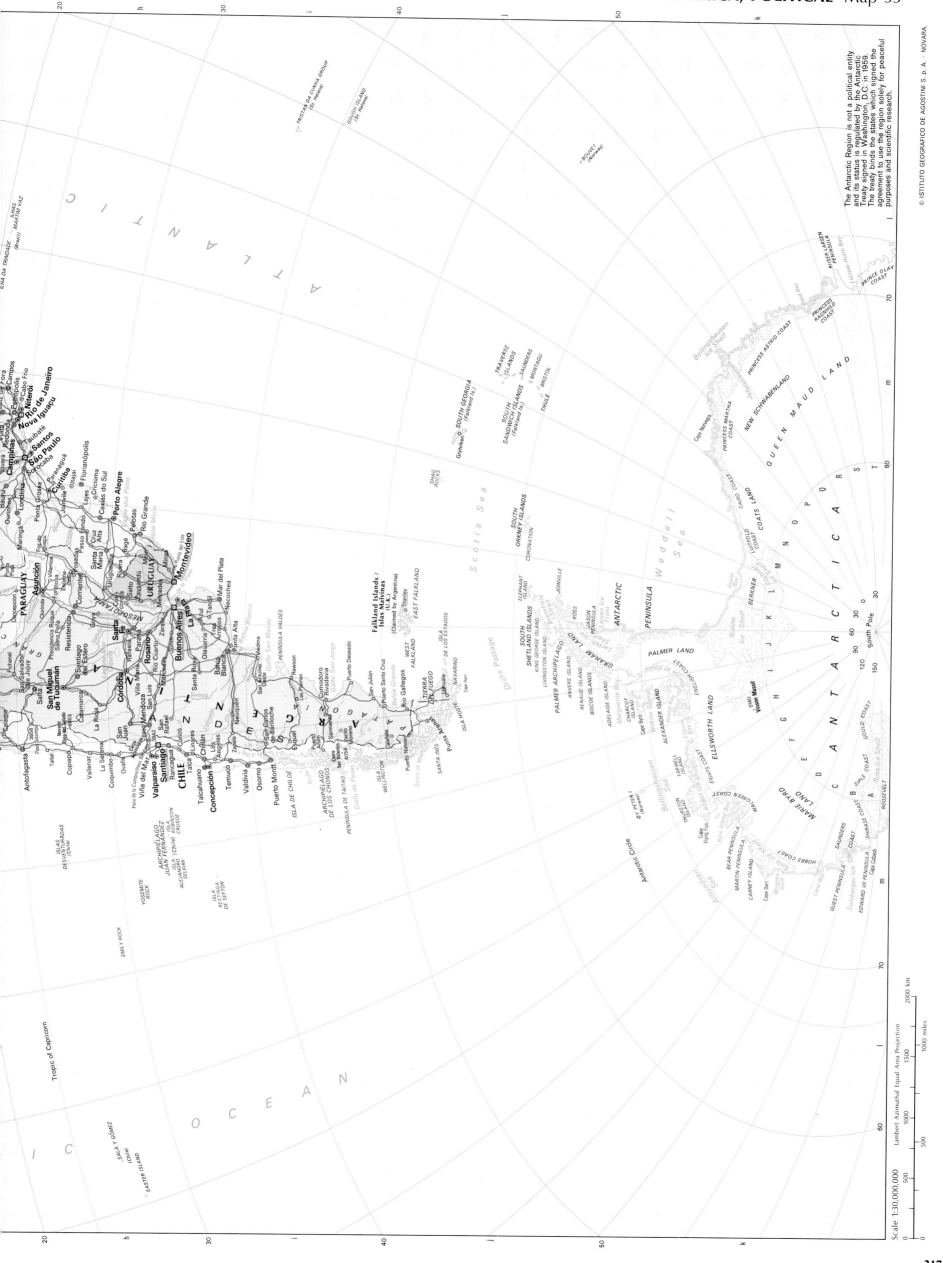

The Antarctic Region is not a political entity and its status is regulated by the Antarctic Treaty signed in Washington, D.C. in 1959. The treaty binds the states which signed the agreement to use the region solely for peaceful purposes and scientific research.

© ISTITUTO GEOGRAFICO DE AGOSTINI S. p. A. - NOVARA.

Scale 1:30,000,000

Lambert Azimuthal Equal Area Projection

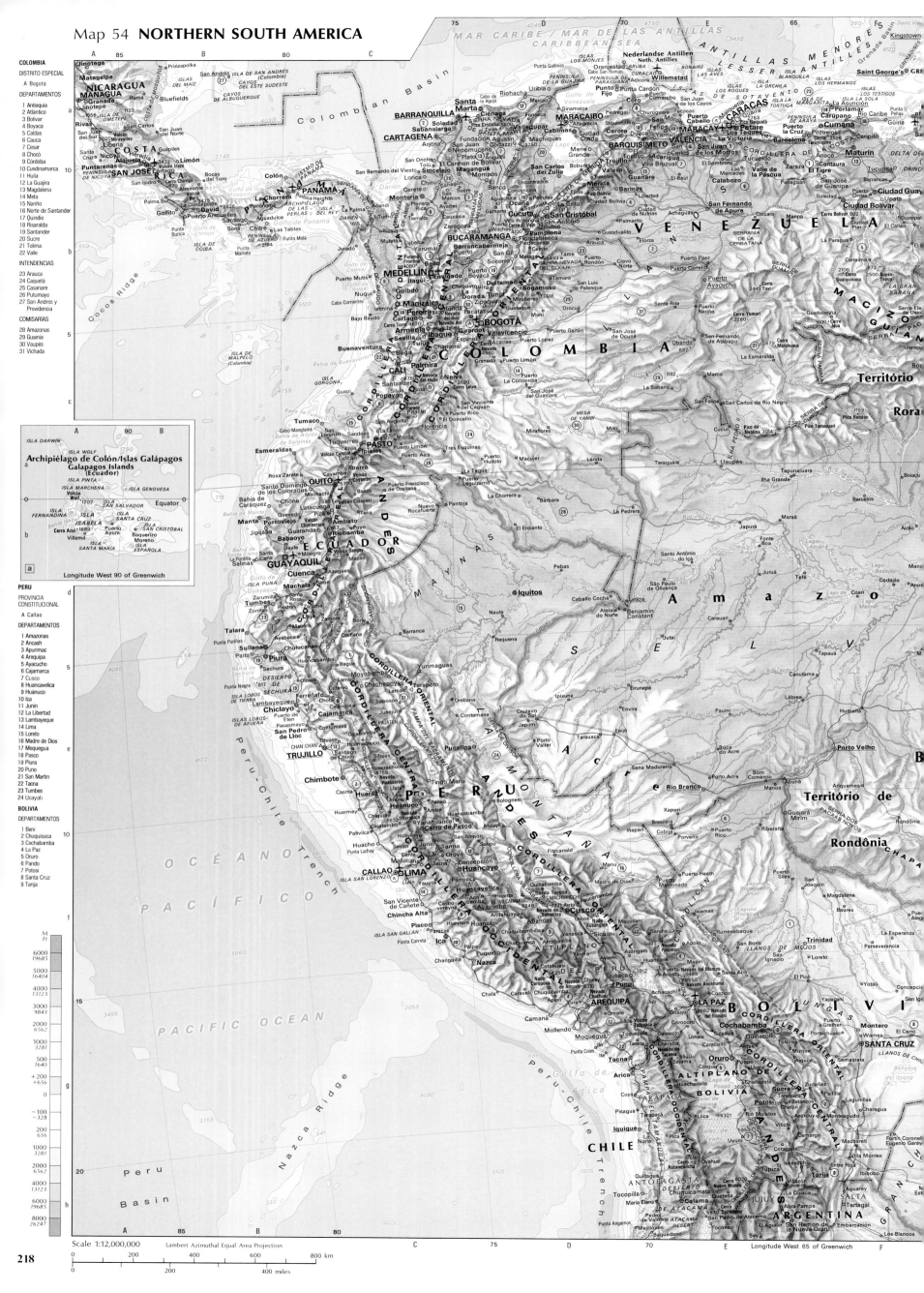

Map 54 NORTHERN SOUTH AMERICA
COLOMBIA
DISTRITO ESPECIAL
A Bogotá
DEPARTAMENTOS
1 Antioquia
2 Atlántico
3 Bolívar
4 Boyacá
5 Caldas
6 Cauca
7 Cesar
8 Chocó
9 Córdoba
10 Cundinamarca
11 Huila
12 La Guajira
13 Magdalena
14 Meta
15 Nariño
16 Norte de Santander
17 Quindío
18 Risaralda
19 Santander
20 Sucre
21 Tolima
22 Valle
INTENDENCIAS
23 Arauca
24 Caquetá
25 Casanare
26 Putumayo
27 San Andrés y Providencia
COMISARÍAS
28 Amazonas
29 Guainía
30 Vaupés
31 Vichada
PERU
PROVINCIA CONSTITUCIONAL
A Callao
DEPARTAMENTOS
1 Amazonas
2 Ancash
3 Apurímac
4 Arequipa
5 Ayacucho
6 Cajamarca
7 Cusco
8 Huancavelica
9 Huánuco
10 Ica
11 Junín
12 La Libertad
13 Lambayeque
14 Lima
15 Loreto
16 Madre de Dios
17 Moquegua
18 Pasco
19 Piura
20 Puno
21 San Martín
22 Tacna
23 Tumbes
24 Ucayali
BOLIVIA
DEPARTAMENTOS
1 Beni
2 Chuquisaca
3 Cochabamba
4 La Paz
5 Oruro
6 Pando
7 Potosí
8 Santa Cruz
9 Tarija
Archipiélago de Colón/Islas Galápagos
Galapagos Islands
(Ecuador)
Longitude West 90 of Greenwich
Scale 1:12,000,000
Lambert Azimuthal Equal Area Projection
Longitude West 65 of Greenwich

VENEZUELA

DISTRITO FEDERAL
A Caracas

ESTADOS
1 Anzoátegui
2 Apure
3 Aragua
4 Barinas
5 Bolívar
6 Carabobo
7 Cojedes
8 Falcón
9 Guárico
10 Lara
11 Mérida
12 Miranda
13 Monagas
14 Nueva Esparta
15 Portuguesa
16 Sucre
17 Táchira
18 Trujillo
19 Yaracuy
20 Zulia

TERRITORIOS
FEDERALES

21 Amazonas
22 Delta Amacuro

23 DEPENDENCIAS
FEDERALES
Islas Los Monjes
Islas La Tortuga
Islas Los Frailes
Isla La Sola
Islas Los Testigos
Islas Las Aves
Islas Los Roques
Isla La Orchila
Isla Blanquilla
Islas Los Hermanos
Isla de Patos
Isla de Aves

Map 55 **EAST-CENTRAL SOUTH AMERICA**

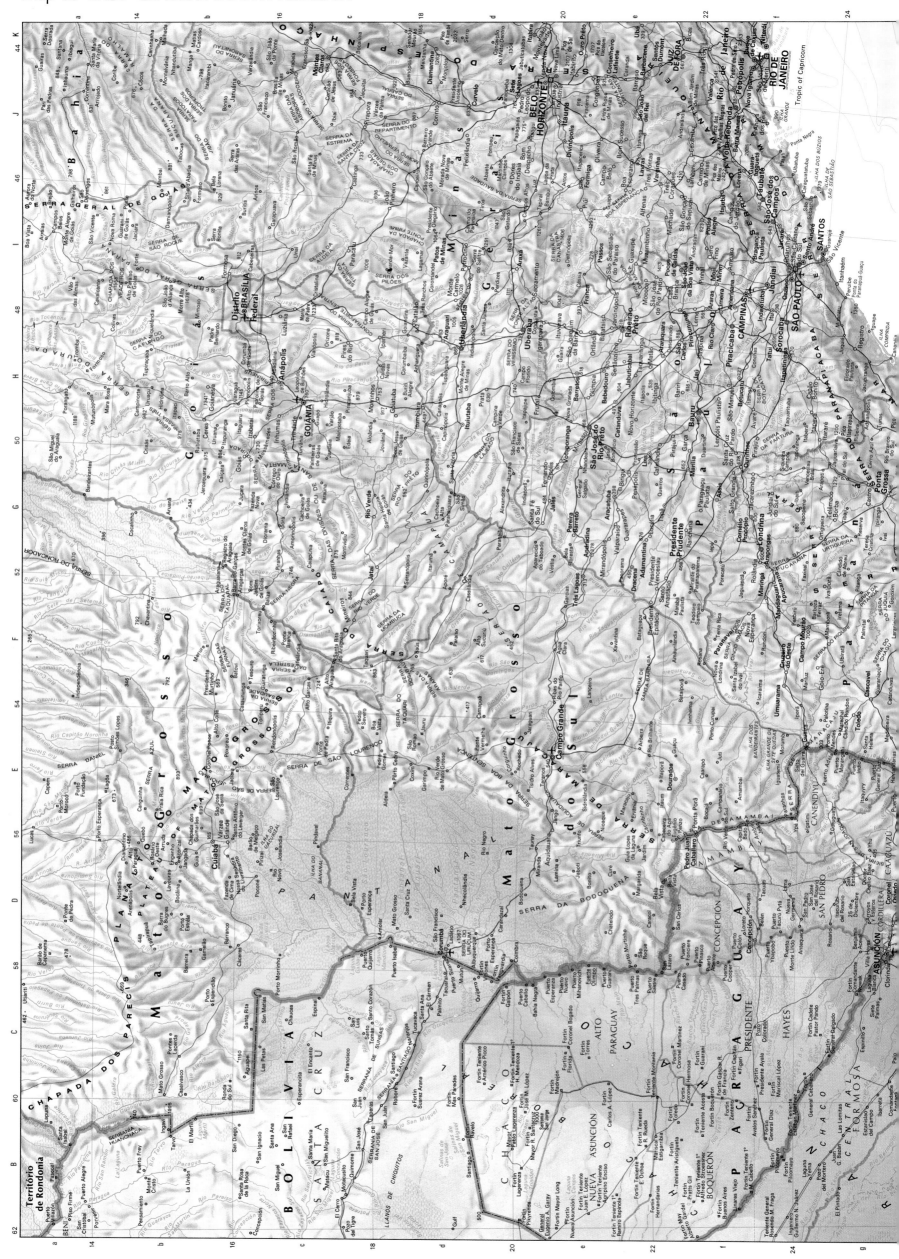

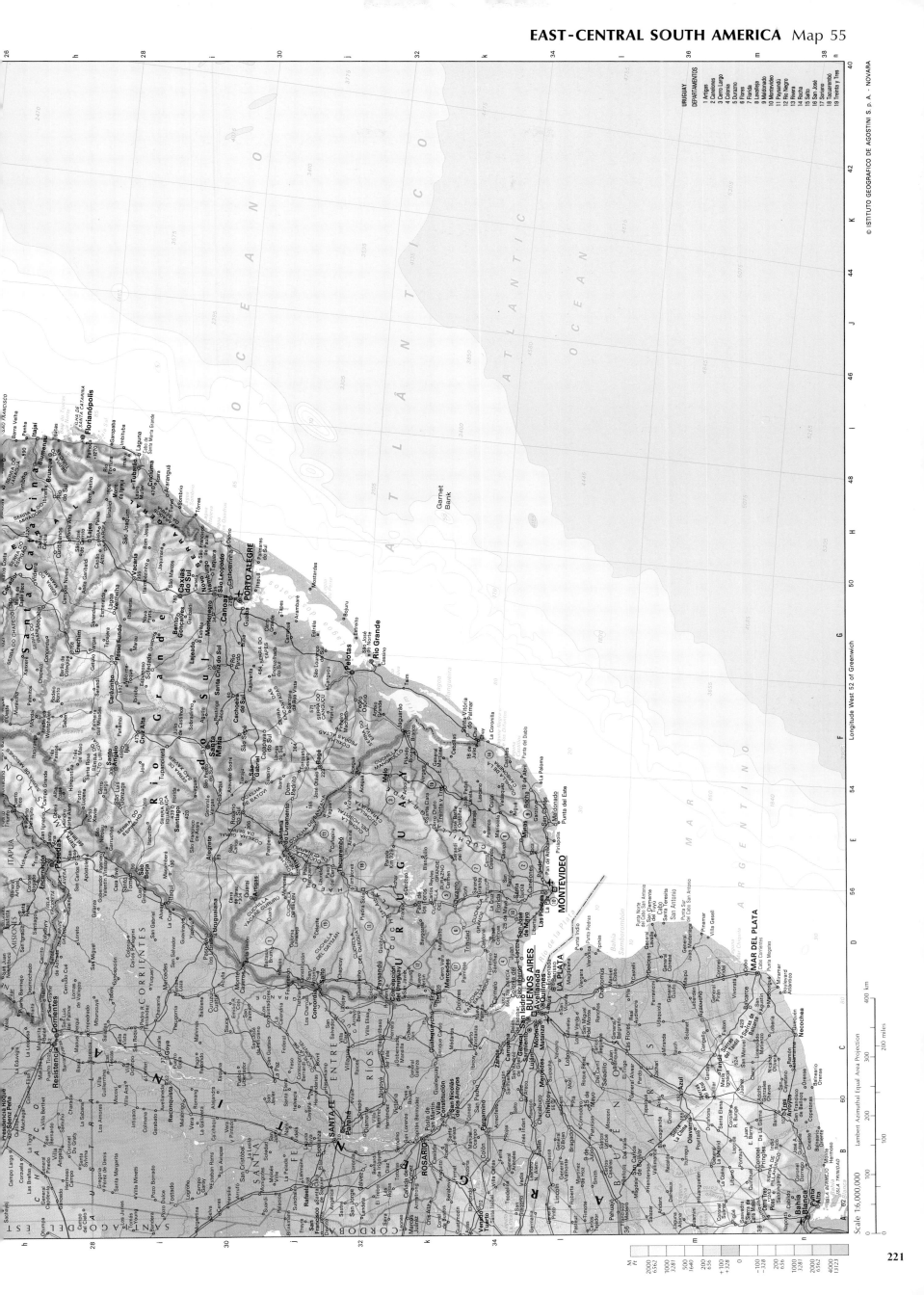
URUGUAY
DEPARTAMENTOS
1 Artigas
2 Canelones
3 Cerro Largo
4 Colonia
5 Durazno
6 Flores
7 Florida
8 Lavalleja
9 Maldonado
10 Montevideo
11 Paysandú
12 Río Negro
13 Rivera
14 Rocha
15 Salto
16 San José
17 Soriano
18 Tacuarembó
19 Treinta y Tres
© ISTITUTO GEOGRAFICO DE AGOSTINI S. p. A. - NOVARA
Longitude West 52 of Greenwich
Scale 1:6,000,000
Lambert Azimuthal Equal Area Projection
O C E A N O
A T L Â N T I C O
A T L A N T I C
O C E A N
M A R
A R G E N T I N O
Garnet Bank
Florianópolis
Blumenau
Itajaí
Laguna
Criciúma
Lajes
Caxias do Sul
PORTO ALEGRE
Pelotas
Rio Grande
Santa Maria
Passo Fundo
Erechim
Uruguaiana
Posadas
Encarnación
Corrientes
Resistencia
Santa Fe
Paraná
ROSARIO
Salto
Paysandú
Tacuarembó
Artigas
Rivera
Melo
Minas
Maldonado
Punta del Este
MONTEVIDEO
BUENOS AIRES
LA PLATA
MAR DEL PLATA
Necochea
Tandil
Azul
Olavarría
Bahía Blanca
Junín
Pergamino
Venado Tuerto
Colón
Dolores
Chascomús
Santa Catarina
Rio Grande do Sul
U R U G U A Y
E N T R E R Í O S
C O R R I E N T E S
S A N T A F E
B U E N O S A I R E S
M I S I O N E S
Lagoa dos Patos
Lagoa Mirim
Rio de la Plata
Bahía Samborombón
400 km
200 miles

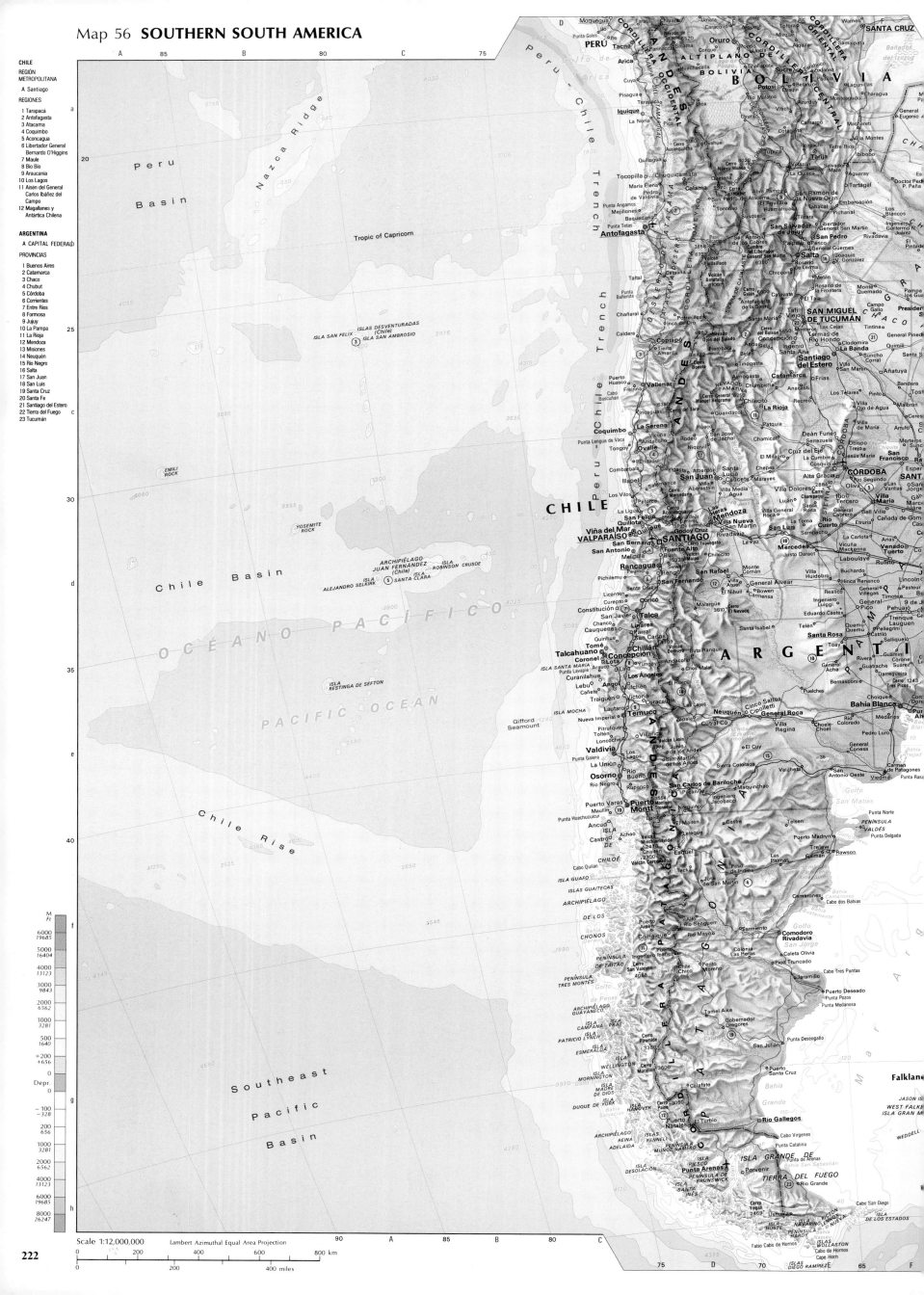

Map 56 SOUTHERN SOUTH AMERICA
CHILE
REGIÓN METROPOLITANA
A Santiago
REGIONES
1 Tarapacá
2 Antofagasta
3 Atacama
4 Coquimbo
5 Aconcagua
6 Libertador General Bernardo O'Higgins
7 Maule
8 Bío Bío
9 Araucania
10 Los Lagos
11 Aisén del General Carlos Ibáñez del Campo
12 Magallanes y Antártica Chilena
ARGENTINA
A CAPITAL FEDERAL
PROVINCIAS
1 Buenos Aires
2 Catamarca
3 Chaco
4 Chubut
5 Córdoba
6 Corrientes
7 Entre Ríos
8 Formosa
9 Jujuy
10 La Pampa
11 La Rioja
12 Mendoza
13 Misiones
14 Neuquén
15 Río Negro
16 Salta
17 San Juan
18 San Luis
19 Santa Cruz
20 Santa Fe
21 Santiago del Estero
22 Tierra del Fuego
23 Tucumán
M
Ft
6000 19685
5000 16404
4000 13123
3000 9843
2000 6562
1000 3281
500 1640
+200 +656
0
Depr.
0
−100 −328
200 656
1000 3281
2000 6562
4000 13123
6000 19685
8000 26247
Peru Basin
Nazca Ridge
Peru - Chile Trench
Tropic of Capricorn
ISLAS DESVENTURADAS (Chile)
ISLA SAN FELIX
ISLA SAN AMBROSIO
EMILI ROCK
YOSEMITE ROCK
ARCHIPIÉLAGO JUAN FERNÁNDEZ (Chile)
ISLA ROBINSON CRUSOE
ISLA ALEJANDRO SELKIRK
ISLA SANTA CLARA
Chile Basin
OCÉANO PACÍFICO
PACIFIC OCEAN
ISLA RESTINGA DE SEFTON
Gifford Seamount
Chile Rise
Southeast Pacific Basin
CHILE
PERÚ
BOLIVIA
ARGENTINA
ALTIPLANO
ANDES
PATAGONIA
SANTIAGO
VALPARAÍSO
Antofagasta
CÓRDOBA
SAN MIGUEL DE TUCUMÁN
Mendoza
Concepción
Bahía Blanca
Comodoro Rivadavia
Río Gallegos
Punta Arenas
ISLA GRANDE DE TIERRA DEL FUEGO
Falkland
Scale 1:12,000,000
Lambert Azimuthal Equal Area Projection
0 200 400 600 800 km
0 200 400 miles
222

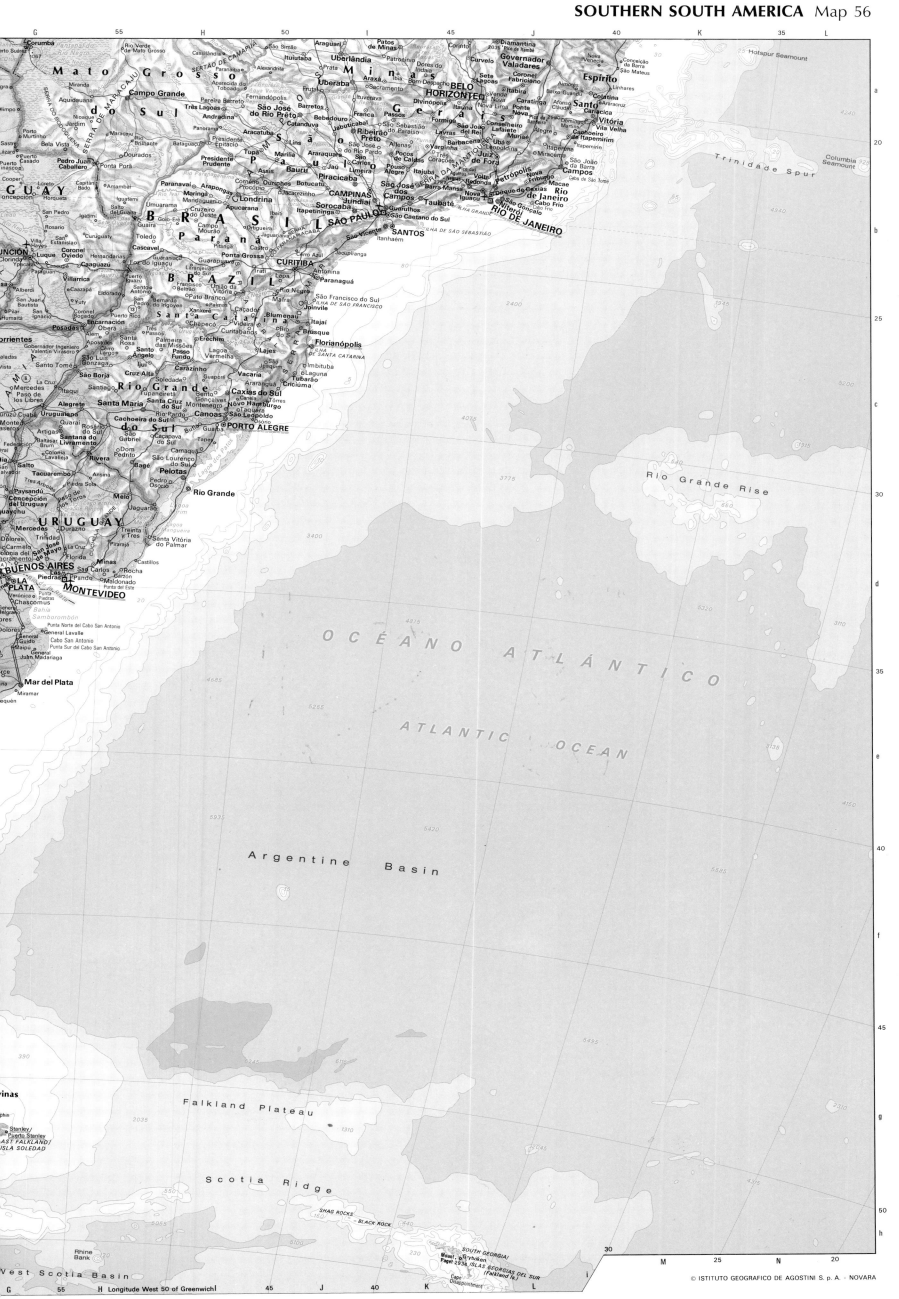
OCÉANO ATLÁNTICO
ATLANTIC OCEAN
Argentine Basin
Rio Grande Rise
Trinidade Spur
Hotspur Seamount
Columbia Seamount
Falkland Plateau
Scotia Ridge
West Scotia Basin
Rhine Bank
SHAG ROCKS
BLACK ROCK
SOUTH GEORGIA/ ISLAS GEORGIAS DEL SUR (Falkland Is.)
Grytviken
Cape Disappointment
Stanley/ Puerto Stanley
EAST FALKLAND/ ISLA SOLEDAD
BRASIL
BRAZIL
URUGUAY
Mato Grosso do Sul
Minas Gerais
São Paulo
Paraná
Santa Catarina
Rio Grande do Sul
Espírito Santo
BELO HORIZONTE
RIO DE JANEIRO
SÃO PAULO
CURITIBA
PORTO ALEGRE
MONTEVIDEO
BUENOS AIRES
LA PLATA
Campo Grande
Vitória
Campinas
Santos
Florianópolis
Rio Grande
Pelotas
Londrina
Uberlândia
Uberaba
Juiz de Fora
Petrópolis
Niterói
Joinvile
Blumenau
Caxias do Sul
Novo Hamburgo
Santa Maria
Mar del Plata
Posadas
Encarnación
Rivera
Melo
Maldonado
Punta del Este
Bahía Samborombón
Longitude West 50 of Greenwich

Map 57 AUSTRALIA AND OCEANIA, PHYSICAL

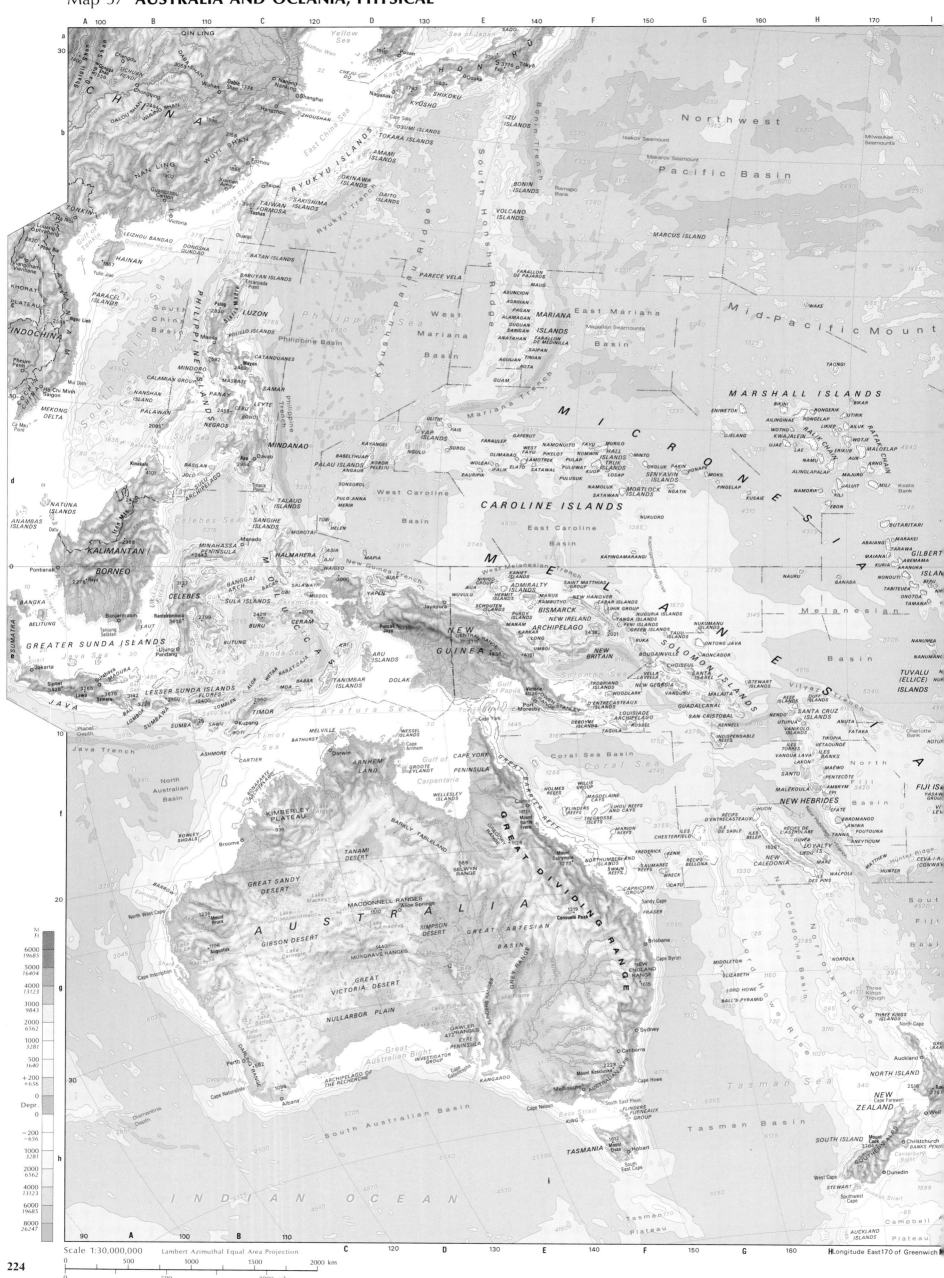

Scale 1:30,000,000 — Lambert Azimuthal Equal Area Projection

PACIFIC OCEAN

Murray Fracture Zone

Northeast

Pacific Basin

Clarion Fracture Zone

Clipperton Fracture Zone

CLIPPERTON

HAWAIIAN ISLANDS

Tropic of Cancer

Musicians Seamounts

MIDWAY ISLANDS
PEARL AND HERMES
LISIANSKI
LAYSAN
MARO
Northampton Seamounts
GARDNER PINNACLES
FRENCH FRIGATE SHOALS
NECKER
NIHOA
KAUAI
NIIHAU
KAULA
OAHU
Honolulu
MOLOKAI
LANAI
MAUI
KAHOOLAWE
Mauna Kea
HAWAII

Hawaiian Ridge

Christmas Ridge

Hess Tablemount
Horizon Tablemount
Pensacola Seamount

Cape Johnson Tablemount
Vityaz Seamount

JOHNSTON

KINGMAN
PALMYRA
TERAINA (WASHINGTON)
TABUAERAN (FANNING)
KIRITIMATI (CHRISTMAS)

LINE ISLANDS

Equator

BAKER
JARVIS

WINSLOW
PHOENIX ISLANDS
KANTON
ENDERBURY
North Tokelau Trough
MCKEAN
BIRNIE
RAWAKI (PHOENIX)
ORONA (HULL)
MANRA (SYDNEY)
UMAROA
GARDNER
CARONDELET

POLYNESIA

MALDEN

STARBUCK

VOSTOK
FLINT
CAROLINE

MARQUESAS ISLANDS
EIAO
HATUTAA
NUKU HIVA
UA HUKA
UA POU
FATU HUTU
HIVA OA
TAHUATA
ROCHER THOMASSET
FATU HIVA

ATAFU
TOKELAU ISLANDS
NUKUNONU
FAKAOFO
RAKAHANGA
MANIHIKI
PENRHYN

UVEA
SAMOA ISLANDS
SAVAI'I
MANUA ISLANDS
UPOLU
TUTUILA
Robbie Bank
SWAINS
PUKAPUKA
NASSAU
NORTHERN COOK ISLANDS
SUWARROW

NIUAFO'OU
NIUATO PUTAPU
TAFAHI

FONUALEI
TONGA ISLANDS
VAVA'U GROUP
HA'APAI GROUP
NOMUKA GROUP
ANTIOPE
MANUAE
MAUPIHAA
MAUPITI
BORA BORA
HUAHINE
TETIAROA
RAIATEA
TAHAA
MOOREA
TAHITI
MAIAO
MOTUTUNGA
WINDWARD ISLANDS

COOK ISLANDS

PALMERSTON
AITUTAKI
MANUAE
TAKUTEA
MITIARO
NIUE
BEVERIDGE
SOUTHERN COOK ISLANDS
RAROTONGA
ATIU
MAUKE

MOTU ONE
LEEWARD ISLANDS
MATAIVA
ILES PALLISER
MAKATEA
RANGIROA
AHE
MANIHI
ILES DU ROI GEORGES
APATAKI
ARATIKA
ARAKARA
TAKUME
TANGATAU
TAKAROA
RAROIA
FAKAHINA
NIHIRU
TEHUATA
MARUTEA
AMANU
TATAKOTO
PUKARUHA
REAO

ILES DU DESAPPOINTEMENT
NAPUKA
PUKAPUKA

TUAMOTU ARCHIPELAGO

Tuamotu Ridge

MANGAIA
MARIA
RURUTU
RIMATARA
TUBUAI ISLANDS
TUBUAI
RAEVAVAE

President Thiers Seamount

TONGATAPU GROUP
ATA
Vityaz II Depth

Tropic of Capricorn

HEREHERETUE
ILES DU DUC DE GLOUCESTER
TEMATANGI
MURUROA
FAGATAUFA
MORANE
GAMBIER ISLANDS
MANGAREVA
TEMOE
OENO
HENDERSON
DUCIE
PITCAIRN

HARAIKI
RETORU
RAVAHERE
NEGONEGO
MANUANGI
PARAOA
AHUNUI
VAHITAHI
PINAKI
AKIAKI
VANAVANA
TUPEIA
MARUTEA
MARIA

RAPA
ILOTS DE BASS

East Pacific Rise

SALA Y GÓMEZ
EASTER ISLAND

CHATHAM ISLANDS

Wachusett Seamount

ERNEST LEGOUVE

MARIA THERESA

Southwest

Pacific

Basin

PACIFIC OCEAN

French Trench
Tonga Trench
Vityaz III Depth

CHANNEL ISLANDS
Point Conception
Mount Pinos
Los Angeles
San Gorgonio
El Paso
Edwards Plateau
BOLSÓN DE MAPIMÍ
Jasper Seamount
ISLA DE GUADALUPE
ISLA CEDROS
Punta Eugenia
Vizcaíno
Bahía Sebastián Vizcaíno
LOWER CALIFORNIA
DESIERTO DE ALTAR
Gulf of California
SIERRA MADRE OCCIDENTAL
Torreón
Cabo San Lucas
La Paz
ISLAS MARÍAS
Cabo Corrientes
ISLAS REVILLAGIGEDO

Map 58 **AUSTRALIA AND OCEANIA, POLITICAL**

Scale 1:30,000,000

Lambert Azimuthal Equal Area Projection

Longitude East 170 of Greenwich

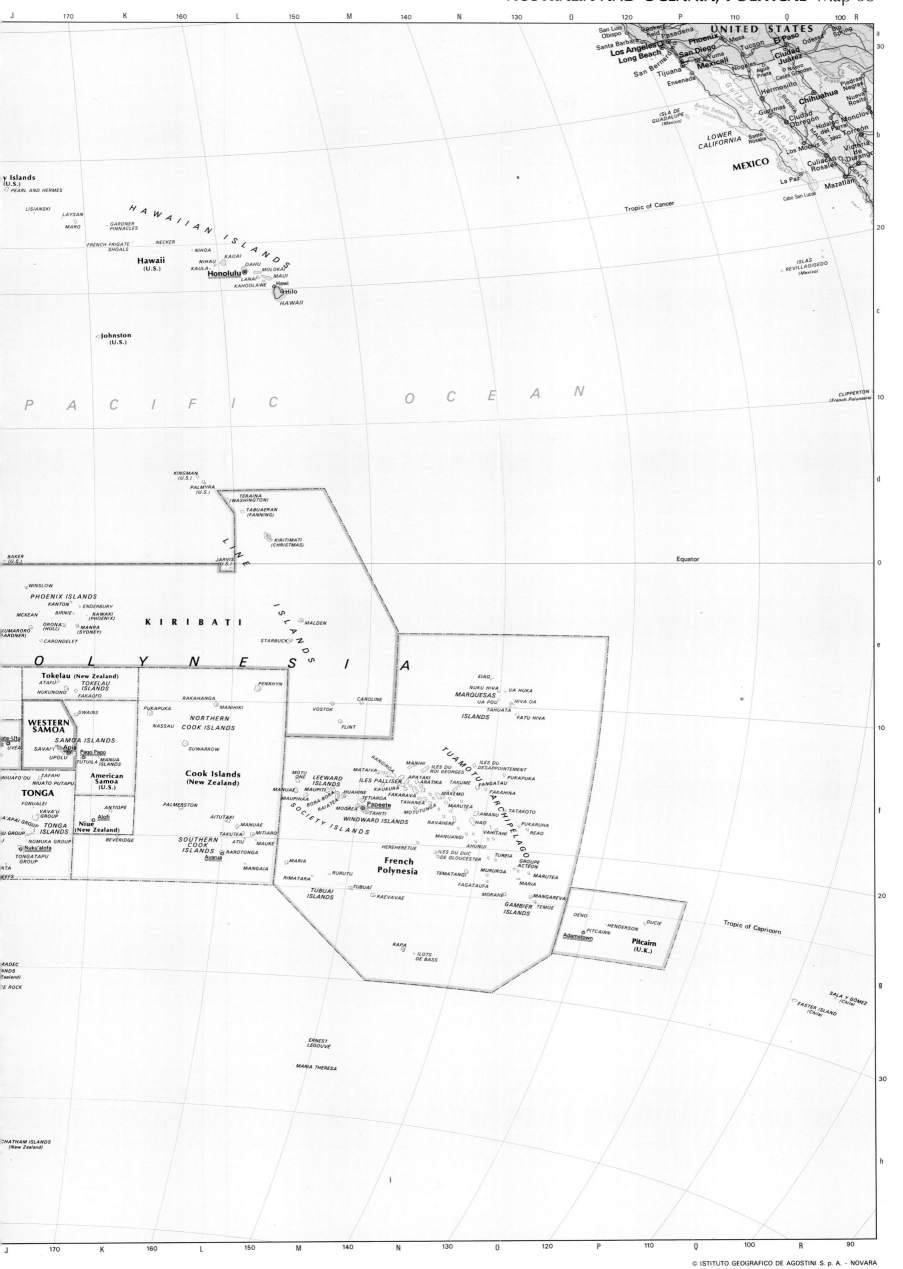
UNITED STATES
MEXICO
LOWER CALIFORNIA
Los Angeles
Long Beach
San Diego
Phoenix
Tijuana
Mexicali
Tucson
El Paso
Ciudad Juárez
Hermosillo
Chihuahua
Ciudad Obregón
Culiacán Rosales
Mazatlán
La Paz
Torreón
Tropic of Cancer
HAWAIIAN ISLANDS
Hawaii (U.S.)
Honolulu
Hilo
HAWAII
Johnston (U.S.)
PACIFIC OCEAN
KINGMAN (U.S.)
PALMYRA (U.S.)
TERAINA (WASHINGTON)
TABUAERAN (FANNING)
KIRITIMATI (CHRISTMAS)
JARVIS (U.S.)
LINE ISLANDS
Equator
PHOENIX ISLANDS
KIRIBATI
MALDEN
STARBUCK
POLYNESIA
Tokelau (New Zealand)
TOKELAU ISLANDS
WESTERN SAMOA
SAMOA ISLANDS
Apia
Pago Pago
American Samoa (U.S.)
TONGA
Nuku'alofa
Niue (New Zealand)
Alofi
NORTHERN COOK ISLANDS
Cook Islands (New Zealand)
SOUTHERN COOK ISLANDS
Avarua
RAROTONGA
MARQUESAS ISLANDS
TUAMOTU ARCHIPELAGO
LEEWARD ISLANDS
WINDWARD ISLANDS
SOCIETY ISLANDS
Papeete
TAHITI
French Polynesia
TUBUAI ISLANDS
GAMBIER ISLANDS
Pitcairn (U.K.)
Adamstown
Tropic of Capricorn
EASTER ISLAND (Chile)
SALA Y GÓMEZ (Chile)
CLIPPERTON (French Polynesia)
ISLAS REVILLAGIGEDO (Mexico)
ERNEST LEGOUVÉ
MARIA THERESA
CHATHAM ISLANDS (New Zealand)

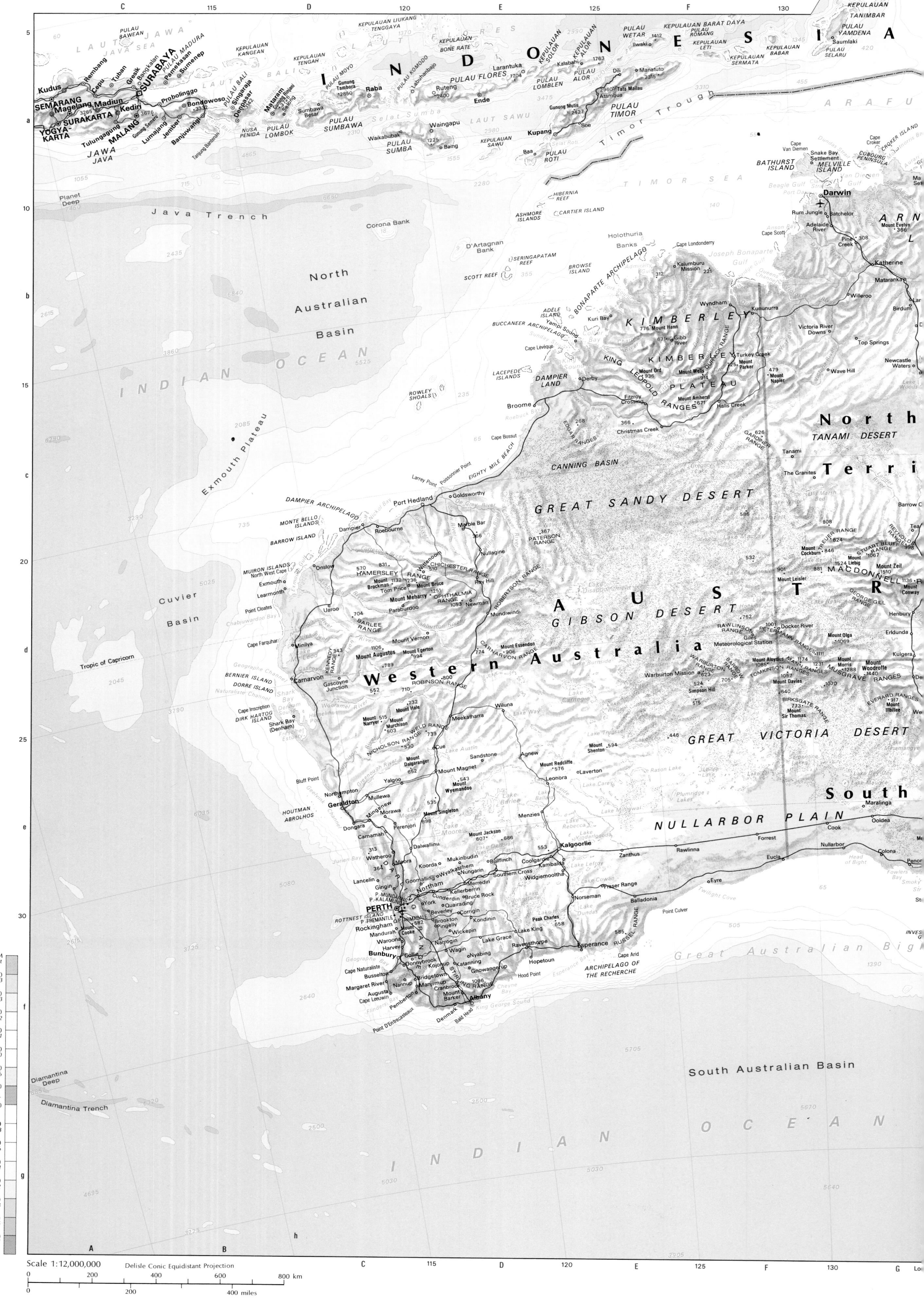

Map 59 AUSTRALIA

INDONESIA

SEMARANG **SURABAYA** **MALANG** **YOGYAKARTA**
Kudus · Rembang · Cepu · Tuban · Gresik
Magelang · Madiun · Kedin
SURAKARTA · Tulungagung · Lumajang · Jember · Banjuwangi
Probolinggo · Bondowoso
PULAU MADURA · Pamekasan · Sumenep
Mataram · Raba · Ende · Ruteng · Larantuka
KEPULAUAN KANGEAN
KEPULAUAN TENGAH
Waikabubak · Waingapu · Baing
PULAU SUMBAWA · PULAU SUMBA · PULAU LOMBOK
NUSA PENIDA
JAWA / JAVA · LAUT JAWA / JAVA SEA · LAUT BALI · LAUT FLORES
PULAU JAWA · PULAU BAWEAN
KEPULAUAN UJUNG TENGGAYA · KEPULAUAN UUKANG TENGGAYA
BONE RATE · PULAU KOMODO · Gunung Tambora
Kupang · PULAU TIMOR · PULAU ROTI · PULAU SAWU · KEPULAUAN SAWU
Baa · Soe · Atambua · Dili · Manatuto · Tata Mailau
Gunung Mutis
PULAU WETAR · PULAU SOLOR · PULAU ALOR · PULAU LOMBLEN
Kalabahi · Ilwaki · Iliwaki
KEPULAUAN BARAT DAYA · PULAU ROMANG · PULAU DAMAR
KEPULAUAN SERMATA · PULAU LETI · PULAU BABAR
LAUT SAWU · Selat Sumba

KEPULAUAN KAI · KEPULAUAN TANIMBAR · PULAU YAMDENA · PULAU SELARU · Saumlaki
ARAFU...

TIMOR SEA · Timor Trough · Timor Sea
HIBERNIA REEF · ASHMORE ISLANDS · CARTIER ISLAND
SCOTT REEF · SERINGAPATAM REEF · D'Artagnan Bank · Corona Bank
Holothuria Banks · Cape Londonderry · BROWSE ISLAND · ADELE ISLAND

BATHURST ISLAND · MELVILLE ISLAND · Cape Van Diemen · Snake Bay Settlement · COBOURG PENINSULA · Cape Croker
Darwin · Rum Jungle · Batchelor · Adelaide River · Pine Creek · Katherine · Matarnka · ARN...
Beagle Gulf · Cape Scott · Mount Evelyn
Joseph Bonaparte Gulf · Wyndham · Kununurra · Willeroo · Birdum
Kalumburu Mission · Kuri Bay · Victoria River Downs · Top Springs
Yampi Sound · KIMBERLEY · Mount Hann · Gibb River · Turkey Creek · Wave Hill
BUCCANEER ARCHIPELAGO · BONAPARTE ARCHIPELAGO
KING LEOPOLD RANGES · DURACK RANGE · Mount Ord · Mount Wells · Mount Parker · Mount Napier
Derby · Fitzroy Crossing · Halls Creek · Newcastle Waters
LACEPEDE ISLANDS · DAMPIER LAND · Cape Leveque
Broome · Christmas Creek · Tanami · The Granites
KIMBERLEY PLATEAU · KING LEOPOLD RANGES · Mount Amherst
ERD RANGES · GARDNER RANGE
North · TANAMI DESERT · **Terri...**

INDIAN OCEAN

North Australian Basin

Java Trench

Planet Deep

Exmouth Plateau

ROWLEY SHOALS

CANNING BASIN · GREAT SANDY DESERT

Cuvier Basin

Larrey Point · Postmonson Point · EIGHTY MILE BEACH · Cape Bossut
Port Hedland · Goldsworthy · Marble Bar · Nullagine
DAMPIER ARCHIPELAGO · MONTE BELLO ISLANDS · BARROW ISLAND
Dampier · Roebourne · Roy Hill · PATERSON RANGE
MUIRON ISLANDS · North West Cape · Onslow · CHICHESTER RANGE · Whittenoom
HAMERSLEY RANGE · Mount Bruce · Wittenoom · ROBERTSON RANGE
Exmouth · Learmonth · Tom Price · Brockman · Mount Meharry · Paraburdoo · Newman · Mundiwindi
Point Cloates · Uaroo · OPHTHALMIA RANGE · Mount Egerton

GIBSON DESERT · Lake Disappointment
Lake Dora

A U S T R ...
MACDONNELL RANGES · Mount Leisler · Mount Liebig · Mount Zeil · Mount Conway
PETERMANN RANGES · Docker River · Mount Olga · Erldunda · Henbury
RAWLINSON RANGE · Giles Meteorological Station · Kulgera
WARBURTON RANGE · Warburton Mission · MUSGRAVE RANGES · Mount Woodroffe · Mount Davies
Simpson Hill · Mount Sir Thomas · BIRKSGATE RANGE · Mount Illbillee · EVERARD RANGES
SCHWERIN RANGE · GEORGE GILL RANGE

Western Australia

BARLEE RANGE · KENNEDY RANGE · CARNARVON RANGE
Mount Vernon · Mount Augustus · Mount Essendon
Cape Farquhar · Minilya · ROBINSON RANGE
Carnarvon · Gascoyne Junction · Mount Hale · Mount Murchison
Geographe Channel · Wooramel River
BERNIER ISLAND · DORRE ISLAND · Cape Inscription · Mount Narryer
DIRK HARTOG ISLAND · Shark Bay (Denham) · WELD RANGE
Naturaliste Channel · Chabuwardoo Bay
Shark Bay · Bluff Point
Cape Farquhar

GREAT VICTORIA DESERT
Lake Carnegie · Lake Wells · Lake Throssell
Wiluna · Lake Way · Meekatharra · Lake Austin
Sandstone · Agnew · Mount Redcliffe · Laverton · Lake Carey
Cue · Mount Magnet · Leonora · Lake Rebecca
Yalgoo · Mount Wyemandoo · Menzies · Lake Rason
Northampton · Mount Shenton
NICHOLSON RANGE · Mount Dalgaranger
Mullewa · Mount Singleton · Lake Barlee · Lake Carey
Geraldton · Morawa · Lake Moore · Kalgoorlie · Zanthus
Dongara · Mingenew · Perenjori · Mount Jackson · Kambalda · Lake Lefroy
Carnamah · Dalwallinu · Mukinbudin · Southern Cross · Coolgardie · Widgiemooltha · Fraser Range
Three Springs · Koorda · Wyalkatchem · Bullfinch · Norseman · Lake Dundas · Balladonia
Perth · Moora · Goomalling · Merredin · Nungarin
HOUTMAN ABROLHOS · Lancelin · Gingin · Northam · Kellerberrin · Point Culver
Julien Bay · Watheroo · Cunderdin · Quairading · Bruce Rock · Peak Charles · Esperance
PERTH · York · Beverley · Corrigin · Lake Grace · Ravensthorpe · Cape Arid
ROTTNEST ISLAND · P. FREMANTLE · Brookton · Pingelly · Wickepin · Kondinin · Hopetoun
Rockingham · Mandurah · Waroona · Narrogin · Wagin · Nyabing · Gnowangerup · Hood Point
Harvey · Collie · Kojonup · Katanning · Cranbrook · ARCHIPELAGO OF THE RECHERCHE
Bunbury · Donnybrook · Bridgetown · Mount Barker · STIRLING RANGE · Esperance Bay
Cape Naturaliste · Busselton · Manjimup · **Albany** · Cheyne Beach
Margaret River · Augusta · Nannup · Pemberton · Denmark · Bad Head · King George Sound
Cape Leeuwin · Point D'Entrecasteaux

NULLARBOR PLAIN · Cook · Oodnadatta · Maralinga
Forrest · Rawlinna · Eucla · Nullarbor · Cocklebiddy
South · Head of Bight
GREAT AUSTRALIAN BIGHT · Fowlers Bay
Twilight Cove · INVES...

INDIAN OCEAN

South Australian Basin

Diamantina Deep
Diamantina Trench

Tropic of Capricorn

Scale 1:12,000,000
Delisle Conic Equidistant Projection
0   200   400   600   800 km
0   200   400 miles

M / Ft
4000 / 13123
3000 / 9843
2000 / 6562
1000 / 3281
500 / 1640
+200 / +656
0
Depr.
−100 / −328
200 / 656
1000 / 3281
2000 / 6562
4000 / 13123
6000 / 19685
8000 / 26247

PULAU IRIAN
NEW GUINEA
PAPUA NEW GUINEA
PULAU DOLAK
PULAU KOMORAN
Merauke
Port Moresby
Gulf of Papua
Lae
HUON PENINSULA
Popondetta
Alotau
Torres Strait
Thursday Island
BANKS ISLAND
PRINCE OF WALES ISLAND
Gulf of Carpentaria
CAPE YORK PENINSULA
Weipa
Cooktown
Cairns
Townsville
Mackay
Rockhampton
Gladstone
Bundaberg
Maryborough
Gympie
BRISBANE
Gold Coast
Toowoomba
Ipswich
GROOTE EYLANDT
MORNINGTON ISLAND
WELLESLEY ISLANDS
BENTINCK ISLAND
Mount Isa
Cloncurry
Julia Creek
Richmond
Hughenden
Charters Towers
Longreach
Winton
Barcaldine
Blackall
Emerald
Charleville
Roma
Cunnamulla
Birdsville
Boulia
Queensland
GREAT DIVIDING RANGE
GREAT ARTESIAN BASIN
DARLING DOWNS
STURT DESERT
New South Wales
Broken Hill
Bourke
Moree
Tamworth
Armidale
Dubbo
Orange
Bathurst
Newcastle
SYDNEY
Wollongong
Canberra
Australian Capital Territory
Wagga Wagga
Albury
Griffith
Mildura
Port Macquarie
Coffs Harbour
Grafton
Lismore
Victoria
MELBOURNE
Geelong
Ballarat
Bendigo
Shepparton
Wangaratta
Horsham
Hamilton
Warrnambool
Portland
Mount Gambier
ADELAIDE
Whyalla
Port Pirie
Port Augusta
KANGAROO ISLAND
WILSONS PROMONTORY
Bass Strait
KING ISLAND
FLINDERS ISLAND
FURNEAUX GROUP
Tasmania
Launceston
Devonport
Burnie
Hobart
Queenstown
Strahan
Port Arthur
BRUNY ISLAND
Coral Sea Islands Territory
CORAL SEA
Coral Sea Basin
GREAT BARRIER REEF
WILLIS GROUP
MAGDELAINE CAYS
CORINGA ISLETS
HERALDS CAYS
FLINDERS REEFS
HOLMES REEFS
BOUGAINVILLE REEF
OSPREY REEF
LIHOU REEFS AND CAYS
TREGROSSE ISLETS
MARION REEFS
MELLISH REEF
FREDERICK REEF
SAUMAREZ REEFS
KENN REEF
WRECK REEF
CATO ISLAND
CAPRICORN GROUP
BUNKER GROUP
FRASER ISLAND
MORETON ISLAND
NORTH STRADBROKE ISLAND
Tropic of Capricorn
Kelso Bank
Kejpel Bank
PACIFIC OCEAN
Nouvelle-Calédonie
New Caledonia
(France)
RÉCIFS ET ILES CHESTERFIELD
ILE DE SABLE
RÉCIFS BELLONA
MIDDLETON REEF (Australia)
ELIZABETH REEF (Australia)
LORD HOWE ISLAND (Australia)
BALL'S PYRAMID
TASMAN SEA
Tasman Basin
Solomon Basin
SOLOMON SEA
New Britain Trench
NEW BRITAIN
NEW IRELAND ISLAND
BISMARCK ARCHIPELAGO
BOUGAINVILLE ISLAND
SOLOMON ISLANDS
CHOISEUL ISLAND
SANTA ISABEL ISLAND
NEW GEORGIA ISLANDS
GUADALCANAL ISLAND
Honiara
MALAITA ISLAND
SAN CRISTOBAL ISLAND
RENNELL ISLAND
INDISPENSABLE REEFS (Vanuatu)
ONTONG JAVA
TROBRIAND ISLANDS
WOODLARK ISLAND
D'ENTRECASTEAUX ISLANDS
LOUISIADE ARCHIPELAGO
ROSSEL ISLAND
POCKLINGTON REEF
140
155
160
165

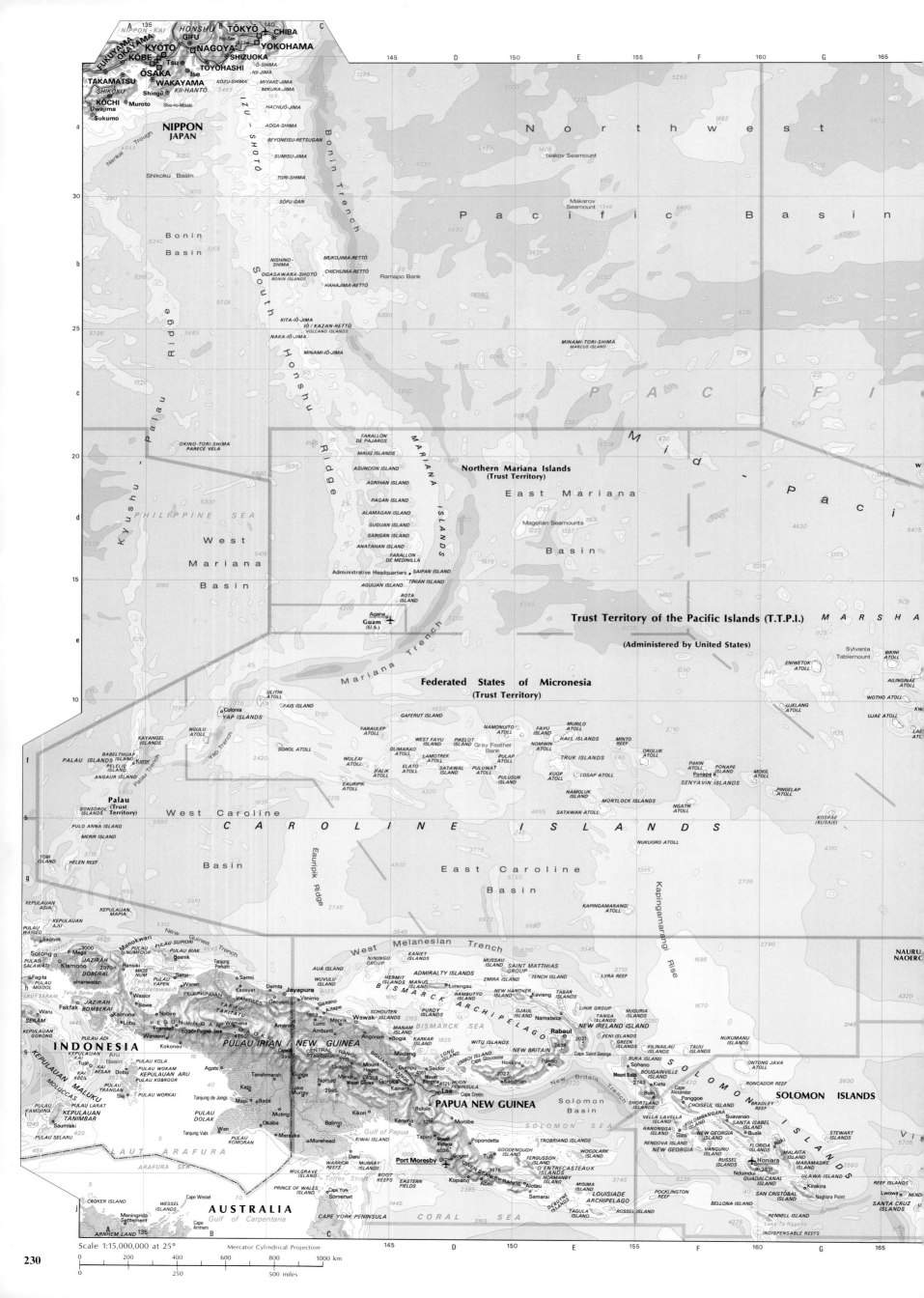

NIPPON
JAPAN

NIPPON-KAI
HONSHU
FUKUYAMA
OKAYAMA
GIFU
TŌKYŌ
CHIBA
KYŌTO
NAGOYA
YOKOHAMA
KŌBE
Tsu
SHIZUOKA
ŌSAKA
TOYOHASHI
WAKAYAMA
Ise
TAKAMATSU
SHIKOKU
Kii-HANTŌ
KŌCHI
Shingū
Muroto
Uwajima
Shio-no-Misaki
Sukumo

Shikoku Basin

Nankai Trough

Izu-shotō

Bonin Trough

Bonin Basin

Ogasawara-shotō
Bonin Islands

South Honshu Ridge

Palau-Kyushu Ridge

PHILIPPINE SEA

West Mariana Basin

Mariana Ridge

Mariana Islands

Northern Mariana Islands
(Trust Territory)

East Mariana Basin

Magellan Seamounts

Administrative Headquarters • SAIPAN ISLAND
TINIAN ISLAND
AGUIJAN ISLAND
ROTA ISLAND

Agana
Guam (U.S.)

Mariana Trench

Trust Territory of the Pacific Islands (T.T.P.I.)

(Administered by United States)

Federated States of Micronesia
(Trust Territory)

Northwest

Pacific Basin

Isakov Seamount

Makarov Seamount

Ramapo Bank

Minami-Tori-Shima
Marcus Island

Mid-Pacific

MARSHA

Sylvania Tablemount

ENIWETOK ATOLL

BIKINI ATOLL

AILINGINAE ATOLL

WOTHO ATOLL

UJELANG ATOLL

UJAE ATOLL

CAROLINE ISLANDS

ULITHI ATOLL
FAIS ISLAND
Colonia
YAP ISLANDS

GAFERUT ISLAND

NAMONUITO ATOLL
WEST FAYU ISLAND
PIKELOT ISLAND
Gray Feather Bank
FAYU ATOLL
MURILO ATOLL
HALL ISLANDS
MINTO REEF

FARAULEP ATOLL

NGULU ATOLL

KAYANGEL ISLANDS

BABELTHUAP ISLAND
PALAU ISLANDS
Koror
PELELIU ISLAND
ANGAUR ISLAND

Palau
(Trust Territory)

SONSOROL ISLANDS

PULO ANNA ISLAND

MERIR ISLAND

TOBI ISLAND

HELEN REEF

OLIMARAO ATOLL
LAMOTREK ATOLL
WOLEAI ATOLL
IFALIK ATOLL
ELATO ATOLL
SATAWAL ISLAND
PULUWAT ATOLL
EAURIPIK ATOLL
PULAP ATOLL
PULUSUK ISLAND

SOROL ATOLL

NOMWIN ATOLL

TRUK ISLANDS

KUOP ATOLL
LOSAP ATOLL

NAMOLUK ATOLL

MORTLOCK ISLANDS

SATAWAN ATOLL

NGATIK ATOLL

OROLUK ATOLL

PAKIN ATOLL
PONAPE ISLAND
Ponape
SENYAVIN ISLANDS
MOKIL ATOLL

PINGELAP ATOLL

KOSRAE (KUSAIE)

West Caroline Basin

Yap Trench

Palau Trench

Eauripik Ridge

East Caroline Basin

NUKUORO ATOLL

KAPINGAMARANGI ATOLL

Kapingamarangi Rise

West Melanesian Trench

New Guinea Trench

KEPULAUAN ASIA
KEPULAUAN MAPIA
PULAU AJU
PULAU WAIGEO
Saonek
PULAU SALAWATI
Sorong
Mega
Klamono
Manokwari
NUMFOOR
PULAU SUPIORI
PULAU BIAK
JAZIRAH
DOBERAI
Ransiki
Teluk Berau
Inanwatan
Wasior
Cenderawasih
PULAU YAPEN
Serui
Waren
Nabire
Kansyat
Demta
Genyem
Jayapura
Vanimo

NININGO GROUP
KANIET ISLANDS
HERMIT ISLANDS
AUA ISLAND
WUVULU ISLAND
ADMIRALTY ISLANDS
MUSSAU ISLAND
SAINT MATTHIAS GROUP
EMIRA ISLAND
MANUS ISLAND
Lorengau
TENCH ISLAND
RAMBUTYO ISLAND
PURDY ISLANDS
NEW HANOVER ISLAND
Kavieng
Namatanai
TABAR ISLANDS
LIHIR GROUP
TANGA ISLANDS
NUGURIA ISLANDS
LYRA REEF

BISMARCK ARCHIPELAGO

SCHOUTEN ISLANDS
Wewak
Aitape
MANAM ISLAND
Bogia
Angoram
Maprik
DJAUL ISLAND
NEW IRELAND ISLAND
FENI ISLANDS
TAUU ISLANDS
GREEN ISLANDS
NISSAN
KARKAR ISLAND
LONG ISLAND
WITU ISLANDS

BISMARCK SEA

Dumpu
Madang
Saidor
UMBOI ISLAND
Cape Gloucester
Rabaul
NUKUMANU ISLANDS
ONTONG JAVA ATOLL
KILINAILAU ISLANDS
BUKA ISLAND
Sohano

INDONESIA

SERAM
LAUT SERAM
Fakfak
Kaimana
JAZIRAH BOMBERAI
Wanapiri
Kokonau
Enarotali
PEGUNUNGAN MAOKE
Puncak Jaya
PEGUNUNGAN
PULAU IRIAN / NEW GUINEA
Wamena
PAPUA NEW GUINEA

TAMRAU-TARITATU

Amanab
Lumi
Ambunti
Telefomin
CENTRAL RANGE
Mount Hagen
Mendi
Mount Giluwe
Gorōka
Kainantu
Mount Wilhelm
STAR RANGE
Lae
Morobe
Cape Cretin
HUON PENINSULA
Finschhafen
NEW BRITAIN
Hoskins
Pomio
Cape Saint George
Kandrian

NEW BRITAIN

Mount Balbi
Buin

SHORTLAND ISLANDS

BOUGAINVILLE ISLAND

Solomon Basin

SOLOMON ISLANDS

RONCADOR REEF

Cape Alexander
Panggoe
CHOISEUL ISLAND
KOLOMBANGARA
VELLA LAVELLA
RANONGGA ISLAND
Gizo
Kieta
VANGUNU
NEW GEORGIA
RENDOVA ISLAND
RUSSELL ISLANDS
Nduindui
SANTA ISABEL ISLAND
FLORIDA ISLANDS
MALAITA
Honiara
MARAMASIKE ISLAND
GUADALCANAL ISLAND
ULAWA ISLAND
Kirakira
SAN CRISTÓBAL ISLAND

Naghora Point

REEF ISLANDS

SANTA CRUZ ISLANDS

CORAL SEA

KEPULAUAN MALUKU
MOLUCCAS
PULAU GOROM
KEPULAUAN GORONG
PULAU ADI
SERAM
Waru
Fagita
Tual
KAI BESAR
PULAU KOLA
KEPULAUAN ARU
KEPULAUAN TANIMBAR
PULAU WOKAM
PULAU KOBROOR
Dobo
PULAU TRANGAN
PULAU LARAT
PULAU WORKAI
Saumlaki
KEPULAUAN TANIMBAR
PULAU SELARU
WESSEL ISLANDS
CROKER ISLAND
Maningrida Settlement

LAUT ARAFURA

Tanjung Vals
PULAU DOLAK
PULAU KOMORAN

Agats
Tanahmerah
Mapi
Muting
Okaba
Merauke

Tanjung de Jongs

ARAFURA SEA

Morehead
Daru
Kikori
Kerema
Balimo
Bulolo
Tapini
Mount Victoria
OWEN STANLEY RANGE
Sogeri
Port Moresby
Kupiano
Abau

Gulf of Papua

WARRIOR REEFS
MURRAY ISLANDS
MULGRAVE ISLAND
PRINCE OF WALES ISLAND
Cape York
Somerset
BOOT REEFS
EASTERN FIELDS
Toffees Strait

Popondetta
Tufi
Kokoda
TROBRIAND ISLANDS
GOODENOUGH ISLAND
FERGUSSON ISLAND
WOODLARK ISLAND
D'ENTRECASTEAUX ISLANDS
NORMANBY ISLAND
Samarai
MISIMA ISLAND
LOUISIADE ARCHIPELAGO
TAGULA ISLAND
DEBOYNE ISLANDS
ROSSEL ISLAND

POCKLINGTON REEF

BELLONA ISLAND

RENNELL ISLAND

INDISPENSABLE REEFS

AUSTRALIA
Gulf of Carpentaria

CAPE YORK PENINSULA
ARNHEM LAND
Cape Wessel
Cape Arnhem

NAURU
NAOERO

Scale 1:15,000,000 at 25°   Mercator Cylindrical Projection

0   200   400   600   800   1000 km

0   250   500 miles

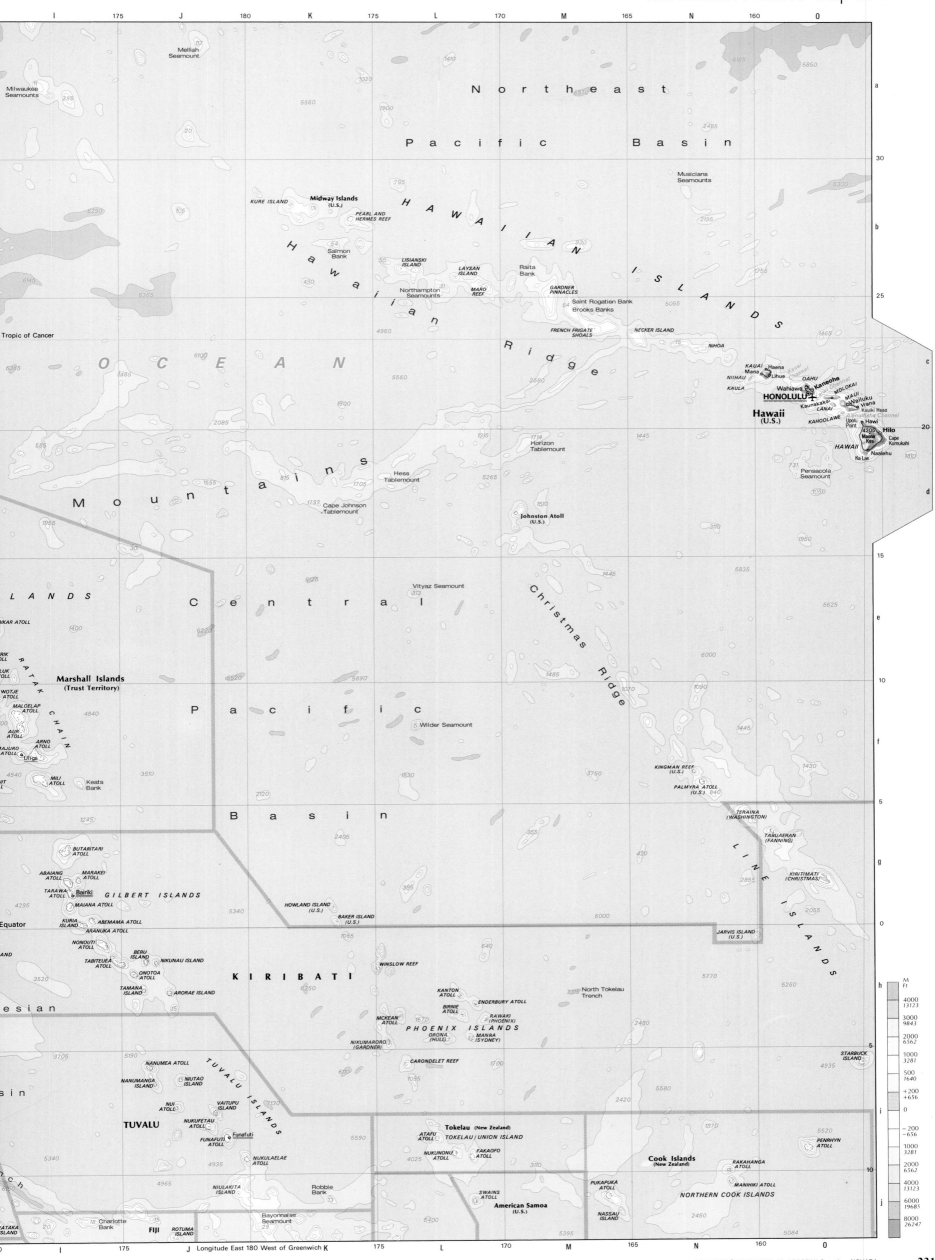
Northeast Pacific Basin
HAWAIIAN ISLANDS
Hawaiian Ridge
OCEAN
Mountains
Central Pacific Basin
Christmas Ridge
LINE ISLANDS
Midway Islands (U.S.)
KURE ISLAND
PEARL AND HERMES REEF
Salmon Bank
LISIANSKI ISLAND
LAYSAN ISLAND
Raita Bank
MARO REEF
Northampton Seamounts
GARDNER PINNACLES
Saint Rogatien Bank
Brooks Banks
FRENCH FRIGATE SHOALS
NECKER ISLAND
NIHOA
KAUAI
NIIHAU
KAULA
OAHU
MOLOKAI
LANAI
KAHOOLAWE
MAUI
HAWAII
Haena
Mana
Lihue
Wahiawa
Kaneohe
HONOLULU
Kaunakakai
Wailuku
Hana
Kauiki Head
Upolu Point
Hawi
Hilo
Mauna Kea
Cape Kumukahi
Naalehu
Ka Lae
Hawaii (U.S.)
Pensacola Seamount
Musicians Seamounts
Mellish Seamount
Milwaukee Seamounts
Tropic of Cancer
Horizon Tablemount
Hess Tablemount
Cape Johnson Tablemount
Johnston Atoll (U.S.)
Vityaz Seamount
Wilder Seamount
Marshall Islands (Trust Territory)
RATAK CHAIN
BIKAR ATOLL
WOTJE ATOLL
MALOELAP ATOLL
AUR ATOLL
ARNO ATOLL
MAJURO ATOLL
Uliga
MILI ATOLL
Keats Bank
KINGMAN REEF (U.S.)
PALMYRA ATOLL (U.S.)
TERAINA (WASHINGTON)
TABUAERAN (FANNING)
KIRITIMATI (CHRISTMAS)
JARVIS ISLAND (U.S.)
BUTARITARI ATOLL
MARAKEI ATOLL
ABAIANG ATOLL
TARAWA ATOLL
Bairiki
GILBERT ISLANDS
MAIANA ATOLL
KURIA ISLAND
ABEMAMA ATOLL
ARANUKA ATOLL
Equator
NONOUTI ATOLL
BERU ISLAND
NIKUNAU ISLAND
TABITEUEA ATOLL
ONOTOA ATOLL
TAMANA ISLAND
ARORAE ISLAND
KIRIBATI
HOWLAND ISLAND (U.S.)
BAKER ISLAND (U.S.)
WINSLOW REEF
KANTON ATOLL
ENDERBURY ATOLL
BIRNIE ATOLL
RAWAKI (PHOENIX)
MCKEAN ATOLL
PHOENIX ISLANDS
ORONA (HULL)
MANRA (SYDNEY)
NIKUMARORO (GARDNER)
North Tokelau Trench
CARONDELET REEF
STARBUCK ISLAND
NANUMEA ATOLL
TUVALU ISLANDS
NANUMANGA ISLAND
NIUTAO ISLAND
NUI ATOLL
VAITUPU ISLAND
TUVALU
NUKUFETAU ATOLL
FUNAFUTI ATOLL
Funafuti
NUKULAELAE ATOLL
NIULAKITA ISLAND
Tokelau (New Zealand)
ATAFU ATOLL
TOKELAU / UNION ISLAND
NUKUNONU ATOLL
FAKAOFO ATOLL
Cook Islands (New Zealand)
PENRHYN ATOLL
RAKAHANGA ATOLL
MANIHIKI ATOLL
NORTHERN COOK ISLANDS
PUKAPUKA ATOLL
NASSAU ISLAND
SWAINS ATOLL
American Samoa (U.S.)
Robbie Bank
Bayonnaise Seamount
Charlotte Bank
FIJI
ROTUMA ISLAND
FATAKA ISLAND
Longitude East 180 West of Greenwich
M
Ft
4000 13123
3000 9843
2000 6562
1000 3281
500 1640
+200 +656
0
−200 −656
1000 3281
2000 6562
4000 13123
6000 19685
8000 26247

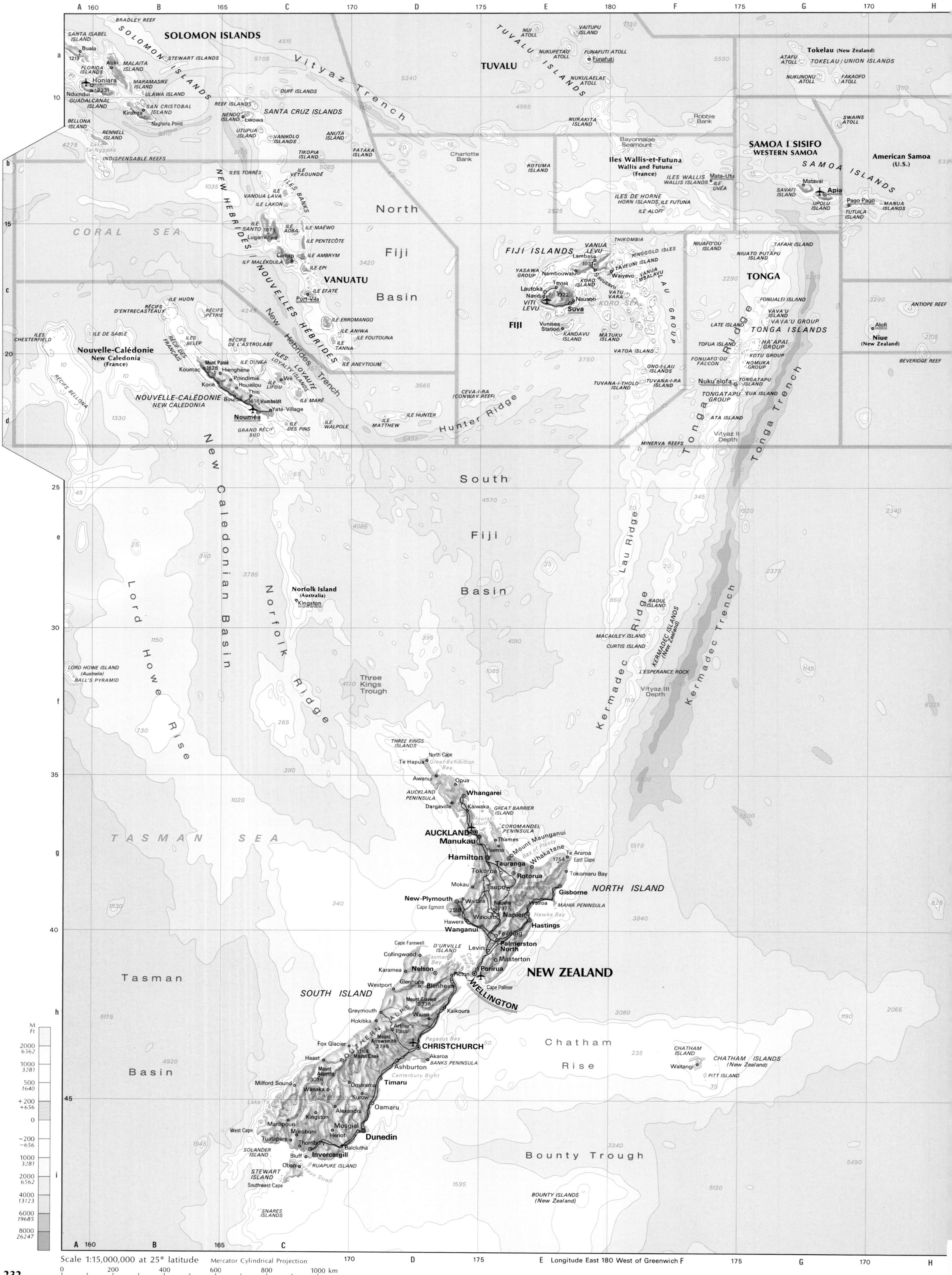

Map 61 **THE SOUTH PACIFIC**

SOLOMON ISLANDS

TUVALU

Tokelau (New Zealand)
TOKELAU / UNION ISLANDS

SAMOA I SISIFO
WESTERN SAMOA

American Samoa
(U.S.)

Vityaz Trench

North
Fiji
Basin

VANUATU

NOUVELLES-HÉBRIDES
New Hebrides

Iles Wallis-et-Futuna
Wallis and Futuna
(France)

FIJI ISLANDS

TONGA

CORAL SEA

Nouvelle-Calédonie
New Caledonia
(France)

NOUVELLE-CALÉDONIE
NEW CALEDONIA

Nouméa

FIJI

Suva

Niue
(New Zealand)

ANTIOPE REEF

Tonga Ridge

Nuku'alofa

TONGA ISLANDS

Hunter Ridge

South
Fiji
Basin

Lau Ridge

Kermadec Ridge

KERMADEC ISLANDS
(New Zealand)

Kermadec Trench

New Caledonian Basin

Norfolk Ridge

Norfolk Island
(Australia)
Kingston

Lord Howe Rise

Three Kings Trough

THREE KINGS ISLANDS

LORD HOWE ISLAND
(Australia)
BALL'S PYRAMID

North Cape

TASMAN SEA

AUCKLAND PENINSULA

Whangarei

GREAT BARRIER ISLAND

COROMANDEL PENINSULA

AUCKLAND
Manukau

Hamilton

Tauranga
Rotorua

Whakatane
Bay of Plenty
East Cape

NORTH ISLAND

New-Plymouth

Cape Egmont

Gisborne

Napier
Hastings

Wanganui

MAHIA PENINSULA
Hawke Bay

NEW ZEALAND

Palmerston North
Masterton
Porirua

Nelson
Blenheim

WELLINGTON

Cape Palliser

Tasman
Basin

SOUTH ISLAND

SOUTHERN ALPS

Greymouth
Hokitika
Arthur's Pass

Mount Cook

CHRISTCHURCH
BANKS PENINSULA
Pegasus Bay

Chatham
Rise

CHATHAM ISLANDS
(New Zealand)
Waitangi

Timaru

Oamaru

Dunedin

Invercargill
Bluff

STEWART ISLAND

Bounty Trough

SNARES ISLANDS

BOUNTY ISLANDS
(New Zealand)

Scale 1:15,000,000 at 25° latitude   Mercator Cylindrical Projection

0   200   400   600   800   1000 km
0   250   500 miles

Longitude East 180 West of Greenwich

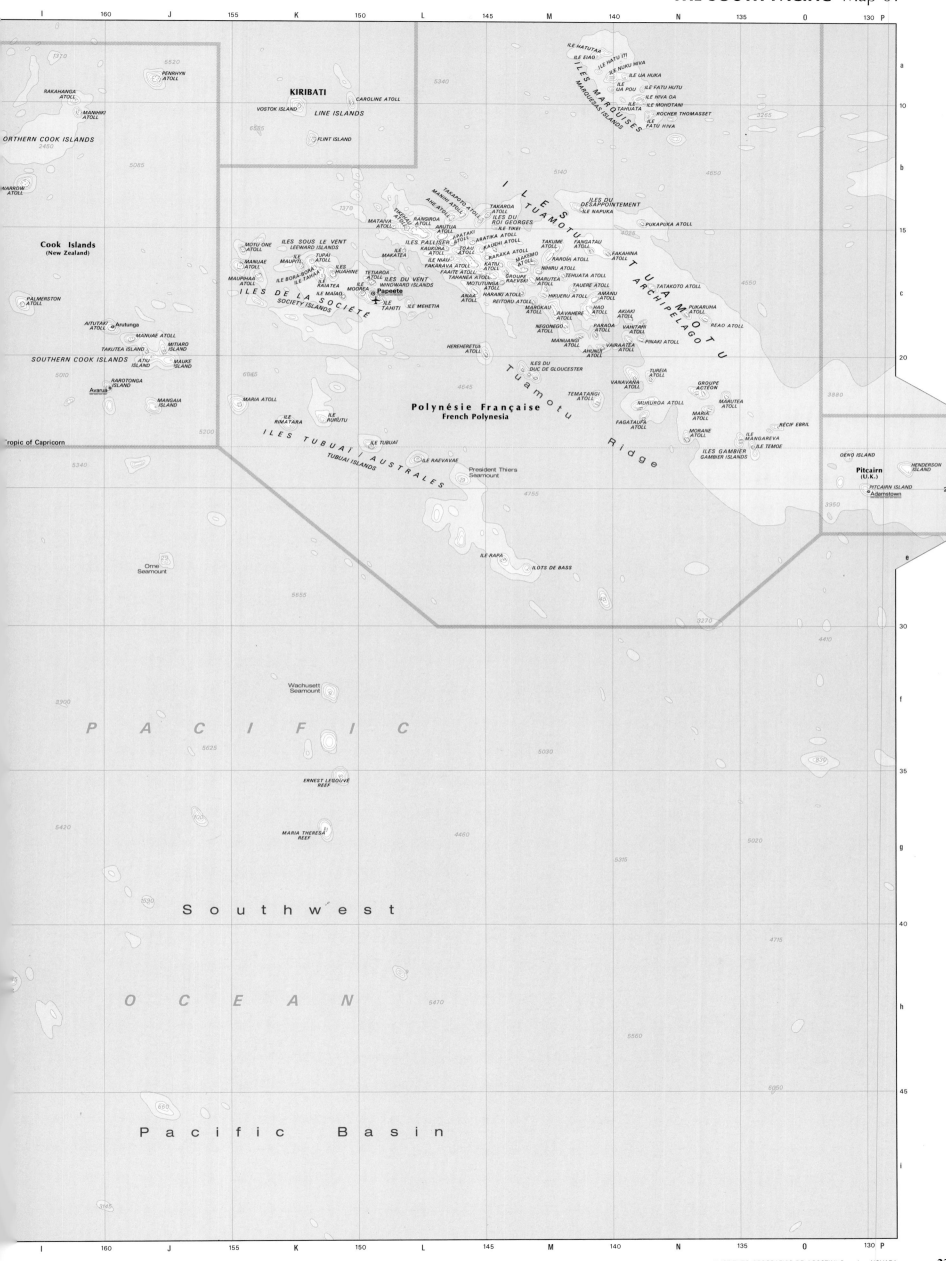

RAKAHANGA ATOLL

PENRHYN ATOLL

MANIHIKI ATOLL

ORTHERN COOK ISLANDS

NARROW ATOLL

KIRIBATI

VOSTOK ISLAND

CAROLINE ATOLL

LINE ISLANDS

FLINT ISLAND

Cook Islands
(New Zealand)

PALMERSTON ATOLL

AITUTAKI ATOLL   Arutunga

MANUAE ATOLL

MAUPIHAA ATOLL

MITIARO ISLAND

TAKUTEA ISLAND   ATIU ISLAND   MAUKE ISLAND

SOUTHERN COOK ISLANDS

RAROTONGA ISLAND

Avarua

MANGAIA ISLAND

MARIA ATOLL

ILE RIMATARA

ILE RURUTU

Tropic of Capricorn

ILES TUBUAI / AUSTRALES
TUBUAI ISLANDS

ILE TUBUAI

ILE RAEVAVAE

President Thiers Seamount

ILE HATUTAA
ILE EIAO
ILE HATU ITI
ILE NUKU HIVA
ILE UA HUKA
ILE UA POU   ILE FATU HUTU
ILE HIVA OA
ILE TAHUATA
ILE MOHOTANI
ROCHER THOMASSET
ILE FATU HIVA

ILES MARQUISES
MARQUESAS ISLANDS

I L E S   T U A M O T U

TAKAPOTO ATOLL
MANIHI ATOLL
AHE ATOLL
TAKAROA ATOLL
ILES DU ROI GEORGES
ILES DU DÉSAPPOINTEMENT
ILE NAPUKA
PUKAPUKA ATOLL

MATAIVA ATOLL
TIKEHAU ATOLL
RANGIROA ATOLL
ARUTUA ATOLL
APATAKI ATOLL
ILE TIKEI

MOTU ONE ATOLL
ILES SOUS LE VENT
LEEWARD ISLANDS
ILES PALLISER
ARATIKA ATOLL
TAKUME ATOLL
FANGATAU ATOLL

MANUAE ATOLL
ILE MAUPITI
TUPAI ATOLL
ILE MAKATEA
KAUKURA ATOLL
TOAU ATOLL
KAUEHI ATOLL
RARAKA ATOLL
MAKEMO ATOLL
RAROIA ATOLL
FAKAHINA ATOLL

ILE BORA-BORA
ILE TAHAA
ILE HUAHINE
ILE NIAU
KATIU ATOLL
NIHIRU ATOLL

ILE RAIATEA
ILE MAIAO
TETIAROA ATOLL
FAKARAVA ATOLL
FAAITE ATOLL
GROUPE RAEVSKI
MARUTEA ATOLL
TEHUATA ATOLL

MAUPIHAA ATOLL
ILE MOOREA
ILES DU VENT
WINDWARD ISLANDS
TAHANEA ATOLL
MOTUTUNGA ATOLL
HIKUERU ATOLL
TAUERE ATOLL

ILES DE LA SOCIÉTÉ
SOCIETY ISLANDS
Papeete
ILE TAHITI
ANAA ATOLL
HARAIKI ATOLL
REITORU ATOLL
MAROKAU ATOLL
HAO ATOLL
AKIAKI ATOLL

ILE MEHETIA
RAVAHERE ATOLL
PARAOA ATOLL
VAHITARI ATOLL
AMANU ATOLL
PINAKI ATOLL

NEGONEGO ATOLL
MANUANGI ATOLL
VAIRAATEA ATOLL
REAO ATOLL

HEREHERETUE ATOLL
AHUNUI ATOLL

ILES DU DUC DE GLOUCESTER
TUREIA ATOLL
TATAKOTO ATOLL
PUKARUHA ATOLL

VANAVANA ATOLL
GROUPE ACTÉON

TEMATANGI ATOLL
MARUTEA ATOLL

Polynésie Française
French Polynesia
MURUROA ATOLL
MARIA ATOLL
RÉCIF EBRIL

FAGATAUFA ATOLL
MORANE ATOLL
ILE MANGAREVA
ILE TEMOE

ILES GAMBIER
GAMBIER ISLANDS

OENO ISLAND

HENDERSON ISLAND

Pitcairn
(U.K.)

PITCAIRN ISLAND
Adamstown

T U A M O T U   A R C H I P E L A G O

Tuamotu Ridge

ILE RAPA   ILOTS DE BASS

Orne Seamount

Wachusett Seamount

ERNEST LEGOUVÉ REEF

MARIA THERESA REEF

P A C I F I C

S o u t h w e s t

O C E A N

Pacific Basin

Map 62 **NEW ZEALAND**

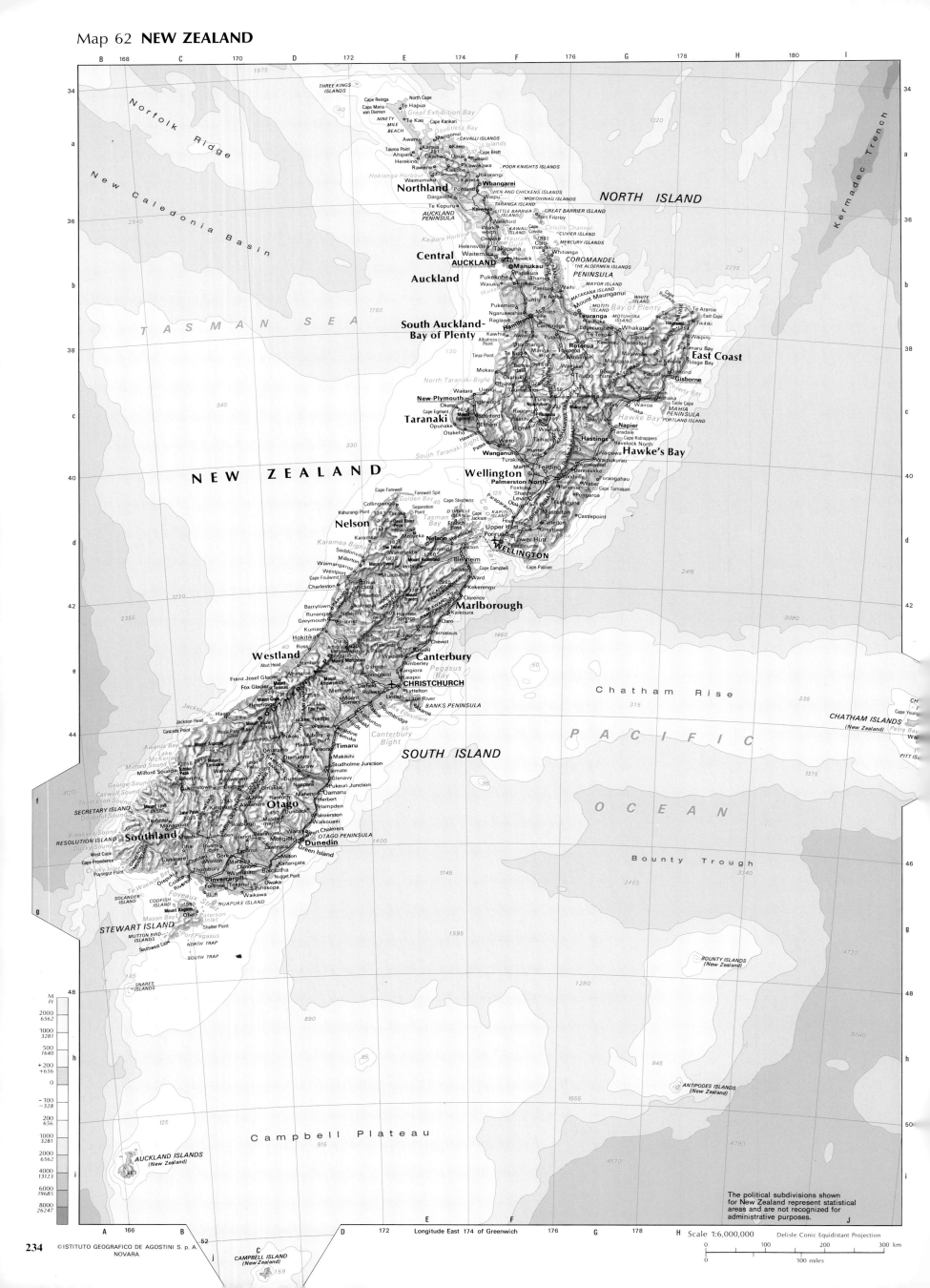

NEW ZEALAND

NORTH ISLAND

Northland

Central
Auckland
AUCKLAND

Auckland

South Auckland-
Bay of Plenty

Taranaki

New Plymouth

COROMANDEL
PENINSULA

Tauranga

Rotorua

Taupo

East Coast

Gisborne

Hawke's Bay

Napier

Hastings

Wanganui

Wellington

Palmerston North

SOUTH ISLAND

Nelson

Upper Hutt

WELLINGTON

Blenheim

Marlborough

Westland

Canterbury

CHRISTCHURCH

Timaru

Otago

Southland

Dunedin

Invercargill

STEWART ISLAND

NORTH ISLAND

TASMAN SEA

PACIFIC OCEAN

Chatham Rise

CHATHAM ISLANDS
(New Zealand)

Bounty Trough

BOUNTY ISLANDS
(New Zealand)

ANTIPODES ISLANDS
(New Zealand)

Campbell Plateau

AUCKLAND ISLANDS
(New Zealand)

CAMPBELL ISLAND
(New Zealand)

Norfolk Ridge

New Caledonia Basin

Kermadec Trench

The political subdivisions shown
for New Zealand represent statistical
areas and are not recognized for
administrative purposes.

©ISTITUTO GEOGRAFICO DE AGOSTINI S. p. A.
NOVARA

Longitude East 174 of Greenwich

Scale 1:6,000,000

Delisle Conic Equidistant Projection

0   100   200   300 km

0   100 miles

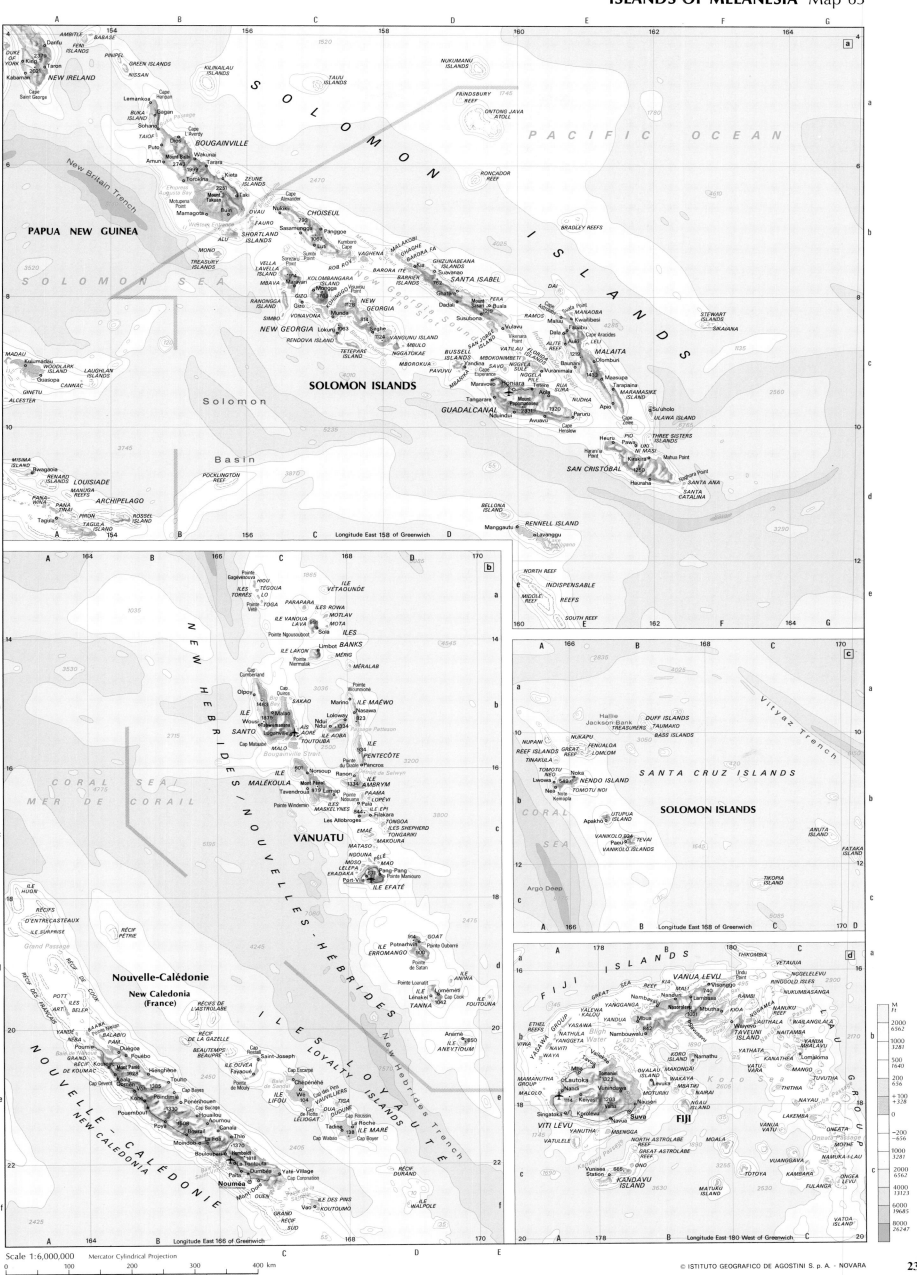
SOLOMON ISLANDS
PACIFIC OCEAN
PAPUA NEW GUINEA
SOLOMON SEA
Solomon Basin
NEW IRELAND
BOUGAINVILLE
CHOISEUL
SANTA ISABEL
NEW GEORGIA
MALAITA
GUADALCANAL
Honiara
SAN CRISTÓBAL
RENNELL ISLAND
ONTONG JAVA ATOLL
LOUISIADE ARCHIPELAGO
New Britain Trench
Longitude East 158 of Greenwich
NEW HEBRIDES / NOUVELLES-HÉBRIDES
VANUATU
BANKS
SANTO
MALÉKOULA
AMBRYM
PENTECÔTE
ILE EFATÉ
Port-Vila
ERROMANGO
TANNA
ANEYTIOUM
CORAL SEA
MER DE CORAIL
Nouvelle-Calédonie
New Caledonia (France)
NOUVELLE-CALÉDONIE
NEW CALEDONIA
Nouméa
ILES LOYAUTÉ
LOYALTY ISLANDS
New Hebrides Trench
Longitude East 166 of Greenwich
SANTA CRUZ ISLANDS
SOLOMON ISLANDS
Vityaz Trench
DUFF ISLANDS
NENDO ISLAND
UTUPUA ISLAND
VANIKOLO ISLANDS
TIKOPIA ISLAND
ANUTA ISLAND
Longitude East 168 of Greenwich
FIJI ISLANDS
VANUA LEVU
VITI LEVU
Suva
FIJI
TAVEUNI ISLAND
KANDAVU ISLAND
Koro Sea
LAU GROUP
YASAWA GROUP
Longitude East 180 West of Greenwich
Scale 1:6,000,000
Mercator Cylindrical Projection
0 100 200 300 400 km
0 100 200 miles

Map 64 **ISLANDS OF MICRONESIA-POLYNESIA**

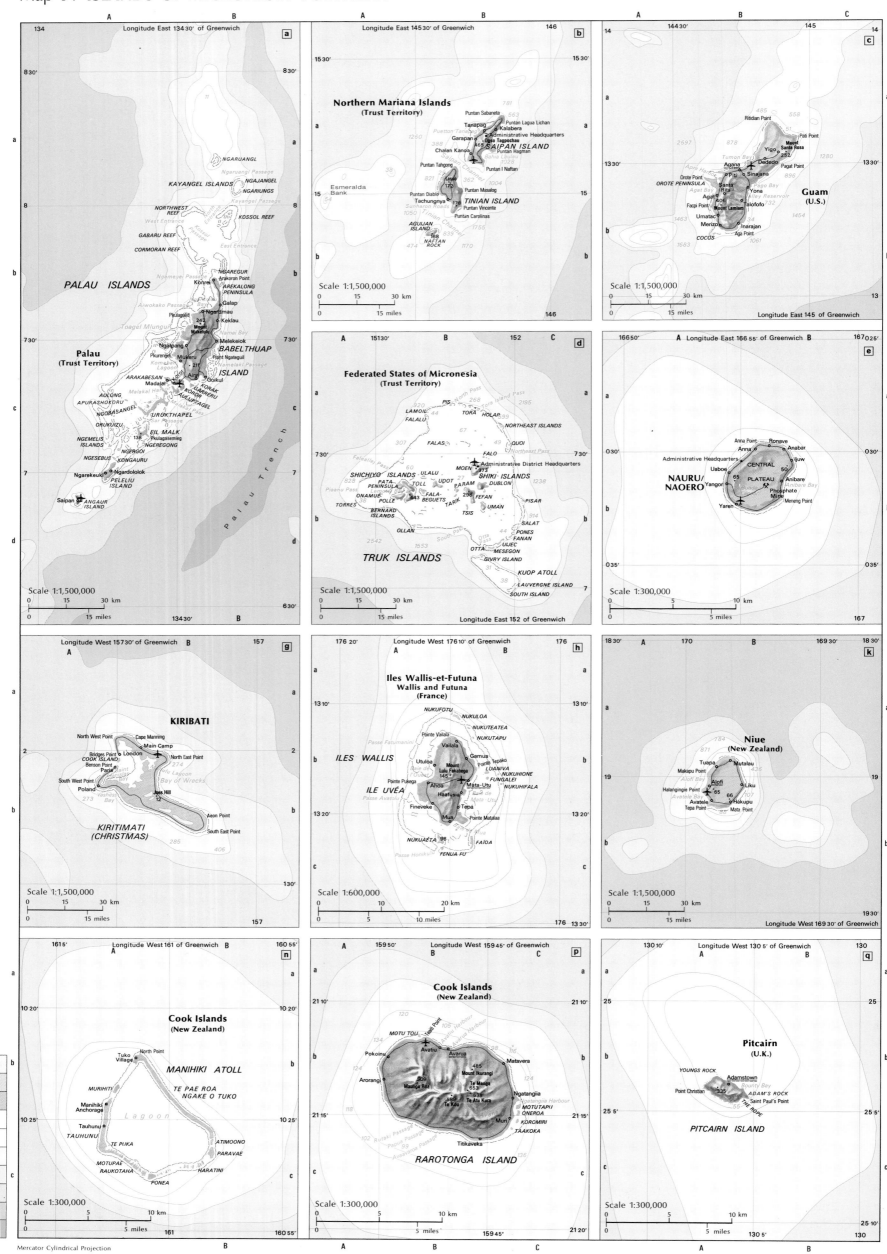

Mercator Cylindrical Projection

© ISTITUTO GEOGRAFICO DE AGOSTINI S. p. A. - NOVARA

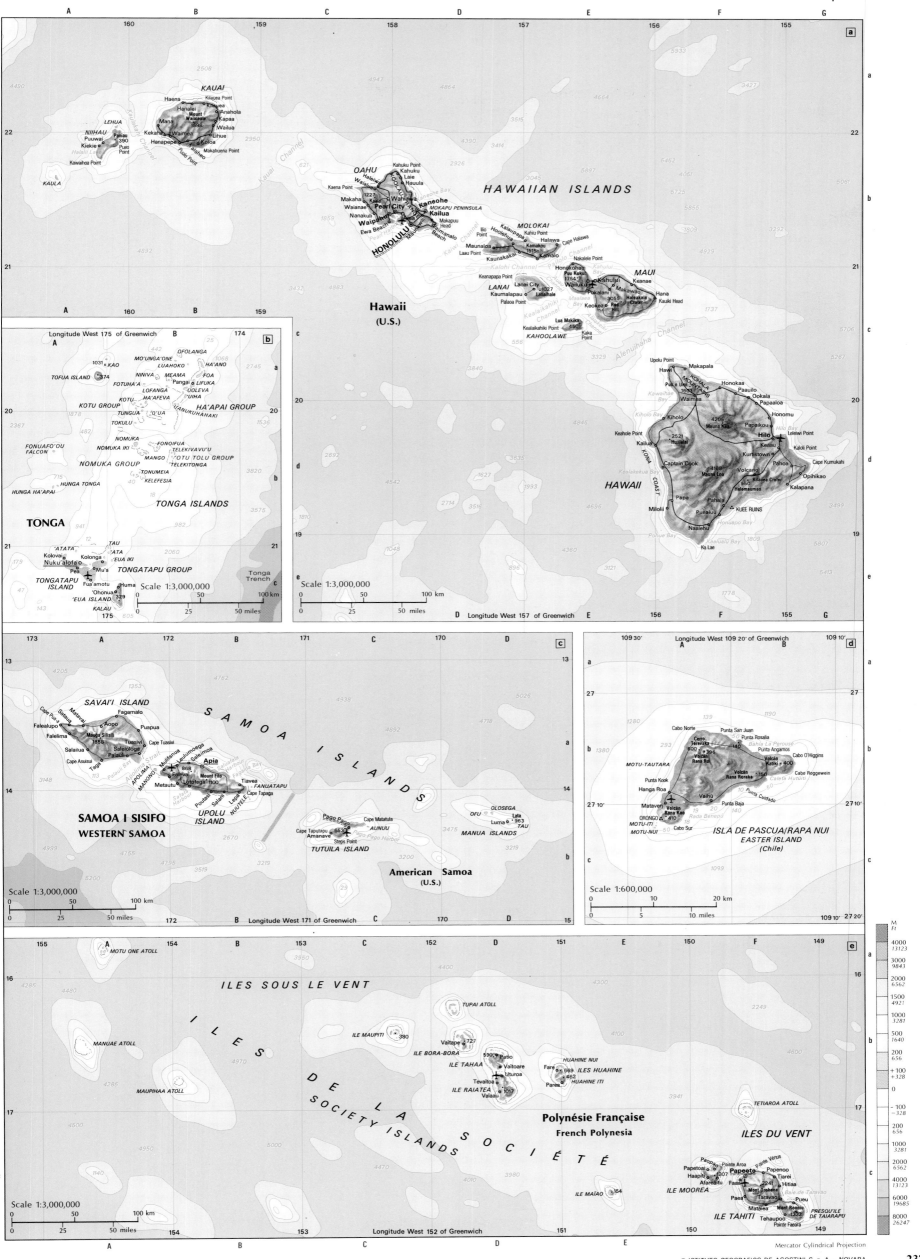

Map a — Hawaiian Islands

KAUAI

Haena · Kilauea Point · Anahola
Hanalei · Kilauea · Anahola
Mana · Mount · Waikaea · Kapaa
Kekaha · Waimea 1598 · Waila
Waimea · Koloa · Lihue
Hanapepe · Makahuena Point

NIIHAU
Puuwai · 390
Kiekie · Pueo Point
Kawaihoa Point

LEHUA

KAULA

OAHU

Kahuku Point
Kahuku
Laie
Hauula
Kaena Point · Waialua
Makaha · 1227 · Wahiawa · Kaneohe
Waianae · MOKAPU PENINSULA
Nanakuli · Pearl City · Kailua
Ewa Beach · Waipahu · Makapuu Head
Pearl Harbor · HONOLULU · Waimanalo Beach

HAWAIIAN ISLANDS

MOLOKAI
Ilio Point · Kahiku Point · Cape Halawa
Hoolehua · Kamakou 1515 · Kamalo
Maunaloa · Kaunakakai · Laau Point · Kalaupapa
Kalaupapa Point

LANAI
Lanai City · 1027
Kaumalapau · Lanaihale
Palaoa Point

MAUI
Keanapapa Point · Kahului · Kaanae
Pau Kukui · Makawao · Hana
1764 · Pukalani · Kauiki Head
Keokea · Haleakala Crater
Kahoolawe · 3055 · Red Hill
Lua Makika · 490 · Red Hill
Kealaikahiki Point · Kaka Point
KAHOOLAWE

Hawaii
(U.S.)

HAWAII

Upolu Point · Makapala
Hawi · Honokaa
KOHALA MTNS · Paauilo
1603 · Waimea · Ookala · Papaaloa
Kawaihae Bay · Honomu
Kiholo Bay · Kiholo
Keahole Point · 4205 · Papaikou
Mauna Kea · Hilo · Leleiwi Point
2521 · Hualalai · Kedsu
Kailua · Keaau
Captain Cook · 4169 · Kaloli Point
KONA COAST · Mauna Loa · Volcano · Cape Kumukahi
Papa · 950 · Kilauea Crater · Pahoa
Pahala · Halemaumau · Opihikao
Miloli · Punaluu · Kalapana
KIUE RUINS
Naalehu
Honuapo Bay
Ka Lae

Scale 1:3,000,000
0   50   100 km
0   25   50 miles

Longitude West 157 of Greenwich

Map b — Tonga

Longitude West 175 of Greenwich

OFOLANGA
MO'UNGA'ONE · LUAHOKO · HA'ANO
1031 · KAO · NINIVA · MEAMA · FOA
TOFUA ISLAND · 374 · FOTUHA'A · Pangai · LIFUKA
LOFANGA · HA'AFEVA · UOLEVA
KOTU GROUP · KOTU · 'O'UA · 'UIHA
TUNGUA · NUKUNUKUHAHAKI
HA'APAI GROUP

FONUAFO'OU · NOMUKA · FONOIFUA
FALCON · NOMUKA IKI · MANGO · TELEKIVAVU'U
NOMUKA GROUP · TELEKITONGA · OTU TOLU GROUP
TONUMEIA
HUNGA TONGA · KELEFESIA
HUNGA HA'APAI

TONGA ISLANDS

TONGA

'ATATA · TAU
'ATA · 'EUA IKI
Kolovai · Kolonga
Nuku'alofa · Mu'a
Pea
TONGATAPU · Fua amotu · Huma
ISLAND · TONGATAPU GROUP
'Ohonua · 329
KALAU · 'EUA ISLAND

Tonga Trench

Scale 1:3,000,000
0   50   100 km
0   25   50 miles

Map c — Samoa

SAVAI'I ISLAND
Cape Pua'a · Sataua · Matavai
Falealupo · Aopo
Faleolima · Mauga Silisili · Tuasivi · Cape Tuasivi
Salailua · 1858 · Salelologa
Cape Asuisui · Taga · Palauli
Safata Bay

SAMOA ISLANDS

Lelumoega · Saleimoa
APOLIMA · Mulifanua · Apia · Tiavea
MANONO · 868 · FANUATAPU
Metautu · Mount Fito · Lepa · Cape Tapaga
Poutasi · 1100 · Salani
UPOLU ISLAND · NUUTELE

SAMOA I SISIFO
WESTERN SAMOA

OFU · OLOSEGA
Pago Pago · Cape Matatula · Lata · 963 · TAU
Cape Taputapu · 653 · AUNUU · Luma
Amanave · Pago Pago Harbor · MANUA ISLANDS
Steps Point
TUTUILA ISLAND

American Samoa
(U.S.)

Scale 1:3,000,000
0   50   100 km
0   25   50 miles

Longitude West 171 of Greenwich

Map d — Easter Island

Longitude West 109 20' of Greenwich

Cabo Norte · Punta San Juan
Punta Rosalia
Cerro · 139 · Punta Angamos
MOTU-TAUTARA · Terevaka · Cabo O'Higgins
293 · 390 · Volcán
Volcán · Rana Roi · Volcán · 400
Punta Koek · Rana Raraka · Cabo Reggewein
Hanga Roa · Vaihu · Caleta Hutuiti
Mataveri · Punta Baja · Punta Cuidado
Volcán · Rana Kao
ORONGO · 410 · Raoa Beineui
MOTU-ITI · Cabo Sur
MOTU-NUI

ISLA DE PASCUA/RAPA NUI
EASTER ISLAND
(Chile)

Scale 1:600,000
0   5   10   20 km
0   5   10 miles

Map e — French Polynesia

MOTU ONE ATOLL

ILES SOUS LE VENT

ILE MAUPITI · 380
TUPAI ATOLL

MANUAE ATOLL
Vaitape · 727
ILE BORA-BORA
MAUPIHAA ATOLL · ILE TAHAA · 590 · Patio
Tevaitoa · Vaitoare · HUAHINE NUI
ILE RAIATEA · Uturoa · Fare · 669
Valaiu · 1017 · 462 · HUAHINE ITI
Parea

ILES DE LA SOCIÉTÉ
SOCIETY ISLANDS

Polynésie Française
French Polynesia

TETIAROA ATOLL

ILES DU VENT

Papaoa · Pointe Aroa · Pointe Venus
Papetoai · Papeete · Papenoo
Haapiti · 1207 · Tiarei
Afareaitu · Taravao · Hitiaa
ILE MOOREA · Faaa · 2241
Paea · Mont Orohena
Mataiea · 1332 · Pueu
ILE MAIAO · 154 · Mont Roonui
Tehaupoo · PRESQU'ILE DE TAIARAPU
ILE TAHITI · Pointe Fasara

Scale 1:3,000,000
0   50   100 km
0   25   50 miles

Longitude West 152 of Greenwich

Mercator Cylindrical Projection

M / ft
4000 / 13123
3000 / 9843
2000 / 6562
1500 / 4921
1000 / 3281
500 / 1640
200 / 656
+100 / +328
0
-100 / -328
200 / 656
1000 / 3281
2000 / 6562
4000 / 13123
6000 / 19685
8000 / 26247

Map 66 **ANTARCTIC REGION**

AUSTRALIA

TASMANIA

NEW ZEALAND

NEW SOUTH WALES

VICTORIA

QUEENSLAND

PAPUA NEW GUINEA

NEW CALEDONIA (France)

FIJI

VANUATU (NEW HEBRIDES)

NORTH ISLAND

SOUTH ISLAND

Melbourne
Sydney
Canberra
Adelaide
Brisbane
Newcastle
Wollongong
Hobart
Launceston
Christchurch
Wellington
Dunedin
Invercargill
Auckland
Hamilton
New Plymouth
Napier
Gisborne
Nelson
Timaru
Whangarei
Noumea
Nouméa
Norfolk

WILKES LAND

VICTORIA LAND

MARIE BYRD LAND

ANTARCTIC MOUNTAINS

TRANSANTARCTIC MOUNTAINS

Ross Sea
Ross Ice Shelf
Amundsen Sea
Dumont d'Urville Sea
TERRE ADÉLIE

ROCKEFELLER PLATEAU

EDWARD VII PENINSULA

South Magnetic Pole (1980)

Antarctic Circle

Tropic of Capricorn

Tasman Sea
Tasman Basin

Lord Howe Rise

New Caledonia Basin

Norfolk Ridge

Three Kings Islands

Campbell Plateau

Chatham Rise
Bounty Trough
CHATHAM ISLANDS (New Zealand)
ANTIPODES ISLANDS (New Zealand)
BOUNTY ISLANDS
AUCKLAND ISLANDS
CAMPBELL I. (N.Z.)
MACQUARIE I. (Austl.)

Southwest Pacific Basin

PACIFIC OCEAN

Pacific-Antarctic Ridge

Southeast Indian Ridge

South Indian Basin

Southeast Pacific Basin

East Pacific Rise

South Indian Ridge

South Australian Basin

Great Australian Bight

NULLARBOR PLAIN

SIMPSON DESERT

GREAT DIVIDING RANGE

GREAT BARRIER REEF

Coral Sea

Gulf of Carpentaria

Summer limit of pack ice (March)
Winter limit of pack ice (September)
Limit of icebergs

KERMADEC ISLANDS (New Zealand)

Kermadec Trench

Tonga Trench

TONGA

COOK ISLANDS (New Zealand)

SOUTHERN COOK ISLANDS

TUBUAI ISLANDS

SOCIETY ISLANDS

TUAMOTU ARCHIPELAGO

GAMBIER ISLANDS

French Polynesia

KIRIBATI

LINE ISLANDS

Tuamotu Ridge

The Antarctic region is not a political entity and its status is regulated by the Antarctic
Treaty signed in Washington, D.C. in 1959. The treaty binds the states which signed
the agreement to use the region solely for peaceful purposes and scientific research.

Longitude West 180 East of Greenwich

Scale 1:30,000,000

Polar Azimuthal Projection

© ISTITUTO GEOGRAFICO DE AGOSTINI S. p. A. — NOVARA

Map 67 **ARCTIC REGION**

Scale 1:30,000,000   Polar Azimuthal Projection   Longitude West 0 East of Greenwich

GEOGRAPHICAL INFORMATION AND INTERNATIONAL MAP INDEX

World Nations

This table gives the area, population, population density, form of government, capital and location of every country in the world.

Area figures include inland water.

The populations are estimates made by Rand McNally and Company on the basis of official data, United Nations estimates and other available information.

Besides specifying the form of government for all political areas, the table classifies them into five groups according to their political status. Units labeled A are independent sovereign nations. (Several of these are designated as members of the British Commonwealth of Nations.) Units labeled B are independent as regards internal affairs, but for purposes of foreign affairs they are under the protection of another country. Units labeled C are colonies, overseas territories, dependencies, etc. of other countries. Units labeled D are states, provinces or other major administrative subdivisions of important countries. Units in the table with no letter designation are regions, islands or other areas that do not constitute separate political units by themselves.

Map Plate numbers refer to the International Map section of the Atlas.

Country, Division, or Region English (Conventional)	Local Name	Area km²	Area sq mi	Population 1/1/82	Population Density per km²	Population Density per sq mi	Form of Government and Political Status		Capital	Continent and Map Plate	
Afars and Issas, see Djibouti	...										
†AFGHANISTAN	Afghanistan	647,497	250,000	13,220,000	20	53	Socialist Republic	A	Kābul	Asia	23
AFRICA	...	30,323,000	11,708,000	490,300,000	16	42				Africa	30–31
Alabama, U.S.	Alabama	133,667	51,609	3,975,000	30	77	State (U.S.)	D	Montgomery	N. Amer.	44
Alaska, U.S.	Alaska	1,527,470	589,759	415,000	0.3	0.7	State (U.S.)	D	Juneau	N. Amer.	40
†ALBANIA	Shqiperia	28,748	11,100	2,820,000	98	254	Socialist Republic	A	Tirana	Europe	15
Alberta, Can.	Alberta	661,185	255,285	2,190,000	3.3	8.6	Province (Canada)	D	Edmonton	N. Amer.	42
†ALGERIA	Al Jazā'ir	2,381,741	919,595	19,270,000	8.1	21	Socialist Republic	A	Algiers (Al Jazā'ir)	Africa	32
American Samoa (U.S.)	American Samoa	197	76	34,000	173	447	Unincorporated Territory (U.S.)	C	Pago Pago	Oceania	65
Andaman and Nicobar Islands, India	Andaman and Nicobar	8,293	3,202	195,000	24	61	Territory of India	D	Port Blair	Asia	25
ANDORRA	Andorra	453	175	40,000	88	229	Co-Principality (Spanish and French protection)	B	Andorra la Vella	Europe	13
†ANGOLA	Angola	1,246,700	481,353	7,335,000	5.9	15	Socialist Republic	A	Luanda	Africa	36
ANGUILLA	Anguilla	90	34	7,900	90	232	Associated State (U.K.)	B	The Valley	N. Amer.	51
Anhwei, China	Anhui	139,859	54,000	49,055,000	351	908	Province (China)	D	Hefei	Asia	28
ANTARCTICA	...	14,000,000	5,405,000	...(1)	...	...				Ant.	66
†ANTIGUA (incl. Barbuda)	Antigua	440	170	77,000	175	453	Parliamentary State (Comm. of Nations)	A	Saint John's	N. Amer.	51
Arabian Peninsula	...	3,003,200	1,159,500	21,050,000	7.0	18				Asia	23
†ARGENTINA	Argentina	2,776,889	1,068,301	28,420,000	10	27	Federal Republic	A	Buenos Aires	S. Amer.	56
Arizona, U.S.	Arizona	295,024	113,909	2,795,000	9.5	25	State (U.S.)	D	Phoenix	N. Amer.	46
Arkansas, U.S.	Arkansas	137,539	53,104	2,335,000	17	44	State (U.S.)	D	Little Rock	N. Amer.	45
Armenian S.S.R., U.S.S.R.	Armjanskaja S.S.R.	29,800	11,506	3,115,000	105	271	Soviet Socialist Republic (U.S.S.R.)	D	Jerevan	Asia	16
Aruba (Neth. Ant.)	Aruba	193	75	67,000	347	893	Division of Netherlands Antilles		Oranjestad	N. Amer.	49
Ascension (U.K.)	Ascension	88	34	1,000	11	29	Dependency of St. Helena (U.K.)	C	Georgetown	Africa	30–31
ASIA	...	44,798,000	17,297,000	2,724,900,000	61	158				Asia	21–22
†AUSTRALIA	Australia	7,686,850	2,967,909	14,910,000	1.9	5.0	Parliamentary State (Federal) (Comm. of Nations)	A	Canberra	Oceania	59
Australian Capital Territory, Austl.	Australian Capital Territory	2,432	939	235,000	97	250	Territory (Australia)	D	Canberra	Oceania	59
†AUSTRIA	Österreich	83,850	32,375	7,510,000	90	232	Federal Republic	A	Vienna (Wien)	Europe	14
Azerbaidzhan S.S.R., U.S.S.R.	Azerbajdžanskaja S.S.R.	86,600	33,436	6,210,000	72	186	Soviet Socialist Republic (U.S.S.R.)	D	Baku	Asia	16
Azores (Port.)	Açores	2,335	902	235,000	101	261	Part of Portugal (3 districts)			Africa	32
†BAHAMAS	Bahamas	13,939	5,382	235,000	17	44	Parliamentary State (Comm. of Nations)	A	Nassau	N. Amer.	47
†BAHRAIN	Al Baḥrayn	662	256	400,000	604	1,563	Constitutional Monarchy	A	Al Manāmah	Asia	24
Balearic Islands, Spain	Islas Baleares	5,014	1,936	730,000	146	377	Province of Spain (Baleares)	D	Palma	Europe	13
Baltic Republics (U.S.S.R.)	...	174,000	67,182	7,555,000	43	112	Part of U.S.S.R. (3 republics)			Europe	8
†BANGLADESH	Bangladesh	143,998	55,598	91,860,000	638	1,652	Republic (Comm. of Nations)	A	Dacca	Asia	25
†BARBADOS	Barbados	430	166	260,000	605	1,566	Parliamentary State (Comm. of Nations)	A	Bridgetown	N. Amer.	51
†BELGIUM	Belgique (French) België (Flemish)	30,513	11,781	9,880,000	324	839	Constitutional Monarchy	A	Brussels (Bruxelles)	Europe	12
†BELIZE	Belize	22,963	8,866	160,000	7.0	18	Parliamentary State (Comm. of Nations)	A	Belmopan	N. Amer.	49
Benelux	...	74,259	28,672	24,535,000	330	856	Economic Union			Europe	12
†BENIN	Bénin	112,622	43,484	3,715,000	33	85	Socialist Republic	A	Porto-Novo	Africa	34
Bermuda (U.K.)	Bermuda	53	21	69,000	1,302	3,286	Colony (U.K.)	C	Hamilton	N. Amer.	47
†BHUTAN	Druk	47,000	18,147	1,345,000	29	74	Monarchy (Indian protection)	B	Thimphu	Asia	25
Bioko, Equat. Gui.	Bioko	2,034	785	94,000	46	120	Province of Equatorial Guinea		Malabo	Africa	34
†BOLIVIA	Bolivia	1,098,581	424,164	5,845,000	5.3	14	Republic	A	Sucre and La Paz	S. Amer.	54
Borneo, Indonesian	Kalimantan	539,460	208,287	6,815,000	13	33	Part of Indonesia (4 provinces)			Asia	26
†BOTSWANA	Botswana	600,372	231,805	875,000	1.5	3.8	Republic (Comm. of Nations)	A	Gaborone	Africa	37
†BRAZIL	Brasil	8,511,965	3,286,487	124,760,000	15	38	Federal Republic	A	Brasília	S. Amer.	54–56
British Columbia, Can.	British Columbia	948,596	366,255	2,725,000	2.9	7.4	Province (Canada)	D	Victoria	N. Amer.	42
British Honduras, see Belize	...										
British Indian Ocean Territory (U.K.)	British Indian Ocean Territory	60	23	...(1)	...	...	Colony (U.K.)	C	...	Africa	22
British Solomon Islands, see Solomon Islands	...										
BRUNEI	Brunei	5,765	2,226	245,000	42	110	Constitutional Monarchy (U.K. protection)	B	Bandar Seri Begawan	Asia	26
†BULGARIA	Balgarija	110,912	42,823	8,915,000	80	208	Socialist Republic	A	Sofia (Sofija)	Europe	15
†BURMA	Burma	676,577	261,228	35,710,000	53	137	Socialist Republic	A	Rangoon	Asia	25
†BURUNDI	Burundi	27,834	10,747	4,705,000	169	438	Republic	A	Bujumbura	Africa	36
†Byelorussian S.S.R., U.S.S.R.	Belorusskaja S.S.R.	207,600	80,155	9,755,000	47	122	Soviet Socialist Republic (U.S.S.R.)	D	Minsk	Europe	16
California, U.S.	California	411,015	158,694	24,155,000	59	152	State (U.S.)	D	Sacramento	N. Amer.	46
Cambodia, see Kampuchea	...										
†CAMEROON	Cameroun	475,442	183,569	8,860,000	19	48	Republic	A	Yaoundé	Africa	34
†CANADA	Canada	9,922,330	3,831,033	24,335,000	2.5	6.4	Parliamentary State (Federal) (Comm. of Nations)	A	Ottawa	N. Amer.	42
Canary Islands (Sp.)		7,273	2,808	1,685,000	232	600	Part of Spain (2 provinces)			Africa	32
†CAPE VERDE	Cabo Verde	4,033	1,557	330,000	82	212	Republic	A	Praia	Africa	32
Cayman Islands (U.K.)	Cayman Islands	259	100	18,000	69	180	Colony (U.K.)	C	Georgetown	N. Amer.	49
Celebes (Indonesia)	Sulawesi	189,216	73,057	10,755,000	57	147	Part of Indonesia (4 provinces)			Asia	26
†CENTRAL AFRICAN REPUBLIC	Centrafrique	622,984	240,535	2,300,000	3.7	9.6	Republic	A	Bangui	Africa	35
Central America	...	523,000	202,000	23,970,000	46	119				N. Amer.	49
Central Asia, Soviet (U.S.S.R.)	...	1,277,100	493,090	26,495,000	21	54	Part of U.S.S.R. (4 republics)			Asia	19
Ceylon, see Sri Lanka	...										

A · 2

Country, Division, or Region English (Conventional)	Local Name	Area km²	Area sq mi	Population 1/1/82	Population Density per km²	Population Density per sq mi	Form of Government and Political Status		Capital	Continent and Map Plate	
°CHAD	Tchad	1,284,000	495,755	4,675,000	3.6	9.4	Republic	A	N'djamena	Africa	35
Channel Islands (U.K.)	Channel Islands	195	75	133,000	682	1,773	. . .		. . .	Europe	9
Chekiang, China	Zhejiang	101,787	39,300	38,115,000	374	970	Province (China)	D	Hangzhou	Asia	27
°CHILE	Chile	756,626	292,135	11,375,000	15	39	Republic	A	Santiago	S. Amer.	56
°CHINA (excl. Taiwan)	Zhonghua Renmin Gongheguo	9,560,939	3,691,500	995,000,000	104	270	Socialist Republic	A	Peking (Beijing)	Asia	27
China (Nationalist), see Taiwan	. . .	. . .	. . .	. . .	. . .	. . .					
Christmas Island (Austl.)	Christmas Island	140	54	3,200	23	60	External Territory (Australia)	C	Flying Fish Cove	Oceania	26
Cocos (Keeling) Islands (Austl.)	Cocos (Keeling) Islands	14	5.4	400	29	74	External Territory (Australia)	C	. . .	Oceania	22
°COLOMBIA	Colombia	1,138,914	439,737	28,185,000	25	64	Republic	A	Bogotá	S. Amer.	54
Colorado, U.S.	Colorado	270,000	104,248	2,960,000	11	28	State (U.S.)	D	Denver	N. Amer.	45
Commonwealth of Nations	. . .	27,629,000	10,667,000	1,106,308,000	40	104	Political Union		. . .	. . .	. . .
°COMOROS	Comores	2,171	838	380,000	175	453	Republic	A	Moroni	Africa	37
°CONGO	Congo	342,000	132,047	1,595,000	4.7	12	Socialist Republic	A	Brazzaville	Africa	36
Connecticut, U.S.	Connecticut	12,973	5,009	3,165,000	244	632	State (U.S.)	D	Hartford	N. Amer.	44
°COOK ISLANDS	Cook Islands	236	91	18,000	76	198	Self-governing Territory (New Zealand protection)	B	Avarua	Oceania	61
Corsica (Fr.)	Corse	8,681	3,352	184,000	21	55	Part of France (2 departments)		. . .	Europe	11
°COSTA RICA	Costa Rica	51,100	19,730	2,340,000	46	119	Republic	A	San José	N. Amer.	49
°CUBA	Cuba	114,524	44,218	9,805,000	86	222	Socialist Republic	A	Havana (La Habana)	N. Amer.	49
Curaçao (Neth. Ant.)	Curaçao	444	171	170,000	383	994	Division of Netherlands Antilles		Willemstad	N. Amer.	49
°CYPRUS	Kypros (Greek) Kıbrıs (Turkish)	9,251	3,572	650,000	70	182	Republic (Comm. of Nations)	A	Nicosia (Levkosia)	Asia	24
°CZECHOSLOVAKIA	Československo	127,877	49,374	15,345,000	120	311	Socialist Republic	A	Prague (Praha)	Europe	10
Dahomey, see Benin	. . .	. . .	. . .	. . .	. . .	. . .					
Delaware, U.S.	Delaware	5,328	2,057	600,000	113	292	State (U.S.)	D	Dover	N. Amer.	44
°DENMARK	Danmark	43,080	16,633	5,150,000	120	310	Constitutional Monarchy	A	Copenhagen (København)	Europe	8
Denmark and Possessions	. . .	2,220,079	857,177	5,246,000	2.4	6.1	. . .		Copenhagen (København)	. . .	. . .
District of Columbia, U.S.	District of Columbia	174	67	640,000	3,678	9,552	District (U.S.)	D	Washington	N. Amer.	44
°DJIBOUTI	Djibouti	23,000	8,880	124,000	5.4	14	Republic	A	Djibouti	Africa	35
°DOMINICA	Dominica	752	290	75,000	100	259	Republic (Comm. of Nations)	A	Roseau	N. Amer.	51
°DOMINICAN REPUBLIC	República Dominicana	48,442	18,704	5,660,000	117	303	Republic	A	Santo Domingo	N. Amer.	49
°ECUADOR	Ecuador	283,561	109,483	8,725,000	31	80	Republic	A	Quito	S. Amer.	54
°EGYPT	Mişr	1,001,400	386,643	43,565,000	44	113	Socialist Republic	A	Cairo (Al Qāhirah)	Africa	33
Ellice Islands, see Tuvalu	. . .	. . .	. . .	. . .	. . .	. . .					
°EL SALVADOR	El Salvador	21,041	8,124	5,270,000	250	649	Republic	A	San Salvador	N. Amer.	49
England, U.K.	England	130,439	50,362	46,575,000	357	925	Administrative division of U.K.	D	London	Europe	9
°EQUATORIAL GUINEA	Guinea Ecuatorial	28,051	10,831	375,000	13	35	Republic	A	Malabo	Africa	36
Estonian S.S.R., U.S.S.R.	Eest: N.S.V.	45,100	17,413	1,505,000	33	86	Soviet Socialist Republic (U.S.S.R.)	D	Tallinn	Europe	8
°ETHIOPIA	Itiopya	1,223,600	472,434	30,370,000	25	64	Monarchy.	A	Ādīs Ābeba	Africa	35
Eurasia	. . .	54,730,000	21,132,000	3,291,300,000	60	156			. . .	. . .	. . .
EUROPE	. . .	9,932,000	3,835,000	666,400,000	67	174			. . .	Europe	5–6
FAEROE ISLANDS	Føroyar (Faeroese) Færøerne (Danish)	1,399	540	45,000	32	83	Part of Danish Realm	B	Tórshavn	Europe	6
Falkland Islands (Islas Malvinas) (excl. Dependencies) (U.K.)[3]	Falkland Islands	12,173	4,700	1,900	0.2	0.4	Colony (U.K.)	C	Stanley	S. Amer.	56
†FIJI	Fiji	18,272	7,055	645,000	35	91	Parliamentary State (Comm. of Nations)	A	Suva	Oceania	63
†FINLAND	Suomi (Finnish) Finland (Swedish)	337,032	130,129	4,805,000	14	37	Republic	A	Helsinki (Helsingfors)	Europe	7
Florida, U.S.	Florida	151,670	58,560	10,215,000	67	174	State (U.S.)	D	Tallahassee	N. Amer.	44
†FRANCE	France	547,026	211,208	54,045,000	99	256	Republic	A	Paris	Europe	11
France and Possessions	. . .	675,114	260,661	55,618,000	82	213	. . .		Paris	. . .	. . .
Franklin (Can.)	Franklin	1,422,559	549,253	8,000	0.01	0.01	District of Northwest Territories (Canada)		. . .	N. Amer.	42
French Guiana (Fr.)	Guyane Française	91,000	35,135	66,000	0.7	1.9	Overseas Department (France)	D	Cayenne	S. Amer.	54
French Polynesia (Fr.)	Polynésie Française	4,000	1,544	150,000	38	97	Overseas Territory (France)	C	Papeete	Oceania	61
French West Indies	. . .	2,879	1,112	620,000	215	558	. . .		. . .	N. Amer.	50
Fukien, China	Fujian	123,024	47,500	22,490,000	183	474	Province (China)	D	Fuzhou	Asia	27
†GABON	Gabon	267,667	103,347	560,000	2.1	5.4	Republic	A	Libreville	Africa	36
Galapagos Islands, Ecuador	Archipiélago de Colón	7,964	3,075	6,100	0.8	2.0	Province of Ecuador (Galápagos)	D	Baquerizo Moreno	S. Amer.	54
†GAMBIA	Gambia	11,295	4,361	625,000	55	143	Republic (Comm. of Nations)	A	Banjul	Africa	34
Georgia, U.S.	Georgia	152,489	58,876	5,570,000	37	95	State (U.S.)	D	Atlanta	N. Amer.	44
Georgian S.S.R., U.S.S.R.	Gruzinskaja S.S.R.	69,700	26,911	5,135,000	74	191	Soviet Socialist Republic (U.S.S.R.)	D	Tbilisi	Asia	16
†GERMAN DEMOCRATIC REPUBLIC	Deutsche Demokratische Republik	108,179	41,768	16,750,000	155	401	Socialist Republic	A	East Berlin (Ost-Berlin)	Europe	10
†GERMANY, FEDERAL REPUBLIC OF (incl. West Berlin)	Bundesrepublik Deutschland	248,650	96,004	61,680,000	248	642	Federal Republic	A	Bonn	Europe	10
Germany (Entire)	Deutschland	356,829	137,772	78,430,000	220	569			. . .	Europe	10
†GHANA	Ghana	238,537	92,100	11,730,000	49	127	Republic (Comm. of Nations)	A	Accra	Africa	34
†Gibraltar (U.K.)	Gibraltar	6.0	2.3	30,000	5,000	13,043	Colony (U.K.)	C	Gibraltar	Europe	13
Gilbert Islands, see Kiribati	. . .	. . .	. . .	. . .	. . .	. . .			. . .	. . .	. . .
Great Britain, see United Kingdom	. . .	. . .	. . .	. . .	. . .	. . .			. . .	. . .	. . .
†GREECE	Ellas	131,944	50,944	9,840,000	75	193	Republic	A	Athens (Athínai)	Europe	15
GREENLAND	Grønland (Danish) Kalaallit Nunaat (Eskimo)	2,175,600	840,003	51,000	0.02	0.06	Part of Danish Realm	B	Godthåb	N. Amer.	41
†GRENADA	Grenada	344	133	112,000	326	842	Parliamentary State (Comm. of Nations)	A	Saint George's	N. Amer.	51
Guadeloupe (incl. Dependencies) (Fr.)	Guadeloupe	1,779	687	320,000	180	466	Overseas Department (France)	D	Basse-Terre	N. Amer.	51
Guam (U.S.)	Guam	549	212	110,000	200	519	Unincorporated Territory (U.S.)	C	Agana	Oceania	64
†GUATEMALA	Guatemala	108,889	42,042	7,375,000	68	175	Republic	A	Guatemala	N. Amer.	49
Guernsey (incl. Dependencies) (U.K.)	Guernsey	77	30	55,000	714	1,833	Bailiwick (U.K.)	C	St. Peter Port	Europe	9
†GUINEA	Guinée	245,857	94,926	5,200,000	21	55	Republic	A	Conakry	Africa	34
†GUINEA-BISSAU	Guiné-Bissau	36,125	13,948	820,000	23	59	Republic	A	Bissau	Africa	34
†GUYANA	Guyana	214,969	83,000	925,000	4.3	11	Republic (Comm. of Nations)	A	Georgetown	S. Amer.	54
†HAITI	Haïti	27,750	10,714	5,145,000	185	480	Republic	A	Port-au-Prince	N. Amer.	49
Hawaii, U.S.	Hawaii	16,706	6,450	995,000	60	154	State (U.S.)	D	Honolulu	N. Amer.	60
Heilungkiang, China	Heilongjiang	705,254	272,300	31,340,000	44	115	Province (China)	D	Harbin	Asia	27
Hispaniola	La Española	76,192	29,418	10,805,000	142	367	. . .		. . .	N. Amer.	49
Holland, see Netherlands	. . .	. . .	. . .	. . .	. . .	. . .			. . .	. . .	. . .

Country, Division, or Region: English (Conventional)	Local Name	Area km²	Area sq mi	Population 1/1/82	Population Density per km²	Population Density per sq mi	Form of Government and Political Status	Capital	Continent	Map Plate
Honan, China	Henan	166,795	64,400	71,840,000	431	1,116	Province (China)	D Chengchow (Zhengzhou)	Asia	27
†HONDURAS	Honduras	112,088	43,277	3,880,000	35	90	Republic	A Tegucigalpa	N. Amer.	49
Hong Kong (U.K.)	Hong Kong	1,061	410	5,375,000	5,066	13,110	Colony (U.K.)	C Victoria	Asia	27
Hopeh, China	Hebei	192,954	74,500	59,925,000	311	804	Province (China)	D Shijiazhuang	Asia	28
Hunan, China	Hunan	210,566	81,300	52,435,000	249	645	Province (China)	D Changsha	Asia	27
†HUNGARY	Magyarország	93,036	35,921	10,715,000	115	298	Socialist Republic	A Budapest	Europe	10
Hupeh, China	Hubei	187,515	72,400	46,665,000	249	645	Province (China)	D Wuhan	Asia	27
†ICELAND	Ísland	103,000	39,769	230,000	2.2	5.8	Republic	A Reykjavík	Europe	7
Idaho, U.S.	Idaho	216,413	83,557	975,000	4.5	12	State (U.S.)	D Boise	N. Amer.	46
Illinois, U.S.	Illinois	150,028	57,926	11,650,000	78	201	State (U.S.)	D Springfield	N. Amer.	45
†INDIA (incl. part of Jammu and Kashmir)	Bhārat	3,203,975	1,237,061	695,230,000	217	562	Federal Socialist Republic (Comm. of Nations)	A New Delhi	Asia	25
Indiana, U.S.	Indiana	94,585	36,519	5,595,000	59	153	State (U.S.)	D Indianapolis	N. Amer.	44
†INDONESIA	Indonesia	1,919,270	741,034	151,500,000	79	204	Republic	A Jakarta	Asia	26
Inner Mongolia, China	Nei Mongol	424,499	163,900	8,555,000	20	52	Autonomous Region (China)	D Hohhot	Asia	27
Iowa, U.S.	Iowa	145,791	56,290	2,980,000	20	53	State (U.S.)	D Des Moines	N. Amer	45
†IRAN	Īrān	1,648,000	636,296	38,565,000	23	61	Republic	A Tehrān	Asia	23
†IRAQ	Al 'Irāq	434,924	167,925	13,465,000	31	80	Socialist Republic	A Baghdād	Asia	24
†IRELAND	Eire	70,283	27,136	3,495,000	50	129	Republic	A Dublin (Baile Átha Cliath)	Europe	9
ISLE OF MAN	Isle of Man	588	227	66,000	112	291	Self-governing Territory (U.K. protection)	B Douglas	Europe	9
†ISRAEL	Yisra'el	20,325	7,848	3,980,000	196	507	Republic	A Jerusalem (Yerushalayim)	Asia	24
Israeli Occupied Areas	...	7,000	2,703	1,235,000	176	457	...	...	Asia	24
†ITALY	Italia	301,262	116,318	57,270,000	190	492	Republic	A Rome (Roma)	Europe	14
†IVORY COAST	Côte d'Ivoire	320,763	123,847	8,145,000	25	66	Republic	A Abidjan	Africa	34
†JAMAICA	Jamaica	10,991	4,244	2,235,000	203	527	Parliamentary State (Comm. of Nations)	A Kingston	N. Amer.	49
†JAPAN	Nippon	372,313	143,751	118,650,000	319	825	Constitutional Monarchy	A Tōkyō	Asia	29
Java (incl. Madura) (Indon.)	Jawa	132,187	51,038	93,780,000	709	1,837	Part of Indonesia (5 provinces)	...	Asia	26
Jersey (U.K.)	Jersey	117	45	78,000	667	1,733	Bailiwick (U.K.)	C St. Helier	Europe	9
†JORDAN	Al Urdun	91,000	35,135	2,300,000	25	65	Constitutional Monarchy	A 'Ammān	Asia	24
†KAMPUCHEA	Kampuchea Prâcheathipâtéyy	181,035	69,898	6,965,000	38	100	Socialist Republic	A Phnum Pénh	Asia	26
Kansas, U.S.	Kansas	213,064	82,264	2,405,000	11	29	State (U.S.)	D Topeka	N. Amer.	45
Kansu, China	Gansu	720,276	278,100	20,895,000	29	75	Province (China)	D Lanzhou	Asia	27
Kashmir, Jammu and	Jammu and Kashmīr	222,802	86,024	9,920,000	45	115	In dispute (India and Pakistan)	... Srīnagar and Jammu	Asia	25
Kazakh S.S.R., U.S.S.R.	Kazahskaja S.S.R.	2,717,300	1,049,155	15,105,000	5.6	14	Soviet Socialist Republic (U.S.S.R.)	D Alma-Ata	Asia	19
Keewatin (Can.)	Keewatin	590,932	228,160	5,000	0.01	0.02	District of Northwest Territories (Canada)	...	N. Amer.	42
Kentucky, U.S.	Kentucky	104,623	40,395	3,745,000	36	93	State (U.S.)	D Frankfort	N. Amer.	44
†KENYA	Kenya	582,646	224,961	17,790,000	31	79	Republic (Comm. of Nations)	A Nairobi	Africa	36
Kerguelen Islands (Fr.)	Iles Kerguèlen	6,993	2,700	90	0.01	0.03	Part of French Southern and Antarctic Territory (France)	C ...	S. Amer.	30–31
Kiangsi, China	Jiangxi	164,723	63,600	28,260,000	172	444	Province (China)	D Nanchang	Asia	27
Kiangsu, China	Jiangsu	92,981	35,900	67,105,000	722	1,869	Province (China)	D Nanjing	Asia	28
Kirghiz S.S.R., U.S.S.R.	Kirgizskaja S.S.R.	198,500	76,641	3,655,000	18	48	Soviet Socialist Republic (U.S.S.R.)	D Frunze	Asia	18
KIRIBATI	Kiribati	754	291	59,000	78	203	Republic (Comm. of Nations)	A Bairiki	Oceania	60
Kirin, China	Jilin	271,690	104,900	22,385,000	82	213	Province (China)	D Changchun	Asia	27
KOREA, NORTH	Chosŏn Minjujuŭi In'min Konghwaguk	120,538[4]	46,540[4]	18,540,000	154	398	Socialist Republic	A P'yŏngyang	Asia	28
KOREA, SOUTH	Taehan-Min'guk	98,484[4]	38,025[4]	40,755,000	414	1,072	Republic	A Seoul (Sŏul)	Asia	28
Korea (Entire)	Chosŏn	220,284	85,052	59,295,000	269	697	...	...	Asia	28
†KUWAIT	Al Kuwayt	17,818	6,880	1,480,000	83	215	Constitutional Monarchy	A Al Kuwayt	Asia	24
Kwangsi, China	Guangxi	240,092	92,700	32,040,000	133	346	Province (China)	D Nanning	Asia	27
Kwangtung, China	Guangdong	211,602	81,700	54,725,000	259	670	Province (China)	D Canton (Guangzhou)	Asia	27
Kweichow, China	Guizhou	174,047	67,200	26,565,000	153	395	Province (China)	D Guiyang	Asia	27
Labrador (Can.)	Labrador	292,218	112,826	35,000	0.1	0.3	Part of Newfoundland Province (Canada)	...	N. Amer.	42
†LAOS	Laos	236,800	91,429	3,850,000	16	42	Socialist Republic	A Viangchan	Asia	26
Latin America	...	20,561,900	7,938,600	571,655,000	18	47	...	...	N.A., S.A.	52–53
Latvian S.S.R., U.S.S.R.	Latvijas P.S.R.	63,700	24,595	2,580,000	41	105	Soviet Socialist Republic (U.S.S.R.)	D Rīga	Europe	8
†LEBANON	Lubnān	10,400	4,015	3,275,000	315	816	Republic	A Beirut (Bayrūt)	Asia	24
†LESOTHO	Lesotho	30,355	11,720	1,385,000	46	118	Monarchy (Comm. of Nations)	A Maseru	Africa	37
Liaoning, China	Liaoning	229,473	88,600	45,970,000	200	519	Province (China)	D Mukden (Shenyang)	Asia	28
†LIBERIA	Liberia	111,369	43,000	1,975,000	18	46	Republic	A Monrovia	Africa	34
†LIBYA	Lībiyā	1,759,540	679,362	3,155,000	1.8	4.6	Socialist Republic	A Tripoli (Tarābulus)	Africa	33
LIECHTENSTEIN	Liechtenstein	169	62	27,000	169	435	Constitutional Monarchy	A Vaduz	Europe	14
Lithuanian S.S.R., U.S.S.R.	Lietuvos T.S.R.	65,200	25,174	3,470,000	53	138	Soviet Socialist Republic (U.S.S.R.)	D Vilnius	Europe	8
Louisiana, U.S.	Louisiana	125,675	48,523	4,300,000	34	89	State (U.S.)	D Baton Rouge	N. Amer.	45
†LUXEMBOURG	Luxembourg	2,586	999	355,000	137	355	Constitutional Monarchy	A Luxembourg	Europe	12
Macao (Port.)	Macau	16	6.0	275,000	17,188	45,833	Overseas Province (Portugal)	D Macau	Asia	27
Macias Nguema Biyogo, *see* Bioko	...	...	...	...	...	...	...	...	...	...
†Mackenzie (Can.)	Mackenzie	1,366,193	527,490	36,000	0.03	0.07	District of Northwest Territories (Canada)	...	N. Amer.	42
†MADAGASCAR	Madagasikara	587,041	226,658	9,085,000	15	40	Republic	A Antananarivo	Africa	37
Madeira Islands, Port.	Arquipélago da Madeira	796	307	265,000	333	863	District of Portugal (Madeira)	D Funchal	Africa	32
Maine, U.S.	Maine	86,027	33,215	1,115,000	13	34	State (U.S.)	D Augusta	N. Amer.	44
Malagasy Republic, see Madagascar	...	...	...	...	...	...	...	...	...	...
†MALAWI	Malawi	118,484	45,747	6,200,000	52	136	Republic (Comm. of Nations)	A Lilongwe	Africa	36
Malaya	Malaya	131,312	50,700	12,235,000	93	241	Part of Malaysia (11 States)	...	Asia	26
†MALAYSIA	Malaysia	332,632	128,430	14,495,000	44	113	Constitutional Monarchy (Comm. of Nations)	A Kuala Lumpur	Asia	26
†MALDIVES	Maldives	298	115	155,000	520	1,348	Republic	A Male	Asia	25
†MALI	Mali	1,240,000	478,766	7,175,000	5.8	15	Republic	A Bamako	Africa	34
†MALTA	Malta	316	122	360,000	1,139	2,951	Republic (Comm. of Nations)	A Valletta	Europe	14
Manitoba, Can.	Manitoba	650,087	251,000	1,045,000	1.6	4.2	Province (Canada)	D Winnipeg	N. Amer	42
Maritime Provinces (excl. Newfoundland) (Can.)	Maritime Provinces	134,584	51,963	1,677,000	12	32	Part of Canada (3 provinces)	...	N. Amer.	42
Marshall Islands (T.T.P.I.)	Marshall Islands	181	70	31,000	171	443	Part of Trust Territory of the Pacific Islands (U.S. administration)	C Uliga	Oceania	60

Country, Division, or Region English (Conventional)	Local Name	Area km²	sq mi	Population 1/1/82	Population Density per km²	sq mi	Form of Government and Political Status		Capital	Continent and Map Plate	
Martinique (Fr.)	Martinique	1,100	425	300,000	273	706	Overseas Department (France)	D	Fort-de-France	N. Amer. .	51
Maryland, U.S.	Maryland	27,394	10,577	4,300,000	157	407	State (U.S.)	D	Annapolis	N. Amer. .	44
Massachusetts, U.S.	Massachusetts	21,386	8,257	5,800,000	271	702	State (U.S.)	D	Boston	N. Amer. .	44
MAURITANIA	Mūrītāniyā	1,030,700	397,955	1,730,000	1.7	4.3	Republic	A	Nouakchott	Africa . . .	32
MAURITIUS (incl. Dependencies)	Mauritius	2,045	790	985,000	482	1,247	Parliamentary State (Comm. of Nations)	A	Port-Louis	Africa . . .	37
Mayotte (Fr.)	Mayotte	374	144	54,000	144	375	Overseas Department (France)	D	Dzaoudzi	Africa . . .	37
MEXICO	México	1,972,547	761,604	70,515,000	36	93	Federal Republic	A	Mexico (Ciudad de México)	N. Amer. .	48
Michigan, U.S.	Michigan	250,687	96,791	9,455,000	38	98	State (U.S.)	D	Lansing	N. Amer. .	44
Micronesia, Federated States of (T.T.P.I.)	Federated States of Micronesia	694	268	71,000			Part of Trust Territory of the Pacific Islands (U.S. administration).	C	Ponape	Oceania. .	60
Middle America	. . .	2,703,900	1,055,600	123,855,000	46	117	. . . .			N. Amer. .	47
Midway Islands (U.S.)	Midway Islands	5.2	2.0	1,500	288	750	Unincorporated Territory (U.S.)	C	. . .	Oceania. .	60
Minnesota, U.S.	Minnesota	223,465	86,280	4,160,000	19	48	State (U.S.)	D	St. Paul	N. Amer. .	45
Mississippi, U.S.	Mississippi	123,584	47,716	2,565,000	21	54	State (U.S.)	D	Jackson	N. Amer. .	45
Missouri, U.S.	Missouri	180,487	69,686	5,015,000	28	72	State (U.S.)	D	Jefferson City	N. Amer. .	45
Moldavian S.S.R., U.S.S.R.	Moldavskaja S.S.R.	33,700	13,012	4,030,000	120	310	Soviet Socialist Republic (U.S.S.R.)	D	Kišinev	Europe . .	16
MONACO	Monaco	1.5	0.6	27,000	18,000	45,000	Constitutional Monarchy	A	Monaco	Europe . .	11
MONGOLIA	Mongol Ard Uls	1,565,000	604,250	1,750,000	1.1	2.9	Socialist Republic	A	Ulan-Bator	Asia . . .	27
Montana, U.S.	Montana	381,087	147,138	810,000	2.1	5.5	State (U.S.)	D	Helena	N. Amer. .	46
Montserrat (U.K.)	Montserrat	103	40	12,000	117	300	Colony (U.K.)	C	Plymouth	N. Amer. .	51
MOROCCO (excl. Western Sahara)	Al Maghrib	446,550	172,414	21,795,000	49	126	Constitutional Monarchy	A	Rabat	Africa . . .	32
MOZAMBIQUE	Moçambique	783,030	302,329	12,385,000	16	41	Socialist Republic	A	Maputo	Africa . . .	37
Muscat and Oman, see Oman	. . .	. . .	. . .	. . .	. . .	. . .	. . . .			. . . .	. . .
Namibia (excl. Walvis Bay) (S. Afr.)(5)	Namibia	824,292	318,261	1,070,000	1.3	3.4	Under South African Administration	C	Windhoek	Africa . . .	37
NAURU	Nauru (English) Naoero (Nauruan)	21	8.2	7,900	376	963	Republic (Comm. of Nations)	A	Domaneab	Oceania. .	64
Nebraska, U.S.	Nebraska	200,018	77,227	1,595,000	8.0	21	State (U.S.)	D	Lincoln	N. Amer. .	45
NEPAL	Nepal	140,797	54,362	15,520,000	110	285	Constitutional Monarchy	A	Kathmandu	Asia	25
NETHERLANDS	Nederland	41,160	15,892	14,300,000	347	900	Constitutional Monarchy	A	Amsterdam	Europe . .	12
Netherlands Guiana, see Suriname	. . .	. . .	. . .	. . .	. . .	. . .	. . . .			. . . .	. . .
NETHERLANDS ANTILLES	Nederlandse Antillen	993	383	260,000	262	679	Self-governing Territory (Netherlands protection).	B	Willemstad	N. Amer. .	50
Nevada, U.S.	Nevada	286,299	110,541	855,000	3.0	7.7	State (U.S.)	D	Carson City	N. Amer. .	46
New Brunswick, Can.	New Brunswick	73,436	28,354	705,000	9.6	25	Province (Canada)	D	Fredericton	N. Amer. .	42
New Caledonia (incl. Dependencies) (Fr.)	Nouvelle-Calédonie	19,058	7,358	140,000	7.3	19	Overseas Territory (France)	C	Nouméa	Oceania. .	63
New England (U.S.)	New England	172,514	66,608	12,550,000	73	188	Part of U.S. (6 states).			N. Amer. .	43
Newfoundland, Can.	Newfoundland	404,517	156,185	585,000	1.4	3.7	Province (Canada)	D	St. John's	N. Amer. .	42
Newfoundland (excl. Labrador) (Can.)	Newfoundland	112,299	43,359	550,000	4.9	13	Part of Newfoundland Province, Canada .			N. Amer. .	42
New Hampshire, U.S.	New Hampshire	24,097	9,304	950,000	39	102	State (U.S.)	D	Concord	N. Amer. .	44
New Hebrides, see Vanuatu	. . .	. . .	. . .	. . .	. . .	. . .	. . . .			. . . .	. . .
New Jersey, U.S.	New Jersey	20,295	7,836	7,515,000	370	959	State (U.S.)	D	Trenton	N. Amer. .	44
New Mexico, U.S.	New Mexico	315,115	121,667	1,350,000	4.3	11	State (U.S.)	D	Santa Fe	N. Amer. .	45
New South Wales, Austl.	New South Wales	801,428	309,433	5,245,000	6.5	17	State (Australia).	D	Sydney	Oceania. .	59
New York, U.S.	New York	137,795	53,203	17,680,000	128	332	State (U.S.)	D	Albany	N. Amer. .	44
NEW ZEALAND	New Zealand	269,057	103,883	3,195,000	12	31	Parliamentary State (Comm. of Nations)	A	Wellington	Oceania. .	62
NICARAGUA	Nicaragua	130,000	50,193	3,035,000	23	60	Republic	A	Managua	N. Amer. .	49
NIGER	Niger	1,267,000	489,191	5,538,000	4.4	11	Republic	A	Niamey	Africa . . .	34
NIGERIA	Nigeria	923,768	356,669	80,765,000	87	226	Federal Republic (Comm. of Nations).	A	Lagos	Africa . . .	34
Ningsia, China	Ningxia	66,304	25,600	2,985,000	45	117	Autonomous Region (China).	D	Yinchuan	Asia	27
NIUE	Niue	263	102	3,000	11	29	Self-governing Territory (New Zealand)	B	Alofi	Oceania. .	64
Norfolk Island (Austl.)	Norfolk Island	36	14	2,300	64	164	External Territory (Australia).	C	Kingston	Oceania. .	61
NORTH AMERICA	. . .	24,360,000	9,406,000	379,400,000	16	40	. . . .			N. Amer. .	38–39
North Borneo, see Sabah	. . .	. . .	. . .	. . .	. . .	. . .	. . . .			. . . .	. . .
North Carolina, U.S.	North Carolina	136,198	52,586	5,985,000	44	114	State (U.S.)	D	Raleigh	N. Amer. .	44
North Dakota, U.S.	North Dakota	183,022	70,665	670,000	3.7	9.5	State (U.S.)	D	Bismarck	N. Amer. .	45
Northern Ireland, U.K.	Northern Ireland	14,120	5,452	1,545,000	109	283	Administrative division of United Kingdom.	D	Belfast	Europe . .	9
Northern Mariana Islands (T.T.P.I.)	Northern Mariana Islands	474	183	18,000	38	98	Part of Trust Territory of the Pacific Islands (U.S. administration).	C	Saipan (island)	Oceania. .	60
Northern Territory, Austl.	Northern Territory	1,375,519	520,280	125,000	0.09	0.2	Territory (Australia)	D	Darwin	Oceania. .	59
Northwest Territories, Can.	Northwest Territories	3,379,684	1,304,903	49,000	0.01	0.04	Territory (Canada)	D	Yellowknife	N. Amer. .	42
NORWAY (incl. Svalbard and Jan Mayen)	Norge	386,317	149,158	4,115,000	13	33	Constitutional Monarchy	A	Oslo	Europe . .	7
Nova Scotia, Can.	Nova Scotia	55,491	21,425	850,000	15	40	Province (Canada)	D	Halifax	N. Amer. .	42
OCEANIA (incl. Australia)	. . .	8,513,000	3,287,000	23,200,000	2.7	7.1	. . . .			Oceania. .	57–58
Ohio, U.S.	Ohio	115,799	44,679	11,025,000	95	247	State (U.S.)	D	Columbus	N. Amer. .	44
Oklahoma, U.S.	Oklahoma	181,090	69,919	3,100,000	17	44	State (U.S.)	D	Oklahoma City	N. Amer. .	45
OMAN	'Umān	212,457	82,030	930,000	4.4	11	Monarchy.	A	Muscat (Masqaṭ)	Asia	23
Ontario, Can.	Ontario	1,068,582	412,582	8,665,000	8.1	21	Province (Canada)	D	Toronto	N. Amer. .	42
Oregon, U.S.	Oregon	251,181	96,981	2,680,000	11	28	State (U.S.)	D	Salem	N. Amer. .	46
Orkney Islands (U.K.)	Orkney Islands	974	376	19,000	20	51	Part of Scotland, U.K. (Orkney Island Area)	. . .	Kirkwall	Europe . .	9
PAKISTAN (incl. part of Jammu and Kashmir)	Pākistān	828,453	319,867	92,070,000	111	288	Federal Republic	A	Islāmābād	Asia	25
Palau (T.T.P.I.)	Palau	461	178	14,000	. . .	. . .	Part of Trust Territory of the Pacific Islands (U.S. administration). .	C	Koror	Oceania. .	60
PANAMA	Panamá	77,082	29,762	1,910,000	25	64	Republic	A	Panamá	N. Amer. .	49
PAPUA NEW GUINEA	Papua New Guinea	462,840	178,703	3,115,000	6.7	17	Parliamentary State (Comm. of Nations)	A	Port Moresby	Oceania. .	60
PARAGUAY	Paraguay	406,752	157,048	3,205,000	7.9	20	Republic	A	Asunción	S. Amer. .	56
Peking, China	Beijing	17,094	6,600	8,000,000	468	1,212	Autonomous City (China)	D	Beijing	Asia	28
Pennsylvania, U.S.	Pennsylvania	119,316	46,068	11,995,000	101	260	State (U.S.)	D	Harrisburg	N. Amer. .	44

A • 5

Country, Division, or Region English (Conventional)	Local Name	Area km²	Area sq mi	Population 1/1/82	Population Density per km²	Population Density per sq mi	Form of Government and Political Status		Capital	Continent and Map Plate	
Persia, see Iran	. . .									. . .	
†PERU	Peru	1,285,216	496,224	18,510,000	14	37	Republic	A	Lima	S. Amer. .	54
†PHILIPPINES	Pilipinas	300,000	115,831	50,960,000	170	440	Republic	A	Manila	Asia	26
Pitcairn (excl. Dependencies) (U.K.)	Pitcairn	4.7	1.8	65	14	36	Colony (U.K.)	C	Adamstown	Oceania. .	61
†POLAND	Polska	312,683	120,728	36,035,000	115	298	Socialist Republic	A	Warsaw (Warszawa)	Europe . .	10
†PORTUGAL	Portugal	88,940	34,340	10,050,000	113	293	Republic	A	Lisbon (Lisboa)	Europe . .	13
Portuguese Guinea, see Guinea-Bissau	. . .										
Prairie Provinces (Can.)	Prairie Provinces	1,963,172	757,985	4,235,000	2.2	5.6	Part of Canada (3 provinces)			N. Amer. .	42
Prince Edward Island, Can.	Prince Edward Island	5,657	2,184	122,000	22	56	Province (Canada)	D	Charlottetown	N. Amer. .	42
PUERTO RICO	Puerto Rico	8,897	3,435	3,270,000	368	952	Commonwealth (U.S. protection)	B	San Juan	N. Amer. .	51
†QATAR	Qaṭar	11,000	4,247	235,000	21	55	Monarchy	A	Ad Dawḩah (Doha)	Asia	24
Quebec, Can.	Québec	1,540,680	594,860	6,375,000	4.1	11	Province (Canada)	D	Québec	N. Amer. .	42
Queensland, Austl.	Queensland	1,727,522	667,000	2,310,000	1.3	3.5	State (Australia)	D	Brisbane	Oceania. .	59
Reunion (Fr.)	Réunion	2,510	969	525,000	209	542	Overseas Department (France)	D	Saint-Denis	Africa . . .	37
Rhode Island, U.S.	Rhode Island	3,144	1,214	950,000	302	783	State (U.S.)	D	Providence	N. Amer. .	44
Rhodesia, see Zimbabwe	. . .										
Rodrigues (Maur.)	Rodrigues	109	42	32,000	294	762	Part of Mauritius			Africa . . .	30–31
†ROMANIA	România	237,500	91,699	22,445,000	95	245	Socialist Republic	A	Bucharest (Bucureşti)	Europe . .	15
Russian Soviet Federated Socialist Republic, U.S.S.R.	Rossijskaja S.F.S.R.	17,075,400	6,592,846	140,580,000	8.2	21	Soviet Federated Socialist Republic (U.S.S.R.)	D	Moscow (Moskva)	Eur./Asia .	19–20
†RWANDA	Rwanda	26,338	10,169	5,175,000	196	509	Republic	A	Kigali	Africa . . .	36
Sabah, Malaysia	Sabah	76,115	29,388	915,000	12	31	State of Malaysia	D	Kota Kinabalu	Asia	26
St. Christopher-Nevis	St. Christopher-Nevis	269	104	41,000	152	394	Associated State (U.K.)	B	Basseterre	N. Amer. .	51
St. Helena (incl. Dependencies) (U.K.)	St. Helena	419	162	6,600	16	41	Colony (U.K.)	C	Jamestown	Africa . . .	31
†SAINT LUCIA	Saint Lucia	616	238	124,000	201	521	Parliamentary State (Comm. of Nations)	A	Castries	N. Amer. .	51
St. Pierre and Miquelon (Fr.)	St.-Pierre et Miquelon	242	93	6,700	28	72	Overseas Department (France)	D	Saint-Pierre	N. Amer. .	42
†ST. VINCENT	St. Vincent	389	150	128,000	329	853	Parliamentary State (Comm. of Nations)	A	Kingstown	N. Amer. .	50
Samoa (entire)	Samoa Islands	3,039	1,173	189,000	62	161				Oceania. .	65
SAN MARINO	San Marino	61	24	24,000	393	1,000	Republic	A	San Marino	Europe . .	14
†SAO TOME AND PRINCIPE	São Tomé e Príncipe	964	372	89,000	92	239	Republic	A	São Tomé	Africa . . .	34
Sarawak, Malaysia	Sarawak	125,205	48,342	1,345,000	11	28	State of Malaysia	D	Kuching	Asia	26
Sardinia	Sardegna	24,090	9,301	1,605,000	67	173	Part of Italy (Sardegna Autonomous Region)	D	Cagliari	Europe . .	14
Saskatchewan, Can.	Saskatchewan	651,900	251,700	1,000,000	1.5	4.0	Province (Canada)	D	Regina	N. Amer. .	42
†SAUDI ARABIA	Al 'Arabīyah as Sa'ūdīyah	2,149,690	830,000	8,755,000	4.1	11	Monarchy	A	Riyadh (Ar Riyāḍ)	Asia	23
Scandinavia (incl. Finland and Iceland)	. . .	1,320,900	510,000	22,680,000	17	44				Europe . .	7
Scotland, U.K.	Scotland	78,775	30,416	5,135,000	65	169	Administrative division of U.K.	D	Edinburgh	Europe . .	9
†SENEGAL	Sénégal	196,722	75,955	5,880,000	30	77	Republic	A	Dakar	Africa . . .	34
Senegambia	Senegambia	208,067	80,316	6,505,000	31	81	Economic Union			Africa . . .	34
†SEYCHELLES	Seychelles	443	171	68,000	153	398	Republic (Comm. of Nations)	A	Victoria	Africa . . .	37
Shanghai, China	Shanghai	5,698	2,200	11,300,000	1,893	5,136	Autonomous City (China)	D	Shanghai	Asia	28
Shansi, China	Shanxi	157,212	60,700	24,575,000	156	405	Province (China)	D	Taiyuan	Asia	27
Shantung, China	Shandong	153,586	59,300	83,380,000	543	1,406	Province (China)	D	Jinan	Asia	28
Shensi, China	Shaanxi	195,803	75,600	29,650,000	151	392	Province (China)	D	Xi'an	Asia	27
Shetland Islands (U.K.)	Shetland Islands	1,427	551	24,000	17	44	Part of Scotland, U.K. (Shetland Island Area)		Lerwick	Europe . .	9
Siam, see Thailand	. . .									. . . .	
Sicily	Sicilia	25,708	9,926	5,040,000	196	508	Part of Italy (Sicilia Autonomous Region)	D	Palermo	Europe . .	14
†SIERRA LEONE	Sierra Leone	72,325	27,925	3,615,000	50	129	Republic (Comm. of Nations)	A	Freetown	Africa . . .	34
†SINGAPORE	Singapore (English) Singapura (Malay)	581	224	2,860,000	4,923	12,768	Republic (Comm. of Nations)	A	Singapore	Asia	26
Sinkiang, China	Xinjiang	1,646,714	635,800	9,550,000	5.8	15	Autonomous Region (China)	D	Ürümqi	Asia	27
†SOLOMON ISLANDS	Solomon Islands	29,800	11,500	235,000	7.9	20	Parliamentary State (Comm. of Nations)	A	Honiara	Oceania. .	63
†SOMALIA	Soomaaliya	637,657	246,200	5,100,000	8.0	21	Socialist Republic	A	Mogadishu (Muqdisho)	Africa . . .	35
†SOUTH AFRICA (incl. Walvis Bay)	South Africa (English) Suid-Afrika (Afrikaans)	1,221,042	471,447	30,495,000	25	65	Republic	A	Pretoria and Cape Town	Africa . . .	37
SOUTH AMERICA		17,828,000	6,883,000	247,800,000	14	36				S. Amer. .	52–53
South Australia, Austl.	South Australia	984,377	380,070	1,315,000	1.3	3.5	State (Australia)	D	Adelaide	Oceania. .	59
South Carolina, U.S.	South Carolina	80,432	31,055	3,190,000	40	103	State (U.S.)	D	Columbia	N. Amer. .	44
South Dakota, U.S.	South Dakota	199,552	77,047	695,000	3.5	9.0	State (U.S.)	D	Pierre	N. Amer. .	45
Southern Yemen, see Yemen, People's Democratic Republic of	. . .										
South Georgia (incl. Dependencies) (U.K.)(3)	South Georgia	4,092	1,580	20	.005	0.01	Dependency of Falkland Islands (U.K.)	C	. . .	S. Amer. .	56
South West Africa, see Namibia	. . .									. . . .	
Soviet Union, see Union of Soviet Socialist Republics	. . .									. . . .	
†SPAIN	España	504,741	194,882	37,865,000	75	194	Constitutional Monarchy	A	Madrid	Europe . .	13
Spanish North Africa (Sp.)(2)	Plazas de Soberanía en el Norte de África	32	12	127,000	3,969	10,583	Five Possessions (No Central Government)	C	. . .	Africa . . .	13
Spanish Sahara, see Western Sahara										. . . .	
†SRI LANKA	Sri Lanka	65,000	25,097	15,605,000	240	622	Socialist Republic (Comm. of Nations)	A	Colombo	Asia	25
†SUDAN	As Sūdān	2,505,813	967,500	20,180,000	8.1	21	Republic	A	Khartoum (Al Kharṭūm)	Africa . . .	35
Sumatra	Sumatera	473,606	182,860	23,785,000	50	130	Part of Indonesia (7 provinces)			Asia	26
†SURINAME	Suriname	163,265	63,037	365,000	2.2	5.8	Republic	A	Paramaribo	S. Amer. .	54
†SWAZILAND	Swaziland	17,364	6,704	580,000	33	87	Monarchy (Comm. of Nations)	A	Mbabane	Africa . . .	37
†SWEDEN	Sverige	450,089	173,780	8,335,000	19	48	Constitutional Monarchy	A	Stockholm	Europe . .	7
SWITZERLAND	Schweiz (German) Suisse (French) Svizzera (Italian)	41,293	15,943	6,315,000	153	396	Federal Republic	A	Bern (Berne)	Europe . .	14
†SYRIA	Sūrīyah	185,180	71,498	9,475,000	51	133	Socialist Republic	A	Damascus (Dimashq)	Asia	24
Szechwan, China	Sichuan	569,020	219,700	106,765,000	188	486	Province (China)	D	Chengdu	Asia	27
Tadzhik S.S.R., U.S.S.R.	Tadžikskaja S.S.R.	143,100	55,251	3,950,000	28	71	Soviet Socialist Republic (U.S.S.R.)	D	Dušanbe	Asia	18

Country, Division, or Region English (Conventional)	Local Name	Area km²	sq mi	Population 1/1/82	Population Density per km²	sq mi	Form of Government and Political Status		Capital	Continent and Map Plate	
⊩TAIWAN	Taiwan	35,989	13,895	18,365,000	510	1,322	Republic	A	Taipei	Asia	27
⊩TANZANIA	Tanzania	945,087	364,900	19,115,000	20	52	Republic (Comm. of Nations)	A	Dodoma	Africa	36
Tasmania, Austl.	Tasmania	68,332	26,383	430,000	6.3	16	State (Australia)	D	Hobart	Oceania	59
Tennessee, U.S.	Tennessee	109,412	42,244	4,690,000	43	111	State (U.S.)	D	Nashville	N. Amer.	44
Texas, U.S.	Texas	692,405	267,339	14,520,000	21	54	State (U.S.)	D	Austin	N. Amer.	45
⊩THAILAND	Muang Thai	513,113	198,114	48,860,000	95	247	Constitutional Monarchy	A	Bangkok (Krung Thep)	Asia	26
Tibet, China	Xizang	1,221,697	471,700	1,690,000	1.4	3.6	Autonomous Region (China)	D	Lhasa	Asia	27
Tientsin, China	Tianjin	4,144	1,600	7,000,000	1,689	4,375	Autonomous City (China)	D	Tianjin	Asia	28
⊩TOGO	Togo	56,785	21,925	2,730,000	48	125	Republic	A	Lomé	Africa	34
Tokelau (N.Z.)	Tokelau	10	3.9	1,600	160	410	Island Territory (New Zealand)	C	. . .	Oceania	61
⊩TONGA	Tonga	699	270	101,000	144	374	Constitutional Monarchy (Comm. of Nations)	A	Nuku'alofa	Oceania	61
Transcaucasia (U.S.S.R.)	. . .	186,100	71,853	14,460,000	78	201	Part of U.S.S.R. (3 republics)		. . .	Asia	16
⊩TRINIDAD AND TOBAGO	Trinidad and Tobago	5,128	1,980	1,165,000	227	588	Republic (Comm. of Nations)	A	Port of Spain	N. Amer.	50
Tristan da Cunha (U.K.)	Tristan da Cunha	104	40	300	2.9	7.5	Dependency of St. Helena (U.K.)	C	Edinburgh	Africa	30–31
Trucial States, see United Arab Emirates	. . .	. . .	. . .	. . .						. . . .	
Trust Territory of the Pacific Islands	Trust Territory of the Pacific Islands	1,810	699	140,000	77	200	U.N. Trusteeship administered by U.S.	C	Saipan (island)	Oceania	60
Tsinghai, China	Qinghai	721,053	278,400	3,880,000	5.4	14	Province (China)	D	Xining	Asia	27
⊩TUNISIA	Tūnis	163,610	63,170	6,585,000	40	104	Republic	A	Tūnis	Africa	32
⊩TURKEY	Türkiye	779,452	300,948	46,435,000	60	154	Republic	A	Ankara	Eur./As.	24
Turkey in Europe	. . .	23,764	9,175	4,005,000	169	437	Part of Turkey		. . .	Europe	24
Turkmen S.S.R., U.S.S.R.	Turkmenskaja S.S.R.	488,100	188,456	2,875,000	5.9	15	Soviet Socialist Republic (U.S.S.R.)	D	Ašhabad	Asia	19
Turks and Caicos Islands (U.K.)	Turks and Caicos Islands	430	166	7,700	18	46	Colony (U.K.)	C	Grand Turk	N. Amer.	49
⊩TUVALU	Tuvalu	26	10	8,100	312	810	Parliamentary State (Comm. of Nations)	A	Funafuti	Oceania	60
⊩UGANDA	Uganda	236,036	91,134	13,440,000	57	147	Republic (Comm. of Nations)	A	Kampala	Africa	36
Ukrainian S.S.R., U.S.S.R.	Ukrainskaja S.S.R.	603,700	233,090	50,760,000	84	218	Soviet Socialist Republic (U.S.S.R)	D	Kiev (Kijev)	Europe	16
⊩UNION OF SOVIET SOCIALIST REPUBLICS	Sojuz Sovetskih Socialističeskih Respublik	22,274,900	8,600,383	268,740,000	12	31	Federal Socialist Republic	A	Moscow (Moskva)	Eur./Asia	19–20
U.S.S.R. in Europe	. . .	4,974,818	1,920,789	174,790,000	35	91	Part of U.S.S.R.		. . .	Europe	19
⊩UNITED ARAB EMIRATES	Al Imārāt al 'Arabīyah al Muttaḥidah	83,600	32,278	1,050,000	13	33	Federation of Monarchs	A	Abū Ẓaby	Asia	23
United Arab Republic, see Egypt	. . .	. . .	. . .	. . .	. . .	. . .				. . . .	
⊩UNITED KINGDOM	United Kingdom	244,102	94,249	56,035,000	230	595	Constitutional Monarchy (Comm. of Nations)	A	London	Europe	9
United Kingdom and Possessions	. . .	294,415	113,676	62,049,000	211	546	. . . .		London	. . . .	
⊩UNITED STATES	United States	9,528,318	3,678,896	231,160,000	24	63	Federal Republic	A	Washington, D.C.	N. Amer.	43
United States and Possessions	. . .	9,540,129	3,683,456	234,817,000	25	64	. . . .		Washington	. . . .	
⊩UPPER VOLTA	Haute-Volta	274,200	105,869	7,180,000	26	68	Republic	A	Ouagadougou	Africa	34
⊩URUGUAY	Uruguay	176,215	68,037	2,930,000	17	43	Republic	A	Montevideo	S. Amer.	55
Utah, U.S.	Utah	219,932	84,916	1,510,000	6.9	18	State (U.S.)	D	Salt Lake City	N. Amer.	46
Uzbek S.S.R., U.S.S.R.	Uzbekskaja S.S.R.	447,400	172,742	16,015,000	36	93	Soviet Socialist Republic (U.S.S.R.)	D	Taškent	Asia	19
⊩VANUATU	Vanuatu	14,800	5,714	120,000	8.1	21	Parliamentary State (Comm. of Nations)	A	Port-Vila	Oceania	63
⊩VATICAN CITY	Città del Vaticano	0.4	0.2	1,000	2,500	5,000	Ecclesiastical State	A	Vatican City (Città del Vaticano)	Europe	14
⊩VENEZUELA	Venezuela	912,050	352,144	14,515,000	16	41	Federal Republic	A	Caracas	S. Amer.	54
Vermont, U.S.	Vermont	24,887	9,609	530,000	21	55	State (U.S.)	D	Montpelier	N. Amer.	44
Victoria, Austl.	Victoria	227,619	87,884	3,955,000	17	45	State (Australia)	D	Melbourne	Oceania	59
⊩VIETNAM	Viet-nam Dan-chu Cong-hoa	329,556	127,242	55,455,000	168	436	Socialist Republic	A	Hanoi	Asia	26
Virginia, U.S.	Virginia	105,716	40,817	5,455,000	52	134	State (U.S.)	D	Richmond	N. Amer.	44
Virgin Islands (U.S.)	Virgin Islands	344	133	101,000	294	759	Unincorporated Territory (U.S.)	C	Charlotte Amalie	N. Amer.	51
Virgin Islands, British (U.K.)	British Virgin Islands	153	59	11,000	72	186	Colony (U.K.)	C	Road Town	N. Amer.	51
Wake Island (U.S.)	Wake Island	7.8	3.0	200	26	67	Unincorporated Territory (U.S.)	C	. . .	Oceania	60
Wales, U.K.	Wales	20,768	8,019	2,780,000	134	347	Administrative division of U.K.	D	Cardiff	Europe	9
Wallis and Futuna (Fr.)	Iles Wallis-et-Futuna	255	98	11,000	43	112	Overseas Territory (France)	C	Mata-Utu	Oceania	61
Washington, U.S.	Washington	176,617	68,192	4,205,000	24	62	State (U.S.)	D	Olympia	N. Amer.	46
Western Australia, Austl.	Western Australia	2,527,621	975,920	1,295,000	0.5	1.3	State (Australia)	D	Perth	Oceania	59
Western Sahara	. . .	266,000	102,703	120,000	0.5	1.2	Occupied by Morocco	C	El Aaiún	Africa	32
⊩WESTERN SAMOA	Samoa i Sisifo	2,842	1,097	155,000	55	141	Constitutional Monarchy (Comm. of Nations)	A	Apia	Oceania	65
West Indies	West Indies (English) Indias Occidentales (Spanish)	238,200	92,000	29,370,000	123	319	. . . .		. . .	N. Amer.	47
West Virginia, U.S.	West Virginia	62,629	24,181	1,990,000	32	82	State (U.S.)	D	Charleston	N. Amer.	44
White Russia, see Byelorussian S.S.R.	. . .	. . .	. . .	. . .	. . .	. . .			Madison	. . . .	. . .
Wisconsin, U.S.	Wisconsin	171,499	66,216	4,810,000	28	73	State (U.S.)	D	Madison	N. Amer.	45
Wyoming, U.S.	Wyoming	253,597	97,914	485,000	1.9	5.0	State (U.S.)	D	Cheyenne	N. Amer.	46
⊩YEMEN	Al Yaman	195,000	75,290	6,140,000	31	82	Republic	A	Şan'ā'	Asia	23
⊩YEMEN, PEOPLE'S DEMOCRATIC REPUBLIC OF	Al Yaman ad Dīmuqrāṭīyah	332,968	128,560	2,060,000	6.2	16	Socialist Republic	A	Aden (Baladiyat 'Adan)	Asia	23
⊩YUGOSLAVIA	Jugoslavija	255,804	98,766	22,635,000	88	229	Federal Socialist Republic	A	Belgrade (Beograd)	Europe	14–15
Yukon Territory, Can.	Yukon Territory	482,515	186,300	24,000	0.05	0.1	Territory (Canada)	D	Whitehorse	N. Amer.	42
Yunnan, China	Yunnan	436,154	168,400	27,860,000	64	165	Province (China)	D	Kunming	Asia	27
⊩ZAIRE	Zaïre	2,345,409	905,567	29,060,000	12	32	Republic	A	Kinshasa (Léopoldville)	Africa	36
⊩ZAMBIA	Zambia	752,614	290,586	5,905,000	7.8	20	Republic (Comm. of Nations)	A	Lusaka	Africa	36
Zanzibar	Zanzibar	2,461	950	520,000	211	547	Part of Tanzania	D	Zanzibar	Africa	36
⊩ZIMBABWE	Zimbabwe	390,580	150,804	7,700,000	20	51	Republic (Comm. of Nations)	A	Harare	Africa	37
WORLD	. . .	149,754,000	57,821,000	4,532,000,000	30	78	. . . .			. . . .	1–2

† Member of the United Nations (1981).
. . . None, or not applicable.
(1) No permanent population.
(2) Comprises Ceuta, Melilla, and several small islands.
(3) Claimed by Argentina.
(4) The 1,262 km² or 487 sq mi of the demilitarized zone are not included in either North or South Korea.
(5) In October 1966 the United Nations terminated the South African mandate over Namibia, a decision which South Africa did not accept.

World Geographical Tables

The Earth: Land and Water

	Total Area km²	sq mi	Area of Land km²	sq mi	%	Area of Oceans and Seas km²	sq mi	%
Earth	510,100,000	197,000,000	149,400,000	57,700,000	29.3	360,700,000	139,300,000	70.7
N. Hemisphere	255,050,000	98,500,000	106,045,650	40,950,000	41.6	149,004,350	57,550,000	58.4
S. Hemisphere	255,050,000	98,500,000	43,354,350	16,750,000	17.0	211,695,650	81,750,000	83.0

The Continents

Continent	Area km² sq mi	Population Estimate (1/1/82)	Population per km² sq mi	Mean Elevation m ft *	Highest Elevation m/ft	Lowest Elevation m/ft (below sea level)	Highest Recorded Temperature °C/°F	Lowest Recorded Temperature °C/°F
Europe	9,932,000 3,835,000	666,400,000	67 174	340 1,000	Mt. Elbrus, U.S.S.R. 5,642/18,510	Caspian Sea, U.S.S.R.-Iran −28/−92	Sevilla, Spain 50°/122°	Ust-Ščugor, U.S.S.R. −55°/−67°
Asia	44,798,000 17,297,000	2,724,900,000	61 158	960 3,150	Mt. Everest, China-Nepal 8,848/29,029	Dead Sea, Israel-Jordan −395/−1,296	Tirat Zevi, Israel 54°/129°	Ojmjakon, U.S.S.R.; Verkhoyansk U.S.S.R. −68°/−90°
Africa	30,323,000 11,708,000	490,300,000	16 42	750 2,450	Kilimanjaro, Tanzania 5,895/19,341	Lac Assal, Djibouti −155/−509	Al 'Azīzīyah, Libya 58°/136°	Ifrane, Morocco −24°/−11°
North America	24,360,000 9,406,000	379,400,000	16 40	720 2,350	Mt. McKinley, United States 6,194/20,320	Death Valley, United States −86/−282	Death Valley, United States 57°/134°	Northice, Greenland −66°/−87°
South America	17,828,000 6,883,000	247,800,000	14 36	590 1,940	Aconcagua, Argentina 6,960/22,835	Salinas Chicas, Argentina −42/−138	Rivadavia, Argentina 49°/120°	Sarmiento, Argentina −33°/−27°
Oceania, incl. Australia	8,513,000 3,287,000	23,200,000	3 7	. . . .	Mt. Wilhelm, Papua N. Gui. 4,509/14,793	Lake Eyre, Australia −12/−39	Cloncurry, Australia 53°/128°	Charlotte Pass, Australia −22°/−8°
Australia	7,686,850 2,967,909	14,910,000	2 5	340 1,100	Mt. Kosciusko, Australia 2,228/7,310	Lake Eyre, Australia −12/−39	Cloncurry, Australia 53°/128°	Charlotte Pass, Australia −22°/−8°
Antarctica	14,000,000 5,405,000	. . . .	. . .	2,600 8,550	Vinson Massif 5,140/16,864	unknown	Esperanza 14°/58°	Vostok −90°/−127°
World	149,754,000 57,821,000	4,532,000,000	30 78	840 2,750	Mt. Everest, China-Nepal 8,848/29,029	Dead Sea, Israel-Jordan −395/−1,296	Al 'Azīzīyah, Libya 58°/136°	Vostok −90°/−127°

All temperatures are rounded to the nearest degree.   * Elevations in feet are converted from metric equivalents and rounded.

Principal Mountains

Mountain	Country	Height M	Ft
Europe			
Elbrus, Mount	U.S.S.R.	5,642	18,510
Dyhtau	U.S.S.R.	5,203	17,070
Blanc, Mont	△France-△Italy	4,810	15,781
Rosa, Monte	Italy-△Switzerland	4,633	15,200
Matterhorn	Italy-Switzerland	4,478	14,692
Jungfrau	Switzerland	4,158	13,642
Grossglockner	△Austria	3,797	12,457
Teide, Pico de	△Spain (Canary Is.)	3,718	12,198
Mulhacén	Spain	3,478	11,411
Aneto, Pico de	Spain	3,404	11,168
Etna, Mount	Italy	3,340	10,958
Corno Grande	Italy	2,914	9,560
Gerlachovský štít	△Czechoslovakia	2,655	8,711
Glittertind	△Norway	2,470	8,104
Narodnaja, gora	U.S.S.R.	1,894	6,214
Nevis, Ben	△United Kingdom	1,343	4,406
Snowdon	United Kingdom	1,085	3,560
Asia			
Everest, Mount	△China-△Nepal	8,848	29,029
K2 (Godwin Austen)	China-△Pakistan	8,611	28,251
Kānchenjunga	△India-Nepal	8,598	28,207
Dhaulagiri	Nepal	8,172	26,811
Annapurna	Nepal	8,078	26,503
Muztag	China	7,723	25,338
Tirich Mīr	Pakistan	7,690	25,230
Communism Peak (pik Kommunizma)	△U.S.S.R.	7,495	24,590
Pobeda Peak (pik Pobedy)	China-U.S.S.R.	7,439	24,406
Demavend, Mount (Qolleh-ye Damāvand)	△Iran	5,670	18,602
Ararat, Mount (Büyük Ağrı Dağı)	△Turkey	5,165	16,946
Jaya, Puncak	△Indonesia	5,030	16,503
Klyuchevskaya Sopka (vulkan Ključevskaja Sopka)	U.S.S.R.	4,750	15,584
Kinabalu, Gunong	△Malaysia	4,101	13,455
Yu Shan	△Taiwan	3,997	13,114
Kerinci, Gunong	Indonesia	3,800	12,467
Fuji-San	△Japan	3,776	12,388
Nabī Shu'ayb, Jabal an	△Yemen	3,760	12,336
Sauda, Qurnet es	△Lebanon	3,083	10,115
Shām, Jabal ash	△Oman	3,017	9,898
Apo, Mount	△Philippines	2,954	9,692
Hermon, Mount	Lebanon-△Syria	2,814	9,232
Mayon, Mount	Philippines	2,462	8,077

Mountain	Country	Height M	Ft
Africa			
Kilimanjaro	△Tanzania	5,895	19,341
Kirinyaga (Mount Kenya)	△Kenya	5,199	17,057
Margherita Peak (Ruwenzori Range)	△Uganda-△Zaire	5,119	16,795
Ras Dashen	△Ethiopia	4,620	15,157
Toubkal, Jebel	△Morocco	4,167	13,671
Cameroun, Mont	△Cameroon	4,070	13,353
North America			
McKinley, Mount	△U.S.	6,194	20,320
Logan, Mount	△Canada	6,050	19,849
Orizaba, Pico de (Volcán Citlaltépetl)	△Mexico	5,700	18,701
Popocatépetl, Volcán	Mexico	5,452	17,887
Whitney, Mount	U.S.	4,418	14,494
Elbert, Mount	U.S.	4,399	14,433
Rainier, Mount	U.S.	4,392	14,410
Shasta, Mount	U.S.	4,317	14,162
Pikes Peak	U.S.	4,301	14,110
Tajumulco, Volcán	△Guatemala	4,220	13,845
Kea, Mauna	U.S.	4,205	13,796
Grand Teton	U.S.	4,197	13,770
Waddington, Mount	Canada	3,994	13,104
Chirripó, Cerro	△Costa Rica	3,820	12,533
Hood, Mount	U.S.	3,426	11,239
Duarte, Pico	△Dominican Republic	3,175	10,417
Mitchell, Mount	U.S.	2,037	6,684
Clingmans Dome	U.S.	2,025	6,643
Washington, Mount	U.S.	1,917	6,288
South America			
Aconcagua, Cerro	△Argentina	6,960	22,835
Ojos del Salado, Nevado	Argentina-△Chile	6,863	22,516
Huascarán, Nevado	△Peru	6,768	22,205
Chimborazo, Volcán	△Ecuador	6,267	20,561
Cristóbal Colón, Pico	△Colombia	5,800	19,029
Bolívar, Pico	△Venezuela	5,007	16,427
Neblina, Pico da	△Brazil	3,014	9,888
Oceania			
Wilhelm, Mount	△Papua New Guinea	4,509	14,793
Cook, Mount	△New Zealand	3,764	12,349
Kosciusko, Mount	△Australia	2,228	7,310
Antarctica			
Vinson Massif	△Antarctica	5,140	16,864
Jackson, Mount	Antarctica	4,191	13,750
△Highest mountain in country.			

Oceans, Seas, and Gulfs

Name	Area km²	Area sq mi	Greatest Depth m	Greatest Depth ft
Pacific Ocean	165,200,000	63,800,000	11,022	36,161
Atlantic Ocean	82,400,000	31,800,000	9,220	30,249
Indian Ocean	74,900,000	28,900,000	7,450	24,442
Arctic Ocean	14,000,000	5,400,000	5,450	17,881
Arabian Sea	3,863,000	1,492,000	5,800	19,029
South China Sea	3,447,000	1,331,000	5,560	18,241
Caribbean Sea	2,754,000	1,063,000	7,680	25,197
Mediterranean Sea	2,505,000	967,000	5,020	16,470
Bering Sea	2,270,000	876,000	4,191	13,750
Bengal, Bay of	2,172,000	839,000	5,258	17,251
Okhotsk, Sea of	1,580,000	610,000	3,372	11,063
Norwegian Sea	1,547,000	597,000	4,020	13,189
Mexico, Gulf of	1,544,000	596,000	4,380	14,370
Hudson Bay	1,230,000	475,000	259	850
Greenland Sea	1,205,000	465,000	4,846	15,899

Waterfalls

Waterfall	Country	River	Height m	Height ft
Angel	Venezuela	Churún	972	3,189
Tugela	South Africa	Tugela	948	3,110
Yosemite	United States	Yosemite Creek	739	2,425
Sutherland	New Zealand	Arthur	579	1,900
Gavarnie	France	Gave de Pau	421	1,381
Lofoi	Zaire	Lofoi	384	1,260
Krimml	Austria	Krimml	381	1,250
Takakkaw	Canada	Yoho	380	1,248
Staubbach	Switzerland	Staubbach	305	1,001
Mardalsfoss	Norway	. . .	297	974
Gersoppa	India	Sharavati	253	830
Kaieteur	Guyana	Potaro	247	810

Principal Rivers

River	Location	Length km	Length mi
Nile-Kagera	Africa	6,671	4,145
Yangtze (Chang Jiang)	China	6,300	3,915
Amazon-Ucayali	Brazil-Peru	6,280	3,902
Mississippi-Missouri-Red Rock	U.S.	6,019	3,741
Yellow (Huang He)	China	5,464	3,395
Ob-Irtysh	China-U.S.S.R.	5,410	3,362
Río de la Plata-Paraná	South America	4,700	2,920
Mekong	Asia	4,500	2,796
Paraná	South America	4,500	2,796
Amur	China-U.S.S.R.	4,416	2,744
Lena	U.S.S.R.	4,400	2,734
Mackenzie	Canada	4,241	2,635
Congo (Zaire)	Africa	4,200	2,610
Niger	Africa	4,160	2,585
Yenisey (Jenisej)	U.S.S.R.	4,092	2,543
Mississippi	U.S.	3,778	2,348
Missouri	U.S.	3,725	2,315
Ob	U.S.S.R.	3,680	2,287
Volga	U.S.S.R.	3,531	2,194
Murray-Darling	Australia	3,490	2,169
Madeira-Mamoré	Bolivia-Brazil	3,200	1,988
Purus	Brazil-Peru	3,200	1,988
Yukon	Canada-U.S.	3,185	1,979
Indus	Asia	3,180	1,976
Rio Grande	Mexico-U.S.	3,033	1,885
Syr Darya (Syrdarja)	U.S.S.R.	2,991	1,859
Brahmaputra	Asia	2,900	1,802
São Francisco	Brazil	2,900	1,802
Danube	Europe	2,860	1,777
Salween	Asia	2,849	1,770
Euphrates	Asia	2,760	1,715
Orinoco	Colombia-Venezuela	2,736	1,700
Darling	Australia	2,720	1,690
Ganges	Bangladesh-India	2,700	1,678
Saskatchewan	Canada	2,672	1,660
Zambezi	Africa	2,660	1,653
Tocantins	Brazil	2,640	1,640
Amu Darya (Amudarja)	Afghanistan-U.S.S.R.	2,600	1,616
Murray	Australia	2,589	1,609
Kolyma	U.S.S.R.	2,575	1,600
Paraguay	South America	2,549	1,584
Ural	U.S.S.R.	2,428	1,509
Arkansas	U.S.	2,333	1,450
Colorado	Mexico-U.S.	2,333	1,450
Irrawaddy	Burma	2,293	1,425
Dnepr	U.S.S.R.	2,201	1,368
Araguaia	Brazil	2,199	1,367
Kasai	Angola-Zaire	2,153	1,338
Tarim	China	2,137	1,328
Brazos	U.S.	2,106	1,309

Principal Islands

Island	Area km²	Area sq mi	Name	Highest Point m	Highest Point ft
Greenland (Grønland)	2,175,600	840,004	Gunnbjørns Fjeld	3,700	12,139
New Guinea	785,000	303,090	Puncak Jaya	5,030	16,503
Borneo	746,545	288,243	Gunong Kinabalu	4,101	13,455
Madagascar	587,041	226,658	Maromokotro	2,876	9,436
Baffin	476,065	183,810	unnamed	2,147	7,045
Sumatra (Sumatera)	473,606	182,860	Kerinci	3,800	12,467
Great Britain	227,581	87,870	Ben Nevis	1,343	4,406
Honshū	227,414	87,805	Fuji	3,776	12,388
Ellesmere	212,687	82,119	Barbeau Peak	2,604	8,543
Victoria	212,198	81,930	unnamed	655	2,150
Celebes (Sulawesi)	189,216	73,057	Rantekombola	3,455	11,335
South Island	150,461	58,093	Cook	3,764	12,349
Java (Jawa)	132,187	51,038	Semeru	3,676	12,060
North Island	114,728	44,297	Ruapehu	2,797	9,177
Cuba	114,524	44,218	Pico Turquino	1,994	6,542
Newfoundland	112,299	43,359	Lewis Hills	814	2,671
Luzon	104,687	40,420	Pulog	2,930	9,613
Iceland (Ísland)	103,000	39,769	Hvannadalshnúkur	2,119	6,952
Mindanao	94,630	36,537	Apo	2,954	9,692
Ireland	84,403	32,588	Carrantuohill	1,041	3,415
Hokkaidō	78,073	30,144	Daisetzu-Zan	2,290	7,513
Sakhalin (Sahalin)	76,400	29,498	Lopatina	1,609	5,279
Hispaniola	76,192	29,418	Pico Duarte	3,175	10,417
Banks	70,028	27,038	Durham	747	2,450
Tasmania	68,332	26,383	Ossa	1,617	5,305
Sri Lanka (Ceylon)	65,000	25,097	Pidurutalagala	2,524	8,281
Devon	55,247	21,331	Treuter	1,887	6,191
Novaya Zemlya (N. part)	48,904	18,882	unnamed	1,547	5,075
Tierra del Fuego	48,174	18,600	Yogan	2,469	8,100
Kyūshū	41,997	16,215	Kuju-San	1,787	5,863

Major Lakes

Lake	Country	Area km²	Area sq mi	Depth m	Depth ft
Caspian Sea	Iran-U.S.S.R	371,000	143,200	1,025	3,363
Superior	Canada-U.S.	82,414	31,820	406	1,333
Victoria	Africa	68,100	26,293	80	262
Aral Sea (Aral'skoje more)	U.S.S.R.	66,500	25,676	68	223
Huron	Canada-U.S.	59,596	23,010	229	750
Michigan	U.S.	58,016	22,400	281	923
Tanganyika	Africa	32,893	12,700	1,436	4,711
Baikal (ozero Bajkal)	U.S.S.R.	31,500	12,162	1,620	5,315
Great Bear	Canada	31,328	12,096	413	1,356
Nyasa	Africa	30,800	11,892	678	2,224
Great Slave	Canada	28,570	11,031	559	1,834
Erie	Canada-U.S.	25,745	9,940	64	210
Winnipeg	Canada	24,390	9,417	18	60
Ontario	Canada-U.S.	19,529	7,540	244	802
Ladoga (Ladožskoje ozero)	U.S.S.R.	18,400	7,104	225	738
Balkhash (ozero Balhaš)	U.S.S.R.	18,200	7,027	26	85
Chad (Lac Tchad)	Africa	16,300	6,293	4	13
Onega (Onežskoje ozero)	U.S.S.R.	9,610	3,710	120	393
Eyre	Australia	9,583	3,700	1	4
Rudolf	Ethiopia-Kenya	8,600	3,320	61	200
Nicaragua	Nicaragua	8,430	3,255	43	141
Titicaca	Bolivia-Peru	8,300	3,205	272	892
Athabasca	Canada	7,936	3,064	124	407
Gairdner	Australia	7,700	2,973	☆	☆
Reindeer	Canada	6,651	2,568	219	720
Issyk-Kul	U.S.S.R.	6,280	2,425	702	2,303
Urmia (Daryācheh-ye Orūmīyeh)	Iran	5,800	2,239	15	49
Torrens	Australia	5,776	2,230	☆	☆
Vänern	Sweden	5,585	2,156	100	328
Winnipegosis	Canada	5,374	2,075	12	38

☆Intermittently dry lake

Drainage Basins

Name	Continent	Area km²	Area sq mi
Amazon-Ucayali	South America	7,050,000	2,722,000
Congo (Zaire)	Africa	3,690,000	1,425,000
Mississippi-Missouri	North America	3,221,000	1,243,700
Río de la Plata-Paraná	South America	3,140,000	1,212,000
Ob	Asia	2,975,000	1,149,000
Nile	Africa	2,867,000	1,107,000
Yenisey (Jenisej)	Asia	2,580,000	996,000
Lena	Asia	2,490,000	961,000
Niger	Africa	2,092,000	808,000
Amur	Asia	1,855,000	716,000
Yangtze (Chang Jiang)	Asia	1,807,000	698,000
Mackenzie	North America	1,760,000	680,000
Saint Lawrence-Great Lakes	North America	1,463,000	565,000
Volga	Europe	1,360,000	525,000

World Geographical Tables

Historical Population of the World

AREA	1650	1750	1800	1850	1900	1914	1920	1939	1950	1982*
Europe	100,000,000	140,000,000	190,000,000	265,000,000	400,000,000	470,000,000	453,000,000	526,000,000	530,000,000	666,400,000
Asia	335,000,000	476,000,000	593,000,000	754,000,000	932,000,000	1,006,000,000	1,000,000,000	1,247,000,000	1,418,000,000	2,724,900,000
Africa	100,000,000	95,000,000	90,000,000	95,000,000	118,000,000	130,000,000	140,000,000	170,000,000	199,000,000	490,300,000
North America	5,000,000	5,000,000	13,000,000	39,000,000	106,000,000	141,000,000	147,000,000	186,000,000	219,000,000	379,400,000
South America	8,000,000	7,000,000	12,000,000	20,000,000	38,000,000	55,000,000	61,000,000	90,000,000	111,000,000	247,800,000
Oceania, incl. Australia	2,000,000	2,000,000	2,000,000	2,000,000	6,000,000	8,000,000	9,000,000	11,000,000	13,000,000	23,200,000
Australia					4,000,000	5,000,000	6,000,000	7,000,000	8,000,000	14,910,000
World	550,000,000	725,000,000	900,000,000	1,175,000,000	1,600,000,000	1,810,000,000	1,810,000,000	2,230,000,000	2,490,000,000	4,532,000,000

* Figures prior to 1982 are rounded to the nearest million. *Figures in italics represent very rough estimates.*

Largest Countries: Population

	Country	Population 1/1/82
1.	China	995,000,000
2.	India	695,230,000
3.	U.S.S.R	268,740,000
4.	United States	231,160,000
5.	Indonesia	151,500,000
6.	Brazil	124,760,000
7.	Japan	118,650,000
8.	Pakistan	92,070,000
9.	Bangladesh	91,860,000
10.	Nigeria	80,765,000
11.	Mexico	70,515,000
12.	Germany, Fed. Rep.	61,680,000
13.	Italy	57,270,000
14.	United Kingdom	56,035,000
15.	Vietnam	55,455,000
16.	France	54,045,000
17.	Philippines	50,960,000
18.	Thailand	48,860,000
19.	Turkey	46,435,000
20.	Egypt	43,565,000
21.	Korea, South	40,755,000
22.	Iran	38,565,000
23.	Spain	37,865,000
24.	Poland	36,035,000
25.	Burma	35,710,000
26.	South Africa	30,495,000
27.	Ethiopia	30,370,000
28.	Zaire	29,060,000
29.	Argentina	28,420,000
30.	Colombia	28,185,000
31.	Canada	24,335,000
32.	Yugoslavia	22,635,000
33.	Romania	22,445,000
34.	Morocco	21,795,000
35.	Sudan	20,180,000
36.	Algeria	19,270,000
37.	Tanzania	19,115,000
38.	Korea, North	18,540,000
39.	Peru	18,510,000
40.	Taiwan	18,365,000
41.	Kenya	17,790,000
42.	German Dem. Rep.	16,750,000
43.	Sri Lanka	15,605,000
44.	Nepal	15,520,000
45.	Czechoslovakia	15,345,000

Largest Countries: Area

	Country	km²	sq mi
1.	U.S.S.R	22,274,900	8,600,383
2.	Canada	9,922,330	3,831,033
3.	China	9,560,939	3,691,500
4.	United States	9,528,318	3,678,896
5.	Brazil	8,511,965	3,286,487
6.	Australia	7,686,850	2,967,909
7.	India	3,203,975	1,237,061
8.	Argentina	2,766,889	1,068,301
9.	Sudan	2,505,813	967,500
10.	Algeria	2,381,741	919,595
11.	Zaire	2,345,409	905,567
12.	Greenland	2,175,600	840,004
13.	Saudi Arabia	2,149,690	830,000
14.	Mexico	1,972,547	761,604
15.	Indonesia	1,919,270	741,034
16.	Libya	1,759,540	679,362
17.	Iran	1,648,000	636,296
18.	Mongolia	1,565,000	604,250
19.	Peru	1,285,216	496,224
20.	Chad	1,284,000	495,755
21.	Niger	1,267,000	489,191
22.	Angola	1,246,700	481,353
23.	Mali	1,240,000	478,766
24.	Ethiopia	1,223,600	472,434
25.	South Africa	1,221,042	471,447
26.	Colombia	1,138,914	439,737
27.	Bolivia	1,098,581	424,164
28.	Mauritania	1,030,700	397,955
29.	Egypt	1,001,400	386,643
30.	Tanzania	945,087	364,900
31.	Nigeria	923,768	356,669
32.	Venezuela	912,050	352,144
33.	Pakistan	828,453	319,867
34.	Mozambique	783,030	302,329
35.	Turkey	779,452	300,948
36.	Chile	756,626	292,135
37.	Zambia	752,614	290,586
38.	Burma	676,577	261,228
39.	Afghanistan	647,497	250,000
40.	Somalia	637,657	246,200
41.	Central African Republic	622,984	240,535
42.	Botswana	600,372	231,805
43.	Madagascar	587,041	226,658
44.	Kenya	582,646	224,961
45.	France	547,026	211,208

Smallest Countries: Population

	Country	Population 1/1/82
1.	Vatican City	1,000
2.	Niue	3,000
3.	Anguilla	7,900
	Nauru	7,900
4.	Tuvalu	8,100
5.	Cook Islands	18,000
6.	San Marino	24,000
7.	Liechtenstein	27,000
	Monaco	27,000
8.	Andorra	40,000
9.	St. Kitts-Nevis	41,000
10.	Faeroe Islands	45,000
11.	Greenland	51,000
12.	Kiribati	59,000
13.	Isle of Man	66,000
14.	Seychelles	68,000
15.	Dominica	75,000
16.	Antigua	77,000
17.	Sao Tome and Principe	89,000
18.	Tonga	101,000
19.	Grenada	112,000
20.	Vanuatu	120,000
21.	Djibouti	124,000
	Saint Lucia	124,000
22.	St. Vincent	128,000
23.	Maldives	155,000
	Western Samoa	155,000
24.	Belize	160,000
25.	Iceland	230,000
26.	Bahamas	235,000
	Qatar	235,000
	Solomon Is.	235,000
27.	Brunei	245,000
28.	Barbados	260,000
	Netherlands Antilles	260,000
29.	Cape Verde	330,000
30.	Luxembourg	355,000
31.	Malta	360,000
32.	Suriname	365,000
33.	Equatorial Guinea	375,000
34.	Comoros	380,000
35.	Bahrain	400,000
36.	Gabon	560,000
37.	Swaziland	580,000
38.	Gambia	625,000

Smallest Countries: Area

	Country	km²	sq mi
1.	Vatican City	0.4	0.2
2.	Monaco	1.5	0.6
3.	Nauru	21	8.2
4.	Tuvalu	26	10
5.	San Marino	61	24
6.	Anguilla	88	34
7.	Liechtenstein	160	62
8.	Cook Islands	236	91
9.	Niue	263	102
10.	St. Kitts-Nevis	269	104
11.	Maldives	298	115
12.	Malta	316	122
13.	Grenada	344	133
14.	St. Vincent	389	150
15.	Barbados	430	166
16.	Antigua	440	170
17.	Seychelles	443	171
18.	Andorra	453	175
19.	Singapore	581	224
20.	Isle of Man	588	227
21.	Saint Lucia	616	238
22.	Bahrain	662	256
23.	Tonga	699	270
24.	Dominica	752	290
25.	Kiribati	754	291
26.	Sao Tome and Principe	964	372
27.	Netherlands Antilles	993	383
28.	Faeroe Islands	1,399	540
29.	Mauritius	2,045	790
30.	Comoros	2,171	838
31.	Luxembourg	2,586	999
32.	Western Samoa	2,842	1,097
33.	Cape Verde	4,033	1,557
34.	Trinidad and Tobago	5,128	1,980
35.	Brunei	5,765	2,226
36.	Puerto Rico	8,897	3,435
37.	Cyprus	9,251	3,572
38.	Lebanon	10,400	4,015
39.	Jamaica	10,991	4,244
40.	Qatar	11,000	4,247
41.	Gambia	11,295	4,361
42.	Bahamas	13,939	5,382
43.	Vanuatu	14,800	5,714
44.	Swaziland	17,364	6,704
45.	Kuwait	17,818	6,880

Highest Population Densities

	Country	Density per km²	sq mi		Country	Density per km²	sq mi
1.	Monaco	18,000	45,000	16.	St. Vincent	329	853
2.	Singapore	4,923	12,768	17.	Grenada	326	842
3.	Vatican City	2,500	5,000	18.	Belgium	324	839
4.	Malta	1,139	2,951	19.	Japan	319	825
5.	Bangladesh	638	1,652	20.	Lebanon	315	816
6.	Barbados	605	1,566	21.	Tuvalu	312	810
7.	Bahrain	604	1,563	22.	Netherlands Antilles	262	679
8.	Maldives	520	1,348	23.	El Salvador	250	649
9.	Taiwan	510	1,322	24.	Germany, Fed. Rep. of	248	642
10.	Mauritius	482	1,247	25.	Sri Lanka	240	622
11.	Korea, South	414	1,072	26.	United Kingdom	230	595
12.	San Marino	393	1,000	27.	Trinidad and Tobago	227	588
13.	Nauru	376	963	28.	India	217	562
14.	Puerto Rico	368	952	29.	Jamaica	203	527
15.	Netherlands	347	900	30.	Saint Lucia	201	521

Lowest Population Densities

	Country	Density per km²	sq mi		Country	Density per km²	sq mi
1.	Greenland	0.02	0.06		Oman	4.4	11
2.	Mongolia	1.1	2.9	15.	Congo	4.7	12
3.	Botswana	1.5	3.8	16.	Bolivia	5.3	14
4.	Mauritania	1.7	4.3	17.	Djibouti	5.4	14
5.	Libya	1.8	4.6	18.	Mali	5.8	15
6.	Australia	1.9	5.0	19.	Angola	5.9	15
7.	Gabon	2.1	5.4	20.	Yemen, P.D.R. of	6.2	16
8.	Iceland	2.2	5.8	21.	Papua New Guinea	6.7	17
	Suriname	2.2	5.8	22.	Belize	7.0	18
9.	Canada	2.5	6.4	23.	Zambia	7.8	20
10.	Chad	3.6	9.4	24.	Paraguay	7.9	20
11.	Central African Republic	3.7	9.6		Solomon Islands	7.9	20
12.	Saudi Arabia	4.1	11	25.	Somalia	8.0	21
13.	Guyana	4.3	11	26.	Algeria	8.1	21
14.	Niger	4.4	11		Vanuatu	8.1	21

Major Metropolitan Areas of the World

This table lists the major metropolitan areas of the world according to their estimated population on January 1, 1982. For convenience in reference, the areas are grouped by major region, and the number of areas in each region and size group is given.

There are 29 areas with more than 5,000,000 population each; these are listed in rank order of estimated population, with the world rank given in parentheses following the name. For example, New York's 1982 rank is second. Below the 5,000,000 level, the metropolitan areas are listed alphabetically within region, not in order of size.

For ease of comparison, each metropolitan area has been defined by Rand McNally & Company according to consistent rules. A metropolitan area includes a central city, surrounding communities linked to it by continuous built-up areas and more distant communities if the bulk of their population is supported by commuters to the central city. Some metropolitan areas have more than one central city, for example Tōkyō–Yokohama or San Francisco–Oakland–San Jose.

POPULATION CLASSIFICATION	UNITED STATES and CANADA	LATIN AMERICA	EUROPE (excl. U.S.S.R.)	U.S.S.R	ASIA	AFRICA-OCEANIA
Over 15,000,000 (4)	New York, U.S. (2)	Mexico City, Mex. (3)			Tōkyō-Yokohama, Jap. (1) Ōsaka-Kōbe-Kyōto, Jap. (4)	
10,000,000–15,000,000 (8)	Los Angeles, U.S. (12)	São Paulo, Braz. (5) Buenos Aires, Arg. (9)	London, U.K. (10)	Moscow (6)	Seoul, Kor. (7) Calcutta, India (8) Bombay, India (11)	
5,000,000–10,000,000 (17)	Chicago, U.S. (16) Philadelphia–Trenton– Wilmington, U.S. (26)	Rio de Janeiro, Braz. (15)	Paris, Fr. (13) Essen–Dortmund– Duisburg (The Ruhr), Ger., Fed. Rep. of (27) İstanbul, Tur. (29)	Leningrad (23)	Shanghai, China, (17) Delhi–New Delhi, India (18) Manila, Phil. (19) Jakarta, Indon. (20) Peking (Beijing), China (21), Tehrān, Iran (22) Bangkok, Thai. (24) Karāchi, Pak. (25) Tientsin (Tianjin), China (28)	Cairo, Eg. (14)
3,000,000–5,000,000 (32)	Boston, U.S. Detroit, U.S.– Windsor, Can. Montréal, Can. San Francisco– Oakland– San Jose, U.S. Toronto, Can. Washington, U.S.	Bogotá, Col. Caracas, Ven. Lima, Peru Santiago, Chile	Athens, Greece Barcelona, Sp. Berlin, Ger. Madrid, Sp. Milan, It. Rome, It.		Baghdād, Iraq Bangalore, India Chungking (Chongqing), China Dacca, Bngl. Lahore, Pak. Madras, India Mukden (Shenyang), China Nagoya, Jap. Pusan, Kor. Rangoon, Bur. Taipei, Taiwan Victoria, Hong Kong Wuhan, China	Alexandria, Eg. Johannesburg, S. Afr. Sydney, Austl.
2,000,000–3,000,000 (46)	Atlanta, U.S. Cleveland, U.S. Dallas– Fort Worth, U.S. Houston, U.S. Miami–Fort Lauderdale, U.S. Minneapolis–St. Paul, U.S. Pittsburgh, U.S. St. Louis, U.S. San Diego, U.S.– Tijuana, Mex. Seattle– Tacoma, U.S.	Belo Horizonte, Braz. Guadalajara, Mex. Havana, Cuba Medellín, Col. Monterrey, Mex. Porto Alegre, Braz. Recife, Braz.	Birmingham, U.K. Brussels, Bel. Bucharest, Rom. Budapest, Hung. Hamburg, Ger., Fed. Rep. of Katowice–Bytom– Gliwice, Pol. Lisbon, Port. Manchester, U.K. Naples, It. Warsaw, Pol.	Donetsk–Makeyevka Kiev Tashkent	Ahmadābād, India Ankara, Tur. Canton (Guangzhou), China Chengtu (Chendu), China Hanoi, Viet. Harbin, China Ho Chi Minh City (Saigon), Viet. Hyderābād, India Sian (Xi'an) China Singapore, Singapore Surabaya, Indon.	Algiers, Alg. Casablanca, Mor. Kinshasa, Zaire Lagos, Nig. Melbourne, Austl.
1,500,000–2,000,000 (37)	Baltimore, U.S. Phoenix, U.S.	Fortaleza, Braz. Salvador, Braz. San Juan, P.R.	Amsterdam, Neth. Cologne, Ger., Fed. Rep. of Copenhagen, Den. Frankfurt am Main, Ger., Fed. Rep. of Glasgow, U.K. Leeds–Bradford, U.K. Liverpool, U.K. Munich, Ger., Fed. Rep. of Stuttgart, Ger., Fed. Rep. of Turin, It. Vienna, Aus.	Baku Dnepropetrovsk Gorki Kharkov Novosibirsk	Bandung, Indon. Chittagong, Bngl. Colombo, Sri Lanka Damascus, Syria Fukuoka, Jap. Hiroshima–Kure, Jap. Kānpur, India Kaohsiung, Taiwan Kitakyūshū– Shimonoseki, Jap. Medan, Indon. Nanking (Nanjing), China Pune, India Sapporo, Jap. Taegu, Kor.	Cape Town, S. Afr. Durban, S. Afr.
1,000,000–1,500,000 (90)	Buffalo–Niagara Falls, U.S.–St. Catharines– Niagara Falls, Can. Cincinnati, U.S. Denver, U.S. El Paso, U.S.–Ciudad Juárez, Mex. Hartford–New Britain, U.S. Indianapolis, U.S. Kansas City, U.S. Milwaukee, U.S. New Orleans, U.S. Portland, U.S. San Antonio, U.S. Vancouver, Can.	Barranquilla, Col. Belém, Braz. Brasília, Braz. Cali, Col. Córdoba, Arg. Curitiba, Braz. Guatemala, Guat. Guayaquil, Ec. Montevideo, Ur. Rosario, Arg. Santo Domingo, Dom. Rep.	Antwerp, Bel. Belgrade, Yugo. Bilbao, Sp. Dublin, Ire. Düsseldorf, Ger., Fed. Rep. of Hannover, Ger., Fed. Rep. of Lille, Fr. Łódź, Pol. Lyon, Fr. Mannheim, Ger., Fed. Rep. of Marseille, Fr. Newcastle– Sunderland, U.K. Nürnberg, Ger., Fed. Rep. of Porto, Port. Prague, Czech. Rotterdam, Neth. Sofia, Bul. Stockholm, Swe. Valencia, Sp.	Alma-Ata Chelyabinsk Kazan Kuybyshev Minsk Odessa Omsk Perm Rostov-na-Donu Saratov Sverdlovsk Tbilisi Ufa Volgograd Yerevan	Anshan, China Asansol, India Beirut, Leb. Changchun, China Chengchou (Zhengzhou), China Faisalabad (Lyallpur), Pak. Fushun, China İzmir, Tur. Jaipur, India Kābul, Afg. Kuala Lumpur, Mala. Kunming, China Kuwait, Kuw. Lanchou (Lanzhou), China Lucknow, India Lüta (Dairen), China Nāgpur, India Patna, India P'yŏngyang, Kor. Rāwalpindi– Islāmābād, Pak. Riyadh, Sau. Ar. Semarang, Indon. Shihchiachuang (Shijiazhuang), China Surat, India Taiyuan, China Tel Aviv-Yafo, Isr. Tsinan (Jinan), China Tsingtao (Qingdao), China	Abidjan, I.C. Addis Ababa, Eth. Brisbane, Austl. Khartoum, Sud. Tunis, Tun.
Total by Region (234)	34	29	50	25	80	16

Populations of Major Cities

The largest and most important of the world's major cities are listed in the following table. Also included are some smaller cities because of their regional significance.

Local official name forms have been used throughout the table. When a commonly used "conventional" name form exists, it has been featured, with the official name following, within parentheses. Former names are identified by italics. Each city name is followed by the English name of its country. Whenever two well-known cities of the same name are in the same country, the state or province name has been added for identification.

Many cities have population figures within parentheses following

the country name. These are metropolitan populations, comprising the central city and its suburbs. When a city is within the metropolitan area of another city the name of the metropolitan central city is specified in parentheses preceded by an (*). The symbol (†) identifies a political district population which includes some rural population. For these cities the estimated city population has been based upon the district figure.

The population of each city has been dated for ease of comparison. The date is followed by a letter designating: Census (C); Official Estimate (E); and in a few instances Unofficial Estimates (UE).

City and Country	Population	Date
Aachen, Fed. Rep. of Ger. (540,000)	242,971	79E
Abidjan, Ivory Coast	1,100,000	78E
Acapulco [de Juárez], Mexico	421,000	78E
Accra, Ghana (738,498)	633,880	70C
Adelaide, Australia (933,300)	13,400	79E
Aden (Baladīyat 'Adan), People's Dem. Rep. of Yemen	271,600	77E
Addis Ababa (Ādīs Ābeba), Ethiopia	1,125,340	78E
Āgra, India (770,352)	723,676	81C
Ahmadābād, India (2,400,000)	2,024,917	81C
Aleppo (Halab), Syria	878,000	78E
Alexandria (Al Iskandarīyah); Egypt (2,850,000)	2,409,000	78E
Algiers (Al Jazā'ir), Algeria (1,800,000)	1,503,720	74E
Allahābād, India (642,420)	609,232	81C
Alma-Ata, U.S.S.R. (970,000)	928,000	80E
'Ammān, Jordan	648,587	79E
Amritsar, India	589,227	81C
Amsterdam, Netherlands (1,810,000)	716,919	80E
Ankara, Turkey (2,290,000)	2,203,729	80C
Anshan, China	1,050,000	75UE
Antananarivo, Madagascar	484,000	77E
Antwerp, (Antwerpen, Anvers), Belgium (1,105,000)	194,073	80E
Asansol, India (1,050,000)	187,039	81C
Asunción, Paraguay (655,000)	463,700	78E
Athens (Athinai), Greece (2,540,241)	867,023	71C
Atlanta, U.S. (1,950,600)	425,022	80C
Auckland, New Zealand (775,000)	147,600	79E
Augsburg, Fed. Rep. of Ger. (390,000)	245,940	79E
Austin, U.S. (422,700)	345,496	80C
Baghdād, Iraq (2,183,800)	1,300,000	70E
Baku, U.S.S.R. (1,800,000)	1,030,000	80E
Baltimore, U.S. (1,883,100)	786,775	80C
Bamako, Mali	404,022	76C
Bandung, Indonesia (1,525,000)	1,462,637	80C
Bangalore, India (2,950,000)	2,482,507	81C
Bangkok (Krung Thep), Thailand (3,375,000)	3,133,834	72E
Barcelona, Spain (3,975,000)	1,902,713	78E
Barranquilla, Colombia (950,000)	859,000	73C
Basel, Switzerland (580,000)	182,143	80C
Basra, Iraq (Al Baṣrah), Iraq	370,900	70C
Beirut (Bayrūt), Lebanon (1,010,000)	474,870	70E
Belém, Brazil (660,000)	565,097	70C
Belfast, U.K. (710,000)	354,400	78E
Belgrade (Beograd), Yugoslavia (1,150,000)	770,140	71C
Belo Horizonte, Brazil (2,450,000)	1,814,990	80C
Berlin, East (Ost), Ger. Dem. Rep. (*Berlin)	1,128,983	78E
Berlin, West, Fed. Rep. of Ger. (3,775,000)	1,902,250	79E
Bern, Switzerland (286,903)	145,254	80C
Bhopāl, India	672,329	81C
Bielefeld, Fed. Rep. of Ger. (525,000)	312,357	79E
Bilbao, Spain (995,000)	452,921	78E
Birmingham, U.K. (2,660,000)	1,033,900	79E
Birmingham, U.S. (697,900)	284,413	80C
Bogotá, Colombia (4,150,000)	4,067,000	79E
Bologna, Italy (550,000)	471,554	79E
Bombay, India (9,950,000)	8,227,332	81C
Bonn, Fed. Rep. of Ger. (555,000)	286,184	79E
Bordeaux, France (612,456)	223,131	75C
Boston, U.S. (3,738,800)	562,994	80C
Brasília, Brazil	1,202,683	80C
Brazzaville, Congo	175,000	70C
Bremen, Fed. Rep. of Ger. (800,000)	556,128	79E
Bremerhaven, Fed. Rep. of Ger. (190,000)	138,987	79E
Brisbane, Australia (1,014,700)	702,000	79E
Bristol, U.K. (635,000)	408,000	79E

City and Country	Population	Date
Brussels (Bruxelles, Brussel), Belgium (2,400,000)	143,957	80C
Bucharest (Bucureşti), Romania (2,050,000)	1,858,418	78E
Budapest, Hungary (2,600,000)	2,060,000	80C
Buenos Aires, Argentina (10,700,000)	2,908,001	80C
Buffalo, U.S. (1,154,600)	357,870	80C
Bursa, Turkey	466,178	80C
Cairo (Al Qāhirah), Egypt (8,500,000)	5,278,000	78E
Calcutta, India (11,100,000)	3,291,655	81C
Cali, Colombia (1,340,000)	1,293,000	79E
Canberra, Australia (241,500)	221,000	79E
Canton (Guangzhou), China	2,500,000	75UE
Cape Town (Kaapstad), South Africa (1,125,000)	697,514	70C
Caracas, Venezuela (2,475,000)	1,658,500	71C
Cardiff, U.K. (625,000)	282,000	79E
Casablanca (Dar-el-Beida), Morocco (1,575,000)	1,506,373	71C
Catania, Italy (515,000)	398,426	79E
Cebu, Philippines (500,000)	413,025	75C
Changchun, China	1,300,000	75UE
Changsha, China	840,000	75UE
Charleroi, Belgium (495,000)	221,911	80E
Chelyabinsk (Čeljabinsk), U.S.S.R. (1,215,000)	1,042,000	80E
Chengchou (Zhengzhou), China	1,100,000	75UE
Chengtu, (Chendu), China	1,800,000	75UE
Chicago, U.S. (7,803,800)	3,005,072	80C
Chittagong, Bangladesh (1,388,476)	980,000	81C
Chungking (Chongqing), China	2,900,000	75UE
Cincinnati, U.S. (1,476,600)	385,457	80C
Ciudad Juárez, Mexico (*El Paso, U.S.)	597,100	78E
Cleveland, U.S. (2,218,300)	573,822	80C
Cochin, India (552,408)	513,081	81C
Coimbatore, India (965,000)	700,923	81C
Cologne, (Köln), Fed. Rep. of Ger. (1,815,000)	976,136	79E
Colombo, Sri Lanka (1,540,000)	616,000	77E
Columbus, Ohio, U.S. (943,300)	564,871	80C
Copenhagen (København), Denmark (1,470,000)	498,850	80E
Córdoba, Argentina (1,070,000)	1,052,147	80C
Coventry, U.K. (655,000)	339,300	79E
Curitiba, Brazil (1,300,000)	1,052,147	80C
Dacca, Bangladesh (3,458,602)	1,850,000	81C
Dakar, Senegal	798,792	76C
Dallas, U.S. (2,811,800)	904,078	80C
Damascus (Dimashq), Syria (1,550,000)	1,156,000	79E
Dar es Salaam, Tanzania	870,000	78C
Dayton, U.S. (898,000)	203,588	80C
Delhi, India (7,200,000)	4,865,077	81C
Denver, U.S. (1,414,200)	491,396	80C
Detroit, U.S. (4,399,000)	1,203,339	80C
Dnepropetrovsk, U.S.S.R. (1,460,000)	1,083,000	80E
Donetsk (Doneck), U.S.S.R. (2,075,000)	1,032,000	80E
Dortmund, Fed. Rep. of Ger. (*Essen)	609,954	79E
Douala, Cameroon	458,246	76C
Dresden, Ger. Dem. Rep. (640,000)	514,508	78E
Dublin (Baile Atha Cliath), Ireland (1,110,000)	544,586	79C
Duisburg, Fed. Rep. of Ger. (*Essen)	559,066	79E
Durban, South Africa (1,040,000)	736,852	70C
Düsseldorf, Fed. Rep. of Ger. (1,225,000)	594,770	79E
Edinburgh, U.K. (635,000)	455,126	79E
Edmonton, Canada (554,228)	461,361	76C
El Paso, U.S. (1,122,300)	425,259	80C
Essen, Fed. Rep. of Ger. (5,125,000)	652,501	79E

City and Country	Population	Date
Faisalabad, (Lyallpur), Pakistan	823,343	72C
Florence (Firenze), Italy (660,000)	462,690	79E
Fortaleza, Brazil (1,490,000)	1,338,733	80C
Frankfurt am Main, Fed. Rep. of Ger. (1,880,000)	628,203	79E
Freetown, Sierra Leone (335,000)	274,000	74C
Frunze, U.S.S.R.	543,000	80E
Fukuoka, Japan (1,575,000)	1,088,617	80C
Fushun, China	1,150,000	75UE
Gdańsk (Danzig), Poland (820,000)	449,200	79E
Geneva (Genève), Switzerland (435,000)	156,505	80C
Genoa (Genova), Italy (855,000)	782,476	79E
Gent, Belgium (470,000)	241,695	80E
Giza (Al Jizah), Egypt (*Cairo)	1,246,713	76C
Glasgow, U.K. (1,830,000)	794,316	79E
Gorki, U.S.S.R. (1,900,000)	1,358,000	80E
Göteborg, Sweden (665,000)	434,699	79E
Graz, Austria (275,000)	250,900	76E
Guadalajara, Mexico (2,350,000)	1,813,100	78E
Guatemala, Guatemala (945,000)	717,322	73C
Guayaquil, Ecuador	1,022,010	78E
Haifa (Hefa), Israel (415,000)	229,300	79E
Hamburg, Fed. Rep. of Ger. (2,260,000)	1,653,043	79E
Hangchou (Hangzhou), China	900,000	75UE
Hannover, Fed. Rep. of Ger. (1,005,000)	535,854	79E
Hanoi, Vietnam	1,600,000	71E
Harare (Salisbury), Zimbabwe (633,000)	118,500	79E
Harbin, China	2,400,000	75UE
Hartford, U.S. (1,055,700)	136,392	80C
Havana (La Habana), Cuba (2,000,000)	1,961,674	76E
Helsinki, Finland (885,000)	484,879	78E
Hiroshima, Japan (1,525,000)	899,394	80C
Ho Chi Minh City (Saigon), Vietnam (2,750,000)	1,804,900	71E
Honolulu, U.S. (762,900)	324,871	80C
Houston, U.S. (2,689,200)	1,594,086	80C
Hyderābād, India (2,750,000)	2,142,087	81C
Hyderābād, Pakistan (660,000)	600,796	72C
Ibadan, Nigeria	847,000	75C
Inch'ŏn, South Korea (*Seoul)	1,084,730	80C
Indianapolis, U.S. (1,104,200)	700,807	80C
Innsbruck, Austria (150,000)	120,400	76E
Irkutsk, U.S.S.R.	561,000	80E
İstanbul, Turkey (4,765,000)	2,853,539	80C
İzmir, Turkey (1,190,000)	753,749	80C
Jacksonville, Florida, U.S. (615,300)	540,898	80C
Jaipur, India (1,025,000)	966,677	81C
Jakarta, Indonesia (6,700,000)	6,503,449	80C
Jerusalem (Yerushalayim), Israel (420,000)	398,200	79E
Jiddah, Saudi Arabia	561,104	74C
Johannesburg, South Africa (2,550,000)	654,232	70C
Kābul, Afghanistan	749,000	75E
Kananga, Zaire	601,000	74C
Kano, Nigeria	399,000	75E
Kānpur, India (1,875,000)	1,531,345	81C
Kansas City, Missouri, U.S. (1,254,600)	448,159	80C
Kaohsiung, Taiwan (1,480,000)	1,172,977	77E
Karāchi, Pakistan (4,500,000)	2,800,000	75E
Karaganda, U.S.S.R.	577,000	80E
Kathmandu, Nepal (215,000)	150,402	71C
Katowice, Poland (2,590,000)	351,300	79E
Kawasaki, Japan (*Tōkyō)	1,040,698	80C
Kazan', U.S.S.R. (*1,050,000)	1,002,000	80E
Khabarovsk (Habarovsk), U.S.S.R.	538,000	80E
Khar'kov (Harkov), U.S.S.R. (1,750,000)	1,464,000	80E

A • 12

City and Country	Population	Date
Khartoum (Al Kharṭūm), Sudan (790,000)	333,921	73C
Kiel, Fed. Rep. of Ger. (335,000)	250,750	79E
Kiev, (Kijev), U.S.S.R. (2,430,000)	2,192,000	80E
Kingston, Jamaica	665,050	78E
Kinshasa, Zaire	2,202,000	75E
Kishinev (Kišinev), U.S.S.R.	519,000	80E
Kitakyūshū, Japan (1,515,000)	1,065,084	80C
Kōbe, Japan (*Ōsaka)	1,367,392	80C
Kowloon, Hong Kong (*Victoria)	749,600	76C
Kraków, Poland (708,000)	706,100	79E
Krasnoyarsk (Krasnojarsk), U.S.S.R.	807,000	80E
Kuala Lumpur, Malaysia (750,000)	451,728	70C
Kueiyang (Guiyang), China	800,000	75UE
Kunming, China	1,225,000	75UE
Kuwait (Al Kuwayt), Kuwait (780,000)	78,116	75C
Kuybyshev (Kujbyšev), U.S.S.R. (1,440,000)	1,226,000	80E
Kwangju, South Korea	727,627	80C
Kyōto, Japan (*Ōsaka)	1,472,993	80C
Lagos, Nigeria (1,450,000)	1,060,800	75E
Lahore, Pakistan (2,200,000)	2,022,577	72C
Lanchou (Lanzhou), China	950,000	75UE
La Paz, Bolivia	654,713	76C
Leeds, U.K. (1,540,000)	724,300	79E
Leipzig, Ger. Dem. Rep. (710,000)	563,980	78E
Leningrad, U.S.S.R. (5,360,000)	4,119,000	80E
León, Mexico	590,000	78E
Liège, Belgium (765,000)	220,183	80E
Lille, France (1,015,000)	172,280	75C
Lima, Peru (3,350,000)	340,339	72C
Linz, Austria (290,000)	208,000)	76E
Lisbon, (Lisboa), Portugal (1,950,000)	829,900	75E
Liverpool, U.K. (1,535,000)	520,200	79E
Łódź, Poland (1,025,000)	830,800	79E
Lomas de Zamora, Argentina (*Buenos Aires)	508,620	80C
London, U.K. (11,050,000)	6,877,100	79E
Los Angeles, U.S. (9,840,200)	2,966,763	80C
Louisville, U.S. (881,100)	298,451	80C
Luanda, Angola	475,328	70C
Lubumbashi, Zaire	404,000	74E
Lucknow, India (1,060,000)	895,947	81C
Ludhiāna, India	606,250	81C
Lusaka, Zambia	641,000	80E
Lüta *(Dairen)*, China (1,700,000†)	1,100,000	75UE
Lvov, U.S.S.R.	676,000	80E
Lyon, France (1,170,660)	456,716	75C
Madras, India (4,475,000)	3,266,034	81C
Madrid, Spain (4,415,000)	3,367,438	78E
Madurai, India (960,000)	817,562	80C
Managua, Nicaragua	552,900	78E
Manchester, U.K. (2,800,000)	479,100	79E
Mandalay, Burma	458,000	77E
Manila, Philippines (5,500,000)	1,479,116	75C
Mannheim, Fed. Rep. of Ger. (1,395,000)	303,247	79E
Maputo *(Lourenço Marques)*, Mozambique	341,922	70C
Maracaibo, Venezuela	651,574	71C
Marseille, France (1,070,912)	908,600	75C
Mecca (Makkah), Saudi Arabia	366,801	74C
Medan, Indonesia (1,450,000)	1,378,955	80C
Medellín, Colombia (2,025,000)	1,477,000	79E
Melbourne, Australia (2,739,700)	65,800	79E
Memphis, U.S. (843,200)	646,356	80C
Mexico City (Ciudad de México), Mexico (14,400,000)	8,988,200	78E
Miami, U.S. (2,689,100)	346,931	80C
Milan (Milano), Italy (3,800,000)	1,677,109	79E
Milwaukee, U.S. (1,358,600)	636,212	80C
Minneapolis, U.S. (1,978,000)	370,951	80C
Minsk, U.S.S.R. (1,330,000)	1,295,000	80E
Mombasa, Kenya	342,000	79C
Monrovia, Liberia	204,210	74C
Monterrey, Mexico (1,925,000)	1,054,000	78E
Montevideo, Uruguay (1,350,000)	1,229,748	75C
Montréal, Canada (2,802,485)	1,080,546	76C
Morón, Argentina (*Buenos Aires)	596,769	80C
Moscow (Moskva), U.S.S.R. (11,950,000)	7,915,000	80E
Mukden (Shenyang), China	3,300,000	75UE
Multān, Pakistan (538,000)	504,365	72C
Munich (München), Fed. Rep. of Ger. (1,940,000)	1,299,693	79E
Mysore, India (476,446)	439,185	80C
Nagoya, Japan (3,700,000)	2,087,884	80C
Nāgpur, India (1,325,000)	1,215,425	81C
Nairobi, Kenya	835,000	79C
Nanking (Nanjing), China	1,800,000	75UE
Nantes, France (453,500)	256,693	75C
Naples (Napoli), Italy (2,740,000)	1,223,228	79E
Nashville, U.S. (608,400)	455,651	80C
Newcastle upon Tyne, U.K. (1,295,000)	287,300	79E
New Delhi, India (*Delhi)	271,990	81C
New Kowloon, Hong Kong (*Victoria)	1,628,880	76C
New Orleans, U.S. (1,175,800)	557,482	80C
New York, U.S. (16,573,600)	7,071,030	80C
Niamey, Niger	225,300	77E
Norfolk, U.S. (795,600)	219,214	80C
Nottingham, U.K. (645,000)	278,600	79E
Novokuznetsk (Novokuzneck), U.S.S.R.	545,000	80E
Novosibirsk, U.S.S.R. (1,460,000)	1,328,000	80E
Nürnberg, Fed. Rep. of Ger. (1,025,000)	484,184	79E
Odessa, U.S.S.R. (1,120,000)	1,057,000	80E
Okayama, Japan	545,737	80C
Oklahoma City, U.S. (742,000)	403,213	80C
Omaha, U.S. (548,400)	311,681	80C
Omsk, U.S.S.R. (1,040,000)	1,028,000	80E
Orlando, U.S. (568,300)	128,394	80C
Ōsaka, Japan (15,200,000)	2,648,158	80C
Oslo, Norway (725,000)	454,819	80E
Ostrava, Czechoslovakia (745,000)	325,473	79E
Ottawa, Canada (693,288)	304,462	76C
Palermo, Italy	693,949	79E
Panamá, Panama (645,000)	439,800	78E
Paris, France (9,450,000)	2,050,500	80E
Patna, India (1,025,000)	773,720	81C
Peking (Beijing), China (8,500,000†)	5,700,000	78E
Perm, U.S.S.R. (1,075,000)	1,008,000	80E
Perth, Australia (883,600)	88,850	79E
Philadelphia, U.S. (5,153,400)	1,688,210	80C
Phnom Penh (Phnum Pénh), Kampuchea	393,995	62C
Phoenix, U.S. (1,483,500)	764,911	80C
Pittsburgh, U.S. (2,165,100)	423,938	80C
Port-au-Prince, Haiti (800,000)	745,700	78E
Portland, Oregon, U.S. (1,220,000)	366,383	80C
Porto, Portugal (1,150,000)	335,700	75E
Porto Alegre, Brazil (2,225,000)	1,158,709	80C
Portsmouth, U.K. (490,000)	191,000	79E
Poznan', Poland (610,000)	545,600	79E
Prague (Praha), Czechoslovakia (1,275,000)	1,193,345	79E
Pretoria, South Africa (575,000)	545,450	70C
Providence, U.S. (897,000)	156,804	80C
Puebla [de Zaragoza], Mexico	678,000	78E
Pune, India (1,775,000)	1,202,848	81C
Pusan, South Korea	3,160,276	80C
P'yŏngyang, North Korea	840,000	67E
Québec, Canada (542,158)	177,082	76C
Quezon City, Philippines (*Manila)	956,864	75C
Quito, Ecuador	742,858	78E
Rabat, Morocco (540,000)	367,620	71C
Rangoon, Burma (3,000,000)	2,276,000	77E
Rāwalpindi, Pakistan (725,000)	372,919	72C
Recife *(Pernambuco)*, Brazil (2,300,000)	1,240,897	80C
Richmond, Virginia, U.S. (548,100)	219,214	80C
Rīga, U.S.S.R. (920,000)	843,000	80E
Rio de Janeiro, Brazil (8,975,000)	5,184,292	80C
Riyadh (Ar Riyāḍ), Saudi Arabia	666,840	74C
Rochester, New York, U.S. (809,500)	241,741	80C
Rome (Roma), Italy (3,195,000)	2,911,671	79E
Rosario, Argentina (1,045,000)	935,471	80C
Rostov-na-Donu, U.S.S.R. (1,075,000)	946,000	80E
Rotterdam, Netherlands (1,085,000)	579,194	80E
Saarbrücken, Fed. Rep. of Ger. (390,000)	194,452	79E
Sacramento, U.S. (848,800)	275,741	80C
St. Louis, U.S. (2,216,100)	453,085	80C
St. Paul, U.S. (*Minneapolis)	270,230	80C
St. Petersburg, U.S. (699,800)	236,893	80C
Sakai, Japan (*Ōsaka)	810,120	80C
Salt Lake City, U.S. (686,200)	163,033	80C
Salvador, Brazil (1,725,000)	1,525,831	80C
Samarkand, U.S.S.R.	481,000	80E
San Antonio, U.S. (1,012,300)	785,410	80C
San Bernardino, U.S. (715,300)	118,057	80C
San Diego, U.S. (1,597,000)	875,504	80C
San Francisco, U.S. (4,665,500)	678,974	80C
San José, Costa Rica (519,400)	239,800	78E
San Juan, Puerto Rico (1,535,000)	422,701	80C
San Justo, Argentina (*Buenos Aires)	946,715	80C
San Salvador, El Salvador (720,000)	397,100	77E
Santiago, Chile (2,925,000)	517,473	70C
Santo Domingo, Dominican Rep.	979,608	76E
Santos, Brazil (610,000)	341,317	70C
São Paulo, Brazil (12,525,000)	8,584,896	80C
Sapporo, Japan (1,450,000)	1,401,758	80C
Saragossa (Zaragoza), Spain	563,375	78E
Saratov, U.S.S.R. (1,090,000)	864,000	80E
Seattle, U.S. (2,077,100)	493,846	80C
Semarang, Indonesia (1,050,000)	1,026,671	80C
Sendai, Japan (925,000)	664,799	80C
Seoul (Sŏul), South Korea (11,200,000)	8,366,756	80C
Sevilla, Spain (740,000)	630,329	78E
Shanghai, China (10,980,000†)	8,100,000	78E
Sheffield, U.K. (705,000)	544,200	79E
Shihchiachuang (Shijiazhuang), China	940,000	75UE
Sian (Xi'an), China	1,900,000	75UE
Singapore (Singapura), Singapore (2,600,000)	2,390,800	80E
Sofia (Sofija), Bulgaria (1,133,733)	1,047,920	79E
Southampton, U.K. (410,000)	207,800	79E
Stockholm, Sweden (1,384,310)	649,384	79E
Stuttgart, Fed. Rep. of Ger. (1,935,000)	581,989	79E
Suchow (Xuzhou), China	800,000	75UE
Suez (As Suways), Egypt	204,000	78E
Surabaya, Indonesia (2,150,000)	2,027,913	80C
Surat, India (960,000)	775,711	81C
Sverdlovsk, U.S.S.R. (1,450,000)	1,225,000	80E
Sydney, Australia (3,193,300)	49,750	79E
Taegu, South Korea	1,607,458	80C
Taichung, Taiwan	585,205	77E
Tainan, Taiwan	572,590	77E
Taipei, Taiwan (3,825,000)	2,196,237	77E
Taiyuan, China	1,350,000	75UE
Tallinn, U.S.S.R.	436,000	80E
Tampa, U.S. (573,100)	271,523	80C
Tashkent (Taškent), U.S.S.R. (2,015,000)	1,816,000	80E
Tbilisi, U.S.S.R. (1,240,000)	1,080,000	80E
Tegucigalpa, Honduras	316,800	77E
Tehrān, Iran (4,700,000)	4,496,159	76C
Tel Aviv-Yafo, Israel (1,350,000)	336,300	79E
The Hague ('s-Gravenhage), Netherlands (775,000)	456,886	80E
Thessaloníki *(Salonika)*, Greece (557,360)	345,799	71C
Tientsin (Tianjin), China (7,210,000†)	4,650,000	78E
Tirana, Albania	192,300	76E
Tōkyō, Japan (25,800,000)	8,349,209	80C
Toledo, U.S. (571,200)	354,635	80C
Toronto, Canada (2,803,101)	633,318	76C
Tripoli (Tarābulus), Libya	264,000	70E
Tsinan (Jinan), China	1,125,000	75UE
Tsingtao (Qingdao), China	1,200,000	75UE
Tsitsihar (Qiqihar), China	850,000	75UE
Tucson, U.S. (495,200)	330,537	80C
Tula, U.S.S.R. (615,000)	518,000	80E
Tulsa, U.S. (569,100)	360,919	80C
Tūnis, Tunisia (915,000)	550,404	75C
Turin (Torino), Italy (1,670,000)	1,160,686	79E
Ufa, U.S.S.R. (1,000,000)	986,000	80E
Ujung Pandang *(Makasar)*, Indonesia	709,038	80C
Ulan-Bator, Mongolia	287,000	70E
Vadodara, India (744,043)	733,656	81C
Valencia, Spain (1,140,000)	750,994	78E
Valparaiso, Chile (530,000)	250,358	70C
Vancouver, Canada (1,166,348)	410,188	76C
Vārānasi *(Benares)*, India (925,000)	704,772	81C
Venice (Venezia), Italy (445,000)	355,865	79E
Victoria, Hong Kong (3,975,000)	1,026,870	76C
Vienna (Wien), Austria (1,925,000)	1,572,300	79E
Vladivostok, U.S.S.R.	558,000	80E
Volgograd *(Stalingrad)*, U.S.S.R. (1,230,000)	939,000	80E
Voronezh (Voronež), U.S.S.R.	796,000	80E
Warsaw (Warszawa), Poland (2,080,000)	1,576,600	79E
Washington, U.S. (3,220,700)	637,651	80C
Wellington, New Zealand (349,900)	137,600	79E
Wiesbaden, Fed. Rep. of Ger. (795,000)	273,267	79E
Winnipeg, Canada (578,217)	560,874	76C
Wrocław *(Breslau)*, Poland	609,100	79E
Wuhan, China	3,000,000	75UE
Wuppertal, Fed. Rep. of Ger. (870,000)	394,605	79E
Yaoundé, Cameroon	313,706	76C
Yerevan, (Jerevan), U.S.S.R. (1,155,000)	1,036,000	80E
Yokohama, Japan (*Tōkyō)	2,773,322	80C
Zagreb, Yugoslavia	566,084	71C
Zaporozhye (Zaporožje), U.S.S.R.	799,000	80E
Zhdanov (Ždanov), U.S.S.R.	507,000	80E
Zürich, Switzerland (780,000)	369,522	80C

Metropolitan area populations are shown in parentheses.
* City is located within the metropolitan area of another city; for example, Kyōto, Japan (*Ōsaka).
† Population of entire municipality or district, including rural area.

C Census
E Official Estimate
UE Unofficial Estimate

Sources

The maps in the Atlas have been compiled from diverse source materials, which are cited in the following lists. The citations are organized by continent and region or country. Within each regional or country group, atlases are listed alphabetically by title and then followed by maps, which are listed according to scale, from the smallest to the largest. Other sources, listed alphabetically by title, follow the map listings.

GENERAL SOURCES

Atlante dei confini sottomarini, *A. Giuffrè Editore, Milano 1979*
Atlante Internazionale del Touring Club Italiano, *TCI, Milano 1977*
Atlas Mira, *G.U.G.K. Moskva 1967*
Atlas Okeanov-Atlantičeski i Indijski Okeany, *Ministerstvo Oborony SSSR-Vojenno-Morskoj Flot, Moskva 1977*
Atlas Okeanov-Tihi Okean, *Ministerstvo Oborony SSSR-Vojenno-Morskoj Flot, Moska 1974*
Atlas of the World, *National Geographic Society (N.G.S.), Washington 1981*
Atlas zur Ozeanographie, *Bibliographisches Institut, Mannheim 1971*
Bertelsmann Atlas International, *C. Bertelsmann Verlag GmbH, München 1963*
Grande Atlante degli Oceani, *Instituto Geografico De Agostini (I.G.D.A.), Novara 1978*
Meyers Neuer Geographischer Handatlas, *Bibliographisches Institut, Mannheim 1966*
The New International Atlas, *Rand McNally & Company, Chicago 1980*
The Odyssey World Atlas, *Western Publishing Company Inc., New York 1966*
The Times Atlas of the World, *John Bartholomew & Son Ltd, Edinburgh 1980*
The World Book Atlas, *World Book Encyclopedia Inc, 1979*
The World Shipping Scene, *Weststadt-Verlag, München 1963*
Weltatlas Erdöl und Erdgas, *George Westermann Verlag, Braunschweig 1976*
Pacific Ocean Floor 1:36,432,000, *N.G.S., Washington 1969*
Atlantic Ocean Floor 1:30,580,000, *N.G.S., Washington 1973*
Indian Ocean 1:25,720,000, *N.G.S. Washington 1967*
Deutsche Meereskarte 1:25,000,000, *Kartographisches Institut Meyer*
Carte générale du Monde 1:10,000,000, *Institut Géographique National (I.G.N.), Paris*
Artic Ocean Floor 1:9,757,000, *N.G.S., Washington 1971*
Carte du Monde 1:5,000,000, *I.G.N., Paris*
Karta Mira 1:2,500,000, *G.U.G.K., Moskva*
Carte Internationale du Monde 1:1,000,000, *Geographical Survey Institute*
Carte Aéronautique du Monde 1:1,000,000, *I.G.N., Paris*
Calendario Atlante, *I.G.D.A., Novara 1982*
Cartactual, *Cartographia, Budapest*
Demographic Yearbook, *United Nations, New York, 1978*
Duden Wörterbuch Geographischer Namen, *Bibliographisches Institut, Mannheim 1966*
Gazetteers (Various), *U.S. Board on Geographical Names, Washington*
Meyers Enzyklopädisches Lexikon, *Bibliographisches Institut, Mannheim 1972–81*
Schtag nach!-Die Staaten der Erde, *Bibliographisches Institut, Mannheim 1977*
Statistical Yearbook, *United Nations, New York, 1978*
Statistik des Auslandes-Länderkurzberichte, *Statistisches Bundesamt, Wiesbaden*
The Columbia Lippincott Gazetteer of the World, *Columbia University Press, New York 1961*
The Europa Year Book 1981, *Europa Publication Ltd., London*
The Statesman's Yearbook 1981–82, *The Macmillan Press Ltd., London*
Webster's New Geographical Dictionary, *G & C Merriam Co, Springfield 1972*

EUROPE

ALBANIA

Shqiperia-Hartë Fizike 1:500,000, *MMS "Hamid Shijaku", Tirana 1970*
Shqiperia Politiko Administrative 1:500,000, *MMS "Hamid Shijaku", Tirana 1969*
Gjeografia e Shqiperise per shkollat e mesme, *Shtëpia Botuese e Librit Shkollor, Tirana 1970*

AUSTRIA

Neuer Schulatlas, *Freytag-Berndt und Artaria KG, Wien 1971*
Generalkarte Österreich 1:200,000, *Mairs Geographischer Verlag, Stuttgart 1974*
Gemeindeverzeichnis von Österreich, *Österreichischen Statistischen Zentralamt, Wien 1970*
Geographisches Namenbuch Österreichs, *Verlag der Österreichischen Akademie der Wissenschaften, Wien 1975*
Statistisches Handbuch für die Republik Österreich, *Österreichischen Statistischen Zentralamt, Wien 1978*

BELGIUM

Atlas de Belgique-Atlas van België, *Comité National de Géographie, Bruxelles 1974*
België, Luxemburg, Belgien 1:350,000, *Pneu. Michelin, Bruxelles 1976*
Belgique, Grand-Duché de Luxembourg, *Pneu. Michelin, Paris 1978*
Lista Alphabetique des Communes-fusion de 1963 à 1977, *Institut National de Statistique, Bruxelles*
Statistique Demographiques 1980, *Institut National de Statistique, Bruxelles*

BULGARIA

Atlas Narodna Republika Bulgarija, *Glavno Upravlenie po Geodezija i Kartografija, Sofija 1973*
Bulgaria 1:1,000,000, *PPWK, Warszawa 1977*
Statističeski Godišnik na Narodna Republika Bălgarija 1973, *Ministerstvo na Informacijata i Săobšenijata, Sofija*

CZECHOSLOVAKIA

Atlas ČSSR, *Kartografie, Praha 1972*
Školní Zeměpisný Atlas Čescoslovenské Socialistické Republiky, *Kartografické Nakladatelství, Praha 1970*
Auto Atlas Č.S.S.R., *Kartografie, Praha 1971*
Č.S.S.R.-Fyzická Mapa 1:500,000, *Ústřední Správa Geodezie a Kartografie, Praha 1963*
Statistická Ročenka Č.S.S.R., *Federální Statistický Úřad, Praha 1980*

DENMARK

Haases Atlas, *P. Haase & Søns Forlag, København 1972*
Opgivne og Tilplantede Landbrugsarealer i Jylland, *Det Kongelige Danske Geografiske Selskab, København 1976*
Danmark 1:300,000, *Geodætisk Institut, København 1972*
Statistisk Årbog Danmark 1980, *Danmarks Statistik, København*

FINLAND

Oppikoulun Kartasto, *Werner Söderström Osakeyhtiö, Porvoo 1972*
Suomi-Finland 1:1,000,000, *Naanmittaushallituksen Kivipaino, Helsinki 1972*
Finland-Suomi 1:1,000,000, *Kümmerly & Frey, Bern 1981*
Suomen Tilastollinen Vuosikirja 1975, *Tilastokeskus, Helsinki*

FRANCE

Atlas Général Larousse, *Librairie Larousse, Paris 1976*
Atlas Général Bordas, *Bordas, Paris 1972*
Atlas Géographique Alpha, *I.G.D.A., Novara 1972*
Atlas Moderne Larousse, *Librairie Larousse-I.G.D.A., Paris 1976*
Carte Administrative de la France 1:1,400,000, *I.G.N., Paris 1977*
Carte de la France 1:1,000,000, *I.G.N., Paris 1971*
France: Routes-Autoroutes 1:1,000,000, *I.G.N., Paris 1978*
Carte Touristique 1:250,000, *I.G.N., Paris 1978*
France 1:200,000, *Pneu. Michelin, Paris*
Carte Touristique 1:100,000, *I.G.N., Paris*
Michelin 1977-France, *Pneu. Michelin, Paris*
Population de la France-Recensement 1975, *Institut National de la Statistique et des Études Économiques, Paris*

GERMAN DEMOCRATIC REPUBLIC

Haack Weltatlas, *V.E.B. Hermann Haack Geographisch-Kartographische Anstalt, Gotha-Leipzig 1972*
Weltatlas-Die Staaten der Erde und ihre Wirtschaft, *V.E.B. Hermann Haack Geographisch-Kartographische Anstalt, Gotha-Leipzig 1972*
Autokarte der D.D.R. 1:600,000, *V.E.B. Landkartenverlag, Berlin 1972*
Statistisches Jahrbuch der Deutschen Demokratischen Republik 1981, *Staatsverlag der D.D.R., Berlin*

GERMANY, FEDERAL REPUBLIC OF

Diercke Weltatlas, *Westermann Verlag, Braunschweig 1977*
Der Grosse Shell Atlas, *Mairs Geographischer Verlag, Stuttgart 1981–82*
Der Neue Weltatlas, *I.G.D.A., Novara 1977*
Deutschland-Strassenkarte 1:1,000,000, *Kümmerly & Frey, Bern 1981*
Bundesrepublik Deutschland-Übersichtskarte 1:500,000, *Institut für Angewandte Geodäsie, Frankfurt 1978*
Topographische Übersichtskarte 1:200,000, *Institut für Angewandte Geodäsie, Frankfurt*
Bevölkerung der Gemeinden, *Statistisches Bundesamt, Wiesbaden 1979*
Statistisches Jahrbuch für die B.R.D. 1980, *Statistisches Bundesamt, Wiesbaden*

GREECE

Greece-Autokarte 1:1,000,000, *Kümmerly & Frey, Bern*
Greece-Autokarte 1:650,000, *Freytag & Berndt, Wien*
Genikos Chartis tis Hellados 1:400,000, *Geografiki Hypiresia Stratoy, Athínai*
Etniki Statistiki Hypiresia tis Hellados 1:200,000, *E.S.Y.E., Athínai*
Statistiki Epetiris tis Hellados 1979, *E.S.Y.E., Athínai*

HUNGARY

Földrajzi Atlas a Középiskolák Számára, *Kartográfiai Vallalat, Budapest 1980*
A Magyar Népköztársaság 1:400,000, *Kartográfiai Vallalat, Budapest 1974*
Magyarorszag Domborzata és Vizei 1:350,000, *Kartográfiai Vallalat, Budapest 1961*
Megye Térképe, *Cartographia, Budapest 1979–80*
A Magyar Népköztársaság Helységnévtára 1973, *Statisztikai Kiadó Vállalat, Budapest*
Statistical Pocket Book of Hungary 1980, *Statistical Publishing House, Budapest*

ICELAND

Landabréfabok, *Ríkisutgáfa Námsbóka, Reykjavik 1970*
Iceland-Road Guide, *Örn & Örlygur H.F., Reykjavik 1975*

IRELAND

Irish Student's Atlas, *Educational Company of Ireland, Dublin-Cork 1971*
Ireland 1:575,000, *Ordnance Survey Office, Dublin 1979*
Ireland 1:250,000, *Ordnance Survey Office, Dublin 1962*
Census of Population of Ireland 1979, *The Stationery Office, Dublin*

ITALY

Atlante Metodico, *I.G.D.A., Novara 1981*
Atlante Stradale d'Italia 1:200,000, *Touring Club Italiano, Milano*
Carta d'Italia 1:1,250,000, *Instituto Geografico Militare, Firenze 1972*
Carte batimetriche, *Istituto Idrografico della Marina, Genova*
Carta Generale d'Italia 1:500,000, *Touring Club Italiano, Milano 1979*
Carta Generale d'Italia 1:200,000, *I.G.M., Firenze*
Enciclopedia Italiana, *Istituto della Enciclopedia Italiana G. Treccani, Roma*
Il Mare, *I.G.D.A., Novara*
La Montagna, *I.G.D.A., Novara*
XI Censimento Generale della Popolazione 24 ottobre 1971, *Istituto Centrale di Statistica, Roma*
XII Censimento Generale della Popolazione 25 ottobre 1981, *Istituto Centrale di Statistica, Roma*

LUXEMBOURG

Grand-Duché de Luxembourg 1:100,000, *I.G.N., Paris 1970*
Annuaire Statistique-Luxembourg 1981–82, *Service Central de la Statistique et des Études Économiques, Paris*

NETHERLANDS

Atlas van Nederland, *Staatsdrukkerij-en Uitgeverijbedrijf,'s-Gravenhage*
De Grote Vara Gezinsatlas, *Vara Omroepvereniging, Hilversum 1975*
Der Kleine Bosatlas, *Wolter-Noordhoff, Groningen 1974*
Pays-Bas/Nederland 1:400,000, *Pneu. Michelin, Paris 1981*
Gegevens per Gemeente Betreffende de Loop der Bevolking in het Jaar 1980, *Centraal Bureau voor de Statistik, Amsterdam*

NORWAY

Atlas-Større Utgave for Gymnaset, *J. W. Cappelens Forlag A.S., Oslo 1969*
Bilkart Bok Road Atlas, *J. W. Cappelens Forlag A.S., Oslo 1967*
Norge-Bit-Og Turistkart 1:400,000, *J. W. Cappelens Forlag A.S., Oslo 1965*
Folketallet i Kommunene 1972–73, *Statistik Sentralbyraå, Oslo*
Statistisk Årbok 1981, *Statistik Sentralbyrå, Oslo*

POLAND

Atlas Geograficzny, *PPWK, Warszawa 1979*
Narodowy Atlas Polski, *Polska Akademia Nauk, Warszawa 1978*
Polska Kontynenty Świat, *P.P.W.K., Warszawa 1977*
Powszechny Atlas Świat, *P.P.W.K. Warszawa 1981*
Polska Rzeczpospolito. Ludowa-Mapa Administracyjna 1:500,000, *P.P.W.K., Warszawa 1980*
Rocznik Statystyczny 1978, *Glówny Urzad Statystyczny, Warszawa*

PORTUGAL

Portugal 1:1,500,000, *Pneu. Michelin, Paris 1981*
Mapa do Estado das Estradas de Portugal 1:550,000, *Automovel Club de Portugal, Lisboa 1979*
Carto. Corográfica de Portugal 1:400,000, *Instituto Geografico e Cadastral, Lisboa 1968*
Anuário Estatístico-Portugal 1974, *Instituto Nacional de Estatística, Lisboa*

ROMANIA

Atlas Geografic General, *Editura Didactica si Pedagogica, Bucureşti 1974*
Atlasul Republicii Socialiste România, *Institutul de Geologie si Geofizica, Bucureşti*
Rumanien-Bulgarien 1:1,000,000, *Freytag-Berndt und Artaria K.G., Wien*
Anuarul Statistic al Republicii Socialiste România 1980, *Direcţia Centrala de Statistică, Bucureşti*

SPAIN

Atlas Bachillerato Universal y de España, *Aguilar, Madrid 1968*
Atlas Básico Universal, *I.G.D.A. Teide, Novara 1969*
Gran Atlas Aguilar, *Aguilar, Madrid 1969*
Peninsula Iberica, Baleares y Canarias 1:1,000,000, *Instituto Geografico y Catastral, Madrid 1966*
Mapa Militar de España 1:800,000, *Servicio Geografico del Ejercito, Madrid 1971*
España 1:500,000, *Firestone Hispania, Madrid*
España-Mapa Oficial de Carreteras 1:400,000 *Ministerio de Obras Publica, Madrid*
España-Anuario Estadistico 1979, *Instituto Nacional de Estadistica, Madrid*

SWEDEN

Atlas Över Välden, *Generalstabens Litografiska Anstalt, Stockholm 1972*
Atlas Över Välden, *Natur Miljö Befolkning, Stockholm 1974*
Kak Bil Atlas, *Generalstabens Litografiska Anstalt, Stockholm 1973*
Sverige-Bilkarta 1:625,000, *A.B. Kartlitografen, Stockholm 1972*
Statistisk Årsbok 1980, *Statistiska Centralbyrån, Stockholm*

SWITZERLAND

Atlas der Schweiz, *Verlag des Bundesamtes fur Landestopographie, Wabern-Bern*
Schweizerischer Mittelschulatlas, *Konferenz der Kantonalen Erziehungsdirektoren, Zürich 1976*
Switzerland 1:300,000, *Kümmerly & Frey, Bern 1979*
Carte Nazionale de la Suisse 1:200,000, *Service Topographique Federale, Wabern-Bern*

U.S.S.R.

Atlas Avtomobilnyh Dorog, *G.U.G.K., Moskva 1976*
Atlas Obrazovanie i Razvitie Sojuza S.S.R., *G.U.G.K., Moskva 1972*
Malyi Atlas S.S.S.R., *G.U.G.K., Moskva 1973*
SSSR 1:8,000,000, *G.U.G.K., Moskva 1980*
SSSR 1:4,000,000, *G.U.G.K., Moskva 1972*
Latvijskaja SSR 1:600,000, *G.U.G.K., Moskva 1967*
Litovskaja SSR 1:600,000, *G.U.G.K., Moskva 1969*
S.S.S.R. Administrativno-Territorialnoje Delenie Sojuznyh Respublik, *Prezidium Verhovnogo Soveta Sojuza Sovetskih Socialističeskih Respublik Moskva 1971*

UNITED KINGDOM

Philips' Modern School Economic Atlas, *George Philip & Son Ltd, London 1981*
Roads Atlas of Great Britain and Ireland, *George Philip & Son Ltd, London 1971*
The Atlas of Britain and Northern Ireland, *Clarendon Press, Oxford 1963*
Route Planning Map 1:625,000, *Ordnance Survey, Southampton 1973*
Cartes 1:400,000, *Michelin Tyre Co. Ltd., London 1981*

YUGOSLAVIA

Atlas, *Izrađenou u Oour Kartografiji Tlos "Učila", Zagreb 1980*
Jugoslavija-Auto Atlas, *Jugoslavenski Leksikografski Zavod, Zagreb 1972*
Školki Atlas, *Izrađenou u Oour Kartografiji Tlos "Učila", Zagreb 1975*
Jugoslavija 1:1,000,000, *Grafički Zavod Hrvatske, Zagreb 1980*
Statistički Godišnjak Jugoslavije 1975, *Savezni Zavod za Statistiku, Beograd*

ASIA

ARABIAN PENINSULA

The Oxford Map of Saudi Arabia 1:2,600,000, *GEO-projects, Beirut 1981*
Arabian Peninsula 1:2,000,000, *United States Geological Survey, Washington 1963*
Arabische Republik Jemen 1:1,000,000, *Deutsch-Jemenitische Gesellschaft e V, Schwaig 1976*
The United Arab Emirates 1:750,000, *GEO-projects, Beirut 1981*

MIDDLE EAST

Atlas of Iran, *"Sahab" Geographic & Drafting Institute, Tehrān 1971*
Modern Büyük Atlas, *Arkin Kitabevi-I.G.D.A., Istanbul 1981*
The New Israel Atlas-Zev Vilnay, *Israel Universities Press, Yerushalaym 1968*
Iran 1:2,500,000, *Imperial Government of Iran, Tehrān 1968*
Guide Map of Iran 1:2,250,000, *Gita Shenassi Co. Ltd, Tehrān*
Guide Map of Iraq 1:2,000,000, *"Sahab" Geographic & Drafting Institute, Tehrān 1971*
Türkiye 1:2,000,000, *Ravenstein Verlag GmbH, Frankfurt 1975*
Iran 1:1,500,000, *Imperial Government of Iran, Tehrān 1968*
Iraq Tourist Map 1:1,500,000, *Summer Resorts and Tourism Service, Baghdād 1967*
The Oxford Map of Syria 1:1,000,000, *GEO-projects, Beirut 1980*
Turkey-Road Map 1:1,000,000, *Kümmerly & Frey, Bern 1980*
Türkei und Naher Osten 1:800,000, *Reis und Verkehrsverlag, Berlin-Stuttgart 1977*
Israel und Angrenzende Länder-Strassenkarte 1:750,000, *Kümmerly & Frey, Bern 1981*
The Oxford Map of Jordan 1:730,000, *GEO-projects, Beirut 1979*
Map of Israel 1:500,000, *Survey of Israel, Yerushalaym 1979*
The Oxford Map of Kuwait 1:500,000, *GEO-projects, Beirut 1980*
The Oxford Map of Qatar 1:270,000, *GEO-projects, Beirut 1980*
Israel Map of the Cease-Fire Lines 1:250,000, *Survey of Israel, Yerushalaym 1973*
Qatar-Visitor's Map 1:250,000, *Ministry of Information, Doha 1979*
Carte Générale du Liban 1:200,000, *Ministère de la Défense Nationale, Beirut 1967*
Qatar 1:200,000, *Hunting Surveys Ltd., Borchamwood 1975*
Bahrain Islands 1:63,360, *Public Works Department, Al Manāmah 1968*
The Oxford Map of Bahrain 1:57,750, *GEO-projects, Beirut 1980*
Bahrain—A Map for Visitors 1:50,000, *Ministry of Information, Al Manāmah 1976*
Annual Abstract of Statistics 1978, *Central Statistical Organization, Baghdād*
Genel Nüfus Sayımı 12 ekim 1980, *Başbakanlik Devlet İstatistik Enstitüsü, Ankara*
Kuwait—Annual Statistical Abstract, *Central Statistical Office-Ministry of Planning, Al Kuwayt 1976*
List of Localities—Geographical Information and Population 1948–1961–1972–1975, *Central Bureau of Statistics, Yerushalaym*
Recueil de Statistiques Libanaises No. 8-1972, *Direction Centrale de la Statistique, Bayrūt*
Republic of Cyprus—Statistical Abstract 1973, *The Statistics and Research Department, Levkosia*
Statistical Abstract—Syrian Arab Republic 1973, *Central Bureau of Statistics, Dimashq*
Statistical Abstract of Israel 1979, *Central Bureau of Statistics, Yerushalaym*
The Hashemite Kingdom of Jordan, Statistical Yearbook 1976, *Department of Statistics, Ammān*
Türkiye İstatistik Yıllığı 1975, *Başbakanlik Devlet İstatistik Enstitüsü, Ankara*

SOUTH ASIA

National Atlas of India, *National Atlas & Thematic Mapping Organization, Calcutta*
Oxford School Atlas for Pakistan, *Oxford University Press—Pakistan Branch, Karachi 1973*
Tourist Atlas of India, *National Atlas Organization, Calcutta*
Physical Map of India 1:4,500,000, *Survey of India, Calcutta 1974*
Political Map of India 1:4,500,000, *Survey of India, Calcutta 1972*
Railway Map of India 1:3,500,000, *Government of India, Calcutta 1971*
Pākistān 1:3,168,000, *Survey of Pākistān, Rāwalpindi 1966*
Bangladesh 1:2,800,000, *Survey of Bangladesh, Dacca 1979*
Burma 1:2,000,000, *Army Map Service, Washington 1963*
Physical and Political Map of Afghanistan 1:1,500,000, *Afghan Cartographic Institute, Kabul 1968*
Ceylon Physical 1:1,000,000, *Survey Department, Colombo 1973*
New Map of Afghanistan 1:1,000,000, *"Sahab" Geographic & Drafting Institute, Tehrān*
Pākistān 1:1,000,000, *Survey of Pākistān, Rāwalpindi 1968*
Motor Map of Ceylon 1:506,880, *Survey Department, Colombo 1973*
Nepal 1:506,880, *Ministry of Defence, London 1967*
Nepal 1:408,000, *Kümmerly & Frey, Bern 1980*
Bangladesh Population Census Report 1974, *Statistics Division-Ministry of Planning, Dacca*
Geomedical Monograph Series—Afghanistan, *Springer-Verlag, Berlin 1968*
Pakistan Statistical Yearbook 1978, *Statistics Division, Karachi*
Statistical Pocket Book of the Democratic Socialist Republic of Sri Lanka 1979, *Department of Census and Statistics, Colombo*

SOUTHEAST ASIA

Atlas Indonesia, *Yayasan Dwidjendra, Denpasar-Jakarta 1977*
Atlas of Thailand, *Royal Thai Survey Department, Bangkok 1974*
Secondary Atlas for Malaysia and Singapore, *Niugini Press Pty. Ltd., Port Moresby 1975*
Secondary School Atlas for Malaysia, *McGraw-Hill Far Eastern Publishers Ltd., Singapore 1970*
Hành Chính Viet Nam 1:2,500,000, *Hồ Chí Minh 1976*
Maluku dan Irian Jaya 1:2,250,000, *Pembina, Jakarta 1975–76*
Bàu-dô Viet Nam 1:2,000,000, *Saigon 1972*
Laos Administratif 1:2,000,000, *Service Géographique National du Laos, Vientiane 1968*
Malaysia 1:2,000,000, *Jabatanarah Pemetaan Negara, 1976*
Map of Thailand and Bangkok 1:2,000,000, *The Shell Company of Thailand Ltd., Bangkok*
Vietnam 1:2,000,000, *G.U.G.K., Moskva 1972*
Kalimantan 1:1,500,000, *Pembina, Jakarta 1975–76*
Philippines 1:1,500,000, *Philippine Coast and Geodetic Survey, Manila 1968*
Cambodia & South Vietnam—Southeast Asia 1:1,250,000, *Army Map Service, Washington 1966*
Carte Générale du Laos, *Service Géographique National du Laos, Vientiane 1968*
Sumatera 1:790,000, *Pembina, Jakarta 1975–76*
Malaysia Barat—West Malaysia 1:760,000, *Jabatanarah Pemetaan Negara, 1968*
Jawa Barat & D.K.I. Jakarta 1:500,000, *Pembina, Jakarta 1974–75*
Jawa Tengah & D.I. Yogyakarta 1:500,000, *Pembina, Jakarta 1974–75*
Jawa Timur 1:500,000, *Pembina, Jakarta 1974–75*

Sabah 1:500,000, *Jabatanarah Pemetaan Negara, 1976*
Nusa Tenggara Barat & Nusa Tenggara Timur 1:330,000, *Pembina, Jakarta 1975*
Jawa Madura 1:225,000, *Pembina, Jakarta 1975–76*
Sulawesi 1:220,000, *Pembina, Jakarta 1975–76*
Gulongan Masharakat-Banchi Pendudok dan Perumahan Malaysia 1970, *Jabatan Perangkaan, Kuala Lumpur*
Sensus Penduluk 1971, *Biro Pusat Statistik, Jakarta*
Statistical Summary of Thailand 1978, *Statistical Reports Division, Bangkok*
Statistik Indonesia 1974–75, *Biro Pusat Statistik, Jakarta*

CHINA, MONGOLIA
Zhonghua Renmin Gongheguo Fen Sheng Dituji, *Ditu Chubanshe, Beijing 1977*
Zhonghua Renmin Gongheguo Ditu 1:6,000,000, *Ditu Chubanshe, Beijing 1980*
China 1:5,500,000, *Cartographia, Budapest 1967*
Zhonghua Renmin Gongheguo Ditu 1:4,000,000, *Ditu Chubanshe, Beijing 1980*
Mongolskaja Narodnaja Respublika 1:3,000,000, *G.U.G.K., Moskva 1972*
Taiwan/Formosa 1:500,000, *Army Map Service, Washington 1964*
China's Changing Map, *Methuen & Co., London 1972*

JAPAN, KOREA
Japan—The Pocket Atlas, *Heibonsha Ltd., Tōkyō 1970*
The National Atlas of Japan, *Geographical Survey Institute, Tōkyō 1977*
Teikoku's Complete Atlas of Japan, *Teikoku Shoin Company Ltd., Tōkyō 1977*
Tourist Map of Japan 1:5,300,000, *Japan National Tourist Organisation, Tōkyō 1974*
Republic of Korea 1:1,000,000, *Chungang Map & Chart Service, Sŏul 1973*
Northern Korea—Road Map of Korea, *Republic of Korea Army Map Service, Sŏul 1971*
Southern Korea 1:700,000, *Republic of Korea Army Map Service, Sŏul 1977*

AFRICA
The Atlas of Africa, *Editions Jeune Afrique, Paris 1973*
Africa 1:14,000,000, *N.G.S., Washington 1980*
Africa 1:9,000,000, *V.E.B. Hermann Haack, Gotha-Leipzig 1977*
Afrique/Africa 1:4,000,000, *Pneu. Michelin, Paris-London*
Africa 1:2,000,000, *Army Map Service, Washington*

NORTH WEST AFRICA
Atlas International de l'Ouest Africain 1:2,500,000, *Organisation de l'Unité Africaine, Dakar 1971*
Mauritanie 1:2,500,000, *I.G.N., Paris 1978*
Algérie-Tunisie 1:1,000,000, *Pneu. Michelin, Paris 1975*
Maroc 1:1,000,000, *Pneu. Michelin, Paris 1975*
Generalkarte Gran Canaria-Tenerife 1:150,000, *Mairs Geographischer Verlag, Stuttgart 1979*
Annuaire Statistique du Maroc, *Direction de la Statistique, Rabat 1976*
Code Géographique National—Code des Communes, *Secretariat d'État au Plan, Alger 1975*
Recensement Général de la Population et des Logements 1975, *Institut National de la Statistique, Tūnis*

NORTH EAST AFRICA
Egypte 1:750,000, *Kummerly & Frey, Bern 1977*
Population Census 1973, *Census and Statistical Department, Tarābulus*

WEST AFRICA
Atlas de Côte d'Ivoire, *Institut de Géographie Tropicale-Université d'Abidjan, Abidjan 1971*
Atlas de Haute-Volta, *Centre Voltaïque de la Recherche Scientifique, Ouagadougou 1969*
Atlas du Cameroun, *Institut de Recherches Scientifiques du Cameroun, Yaoundé*
Atlas for the United Republic of Cameroon, *Collins-Longman, Glasgow 1977*
Ghana Junior Atlas, *E. A. Boateng-Thomas Nelson and Sons Ltd., London 1965*
Liberia in Maps, *Stefan von Gnielinski, Hamburg 1972*
Oxford Atlas for Nigeria, *Oxford University Press, London-Ibadan 1971*
School Atlas for Sierra Leone, *Collins-Longman, Glasgow 1975*
République du Mali 1:2,500,000, *I.G.N., Paris 1971*
Ghana-Administrative 1:2,000,000, *Survey of Ghana, Accra 1968*
Road Map of Nigeria 1:585,000, *Federal Surveys, Lagos 1969*
République Unie du Cameroun 1:1,000,000, *I.G.N., Paris 1972*
République de Haute-Volta-Carte Routière 1:1,000,000, *I.G.N., Paris 1968*
Philips' School Room Map of Ghana 1:1,000,000, *George Philip & Son Ltd., London 1963*
Sénégal 1:1,000,000, *I.G.N., Paris 1974*
Sénégal-Carte Administrative 1:1,000,000, *I.G.N., Paris 1966*
Physical Map of Nigeria 1:1,000,000, *Federal Surveys, Lagos 1965*
République du Côte d'Ivoire 1:1,000,000, *I.G.N., Paris 1970*
Côte d'Ivoire 1:800,000, *Pneu. Michelin, Paris 1978*
Mapa da Guiné 1:650,000, *J. R. Silva, Lisboa 1969*
République du Dahomey-Carte Routière et Touristique 1:500,000, *I.G.N., Paris 1968*
Road Map of Ghana 1:500,000, *Survey of Ghana, Accra 1970*
The Gambia Road Map 1:500,000, *Survey Department The Gambia, Banjul 1973*
Nigeria-Digest of Statistics 1973, *Federal Office of Statistics, Lagos*

EAST AND CENTRAL AFRICA
Atlas Pratique du Tchad, *Institut Tchadien pour les Sciences Humaines, Paris 1972*
Sudan Roads 1:4,000,000, *Sudan Survey Department, Khartoum 1976*
Äthiopie/Ethiopia 1:4,000,000, *Medizinische Länderkunde/Geomedical Monograph Series, Berlin 1972*
Carte de l'Afrique Centrale 1:2,500,000, *I.G.N., Paris 1968*
Highway Map of Ethiopia 1:2,000,000, *Imperial Ethiopian Government, Addis Ababa 1961*
République du Tchad-Carte Routière 1:1,500,000, *I.G.N., Paris 1968*
République Centrafricaine-Carte Routière 1:1,500,000, *I.G.N., Paris 1969*
Territoire Française des Afars et des Issas 1:400,000, *Office Developpement du Tourisme, Djibouti 1970*
Ethiopia-Statistical Abstract 1976, *Central Statistical Office, Addis Ababa*

EQUATORIAL AFRICA
Atlas du Congo, *Office de la Recherche Scientifique et Techique Outre-Mer, Brazzaville 1969*
Atlas for Malawi, *Collins-Longman, Glasgow 1969*
Atlas of Uganda, *Department of Lands and Surveys, Kampala 1967*
Malawi in Maps, *University of London Press Ltd., London 1972*
Tanzania in Maps, *University of London Press, Ltd., London 1975*
The First Kenya Atlas, *George Philip & Son Ltd., London 1973*
Carte de l'Afrique Centrale 1:2,500,000, *I.G.N., Paris 1968*
Carta Rodoviária de Angola 1:2,000,000, *Lello S.A.R.L., Luanda 1974*
Republic of Zambia 1:1,500,000, *Surveyor General, Ministry of Lands and Natural Resources, Lusaka 1972*
Tanzania 1:1,250,000, *Shell & B.P. Tanzania Ltd., Dar es Salaam 1973*
Malawi 1:1,000,000, *Malawi Government, Blantyre 1971*
Road Map of Kenya 1:1,000,000, *George Philip & Son Ltd., London 1972*
République Populaire du Congo 1:1,000,000, *I.G.N., Paris 1973*
Gabon 1:1,000,000, *I.G.N., Paris 1975*
Statistical Abstract 1979, *Central Bureau of Statistics, Nairobi*

SOUTHERN AFRICA
Large Print Atlas for Southern Africa, *George Philip & Son Ltd., London 1976*
Atlas de Madagascar, *Association des Géographes de Madagascar, Antananarivo 1971*
Atlas for Mauritius, *Macmillan Education Ltd., London 1971*
Ontwikkelingsatlas-Development Atlas, *Republic of South Africa-Department of Planning, Pretoria 1966*
Botswana Road Map and Climate Chart 1:6,000,000, *Department of Surveys and Lands, Gaborone 1980*
Madagascar et Comores 1:4,000,000, *I.G.N., Paris 1970*
Suidelike Afrika/Southern Africa 1:2,500,000, *The Government Printer, Pretoria 1973*
Roads of Zimbabwe 1:2,100,000, *Shell Zimbabwe Ltd., Salisbury, 1980*
Carta de Moçambique 1:2,000,000, *Ministerio do Ultramar, Lisboa 1971*
Mapa Rodoviário de Maçambique 1:2,000,000, *J.A.E.M. 1972*
The Black Homelands of South Africa 1:1,900,000, *Perskor Boeke Tekenkantoor, Johannesburg*
Road Map of Zimbabwe 1:1,800,000, *A.A. of Zimbabwe, Salisbury 1980*
Zimbabwe-Mobil 1:1,470,000, *M.O. Collins Ltd., Salisbury 1976*
Rhodesia Relief 1:1,000,000, *Surveyor General, Salisbury 1973*
Lafatsche La Botsvana/Republic of Botswana 1:1,000,000, *Department of Surveys and Lands, Gaborone 1970*
Suid Afrika/South Africa 1:500,000, *The Government Printer, Pretoria*
Lesotho, 1:250,000, *Government Overseas Surveys, Maseru 1969*
Île Maurice-Carte Touristique 1:100,000, *I.G.N., Paris 1978*
La Réunion-Carte Touristique 1:100,000, *I.G.N., Paris 1978*
Annual Statistical Bulletin 1973, *The Bureau of Statistics, Maseru*
Bi-Annual Digest of Statistics 1976, *Central Statistical Office, Port Louis*
Population Census 1970, *Department of Statistics, Pretoria*
Population de Madagascar au Ier Janvier 1972, *Direction Général du Gouvernement, Antananarivo*
South Africa 1980–81-Official Yearbook, *Chris van Rensburg Publications Ltd., Johannesburg*

NORTH AMERICA
CANADA
Atlas Larousse Canadien, *Les Editions Françaises Inc., Québec - Montréal 1971*
Oxford Regional Economic Atlas - United States & Canada, *Clarendon Press, Oxford 1967*
Road Atlas United States - Canada - Mexico, *Rand McNally & Co., Chicago 1981*
The National Atlas of Canada, *Department of Energy, Mines and Resources, Ottawa 1972*
Northwest Territories - Yukon Territory 1:4,000,000, *Department of Energy, Mines and Resources, Ottawa 1974*
Quebec and Newfoundland 1:3,700,000, *N.G.S., Washington 1980*
British Columbia, Alberta and the Yukon Territory 1:3,500,000, *N.G.S., Washington 1978*
Ontario 1:3,000,000, *N.G.S., Washington 1980*
Saskatchewan and Manitoba 1:2,600,000, *N.G.S., Washington 1979*
Canada Year Book 1978-79, *Minister of Industry, Trade and Commerce, Ottawa*

UNITED STATES
Oxford Regional Economic Atlas - United States & Canada, *Clarendon Press, Oxford 1967*
Road Atlas United States - Canada - Mexico, *Rand McNally & Co., Chicago 1981*
Transportation Map of the United States, *U.S. Department of Transportation, Washington 1976*
National Energy Transportation System 7,500,000, *U.S. Geological Survey, Reston, Virginia 1977*
Close-up: Alaska 1:3,295,000, *N.G.S., Washington 1975*
Close-up: The Southwest 1:2,124,000, *N.G.S., Washington 1977*
Close-up: The Northwest 1:2,000,000, *N.G.S., Washington 1973*
Close-up: The Southeast 1:1,780,000, *N.G.S., Washington 1975*
Close-up: California and Nevada 1:1,700,000, *N.G.S., Washington 1978*
Close-up: Florida 1:1,331,000, *N.G.S., Washington 1973*
Close-up: Illinois, Indiana, Ohio and Kentucky 1:1,267,000, *N.G.S., Washington 1977*
Close-up: The Northeast 1:1,215,000, *N.G.S., Washington 1978*
Close-up: The Mid-Atlantic States 1:886,000, *N.G.S., Washington 1973*
Topographic Maps 1:500,000, *U.S. Geological Survey, Washington*
Topographic Maps 1:250,000, *U.S. Geological Survey, Washington*
Togographic Maps 1:24,000, *U.S. Geological Survey, Washington*
Census of Population and Housing 1980, *Bureau of the Census, Washington*

MEXICO
Atlas of Mexico, *Bureau of Business Research, University of Texas, Austin 1975*
Road Atlas United States - Canada - Mexico, *Rand McNally & Co., Chicago 1981*
Mapas de los Estados-Serie Patria, *Libreria Patria S.A., México*
Carta Geografica de México 1:2,500,000, *Asociación Nacional Automovilística, Ciudad de México 1976*
Archeological Map of Middle America 1:2,250,000, *N.G.S., Washington 1968*

CENTRAL AMERICA AND THE CARIBBEAN
Atlas for Barbados, Windwards and Leewards, *Macmillan Education Ltd., London 1974*
Atlas for Guyana & Trinidad & Tobago, *Macmillan Education Ltd, London 1973*
Atlas for the Eastern Caribbean, *Collins-Longman, London 1977*
Atlas Nacional de Cuba, *Academia de Ciencias de Cuba, La Habana 1970*
Atlas of the Commonwealth of the Bahamas, *Kingston Publishers Ltd.-Ministry of Education, Kingston-Nassau 1976*
Jamaica in Maps, *University of London Press Ltd., London 1974*
West Indies and Central Amerika 1:4,500,000, *N.G.S., Washington 1981*
Mapa General-República de Honduras 1:1,000,000, *Instituto Geográfico Nacional, Tegucigalpa 1980*
Mapa Oficial de la República de Panamá 1:1,000,000, *Instituto Geográfico Nacional, Panamá 1979*
Mapa Preliminar de la República de Guatemala 1:1,000,000, *Instituto Geográfico Nacional, Guatemala 1976*
República de Nicaragua 1:1,000,000, *Instituto Geográfico Nacional, Managua 1975*
Belize 1:800,000, *Directorate of Overseas Surveys, London 1974*
Mapa de la República Dominicana 1:600,000, *Instituto Geográfico Universitario, Santo Domingo 1979*
Costa Rica - Mapa Fisico-Politico 1:500,000, *Instituto Geográfico de Costa Rica, San José 1974*
El Salvador 1:500,000, *Ministerio de Obras Públicas, San Salvador 1978*
Mapa Hipsométrico de la República de Guatemala 1:500,000, *Instituto Geográfico Nacional, Guatemala 1979*
Jamaica 1:280,000, *Fairey Surveys Ltd., Maidenhead 1974*
Mapa de Carreteras Estatales de Puerto Rico 1:250,000, *Autoridad de Carreteras Estatales, San Juan 1972*
Nicaragua-Costa Rica 1:250,000, *Instituto Geográfico Nacional, Managua 1972*
Puerto Rico e Islas Limitrofes 1:240,000, *U.S. Geological Survey, Washington 1970*
Turks & Caicos Islands 1:200,000, *Directorate of Overseas Surveys, London 1971*
Cayman Islands 1:150,000, *Directorate of Overseas Surveys, London 1972*
Trinidad 1:150,000, *Director of Surveys-Ministry of Defense, London 1970*
Guadeloupe-Carte Touristique 1:100,000, *I.G.N., Paris 1978*
Martinique-Carte Touristique 1:100,000, *I.G.N., Paris 1977*
Lesser Antilles-Antigua 1:50,000, *Directorate of Overseas Surveys, London 1973*
Tourist Map of Tobago 1:50,000, *Lands & Surveys Department, Port of Spain 1969*
Dominica 1:25,000, *Directorate of Overseas Surveys, London 1978*
Lesser Antilles-Barbuda 1:25,000, *Directorate of Overseas Surveys, London 1970*
Annuario Estadístico de Costa Rica 1977, *Dirección General de Estadística, San José*
Annuario Estadístico de Cuba 1973, *Dirección Central de Estadística, La Habana*
Caribbean Year Book 1978-80, *Caribook Ltd., Toronto*
Fact Sheets on the Commonwealth-Antigua, *British Information Services, London 1974*
Fact Sheets on the Commonwealth-Belize, *British Information Services, London 1976*
Guatemala-III Censo de Habitación 26 de marzo de 1973, *Dirección General de Estadística, Guatemala*
Honduras-Annuario Estadístico 1978, *Dirección General de Estadística, Censos, Tegucigalpa*
Nicaragua-Annuario Estadístico 1975, *Oficina Ejecutiva de Encuestas y Censos, Managua*
Statistical Yearbook for Latin America, *United Nations, New York 1976*
Zentralamerika-Karten zur Bevölkerungs und Wirtschaftsstruktur 1975, *H. Nuhn, P. Krieg & W. Schlick, Hamburg*

SOUTH AMERICA
NORTHERN SOUTH AMERICA
Atlas Basico de Colombia, *Instituto Geográfico Agustin Codazzi, Bogotá 1970*
Atlas de Colombia, *Instituto Geográfico Agustin Codazzi, Bogotá 1979*
Atlas de Venezuela, *Ministerio de Obras Públicas, Caracas 1970*
Atlas for Guyana, Trinidad & Tobago, *Macmillan Education Ltd., London 1973*
Atlas Histórico Geográfico y de Paisajes Peruanos, *Instituto Nacional de Planificación, Lima 1970*
Atlas Nacional do Brasil, *Instituto Brasileiro de Geografia*
Atlas Universal y del Perú, *Thomas Nelson & Sons Ltd., Sunbury on Thames 1968*
Brasil-Didáctico, Rodoviário, Turístico 1:5,000,000, *Gr. Editôra e Publicidade Ltda., Rio de Janeiro*
Mapa de la República de Bolivia 1:4,000,000, *Instituto Geográfico Militar, La Paz 1974*
Mapa Politico del Perú 1:2,400,000, *Editorial "Navarrete", Lima 1975*
Mapa de Carreteras del Perú 1:2,200,000, *Instituto Geográfico Militar, Lima 1979*
Mapa Fisico-Politico 1:2,000,000, *Instituto Geográfico Militar, Lima 1970*
Mapa Fisico de la República de Venezuela 1:2,000,000, *Ministerio de Obras Públicas, Bogotá 1975*
Brasil-Mapa Rodoviário 1:2,000,000, *Ministério dos Transportes, 1971*
Carte de la Guyane Française 1:1,500,000, *I.G.N., Paris 1973*
República de Colombia 1:1,500,000, *Ministerio de Hacienda y Credito Público, Bogotá 1979*
Ecuador 1:1,000,000, *Instituto Geográfico Militar, Quito 1971*
Kaart van Suriname 1:1,000,000, *C. Kersten & Co. N.V., Paramaribo*
Mapa de Bolivia 1:1,000,000, *Instituto Geográfico Militar, La Paz 1973*
Mapa Vial 1:1,000,000, *Ministerio de Obras Públicas, Caracas 1970*
República del Perú-Mapa Fisico-Politico, 1:1,000,000, *Instituto Geográfico Militar, Lima 1978*
Carte de la Guyane Française 1:500,000, *I.G.N., Paris 1976*
Suriname 1:500,000, *Uitgave Centraal Bureau Luchtkartering, 1969*
Guyana 1:500,000, *Ordnance Survey, Georgetown 1972*
Annuário Estatístico do Brasil 1978, *Fundacão Instituto Brasileiro de Geografia e Estatística, Rio de Janeiro*
Boletín Mensual de Estadística-agosto 1977, *D.A.N.E., Bogotá*
Dicionário Geográfico Brasileiro, *Editora Globo, Pôrto Alegre 1972*
Discover Bolivia, *Los Amigos del Libro, La Paz 1972*
Venezuela-Annuário Estadístico 1976, *Oficina Central de Estadística e Informatica, Caracas*

SOUTHERN SOUTH AMERICA
Atlas de la República Argentina, *Instituto Geográfico Militar, Buenos Aires 1972*
Atlas de la República Argentina, *Instituto Geográfico Militar, Santiago 1976*
Atlas de la República de Chile, *Instituto Geográfico Militar, Santiago 1970*
Atlas Escolar de Chile, *Instituto Geográfico Militar, Santiago 1978*
Atlas Universal y de la República Argentina, *Aguilar Argentina S.A. de Ediciones, Buenos Aires 1972*
Mapa de la República Argentina 1:5,000,000, *Instituto Geográfico Militar, Buenos Aires 1973*
Paraguay 1:1,000,000, *Instituto Geográfico Militar, Asuncion 1974*
República Oriental del Uruguay 1:500,000, *Servicio Geográfico Militar, Montevideo 1961*
Uruguay-Moyennes et Petites Villes 1972, *Institut des Hautes Etudes de l'Amerique Latine, Paris*

AUSTRALIA AND OCEANIA
Atlas of Australian Resources, *Division of National Mapping, Canberra 1980*
New Zealand-Mobil Travel Map, *Mobil Oil New Zealand Ltd., Wellington 1973*
New Zealand Atlas, *A.R. Shearer Government Printer, Wellington 1976*
The Jacaranda Atlas, *Jacaranda Press Pty. Ltd., 1971*
The Jacaranda Atlas For New Zealand, *Jacaranda Press Pty. Ltd., 1971*
Australia-Geographic Map 1:2,500,000, *Minister for National Development, Canberra 1967*
Territory of Papua and New Guinea 1:2,500,000, *Division of National Mapping, Canberra 1970*
Carte de l'Océanie Française 1:2,000,000, *I.G.N., Paris 1971*
Îles Tuamotu-Îles Marquises 1:2,000,000, *I.G.N., Paris 1969*
New Zealand-Map Guide 1:1,900,000, *New Zealand Tourist and Publicity Department, Wellington 1978*
Mobil New Zealand Road Map, *Mobil Oil New Zealand Ltd., Wellington 1973*
Fiji Islands-World Aeronautical Chart 1:1,000,000, *Ordnance Survey, Southampton 1970*
Close-up: Hawaii 1:675,000, *N.G.S., Washington 1978*
Archipel des Nouvelles-Hébrides 1:500,000, *I.G.N., Paris 1976*
New Zealand 1:500,000, *Department of Lands and Survey, Wellington 1976*
Nouvelle Calédonie 1:500,000, *I.G.N., Paris 1978*
Palau Islands 1:165,000, *Defense Mapping Agency Hydrographic Center, Washington 1973*
General Map of Tokelau Islands 1:100,000, *Department of Lands & Survey, Wellington 1969*
Tahiti-Carte Touristique 1:100,000, *I.G.N., Paris 1977*
Christmas Islands - Gilbert and Ellice Islands Colony 1:50,000, *Directorate of Overseas Survey, London 1970*
Tuvalu, *Government of Tuvalu 1979*
Annual Statistical Abstract-Fiji 1970-71, *Bureau of Statistics, Suva*
Australia - Population and Dwellings in Local Government Areas and Urban Centres 1976, *Australian Bureau of Statistics, Canberra*
Fact Sheet - Pitcairn Islands Group, *British Information Services, London 1974*
Fact Sheet - The Gilbert Islands, *British Information Services, London 1977*
Fact Sheet - The New Hebrides, *British Information Services, London 1976*
Fact Sheet - The Solomon Islands, *British Information Services, London 1976*
Fact Sheet - Tuvalu, *British Information Services, London 1977*
New Zealand Pocket Digest of Statistics 1979, *Department of Statistics, Wellington*
New Zealand Official Yearbook 1978, *Department of Statistics, Wellington*

POLAR REGIONS
Antarctica 1:11,250,000, *U.S. Naval Oceanographic Office, Washington 1965*
Antarctica 1:10,000,000, *American Geographical Society, New York 1970*
Antarctica 1:10,000,000, *Division of National Mapping, Canberra 1979*
Antarctica 1:5,000,000, *American Geographical Society, New York 1970*
Map of the Artic Region 1:5,000,000, *American Geographical Society, New York 1975*

Transliteration Systems

Toponymy: Criteria Used for the Writing of Names on the Maps

The language of geography is a language which defines geographic features in universally recognized terms. In creating this language, toponymy experts and cartographers have confronted complex problems in finding terms which are universally acceptable. So that the reader can fully understand the maps in this atlas, here is a brief explanation of how the toponyms (place-names for geographic features) have been written, particularly those relating to regions or countries where the Roman alphabet is not used. Among these are the Slavic-speaking nations such as the Soviet Union, Yugoslavia and Bulgaria; and China and Japan, which use ideographic characters. Of the European countries, Greece has its own alphabet, which is totally different from the Roman alphabet. Many of the Islamic countries use Arabic, with variations derived from local dialects.

There are two basic systems for Romanizing writing. The first is by phonetic transcription, using combinations of different alphabetical signs for each language when the phonetic sound in other languages should be maintained. For example, the Italian sound "sc" (which must be followed by an "e" or "i" to remain soft) in French is "ch," in English is "sh," and in German is "sch."

The second system is transliteration, in which the words, letters or characters of one language are represented or spelled in the letters or characters of another language.

Chinese, Japanese and Arabic Languages

Various Asian and African countries use non-Roman forms in their writing. For example, the Chinese and Japanese languages use ideographic characters instead of an alphabet, and these ideographic characters are transformed into the Roman alphabet through phonetic transcription. Until recently, one of the methods used for transforming Chinese was the Wade-Giles system, named for its English authors. Used in this atlas is the Pinyin system, which was approved by the Chinese government in 1958 and has been incorporated into the official maps of the People's Republic of China. The Pinyin system also has been adopted by the United States Board on Geographic Names and is used in official United Nations documents. The Pinyin names, however, often are accompanied by the Wade-Giles form, as the latter was widely known.

In Japan, ideographic characters are used, although the Roman alphabet is used in many Japanese scientific works. Japan uses two principal systems for standardizing names. They are the Kunreisiki, used by the government in official publications, and the Hepburn method. Adopted for this atlas is the Hepburn method, the system used in international English-language publications and by the United States Board on Geographic Names.

Romanization of the Arabic alphabet, which is used in many Islamic countries, is by transliteration. Since English and French are still used as an international language in many Arab countries, the name forms proposed by the major English and French sources have been taken into consideration. Generally, the systems proposed by the United States Board on Geographic Names and the Permanent Committee on Geographical Names have been used for most Asian countries and Arab-speaking countries.

Greek, Russian and Other Slavic Languages

Practically all written languages in Europe use the Roman alphabet. The differences in phonetics and grammar are shown by the use of diacritical marks and by groupings of consonants, vocals and syllables which give meaning to the various tones in the language. According to a centuries-old tradition, each written language maintains its formal characters, using the translated form rather than the phonetic transcription when a geographical term must be given in another language. This system, therefore, makes it more a translation than a transliteration.

In the Aegean area, Greek and the Greek alphabet are particularly significant because of historical links to the beginning of European civilization. The 1962 United States Board on Geographic Names and the Permanent Committee on Geographical Names systems, based on modern Greek pronunciation, have been used in transcribing toponyms from official sources for these maps. (The table that follows has an example indicating essential norms for Romanizing the modern Greek alphabet.)

A different situation arises in countries using the Cyrillic alphabet. Six principal Slavic languages using this alphabet are Russian, Byelorussian, Ukrainian, Bulgarian, Serbian, and Macedonian. The Cyrillic alphabet also is used by the non-Slavic people of the central Soviet Union. The nomenclature of these regions has been transliterated in accordance with the system proposed by the International Organization for Standardization, taking into consideration sounds and letters and uses of the diacritical marks normal in Slavic languages. The International Organization for Standardization method is accepted and used in bibliographical works and international documents. (The table which follows gives the relationship between the letters of the Cyrillic and Roman alphabets for the above six languages.) An exception to this transliteration is made by the Soviet Balkan republics of Estonia, Latvia and Lithuania. Here the name forms deriving from the national languages have been adopted, using the Roman alphabet.

Special Cases: Conventional Forms and Multilinguals

Cartographic nomenclature generally derives from the official nomenclature of the sovereign and nonsovereign countries, although a number of cases need an explanation.

In numerous situations, English conventional forms are used along with the local or conventional name in referring to a geographical entity used outside the official language area. For example, Vienna, Prague, Copenhagen and Moscow are English forms for Wien, Praha, København and Moskva, respectively. There have been cases, however, where the conventional or historical form commonly used in English cartography has been applied with the same meaning. Thus, Peking and Nanking are the English conventional forms for Beijing and Nanjing, while Tsinan, Tientsin and Mukden are the former conventional spellings or names for Jinan, Tianjin and Shenyang, respectively. Other examples are Saigon, the former name for Ho Chi Minh, Vietnam; and Bangkok, the name for Krung Thep, which is used in Thailand.

The lack of reliable data for countries, especially ex-colonies without a firm national cartographic tradition, has made it necessary to utilize mapping skills of former colonist nations such as France, the United Kingdom and Belgium. A lack of data has led to the adoption of French and British forms in many areas, as these two languages are widely used for official purposes.

Another special case is that of the multilingual areas. Many countries and areas officially recognize two or more written and spoken languages; therefore, all of the principal written forms appear on the maps. This is true, for example, of Belgium where the official languages are French and Dutch (e.g. Bruxelles/Brussel) and of Italian regions such as Valle d'Aosta and Alto Adige, where French, German and Italian are used (e.g. Aosta/Aoste) (Bolzano/Bozen).

In preparing this atlas, each of these special cases has been taken into full consideration within the limits of the scale, space and readability of the maps.

Transliteration of the Cyrillic Alphabet
(International System—ISO)

Cyrillic Letter		Roman Letter		Cyrillic Letter		Roman Letter	
А	а	a		О	о	o	
Б	б	b		П	ń	p	
В	в	v		Р	р	r	
Г	г	g		С	с	s	
Д	д	d		Т	т	t	
Е	е	e	initially, after a vowel or after the mute sign "Ъ", becomes "je"	У	у	u	
				Ф	ф	f	
				Х	х	h	
Ё	ё	ё		Ц	ц	c	
Ж	ж	ž		Ч	ч	č	
З	з	z		Ш	ш	š	
И	и	i		Щ	щ	šč	
Й	й	j	not written if preceded by "И" or "Ы"	Ъ	ъ	—	not written
				Ы	ы	y	
К	к	k		Ь	ь	—	not written
Л	л	l		Э	э	e	
М	м	m		Ю	ю	ju	
Н	н	n		Я	я	ja	

Transcription of Modern Greek
(U.S. B. G. N./P.C.G.N.)

Greek Letter (or combination)		Roman Letter (or combination)		Greek Letter (or combination)		Roman Letter (or combination)	
A	α	a			$\mu\pi$	b	beginning a word
	$\alpha\iota$	ai				mb	within a word
	$\alpha\upsilon$	av		N	ν	n	
B	β	v			$\nu\tau$	d	beginning a word
Γ	γ	g				nd	within a word
	$\gamma\gamma$	ng		Ξ	ξ	x	
	$\gamma\kappa$	g	beginning a word	O	o	o	
					$o\iota$	oi	
		ng	within a word		$o\upsilon$	ou	
Δ	δ	d		Π	π	p	
E	ϵ	e		P	ρ	r	
	$\epsilon\iota$	i		Σ	σ	s	
	$\epsilon\upsilon$	ev			ς	s	ending a word
Z	ζ	z		T	τ	t	
H	η	i			$\tau\zeta$	tz	
	$\eta\upsilon$	iv		Y	υ	i	
Θ	θ	th			$\upsilon\iota$	i	
I	ι	i		Φ	ϕ	f	
K	κ	k		X	χ	kh	
Λ	λ	l		Ψ	ψ	ps	
M	μ	m		Ω	ω	o	

The "Geographical Glossary" lists the principal geographical terms used on the maps. All of these terms, including abbreviations, prefixes and suffixes, appear in the cartographic table as they appear on the maps. Terms are listed in accordance with the English alphabet, without consideration of diacritical marks on letters or of particular groups of letters.
Prefixes and suffixes relating to principal names or forming part of geographical toponyms are followed or preceded by a dash and the language to which they refer: e.g. Chi-/Dan. (Chi, a Danish prefix, means large); -bor/Slvn. (-bor, a Slovakian suffix, means city). Suffixes can also appear as words in themselves. In this case, the suffix and primary word are coupled together: e.g. Berg, -berg (Berg, which means mountain, can be used alone or as part of another word, such as Hapsberg).

Certain terms are followed or preceded by their abbreviation used on the maps. Both instances are listed: e.g. Fjord, Fj. and Fj., Fjord.
All geographical terms are identified by the language or languages to which each belongs. The language or languages in italics follows the term: e.g. Abbey/Eng.; -bad/Nor., Dut., Swed., Germ. Each term is translated into a corresponding English term or terms.
Below is a table identifying the abbreviations of various language names used on the maps. Note that certain abbreviations represent a group of languages, instead of one language: e.g. Ural. is the abbreviation for Uralic, a group word for Udmurt, Komi, and Nenets.
Alt. = Altaic (Turkmen, Tatar, Bashkir, Kazakh, Karalpak, Nogai, Kirghiz, Uzbek, Uigur, Altaic, Yakut, Khakass)
Ban. = Bantu (KiSwahili, ChiLuba, Lingala, KiKongo)

Cauc. = Caucasian (Chechen, Ingush, Kalmuck, Georgian)
Iran. = Iranian (Baluchi, Tagus)
Mel. = Melanesian (Fijian, New Caledonian, Micronesian, Nauruan)
Mong. = Mongolian (Buryat, Khalka Mongol)
Poly. = Polynesian (Maori, Samoan, Tongan, Tahitian, Hawaiian)
Sah. = Saharan (Kanuri, Tubu)
Som. = Somalian (Somali, Galla)
Sud. = Sudanese (Peul, Ehoué, Mossi, Yoruba, Ibo)
Ural. = Uralic (Udmurt, Komi, Nenets).
Because of their technical application to geography, some geographical terms may not fully correspond with the meaning given for them in some dictionaries.

Abbreviations of Language Names

Abbreviations in English	English	Abbreviations in English	English	Abbreviations in English	English	Abbreviations in English	English	Abbreviations in English	English	Abbreviations in English	English
Afr.	Afrikaans	Bulg.	Bulgarian	Fr.	French	Khm.	Khmer	Pers.	Persian	Som.	Somalian
A.I.	American Indian	Burm.	Burmese	Gae.	Gaelic	Kor.	Korean	Pol.	Polish	Sp.	Spanish
Alb.	Albanian	Cat.	Catalan	Georg.	Georgian	K.S.	Khoi-San	Poly.	Polynesian	Sud.	Sudanese
Alt.	Altaic	Cauc.	Caucasian	Germ.	German	Laot.	Laotian	Port.	Portuguese	Swa.	Swahili
Amh.	Amharic	Chin.	Chinese	Gr.	Greek	Lapp.	Lappish	Prov.	Provençal	Swed.	Swedish
Ar.	Arabic	Cz.	Czech	Hebr.	Hebrew	Latv.	Latvian	Rmsh.	Romansh	Tam.	Tamil
Arm.	Armenian	Dan.	Danish	Hin.	Hindi	Lith.	Lithuanian	Rom.	Romanian	Thai	Thai
Az.	Azerbaidzhani	Dut.	Dutch	Hung.	Hungarian	Mal.	Malay	Rus.	Russian	Tib.	Tibetan
Ban.	Bantu	Eng.	English	Icel.	Icelandic	Malag.	Malagasy	Sah.	Saharan	Tur.	Turkish
Bas.	Basque	Esk.	Eskimo	Indon.	Indonesian	Mel.	Melanesian	S.C.	Serbo-Croatian	Ural.	Uralic
Beng.	Bengali	Est.	Estonian	Ir.	Irish	Mong.	Mongolian			Urdu	Urdu
Ber.	Berber	Far.	Faroese	Iran.	Iranian	Nep.	Nepalese	Sin.	Sinhalese	Viet.	Vietnamese
Br.	Breton	Finn.	Finnish	It.	Italian	Nor.	Norwegian	Slvk.	Slovak	Wall.	Walloon
		Fle.	Flemish	Jap.	Japanese	Pash.	Pashto	Slvn.	Slovene	Wel.	Welsh

Glossary of Geographical Terms

Local Form	English	Local Form	English	Local Form	English	Local Form	English
A		Ait / Ar.; Ber.	sons	Ard- / Gae.	high	Badwĕynta / Som.	ocean
		Aiví, -aivi / Lapp.	mountain	Areg / Ar.	dune	Badyarada / Som.	gulf
A- / Ban.	people	Ak / Tur.	white	Areia / Port.	beach	Baeg / Kor.	white
A' / Icel.	river	'Aklé / Ar.	dunes	Arena / Sp.	beach	Bæk / Dan.	brook
Å / Dan.; Nor.; Swed.	stream	Akmeņs / Latv.	stone	Argent / Fr.	silver	Bælt / Dan.	strait
a., an / Germ.	on	Ákra / Gr.	point	Arhipelag / Rus.	archipelago	Bagni / It.	thermal springs
Aa / Germ.	stream	Akti / Gr.	coast	Arkhaios / Gr.	old, antique	Baharu / Mal.	new
Aache / Germ.	stream	Ala / Malag.	forest	Arm / Eng.; Germ.	branch	Bahia / Port.	bay
Aaiún / Ar.	springs	Ala / Finn.	low, lower	Arquipélago / Port.	archipelago	Bahía / Sp.	bay
Aan / Dut.; Fle.	on	Alan / Tur.	field	Arr., Arroyo / Sp.	stream	Bahir / Ar.	river, lake, sea
Ăb / Pers.	stream	Alb / Rom.	white	Arrecife / Sp.	reef	Bahnhof / Germ.	railway station
Ăbăd / Pers.	city, town	Albo / Sp.	white	Arroio / Port.	stream	Bahr / Ar.	wadi
Abad, -abad / Pers.	city, town	Albufera / Sp.	lagoon	Art / Tur.	pass, watershed	Baḥr / Ar.	river, lake, sea
Ăbăr / Ar.	spring	Alcalá / Sp.	castle	Aru / Sin.; Tam.	river	Baḥrat / Ar.	lake
Abbadia / It.	abbey	Alcázar / Sp.	castle	Ås / Dan.; Nor.; Swed.	hills	Bahri / Ar.	north, northern
Abbaye / Fr.	abbey	Aldea / Sp.	village	Asfar / Ar.	yellow	Baḥri / Ar.	north
Abbazia / It.	abbey	Alföld / Hung.	lowland	Asif / Ber.	river	Baḥrīyah / Ar.	northern
Abbi / Amh.	great	Ali / Amh.	mountain	Asky / Alt.	lower	Bai / Chin.	white
Abd / Ar.	servant	Alia / Poly.	stream	Áspros / Gr.	white	Băi / Rom.	thermal springs
Abeba / Amh.	flower	Alin / Mong.	range	Assa / Ber.	wadi	Baia / Port.	bay
Aber / Br.; Wel.	estuary	Alm / Germ.	mountain pasture	Atalaya / Sp.	frontier	Baie / Fr.	bay
Abhang / Germ.	slope			Áth / Gae.	ford	Baigne / Fr.	seaside resort
Abū / Ar.	father, master	Alor / Mal.	river	Átha / Gae.	ford	Baile / Gae.	city, town
Abyad / Ar.	white	Alp / Germ.	mountain pasture	Atol / Port.	atoll	Bain / Fr.	thermal springs
Abyaḍ / Ar.	white			Au / Germ.	meadow	Bains / Fr.	thermal springs
Abyăr / Ar.	well	Alpe / Germ.; Fr.; It.	mountain pasture	Aue / Germ.	irrigated field	Baixo / Port.	low, lower
Abyss / Eng.	ocean depth, deep	Alps / Eng.	mountains	Aust / Nor.	east	Bajan / Mong.	rich
Ach / Germ.	stream	Alsó / Hung.	low, lower	Austur / Icel.	east	Bajo / Sp.	low
Achaïf / Ar.	dunes	Alt / Germ.	old	Ava / Poly.	canal	Bajrak / Alt.	tribe
Ache / Germ.	stream	Altin / Tur.	lower	Aven / Fr.	doline, sink	Bakhtīyārī / Pers.	western
Achter / Afr.; Dut.; Fle.	back	Altiplano / Sp.	plateau	Awa / Poly.	bay	Bakki / Icel.	hill
Acqua / It.	water	Alto / Sp.; It.; Port.	high	Áyios / Gr.	saint	Bālă / Pers.	high
Açu / A.I.	great	Altopiano / It.	plateau	'Ayn / Ar.	spring, well	Bald / Eng.	peak
Açude / Port.	reservoir, dam	Älv / Swed.	river	'Ayoún / Ar.	springs, wells	Balka / Rus.	gorge
Ada / Tur.	island	Am / Kor.	mountain, peak	'Ayoûn / Ar.	spring	Balkan / Bulg.; Tur.	mountain range
Adalar / Tur.	archipelago	Amane / Ber.	water	Aza / Ber.	wadi	Ballin / Gae.	mouth
Adasr / Tur.	island	Amba / Amh.	mountain	Azraq / Ar.	light blue	Ballon / Fr.	dome
Addis / Amh.	new	Ambato / Malag.	rock	Azul / Port.; Sp.	light blue	Bally / Gae.	city, town
Adi / Amh.	village	An / Gae.	of	Azur / Fr.	light blue	Balta / Rom.	marsh
Adrar / Ber.	mount, mountains	An, a. / Germ.	on			Báltos / Gr.	marsh
		Ana / Poly.	grotto	**B**		Ban / Laot.	village
Aéroport / Fr.	airport	Anatolikós / Gr.	eastern			Bana / Jap.	promontory
Aeroporto / It.; Port.	airport	Äng / Swed.	meadow	B., Bay / Eng.	bay	Baña / Slvk.	mine
Aeropuerto / Sp.	airport	Angra / Port.	bay, anchorage	b., bei / Germ.	by	Bañados / Sp.	marsh
Af / Som.	mouth, gorge	Ani- / Malag.	center	B., Bucht / Germ.	bay	Banc / Fr.	bank
Afsluitdijk / Dut.	dam	Áno / Gr.	upper	Ba / Sud.	river	Banco / It.; Sp.	bank
Agadir / Ber.	castle	Ánou / Ber.	well	Ba- / Ban.	people	Band / Pers.	dam, mountain range
Aĝiz / Tur.	mouth	Anse / Fr.	inlet	Ba / Mel.	hill, mountain		
Agro / Sp.; It.	plain	Ant- / Malag.	center	Baai / Afr.	bay	Bandao / Chin.	peninsula
Agua / Sp.	water	Ao / Chin.; Khm.; Thai	gulf	Bab / Ar.	gate	Bandar / Ar.; Mal.; Pers.	port, market
Aguja / Sp.	needle	'Āouâna / Ar.	well	Bac / Viet.	north	Bang / Indon.; Mal.	stream
Agulha / Port.	needle, promontory	Apă / Rom.	water	Bach / Germ.	brook, torrent	Bangou / Sah.	well
Ahal / Georg.	new	'Aqabat / Ar.	pass	Bacino / It.	reservoir	Banhado / Port.	marsh
Aḥmar / Ar.	red	Aqueduc / Fr.	aqueduct	Back / Eng.	ridge	Bani / Ar.	sons
Ahrămăt / Ar.	pyramids	Ar / Mong.	north	Bäck / Swed.	brook	Banja / Bulg.; S.C.; Slvn.	thermal springs
Ahzar / Ber.	wadi	Ar / Sin.; Tam.	river	Backe / Swed.	brook	Banjaran / Mal.	mountain range
Aigialós / Gr.	coast	'Arâguîb / Ar.	hills	Backe / Swed.	hill	Banka / Rus.	sandbank
Aigue / Prov.	water	Arba / Amh.	mount	Bad, -bad / Dan.; Germ.; Nor.; Swed.	thermal springs	Banke / Dan.	bank
Aiguille / Fr.	needle	Arbore / Rom.	tree	Baden, -baden / Germ.	thermal springs	Baño / Sp.	thermal springs
Ain / Ar.	spring	Archipiélago / Sp.	archipelago	Bādiyat / Ar.	desert	Banský / Cz.	upper
		Arcipelago / It.	archipelago			Bánya / Hung.	mine
		Ard / Ar.	region			Bar / Gae.	peak
						Bar / Eng.	sandbar

Geographical Glossary

Local Form	English
Bar / Hin.	great
Bāra / Hin.	great
Bara / S.C.	pond
Barā / Urdu	great
Barajı / Tur.	dam
Barat / Indon.; Mal.	west, western
Barkas / Lith.	castle, city, town
Barlovento / Sp.	windward
Barq / Ar.	hill
Barra / Port.; Sp.	bar, bank
Barrage / Fr.	dam
Barragem / Port.	reservoir
Barranca / Sp.	gorge
Barranco / Port.; Sp.	gorge
Barre / Fr.	bar
Barun / Mong.	western
Bas / Fr.	low
-bas / Rus.	reservoir
Bassa / Port.	flat
Bassejn / Rus.	reservoir
Bassin / Fr.	basin
Bassure / Fr.	flat
Bassurelle / Fr.	flat
Bašta / S.C.	garden
Bataille / Fr.	battle
Batalha / Port.	battle
Batang / Indon.; Mal.	river
Batha / Sah.	stream
Baṭin / Ar.	depression
Bāṭlāq / Pers.	marsh
Batu / Mal.	rock
Bayan / Mong.	rich
Bayır / Tur.	mountain, slope
Bayou / Fr.	branch, stream
Bayt / Ar.	house
Bazar / Pers.	market
Be / Malag.	great
Beau / Fr.	beautiful
Becken / Germ.	basin
Bed / Eng.	river bed
Beek / Dut.	creek
Be'er / Hebr.	spring
Bei / Chin.	north
Bei, b. / Germ.	by
Beida / Ar.	white
Beinn / Gae.	mount
Bel / Ar.	son
Bel / Bulg.	white
Bel / Tur.	pass
Beled / Ar.	village
Belen / Tur.	mount
Belet / Ar.	village
Beli / S.C.; Slvn.	white
Beli / Tur.	pass
Bellah / Sah.	well
Belogorje / Rus.	mountains
Belt / Dan.; Germ.	strait
Bely / Rus.	white
Bělý / Cz.	white
Ben / Ar.	son
Ben / Gae.	mount
Bender / Pers.	port, market
Bendi / Tur.	dam
Beni / Ar.	son
Beo / S.C.	white
Bereg / Rus.	bank
Berg, -berg / Afr.; Dut.; Fle.; Germ.; Nor.; Swed.	mount
Berge / Afr.	mountain
Bergen / Dut.; Fle.	dunes
Bergland / Germ.	upland
Bermejo / Sp.	red
Besar / Mal.	great
Betsu / Jap.	river
Betta / Tam.	mountain
Bhani / Hin.	community
Bharu / Mal.	new
Bheag / Gae.	little
Bīābān / Pers.	desert
Biały / Pol.	white
Bianco / It.	white
Bien / Viet.	lake
Bight / Eng.	bay
Bijeli / S.C.	white
Bill / Eng.	promontory
Bilo / S.C.	range
Bilý / Cz.	white
Binnen / Dut.; Fle.; Germ.	inner
Biqā' / Ar.	valley
Bir / Ar.	well
Bi'r / Ar.	well
Birkat / Ar.	pond
Bistrica / Bulg.; S.C.; Slvn.	stream
Bjarg / Icel.	rock
Bjerg / Dan.	mount
Bjeshkët / Alb.	mountain pasture
Blaauw / Afr.	blue
Blanc / Fr.	white
Blanco / Sp.	white
Blau / Germ.	blue
Bleu / Fr.	blue
Bluff / Eng.	cliff
Bo- / Ban.	people
Bo / Chin.	white
Bo / Swed.	habitation
Boca / Sp.	gap, mouth
Bôca / Port.	gap, mouth
Bocage / Fr.	forest
Bocca / It.	gap, pass
Bocchetta / It.	gap, pass
Bodden / Germ.	bay, lagoon
Boden / Germ.	soil
Bœng / Khm.	lake, marsh
Bog / Eng.	marsh
Bogaz / Alt.; Az.; Tur.	strait
Bogāzi / Tur.	strait
Bogdo / Mong.	high
Bogen / Nor.	bay
Bois / Fr.	forest
Boka / S.C.	channel
Boloto / Rus.	marsh
Bolšoj / Rus.	great
Bolsón / Sp.	basin
Bom / Port.	good
Bong / Kor.	peak
Bongo / Malag.	upland
Bor / Cz.; Rus.	coniferous forest
Bór / Pol.	forest
-bor / Slvn.	city, town
Bóras / Gr.	north
Börde / Germ.	fertile plain
Bordj / Ar.	fort
Bóreios / Gr.	northern
Borg, -borg / Dan.; Nor.; Swed.	castle
Borgo / It.	village
Born / Germ.	spring
Bory / Pol.	forest
Bosch / Dut.; Fle.	forest
Bosco / It.	wood
Bosque / Sp.	forest
Bosse / Fr.	hill
Botn / Nor.	bay
Bou / Ar.	father, master
Bouche / Fr.	mouth
Boula / Sud.	well
Bourg / Fr.	city, town
Bourne, - bourne / Eng.	frontier
Boven / Afr.	upper
Boz / Tur.	grey
Bozorg / Pers.	great
Brána / Cz.	gate
Braña / Sp.	mountain pasture
Branche / Fr.	branch
Branco / Port.	white
Braţul / Rom.	branch
Bravo / Sp.	wild
Brazo / Sp.	branch
Brdo / Cz.; S.C.	hill
Bre / Nor.	glacier
Bredning / Dan.	bay
Breg / Alb.; Bulg.; S.C.	hill, coast
Brjag / Bulg.	bank
Bro / Dan.; Nor.; Swed.	bridge
Brod / Bulg.; Cz.; Rus.; S.C.; Slvk.; Slvn.	ford
Bród / Pol.	ford
Bron / Afr.	spring
Bronn / Germ.	spring
Bru / Nor.	bridge
Bruch / Germ.	peat-bog
Bruchzone / Germ.	fracture zone
Bruck, -bruck / Germ.	bridge
Brücke / Germ.	bridge
Brug / Dut.; Fle.	bridge
Brugge / Dut.; Fle.	bridge
Bruk / Nor.	factory
Brunn / Swed.	spring
-brunn / Germ.	spring
Brunnen / Germ.	spring
Brygg / Swed.	bridge
Brzeg / Pol.	coast
Bü / Ar.	father, master
Bucht, B. / Germ.	bay
Bugt / Dan.	bay
Buḥayrat / Ar.	lake, lagoon
Bühel / Germ.	hill
Bühl / Germ.	hill
Buhta / Rus.	bay
Bukit / Mal.	mountain, peak
Bukt / Nor.; Swed.	bay
Buku / Indon.	hill, mountain
Bulag / Mong.; Tur.	spring
Bulak / Mong.; Tur.	spring
Būlāq / Tur.	spring
Bult / Afr.	hill
Bulu / Indon.	mountain
Bur / Som.	mount
Bür / Ar.	port
Burg, - burg / Afr.; Ar.; Dut.; Eng.; Germ.	castle
Burgh / Eng.	city, town
Burgo / Sp.	village
Burha / Hin.	old
Buri / Thai	city, town
Burj / Ar.	village
Burn / Eng.	stream
Burnu / Tur.	promontory
Burqat / Ar.	mount, marsh
Burun / Tur.	cape
Busen / Germ.	bay
Busu / Ban.	land
Būtat / Ar.	lake, pond
Butte / Eng.; Fr.	flat-topped hill
Büyük / Tur.	great
By / Eng.	near
By, -by / Dan.; Nor.; Swed.	city, town
Bystrica / Cz.; Slvk.	stream
Bystrzyca / Pol.	stream

C

Local Form	English
C., Cap / Cat.; Fr.; Rom.	cape
C., Cape / Eng.	cape
C., Colle / It.	pass
Caatinga / A.I.	forest
Cabeça / Port.	peak
Cabeço / Port.	peak
Cabeza / Sp.	peak
Cabezo / Sp.	peak, mountain
Cabo / Port.; Sp.	cape
Cachoeira / Port.	waterfall, rapids
Cachopo / Port.	reef
Cadena / Sp.	range
Caer / Wel.	castle
Cagan / Cauc.; Mong.	white
Cairn / Gae.	hill
Čaj / Az.; Tur.	river
Cajdam / Mong.	salt marsh
Caka / Chin.	lake
Cala / Sp.; It.	inlet
Calar / Sp.	plateau
Caldas / Sp.; Port.	thermal springs
Caleta / Sp.	inlet
Camp / Cat.; Fr.; Eng.	field
Campagna / It.	plain
Campagne / Fr.	plain
Campo / Sp.; It.; Port.	field
Cañada / Sp.	gorge, ravine
Canale / It.	canal, channel
Caño / Sp.	branch
Cañón / Sp.	gorge
Canyon / Eng.	gorge
Cao / Viet.	mountain
Cap, C. / Cat.; Fr.; Rom.	cape
Car / Gae.	castle
Càrn / Gae.	peak
Carrera / Sp.	road
Carrick / Gae.	rock
Casale / It.	hamlet
Cascada / Sp.	waterfall
Cascata / It.	waterfall
Castel / It.	castle
Castell / Cat.	castle
Castello / It.	castle
Castelo / Port.	castle
Castillo / Sp.	castle
Castro / Sp.; It.	village
Catarata / Sp.	cataract
Catena / It.	mountain range
Catinga / Port.	degraded forest
Cauce / Sp.	river bed
Causse / Fr.	highland
Cava / It.	stone quarry
Çay / Tur.	river
Cay / Eng.	islet, island
Caye / Fr.	island
Cayo / Sp.	islet, island
Ceann / Gae.	promontory
Centralny / Rus.	middle
Čeren / Alb.	black
Černi / Bulg.	black
Černý / Cz.	black
Čërny / Rus.	black
Cerrillo / Sp.	hill
Cerrito / Sp.	hill
Cerro / Sp.; Port.	hill, mountain
Cêrro / Port.	hill, mountain
Červen / Bulg.	red
Červony / Rus.	red
Cetate / Rom.	city, town
Chaco / Sp.	scrubland
Chāh / Pers.	well
Chaïf / Ar.	dunes
Chaîne / Fr.	mountain range
Champ / Fr.	field
Chang / Chin.	highland
Chapada / Port.	highland
Chapadão / Port.	highland
Château / Fr.	castle
Châtel / Fr.	castle
Chāy / Tur.	river
Chedo / Kor.	archipelago
Chenal / Fr.	canal
Cheng / Chin.	city, town, wall
Cheon / Kor.	city, river
Chergui / Ar.	eastern
Cherry, -cherry / Hin.; Tam.	city, town
Chew / Amh.	salt mine, salt
Chhâk / Khm.	bay
Chhotla / Hin.	little
Chi- / Ban.	great
Chi / Chin.	marsh, lake
Chi / Kor.	lake, pond
Chi- / Swa.	land
Chiang / Thai	city, town
Chico / Sp.	little
Chine / Eng.	ridge
Ch'on / Kor.	station
Ch'ŏn / Kor.	river
Chŏsuji / Kor.	reservoir
Chott / Ar.	salt marsh
Chu / Chin.; Viet.	mountain, hill
Chuôr phnum / Khm.	mountain range
Chute / Fr.	waterfall
Chutes / Fr.	waterfalls
Cidade / Port.	city, town
Ciems / Latv.	village
Čierny / Slvk.	black
Cime / Fr.	peak
Cîmp / Rom.	field
Cîmpie / Rom.	plain
Cinco / Sp.; Port.	five
Citeli / Georg.	red
Città / It.	city, town
Ciudad / Sp.	city, town
Ckali / Georg.	water
Ckaro / Georg.	spring
Co / Chin.	lake
Col / Cat.; Fr.	pass
Colina / Port.; Sp.	hill
Coll / Cat.	hill
Collado / Sp.	pass
Colle, C. / It.	pass
Collina / It.	hill
Colline / Fr.	hill
Colonia / Sp.; It.	colony
Coma / Sp.	hill country
Comb / Eng.	basin
Comba / Sp.	basin
Combe / Fr.	basin
Comté / Fr.	county, shire
Con / Viet.	island
Conca / It.	depression
Condado / Sp.	county, shire
Cone / Eng.	volcanic cone
Cône / Fr.	volcanic cone
Contraforte / Port.	front range
Cordal / Sp.	crest
Cordilheira / Port.	mountain range
Cordillera / Sp.	mountain range
Coring / Chin.	lake
Corixa / A.I.	stream
Corno / It.	peak
Cornone / It.	peak
Corrente / It.; Port.	stream
Corriente / Sp.	stream
Costa / Sp.; It.; Port.	coast
Côte / Fr.	coast
Coteau / Fr.	height, slope
Coxilha / Port.	ridge
Craig / Gae.	rock
Cratère / Fr.	crater
Cresta / Sp.; It.	crest
Crêt / Fr.	crest
Crête / Fr.	crest
Crkva / S.C.	church
Crni / S.C.; Slvn.	black
Crven / S.C.	red
Csatorna / Hung.	canal
Cuchilla / Sp.	ridge
Cuenca / Sp.	basin
Cuesta / Sp.	escarpment
Cueva / Sp.	cave
Čuka / Bulg.; S.C.	peak
Çukur / Tur.	well
Cu Lao / Viet.	island
Cumbre / Sp.	peak
Cun / Chin.	village
Cura / A.I.	stone
Curr / Alb.	rock
Cy., City / Eng.	city, town
Czarny / Pol.	black

D

Local Form	English
Da / Chin.	great
Da / Viet.	mountain, peak
Daal / Dut.; Fle.	valley
Daba / Mong.	pass
Daba / Som.	hill
Daban / Chin.; Mong.	pass
Dae / Kor.	great
Dağ / Tur.	mountain
Dağ., Daği / Tur.	mountain
Dāgh / Pers.; Tur.	mountain
Daği, Dağ. / Tur.	mountain
Dağları / Tur.	mountain range
Dahar / Ar.	hill
Dahr / Ar.	plateau, escarpment
Dai / Chin.; Jap.	great
Daiet / Ar.	marsh
Dak / Viet.	stream
Dake / Jap.	mountain
Dakhla / Ar.	depression
Dakhlet / Ar.	depression, bay
Dal, -dal / Afr.; Dan.; Dut.; Fle.; Nor.; Swed.	valley
Dala / Alt.	steppe, plain
Dalaj / Mong.	lake, sea
Dalan / Mong.	wall
Dallol / Sud.	valley, torrent
Dalur / Icel.	valley
Damm / Germ.	dam
Dan / Kor.	point

Local Form	English
Danau / *Indon.*	lake
Danda / *Nep.*	mountains
Dao / *Chin.*	island, peninsula
Dao / *Viet.*	island
Dar / *Ar.*	house, region
Dar / *Swa.*	port
Dara / *Tur.*	torrent, valley
Darb / *Ar.*	track
Darja / *Alt.*	river, sea
Darya, Daryā / *Pers.*	river, sea
Daryācheh / *Pers.*	lake, sea
Daš / *Alt.; Az.*	rock
Dasht / *Pers.*	desert, plain
Dawḥat / *Ar.*	bay
Dayr / *Ar.*	convent
De / *Sp.; Fr.*	of
Deal / *Rom.*	hill
Dearg / *Gae.*	red
Debre / *Amh.*	hill, monastery
Dega / *Som.*	stone
Deh / *Pers.*	village
Dēḥ / *Som.*	stream
Deich / *Germ.*	dike
Dél / *Hung.*	south
Delft / *Dut.; Fle.*	deep
Delger / *Mong.*	wide, market
-den / *Eng.*	city, town
Deniz / *Tur.*	sea
Denizi / *Tur.*	sea
Dent / *Fr.*	peak
Deo / *Laot.; Viet.*	pass
Dépression / *Fr.*	depression
Depressione / *It.*	depression
Der / *Som.*	high
Dera / *Hin.; Urdu*	temple
Derbent / *Tur.*	gorge, pass
Dere / *Tur.*	river, valley
Désert / *Fr.*	desert
Desfiladero / *Sp.*	pass
Desh / *Hin.*	land, country
Desierto / *Sp.*	desert
Det / *Alb.*	sea
Détroit / *Fr.*	strait
Deux / *Fr.*	two
Dezh / *Pers.*	castle
Dhar / *Ar.*	heights, hills
Dhār / *Hin.; Urdu*	mountain
Dhitikós / *Gr.*	western
Dien / *Khm.; Viet.*	rice-field
Diep / *Dut.; Fle.*	deep, strait
Dijk, -dijk / *Dut.; Fle.*	dam
Ding / *Chin.*	mountain, peak
Dique / *Sp.*	dam
Di Sopra / *It.*	upper
Di Sotto / *It.*	lower
Distrito / *Sp.; Port.*	district
Diu / *Hin.*	island
Diz / *Pers.*	castle
Djebel / *Ar.*	mountain
Dji / *Ban.*	water
Djup / *Swed.*	deep
Do / *Kor.*	Island
Do / *S.C.*	valley
Dō / *Jap.*	island, administrative division
Dōho / *Som.*	valley
Doi / *Thai*	mountain, peak
Dol / *Bulg.; Cz.; Rus.; S.C.*	valley
Doł / *Pol.*	valley
Dolen / *Bulg.*	low
Dolgi / *Rus.*	long
Dolina / *Bulg.; Cz.; Pol.; Rus.; S.C.; Slvn.*	valley
Dolni / *Bulg.*	low
Dolni / *Pol.*	lower
Dolny / *Pol.*	lower
Domb / *Hung.*	hill
Dôme / *Fr.*	dome
Dong / *Chin.; Viet.*	east
Dong / *Kor.*	city, town
Dong / *Thai*	mountain
Dong / *Viet.*	marsh, plain
Donji / *S.C.*	low, lower
Dorf, -dorf / *Germ.*	village
Doroga / *Rus.*	road
Dorp, -dorp / *Afr.; Dut.; Fle.*	village
Dos / *Rom.*	ridge
Dos / *Sp.*	two
Douarn / *Br.*	land
Dougou / *Sud.*	settlement
Doukou / *Sud.*	settlement
Down / *Eng.*	hill
Drâa / *Ar.*	dunes, hills
Dracht / *Germ.*	sandbank
Draw / *Eng.*	ravine, valley
Drif / *Afr.*	ford
Drift / *Afr.*	ford
Droichead / *Gae.*	bridge
Droûs / *Ar.*	crest
Dry / *Pash.*	river
Dubh / *Gae.*	black
Dugi / *S.C.*	long
Dugu / *Sud.*	settlement
Dun / *Gae.*	castle
Duna / *Sp.; It.*	dune
Düne / *Germ.*	dune
Dungar / *Hin.*	mountain
Düngar / *Hin.*	mountain
Duong / *Viet.*	stream
Durchbruch / *Germ.*	gorge
Ḍurg / *Hin.*	castle
-durga / *Hin.*	castle
Duży / *Pol.*	great
Dvor / *Cz.*	court
Dvorec / *Rus.*	castle
Dvůr / *Cz.*	castle
Dwór / *Pol.*	court
Džebel / *Bulg.*	mountain
Dzong / *Tib.*	fort, monastery

E

Local Form	English
Ea / *Thai*	river
Eau / *Fr.*	water
Ebe / *Ban.*	forest
Ebene / *Germ.*	plain
Eck / *Germ.*	point
Eclusa / *Sp.*	lock
Écluse / *Fr.*	lock
Écueil / *Fr.*	cliff
Edeien / *Ber.*	sand desert
Edjérir / *Ber.*	wadi
Egg / *Germ.; Nor.*	crest, point
Eglab / *Ar.*	hills
Ehi / *Sah.*	mountain
Eid / *Nor.*	isthmus
Eiland / *Afr.*	island
Eisen / *Germ.*	iron
Eisenerz / *Germ.*	iron ore
El / *Amh.*	well
Elv, -elv / *Nor.*	river
Embalse / *Sp.*	reservoir
Embouchure / *Fr.*	mouth
Emi / *Sah.*	mountain
En / *Fr.*	in
Ende / *Germ.*	end
Enneri / *Sah.*	stream
Ennis / *Gae.*	island
Enseada / *Port.*	Bay, inlet
Ensenada / *Sp.*	bay, inlet
Ér / *Hung.*	stream
Erdő / *Hung.*	forest
Erg / *Ar.*	sand desert
Erz / *Germ.*	ore
Espigão / *Port.*	plateau
Ēstān / *Pers.*	land
Este / *Sp.*	east
Estero / *Sp.*	estuary, marsh
Estrecho / *Sp.*	strait
Estreito / *Port.*	strait
Estuaire / *Fr.*	estuary
Estuário / *Port.*	estuary
Estuario / *Sp.; It.*	estuary
Észak / *Hung.*	north
Étang / *Fr.*	pond
Ewaso / *Ban.*	river
Ey / *Icel.*	island
Eyja / *Icel.*	island
Eyjar / *Icel.*	islands
Eylandt / *Dut.*	island
Ežeras / *Lith.*	lake
Ezers / *Latv.*	lake

F

Local Form	English
Fa / *Mel.*	stream
Falaise / *Fr.*	cliff
Fall, -fall / *Germ.; Eng.; Swed.*	waterfall
Falls / *Eng.*	waterfall
Falu / *Hung.*	village
-falva / *Hung.*	village
Fan / *Sah.*	village
Faraglione / *It.*	cliff
Farallón / *Sp.*	cliff
Faro / *Sp.; It.*	lighthouse
Farvand / *Dan.*	strait
Fehér / *Hung.*	white
Fehn / *Germ.*	peat fen, peat-bog
Fekete / *Hung.*	black
Feld / *Dan.; Germ.*	field
Fell / *Eng.*	upland moor
Fell / *Icel.*	mountain
Fels / *Germ.*	rock
Fen / *Eng.*	marsh, peat-bog
Feng / *Chin.*	mountain, peak
Feste / *Germ.*	fort
Festung / *Germ.*	fort
Fier / *Rom.*	iron
Firn / *Germ.*	snow-field
Firth / *Eng.*	estuary, fjord
Fiume / *It.*	river
Fjäll / *Swed.*	mountain
Fjärd / *Swed.*	fjord
Fjell / *Nor.*	mountain
Fjöll / *Icel.*	mountain
Fjord, Fj. / *Dan.; Nor.; Swed.*	fjord
Fjörður / *Icel.*	fjord, bay
Fleuve / *Fr.*	river
Fließ / *Germ.*	torrent
Fljót / *Icel.*	river
Flói / *Icel.*	bay, gulf
Floresta / *Sp.; Port.*	forest
Flow / *Eng.*	strait
Flughafen / *Germ.*	airport
Fluß / *Germ.*	river
Fo / *Mel.*	stream
Foa / *Mel.*	stream
Foa / *Poly.*	cove
Foce / *It.*	mouth
Föld / *Hung.*	plain
Fonn / *Nor.*	glacier
Fontaine / *Fr.*	fountain
Fonte / *It.; Port.*	spring
Fontein / *Afr.; Dut.*	spring
Foort / *Afr.; Dut.*	ford
Forca / *It.*	pass
Forcella / *It.*	defile
Ford / *Rus.*	fjord
Förde / *Germ.*	fjord, gulf
Foreland / *Eng.*	promontory
Foresta / *It.*	forest
Forêt / *Fr.*	forest
Fors / *Swed.*	rapids, waterfall
Forst / *Germ.; Dut.*	forest
Forte / *It.; Port.*	fort
Fortin / *Sp.*	fort
Fosa / *Sp.*	trench
Foss / *Icel.; Nor.*	rapids, waterfall
Fossé / *Fr.*	trench
Foum / *Ar.*	pass
Fourche / *Fr.*	pass
Foz / *Sp.; Port.*	mouth
Frei / *Germ.*	free
Fronteira / *Port.*	frontier
Frontera / *Sp.*	frontier
Frontón / *Sp.*	promontory
Fuente / *Sp.*	spring
Fuerte / *Sp.*	fort
Fuji / *Jap.*	mountain
Fūlat / *Ar.*	marsh
Furt / *Germ.*	ford
Fushë / *Alb.*	plain

G

Local Form	English
G., Gora / *Bulg.; Rus.; S.C.*	mountain, hill
G., Gunung / *Indon.*	mountain
Ga / *Jap.*	bay
Ga / *Mel.*	mountain, peak
Gabel / *Germ.*	pass
Gaissa / *Lapp.*	mountain
Gala / *Sin.; Tam.*	mountain
Gam / *Hin.; Urdu*	village
Gamle / *Nor.; Swed.*	old
Gana / *Sud.*	little
Gang / *Germ.*	passage
Gang / *Chin.*	port, bay
Gang / *Kor.*	stream, bay
Gang / *Tib.*	glacier
Ganga / *Hin.*	river
Ganj / *Hin.; Urdu*	market
-gaon / *Hin.*	city, town
Gaoyuan / *Chin.*	plateau
Gap / *Kor.*	point
Gar / *Hin.*	house
Gara / *Bulg.*	station
Gara / *Ar.*	hills, range
Gară / *Rom.*	station
Garaet / *Ar.*	marsh, intermittent lake
Garam / *Beng.; Hin.; Urdu*	village
-gard / *Pol.*	city, town
Gård, -gård / *Dan.; Nor.; Swed.*	farmhouse
Gardaneh / *Pers.*	pass
Gare / *Fr.*	railway station
Garet / *Ar.*	hill
Garh, -garh / *Hin.; Urdu*	castle
Garhi / *Hin.; Nep.; Urdu*	fort
Garten / *Germ.*	garden
Gat / *Dan.; Fle.; Dut.*	strait
Gata / *Jap.*	bay, lake
Gau, -gau / *Germ.*	district
Gäu, -gäu / *Germ.*	district
Gavan / *Rus.*	port
Gave / *Bas.*	torrent
Gawa / *Jap.*	river
Geb., Gebirge / *Germ.*	mountain range
Gebergte / *Afr.; Dut.*	mountain range
Gebirge, Geb. / *Germ.*	mountain range
Geç., Geçit / *Tur.*	pass
Geçidi / *Tur.*	pass
Geçit, Geç. / *Tur.*	pass
Geysir / *Icel.*	geyser
Ghar / *Hin.; Urdu*	house
Ghar / *Pash.*	mountain, mountain range
Gharbīyah / *Ar.*	western
Ghat / *Hin.; Nep.; Urdu*	pass
Ghubbat / *Ar.*	bay
Ghurd / *Ar.*	dune
Gi / *Kor.*	peninsula
Giang / *Viet.*	stream
Giri / *Hin.; Urdu*	mountain, hill
Girlo / *Rus.*	branch
Gjebel / *Ar.*	mountain
Gji / *Alb.*	bay
Glace / *Fr.*	ice
Glaciar / *Sp.*	glacier
Glacier / *Eng.; Fr.*	glacier
Glen / *Gae.*	valley
Gletscher / *Germ.*	glacier
Gobi / *Mong.*	desert
Godār / *Pers.*	ford
Gok / *Kor.*	river
Gök / *Tur.*	blue
Gol / *Cauc.; Mong.*	river
Göl / *Tur.*	lake
Gola / *It.*	gorge
Gold / *Germ.; Eng.*	gold
Golet / *S.C.*	mountain
Golf / *Germ.*	gulf
Golfe / *Fr.*	gulf
Golfete / *Sp.*	inlet
Golfo / *Sp.; It.; Port.*	gulf
Goljam / *Bulg.*	great
Gölü / *Tur.*	lake
Gong / *Tib.*	high
Gonggar / *Tib.*	mountain
Gongo / *Ban.*	mountain
Góra / *Pol.*	mountain
Gora, G. / *Bulg.; Rus.; S.C.*	mountain, hill
Gorica / *S.C.; Slvn.*	hill
Gorje / *S.C.*	mountain range
Gorlo / *Rus.*	gorge
Gorm / *Gae.*	blue
Gorni / *Bulg.; S.C.; Slvn.*	upper
Gornji / *S.C.; Slvn.*	upper
Górny / *Pol.*	high
Gorod / *Rus.*	city, town
Gorodok / *Rus.*	village
Gorski / *Bulg.*	upper
Gory / *Rus.*	mountains
-gou / *Chin.*	river
Goulbi / *Sud.*	river, lake
Goulbin / *Sud.*	wadi
Goulet / *Fr.*	gap
Gour / *Ar.*	hills, range
Gourou / *Sud.*	wadi
Goz / *Sah.*	dune
Graafschap / *Dut.*	county, shire
Graben / *Germ.*	ditch, canal
Gracht / *Dut.*	canal
Grad, -grad / *Bulg.; Rus.; S.C.; Slvn.*	city, town, castle
Gradac / *S.C.*	castle
Gradec / *Bulg.*	village
Gradec / *Slvn.*	castle
Græn / *Icel.*	green
Gran / *Sp.; It.*	great
Grande / *Sp.; It.; Port.*	great
Grao / *Cat.; Sp.*	gap
Grat / *Germ.*	crest
Grève / *Fr.*	beach
Grind / *Germ.*	peak
Grjada / *Rus.*	range
Gród, -gród / *Pol.*	castle, city, town
Grön / *Icel.*	green
Grond / *Afr.*	soil
Gronden / *Dut.; Fle.*	flat
Groot / *Afr.; Dut.; Fle.*	great
Groß / *Germ.*	great
Grotta / *It.*	grotto
Grotte / *Fr.; Germ.*	grotto
Grube / *Germ.*	mine
Grün / *Germ.*	green
Grunn / *Nor.*	ground
Gruppe / *Germ.*	mountain system
Gruppo / *It.*	mountain system
Gua / *Mal.*	cave
Guaçu / *A.I.*	great
Guan / *Chin.*	pass
Guazú / *A.I.*	great
Guba / *Rus.*	bay
Guchi / *Jap.*	strait
Guelb / *Ar.*	hill, mountain
Guelta / *Ar.*	well
Guic / *Br.*	village
Güney / *Tur.*	south, southern
Gunong / *Mal.*	mountain
Guntō / *Jap.*	archipelago
Gunung, G. / *Indon.*	mountain
Guo / *Chin.*	state, land
Gur / *Rom.*	mountain
Guri / *Jap.*	cliff
Gurud / *Ar.*	hills, dunes
Gyár / *Hung.*	factory

H

Local Form	English
Haag / *Dut.; Fle.*	hedge
-håb / *Dan.*	port
Haḍabat / *Ar.*	highland
Hadd / *Ar.*	point
Hadjer / *Ar.*	hill, mountain
Hae / *Kor.*	bay, sea
Haehyeop / *Kor.*	strait

Local Form	English
Haf / Icel.	sea
Ḩafar / Ar.	well
Hafen / Germ.	port
Haff / Germ.	lagoon
Hafir / Ar.	spring, ditch
Hafnar / Icel.	port
Häfūn / Som.	bay
Hage / Dan.	point
Hage / Dut.; Fle.	hedge
Hågna / Swed.	peak
Hai / Chin.	sea, lake, bay
Hain / Germ.	forest
Haixia / Chin.	strait
Ḩajar / Ar.	hill, mountain
Hajar / Ar.	hill country
Halbinsel / Germ.	peninsula
Halma / Hung.	hill
Halom / Hung.	hill
Halq / Ar.	gap
Hals / Nor.	peninsula
Halvø / Dan.	peninsula
Halvøy / Nor.	peninsula
Hama / Jap.	beach
Hamāda / Ar.	rocky desert
Ḩamādah / Ar.	plateau
Ḩamādat / Ar.	plateau
Hammam / Ar.	thermal springs
Ḩammām / Ar.	well
Hamn / Nor.; Swed.	port
Hamrā' / Ar.	red
Hāmūn / Jap.	salt lake
Hana / Jap.	cape
Hana / Poly.	bay
Hane / Tur.	house
Hang / Kor.	port
Hank / Ar.	escarpment, plateau
Hantō / Jap.	peninsula
Har / Hebr.	mountain
Hara / Mong.	black
Harar / Swa.	well
Ḩarrah / Ar.	lava field
Ḩarrat / Ar.	lava field
Hasi / Ar.	well
Ḩasi / Ar.	well
Hassi / Ar.	well
Ḩasy / Ar.	well
Haug / Nor.	hill
Haupt- / Germ.	principal
Haure / Lapp.	lake
Haus / Germ.	house
Hausen / Germ.	village
Haut / Fr.	high
Hauteur / Fr.	hill
Hauts Plateaux / Fr.	highlands
Hauz / Pers.	reservoir
Hav / Dan.; Nor.; Swed.	sea, gulf
Haven / Eng.; Fle.; Dut.	port
Havn / Dan.; Nor.	port
Havre / Fr.	port
Hawr / Ar.	lake, marsh
Ház / Hung.	house
-háza / Hung.	house
Hazm / Ar.	height, mountain range
He / Chin.	river
Head / Eng.	headland
Hed / Dan.; Swed.	heath
Hegy / Hung.	mountain
Hegység / Hung.	mountain
Hei / Nor.	heath
Heide / Germ.	heath
Heijde / Dut.; Fle.	heath
Heilig / Germ.	saint
Heim, -heim / Germ.; Nor.	house
Heiya / Jap.	plain
-hely / Hung.	locality
Hem / Swed.	home
Hen / Br.	old
Higashi / Jap.	east, eastern
Hima / Hin.	ice
Himal / Nep.	peak
Hisar / Tur.	castle
Ho / Chin.	reservoir, river
Ho / Kor.	river, reservoir
Hō / Jap.	mountain
Hoch / Germ.	high, upper
Hochland / Germ.	highland
Hochplato / Afr.	highland
Hodna / Ar.	highland
Hoek / Dut.; Fle.	cape
Hof / Dut.; Germ.	court
Höfn / Icel.	port
Høg / Nor.	peak
Hög / Swed.	mountain
Hogna / Nor.	peak
Höhe / Germ.	peak
Høj / Dan.	hill
Hoj / Ural.	mountain range
Hok / Jap.	north
Hoku / Jap.	north, northern
Holm / Dan.; Nor.; Swed.	island
Holz / Germ.	forest
Hon / Viet.	island, point
Hong / Chin.; Viet.	red
Hono / Poly.	bay, anchorage
Hoog / Afr.; Dut.; Fle.	high
Hook / Eng.	point
Hoorn / Afr.; Dut.; Fle.	cape, point
Hora / Cz.; Slvk.	point
Horn / Eng.; Germ.; Icel.; Nor.; Swed.	point
Horni / Cz.	high
Horný / Slvk.	upper
Horst / Germ.	mountain
Horvot / Hebr.	ruins
Hory / Cz.; Slvk.	mountain range
Hout / Dut.; Fle.	forest
Hovd, -hovd / Dan.; Nor.	cape
Ḩowz / Pers.	basin
Hrad / Cz.; Slvk.	castle, city, town
Hradiště / Cz.	citadel
Hřeben / Cz.	crest
Hrebet / Rus.	mountain range
Hu / Rmsh.	lake
Huang / Chin.	yellow
Hude / Germ.	pasture
Huerta / Sp.	market garden
Hügel / Germ.	hill
Hügelland / Germ.	hill country
Huis, -huis / Afr.; Dut.; Fle.	house
Huisie / Afr.	house
Huizen, -huizen / Dut.	houses
Huk / Afr.; Dan.; Swed.	cape
Hum / S.C.	hill
Hurst / Eng.	grove
Hus / Dut.; Nor.; Swed.	house
Huta / Pol.; Slvk.	hut
Hütte / Germ.	hut
Hver / Icel.	crater
Hvit / Icel.	white
Hvost / Rus.	spit

I

Local Form	English
I., Island / Eng.	island
Ierós / Gr.	holy
Igarapé / A.I.	river
Ighazer / Ber.	torrent
Ighil / Ber.	hill
Iguidi / Ber.	dunes
Ih / Mong.	great
Ike / Jap.	pond
Ile / Fr.	island
Ilha / Port.	island
Iller / Tur.	administrative division
Ilot / Fr.	islet
Imi / Ar.	spring
I-n / Ber.	well
Inch / Gae.	island
Inder / Dan.; Nor.	inner
Indre / Nor.	inner
Inferiore / It.	lower
Inish / Gae.	island
Insel / Germ.	island
Insulă / Rom.	island
Inver / Gae.	mouth
Irhazér / Ber.	wadi
Irmak / Tur.	river
'Irq / Ar.	dunes
Is / Nor.	glacier
Ís / Icel.	ice
Isblink / Dan.	glacier
Ishi / Jap.	rock
Iske / Alt.	old
Isla / Sp.	island
Iso / Finn.	great
Iso / Jap.	cliff
Isola / It.	island
Isthmós / Gr.	isthmus
Istmo / Sp.; It.	isthmus
Ita / A.I.	stone
Itä / Finn.	east
Itivdleq / Esk.	isthmus
Iwa / Jap.	rock, cliff
Iztočni / Bulg.	eastern
Izvor / Bulg.; Rom.; S.C.; Slvn.	spring

J

Local Form	English
J., Jazīrat / Ar.	island
J., Jiang / Chin.	river
Jabal / Ar.	mountain
Jaha / Ural.	river
Jam / Ural.	lake, river
Jama / Rus.	cave
Jan / Alt.	great
Janga / Tur.	north
Jangi / Alt.; Iran.	new
Janūbīyah / Ar.	southern
Jar / Rus.	bank
Järv / Est.	lake
Järve / Finn.	lake
Järvi / Finn.	lake
Jasirēd / Som.	island
Jaun / Latv.	new
Jaur / Lapp.	lake
Jaure / Lapp.	lake
Javr / Lapp.	lake
Javrre / Lapp.	lake
Jazā'ir / Ar.	islands
Jazīrat, J. / Ar.	island
Jazovir / Bulg.	reservoir
Jbel / Ar.	mountain
Jebel / Ar.	mountain
Jedid / Ar.	new
Jedo / Kor.	archipelago
Jezero / S.C.; Slvn.	lake
Jezioro / Pol.	lake
Jhil / Hin.; Urdu	lake
Jian / Chin.	mountain
Jiang, J. / Chin.	river
Jiao / Chin.	cape, cliff
Jibāl / Ar.	mountain
Jih / Cz.	south
Jima / Jap.	island
Jin / Kor.	cove
Jing / Chin.	spring
Jisr / Ar.	bridge
Joch / Germ.	pass
Jõgi / Est.	river
Jøkel / Nor.	glacier
Joki / Finn.	river
Jokka / Lapp.	river
Jökull / Icel.	glacier
Jord, -jord / Nor.	earth
Ju / Ural.	river
Judeţ / Rom.	district
Jugan / Ural.	river
Jura / Lith.	sea
Jūra / Latv.	sea
Jūras Līcis / Latv.	bay
Jūrmala / Latv.	beach
Jurt / Cauc.	village
Južni / Bulg.; S.C.; Slvn.	southern
Južny / Rus.	southern
Juzur / Ar.	islands

K

Local Form	English
Ka / Poly.	lake
Kaap / Afr.	cape
Kabīr / Ar.	great
Kae / Kor.	inlet
Kāf / Ar.	peak, mountain
Kafr / Ar.	village
Kaga / Ban.	hills, mountain range
Kahal / Ar.	plateau, escarpment
Kai / Jap.	sea
Kaikyō / Jap.	strait
Kaise / Lapp.	mountain
Kal / Pers.	stream
Kala / Az.; Kor.	fort
Kala / Finn.	river
Kala / Hin.	black
Kala / Tur.	castle
Kalaa / Ar.	castle
Kalaki / Georg.	city, town
Kale / Tur.	castle
Kali / Hin.	black
Kali / Indon.; Mal.	bay, river
Kallio / Finn.	rock
Kaln / Latv.	mountain
Kalós / Gr.	beautiful, good
Kamen / Bulg.; Rus.; S.C.; Slvn.	mountain, peak
Kámen / Cz.	rock
Kameň / Slvk.	rock
Kami / Jap.	upper
Kamień / Pol.	rock
Kamm / Germ.	crest
Kamp / Germ.	field
Kâmpóng / Khm.	village
Kámpos / Gr.	field
Kampung / Indon.; Mal.	village
Kan., Kanal / Alb.; Dan.; Germ.; Nor.; Rus.; S.C.; Slvn.; Swed.; Tur.	canal, channel
Kanaal / Dut.; Fle.	canal
Kanal / Pol.	canal
Kanal, Kan. / Alb.; Dan.; Germ.; Nor.; Rus.; S.C.; Slvn.; Swed.; Tur.	canal, channel
Kand, -kand / Pers.; Tur.	city, town
Kang / Chin.; Kor.	bay, river
Kangas / Fle.	heath
Kange / Esk.	east
Kangri / Tib.	snow-capped mountain
Kantara / Ar.	bridge
Kaôh / Khm.	island
Kap / Dan.; Germ.	cape
Kapija / S.C.	gate, gorge
Kapp / Nor.	cape
Kar / Tib.	white
Kar / Ural.	city, town
Kara / Tur.	black
Karang / Indon.; Mal.	sandbank, cliff
Kari / Finn.	cliff
Kariba / Ban.	gorge
Kariet / Ar.	village
Karki / Finn.	peninsula
Kastel / Ar.	castle
Kástron / Gr.	fort, city, town
Káto / Gr.	lower
Kaupstadur / Icel.	city, town
Kaupunki / Finn.	city, town
Kavīr / Pers.	salt desert
Kawa / Jap.	river
Kawm / Ar.	hill
Kebir / Ar.	great
Kedi / Georg.	mountain range
Kédia / Ar.	mountain, plateau
Kedim / Ar.	old
Kef / Ar.	mountain
Kefála / Gr.	mountain, peak
Kefar / Hebr.	village
Kei / Gae.	river
Kelet / Hung.	east
Ken / Gae.	cape
Kent / Alt.; Iran.; Tur.	city, town
Kenya / Swa.	fog
Kep / Alb.	cape
Kep., Kepulauan / Mal.	archipelago
Kepulauan, Kep. / Mal.	archipelago
Kereszt / Hung.	cross
Kerk / Dut.; Fle.	church
Keski / Finn.	middle
Kette / Germ.	mountain range
Keur / Sud.	village
Key / Eng.	coral island
Kha / Tib.	valley
Khal / Hin.	canal
Khalīj / Ar.	gulf
Khand / Hin.	district
Khao / Thai	hill, mountain
Kharābeh / Pers.	ruins
Khashm / Ar.	promontory
Khatt / Ar.	wadi
Khawr / Ar.	mouth, bay
Khazzān / Ar.	dam
Khemis / Ar.	fifth
Khersónisos / Gr.	peninsula
Khirbat / Ar.	ruins
Khlong / Thai	stream, mouth
Khokhok / Thai	isthmus
Khor / Ar.	mouth, bay
Khóra / Gr.	land
Khorion / Gr.	village
Khowr / Pers.	bay
Khrisós / Gr.	gold
Ki- / Ban.	little
Kibali / Sud.	river
Kil / Gae.	church
Kilde / Dan.	spring
Kilima / Swa.	mountain
Kill / Gae.	strait
Kilwa / Ban.	lake
Kin / Gae.	cape
Kinn / Nor.	cape, point
Kirche / Germ.	church
Kirk / Eng.	church
Kis / Hung.	little
Kisiwa / Swa.	island
Kita / Jap.	north, northern
Kızıl / Tur.	red
Klein / Afr.; Dut.; Germ.	little
Kliff / Germ.	cliff
Klint / Dan.	reef
Klip / Afr.; Dut.	rock, cliff
Klit / Dan.	dune
Kloof / Afr.; Dut.	gorge
Kloster / Dan.; Germ.; Nor.; Swed.	convent
Knob / Eng.	mountain
Knock / Gae.	mountain, hill
Ko / Jap.	bay, lake, little
Ko / Sud.	stream
Ko / Thai	island, point
Købing / Dan.	town
Kogel / Germ.	dome
Kōgen / Jap.	plateau
Koh / Hin.; Pers.	mountain, mountain range
Kol / Alt.	river, valley
Kol / Alt.; Tur.	lake
Koll / Nor.	peak
Kólpos / Gr.	gulf
Kong / Dan.; Nor.; Swed.	king
Kong / Indon.; Mal.	mountain
Kong / Viet.	mountain, hill
Konge / Ban.	river
König / Germ.	king
Koog / Germ.	polder
Kop / Afr.	hill
Kopec / Cz.; Slvk.	hill
Kopf / Germ.	peak
Köping / Swed.	town
Köprü / Tur.	bridge
Körfezi / Tur.	gulf
Korfi / Gr.	rock
Koro / Mel.	mountain, island
Koro / Sud.	old
Koru / Tur.	forest
Kosa / Rus.	spit
Koška / Rus.	cliff
Koski / Finn.	rapids
Kosui / Jap.	lake
Kot / Urdu	castle
Kota / Mal.	city, town
Kotal / Pash.; Pers.	pass
Kotar / S.C.	cultivated area
Kotlina / Pol.	basin

Local Form	English
Kotlovina / Rus.	basin, plain
Kou / Chin.	mouth, pass
Kourou / Sud.	well
Kowr / Pers.	river
Kowtal / Pers.	pass
Koy / Tur.	bay
Köy / Tur.	village
Kraal / Afr.	village
Kraina / Pol.	land
Kraj / Rus.; S.C.	land
Kraj / Rus.	administrative division
Krajina / S.C.	land
Krak / Ar.	hill, castle
Krans / Afr.	mountain
Kras / S.C.; Slvn.	karst landscape
Krasny / Rus.	red
Kreb / Ar.	hills, mountain range
Kriaž / Ar.	mountain range
Krš / S.C.	karst area, limestone area
Krung / Thai	city, town
Ksar / Ar.	castle
Ksour / Ar.	fortified village
Ku- / Ban.	river branch
Kuala / Mal.	river, mouth
Kubra / Ar.	bridge
Küçük / Tur.	little
Kuduk / Tur.	spring
Küh / Pers.	mountain
Kühhā / Pers.	mountain range
Kul / Alt.; Iran.; Tur.	lake
Kulam, -kulam / Hin.; Tam.	pond
Kulle / Swed.	hill
Kulm / Germ.	peak
Kultuk / Rus.	bay
Kum / Tur.	dunes, sand desert
Kuppe / Germ.	dome, seamount
Kurayb / Ar.	hill
Kurgan / Alt.	hill
Kurgan / Tur.	fort
Kuro / Jap.	black
Kurort / Bulg.; Germ.; Rus.	spa
Kust / Dut.; Fle.	coast
Kust- / Swed.	coast
Küste / Germ.	coast
Kút / Hung.	spring
Kuyu / Tur.	spring
Kvemo / Georg.	low, lower
Kwa / Ban.	village
Kylä / Finn.	village
Kyle / Gae.	strait, channel
Kyō / Jap.	strait
Kyrka / Swed.	church
Kyst / Dan.; Nor.	coast
Kyun / Burm.	island
Kyūryō / Jap.	hills, mountains
Kyzyl / Tur.	red
Kzyl / Tur.	red

L

Local Form	English
L., Lake, Lago / Eng.; It.; Port.; Sp.	lake
La / Tib.	pass
Laagte / Afr.	stream, valley
Labuan / Indon.; Mal.	bay, port
Lac / Fr.	lake
Lach / Som.	stream, wadi
Lacul / Rom.	lake
Lae / Poly.	cape, point
Laem / Thai	bay, port
Låg / Nor.; Swed.	low, lower
Lag / Swed.	stream, wadi
Läge / Swed.	beach
Lagh / Som.	stream, wadi
Lago, L. / It.; Port.; Sp.	lake
Lagoa / Port.	lagoon
Laguna / Alb.; It.; Rus.; Sp.	lagoon, lake
Lagune / Fr.	lagoon
Laht / Est.	bay
Lahti / Finn.	bay, gulf
Laks / Finn.	bay
Lalla / Ar.	saint
Lampi / Finn.	pond
Lande / Fr.	heath
Lang / Afr.; Dut.; Germ.	long
Lang / Viet.	village
Lao / Chin.	old
Lapa / Poly.	mountain range, peak
Largo / Port.; Sp.	basin
Las / Pol.	forest
Las, Läs / Som.	well
Laut / Mal.	sea
Law / Gae.	hill, mountain
Lázně / Cz.	thermal springs
Lednik / Rus.	glacier
Leite / Germ.	coast
Lekh / Nep.	mountain range

Local Form	English
Les / Bulg.; Cz.; Rus.; Slvk.	forest
Leso / Rus.	forested
Levante / It.; Sp.	eastern
Levkós / Gr.	white
Levy / Rus.	left
Lha / Tib.	temple
Lhari / Hin.; Nep.	mountain
Lho / Tib.	south
Lido / It.	sandbar
Liedao / Chin.	archipelago
Liehtao / Chin.	archipelago
Liels / Latv.	great
Lilla / Swed.	little
Lille / Dan.; Nor.	little
Liman / Alb.; Rus.; Tur.	lagoon, bay
Liman / Tur.	bay, port
Limín / Gr.	port
Limni / Gr.	lake
Ling / Chin.	mountain range, peak
Linna / Finn.	castle
Liqen / Alb.	lake
Lithos / Gr.	stone
Litoral / Port.; Sp.	littoral
Litorale / It.	littoral
Llan / Wel.	church
Llano / Sp.	plain
Llanura / Sp.	plain
Lo- / Ban.	river
Loch / Gae.	lake, inlet
Loch / Germ.	grotto
Loka / Slvn.	forest
Loma / Sp.	hill
Long / Indon.	stream
Loo / Dut.; Fle.	clearing
Lough / Gae.	lake
Loutrá / Gr.	thermal springs
Ložbina / Rus.	depression
Lu- / Ban.	river
Lua / Ban.	river
Lua / Mel.	island, reef
Lua / Poly.	crater
Luang / Thai	yellow
Luch / Germ.	peat-bog
Lücke / Germ.	pass
Lug / Rus.	meadow
Luka / S.C.; Slvn.	port
Lule / Lapp.	east, eastern
Lum / Alb.	river
Lund / Dan.; Swed.	forest
Lung / Rom.	long
Lung / Tib.	valley
Luoto / Finn.	shoal
Lurg / Pers.	salt flat
Lut / Pers.	desert

M

Local Form	English
M., Monte / It.; Port.; Sp.	mountain
Ma / Ar.	water
Ma- / Ban.	people
Maa / Est.; Finn.	island, land
Ma'arrat / Ar.	height
Machi / Jap.	district
Macizo / Sp.	massif
Madhya / Ar.	central
Madīnah / Ar.	city, town
Madīq / Ar.	strait
Mado / Swa.	well
Madu / Tam.	pond
Mae / Thai	stream
Mae nam / Thai	stream, mouth
Magh / Gae.	plain
Mägi / Est.	mountain
Măgura / Rom.	height
Mahā / Hin.	great
Mahal / Hin.; Urdu	palace
Mai / Amh.; Ban.	stream
Majdan / S.C.	quarry
Mäki / Finn.	mountain, hill
Makrós / Gr.	long
Mala / Hin.; Tam.	mountain
Malai / Hin.; Tam.	mountain
Malal / A.I.	fence
Malhão / Port.	dome
Mali / Alb.	mountain
Mali / S.C.; Slvn.	little
Malki / Bulg.	little
Malla / Tam.	mountain
Maly / Rus.	little
Malý / Cz.; Slvk.	little
Mały / Pol.	little
Man / Kor.	bay
Manastir / Bulg.; S.C.	monastery
Manche / Fr.	channel
Mar / It.; Port.; Sp.	sea
Mar / Tib.	red
Mar / Ural.	city, town
Marais / Fr.	marsh
Marché / Fr.	market
Mare / Fr.	pond
Mare / It.; Rom.	sea
Mare / Rom.	great
Marea / Rom.	sea
Marécage / Fr.	marsh
Marios / Lith.	reservoir

Local Form	English
Marisma / Sp.	marsh
Mark / Dan.; Nor.; Swed.	land
Markt / Germ.	market
Marsa / Ar.	anchorage, bay
Marsch / Germ.	marsh
Maru / Jap.	mountain
Mas / Prov.	farmhouse
Maşabb / Ar.	mouth
Mashra' / Ar.	landing, pier
Masivul / Rom.	massif
Massiv / Germ.; Rus.	massif
Mata / Poly.	point
Mata / Port.; Sp.	forest
Mata / Som.	waterfall
Mato / Port.; Sp.	forest
Matsu / Jap.	point
Mauna / Poly.	mountain
Mávros / Gr.	black
Mayo / Sud.	river
Maza / Lith.	little
Mazar / Pers.; Tur.	sanctuary
Mazs / Latv.	little
Me / Khm.	river
Me / Mel.	hill, mountain
Me / Thai	great
Medina / Ar.	city, town
Medjez / Ar.	ford
Meer / Dut.; Fle.	lake
Meer / Germ.	lake, sea
Megálos / Gr.	great
Mégas / Gr.	great
Megye / Hung.	district
Mélas / Gr.	black
Melkosopočnik / Rus..	hill country
Mellan / Swed.	central
Men / Chin.	gate, channel
Ménez / Br.	mountain
Menzel / Ar.	bivouac
Meos / Indon.	island
Mer / Fr.	sea
Mercato / It.	market
Merdja / Ar.	lagoon, marsh
Meri / Est.; Finn.	sea
Meridional / Rom.; Sp.	southern
Merin / A.I.	little
Merja / Ar.	lagoon, marsh
Mers / Ar.	port
Mersa / Ar.	port
Mesa / Sp.	mesa, tableland
Meseta / Sp.	plateau
Mésos / Gr.	central
Mesto / Bulg.; S.C.; Slvk.; Slvn.	city, town
Město / Cz.	city, town
Mestre / Port.	principal
Meydan / Tur.	square
Mezad / Hebr.	castle
Mező / Hung.	field
Mgne., Montagne / Fr.	mountain
Mgnes., Montagnes / Fr.	mountains
Miao / Chin.	temple
Miasto / Pol.	city, town
Mic / Rom.	little
Middel / Afr.; Dut.; Fle.	middle
Midi / Fr.	noon, south
Między / Pol.	central
Miedzyrzecze / Pol.	interfluve
Mierzeja / Pol.	sand spit
Mifraz / Hebr.	bay, gulf
Miftah / Ar.	gorge
Mikrós / Gr.	little
Mina / Port.; Sp.	mine
Mīnā' / Ar.	port
Minami / Jap.	south, southern
Minamoto / Jap.	spring
Minato / Jap.	port
Mine / Jap.	peak
Mirim / A.I.	little
Misaki / Jap.	cape
Mittel- / Germ.	middle
Mo / Chin.	sand desert
Mo / Nor.; Swed.	heath
Moana / Poly.	lake
Mogila / Bulg.; Rus.	hill
Moku / Poly.	island
Mølle / Dan.	mill
Monasterio / Sp.	monastery
Mond / Afr.; Dut.; Fle.	mouth
Mong / Burm.; Thai; Viet.	city, town
Moni / Gr.	monastery
Mont / Cat.; Fr.	mountain
Montagna / It.	mountain
Montagne, Mgne. / Fr.	mountain
Montagnes, Mgnes. / Fr.	mountains
Montaña / Sp.	mountain
Monte, M. / It.; Port.; Sp.	mountain
Monts, Mts. / Fr.	mountains
Moos / Germ.	moor
Mór / Gae.	great
More / Bulg.; Rus.; S.C.	sea
More / Gae.	great
Mori / Jap.	mountain, forest
Morne / Fr.	mountain
Moron / Mong.	river
Morro / Port.; Germ.	hill, peak
Morrón / Sp.	mountain
Morze / Pol.	sea

Local Form	English
Most / Bulg.; Cz.; Pol.; Rus.; S.C.; Slvn.	bridge
Moto / Jap.	spring
Motte / Fr.	hill
Motu / Mel.; Poly.	island, rock
Moutier / Fr.	monastery
Movilă / Rom.	hill
Moyen / Fr.	central
Mta / Georg.	mountain
Mts., Monts, Mountains / Eng.; Fr.	mountains
Muang / Laot.; Thai	city, town, land
Muara / Indon.; Mal.	mouth
Muela / Sp.	mountain
Mühle / Germ.	mill
Mui / Mel.	point
Mui / Viet.	point, cape
Muiden / Dut.; Fle.	mouth
Muir / Gae.	sea
Mukh / Hin.	mouth
Mull / Gae.	promontory
Münde / Germ.	mouth
Mündung / Germ.	mouth
Municipiul / Rom.	commune
Munkhafaḍ / Ar.	depression
Münster / Germ.	monastery
Munte / Rom.	mountain
Muntelé / Rom.	mountain
Munţii / Rom.	mountain range
Muren / Mong.	river
Mushāsh / Ar.	spring
Muz / Tur.	ice
Muztagh / Tur.	snow-capped mountain
Mwambo / Ban.	rock, cliff
Myit / Burm.	stream
Mynydd / Wel.	mountain
Myo / Burm.	city, town
Mýri / Icel.	marsh
Mys / Rus.	cape

N

Local Form	English
Na / Cz.; Pol.; Rus.; S.C.; Slvn.	on
Nab / Ar.	spring
Nad / Cz.; Pol.; Rus.	on
Nada / Jap.	bay, sea
Nadi, -nadi / Hin.; Urdu	river
Næs / Dan.	point
Nafūd / Ar.	dunes
Nag / Tib.	black
Nagar, -nagar / Hin.; Tib.	city, town
Nagaram / Hin.; Tam.	city, town
Nagorje / Rus.	plateau, mountains
Nagy / Hung.	great
Nahr / Ar.	river
Naikai / Jap.	sea
Naka / Jap.	central
Nakhon / Thai	city, town
Nam / Burm.; Laot.; Thai	river
Nam / Kor.	south
Namakzar / Pers.	salt desert
Nan / Chin.	south
Narrows / Eng.	strait
Narssaq / Esk.	plain, valley
Näs / Swed.	cape
Nationalpark / Swed.; Germ.	national park
Nau / Lith.	new
Nauja / Lith.	new
Navolok / Rus.	cape, promontory
Ne / Jap.	cliff
Neder / Fle.; Dut.	low
Neem / Est.	cape
Negro / Port.; Sp.	black
Negru / Rom.	black
Nehir / Tur.	river
Nei / Chin.	inner
Nene, -nene / Ban.	great
Néos / Gr.	new
Nero / It.	black
Nes / Icel.; Nor.	cape
Ness / Gae.	promontory
Neu / Germ.	new
Neuf / Fr.	new
Nevado / Sp.	snow-capped mountain
Nez / Fr.	cape
Ngok / Viet.	mountain, peak
Ngolo / Ber.	great
Ni / Kor.	village
Niecka / Pol.	basin
Niemi / Finn.	peninsula
Nieuw / Fle.; Dut.	new
Nij / Dut.	new
Nil / Hin.	blue
Nishi / Jap.	west
Niski / Pol.	lower
Nisko / S.C.	low
Nisoi / Gr.	islands
Nisos / Gr.	island
Nizina / Pol.	lowland
Nižina / Cz.	depression
Nizký / Cz.	low, lower

Geographical Glossary

Local Form	English
Nizmennost / Rus.	lowland, depression
Nižni / Rus.	low, lower
Nižný / Slvk.	low, lower
No / Mel.	stream
Nock / Gae.	ridge
Noir / Fr.	black
Non / Thai	hill
Nong / Thai	lake, marsh
Noord / Afr.; Fle.; Dut.	north
Noordoost / Afr.; Fle.; Dut.	northeast
Nor / Arm.	new
Nord / Fr.; It.; Germ.	north
Nördlich / Germ.	northern
Nørdre / Dan.; Nor.	northern
Norra / Swed.	northern
Nørre / Dan.	northern
Norte / Sp.	north
Nos / Bulg.; Rus.; S.C.; Slvn.	cape
Nosy / Malag.	island
Nótios / Gr.	southern
Nou / Rom.	new
Novi / Bulg.; S.C.; Slvn.	new
Novo / Port.	new
Novy / Rus.	new
Nový / Cz.; Slvk.	new
Now / Pers.	new
Nowy / Pol.	new
Nudo / Sp.	mountain
Nuevo / Sp.	new
Nui / Viet.	mountain
Numa / Jap.	marsh, lake
Nummi / Finn.	heath
Nunatak / Esk.	peak
Nuovo / It.	new
Nur / Chin.	lake
Nusa / Mal.	island
Nut, -nut / Nor.	peak
Nuwara / Sin.; Tam.	city, town
Nuwe / Afr.	new
Nyanza / Ban.	water, river, lake
Nyasa / Ban.	lake
Nyeong / Kor.	pass
Nyika / Ban.	upland
Nyŏng / Kor.	mount, pass
Nyugat / Hung.	west

O

Local Form	English
Ō / Jap.	great
Ó / Hung.	old
Ö / Swed.	island
Ø, -ø / Dan.; Nor.	island
Öar / Swed.	islands
Ober / Germ.	upper
Oblast / Rus.	province
Obo / Mong.	mountain, hill
Occidental / Fr.; Rom.; Sp.	western
Océan / Fr.	ocean
Océano / Sp.	ocean
Oceano / It.; Port.	ocean
Ocnă / Rom.	salt mine
Odde / Dan.; Nor.	promontory
Oeste / Port.; Sp.	west
Oever / Fle.; Dut.	bank
Oewer / Afr.	bank
Oie / Germ.	islet
Ojos / Sp.	spring
Oka / Jap.	coast
Oke / Sud.	height
Okean / Rus.	ocean
Oki / Jap.	bay
Okrug / Rus.	district
Ola / Alt.	city, town
Omuramba / K.S.	stream
Onder / Afr.	under
Oni / Malag.	river
Oos / Afr.	east
Oost / Fle.; Dut.	east
Oostelijk / Dut.	eastern
Opatija / Slvn.	abbey
Or / Fr.	gold
Oraş / Rom.	city, town
Óri / Gr.	mountains
Oriental / Fr.; Port.; Rom.; Sp.	eastern
Orientale / It.	eastern
Orilla / Sp.	bank
Órmos / Gr.	bay
Óros / Gr.	mountain
Ország / Hung.	land
Ort / Germ.	cape
Orta / Tur.	central
Orto / Alt.	central
Oseaan / Afr.	ocean
Ōshima / Jap.	large island
Ost / Dan.; Germ.	east
Öst / Swed.	east
Ostän, -ostän / Pers.	province
Øster / Dan.; Nor.	east, eastern
Öster / Swed.	east, eastern
Östlich / Germ.	eastern
Ostrog / Rus.	castle
Ostrov / Rus.	island
Ostrovul / Rom.	island
Ostrów / Pol.	island
Ostrvo / S.C.	island
Otok / S.C.; Slvn.	island
Otrog / Rus.	front range (mountains)
Oua / Mel.	stream
Ouar / Ar.	rocky desert
Oud / Fle.; Dut.	old
Oued / Ar.	wadi
Ouest / Fr.	west
Ouled / Ar.	son
Oum / Ar.	mother
Ouro / Port.	gold
Outu / Poly.	cape
Ova / Ban.	people
Ova / Tur.	plain
Ovasi / Tur.	plain
Øver / Nor.	over
Över / Swed.	over
Övre / Swed.	over
Øy / Dan.; Nor.	island
oz., Ozero / Rus.	lake
Ozek / Alt.	hollow
Ozera / Rus.	lakes
Ozero, oz. / Rus.	lake

P

Local Form	English
P., Pulau / Mal.; Indon.	island
Pää / Finn.	principal
Pad / Rus.	valley
Padang / Indon.	plain
Padiş / Rom.	upland
Padół / Pol.	valley
Pădure / Rom.	forest
Pahorek / Cz.	hill
Pahorkatina / Cz.	plateau, hills
Pais / Port.; Sp.	land, country
Pak / Thai	mouth
Pala / It.	peak
Palaiós / Gr.	old
Palanka / S.C.	village
Pali / Poly.	cliff
-palli / Hin.	village
Pampa / Sp.	plain, prairie
Panda / Swa.	junction
Panev / Cz.	basin
Pantanal / Sp.	swamp
Pantano / Sp.	swamp, lake
Pao / Mel.	hill
Pará / A.I.	river
Paramera / Sp.	desert highland
Páramo / Sp.	moor
Paraná / A.I.	river
Parbat / Hin.; Urdu	mountain
Parc / Fr.	park
Parco / It.	park
Parco Nazionale / It.	national park
Pardo / Port.	grey
Parque / Sp.	park
Parque Nacional / Sp.; Port.	national park
Pas / Fr.; Rom.	pass, strait
Pasaje / Sp.	passage
Pasir / Mal.	sand, beach
Paso / Sp.	pass
Passágem / Port.	passage
Passe / Fr.	pass
Passo / It.; Port.	pass
Pasul / Rom.	pass
Patak / Hung.	stream
Patam, -patam / Hin.	city, town
Patnā / Hin.	city, town
Patnam, -patnam / Hin.	city, town
Pattinam, -pattinam / Hin.	city, town
Pays / Fr.	land, country
Pazar / Tur.	market
Pea / Est.	cape
Pech / Cat.	hill
Pedhiás / Gr.	plain
Pedra / Port.	rock, mountain
Peg., Pegunungan / Mal.; Indon.	mountain range
Pegunungan, Peg. / Mal.; Indon.	mountain range
Pélagos / Gr.	sea
Pele / Poly.	peak, hill
Pen / Br.	principal
Pen / Br.; Gae.	cape, mountain
Peña / Sp.	peak
Pendi / Chin.	basin
Pendiente / Sp.	slope
Penha / Port.	peak
Península / Port.; Sp.	peninsula
Péninsule / Fr.	peninsula
Penisola / It.	peninsula
Peñon / Sp.	rock, island
Pente / Fr.	slope
Perekop / Rus.	channel
Pereval / Rus.	pass
Perevoz / Rus.	ford
Pertuis / Fr.	strait
Peščara / S.C.	sandy soil
Peski / Rus.	sand desert
Petit / Fr.	little
Pétra / Gr.	rock
Phanom / Thai; Khm.	mountain range, mountain
Phau / Laot.	mountain
Phnum / Khm.	hill, mountain
Phu / Viet.	mountain, hill
Phum / Thai	forest
Phumi / Khm.	village
Pi / Chin.	cape
Piana, Pianura / It.	plain
Piano / It.	plain
Piatră / Rom.	stone
Pic / Cat.; Fr.	peak
Picacho / Sp.	peak
Piccolo / It.	little
Pico / Port.; Sp.	peak
Piedra / Sp.	rock, cliff
Pietra / It.	stone
Pieve / It.	parish
Pik / Rus.	peak
Pils / Latv.	city, town
Pinar / Sp.	pine forest
Pingyuan / Chin.	plain
Pioda / It.	crest
Pirgos / Gr.	tower, peak
Pish / Pers.	anterior, before
Pitkä / Finn.	great
Piton / Fr.	mountain, peak
Piz / Rmsh.	peak
Pizzo / It.	peak
Pjasăci / Bulg.	beach
Plaat / Fle.; Dut.	sandbank
Plage / Fr.	beach
Plaine / Fr.	plain
Plan / Fr.	plain
Planalto / Port.	plateau
Planina / Bulg.	mountain
Plano / Sp.	plain
Plas / Dut.; Fle.	lake, marsh
Plato / Bulg.; Rus.	plateau
Platosu / Tur.	plateau
Platte / Germ.	plain, plateau
Plav / S.C.	blue
Plavnja / Rus.	marsh
Playa / Sp.	beach
Ploskogorje / Rus.	plateau
Plou / Br.	church
Po / Kor.	port
Po / Chin.	lake, white
P'o / Kor.	bay, lake
Poa / Mel.	hill
Poarta / Rus.	pass
Poartă / Rom.	gate
Pobla / Cat.	village
Pobrzeże / Pol.	littoral, coast
Poço / Port.	well
Poço / Port.	point
Pod / Cz.; Pol.; Rus.; S.C.; Slvn.	bridge
Podkamenny / Rus.	stony
Poggio / It.	hill
Pohja / Finn.	north, northern
Pohjois- / Finn.	north
Pojezierze / Pol.	lake region
Pol / Pers.	bridge
Pol, -pol / Rus.	city, town
Pola / Port.; Sp.	village
Polder / Fle.; Dut.	reclaimed land
Pole / Pol.	field
Pólis / Gr.	city, town
Poljana / Bulg.; Rus.; S.C.; Slvn.	field, terrace
Poljarny / Rus.	polar
Polje / S.C.; Slvn.	valley, field, basin
Poluostrov / Rus.	peninsula
Pomorije / Bulg.	littoral
Pomorze / Pol.	littoral
Ponente / It.	western
Pont / Cat.; Fr.	bridge
Ponta / Port.	point
Ponte / It.; Port.	bridge
Póntos / Gr.	sea
Poort / Afr.; Fle.; Dut.	pass
Pore, -pore / Hin.; Urdu	city, town
Porog / Rus.	rapids
Porte / Fr.	gate
Portile / Rom.	gorge
Portillo / Sp.	pass
Portiţa / Rom.	small gate
Porto / It.	port
Pôrto / Port.	port
Posht / Pers.	back, posterior
Potjo / Indon.	peak
Potok / Bulg.; Cz.; Pol.; Rus.; S.C.; Slvn.	stream
Póvoa / Port.	village
Pozo / Sp.	well
Pozzo / It.	well
Pradesh / Hin.	region, state
Prado / Sp.	meadow
Praia / Port.	beach
Prato / It.	meadow
Pré / Fr.	meadow
Prealpi / It.	prealps
Presa / Sp.	reservoir
Presqu'ile / Fr.	peninsula
Prêto / Port.	black
Priehradni nádrž / Cz.	reservoir
Pripoljarny / Rus.	subpolar
Pristan / Rus.	port
Prohod / Bulg.	pass
Proliv / Rus.	strait
Promontoire / Fr.	promontory
Průchod / Cz.	pass
Przedgorze / Pol.	front range (mountains)
Przełęcz / Pol.	pass
Przemysł / Pol.	industry
Przylądek / Pol.	cape
Pua / Mel.	hill
Puebla / Sp.	village
Puente / Sp.	bridge
Puerto / Sp.	port, pass
Puig / Cat.	peak
Puits / Fr.	well
Pul / Pash.	bridge
Pulau, P. / Mal.; Indon.	island
Pulau Pulau / Mal.	islands
Pulo / Mal.; Indon.	island
Puna / A.I.	upland
Puncak / Indon.	mountain
Punjung / Mal.; Indon.	mountain
Punt / Afr.	point
Punta / It.; Sp.	point
Pur, -pur / Hin.; Urdu	city, town
-pura / Hin.; Urdu	city, town
Pura / Indon.	city, town, temple
Puri, -puri / Hin.; Urdu	city, town
Pus / Alb.	spring
Pušča / Rus.	forest
Pustynja / Rus.	desert
Puszcza / Pol.	heath
Puszta / Hung.	lowland
Put / Afr.	well
Put / Rus.; S.C.	road
Putra, -putra / Hin.	son
Puu / Poly.	mountain, volcano
Puy / Fr.	peak
Pwell / Wel.	pond
Pyeong / Kor.	plain
Pyhä / Finn.	saint

Q

Local Form	English
Qagan / Mong.	white
Qala / Pash.	fortified town
Qal'at / Ar.	castle
Qalb / Ar.	hill
Qalib / Ar.	spring
Qaliq / Ar.	spring
Qanāt / Ar.	canal
Qantara / Ar.	bridge
Qaqortoq / Esk.	white
Qar / Som.	mountain
Qara / Pers.	black
Qarah / Tur.	black
Qārat / Ar.	height, mountain
Qāret / Ar.	village, hill
Qaryah / Ar.	village
Qaryat / Ar.	village
Qaşr / Ar.	castle
Qawz / Ar.	dunes
Qeqertarssuaq / Esk.	peninsula
Qezel / Tur.	red
Qi / Chin.	river
Qing / Chin.	blue, green
Qiryat / Hebr.	city, town
Qolleh / Pers.	mountain, peak
Qu / Chin.	river, canal
Quan dao / Viet.	islands
Quebracho / Sp.	stream
Quebrada / Sp.	gorge, stream
Quedas / Port.	waterfalls
Qulbān / Ar.	well
Qundao / Chin.	archipelago
Qūr / Ar.	height, hill
Qytet / Alb.	city, town
Qyteti / Alb.	city, town

R

Local Form	English
R., Rio, River / Eng.; Sp.	river
Rada / It.; Sp.	anchorage
Rade / Fr.	anchorage
Rags / Latv.	cape
Rahad / Ar.	lake, pond
Rajon / Rus.	district
Rak / Fle.; Dut.	strait
Rakai / Poly.	reef
Ramla / Ar.	sand
Rancho / Port.; Sp.	farm, ranch
Rand / Afr.; Germ.	escarpment
Range / Eng.	mountain range
Rann / Urdu	marsh
Rano / Malag.	water
Ranta / Finn.	bank, beach
Rapide / Fr.	rapids
Ras / Amh.	peak
Rās / Ar.	point, cape

Local Form	English
Ras, Ràs / Ar.	promontory, peak
Rãsiga / Som.	promontory
Rass / Ar.	promontory, peak
Rassa / Lapp.	mountain
Ráth / Gae.	castle
Raunina / Bulg.; Rus.	plain
Raz / Fr.	strait
Razliv / Rus.	flood plain
Récif / Fr.	reef
Recife / Port.	reef
Reede / Germ.; Dut.; Slvn.	anchorage
Reek / Afr.; Gae.	mountain range
Reg / Pash.	dunes
Région / Fr.	region
Rei / Port.	king
Reka / Bulg.; Rus.; S.C.; Slvn.	river
Řeka / Cz.	river
Réma / Gr.	torrent
Renne / Dan.; Nor.	deep
Reprêsa / Port.	dam, reservoir
Represa / Sp.	dam, reservoir
República / Port.; Sp.	republic
République / Fr.	republic
Rés., Réservoir / Fr.	reservoir
Res., Reservoir / Eng.	reservoir
Réservoir, Rés. / Fr.	reservoir
Reshteh / Pers.	mountain range
Respublika / Rus.	republic
Restinga / Port.	cliff, sandbank
Retsugan / Jap.	reef
Rettō / Jap.	archipelago
Rev / Dan.; Nor.; Swed.	reef
Rey / Sp.	king
Ri / Tib.	mountain
Ria / Sp.	estuary
Riacho / Port.	stream
Rialto / It.	plateau
Rialto / It.	rise
Riba / Port.	bank
Ribeira / Port.	river
Ribeirão / Port.	stream
Ribeiro / Port.	stream
Ribera / Sp.	coast
Ribnik / Slvn.	pond
Rid / Bulg.	mountain range
Rif / Icel.	cliff
Riff / Germ.	reef
Rīg / Pash.	dunes
Rijeka / S.C.	river
Rimāl / Ar.	sand desert
Rincón / Sp.	peninsula, between two rivers
Ring / Tib.	long
Rinne / Germ.	trench
Rio / Port.	river
Rio, R. / Sp.	river
Riu / Rom.	river
Riva / It.	bank
Rive / Fr.	bank
Rivera / Sp.	brook, stream
Rivier, -rivier / Afr.; Dut.; Fle.	river
Riviera / It.	coast
Rivière / Fr.	river
Roads / Eng.	anchorage
Roc / Fr.	rock
Roca / Port.; Sp.	rock
Rocca / It.	castle
Roche / Fr.	rock
Rocher / Fr.	rock
Rock / Eng.	rock
Rod / Pash.	river
Rode / Germ.	tilled soil
Rodnik / Rus.	spring
Rog / Rus.; S.C.; Slvn.	peak
Roi / Fr.	king
Rojo / Sp.	red
Roque / Sp.	rock
Rot / Germ.	red
Roto / Poly.	lake
Rouge / Fr.	red
Równina / Pol.	plain
Rt / S.C.; Slvn.	cape
Ru / Tib.	mountain
Ruck / Germ.	ridge
Rücken / Germ.	ridge
Rud / Pers.	river
Ruda / Cz.; Slvk.	mine
Ruda / Pol.	ore
Rüdbār / Pers.	river
Rudha / Gae.	point
Rudnik / Rus.; S.C.; Slvn.	mine
Rug / Fle.; Dut.	ridge
Ruggen / Afr.	ridge
Ruina / Sp.	ruins
Ruine / Fr.; Dut.; Germ.	ruins
Rujm / Ar.	hill
Run / Eng.	stream

S

Local Form	English
S., See / Germ.	lake, sea
Saar / Est.	island
Saari / Finn.	island
Sabbia / It.	sand
Sabkhat / Ar.	salt flat, salt marsh
Sable / Fr.; Eng.	beach
Sacca / It.	anchorage
Saco / Port.	bay
Sad / Cz.; Slvk.	park
Sad / Pers.	wall
Sadd / Ar.; Pers.	cataract, dam
Safīd / Pash.; Urdu; Hin.	white
Şafrā' / Ar.	desert
Sāgar / Hin.	reservoir
Saguia / Ar.	irrigation canal
Sahara / Ar.	desert
Sahel / Ar.	plain, coast
Sahr / Iran.	city, town
Şaḥrā' / Ar.	desert
Said / Ar.	sweet
Saj / Alt.	stream, valley
Saki / Jap.	point
Sala / Latv.; Lith.	island
Saladillo / Sp.	salt desert
Salar / Sp.	salt lake
Sale / Ural.	village
Salina / It.; Sp.	salt flat, salt marsh
Saline / Dut.; Fr.; Germ.	salt flat, salt marsh
Salmi / Finn.	strait
Salseleh-ye Kūh / Pers.	mountain range
Salto / Port.; Sp.	waterfall, rapids
Salz / Germ.	salt
Samudera / Indon.	ocean
Samudra / Hin.	lake
Samut / Thai	sea
San / Jap.; Kor.	mountain
San / It.; Sp.	saint
Sanchi / Jap.	mountain range
Sand / Dan.; Eng.; Nor.; Swed.; Germ.	beach
Šand / Mong.	spring
Sandur / Icel.	sand
Sank / Pers.	rock
Sankt, St. / Germ.; Swed.	saint
Sanmaeg / Kor.	mountain range
Sanmyaku / Jap.	mountain range
Sansanné / Sud.	campsite
Santo / It.; Port.; Sp.	saint
Santuario / It.	sanctuary
São / Port.	saint
Sar / Pers.	cape; peak
Šar / Rus.; Tur.	strait
Saraf / Ar.	well
Sari / Latv.	island
Sari / Tur.	yellow
Sarīr / Ar.	rocky desert
Sary / Tur.	yellow
Sasso / It.	stone
Sat / Rom.	village
Sattel / Germ.	pass
Saurum / Latv.	strait
Schleuse / Germ.	lock
Schloß / Germ.	castle
Schlucht / Germ.	gorge
Schnee / Germ.	snow
Schwarz / Germ.	black
Scoglio / It.	cliff
Se / Jap.	bank, shoal
Sebkha / Ar.	salt flat
Sebkhet / Ar.	salt flat
Sed / Ar.	dam
Seda / Ural.	mountain
See, S. / Germ.	lake, sea
Sefra / Ar.	yellow
Segara / Indon.	lagoon
Şehir / Tur.	city, town
Seki / Jap.	dam
Selat / Mal.; Indon.	strait
Selatan / Indon.	southern
Selkä / Finn.	ridge, lake
Sella / It.	pass
Selo / Bulg.; Rus.; S.C.; Slvn.	village
Selsela Kohe / Pers.	mountain range
Selva / It.; Sp.	forest
Semenanjung / Mal.	peninsula
Sen / Jap.	mountain
Seong / Kor.	castle
Sep / Alt.	canal
Serīr / Ar.	rocky desert
Serra / Cat.; Port.	mountain range
Serra / It.	mountain
Serrania / Sp.	mountain range
Sertão / Port.	steppe
Seto / Jap.	strait
Sett., Settentrionale / It.	northern
Settentrionale, Sett. / It.	northern
Seuil / Fr.	sill
Sev / Arm.	black
Sever / Rus.	north
Severny / Rus.	northern
Sfint / Rom.	saint
Sfintu / Rom.	saint
Sgeir / Gae.	cliff
Sha'b / Ar.	cliff
Shahr / Pers.; Hin.	city, town
Sha'ib / Ar.	stream
Shallāl / Ar.	cataract
Shām / Ar.	north; northern
Shamo / Chin.	sand desert
Shan / Chin.	mountain, mountain range
Shan / Gae.	old
Shand / Mong.	spring
Shankou / Chin.	pass
Shaqq / Ar.	wadi
Sharm / Ar.	bay
Sharqī / Ar.	east, eastern
Sharqīyah / Ar.	eastern
Shatt / Ar.	river, salt lake
Shatt / Tur.	stream
Shën / Alb.	saint
Sheng / Chin.	province
Shi / Chin.	city, town
Shibīn / Chin.	village
Shih / Chin.	rock
Shima / Jap.	island
Shimo / Jap.	lower
Shin / Jap.	new
Shō / Jap.	island
Shotō / Jap.	archipelago
Shū / Jap.	administrative division
Shui / Chin.	river
Shuiku / Chin.	reservoir
Shur / Pers.	salt
Sidhiros / Gr.	iron
Sidi / Ar.	master
Sieben / Germ.	seven
Sierra / Sp.	mountain range
Sikt / Ural.	village
Sillon / Fr.	furrow
Šine / Mong.	new
Sink / Eng.	depression
Sinn / Ar.	point
Sint / Dut.; Fle.	saint
Sirt / Tur.	mountain range
Sirtlar / Tur.	mountain range
Sistema / It.; Sp.	mountain system
Sīyāh / Pers.	black
Sjø / Nor.	lake
Sjö / Swed.	lake, sea
Skag / Icel.	peninsula
Skala / Bulg.; Rus.	rock
Skála / Slvk.	rock
Skar / Nor.	pass
Skär / Swed.	cliff
Skeir / Gae.	cliff
Skerry / Gae.	cliff
Skog / Nor.; Swed.	forest
Skóg / Icel.	forest
Skov / Dan.; Nor.	forest
Slatina / S.C.; Slvn.	mineral water
Slätt / Swed.	plain
Slieve / Gae.	mountain
Slot / Dan.; Fle.	castle
Slott / Nor.; Swed.	castle
Slough / Eng.	creek, pond, marsh
Sluis / Dut.; Fle.	sluice
Små / Swed.	little
Sne / Nor.	snow
Sneeuw / Afr.; Dut.	snow
Snežny / Rus.	snowy
Snø / Nor.	snow
So / Kor.	little
Sø / Dan.; Nor.	lake; sea
So / Ural.	passage
Söder / Swed.	south
Södra / Swed.	southern
Solončak / Rus.	salt flat
Sommet / Fr.	peak
Son / Viet.	mountain
Sønder / Dan.; Nor.	southern
Søndre / Dan.	southern
Sone / Jap.	bank
Song / Viet.	river
Sopka / Rus.	volcano
Sopočnik / Rus.	mountain system
Soprana / It.	upper
Šor, Sor / Alt.	salt marsh
Sos / Sp.	upon
Sotavento / Sp.	leeward
Sotoviento / Sp.	leeward
Sottana / It.	lower
Souk / Ar.	market
Souq / Ar.	market
Sour / Ar.	rampart
Source / Eng.; Fr.	spring
Souto / Port.	forest
Spitze / Germ.	peak
Spruit / Afr.	current
Sreden / Bulg.	central
Sredni / Rus.	central
Średni / Pol.	central
Srednji / S.C.; Slvn.	central
St., Saint, Sankt / Eng.; Fr.; Germ.; Swed.	saint
Stadhur / Icel.	city, town
Stadt, -stadt / Germ.	city, town
Stag / Eng.	city, town
Stagno / It.	pond
-stan / Hin.; Pers.; Urdu	land
Star / Bulg.	old
Stari / S.C.; Slvn.	old
Stary / Pol.; Rus.	old
Stary / Cz.; Slvk.	old
Stat / Afr.; Dan.; Fle.; Nor.; Dut.; Swed.	city, town
Stathmós / Gr.	railway station
Stausee / Germ.	reservoir
Stavrós / Gr.	cross
Sted / Dan.; Nor.	place
Stedt / Germ.	place
Stein, -stein / Nor.; Germ.	stone
Sten / Nor.; Swed.	stone
Stena / S.C.; Slvn.	rock
Stěna / Cz.	mountain range
Stenón / Gr.	strait, pass
Step / Rus.	steppe
-sthän / Hin.; Pers.; Urdu	land
Stift / Germ.	foundation
Štít / Cz.; Slvk.	peak
Stock / Germ.	massif
Stok / Pol.	slope
Stor / Dan.; Nor.; Swed.	great
Store / Dan.	great
Stræde / Dan.	strait
Strana / Rus.	land
Strand / Germ.; Nor.; Swed.; Afr.; Dan.	beach
Straße / Germ.	street, road
Strath / Gae.	valley
Straum / Nor.; Swed.	stream
Střední / Cz.	central
Stredný / Slvk.	central
Strelka / Rus.	spit
Stret / Nor.	strait
Stretto / It.	strait
Strom / Germ.	stream
Strøm / Nor.	stream
Ström / Swed.	stream
Stroom / Dut.	stream
Su / Jap.	sandbank
Su / Tur.	river
Suando / Finn.	pond
Suid / Afr.	south
Suidō / Jap.	strait
Sul / Port.	south
Sund / Dan.; Nor.; Swed.; Germ.	strait
Sungai / Mal.	river
Sunn / Nor.	south
Sūq / Ar.	market
Sur / Fr.	on
Sur / Sp.	south
Surkh / Pers.	red
Suu / Finn.	mouth, river mouth
Suur / Cat.	great
Svart / Nor.; Swed.	black
Sveti / S.C.; Slvn.	saint
Swa / Ban.	great
Swart / Afr.	black
Święty / Pol.	saint
Syrt / Alt.	ridge
Szállás / Hung.	village
Szczyt / Pol.	peak
Szeg / Hung.	bend
Székes / Hung.	residence
Szent / Hung.	saint
Sziget / Hung.	river island

T

Local Form	English
Tadi / Ban.	rock, cliff
Tae / Kor.	great
Tafua / Poly.	mountain
Tag / Alt.; Tur.	mountain
Tahta / Ar.	lower
Tahti / Ar.	lower
Tai / Chin.; Jap.	great
Taipale / Finn.	isthmus
Tajga / Rus.	forest
Take / Jap.	mountain
Tal / Germ.	valley
Tala / Mong.	plain, steppe
Tala / Ber.	spring
Tall / Ar.	hill
Talsperre / Germ.	dam
Tam / Viet.	stream
Tamgout / Ber.	peak
Tan / Chin.; Kor.	sandbank
Tana / Malag.	city, town
Tanana / Malag.	city, town
Tandjung / Mal.	cape, point
Tanezrouft / Ber.	desert
Tang / Chin.	upland
Tangeh / Pers.	strait
Tanjong / Mal.	cape, point
Tanjung, Tg. / Indon.	cape, point
Tanout / Ber.	well
Tao / Chin.	island
Taourirt / Ber.	peak
Targ / Pol.	market
Tärg / Bulg.	market
Tarn / Eng.	glacial lake
Tarso / Sah.	crater
Taš / Alt.	stone

Geographical Glossary

Local Form	English	Local Form	English	Local Form	English	Local Form	English
Tassili / Ber.	upland	Uebi / Som.	river	Vidda / Nor.	upland	Woda / Pol.	water
Tau / Tur.	mountain	Új- / Hung.	new	Vidde / Nor.	upland	Woestyn / Afr.	desert
Taung / Burm.	mountain	Ujście / Pol.	mouth	Viejo / Sp.	old	Wold / Dut.; Fle.; Eng.	forest
Ţawîl / Ar.	hill	Ujung / Indon.	point, cape	Vier / Germ.	four	Wörth / Germ.	river island
Tégi / Sah.	hill	Ul / Chin.; Mong.	mountain, mountain range	Viertel / Germ.	quarter	Woud / Dut.; Fle.	forest
Teguidda / Ber.	well			Vieux / Fr.	old	Wschodni / Pol.	eastern
Tehi / Ber.	pass, mountain	Ula / Mong.	mountain range	Vig / Dan.	bay	Wysoczyzna / Pol.	upland
Teich / Germ.	pond	Ulan / Mong.	red	Vík / Icel.; Nor.; Swed.	gulf, bay	Wysoki / Pol.	upper
Tell / Tur.	hill	Uls / Mong.	state	Vila / Port.	city, town	Wyspa / Pol.	island
Telok / Mal.	bay, port	Umi / Jap.	bay	Villa / Sp.	city, town	Wyżyna / Pol.	highland
Teluk / Mal.	bay, port	Umm / Ar.	mother, spring	Ville, -ville / Eng.; Fr.	city, town	Wzgórze / Pol.	hill
Tempio / It.	temple	Umne / Mong.	south	Vinh / Viet.	bay		
Ténéré / Ber.	rocky desert	Under / Mong.	mountain, peak	Virful / Rom.	peak, mountain		
Tengah / Indon.; Mal.	central					**X**	
Tepe / Tur.	hill	Ungur / Alt.	cave	Virta / Finn.	river		
Tepesi / Tur.	hill	Unter-, U. / Germ.	under, lower	Višni / Rus.	high	Xi / Chin.	west
Termas / Sp.	thermal springs	Upar / Hin.	river	Visok / S.C.	high	Xia / Chin.	gorge, strait
Terme / It.	thermal springs	'Uqlat / Ar.	well	Viz / Hung.	water	Xian / Chin.	county, shire
Terra / It.; Dut.	land, earth	Ür / Tam.	city, town	Viztároló / Hung.	reservoir	Xiang / Chin.	village
Terrazzo / It.	guyot, tablemount	Ura / Jap.	bay, coast	Vlakte / Dut.; Fle.	plain	Xiao / Chin.	little
		Ura / Alt.	depression	Vlei / Afr.	pond	Xin / Chin.	new
Terre / Fr.	land, earth	Urd / Mong.	south	Vliet / Dut.; Fle.	river	Xu / Chin.	island
Teso / Cat.	hill	Uru / Tam.	city, town	Vloer / Afr.	depression		
Téssa / Ber.	wadi, depression	Ušće / S.C.	mouth	Voda / Bulg.; Cz.; Rus.; S.C.; Slvn.	water		
Testa / It.	point	Uske / Alt.	upper			**Y**	
Tête / Fr.	peak	Ust / Rus.	mouth	Vodny put / Rus.	stream, canal		
Tetri / Georg.	white	Ústí / Cz.	mouth	Vodohranilišče, vdhr. / Rus.	reservoir	Yam / Hebr.	lake, sea
Teu / Poly.	reef	Ustup / Rus.	terrace			Yama / Jap.	mountain
Teze / Alt.	new	Utan / Indon.; Mal.	forest	Vodopad / Rus.	waterfall	Yan / Chin.	mountain
Tg., Tanjung / Indon.	cape, point	Utara / Indon.	north, northern	Volcan / Fr.	volcano	Yang / Chin.	strait, ocean
Thaba / Ban.	mountain			Volcán / Sp.	volcano	Yani / Tur.	new
Thabana / Ban.	mountain	Uusi / Finn.	new	Voll / Nor.	meadow	Yar / Tur.	gorge
Thal / Germ.	valley	Uval / Rus.	height	Vórios / Gr.	northern	Yarimada / Tur.	peninsula
Thálassa / Gr.	sea	Úval / Cz.	mountain	Vorota / Rus.	gate	Yazı / Tur.	plain
Thale / Thai	lagoon	'Uwaynāt / Ar.	well	Vorrás / Hung.	north	Yegge / Sah.	well
Thamad / Ar.	well	Uzboj / Alt.	river bed	Vostočny / Rus.	eastern	Yeni / Tur.	new
Theós / Gr.	god	Uzun / Tur.	long	Vostok / Rus.	east	Yeon / Kor.	sea
Thermes / Fr.	thermal springs	Užürekis / Lith.	gulf	Vötn / Icel.	lake, water	Yeong / Kor.	mountain
Thog / Tib.	high, upper			Vož / Ural.	mouth	Yeşil / Tur.	green
Tian / Chin.	field			Vozvyšennost / Rus.	upland	Ylä / Finn.	upper
Tiefe / Germ.	deep	**V**		Vpadina / Rus.	depression	Yli- / Finn.	upper
Tierra / Sp.	land, earth			Vrah / Bulg.	peak	Yō / Jap.	ocean
Timur / Indon.; Mal.	eastern	Va / Alb.	ford	Vrata / Bulg.; S.C.; Slvn.	pass	Yobe / Sud.	great
Tind / Nor.	mountain	Va / Ural.	water, river	Vrch / Cz.; Slvk.	mountain	Yōm / Kor.	island
Tinto / Sp.	black			Vrch / S.C.; Slvn.	peak	Yoma / Burm.	mountain range
Tirg / Rom.	market	Vaara / Finn.	mountain	Vrchni / Cz.	upper	Yŏn / Kor.	lake, pond
Tis / Amh.	new	Väärti / Finn.	bay	Vrchovina / Cz.	upland	Yŏng / Kor.	mountain, peak
Tizgui / Ber.	forest	Vad / Rom.	ford	Vulcan / Rom.; Rus.	volcano	Ytter / Nor.; Swed.	outer
Tizi / Ber.	pass	Vær / Nor.	port	Vulcano / It.	volcano	Yttre / Swed.	outer
Tjåkko / Lapp.	mountain	Våg / Nor.	bay	Vulkan / Germ.; Rus.	volcano	Yu / Chin.	old
Tjärn / Swed.	tarn, glacial lake	Vähä / Finn.	little	Vuopio / Lapp.	bend	Yu / Chin.	island
Tji / Mal.	stream	Väike / Est.	little	Vuori / Finn.	rock	Yu / Jap.	thermal spring
To / Kor.	island	Väin / Est.	strait	Východný / Cz.	eastern	Yüan / Chin.	spring, river
To / Mel.	stream	Val / Fr.; It.	valley	Vyšný / Slvk.	upper	Yunhe / Chin.	canal
Tō / Jap.	island	Val / Rom.; Rus.	wall	Vysoki / Rus.	high		
Tó / Hung.	lake	Valico / It.	pass	Vysoky / Cz.; Slvk.	high		
To / Ural.	lake	Vall / Cat.	valley	Vyšši / Cz.	high	**Z**	
Tobe / Tur.	hill	Vall / Swed.	pasture				
Tofua / Poly.	mountain	Valle / It.; Sp.	valley			Zāb / Ar.	river
Tog / Som.	valley	Vallée / Fr.	valley	**W**		Zachodni / Pol.	western
Tōge / Jap.	pass	Vallei / Afr.	valley			Zaki / Jap.	cape
Tokoj / Alt.	forest	Vallo / It.	wall	W., Wādī / Ar.	wadi	Zalew / Pol.	gulf
Tônle / Khm.	stream, lake	Valta / Finn.	cape	Wa / Ban.	people	Zaliv / Bulg.; Rus.; S.C.; Slvn.	gulf
Tope / Dut.	peak	Váltos / Gr.	marsh	Wabe / Amh.	stream		
Toplice / S.C.; Slvn.	thermal springs	Valul / Rom.	wall	Wad / Ar.	wadi	Zaljev / Slvn.	bay
Topp / Nor.	peak	Vann / Dan.; Nor.	water, lake	Wad / Dut.	tidal flat	Zámek / Cz.	castle
Tor / Gae.	rock	Vanua / Mel.	land	Wādī, W. / Ar.	wadi	Zan / Jap.	mountain
Tor / Germ.	gate	Vár / Hung.	fort	Wāhāt / Ar.	oasis	Zand / Dut.; Fle.	sand
Torbat / Pers.	tomb	Vara / Finn.	mountain	Wai / Mel.; Poly.	stream	Zandt / Dut.; Fle.	sand
Törl / Germ.	pass	Varoš / S.C.	city, town	Wal / Afr.	wall	Zangbo / Chin.	river
Torp / Swed.	hut	Város / Hung.	city, town	Wala / Hin.	mountain range	Zapad / Rus.	west
Torre / Cat.; It.; Sp.; Port.	tower	Varre / Lapp.	mountain	Wald / Germ.	forest	Zapaden / Bulg.	western
Torrente / It.; Sp.	torrent, stream	Vary / Cz.	spring	Wan / Burm.	village	Zapadni / S.C.; Slvn.	western
		Vas / S.C.; Slvn.	village	Wan / Chin.; Jap.	bay	Západní / Cz.	western
Tossa / Cat.	mountain, peak	Vásár / Hung.	market	Wand / Germ.	bluff	Zapadny / Rus.	western
Tota / Sin.	port	Väst / Swed.	west	War / Som.	pond	Zapovednik / Rus.	reserve
Tour / Fr.	tower	Väster / Swed.	western	Wār / Ar.	desert	Zatoka / Pol.	gulf
Traforo / It.	tunnel	Vatn / Icel.; Nor.	lake	-waram / Hin.; Tam.	village	Zavod / Rus.	roadstead
Träsk / Swed.	lake	Vatten / Swed.	water, lake	Wasser / Germ.	water	Zāwiyat / Ar.	monastery
Trg / S.C.	market	Vatu / Mel.; Poly.	island, reef	Wat / Pol.	wall	Zdrój / Pol.	thermal springs
Trog / Germ.	trough, trench	Vdhr., Vodohranilišče / Rus.	reservoir	Wat / Thai	church	Ze / Jap.	islet
Trois / Fr.	three			Waterval / Afr.; Dut.	waterfall	Zee / Dut.; Fle.	sea
Trung / Viet.	central	Vechiu / Rom.	old	Watt / Germ.	tidal flat	Zelёny / Rus.	green
Tse / Tib.	peak, point	Vecs / Latv.	old	Wāw / Ar.	oasis	Žem / Lith.	land, country
Tsi / Chin.	pond	Vega / Sp.	irrigated crops	Weald / Eng.	wooded country	Zemé / Cz.; Slvk.	land, country
Tskali / Georg.	river	Veld / Afr.; Dut.; Fle.	field	Webi / Som.	stream	Zemlja / Rus.	land
Tsu / Jap.	bay	Veli / S.C.; Slvn.	great	Weg / Germ.	way, road	Zen / Jap.	mountain
Tulūl / Ar.	hills	Velik / Bulg.	great	Wei / Chin.	cape, point	Zhan / Chin.	mountain
Tünel / Pers.	tunnel	Veliki / Rus.; S.C.; Slvn.	great	Weide / Germ.	pasture	Zhen / Chin.	market
Tunturi / Lapp.	mountain, tundra	Veliký / Cz.	great	Weiler / Germ.	village	Zhong / Chin.	central
		Velký / Cz.	great	Weiß / Germ.	white	Zhou / Chin.	quarter, district
Tur'ah / Ar.	irrigation canal	Vel'ky / Slvk.	great	Weon / Kor.	field		
Turm / Germ.	tower	Vella / Cat.	old	Wer / Som.	pond	Zhuang / Chin.	village
Turn / Rom.	tower	Ver / Ural.	forest	Werder / Germ.	river island	Ziemia / Pol.	land
Turó / Cat.	dome	Verde / It.; Sp.	green	Werk / Germ.	factory	Zigos / Gr.	pass
Tuz / Tur.	salt	Verh / Rus.	peak	Wes / Afr.	west	Zipfel / Germ.	tip, point
Týn / Cz.	fortress	Verhni / Rus.	upper	Westlich / Germ.	western	Ziwa / Swa.	marsh
		Verk / Swed.	factory	Westr- / Sca.	western	Zizhiqu / Chin.	autonomous region
		Vermelho / Port.	red	Wëyn / Som.	great		
U		Vert / Fr.	green	Wëyne / Som.	great	Zlato / Bulg.	gold
		Ves / Cz.	village	Wick / Eng.	village	Zuid / Dut.; Fle.	south
U., Unter-, Upon / Eng.; Germ.	under, lower	Vesi / Finn.	water, lake	Wiek / Germ.	bay	Zuidelijk / Dut.	southern
		Vest / Dan.; Nor.	west	Wielki / Pol.	great	Żuława / Pol.	marsh
Uaimh / Gae.	cave	Vester / Dan.; Nor.	western	Wieś / Pol.	village	Zun / Mong.	east
Uchi / Jap.	bay	Vestur / Icel.	west	Wijk / Dut.; Fle.	quarter, district	Zwart / Dut.	black
Udde / Swed.	cape	Vetta / It.	summit	-willer / Germ.	village	Zwei / Germ.	two
Údolní nádrž / Cz.	reservoir	Viaduc / Fr.	viaduct				

International Map Index

All of the toponyms (place-names) which appear on the maps are listed in the International Map Index. Each entry includes the following: Place-name and, where applicable, other forms by which it is written or known; a symbol, where applicable, indicating what kind of feature it is; the number of the map on which it appears; and the map-reference letters and geographical coordinates indicating its location on the map.

Toponyms

Each toponym, or place-name, is written in full, with accents and diacritical marks. Since many countries have more than one official language, many of these forms are included on the maps. For example, many Belgian place-names are listed as follows: Bruxelles/Brussel; Antwerpen/Anvers, and vice versa, Brussel/Bruxelles; Anvers/Antwerpen. In Italy, certain regions have a special status—they are largely autonomous and officially bilingual. As a result, Index listings appear as follows: Aosta/Aoste; Alto Adige/Sud Tirol, and vice versa. One name, however, may be the only name on the map.

In China, the written forms of commonly used regional languages have been taken into account. These forms are enclosed in parenthesis following the official name: e.g. Xiangshan (Dancheng). However, when the regional is listed first, it is linked to the official name with an →: e.g. Dancheng→Xiangshan. The same style is used for former or historical name forms: e.g. Rhodesia→Zimbabwe and Zimbabwe (Rhodesia).

Place-names for major features (countries, major cities, and large physical features), where applicable, include the English conventional form identified by (EN) and linked in the local name or names with an = sign: e.g. Italia=Italy (EN), and vice versa, Italy (EN)=Italia. Former English names are linked in the Index to the conventional form by an →.

Symbols

The last component with the place-name is a symbol, where applicable, specifying the broad category of the feature named. A table preceding the Index lists all of the symbols used and their meanings; this information also appears as a footnote on each page of the Index. Place-names without symbols are cities and towns.

Alphabetization

Place-names are listed in English alphabetical order—26 letters, from A to Z—because of its international usage. Names including two or more words are listed alphabetically according to the first letter of the word: e.g. De Ruyter is listed under D; Le Havre is listed under L. Names with the prefix Mc are listed as if spelled Mac. The generic portion of a name (lake, sierra, mountain, etc.) is placed after the name: e.g. Lake Erie is listed as Erie, Lake; Sierra Morena is listed as Morena, Sierra. In Spanish, "ch" and "ll" groups and the letter "n" are included respectively under C, L, and N, without any distinction.

The same place-name sometimes is listed in the Index several times. It may because of the various translations of a name, or it may be that several places have the same name.

Various translations of a name appear as follows:

Danube (EN) = Dunav   Danube (EN) = Donau
Danube (EN) = Dunărea   Danube (EN) = Dunaj

Several places with the same name appear as follows; however, only in these cases is the location—abbreviated and enclosed in brackets—included. A table of these abbreviations precedes the Index.

Abbeville [U.S.]   Aberdeen [Scot.-U.K.]
Abbeville [Fr.]   Aberdeen [N.C.-U.S.]
Aberdeen [S. Afr.]

Map Number

Each map in the atlas is identified by a number. Where multiple maps are on one page, each map is additionally identified by a boxed letter in the upper-right-hand corner of the map. In the Index listing following the place-name and its variations in language and spelling, where applicable, is the number of the map on which it appears. If the map is one of several on a page, the Index listing includes the map number and letter.

Although a place-name may appear on one or more maps, it is indexed to only one map. Most places are indexed to the regional maps. However, if a place-name appears on either the physical or political continental maps, it is indexed to one of the two types of map. For example, a river or mountain would be indexed to a physical continental map; a city or state would be indexed to a political continental map.

Map-Reference Letters and Geographical Coordinates

The next elements in the Index listing are the map-reference letters and the geographical coordinates, respectively, locating the place on the map.

Map-reference letters consist of a capital and a lowercase letter. Capital letters are across the top and bottom of the maps; lowercase letters are down the sides. The map-reference letters assigned to each place-name refer to the location of the name within the area formed by grid lines connecting the geographical coordinates on either sides of the letters.

Geographical coordinates are the latitude (N for North, S for South) and longitude (E for East, W for West) expressed in degrees and minutes and based on the prime meridian, Greenwich.

Map-reference letters and coordinates for extensive geographical features, such as mountain ranges and countries, are given for the approximate central point of the area. Those for waterways, such as canals and rivers, are given for the mouth of the river, the point where it enters another river or where the feature reaches the map margin. On this page are sample maps showing points to which features are indexed according to map-reference letters and coordinates.

On most maps there is not enough space to place all of the names of administrative subdivisions. In these cases the location of the place is shown on the map by a circled letter or number and the place-name and circled letter or number are listed in the map margin. The map-reference numbers and coordinates for these places refer to the location of the circled letter or number on the map.

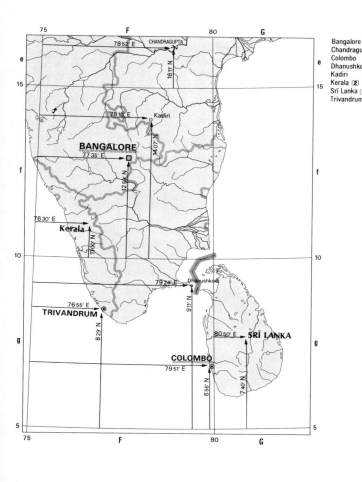

Bangalore	25	Ff	12°59'N	77°35'E
Chandragupta	35	Fe	16°11'N	78°52'E
Colombo	25	Fg	6°56'N	79°51'E
Dhanushkodi	25	Fg	9°11'N	79°24'E
Kadiri	25	Ff	14°07'N	78°10'E
Kerala	25	Ff	11°00'N	76°30'E
Sri Lanka	25	Gg	7°40'N	80°50'E
Trivandrum	25	Fg	8°29'N	76°55'E

Alaska	38	Dc	65°00'N	153°00'W
Alaska, Gulf of	38	Ed	58°00'N	146°00'W
Alexander Archipelago	38	Fd	56°30'N	134°00'W
Barrow, Point	38	Db	71°23'N	156°30'W
Bering Strait	38	Cc	65°30'N	169°00'W
Coast Mountains	38	Gd	55°00'N	129°00'W
Kodiak	38	Dd	57°30'N	153°30'W
Yukon	38	Cc	62°33'N	163°59'W

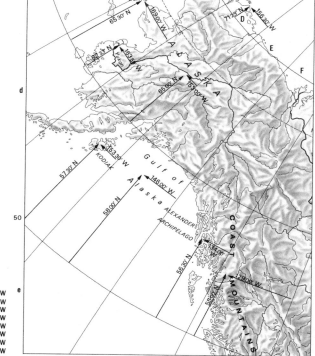

List of Abbreviations

Abz.-U.S.S.R. Azerbaidzhan S.S.R., U.S.S.R.
Afg. Afghanistan
Afr. Africa
Agl. Anguilla
Ak.-U.S. Alaska, U.S.
Al.-U.S. Alabama, U.S.
Alb. Albania
Alg. Algeria
Alta.-Can. Alberta, Canada
Am. Sam. American Samoa
And. Andorra
Ang. Angola
Ant. Antarctica
Ar.-U.S. Arkansas, U.S.
Arg. Argentina
Arm.-U.S.S.R. Armenian S.S.R., U.S.S.R.
Asia Asia
Atg. Antigua
Aus. Austria
Austl. Australia
Az.-U.S. Arizona, U.S.
Azr. Azores
Bah. Bahamas
Bar. Barbados
B.A.T. British Antarctic Territory
B.C.-Can. British Columbia, Canada
Bel. Belgium
Ben. Benin
Ber. Bermuda
Bhr. Bahrain
Bhu. Bhutan
Blz. Belize
Bnd. Burundi
Bngl. Bangladesh
Bol. Bolivia
Bots. Botswana
Braz. Brazil
Bru. Brunei
Bul. Bulgaria
Bur. Burma
B.V.I. British Virgin Islands
Bye.-U.S.S.R. Byelorussian S.S.R., U.S.S.R.
Ca.-U.S. California, U.S.
Cam. Cameroon
C. Amer. Central America
Can. Canada
Can. Is. Canary Islands
C.A.R. Central African Republic
Cay. Is. Cayman Islands
Chad Chad
Chan. Is. Channel Islands
Chile Chile
China China
Co.-U.S. Colorado, U.S.
Cocos Is. Cocos Islands
Col. Colombia
Con. Congo
Cook Cook Islands
Cor. Sea Is. Coral Sea Islands
C.R. Costa Rica
Ct.-U.S. Connecticut, U.S.
Cuba Cuba
C.V. Cape Verde
Cyp. Cyprus

Czech. Czechoslovakia
D.C.-U.S. District of Columbia, U.S.
De.-U.S. Delaware, U.S.
Den. Denmark
Dji. Djibouti
Dom. Dominica
Dom. Rep. Dominican Republic
Ec. Ecuador
Eg. Egypt
El Sal. El Salvador
Eng.-U.K. England, U.K.
Eq. Gui. Equatorial Guinea
Est.-U.S.S.R. Estonian S.S.R., U.S.S.R.
Eth. Ethiopia
Eur. Europe
Falk. Is. Falkland Islands
Far. Is. Faeroe Islands
Fiji Fiji
Fin. Finland
Fl.-U.S. Florida, U.S.
Fr. France
F.R.G. Federal Republic of Germany
Fr. Gui. French Guiana
Fr. Poly. French Polynesia
F.S.M. Federated States of Micronesia
Ga.-U.S. Georgia, U.S.
Gabon Gabon
Gam. Gambia
G.D.R. German Democratic Republic
Geo.-U.S.S.R. Georgian S.S.R., U.S.S.R.
Ghana Ghana
Gib. Gibraltar
Grc. Greece
Gren. Grenada
Grld. Greenland
Guad. Guadeloupe
Guam Guam
Guat. Guatemala
Gui. Guinea
Gui. Bis. Guinea Bissau
Guy. Guyana
Haiti Haiti
Hi.-U.S. Hawaii, U.S.
H.K. Hong Kong
Hond. Honduras
Hun. Hungary
Ia.-U.S. Iowa, U.S.
I.C. Ivory Coast
Ice. Iceland
Id.-U.S. Idaho, U.S.
Il.-U.S. Illinois, U.S.
In.-U.S. Indiana, U.S.
India India
Indon. Indonesia
I. of M. Isle of Man
Iran Iran
Iraq Iraq
Ire. Ireland
Isr. Israel
It. Italy
Jam. Jamaica
Jap. Japan
Jor. Jordan
Kam. Kampuchea

Kaz.-U.S.S.R. Kazakh S.S.R., U.S.S.R.
Kenya Kenya
Ker. Is. Kermadec Islands
Kir. Kiribati
Kirg.-U.S.S.R. Kirghiz S.S.R., U.S.S.R.
Ks.-U.S. Kansas, U.S.
Kuw. Kuwait
Ky.-U.S. Kentucky, U.S.
La.-U.S. Louisiana, U.S.
Laos Laos
Lat.-U.S.S.R. Latvian S.S.R., U.S.S.R.
Lbr. Liberia
Leb. Lebanon
Les. Lesotho
Lib. Libya
Liech. Liechtenstein
Lith.-U.S.S.R. Lithuanian S.S.R., U.S.S.R.
Lux. Luxembourg
Ma.-U.S. Massachusetts, U.S.
Mac. Macao
Mad. Madagascar
Mala. Malaysia
Mald. Maldives
Mali Mali
Malta Malta
Man.-Can. Manitoba, Canada
Mar. Is. Marshall Islands
Mart. Martinique
Maur. Mauritius
May. Mayotte
Mco. Monaco
Md.-U.S. Maryland, U.S.
Me.-U.S. Maine, U.S.
Mex. Mexico
Mi.-U.S. Michigan, U.S.
Mid. Is. Midway Islands
Mn.-U.S. Minnesota, U.S.
Mo.-U.S. Missouri, U.S.
Mold.-U.S.S.R. Moldavian S.S.R., U.S.S.R.
Mong. Mongolia
Mont. Montserrat
Mor. Morocco
Moz. Mozambique
Ms.-U.S. Mississippi, U.S.
Mt.-U.S. Montana, U.S.
Mtna. Mauritania
Mwi. Malawi
Nam. Namibia
N. Amer. North America
Nauru Nauru
N.B.-Can. New Brunswick, Canada
Nb.-U.S. Nebraska, U.S.
N.C.-U.S. North Carolina, U.S.
N. Cal. New Caledonia
N.D.-U.S. North Dakota, U.S.
Nep. Nepal
Neth. Netherlands
Neth. Ant. Netherlands Antilles
Newf.-Can. Newfoundland, Canada
N.H.-U.S. New Hampshire, U.S.

Nic. Nicaragua
Nig. Nigeria
Niger Niger
N. Ire.-U.K. Northern Ireland, U.K.
N.J.-U.S. New Jersey, U.S.
N. Kor. North Korea
N.M.-U.S. New Mexico, U.S.
N.M. Is. Northern Mariana Islands
Nor. Norway
Nor. I. Norfolk Island
N.S.-Can. Nova Scotia, Canada
Nv.-U.S. Nevada, U.S.
N.W.T.-Can. Northwest Territories, Canada
N.Y.-U.S. New York, U.S.
N.Z. New Zealand
Ocn. Oceania
Oh.-U.S. Ohio, U.S.
Ok.-U.S. Oklahoma, U.S.
Oman Oman
Ont.-Can. Ontario, Canada
Or.-U.S. Oregon, U.S.
Pa.-U.S. Pennsylvania, U.S.
Pak. Pakistan
Pal. Palau
Pan. Panama
Pap. N. Gui. Papua New Guinea
Par. Paraguay
Pas. Pascua
P.D.R.Y. People's Democratic Republic of Yemen
P.E.I.-Can. Prince Edward Island, Canada
Peru Peru
Phil. Philippines
Pit. Pitcairn
Pol. Poland
Port. Portugal
P.R. Puerto Rico
Qatar Qatar
Que.-Can. Quebec, Canada
Reu. Reunion
R.I.-U.S. Rhode Island, U.S.
Rom. Romania
R.S.F.S.R.- Russian U.S.S.R. Soviet Federated Socialist Republic, U.S.S.R.
Rwn. Rwanda
S. Afr. South Africa
S. Amer. South America
Sao T.P. Sao Tome and Principe
Sask.-Can. Saskatchewan, Canada
Sau. Ar. Saudi Arabia
S.C.-U.S. South Carolina, U.S.
Scot.-U.K. Scotland, U.K.
S.D.-U.S. South Dakota, U.S.
Sen. Senegal
Sey. Seychelles
Sing. Singapore
S. Kor. South Korea
S.L. Sierra Leone
S. Lan. Sri Lanka
S.M. San Marino
S.N.A. Spanish North Africa

Sol. Is. Solomon Islands
Som. Somalia
Sp. Spain
St. C.N. Saint Christopher-Nevis
St. Hel. Saint Helena
St. Luc. Saint Lucia
St. P.M. Saint Pierre and Miquelon
St. Vin. Saint Vincent
Sud. Sudan
Sur. Suriname
Sval. Svalbard
Swe. Sweden
Switz. Switzerland
Syr. Syria
Tad.-U.S.S.R. Tadzhik S.S.R., U.S.S.R.
Tai. Taiwan
Tan. Tanzania
T.C. Is. Turks and Caicos Islands
Thai. Thailand
Tn.-U.S. Tennessee, U.S.
Togo Togo
Ton. Tonga
Trin. Trinidad and Tobago
T.T.P.I. Trust Territory of the Pacific Islands
Tun. Tunisia
Tur. Turkey
Tur.-U.S.S.R. Turkman S.S.R., U.S.S.R.
Tuv. Tuvalu
Tx.-U.S. Texas, U.S.
U.A.E. United Arab Emirates
Ug. Uganda
U.K. United Kingdom
Ukr.-U.S.S.R. Ukrainian S.S.R., U.S.S.R.
Ur. Uruguay
U.S. United States
U.S.S.R. Union of Soviet Socialist Republics
Ut.-U.S. Utah, U.S.
U.V. Upper Volta
Uzb.-U.S.S.R. Uzbek S.S.R., U.S.S.R.
Va.-U.S. Virginia, U.S.
Van. Vanuatu
V.C. Vatican City
Ven. Venezuela
Viet. Vietnam
V.I.U.S. Virgin Islands of the U.S.
Vt.-U.S. Vermont, U.S.
Wa.-U.S. Washington, U.S.
Wake Wake Island
Wales-U.K. Wales, U.K.
W.F. Wallis and Futuna
Wi.-U.S. Wisconsin, U.S.
W. Sah. Western Sahara
W. Sam. Western Samoa
W.V.-U.S. West Virginia, U.S.
Wy.-U.S. Wyoming, U.S.
Yem. Yemen
Yugo. Yugoslavia
Yuk.-Can. Yukon, Canada
Zaire Zaire
Zam. Zambia
Zimb. Zimbabwe

List of Symbols

Plains and Associated Features
Plain, Basin, Lowland
Delta
Salt Flat

Valleys and Depressions
Valley, Gorge, Ravine, Canyon
Cave, Crater, Quarry
Karst Features
Depression
Polder, Reclaimed Marsh

Vegetational Features
Desert, Dunes
Forest, Woods
Heath, Steppe, Tundra, Moor
Oasis

Political/Administrative Units
[1] Independent Nation
[2] State, Canton, Region
[3] Province, Department, County, Territory, District
[4] Municipality
[5] Colony, Dependency, Administered Territory

Geographical Regions
Continent
Physical Region
Historical or Cultural Region

Mountain Features
Mount, Mountain, Peak
Volcano
Hill
Mountains, Mountain Range
Hills, Escarpment
Plateau, Highland, Upland
Pass, Gap

Coastal Features
Cape, Point
Coast, Beach
Cliff
Peninsula, Promontory
Isthmus
Sandbank, Tombolo, Sandbar

Islands Rocks, Reefs
Island
Atoll
Rock, Reef
Islands, Archipelago
Rocks, Reefs
Coral Reef

Hydrographic Features
Well, Spring
Geyser, Fumarole
River, Stream, Brook
Waterfall, Rapids, Cataract
River Mouth, Estuary
Lake
Salt Lake
Intermittent Lake, Dry Lake Bed
Reservoir, Artificial Lake
Swamp, Marsh, Pond
Irrigation Canal, Navigable Canal, Ditch, Aqueduct

Ice Features
Glacier, Snowfield
Ice Shelf, Pack Ice

Marine Features
Ocean
Sea
Gulf, Bay
Strait, Fjord, Sea Channel
Lagoon, Anchorage

Submarine Features
Bank, Shoal
Seamount
Rise, Plateau, Tablemount
Seamount Chain, Ridge
Platform, Shelf
Basin, Depression
Escarpment, Slope, Sea Scarp
Fracture
Trench, Abyss, Valley, Canyon

Other Features
National Park, Nature Reserve
Scenic Area, Point of Interest
Recreation Site, Sports Arena
Cave, Cavern
Historic Site, Memorial, Mausoleum, Museum
Ruins
Wall, Walls, Tower, Castle, Fortress
Church, Abbey, Cathedral, Sanctuary
Temple, Synagogue, Mosque
Research or Scientific Station
Airport, Heliport
Port, Dock
Lighthouse
Mine
Tunnel
Dam, Bridge

Index Symbols

Independent Nation	Historical or Cultural Region	Pass, Gap
State, Region	Mount, Mountain	Plain, Lowland
District, County	Volcano	Delta
Municipality	Hill	Salt Flat
Colony, Dependency	Mountains, Mountain Range	Valley, Canyon
Continent	Hills, Escarpment	Crater, Cave
Physical Region	Plateau, Upland	Karst Features

Depression	Coast, Beach	Rock, Reef	Waterfall Rapids	Canal
Polder	Cliff	Islands, Archipelago	River Mouth, Estuary	Glacier
Desert, Dunes	Peninsula	Rocks, Reefs	Lake	Ice Shelf, Pack Ice
Forest, Woods	Isthmus	Coral Reef	Salt Lake	Ocean
Heath, Steppe	Sandbank	Well, Spring	Intermittent Lake	Sea
Oasis	Island	Geyser	Reservoir	Gulf, Bay
Cape, Point	Atoll	River, Stream	Swamp, Pond	Strait, Fjord

Lagoon	Escarpment, Sea Scarp	Historic Site	Port
Bank	Fracture	Ruins	Lighthouse
Seamount	Trench, Abyss	Wall, Walls	Mine
Tablemount	National Park, Reserve	Church, Abbey	Tunnel
Ridge	Point of Interest	Temple	Dam, Bridge
Shelf	Recreation Site	Scientific Station	
Basin	Cave, Cavern	Airport	

Aginski Burjatski Nacionalny Okrug [3] 20 Gf 51.00N 114.30 E
Aginskoje 20 Gf 51.03N 114.33 E
Agnew 59 Ee 28.01S 120.30 E
Agnibilékrou 34 Ed 7.08N 3.12W
Agnita 15 Hd 45.58N 24.37 E
Agno 14 Fe 45.32N 11.21 E
Agnone 14 Ii 41.48N 14.22 E
Ago 29 Ed 34.19N 136.50 E
Agoare 34 Fd 8.30N 3.25 E
Agogna 14 Ce 45.04N 8.54 E
Agön 8 Gc 61.35N 17.25 E
Agordat 31 Kg 15.32N 37.53 E
Agordo 14 Gd 46.17N 12.02 E
Agout 11 Hk 43.47N 1.41 E
Āgra 22 Jg 27.11N 78.01 E
Agrahanski Poluostrov 16 Oh 43.45N 47.35 E
Agramunt 13 Nc 41.47N 1.06 E
Agreda 13 Kc 41.51N 1.56W
Agri 14 Kj 40.13N 16.44 E
Agričaj 16 Oi 41.17N 46.43 E
Agrigento 6 Hh 37.19N 13.34 E
Agrihan Island 57 Fc 18.46N 145.40 E
Agrij 15 Gb 47.15N 23.16 E
Agrinion 15 Ek 38.38N 21.25 E
Agropoli 14 Ij 40.21N 14.59 E
Agro Pontino 14 Gi 41.25N 12.55 E
Agryz 7 Mh 56.31N 53.01 E
Agto 41 Ge 67.37N 53.49W
Agua Brava, Laguna- 48 Gf 22.10N 105.32W
Agua Caliente, Cerro- 47 Cc 26.27N 106.12W
Aguachica 54 Db 8.18N 73.38W
Agua Clara 55 Fe 20.27S 52.52W
Aguada de Pasajeros 49 Gb 22.23N 80.51W
Aguadez, Irhazer Oua-n- 34 Gb 17.28N 6.26 E
Aguadilla 49 Nd 18.26N 67.09W
Aguadulce 49 Gi 8.15N 80.33W
Agua Fria River 46 Ij 33.23N 112.21W
Agua Limpa, Rio- 55 Gb 14.58S 51.20W
Aguán, Rio- 49 Ef 15.57N 85.44W
Aguanaval, Rio- 48 Hf 25.28N 102.53W
Aguapei 55 Cc 16.12S 59.43W
Aguapei, Rio- 56 Jb 21.03S 51.47W
Aguapei, Rio- 55 Cb 15.53S 58.25W
Agua Prieta 39 If 31.18N 109.34W
Aguaray 56 Hb 22.16S 63.44W
Aguaray Guazú, Rio- [Par.] 55 Dg 24.05S 56.40W
Aguaray Guazú, Rio- [Par.] 55 Dg 24.47S 57.19W
Aguasay 50 Eh 9.25N 63.44W
Aguascalientes 39 Ig 21.53N 102.18W
Aguascalientes [2] 47 Dd 22.00N 102.30W
Aguasvivas 13 Lc 41.20N 0.25W
Água Verde, Rio- 55 Da 13.42S 56.43W
Agua Vermelha, Reprêsa- 56 Ja 19.53S 50.17W
Agudo [Braz.] 55 Fi 29.38S 53.15W
Agudo [Sp.] 13 Hf 38.59N 4.52W
Agueda 13 Fc 41.02N 6.56W
Águeda 13 Dd 40.34N 8.27W
Aguelhok 34 Fb 19.28N 0.51 E
Agüenit 32 Ee 22.11N 13.08W
Aguerguer 30 Ff 23.09N 16.01W
Aguijan Island 57 Fc 14.51N 145.34 E
Aguilar de Campóo 13 Hb 42.48N 4.16W
Aguilar de la Frontera 13 Hg 37.31N 4.39W
Aguilas 13 Kg 37.24N 1.35W
Aguililla 48 Hh 18.44N 102.44W
Aguirre, Rio- 50 Fh 8.28N 61.02W
Aguja, Cabo de la- 54 Da 11.21N 73.59W
Agujereada, Punta- 51a Ab 18.31N 67.08W
Agul 20 Ee 55.40N 95.45 E
Agulhas, Cape-(EN)= Agulhas, Kaap- 30 Jl 34.50S 20.00 E
Agulhas, Kaap-=Agulhas, Cape-(EN) 30 Jl 34.50S 20.00 E
Agulhas Bank (EN) 37 Cg 35.30S 21.00 E
Agulhas Basin (EN) 3 En 47.00S 20.00 E
Agulhas Negras, Pico das- 52 Lh 22.23S 44.38W
Agulhas Plateau (EN) 30 Jm 40.00S 26.00 E
Agung, Gunung- 26 Gh 8.21S 115.30 E
Aguni-Shima 27 Mf 26.35N 127.15 E
Agupey, Rio- 55 Di 29.07S 56.36W
Agustin Codazzi 54 Da 10.02N 73.15W
Ağva 24 Cb 41.05N 29.50 E
Ahaggar 30 Hf 23.10N 5.50 E
Ahaggar, Tassili-oua-n- 30 Hf 20.30N 5.00 E
Aha Hills 37 Cc 19.45S 21.10 E
Ahalcihe 19 Eg 41.38N 42.59 E
Ahalkalaki 19 Eg 41.25N 43.29 E
Ahangaran 18 Gd 40.57N 69.37 E
Ahar 23 Gb 38.28N 47.04 E
Ahat 15 Mk 38.39N 29.47 E
Ahaus 10 Cd 52.04N 7.00 E
Ahe Atoll 57 Mf 14.30S 146.18W
Ahenet, Tanezrouft-n- 32 He 22.00N 1.00 E
Ahini 20 Ff 53.18N 105.01 E
Ahipara 62 Ea 35.10S 173.09 E
Ahja Jōgi 8 Lf 58.19N 27.15 E
Ahlat 24 Jc 38.45N 42.29 E
Ahlen 10 De 51.45N 7.55 E
Ahmadābād 22 Jg 23.02N 72.37 E
Aḩmadī 24 Qi 27.56N 56.42 E
Ahmadnagar 25 Ee 19.05N 74.44 E
Ahmadpur East 25 Ec 29.09N 71.16 E
Ahmar 30 Lh 9.23N 41.13 E
Aḩmar, Al Baḩr al-=Red Sea (EN) 30 Kf 25.00N 38.00 E
Ahmeta 16 Nh 42.02N 45.11 E
Ahmetli 15 Kk 38.31N 27.57 E
Ahnet 32 He 24.35N 3.15 E
Ahoa 64h Ab 13.17S 176.12W
Ahome 48 Ee 25.55N 109.11W
Ahon, Tarso- 35 Ba 20.23N 18.18 E
Ahr 10 Df 50.33N 7.17 E
Ahram 24 Nh 28.52N 51.16 E
Ahrāmāt al Jīzah 33 Fd 29.55N 31.05 E
Ahrensburg 10 Gc 53.41N 10.15 E
Ahrgebirge 12 Id 50.31N 6.54 E
Ahse 12 Jc 51.42N 7.51 E
Ahsu 16 Pi 40.35N 48.26 E
Ähtäri 7 Ee 62.02N 21.20 E
Ähtärinjarvi 8 Kb 62.40N 24.05 E
Ähtävänjoki 7 Fe 63.38N 22.48 E
Ahtopol 15 Kg 42.06N 27.57 E
Ahtuba 5 Kf 46.42N 48.00 E
Ahtubinsk 6 Kf 48.14N 46.14 E
Ahtyrka 19 De 50.19N 34.55 E
Ahuacapán 49 Cg 13.55N 89.51W
Ahuazotepec 48 Jg 20.03N 98.09W
Ahunui Atoll 57 Mf 19.35S 140.28W
Åhus 7 Di 55.55N 14.17 E
Ahvāz 22 Gf 31.19N 48.42 E
Ahvenanmaa/Åland [2] 7 Ef 60.15N 20.00 E
Ahvenanmaa/Åland=Aland Islands (EN) 5 Hc 60.15N 20.00 E
Ahvenanmeri 8 Hd 60.00N 19.30 E
Aḩwar 23 Gg 13.31N 46.42 E
Aibag Gol 28 Ad 41.42N 110.24 E
Aibetsu 29a Cb 43.55N 142.33 E
Aichach 10 Hh 48.28N 11.08 E
Aichi Ken [2] 28 Ng 35.00N 137.07 E
Aiea 65a Db 21.23N 157.56W
Aigle 14 Ad 46.20N 6.59 E
Aigoual, Mont- 11 Jj 44.07N 3.35 E
Aiguá 55 El 34.12S 54.45W
Aigues 11 Kj 44.07N 4.43 E
Aigues-Mortes 11 Kk 43.34N 4.11 E
Aiguilles 11 Mj 44.47N 6.52 E
Aiguillon 11 Gj 44.18N 0.21 E
Aigurande 11 Hh 46.26N 1.50 E
Ai He 28 Hd 40.13N 124.30 E
Aihui (Heihe) 22 Od 50.13N 127.26 E
Aikawa 29 Fb 38.02N 138.14 E
Aiken 43 Ke 33.34N 81.44W
Ailao Shan 49 Hg 23.15N 102.20 E
Ailette 12 Fe 49.35N 3.10 E
Ailinginae Atoll 57 Hc 11.08N 166.24 E
Aillte an Mhothair/Moher, Cliffs of- 9 Di 52.58N 9.27W
Ailly-le-Haut-Clocher 12 Dd 50.05N 1.59 E
Ailly-sur-Noye 12 Ee 49.45N 2.22 E
Ailsa Craig 9 Hf 55.16N 5.07W
Ailuk Atoll 57 Hc 10.20N 169.56 E
Aim 20 Ie 58.48N 134.12 E
Aimogasta 56 Gc 28.33S 66.49W
Aimorés 54 Jg 19.30S 41.04W
Ain [3] 11 Lh 46.10N 5.20 E
Ain 11 Li 45.48N 5.10 E
Ainazi/Ajnazi 7 Fh 57.52N 24.25 E
Aïn Beïda 32 Ib 35.48N 7.24 E
Aïn Beni Mathar 32 Gc 34.01N 2.01W
Aïn Bessem 13 Ph 36.18N 3.40 E
Aïn Boucif 13 Pi 35.53N 3.09 E
Aïn Defla 13 Nh 36.16N 1.58 E
Aïn el Berd 13 Li 35.21N 0.31W
Aïn el Hammam 13 Qh 36.34N 4.19 E
Aïn el Turck 13 Li 35.44N 0.46W
Ain Galakka 35 Bb 18.05N 18.31 E
Ainos Óros 15 Dk 38.07N 20.40 E
Aïn Oulmene 13 Ri 35.55N 5.18 E
Aïn Oussera 13 Oi 35.27N 2.54 E
Aïn Sefra 31 Ge 32.45N 0.35W
Ainsworth 45 Ge 42.33N 99.52W
Aïn Taghrout 13 Rh 36.08N 5.05 E
Aïn Tedeles 13 Mh 36.00N 0.18 E
Aïn Témouchent 32 Gb 35.18N 1.08W
Aïn Tolba 13 Ki 35.15N 1.15W
Aioi 29 Dd 34.49N 134.28 E
Aiquile 54 Eg 18.10S 65.10W
Aïr/Azbine 30 Hg 18.00N 8.30 E
Airabu, Pulau- 26 Ef 2.46N 106.14 E
Airai 64a Bc 7.21N 134.34 E
Airaines 12 De 49.58N 1.57 E
Airão 54 Fd 1.56S 61.22W
Airbangis 26 Cf 0.12N 99.23 E
Airdrie 46 Ha 51.18N 114.02W
Aire 11 Id 50.38N 2.24 E
Aire [Eng.-U.K.] 9 Mh 53.44N 0.54W
Aire [Fr.] 11 Ke 49.19N 4.49 E
Aire, Canal d'- 11 Id 50.38N 2.25 E
Aire, Isla del- 13 Qe 39.47N 4.16 E
Aire-sur-l'Adour 11 Fk 43.42N 0.16W
Air Force 42 Kc 67.55N 74.05W
Airolo 14 Cd 46.33N 8.35 E
Ais 63b Cb 15.26S 167.15 E
Aisch 10 Hg 49.46N 11.01 E
Aisén del General Carlos Ibáñez del Campo [2] 56 Fg 46.00S 73.00W
Aishihik 42 Dd 61.34N 137.30W
Ai-Shima 29 Bd 34.30N 131.18 E
Aisne [3] 11 Je 49.30N 3.30 E
Aisne 11 Ie 49.26N 2.50 E
Aisne à la Marne, Canal de l'- 11 Je 49.24N 3.55 E
Aïssa, Djebel- 32 Gc 32.51N 0.30W
Aitana, Pico- 13 Lf 38.39N 0.16W
Aitape 60 Ch 3.08S 142.21 E
Aitolikón 15 Ek 38.26N 21.21 E
Aitutaki Atoll 57 Lf 18.52S 159.45W
Ait Youssef ou Ali 13 Ii 35.09N 3.55W
Aiud 15 Gc 46.18N 23.43 E
Aiviekste 7 Fh 56.36N 25.44 E
Aiviekste/Ajviekste 7 Fh 56.36N 25.44 E
Aiwokako Passage 64a Bb 7.39N 134.33 E
Aix, Ile d'- 11 Eh 46.01N 1.10W
Aix-en-Provence 11 Lk 43.32N 5.26 E
Aix-sur-Vienne 11 Hi 45.48N 1.08 E
Aix-les-Bains 11 Li 45.42N 5.55 E
Aiyaíon Pélagos=Aegean Sea (EN) 5 Ih 39.00N 25.00 E
Aiyina 15 Gl 37.45N 23.26 E
Aíyina = Aegina (EN) 15 Gl 37.40N 23.30 E
Aiyínion 15 Fi 40.30N 22.33 E
Aíyion 15 Fk 38.15N 22.05 E
Aizawl 25 Id 23.44N 92.43 E
Aizenay 11 Eh 46.44N 1.37W
Aizpute/Ajzpute 7 Eh 56.45N 21.39 E
Aizubange 29 Fc 37.34N 139.49 E
Aizutakada 29 Fc 37.29N 139.48 E
Aizuwakamatsu 28 Of 37.30N 139.56 E
Ajā', Jabal- 24 Ii 27.30N 41.30 E
'Ajab Shīr 24 Kd 37.28N 45.54 E
Ajaccio 6 Gg 41.55N 8.44 E
Ajaccio, Golfe d'- 11a Ab 41.50N 8.41 E
Ajaguz 22 Ke 47.58N 80.27 E
Ajakli 20 Eb 70.13N 95.55 E
Ajan [R.S.F.S.R.] 20 Fe 59.38N 106.45 E
Ajan [R.S.F.S.R.] 20 Ie 56.27N 138.10 E
Ajanka 20 Ld 63.40N 167.30 E
Ajanta Range 25 Fd 20.30N 76.00 E
Ajat 17 Kj 52.54N 62.50 E
Ajax Peak 46 Id 45.20N 113.40W
Ajdābiyā 31 Je 30.46N 20.14 E
Ajdabul 19 Ge 52.42N 69.01 E
Ajdar 16 Ke 48.42N 39.13 E
Ajdar, Soloncak- 18 Fd 40.50N 66.50 E
Ajdovščina 14 He 45.53N 13.53 E
Ajdyrlinski 17 Ij 52.03N 59.50 E
Ajhal 20 Gc 66.00N 111.32 E
Ajigasawa 28 Pd 40.47N 140.12 E
Aji-Shima 29 Gb 38.15N 141.30 E
Ajjer, Tassili-n- 30 Hf 25.30N 9.00 E
Ajka 10 Ni 47.06N 17.34 E
Ajke, Ozero- 16 Vd 50.55N 61.35 E
Ajkino 17 De 62.15N 49.56 E
'Ajlūn 24 Ff 32.20N 35.45 E
'Ajmah, Jabal al- 24 Fh 29.12N 34.02 E
'Ajmān 23 Id 25.25N 55.27 E
Ajmer 22 Jg 26.27N 74.38 E
Ajnaži/Ainaži 7 Fh 57.52N 24.25 E
Ajni 18 Ge 39.23N 68.36 E
Ajo 43 Ee 32.22N 112.52W
Ajo, Cabo de- 13 Ia 43.31N 3.35W
Ajon, Ostrov- 21 Sc 69.50N 168.40 E
Ajoupa-Bouillon 51h Ab 14.50N 61.08W
Ajsary 19 He 53.05N 71.00 E
Ajtos 15 Kg 42.42N 27.15 E
Aju, Kepulauan- 26 Jf 0.28N 131.03 E
'Ajūz, Jabal al- 24 Dj 25.49N 30.43 E
Ajviekste 7 Fh 56.36N 25.44 E
Ajviekste/Aiviekste 7 Fh 56.36N 25.44 E
Ajzpute/Aizpute 7 Eh 56.45N 21.39 E
Akaba 34 Fd 7.57N 1.03 E
Akabira 28 Qc 43.30N 142.04 E
Akabli 32 Hd 26.42N 1.22 E
Akademika Obručeva, Hrebet- 20 Ef 51.30N 96.45 E
Akadomari 29 Fc 37.54N 138.24 E
Aka-Gawa 29 Fb 38.54N 139.50 E
Akagi-San 29 Fc 36.33N 139.11 E
Akaishi-Dake 29 Fd 35.27N 138.09 E
Akaishi-Sanmyaku 29 Fd 35.25N 138.10 E
Akajaure 7 Dc 67.42N 17.30 E
Aka-Jima 29b Ab 26.14N 127.17 E
Akaki 35 Fd 8.51N 38.48 E
Akala 35 Fb 15.38N 36.12 E
Akan 29a Db 43.08N 144.07 E
Akan-Gawa 29a Db 43.00N 144.16 E
Akanthou 24 Ee 35.22N 33.45 E
Akar 24 Dc 38.38N 31.06 E
Akarnaniká Óri 15 Dk 38.45N 21.00 E
Akaroa 61 Dh 43.48S 172.59 E
Akasaki 29 Cd 35.31N 133.38 E
'Akasha East 35 Ea 21.05N 30.43 E
Akashi 28 Mg 34.38N 134.59 E
Akbaba Tepe 24 Hc 39.32N 39.33 E
Akbajtal, Pereval- 19 Hh 38.31N 73.41 E
Akbou 13 Qh 36.28N 4.32 E
Akbulak 19 Fe 51.03N 55.37 E
Akbura 18 Id 40.34N 72.45 E
Akçaabat 24 Hb 40.59N 39.34 E
Akçadağ 24 Gc 38.21N 37.59 E
Akçakale 24 Hd 36.41N 38.56 E
Akçakara Dağı 24 Ic 38.40N 40.52 E
Akçakoca 24 Db 41.05N 31.09 E
Akçaova [Tur.] 15 Mh 41.03N 29.57 E
Akçaova [Tur.] 15 Ll 37.30N 28.02 E
Akčatau 19 Hf 47.59N 74.02 E
Akçay 15 Ll 37.50N 28.15 E
Akçay 15 Mm 36.36N 29.45 E
Akchâr 30 Ff 20.20N 14.28W
Ak Dağ [Tur.] 24 Ib 40.35N 41.46 E
Ak Dağ [Tur.] 23 Cb 36.32N 29.34 E
Akdağ [Tur.] 24 Gd 37.53N 37.56 E
Akdağ [Tur.] 24 Fb 40.57N 35.55 E
Akdağ [Tur.] 24 Cc 39.15N 28.49 E
Akdağ [Tur.] 15 Ll 37.42N 28.56 E
Akdağ [Tur.] 15 Mk 38.18N 29.58 E
Akdağ [Tur.] 15 Jk 38.33N 26.30 E
Ak Dağlar 24 Gc 39.30N 36.00 E
Ak Dağları 24 Ic 38.40N 40.12 E
Akdağmadeni 24 Fc 39.40N 35.54 E
Akdeniz=Mediterranean Sea (EN) 5 Hh 35.00N 20.00 E
Ak-Dovurak 20 Ef 51.10N 90.40 E
Akechi 29 Ed 35.18N 137.22 E
Ake Eze 34 Gd 5.55N 7.40 E
Akera 16 Oj 39.09N 46.48 E
Åkersberga 8 He 59.29N 18.18 E
Akershus [2] 7 Cf 60.00N 11.10 E
Aketi 31 Jh 2.44N 23.46 E
Akharnai 15 Gk 38.05N 23.44 E
Akhdar, al Jabal al- 21 Hg 23.30N 57.00 E
Akhḑar, Al Jabal al- 30 Je 32.30N 21.30 E
Akhḑar, Wādī al- 24 Gh 28.35N 36.35 E
Akhelóös 15 Ej 38.18N 21.10 E
Akhisar 23 Cb 38.55N 27.51 E
Akhmīm 33 Fd 26.34N 31.44 E
Akhtarīn 24 Gd 36.31N 37.20 E
Aki 29 Ce 33.30N 133.53 E
Akiaki Atoll 61 Nc 18.30S 139.12W
Akiéni 36 Bc 1.11S 13.53 E
Akimiski 38 Kd 53.00N 81.20W
Akimovka 16 If 46.42N 35.09 E
Aki-Nada 29 Cd 34.05N 132.40 E
Åkirkeby 8 Fi 55.04N 14.56 E
Akita 22 Qf 39.43N 140.07 E
Akita Ken [2] 28 Pe 39.45N 140.20 E
Akjoujt 31 Fg 19.44N 14.22W
Akka 32 Fd 29.25N 8.15W
Akkanburluk 17 Mj 52.46N 66.35 E
'Akko 23 Ec 32.55N 35.05 E
Akkol 18 Hc 43.25N 70.47 E
Akköy 24 Bd 37.29N 27.15 E
Akkystau 19 Ff 47.17N 51.03 E
Aklavik 42 Dc 68.14N 135.02W
Aklé Mseïguîlé 34 Eb 16.20N 4.45W
Akmenė/Akmene 8 Jh 56.14N 22.43 E
Akmene/Akmenė 8 Jh 56.14N 22.43 E
Akmenrags/Akmeņrags 8 Ih 56.54N 20.55 E
Akmeņrags/Akmenrags 8 Ih 56.54N 20.55 E
Akmeqit 27 Cd 37.05N 76.55 E
Akniste 8 Kh 56.10N 25.54 E
Akō 29 Dd 34.45N 134.23 E
Akobo 30 Kh 7.48N 33.03 E
Akobo 31 Kh 7.47N 33.01 E
Akola 22 Jg 20.44N 77.00 E
Akonolinga 34 He 3.46N 12.15 E
Akosombo Dam 34 Fd 6.16N 0.03 E
Akpatok 42 Kd 60.24N 68.05W
Akqi 27 Cc 40.50N 78.01 E
Ákra Ámbelos 15 Gj 39.56N 23.56 E
Ákra Kambanós 15 Hl 37.59N 24.45 E
Akranes 7a Ab 64.19N 22.06W
Ákra Spathí 15 Gl 37.27N 23.31 E
Åkrehamn 7 Ag 59.16N 5.11 E
Akrítas, Ákra- = Akritas, Cape- (EN) 15 Em 36.43N 21.53 E
Akritas Cape- (EN) = Akrítas, Ákra- 15 Em 36.43N 21.53 E
Akron [Co.-U.S.] 45 Ef 40.10N 103.13W
Akron [Oh.-U.S.] 43 Kc 41.04N 81.31W
Akrotiri 24 Ee 34.36N 32.57 E
Akša 20 Gf 50.17N 113.17 E
Aksaj 16 Oh 43.32N 46.55 E
Aksaj [Kaz.-U.S.S.R.] 19 Fe 51.13N 53.01 E
Aksaj [R.S.F.S.R.] 16 Kf 47.15N 39.52 E
Aksakal 15 Li 40.09N 28.07 E
Aksakovo 17 Gi 54.02N 54.09 E
Aksaray 23 Db 38.23N 34.03 E
Aksay 27 Fd 39.28N 94.15 E
Akşehir 23 Db 38.21N 31.25 E
Aksehir Gölü 24 Dc 38.30N 31.28 E
Akseki 24 Dd 37.02N 31.48 E
Aksenovo-Zilovskoje 20 Gf 53.00N 117.35 E
'Aks-e Rostam 24 Ph 28.23N 54.52 E
Aksoran, Gora 19 Hf 48.25N 75.30 E
Akstafa 16 Ni 41.13N 45.27 E
Akstafa 16 Ni 41.06N 45.28 E
Aksu [China] 22 Ke 41.09N 80.15 E
Aksu [Kaz.-U.S.S.R.] 19 He 52.28N 71.59 E
Aksu [Kaz.-U.S.S.R.] 18 Lb 45.34N 79.30 E
Aksu [Kaz.-U.S.S.R.] 19 Hf 46.20N 78.15 E
Aksu [Tur.] 15 Ll 37.56N 28.56 E
Aksu [Tur.] 24 Dd 36.51N 30.54 E
Aksuat 19 If 47.48N 82.50 E
Aksubajevo 7 Mi 54.52N 50.50 E
Aksu He 21 Ke 40.28N 80.52 E
Aksum 35 Fc 14.07N 38.44 E
Ak-Šyjrak 18 Ld 41.49N 78.44 E
Aktag 27 Dd 36.45N 84.40 E
Aktaš [R.S.F.S.R.] 20 Df 50.18N 87.44 E
Aktaš [Uzb.-U.S.S.R.] 19 Gh 39.55N 65.53 E
Aktau 19 He 50.16N 73.07 E
Aktau, Gora- 19 Gg 41.45N 64.30 E
Aktjubinsk 6 Le 50.17N 57.10 E
Aktjubinskaja Oblast [3] 19 Ff 48.00N 58.00 E
Ak-Tjuz 18 Kc 42.50N 76.07 E
Akto 27 Cd 39.05N 76.02 E
Aktogaj 19 Hf 47.01N 79.40 E
Akula 36 Db 2.22N 20.11 E
Akun 40a Eb 54.12N 165.35W
Akune 28 Kh 32.01N 130.11 E
Akure 34 Gd 7.15N 5.12 E
Akureyri 6 Eb 65.40N 18.06W
Akuseki-Jima 28 Jj 29.28N 129.33 E
Akutan 40a Eb 54.10N 165.55W
Akutan 40a Eb 54.08N 165.46W
Akyab → Sittwe 22 Lg 20.09N 92.54 E
Akyazı 24 Db 40.41N 30.37 E
Akžajkyn, Ozero- 18 Fb 44.55N 67.45 E
Akzāl 19 If 49.13N 81.30 E
Ål 8 Cd 60.38N 8.34 E
Alà, Monti di- 14 Dj 40.35N 9.16 E
Alabama 38 Kf 31.08N 87.57W
Alabama [2] 43 Je 32.50N 87.30W
Al'Abbāsīyah 35 Ec 12.10N 31.18 E
Alaca 24 Fb 40.10N 34.51 E
Alaçam Dağlari 15 Lj 39.20N 28.32 E
Alaçan 24 Fb 41.37N 35.37 E
Alaçati 15 Jk 38.16N 26.23 E
Aladağ 24 Jc 43.35N 39.20 E
Ala Dağ [Tur.] 24 Jb 40.11N 42.49 E
Ala Dağ [Tur.] 24 Ed 37.58N 32.04 E
Alādāgh, Kūh-e- 24 Qd 37.13N 57.30 E
Ala Dağları 24 Fd 37.55N 35.13 E
Aladža 16 Rj 39.21N 53.12 E
Aladža Manastir 15 Lf 43.17N 28.01 E
Alagir 16 Nh 43.01N 44.12 E
Alagna Valsesia 14 Be 45.51N 7.56 E
Alagnon 11 Ji 45.27N 3.19 E
Alagoas [2] 54 Ke 9.30S 36.30W
Alagoinhas 53 Mg 12.07S 38.26W
Alagón 13 Kc 41.46N 1.07W
Alagón 13 Fe 39.44N 6.53W
Ala Gou 27 Ec 42.42N 89.
Alahanpanjang 26 Dg 1.05S 100.
Alahärmä 7 Fe 63.14N 22.
Al Aḩmadī 24 Mh 29.05N 48.
Alaid, Vulkan 20 Kf 50.50N 155.
Alajärvi 7 Fe 63.00N 23.
Alajku 19 Hg 40.18N 74.
Alajski Hrebet 21 Jf 39.45N 72.
Alajuela [3] 49 Eh 10.30N 84.
Alajuela 47 Hf 10.01N 84.
Alajuela, Lago- 49 Hi 9.05N 79.
Alakol, Ozero- 21 Ke 46.05N 81.
Alakurtti 7 Hc 66.59N 30.
Alalakeiki Channel 65a Ec 20.35N 156.
Al 'Alamayn 31 Je 30.49N 28.
Alalau, Rio- 54 Fd 0.30S 61.
Al Amādīyah 24 Jd 37.06N 43.
Alamagan Island 57 Fc 17.36N 145.
Al 'Amārah 23 Gc 31.50N 47.
'Alam ar Rūm, Ra's- 24 Bg 31.22N 27.
Alāmarvdasht 24 Oi 27.52N 52.
Alamashindo 35 Ge 4.51N 42.
Alamata 35 Fc 12.25N 39.
Alameda 45 Ci 35.11N 106.
Alaminos 26 Gc 16.10N 119.
Al 'Āmirīyah 24 Cg 31.01N 29.
Alamito Creek 45 Dl 29.31N 104.
Alamitos, Sierra de los- 48 Hd 26.20N 102.
'Alāmo 35 Ge 4.23N 43.
Alamo 46 Hh 37.22N 115.
Alamogordo 43 Fe 32.54N 105.
Alamos 47 Cc 27.01N 108.
Alamos, Sierra- 48 Gc 28.25N 105.
Alamosa 43 Fd 37.28N 105.
Al Anbār [3] 24 If 34.00N 42.
Åland/Ahvenanmaa [2] 7 Ef 60.15N 20.
Åland/Ahvenanmaa=Aland Islands (EN) 5 Hc 60.15N 20.
Aland Islands (EN)= Ahvenanmaa/Åland 5 Hc 60.15N 20.
Aland Islands (EN)=Åland/ Ahvenanmaa 5 Hc 60.15N 20.
Älandsbro 8 Gb 62.40N 17.
Ålandshav 8 Hd 60.00N 19.
Alange 13 Ff 38.47N 6.
Alanje 49 Fi 8.24N 82.
Alanya 23 Db 36.33N 32.
Alaotra, Lac- 37 Hc 17.30S 48.
Alapaha River 44 Fj 30.26N 83.
Alapajevsk 19 Gd 57.52N 61.
Alaplı 24 Db 41.08N 31.
Al 'Aqabah=Aqaba (EN) 23 Dd 29.31N 35.
Al 'Aqabah aş Şaghīrah 24 Ej 24.14N 32.
Al 'Arabīyah As-Su'ūdīyah= Saudi Arabia (EN) [1] 22 Gg 25.00N 45.
Alarcón, Embalse de- 13 Je 39.45N 2.
Al 'Arish 33 Fc 31.08N 33.
Al 'Armah 24 Lj 25.30N 46.
Al Arţāwīyah 24 Ki 26.30N 45.
Alas, Selat- 26 Gh 8.40S 116.
Al 'Aşab 24 Pk 23.20N 54.
Alaşehir 24 Cc 38.21N 28.
Al Ashkharah 23 Ie 21.47N 59.
Al 'Āshūrīyah 24 Jg 31.02N 43.
Alaska [2] 40 Ic 65.00N 153.
Alaska 38 Dc 65.00N 153.
Alaska, Gulf of- 38 Ed 58.00N 146.
Alaska Peninsula 38 Dd 57.00N 158.
Alaska Range 38 Ec 62.30N 150.
Alassio 14 Cf 44.00N 8.
Alastaro 8 Jd 60.57N 22.
Alat 18 De 39.26N 63.
Alataw Shan 27 Cb 45.00N 80.
Alataw Shankou= Dzungarian Gate (EN) 21 Ke 45.25N 82.
Al 'Athāmīn 24 Jg 30.35N 43.
Alatri 14 Hi 41.43N 13.
Al 'Aţrun 31 Jg 18.11N 26.
Alatyr 7 Li 54.52N 46.
Alatyr 19 Ee 54.50N 46.
Alava [3] 13 Jb 42.50N 2.
Alava, Cape- 46 Cb 48.10N 124.
Alaverdi 19 Eg 41.08N 44.
Alavijeh 24 Nf 33.03N 51.
Alavo/Alavus 7 Fe 62.35N 23.
Alavus/Alavo 7 Fe 62.35N 23.
Al 'Awāliq 23 Gg 14.15N 46.
Al 'Awāriq 35 Ha 20.25N 48.
Al 'Awsajīyah 24 Ki 26.04N 44.
'Ālayh 24 Ff 33.48N 35.
Al 'Ayn [Sau.Ar.] 24 Hj 25.04N 38.
Al 'Ayn [U.A.E.] 24 Pj 24.13N 55.
Alayor 13 Qe 39.56N 4.
Al 'Ayyūţ 24 Dh 29.37N 31.
Al A'ẓamīyah 24 Kf 33.23N 44.
Alazani 16 Oi 41.03N 46.
Alazeja 20 Kb 70.55N 153.
Al'Azīzīyah 33 Bc 32.32N 13.
Alazores, Puerto de los- 13 Hg 37.05N 4.
Alb [Eur.] 10 Ei 47.35N 8.
Alb [F.R.G.] 12 Ke 49.04N 8.
Alba [2] 15 Gc 46.08N 23.
Alba 14 Cf 44.42N 8.
Alba Adriatica 14 Hh 42.50N 13.
Al Bāb 24 Gd 36.22N 37.
Albac 15 Fc 46.27N 22.
Albacete 6 Fh 38.59N 1.
Albacete [3] 13 Kf 38.50N 2.
Al Badārī 33 Fd 26.59N 31.
Alba de Tormes 13 Gd 40.49N 5.
Al Badi 33 Ie 22.02N 46.
Al Bādi 24 Ie 35.56N 41.
Ålbæk 8 Dg 57.36N 10.
Ålbæk Bugt 8 Dg 57.35N 10.
Al Bahrah 24 Lh 29.40N 47.
Al Baḩr al Aḩmar [3] 35 Fb 19.50N 35.
Al Baḩrayn 21 Hg 26.00N 50.

Index Symbols

[1] Independent Nation
[2] State, Region
[3] District, County
[4] Municipality
[5] Colony, Dependency
Continent
Physical Region
Historical or Cultural Region
Mount, Mountain
Volcano
Hill
Mountains, Mountain Range
Hills, Escarpment
Plateau, Upland
Pass, Gap
Plain, Lowland
Delta
Salt Flat
Valley, Canyon
Crater, Cave
Karst Features
Depression
Polder
Desert, Dunes
Forest, Woods
Heath, Steppe
Oasis
Cape, Point
Coast, Beach
Cliff
Peninsula
Isthmus
Sandbank
Island
Atoll
Rock, Reef
Islands, Archipelago
Rocks, Reefs
Coral Reef
Well, Spring
Geyser
River, Stream
Waterfall Rapids
River Mouth, Estuary
Lake
Salt Lake
Intermittent Lake
Reservoir
Swamp, Pond
Canal
Glacier
Ice Shelf, Pack Ice
Ocean
Sea
Gulf, Bay
Strait, Fjord
Lagoon
Bank
Seamount
Tablemount
Ridge
Shelf
Basin
Escarpment, Sea Scarp
Fracture
Trench, Abyss
National Park, Reserve
Point of Interest
Recreation Site
Cave, Cavern
Historic Site
Ruins
Wall, Walls
Church, Abbey
Temple
Scientific Station
Airport
Port
Lighthouse
Mine
Tunnel
Dam, Bridge

ahrayn=Bahrain (EN) 22 Hg 26.00N 50.29 E
ida 13 Lf 38.51N 0.31W
lulia 15 Gc 46.04N 23.35 E
late del Arzobispo 13 Lc 41.07N 0.31W
alyanā 33 Fd 26.14N 32.00 E
n 11 Ik 43.54N 2.28 E
nel, Lac- 42 Kf 51.05N 73.05W
ni, Colli- 14 Gi 41.45N 12.45 E
nia (EN)=Shqiperia 6 Hg 41.00N 20.00 E
no, Lago- 14 Gi 41.45N 12.40 E
no Laziale 14 Gi 41.44N 12.39 E
ny 38 Kd 52.17N 81.31W
ny [Austl.] 58 Ch 35.02 S 117.53 E
ny [Ga.-U.S.] 43 Ke 31.35N 84.10W
ny [Ky.-U.S.] 44 Eg 36.42N 85.08W
ny [N.Y.-U.S.] 39 Le 42.39N 73.45W
ny [Or.-U.S.] 43 Cc 44.38N 123.06W
Posse 55 Eh 27.33 S 54.42W
rche 13 He 39.58N 4.46W
rdón 56 Gd 31.26 S 68.32W
rracin 13 Kd 40.25N 1.26W
rracín, Sierra de- 13 Kd 40.30N 1.30W
aşalīyah Qiblī 24 Ej 25.06N 32.47 E
aşrah 24 Lg 30.30N 47.27 E
aşrah=Basra (EN) 22 Gf 30.30N 47.47 E
athā' 24 Kg 31.07N 45.54 E
ātın 24 Lh 29.00N 46.35 E
ātinah 21 Hg 23.45N 57.20 E
tross Bank (EN) 40 Ie 56.10N 152.20W
tross Bay 59 Ib 12.45 S 141.43 E
tross Plateau (EN) 3 Mi 10.00N 103.00W
tross Point 62 Fc 38.07 S 174.40 E
atrūn 24 Fe 34.15N 35.39 E
awīţī 33 Ed 28.21N 28.52 E
ayād 21 Gg 22.00N 47.00 E
aydā' 33 Dc 32.00N 21.30 E
aydā' 33 Cd 28.21N 18.58 E
aydā' 31 Je 32.46N 21.43 E
aydā' 33 Ig 13.58N 45.35 E
gna 14 Fh 42.30N 11.11 E
marle 44 Gh 35.21N 80.12W
marle Sound 43 Ld 36.03N 76.12W
nga 14 Cf 44.03N 8.13 E
rdi 56 Ic 26.10 S 58.09W
res, Chaîne des- 11 Il 42.28N 2.56 E
res, Montes-/Les beres 11 Il 42.28N 2.56 E
rgaria-a-Velha 13 Dd 40.42N 8.29W
rique 13 Le 39.07N 0.31W
robello 14 Lj 40.47N 17.16 E
rt 11 Id 50.00N 2.39 E
rt, Canal-/Albert Kanaal Albert Canal (EN) 11 Ld 50.39N 5.37 E
rt, Lake- [Afr.] 30 Kh 1.40N 31.00 E
rt, Lake- [Or.-U.S.] 46 Ee 42.38N 120.13W
rt, Lake- (EN)=Mobuto se Seko, Lac- 30 Kh 1.40N 31.00 E
rta 42 Gf 55.00N 115.00W
rt Canal (EN)=Albert, nal-/Albert Kanaal 11 Ld 50.39N 5.37 E
rt Canal (EN)=Albert naal/Albert, Canal- 11 Ld 50.39N 5.37 E
rt Edward, Mount- 59 Ja 8.23 S 147.27 E
rt Edward Bay 42 Hc 69.35N 103.10W
rti 56 He 35.02 S 60.16W
rtirsa 10 Pi 47.15N 19.37 E
rt Kanaal/Albert, Canal- Albert Canal (EN) 11 Ld 50.39N 5.37 E
rt Lea 43 Ic 43.39N 93.22W
rt Nile 30 Kh 3.36N 32.02 E
rtville [Al.-U.S.] 44 Dh 34.16N 86.12W
rtville [Fr.] 11 Mi 45.41N 6.23 E
stroff 12 If 48.56N 6.51 E
11 Ik 43.56N 2.09 E
a 45 Jf 41.02N 92.48W
id' 24 Fh 28.28N 35.01 E
na 54 Hb 5.30N 54.03W
na, Ponta- 30 Ij 15.51 S 11.44 E
no 14 De 45.46N 9.47 E
on [Mi.-U.S.] 44 Ed 42.15N 84.45W
on [Nb.-U.S.] 45 Hf 41.42N 98.00W
on [N.Y.-U.S.] 44 Hd 43.15N 78.12W
iqa' 24 Ge 34.10N 36.10 E
i'r 23 Ed 28.51N 36.15 E
i'r al Jadīd 23 Ed 26.01N 38.29 E
irk 23 Ff 18.13N 41.33 E
s 14 Cc 47.20N 8.30 E
, Monte- 14 Dj 40.32N 9.35 E
ocácer/Albocasser 13 Md 40.21N 0.02 E
ocasser/Albocácer 13 Md 40.21N 0.02 E
rán, Isla de- 5 Fh 35.58N 3.02W
ran Basin (EN) 13 Ii 36.00N 4.00W
rg 6 Gd 57.03N 9.56 E
rg Bugt 7 Ch 56.45N 10.30 E
rz, Reshteh-ye Kūhhā- -=Elburz Mountains N) 21 Hf 36.00N 53.00 E
x 13 Jg 37.23N 2.08W
et, Pays d'- 11 Fj 44.10N 0.20W
'Alī 24 Je 34.49N 43.35 E
feira 13 Dg 37.05N 8.15W
Gharz, Sabkhat- 24 Ie 34.45N 41.15 E
uheyrat 35 Dd 7.00N 29.30 E
umbah 33 Dc 32.13N 23.00 E
uñol 13 Ih 36.47N 3.12W
uquerque [Braz.] 55 Dd 19.23 S 57.26W
uquerque [N.M.-U.S.] 39 If 35.05N 106.40W
uquerque, Cayos de- 47 Hf 12.10N 81.50W
urayj 24 Ge 34.15N 36.46 E
uraymī 23 Ie 24.15N 55.45 E
urmah 32 Ic 31.45N 9.02 E
urquerque 13 Fe 39.13N 7.00W
ury [Austl.] 58 Fh 36.05 S 146.55 E
ury [N.Z.] 62 Df 44.14 S 170.53 E
uţanah 30 Kg 15.00N 35.00 E
uţayn 24 Kj 25.52N 45.50 E

Alby 8 Fb 62.30N 15.28 E
Alcácer do Sal 13 Df 38.22N 8.30W
Alcáçovar 13 Df 38.25N 8.13W
Alcalá de Chivert 13 Md 40.18N 0.14 E
Alcalá de Guadaira 13 Gg 37.20N 5.50W
Alcalá de Henares 13 Id 40.29N 3.22W
Alcalá del Júcar 13 Ke 39.12N 1.26W
Alcalá de los Gazules 13 Gh 36.28N 5.44W
Alcalá del Río 13 Gg 37.31N 5.59W
Alcalá la Real 13 Ig 37.28N 3.56W
Alcamo 14 Gm 37.59N 12.58 E
Alcanandre 13 Mc 41.37N 0.12 E
Alcañices 13 Fc 41.42N 6.21W
Alcañiz 13 Lc 41.03N 0.08W
Alcántara 13 Fe 39.43N 6.53W
Alcântara 54 Jd 2.24 S 44.24W
Alcantara 14 Jm 37.49N 15.16 E
Alcántara, Embalse de- 13 Fe 39.45N 6.48W
Alcantarilla 13 Kg 37.58N 1.13W
Alcaraz 13 Jf 38.40N 2.29W
Alcaraz, Sierra de- 13 Jf 38.35N 2.25W
Alcaudete 13 Hg 37.36N 4.05W
Alcázar de San Juan 13 Ie 39.24N 3.12W
Alcester 63a Ac 9.33 S 152.25 E
Alcira/Alzira 13 Le 39.09N 0.26W
Alcobaça [Braz.] 54 Kg 17.30 S 39.13W
Alcobaça [Port.] 13 De 39.33N 8.59W
Alcobendas 13 Id 40.32N 3.38W
Alcoi/Alcoy 13 Lf 38.42N 0.28W
Alcolea del Pinar 13 Jc 41.02N 2.28W
Alcorta 55 Bk 33.32 S 61.07W
Alcoutim 13 Eg 37.28N 7.28W
Alcova 46 Le 42.37N 106.36W
Alcoy/Alcoi 13 Lf 38.42N 0.28W
Alcubierre, Sierra de- 13 Lc 41.44N 0.29W
Alcudia 13 Pe 39.52N 3.07 E
Alcúdia, Badia d'-/Alcudia, Bahía de- 13 Pe 39.48N 3.13 E
Alcudia, Bahía de-/Alcúdia, Badia d'- 13 Pe 39.48N 3.13 E
Alcudia, Sierra de- 13 Hf 38.35N 4.35W
Aldabra Group 37b Ab 9.25 S 46.22 E
Aldabra Islands 30 Li 9.25 S 46.22 E
Aldama [Mex.] 48 Jf 22.55N 98.04W
Aldama [Mex.] 47 Cc 28.51N 105.54W
Aldan 22 Od 58.37N 125.24 E
Aldan [R.S.F.S.R.] 20 Hd 63.20N 129.25 E
Aldan [U.S.S.R.] 21 Oc 63.28N 129.35 E
Aldan Plateau (EN)= Aldanskoje Nagorje 21 Od 57.30N 127.30 E
Aldanskoje Nagorje=Aldan Plateau (EN) 21 Od 57.30N 127.30 E
Aldarhan 27 Gb 47.42N 96.36 E
Alde 12 Db 52.10N 1.32 E
Aldeburgh 9 Oi 52.09N 1.35 E
Aldeia 55 Ed 18.12 S 55.10W
Aldeia, Serra da- 55 Ic 17.00 S 46.50W
Alderney 9 Kl 49.43N 2.12W
Aldershot 12 Bc 51.15N 0.46W
Alderson 46 Ja 50.18N 111.26W
Aledo 45 Kf 41.12N 90.45W
Aleg 31 Fg 17.03N 13.53W
Alegranza 32 Ed 29.23N 13.30W
Alegre 54 Jh 20.46 S 41.32W
Alegre, Rio- 55 Cb 15.14 S 59.58W
Alegrete 56 Ic 29.46 S 55.46W
Alej 20 Df 52.50N 83.35 E
Alejandra 55 Ci 29.54 S 59.50W
Alejandro Selkirk, Isla- 52 Hi 33.45 S 80.46W
Alejsk 20 Df 52.28N 82.45 E
Aleksandrija 16 He 48.40N 33.07 E
Aleksandrov 19 Dd 56.25N 38.42 E
Aleksandrov Gaj 19 Ee 50.08N 48.32 E
Aleksandrovka 16 He 48.59N 32.13 E
Aleksandrovsk 17 Hg 59.10N 57.35 E
Aleksandrovskoje 16 Mg 44.39N 43.00 E
Aleksandrovsk-Sahalinsk 22 Qd 50.54N 142.10 E
Aleksandrów Kujawski 10 Od 52.52N 18.42 E
Aleksandrów Łódzki 10 Pe 51.49N 19.19 E
Aleksandry, Zemlja- 21 Ga 80.45N 46.00 E
Aleksejevka [Kaz.-U.S.S.R.] 19 If 48.26N 85.40 E
Aleksejevka [Kaz.-U.S.S.R.] 19 He 51.58N 70.59 E
Aleksejevka [Kaz.-U.S.S.R.] 17 Nj 53.31N 69.28 E
Aleksejevka [R.S.F.S.R.] 19 De 50.39N 38.42 E
Aleksejevsk 20 Fe 57.50N 108.23 E
Aleksejevskoje 7 Mi 55.19N 50.03 E
Aleksin 16 Jb 54.31N 37.07 E
Aleksinac 15 Ef 43.32N 21.43 E
Alem 56 Ic 27.31 S 55.15W
Ålem 7 Dh 56.57N 16.23 E
Alem Maya 35 Gd 9.27N 41.58 E
Ålen 8 Db 62.51N 11.17 E
Alençon 11 Gf 48.26N 0.05 E
Alenquer 54 Hd 1.56 S 54.46W
Alenuihaha Channel 60 Oc 20.26N 156.00W
Alépé 34 Ed 5.30N 3.39W
Aleppo (EN)=Ḩalab 22 Ff 36.12N 37.10 E
Aléria 11a Ba 42.06N 9.31 E
Aléria, Plaine d'- 11a Ba 42.05N 9.30 E
Alert 39 Ma 82.30N 62.00W
Alert Bay 46 Ba 50.35N 126.55W
Alès 11 Kj 44.08N 4.05 E
Aleşd 15 Fb 47.04N 22.25 E
Alessandria 14 Cf 44.54N 8.37 E
Ålestrup 8 Ch 56.42N 9.30 E
Ålesund 6 Gc 62.28N 6.09 E
Aleutian Basin (EN) 38 Ad 57.00N 177.00 E
Aleutian Islands 38 Bd 52.00N 176.00W
Aleutian Range 38 Dd 59.00N 155.00W
Aleutian Trench (EN) 3 Je 51.00N 179.00 E
Alexander, Cape- 60 Fi 6.35 S 156.30 E
Alexander, Kap- 41 Ec 78.10N 72.45W
Alexander Archipelago 38 Fd 56.30N 134.00W
Alexanderbaai 37 Be 28.40 S 16.30 E
Alexander City 43 Je 32.56N 85.57W
Alexander Island 66 Qe 71.00 S 70.00W
Alexandra 61 Ci 45.15 S 169.24 E

Alexandra Fiord 42 Ka 79.17N 75.00W
Alexandretta (EN)= İskenderun 22 Ff 36.37N 36.07 E
Alexandretta, Gulf of- (EN) =İskenderun Körfezi 23 Eb 36.30N 35.40 E
Alexándria 15 Fi 40.38N 22.27 E
Alexandria [Austl.] 59 Hc 19.05 S 136.40 E
Alexandria [La.-U.S.] 39 Jf 31.18N 92.27W
Alexandria [Mn.-U.S.] 43 Hb 45.53N 95.22W
Alexandria [Rom.] 15 If 43.59N 25.20 E
Alexandria [S.Afr.] 37 Df 33.39 S 26.24 E
Alexandria [Va.-U.S.] 44 If 38.49N 77.06W
Alexandria (EN)=Al Iskandarīyah [Eg.] 31 Je 31.12N 29.54 E
Alexandria Bay 44 Jc 44.20N 75.55W
Alexandrina, Lake- 59 Hg 35.25 S 139.10 E
Alexandrita 54 Hg 19.42 S 50.27W
Alexandroúpolis 6 Ig 40.51N 25.52 E
'Aleyak, Godār-e- 24 Qd 36.30N 57.45 E
Alf 10 Df 50.03N 7.07 E
Alfabia, Sierra de- 13 Oe 39.45N 2.48 E
Alfambra 13 Kd 40.21N 1.07W
Al Fardah 35 Hc 14.51N 48.26 E
Alfaro 13 Kb 42.11N 1.45W
Al Fāshir 31 Jg 13.38N 25.21 E
Al Fashn 33 Fd 28.49N 30.54 E
Alfatar 15 Kf 43.57N 27.17 E
Al Fathah 24 Je 35.04N 43.34 E
Al Fāw 23 Gd 29.58N 48.29 E
Al Fawwārah 24 Ji 26.03N 43.05 E
Al Fayyūm 31 Kf 29.19N 30.58 E
Alfbach 12 Jd 50.03N 7.08 E
Alfeld 10 Fe 51.59N 9.50 E
Alfenas 54 Ih 21.26 S 45.57W
Al Fifi 35 Dc 10.03N 25.01 E
Alfiós 15 El 37.37N 21.27 E
Alföld 5 If 47.15N 20.25 E
Alfonsine 14 Gf 44.30N 12.03 E
Alford 12 Ca 53.15N 0.11 E
Ålfotbreen 8 Ac 61.45N 5.40 E
Alfreton 12 Aa 53.06N 1.23W
Alfta 7 Df 61.21N 16.05 E
Al Fuḩayḩīl 23 Gd 29.05N 48.08 E
Al Fuhūd 24 Lg 30.58N 46.43 E
Al Fujayrah 23 Id 25.06N 56.21 E
Al Fūlah 35 Dc 11.48N 28.24 E
Al Fuqahā' 33 Cd 27.50N 16.21 E
Al Furāt=Euphrates (EN) 21 Gf 31.00N 47.25 E
Al Fuwayriţ 24 Ni 26.02N 51.22 E
Alga 19 Ff 49.55N 57.20 E
Algador 13 Ie 39.55N 3.53W
Al Gārah 24 Ih 29.52N 40.15 E
Algarås 8 Ff 58.48N 14.14 E
Ålgård 8 Af 58.46N 5.51 E
Algarrobo 49 Jh 10.12N 74.04W
Algarve 13 Dg 37.10N 8.15W
Algarve 5 Fh 37.10N 8.15W
Algeciras 6 Fh 36.08N 5.30W
Algeciras, Bahía de- 13 Gh 36.09N 5.25W
Algena 35 Fb 17.20N 38.34 E
Algeria (EN)=Al Jazā'ir 31 Hf 28.00N 3.00 E
Algerian Basin (EN) 5 Gh 39.00N 5.00 E
Al Gharaq as Sulţānī 24 Dh 29.08N 30.42 E
Al Gharbi 32 Jc 34.40N 11.13 E
Al Ghāţ 24 Ki 26.00N 45.03 E
Al Ghaydah 23 Hf 16.12N 52.15 E
Alghero 14 Cj 40.33N 8.19 E
Alghero, Rada d'- 14 Cj 40.35N 8.20 E
Älghult 8 Fg 57.01N 15.34 E
Al Ghurāb 24 Dj 25.20N 30.20 E
Al Ghurayfah 24 Qk 23.59N 56.29 E
Al Ghurdaqah 33 Fd 27.14N 33.50 E
Algiers (EN)=Al Jazā'ir 31 He 36.47N 3.03 E
Algiers (EN)=Al Jazā'ir 32 Hb 36.35N 3.00 E
Algoa Bay 30 Jl 33.50 S 25.50 E
Algodoeiro, Serra do- 55 Jc 16.30 S 44.45W
Algoma 45 Md 44.36N 87.27W
Algoma Uplands 44 Fb 47.00N 83.35W
Algona 45 Ie 43.04N 94.14W
Algonquin Park 44 Hc 45.27N 78.26W
Algrange 12 Ie 49.21N 6.03 E
Al Ḩabakah 24 Jh 29.51N 42.16 E
Al Ḩadd 23 Ie 22.29N 59.58 E
Al Ḩadīdah 35 Ia 21.31N 50.28 E
Al Ḩadīthah 23 Fc 34.07N 42.23 E
Al Ḩadithah 24 Gg 31.28N 37.08 E
Al Ḩaḑr 24 Je 35.35N 42.44 E
Al Haffah 24 Ge 35.35N 36.02 E
Al Ḩahjarah 23 Fc 30.25N 44.30 E
Al Ḩā'ır 24 Lj 24.23N 46.50 E
Al Ḩajar 35 Hb 16.08N 47.50 E
Al Hajar 23 Ie 23.15N 57.30 E
Al Halfāyah 24 Lg 31.49N 47.26 E
Alhama 13 Kb 42.11N 1.45W
Al Ḩamād 21 Ff 32.00N 39.30 E
Alhama de Granada 13 Ih 37.00N 3.59W
Alhama de Murcia 13 Kg 37.51N 1.25W
Alhamilla, Sierra- 13 Jh 36.58N 2.20W
Al Ḩammāh 32 Ic 33.54N 9.48 E
Al Ḩammām [Eg.] 24 Cg 30.50N 29.23 E
Al Ḩammām [Iraq] 24 Kg 31.08N 44.04 E
Al Ḩamrā 24 Pj 25.42N 55.47 E
Al Hanīyah 24 Kh 29.10N 45.50 E
Al Ḩarrah 24 Ch 28.20N 29.07 E
Al Ḩarrah 24 Hg 31.00N 38.40 E
Al Harūj al Aswad 30 If 27.00N 17.10 E
Al Ḩasā 24 Fg 30.49N 35.59 E
Al Hasā' 21 Gg 26.35N 48.10 E
Al Ḩasakah 23 Fb 36.29N 40.45 E
Al Ḩasan 24 Je 34.39N 43.43 E
Al Ḩasānī 24 Gj 24.58N 37.05 E
Alhaurín el Grande 13 Hh 36.38N 4.41W
Al Ḩawāmidīyah 24 Dh 29.54N 31.15 E
Al Ḩawātah 35 Ec 13.25N 34.38 E
Al Ḩawjā' 24 Hh 28.59N 38.34 E
Al Ḩawrah 35 Hc 13.49N 47.35 E

Al Hayy 23 Gc 32.10N 46.03 E
Al Ḩayz 33 Ed 28.02N 28.39 E
Al Hibāk 23 He 20.20N 53.10 E
Al Ḩijāz 21 Fg 24.30N 38.30 E
Al Hillah 33 Ie 23.50N 46.51 E
Al Ḩillah 23 Fc 32.29N 44.25 E
Al Ḩināķīyah 23 Fe 24.51N 40.31 E
Al Hindiyah 24 Kf 32.32N 44.13 E
Al Ḩınnāh 24 Mi 26.56N 48.45 E
Al Hirmil 24 Ge 34.23N 36.23 E
Al Hoceima 32 Gb 35.15N 3.55W
Al Hoceima 32 Gb 35.00N 4.15W
Alhucemas, Peñón de- 13 Ii 35.13N 3.53W
Al Ḩudaydah 22 Gh 14.48N 42.57 E
Al Ḩufrah 33 Cd 29.30N 17.55 E
Al Hufrah 23 Ed 28.49N 38.15 E
Al Hufūf 22 Gg 25.22N 49.34 E
Al Hūj 24 Hh 29.00N 38.25 E
Al Ḩunayy 24 Mj 24.48N 48.45 E
Al Ḩuşayḩişah 35 Ec 14.44N 33.18 E
Al Ḩuwaimī 23 Fg 13.58N 47.40 E
Al Ḩuwayyiţ 24 Ij 25.36N 40.23 E
Al Ḩyyānīyah 24 Jh 28.42N 42.18 E
'Alīābād [Iran] 23 Id 28.37N 55.51 E
'Alīābād [Iran] 24 Le 35.04N 46.58 E
'Alīābād [Iran] 24 Nd 36.37N 51.33 E
Aliābād 24 Pd 36.56N 54.50 E
Alīābād, Kūh-e- 23 Hc 34.13N 50.46 E
Aliaga 13 Ld 40.40N 0.42W
Aliağa 24 Bc 38.48N 26.59 E
Aliákmon 15 Fi 40.30N 22.40 E
'Alī al Gharbī 24 Lf 32.27N 46.41 E
'Alī ash Sharqī 24 Lf 32.07N 46.44 E
Ali-Bajramly 19 Eh 39.55N 48.57 E
Alibej, Ozero- 15 Nd 45.50N 30.00 E
Alibey Adasi 15 Jj 39.20N 26.38 E
Alibo 35 Fd 9.53N 37.05 E
Alibori 34 Fc 11.56N 3.17 E
Alibunar 15 Dd 45.04N 20.58 E
Alicante 6 Fh 38.21N 0.29W
Alicante 13 Lf 38.30N 0.30W
Alicante, Golfo de- 13 Lf 38.20N 0.15W
Alice [S.Afr.] 37 Df 32.47 S 26.50 E
Alice [Tx.-U.S.] 43 Hf 27.45N 98.04W
Alice, Punta- 14 Lk 39.12N 17.09 E
Alice Springs 58 Eg 23.42 S 133.53 E
Aliceville 44 Ci 33.08N 88.09W
Alicudi 14 Il 38.30N 14.20 E
Alīgarh 22 Jg 28.02N 78.17 E
Alīgūdarz 24 Mf 33.24N 49.41 E
Alihe→Oroqen Zizhiqi 27 La 50.35N 123.42 E
Alijó 13 Ec 41.16N 7.28W
Alijos, Rocas- 47 Ad 24.57N 115.44W
'Al Ijūq, Kūh-e- 24 Ng 31.30N 51.45 E
Al Ikhwan 21 Hh 12.08N 53.10 E
Al Ikhwān 24 Fi 26.19N 34.52 E
Alima 30 Ii 1.36 S 16.36 E
Al Imārāt al 'Arabīyah al Muttaḩidah=United Arab Emirates (EN) 22 Hg 24.00N 54.00 E
Alimiá 15 Km 36.16N 27.43 E
Alindao 35 Cd 5.02N 21.13 E
Alinglapalap Atoll 57 Hd 7.08N 168.16 E
Alingsås 7 Ch 57.56N 12.31 E
Aliquippa 44 Ge 40.38N 80.16W
Al 'Irāq=Iraq (EN) 22 Gf 33.00N 44.00 E
Al'Irq 33 Dd 29.01N 21.31 E
Al 'Irqah 23 Gg 13.40N 47.18 E
Ali-Sabjeh 35 Gc 11.08N 42.43 E
'Alī Shāh 'Avaz 24 Ne 35.39N 51.04 E
Al Iskandarīyah [Eg.] = Alexandria (EN) 31 Je 31.12N 29.54 E
Al Iskandarīyah [Iraq] 24 Kf 32.53N 44.21 E
Aliskerovo 20 Lc 67.52N 167.40 E
Al Ismā'īlīyah=Ismailia (EN) 33 Fc 30.35N 32.16 E
Al Istiwā'īyah al Gharbīyah 35 Dd 5.20N 28.30 E
Al Istiwā'īyah al Sharkīyah 35 Ed 5.20N 33.50 E
Alistráti 15 Gh 41.04N 23.58 E
Alitak, Cape- 40 Ie 56.51N 154.21W
Alite Reef 63a Ec 8.53 S 160.38 E
Alitus/Alytus 19 Ce 54.25N 24.08 E
Alivérion 15 Hk 38.25N 24.02 E
Aliwal North 31 Jl 30.44 S 26.40 E
Al Jabalayn 35 Ec 12.36N 32.48 E
Al Jadīdah [Eg.] 24 Cj 25.34N 28.51 E
Al Jadīdah [Sau.Ar.] 24 Mj 25.39N 49.32 E
Al Jafr 24 Gg 30.18N 36.13 E
Al Jāfūrah 35 Ia 23.25N 50.17 E
Al Jāfūrah 24 Nj 25.00N 50.15 E
Al Jaghbūb 31 Jf 29.45N 24.31 E
Al Jahrah 23 Gc 29.20N 47.40 E
Al Jalāmīd 24 Ig 31.17N 40.06 E
Al Jamalīyah 24 Nj 25.37N 51.05 E
Al Jamm 32 Jb 35.18N 10.43 E
Al Janā'in 32 Jc 31.44N 10.09 E
Aljat 16 Pj 39.58N 49.27 E
Al Jawf [Lib.] 31 Jf 24.12N 23.18 E
Al Jawf [Sau.Ar.] 22 Fg 29.50N 39.52 E
Al Jazā'ir=Algeria (EN) 31 Hf 28.00N 3.00 E
Al Jazā'ir=Algiers (EN) 32 Hb 36.35N 3.00 E
Al Jazā'ir=Algiers (EN) 31 He 36.47N 3.03 E
Al Jazā'ir-El Harrach 13 Ph 36.43N 3.08 E
Al Jazīrah 35 Ec 14.40N 33.30 E
Al Jazīrah [Asia] 21 Gf 35.10N 42.00 E
Al Jazīrah [Sud.] 30 Kg 14.25N 33.00 E
Aljezur 13 Dg 37.19N 8.48W
Aljibe 13 Gh 36.31N 5.37W
Al Jifārah 30 Ie 32.30N 11.45 E
Al Jiwā' 23 He 23.00N 54.00 E
Al Jīzah=Giza (EN) 31 Ke 30.01N 31.13 E
Al Jubayl 23 Gd 27.01N 49.40 E
Al Jubaylah 24 Lj 24.54N 46.27 E
Al Junaynah [Sau.Ar.] 33 He 20.17N 42.48 E
Al Junaynah [Sud.] 31 Jg 13.27N 22.27 E
Al Juraid 24 Mi 27.11N 49.52 E

Aljustrel 13 Dg 37.52N 8.10W
Alką 40a Db 52.15N 174.30W
Al Kaba'ish 24 Lg 30.58N 47.00 E
Al Kāf 32 Ib 36.00N 9.00 E
Al Kāf 32 Ib 36.11N 8.43 E
Alkali Lake 46 Ff 41.42N 119.50W
Al Kamāsin 23 Fe 20.25N 44.48 E
Al Kāmilīn 35 Eb 15.05N 33.11 E
Al Karak 24 Fg 31.11N 35.42 E
Al Karkh 24 Kf 33.20N 44.20 E
Al Karnak 33 Fd 25.43N 32.39 E
Al Kawah 35 Ec 13.44N 32.30 E
Al Kāẓimīyah 24 Kf 33.22N 44.20 E
Alken 12 Hd 50.52N 5.18 E
Al Khabrā' 23 Fd 26.04N 43.33 E
Al Khābūra 23 Ie 23.50N 57.18 E
Al-Khalīj al- 'Arabi=Persian Gulf (EN) 21 Hg 27.00N 51.00 E
Al Khalīl 24 Fg 31.32N 35.06 E
Al Khālis 24 Kf 33.51N 44.32 E
Al Khandaq 35 Eb 18.36N 30.34 E
Al Khārijah 31 Kf 25.26N 30.33 E
Al Kharj 24 Lj 24.10N 47.30 E
Al Kharţūm=Khartoum (EN) 35 Eb 15.50N 33.00 E
Al Kharţūm=Khartoum (EN) 31 Kg 15.36N 32.32 E
Al Kharţūm Baḩrī= Khartoum North (EN) 31 Kg 15.38N 32.33 E
Al Khaşab 24 Qi 26.12N 56.15 E
Al Khaţţ 24 Qk 25.37N 56.01 E
Al Khawr 23 Hd 25.40N 51.30 E
Al Khidr 24 Kg 31.12N 45.33 E
Al Khubar 23 Hd 26.17N 50.12 E
Al Khufayfīyah 23 Fe 24.55N 44.42 E
Al Khums 33 Bc 31.20N 14.10 E
Al Khums 31 Ie 32.39N 14.16 E
Al Khunn 35 Ha 23.18N 49.15 E
Al Khuwayr 24 Ni 26.04N 51.05 E
Al Kidn 35 Ia 22.30N 54.00 E
Al Kilḩ Sharq 24 Ej 25.03N 32.52 E
Alkionidhon, Kólpos- 15 Fk 38.05N 23.00 E
Al Kır'ānah 24 Nj 25.00N 51.03 E
Alkmaar 11 Kb 52.37N 4.44 E
Al Kūfah 24 Kf 32.02N 44.24 E
Al Kumayt 24 Lf 32.02N 46.52 E
Al Kuntillah 33 Fc 30.00N 34.41 E
Al Kushḩ 24 Ei 26.14N 32.05 E
Al Kut 23 Gc 32.30N 45.49 E
Al Kuwayt=Kuwait (EN) 22 Gg 29.30N 47.45 E
Al Kuwayt=Kuwait (EN) 22 Gg 29.20N 47.59 E
Al Labbah 24 Ih 29.20N 41.30 E
Al Lādhiqīyah=Latakia (EN) 22 Ff 35.31N 35.07 E
Allagash River 44 Mb 47.05N 69.20W
Al Lagowa 35 Dc 11.24N 29.08 E
Allahābād 22 Kg 25.27N 81.51 E
Allah-Jun 20 Id 60.27N 134.57 E
Allah-Jun 20 Id 61.08N 137.59 E
Allahüekber DaGı 24 Jb 40.35N 42.32 E
Allakaket 40 Ic 66.34N 152.41W
Allanmyo 25 Je 19.22N 95.13 E
Allariz 13 Eb 42.11N 7.48W
All-Awash Island 51n Bb 12.55N 61.10W
Alldays 37 Dd 22.41 S 29.06 E
Ålleberg 8 Ef 58.08N 13.36 E
Allegan 44 Ed 42.32N 85.51W
Allegheny Mountains 38 Lf 38.30N 80.00W
Allegheny Plateau 38 Le 41.30N 78.00W
Allegheny Reservoir 44 He 42.00N 78.56W
Allegheny River 43 Lc 40.27N 80.00W
Allègre, Pointe- 51e Ab 16.22N 61.45W
Allen 26 Hd 12.30N 124.17 E
Allen, Bog of- 9 Gh 53.20N 7.00W
Allen, Lough-/Loch Aillionn 9 Eg 54.08N 8.08W
Allendale 44 Gi 33.01N 81.19W
Allende 47 Dc 28.20N 100.51W
Allendorf (Eder) 12 Kc 51.02N 8.40 E
Allendorf (Lumda) 12 Kd 50.41N 8.50 E
Allentown 43 Lc 40.37N 75.30W
Alleppey 22 Ji 9.29N 76.19 E
Aller 10 Fd 52.57N 9.11 E
Allevard 11 Mi 45.24N 6.04 E
Allgäuer Alpen 10 Gi 47.20N 10.25 E
Alliance [Nb.-U.S.] 43 Gc 42.06N 102.52W
Alliance [Oh.-U.S.] 44 Ge 40.56N 81.06W
Allier 11 Ih 46.30N 3.00 E
Allier 5 Gf 46.57N 3.05 E
Al Līfīyah 23 Fc 30.35N 43.09 E
Al Lişāfah 24 Li 27.37N 46.52 E
Alliston 44 Hc 44.09N 79.52W
Al Līth 23 Fe 20.09N 40.16 E
Alloa 9 Je 56.07N 3.49W
Allonnes 11 Gg 47.58N 0.09 E
Allos 11 Mj 44.14N 6.38 E
All Saints 51d Bb 17.03N 61.48W
Al Luḩayyah 23 Ff 15.43N 42.42 E
Al Luwaymī 23 Fd 27.54N 42.22 E
Alm 14 Hb 48.05N 13.55 E
Alma [Ga.-U.S.] 44 Fj 31.33N 82.28W
Alma [Mi.-U.S.] 44 Ed 43.23N 84.39W
Alma [Nb.-U.S.] 45 Gf 40.06N 99.22W
Alma [Que.-Can.] 42 Kg 48.32N 71.40W
Alma-Ata 22 Je 43.15N 76.57 E
Alma-Atinskaja Oblast 19 Hg 44.00N 77.00 E
Almada 13 Cf 38.41N 9.09W
Almadén 13 Hf 38.46N 4.50W
Al Madīnah [Iraq] 24 Lg 30.57N 47.16 E
Al Madīnah [Sau.Ar.] = Medina (EN) 22 Fg 24.28N 39.36 E
Al Madīnah al Fikrīyah 24 Di 27.56N 30.49 E
'Al Madōw 35 Hc 10.59N 48.42 E
Al Mafraq 24 Gf 32.21N 36.12 E
Al Maghrib=Morocco (EN) 31 Ge 32.00N 5.50W
Almagro 13 If 38.53N 3.43W
Almagrundet 8 He 59.06N 19.00 E

dex Symbols

Independent Nation
State, Region
District, County
Municipality
Colony, Dependency
Continent
Physical Region
Historical or Cultural Region
Mount, Mountain
Volcano
Hill
Mountains, Mountain Range
Hills, Escarpment
Plateau, Upland
Pass, Gap
Plain, Lowland
Delta
Salt Flat
Valley, Canyon
Crater, Cave
Karst Features
Depression
Polder
Desert, Dunes
Forest, Woods
Heath, Steppe
Oasis
Cape, Point
Coast, Beach
Cliff
Peninsula
Isthmus
Sandbank
Island
Atoll
Rock, Reef
Islands, Archipelago
Rocks, Reefs
Coral Reef
Well, Spring
Geyser
River, Stream
Waterfall Rapids
River Mouth, Estuary
Lake
Salt Lake
Intermittent Lake
Reservoir
Swamp, Pond
Canal
Glacier
Ice Shelf, Pack Ice
Ocean
Sea
Gulf, Bay
Strait, Fjord
Lagoon
Bank
Seamount
Tablemount
Ridge
Shelf
Basin
Escarpment, Sea Scarp
Fracture
Trench, Abyss
National Park, Reserve
Point of Interest
Recreation Site
Cave, Cavern
Historic Site
Ruins
Wall, Walls
Church, Abbey
Temple
Scientific Station
Airport
Port
Lighthouse
Mine
Tunnel
Dam, Bridge

Al Maḩallah al Kubrá 33 Fc 30.58N 31.10 E
Al Maḩāriq 33 Fd 25.37N 30.39 E
Al Mahdīyah 32 Jb 35.30N 11.04 E
Al Mahdīyah [3] 32 Jb 35.35N 11.00 E
Al Maḩfid 33 Ig 14.03N 46.55 E
Al Mahrah 23 Hf 16.56N 52.15 E
Al Maḩras 32 Jc 34.32N 10.30 E
Al Majarr al Kabīr 24 Lg 31.34N 47.10 E
Almajului, Munţii- 15 Fe 44.43N 22.12 E
Al Maks al Qiblī 33 Fe 24.35N 30.38 E
Almalyk 19 Gg 40.49N 69.38 E
Al Manādir 24 Pk 23.10N 55.10 E
Al Manāmah=Manama (EN) 22 Hg 26.13N 50.35 E
Al Manāqil 35 Ec 14.15N 32.59 E
Almanor, Lake- 46 Ef 40.15N 121.08W
Almansa 13 Kf 38.52N 1.05W
Almansa, Puerto de- 13 Lf 38.49N 0.58W
Al Manshāh 33 Fd 26.28N 31.48 E
Almansor 13 Df 38.56N 8.54W
Al Manşūrah 33 Fc 31.03N 31.23 E
Al Manzilah 24 Dg 31.09N 31.56 E
Almanzor, Pico de- 13 Gd 40.15N 5.18W
Almanzora 13 Jg 37.21N 2.08W
Al Ma'qil 24 Lg 30.33N 47.48 E
Al Maqnah 24 Fh 28.24N 34.45 E
Al Maqta' 24 Pj 24.25N 54.29 E
Almar 24 Gd 40.54N 5.29W
Al Marāghah 24 Di 26.42N 31.36 E
Al Marsá 14 En 36.53N 10.20 E
Al Mary 31 Je 32.30N 20.54 E
Almaş 15 Gb 47.14N 23.19 E
Almas, Picos de- 52 Lg 13.33 S 41.56W
Almas, Rio das- 54 If 14.35 S 49.02W
'Al Maskād 35 Hc 11.18N 49.41 E
Al Maţarīyah 33 Fc 31.11N 32.02 E
Al Mawşil=Mosul (EN) 22 Gf 36.20N 43.08 E
Al Mayādīn 24 Ie 35.01N 40.27 E
Al Mayyāh 24 Ji 27.51N 42.47 E
Almazán 13 Jc 41.29N 2.32W
Al Mazār 24 Eg 31.23N 33.23 E
Almazny 20 Gd 62.19N 114.04 E
Almazora 13 Le 39.57N 0.03W
Al Mazra'ah 24 Fg 31.16N 35.31 E
Alme, Brilon- 12 Kc 51.27N 8.37 E
Almeida 13 Fc 41.16N 6.04W
Almeirim [Braz.] 54 Hd 1.32 S 52.34W
Almeirim [Port.] 13 De 39.12N 8.38W
Al Mellem 35 Dd 9.49N 28.45 E
Almelo 11 Mb 52.21N 6.39 E
Almenara, Sierra de la- 13 Kg 37.35N 1.31W
Almendra, Embalse de- 13 Fc 41.13N 6.10W
Almendralejo 13 Ff 38.41N 6.24W
Almería [3] 13 Jg 37.10N 2.20W
Almería 6 Fh 36.50N 2.27W
Almería, Golfo de- 13 Jh 36.46N 2.30W
Almetjevsk 19 Fe 54.54N 52.20 E
Al Metlaoui 32 Ic 34.20N 8.24 E
Älmhult 7 Dh 56.33N 14.08 E
Almijara, Sierra de- 13 Ih 36.55N 3.55W
Almina, Punta- 13 Gi 35.54N 5.17W
Al Minyā [Eg.] 24 Dh 29.45N 31.18 E
Al Minyā [Eg.] 31 Kf 28.06N 30.45 E
Al Miqdādīyah 24 Kf 33.59N 44.56 E
Almirante 49 Fi 9.18N 82.24W
Almirante Brown 66 Qe 64.53 S 62.53W
Almirós 15 Fj 39.11N 22.46 E
Almiroú, Órmos- 15 Hn 35.23N 24.20 E
Almodôvar 13 Dg 37.31N 8.04W
Almodóvar del Campo 13 Hf 38.43N 4.10W
Almodóvar del Río 13 Gg 37.48N 5.01W
Almonte 13 Fg 37.15N 6.31W
Almonte 13 Fe 39.42N 6.28W
Almora 25 Fc 29.37N 79.40 E
Almoustarat 34 Fb 17.22N 0.07 E
Älmsta 8 He 59.58N 18.48 E
Al Mubarraz 23 Gd 25.25N 49.35 E
Al Mudawwarah 24 Fh 29.19N 35.59 E
Al Mudharī, Rujm- 24 Hf 32.45N 39.08 E
Al Mughayrā' [Sau.Ar.] 24 Gh 29.17N 37.41 E
Al Mughayrā' [U.A.E.] 24 Oj 24.05N 53.32 E
Al Muglad 31 Jg 11.02N 27.44 E
Al Muḩarraq 24 Ni 26.16N 50.37 E
Al Mukallā 22 Gh 14.32N 49.08 E
Al Mukhā 23 Fg 13.19N 43.15 E
Al Munastīr [3] 32 Jb 35.40N 10.50 E
Al Munastīr 32 Jb 35.47N 10.50 E
Almuñécar 13 Ih 36.43N 3.41W
Al Murabba' 24 Kj 25.43N 44.18 E
Almus 24 Gb 40.23N 36.55 E
Al Musannāh 24 Lh 29.02N 47.12 E
Al Muşawwarāt aş Şafra' 35 Eb 16.25N 33.22 E
Al Musayjīd 24 Hj 24.05N 39.06 E
Al Musayyib 24 Kf 32.47N 44.18 E
Al Mustawī 24 Kj 25.55N 44.40 E
Al Muthanna [3] 24 Kg 30.50N 45.20 E
Al Muwayh 33 He 22.45N 41.35 E
Al Muwaylih 24 Fi 27.41N 35.28 E
Alnön 8 Gb 62.25N 17.25 E
Alnwick 9 Lf 55.25N 1.42W
Ålö 8 Jd 60.20N 22.15 E
Aloândia 55 Hc 17.43 S 49.29W
Alofi 58 Kf 19.03 S 169.56W
Alofi, Ile- 57 Jf 14.19 S 178.02W
Alofi Bay 64k Bb 19.01 S 169.56W
Aloja 7 Fh 57.44N 24.59 E
Along 25 Ic 28.10N 94.46 E
Alónnisos 15 Gj 39.13N 23.55 E
Alonsa 45 Ga 50.47N 99.00W
Alonso, Rio- 55 Gg 24.05 S 51.35W
Alor, Kepulauan- 26 Hh 8.15 S 124.30 E
Alor, Pulau- 21 Oj 8.15 S 124.45 E
Alora 13 Hh 36.48N 4.42W
Alor Setar 22 Mi 6.07N 100.22 E
Alost/Aalst 11 Kd 50.56N 4.02 E
Alotau 60 Ej 10.31 S 150.43 E
Aloysius, Mount- 59 Fe 26.00 S 128.34 E
Alpen = Alps (EN) 5 Gf 46.25N 10.00 E
Alpena 43 Kb 45.04N 83.26W
Alpera 13 Kf 38.58N 1.13W
Alpes=Alps (EN) 5 Gf 46.25N 10.00 E
Alpes Bernoises/Berner Alpen=Bernese Alps (EN) 14 Bd 46.25N 7.30 E
Alpes Cottiennes 14 Af 44.45N 7.00 E
Alpes de Haute-Provence [3] 11 Lj 44.10N 6.00 E
Alpes Grées/Alpi Graie 14 Be 45.30N 7.10 E
Alpes Mancelles 11 Ff 48.25N 0.10W
Alpes Maritimes 14 Bf 44.15N 7.10 E
Alpes-Maritimes [3] 11 Nk 44.00N 7.10 E
Alpes Pennines/Alpi Pennine 14 Bd 46.05N 7.50 E
Alpes Valaisannes/Walliser Alpen 14 Bd 46.10N 7.30 E
Alpha Cordillera (EN) 67 Re 85.30N 125.00W
Alphen aan der Rijn 12 Gb 52.08N 4.42 E
Alphonse Island 30 Mi 7.00 S 52.45 E
Alpi=Alps (EN) 5 Gf 46.25N 10.00 E
Alpi Apuane 14 Ef 44.05N 10.20 E
Alpi Aurine 10 Hi 47.00N 11.55 E
Alpi Carniche 14 Gd 46.40N 13.00 E
Alpi Cozie 14 Af 44.45N 7.00 E
Alpi Graie/Alpes Grées 14 Be 45.30N 7.10 E
Alpi Lepontine 14 Cd 46.25N 8.40 E
Alpi Liguri 14 Cf 44.10N 8.05 E
Alpi Marittime 14 Bf 44.15N 7.10 E
Alpine [Az.-U.S.] 46 Kj 33.51N 109.09W
Alpine [Tx.-U.S.] 43 Ge 30.22N 103.40W
Alpine [Wy.-U.S.] 46 Je 43.15N 110.59W
Alpi Orobie 14 Dd 46.00N 10.00 E
Alpi Pennine/Alpes Pennines 14 Bd 46.05N 7.50 E
Alpi Retiche=Rhaetian Alps (EN) 14 Dd 46.30N 10.00 E
Alpi Ticinesi 14 Cd 46.20N 8.45 E
Alpi Venoste 10 Gj 46.45N 10.55 E
Alprech, Cap d'- 12 Dd 50.42N 1.34 E
Alps (EN) = Alpen 5 Gf 46.25N 10.00 E
Alps (EN)=Alpes 5 Gf 46.25N 10.00 E
Alps (EN)=Alpi 5 Gf 46.25N 10.00 E
Al qa 'Āmīyāt 35 Hb 18.50N 48.30 E
Al Qābil 24 Pk 23.56N 55.49 E
Al Qaḑārif 31 Kg 14.02N 35.24 E
Al Qaḑīmah 23 Ee 22.21N 39.09 E
Al Qādisīya [3] 24 Kg 31.50N 45.00 E
Al Qādisīya 24 Kg 31.42N 44.28 E
Al Qadmūs 24 Ge 35.05N 36.10 E
Al Qaffāy 24 Nj 24.35N 51.44 E
Al Qāhirah=Cairo (EN) 31 Ke 30.03N 31.15 E
Al Qāhirah-Imbabah 33 Fc 30.05N 31.13 E
Al Qāhirah-Mişr al Jadīdah 33 Fc 30.06N 31.20 E
Al Qā'īyah 24 Ki 26.27N 45.35 E
Al Qal'ah al Kubrá 14 Eo 35.52N 10.32 E
Al Qalībah 23 Ed 28.24N 37.42 E
Al Qāmishlī 23 Fb 37.02N 41.14 E
Al Qanţarah 33 Fc 30.52N 32.19 E
Al Qaryah ash Sharqīyah 33 Bc 30.24N 13.36 E
Al Qaryatayn 24 Ge 34.14N 37.14 E
Al Qaşab 24 Kj 25.18N 45.30 E
Al Qaşabāt 33 Bc 32.35N 14.03 E
Al Qa'şah 24 Ch 28.25N 28.56 E
Al Qash 35 Fb 16.48N 35.51 E
Al Qaşr 33 Ed 25.42N 28.53 E
Al Qaşrayn 32 Ib 35.11N 8.48 E
Al Qaşrayn [3] 32 Ib 35.15N 9.00 E
Al Qaţīf 24 Mi 26.33N 50.00 E
Al Qaţrānī 24 Gg 31.15N 36.03 E
Al Qaţrūn 33 Be 24.56N 14.38 E
Al Qay'īyah 23 Fe 24.18N 43.30 E
Al Qayrawān 32 Jb 35.41N 10.07 E
Al Qayrawān [3] 32 Ib 35.30N 10.00 E
Al Qayşūmah [Sau.Ar.] 24 Jh 29.11N 42.58 E
Al Qayşūmah [Sau.Ar.] 23 Gd 28.16N 46.03 E
Alqōsh 24 Jd 36.44N 43.06 E
Al Qubayyāt 24 Ge 34.34N 36.17 E
Al Qunayţirah 23 Ec 33.07N 35.49 E
Al Qunfudhah 23 Ff 19.08N 41.05 E
Al Qurayyah 24 Gh 28.45N 36.12 E
Al Qurnah 24 Lg 31.00N 47.26 E
Al Quşaymah 33 Fc 30.40N 34.22 E
Al Quşayr [Eg.] 31 Kf 26.06N 34.17 E
Al Quşayr [Syr.] 24 Ge 34.31N 36.35 E
Al Qūşīyah 33 Fd 27.26N 30.49 E
Al Quşūr 14 Co 35.54N 8.53 E
Al Quţayfah 24 Gf 33.44N 36.36 E
Al Quwārah 24 Ji 26.47N 43.28 E
Al Quwayr 24 Jd 36.03N 43.30 E
Al Quzah 35 Hb 15.06N 49.08 E
Als 8 Ci 55.00N 9.55 E
Alsace 11 Nf 48.30N 7.30 E
Alsace, Ballon d'- 11 Mg 47.50N 6.51 E
Alsasua 13 Jb 42.54N 2.10W
Alsdorf 12 Id 50.53N 6.10 E
Alsea River 46 Cd 44.26N 124.05W
Alsenz 12 Je 49.49N 7.51 E
Alsfeld 10 Ff 50.45N 9.16 E
Alsina, Laguna- 55 Am 36.52 S 62.07W
Alsten 7 Cd 65.57N 12.36 E
Alsterån 8 Gh 56.55N 16.26 E
Alsunga 8 Ig 57.02N 21.28 E
Alta 7 Fb 69.58N 23.14 E
Altaelva 7 Fb 69.58N 23.23 E
Altafjorden 7 Fa 70.12N 23.06 E
Altagracia 54 Da 10.07N 71.14W
Alta Gracia 56 Hd 31.40 S 64.26W
Altagracia de Orituco 50 Ch 9.52N 66.23W
Altai (EN)= Altay Shan 21 Le 46.30N 93.00 E
Altaj 22 Le 46.20N 96.17 E
Altaj 21 Kd 51.30N 90.00 E
Altajski 20 Df 51.58N 85.30 E
Altajski Kraj [3] 20 Df 52.00N 82.30 E
Altamaha River 45 Kk 31.19N 81.17W
Altamira 53 Kf 3.12 S 52.12W
Altamira, Cuevas de- 13 Ha 43.23N 4.05W
Altamira, Sierra de- 13 Ge 39.35N 5.10W
Altamirano 48 Mi 16.53N 92.09W
Altamont 46 Ee 42.12N 121.44W
Altamura 14 Kj 40.49N 16.33 E
Altamura, Isla de- 48 Ee 25.00N 108.10W
Altan Bulag 27 Jc 44.19N 113.28 E
Altan-Emel → Xin Barag Youqi 27 Kb 48.41N 116.47 E
Altan Xiret → Ejin Horo Qi 27 Id 39.31N 109.45 E
Altar 48 Db 30.43N 111.44W
Altar, Desierto de- 38 Hf 31.50N 114.15W
Altar, Rio- 48 Db 30.39N 111.55W
Altar de los Sacrificios 49 Be 16.28N 90.32W
Altata 47 Cd 24.38N 107.55W
Alta Verapaz [3] 49 Bf 15.40N 90.00W
Altavista 44 Hg 37.07N 79.18W
Altay 22 Ke 47.52N 88.07 E
Altay Shan=Altai (EN) 21 Le 46.30N 93.00 E
Altdorf 14 Cd 46.53N 8.40 E
Altea 13 Lf 38.36N 0.03W
Altena 10 De 51.18N 7.40 E
Altenberge 12 Jb 52.03N 7.28 E
Altenburg 10 If 50.59N 12.27 E
Altenglan 12 Je 49.33N 7.28 E
Altenkirchen (Westerwald) 12 Jd 50.42N 7.39 E
Alter do Chão 13 Ee 39.12N 7.40W
Altevatnet 7 Eb 68.32N 19.30 E
Altındağ 24 Ec 39.56N 32.52 E
Altınoluk 15 Jj 39.34N 26.44 E
Altinova 15 Jj 39.13N 26.47 E
Altıntaş 24 Dc 39.04N 30.07 E
Altinyayla 15 Mm 36.59N 29.33 E
Altkirch 11 Ng 47.37N 7.15 E
Altmark 10 Hd 52.40N 11.20 E
Altmühl 10 Hh 48.55N 11.52 E
Alto, Morro- 55 Ib 13.46 S 46.50W
Alto, Pico- 54 Kd 4.20 S 39.00W
Alto Alentejo 13 Ef 38.50N 7.40W
Alto Araguaia 54 Hg 17.19 S 53.12W
Alto Coité 55 Eb 15.47 S 54.20W
Alto Garças 55 Fc 16.56 S 53.32W
Alto Hama 36 Ce 12.14 S 15.34 E
Alto Longá 54 Je 5.15 S 42.12W
Alto Molócuè 37 Fc 15.38 S 37.42 E
Altomonte 14 Kk 39.42N 16.08 E
Alton [Eng.-U.K.] 12 Bc 51.08N 0.59W
Alton [Il.-U.S.] 43 Id 38.54N 90.10W
Altona, Hamburg- 10 Fc 53.33N 9.57 E
Altoona 43 Lc 40.32N 78.23W
Alto Paraguai 54 Gf 14.30 S 56.31W
Alto Paraguay [3] 55 Ce 21.00 S 59.00W
Alto Paraíso de Goiás 55 Ib 14.12 S 47.38W
Alto Paraná [3] 55 Eg 25.00 S 54.50W
Alto Parnaíba 54 Ie 9.06 S 45.57W
Alto Purús, Río- 54 De 9.34 S 70.36W
Alto Rio Senguerr 56 Fg 45.02 S 70.50W
Altos 54 Jd 5.03 S 42.28W
Alto Sucuriú 55 Fd 19.19 S 52.47W
Altötting 10 Ih 48.14N 12.41 E
Alto Uruguai, Serra do- 55 Fh 27.35 S 53.40W
Altun Ha 49 Ce 17.50N 88.20W
Āltūn Kūprī 24 Ke 35.45N 44.09 E
Altun Shan 21 Kf 38.00N 88.00 E
Alturas 43 Cc 41.29N 120.32W
Alturitas 49 Ki 9.45N 72.25W
Altus 43 He 34.38N 99.20W
Altynkan 18 Hd 41.03N 70.43 E
Altynkul 18 Bc 43.07N 58.55 E
Alu 63a Bb 7.05 S 155.47 E
Al 'Ubaylah 35 Ia 21.59N 50.57 E
Al Ubayyiḑ 31 Kg 13.11N 30.13 E
Alucra 24 Hb 40.20N 38.46 E
Al 'Udaysāt 24 Ej 25.35N 32.29 E
Al Uḑayyah 35 Dc 12.03N 28.17 E
Alūksne/Aluksne 7 Gh 57.26N 27.01 E
Aluksne/Alūksne 7 Gh 57.26N 27.01 E
Aluksne Ozero 8 Lg 57.22N 27.10 E
Aluksne Ozero/Alūksnes Ezers 8 Lg 57.22N 27.10 E
Alūksnes Ezers/Aluksne Ozero 8 Lg 57.22N 27.10 E
'Alūla 35 Ic 11.58N 50.48 E
Al 'Ulā 23 Ed 26.37N 37.52 E
Al Umm 33 Hf 18.18N 40.45 E
Alunda 8 Hd 60.04N 18.05 E
Alupka 19 Dg 44.24N 34.03 E
Al'Uqaylah 33 Cc 30.16N 19.12 E
Al 'Uqaylāt 24 Ii 26.43N 41.43 E
Al 'Uqayr 24 Nj 25.39N 50.13 E
Al Uqşur=Luxor (EN) 33 Fd 25.41N 32.39 E
Al Urayq 24 Hh 29.00N 39.10 E
Al Urdun=Jordan (EN) [1] 22 Ff 31.00N 36.00 E
Al 'Urūq al Mu'Tariḑah 35 Ia 21.00N 54.00 E
Ālūs 24 Ie 34.02N 42.26 E
Alušta 19 Dg 44.42N 34.20 E
Al 'Uthmānīyah 24 Mj 25.15N 49.22 E
Al 'Uwaynāt 33 Bd 25.48N 10.33 E
Al 'Uwaynidhīyah 24 Gi 26.38N 36.05 E
Al 'Uwayqīlah 24 Jg 30.21N 42.14 E
Al 'Uyūn 24 Hj 24.33N 39.35 E
Al Uzayin 24 Ke 34.02N 44.20 E
Al 'Uzayr 24 Lg 31.19N 47.25 E
Alva 43 Hd 36.48N 98.40W
Alva 13 Dd 40.18N 8.15W
Alvand, Kūh-e- 24 Me 34.41N 48.28 E
Älvängen 8 Eg 57.56N 12.09 E
Alvaro Obregón, Presa 48 Ed 28.00N 109.45W
Alvdal 7 Ce 62.07N 10.39 E
Älvdalen 8 Ed 60.30N 13.00 E
Älvdalen 7 Df 61.14N 14.02 E
Alvear 55 Di 29.06 S 56.33W
Alvelos, Serra de- 13 De 39.55N 8.01W
Alvesta 7 Dh 56.54N 14.33 E
Alvik 8 Gb 62.25N 17.24 E
Älvik 7 Bf 60.26N 6.26 E
Alvin 45 Il 29.25N 95.15W
Älvkarleby 7 Df 60.34N 17.27 E
Alvord Valley 46 Fe 42.45N 118.25W
Alvøy 8 Ad 60.35N 4.50 E
Älvros 8 Fb 62.03N 14.39 E
Älvsborg [2] 7 Cg 58.00N 12.30 E
Älvsbyn 7 Ed 65.40N 21.00 E
Al Wāḩidī 23 Gg 14.20N 47.50 E
Al Wajh 22 Fg 26.14N 36.28 E
Al Wakrah 24 Nj 25.10N 51.36 E
Al Wannān 24 Mi 26.55N 48.24 E
Alwar 25 Fc 27.34N 76.36 E
Al Wari'ah 24 Li 27.50N 47.29 E
Al Wāsiţah 33 Fd 29.20N 31.12 E
Al Waslātīyah 14 Do 35.51N 9.35 E
Al Wati'ah 33 Bc 32.28N 11.46 E
Al Wazz 35 Eb 15.01N 30.10 E
Al Widyān 21 Gf 31.10N 40.45 E
Alxa Youqi (Ehen Hudag) 27 Hd 39.12N 101.40 E
Alxa Zuoqi (Bayan Hot) 27 Id 38.50N 105.32 E
Al Yaman=Yemen (EN) [1] 22 Gh 15.00N 44.00 E
Al Yaman ad Dīmuqrāţīyah =Yemen, People's Democratic Republic of- (EN) [1] 22 Gh 14.00N 46.00 E
Alyangula 59 Hb 13.50 S 136.25 E
Alygdžer 20 Ef 53.38N 98.16 E
Alymka 17 Ng 59.01N 68.40 E
Alytus/Alitus 19 Ce 54.25N 24.08 E
Alz 10 Ih 48.10N 12.48 E
Alzamaj 20 Ee 55.33N 98.39 E
Alzey 10 Eg 49.45N 8.07 E
Alzira/Alcira 13 Le 39.09N 0.26W
Amachkalo Ahzar 34 Fb 15.30N 3.20 E
Amacuro, Río- 54 Fb 8.32N 60.28W
Amada 33 Fe 22.45N 32.10 E
Amadeus, Lake- 57 Eg 24.50 S 130.45 E
Amadi [Sud.] 35 Ed 5.31N 30.20 E
Amadi [Zaire] 36 Eb 3.35N 26.47 E
Amadjuak Lake 42 Kd 64.55N 71.00W
Amadora 13 Cf 38.45N 9.14W
Amadror 32 Ie 24.50N 6.25 E
Amadror 32 Id 26.00N 5.21W
Amagasaki 29 Dd 34.42N 135.25 E
Amager 8 Ei 55.35N 12.35 E
Amagi [Jap.] 29 Be 33.26N 130.39 E
Amagi [Jap.] 29b Bb 27.47N 128.52 E
Amagi-San 29 Fd 34.51N 139.00 E
Amaha 29 Fd 35.13N 139.51 E
Amahai 26 Ig 3.20 S 128.55 E
Amain, Monts d'- 11 Gf 48.39N 0.20 E
Amajac, Río- 48 Jg 21.15N 98.46W
Amakusa-Nada 28 Jh 32.25N 129.40 E
Amakusa-Shotō 28 Kh 32.22N 130.12 E
Amal 33 Dd 29.25N 21.10 E
Åmål 7 Cg 59.03N 12.42 E
Amalfi 14 Ij 40.38N 14.36 E
Amaliás 15 El 37.48N 21.21 E
Amalner 25 Fd 21.03N 75.04 E
Amambai 54 Gh 23.05 S 55.13W
Amambai, Rio- 55 Ff 23.22 S 53.56W
Amambai, Serra de- 55 Ef 23.10 S 55.30W
Amambay [3] 55 Df 23.00 S 56.00W
Amami Islands (EN)= Amami-Shotō 21 Og 28.16N 129.21 E
Amami-Ō-Shima 27 Mf 28.15N 129.20 E
Amami-Shotō=Amami Islands (EN) 21 Og 28.16N 129.21 E
Amån 8 Fc 61.12N 14.45 E
Amanã, Lago- 54 Fd 2.35 S 64.40W
Amana, Rio- 50 Eh 9.45N 62.39W
Amanave 65c Cb 14.19 S 170.49W
Amangeldy 19 Ge 50.10N 65.13 E
Amankaragaj 17 Lj 52.27N 64.08 E
Amantea 14 Kk 39.07N 16.08 E
Amanu Atoll 57 Mf 17.48 S 140.46W
Amanzimtoti 37 Ef 30.05 S 30.53 E
Amapá 53 Ke 2.03N 50.48W
Amapá, Território do- [2] 54 Hc 1.30N 52.00W
Amapala 49 Dg 13.17N 87.40W
Amara' 15 Ke 44.37N 27.19 E
Amara 30 Kg 11.30N 37.45 E
Amaradia 15 Ge 44.22N 23.43 E
'Amara East 35 Ea 20.48N 30.23 E
Amarante [Braz.] 54 Je 6.14 S 42.50W
Amarante [Port.] 13 Dc 41.16N 8.05W
Amaranth 45 Ga 50.36N 98.43W
Amargosa 46 Gh 36.18N 116.25W
Amargosa Desert 46 Gh 36.40N 116.30W
Amargosa Range 46 Gh 36.30N 116.45W
Amargosa River 46 Gh 36.13N 116.48W
Amarillo 39 If 35.13N 101.49W
Amárion 15 Hn 35.14N 24.39 E
Amarume 29 Fb 38.50N 139.54 E
Amasra 24 Eb 41.45N 32.34 E
Amasya 23 Ea 40.39N 35.51 E
Amathus 24 Ee 34.42N 33.08 E
Amatique, Bahía de- 49 Cf 15.55N 88.45W
Amatlán de Cañas 48 Gg 20.52N 104.27W
Amatrice 14 Hh 42.38N 13.17 E
Amaurilandia 55 Ff 22.10 S 52.38W
Amay 12 Hd 50.33N 5.19 E
Amazar 20 Hf 53.54N 120.57 E
Amazon (EN)=Amazonas, Rio- (Solimões) 52 Lf 0.10 S 49.00W
Amazon, Mouths of the- (EN) 52 Le 0.10 S 49.00W
Amazonas [Braz.] [2] 54 Fd 5.00 S 63.00W
Amazonas [Col.] [2] 54 Dd 1.00N 72.00W
Amazonas [Peru] [2] 54 Ce 5.00 S 77.00W
Amazonas [Ven.] [2] 54 Ec 3.30N 66.00W
Amazonas, Rio-=Amazon (EN) 52 Lf 0.10 S 49.00W
Amazonas, Rio- (Solimões) =Amazon (EN) 52 Lf 0.10 S 49.00W
Amazon Cone (EN) 52 Ke 4.30N 52.00W
Amba Ferit 35 Fc 10.55N 38.55 E
Ambāla 25 Fb 30.21N 76.50 E
Ambalangoda 25 Gg 6.14N 80.
Ambalavao 37 Hd 21.50 S 46.
Ambam 34 He 2.23N 11.
Ambanja 37 Hb 13.39 S 48.
Ambarčik 22 Sc 69.39N 162.
Ambarès-et-Lagrave 11 Fj 44.55N 0
Ambargasta, Salinas de- 56 Hc 29.20 S 64.
Ambarny 19 Db 65.54N 33.
Ambasamudram 25 Fg 8.42N 77.
Ambato 53 If 1.15 S 78.
Ambato-Boéni 37 Hc 16.28 S 46
Ambatofinandrahana 37 Hd 20.33 S 46.
Ambatolampy 37 Hc 19.23 S 47.
Ambatondrazaka 31 Lj 17.48 S 48
Ambatosoratra 37 Hc 17.36 S 48.
Ambelau, Pulau- 26 Ig 3.51 S 127.
Amberg 10 Hg 49.27N 11.
Ambergris Cay 49 Dd 18.03N 87.
Ambergris Cays 49 Lc 21.18N 71.
Ambérieu-en-Bugey 11 Li 45.57N 5.
Amberley [Eng.-U.K.] 12 Bd 50.55N 0.
Amberley [N.Z.] 62 Ee 43.09 S 172.
Ambert 11 Ji 45.33N 3.
Ambikāpur 25 Gd 23.07N 83.
Ambila 37 Hd 21.58 S 47.
Ambilobe 37 Hb 13.11 S 49.
Ambitle 63a Aa 4.05 S 153.
Ambjörby 8 Ed 60.30N 13.
Ambla 8 Ke 59.10N 25.
Amblève 11 Ld 50.28N 5.
Amblève/Amel 12 Id 50.21N 6.
Ambo 54 Cf 10.07 S 76.
Amboasary Sud 37 He 25.01 S 46
Ambodifototra 37 Hc 16.58 S 49
Ambohimahasoa 37 Hd 21.08 S 47.
Ambohimanarina 37 Hc 18.52 S 47.
Ambohitralanana 37 Ic 15.15 S 50.
Amboise 11 Gg 47.25N 0.
Ambon 58 De 3.43 S 128.
Ambon, Pulau- 26 Ig 3.40 S 128.
Ambongo 37 Gc 16.50 S 45.
Amboseli, Lake- 36 Gc 2.37 S 37.
Ambositra 31 Lk 20.30 S 47.
Ambovombe 37 He 25.09 S 46.
Ambre, Cap d'-=Ambre, Cape d'-(EN) 30 Lj 11.57 S 49.
Ambre, Cape d'-(EN)= Ambre, Cap d'- 30 Lj 11.57 S 49.
Ambre, Montagne d'- 37 Hb 12.30 S 49.
Ambriz 31 Ii 7.50 S 13.
Ambrolauri 16 Mh 42.31N 43.
Ambrym, Ile- 57 Hf 16.15 S 168.
Ambunti 60 Ch 4.14 S 142.
Āmbūr 25 Ff 12.47N 78.
Amchitka 40a Bb 51.30N 179.
Amchitka Pass 40a Cb 51.30N 179.
Am Dafok 35 Cc 10.28N 23.
Am Dam 35 Cc 12.46N 20.
Amded 32 He 22.10N 3.
Amderma 19 Gb 69.45N 61.
Am Djéména 35 Bc 13.06N 17.
Amdo 27 Fe 32.29N 91.
Ameca 47 Dd 20.33N 104.
Ameca, Río- 48 Gg 20.41N 105.
Amel/Amblève 12 Id 50.21N 6.
Ameland 12 Ha 53.26N 5.
Ameland 11 La 53.25N 5.
Ameland- Nes 12 Ha 53.26N 5.
Amelia Island 44 Gj 30.37N 81.
Amélie-les-Bains-Palaloa 11 Il 42.28N 2.
Amendola 14 Hh 42.59N 13.
Amendolara 14 Kk 39.57N 16.
'Āmerī 24 Nh 28.30N 51.
Americana 55 If 22.45 S 47.
American Falls 46 Ie 42.47N 112.
American Falls Reservoir 46 Ie 43.00N 113.
American Fork 46 Jf 40.23N 111.
American Highland 66 Ff 72.30 S 78.
American Samoa [5] 58 Kf 14.50 S 170.
Americus 43 Ke 32.04N 84.
Amersfoort 11 Lb 52.09N 5.
Amery Ice Shelf 66 Fe 69.30 S 72.
Ames 43 Ic 42.02N 93.
Amfilokhia 15 Ek 38.52N 21.
Amfissa 15 Fk 38.32N 22.
Amfreville-la-Campagne 12 Ce 49.13N 0.
Amga 20 Id 60.52N 131.
Amga 21 Pc 62.40N 134.
Amgalang→Xin Barag Zuoqi 27 Kb 48.13N 118.
Am Géréda 35 Cc 12.52N 21.
Amgu 28 Nb 45.51N 137.
Amguema 20 Nc 68.03N 177.
Amguid 32 Id 26.30N 5.
Amguid 31 Hf 26.26N 5.
Amgun 21 Pd 52.56N 139.
Amherst 42 Lg 45.49N 64.
Amherst, Mount- 59 Fc 18.11 S 126.
Amherst Island 44 Ic 44.12N 76.
Amiata, Monte- 14 Fh 42.53N 11.
Amiens 6 Gf 49.54N 2.
Āmij, Wādī- 24 If 33.48N 41.
Amik Gölü 24 Gd 36.22N 36.
Amik Ölü 24 Gd 36.15N 36.
Amili 25 Jc 28.26N 95.
Amīndīvi Islands 25 Ef 11.23N 72.
Aminuis 37 Bd 23.43 S 19.
'Āmir, Ra's- 30 Je 32.57N 21.
Amirante Islands 30 Mi 6.00 S 53.
Amirante Trench (EN) 37 Bb 6.00 S 52.
Amisk Lake 42 Hf 54.35N 102.
Amistad, Presa de la- 45 Fl 28.34N 101.
Amistad Reservoir 45 Gl 28.34N 101.
Amite 45 Kk 30.44N 90.
Amlekhganj 25 Gc 27.17N 84.
Amlia 40a Db 52.06N 173.
Amlwch 9 Ih 53.25N 4.

Index Symbols

[1] Independent Nation
[2] State, Region
[3] District, County
[4] Municipality
[5] Colony, Dependency
Continent
Physical Region
Historical or Cultural Region
Mount, Mountain
Volcano
Hill
Mountains, Mountain Range
Hills, Escarpment
Plateau, Upland
Pass, Gap
Plain, Lowland
Delta
Salt Flat
Valley, Canyon
Crater, Cave
Karst Features
Depression
Polder
Desert, Dunes
Forest, Woods
Heath, Steppe
Oasis
Cape, Point
Coast, Beach
Cliff
Peninsula
Isthmus
Sandbank
Island
Atoll
Rock, Reef
Islands, Archipelago
Rocks, Reefs
Coral Reef
Well, Spring
Geyser
River, Stream
Waterfall Rapids
River Mouth, Estuary
Lake
Salt Lake
Intermittent Lake
Reservoir
Swamp, Pond
Canal
Glacier
Ice Shelf, Pack Ice
Ocean
Sea
Gulf, Bay
Strait, Fjord
Lagoon
Bank
Seamount
Tablemount
Ridge
Shelf
Basin
Escarpment, Sea Scarp
Fracture
Trench, Abyss
National Park, Reserve
Point of Interest
Recreation Site
Cave, Cavern
Historic Site
Ruins
Wall, Walls
Church, Abbey
Temple
Scientific Station
Airport
Port
Lighthou
Mine
Tunnel
Dam, Bri

m Adām 35 Fb 16.22N 36.09 E
mān 22 Ff 31.57N 35.56 E
manford 9 Jj 51.48N 3.59W
marnäs 7 Dd 65.58N 16.12 E
meberg 8 Ff 58.52N 15.00 E
mer 10 Hi 47.57N 11.08 E
merån 8 Ga 63.09N 16.13 E
merland 10 Dc 53.15N 8.00 E
mersee 10 Hi 48.00N 11.08 E
mi-Moussa 13 Ni 35.52N 1.07 E
möchöstos=Famagusta
N) 23 Dc 35.07N 33.57 E
nja 17 Me 63.45N 67.07 E
nok-kang 27 Ld 39.55N 124.20 E
ol 23 Hb 36.23N 52.20 E
olar 55 Dd 18.01S 57.30W
orgós 15 Im 36.50N 25.53 E
orgós 15 Im 36.50N 25.59 E
orinópolis 55 Gc 16.36S 51.08W
ory 45 Lj 33.59N 88.29W
os 42 Jg 48.34N 78.07W
ot [Nor.] 8 Be 59.35N 8.00 E
ot [Nor.] 7 Bg 59.54N 9.54 E
otfors 8 Ee 59.46N 12.22 E
oucha 13 Rh 36.23N 5.25 E
ouliani 15 Gi 40.20N 23.55 E
our, Djebel- 32 Hc 33.45N 1.45 E
ourj 32 Ff 16.10N 7.35W
oanihy 37 Gd 24.40S 44.45 E
oarafaravola 37 Hc 17.36S 48.12 E
oaro 55 If 22.42S 46.47W
oer 10 Hh 48.10N 11.50 E
oère Seamount
N) 5 Eh 35.05N 12.13W
ohitrite Point 46 Cb 48.56N 125.35W
oosta 13 Md 40.43N 0.35 E
othill 12 Bb 52.02N 0.29W
ourdán/L'Empordà 13 Ob 42.12N 2.45 E
ourias 13 Pb 42.10N 3.05 E
qui 44 Na 48.28N 67.26W
rān 23 Ff 15.41N 43.55 E
ravati 22 Jg 20.56N 77.45 E
Raya 35 Bc 14.05N 16.30 E
itsar 22 Jf 31.35N 74.53 E
um 8 Cj 54.40N 8.20 E
saga 32 Ee 20.07N 14.10W
sittene, Jebel- 32 Fc 31.11N 9.40W
stel 12 Gb 52.22N 4.56 E
stelveen 12 Gb 52.18N 4.53 E
sterdam 30 Ol 37.57S 77.40 E
sterdam [Neth.] 6 Ge 52.22N 4.54 E
sterdam [N.Y.-U.S.] 44 Jd 42.56N 74.12W
sterdam-Rijnkanaal 12 Hc 51.57N 5.25 E
stetten 14 Ib 48.07N 14.52 E
Timan 31 Jg 11.02N 20.17 E
ūd, Jabal al- 23 Ec 30.59N 39.20 E
ūdā 24 Id 37.05N 40.54 E
u-Darja 18 Ef 37.57N 65.15 E
udarja=Amu Darya (EN)
21 He 43.40N 59.01 E
ū Daryā=Amu Darya
N) 21 He 43.40N 59.01 E
u Darya (EN)=
nudarja 21 He 43.40N 59.01 E
u Darya (EN)=Āmū
aryā 21 He 43.40N 59.01 E
udat 36 Fb 1.58N 34.56 E
ukta Pass 40a Db 52.25N 172.00W
un 63a Ba 5.57S 154.45 E
und Ringnes 42 Ha 78.15N 97.00W
undsen Bay 66 Ee 66.55S 50.00 E
undsen Coast 66 Mg 85.30S 159.00W
undsen Glacier 66 Mg 85.35S 159.00W
undsen Gulf 38 Gb 71.00N 124.00W
undsen-Scott Station 66 Bg 90.00S 0.00
undsen Sea (EN) 66 Of 72.30S 112.00W
ungen 8 Fc 61.10N 15.40 E
untai 22 Nj 2.26S 115.15 E
ur 21 Qd 52.56N 141.10 E
ūr, Wādī 35 Eb 18.56N 33.34 E
urang 26 Hf 1.11N 124.35 E
ursk 20 If 50.16N 136.55 E
urskaja Oblast 20 Hf 54.00N 128.00 E
urzet 20 Ig 47.41N 131.07 E
vrakia, Gulf of- (EN) =
nvrakikós Kólpos 15 Dk 39.00N 21.00 E
nvrakikós Kólpos =
nvrakia, Gulf of- (EN) 15 Dk 39.00N 21.00 E
vrosijevka 16 Kf 47.44N 38.31 E
Zoer 35 Cc 14.13N 21.23 E
na Atoll 61 Lc 17.25S 145.30W
abar 64e Ba 0.29S 166.57 E
abar 21 Nb 73.08N 113.36 E
abarskoje Ploskogorje 21 Mc 70.00N 108.00 E
Abhainn Dubh/
ackwater 9 Gh 53.39N 6.43W
Abhainn Mhór/
ackwater [Ire.] 9 Fj 51.51N 7.50W
Abhainn Mhór/
ackwater [N.Ire.-U.K.] 9 Gg 54.30N 6.35W
abuki 29 Dd 34.02N 134.11 E
nasti 56 Gc 28.49S 65.30W
aco 54 Fb 9.27N 64.28W
aconda 43 Eb 46.08N 112.57W
acortes 46 Db 48.30N 122.37W
adarko 45 Gi 35.04N 98.15W
adolu=Anatolia (EN) 21 Ff 39.00N 35.00 E
adyr 21 Tc 64.55N 176.05 E
adyr 22 Tc 64.45N 177.29 E
adyr Gulf (EN)=
nadyrskij Zaliv 21 Uc 64.00N 179.00W
adyr Range (EN)=
nadyrskoje
oskogorje 21 Tc 67.00N 174.00 E
adyrski Liman 20 Md 64.30N 178.00 E
adyrski Zaliv=Anadyr
ulf (EN) 21 Uc 64.00N 179.00W

Anadyrskoje Ploskogorje=
Anadyr Range (EN) 21 Tc 67.00N 174.00 E
Anáfi 15 Im 36.22N 25.47 E
Anaghit 35 Fb 16.20N 38.39 E
Anagni 14 Hi 41.44N 13.09 E
'Ānah 23 Fc 34.28N 41.56 E
Anaheim 46 Gj 33.51N 117.57W
Anahola 65a Ba 22.09N 159.19W
Anáhuac 48 Id 27.14N 100.09W
Anahuac, Meseta de- 47 Dd 21.30N 101.00W
An Aird/Ards Peninsula 9 Hg 54.30N 5.30W
Anaj Mudi 21 Jh 10.10N 77.04 E
Anaktuvuk Pass 40 Ic 68.10N 151.50W
Analalava 37 Hb 14.38S 47.45 E
Analavelona 37 Gd 22.37S 44.10 E
Ana Maria, Golfo de- 49 Hc 21.25N 78.40W
Anambas, Kepulauan-=
Ahambas Islands (EN) 21 Mi 3.00N 106.00 E
Anambas Islands (EN)=
Anambas, Kepulauan- 21 Mi 3.00N 106.00 E
Anambra 34 Gd 6.30N 7.30 E
Anamé 63b De 20.08S 169.49 E
Anamizu 28 Nf 37.14N 136.54 E
Anamur 23 Db 36.06N 32.50 E
Anamur Burun 23 Db 36.03N 32.48 E
Anan [Jap.] 28 Mh 33.55N 134.39 E
Anan [Jap.] 28 Id 35.19N 137.48 E
Anane, Djebel- 13 Mi 35.12N 0.47 E
Anánes 15 Hm 36.31N 24.08 E
Ananjev 16 Ff 47.43N 29.59 E
Anankwin 25 Je 15.41N 97.59 E
Anantapur 25 Ff 14.41N 77.36 E
Anantnāg (Islāmābād) 25 Fb 33.44N 75.09 E
Anapa 19 Dg 44.53N 37.19 E
Anapo 14 Jm 37.03N 15.16 E
Anápolis 53 Lg 16.20S 48.58W
Anapu, Rio- 54 Hd 2.15S 51.30W
Anār 23 Ic 30.53N 55.18 E
Anārak 23 Hc 33.20N 53.42 E
Anare Station 66 Jd 54.30S 158.55 E
Anaro, Rio- 49 Lj 7.48N 70.12W
Añasco 51a Ab 18.17N 67.10W
Anatahan Island 57 Fc 16.22N 145.40 E
Anatolia (EN)=
Anadolu 21 Ff 39.00N 35.00 E
Anatoliki Rodhópi 15 Ih 41.44N 25.31 E
Añatuya 56 Hc 28.28S 62.50W
Anauá, Rio- 54 Fc 0.58N 61.21W
Anazarba 24 Fd 37.15N 35.45 E
An Baile Meánach/
Ballymena 9 Gg 54.52N 6.17W
An Bhanna/Bann 9 Gf 55.10N 6.46W
An Bhearú/Barrow 9 Gi 52.10N 7.00W
An Bhinn Bhui/Benwee
Head 9 Dg 54.21N 9.48W
An Bhograch/Boggeragh
Mountains 9 Ei 52.05N 9.00W
An Bhóinn/Boyne 9 Gh 53.43N 6.15W
An Bhrosnach/Brosna 9 Fh 53.13N 7.58W
An Blascaod Mór/Great
Blasket 9 Ci 52.05N 10.32W
Anbyŏn 28 Ie 39.02N 127.32 E
An Cabhán/Cavan 9 Fh 53.55N 7.30W
An Cabhán/Cavan 9 Fg 54.00N 7.21W
An Caisleán Nua/Newcastle 9 Hg 54.12N 5.54W
An Caisleán Nua/Newcastle
West 9 Di 52.27N 9.03W
An Caisleán Riabhach/
Castlerea 9 Eh 53.46N 8.29W
An Caoláire Rua/Killary
Harbour 9 Dh 53.38N 9.55W
Ancares, Sierra de- 13 Fb 42.46N 6.54W
Ancash 54 Ce 9.30S 77.45W
Ancenis 11 Eg 47.22N 1.10W
An Chathair/Caher 9 Fi 52.22N 7.55W
An Cheacha/Caha
Mountains 9 Dj 51.45N 9.45W
Anchorage 39 Ec 61.13N 149.53W
An Chorr Chríochach/
Cookstown 9 Gg 54.39N 6.45W
Anci (Langfang) 27 Kd 39.29N 116.40 E
An Clár/Clare 9 Ei 52.50N 9.00W
An Cóbh/Cóbh 9 Ej 51.51N 8.17W
Ancohuma, Nevado- 54 Eg 15.51S 68.36W
Ancona 6 Hg 43.38N 13.30 E
Ancón de Sardinas, Bahia
de- 54 Cc 1.30N 79.50W
Ancre 11 Ie 49.54N 2.28 E
Ancuabe 37 Fb 12.58S 39.51 E
Ancud 56 Ff 41.52S 73.50W
Ancud, Golfo de- 56 Ff 42.05S 73.00W
Anda 27 Mb 46.24N 125.20 E
Anda (Sartu) 28 Ha 46.35N 125.00 E
Andacollo [Arg.] 56 Fe 37.11S 70.41W
Andacollo [Chile] 56 Fd 30.14S 71.06W
Andahuaylas 54 Df 13.39S 73.23W
An Daingean/Dingle 9 Ci 52.08N 10.15W
Andalgalá 56 Gc 27.36S 66.19W
Åndalsnes 7 Be 62.34N 7.42 E
Andalucia=Andalusia (EN)
13 Hg 37.30N 4.30W
Andalucia=Andalusia (EN)
5 Fh 37.30N 4.30W
Andalusia 43 Je 31.19N 86.29W
Andalusia (EN)=
Andalucia 13 Hg 37.30N 4.30W
Andalusia (EN)=
Andalucia 5 Fh 37.30N 4.30W
Andaman and Nicobar 25 If 12.30N 92.45 E
Andaman Basin (EN) 21 Lh 10.00N 94.00 E
Andaman Islands 21 Lh 12.30N 92.43 E
Andaman Sea (EN) 21 Lh 10.00N 95.00 E
Andamooka 59 Hf 30.27S 137.12 E
'Andān, Wādī- 23 Ie 21.05N 58.23 E
Andant 55 Am 36.34S 62.07W
Andapa 37 Hb 14.38S 49.33 E
Andara 37 Cc 18.03S 21.27 E

Andelle 12 De 49.19N 1.14 E
Andenes 7 Db 69.19N 16.08 E
Andenne 12 Hd 50.29N 5.06 E
Andenne-Namêche 12 Hd 50.28N 5.00 E
Andéranboukane 34 Fb 15.26N 3.02 E
Anderlecht 12 Gd 50.50N 4.18 E
Anderlues 12 Gd 50.24N 4.16 E
Andermatt 14 Cd 46.38N 8.37 E
Andernach 10 Df 50.26N 7.24 E
Andernos-les-Bains 11 Ej 44.44N 1.06W
Anderson 42 Ec 69.42N 129.01W
Anderson [Ca.-U.S.] 46 Df 40.27N 122.18W
Anderson [In.-U.S.] 43 Jc 40.10N 85.41W
Anderson [S.C.-U.S.] 43 Ke 34.30N 82.39W
Anderstorp 8 Eg 57.17N 13.38 E
Andes (EN) = Andes,
Cordillera de los- 52 Jh 20.00S 67.00W
Andes, Cordillera de los- =
Andes (EN) 52 Jh 20.00S 67.00W
Andevoranto 37 Hc 18.48S 49.02 E
Andfjorden 7 Db 69.10N 16.20 E
Andhra Pradesh 25 Fe 16.00N 79.00 E
Andia, Sierra de- 13 Kb 42.45N 2.00W
Andikhásia Ōri 15 Ej 39.47N 21.55 E
Andikira 15 Fk 38.23N 22.38 E
Andikithira = Andikithira
(EN) 15 Gn 35.52N 23.18 E
Andikithira (EN) =
Andikithira 15 Gn 35.52N 23.18 E
Andikithiron, Stenón- 15 Gn 35.45N 23.25 E
Andilamena 37 Hc 17.01S 48.35 E
Andilanatoby 37 Hc 17.56S 48.14 E
Andimeshk 24 Mf 32.27N 48.21 E
Andimilos 15 Hm 36.47N 24.14 E
Andiparos 15 Il 37.00N 25.03 E
Andipaxoi 15 Dj 39.08N 20.14 E
Andipsara 15 Ik 38.33N 25.24 E
Andir He 27 Dd 38.00N 83.36 E
Andiria Burun 24 Fe 35.42N 34.35 E
Andirin 24 Gd 37.34N 36.20 E
Andirlangar 27 Dd 37.36N 83.50 E
Andirrion 15 Ek 38.20N 21.46 E
Andítilos 15 Km 36.22N 27.28 E
Andižan 22 Je 40.45N 72.22 E
Andižanskaja Oblast 19 Hg 40.45N 72.20 E
Andkhvoy 23 Kb 36.56N 65.08 E
Andŏng 27 Md 36.36N 128.44 E
Andorra (Valls d'Andorra)
6 Gg 42.30N 1.30 E
Andorra la Vella 6 Gg 42.31N 1.31 E
Andover 9 Lj 51.13N 1.28W
Andøya 7 Db 69.08N 15.50 E
Andradas 55 If 22.05S 46.35W
Andradina 56 Jb 20.54S 51.23W
Andraitx 13 Oe 39.35N 2.25 E
Andreanof Islands 38 Bd 52.00N 176.00W
Andreapol 7 Hh 56.39N 32.16 E
Andrées Land 41 Jd 73.20N 26.30W
Andrejevka [Kaz.-U.S.S.R.] 19 If 45.47N 80.35 E
Andrejevka [Ukr.-U.S.S.R.] 16 Je 49.32N 36.40 E
Andrejevo-Ivanovka 15 Nb 47.31N 30.21 E
Andrejevsk 20 Ge 58.10N 114.15 E
Andrelândia 55 Je 21.44S 44.18W
Andresito 55 Dk 33.08S 57.09W
Andrespol 10 Pe 51.43N 19.40 E
Andrews 45 Ej 32.19N 102.33W
Andria 14 Ki 41.13N 16.17 E
Andriamena 37 Hc 17.28S 47.29 E
Andriba 37 Hc 17.36S 46.53 E
Andrijevica 15 Cg 42.44N 19.48 E
Andringitra 30 Lk 22.20S 46.55 E
Andritsaina 15 El 37.29N 21.54 E
Androka 37 Gd 24.59S 44.04 E
Androna, Plateau de l'- 37 Hc 15.30S 48.20 E
Ándros 5 Ih 37.50N 24.50 E
Andros 38 Lg 24.25N 78.00W
Ándros 15 Hl 37.50N 24.56 E
Androscoggin River 44 Md 43.55N 69.55W
Androssan 9 If 55.40N 4.55W
Andros Town 47 Id 24.43N 77.47W
Androth Island 25 Ef 10.50N 73.41 E
Androy 30 Lk 25.00S 45.40 E
Andruševka 16 Fd 49.59N 29.01 E
Andrychów 10 Pg 49.52N 19.21 E
Andselv 7 Eb 69.04N 18.30 E
Andudu 36 Eb 2.29N 28.41 E
Andújar 13 Hf 38.03N 4.04W
Andulo 36 Ce 11.28S 16.43 E
Andu Tan 26 Fe 7.35N 114.15 E
Anduze 11 Jj 44.03N 3.59 E
An Ea agail/Errigal 9 Ef 55.02N 8.07W
Aneby 8 Fg 57.50N 14.48 E
Anéfis 34 Fb 18.03N 0.36 E
Anegada 47 Le 18.45N 64.20W
Anegada, Bahia- 56 Hf 40.15S 62.15W
Anegada Passage 47 Le 18.30N 63.40W
Aného 34 Fd 6.14N 1.36 E
An Éirne/Erne 9 Eg 54.30N 8.15W
An Eithne/Inny 9 Fh 53.35N 7.50W
An Eoghanach/Annalee 9 Fg 54.02N 7.25W
Anet 12 Df 48.51N 1.26 E
Aneto, Pico de- 5 Gg 42.38N 0.40 E
Aney 34 Hb 19.24N 12.56 E
Aneytioum, Ile- 57 Hg 20.12S 169.49 E
An Feabhal 9 Ff 55.04N 7.15W
An Fhéil/Feale 9 Di 52.28N 9.40W
An Fheoir/Nore 9 Gi 52.25N 6.58W
Angamos, Punta- [Chile] 56 Fb 23.01S 70.32W
Angamos, Punta- [Pas.] 65d Bb 27.04S 109.17W
Angara 21 Ld 58.06N 93.00 E
Angarsk 22 Md 52.34N 103.54 E
Angarski, Pereval- 16 Ig 44.47N 34.25 E
Angarski Krjaž 20 Fe 57.30N 103.00 E
Angathonisi 15 Jl 37.28N 27.00 E
Angaur Island 57 Ed 6.54N 134.09 E
Ånge 7 De 62.31N 15.37 E
Änge 8 Fa 63.27N 14.03 E

An Gearran/
Garron Point 9 Hf 55.05N 5.58W
Ángel, Cerro- 48 Hf 22.49N 102.34W
Ángel, Salto-=Angel Falls
(EN) 52 Je 5.57N 62.30W
Angelburg 12 Kd 50.47N 8.25 E
Angel de la Guarda, Isla- 47 Bc 29.20N 113.25W
Angeles 26 Hc 15.09N 120.35 E
Ángeles, Sierra de los- 48 Jf 23.10N 99.20W
Angel Falls (EN)=Ángel,
Salto- 52 Je 5.57N 62.30W
Angel Falls (EN)=Churún
Merú 52 Je 5.57N 62.30W
Ängelholm 7 Ch 56.15N 12.51 E
Angélica 55 Bj 31.33S 61.33W
Angeln 10 Fb 54.40N 9.45 E
Ängelsberg 8 Ge 59.58N 16.02 E
Anger 35 Fd 9.40N 36.06 E
Angereb 35 Fc 13.44N 36.28 E
Ångermanälven 5 Hc 62.48N 17.56 E
Angermünde 10 Jc 53.02N 14.00 E
Angers 6 Ff 47.28N 0.33W
Angkor 25 Kf 13.26N 103.52 E
Angikuni Lake 42 Hd 62.10N 99.55W
Angistrion 15 Gl 37.40N 23.20 E
Anglem, Mount- 62 Bg 46.44S 167.54 E
Anglès 13 Oc 41.57N 2.39 E
Anglesey 5 Fe 53.18N 4.20W
Anglet 11 Ek 43.29N 1.32W
Angleton 45 Il 29.10N 95.26W
Anglin 11 Gh 46.42N 0.52 E
Anglona 14 Cj 40.45N 8.45 E
Angmagssalik 67 Mc 65.45N 37.30W
Ango 36 Eb 4.02N 25.52 E
Angoche 31 Kj 16.12S 39.54 E
Angoche, Ilha- 30 Kj 16.20S 39.51 E
Angol 56 Fe 37.48S 72.43W
Angola 31 Ij 12.30S 18.30 E
Angola 44 Ee 41.38N 85.00W
Angola Basin (EN) 3 Ek 15.00S 3.00 E
Angoram 60 Ch 4.04S 144.04 E
Angostura 48 Ee 25.22N 108.11W
Angostura, Presa de la- 48 Mi 16.30N 92.30W
Angostura, Salto- 54 Dc 2.43N 70.57W
Angostura Reservoir 45 Ee 43.18N 103.27W
Angoulême 11 Gi 45.39N 0.09 E
Angoumois 11 Fi 45.30N 0.10W
Angra do Heroismo 32 Bb 38.42N 27.15W
Angra do Heróismo 31 Ee 38.39N 27.13W
Angra dos Reis 55 Jf 23.00S 44.18W
Angren 19 Hg 41.03N 70.10 E
Angu 36 Db 3.33N 24.28 E
Anguang 28 Gb 45.36N 123.48 E
Anguilla 39 Mh 18.15N 63.05W
Anguilla 38 Mh 18.15N 63.05W
Anguilla, Canal de l'- =
Anguilla Channel (EN) 51b Ab 18.09N 63.04W
Anguilla Bank (EN) 51b Ab 18.30N 63.03W
Anguilla Cays 49 Hb 23.31N 78.33W
Anguilla Channel (EN)=
Anguilla, Canal de l'- 51b Ab 18.09N 63.04W
Anguli Nur 28 Cd 41.23N 114.30 E
Anguo 28 Ce 38.25N 115.20 E
Anhanca 36 Cf 16.47S 15.33 E
Anhanguera 55 Hd 18.21S 48.17W
An Hoa 25 Le 15.46N 108.03 E
Anholt 7 Ch 56.40N 11.35 E
Anhua (Dongping) 27 Jf 28.27N 111.15 E
Anhui Sheng (An-hui
Sheng)=Anhwei (EN) 27 Ke 32.00N 117.00 E
An-hui Sheng→Anhui
Sheng=Anhwei (EN) 27 Ke 32.00N 117.00 E
Anhwei (EN)=Anhui Sheng
(An-hui Sheng) 27 Ke 32.00N 117.00 E
Anhwei (EN)=An-hui
Sheng→Anhui Sheng 27 Ke 32.00N 117.00 E
Ani 29 Gb 39.59N 140.25 E
Aniak 40 Hd 61.34N 159.30W
An Iarmhí/Westmeath 9 Fh 53.30N 7.30W
Anibare 64e Bb 0.32S 166.57 E
Anibare Bay 64e Bb 0.32S 166.57 E
Aniche 12 Fd 50.20N 3.15 E
Ánidros 15 Im 36.37N 25.41 E
Anié 34 Fd 7.45N 1.12 E
Anie, Pic d'- 11 Fl 42.57N 0.43W
Aniene 14 Gi 41.56N 12.30 E
Anjiangying → Luanping 28 Dd 40.55N 117.19 E
Anikščiaj/Anykščiai 7 Fi 55.31N 25.08 E
Animas Peak 45 Bk 31.35N 108.47W
Anina 15 Ed 45.05N 21.51 E
Anita Garibaldi 55 Gh 27.37S 51.05W
Anittepe 15 Kh 41.21N 27.42 E
Aniva 20 Jg 46.41N 142.35 E
Aniva, Zaliv- 20 Jg 46.20N 142.40 E
Anivorano Nord 37 Hb 12.43S 49.12 E
Aniwa, Ile- 57 Hf 19.16S 169.35 E
Anizy-le-Château 12 Fe 49.30N 3.27 E
Anjala 7 Gf 60.41N 26.50 E
Anji 28 Ei 30.39N 119.41 E
Anjiang → Qianyang 27 Jf 27.19N 110.13 E
Anjō 29 Ed 34.57N 137.05 E
Anjou 11 Fg 47.20N 0.30W
Anjou, Ostrova-=Anjou
Islands (EN) 21 Qb 75.30N 143.00 E
Anjouan/Nzwali 30 Lj 12.15S 44.25 E
Anjou Islands (EN)=Anjou,
Ostrova- 21 Qb 75.30N 143.00 E
Anjozorobe 37 Hc 18.24S 47.52 E
Anju 27 Md 39.37N 125.40 E
Anjuj 20 Ig 49.20N 136.20 E
Anjujski Hrebet 20 Lc 67.20N 166.00 E
Anjou, Val d'- 11 Fg 47.25N 0.15W
Anka 34 Gc 12.07N 5.55 E
Ankang (Xing'an) 22 Mf 32.37N 109.03 E
Ankara 22 Ff 39.56N 32.52 E
Ankaratra 30 Lj 19.25S 47.12 E
Ankarsrum 7 Dh 57.42N 16.19 E

Ankavandra 37 Hc 18.45S 45.18 E
Ankazoabo 37 Gd 22.16S 44.30 E
Ankazobe 37 Hc 18.17S 47.05 E
Ankeny 45 Jf 41.44N 93.36W
'Ankhor 35 Hc 10.47N 46.18 E
Anklam 10 Jc 53.52N 13.42 E
Ankober 35 Fd 9.40N 39.44 E
Ankoro 36 Ed 6.45S 26.57 E
Ankum 12 Jb 52.33N 7.53 E
An Laoi/Lee 9 Ej 51.55N 8.30W
Anlong 27 If 25.02N 105.30 E
An Longfort/Longford 9 Fh 53.40N 7.40W
An Longfort/Longfort 9 Fh 53.44N 7.47W
An Lorgain/Lurgan 9 Gg 54.28N 6.20W
Anlu 27 Je 31.12N 113.46 E
An Mhi/Meath 9 Gh 53.35N 6.40W
An Mhuaidh/Moy 9 Dg 54.12N 9.08W
An Mhuir Cheilteach=Celtic
Sea (EN) 5 Fe 51.00N 7.00W
An Muileann gCearr/
Mullingar 9 Fh 53.32N 7.20W
An Muirthead/Mullet
Peninsula 9 Cg 54.15N 10.04W
Ånn 7 Ce 63.15N 12.35 E
Ånn 8 Ea 63.19N 12.33 E
Ann, Cape- [Ant.] 66 Ee 66.10S 51.22 E
Ann, Cape- [Ma.-U.S.] 44 Ld 42.39N 70.38W
Anna [Il.-U.S.] 45 Lh 37.28N 89.15W
Anna [Nauru] 64e Ba 0.29S 166.56 E
Anna [R.S.F.S.R.] 19 Ee 51.29N 40.26 E
Annaba 31 He 36.54N 7.46 E
Annaba 32 Ib 35.35N 8.00 E
An Nabatiyah at Taḩtā 24 Gf 33.23N 35.29 E
Annaberg-Buchholz 10 If 50.34N 13.00 E
An Nabī Şāliḩ 24 Eh 28.38N 33.59 E
An Nabk 23 Ec 34.01N 36.44 E
An Nabk Abū Qaşr 24 Hg 30.21N 38.34 E
An Nafiḑah 14 En 36.08N 10.23 E
An Nafūd 21 Gg 28.30N 41.00 E
An Najaf 22 Gf 31.59N 44.20 E
An Najaf 24 Kg 31.20N 44.07 E
An Nakhl 33 Fd 29.55N 33.45 E
Annalee/An Eoghanach 9 Fg 54.02N 7.25W
Annam (EN)=Trung
Phan 21 Me 15.00N 108.00 E
Annamitique, Chaîne- 25 Le 17.00N 106.00 E
Annan 9 Jg 54.59N 3.16W
Annan 9 Jg 55.00N 3.16W
Anna Paulowna 12 Gb 52.52N 4.52 E
Anna Paulowna-Kleine
Sluis 12 Gb 52.52N 4.52 E
Anna Point 64e Ba 0.29S 166.56 E
Annapolis 39 Lf 38.59N 76.30W
Annapolis Royal 44 Oc 44.45N 65.31W
Annapurna 21 Kg 28.34N 83.50 E
Ann Arbor 43 Kc 42.18N 83.45W
Anna Regina 50 Gi 7.16N 58.30W
An Nás/Naas 9 Gh 53.13N 6.39W
An Nashshāsh 24 Pk 23.05N 54.02 E
An Nashwah 24 Lg 30.49N 47.36 E
An Nāşirīyah 23 Gc 31.02N 46.16 E
An Nasser 24 Ej 24.36N 32.58 E
An Nawfalīyah 33 Cc 30.47N 17.50 E
Annecy 11 Mi 45.54N 6.07 E
Annecy, Lac d'- 11 Mi 45.51N 6.11 E
Annemasse 11 Mh 46.12N 6.15 E
Annevoie-Rouillon 12 Gd 50.21N 4.50 E
An Nil 35 Ea 20.10N 33.00 E
An Nil al Azraq 35 Ed 12.20N 34.15 E
Anning 27 Hg 24.58N 102.29 E
Anniston 43 Je 33.40N 85.50W
Annobón 30 Hi 1.32S 5.38 E
Annonay 11 Ki 45.14N 4.40 E
Annotto Bay 49 Id 18.16N 76.46W
An Nu'ayriyah 24 Mi 27.28N 48.27 E
An Nuhūd 31 Jg 12.42N 28.26 E
An Nu' Mān 24 Fi 27.06N 35.46 E
An Nu'mānīyah 24 Kf 32.32N 45.25 E
Annweiler am Trifels 12 Je 49.12N 7.58 E
Anoia/Noya 13 Nc 41.28N 1.56 E
Anoka 45 Jd 45.11N 93.23W
An Ómaigh/Omagh 9 Fg 54.36N 7.18W
Anori 54 Fd 3.47S 61.38W
Anosyennes, Chaînes- 37 Hd 24.20S 47.00 E
Ānou Makarene 34 Gb 18.07N 7.35 E
Áno Viánnos 15 In 35.03N 25.25 E
Anóyia 15 Hn 35.15N 24.54 E
Anping [China] 28 Ce 38.13N 115.32 E
Anping [China] 28 Gd 41.10N 123.25 E
An Pointe/Warrenpoint 9 Gg 54.06N 6.15W
Anpu 27 Ig 21.30N 110.00 E
Anpu Gang 27 Ig 21.25N 109.40 E
Anqing 22 Nf 30.32N 116.59 E
Anqiu 28 Ef 36.25N 119.12 E
An Ráth/Ráth Luirc 9 Ei 52.21N 8.41W
An Ribhéar/Kenmare
River 9 Dj 51.50N 9.50W
Anröchte 12 Kc 51.34N 8.20 E
Ans 12 Hd 50.39N 5.32 E
Anşāb 23 Fd 29.11N 44.43 E
Ansauvillers 12 Ee 49.34N 2.24 E
Ansbach 10 Gg 49.18N 10.35 E
An Sciobairín/Skibbereen 9 Dj 51.33N 9.15W
An Seancheann/Kinsale, Old
Head of- 9 Ej 51.36N 8.32W
Anse-à-Veau 49 Kd 18.30N 73.19W
Anse-Bertrand 51e Ab 16.29N 61.31W
Anse-d'Hainault 49 Jd 18.30N 74.27W
Anse la Raye 51k Ab 13.57N 61.03W
Anshan 22 Oe 41.08N 122.59 E
Anshun 22 Mg 26.15N 105.58 E
Ansina 56 Id 31.54S 55.28W
Ansley 45 Gf 41.18N 99.23W
Anson Bay 59 Gb 13.20S 130.05 E
Ansongo 34 Fb 15.40N 0.31 E
An Srath Bán/Strabane 9 Fg 54.49N 7.27W
Anta 54 Df 13.29S 72.09W

dex Symbols

Independent Nation
State, Region
District, County
Municipality
Colony, Dependency
Continent
Physical Region
Historical or Cultural Region
Mount, Mountain
Volcano
Hill
Mountains, Mountain Range
Hills, Escarpment
Plateau, Upland
Pass, Gap
Plain, Lowland
Delta
Salt Flat
Valley, Canyon
Crater, Cave
Karst Features
Depression
Polder
Desert, Dunes
Forest, Woods
Heath, Steppe
Oasis
Cape, Point
Coast, Beach
Cliff
Peninsula
Isthmus
Sandbank
Island
Atoll
Rock, Reef
Islands, Archipelago
Rocks, Reefs
Coral Reef
Well, Spring
Geyser
River, Stream
Waterfall Rapids
River Mouth, Estuary
Lake
Salt Lake
Intermittent Lake
Reservoir
Swamp, Pond
Canal
Glacier
Ice Shelf, Pack Ice
Ocean
Sea
Gulf, Bay
Strait, Fjord
Lagoon
Bank
Seamount
Tablemount
Ridge
Shelf
Basin
Escarpment, Sea Scarp
Fracture
Trench, Abyss
National Park, Reserve
Point of Interest
Recreation Site
Cave, Cavern
Historic Site
Ruins
Wall, Walls
Church, Abbey
Temple
Scientific Station
Airport
Port
Lighthouse
Mine
Tunnel
Dam, Bridge

Antabamba	54	Df	14.19S	72.55W
Antakya=Antioch (EN)	23	Eb	36.14N	36.07 E
Antalaha	31	Mj	14.55S	50.15 E
Antalya	22	Ff	36.53N	30.42 E
Antalya, Gulf of- (EN)= Antalya Körfezi [C]				
Antalya Körfezi=Antalya, Gulf of- (EN) [C]	23	Db	36.30N	31.00 E
An Tan	25	Le	15.26N	108.39 E
Antananarivo	31	Lj	18.55S	47.30 E
Antananarivo [3]	37	Hc	19.00S	46.40 E
Antanimora	37	Hd	24.48S	45.39 E
An tAonach/Nenagh	9	Ei	52.52N	8.12W
Antarctica (EN)	66	Bg	90.00S	0.00
Antarctic Peninsula (EN)	66	Qe	69.30S	65.00W
Antas, Cachoeira das-	55	Ha	13.06S	48.09W
Antas, Rio das-	55	Gi	29.04S	51.21W
An Teampall Mór/ Templemore	9	Fi	52.48N	7.50W
Antela, Laguna de-	13	Eb	42.07N	7.41W
Antelao	14	Gd	46.27N	12.16 E
Antelope Creek	46	Me	43.29N	105.23W
Anten	8	Ef	58.03N	12.30 E
Antequera [Par.]	55	Dg	24.08S	57.07W
Antequera [Sp.]	13	Hg	37.01N	4.33W
Anthony	45	Cj	32.00N	106.34W
Anti-Atlas	30	Ge	30.00N	8.30W
Antibes	11	Nk	43.55N	7.07 E
Antibes, Cap d'-	11	Nk	43.32N	7.07 E
Antica, Isla-	50	Eg	10.24N	62.43W
Anticosti, Ile d'-	38	Me	49.30N	63.00W
Antigo	45	Ld	45.09N	89.09W
Antigonish	42	Lg	45.37N	61.58W
Antigua	38	Mh	17.03N	61.48W
Antigua [1]	39	Mh	17.03N	61.48W
Antigua Guatemala	47	Ff	14.34N	90.44W
Antiguo Cauce del Río Bermejo	56	Hc	25.39S	60.11W
Antiguo Morelos	48	Jf	22.30N	99.05W
Antilla	49	Jc	20.50N	75.45W
Antillas, Mar de las-/Caribe, Mar-=Caribbean Sea (EN)	38	Lh	15.00N	73.00W
Antillas Mayores=Greater Antilles (EN) [C]	38	Lh	20.00N	74.00W
Antillas Menores=Lesser Antilles (EN) [C]	38	Mh	15.00N	61.00W
Antillas, Mer des-/Caraïbe, Mer-=Caribbean Sea (EN)	38	Lh	15.00N	73.00W
An tInbhear Mór/Arklow	9	Gi	52.48N	6.09W
Antioch	46	Eg	38.00N	121.49W
Antioch (EN)=Antakya	23	Eb	36.14N	36.07 E
Antioche, Pertuis d'-	11	Eh	46.05N	1.20W
Antiope Reef	57	Kf	18.18S	168.40W
Antioquia [2]	54	Cb	7.00N	75.30W
Antipajëta	20	Cc	69.09N	77.00 E
Antipodes Islands [C]	57	Ii	49.40S	178.50 E
Antiques, Pointe d'-	51e	Ab	16.26N	61.33W
An t-Iúr/Newry	9	Gg	54.11N	6.20W
Antler River	45	Fb	49.08N	101.00W
Antlers	45	Ii	34.14N	95.37W
Antofagasta [2]	56	Gb	23.30S	69.00W
Antofagasta	56	Gb	23.39S	70.24W
Antofagasta de la Sierra	56	Gc	26.04S	67.25W
Antofalla, Salar de-	56	Gc	25.44S	67.45W
Antofalla, Volcán-	56	Gc	25.34S	67.55W
Antoing	12	Fd	50.34N	3.27 E
Antón	49	Gi	8.24N	80.16W
Anton Dohrn Seamount (EN) [C]	9	Cd	57.30N	11.00W
Antongil, Baie d'- [C]	30	Lj	15.45S	49.50 E
Antonina	56	Kc	25.27S	48.43W
Antônio João	55	Ef	23.15S	55.31W
Antonito	45	Dh	37.05N	106.00W
Antony	12	Ef	48.45N	2.18 E
Antopol	10	Ud	52.12N	24.53 E
Antracit	16	Ke	48.06N	39.06 E
Antreff	12	Ld	50.52N	9.15 E
Antrim/Aontroim	9	Gg	54.43N	6.13W
Antrim Mountains	9	Gf	55.00N	6.10W
Antrodoco	14	Hh	42.25N	13.05 E
Antsakabary	37	Hc	15.03S	48.56 E
Antsalova	37	Ge	18.42S	44.33 E
Antseranana [3]	37	Hb	13.40S	49.15 E
Antseranana	31	Lj	12.17S	49.17 E
An tSionainn/Shannon	5	Fe	52.36N	9.41W
Antsirabe	31	Lj	19.51S	47.01 E
An tSiúir/Suir	9	Gi	52.15N	7.00W
Antsla	7	Gh	57.52N	26.33 E
An tSláine/Slaney	9	Gi	52.21N	6.30W
Antsohihy	31	Lj	14.52S	47.58 E
An tSuca/Suck	9	Fh	53.16N	8.03W
Anttola	8	Lc	61.35N	27.39 E
Antu (Songjiang)	28	Jc	42.33N	128.20 E
An Tuc	25	Lf	13.57N	108.39 E
Antufash, Jazirat-	33	Hf	15.42N	42.25 E
An Tulach/Tullow	9	Gi	52.48N	6.44W
An Tulach Mhór/Tullamore	9	Fh	53.16N	7.30W
Antwerp (EN)=Antwerpen/ Anvers	6	Ge	50.38N	5.34 E
Antwerp (EN)=Anvers-/ Antwerpen	6	Ge	50.38N	5.34 E
Antwerpen [3]	12	Gc	51.10N	4.30 E
Antwerpen/Anvers= Antwerp (EN)	6	Ge	50.38N	5.34 E
Antwerpen-Ekeren	11	Kc	51.17N	4.25 E
Antwerpen-Hoboken	12	Gc	51.10N	4.21 E
Antwerpen-Merksem	12	Gc	51.10N	4.21 E
Antykan	20	If	54.55N	135.13 E
An Uaimh/Navan	9	Gh	53.39N	6.41W
Anuradhapura	25	Gg	8.21N	80.23 E
Anuta Island	57	Hf	11.38S	169.50 E
Anvers/Antwerpen= Antwerp (EN)	6	Ge	50.38N	5.34 E
Anvers Island	66	Qe	64.33S	63.35W

Anvik	40	Gd	62.40N	160.12W
Anxi	22	Le	40.30N	96.00 E
Anxiang	27	Jf	29.26N	112.11 E
Anxin	28	Ce	38.55N	115.56 E
Anxious Bay [C]	59	Gf	33.25S	134.35 E
Anyang (Zhangde)	22	Nf	36.01N	114.25 E
A'nyêmaqen Shan	21	Lf	34.30N	100.00 E
Anyi	28	Cj	28.50N	115.31 E
Anykščiai/Anikščaj	7	Fi	55.31N	25.08 E
Anyva, Mys-	20	Jg	46.00N	143.25 E
Anza	14	Ce	46.00N	8.17 E
Anze	28	Bf	36.09N	112.14 E
Anzegem	12	Fd	50.50N	3.28 E
Anžero-Sudžensk	22	Kd	56.07N	86.00 E
Anzi	36	Dc	0.52S	23.24 E
Anzio	14	Gi	41.27N	12.37 E
Anzoátegui [2]	54	Fb	9.00N	64.30W
Anzob, Pereval-	18	Ge	39.07N	68.53 E
Aoba, Ile-	61	Cc	15.25S	167.50 E
Ao Ban Don [C]	25	Jg	9.20N	99.25 E
Aoga-Shima	27	Oe	32.30N	139.50 E
Aohan Qi (Xinhui)	28	Ec	42.18N	119.53 E
Aoiz	13	Kb	42.47N	1.22W
Aoji	28	Kc	42.31N	130.24 E
Aola	63a	Ec	9.32S	160.29 E
Aomen/Macau=Macao (EN) [5]	25	Ng	22.10N	113.33 E
Aomen/Macau=Macao (EN)	27	Jg	22.12N	113.33 E
Aomori	22	Qe	40.49N	140.45 E
Aomori Ken [2]	28	Pd	40.40N	140.40 E
Aono-Yama	29	Bd	34.27N	131.48 E
Aontroim/Antrim	9	Gg	54.43N	6.13W
Aoral, Phnum-	25	Kf	12.02N	104.10 E
Aoré [C]	63b	Cb	15.35S	167.10 E
Aosta / Aoste	14	Be	45.44N	7.20 E
Aosta, Val d'- [C]	14	Be	45.45N	7.20 E
Aoste / Aosta	14	Be	45.44N	7.20 E
Aouk, Bahr-	30	Ih	8.51N	18.53 E
Aoukalé	35	Cd	9.10N	20.30 E
Aoukâr [Afr.]	32	Ge	24.00N	2.30W
Aoukâr [Mtna.]	30	Gg	17.30N	9.30W
Aoulef	32	Hd	26.58N	1.05 E
Aoumou	63b	Be	21.24S	165.49 E
Aourou	34	Cc	14.28N	11.34W
Aoya	29	Cc	35.32N	133.59 E
Aozou	31	If	21.49N	17.25 E
Apa, Rio-	56	Ib	22.06S	58.00W
Apača	20	Kf	52.50N	157.10 E
Apache	46	Kk	31.44N	109.07W
Apache Junction	46	Jj	33.26N	111.32W
Apahida	15	Gc	46.49N	23.45 E
Apakho	63c	Ec	11.25S	166.32 E
Apalachee Bay [C]	38	Kg	29.30N	84.00W
Apalachicola	44	Ek	29.44N	84.59W
Apalachicola River	44	Ek	29.44N	84.59W
Apan	48	Jh	19.43N	98.25W
Apaporis, Rio-	52	Jf	1.23S	69.25W
Aparecida do Taboado	55	Fe	20.05S	51.05W
Apataki Atoll [C]	57	Mf	15.26S	146.20W
Apatin	15	Bd	45.40N	18.59 E
Apatity	6	Jb	67.34N	33.18 E
Apatzingán de la Constitución	47	De	19.05N	102.21W
Apaxtla de Castrejón	48	Jh	18.09N	99.52W
Ape	7	Gh	57.32N	26.42 E
Apeldoorn	11	Lb	52.13N	5.58 E
Apeldoorn-Nieuw Milligen	12	Hb	52.14N	5.45 E
Apen	12	Ja	53.13N	7.48 E
Apennines (EN)= Appennini	5	Hg	43.00N	13.00 E
Apere, Rio-	54	Ef	13.44S	65.18W
Aphrodisias	24	Cd	37.45N	28.40 E
Api	24	Kf	30.00N	80.57 E
Api	36	Bb	3.40N	25.26 E
Apia	58	Jf	13.50S	171.44W
Apiacás, Serra dos-	54	Gf	10.15S	57.15W
Apio	63a	Ec	9.39S	161.23 E
Apipé Grande, Isla-	55	Di	27.30S	56.54W
Apizaco	48	Jh	19.25N	98.09W
Aplao	54	Be	16.05S	72.31W
Apo, Mount-	21	Oi	6.59N	125.16 E
Apodi	54	Ke	5.39S	37.48W
Apolda	10	He	51.01N	11.30 E
Apolima Strait	65c	Aa	13.49S	172.07W
Apollo Bay	59	Ig	38.45S	143.40 E
Apollonia [Alb.]	15	Ci	40.43N	19.27 E
Apollonia [Lib.]	33	Dc	32.54N	21.58 E
Apolo	54	Ef	14.43S	68.31W
Apón, Rio-	49	Kh	10.06N	72.23W
Apopka, Lake-	44	Gk	28.37N	81.38W
Aporé	55	Fd	18.58S	51.01W
Aporé, Rio-	52	Kg	19.27S	50.57W
Apostle Islands [C]	43	Ib	46.50N	90.30W
Apóstoles	56	Ic	27.55S	55.46W
Apostolovo	16	Hf	47.39N	33.43 E
Apoteri	54	Ka	4.02N	58.34W
Apôtres, Iles des- [C]	30	Mm	45.50S	50.20 E
Appalachia	44	Fg	36.54N	82.48W
Appalachian Mountains	38	Lc	41.00N	77.00W
Äppelbo	8	Ed	60.30N	14.00 E
Appennini=Apennines (EN)	5	Hg	43.00N	13.00 E
Appennino Abruzzese	14	Hh	42.00N	13.55 E
Appennino Calabro	14	Kl	39.00N	16.30 E
Appennino Campano	14	Ii	40.50N	15.00 E
Appennino Ligure	14	Cf	44.30N	9.00 E
Appennino Lucano	14	Jj	40.30N	16.00 E
Appennino Tosco- Emiliano	14	Fg	44.00N	11.30 E
Appennino Umbro- Marchigiano	14	Gg	43.20N	12.55 E
Appenzell	14	Dc	47.20N	9.25 E
Appenzell Ausser- Rhoden [2]	14	Dc	47.20N	9.20 E

Appenzell Inner-Rhoden [2]	14	Dc	47.15N	9.25 E
Appingedam	12	Ia	53.19N	6.52 E
Appleby	9	Kg	54.36N	2.29W
Appleton	43	Jc	44.16N	88.25W
Appomattox	44	Hg	37.21N	78.51W
Apra Harbor [C]	64c	Bb	13.27N	144.38 E
Apricena	14	Ji	41.47N	15.27 E
Aprilia	14	Gi	41.36N	12.39 E
Apšeronsk	19	Dg	44.27N	39.44 E
Apšeronski Poluostrov= Apsheron Peninsula (EN)	5	Lg	41.00N	50.50 E
Apsheron Peninsula (EN)= Apšeronski Poluostrov	5	Lg	41.00N	50.50 E
Apt	11	Lk	43.53N	5.24 E
Apucarana	56	Jb	23.33S	51.29W
Apucarana, Serra da-	55	Gf	23.50S	51.20W
Apuka	20	Ld	60.23N	169.45 E
Apulia (EN)= Puglia [2]	14	Ki	41.15N	16.15 E
Apurashokoru	64a	Ac	7.10N	134.18 E
Apure [2]	54	Fb	7.10N	68.50W
Apure, Rio-	52	Je	7.37N	66.25W
Apurimac	54	Df	14.00S	73.00W
Apurimac, Rio-	52	Je	12.17S	73.56W
Apurito	50	Bi	7.56N	68.27W
Aqaba (EN)=Al 'Aqabah	24	Dd	29.31N	35.00 E
Aqaba, Gulf of- (EN)= 'Aqabah, Khalij al-	30	Kf	29.00N	34.40 E
Aqā Bāba	24	Md	36.20N	49.46 E
'Aqabah, Khalij al-=Aqaba, Gulf of- (EN) [C]	30	Kf	29.00N	34.40 E
Āqcheh	23	Kb	36.56N	66.11 E
'Aqdā	24	Of	32.26N	53.37 E
'Aqiq	35	Fb	18.14N	38.12 E
'Aqiq	27	Fc	41.49N	90.38 E
Āqotāq	24	Lf	37.10N	47.05 E
Āq Qal'eh	24	Pd	37.01N	54.30 E
Aqqikkol Hu	27	Hd	37.00N	88.20 E
'Aqrah	24	Jd	36.45N	43.54 E
Aqrin, Jabal-	24	Mj	31.32N	38.18 E
Āq Sū	24	Ke	34.35N	44.31 E
Aquidabã, Rio-	55	De	20.58S	57.50W
Aquidabán, Rio-	55	Df	23.11S	57.32W
Aquidauana	56	Jb	20.28S	55.48W
Aquidauana, Rio-	54	Gg	19.44S	56.50W
Aquidauana, Serra de-	55	Ee	20.50S	55.30W
Aquiles Serdán	48	Gc	28.36N	105.53W
Aquin	49	Kd	18.16N	73.24W
Aquitaine, Bassin d'-= Aquitane Basin (EN)	5	Fg	44.00N	0.10W
Aquitane Basin (EN)= Aquitaine, Bassin d'-	5	Fg	44.00N	0.10W
Ara	13	Mb	42.25N	0.09 E
'Arab, Bahr al-	30	Jh	9.02N	29.28 E
'Arab, Khalij al-	33	Dc	30.55N	29.05 E
'Arab, Shatt al-	21	Gf	30.28N	47.59 E
'Arabah, Wādi-	24	Eh	29.07N	32.39 E
'Arabah, Wādi al-	24	Dg	30.58N	32.24 E
Arabatskaja Strelka, Kosa-	16	Ig	45.40N	35.05 E
'Arabestān	24	Mg	30.30N	50.00 E
Arabian Basin (EN)	3	Gh	11.30N	65.00 E
Arabian Desert (EN)= Sharqiyah, Aş Şahrā' ash-	30	Kf	28.00N	32.00 E
Arabian Peninsula (EN)	21	Gg	25.00N	45.00 E
Arabian Sea (EN)	21	Ih	15.00N	65.00 E
Araç	24	Eb	41.15N	33.21 E
Aracá, Rio-	54	Fd	0.25S	62.55W
Aracaju	53	Mg	10.55S	37.04W
Aracataca	49	Jh	10.35N	74.13W
Aracati	54	Kd	4.34S	37.46W
Araçatuba	53	Kh	21.12S	50.25W
Aracena, Sierra de-	13	Fg	37.53N	6.33W
Aracides, Cape-	63a	Ec	8.39S	161.01 E
Aracruz	55	Jd	19.49S	40.16W
Araçuai	55	Jg	16.52S	42.04W
Arad	6	If	46.11N	21.19 E
'Arad	24	Ee	31.15N	35.13 E
Arad [2]	15	Ec	46.11N	21.25 E
'Arādah	35	Lb	22.59N	53.26 E
Arafali	35	Fb	15.04N	39.45 E
Ara Fana	35	Gd	6.01N	41.11 E
Arafune-Yama	29	Fc	36.12N	138.38 E
Arafura, Laut-=Arafura Sea (EN)	57	De	9.00S	133.00 E
Arafura, Sea (EN)=Arafura, Laut-	57	De	9.00S	133.00 E
Aragac, Gora-	5	Kg	40.31N	44.10 E
Aragarças	53	Jg	15.55S	52.15W
Aragón	13	Kb	42.13N	1.44W
Aragón [2]	5	Fg	41.00N	1.00W
Aragón [2]	13	Lc	41.00N	1.00W
Aragona	14	Hm	37.24N	13.37 E
Aragua [2]	54	Ie	10.00N	67.10W
Araguacema	54	Ie	8.50S	49.34W
Aragua de Barcelona	50	Dh	9.28N	64.49W
Aragua de Maturin	49	Mh	9.58N	63.29W
Araguaia, Rio-	52	Lf	5.21S	48.41W
Araguaiana	54	Ie	16.49S	53.05W
Araguaina	54	Ie	7.12S	48.12W
Araguao, Boca-	50	Fb	9.29N	60.50W
Araguao, Caño-	50	Fb	9.29N	60.50W
Araguapiche, Punta-	50	Fb	9.29N	60.15W
Araguari	53	Kg	18.38S	48.11W
Araguari, Rio- [Braz.]	52	Le	1.15S	49.55W
Araguari, Rio- [Braz.]	55	Hd	18.21S	48.40W
Araguatins	54	Ie	5.38S	48.07W

'Arāguib [C]	32	Ff	18.50N	7.45W
Aragvi	16	Ni	41.50N	44.43 E
Arai	28	Of	37.09N	138.06 E
Arainn/ [C]	5	Hg	42.45N	10...
Inishmore	5	Ee	53.07N	9.45W
Arainn Mhór/Aran Island	9	Ef	55.00N	8.30W
Araioses	54	Jd	2.53S	41.55W
Arāk	22	Gf	34.05N	49.41 E
Arak	32	Hd	25.18N	3.45 E
Arakabesan	64a	Ac	7.21N	134.27 E
Arakan [2]	25	Ie	19.00N	94.15 E
Arakan Yoma	21	Lh	19.00N	94.40 E
Arakawa	29	Fb	38.09N	139.25 E
Ara-Kawa [Jap.]	29	Fb	38.09N	139.23 E
Ara-Kawa [Jap.]	29	Fc	37.11N	138.15 E
Arākhthos	15	Ej	39.01N	21.03 E
Aral [China]	22	Jd	60.25N	169.35 E
Aral [Kirg.-U.S.S.R.]	19	Hg	41.48N	74.25 E
Aral Sea (EN)=Aralskoje More	21	Hg	45.00N	60.00 E
Aralsk	22	Ie	46.48N	61.40 E
Aralskoje More=Aral Sea (EN)	21	Hg	45.00N	60.00 E
Arālsor, Ozero-	16	Pe	49.05N	48.15 E
Aralsulfat	19	Gf	46.50N	61.59 E
Aramac	59	Jd	22.59S	145.14 E
Arambaré	55	Gj	30.55S	51.29W
Aran	24	Ne	34.03N	51.30 E
Aranda de Duero	13	Ic	41.41N	3.41W
Arandelovac	15	De	44.18N	20.35 E
Arandilla	13	Ic	41.40N	3.41W
Aran Island/Arainn Mhór	9	Dh	53.07N	9.43W
Aran Islands	5	Ee	55.00N	8.30W
Aranjunez	13	Id	40.02N	3.36W
Aranos	37	Bd	24.09S	19.09 E
Arañuelo, Campo-	13	Ge	39.55N	5.30W
Aranuka Atoll [C]	57	Id	0.11N	173.36 E
Arao	29	Be	32.59N	130.27 E
Araouane	31	Gg	18.53N	3.35W
Arapahoe	45	Gf	40.18N	99.54W
Arapey Grande, Rio-	55	Dj	30.55S	57.49W
Arapiraca	54	Ke	9.45S	36.39W
Arápis, Ákra-	15	Gi	40.27N	24.00 E
Arapkir	24	Hc	39.03N	38.30 E
Arapoim, Rio-	55	Kb	15.45S	43.39W
Arapongas	56	Jb	23.23S	51.27W
Arapoti	56	Jb	24.08S	49.50W
'Ar'ar	24	Ig	30.59N	41.02 E
'Ar'ar, Wādi	24	Jg	31.23N	42.26 E
Araranguá	56	Kc	28.56S	49.29W
Araraquara	53	Lh	21.47S	48.10W
Araras	55	If	22.22S	47.23W
Araras, Açude-	54	Jd	4.20S	40.30W
Araras, Serra das-	55	Fd	18.45S	53.30W
Ararat [Arm.-U.S.S.R.]	19	Eh	39.50N	44.43 E
Ararat, Mount- (EN)=Büyük Ağrı Dağı	21	Gf	39.40N	44.24 E
Arari	24	Jg	31.28S	44.47W
Arari, Lago-	54	Id	0.37S	49.07W
Aras	21	Gf	39.56N	48.20 E
Aras Dağları	24	Jc	40.00N	43.00 E
Aratika Atoll [C]	57	Mf	15.32S	145.32W
Aratürük/Yiwu	22	Kc	43.15N	94.35 E
Arauca [2]	54	Db	6.30N	71.00W
Arauca	52	Je	7.03N	70.47W
Arauca, Rio-	52	Je	7.24N	66.35W
Araucania [2]	56	Ee	37.50S	73.15W
Arauco	56	Fe	37.15S	73.19W
Ar Dubal Khâfi [C]	21	Bh	21.00N	69.15W
Aravaca, Madrid-	13	Id	40.27N	3.47W
Aravis	11	Mi	45.53N	6.28 E
Arawalli Range	21	Jg	25.00N	73.30 E
Araxá	54	Lg	19.35S	46.55W
Áraxos, Ákra-	15	Ek	38.10N	21.23 E
Araya	50	Dh	10.34N	64.15W
Araya, Peninsula de-	50	Dh	10.34N	64.15W
Arba'in, Darb al-	24	Di	26.40N	30.50 E
Arbaj-Here	27	Hb	46.15N	102.48 E
Arba Minch	35	Kh	5.59N	37.38 E
'Arbat	24	Ke	35.25N	45.35 E
Arbatax	14	Dk	39.56N	9.42 E
Arboga	6	Dg	59.24N	15.50 E
Arbogaān	8	Ge	59.26N	16.04 E
Arbois	11	Lh	46.54N	5.46 E
Arboletes	49	Ii	8.52N	76.25W
Arbolito	54	Ee	32.39S	54.15W
Arbon	14	Dc	47.30N	9.25 E
Arbore	35	Jh	4.58N	36.21 E
Arborea	14	Ck	39.46N	8.35 E
Arboriea [C]	14	Ck	39.46N	8.35 E
Arborg	45	Ha	50.55N	97.15W
Arbra	7	Dc	61.29N	16.23 E
Arbroath	9	Ke	56.34N	2.35W
Arbus	14	Ck	39.32N	8.36 E
Arc [Fr.]	11	Mi	45.34N	6.12 E
Arc [Fr.]	13	Kb	43.31N	5.07 E
Arcachon	6	Fg	44.39N	1.10W
Arcachon, Bassin d'- [C]	11	Ej	44.42N	1.09W
Arcadia [Fl.-U.S.]	44	Gl	27.14N	81.52W
Arcadia [La.-U.S.]	45	Jj	32.33N	92.55W
Aragaly-Ajat	17	Jj	53.00N	61.50 E
Arcas, Cayos-	38	Jg	20.12N	91.58W
Arcata	46	Cf	40.52N	124.05W
Arcelia	48	Ih	18.17N	100.16W
Arcen, Areen en Velden-	12	Ic	51.28N	6.11 E
Arcevia	14	Gg	43.30N	12.56 E
Archangelsk	6	Kc	64.34N	40.32 E
Archaringa Creek	59	Hd	28.10S	134.50 E
Archer River	59	Ib	13.28S	141.41 E
Archer's Post	36	Gb	0.39N	37.41 E
Archidona	13	Hg	37.05N	4.23W
Arcidosso	14	Fh	42.52N	11.33 E

Arcipelago Campano [C]	5	Hg	40.30N	13.
Arcipelago Toscano= Tuscan Archipelago (EN)	5	Hg	42.45N	10.
Arcis-sur-Aube	11	Kf	48.32N	4.
Arciz	45	Gi	45.59N	29.
Arco [Id.-U.S.]	46	Ie	43.38N	113.
Arco [It.]	14	Ge	45.55N	10.
Arconce	11	Jh	46.27N	4.
Arcos	55	Je	20.17S	45.
Arcos de Jalón	13	Jc	41.13N	2.
Arcos de la Frontera	13	Gh	36.45N	5.
Arcos de Valdevez	13	Dc	41.51N	8.
Arcoverde	53	Mf	8.25S	37.
Arctic Bay	39	Kb	73.02N	85.
Arctic Ocean	67	Be	85.00N	170.
Arctic Ocean (EN)= Ishavet	67	Be	85.00N	170.
Arctic Ocean (EN)=Severny Ledovity Okean	67	Be	85.00N	170.
Arctic Red River	42	Ec	67.27N	133.
Arctic Red River	42	Ec	67.22N	133.
Arctic Village	40	Jc	68.08N	145.
Arda [Eur.]	15	Jh	41.39N	26.
Arda [It.]	14	Ee	45.02N	10.
Ardabil [Iran]	22	Gf	38.15N	48.
Ardabil [Iraq]	24	Ie	34.24N	40.
Ardahan	24	Jb	41.07N	42.
Ardakāh	23	Hc	32.19N	53.
Ardakān	24	Og	30.16N	52.
Ardal	24	Ng	31.59N	50.
Ardales	13	Hh	36.52N	4.
Ardalsfjorden	8	Bc	61.15N	7.
Ardalstangen	7	Bf	61.14N	7.
Ardanuç	24	Jb	41.08N	42.
Ardatov [R.S.F.S.R.]	7	Ki	55.17N	43.
Ardatov [R.S.F.S.R.]	7	Li	54.53N	46.
'Arde	35	Hd	9.58N	46.
Ardèche	11	Kj	44.16N	4.
Ardèche	11	Kj	44.40N	4.
Ardee/Béal Átha Fhirdhia	9	Gh	53.52N	6.
Ardencaple Fjord	41	Jd	75.15N	20.
Ardenne, Plateau de l'-/ Ardennes, Plateau van der- =Ardennes (EN)	5	Ge	50.10N	5.
Ardennes, Plateau van der-/ Ardenne, Plateau de l'-= Ardennes (EN)	5	Ge	50.10N	5.
Ardennes [3]	11	Ke	49.40N	4.
Ardennes (EN)=Ardenne, Plateau de l'-/Ardennes, Plateau van der-	5	Ge	50.10N	5.
Ardennes (EN)=Ardennes, Plateau van der-/Ardenne, Plateau de l'-	5	Ge	50.10N	5.
Ardennes, Canal des-	11	Ke	49.26N	4.
Ardennes, Forêt des-	12	Ge	49.48N	4.
Ardentes	11	Hh	46.45N	1.
Ardesen	24	Ib	41.12N	41.
Ardestän	24	Of	33.22N	52.
Ardhas	15	Jh	41.39N	26.
Ardila	13	Ef	38.12N	7.
Ard Mhacha/Armagh	9	Gg	54.21N	6.
Ardmore	43	He	34.10N	97.
Ardnamurchan, Point of-	9	Ge	56.45N	6.
Ardon	16	Nh	43.07N	44.
Ardooie	12	Fd	50.59N	3.
Ardre	12	Fe	49.18N	3.
Ardres	12	Dd	50.51N	1.
Ards Peninsula/An Aird	9	Hg	54.30N	5.
Ar Dubal Khâfi [C]	21	Mj	21.00N	55.
Ardud	15	Fb	47.38N	22.
Arebi	36	Eb	2.50N	29.
Arecibo	47	Le	18.28N	66.
Areen en Velden-Arcen	12	Ic	51.28N	6.
Arena, Cayo-	47	Fd	22.08N	91.
Arenas, Punta de-	56	Gh	53.09S	68.
Arenas de San Pedro	13	Gd	40.12N	5.
Arenberg	12	Jb	52.42N	7.
Arendal	7	Bg	58.27N	8.
Arendonk	12	Hc	51.19N	5.
Arenys de Mar/Arenys de Mar	13	Oc	41.35N	2.
Arenys de Mar/Arenys de Mar	13	Oc	41.35N	2.
Areópolis	15	Fm	36.40N	22.
Areq, Sebkha bou-	13	Ji	35.10N	2.
Arequipa	53	Ie	16.24S	71.
Arequipa [2]	54	Dg	16.00S	72.
Arequito	55	Di	33.09S	61.
Arero	35	Fe	4.44N	38.
Áreskutan	7	Cc	63.26N	13.
Areskutan	7	Cc	63.24N	13.
Arévalo	13	Hc	41.04N	4.
Arezzo	14	Fg	43.25N	11.
Arga	13	Kb	42.35N	1.
Argajas	7	Ji	55.31N	60.
Argamasilla de Alba	13	Ie	39.07N	3.
Argan	27	Ec	40.09N	88.
Argens	11	Mk	43.24N	6.

Index Symbols

[1] Independent Nation	Historical or Cultural Region	Pass, Gap	Depression
[2] State, Region	Mount, Mountain	Plain, Lowland	Polder
[3] District, County	Volcano	Delta	Desert, Dunes
[4] Municipality	Hill	Salt Flat	Forest, Woods
[5] Colony, Dependency	Mountains, Mountain Range	Valley, Canyon	Heath, Steppe
Continent	Hills, Escarpment	Crater, Cave	Oasis
Physical Region	Plateau, Upland	Karst Features	Cape, Point

Coast, Beach	Rock, Reef	Waterfall Rapids	Canal
Cliff	Rocks, Reefs	River Mouth, Estuary	Bank
Islands, Archipelago	Coral Reef	Lake	Seamount
Peninsula	Well, Spring	Salt Lake	Tablemount
Isthmus	Geyser	Intermittent Lake	Ridge
Sandbank	River, Stream	Reservoir	Shelf
Island		Swamp, Pond	Strait, Fjord
Atoll			Basin

Lagoon	Escarpment, Sea Scarp	Historic Site	Port
Glacier	Fracture	Ruins	Lighthouse
Ice Shelf, Pack Ice	Trench, Abyss	Wall, Walls	Mine
Ocean	National Park, Reserve	Church, Abbey	Tunnel
Sea	Point of Interest	Temple	Dam, Bridge
Gulf, Bay	Recreation Site	Scientific Station	
	Cave, Cavern	Airport	

nt, Côte d'- 11 Ej 44.00N 1.30W
nta 14 Ff 44.37N 11.50 E
ntan 11 Ff 48.45N 0.01W
ntario, Monte- 14 Fh 42.24N 11.09 E
ntat 11 Hi 45.06N 1.56 E
ntera 14 Bf 44.10N 7.18 E
nteuil 11 If 48.57N 2.15 E
ntiera,
o dell'- 14 Cj 40.44N 8.08 E
ntina 55 Ai 29.33S 62.17W
ntina 53 Ji 34.00S 64.00W
ntine Basin (EN) 3 Cn 45.00S 45.00W
ntino, Lago- 52 Ik 50.13S 72.25W
ntino, Mar- 52 Kj 46.00S 59.40W
nton 11 Fg 47.05N 0.13W
nton-Château 11 Fh 46.59N 0.27W
nton-sur-Creuse 11 Hh 46.35N 1.31 E
s 15 Jd 44.04N 26.37 E
s (2) 15 Hd 45.00N 24.50 E
andāb 23 Jc 31.27N 64.23 E
35 Eb 19.31N 30.25 E
Depth (EN) 3 Jk 12.10S 165.40W
ikós Kólpos = Argolis,
of- (EN) 15 Fl 37.20N 22.55 E
is, Gulf of- (EN) =
olikós Kólpos 15 Fl 37.20N 22.55 E
ne 12 He 49.30N 5.00 E
ne 11 Ke 49.30N 5.00 E
s 15 Fl 37.38N 22.44 E
s Orestikón 15 Ei 40.30N 21.16 E
stólion 15 Dk 38.11N 20.29 E
edas 13 Kb 42.10N 1.36W
eil-Fry 12 De 49.37N 1.31 E
ello, Point- 46 Ei 34.35N 120.39W
enon 11 Df 48.35N 2.13W
h 16 Nh 43.16N 45.52 E
n 21 Od 53.20N 121.28 E
ngu 34 Fc 12.45N 4.31 E
e 51n Ba 13.10N 61.10W
e, Lake- 57 Df 16.15S 128.40 E
l 9 Ie 56.20N 5.00W
ngelsk=Archangel
) 6 Kc 64.34N 40.32 E
ngelskaja Oblast (3) 19 Ec 63.30N 43.00 E
ra 20 Ig 49.30N 130.09 E
vi 24 Ib 41.22N 41.16 E
lma 8 He 59.50N 19.05 E
orqin Qi
nshan) 27 Lc 43.55N 120.05 E
s (2) 8 Dh 56.10N 10.15 E
s 6 Hd 56.09N 10.13 E
s Bugt 8 Dh 56.10N 10.20 E
st 27 Ib 47.42N 107.50 E
noje 20 Ig 45.08N 134.25 E
e-Kai 28 Kh 32.55N 130.27 E
nsvlei 37 Be 28.08S 19.50 E
o Irpino 14 Ji 41.09N 15.05 E
, Rio- 54 Dc 2.35N 72.47W
56 Hd 33.38S 62.25W
toll 25a Bb 3.30N 72.45 E
nda 34 Ec 14.14N 0.52W
53 Ig 18.29S 70.20W
, Golfo de- 52 Ig 18.30S 70.30W
una 50 Ci 7.42N 67.08W
Cape- 59 Ef 34.00S 123.09 E
28 Mg 34.05N 135.07 E
-Gawa 29 Dd 34.05N 135.06 E
aia 15 Fi 40.59N 22.04 E
ge 11 Hk 43.31N 1.25 E
ge (3) 11 Hk 43.00N 1.30 E
55 Cm 36.32S 59.54W
15 Gc 46.26N 23.59 E
uaní 54 Db 9.50N 74.01W
uani, Rio- 49 Ki 9.35N 73.46W
[Jor.] 24 Fg 31.52N 35.27 E
[Syr.] 24 Ge 35.48N 36.36 E
aree River 45 Ff 40.01N 101.56W
awa 29 Ae 32.59N 129.07 E
15 Df 43.45N 20.06 E
a 54 Fa 10.38N 61.17W
os 55 Ib 15.55S 46.04W
os, Rio- 52 Kg 10.25S 58.20W
os Novo, Rio- 55 Db 14.14S 56.01W
gala/Arėgala 8 Ji 55.13N 23.30 E
uanã 54 Fe 9.10S 60.38W
uanã, Rio- 52 Jf 5.07S 60.24W
uemes 54 Fe 9.56S 63.04W
35 Gc 11.11N 41.38 E
h, Wādī al- 24 Eg 31.09N 33.49 E
nendi 49 Mi 8.29N 68.22W
29 Ae 33.11N 129.52 E
o 14 Dk 39.57N 9.12 E
ang/Wenquan 27 Dc 44.59N 81.04 E
13 Jc 41.19N 2.03W
aro, Salar de- 56 Gb 24.42S 67.45W
, Massif de l'- 11 Hl 42.50N 1.30 E
ona (2) 43 Ee 34.00N 112.00W
pe 48 Db 30.20N 110.10W
ng 7 Cg 59.23N 12.08 E
plog 7 Dc 66.03N 17.54 E
35 Fd 8.45N 36.30 E
na 54 Ca 10.15N 75.21W
adak 19 Ee 51.58N 43.28 E
adelphia 43 Ie 34.07N 93.04W
alyk 22 Id 50.13N 66.50 E
ansas 38 Jf 33.48N 91.04W
ansas (2) 43 Id 34.50N 93.40W
ansas City 43 Hd 37.04N 97.02W
anū, Jabal- 33 De 22.15N 24.45 E
atag 21 Kf 36.45N 89.10 E
ángelos 15 Lm 36.12N 28.08 E
15 Jl 37.22N 26.45 E
ow/An tInbhear Mór 9 Gi 52.48N 6.09W
ona, Kap- 10 Jb 54.41N 13.26 E
onam 25 Ff 13.06N 79.40 E
ösund 8 Gf 58.30N 16.56 E
oúdhion 15 Dk 38.33N 20.43 E

Arktičeskoga Instituta,
Ostrova-=Arkticheski
Institut Islands (EN) 20 Da 75.20N 81.50 E
Arkticheski Institut Islands
(EN)=Arktičeskoga
Instituta, Ostrova- 20 Da 75.20N 81.50 E
Arlan, Gora- 16 Sj 39.43N 54.40 E
Arlanza 13 Hb 42.06N 4.09W
Arlanzón 13 Hb 42.03N 4.17W
Arlberg 14 Ec 47.08N 10.12 E
Arles 11 Kk 43.40N 4.38 E
Arlington [Or.-U.S.] 46 Ed 45.46N 120.13W
Arlington [Tx.-U.S.] 45 Hj 32.44N 97.07W
Arlington [Va.-U.S.] 44 Id 38.52N 77.05W
Arlington Heights 45 Me 42.05N 87.59W
Arlit 31 Hg 19.00N 7.38 E
Arlon/Aarlen 11 Le 49.41N 5.49 E
Arlöv 8 Ei 55.39N 13.05 E
Arly 34 Fc 11.35N 1.28 E
Armagh/Ard Mhacha 9 Gg 54.21N 6.39W
Armagnac 11 Gk 43.45N 0.10 E
Armagnac, Collines de l'- 11 Gk 43.30N 0.30 E
Armah, Wādī- 23 Hf 18.12N 51.02 E
Arman 20 Ke 59.43N 150.12 E
Armançon 11 Jg 47.57N 3.30 E
Armandale, Perth- 59 Df 32.09S 116.00 E
Armant 33 Fd 25.37N 32.32 E
Armáthia 15 Jn 35.26N 26.52 E
Armavir 6 Kf 45.00N 41.08 E
Armenia 53 Ie 4.31N 75.41W
Armenia (EN)=
Ermenistan 23 Fb 39.10N 43.00 E
Armenia (EN)=
Ermenistan 21 Gf 39.10N 43.00 E
Armenian SSR (EN)=
Armjanskaja SSR (2) 19 Eg 40.00N 45.00 E
Armentières 11 Id 50.41N 2.53 E
Armeria 48 Gh 18.56N 103.58W
Armi, Capo dell'- 14 Jm 37.57N 15.41 E
Armidale 58 Gh 30.31S 151.39 E
Armisvesi 8 Lb 62.30N 26.35 E
Armjansk 16 Hf 46.05N 33.41 E
Armjanskaja Sovetskaja
Socialističeskaja
Respublika (2) 19 Eg 40.00N 45.00 E
Armjanskaja SSR/Haikakan
Sovetakan Socialistakan
Respublika (2) 19 Eg 40.00N 45.00 E
Armjanskaja SSR=Armenian
SSR (EN) (2) 19 Eg 40.00N 45.00 E
Armoricain, Massif-=
Armorican Massif (EN) 5 Ff 48.00N 3.00W
Armorican Massif (EN)=
Armoricain, Massif- 5 Ff 48.00N 3.00W
Armour 45 Ge 43.19N 98.21W
Arm River 46 Ma 50.46N 105.00W
Armstrong [Arg.] 56 Hd 32.47S 61.36W
Armstrong [B.C.-Can.] 46 Fa 50.27N 119.12W
Armstrong [Ont.-Can.] 42 If 50.18N 89.02W
Ārmūdiū 24 Qd 37.15N 56.05 E
Armutçuk Dağ 15 Ki 40.05N 27.23 E
Armutlu 15 Li 40.31N 28.50 E
Armutova 15 Jj 39.23N 26.50 E
Arnaia 15 Gi 40.29N 23.36 E
Arnaud 42 Kd 60.00N 69.55W
Arnautis, Akrotérion- 24 Ee 35.06N 32.17 E
Arnay-le-Duc 11 Kg 47.08N 4.29 E
Arnedo 13 Jb 42.13N 2.06W
Årnes 7 Cf 60.09N 11.28 E
Arnhem 11 Lc 51.59N 5.55 E
Arnhem, Cape- 57 Ef 12.21S 136.21 E
Arnhem Bay 59 Hb 12.20S 136.10 E
Arnhem Land 57 Ef 13.10S 134.30 E
Arno 5 Hg 43.41N 10.17 E
Arno Atoll 57 Id 7.05N 171.41 E
Arnold 12 Aa 53.00N 1.08W
Arnon 11 Ig 47.13N 2.01 E
Arnøy 7 Ea 70.08N 20.36 E
Arnprior 44 Ic 45.26N 76.21W
Arnsberg 10 Ee 51.23N 8.05 E
Arnsberger Wald 12 Kc 51.26N 8.10 E
Arnsberg-Oeventrop 12 Kc 51.24N 8.08 E
Arnsburg 12 Kd 50.29N 8.48 E
Arnstadt 10 Gf 50.50N 10.57 E
Aro, Rio- 50 Di 8.01N 64.11W
Aroa 50 Bg 10.26N 68.54W
Aroa, Pointe- 65e Fc 17.28S 149.46W
Aroa, Rio- 50 Bg 10.41N 68.18W
Aroa, Sierra de- 50 Bg 10.15N 68.55W
Aroab 37 Be 26.47S 19.40 E
Aroánia Óri 15 Fl 37.57N 22.13 E
Aroche 13 Fg 37.57N 6.57W
Aroche, Pico de- 13 Ff 38.01N 6.56W
Aroeira 55 Ee 21.41S 54.25W
Arolsen 10 Ff 51.22N 9.01 E
Aroma 35 Fb 15.49N 36.08 E
Aron 11 Jh 46.50N 3.27 E
Arona 14 Ce 45.46N 8.34 E
Aroostook River 44 Nb 46.48N 67.45W
Arorae Island 57 Ie 2.38S 176.49 E
Arorangi 64p Bb 21.13S 159.49W
Aros, Rio- 48 Ec 29.30N 109.15W
Arosa 14 Dd 46.47N 9.40 E
Arosa, Ria de- 13 Db 42.28N 8.57W
Aros Papigochic, Rio- 48 Ec 29.09N 108.35W
Årøsund 8 Ci 55.15N 9.43 E
Arouca 13 Dd 40.56N 8.15W
Arpaçay 24 Jb 40.45N 43.25 E
Arpajon 11 If 48.35N 2.15 E
Arpino 14 Hi 41.39N 13.36 E
Arquata Scrivia 14 Cf 44.41N 8.53 E
Arque 54 Eg 17.48S 66.23W
Arques-la-Bataille 12 De 49.53N 1.08 E
Ar Rachidiya 32 Gc 31.55N 4.40W
Ar Rachidiya (3) 32 Gc 31.00N 4.00W
Ar Radīsiyah Baḥrī 33 Fe 24.57N 32.53 E
Arrah 25 Gc 25.34N 84.40 E

Ar Rahad 35 Ec 12.43N 30.39 E
Ar Rahad 30 Kg 14.28N 33.31 E
Arraias 54 If 12.56S 46.57W
Arraias, Rio- [Braz.] 54 Hf 11.10S 53.35W
Arraias, Rio- [Braz.] 55 Ia 12.28S 47.18W
Arraiolos 13 Ef 38.43N 7.59W
Ar Ramādī 23 Fc 33.25N 43.17 E
Ar Ramlah 24 Fh 29.32N 35.57 E
Ar Ramlī al Kabīr 33 Dd 26.30N 22.10 E
Arran, Island of- 9 Hf 55.35N 5.15W
Ar Rank 35 Ec 11.45N 32.48 E
Ar Raqqah 23 Eb 35.56N 39.01 E
Arras 11 Id 50.17N 2.47 E
Ar Rāshidah 24 Cj 25.35N 28.56 E
Ar Rass 24 Jj 25.52N 43.28 E
Ar Rastān 24 Ge 34.55N 36.44 E
Arrats 11 Gj 44.06N 0.52 E
Ar Rawḍah [Sau.Ar.] 33 He 21.16N 42.50 E
Ar Rawḍah [Alg.] 13 Ki 35.23N 1.05W
Ar Rawḍah [P.D.R.Y.] 33 Ig 14.28N 47.17 E
Ar Rawḍatayn 24 Lh 29.53N 47.44 E
Ar Rayḥānī 24 Pk 23.37N 55.58 E
Arrecife 32 Ed 28.57N 13.32W
Arrecife Alacrán 47 Gd 22.24N 89.42W
Arrecifes 56 Hd 34.03S 60.07W
Arrecifes, Rio- 55 Ck 33.46S 59.31W
Arrée, Montagnes d'-
11 Cf 48.26N 3.55W
Arresø 8 Ei 55.55N 12.05 E
Arriaga 48 Mi 16.14N 93.54W
Ar Rifā'ī 24 Lg 31.43N 46.07 E
Ar Rihāb 24 Kg 30.52N 45.30 E
Ar Rimāh 24 Lj 25.34N 47.09 E
Ar Rimāl 21 Hg 22.00N 52.50 E
Ar Riyāḍ=Riyadh (EN) 22 Gg 24.38N 46.43 E
Arrochar 9 Ie 56.12N 4.45W
Arroio Grande 55 Fk 32.14S 53.05W
Arrojado 55 Ja 13.29S 44.37W
Arrojado, Rio- 55 Ja 13.24S 44.20W
Arromanches-les-Bains 12 Be 49.20N 0.37W
Arros 11 Gk 43.40N 0.02 E
Arroscia 14 Cg 44.03N 8.11 E
Arroux 11 Jh 46.29N 3.58 E
Arrow, Lough-/Loch
Arabhach 9 Eg 54.05N 8.20W
Arrowsmith, Mount- 61 Dh 43.21S 170.59 E
Arrowtown 62 Cf 44.56S 168.50 E
Arroyo Barú 55 Cj 31.52S 58.26W
Arroyo de la Luz 13 Fe 39.29N 6.35W
Arroyo Grande 46 Ei 35.07N 120.34W
Arroyos y Esteros 55 Dg 25.04S 57.06W
Arruda 55 Db 15.02S 56.07W
Arrufó 56 Hd 30.15S 61.45W
Ar Rumaythah 24 Kg 31.32N 45.12 E
Ar Ruq'ī 24 Lh 29.01N 46.33 E
Ar Rusāfah 24 He 35.02N 36.17 E
Ar Ruṣayriṣ 31 Kg 11.51N 34.23 E
Ar Rutbah 23 Fc 33.02N 40.17 E
Ar Ruwaydah 24 Ki 26.23N 44.14 E
Ar Ruways [Qatar] 23 Hd 26.08N 51.13 E
Ar Ruways [U.A.E.] 23 He 24.08N 52.45 E
Ar Ruzayqāt 24 Ej 25.35N 32.28 E
Års 8 Ch 56.48N 9.32 E
Arsenjān 24 Oh 29.56N 53.18 E
Arsenjev 20 Ih 44.12N 133.20 E
Arsi (3) 35 Fd 7.10N 40.00 E
Arsk 7 Lh 56.07N 49.52 E
Årskogen 8 Gb 62.05N 17.20 E
Arslanköy 24 Fd 37.01N 34.17 E
Ars-sur-Moselle 12 Ie 49.05N 6.04 E
Arsuk 41 Hf 61.11N 48.30W
Årsunda 8 Gd 60.32N 16.44 E
Art 63b Ad 19.43S 163.39 E
Artá 13 Pe 39.42N 3.21 E
Arta 35 Gc 11.31N 42.50 E
Árta 15 Dj 39.09N 20.59 E
Artá, Cuevas de- 13 Pe 39.40N 3.24 E
Artašat 16 Nj 39.59N 44.33 E
Arteaga 48 Hh 18.28N 102.25W
Artem 20 Ih 43.23N 132.10 E
Artemisa 47 Hd 22.49N 82.46W
Artemón 15 Hm 36.57N 24.43 E
Artem-Ostrov 19 Fg 40.28N 50.18 E
Artemovsk [R.S.F.S.R.] 20 Ef 54.23N 93.30 E
Artemovsk [Ukr.-U.S.S.R.] 16 Ke 48.33N 38.03 E
Artemovski 17 Jh 57.25N 61.58 E
Artesa de Segre 13 Nc 41.54N 1.03 E
Artesia 43 Ge 32.51N 104.24W
Arthur 45 Ff 41.35N 101.31W
Arthur Creek 59 Hd 23.00S 136.58 E
Arthur River 59 Ih 41.00S 144.55 E
Arthur's Pass 61 Dh 42.57S 171.34 E
Arthur's Pass 62 De 42.54S 171.34 E
Arthur's Town 49 Ja 24.38N 75.32W
Arti 17 Ih 56.26N 58.32 E
Artibonite, Rivière de l'- 49 Kd 19.15N 72.47W
Artigas 56 Id 30.42S 56.28W
Artigas (2) 55 Dj 30.35S 57.00W
Artijarvi/Artsjö 8 Ld 60.45N 26.05 E
Artik 16 Mi 40.36N 43.58 E
Artillery Lake 42 Gd 63.08N 107.45W
Artois 11 Id 50.10N 2.30 E
Artois, Collines de l'- 11 Id 50.30N 2.15 E
Artoli 35 Eb 18.19N 33.54 E
Artsjö/Artijarvi 8 Ld 60.45N 26.05 E
Artux 27 Cd 39.40N 76.10 E
Artvin 23 Fa 41.11N 41.49 E
Artyk 20 Jd 64.12N 145.15 E
Aru 36 Fb 2.52N 30.51 E
Aru, Kepulauan-=Aru
Islands (EN) 57 Ee 6.00S 134.30 E
Arua 31 Kh 3.01N 30.55 E
Aruanã 55 Gb 14.54S 51.05W
Aruba 54 Ea 12.30N 70.00W
Aru Bassin (EN) 26 Jg 5.00S 134.00 E
Aru Islands (EN)=Aru,
Kepulauan- 57 Ee 6.00S 134.30 E

Arukoron Point 64a Bb 7.43N 134.38 E
Arun 9 Mk 50.48N 0.33W
Arunāchal Pradesh (3) 25 Ic 27.50N 94.50 E
Arundel 12 Bd 50.51N 0.33W
Arun He 27 Lb 47.36N 124.06 E
Arun Qi 27 Lb 48.09N 123.29 E
Arus, Tanjung- 26 Hf 1.24N 125.06 E
Arusha (3) 36 Gc 3.30S 36.00 E
Arusha 31 Ki 3.22S 36.41 E
Arutua Atoll 61 Lc 15.18S 146.44W
Arutunga 61 Jc 18.52S 159.46W
Aruwimi 30 Jh 1.13N 23.36 E
Arvada [Co.-U.S.] 45 Dg 39.50N 105.05W
Arvada [Wy.-U.S.] 46 Ld 44.40N 106.03W
Arve 11 Mh 46.12N 6.08 E
Arvert, Presqu'île d'- 11 Ei 45.45N 1.05W
Arvida 42 Kg 48.26N 71.11W
Arvidsjaur 7 Ed 65.35N 19.10 E
Arvika 7 Cg 59.39N 12.36 E
Årviksand 7 Ea 70.12N 20.32 E
Arvin 46 Fi 35.12N 118.50W
Aryānah 14 En 36.52N 10.11 E
Arys 18 Gc 42.48N 68.15 E
Arys 19 Gg 42.26N 68.48 E
Arys, Ozero- 18 Fb 45.50N 66.20 E
Arz 11 Dg 47.39N 2.06W
Arzachena 14 Di 41.05N 9.23 E
Arzamas 19 Ed 55.23N 43.50 E
Arzanah 24 Oj 24.47N 52.34 E
Aržano 14 Kg 43.35N 16.59 E
Arzew 32 Gb 35.51N 0.19W
Arzew, Golfe d'- 13 Li 35.50N 0.10W
Arzew, Salines d'- 13 Li 35.42N 0.18W
Arzfeld 12 Id 50.05N 6.16 E
Arzgir 19 Ef 45.22N 44.13 E
Arzúa 13 Db 42.56N 8.09W
As 12 Hc 51.01N 5.35 E
Ås 8 De 59.40N 10.48 E
Aš 10 If 50.13N 12.12 E
Aša 19 Fd 55.02N 57.18 E
Aså 8 Dg 57.09N 10.25 E
Asab 37 Be 25.29S 17.59 E
Asaba 34 Gd 6.11N 6.45 E
Asad, Buḥayrat al- 24 He 35.57N 38.10 E
Asadābād [Afg.] 23 Lc 34.52N 71.09 E
Asadābād [Iran] 24 Me 34.47N 48.07 E
Asafik 35 Bc 13.10N 19.26 E
Asahi [Jap.] 29 Fb 38.15N 139.30 E
Asahi [Jap.] 29a Ca 44.08N 142.35 E
Asahi [Jap.] 29 Gd 35.43N 140.35 E
Asahi [Jap.] 29 Ec 36.57N 137.34 E
Asahi-Dake 29 Fb 38.16N 139.55 E
Asahi-Gawa 29 Cd 34.36N 133.58 E
Asahikawa 22 Qe 43.46N 142.22 E
Asaka-Drainage 29 Gc 37.30N 140.15 E
Asale, Lake- 35 Gc 14.00N 40.20 E
'Asalūyeh 24 Oi 27.28N 52.37 E
Asama-Yama 28 Of 36.27N 138.30 E
Asan-Man 28 If 36.56N 126.51 E
Asansol 22 Kg 23.41N 86.59 E
Asarna 7 De 62.39N 14.21 E
Asarum 8 Fh 56.12N 14.50 E
'Asāyr=Guardafui, Cape-
(EN) 30 Mg 11.49N 51.15 E
Asayta 35 Gc 11.33N 41.27 E
Asbest 17 Jh 57.01N 61.31 E
Asbestos 44 Lc 45.46N 71.57W
Asbe Teferi 35 Gd 9.05N 40.51 E
Asbury Park 44 Je 40.14N 74.01W
Ascension 30 Fi 7.57S 14.22W
Ascensión, Bahía de la- 47 Ge 19.40N 87.30W
Ascensión, Bahía de la- 48 Ph 19.40N 87.30W
Ascensión, Laguna de la- 48 Fb 31.05N 107.55W
Aschaffenburg 10 Fg 49.59N 9.09 E
Ascheberg 12 Jc 51.47N 7.37 E
Aschendorf (Ems),
Papenburg- 12 Ja 53.04N 7.22 E
Aschersleben 10 He 51.45N 11.28 E
Aščikol, Ozero- 18 Fb 45.05N 67.20 E
Aščiozek 16 Pe 49.12N 48.06 E
Ascoli Piceno 14 Hh 42.51N 13.34 E
Ascoli Satriano 14 Ji 41.12N 15.34 E
Ascot 12 Bc 51.24N 0.40W
Aseb 31 Lg 13.00N 42.44 E
Åseda 7 Dh 57.10N 15.20 E
Asedjrad 30 Hf 24.42N 1.40 E
Asekejevo 16 Rc 53.36N 52.51 E
Asela 31 Kh 7.58N 39.08 E
As Ela 35 Gc 11.06N 42.06 E
Åsele 7 Dd 64.10N 17.20 E
Åsen [Nor.] 7 Ce 63.36N 11.03 E
Åsen [Swe.] 7 Cf 61.17N 13.50 E
Asendabo 35 Fd 9.47N 37.36 E
Asendorf 12 Kb 52.46N 9.00 E
Asenovgrad 15 Hg 42.01N 24.52 E
Åsensbruk 8 Ef 58.48N 12.25 E
Åseral 8 Bf 58.37N 7.25 E
Aseri/Azeri 7 Gg 59.29N 26.51 E
Asfeld 12 Ge 49.28N 4.07 E
Asfūn al Maṭā'inah 24 Ej 25.23N 32.32 E
Asgårdstrand 8 De 59.21N 10.28 E
Ašhabad 22 Hf 37.57N 58.23 E
Ašhabadskaja Oblast (3) 19 Fh 38.30N 59.00 E
Ashanti (3) 34 Ed 6.45N 1.30W
Ashburn 44 Fj 31.43N 83.39W
Ashburton 61 Dh 43.54S 171.45 E
Ashburton River 57 Cg 21.40S 114.56 E
Ashdod 24 Fg 31.49N 34.39 E
Ashdown 45 Ij 33.41N 94.08W
Asheboro 44 Hh 35.42N 79.49W
Asheroft 46 Ea 50.43N 121.17W
Asheville 43 Kd 35.34N 82.33W
Ashford 9 Nj 51.09N 0.53 E
Ashford Airport 12 Cc 51.10N 0.59 E
Ash Fork 46 Ii 35.13N 112.29W
Ashibetsu 28 Qc 43.31N 142.11 E
Ashikaga 29 Fc 36.21N 139.27 E

Ashington 9 Lf 55.11N 1.34W
Ashiro 29 Ga 40.06N 141.01 E
Ashiya 29 Be 33.53N 130.40 E
Ashizuri-Misaki 28 Lh 32.44N 133.01 E
Ashkal, Qar'at al- 14 Dm 37.10N 9.40 E
Āshkhāneh 24 Qd 37.28N 57.00 E
Ashland [Ks.-U.S.] 45 Gh 37.11N 99.46W
Ashland [Ky.-U.S.] 43 Kd 38.28N 82.38W
Ashland [Mt.-U.S.] 46 Ld 45.35N 106.16W
Ashland [Oh.-U.S.] 44 Fe 40.52N 82.19W
Ashland [Or.-U.S.] 43 Cc 42.12N 122.42W
Ashland [Wi.-U.S.] 43 Ib 46.35N 90.53W
Ashland, Mount- 46 De 42.05N 122.43W
Ashley 45 Gc 46.02N 99.22W
Ashmore Islands 57 Df 12.15S 123.05 E
Ashmūn 24 Dg 30.18N 30.58 E
Ashoro 29a Cb 43.14N 143.31 E
Ashqelon 24 Fg 31.40N 34.35 E
Ash Shabakah 24 Jg 30.49N 43.39 E
Ash Shabb 33 Ee 22.19N 29.46 E
Ash Shā'ib 24 Gh 28.59N 37.07 E
Ash Sha'm 23 Id 26.02N 56.05 E
Ash Shamālīyah (3) 35 Db 18.40N 30.00 E
Ash 'Shāmīyah 24 Kg 31.57N 44.36 E
Ash Shāmīyah 24 Lg 30.15N 46.55 E
Ash Shaqq 24 Lh 28.20N 47.30 E
Ash Shaqrā' 23 Gd 25.15N 45.15 E
Ash Sha'rā' 24 Kj 24.16N 44.11 E
Ash Sharīqah 23 Id 25.22N 55.23 E
Ash Sharqāṭ 23 Fb 35.27N 43.16 E
Ash Sharqī 24 Jc 34.45N 11.15 E
Ash Sharqī 24 Ge 34.00N 36.30 E
Ash Sharqīyah 23 Ie 22.15N 58.30 E
Ash Shatrah 24 Lg 31.25N 46.10 E
Ash Shawbak 24 Fg 30.32N 35.34 E
Ash Shaykh Ḥumayd 24 Fh 28.07N 34.34 E
Ash Shifā 24 Fh 28.30N 35.30 E
Ash Shiḥr 23 Gg 14.44N 49.35 E
Ash Shināfīyah 24 Kg 31.35N 44.39 E
Ash Shu'aybah [Kuw.] 24 Mh 29.03N 48.08 E
Ash Shu'aybah [Sau.Ar.] 24 Ji 27.53N 42.43 E
Ash Shu'bah 24 Kh 28.54N 44.44 E
Ash Shumlūl 24 Li 26.31N 47.20 E
Ash Shuqayq 23 Ff 17.44N 42.01 E
Ash Shurayk 35 Eb 18.48N 33.34 E
Ash Shuwayhāt 24 Oj 24.05N 52.28 E
Ash Shuwaykh 24 Lh 29.21N 47.55 E
Ashtabula 43 Kc 41.53N 80.47W
Ashtabula, Lake- 45 Hc 47.11N 97.58W
Ashtīyān 24 Me 34.30N 49.55 E
Ashton [Id.-U.S.] 46 Jd 44.04N 111.27W
Ashton [St.Vin.] 51n Bb 12.36N 61.27W
Ashuanipi 42 Kf 52.55N 66.00W
Ashuanipi Lake 42 Kf 52.45N 66.10W
Asia 21 Ke 40.00N 85.00 E
Asia, Kepulauan- 26 Jf 1.03N 131.18 E
Asiago 14 Fe 45.52N 11.30 E
Asiago, Altopiano di- 14 Fe 45.54N 11.30 E
Asilah 32 Fb 35.28N 6.02W
Asinara 5 Gg 41.04N 8.15 E
Asinara, Golfo dell'- 14 Cj 41.00N 8.35 E
Asino 20 De 56.58N 86.09 E
'Asir 23 Ff 19.00N 42.00 E
Aškadar 17 Hi 53.37N 56.01 E
Aşkale 24 Ic 39.55N 40.42 E
Askanija-Nova 16 Hf 46.27N 33.52 E
Asker 8 De 59.50N 10.26 E
Askersund 7 Dg 58.53N 14.54 E
Askī Al Mawṣil 24 Jd 36.34N 42.42 E
Askim [Nor.] 8 De 59.35N 11.10 E
Askim [Swe.] 8 Dg 57.38N 11.56 E
Áskion Óros 15 Ei 40.22N 21.34 E
Askiz 20 Ef 53.08N 90.32 E
Askja 5 Eb 65.03N 16.48W
Askola 8 Kd 60.32N 25.36 E
Asköping 8 Ge 59.09N 16.04 E
Askøy 8 Ad 60.30N 5.05 E
Askøy 8 Ad 60.24N 5.11 E
Askrova 8 Ac 61.30N 4.55 E
Askvoll 7 Af 61.21N 5.04 E
Asl 24 Eh 29.30N 32.43 E
Aslanapa 15 Mj 39.13N 29.52 E
Asmara (EN)=Asmera 31 Kg 15.19N 38.57 E
Asmera=Asmara (EN) 31 Kg 15.19N 38.57 E
Åsnen 8 Fh 56.40N 14.40 E
Asni 32 Fc 31.15N 7.59W
Asnières-sur-Seine 12 Ef 48.55N 2.17 E
Aso 14 Hg 43.06N 13.51 E
Aso 29 Be 32.58N 131.02 E
Asola 14 Ee 45.13N 10.24 E
Asosa 31 Kg 10.02N 34.32 E
Aso-San 29 Be 32.53N 131.06 E
Asoteriba, Jabal- 35 Fa 21.51N 36.30 E
Asouf Mellene 32 Hd 25.40N 2.08 E
Asō-Wan 29 Ad 34.20N 129.15 E
Āspās 24 Og 30.40N 52.24 E
Aspe 13 Lf 38.21N 0.46W
Aspen 43 Fd 39.11N 106.49W
Aspermont 45 Fj 33.08N 100.14W
Aspiring, Mount- 61 Ch 44.23S 168.44 E
Aspromonte 14 Jl 38.10N 16.00 E
Assa 32 Fd 28.37N 9.25W
Aş Şadr 23 He 24.40N 54.41 E
Aş Şaff 24 Dh 29.34N 31.17 E
Aş Şāfī 24 Fg 31.02N 35.28 E
Aş Safirah 24 Gd 36.04N 37.22 E
Aş Şaḥm 24 Qj 24.10N 56.53 E
Assahoun 34 Fd 6.27N 0.55 E
Aş Şa'īd 30 Kf 26.00N 32.00 E
Assal, Lac- 35 Gc 11.40N 42.22 E
As Salamīyah [Sau.Ar.] 23 Ge 24.12N 47.23 E
As Salamīyah [Syr.] 24 Ge 35.01N 37.03 E
Aş Şāliḥīyah 24 Dg 30.47N 31.55 E
As Sallūm 31 Je 31.34N 25.09 E
As Salmān 24 Kg 30.26N 44.30 E
As Salt 24 Ff 32.03N 35.44 E
As Salwá 23 He 24.45N 50.49 E

lex Symbols

ndependent Nation
State, Region
District, County
Municipality
Colony, Dependency
Continent
Physical Region
Historical or Cultural Region
Mount, Mountain
Volcano
Hill
Mountains, Mountain Range
Hills, Escarpment
Plateau, Upland
Pass, Gap
Plain, Lowland
Delta
Salt Flat
Valley, Canyon
Crater, Cave
Karst Features
Depression
Polder
Desert, Dunes
Forest, Woods
Heath, Steppe
Oasis
Cape, Point
Coast, Beach
Cliff
Peninsula
Isthmus
Sandbank
Island
Atoll
Rock, Reef
Islands, Archipelago
Rocks, Reefs
Coral Reef
Well, Spring
Geyser
River, Stream
Waterfall Rapids
River Mouth, Estuary
Lake
Salt Lake
Intermittent Lake
Reservoir
Swamp, Pond
Canal
Glacier
Ice Shelf, Pack Ice
Ocean
Sea
Gulf, Bay
Strait, Fjord
Lagoon
Bank
Seamount
Tablemount
Ridge
Shelf
Basin
Escarpment, Sea Scarp
Fracture
Trench, Abyss
National Park, Reserve
Point of Interest
Recreation Site
Cave, Cavern
Historic Site
Ruins
Wall, Walls
Church, Abbey
Temple
Scientific Station
Airport
Port
Lighthouse
Mine
Tunnel
Dam, Bridge

Name	Map	Grid	Lat.	Long.
Assam ▨	21	Lg	26.50N	94.00 E
Assam ▣	25	Ic	26.00N	93.00 E
Assamakka	34	Gb	19.21N	5.38 E
As Samawah	23	Gc	31.18N	45.17 E
As Sanām ▨	35	Ia	22.00N	51.10 E
Assaouas	34	Gb	16.52N	7.27 E
As Sars	14	Dn	36.05N	9.01 E
As Sayl al Kabīr	33	He	21.38N	40.25 E
Asse	12	Gd	50.56N	4.12 E
Asse ▷	11	Lk	43.53N	5.53 E
Assebroek, Brugge-	12	Fc	51.12N	3.16 E
Assekkârai ▨	34	Fb	15.50N	2.52 E
Assemini	14	Dk	39.17N	9.01 E
Assen	11	Ma	53.00N	6.34 E
Assenede	12	Fc	51.14N	3.45 E
Assens	8	Ci	55.16N	9.55 E
As Sibā'īyah	24	Ej	25.11N	32.41 E
As Sidr	31	Ie	30.39N	18.22 E
As Sidrah = Sirte Desert (EN) ▨	30	Ie	30.30N	17.30 E
As Sila'	23	He	24.02N	51.46 E
As Simbillâwayn	24	Dg	30.53N	31.27 E
Assiniboia	42	Gg	49.38N	105.59W
Assiniboine ▷	38	Je	49.53N	97.08W
Assiniboine, Mount-	38	Hd	50.52N	115.39W
Assis	56	Jb	22.40S	50.25W
Assisi	14	Gg	43.04N	12.37 E
Aßlar	12	Kd	50.36N	8.28 E
Assos ▷	15	Jj	39.31N	26.20 E
As Sslimīyah	24	Mh	29.20N	48.04 E
As Subaykhah	14	Eo	35.56N	10.01 E
As Subū' ▷	33	Fe	22.45N	32.34 E
As Sūdān = Sudan (EN) ▣	31	Jg	15.00N	30.00 E
As Sudd ▨	30	Kh	8.00N	31.00 E
As Sufāl	35	Hc	14.06N	48.43 E
Aş Şufuq	24	Nk	23.52N	51.45 E
Aş Şukhayrah	32	Jc	34.17N	10.06 E
Aş Şukhnah	24	He	34.52N	38.52 E
As Sulaymī	24	Ii	26.17N	41.21 E
Aş Şulayyil	23	Ge	20.27N	45.34 E
Aş Şulb ▨	24	Mj	25.42N	48.25 E
Aş Şumayḥ	35	Dd	9.49N	27.39 E
Aş Şummān ▨	33	Ie	23.00N	48.00 E
Aş Şummān ▨	24	Li	27.00N	47.00 E
Assumption Island	30	Li	9.45S	46.30 E
As Sūq	33	He	21.54N	42.03 E
Assur ▨	24	Je	35.25N	43.16 E
Aş Şuwār	24	Ie	35.30N	40.39 E
Aş Şuwaydā'	23	Ec	32.42N	36.34 E
Aş Şuwayrah	24	Kf	32.55N	44.47 E
As Suways = Suez (EN)	31	Kf	29.58N	32.33 E
Astakidha	15	Jn	35.53N	26.50 E
Astakós	15	Ek	38.32N	21.05 E
Astáneh [Iran]	24	Md	37.17N	49.59 E
Astáneh [Iran]	24	Mf	33.53N	49.22 E
Astárā	23	Gb	38.26N	48.52 E
Astara	6	Kh	38.28N	48.52 E
Aştarak	16	Ni	40.16N	44.18 E
Asten	12	Hc	51.24N	5.45 E
Asti	14	Cf	44.54N	8.12 E
Astico ▷	14	Fe	45.37N	11.37 E
Astipálaia	15	Jm	36.33N	26.21 E
Astipálaia ▷	15	Jm	36.35N	26.20 E
Asto, Monte- ▨	11a	Ba	42.30N	9.15 E
Astola Island	25	Cc	25.07N	63.51 E
Astorga	13	Fb	42.27N	6.03W
Astoria	43	Cb	46.11N	123.50W
Åstorp	8	Eh	56.08N	13.00 E
Astove Island	30	Lj	10.06 S	47.45 E
Astrahan	6	Kf	46.21N	48.03 E
Astrahanskaja Oblast ▣	19	Ef	47.10N	47.30 E
Astrolabe, Cape-	63a	Ec	8.20 S	160.34 E
Astrolabe, Récifs de l'- ▷	57	Hf	19.49 S	165.35 E
Astudillo	13	Hb	42.12N	4.18W
Asturias ▣	13	Ga	43.20N	6.00W
Asuisui, Cape-	65c	Aa	13.47 S	172.29W
Asunción	53	Kh	25.16 S	57.40W
Asunción, Bahía- ▷	48	Bd	27.05N	114.10W
Asunción, Cerro de la- ▨	48	Je	24.15N	99.56W
Asunción Island	57	Fc	19.40N	145.24 E
Asunción Mita	49	Cf	14.20N	89.43W
Asunción Nochixtlán	48	Ki	17.28N	97.14W
Asunden	8	Fg	58.00N	15.50 E
Åsunden	8	Eg	57.44N	13.22 E
Aswa ▷	36	Fb	3.43N	31.55 E
Aswân	31	Kf	24.05N	32.53 E
Aswân, Sadd al- = First Cataract (EN) ▨	30	Kf	24.01N	32.52 E
Asyūṭ	31	Kf	27.11N	31.11 E
Asyūṭī, Wādī al- ▷	24	Di	27.10N	31.16 E
Aszód	10	Pi	47.39N	19.30 E
'Ata ▣	65b	Bc	21.03 S	174.59W
Atacama ▣	56	Gc	27.30 S	70.00W
Atacama, Desierto de- = Atacama Desert (EN) ▨	52	Jh	22.30 S	69.15W
Atacama, Salar de- ▨	52	Jh	23.30 S	68.15W
Atacama Desert (EN) = Atacama, Desierto de- ▨	52	Jh	22.30 S	69.15W
Atacama Trench (EN) ▨	3	Nm	30.00 S	73.00W
Atafu Atoll ▷	57	Je	8.33 S	172.30W
Atagaj	20	Ee	55.06N	99.25 E
Ata Island ▷	57	Jg	21.03 S	175.00W
Atakor ▨	30	Hf	23.13N	5.40 E
Atakora ▣	34	Fc	10.00N	1.35 E
Atakora ▷	34	Fc	10.45N	1.30 E
Atakpamé	31	Hh	7.32N	1.08 E
Atalaia do Norte	54	Dd	4.20 S	70.12W
Atalándi	15	Fk	38.39N	23.00 E
Atalaya	54	Df	10.44 S	73.45W
Atalayasa ▨	13	Nf	38.55N	1.15 E
Atambua	26	Hh	9.07 S	124.54 E
Atami	29	Fd	35.05N	139.02 E
Atangmik	41	Gf	64.53N	52.00W
Aṭār	31	Ff	20.30N	13.03W
Atas-Bogdo-Ula ▨	27	Gc	43.20N	96.30 E
Atascadero	46	Ei	35.29N	120.41W
Atasu	19	Hf	48.42N	71.38 E
'Atata ▷	65b	Ac	21.03 S	175.15W
Atauat, Phou- ▨	25	Le	16.01N	107.23 E
Atauro, Pulau- ▷	26	Ih	8.13 S	125.35 E
Atáviros ▨	15	Km	36.12N	27.52 E
Ataway	35	Md	9.59N	18.38 E
Atbara	35	Eb	17.40N	33.56 E
'Aṭbarah ▷	30	Kg	17.40N	33.56 E
'Aṭbarah	31	Kg	17.42N	33.59 E
Atbasar	22	Id	51.48N	68.20 E
At-Baši	19	Hg	41.08N	75.51 E
Atça	15	Ll	37.53N	28.13 E
Atchafalaya Bay ▷	43	If	29.25N	91.20W
Atchison	43	Hd	39.34N	95.07W
Atebubu	34	Ed	7.45N	0.59W
Ateca	13	Kc	41.20N	1.47W
Aterno ▷	14	Hg	42.11N	13.51 E
Atessa	14	Ih	42.04N	14.27 E
Ath/Aat	11	Jd	50.38N	3.47 E
Athabasca ▷	38	Hd	58.40N	110.50W
Athabasca	42	Gf	54.43N	113.17W
Athabasca, Lake- ▨	38	Id	59.07N	110.00W
Athamánon, Óri- ▨	15	Ej	39.27N	21.08 E
Athamánon Óri ▨	15	Ej	39.27N	21.08 E
Athens [Al.-U.S.]	44	Dh	34.48N	86.58W
Athens [Ga.-U.S.]	43	Ke	33.57N	83.23W
Athens [Oh.-U.S.]	44	Ff	39.20N	82.06W
Athens [Tn.-U.S.]	44	Eh	35.28N	84.35W
Athens [Tx.-U.S.]	45	Ij	32.12N	95.51W
Athens (EN) = Athínai	6	Ih	37.59N	23.44 E
Athéras ▨	15	Jl	37.36N	20.46 E
Atherton	59	Jc	17.16 S	145.29 E
Athi ▷	36	Gc	2.59 S	38.31 E
Athies-sous-Laon	12	Fe	49.34N	3.41 E
Athínai = Athens (EN)	6	Ih	37.59N	23.44 E
Athi River	36	Gc	1.27 S	36.59 E
Athis-de-l'Orne	12	Bf	48.49N	0.30W
Athlone/Baile Átha Luain	9	Fh	53.25N	7.56W
Athol	44	Kd	42.36N	72.14W
Áthos	15	Hi	40.10N	24.20 E
Athos, Mount- (EN) = Áyion Óros ▣	15	Hi	40.15N	24.15 E
Ath Thamad	24	Fh	29.41N	34.18 E
Ath Thumāmī	24	Ki	27.42N	44.59 E
Athus, Aubange-	12	He	49.34N	5.50 E
Athy	9	Gi	53.00N	7.00W
Ati	31	Ig	13.13N	18.20 E
Atiak	36	Fb	3.16N	32.07 E
Atiamuri	62	Gc	38.23 S	176.02 E
Atibaia, Rio- ▷	55	If	22.42 S	47.17W
Atienza	13	Jc	41.12N	2.52W
Atikokan	42	Ig	48.45N	91.37W
Atikonak Lake ▨	42	Lf	52.40N	64.35W
Atimoono ▷	64n	Bc	10.26 S	160.58W
Atitlán, Lago de- ▨	49	Bf	14.42N	91.12W
Atitlán, Volcán- ▨	47	Ff	14.35N	91.11W
Atiu Island ▷	57	Lg	20.02 S	158.07W
'Atk, Wādī al- ▷	24	Li	26.03N	46.30 E
Atka ▷	38	Bd	52.15N	174.30W
Atka [Ak.-U.S.]	40a	Db	52.12N	174.12W
Atka [R.S.F.S.R.]	20	Kd	60.49N	151.58 E
Atka Iceport	66	Bf	70.35 S	7.45W
Atkarsk	19	Ee	51.52N	44.59 E
Atkasook	40	Hb	70.28N	157.24W
Atkinson	45	Ge	42.32N	98.59W
Atlacomulco de Fabela	48	Jh	19.48N	99.53W
Atlanta [Ga.-U.S.]	39	Kf	33.45N	84.23W
Atlanta [Mi.-U.S.]	44	Ec	45.00N	84.09W
Atlanta [Tx.-U.S.]	45	Ij	33.07N	94.10W
Atlanterhavet = Atlantic Ocean (EN) ▨	3	Di	2.00N	25.00W
Atlantic [Ia.-U.S.]	45	If	41.24N	95.01W
Atlantic [N.C.-U.S.]	44	Ih	34.54N	76.20W
Atlantic City	39	Lf	39.27N	74.35W
Atlantic Coastal Plain ▨	38	Lf	34.00N	79.00W
Atlantic-Indian Basin (EN) ▨	3	Eo	60.00 S	15.00 E
Atlantic-Indian Ridge (EN) ▨	3	Eo	52.00 S	25.00 E
Atlántico ▣	54	Da	10.40N	75.00W
Atlántico, Océano- = Atlantic Ocean (EN) ▨	3	Di	2.00N	25.00W
Atlántico, Oceano- = Atlantic Ocean (EN) ▨	3	Di	2.00N	25.00W
Atlantic Ocean (EN) = Atlanterhavet ▨	3	Di	2.00N	25.00W
Atlantic Ocean (EN) = Atlántico, Oceano- ▨	3	Di	2.00N	25.00W
Atlantic Ocean (EN) = Atlantique, Océan- ▨	3	Di	2.00N	25.00W
Atlantic Ocean (EN) = Atlantiese Oseaan ▨	3	Di	2.00N	25.00W
Atlantic Ocean (EN) = Atlantshaf ▨	3	Di	2.00N	25.00W
Atlantic Ocean (EN) = Muhīt, Al Baḥr al- ▨	3	Di	'2.00N	25.00W
Atlántida ▣	49	Df	15.30N	87.00W
Atlantiese Oseaan = Atlantic Ocean (EN) ▨	3	Di	2.00N	25.00W
Atlantique, Océan- = Atlantic Ocean (EN) ▨	3	Di	2.00N	25.00W
Atlantshaf = Atlantic Ocean (EN) ▨	3	Di	2.00N	25.00W
Atlas = Atlas Mountains (EN) ▨	30	Ge	32.00N	2.00W
Atlas Mountains (EN) = Atlas ▨	30	Ge	32.00N	2.00W
Atlasova, Ostrov- ▷	20	Kf	50.50N	155.25 E
Atlasovo	20	Jg	46.00N	142.09 E
Atlas Saharien = Saharan Atlas (EN) ▨	30	He	34.00N	2.00 E
Atlas Tellien = Tell Atlas (EN) ▨	30	He	36.00N	2.00 E
Atlin	42	Ee	59.35N	133.42W
Atlin Lake ▨	42	Ee	59.35N	133.43W
Atlixco	47	Ee	18.54N	98.26W
Atley ▷	8	Ac	61.20N	4.55 E
Atmore	44	Dj	31.02N	87.29W
Atna ▷	8	Dc	61.44N	10.49 E
Atna Peak ▨	42	Ef	53.57N	128.04W
Atô	29	Bd	34.04N	131.43 E
Atoka	45	Hi	34.23N	96.08W
Átokos ▷	15	Dk	38.29N	20.49 E
Atotonilco el Alto	48	Hg	20.33N	102.31W
Atoui, Khatt- ▷	32	De	20.04N	15.58W
Atouila, 'Erg- ▨	30	Gf	21.15N	3.20W
Atoyac, Rio- ▷	48	Ki	16.30N	97.31W
Atoyac de Alvarez	48	Ii	17.12N	100.26W
Ātran ▷	8	Eh	56.53N	12.30 E
Atrato, Rio- ▷	52	Ie	8.17N	76.58W
Atrek ▷	21	Hf	37.23N	53.57 E
Atri	14	Hg	42.35N	13.59 E
Atsugi	29	Fd	35.26N	139.20 E
Atsukeshi	28	Rc	43.02N	144.51 E
Atsukeshi-Wan ▷	28a	Db	43.00N	144.45 E
Atsumi [Jap.]	28	Oe	38.37N	139.35 E
Atsumi [Jap.]	29	Ed	34.37N	137.05 E
Atsumi-Hantō ▷	29	Ed	34.40N	137.15 E
Atsumi-Wan ▷	29	Ed	34.45N	137.15 E
Atsuta	29a	Bb	43.24N	141.25 E
Atsutoko	29a	Db	43.15N	145.13 E
Aṭ Ṭaff ▨	23	He	23.55N	54.25 E
Aṭ Ṭafilah	24	Fg	30.50N	35.36 E
Aṭ Ṭā'if	22	Gg	21.16N	40.25 E
Aṭ Tāj	33	De	24.13N	23.18 E
Aṭ Ṭallāb	33	De	24.01N	23.10 E
At Ta'mīm ▣	24	Ke	36.00N	44.00 E
Attapu	25	Lf	14.48N	106.50 E
Aṭ Ṭārmīyah	24	Kf	33.40N	44.24 E
Attawapiskat ▷	38	Kd	52.57N	82.18W
Attawapiskat	39	Kd	52.55N	82.26W
Attawapiskat Lake ▨	42	If	52.15N	87.50W
At Tawīl ▨	24	Hh	29.20N	39.35 E
At Taysiyaḥ ▨	24	Jh	28.00N	44.00 E
Aṭ Ṭayyārah	35	Cb	13.12N	30.47 E
Attendorn	12	Jc	51.07N	7.54 E
Attersee ▨	14	Hc	47.55N	13.33 E
Attert ▷	12	Ie	49.49N	6.05 E
Attica	44	De	40.17N	87.15W
Attichy	12	Fe	49.25N	3.03 E
Attigny	12	Ge	49.29N	4.35 E
At Tīh Desert (EN) = Tīh, Ṣaḥrā' at- ▨	33	Fc	30.05N	34.00 E
Attikamagen Lake ▨	42	Ke	55.00N	66.30W
Attleboro	44	Le	41.56N	71.17W
Attleborough	12	Db	52.31N	1.01 E
Attre ▨	12	Fd	50.37N	3.50 E
Attu	40a	Ab	52.56N	173.15 E
Attu ▷	40a	Ab	52.55N	173.00 E
Aṭ Ṭulayḥī	24	Ki	27.33N	44.08 E
Aṭ Ṭūr	24	Eh	28.14N	33.37 E
Aṭ Ṭurayf	23	Ec	31.44N	38.33 E
At Turbah	23	Fg	12.40N	43.30 E
Aṭ Ṭuwayshah	35	Dc	12.21N	26.32 E
Atuel, Rio- ▷	52	Ji	36.17 S	66.50W
Åtvidaberg	7	Dg	58.12N	16.00 E
Atwater	46	Fh	37.21N	120.36W
Atwood	45	Fg	39.45N	101.03W
Aua Island ▷	57	Fc	1.27 S	143.04 E
Auasbila	49	Ef	14.52N	84.40W
Auatu ▣	35	Gd	7.17N	41.03 E
Auau Channel ▷	65a	Ec	20.51N	156.45W
Aubagne	11	Lk	43.17N	5.34 E
Aubange	12	He	49.35N	5.48 E
Aubange-Athus	12	He	49.34N	5.50 E
Aube ▣	11	Kf	48.15N	4.05 E
Aube ▷	11	Kf	48.34N	3.43 E
Aubel	12	Hd	50.42N	5.51 E
Aubenas	11	Kj	44.37N	4.23 E
Aubenton	12	Ge	49.50N	4.12 E
Aubetin ▷	12	Ff	48.49N	3.01 E
Aubigny-en-Artois	12	Ed	50.21N	2.35 E
Aubigny-sur-Nère	11	Jg	47.29N	2.26 E
Aubin	11	Jj	44.32N	2.15 E
Aubrac, Monts d'- ▨	11	Jj	44.38N	3.00 E
Aubry, Lake- ▨	38	Ec	67.25N	126.30W
Auburn [Al.-U.S.]	44	Ei	32.36N	85.29W
Auburn [Ca.-U.S.]	46	Fg	38.54N	121.04W
Auburn [In.-U.S.]	44	Ee	41.22N	85.04W
Auburn [Me.-U.S.]	44	Lc	44.06N	70.14W
Auburn [Nb.-U.S.]	45	If	40.23N	95.51W
Auburn [N.Y.-U.S.]	44	If	42.57N	76.34W
Auburn [Wa.-U.S.]	43	Dc	47.18N	122.13W
Auburn Range ▨	59	Ke	25.10 S	150.30 E
Aubusson	11	Ii	45.57N	2.10 E
Aucanquilcha, Cerro- ▨	52	Jh	21.14 S	68.28W
Auce	11	Jk	45.56N	3.36 E
Auch	6	Gg	43.39N	0.35 E
Auchel	12	Ed	50.30N	2.28 E
Auchi	34	Fd	7.04N	6.16 E
Auckland	58	Ih	36.52 S	174.45 E
Auckland Islands ▣	57	Ik	50.35 S	166.00 E
Auckland Peninsula	62	Eb	36.15 S	174.00 E
Aude ▣	11	Jk	43.13N	3.14 E
Aude ▷	11	Ik	43.05N	2.30 E
Auden	45	Ma	50.13N	87.47W
Audenarde/Oudenaarde	12	Fd	50.51N	3.36 E
Audierne	11	Af	48.01N	4.32W
Audierne, Baie d'- ▷	11	Af	47.57N	4.28W
Audo ▨	35	Gd	6.09N	41.53 E
Audresselles	12	Dd	50.49N	1.35 E
Audru	8	Kf	58.20N	24.19 E
Audruicq	12	Ed	50.53N	2.05 E
Audubon	45	If	41.43N	94.55W
Audun-le-Roman	12	He	49.22N	5.54 E
Audun-le-Tiche	12	He	49.28N	5.57 E
Aue	10	If	50.35N	12.42 E
Aue [F.R.G.] ▷	12	Kb	52.16N	8.59 E
Aue [F.R.G.] ▷	10	Fd	52.33N	9.05 E
Auerbach	10	If	50.31N	12.24 E
Auezov	19	If	49.40N	81.40 E
Auffay	12	De	49.43N	1.06 E
Augathella	58	Fg	25.48 S	146.35 E
Auge, Pays d'- ▨	12	Ge	49.05N	0.10 E
Augpilagtoq	41	Gd	72.45N	55.35W
Augrabies Falls ▷	30	Jk	28.35 S	20.23 E
Augsburg	6	Hf	48.22N	10.53 E
Augusta [Ar.-U.S.]	45	Ki	35.17N	91.22W
Augusta [Austl.]	58	Ch	34.10 S	115.10 E
Augusta [Ga.-U.S.]	39	Kf	33.29N	81.57W
Augusta [It.]	14	Jm	37.13N	15.13 E
Augusta [Ks.-U.S.]	45	Hh	37.41N	96.58W
Augusta [Me.-U.S.]	39	Me	44.19N	69.47W
Augusta [Mt.-U.S.]	46	Ic	47.30N	112.24W
Augusta, Golfo di- ▷	14	Jm	37.10N	15.15 E
Augustów	10	Sc	53.51N	22.59 E
Augustowski, Kanał- ▨	10	Tc	53.54N	23.26 E
Augustus, Mount- ▨	57	Cg	24.20 S	116.50 E
Auki	58	He	8.45 S	160.42 E
Auld, Lake- ▨	59	Ed	22.30 S	123.45 E
Aulla	14	Df	44.12N	9.58 E
Aulne ▷	11	Bf	48.17N	4.16W
Aulneau Peninsula ▨	45	Ib	49.23N	94.29W
Aulnoye-Aymeries	12	Fd	50.12N	3.50 E
Aulong ▷	64a	Ac	7.17N	134.17 E
Ault	12	Dd	50.06N	1.27 E
Auluptagel ▷	64a	Ac	7.19N	134.29 E
Aulus-les-Bains	11	Hl	42.48N	1.20 E
Aumale	11	He	49.46N	1.45 E
Auna	34	Fc	10.11N	4.43 E
Aunay-sur-Odon	12	Be	49.01N	0.38W
Auneau	12	Ee	49.22N	2.00 E
Auneuil	12	Ee	49.22N	2.00 E
Auning	7	Ch	56.26N	10.23 E
Aunis ▨	11	Fh	46.10N	1.00W
Aunuu ▷	65c	Cb	14.17 S	170.33W
Auob ▷	36	Bb	26.27 S	20.38 E
Aura	8	Jf	60.36N	22.34 E
Aurangābād	25	Fe	19.53N	75.20 E
Aurari Bay ▷	59	Gb	11.40 S	133.40 E
Aur Atoll ▷	57	Id	8.16N	171.06 E
Auray	11	Dg	47.40N	2.59W
Aurdal	7	Bf	60.56N	9.24 E
Aure ▷	12	Ie	49.49N	6.05 E
Aure [Nor.]	7	Be	63.13N	8.32 E
Aure [Nor.]	8	Bb	62.24N	6.36 E
Aurejärvi	8	Jb	62.05N	23.25 E
Aurès, Massif de l'- ▨	30	He	35.14N	6.10 E
Aurich	10	Dc	53.28N	7.29 E
Aurillac	11	Ij	44.55N	2.27 E
Aurlandsfjorden	8	Bc	61.05N	7.05 E
Aurlandsvangen	7	Bf	60.54N	7.11 E
Auron	11	Mj	44.10N	6.56 E
Auron ▷	11	Ig	47.06N	2.24 E
Aurora [Co.-U.S.]	43	Gd	39.44N	104.52W
Aurora [Il.-U.S.]	43	Jc	42.46N	88.19W
Aurora [Mo.-U.S.]	45	Jh	36.58N	93.43W
Aurora [Phil.]	26	He	7.57N	123.36 E
Aurora do Norte	55	Ia	12.38 S	46.23W
Aursjøen ▨	8	Cb	62.20N	8.40 E
Aursunden ▨	8	Db	62.40N	11.40 E
Aurukun Mission	59	Ib	13.19 S	141.45 E
Aus	37	Be	26.40 S	16.15 E
Au Sable River ▷	44	Fc	44.25N	83.20W
Ausiait/Egedesminde	67	Nc	68.50N	52.45W
Ausoni, Monti- ▨	14	Hh	41.35N	13.20 E
Aust-Agder ▣	7	Bg	58.50N	8.00 E
Austfonna ▨	41	Oc	79.55N	25.00 E
Austin [Mn.-U.S.]	43	Ic	43.40N	92.59W
Austin [Nv.-U.S.]	43	Dd	39.30N	117.04W
Austin [Tx.-U.S.]	39	Jf	30.16N	97.45W
Austral, Chaco- ▨	52	Jh	25.00 S	61.00W
Australes, Iles -Tubuaï, Iles- = Tubuai Islands (EN) ▷	57	Lg	23.00 S	150.00W
Australia ▣	58	Eg	25.00 S	135.00 E
Australian Alps ▨	57	Fh	37.00 S	148.00 E
Australian Capital Territory	59	Jg	35.30 S	149.00 E
Österreich ▣	6	Hf	47.30N	14.00 E
Austvågøy ▷	7	Db	68.20N	14.36 E
Autazes	54	Gd	3.35 S	59.08W
Autheuil-Authouillet	12	De	49.06N	1.17 E
Authie ▷	11	Hd	50.21N	1.38 E
Autlán de Navarro	47	De	19.46N	104.22W
Autun	11	Kh	46.57N	4.18 E
Auve	12	Ge	49.02N	4.42 E
Auvergne ▨	11	Ji	45.30N	2.45 E
Auvergne, Monts d'- ▨	11	Ji	45.30N	2.45 E
Auvézère ▷	11	Gi	45.12N	0.50 E
Auvillers-lès-Forges-Mon Idée	12	Ge	49.52N	4.21 E
Auxerre	11	Jg	47.48N	3.33 E
Auxi-le-Château	11	Id	50.14N	2.07 E
Auxois ▨	11	Kg	47.20N	4.18 E
Auxonne	11	Lg	47.12N	5.23 E
Auyán-Tepuy ▨	52	Jf	5.55N	62.32W
Auzances	11	Ih	46.01N	2.30 E
Avaavaroa Passage ▷	64p	Bc	21.16 S	159.47W
Availles-Limouzine	11	Gh	46.07N	0.39 E
Avala ▨	15	De	44.42N	20.31 E
Avaldsnes	8	Ae	59.21N	5.16 E
Avallon	11	Kg	47.29N	3.54 E
Avalon Peninsula ▨	42	Mg	47.30N	53.30W
Avan	11	Ge	49.29N	4.35 E
Avaré	55	Hf	23.05 S	48.55W
Avarua Harbour ▷	64p	Bb	21.11 S	159.46W
Avatele	64k	Bb	19.06 S	169.55W
Avatele Bay ▷	64k	Bb	19.05 S	169.56W
Avatiu	64p	Bb	21.12 S	159.47W
Avatiu Harbour	64p	Bb	21.11 S	159.46W
Avatolu, Passe- ▷	64h	Ab	13.19 S	176.—
Ávdhira	15	Hi	40.59N	24.—
Ave ▷	13	Dc	41.20N	8.—
Aveh	24	Ne	34.47N	50.—
Aveh, Gardaneh-ye- ▨	24	Me	35.32N	49.—
Aveiro ▣	13	Dd	40.45N	8.—
Aveiro [Braz.]	54	Gd	3.15 S	55.—
Aveiro [Port.]	13	Dd	40.38N	8.—
Āvej	24	Me	35.34N	49.—
Avelgem	12	Fd	50.46N	3.—
Avellaneda [Arg.]	56	Ic	29.07 S	59.—
Avellaneda [Arg.]	56	Id	34.39 S	58.—
Avellino	14	Ij	40.54N	14.—
Aven Armand ▨	11	Jj	44.15N	3.—
Averbode ▨	12	Gc	51.02N	4.—
Avereest	12	Ib	52.37N	6.—
Avereest-Dedemsvaart	12	Ib	52.37N	6.—
Averøya ▷	7	Be	63.00N	7.—
Aversa	14	Ij	40.58N	14.—
Avesnes-le-Compte	12	Ed	50.17N	2.—
Avesnes-sur-Helpe	12	Fd	50.12N	3.—
Aves Ridge (EN) ▨	47	Lf	14.00N	63.—
Avesta	7	Df	60.09N	16.—
Aveyron ▷	11	Hj	44.05N	1.—
Aveyron ▣	11	Ij	44.15N	2.—
Avezzano	14	Hh	42.02N	13.—
Avgan	15	Mk	38.25N	29.—
Avgó [Grc.] ▷	15	In	35.36N	25.—
Avgó [Grc.] ▷	15	Jn	35.55N	26.—
Aviemore	9	Jd	57.12N	3.—
Avigait	41	Gf	62.15N	50.—
Avigliano	14	Jj	40.44N	15.—
Avignon	6	Gg	43.57N	4.—
Ávila	13	Hd	40.39N	4.—
Ávila ▣	13	Hd	40.35N	5.—
Ávila, Sierra de- ▨	13	Gd	40.35N	5.—
Avilés	13	Ga	43.33N	5.—
Avinurme	8	Lf	58.55N	26.—
Avion	12	Ed	50.24N	2.—
Ávios Theódhoros ▷	15	Gn	35.32N	23.—
Avioth	12	He	49.34N	5.—
Avis	13	Ee	39.03N	7.—
Avisio ▷	14	Hd	46.07N	11.—
Avize	12	Gf	48.58N	4.—
Avlaka Burun ▷	15	Ii	40.07N	25.—
Avola [B.C.-Can.]	46	Fa	51.47N	119.—
Avola [It.]	14	Jn	36.54N	15.—
Avon ▷	9	Kj	51.30N	2.—
Avon [Eng.-U.K.] ▷	9	Kj	51.59N	2.—
Avon [Eng.-U.K.] ▷	9	Kj	51.30N	2.—
Avon [Eng.-U.K.] ▷	9	Lk	50.43N	1.—
Avon Downs	58	Eg	20.05 S	137.—
Avon Park	44	Gl	27.36N	81.—
Avon River ▷	59	Df	31.40 S	116.—
Avranches	11	Je	48.41N	1.—
Avre [Fr.] ▷	11	Ie	49.53N	2.—
Avre [Fr.] ▷	11	Hf	48.47N	1.—
Avrig	15	Hd	45.43N	24.—
Avron ▷	11	Ki	45.15N	4.—
Avşa Adası ▷	15	Ki	40.30N	27.—
Avuavu	63a	Ec	9.50 S	160.—
Awaji ▷	28	Mg	34.35N	135.—
Awaji-Shima ▷	28	Mg	34.25N	134.—
Awanui	61	—	35.03 S	173.—
Awara Plain ▨	36	Hb	3.45N	41.—
Aware	35	Gd	8.14N	44.—
Awarua Bay ▷	62	Cf	44.20 S	168.—
Awasa	31	Kh	7.02N	38.—
Awash	35	Gd	9.00N	40.—
Awash ▷	30	Lg	11.12N	41.—
Awa-Shima ▷	28	Oe	38.27N	139.—
Awaso	34	Ed	6.14N	2.—
Awat	27	Dc	40.38N	80.—
Awata ▷	35	Fe	4.45N	39.—
Awatere ▷	62	Fd	41.36 S	174.—
Awbārī	31	If	26.35N	12.—
Awbārī ▣	33	Bd	26.35N	12.—
Awbārī, Şaḥrā' ▨	30	If	27.30N	11.—
Awdégle	35	Ge	1.58N	44.—
Awe, Loch- ▨	9	He	56.15N	5.—
Awjilah	31	Jf	29.06N	21.—
Axel	12	Fc	51.16N	3.—
Axel Heiberg ▷	38	Ja	80.30N	92.—
Axim	34	Ed	4.52N	2.—
Axiós ▷	15	Fi	40.35N	22.—
Axixá	54	Jd	2.51 S	44.—
Ax-les-Thermes	11	Hl	42.43N	1.—
Ayabaca	54	Cd	4.38 S	79.—
Ayabe	28	Mg	35.18N	135.—
Ayachi, Ari n'- ▨	32	Gc	32.30N	4.—
Ayacucho [Arg.]	56	Ie	37.09 S	58.—
Ayacucho [Peru]	53	Ig	13.07 S	74.—
Ayakita-Gawa ▷	29	Bf	31.58N	131.—
Ayakkum Hu ▨	27	Ed	37.30N	89.—
Ayamé	34	Ed	5.36N	3.—
Ayamonte	13	Eg	37.13N	7.—
Ayangba	34	Fd	7.31N	7.—
Ayapel	54	Cb	8.18N	75.—
Ayaviri	54	Df	14.52 S	70.—
Āybak	23	Kb	36.16N	68.—
Aybastı	24	Gb	40.41N	37.—
'Aydim, Wādī- ▷	9	Lg	54.36N	1.—
Aydın	23	Cb	37.51N	27.—
Aydıncik	24	Ec	36.08N	33.—
Aydıngkol Hu ▨	27	Ec	42.40N	89.—
Aydınkent	24	Ec	37.06N	31.—
Aydos Dağı ▨	24	Fd	37.21N	34.—
Ayerbe	13	La	42.17N	0.—
Ayer Hitam	26	Df	1.55N	103.—

Index Symbols

- ▢ Independent Nation
- ▣ State, Region
- ▤ District, County
- ▥ Municipality
- ▦ Colony, Dependency
- ■ Continent
- ▨ Physical Region
- ▧ Historical or Cultural Region
- ▲ Mount, Mountain
- Volcano
- Hill
- Mountains, Mountain Range
- Hills, Escarpment
- Plateau, Upland
- Pass, Gap
- Plain, Lowland
- Delta
- Salt Flat
- Valley, Canyon
- Crater, Cave
- Karst Features
- Depression
- Polder
- Cliff
- Desert, Dunes
- Forest, Woods
- Heath, Steppe
- Oasis
- Cape, Point
- Coast, Beach
- Islands, Archipelago
- Rocks, Reefs
- Coral Reef
- Well, Spring
- Island
- Atoll
- Waterfall Rapids
- River Mouth, Estuary
- Lake
- Intermittent Lake
- Geyser
- Reservoir
- River, Stream
- Swamp, Pond
- Canal
- Glacier
- Ice Shelf, Pack Ice
- Ocean
- Sea
- Gulf, Bay
- Strait, Fjord
- Lagoon
- Bank
- Seamount
- Tablemount
- Ridge
- Shelf
- Basin
- Escarpment, Sea Scarp
- Fracture
- Trench, Abyss
- National Park, Reserve
- Point of Interest
- Recreation Site
- Cave, Cavern
- Historic Site
- Ruins
- Wall, Walls
- Church, Abbey
- Temple
- Scientific Station
- Airport
- Port
- Lighthouse
- Mine
- Tunnel
- Dam, Bridge

ā 15 Fj 39.43N 22.46 E
a Marina 15 Jl 37.09N 26.52 E
isos 15 Jj 39.06N 26.22 E
a Triás 15 Hn 35.04N 24.45 E
na 36 Bb 1.48N 13.10 E
on Óros 15 Hi 40.15N 24.15 E
on Óros=Athos, Mount-
N) 15 Hi 40.15N 24.15 E
os Evstrátios 15 Hj 39.31N 25.00 E
os Ioánnis, Ákra- 15 In 35.20N 25.46 E
os Kírikos 15 Jl 37.35N 26.14 E
os Minás 15 Jl 37.36N 26.34 E
os Nikólaos 15 In 35.11N 25.43 E
os Yeóryios 15 Jl 37.28N 23.56 E
iota 35 Fb 15.10N 37.03 E
esbury 9 Mj 51.50N 0.50W
ón, Sierra de- 13 Ic 41.15N 3.25W
ner Lake 42 Gd 64.05N 108.30W
sham 12 Db 52.47N 1.15 E
a 13 Jf 38.33N 2.05W
nabo 35 Hd 8.57N 46.30 E
n ad Darāhim 14 Cn 36.47N 8.42 E
n al Bayḍā 24 Ge 34.32N 37.55 E
n al Ghazāl [Eg.] 24 Dj 25.46N 30.38 E
n al Ghazāl [Lib.] 31 Jf 21.50N 24.55 E
n al Shigi 24 Ci 27.01N 28.02 E
n al Wādī 24 Ci 27.23N 28.13 E
n Bū Sālim 14 Cn 36.37N 8.59 E
n Dāllah 33 Ed 27.19N 27.20 E
n Dār 24 Mj 25.58N 49.14 E
n Dīwār 24 Jd 37.17N 42.11 E
n Ilwān 24 Dj 25.44N 30.25 E
n Khalīfah 24 Bi 26.46N 27.47 E
n Sifnī 24 Jd 36.42N 43.21 E
n Sukhnah 33 Fd 29.30N 32.10 E
nūnah 23 Ed 28.05N 35.08 E
d 35 Ed 8.08N 31.24 E
ra 13 Ke 39.04N 1.03W
rou 34 Fc 14.44N 0.55 E
oûn el 'Atroûs 31 Gg 16.38N 9.36W
9 If 55.29N 4.28W
[Austl.] 59 Jc 19.35S 147.24 E
[Scot.-U.K.] 9 If 55.28N 4.38W
e, Point of- 9 Ig 54.26N 4.22W
olle, Étang de l'- 11 Jk 43.16N 3.30 E
sha 35 Gc 10.45N 42.35 E
ré 11 Eh 46.08N 1.06W
atla 48 Gg 20.07N 104.22W
atla de los Libres 48 Ji 16.54N 99.13W
acık 24 Gb 41.00N 36.45 E
acik 15 Jj 39.36N 26.24 E
alık 23 Cb 39.18N 26.41 E
vaille 12 Hd 50.28N 5.40 E
idshahr 24 Pd 37.05N 55.08 E
ahar, Costa del- 13 Me 39.58N 0.01 E
aila 13 Lc 41.17N 0.29W
ambuja 13 De 39.04N 8.52W
amgarh 25 Gc 26.04N 83.11 E
angaro 54 Df 14.55S 70.13W
annes-et-Soumazannes 12 He 49.18N 5.28 E
aouâd=Azaouad (EN) 30 Gg 19.00N 3.00W
aouad (EN)=Azaouâd 30 Gg 19.00N 3.00W
aouak 34 Fb 15.30N 3.18 E
aouak 30 Hg 15.20N 4.55 E
aouak, Vallée de l'- 30 Hg 17.30N 3.40 E
ar 34 Fb 16.02N 4.04 E
arbāijān-e Gharbī 23 Fb 37.00N 45.00 E
arbāijān-e Sharqī 23 Gb 37.00N 47.00 E
arbaijčan Sovet
ocialistik Respublicasy/
zerbajdžanskaja SSR 19 Eg 40.30N 47.30 E
are 34 Hc 11.41N 10.12 E
ār Shahr 24 Kd 37.45N 45.59 E
ay-le-Rideau 11 Gg 47.16N 0.28 E
zāz 24 Gd 36.35N 37.03 E
azga 13 Qh 36.44N 4.22 E
bine/Air 30 Hg 18.00N 8.30 E
daak, Gora- 16 Ni 40.13N 44.59 E
davay 24 Eb 41.39N 33.18 E
efal 30 Ff 21.00N 14.45W
effoun 13 Qh 36.53N 4.25 E
emmour 32 Fc 33.17N 8.21W
erbaidzhan (EN) 21 Gf 37.00N 46.00 E
erbaidzhan SSR (EN)=
zerbajdžanskaja SSR 19 Eg 40.30N 47.30 E
erbajdžanskaja
ovetskaja
ocialističeskaja
espublika 19 Eg 40.30N 47.30 E
erbajdžanskaja SSR/
zarbaijčan Sovet
ocialistik Respublicasy 19 Eg 40.30N 47.30 E
erbajdžanskaja SSR=
zerbaidzhan SSR (EN) 19 Eg 40.30N 47.30 E
eri/Aseri 7 Gg 59.29N 26.51 E
evedo Sodré 55 Ej 30.04S 54.36W
ezo 35 Fc 12.33N 37.25 E
ilal 32 Fc 32.09N 6.05W
ilal 32 Fc 31.58N 6.35W
nā 24 Mf 33.56N 49.24 E
nakajevo 7 Mi 54.56N 53.04 E
ogues 54 Cd 2.44S 78.48W
ores (EN)=Açores 31 Ee 38.30N 28.00W
ores (EN)=Açores,
Arquipélago dos- 30 Ee 38.30N 28.00W
ores-Gibraltar Ridge (EN)
3 Df 37.00N 16.00W
oum, Bahr- 30 Jg 10.53N 20.15 E
ov 19 Df 47.05N 39.25 E
ov, Sea of- (EN)=
Azovskoje More 5 Jf 46.00N 36.00 E
ovskoje More=Azov, Sea
of- (EN) 5 Jf 46.00N 36.00 E
peitia 13 Ja 43.11N 2.16W
rak, Bahr- 35 Bc 10.50N 19.50 E
raq, Al Baḥr al-=Blue
Nile (EN) 30 Kg 15.38N 32.31 E
Azraq ash Shīshān 24 Gg 31.50N 36.49 E
Azrou 32 Fc 33.26N 5.13W
Aztec 45 Ch 36.49N 107.59W
Aztec Ruins 46 Kh 36.51N 108.10W
Azua 49 Ld 18.27N 70.44W
Azuaga 13 Gf 38.16N 5.41W
Azuar 13 Ie 39.08N 3.36W
Azuero, Peninsula de-=
Azuero Peninsula (EN) 38 Ki 7.40N 80.30W
Azuero Peninsula (EN)=
Azuero, Peninsula de- 38 Ki 7.40N 80.30W
Azul 53 Ki 36.45S 59.50W
Azul, Arroyo del- 55 Cm 36.15S 59.07W
Azul, Cerro- 54a Ab 0.54S 91.21W
Azul, Cordillera- 54 Ce 8.30S 76.00W
Azul, Rio- 48 Oi 17.54N 88.52W
Azul, Serra- 55 Eb 14.50S 54.50W
Azul, Sierras del- 55 Cm 37.02S 59.55W
Azūm 35 Cc 10.53N 20.15 E
Azuma-San 29 Gc 37.44N 140.08 E
Azur, Côte d'- 11 Mk 43.30N 7.00 E
Azurduy 54 Fg 19.59S 64.29W
Azzaba 32 Ib 36.44N 7.06 E
Az Zāb al Kabīr 23 Fb 36.00N 43.21 E
Az Zāb aş Şaghīr 23 Fb 35.12N 43.25 E
Az Zabdānī 24 Gf 33.43N 36.05 E
Az Zabū 24 Ch 28.22N 28.56 E
Az Ẓafīr 23 Ff 19.57N 41.30 E
Az Zaghāwa 35 Cb 15.15N 23.14 E
Az Ẓāhirah 24 Qk 23.30N 56.15 E
Az Zallāq 24 Ni 26.03N 50.29 E
Az Zaqāzīq 33 Fc 30.35N 31.31 E
Az Zarqā' 24 Oj 24.53N 53.04 E
Az Zarqā' 24 Gf 32.05N 36.06 E
Az Zāwiyah 33 Bc 32.40N 12.10 E
Az Zāwiyah 33 Bc 32.45N 12.44 E
Az Zaytūn 33 Ed 29.09N 25.47 E
Azzel Matti, Sebkha- 30 Hf 26.00N 0.55 E
Az Zilfī 24 Ki 26.18N 44.48 E
Az Zubayr 24 Lg 30.23N 47.43 E

B

Baa 26 Hi 10.43S 123.03 E
Baaba 63b Ae 20.03S 163.58 E
Ba'ādwēyn 35 Hd 7.12N 47.24 E
Ba an Daingin/Dingle
Bay 9 Ci 52.05N 10.15W
Baar 10 Ei 48.00N 8.30 E
Baarle-Hertog 12 Gc 51.27N 4.56 E
Baarn 12 Hb 52.14N 5.17 E
Baas, Bassure de- 12 Dd 50.30N 1.15 E
Bāb 24 Ok 23.55N 53.45 E
Baba 35 Bd 6.25N 17.07 E
Baba 15 Ei 40.55N 21.10 E
Baba Burun [Tur.] 24 Db 41.18N 31.26 E
Baba Burun [Tur.] 24 Bc 39.29N 26.04 E
Babadağ 15 Ll 37.48N 28.52 E
Baba Dağ 15 Mm 36.32N 29.10 E
Babadag 15 Le 44.54N 28.43 E
Babadag, Gora- 16 Pi 41.01N 48.29 E
Babaeski 24 Bb 41.26N 27.06 E
Bābā-Ḥeydar 24 Nf 32.20N 50.28 E
Babajevo 19 Dd 59.24N 35.55 E
Babajtag, Gora- 18 Hd 41.13N 70.16 E
Babajurt 16 Oh 43.35N 46.47 E
Bāb al Māndab=Bab el
Mandeb (EN) 30 Lg 12.35N 43.25 E
Babanūsah 35 Dc 11.20N 27.48 E
Babao → Qilian 27 Hd 38.14N 100.15 E
Babaoyo 54 Cd 1.50S 79.30W
Babar, Kepulauan- 26 Ih 7.50S 129.45 E
Babar, Pulau- 57 De 7.55S 129.45 E
Babase 63a Aa 4.01S 153.42 E
Babatag, Hrebet- 18 Ge 38.00N 68.10 E
Babati 36 Gc 4.13S 35.45 E
Babbitt 45 Kc 47.43N 91.57W
B'abdā 24 Ff 33.50N 35.32 E
Bab el Mandeb (EN)=Bāb
al Māndab 30 Lg 12.35N 43.25 E
Babelthuap Island 57 Ed 7.30N 134.36 E
Babenhausen [F.R.G.] 12 Ke 49.58N 8.57 E
Babenhausen [F.R.G.] 10 Gh 48.09N 10.15 E
Babeni 15 He 44.59N 24.15 E
Baberton 44 Ge 41.02N 81.38W
Bá Bheanntrai/Bantry
Bay 9 Dj 51.38N 9.48W
Babian Jiang=Black River
(EN) 21 Mg 20.17N 106.34 E
Babil 24 Kf 32.40N 44.50 E
Babine Lake 42 Ef 54.45N 126.00W
Babino Polje 14 Lh 42.43N 17.33 E
Babit Point 51b Ab 18.03N 63.02W
Babo 26 Jg 2.33S 133.25 E
Bābol 23 Hb 36.34N 52.42 E
Babol Sar 24 Od 36.43N 52.39 E
Baboquivari Peak 46 Jk 31.46N 111.35W
Babor, Djebel- 13 Rh 36.32N 5.28 E
Baborigame 48 Fd 26.27N 107.16W
Baboua 35 Ad 5.48N 14.49 E
Babozero, Ozero- 7 Ic 66.30N 37.25 E
Babu → Hexian 27 Jg 24.28N 111.34 E
Babuna 15 Eh 41.30N 21.40 E
Babuyan 26 Hc 19.32N 121.57 E
Babuyan 26 Gd 10.01N 118.58 E
Babuyan Channel 26 Hc 18.44N 121.40 E
Babuyan Islands 21 Oh 19.15N 121.40 E
Babylon 23 Fc 32.32N 44.25 E
Bač 15 Cd 45.23N 19.14 E
Bacabachi 48 Ed 26.55N 109.24W
Bacabal 53 Lf 4.14S 44.47W
Ba-Cagan 27 Gb 45.40N 99.30 E
Bacajá, Rio- 54 Hd 3.25S 51.50W
Bacalar 48 Oh 18.43N 88.27W
Bacalar, Laguna de- 48 Oh 18.43N 88.22W
Bacalar Chico, Boca- 49 Dd 18.12N 87.53W
Bacan, Kepulauan- 26 Ig 0.35S 127.30 E
Bacan, Pulau- 26 Ig 0.35S 127.30 E
Bacău 15 Jc 46.36N 27.00 E
Bacău 6 If 46.34N 26.54 E
Baccarat 11 Mf 48.27N 6.45 E
Bacchiglione 14 Ge 45.11N 12.14 E
Baceşti 15 Kc 46.51N 27.14 E
Bachaquero 49 Li 9.56N 71.08W
Bacharach 12 Jd 50.04N 7.46 E
Bacheli 25 Ge 18.40N 81.15 E
Bachiniva 48 Fc 28.45N 107.15W
Bachu/Maralwexi 27 Cd 39.46N 78.15 E
Back 38 Jd 67.15N 95.15W
Bačka 15 Cd 45.50N 19.30 E
Bac Kan 25 Ld 22.08N 105.49 E
Bačka Palanka 15 Cd 45.15N 19.22 E
Bačka Topola 15 Cd 45.49N 19.39 E
Bäckefors 8 Ef 58.48N 12.10 E
Bäckhammar 8 Fe 59.10N 14.11 E
Backnang 10 Fh 48.57N 9.26 E
Bačkovski Manastir 15 Hh 41.56N 24.51 E
Bac Lieu 25 Lg 9.17N 105.43 E
Bac Ninh 25 Ld 21.11N 106.03 E
Bacolet 51p Bb 12.02N 61.41W
Bacolod 22 Oh 10.40N 122.57 E
Bac-Phan=Tonkin (EN) 21 Mg 22.00N 105.00 E
Bacqueville, Lac- 42 Ke 58.00N 74.00W
Bacqueville-en Caux 12 Ce 49.47N 1.00 E
Bácsalmás 10 Pj 46.08N 19.20 E
Bács-Kiskun 10 Pj 46.30N 19.25 E
Bacton 12 Db 52.51N 1.28 E
Bād 23 Hc 33.41N 52.01 E
Badagara 25 Ff 11.36N 75.35 E
Badagri 34 Fd 6.25N 2.53 E
Badain Jaran Shamo 21 Me 40.20N 101.40 E
Badajós, Lago- 54 Fd 3.15S 62.45W
Badajoz 6 Fh 38.53N 6.58W
Badajoz 13 Ff 38.40N 6.10W
Badakhshan 23 Lb 36.45N 72.00 E
Badalona 13 Oc 41.27N 2.15 E
Badanah 23 Fc 30.59N 41.02 E
Badaohao 28 Fd 41.50N 121.59 E
Badas, Kepulauan- 26 Ef 0.35N 107.06 E
Bad Aussee 14 Hc 47.36N 13.47 E
Bad Axe 44 Fd 43.48N 83.00W
Bad Bergzabern 10 Dg 49.06N 8.00 E
Bad Berleburg 12 Kc 51.04N 8.24 E
Bad Bertrich 12 Jd 50.03N 7.02 E
Bad Bramstedt 10 Fc 53.55N 9.53 E
Bad Brückenau 10 Ff 50.18N 9.45 E
Badda 35 Fd 7.55N 39.23 E
Baddo 25 Cc 27.59N 64.21 E
Bad Doberan 10 Hb 54.06N 11.54 E
Bad Driburg 12 Lc 51.44N 9.01 E
Bad Düben 10 Ie 51.36N 12.35 E
Bad Dürkheim 12 Ke 49.28N 8.12 E
Bade 26 Kh 7.10S 139.35 E
Bademli 15 Lk 38.04N 28.04 E
Baden [Aus.] 14 Kb 48.01N 16.14 E
Baden [Switz.] 14 Cc 47.28N 8.18 E
Baden-Baden 10 Eh 48.45N 8.15 E
Badenoch 9 Je 56.50N 4.00W
Baden-Württemberg 10 Eh 48.30N 9.00 E
Bad Essen 12 Kb 52.19N 8.20 E
Bad Freienwalde 10 Kd 52.47N 14.02 E
Badgastein 14 Hc 47.07N 13.08 E
Bādghīsat 23 Jc 35.00N 63.45 E
Bad Gleichenberg 14 Jd 46.52N 15.54 E
Bad Godesberg, Bonn- 10 Df 50.41N 7.09 E
Bad Hall 14 Ib 48.02N 14.12 E
Bad Harzburg 10 Ge 51.53N 10.34 E
Bad Herrenalb 12 Kf 48.48N 8.25 E
Bad Hersfeld 10 Ff 50.52N 9.42 E
Bad Homburg 10 Ef 50.13N 8.37 E
Bad Honnef 12 Jd 50.38N 7.12 E
Bá Dhún na nGall/Donegal
Bay 5 Fe 54.30N 8.30W
Badhyz 18 Cg 35.50N 62.00 E
Badiraguato 48 Fe 25.22N 107.31W
Bad Ischl 14 Hc 47.43N 13.37 E
Bad Kissingen 10 Gf 50.12N 10.05 E
Bad Kreuznach 10 Dg 49.50N 7.52 E
Badlands [S.D.-U.S.] 45 Ee 43.30N 102.20W
Badlands [U.S.] 43 Gb 46.45N 103.30W
Bad Langensalza 10 Ge 51.06N 10.39 E
Bad Lautenberg am Harz 10 Ge 51.38N 10.28 E
Bad Liebenwerda 10 Je 51.31N 13.24 E
Bad Liebenzel 12 Kf 48.46N 8.44 E
Bad Mergentheim 10 Fg 49.29N 9.46 E
Bad Mondorf/Mondorf-les-
Bains 12 Ie 49.30N 6.17 E
Bad Münster am Stein
Ebernburg 12 Je 49.49N 7.51 E
Bad Münstereifel 12 Id 50.34N 6.45 E
Bad Muskau 10 Ke 51.33N 14.43 E
Bad Nauheim 12 Kd 50.22N 8.45 E
Bad Neuenahr-Ahrweiler 10 Df 50.33N 7.08 E
Bad Neustadt an der Saale 10 Gf 50.20N 10.13 E
Bad Oeynhausen 12 Kb 52.12N 8.48 E
Bad Oldesloe 10 Gc 53.49N 10.23 E
Ba Don 25 Le 17.45N 106.27 E
Badou [China] 28 Df 36.27N 117.56 E
Badou [Togo] 34 Fd 7.35N 0.36 E
Bad Pyrmont 10 Fe 51.59N 9.15 E
Bad Ragaz 14 Dc 47.00N 9.30 E
Badrah 24 Kf 33.06N 45.58 E
Bad Reichenhall 10 Ii 47.44N 12.53 E
Badr Ḥunayn 23 Ee 23.44N 38.46 E
Bad River 45 Fd 44.22N 100.22W
Bad Salzuflen 12 Kb 52.05N 8.46 E
Bad Salzungen 10 Gf 50.49N 10.14 E
Bad Schwartau 10 Gc 53.55N 10.42 E
Bad Segeberg 10 Gc 53.56N 10.19 E
Bad Tölz 10 Hi 47.46N 11.34 E
Badulla 25 Gg 6.59N 81.03 E
Bad Wildungen 10 Fe 51.07N 9.07 E
Bad Wimpfen 10 Fg 49.14N 9.08 E
Baena 13 Hg 37.37N 4.19W
Baeza [Ec.] 54 Cd 0.28S 77.53W
Baeza [Sp.] 13 Ig 37.59N 3.28W
Baf/Paphos 24 Ee 34.50N 32.35 E
Bafang 34 Hd 5.09N 10.11 E
Bafatá 31 Fg 12.10N 14.40W
Bafélé 34 Cc 10.09N 10.08W
Baffin 38 Mc 68.00N 70.00W
Baffin Bay 38 Mb 73.00N 65.00W
Bafia 34 He 4.45N 11.14 E
Bafilo 34 Fd 9.21N 1.16 E
Bafing [Afr.] 30 Fg 13.49N 10.50W
Bafing [I.C.] 34 Dd 7.52N 7.07W
Bafoulabé 34 Cc 13.48N 10.50W
Bafoussam 31 Ih 5.28N 10.25 E
Bāfq 23 Ic 31.35N 55.24 E
Bāfq, Kūh-e- 24 Pg 31.20N 55.10 E
Bafra 23 Ea 41.34N 35.56 E
Bafra Burnu 24 Fb 41.44N 35.58 E
Bāft 24 Qh 29.14N 56.38 E
Bafwaboli 36 Eb 0.39N 26.10 E
Bafwasende 36 Eb 1.05N 27.16 E
Baga 34 Hc 13.06N 13.50 E
Bagaces 49 Eh 10.31N 85.15W
Bagagem, Rio- 55 Ha 13.58S 48.21W
Bagajevski 16 Lf 47.19N 40.25 E
Bāgalkot 25 Fe 16.11N 75.42 E
Bagamoyo 36 Gd 6.26S 38.54 E
Bagansiapi-Api 26 Df 2.09N 100.49 E
Bağarasi 15 Kl 37.42N 27.33 E
Baga Sola 35 Ac 13.32N 14.19 E
Bagata 36 Cc 3.44S 17.57 E
Bagdad 48 Ke 25.57N 97.09W
Bagdarin 20 Gf 54.30N 113.36 E
Bağdere 24 Ic 38.10N 40.45 E
Bagé 53 Ki 31.20S 54.06W
Bages et de Sigean, Étang
de- 11 Jk 43.05N 3.01 E
Baggs 46 Lf 41.02N 107.39W
Bāgh Baile na Sgealg/
Ballinskelligs Bay 9 Cj 51.50N 10.15W
Baghdād 24 Kf 33.18N 44.36 E
Baghdād 22 Gf 33.21N 44.23 E
Baghdādī, Ra's- 24 Fj 24.40N 35.06 E
Bāgh-e Chenar 24 Qh 28.11N 56.54 E
Bāgh-e-Malek 24 Mg 31.32N 49.55 E
Bagheria 14 Hl 38.05N 13.30 E
Bāghīn 23 Ic 30.12N 56.48 E
Baghlān 23 Kb 35.45N 69.00 E
Baghlān 23 Kb 36.13N 68.46 E
Bāglung 25 Gc 28.16N 83.36 E
Bagn 8 Cd 60.49N 9.34 E
Bagnara Calabra 14 Jl 38.17N 15.48 E
Bagnères-de-Bigorre 11 Gk 43.04N 0.09 E
Bagnères-de-Luchon 11 Gl 42.47N 0.36 E
Bagni di Lucca 14 Ef 44.01N 10.35 E
Bagno di Romagna 14 Fg 43.50N 11.57 E
Bagnolo Mella 14 Ee 45.26N 10.10 E
Bagnols-sur-Cèze 11 Kj 44.10N 4.37 E
Bagoé 30 Gg 12.36N 6.34W
Bagolino 14 Ee 45.49N 10.28 E
Bagrationovsk 8 Ij 54.23N 20.40 E
Bagrax/Bohu 27 Ec 41.58N 86.29 E
Bagrax Hu/Bosten 21 Ke 42.00N 87.00 E
Bagua 54 Ce 5.40S 78.31W
Baguio 22 Oh 16.25N 120.36 E
Baguirmi 30 Ig 11.40N 16.20 E
Bagzane, Monts- 30 Hg 17.43N 8.45 E
Bahama Islands 38 Lg 24.15N 76.00W
Bahamas 39 Lg 24.15N 76.00W
Bahamas, Canal Viejo de-=
Old Bahama Channel (EN)
49 Ib 22.30N 78.05W
Bahār 24 Me 34.54N 48.26 E
Baharden 19 Fh 38.28N 57.28 E
Bahardok 19 Fh 38.51N 58.24 E
Bahariyah, Wāḥāt al- 33 Ed 28.10N 29.00 E
Baḥariyah, Wāḥāt al-=
Bahariya Oasis (EN) 33 Ed 28.15N 28.57 E
Bahariya Oasis (EN)=
Baḥariyah, Wāḥāt al- 33 Ed 28.15N 28.57 E
Bahaur 26 Fg 3.20N 114.00 E
Bahāwalnagar 25 Ec 29.59N 73.16 E
Bahāwalpur 22 Jg 29.24N 71.41 E
Bahčisaraj 16 Hg 44.45N 33.51 E
Bahçe 24 Gd 37.14N 36.34 E
Bahi 36 Gd 5.39S 35.19 E
Bahia 54 Jf 12.00S 42.00W
Bahia, Islas de la- 47 Ge 16.20N 86.30W
Bahia Blanca 53 Ji 38.44S 62.16W
Bahia de Caráquez 54 Bd 0.37S 80.25W
Bahia Kino 47 Bc 28.50N 111.55W
Bahia Negra 56 Ib 20.15S 58.12W
Bahias, Cabo dos- 52 Jj 44.55S 65.32W
Bahīj 24 Cg 30.56N 29.35 E
Bahinga 36 Ed 5.57S 27.06 E
Bahi Swamp 36 Gd 6.05S 35.10 E
Bahlui 15 Kb 47.08N 27.44 E
Bahmač 16 Ge 51.11N 32.50 E
Bahoruco, Sierra de- 49 Ld 18.10N 71.25W
Bahraich 25 Gc 27.35N 81.36 E
Bahrain (EN)=Al
Baḥrayn 22 Hg 26.00N 50.29 E
Baḥr al Ghazāl 35 Dd 8.15N 26.50 E
Bahr ar Ramla al Kabīr 33 Ed 27.00N 26.00 E
Baḥrayn, Khalij al- 24 Nj 25.45N 50.40 E
Bahr Dar 31 Kg 11.36N 37.22 E
Bahta 20 Dd 62.20N 89.15 E
Bahusi 15 Jc 46.43N 26.42 E
Baia 15 Le 44.43N 28.40 E
Baia de Aramă 15 Fe 45.00N 22.50 E
Baia de Fier 15 Gd 45.10N 23.46 E
Baia dos Tigres 36 Bf 16.35S 11.43 E
Baia Farta 36 Be 12.37S 13.26 E
Baia Mare 15 Gb 47.40N 23.35 E
Baião 54 Id 2.41S 49.41W
Baia Sprie 15 Gb 47.40N 23.42 E
Baibiene 55 Ci 29.36S 58.10W
Baïbokoum 35 Bd 7.45N 15.41 E
Baicheng 22 Oe 45.34N 122.49 E
Baicheng/Bay 27 Dc 41.46N 81.52 E
Băicoi 15 Id 45.02N 25.51 E
Băiculeşti 15 Hd 45.04N 24.42 E
Baidou 35 Cc 5.52N 20.41 E
Baie-Comeau 39 Me 49.13N 68.10W
Baie-du-Poste 42 Kf 50.30N 74.00W
Baie-Mahault 50 Fd 16.16N 61.35W
Baie-Saint-Paul 42 Kg 47.27N 70.30W
Baie-Trinité 44 Na 49.24N 67.19W
Baie Verte 42 Lg 49.55N 56.11W
Baiguan → Shangyu 28 Fi 30.01N 120.53 E
Baihe 27 Je 32.46N 110.06 E
Bai He [China] 28 Bh 32.10N 112.20 E
Bai He [China] 28 Dd 40.43N 116.33 E
Baikal, Lake- (EN)=Bajkal,
Ozero- 21 Md 53.00N 107.40 E
Baikal Range (EN)=
Bajkalski Hrebet 21 Md 55.00N 108.40 E
Baile an Chaistil/Ballycastle 9 Gf 55.12N 6.15W
Baile an Róba/Ballinrobe 9 Dh 53.37N 9.13W
Baile Átha Cliath/Dublin 9 Gh 53.20N 6.15W
Baile Átha Cliath/Dublin 6 Fe 53.20N 6.15W
Baile Átha Luain/Athlone 9 Fh 53.25N 7.56W
Baile Átha Troim/Trim 9 Gh 53.34N 6.47W
Băile Borşa 15 Hb 47.41N 24.43 E
Baile Brigín/Balbriggan 9 Gh 53.37N 6.11W
Băile Govora 15 Hd 45.05N 24.11 E
Baile Locha Riach/Loughrea 9 Eh 53.12N 8.34W
Baile Mhistéala/
Mitchelstown 9 Ei 52.16N 8.16W
Bailén 13 If 38.06N 3.46W
Baile na Mainistreach/
Newtownabbey 9 Hg 54.42N 5.54W
Baile Nua na hArda/
Newtownards 9 Hg 54.36N 5.41W
Băile Olăneşti 15 Hd 45.12N 24.14 E
Băileşti 15 Ge 44.01N 23.21 E
Bailleul 12 Ce 49.12N 0.26 E
Bailleul 12 Ed 50.44N 2.44 E
Ba Illi 35 Bc 10.31N 16.29 E
Bailong Jiang 27 Ie 32.42N 105.15 E
Bailundo 36 Ce 12.10S 15.56 E
Baima 27 He 33.05N 100.29 E
Bain 12 Ba 53.04N 0.12W
Bainbridge 43 Ke 30.54N 84.34W
Bain-de-Bretagne 11 Eg 47.50N 1.41W
Baines Drift 37 Dd 22.30S 28.43 E
Baing 26 Hi 10.14S 120.34 E
Baingoin 27 Ee 31.36N 89.48 E
Baiquan 27 Mb 47.38N 126.04 E
Bā'ir 24 Gg 30.46N 36.41 E
Bā'ir, Wādī- 24 Gg 31.12N 37.31 E
Baird 45 Gj 32.24N 99.24W
Baird Inlet 40 Gd 60.45N 164.00W
Baird Mountains 40 Gc 67.35N 161.30W
Baird Peninsula 42 Jc 69.00N 75.15W
Bairiki 58 Id 1.20N 173.01 E
Bairin Youqi (Daban) 27 Kc 43.30N 118.37 E
Bairin Zuoqi (Lindong) 27 Kc 43.59N 119.22 E
Bairnsdale 58 Fh 37.50S 147.38 E
Bais 26 He 9.35N 123.07 E
Bai Shan 27 Fe 40.53N 93.48 E
Baisogala/Bajsogala 8 Ji 55.35N 23.44 E
Baitou Shan 21 Oe 42.00N 128.00 E
Baitoushan Tian Chi 28 Jc 42.00N 128.03 E
Baixiang 28 Cf 37.29N 114.44 E
Baixo Alentejo 13 Dg 37.55N 8.10W
Baixo Guandu 54 Jg 19.31S 41.01W
Baixo Longa 36 Cf 15.42S 18.38 E
Baiyanghe 27 Ec 43.12N 88.28 E
Baiyü 27 Ge 31.13N 98.51 E
Baja 10 Oj 46.11N 18.58 E
Baja, Punta- [Mex.] 48 Dc 28.25N 111.45W
Baja, Punta- [Pas.] 65d Ab 27.10S 109.22W
Baja California=Lower
California (EN) 38 Hg 28.00N 112.00W
Baja California Norte 47 Ac 30.00N 115.00W
Baja California Sur 47 Bd 25.50N 111.50W
Bājah 32 Ib 36.30N 9.30 E
Bājah 32 Ib 36.44N 9.11 E
Bajalān 24 Md 37.18N 48.47 E
Bajan 27 Jb 49.15N 111.58 E
Bajanaul 19 He 50.47N 75.42 E
Bajandaj 20 Ff 53.04N 105.30 E
Bajan-Delger 27 Jb 45.55N 112.15 E
Bajangol 20 Ff 50.40N 103.25 E
Bajan-Hongor 22 Me 46.20N 100.40 E
Bajan-Ula [Mong.] 27 Jb 49.07N 112.45 E
Bajan-Ula [Mong.] 27 Gb 47.05N 95.15 E
Bajan-Under 27 Gc 44.45N 98.45 E
Baja Verapaz 49 Bf 15.05N 90.20W
Bajawa 26 Hh 8.47S 120.59 E
Bajčunas 16 Rf 47.17N 53.03 E
Bajdarackaja Guba 20 Bc 69.00N 67.30 E
Bajdarata 17 Nb 68.12N 68.18 E
Bajdrag Gol 27 Hb 45.10N 100.45 E
Bājgīrān 24 Rd 37.36N 58.24 E
Baj-Haak 20 Ef 51.07N 94.34 E
Bajiazi 28 Jc 42.41N 129.13 E
Bajina Bašta 15 Cf 43.58N 19.34 E
Bajkal 20 Ff 51.53N 104.47 E
Bajkal, Ozero-=Baikal,
Lake- (EN) 21 Md 53.00N 107.40 E
Bajkalovo 17 Kh 57.24N 63.40 E
Bajkalsk 20 Ff 51.30N 104.05 E
Bajkalski Hrebet=Baikal
Range (EN) 21 Md 55.00N 108.40 E
Bajkit 20 Ed 61.41N 96.25 E
Bajkonur 19 Gf 47.50N 66.07 E
Bajmak 19 Fe 52.36N 58.19 E
Bajmba, Mount- 59 Ke 29.20S 152.05 E
Bajmok 15 Cd 45.58N 19.26 E
Bajo Baudó 54 Cc 4.58N 77.22W

ndex Symbols

Independent Nation
State, Region
District, County
Municipality
Colony, Dependency
Continent
Physical Region
Historical or Cultural Region
Mount, Mountain
Volcano
Hill
Mountains, Mountain Range
Hills, Escarpment
Plateau, Upland
Pass, Gap
Plain, Lowland
Delta
Salt Flat
Valley, Canyon
Crater, Cave
Karst Features
Depression
Polder
Desert, Dunes
Forest, Woods
Heath, Steppe
Oasis
Cape, Point
Coast, Beach
Cliff
Peninsula
Isthmus
Sandbank
Island
Atoll
Rock, Reef
Islands, Archipelago
Rocks, Reefs
Coral Reef
Well, Spring
Geyser
River, Stream
Waterfall Rapids
River Mouth, Estuary
Lake
Salt Lake
Intermittent Lake
Reservoir
Swamp, Pond
Canal
Glacier
Ice Shelf, Pack Ice
Ocean
Sea
Gulf, Bay
Strait, Fjord
Lagoon
Bank
Seamount
Tablemount
Ridge
Shelf
Basin
Escarpment, Sea Scarp
Fracture
Trench, Abyss
National Park, Reserve
Point of Interest
Recreation Site
Cave, Cavern
Historic Site
Ruins
Wall, Walls
Church, Abbey
Temple
Scientific Station
Airport
Port
Lighthouse
Mine
Tunnel
Dam, Bridge

Index Symbols

- [1] Independent Nation
- [2] State, Region
- [3] District, County
- [4] Municipality
- [5] Colony, Dependency
- ◻ Continent
- ☒ Physical Region
- ◨ Historical or Cultural Region
- ▲ Mount, Mountain
- ▲ Volcano
- ▲ Hill
- ▲ Mountains, Mountain Range
- ▨ Hills, Escarpment
- ☒ Plateau, Upland
- ☒ Pass, Gap
- ☒ Plain, Lowland
- ☒ Delta
- ☒ Salt Flat
- ☒ Valley, Canyon
- ☒ Crater, Cave
- ☒ Karst Features
- ☐ Depression
- ☐ Polder
- ☐ Desert, Dunes
- ☐ Forest, Woods
- ☐ Marsh, Steppe
- ☒ Oasis
- ▶ Cape, Point
- ☒ Coast, Beach
- ☐ Cliff
- ☐ Peninsula
- ☐ Isthmus
- ☐ Sandbank
- ☒ Island
- ☐ Atoll
- ☒ Rock, Reef
- ☐ Islands, Archipelago
- ☒ Rocks, Reefs
- ☒ Coral Reef
- ☐ Well, Spring
- ☐ Geyser
- ☐ River, Stream
- ☐ Waterfall Rapids
- ☐ River Mouth, Estuary
- ☐ Lake
- ☐ Salt Lake
- ☐ Intermittent Lake
- ☐ Reservoir
- ☐ Swamp, Pond
- ☐ Canal
- ☐ Glacier
- ☐ Ice Shelf, Pack Ice
- ☐ Ocean
- ☐ Sea
- ☐ Gulf, Bay
- ☐ Strait, Fjord
- ☐ Basin
- ☐ Lagoon
- ☐ Bank
- ☐ Seamount
- ☐ Tablemount
- ☐ Ridge
- ☐ Shelf
- ☐ Escarpment, Sea Scarp
- ☐ Fracture
- ☐ Trench, Abyss
- ☐ National Park, Reserve
- ☒ Point of Interest
- ☒ Recreation Site
- ☐ Cave, Cavern
- ☐ Historic Site
- ☐ Ruins
- ☐ Wall, Walls
- ☐ Church, Abbey
- ☐ Temple
- ☒ Scientific Station
- ☒ Airport
- ☒ Port
- ☒ Lighthouse
- ☒ Mine
- ☒ Tunnel
- ☒ Dam, Bridge

ranoviči 6 Ie 53.08N 26.02 E
ranovka 16 Ed 50.18N 27.41 E
ranya [2] 10 Oj 46.05N 18.15 E
rão de Capanema 55 Da 13.19S 57.52W
rão de Cotegipe 55 Fh 27.37S 52.23W
rão de Grajaú 54 Je 6.45S 43.01W
rão de Melgaço 54 Gg 16.13S 55.58W
raque de Fraiture 11 Ld 50.15N 5.45 E
ratang 25 If 12.13N 92.45 E
rataria Bay 45 Ll 29.22N 89.57W
rat Daja, Kepulauan- 21 Oj 7.25S 128.00 E
räwe 31 Lh 1.09N 44.03 E
rbacena 53 Lh 21.14S 43.46W
rbacoas [Ven.] 49 Li 9.49N 70.03W
rbacoas [Ven.] 50 Ch 9.29N 66.58W
rbacoas, Bahía de- 49 Jh 10.10N 75.35W
rbado, Rio- 55 Cb 15.12S 58.58W
rbados [1] 39 Nh 13.10N 59.32W
rbados 38 Nh 13.10N 59.32W
rbados Ridge (EN) 50 Gf 12.45N 59.35W
rbagia 14 Dj 40.10N 9.10 E
rbar 35 Eb 18.01N 33.59 E
rbara 54 Dd 0.52S 72.30W
rbaros 15 Ki 40.54N 27.27 E
rbas, Cabo- 32 De 22.18N 16.41W
rbastro 13 Mb 42.02N 0.08 E
rbate de Franco 13 Gh 36.12N 5.55W
rbeau Peak 38 La 81.54N 75.01W
rbeton 37 Ee 25.48S 31.03 E
rbezieux 11 Fi 45.28N 0.09W
rbourville 44 Fg 36.52N 83.53W
rboza Ferraz 55 Fg 24.04S 52.03W
rbuda 38 Mh 17.38N 61.48W
rcaldine 58 Fg 23.33S 145.17 E
rcarrota 13 Ff 38.31N 6.51W
rcău 15 Ec 46.59N 21.07 E
rcellona Pozzo di Gotto 14 Jl 38.09N 15.13 E
rcelona [3] 13 Nc 41.40N 2.00 E
rcelona [Sp.] 6 Gg 41.23N 2.11 E
rcelona [Ven.] 54 Fa 10.08N 64.42W
rcelonnette 11 Mj 44.23N 6.39 E
rcelos [Braz.] 54 Fd 0.58S 62.57W
rcelos [Port.] 13 Dc 41.32N 8.37W
rcin 10 Nd 52.52N 17.57 E
rcoo River 59 Ie 25.30S 142.50 E
rcs 10 Nk 45.58N 17.28 E
rda 16 Oi 40.25N 47.05 E
rdagé 35 Ba 22.06N 16.28 E
rdaï 31 If 21.21N 16.59 E
rdăr Shāh 24 Ld 36.45N 47.15 E
rdaw 14 En 36.49N 10.08 E
rdawīl, Sabkhat al- 24 Eg 31.10N 33.10 E
rdejov 10 Rg 49.18N 21.16 E
rdêre 31 Lh 2.20N 42.20 E
rdeskan 24 Qe 35.12N 57.58 E
rdīyah 33 Ed 31.46N 25.06 E
rdonecchia 14 Ae 45.05N 6.42 E
rdsey 9 Ii 52.45N 4.45W
rdstown 44 Eg 37.49N 85.28W
rēda 31 Mg 11.52N 51.03 E
reilly 22 Jg 28.25N 79.23 E
rencevo More = Barents
ea (EN) 67 Jd 74.00N 36.00 E
rentin 11 Ge 49.33N 0.57 E
rentsburg 67 Kd 78.04N 14.14 E
rentshav = Barents Sea
EN) 67 Jd 74.00N 36.00 E
rentsøya 41 Oc 78.27N 21.15 E
rents Sea (EN) =
arencevo More 67 Jd 74.00N 36.00 E
rents Sea (EN) =
arentshav 67 Jd 74.00N 36.00 E
rents Trough (EN) 5 Ia 73.00N 29.00 E
rentu 35 Fb 15.06N 37.36 E
rfleur 11 Ee 49.40N 1.15W
rfleur, Pointe de- 11 Ee 49.42N 1.16W
rga 22 Kf 30.48N 81.17 E
rgal 35 Ic 11.18N 51.07 E
rgarh 25 Gd 21.20N 83.37 E
rguelonne 11 Gj 44.07N 0.50 E
rguzin 20 Ff 53.27N 108.58 E
rguzinski Hrebet 20 Ff 54.30N 110.00 E
r Harbor 44 Mc 44.23N 68.13W
rhi 25 Hd 24.18N 85.25 E
ri [3] 35 Hd 10.00N 50.00 E
ri 6 Hg 41.08N 16.51 E
ri, Terra di- 14 Kj 41.05N 16.50 E
Ria 25 Lf 10.30N 107.10 E
rīdī, Ra's- 24 Gj 24.17N 37.31 E
rika 13 Ri 35.22N 5.05 E
rim 33 Hg 12.39N 43.25 E
rima, Rio- 50 Fh 8.35N 60.25W
rima River 50 Fh 8.35N 60.25W
rinas 54 Db 8.38N 70.12W
rinas [2] 54 Eb 8.10N 70.00W
ring, Cape- 42 Fb 70.01N 117.28W
ringa 36 Db 0.45N 20.52 E
rinitas 49 Li 8.45N 70.25W
ripāda 25 Hd 21.56N 86.43 E
riri 55 Hf 22.04S 48.44W
riri, Reprêsa- 55 Hf 22.21S 48.39W
rīs 33 Fe 24.40N 30.36 E
ri Sādri 25 Ed 24.25N 74.28 E
risāl 25 Id 22.42N 90.22 E
risan, Pegunungan- =
Barisan Mountains (EN) 21 Mj 3.00S 102.15 E
risan Mountains (EN) =
Barisan, Pegunungan-
21 Mj 3.00S 102.15 E
rito 21 Nj 3.32S 114.29 E
rjols 11 Lk 43.33N 6.00 E
rkā' 23 Ie 23.35N 57.55 E
rkam 27 He 31.45N 102.32 E
rkan, Ra's-e- 24 Mg 30.01N 49.35 E
rkava 8 Lh 56.40N 26.45 E
rkley, Lake- 43 Jd 36.40N 87.55W
rkley Sound 46 Cb 48.53N 125.20W
Barkly East 37 Df 30.58S 27.33 E
Barkly Tableland 57 Ef 19.00S 138.00 E
Barkly West 37 Ce 28.05S 24.31 E
Barkol 27 Fc 43.35N 92.51 E
Barkol Hu 27 Fc 43.40N 92.39 E
Barlavento [3] 32 Cf 16.10N 24.40W
Bar-le-Duc 11 Lf 48.47N 5.10 E
Barlee, Lake- 57 Cg 29.10S 119.30 E
Barlee Range 59 Dd 23.35S 116.00 E
Barletta 14 Ki 41.19N 16.17 E
Barlinek 10 Lc 53.00N 15.12 E
Barlovento, Islas de- =
Windward Islands (EN) 38 Mh 15.00N 61.00W
Barma 26 Jg 1.54S 133.00 E
Barmer 25 Ec 25.45N 71.23 E
Barmera 59 If 34.15S 140.28 E
Barmouth 9 Ii 52.43N 4.03W
Barnard Castle 9 Lg 54.33N 1.55W
Barnaul 22 Kd 53.22N 83.45 E
Barnes Ice Cap 42 Kc 70.00N 73.30W
Barnesville [Ga.-U.S.] 44 Ei 33.04N 84.09W
Barnesville [Mn.-U.S.] 45 Hc 46.39N 96.25W
Barnet, London- 12 Bc 51.39N 0.12W
Barneveld 12 Hb 52.08N 5.34 E
Barnim 10 Jd 52.40N 13.45 E
Barnsley 9 Lh 53.34N 1.28W
Barnstaple 9 Ij 51.05N 4.04W
Barnstaple (Bideford Bay)
9 Ij 51.05N 4.20W
Barnstorf 12 Kb 52.43N 8.30 E
Barntrup 12 Lc 51.59N 9.07 E
Barnwell 44 Gi 33.14N 81.21W
Baro 30 Kh 8.26N 33.14 E
Baro [Chad] 35 Bc 12.12N 18.58 E
Baro [Nig.] 34 Gd 8.36N 6.25 E
Baronnies 11 Lj 44.15N 5.30 E
Barora Fa 63a Db 7.30S 158.20 E
Barora Ite 63a Db 7.36S 158.24 E
Barotseland 36 Df 15.05S 24.00 E
Barqah = Cyrenaica (EN) 33 Dc 31.00N 22.30 E
Barqah = Cyrenaica (EN) 30 Je 31.00N 23.00 E
Barqah, Jabal al- 24 Ej 24.24N 32.34 E
Barqah al Bahrīyah =
Marmarica (EN) 30 Je 31.40N 24.30 E
Barqū, Jabal- 14 Dn 36.04N 9.37 E
Barques, Pointe aux- 44 Fc 44.04N 82.58W
Barquisimeto 53 Jd 10.04N 69.19W
Barr 11 Nf 48.24N 7.27 E
Barr, Ra's al- 24 Nj 25.47N 50.34 E
Barra 53 Lg 11.05S 43.10W
Barra 9 Fd 57.00N 7.30W
Barra, Ponta da- 30 Kk 23.47S 35.32 E
Barra, Sound of- 9 Fd 57.10N 7.20W
Barraba 59 Kf 30.22S 150.36 E
Barra Bonita, Reprêsa- 55 Hf 22.38S 48.20W
Barra de Navidad 47 De 19.12N 104.41W
Barra do Bugres 54 Gg 15.05S 57.11W
Barra do Corda 54 Ie 5.30S 45.15W
Barra do Cuanza 36 Bd 9.18S 13.09 E
Barra do Dande 36 Bd 8.28S 13.22 E
Barra do Garças 54 Hg 15.53S 52.15W
Barra Falsa, Ponta da- 30 Kk 22.55S 35.37 E
Barra Head 9 Fe 56.46N 7.36W
Barra Mansa 54 Jh 22.32S 44.11W
Barrāmīyah, Wādī al- 24 Ej 25.00N 33.23 E
Barranca 54 Cd 4.50S 76.42W
Barrancabermeja 53 Ie 7.03N 73.52W
Barrancas [Col.] 49 Kh 10.57N 72.50W
Barrancas [Ven.] 54 Fb 8.42N 62.11W
Barrancas, Arroyo- 55 Cj 30.19S 59.25W
Barranco 55 Db 15.56S 57.41W
Barrancos 13 Ff 38.08N 6.59W
Barranqueras 56 Ic 27.29S 58.56W
Barranquilla 53 Id 10.59N 74.48W
Barranquitas 51a Bb 18.12N 66.23W
Barra Patuca 49 Ef 15.50N 84.17W
Barras 54 Jd 4.15S 42.18W
Barra Velha 55 Hh 26.39S 48.43W
Barre 44 Kc 44.12N 72.30W
Barreira 55 Db 15.24S 57.52W
Barreiras 53 Lg 12.08S 45.00W
Barreirinha 54 Gd 2.47S 57.03W
Barreirinhas 54 Jd 2.45S 42.50W
Barreiro 13 Cf 38.40N 9.04W
Barreiro, Rio- 55 Fb 15.43S 52.45W
Barreiro Grande 55 Jd 18.12S 45.10W
Barreiros 54 Ke 8.49S 35.12W
Barren 25 If 12.16N 93.51 E
Barren, Iles- 37 Gc 18.25S 43.40 E
Barren Islands 40 Ie 58.55N 152.15W
Barretos 56 Kb 20.33S 48.33W
Barrie 44 Hc 44.24N 79.40W
Barrier Bay 66 Ge 67.45S 81.10 E
Barrier Islands 63a Db 7.44S 158.32 E
Barrington Tops 59 Kf 32.00S 151.28 E
Barro Alto 55 Hb 15.04S 48.58W
Barrois, Plateau du- 11 Kf 48.45N 5.00 E
Barros, Lagoa dos- 55 Gi 29.56S 50.23W
Barros, Tierra de- 13 Ff 38.40N 6.25W
Barroso 55 Ke 21.11S 43.58W
Barrouallie 51n Ba 13.14N 61.17W
Barrow [Ak.-U.S.] 39 Db 71.17N 156.47W
Barrow [Arg.] 55 Bn 38.18S 60.14W
Barrow/An Bhearú 9 Gi 52.10N 7.00W
Barrow, Point- 38 Db 71.23N 156.30W
Barrow Creek 58 Eg 21.33S 133.53 E
Barrow-in-Furness 9 Jg 54.07N 3.14W
Barrow Island 57 Cg 20.50S 115.25 E
Barrow Range 59 Fe 26.05S 127.30 E
Barrow Strait 38 Jb 74.21N 94.10W
Barru 26 Gg 4.25S 119.37 E
Barry 9 Jj 51.24N 3.18W
Barrytown 62 De 42.14S 171.20 E
Barsakelmes, Ostrov- 18 Bb 45.40N 59.55 E
Barsalogo 34 Ec 13.25N 1.03W
Barsatas 19 Hf 48.13N 78.33 E
Baršć/Forst 10 Ke 51.44N 14.38 E
Bärsi 25 Fe 18.14N 75.42 E
Barsinghausen 10 Fd 52.18N 9.27 E
Barstow 43 De 34.54N 117.01W
Bar-sur-Aube 11 Kf 48.14N 4.43 E
Bar-sur-Seine 11 Kf 48.07N 4.22 E
Baršyn 19 Gf 49.45N 69.36 E
Bārta/Barta 8 Ih 56.57N 20.57 E
Barta/Bārta 8 Ih 56.57N 20.57 E
Bartallah 24 Jd 36.23N 43.25 E
Bartang 18 Hf 37.55N 71.33 E
Barth 10 Ib 54.22N 12.44 E
Bartholomew, Bayou- 45 Jj 32.43N 92.04W
Bartica 54 Gb 6.24N 58.37W
Bartın 24 Eb 41.38N 32.21 E
Bartle Frere, Mount- 57 Ff 17.23S 145.49 E
Bartlesville 43 Hd 36.45N 95.59W
Bartlett 45 Gf 41.53N 98.33W
Bartoszyce 10 Qb 54.16N 20.49 E
Bartow 44 Gl 27.54N 81.50W
Barú, Isla- 49 Jh 10.26N 75.35W
Barú, Volcán 47 Hg 8.48N 82.33W
Bārūd, Ra's- 24 Ei 26.47N 33.39 E
Barumini 14 Dk 39.42N 9.01 E
Barun-Bogdo-Ula 27 Hb 45.00N 100.20 E
Bāruni 25 Hc 25.29N 85.59 E
Barun-Šabartuj, Gora- 20 Fg 49.43N 109.58 E
Barun-Urt 27 Jb 46.40N 113.12 E
Barwice 10 Mc 53.45N 16.22 E
Barwon River 57 Fg 30.00S 148.05 E
Barycz 10 Me 51.42N 16.15 E
Baryš 7 Lj 53.40N 47.08 E
Baryš 7 Li 54.35N 46.47 E
Bāsa'īdū 24 Pi 26.39N 55.17 E
Basail 55 Ch 27.52S 59.18W
Basankusu 36 Cb 1.14N 19.48 E
Basarai, Ostrov- 18 Ib 45.25N 73.45 E
Basauri 13 Ja 43.13N 2.53W
Basavilbaso 55 Ck 32.22S 58.53W
Bas Champs 12 Dd 50.20N 1.41 E
Basco 26 Hb 20.27N 121.58 E
Bascuñán, Cabo- 56 Fc 28.51S 71.30W
Base 11 Gj 44.17N 0.18 E
Basel [2] 14 Bc 47.35N 7.40 E
Basel/Bâle 6 Gf 47.30N 7.30 E
Baselland [2] 14 Bc 47.30N 7.45 E
Basentello 14 Kj 40.40N 16.23 E
Basento 14 Kj 40.20N 16.49 E
Başeu 15 Kb 47.44N 27.15 E
Basey 26 Id 11.17N 125.04 E
Bashi Channel (EN) = Bashi
Haixia 27 Lg 22.00N 121.00 E
Bashi Haixia = Bashi
Channel (EN) 27 Lg 22.00N 121.00 E
Bāsht 24 Ng 30.21N 51.09 E
Ba Shui 28 Ci 30.25N 115.02 E
Basilan 21 Oi 6.34N 122.03 E
Basilan City (Isabela) 22 Oi 6.42N 121.58 E
Basilan Strait 26 He 6.49N 122.05 E
Basildon 9 Nj 51.34N 0.25 E
Basilicata [2] 14 Kj 40.30N 16.30 E
Basingstoke 9 Lj 51.16N 1.05W
Basjanovski 17 Jg 58.19N 60.44 E
Başkale 24 Jc 38.02N 44.00 E
Baskatong, Réservoir- 42 Jg 46.47N 75.50W
Baškaus 20 Df 51.09N 87.43 E
Baskil 24 Hc 38.35N 38.40 E
Baškirskaja ASSR [3] 19 Fe 55.00N 56.00 E
Baskunčak, Ozero- 16 Oe 48.10N 46.55 E
Bašmakovo 16 Mc 53.12N 43.03 E
Bäsmenj 24 Ld 37.59N 46.29 E
Basoko 36 Db 1.14N 23.36 E
Basongo 36 Dc 4.20S 20.24 E
Basque Provinces (EN) =
Euzkadi/Vascongadas 13 Ja 43.00N 2.30W
Basque Provinces (EN) =
Vascongadas/Euzkadi 13 Ja 43.00N 2.30W
Basra (EN) = Al Başrah 22 Gf 30.30N 47.47 E
Bas Rhin [3] 11 Nf 48.35N 7.40 E
Bass, Ilots de- 57 Mg 27.55S 143.26W
Bassano 46 Ia 50.47N 112.28W
Bassano del Grappa 14 Fe 45.46N 11.44 E
Bassar 34 Fd 9.15N 0.47 E
Bassas da India 30 Lk 21.25S 39.42 E
Bassein 22 Lh 16.47N 94.44 E
Bassein → Vasai 25 Ee 19.21N 72.48 E
Basse-Kotto [3] 35 Ce 5.00N 21.30 E
Basse-Pointe 51h Ab 14.52N 61.07W
Basses, Pointe des- 51e Bc 15.52N 61.17W
Basse-Sambre 12 Gd 50.27N 4.37 E
Basse Santa Su 34 Cc 13.19N 14.13W
Basse-Terre 50 Fd 16.10N 61.40W
Basse-Terre 47 Le 16.00N 61.44W
Basseterre 47 Le 17.18N 62.43W
Bassett 45 Ge 42.35N 99.32W
Bassigny 11 Lf 48.00N 5.30 E
Bassikounou 32 Ff 15.52N 5.58W
Bassila 34 Fd 9.01N 1.40 E
Bass Islands 63c Ba 9.58S 167.17 E
Basso,
Plateau de- 30 Jg 17.20N 22.40 E
Bass Strait 57 Fh 39.20S 145.30 E
Bassum 12 Kb 52.51N 8.44 E
Basswood Lake 45 Kb 48.05N 91.35W
Båstad 7 Ch 56.26N 12.51 E
Bastak 24 Pi 27.14N 54.22 E
Bastām 24 Pd 36.29N 55.04 E
Bastenaken/Bastogne 11 Le 50.00N 5.43 E
Bastia [Fr.] 6 Gg 42.42N 9.27 E
Bastia [It.] 14 Gg 43.04N 12.33 E
Bastogne/Bastenaken 11 Le 50.00N 5.43 E
Bastrop 45 Kj 32.47N 91.55W
Basudan Ula 27 Fe 33.05N 91.00 E
Basuo → Dongfang 27 Ih 19.14N 108.39 E
Basuto 37 Dc 19.52S 26.32 E
Bas-Zaïre [2] 36 Bd 5.30S 14.30 E
Bata 31 Hh 1.51N 9.45 E
Batabanó, Golfo de- 47 Hd 22.15N 82.30W
Batagaj 20 Ic 67.38N 134.38 E
Batagaj-Alyta 20 Ic 67.53N 130.31 E
Bataguaçu 54 Hh 21.42S 52.22W
Bataiporã 55 Ff 22.20S 53.17W
Batajnica 15 De 44.54N 20.17 E
Batajsk 19 Df 47.05N 39.46 E
Batak 15 Hh 41.57N 24.13 E
Bataklık Gölü 24 Ed 37.42N 33.07 E
Batala 25 Fb 31.48N 75.12 E
Batalha 13 De 39.39N 8.50W
Batama 36 Eb 0.56N 26.39 E
Batamaj 20 Hd 63.30N 129.25 E
Batamšinski 19 Fe 50.36N 58.17 E
Batan 26 Hb 20.30N 121.50 E
Batang 27 Ge 30.02N 99.10 E
Batanga 36 Ac 0.21S 9.18 E
Batangafo 35 Bd 7.18N 18.18 E
Batangas 22 Oh 13.45N 121.03 E
Batanghari 26 Mj 1.00S 104.00 E
Batan Islands 21 Og 20.30N 121.50 E
Batanta, Pulau- 26 Jg 0.50S 130.40 E
Bátaszék 10 Oj 46.11N 18.44 E
Batatais 55 Ie 20.53S 47.37W
Batavia 44 Hd 43.00N 78.11W
Bat-Cengel 27 Hb 47.47N 101.58 E
Batchawana 44 Eb 46.55N 84.34W
Batchelor 59 Gb 13.04S 131.01 E
Bătdâmbâng 22 Mh 13.06N 103.12 E
Batéké, Plateaux- 36 Cc 3.30S 15.45 E
Batel, Esteros del- 55 Ci 28.30S 58.20W
Batemans Bay 59 Kg 35.43S 150.11 E
Batesburg 44 Gi 33.56N 81.33W
Batesville [Ar.-U.S.] 45 Ki 35.46N 91.39W
Batesville [Ms.-U.S.] 45 Li 34.18N 90.00W
Bath [Eng.-U.K.] 9 Kj 51.23N 2.22W
Bath [Me.-U.S.] 44 Md 43.55N 69.49W
Bath [N.B.-Can.] 44 Nb 46.32N 67.33W
Bath [St.C.N.] 51c Ab 17.08N 62.37W
Batha 30 Ig 12.47N 17.34 E
Batha [3] 35 Bc 14.00N 19.00 E
Bá Thrá Li/Tralee Bay 9 Di 52.15N 9.59W
Bathsheba 50 Gf 13.13N 59.31W
Bá Thuath Reanna/
Liscannor Bay 9 Di 52.55N 9.25W
Bathurst 38 Ib 76.00N 100.30W
Bathurst [Austl.] 59 Jf 33.25S 149.35 E
Bathurst [N.B.-Can.] 39 Me 47.36N 65.39W
Bathurst, Cape- 38 Gb 70.35N 128.00W
Bathurst Inlet 38 Ic 68.10N 108.50W
Bathurst Inlet 39 Ic 66.50N 108.01W
Bathurst Island 57 Ef 11.35S 130.25 E
Bati 35 Gc 11.13N 40.01 E
Batié 34 Ed 9.53N 2.55W
Bāṭin, Wādī al- 23 Gc 30.25N 47.35 E
Batman 23 Fb 37.52N 41.07 E
Batman 24 Id 37.45N 41.00 E
Batna [3] 32 Ib 35.10N 6.00 E
Batna 31 He 35.34N 6.11 E
Ba To 25 Lf 14.46N 108.44 E
Bato Bato 26 Ge 5.06N 119.50 E
Batoka 36 Ef 16.47S 27.15 E
Baton Rouge 39 Jf 30.23N 91.11W
Batopilas 48 Fd 27.01N 107.44W
Batouri 34 He 4.26N 14.22 E
Batovi 55 Fb 15.53S 53.24W
Batovi, Coxilha de- 55 Ej 30.33S 54.27W
Båtsfjord 7 Ga 70.38N 29.44 E
Bat-Sumber 27 Ib 48.25N 106.42 E
Batticaloa 25 Gg 7.43N 81.42 E
Batti Maly 25 Ig 8.50N 92.51 E
Battipaglia 14 Ij 40.37N 14.58 E
Battle 12 Cd 50.55N 0.30 E
Battle 42 Gf 52.42N 108.15W
Battle Creek 46 Kb 48.36N 109.11W
Battle Creek 43 Jc 42.19N 85.11W
Battle Harbour 39 Nd 52.17N 55.35W
Battle Mountain 43 Dc 40.38N 116.56W
Battonya 10 Rj 46.17N 21.01 E
Battowia Island 51n Bb 12.58N 61.09W
Batu 35 Fd 6.59N 39.37 E
Batu, Kepulauan- = Batu
Islands (EN) 21 Lj 0.18S 98.28 E
Batuasa 26 Jg 3.32S 130.08 E
Batuata, Pulau- 26 Hh 6.12S 122.42 E
Batudaka, Pulau- 26 Hg 0.28S 121.48 E
Batui 26 Hg 1.17S 122.33 E
Batu Islands (EN) = Batu,
Kepulauan- 21 Lj 0.18S 98.28 E
Batumi 6 Kg 41.38N 41.38 E
Batu Pahat 26 Df 1.51N 102.56 E
Baturaja 26 Dg 4.08S 104.10 E
Baturino 20 De 57.45N 85.12 E
Baturité 54 Kd 4.20S 38.53W
Batz, Ile de- 11 Bf 48.45N 4.01W
Bau 26 Ff 1.25N 110.09 E
Baubau 22 Oj 5.28S 122.38 E
Baucau 26 Ih 8.27S 126.27 E
Bauchi 31 Hg 10.19N 9.50 E
Bauchi [2] 34 Hc 10.40N 10.00 E
Bauchi Plateau 34 Gc 10.00N 9.30 E
Baud 11 Cg 47.52N 3.01W
Baudette 45 Ib 48.43N 94.36W
Baudo, Serrania de- 54 Cb 6.00N 77.05W
Baudour, Saint-Ghislain- 12 Fd 50.29N 3.49 E
Baugé 11 Fg 47.33N 0.06W
Bauges 11 Mi 45.38N 6.10 E
Baúl, Cerro- 48 Ii 17.38N 100.19W
Baula 26 Hg 4.09S 121.41 E
Bauld, Cape- 38 Nd 51.38N 55.25W
Bauman Fiord 42 Ia 77.45N 86.00W
Baume-les-Dames 11 Mg 47.21N 6.22 E
Baunach 10 Gg 49.59N 10.51 E
Baunani 63a Ec 9.08S 160.51 E
Baunei 14 Dj 40.02N 9.40 E
Baures 54 Ff 13.35S 63.35W
Bauru 53 Lh 22.19S 49.04W
Baús 55 Fd 18.19S 53.10W
Baús, Serra dos- 55 Fd 18.20S 53.25W
Bauska 7 Fh 56.24N 24.13 E
Bautzen/Budyšin 10 Ke 51.11N 14.26 E
Bavaria (EN) = Bayern [2] 10 Hg 49.00N 11.30 E
Bavaria (EN) = Bayern 5 Hf 49.00N 11.30 E
Bavarian Forest (EN) =
Bayerischer Wald 10 Ig 49.00N 12.55 E
Bavay 12 Fd 50.18N 3.47 E
Båven 8 Ge 59.00N 16.55 E
Bavispe 48 Eb 30.24N 108.50W
Bavispe, Rio de- 48 Ec 29.15N 109.11W
Bavly 7 Mi 54.26N 53.18 E
Bawah, Pulau- 26 Ef 2.31N 106.03 E
Bawal, Pulau- 26 Fg 2.44S 110.06 E
Bawe 58 Ee 2.59S 134.43 E
Bawean, Pulau- 26 Fh 5.46S 112.40 E
Bawku 34 Ec 11.03N 0.15W
Baxian 27 Kd 39.03N 116.24 E
Baxoi 27 Ge 30.07N 96.56 E
Bay [3] 35 Ge 2.50N 43.30 E
Bay/Baicheng 27 Dc 41.46N 81.52 E
Bayamo 47 Id 20.23N 76.39W
Bayamón 49 Nd 18.24N 66.09W
Bayan 28 Ia 46.05N 127.24 E
Bayanbulak 27 Dc 43.05N 84.05 E
Bayanga 35 Be 2.53N 16.19 E
Bayan Gol 27 Gd 37.18N 96.50 E
Bayan Gol → Dengkou 22 Me 40.25N 106.59 E
Bayan Har Shan 21 Lf 34.20N 97.00 E
Bayan Har Shankou 27 Ge 34.06N 97.38 E
Bayan Hot → Alxa Zuoqi 27 Id 38.50N 105.32 E
Bayan Hure → Chen Barag Qi 27 Kb 49.21N 119.25 E
Bayan Huxu → Horqin Youyi
Zhongqi 27 Lb 45.04N 121.27 E
Bayano, Lago de- 49 Hi 9.00N 78.30W
Bayan Obo 27 Ic 41.50N 109.58 E
Bayan Qagan 28 Ga 46.11N 123.59 E
Bayan Qagan → Qahar
Youyi Houqi 28 Bd 41.28N 113.10 E
Bayan Ul Hot → Xi Ujimqin
Qi 27 Kc 44.31N 117.33 E
Bayas 48 Gf 23.32N 104.50W
Bayat 24 Fb 40.39N 34.15 E
Bayauca 55 Bl 34.51S 61.18W
Bayawan 26 He 9.20N 123.00 E
Bayāz 24 Pg 30.42N 55.28 E
Bayāzeh 24 Pf 30.42N 55.28 E
Baybay 26 Hd 10.41N 124.48 E
Bayburt 23 Fa 40.16N 40.15 E
Bay City [Mi.-U.S.] 43 Kc 43.36N 83.53W
Bay City [Tx.-U.S.] 43 Hf 29.09N 95.39W
Bayerische Alpen 10 Hi 47.30N 11.30 E
Bayerischer Wald = Bavarian
Forest (EN) 10 Ig 49.00N 12.55 E
Bayern = Bavaria (EN) 5 Hf 49.00N 11.30 E
Bayern = Bavaria (EN) [2] 10 Hg 49.00N 11.30 E
Bayes, Cap- 63b Be 20.57S 165.25 E
Bayeux 11 Fe 49.16N 0.42W
Bayfield 45 Kc 46.49N 90.49W
Bay Fiord 42 Ja 79.00N 84.00W
Baygorria 55 Dk 32.52S 56.44W
Baygorria, Lago
Artificial de- 55 Dk 33.05S 57.00W
Bayḥān al Qiṣāb 33 Ig 14.48N 45.44 E
Bayındır 24 Bc 38.13N 27.40 E
Bayjī 24 Je 34.56N 43.29 E
Bay Minette 44 Dj 30.53N 87.47W
Baynūnah 24 Ok 23.50N 52.50 E
Bayombong 26 Hc 16.29N 121.09 E
Bayona 13 Db 42.07N 8.51W
Bayonnaise Seamount (EN)
57 Jf 12.00S 179.30W
Bayonne 6 Fg 43.29N 1.29W
Bayou Bodcau Lake 45 Jj 32.58N 93.30W
Bayou D'Arbonne
Lake 45 Jj 32.45N 92.27W
Bayramiç 15 Jj 39.48N 26.37 E
Bayreuth 10 Hg 49.57N 11.35 E
Bayrūt = Beirut (EN) 22 Ff 33.53N 35.30 E
Bay Saint Louis 45 Lk 30.19N 89.20W
Bay Springs 45 Lk 31.59N 89.17W
Bayt al Faqīh 23 Fg 14.31N 43.17 E
Baytik Shan 27 Fb 45.15N 90.50 E
Bayt Laḥm = Bethlehem (EN) 24 Fg 31.43N 35.12 E
Baytown 43 If 29.44N 94.58W
Bayuda Desert (EN) =
Bayyūḍah, Ṣaḥrā'- 30 Kg 18.00N 33.00 E
Bayunglencir 26 Dg 2.03S 103.41 E
Bayview 46 Gc 48.00N 116.30W
Bay View 62 Gc 39.26S 176.52 E
Bayy al Kabīr 33 Cc 31.11N 15.53 E
Bayyūḍah, Ṣaḥrā'- = Bayuda
Desert (EN) 30 Kg 18.00N 33.00 E
Baza 13 Jg 37.29N 2.46W
Baza, Sierra de- 13 Jg 37.15N 2.45W
Bazardjuzju, Gora- 5 Kg 41.13N 47.51 E
Bazaruto, Ilha do- 37 Fd 21.40S 35.25 E
Bazas 11 Fj 44.26N 0.13W
Bazhong 27 Ie 31.54N 106.42 E
Bazoches-sur-Vesle 12 Fe 49.19N 3.37 E
Baztán 13 Ka 43.09N 1.31W
Beach 43 Gb 46.55N 103.52W
Beachy Head 9 Nk 50.44N 0.16 E
Beacon 44 Ke 41.31N 73.59W
Beaconsfield [Austl.] 59 Jh 41.12S 146.48 E
Beaconsfield [Eng.-U.K.] 12 Bc 51.36N 0.38W
Beagle, Canal- 56 Gh 54.53S 68.10W
Beagle Gulf 59 Gb 12.00S 130.20 E
Bealach an Doirin/
Ballaghaderreen 9 Eh 53.55N 8.35W
Béalanana 37 Hb 14.33S 48.44 E
Béal an Átha/Ballina 9 Dg 54.07N 9.09W
Béal an Bheara/Gweebarra
Bay 9 Eg 54.52N 8.20W
Béal Átha Fhirdhia/Ardee 9 Gh 53.52N 6.33W
Béal Átha hAmhnais/
Ballyhaunis 9 Eh 53.46N 8.46W

ndex Symbols

Independent Nation; State, Region; District, County; Municipality; Colony, Dependency; Continent; Physical Region

Historical or Cultural Region; Mount, Mountain; Volcano; Hill; Mountains, Mountain Range; Hills, Escarpment; Plateau, Upland

Pass, Gap; Plain, Lowland; Delta; Salt Flat; Valley, Canyon; Crater, Cave; Karst Features

Depression; Polder; Desert, Dunes; Forest, Woods; Heath, Steppe; Oasis; Cape, Point

Coast, Beach; Cliff; Peninsula; Isthmus; Sandbank; Island; Atoll

Rock, Reef; Islands, Archipelago; Rocks, Reefs; Coral Reef; Well, Spring; Geyser; River, Stream

Waterfall Rapids; River Mouth, Estuary; Lake; Salt Lake; Intermittent Lake; Reservoir; Swamp, Pond

Canal; Glacier; Ice Shelf, Pack Ice; Ocean; Sea; Gulf, Bay; Strait, Fjord

Lagoon; Bank; Seamount; Tablemount; Ridge; Shelf; Basin

Escarpment, Sea Scarp; Fracture; Trench, Abyss; National Park, Reserve; Point of Interest; Recreation Site; Cave, Cavern

Historic Site; Ruins; Wall, Walls; Church, Abbey; Temple; Scientific Station; Airport

Port; Lighthouse; Mine; Tunnel; Dam, Bridge

Béal Átha na Muice/ Swinford 9 Eh 53.57N 8.57W
Béal Átha na Sluaighe/ Ballinasloe 9 Eh 53.20N 8.13W
Béal Átha Seanaidh/ Ballyshannon 9 Eg 54.30N 8.11W
Beale, Cape- 46 Cb 48.44N 125.20W
Béal Easa/Foxford 9 Dh 53.59N 9.07W
Béal Feirste/Belfast 6 Fe 54.35N 5.55W
Beal Range 59 Ie 25.30S 141.30 E
Béal Tairbirt/Belturbet 9 Fg 54.06N 7.26W
Beanna Boirche/Mourne Mountains 9 Gg 54.10N 6.04W
Beannchar/Bangor 9 Hg 54.40N 5.40W
Beanntrai/Bantry 9 Dj 51.41N 9.27W
Bear Bay 42 Ia 75.45N 86.30W
Beardmore 45 Mb 49.36N 87.57W
Beardstown 45 Kg 39.59N 90.26W
Bear Island (EN)= Björnöya 5 Ha 74.30N 19.00 E
Bear Islands (EN)=Medveži, Ostrova- 21 Sb 70.52N 161.26 E
Bear Lake 43 Ec 42.00N 111.20W
Bear Lodge Mountains 45 Dd 44.35N 104.15W
Béarn 11 Fk 43.20N 0.45W
Bearpaw Mountains 46 Kb 48.15N 109.30W
Bear Peninsula 66 Of 74.36S 110.50W
Bear River 46 If 41.30N 112.08W
Bearskin Lake 42 If 53.57N 90.59W
Beās 25 Eb 31.10N 74.59 E
Beas de Segura 13 Jf 38.15N 2.53W
Beata, Cabo- 47 Je 17.36N 71.25W
Beata, Isla- 49 Le 17.35N 71.31W
Beata Ridge (EN) 47 Je 16.00N 72.30W
Beatrice 43 Hc 40.16N 96.44W
Beatrice, Cape- 59 Hb 14.15S 137.00 E
Beatton 42 Fe 56.06N 120.22W
Beatton River 42 Fe 56.10N 120.25W
Beatty 43 Dd 36.54N 116.46W
Beattyville 44 Ia 48.52N 77.10W
Beatys Butte 46 Fe 42.23N 119.20W
Beau-Bassin 37a Bb 20.13S 57.27 E
Beaucaire 11 Kk 43.48N 4.38 E
Beaucamps-le-Vieux 12 De 49.50N 1.47 E
Beaucanton 44 Ha 49.05N 79.15W
Beauce 11 Hf 48.22N 1.50 E
Beaudesert 59 Ke 27.59S 153.00 E
Beaufort [Mala.] 26 Ge 5.20N 115.45 E
Beaufort [S.C.-U.S.] 44 Gi 32.26N 80.40W
Beaufort/Befort 12 Ie 49.50N 6.18 E
Beaufort, Massif de- 11 Mi 45.50N 6.40 E
Beaufort Island 66 Kf 76.57S 166.56 E
Beaufort Sea 67 Eb 73.00N 140.00W
Beaufort West 31 Jl 32.20S 22.33 E
Beaugency 11 Hg 47.47N 1.38 E
Beaujolais, Monts du- 11 Kh 46.00N 4.22 E
Beauly 9 Id 57.29N 4.29W
Beaumesnil 12 Ce 49.01N 0.43 E
Beaumetz-lès-Loges 12 Ed 50.14N 2.39 E
Beaumont [Bel.] 12 Gd 50.14N 4.14 E
Beaumont [Fr.] 11 Gj 44.46N 0.46 E
Beaumont [Fr.] 11 Ee 49.40N 1.51W
Beaumont [Fr.] 12 Hf 48.51N 5.47 E
Beaumont [Ms.-U.S.] 45 Lk 31.11N 88.55W
Beaumont [N.Z.] 62 Cf 45.49S 169.32 E
Beaumont [Tx.-U.S.] 39 Jf 30.05N 94.06W
Beaumont-de-Lomagne 11 Gk 43.53N 0.59 E
Beaumont-en-Argonne 12 He 49.32N 5.03 E
Beaumont-le-Roger 12 Ce 49.05N 0.47 E
Beaumont-sur-Oise 12 Ee 49.08N 2.17 E
Beaumont-sur-Sarthe 11 Gf 48.13N 0.08 E
Beaune 11 Kg 47.02N 4.50 E
Beaupré 44 Lb 47.03N 70.53W
Beauraing 12 Gd 50.07N 4.48 E
Beaurepaire 11 Li 45.20N 5.03 E
Beausejour 42 Hf 50.04N 96.33W
Beautemps Beaupré 63b Ce 20.25S 166.08 E
Beauvais 11 Ie 49.26N 2.05 E
Beauval 12 Ed 50.06N 2.20 E
Beauvoir-sur-Mer 11 Dh 46.55N 2.03W
Beaver [Ak.-U.S.] 40 Jc 66.22N 147.24W
Beaver [Ok.-U.S.] 45 Fh 36.48N 100.30W
Beaver [Ut.-U.S.] 43 Ed 38.17N 112.38W
Beaver Creek [Co.-U.S.] 45 Ef 40.20N 103.33W
Beaver Creek [U.S.] 45 Ec 47.20N 103.39W
Beaver Creek [U.S.] 45 Gf 40.04N 99.20W
Beaver Creek [U.S.] 45 Ee 43.25N 103.59W
Beaver Dam 45 Le 43.28N 88.50W
Beaver Falls 44 Ge 40.45N 80.21W
Beaverhead Mountains 46 Id 45.00N 113.20W
Beaver Island 44 Ec 45.40N 85.31W
Beaver Lake 45 Jh 36.20N 93.55W
Beaver River [U.S.] 45 Gh 36.10N 98.45W
Beaver River [Ut.-U.S.] 46 Ig 39.10N 112.57W
Beaverton 46 Dd 45.29N 122.48W
Beāwar 25 Ec 26.06N 74.19 E
Bebedouro 56 Kb 20.56S 48.28W
Becan 48 Oh 18.37N 89.35W
Becanchén 48 Oh 19.50N 89.22W
Beccles 9 Oi 52.28N 1.34 E
Bečej 15 Dd 45.37N 20.03 E
Beceni 15 Jd 45.23N 26.47 E
Becerreá 13 Eb 42.51N 7.10W
Becerro, Cayos- 49 Ff 15.57N 83.17W
Béchar 31 Ge 31.37N 2.13W
Béchar [3] 32 Gd 30.00N 2.00W
Becharof Lake 40 He 58.00N 156.30W
Bechet 15 Gf 43.46N 23.57 E
Bechevin Bay 40 Ge 55.00N 163.27W
Bechyně 10 Kg 49.18N 14.28 E
Beckingen 12 Ie 49.24N 6.42 E
Beckley 43 Kd 37.46N 81.12W
Beckum 10 Ee 51.45N 8.02 E
Beckumer Berge 12 Kc 51.43N 8.10 E
Beclean 15 Hb 47.11N 24.11 E
Bédarieux 11 Jk 43.37N 3.09 E
Bedburg-Hau 12 Ic 51.46N 6.11 E
Bedele 35 Fd 8.27N 36.22 E
Bedesa 35 Gd 8.53N 40.46 E
Bedford 9 Mi 52.10N 0.50W
Bedford [Eng.-U.K.] 9 Mi 52.08N 0.29W
Bedford [In.-U.S.] 44 Df 38.52N 86.29W
Bedford [Pa.-U.S.] 44 He 40.00N 78.31W
Bedford [Va.-U.S.] 44 Hg 37.20N 79.31W
Bedford Level 9 Ni 52.30N 0.05 E
Bedford Point 51p Bb 12.13N 61.36W
Bedfordshire [3] 9 Mi 52.05N 0.20W
Bednja 14 Kd 46.18N 16.45 E
Bednodemjanovsk 16 Mc 53.55N 43.12 E
Bedourie 59 Hd 24.21S 139.28 E
Bedum 12 Ia 53.18N 6.39 E
Beech Grove 44 Df 39.43N 86.03W
Beecroft Head 59 Kg 35.01S 150.50 E
Beef Island 51a Db 18.27N 64.31W
Beelitz 10 Id 52.14N 12.58 E
Beemster 12 Gb 52.34N 4.56 E
Beerfelden 12 Ke 49.34N 8.59 E
Beernem 12 Fc 51.09N 3.20 E
Beerse 12 Gc 51.19N 4.52 E
Beersel 12 Gd 50.46N 4.18 E
Beersheba (EN)=Be'er Shevà 23 Dc 31.14N 34.47 E
Be'er Shevà=Beersheba (EN) 23 Dc 31.14N 34.47 E
Beerze 12 Hc 51.36N 5.19 E
Beeskow 10 Kd 52.10N 14.14 E
Beestekraal 37 De 25.23S 27.38 E
Beeston 9 Li 52.56N 1.12W
Beethoven Peninsula 66 Qf 71.40S 73.45W
Beetsterzwaag, Opsterland- 12 Ia 53.03N 6.04 E
Beeville 43 Hf 28.24N 97.45W
Befale 36 Db 0.28N 20.58 E
Befandriana Nord 37 Hc 15.15S 48.32 E
Befandriana Sud 37 Gd 22.06S 43.54 E
Befori 36 Db 0.06N 22.17 E
Befort/Beaufort 12 Ie 49.50N 6.18 E
Bega 15 Dd 45.13N 20.19 E
Bega 58 Fh 36.40S 149.50 E
Bégard 11 Cf 48.38N 3.18W
Begejski kanal 15 Dd 45.27N 20.27 E
Beggars Point 51d Bb 17.10N 61.48W
Bègle 11 Fj 44.48N 0.32W
Begna 7 Bf 60.35N 10.00 E
Begoml 8 Mj 54.46N 28.14 E
Begunicy 8 Me 59.31N 29.30 E
Behābād 24 Pg 31.52N 55.57 E
Behbehān 23 Hc 30.35N 50.14 E
Behring Point 49 Ia 24.27N 77.43W
Behshahr 23 Hb 36.43N 53.34 E
Bei'an 22 Oe 48.16N 126.29 E
Beibu Wan=Tonkin, Gulf of- (EN) 21 Mh 20.00N 108.00 E
Beida He 27 Gc 40.18N 99.01 E
Beihai 22 Mg 21.31N 109.07 E
Bei Hulsan Hu 27 Gd 36.55N 95.55 E
Bei Jiang 27 Jg 23.02N 112.58 E
Beijing=Peking (EN) 22 Nf 39.55N 116.23 E
Beijing Shi (Pei-ching Shih) [5] 27 Kc 40.15N 116.30 E
Beila 32 Df 18.10N 15.53W
Beilen 12 Ib 52.52N 6.32 E
Beiliutang He 28 Eg 34.12N 119.33 E
Beilstroom 12 Ib 52.41N 6.12 E
Beilstein 12 Jd 50.07N 7.15 E
Beilu He 27 Fe 34.34N 94.00 E
Beinamar 35 Bd 8.40N 15.23 E
Beine-Nauroy 12 Ge 49.15N 4.13 E
Beipiao 27 Lc 41.49N 120.45 E
Beira 31 Kj 19.50S 34.52 E
Beira Alta 13 Ed 40.40N 7.35W
Beira Baixa 13 Ee 39.55N 7.30W
Beira Litoral 13 Dd 40.15N 8.25W
Beiru He 28 Bh 33.40N 113.35 E
Beirut (EN)=Bayrūt 22 Ff 33.53N 35.30 E
Bei Shan 22 Le 41.30N 96.00 E
Beitstad 7 Cd 64.05N 11.22 E
Beiuş 15 Fc 46.40N 22.21 E
Beiwei Tan 27 Kg 21.10N 116.10 E
Beizhen [China] 27 Kd 37.24N 117.59 E
Beizhen [China] 28 Fd 41.36N 121.47 E
Beja 13 Ef 38.01N 7.52W
Beja [2] 13 Eg 37.58N 7.50W
Bejaïa [3] 32 Ib 36.40N 5.10 E
Bejaïa 31 He 36.45N 5.05 E
Bejaïa, Golfe de- 13 Rh 36.45N 5.20 E
Béjar 13 Gd 40.23N 5.46W
Beji 25 Dc 29.47N 67.58 E
Bejneu 19 Ff 45.15N 55.05 E
Bejsug 16 Kf 46.02N 38.35 E
Bejsugski Liman 16 Kf 46.05N 38.25 E
Bekabad 19 Gg 40.13N 69.14 E
Bekasi 26 Eh 6.14S 106.59 E
Bekdaš 16 Fg 41.31N 52.40 E
Békés 10 Rj 46.46N 21.08 E
Békés [2] 10 Qj 46.45N 21.00 E
Békéscsaba 10 Rj 46.41N 21.06 E
Bekilli 15 Mk 38.14N 29.26 E
Bekily 37 Hd 24.12S 45.18 E
Bekkai 29a Db 43.25N 145.07 E
Bekoji 35 Fd 7.32N 39.15 E
Bekopaka 37 Gc 19.08S 44.45 E
Bekovo 16 Mc 52.29N 43.45 E
Bela [India] 25 Gc 25.56N 81.59 E
Bela [Pak.] 25 Dc 26.14N 66.19 E
Bélabo 34 He 4.52N 13.10 E
Bela Crkva 15 Ee 44.54N 21.26 E
Bela Dila 25 Ge 18.40N 80.55 E
Bela Floresta 55 Ge 20.36S 51.16W
Belaga 26 Ff 2.42N 113.47 E
Belaja [R.S.F.S.R.] 20 Mc 65.30N 173.15 E
Belaja [R.S.F.S.R.] 5 Ld 56.00N 54.32 E
Belaja [R.S.F.S.R.] 16 Kg 45.03N 39.25 E
Belaja Cerkov 6 Jf 49.49N 30.07 E
Belaja Gora 20 Jc 68.30N 146.15 E
Belaja Holunica 19 Fd 58.53N 50.50 E
Belaja Kalitva 19 Ef 48.09N 40.49 E
Bela Krajina 14 Je 45.35N 15.15 E
Bela Lorena 55 Ib 15.13S 46.01W
Belang 26 Hf 0.57N 124.47 E
Bela Palanka 15 Ff 43.13N 22.19 E
Belarbi 13 Li 35.09N 0.27W
Belaruskaja Sovetskaja Socialistyčnaja Respublika /Belorusskaja SSR [2] 19 Ce 53.50N 28.00 E
Belasica 15 Fh 41.21N 22.50 E
Bela Vista [Ang.] 36 Ce 12.33S 16.14 E
Bela Vista [Braz.] 54 Gh 22.06S 56.31W
Bela Vista [Braz.] 55 Dc 17.37S 57.01W
Bela Vista [Moz.] 37 Ee 26.20S 32.40 E
Belawan 26 Cf 3.47N 98.41 E
Běła Woda/Weißwasser 10 Ke 51.31N 14.38 E
Belayan 26 Gg 0.14S 116.36 E
Belbo 14 Cf 44.54N 8.31 E
Bełchatow 10 Pe 51.22N 19.21 E
Belcher Channel 42 Ia 77.20N 94.30W
Belcher Islands 38 Ld 56.20N 79.30W
Belchite 13 Lc 41.18N 0.45W
Belcy 19 Cf 47.46N 27.55 E
Bełczyna 10 Ne 51.25N 17.50 E
Belebej 19 Fe 54.10N 54.07 E
Belecke, Warstein- 12 Kc 51.29N 8.20 E
Beled 10 Ni 47.28N 17.06 E
Beled Wěyne 31 Lh 4.47N 45.12 E
Bélel 34 Hd 7.03N 14.26 E
Belém [Moz.] 37 Fb 14.08S 35.58 E
Belém [Braz.] 53 Lf 1.27S 48.29W
Belem [Mex.] 48 Dd 27.45N 110.28W
Belém de São Francisco 54 Ke 8.46S 38.58W
Belen 43 Fe 34.40N 106.46W
Belén [Arg.] 56 Gc 27.39S 67.02W
Belén [Nic.] 49 Eh 11.30N 85.53W
Belén [Par.] 55 Df 23.30S 57.06W
Belén [Ur.] 55 Dj 30.47S 57.47W
Belén, Cuchilla de- 55 Dj 30.55S 56.30W
Belén de Escobar 55 Cl 34.21S 58.47W
Belene 15 If 43.39N 25.07 E
Bélep, Iles- 57 Hf 19.45S 163.40 E
Beles 35 Fc 10.55N 35.10 E
Belev 16 Jc 53.50N 36.10 E
Beleye 35 Fc 11.24N 36.10 E
Belfast [Me.-U.S.] 44 Mc 44.27N 69.01W
Belfast [S.Afr.] 37 Ee 25.43S 30.03 E
Belfast/Béal Feirste 6 Fe 54.35N 5.55W
Belfast Lough/Loch Lao 9 Hg 54.40N 5.50W
Belfield 45 Ec 46.53N 103.12W
Belford 9 Lf 55.36N 1.49W
Belfort 11 Mg 47.45N 7.00 E
Belgaum 25 Jh 15.52N 74.30 E
Belgica Bank (EN) 67 Ld 78.28N 15.00W
Belgicafjella 66 Df 72.35S 31.10 E
België/Belgique=Belgium (EN) [1] 6 Ge 50.30N 4.30 E
Belgique/België=Belgium (EN) [1] 6 Ge 50.30N 4.30 E
Belgium (EN)=België/Belgique [1] 6 Ge 50.30N 4.30 E
Belgium (EN)=Belgique/België [1] 6 Ge 50.30N 4.30 E
Belgorod 6 Je 50.36N 36.35 E
Belgorod-Dnestrovski 19 Df 46.12N 30.17 E
Belgorodskaja Oblast [3] 19 De 50.45N 37.30 E
Belgrade (EN)=Beograd 6 Ig 44.50N 20.30 E
Bel Haïrane 32 Ic 31.17N 6.20 E
Beli 34 Hd 7.52N 10.58 E
Belice 14 Gm 37.35N 12.52 E
Beli Drim 15 Dg 42.05N 20.20 E
Belidži 16 Pi 41.53N 48.20 E
Beli Lom 15 If 43.41N 26.00 E
Beli Manastir 14 Me 45.46N 18.37 E
Belimbegovo 15 Eh 42.00N 21.35 E
Belin 11 Fj 44.30N 0.47W
Belinga 36 Bb 1.04N 13.12 E
Belinski 16 Mc 52.58N 43.29 E
Belinyu 26 Eg 1.38S 105.46 E
Beliş 15 Gc 46.39N 23.02 E
Beli Timok 15 Ff 43.55N 22.18 E
Belize [1] 39 Kh 17.15N 88.45W
Belize (British Honduras) 49 Ce 17.35N 88.35W
Belize City 39 Kh 17.30N 88.12W
Belize River 49 Ce 17.32N 88.14W
Beljajevka 16 Gf 46.29N 30.14 E
Beljanica 15 Ee 44.07N 21.43 E
Belka 8 Mg 57.40N 29.47 E
Belkovski, Ostrov- 20 Ia 75.30N 136.00 E
Bellac 11 Hh 46.07N 1.03 E
Bella Coola 42 Ef 52.22N 126.46W
Bellagio 14 De 45.59N 9.15 E
Bellaire [Oh.-U.S.] 44 Ge 40.02N 80.46W
Bellaire [Tx.-U.S.] 45 Il 29.43N 95.28W
Bellaria-Igea Marina 14 Gf 44.09N 12.28 E
Bellary 22 Jh 15.09N 76.56 E
Bella Unión 55 Dj 30.15S 57.35W
Bella Vista [Arg.] 56 Ic 28.30S 59.03W
Bella Vista [Par.] 55 Df 22.08S 56.31W
Bellavista, Capo- 14 Dk 39.56N 9.43 E
Bell Bay 42 Jb 71.10N 84.55W
Belle-Anse 49 Kd 18.14N 72.04W
Belledonne 11 Mi 45.18N 6.08 E
Bellefontaine [Mart.] 51h Ab 14.40N 61.10W
Bellefontaine [Oh.-U.S.] 44 Fe 40.22N 83.45W
Belle Fourche 43 Gc 44.40N 103.51W
Belle Fourche River 45 Ed 44.26N 102.19W
Bellegarde 11 If 47.59N 2.26 E
Bellegarde-sur-Valserine 11 Lh 46.06N 5.49 E
Belle Glade 44 Gl 26.41N 80.40W
Belle Ile 5 Ff 47.19N 3.11W
Belle Isle 42 Lf 51.55N 55.20W
Belle Isle, Strait of- 38 Nd 51.35N 56.30W
Bellencombre 12 De 49.42N 1.14 E
Belleplaine 51q Ab 13.15N 59.34W
Belleville [Fr.] 11 Kh 46.06N 4.45 E
Belleville [Il.-U.S.] 45 Lg 38.31N 90.00W
Belleville [Ks.-U.S.] 45 Hg 39.49N 97.38W
Belleville [Ont.-Can.] 42 Jh 44.10N 77.23W
Bellevue [Nb.-U.S.] 45 If 41.09N 95.54W
Bellevue [Wa.-U.S.] 46 Dc 47.37N 122.12W
Belley 11 Li 45.46N 5.41 E
Bellheim 12 Ke 49.12N 8.17 E
Bellin 39 Lc 60.00N 70.01W
Bellingham [Eng.-U.K.] 9 Kf 55.09N 2.16W
Bellingham [Wa.-U.S.] 39 Ge 48.46N 122.29W
Bellingsfors 8 Ef 58.59N 12.15 E
Bellingshausen 66 Re 62.12S 58.56W
Bellingshausen Ice Shelf 66 Ce 71.00S 89.00W
Bellingshausen Sea (EN) 66 Pf 71.00S 85.00W
Bellinzona 14 Dd 46.11N 9.02 E
Bello 54 Cb 6.19N 75.34W
Bellocq 55 Bl 35.55S 61.32W
Bellona, Récifs- 57 Gg 21.00S 159.00 E
Bellona Island 60 Fj 11.17S 159.47 E
Bellot Strait 42 Ib 72.00N 94.30W
Bellow Falls 44 Kd 43.08N 72.28W
Bell Peninsula 42 Jd 63.45N 81.30W
Bell River 42 Jg 49.49N 77.39W
Bell Rock→Inchcape 9 Ke 56.26N 2.24W
Bellsund 41 Nc 77.39N 14.15 E
Belluno 14 Gd 46.09N 12.13 E
Bell Ville 56 Hd 32.37S 62.42W
Bellville 37 Bf 33.53S 18.36 E
Belmond 45 Je 42.51N 93.37W
Belmont 44 Hd 42.14N 78.02W
Belmonte [Braz.] 54 Kg 15.51S 38.54W
Belmonte [Port.] 13 Ed 40.21N 7.21W
Belmonte [Sp.] 13 Je 39.34N 2.42W
Belmopan 39 Kh 17.15N 88.46W
Beloeil 12 Fd 50.35N 3.43 E
Belogorsk [R.S.F.S.R.] 22 Od 50.57N 128.25 E
Belogorsk [Ukr.-U.S.S.R.] 16 Ig 45.01N 34.33 E
Belogradčik 15 Ff 43.38N 22.41 E
Belogradčiški 15 Ff 43.38N 22.28 E
Belo Horizonte 53 Lg 19.55S 43.56W
Beloit [Ks.-U.S.] 45 Gg 39.28N 98.06W
Beloit [Wi.-U.S.] 43 Jc 42.31N 89.02W
Belojarovo 20 Hf 51.35N 128.55 E
Belojarski 19 Gc 63.40N 66.45 E
Beloje More=White Sea (EN) 5 Kb 66.00N 44.00 E
Beloje Ozero=White Lake (EN) 5 Jc 60.11N 37.35 E
Belokany 16 Oi 41.43N 46.28 E
Belomorsk 6 Jc 64.29N 34.43 E
Belomorsko-Baltijski Kanal =White Sea-Baltic Canal (EN) 5 Jc 63.30N 34.48 E
Belomorsko-Kulojskoje Plato 7 Jd 65.20N 41.50 E
Beloozersk 16 Dc 52.28N 25.13 E
Belopolje 19 De 51.09N 34.18 E
Beloreč'ensk 16 Kg 44.43N 39.52 E
Beloreck 19 Fe 53.58N 58.24 E
Belorusskaja Grjada 16 Ec 53.50N 27.00 E
Belorusskaja Sovetskaja Socialističeskaja Respublika [2] 19 Ce 53.50N 28.00 E
Belorusskaja SSR/ Belaruskaja Sovetskaja Socialistyčnaja Respublika [2] 19 Ce 53.50N 28.00 E
Belorusskaja SSR= Byelorussian SSR (EN) [2] 19 Ce 53.50N 28.00 E
Belo-sur-Mer 37 Gd 20.44S 44.00 E
Belo-sur-Tsiribihina 37 Gc 19.39S 44.32 E
Belot, Lac- 42 Ec 66.50N 126.20W
Belovo 20 Df 54.25N 86.18 E
Belovodsk 16 Ke 49.10N 39.33 E
Belovodskoe 18 Jc 42.47N 74.13 E
Belozersk 19 Dd 60.03N 37.48 E
Belper 12 Aa 53.02N 1.28W
Belted Range 46 Gh 37.25N 116.10W
Belton [Mo.-U.S.] 45 Ig 38.49N 94.32W
Belton [Tx.-U.S.] 45 Hk 31.04N 97.28W
Belton Lake 45 Hk 31.08N 97.32W
Belturbet/Béal Tairbirt 9 Fg 54.06N 7.26W
Beluha 21 Ke 49.48N 86.35 E
Belvedere Marittimo 14 Jk 39.37N 15.52 E
Belvidere 45 Le 42.15N 88.50W
Bely 7 Hi 55.50N 32.58 E
Bely, Ostrov-=Bely Island (EN) 21 Jb 73.10N 70.45 E
Belyando River 59 Jd 21.38S 146.50 E
Bely Čeremoš 15 Ia 48.06N 25.04 E
Bely Island (EN)=Bely, Ostrov- 21 Jb 73.10N 70.45 E
Bely Jar 20 De 58.26N 85.03 E
Belyje Berega 16 Ic 53.12N 34.42 E
Belz 16 Dd 50.23N 24.03 E
Bełżec 10 Tf 50.24N 23.26 E
Belzoni 45 Kj 33.11N 90.29W
Bełżyce 10 Se 51.11N 22.18 E
Bemaraha, Plateau de- 30 Lj 19.00S 45.15 E
Bembe 36 Bd 7.02S 14.18 E
Bembéréké 34 Fc 10.13N 2.40 E
Bembézar 13 Gg 37.45N 5.13W
Bembridge 12 Ad 50.41N 1.05W
Bemidji 43 Ib 47.29N 94.53W
Ben 24 Nf 32.32N 50.45 E
Benāb 23 Gb 37.18N 46.05 E
Benabarre/Benavarn 13 Mb 42.07N 0.29 E
Bena Dibele 36 Dc 4.07S 22.50 E
Bénaize 11 Hh 46.34N 1.04 E
Benalla 59 Jg 36.33S 145.59 E
Benares→Vārānasi 22 Kg 25.20N 83.00 E
Benasc/Benasque 13 Mb 42.36N 0.32 E
Benasque/Benasc 13 Mb 42.36N 0.32 E
Benavarn/Benabarre 13 Mb 42.07N 0.29 E
Benavente 13 Gc 42.00N 5.41W
Benbecula 9 Fd 57.27N 7.20W
Bencheng→Luannan 28 Ee 39.30N 118.4
Ben-Chicao, Col de- 13 Oh 36.12N 2.5
Bend 43 Cc 44.03N 121.1
Bendaja 34 Cd 7.10N 11.1
Bendel [2] 34 Gd 6.00N 5.5
Bendela 36 Cc 3.18S 17.3
Bender Bäyla 31 Mh 9.30N 50.3
Bendersiyada 35 Hc 11.14N 48.5
Bendery 19 Cf 46.48N 29.2
Bendigo 58 Fh 36.46S 144.1
Bendorf 12 Jd 50.26N 7.3
Bēne/Bene 8 Jh 56.28N 23.0
Bene/Bēne 8 Jh 56.28N 23.0
Bénéna 34 Ec 13.06N 4.2
Benepú, Rada- 65d Ac 27.10S 109.2
Benešov 10 Kg 49.47N 14.4
Benevento 14 Ii 41.08N 14.4
Bengal 21 Kg 24.00N 90.0
Bengal, Bay of- (EN) 21 Kh 15.00N 90.0
Bengamisa 36 Eb 0.57N 25.1
Bengbis 34 He 3.27N 12.2
Bengbu 22 Nf 32.47N 117.2
Benghazi (EN)=Banghāzī 31 Je 32.07N 20.0
Benghazi (EN)= Banghāzī [3] 33 Dd 27.00N 20.3
Benghisa Point 14 Io 35.50N 14.3
Bengkalis 26 Df 1.28N 102.0
Bengkulu [3] 26 Dg 3.48S 102.1
Bengkulu 22 Mj 3.48S 102.1
Bengo, Baía do- 30 Ii 8.43S 13.2
Bengo He 28 Eg 35.04N 118.2
Bengough 46 Mb 49.24N 105.0
Bengtsfors 7 Cg 59.02N 12.1
Benguela 31 Ij 12.35S 13.2
Benguela [3] 36 Be 12.00S 15.0
Benguerir 32 Fc 32.14N 7.5
Benguérua, Ilha- 37 Fd 21.53S 35.2
Bengue Viejo 49 Ce 17.05N 89.0
Bengut, Cap- 32 Hb 36.55N 3.5
Beni 31 Jh 0.30N 29.2
Beni [2] 54 Ef 14.00S 65.3
Beni, Río- 52 Jg 10.23S 65.2
Beni Abbes 32 Gc 30.08N 2.1
Beni Baufrah 13 Hi 35.05N 4.1
Benicarló 13 Md 40.25N 0.2
Benicasim 13 Md 40.03N 0.0
Beni Chougran, Monts des- 13 Mi 35.30N 0.15
Benidorm 13 Lf 38.32N 0.08
Beni Enzar 13 Ji 35.14N 2.57
Beni Haoua 13 Nh 36.32N 1.34
Beni Mellal 31 Ge 32.20N 6.21
Beni Mellal [3] 32 Fc 32.30N 6.30
Benin 34 Gd 5.45N 5.04
Bénin=Benin (EN) [1] 31 Hh 9.30N 2.15
Bénin (Dahomey) [1] 31 Hh 9.30N 2.15
Benin (EN)=Bénin [1] 31 Hh 9.30N 2.15
Benin, Bight of- 30 Hh 5.30N 4.00
Benin City 31 Hh 6.20N 5.38
Beni Ounif 32 Gc 32.03N 1.15
Benisa 13 Mf 38.43N 0.03
Beni Saf 13 Ki 35.19N 1.23
Benisheikh 34 Hc 11.48N 12.29
Benito Juárez 48 Mi 17.50N 92.32
Benito Juárez, Presa- 48 Li 16.27N 95.30
Benjamen Island 37b Bb 5.27S 53.21
Benjamin 45 Gj 33.35N 99.48
Benjamín Aceval 55 Dg 24.58S 57.34
Benjamin Constant 53 If 4.22S 70.02
Benjamin Hill 48 Db 30.10N 111.10
Benkei-Misaki 29a Bb 42.50N 140.11
Benkelman 45 Ff 40.03N 101.32
Benkovac 14 Jf 44.02N 15.37
Ben Mehidi 14 Bn 36.46N 7.54
Bennett, Lake- 59 Gd 23.50S 131.00
Bennett, Ostrov- 20 Ja 76.45N 149.00
Benneydale 62 Fc 38.31S 175.21
Bennichab 32 Df 19.26N 15.21
Bennington 44 Kd 42.53N 73.12
Benom 26 Df 3.50N 102.06
Benoni 31 Jk 26.19S 28.27
Bénoué=Benue (EN) 30 Hh 7.48N 6.46
Benoy 35 Bd 8.59N 16.19
Benrath 12 Ic 51.10N 6.52
Bensekrane 13 Ki 35.04N 1.13
Bensheim 10 Eg 49.41N 8.37
Ben Slimane 32 Fc 33.37N 7.07
Benson [Az.-U.S.] 46 Jk 31.58N 110.18
Benson [Mn.-U.S.] 45 Id 45.19N 95.36
Benson Point 64g Ab 1.56N 157.30
Bent 23 Id 26.17N 59.31
Benteng [Indon.] 26 Hg 0.24S 121.59
Benteng [Indon.] 26 Hh 6.08N 120.27
Bentheim 10 Dd 52.19N 7.10
Bentiaba 36 Be 14.29S 12.50
Bentinck 25 Jf 11.45N 98.03
Bentinck Island 59 Hc 17.05S 139.30
Bentiu 35 Dd 9.14N 29.50
Bento Conçalves 56 Jc 29.10S 51.31
Bento Gomes, Rio- 55 Dc 16.40S 57.12
Benton [Ar.-U.S.] 45 Ji 34.34N 92.35
Benton [Il.-U.S.] 45 Lg 38.01N 88.55
Bentong 26 Df 3.32N 101.55
Benton Harbor 44 Dd 42.07N 86.27
Bentonville 45 Ih 36.22N 94.13
Benua, Pulau- 26 Ef 0.56N 107.27
Benue [2] 34 Gd 7.15N 8.20
Benue 30 Hh 7.48N 6.46
Benue (EN)=Bénoué 30 Hh 7.48N 6.46
Benwee Head/An Bhinn Bhuí 9 Dg 54.21N 9.48W
Benxi 22 Oe 41.16N 123.48
Beo 26 If 4.15N 126.48
Beograd = Belgrade (EN) 6 Ig 44.50N 20.30
Beograd-Krnjača 15 De 44.52N 20.28
Beograd-Zemun 15 De 44.53N 20.25
Béoumi 34 Dd 7.40N 5.34W

Index Symbols

- [1] Independent Nation
- [2] State, Region
- [3] District, County
- [4] Municipality
- [5] Colony, Dependency
- Continent
- Physical Region
- Historical or Cultural Region
- Mount, Mountain
- Volcano
- Hill
- Mountains, Mountain Range
- Hills, Escarpment
- Plateau, Upland
- Pass, Gap
- Plain, Lowland
- Delta
- Salt Flat
- Valley, Canyon
- Crater, Cave
- Karst Features
- Depression
- Polder
- Desert, Dunes
- Forest, Woods
- Heath, Steppe
- Oasis
- Cape, Point
- Coast, Beach
- Cliff
- Peninsula
- Isthmus
- Sandbank
- Island
- Atoll
- Rock, Reef
- Islands, Archipelago
- Rocks, Reefs
- Coral Reef
- Well, Spring
- Geyser
- River, Stream
- Waterfall Rapids
- River Mouth, Estuary
- Lake
- Salt Lake
- Intermittent Lake
- Reservoir
- Swamp, Pond
- Canal
- Glacier
- Ice Shelf, Pack Ice
- Ocean
- Sea
- Gulf, Bay
- Strait, Fjord
- Lagoon
- Bank
- Seamount
- Tablemount
- Ridge
- Shelf
- Basin
- Escarpment, Sea Scarp
- Fracture
- Trench, Abyss
- National Park, Reserve
- Point of Interest
- Recreation Site
- Cave, Cavern
- Historic Site
- Ruins
- Wall, Walls
- Church, Abbey
- Temple
- Scientific Station
- Airport
- Port
- Lighthouse
- Mine
- Tunnel
- Dam, Bridge

pu	27	Ne	33.17N	131.30 E
pu-Wan ◐	29	Be	33.20N	131.35 E
uia Head ►	51n	Ba	13.03N	61.12W
uia Island ◆	50	Ff	13.01N	61.13W
aketa	37	Hd	24.11S	45.42 E
ati	15	Ci	40.42N	19.57 E
atus, Gunung- ▲	26	Gg	1.02S	116.20 E
au, Teluk-=McCluer Gulf N) ◐	26	Jg	2.30S	132.30 E
berä	31	Lg	10.25N	45.02 E
bérati	31	Ih	4.16N	15.47 E
beria, Cabo- ►	13	Nf	38.38N	1.23 E
bice River ∿	54	Gb	6.17N	57.32W
ca	15	Jd	45.17N	26.41 E
chères-sur-Vesgre	12	Df	48.51N	1.33 E
chtesgaden	10	Ii	47.38N	13.00 E
ck [Fr.]	12	Dd	50.24N	1.36 E
ck [Fr.]	11	Hd	50.24N	1.34 E
ck- Berck Plage	12	Dd	50.24N	1.34 E
ck-Plage, Berck-	12	Dd	50.24N	1.34 E
da ∿	16	Jf	46.47N	36.52 E
dāle	35	Hd	7.04N	47.51 E
dičev	19	Cf	49.53N	28.36 E
digestjah	20	Hd	62.03N	126.50 E
djansk	19	Df	46.43N	36.48 E
dsk	20	Df	54.47N	83.05 E
egomet	15	Ia	48.10N	25.24 E
egovo	19	Cf	48.13N	22.41 E
eku	36	Gc	4.27S	35.44 E
ekua	50	Fe	15.14N	61.19W
ekum	34	Ed	7.27N	2.35W
ens ∿	42	Hf	52.21N	97.01W
ens River	42	Hf	52.22N	97.02W
esford	45	He	43.05N	96.47W
estečko	10	Vf	50.16N	25.14 E
eşti	15	Kc	46.06N	27.53 E
ettyó ∿	15	Ec	46.59N	21.07 E
ettyóújfalu	10	Ri	47.13N	21.33 E
eza	19	Ce	52.33N	24.58 E
ezan	16	Gd	50.19N	31.31 E
ežany	16	De	49.29N	25.00 E
ezina [Bye.-U.S.S.R.] ∿	16	Dc	53.48N	25.59 E
ezina [U.S.S.R.] ∿	5	Je	52.33N	30.14 E
ezino [Bye.-U.S.S.R.]	16	Fc	53.51N	29.00 E
ezino [Bye.-U.S.S.R.]	8	Mj	54.55N	28.16 E
ezino [Ukr.-U.S.S.R.]	15	Mc	46.16N	29.11 E
eznegovatoje	16	Hf	47.20N	32.49 E
eznik	19	Ec	62.53N	42.42 E
ezniki	6	Ld	59.24N	56.46 E
ezno	16	Ed	51.01N	26.45 E
ezovka [Bye.-U.S.S.R.]	10	Vc	53.40N	25.37 E
ezovka [R.S.F.S.R.]	17	Hd	64.59N	56.29 E
ezovka [Ukr.-U.S.S.R.]	19	Df	47.12N	30.56 E
ezovka Višerka ∿	17	Hf	60.55N	56.50 E
ezovo	19	Gc	63.58N	65.00 E
ezovski [R.S.F.S.R.]	17	Jh	56.55N	60.50 E
ezovski [R.S.F.S.R.]	20	De	55.39N	86.16 E
ezovy	20	If	51.41N	135.52 E
ga [Sp.]	13	Nb	42.06N	1.51 E
ga [Swe.]	8	Gg	57.13N	16.02 E
gama	23	Cb	39.07N	27.10 E
gamo	14	De	45.41N	9.43 E
gantiños ⊠	13	Da	43.20N	8.45W
gby	7	Df	60.56N	17.02 E
gen [G.D.R.]	10	Jb	54.25N	13.26 E
gen [Neth.]	12	Gb	52.40N	4.42 E
gen [Nor.]	6	Gc	60.23N	5.20 E
gen/Mons	11	Jd	50.27N	3.56 E
gen aan Zee, Bergen-	12	Gb	52.40N	4.38 E
gen-Bergen aan Zee	12	Gb	52.40N	4.38 E
gen op Zoom	11	Kc	51.30N	4.17 E
gerac	11	Gj	44.51N	0.29 E
geyk	12	Hc	51.19N	5.22 E
gh	12	Ic	51.53N	6.16 E
gheim	10	Cf	50.58N	6.39 E
gh-s'Heerenberg	12	Ic	51.53N	6.16 E
gisches Land ⊠	10	De	51.07N	7.10 E
gisch Gladbach	10	Df	50.59N	7.08 E
gkvara	8	Gh	56.23N	16.05 E
gneustadt	12	Jc	51.02N	7.39 E
gö ◆	8	Ib	62.55N	21.10 E
gsjö	7	Df	61.59N	17.04 E
gslagen ⊠	8	Fd	60.05N	14.30 E
gstraße ⊠	12	Ke	49.40N	8.40 E
gues	12	Ed	50.58N	2.26 E
gum, Tietjerksteradeel-	12	Ha	53.12N	6.00 E
gviken ≈	8	Gc	61.10N	16.45 E
gville	37	De	28.52S	29.18 E
h	27	Jb	47.45N	111.07 E
hala, Selat- ═	26	Dg	0.48S	104.25 E
hampore	25	Hd	24.06N	88.15 E
hampur	22	Kh	19.19N	84.47 E
ici, Monti- ⛰	14	Fe	45.26N	11.31 E
ikān	24	Nh	28.17N	51.14 E
ikulski	20	De	55.32N	88.08 E
inga, Ostrov-=Bering sland (EN) ◆	20	Lf	55.00N	166.10 E
ingen	12	Hc	51.03N	5.13 E
ing Glacier ❄	40	Kd	60.15N	143.30W
ing Island (EN)= Beringa, Ostrov- ◆	20	Lf	55.00N	166.10 E
ingovo More=Bering Sea (EN) ≡	38	Bd	60.00N	175.00W
ingovski	22	Tc	63.07N	179.19 E
ing Proliv=Bering Strait EN) ═	38	Cc	65.30N	169.00W
ing Sea ≡	38	Bd	60.00N	175.00W
ing Sea (EN)=Beringovo More ≡	38	Bd	60.00N	175.00W
ing Strait ═	38	Cc	65.30N	169.00W
ing Strait (EN)=Bering Proliv ═	38	Cc	65.30N	169.00W
islav	16	Hf	46.51N	33.29 E
isso	55	Dl	34.52S	57.53W
it Dağı ▲	24	Gc	38.01N	36.52 E
īzak	24	Qi	26.06N	57.15 E
ja	13	Jh	36.51N	2.57W
Berkåk	7	Be	62.50N	10.00 E
Berkane	32	Gc	34.56N	2.20W
Berkel ∿	10	Cd	52.09N	6.12 E
Berkeley	43	Cd	37.57N	122.18W
Berkhamsted	12	Bc	51.45N	0.33W
Berkner Island ◆	66	Rf	79.30S	49.30W
Berkovica	15	Gf	43.14N	23.07 E
Berks ▣	9	Lj	51.15N	1.20W
Berkshire ③	9	Lj	51.30N	1.10W
Berkshire Downs ⌓	9	Lj	51.35N	1.25W
Berkshire Hills ⌓	44	Kd	42.20N	73.10W
Berlaimont	12	Fd	50.12N	3.49 E
Berlanga de Duero	13	Jc	41.28N	2.51W
Berlengas, Ilhas- ❖	13	Ce	39.25N	9.30W
Berlevåg	7	Ga	70.51N	29.06 E
Berlin	43	Mc	44.29N	71.10W
Berlin (Ost)=East Berlin (EN) ②	10	Jd	52.30N	13.25 E
Berlin (Ost)=East Berlin (EN)	6	He	52.31N	13.24 E
Berlin (West)=West Berlin (EN)	6	He	52.31N	13.24 E
Berlin-Pankow	10	Jd	52.34N	13.24 E
Bermeja, Sierra- ⛰	13	Gh	36.30N	5.15W
Bermejillo	47	Dc	25.53N	103.37W
Bermejito, Río- ∿	55	Bg	25.39S	60.11W
Bermejo, Isla- ◆	55	An	39.01S	62.01W
Bermejo, Paso-/Cumbre, Paso de la- ⌵	52	Ii	32.50S	70.05W
Bermejo, Río- [Arg.] ∿	52	Ji	31.52S	67.22W
Bermejo, Río- [S.Amer.] ∿	52	Kh	26.52S	58.23W
Bermen, lac- ≈	42	Kf	53.35N	68.55W
Bermeo	13	Ja	43.26N	2.43W
Bermillo de Sayago	13	Fc	41.22N	6.06W
Bermuda ⑤	39	Mf	32.20N	64.45W
Bermuda Islands ❖	39	Mf	32.20N	64.45W
Bermuda Rise (EN) ⋀	38	Mf	32.30N	65.00W
Bern ②	14	Bd	46.55N	7.40 E
Bern/Berne	6	Gf	46.55N	7.30 E
Bernalda	14	Kj	40.24N	16.41 E
Bernalillo	45	Ci	35.18N	106.33W
Bernard Islands ❖	64d	Bb	7.18N	151.32 E
Bernardo de Irigoyen	55	Bk	32.10S	61.09W
Bernardo do Irigoyen	56	Jc	26.15S	53.39W
Bernasconi	56	He	37.54S	63.43W
Bernau bei Berlin	10	Jd	52.40N	13.35 E
Bernaville	12	Ed	50.08N	2.10 E
Bernay	11	Ge	49.06N	0.36 E
Bernburg	10	He	51.48N	11.44 E
Berndorf	14	Kc	47.57N	16.06 E
Berne [F.R.G.]	12	Ka	53.11N	8.29 E
Berne [In.-U.S.]	44	Ee	40.39N	84.57W
Berne/Bern	6	Gf	46.55N	7.30 E
Berner Alpen/Alpes Bernoises=Bernese Alps (EN) ⛰	14	Bd	46.25N	7.30 E
Berneray ◆	9	Fd	57.43N	7.15W
Bernese Alps (EN)=Alpes Bernoises/Berner Alpen ⛰	14	Bd	46.25N	7.30 E
Bernese Alps (EN)=Berner Alpen/Alpes Bernoises ⛰	14	Bd	46.25N	7.30 E
Bernesga ∿	13	Gb	42.28N	5.31W
Bernesq	12	Be	49.16N	0.56W
Bernier Bay ◐	42	Ib	71.08N	88.00W
Bernier Island ◆	59	Cd	24.50S	113.10 E
Bernina ⌵	14	Ed	46.25N	10.01 E
Bernina ▲	5	Gf	46.22N	9.50 E
Berninapaß ⌵	14	Ed	46.25N	10.01 E
Bernissart	12	Fd	50.28N	3.38 E
Bernkastel-Kues	10	Dg	49.55N	7.04 E
Bernstorffs Isfjord ═	41	Hf	63.10N	40.45W
Berón de Astrada	55	Dh	27.33S	57.32W
Beroroha	37	Hd	21.39S	45.10 E
Béroubouay	34	Fc	10.32N	2.44 E
Beroun	10	Kg	49.58N	14.04 E
Berounka ∿	10	Kg	50.00N	14.24 E
Berovo	15	Fh	41.43N	22.51 E
Berre, Étang de- ≋	11	Lk	43.27N	5.08 E
Berriane	32	Hc	32.50N	3.46 E
Berrouaghia	13	Oh	36.08N	2.55 E
Berry ▣	11	Hh	47.00N	2.00 E
Berry-au-Bac	12	Fe	49.24N	3.54 E
Berryessa, Lake- ≈	46	Dg	38.37N	122.16W
Berry Head ►	9	Jk	50.24N	3.29W
Berry Islands ❖	47	Ic	25.34N	77.45W
Berry River ∿	46	Ja	50.50N	111.36W
Beršad	19	Cf	48.23N	29.33 E
Berseba	37	Be	26.01S	17.41 E
Bersenbrück	12	Jb	52.33N	7.56 E
Berthierville	44	Kb	46.05N	73.11W
Bertincourt	12	Ed	50.05N	2.59 E
Bertogne	12	Hd	50.05N	5.40 E
Bertolinia	54	Je	7.38S	43.57W
Bertoua	31	Ih	4.35N	13.41 E
Bertraghboy Bay ◐	9	Dh	53.23N	9.50W
Bertrix	12	He	49.51N	5.15 E
Beru Island ◆	57	Ie	1.20S	176.00 E
Berwick-upon-Tweed	9	Lf	55.46N	2.00W
Berwyn ⛰	9	Ji	52.53N	3.24W
Besalampy	37	Gc	16.44S	44.24 E
Besançon	6	Gf	47.15N	6.02 E
Besar, Gunung- ▲	26	Gg	1.25S	115.39 E
Besbre ∿	11	Jh	46.33N	3.44 E
Besed ∿	16	Gc	52.38N	31.11 E
Besikama	26	Hh	9.36S	124.57 E
Beskid Mountains (EN) ⛰	5	Hf	49.40N	20.00 E
Beskid Niski ⛰	10	Rg	49.20N	21.30 E
Beskid Średni ⛰	10	Pg	49.45N	19.20 E
Beskid Wysoki ⛰	10	Pg	49.32N	20.00 E
Beskidy Wschodnie ⛰	10	Sg	49.20N	22.30 E
Beskidy Zachodnie ⛰	10	Pg	49.30N	19.30 E
Beskol	18	Ma	46.06N	81.01 E
Beslan	19	Eg	43.10N	44.35 E
Besna Kobila ▲	15	Fg	42.32N	22.14 E
Besni	24	Gd	37.41N	37.52 E
Besparmak Dağ ▲	15	Kl	37.30N	27.35 E
Bessao	35	Bd	7.53N	15.59 E
Bessarabia (EN)= Bessarabija ▣	15	Lb	47.00N	28.30 E
Bessarabija=Bessarabia (EN) ▣	15	Lb	47.00N	28.30 E
Bessarabka	16	Ff	46.20N	28.59 E
Bessèges	11	Kj	44.17N	4.06 E
Bessemer	43	Je	33.25N	86.57W
Bessin ⊠	11	Fe	49.10N	1.00W
Bessines-sur-Gartempe	11	Hh	46.06N	1.22 E
Bessoki, Gora- ▲	16	Rh	43.57N	52.30 E
Best	12	Hc	51.30N	5.24 E
Bestjah [R.S.F.S.R.]	20	Hc	66.00N	123.35 E
Bestjah [R.S.F.S.R.]	20	Hd	61.17N	128.50 E
Bestobe	19	He	52.30N	73.05 E
Bestwig	12	Kc	51.22N	8.24 E
Betafo	37	Hc	19.49S	46.50 E
Betanzos [Bol.]	54	Eg	19.34S	65.27W
Betanzos [Sp.]	13	Da	43.17N	8.12W
Betanzos, Ría de- ⋎	13	Da	43.23N	8.15W
Bétaré Oya	34	Hd	5.36N	14.05 E
Bétérou	34	Fd	9.12N	2.16 E
Beteta	13	Jd	40.34N	2.04W
Bethal	37	De	26.27S	29.28 E
Bethanien ③	37	Be	26.30S	17.00 E
Bethanien	31	Ik	26.32S	17.11 E
Bethany [Mo.-U.S.]	45	If	40.16N	94.02W
Bethany [Ok.-U.S.]	45	Hi	35.31N	97.38W
Bethel	39	Cc	60.48N	161.46W
Bétheniville	12	Ge	49.18N	4.22 E
Bethlehem [Pa.-U.S.]	44	Je	40.36N	75.22W
Bethlehem [S.Afr.]	31	Jk	28.15S	28.15 E
Bethlehem (EN)=Bayt Laḩm	24	Fg	31.43N	35.12 E
Bethulie	37	Df	30.32S	25.59 E
Béthune	11	Id	50.32N	2.38 E
Béthune ∿	11	He	49.53N	1.09 E
Betioky	37	Gd	23.42S	44.22 E
Betong	25	Kg	5.45N	101.05 E
Betor	35	Fc	11.37N	39.00 E
Bétou	36	Cb	3.03N	18.31 E
Betpak-Dala ψ	21	Ie	46.00N	70.00 E
Betroka	37	Hd	23.15S	46.05 E
Bet She'an	24	Ff	32.30N	35.30 E
Betsiamites, Rivière- ∿	42	Kg	48.56N	68.38W
Betsiboka ∿	30	Lj	16.03S	46.36 E
Bette ▲	30	If	22.00N	19.12 E
Bettembourg/Bettemburg	12	Ie	49.31N	6.06 E
Bettemburg/Bettembourg	12	Ie	49.31N	6.06 E
Bettendorf	45	Kf	41.32N	90.30W
Bettles Field	40	Ic	66.53N	151.51W
Bettna	8	Gf	58.55N	16.38 E
Bettola	14	Df	44.47N	9.36 E
Betūl	25	Fd	21.55N	77.54 E
Betuwe ⊠	11	Lc	51.55N	5.30 E
Betwa ∿	25	Hc	25.55N	80.12 E
Betz	12	Ee	49.09N	2.57 E
Betzdorf	10	Df	50.47N	7.53 E
Beulah	44	Dc	44.38N	86.06W
Beult ∿	12	Cc	51.13N	0.26 E
Beuvron ∿	11	Hg	47.29N	1.15 E
Beuzeville	12	Ce	49.20N	0.21 E
Beveland ⊠	11	Jc	51.30N	3.40 E
Beveren	12	Gc	51.13N	4.15 E
Beveridge Reef ✹	57	Kg	20.00S	168.00W
Beverley [Austl.]	59	Df	32.06S	116.56 E
Beverley [Eng.-U.K.]	9	Mh	53.51N	0.26W
Beverwijk	11	Kb	52.28N	4.40 E
Bewsher, Mount- ▲	66	Ff	70.54S	65.28 E
Bexhill	9	Nk	50.50N	0.29 E
Bexley, London-	12	Cc	51.26N	0.09 E
Beyağaç	15	Ll	37.13N	28.57 E
Beyānlū	24	Ld	36.02N	47.53 E
Bey Dağı ▲	24	Hc	38.15N	38.22 E
Bey Dağlari ⛰	23	Db	36.40N	30.15 E
Beykoz	24	Cb	41.08N	29.05 E
Beyla	34	Dd	8.41N	8.38W
Beyoğlu, İstanbul	15	Lh	41.02N	28.59 E
Beyoneisu-Retsugan ✱	27	Oe	31.55N	139.55 E
Beypazari	24	Db	40.10N	31.55 E
Beyra	35	Hd	6.57N	47.19 E
Beyram	24	Oi	27.26N	53.31 E
Beyşehir	24	Dd	37.41N	31.43 E
Beyşehir Gölü ≈	23	Db	37.40N	31.30 E
Bezaha	37	Gd	23.29S	44.30 E
Bežanickaja Vozvyšennost ▬	7	Gh	56.45N	29.30 E
Bežanicy	7	Gh	56.58N	29.57 E
Bezdan	15	Bd	45.51N	18.56 E
Bezděz ▲	10	Kf	50.32N	14.43 E
Bezdež	10	Vd	52.18N	25.20 E
Bežeck	19	Dd	57.50N	36.41 E
Bezenčuk	7	Lj	53.01N	49.24 E
Bezerra, Rio- ∿	55	Ia	13.16S	47.31W
Bezerros	54	Ke	8.14S	35.45W
Beziers	11	Jk	43.21N	3.15 E
Bezmein	19	Fh	38.05N	58.12 E
Bežta	19	Eg	42.08N	46.08 E
Bhadrakh	25	Hd	21.04N	86.30 E
Bhadrāvati	25	Ff	13.52N	75.43 E
Bhāgalpur	22	Kg	25.15N	87.00 E
Bhairawa	25	Gc	27.31N	83.24 E
Bhaironghati	25	Fb	31.01N	78.53 E
Bhakkar	25	Eb	31.38N	71.04 E
Bhamo	25	Jd	24.16N	97.14 E
Bhandāra	25	Fd	21.10N	79.39 E
Bhanjan	25	Gc	25.47N	83.36 E
Bhārat Juktarashtra=India (EN) ①	22	Jh	20.00N	77.00 E
Bharatpur	25	Fc	27.13N	77.29 E
Bharūch	25	Ed	21.46N	72.54 E
Bhatinda	25	Eb	30.12N	74.57 E
Bhātpāra	25	Hd	22.52N	88.24 E
Bhaunagar	22	Jg	21.46N	72.09 E
Bhera	25	Eb	32.29N	72.55 E
Bheri ∿	25	Gc	28.44N	81.16 E
Bhīlwāra	25	Ec	25.21N	74.38 E
Bhīma ∿	21	Jh	16.25N	77.17 E
Bhind	25	Fc	26.34N	78.48 E
Bhiwāni	25	Fc	28.47N	76.08 E
Bhopāl	22	Jg	23.16N	77.24 E
Bhubaneswar	22	Kg	20.14N	85.50 E
Bhuj	25	Dd	23.16N	69.40 E
Bhusāwal	25	Fd	21.03N	75.46 E
Bhutan (Druk-Yul) ①	22	Lg	27.30N	90.30 E
Bia ∿	34	Ed	5.21N	3.11W
Bia, Phou- ▲	21	Mh	18.36N	103.01 E
Biá, Rio- ∿	54	Ed	3.28S	67.23W
Bīābān, Kūh-e- ⛰	24	Qi	26.30N	57.25 E
Biabou	51n	Ba	13.12N	61.09W
Biafra ⊠	30	Hh	5.00N	7.30 E
Biafra, Bight of- ◐	30	Hh	3.20N	9.20 E
Biak	26	Kg	1.10S	136.06 E
Biak, Pulau- ◆	57	Ee	1.00S	136.00 E
Biała Piska	10	Sc	53.37N	22.04 E
Biała Podlaska ②	10	Td	52.00N	23.05 E
Biała Podlaska	10	Td	52.02N	23.06 E
Białobrzegi	10	Qe	51.40N	20.57 E
Białogard	10	Lb	54.01N	16.00 E
Białostocka, Wysoczyzna- ▬	10	Tc	53.23N	23.10 E
Białowieża	10	Td	52.41N	23.50 E
Białystok	6	Ie	53.09N	23.09 E
Białystok ②	10	Tc	53.10N	23.10 E
Biancavilla	14	Im	37.38N	14.52 E
Bianco	14	Kl	38.05N	16.09 E
Bianco, Monte- ▲	5	Gf	45.50N	6.52 E
Biankouma	34	Dd	7.44N	7.37W
Biankouma ③	34	Dd	7.43N	7.40W
Bianzhuang → Cangshan	28	Eg	34.51N	118.03 E
Biaro, Pulau- ◆	26	If	2.05N	125.20 E
Biarritz	11	Ek	43.29N	1.34W
Biasca	14	Cd	46.22N	8.57 E
Bibā	33	Fd	28.55N	30.59 E
Bibai	27	Pc	43.19N	141.52 E
Bibala	36	Be	14.50S	13.30 E
Biban, Chaine des- ⛰	13	Qh	36.12N	4.25 E
Bibbiena	14	Fg	43.42N	11.49 E
Biberach an der Riß	10	Fh	48.06N	9.48 E
Bibiani	34	Ed	6.28N	2.20W
Bic	44	Ma	48.22N	68.42W
Bicaj	15	Dh	41.59N	20.25 E
Bicas	55	Ke	21.43S	43.04W
Bicaz	15	Jc	46.55N	26.04 E
Bicaz, Pasul- ⌵	15	Ic	46.49N	25.52 E
Bičenekski, Pereval- ⌵	16	Nj	39.33N	45.48 E
Bicester	9	Lj	51.54N	1.09W
Bichena	35	Fc	10.21N	38.14 E
Bickerton Island ◆	59	Hb	13.45S	136.10 E
Bicske	10	Oi	47.29N	18.38 E
Bičura	20	Ff	50.36N	107.35 E
Bīd	24	Qd	36.33N	57.35 E
Bida	31	Hh	9.05N	6.01 E
Bīdar	25	Fe	17.54N	77.33 E
Bidasoa ∿	13	Ka	43.22N	1.47W
Biddeford	43	Mc	43.30N	70.26W
Bideford	9	Ij	51.01N	4.13W
Bideford Bay → Barnstaple ◐	9	Ij	51.05N	4.20W
Bidon V/Poste Maurice Cortier	32	He	22.18N	1.05 E
Bié ③	36	Ce	13.00S	17.30 E
Bié, Planalto do-	30	Ij	13.30S	17.02 E
Biebrza ∿	10	Sc	53.13N	22.28 E
Biecz	10	Rg	49.44N	21.14 E
Biedenkopf	10	Ef	50.55N	8.32 E
Biei	29a	Cb	43.35N	142.28 E
Biel/Bienne	14	Bc	47.10N	7.15 E
Bielefeld	10	Ed	52.02N	8.32 E
Bielefeld-Brackwede	12	Kc	51.59N	8.31 E
Bielefeld-Sennestadt	12	Kc	51.57N	8.35 E
Biella	14	Ce	45.34N	8.03 E
Bielsk	10	Pd	52.40N	19.49 E
Bielska, Wysoczyzna- ▬	10	Sd	52.35N	23.00 E
Bielsko ②	10	Og	49.50N	19.00 E
Bielsko-Biała	10	Pg	49.49N	19.02 E
Bielsk Podlaski	10	Td	52.47N	23.12 E
Bien Dong=South China Sea (EN) ≡	21	Ni	10.00N	113.00 E
Bien Hoa	25	Lf	10.57N	106.49 E
Bienne ∿	11	Lh	46.20N	5.38 E
Bienne/Biel	14	Bc	47.10N	7.15 E
Bienvenida ▲	13	Jd	40.30N	2.30W
Bienville, Lac - ≈	42	Ke	55.20N	72.40W
Bierbeek	12	Gd	50.50N	4.46 E
Bieszczady ⛰	10	Sg	49.10N	22.35 E
Bièvre	12	He	49.56N	5.01 E
Biferno ∿	14	Ji	41.59N	15.02 E
Bifoum	36	Bc	0.20S	10.23 E
Bifuka	28	Qb	44.29N	142.21 E
Biga	24	Bb	40.13N	27.14 E
Bigadiç	24	Cc	39.23N	28.08 E
Big Bald Mountain ▲	44	Nb	47.37N	66.38W
Big Baldy Mountain ▲	46	Jc	46.58N	110.37W
Big Bay [Mi.-U.S.]	44	Db	46.49N	87.44W
Big Bay [Van.]	63b	Cb	15.05S	166.54 E
Big Beaver House	42	If	52.58N	89.57W
Big Belt Mountains ⛰	46	Jc	46.40N	111.25W
Big Black River ∿	45	Kj	32.00N	91.05W
Big Blue River ∿	43	Hd	39.11N	96.32W
Big Creek Peak ▲	46	Id	44.28N	113.32W
Big Dry Creek ∿	46	Lc	47.30N	106.19W
Big Falls	45	Jb	48.11N	93.46W
Biggar	42	Gf	52.04N	108.00W
Biggenden	59	Ke	25.30S	152.00 E
Biggleswade	9	Mi	52.05N	0.17W
Big Hatchet Peak ▲	45	Bk	31.37N	108.20W
Big Hole River ∿	46	Id	45.34N	112.20W
Bighorn Basin ◡	43	Fc	44.15N	108.10W
Bighorn Lake ≈	46	Kd	45.08N	108.10W
Bighorn Mountains ⛰	38	Ie	44.00N	107.30W
Bighorn River ∿	43	Fb	46.09N	107.28W
Bight, Head of- ◐	59	Gf	31.30S	131.10 E
Big Island ◆	42	Kd	62.43N	70.40W
Big Lake ≈	44	Nc	45.10N	67.40W
Big Lake	45	Fk	31.12N	101.28W
Big Lost River ∿	46	Ie	43.50N	112.44W
Big Muddy Creek ∿	46	Mb	48.08N	104.36W
Big Muddy Lake ≈	46	Mb	49.08N	104.54W
Bignona	34	Bc	12.49N	16.14W
Bigorre ⊠	11	Gk	43.06N	0.05 E
Big Porcupine Creek ∿	46	Lc	46.17N	106.47W
Big Quill Lake ≈	42	Hf	51.51N	104.18W
Big Rapids	44	Ed	43.42N	85.29W
Big River	42	Gf	53.50N	107.01W
Big River ∿	42	Fb	72.50N	125.00W
Big Sand Lake ≈	42	He	57.45N	99.45W
Big Sandy	46	Jb	48.11N	110.07W
Big Sandy Creek ∿	45	Eg	38.06N	102.29W
Big Sandy River [Az.-U.S.] ∿	46	Ii	34.19N	113.31W
Big Sandy River [Wy.-U.S.] ∿	46	Kf	41.50N	109.48W
Big Sheep Mountains ⛰	46	Mc	47.03N	105.43W
Big Sioux River ∿	43	Hc	42.30N	96.25W
Big Smoky Valley ▽	43	Dd	38.30N	117.15W
Big Snowy Mountains ⛰	46	Kc	46.50N	109.30W
Big Spring	39	If	32.15N	101.28W
Big Spruce Knob ▲	44	Gf	38.16N	80.12W
Big Stone Lake ≈	45	Hd	45.25N	96.40W
Big Timber	46	Kd	45.50N	109.57W
Big Trout Lake ≈	42	If	53.45N	90.00W
Biguglia, Étang de- ≋	11a	Ba	42.36N	9.29 E
Big Wood Cay ◆	49	Ia	24.21N	77.44W
Big Wood River ∿	46	He	42.52N	114.55W
Bihać	14	Jf	44.49N	15.52 E
Bihār ③	25	Hd	25.00N	86.00 E
Bihār	25	Hc	25.11N	85.31 E
Biharamulo	36	Fc	2.38S	31.20 E
Bihor ②	15	Ec	47.00N	22.00 E
Bihoro	27	Pc	43.49N	144.07 E
Bihorului, Munţii- ⛰	15	Fc	46.40N	22.45 E
Bija ∿	21	Kd	52.25N	85.05 E
Bijagós, Arquipélago dos-= Bijagos Islands (EN) ❖	30	Fg	11.15N	16.05W
Bijagós Islands (EN)= Bijagós, Arquipélago dos- ❖	30	Fg	11.15N	16.05W
Bijapur	25	Fe	16.50N	75.42 E
Bījār	23	Gb	35.52N	47.36 E
Bijeljina	14	Nf	44.45N	19.13 E
Bijelo Polje	15	Cf	43.02N	19.45 E
Bijiang (Zhiziluo)	27	Gf	26.39N	99.00 E
Bijie	27	If	27.15N	105.16 E
Bijlikol, Ozero- ≈	18	Hc	43.05N	70.40 E
Bijou Creek ∿	45	Ef	40.17N	103.52W
Bijoutier Island ◆	37b	Bb	7.04S	52.45 E
Bijsk	22	Kd	52.34N	85.15 E
Bīkāner	22	Jg	28.01N	73.18 E
Bikar Atoll ⊙	57	Ic	12.15N	170.06 E
Bikeqi	28	Ad	40.45N	111.17 E
Bikin ∿	20	Ig	46.43N	134.02 E
Bikin	20	Ig	46.51N	134.02 E
Bikini Atoll ⊙	57	Hc	11.35N	165.23 E
Bikoro	31	Ii	0.45S	18.07 E
Bilād Ghāmid ⊠	33	Hf	19.58N	41.38 E
Bilād Zahrān ⊠	33	He	20.15N	41.15 E
Bilāspur	22	Kg	22.03N	82.10 E
Bilate ∿	35	Fd	6.34N	38.01 E
Bilauktaung Range ⛰	21	Lh	13.00N	99.00 E
Bilbao	6	Fg	43.15N	2.58W
Bilbays	33	Fc	30.25N	31.34 E
Bileća	14	Mh	42.53N	18.26 E
Bilecik	23	Ca	40.09N	29.59 E
Bīlehsavār	24	Mc	39.28N	48.20 E
Bilé Karpaty=White Carpathians (EN) ⛰	10	Nh	48.55N	17.50 E
Bilesha Plain ▭	36	Hb	0.35N	40.45 E
Biłgoraj	10	Sf	50.34N	22.43 E
Bili ∿	36	Db	4.50N	22.29 E
Bili	36	Eb	4.09N	25.10 E
Bilibino	22	Sc	68.03N	166.20 E
Biliran ◆	26	Hd	11.35N	124.28 E
Bilishti	15	Di	40.37N	20.59 E
Biliu He ∿	28	Ge	39.30N	122.36 E
Bill Baileys Bank (EN) ▤	9	Ca	60.40N	10.20W
Billerbeck	12	Jc	51.58N	7.18 E
Billericay	12	Cc	51.37N	0.35 E
Billingen ▬	8	Ef	58.24N	13.45 E
Billings	39	Jf	37.04N	93.33W
Billings, Reprêsa- ≈	55	If	23.45S	46.40W
Billingshurst	12	Bc	51.01N	0.27W
Bill Williams River ∿	46	Hi	34.17N	114.03W
Billy Chinook, Lake- ≈	46	Ed	44.33N	121.20W
Bilma	31	Ig	18.41N	12.56 E
Biloela	59	Kd	24.24S	150.30 E
Bilo Gora ⛰	14	Le	45.50N	17.10 E
Biloku	54	Gc	1.46N	58.33W
Biloxi	43	Je	30.24N	88.53W
Bilqās Qism Awwal	24	Dg	31.13N	31.21 E
Bîlteni	15	Ge	44.52N	23.17 E
Biltine	35	Cc	14.32N	20.55 E
Biltine ③	35	Cc	15.00N	21.00 E
Bilzen	12	Hd	50.51N	5.31 E
Bima ∿	36	Eb	3.23N	25.09 E
Bimbān	24	Ej	24.26N	32.53 E
Bimberi Peak ▲	59	Jg	35.40S	148.47 E
Bimbila	34	Fd	8.51N	0.04 E
Bimbo	35	Be	4.18N	18.33 E
Bimini Islands ❖	47	Ic	25.44N	79.15W
Bināb	24	Md	36.35N	48.41 E
Binačka Morava ∿	15	Eg	42.27N	21.47 E
Binaiya, Gunung- ▲	26	Ig	3.11S	129.26 E
Binatang	26	Ff	2.10N	111.38 E
Bınboga Dağı ▲	24	Gc	38.21N	36.32 E
Binche	12	Gd	50.24N	4.10 E
Binder	27	Jb	48.35N	110.36 E
Bindura	31	Kj	17.17S	31.20 E
Bine el Ouidane	32	Fc	32.08N	6.28W
Binéfar	13	Mc	41.51N	0.18 E
Binem ∿	35	Bb	18.43N	19.40 E
Binga [Zaire]	36	Db	2.23N	20.30 E
Binga [Zimb.]	37	Dc	17.37S	27.20 E

ndex Symbols

■ Independent Nation	▣ Historical or Cultural Region	⌵ Pass, Gap	◡ Depression	▥ Coast, Beach	✱ Rock, Reef	∿ Waterfall Rapids	▭ Canal	⊡ Lagoon	◩ Escarpment, Sea Scarp	▲ Historic Site	⚓ Port
☐ State, Region	▲ Mount, Mountain	▭ Plain, Lowland	◡ Polder	◧ Cliff	❖ Islands, Archipelago	⋎ River Mouth, Estuary	❄ Glacier	▤ Bank	◩ Fracture	⁘ Ruins	⌖ Lighthouse
☐ District, County	▲ Volcano	◣ Delta	◢ Desert, Dunes	⊟ Peninsula	✱ Rocks, Reefs	≈ Lake	◪ Ice Shelf, Pack Ice	⊠ Seamount	◡ Trench, Abyss	▬ Wall, Walls	⚒ Mine
☐ Municipality	⌓ Hill	▭ Salt Flat	♣ Forest, Woods	⊟ Isthmus	✹ Coral Reef	≈ Salt Lake	≡ Ocean	▲ Tablemount	◭ National Park, Reserve	⛪ Church, Abbey	⌒ Tunnel
☐ Colony, Dependency	⛰ Mountains, Mountain Range	▽ Valley, Canyon	ψ Heath, Steppe	▭ Sandbank	⊙ Well, Spring	◻ Intermittent Lake	≡ Sea	⋀ Ridge	◆ Point of Interest	▲ Temple	⟋ Dam, Bridge
■ Continent	⌓ Hills, Escarpment	◡ Crater, Cave	✿ Oasis	◆ Island	◫ Geyser	≈ Reservoir	◐ Gulf, Bay	▭ Shelf	✚ Recreation Site	⊛ Scientific Station	
☐ Physical Region	▬ Plateau, Upland	✪ Karst Features	► Cape, Point	⊙ Atoll	∿ River, Stream	≋ Swamp, Pond	═ Strait, Fjord	◡ Basin	◠ Cave, Cavern	✈ Airport	

Bingen 10 Dg 49.58N 7.54 E
Bingham [Me.-U.S.] 44 Mc 45.03N 69.53W
Bingham [N.M.-U.S.] 45 Cj 33.56N 106.17W
Binghamton 43 Lc 42.06N 75.55W
Bin Ghunaymah, Jabal- 30 If 25.00N 15.30 E
Bing Inlet 44 Gc 45.13N 80.30W
Bingöl 23 Fb 38.53N 40.29 E
Bingöl Dağları 24 Ic 39.20N 41.20 E
Binhai (Dongkan) 27 Ke 34.00N 119.52 E
Binjai 26 Cf 3.36N 98.30 E
Binkiliç 15 Lh 41.25N 28.11 E
Binongko, Pulau- 26 Hh 5.57S 124.02 E
Bin Qirdān 32 Jc 33.08N 11.13 E
Bintan, Pulau- 26 Df 1.05N 104.30 E
Bintuhan 26 Dg 4.48S 103.22 E
Bintulu 26 Ff 3.10N 113.02 E
Bin Walid, Jabal- 14 En 36.52N 10.47 E
Binxian 28 Df 37.22N 117.57 E
Binxian (Binzhou) [China] 27 Mb 45.45N 127.27 E
Binxian (Binzhou) [China] 27 Id 35.02N 108.06 E
Binzhou → Binxian [China] 27 Id 35.02N 108.06 E
Binzhou → Binxian [China] 27 Mb 45.45N 127.27 E
Bioara 25 Fd 23.58N 76.55 E
Biobío 56 Fe 36.49S 73.10W
Bio Bio [2] 56 Fe 37.45S 72.00W
Biograd na Moru 14 Jg 43.57N 15.27 E
Bioko [3] 34 Ge 3.00N 8.40 E
Bioko 30 Hh 4.30N 9.30 E
Biokovo 14 Lg 43.18N 17.02 E
Biorra/Birr 9 Fh 53.05N 7.54W
Bippen 12 Jb 52.35N 7.44 E
Bir 25 Fe 18.59N 75.46 E
Bira 20 Ig 49.03N 132.27 E
Bi'r Abraq 33 Fe 23.35N 34.48 E
Bi'r Abū al Ḩuşayn 33 Ee 22.53N 29.55 E
Bi'r Abū Gharādiq 24 Cg 30.06N 28.06 E
Bi'r Abū Hashim 33 Fe 23.42N 34.08 E
Bi'r Abū Minqat 33 Ed 26.30N 27.35 E
Bīrah Kaprah 24 Kd 36.52N 44.01 E
Birāk 33 Bd 27.39N 14.17 E
Birakan 20 Ig 49.02N 131.40 E
Bi'r al 'Abd 24 Eg 31.22N 32.58 E
Bi'r al Ghuzaylah 33 Bd 28.50N 10.45 E
Bi'r al Ḩakīm 33 Dc 31.36N 23.29 E
Bi'r al Hasa 35 Fa 22.58N 35.40 E
Bi'r al Khamsah 33 Ec 30.57N 25.46 E
Bi'r 'Allāq 33 Bc 31.10N 11.55 E
Bi'r al Mushayqīq 32 Jc 30.53N 10.18 E
Bi'r al Qurayyah 24 Ei 26.22N 33.01 E
Bi'r al Uzam 33 Dc 31.46N 23.59 E
Bi'r al Wa'r 31 Be 22.39N 14.10 E
Bi'r al Washkah 33 Cd 28.52N 15.35 E
Birao 31 Jg 10.17N 22.47 E
Bi'r 'Arjā' 24 Ij 25.17N 40.58 E
Bi'r ar Rāh 24 If 33.27N 40.25 E
Bi'r ar Rūmān 32 Ic 32.31N 8.21 E
Birātnagar 25 Hc 26.29N 87.17 E
Biratori 28 Qc 42.35N 142.12 E
Bi'r Baylī 33 Ec 30.32N 25.08 E
Bi'r Bayzaḩ 24 Fj 25.10N 34.05 E
Bi'r Bū Ḩawsh 33 Dd 24.34N 22.07 E
Bi'r Bū Zurayyq 33 Dd 24.32N 22.38 E
Bîrca 15 Gf 43.58N 23.37 E
Birch 42 Ge 58.28N 112.17W
Birch Mountains 42 Ge 57.20N 112.55W
Bird 42 Ie 56.30N 94.14W
Bi'r Dibs 33 Ee 22.12N 29.32 E
Bird Island [Gren.] 51p Bb 12.12N 61.33W
Bird Island [Sey.] 37b Ca 3.43S 55.12 E
Birdsville 59 He 25.54S 139.22 E
Birdum 59 Gc 15.39S 133.13 E
Birecik 24 Gd 37.02N 37.58 E
Bir El Ater 32 Ic 34.44N 8.03 E
Bir el Mrabba'ab 24 He 34.30N 39.07 E
Bir Enzarán 32 Ee 23.53N 14.32W
Bireuen 26 Ce 5.12N 96.41 E
Bi'r Fajr 24 Gh 28.54N 37.54 E
Bi'r Fu'ād 33 Ec 30.27N 26.27 E
Bir Gandús 32 De 21.36N 16.30W
Birganj 25 Gc 27.00N 84.52 E
Bir Gara 35 Bc 13.11N 15.58 E
Bir-Ghbalou 13 Ph 36.16N 3.35 E
Birgi 15 Lk 38.15N 28.05 E
Bi'r Ḩasanah 24 Eg 30.28N 33.47 E
Bi'r Ḩaymir 24 Hj 24.41N 38.04 E
Bi'r Ḩulayyi 24 Fj 24.06N 34.32 E
Birigui 55 Ge 21.18S 50.19W
Biriliussy 20 Ee 57.07N 90.42 E
Bīrīn 24 Ge 35.01N 36.40 E
Birine 13 Pi 35.37N 3.13 E
Bīrjand 22 Hf 32.53N 59.13 E
Birjusa 21 Ld 57.43N 95.24 E
Birjusinsk 20 Ee 55.55N 97.55 E
Bi'r Karawayn 24 Ci 27.06N 28.32 E
Birkeland 7 Bg 58.20N 8.14 E
Birkenfeld 10 Dg 49.39N 7.11 E
Birkenhead 9 Jh 53.24N 3.02W
Birkerød 8 Ei 55.50N 12.26 E
Bi'r Khālidah 24 Bg 30.50N 27.15 E
Birksgate Range 59 Fe 27.10S 129.45 E
Birlad 15 Kc 46.14N 27.40 E
Birlad 15 Kc 45.36N 27.31 E
Bir Lehlú 32 Fd 26.21N 9.34W
Bi'r Ma'sūr 24 Fj 24.31N 34.12 E
Birmingham [Al.-U.S.] 39 Kf 33.31N 86.49W
Birmingham [Eng.-U.K.] 6 Fe 52.30N 1.50W
Bi'r Misāḩah 33 Ee 22.12N 27.57 E
Bi'r Murr 33 Fe 23.21N 30.05 E
Bi'r Murrah 33 Fe 22.32N 33.54 E
Bi'r Nāhid 33 Ec 30.13N 28.52 E
Bi'r Naşīf 23 Ee 24.51N 39.11 E
Birnie Atoll 57 Je 3.35S 171.31W
Birnin Gaouré 34 Fc 13.05N 2.54 E
Birnin Gwari 34 Gc 11.02N 6.47 E
Birnin Kebbi 34 Fc 12.28N 4.12 E
Birni Nkonni 31 Hg 13.48N 5.15 E
Birnin Kudu 34 Gc 11.27N 9.30 E
Birni Yauri 34 Fc 10.47N 4.49 E
Bi'r Nukhaylah 24 Dj 24.01N 30.52 E
Birobidžan 22 Pe 48.48N 132.57 E
Birr/Biorra 9 Fh 53.05N 7.54W
Birs 14 Bc 47.26N 7.33 E
Bi'r Safājah 33 Fd 26.50N 34.54 E
Bi'r Sayyālah 24 Ei 26.07N 33.56 E
Bi'r Shalatayn 33 Ge 23.08N 35.36 E
Birsk 19 Fd 55.25N 55.32 E
Birštonas 8 Kj 54.33N 24.07 E
Bi'r Ţarfāwī 33 Ee 22.55N 28.53 E
Biru 27 Fe 31.30N 93.50 E
Bi'r Umm al 'Abbās 24 Ei 26.57N 32.34 E
Bi'r Umm Fawākhīr 24 Ei 26.01N 33.38 E
Bi'r Umm Sa'īd 24 Eh 29.40N 33.34 E
Bi'r Umm Ţunaydibah 24 Ej 25.16N 33.06 E
Biruni 19 Gg 41.42N 60.45 E
Biržai/Biržaj 19 Cd 56.12N 24.48 E
Biržaj/Biržai 19 Cd 56.12N 24.48 E
Bîrzava 15 Ec 46.07N 21.59 E
Bîrzava 15 Dd 45.16N 20.49 E
Birzebbuga 14 Io 35.49N 14.32 E
Bisa, Pulau- 26 Ig 1.15S 127.28 E
Bisaccia 14 Ji 41.01N 15.22 E
Bisacquino 14 Hm 37.42N 13.15 E
Bisbee 43 Fe 31.27N 109.55W
Biscarrosse, Étang de- 11 Ej 44.21N 1.10W
Biscay, Bay of- (EN) = Gascogne, Golfe de- 5 Fg 44.00N 4.00W
Bisceglie 14 Ki 41.14N 16.30 E
Bischofslofen 10 Jc 47.25N 13.13 E
Bischofswerda/Biskopicy 10 Ke 51.07N 14.11 E
Biscoe Islands 66 Qe 66.00S 66.30W
Biscotasi Lake 44 Fb 47.20N 82.05W
Biscucuy 50 Bh 9.22N 69.59W
Bisert 17 Hh 56.39N 57.59 E
Bisert 19 Fd 56.52N 59.03 E
Biševiski Kanal 14 Kg 43.00N 16.03 E
Biševo 14 Kh 42.59N 16.01 E
Bisha 35 Fb 15.28N 37.33 E
Bishārah 33 De 22.58N 22.39 E
Bishārīyīn, Barq al- 35 Eb 19.26N 32.22 E
Bishnupur 25 Hd 23.05N 87.19 E
Bishop 43 Dd 37.22N 118.24W
Bishop Auckland 9 Lg 54.40N 1.40W
Bishop Rock 9 Gl 49.53N 6.25W
Bishop's Falls 42 Lg 49.01N 55.30W
Bishop's Stortford 9 Nj 51.53N 0.09 E
Bishop's Waltham 12 Ad 50.57N 1.13W
Bishrī, Jabal- 24 He 35.20N 39.20 E
Bishui 27 La 52.07N 123.43 E
Biskopicy/Bischofswerda 10 Ke 51.07N 14.11 E
Biskra 31 He 34.51N 5.44 E
Biskra [3] 32 Ic 34.40N 6.00 E
Biskupiec 10 Qc 53.52N 20.27 E
Bislig 26 Ie 8.13N 126.19 E
Bismarck 39 Ie 46.48N 100.47W
Bismarck, Kap- 41 Kc 76.40N 18.40W
Bismarck Archipelago 57 Fe 5.00S 150.00 E
Bismarck Sea 60 Dh 4.00S 147.30 E
Bismark Range 60 Ci 5.30S 144.45 E
Bismil 24 Id 37.51N 40.40 E
Bison 45 Ed 45.31N 102.28W
Bisotūn 24 Le 34.23N 47.26 E
Bispfors 8 Ga 63.02N 16.37 E
Bissau 31 Fg 11.51N 15.35W
Bissaula 34 Hd 7.01N 10.27 E
Bissett 44 Hb 46.13N 78.02W
Bisson, Banc du- 37 Hb 12.00S 46.25 E
Bistcho Lake 42 Fe 59.45N 118.50W
Bistineau, Lake- 45 Jj 32.25N 93.22W
Bistra 15 Fd 45.29N 22.11 E
Bistra 15 Dh 41.37N 20.44 E
Bistreț 15 Gf 43.54N 23.30 E
Bistrica 15 Dg 42.09N 20.59 E
Bistrica 15 Cf 43.28N 19.42 E
Bistrița 15 Hb 47.08N 24.29 E
Bistrița [Rom.] 15 Jc 46.30N 26.57 E
Bistrița [Rom.] 15 Hb 47.04N 24.25 E
Bistrița-Năsăud [2] 15 Hb 47.05N 24.35 E
Bitam 36 Bb 2.05N 11.29 E
Bitam 13 Ri 35.15N 5.11 E
Bitburg 10 Cg 49.58N 6.32 E
Bitche 11 Ne 49.03N 7.26 E
Biteá 35 Cc 13.11N 20.10 E
Bithia 14 Cl 38.55N 8.52 E
Bithynia 15 Mi 40.20N 29.30 E
Bitjug 16 Kd 50.37N 39.55 E
Bitkine 35 Bc 11.59N 18.13 E
Bitlis 23 Fb 38.22N 42.06 E
Bitola 6 Ig 41.02N 21.20 E
Bitonto 14 Ki 41.06N 16.41 E
Bitterfeld 10 Ie 51.37N 12.19 E
Bitterfontein 31 Il 31.00S 18.32 E
Bitterroot Range 38 He 47.06N 115.10W
Bitterroot River 46 Hc 46.52N 114.06W
Bitti 14 Dj 40.29N 9.23 E
Bitung 26 If 1.27N 125.11 E
Biu 31 Ig 10.37N 12.12 E
Bivolari 15 Kb 47.32N 27.26 E
Bivolu, Vîrful- 15 Ib 47.15N 25.56 E
Bivona 14 Hm 37.37N 13.26 E
Biwa-ko 28 Ng 35.13N 136.05 E
Bixad [Rom.] 15 Ic 46.06N 25.52 E
Bixad [Rom.] 15 Fb 47.56N 23.24 E
Bixby 45 Ii 35.57N 95.53W
Biyalā 24 Dg 31.10N 31.13 E
Biyang 27 Je 32.40N 113.21 E
Biyārjomand 24 Pd 36.06N 55.53 E
Bižbuljak 17 Gj 53.43N 54.16 E
Bižeе 18 Kb 45.10N 77.58 E
Bizen 28 Mg 34.44N 134.09 E
Bizerte (EN) = Banzart 31 He 37.17N 9.52 E
Bjala 15 If 43.27N 25.44 E
Bjala Slatina 15 Gf 43.28N 23.56 E
Bjargtangar 5 Db 65.30N 24.32W
Bjärna/Perniö 7 Ff 60.12N 23.08 E
Bjärnum 8 Eh 56.17N 13.42 E
Bjästa 8 Ha 63.12N 18.30 E
Bjelašnica [Yugo.] 14 Mg 43.43N 18.09 E
Bjelašnica [Yugo.] 14 Mh 42.51N 18.09 E
Bjelašnica [Yugo.] 14 Mg 43.09N 18.23 E
Bjelolasica 14 Ie 45.16N 14.58 E
Bjelovar 14 Ke 45.54N 16.51 E
Bjerkvik 7 Db 68.33N 17.34 E
Bjerringbro 8 Ch 56.23N 9.40 E
Bjervamoen 8 Ce 59.25N 9.04 E
Bjeshkët e Nemuna 15 Cg 42.30N 19.50 E
Björdo 8 Fd 60.28N 14.42 E
Bjørkelangen 8 De 59.53N 11.34 E
Björkfors 8 Ff 58.01N 15.54 E
Björklinge 8 Gd 60.02N 17.33 E
Björkö 8 Eg 59.55N 19.00 E
Björna 7 Ee 63.34N 18.33 E
Bjørnafjorden 8 Ad 60.05N 5.20 E
Björneborg 8 Fe 59.15N 14.15 E
Björneborg/Pori 6 Ic 61.29N 21.47 E
Bjorne Peninsula 42 Ia 77.30N 87.00W
Bjørnesfjorden 8 Bd 60.10N 7.40 E
Bjørnevatn 7 Gb 69.40N 30.00 E
Bjørnøya 67 Kd 74.30N 19.00 E
Björnöya = Bear Island (EN) 5 Ha 74.30N 19.00 E
Bjurholm 7 Ee 63.56N 19.13 E
Bjuröklubb 7 Ed 64.28N 21.35 E
Bjuv 8 Eh 56.05N 12.54 E
Bla 34 Dc 12.56N 5.45W
Blace 15 Ef 43.18N 21.18 E
Blackall 58 Gf 24.25S 145.28 E
Black Bank (EN) = Zwarte Bank 12 Fa 53.15N 3.55 E
Black Bay 45 Lb 48.40N 88.30W
Blackburn 9 Kh 53.45N 2.29W
Blackburn, Mount- 38 Ec 61.44N 143.26W
Black Butte Lake 46 Dg 39.45N 122.20W
Black Coast 66 Qf 71.45S 62.00W
Blackdown Hills 9 Jk 50.57N 3.09W
Blackduck 45 Ic 47.44N 94.33W
Blackfoot 43 Ec 43.11N 112.20W
Blackfoot Reservoir 46 Je 42.55N 111.35W
Black Forest (EN) = Schwarzwald 5 Gf 48.00N 8.15 E
Black Head 9 Hk 50.01N 5.03W
Black Hills 38 Ie 44.00N 104.00W
Black Isle 9 Id 57.35N 4.20W
Black Lake 42 Ge 59.11N 105.20W
Blackman's 51q Ab 13.11N 59.32W
Black Mesa 46 Jh 36.35N 110.20W
Blackmoor 9 Ik 50.23N 4.50W
Black Mountain 43 Kd 36.54N 82.54W
Black Mountains [U.S.] 46 Hi 35.30N 114.30W
Black Mountains [Wales-U.K.] 9 Jj 51.57N 3.08W
Blackpool 9 Jh 53.50N 3.03W
Black Range 43 Fe 33.20N 107.50W
Black River 49 Id 18.01N 77.51W
Black River [Az.-U.S.] 46 Jj 33.44N 110.13W
Black River [Mi.-U.S.] 44 Fd 43.00N 82.25W
Black River [N.Y.-U.S.] 44 Id 43.59N 76.04W
Black River [U.S.] 45 Ki 35.38N 91.19W
Black River [Wi.-U.S.] 45 Ke 43.57N 91.22W
Black River (EN) = Babian Jiang 21 Mg 20.17N 106.34 E
Black River (EN) = Da, Sông- 21 Mg 20.17N 106.34 E
Black River Falls 45 Kd 44.16N 90.52W
Black Rock 56 Lh 53.39S 41.48W
Black Rock [Ire.] 9 Cg 54.05N 10.20W
Black Rock [Phil.] 26 Ge 8.48N 119.50 E
Black Rock Desert 43 Dc 41.10N 119.00W
Blacksburg 44 Gg 37.15N 80.25W
Black Sea (EN) = Černoje More 5 Jg 43.00N 35.00 E
Black Sea (EN) = Černo More 5 Jg 43.00N 35.00 E
Black Sea (EN) = Karadeniz 5 Jg 43.00N 35.00 E
Black Sea (EN) = Neagră, Marea- 5 Jg 43.00N 35.00 E
Blacksod Bay/Cuan an Fhóid Duibh 9 Dg 54.08N 10.00W
Blackstairs Mountains/Na Staighri Dubha 9 Gi 52.33N 6.49W
Blackstone 44 Hg 37.04N 78.01W
Blackville 44 Ob 46.44N 65.54W
Black Volta 30 Gh 8.38N 1.30W
Black Volta (EN) = Volta Noire 30 Gh 8.38N 1.30W
Black Volta (EN) = Volta Noire 34 Ec 12.30N 4.00W
Blackwater 12 Cc 51.43N 0.28 E
Blackwater/An Abhainn Dubh 9 Gh 53.39N 6.43W
Blackwater/An Abhainn Mhór [Ire.] 9 Fj 51.51N 7.50W
Blackwater/An Abhainn Mhór [N.Ire.-U.K.] 9 Gg 54.30N 6.35W
Blackwell 45 Hh 36.48N 97.17W
Blackwood River 59 Df 34.35S 115.02 E
Blagnac 11 Hk 43.38N 1.24 E
Blagodarny 19 Ef 45.04N 43.24 E
Blagojevgrad 15 Gg 42.01N 23.06 E
Blagojevgrad [2] 15 Gh 41.45N 23.25 E
Blagoveščenka 20 Cf 52.50N 79.55 E
Blagoveščensk [R.S.F.S.R.] 19 Fd 55.01N 55.59 E
Blagoveščensk [R.S.F.S.R.] 22 Od 50.17N 127.32 E
Blåhø 8 Cb 62.45N 9.19 E
Blain 11 Eg 47.29N 1.45W
Blaine [Mn.-U.S.] 45 Jd 45.11N 93.14W
Blaine [Wa.-U.S.] 46 Db 48.59N 122.44W
Blair 45 Hf 41.33N 96.08W
Blair Athol 59 Jd 22.42S 147.33 E
Blairgowrie 9 Je 56.36N 3.21W
Blairmore 46 Hb 49.36N 114.26W
Blaise 11 Kf 48.38N 4.43 E
Blaj 15 Gc 46.11N 23.55 E
Blake Basin (EN) 43 Mf 29.00N 76.00W
Blakely 44 Ej 31.23N 84.56W
Blakeney Point 9 Ni 52.59N 1.00 E
Blake Plateau (EN) 38 Lf 31.00N 79.00W
Blake Ridge (EN) 38 Lg 29.00N 73.30W
Blakstad 7 Bg 58.30N 8.39 E
Blanc, Cape- (EN) = Abyaḑ, Ra's al- 30 He 37.20N 9.50 E
Blanc, Cape- (EN) = Nouâdhibou, Râs- 30 Ff 20.46N 17.03W
Blanc, Lac- 44 Kb 47.45N 73.12W
Blanc, Mont- 5 Gf 45.50N 6.52 E
Blanca, Bahía- 52 Ji 38.55S 62.10W
Blanca, Cerro- 49 Gi 8.40N 80.35W
Blanca, Cordillera- 54 Ce 9.10S 77.35W
Blanca, Costa- 13 Lg 37.38N 0.40W
Blanca, Isla- 48 Pg 21.24N 86.50W
Blanca, Punta- 48 Bc 29.05N 114.45W
Blancagrande 55 Bm 36.32S 60.53W
Blanca Peak [Co.-U.S.] 43 Fd 37.34N 105.29W
Blanca Peak [U.S.] 38 If 37.35N 105.29W
Blanche, Lake- [Austl.] 59 Ed 22.25S 123.15 E
Blanche, Lake- [Austl.] 59 He 29.15S 139.40 E
Blanche, Point- 51b Ac 18.00N 63.03W
Blanche Channel 63a Cc 8.30S 157.30 E
Blanc-Nez, Cap- 12 Dd 50.56N 1.42 E
Blanco, Cabo- [C.R.] 47 Gg 9.33N 85.06W
Blanco, Cabo- [Sp.] 13 Oe 39.22N 2.46 E
Blanco, Cape- 43 Cc 42.50N 124.34W
Blanco, Cerro- 48 Fe 25.43N 107.39W
Blanco, Río- 54 Ff 12.30S 64.18W
Blanco del Sur, Cayo- 49 Gb 22.02N 81.24W
Blanda 7a Bb 65.39N 20.18W
Blanding 46 Kh 37.37N 109.29W
Blanes 13 Oc 41.41N 2.48 E
Blangy-le-Château 12 Ce 49.14N 0.17 E
Blangy-sur-Bresle 11 He 49.56N 1.38 E
Blanice [Czech.] 10 Kg 49.48N 14.58 E
Blanice [Czech.] 10 Kg 49.17N 14.09 E
Blankaholm 8 Gg 57.35N 16.31 E
Blankenberge 11 Jc 51.19N 3.08 E
Blankenheim 12 Id 50.26N 6.39 E
Blanquilla, Isla- 54 Fa 11.51N 64.37W
Blanquillo 55 Ek 32.55S 55.40W
Blansko 10 Mg 49.22N 16.39 E
Blantyre 31 Ki 15.47S 35.00 E
Blantyre-Limbe 36 Gf 15.49S 35.03 E
Blåskavlen 8 Bd 60.58N 7.18 E
Błaszki 10 Oe 51.39N 18.27 E
Blatná 10 Jg 49.26N 13.53 E
Blato 14 Kh 42.56N 16.48 E
Blåvands Huk 5 Gd 55.33N 8.05 E
Blavet [Fr.] 11 Cf 48.13N 3.10W
Blavet [Fr.] 11 Cg 47.46N 3.18W
Blaye 11 Fi 45.08N 0.40W
Blaye-les-Mines 11 Ij 44.01N 2.08 E
Bled 14 Id 46.22N 14.08 E
Blefjell 8 Ce 59.48N 9.10 E
Bleialf 12 Id 50.14N 6.17 E
Blekinge [2] 7 Dh 56.20N 15.20 E
Blenheim 58 Ii 41.31S 173.57 E
Bletchley 9 Mj 52.00N 0.46W
Bleus, Monts- 36 Fb 1.30N 30.30 E
Bhārshāh 25 Fe 19.50N 79.22 E
Blida [3] 32 Hb 36.35N 2.30 E
Blida 31 He 36.34N 2.55 E
Blidö 8 He 59.35N 18.55 E
Blidsberg 8 Eg 57.56N 13.29 E
Blies 12 Je 49.07N 7.04 E
Blieskastel 12 Je 49.14N 7.15 E
Bligh Water 63d Ab 17.00S 178.00 E
Blind River 42 Jg 46.10N 82.58W
Blitar 26 Fh 8.06S 112.09 E
Blitta 34 Fd 8.19N 0.59 E
Block Island 44 Le 41.11N 71.35W
Bloemfontein 31 Jk 29.12S 26.07 E
Bloemhof 37 De 27.38S 25.32 E
Blois 11 Hg 47.35N 1.20 E
Blokhus 8 Cg 57.15N 9.35 E
Blomberg 12 Lc 51.56N 9.05 E
Blönduós 7a Bb 65.40N 20.18W
Bloody Foreland/Cnoc Fola 9 Ef 55.09N 8.17W
Bloomfield [Ia.-U.S.] 45 Jf 40.45N 92.25W
Bloomfield [In.-U.S.] 44 Df 39.01N 86.56W
Bloomington [Il.-U.S.] 43 Jc 40.29N 88.59W
Bloomington [In.-U.S.] 43 Jd 39.10N 86.32W
Bloomington [Mn.-U.S.] 45 Jd 44.50N 93.17W
Bloomsburg 44 Ie 41.01N 76.27W
Blosseville Kyst 41 Je 68.45N 27.25W
Blötberget 8 Fd 60.07N 15.04 E
Blountstown 44 Ej 30.29N 85.03W
Bludenz 14 Dc 47.09N 9.49 E
Blue Earth 45 Ie 43.38N 94.06W
Bluefield 43 Kd 37.14N 81.17W
Bluefields 39 Kh 12.00N 83.45W
Bluefields, Bahía de- 49 Fg 12.02N 83.44W
Blue Mesa Reservoir 45 Cg 38.28N 107.15W
Blue Mountain 44 Ie 40.15N 77.30W
Blue Mountain [Or.-U.S.] 46 Ge 42.25N 117.50W
Blue Mountain [U.S.] 45 Ii 34.41N 94.03W
Blue Mountain Lake 44 Jd 43.53N 74.26W
Blue Mountain Pass 46 Ge 42.18N 117.45W
Blue Mountain Peak 47 Ie 18.03N 76.35W
Blue Mountains [Austl.] 59 Kf 33.35S 150.15 E
Blue Mountains [U.S.] 43 Ec 44.35N 118.25W
Blue Mud Bay 59 Hb 13.25S 135.55 E
Blue Nile (EN) = Abay 30 Kg 15.38N 32.31 E
Blue Nile (EN) = Azraq, Al Baḩr al- 30 Kg 15.38N 32.31 E
Bluenose Lake 42 Fc 68.00N 121.00W
Blue Ridge 44 Eh 34.52N 84.20W
Blue Ridge 38 Kf 37.00N 82.00W
Blue Stack/Na Cruacha 9 Eg 54.45N 8.06W
Bluestone Lake 44 Gg 37.30N 80.50W
Bluff [N.Z.] 61 Ci 46.36S 168.2
Bluff [Ut.-U.S.] 46 Kh 37.17N 109.3
Bluff Point 59 Ce 27.50S 114.0
Bluffton 44 Ee 40.44N 85.1
Blumberg 10 Ei 47.50N 8.3
Blumenau 56 Kc 26.56S 49.0
Blyth 12 Db 52.19N 1.4
Blyth 9 Lf 55.07N 1.3
Blythe 43 Ee 33.37N 114.3
Blytheville 43 Jd 35.56N 89.5
Bø 7 Bg 59.25N 9.0
Bo 31 Fh 7.58N 11.4
Boa 34 Dd 8.26N 7.1
Boac 26 Hd 12.28N 122.2
Boaco [3] 49 Eg 12.35N 85.2
Boaco 49 Eg 12.28N 85.4
Boa Esperança 55 Je 21.05S 45.3
Boa Esperança, Represa- 54 Je 6.50S 44.0
Boa Esperança, Serra da- 55 Je 20.57S 45.4
Bo'ai 28 Bg 35.10N 113.0
Boal 13 Fa 43.26N 6.4
Boali 35 Be 4.48N 18.0
Boano, Pulau- 26 Ig 2.56S 127.5
Boardman 46 Fd 45.51N 119.4
Boa Sentença, Serra da- 55 Ed 19.13S 57.3
Boa Vista 30 Eg 16.05N 22.5
Boa Vista [Braz.] 55 Ec 17.51S 54.1
Boa Vista [Braz.] 55 Ia 12.40S 46.5
Boa Vista [Braz.] 53 Je 2.49N 60.4
Bobai 27 Ig 22.15N 109.5
Bobali, Cerros de- 49 Ki 8.53N 73.2
Bobali, Cerros de- 49 Ki 8.53N 73.2
Bobbio 14 Df 44.46N 9.2
Bobigny 11 If 48.54N 2.2
Bobo Dioulasso 31 Gg 11.12N 4.1
Bobojod, Gora- 18 Hd 40.50N 70.2
Bobolice 10 Mc 53.57N 16.3
Bobonong 37 Dd 21.58S 28.2
Bobovdol 15 Fg 42.22N 23.0
Bóbr 10 Ld 52.04N 15.0
Bobrik 16 Ec 52.08N 26.4
Bobrinec 16 He 48.04N 32.0
Bobrka 10 Ug 49.34N 24.2
Bobrov 19 Ee 51.06N 40.0
Bobrovica 16 Gd 50.43N 31.2
Bobrowniki 10 Tc 53.08N 23.5
Bobrujsk 6 Ie 53.09N 29.1
Bobures 54 Db 9.15N 71.1
Boby, Pic- 37 Hd 22.12S 46.5
Boca del Ric 48 Ee 25.20N 108.2
Boca de Pozo 50 Dg 11.00N 64.2
Boca do Acre 53 Jf 8.45S 67.2
Bocage, Cap- 63b Be 21.12S 165.3
Bocaina 15 Db 15.16S 56.4
Bocaiúva 55 Kc 17.07S 43.4
Bocajá 55 Ef 22.45S 55.1
Bocaranga 35 Bd 6.59N 15.3
Boca Raton 43 Kf 26.21N 80.0
Bocas del Toro 47 Hg 9.20N 82.1
Bocas del Toro [3] 49 Fi 8.50N 82.1
Bocas del Toro, Archipiélago de- 49 Fi 9.20N 82.1
Bocay 49 Ef 14.19N 85.1
Bochaine 11 Lj 44.20N 5.5
Bochnia 10 Qg 49.58N 20.2
Bocholt [Bel.] 12 Hc 51.10N 5.3
Bocholt [F.R.G.] 10 Ce 51.50N 6.3
Bochum 10 De 51.29N 7.1
Bocognano 11a Ba 42.05N 9.0
Bocoio 36 Be 12.28S 14.0
Boconó 49 Li 9.15N 70.1
Boçsa 15 Ed 45.23N 21.4
Boda 35 Be 4.19N 17.2
Boda 8 Fc 61.01N 15.1
Böda 8 Gg 57.15N 17.0
Bodafors 8 Fg 57.30N 14.4
Bodajbo 22 Nd 57.51N 114.1
Bodalangi 36 Db 3.14N 22.1
Bode 10 Hd 52.01N 11.1
Bödefeld-Freiheit, Schmallenberg- 12 Kc 51.15N 8.2
Bodegraven 12 Gb 52.06N 4.4
Bodélé 30 Ig 16.30N 17.3
Boden 6 Ib 65.50N 21.4
Bodenheim 12 Ke 49.56N 8.1
Bodensee = Constance, Lake- (EN) 5 Gf 47.35N 9.2
Boderg, Lough- 9 Fh 53.52N 8.0
Bodmin 9 Ik 50.29N 4.4
Bodmin Moor 9 Ik 50.35N 4.4
Bodø 6 Hb 67.17N 14.2
Bodoquena 55 De 20.12S 56.4
Bodoquena, Serra da- 54 Gh 21.00S 56.5
Bodrog 10 Rh 48.07N 21.2
Bodrogköz 10 Rh 48.15N 21.4
Bodrum 23 Cb 37.02N 27.0
Bodrum Yarimadasi 15 Kl 37.05N 27.3
Bodva 10 Qh 48.12N 20.4
Boën 11 Ji 45.44N 4.0
Boende 31 Ji 0.13S 20.5
Boeo, Capo- (Lilibeo, Capo-) 14 Gm 37.34N 12.4
Boerne 45 Gl 29.47N 98.4
Boesmanland = Bushman-land (EN) 37 Be 29.30S 19.0
Boffa 34 Cc 10.10N 14.0
Boga 15 Cg 42.24N 19.3
Bogale 25 Je 16.17N 95.2
Bogalusa 45 Lk 30.47N 89.5
Bogandé 34 Ec 12.59N 0.0
Bogangolo 35 Bd 5.34N 18.1
Bogatić 15 Ce 44.51N 19.2
Bogatynia 10 Kf 50.55N 14.5
Boğazkale 24 Fb 40.01N 34.3
Boğazlıyan 24 Fc 39.12N 35.1
Bogbonga 36 Cb 1.35N 19.2

Index Symbols

[1] Independent Nation
[2] State, Region
[3] District, County
[4] Municipality
[5] Colony, Dependency
Continent
Physical Region
Historical or Cultural Region
Mount, Mountain
Volcano
Hill
Mountains, Mountain Range
Hills, Escarpment
Plateau, Upland
Pass, Gap
Plain, Lowland
Delta
Salt Flat
Valley, Canyon
Crater, Cave
Karst Features
Depression
Polder
Desert, Dunes
Forest, Woods
Heath, Steppe
Oasis
Cape, Point
Coast, Beach
Cliff
Peninsula
Isthmus
Sandbank
Island
Atoll
Rock, Reef
Islands, Archipelago
Rocks, Reefs
Coral Reef
Well, Spring
Geyser
River, Stream
Waterfall Rapids
River Mouth, Estuary
Lake
Salt Lake
Intermittent Lake
Reservoir
Swamp, Pond
Canal
Glacier
Ice Shelf, Pack Ice
Ocean
Sea
Gulf, Bay
Strait, Fjord
Lagoon
Bank
Seamount
Tablemount
Ridge
Shelf
Basin
Escarpment, Sea Scarp
Fracture
Trench, Abyss
National Park, Reserve
Point of Interest
Recreation Site
Cave, Cavern
Historic Site
Ruins
Wall, Walls
Church, Abbey
Temple
Scientific Station
Airport
Port
Lighthouse
Mine
Tunnel
Dam, Bridg

- Bogcang Zangbo 27 Ee 31.56N 87.24 E
- Bogda Feng 27 Ec 43.45N 88.32 E
- Bogdan 15 Hg 42.37N 24.28 E
- Bogdanovka 16 Mi 41.15N 43.36 E
- Bogda Shan 21 Ke 43.35N 90.00 E
- Bogen 7 Db 68.32N 17.00 E
- Bogenfels 37 Be 27.23S 15.22 E
- Bogense 8 Di 55.34N 10.06 E
- Boggeragh Mountains/An Bhograch 9 Ei 52.05N 9.00W
- Boggy Peak 51d Bb 17.03N 61.51W
- Boghar 13 Oi 35.55N 2.43 E
- Boghni 13 Ph 36.32N 3.57 E
- Bogia 60 Ch 4.16S 144.58 E
- Bognor Regis 12 Bd 50.47N 0.39W
- Bogny-sur-Meuse 12 Ge 49.54N 4.43 E
- Bogoduhov 16 Id 50.12N 35.31 E
- Bogomila 15 Eh 41.36N 21.28 E
- Bogor 22 Mj 6.35S 106.47 E
- Bogoridick 19 De 53.50N 38.08 E
- Bogorodčany 10 Uh 48.45N 24.40 E
- Bogorodsk 7 Kh 56.09N 43.32 E
- Bogorodskoje [R.S.F.S.R.] 7 Mh 57.51N 50.48 E
- Bogorodskoje [R.S.F.S.R.] 20 Jf 52.22N 140.30 E
- Bogotá 53 Ie 4.36N 74.05W
- Bogotol 20 De 56.17N 89.43 E
- Bogøy 7 Dc 67.54N 15.11 E
- Bogra 25 Hd 24.51N 89.22 E
- Bogučany 20 Ee 58.23N 97.39 E
- Bogučar 16 Le 49.57N 40.33 E
- Bogué 32 Ef 16.36N 14.15W
- Boguševsk 7 Hi 54.50N 30.13 E
- Boguslav 19 Df 49.33N 30.54 E
- Bo Hai=Chihli, Gulf of- (EN) 21 Nf 38.30N 120.00 E
- Bohai Haixia 27 Ld 38.00N 121.30 E
- Bohain-en-Vermandois 12 Fe 49.59N 3.27 E
- Bohemia (EN)=Čechy 5 Hf 50.00N 14.30 E
- Bohemia (EN)=Čechy 10 Kf 50.00N 14.30 E
- Bohemian Forest (EN)= Böhmerwald 5 Hf 49.00N 13.30 E
- Bohemian Forest (EN)= Český Les 10 Ig 49.50N 12.30 E
- Bohemian Forest (EN)= Oberpfälzer Wald 10 Ig 49.50N 12.30 E
- Bohemian Forest (EN)= Šumava 5 Hf 49.00N 13.30 E
- Bohicon 34 Fd 7.12N 2.04 E
- Böhmerwald=Bohemian Forest (EN) 5 Hf 49.00N 13.30 E
- Bohmte 12 Kb 52.22N 8.19 E
- Bohodoyou 34 Dd 9.46N 9.04W
- Bohol 21 Oi 9.50N 124.10 E
- Böhönye 10 Nj 46.24N 17.24 E
- Bohor 14 Jd 46.04N 15.26 E
- Bohu/Bagrax 27 Ec 41.58N 86.29 E
- Bohus 8 Eg 57.51N 12.01 E
- Bohuslän 8 Df 58.15N 11.50 E
- Boiaçu 54 Fd 0.27S 61.46W
- Boiano 14 Ii 41.29N 14.29 E
- Boina 30 Lj 16.00S 46.30 E
- Bois, Lac des- 42 Ec 66.50N 125.15W
- Bois, Rio dos- [Braz.] 55 Gd 18.35S 50.02W
- Bois, Rio dos- [Braz.] 55 Ha 13.55S 49.51W
- Bois Blanc Island 44 Ec 45.45N 84.28W
- Boischaut 11 Hh 46.40N 1.45 E
- Boise 39 He 43.37N 116.13W
- Boise City 45 Eh 36.44N 102.31W
- Boise River 46 Ge 43.49N 117.01W
- Boissay 12 De 49.31N 1.21 E
- Boissevain 42 Hg 49.14N 100.03W
- Boizenburg 10 Gc 53.23N 10.43 E
- Bojador, Cabo- 30 Ff 26.08N 14.30W
- Bojana 15 Ch 41.52N 19.22 E
- Bojanowo 10 Me 51.42N 16.44 E
- Bojarka 19 De 50.19N 30.20 E
- Bojčinovci 15 Gf 43.28N 23.20 E
- Bojnūrd 23 Ib 37.28N 57.19 E
- Bojonegoro 26 Fh 7.09S 111.52 E
- Bojuru 55 Gj 31.38S 51.26W
- Bokatola 36 Cc 0.38S 18.46 E
- Boké 34 Cc 10.56N 14.13W
- Bokhara River 59 Je 29.55S 146.42 E
- Bokn 8 Ae 59.15N 5.25 E
- Boknafjorden 5 Gd 59.10N 5.35 E
- Boko 36 Bc 4.47S 14.38 E
- Bokol Mayo 35 Ge 4.31N 41.32 E
- Bokoro 35 Bc 12.23N 17.03 E
- Bokote 35 Dc 0.05S 20.08 E
- Bokpyin 25 Jf 11.16N 98.46 E
- Boksitogorsk 19 Dd 59.29N 33.52 E
- Bokungu 36 Dc 0.41S 22.19 E
- Bol [Chad] 35 Ac 13.30N 14.41 E
- Bol [Yugo.] 14 Kg 43.16N 16.40 E
- Bola, Bahr- 35 Bd 9.50N 18.59 E
- Bolama 34 Bc 11.35N 15.28W
- Bolands 51d Bb 17.02N 61.53W
- Bolaños, Río- 48 Gg 21.14N 104.08W
- Bolattau, Gora- 18 Ha 46.44N 71.54 E
- Bolayir 15 Ji 40.31N 26.45 E
- Bolbec 11 Ge 49.34N 0.29 E
- Bolda 16 Pg 45.58N 48.35 E
- Bole [Eth.] 35 Fd 6.37N 37.22 E
- Bole [Ghana] 34 Ed 9.02N 2.29W
- Bole/Bortala 27 Dc 44.59N 81.57 E
- Bolehov 16 Ce 49.03N 23.50 E
- Bolesławiec 10 Le 51.16N 15.34 E
- Bolgatanga 31 Gg 10.47N 0.51W
- Bolgrad 16 Fg 45.40N 28.38 E
- Bolhov 19 De 53.30N 36.01 E
- Boli 27 Nb 45.46N 130.31 E
- Bolia 36 Cc 1.36S 18.23 E
- Boliden 7 Ed 64.52N 20.23 E
- Bolinao, Cape- 26 Gc 16.22N 119.50 E
- Bolintin Vale 15 Ie 44.27N 25.46 E
- Bolivar [Col.] 54 Db 9.00N 74.40W
- Bolivar [Mo.-U.S.] 45 Jh 37.37N 93.25W
- Bolivar [Tn.-U.S.] 44 Ch 35.15N 88.59W
- Bolivar [Ven.] 54 Fb 6.20N 63.30W
- Bolivar, Cerro- 54 Fb 7.28N 63.25W
- Bolivar, Pico- 52 Ie 8.30N 71.02W
- Bolivia 53 Jg 17.00S 65.00W
- Bolivia, Altiplano de- 52 Jg 18.00S 68.00W
- Boljevac 15 Ef 43.50N 21.58 E
- Bollendorf 12 Ie 49.51N 6.22 E
- Bollène 11 Kj 44.17N 4.45 E
- Bollnäs 7 Df 61.21N 16.25 E
- Bollon 59 Je 28.02S 147.28 E
- Bollstabruk 8 Ga 63.00N 17.41 E
- Bollullos par del Condado 13 Fg 37.20N 6.32W
- Bolmen 7 Ch 56.55N 13.40 E
- Bolnisi 16 Ni 41.28N 44.31 E
- Bolobo 36 Cc 2.10S 16.14 E
- Bolodek 20 If 53.43N 133.09 E
- Bologna 6 Hg 44.29N 11.20 E
- Bolognesi 54 Df 10.01S 74.05W
- Bologoje 6 Jd 57.54N 34.02 E
- Bolohovo 16 Jb 54.05N 37.52 E
- Bolomba 36 Cb 0.29N 19.12 E
- Bolombo 36 Dc 3.59S 21.22 E
- Bolon 20 Ig 49.58N 136.04 E
- Bolotnoje 20 De 55.41N 84.33 E
- Bolovens, Plateau des- 25 Le 15.20N 106.20 E
- Bolšaja Balahnja 20 Fb 73.37N 107.05 E
- Bolšaja Berestovica 10 Uc 53.09N 24.02 E
- Bolšaja Černigovka 7 Mj 52.08N 50.48 E
- Bolšaja Glušica 7 Mj 52.24N 50.29 E
- Bolšaja Ižora 8 Me 59.55N 29.40 E
- Bolšaja Kinel 7 Mj 53.14N 50.32 E
- Bolšaja Koksaga 7 Lh 56.07N 47.48 E
- Bolšaja Kuonamka 20 Gc 70.50N 113.20 E
- Bolšaja Oju 17 Jb 69.42N 60.42 E
- Bolšaja Rogovaja 17 Jc 66.30N 60.40 E
- Bolšaja Synja 17 Id 65.58N 58.01 E
- Bolšaja Tap 17 Lg 59.55N 65.42 E
- Bolšaja Ussurka 20 Ig 46.00N 133.30 E
- Bolšaja Vladimirovka 19 He 50.53N 79.30 E
- Bolšakovo 8 Ij 54.50N 21.36 E
- Bolsena 14 Fh 42.39N 11.59 E
- Bolsena, Lago di- 14 Fh 42.35N 11.55 E
- Bolšerečje 19 Hd 56.06N 74.38 E
- Bolšereck 20 Kf 52.22N 156.24 E
- Bolšeustikinskoje 17 Ii 55.57N 58.20 E
- Bolševik 20 Jd 62.40N 147.30 E
- Bolševik, Ostrov-=Bolshevik Island (EN) 21 Mb 78.40N 102.30 E
- Bolšezemelskaja Tundra 19 Fb 67.30N 58.30 E
- Bolshevik Island (EN)= Bolševik, Ostrov- 21 Mb 78.40N 102.30 E
- Bolšije Uki 19 Hd 56.57N 72.37 E
- Bolšoj Anjuj 20 Lc 68.30N 160.50 E
- Bolšoj Begičev, Ostrov- 20 Gb 74.20N 112.30 E
- Bolšoj Berezovy, Ostrov- 8 Md 60.15N 28.35 E
- Bolšoj Boktybaj, Gora- [Kaz.-U.S.S.R.] 19 Ff 48.30N 58.20 E
- Bolšoj Boktybaj, Gora- [U.S.S.R.] 16 Ue 48.30N 58.25 E
- Bolšoj Bolvanski Nos, Mys- 17 Ia 70.27N 59.05 E
- Bolšoj Čeremšan 7 Li 54.12N 49.40 E
- Bolšoje Muraškino 7 Ki 55.47N 44.46 E
- Bolšoje Vlasjevo 20 Jf 53.25N 140.55 E
- Bolšoje Zagorje 8 Mg 57.47N 28.58 E
- Bolšoj Gašun 16 Mf 47.22N 42.42 E
- Bolšoj Ik 17 Hj 51.47N 56.20 E
- Bolšoj Irgiz 19 Ee 52.01N 47.24 E
- Bolšoj Jenisej 20 Ef 51.40N 94.26 E
- Bolšoj Jugan 19 Hc 60.55N 73.40 E
- Bolšoj Kamen 20 Ih 43.08N 132.28 E
- Bolšoj Klimecki, Ostrov- 7 Ie 62.00N 35.15 E
- Bolšoj Kujalnik 16 Gf 46.46N 30.38 E
- Bolšoj Kumak 16 Ud 51.22N 58.55 E
- Bolšoj Ljahovski, Ostrov- 20 Jb 73.35N 142.00 E
- Bolšoj Murta 20 Ee 56.55N 93.10 E
- Bolšoj Nimnyr 20 He 58.08N 125.45 E
- Bolšoj Pit 20 Ee 59.02N 91.40 E
- Bolšoj Tjuters, Ostrov- 8 Le 59.50N 27.10 E
- Bolšoj Uluj 20 Ee 56.45N 90.46 E
- Bolšoj Uvat, Ozero- 17 Oh 57.35N 70.30 E
- Bolšoj Uzen 5 Kf 48.50N 49.40 E
- Bolsón, Cerro del- 52 Jh 27.13S 66.06W
- Bolšovcy 10 Ug 49.08N 24.47 E
- Bolsward 12 Ha 53.04N 5.30 E
- Boltaña 13 Mb 42.27N 0.04 E
- Bolton 9 Kh 53.35N 2.26W
- Bolu 23 Da 40.44N 31.37 E
- Bolu Dağları 24 Eb 41.05N 32.05 E
- Bolungarvik 7a Aa 66.09N 23.15W
- Boluntay 27 Fd 36.29N 92.18 E
- Bolva 16 Ic 53.17N 34.20 E
- Bolvadin 24 Dc 38.42N 31.04 E
- Bolzano/Bozen 6 Hf 46.31N 11.22 E
- Boma 31 Ii 5.51S 13.03 E
- Bomassa 36 Cb 2.12N 16.12 E
- Bombala 59 Jg 36.54S 149.14 E
- Bombarral 13 Ce 39.16N 9.09W
- Bombay 22 Jh 18.58N 72.50 E
- Bomberai, Jazirah- 26 Jg 3.00S 133.00 E
- Bombo 36 Fb 0.35N 32.32 E
- Bomboma 36 Cb 2.26N 18.57 E
- Bom Comércio 54 Ee 9.45S 65.54W
- Bom Conselho 54 Ke 9.10S 36.41W
- Bom Despacho 54 Ig 19.43S 45.15W
- Bomdila 25 Ic 27.16N 92.23 E
- Bomi/Bowo 27 Ge 30.02N 95.39 E
- Bomi Hills 31 Fh 6.52N 10.45W
- Bomili 36 Eb 1.40N 27.01 E
- Bom Jardim de Goiás 55 Fc 16.17S 52.07W
- Bom Jardim de Minas 55 Je 21.57S 44.11W
- Bom Jesus 55 Gi 28.42S 50.24W
- Bom Jesus da Lapa 53 Lg 13.15S 43.25W
- Bom Jesus de Goiás 55 Hd 18.12S 49.37W
- Bømlafjorden 8 Ae 59.40N 5.20 E
- Bømlo 7 Ag 59.45N 5.10 E
- Bomokandi 36 Eb 3.30N 26.08 E
- Bomongo 36 Cb 1.22N 18.21 E
- Bom Retiro 55 Hh 27.48S 49.31W
- Bom Sucesso 55 Je 21.02S 44.46W
- Bomu 30 Jh 4.08N 22.26 E
- Bomu (EN)=Mbomou 30 Jh 4.08N 22.26 E
- Bomu (EN)=Mbomou 35 Cd 5.30N 23.30 E
- Bon, Cape- (EN)=Ţīb, Ra's At- 30 Ie 37.05N 11.03 E
- Bona, Mount- 40 Kd 61.20N 141.50W
- Bonaire 54 Ea 12.10N 68.15W
- Bonaire Basin (EN) 50 Cg 11.25N 67.30W
- Bonampak 48 Ni 16.43N 91.05W
- Bonanza 49 Ef 14.01N 84.35W
- Bonanza Peak 46 Eb 48.14N 120.52W
- Bonao 49 Ld 18.56N 70.25W
- Bonaparte, Mount- 46 Fb 48.45N 119.08W
- Bonaparte Archipelago 57 Df 14.20S 125.20 E
- Bonaparte Lake 46 Ea 51.16N 120.35W
- Bonaparte Rocks 51p Cb 12.24N 61.30W
- Bonasse 50 Fg 10.05N 61.52W
- Bonavista 42 Mg 48.39N 53.07W
- Bonavista Bay 42 Mg 49.00N 53.20W
- Bon-Cagan-Nur 27 Gb 45.35N 99.15 E
- Bondeno 14 Ff 44.53N 11.25 E
- Bondo 31 Jh 3.49N 23.40 E
- Bondoukou 34 Ed 8.02N 2.48W
- Bondoukou 34 Ed 8.20N 2.55W
- Bondowoso 26 Fh 7.55S 113.49 E
- Bone, Gulf of- (EN)=Bone, Teluk- 21 Oj 4.00S 120.40 E
- Bone, Teluk-=Bone, Gulf of- (EN) 21 Oj 4.00S 120.40 E
- Bone Bay 51a Db 18.45N 64.22W
- Bonelohe 26 Hh 5.48S 120.27 E
- Bönen 12 Jc 51.36N 7.46 E
- Bone Rate, Kepulauan- 26 Hh 7.00S 121.00 E
- Bone Rate, Pulau- 26 Hh 7.22S 121.08 E
- Bonete, Cerro- 56 Gc 27.51S 68.47W
- Bong 34 Cd 6.49N 10.19W
- Bong 34 Dd 7.00N 9.40W
- Bonga 35 Fd 7.16N 36.14 E
- Bongabong 26 Hd 12.45N 121.29 E
- Bongandanga 36 Db 1.30N 21.03 E
- Bongo, Massif des- 35 Cd 8.40N 22.25 E
- Bongolava 37 Hc 18.35S 45.20 E
- Bongor 31 Ig 10.17N 15.22 E
- Bongouanou 34 Ed 6.43N 4.12W
- Bongouanou 34 Ed 6.39N 4.12W
- Bonham 45 Hj 33.35N 96.11W
- Bonheiden 12 Gc 51.02N 4.32 E
- Bonhomme, Col du- 11 Nf 48.10N 7.06 E
- Bonhomme, Pic- 49 Kd 19.05N 72.15W
- Bonifacio 11a Bb 41.23N 9.09 E
- Bonifacio, Bocche di-= Bonifacio, Strait of- (EN) 5 Gg 41.18N 9.15 E
- Bonifacio, Strait of- (EN)= Bonifacio, Bocche di- 5 Gg 41.18N 9.15 E
- Bonifati, Capo- 14 Jk 39.33N 15.52 E
- Bonin Basin (EN) 60 Bb 29.00N 137.00 E
- Bonin Islands (EN)= Ogasawara-Shotō 21 Qg 27.00N 142.10 E
- Bonin Trench (EN) 3 If 30.00N 145.00 E
- Bonita Springs 44 Gl 26.21N 81.47W
- Bonito [Braz.] 55 Jb 15.20S 44.46W
- Bonito [Braz.] 55 De 21.08S 56.28W
- Bonito, Pico- 49 Ge 15.38N 86.55W
- Bonito, Rio- [Braz.] 55 Hb 15.18S 49.36W
- Bonito, Rio- [Braz.] 55 Gc 16.31S 51.23W
- Bonn 6 Ge 50.44N 7.06 E
- Bonn-Bad Godesberg 10 Df 50.41N 7.09 E
- Bonnebosq 12 Ce 49.12N 0.05 E
- Bonnechère River 44 Ic 45.31N 76.33W
- Bonners Ferry 46 Gb 48.41N 116.18W
- Bonnet, Lac du- 45 Ia 50.22N 95.55W
- Bonnétable 11 Gf 48.11N 0.26 E
- Bonnet Plume 42 Ec 65.53N 134.58W
- Bonneval 11 Hf 48.11N 1.24 E
- Bonneville 11 Mh 46.05N 6.25 E
- Bonneville Salt Flats 46 If 40.45N 113.50W
- Bonnières-sur-Seine 12 De 49.02N 1.35 E
- Bonningues-lès-Ardres 12 Ed 50.47N 2.01 E
- Bonny 34 Ge 4.25N 7.10 E
- Bono 14 Dj 40.25N 9.02 E
- Bō-no-Misaki 29 Bf 31.15N 130.13 E
- Bonorva 14 Cj 40 25N 8.46 E
- Bontang 26 Gf 0.08N 117.30 E
- Bonthain 26 Gh 5.32S 119.56 E
- Bonthe 34 Cd 7.32N 12.30W
- Bontoc 26 Hc 17.05N 120.58 E
- Bonyhád 10 Oj 46.18N 18.32 E
- Boo, Kepulauan- 26 Ig 1.12S 129.24 E
- Boola 34 Dd 8.22N 8.43W
- Booligal 59 If 33.52S 144.53 E
- Boone [Ia.-U.S.] 45 Je 42.04N 93.53W
- Boone [N.C.-U.S.] 44 Gg 36.13N 81.41W
- Booneville [Ar.-U.S.] 45 Ji 35.08N 93.55W
- Booneville [Ms.-U.S.] 45 Li 34.39N 88.34W
- Boon Point 51d Bb 17.10N 61.50W
- Boonville [In.-U.S.] 44 Df 38.03N 87.16W
- Boonville [Mo.-U.S.] 45 Jg 38.58N 92.44W
- Boos 12 De 49.23N 1.12 E
- Boothia, Gulf of- 38 Jb 71.00N 91.00W
- Boothia Peninsula 38 Jb 70.30N 95.00W
- Boot Reefs 60 Cj 10.00S 144.35 E
- Booué 36 Bc 0.06S 11.56 E
- Bophuthatswana 37 De 26.00S 25.30 E
- Bopolu 34 Cd 7.04N 10.29W
- Boppard 12 Jd 50.14N 7.36 E
- Boquerón 55 Bf 23.00S 61.00W
- Boquerón 51a Ab 18.03N 67.09W
- Boquilla, Presa de la- 48 Gd 27.30N 105.30W
- Boquillas del Carmen 48 Hc 29.17N 102.53W
- Bor [Czech.] 10 Ig 49.43N 12.47 E
- Bor [R.S.F.S.R.] 19 Ed 56.23N 44.07 E
- Bor [Sud.] 31 Kh 6.12N 31.33 E
- Bor [Swe.] 8 Fg 57.07N 14.10 E
- Bor [Tur.] 24 Fd 37.54N 34.34 E
- Bor [Yugo.] 15 Fe 44.06N 22.06 E
- Bora-Bora, Île- 57 Lf 16.30S 151.45W
- Borah Peak 38 He 44.08N 113.14W
- Boraldaj 18 Gc 42.30N 69.05 E
- Bora Marina 14 Jm 37.56N 15.55 E
- Bōramo 35 Gd 9.58N 43.07 E
- Borås 7 Ch 57.43N 12.55 E
- Borāzjān 24 Nh 29.16N 51.12 E
- Borba [Braz.] 54 Gd 4.24S 59.35W
- Borba [Port.] 13 Ef 38.48N 7.27W
- Borborema, Planalto da- 52 Mf 7.00S 37.00W
- Borca 15 Ib 47.11N 25.46 E
- Borcea 15 Ke 44.20N 27.45 E
- Borcea, Braţul- 15 Ke 44.40N 27.53 E
- Borchgrevink Coast 66 Kf 73.00S 171.00 E
- Borçka 24 Ib 41.22N 41.40 E
- Borculo 12 Ib 52.07N 6.31 E
- Borda da Mata, Serra- 55 Ie 21.18S 47.06W
- Bordeaux 6 Fg 44.50N 0.34W
- Borden 42 Ga 78.30N 110.30W
- Borden Peninsula 38 Kb 73.00N 83.00W
- Borders 9 Kf 55.35N 3.00W
- Bordertown 58 Fh 36.19S 140.47 E
- Bordighera 14 Bg 43.46N 7.39 E
- Bordj Bou Arreridj 32 Hb 36.04N 4.46 E
- Bordj el Emir Abdelkader 13 Oi 35.52N 2.16 E
- Bordj Fly Sainte Marie 32 Gd 27.18N 2.59W
- Bordj-Menaïel 13 Ph 36.44N 3.43 E
- Bordj Messouda 32 Ic 30.12N 9.25 E
- Bordj Moktar 31 Hf 21.20N 0.56 E
- Bordj Omar Driss 31 Hf 28.09N 6.49 E
- Bord Khūn-e Now 24 Nh 28.03N 51.28 E
- Bordon Camp 12 Bc 51.07N 0.51W
- Boreal, Chaco- 52 Kh 23.00S 60.00W
- Boren 8 Ff 58.35N 15.10 E
- Borensberg 8 Ff 58.34N 15.17 E
- Borgå/Porvoo 7 Ff 60.24N 25.40 E
- Borgarnes 7a Bb 64.32N 21.55W
- Børgefjell 7 Cd 65.23N 13.50 E
- Borgentreich 12 Lc 51.34N 9.15 E
- Borger [Neth.] 12 Ib 52.55N 6.48 E
- Borger [Tx.-U.S.] 43 Gd 35.39N 101.24W
- Borgholm 7 Dh 56.53N 16.39 E
- Borghorst, Steinfurt- 12 Jb 52.08N 7.25 E
- Borgia 14 Kl 38.49N 16.30 E
- Borgloon 12 Hd 50.48N 5.20 E
- Borgomanero 14 Ce 45.42N 8.28 E
- Borgorose 14 Hh 42.11N 13.15 E
- Borgo San Dalmazzo 14 Bf 44.20N 7.30 E
- Borgo San Lorenzo 14 Fg 43.57N 11.23 E
- Borgosesia 14 Ce 45.43N 8.16 E
- Borgou 34 Fc 10.30N 2.50 E
- Borgo Val di Taro 14 Df 44.29N 9.46 E
- Borgo Valsugana 14 Fd 46.03N 11.27 E
- Borgu 30 Hg 10.35N 3.40 E
- Borgworm/Waremme 11 Ld 50.42N 5.15 E
- Bori 34 Ge 4.42N 7.21 E
- Borinquen, Punta- 51a Ab 18.30N 67.10W
- Borislav 19 Cf 49.18N 23.27 E
- Borisoglebsk 6 Ke 51.23N 42.06 E
- Borisov 19 Ce 54.15N 28.30 E
- Borisovka 16 Jd 50.36N 36.06 E
- Borispol 19 De 50.23N 30.59 E
- Bo River 35 Dd 6.48N 27.55 E
- Borja 14 Lf 44.31N 17.44 E
- Borja [Peru] 54 Cd 4.26S 77.33W
- Borja [Sp.] 13 Kc 41.50N 1.32W
- Borjas Blancas/Les Borges Blanques 13 Mc 41.31N 0.52 E
- Borken 10 Ce 51.51N 6.52 E
- Borkou 30 Ig 18.15N 18.50 E
- Borkou-Ennedi-Tibesti 35 Bb 18.00N 19.00 E
- Borkoviči 8 Mi 55.38N 28.23 E
- Borkum 10 Cc 53.35N 6.41 E
- Borlänge 7 Df 60.29N 15.25 E
- Borlu 24 Cc 38.44N 28.27 E
- Bormida 14 Cf 44.56N 8.40 E
- Bormio 14 Ed 46.28N 10.22 E
- Born 11 Fj 44.30N 1.00W
- Borna 10 Ie 51.07N 12.30 E
- Borndiep 12 Ha 53.25N 5.35 E
- Borne 12 Ib 52.18N 6.45 E
- Borneo/Kalimantan 21 Ni 1.00N 114.00 E
- Bornheim 12 Id 50.46N 7.00 E
- Bornholm 5 Hd 55.10N 15.00 E
- Bornholm 8 Fi 55.10N 15.00 E
- Bornos 13 Gh 36.48N 5.44W
- Bornova, İzmir- 24 Bc 38.27N 27.14 E
- Bornu 34 Hc 12.00N 12.40 E
- Bornu 30 Ig 12.30N 13.00 E
- Boro 30 Jh 8.52N 26.11 E
- Borodino [R.S.F.S.R.] 7 Ii 55.32N 35.49 E
- Borodino [R.S.F.S.R.] 20 Ee 55.57N 95.03 E
- Borodinskoje 8 Md 61.00N 29.29 E
- Borogoncy 20 Id 62.39N 131.08 E
- Borohoro Shan 21 Ke 42.00N 85.00 E
- Boromo 34 Ec 11.45N 2.56W
- Borongan 26 Id 11.37N 125.26 E
- Borotou 34 Dd 8.44N 7.30W
- Borovan 15 Gf 43.26N 23.45 E
- Borovec 15 Gg 42.16N 23.35 E
- Boroviči 19 Dd 58.24N 33.56 E
- Borovici 8 Mg 57.58N 29.47 E
- Borovljanka 20 Df 52.38N 84.35 E
- Borovo 14 Me 45.24N 18.58 E
- Borovski 19 Gd 57.03N 65.44 E
- Borovskoj 19 Ge 53.48N 64.17 E
- Borrachas, Islas- 50 Dg 10.18N 64.44W
- Borrān 35 Hc 10.11N 48.53 E
- Borrby 8 Fi 55.27N 14.10 E
- Borroloola 58 Ef 16.04S 136.17 E
- Borş 15 Eb 47.07N 21.49 E
- Borşa 15 Hb 47.39N 24.40 E
- Borščovočny Hrebet= Borshchovochny Range (EN) 20 Gf 52.00N 118.30 E
- Borsec 15 Ic 46.57N 25.34 E
- Borshchovochny Range (EN) =Borščovočny Hrebet 20 Gf 52.00N 118.30 E
- Borsod-Abaúj-Zemplén 10 Qh 48.15N 21.00 E
- Bortala/Bole 27 Dc 44.59N 81.57 E
- Bortala He 27 Dc 44.53N 82.45 E
- Bort-les-Orgues 11 Ii 45.24N 2.30 E
- Borūjen 24 Ng 31.59N 51.18 E
- Borūjerd 23 Gc 33.54N 48.46 E
- Borzja 22 Nd 50.24N 116.31 E
- Borzna 16 Hd 51.15N 32.29 E
- Boržomi 16 Mi 41.50N 43.25 E
- Borzsöny 10 Oi 47.55N 19.00 E
- Borzyszkowy 10 Nb 54.03N 17.22 E
- Bosa 14 Cj 40.18N 8.30 E
- Bosanska Dubica 14 Ke 45.11N 16.48 E
- Bosanska Gradiška 14 Le 45.09N 17.15 E
- Bosanska Krupa 14 Kf 44.53N 16.10 E
- Bosanski Brod 14 Me 45.08N 18.01 E
- Bosanski Novi 14 Ke 45.03N 16.22 E
- Bosanski Petrovac 14 Kf 44.34N 16.21 E
- Bosanski Šamac 14 Me 45.04N 18.28 E
- Bosansko Grahovo 23 Ff 44.11N 16.22 E
- Bōsāso 31 Lg 11.13N 49.08 E
- Bosavi, Mount- 59 Ia 6.35S 142.50 E
- Bosbeek 12 Hc 51.06N 5.48 E
- Bose 22 Mg 24.01N 106.32 E
- Boshan 27 Kd 36.30N 117.50 E
- Boshrūyeh 24 Qf 33.53N 57.26 E
- Bosilegrad 15 Fg 42.30N 22.28 E
- Bosingfeld, Extertal- 12 Lb 52.04N 9.07 E
- Bosna 14 Me 45.04N 18.28 E
- Bosna 15 Kg 42.11N 27.27 E
- Bosna=Bosnia (EN) 5 Hg 44.00N 18.00 E
- Bosna = Bosnia (EN) 14 Lf 44.00N 18.00 E
- Bosna i Hercegovina = Bosnia-Hercegovina (EN) 14 Lf 44.15N 17.50 E
- Bosnia (EN) = Bosna 14 Lf 44.00N 18.00 E
- Bosnia (EN)=Bosna 5 Hg 44.00N 18.00 E
- Bosnia-Hercegovina (EN) = Bosna i Hercegovina 14 Lf 44.15N 17.50 E
- Bosnik 26 Kg 1.10S 136.14 E
- Bošnjakovo 20 Jg 49.41N 142.10 E
- Bosobolo 36 Cb 4.11N 19.54 E
- Bōsō-Hantō 28 Pg 35.20N 140.10 E
- Bosporus (EN)=İstanbul Boğazi 15 Lg 41.00N 29.00 E
- Bosque Bonito 48 Gb 30.42N 105.06W
- Bossangoa 31 Ih 6.29N 17.27 E
- Bossé Bangou 34 Fc 13.21N 1.18 E
- Bossembélé 35 Bd 5.16N 17.39 E
- Bossemtélé II 35 Bd 5.41N 16.38 E
- Bossier City 43 Ie 32.31N 93.43W
- Bosso 34 Hc 13.42N 13.19 E
- Bosso, Dallol- 30 Hg 12.25N 2.50 E
- Bossut, Cape- 59 Ec 18.43S 121.38 E
- Bostān 25 Db 30.26N 67.02 E
- Bostānābād 24 Ld 37.50N 46.50 E
- Bosten/Bagrax Hu 21 Ke 42.00N 87.00 E
- Boston [Eng.-U.K.] 9 Mi 52.59N 0.01W
- Boston [Ma.-U.S.] 39 Le 42.21N 71.04W
- Boston Bar 46 Eb 49.52N 121.26W
- Boston Deeps 12 Ca 53.00N 0.15 E
- Boston Mountains 43 Id 35.50N 93.20W
- Botan 24 Id 37.44N 41.48 E
- Botas, Ribeirão das- 55 Fe 20.26S 53.43W
- Botesdale 12 Db 52.20N 1.01 E
- Botev 15 Hg 42.43N 24.55 E
- Botevgrad 15 Gg 42.54N 23.47 E
- Bothnia, Gulf of- (EN)= Bottniska viken 5 Hc 63.00N 20.00 E
- Bothnia, Gulf of- (EN)= Pohjanlahti 5 Hc 63.00N 20.00 E
- Boticas 13 Ec 41.41N 7.40W
- Botletle 37 Cd 21.07S 24.42 E
- Botlih 16 Oh 42.41N 46.13 E
- Botna 15 Mc 46.48N 29.30 E
- Botoşani 15 Jb 47.40N 26.43 E
- Botoşani 15 Jb 47.45N 26.40 E
- Botrange 11 Md 50.30N 6.08 E
- Botswana 31 Jk 22.00S 24.00 E
- Botte Donato 14 Kk 39.17N 16.27 E
- Bottineau 43 Gb 48.50N 100.27W
- Bottniska viken=Bothnia, Gulf of- (EN) 5 Hc 63.00N 20.00 E
- Bottrop 10 Ce 51.31N 6.55 E
- Botucatu 56 Kb 22.52S 48.26W
- Botucatu, Serra de- 55 Hf 23.00S 48.20W
- Botwood 42 Lg 49.08N 55.21W
- Bouaflé 34 Dd 6.59N 5.45W
- Bouaflé 34 Dd 7.03N 5.48W
- Bouaké 31 Gh 7.41N 5.02W
- Bouaké 34 Dd 7.45N 5.02W
- Bou Anane 32 Gc 32.02N 3.03W
- Bouar 31 Ih 5.57N 15.36 E
- Bou Arfa 32 Gc 32.32N 1.57W
- Boubin 10 Jh 48.58N 13.50 E
- Bouca 31 Ih 6.30N 18.17 E
- Bouchain 12 Fd 50.17N 3.19 E
- Bouchegouf 14 Bn 36.28N 7.44 E
- Bouche Island 51k Bb 13.57N 60.53W
- Bouches-du-Rhône 11 Kk 43.30N 5.00 E
- Boudenib 32 Gc 31.57N 3.36W
- Boudeuse Cay 37b Bb 6.05S 52.51 E
- Boû Djébéha 34 Eb 18.33N 2.45W
- Bouenza 36 Bc 3.00S 13.00 E
- Boufarik 13 Oh 36.34N 2.55 E
- Bougaa 13 Rh 36.20N 5.05 E
- Bougainville Island 57 Ge 6.00S 155.00 E
- Bougainville Reef 59 Jc 15.30S 147.05 E
- Bougainville Strait [Ocn.] 63a Cb 6.40S 156.10 E
- Bougainville Strait [Van.] 63b Cb 15.50S 167.10 E
- Bougouni 31 Gg 11.25N 7.28W

Index Symbols

- [1] Independent Nation
- [2] State, Region
- [3] District, County
- [4] Municipality
- [5] Colony, Dependency
- Continent
- Physical Region
- Historical or Cultural Region
- Mount, Mountain
- Volcano
- Hill
- Mountains, Mountain Range
- Hills, Escarpment
- Plateau, Upland
- Pass, Gap
- Plain, Lowland
- Delta
- Salt Flat
- Valley, Canyon
- Crater, Cave
- Karst Features
- Depression
- Polder
- Desert, Dunes
- Forest, Woods
- Heath, Steppe
- Oasis
- Cape, Point
- Coast, Beach
- Cliff
- Peninsula
- Isthmus
- Sandbank
- Island
- Atoll
- Rock, Reef
- Islands, Archipelago
- Rocks, Reefs
- Coral Reef
- Well, Spring
- Geyser
- River, Stream
- Waterfall Rapids
- River Mouth, Estuary
- Lake
- Salt Lake
- Intermittent Lake
- Reservoir
- Swamp, Pond
- Canal
- Glacier
- Ice Shelf, Pack Ice
- Ocean
- Sea
- Gulf, Bay
- Strait, Fjord
- Lagoon
- Bank
- Seamount
- Tablemount
- Ridge
- Shelf
- Basin
- Escarpment, Sea Scarp
- Fracture
- Trench, Abyss
- National Park, Reserve
- Point of Interest
- Recreation Site
- Cave, Cavern
- Historic Site
- Ruins
- Wall, Walls
- Church, Abbey
- Temple
- Scientific Station
- Airport
- Port
- Lighthouse
- Mine
- Tunnel
- Dam, Bridge

Name	Grid	Lat.	Long.
Bougtob	32 Hc	34.02N	0.05 E
Bouguenais	11 Eg	47.11N	1.37W
Bougzoul	13 Oi	35.42N	2.51 E
Bou Hadjar	14 Cn	36.30N	8.06 E
Bouhalla, Jbel- ▲	13 Gi	35.06N	5.07W
Bou Hamed	13 Hi	35.19N	4.58W
Bouillante	51e Ab	16.08N	61.46W
Bouillon	11 Le	49.48N	5.04 E
Bouira	32 Hb	36.23N	3.54 E
Bouira ③	32 Hb	36.15N	4.10 E
Bou Ismail	13 Oh	36.38N	2.41 E
Bou Izakarn	32 Fd	29.10N	9.44W
Bou Kadir	13 Nh	36.04N	1.07 E
Boukombé	34 Fc	10.11N	1.06 E
Boulay-Moselle	11 Le	49.11N	6.30 E
Boulder [Co.-U.S.]	39 Ie	40.01N	105.17W
Boulder [Mt.-U.S.]	46 Ic	46.14N	112.07W
Boulder City	46 Hi	35.59N	114.50W
Boulemane	32 Gc	33.22N	4.45W
Boulemane ③	32 Gc	33.02N	4.04W
Boulevard Atlántico	55 Dn	38.19S	57.59W
Boulia	59 Hd	22.54S	139.54 E
Bouligny	11 Le	49.17N	5.45 E
Boulogne ⟶	11 Eg	47.05N	1.40W
Boulogne-Billancourt	11 If	48.50N	2.15 E
Boulogne-sur-Mer	11 Hd	50.43N	1.37 E
Boulonnais ◨	11 Hd	50.42N	1.40 E
Bouloupari	63b Ce	21.52S	166.03 E
Boulsa	34 Ec	12.39N	0.34W
Boultoum	34 Hc	14.40N	10.18 E
Bou Maad, Djebel- ▲	13 Oh	36.26N	2.08 E
Boumba ⟶	34 Ie	2.02N	15.12 E
Boumdeid	32 Ef	17.26N	11.21W
Boum Kabir	35 Bc	10.11N	19.24 E
Boumort ▲	13 Nb	42.14N	1.08 E
Bouna	31 Gh	9.16N	3.00W
Bouna ③	34 Ed	9.15N	3.20W
Boû Nâga	32 Df	19.00N	13.13W
Bou Nasser, Adrar- ▲	32 Gc	33.35N	3.53W
Boundary Peak ▲	46 Fh	37.51N	118.21W
Boundiali	34 Dd	9.23N	6.32W
Boundiali ③	34 Dd	9.31N	6.29W
Boundji	36 Cc	1.03S	15.22 E
Boungou ⟶	35 Cc	6.45N	22.06 E
Bountiful	43 Ec	40.53N	111.53W
Bounty Bay ◪	64q Ab	25.03S	130.05W
Bounty Islands ▣	57 Ii	47.45S	179.05 E
Bounty Trough (EN) ▭	3 Jn	46.00S	178.00 E
Bourail	61 Cd	21.34S	165.30 E
Bourbon-Lancy	11 Jh	46.37N	3.47 E
Bourbonnais ◨	11 Ih	46.30N	3.00 E
Bourbonne-les-Bains	11 Lg	47.57N	5.45 E
Bourbourg	12 Ed	50.57N	2.12 E
Bourbre ⟶	11 Li	45.47N	5.11 E
Bourem	34 Eb	16.58N	0.21W
Bouressa	34 Fa	20.01N	2.18 E
Bourg-Achard	12 Ce	49.21N	0.49 E
Bourganeuf	11 Hi	45.57N	1.45 E
Bourgar'oûn, Cap- ▶	32 Ib	37.06N	6.28 E
Bourg-de-Péage	11 Li	45.02N	5.03 E
Bourg-en-Bresse	11 Lh	46.12N	5.13 E
Bourges	6 Gf	47.05N	2.24 E
Bourget, Lac du- ◪	11 Li	45.44N	5.52 E
Bourgneuf, Baie de- ◪	11 Dg	47.02N	2.13W
Bourgogne	12 Ge	49.21N	4.04 E
Bourgogne = Burgundy (EN) ◨	5 Gf	47.00N	4.30 E
Bourgogne = Burgundy (EN) ◨	11 Kg	47.00N	4.30 E
Bourgogne, Canal de- ▭	11 Jg	47.58N	3.30 E
Bourgogne, Porte de- ▭	11 Mg	47.38N	6.52 E
Bourgoin-Jallieu	11 Li	45.35N	5.17 E
Bourgtheroulde-Infreville	12 Ce	49.18N	0.53 E
Bourguébus	12 Be	49.07N	0.18W
Boû Rjeimat	32 Df	19.04N	15.08W
Bourke	58 Fh	30.05S	145.56 E
Bourne	12 Bb	52.46N	0.23W
Bournemouth	9 Lk	50.43N	1.54W
Bourtanger Moor ⟶	12 Jb	52.50N	7.06 E
Bourth	12 Cf	48.46N	0.49 E
Bou Saâda	32 Hb	35.12N	4.11 E
Bou Sellam ⟶	13 Qh	36.26N	4.34 E
Boussac	34 Ec	12.39N	1.53W
Boussens	11 Gk	43.11N	0.58 E
Bousso	35 Bc	10.29N	16.43 E
Bouthaleb, Djebel- ▲	13 Ri	35.48N	5.12 E
Boutilimit	32 Ef	17.33N	14.42W
Bou-Tlélis	13 Lk	35.34N	0.54W
Boutonne ⟶	11 Fi	45.55N	0.49W
Bouvet ◪	66 Cd	54.26S	3.24 E
Bouxwiller	12 Jf	48.49N	7.29 E
Bouza	34 Gc	14.25N	6.02 E
Bouzanne ⟶	11 Hh	46.38N	1.28 E
Bouzghaïa	13 Nh	36.20N	1.15 E
Bouzonville	12 Ie	49.17N	6.32 E
Bovalino	14 Kl	38.09N	16.11 E
Bovec	14 Hd	46.20N	13.33 E
Bovenkarspel	12 Hb	52.42N	5.17 E
Boves	12 Ee	49.51N	2.23 E
Bovino	14 Ji	41.15N	15.20 E
Bovril	55 Cj	31.21S	59.26W
Bowa ⟶ Muli	27 Hf	27.55N	101.13 E
Bowen [Arg.]	56 Ge	35.02S	67.31W
Bowen [Austl.]	58 Fg	20.01S	148.15 E
Bowers Bank (EN) ▭	40a Bb	54.00N	180.00
Bowers Ridge (EN) ▭	40a Bb	54.30N	180.00
Bowie	45 Hj	33.34N	97.51W
Bowkān	36 Hj	36.31N	46.12 E
Bowland, Forest of- ⟶	9 Kh	54.00N	2.30W
Bowling Green [Ky.-U.S.]	43 Jd	37.00N	86.27W
Bowling Green [Oh.-U.S.]	44 Fe	41.22N	83.40W
Bowman	43 Hb	46.11N	103.24W
Bowman Bay ◪	42 Kc	65.33N	73.40W
Bowman Island ◪	66 He	65.17S	103.08 E
Bowman, Mount- ▲	46 Eg	51.10N	121.55W
Bowo/Bomi	27 Ge	30.02N	95.39 E
Bowokan, Kepulauan- ▣	26 Hg	2.05S	123.35 E
Bowral	59 Kf	34.28S	150.25 E
Bow River ⟶	42 Gg	49.56N	111.42W
Box Elder Creek ⟶	46 Kc	46.57N	108.04W
Boxelder Creek ⟶	46 Nd	45.59N	103.57W
Boxholm	7 Dg	58.12N	15.03 E
Boxian	27 Ke	33.46N	115.44 E
Boxing	27 Kd	37.07N	118.04 E
Boxmeer	12 Hc	51.39N	5.57 E
Boxtel	11 Lc	51.35N	5.20 E
Boyabat	24 Fb	41.28N	34.47 E
Boyabo	36 Cb	3.43N	18.46 E
Boyacá ②	54 Db	5.30N	72.50W
Boyang	27 Kf	29.00N	116.41 E
Boyer, Cap- ▶	63b De	21.37S	168.07 E
Boyer Ahmadí-ye Sardsír va Kohkilúyeh ③	23 Nc	31.00N	50.30 E
Boyle/Mainistir na Búille	9 Eh	53.58N	8.18W
Boyne/An Bhóinn ⟶	9 Fh	53.43N	6.15W
Boyne City	44 Ec	45.13N	85.01W
Boynes, Iles de- ▣	30 Nm	49.58S	69.59 E
Boynton Beach	44 GI	26.32N	80.03W
Boysen Reservoir ⟶	46 Kg	43.19N	108.11W
Boz, Küh-e- ▲	24 Pi	27.46N	55.54 E
Bozburun ▶	15 Li	40.32N	28.46 E
Bozburun Dağı ▲	15 Lm	36.41N	28.04 E
Bozcaada	24 Bc	39.50N	26.04 E
Bozcaada ◪	24 Bc	39.49N	26.03 E
Bozdağ	15 Lk	38.20N	28.06 E
Boz Dağı [Tur.] ▲	24 Cd	37.18N	29.12 E
Boz Dağı [Tur.] ▲	24 Cc	38.19N	28.08 E
Bozdoğan	15 Kj	38.20N	27.45 E
Bozdoğan	15 Ll	37.40N	28.19 E
Bozeman	39 He	45.41N	111.02W
Bozen / Bolzano	6 Hf	46.31N	11.22 E
Bozene	36 Cb	2.56N	19.12 E
Bozene	28 Be	38.04N	116.34 E
Bozkol, Zaliv- ◪	18 Cb	45.01N	61.45 E
Bozkurt	24 Fb	41.57N	34.01 E
Bozok Platosu ⟶	24 Fc	39.05N	35.05 E
Bozouls	11 Ij	44.28N	2.43 E
Bozoum	31 Ih	6.19N	16.23 E
Bozova	24 Hd	37.22N	38.31 E
Bozovici	15 Ke	44.56N	22.00 E
Bozqüsh, Küh-e- ▲	24 Ld	37.45N	47.40 E
Bra	14 Bf	44.42N	7.51 E
Brås	9 Gf	57.04N	15.03 E
Braathen, Cape- ▶	66 Pf	71.48S	96.05W
Brabant ⊟	11 Lc	51.10N	5.05 E
Brabant ③	12 Gd	50.45N	4.30 E
Brabant-les-Villers	12 Gf	48.51N	4.59 E
Brábich ◨	34 Eb	17.30N	3.00W
Brač ◪	14 Kg	43.19N	16.40 E
Bracadale, Loch- ◪	9 Gd	57.20N	6.35W
Bracciano	14 Gh	42.06N	12.40 E
Bracciano, Lago di- ◪	14 Gh	42.05N	12.15 E
Bräcke	7 De	62.43N	15.27 E
Brackettville	45 Fl	29.19N	100.24W
Brački Kanal ⟶	14 Kg	43.24N	16.40 E
Bracknell	9 Mj	51.26N	0.46W
Brackwede, Bielefeld-	12 Kc	51.59N	8.31 E
Brad	15 Ke	46.08N	22.47 E
Bradano ⟶	14 Kj	40.23N	16.51 E
Bradenton	43 Kf	27.29N	82.34W
Bradford [Eng.-U.K.]	9 Lh	53.48N	1.45W
Bradford [Pa.-U.S.]	44 Hf	41.57N	78.39W
Bradley Reef ◪	60 Gi	6.52S	160.48 E
Brady	43 He	31.08N	99.20W
Brady Mountains ▲	45 Gk	31.20N	99.40W
Brædstrup	8 Ci	55.58N	9.37 E
Braemar	9 Jd	57.01N	3.24W
Braga	13 Dc	41.35N	8.25W
Braga ②	6 Fg	41.33N	8.26W
Bragadiru	15 If	43.46N	25.31 E
Bragado	56 He	35.08S	60.30W
Bragança [Braz.]	53 Lf	1.03S	46.46W
Bragança [Port.]	13 Ff	41.49N	6.45W
Bragança Paulista	55 If	22.57S	46.34W
Brahestad/Raahe	7 Fd	64.41N	24.29 E
Brahmanbāria	25 Id	23.59N	91.07 E
Brahmani ⟶	21 Kg	20.39N	86.46 E
Brahmaputra ⟶	21 Lg	24.02N	90.59 E
Brăila	15 Kd	45.16N	27.59 E
Brăila ②	15 Ke	45.00N	28.00 E
Brăilei, Balta- ⟶	15 Ke	45.00N	28.00 E
Braine	12 Fe	49.20N	3.32 E
Braine-l'Alleud/Eigenbrakel	12 Gd	50.41N	4.22 E
Brainerd	43 He	46.21N	94.12W
Braintree	12 Cc	51.53N	0.34 E
Braithwaite Point ▶	59 Gb	11.58S	134.00 E
Brake	12 Fd	53.20N	8.29 E
Brakel [Bel.]	12 Fd	50.47N	3.45 E
Brakel [F.R.G.]	12 Kc	51.43N	9.11 E
Brakna ③	32 Ef	17.30N	13.30W
Brålanda	8 Ef	58.34N	12.22 E
Bralorne	46 Da	50.47N	122.49W
Bramming	8 Ci	55.28N	8.42 E
Brämön ◪	8 Gb	62.10N	17.40 E
Brampton	44 Hd	43.41N	79.46W
Bramsche	10 Dd	52.24N	7.59 E
Bran, Pasul- ⟶	15 Id	45.26N	25.17 E
Branco ⟶	52 Cf	16.39N	24.41W
Branco ⟶	52 Mf	7.09S	34.47W
Branco, Cabo- ▶	54 Jc	1.24S	61.51W
Branco ou Cabixi, Rio- ⟶	55 Ba	13.55S	60.10W
Brandberg ▲	30 Ik	21.08S	14.35 E
Brande	8 Bi	55.57N	9.07 E
Brandenburg	10 Jd	52.25N	12.33 E
Brandenburg	10 Jd	52.10N	13.30 E
Brändö ◪	8 Jd	60.25N	21.05 E
Brandon [Eng.-U.K.]	9 'Cb	52.27N	0.37 E
Brandon [Fl.-U.S.]	44 Fl	27.56N	82.17W
Brandon [Man.-Can.]	39 Je	49.50N	99.57W
Brandon [Vt.-U.S.]	44 Kd	43.47N	73.05W
Brandon Head/Na Machairí	9 Ci	52.16N	10.15W
Brandon Mount/Cnoc Bréanainn ▲	9 Ci	52.14N	10.15W
Brandval	8 Ed	60.19N	12.02 E
Brandvlei	37 Cf	30.25S	20.30 E
Brandýs nad Labem-Stará Boleslav	10 Kf	50.11N	14.40 E
Brăneşti	15 Je	44.27N	26.20 E
Braniewo	10 Pb	54.24N	19.50 E
Bransby Point ▶	51c Bc	16.43N	62.14W
Bransfield Strait ⟶	66 Re	63.00S	59.00W
Brańsk	10 Sd	52.45N	22.51 E
Branson	45 Jh	36.39N	93.13W
Brantevik	8 Fi	55.31N	14.21 E
Brantford	42 Lg	43.08N	80.16W
Brantôme	11 Gi	45.22N	0.39 E
Bras d'Or Lake ◪	42 Lg	45.50N	60.50W
Brasil = Brazil (EN) ①	53 Kf	9.00S	53.00W
Brasil, Planalto do- ⟶ Brazilian Highlands (EN)			
Brasiléia	54 Ef	11.00S	68.44W
Brasília	53 Jg	15.47S	47.55W
Brasília de Minas	55 Jc	16.12S	44.26W
Braslă ⟶	8 Kg	57.08N	24.50 E
Braslav	7 Gj	55.37N	27.05 E
Braşov ②	15 Id	45.40N	25.10 E
Braşov	9 If	45.38N	25.35 E
Brass	34 Ge	4.19N	6.14 E
Brassac	11 Ik	43.38N	2.30 E
Brasschaat	12 Gc	51.17N	4.27 E
Brasstown Bald ▲	44 Fh	34.52N	83.48W
Brastavățu	15 Hf	43.55N	24.24 E
Brataj	15 Gi	40.16N	19.40 E
Bråte	8 De	59.43N	11.27 E
Bratea	15 Fc	46.56N	22.37 E
Bratislava	6 Hf	48.09N	17.07 E
Bratsk	22 Md	56.05N	101.48 E
Bratskoje Vodohranilišče = Bratsk Reservoir (EN) =	20 Fe	56.30N	102.00 E
Bratsk Reservoir (EN) = Bratskoje Vodohranilišče =	20 Fe	56.30N	102.00 E
Brattleboro	44 Kd	42.51N	72.36W
Brattvåg	8 Bb	62.36N	6.27 E
Braubach	12 Jd	50.17N	7.40 E
Braunau am Inn	14 Hb	48.16N	13.02 E
Braunschweig	10 Gd	52.16N	10.32 E
Brava	30 Ng	14.52N	24.43W
Brava, Costa- ◪	13 Pc	41.45N	3.04 E
Bråviken ◪	8 Gf	58.40N	16.30 E
Bravo del Norte, Rio-= Grande, Rio- (EN) ⟶	38 Jg	25.57N	97.09W
Brawley	43 De	32.59N	115.34W
Bray ⊞	37 Gc	25.26S	23.38 E
Bray/Brè	9 Gh	53.12N	6.06W
Bray, Pays de- ⟶	11 He	49.46N	1.26 E
Bray-Dunes	12 Ec	51.05N	2.31 E
Braye ⟶	11 Gg	47.45N	0.42 E
Bray Head ▶	9 Cj	51.53N	10.25W
Bray-sur-Somme	12 Ee	49.56N	2.43 E
Brazi	15 Je	44.52N	26.01 E
Brazil	44 Df	39.32N	87.08W
Brazil (EN) = Brasil ①	53 Kf	9.00S	53.00W
Brazil Basin (EN) ▭	3 Dk	15.00S	25.00W
Brazilian Highlands (EN) = Brasil, Planalto do- ⟶	52 Lg	17.00S	45.00W
Brazos ⟶	38 Jg	28.53N	95.23W
Brazos Santiago Pass ⟶	45 Hm	26.05N	97.16W
Brazzaville	31 Ii	4.16S	15.17 E
Brčko	14 Mf	44.52N	18.49 E
Brda ⟶	10 Oc	53.07N	18.08 E
Brdy ▲	10 Jg	49.35N	13.50 E
Bré/Bray	9 Gh	53.12N	6.06W
Brea, Punta- ▶	51a Bc	17.54N	66.55W
Breaden, Lake- ◪	59 Ee	25.45S	125.40 E
Breaksea Sound ◪	62 Bf	45.35S	166.40 E
Breaza [Rom.]	15 Id	45.11N	25.40 E
Breaza [Rom.]	15 Ib	47.37N	25.20 E
Breaza, Virful- ▲	15 Hb	47.22N	24.02 E
Brebes	10 Eh	6.53S	109.03 E
Brèche ⟶	12 Ee	49.16N	2.30 E
Brechin	9 Ke	56.44N	2.40W
Brecht	12 Gc	51.21N	4.38 E
Břeclav	10 Mh	48.46N	16.54 E
Brecon Beacons ▲	9 Jj	51.53N	3.31W
Breda	11 Kc	51.35N	4.46 E
Bredaryd	8 Eg	57.10N	13.44 E
Bredasdorp	31 Jl	34.32S	20.02 E
Brede ⟶	12 Cd	50.55N	0.43 E
Bredene	12 Fc	51.14N	2.58 E
Bredstedt	10 Eb	54.37N	8.59 E
Bredy	19 Ge	52.26N	60.21 E
Bree	12 Hc	51.08N	5.36 E
Breg ⟶	10 Ei	47.57N	8.31 E
Bregalnica ⟶	15 Eh	41.36N	21.56 E
Bregenz	14 Hb	47.30N	9.46 E
Bréhat, Ile de- ◪	11 Df	48.51N	3.00W
Breiðafjörður ◪	7a Bb	65.15N	23.15W
Breisach am Rhein	10 Dh	48.02N	7.35 E
Breisund ⟶	8 Ab	62.30N	6.00 E
Breit Bridge	37 Dd	22.12S	29.59 E
Breivikbotn	7 Fa	70.37N	22.29 E
Brejão	55 Ia	12.59S	46.28W
Brekken	7 Ce	62.39N	11.53 E
Brekstad	7 Be	63.41N	9.41 E
Bremangerlandet ◪	7 Af	61.50N	5.00 E
Brembana, Val- ⟶	14 De	45.55N	9.40 E
Brembo ⟶	14 De	45.35N	9.32 E
Bremen ②	10 Ec	53.05N	8.50 E
Bremen [F.R.G.]	6 Ge	53.05N	8.48 E
Bremen [In.-U.S.]	44 De	41.27N	86.09W
Bremerhaven	6 Ge	53.33N	8.35 E
Bremerton	43 Cb	47.34N	122.38W
Bremervörde	10 Fc	53.29N	9.08 E
Brendel	46 Kg	38.57N	109.50W
Brenham	45 Hk	30.10N	96.24W
Brenne ⟶	11 Hh	46.44N	1.14 E
Brennero, Passo del-=Brenner Pass (EN) ▭	5 Hf	47.00N	11.30 E
Brennerpaß=Brenner Pass (EN) ▭	5 Hf	47.00N	11.30 E
Brenner Pass (EN)=Brennero, Passo del- ▭	5 Hf	47.00N	11.30 E
Brenner Pass (EN)=Brennerpaß ▭	5 Hf	47.00N	11.30 E
Brenta ⟶	14 Ge	45.11N	12.18 E
Brentwood	9 Nj	51.38N	0.18 E
Brescia	6 Hf	45.33N	10.15 E
Breskens	12 Fc	51.24N	3.33 E
Breslau (EN)=Wrocław	6 He	51.06N	17.00 E
Bresle ⟶	11 Hd	50.04N	1.22 E
Bressanone / Brixen	14 Fd	46.43N	11.39 E
Bressay ◪	9 La	60.08N	1.05W
Bresse ⟶	11 Lh	46.30N	5.15 E
Bressuire	11 Fh	46.51N	0.29W
Brest [Bye.-U.S.S.R.]	6 Ie	52.06N	23.42 E
Brest [Fr.]	6 Ff	48.24N	4.29W
Brestova	14 Je	45.08N	14.14 E
Brestskaja Oblast ③	19 Ce	52.20N	25.30 E
Bretagne=Brittany (EN) ◨	11 Df	48.00N	3.00W
Bretagne=Brittany (EN) ◨	5 Ff	48.00N	3.00W
Bretçu	15 Jc	46.03N	26.18 E
Breteuil [Fr.]	12 Cf	48.50N	0.55 E
Breteuil [Fr.]	11 Je	49.38N	2.18 E
Breton, Marais- ⟶	11 Eh	46.50N	2.00W
Breton, Pertuis- ⟶	11 Eh	46.15N	1.22W
Breton Sound ⟶	45 Ll	29.30N	89.30W
Brett ⟶	12 Cc	51.58N	0.57 E
Brett, Cape- ▶	62 Fa	35.10S	174.20 E
Bretten	12 Ke	49.02N	8.42 E
Bretteville-sur-Laize	12 Be	49.03N	0.20W
Breuh, Pulau- ◪	26 Be	5.41N	95.05 E
Breuil Cervinia	14 Be	45.56N	7.38 E
Breukelen	12 Hb	52.10N	5.01 E
Breuna	12 Lc	51.25N	9.11 E
Breves	54 Hd	1.40S	50.29W
Brevik	8 Bj	59.04N	9.42 E
Brevoort ▶	42 Ld	63.30N	64.20W
Brewarrina	59 Je	29.57S	146.52 E
Brewerville	34 Cd	6.32N	10.47W
Brewster	46 Fb	48.06N	119.47W
Brewster, Kap- ▶	67 Md	70.10N	21.30W
Brewton	45 Je	31.07N	87.04W
Brežice	14 Je	45.54N	15.35 E
Březnica	32 Hc	33.05N	1.16 E
Breznik	15 Gg	42.44N	22.54 E
Brezno	10 Ph	48.49N	19.39 E
Brezoi	15 Hd	45.21N	24.15 E
Brezolles	12 Cf	48.41N	1.04 E
Brezovo	15 Ig	42.21N	25.05 E
Bria	31 Je	6.32N	21.59 E
Briance ⟶	11 Hi	45.47N	1.12 E
Briançon	11 Mi	44.54N	6.39 E
Brianza ◨	14 De	45.40N	9.15 E
Briare, Canal de- ▭	11 If	48.02N	2.43 E
Bribie Island ◪	59 Ke	27.00S	153.05 E
Bričany	15 Ka	48.18N	27.04 E
Bride ⟶	9 Fi	51.31N	3.35W
Bridgend	9 Jj	51.31N	3.35W
Bridgeport [Ca.-U.S.]	46 Fg	38.10N	119.13W
Bridgeport [Ct.-U.S.]	43 Mc	41.11N	73.11W
Bridgeport [Nb.-U.S.]	45 Ef	41.40N	103.06W
Bridge River ⟶	46 Ea	50.45N	121.40W
Bridger Peak ▲	46 Lf	41.12N	107.02W
Bridges Point ▶	64g Bb	51.58S	57.28W
Bridgeton	44 Jf	39.26N	75.14W
Bridgetown [Austl.]	59 Df	33.57S	116.08 E
Bridgetown [Bar.]	39 Nh	13.06N	59.37W
Bridgewater	42 Kg	44.23N	64.31W
Bridgnorth	9 Ki	52.33N	2.25W
Bridgwater	9 Jj	51.08N	3.00W
Bridgwater Bay ◪	9 Jj	51.16N	3.12W
Bridlington	9 Mg	54.05N	0.12W
Bridlington Bay ◪	9 Mg	54.04N	0.08W
Bridport	9 Kk	50.44N	2.46W
Brie ◨	11 Jf	48.40N	3.30 E
Brielle	12 Gc	51.54N	4.10 E
Brienne-le-Château	11 Kf	48.24N	4.32 E
Brienzer-See ◪	14 Cc	46.45N	7.55 E
Briey	11 Le	49.15N	5.56 E
Brig	14 Cd	46.19N	7.59 E
Brigach ⟶	10 Ei	47.58N	8.30 E
Brigham City	43 Ec	41.31N	112.01W
Brighstone	12 Ad	50.38N	1.23W
Bright	59 Jg	36.44S	146.58 E
Brightlingsea	12 Cc	51.49N	1.02 E
Brighton [Co.-U.S.]	45 Dg	39.59N	104.49W
Brighton [Eng.-U.K.]	6 Ge	50.50N	0.08W
Brignoles	11 Mk	43.24N	6.04 E
Brihuega	13 Jd	40.45N	2.52W
Brijuni ◪	14 Hf	44.55N	13.46 E
Brikama	34 Bc	13.16N	16.39W
Brilhante, Rio- ⟶	55 Be	21.58S	54.18W
Brilon	12 Kc	51.24N	8.35 E
Brilon-Alme	12 Kc	51.29N	8.40 E
Brimstone Hill ◪	51c Ab	17.21N	62.49W
Brindisi	6 Ih	40.38N	17.56 E
Brinkley	45 Ki	34.53N	91.12W
Brinkmann	55 Aj	30.52S	62.02W
Brioude	11 Ji	45.18N	3.24 E
Brisbane	58 Gg	27.28S	153.02 E
Brisighella	14 Ff	44.13N	11.46 E
Bristol ◨	66 Ad	59.02S	26.31W
Bristol [Eng.-U.K.]	6 Fe	51.27N	2.35W
Bristol [Tn.-U.S.]	44 Fg	36.36N	82.11W
Bristol Bay ◪	38 Bd	58.00N	159.00W
Bristol Channel ⟶	5 Fe	51.20N	4.00W
Bristol Lake ◪	46 Hi	34.28N	115.41W
Bristow	45 Hi	35.50N	96.23W
Britannia Range ▲	66 Jf	80.00S	158.00 E
British Columbia ③	38 Fc	55.00N	125.00W
British Honduras → Belize	49 Ce	17.35N	88.35W
British Indian Ocean Territory ⑤	22 Jj	7.00S	72.00 E
British Isles ◨	5 Fd	54.00N	4.00W
British Mountains ▲	40 Kc	69.20N	140.20W
British Solomon Islands → Solomon Islands ①	58 Ge	8.00S	159.00 E
British Virgin Islands ⑤	39 Mh	18.20N	64.50W
Brits	37 De	25.40S	27.46 E
Britstown	37 Cf	30.37S	23.30 E
Britt	45 Ja	46.03N	93.48W
Brittany (EN) = Bretagne ◨	5 Ff	48.00N	3.00W
Brittany (EN) = Bretagne ◨	11 Df	48.00N	3.00W
Britton	45 Hd	45.48N	97.45W
Brive-la-Gaillarde	11 Hi	45.09N	1.32 E
Briviesca	13 Ib	42.33N	3.19W
Brixen / Bressanone	14 Fd	46.43N	11.39 E
Brixham	9 Jk	50.24N	3.30W
Brjansk	6 Je	53.15N	34.22 E
Brjanskaja Oblast ③	19 De	52.56N	33.20 E
Brjuhoveckaja	16 Kg	45.46N	39.01 E
Brjukovići	10 Wg	49.52N	24.00 E
Brno	6 Hf	49.12N	16.37 E
Broa, Ensenada de la- ◪	49 Fb	22.35N	82.00W
Broad Bay ◪	9 Gc	58.15N	6.15W
Broadford	9 Hd	57.14N	5.54W
Broad Sound ⟶	59 Jd	22.10S	149.45 E
Broadstairs	12 Dc	51.22N	1.27 E
Broadus	43 Hb	45.27N	105.25W
Brocēni/Broceny	8 Jh	56.41N	22.30 E
Broceny/Brocēni	8 Jh	56.41N	22.30 E
Brochet	42 He	57.53N	101.40W
Brochu, Lac- ◪	44 Ja	48.26N	74.15W
Brocken ▲	10 Ge	51.48N	10.36 E
Brockman, Mount- ▲	59 Dd	22.28S	117.18 E
Brockton	44 Ld	42.05N	71.01W
Brockville ◪	44 Jd	44.35N	75.41W
Brod	15 Eh	41.31N	21.14 E
Brodarevo	15 Cf	43.14N	19.43 E
Broderick Falls	36 Fb	0.37N	34.46 E
Brodeur Peninsula ⟶	38 Kb	73.00N	88.00W
Brodick	9 Hf	55.35N	5.09W
Brodnica	10 Pc	53.16N	19.23 E
Brody	16 Cd	50.04N	25.12 E
Broglie	12 Ce	49.01N	0.32 E
Brok	10 Rd	52.43N	21.52 E
Brokę ⟶	42 Ga	77.55N	114.30W
Bromley, London-	12 Cc	51.25N	0.01 E
Bromölla	7 Dh	56.04N	14.28 E
Brønderslev	8 Cg	57.16N	9.58 E
Brong-Ahafo ③	34 Ed	7.45N	1.30W
Bronnikovo	17 Ng	58.29N	68.27 E
Brønnøysund	7 Cd	65.28N	12.13 E
Bronte	14 Im	37.47N	14.50 E
Brooke's Point	26 Gp	8.47N	117.50 E
Brookfield	45 Jg	39.47N	93.04W
Brookhaven	45 Kk	31.35N	90.26W
Brookings [Or.-U.S.]	46 Cf	42.03N	124.17W
Brookings [S.D.-U.S.]	43 Hc	44.19N	96.48W
Brooks	42 Gf	50.35N	111.53W
Brooks Banks (EN) ▭	60 Mc	24.05N	166.50W
Brooks Range ▲	38 Cb	68.00N	154.00W
Brookston	45 Jc	46.50N	92.32W
Brooksville	44 Fk	28.33N	82.23W
Brookton	59 Df	32.22S	117.01 E
Brookville [In.-U.S.]	44 Ef	39.25N	85.01W
Brookville [Pa.-U.S.]	44 Hf	41.10N	79.06W
Broom ⟶	9 Hd	57.45S	5.05W
Broom, Loch- ◪	9 Hd	57.55N	5.15W
Broome	58 Df	17.58S	122.14 E
Brora	9 Jc	58.01N	3.51W
Brora ⟶	9 Jc	58.01N	3.51W
Brosna/An Bhrosnach ⟶	9 Fh	53.13N	7.58W
Broșteni	15 Ib	47.14N	25.42 E
Brou	11 Hf	48.13N	1.11 E
Brough	9 Kg	54.32N	2.19W
Broughton Island	39 Mc	67.35N	63.50W
Broussard	45 Kk	30.09N	91.58W
Brovary	16 Ed	50.30N	30.48 E
Brovst	8 Cg	57.06N	9.32 E
Brown Bank (EN) = Bruine Bank ▭	12 Fb	52.35N	3.20 E
Brownfield	43 Ge	33.11N	102.16W
Browning	43 Eb	48.34N	113.01W
Browns Bank (EN) ▭	42 Kh	42.40N	65.50W
Brownsville [Tn.-U.S.]	45 Ch	35.36N	89.15W
Brownsville [Tx.-U.S.]	39 Jg	25.54N	97.30W
Brownwood	43 Ie	31.43N	98.59W
Browse Island ◪	59 Eb	14.05S	123.35 E
Broye ⟶	14 Bc	46.54N	7.02 E
Bruay-en-Artois	11 Id	50.29N	2.33 E
Bruay-sur-l'Escaut	12 Fd	50.26N	3.33 E
Bruce, Mount- ▲	57 Cg	22.36S	118.08 E
Bruce Crossing	45 Lb	46.33N	89.11W
Bruce Peninsula ⟶	42 Jh	44.59N	81.20W
Bruce Rock	59 Df	31.53S	118.09 E
Bruche ⟶	11 Nf	48.34N	7.43 E

Index Symbols

① Independent Nation	▱ Historical or Cultural Region	▱ Pass, Gap	▱ Depression	▱ Coast, Beach	▱ Rock, Reef
② State, Region	▲ Mount, Mountain	▱ Plain, Lowland	▱ Polder	▱ Cliff	▱ Islands, Archipelago
③ District, County	▲ Volcano	▱ Delta	▱ Desert, Dunes	▱ Peninsula	▱ Rocks, Reefs
④ Municipality	⬤ Hill	▱ Salt Flat	▱ Forest, Woods	▱ Isthmus	▱ Coral Reef
⑤ Colony, Dependency	▲ Mountains, Mountain Range	▱ Valley, Canyon	▱ Heath, Steppe	▱ Sandbank	▱ Atoll
■ Continent	▰ Hills, Escarpment	▱ Crater, Cave	▱ Oasis	▱ Island	▱ River, Stream
◨ Physical Region	⬢ Plateau, Upland	▱ Karst Features	▶ Cape, Point		

⟶ Waterfall Rapids	▱ Canal	▱ Lagoon	▱ Escarpment, Sea Scarp	▱ Historic Site	▱ Port
⟶ River Mouth, Estuary	▱ Glacier	▱ Bank	▱ Fracture	▱ Ruins	▱ Lighthouse
⟶ Lake	▱ Ice Shelf, Pack Ice	▱ Seamount	▱ Trench, Abyss	▱ Wall, Walls	▱ Mine
⟶ Salt Lake	▱ Ocean	▱ Tablemount	▱ National Park, Reserve	▱ Church, Abbey	▱ Tunnel
▱ Well, Spring	▱ Sea	▱ Ridge	▱ Point of Interest	▱ Temple	▱ Dam, Bridge
◪ Intermittent Lake	◪ Gulf, Bay	▱ Shelf	▱ Recreation Site	▱ Scientific Station	
▱ Reservoir	▱ Strait, Fjord	▱ Basin	▱ Cave, Cavern	▱ Airport	
⟶ Swamp, Pond					

Bruchhausen Vilsen 12 Lb 52.50N 9.01 E
Bruchmühlbach Miesau 12 Je 49.23N 7.28 E
Bruchsal 10 Eg 49.08N 8.36 E
Bruck an der Leitha 14 Kb 48.01N 16.46 E
Bruck an der Mur 14 Jc 47.25N 15.17 E
Brue 9 Kj 51.13N 3.00W
Bruges/Brugge 11 Jc 51.13N 3.14 E
Brugg 14 Cc 47.29N 8.12 E
Brugge/Bruges 11 Jc 51.13N 3.14 E
Brugge-Assebroek 12 Fc 51.12N 3.16 E
Brüggen 12 Ic 51.15N 6.11 E
Brugge-Sint-Andries 12 Fc 51.12N 3.10 E
Brühl [F.R.G.] 12 Id 50.50N 6.54 E
Brühl [F.R.G.] 12 Ke 49.24N 8.32 E
Bruine Bank=Brown Bank (EN) 12 Fb 52.35N 3.20 E
Bruin Point 43 Ed 39.39N 110.22W
Brule River 44 Cc 45.57N 88.12W
Brumado 54 Jf 14.13S 41.40W
Brummen 12 Ib 52.06N 6.10 E
Brummo 8 Ef 58.50N 13.40 E
Brumunddal 7 Cf 60.53N 10.56 E
Bruna 14 Eh 42.45N 10.53 E
Brune 12 Fe 49.45N 3.47 E
Bruneau 46 He 42.53N 115.48W
Bruneau River 46 He 42.57N 115.58W
Bruneck / Brunico 14 Fd 46.48N 11.56 E
Brunehamel 12 Ge 49.46N 4.11 E
Brunei 22 Ni 4.30N 114.40 E
Brunei, Teluk- 21 Ni 5.05N 115.18 E
Brunette Downs 59 Hc 18.38S 135.57 E
Brunflo 8 Fa 63.05N 14.49 E
Brunico / Bruneck 14 Fd 46.48N 11.56 E
Brunna 8 Ge 59.52N 17.25 E
Brunner 62 De 42.26S 171.19 E
Brunner, Lake- 62 De 42.35S 171.25 E
Brunnsberg 8 Ec 61.17N 13.55 E
Brunsbüttel 10 Fc 53.54N 9.07 E
Brunssum 12 Hd 50.57N 5.57 E
Brunswick [Ga.-U.S.] 43 Ke 31.10N 81.29W
Brunswick [Me.-U.S.] 43 Nc 43.55N 69.58W
Brunswick, Peninsula de- 52 Ik 53.30S 71.25W
Brunswick Lake 44 Fa 49.00N 83.23W
Bruntál 10 Ng 49.59N 17.28 E
Bruny Island 59 Jh 43.30S 147.05 E
Brus 15 Ef 43.23N 21.02 E
Brus, Laguna de- 49 Ef 15.50N 84.35W
Brush 43 Gc 40.15N 103.37W
Brus Laguna 49 Ef 15.47N 84.35W
Brusque 56 Kc 27.06S 48.56W
Brussel/Bruxelles=Brussels (EN) 6 Ge 50.50N 4.20 E
Brussels (EN)=Brussel/Bruxelles 6 Ge 50.50N 4.20 E
Brussels (EN)=Bruxelles/Brussel 6 Ge 50.50N 4.20 E
Brusset, 'Erg- 34 Hb 18.55N 10.30 E
Brusturi 15 Fb 47.09N 22.15 E
Brusy 10 Nc 53.53N 17.45 E
Bruxelles/Brussel=Brussels (EN) 6 Ge 50.50N 4.20 E
Bruzual 50 Bh 8.03N 69.19W
Bryan [Oh.-U.S.] 44 Ee 41.30N 84.34W
Bryan [Tx.-U.S.] 43 He 30.40N 96.22W
Bryan Coast 66 Pf 73.35S 84.00W
Bryne 7 Ag 58.44N 5.39 E
Brza Palanka 15 Fe 44.28N 22.27 E
Brzava kanal 15 Dd 45.16N 20.49 E
Brzeg 10 Nf 50.52N 17.27 E
Brzeg Dolny 10 Me 51.15N 16.40 E
Brzeziny 10 Pe 51.48N 19.46 E
Brzozów 10 Sg 49.42N 22.02 E
Bsharrī 24 Ge 34.15N 36.01 E
Bū 12 Df 48.48N 1.30 E
Bua 8 Eg 57.14N 12.07 E
Buada Lagoon 64e Ab 0.32S 166.54 E
Buala 58 Ge 8.10S 159.35 E
Bū al Ḥidān, Wādī- 33 Cd 27.25N 19.22 E
Buapinang 26 Hg 4.46S 121.34 E
Buatan 26 Df 0.44N 101.51 E
Bū aṭ Ṭifl 33 Dd 28.54N 22.30 E
Bua Yai 25 Ke 15.34N 102.24 E
Bu'ayrāt al Ḥasūn 33 Cc 31.24N 15.44 E
Bubanza 36 Ec 3.06S 29.23 E
Bubaque 34 Bc 11.17N 15.50W
Būbīyan 24 Mh 29.45N 48.15 E
Bubu 36 Gd 6.03S 35.19 E
Bubye 37 Ed 22.20S 31.07 E
Buca 15 Kk 38.22N 27.11 E
Bučač 16 De 49.04N 25.23 E
Bucačača 20 Gf 52.59N 116.55 E
Buçaco 36 De 11.27S 20.12 E
Bucak 24 Dd 37.28N 30.36 E
Bucaramanga 53 Ie 7.08N 73.09W
Bucas Grande 26 Ie 9.40N 125.58 E
Buccament Bay 51n Ba 13.12N 61.17W
Buccaneer Archipelago 59 Ec 16.17S 123.20 E
Bucecea 15 Jb 47.46N 26.26 E
Buchanan 34 Cd 5.53N 10.03W
Buchanan, Lake- [Austl.] 59 Jd 21.30S 145.50 E
Buchanan, Lake- [Tx.-U.S.] 45 Gk 30.48N 98.25W
Buchanan Bay 42 Ka 78.55N 75.00W
Buchan Gulf 42 Kb 71.48N 74.06W
Buchardo 56 Hd 34.43S 63.31W
Bucharest (EN)=București 6 Ig 44.26N 26.06 E
Buchen 10 Fg 49.31N 9.20 E
Buchholz in der Nordheide 10 Fc 53.20N 9.52 E
Buchon, Point- 46 Ei 35.15N 120.54W
Buchs 14 Dc 47.10N 9.30 E
Buchy 12 De 49.35N 1.22 E
Bückeburg 12 Lb 52.16N 9.03 E
Buckeye 46 Ij 33.22N 112.35W
Buckhaven 9 Je 56.11N 3.03W
Buckie 9 Kd 57.40N 2.58W
Buckingham [Eng.-U.K.] 12 Bb 52.00N 0.59W
Buckingham [Que.-Can.] 44 Jc 45.35N 75.25W
Buckingham Bay 59 Hb 12.10S 135.46 E
Buckinghamshire 9 Mj 51.50N 0.55W
Buckland 40 Gc 66.16N 161.20W
Buckle Island 66 Ke 66.47S 163.14 E
Buckley Bay 66 Je 68.16S 148.12 E
Bucks 9 Mj 51.50N 0.55W
Bucksport 44 Mc 44.34N 68.48W
Buco Zau 36 Bc 4.50S 12.33 E
Bu Craa 32 Ed 26.17N 12.46W
Bucureşti 15 Je 44.30N 26.05 E
Bucureşti=Bucharest (EN) 6 Ig 44.26N 26.06 E
Bucy-lès-Pierrepont 12 Fe 49.39N 3.54 E
Bucyrus 44 Fe 40.47N 82.57W
Bud 7 Be 62.55N 6.55 E
Budacu, Virful- 15 Ib 47.07N 25.41 E
Buda-Koševelo 16 Gc 52.43N 30.39 E
Budapest 10 Pi 47.30N 19.05 E
Budapest 6 Hf 47.30N 19.05 E
Búdardalur 7a Bb 65.07N 21.46W
Budaun 25 Fc 28.03N 79.07 E
Budbud 35 He 4.13N 46.31 E
Budd Coast 66 He 66.30S 113.00 E
Buddusò 14 Di 40.35N 9.15 E
Bude [Eng.-U.K.] 9 Ik 50.50N 4.33W
Bude [Ms.-U.S.] 45 Kk 31.28N 90.51W
Bude Bay 9 Ik 50.50N 4.37W
Budel 12 Hc 51.16N 5.30 E
Budennovsk 19 Eg 44.45N 44.08 E
Budeşti 15 Je 44.14N 26.27 E
Budia 13 Jd 40.38N 2.45W
Büdingen 10 Ff 50.18N 9.07 E
Búdir 7a Cb 64.56N 14.01W
Budjala 36 Cb 2.39N 19.42 E
Budkowiczanka 10 Nf 50.52N 17.33 E
Budogošč 7 Hg 59.19N 32.29 E
Budrio 14 Ff 44.32N 11.32 E
Budslav 8 Lj 54.49N 27.32 E
Budva 15 Bg 42.17N 18.51 E
Budyšin/Bautzen 10 Ke 51.11N 14.26 E
Budžjak 15 Lc 46.15N 28.45 E
Buea 34 Ge 4.09N 9.14 E
Buech 11 Lj 44.12N 5.57 E
Buenaventura [Col.] 53 Ie 3.53N 77.04W
Buenaventura [Mex.] 47 Cc 29.51N 107.29W
Buenaventura, Bahia de- 54 Cc 3.45N 77.15W
Buenavista 48 Ef 23.39N 109.42W
Buena Vista [Co.-U.S.] 45 Cg 38.50N 106.08W
Buena Vista [Mex.] 48 Mi 16.05N 93.00W
Buena Vista [Mex.] 48 Bb 31.10N 115.40W
Buena Vista [Ven.] 50 Eh 9.02N 63.49W
Buenavista, Bahia de- 49 Hb 22.30N 79.08W
Buendia, Embalse de- 13 Jd 40.25N 2.43W
Buenópolis 55 Jc 17.54S 44.11W
Buenos Aires 56 Ie 36.00S 60.00W
Buenos Aires [Arg.] 53 Ki 34.36S 58.27W
Buenos Aires [C.R.] 49 Fi 10.04N 84.26W
Buenos Aires, Lago- 52 Ij 46.30S 72.00W
Buffalo 42 Fe 60.52N 115.03W
Buffalo [N.Y.-U.S.] 39 Le 42.54N 78.53W
Buffalo [Ok.-U.S.] 45 Gh 36.50N 99.38W
Buffalo [S.D.-U.S.] 43 Gb 45.35N 103.33W
Buffalo [Tx.-U.S.] 45 Hk 31.28N 96.04W
Buffalo [Wy.-U.S.] 43 Fc 44.21N 106.42W
Buffalo Bill Reservoir 46 Kd 44.29N 109.13W
Buffalo Lake 42 Fd 60.12N 115.25W
Buffalo Narrows 42 Ge 55.51N 108.30W
Buffalo Pound Lake 46 Ma 50.38N 105.20W
Buffels 37 Be 29.41S 17.04 E
Bū Fishah 14 En 36.18N 10.28 E
Buford 44 Fh 34.07N 84.00W
Buftea 15 Ie 44.34N 25.57 E
Bug 5 Ie 52.31N 21.05 E
Buga 54 Cc 3.55N 76.18W
Bugarach, Pech de- 11 Il 42.52N 2.23 E
Bugeat 11 Hi 45.36N 1.56 E
Bugene 36 Fc 1.35S 31.08 E
Bugey 11 Li 45.48N 5.30 E
Bugojno 23 Ff 44.03N 17.27 E
Bugøynes 7 Gb 69.58N 29.39 E
Bugrino 17 Db 68.48N 49.09 E
Bugsuk 26 Ge 8.15N 117.18 E
Bugt 27 Lb 48.47N 121.55 E
Bugulma 19 Fe 54.33N 52.48 E
Bugun 18 Hc 43.22N 70.10 E
Bugun 18 Gc 42.56N 68.36 E
Bügür/Luntai 27 Dc 41.46N 84.10 E
Buguruslan 19 Fe 53.39N 52.30 E
Buhara 22 If 39.49N 64.25 E
Buharskaja Oblast 19 Gg 41.20N 64.20 E
Bū Ḥaṣā' 24 Ok 23.20N 53.20 E
Buhera 37 Ec 19.18S 31.29 E
Buh He 27 Gd 36.58N 99.48 E
Buhl 46 He 42.36N 114.46W
Bühl 10 Eh 48.42N 8.09 E
Bühödle 35 Hd 8.15N 46.20 E
Buhtarminskoje Vodohranilišče 19 If 49.10N 84.00 E
Bui Dam 34 Ed 8.22N 2.15W
Builth Wells 9 Ji 52.09N 3.24W
Buin [Chile] 56 Fd 33.44S 70.44W
Buin [Pap.N.Gui.] 60 Fi 6.50S 155.44 E
Buinsk 19 Ee 54.59N 48.17 E
Buir Nur 27 Kb 47.48N 117.42 E
Buitrago del Lozoya 13 Id 41.00N 3.38W
Buj 17 Gh 56.15N 54.12 E
Buj 19 Ed 58.29N 41.31 E
Bujalance 13 Hg 37.54N 4.22W
Bujanovac 15 Eg 42.28N 21.47 E
Bujaraloz 13 Lc 41.30N 0.09W
Buje 14 He 45.24N 13.40 E
Bujnaksk 19 Eg 42.49N 47.07 E
Bujukly 20 Jg 49.33N 142.55 E
Bujumbura 31 Ji 3.23S 29.22 E
Bujunda 20 Kd 62.00N 153.30 E
Buk 10 Md 52.22N 16.31 E
Bük 10 Mi 47.23N 16.45 E
Buk 10 Hb 54.10N 11.42 E
Buka Island 57 Ge 5.15S 154.35 E
Bukakata 36 Fc 0.18S 32.02 E
Bukama 31 Ji 9.12S 25.51 E
Buka Passage 63a Ba 5.25S 154.41 E
Bukavu 31 Ji 2.30S 28.52 E
Bukene 36 Fc 4.14S 32.53 E
Bukhā 24 Qi 26.10N 56.09 E
Bukit Besi 26 Df 4.46N 103.12 E
Bukit Mertajam 26 De 5.22N 100.28 E
Bukittinggi 22 Mj 0.19S 100.22 E
Bükk 10 Qh 48.05N 20.30 E
Bukoba 31 Ki 1.20S 31.49 E
Bukovina 15 Ia 48.00N 25.30 E
Bukowiec 10 Ld 52.23N 15.20 E
Bukuru 34 Gd 9.48N 8.52 E
Būl, Kūh-e- 23 Hc 30.48N 52.45 E
Bulajevo 19 He 54.53N 70.26 E
Bulan 26 Hd 12.40N 123.52 E
Bulanaš 17 Kh 57.16N 62.02 E
Bulancak 24 Hb 40.57N 38.14 E
Bulanık 24 Jc 39.05N 42.15 E
Būlāq 33 Fd 25.12N 30.32 E
Bulawayo 31 Jk 20.09S 28.34 E
Buldan 24 Cc 38.03N 28.51 E
Buldir 40a Bb 52.21N 175.54 E
Bulgan [Mong.] 27 Hc 44.05N 103.32 E
Bulgan [Mong.] 27 Hb 48.45N 103.34 E
Bulgan [Mong.] 27 Fb 46.05N 91.34 E
Bulgaria (EN)=Bâlgarija 6 Ig 43.00N 25.00 E
Buli 26 If 0.53N 128.18 E
Buli, Teluk- 26 If 0.45N 128.30 E
Buliluyan, Cape- 26 Ge 8.20N 117.11 E
Bulki 35 Fd 6.01N 36.36 E
Bullahār 35 Gc 10.23N 44.27 E
Bullange/Büllingen 12 Id 50.25N 6.16 E
Bullaque 13 Hf 38.59N 4.17W
Bulla Regia 14 Cn 36.33N 8.45 E
Bullas 13 Kf 38.03N 1.40W
Bulle 14 Bd 46.37N 7.04 E
Buller 62 Dd 41.44S 171.35 E
Bullfinch 59 Df 30.59S 119.06 E
Büllingen/Bullange 12 Id 50.25N 6.16 E
Bullion Mountains 46 Hi 34.25N 116.00W
Bulloo River 57 Fg 28.43S 142.30 E
Bull Point [Eng.-U.K.] 9 Ij 51.12N 4.10W
Bull Point [Falk.Is.] 56 Ih 52.19S 59.18W
Bulls 62 Fd 40.10S 175.23 E
Bulls Bay 44 Hi 32.59N 79.33W
Bull Shoals Lake 45 Jh 36.30N 92.50W
Bully Choop Mountain 46 Df 40.35N 122.45W
Bully-les-Mines 12 Ed 50.26N 2.43 E
Bulo Berde 35 He 3.52N 45.40 E
Bulolo 60 Di 7.12S 146.39 E
Bulqiza 15 Dh 41.30N 20.21 E
Bulter 45 Ig 38.16N 94.20W
Bultfontein 37 De 28.20S 26.05 E
Bulukumba 26 Hh 5.33S 120.11 E
Bulungu [Zaire] 36 Cc 4.33S 18.36 E
Bulungu [Zaire] 36 Dd 6.04S 21.54 E
Bumba 31 Jh 2.11N 22.28 E
Bumbah, Khalīj al- 33 Dc 32.25N 23.06 E
Buna 15 Ch 41.52N 19.22 E
Buna 36 Gb 2.47N 39.31 E
Bunbury 58 Ch 33.19S 115.38 E
Buncrana/Bun Cranncha 9 Ff 55.08N 7.27W
Bun Cranncha/Buncrana 9 Ff 55.08N 7.27W
Bunda 36 Fc 2.03S 33.52 E
Bundaberg 58 Gg 24.52S 152.21 E
Bünde 10 Ed 52.12N 8.35 E
Bundesrepublik Deutschland =Germany, Federal Republic of- (EN) 6 Ge 51.00N 9.00 E
Bun Dobhráin/Bundoran 9 Eg 54.28N 8.17W
Bundoran/Bun Dobhráin 9 Eg 54.28N 8.17W
Bungay 12 Db 52.27N 1.27 E
Bungku 26 Hg 2.33S 121.58 E
Bungo 36 Cd 7.26S 15.24 E
Bungo Strait (EN)=Bungo-Suidō 28 Lh 32.40N 132.18 E
Bungo-Suidō=Bungo Strait (EN) 28 Lh 32.40N 132.18 E
Bungotakada 29 Be 33.33N 131.27 E
Bungsberg 10 Gb 54.12N 10.43 E
Bunguran, Kepulauan-=Natuna Islands (EN) 21 Mi 2.45N 109.00 E
Buni 34 Hc 11.12N 12.02 E
Bunja 31 Kh 1.34N 30.15 E
Bunji 25 Ea 35.40N 74.36 E
Bunker 45 Kh 37.27N 91.13W
Bunker Group 59 Kd 23.50S 152.20 E
Bunkeya 36 Ee 10.24S 26.58 E
Bunkie 45 Jk 30.57N 92.11W
Bunnerfjällen 8 Ea 63.10N 12.34 E
Buñol 13 Le 39.25N 0.47W
Bunschoten 12 Hb 52.14N 5.24 E
Buntingford 12 Bc 51.57N 0.01W
Buntok 26 Fg 1.42S 114.48 E
Bünyan 24 Fc 38.51N 35.52 E
Bunyu, Pulau- 26 Gf 3.30N 117.50 E
Buor-Haja, Guba- 20 Ib 71.00N 131.00 E
Buotama 20 Hd 61.17N 128.55 E
Buqayq 23 Gd 25.56N 49.40 E
Buqda Kōsār 35 Ge 4.31N 44.49 E
Bur 20 Hb 71.40N 123.40 E
Bura 36 Gc 1.06S 39.57 E
Buram 31 Jg 10.49N 25.10 E
Buran 19 If 48.04N 85.15 E
Burang 27 De 30.18N 81.08 E
Burāq 24 Gf 33.10N 36.29 E
Buras 45 Ll 29.21N 89.32W
Buraydah 22 Gg 26.20N 43.59 E
Burbach 12 Kd 50.43N 8.03 E
Būrdab 35 Hd 9.05N 46.30 E
Burdekin River 59 Jc 19.39S 147.30 E
Burdère 35 He 3.30N 45.37 E
Burdur 23 Db 37.43N 30.17 E
Burdur Gölü 24 Dd 37.44N 30.12 E
Burdwān 25 Ad 23.15N 87.51 E
Burdwood Bank (EN) 56 Ih 54.15S 59.00W
Bure 12 Db 52.38N 1.45 E
Bure [Eth.] 35 Fd 8.20N 35.08 E
Bure [Eth.] 35 Fc 10.43N 37.03 E
Bureå 7 Ed 64.37N 21.12 E
Bureinski Hrebet=Bureya Range (EN) 21 Pd 50.40N 134.00 E
Bureja 20 Hg 49.43N 129.51 E
Bureja 20 Ie 49.25N 129.35 E
Büren 10 Ee 51.33N 8.34 E
Buren-Cogt 27 Jb 46.45N 111.30 E
Bureya Range (EN)=Bureinski Hrebet 21 Pd 50.40N 134.00 E
Burfjord 7 Fb 69.56N 22.03 E
Būr Gābo 35 Gf 1.10S 41.50 E
Burgas 6 Ig 42.30N 27.28 E
Burgas 15 Kg 42.30N 27.20 E
Burgas, Gulf of- (EN)=Burgaski Zaliv 15 Kg 42.30N 27.33 E
Burgaski Zaliv=Burgas, Gulf of- (EN) 15 Kg 42.30N 27.33 E
Burg auf Fehmarn 10 Hb 54.26N 11.12 E
Burg auf Fehmarn-Puttgarden 10 Hb 54.30N 11.13 E
Burgaw 44 Ih 34.33N 77.56W
Burgaz Daği 15 Mk 38.25N 29.46 E
Burg bei Magdeburg 10 Hd 52.16N 11.51 E
Burgdorf [F.R.G.] 10 Gd 52.27N 10.01 E
Burgdorf [Switz.] 14 Bc 47.04N 7.37 E
Burgenland 14 Kc 47.30N 16.25 E
Burgersdorp 37 Df 31.00S 26.20 E
Burgess Hill 12 Bd 50.58N 0.08W
Burgfjället 7 Dd 64.56N 15.03 E
Burghausen 10 Ih 48.10N 12.50 E
Burghūth, Sabkhat al- 24 Ie 34.58N 41.06 E
Burglengenfeld 10 Ig 49.12N 12.02 E
Burgos 13 Ib 42.20N 3.40W
Burgos [Mex.] 48 Je 24.57N 98.57W
Burgos [Sp.] 6 Fg 42.21N 3.42W
Burg-Reuland 12 Id 50.12N 6.09 E
Burgsvik 7 Eh 57.03N 18.16 E
Burgundy (EN)=Bourgogne 5 Gf 47.00N 4.30 E
Burgundy (EN)=Bourgogne 11 Kg 47.00N 4.30 E
Burgwald 12 Kd 50.57N 8.48 E
Būr Hakkaba 35 Ge 2.43N 44.10 E
Burhaniye 24 Bc 39.30N 26.58 E
Burhānpur 22 Jg 21.18N 76.14 E
Burias 26 Hd 12.57N 123.08 E
Buribaj 17 Ij 51.57N 58.11 E
Burica, Punta- 47 Hg 8.03N 82.53W
Burien 46 Dc 47.27N 122.21W
Burin Peninsula 42 Lg 47.00N 55.40W
Buriram 25 Kf 14.59N 103.08 E
Buriti, Rio- 55 Ca 12.50S 58.28W
Buriti Alegre 55 Hd 18.09S 49.03W
Buriti Bravo 54 Je 5.50S 43.50W
Buriti dos Lopes 54 Jd 3.10S 41.52W
Buritis 55 Ib 15.37S 46.26W
Burj al Ḥaṭṭābah 32 Ic 30.20N 9.30 E
Burjasot 13 Le 39.31N 0.25W
Burjatskaja ASSR 20 Ff 53.00N 110.00 E
Burj Şāfitā 24 Ge 34.49N 36.07 E
Burkandja 20 Jd 63.27N 147.27 E
Burkburnett 45 Gi 34.06N 98.34W
Burke 45 Ge 43.11N 99.18W
Burke, Mount- 46 Ha 50.18N 114.30W
Burke Island 66 Of 73.08S 105.06W
Burke River 59 Hd 23.12S 139.33 E
Burkesville 44 Eg 36.48N 85.22W
Burketown 58 Ef 17.44S 139.22 E
Burley 43 Ec 42.32N 113.48W
Burli 16 Rd 51.28N 52.44 E
Burlingame 45 Ig 38.45N 95.50W
Burlington [Co.-U.S.] 43 Gd 39.18N 102.16W
Burlington [Ia.-U.S.] 43 Ic 40.49N 91.07W
Burlington [Ks.-U.S.] 45 Ig 38.12N 95.45W
Burlington [N.C.-U.S.] 44 Hg 36.06N 79.26W
Burlington [Ont.-Can.] 44 Hd 43.19N 79.43W
Burlington [Vt.-U.S.] 43 Mc 44.28N 73.14W
Burlington [Wi.-U.S.] 45 Le 42.41N 88.17W
Burma 22 Lg 22.00N 98.00 E
Burma (Myanma-Nainggan-Daw) 22 Lg 22.00N 98.00 E
Burnazului, Cîmpia- 15 Ie 44.10N 25.50 E
Burnett River 59 Kd 24.46S 152.25 E
Burney 46 Ef 40.53N 121.40W
Burnham Market 12 Cb 52.57N 0.44 E
Burnham-on-Crouch 12 Cc 51.37N 0.50 E
Burnie 59 Jh 41.04S 145.54 E
Burnley 9 Kh 53.48N 2.14W
Burns 43 Dc 43.35N 119.03W
Burnside 42 Gc 66.51N 108.04W
Burnside, Lake- 59 Ee 25.20S 123.10 E
Burns Lake 42 Ef 54.14N 125.46W
Burnsville 44 Fh 35.55N 82.18W
Burnt Lava Flow 46 Ef 41.35N 121.35W
Burnt River 44 Hc 44.35N 78.46W
Burntwood 42 He 56.08N 96.33W
Bur'o 31 Lh 9.30N 45.34 E
Burqin 27 Eb 47.43N 86.53 E
Burqin He 27 Eb 47.42N 86.50 E
Burqūm, Ḥarrat al- 33 He 20.54N 42.00 E
Burra 59 Hf 33.40S 138.56 E
Burragorang Lake 59 Kf 34.00S 150.25 E
Burreli 15 Ch 41.37N 20.00 E
Burrendong Reservoir 59 Jf 32.40S 149.10 E
Burriana 13 Le 39.53N 0.05W
Burro, Serranias del 48 Ic 28.50N 101.35W
Burrow Head 9 Ig 54.41N 4.24W
Bursa 22 Ee 40.11N 29.04 E
Būr Sa'īd=Port Said (EN) 31 Ke 31.16N 32.18 E
Burscheid 12 Jc 51.06N 7.07 E
Bürstadt 12 Ke 49.38N 8.27 E
Burštyn 16 De 49.16N 24.37 E
Būr Sūdān=Port Sudan (EN) 31 Kg 19.37N 37.14 E
Burt Lake 44 Ec 45.27N 84.40W
Burtnieku, Ozero- 8 Kg 57.35N 25.10 E
Burtnieku, Ozero-/Burtnieku Ezers 8 Kg 57.35N 25.10 E
Burtnieku Ezers 8 Kg 57.35N 25.10 E
Burtnieku Ezers/Burtnieku, Ozero- 8 Kg 57.35N 25.10 E
Burton 44 Fd 43.02N 83.36W
Burton Latimer 12 Bb 52.21N 0.40W
Burton-upon-Trent 9 Li 52.49N 1.36W
Burträsk 7 Ed 64.31N 20.39 E
Buru, Pulau- 57 De 3.24S 126.40 E
Burullus, Buḥayrat al- 24 Dg 31.30N 30.50 E
Burultokay/Fuhai 27 Eb 47.06N 87.23 E
Burum Gana 34 Hc 13.00N 11.57 E
Burūn, Ra's- 24 Eg 31.14N 33.04 E
Burundaj 19 Hg 43.20N 76.49 E
Burundi 31 Ki 3.15S 30.00 E
Bururi 36 Ec 3.57S 29.37 E
Burutu 34 Gd 5.21N 5.31 E
Bury 9 Kh 53.36N 2.17W
Burylbajtal 18 Ib 44.56N 73.59 E
Buryn 16 Hd 51.13N 33.48 E
Bury Saint Edmunds 9 Ni 52.15N 0.43 E
Burzil Pass 25 Ff 34.54N 75.06 E
Busalla 14 Cf 44.34N 8.57 E
Busanga [Zaire] 36 Ee 10.12S 25.23 E
Busanga [Zaire] 36 Dc 0.51S 22.04 E
Busanga Swamp 36 Ee 14.10S 25.50 E
Buşayrah 24 Ie 35.09N 40.26 E
Būsh 24 Dh 29.09N 31.08 E
Būshehr 23 Hd 28.00N 52.00 E
Būshehr 22 Hg 28.59N 50.50 E
Būshgān 24 Nh 28.48N 51.42 E
Bushimaie 29 Ji 6.02S 23.45 E
Bushmanland (EN)=Boesmanland 37 Be 29.30S 19.00 E
Busia 36 Fb 0.28N 34.06 E
Busigny 12 Fd 50.02N 3.28 E
Businga 36 Db 3.20N 20.53 E
Busira 30 Ii 0.15S 18.59 E
Busk 16 Dd 50.01N 24.37 E
Buskerud 7 Bf 60.30N 9.10 E
Busko-Zdrój 10 Qf 50.28N 20.44 E
Busoga 36 Fb 0.45N 33.30 E
Buşrá ash Shām 24 Gf 32.31N 36.29 E
Busselton 59 Df 33.39S 115.20 E
Bussum 11 Lb 52.16N 5.10 E
Bustamante, Bahía- 56 Gg 45.07S 66.27W
Buşteni 15 Id 45.24N 25.32 E
Busto Arsizio 14 Ce 45.37N 8.51 E
Buştyna 10 Th 48.03N 23.28 E
Busuanga 26 Hd 12.05N 120.05 E
Busu-Djanoa 36 Db 1.43N 21.23 E
Büsum 10 Eb 54.08N 8.51 E
Buta 31 Jh 2.48N 24.44 E
Butajira 35 Fd 8.08N 38.27 E
Buta Ranquil 56 Ge 37.03S 69.50W
Butare 36 Ec 2.36S 29.44 E
Butaritari Atoll 57 Id 3.03N 172.49 E
Bute, Island of- 9 Hf 55.50N 5.05W
Bute Inlet 46 Ca 50.37N 124.53W
Butembo 31 Jh 0.09N 29.17 E
Butera 14 Im 37.11N 14.11 E
Butere 36 Fb 0.13N 34.30 E
Butha Qi (Zalantum) 27 Lb 48.02N 122.42 E
Buthidaung 25 Id 20.52N 92.32 E
Butiá 56 Jd 30.07S 51.58W
Butiaba 36 Fb 1.49N 31.19 E
Butler 44 He 40.51N 79.55W
Butser Hill 12 Bd 50.57N 0.59W
Butte 39 He 46.00N 112.32W
Butterworth [Mala.] 26 Df 5.25N 100.24 E
Butterworth [S.Afr.] 37 Df 32.23S 28.04 E
Button Bay 42 Ie 58.45N 94.25W
Butuan 22 Oi 8.57N 125.33 E
Butung, Palau- 21 Oj 5.00S 122.55 E
Buturlinovka 16 Ld 50.48N 40.45 E
Butzbach 12 Kd 50.26N 8.41 E
Bützow 10 Hc 53.50N 11.59 E
Buxtehude 10 Fc 53.27N 9.42 E
Buxton [Eng.-U.K.] 9 Lh 53.15N 1.55W
Buxton [N.C.-U.S.] 44 Jh 35.16N 75.32W
Buyo 34 Dd 6.16N 7.03W
Büyük Ağri Daği=Ararat, Mount- (EN) 21 Gf 39.40N 44.24 E
Büyükanafarta 15 Ji 40.17N 26.22 E
Büyükçekmece 15 Lh 41.01N 28.34 E
Büyükkariştiran 15 Kh 41.18N 27.32 E
Büyük Kemikli Burun 15 Ji 40.18N 26.14 E
Büyük Mahya 15 Kh 41.47N 27.36 E
Büyük Menderes 23 Cb 37.57N 28.58 E
Büyükorhan 15 Lj 39.45N 28.55 E
Buyun Shan 27 Lc 40.06N 122.42 E
Buzači, Poluostrov- 19 Ff 45.00N 52.00 E
Buzan 16 Pf 46.18N 49.06 E
Buzançais 11 Hh 46.53N 1.25 E
Buzancy 12 Ge 49.25N 4.57 E
Buzău 15 Jd 45.09N 26.50 E
Buzău 15 Jd 45.09N 26.50 E
Buzău 15 Kd 45.26N 27.44 E
Buzaymah 33 De 24.55N 22.02 E
Buzen 29 Be 33.37N 131.08 E
Buzet 14 He 45.24N 13.59 E
Būzhān 24 Le 34.09N 47.05 E
Būzi 37 Ec 19.51S 34.30 E
Būzi 37 Ec 19.52S 34.46 E
Buziaş 15 Ed 45.39N 21.36 E
Búzios, Ilha dos- 55 Jf 23.48S 45.08W
Bužora, Gora- 10 Th 48.24N 23.15 E
Buzuluk 19 Fe 52.46N 52.17 E
Buzuluk [R.S.F.S.R.] 16 Md 50.13N 42.12 E
Buzuluk [R.S.F.S.R.] 16 Rc 52.47N 52.16 E
Buzzards Bay 44 Le 41.33N 70.47W

Index Symbols

Independent Nation; State, Region; District, County; Municipality; Colony, Dependency; Continent; Physical Region; Historical or Cultural Region; Mount, Mountain; Volcano; Hill; Mountains, Mountain Range; Hills, Escarpment; Plateau, Upland; Pass, Gap; Plain, Lowland; Delta; Salt Flat; Valley, Canyon; Crater, Cave; Karst Features; Depression; Polder; Desert, Dunes; Forest, Woods; Heath, Steppe; Oasis; Cape, Point; Coast, Beach; Cliff; Peninsula; Isthmus; Sandbank; Island; Atoll; Rock, Reef; Islands, Archipelago; Rocks, Reefs; Coral Reef; Well, Spring; Geyser; River, Stream; Waterfall Rapids; River Mouth, Estuary; Lake; Salt Lake; Intermittent Lake; Reservoir; Swamp, Pond; Canal; Glacier; Ice Shelf, Pack Ice; Ocean; Sea; Gulf, Bay; Strait, Fjord; Lagoon; Bank; Seamount; Tablemount; Ridge; Shelf; Basin; Escarpment, Sea Scarp; Fracture; Trench, Abyss; National Park, Reserve; Point of Interest; Recreation Site; Cave, Cavern; Historic Site; Ruins; Wall, Walls; Church, Abbey; Temple; Scientific Station; Airport; Port; Lighthouse; Mine; Tunnel; Dam, Bridge

Bwagaoia 63a Ad 10.42 S 152.50 E
Byälven 8 Ee 59.06N 12.54 E
Byam Martin 42 Ha 75.15N 104.15W
Byam Martin Channel 42 Ha 76.00N 105.00W
Bychawa 10 Se 51.01N 22.32 E
Byczyna 10 Oe 51.07N 18.11 E
Bydgoszcz 10 Nc 53.10N 18.00 E
Bydgoszcz 6 He 53.08N 18.00 E
Byelorussian SSR (EN)= Belorusskaja SSR 19 Ce 53.50N 28.00 E
Bygdin 8 Cc 61.20N 8.35 E
Bygland [Nor.] 7 Bg 58.51N 7.51 E
Bygland [Nor.] 8 Bf 58.41N 7.48 E
Byglandsfjorden 8 Bf 58.50N 7.50 E
Byhov 19 De 53.31N 30.15 E
Byk 15 Mc 46.55N 29.25 E
Bykovec 15 Lb 47.12N 28.18 E
Bykovo 16 Ne 49.47N 45.25 E
Bykovski 20 Hb 71.56N 129.05 E
Bylot 38 Lb 73.13N 78.34W
Byrd, Cape- 66 Qe 69.38S 76.07W
Byrdbreen 66 Df 71.35S 26.00 E
Byrd Glacier 66 Jg 80.15S 160.20 E
Byron, Cape- 57 Gg 28.39S 153.38 E
Byron Bay 42 Gc 68.55N 108.25W
Byron Bay 59 Ke 28.39S 153.37 E
Byrranga Gory=Byrranga Mountains (EN) 21 Mb 75.00N 104.00 E
Byrranga Mountains (EN)= Byrranga Gory 21 Mb 75.00N 104.00 E
Bystraja 20 Kf 52.40N 156.10 E
Bystreyca 10 Se 51.40N 22.33 E
Bystřice 10 Lf 50.11N 15.30 E
Bystrovka 18 Jc 42.45N 75.43 E
Bystrzyca [Pol.] 10 Se 51.16N 22.45 E
Bystrzyca [Pol.] 10 Me 51.13N 16.54 E
Bystrzyca Kłodzka 10 Mf 50.19N 16.39 E
Bytantaj 20 Ic 68.40N 134.50 E
Bytča 10 Og 49.14N 18.35 E
Byten 10 Vd 52.49N 25.33 E
Bytom 10 Of 50.22N 18.54 E
Bytów 10 Nb 54.11N 17.30 E
Byumba 36 Fc 1.35S 30.04 E
Byxelkrok 7 Dh 57.20N 17.00 E
Bzura 10 Qd 52.23N 20.09 E
Bzyb 16 Lh 43.12N 40.15 E

C

Cà, Sông- 25 Le 18.40N 105.40 E
Caacupé 56 Ic 25.23S 57.09W
Čaadajevka 16 Nc 53.09N 45.56 E
Caaguazú 56 Ic 25.26S 56.02W
Caaguazú 55 Eg 25.00S 55.45W
Caála 36 Ce 12.55S 15.35 E
Caapucú 55 Dh 26.13S 57.12W
Caarapó 55 Ef 22.38S 54.48W
Caatinga 54 Ig 17.10S 45.53W
Caatinga 52 Lf 9.00S 42.00W
Caatinga, Rio- 55 Jc 17.10S 45.52W
Caazapá 55 Dh 26.10S 56.00W
Caazapá 56 Ic 26.09S 56.24W
Cabaçal, Rio- 55 Db 16.00S 57.42W
Cabadbaran 26 Ie 9.10N 125.38 E
Cabaiguán 49 Hb 22.05N 79.30W
Caballeria, Cabo de- 13 Qd 40.05N 4.05 E
Caballo Cocha 54 Dd 3.54S 70.32W
Caballo Reservoir 45 Cj 32.58N 107.18W
Cabañas 13 Jg 37.40N 3.00W
Cabanatuan 22 Oh 15.29N 120.58 E
Cabano 44 Mb 47.41N 68.54W
Čabar 14 Ie 45.36N 14.39 E
Cabeceira do Apa 55 Ef 22.01S 55.46W
Cabeceiras 55 Ib 15.48S 46.59W
Cabeceiras de Basto 13 Ec 41.31N 7.59W
Cabeza, Arrecife- 48 Lh 19.04N 95.50W
Cabeza de Buey 13 Gf 38.43N 5.13W
Cabildo 55 Bn 38.29S 61.54W
Cabimas 53 Id 10.23N 71.28W
Cabinda 31 Ii 5.35S 12.13 E
Cabinda 36 Bd 5.00S 12.30 E
Cabinet Mountains 46 Hb 48.08N 115.46W
Cabo Bojador 32 Ed 26.08N 14.30W
Cabo Frio 53 Lh 22.53S 42.01W
Cabo Gracias a Dios 49 Ff 14.59N 83.10W
Cabonga, Réservoir- 42 Jg 47.20N 76.35W
Caboolture 59 Ke 27.05S 152.50 E
Cabora Bassa, Dique de- 37 Ec 15.34S 32.42 E
Cabora Bassa, Lago-= Cabora Bassa, Lake-(EN) 30 Kj 15.40S 31.40 E
Cabora Bassa, Lake-(EN)= Cabora Bassa, Lago- 30 Kj 15.40S 31.40 E
Caborca 47 Bb 30.37N 112.06W
Cabot Strait 38 Ne 47.20N 59.30W
Cabourg 11 Fe 49.17N 0.08W
Cabo Verde=Cape Verde (EN) 31 Eg 16.00N 24.00W
Cabo Verde, Ilhas do-=Cape Verde Islands (EN) 30 Eg 16.00N 24.10W
Cabra 13 Hg 37.28N 4.27W
Cabral, Serra do- 55 Jc 17.45S 44.22W
Cabras 14 Ck 39.56N 8.32 E
Cabras, Stagno di- 14 Ck 39.55N 8.30 E
Cabreira 13 Dc 41.39N 8.04W
Cabrejas, Puerto de- 13 Jd 40.08N 2.25W
Cabrera 49 Md 19.38N 69.54W
Cabrera, Isla- 13 Oe 39.09N 2.56 E
Cabrera, Sierra de la- 13 Fb 42.10N 6.25W
Cabri 46 Ka 50.37N 108.28W
Cabriel 13 Ke 39.14N 1.03W
Cabrit, Ilet 'a- 51e Ac 15.53N 61.36W
Cabrits, Ilet- 51h Bc 14.23N 60.52W
Cabrón, Cabo- 49 Md 19.22N 69.12W
Cabruta 50 Ci 7.38N 66.15W
Čabulja 14 Lg 43.30N 17.35 E
Cabure 49 Mh 11.08N 69.38W
Cacacas, Islas- 50 Dg 10.22N 64.26W
Caçador 56 Jc 26.47S 51.00W
Čačak 15 Df 43.54N 20.21 E
Caçapava dó Sul 56 Jd 30.30S 53.30W
Caccamo 14 Hm 37.56N 13.40 E
Caccia, Capo- 14 Cj 40.34N 8.09 E
Cacequi 55 Ei 29.53S 54.49W
Cáceres 13 Ge 39.40N 6.00W
Cáceres [Braz.] 53 Kg 16.04S 57.41W
Cáceres [Sp.] 13 Fe 39.29N 6.22W
Cáceres, Laguna- 55 Dd 18.56S 57.48W
Cachari 56 Ie 36.24S 59.32W
Cache Peak 46 Ie 42.11N 113.40W
Čacheu 34 Bc 12.10N 16.21W
Cachimbo 53 Kf 9.08S 55.10W
Cachimbo, Serra do- 52 Kf 8.30S 55.50W
Cachimo 36 Dd 8.20S 21.21 E
Cáchira 49 Kj 7.46N 73.03W
Cáchira, Rio- 49 Kj 7.52N 73.40W
Cachoeira 54 Kf 12.36S 38.58W
Cachoeira Alta 55 Gd 18.48S 50.58W
Cachoeira de Goiás 55 Gc 16.44S 50.38W
Cachoeira do Arari 54 Id 1.01S 48.58W
Cachoeira do Sul 56 Jc 29.58S 52.54W
Cachoeira Dourada, Reprêsa de- 54 Ig 18.30S 49.00W
Cachoeirinha 55 Gi 29.57S 51.05W
Cachoeiro de Itapemirim 54 Jh 20.51S 41.06W
Cacinbinho 55 Ee 21.50S 55.43W
Căciulaţi 15 Je 44.38N 26.10 E
Cacolo 36 Ce 10.08S 19.18 E
Caconda 36 Ce 13.45S 15.05 E
Cacuaco 36 Bd 8.47S 13.21 E
Cacuchi 36 Ce 14.23S 16.59 E
Cacula 36 Be 14.29S 14.10 E
Caculé 54 Jf 14.30S 42.13W
Caculuvar 36 Bf 16.46S 14.56 E
Cacuso 36 Cd 9.26S 15.45 E
Čadan 20 Ef 51.17N 91.40 E
Cadaqués 13 Pb 42.17N 3.17 E
Čadca 10 Og 49.26N 18.48 E
Caddo Lake 45 Ij 32.42N 94.01W
Cadena Costero Catalana/ Serralada Litoral Catalana =Catalan Coastal Range (EN) 5 Gg 41.35N 1.40 E
Cadereyta Jiménez 48 Ie 25.36N 100.00W
Cadí, Serra del-/Cadí, Sierra del- 13 Nb 42.17N 1.42 E
Cadibarrawirracanna, Lake- 59 He 28.50S 135.25 E
Cadibona, Colle di- 14 Cf 44.20N 8.22 E
Cadillac [Fr.] 11 Fj 44.38N 0.19W
Cadillac [Mi.-U.S.] 43 Jc 44.15N 85.24W
Cadí, Sierra del/Cadí, Serra del- 13 Nb 42.17N 1.42 E
Cadiz 26 Hd 10.57N 123.18 E
Cádiz 13 Gh 36.30N 5.45W
Cádiz 6 Fh 36.32N 6.18W
Cadiz [Ca.-U.S.] 46 Hi 34.30N 115.30W
Cadiz [Ky.-U.S.] 44 Dg 36.52N 87.50W
Cádiz, Bahía de- 13 Fh 36.32N 6.16W
Cádiz, Golfo de- 5 Fh 36.50N 7.10W
Cadiz Lake 46 Hi 34.18N 115.24W
Cadore 14 Gd 46.30N 12.20 E
Cadwell 43 Dc 43.40N 116.41W
Čadyr-Lunga 16 Ff 46.04N 28.52 E
Caen 6 Ff 49.11N 0.21W
Caen, Campagne de- 11 Fe 49.05N 0.20W
Caernarvon 9 Ih 53.08N 4.16W
Caernarvon Bay 9 Ih 53.05N 4.30W
Caerphilly 9 Jj 51.35N 3.14W
Caetité 54 Jf 14.04S 42.29W
Cafayate 56 Gc 26.05S 65.58W
Cafelândia [Braz.] 55 Fe 16.40S 53.25W
Cafelândia [Braz.] 55 Ie 21.49S 49.35W
Cafundó, Serra do- 55 Hb 14.40S 48.23W
Čagan 19 He 50.30N 79.10 E
Cagan-Aman 19 Ef 47.32N 46.43 E
Cagan-Nur [Mong.] 27 Eb 49.40N 89.55 E
Cagan-Nur [Mong.] 27 Ia 50.25N 105.15 E
Cagan-Ula 27 Gb 49.35N 98.25 E
Cagatá, Arroyo- 55 Df 23.26S 56.36W
Cagayan 26 Hc 18.22N 121.37 E
Cagayan de Oro 22 Oi 8.29N 124.39 E
Cagayan Islands 26 He 9.40N 121.16 E
Cagayan Sulu 26 Ge 7.01N 118.30 E
Čagda 20 Ie 58.42N 130.37 E
Cageri 16 Mh 42.39N 42.42 E
Çağiş 15 Lj 39.30N 28.01 E
Cagli 14 Gg 43.33N 12.39 E
Cagliari 6 Gh 39.13N 9.07 E
Cagliari, Golfo di- 14 Dk 39.10N 9.10 E
Cagliari, Stagno di- 14 Dk 39.15N 9.05 E
Čaglinka 17 Nj 53.59N 69.47 E
Cagnes-sur-Mer 11 Nk 43.40N 7.09 E
Čagoda 7 Ig 59.12N 35.13 E
Čagodošča 7 Ig 58.58N 36.37 E
Caguas 47 Ke 18.14N 66.02W
Çagyl 19 Fg 40.43N 55.25 E
Cahama 36 Bf 16.16S 14.17 E
Caha Mountains/An Cheacha 9 Dj 51.45N 9.45W
Caher/An Chathair 9 Fi 52.22N 7.55W
Cahersiveen/Cathair Saidhbhín 9 Cj 51.57N 10.13W
Cahore Point/Rinn Chathóir 9 Gi 52.34N 6.11W
Cahors 11 Hj 44.26N 1.26 E
Cai, Rio- 55 Gi 29.56S 51.16W
Caia 37 Fc 17.49S 35.20 E
Caia 13 Ef 38.50N 7.05W
Caiabis, Serra dos- 54 Gf 11.40S 56.30W
Caiapó, Rio- 55 Gb 15.49S 51.53W
Caiapó, Serra do- 52 Kg 17.00S 52.00W
Caiapônia 55 Gc 16.57S 51.49W
Caibarién 47 Id 22.31N 79.28W
Caiçara 55 Gb 15.34S 50.12W
Caicara 54 Eb 7.37N 66.10W
Caicara de Maturín 50 Eh 9.49N 63.36W
Caicó 54 Ke 6.27S 37.06W
Caicos Bank (EN) 47 Jd 21.35N 71.55W
Caicos Islands 38 Lg 21.45N 71.35W
Caicos Passage 47 Jd 22.00N 72.30W
Caille Island 51p Bb 12.17N 61.35W
Caimanera 49 Jd 19.59N 75.09W
Caine, Rio- 54 Eg 18.23S 65.21W
Cai Nuoc 25 Lg 8.56N 105.01 E
Caird Coast 66 Af 76.00S 24.30W
Cairngorms Mountains 9 Jd 57.06N 3.30W
Cairns 58 Ff 16.55S 145.46 E
Cairo [Ga.-U.S.] 44 Ej 30.53N 84.12W
Cairo [Il.-U.S.] 43 Jd 37.00N 89.11W
Cairo (EN)=Al Qāhirah 31 Ke 30.03N 31.15 E
Cairo Montenotte 14 Cf 44.24N 8.16 E
Caiseal/Cashel 9 Fi 52.31N 7.53W
Caisleán an Bharraigh/ Castlebar 9 Dh 53.52N 9.17W
Caister-on-Sea 12 Db 52.40N 1.45 E
Caiundo 36 Cf 15.42S 17.27 E
Caiúva, Lagoa- 55 Fk 32.24S 52.30W
Caiyuanzhen → Shengsi 28 Gi 30.42N 122.29 E
Caizi Hu 28 Di 30.48N 117.05 E
Čaja 20 De 58.17N 82.45 E
Cajabamba 54 Ce 7.58S 77.59W
Caja de Muertos, Isla- 51a Bc 17.53N 66.31W
Cajamarca 53 If 7.10S 78.31W
Cajamarca 54 Ce 6.15S 78.50W
Cajapió 54 Jd 2.58S 44.48W
Cajarc 11 Hj 44.29N 1.51 E
Cajatambo 54 Cf 10.29S 77.02W
Čajkovski 19 Fd 56.47N 54.09 E
Çakırgöl Dağ 24 Hb 40.34N 39.42 E
Cakmak 24 Fd 37.37N 34.19 E
Çakmak Dağı 24 Jc 39.46N 42.12 E
Čakor 15 Dg 42.40N 20.02 E
Čakovec 14 Kd 46.23N 16.26 E
Cakrani 15 Ci 40.36N 19.37 E
Çal 24 Cc 38.05N 29.24 E
Cal, Rio de la- 55 Cc 17.27S 58.15W
Calabar 31 Hh 4.57N 8.19 E
Calabozo 54 Eb 8.56N 67.26W
Calabozo, Ensenada de- 49 Lh 11.30N 71.45W
Calabria 14 Kl 39.00N 16.30 E
Calaburras, Punta de- 13 Hh 36.30N 4.38W
Calacoto 54 Eg 17.18S 68.39W
Calacuccia 11a Ba 42.20N 9.01 E
Calaf 13 Nc 41.44N 1.31 E
Calafat 15 Ff 43.59N 22.56 E
Calafate 53 Ik 50.20S 72.16W
Cala Figuera, Cabo de- 13 Oe 39.27N 2.31 E
Calagua Islands 26 Hd 14.27N 122.55 E
Calahorra 13 Kb 42.18N 1.58W
Calai 36 Cf 17.50S 19.20 E
Calais [Fr.] 6 Ge 50.57N 1.50 E
Calais [Me.-U.S.] 44 Nc 45.11N 67.17W
Calais, Pas de-=Dover, Strait of- (EN) 5 Ge 51.00N 1.30 E
Calakmul 48 Oh 18.05N 89.55W
Calalaste, Sierra de- 56 Gc 25.30S 67.30W
Calama 53 Jh 22.28S 68.56W
Calamar 49 Jh 10.14N 74.56W
Calamian Group 21 Nh 12.00N 120.00 E
Calamocha 13 Kd 40.55N 1.18W
Călan 15 Fd 45.44N 22.59 E
Calanda 13 Ld 40.56N 0.14W
Calang 26 Cf 4.30N 95.40 E
Calangiánus 14 Dj 40.56N 9.11 E
Calapan 26 Hd 13.25N 121.10 E
Calar Alto 13 Jg 37.15N 2.25W
Călăraşi 15 Ke 44.12N 27.20 E
Cala Ratjada 13 Pe 39.42N 3.25 E
Calar del Mundo 13 Jf 38.31N 2.28W
Calatafimi 14 Gm 37.55N 12.52 E
Calatañazor 13 Jc 41.42N 2.49W
Calatayud 13 Kc 41.21N 1.38W
Calatrava 13 If 38.35N 3.48W
Calatrava, Campo de- 13 Hf 38.50N 4.15W
Calavà, Capo- 14 Il 38.10N 14.55 E
Calavon 11 Kk 43.51N 5.00 E
Calayan 26 Hc 19.20N 121.27 E
Calbayog 22 Oh 12.04N 124.36 E
Calchaquí 56 Hc 29.54S 60.18W
Calçoene 54 Hc 2.30N 50.57W
Calcutta 22 Kg 22.32N 88.22 E
Caldaro / Kaltern 14 Fd 46.25N 11.14 E
Caldas 54 Cb 5.15N 75.30W
Caldas da Rainha 13 Ce 39.24N 9.08W
Caldas Novas 55 Hc 17.45S 48.38W
Caldeirão, Serra de- 13 Dg 37.19N 8.04W
Calder 9 Lh 53.44N 1.21W
Caldera 56 Fc 27.04S 70.50W
Calderina, Sierra de la- 13 Ie 39.19N 3.48W
Caldes de Mombúy 13 Oc 41.38N 2.10 E
Caldwell 44 Gf 39.44N 81.32W
Caledon 37 Bf 34.12S 19.23 E
Caledon 30 Jl 30.32S 26.05 E
Caledonia [Blz.] 49 Cd 18.14N 88.29W
Caledonia [Mn.-U.S.] 45 Ke 43.38N 91.29W
Caledonian Canal 9 Id 57.20N 4.30W
Calella 13 Oc 41.37N 2.40 E
Caleta Olivia 56 Gg 46.26S 67.32W
Calexico 46 Hj 32.40N 115.30W
Çalgal Dağı 24 Hc 39.06N 38.05 E
Calgary 39 Hd 51.03N 114.05W
Calhoun 44 Eh 34.30N 84.57W
Cali 53 Ie 3.27N 76.31W
Calicut (Kozhikode) 22 Jh 11.19N 75.46 E
Caliente 43 Ed 37.37N 114.31W
California 43 Dd 37.30N 119.30W
California, Golfo de-= California, Gulf of- (EN) 38 Hg 28.00N 112.00W
California, Gulf of- (EN)= California, Golfo de- 38 Hg 28.00N 112.00W
Căliman, Munţii- 15 Ib 47.07N 25.03 E
Călimăneşti 15 Hd 45.14N 24.20 E
Calimere, Point- 25 Ff 10.18N 79.52 E
Calingasta 56 Gd 31.19S 69.25W
Calispell Peak 46 Gb 48.26N 117.30W
Calitri 14 Jj 40.54N 15.26 E
Calitzdorp 37 Cf 33.33S 21.42 E
Caliviny 51p Bb 12.01N 61.43W
Calixtlahuaca 48 Jh 19.15N 99.45W
Calka 16 Ni 41.35N 44.05 E
Calkini 48 Ng 20.22N 90.03W
Callabonna, Lake- 59 Ie 29.45S 140.05 E
Callac 11 Cf 48.24N 3.26W
Callaghan, Mount- 46 Gg 39.42N 116.57W
Callainn/Callan 9 Fi 52.33N 7.23W
Callan/Callainn 9 Fi 52.33N 7.23W
Callander [Ont.-Can.] 44 Hb 46.13N 79.23W
Callander [Scot.-U.K.] 9 Ie 56.15N 4.13W
Callantsoog 12 Gb 52.50N 4.41 E
Callao 53 Ig 12.02S 77.05W
Callao 54 Cf 2.04S 77.09W
Calliaqua 51n Ba 13.08N 61.12W
Callosa de Ensarriá 13 Lf 38.39N 0.07W
Callosa de Segura 13 Lf 38.08N 0.52W
Calmalli 48 Cc 28.14N 113.33W
Călmăţui [Rom.] 15 If 43.46N 25.10 E
Călmăţui [Rom.] 15 Ke 44.50N 27.50 E
Calonne 12 Ce 49.17N 0.12 E
Calore 14 Ii 41.11N 14.28 E
Čalovo 10 Ni 47.52N 17.47 E
Calpe 13 Mf 38.39N 0.03 E
Caltabellotta 14 Hm 37.34N 13.13 E
Caltagirone 14 Im 37.14N 14.31 E
Caltanissetta 14 Im 37.29N 14.04 E
Caltilibük 15 Lj 39.57N 28.36 E
Čaltyr 16 Kf 47.17N 39.29 E
Caluago 36 Cd 8.15S 19.38 E
Calucinga 36 Ce 11.19S 16.13 E
Călugareni 15 Ie 44.11N 25.59 E
Calulo 36 Bd 9.59S 14.54 E
Caluquembe 36 Be 13.46S 14.41 E
Calvados 11 Fe 49.10N 0.30W
Calvados, Côte du- 11 Fe 49.22N 0.30W
Calvert Island 46 Ba 51.35N 128.00W
Calvert River 59 Hc 16.17S 137.44 E
Calvi 11a Aa 42.34N 8.45 E
Calvillo 48 Hg 21.51N 102.43W
Calvinia 31 Il 31.25S 19.45 E
Calvitero 13 Gd 40.20N 5.43W
Cam 9 Ni 52.21N 0.15 E
Camabatela 36 Cd 8.13S 15.23 E
Camacá 54 Kg 15.24S 39.30W
Camacupa 36 Ce 12.01S 17.22 E
Camaguán 50 Ch 8.06N 67.36W
Camagüey 49 Ic 21.30N 78.10W
Camagüey 39 Lg 21.23N 77.55W
Camagüey, Archipiélago de- 47 Id 22.18N 78.00W
Camaiore 14 Eg 43.56N 10.18 E
Camajuaní 49 Hb 22.28N 79.44W
Camamu 54 Kf 13.57S 39.07W
Camaná 54 Dg 16.37S 72.42W
Camapuã 55 Ed 19.30S 54.05W
Camapuã, Sertão de- 52 Kg 19.00S 51.30W
Camaquã 56 Jd 30.51S 51.49W
Camaquã, Rio- 55 Gj 31.17S 51.47W
Camarat, Cap- 11 Mk 43.12N 6.41 E
Camargo [Bol.] 54 Eh 20.39S 65.13W
Camargo [Sp.] 13 Ia 43.24N 3.54W
Camargos, Reprêsa- 55 Je 21.20S 44.30W
Camargue 11 Kk 43.31N 4.34 E
Camariñas 13 Ca 43.07N 9.10W
Camarón, Cabo- 47 He 16.00N 85.04W
Camarones 56 Gf 44.48S 65.42W
Camarones, Bahía- 56 Gf 44.45S 65.34W
Camas [Sp.] 13 Fg 37.24N 6.02W
Camas [Wa.-U.S.] 46 Dd 45.35N 122.24W
Camatagua, Embalse de- 50 Ch 9.48N 66.55W
Ca Mau, Mui-=Ca Mau Point (EN) 21 Mi 8.38N 104.44 E
Ca Mau Point (EN)=Ca Mau, Mui- 21 Mi 8.38N 104.44 E
Cambados 13 Db 42.30N 8.48W
Camberg 12 Kd 50.18N 8.16 E
Camberley 12 Bc 51.21N 0.44W
Cambo 36 Cd 7.40S 17.17 E
Cambodia → Kampuchea 22 Mh 13.00N 105.00 E
Cambo-les-Bains 11 Ek 43.22N 1.24W
Camboriú, Ponta- 55 Ig 25.10S 47.55W
Cambrai 11 Jd 50.10N 3.14 E
Cambremer 12 Ce 49.09N 0.03 E
Cambrésis 12 Fd 50.15N 3.05 E
Cambrian Mountains 5 Fe 52.35N 3.35W
Cambridge 9 Ni 52.25N 0.10 E
Cambridge [Eng.-U.K.] 9 Ni 52.12N 0.07 E
Cambridge [Id.-U.S.] 46 Gd 44.34N 116.41W
Cambridge [Ma.-U.S.] 44 Ld 42.22N 71.06W
Cambridge [Md.-U.S.] 44 If 38.34N 76.04W
Cambridge [Mn.-U.S.] 45 Jd 45.31N 93.14W
Cambridge [N.Z.] 62 Fb 37.53S 175.28 E
Cambridge [Oh.-U.S.] 44 Ge 40.02N 81.36W
Cambridge Airport 12 Cb 52.10N 0.08 E
Cambridge Bay 39 Ic 69.03N 105.05W
Cambridge Gulf 59 Fb 14.55S 128.15 E
Cambridgeshire 9 Mi 52.25N 0.05W
Cambutal, Cerro- 49 Gj 7.16N 80.36W
Camden [Al.-U.S.] 44 Dj 32.00N 87.17W
Camden [Ar.-U.S.] 43 Ie 33.35N 92.50W
Camden [N.J.-U.S.] 44 Jf 39.57N 75.07W
Camden [S.C.-U.S.] 44 Gh 34.16N 80.36W
Camden [Tn.-U.S.] 44 Cg 36.04N 88.06W
Camden Bay 40 Kb 70.00N 145.00W
Camdenton 45 Jg 38.00N 92.45W
Camel 9 Ik 50.33N 4.55W
Çameli 24 Cd 37.05N 29.20 E
Camerino 14 Hg 43.08N 13.04 E
Cameron 42 Ha 76.15N 104.00W
Cameron [Az.-U.S.] 46 Ji 35.51N 111.25W
Cameron [La.-U.S.] 45 Jl 29.48N 93.19W
Cameron [Mo.-U.S.] 45 Ig 39.44N 94.14W
Cameron [Tx.-U.S.] 45 Hk 30.51N 96.59W
Cameron [Wi.-U.S.] 45 Kd 45.25N 91.44W
Cameron Hills 42 Fe 60.00N 118.00W
Cameron Mountains 62 Bf 46.00S 166.55 E
Cameroon (EN)= Cameroun 31 Ih 6.00N 12.00 E
Cameroon, Mount- (EN)= Cameroun 30 Hh 4.12N 9.11 E
Camerota 14 Jj 40.02N 15.22 E
Cameroun=Cameroon (EN) 31 Ih 6.00N 12.00 E
Cameroun=Cameroon, Mount-(EN) 30 Hh 4.12N 9.11 E
Cametá 54 Id 2.15S 49.30W
Camiguin [Phil.] 26 He 9.11N 124.42 E
Camiguin [Phil.] 26 Hc 18.56N 121.55 E
Camiling 26 Hc 15.42N 120.24 E
Camilla 44 Ej 31.14N 84.12W
Caminha 13 Dc 41.52N 8.50W
Camoapa 49 Eg 12.23N 85.31W
Camocim 53 Lf 2.54S 40.50W
Camonica, Val- 14 Ed 46.00N 10.20 E
Camooweal 59 Hc 19.55S 138.07 E
Camopi 54 Hc 3.13N 52.28W
Camorta 25 Ig 8.08N 93.30 E
Campagne-lès-Hesdin 12 Dd 50.24N 1.52 E
Campana 55 Cl 34.10S 58.57W
Campana, Isla- 52 Ij 48.20S 75.15W
Campanario 13 Gf 38.52N 5.37W
Campanário 55 Ef 22.48S 55.03W
Campania 14 Ii 41.00N 14.30 E
Campanquiz, Cerros- 54 Cd 4.30S 77.40W
Campbell, Cape- 62 Fd 41.44S 174.16 E
Campbell Island 62 Ci 52.30S 169.10 E
Campbell Plateau (EN) 57 Ij 51.00S 170.00 E
Campbell River 42 Ef 50.01N 125.15W
Campbellsville 44 Eg 37.21N 85.20W
Campbellton 42 Kg 48.00N 66.40W
Campbelltown, Sydney- 59 Kf 34.04S 150.49 E
Campbeltown 9 Hf 55.26N 5.36W
Campeche 39 Jh 19.51N 90.32W
Campeche 47 Fe 19.00N 90.30W
Campeche, Bahía de-= Campeche, Gulf of- (EN) 38 Jg 20.00N 94.00W
Campeche, Gulf of- (EN)= Campeche, Bahía de- 38 Jg 20.00N 94.00W
Campeche Bank (EN) 47 Fd 22.00N 90.00W
Campechuela 49 Ic 20.14N 77.17W
Camperdown 59 Ig 38.14S 143.09 E
Campidano 14 Ck 39.30N 8.45 E
Campiglia Marittima 14 Eg 43.03N 10.37 E
Campillos 13 Hg 37.03N 4.51W
Campina Grande 53 Mf 7.13S 35.53W
Campinas 53 Lh 22.54S 47.05W
Campina Verde 55 Hd 19.31S 49.28W
Campine/Kempen 11 Lc 51.10N 5.20 E
Campinorte 55 Hb 14.20S 49.08W
Campione d'Italia 14 Ce 45.59N 8.59 E
Campo 34 Ge 2.22N 9.49 E
Campo Alegre 50 Bh 9.15N 68.25W
Campo Alegre de Goiás 55 Ic 17.36S 47.46W
Campobasso 14 Ii 41.34N 14.39 E
Campo Belo 55 Je 20.53S 45.16W
Campo de Criptana 13 Ie 39.24N 3.07W
Campo de la Cruz 49 Jh 10.23N 74.52W
Campo del Cielo 55 Bh 27.53S 61.49W
Campo Florido 55 Hd 19.46S 48.34W
Campo Formoso 54 Jf 10.31S 40.20W
Campo Gallo 56 Hc 26.35S 62.51W
Campo Garay 55 Bi 29.41S 61.37W
Campo Grande [Arg.] 55 Eh 27.13S 54.58W
Campo Grande [Braz.] 53 Kh 20.27S 54.37W
Campo Largo [Arg.] 55 Bh 26.48S 60.50W
Campo Largo [Braz.] 55 Hg 25.26S 49.32W
Campo Maior [Braz.] 54 Jd 4.49S 42.10W
Campo Maior [Port.] 13 Ee 39.01N 7.04W
Campomarino 14 Ji 41.57N 15.02 E
Campo Mourão 56 Jb 24.03S 52.22W
Campos 53 Lh 21.45S 41.18W
Campos [Braz.] 52 Lg 15.00S 44.30W
Campos [Braz.] 52 Kh 21.00S 51.00W
Campos, Laguna- 55 Be 20.50S 61.31W
Campos, Tierra de- 13 Hb 42.10N 4.50W
Campos Altos 55 Id 19.41S 46.10W
Campos Belos 55 Ia 13.03S 46.53W
Campos do Jordão 55 Jf 22.44S 45.35W
Campos Novos 55 Gh 27.24S 51.12W
Campos Sales 54 Je 7.04S 40.23W
Campo Tures / Sand in Taufers 14 Fd 46.55N 11.57 E
Camp Verde 43 Ee 34.34N 111.51W
Cam Ranh 25 Lf 11.54N 109.13 E
Camrose 42 Gf 53.01N 112.50W
Camseil 42 Fc 65.40N 118.07W
Camsell Portage 42 Ge 59.38N 109.42W
Çan 24 Bb 40.02N 27.03 E
Canaan [Ct.-U.S.] 44 Kd 42.02N 73.20W
Canaan [Trin.] 50 Fg 11.09N 60.49W
Canaan Mountain 46 Jh 37.45N 111.51W
Cana Brava, Ribeirão- 55 Ic 16.35S 46.34W
Cana Brava, Rio- [Braz.] 55 Ib 14.40S 47.07W
Cana Brava, Rio- [Braz.] 55 Ha 12.12S 48.40W
Cana Brava, Rio- [Braz.] 55 Ha 13.11S 48.11W
Canada 39 Jc 60.00N 95.00W
Cañada 13 Fb 42.50N 6.05W
Canada Basin (EN) 67 Ad 80.00N 145.00W
Cañada de Gomez 56 Hd 32.49S 61.24W
Canadian 45 Fi 35.55N 100.23W
Canadian River 38 Jf 35.27N 95.03W
Canaguá, Río- 49 Mj 7.57N 69.36W
Canaima 54 Db 9.49N 70.56W

Index Symbols

Independent Nation; State, Region; District, County; Municipality; Colony, Dependency; Continent; Physical Region

Historical or Cultural Region; Mount, Mountain; Volcano; Hill; Mountains, Mountain Range; Hills, Escarpment; Plateau, Upland

Pass, Gap; Plain, Lowland; Delta; Salt Flat; Valley, Canyon; Crater, Cave; Karst Features

Depression; Polder; Desert, Dunes; Forest, Woods; Heath, Steppe; Oasis; Cape, Point

Coast, Beach; Cliff; Peninsula; Isthmus; Sandbank; Island; Atoll

Rock, Reef; Islands, Archipelago; Rocks, Reefs; Coral Reef; Well, Spring; Geyser; River, Stream

Waterfall Rapids; River Mouth, Estuary; Lake; Salt Lake; Intermittent Lake; Reservoir; Swamp, Pond

Canal; Glacier; Ice Shelf, Pack Ice; Ocean; Sea; Gulf, Bay; Strait, Fjord

Lagoon; Bank; Seamount; Tablemount; Ridge; Shelf; Basin

Escarpment, Sea Scarp; Fracture; Trench, Abyss; National Park, Reserve; Point of Interest; Recreation Site; Cave, Cavern

Historic Site; Ruins; Wall, Walls; Church, Abbey; Temple; Scientific Station; Airport

Port; Lighthouse; Mine; Tunnel; Dam, Bridge

Çanakkale Boğazi = Dardanelles (EN) 5 Ig 40.15N 26.25 E
Canala 63b Be 21.32S 165.57 E
Canandaigua 44 Id 42.53N 77.19W
Cananea 47 Bb 30.57N 110.18W
Cananéia 55 Ig 25.01S 47.57W
Canapolis 55 Hd 18.44S 49.13W
Canarias, Islas- = Canary Islands (EN) 31 Ff 28.00N 15.30W
Canarias, Islas- = Canary Islands (EN) 30 Ff 28.00N 15.30W
Canaries 51k Ab 13.55N 61.04W
Canaronero, Laguna- 48 Ff 23.00N 106.15W
Canarreos, Archipiélago de los- 47 Hd 21.50N 82.30W
Canary Basin (EN) 3 Dg 30.00N 25.00W
Canary Islands (EN) = Canarias, Islas- 30 Ff 28.00N 15.30W
Canary Islands (EN) = Canarias, Islas- 31 Ff 28.00N 15.30W
Cañas [C.R.] 49 Eh 10.25N 85.07W
Cañas [Pan.] 49 Gj 7.27N 80.16W
Canastra, Serra da- 55 Ie 20.00S 46.20W
Canatlán 48 Ge 24.31N 104.47W
Cañaveral 13 Fe 39.47N 6.23W
Canaveral, Cape- 38 Kg 28.30N 80.35W
Canavese 14 Be 45.20N 7.40 E
Canavieiras 54 Kg 15.39S 38.57W
Canazei 14 Fd 46.28N 11.46 E
Canberra 58 Fh 35.17S 149.08 E
Canby [Mn.-U.S.] 45 Hd 44.43N 96.16W
Canby [Or.-U.S.] 46 Dd 45.16N 122.42W
Cance 11 Ki 45.12N 4.48 E
Canche 11 Hd 50.31N 1.39 E
Cancon 11 Gj 44.32N 0.37 E
Cancún 47 Gd 21.05N 86.46W
Cancún, Isla- 48 Pg 21.05N 86.46W
Çandarli 15 Jk 38.56N 26.56 E
Çandarli Körfezi 15 Jk 38.52N 26.55 E
Candé 11 Eg 47.34N 1.02W
Candela 48 Id 26.50N 100.40W
Candelaria 48 Nh 18.18N 91.21W
Candelaria, Cerro- 48 Hf 23.25N 103.43W
Candelaria, Río- [Bol.] 55 Cc 17.17S 58.39W
Candelaria, Río- [Mex.] 48 Nh 18.38N 91.15W
Candelaro 14 Ji 41.34N 15.53 E
Cândido de Abreu 55 Gg 24.35S 51.20W
Cândido Mendes 54 Id 1.27S 45.43W
Candlemas Islands 66 Ad 57.03S 26.40W
Candói 55 Fg 25.43S 52.11W
Çandyr 16 Jj 38.13N 55.44 E
Canela 56 Jc 29.22S 50.50W
Canelli 14 Cf 44.43N 8.17 E
Canelones 55 El 34.35S 56.00W
Canelones 55 Dl 34.32S 56.17W
Canendiyu 55 Eg 24.20S 55.00W
Cañete [Chile] 56 Fe 37.48S 73.24W
Cañete [Sp.] 13 Kd 40.03N 1.39W
Cangallo 55 Cm 37.13S 58.42W
Cangamba 36 Ce 13.44S 19.53 E
Cangas 13 Db 42.16N 8.47W
Cangas de Narcea 13 Fa 43.11N 6.33W
Cangas de Onís 13 Ga 43.21N 5.07W
Cangola 36 Cd 7.58S 15.53 E
Cangombe 36 Ce 14.24S 19.59 E
Cangshan (Bianzhuang) 28 Eg 34.51N 118.03 E
Canguçu 55 Fj 31.24S 52.41W
Canguçu, Serra do- 55 Fj 31.20S 52.40W
Canguinha 55 Eb 14.42S 55.40W
Cangumbe 36 Ce 12.00S 19.09 E
Cangyuan 27 Gg 23.10N 99.15 E
Cangzhou 27 Kd 38.14N 116.58 E
Cani, Iles- 14 Em 37.21N 10.07 E
Caniapiscau 38 Md 57.40N 69.30W
Caniapiscau, Lac- 42 Kf 54.00N 70.10W
Canicatti 14 Hm 37.21N 13.51 E
Canigou, Pic du- 11 Il 42.31N 2.27 E
Canik Dağlari 24 Gb 40.50N 37.10 E
Canim Lake 46 Ea 51.52N 120.45W
Canindé 54 Kd 4.22S 39.19W
Canindé, Rio- 54 Je 6.15S 42.52W
Cañitas de Felipe Pescador 48 Hf 23.36N 102.43W
Çankaya 24 Ec 39.56N 32.52 E
Çankırı 23 Da 40.36N 33.37 E
Canna 9 Gd 57.03N 6.33W
Cannac 63a Ac 9.15S 153.29 E
Çannakale 23 Ca 40.09N 26.24 E
Cannanore 25 Ff 11.51N 75.22 E
Cannanore Islands 25 Ef 10.05N 72.10 E
Cannes 11 Nk 43.33N 7.01 E
Cannich 9 Id 57.20N 4.45W
Canning Basin 59 Ed 20.10S 123.00 E
Cannobio 14 Cd 46.04N 8.42 E
Cannock 9 Ki 52.42N 2.01W
Cannonball River 45 Fc 46.26N 100.38W
Cann River 59 Jg 37.34S 149.10 E
Caño, Isla del- 49 Fi 8.44N 83.53W
Canoas 56 Jc 29.56S 51.11W
Canoas, Punta- 48 Bc 29.25N 115.10W
Canoas, Rio- 56 Jc 27.36S 51.25W
Canoeiros 54 Ig 18.02S 45.31W
Canoinhas 56 Jh 26.10S 50.24W
Canoinhas, Rio- 55 Gh 26.07S 50.22W
Cañoles 13 Le 39.02N 0.29W
Canon City 43 Fd 38.27N 105.14W
Canon Fiord 42 Ja 80.15N 83.00W
Canonnier, Pointe du- 51b Ab 18.04N 63.10W
Canora 42 Hf 51.37N 102.26W
Canosa di Puglia 14 Ki 41.13N 16.04 E
Canouan Island 50 Ff 12.43N 61.20W
Canourgue 11 Jj 44.25N 3.13 E
Canso, Strait of - 42 Lg 45.35N 61.23W
Canta 54 Cf 11.25S 76.38W
Cantabrian Mountains (EN) = Cantábrica, Cordillera- 5 Fg 43.00N 5.00W
Cantábrica, Cordillera- = Cantabrian Mountains (EN) 5 Fg 43.00N 5.00W
Cantal 5 Gf 45.10N 2.50 E
Cantal 11 Ii 45.05N 2.40 E
Cantalejo 13 Ic 41.15N 3.55W
Cantanhede 13 Dd 40.21N 8.36W
Cantaura 54 Fb 9.19N 64.21W
Cantavieja 13 Ld 40.32N 0.24W
Cantavir 15 Cd 45.55N 19.46 E
Canterbury 62 De 43.30S 171.50 E
Canterbury 9 Oj 51.17N 1.05 E
Canterbury Bight 57 Ii 44.10S 172.00 E
Can Tho 22 Mi 10.02N 105.47 E
Cantiles, Cayo- 49 Fc 21.36N 82.02W
Canto do Buriti 54 Je 8.07S 42.58W
Canton [Il.-U.S.] 45 Kf 40.33N 90.02W
Canton [Mo.-U.S.] 45 Kf 40.08N 91.32W
Canton [Ms.-U.S.] 45 Kj 32.37N 90.02W
Canton [N.Y.-U.S.] 44 Jc 44.37N 75.11W
Canton [Oh.-U.S.] 43 Kc 40.48N 81.23W
Canton [S.D.-U.S.] 45 He 43.18N 96.35W
Canton (EN) = Guangzhou 22 Ng 23.07N 113.18 E
Cantù 14 De 45.44N 9.08 E
Cantwell 40 Jd 63.23N 148.57W
Cañuelas 55 Cl 35.03S 58.44W
Canumã, Rio- 52 Kf 3.55S 59.10W
Canutama 54 Fe 6.32S 64.20W
Canvey 12 Cc 51.31N 0.36 E
Çany 20 Ce 55.19N 76.56 E
Çany, Ozero- 21 Jd 54.50N 77.30 E
Cany-Barville 12 Ce 49.47N 0.38 E
Canyon [Mn.-U.S.] 45 Jc 47.02N 92.29W
Canyon [Tx.-U.S.] 43 Ge 34.59N 101.55W
Canyon [Wy.-U.S.] 46 Jd 44.44N 110.30W
Canyon Lake 45 Gl 29.52N 98.16W
Canzar 36 Dd 7.36S 21.33 E
Cao Bang 25 Ld 22.40N 106.15 E
Caojiahe → Qichun 28 Ci 30.15N 115.26 E
Caojian 27 Gf 25.38N 99.07 E
Caombo 36 Cd 8.42S 16.33 E
Caorle 14 Ge 45.36N 12.53 E
Caoxian 28 Cg 34.49N 115.33 E
Caozhou → Heze 27 Kd 35.14N 115.28 E
Capaccio 14 Jj 40.25N 15.05 E
Čapajev 19 Fe 50.14N 51.08 E
Čapajevsk 19 Ee 53.01N 49.36 E
Capanaparo, Río- 54 Eb 7.01N 67.07W
Capanema [Braz.] 54 Id 1.12S 47.11W
Capanema [Braz.] 55 Fg 25.40S 53.48W
Capanema, Serra do- 55 Fh 26.05S 53.16W
Capão Alto 55 Gh 27.56S 50.30W
Capão Bonito 55 Hf 24.01S 48.20W
Capão Doce, Morro do- 55 Gh 26.43S 51.25W
Caparo, Río- 49 Lj 7.46N 70.23W
Capatárida 49 Lh 11.11N 70.37W
Capbreton 11 Ek 43.38N 1.26W
Cap Breton Canyon (EN) 11 Ek 43.40N 1.50W
Čapčama, Pereval- 18 Hd 41.34N 70.50 E
Cap-Chat 44 Na 49.06N 66.42W
Capcir 11 Il 42.45N 2.10 E
Cap-de-la-Madeleine 42 Kg 46.22N 72.32W
Capdenac-Gare 11 Ij 44.34N 2.05 E
Cape Barren Island 59 Jh 40.25S 148.10 E
Cape Basin (EN) 3 Em 37.00S 7.00 E
Cape Breton Island 38 Me 46.00N 60.30W
Cape Charles 44 Jg 37.17N 76.00W
Cape Coast 31 Gh 5.06N 1.15W
Cape Cod Bay 44 Le 41.52N 70.22W
Cape Coral 44 Gl 26.33N 81.58W
Cape Dorset 39 Lc 64.14N 76.32W
Cape Dyer 39 Mc 66.30N 61.18W
Cape Fear River 44 Ii 33.53N 78.00W
Cape Girardeau 43 Jd 37.19N 89.32W
Cape Johnson Tablemount (EN) 57 Jc 17.08N 177.15W
Capel 12 Bc 51.08N 0.19W
Cape Lisburne 40 Fc 68.52N 166.05W
Capelka 8 Mf 58.02N 29.07 E
Capelongo 36 Ce 14.53S 16.18 E
Capem 55 Ea 13.14S 55.14W
Cape May 44 Jf 38.56N 74.54W
Cape Mount 34 Cd 7.05N 10.50W
Cape Province/Kaapprovinsie 37 Cf 32.00S 22.00 E
Cape Rise (EN) 3 En 42.00S 15.00 E
Cape Smith 42 Jd 60.44N 78.29W
Capesterre 51e Bc 15.54N 61.13W
Capesterre-Belle-Eau 50 Fd 16.03N 61.34W
Cape Town / Kaapstad 31 Il 33.55S 18.22 E
Cape Verde (EN) = Cabo Verde 31 Eg 16.00N 24.00W
Cape Verde (EN) = Cap Vert 34 Bc 14.45N 17.20W
Cape Verde Basin (EN) 3 Ch 15.00N 30.00W
Cape Verde Islands (EN) = Cabo Verde, Ilhas do- 30 Eg 16.00N 24.10W
Cape Yakataga 40 Kd 60.04N 142.26W
Cape York Peninsula 57 Ff 14.00S 142.30 E
Cap-Haïtien 39 Lh 19.45N 72.15W
Capiibary, Arroyo- 55 Dg 24.06S 56.26W
Capiibary, Rio- 55 Eg 25.30S 55.33W
Capim, Rio- 52 Lf 1.40S 47.47W
Capinópolis 55 Hd 18.41S 49.35W
Capira 49 Hi 8.45N 79.53W
Capital Federal 56 Id 34.36S 58.27W
Capitán Arturo Prat 66 Re 62.29S 59.39W
Capitán Bado 56 Ib 23.16S 55.32W
Capitán Bermúdez 55 Bk 32.49S 60.43W
Capitán Sarmiento 55 Cl 34.10S 59.48W
Capitão Noronha, Rio- 55 Ea 13.19S 54.36W
Capivara, Represa da- 55 Gf 22.40S 50.57W
Capivari, Rio- 55 Dd 19.16S 57.10W
Capivarita 55 Fj 30.18S 52.19W
Cap Lopez, Baie du- 36 Ac 0.40S 9.00 E
Čaplygin 16 Kc 53.17N 39.59 E
Cappeln (Oldenburg) 12 Kb 52.49N 8.07 E
Cap Point 50 Fe 14.07N 60.57W
Capraia 14 Dg 43.05N 9.50 E
Caprara, Punta- 14 Ci 41.07N 8.19 E
Capreol 44 Gb 46.43N 80.56W
Caprera 14 Di 41.10N 9.30 E
Capri 14 Ij 40.35N 14.15 E
Capri 14 Ij 40.33N 14.14 E
Capricorn, Cape- 59 Kd 23.30S 151.15 E
Capricorn Channel 59 Kd 22.15S 151.30 E
Capricorn Group 57 Gg 23.30S 152.00 E
Caprivi Strip (EN) = Caprivi Zipfel 30 Jj 18.00S 23.00 E
Caprivi Zipfel = Caprivi Strip (EN) 30 Jj 18.00S 23.00 E
Captain Cook 65a Fd 19.30N 155.55W
Captains Flat 59 Jg 35.35S 149.27 E
Captieux 11 Fj 44.17N 0.15W
Capua 14 Ii 41.06N 14.12 E
Capuchin, Cape- 51g Ba 15.38N 61.28W
Capunda 36 Ce 10.41S 17.23 E
Cap Vert = Cape Verde (EN) 34 Bc 14.45N 17.20W
Caquetá 54 Dc 1.00N 74.00W
Čara 21 Oc 60.17N 120.40 E
Čara [R.S.F.S.R.] 20 Ge 56.58N 118.17 E
Čara [R.S.F.S.R.] 20 Ge 58.54N 118.12 E
Carabobo 54 Ea 10.10N 68.05W
Caracal 15 He 44.07N 24.21 E
Caracaraí 54 Fc 1.50N 61.08W
Caracas 53 Jd 10.30N 66.56W
Carache 49 Li 9.38N 70.14W
Caracol 55 De 21.59S 57.02W
Caracol, Rio- 55 Df 22.13S 57.03W
Caracollo 54 Eg 17.39S 67.10W
Cara Droma Rúisc/Carrick-on-Shannon 9 Eh 53.57N 8.05W
Caraguatá, Cuchilla- 55 Ek 32.05S 54.54W
Caraguatatuba 55 Jf 23.37S 45.25W
Caraïbe, Mer-/Antilles, Mer des- = Caribbean Sea (EN) 38 Lh 15.00N 73.00W
Carajas, Serra dos- 54 He 6.00S 51.20W
Caramoan Peninsula 26 Hd 13.48N 123.40 E
Caramulo, Serra do- 13 Dd 40.34N 8.11W
Caraná, Rio- 55 Ca 13.20S 59.17W
Carandai 55 Ke 20.57S 43.48W
Carandazal 55 Dd 19.50S 57.09W
Caransebeş 15 Fd 45.25N 22.13 E
Carapá, Rio- 55 Eg 24.30S 54.20W
Carapelle 14 Ji 41.30N 15.55 E
Caraş 15 Ee 44.49N 21.20 E
Caraş Severin 15 Ed 45.20N 22.00 E
Caratasca, Cayo- 49 Fe 16.02N 83.20W
Caratasca, Laguna de- 47 He 15.20N 83.50W
Caratinga 54 Jg 19.47S 42.08W
Carauari 54 Ed 4.52S 66.54W
Caraúbas 54 Ke 5.47S 37.34W
Caravaca 13 Kf 38.06N 1.51W
Caravelas 53 Mg 17.45S 39.15W
Caraveli 54 Dg 15.46S 73.22W
Caravelle, Presqu'île de la- 51h Bb 14.45N 60.55W
Caravelle, Rocher de la- 51h Bb 14.48N 60.53W
Caràzinho 56 Jc 28.18S 52.48W
Carazo 49 Dh 11.45N 86.15W
Carballino 13 Db 42.26N 8.04W
Carballo 13 Da 43.13N 8.41W
Carberry 45 Gb 49.52N 99.20W
Carbet, Pitons du- 51h Ab 14.42N 61.07W
Carbon, Cap- [Alg.] 13 Rh 36.47N 5.06 E
Carbon, Cap- [Alg.] 13 Li 35.54N 0.20W
Carbonara, Capo- 14 Dk 39.06N 9.31 E
Carbondale [Il.-U.S.] 43 Jd 37.44N 89.13W
Carbondale [Pa.-U.S.] 44 Je 41.35N 75.31W
Carbonera, Cuchilla de la- 55 El 34.10S 54.00W
Carboneras 13 Kh 36.59N 1.54W
Carboneras, Cerro- 48 Ih 18.10N 101.10W
Carbones 13 Gg 37.36N 5.39W
Carbonia 14 Ck 39.10N 8.31 E
Carcans, Étang de- 11 Ei 45.06N 1.07W
Carcar 26 Hd 10.06N 123.38 E
Carcarañá, Río- 55 Bk 32.27S 60.48W
Carcassonne 11 Ik 43.13N 2.21 E
Carcross 42 Ed 60.10N 134.42W
Çardak [Tur.] 15 Ji 40.22N 26.43 E
Çardak [Tur.] 24 Cd 37.48N 29.40 E
Čardara 19 Gg 41.15N 68.01 E
Čardarinskoje Vodohranilišče 18 Gd 41.05N 68.15 E
Cárdenas [Cuba] 47 Hd 23.02N 81.12W
Cárdenas [Mex.] 47 Ed 22.00N 99.40W
Cárdenas [Mex.] 48 Mi 17.59N 93.22W
Cárdenas, Bahía de- 49 Gb 23.05N 81.10W
Cardener/Cardoner 13 Nc 41.41N 1.51 E
Cardiel, Lago- 56 Fg 48.55S 71.15W
Cardiff 6 Fe 51.30N 3.13W
Cardigan 9 Ii 52.06N 4.40W
Cardigan Bay 5 Fe 52.30N 4.20W
Cardona [Sp.] 13 Nc 41.55N 1.41 E
Cardona [Ur.] 55 Dk 33.54S 57.22W
Cardoner/Cardener 13 Nc 41.41N 1.51 E
Cardozo 55 Dk 32.38S 56.21W
Cardston 42 Gg 49.12N 113.18W
Čardžou 22 If 39.06N 63.34 E
Čardžouskaja Oblast 19 Gh 39.00N 63.00 E
Carei 15 Fb 47.41N 22.28 E
Careiro 54 Gd 3.12S 59.45W
Carentan 11 Ee 49.18N 1.14W
Carey 46 Ie 43.20N 113.58W
Carey, Lake- 57 Dg 29.05S 122.15 E
Cargados Carajos Islands 30 Mj 16.35S 59.40 E
Cargese 11a Aa 42.08N 8.35 E
Carhaix-Plouguer 11 Cf 48.17N 3.35W
Cari 14 Hi 41.23N 13.50 E
Caria 15 Ll 37.30N 29.00 E
Cariacica 54 Jh 20.16S 40.25W
Cariaco 55 Eg 10.29N 63.33W
Cariaco, Golfo de- 50 Eg 10.30N 64.00W
Cariaco Basin (EN) 50 Dg 10.37N 65.10W
Cariati 14 Kk 39.30N 16.57 E
Caribana, Punta- 49 Ii 8.37N 76.52W
Caribbean Sea 38 Lh 15.00N 73.00W
Caribbean Sea (EN) = Antillas, Mar de las-/Caribe, Mar- 38 Lh 15.00N 73.00W
Caribbean Sea (EN) = Antilles, Mer des-/Caraïbe, Mer- 38 Lh 15.00N 73.00W
Caribbean Sea (EN) = Caribe, Mar-/Antillas, Mar de las- 38 Lh 15.00N 73.00W
Caribe, Mar-/Antillas, Mar de las- = Caribbean Sea (EN) 38 Lh 15.00N 73.00W
Cariboo Mountains 42 Ff 53.00N 121.00W
Caribou 42 Ie 59.20N 94.45W
Caribou 44 Mb 46.52N 68.01W
Caribou Island 44 Eb 47.27N 85.52W
Caribou Lake 45 La 50.25N 89.00W
Caribou Mountains 38 Hd 59.12N 115.40W
Caribou Range 46 Je 43.05N 111.15W
Caričin Grad 15 Eg 42.57N 21.45 E
Carignan 11 Le 49.38N 5.10 E
Carignano 14 Bf 44.55N 7.40 E
Cariñena 13 Kc 41.20N 1.13W
Carinhanha 54 Jf 14.08S 43.47W
Carinhanha, Rio- 55 Kb 14.20S 43.47W
Carini 14 Hl 38.08N 13.11 E
Carinola 14 Hi 41.11N 13.58 E
Carinthia (EN) = Kärnten 14 Hd 46.45N 14.00 E
Carinthia (EN) = Kärnten 14 Hd 46.45N 14.00 E
Caripe 50 Eg 10.21N 63.29W
Caripito 54 Fa 10.08N 63.06W
Caris, Rio- 50 Eh 8.09N 63.46W
Carlet 13 Le 39.14N 0.31W
Carleton Place 44 Ic 45.07N 76.08W
Carletonville 37 De 26.23S 27.22 E
Carlin 46 Gf 40.43N 116.07W
Carling 12 Ie 49.10N 6.43 E
Carlingford Lough/Loch Cairlinn 9 Gg 54.05N 6.14W
Carlinville 45 Lg 39.17N 89.53W
Carlisle [Eng.-U.K.] 6 Fe 54.54N 2.55W
Carlisle [Pa.-U.S.] 44 Ie 40.12N 77.12W
Carlisle Bay 51q Ab 13.05N 59.37W
Carloforte 14 Ck 39.08N 8.18 E
Carlos Beguerie 55 Cl 35.29S 59.06W
Carlos Casares 56 He 35.38S 61.21W
Carlos Chagas 54 Jg 17.43S 40.45W
Carlos Reyles 55 Dk 33.03S 56.29W
Carlos Tejedor 55 Al 35.23S 62.25W
Carlow/Ceatharlach 9 Gi 52.50N 6.55W
Carlow/Ceatharlach 9 Gi 52.50N 7.00W
Carloway 9 Gc 58.17N 6.47W
Carlsbad [Ca.-U.S.] 46 Gj 33.10N 117.21W
Carlsbad [N.M.-U.S.] 39 If 32.25N 104.14W
Carlyle 42 Hg 49.38N 102.16W
Carlyle Lake 45 Lg 38.40N 89.18W
Carmacks 42 Dd 62.05N 136.18W
Carmagnola 14 Bf 44.51N 7.43 E
Carmarthen 9 Ij 51.52N 4.19W
Carmarthen Bay 9 Ij 51.40N 4.30W
Carmaux 11 Ij 44.03N 2.09 E
Carmel Head 9 Ih 53.24N 4.34W
Carmelita 49 Be 17.21N 90.10W
Carmelo 56 Id 34.00S 58.17W
Carmen 55 Dk 33.15S 56.01W
Carmen, Isla- 47 Bc 25.57N 111.12W
Carmen, Isla del- 48 Nh 18.42N 91.40W
Carmen, Laguna del- 48 Mh 18.15N 93.50W
Carmen, Rio del- 48 Fb 30.42N 106.29W
Carmen, Sierra del- 48 Hc 29.00N 102.30W
Carmen de Patagones 56 Hf 40.48S 62.59W
Carmensa 56 Ge 35.08S 67.38W
Carmi 45 Lg 38.07N 88.10W
Carmichael 46 Eg 38.38N 121.19W
Carmo de Minas 55 Jf 22.07S 45.08W
Carmo do Paranaíba 55 Id 18.59S 46.21W
Carmona 13 Gg 37.28N 5.38W
Carnac 11 Cg 47.35N 3.05W
Carnamah 59 De 29.42S 115.53 E
Carnarvon [Austl.] 58 Cg 24.53S 113.40 E
Carnarvon [S.Afr.] 31 Jl 30.56S 22.08 E
Carnarvon Range 59 Ee 25.10S 121.00 E
Carnatic (EN) 21 Jh 10.30N 79.00 E
Carnegie, Lake- 57 Dg 26.10S 122.30 E
Carnegie Ridge (EN) 3 Nj 1.00S 85.00W
Carn Eige 9 Hd 57.30N 5.05W
Carney Island 66 Nf 73.57S 121.00W
Carnia 14 Gd 46.25N 13.00 E
Car Nicobar 25 Ig 9.10N 92.47 E
Carnot 35 Be 4.48N 16.03 E
Carnoustie 9 Ke 56.30N 2.44W
Carnsore Point/Ceann an Chairn 9 Gi 52.10N 6.22W
Carn Ui Néid/Mizen Head 5 Fe 51.27N 9.49W
Caro 44 Fd 43.29N 83.24W
Carol City 44 Gm 25.56N 80.16W
Carolina [Braz.] 53 Lf 7.20S 47.28W
Carolina [P.R.] 51a Cb 18.24N 65.57W
Carolina [S.Afr.] 37 Ee 26.05S 30.06 E
Carolina Beach 44 Ih 34.02N 77.54W
Carolinas, Puntan- 64b Bb 14.54N 145.38 E
Caroline Atoll 57 Le 9.58S 150.13W
Caroline Islands 57 Fd 8.00N 147.00 E
Carondelet Reef 57 Je 5.34S 173.51W
Caroni, Rio- 52 Je 8.21N 62.43W
Caronie → Nebrodi 14 Im 37.55N 14.35 E
Carora 54 Da 10.11N 70.05W
Carpathian Mountains (EN) 5 If 48.00N 24.00 E
Carpathian Mountains (EN) = Carpaţii Occidentali 15 Fc 46.30N 22.10 E
Carpathian Mountains (EN) = Carpaţii Orientali 15 Ib 47.30N 25.30 E
Carpaţii Meridionali = Transylvanian Alps (EN) 5 If 45.30N 22.10 E
Carpaţii Occidentali = Carpathian Mountains (EN) 15 Fc 46.30N 22.10 E
Carpaţii Orientali = Carpathian Mountains (EN) 15 Ib 47.30N 25.30 E
Carpen 15 Ge 44.20N 23.15 E
Carpentaria, Gulf of- 57 Ef 14.00S 139.00 E
Carpentras 11 Lj 44.03N 5.03 E
Carpi 14 Ef 44.47N 10.53 E
Carpina 54 Ke 7.51S 35.15W
Carr, Cape- 66 Ie 66.07S 130.51 E
Carraig Fhearghais/Carrickfergus 9 Hg 54.43N 5.44W
Carraig na Siúire/Carrick-on-Suir 9 Fi 52.21N 7.25W
Carrantuohill 5 Fe 52.00N 9.45W
Carrara 14 Ef 44.05N 10.06 E
Carreiro, Rio- 55 Gi 29.07S 51.43W
Carreño 13 Ga 43.35N 5.46W
Carreta, Punta- 54 Cf 14.13S 76.18W
Carretero, Puerto- 13 Ig 37.28N 3.40W
Carriacou 50 Ff 12.30N 61.27W
Carrick 9 If 55.15N 4.40W
Carrickfergus/Carraig Fhearghais 9 Hg 54.43N 5.44W
Carrick-on-Shannon/Cara Droma Rúisc 9 Eh 53.57N 8.05W
Carrick-on-Suir/Carraig na Siúire 9 Fi 52.21N 7.25W
Carrington 43 Hb 47.27N 99.08W
Carrión 13 Hc 41.53N 4.32W
Carrión de los Condes 13 Hb 42.20N 4.36W
Carrizal 49 Kh 11.58N 72.12W
Carrizo Peak 45 Dj 33.20N 105.38W
Carrizos 48 Gc 29.58N 105.16W
Carrizo Springs 45 Gl 28.31N 99.52W
Carrizo Wash 46 Ki 34.36N 109.26W
Carrizozo 45 Dj 33.38N 105.53W
Carroll 45 Ie 42.04N 94.52W
Carroll Inlet 66 Qf 73.18S 78.30W
Carrollton [Ga.-U.S.] 44 Ei 33.35N 85.05W
Carrollton [Il.-U.S.] 45 Kg 39.18N 90.24W
Carrollton [Ky.-U.S.] 44 Ef 38.41N 85.11W
Carrollton [Mo.-U.S.] 45 Jg 39.22N 93.30W
Carron, Loch- 9 Hd 57.30N 5.40W
Carrot 42 Hf 53.50N 101.18W
Carrowmore Lough 9 Dg 54.12N 9.47W
Çarşamba 24 Gb 41.12N 36.44 E
Çarşamba 24 Ed 37.53N 32.37 E
Čaršanga 19 Gh 37.31N 66.03 E
Čarsk 19 If 49.35N 81.05 E
Carson 46 Ed 45.44N 121.49W
Carson City 39 Hf 39.10N 119.46W
Carson Lake 46 Fg 39.19N 118.43W
Carson Sink 46 Fg 39.45N 118.30W
Cartagena [Col.] 53 Id 10.25N 75.32W
Cartagena [Sp.] 6 Fh 37.36N 0.59W
Cartago 49 Fi 9.50N 83.45W
Cartago [Col.] 54 Cc 4.46N 75.56W
Cartago [C.R.] 47 Hg 9.52N 83.55W
Cartaxo 13 De 39.09N 8.47W
Carter, Mount- 59 Ib 13.05S 143.15 E
Carteret 11 Ee 49.23N 1.47W
Cartersville 44 Eh 34.10N 85.05W
Carterton 62 Fd 41.01S 175.31 E
Carthage [Mo.-U.S.] 45 Ih 37.11N 94.19W
Carthage [Tx.-U.S.] 45 Ij 32.09N 94.20W
Cartier 44 Gb 46.42N 81.32W
Cartier Island 57 Df 12.30S 123.30 E
Caruaru 53 Mf 8.17S 35.58W
Carúpano 54 Fa 10.40N 63.14W
Carutapera 54 Id 1.13S 46.01W
Čarvak 18 Gd 41.38N 69.56 E
Carvin 12 Ed 50.29N 2.58 E
Carvoeiro, Cabo- 13 Ce 39.21N 9.24W
Čaryn 18 Lc 43.50N 79.12 E
Čaryš 20 Df 52.22N 83.45 E
Casablanca 32 Fc 33.37N 7.35W
Casablanca 31 Ge 33.36N 7.37W
Casa Branca 55 Ie 21.46S 47.05W
Casa Grande 43 Ee 32.53N 111.45W
Casalbordino 14 Ih 42.09N 14.35 E
Casale Monferrato 14 Ce 45.08N 8.27 E
Casalmaggiore 14 Ef 44.59N 10.26 E
Casalvasco 55 Cb 15.19S 59.59W
Casal Velino 14 Jj 40.11N 15.06 E
Casamance 34 Bc 12.33N 16.46W
Casamance 34 Bc 12.55N 15.00W
Casanare 54 Db 5.20N 72.00W
Casanare, Rio- 54 Eb 6.02N 69.51W
Casanay 50 Eg 10.30N 63.25W
Casa Nova 54 Je 9.25S 41.08W
Casarano 14 Mj 40.00N 18.10 E
Casas Grandes, Rio- 48 Eb 30.22N 107.31W
Casas-Ibáñez 13 Ke 39.17N 1.28W
Casca, Rio da- 55 Eb 14.52S 55.52W
Cascade 46 Hd 44.31N 115.59W
Cascade Point 62 Cf 44.01S 168.22 E
Cascade Range 38 Ge 45.00N 121.30W
Cascais 13 Cf 38.42N 9.25W
Cascavel 56 Jb 24.57S 53.28W
Cascia 14 Hh 42.43N 13.01 E
Casciana Terme 14 Eg 43.32N 10.38 E
Cascina 14 Eg 43.41N 10.33 E
Casentino 14 Fg 43.40N 11.50 E

Index Symbols

Independent Nation · State, Region · District, County · Municipality · Colony, Dependency · Continent · Physical Region · Historical or Cultural Region · Mount, Mountain · Volcano · Hill · Mountains, Mountain Range · Hills, Escarpment · Plateau, Upland · Pass, Gap · Plain, Lowland · Delta · Salt Flat · Valley, Canyon · Crater, Cave · Karst Features · Depression · Polder · Desert, Dunes · Forest, Woods · Heath, Steppe · Oasis · Cape, Point · Coast, Beach · Cliff · Peninsula · Isthmus · Sandbank · Island · Atoll · Rock, Reef · Islands, Archipelago · Rocks, Reefs · Coral Reef · Well, Spring · Geyser · River, Stream · Waterfall Rapids · River Mouth, Estuary · Lake · Salt Lake · Intermittent Lake · Reservoir · Swamp, Pond · Canal · Glacier · Ice Shelf, Pack Ice · Ocean · Sea · Gulf, Bay · Strait, Fjord · Lagoon · Bank · Seamount · Tablemount · Ridge · Shelf · Basin · Escarpment, Sea Scarp · Fracture · Trench, Abyss · National Park, Reserve · Point of Interest · Recreation Site · Cave, Cavern · Historic Site · Ruins · Wall, Walls · Church, Abbey · Temple · Scientific Station · Airport · Port · Lighthouse · Mine · Tunnel · Dam, Bridge

Case-Pilote 51h Ab 14.38N 61.08W
Caserta 14 Ii 41.04N 14.20 E
Casey 66 He 66.17S 110.32 E
Casey Bay 66 Ee 67.00S 48.00 E
Cashel/Caiseal 9 Fi 52.31N 7.53W
Casigua 49 Ki 8.46N 72.30W
Casilda 56 Hd 33.03S 61.10W
Casimcea 15 Le 44.24N 28.33 E
Casino 59 Ke 28.52S 153.03 E
Casiquiare, Brazo- 54 Ec 2.01N 67.07W
Čáslav 10 Lg 49.55N 15.25 E
Casma 54 Ce 9.28S 78.19W
Časnačorr, Gora- 7 Hc 67.45N 33.29 E
Čašniki 7 Gi 54.52N 29.08 E
Casoli 14 Ih 42.07N 14.18 E
Casoria 14 Ij 40.54N 14.17 E
Caspe 13 Lc 41.14N 0.02W
Casper 39 Ie 42.51N 106.19W
Caspian Depression (EN)= Prikaspijskaja Nizmennost 5 Lf 48.00N 52.00 E
Caspian Sea (EN)= Kaspijskoje More 5 Lg 42.00N 50.30 E
Caspian Sea (EN)= Māzandarān, Daryā-ye- 5 Lg 42.00N 50.30 E
Cassai 30 Ii 3.02S 16.57 E
Cassamba 36 De 13.04S 20.25 E
Cassange, Rio- 55 Dc 17.06S 57.23W
Cassano allo Ionio 14 Kk 39.47N 16.19 E
Cass City 44 Fd 43.36N 83.10W
Cassel 12 Ed 50.47N 2.29 E
Casselton 45 Hc 46.54N 97.13W
Cássia 55 Ie 20.36S 46.56W
Cassiar 42 Ee 59.16N 129.40W
Cassiar Mountains 38 Gd 59.00N 129.00W
Cassilândia 54 Hg 19.09S 51.45W
Cassino [Braz.] 55 Fk 32.11S 52.10W
Cassino [It.] 14 Hi 41.30N 13.49 E
Cassis 11 Lk 43.13N 5.32 E
Cass Lake 45 Ic 47.23N 94.36W
Cass River 44 Fd 43.23N 83.59W
Cassununga 55 Fc 16.03S 53.38W
Castagneto Carducci 14 Eg 43.10N 10.36 E
Castagniccia 11a Ba 42.25N 9.30 E
Castañar, Sierra del- 13 He 39.35N 4.10W
Castanhal 54 Id 1.18S 47.55W
Castaños 48 Id 26.47N 101.25W
Castelbuono 14 Im 37.56N 14.05 E
Castel di Sangro 14 Ii 41.47N 14.06 E
Castelfidardo 14 Hg 43.28N 13.33 E
Castelfranco Veneto 14 Fe 45.40N 11.55 E
Casteljaloux 11 Gj 44.19N 0.06 E
Castellabate 14 Ij 40.17N 14.57 E
Castellammare, Golfo di- 14 Gl 38.10N 12.55 E
Castellammare del Golfo 14 Gl 38.01N 12.53 E
Castellammare di Stabia 14 Ij 40.42N 14.29 E
Castellana Grotte 14 Lj 40.53N 17.10 E
Castellane 11 Mk 43.51N 6.31 E
Castellaneta 14 Kj 40.38N 16.56 E
Castelldefels 13 Nc 41.17N 1.58 E
Castelli [Arg.] 56 Hc 25.57S 60.37W
Castelli [Arg.] 55 Dm 36.06S 57.47W
Castelló de la Plana/ Castellón de la Plana 6 Fh 39.59N 0.02W
Castellón 13 Ld 40.10N 0.10W
Castellón de la Plana/ Castelló de la Plana 6 Fh 39.59N 0.02W
Castellón de la Plana-El Grao 13 Me 39.58N 0.01 E
Castellote 13 Ld 40.48N 0.19W
Castelnaudary 11 Hk 43.19N 1.57 E
Castelnau-de-Médoc 11 Fi 45.02N 0.48W
Castelnovo ne' Monti 14 Ef 44.26N 10.24 E
Castelo Branco 13 Ee 40.00N 7.30W
Castelo Branco 13 Ee 39.49N 7.30W
Castelo de Vide 13 Ee 39.25N 7.27W
Castelo do Piauí 54 Je 5.20S 41.33W
Castel San Giovanni 14 De 45.04N 9.26 E
Castelsardo 14 Cj 40.55N 8.43 E
Castelsarrasin 11 Hj 44.02N 1.06 E
Casteltermini 14 Hm 37.32N 13.39 E
Castelvetrano 14 Gm 37.41N 12.47 E
Castets 11 Ek 43.53N 1.09W
Castiglione del Lago 14 Gg 43.07N 12.03 E
Castiglione della Pescaia 14 Eh 42.46N 10.53 E
Castiglion Fiorentino 14 Fg 43.20N 11.55 E
Castilla la Nueva=New Castile (EN) 13 Id 40.00N 3.45W
Castilla la Vieja=Old Castile (EN) 13 Ic 41.30N 4.00W
Castillejo 13 Gc 41.14N 5.30W
Castillon-la-Bataille 11 Fj 44.51N 0.02W
Castillonnès 11 Gj 44.39N 0.36 E
Castillos 56 Jd 34.12S 53.50W
Castillos, Laguna de- 55 Fl 34.20S 53.54W
Castlebar/Caisleán an Bharraigh 9 Dh 53.52N 9.17W
Castle Bruce 51g Bb 15.26N 61.16W
Castle Dome Peak 46 Hj 33.05N 114.08W
Castle Douglas 9 Jg 54.57N 3.56W
Castlegar 42 Fg 49.19N 117.40W
Castleisland/Oiléan Ciarrai 9 Di 52.14N 9.27W
Castlemaine 59 Ig 37.04S 144.13 E
Castle Peak 46 Hd 44.03N 114.32W
Castlepoint 62 Gd 40.55S 176.13 E
Castlepollard 9 Fh 53.41N 7.17W
Castlerea/An Caisleán Riabhach 9 Eh 53.46N 8.29W
Castlereagh Bay 59 Hb 12.10S 135.10 E
Castle Rock Butte 45 Ed 45.00N 103.27W
Castle Rock Lake 45 Le 43.56N 89.58W
Častoozerje 17 Mi 55.34N 67.53 E
Castor 46 Ja 52.13N 111.53W
Castres 11 Ik 43.36N 2.15 E
Castricum 12 Gb 52.33N 4.42 E
Castries 39 Mh 14.01N 61.00W
Castrignano del Capo 14 Mk 39.50N 18.20 E
Castro [Braz.] 56 Jb 24.47S 50.03W
Castro [Chile] 56 Ff 42.29S 73.46W
Castro Alves 54 Kf 12.45S 39.26W
Castrocaro Terme e Terra del Sole 14 Ff 44.10N 11.57 E
Castro Daire 13 Ed 40.54N 7.56W
Castro del Río 13 Hg 37.41N 4.28W
Castrojeriz 13 Hb 42.17N 4.08W
Castropol 13 Ea 43.32N 7.02W
Castrop-Rauxel 12 Jc 51.33N 7.19 E
Castro Urdiales 13 Ia 43.23N 3.13W
Castro Verde 13 Dg 37.42N 8.05W
Castrovillari 14 Kk 39.49N 16.12 E
Castrovirreyna 54 Cf 13.16S 75.19W
Castuera 13 Gf 38.43N 5.33W
Častyje 17 Gh 57.19N 54.59 E
Casupá 55 El 34.09S 55.38W
Caswell Sound 62 Bf 45.00S 167.10 E
Çat 24 Ic 39.40N 41.02 E
Cata 10 Oi 47.58N 18.40 E
Catacamas 49 Ef 14.54N 85.56W
Catahoula Lake 45 Jk 31.30N 92.06W
Çatak 24 Jc 38.01N 43.07 E
Çatak 24 Jd 37.53N 42.39 E
Catalan Coastal Range (EN) =Cadena Costero Catalana /Serralada Litoral Catalana 5 Gg 41.35N 1.40 E
Catalan Coastal Range (EN) =Serralada Litoral Catalana/Cadena Costero Catalana 5 Gg 41.35N 1.40 E
Catalão 54 Ig 18.10S 47.57W
Çatal Balkan 15 Jg 42.46N 27.00 E
Çatalca 15 Lh 41.09N 28.27 E
Çatal Dağ 15 Lj 39.51N 28.20 E
Catalina 56 Gc 25.13S 69.43W
Catalina, Isla- 49 Md 18.21N 69.00W
Catalina, Punta- 56 Gh 52.32S 68.47W
Catalonia (EN)=Cataluña/ Catalunya 5 Gg 42.00N 2.00 E
Catalonia (EN)=Cataluña/ Catalunya 13 Nc 42.00N 2.00 E
Catalonia (EN)=Catalunya/ Cataluña 5 Gg 42.00N 2.00 E
Catalonia (EN)=Catalunya/ Cataluña 13 Nc 42.00N 2.00 E
Cataluña/Catalunya= Catalonia (EN) 5 Gg 42.00N 2.00 E
Cataluña/Catalunya= Catalonia (EN) 13 Nc 42.00N 2.00 E
Catalunya/Cataluña= Catalonia (EN) 13 Nc 42.00N 2.00 E
Catalunya/Cataluña= Catalonia (EN) 5 Gg 42.00N 2.00 E
Çatalzeytin 24 Fb 41.57N 34.13 E
Catamarca 53 Jh 28.30S 65.45W
Catamarca 56 Gc 27.00S 67.00W
Catanduanes 21 Oh 13.45N 124.15 E
Catanduva 56 Kb 21.08S 48.58W
Catanduvas 55 Fg 25.12S 53.08W
Catania 6 Hh 37.30N 15.06 E
Catania, Golfo di- 14 Jm 37.25N 15.10 E
Catania, Piana di- 14 Im 37.25N 14.50 E
Catanzaro 6 Hh 38.54N 16.35 E
Catarman 26 Hd 12.30N 124.38 E
Catastrophe, Cape- 57 Eh 35.00S 136.00 E
Catatumbo, Río- 49 Li 9.21N 71.45W
Catbalogan 26 Hd 11.46N 124.53 E
Catemaco, Lago- 48 Lh 18.25N 95.05W
Catete 36 Bd 9.07S 13.41 E
Cathair na Mart/Westport 9 Dh 53.48N 9.32W
Cathair Saidhbhín/ Cahersiveen 9 Cj 51.57N 10.13W
Cathcart 37 Df 32.18S 27.09 E
Catherine, Mount- 46 Ig 39.05N 112.04W
Catholic Island 51n Bb 12.40N 61.24W
Catio 34 Bc 11.17N 15.15W
Cat Island 38 Lg 24.30N 75.30W
Čatkal 18 Hd 41.36N 70.05 E
Čatkalski Hrebet 19 Hg 41.30N 70.50 E
Cat Lake 42 If 51.40N 91.52W
Catoche, Cabo- 38 Kg 21.36N 87.07W
Cato Island 57 Gg 23.15S 155.35 E
Catolé do Rocha 54 Ke 6.21S 37.45W
Catoute 13 Fb 42.45N 6.20W
Catria 14 Gg 43.28N 12.42 E
Catriló 56 He 36.26S 63.24W
Catrimani, Rio- 54 Fc 0.28N 61.44W
Catskill Mountains 44 Jd 42.10N 74.30W
Cattenom 12 Ie 49.25N 6.15 E
Cattolica 14 Gg 43.58N 12.44 E
Catu 54 Kf 12.21S 38.23W
Catuane 37 Ee 26.48S 32.14 E
Catumbela 36 Be 12.27S 13.29 E
Catur 37 Fb 13.45S 35.37 E
Catwick, Iles- 25 Lg 10.00N 109.00 E
Catwright 39 Nd 53.50N 56.45W
Čatyrkël, Ozero- 18 Jd 40.35N 75.20 E
Čatyrtaš 18 Kd 40.52N 76.23 E
Cauca 54 Cc 2.30N 77.00W
Cauca, Río- 52 Ie 8.54N 74.28W
Caucasia 54 Cb 7.59N 75.13W
Caucasus (EN)=Kavkaz, Bolšoj- 5 Kg 42.30N 45.00 E
Caucete 56 Gd 31.38S 68.16W
Caudebec-en-Caux 12 Ce 49.32N 0.44 E
Caudete 13 Lf 38.42N 0.59W
Caudry 11 Jd 50.08N 3.25 E
Caulonia 14 Kl 38.23N 16.24 E
Caumont-l'Eventé 12 Be 49.05N 0.48W
Caungula 31 Ii 8.26S 18.37 E
Čaunskaja Guba 20 Lc 69.30N 170.00 E
Caupolican 54 Ef 13.30S 68.30W
Cauquenes 56 Fe 35.58S 72.21W
Caura, Río- 52 Je 7.38N 64.53W
Causapscal 44 Na 48.22N 67.14W
Caussade 11 Hj 44.10N 1.32 E
Čausy 16 Gc 53.50N 30.59 E
Cauterets 11 Fl 42.53N 0.07W
Cauto, Río- 49 Ic 20.33N 77.15W
Cauvery 21 Jh 11.09N 78.52 E
Caux, Pays de- 11 Ge 49.40N 0.40 E
Cávado 13 Dc 41.32N 8.48W
Cavaillon 11 Lk 43.50N 5.02 E
Cavalcante 55 Ia 13.48S 47.30W
Cavalese 14 Fd 46.17N 11.27 E
Cavalli Islands 62 Ea 35.00S 173.55 E
Cavallo, Isola- 11a Bb 41.22N 9.16 E
Cavallo Pass 45 Hl 28.25N 96.26W
Cavally 30 Gh 4.22N 7.32W
Cavan/An Cabhán 9 Fg 54.00N 7.21W
Cavan/An Cabhán 9 Fh 53.55N 7.30W
Cavarzere 14 Ge 45.08N 12.05 E
Çavdarhisar 15 Mj 39.12N 29.37 E
Çavdir 15 Ml 37.09N 29.42 E
Caviana, Ilha- 54 Hc 0.10N 50.05W
Cavili 26 He 9.17N 120.50 E
Cavour, Canale- 14 Be 45.11N 7.54 E
Cavtat 14 Mh 42.35N 18.13 E
Caxambu 55 Je 21.59S 44.56W
Caxias 53 Lf 4.50S 43.21W
Caxias do Sul 53 Kh 29.10S 51.11W
Caxito 36 Bd 8.34S 13.40 E
Çay 24 Dc 38.35N 31.02 E
Cayambe 54 Cc 0.05N 78.08W
Cayambe, Volcán- 52 Ie 0.02N 77.59W
Cayastá 55 Bj 31.12S 60.10W
Cayce 44 Gi 33.59N 81.04W
Çaycuma 24 Eb 41.25N 32.05 E
Çayeli 24 Ib 41.05N 40.44 E
Cayenne 53 Ke 4.56N 52.20W
Cayeux-Sur-Mer 12 Dd 50.11N 1.29 E
Cayey 49 Nd 18.07N 66.10W
Çayırlı 24 Ic 39.48N 40.01 E
Çaykara 24 Ib 40.45N 40.19 E
Caylus 11 Hj 44.14N 1.47 E
Cayman Brac 47 Ie 19.43N 79.49W
Cayman Islands 39 Kh 19.30N 80.30W
Cayman Islands 38 Kh 19.30N 80.30W
Cayman Ridge (EN) 47 He 19.30N 80.30W
Cayman Trench (EN) 3 Bh 19.00N 80.00W
Cayo 49 Ce 17.10N 88.50W
Cayon 51c Ab 17.21N 62.43W
Cayones, Cayos- 49 Fe 16.05N 83.12W
Cay Sal Bank 47 Hd 23.45N 80.00W
Cayuga Lake 44 Id 42.45N 76.45W
Cazalla de la Sierra 13 Gg 37.56N 5.45W
Caza Pava 55 Di 28.17S 56.07W
Cazaux, Étang de- 11 Ej 44.29N 1.10W
Cazombo 31 Jj 11.54S 22.53 E
Cazorla 13 Jg 37.55N 3.00W
Cazorla, Sierra de- 13 Jf 37.55N 2.55W
Cea 13 Gb 42.00N 5.36W
Ceahlău 15 Ib 47.03N 25.58 E
Ceanannas Mór/Kells 9 Gh 53.44N 6.53W
Ceanna Cailllighe/Hags Head 9 Di 52.57N 9.28W
Ceann Acla/Achill Head 9 Ch 53.59N 10.13W
Ceann an Chairn/Carnsore Point 9 Gi 52.10N 6.22W
Ceann Chill Mhantáin/ Wicklow Head 9 Hi 52.58N 6.00W
Ceann Gólaim/Slyne Head 9 Ch 53.24N 10.13W
Ceann Iorrais/Erris Head 5 Fe 54.19N 10.00W
Ceann Léime/Loop Head 9 Di 52.34N 9.56W
Ceann Ros Eoghain/Rossan Point 9 Eg 54.42N 8.48W
Ceann Sléibhe/Slea Head 9 Ci 52.06N 10.27W
Ceann Toirc/Kanturk 9 Ei 52.10N 8.55W
Ceará 54 Kd 5.00S 39.30W
Ceará-Mirim 54 Ke 5.38S 35.26W
Ceatharlach/Carlow 9 Gi 52.50N 7.00W
Ceatharlach/Carlow 9 Gi 52.50N 6.55W
Cébaco, Isla- 49 Gj 7.32N 81.09W
Ceballos 48 Gd 26.32N 104.09W
Čebarkul 17 Ji 54.58N 60.25 E
Čeboksary 6 Kd 56.09N 47.15 E
Cebollati 55 Fk 33.16S 53.47W
Cebollati, Río- 55 Fk 33.09S 53.38W
Cebollera, Sierra- 13 Jc 42.00N 2.40W
Ceboruco, Volcán- 48 Gg 21.09N 104.30W
Cebreros 13 Hd 40.27N 4.28W
Cebrikovo 15 Nb 47.09N 30.02 E
Cebu 21 Oh 10.20N 123.45 E
Cebu 22 Oh 10.18N 123.54 E
Cece 10 Oj 46.46N 18.39 E
Čečen, Ostrov- 16 Og 44.00N 47.45 E
Čečeno-Ingušskaja ASSR 19 Eg 43.15N 45.30 E
Cecen-Ula 27 Gb 48.45N 95.55 E
Cecerleg 22 Me 47.30N 101.27 E
Čečersk 16 Gc 52.56N 30.58 E
Čechy=Bohemia (EN) 5 Hf 50.00N 14.30 E
Čechy=Bohemia (EN) 10 Kf 50.00N 14.30 E
Cecina 14 Eg 43.18N 10.29 E
Cecina 14 Eg 43.10N 10.31 E
Čečuisk 20 Fe 58.07N 108.32 E
Cedar City 39 Hf 37.41N 113.04W
Cedar Creek 46 Fc 46.07N 101.18W
Cedar Creek Reservoir 45 Hj 32.20N 96.10W
Cedar Falls 43 Ic 42.32N 92.27W
Cedar Grove 51d Bb 17.10N 61.49W
Cedar Lake 42 Hf 53.25N 100.00W
Cedar Rapids 39 Je 41.59N 91.40W
Cedar River [Nb.-U.S.] 45 Hf 41.22N 97.57W
Cedar River [U.S.] 43 Ic 41.17N 91.20W
Cedartown 44 Eh 34.01N 85.15W
Cedar-Tree Point 51d Ba 17.42N 61.53W
Cedeira 13 Da 43.39N 8.03W
Cedral 48 If 23.48N 100.44W
Cedrino 14 Dj 40.23N 9.44 E
Cedro 54 Ke 6.36S 39.03W
Cedrón 13 Ie 39.48N 3.33W
Cedros, Isla- [Mex.] 47 Ac 28.12N 115.15W
Cedros, Isla [Mex.]=Cedros Island (EN) 38 Hg 28.10N 115.15W
Cedros Island (EN)=Cedros, Isla [Mex.] 38 Hg 28.10N 115.15W
Cedros Trench (EN) 47 Ac 27.45N 115.45W
Ceduna 59 Gf 32.07S 133.40 E
Cedynia 10 Kd 52.50N 14.14 E
Cefalù 14 Il 38.02N 14.01 E
Cega 13 Hc 41.33N 4.46W
Čegdomyn 22 Pd 51.07N 133.05 E
Čegem 16 Mh 43.36N 43.48 E
Cegléd 10 Pi 47.10N 19.48 E
Ceglie Messapico 14 Lj 40.39N 17.31 E
Cehegín 13 Kf 38.06N 1.48W
Cehotina 15 Bf 43.31N 18.45 E
Čehov [R.S.F.S.R.] 7 Ii 55.11N 37.29 E
Čehov [R.S.F.S.R.] 20 Jg 47.24N 142.05 E
Ceica 15 Fc 46.51N 22.11 E
Çekerek 24 Fb 40.34N 35.46 E
Çekerek 24 Fb 40.04N 35.31 E
Čekmaguš 17 Gi 55.10N 54.40 E
Cela 36 Ce 11.25S 15.07 E
Celano 14 Hh 42.05N 13.33 E
Celaya 47 Dd 20.31N 100.37W
Čelbas 16 Kf 46.06N 38.59 E
Célé 11 Hj 44.28N 1.38 E
Celebes/Sulawesi 21 Oj 2.00S 121.10 E
Celebes Basin (EN) 26 Hf 4.00N 122.00 E
Celebes Sea (EN)= Sulawesi, Laut- 21 Oj 3.00N 122.00 E
Čeleken 19 Fh 39.27N 53.10 E
Čeleken, Poluostrov- 16 Rj 39.25N 53.35 E
Celendín 54 Ce 6.52S 78.09W
Celerain, Punta- 48 Pg 20.16N 86.59W
Celeste 55 Dj 31.18S 57.04W
Celestún 48 Ng 20.52N 90.24W
Celinograd 22 Jd 51.10N 71.30 E
Celinogradskaja Oblast 19 Gh 51.00N 70.00 E
Čeljabinsk 22 Id 55.10N 61.24 E
Čeljabinskaja Oblast 19 Ge 54.00N 61.00 E
Celje 14 Jd 46.14N 15.16 E
Čeljuskin, Mys- 21 Mb 77.45N 104.20 E
Čelkar 19 Ff 47.50N 59.29 E
Celldömölk 10 Ni 47.15N 17.09 E
Celle 10 Gd 52.37N 10.05 E
Celles 12 Fd 50.43N 3.27 E
Celles, Houyet- 12 Hd 50.19N 5.01 E
Cellina 14 Ge 46.02N 12.47 E
Celone 14 Ji 41.36N 15.41 E
Celorico da Beira 13 Ed 40.38N 7.23W
Celtic Sea 5 Fe 51.00N 7.00W
Celtic Sea (EN)=An Mhuir Cheilteach 5 Fe 51.00N 7.00W
Cemaes Head 9 Ii 52.07N 4.44W
Čemal 20 Df 51.25N 86.05 E
Čemdalsk 20 Fe 59.45N 103.18 E
Cemernica 14 Lf 44.30N 17.15 E
Cemerno 15 Df 43.36N 20.26 E
Çemişkezek 24 Hc 39.04N 38.55 E
Cenajo, Embalse de- 13 Kf 38.20N 1.55W
Cenderawasih, Teluk- 26 Kg 2.25S 135.10 E
Cengel 27 Eb 48.56N 89.10 E
Çengel Geçidi 24 Kc 39.45N 44.02 E
Ceno 14 Ef 44.41N 10.05 E
Centenary 37 Ec 16.44S 31.07 E
Centennial 46 Lf 41.51N 106.07W
Centennial Lake 44 Ic 45.15N 77.00W
Centennial Mountains 46 Jd 44.35N 111.55W
Center 45 Ik 31.48N 94.11W
Center Hill Lake 44 Eg 36.00N 85.45W
Centerville 45 Jf 40.43N 92.52W
Centinela, Farallón- 50 Cg 10.49N 66.05W
Centinela, Picacho del- 47 Dc 29.07N 102.27W
Cento 14 Ff 44.43N 11.17 E
Centrafrique=Central African Republic (EN) 31 Jh 7.00N 21.00 E
Central [Bots.] 37 Dd 21.30S 26.00 E
Central [Ghana] 34 Ed 5.30N 1.00W
Central [Kenya] 36 Gc 0.45S 37.00 E
Central [Mwi.] 36 Fe 13.30S 34.00 E
Central [Par.] 55 Dg 25.30S 57.30W
Central [Scot.-U.K.] 9 Ie 56.15N 4.10W
Central [Ug.] 36 Fb 0.10N 32.05 E
Central [Zam.] 36 Ee 15.00S 29.00 E
Central, Chaco- 52 Kh 25.00S 59.45W
Central, Cordillera- [Dom.Rep.] 47 Je 18.45N 70.30W
Central, Cordillera- [P.R.] 49 Nd 18.10N 66.35W
Central, Massif- 5 Gf 45.00N 3.10 E
Central, Meseta- 38 Ig 23.00N 103.00W
Central African Republic (EN)=Centrafrique 31 Jh 7.00N 21.00 E
Central Auckland 62 Fb 36.45S 174.40 E
Central Brāhui Range 25 Dc 29.20N 66.55 E
Central City 45 Hf 41.07N 98.00W
Centralia [Il.-U.S.] 45 Lg 38.31N 89.08W
Centralia [Wa.-U.S.] 43 Cb 46.43N 122.58W
Central Lowland 38 Ke 40.20N 90.00W
Central Makrān Range 21 Ig 26.40N 64.30 E
Centralno Tungusskoje Plato 20 Fd 61.15N 102.00 E
Centralny-Kospašski 17 Hg 59.03N 57.50 E
Central Pacific Basin (EN) 3 Ki 5.00N 175.00W
Central Plateau 64e Bb 0.32S 166.56 E
Central Point 46 De 42.23N 122.57W
Central Range 57 Fe 5.00S 142.30 E
Central Russian Uplands (EN)=Srednerusskaja Vozvyšennost 5 Je 52.00N 38.00 E
Central Siberian Uplands (EN)=Srednesibirskoje Ploskogorje 21 Mc 65.00N 105.00 E
Central Urals (EN)=Sredni Ural 5 Ld 58.00N 59.00 E
Centre [Togo] 34 Fd 9.15N 1.00 E
Centre [U.V.] 34 Ec 12.00N 1.00W
Centre, Canal du- 11 Jh 46.28N 3.59 E
Centre-Est 34 Ec 11.30N 0.20W
Centre-Nord 34 Ec 13.20N 0.55W
Centre-Ouest 34 Ec 12.00N 2.20W
Centre-Sud 34 He 3.30N 11.50 E
Centro, Cayo- 48 Ph 18.35N 87.20W
Centuripe 14 Im 37.37N 14.44 E
Čepca 19 Fd 58.35N 50.05 E
Cepelare 15 Hh 41.44N 24.41 E
Cephalonia (EN)= Kefallinía 5 Ih 38.15N 20.35 E
Čepin 14 Me 45.32N 18.34 E
Ceplenița 15 Jb 47.23N 26.58 E
Cepu 26 Fh 7.09S 111.35 E
Cer 15 Ce 44.37N 19.28 E
Ceram Sea (EN)=Seram, Laut- 57 De 2.30S 128.00 E
Cerbatana, Serranía de la- 54 Eb 6.50N 66.15W
Cerbicales, Iles- 11a Bb 41.33N 9.22 E
Cercal 13 Dg 37.47N 8.40W
Čerchov 10 Rg 49.10N 21.05 E
Čerdakly 7 Li 54.23N 48.51 E
Čerdyn 17 Hf 60.25N 56.29 E
Cère 11 Hj 44.55N 1.49 E
Čereha 7 Gh 57.47N 28.22 E
Čeremhovo 22 Md 53.09N 103.05 E
Čerepanovo 20 Df 54.13N 83.32 E
Čerepovec 6 Jd 59.08N 37.54 E
Ceres [Arg.] 56 Hc 29.53S 61.57W
Ceres [Braz.] 54 Ig 15.17S 49.35W
Ceres [S.Afr.] 37 Bf 33.21S 19.18 E
Céret 11 Il 42.29N 2.45 E
Cereté 54 Cb 8.53N 75.47W
Cerf Island 30 Mi 9.31S 51.01 E
Cerfontaine 12 Gd 50.10N 4.25 E
Cergy 12 Ee 49.02N 2.04 E
Cerignola 14 Ji 41.16N 15.54 E
Čerikov 16 Gc 53.35N 31.25 E
Cérilly 11 Ih 46.37N 2.50 E
Čerkasskaja Oblast 19 Df 49.15N 31.15 E
Čerkassy 19 Df 49.26N 32.04 E
Çerkeş 24 Eb 40.50N 32.54 E
Čerkessk 19 Eg 44.14N 42.04 E
Çerkezköy 15 Kh 41.17N 28.00 E
Čerlak 19 He 54.09N 74.58 E
Čerlakski 19 He 53.47N 74.31 E
Čermasan 17 Gi 55.10N 55.20 E
Cermei 15 Ec 46.33N 21.51 E
Čermenika 15 Dh 41.03N 20.20 E
Čermoz 17 Hg 58.47N 56.10 E
Cerna [Rom.] 15 Ge 44.37N 23.57 E
Cerna [Rom.] 15 Fd 44.42N 22.25 E
Cerna [Rom.] 15 Fe 45.53N 22.58 E
Černaja 17 Hb 68.35N 56.31 E
Černaja [R.S.F.S.R.] 17 Hb 68.35N 56.30 E
Černaja [Ukr.-U.S.S.R.] 15 Mb 47.39N 29.11 E
Černa Skala, Prohod- 15 Fg 42.02N 22.47 E
Černatica 15 Hh 41.53N 24.33 E
Černavčicy 10 Td 52.11N 23.47 E
Cernavoda 15 Le 44.22N 28.01 E
Cernay 11 Ng 47.49N 7.10 E
Cernay-en-Dormois 12 Ge 49.13N 4.46 E
Černevo 8 Mf 58.35N 28.23 E
Černigov 6 Je 51.30N 31.18 E
Černigovskaja Oblast 19 De 51.20N 32.00 E
Černi Lom 15 If 43.33N 25.57 E
Černi vrăh 15 Gg 42.35N 23.15 E
Černjahovsk 19 Ce 54.38N 21.48 E
Černjanka 16 Jd 50.55N 37.49 E
Černobyl 19 De 51.17N 30.13 E
Černogorsk 20 Ef 53.45N 91.18 E
Černoje More=Black Sea (EN) 5 Jg 43.00N 35.00 E
Černo More=Black Sea (EN) 5 Jg 43.00N 35.00 E
Černomorskoje 16 Hg 45.31N 32.42 E
Černovcy 6 If 48.18N 25.56 E
Černovickaja Oblast 19 Cf 48.20N 26.10 E
Černuška 19 Fd 56.31N 56.03 E
Černy Jar 16 Oe 48.03N 46.05 E
Černyje Zemli 16 Nf 45.55N 46.00 E
Černyševa, Grjada- 17 Ic 66.20N 59.45 E
Černyševa, Zaliv- 18 Bb 45.50N 59.10 E
Černyševsk 20 Gf 52.35N 117.02 E
Černyševski 20 Gd 62.58N 112.15 E
Černyškovski 16 Me 48.27N 42.14 E
Cérou 11 Hj 44.08N 1.52 E
Cerralvo 48 Jd 26.06N 99.37W
Cerralvo, Isla- 47 Cd 24.15N 109.55W
Cerredo, Torre de- 13 Ha 43.13N 4.50W
Cerriku 15 Ch 41.02N 19.57 E
Cerrito [Col.] 54 Db 6.51N 72.42W
Cerrito [Par.] 55 Dh 27.19S 57.40W
Cerritos 47 Dd 22.26N 100.17W
Cerro Azul 48 Kg 21.12N 97.44W
Cêrro Azul 56 Kb 24.50S 49.15W
Cerro Chato 55 Ek 33.06S 55.08W
Cerro Colorado 55 Ek 33.52S 55.33W
Cerro de las Mesas 48 Kh 18.47N 96.05W
Cerro de Pasco 53 Ig 10.41S 76.16W
Cêrro Grande 55 Gj 30.36S 51.45W
Cerro Largo 56 Jc 28.09S 54.45W
Cerro Largo 55 Ek 32.20S 54.20W
Cerron, Cerro- 49 Lh 10.19N 70.39W
Cerro San Valentín 52 Ij 46.36S 73.20W
Cerros Colorados, Embalse- 56 Ge 38.35S 68.40W
Cerro Vera 55 Dk 33.11S 57.28W
Cerrudo Cué 55 Dh 27.34S 57.57W
Čerski 22 Sc 68.45N 161.45 E
Čerskogo, Hrebet- [R.S.F.S.R.] 20 Gf 52.00N 114.00 E
Čerskogo, Hrebet- [R.S.F.S.R.]=Cherski Mountains (EN) 21 Qc 65.00N 145.00 E

Index Symbols

Independent Nation
State, Region
District, County
Municipality
Colony, Dependency
Continent
Physical Region
Historical or Cultural Region
Mount, Mountain
Volcano
Hill
Mountains, Mountain Range
Hills, Escarpment
Plateau, Upland
Pass, Gap
Plain, Lowland
Delta
Salt Flat
Valley, Canyon
Crater, Cave
Karst Features
Depression
Polder
Desert, Dunes
Forest, Woods
Heath, Steppe
Oasis
Cape, Point
Coast, Beach
Cliff
Peninsula
Isthmus
Sandbank
Island
Atoll
Rock, Reef
Islands, Archipelago
Rocks, Reefs
Coral Reef
Well, Spring
Geyser
River, Stream
Waterfall Rapids
River Mouth, Estuary
Lake
Salt Lake
Intermittent Lake
Reservoir
Swamp, Pond
Canal
Glacier
Ice Shelf, Pack Ice
Ocean
Sea
Gulf, Bay
Strait, Fjord
Lagoon
Bank
Seamount
Tablemount
Ridge
Shelf
Basin
Escarpment, Sea Scarp
Fracture
Trench, Abyss
National Park, Reserve
Point of Interest
Recreation Site
Cave, Cavern
Historic Site
Ruins
Wall, Walls
Church, Abbey
Temple
Scientific Station
Airport
Port
Lighthouse
Mine
Tunnel
Dam, Bridge

Certaldo 14 Fg 43.33N 11.02 E
Čertkovo 16 Le 49.20N 40.12 E
Cervaro 14 Ji 41.30N 15.52 E
Cervati 14 Jj 40.17N 15.29 E
Červeh 15 Jf 43.37N 26.02 E
Červen 16 Fc 53.43N 28.29 E
Červen brjag 15 Hf 43.16N 24.06 E
Cervera 13 Nc 41.40N 1.17 E
Cervera del Río Alhama 13 Kb 42.01N 1.57W
Cervera de Pisuerga 13 Hb 42.52N 4.30W
Cerveteri 14 Gh 42.00N 12.06 E
Cervia 14 Gf 44.15N 12.22 E
Cervin/Cervino 14 Be 45.58N 7.39 E
Cervino/Cervin 14 Be 45.58N 7.39 E
Cervione 11a Ba 42.20N 9.29 E
Červonoarmejsk 10 Vf 50.03N 25.18 E
Červonoarmejskoje 15 Ld 45.50N 28.38 E
Červonograd 19 Ce 50.24N 24.12 E
Cesano 14 Hg 43.45N 13.10 E
Cesar 54 Db 9.50N 73.30W
César, Rio- 49 Ki 9.00N 73.58W
Cesena 14 Gf 44.08N 12.15 E
Cesenatico 14 Gf 44.12N 12.24 E
Cēsis/Cesis 19 Cd 57.18N 25.18 E
Cesis/Cēsis 19 Cd 57.18N 25.18 E
Česká Lípa 10 Kf 50.42N 14.32 E
Česká Třebová 10 Mg 49.54N 16.27 E
České Budějovice 10 Kh 48.58N 14.29 E
České středohoří 10 Jf 50.35N 14.00 E
České země 10 Kg 49.45N 15.00 E
Českomoravská Vrchovina= Moravian Upland (EN) 5 Hf 49.20N 15.30 E
Československá Socialistická Republika (ČSSR) 6 Hf 49.30N 17.00 E
Československo= Czechoslovakia (EN) 6 Hf 49.30N 17.00 E
Český Krumlov 10 Kh 48.49N 14.19 E
Český Les=Bohemian Forest (EN) 10 Ig 49.50N 12.30 E
Cesma 14 Kf 45.35N 16.29 E
Česma 17 Jj 53.50N 60.40 E
Çeşme 24 Bc 38.18N 26.19 E
Çeşme Yarimadasi 15 Jk 38.30N 26.30 E
Češskaja Guba=Chesha Bay (EN) 5 Kb 67.20N 46.30 E
Cessnock 59 Kf 32.50S 151.21 E
Cestos 30 Gh 5.27N 9.35W
Cesvaine/Cesvajne 8 Lh 56.55N 26.20 E
Cesvajne/Cesvaine 8 Lh 56.55N 26.20 E
Cetate 15 Ge 44.06N 23.03 E
Cetina 14 Kg 43.27N 16.42 E
Cetinje 15 Bg 42.24N 18.55 E
Çetinkaya 24 Gc 39.15N 37.38 E
Cetraro 14 Jk 39.31N 15.56 E
Cetynia 10 Sd 52.33N 22.26 E
Ceuta 31 Ge 35.53N 5.19W
Ceva-i-Ra (Conway Reef) 57 Ig 21.45S 174.35 E
Cevedale/Zufallspitze 14 Ed 46.27N 10.37 E
Cévennes 5 Gg 44.40N 4.00 E
Ceyhan 23 Eb 36.45N 35.42 E
Ceyhan 23 Eb 37.04N 35.47 E
Ceylanpınar 24 Id 36.51N 40.02 E
Ceylon 21 Ki 7.30N 80.30 E
Ceylon→Srī Lanka 22 Ki 7.40N 80.50 E
Cézallier 11 Ii 45.20N 3.00 E
Cèze 11 Kj 44.06N 4.42 E
Chaalis, Abbaye de- 12 Ee 49.10N 2.40 E
Cha-am 25 Jf 12.48N 99.58 E
Chabanais 11 Gi 45.52N 0.43 E
Chabjuwardoo Bay 59 Cd 22.55S 113.50 E
Chablais 11 Mh 46.20N 6.30 E
Chăboksar 24 Nd 36.58N 50.34 E
Chabówka 10 Pg 49.34N 19.58 E
Chacabuco 56 Hd 34.38S 60.29W
Chachan, Nevado- 54 Dg 16.12S 71.33W
Chachapoyas 54 Ce 6.13S 77.51W
Chachoengsao 25 Kf 13.41N 101.03 E
Chaco 56 Hc 26.00S 60.30W
Chaco 55 Bd 20.00S 60.30W
Chaco, Gran- 52 Jh 23.00S 60.00W
Chaco Mesa 45 Ci 35.50N 107.35W
Chaco River 45 Bh 36.46N 108.39W
Chad (EN)=Tchad 31 Ig 15.00N 19.00 E
Chad, Lake- (EN)=Tchad, Lac- 30 Ig 13.20N 14.00 E
Chādegān 24 Nf 32.46N 50.38 E
Chadileuvú, Rio- 56 Ee 38.49S 64.57W
Chadiza 36 Fe 14.04S 32.26 E
Chadron 43 Gc 42.50N 103.02W
Chaeryŏng 28 He 38.24N 125.37 E
Chafarinas, Islas- 13 Ji 35.11N 2.26W
Chāgai Hills 21 Ig 29.30N 64.15 E
Chagang-Do 28 Ie 40.50N 126.30 E
Chaghcharān 22 If 34.31N 65.15 E
Chagny 11 Kh 46.55N 4.45 E
Chagos Archipelago 21 Jj 6.00S 72.00 E
Chagos-Laccadive Plateau (EN) 3 Gi 3.00N 73.00 E
Chagu, Serra do- 55 Fg 25.10S 52.40W
Chaguaramas 50 Ch 9.20N 66.16W
Chahār Borjak 23 Jc 30.17N 62.03 E
Chāh Bahār 23 Jd 25.18N 60.37 E
Chahbounia 13 Oi 35.33N 2.36 E
Ch'aho 28 Jd 40.12N 128.38 E
Chai Badan 25 Ke 15.05N 101.04 E
Chaibāsa 25 Hd 22.34N 85.49 E
Chaigoubu → Huai'an 28 Cd 40.40N 114.25 E
Chai He 28 Gc 42.20N 123.51 E
Chaillu, Massif du- 30 Ii 2.32S 11.10 E
Chainat 25 Ke 15.10N 100.10 E
Chaitén 56 Ff 42.55S 72.43W
Chaiyaphum 25 Ke 16.09N 102.02 E
Chajul 49 Bf 15.30N 91.02W
Chakari 37 Dc 18.09S 29.52 E
Chak Chak 35 Dd 8.40N 26.54 E
Chake Chake 31 Ki 5.15S 39.46 E
Chakhānsūr 23 Jc 31.10N 62.04 E
Chala 54 Dg 15.52S 74.16W
Chalais 11 Gi 45.17N 0.02 E
Chalaltenango 49 Cf 14.03N 88.56W
Chalan Kanoa 64b Ba 15.08N 145.43 E
Chālās 22 Gf 37.16N 49.36 E
Chalbi Desert 30 Kh 3.00N 37.20 E
Chalchuapa 49 Cg 13.59N 89.41W
Chalcidice (EN)= Khalkidhiki 5 Ig 40.25N 23.25 E
Chālesbān 24 Ne 35.18N 50.03 E
Chaleur Bay 42 Kg 47.50N 65.30W
Chalhuanca 54 Df 14.17S 73.15W
Chaling 27 Jf 26.47N 113.32 E
Chalky Inlet 62 Bg 46.05S 166.30 E
Challans 11 Eh 46.51N 1.53W
Challapata 54 Eg 18.54S 66.47W
Challis 46 Hd 44.30N 114.14W
Chalmette 45 Ll 29.56N 89.58W
Châlons-sur-Marne 11 Kf 48.57N 4.22 E
Chalon-sur-Saône 11 Kh 46.47N 4.51 E
Chaltubo 16 Mh 42.19N 42.34 E
Chālūs 23 Hb 36.38N 51.26 E
Châlus 11 Gi 45.39N 0.59 E
Cham 10 Ig 49.13N 12.40 E
Chama 36 Fe 11.12S 33.10 E
Chama, Rio- 45 Ch 36.03N 106.05W
Chama, Rio- 49 Li 9.03N 71.37W
Chaman 25 Db 30.55N 66.27 E
Chaman Bīd 24 Qd 37.25N 56.38 E
Chamba [India] 25 Fb 32.34N 76.08 E
Chamba [Tan.] 36 Ge 11.35S 36.58 E
Chambal 21 Jg 26.29N 79.15 E
Chambaran, Plateau de- 11 Li 45.10N 5.20 E
Chambas 49 Hb 22.12N 78.55W
Chamberlain 43 Hc 43.49N 99.20W
Chamberlain Lake 44 Mb 46.17N 69.20W
Chamberlain River 59 Fc 15.35S 127.51 E
Chambersburg 44 If 39.57N 77.40W
Chambéry 11 Li 45.34N 5.56 E
Chambeshi 30 Jj 11.53S 29.48 E
Chambley-Bussières 12 He 49.03N 5.54 E
Chambly 12 Ee 49.10N 2.15 E
Chambois 12 Cf 48.48N 0.07 E
Chambon, Lac de- 11 Ih 45.35N 2.55 E
Chambord 11 Hg 47.37N 1.31 E
Chamchamal 24 Ke 35.32N 44.50 E
Chame, Punta- 49 Hi 8.39N 79.42W
Chamela 48 Gh 19.32N 105.05W
Chamela, Bahía- 48 Gh 19.30N 105.10W
Chamelecón, Río- 49 Df 15.51N 87.49W
Chamical 56 Gd 30.21S 66.19W
Chamiss Bay 46 Ba 50.07N 127.22W
Chamoli 25 Fb 30.24N 79.21 E
Chamonix-Mont-Blanc 11 Mi 45.55N 6.52 E
Chamouchouane, Rivière- 44 Ka 48.40N 72.20W
Champagne 5 Gf 49.00N 4.30 E
Champagne 11 Kf 49.00N 4.30 E
Champagne Berrichonne 11 Hh 47.00N 2.00 E
Champagne Humide 11 Kf 48.20N 4.30 E
Champagne Pouilleuse 11 Kf 48.40N 4.20 E
Champagnole 11 Lh 46.45N 5.55 E
Champaign 43 Jc 40.07N 88.14W
Champaqui, Cerro- 52 Ji 31.59S 64.56W
Champasak 25 Lf 14.53N 105.52 E
Champaubert 12 Ff 48.53N 3.47 E
Champdoré, Lac- 42 Ke 55.55N 65.45W
Champeigne 11 Gg 47.15N 0.50 E
Champerico 49 Bf 14.18N 91.55W
Champlain, Lake- 43 Mc 44.45N 73.15W
Champlitte-et-le-Prélot 11 Lg 47.37N 5.31 E
Champotón 47 Fe 19.21N 90.43W
Champsaur 11 Mj 44.45N 6.10 E
Chāmrājnagar 25 Ff 11.55N 76.57 E
Chañaral 56 Fc 26.21S 70.37W
Chança 13 Eg 37.33N 7.31W
Chan Chan 54 Ce 8.07S 79.02W
Chanco 56 Fe 35.44S 72.32W
Chandalar 40 Jc 66.36N 145.48W
Chandalar 40 Jc 67.30N 148.30W
Chandausi 25 Fc 28.27N 78.46 E
Chandeleur Islands 43 Jf 29.48N 88.51W
Chandeleur Sound 45 Ll 29.55N 89.10W
Chandīgarh 22 Jf 30.44N 76.55 E
Chandler 42 Lg 48.21N 64.41W
Chandless, Rio 54 Ee 9.08S 69.51W
Chāndpur 25 Id 23.13N 90.39 E
Chandragupta 25 Fe 16.11N 78.52 E
Chandrapur 22 Jh 19.57N 79.18 E
Chang, Ko- 25 Kf 12.00N 102.23 E
Changajn Nuruu → Hangaj, Hrebet-=Khangai Mountains (EN) 21 Le 47.30N 100.00 E
Chang'an → Rong'an 27 If 25.16N 109.23 E
Changane 30 Kk 24.43S 33.32 E
Changbai 28 Jd 41.25N 128.11 E
Changbai Shan 21 Oe 42.00N 128.00 E
Changchun 22 Oe 43.51N 125.20 E
Changdao(Sihou) 28 Ff 37.56N 120.42 E
Changde 22 Ng 29.04N 111.42 E
Ch'angdo 28 Ie 38.30N 127.45 E
Changfeng (Shuijiahu) 28 Dh 32.29N 117.10 E
Changge 28 Bg 34.12N 113.45 E
Changhang 28 If 36.01N 126.42 E
Chang He 28 Ei 31.21N 118.21 E
Changhowŏn 28 If 37.07N 127.38 E
Changhua 27 Lg 24.05N 120.32 E
Changhŭng 28 Ig 34.40N 126.54 E
Changji 27 Ec 44.01N 87.16 E
Chang Jiang 28 Dj 28.59N 116.42 E
Changjiang (Shiliu) 27 Ih 19.20N 109.03 E
Chang Jiang (Yangtze Kiang) 21 Of 31.48N 121.10 E
Changjiang Kou 27 Le 31.24N 121.59 E
Changjin-gang 28 Id 40.30N 127.12 E
Changjin-ho 28 Id 40.30N 127.12 E
Changjin-ŭp 27 Mc 40.23N 127.15 E
Changli 28 Ee 39.43N 119.10 E
Changling 27 Lc 44.15N 123.58 E
Changlung 25 Fb 34.56N 77.29 E
Changping 28 Dd 40.14N 116.13 E
Changsha 22 Ng 28.12N 113.02 E
Changshan 28 Ej 28.55N 118.31 E
Changshan Qundao 28 Ge 39.10N 122.34 E
Changshu 28 Fi 31.38N 120.44 E
Changsŏng 28 Ig 35.19N 126.48 E
Changting 28 Jb 44.27N 128.50 E
Changtu 28 Hc 42.47N 124.08 E
Changuillo 54 Cf 14.40S 75.12W
Changuinola 49 Fi 9.26N 82.31W
Changwu 27 Id 35.17N 107.52 E
Changxing 28 Ei 31.01N 119.55 E
Changxing Dao 28 Fe 39.35N 121.42 E
Changyi 28 Ef 36.52N 119.25 E
Changyŏn 27 Md 38.15N 125.05 E
Changyuan 28 Cg 35.12N 114.40 E
Changzhi 27 Jd 36.07N 113.10 E
Changzhou 28 Ei 31.46N 119.56 E
Channel Islands 9 Kl 49.20N 2.20W
Channel Islands [Chan.Is.] 5 Ff 49.20N 2.20W
Channel Islands [U.S.] 38 Hf 34.00N 120.00W
Channel Port-aux-Basques 39 Ne 47.35N 59.11W
Channel Rock 49 Ib 23.00N 77.55W
Channing 45 Ei 35.41N 102.20W
Chantada 13 Eb 42.37N 7.46W
Chantengo, Laguna- 48 Ji 16.35N 99.10W
Chanthaburi 25 Kf 12.35N 102.06 E
Chantilly 11 Ie 49.12N 2.28 E
Chantonnay 11 Eh 46.41N 1.03W
Chantrey Inlet 38 Jc 67.48N 96.20W
Chanute 45 Ih 37.41N 95.27W
Chanza 13 Eg 37.33N 7.31W
Chao'an (Chaozhou) 27 Kg 23.41N 116.37 E
Chaobai Xinhe 28 De 39.07N 117.41 E
Chao He 28 Dd 40.36N 117.08 E
Chao Hu 28 Di 31.31N 117.33 E
Chao Phraya 21 Mh 13.32N 100.36 E
Chaor He 27 Lb 46.49N 123.45 E
Chaoxian 27 Ke 31.37N 117.49 E
Chaoyang [China] 22 Oe 41.35N 120.26 E
Chaoyang [China] 27 Kg 23.17N 116.37 E
Chaoyang → Huinan 28 Ic 42.41N 126.03 E
Chaoyang → Jiayin 27 Nb 48.52N 130.21 E
Chaoyangchuan 28 Jc 42.53N 129.23 E
Chaoyangcun 27 La 50.01N 124.22 E
Chaozhong 27 La 50.53N 121.23 E
Chaozhou → Chao'an 27 Kg 23.41N 116.37 E
Chapada dos Guimarães 54 Gg 15.26S 55.45W
Chapadinha 54 Jd 3.44S 43.21W
Chapais 44 Ja 49.47N 74.56W
Chapala 48 Hg 20.18N 103.12W
Chapala, Lago de- 38 Ig 20.15N 103.00W
Chaparral 54 Cc 3.43N 75.28W
Chapecó 56 Jc 27.06S 52.36W
Chapecó, Rio- 55 Fh 27.06S 53.01W
Chapecó, Serra do- 55 Gh 26.44S 51.54W
Chapel Hill 44 Hh 35.55N 79.04W
Chapicuy 55 Dj 31.40S 57.55W
Chapleau 42 Jg 47.50N 83.24W
Chaplin 46 La 50.28N 106.40W
Chaplin Lake 46 La 50.18N 106.35W
Chapman, Cape - 42 Ic 69.15N 89.27W
Chappell 45 Ef 41.06N 102.28W
Chāpra 25 Gc 25.46N 84.45 E
Chapultepec 48 Hf 23.27N 103.04W
Chaqui 54 Eg 19.36S 65.32W
Char 32 Ee 21.31N 12.51W
Charadai 55 Ch 27.38S 59.54W
Charagua 54 Fg 19.48S 63.13W
Charām 24 Ng 30.45N 50.44 E
Charaña 54 Eg 17.36S 69.28W
Charcas 48 If 23.08N 101.07W
Charco de la Aguja 48 Gc 28.25N 104.01W
Charcot Island 66 Qe 69.45S 75.15W
Chard [Alta.-Can.] 42 Ge 55.48N 111.10W
Chard [Eng.-U.K.] 9 Kk 50.53N 2.58W
Chardāvol 24 Lf 33.45N 46.38 E
Chardonnières 49 Jd 18.16N 74.10W
Charente 11 Gi 45.40N 0.05 E
Charente 11 Ei 45.57N 1.05W
Charente-Maritime 11 Fi 45.30N 0.45W
Charentonne 12 Ce 49.07N 0.44 E
Chari 30 Ig 12.58N 14.31 E
Chari-Baguirmi 35 Bc 12.00N 17.00 E
Chārīkār 23 Kb 35.01N 69.11 E
Charing 12 Cc 51.12N 0.48 E
Chariton 45 Jf 41.00N 93.19W
Chariton River 45 Jg 39.19N 92.57W
Charity 54 Gb 7.24N 58.36W
Charleroi 11 Kd 50.25N 4.26 E
Charleroi-Jumet 11 Kd 50.27N 4.26 E
Charleroi-Marcinelle 12 Gd 50.25N 4.28 E
Charles 42 Kd 62.38N 74.15W
Charles, Cape- [Can.] 38 Nd 52.13N 55.40W
Charles, Cape- [Va.-U.S.] 43 Ld 37.08N 75.58W
Charles, Peak- 59 Ef 32.52S 121.11 E
Charlesbourg 44 Lb 46.52N 71.16W
Charles City 43 Ic 43.04N 92.40W
Charles de Gaulle, Aéroport- =Charles de Gaulle Airport (EN) 12 Ee 49.02N 2.35 E
Charles de Gaulle Airport (EN)=Charles de Gaulle, Aéroport- 12 Ee 49.02N 2.35 E
Charleston [Il.-U.S.] 45 Lg 39.30N 88.10W
Charleston [Mo.-U.S.] 45 Lh 36.55N 89.21W
Charleston [Ms.-U.S.] 45 Ki 34.01N 90.04W
Charleston [N.Z.] 62 Dd 41.54S 171.27 E
Charleston [S.C.-U.S.] 39 Lf 32.48N 79.57W
Charleston [W.V.-U.S.] 39 Kf 38.21N 81.38W
Charleston Peak 43 Dd 36.16N 115.42W
Charles Town 44 If 39.18N 77.52W
Charlestown 50 Ed 17.12N 62.35W
Charleval 12 De 49.22N 1.23 E
Charleville 58 Fg 26.24S 146.15 E
Charleville-Mézières 11 Ke 49.46N 4.43 E
Charleville Mézières-Mohon 12 Ge 49.46N 4.43 E
Charlevoix 44 Ec 45.19N 85.16W
Charlieu 11 Kh 46.09N 4.11 E
Charlotte [Mi.-U.S.] 44 Ed 42.36N 84.50W
Charlotte [N.C.-U.S.] 39 Kf 35.14N 80.50W
Charlotte Amalie 47 Le 18.21N 64.56W
Charlotte Bank (EN) 57 If 11.47S 173.13 E
Charlotte Harbor 44 Fl 26.45N 82.12W
Charlottenberg 8 Ee 59.53N 12.17 E
Charlottesville 43 Ld 38.02N 78.29W
Charlottetown 39 Me 46.14N 63.08W
Charlton 59 Ig 36.16S 143.21 E
Charlton 42 Jf 52.00N 79.26W
Charly 12 Ff 48.58N 3.17 E
Charmes 11 Mf 48.22N 6.17 E
Charnley River 59 Ec 16.20S 124.53 E
Charny-sur-Meuse 12 He 49.12N 5.22 E
Charollais 11 Kh 46.26N 4.16 E
Charouine 32 Gd 29.01N 0.16W
Charroux 11 Gh 46.09N 0.24 E
Chārsadda 25 Eb 34.09N 71.44 E
Charters Towers 58 Fg 20.05S 146.16 E
Chartres 11 Hf 48.27N 1.30 E
Charzykowskie, Jezioro- 10 Nc 53.47N 17.30 E
Chascomus 56 Ie 35.34S 58.01W
Chase 46 Fa 50.49N 119.41W
Chasŏng 28 Id 41.25N 126.35 E
Chassengue 36 Ce 10.26S 18.32 E
Chassezac 11 Kj 44.26N 4.19 E
Chassiron, Pointe de- 11 Eh 46.03N 1.24W
Chat 24 Pd 37.59N 55.16 E
Châtaigneraie 11 Ij 44.45N 2.20 E
Châtāl 24 Pd 37.40N 55.45 E
Château-Arnoux 11 Lj 44.06N 6.00 E
Châteaubelair 51n Ba 13.17N 61.15W
Châteaubriant 11 Eg 47.43N 1.23W
Château-Chinon 11 Jg 47.04N 3.56 E
Château-du-Loir 11 Gg 47.42N 0.25 E
Châteaudun 11 Hf 48.05N 1.20 E
Château-Gontier 11 Fg 47.50N 0.42W
Châteaulin 11 Bf 48.12N 4.05W
Châteaulin, Bassin de- 11 Cf 48.18N 3.50W
Châteaumeillant 11 Ih 46.34N 2.12 E
Châteauneuf-de-Randon 11 Jj 44.39N 3.04 E
Châteauneuf-sur-Cher 11 Ih 46.51N 2.19 E
Châteauneuf-sur-Loire 11 Ig 47.52N 2.14 E
Château-Porcien 12 Ge 49.32N 4.15 E
Châteaurenard 11 Kk 43.53N 4.51 E
Château-Renault 11 Gg 47.35N 0.54 E
Châteauroux 11 Hh 46.49N 1.42 E
Château-Salins 11 Mf 48.49N 6.30 E
Château-Thierry 11 Je 49.03N 3.24 E
Châteaux, Pointe des- 51e Bb 16.15N 61.11W
Châtelaillon-Plage 11 Eh 46.04N 1.05W
Châtelet 12 Gd 50.24N 4.31 E
Châtelguyon 11 Ji 45.55N 3.04 E
Châtellerault 11 Gh 46.48N 0.32 E
Chatelodo 55 De 21.19S 57.28W
Chatham [Eng.-U.K.] 9 Nj 51.23N 0.32 E
Chatham [N.B.-Can.] 42 Kg 47.02N 65.26W
Chatham [Ont.-Can.] 42 Jh 42.24N 82.11W
Chatham [Va.-U.S.] 44 Hg 36.49N 79.26W
Chatham Island 57 Ji 44.00S 176.30W
Chatham Islands 57 Ji 44.00S 176.30W
Chatham Rise (EN) 57 Ii 43.30S 180.00
Chatham Strait 40 Me 57.30N 134.45W
Châtillon-en-Bazois 11 Jg 47.03N 3.40 E
Châtillon-sur-Indre 11 Hh 46.59N 1.10 E
Châtillon-sur-Marne 12 Fe 49.06N 3.45 E
Châtillon-sur-Seine 11 Kg 47.51N 4.33 E
Chatom 44 Cj 31.28N 88.16W
Chatsworth 37 Ec 19.38S 30.50 E
Chattahoochee 44 Ej 30.42N 84.51W
Chattahoochee 38 Kf 30.52N 84.57W
Chattanooga 39 Kf 35.03N 85.19W
Chatteris 12 Cb 52.27N 0.03 E
Chaucas 55 Cc 16.46S 58.44W
Chaudfontaine 12 Hd 50.35N 5.38 E
Chaudière, Rivière- 44 Lb 46.43N 71.17W
Chauk 25 Id 20.53N 94.49 E
Chaulnes 12 Ee 49.49N 2.48 E
Chaumont 11 Lf 48.07N 5.08 E
Chaumont-en-Vexin 12 De 49.16N 1.53 E
Chaumont-Gistoux 12 Gd 50.41N 4.44 E
Chaumont-Porcien 12 Ge 49.39N 4.15 E
Chaumont-sur-Aire 12 Hf 48.56N 5.15 E
Chaumont-sur-Loire 11 Hg 47.29N 1.11 E
Chauny 11 Je 49.37N 3.13 E
Chau Phu 25 Lf 10.42N 105.07 E
Chausey, Iles- 11 Ef 48.53N 1.50W
Chauvigny 11 Gh 46.34N 0.39 E
Chavantina 54 Hf 14.40S 52.21W
Chavarría 55 Ci 28.57S 58.35W
Chaves [Braz.] 54 Id 0.10S 49.55W
Chaves [Port.] 13 Ec 41.44N 7.28W
Chavigny, Lac - 42 Je 58.00N 75.05W
Chavuma 36 De 13.05S 22.42 E
Chazelles-sur-Lyon 11 Ki 45.38N 4.23 E
Chbar 25 Lf 12.46N 107.10 E
Cheaha Mountain 44 Ei 33.30N 85.47W
Cheat River 44 Hf 39.45N 79.55W
Cheb 10 If 50.04N 12.23 E
Cheboygan 43 Kb 45.39N 84.29W
Chech, 'Erg- 30 Gf 25.00N 3.00W
Chechaouene 32 Fb 35.00N 5.00W
Chechaouene 32 Fb 35.10N 5.16W
Checheng 27 Lg 22.05N 120.42 E
Che-Chiang Sheng→Zhejiang Sheng 27 Kf 29.00N 120.00 E
Chech'ŏn 28 Jf 37.08N 128.12 E
Chęciny 10 Qf 50.48N 20.28 E
Cheddar Gorge 9 Kj 51.13N 2.47W
Cheduba 25 Ie 18.48N 93.38 E
Chée 12 Gf 48.45N 4.39 E
Cheektowaga 44 Hd 42.57N 78.38W
Chefu 37 Ed 22.27S 32.45 E
Chegga 31 Gf 25.22N 5.49W
Cheghelvandī 24 Mf 33.42N 48.25 E
Chehel Pāyeh 24 Qg 31.54N 57.14 E
Cheju 27 Me 33.31N 126.32 E
Cheju-Do 21 Of 33.25N 126.30 E
Cheju-Do 28 Ih 33.25N 126.30 E
Cheju-Haehyŏp 28 Ih 33.40N 126.28 E
Chela, Serra da- 30 Ij 16.00S 13.10 E
Chelan 46 Ec 47.51N 120.01W
Chelan, Lake- 46 Eb 48.05N 120.30W
Chelforó, Arroyo- 55 Cm 36.55S 58.12W
Cheliff 32 Hb 36.10N 1.45 E
Cheliff 30 He 36.02N 0.08 E
Cheliff 32 Hb 36.10N 1.20 E
Cheliff, Plaine du- 13 Mi 35.57N 0.45 E
Chellalat el Adhaouara 13 Pi 35.56N 3.25 E
Chelleh Khāneh, Kūh-e- 24 Md 36.52N 48.36 E
Chełm 10 Te 51.10N 23.30 E
Chełm 10 Te 51.10N 23.28 E
Chelmer 12 Cc 51.44N 0.42 E
Chełmińskie, Pojezierze- 10 Oc 53.20N 19.00 E
Chełmno 10 Oc 53.22N 18.26 E
Chelmsford 9 Nj 51.44N 0.28 E
Chełmża 10 Oc 53.12N 18.37 E
Cheltenham 9 Kj 51.54N 2.04W
Chelva 13 Le 39.45N 0.59W
Chemainus 46 Db 48.55N 123.43W
Chemāma 32 Ef 16.50N 14.00 E
Chemba 37 Ec 17.09S 34.53 E
Chembe 36 Ee 11.58S 28.45 E
Chemillé 11 Fg 47.13N 0.43W
Chemult 46 Ee 43.13N 121.47W
Chenāb 21 Jg 29.13N 70.49 E
Chenachane 32 Gd 26.00N 4.15W
Chenachane 32 Gd 25.17N 3.10W
Chenārbāshi 24 Lf 33.20N 46.20 E
Chen Barag Qi (Bayan Hure) 27 Kb 49.21N 119.25 E
Chencha 35 Fd 6.17N 37.40 E
Chencoyi 48 Nh 19.48N 90.14W
Cheney 46 Gc 47.29N 117.34W
Cheney Reservoir 45 Hh 37.45N 97.50W
Cheng'an 28 Cf 36.27N 114.41 E
Chengde 27 Kc 41.00N 117.57 E
Chengdu 22 Mf 30.45N 104.04 E
Chengkou 27 Ie 31.54N 108.37 E
Chengmai 27 Ih 19.50N 109.59 E
Chengshan Jiao 27 Ld 37.24N 122.42 E
Chengxi Hu 28 Dh 32.22N 116.12 E
Chengzitan 27 Ld 39.31N 122.28 E
Chenisckali 16 Mh 42.06N 42.16 E
Chenjiagang 28 Eg 34.22N 119.48 E
Chenonceaux 11 Hg 47.20N 1.04 E
Chenxi 27 Jf 28.02N 110.15 E
Chenxian 27 Jf 25.49N 113.05 E
Chenying → Wannian 28 Dj 28.42N 117.04 E
Chépénéhé 63b Ce 20.47S 167.09 E
Chepes 56 Gd 31.21S 66.36W
Chepo 49 Hi 9.10N 79.06W
Cher 11 Ig 47.00N 2.30 E
Cher 5 Gf 47.21N 0.29 E
Cheradi, Isole- 14 Lj 40.25N 17.10 E
Cherangany Hills 36 Gb 1.15N 35.27 E
Cheraw 44 Hh 34.42N 79.53W
Cherbaniani Reef 25 Ef 12.18N 71.53 E
Cherbourg 6 Ff 49.39N 1.39W
Cherchell 32 Hb 36.36N 2.12 E
Chère 11 Eg 47.42N 1.50W
Chergui, Chott Ech- 30 He 34.21N 0.30 E
Chéri 34 Hc 13.26N 11.21 E
Cherlen → Kerulen 21 Ne 48.48N 117.00 E
Cherokee 45 Ie 42.45N 95.33W
Cherokees, Lake O' the- 45 Ih 36.39N 94.49W
Cherski Mountains (EN)= Čerskogo, Hrebet- [R.S.F.S.R.] 21 Qc 65.00N 145.00 E
Chersterfield Inlet 39 Jc 63.21N 90.42W
Chertsey 12 Bc 51.23N 0.30W
Cherwell 9 Lj 51.44N 1.15W
Chesapeake 44 Ig 36.45N 76.15W
Chesapeake Bay 38 Lf 38.40N 76.25W
Chesapeake Bay Bridge-Tunnel 44 Ig 37.00N 76.02W
Chesha Bay (EN)=Češskaja Guba 5 Kb 67.20N 46.30 E
Chesham 12 Bc 51.42N 0.36W
Cheshire 9 Kh 53.15N 2.30W
Cheshire Plain 9 Kh 53.20N 2.40W
Cheshunt 12 Bc 51.42N 0.02W
Chester 9 Kh 53.10N 2.55W
Chester [Eng.-U.K.] 9 Kh 53.12N 2.54W
Chester [Il.-U.S.] 45 Lh 37.55N 89.49W
Chester [Mt.-U.S.] 46 Jb 48.31N 110.58W
Chester [Pa.-U.S.] 44 Jf 39.50N 75.23W
Chester [S.C.-U.S.] 44 Gh 34.40N 81.12W
Chesterfield 9 Lh 53.15N 1.25W
Chesterfield, Ile- 37 Gc 16.20S 43.58 E
Chesterfield, Récifs et Iles- =Chesterfield Reefs and Islands (EN) 57 Gf 20.00S 159.00 E
Chesterfield Inlet 38 Jc 63.25N 90.45W
Chesterfield Reefs and Islands (EN)=Chesterfield, Récifs et Iles- 57 Gf 20.00S 159.00 E
Chesterton Range 59 Je 25.30S 147.30 E
Chestnut Ridge 44 He 40.10N 79.25W
Chesuncook Lake 44 Mb 46.00N 69.20W
Chetaibi 32 Ib 37.04N 7.23 E
Chetumal 39 Kh 18.35N 88.07W
Chetumal, Bahía de 47 Ge 18.20N 88.05W
Cheviot 62 Ee 42.49S 173.16 E
Chew Bahir=Stefanie, Lake- (EN) 30 Kh 4.38N 36.50 E
Chewelah 46 Gb 48.17N 117.43W
Cheyenne [Ok.-U.S.] 45 Gi 35.37N 99.40W

Index Symbols

Independent Nation
State, Region
District, County
Municipality
Colony, Dependency
Continent
Physical Region
Historical or Cultural Region
Mount, Mountain
Volcano
Hill
Mountains, Mountain Range
Hills, Escarpment
Plateau, Upland
Pass, Gap
Plain, Lowland
Delta
Salt Flat
Valley, Canyon
Crater, Cave
Karst Features
Depression
Polder
Desert, Dunes
Forest, Woods
Heath, Steppe
Oasis
Cape, Point
Coast, Beach
Cliff
Peninsula
Isthmus
Sandbank
Island
Atoll
Rock, Reef
Islands, Archipelago
Rocks, Reefs
Coral Reef
Well, Spring
Geyser
River, Stream
Waterfall Rapids
River Mouth, Estuary
Lake
Salt Lake
Intermittent Lake
Reservoir
Swamp, Pond
Canal
Glacier
Ice Shelf, Pack Ice
Ocean
Sea
Gulf, Bay
Strait, Fjord
Lagoon
Bank
Seamount
Tablemount
Ridge
Shelf
Basin
Escarpment, Sea Scarp
Fracture
Trench, Abyss
National Park, Reserve
Point of Interest
Recreation Site
Cave, Cavern
Historic Site
Ruins
Wall, Walls
Church, Abbey
Temple
Scientific Station
Airport
Port
Lighthouse
Mine
Tunnel
Dam, Bridge

Index Symbols

[1] Independent Nation
[2] State, Region
[3] District, County
[4] Municipality
[5] Colony, Dependency
[C] Continent
[P] Physical Region

Historical or Cultural Region
Mount, Mountain
Volcano
Hill
Mountains, Mountain Range
Hills, Escarpment
Plateau, Upland

Pass, Gap
Plain, Lowland
Delta
Salt Flat
Valley, Canyon
Crater, Cave
Karst Features

Depression
Polder
Desert, Dunes
Forest, Woods
Heath, Steppe
Oasis
Cape, Point

Coast, Beach
Cliff
Peninsula
Isthmus
Sandbank
Island
Atoll

Rock, Reef
Islands, Archipelago
Rocks, Reefs
Coral Reef
Well, Spring
Geyser
River, Stream

Waterfall Rapids
River Mouth, Estuary
Lake
Salt Lake
Intermittent Lake
Reservoir
Swamp, Pond

Canal
Glacier
Ice Shelf, Pack Ice
Ocean
Sea
Gulf, Bay
Strait, Fjord

Lagoon
Bank
Seamount
Tablemount
Ridge
Shelf
Basin

Escarpment, Sea Scarp
Fracture
Trench, Abyss
National Park, Reserve
Point of Interest
Recreation Site
Cave, Cavern

Historic Site
Ruins
Wall, Walls
Church, Abbey
Temple
Scientific Station
Airport

Port
Lighthouse
Mine
Tunnel
Dam, Bridge

Feature	Map	Grid	Lat	Long
Citeli-Ckaro	16	Oi	41.28N	46.06 E
Čitinskaja Oblast [3]	20	Gf	52.30N	117.30 E
Citlaltépetl, Volcán- → Orizaba, Pico de- ▲	38	Jh	19.01N	97.16W
Citrusdale	37	Bf	32.36 S	19.00 E
Città del Vaticano = Vatican City (EN) [1]	6	Hg	41.54N	12.27 E
Città di Castello	14	Gg	43.27N	12.14 E
Cittanova	14	Kl	38.21N	16.05 E
Ciucaşu, Vîrful- ▲	15	Id	45.31N	25.55 E
Ciucea	15	Fd	46.57N	22.49 E
Ciudad	48	Gf	23.44N	105.44W
Ciudad Acuña	47	Dc	29.18N	100.55W
Ciudad Altamirano	48	Ih	18.20N	100.40W
Ciudad Bolívar	53	Je	8.08N	63.33W
Ciudad Bolivia	54	Db	8.21N	70.34W
Ciudad Camargo [Mex.]	47	Ec	26.19N	98.50W
Ciudad Camargo [Mex.]	47	Cc	27.40N	105.10W
Ciudad Dario	49	Dg	12.43N	86.08W
Ciudad de Areco	55	Cl	34.18 S	59.46W
Ciudad de Dolores Hidalgo	48	Ig	21.10N	100.56W
Ciudad de la Habana [3]	49	Fb	23.10N	82.10W
Ciudad del Carmen	47	Fe	18.38N	91.50W
Ciudad del Maíz	48	Jf	22.24N	99.36W
Ciudad de México = Mexico City (EN)	39	Jh	19.24N	99.09W
Ciudad de Nutrias	54	Eb	8.07N	69.19W
Ciudad de Rio Grande	47	Dd	23.50N	103.02W
Ciudadela/Ciutadella	13	Pd	40.02N	3.50 E
Ciudad Guayana	53	Je	8.22N	62.40W
Ciudad Guerrero	47	Cc	28.33N	107.30W
Ciudad Guzmán	48	De	19.41N	103.29
Ciudad Hidalgo [Mex.]	48	Mj	14.41N	92.09W
Ciudad Hidalgo [Mex.]	48	Ih	19.41N	100.34W
Ciudad Juárez	39	If	31.44N	106.29W
Ciudad Lerdo	47	Dc	25.32N	103.32W
Ciudad Madero	39	Jg	22.16N	97.50W
Ciudad Mante	47	Ed	22.44N	98.57W
Ciudad Mendoza	48	Kh	18.48N	97.11W
Ciudad Obregón	39	Ig	27.59N	109.56W
Ciudad Ojeda	54	Da	10.12N	71.19W
Ciudad Piar	54	Fb	7.27N	63.19W
Ciudad Real	13	If	38.59N	3.56W
Ciudad Real [3]	13	If	39.00N	4.00W
Ciudad Rio Bravo	47	Ec	25.59N	98.06W
Ciudad-Rodrigo	13	Fd	40.36N	6.32W
Ciudad Valles	47	Ed	21.59N	99.01W
Ciudad Victoria	39	Jg	23.44N	99.08W
Ciutadella/Ciudadela	13	Pd	40.02N	3.50 E
Civa Burnu ▶	24	Gb	41.22N	36.35 E
Cividale del Friuli	14	Hd	46.06N	13.25 E
Civilsk	7	Li	55.53N	47.29 E
Civita Castellana	14	Gg	42.17N	12.25 E
Civitanova Marche	14	Hg	43.18N	13.44 E
Civitavecchia	14	Fh	42.06N	11.48 E
Civitella del Tronto	14	Hh	42.46N	13.40 E
Çivril	24	Cc	38.56N	35.29 E
Cixerri ⌐	14	Ck	39.17N	8.59 E
Cixian	28	Cf	36.22N	114.22 E
Cixi (Hushan)	28	Fi	30.10N	121.14 E
Čiža	19	Eb	67.06N	44.19 E
Cizre	23	Fb	37.20N	42.12 E
Cjurupinsk	16	Hf	46.37N	32.43 E
Čkalovsk	7	Kh	56.47N	43.17 E
Clacton-on-Sea	9	Oj	51.48N	1.09 E
Clain ⌐	11	Gh	46.47N	0.33 E
Claire, Côte- ⌐	66	Ie	66.30 S	133.00 E
Claire, Lake- ⌐	42	Ge	58.30N	112.00W
Clair Engle Lake ⌐	46	Df	40.52N	122.43W
Claire	3	Gh	46.56N	0.42 E
Clamecy	11	Jg	47.27N	3.31 E
Clan Alpine Mountains ▲	46	Gg	39.40N	117.55W
Clanton	44	Di	32.50N	86.38W
Clanwilliam	37	Bf	32.11 S	18.54 E
Claraz	55	Cm	37.54 S	59.17W
Clár Chlainne Mhuiris/ Claremorris	9	Eh	53.44N	9.00W
Clare [Austl.]	59	Hf	33.50 S	138.36 E
Clare [Mi.-U.S.]	44	Ed	43.49N	84.46W
Clare/Abhainn an Chláir ⌐	9	Dh	53.20N	9.03W
Clare/An Clár ⌐	9	Ei	52.50N	9.00W
Clare/Cliara ⌐	9	Dh	53.49N	10.00W
Claremont	44	Kd	43.23N	72.21W
Claremore	45	Ih	36.19N	95.36W
Claremorris/Clár Chlainne Mhuiris	9	Eh	53.44N	9.00W
Clarence ⌐	62	Ee	42.10 S	173.57 E
Clarence	62	Ee	42.10 S	173.56 E
Clarence, Cape - ▶	42	Ib	73.55N	90.10W
Clarence Cannon Reservoir ⌐	45	Kg	39.31N	91.45W
Clarence Island ⌐	66	Re	61.12S	54.05W
Clarence River ⌐	59	Ke	29.25 S	153.22 E
Clarence Strait [Ak.-U.S.] ⌐	40	Me	55.25N	132.00W
Clarence Strait [Austl.] ⌐	59	Gb	12.00 S	131.00 E
Clarence Town	49	Jb	23.06N	74.59W
Clarendon	45	Fi	34.56N	100.53W
Clarenville	42	Mg	48.90N	53.58W
Claresholm	42	Gf	50.02N	113.35W
Clarinda	45	If	40.44N	95.02W
Clarines	50	Dh	9.56N	65.10W
Clarion, Isla- ⌐	47	Be	18.22N	114.44W
Clarion Fracture Zone (EN) ⌐	3	Lh	18.00N	130.00W
Clarion River ⌐	44	Hf	41.07N	79.41W
Clark	45	Hd	44.53N	97.44W
Clark, Lake- ⌐	40	Id	60.15N	154.15W
Clark, Mount - ▲	46	Ii	33.46N	112.03W
Clarke Range ▲	59	Jd	20.50 S	148.35 E
Clark Fork ⌐	38	He	48.09N	116.15W
Clark Hill Lake ⌐	44	Fi	33.50N	82.15W
Clark Mountain ▲	46	Hi	35.32N	115.35W
Clarksburg	43	Kd	39.17N	80.21W
Clarksdale	43	Ie	34.12N	90.34W
Clarks Fork ⌐	46	Kd	45.39N	108.43W
Clark's Harbour	44	Od	43.26N	65.38W
Clarkston	46	Gc	46.30N	117.03W
Clarksville [Ar.-U.S.]	45	Ji	35.28N	93.28W
Clarksville [Tn.-U.S.]	43	Jd	36.32N	87.21W
Clarksville [Tx.-U.S.]	45	Ji	33.37N	95.03W
Claro, Rio- [Braz.] ⌐	54	Hg	19.08 S	50.40W
Claro, Rio- [Braz.] ⌐	54	Hg	15.28 S	51.45W
Clary	12	Fd	50.00N	3.24 E
Claude	45	Fi	35.07N	101.22W
Claustra/Klosters	14	Dd	46.52N	9.52 E
Clavering ⌐	41	Jd	74.20N	21.10W
Claxton	44	Gi	32.10N	81.55W
Clay Belt ⌐	38	Kd	51.50N	82.00W
Clay Center	45	Hg	39.23N	96.08W
Clay Cross	12	Aa	53.09N	1.25W
Claye Souilly	12	Ef	48.57N	2.42 E
Clayton	43	Gg	36.27N	103.11W
Clear, Cape- ▶	9	Dj	51.26N	9.31W
Clear Boggy Creek ⌐	45	Ii	34.03N	95.47W
Clear Creek [Az.-U.S.] ⌐	46	Ji	34.59N	110.38W
Clear Creek [U.S.] ⌐	46	Ld	44.53N	106.04W
Clearfield [Pa.-U.S.]	44	He	41.02N	78.27W
Clearfield [Ut.-U.S.]	46	If	41.07N	112.01W
Clear Fork Brazos ⌐	45	Gj	33.01N	98.40W
Clear Lake	43	Cd	39.02N	122.50W
Clear Lake [Ia.-U.S.]	45	Je	43.08N	93.23W
Clear Lake [S.D.-U.S.]	45	Hd	44.45N	96.41W
Clear Lake Reservoir ⌐	46	Ef	41.52N	121.08W
Clearwater	42	Ge	56.45N	111.22W
Clearwater	43	Kf	27.58N	82.48W
Clearwater Mountains ▲	43	Db	46.00N	115.30W
Clearwater River [Alta.-Can.] ⌐	46	Ha	52.23N	114.50W
Clearwater River [U.S.] ⌐	46	Gc	46.25N	117.02W
Cleburne	43	He	32.21N	97.23W
Clécy	12	Bf	48.55N	0.29W
Clee Hills ▲	9	Ki	52.25N	2.35W
Cleethorpes	9	Mh	53.34N	0.02W
Clères	12	De	49.36N	1.07 E
Clerf/Clervaux ⌐	12	Id	50.03N	6.02 E
Clermont [Austl.]	59	Jd	22.49 S	147.39 E
Clermont [Fr.]	11	Ie	49.23N	2.24 E
Clermont-en-Argonne	12	He	49.06N	5.04 E
Clermont-Ferrand	6	Gf	45.47N	3.05 E
Clermont-l'Hérault	11	Jk	43.37N	3.26 E
Clervaux/Clerf	12	Id	50.03N	6.02 E
Clervé ⌐	12	Ie	49.57N	6.01 E
Cles	14	Fd	46.22N	11.02 E
Clevedon	9	Kj	51.27N	2.51W
Cleveland ▲	9	Lg	54.25N	1.05W
Cleveland [3]	9	Mg	54.40N	1.00W
Cleveland [Ms.-U.S.]	45	Kj	33.45N	90.50W
Cleveland [Oh.-U.S.]	39	Kf	41.30N	81.41W
Cleveland [Tn.-U.S.]	43	Kd	35.10N	84.53W
Cleveland [Tx.-U.S.]	45	Ik	30.21N	95.05W
Cleveland, Mount- ▲	43	Eb	48.56N	113.51W
Cleveland Heights	44	Ge	41.30N	81.34W
Cleveländia	55	Fh	26.24 S	52.21W
Cleveland Mountain	46	Ic	46.37N	113.47W
Clew Bay/Cuan Mó ⌐	9	Dh	53.50N	9.50W
Cliara/Clare ⌐	9	Dh	53.49N	10.00W
Cliff	45	Bj	32.59N	108.36W
Clifton [Az.-U.S.]	43	Fe	33.03N	109.18W
Clifton [St.Vin.]	51n	Bb	12.36N	61.26W
Clifton [Tx.-U.S.]	45	Hk	31.47N	97.35W
Clinch River ⌐	44	Ba	36.43N	84.29W
Cline, Mount- ▲	46	Ga	52.10N	116.40W
Clines Corners	45	Di	35.01N	105.34W
Clingmans Dome ▲	44	Db	35.35N	83.30W
Clinton [Ar.-U.S.]	45	Ji	35.36N	92.28W
Clinton [B.C.-Can.]	42	Ff	51.05N	121.35W
Clinton [Ia.-U.S.]	43	Ic	41.51N	90.12W
Clinton [Il.-U.S.]	45	Lf	40.09N	88.57W
Clinton [Mo.-U.S.]	45	Jg	38.22N	93.46W
Clinton [Ms.-U.S.]	45	Kj	32.20N	90.20W
Clinton [N.C.-U.S.]	44	Hh	34.59N	78.20W
Clinton [N.Z.]	62	Cg	46.13S	169.23 E
Clinton [Ok.-U.S.]	43	Hd	35.31N	98.59W
Clinton-Colden Lake ⌐	42	Gd	63.55N	107.30W
Clintonville	45	Ld	44.37N	88.46W
Clipperton ⌐	38	Ih	10.17N	109.13W
Clipperton, Fracture Zone (EN) ⌐	3	Mi	10.00N	115.00W
Clisson	11	Eg	47.05N	1.17W
Cloates, Point- ▶	59	Cd	22.45 S	113.40 E
Clochán an Aifir/ Giant's Causeway	9	Gf	55.15N	6.35W
Clodomira	56	Hc	27.35 S	64.08W
Cloich na Coillte/Clonakilty	9	Ej	51.37N	8.54W
Clonakilty/Cloich na Coillte	9	Ej	51.37N	8.54W
Cloncurry	58	Fg	20.42 S	140.30 E
Clones/Cluain Eois	9	Fi	52.21N	7.42W
Clonmel/Cluain Meala	9	Fi	52.21N	7.42W
Cloppenburg	10	Ed	52.51N	8.03 E
Cloquet	43	Ib	46.43N	92.28W
Clorinda	53	Kh	25.20 S	57.40W
Cloud Peak ▲	43	Fc	44.25N	107.10W
Clouère ⌐	11	Gh	46.26N	0.17 E
Cloverdale	46	Dg	38.48N	123.01W
Clovis [Ca.-U.S.]	46	Fh	36.49N	119.42W
Clovis [N.M.-U.S.]	39	If	34.24N	103.12W
Cluain Meala/Clonmel	9	Fi	52.21N	7.42W
Cluain Eois/Clones	9	Fg	54.11N	7.14W
Cluj [3]	15	Gc	46.49N	23.35 E
Cluj Napoca	6	If	46.46N	23.36 E
Cluny	11	Kh	46.26N	4.39 E
Cluses	11	Mh	46.04N	6.36 E
Clusone	14	Ee	45.54N	9.57 E
Clutha ⌐	62	Cg	46.21 S	169.48 E
Clwyd ⌐	9	Jh	53.10N	3.15W
Clwyd [3]	9	Jh	53.10N	3.15W
Clyde	9	If	55.56N	4.29W
Clyde [N.W.T.-Can.]	39	Mb	70.25N	68.30W
Clyde [N.Z.]	62	Cf	45.11 S	169.19 E
Clyde, Firth of- ⌐	9	If	55.42N	5.00W
Clyde Inlet ⌐	42	Kb	70.20N	68.20W
Cna ⌐	5	Ke	54.32N	42.05 E
Cnoc Bréanainn/Brandon Mount ▲	9	Ci	52.14N	10.15W
Cnoc Fola/Bloody Foreland ▶	9	Ef	55.09N	8.17W
Cnoc Mhaoldonn/ Knockmealdown Mountains ▲	9	Fi	52.15N	8.00W
Cnori	16	Ni	41.35N	45.59 E
Cnossus (EN) = Knosós ⌐	15	Jn	35.18N	25.10 E
Côa ⌐	13	Ec	41.05N	7.06W
Coachella Canal ⌐	46	Hj	33.34N	116.00W
Coahuayana	48	Hh	18.44N	103.41W
Coahuila [3]	47	Dc	27.20N	102.00W
Coalcomán, Sierra de- ▲	47	De	18.30N	102.55W
Coalcomán de Matamoros	48	Hh	18.47N	103.09W
Coaldale	46	Ib	49.43N	112.37W
Coalgate	45	Hi	34.32N	96.13W
Coalinga	46	Eh	36.09N	120.21W
Coalville	9	Li	52.44N	1.20W
Coamo	49	Nd	18.05N	66.22W
Coari	54	Fd	4.05 S	63.08W
Coari, Lago de- ⌐	54	Fd	4.15 S	63.25W
Coari, Rio- ⌐	52	Jf	4.30 S	63.33W
Coast	36	Gc	3.00 S	39.30 E
Coast Mountains ▲	38	Gd	55.00N	129.00W
Coast Plain (EN) = Kustvlakte ⌐	11	Ic	51.00N	2.30 E
Coast Ranges ▲	38	Ge	41.00N	123.30W
Coatbridge	9	If	55.52N	4.01W
Coatepec	48	Kh	19.27N	96.58W
Coatepec, Cerro- ▲	48	Kh	18.25N	97.35W
Coatepeque	49	Bf	14.42N	91.52W
Coats ⌐	38	Kc	62.30N	83.00W
Coats Land (EN) ⌐	66	Af	77.00 S	28.00W
Coatzacoalcos	39	Jh	18.09N	94.25W
Coatzacoalcos, Bahía- ⌐	48	Lh	18.10N	94.27W
Coatzacoalcos, Rio- ⌐	48	Lh	18.09N	94.24W
Coba ⌐	47	Gd	20.36N	87.35W
Cobadin	15	Lc	44.05N	28.13 E
Cobalt	42	Kf	47.24N	79.41W
Cobán	47	Fe	15.29N	90.19W
Cobb, Mount- ▲	46	Dg	38.45N	122.40W
Cobb Seamount (EN) ⌐	38	Fe	46.46N	130.43W
Cóbh/An Cóbh	9	Ej	51.51N	8.17W
Cobija	54	Ef	11.02 S	68.44W
Cobo	55	Dm	37.48 S	57.38W
Cobourg	42	Kf	43.58N	78.10W
Cobourg Peninsula ⌐	59	Gb	11.20 S	132.15 E
Cóbué	37	Eb	12.07 S	34.52 E
Coburg	42	Ja	75.57N	79.00W
Coburn Mountain ▲	44	Lc	45.28N	70.06W
Coca, Pizzo di- ▲	14	Ed	46.04N	10.01 E
Cocalinho	54	Hf	14.22 S	51.00W
Cocentaina	13	Lf	38.45N	0.26W
Cochabamba [2]	54	Eg	17.30 S	65.40W
Cochabamba	53	Jg	17.24 S	66.09W
Coche, Isla- ⌐	50	Eg	10.47N	63.56W
Cochem	10	Df	50.08N	7.09 E
Cochin	22	Ji	9.58N	76.14 E
Cochin China (EN) = Nam Phan ⌐	21	Mg	11.00N	107.00 E
Cochinos, Bahía de- = Pigs, Bay of- (EN) ⌐	49	Gb	22.07N	81.10W
Cochons, Ile aux- ⌐	30	Mm	46.05 S	50.08 E
Cochran	44	Fi	32.23N	83.21W
Cochrane [Alta.-Can.]	46	Ha	51.11N	114.28W
Cochrane [Ont.-Can.]	39	Ke	49.04N	81.01W
Cockburn, Canal- ⌐	56	Fh	54.20 S	71.30W
Cockburn, Mount- ▲	59	Gd	22.46 S	130.36 E
Cockburn Bank ⌐	9	El	49.40N	8.50W
Cockburn Island ⌐	44	Fc	45.55N	83.22W
Cockburn Town	49	Ja	24.02N	74.31W
Cockermouth	9	Jg	54.40N	3.21W
Coclé [3]	49	Gi	8.30N	80.15W
Coco, Cayo- ⌐	49	Hb	22.30N	78.28W
Coco, Ile- ⌐	50	Eg	17.52N	62.49W
Coco, Isla del- ⌐	38	Ki	5.32N	87.04W
Coco, Rio-o Segovia, Rio- ⌐	38	Kh	15.00N	83.08W
Cocoa	44	Gk	28.21N	80.44W
Cocoa Beach	44	Gk	28.19N	80.36W
Cocoa Point ▶	51d	Ba	17.33N	61.46W
Cocobeach	36	Bb	0.59N	9.36 E
Coco Channel ⌐	25	If	14.00N	93.00 E
Coco Islands ⌐	25	If	14.05N	93.18 E
Coconino Plateau ⌐	46	Ii	35.50N	112.30W
Cocorocuma, Cayos- ⌐	49	Ff	15.45N	83.00W
Cocos	54	Jf	14.10 S	44.33W
Cocos Islands (Keeling Islands) ⌐	21	Lk	12.10 S	96.55 E
Cocos Islands (Keeling Islands) ⌐	2	Lk	12.10 S	96.55 E
Cocos Ridge (EN) ⌐	3	Ni	5.30N	86.00W
Cocula	48	Hg	20.23N	103.50W
Cocuzzo ▲	14	Kk	39.13N	16.08 E
Cod, Cape- ▶	44	Me	41.50N	70.00W
Coda Cavallo, Capo- ▶	14	Dj	40.51N	9.43 E
Codaeştl	45	Kc	46.52N	27.45 E
Codajás	54	Fd	3.50 S	62.05W
Codera, Cabo- ▶	50	Cg	10.35N	66.04W
Codfish Island ⌐	62	Bg	46.45 S	167.40 E
Codigoro	14	Gf	44.49N	12.08 E
Codlea	15	Id	45.42N	25.27 E
Codó	54	Jd	4.29 S	43.53W
Codogno	14	Ee	45.09N	9.42 E
Codrington	51d	Ba	17.38N	61.50W
Codrington Lagoon ⌐	51d	Ba	17.43N	61.49W
Codrului, Munţii ▲	15	Fc	46.35N	22.10 E
Cody	43	Fc	44.32N	109.05W
Coen	58	Gf	13.56N	143.12 E
Coesfeld	10	De	51.56N	7.09 E
Coetivy Island ⌐	30	Mi	7.08 S	56.16 E
Coeur d'Alene	43	Db	47.41N	116.46W
Coevorden	11	Mb	52.40N	6.45 E
Coffeyville	45	Ih	37.02N	95.37W
Coffs Harbour	58	Gh	30.18 S	153.08 E
Cofre de Perote, Cerro- (Nauhcampatépetl) ▲	48	Kh	19.29N	97.08W
Cofrentes	13	Ke	39.14N	1.04W
Coggeshall	12	Cc	51.52N	0.41 E
Coghinas ⌐	14	Cj	40.56N	8.48 E
Coghinas, Lago del- ⌐	14	Dj	40.45N	9.05 E
Coglians ▲	14	Gd	46.37N	12.53 E
Cognac	11	Fi	45.42N	0.20W
Cogne	14	Be	45.37N	7.21 E
Cogolludo	13	Id	40.57N	3.05W
Čograjskoje Vodohranilišče ⌐	16	Ng	45.30N	44.30 E
Coiba, Isla de- ⌐	47	Hg	7.27N	81.45W
Coig, Rio- (Coyle) ⌐	56	Gh	50.58 S	69.11W
Coihaique	56	Fg	45.34 S	72.04W
Coimbatore	22	Jh	11.00N	76.58 E
Coimbra	13	Dd	40.12N	8.25W
Coimbra [Braz.]	55	Dd	19.55 S	57.47W
Coimbra [Port.]	6	Fg	40.12N	8.25W
Coín	13	Hh	36.40N	4.45W
Coipasa, Salar de- ⌐	54	Eg	19.30 S	68.10W
Cojedes	50	Bh	9.37N	68.55W
Cojedes [2]	54	Eb	9.20N	68.20W
Cojedes, Rio- ⌐	50	Bh	8.44N	68.15W
Cojutepeque	49	Cg	13.43N	88.56W
Čoka	15	Dd	45.56N	20.09 E
Cokeville	46	Je	42.05N	110.57W
Cokover River ⌐	59	Ed	20.40 S	120.45 E
Čokurdah	20	Jb	70.38N	147.55 E
Colac [Austl.]	59	Jg	38.20 S	143.35 E
Colac [N.Z.]	62	Bg	46.22 S	167.53 E
Colatina	53	Lg	19.32 S	40.37W
Colbeck, Cape- ▶	66	Mf	77.06 S	157.48W
Colbitz-Letzlinger Heide ⌐	10	Hd	52.27N	11.35 E
Colby	45	Fg	39.24N	101.03W
Colchester	9	Nj	51.54N	0.54 E
Cold Bay	40	Ge	55.11N	162.30W
Cold Lake	42	Gd	54.27N	110.10W
Coldstream	9	Kf	55.39N	2.15W
Coldwater [Ks.-U.S.]	45	Gh	37.16N	99.19W
Coldwater [Mi.-U.S.]	44	Ee	41.57N	85.00W
Colebrook	44	Lc	44.53N	71.30W
Coleman	45	Gk	31.50N	99.26W
Coleraine ⌐	59	Ic	15.06 S	141.38 E
Coleraine/Cúil Raithin	9	Gf	55.08N	6.40W
Coleridge, Lake- ⌐	62	De	43.20 S	171.30 E
Coles, Punta- ▶	54	Dg	17.42 S	71.23W
Colesberg	37	Df	30.45 S	25.05 E
Colfax [La.-U.S.]	45	Jk	31.31N	92.42W
Colfax [Wa.-U.S.]	46	Gc	46.53N	117.22W
Colfontaine	12	Fd	50.25N	3.50 E
Colhué Huapi, Lago- ⌐	56	Gg	45.30 S	68.48W
Colibași	15	He	44.56N	24.54 E
Colibris, Pointe des- ▶	51e	Bb	16.17N	61.06W
Colima	47	De	19.10N	104.00W
Colima [2]	39	Ih	19.10N	103.40W
Colima, Nevado de- ▲	38	Jh	19.33N	103.38W
Colinas	55	He	14.12 S	48.03W
Coll ⌐	9	Ge	56.40N	6.35W
Collado Bajo ▲	13	Kd	40.14N	1.50W
Colladara ⌐	13	Lb	42.43N	0.29W
Colle di Val d'Elsa	14	Fg	43.25N	11.07 E
Colleferro	14	Gi	41.44N	12.59 E
College	40	Jd	64.51N	147.47W
College Place	46	Fc	46.03N	118.23W
College Station	45	Hk	30.37N	96.21W
Collegno	14	Be	45.05N	7.34 E
Collie	58	Df	33.21 S	116.09 E
Collier Bay ⌐	59	Ec	16.10 S	124.15 E
Collierville	44	Ch	35.03N	89.40W
Collingwood [N.Z.]	62	Db	40.41 S	172.41 E
Collingwood [Ont.-Can.]	44	Gc	44.29N	80.13W
Collinson Peninsula ⌐	42	Hb	70.00N	101.10W
Collinsville	59	Jd	20.34 S	147.51 E
Collmberg ▲	10	Je	51.15N	13.02 E
Colmar	11	Nf	48.05N	7.22 E
Colmena	55	Bi	28.45 S	60.06W
Colmenar	13	Hh	36.54N	4.20W
Colmenar Viejo	13	Id	40.40N	3.46W
Colne ⌐	12	Cc	51.51N	0.59 E
Colne Point ▶	12	Dc	51.46N	1.03 E
Colnett, Punta- ▶	48	Ab	31.00N	116.20W
Cologne (EN) = Köln	6	Ge	50.56N	6.57 E
Colombia	53	He	4.00N	72.00W
Colômbia	54	He	20.10 S	48.40W
Colombian Basin (EN) ⌐	38	Lh	13.00N	76.00W
Colombier, Pointe à- ▶	51e	Bc	17.55N	62.53W
Colombo	22	Ji	6.56N	79.51 E
Colón [Arg.]	56	Id	33.53 S	61.07W
Colón [Arg.]	56	Id	32.13 S	58.08W
Colón [Cuba]	49	Fb	22.43N	80.54W
Colón [Hond.] [3]	49	Ef	15.20N	84.30W
Colón [Pan.] [2]	49	Hi	9.30N	79.55W
Colón [Pan.]	39	Li	9.22N	79.54W
Colón [Ur.]	55	Ek	33.53 S	54.43W
Colón, Archipiélago de-/ Galápagos, Islas- = Galapagos Islands (EN) ⌐	52	Gf	0.30 S	90.30W
Colón, Montañas de- ▲	49	Ef	14.55N	84.45W
Colona	59	Gf	31.38 S	132.05 E
Colonarie	51n	Ba	13.14N	61.08W
Colonarie ⌐	51n	Ba	13.14N	61.08W
Colonel Hill	49	Jb	23.14N	74.15W
Colonia agrícola de Turén	50	Bh	9.15N	69.05W
Colonia Carlos Pellegrini	55	Dh	28.32 S	57.10W
Colonia del Sacramento	56	Id	34.28 S	57.51W
Colonia Elisa	55	Ch	26.56 S	59.32W
Colonia Juárez	48	Db	30.19N	108.00W
Colonia Las Heras	56	Gg	46.33 S	68.57W
Colonia Lavalleja	56	Id	31.06 S	57.01W
Colonial Heights	44	Ig	37.15N	77.25W
Colonia Morelos	48	Eb	30.50N	109.10W
Colonne, Capo- ▶	14	Lk	39.02N	17.12 E
Colonsay ⌐	9	Ge	56.05N	6.10W
Colorado	49	Fh	10.46N	83.35W
Colorado [2]	39	Ef	39.30N	105.30W
Colorado, Cerro- ▲	48	Bb	31.31N	115.31W
Colorado, Rio- [Arg.] ⌐	52	Ji	39.50 S	62.08W
Colorado, Rio- [N.Amer.] ⌐	38	Hf	31.45N	114.40W
Colorado City	45	Fj	32.24N	100.52W
Colorado Plateau ⌐	38	Hf	36.30N	108.00W
Colorado River [N.Amer.] ⌐	38	Hf	31.45N	114.40W
Colorado River [U.S.] ⌐	38	Jg	28.36N	95.58W
Colorado Springs	39	If	38.50N	104.49W
Colotlán	48	Kc	22.03N	103.16W
Colpon-Ata	18	Kc	42.39N	77.06 E
Coltishall	12	Db	52.44N	1.22 E
Colui ⌐	36	Cf	15.10 S	16.40 E
Columbia [Ky.-U.S.]	44	Eg	37.06N	85.18W
Columbia [Mo.-U.S.]	43	Id	38.57N	92.20W
Columbia [Ms.-U.S.]	45	Lk	31.15N	89.56W
Columbia [Pa.-U.S.]	44	Ie	40.02N	76.30W
Columbia [S.C.-U.S.]	39	Kf	34.00N	81.03W
Columbia [Tn.-U.S.]	44	Dh	35.37N	87.02W
Columbia, Cape- ▶	38	La	83.05N	70.35W
Columbia, Mount- ▲	38	Hd	57.00N	117.00W
Columbia Basin ⌐	43	Db	46.45N	119.05W
Columbia Falls	46	Hb	48.23N	114.11W
Columbia Mountains ▲	38	Hd	52.00N	119.00W
Columbia Plateau ⌐	38	He	44.00N	113.00W
Columbia Seamount (EN) ⌐	54	Lh	20.40 S	31.30W
Columbine, Cape- ▶	30	Il	32.49 S	17.51 E
Columbretes, Els- ⌐	13	Me	39.52N	0.40 E
Columbretes, Els-/ Columbretes, Islas- ⌐	13	Me	39.52N	0.40 E
Columbus [Ga.-U.S.]	39	Kf	32.29N	84.59W
Columbus [In.-U.S.]	43	Jd	39.13N	85.55W
Columbus [Ks.-U.S.]	45	Ih	37.10N	94.50W
Columbus [Mt.-U.S.]	46	Kd	45.38N	109.15W
Columbus [Nb.-U.S.]	43	Hc	41.25N	97.22W
Columbus [N.M.-U.S.]	45	Ck	31.50N	107.38W
Columbus [Tx.-U.S.]	45	Hl	29.42N	96.33W
Columbus Point ▶	49	Ja	24.08N	75.16W
Colville ⌐	38	Dc	70.25N	150.30W
Colville, Cape- ▶	62	Fb	36.28 S	175.21 E
Colville Channel ⌐	62	Fb	36.25 S	175.30 E
Colville Lake ⌐	42	Ec	67.10N	126.00W
Colville Lake	42	Ec	67.06N	126.00W
Col Visentin ▲	14	Gd	46.05N	12.20 E
Colwyn Bay	9	Jh	53.18N	3.43W
Coma	35	Fd	8.27N	36.55 E
Comacchio	14	Gf	44.42N	12.11 E
Comacchio, Valli di- ⌐	14	Gf	44.40N	12.05 E
Comai (Damxoi)	27	Gf	28.26N	91.32 E
Comala	48	Hh	19.19N	103.45W
Comalcalco	47	Fe	18.16N	93.13W
Coman, Mount- ▲	66	Qf	73.49 S	64.18W
Comanche [Mt.-U.S.]	46	Kc	46.02N	108.54W
Comanche [Tx.-U.S.]	45	Gk	31.54N	98.36W
Comandante Fontana	55	Cg	25.20 S	59.41W
Comandău	15	Jd	45.46N	26.16 E
Comăneşti	15	Jc	46.25N	26.26 E
Comayagua	47	Fc	14.25N	87.37W
Comayagua [3]	49	Df	14.30N	87.40W
Combarbalá	56	Fc	31.11 S	71.02W
Combeaufontaine	11	Lg	47.43N	5.53 E
Combermere Bay ⌐	25	Ie	19.37N	93.34 E
Combles	12	Fd	50.28N	5.35 E
Combourg	11	Ef	50.01N	2.52 E
Combrailles ⌐	11	Ih	46.30N	3.10 E
Combrailles ⌐	11	If	48.25N	1.45W
Comeragh Mountains/Na Comaraigh ▲	9	Fi	52.13N	7.35W
Comilla	25	Id	23.27N	91.12 E
Comines	12	Fd	50.46N	3.01 E
Comines/Komen	14	Id	50.46N	2.59 E
Comino, Capo- ▶	14	Dj	40.32N	9.49 E
Comiso	14	Jm	36.56N	14.36 E
Comitán de Domínguez	47	Fe	16.15N	92.08W
Commentry	11	Ih	46.17N	2.45 E
Commerce	45	Ij	33.15N	95.54W
Commiges	11	Lf	48.45N	5.35 E
Commiges ⌐	11	Lf	43.15N	3.15W
Committee Bay ⌐	38	Kc	68.30N	86.30W
Commonwealth Bay ⌐	66	Je	66.54 S	142.40 E
Communism Peak (EN) = Kommunizma, Pik- ▲	21	Jf	38.57N	72.08 E
Como [China]	27	Fe	31.28N	86.21 E
Como [It.]	14	De	45.47N	9.05 E
Como, Lago di- ⌐	14	Dd	46.00N	9.15 E
Comodoro	55	Bl	35.19 S	60.31W
Comodoro Rivadavia	53	Jj	45.50 S	67.30W
Comondú	48	Bc	26.03N	111.46W
Comores/Comoros [1]	31	Lj	12.10 S	44.10 E
Comoro Islands (EN) = Comores/Comoros [1]	30	Lj	12.10 S	44.15 E
Comorin, Cape- ▶	21	Ji	8.04N	77.34 E
Comoro Islands (EN) = Comores, Archipel des- ⌐	30	Lj	12.10 S	44.10 E
Comox	46	Cb	49.40N	124.55W
Compiègne	11	Je	49.25N	2.50 E
Composteia	47	Dd	21.14N	104.55W
Compton	46	Fj	33.54N	118.13W
Comstock	45	Fl	29.41N	101.11W
Comtal, Cause du- ⌐	11	Ij	44.26N	2.38 E

Index Symbols

[1]	Independent Nation
[2]	State, Region
[3]	District, County
	Municipality
	Colony, Dependency
	Continent
	Physical Region
	Historical or Cultural Region
	Mount, Mountain
	Volcano
	Hill
	Mountains, Mountain Range
	Hills, Escarpment
	Plateau, Upland
	Pass, Gap
	Plain, Lowland
	Delta
	Salt Flat
	Valley, Canyon
	Crater, Cave
	Karst Features
	Depression
	Polder
	Desert, Dunes
	Forest, Woods
	Heath, Steppe
	Oasis
	Cape, Point
	Coast, Beach
	Cliff
	Peninsula
	Isthmus
	Sandbank
	Island
	Atoll
	Rock, Reef
	Islands, Archipelago
	Rocks, Reefs
	Coral Reef
	Well, Spring
	Geyser
	River, Stream
	Waterfall Rapids
	River Mouth, Estuary
	Lake
	Salt Lake
	Intermittent Lake
	Sea
	Swamp, Pond
	Canal
	Glacier
	Ice Shelf, Pack Ice
	Ocean
	Ridge
	Shelf
	Strait, Fjord
	Lagoon
	Bank
	Seamount
	Tablemount
	Trench, Abyss
	Basin
	Gulf, Bay
	Escarpment, Sea Scarp
	Fracture
	Trench, Abyss
	National Park, Reserve
	Point of Interest
	Recreation Site
	Cave, Cavern
	Historic Site
	Ruins
	Wall, Walls
	Church, Abbey
	Temple
	Scientific Station
	Airport
	Port
	Lighthouse
	Mine
	Tunnel
	Dam, Bridge

Cona 21 Mc 62.00N 110.00 E
Cona 27 Ff 28.01N 91.57 E
Co Nag 27 Fe 32.00N 91.25 E
Conakry 31 Fh 9.31N 13.43W
Conara Junction 59 Jh 41.50S 147.26 E
Concarneau 11 Cg 47.52N 3.55W
Conceição da Barra 54 Kg 18.35S 39.45W
Conceição do Araguaia 54 Ie 8.15S 49.17W
Conceição do Mato Dentro 55 Kd 19.01S 43.25W
Concepción [3] 55 Df 23.00S 57.00W
Concepción [Arg.] 56 Gc 27.20S 65.35W
Concepción [Arg.] 55 Di 28.23S 57.53W
Concepción [Bol.] 54 Fg 16.15S 62.04W
Concepción [Chile] 53 Ii 36.50S 73.03W
Concepción [Par.] 53 Kh 23.25S 57.17W
Concepción [Peru] 54 Cf 11.55S 75.17W
Concepción [Ven.] 49 Lh 10.25N 71.41W
Concepción, Bahía- 48 Dd 26.40N 111.48W
Concepción, Laguna- 54 Fg 17.30S 61.25W
Concepción, Punta- 48 Dd 26.50N 111.50W
Concepción, Río- 55 Ab 15.46S 62.10W
Concepción del Bermejo 55 Bh 26.36S 60.57W
Concepción del Oro 47 Dd 24.38N 101.25W
Concepción del Uruguay 56 Id 32.29S 58.14W
Conception, Point- 46 Ei 34.27N 120.27W
Conception Bay 42 Mg 48.00N 52.50W
Conception Island 49 Jb 23.52N 75.03W
Concha 49 Li 9.02N 71.45W
Conchas 55 Hf 23.01S 48.00W
Conchas Dam 45 Di 35.22N 104.11W
Conchas Lake 45 Di 35.25N 104.14W
Conches-en-Ouche 11 Gf 48.58N 0.56 E
Concho River 45 Gk 31.32N 99.43W
Conchos, Río- 38 Ig 29.35N 104.25W
Concoran 46 Fh 36.06N 119.33W
Concord [Ca.-U.S.] 46 Eh 37.59N 122.00W
Concord [N.H.-U.S.] 39 Le 43.12N 71.32W
Concordia [Arg.] 53 Ki 31.24S 58.02W
Concordia [Braz.] 55 Fh 27.14S 52.01W
Concordia [Ks.-U.S.] 45 Hg 39.34N 97.39W
Concordia [Mex.] 48 Ff 23.17N 106.04W
Concordia Baai 51c Aa 17.31N 62.58W
Con Cuong 25 Ke 19.02N 104.54 E
Conda 36 Be 11.06S 14.20 E
Condamine River 59 Je 27.00S 149.50 E
Condat 11 Ii 45.22N 2.46 E
Conde 54 Kf 11.49S 37.37W
Condé-en-Brie 12 Fe 49.01N 3.33 E
Condega 49 Dg 13.21N 86.24W
Condé-sur-l'Escaut 12 Fd 50.27N 3.35 E
Condé-sur-Marne 12 Ge 49.03N 4.11 E
Condé-sur-Noireau 11 Ff 48.51N 0.33W
Condobolin 59 Jf 33.05S 147.09 E
Condom 11 Gk 43.58N 0.22 E
Condon 46 Ed 45.14N 120.11W
Condor, Cordillera del- 54 Cd 4.20S 78.30W
Condroz/Condruzisch Plateau 11 Kd 50.25N 5.00 E
Condruzisch Plateau/Condroz 11 Kd 50.25N 5.00 E
Conecuh River 44 Dj 30.58N 87.14W
Conegliano 14 Ge 45.53N 12.18 E
Conejera, Isla- [Sp.] 13 Nf 38.59N 1.12 E
Conejera, Isla- [Sp.] 13 Oe 39.11N 2.57 E
Conejo 48 De 24.05N 111.00W
Conejo, Cerro- 48 Jg 21.24N 99.06W
Conero 14 Hg 43.33N 13.36 E
Conesa 55 Bk 33.36S 60.21W
Conference Island 51p Bb 12.09N 61.35W
Conflans-en-Jarnisy 12 He 49.10N 5.51 E
Conflans-Sainte-Honorine 12 Ef 48.59N 2.06 E
Confolens 11 Gh 46.01N 0.40 E
Confuso, Río- 55 Dg 25.09S 57.34W
Conghua 27 Jg 23.31N 113.30 E
Congo [1] 31 Ii 1.00S 15.00 E
Congo 30 Ii 6.04S 12.24 E
Congo, Dem. Rep. of the-→Zaïre [1] 31 Ji 1.00S 25.00 E
Congo Basin (EN) 30 Ih 0.00 17.00 E
Congonhas 55 Ke 20.30S 43.52W
Conil de la Frontera 13 Fh 36.16N 6.05W
Coniston 44 Gb 46.29N 80.51W
Conn, Lough-/Loch Con 9 Dg 54.04N 9.20W
Connacht/Connaught 9 Eh 53.30N 9.00W
Connaught/Connacht 9 Eh 53.30N 9.00W
Conneaut 44 Ge 41.58N 80.34W
Connecticut [2] 43 Mc 41.45N 72.45W
Connecticut River 43 Mc 41.17N 72.21W
Connell 46 Fc 46.40N 118.52W
Connellsville 44 He 40.02N 79.38W
Connemara, Mountains of- 9 Dh 53.30N 9.45W
Connersville 44 Ef 39.39N 85.08W
Conn Lake 42 Kb 70.30N 73.30W
Connors Range 59 Jd 21.40S 149.10 E
Conon 9 Id 57.35N 4.30W
Conquista 55 Id 19.56S 47.33W
Conrad 46 Jb 48.10N 111.57W
Conroe 45 Ik 30.19N 95.27W
Conroe Lake 45 Ik 30.25N 95.37W
Conscripto Bernardi 55 Cj 31.03S 59.05W
Conselheiro Lafaiete 54 Jh 20.40S 43.48W
Conselice 14 Ff 44.31N 11.49 E
Consett 9 Lg 54.51N 1.49W
Consolación del Sur 49 Fb 22.30N 83.31W
Con Son 25 Lg 8.43N 106.36 E
Constance, Lake- (EN)=Bodensee 5 Gf 47.35N 9.25 E
Constanța [2] 15 Le 44.30N 28.30 E
Constanța 6 Ig 44.11N 28.39 E
Constantina 13 Gg 37.52N 5.37W
Constantine [3] 32 Ib 36.20N 6.35 E
Constantine 31 He 36.22N 6.37 E
Constantine, Cape- 40 He 58.25N 158.50W
Constitución [Chile] 56 Fe 35.20S 72.25W
Constitución [Ur.] 55 Dj 31.05S 57.50W
Consuegra 13 Ie 39.28N 3.36W
Consuelo Peak 57 Fg 24.58S 148.10 E
Contamana 54 De 7.15S 74.54W
Contas, Rio de- 52 Mg 14.17S 39.01W
Contoy, Isla- 48 Pg 21.30N 86.48W
Contraforte Central, Serra do- 55 Ic 17.15S 47.50W
Contramaestre 49 Ic 20.18N 76.15W
Contraviesa, Sierra- 13 Ih 36.50N 3.10W
Contreras, Embalse de- 13 Ke 39.32N 1.30W
Contreras, Islas- 49 Gj 7.50N 81.47W
Contreras, Puerto de- 13 Ke 39.32N 1.30W
Contres 11 Hg 47.25N 1.26 E
Contumazá 54 Ce 7.22S 78.49W
Contursi 14 Jj 40.39N 15.14 E
Contwig 12 Je 49.15N 7.26 E
Contwoyto Lake 42 Gc 65.40N 110.40W
Conty 12 Ee 49.44N 2.09 E
Convención 54 Db 8.28N 73.20W
Conversano 14 Lj 40.58N 17.07 E
Conway 9 Jh 53.17N 3.50W
Conway [Ar.-U.S.] 43 Id 35.05N 92.26W
Conway [N.H.-U.S.] 44 Ld 43.58N 71.07W
Conway [S.C.-U.S.] 44 Hi 33.51N 79.04W
Conway [Wales-U.K.] 9 Jh 53.17N 3.50W
Conway, Mount- 59 Gd 23.45S 133.25 E
Conway Reef→Ceva-i-Ra 57 Ig 21.45S 174.35 E
Conyers 44 Fi 33.40N 84.00W
Conza, Sella di- 14 Jj 40.50N 15.18 E
Coober Pedy 58 Eg 29.01S 134.43 E
Cooch Behār 25 Hc 26.19N 89.26 E
Cook 66 Ad 59.27S 27.10W
Cook 59 Gf 30.37S 130.25 E
Cook, Bahía- 56 Fi 55.10S 70.10W
Cook, Cap- 63b Dd 19.32S 169.30 E
Cook, Cape- 46 Ba 50.08N 127.55W
Cook, Mount- 57 Hi 43.36S 170.09 E
Cook, Récif de- 63b Ad 19.25S 163.50 E
Cooke, Mount- 59 Df 32.25S 116.18 E
Cookes Peak 45 Cj 32.32N 107.44W
Cookeville 44 Eg 36.10N 85.31W
Cook Ice Shelf 66 Je 68.40S 152.30 E
Cook Inlet 38 Dc 60.30N 152.00W
Cook Island 64g Bb 1.57N 157.28W
Cook Islands [5] 58 Lf 20.00S 158.00W
Cookstown/An Chorr Chriochach 9 Gg 54.39N 6.45W
Cook Strait 57 Ii 41.20S 174.25 E
Cooktown 58 Ff 15.28S 145.15 E
Coolgardie 59 Ef 30.57S 121.10 E
Coolidge [Az.-U.S.] 43 Ee 32.59N 111.31W
Coolidge [Ks.-U.S.] 45 Fg 38.03N 101.59W
Coolidge Dam 46 Jj 33.12N 110.32W
Cooma 59 Jg 36.14S 149.08 E
Coonabarabran 59 Jf 31.16S 149.17 E
Coonamble 59 Jf 30.57S 148.23 E
Coonoor 25 Ff 11.21N 76.49 E
Coon Rapids 45 Jd 45.09N 93.18W
Cooper 45 Ij 33.23N 95.35W
Cooper, Mount- 46 Ga 50.13N 117.12W
Cooper Creek 57 Eg 28.29S 137.46 E
Cooper's Town 44 Ii 26.51N 77.31W
Cooperstown [N.D.-U.S.] 45 Gc 47.27N 98.07W
Cooperstown [N.Y.-U.S.] 44 Jd 42.43N 74.56W
Coosa River 44 Di 32.30N 86.16W
Coos Bay 43 Cc 43.22N 124.13W
Coos Bay 46 Ce 43.23N 124.16W
Cootamundra 59 Jf 34.39S 148.02 E
Čop 10 Sh 48.26N 22.14 E
Copaiapó, Río- 56 Fc 27.19S 70.56W
Copainalá 48 Mi 17.05N 93.12W
Copán [3] 49 Cf 14.50N 89.00W
Copan 39 Kh 14.50N 89.09W
Copán 49 Cf 14.50N 89.12W
Copenhagen (EN)=København 6 Hi 55.40N 12.35 E
Copertino 14 Mj 40.16N 18.03 E
Copetonas 55 Bn 38.43N 60.27W
Copiapó 53 Ih 27.22S 70.20W
Čöpköy 15 Jh 41.13N 26.49 E
Coporito 50 Fh 8.56N 62.00W
Coporolo 36 Be 12.56S 13.00 E
Copparo 14 Ff 44.54N 11.49 E
Copper 40 Kd 60.30N 144.50W
Copperbelt [3] 36 Ee 13.00S 28.00 E
Copper Center 40 Jd 61.58N 145.19W
Copper Cliff 42 Jg 46.28N 81.04W
Copper Harbor 44 Db 47.27N 87.53W
Coppermine 39 Hc 67.50N 115.05W
Coppermine 38 Hc 67.49N 115.04W
Coppermine Point 44 Eb 46.59N 84.47W
Copper Queen 37 Dc 17.31S 29.20 E
Coqên (Maindong) 27 Ee 31.15N 85.13 E
Coquet 9 Lf 55.22N 1.37W
Coquetá, Río- 52 Jf 3.08S 64.46W
Coquille 46 Ce 43.11N 124.11W
Coquimbo [2] 56 Fd 31.00S 71.00W
Coquimbo 53 Ih 29.58S 71.21W
Corabia 15 Hf 43.47N 24.30 E
Coracão de Jesus 55 Jc 16.42S 44.22W
Coradi o Cheradi, Isole- 14 Lj 40.27N 17.09 E
Corail 49 Kd 18.34N 73.53W
Corail, Mer de-=Coral Sea (EN) 57 Gf 20.00S 158.00 E
Coral, Cabeza de- 48 Ph 18.47N 87.19W
Coral Gables 43 Kf 25.45N 80.16W
Coral Harbour 39 Kc 64.08N 83.10W
Coral Sea 57 Gf 20.00S 158.00 E
Coral Sea (EN)=Corail, Mer de- 57 Gf 20.00S 158.00 E
Coral Sea Basin (EN) 57 Gf 14.00S 152.00 E
Coral Sea Islands Territory 59 Lc 18.00S 158.00 E
Coralville 45 Kf 41.40N 91.35W
Coralville Lake 45 Kf 41.47N 91.48W
Corantijn River 52 Ke 5.55N 57.05W
Corato 14 Ki 41.09N 16.25 E
Corbara, Lago di- 14 Gh 42.45N 12.15 E
Corbeil-Essones 11 If 48.36N 2.29 E
Corbie 12 Ee 49.55N 2.30 E
Corbières 11 Il 42.55N 2.38 E
Corbigny 11 Jg 47.15N 3.40 E
Corby 9 Mi 52.29N 0.40W
Corcaigh/Cork [2] 9 Ej 52.00N 8.30W
Corcaigh/Cork 6 Fe 51.54N 8.28W
Corcoran 46 Gi 35.45N 117.23W
Corcovado, Cerro- 48 Bb 30.40N 114.55W
Corcovado, Golfo 56 Ff 43.30S 73.30W
Corcovado, Golfo- 52 Ij 43.30S 73.30W
Corcovado, Volcán- 52 Ij 43.12S 72.48W
Corcubión 13 Cb 42.57N 9.11W
Corcubión, Ría de- 13 Cb 42.54N 9.09W
Cordele 43 Ke 31.58N 83.47W
Cordes 11 Hj 44.04N 1.57 E
Cordevole 14 Gd 46.05N 12.04 E
Cordilheiras, Serra das- 54 Ie 7.30S 48.30W
Cordillera [3] 55 Dg 25.15S 57.00W
Cordillera Central [Phil.] 26 Hc 17.20N 120.57 E
Cordillera Central [S.Amer.] 52 If 8.00S 77.00W
Cordillera Occidental 52 Ig 14.00S 74.00W
Cordillera Oriental 52 If 7.00S 76.00W
Córdoba [3] 13 Hf 38.00N 4.50W
Córdoba [Arg.] [2] 56 Hd 32.00S 64.00W
Córdoba [Arg.] 53 Ji 31.25S 64.10W
Córdoba [Col.] [2] 54 Cb 8.20N 75.40W
Córdoba [Mex.] 47 Ee 18.53N 96.56W
Córdoba [Sp.] 6 Fh 37.53N 4.46W
Córdoba, Sierras de- 52 Ji 31.15S 64.00W
Cordova 39 Ec 60.33N 145.46W
Corfu (EN)=Kérkira 5 Hh 39.40N 19.45 E
Corfu, Strait of- (EN)=Kerkiras, Stenón- 15 Dj 39.35N 20.05 E
Corguinho 55 Ed 19.53S 54.52W
Coria 13 Fe 39.59N 6.32W
Coria del Rio 13 Fg 37.16N 6.03W
Coribe 55 Ja 13.50S 44.28W
Coricudgy, Mount- 59 Kf 32.50S 150.22 E
Corigliano Calabro 14 Kk 39.36N 16.31 E
Coringa Islets 59 Jc 17.00S 150.00 E
Corinne 46 Ma 50.06N 104.32W
Corinth 43 Je 34.56N 88.31W
Corinth (EN)=Kórinthos 15 Fl 37.55N 22.53 E
Corinth, Gulf of- (EN)=Korinthiakós Kólpos 5 Ih 38.12N 22.30 E
Corinth Canal (EN)=Korinthou, Dhiórix- 15 Fl 37.57N 22.58 E
Corinto [Braz.] 54 Jg 18.21S 44.27W
Corinto [Nic.] 49 Dg 12.29N 87.10W
Corisco 34 Ge 0.55N 9.19 E
Cork/Corcaigh 6 Fe 51.54N 8.28W
Cork/Corcaigh [2] 9 Ej 52.00N 8.30W
Cork Harbour 9 Ej 51.45N 8.15W
Corleone 14 Hm 37.49N 13.18 E
Çorlu 23 Ca 41.09N 27.48 E
Çorlu 15 Kh 41.12N 27.28 E
Cormeilles 12 Ce 49.15N 0.23 E
Cormoran Reef 64a Bb 7.50N 134.32 E
Cornelio 48 Dc 29.55N 111.08W
Cornélio Procopio 56 Jb 23.08S 50.39W
Cornelius Grinnel Bay 42 Ld 63.20N 64.50W
Corner Brook 39 Ne 48.57N 57.57W
Corner Seamounts (EN) 38 Nf 35.30N 51.30W
Cornia 14 Eh 42.57N 10.33 E
Corning [Ar.-U.S.] 45 Kh 36.24N 90.35W
Corning [Ca.-U.S.] 46 Dg 39.56N 122.11W
Corning [N.Y.-U.S.] 44 Id 42.10N 77.04W
Corno Grande 14 Hh 42.28N 13.34 E
Cornouaille 11 Cg 48.00N 4.00W
Cornwall [3] 9 Ik 50.30N 4.30W
Cornwall 42 Kg 45.02N 74.44W
Cornwall 42 Ia 73.30N 95.00W
Cornwall 9 Hk 50.20N 5.05W
Cornwall 5 Fe 50.30N 4.40W
Cornwall, Cape- 9 Hk 50.08N 5.43W
Cornwallis 42 Ia 75.15N 95.00W
Coro 53 Jd 11.25N 69.41W
Coro, Golfete de- 49 Mh 11.34N 69.53W
Corocoro 54 Eg 17.12S 68.28W
Corocoro, Isla- 50 Fh 8.31N 60.05W
Corod 15 Kd 45.54N 27.37 E
Čoroh 23 Fa 41.36N 41.35 E
Coroico 54 Eg 16.10S 67.44W
Coromandel [Braz.] 55 Id 18.28S 47.13W
Coromandel [N.Z.] 62 Fb 36.46S 175.30 E
Coromandel Coast 21 Kh 14.00N 80.10 E
Coromandel Peninsula 61 Eg 36.50S 175.35 E
Coromandel Range 62 Fb 37.00S 175.40 E
Coron 26 Hd 12.00N 120.12 E
Corona 45 Di 34.15N 105.36W
Corona Bank (EN) 59 Db 12.20S 118.30 E
Coronado, Bahía de- 38 Ki 9.00N 83.50W
Coronado, Isla- 48 Aa 32.25N 117.15W
Coronados, Isla- 48 Dd 26.07N 111.17W
Coronation 66 Re 60.37S 45.35W
Coronation 46 Ja 52.05N 111.27W
Coronation, Cap- 63b Cf 22.15S 167.02 E
Coronation Gulf 38 Ic 68.25N 110.00W
Coronda 55 Bj 31.58S 60.55W
Coronda, Laguna- 55 Bk 32.06S 60.52W
Coronel 56 Fe 37.01S 73.08W
Coronel Bogado 56 Ic 27.11S 56.18W
Coronel Dorrego 56 He 38.42S 61.17W
Coronel du Graty 55 Bh 27.40S 60.56W
Coronel Fabriciano 55 Jg 19.31S 42.38W
Coronel Oviedo 56 Ic 25.25S 56.27W
Coronel Ponce 55 Eb 15.34S 55.01W
Coronel Pringles 56 He 37.58S 61.22W
Coronel Rodolfo Bunge 55 Bm 37.34S 60.08W
Coronel Suárez 56 He 37.28S 61.55W
Coronel Vidal 55 Dm 37.27S 57.43W
Coronel Vivida 55 Fg 25.58S 52.34W
Coropuna, Nudo- 52 Ig 15.30S 72.41W
Çorovoda 15 Di 40.30N 20.13 E
Corozal [Blz.] 49 Cd 18.24N 88.24W
Corozal [Blz.] 49 Cd 18.15N 88.17W
Corozal [Col.] 49 Ji 9.18N 75.17W
Corpus Christi 39 Jg 27.48N 97.24W
Corpus Christi, Lake- 45 Hl 28.10N 97.53W
Corpus Christi Bay 45 Hm 27.48N 97.20W
Corque 54 Eg 18.21S 67.42W
Corral de Bustos 55 Ak 33.17S 62.12W
Corrèggio 14 Ef 44.46N 10.47 E
Córrego do Ouro 55 Gc 16.18S 50.32W
Corrente 54 If 10.27S 45.10W
Corrente, Rio- [Braz.] 54 Hg 19.19S 50.50W
Corrente, Rio- [Braz.] 55 Ka 13.08S 43.28W
Corrente, Rio- [Braz.] 55 Ib 14.14S 46.58W
Correntes 55 Ec 17.37S 54.59W
Correntes, Rio- 55 Ec 17.38S 55.08W
Correnti, Capo delle- 5 Hh 36.40N 15.05 E
Correntina 54 Jf 13.20S 44.39W
Corrèze 11 Hi 45.10N 1.28 E
Corrèze [3] 11 Hi 45.15N 1.50 E
Corrib, Lough-/Loch Coirib 9 Dh 53.05N 9.10W
Corrientes [2] 56 Ic 29.00S 58.00W
Corrientes 53 Kh 27.30S 58.50W
Corrientes, Cabo- [Arg.] 55 Dn 38.01S 57.32W
Corrientes, Cabo- [Col.] 54 Cb 5.30N 77.34W
Corrientes, Cabo- [Cuba] 49 Ec 21.45N 84.31W
Corrientes, Cabo- [Mex.] 38 Ig 20.25N 105.42W
Corrientes, Ensenada de- 49 Ec 21.45N 84.31W
Corrientes, Río- [Arg.] 55 Cj 30.21S 59.33W
Corrientes, Río- [Peru] 54 Dd 3.43S 74.40W
Corrieyairack Pass 9 Id 57.05N 4.40W
Corrigan 45 Ik 31.00N 94.50W
Corrigin 59 Df 32.21S 117.52 E
Corry 44 He 41.56N 79.39W
Corryong 59 Jg 36.12S 147.54 E
Corse=Corsica (EN) 5 Gg 42.00N 9.00 E
Corse, Cap- 5 Gg 43.00N 9.23 E
Corse-du-Sud [3] 11a Ab 41.50N 9.00 E
Corsewall Point 9 Hf 55.02N 5.05W
Corsica (EN)=Corse 5 Gg 42.00N 9.00 E
Corsica, Canale di- 14 Dh 42.45N 9.45 E
Corsicana 43 He 32.06N 96.28W
Cort Adelaer, Kap- 41 Hf 61.45N 42.00W
Corte 11a Ba 42.18N 9.09 E
Cortegana 13 Fg 37.55N 6.49W
Cortés [3] 49 Cf 15.30N 88.00W
Cortes 13 Kc 41.55N 1.25W
Cortez 43 Fd 37.21N 108.35W
Cortina d'Ampezzo 14 Gd 46.32N 12.08 E
Čortkov 16 De 48.59N 25.50 E
Cortland 44 Id 42.36N 76.10W
Cortona 14 Fg 43.16N 11.59 E
Corubal 34 Bc 11.57N 15.06W
Coruche 13 Df 38.57N 8.31W
Çoruh 23 Fa 41.36N 41.35 E
Çorum 24 Fb 40.29N 35.36 E
Çorum 23 Da 40.33N 34.58 E
Corumbá 53 Kg 19.01S 57.39W
Corumbá, Rio- 54 Ig 18.19S 48.55W
Corumbá de Goiás 55 Hb 15.55S 48.48W
Corumbáiba 55 Hd 18.09S 48.34W
Corumo, Rio- 50 Fi 6.49N 60.52W
Corvallis 43 Cc 44.34N 123.16W
Corvo 30 De 39.42N 31.06W
Corzuela 55 Bh 26.57S 60.58W
Cosalá 48 Fe 24.23N 106.41W
Cosamaloapan 48 Lh 18.22N 95.48W
Cosenza 6 Hh 39.18N 16.15 E
Coshocton 44 Ge 40.16N 81.53W
Cosigüina, Punta- 49 Dg 12.54N 87.41W
Cosmoledo Group 30 Li 9.43S 47.35 E
Cosne-sur-Loire 11 Ig 47.24N 2.55 E
Cosquín 56 Hd 31.15S 64.29W
Cossato 14 Ce 45.34N 8.10 E
Costa, Cordillera de la- 52 Je 9.50N 66.00W
Costa Rica [1] 39 Ki 10.00N 84.00W
Costa Verde 13 Ga 43.40N 5.40W
Costești 15 He 44.40N 24.53 E
Costiera, Catena- 14 Kk 39.25N 16.10 E
Coswig 10 Je 51.08N 13.35 E
Cotabato 26 He 7.13N 124.15 E
Cotagaita 54 Eh 20.50S 65.41W
Cotahuasi 54 Dg 15.12S 72.56W
Côte d'Ivoire=Ivory Coast (EN) [1] 31 Gh 8.00N 5.00W
Côte d'Or 11 Kg 47.10N 4.50 E
Côte-d'Or [3] 11 Kg 47.30N 4.50 E
Cotentin 5 Ff 49.30N 1.30W
Côtes-du-Nord [3] 11 Df 48.25N 2.40W
Cotiella 13 Mb 42.31N 0.19 E
Cotmeana 15 He 44.24N 24.45 E
Cotmeana 15 He 44.58N 24.37 E
Cotonou 31 Hh 6.21N 2.26 E
Cotopaxi, Volcán- 52 If 0.40S 78.26W
Cotswold Hills 9 Kj 51.45N 2.10W
Cottage Grove 46 De 43.48N 123.03W
Cottbus [2] 10 Je 51.45N 14.00 E
Cottbus/Chośebuz 10 Ke 51.46N 14.20 E
Cottenham 12 Cb 52.17N 0.08 E
Cottondale 44 Ej 30.48N 85.23W
Cottonwood Wash 46 Ji 35.05N 110.22W
Cotuí 49 Ld 19.03N 70.09W
Cotulla 45 Gl 28.26N 99.14W
Coubre, Pointe de la- 11 Ei 45.42N 1.14W
Couburg 10 Gf 50.15N 10.58 E
Coucy-le-Château-Auffrique 12 Fe 49.31N 3.19 E
Coudekerque-Branche 12 Ec 51.02N 2.24 E
Coudersport 44 He 41.46N 78.01W
Couedic, Cape du- 59 Hg 36.10S 136.40 E
Couesnon 11 Ef 48.37N 1.31W
Couhé 11 Gh 46.18N 0.11 E
Couilly-Pont-aux-Dames 12 Ef 48.53N 2.52 E
Coulee Dam 46 Fb 48.00N 118.59W
Coulihaut 51g Bb 15.30N 61.29W
Coulman Island 66 Kf 73.28S 169.45 E
Coulogne 12 Dd 50.55N 1.53 E
Coulommiers 11 Jf 48.49N 3.05 E
Coulonge, Rivière- 44 Ic 45.51N 76.45
Coulounieix-Chamiers 11 Gi 45.10N 0.42
Council 46 Gd 44.44N 116.26
Council Bluffs 43 Hc 41.16N 95.52
Courcelles 12 Gd 50.28N 4.22
Courcelles-Chaussy 12 Ie 49.07N 6.24
Courland (EN)=Kurzeme 5 Id 57.00N 20.30
Courmayeur 14 Ae 45.47N 6.58
Cours 11 Kh 46.06N 4.19
Courseulles-sur-Mer 12 Be 49.20N 0.27
Courtenay 42 Fg 49.41N 125.00
Courtisols 12 Gf 48.59N 4.31
Courtrai/Kortrijk 11 Jd 50.50N 3.16
Coushatta 45 Jj 32.00N 93.21
Cousin 11 Kh 46.58N 4.15
Coutances 11 Ee 49.03N 1.26
Couto de Magalhães, Rio- 55 Fa 13.37S 53.09
Coutras 11 Fi 45.02N 0.08
Couture, Lac- 42 Jd 60.05N 75.20
Couvin 11 Kd 50.03N 4.20
Couvin-Mariembourg 12 Gd 50.06N 4.31
Covarrubias 13 Ib 42.04N 3.31
Covasna [2] 15 Id 46.00N 26.00
Covasna 15 Jd 45.51N 26.11
Coveñas 49 Ji 9.25N 75.42
Coventry 9 Li 52.25N 1.30
Covilhã 13 Ed 40.17N 7.30
Covington [Ga.-U.S.] 44 Fi 33.37N 83.51
Covington [Ky.-U.S.] 43 Kd 39.05N 84.30
Covington [La.-U.S.] 45 Kk 30.29N 90.06
Covington [Tn.-U.S.] 44 Ch 35.34N 89.39
Covington [Va.-U.S.] 44 Hg 37.48N 79.59
Cowal 9 He 56.05N 5.10
Cowan, Lake- 59 Ef 31.50S 121.50
Cowan Knob 45 Ji 35.52N 93.29
Cowell 59 Hf 33.41S 136.55
Cowes 12 Ad 50.46N 1.18
Cowichan Lake 46 Cb 48.54N 124.20
Cowra 59 Jf 33.50S 148.41
Coxim 53 Kg 18.30S 54.45
Coxim, Rio- 55 Ed 18.34S 54.46
Cox's Bāzār 25 Id 21.26N 91.59
Coyah 34 Cd 9.43N 13.23
Coyame 48 Gc 29.28N 105.06
Coyanosa Draw 45 Ek 31.18N 103.06
Coycoyan, Sierra de- 48 Ji 17.30N 98.20
Coyle—Coig, Río- 56 Gh 50.58S 69.11
Coyote, Río- 48 Cb 30.48N 112.35
Coyotitán 48 Ff 23.47N 106.35
Coyuca, Laguna de- 48 Ii 16.57N 100.05
Cozia, Pasul- 15 Hd 45.15N 24.15
Cozumel 48 Pg 20.31N 86.55
Cozumel, Isla de- 47 Gd 20.25N 86.55
Cradock 31 Jl 32.08S 25.36
Craig [Ak.-U.S.] 40 Me 55.29N 133.09
Craig [Co.-U.S.] 43 Fc 40.31N 107.33
Craigmont 46 Gc 46.15N 116.28
Craigs Range 59 Ke 26.40S 151.30
Crailsheim 10 Gg 49.09N 10.05
Craiova 6 Ig 44.19N 23.48
Cranbrook [Austl.] 59 Df 34.18S 117.32
Cranbrook [B.C.-Can.] 42 Fg 49.31N 115.46
Cranbrook [Eng.-U.K.] 12 Cc 51.05N 0.32
Crandon 45 Ld 45.34N 88.54
Crane [Or.-U.S.] 46 Fe 43.25N 118.35
Crane [Tx.-U.S.] 45 Ek 31.24N 102.21
Crane Lake 45 Jb 48.16N 92.28
Crane Lake 46 Ka 50.06N 109.06
Cranleigh 12 Bc 51.08N 0.29
Craon 11 Fg 47.51N 0.57
Craonne 12 Fe 49.26N 3.47
Crapaud, Puy- 11 Fh 46.40N 0.40
Crary Mountains 66 Of 76.48S 117.40
Crasna 15 Fb 48.09N 22.20
Crasna [Rom.] 15 Kc 46.31N 27.51
Crasna [Rom.] 15 Fb 47.10N 22.54
Crater Lake [Or.-U.S.] 43 Cc 42.56N 122.06
Crater Lake [St.Vin.] 51n Ba 13.19N 61.11
Crateús 53 Lf 5.10S 40.40
Crati 14 Kk 39.43N 16.31
Crato [Braz.] 54 Ke 7.14S 39.23
Crato [Port.] 13 Ee 39.17N 7.39
Crau 11 Kk 43.36N 4.50
Crauford, Cape- 42 Jb 73.44N 84.51
Cravo Norte 54 Db 6.17N 70.12
Crawford 45 Ee 42.41N 103.25
Crawfordsville 44 De 40.02N 86.54
Crawley 9 Mj 51.07N 0.12
Crazy Mountains 46 Jc 46.08N 110.20
Crazy Peak 43 Eb 46.01N 110.16
Creciente, Isla- 48 De 24.23N 111.37
Crécy-en-Ponthieu 12 Dd 50.15N 1.53
Crécy-la-Chapelle 12 Ef 48.51N 2.55
Crécy-sur-Serre 12 Fe 49.42N 3.37
Crediton 9 Jk 50.47N 3.39
Cree [Sask.-Can.] 42 Ge 58.50N 105.40
Cree [Scot.-U.K.] 9 Ig 54.52N 4.20
Creede 45 Ch 37.51N 106.56
Creel 47 Cc 27.45N 107.38
Cree Lake 42 Ge 57.30N 106.30
Creglingen 10 Gg 49.28N 10.02
Creil 11 Ie 49.16N 2.29
Crema 14 De 45.22N 9.41
Cremenea, Bratul- 15 Ke 44.57N 27.54
Crémieu, Plateau de- 11 Li 45.40N 5.30
Cremona 14 Ee 45.07N 10.02
Crepaja 15 Dd 45.01N 20.39
Crepori, Rio- 54 Ge 5.42S 57.08
Crépy-en-Valois 11 Ie 49.14N 2.54
Cres [Yugo.] 14 If 44.40N 14.25
Cres [Yugo.] 14 If 44.58N 14.24
Crescent 46 Ee 43.29N 121.41
Crescent City 43 Cc 41.45N 124.12
Crescent Lake 44 Gk 29.28N 81.30
Crespo 55 Bk 32.02S 60.19

Index Symbols

[1] Independent Nation
[2] State, Region
[3] District, County
[4] Municipality
[5] Colony, Dependency
Continent
Physical Region
Historical or Cultural Region
Mount, Mountain
Volcano
Hill
Mountains, Mountain Range
Hills, Escarpment
Plateau, Upland
Pass, Gap
Plain, Lowland
Delta
Salt Flat
Valley, Canyon
Crater, Cave
Karst Features
Depression
Polder
Desert, Dunes
Forest, Woods
Heath, Steppe
Oasis
Cape, Point
Coast, Beach
Cliff
Peninsula
Isthmus
Sandbank
Island
Atoll
Rock, Reef
Islands, Archipelago
Rocks, Reefs
Coral Reef
Well, Spring
Geyser
River, Stream
Waterfall Rapids
River Mouth, Estuary
Lake
Salt Lake
Intermittent Lake
Reservoir
Swamp, Pond
Canal
Glacier
Ice Shelf, Pack Ice
Ocean
Sea
Gulf, Bay
Strait, Fjord
Lagoon
Bank
Seamount
Tablemount
Ridge
Shelf
Basin
Escarpment, Sea Scarp
Fracture
Trench, Abyss
National Park, Reserve
Point of Interest
Recreation Site
Cave, Cavern
Historic Site
Ruins
Wall, Walls
Church, Abbey
Temple
Scientific Station
Airport
Port
Lighthouse
Mine
Tunnel
Dam, Bridg

Crest 11 Lj 44.44N 5.02 E
Crested Butte 45 Cg 38.52N 106.59W
Creston [B.C.-Can.] 46 Gb 49.06N 116.31W
Creston [Ia.-U.S.] 43 Ic 41.04N 94.22W
Crestone Peak 45 Dh 37.58N 105.36W
Crestview 43 Je 30.46N 86.34W
Creswell 44 Ih 35.52N 76.23W
Creswell Bay 42 Ib 72.40N 93.30W
Creswell Creek 59 Hc 18.10S 135.11 E
Crete 45 Hf 40.38N 96.58W
Crete (EN) = Kriti 5 Ih 35.15N 24.45 E
Crete (EN) = Kriti 15 Hn 35.35N 25.00 E
Crete, Sea of- (EN) = Kritikón Pélagos 15 Hn 36.00N 25.00 E
Créteil 11 If 48.47N 2.28 E
Cretin, Cape- 60 Di 6.40S 147.52 E
Creus, Cabo de-/Creus, Cap de- 5 Gg 42.19N 3.19 E
Creus, Cap de-/Creus, Cabo de- 5 Gg 42.19N 3.19 E
Creuse 11 Hh 46.05N 2.00 E
Creuse 11 Gg 47.00N 0.34 E
Creutzwald 11 Me 49.12N 6.41 E
Crevecoeur-en-Auge 12 Ce 49.07N 0.01 E
Crèvecoeur-le-Grand 12 Ee 49.36N 2.05 E
Crevillente 13 Lf 38.15N 0.48W
Crewe 9 Kh 53.05N 2.27W
Crézancy 12 Fe 49.03N 3.30 E
Criciúma 53 Lh 28.40S 49.23W
Cricket Mountains 46 Ig 38.50N 113.00W
Crieff 9 Je 56.23N 3.52W
Criel-sur-Mer 12 Dd 50.01N 1.19 E
Criel sur Mer-Mesnil Val 12 Dd 50.03N 1.20 E
Crikvenica 14 Ie 45.11N 14.42 E
Crillon 12 De 49.31N 1.56 E
Crimea (EN)=Krymski Poluostrov 5 Jf 45.00N 34.00 E
Crimean Mountains (EN)= Krymskije Gory 5 Jg 44.45N 34.30 E
Crimmitschau 10 If 50.49N 12.23 E
Criquetot-l'Esneval 12 Ce 49.39N 0.16 E
Crissolo 14 Bf 44.42N 7.09 E
Cristal, Monts de- 36 Bb 0.30N 10.30 E
Cristal, Serra del- 49 Jc 20.33N 75.31W
Cristalândia 54 If 10.36S 49.11W
Cristalina 54 Ig 16.45S 47.36W
Cristalino, Rio- 54 Hf 12.40S 50.40W
Cristallo 14 Gd 46.34N 12.12 E
Cristóbal Colón, Pico 52 Id 10.50N 73.45W
Cristuru Secuiesc 15 Ic 46.35N 25.47 E
Crişu Alb 15 Ec 46.42N 21.16 E
Crişu Negru 15 Ec 46.42N 21.16 E
Crişu Repede 15 Dc 46.55N 20.59 E
Crixás 55 Hb 14.27S 49.58W
Crixás-Açu, Rio- 55 Hb 13.19S 50.36W
Crixás Mirim, Rio- 55 Ga 13.28S 50.36W
Crkvena Planina 15 Fg 42.48N 22.22 E
Crna Gora 15 Eg 42.16N 21.35 E
Crna Gora 15 Ce 44.05N 19.50 E
Crna Gora = Montenegro (EN) 15 Cg 42.30N 19.18 E
Crna Gora=Montenegro (EN) 15 Cg 42.30N 19.18 E
Crna Reka 15 Ef 43.50N 21.55 E
Crna reka 15 Eh 41.33N 21.59 E
Crni Drim 15 Dg 42.05N 20.23 E
Crni Timok 15 Ff 43.55N 22.18 E
Crni Vrh 14 Jd 46.29N 15.14 E
Crni vrh 14 Kf 44.36N 16.30 E
Črnomelj 14 Je 45.34N 15.12 E
Croatia (EN) = Hrvatska 14 Jf 45.00N 15.30 E
Croatia (EN) = Hrvatska 5 Hf 45.00N 15.30 E
Croatia (EN) = Hrvatska 14 Je 45.00N 15.30 E
Crocker, Banjaran- 26 Ge 5.40N 116.20 E
Crockett 45 Ik 31.19N 95.28W
Crocq 11 Ii 45.52N 2.22 E
Crocus Bay 51b Ab 18.13N 63.05W
Croisette, Cap- 11 Lk 43.13N 5.20 E
Croisic, Pointe du- 11 Dg 47.17N 2.33W
Croisilles 12 Ed 50.12N 2.53 E
Croissy-sur-Celle 12 Ee 49.42N 2.11 E
Croix, Lac la- 45 Jb 48.21N 92.05W
Croix-Haute, Col de la- 11 Lj 44.43N 5.40 E
Croker, Cape- 59 Gb 10.58S 132.35 E
Croker Bay 42 Jb 74.38N 83.15W
Croker Island 59 Gb 11.10S 132.30 E
Cromarty 9 Id 57.40N 4.02W
Cromer 9 Oi 52.56N 1.18 E
Cromwell 62 Cf 45.03S 169.14 E
Crooked Island 47 Jd 22.45N 74.13W
Crooked Island Passage 47 Jd 22.55N 74.35W
Crooked River 46 Ed 44.34N 121.16W
Crookston 43 Hb 47.47N 96.37W
Crosby [Mn.-U.S.] 45 Jc 46.28N 93.57W
Crosby [N.D.-U.S.] 45 Eb 48.55N 103.18W
Cross 34 Ge 4.55N 8.15 E
Cross City 44 Fk 29.32N 83.07W
Crossett 45 Kj 33.08N 91.58W
Cross Fell 9 Kg 54.42N 2.29W
Cross Lake 47 Hf 54.47N 97.22W
Crossman Peak 46 Hi 34.32N 114.07W
Cross River 34 Gd 5.40N 8.10 E
Cross Sound 40 Le 58.10N 136.30W
Crotone 14 Lk 39.05N 17.08 E
Crotto 55 Bm 36.35S 60.10W
Crouch 12 Cc 51.37N 0.53 E
Crow Agency 46 Ld 45.36N 107.27W
Crowborough 12 Cc 51.03N 0.09 E
Crow Creek 45 Df 40.23N 104.29W
Crowell 45 Gj 33.59N 99.43W
Crow Lake 45 Jb 49.12N 93.57W
Crowley 45 Jk 30.13N 92.22W
Crowley, Lake- 46 Fh 37.37N 118.44W
Crowley Ridge 45 Ki 35.45N 90.45W
Crownpoint 45 Bi 35.42N 108.07W
Crown Prince Frederik 42 Ic 70.05N 86.40W
Crowsnest Pass 42 Gg 49.00N 114.30W
Crows Nest Peak 45 Ed 44.03N 103.58W
Croydon 59 Ic 18.12S 142.14 E
Croydon, London- 9 Mj 51.23N 0.07W
Crozet, Iles- 30 Mm 46.30S 51.00 E
Crozet Basin (EN) 3 Gm 39.00S 60.00 E
Crozet Ridge (EN) 3 Fn 45.00S 45.00 E
Crozon 11 Bf 48.15N 4.29W
Crozon, Presqu'île de- 11 Bf 48.15N 4.25W
Crucero, Cerro- 48 Gg 21.41N 104.25W
Cruces 49 Gb 22.21N 80.16W
Crump Lake 46 Fe 42.17N 119.50W
Crumpton Point 51g Ba 15.35N 61.19W
Cruz, Cabo- 47 Ie 19.51N 77.44W
Cruz Alta [Arg.] 55 Bk 33.01S 61.49W
Cruz Alta [Braz.] 53 Kh 28.39S 53.36W
Cruz del Eje 56 Hd 30.44S 64.48W
Cruzeiro do Oeste 56 Jb 23.46S 53.04W
Cruzeiro do Sul 53 If 7.38S 72.36W
Cruzen Island 66 Mf 74.47S 140.42W
Cruz Grande 48 Ji 16.44N 99.08W
Crvanj 14 Mg 43.25N 18.11 E
Crvenka 15 Cd 45.39N 19.28 E
Crystal Brook 59 Hf 33.21S 138.13 E
Crystal City [Man.-Can.] 45 Gb 49.08N 98.57W
Crystal City [Tx.-U.S.] 45 Gl 28.41N 99.50W
Crystal Falls 44 Cb 46.06N 88.20W
Crystal Springs 45 Kk 31.59N 90.21W
Csákvár 10 Oi 47.24N 18.27 E
Cserhat 10 Pi 47.55N 19.30 E
Csongrád 10 Qj 46.25N 20.15 E
Csongrad 10 Qj 46.42N 20.09 E
Csorna 10 Ni 47.37N 17.15 E
ČSSR→ Československá Socialistická Republika 6 Hf 49.30N 17.00 E
Csurgó 10 Nj 46.16N 17.06 E
Ctesiphon 24 Kf 33.05N 44.35 E
Ču 21 Ie 45.00N 67.44 E
Ču 22 Je 43.33N 73.45 E
Cuajinicuilapa 48 Ji 16.28N 98.25W
Cuale 36 Cd 7.40S 17.01 E
Cuamba 31 Kj 14.49S 36.33 E
Cuan an Fhóid Duibh/ Blacksod Bay 9 Dg 54.08N 10.00W
Cuanavale 36 Cf 15.07S 19.14 E
Cuan Bhaile Átha Cliath/ Dublin Bay 9 Gh 53.20N 6.06W
Cuan Chill Ala/Killala Bay 9 Dg 54.15N 9.10W
Cuan Dhun Dealgan/ Dundalk Bay 9 Gh 53.57N 6.17W
Cuan Dhún Droma/Dundrum Bay 9 Hg 54.13N 5.45W
Cuando 30 Jj 18.27S 23.32 E
Cuando-Cubango 36 Df 16.00S 20.30 E
Cuan Eochaille/Youghal Harbour 9 Fj 51.52N 7.50W
Cuangar 36 Cf 17.36S 18.37 E
Cuango 30 Ii 3.14S 17.22 E
Cuango [Ang.] 36 Cd 9.07S 18.05 E
Cuango [Ang.] 36 Cd 6.17S 16.41 E
Cuan Loch Garman/Wexford Harbour 9 Gi 52.20N 6.25W
Cuan Mó/Clew Bay 9 Dh 53.50N 9.50W
Cuan na Gaillimhe/Galway Bay 5 Fe 53.10N 9.15W
Cuan na gCaorach/Sheep Haven 9 Ff 55.10N 7.52W
Cuan Phort Láirge/ Waterford Harbour 9 Gi 52.10N 6.57W
Cuan Shligigh/Sligo Bay 9 Eg 54.20N 8.40W
Cuanza 30 Ii 9.19S 13.08 E
Cuanza Norte 36 Bd 8.50S 14.30 E
Cuanza Sul 36 Be 10.50S 14.50 E
Cuareim, Arroyo- 55 Dj 30.12S 57.36W
Cuaró 55 Dj 30.37S 56.54W
Cuaró Grande, Arroyo- 55 Dj 30.18S 57.12W
Cuarto, Rio- 56 Hd 33.25S 63.02W
Cuatir 36 Cf 17.01S 18.09 E
Cuatro Ciénegas de Carranza 48 Hd 26.59N 102.05W
Cuauhtémoc 47 Cc 28.25N 106.52W
Cuautitlán 48 Jh 19.40N 99.11W
Cuay Grande 55 Di 28.40S 56.17W
Cuba 38 Lg 21.30N 80.00W
Cuba 39 Lg 21.30N 80.00W
Cuba [Mo.-U.S.] 45 Kg 38.04N 91.24W
Cuba [N.M.-U.S.] 45 Ch 36.01N 107.04W
Cuba [Port.] 13 Ef 38.10N 7.53W
Cubabi, Cerro- 48 Cb 31.42N 112.46W
Cubagua, Isla- 50 Dg 10.49N 64.11W
Cubal 36 Be 13.03S 14.15 E
Cubal [Ang.] 36 Be 11.29S 13.48 E
Cubal [Ang.] 36 Bf 15.22S 12.39 E
Cubango 30 Jj 18.53N 22.24 E
Çubuk 24 Eb 40.59N 32.05 E
Čubukulah, Gora- 20 Kc 66.23N 153.59 E
Cucalón, Sierra de- 13 Kd 40.59N 1.10W
Cuchi 36 Ce 14.40S 16.52 E
Cuchi 30 Ij 15.28S 17.21 E
Cuchibi 36 De 15.00S 20.45 E
Cuchilla Áquila, Cerro- 48 Ig 21.27N 101.03W
Cuchivero, Rio- 50 Di 7.40N 65.57W
Cuchumatanes, Sierra de los- 49 Bf 15.35N 91.25W
Cuckfield 12 Bc 51.01N 0.08W
Cuckmere 12 Cd 50.45N 0.09 E
Cucui 54 Ec 1.12N 66.50W
Cucumbi 36 Ce 10.17S 19.03 E
Cucurpe 48 Db 30.20N 110.43W
Cúcuta 53 Ie 7.54N 72.31W
Cudahy 45 Me 42.57N 87.52W
Cudalbi 15 Kd 45.47N 27.42 E
Cuddalore 22 Jh 11.45N 79.45 E
Cuddapah 25 Ff 14.28N 78.49 E
Čudovo 19 Dd 59.08N 31.41 E
Čudskoje Ozero=Peipus, Lake- (EN) 5 Id 58.45N 27.30 E
Cue 59 De 27.25S 117.54 E
Cuebe 36 Cf 15.48S 17.30 E
Cuelei 36 Cf 15.33S 17.21 E
Cuéllar 13 Hc 41.29N 4.19W
Cuemba 36 Ce 12.09S 18.07 E
Cuenca 13 Ke 40.00N 2.00W
Cuenca [Ec.] 53 If 2.53S 78.59W
Cuenca [Sp.] 13 Jd 40.04N 2.08W
Cuenca, Serrania de- 5 Fg 40.10N 1.55W
Cuencamé de Ceniceros 48 He 24.53N 103.42W
Cuera/Chur 14 Dd 46.50N 9.35 E
Cuerda del Pozo, Embalse de la- 13 Jc 41.51N 2.44W
Cuernavaca 39 Jh 18.55N 99.15W
Cuero 45 Hl 29.06N 97.18W
Cuevas del Almanzora 13 Kg 37.18N 1.53W
Cugir 15 Gd 45.50N 23.22 E
Cugo 36 Cd 7.22S 17.06 E
Čugujev 16 Je 49.50N 36.41 E
Čugujevka 28 Mb 44.08N 133.53 E
Čuhloma 19 Ed 58.47N 42.41 E
Cuiabá 53 Kg 15.35S 56.05W
Cuiabá, Rio- 52 Kg 17.05S 56.36W
Cuiabá Mirim, Rio- 55 Ec 16.20S 55.55W
Cuidado, Punta- 65d Bb 27.08S 109.19W
Cuijk, Cuijk en Sint Agatha- 12 Hc 51.44N 5.52 E
Cuijk en Sint Agatha-Cuijk 12 Hc 51.44N 5.52 E
Cuilapa 49 Bf 14.17N 90.18W
Cuillin Hills 9 Gd 57.14N 6.15W
Cuilo 30 Ii 3.22S 17.22 E
Cúil Raithin/Coleraine 9 Gf 55.08N 6.40W
Cuiluan 27 Mb 47.39N 128.34 E
Cuima 36 Ce 13.14S 15.38 E
Cuito 30 Jj 18.01S 20.48 E
Cuito Cuanavale 31 Ij 15.13S 19.08 E
Cuitzeo, Lago de- 48 Ih 19.55N 101.05W
Cuiuni, Rio- 54 Fd 0.45S 63.07W
Cujmir 15 Fe 44.13N 22.56 E
Čukata 15 Ih 41.50N 25.15 E
Čukotski Nacionalny okrug 20 Mc 66.00N 172.30 E
Čukotski Poluostrov= Chukchi Peninsula (EN) 21 Uc 66.00N 175.00W
Čukotskoje More=Chukchi Sea (EN) 67 Bd 69.00N 171.00W
Çukurca 24 Jd 37.15N 43.37 E
Çukurdağı 15 Ll 37.58N 28.44 E
Čulakkurgan 19 Gg 43.48N 69.12 E
Culan 11 Ih 46.33N 2.21 E
Cu Lao, Hon- 25 Lf 10.30N 109.13 E
Culasi 26 Hd 11.26N 122.03 E
Culbertson 46 Mb 48.09N 104.31W
Culebra, Isla de- 49 Od 18.19N 65.17W
Culebra, Sierra de la- 13 Fc 41.55N 6.20W
Culebra Peak 45 Dh 37.06N 105.10W
Culemborg 12 Hc 51.57N 5.14 E
Culiacán, Rio de- 48 Fe 24.31N 107.41W
Culiacán Rosales 39 Ig 24.48N 107.24W
Culion 26 Gd 11.50N 119.55 E
Culion 26 Hd 11.53N 120.01 E
Culiseu, Rio- 54 Hf 12.14S 53.17W
Cullera 13 Le 39.10N 0.15W
Cullman 43 Je 34.11N 86.51W
Čulman 22 Od 56.52N 124.52 E
Culpeper 44 Hf 38.28N 78.01W
Culuene, Rio- 52 Kg 12.56S 52.51W
Culukidze 16 Mh 42.18N 42.25 E
Culver, Point- 59 Ef 32.54S 124.43 E
Culverden 62 Ee 42.46S 172.51 E
Čulym 20 De 55.06N 80.58 E
Čulym 21 Kd 57.40N 83.50 E
Čulyšman 20 Df 51.20N 87.45 E
Cuma 36 Ce 12.52S 15.04 E
Cumaná 53 Jd 10.28N 64.10W
Cumanacoa 50 Eg 10.15N 63.55W
Cumaovası 15 Kk 38.15N 27.09 E
Cumbal, Volcán- 54 Cc 0.57N 77.52W
Cumberland 9 Kg 54.40N 2.50W
Cumberland 38 Kf 37.09N 88.25W
Cumberland [B.C.-Can.] 46 Cb 49.37N 125.01W
Cumberland [Md.-U.S.] 43 Ld 39.39N 78.46W
Cumberland [Va.-U.S.] 44 Hg 37.31N 78.16W
Cumberland, Cap- 63b Cb 14.39S 166.37 E
Cumberland, Lake- 44 Eg 36.57N 84.55W
Cumberland Bay 51n Ba 13.16N 61.17W
Cumberland Island 44 Gj 30.51N 81.27W
Cumberland Islands 59 Jd 20.40S 149.10 E
Cumberland Lake 42 Hf 54.00N 102.20W
Cumberland Peninsula 38 Mc 66.50N 64.00W
Cumberland Plateau 38 Kf 36.00N 85.00W
Cumberland Sound 38 Mc 65.10N 65.30W
Cumbernauld 9 Jf 55.58N 3.59W
Cumbre, Paso de la-/ Bermejo, Paso- 52 Ii 32.50S 70.05W
Cumbria 9 Kg 54.35N 2.45W
Cumbrian Mountains 9 Jg 54.30N 3.05W
Čumerna 15 Ig 42.47N 25.58 E
Čumikan 20 If 54.42N 135.19 E
Cummins 59 Hf 34.16S 135.44 E
Cumnock 9 If 55.27N 4.16W
Cumpas 48 Eb 30.02N 109.48W
Çumra 24 Ed 37.34N 32.48 E
Čumyš 20 Df 53.30N 83.10 E
Cuna 21 Ld 57.42N 95.35 E
Cunagua 49 Hb 22.05N 78.20W
Cuñapirú 55 Ej 31.32S 55.35W
Cuñapirú, Arroyo- 55 Ej 31.12S 55.31W
Cuñapirú, Cuchilla de- 55 Ej 31.12S 55.36W
Cunaviche, Rio- 50 Ci 7.19N 67.11W
Cunderdin 59 Df 31.39S 117.15 E
Cundinamarca 54 Db 5.00N 74.00W
Čundža 19 Hg 43.32N 79.28 E
Cunene 36 Cf 16.30S 15.00 E
Cunene=Kunene (EN) 30 Ij 17.20S 11.50 E
Cuneo 14 Bf 44.23N 7.32 E
Čunja 21 Lc 61.30N 96.20 E
Cunnamulla 58 Fg 28.04S 145.41 E
Čunski [R.S.F.S.R.] 20 Ee 56.03N 99.48 E
Čunski [R.S.F.S.R.] 20 Ee 57.23N 97.40 E
Cuorgné 14 Be 45.23N 7.39 E
Čupa 19 Db 66.17N 33.01 E
Cupar 9 Je 56.19N 3.01W
Cupica, Golfo de- 54 Cb 6.35N 77.30W
Ćuprija 15 Ef 43.56N 21.22 E
Cupula, Pico- 48 De 24.47N 110.50W
Čur 7 Mh 57.11N 53.01 E
Curaçá 54 Ke 8.59S 39.54W
Curacao 52 Jd 12.11N 69.00W
Curacautín 56 Fe 38.26S 71.53W
Cura Malal, Sierra de- 55 Am 37.44S 62.16W
Curanilahue 56 Fe 37.28S 73.21W
Čurapča 20 Id 61.56N 132.18 E
Curaray, Rio- 54 Dd 2.20S 74.05W
Curcŭbata, Vîrful- 15 Fc 46.25N 22.35 E
Curdimurka 58 Eg 29.30S 137.10 E
Curé 55 De 21.25S 56.25W
Cure 11 Jg 47.40N 3.41 E
Curepipe 37a Bb 20.19S 57.31 E
Curepto 56 Fe 35.05S 72.01W
Curiapo 54 Fb 8.33N 61.00W
Curicó 53 Ii 34.59S 71.14W
Curicuriari, Rio- 54 Ed 0.14S 66.48W
Curitabanos 56 Jc 27.18S 50.36W
Curitiba 53 Lh 25.25S 49.15W
Curoca 36 Bf 15.43S 11.55 E
Currais Novos 54 Ke 6.15S 36.31W
Curralinho 54 Id 1.48S 49.47W
Curral-Velho 32 Cf 15.59N 22.48W
Current River 45 Kh 36.15N 90.57W
Currie 59 Ig 39.56S 143.52 E
Curtea de Argeş 15 Hd 45.08N 24.41 E
Curtici 15 Ec 46.21N 21.18 E
Curtis 45 Ff 40.38N 100.31W
Curtis Channel 59 Kd 23.55S 152.05 E
Curtis Island 57 Jh 30.35S 178.36W
Curtis Island [Austl.] 59 Kd 23.40S 151.10 E
Curuá, Rio- [Braz.] 55 Ga 13.26S 51.24W
Curuá, Rio- [Braz.] 54 Gd 1.55S 55.07W
Curuá, Rio- [Braz.] 52 Kf 5.23S 54.22W
Curuçá 54 Id 0.43S 47.50W
Curuçá, Rio- 54 Dd 4.27S 71.23W
Curuguaty 56 Ib 24.31S 55.42W
Curuguaty, Arroyo- 55 Dg 24.06S 56.02W
Curup 26 Dg 3.28S 102.32 E
Curupira, Sierra de- 54 Fc 1.25N 64.30W
Cururupu 54 Jd 1.50S 44.52W
Curuzú Cuatiá 56 Ic 29.47S 58.03W
Curvelo 54 Jg 18.45S 44.25W
Cusco 53 Ig 13.31S 71.59W
Cushing 45 Hi 35.59N 96.46W
Cushing, Mount- 42 Ee 57.36N 126.51W
Čusovaja 5 Ld 58.13N 56.30 E
Čusovoj 19 Fd 58.17N 57.50 E
Cusset 11 Jh 46.08N 3.28 E
Cusseta 44 Ei 32.18N 84.47W
Čust 18 Hd 41.00N 71.15 E
Custer 45 Ee 43.46N 103.36W
Cutato 36 Ce 10.33S 16.48 E
Cut Bank 43 Eb 48.38N 112.20W
Cutervo 54 Ce 6.22S 78.51W
Cuthbert 44 Ej 31.46N 84.48W
Cutral Có 56 Ge 38.56S 69.14W
Cutro 14 Kk 39.02N 16.59 E
Cuttack 22 Kg 20.30N 85.50 E
Čuvašskaja ASSR 19 Ed 55.30N 47.10 E
Cuvelai 36 Cf 15.40S 15.47 E
Cuvette 36 Cc 0.10S 15.30 E
Cuvier Basin (EN) 59 Cd 22.00S 111.00 E
Cuvier Island 62 Fb 36.25S 175.45 E
Cuvo ou Queve 30 Ij 10.50S 13.47 E
Cuxhaven 10 Ec 53.53N 8.42 E
Cuya 56 Fa 19.07S 70.08W
Cuyahoga Falls 44 Ge 41.08N 81.55W
Cuyo Islands 26 Hd 11.04N 120.57 E
Cuyubini, Rio- 50 Fh 8.20N 60.20W
Cuyuni, Rio- 52 Ke 6.23N 58.41W
Cuyuni River 52 Kf 6.23N 58.41W
Cuyutlán, Laguna- 48 Gh 19.00N 104.10W
Cuzco 54 Df 12.30S 72.30W
Cuzna 13 Hf 38.04N 4.41W
Cvikov 10 Kf 50.48N 14.40 E
Čvrsnica 14 Lg 43.35N 17.35 E
Cyangugu 36 Ec 2.29S 28.54 E
Cybinka 10 Kd 52.12N 14.48 E
Cyclades (EN) = Kikládhes 5 Ih 37.00N 25.10 E
Čyjyrčyk, Pereval- 18 Id 40.15N 73.20 E
Cypress Hills 38 Ie 49.40N 110.30W
Cypress Lake 46 Kb 49.28N 109.29W
Cyprus (EN)=Kıbrıs/ Kypros 22 Ff 35.00N 33.00 E
Cyprus (EN)=Kıbrıs/ Kypros 21 Ff 35.00N 33.00 E
Cyprus (EN)=Kypros/ Kıbrıs 22 Ff 35.00N 33.00 E
Cyprus (EN)=Kypros/ Kıbrıs 21 Ff 35.00N 33.00 E
Cyrenaica (EN)=Barqah 33 Dc 31.00N 22.30 E
Cyrenaica (EN)=Barqah 30 Je 31.00N 23.00 E
Cyrene 33 Dc 32.48N 21.59 E
Cyrus Field Bay 42 Ld 62.50N 65.00W
Cysoing 12 Fd 50.34N 3.13 E
Cythera (EN)=Kithira 15 Fm 36.09N 23.00 E
Czaplinek 10 Mc 53.34N 16.14 E
Czarna [Pol.] 10 Pe 51.12N 19.53 E
Czarna [Pol.] 10 Rf 50.30N 21.15 E
Czarna Białostocka 10 Tc 53.18N 23.19 E
Czarna Dąbrówka 10 Nb 54.20N 17.32 E
Czarna Hańcza 10 Tc 53.50N 23.47 E
Czarnków 10 Md 52.55N 16.34 E
Czchów 10 Qg 49.50N 20.39 E
Czechoslovakia (EN)= Československo 6 Hf 49.30N 17.00 E
Czechowice-Dziedzice 10 Og 49.54N 19.00 E
Czeremcha 10 Td 52.32N 23.15 E
Czersk 10 Nc 53.48N 18.00 E
Częstochowa 6 He 50.49N 19.06 E
Częstochowa 10 Pf 50.50N 19.05 E
Człopa 10 Mc 53.06N 16.08 E
Człuchów 10 Nc 53.41N 17.21 E

D

Da, Sông- = Black River (EN) 21 Mg 20.17N 106.34 E
Da'an (Dalai) 27 Lb 45.35N 124.16 E
Dabaga 36 Gd 8.07S 35.55 E
Dabakala 34 Ed 8.22N 4.26W
Dabakala 34 Ed 8.27N 4.28W
Daban→Bairin Youqi 27 Kc 43.30N 118.37 E
Dabas 10 Pi 47.11N 19.19 E
Daba Shan 21 Mf 32.15N 109.00 E
Dabat 35 Fc 12.58N 37.45 E
Dabay Sima 35 Gc 12.43N 42.17 E
Dabba/Daocheng 27 Hf 29.01N 100.26 E
Dabbāgh, Jabal- 23 Ed 27.52N 35.45 E
Dabeiba 54 Cb 7.02N 76.16W
Dąbie 10 Od 52.06N 18.49 E
Dabie, Jezioro- 10 Kc 53.29N 14.40 E
Dabie Shan 21 Nf 31.15N 115.00 E
Dabl, Wādī- [Sau.Ar.] 24 Gh 28.35N 39.04 E
Dabl, Wādī- [Sau.Ar.] 24 Gh 29.05N 36.14 E
Dabnou 34 Gc 14.09N 5.22 E
Dabola 34 Cc 10.45N 11.07W
Daborow 35 Hd 6.11N 48.22 E
Dabou 34 Ed 5.19N 4.23W
Dabqig→Uxin Qi 27 Id 38.27N 109.08 E
Dabraš 15 Gh 41.40N 23.50 E
Dabrowa Białostocka 10 Tc 53.40N 23.20 E
Dąbrowa Górnicza 10 Pf 50.20N 19.11 E
Dąbrowa Tarnowska 10 Qf 50.11N 21.00 E
Dabsan Hu 27 Fd 36.58N 95.00 E
Dăbuleni 15 Hf 43.48N 24.05 E
Dabus 35 Fc 10.38N 35.10 E
Dacata 35 Gd 7.16N 42.15 E
Dacca 22 Lg 23.43N 90.25 E
Dachangzhen 28 Eh 32.13N 118.44 E
Dachau 10 Hh 48.16N 11.26 E
Dachen Dao 28 Fj 28.29N 121.53 E
Dachstein 14 Hc 47.30N 13.36 E
Dacia Seamount (EN) 5 Ei 31.10N 13.42W
Dačice 10 Lg 49.05N 15.26 E
Dac Lac, Caonguyen- 25 Lf 12.50N 108.05 E
Ðacovica 15 Dg 42.23N 20.26 E
Dadali 63a Dc 8.07S 159.06 E
Dadanawa 54 Gc 2.50N 59.30W
Daday 24 Eb 41.28N 33.28 E
Dade City 44 Fk 28.22N 82.12W
Dadou 11 Hk 43.44N 1.49 E
Dādra and Nagar Haveli 25 Ed 20.20N 72.50 E
Dadu 25 Dc 26.44N 67.47 E
Dadu He 21 Mg 29.32N 103.44 E
Dadukou 28 Di 30.30N 117.03 E
Dāeni 15 Le 44.50N 28.07 E
Daet 26 Hd 14.05N 122.55 E
Dafang 27 If 27.06N 105.32 E
Dafeng (Dazhongji) 28 Fh 33.11N 120.27 E
Dagana 34 Bb 16.31N 15.30W
Dagana 35 Bc 13.05N 16.00 E
Daga Post 35 Ed 9.13N 33.58 E
Dağardi 15 Lj 39.26N 29.00 E
Dagash 35 Eb 19.22N 33.24 E
Dagda 8 Lh 56.04N 27.36 E
Dagdan-Daba 27 Gb 48.20N 96.50 E
Dagéla 35 Bc 10.40N 18.26 E
Dagestanskaja 19 Eg 43.00N 47.00 E
Dagestanskije Ogni 19 Eg 42.06N 48.12 E
Dagezhen → Fengning 28 Dd 41.12N 116.39 E
Dagu 28 De 38.58N 117.40 E
Daguan 27 Hf 27.48N 103.54 E
Dagu He 28 Ff 37.34N 121.17 E
Daguokui Shan 28 Jb 45.19N 129.50 E
Dagupan 26 Hc 16.03N 120.20 E
Dagxoi → Yidun 27 Ge 30.25N 99.28 E
Dagzê 27 Ff 29.41N 91.24 E
Dagzê Co 27 Ee 31.54N 87.29 E
Daheiding Shan 27 Mb 47.58N 129.10 E
Dahei He 28 Ad 40.34N 111.05 E
Da Hinggan Ling=Greater Khingan Range (EN) 21 Oe 49.00N 122.00 E
Dahlak Archipelago 30 Lg 15.40N 40.30 E
Dahlak Kebir 35 Gb 15.38N 40.11 E
Daḥl al Furayy 24 Li 26.45N 47.03 E
Dahlem 12 Id 50.23N 6.33 E
Dahlonega Plateau 44 Fh 34.30N 83.45W
Dahm, Ramlat- 33 If 16.25N 45.45 E
Dahme 10 Je 51.52N 13.26 E
Dahmouni 13 Ni 35.25N 1.29 E
Dahn 12 Je 49.09N 7.47 E
Dahomey→Bénin 31 Hh 9.30N 2.15 E
Dahongliutan 27 Cd 36.00N 79.12 E
Dahra 13 Mh 36.18N 0.55 E
Dahra [Lib.] 33 Cd 29.40N 17.40 E
Dahra [Sen.] 34 Bb 15.21N 15.29W
Dahra, Massif de- 13 Oh 36.30N 2.05 E
Dahūk 24 Jd 36.57N 43.00 E
Dahūk 24 Jd 36.52N 43.00 E
Dahushan 28 Gd 41.37N 122.09 E
Daḥy, Nafūd ad- 33 Ie 22.00N 45.25 E
Dai 63a Eb 7.53S 160.37 E
Daia 15 If 44.00N 25.59 E
Daïa, Région des- 32 Hc 33.30N 3.25 E
Daicheng 28 De 38.42N 116.37 E
Daigo 28 Pf 36.46N 140.21 E
Dai Hai 28 Bd 40.31N 112.43 E
Dailekh 25 Gc 28.50N 81.44 E
Daimanji-San 29 Cc 36.15N 133.19 E
Daimiel 13 Ie 39.04N 3.37W

Index Symbols

Independent Nation
State, Region
District, County
Municipality
Colony, Dependency
Continent
Physical Region
Historical or Cultural Region
Mount, Mountain
Volcano
Hill
Mountains, Mountain Range
Hills, Escarpment
Plateau, Upland
Pass, Gap
Plain, Lowland
Delta
Salt Flat
Valley, Canyon
Crater, Cave
Karst Features
Depression
Polder
Desert, Dunes
Forest, Woods
Heath, Steppe
Oasis
Cape, Point
Coast, Beach
Cliff
Peninsula
Isthmus
Sandbank
Island
Atoll
Rock, Reef
Islands, Archipelago
Rocks, Reefs
Coral Reef
Well, Spring
Geyser
River, Stream
Waterfall Rapids
River Mouth, Estuary
Lake
Salt Lake
Intermittent Lake
Reservoir
Swamp, Pond
Canal
Glacier
Ice Shelf, Pack Ice
Ocean
Sea
Gulf, Bay
Strait, Fjord
Lagoon
Bank
Seamount
Tablemount
Ridge
Shelf
Basin
Escarpment, Sea Scarp
Fracture
Trench, Abyss
National Park, Reserve
Point of Interest
Recreation Site
Cave, Cavern
Historic Site
Ruins
Wall, Walls
Church, Abbey
Temple
Scientific Station
Airport
Port
Lighthouse
Mine
Tunnel
Dam, Bridge

Dainanji-San 29 Ec 36.36N 137.42 E
Dainichi-San 29 Ec 36.09N 136.30 E
Dainkog 27 Ge 32.31N 97.59 E
Daiō-Zaki 28 Ng 34.22N 136.53 E
Dairan (EN)=Dalian (Luda) 22 Of 38.55N 121.39 E
Dairan (EN) = Lüda→Dalian 22 Of 38.55N 121.39 E
Dairbhre/Valentia 9 Cj 51.55N 10.20W
Daireaux 55 Bm 36.36 S 61.45W
Dai-Sen 29 Cd 35.24N 133.34 E
Daisengen-Dake 29a Bc 41.35N 140.09 E
Daishan (Gaotingzhen) 28 Gi 30.15N 122.13 E
Daitō [Jap.] 29 Cd 35.19N 132.58 E
Daitō [Jap.] 29 Gb 39.02N 141.22 E
Daito Islands (EN)=Daitō Shotō 21 Pg 25.00N 131.15 E
Daitō Shotō=Daito Islands (EN) 21 Pg 25.00N 131.15 E
Daitō-Zaki 29 Gd 35.18N 140.24 E
Daixian 28 Be 39.03N 112.57 E
Daiyue→Shanyin 28 Be 39.30N 112.48 E
Dajabón 49 Ld 19.33N 71.42W
Dajarra 58 Eg 21.42 S 139.31 E
Dajtit, Mali i- 15 Ch 41.22N 19.55 E
Daka 34 Ed 8.19N 0.13W
Dakar 31 Fg 14.40N 17.26W
Dākhilah, Wāḩāt al-= Dakhla Oasis (EN) 30 Jf 25.30N 29.10 E
Dakhla Oasis (EN)= Dākhilah, Wāḩāt al- 30 Jf 25.30N 29.10 E
Dakhlet Nouâdhibou 32 De 20.30N 16.00W
Dakla 31 Ff 23.42N 15.56W
Dakoro 34 Gc 14.30N 6.25 E
Đakovo 14 Me 45.19N 18.25 E
Daksti 8 Kg 57.38N 25.32 E
Dak To 25 Lf 14.42N 107.51 E
Dal 8 Dd 60.15N 11.12 E
Dal, Jökulsá á- 7a Cb 65.40N 14.20W
Đala 15 Dc 46.09N 20.07 E
Dala [Ang.] 36 De 11.03 S 20.17 E
Dala [Sol.Is.] 63a c 8.36 S 160.41 E
Dalaba 34 Cc 10.42N 12.15W
Dalai → Da'an 27 Lb 45.35N 124.16 E
Dalai Nur 27 Kc 43.18N 116.15 E
Dala-Järna 8 Fd 60.33N 14.21 E
Dālakī 24 Nh 29.19N 51.06 E
Dalälven 5 Hc 60.38N 17.27 E
Dalaman 24 Cd 36.40N 28.45 E
Dalaman 15 Lm 36.44N 28.49 E
Dalāmī 35 Ec 11.52N 30.28 E
Dalān 24 Kj 24.15N 45.47 E
Dalan-Dzadgad 22 Me 43.47N 104.29 E
Dalane 8 Bf 58.35N 6.20 E
Dalarna 8 Fd 61.00N 14.05 E
Dalarö 8 He 59.08N 18.24 E
Da Lat 22 Mh 11.56N 108.25 E
Dālbandin 25 Cc 28.53N 64.25 E
Dalbosjön 8 Ef 58.45N 12.50 E
Dalboslätten 8 Ef 58.35N 12.25 E
Dalby 59 Ke 27.11 S 151.16 E
Dale [Nor.] 7 Af 60.35N 5.49 E
Dale [Nor.] 7 Af 61.22N 5.25 E
Dale Hollow Lake 44 Eg 36.36N 85.19W
Dalen 7 Bg 59.27N 8.00 E
Dalfsen 12 Ib 52.30N 6.14 E
Dalgaranger, Mount- 59 De 27.51 S 117.06 E
Dalgopol 15 Kf 43.03N 27.21 E
Dalhart 43 Gd 36.04N 102.31W
Dalhousie 42 Kg 48.04N 66.23W
Dalhousie, Cape- 42 Eb 70.15N 129.41W
Dali [China] 22 Mg 25.43N 100.07 E
Dali [China] 27 Ie 34.55N 110.00 E
Dalian (Lüda) = Dairan (EN) 22 Of 38.55N 121.39 E
Dalias 13 Jh 36.49N 2.52W
Daling He 28 Fd 40.56N 121.44 E
Dalizi 27 Mc 41.45N 126.50 E
Dalj 14 Me 45.29N 18.59 E
Daljā' 33 Fd 27.39N 30.42 E
Dalkowskie, Wzgórza- 10 Le 51.35N 15.50 E
Dall [Ak.-U.S.] 40 Mf 54.50N 132.55W
Dall [Can.] 2 Ef 55.00N 133.00W
Dallas [Or.-U.S.] 46 Dd 44.55N 123.19W
Dallas [Tx.-U.S.] 39 Jf 32.47N 96.48W
Dalmā' 24 Oj 24.30N 52.20 E
Dalmā', Qārat- 33 Dd 25.32N 23.57 E
Dalmacija 14 Kg 43.00N 17.00 E
Dalmacija = Dalmatia (EN) 5 Hg 43.00N 17.00 E
Dalmaj, Hawr- 24 Kf 32.20N 45.28 E
Dalmally 9 Ie 56.24N 4.58W
Dalmatia (EN) = Dalmacija 5 Hg 43.00N 17.00 E
Dalmatovo 17 Kh 56.16N 63.00 E
Dalnegorsk 22 Pe 44.31N 135.31 E
Dalnerečensk 22 Pe 45.55N 133.45 E
Dalni [R.S.F.S.R.] 20 Kf 53.15N 157.30 E
Dalni [R.S.F.S.R.] 20 Ih 44.57N 135.03 E
Dalnjaja, Gora- 20 Mc 68.08N 179.53 E
Daloa 34 Dd 6.58N 6.23W
Daloa 31 Gh 6.53N 6.27W
Dalou Shan 21 Mg 28.00N 106.40 E
Dalqū 35 Ea 20.07N 30.35 E
Dalrymple, Mount- 57 Fg 21.02 S 148.38 E
Dalsbruk 8 Jd 60.02N 22.31 E
Dalsbruk/Taalintendas 8 Jd 60.02N 22.31 E
Dalsfjorden 8 Ac 61.20N 5.05 E
Dalsjöfors 8 Eg 57.43N 13.05 E
Dalsland 8 Ef 58.35N 12.55 E
Dalslands kanal 8 Ef 58.50N 12.25 E
Dals Långed 7 Cg 58.55N 12.18 E
Dalton 44 Eh 34.47N 84.58W
Daltonganj 25 Gd 24.02N 84.04 E
Dalul 35 Gc 14.22N 40.21 E
Daluo 27 Hg 21.38N 100.15 E
Dalupiri 26 Hc 19.05N 121.12 E
Dalvik 7a Bb 65.58N 18.32W
Dalwallinu 59 Df 30.17 S 116.40 E
Dalyan 15 Lm 36.50N 28.39 E
Daly Bay 42 Id 64.00N 89.40W
Daly City 46 Dh 37.42N 122.29W
Daly River 57 Ef 13.20 S 130.19 E
Daly Waters 59 Gc 16.15 S 133.22 E
Damā, Wādī- 24 Fi 27.09N 35.47 E
Damagarim 34 Gc 13.42N 9.00 E
Damān 25 Ed 20.10N 73.00 E
Damanhūr 33 Fc 31.02N 30.28 E
Damar, Pulau- 26 Ih 7.09 S 128.40 E
Damara 35 Be 4.58N 18.42 E
Damaraland 37 Bd 21.00 S 17.30 E
Damas Cays 49 Hb 23.58N 79.55W
Damascus (EN)=Dimashq 22 Ff 33.30N 36.15 E
Dāmāsh 24 Md 36.46N 49.46 E
Damaturu 34 Hc 11.45N 11.58 E
Damāvand 24 He 35.56N 52.08 E
Damāvand, Qolleh-ye- 21 Hf 35.56N 52.08 E
Damba 36 Cd 6.50 S 15.07 E
Dambaslar 15 Kh 41.13N 27.14 E
Dame Marie, Cap- 47 Je 18.36N 74.26W
Damergou 30 Hg 15.00N 9.00 E
Dāmghān 24 Pd 36.09N 54.22 E
Damianópolis 55 Ib 14.33 S 46.10W
Damiao 27 He 30.52N 104.38 E
Damietta (EN)=Dumyāṭ 31 Ke 31.25N 31.48 E
Daming 28 Cf 36.17N 115.09 E
Daming Shan 27 Ig 23.23N 108.30 E
Damīr Qābū 24 Id 36.54N 41.47 E
Dammartin en Goële 12 Ee 49.03N 2.41 E
Dammastock 14 Cd 46.38N 8.25 E
Damme [Bel.] 12 Fc 51.15N 3.17 E
Damme [F.R.G.] 12 Kb 52.31N 8.12 E
Dammer Berge 12 Kb 52.35N 8.17 E
Damoh 25 Fd 23.50N 79.27 E
Damongo 34 Ed 9.05N 1.49W
Damous 13 Nh 36.33N 1.42 E
Dampier 58 Cg 20.39 S 116.45 E
Dampier, Selat-=Dampier Strait (EN) 26 Jg 0.40 S 130.40 E
Dampier Archipelago 59 Dd 20.35 S 116.35 E
Dampier Land 59 Ec 17.30 S 122.55 E
Dampierre 12 Df 48.42N 1.59 E
Dampier Strait 59 Ja 5.36 S 148.12 E
Dampier Strait (EN)= Dampier, Selat- 26 Jg 0.40 S 130.40 E
Damqawt 23 Hf 16.34N 52.50 E
Damqog Kanbab/Maquan He 27 Df 29.36N 84.09 E
Dam Qu 27 Fe 33.56N 92.41 E
Damville 12 Df 48.52N 1.04 E
Damvillers 12 He 49.20N 5.24 E
Damwoude, Dantumadeel- 12 Ha 53.18N 5.59 E
Damxoi → Comai 27 Ff 28.26N 91.32 E
Damxung 27 Fe 30.34N 91.16 E
Danakil=Danakil Plain (EN) 30 Lg 12.25N 40.30 E
Danakil Plain (EN)= Danakil 30 Lg 12.25N 40.30 E
Danané 34 Dd 7.25N 8.10W
Danané 34 Dd 7.16N 8.09W
Da Nang 22 Mh 16.04N 108.13 E
Danba/Rongzhag 27 He 30.48N 101.54 E
Danbury 44 Ke 41.23N 73.27W
Danby Lake 46 Hi 34.14N 115.07W
Dancheng 28 Ch 33.36N 115.14 E
Dancheng→Xiangshan 27 Lf 29.29N 121.52 E
Dandarah 33 Fd 26.10N 32.39 E
Dandeldhura 25 Gc 29.18N 80.35 E
Dandenong, Melbourne- 59 Jg 37.59 S 145.12 E
Dandong 22 Oe 40.10N 124.15 E
Daneborg 41 Jd 74.25N 20.10W
Danells Fjord 41 Hf 60.45N 42.45W
Daneţi 15 Hf 43.59N 24.03 E
Danfeng (Longjuzhai) 27 Je 33.44N 110.22 E
Danforth Hills 45 Cf 40.15N 108.00W
Danfu 63a Aa 4.12 S 153.04 E
Dangara 19 Gh 38.09N 69.22 E
Dangchengwan → Subei 27 Fd 39.36N 94.58 E
Dang He 27 Fc 40.30N 94.42 E
Dangjin Shankou 21 Lf 39.15N 94.30 E
Dangla 35 Fc 11.16N 36.50 E
Dangla Shan→Tanggula Shan 21 Lf 33.00N 92.00 E
Dangoura, Mount- 35 Dd 6.12N 26.27 E
Dangrek Range (EN)=Dong Rak, Phanom- 21 Mh 14.25N 104.30 E
Dangshan 27 Ke 34.22N 116.21 E
Dangtu 28 Ei 31.33N 118.30 E
Dangu 12 De 49.15N 1.42 E
Dangyang 28 Ai 30.49N 111.47 E
Dan He 28 Bg 35.05N 112.59 E
Daniel 46 Je 42.52N 110.04W
Daniel, Serra- 55 Ea 13.40 S 54.55W
Danielskuil 37 Ce 28.11 S 23.33 E
Danilov 19 Ed 58.12N 40.13 E
Danilovgrad 15 Cg 42.33N 19.07 E
Danilovka 16 Nd 50.21N 44.06 E
Daning 27 Jd 36.31N 110.45 E
Danjiang → Junxian 27 Je 32.31N 111.32 E
Danjiangkou Shuiku 27 Je 32.37N 111.30 E
Danjo-Guntō 27 Me 32.00N 128.20 E
Dank 24 Qk 23.33N 56.16 E
Dankov 16 Kc 53.16N 39.07 E
Danli 47 Df 14.00N 86.35W
Danmark=Denmark (EN) 6 Gd 56.00N 10.00 E
Danmark Fjord 67 Me 81.10N 23.20W
Danmarks Havn 67 Ld 76.50N 18.30W
Danmarksstraedet= Denmark Strait (EN) 38 Qc 67.00N 25.00W
Dannenberg 10 Hc 53.06N 11.06 E
Dannevirke 62 Gd 40.12 S 176.06 E
Danot 35 Hd 7.33N 45.17 E
Dantumadeel 12 Ha 53.18N 5.59 E
Dantumadeel-Damwoude 12 Ha 53.18N 5.59 E
Danube (EN)=Donau 5 If 45.20N 29.40 E
Danube (EN)=Duna 5 If 45.20N 29.40 E
Danube (EN)=Dunaj 5 If 45.20N 29.40 E
Danube (EN)=Dunărea 5 If 45.20N 29.40 E
Danube (EN)=Dunav 5 If 45.20N 29.40 E
Danube, Mouths of the- (EN) = Dunării, Delta- 5 If 45.30N 29.45 E
Danville [Ar.-U.S.] 45 Ji 35.03N 93.24W
Danville [Il.-U.S.] 43 Jc 40.08N 87.37W
Danville [In.-U.S.] 44 Df 39.46N 86.32W
Danville [Ky.-U.S.] 43 Kd 37.39N 84.46W
Danville [Va.-U.S.] 43 Ld 36.34N 79.25W
Danxian (Nada) 27 Ih 19.38N 109.32 E
Danyang 28 Eh 32.00N 119.33 E
Danzig (EN)=Gdańsk 6 He 54.23N 18.40 E
Dao 26 Hd 10.31N 121.57 E
Dão 13 Dd 40.20N 8.11W
Daocheng/Dabba 27 Hf 29.01N 100.26 E
Daokou → Huaxian 28 Cg 35.33N 114.30 E
Daosa 25 Fc 26.53N 76.20 E
Dao Shui 28 Ci 30.42N 114.40 E
Dao Timni 34 Ha 20.38N 13.39 E
Daora 32 Gd 29.03N 4.33W
Daoxian 27 Jf 25.37N 111.36 E
Dapaong 34 Fc 10.52N 0.12 E
Dapchi 34 Hc 12.29N 11.29 E
Daqing Shan 28 Ad 41.00N 111.00 E
Daqin Tal→Naiman Qi 27 Lc 42.49N 120.38 E
Daquing Shan 28 Ed 40.30N 119.38 E
Dar'ā 23 Ec 32.37N 36.06 E
Dārāb 24 Ph 28.45N 54.34 E
Darabani 15 Ja 48.11N 26.35 E
Daraçya Yarimadasi 15 Lm 36.40N 28.10 E
Darāfisah 35 Ec 13.23N 31.59 E
Dārān 24 Nf 32.59N 50.24 E
Darasun 20 Gf 51.39N 113.59 E
Đaravica 15 Dg 42.32N 20.08 E
Darāw 24 Ej 24.25N 32.56 E
Darazo 34 Hc 11.00N 10.25 E
Darband 23 Ic 31.38N 57.02 E
Darband, Kūh-e- 24 Qg 31.34N 57.08 E
Darbandī Khān, Sad ad- 24 Ke 35.07N 45.50 E
Darbat Alī, Ra's- 23 Hf 16.43N 53.33 E
Darbėnai/Darbenaj 8 Ih 56.02N 21.08 E
Dar Ben Karriche el Bahri 13 Gi 35.51N 5.21W
Darbhanga 25 Hc 26.10N 85.54 E
Dārboruk 35 Gd 9.44N 44.31 E
Darby 46 Hc 46.01N 114.11W
Darchan → Darhan 22 Me 49.33N 106.21 E
Darda 14 Me 45.38N 18.42 E
Dardanelle Lake 45 Ji 35.25N 93.20W
Dardanelles (EN)= Çanakkale Boğazi 5 Ig 40.15N 26.25 E
Dardo/Kangding 27 He 30.01N 101.58 E
Dar el Kouti 30 Jh 8.50N 21.50 E
Darende 24 Gc 38.34N 37.30 E
Dar es Salaam 36 Gd 6.50 S 39.02 E
Dar es Salaam 31 Ki 6.48 S 39.17 E
Darfield 62 Ee 43.29 S 172.07 E
Darfo Boario Terme 14 Ee 45.53N 10.11 E
Dārfūr 30 Jg 12.40N 24.20 E
Dārfūr al Janūbīyah 35 Dc 11.30N 25.10 E
Dārfūr ash Shamālīyah 35 Db 16.00N 25.30 E
Dargan-Ata 19 Gg 40.29N 62.12 E
Dargaville 61 Dg 35.56 S 173.52 E
Darhan (Darchan) 22 Me 49.33N 106.21 E
Darhan Muminggan Lianheqi 27 Jc 41.45N 110.24 E
Darica [Tur.] 15 Kj 40.00N 27.50 E
Darica [Tur.] 15 Mi 40.45N 29.23 E
Darién 47 Ig 8.30N 77.30W
Darien 44 Gj 31.22N 81.26W
Darién 49 Ii 8.10N 77.45W
Darién, Golfo de- 52 Ie 8.25N 76.53W
Darién, Serrania del- 47 Ig 8.30N 77.30W
Dariense, Cordillera- 49 Eg 12.55N 85.30W
Darja 18 Ee 38.13N 65.46 E
Darjalyk 18 Ac 42.00N 57.45 E
Darjeeling 25 Hc 27.02N 88.16 E
Dar-Kebdani 13 Ii 35.07N 3.21W
Dark Head 51n Ba 13.17N 61.17W
Dārkhovīn 24 Mg 30.45N 48.25 E
Darlag 27 Ge 33.49N 99.08 E
Darling 37 Bf 33.23 S 18.23 E
Darling Downs 59 Ke 27.30 S 150.30 E
Darling Range 57 Ch 32.00 S 116.30 E
Darling River 57 Fh 34.07 S 141.55 E
Darlington [Eng.-U.K.] 9 Lg 54.31N 1.34W
Darlington [S.C.-U.S.] 44 Hh 34.19N 79.53W
Darłowo 10 Mb 54.26N 16.23 E
Darmouth 9 Jk 50.21N 3.35W
Darmstadt 10 Eg 49.52N 8.39 E
Darnah 31 Je 32.46N 22.39 E
Darnah 33 Dc 31.00N 23.40 E
Darnétal 12 De 49.27N 1.09 E
Darney 11 Mf 48.05N 6.03 E
Darnley, Cape- 66 Fe 67.43 S 69.30 E
Darnley Bay 42 Fc 69.45N 123.45W
Daroca 13 Kc 41.07N 1.25W
Darou Khoudos 34 Bb 15.06N 16.50W
Darovskoj 7 Lg 58.47N 47.59 E
Darrah, Mount- 46 Hb 49.28N 114.35W
Darregueira 56 He 37.42 S 63.10W
Darrehshahr 24 Lf 33.10N 47.18 E
D'Arros Island 37b Bb 5.24 S 53.18 E
Dar Rounga 30 Jg 10.45N 22.20 E
Dar Sila 35 Cc 12.11N 21.21 E
Darss 10 Ib 54.25N 12.31 E
Darßer Ort 10 Ib 54.29N 12.31 E
Dart 9 Jk 50.20N 3.33W
Dart, Cape- 66 Nf 73.06 S 126.20W
D'Artagnan Bank (EN) 59 Eb 13.00 S 121.00 E
Dartang → Baqên 27 Fe 31.58N 94.00 E
Dartford 12 Cc 51.27N 0.13 E
Dartmoor 9 Jk 50.35N 4.00W
Dartmouth 42 Lh 44.40N 63.34W
Dartuch, Cabo- 13 Pe 39.56N 3.48 E
Daru 60 Ci 9.04 S 143.12 E
Daruneh 24 Qe 35.10N 57.18 E
Daruvar 14 Le 45.35N 17.14 E
Darvaza 19 Fg 40.15N 58.24 E
Darvel, Teluk- 26 Gf 4.50N 118.30 E
Darwin 58 Ef 12.28 S 130.50 E
Darwin, Bahía- 56 Fg 45.27 S 74.40W
Darwin, Isla- 54a Aa 1.39N 92.00W
Darwin, Port- 59 Gb 12.20 S 130.40 E
Dar Zagaoua 35 Cb 15.15N 23.14 E
Dar Zebada 35 Bc 13.45N 18.50 E
Dās 24 Oj 25.09N 52.53 E
Dašava 10 Ug 49.13N 24.05 E
Daš-Balbar 27 Jb 49.31N 114.21 E
Dasha He 28 Ce 38.27N 114.39 E
Dashengtang Shan 28 Dc 42.07N 117.12 E
Dashennongjia 27 Je 31.47N 114.12 E
Dashennongjia 27 Je 31.26N 110.18 E
Dashiqiao → Yingkou 28 Gd 40.39N 122.31 E
Dashitou 28 Jc 43.18N 128.29 E
Dasht 24 Qd 37.17N 56.04 E
Dasht Āb 24 Qh 28.59N 56.32 E
Dashtak 24 Og 30.23N 52.30 E
Dasht-e-Āzādegan 24 Mg 31.32N 48.10 E
Daškesan 16 Oi 40.30N 46.03 E
Dasseneiland 37 Bf 33.26 S 18.05 E
Dastgardān 24 Qe 34.19N 56.51 E
Dastjerd-e Qaddādeh 24 Nf 32.44N 51.32 E
Datça 24 Bd 36.45N 27.40 E
Date 28 Pc 42.27N 140.51 E
Dāth, Sha'īb ad- 24 Jj 25.45N 43.10 E
Datia 25 Fc 25.40N 78.28 E
Datian Ding 27 Jg 22.17N 111.13 E
Datil 45 Ci 34.09N 107.47W
Datong [China] 27 Hd 36.56N 101.40 E
Datong [China] 22 Ne 40.09N 113.17 E
Datteln 12 Jc 51.40N 7.23 E
Datteln-Hamm Kanal 12 Jc 51.39N 7.21 E
Datu 21 Mi 2.05N 109.39 E
Datu, Teluk- 21 Ni 2.00N 111.00 E
Datu Plang 26 He 6.58N 124.40 E
Dāūd Khel 25 Eb 32.53N 71.34 E
Daudzeva 8 Kh 56.28N 25.18 E
Daugaard-Jensen Land 41 Fb 80.10N 63.30W
Daugai/Daugaj 8 Kj 54.20N 24.28 E
Daugaj/Daugai 8 Kj 54.20N 24.28 E
Daugava=Dvina(EN) 19 Cd 57.04N 24.03 E
Daugavpils 6 Id 55.53N 26.32 E
Daule 54 Cd 1.50 S 79.57W
Daun 10 Cf 50.12N 6.50 E
Daung Kyun 25 Jf 12.14N 98.05 E
Daunia, Monti della- 14 Ji 41.25N 15.05 E
Dauphin 42 Hf 51.09N 100.03W
Dauphiné 11 Lj 44.50N 6.00 E
Dauphin Lake 42 Hf 51.15N 99.45W
Daura 34 Gc 13.02N 8.18 E
Dautphetal 12 Kd 50.52N 8.33 E
Dāvangere 25 Ff 14.28N 75.55 E
Davao 22 Oi 7.04N 125.36 E
Davao Gulf 21 Oi 6.40N 125.55 E
Dāvarān, Kūh-e- 24 Qg 30.40N 56.15 E
Dāvar Panāh 23 Jd 27.21N 62.21 E
Dāvarzan 24 Qd 36.23N 56.50 E
Đavat 15 Eh 41.04N 21.06 E
Davenport [Ia.-U.S.] 39 Je 41.32N 90.41W
Davenport [Wa.-U.S.] 46 Fc 47.39N 118.09W
Davenport Range 59 Gd 20.45 S 134.50 E
Daventry 12 Ab 52.15N 1.10W
Davert 12 Jc 51.51N 7.36 E
Davey, Port- 59 Jh 43.20 S 145.55 E
David 39 Ki 8.25N 82.27W
David City 45 Hf 41.15N 97.08W
David-Gorodok 16 Ec 52.03N 27.13 E
David Point 51p Bb 12.14N 61.39W
Davidson 46 Ma 51.18N 105.59W
Davidson Mountains 40 Kc 68.45N 142.10W
Davies, Mount- 59 Fe 26.14 S 129.16 E
Davis 43 Cd 38.33N 121.44W
Davis 66 Fe 68.35 S 77.58 E
Davis, Cape- 66 Ee 66.24 S 56.50 E
Davis, Mount- 44 Hf 39.47N 79.10W
Davis Bay 66 Ie 66.08 S 134.05 E
Davis Inlet 42 Le 56.00N 61.30W
Davis Mountains 45 Ek 30.35N 104.00W
Davis Sea (EN) 66 Ge 66.00 S 92.00 E
Davisstrædet = Davis Strait (EN) 38 Nc 68.00N 58.00W
Davis Strait 38 Nc 68.00N 58.00W
Davis Strait (EN) = Davisstrædet 38 Nc 68.00N 58.00W
Davlekanovo 19 Fe 54.13N 55.03 E
Davo 34 Dd 5.00N 6.08W
Davos/Tavau 14 Dd 46.47N 9.50 E
Davutlar 15 Kl 37.43N 27.17 E
Dawa 28 Gd 40.58N 122.01 E
Dawanlé 35 Gc 11.06N 42.38 E
Dawāsir, Wādī ad- 21 Gg 20.24N 46.29 E
Dawen He 28 Dg 35.37N 116.23 E
Dawes Range 59 Kd 24.30 S 151.10 E
Dawḩarab 33 Hf 16.17N 41.57 E
Dawson [Ga.-U.S.] 44 Ej 31.47N 84.26W
Dawson [Yuk.-Can.] 39 Fc 64.04N 139.25W
Dawson, Mount- 46 Ga 51.09N 117.25W
Dawson Creek 39 Gd 55.45N 120.07W
Dawson-Lambton Glacier 66 Af 76.15 S 27.30W
Dawson Range 42 Dd 65.15N 137.45W
Dawson River 59 Jd 23.38 S 149.46 E
Dawu 27 He 30.45N 101.11 E
Dawu (Erlangdian) 28 Ci 31.33N 114.07 E
Dawu→Maqên 27 He 34.29N 100.01 E
Dawukou → Shizuishan 27 Id 39.03N 106.24 E
Dax 11 Ek 43.43N 1.03W
Da Xi 27 Lf 28.10N 120.14 E
Daxian 27 Ie 31.15N 107.28 E
Daxin 27 Ig 22.52N 107.14 E
Daxing 28 De 39.45N 116.19 E
Daxinggou 28 Jc 43.23N 129.39 E
Daxue Shan 21 Mf 30.30N 101.30 E
Dayan → Lijiang 22 Mg 26.56N 100.15 E
Dayang He 28 Ge 39.52N 123.40
Dayao 27 Hf 25.49N 101.18
Daye 28 Ci 30.05N 114.58
Dayishan → Guanyun 28 Eg 34.18N 119.14
Daymán, Cuchilla del- 55 Dj 31.38 S 57.10
Daymán, Rio- 55 Dj 31.40 S 58.02
Daym Zubayr 35 Dd 7.43N 26.13
Dayong 27 Jf 29.09N 110.30
Dayr, Jabal ad- 35 Ec 12.27N 30.45
Dayr az Zawr 22 Gf 35.20N 40.09
Dayr Hāfir 24 Gd 36.09N 37.42
Dayr Kātrīnā = Saint Catherine Monastery of- (EN) 33 Fd 28.31N 33.57
Dayr Mawās 24 Di 27.38N 30.51
Dayrūṭ 33 Fd 27.33N 30.49
Dayton [Oh.-U.S.] 39 Kf 39.45N 84.15
Dayton [Wa.-U.S.] 46 Gc 46.19N 117.59
Daytona Beach 39 Kg 29.12N 80.59
Dayu 27 Jf 25.29N 114.22
Da Yunhe=Grand Canal (EN) 21 Nf 39.54N 116.44
Dayville 46 Fd 44.28N 119.3
Dayyīnah 24 Oj 24.57N 52.2
Dazhongji → Dafeng 28 Fh 33.11N 120.22
Dazhu 27 Ie 30.42N 107.1
Dazjā 24 Pe 35.50N 55.4
Dazkırı 24 Cd 37.54N 29.4
De Aar 31 Jl 30.39 S 24.0
Dead 9 Ei 52.40N 8.3
Deadhorse 40 Jb 70.11N 148.2
Deadmans Cay 49 Jb 23.14N 75.1
Dead Sea (EN)=Mayyit, Al Baḩr al- 21 Ff 31.30N 35.3
Deadwood 45 Ed 44.23N 103.4
Deal 12 Dc 51.13N 1.2
Dealu Mare 15 Jb 47.27N 26.4
De'an 28 Cj 29.18N 115.4
Deán Funes 56 Hd 30.26 S 64.2
Dearborn 44 Fd 42.18N 83.1
Dearg, Beinn- 9 Id 57.48N 4.5
Deary 46 Gc 46.52N 116.3
Dease 42 Ee 59.55N 128.2
Dease Arm 42 Fc 66.50N 120.0
Dease Lake 39 Fd 58.35N 130.0
Dease Strait 42 Gc 69.00N 107.0
Death Valley 38 Hf 36.30N 117.0
Death Valley 46 Gh 36.20N 116.5
Deauville 11 Ge 49.22N 0.0
Debak 26 Ff 1.34N 111.2
Debalcevo 16 Ke 48.20N 38.2
Debao 27 Ig 23.17N 106.2
Debar 15 Dh 41.32N 20.3
Debark 35 Fc 13.08N 37.5
Debdou 32 Gc 33.59N 3.0
Debed 16 Ni 41.22N 44.5
Deben 12 Db 52.01N 1.2
De Beque 45 Bg 39.20N 108.1
Dębica 10 Rf 50.04N 21.2
De Bilt 12 Hb 52.06N 5.
Debin 20 Kd 62.18N 150.4
Dęblin 10 Re 51.35N 21.
Dębno 10 Kd 52.45N 14.4
Débo, Lac- 34 Eb 15.18N 4.0
Deborah East, Lake- 59 Df 30.45 S 119.
Deborah West, Lake- 59 Df 30.45 S 119.
Deboyne Islands 57 Gf 10.43 S 152.
Debrc 15 Ce 44.37N 19.
Debre Berhan 35 Fd 9.41N 39.
Debrecen 6 If 47.32N 21.
Debrecen 10 Ri 47.31N 21.
Debre Libanos 35 Fd 9.43N 38.
Debre Markós 31 Kg 10.10N 37
Debre Sina 35 Fd 9.51N 39
Debre Tabor 35 Fc 11.51N 38.
Debre Zeyt 31 Kh 8.47N 39.
De-Buka, Glacier- 66 Nf 76.00 S 131
Decatur [Al.-U.S.] 43 Je 34.36N 8
Decatur [Ga.-U.S.] 44 Ei 33.46N 84.
Decatur [Il.-U.S.] 43 Jd 39.51N 89
Decatur [In.-U.S.] 44 Ee 40.50N 84
Decatur [Tx.-U.S.] 45 Hj 33.14N 97
Decazeville 11 Ij 44.33N 2.
Deccan 21 Jh 14.00N 77
Decelles, Reservoir- 44 Hb 47.40N 78
Deception Bay 59 Ia 7.07 S 144.
Dechang 27 Hf 27.22N 102.
Děčín 10 Kf 50.47N 14.
Decize 11 Jh 46.50N 3
Decorah 45 Ke 43.18N 91.
Deda 15 Hc 46.56N 24
Dededo 64c Ba 13.31N 144
Dedegöl Dağı 24 Dd 37.39N 31
Dedemsvaart, Avereest- 12 Ib 52.37N 6
Dédougou 34 Ec 12.28N 3.
Dedoviči 7 Gh 57.33N 29
Dedza 36 Fe 14.22 S 34
Dee [Eng.-U.K.] 9 Jh 53.19N 3
Dee [Scot.-U.K.] 9 Kd 57.08N 2
Dee [Scot.-U.K.] 9 Ig 54.50N 4
Deep Creek Range 46 If 40.00N 113
Deering 40 Gc 66.05N 162
Deer Isle 44 Mc 44.13N 68
Deer Lake [Newf.-Can.] 42 Lg 49.10N 57
Deer Lake [Ont.-Can.] 42 If 52.40N 94
Deer Park 46 Gc 47.57N 117
Defiance 44 Ee 41.17N 84
Defla 13 Qi 35.14N 4
De Funiak Springs 44 Dj 30.43N 86
Dega Ahmedo 35 Gd 7.50N 42
Dêgê 27 Ge 31.52N 98
Degebe 13 Ef 38.13N 7
Degeh Bur 35 Gd 8.13N 43
Degema 34 Ge 4.45N 6
Degerby 8 Id 60.02N 20
Degerfors 7 Dg 59.14N 14
Degerhamn 7 Dh 56.21N 16
Deggendorf 10 Ih 48.50N 12

Index Symbols

1 Independent Nation
2 State, Region
3 District, County
4 Municipality
5 Colony, Dependency
Continent
Physical Region
Historical or Cultural Region
Mount, Mountain
Volcano
Hill
Mountains, Mountain Range
Hills, Escarpment
Plateau, Upland
Pass, Gap
Plain, Lowland
Delta
Salt Flat
Valley, Canyon
Crater, Cave
Karst Features
Depression
Polder
Desert, Dunes
Forest, Woods
Heath, Steppe
Oasis
Cape, Point
Coast, Beach
Cliff
Peninsula
Isthmus
Sandbank
Island
Atoll
Rock, Reef
Islands, Archipelago
Rocks, Reefs
Coral Reef
Well, Spring
Geyser
River, Stream
Waterfall Rapids
River Mouth, Estuary
Lake
Salt Lake
Intermittent Lake
Reservoir
Swamp, Pond
Canal
Glacier
Ice Shelf, Pack Ice
Ocean
Sea
Gulf, Bay
Strait, Fjord
Lagoon
Bank
Seamount
Tablemount
Ridge
Shelf
Basin
Escarpment, Sea Scarp
Fracture
Trench, Abyss
National Park, Reserve
Point of Interest
Recreation Site
Cave, Cavern
Historic Site
Ruins
Wall, Walls
Church, Abbey
Temple
Scientific Station
Airport
Port
Lighth
Mine
Tunne
Dam,

Name	Map	Grid	Lat.	Long.
Değirmendere	15	Kk	38.06N	27.09 E
De Gray Lake	45	Ji	34.15N	93.15W
De Grey River	59	Dd	20.12S	119.11 E
Degtarsk	17	Jh	56.42N	60.06 E
De Haan	12	Fc	51.16N	3.02 E
Dēh 'Ain	35	Hd	8.55N	46.15 E
Dehaj	24	Pg	30.42N	54.53 E
Dehaq	24	Nf	32.55N	50.57 E
Deh Bārez	24	Qi	27.26N	57.12 E
Deh Bīd	24	Og	30.38N	53.13 E
Deh Dasht	24	Ng	30.47N	50.34 E
Dehdez	24	Ng	31.43N	50.17 E
Deh-e Namak	24	Oe	35.25N	52.50 E
Deh-e Shīr	24	Og	31.29N	53.45 E
Deh-e Ziyār	24	Qg	30.40N	57.00 E
Dehgolān	24	Le	35.17N	47.25 E
Dehlorān	24	Lf	32.41N	47.16 E
Deh Now	24	Qf	33.01N	57.41 E
Dehra Dūn	25	Fb	30.19N	78.02 E
Dehui	27	Mc	44.33N	125.38 E
Deinze	11	Jd	50.59N	3.32 E
Dej	15	Gb	47.09N	23.52 E
Deje	8	Ee	59.36N	13.28 E
Dejen	35	Fc	10.05N	38.11 E
Dejës, Mali i-	15	Dh	41.42N	20.10 E
Dejnau	19	Gh	39.18N	63.11 E
De Jongs, Tanjung-	26	Kh	6.56S	138.32 E
De Kalb	45	Lf	41.56N	88.45W
Dekar	37	Cd	21.30S	21.58 E
Dekese	31	Ji	3.27S	21.24 E
Dekina	34	Gd	7.42N	7.01 E
Dékoa	35	Bd	6.19N	19.04 E
De Koog, Texel-	12	Ga	53.07N	4.46 E
De La Garma	55	Bm	37.58S	60.25W
De Land	44	Gk	29.02N	81.18W
Delano	43	Dd	35.41N	119.15W
Delano Peak	43	Ed	38.22N	112.23W
Delārām	23	Jc	32.11N	63.25 E
Delarof Islands	40a	Cb	51.30N	178.45W
Delaware	44	Fe	40.18N	83.06W
Delaware	45	Ek	32.00N	104.00W
Delaware [2]	43	Ld	39.10N	75.30W
Delaware Bay	38	Lc	39.05N	75.15W
Delaware River	43	Ld	39.20N	75.25W
Delbrück	12	Kc	51.46N	8.34 E
Del Carril	55	Cl	35.31S	59.30W
Delčevo	15	Fh	41.58N	22.47 E
Del City	45	Hi	35.27N	97.27W
Delegate	59	Jg	37.03S	148.58 E
Delémont/Delsberg	14	Bc	47.22N	7.21 E
Delet/Teili	8	Id	60.15N	20.35 E
Delfinópolis	55	Ie	20.20S	46.51W
Delft	11	Kb	52.00N	4.21 E
Delfzijl	11	Ma	53.19N	6.56 E
Delgada, Punta-	52	Jj	42.46S	63.38W
Delgado, Cabo-=Delgado, Cape-(EN)	30	Lj	10.40S	40.38 E
Delgado, Cabo-=Delgado, Cape-(EN) [3]	37	Fb	12.30S	39.00 E
Delgado, Cape-(EN)= Delgado, Cabo-	30	Lj	10.40S	40.38 E
Delgado, Cape-(EN)= Delgado, Cabo- [3]	37	Fb	12.30S	39.00 E
Delger Muren	27	Hb	49.17N	100.40 E
Delhi [Co.-U.S.]	45	Eh	37.42N	103.58W
Delhi [India]	25	Jg	28.40N	77.13 E
Delhi [N.Y.-U.S.]	44	Jd	42.17N	74.57W
Deliblatska Peščara	15	Dd	45.00N	21.00 E
Delice	24	Fc	39.58N	34.02 E
Deliceırmak	24	Fb	40.28N	34.10 E
Delicias [Cuba]	49	Ic	21.11N	76.34W
Delicias [Mex.]	47	Cc	28.13N	105.28W
Deljān	24	Nf	33.59N	50.40 E
Delingha	27	Gd	37.26N	97.25 E
Dēliņkalns/Delinkalns, Gora-	8	Lg	57.30N	27.02 E
Delinkalns, Gora-/ Dēliņkalns	8	Lg	57.30N	27.02 E
Delitzsch	10	Ie	51.32N	12.21 E
Deljatin	15	Ha	48.29N	24.45 E
Delle	11	Mg	47.30N	7.00 E
Dell Rapids	45	He	43.50N	96.43W
Dellys	32	Hb	36.55N	3.55 E
Delmarva Peninsula	38	Lf	38.50N	75.30W
Delme	12	Ka	53.05N	8.40 E
Delme	12	If	48.53N	6.24 E
Delmenhorst	10	Ec	53.03N	8.37 E
Delnice	14	Ie	45.24N	14.48 E
Delo	35	Fd	5.49N	37.57 E
De Long Strait (EN)= Longa, Proliv-	21	Tb	70.20N	178.00 E
De-Longa, Ostrova-=De Long Islands (EN)	21	Rb	76.30N	153.00 E
De Long Islands (EN)=De-Longa, Ostrova-	21	Rb	76.30N	153.00 E
De Long Mountains	40	Gc	68.20N	162.00W
Deloraine	59	Jh	41.31S	146.39 E
Delorme, Lac-	42	Kf	54.35N	69.55W
Delphi (EN) = Dhelfoí	15	Fk	38.29N	22.30 E
Del Rio	43	Gf	29.22N	100.54W
Delsberg/Delémont	14	Bc	47.22N	7.21 E
Delsbo	7	Dc	61.48N	16.35 E
Delta [Co.-U.S.]	43	Fd	38.44N	108.04W
Delta [Ut.-U.S.]	43	Ed	39.21N	112.35W
Delta Amacuro [2]	54	Fb	8.30N	61.30W
Delta Junction	40	Jd	64.02N	145.41W
Delvāda	25	Ed	20.46N	71.02 E
Del Valle	55	Bl	35.54S	60.43W
Delvina	15	Dj	39.57N	20.06 E
Dēma	17	Gi	54.42N	55.58 E
Demanda, Sierra de la-	13	Ib	42.15N	3.05W
Demba	36	Dd	5.30S	22.16 E
Dembi	35	Fd	8.05N	36.28 E
Dembia	35	Cd	5.07N	24.25 E
Dembi Dolo	35	Ed	8.32N	34.49 E
De Medinilla, Farallon-	57	Fc	16.01N	146.04 E
Demer	11	Kd	50.58N	4.45 E
Demerara Plateau (EN)	52	Le	4.30N	44.00W
Demerara River	50	Gi	6.48N	58.10W
Demidov	16	Gb	55.15N	31.29 E
Demidovka	10	Vf	50.20N	25.27 E
Deming	43	Fe	32.16N	107.45W
Demini, Rio-	54	Fd	0.46S	62.56W
Demirci	24	Cc	39.03N	28.40 E
Demir Kapija	15	Fh	41.25N	22.15 E
Demirköy	15	Kh	41.49N	27.45 E
Demirtaş	15	Mi	40.16N	29.06 E
Demjanka	19	Gd	59.34N	69.20 E
Demjansk	7	Hh	57.38N	32.29 E
Demjanskoje	19	Gd	59.36N	69.18 E
Demmin	10	Jc	53.54N	13.02 E
Demopolis	44	Di	32.31N	87.50W
Dempo, Gunung-	21	Mj	4.02S	103.09 E
Demta	26	Lg	2.20S	140.08 E
Denain	11	Jd	50.20N	3.23 E
Denan	35	Gd	6.30N	43.30 E
Denau	19	Gh	38.18N	67.55 E
Den Bosch/'s-Hertogenbosch	11	Lc	51.41N	5.19 E
Den Burg, Texel-	12	Ga	53.03N	4.47 E
Den Chai	25	Ke	17.59N	100.04 E
Dendang	26	Eg	3.05S	107.54 E
Dender/Dendre	11	Kc	51.02N	4.06 E
Dendermonde/Termonde	12	Gc	51.02N	4.07 E
Dendre/Dender	11	Kc	51.02N	4.06 E
Dendtler Island	66	Pf	72.58S	89.57W
Denekamp	12	Jb	52.23N	7.00 E
Deneżkin Kamen, Gora-	19	Fc	60.25N	59.31 E
Dengarh	25	Hd	23.50N	81.42 E
Dêngkagoin→Têwo	27	He	34.03N	103.21 E
Dengkou (Bayan Gol)	22	Me	40.25N	106.59 E
Dêngqên	27	Ge	31.29N	95.32 E
Dengzhou→Penglai	27	Ld	37.44N	120.45 E
Den Haag/'s-Gravenhage= The Hague (EN)	6	Ge	52.06N	4.18 E
Den Ham	12	Ib	52.28N	6.32 E
Denham→Shak Bay	59	Ce	25.55S	113.32 E
Denham, Mount-	49	Id	18.13N	77.32W
Denham Range	59	Jd	21.55S	147.45 E
Denham Sound	59	Ce	25.40S	113.15 E
Den Helder	11	Kb	52.54N	4.45 E
Denia	13	Mf	38.51N	0.07 E
Deniliquin	59	Ig	35.32S	144.58 E
Denio	46	Ff	41.59N	118.39W
Denis Island	37b	Ca	3.48S	55.40 E
Denison [Ia.-U.S.]	43	Hc	42.01N	95.20W
Denison [Tx.-U.S.]	43	He	33.45N	96.33W
Denison, Mount-	40	Ie	58.25N	154.27W
Denizli	23	Cb	37.46N	29.06 E
Denklingen, Reichshoft-	12	Jd	50.55N	7.39 E
Denman Glacier	66	Ge	66.45S	99.25 E
Denmark [Austl.]	59	Df	34.57S	117.21 E
Denmark [S.C.-U.S.]	44	Gi	33.19N	81.09W
Denmark (EN)=Danmark [1]	6	Gd	56.00N	10.00 E
Denmark Strait (EN)= Danmarksstraedet	38	Qc	67.00N	25.00W
Dennery	51k	Bb	13.55N	60.54W
Den Oever, Wieringen-	12	Hb	52.56N	5.02 E
Denpasar	22	Nj	8.39S	115.13 E
Denton	43	He	33.13N	97.08W
D'Entrecasteaux, Point-	59	Df	34.50S	116.00 E
D'Entrecasteaux Islands	57	Ge	9.35S	150.40 E
Denver	39	If	39.43N	105.01W
Deoghar	25	Hd	24.29N	86.42 E
Deolāli	25	Ee	19.54N	73.50 E
De Pajaros, Farallon-	57	Fb	20.32N	144.54 E
De Panne/La Panne	12	Ec	51.06N	2.35 E
De Pere	45	Ld	44.27N	88.04W
Deputatski	20	Ic	69.13N	139.55 E
Dêqên	27	Gf	28.32N	98.50 E
Deqing	27	Jg	23.14N	111.42 E
De Queen	45	Ii	34.02N	94.21W
De Quincy	45	Jk	30.27N	93.26W
Deqing	28	Fi	30.34N	120.05 E
Dera, Lach-	35	Ge	0.15N	42.17 E
Dera, Laghi-	30	Lh	0.15N	42.17 E
Dera Bugti	25	Dc	29.02N	69.09 E
Dera Ghāzi Khan	22	Jf	30.03N	70.38 E
Dera Ismāil Khan	25	Eb	31.50N	70.54 E
Derbent [R.S.F.S.R.]	6	Kg	42.00N	48.18 E
Derbent [Tur.]	15	Lk	38.11N	28.33 E
Derby	9	Lh	53.05N	1.40W
Derby [Austl.]	58	Df	17.18S	123.38 E
Derby [Eng.-U.K.]	9	Li	52.55N	1.30W
Derby [Ks.-U.S.]	45	Hh	37.33N	97.16W
Derbyshire [3]	9	Lh	53.10N	1.35W
Đerdap	15	Fe	44.41N	22.10 E
Derecske	10	Ri	47.21N	21.34 E
Dereköy	15	Kh	41.56N	27.21 E
Dereli	24	Hb	40.45N	38.27 E
Derg/Abhainn na Deirge	9	Fg	54.40N	7.25W
Derg, Lough-/Loch Deirgeirt	9	Ei	53.00N	8.20W
Dergači [R.S.F.S.R.]	16	Pd	51.13N	48.46 E
Dergači [Ukr.-U.S.S.R.]	16	Jd	50.09N	36.09 E
Der Grabow	10	Ib	54.23N	12.50 E
De Ridder	45	Jk	30.51N	93.17W
Derik	24	Id	37.22N	40.17 E
Derkul	16	Qd	51.17N	51.15 E
Dermott	45	Kj	33.32N	91.26W
Dernieres, Isles-	45	Kl	29.02N	90.47W
Derong	27	Gf	28.44N	99.18 E
De Rose Hill	59	Ge	26.25S	133.15 E
Déroute, Passage de la-	11	Ee	49.12N	1.51W
Dersa, Eglab-	32	Gd	26.45N	4.26W
Dersca	15	Jb	47.59N	26.12 E
Dersingham	12	Cb	52.51N	0.30 E
Derudeb	35	Fb	17.32N	36.06 E
Derventa	14	Lf	44.59N	17.55 E
Derwent [Eng.-U.K.]	9	Mg	54.10N	0.40W
Derwent [Eng.-U.K.]	12	Ab	52.53N	1.17W
Derwent River	59	Jh	43.03S	147.22 E
Deržavinsk	19	Ge	51.03N	66.19 E
Desaguadero, Rio-	52	Ji	34.13S	66.47W
Désappointement, Iles du-	57	Mf	14.10S	141.20W
Des Arc	45	Ki	34.58N	91.30W
Desborough	12	Bb	52.26N	0.49W
Descalvado	55	Ie	21.54S	47.37W
Descartes	11	Gh	46.58N	0.45 E
Deschambault Lake	42	Hf	54.50N	103.30W
Deschutes River	43	Cb	45.38N	120.54W
Descoberto, Rio-	55	Hc	16.20S	48.19W
Dese	31	Kg	11.07N	39.38 E
Deseado, Rio-	52	Jj	47.45S	65.54W
Desecheo, Isla-	51a	Ab	18.25N	67.28W
Desengaño, Punta-	56	Gg	49.15S	67.37W
Desenzano del Garda	14	Ee	45.28N	10.32 E
Desert Center	46	Hj	33.42N	115.26W
Desert Peak	46	If	40.28N	112.38W
Deshaies [Guad.]	51e	Ab	16.18N	61.48W
Deshaies [Guad.]	51e	Ab	16.18N	61.47W
Desiderio, Rio-	55	Ja	12.20S	44.50W
Desmaraisville	44	Ia	49.31N	76.10W
De Smet	45	Hd	44.23N	97.33W
Desmochado	55	Ch	27.07S	58.06W
Des Moines	38	Je	40.22N	91.26W
Des Moines [Ia.-U.S.]	39	Je	41.35N	93.37W
Des Moines [N.M.-U.S.]	45	Eh	36.46N	103.50W
Desmoronado, Cerro-	47	Dd	20.21N	105.01W
Desna	5	Je	50.33N	30.32 E
Desnăţui	15	Ge	43.53N	23.35 E
Desolación, Isla-	52	Ik	53.00S	74.10W
De Soto	45	Kg	38.08N	90.33W
Despeñaperros, Desfiladero de-	13	If	38.24N	3.30W
Des Roches, Ile-	37b	Bb	5.41S	53.41 E
Dessau	10	Ie	51.50N	12.15 E
Destruction Bay	42	Dd	61.20N	139.00W
Desventuradas, Islas-	52	Ih	26.45S	80.00W
Desvres	11	Hd	50.40N	1.50 E
Deta	15	Ed	45.24N	21.14 E
Detmold	10	Ee	51.56N	8.53 E
Detour, Point-	44	Dc	45.36N	86.37W
Detroit [Mi.-U.S.]	39	Ke	42.20N	83.03W
Detroit [Or.-U.S.]	46	Dd	44.42N	122.10W
Detroit Lakes	45	Ic	46.49N	95.51W
Dett	37	Dc	18.37S	26.51 E
Dettifoss	7a	Cb	65.49N	16.24W
Detva	10	Ph	48.34N	19.25 E
Deûle	12	Ed	50.44N	2.56 E
Deurdeur	13	Oh	36.14N	2.16 E
Deurne	12	Hc	51.28N	5.48 E
Deutsche Bucht	10	Db	54.30N	7.30 E
Deutsche Demokratische Republik=German Democratic Republic (EN) [1]	6	He	52.00N	12.30 E
Deutschlandsberg	14	Jd	46.49N	15.13 E
Deux-Bassins, Col des-	13	Ph	36.27N	3.18 E
Deux Sèvres [3]	11	Fh	46.30N	0.15W
Deva	15	Fd	45.53N	22.54 E
Dévaványa	10	Qi	47.02N	20.58 E
Deveci Dağları	24	Gb	40.05N	36.00 E
Devecser	10	Ni	47.06N	17.26 E
Develi	24	Fc	38.22N	35.06 E
Deventer	11	Mb	52.15N	6.10 E
Deverd, Cap-	63b	Be	20.46S	164.22 E
Deveron	9	Kd	57.40N	2.30W
Devès, Monts du-	11	Jj	44.57N	3.46 E
Devetak	14	Mg	43.58N	19.00 E
Devil River Peak	62	Ed	40.58S	172.39 E
Devil's Hole	9	Ne	56.38N	0.40 E
Devil's Island (EN)=Diable, Ile du-	54	Hb	5.17N	52.35W
Devils Lake	43	Hb	48.07N	98.59W
Devils Lake	45	Gb	48.01N	98.52W
Devils Paw	40	Me	58.44N	133.50W
Devils River	45	Fl	29.39N	100.58W
Devils Tower	46	Md	44.31N	104.57W
Devin	15	Hh	41.45N	24.24 E
Devizes	9	Lj	51.22N	1.59W
Devnja	15	Kf	43.13N	27.33 E
Devodi Munda	25	Ge	17.37N	82.57 E
De Volet Point	51n	Ba	13.22N	61.13W
Devolli	15	Ci	40.49N	19.51 E
Devolli	15	Di	40.30N	20.50 E
Dévoluy	11	Lj	44.39N	5.53 E
Devon [3]	9	Jk	50.50N	3.50W
Devon	9	Jk	50.50N	4.00W
Devon	38	Kb	75.00N	87.00W
Devon	12	Ba	53.04N	0.49W
Devonport	57	Fi	41.11S	146.21 E
Devoto	55	Aj	31.24S	62.19W
Devrek	24	Db	41.13N	31.57 E
Devrez	24	Fb	41.06N	34.25 E
Dewa	30	Lh	4.11N	42.06 E
Dewar Lakes	42	Kc	68.00N	73.00W
Dewās	25	Fd	22.58N	76.04 E
Dewa-Sanchi	29	Gb	39.30N	140.15 E
Dewey	45	Ih	36.48N	95.56W
De Witt	45	Ki	34.18N	91.20W
Dexemhare	35	Fb	15.04N	39.03 E
Dexing	28	Dj	28.55N	117.33 E
Dexter	45	Lh	36.48N	89.57W
Deyang	27	He	31.07N	104.25 E
Dey-Dey, Lake-	59	Ge	29.15S	131.05 E
Deyhūk	24	Qf	33.17N	57.30 E
Deyyer	24	Hd	27.50N	51.55 E
Dez	24	Mg	31.39N	48.52 E
Dezfūl	22	Gf	32.23N	48.24 E
Dez Gerd	24	Ng	30.45N	51.57 E
Dezhou	27	Kd	37.28N	116.18 E
Dežneva, Mys-	21	Uc	66.06N	169.45 E
Dhāfnī	15	Fl	37.46N	22.02 E
Dhahab	33	Fd	28.29N	34.32 E
Dhamār	23	Fg	14.37N	44.23 E
Dhamtari	25	Gd	20.41N	81.34 E
Dhānbād	25	Hd	23.48N	86.27 E
Dhanushkodi	25	Fg	9.11N	79.24 E
Dhārwār	25	Fe	15.43N	75.01 E
Dhaulagiri	21	Kg	28.44N	83.25 E
Dhekeleia	24	Ee	35.03N	33.40 E
Dhelfoí = Delphi (EN)	15	Fk	38.29N	22.30 E
Dhelvinákion	15	Dj	39.56N	20.28 E
Dhenkanal	25	Hd	20.40N	85.36 E
Dheskáti	15	Ej	39.55N	21.49 E
Dhespotikó	15	Hm	36.58N	25.00 E
Dhiapóndioi Nisoi	15	Cj	39.50N	19.25 E
Dhībān	24	Fg	31.30N	35.47 E
Dhidhimótikhon	15	Jh	41.21N	26.30 E
Dhikti Óros	15	In	35.15N	25.30 E
Dhílos	15	Il	37.24N	25.16 E
Dhílos	15	Il	37.24N	25.16 E
Dhimitsána	15	Fl	37.36N	22.03 E
Dhionisiádhes, Nisoi-	15	Jn	35.21N	26.10 E
Dhióríx Potidhaia	15	Gi	40.10N	23.20 E
Dhī-Qār [3]	24	Lg	31.10N	46.10 E
Dhī-Qar	24	Kf	32.14N	44.22 E
Dhírfis Óros	15	Gk	38.38N	23.50 E
Dhísoron Óros	15	Fh	41.11N	22.57 E
Dhivounia	15	Jn	35.50N	26.28 E
Dhodhekánisos = Dodecanese (EN)	15	Jm	36.20N	27.00 E
Dhodhóni = Dodona (EN)	15	Dj	39.33N	20.46 E
Dholpur	25	Fc	26.42N	77.54 E
Dhomokós	15	Fj	39.08N	22.18 E
Dhone	25	Fe	15.25N	77.53 E
Dhonoúsa	15	Il	37.10N	25.50 E
Dhorāij	25	Ed	21.44N	70.27 E
Dhoxáton	15	Hh	41.06N	24.14 E
Dhragónisos	15	Il	37.27N	25.29 E
Dhubri	25	Hc	26.02N	89.58 E
Dhule	22	Jg	20.54N	74.47 E
Dhuliān	25	Hd	24.41N	87.58 E
Dia	15	In	35.27N	25.13 E
Diable, Ile du-=Devil's Island (EN)	54	Hb	5.17N	52.35W
Diable, Morne au-	51g	Ba	15.37N	61.27W
Diable, Pointe du- [Mart.]	51h	Bb	14.47N	60.54W
Diable, Pointe du- [Van.]	63b	Dc	16.01S	168.12 E
Diablo, Punta del-	55	Fl	34.22S	53.46W
Diablo, Puntan-	64b	Ba	15.00N	145.34 E
Diablo Range	46	Eh	36.45N	121.20W
Diafarabé	34	Ec	14.10N	5.00W
Dialafara	34	Cc	13.27N	11.23W
Diamant, Pointe du-	51h	Ac	14.27N	61.04W
Diamant, Rocher du-	51h	Ac	14.27N	61.03W
Diamante [Arg.]	56	Hd	32.04S	60.39W
Diamante [It.]	14	Jk	39.41N	15.49 E
Diamante, Punta del-	48	Ji	16.47N	99.52W
Diamantina	54	Jg	18.15S	43.36W
Diamantina, Chapada-	52	Lg	11.30S	41.10W
Diamantina, Rio-	55	Fc	16.42S	52.45W
Diamantina Depth (EN)	3	Hm	33.30S	102.00 E
Diamantina Lakes	59	Id	23.46S	141.09 E
Diamantina River	57	Eg	26.45S	139.10 E
Diamantina Trench (EN)	3	Hm	36.00S	104.00 E
Diamantino	53	Kg	14.25S	56.27W
Diamantino, Rio-	55	Fc	16.08S	52.28W
Diamond Harbour	25	Hd	22.12N	88.12 E
Diamond Island	51p	Bb	12.20N	61.35W
Diamond Jenness Peninsula	42	Fb	71.00N	117.00W
Diamond Peak [Nv.-U.S.]	46	Hg	39.40N	115.48W
Diamond Peak [Or.-U.S.]	46	De	43.33N	122.09W
Diamond Peak [U.S.]	46	Id	44.09N	113.05W
Diamond Peak [U.S.]	46	Gc	46.07N	117.32W
Diamou	34	Cc	14.05N	11.16W
Diana, Baie-	42	Kd	61.00N	70.00W
Dianbai	27	Jg	21.33N	110.58 E
Dianbu → Feidong	28	Di	31.53N	117.29 E
Diancang Shan	27	Hf	25.42N	100.02 E
Dian Chi	27	Hg	24.50N	102.45 E
Diane, Étang de-	11a	Ba	42.07N	9.32 E
Dianjiang	27	Ie	30.19N	107.25 E
Diano Marina	14	Cg	43.54N	8.05 E
Dianópolis	54	If	11.38S	46.50W
Dianra	34	Dd	8.45N	6.18W
Diapaga	34	Fc	12.04N	1.47 E
Diaz	55	Bk	32.22S	61.05W
Dibā, Dawḩat-	24	Qk	25.38N	56.18 E
Dibagah	24	Je	35.52N	43.49 E
Dibang	25	Jc	27.50N	95.32 E
Dibaya	36	Dd	6.30S	22.57 E
Dibaya-Lubue	36	Cc	4.09S	19.52 E
Dibella	34	Hb	17.31N	12.59 E
Dibrugarh	22	Lg	27.29N	94.54 E
Dibs	24	Ke	35.40N	44.04 E
Dibsī Afnān	24	Ee	35.55N	38.16 E
Dickens	45	Fj	33.37N	100.50W
Dickinson	43	Gb	46.53N	102.47W
Dickins Seamount (EN)	40	Lf	54.30N	137.00W
Dickson	44	Dg	36.05N	87.23W
Dicle	24	Ic	38.22N	40.04 E
Dicle=Tigris (EN)	21	Gf	31.00N	47.25 E
Didam	12	Ic	51.56N	6.09 E
Didao	28	Kb	45.22N	130.48 E
Didcot	12	Ac	51.36N	1.15W
Didesa	35	Fd	9.40N	35.32 E
Didiéni	34	Dc	13.23N	8.05W
Didyma	15	Kl	37.21N	27.13 E
Die	11	Lj	44.45N	5.22 E
Dieburg	10	Eg	49.54N	8.51 E
Diecinueve de Abril	55	El	34.22S	54.04W
Dieciocho de Julio	55	Fk	33.41S	53.33W
Diefenbaker Lake	42	Gf	51.00N	107.00W
Diège	11	Ii	45.36N	2.16 E
Diego Garcia	21	Jj	6.20S	72.20 E
Diego Ramírez, Islas	56	Gi	56.30S	68.44W
Diekirch	11	Me	49.53N	6.10 E
Die Lewitz	10	Hc	53.30N	11.30 E
Diéma	34	Dc	14.33N	9.11W
Diemel	10	Fe	51.39N	9.27 E
Diemelsee	12	Kc	51.19N	8.43 E
Diemelstadt	12	Lc	51.27N	9.01 E
Dien Bien Phu	25	Kd	21.23N	103.01 E
Diepenbeek	12	Hd	50.54N	5.24 E
Diepholz	10	Ed	52.36N	8.22 E
Dieppe	11	He	49.56N	1.05 E
Dieppe Bay Town	51c	Ab	17.25N	62.48W
Dierdorf	12	Jd	50.33N	7.40 E
Dieren, Rheden-	12	Ib	52.03N	6.08 E
Di'er Songhua Jiang	27	Lc	45.26N	124.39 E
Diest	12	Hd	50.59N	5.03 E
Dieulefit	11	Lj	44.31N	5.04 E
Dieulouard	12	If	48.51N	6.04 E
Dieuze	11	Mf	48.49N	6.43 E
Dieveniškes	8	Kj	54.10N	25.44 E
Die Ville	12	Id	50.40N	6.55 E
Diez	12	Kd	50.22N	8.01 E
Dif	36	Hb	0.59N	40.57 E
Diffa [2]	34	Hb	16.00N	13.30 E
Diffa	34	Hc	13.19N	12.37 E
Differdange/Differdingen	11	Le	49.32N	5.52 E
Differdingen/Differdange	11	Le	49.32N	5.52 E
Digby	42	Kh	44.40N	65.50W
Dighton	45	Fg	38.29N	100.28W
Digne	11	Mj	44.06N	6.14 E
Digoin	11	Jh	46.29N	3.59 E
Digora	16	Nh	43.07N	44.06 E
Digos	26	Ie	6.45N	125.20 E
Digranes	7a	Ca	66.02N	14.45W
Digul	26	Kh	7.07S	138.42 E
Dihang	25	Jc	27.48N	95.30 E
Dijar	16	Tf	46.33N	56.05 E
Dijlah=Tigris (EN)	21	Gf	31.00N	47.25 E
Dijle	11	Kd	50.53N	4.42 E
Dijon	6	Gf	47.19N	5.01 E
Dik	35	Bd	9.58N	17.31 E
Dikanäs	7	Dd	65.14N	16.00 E
Dikhil	35	Gc	11.06N	42.22 E
Dikili	24	Bc	39.04N	26.53 E
Dikli	8	Kg	57.30N	25.00 E
Diksmuide/Dixmude	11	Ic	51.02N	2.52 E
Dikson	22	Kb	73.30N	80.35 E
Dikwa	34	Hc	12.02N	13.55 E
Dila	35	Fd	6.23N	38.19 E
Dilbeek	12	Gd	50.51N	4.16 E
Dili	22	Oj	8.33S	125.34 E
Di Linh	25	Lf	11.35N	108.04 E
Diližan	16	Ni	40.46N	44.55 E
Dilj	14	Me	45.16N	18.01 E
Dill	12	Kd	50.33N	8.29 E
Dillenburg	10	Ef	50.44N	8.17 E
Dillia	30	Ig	14.09N	12.50 E
Dilling	31	Jg	12.03N	29.39 E
Dillingen (Saar)	12	Ie	49.21N	6.44 E
Dillingham	39	Dd	59.02N	158.29W
Dillon [Mt.-U.S.]	43	Eb	45.13N	112.38W
Dillon [S.C.-U.S.]	44	Hh	34.25N	79.22W
Dilly	34	Dc	14.57N	7.43W
Dilolo	31	Jj	10.42S	22.20 E
Dilsen	12	Hc	51.02N	5.44 E
Dimashq=Damascus (EN)	22	Ff	33.30N	36.15 E
Dimbelenge	36	Dd	5.30S	23.53 E
Dimbokro [3]	34	Ed	6.50N	4.45W
Dimbokro	34	Ed	6.39N	4.42W
Dimboola	59	Ig	36.27S	142.02 E
Dîmbovița	15	Je	44.14N	26.27 E
Dîmbovița [2]	15	Ie	44.55N	25.30 E
Dimbovnic	15	Ie	44.20N	25.40 E
Dimitrovgrad [Bul.]	15	Ig	42.03N	25.36 E
Dimitrovgrad [R.S.F.S.R.]	19	Ee	54.14N	49.42 E
Dimitrovgrad [Yugo.]	15	Fg	43.01N	22.47 E
Dimmitt	45	Ei	34.33N	102.19W
Dimona	24	Fg	31.04N	35.02 E
Dimovo	15	Ff	43.44N	22.44 E
Dinagat	26	Id	10.12N	125.35 E
Dinājpur	25	Hc	25.38N	88.38 E
Dinan	11	Df	48.27N	2.02W
Dinangourou	34	Ec	14.27N	2.14W
Dinant	11	Kd	50.16N	4.55 E
Dinar	24	Dc	38.04N	30.10 E
Dinar, Kūh-e-	24	Ng	30.50N	51.35 E
Dinara	14	Kf	44.04N	16.23 E
Dinara=Dinaric Alps (EN)	5	Hg	43.50N	16.35 E
Dinard	11	Df	48.38N	2.04W
Dinaric Alps (EN)= Dinara	5	Hg	43.50N	16.35 E
Dindar, Nahr ad-	35	Ec	14.06N	33.40 E
Dinder	35	Ec	14.06N	33.40 E
Dindigul	25	Ff	10.21N	77.57 E
Dindima	34	Hc	10.14N	10.09 E
Dinga	36	Cd	5.19S	16.34 E
Dingbian	27	Id	37.35N	107.37 E
Dingden, Hamminkeln-	12	Ic	51.46N	6.37 E
Dinggyê	27	Ef	28.25N	87.45 E
Dinghai	27	Le	30.05N	122.07 E
Dingle	8	Df	58.32N	11.34 E
Dingle/An Daingean	9	Ci	52.08N	10.15W
Dingle Bay/Bá an Daingin	9	Ci	52.05N	10.15W
Dingolfing	10	Ih	48.38N	12.30 E
Dingshuzhen	28	Ei	31.16N	119.50 E
Dingtao	28	Cg	35.04N	115.35 E
Dinguiraye	34	Cc	11.18N	10.43W
Dingwall	9	Id	57.35N	4.26W
Dingxi	27	Hd	35.33N	104.32 E
Dingxian	27	Jd	39.29N	115.00 E
Dingxiang	28	Be	38.32N	112.59 E
Dingxing	27	Kd	39.11N	115.48 E
Dingyuan	28	Dh	32.32N	117.41 E
Dingzi Gang	28	Ff	36.33N	120.59 E
Dinh, Mui-	21	Mh	11.22N	109.01 E
Dinkel	12	Ib	52.30N	6.58 E
Dinosaur	45	Bf	40.15N	109.01W
Dinskaja	16	Kg	45.09N	39.12 E
Dinslaken	12	Ic	51.34N	6.44 E
Ḑinsōr	35	Ge	2.23N	42.58 E
Dintel	12	Gc	51.39N	4.24 E
Dinuba	46	Fh	36.36N	119.27W

Index Symbols

[1] Independent Nation
[2] State, Region
[3] District, County
[4] Municipality
[5] Colony, Dependency
Continent
Physical Region
Historical or Cultural Region
Mount, Mountain
Volcano
Hill
Mountains, Mountain Range
Hills, Escarpment
Plateau, Upland
Pass, Gap
Plain, Lowland
Delta
Salt Flat
Valley, Canyon
Crater, Cave
Karst Features
Depression
Polder
Desert, Dunes
Forest, Woods
Heath, Steppe
Oasis
Cape, Point
Coast, Beach
Cliff
Peninsula
Isthmus
Sandbank
Island
Atoll
Rock, Reef
Islands, Archipelago
Rocks, Reefs
Coral Reef
Well, Spring
Geyser
River, Stream
Waterfall Rapids
River Mouth, Estuary
Lake
Salt Lake
Intermittent Lake
Reservoir
Swamp, Pond
Canal
Glacier
Ice Shelf, Pack Ice
Ocean
Sea
Gulf, Bay
Strait, Fjord
Lagoon
Bank
Seamount
Tablemount
Ridge
Shelf
Basin
Escarpment, Sea Scarp
Fracture
Trench, Abyss
National Park, Reserve
Point of Interest
Recreation Site
Cave, Cavern
Historic Site
Ruins
Wall, Walls
Church, Abbey
Temple
Scientific Station
Airport
Port
Lighthouse
Mine
Tunnel
Dam, Bridge

Dinwiddie 44 Ig 37.05N 77.35W
Dioila 34 Dc 12.28N 6.47W
Diois, Massif du- 11 Lj 44.35N 5.20 E
Dion 34 Dc 10.12N 8.39W
Diorama 55 Gc 16.21S 51.14W
Dios 63a Ba 5.33S 154.58 E
Diosig 15 Eb 47.18N 22.00 E
Dioura 34 Dc 14.51N 5.15W
Diourbel [3] 34 Bc 14.45N 16.10W
Diourbel 34 Bc 14.40N 16.15W
Dipkarpas/Rizokarpásso 24 Fe 35.36N 34.23 E
Dipolog 22 Oi 8.35N 123.20 E
Dīr 25 Ea 35.12N 71.53 E
Dira, Djebel- 13 Ph 36.05N 3.38 E
Diré 34 Eb 16.15N 3.24W
Dire Dawa 31 Lh 9.35N 41.53 E
Diriamba 49 Dh 11.51N 86.14W
Dirico 36 Df 17.58S 20.45 E
Dirj 33 Bc 30.09N 10.26 E
Dirk Hartog Island 59 Ce 25.45S 113.00 E
Dirkou 34 Hb 19.01N 12.53 E
Dirranbandi 58 Fg 28.35S 148.14 E
Dirty Devil River 46 Jh 37.53N 110.24W
Disappointment, Cape- [B.A.T.] 56 Mh 54.53S 36.07W
Disappointment, Cape- [U.S.] 46 Cc 46.18N 124.03W
Disappointment, Lake- 57 Dg 23.30S 122.50 E
Discovery Tablemount (EN) 30 Hm 42.00S 0.10 E
Dishna 33 Fd 26.07N 32.28 E
Disko 67 Nc 69.50N 53.30W
Disko Bay (EN)=Disko Bugt 67 Nc 69.15N 52.30W
Disko Bugt=Disko Bay (EN) 67 Nc 69.15N 52.30W
Diskofjord 41 Ge 69.39N 53.45W
Disna 7 Gi 55.33N 28.12 E
Disna 7 Gi 55.34N 28.12 E
Disnaj, Ozero-/Dysnų Ežeras 7 Gi 55.35N 26.32 E
Dispur 25 Ic 26.07N 91.48 E
Diss 12 Db 52.23N 1.07 E
District of Columbia [2] 43 Ld 38.54N 77.01W
Distrito Federal [Braz.] [2] 54 Ig 15.45S 47.45W
Distrito Federal [Mex.] [2] 47 Ee 19.15N 99.10W
Disūq 24 Dg 31.08N 30.39 E
Dithmarschen 10 Fb 54.10N 9.15 E
Ditrău 15 Ic 46.49N 25.31 E
Dittaino 14 Im 37.25N 15.00 E
Diu [3] 25 Ed 20.42N 70.59 E
Divāndarreh 24 Le 35.55N 47.02 E
Divénié 36 Bc 2.41S 12.05 E
Divenskaja 8 Ne 59.09N 30.09 E
Dives 11 Fe 49.19N 0.05W
Dives-sur-Mer 12 Be 49.17N 0.06W
Diviaka 15 Ci 41.00N 19.32 E
Diviči 16 Pi 42.10N 49.01 E
Divin 10 Ue 51.57N 24.09 E
Divinópolis 53 Lh 20.09S 44.54W
Divion 12 Ed 50.28N 2.30 E
Divisões, Serra das- 54 Hg 16.40S 50.50W
Divisor, Serra de 54 De 8.00S 73.50W
Divnogorsk 20 Ee 55.58N 92.32 E
Divnoje 19 Ef 45.53N 43.22 E
Divo [3] 34 Dd 5.57N 5.15W
Divo 34 Dd 5.50N 5.22W
Divoká Orlice 10 Mf 50.09N 16.06 E
Divor 13 Df 38.59N 8.29W
Divriği 24 Hc 39.23N 38.07 E
Divrūd 24 Nd 36.52N 49.34 E
Dixmude/Diksmuide 11 Ic 51.02N 2.52 E
Dixon [Il.-U.S.] 45 Lf 41.50N 89.29W
Dixon [N.M.-U.S.] 45 Dh 36.11N 105.53W
Dixon Entrance 38 Fd 54.25N 132.30W
Diyālā 21 Gf 33.14N 44.31 E
Diyālā [3] 24 Kf 34.00N 45.00 E
Diyarbakir 23 Fb 37.55N 40.14 E
Dizy 12 Fe 49.04N 3.58 E
Dizy-le-Gros 12 Ge 49.38N 4.01 E
Dja 30 Ih 2.02N 15.12 E
Djado 31 If 21.01N 12.18 E
Djado, Plateau du- 30 If 21.45N 12.50 E
Djakovo 10 Th 48.03N 23.01 E
Djamaa 32 Ic 33.32N 6.00 E
Djambala 31 Ii 2.33S 14.45 E
Djanet 31 Hf 24.34N 9.29 E
Djaret 32 Hd 26.35N 1.38 E
Djatkovo 19 De 53.36N 34.20 E
Djatlovo 16 Dc 53.31N 25.24 E
Djaul Island 60 Eh 2.56S 150.55 E
Djebel Ṭāriq, El Bōghāz-=Gibraltar, Strait of- (EN) 5 Fh 35.57N 5.36W
Djédaa 35 Bc 13.31N 18.34 E
Djedi 30 He 34.39N 5.55 E
Djedoug, Djebel- 13 Qi 35.53N 4.20 E
Djelfa 31 He 34.40N 3.15 E
Djelfa [3] 32 Hc 34.15N 3.30 E
Djéma 31 Jh 6.03N 25.19 E
Djember 35 Bc 10.25N 17.50 E
Djemila 32 Ib 36.19N 5.44 E
Djenane 13 Pi 35.43N 3.59 E
Djenné 34 Ec 13.55N 4.33W
Djerem 34 Hd 5.20N 13.24 E
Dji 35 Cd 6.47N 22.14 E
Djibo 34 Ec 14.06N 1.38W
Djibouti 31 Lg 11.35N 43.08 E
Djibouti (Afars and Issas) [1] 31 Lg 11.30N 43.00 E
Djokupunda 36 Dd 5.27S 20.58 E
Djolu 31 Jh 0.37N 22.21 E
Djoua 36 Bb 1.13N 13.12 E
Djougou 34 Fd 9.42N 1.40 E
Djoum 34 He 2.40N 12.40 E
Djourab, Erg du- [Chad] 35 Bb 17.00N 19.30 E
Djourab, Erg du- [Chad] 35 Bb 16.40N 18.50 E
Djugu 36 Fb 1.55N 30.30 E
Djultydag, Gora- 16 Oi 41.58N 46.56 E
Djup 8 Bd 60.50N 8.00 E
Djúpi vogur 7a Cb 64.39N 14.17W
Djurbeldžin 18 Jd 41.10N 74.59 E
Djurdjura, Djebel- 13 Qh 36.27N 4.15 E
Djurmo 8 Fd 60.33N 15.10 E
Djurö 8 Ef 58.50N 13.30 E
Djursholm 8 He 59.24N 18.05 E
Djursland 8 Dh 56.20N 10.45 E
Djurtjuli 19 Fd 55.29N 54.55 E
Dmitrija Lapteva, Proliv-=Dmitri Laptev Strait (EN) 21 Qb 73.00N 142.00 E
Dmitrijev-Lgovski 16 Ic 52.08N 35.05 E
Dmitri Laptev Strait (EN)=Dmitrija Lapteva, Proliv- 21 Qb 73.00N 142.00 E
Dmitrov 7 Ih 56.26N 37.31 E
Dmitrovsk-Orlovski 16 Ic 52.31N 35.09 E
Dnepr 5 Jf 46.30N 32.18 E
Dneprodzeržinsk 19 Df 48.30N 34.37 E
Dneprodzeržinskoje Vodohranilišče 16 Ie 48.45N 34.10 E
Dnepropetrovsk 6 Jf 48.27N 34.59 E
Dnepropetrovskaja Oblast [3] 19 Df 48.15N 35.00 E
Dneprorudnoje 16 If 47.23N 35.01 E
Dneprovski Liman 16 Gf 46.35N 31.55 E
Dneprovsko-Bugski Kanal 16 Dc 52.03N 25.10 E
Dnepr Upland (EN)=Pridneprovskaja Vozvyšennost 5 Jf 49.00N 32.00 E
Dnestr [U.S.S.R.] 5 Jf 46.18N 30.17 E
Dnestrovsk 15 Mc 46.39N 29.48 E
Dnestrovski Liman 16 Gf 46.15N 30.15 E
Dno 19 Cd 57.49N 29.59 E
Doany 37 Hb 14.22S 49.30 E
Doba 35 Bd 8.39N 16.51 E
Dobbiaco / Toblach 14 Gd 46.44N 12.14 E
Dobele 7 Fh 56.39N 23.16 E
Döbeln 10 Je 51.07N 13.07 E
Doberah, Jazirah- 26 Jg 1.30S 132.30 E
Dobo 26 Jh 5.46S 134.13 E
Doboj 14 Mf 44.44N 18.05 E
Dobra 10 Oe 51.54N 18.37 E
Dobre Miasto 10 Qc 53.59N 20.25 E
Dobreta Turnu Severin 6 Ig 44.38N 22.40 E
Dobrinka 16 Lc 52.08N 40.29 E
Dobříš 10 Kg 49.47N 14.10 E
Dobrjanka 19 Fd 58.29N 56.29 E
Dobrodzień 10 Of 50.44N 18.27 E
Dobrogea=Dobruja (EN) 15 Ke 44.00N 28.00 E
Dobrogea = Dobruja (EN) 5 Ig 44.00N 28.00 E
Dobrogean, Masivul- 15 Le 44.50N 28.30 E
Dobromil 10 Sg 49.34N 22.49 E
Dobropolje 16 Je 48.28N 37.02 E
Dobroteşti 15 He 44.17N 24.53 E
Dobrotvor 10 Uf 50.10N 24.27 E
Dobrudžansko Plato 15 Kf 43.32N 27.50 E
Dobruja (EN)=Dobrogea 15 Ke 44.00N 28.00 E
Dobruja (EN) = Dobrogea 5 Ig 44.00N 28.00 E
Dobruš 16 Gc 52.26N 31.19 E
Dobruška 10 Mf 50.18N 16.10 E
Dobrzyń nad Wisłą 10 Pd 52.38N 19.20 E
Dobrzyńskie, Pojezierze- 10 Pc 53.00N 19.20 E
Dobšiná 10 Qh 48.49N 20.22 E
Doce, Rio- [Braz.] 52 Mg 19.37S 39.49W
Doce, Rio- [Braz.] 55 Gd 18.28S 51.05W
Doce Leguas, Cayos de las- 49 Hc 20.55N 79.05W
Doce Leguas, Laberinto de las- 49 Hc 20.39N 78.35W
Docker River 59 Fd 24.58S 129.03 E
Docksta 8 Ha 63.03N 18.20 E
Doctor Arroyo 48 If 23.40N 100.11W
Doctor Cecilio Baez 55 Dg 25.03S 56.19W
Doctor Pedro P. Peña 56 Hb 22.26S 62.22W
Doctor Petru Groza 15 Fc 46.37N 22.25 E
Doda 25 Fb 33.08N 75.34 E
Doda Betta 25 Ff 11.24N 76.44 E
Dodecanese (EN)=Dhodhekánisos 15 Jm 36.20N 27.00 E
Dodecanese (EN)=Nótioi Sporádhes 5 Ih 36.00N 27.00 E
Dodge City 43 Gd 37.45N 100.00W
Dodgeville 45 Ke 42.58N 90.08W
Dodman Point 9 Ik 50.13N 4.48W
Dodoma [3] 36 Gd 6.00S 36.00 E
Dodoma 31 Ki 6.11S 35.45 E
Dodona (EN)=Dhodhóni 15 Dj 39.33N 20.46 E
Dodurga 15 Mj 39.48N 29.55 E
Doesburg 12 Ib 52.01N 6.08 E
Doetinchem 11 Mc 51.58N 6.17 E
Dofa 26 Ig 1.47S 125.22 E
Dogai Coring 27 Ee 34.30N 89.10 E
Doğanbey 15 Jk 38.04N 26.53 E
Doğanşehir 24 Gc 38.06N 37.53 E
Dog Creek 46 Da 51.35N 122.15W
Dogger Bank 5 Ge 55.00N 3.00 E
Dog Island 50 Ec 18.15N 63.13W
Dog Lake [Man.-Can.] 45 Ga 51.02N 98.30W
Dog Lake [Ont.-Can.] 44 Ea 48.18N 84.10W
Dog Lake [Ont.-Can.] 45 Lb 48.46N 89.32W
Dogliani 14 Bf 44.32N 7.56 E
Dōgo 28 Lf 36.15N 133.17 E
Dogonbadān 23 Hc 30.21N 50.48 E
Dogondoutchi 34 Fc 13.38N 4.02 E
Dōgo-San 29 Cd 35.04N 133.14 E
Dog Rocks 49 Ha 24.05N 79.51W
Doğubayazıt 24 Kc 39.32N 44.08 E
Dogwood Point 51c Ab 17.06N 62.38W
Doha (EN)=Ad Dawḥah 22 Hg 25.17N 51.32 E
Dohad 25 Ed 22.50N 74.16 E
Dohāzāri 25 Id 22.10N 92.04 E
Doi Luang Chinag Dao 25 Je 19.23N 98.54 E
Doilungdêqên 27 Ff 29.47N 90.49 E
Doire/Londonderry 6 Fd 55.00N 7.19W
Doire Baltée/Dora Baltea 14 Ce 45.11N 8.03 E
Doische 12 Gd 50.08N 4.45 E
Dojransko jezero 15 Fh 41.13N 22.44 E
Doka 35 Fc 13.31N 35.46 E
Dokhara, Dunes de- 32 Ic 32.50N 6.00 E
Dokka 8 Dd 60.49N 10.05 E
Dokka 7 Cf 60.50N 10.05 E
Dokkum 11 La 53.19N 6.00 E
Dokšicy 7 Gi 54.56N 27.46 E
Doksy 10 Kf 50.34N 14.40 E
Dokučajevsk 16 Jf 47.43N 37.47 E
Dolak, Pulau- 57 Ee 7.50S 138.30 E
Dolbeau 42 Kg 48.52N 72.14W
Dol-de-Bretagne 11 Ef 48.33N 1.45W
Dôle 11 Lg 47.06N 5.30 E
Doleib Hill 35 Ed 9.22N 31.36 E
Dolenjsko 14 Je 45.50N 15.10 E
Dolgaja, Kosa- 16 Jf 46.40N 37.45 E
Dolgellau 9 Ji 52.44N 3.53W
Dolgi, Ostrov- 17 Ib 69.15N 59.05 E
Dolgi Most 20 Ee 56.45N 96.58 E
Dolianova 14 Dk 39.22N 9.10 E
Dolina 16 De 48.58N 24.01 E
Dolinsk 20 Jg 47.20N 142.50 E
Dolinskaja 19 Df 48.07N 32.44 E
Dolinskoje 15 Mb 47.33N 29.50 E
Dolj [2] 15 Ge 44.10N 23.40 E
Dollart 11 Na 53.17N 7.10 E
Dolly Cays 49 Ib 23.39N 77.22W
Dolni Dăbnik 15 Hf 43.24N 24.26 E
Dolní Dvořiště 10 Kh 48.39N 14.27 E
Dolnomoravský úval 10 Nh 49.00N 17.15 E
Dolnośląskie, Bory- 10 Le 51.25N 15.20 E
Dolný Kubín 10 Pg 49.12N 19.17 E
Dolo 31 Lh 4.11N 42.05 E
Dolomites (EN) = Dolomiti 5 Hf 46.23N 11.51 E
Dolomiti = Dolomites (EN) 14 Fd 46.23N 11.51 E
Dolon, Pereval- 18 Jd 41.48N 75.45 E
Dolonnur/Duolun 27 Kc 42.10N 116.30 E
Dolores [Arg.] 56 Ie 36.20S 57.40W
Dolores [Guat.] 49 Ce 16.31N 89.25W
Dolores [Ur.] 56 Id 33.33S 58.13W
Dolores River 46 Kg 38.49N 109.17W
Dolphin, Cape- 56 Ih 51.15S 58.58W
Dolphin and Union Strait 42 Gc 69.00N 115.00W
Dom, Kūh-e- 24 Of 33.52N 53.00 E
Domačevo 10 Te 51.46N 23.37 E
Domaniç 24 Cc 39.48N 29.37 E
Domantaj/Domantaj 8 Ji 55.57N 23.19 E
Domantaj/Domantai 8 Ji 55.57N 23.19 E
Domart-en-Ponthieu 12 Ed 50.04N 2.07 E
Domasa, údolná nádrž- 10 Rg 49.05N 21.47 E
Domažlice 10 Ig 49.27N 12.56 E
Dombaj-Ulgen, Gora- 16 Lh 43.14N 41.46 E
Dombarovski 19 Fe 50.47N 59.34 E
Dombås 6 Gc 62.05N 9.08 E
Dombe Grande 36 Be 12.56S 13.07 E
Dombes 11 Lh 46.00N 5.03 E
Dombóvár 10 Oj 46.23N 18.07 E
Dombrád 10 Rh 48.14N 21.56 E
Domburg 12 Fc 51.34N 3.30 E
Dôme, Monts- 11 Ii 45.45N 2.55 E
Dôme, Puy de- 11 Ii 45.47N 2.58 E
Domérat 11 Ih 46.21N 2.32 E
Domeyko, Cordillera- 52 Jh 24.30S 69.00W
Domfront 11 Ff 48.36N 0.39W
Domingo M. Irala 55 Eg 25.54S 54.43W
Domingos Martins 54 Jh 20.22S 40.40W
Dominica [1] 39 Mh 15.30N 61.20W
Dominica 38 Mh 15.30N 61.20W
Dominical 49 Fi 9.13N 83.51W
Dominicana, República-=Dominican Republic (EN) [1] 39 Lh 19.00N 70.40W
Dominican Republic (EN)=Dominicana, República- [1] 39 Lh 19.00N 70.40W
Dominica Passage 50 Fe 15.10N 61.15W
Dominica Passage (EN)=Dominique, Canal de la- 50 Fe 15.10N 61.15W
Dominion, Cape - 42 Kc 66.10N 74.30W
Dominique, Canal de la-=Dominica Passage (EN) 50 Fe 15.10N 61.15W
Domino 42 Lf 53.28N 55.46W
Domiongo 36 Dc 4.37S 21.15 E
Dommartin-Varimont 12 Gf 48.59N 4.46 E
Domme 11 Hj 44.48N 1.13 E
Dommel 11 Lc 51.40N 5.20 E
Domneşti 15 Hd 45.12N 24.50 E
Domo 35 Hd 7.57N 46.51 E
Domodedovo 7 Ii 55.27N 37.47 E
Domodossola 14 Cd 46.07N 8.17 E
Domont 12 Ee 49.02N 2.20 E
Dom Pedrito 56 Jd 30.59S 54.40W
Dom Pedro 54 Jd 5.00S 44.27W
Dompierre-sur-Besbre 11 Jh 46.31N 3.41 E
Dompu 26 Gh 8.32S 118.28 E
Domusnovas 14 Ck 39.19N 8.39 E
Domuyo, Volcán- 52 Ii 36.38S 70.26W
Don 48 Ed 26.26N 109.02W
Don [Eng.-U.K.] 9 Mh 53.39N 0.59W
Don [Fr.] 12 Ej 47.40N 1.56W
Don [R.S.F.S.R.] 5 Jf 47.04N 39.18 E
Don [Scot.-U.K.] 9 Kd 57.10N 2.04W
Donaldsonville 45 Kk 30.06N 90.59W
Donau=Danube (EN) 5 If 45.20N 29.40 E
Donaueschingen 10 Ei 47.57N 8.30 E
Donaumoos 10 Hh 48.40N 11.15 E
Donauried 10 Gh 48.35N 10.40 E
Donauwörth 10 Gh 48.42N 10.48 E
Don Benito 13 Gf 38.57N 5.52W
Doncaster 9 Lh 53.32N 1.07W
Dondjušany 15 Ka 48.11N 27.31 E
Dondo [Ang.] 31 Ii 9.40S 14.26 E
Dondo [Moz.] 37 Ec 19.36S 34.44 E
Dondra Head 21 Ki 5.55N 80.35 E
Donec 5 Kf 47.40N 40.50 E
Doneck [R.S.F.S.R.] 16 Ke 48.21N 39.59 E
Doneck [Ukr.-U.S.S.R.] 6 Jf 48.00N 37.48 E
Doneckaja Oblast [3] 19 Df 48.00N 37.45 E
Donecki Krjaž=Donec Ridge (EN) 5 Kh 48.15N 38.45 E
Donec Ridge (EN)=Donecki Krjaž 5 Kh 48.15N 38.45 E
Donegal/Dún na nGall 9 Eg 54.39N 8.06W
Donegal/Dún na nGall [2] 9 Fg 54.50N 8.00W
Donegal Bay/Bá Dhún na nGall 5 Fe 54.30N 8.30W
Donegal Mountains 9 Eg 54.50N 8.10W
Donga 34 Hd 8.19N 10.01 E
Dongara 59 Ce 29.15S 114.56 E
Dongbei Pingyuan 28 Gc 44.00N 124.00 E
Dongchuan (Tangdan) 27 Hf 26.07N 103.05 E
Dongcun → Lanxian 28 Ae 38.17N 111.38 E
Dong Dao 27 Jc 16.45N 113.00 E
Donge 12 Gc 51.41N 4.49 E
Dong'e (Tongcheng) 28 Df 36.19N 116.14 E
Dongen 12 Gc 51.37N 4.57 E
Donges 11 Dg 47.18N 2.04W
Dongfang (Basuo) 27 Ih 19.14N 108.39 E
Dongfanghong 28 La 46.15N 133.07 E
Dongfeng 28 Hc 42.41N 125.33 E
Donggala 26 Gg 0.40S 119.44 E
Donggou 27 Ld 39.55N 124.08 E
Dongguang 28 Df 37.54N 116.32 E
Dong Hai=East China Sea (EN) 21 Og 29.00N 125.00 E
Donghai Dao 27 Jg 21.00N 110.25 E
Dong He 27 Hc 42.12N 101.10 E
Dongjingcheng 25 Le 17.29N 106.36 E
Dong Jang 21 Ng 23.02N 113.31 E
Dongkala 26 Hh 5.18S 122.03 E
Dongkan → Binhai 27 Ke 34.00N 119.52 E
Donglan 27 Ig 24.35N 107.22 E
Dongliao He 28 Gc 43.24N 123.42 E
Dongming 28 Cg 35.17N 115.04 E
Dongnan Qiuling 27 Jg 24.00N 113.00 E
Dongo 36 Ce 14.36S 15.43 E
Dongola (EN)=Dunqulah 31 Kg 19.10N 30.29 E
Dongou 36 Cb 2.02N 18.04 E
Dongoun → Haiyang 28 Ff 36.46N 121.09 E
Dongping 27 Kd 35.51N 116.15 E
Dongping → Anhua 27 Jf 28.27N 111.15 E
Dong Rak, Phanom-=Dangrek Range (EN) 21 Mh 14.25N 104.30 E
Dongsha Dao 27 Kg 20.45N 116.45 E
Dongsha Qundao 21 Ng 20.42N 116.43 E
Dongsheng 27 Id 39.48N 110.00 E
Dongtai 27 Le 32.47N 120.18 E
Dong Taijnar Hu 27 Fd 37.25N 94.00 E
Dongtin Hu 21 Ng 29.18N 112.45 E
Dong Ujimqin Qi (Uliastai) 27 Kc 45.31N 116.58 E
Dongwe 36 De 13.56S 23.53 E
Dongxiang 27 Kf 28.15N 116.38 E
Dongyang 28 Fj 29.16N 120.14 E
Dongying 27 Kd 37.30N 118.30 E
Dongzhi (Yaodu) 28 Di 30.06N 117.01 E
Donington 12 Bb 52.54N 0.12W
Doniphan 45 Kh 36.37N 90.50W
Donja Brela 14 Kg 43.23N 16.55 E
Donji Miholjac 14 Me 45.45N 18.10 E
Donji Vakuf 14 Lf 44.08N 17.24 E
Dønna 7 Cc 66.06N 12.35 E
Donnacona 44 Lb 46.40N 71.47W
Donner Pass 43 Cd 39.19N 120.20W
Donnersberg 12 Je 49.38N 7.55 E
Donner und Blitzen River 46 Fe 43.17N 118.49W
Donnybrook 59 Df 33.35S 115.49 E
Donskaja Grjada=Don Upland (EN) 5 Kf 49.10N 42.00 E
Donskoj 16 Kb 54.01N 38.20 E
Don Upland (EN)=Donskaja Grjada 5 Kf 49.10N 42.00 E
Donuzlav, Ozero- 16 Hg 45.25N 33.10 E
Doolette Bay 66 Je 67.55S 147.00 E
Doon 9 If 55.26N 4.38W
Doonerak, Mount- 40 Ic 67.56N 150.37W
Doorn 12 Hb 52.02N 5.19 E
Doornik/Tournai 11 Jd 50.36N 3.23 E
Door Peninsula 45 Md 44.55N 87.20W
Do Qu 27 He 31.48N 102.09 E
Dora, Lake- 59 Ed 22.05S 122.56 E
Dora Baltea/Doire Baltée 14 Ce 45.11N 8.03 E
Dorada, Costa- 13 Nc 41.08N 1.10 E
Dora Riparia 14 Be 45.05N 7.44 E
Dorbiljin/Emin 27 Db 46.32N 83.39 E
Dorchester 9 Kk 50.43N 2.26W
Dorchester, Cape - 42 Jc 65.28N 77.30W
Dordabis 37 Bd 22.52S 17.38 E
Dordogne 5 Ff 45.02N 0.35W
Dordogne [3] 11 Gi 45.10N 0.50 E
Dordrecht [Neth.] 12 Gc 51.48N 4.40 E
Dordrecht [Neth.] 11 Kc 51.49N 4.40 E
Dordrecht [S.Afr.] 37 Df 31.20S 27.03 E
Dore 11 Ji 46.00N 3.28 E
Dore, Monts- 5 Gf 45.30N 2.45 E
Doré Lake 42 Gf 54.45N 107.20W
Dores do Indaia 54 Ig 19.27S 45.36W
Dorgali 14 Dj 40.17N 9.35 E
Dori 31 Gg 14.02N 0.02W
Doring 30 Il 31.52S 18.39 E
Dorking 12 Bc 51.13N 0.20W
Dormagen 12 Ic 51.06N 6.50 E
Dormans 11 Je 49.04N 3.38 E
Dormidontovka 20 Ig 47.45N 134.58 E
Dornbirn 14 Dc 47.25N 9.44 E
Dornoch 9 Id 57.52N 4.02W
Dornoch Firth 9 Id 57.52N 4.02W
Doro 34 Eb 16.09N 0.51W
Dorog 10 Oi 47.43N 18.44 E
Dorogobuž 16 Hb 54.56N 33.15 E
Dorohoi 15 Jb 47.57N 26.24 E
Dorotea 7 Dd 64.16N 16.24 E
Dorre Island 59 Ce 25.10S 113.05 E
Dorrigo 59 Kf 30.20S 152.45 E
Dorset [3] 9 Kk 50.50N 2.10W
Dorset 9 Kk 50.55N 2.15W
Dorsten 10 Ce 51.40N 6.58 E
Dortmund 6 Ge 51.31N 7.27 E
Dortmund-Ems-Kanal 10 De 51.32N 7.27 E
Doruma 36 Eb 4.44N 27.42 E
Dörverden 12 Lb 52.51N 9.14 E
Doseo, Bar- 35 Bd 9.01N 19.38 E
Dos Hermanas 13 Gg 37.17N 5.55W
Dos Lagunas 49 Ce 17.42N 89.36W
Dospat 15 Hh 41.39N 24.10 E
Dospat 15 Hh 41.23N 24.05 E
Dosse 10 Ic 53.13N 12.20 E
Dosso 31 Hg 13.03N 3.12 E
Dosso [2] 34 Fc 13.30N 3.30 E
Dossor 19 Ff 47.32N 53.01 E
Dostluk 18 Ef 37.45N 65.22 E
Dothan 43 Je 31.13N 85.24W
Dotnuva 8 Ji 55.18N 23.55 E
Dötyol 24 Gd 36.52N 36.12 E
Douai 11 Jd 50.22N 3.04 E
Douala 31 Hh 4.03N 9.42 E
Douaouir 34 Ea 20.45N 2.30W
Douarnenez 11 Bf 48.06N 4.20W
Douarnenez, Baie de- 11 Bf 48.10N 4.25W
Double Mountain Fork Brazos 45 Gj 33.15N 100.00W
Doubrava 10 Lf 50.03N 15.20 E
Doubs 11 Lh 46.54N 5.02 E
Doubs [3] 11 Mg 47.10N 6.25 E
Doubtful Sound 62 Bf 45.15S 166.50 E
Doubtless Bay 62 Ea 34.55S 173.25 E
Douchy-les-Mines 12 Fd 50.18N 3.23 E
Doudeville 12 Ce 49.43N 0.48 E
Doué-la-Fontaine 11 Fg 47.12N 0.17W
Douentza 34 Eb 15.03N 2.57W
Douera 13 Oh 36.40N 2.57 E
Dougga 32 Ib 36.24N 9.13 E
Douglas [Ak.-U.S.] 40 Me 58.16N 134.26W
Douglas [Az.-U.S.] 43 Fe 31.21N 109.33W
Douglas [Ga.-U.S.] 44 Fj 31.31N 82.51W
Douglas [S.Afr.] 37 Ce 29.04S 23.46 E
Douglas [U.K.] 9 Ig 54.09N 4.28W
Douglas [Wy.-U.S.] 43 Fc 42.45N 105.24W
Douglas Lake 44 Fh 36.00N 83.22W
Douglas Range 66 Qf 70.00S 69.35W
Doullens 11 Id 50.09N 2.21 E
Doumé 34 He 4.14N 13.27 E
Douna 34 Ec 14.39N 1.43W
Doupovské hory 10 Jf 50.13N 13.08 E
Dour 12 Fd 50.24N 3.47 E
Dourada, Serra- [Braz.] 55 Gb 16.00S 50.05W
Dourada, Serra- [Braz.] 55 Ha 13.10S 48.45W
Dourados 53 Kh 22.13S 54.48W
Dourados, Rio- [Braz.] 55 Ee 21.58S 54.18W
Dourados, Rio- [Braz.] 55 Id 18.17S 47.36W
Dourbali 35 Bc 11.49N 15.52 E
Dourdan 11 If 48.32N 2.01 E
Douro 5 Fg 41.08N 8.40W
Douro Litoral 13 Dc 41.05N 8.20W
Doushi → Gong'an 27 Je 30.05N 112.12 E
Douve 11 Ee 49.19N 1.44W
Douvres-la-Delivrande 12 Be 49.17N 0.23W
Douze 11 Fk 43.54N 0.30W
Douzy 12 He 49.40N 5.03 E
Dove 9 Li 52.50N 1.35W
Dove Bugt 41 Jd 76.25N 21.00W
Dove Creek 45 Bh 37.46N 108.54W
Dover [De.-U.S.] 39 Lf 39.10N 75.32W
Dover [Eng.-U.K.] 6 Ge 51.08N 1.19 E
Dover [N.H.-U.S.] 44 Ld 43.12N 70.55W
Dover [Oh.-U.S.] 44 Ge 40.32N 81.30W
Dover, Strait of- 5 Ge 51.00N 1.30 E
Dover, Strait of- (EN)=Calais, Pas de- 5 Ge 51.00N 1.30 E
Dover Foxcroft 44 Mc 45.11N 69.13W
Dovey 9 Ji 52.34N 3.59W
Dovre 8 Cc 61.59N 9.15 E
Dovrefjell 5 Gc 62.10N 9.25 E
Dowa 36 Fe 13.39S 33.56 E
Dowagiac 44 De 41.59N 86.06W
Dowlatābād 24 Qh 28.20N 57.13 E
Downey 46 Ie 42.26N 112.07W
Downham Market 12 Cb 52.36N 0.22 E
Downieville 46 Eg 39.34N 120.50W
Downpatrick / Dún Pádraig 9 Hg 54.20N 5.43W
Dow Rūd 23 Gc 33.28N 49.04 E
Dow Sar 24 Me 35.06N 48.02 E
Dōzen 29 Cc 36.05N 132.59 E
Dozois, Reservoir- 44 Ib 47.30N 77.00W
Dozulé 12 Be 49.14N 0.03W
Drâa 30 Ff 28.40N 11.07W
Drâa, Cap- 32 Ed 28.44N 11.05W
Drâa, Hamada du- 30 Gf 28.30N 7.30W
Draa el Baguel 32 Ic 30.17N 6.25 E
Draa el Mizan 13 Ph 36.32N 3.50 E
Drac 11 Li 45.13N 5.41 E
Dracena 55 Ge 21.32S 51.29W
Drach, Cuevas del- 13 Pe 39.32N 3.15 E
Dragalina 15 Kc 44.26N 27.19 E
Dragan 7 Dd 64.00N 15.21 E
Drăgăneşti-Olt 15 He 44.09N 24.42 E
Drăgăneşti-Vlaşca 15 Ie 44.06N 25.36 E
Drăgăşani 15 He 44.39N 24.16 E
Dragobia 15 Cg 42.26N 19.59 E
Dragón, Bocas del-/Dragon's Mouths 54 Fa 10.45N 61.46W
Dragonera, Isla-/Dragonera, Sa- 13 Oe 39.35N 2.19 E
Dragonera, Sa-/Dragonera, Isla- 13 Oe 39.35N 2.19 E

Index Symbols

[1] Independent Nation
[2] State, Region
[3] District, County
[4] Municipality
[5] Colony, Dependency
Continent
Physical Region
Historical or Cultural Region
Mount, Mountain
Volcano
Hill
Mountains, Mountain Range
Hills, Escarpment
Plateau, Upland
Pass, Gap
Plain, Lowland
Delta
Salt Flat
Valley, Canyon
Crater, Cave
Karst Features
Depression
Polder
Desert, Dunes
Forest, Woods
Heath, Steppe
Oasis
Cape, Point
Coast, Beach
Cliff
Peninsula
Isthmus
Sandbank
Island
Atoll
Rock, Reef
Islands, Archipelago
Rocks, Reefs
Coral Reef
Well, Spring
Geyser
River, Stream
Waterfall Rapids
River Mouth, Estuary
Lake
Salt Lake
Intermittent Lake
Reservoir
Swamp, Pond
Canal
Glacier
Ice Shelf, Pack Ice
Ocean
Sea
Gulf, Bay
Strait, Fjord
Lagoon
Bank
Seamount
Tablemount
Ridge
Shelf
Basin
Escarpment, Sea Scarp
Fracture
Trench, Abyss
National Park, Reserve
Point of Interest
Recreation Site
Cave, Cavern
Historic Site
Ruins
Wall, Walls
Church, Abbey
Temple
Scientific Station
Airport
Port
Lighthouse
Mine
Tunnel
Dam, Bridge

Dragon's Mouths/Dragón, Bocas del- 54 Fa 10.45N 61.46W
Dragør 8 Ei 55.36N 12.41 E
Draguignan 11 Mk 43.32N 6.28 E
Drahanska vrchovina 10 Mg 49.30N 16.45 E
Drain 46 De 43.40N 123.19W
Drake 45 Fc 47.55N 100.23W
Drake, Estrecho de-=Drake Passage (EN) 52 Jk 58.00S 70.00W
Drakensberg 30 Jk 29.00S 29.00 E
Drake Passage (EN)=Drake, Estrecho de- 52 Jk 58.00S 70.00W
Dráma 15 Hh 41.09N 24.09 E
Drammen 6 Hd 59.44N 10.15 E
Dramselva 8 De 59.44N 10.14 E
Drangajokull 7a Aa 66.09N 22.15W
Dranse 11 Mh 46.24N 6.30 E
Drau=Drava (EN) 5 Hf 45.33N 18.55 E
Dráva=Drava (EN) 5 Hf 45.33N 18.55 E
Drava (EN)=Drau 5 Hf 45.33N 18.55 E
Drava (EN)=Dráva 5 Hf 45.33N 18.55 E
Dravograd 14 Jd 46.35N 15.01 E
Drawa 10 Ld 52.52N 15.59 E
Drawno 10 Lc 53.13N 15.45 E
Drawsko, Jezioro- 10 Mc 53.33N 16.10 E
Drawsko Pomorskie 10 Lc 53.32N 15.48 E
Drayton Valley 42 Gf 53.13N 115.00W
Drean 14 Bn 36.41N 7.45 E
Dreieich 12 Ke 50.01N 8.43 E
Drenovci 14 Mf 44.55N 18.55 E
Drenthe 12 Ib 52.45N 6.30 E
Dresden 10 Je 51.10N 14.00 E
Dresden 6 He 51.03N 13.45 E
Dreux 11 Hf 48.44N 1.22 E
Drevsjø 7 Cf 61.54N 12.02 E
Drezdenko 10 Ld 52.51N 15.50 E
Dricēni/Driceni 8 Lh 56.39N 27.11 E
Driceni/Dricēni 8 Lh 56.39N 27.11 E
Driffield 9 Mg 54.01N 0.26W
Driggs 46 Je 43.44N 111.14W
Drina 5 Hg 44.53N 19.21 E
Drincea 15 Fe 44.07N 22.59 E
Drin Gulf (EN)=Drinit, Gjiri i- 15 Ch 41.45N 19.28 E
Drini 5 Hg 41.45N 19.34 E
Drini i Zi 15 Dg 42.05N 20.23 E
Drinit, Gjiri i-=Drin Gulf (EN) 15 Ch 41.45N 19.28 E
Drinjača 14 Nf 44.17N 19.10 E
Drinosi 15 Di 40.17N 20.02 E
Drissa 7 Gi 55.47N 27.57 E
Drisvjaty, Ozero-/Drūkšiu Ežeras 8 Lj 55.37N 26.45 E
Driva 8 Cb 62.40N 8.34 E
Drjanovo 15 Ig 42.58N 25.28 E
Drniš 14 Kg 43.52N 16.09 E
Drøbak 7 Cg 59.39N 10.39 E
Drocea, Virful- 15 Fc 46.12N 22.14 E
Drogheda/Droichead Átha 9 Gh 53.43N 6.21W
Drogičin 16 Dc 52.13N 25.10 E
Drogobyč 16 Ce 49.22N 23.33 E
Drohiczyn 10 Sd 52.24N 22.41 E
Droichead Átha/Drogheda 9 Gh 53.43N 6.21W
Droichead na Bandan/Bandon 9 Ej 51.45N 8.45W
Droichead na Banna/Banbridge 9 Gg 54.21N 6.16W
Drokija 16 Ee 48.01N 27.53 E
Drôme 12 Be 49.19N 0.45W
Drôme 11 Lj 44.35N 5.10 E
Drömling 10 Hd 52.29N 11.04 E
Dronero 14 Bf 44.28N 7.22 E
Dronne 11 Fi 45.02N 0.09W
Dronning Fabiola-Fjella 66 Df 71.30S 35.40 E
Dronning Louise Land 41 Jc 76.45N 24.00W
Dronten 11 Lb 52.31N 5.42 E
Dropt 11 Fj 44.35N 0.06W
Drovjanoj 20 Cb 72.25N 72.45 E
Drowning River 45 Na 50.55N 84.35W
Druja 7 Gi 55.47N 27.29 E
Drūkšiu Ežeras/Drisvjaty, Ozero- 8 Lj 55.37N 26.45 E
Druk-Yul→Bhutan 22 Lg 27.30N 90.30 E
Drulingen 12 Jf 48.52N 7.11 E
Drumheller 42 Gf 51.28N 112.42W
Drummond [Mt.-U.S.] 46 Ic 46.40N 113.09W
Drummond [Wi.-U.S.] 45 Kc 46.20N 91.15W
Drummond Island 44 Fb 46.00N 83.40W
Drummond Range 59 Jd 23.30S 147.15 E
Drummondville 42 Kg 45.50N 72.20W
Drummore 9 Ig 54.42N 4.54W
Drumochter, Pass of- 9 Ie 56.50N 4.12W
Drunen 12 Hc 51.41N 5.10 E
Druskininkai/Druskininkaj 7 Fi 54.04N 24.06 E
Druskininkaj/Druskininkai 7 Fi 54.04N 24.06 E
Drut 16 Gc 53.04N 30.35 E
Druten 12 Hc 51.54N 5.38 E
Družba 16 Hc 52.05N 33.59 E
Druzba 19 If 45.18N 82.29 E
Družkovka 16 Je 48.36N 37.33 E
Družnaja Gorka 8 Ne 59.11N 30.10 E
Družnino 17 Ih 56.48N 59.29 E
Družno, Jezioro- 10 Pb 54.08N 19.30 E
Drvar 14 Kf 44.22N 16.23 E
Drvenik 14 Lg 43.09N 17.15 E
Drweca 10 Oc 53.00N 18.42 E
Dryden 42 Ig 49.47N 92.50W
Dry Fork 46 Me 43.30N 105.24W
Drygalski Ice Tongue 66 Kf 75.24S 163.30 E
Drygalski Island 66 Ge 65.45S 92.30 E
Drysdale River 59 Fb 13.59S 126.51 E
Dry Tortugas 43 Kg 24.38N 82.55W
Drzewica 10 Qe 51.27N 20.28 E
Drzewiczka 10 Qe 51.33N 20.35 E
Dschang 34 Hd 5.27N 10.04 E
Dua 36 Db 3.20N 20.53 E
Duaca 54 Ea 10.18N 69.10W
Duancun→Wuxiang 28 Bf 36.50N 112.51 E
Duarte, Pico- 38 Lh 19.00N 71.00W
Duartina 55 Hf 22.24S 49.25W
Dubawnt 42 Hd 64.30N 100.06W
Dubawnt Lake 38 Ic 63.08N 101.30W
Dubay'ah, Ra's- 24 Pj 24.20N 54.09 E
Dubayy 22 Hg 25.18N 55.18 E
Dubbo 58 Fh 32.15S 148.36 E
Dübener Heide 10 Ie 51.40N 12.40 E
Dubenski 16 Td 51.29N 56.38 E
Dubh Artach 9 Ge 56.08N 6.39W
Dubica 14 Ke 45.13N 16.48 E
Dublin 46 Ke 32.32N 82.54W
Dublin/Baile Átha Cliath 9 Gh 53.20N 6.15W
Dublin/Baile Átha Cliath 6 Fe 53.20N 6.15W
Dublin Bay/Cuan Bhaile Átha Cliath 9 Gh 53.20N 6.06W
Dubljany 10 Tg 49.26N 23.16 E
Dublon 64d Bb 7.23N 151.53 E
Dubna 8 Lh 56.20N 26.31 E
Dubna 19 Dd 56.47N 37.10 E
Dubnica nad Váhom 10 Oh 48.58N 18.10 E
Dubno 19 Ce 50.29N 25.46 E
Du Bois 44 He 41.06N 78.46W
Dubois [Id.-U.S.] 46 Id 44.10N 112.14W
Dubois [Wy.-U.S.] 46 Ke 43.33N 109.38W
Dubossary 16 Ff 47.17N 29.10 E
Dubovka 19 Ef 49.03N 44.50 E
Dubovoje 10 Ih 48.08N 23.59 E
Dubreka 34 Cd 9.48N 13.31W
Dubrovica 16 Ed 51.34N 26.34 E
Dubrovnik 6 Hg 42.39N 18.07 E
Dubrovno 7 Hi 54.33N 30.41 E
Dubrovnoje 19 Gd 57.58N 69.25 E
Dubuque 43 Ic 42.30N 90.41W
Dubysa 8 Ji 55.02N 23.27 E
Duc de Gloucester, Iles du-=Duke of Gloucester, Islands (En) 57 Mg 20.38S 143.20W
Duchang 28 Dj 29.16N 116.11 E
Duchesne 46 Jf 40.10N 110.24W
Duchess 59 Hd 21.22S 139.52 E
Ducie Atoll 57 Qg 24.40S 124.47W
Duck River 44 Dg 36.02N 87.52W
Duckwater Peak 46 Hg 38.58N 115.26W
Duclair 12 Ce 49.29N 0.53 E
Duc Lap 25 Lf 12.27N 107.38 E
Ducos 51h Bb 14.34N 60.58W
Dudelange/Düdelingen 12 Ie 49.28N 6.06 E
Duderstadt 10 Ge 51.31N 10.16 E
Dudinka 22 Kc 69.25N 86.15 E
Dudley 9 Ki 52.30N 2.05W
Dūdo 35 Id 9.20N 50.14 E
Dudub 35 Hd 6.55N 46.42 E
Dudune 63b Ce 21.21S 167.44 E
Dudvah 10 Ni 47.58N 17.50 E
Dudweiler, Saarbrücken- 12 Je 49.17N 7.02 E
Düdwéyn 35 Gd 9.19N 44.53 E
Dudypta 20 Db 70.55N 89.50 E
Duékoué 34 Dd 6.45N 7.21W
Dueodde 8 Fj 54.59N 15.05 E
Duerna 13 Gb 42.19N 5.54W
Duero 5 Fg 41.08N 8.40W
Dufek Coast 66 Lg 84.30S 179.00W
Duffer Peak 46 Ff 41.40N 118.44W
Duff Islands 57 He 9.50S 167.10 E
Dugi Otok 14 Ii 44.00N 15.00 E
Dugo Selo 14 Ke 45.48N 16.15 E
Du Gué, Rivière- 42 Ke 57.20N 70.46W
Duhovnickoje 16 Pc 52.29N 48.15 E
Duijan Yan 27 He 31.01N 103.28 E
Duiru→Wuchuan 27 If 28.28N 107.57 E
Duisburg 10 Ce 51.26N 6.45 E
Duitama 54 Db 5.50N 73.02W
Dujūma 35 Ge 1.14N 42.34 E
Dukagjini 15 Cg 42.18N 19.45 E
Dükān 24 Ke 35.56N 44.58 E
Dukan, Sad ad- 24 Kd 36.10N 44.56 E
Dukat 15 Fg 42.26N 22.21 E
Duke of Gloucester Islands (EN)=Duc de Gloucester, Iles du- 57 Mg 20.38S 143.20W
Duke of York 63a Aa 4.10S 152.28 E
Duke of York Bay 42 Jc 65.25N 84.50W
Duk Fadiat 35 Ed 7.45N 31.25 E
Duk Faiwil 35 Ed 7.30N 31.29 E
Dukhān 23 Hd 25.25N 50.48 E
Dukielska, Przełecz- 10 Rg 49.25N 21.42 E
Dukku 34 Hc 10.49N 10.46 E
Dukla 10 Rg 49.34N 21.41 E
Dukou 22 Mg 26.31N 101.44 E
Dūkštas/Dukštas 8 Li 55.32N 26.28 E
Dukštas/Dūkštas 8 Li 55.32N 26.28 E
Dulan (Qagan Us) 22 Lf 36.29N 98.29 E
Dulce, Bahía- 48 Ji 16.30N 98.50W
Dulce, Golfo- 47 Hg 8.36N 83.15W
Dulce, Río- 52 Ji 30.31S 62.32W
Dulce Nombre de Culmi 49 Ef 15.09N 85.37W
Duldurga 20 Gf 50.38N 113.35 E
Dulgalah 20 Pc 67.30N 133.20 E
Dulia 36 Db 2.57N 24.08 E
Dülmen 10 De 51.50N 7.18 E
Dulovka 8 Mg 57.27N 28.29 E
Dulovo 15 Kf 43.49N 27.09 E
Duluth 39 Je 46.47N 92.06W
Dümä 24 Gf 33.35N 36.24 E
Dumaguete 26 He 9.18N 123.18 E
Dumai 26 Df 1.41N 101.27 E
Dumaran 26 Gd 10.33N 119.51 E
Dumaresq River 59 Ke 28.40S 150.28 E
Dumas [Ar.-U.S.] 45 Kj 33.53N 91.29W
Dumas [Tx.-U.S.] 45 Fi 35.52N 101.58W
Dumayr 24 Gf 33.38N 36.40 E
Dumbarton 9 If 55.57N 4.35W
Dumbéa 63b Cf 22.09S 166.27 E
Dumbrăveni [Rom.] 15 Jb 47.39N 26.25 E
Dumbrăveni [Rom.] 15 Hc 46.14N 24.34 E
Dumfries 9 Jf 55.04N 3.37W
Dumfries and Galloway 9 Jf 55.10N 3.35W
Dumka 25 Hd 24.16N 87.15 E
Dumlupinar 15 Mk 38.52N 30.00 E
Dümmer 10 Ed 52.31N 8.19 E
Dumoine, Lac- 44 Ib 46.52N 77.52W
Dumoine, Rivière- 44 Ib 46.13N 77.50W
Dumont d'Urville 66 Je 66.40S 140.01 E
Dumont D'Urville Sea (EN) 66 Je 63.00S 140.00 E
Dumpu 58 Fe 5.52S 145.46 E
Dümrek 15 Lk 38.40N 28.24 E
Dumuhe 28 La 46.21N 133.33 E
Dumyāṭ=Damietta (EN) 31 Ke 31.25N 31.48 E
Dumyāṭ, Maṣabb- 24 Dg 31.27N 31.51 E
Duna=Danube (EN) 5 If 45.20N 29.40 E
Dunaföldvár 10 Oi 46.48N 18.56 E
Dunaharaszti 10 Pi 47.21N 19.05 E
Dunaj 20 Ih 42.57N 132.20 E
Dunaj=Danube (EN) 5 If 45.20N 29.40 E
Dunajec 10 Qf 50.15N 20.44 E
Dunajevcy 16 Ee 48.51N 26.44 E
Dunajská Streda 10 Ni 47.01N 17.38 E
Dunakeszi 10 Pi 47.38N 19.08 E
Dunántúl 10 Nj 47.00N 18.00 E
Dunărea=Danube (EN) 5 If 45.20N 29.40 E
Dunărea Veche 15 Ld 45.17N 28.02 E
Dunării, Delta-=Danube, Mouths of the- (EN) 5 If 45.30N 29.45 E
Duna-Tisza Köze 10 Pj 46.45N 19.30 E
Dunaújváros 10 Oj 46.58N 18.56 E
Dunav=Danube (EN) 5 If 45.20N 29.40 E
Dunavăţu de Jos 15 Me 44.59N 29.13 E
Dunav-Tisa-Dunav kanal 15 Dd 45.10N 20.50 E
Dunback 62 Df 45.23S 170.38 E
Dunbar 9 Kf 56.00N 2.31W
Duncan [Az.-U.S.] 46 Kj 32.43N 109.06W
Duncan [B.C.-Can.] 46 Db 48.47N 123.42W
Duncan [Ok.-U.S.] 43 He 34.30N 97.57W
Duncan Passage 25 If 11.00N 92.00 E
Duncansby Head 5 Fd 58.39N 3.01W
Dundaga 8 Jg 57.31N 22.14 E
Dundalk 44 If 39.15N 76.31W
Dundalk/Dún Dealgan 9 Gg 54.01N 6.25W
Dundalk Bay/Cuan Dhun Dealgan 9 Gh 53.57N 6.17W
Dundas [Grld.] 41 Fc 76.30N 69.00W
Dundas [Ont.-Can.] 44 Hd 43.16N 79.58W
Dundas, Lake- 59 Ef 32.35S 121.50 E
Dundas Peninsula 42 Gb 74.40N 113.00W
Dundas Strait 59 Gb 11.20S 131.35 E
Dún Dealgan/Dundalk 9 Gg 54.01N 6.25W
Dundee [S.Afr.] 37 Ee 28.12S 30.16 E
Dundee [Scot.-U.K.] 6 Fd 56.28N 3.00W
Dund Hot→Zhenglan Qi 28 Cc 42.14N 115.59 E
Dundrum Bay/Cuan Dhún Droma 9 Hg 54.13N 5.45W
Dunedin [Fl.-U.S.] 44 Fk 28.02N 82.47W
Dunedin [N.Z.] 58 Ii 45.53S 170.31 E
Dunfanaghy 9 Ff 55.11N 7.59W
Dunfermline 9 Je 56.04N 3.29W
Dungannon/Dún Geanainn 9 Gg 54.31N 6.46W
Dún Garbhán/Dungarvan 9 Fi 52.05N 7.37W
Düngarpur 25 Ed 23.50N 73.43 E
Dungarvan/Dún Garbhán 9 Fi 52.05N 7.37W
Dungas 34 Gc 13.04N 9.20 E
Dungau 10 Ih 48.45N 12.30 E
Dún Geanainn/Dungannon 9 Gg 54.31N 6.46W
Dungeness 9 Nk 50.55N 0.58 E
Dungu 36 Eb 3.42N 28.40 E
Dungu 36 Eb 3.37N 28.34 E
Dunhua 27 Mc 43.22N 128.12 E
Dunhuang 27 Fc 40.10N 94.50 E
Dunkerque 11 Ic 51.03N 2.22 E
Dunkery Beacon 9 Jj 51.11N 3.35W
Dunkirk 43 Lc 42.29N 79.21W
Dunkwa 34 Ed 5.58N 1.47W
Dún Laoghaire 9 Gh 53.17N 6.08W
Dún Mánmhai/Dunmanway 9 Dj 51.43N 9.07W
Dunmanway/Dún Mánmhai 9 Dj 51.43N 9.07W
Dunn 44 Hh 35.19N 78.37W
Dún na nGall/Donegal 9 Fg 54.50N 8.00W
Dún na nGall/Donegal 9 Eg 54.39N 8.06W
Dunnellon 44 Fk 29.03N 82.28W
Dunnet Head 9 Jc 58.39N 3.23W
Dunning 45 Ff 41.50N 100.06W
Dún Pádraig/Downpatrick 9 Hg 54.20N 5.43W
Dunqulah=Dongola (EN) 31 Kg 19.10N 30.29 E
Dunqulah al Qadīmah 35 Eb 18.13N 30.45 E
Dunqunāb 35 Fa 21.06N 37.05 E
Dunqunāb, Khalīj- 35 Fa 21.05N 37.08 E
Dunrankin 44 Fa 48.39N 83.04W
Duns 9 Kf 55.47N 2.20W
Dünsberg 12 Kd 50.39N 8.35 E
Dunsmuir 46 Df 41.13N 122.16W
Dunstable 12 Bc 51.53N 0.31W
Dunstan Mountains 62 Cf 44.55S 169.30 E
Dun-sur-Auron 11 Ih 46.53N 2.34 E
Dun-sur-Meuse 12 He 49.23N 5.11 E
Duntroon 62 Df 44.51S 170.41 E
Dunvegan 9 Gd 57.26N 6.35W
Duobukur 27 La 50.19N 124.57 E
Duolun/Dolonnur 27 Kc 42.10N 116.30 E
Duong Dong 25 Kf 10.13N 103.58 E
Dupree 45 Fd 45.03N 101.36W
Duqm 22 Hf 19.41N 57.32 E
Duque de Bragança, Quedas- 30 Ii 9.05S 16.10 E
Duque de Caxias 54 Jh 22.47S 43.18W
Duque de York, Isla- 56 Eh 50.40S 75.20W
Du Quoin 45 Lg 38.01N 89.14W
Durack Range 59 Fc 17.00S 128.00 E
Durack River 59 Fc 15.33S 127.52 E
Durağan 24 Fb 41.25N 35.04 E
Durance 5 Gg 43.55N 4.44 E
Durand 45 Kd 44.38N 91.58W
Durand, Récif- 63b Df 22.02S 168.39 E
Durango 47 Dd 24.50N 104.50W
Durango [Co.-U.S.] 39 If 37.16N 107.53W
Durango [Sp.] 13 Ja 43.10N 2.37W
Durañona 55 Bm 37.15S 60.31W
Durant 43 He 33.59N 96.23W
Duras 11 Gj 44.40N 0.11 E
Duratón 13 Hc 41.37N 4.07W
Durazno 56 Id 33.22S 56.31W
Durazno 55 Dk 33.05S 56.05W
Durazno, Cuchilla Grande del- 55 Dk 33.15S 56.15W
Durazzo (EN)=Durresi 15 Ch 41.19N 19.26 E
Durban 31 Kk 29.55S 30.56 E
Durbe 8 Ih 56.39N 21.14 E
Durbet-Daba, Pereval- 27 Eb 49.37N 89.25 E
Ðurbo 35 Ic 11.30N 50.18 E
Durbuy 12 Hd 50.21N 5.28 E
Đurđevac 14 Ld 46.02N 17.04 E
Düren 10 Cf 50.48N 6.29 E
Durg 25 Gd 21.11N 81.17 E
Durgapūr 25 Hd 23.30N 87.15 E
Durgen-Nur 27 Fb 47.40N 93.30 E
Durham 9 Lg 54.45N 1.45W
Durham 9 Lg 54.45N 1.40W
Durham [Eng.-U.K.] 9 Lg 54.47N 1.34W
Durham [N.C.-U.S.] 43 Ld 35.59N 78.54W
Durkee 46 Gd 44.36N 117.28W
Durlas/Thurles 9 Fi 52.41N 7.49W
Ðurmā 23 Ge 24.37N 46.08 E
Durmersheim 12 Kf 48.56N 8.16 E
Durmitor 5 Hg 43.09N 19.02 E
Durnford, Punta- 32 De 23.37N 16.00W
Durresi=Durazzo (EN) 15 Ch 41.19N 19.26 E
Durrësit, Gjiri- 15 Ch 41.16N 19.28 E
Dursey/Oileán Baoi 9 Cj 51.36N 10.12W
Dursunbey 24 Cc 39.35N 28.38 E
Durtal 11 Fg 47.40N 0.15W
Duru→Wuchuan 27 If 28.28N 107.57 E
Duruksi 35 Hd 8.29N 45.38 E
Durusu Gölü 15 Lh 41.20N 28.38 E
Durūz, Jabal ad- 24 Gf 32.40N 36.44 E
D'Urville Island 61 Dh 40.50S 173.50 E
Dušak 18 Cf 37.15N 60.01 E
Dusa Mareb 35 Hd 5.31N 46.24 E
Dušanbe 22 If 38.35N 68.48 E
Dušeti 16 Nh 42.05N 44.42 E
Dusetos 8 Li 55.42N 26.02 E
Dushan 22 Mg 25.55N 107.36 E
Dushan Hu 28 Dg 35.06N 116.48 E
Dusios Ežeras/Dusja, Ozero- 8 Jj 54.15N 23.45 E
Dusja, Ozero-/Dusios Ežeras 8 Jj 54.15N 23.45 E
Dusky Sound 62 Bf 45.45S 166.30 E
Düsseldorf 6 Ge 51.13N 6.46 E
Dusti 18 Gf 37.22N 68.43 E
Dutch Harbor 40a Eb 53.53N 166.32W
Dutlwe 37 Cd 23.58S 23.54 E
Dutton, Mount- 46 Ig 38.01N 112.13W
Duved 8 Ea 63.24N 12.52 E
Duvergé 49 Ld 18.22N 71.31W
Düvertepe 15 Lj 39.14N 28.27 E
Duvno 14 Lg 43.43N 17.14 E
Duwayhin 23 He 24.16N 51.20 E
Duwayhin, Khawr- 24 Nj 24.20N 51.25 E
Duyfken Point 59 Ib 12.35S 141.40 E
Duyun 27 If 26.20N 107.28 E
Düz 32 Ic 33.28N 9.01 E
Düzce 23 Da 40.50N 31.10 E
Dve Mogili 15 If 43.36N 25.52 E
Dvina (EN)=Daugava 19 Cd 57.04N 24.03 E
Dvina Gulf (EN)=Dvinskaja Guba 5 Jb 65.00N 39.45 E
Dvinskaja Guba=Dvina Gulf (EN) 5 Jb 65.00N 39.45 E
Dvor 14 Ke 45.04N 16.23 E
Dvuh Cirkov, Gora- 20 Lc 67.30N 168.20 E
Dvůr Králové nad Labem 10 Lf 50.26N 15.48 E
Dwārka 25 Dd 22.14N 68.58 E
Dworshak Reservoir 46 Hc 46.45N 116.00W
Dyer, Cape- 38 Mc 66.37N 61.18W
Dyero 34 Dc 12.50N 6.30W
Dyer Plateau 66 Qf 70.45S 65.30W
Dyersburg 43 Jd 36.03N 89.23W
Dyfed 9 Ji 52.05N 4.00W
Dyhtau, Gora- 16 Mh 43.05N 43.12 E
Dyje 10 Mh 48.37N 16.56 E
Dyjsko-Svratecký úval 10 Mh 48.56N 16.25 E
Dyle 12 Gd 50.57N 4.40 E
Dylewska Góra 10 Pc 53.34N 19.57 E
Dynów 10 Sg 49.49N 22.14 E
Dyr, Djebel- 14 Cn 36.13N 8.46 E
Dyrhólaey 5 Ec 63.24N 19.08W
Dysny Ežeras/Disnaj, Ozero- 7 Gi 55.35N 26.32 E
Dytike Rodhópi 15 Hh 41.45N 24.05 E
Dzabhan 21 Le 48.54N 93.23 E
Džagdy, Hrebet- 20 If 53.40N 131.00 E
Džalagaš 19 Gf 45.05N 64.40 E
Džalal-Abad 18 Id 40.56N 73.05 E
Džalilabad 19 Eh 39.12N 48.31 E
Džalinda 20 Hf 53.31N 123.59 E
Džambejty 16 Rd 50.14N 52.38 E
Džambul [Kaz.-U.S.S.R.] 22 Je 42.54N 71.22 E
Džambul [Kaz.-U.S.S.R.] 19 Hf 47.17N 71.42 E
Džambulskaja Oblast 19 Hg 44.30N 72.30 E
Džamyn-Ud 27 Jb 43.50N 111.45 E
Džanak 16 Si 40.30N 55.35 E
Džanga 19 Fg 40.01N 53.10 E
Džankoj 19 Df 45.42N 34.22 E
Džansugurov 19 Hf 45.23N 79.29 E
Džanybek 19 Ef 49.24N 46.50 E
Dzaoudzi 31 Lj 12.47S 45.17 E
Džardžan 20 Hc 68.55N 124.05 E
Džargalant 27 Gb 47.20N 99.35 E
Dzargalant 27 Ib 48.35N 105.50 E
Džarkurgan 19 Gh 37.29N 67.25 E
Džava 16 Mh 42.24N 43.53 E
Džebariki-Haja 20 Id 62.23N 135.50 E
Džebel [Bul.] 15 Ih 41.30N 25.18 E
Džebel [Tur.-U.S.S.R.] 16 Sj 39.37N 54.18 E
Džebrail 16 Oj 39.23N 47.01 E
Dzereg 27 Fb 47.08N 92.50 E
Džergalan 18 Lc 42.33N 79.02 E
Dzermuk 16 Nj 39.48N 45.39 E
Dzeržinsk [Bye.-U.S.S.R.] 16 Ec 53.44N 27.08 E
Dzeržinsk [R.S.F.S.R.] 19 Ed 56.16N 43.32 E
Dzeržinsk [Ukr.-U.S.S.R.] 16 Je 48.22N 37.50 E
Dzeržinskaja, Gora- 8 Lk 53.53N 27.10 E
Dzeržinskoje 20 Ee 56.49N 95.18 E
Džetygara 22 Id 52.11N 61.12 E
Džetysaj 18 Gd 40.49N 68.20 E
Džezkazgan [Kaz.-U.S.S.R.] 19 Gf 47.53N 67.27 E
Džezkazgan [Kaz.-U.S.S.R.] 22 Ie 47.47N 67.46 E
Džezkazganskaja Oblast 19 Gf 47.30N 70.00 E
Dzhugdzhur Range (EN)=Džugdžur, Hrebet- 21 Pd 58.00N 136.00 E
Działdówka 10 Qd 52.58N 20.05 E
Działdowo 10 Qc 53.15N 20.10 E
Działoszyce 10 Qf 50.22N 20.21 E
Dzibalchén 48 Oh 19.31N 89.45W
Dzibilchaltún 48 Og 21.05N 89.36W
Dzierzgoń 10 Pc 53.56N 19.21 E
Dzierżoniów 10 Mf 50.44N 16.39 E
Džirgatal 18 He 39.13N 71.12 E
Džizak 19 Gg 40.07N 67.52 E
Džizakskaja Oblast 19 Gg 40.20N 67.40 E
Džugdžur, Hrebet-=Dzhugdzhur Range (EN) 21 Pd 58.00N 136.00 E
Džūkste/Džukste 8 Jh 56.45N 23.10 E
Džukste/Džūkste 8 Jh 56.45N 23.10 E
Džulfa 16 Nj 38.59N 45.35 E
Džuma 18 Fe 39.44N 66.39 E
Dzun-Bajan 27 Jc 44.26N 110.03 E
Dzungarian Basin (EN)=Junggar Pendi 21 Ke 45.00N 88.00 E
Dzungarian Gate (EN)=Alataw Shankou 21 Ke 45.25N 82.25 E
Dzungarian Gate (EN)=Džungarskije Vorota 21 Ke 45.25N 82.25 E
Džungarski Alatau, Hrebet- 21 Ke 45.00N 81.00 E
Džungarskije Vorota=Dzungarian Gate (EN) 21 Ke 45.25N 82.25 E
Dzun-Hara 27 Ib 48.40N 106.40 E
Dzun-Mod 27 Ib 47.50N 106.57 E
Džurak-Sal 16 Mf 47.18N 43.36 E
Džusaly 19 Gf 45.29N 64.05 E
Džvari 16 Mh 42.42N 42.02 E

E

Éadan Doire/Edenderry 9 Fh 53.21N 7.03W
Eads 45 Eg 38.29N 102.47W
Eagle 40 Kd 64.46N 141.16W
Eagle 42 Lf 53.35N 57.25W
Eagle Creek 46 La 52.22N 107.24W
Eagle Lake 44 Mb 47.02N 68.36W
Eagle Lake [Ca.-U.S.] 46 Ef 40.39N 120.44W
Eagle Lake [Me.-U.S.] 44 Mb 46.20N 69.20W
Eagle Lake [Ont.-Can.] 45 Jb 49.42N 93.13W
Eagle Mountain 45 Kc 47.54N 90.33W
Eagle Nest 45 Dh 36.35N 105.14W
Eagle Pass 43 Gf 28.43N 100.30W
Eagle Peak [Ca.-U.S.] 43 Cc 41.17N 120.12W
Eagle Peak [Tx.-U.S.] 45 Dk 30.56N 105.01W
Eagle River [Ak.-U.S.] 40 Jd 61.19N 149.34W
Eagle River [Wi.-U.S.] 45 Ld 45.55N 89.15W
Eagle Summit 40 Jc 65.30N 145.38W
Ealing, London- 12 Bc 51.30N 0.19W
Ear Falls 45 Ja 50.38N 93.13W
Earn 9 Je 56.25N 3.30W
Earn, Loch- 9 Ie 56.25N 4.10W
Earnslaw, Mount- 62 Cf 44.37S 168.25 E
Easley 44 Fh 34.50N 82.36W
East Alligator River 59 Gb 12.08S 132.42 E
East Anglia 9 Ni 52.25N 1.00 E
East Angus 44 Lc 45.29N 71.40W
East Bay [Can.] 42 Jd 64.05N 81.30W
East Bay [U.S.] 45 Ll 29.05N 89.15W
East Berlin (EN)=Berlin (Ost) 10 Jd 52.30N 13.25 E
East Berlin (EN)=Berlin (Ost) 6 He 52.31N 13.24 E
Eastbourne [Eng.-U.K.] 9 Nk 50.46N 0.17 E
Eastbourne [N.Z.] 62 Fd 41.17S 174.54 E
East Caicos 49 Lc 21.41N 71.30W
East Cape [Fl.-U.S.] 44 Gm 25.07N 81.05W
East Cape [N.Z.] 57 Ih 37.41S 178.33 E
East Caroline Basin (EN) 3 Ii 4.00N 146.45 E
East Chicago 44 De 41.38N 87.27W
East China Sea (EN)=Dong Hai 21 Og 29.00N 125.00 E
East China Sea (EN)=Higashi-Shina-Kai 21 Og 29.00N 125.00 E
East Coast 62 Gc 38.20S 177.50 E
East Dereham 9 Ni 52.41N 0.56 E
Eastend 46 Kb 49.31N 108.48W
East Entrance 64a Bb 7.50N 134.40 E
Easter Island (EN)=Pascua, Isla de-/Rapa Nui 57 Qg 27.07S 109.22W
Easter Island (EN)=Rapa Nui/Pascua, Isla de- 57 Qg 27.07S 109.22W
Eastern [Ghana] 34 Ed 6.30N 0.30W
Eastern [Kenya] 36 Gb 0.05N 38.00 E
Eastern [S.L.] 34 Cd 8.15N 11.00W
Eastern [Ug.] 36 Fb 1.30N 33.50 E
Eastern [Zam.] 36 Fe 13.00S 32.15 E
Eastern Fields 60 Dj 10.03S 145.22 E

Index Symbols

1 Independent Nation
2 State, Region
3 District, County
4 Municipality
5 Colony, Dependency
Continent
Physical Region
Historical or Cultural Region
Mount, Mountain
Volcano
Hill
Mountains, Mountain Range
Hills, Escarpment
Plateau, Upland
Pass, Gap
Plain, Lowland
Delta
Salt Flat
Valley, Canyon
Crater, Cave
Karst Features
Depression
Polder
Desert, Dunes
Forest, Woods
Heath, Steppe
Oasis
Cape, Point
Coast, Beach
Cliff
Peninsula
Isthmus
Sandbank
Island
Atoll
Rock, Reef
Islands, Archipelago
Rocks, Reefs
Coral Reef
Well, Spring
Geyser
River, Stream
Waterfall Rapids
River Mouth, Estuary
Lake
Salt Lake
Intermittent Lake
Reservoir
Swamp, Pond
Canal
Glacier
Ice Shelf, Pack Ice
Ocean
Sea
Gulf, Bay
Strait, Fjord
Lagoon
Bank
Seamount
Tablemount
Ridge
Shelf
Basin
Escarpment, Sea Scarp
Fracture
Trench, Abyss
National Park, Reserve
Point of Interest
Recreation Site
Cave, Cavern
Historic Site
Ruins
Wall, Walls
Church, Abbey
Temple
Scientific Station
Airport
Port
Lighthouse
Mine
Tunnel
Dam, Bridge

Index Symbols

[1] Independent Nation
[2] State, Region
[3] District, County
[4] Municipality
[5] Colony, Dependency
Continent
Physical Region

Historical or Cultural Region
Mount, Mountain
Volcano
Hill
Mountains, Mountain Range
Hills, Escarpment
Plateau, Upland

Pass, Gap
Plain, Lowland
Delta
Salt Flat
Valley, Canyon
Crater, Cave
Karst Features

Depression
Polder
Desert, Dunes
Forest, Woods
Heath, Steppe
Oasis
Cape, Point

Coast, Beach
Cliff
Peninsula
Isthmus
Sandbank
Island
Atoll

Rock, Reef
Islands, Archipelago
Rocks, Reefs
Coral Reef
Well, Spring
Geyser
River, Stream

Waterfall Rapids
River Mouth, Estuary
Lake
Salt Lake
Intermittent Lake
Reservoir
Swamp, Pond

Canal
Glacier
Ice Shelf, Pack Ice
Ocean
Sea
Gulf, Bay
Strait, Fjord

Lagoon
Bank
Seamount
Tablemount
Shelf
Ridge
Basin

Escarpment, Sea Scarp
Fracture
Trench, Abyss
National Park, Reserve
Point of Interest
Recreation Site
Cave, Cavern

Historic Site
Ruins
Wall, Walls
Church, Abbey
Temple
Scientific Station
Airport

Port
Lighthouse
Mine
Tunnel
Dam, Bridge

Elm 10 Gd 52.09N 10.53 E
El Macao 49 Md 18.46N 68.33W
Elmadağ 24 Ec 39.55N 33.15 E
Elma Dağı 15 Mk 38.46N 29.32 E
El Maestrat/El Maestrazgo 13 Ld 40.30N 0.10W
El Maestrazgo/El Maestrat 13 Ld 40.30N 0.10W
El Mahia 34 Ea 22.30N 2.30W
El Maitén 56 Ff 42.03S 71.10W
Elmaki 34 Gb 17.55N 8.20 E
El Malah 13 Ph 36.18N 3.14 E
Elmalı 24 Ic 39.25N 40.35 E
Elmali 24 Cd 36.44N 29.56 E
El Manteco 50 Ei 7.27N 62.32W
El Marfil 55 Bb 15.35S 60.19W
El Marsa 13 Mh 36.24N 0.55 E
El Medo 35 Gd 5.41N 41.46 E
El Meghaïer 32 Ic 33.57N 5.56 E
Elmhurst 45 Mf 41.53N 87.56W
El Milagro 56 Gd 31.01S 65.59W
Elmira 43 Lc 42.06N 76.50W
El Mrâyer 32 Fe 21.30N 8.10W
El Mreïti 32 Fe 23.29N 7.52W
El Mreyyé 30 Gg 19.30N 7.00W
Elmshorn 10 Fc 53.45N 9.39 E
Elmstein 12 Je 49.22N 7.56 E
Elne 11 Il 42.36N 2.58 E
El Nevado, Cerro- 56 Ge 35.35S 68.30W
El Niabo 35 Fe 4.33N 39.59 E
El Nihuil 56 Gd 34.58S 68.40W
El Novillo 48 Ec 28.40N 109.30W
El Novillo, Presa- 48 Ec 29.05N 109.45W
El Ochenta y Uno 48 Kg 21.35N 97.57W
Elorn 11 Bf 48.27N 4.16W
Elortondo 55 Bk 33.42S 61.37W
Elorza 54 Eb 7.03N 69.31W
Elota, Rio- 48 Ff 23.52N 106.56W
El Oued 32 Ic 33.20N 6.53 E
Eloy 46 Jj 32.45N 111.33W
El Palmar 50 Fh 8.01N 61.53W
El Palmito 48 Ge 25.40N 104.59W
El Panadés/El Penedès 13 Nc 41.25N 1.30 E
El Pao [Ven.] 50 Eh 8.06N 62.33W
El Pao [Ven.] 50 Bh 9.38N 68.08W
El Paraíso [3] 49 Df 14.10N 86.30W
El Paraíso 49 Dg 13.51N 86.34W
El Páramo 13 Gb 42.25N 5.45W
El Pardo, Madrid- 13 Id 40.32N 3.46W
El Paso [Il.-U.S.] 45 Lf 40.44N 89.01W
El Paso [Tx.-U.S.] 39 If 31.45N 106.29W
El Penedès/El Panadés 13 Nc 41.25N 1.30 E
El Perú 50 Fi 7.19N 61.49W
El Pico 54 Fg 15.57S 64.42W
El Pilar 50 Eg 10.32N 63.09W
El Pintado 56 Hb 24.38S 61.27W
El Porvenir [Hond.] 49 Df 14.41N 87.11W
El Porvenir [Pan.] 49 Hi 9.12N 80.08W
El Porvenir [Ven.] 50 Bi 6.55N 68.42W
El Potosí 48 Ie 24.51N 100.19W
El Prat de Llobregat/Prat de Llobregat 13 Oc 41.20N 2.06 E
El Priorat/El Priorato 13 Mc 41.10N 1.00 E
El Priorato/El Priorat 13 Mc 41.10N 1.00 E
El Progreso [3] 49 Cf 14.50N 90.00W
El Progreso [Guat.] 49 Bf 14.51N 90.04W
El Progreso [Hond.] 47 Ge 15.21N 87.49W
El Puente del Arzobispo 13 Ge 39.48N 5.10W
El Puerto 48 Dc 28.45N 111.20W
El Puerto de Santa María 13 Fh 36.36N 6.13W
El Rastro 50 Ch 9.03N 67.27W
El Real de Santa María 49 Ii 8.08N 77.43W
El Reno 43 Hd 35.32N 97.57W
El Ribeiro 13 Db 42.25N 8.10W
Elrose 46 Ka 51.13N 108.01W
El Saler 13 Le 39.23N 0.20W
El Salto 47 Cd 23.47N 105.23W
El Salvador [1] 39 Kh 13.50N 88.55W
El Samán de Apure 50 Bi 7.55N 68.44W
El Sauce [Mex.] 48 De 24.34N 111.29W
El Sauce [Nic.] 49 Dg 12.53N 86.32W
El Sáuz 48 Fc 29.03N 106.15W
Elsberry 45 Kg 39.10N 90.47W
Elsdorf 12 Id 50.56N 6.34 E
Else 12 Kb 52.12N 8.40 E
El Seibo 49 Md 18.46N 68.52W
Elsen, Paderborn- 12 Kc 51.44N 8.41 E
Elsen Nur 27 Fd 35.08N 92.20 E
'Ēl Shāma 35 Ge 2.46N 41.03 E
El Socorro 50 Dh 8.59N 65.44W
El Sombrero 54 Eb 9.23N 67.03W
Elst 12 Hc 51.55N 5.52 E
Elsterwerda 10 Je 51.27N 13.32 E
El Sueco 47 Cc 29.54N 106.24W
El-Taht 13 Mi 35.27N 0.46 E
El Tajin 47 Ed 20.27N 97.23W
El Tala 56 Gc 26.07S 65.17W
Eltanin Bay 66 Pf 73.40S 82.00W
Eltham 62 Fc 39.26S 174.18 E
El Tigre 53 Je 8.55N 64.15W
El Tigre, Isla- 49 Dg 13.16N 87.38W
El Toboso 13 Je 39.31N 3.00W
El Tocuyo 54 Eb 9.47N 69.48W
Elton 16 Oe 49.08N 46.50 E
Elton, Ozero- 19 Ef 49.10N 46.40 E
El Torcal 13 Hh 36.55N 4.35W
El Trébol 55 Bk 32.12S 61.42W
El Trigo 55 Cl 35.52S 59.24W
El Triunfo [Hond.] 49 Dg 13.06N 87.00W
El Triunfo [Mex.] 48 Df 23.47N 110.08W
El Tuito 48 Gg 20.19N 105.22W
El Turbio 56 Fh 51.41S 72.05W
Eltville am Rhein 12 Kd 50.02N 8.07 E
Eltz 12 Jd 50.12N 7.18 E
Elūru 25 Ge 17.05N 82.15 E
Elva 7 Gg 58.13N 26.25 E
El Valle 49 Gi 8.31N 80.08W
El Valles/Valles 13 Oc 41.35N 2.15 E
Elvas 13 Ef 38.53N 7.10W
El Vejo, Cerro- 54 Db 7.30N 73.05W
El Venado, Isla- 49 Fh 11.57N 83.44W
El Vendrell/Vendrell 13 Nc 41.13N 1.32 E
Elverum 7 Cf 60.53N 11.34 E
El Viejo 49 Dg 12.40N 87.10W
El Viejo, Volcán 38 Kh 12.38N 87.11W
El Vigía 49 Li 8.38N 71.39W
El Vigía, Cerro- 48 Gg 21.25N 104.00W
El Wak 36 Hb 2.49N 40.56 E
Elwell, Lake- 46 Jb 48.22N 111.17W
Elwood 44 Ee 40.17N 85.50W
Ely [Eng.-U.K.] 9 Ni 52.24N 0.16 E
Ely [Mn.-U.S.] 43 Ib 47.54N 91.51W
Ely [Nv.-U.S.] 39 Hf 39.15N 114.53W
Elyria 44 Fe 41.22N 82.06W
El Yunque 51a Cb 18.18N 65.47W
Elz 12 Kd 50.25N 8.02 E
Elzbach 12 Jd 50.12N 7.22 E
Emaé 63b Dc 17.04S 168.22 E
Ema Jõgi/Emajygi 8 Lf 58.20N 27.15 E
Emajygi/Ema Jõgi 8 Lf 58.20N 27.15 E
Emali 36 Gc 2.05S 37.28 E
Emāmshahr [Iran] 23 Ib 36.25N 55.01 E
Emāmshahr [Iran] 22 Hf 36.50N 54.29 E
Emāmzādeh 'Abbās 24 Lf 32.25N 47.55 E
Emån 7 Dh 57.08N 16.30 E
Emba 19 Ff 48.50N 58.10 E
Emba 5 Lf 46.38N 53.04 E
Embaracai, Rio- 55 Ff 23.27S 53.58W
Embarcación 56 Hb 23.13S 64.06W
Embarras Portage 42 Ge 58.25N 111.27W
Embarras River 45 Mg 38.39N 87.37W
Embira, Rio- 54 De 7.19S 70.15W
Embrun 11 Mj 44.34N 6.30 E
Embu 36 Gc 0.32S 37.27 E
Emden 10 Dc 53.22N 7.13 E
Emeldžak 20 He 58.27N 126.57 E
Emerald 58 Fg 23.32S 148.10 E
Emerald 42 Ga 76.50N 114.00W
Emerson 45 Hb 49.00N 97.12W
Emet 24 Cc 39.20N 29.15 E
Emiliano Zapata 48 Ni 17.45N 91.46W
Emilia-Romagna [2] 14 Ef 44.45N 11.00 E
Emilio R. Coni 55 Cj 30.04S 58.16W
Emili Rock 52 Hh 29.40S 87.25W
Emin/Dorbiljin 27 Db 46.32N 83.39 E
Emine, Nos- 15 Kg 42.42N 27.54 E
Emira Island 60 Dh 1.40S 150.00 E
Emirdağ 24 Dc 39.01N 31.10 E
Emisu, Tarso- 30 If 21.13N 18.32 E
Emlichheim 10 Cd 52.37N 6.51 E
Emmaboda 7 Dh 56.38N 15.32 E
Emmaste 7 Fg 58.43N 22.36 E
Emme 14 Bd 47.10N 7.35 E
Emmeloord, Noordoostpolder- 12 Hb 52.42N 5.44 E
Emmelshausen 12 Jd 50.09N 7.34 E
Emmen 11 Mb 52.47N 6.55 E
Emmendingen 10 Dh 48.08N 7.51 E
Emmen-Emmer-Compascuum 12 Jb 52.49N 7.03 E
Emmen-Klazienaveen 12 Jb 52.44N 7.01 E
Emmen-Nieuw Weerdinge 12 Jb 52.52N 7.01 E
Emmental 14 Bd 46.55N 7.45 E
Emmen-Weerdinge 12 Ib 52.49N 6.57 E
Emmer 12 Lb 52.03N 9.23 E
Emmer-Compascuum, Emmen- 12 Jb 52.49N 7.03 E
Emmerich 10 Ce 51.50N 6.15 E
Emmet 59 Id 24.40S 144.28 E
Emmetsburg 45 Ie 43.07N 94.41W
Emmett 46 Ge 43.52N 116.30W
Emmonak 40 Gd 62.46N 164.30W
Emőd 10 Qi 47.56N 20.49 E
Emory 46 Jf 41.05N 111.16W
Emory Peak 43 Gf 29.13N 103.17W
Empalme 47 Bc 27.58N 110.51W
Empangeni 37 Ee 28.50S 31.48 E
Empedrado 56 Ic 27.57S 58.48W
Emperor Seamounts (EN) 3 Je 40.00N 171.00 E
Empoli 14 Eg 43.43N 10.57 E
Emporia [Ks.-U.S.] 43 Hd 38.24N 96.11W
Emporia [Va.-U.S.] 44 Ig 36.42N 77.33W
Emporium 44 He 41.31N 78.14W
Empress Augusta Bay 63a Bb 6.25S 155.05 E
Empress Mine 37 Dc 18.27S 29.27 E
Ems 11 Na 53.19N 7.03 E
Emsbach 12 Kd 50.24N 8.06 E
Emsdetten 10 Dd 52.11N 7.32 E
Ems-Jade-Kanal 10 Dc 53.19N 7.10 E
Emsland 10 Dd 52.50N 7.20 E
Emstek 12 Kb 52.50N 8.09 E
Emumägi/Emumjagi 8 Lf 58.54N 26.23 E
Emumjagi/Emumägi 8 Lf 58.54N 26.23 E
Ena 29 Ed 35.27N 137.24 E
Enånger 7 Df 61.32N 17.00 E
Enaratoli 26 Kg 3.55S 136.21 E
Enard Bay 9 Hc 58.06N 5.20W
Ena-San 29 Ed 35.26N 137.36 E
Enbetsu 28 Pb 44.44N 141.47 E
Encantada, Cerro de la- 38 Hf 31.00N 115.23W
Encantada, Sierra de la- 48 Hc 28.30N 102.20W
Encantadas, Serra das 55 Fj 30.40S 53.00W
Encantado, Cerro- 47 Bc 27.03N 112.30W
Encarnación 53 Kh 27.20S 55.54W
Encarnación de Díaz 48 Hg 21.31N 102.14W
Enchi 34 Ed 5.49N 2.49W
Encinal 45 Gl 28.02N 99.21W
Encinasola 13 Ff 38.08N 6.52W
Encontrados 54 Db 8.46N 72.30W
Encounter Bay 59 Hg 35.35S 138.45 E
Encrucijada 49 Hb 22.37N 79.52W
Encruzilhada do Sul 55 Fj 30.32S 52.31W
Encs 10 Rh 48.20N 21.08 E
Ende 22 Oj 8.50S 121.39 E
Endeavour Strait 59 Ib 10.50S 142.15 E
Endelave 8 Di 55.45N 10.15 E
Enderbury Atoll 57 Je 3.08S 171.05W
Enderby 46 Fa 50.33N 119.08W
Enderby Land 66 Ee 67.30S 53.00 E
Endicott Mountains 40 Ic 67.50N 152.00W
Ené, Rio- 54 Df 11.09S 74.19W
Energetik 19 Fe 51.44N 58.48 E
Enez 24 Bb 40.44N 26.04 E
Enez Körfezi 15 Ii 40.45N 26.00 E
Enfer, Portes d'- 36 Ed 5.05S 27.30 E
Enfield 44 Ig 36.11N 77.47W
Enfield, London- 12 Bc 51.40N 0.04W
Engadin/Engiadin'ota/Engadina 14 Dd 46.35N 10.00 E
Engadina/Engadin/Engiadin'ota 14 Dd 46.35N 10.00 E
Engaño, Cabo- 47 Ke 18.37N 68.20W
Engaru 28 Qb 44.03N 143.31 E
Engelberg 14 Cd 46.50N 8.24 E
Engelhard 44 Jh 35.31N 76.00W
Engels 6 Ke 51.30N 46.07 E
Engelskirchen 12 Jd 50.59N 7.24 E
Engenho 55 Db 15.10S 56.25W
Enger 12 Kb 52.08N 8.34 E
Engeren 8 Ec 61.35N 12.05 E
Engershatu 35 Fb 16.34N 38.15 E
Enggano, Pulau- 21 Mj 5.24S 102.16 E
Enghien/Edingen 12 Gd 50.42N 4.02 E
Engiadin'ota/Engadina/Engadin 14 Dd 46.35N 10.00 E
England 5 Fe 52.30N 1.30W
England [2] 9 Li 52.30N 1.30W
Englehart 42 Jg 47.49N 79.52W
Englewood 45 Dg 39.39N 104.59W
English 44 Df 38.20N 86.28W
English Bāzār 25 Hc 25.00N 88.09 E
English Channel 5 Fe 50.20N 1.00W
English Coast 66 Qf 73.30S 73.00W
English River 45 Ia 50.12N 95.00W
English River 45 Kb 49.13N 90.58W
Engozero, Ozero- 7 Hd 65.45N 33.30 E
Enguera 13 Lf 38.59N 0.41W
Engure/Engures 8 Jg 57.09N 23.06 E
Engures/Engure 8 Jg 57.09N 23.06 E
Engures, Ozero-/Engures Ezers 8 Jg 57.15N 23.10 E
Engures Ezers/Engures, Ozero- 8 Jg 57.15N 23.10 E
Enh-Gajvan 27 Gb 48.05N 97.35 E
Enid 39 Jf 36.19N 97.48W
Enid Lake 45 Li 34.10N 89.50W
Eniwa 28 Pc 42.53N 141.14 E
Eniwa-Dake 29a Bb 42.47N 141.17 E
Eniwetok Atoll 57 Hc 11.30N 162.15 E
Enkeldoorn 37 Ec 19.01S 30.53 E
Enkenbach Alsenborn 12 Je 49.29N 7.53 E
Enkhuizen 11 Lb 52.42N 5.17 E
Enklinge 8 Id 60.20N 20.45 E
Enköping 7 Dg 59.38N 17.04 E
Enna 14 Im 37.34N 14.16 E
Ennadai 42 Hd 61.10N 101.00W
Ennadei Lake 42 Hd 60.55N 101.20W
Enné 35 Bc 14.24N 18.45 E
Ennedi 30 Jg 17.15N 22.00 E
Ennell, Lough-/Loch Ainninn 9 Fh 53.28N 7.24W
Ennepetal 12 Jc 51.18N 7.21 E
Ennigerloh 12 Kc 51.50N 8.01 E
Enning 45 Ed 44.37N 102.31W
Ennis [Mt.-U.S.] 46 Jd 45.21N 111.44W
Ennis [Tx.-U.S.] 45 Hj 32.20N 96.38W
Ennis/Inis 9 Ei 52.50N 8.59W
Enniscorthy/Inis Córthaidh 9 Gi 52.30N 6.34W
Enniskillen/Inis Ceithleann 9 Fg 54.21N 7.38W
Ennistymon/Inis Diomáin 9 Di 52.57N 9.13W
Enns 14 Ib 48.14N 14.28 E
Enns 5 Hf 48.14N 14.30 E
Ennstaler Alpen 14 Ic 47.37N 14.35 E
Eno 7 He 62.48N 30.09 E
Enontekiö 7 Fb 68.23N 23.38 E
Enonvesi [Fin.] 8 Mb 62.10N 28.55 E
Enonvesi [Fin.] 8 Lc 61.20N 26.30 E
Enozero, Ozero- 7 Ib 68.10N 38.00 E
Enrekang 26 Gg 3.34S 119.47 E
Enrique Carbó 55 Ck 33.08S 59.14W
Enriquillo 49 Le 17.54N 71.14W
Enriquillo, Lago- 47 Je 18.27N 71.39W
Enschede 11 Mb 52.12N 6.53 E
Ensenada [Arg.] 55 Dl 34.51S 57.55W
Ensenada [Mex.] 39 Hf 31.52N 116.37W
Enshi 27 Ie 30.16N 109.26 E
Enshū-Nada 29 Ed 34.30N 138.00 E
Entebbe 31 Kh 0.04N 32.28 E
Entenbühl 10 Ig 49.46N 12.24 E
Enterprise [Al.-U.S.] 44 Ej 31.19N 85.51W
Enterprise [N.W.T.-Can.] 42 Fd 60.39N 116.08W
Enterprise [Or.-U.S.] 46 Gd 45.25N 117.17W
Entinas, Punta- 13 Jh 36.41N 2.46W
Entrada, Punta- 47 Ab 30.22N 115.59W
Entraygues-sur-Truyère 11 Ij 44.39N 2.34 E
Entrecasteaux, Récifs d'- 57 Hf 18.20S 163.00 E
Entrepeñas, Embalse de- 13 Jd 40.34N 2.42W
Entre Ríos [2] 56 Id 32.00S 59.00W
Entre Rios 54 Fh 21.32S 64.12W
Entre Rios de Minas 55 Je 20.41S 44.04W
Entrevaux 11 Mk 43.57N 6.49 E
Entroncamento 13 De 39.28N 8.28W
Enugu 31 Hh 6.26N 7.29 E
Enugu Ezike 34 Gd 6.59N 7.27 E
Envermeu 12 De 49.54N 1.16 E
Envigado 54 Cb 6.08N 75.39W
Envira 54 De 7.18S 70.13W
Enyamba 36 Dc 3.40S 24.58 E
Enyélé 36 Cb 2.49N 18.06 E
Enz 10 Fh 49.00N 9.10 E
Enza 14 Ef 44.54N 10.31 E
Enzan 28 Og 34.52N 138.44 E
Enzgau 12 Kf 48.48N 8.37 E
Eo 13 Ea 43.28N 7.03W
Eochaill/Youghal 9 Fj 51.57N 7.50W
Eolie o Lipari, Isole-=Lipari Islands (EN) 5 Hh 38.35N 14.55 E
Epanomi 15 Fi 40.26N 22.56 E
Epazote, Cerro- 47 Cd 24.35N 105.07W
Epe [Neth.] 12 Hb 52.21N 5.59 E
Epe [Nig.] 34 Fd 6.35N 3.59 E
Epéna 36 Cb 1.22N 17.29 E
Epernay 11 Je 49.03N 3.57 E
Epe-Vaassen 12 Hb 52.17N 5.58 E
Ephesus (EN)=Efes 15 Kl 37.55N 27.20 E
Ephraim 46 Jg 39.22N 111.35W
Ephrata 46 Fc 47.19N 119.33W
Epi, Ile- 57 Hf 16.43S 168.15 E
Epidamnus 15 Ch 41.19N 19.26 E
Epidaurus (EN) = Epidhavros 15 Gl 37.38N 23.09 E
Epidhavros = Epidaurus (EN) 15 Gl 37.38N 23.09 E
Epila 13 Kc 41.36N 1.17W
Épinal 11 Mf 48.11N 6.27 E
Epirus (EN)=Ipiros 5 Ih 39.30N 20.40 E
Epirus (EN)=Ipiros 15 Dj 39.30N 20.40 E
Episkopi 24 Ee 34.40N 32.54 E
Epping 12 Cc 51.42N 0.08 E
Eppingen 12 Ke 49.08N 8.54 E
Epsom 9 Mj 51.20N 0.16W
Epte 11 He 49.04N 1.31 E
Epukiro 37 Bd 21.41S 19.08 E
Epukiro 37 Bd 21.28S 19.59 E
Epulu 36 Eb 1.15N 28.21 E
Eqlīd 23 Hc 30.55N 52.39 E
Équateur=Equator (EN) [2] 36 Eb 1.00N 20.00 E
Equator (EN)=Équateur [2] 36 Eb 1.00N 20.00 E
Equatorial Guinea (EN)=Guinea Ecuatorial [1] 1 Hh 2.00N 9.00 E
Equinox Mountain 44 Kd 43.15N 73.10W
Era [It.] 14 Eg 43.40N 10.38 E
Era [Sud.] 35 Dd 5.30N 29.50 E
Eraclea 14 Kj 40.15N 16.40 E
Eraclea Minoa 14 Hm 37.25N 13.18 E
Eradaka 63b Dc 17.39S 168.08 E
Eräjärvi 8 Kc 61.35N 24.34 E
Eratini 15 Fk 38.22N 22.14 E
Erbaa 24 Gb 40.42N 36.36 E
Erbach 10 Eg 49.39N 9.00 E
Erbeskopf 10 Dg 49.44N 7.05 E
Erbil [3] 24 Je 36.10N 44.00 E
Erbil 22 Gf 36.11N 44.01 E
Ercek 24 Jc 38.39N 43.36 E
Erçek Gölü 24 Jc 38.39N 43.32 E
Erciş 24 Jc 39.00N 43.19 E
Erciyas Dağı 21 Ff 38.32N 35.28 E
Ercolano 14 Ij 40.48N 14.21 E
Ercsi 10 Oi 47.15N 18.54 E
Érd 10 Oi 47.22N 18.56 E
Erdaobaihe 27 Mc 42.28N 128.05 E
Erdao Jiang 28 Ic 42.35N 127.10 E
Erdek 24 Bb 40.24N 27.48 E
Erdek Körfezi 24 Bb 40.25N 27.45 E
Erdemli 24 Fd 36.37N 34.18 E
Erdene-Cagan 27 Kb 45.55N 115.30 E
Erdene-Dalaj 27 Hb 46.02N 104.55 E
Erdene-Mandal 27 Hb 48.30N 101.21 E
Erdi 30 Jg 19.05N 22.40 E
Erdi Ma 35 Cb 18.35N 23.30 E
Erding 10 Hh 48.18N 11.56 E
Erdinger Moos 10 Hh 48.20N 11.50 E
Erdre 11 Eg 47.13N 1.32W
Erebus, Mount- 66 Kf 77.32S 167.09 E
Erechim 56 Jc 27.38S 52.17W
Ereğli [Tur.] 23 Db 37.31N 34.04 E
Ereğli [Tur.] 23 Da 41.17N 31.25 E
Erei, Monti- 14 Im 37.35N 14.20 E
Ereke 26 Hg 4.45S 123.10 E
Eren 24 Dd 37.25N 30.05 E
Erenhot 22 Ne 43.35N 112.00 E
Erepecu, Lago do- 54 Gd 1.20S 56.35W
Eresma 13 Hc 41.26N 4.45W
Erétria 15 Gk 38.25N 23.48 E
Erfelek 24 Fb 41.55N 34.57 E
Erfengshan 28 Ag 35.50N 111.47 E
Erfoud 32 Gc 31.26N 4.14W
Erft 10 Ce 51.11N 6.44 E
Erftstadt 12 Id 50.48N 6.49 E
Erfurt 6 He 50.59N 11.02 E
Erfurt [2] 10 Gf 51.00N 11.00 E
Ergani 24 Hc 38.17N 39.46 E
Ergene 24 Bb 41.01N 26.22 E
Erges 13 Ee 39.40N 7.01W
Ergig, Bahr- 35 Bc 11.22N 15.24 E
Ērgļi/Ergli 7 Fh 56.55N 25.41 E
Ergli/Ērgļi 7 Fh 56.55N 25.41 E
Ergun He 21 Od 53.20N 121.28 E
Ergun Youqi (Labudalin) 27 La 50.16N 120.09 E
Ergun Zuoqi (Genhe) 22 Od 50.47N 121.32 E
Er Hai 27 Hf 25.45N 100.10 E
Eria 13 Gb 42.03N 5.44W
Eriba 35 Fb 16.37N 36.04 E
Eriboll, Loch- 9 Ic 58.30N 4.40W
Eric 42 Kf 51.52N 65.45W
Erice 14 Gl 38.02N 12.35 E
Ericeira 13 Cf 38.59N 9.25W
Erichsen Lake 42 Jb 70.38N 80.20W
Ericht, Loch- 9 Ie 56.50N 4.25W
Erick 45 Gi 35.13N 99.52W
Eridu [3] 24 Lg 30.50N 46.00 E
Erie 39 Ke 42.08N 80.04W
Erie, Lake- 38 Ke 42.15N 81.00W
'Erigābo 35 Hc 10.37N 47.24 E
Erīgāt 30 Gg 19.40N 4.50W
Erikoússa 15 Cj 39.53N 19.35 E
Eriksdale 45 Ga 50.52N 98.06W
Eriksenstretet 41 Oc 79.00N 26.00 E
Erikub Atoll 57 Id 9.08N 170.02 E
Erimanthos Óros 15 El 37.58N 21.48 E
Erimo-Misaki 27 Pc 41.55N 143.15 E
Eriskay 9 Fd 57.04N 7.13W
Eritrea 30 Kg 15.00N 40.00 E
Eritrea [3] 35 Fb 15.00N 39.00 E
Eritrea 35 Fb 15.00N 40.00 E
Erjas 13 Ee 39.40N 7.01W
Erkelenz 12 Ic 51.05N 6.19 E
Erken 8 He 59.50N 18.35 E
Erkowit 35 Fb 18.46N 37.07 E
Erlangdian → Dawu 28 Ci 31.33N 114.07 E
Erlangen 10 Hg 49.36N 11.01 E
Erlang Shan 27 Hf 29.58N 102.20 E
Erlauf 14 Jb 48.12N 15.11 E
Erldunda 59 Ge 25.14S 133.12 E
Erlenbach 12 Ke 49.07N 8.11 E
Erlong Shan 27 Mc 43.30N 128.44 E
Ermelo [Neth.] 12 Hb 52.19N 5.37 E
Ermelo [S.Afr.] 37 De 26.34S 29.58 E
Ermenek 24 Ed 36.38N 32.54 E
Ermenistan=Armenia (EN) 23 Fb 39.10N 43.00 E
Ermenistan=Armenia (EN) 21 Gf 39.10N 43.00 E
Ermenonville 12 Ee 49.08N 2.42 E
Ermesinde 13 Dc 41.13N 8.33W
Ermoúpolis 15 Hl 37.27N 24.56 E
Ernākulam 25 Fg 9.59N 76.17 E
Erndtebrück 12 Kd 50.59N 8.16 E
Erne/An Éirne 9 Eg 54.30N 8.15W
Ernée 11 Ff 48.18N 0.56W
Ernest Legouvé Reef 57 Lh 35.12S 150.35W
Ernici, Monti- 14 Hi 41.50N 13.20 E
Erode 25 Ff 11.21N 77.44 E
Eromanga 59 Ie 26.40S 143.16 E
Erongoberg 37 Bd 21.40S 15.40 E
Erpengdianzi 28 Hd 41.12N 125.29 E
Errego 37 Fc 16.02S 37.10 E
Errigal/An Ea agail 9 Ef 55.02N 8.07W
Erris Head/Ceann Iorrais 5 Fe 54.19N 10.00W
Erromango, Ile- 57 Hf 18.48S 169.05 E
Erseka 15 Di 40.20N 20.41 E
Erstein 11 Nf 48.26N 7.40 E
Ertai 27 Fb 46.02N 90.10 E
Ertil 16 Ee 51.50N 40.51 E
Ertix He 21 Ke 47.52N 84.16 E
Erts 37 De 25.08S 29.55 E
Ertvågøy 8 Ca 63.15N 8.25 E
Eruh 24 Jd 37.46N 42.15 E
Ervânia 55 Ee 21.43S 55.32W
Erve 11 Fg 47.50N 0.20W
Ervy-le-Châtel 11 Jf 48.02N 3.55 E
Erwin 44 Fg 36.09N 82.25W
Erwitte 12 Kc 51.37N 8.21 E
Eryuan 27 Gf 26.09N 99.56 E
Erzeni 15 Ch 41.26N 19.27 E
Erzgebirge = Ore Mountains (EN) 5 He 50.30N 13.15 E
Erzin 20 Ef 50.17N 95.10 E
Erzincan 23 Eb 39.44N 39.29 E
Erzurum 22 Gf 39.55N 41.17 E
Esan-Misaki 28 Pd 41.48N 141.12 E
Esashi [Jap.] 28 Pd 41.52N 140.07 E
Esashi [Jap.] 28 Qb 44.56N 142.35 E
Esashi [Jap.] 28 Pe 39.12N 141.09 E
Esbjerg 6 Gd 55.28N 8.27 E
Esbo/Espoo 7 Ff 60.13N 24.40 E
Escalante 46 Jh 37.47N 111.36W
Escalante Desert 46 Ih 37.50N 113.30W
Escalante River 46 Jh 37.17N 110.53W
Escalaplano 14 Dk 39.37N 9.21 E
Escalón 47 Dc 26.45N 104.20W
Escalona 13 Hd 40.10N 4.24W
Escanaba 39 Ke 45.45N 87.04W
Escanaba River 44 Dc 45.47N 87.04W
Escandón, Puerto de- 13 Ld 40.17N 1.00W
Escandorgue 11 Jk 43.46N 3.14 E
Escarpada Point 21 Oh 18.31N 122.13 E
Escarpé, Cap- 63b Ce 20.41S 167.13 E
Escatrón 13 Lc 41.17N 0.19W
Escaut=Schelde (EN) 11 Kc 51.22N 4.15 E
Esch an der Alzette/Esch-sur-Alzette 11 Le 49.30N 5.59 E
Eschkopf 12 Je 49.19N 7.51 E
Esch-sur-Alzette/Esch an der Alzette 11 Le 49.30N 5.59 E
Eschwege 10 Ge 51.11N 10.04 E
Eschweiler 10 Cf 50.49N 6.17 E
Escocesa, Bahía- 49 Md 19.25N 69.45W
Escondida, Punta- 48 Kj 15.49N 97.03W
Escondido 46 Gj 33.07N 117.05W
Escondido, Río- 49 Fg 12.04N 83.45W
Escravos 34 Gd 5.36N 5.11 E
Escudo, Puerto del- 13 Ia 43.05N 3.50W
Escudo de Veraguas, Isla- 49 Gi 9.06N 81.33W
Escuintla [3] 49 Bf 14.10N 91.00W
Escuintla [Guat.] 47 Ff 14.18N 90.47W
Escuintla [Mex.] 48 Mj 15.20N 92.38W
Escuro, Rio- [Braz.] 55 Ic 17.31S 46.39W
Escuro, Rio- [Braz.] 55 Ha 12.50S 49.28W
Ese 36 Eb 4.04N 26.40 E
Ese-Hajja 20 Ic 67.35N 134.55 E
Eséka 34 He 3.39N 10.46 E
Eşen 24 Cd 36.27N 29.16 E
Esendere 24 Kd 37.46N 44.40 E
Esera 13 Mb 42.06N 0.15 E
Esfahān [3] 23 Hc 32.50N 51.50 E
Eşfahān=Isfahan (EN) 22 Hf 32.40N 51.38 E
Esfandārān 24 Og 31.52N 52.32 E
Esfarāyen, Reshteh-ye- 24 Qd 36.46N 57.10 E
Esgueva 13 Hc 41.40N 4.43W

Index Symbols

[1] Independent Nation
[2] State, Region
[3] District, County
[4] Municipality
[5] Colony, Dependency
Continent
Physical Region
Historical or Cultural Region
Mount, Mountain
Volcano
Hill
Mountains, Mountain Range
Hills, Escarpment
Plateau, Upland
Pass, Gap
Plain, Lowland
Delta
Salt Flat
Valley, Canyon
Crater, Cave
Karst Features
Depression
Polder
Desert, Dunes
Forest, Woods
Heath, Steppe
Oasis
Cape, Point
Coast, Beach
Cliff
Peninsula
Isthmus
Sandbank
Island
Atoll
Rock, Reef
Islands, Archipelago
Rocks, Reefs
Coral Reef
Well, Spring
Geyser
River, Stream
Waterfall Rapids
River Mouth, Estuary
Lake
Salt Lake
Intermittent Lake
Reservoir
Swamp, Pond
Canal
Glacier
Ice Shelf, Pack Ice
Ocean
Sea
Gulf, Bay
Strait, Fjord
Lagoon
Bank
Seamount
Tablemount
Ridge
Shelf
Basin
Escarpment, Sea Scarp
Fracture
Trench, Abyss
National Park, Reserve
Point of Interest
Recreation Site
Cave, Cavern
Historic Site
Ruins
Wall, Walls
Church, Abbey
Temple
Scientific Station
Airport
Port
Lighthouse
Mine
Tunnel
Dam, Bridge

Eshowe	37	Ee	28.58 S	31.29 E
Eshtehärd	24	Ne	35.44N	50.23 E
Esino	14	Hg	43.39N	13.22 E
Esk	9	Jg	54.58N	3.04W
Eskifjördur	7a	Cb	65.04N	14.01W
Eskilstuna	7	Dg	59.22N	16.30 E
Eskimo Point	39	Jc	61.07N	94.03W
Eskişehir	22	Ff	39.46N	30.32 E
Esla	13	Fc	41.29N	6.03W
Eslâmâbâd	23	Gc	34.11N	46.35 E
Eşler Daği	15	Ml	37.24N	29.43 E
Eslohe (Sauerland)	12	Kc	51.15N	8.10 E
Eslöv	7	Ci	55.50N	13.20 E
Eşme	24	Cc	38.24N	28.59 E
Esmeralda [Braz.]	55	Gi	28.03 S	51.12W
Esmeralda [Cuba]	49	Hc	21.51N	78.07W
Esmeralda, Isla-	48	Sf	48.57 S	75.25W
Esmeralda Bank (EN)	65b	Ab	14.57N	145.15 E
Esmeraldas	53	Ie	0.59N	79.42W
Esnagami Lake	45	Ma	50.21N	86.48W
Esneux	12	Hd	50.32N	5.34 E
Espada, Punta-	49	Lg	12.05N	71.07W
Espagnol Point	51n	Ba	13.22N	61.09W
Espalion	11	Ij	44.31N	2.46 E
Espalmador, Isla-	13	Nf	38.47N	1.26 E
España = Spain (EN)	6	Fg	40.00N	4.00W
Espanola [N.M.-U.S.]	45	Ch	36.06N	106.02W
Espanola [Ont.-Can.]	44	Gb	46.15N	81.46W
Española, Isla-	54a	Bb	1.25 S	89.42W
Espardell, Isla-	13	Nf	38.47N	1.27 E
Esparta	49	Ei	9.59N	84.40W
Espeland	8	Ad	60.23N	5.28 E
Espelkamp	10	Ed	52.25N	8.37 E
Esperance	58	Dh	33.51 S	121.53 E
Esperance, Cape-	63a	Dc	9.15 S	159.43 E
Esperance Bay	59	Ef	33.50 S	121.55 E
Esperance Harbour	51k	Ba	14.04N	60.55W
Esperancita	55	Bc	16.55 S	60.06W
Esperantina	54	Jd	3.54 S	42.14W
Esperanza	66	Re	63.26 S	57.00W
Esperanza [Arg.]	56	Hd	31.27 S	60.56W
Esperanza [Mex.]	48	Ed	27.35N	109.56W
Esperanza [P.R.]	51a	Cb	18.06N	65.29W
Esperanza, Sierra la-	49	Ef	15.40N	85.45W
Espevær	7	Ag	59.36N	5.10 E
Espichel, Cabo-	13	Cf	38.25N	9.13W
Espiel	13	Gf	38.12N	5.01W
Espigão Serra do-	55	Gh	26.55 S	50.25W
Espinal [Bol.]	55	Cc	17.13 S	58.43W
Espinal [Col.]	54	Dc	4.10N	74.54W
Espinazo del Diablo, Sierra-	48	Ff	24.00N	106.00W
Espinhaço, Serra do-	52	Lg	17.30 S	43.30W
Espinho	13	Dc	41.01N	8.38W
Espinilho, Serra do-	55	Ei	28.30 S	55.06W
Espinillo	55	Cg	24.58 S	58.34W
Espino	50	Dh	8.34N	66.01W
Espinosa	54	Jf	14.56 S	42.50W
Espinouse	11	Ik	43.32N	2.46 E
Espírito Santo	54	Jg	20.00 S	40.30W
Espíritu Santo, Bahía del-	48	Ph	19.20N	87.35W
Espíritu Santo, Isla-	48	De	24.30N	110.22W
Espita	48	Og	21.01N	88.19W
Esplanada	54	Kf	11.47 S	37.57W
Espoo/Esbo	7	Ff	60.13N	24.40 E
Espoo-Tapiola	8	Kd	60.11N	24.49 E
Esposende	13	Dc	41.32N	8.47W
Espuña, Sierra de-	13	Kg	37.52N	1.34W
Espungabera	37	Ed	20.28 S	32.46 E
Esquel	53	Ij	42.55 S	71.20W
Esquina	56	Id	30.01 S	59.32W
Esquinapa de Hidalgo	47	Cd	22.51N	105.48W
Esquipular	49	Cf	14.34N	89.21W
Essandsjøen	8	Da	63.05N	12.00 E
Essaouira	31	Ge	31.31N	9.46W
Essaouira	32	Fc	31.04N	9.03W
Essen [Bel.]	12	Gc	51.28N	4.28 E
Essen [F.R.G.]	6	Ge	51.27N	7.01 E
Essen (Oldenburg)	12	Jb	52.42N	7.55 E
Essendon, Mount-	59	Ed	24.59 S	120.28 E
Essequibo River	52	Ke	6.50N	58.30W
Essex	46	Hi	34.42N	115.12W
Essex	9	Mj	51.50N	0.30 E
Essex	9	Mj	51.50N	0.35W
Essex Mountain	46	Kf	42.02N	109.13W
Esslingen am Neckar	10	Fh	48.45N	9.18 E
Esso	20	Ke	55.55N	158.40 E
Essonne	11	Hf	48.37N	2.29 E
Essonne	11	If	48.36N	2.20 E
Est [Cam.]	34	He	4.00N	14.00 E
Est [U.V.]	34	Fc	12.00N	1.00 E
Est, Canal de l'-	11	Lf	48.45N	5.35 E
Est, Cap-	37	Ic	15.16 S	50.29 E
Est, Ile de l'-	30	Mm	46.15 S	52.05 E
Est, Pointe de l'-	42	Lg	49.08N	61.41W
Estaca de Bares, Punta de la-	5	Fg	43.46N	7.42W
Estados Unidos Mexicanos	39	Ig	23.00N	102.00W
Eştahbänät	24	Ph	29.08N	54.04 E
Estaimpuis	12	Fd	50.42N	3.15 E
Estância	54	Kf	11.16 S	37.26W
Estancias, Sierra de las-	13	Jg	37.35N	2.20W
Estanislao del Campo	55	Bg	25.03 S	60.06W
Estarreja	13	Dd	40.45N	8.34W
Estats, Pica d'-	11	Hn	42.40N	1.24 E
Estats, Pica d'-/Estats, Pico d'-	11	Hn	42.40N	1.24 E
Estats, Pic d'-	11	Hn	42.40N	1.24 E
Estats, Pico d'-	11	Hn	42.40N	1.24 E
Estats, Pico d'-/Estats, Pica d'-	11	Hn	42.40N	1.24 E
Estcourt	37	De	29.01 S	29.52 E
Este	14	Fe	45.14N	11.39 E
Este, Punta-	51a	Cb	18.08N	65.16W
Este, Punta del-	56	Jd	34.59 S	54.57W
Esteban Rams	55	Bi	29.47 S	61.29W
Esteli	47	Gf	13.05N	86.23W
Esteli	49	Dg	13.10N	86.20W
Estella	13	Jb	42.40N	2.02W
Estepa	13	Hg	37.18N	4.54W
Estepona	13	Gh	36.26N	5.08W
Esternay	11	Mk	43.30N	6.50 E
Estérel	12	Ff	48.44N	3.34 E
Esterri d'Aneu/Esterri de Aneu	13	Nb	42.38N	1.08 E
Esterri de Aneu/Esterri d'Aneu	13	Nb	42.38N	1.08 E
Esterwegen	12	Jb	52.59N	7.37 E
Estes Park	45	Df	40.23N	105.31W
Este Sudeste, Cayos del-	47	Hf	12.26N	81.27W
Estevan	45	Ie	49.07N	103.05W
Estherville	45	Ie	43.24N	94.50W
Estissac	11	Jf	48.16N	3.49 E
Eston	46	Ka	51.10N	108.46W
Estonia (EN)	5	Id	59.00N	26.00 E
Estonian SSR (EN) = Eesti NSV	19	Cd	59.00N	26.00 E
Estonskaja Sovetskaja Socialističeskaja Respublika	19	Cd	59.00N	26.00 E
Estonskaja SSR/Eesti Nõukogude Socialistlik Vabarijk	19	Cd	59.00N	26.00 E
Estoril	13	Cf	38.42N	9.24W
Estrées-Saint-Denis	12	Ie	49.26N	2.39 E
Estreito	55	Gj	31.50 S	51.44W
Estreito, Représa do-	55	Ie	20.15 S	47.09W
Estrêla [Braz.]	55	Gi	29.29 S	51.58W
Estrêla [Braz.]	55	Gj	31.15 S	21.45W
Estrela, Arroyo-	55	Df	22.05 S	56.25W
Estrela, Serra da-	5	Fg	40.20N	7.38W
Estrêla do Sul	55	Id	18.21 S	47.49W
Estrella	13	If	38.28N	3.35W
Estrella, Punta-	48	Bb	30.55N	114.40W
Estrema, Serra da-	55	Jc	16.50 S	45.07W
Estremadura	13	Ce	39.15N	9.10W
Estremoz	13	Ef	38.51N	7.35W
Estrondo, Serra do-	54	Ie	9.00 S	48.45W
Estry	12	Bf	48.54N	0.44W
Estuaire	36	Ab	10.00N	10.00 E
Esztergom	10	Oi	47.48N	18.45 E
Etah	41	Ec	78.19N	72.38W
Étain	11	Le	49.13N	5.38 E
Etajima	29	Cd	34.15N	132.29 E
Etalle	12	He	49.41N	5.36 E
Étampes	11	If	48.26N	2.09 E
Étaples	11	Hd	50.31N	1.39 E
Étawah	25	Fc	26.46N	79.02 E
Ethe, Virton-	12	He	49.35N	5.35 E
Ethel Reefs	63d	As	16.5 S	177.13 E
Ethiopia (EN) = Itiopya	31	Kh	9.00N	39.00 E
Ethiopian Plateau (EN)	30	Kg	10.00N	38.10 E
Etive, Loch-	9	He	56.35N	5.15W
Etna	3	Dd	60.50N	10.03 E
Etna	5	Hh	37.50N	14.55 E
Etne	8	Ae	59.40N	5.56 E
Etoile Cay	37b	Bb	5.53 S	53.01 E
Etoile Island	40	Me	56.08N	132.26W
Etolin Strait	40	Fd	60.20N	165.15W
Etomo-Misaki	29a	Bb	42.20N	140.55 E
Etorofu Tõ/Iturup, Ostrov-	21	Qe	44.54N	147.30 E
Etosha Pan	30	Ij	18.50 S	16.20 E
Etoumbi	36	Bb	0.01N	14.57 E
Etrépagny	12	De	49.18N	1.37 E
Étretat	11	Ge	49.42N	0.12 E
Etropole	15	Gg	42.50N	24.00 E
Etruria	56	Hd	32.56 S	63.15W
Etsch/Adige	5	Hf	45.10N	12.20 E
Ettelbrück/Ettelbruck	12	Ie	49.51N	6.07 E
Ettelbruck/Ettelbrück	12	Ie	49.51N	6.07 E
Etten-Leur	12	Gc	51.35N	4.39 E
Ettersberg	10	He	51.03N	11.15 E
Ettlingen	12	Kf	48.57N	8.24 E
Etzna Tixmucuy	48	Nh	19.35N	90.13W
Eu	11	Hd	50.03N	1.25 E
'Eua Iki	65b	Bc	21.07 S	174.59W
Eua Island	61	Gd	21.22 S	174.56W
Euboea (EN) = Évvoia	5	Ih	38.30N	24.00 E
Eucla	58	Dh	31.43 S	128.52 E
Euclid	44	Gd	41.34N	81.33W
Euclides da Cunha	54	Kf	10.31 S	39.01W
Eucumbene, Lake-	59	Jg	36.05 S	148.45 E
Eudora	45	Kj	33.07N	91.16W
Eufaula	44	Ej	31.54N	85.09W
Eufaula Lake	45	Ii	35.17N	95.31W
Euganei, Colli-	14	Fe	45.19N	11.40 E
Eugene	39	Ge	44.02N	123.05W
Eugenia, Punta-	38	Hg	27.50N	115.03W
Eugênio Penzo	55	Ef	22.13 S	55.53W
Eugmo	7	Fe	63.49N	22.45 E
Eunice [La.-U.S.]	45	Jk	30.30N	92.26W
Eunice [N.M.-U.S.]	45	Ej	32.26N	103.09W
Euphrates (EN) = Al Furāt	21	Gf	31.00N	47.25 E
Euphrates (EN) = Firat	21	Gf	31.00N	47.25 E
Eupora	45	Lj	33.32N	89.16W
Eura	7	Fe	61.08N	22.08 E
Eurajoki	8	Ic	61.12N	21.44 E
Eurasia Basin (EN)	67	Ge	87.00N	80.00 E
Eure	11	Ge	49.10N	1.00 E
Eure-et-Loir	11	He	48.18N	1.12 E
Eureka [Ca.-U.S.]	39	Ge	40.47N	124.09W
Eureka [Ks.-U.S.]	45	Hh	37.49N	96.17W
Eureka [Mt.-U.S.]	46	Hb	48.53N	115.03W
Eureka [Nv.-U.S.]	43	Dd	39.31N	115.58W
Eureka [N.W.T.-Can.]	42	Ia	80.00N	85.59W
Eureka [S.D.-U.S.]	45	Gd	45.46N	99.38W
Eureka [Ut.-U.S.]	46	Ig	39.57N	112.07W
Eureka Sound	42	Ia	79.00N	87.00W
Europa	30	Lk	22.20 S	40.22 E
Europa, Picos de-	5	Fg	43.12N	4.48W
Europe	5	Ie	50.00N	20.00 E
Europoort	11	Jc	51.58N	4.00 E
Euskirchen	10	Cf	50.40N	6.47 E
Eustis	44	Gk	28.51N	81.41W
Eutaw	44	Di	32.50N	87.53W
Eutin	10	Gb	54.08N	10.37 E
Euzkadi/Vascongadas = Basque Provinces (EN)	13	Ja	43.00N	2.30W
Evale	36	Cf	16.33 S	15.44 E
Evans, Lac-	42	Jf	50.50N	77.00W
Evans, Mount-	46	Ic	46.05N	113.07W
Evans Strait	42	Jd	63.20N	82.00W
Evanston [Il.-U.S.]	45	Me	42.03N	87.42W
Evanston [Wy.-U.S.]	43	Ec	41.16N	110.58 E
Evansville	39	Kf	37.58N	87.35W
Evant	45	Gk	31.29N	98.09W
Evart	44	Ed	43.54N	85.14W
Evaux-les-Bains	11	Ih	46.10N	2.29 E
Evaz	24	Oi	27.46N	53.59 E
Eveleth	45	Jj	39.46N	26.46 E
Eviler [Tur.]	15	Jj	39.46N	26.46 E
Eviler [Tur.]	15	Mk	38.03N	29.54 E
Evelyn, Mount-	59	Gb	13.36 S	132.53 E
Evenkijski Nac. okrug	20	Ed	65.00N	98.00 E
Evensk	22	Rc	61.57N	159.14 E
Everard, Lake-	59	Hf	31.25 S	135.05 E
Everard Ranges	59	Ge	27.05 S	132.30 E
Everest, Mount- (EN) = Qomolangma Feng	21	Kg	27.59N	86.56 E
Everest, Mount- (EN) = Saragmatha	21	Kg	27.59N	86.56 E
Everett	43	Cb	47.59N	122.13W
Everett Mountains	42	Kd	62.45N	67.10W
Evergem	12	Fc	51.07N	3.42 E
Evergem-Sleidinge	12	Fc	51.08N	3.41 E
Everglades City	44	Gm	25.52N	81.23W
Evergreen	44	Dj	31.26N	86.57W
Evertsberg	8	Ec	61.08N	13.57 E
Evesham	9	Li	52.05N	1.56W
Evesham, Vale of-	9	Li	52.05N	1.50W
Evian-les-Bains	11	Mh	46.23N	6.35 E
Evijärvi	7	Fe	63.22N	23.29 E
Evinayong	34	He	1.27N	10.34 E
Évinos	15	Ek	38.19N	21.32 E
Evje	7	Bg	58.36N	7.51 E
Évora	8	Fh	38.34N	7.54W
Évora	13	Ef	38.35N	7.50W
Evoron	20	If	51.23N	136.23 E
Evowghli	24	Kc	38.43N	45.13 E
Evre	11	Eg	47.22N	1.02W
Evrecy	12	Be	49.06N	0.30W
Evreux	11	He	49.01N	1.09 E
Evron	11	Ff	48.10N	0.24W
Évros	15	Ji	40.52N	26.12 E
Evrótas	15	Fm	36.48N	22.41 E
Evry	11	If	48.38N	2.27 E
Évvoia = Euboea (EN)	5	Ih	38.30N	24.00 E
Évvoia, Gulf of- (EN) = Vórios Evvoïkós Kólpos	15	Gk	38.45N	23.10 E
Evzonoi	15	Fh	41.06N	22.33 E
Ewa Beach	65a	Cb	21.19N	158.00W
Ewing Seamount (EN)	30	Hk	23.20 S	8.45 E
Ewo	36	Bc	0.55 S	14.49 E
Excelsior Mountain	46	Fg	38.02N	119.18W
Excelsior Mountains	46	Fg	38.10N	118.30W
Excelsior Springs	45	Ig	39.20N	94.13W
Exe	9	Jk	50.37N	3.25W
Executive Committee Range	66	Nf	76.50 S	126.00W
Exeter [Eng.-U.K.]	6	Fe	50.43N	3.31W
Exeter [N.H.-U.S.]	44	Ld	42.59N	70.56W
Exeter Sound	42	Lc	66.10N	62.00W
Exmoor	9	Jj	51.10N	3.45W
Exmouth [Austl.]	59	Cd	21.55 S	114.07 E
Exmouth [Eng.-U.K.]	9	Jk	50.37N	3.25W
Exmouth Gulf	57	Cc	22.00 S	114.20 E
Exmouth Plateau (EN)	59	Cc	16.00 S	114.00 E
Expedition Range	59	Jd	24.30 S	149.05 E
Explorer Tablemount (EN)	47	He	16.55N	83.15W
Externsteine	12	Kc	51.52N	8.55 E
Extertal	12	Lb	52.04N	9.07 E
Extertal-Bösingfeld	12	Lb	52.04N	9.07 E
Extremadura	13	Ge	39.00N	6.00W
Exuma Cays	39	Ld	24.00N	76.20W
Exuma Cays	49	Ia	24.20N	76.40W
Exuma Sound	47	Id	24.15N	76.00W
Eyasi, Lake-	30	Ki	3.40 S	35.05 E
Eydehavn	8	Cf	58.31N	8.53 E
Eye	9	Nh	52.19N	1.09 E
Eyemouth	9	Kf	55.52N	2.06W
Eye Peninsula	9	Gc	58.13N	6.05W
Eygurande	11	Ii	45.40N	2.28 E
Eyjafjallajökull	7a	Bc	63.38N	19.36W
Éyl	31	Lh	8.00N	49.51 E
Eymoutiers	11	Hi	45.44N	1.44 E
Eynesil	24	Hb	41.03N	39.08 E
Eyrarbakki	7a	Bc	63.52N	21.09W
Eyre	59	Ff	32.15 S	126.18 E
Eyre, Lake-	57	Ee	28.43 S	137.11 E
Eyre Creek	59	Ge	26.40 S	139.00 E
Eyre Mountains	62	Cf	45.20 S	168.20 E
Eyre North, Lake-	59	He	28.30 S	137.20 E
Eyre Peninsula	57	Ef	34.00 S	135.45 E
Eyre South, Lake-	59	He	29.30 S	137.20 E
Eyrieux	11	Kj	44.48N	4.48 E
Eystrup	12	Lb	52.47N	9.13 E
Eythorne	12	Dc	51.11N	1.17 E
Eyvänaki	24	Oe	35.24N	51.56 E
Ezequiel Ramos Mexia, Embalse-	56	Ge	39.30 S	69.00W
Ezere	8	Jh	56.27N	22.17 E
Ežerelis	8	Jj	54.50N	23.38 E
Ezine	24	Bc	39.47N	26.20 E
Eznas/Jieznas	8	Kj	54.34N	24.17 E
Ežva	17	Ef	61.47N	50.40 E

F

Faaa	65e	Fc	17.33 S	149.36W
Faaite Atoll	61	Lc	16.45 S	145.14W
Fabens	45	Ck	31.30N	106.10W
Fåberg	8	Bc	61.10N	10.24 E
Faber Lake	42	Fd	63.55N	117.15W
Fåborg	7	Ci	55.06N	10.15 E
Fabriano	14	Gg	43.20N	12.54 E
Făcăeni	15	Ke	44.34N	27.54 E
Facatativá	54	Dc	4.49N	74.22W
Facha	33	Cd	29.30N	17.20 E
Fachi	31	Ig	18.06N	11.34 E
Facpi Point	64c	Bb	13.20N	144.38 E
Fada	31	Jj	17.14N	21.33 E
Fada N'Gourma	31	Fg	12.04N	0.21 E
Faddeja, Zaliv-	20	Fa	76.30N	107.30 E
Faddejevski, Ostrov-	20	Ja	75.30N	144.00 E
Fadiffolu Atoll	25a	Ba	5.25N	73.30 E
Făgăli	24	Mi	26.58N	11.34 E
Faeaara, Pointe-	65e	Fc	17.52 S	149.11W
Faenza	14	Ff	44.17N	11.53 E
Færøerne/Føroyar = Faeroe Islands (EN)	9	Ea	60.55N	8.40W
Faeroe-Iceland Ridge (EN)	5	Fc	64.00N	10.00W
Faeroe Islands (EN) = Færøerne/Føroyar	5	Fc	62.00N	7.00W
Faeroe Islands (EN) = Føroyar/Færøerne	6	Fc	62.00N	7.00W
Faeroe Islands (EN) = Føroyar/Færøerne	5	Fc	62.00N	7.00W
Færøerne/Føroyar = Faeroe Islands (EN)	5	Fc	62.00N	7.00W
Færøerne/Føroyar = Faeroe Islands (EN)	6	Fc	62.00N	7.00W
Fafa	35	Bd	7.18N	18.16 E
Fafe	13	Dc	41.27N	8.10W
Fafen	30	Lh	5.47N	44.11 E
Faga	34	Fc	13.45N	0.58 E
Fagaloa Bay	65c	Ba	13.54 S	171.28W
Fagamalo	65c	Aa	13.25 S	172.21W
Fagămaşului, Munţii-	15	Hd	45.35N	25.00 E
Fagataufa Atoll	57	Mg	22.14 S	138.45W
Fågelmara	8	Fh	56.15N	15.57 E
Fagerhult	8	Fg	57.09N	15.40 E
Fagernes	7	Bf	60.59N	9.15 E
Fagersta	7	Df	60.00N	15.47 E
Fåget	15	Kf	45.51N	22.11 E
Fagita	26	Jj	1.48 S	130.25 E
Fagnano, Lago-	56	Gh	54.38 S	68.00W
Fagne	12	Gd	50.10N	4.25 E
Faguibine, Lac-	30	Gg	16.45N	3.54W
Fahlian	24	Mg	30.12N	51.28 E
Fahner Höhe	10	Ge	51.10N	10.45 E
Faial	30	Bc	38.34N	28.42W
Fā'id	24	Eg	30.19N	32.19 E
Faioa	64b	Bc	13.23 S	176.08W
Fairbairn Reservoir	59	Jd	23.40 S	148.00 E
Fairbanks	39	Ec	64.51N	147.43W
Fairborn	44	Ef	39.48N	84.03W
Fairbury	43	Mc	40.08N	97.11W
Fairchild	45	Kd	44.36N	90.58W
Fairfax	44	Di	33.29N	86.55W
Fairfield [Al.-U.S.]	44	Di	33.29N	86.55W
Fairfield [Ca.-U.S.]	46	Dg	38.15N	122.01W
Fairfield [Ia.-U.S.]	45	Kf	40.59N	91.57W
Fairfield [Id.-U.S.]	46	He	43.21N	114.48W
Fairfield [Il.-U.S.]	45	Le	38.23N	88.22W
Fair Isle	9	Lb	59.30N	1.40W
Fairlie	62	Cf	44.06 S	170.50 E
Fairmont [Mn.-U.S.]	43	Ic	43.39N	94.28W
Fairmont [W.V.-U.S.]	43	Jd	39.28N	80.08W
Fair Ness	42	Kd	63.24N	72.05W
Fairview [Austl.]	59	Ib	15.31 S	144.17 E
Fairview [Ok.-U.S.]	45	Gh	36.16N	98.29W
Fairview Peak	46	De	43.35N	122.39W
Fairweather, Mount-	38	Fd	58.54N	137.32W
Fais Island	57	Hd	9.46N	140.31 E
Faistós	15	Hn	35.03N	24.48 E
Faith	43	Gb	45.02N	102.02W
Faizābād	25	Gc	26.47N	82.08 E
Fajardo	49	Od	18.20N	65.39W
Fajou, Ilet 'a-	51e	Ab	16.21N	61.35W
Fakahina Atoll	57	Mf	15.59 S	140.08W
Fakaofo Atoll	57	Je	9.22 S	171.14W
Fakarava Atoll	57	Mf	16.20 S	145.37W
Fakatura	29	Fa	40.38N	139.55 E
Fakel	17	Mh	57.40N	53.05 E
Fakenham	12	Cb	52.50N	0.50 E
Fakfak	26	Jj	2.55 S	132.17 E
Fakhr	24	Pg	31.25N	54.01 E
Fakse Bugt	8	Ei	55.10N	12.15 E
Faksefjell	8	Ei	55.20N	12.52 E
Fakse Ladeplads	8	Ei	55.15N	12.08 E
Faku	28	Gc	42.30N	123.24 E
Falaba	34	Cd	9.51N	11.19W
Fala-Beguets	64d	Bb	7.21N	151.46 E
Falaise	11	Ff	48.54N	0.12W
Falaise de Tiguidit	34	Ge	16.22N	7.45 E
Falakrón Óros	15	Gh	41.19N	24.00 E
Falalu	4d	Ba	7.38N	151.41 E
Falam	25	Id	22.55N	93.41 E
Falas	64d	Ba	7.32N	151.46 E
Fălciu	15	Lc	46.18N	28.08 E
Falcón	54	Ea	11.00N	69.50W
Falcon, Cap-	13	Li	35.46N	0.48W
Falcon, Presa-	45	Gm	26.37N	99.11W
Falconara Marittima	14	Hg	43.37N	13.24 E
Falcone, Punta-	14	Cj	40.58N	8.12 E
Falcon Reservoir	43	Hf	26.37N	99.11W
Faléa	34	Cc	12.16N	11.15W
Faleallej Pass	64d	Bb	7.26N	151.34 E
Falealupo	65c	Aa	13.30 S	172.48W
Falelima	65c	Aa	13.32 S	172.41W
Falémé	30	Fg	14.46N	12.14W
Falenki	7	Mg	58.23N	51.36 E
Falerum	8	Gf	58.09N	16.13 E
Faleshty	16	Ef	47.35N	27.44 E
Falevai	65c	Ba	13.55 S	171.59W
Falfurrias	43	Hf	27.14N	98.09W
Falkenberg	7	Ch	56.54N	12.28 E
Falkensee	10	Jd	52.34N	13.05 E
Falkirk	9	Jf	56.00N	3.48W
Falkland Islands/Malvinas, Islas-	53	Kk	51.45 S	59.00W
Falkland Islands/Malvinas, Islas-	52	Kk	51.45 S	59.00W
Falkland Plateau (EN)	52	Lk	51.00 S	50.00W
Falkland Sound	56	Ih	51.45 S	59.25W
Falkonéra	15	Gm	36.50 S	23.53 E
Falköping	7	Cg	58.10N	13.31 E
Fallingbostel	10	Fd	52.52N	9.42 E
Fallon [Mt.-U.S.]	46	Mc	46.48N	105.00W
Fallon [Nv.-U.S.]	46	Fg	39.28N	118.47W
Fall River	43	Lc	41.43N	71.08W
Falls City	43	Hc	40.03N	95.36W
Falmouth [Atg.]	51d	Bb	17.01N	61.46W
Falmouth [Eng.-U.K.]	9	Hk	50.08N	5.04W
Falmouth [Jam.]	49	Id	18.30N	77.39W
Falmouth [Ky.-U.S.]	44	Ef	38.40N	84.20W
Falmouth Bay	9	Hk	50.05N	5.05W
Falmouth Harbour	51d	Bb	17.01N	61.46W
Falo	64d	Bb	7.29N	151.53 E
False Bay	30	Il	34.15 S	18.35 E
False Pass	40	Gf	54.52N	163.24W
Falset	13	Mc	41.08N	0.49 E
Falso, Cabo- [Dom.Rep.]	49	Le	17.47N	71.41W
Falso, Cabo- [Hond.]	49	Ff	15.12N	83.20W
Falso, Cabo- [Mex.]	47	Cd	22.52N	109.58W
Falso Cabo de Hornos	56	Gi	55.43 S	68.05W
Falster	7	Ci	54.50N	12.00 E
Falsterbo	8	Ei	55.24N	12.50 E
Falterona	14	Fg	43.52N	11.42 E
Fălticeni	15	Jc	47.27N	26.18 E
Falun	6	Hc	60.36N	15.38 E
Famagusta (EN) = Ammókhostos	23	Dc	35.07N	33.57 E
Famagusta (EN) = Magosa	23	Dc	35.07N	33.57 E
Famatina, Nevados de-	56	Gc	29.00 S	67.51W
Famenne	11	Ld	50.15N	5.15 E
Fana	34	Dc	12.45N	6.57W
Fanan	64d	Bb	7.11N	151.59 E
Fanchang	27	Kc	31.00N	118.11 E
Fancy	51n	Ba	13.22N	61.12W
Fandriana	37	Hd	20.13 S	47.20 E
Fangak	35	Ed	9.04N	30.53 E
Fangatau Atoll	57	Mf	15.50 S	140.52W
Fangcheng	27	Je	33.09N	113.05 E
Fangliao	27	Lg	22.22N	120.25 E
Fangshan	28	Ce	39.43N	115.58 E
Fangxian	27	Je	32.03N	110.41 E
Fangzheng	27	Mb	45.50N	128.49 E
Fangzi	28	Ef	36.36N	119.08 E
Fanjiatun	28	Hc	43.42N	125.05 E
Fanjing Shan	27	If	27.57N	108.50 E
Fannårken	8	Bc	61.31N	7.55 E
Fanning → Tabuaeran Atoll	57	Ld	3.52N	159.20W
Fano	14	Hg	43.50N	13.01 E
Fanø	8	Ci	55.25N	8.25 E
Fanø Bugt	8	Ci	55.25N	8.10 E
Fanshi	28	Be	39.11N	113.16 E
Fan Si Pan	21	Lg	22.15N	103.50 E
Fan Si Pan	25	Kd	22.18N	103.46 E
Fanuatapu	65c	Ba	13.59 S	171.20W
Fanxian	28	Cg	35.53N	115.29 E
Fanø	24	Dg	30.44N	31.48 E
Faon	18	Dc	39.12N	63.38 E
Faraba	34	Cc	12.52N	11.23W
Faraday	66	Qe	65.15 S	64.15W
Faraday Seamounts (EN)	30	Eb	39.30N	28.30W
Faradje	36	Eb	3.44N	29.43 E
Faradofay	31	Lk	25.01 S	46.59 E
Farafangana	37	Hd	22.48 S	47.50 E
Farāfirah, Wāḥat al- = Farafra Oasis (EN)	30	Jf	27.15N	28.10 E
Farafra Oasis (EN) = Farāfirah, Wāḥat al-	30	Jf	27.15N	28.10 E
Farāh	21	If	31.29N	61.24 E
Farāh	22	If	32.22N	62.07 E
Farāh	23	Jc	30.00N	62.30 E
Far'ah, Wādī al-	24	Hj	24.02N	38.09 E
Farahābād	24	Od	36.47N	53.06 E
Faranah	34	Cd	10.02N	10.44W
Farasan	23	Ff	16.42N	42.00 E
Farasan, Jazā'ir-	23	Ff	16.48N	41.54 E
Farasān al Kabīr	33	Hf	16.42N	42.00 E
Faraulep Atoll	57	Hd	8.36N	144.33 E
Farcău, Vîrful-	15	Hb	47.55N	24.27 E
Farciennes	12	Gd	50.26N	4.33 E
Fardes	13	Jg	37.33N	3.00W
Fare	65e	Db	16.42 S	151.01W
Fareham	9	Lk	50.51N	1.10W
Farewell, Cape-	57	Ii	40.30 S	172.43 E
Farewell Spit	62	Ed	40.30 S	172.50 E
Färgelanda	8	Df	58.34N	11.59 E
Fargo	39	Je	46.52N	96.48W
Faribault	45	Jd	44.18N	93.16W
Faribault, Lac-	42	Ke	58.00N	72.00W

Index Symbols

[1] Independent Nation	Historical or Cultural Region
[2] State, Region	Mount, Mountain
[3] District, County	Volcano
[4] Municipality	Hill
[5] Colony, Dependency	Mountains, Mountain Range
Continent	Hills, Escarpment
Physical Region	Plateau, Upland

Pass, Gap	Depression
Plain, Lowland	Polder
Delta	Desert, Dunes
Salt Flat	Forest, Woods
Valley, Canyon	Heath, Steppe
Crater, Cave	Oasis
Karst Features	Cape, Point

Coast, Beach	Rock, Reef
Cliff	Islands, Archipelago
Peninsula	Rocks, Reefs
Isthmus	Coral Reef
Sandbank	Well, Spring
Island	Geyser
Atoll	River, Stream

Waterfall Rapids	Canal
River Mouth, Estuary	Bank
Lake	Seamount
Salt Lake	Ocean
Intermittent Lake	Sea
Reservoir	Gulf, Bay
Swamp, Pond	Strait, Fjord

Lagoon	Escarpment, Sea Scarp
Fracture	Ruins
Trench, Abyss	Wall, Walls
Tablemount	National Park, Reserve
Ridge	Point of Interest
Shelf	Recreation Site
Basin	Cave, Cavern

Historic Site	Port
Lighthouse	Mine
Church, Abbey	Temple
Scientific Station	Airport
Dam, Bridge	Tunnel

Farīd, Qarāt al- 24 Ch 28.43N 28.21 E
Faridpur 25 Hd 23.36N 89.50 E
Färila 7 Df 61.48N 15.51 E
Farilhões, Ilhas- 13 Ce 39.28N 9.34W
Farim 34 Bc 12.29N 15.13W
Farini d'Olmo 14 Df 44.43N 9.34 E
Fāris 24 Ej 24.37N 32.54 E
Fariš 18 Fd 40.33N 66.52 E
Fāris 35 Ia 20.11N 50.56 E
Faris Seamount (EN) 40 Jf 54.30N 147.15W
Färjestaden 7 Dh 56.39N 16.27 E
Farkadhón 15 Fj 39.36N 22.04 E
Farmahīn 24 Me 34.30N 49.41 E
Farmakonisi 15 Kl 37.18N 27.08 E
Farmerville 45 Jj 32.47N 92.24W
Farmington [Me.-U.S.] 44 Lc 44.40N 70.09W
Farmington [Mo.-U.S.] 45 Kh 37.47N 90.25W
Farmington [N.M.-U.S.] 43 Fd 36.44N 108.12W
Farmville 44 Hg 37.17N 78.25W
Färnäs 8 Fc 61.00N 14.38 E
Farnborough 12 Bc 51.16N 0.44W
Farne Deep 9 Mf 55.30N 0.50W
Farne Islands 9 Lf 55.38N 1.38W
Farnham [Eng.-U.K.] 12 Bc 51.12N 0.48W
Farnham [Que.-Can.] 44 Kc 45.17N 72.59W
Farnham, Mount- 46 Ga 50.29N 116.30W
Farö 7 Eh 57.55N 19.10 E
Faro 34 Hd 9.21N 12.55 E
Faro [2] 13 Dg 37.12N 8.10W
Faro 6 Fh 37.01N 7.56W
Faro, Punta- 49 Jh 11.07N 74.51W
Faro, Sierra del- 13 Eb 42.37N 7.55W
Faro de Avión 13 Db 42.18N 8.16W
Faro de Chantada 13 Eb 42.37N 7.55W
Farofa, Serra da- 55 Gh 28.00S 50.10W
Farosund 8 Hg 57.55N 19.05 E
Fårösund 7 Eh 57.52N 19.03 E
Farquhar, Cape- 59 Cd 23.35S 113.35 E
Farquhar Group 30 Mj 10.10S 51.10 E
Farrar 9 Id 57.27N 4.35W
Farrāshband 24 Oh 28.53N 52.06 E
Farris 8 Ce 59.05N 10.00 E
Farruch, Cabo- 13 Pe 39.47N 3.21 E
Farrukhābād 25 Fc 27.24N 79.34 E
Fārs 21 Hg 29.00N 53.00 E
Fārs [3] 23 Hd 29.00N 53.00 E
Fārsābād 24 Mc 39.30N 48.05 E
Fársala 15 Fj 39.18N 22.23 E
Farshūţ 24 Ei 26.03N 32.09 E
Farsø 8 Ch 56.47N 9.21 E
Farsund 7 Bg 58.05N 6.48 E
Fartak, Ra's- 23 Hf 15.38N 52.15 E
Fartura, Rio- 55 Gc 16.29S 50.33W
Fartura, Serra da- [Braz.] 55 Hf 23.20S 49.25W
Fartura, Serra da- [Braz.] 55 Fh 26.21S 52.52W
Fārūj 24 Rd 37.14N 58.14 E
Farvel, Kap-/ Ūmánarssuaq 67 Nb 59.50N 43.50W
Farwell Island 66 Pf 72.49S 91.10W
Fāryāb [3] 23 Jb 36.00N 65.00 E
Fasā 24 Oh 28.56N 53.42 E
Fasano 14 Lj 40.50N 17.22 E
Fastnet Rock 9 Dj 51.24N 9.35W
Fastov 19 De 50.06N 30.01 E
Fataka Island 57 If 11.55S 170.12 E
Fatala 34 Cc 10.13N 14.00W
Fatehpur 25 Ec 28.01N 74.58 E
Fatež 16 Ic 52.06N 35.52 E
Father Lake 44 Ja 49.24N 75.18W
Fatick 34 Bc 14.20N 16.25W
Fátima 13 De 39.37N 8.39W
Fatīrah, Wādī- 24 Ei 26.39N 32.58 E
Fatsa 24 Gb 40.59N 37.24 E
Fatu Hiva, Ile- 57 Nf 10.28S 138.38W
Fatu Hutu, Ile- 57 Ne 9.00S 138.50W
Fatumanini, Passe- 64h Ab 13.14S 176.13W
Fatunda 36 Cc 4.08S 17.13 E
Fauabu 63a Ec 8.34S 160.43 E
Faucigny 11 Mh 46.05N 6.35 E
Faucille, Col de la- 11 Mh 46.22N 6.02 E
Faulkton 45 Gd 45.02N 99.08W
Faulquemont 12 Ie 49.03N 6.36 E
Fauquembergues 12 Ed 50.36N 2.05 E
Făurei 15 Kd 45.04N 27.14 E
Fauro 63a Cb 6.55S 156.07 E
Fauske 7 Dc 67.15N 15.24 E
Fauville-en-Caux 12 Ce 49.39N 0.35 E
Faux-Lap 37 He 25.32S 45.30 E
Fåvang 8 Dc 61.26N 10.13 E
Favara 14 Hm 37.19N 13.39 E
Faversham 12 Cc 51.19N 0.54 E
Favignana 14 Gm 37.55N 12.19 E
Favignana 14 Gm 37.56N 12.20 E
Favorite 12 Kf 48.49N 8.16 E
Fawley 12 Ad 50.49N 1.21W
Fawn 42 Ie 55.22N 88.20W
Fa'w Qiblī 24 Ei 26.07N 32.24 E
Faxaflói 5 Dc 64.24N 23.00W
Faxinal 55 Gf 23.59S 51.22W
Faya-Largeau 31 Ig 17.55N 19.07 E
Fayaoué 63b Ce 20.39S 166.32 E
Fayd 24 Ji 27.07N 42.31 E
Fayette [Al.-U.S.] 44 Di 33.42N 87.50W
Fayette [Oh.-U.S.] 44 Ee 41.41N 84.20W
Fayetteville [Ar.-U.S.] 43 Id 36.04N 94.10W
Fayetteville [N.C.-U.S.] 39 Lf 35.03N 78.54W
Fayetteville [Tn.-U.S.] 44 Dh 35.09N 86.35W
Faylakah, Jazīrat- 24 Mh 29.27N 48.20 E
Faysh Khābūr 24 Jd 37.04N 42.23 E
Fayu Island 57 Gd 8.35N 151.22 E
Fazenda de Cima 55 Db 15.56S 56.37W
Fazenda Nova 55 Gc 16.11S 50.48W
Fāzilka 25 Eb 30.24N 74.02 E
Fazrān 24 Mi 26.13N 49.12 E
Fazzān = Fezzan (EN) 33 Bd 25.30N 14.00 E
Fazzān = Fezzan (EN) 30 If 26.00N 14.00 E
Fdérick 31 Ff 22.39N 12.43W
Feale/An Fhéil 9 Di 52.28N 9.40W
Fear, Cape- 43 Le 33.50N 77.58W
Featherston 62 Fd 41.07S 175.19 E
Feathertop, Mount- 59 Jg 36.54S 147.08 E
Fécamp 11 Ge 49.45N 0.22 E
Fecht 11 Nf 48.11N 7.26 E
Federacion 56 Id 31.00S 57.54W
Federal 56 Id 30.55S 58.45W
Federated States of Micronesia [5] 58 Gd 6.30N 152.00 E
Federovka [Kaz.-U.S.S.R.] 19 Ge 53.38N 62.42 E
Federovka [R.S.F.S.R.] 17 Gj 53.10N 55.10 E
Federsee 10 Fh 48.05N 9.38 E
Fedje 7 Af 60.47N 4.42 E
Fedorovka 16 Qd 51.16N 52.00 E
Fefan 64d Bb 7.21N 151.51 E
Fegen 8 Eg 57.11N 13.09 E
Fegen 8 Eg 57.06N 13.02 E
Fehérgyarmat 10 Si 47.59N 22.31 E
Fehmarn 10 Hb 54.30N 11.10 E
Fehmarnbelt 8 Dj 54.35N 11.15 E
Fehrbellin 10 Id 52.48N 12.46 E
Feicheng 28 Df 36.15N 116.46 E
Feidong (Dianbu) 28 Di 31.53N 117.29 E
Fei Huang He 28 Fg 34.15N 120.17 E
Feijó 54 De 8.09S 70.21W
Feilding 61 Eh 40.12S 175.35 E
Feira 36 Ff 15.37S 30.25 E
Feira de Santana 53 Mg 12.15S 38.57W
Feiran Oasis 24 Eh 28.42N 33.38 E
Feistritz 14 Kc 47.01N 16.08 E
Feixi (Shangpaihe) 28 Di 31.42N 117.09 E
Feixian 28 Dg 35.16N 117.59 E
Feixiang 28 Cf 36.32N 114.47 E
Fejão Prêto ou Furtado, Rio- 55 Dc 17.33S 57.23W
Fejér [2] 10 Oi 47.10N 18.35 E
Fejø 8 Dj 54.55N 11.25 E
Feke 24 Fd 37.53N 35.58 E
Fekete-viz 10 Ok 45.47N 18.13 E
Felanitx 13 Pe 39.28N 3.08 E
Feldbach 14 Jd 46.57N 15.53 E
Feldioara 15 Id 45.49N 25.36 E
Feldkirch 14 Dc 47.14N 9.36 E
Feldkirchen 14 Id 46.43N 14.06 E
Feliciano, Arroyo- 55 Cj 31.06S 59.54W
Felidu Atoll 25a Bb 3.30N 73.30 E
Felipe Carrillo Puerto 47 Ge 19.35N 88.03W
Felix, Cape - 42 Hc 69.55N 97.47W
Felixlândia 55 Jd 18.47S 44.55W
Felixstowe 9 Oi 51.58N 1.20 E
Felletin 11 Ii 45.53N 2.11 E
Feltre 14 Fd 46.01N 11.54 E
Femer Bælt 8 Dj 54.35N 11.15 E
Femø 8 Dj 54.55N 11.35 E
Femund 7 Ce 62.15N 11.50 E
Fena Valley Reservoir 64c Bb 13.20N 144.45 E
Fener Burnu 24 Hb 41.07N 39.25 E
Fénérive 37 Hc 17.22S 49.25 E
Fenerwa 35 Fc 13.05N 39.01 E
Fénétrange 12 Jf 48.51N 7.01 E
Fengcheng [China] 27 Lc 40.28N 124.01 E
Fengcheng [China] 28 Cj 28.11N 115.47 E
Fengdu 27 If 29.58N 107.39 E
Fenghua 28 Fj 29.40N 121.24 E
Fengjie 27 He 31.06N 104.30 E
Fenglingdu 27 Je 34.40N 110.19 E
Fengnan (Xugezhuang) 28 Ee 39.34N 118.05 E
Fengning (Dagezhen) 28 Dd 41.12N 116.39 E
Fengqing 27 Gg 24.41N 99.53 E
Fengqiu 28 Cg 35.02N 114.24 E
Fengrun 28 Ee 39.50N 118.09 E
Fengshui Shan 27 La 52.15N 123.30 E
Fengtai [China] 28 Dh 32.43N 116.43 E
Fengtai [China] 28 De 39.51N 116.17 E
Fengweiba → Zhenkang 27 Gg 23.54N 99.00 E
Fengxian 28 Dg 34.42N 116.35 E
Fengxian (Nanqiao) 28 Fi 30.55N 121.27 E
Fengxiang 27 Ie 34.32N 107.34 E
Fengxiang → Luobei 27 Nb 47.36N 130.58 E
Fengxin 28 Cj 28.42N 115.23 E
Fengyang 28 Dh 32.53N 117.33 E
Fengzhen 27 Jc 40.28N 113.09 E
Fen He [China] 27 Jd 35.36N 110.42 E
Fen He [China] 28 Ae 38.06N 111.52 E
Feni Islands 57 Ge 4.05S 153.42 E
Fennimore 45 Ke 42.59N 90.39W
Fensfjorden 8 Ad 60.50N 4.50 E
Fenshui Guan 27 Kf 27.56N 117.50 E
Fenton 44 Fd 42.48N 83.42W
Fenua Fu 64h Ac 13.23S 176.11W
Fenualoa 63c Bb 10.16S 166.15 E
Fenyang 27 Jd 37.17N 111.45 E
Feodosija 19 Df 45.02N 35.23 E
Fer, Cap de- 32 Ib 37.05N 7.10 E
Fer, Point au- 45 Kl 29.20N 91.21W
Feragen 8 Db 62.30N 11.55 E
Férai 15 Ji 40.54N 26.10 E
Ferdows 23 Ic 34.00N 58.09 E
Fère-Champenoise 11 Jf 48.45N 3.59 E
Fère-en-Tardenois 12 Fe 49.12N 3.31 E
Feren 8 Da 63.34N 11.50 E
Ferentino 14 Hi 41.42N 13.15 E
Ferfer [Eth.] 35 Hd 5.06N 45.09 E
Ferfer [Som.] 35 Hd 5.07N 45.07 E
Fergana 22 Je 40.23N 71.46 E
Fergana 21 Je 40.30N 71.00 E
Ferganskaja Oblast [3] 19 Hg 40.30N 71.20 E
Ferganskij Hrebet 19 Hg 41.00N 74.00 E
Fergus Falls 43 Hb 46.17N 96.04W
Ferguson Lake 42 Hc 69.00N 105.00W
Fergusson Island 60 Ei 9.30S 150.40 E
Ferkéssédougou [3] 34 Ed 9.20N 4.55W
Ferkéssédougou 34 Dd 9.36N 5.12W
Ferlo 30 Fg 15.00N 14.00W
Ferlo 30 Fg 15.42N 15.30W
Fermo 14 Hg 43.09N 13.43 E
Fermoselle 13 Fc 41.19N 6.23W
Fermoy/Mainistir Fhear Mai 9 Ei 52.08N 8.16W
Fernandina, Isla- 52 Gf 0.25S 91.30W
Fernandina Beach 44 Gj 30.40N 81.27W
Fernando de Noronha, Ilha- 52 Mf 3.51S 32.25W
Fernando de Noronha, Território de- [2] 54 Ld 3.50S 33.00W
Fernandópolis 56 Kb 20.16S 50.00W
Fernán-Núñez 13 Hg 37.40N 4.43W
Fernelmont 12 Hd 50.35N 5.02 E
Fernie 46 Hb 49.30N 115.03W
Ferrandina 14 Kj 40.29N 16.27 E
Ferrara 14 Ff 44.50N 11.35 E
Ferrat, Cap- 13 Li 35.54N 0.23W
Ferrato, Capo- 14 Dk 39.18N 9.38 E
Ferré 55 Bl 34.08S 61.08W
Ferré, Cap- 51h Bc 14.28N 60.49W
Ferreira do Alentejo 13 Df 38.03N 8.07W
Ferreñafe 54 Ce 6.38S 79.48W
Ferret, Cap- 11 Ej 44.37N 1.15W
Ferriday 45 Kk 31.38N 91.33W
Ferrières 12 Hd 50.24N 5.36 E
Ferro, Capo- 14 Di 41.09N 9.31 E
Ferro, Rio- 55 Ea 12.27S 54.31W
Ferru, Monte- 14 Cj 40.08N 8.36 E
Ferry, Pointe- 51e Ab 16.17N 61.49W
Fertilia 14 Cj 40.36N 8.17 E
Fertő → Neusiedler See 10 Mi 47.50N 16.45 E
Fès 32 Gc 34.02N 4.59W
Fès [3] 32 Gc 34.00N 5.00W
Feshi 36 Cd 6.07S 18.10 E
Fessenden 45 Gc 47.39N 99.38W
Festieux 12 Fe 49.31N 3.45 E
Festus 45 Kg 38.13N 90.24W
Fetești 15 Ke 44.23N 27.50 E
Fethiye 23 Cb 36.37N 29.07 E
Fethiye Körfezi 24 Cd 36.40N 29.00 E
Fetlar 9 Ma 60.37N 0.52W
Fetsund 7 Cg 59.56N 11.10 E
Feuchtwangen 10 Gg 49.10N 10.20 E
Feuilles, Baie aux - 42 Ke 58.55N 69.15W
Feuilles, Rivière aux- 42 Ke 58.46N 70.05W
Feurs 11 Ki 45.45N 4.14 E
Fevik 8 Cf 58.23N 8.42 E
Feyzābād 22 Jf 37.06N 70.34 E
Fezzan (EN) = Fazzān 33 Bd 25.30N 14.00 E
Fezzan (EN) = Fazzān 30 If 26.00N 14.00 E
Fezzane, Emi- 34 Ha 21.42N 14.15 E
Ffestiniog 9 Ji 52.58N 3.55W
Fiambalá 56 Gc 27.41S 67.38W
Fianarantsoa 31 Lk 21.28S 47.05 E
Fianarantsoa [3] 37 Hd 21.30S 47.05 E
Fianga 35 Bd 9.55N 15.09 E
Fiche 35 Fd 9.48N 38.44 E
Fichtelgebirge 10 He 50.00N 12.00 E
Ficksburg 37 De 28.57S 27.50 E
Fidenza 14 Ef 44.52N 10.03 E
Fieni 15 Id 45.08N 25.25 E
Fier 11 Li 45.56N 5.51 E
Fieri 15 Ci 40.43N 19.34 E
Fife [3] 9 Je 56.05N 3.15W
Fife Ness 9 Ke 56.17N 2.36W
Fiffa 34 Dc 11.27N 9.52W
Fifth Cataract (EN) = Khāmis, Ash Shallāl al- 30 Kg 18.23N 33.47 E
Figalo, Cap- 13 Ki 35.35N 1.12W
Figeac 11 Ij 44.36N 2.02 E
Figeholm 8 Gg 57.22N 16.33 E
Figtree 37 Dd 20.22S 28.20 E
Figueira, Baia da- 55 Dc 16.33S 57.25W
Figueira da Foz 13 Dd 40.09N 8.52W
Figueira de Castelo Rodrigo 13 Fd 40.54N 6.58W
Figueras 13 Ob 42.16N 2.58 E
Figueras/Figueres 13 Ob 42.16N 2.58 E
Figueres 13 Ob 42.16N 2.58 E
Figueres/Figueras 13 Ob 42.16N 2.58 E
Figuig [3] 32 Gc 33.00N 2.01W
Figuig 31 Ge 32.06N 1.14W
Fiherenana 37 Gd 23.19S 43.37 E
Fijāj, Shaţţ al- 32 Ic 33.55N 9.10 E
Fiji [1] 58 If 18.00S 178.00 E
Fiji Islands 57 If 18.00S 178.00 E
Fik 35 Gd 8.08N 42.18 E
Filabres, Sierra de los- 13 Jg 37.15N 2.20W
Filabusi 37 Dd 20.32S 29.16 E
Filadélfia 54 Ie 7.21S 47.30W
Filadelfia [C.R.] 49 Eh 10.26N 85.34W
Filadelfia [It.] 14 Kl 38.47N 16.17 E
Filakara 63b Dc 16.49S 168.24 E
Filákovo 10 Ph 48.16N 19.50 E
Filamana 34 Dc 10.30N 7.57W
Filatova Gora 8 Mg 57.39N 28.21 E
Filchner Ice Shelf 66 Af 79.00S 40.00W
Filey 9 Mg 54.12N 0.17W
Filiaşi 15 Ge 44.33N 23.31 E
Filiátai 15 Dj 39.36N 20.49 E
Filiatrá 15 El 37.09N 21.35 E
Filicudi 14 Il 38.35N 14.35 E
Filingué 34 Fc 14.21N 3.19 E
Filiouri 15 Ii 40.57N 25.20 E
Filippiás 15 Dj 39.12N 20.53 E
Filippoi 15 Hh 41.02N 24.20 E
Filippoi = Philippi (EN) 15 Hh 41.02N 24.18 E
Filipstad 7 Dg 59.43N 14.10 E
Fillefjell 8 Cc 61.09N 8.15 E
Filliévres 12 Ed 50.19N 2.10 E
Fillmore 46 Ig 38.58N 112.20W
Fils 10 Fh 48.35N 9.29 E
Filtu 35 Gd 5.06N 40.40 E
Fimaina 15 Jl 37.35N 26.26 E
Fimi 30 Ii 3.01S 16.58 E
Fin [Iran] 24 Pi 27.38N 55.55 E
Fin [Iran] 24 Nf 33.57N 51.24 E
Finale Emilia 14 Ff 44.50N 11.17 E
Finale Ligure 14 Cf 44.10N 8.20 E
Findhorn 9 Jd 57.41N 3.32W
Fındıklı 24 Ib 41.17N 41.09 E
Findlay 43 Kc 41.02N 83.40W
Findlay, Mount- 46 Ga 50.04N 116.28W
Findlay Group 42 Ha 77.15N 104.00W
Fineveke 64h Ab 13.19S 176.12W
Fingoé 37 Ec 15.10S 31.53 E
Finike 24 Dd 36.18N 30.09 E
Finistère [3] 11 Cf 48.20N 4.00W
Finisterre, Cabo de- 5 Fg 42.53N 9.16W
Finisterre Range 59 Ja 5.50S 146.05 E
Finke 58 Eg 25.34S 134.35 E
Finke, Mount- 59 Gf 30.55S 134.02 E
Finke River 57 Eg 27.00S 136.10 E
Finland/Suomi [1] 6 Ic 64.00N 26.00 E
Finland, Gulf of- (EN) = Finski Zaliv 5 Ic 60.00N 27.00 E
Finland, Gulf of- (EN) = Soomenlaht 5 Ic 60.00N 27.00 E
Finland, Gulf of- (EN) = Suomenlahti 5 Ic 60.00N 27.00 E
Finlay 42 Fe 55.59N 123.50W
Finlay Mountains 45 Dk 31.30N 105.35W
Finne 10 He 51.13N 11.19 E
Finngrunden 8 Hc 61.00N 18.19 E
Finnigan, Mount- 59 Jc 15.50S 145.20 E
Finniss, Cape- 59 Gf 33.38S 134.51 E
Finnmark 8 Fc 61.40N 14.45 E
Finnmark [3] 7 Fb 69.50N 24.10 E
Finnmarksvidda 5 Ib 69.30N 24.20 E
Finnøy 8 Ae 59.10N 5.50 E
Finnskogen 8 Ed 60.40N 12.40 E
Finnsnes 7 Eb 69.14N 18.02 E
Finnveden 8 Eh 56.50N 13.40 E
Finote Selam 35 Fc 10.42N 37.12 E
Finschhafen 59 Ja 6.35S 147.50 E
Finse 8 Bd 60.36N 7.30 E
Finski Zaliv = Finland, Gulf of- (EN) 5 Ic 60.00N 27.00 E
Finspång 7 Dg 58.43N 15.47 E
Finstadåa 8 Dc 61.47N 11.10 E
Finsteraarhorn 14 Cd 46.32N 8.08 E
Finsterwalde 10 Je 51.38N 13.43 E
Finström 8 Hd 60.16N 19.50 E
Fiora 14 Fh 42.20N 11.34 E
Fiorenzuola d'Arda 14 Df 44.56N 9.55 E
Firat = Euphrates (EN) 21 Gf 31.00N 47.25 E
Firenze = Florence (EN) 6 Hg 43.46N 11.15 E
Firenzuola 14 Ff 44.07N 11.23 E
Firmat 55 Bk 33.27S 61.29W
Firminópolis 55 Gc 16.40S 50.19W
Firminy 11 Ki 45.23N 4.18 E
Firozābād 25 Fc 27.09N 78.25 E
Firozpur 25 Eb 30.55N 74.36 E
First Cataract (EN) = Aswān, Sadd al- 30 Kf 24.01N 32.52 E
Fīrūzābād 24 Oh 28.50N 52.36 E
Fīrūzābād 24 Pg 31.59N 54.20 E
Fīrūzābād 24 Le 34.09N 46.25 E
Fīrūz Kūh 24 Oe 35.45N 52.47 E
Fischach 12 Je 49.44N 7.24 E
Fischbacher Alpen 14 Jc 47.25N 15.30 E
Fischland 10 Ib 54.22N 12.25 E
Fish [Nam.] 30 Ik 17.11S 28.08 E
Fish [S.Afr.] 37 Cf 31.14S 20.15 E
Fisher Glacier 66 Ef 73.15S 66.00 E
Fisher Peak 44 Gg 36.33N 80.50W
Fisher Strait 42 Jd 63.00N 84.00W
Fishguard 6 Fe 51.59N 4.59W
Fish River' Canyon 37 Be 27.35S 17.35 E
Fiskárdhon 15 Dk 38.28N 20.35 E
Fiskenaes Bank (EN) 41 Gf 63.18N 52.10W
Fiskenæsset 41 Gf 63.10N 50.45W
Fismes 12 Fe 49.18N 3.41 E
Fišt, Gora- 19 Dg 43.57N 39.55 E
Fitchburg 44 Ld 42.35N 71.48W
Fitjar 7 Ag 59.55N 5.20 E
Fito, Mount- 65c Ba 13.55S 171.44W
Fitri, Lac- 35 Bc 12.50N 17.28 E
Fitzcarrald 54 Df 11.49S 71.48W
Fitzgerald [Alta.-Can.] 42 Ge 59.52N 111.40W
Fitzgerald [Ga.-U.S.] 44 Fj 31.43N 83.15W
Fitzroy Crossing 59 Fc 18.11S 125.35 E
Fitzroy River [Austl.] 59 Kc 23.32S 150.52 E
Fitzroy River [Austl.] 57 Df 17.31S 123.35 E
Fitzwilliam Island 44 Gc 45.30N 81.45W
Fiuggi 14 Hi 41.48N 13.13 E
Fiumicino 14 Gi 41.46N 12.14 E
Five Island Harbour 51d Bb 17.06N 61.54W
Fivizzano 14 Ef 44.14N 10.08 E
Fizi 31 Ji 4.18S 28.57 E
Fizuli 19 Eh 39.35N 47.11 E
Fjærlandsfjorden 8 Bc 61.15N 6.40 E
Fjällbacka 8 Df 58.36N 11.17 E
Fjärås 7 Ch 57.26N 12.09 E
Fjerritslev 8 Cg 57.05N 9.16 E
Fjöllum, Jökulsá á- 7a Ca 66.02N 16.27W
Fjugesta 8 Fe 59.10N 14.52 E
Flacq 37a Bb 20.12S 57.43 E
Flade Isblink 41 Kb 81.25N 16.00W
Fladen 8 Dg 57.07N 11.35 E
Fladen 8 Dg 57.10N 11.45 E
Flagler 45 Eg 39.18N 103.04W
Flagstaff 39 Hf 35.12N 111.39W
Flåm 7 Bf 60.50N 7.07 E
Flamborough Head 9 Mg 54.07N 0.04W
Fläming 10 Ie 52.00N 13.00 E
Flaming Gorge Reservoir 46 Kf 41.15N 109.30W
Flamingo 44 Gm 25.09N 80.56W
Flamingo, Teluk- 26 Kh 5.33S 138.00 E
Flanders (EN) = Flandres/Vlaanderen 5 Ge 51.00N 3.20 E
Flanders (EN) = Flandres/Vlaanderen 11 Jc 51.00N 3.20 E
Flanders (EN) = Vlaanderen/Flandres 5 Ge 51.00N 3.20 E
Flanders (EN) = Vlaanderen/Flandres 11 Jc 51.00N 3.20 E
Flanders Plain (EN) = Flandres, Plaine des- 11 Id 50.40N 2.50 E
Flanders Plain (EN) = Vlamse Vlakte 11 Id 50.40N 2.50 E
Flandreau 45 Hd 44.03N 96.36W
Flandres/Vlaanderen = Flanders (EN) 11 Jc 51.00N 3.20 E
Flandres/Vlaanderen = Flanders (EN) 5 Ge 51.00N 3.20 E
Flandres, Plaine des- = Flanders Plain (EN) 11 Id 50.40N 2.50 E
Flannan Isles 9 Fc 58.20N 7.35W
Flåren 8 Fh 57.00N 14.05 E
Flasher 45 Fc 46.27N 101.14W
Fläsjön 7 Dd 64.06N 15.51 E
Flat 40 Hd 62.27N 158.01W
Flatey 7a Ab 65.22N 22.56W
Flateyri 7a Aa 66.03N 23.31W
Flathead Lake 43 Eb 47.52N 114.08W
Flathead Range 46 Ib 48.05N 113.28W
Flathead River 46 Hc 47.22N 114.47W
Flat Point 51b Ab 18.15N 63.05W
Flat River 45 Kh 37.51N 90.31W
Flattery, Cape- 38 Ge 48.23N 124.43W
Flåvatnet 8 Ce 59.20N 8.50 E
Flaxton 45 Eb 48.54N 102.24W
Flaygreen Lake 42 Hf 53.50N 97.20W
Fleckenstein, Château de- 12 Je 49.05N 7.48 E
Fleet 12 Bc 51.17N 0.50W
Fleetwood 9 Jh 53.56N 3.01W
Flekkefjord 7 Bg 58.17N 6.41 E
Flémalle 12 Hd 50.36N 5.29 E
Flemish Bight [Eur.] 11 Dc 51.44N 2.30W
Flemish Bight [U.K.] 9 Pi 52.10N 2.50 E
Flemish Cap (EN) 38 Oe 47.00N 45.00W
Flemsøya 8 Bb 62.40N 6.20 E
Flen 7 Dg 59.04N 16.35 E
Flensborg Fjord 8 Cj 54.50N 9.45 E
Flensburg 6 Ge 54.47N 9.26 E
Flensburger Förde 8 Cj 54.50N 9.45 E
Flers 11 Ff 48.45N 0.34W
Flesberg 8 Ce 59.51N 9.27 E
Fleurance 11 Gk 43.50N 0.40 E
Fleury-sur-Andelle 12 De 49.22N 1.21 E
Fleuve [3] 34 Cb 16.00N 13.50W
Flevoland 11 Lb 52.25N 5.30 E
Flian 8 Ef 58.27N 13.05 E
Flims 14 Dd 46.50N 9.16 E
Flinders Bay 59 Df 34.25S 115.19 E
Flinders Island 57 Fi 40.00S 148.00 E
Flinders Passage 59 Jc 18.50S 149.00 E
Flinders Ranges 57 Eh 31.25S 138.45 E
Flinders Reefs 57 Ff 17.40S 148.30 E
Flinders River 57 Ff 17.36S 140.36 E
Flin Flon 39 Id 54.56N 101.53W
Flint [Mi.-U.S.] 39 Ke 43.01N 83.41W
Flint [Wales-U.K.] 9 Jh 53.15N 3.07W
Flint Hills 45 Hh 37.20N 96.35W
Flint Island 57 Lf 11.26S 151.48W
Flint River 43 Ke 30.52N 84.38W
Flisa 7 Cf 60.37N 12.04 E
Flisa 8 Ed 60.36N 12.01 E
Flisegga 8 Be 59.50N 7.50 E
Flitwick 12 Bb 52.00N 0.29W
Flix 13 Mc 41.14N 0.33 E
Flixecourt 12 Ed 50.01N 2.05 E
Flize 12 Ge 49.42N 4.46 E
Flobecq/Vloesberg 12 Fd 50.44N 3.44 E
Floby 8 Ef 58.08N 13.20 E
Floda [Swe.] 8 Fd 60.26N 14.49 E
Floda [Swe.] 8 Eg 57.48N 12.22 E
Flood Range 66 Nf 76.03S 134.00W
Flora [Il.-U.S.] 45 Lg 38.40N 88.29W
Flora [Nor.] 7 Af 61.36N 5.00 E
Florac 11 Jj 44.19N 3.36 E
Florala 44 Dj 31.00N 86.20W
Florange 12 Ie 49.20N 6.07 E
Florence [Al.-U.S.] 43 Je 34.49N 87.40W
Florence [Ks.-U.S.] 45 Hg 38.15N 96.56W
Florence [Or.-U.S.] 46 Cd 44.01N 124.07W
Florence [S.C.-U.S.] 43 Le 34.12N 79.44W
Florence (EN) = Firenze 6 Hg 43.46N 11.15 E
Florencia [Arg.] 55 Ci 28.02S 59.15W
Florencia [Col.] 53 Ie 1.36N 75.36W
Florencio Sánchez 55 Dk 33.53S 57.24W
Florennes 12 Gd 50.15N 4.37 E
Florentino Ameghino, Embalse- 56 Gf 43.48S 66.25W
Florenville 11 Le 49.42N 5.18 E
Flores [2] 55 Dk 33.35S 56.50W
Flores 30 De 39.26N 31.13W
Flores [Guat.] 47 Ge 16.56N 89.53W
Flores [Guat.] 49 Ce 16.58N 89.50W
Flores, Arroyo de las- 55 Cl 35.36S 59.01W
Flores, Laut- = Flores Sea (EN) 21 Oj 8.00S 121.00 E
Flores, Pulau- 21 Oj 8.30S 121.00 E
Flores Island 46 Bb 49.20N 126.10W
Flores Sea (EN) = Flores, Laut- 21 Oj 8.00S 121.00 E
Florești 16 Ff 47.55N 28.18 E
Floriano 53 Lf 6.47S 43.01W
Florianópolis 53 Lh 27.35S 48.34W
Florida 38 Kg 28.00N 82.00W
Florida [Braz.] 55 Ei 29.15S 54.36W
Florida [Cuba] 47 Id 21.32N 78.14W
Florida [U.S.] [2] 43 Kf 28.00N 82.00W
Florida [Ur.] [2] 55 Ek 33.50S 55.55W
Florida [Ur.] 55 Dk 34.06S 56.13W
Florida, Estrecho de- = Florida, Straits of- (EN) 38 Kg 24.00N 81.00W
Florida, Straits of- 38 Kg 24.00N 81.00W
Florida, Straits of- (EN) = Florida, Estrecho de- 38 Kg 24.00N 81.00W
Florida Bay 44 Gm 25.00N 80.45W
Floridablanca 54 Db 7.04N 73.06W

Index Symbols

[1] Independent Nation
[2] State, Region
[3] District, County
[5] Municipality
Colony, Dependency
Continent
Physical Region
Historical or Cultural Region
Mount, Mountain
Volcano
Hill
Mountains, Mountain Range
Hills, Escarpment
Plateau, Upland
Pass, Gap
Plain, Lowland
Delta
Salt Flat
Valley, Canyon
Crater, Cave
Karst Features
Depression
Polder
Desert, Dunes
Forest, Woods
Heath, Steppe
Oasis
Cape, Point
Coast, Beach
Cliff
Peninsula
Isthmus
Sandbank
Island
Atoll
Rock, Reef
Islands, Archipelago
Rocks, Reefs
Coral Reef
Well, Spring
Geyser
River, Stream
Waterfall Rapids
River Mouth, Estuary
Lake
Salt Lake
Intermittent Lake
Reservoir
Swamp, Pond
Canal
Glacier
Ice Shelf, Pack Ice
Ocean
Sea
Gulf, Bay
Strait, Fjord
Lagoon
Bank
Seamount
Tablemount
Ridge
Shelf
Basin
Escarpment, Sea Scarp
Fracture
Trench, Abyss
National Park, Reserve
Point of Interest
Recreation Site
Cave, Cavern
Historic Site
Ruins
Wall, Walls
Church, Abbey
Temple
Scientific Station
Airport
Port
Lighthouse
Mine
Tunnel
Dam, Bridge

Index Symbols

- [1] Independent Nation
- [2] State, Region
- [3] District, County
- [4] Municipality
- [5] Colony, Dependency
- ■ Continent
- Physical Region
- Historical or Cultural Region
- Mount, Mountain
- Volcano
- Hill
- Mountains, Mountain Range
- Hills, Escarpment
- Plateau, Upland
- Pass, Gap
- Plain, Lowland
- Delta
- Salt Flat
- Valley, Canyon
- Crater, Cave
- Karst Features
- Depression
- Polder
- Desert, Dunes
- Forest, Woods
- Heath, Steppe
- Oasis
- Cape, Point
- Coast, Beach
- Cliff
- Peninsula
- Isthmus
- Sandbank
- Island
- Atoll
- Rock, Reef
- Islands, Archipelago
- Rocks, Reefs
- Coral Reef
- Well, Spring
- Geyser
- River, Stream
- Waterfall Rapids
- River Mouth, Estuary
- Lake
- Salt Lake
- Intermittent Lake
- Reservoir
- Swamp, Pond
- Canal
- Glacier
- Ice Shelf, Pack Ice
- Ocean
- Sea
- Gulf, Bay
- Strait, Fjord
- Lagoon
- Bank
- Seamount
- Tablemount
- Ridge
- Shelf
- Basin
- Escarpment, Sea Scarp
- Fracture
- Trench, Abyss
- National Park, Reserve
- Point of Interest
- Recreation Site
- Cave, Cavern
- Historic Site
- Ruins
- Wall, Walls
- Church, Abbey
- Temple
- Scientific Station
- Airport
- Port
- Lighthouse
- Mine
- Tunnel
- Dam, Bridge

Friesoythe 10 Dc 53.01N 7.51 E
Frigate Island 51p Cb 12.25N 61.29W
Friggesund 8 Gc 61.54N 16.32 E
Frignano 14 Ef 44.20N 10.50 E
Frindsbury Reef 63a Da 5.00S 159.07 E
Frinnaryd 8 Fg 57.56N 14.49 E
Frinton-on-Sea 12 Dc 51.50N 1.15 E
Frio, Cabo- 52 Lh 22.53S 42.00W
Frio, Rio- 49 Eh 11.08N 84.46W
Frio Draw 45 Ei 34.50N 102.08W
Friona 45 Ei 34.38N 102.43W
Frio River 45 Gl 28.30N 98.10W
Frisco Peak 46 Ig 38.31N 113.14W
Frisian Islands (EN) 5 Ge 54.00N 7.00 E
Fristad 8 Eg 57.50N 13.01 E
Fritsla 8 Eg 57.33N 12.47 E
Fritzlar 10 Fe 51.08N 9.17 E
Friuli 14 Ge 46.00N 13.00 E
Friuli-Venezia Giulia 14 Gd 46.00N 13.00 E
Frobisher Bay 39 Mc 63.44N 68.28W
Frobisher Bay 38 Mc 62.30N 66.00W
Frobisher Lake 42 Ge 56.20N 108.20W
Froidchapelle 12 Gd 50.09N 4.20 E
Froissy 12 Ee 49.34N 2.13 E
Frolovo 16 Ef 49.45N 43.39 E
Fromberg 46 Kd 45.23N 108.54W
Frombork 10 Pb 54.22N 19.41 E
Frome 9 Kj 51.14N 2.20W
Frome, Lake- 57 Eh 30.50S 139.50 E
Frondenberg 12 Jc 51.28N 7.46 E
Fronteira 13 Ee 39.03N 7.39W
Fronteiras 54 Je 7.05S 40.37W
Frontera 48 Mh 18.32N 92.38W
Frontera, Punta- 48 Mh 19.36N 92.42W
Fronteras 48 Eb 30.56N 109.31W
Frontignan 11 Jk 43.27N 3.45 E
Frontino, Paramo- 54 Cb 6.28N 76.04W
Front Range 38 If 39.45N 105.45W
Front Royal 44 Hf 38.56N 78.13W
Frosinone 14 Hi 41.38N 13.19 E
Frösö 8 Fa 63.11N 14.32 E
Frostburg 44 Hf 39.39N 78.56W
Frost Glacier 66 Ie 67.05S 129.00 E
Frövi 8 Fe 59.28N 15.22 E
Frøya 7 Be 63.43N 8.42 E
Frøysjøen 8 Ac 61.50N 5.05 E
Frozen Strait 42 Jc 65.50N 84.30W
Fruges 11 Id 50.31N 2.08 E
Frunze [Kirg.-U.S.S.R.] 18 Hd 40.06N 71.45 E
Frunze [Kirg.-U.S.S.R.] 22 Je 42.54N 74.36 E
Frunzovka 15 Mb 47.20N 29.37 E
Fruška Gora 15 Cd 45.10N 19.35 E
Frutal 54 Ih 20.02S 48.55W
Frutigen 14 Bd 46.35N 7.40 E
Fry Canyon 46 Jh 37.38N 110.08W
Frýdek Místek 10 Og 49.41N 18.22 E
Frylinckspan 37 Ce 26.46S 22.28 E
Ftéri 15 Ej 39.09N 21.33 E
Fua'amotu 65b Ac 21.15S 175.08W
Fua Mulaku Island 25a Bc 0.15S 73.30 E
Fu'an 27 Kf 27.10N 119.44 E
Fu-chien Sheng → Fujian Sheng = Fukien (EN) 27 Kf 26.00N 118.00 E
Fuchskauten 10 Ef 50.40N 8.05 E
Fuchū [Jap.] 29 Cd 34.34N 133.14 E
Fuchū [Jap.] 29 Fd 35.41N 139.28 E
Fuchun-Jiang 28 Fi 30.15N 120.15 E
Fuchunjiang-Shuiku 28 Ej 29.29N 119.31 E
Fucino, Conca del- 14 Hj 42.01N 13.31 E
Fudai 29 Ga 40.01N 141.52 E
Fuding 27 Lf 27.19N 120.08 E
Fuengirola 13 Hh 36.32N 4.37W
Fuente Alto 56 Fd 33.37S 70.35W
Fuente del Maestre 13 Ff 38.32N 6.27W
Fuente-Obejuna 13 Gf 38.16N 5.25W
Fuentesaúco 13 Gc 41.14N 5.30W
Fuentes de Andalucía 13 Gg 37.28N 5.21W
Fuentes de Cantos 13 Ff 38.15N 6.18W
Fuerte 47 Cc 25.54N 109.22W
Fuerte, Isla- 49 Ii 9.23N 76.11W
Fuerte, Sierra del- 48 Hd 27.30N 102.45W
Fuerte Olimpo 56 Ib 21.02S 57.54W
Fuerteventura 30 Ff 28.20N 14.00W
Fuga 26 Hc 18.52N 121.22 E
Fugong 27 Gf 27.03N 98.57 E
Fugou 28 Cg 34.04N 114.23 E
Fugu 27 Jd 39.02N 111.03 E
Fuguo → Zhanhua 28 Ef 37.42N 118.08 E
Fuhai/Burultokay 27 Eb 47.06N 87.23 E
Fuhayrī, Wādī- 23 Hf 16.04N 52.11 E
Fu He 28 Dj 28.36N 116.04 E
Fuji 28 Og 35.09N 138.38 E
Fujian Sheng (Fu-chien Sheng) = Fukien (EN) 27 Kf 26.00N 118.00 E
Fujieda 29 Fd 34.51N 138.15 E
Fuji-Gawa 29 Fd 35.07N 138.38 E
Fujin 27 Nb 47.15N 132.01 E
Fujinomiya 29 Fd 35.12N 138.38 E
Fujioka 29 Fc 36.15N 139.03 E
Fuji-San 21 Pf 35.26N 138.43 E
Fujisawa 29 Fd 35.21N 139.27 E
Fuji-yoshida 29 Fd 35.29N 138.47 E
Fukagawa 27 Pc 43.43N 142.03 E
Fūkah 24 Bg 31.04N 27.55 E
Fukang 27 Ec 44.10N 87.59 E
Fuka-Shima 29 Be 32.43N 131.56 E
Fukiage 29 Bf 31.30N 130.20 E
Fukien (EN) = Fu-chien Sheng → Fujian Sheng 27 Kf 26.00N 118.00 E
Fukien (EN) = Fujian Sheng (Fu-chien Sheng) 27 Kf 26.00N 118.00 E
Fukuchiyama 28 Mg 35.18N 135.07 E
Fukue 28 Jh 32.41N 128.50 E
Fukueichiao 27 Lf 25.19N 121.34 E
Fukue-Jima 28 Jh 32.41N 128.48 E
Fukui 27 Od 36.04N 136.13 E
Fukui Ken 28 Ng 36.00N 136.20 E
Fukuma 29 Be 33.47N 130.28 E
Fukuoka 22 Pf 33.35N 130.24 E
Fukuoka Ken 28 Kh 33.28N 130.45 E
Fukuroi 29 Ed 34.45N 137.54 E
Fukushima [Jap.] 27 Pd 37.45N 140.28 E
Fukushima [Jap.] 27 Pc 41.29N 140.15 E
Fukushima Ken 28 Pf 37.25N 140.10 E
Fukuyama 27 Ne 34.29N 133.22 E
Fūlādī, Kūh-e- 23 Kc 34.38N 67.32 E
Fūlād Mahalleh 24 Od 36.02N 53.44 E
Fulanga 63d Cc 19.08S 178.34W
Fulda 5 Ge 51.25N 9.39 E
Fulda 10 Ff 50.33N 9.40 E
Fuliji 28 Dh 33.47N 116.59 E
Fulin → Hanyuan 27 Hf 29.25N 102.12 E
Fuling 27 If 29.40N 107.21 E
Fullerton 45 Hf 41.22N 97.58W
Fulton [Arg.] 55 Cm 37.25S 58.48W
Fulton [Il.-U.S.] 45 Kf 41.52N 90.11W
Fulton [Ky.-U.S.] 44 Cg 36.30N 88.53W
Fulton [Mo.-U.S.] 45 Kg 38.52N 91.57W
Fulton [N.Y.-U.S.] 44 Id 43.20N 76.26W
Fulufjället 8 Ec 61.33N 12.43 E
Fumaiolo 14 Gg 43.47N 12.04 E
Fumay 11 Kd 50.00N 4.42 E
Fumel 11 Gj 44.30N 0.58 E
Funabasi 28 Og 35.42N 139.59 E
Funabiki 29 Gc 37.26N 140.35 E
Funafuti 58 Ie 8.01S 178.00 E
Funafuti Atoll 57 Ie 8.31S 179.08 E
Funagata 29 Gb 38.42N 140.18 E
Funagata-Yama 29 Gb 38.27N 140.37 E
Funakoshi-Wan 29 Hb 39.25N 142.00 E
Funan 28 Ch 32.38N 115.35 E
Funäsdalen 7 Ce 62.32N 12.33 E
Funchal 31 Fe 32.38N 16.54W
Fundación 54 Da 10.29N 74.12W
Fundão 13 Ed 40.08N 7.30W
Fundy, Bay of- 38 Me 45.00N 66.00W
Funeral Peak 46 Gh 36.08N 116.37W
Fungalei 64h Bb 13.17S 176.07W
Funhalouro 37 Ed 23.05S 34.24 E
Funing [China] 27 Ig 23.39N 105.33 E
Funing [China] 28 Eh 33.48N 119.47 E
Funing [China] 28 Ee 39.56N 119.15 E
Funiu Shan 27 Je 33.40N 112.10 E
Funtua 34 Gc 11.32N 7.19 E
Fuping 28 Ce 38.48N 114.15 E
Fuqing 27 Kf 25.47N 119.24 E
Furancungo 37 Eb 14.54S 33.37 E
Furano 29 Qc 43.21N 142.23 E
Füren 29a Ca 44.17N 142.25 E
Furenai 29a Cb 42.43N 142.15 E
Füren-Ko 29a Db 43.20N 145.20 E
Fürg 24 Ph 28.18N 55.13 E
Fur Jiang 28 Hc 42.37N 125.33 E
Furmanov 7 Jh 57.16N 41.07 E
Furnas, Represa de- 54 Ih 21.20S 45.50W
Furnas, Serra das- 55 Fb 15.45S 53.20W
Furneaux Group 57 Fi 40.10S 148.05 E
Furnes/Veurne 11 Ic 51.04N 2.40 E
Furqlus 24 Ge 34.36N 37.05 E
Furrīyānah 32 Ic 34.57N 8.34 E
Fürstenau 12 Jb 52.31N 7.43 E
Furstenauer Berge 12 Jb 52.35N 7.45 E
Fürstenfeld 14 Kc 47.03N 16.05 E
Fürstenfeldbruck 10 Hh 48.11N 11.15 E
Furstenlager 12 Ke 49.42N 8.38 E
Fürstenwalde 10 Kd 52.22N 14.04 E
Fürth [F.R.G.] 10 Gg 49.28N 11.00 E
Fürth [F.R.G.] 12 Ke 49.39N 8.47 E
Furth im Wald 10 Ig 49.18N 12.51 E
Furubira 29a Bb 43.16N 140.39 E
Furudal 7 Df 61.10N 15.08 E
Furukawa 27 Pd 38.34N 140.58 E
Furusund 8 He 59.40N 18.55 E
Fury and Hecla Strait 42 Jc 69.55N 84.00W
Fushan [China] 28 Ff 37.30N 121.15 E
Fushan [China] 28 Ag 35.58N 111.51 E
Fushë-Arëzi 15 Dg 42.04N 20.02 E
Fushë-Lura 15 Dh 41.48N 20.13 E
Fu Shui 28 Cj 29.52N 115.26 E
Fushun 22 Oe 41.46N 123.56 E
Fusong 27 Mc 42.20N 127.17 E
Füsselberg 12 Je 49.32N 7.14 E
Füssen 10 Gi 47.34N 10.42 E
Futa, Passo della- 14 Ff 44.05N 11.17 E
Futago-Yama 29 Be 33.35N 131.38 E
Futaoi-Jima 29 Bd 34.06N 130.47 E
Futog 15 Cd 45.15N 19.42 E
Futuna, Ile- 57 Jf 14.17S 178.09W
Fuwah 24 Dg 31.12N 30.33 E
Fuxian (Wafangdian) 27 Ld 39.38N 121.59 E
Fuxian Hu 27 Hg 24.30N 102.55 E
Fuxin 22 Oe 41.59N 121.38 E
Fuxin Monggolzu Zizhixian 28 Fc 42.06N 121.46 E
Fuyang 27 Ke 32.47N 115.46 E
Fuyang He 28 Dg 38.14N 116.05 E
Fuyang Zhan 28 Ch 32.56N 115.53 E
Fuyu [China] 27 Lb 45.10N 124.52 E
Fuyu [China] 27 Lb 47.48N 124.26 E
Fuyuan [China] 27 Lc 42.44N 124.57 E
Fuyuan [China] 27 Nb 48.21N 134.18 E
Fuyuan [China] 27 Hf 25.43N 104.20 E
Fuyun/Koktokay 22 Ke 47.13N 89.39 E
Füzesabony 10 Qi 47.45N 20.25 E
Fuzhou [China] 22 Ng 26.10N 119.20 E
Fuzhou [China] 27 Kf 27.58N 116.20 E
Fuzhou He 28 Fe 39.36N 121.35 E
Fyllas Bank (EN) 41 Gf 64.00N 53.00W
Fyn 5 Hd 55.20N 10.30 E
Fyn 8 Di 55.20N 10.30 E
Fyne, Loch- 9 He 56.10N 5.20W
Fyresdal 7 Bg 59.11N 8.06 E
Fyresvatn 8 Ce 59.05N 8.10 E
Fzâra, Gara'et- 14 Bn 36.47N 7.30 E

G

Gaasbeek 12 Gd 50.48N 4.10 E
Gaasterland 12 Hb 52.54N 5.36 E
Gaasterland 12 Hb 52.53N 5.35 E
Gaasterland-Balk 12 Hb 52.54N 5.36 E
Gabaru Reef 64a Bb 7.53N 134.31 E
Gabas 11 Fk 43.46N 0.42W
Gabba' 35 Id 8.02N 50.08 E
Gabbs 46 Gg 38.52N 117.55W
Gabela 31 Ij 10.52S 14.23 E
Gabès, Gulf of-(EN) = Qābis, Khalīj- 30 Ie 34.00N 10.25 E
Gabon 36 Ab 0.25N 9.20 E
Gabon 31 Ii 1.00S 11.45 E
Gaborone 31 Jk 24.40S 25.55 E
Gabras 35 Dc 10.16N 26.14 E
Gabriel Strait 42 Kd 61.50N 65.40W
Gabriel y Galán, Embalse de- 13 Fd 40.15N 6.15W
Gabrovo 15 Ig 42.52N 25.19 E
Gabrovo 15 Ig 42.52N 25.19 E
Gacé 11 Gf 48.48N 0.18 E
Gachsārān 24 Ng 30.12N 50.47 E
Gackle 45 Gc 46.38N 99.09W
Gacko 14 Mg 43.10N 18.32 E
Gadag 25 Fe 15.25N 75.37 E
Gäddede 7 Dd 64.30N 14.09 E
Gadê 27 Ge 34.13N 99.29 E
Gadjač 16 Id 50.22N 34.01 E
Gádor, Sierra de- 13 Jh 36.55N 2.45W
Gadsden 43 Je 34.02N 86.02W
Gadūk, Gardaneh-ye- 24 Oe 35.55N 52.55 E
Gadzi 35 Be 4.47N 16.42 E
Gael Hamkes Bugt 41 Jd 74.00N 22.00W
Găeşti 15 Ie 44.43N 25.19 E
Gaeta 14 Hi 41.12N 13.35 E
Gaeta, Golfo di- 14 Hi 41.05N 13.30 E
Gaferut Island 57 Fd 9.14N 145.23 E
Gaffney 44 Gh 35.05N 81.39W
Gagan 63a Ba 5.14S 154.37 E
Gagarin [R.S.F.S.R.] 19 Dd 55.35N 35.01 E
Gagarin [Uzb.-U.S.S.R.] 18 Gd 40.40N 68.05 E
Gagévésouva, Pointe- 63b Ca 13.04S 166.32 E
Gaggenau 12 Kf 48.48N 8.20 E
Gagnef 7 Df 60.35N 15.04 E
Gagnoa 31 Gh 6.08N 5.56W
Gagnoa 34 Dd 6.03N 6.00W
Gagnon 42 Kf 51.55N 68.10W
Gagra 19 Eg 43.17N 40.15 E
Gahkom 24 Ph 28.12N 55.50 E
Gahkom, Kūh-e- 24 Ph 28.10N 55.57 E
Gaiba, Laguna- 55 Dc 17.45S 57.43W
Gail 14 Hd 46.36N 13.53 E
Gaillac 11 Hk 43.54N 1.55 E
Gaillefontaine 12 De 49.39N 1.37 E
Gaillimh/Galway 6 Fe 53.16N 9.03W
Gaillimh/Galway 9 Eh 53.20N 9.00W
Gaillon 12 De 49.10N 1.20 E
Gailtaler Alpen 14 Gd 46.40N 13.00 E
Gaiman 56 Gf 43.17S 65.29W
Găineşti 15 Ib 47.25N 25.55 E
Gainesville [Fl.-U.S.] 39 Kg 29.40N 82.20W
Gainesville [Ga.-U.S.] 43 Ke 34.18N 83.50W
Gainesville [Mo.-U.S.] 45 Jh 36.36N 92.26W
Gainesville [Tx.-U.S.] 43 He 33.37N 97.08W
Gainsborough 9 Mh 53.24N 0.46W
Gairdner, Lake- 57 Eh 31.35S 136.00 E
Gairloch 9 Hd 57.43N 5.40W
Gaizina Kalns/Gajzinkalns 8 Kh 56.50N 25.59 E
Gaj 19 Fe 51.31N 58.30 E
Gajny 19 Fc 60.20N 54.15 E
Gajsin 19 Cf 48.50N 29.27 E
Gajvoron 16 Fe 48.22N 29.52 E
Gajzinkalns/Gaizina Kalns 8 Kh 56.50N 25.59 E
Galaasija 18 Ee 39.52N 64.27 E
Galābovo 15 Ig 42.08N 25.51 E
Gala Gölü 15 Ji 40.45N 26.12 E
Galaico, Macizo- 13 Eb 42.30N 7.20W
Galán, Cerro- 56 Gc 25.55S 66.52W
Galana 30 Li 3.09S 40.08 E
Galanta 10 Nh 48.12N 17.44 E
Galap 64a Bb 7.38N 134.39 E
Galápagos, Islas-/Colón, Archipiélago de- = Galapagos Islands (EN) 52 Gf 0.30S 90.30W
Galapagos Fracture Zone (EN) 3 Mi 0.00 100.00W
Galapagos Islands (EN) = Colon, Archipiélago de-/Galápagos, Islas- 52 Gf 0.30S 90.30W
Galapagos Islands (EN) = Galápagos, Islas-/Colón, Archipiélago de- 52 Gf 0.30S 90.30W
Galarza 55 Di 28.06S 56.41W
Galashiels 9 Kf 55.37N 2.49W
Galaţi 15 Kd 45.33N 27.56 E
Galaţi 6 If 45.27N 28.03 E
Galatina 14 Mj 40.10N 18.10 E
Galatone 14 Mj 40.09N 18.04 E
Galatzó 13 Oe 39.38N 2.29 E
Galdar 32 Dd 28.09N 15.39W
Galdhøpiggen 7 Bf 61.37N 8.17 E
Galeana [Mex.] 48 Fb 30.07N 107.38W
Galeana [Mex.] 48 Ie 24.50N 100.04W
Galeh Dār 24 Oi 27.38N 52.42 E
Galela 58 Dd 1.50N 127.50 E
Galena [Ak.-U.S.] 40 Hd 64.44N 156.57W
Galena [Il.-U.S.] 45 Ke 42.25N 90.26W
Galeota Point 50 Fg 10.08N 60.59W
Galera, Punta- 56 Fe 39.59S 73.43W
Galera, Rio- 55 Bb 14.25S 60.07W
Galera Point 50 Fg 10.49N 60.55W
Galesburg 43 Ic 40.57N 90.22W
Galga 10 Pi 47.33N 19.43 E
Gal Gaduud 35 Hd 5.00N 47.00 E
Galheirão, Rio- 55 Ja 12.23S 45.05W
Galheiros 55 Ia 13.18S 46.25W
Gali 16 Lh 42.36N 41.42 E
Galič [R.S.F.S.R.] 19 Ed 58.23N 42.21 E
Galič [Ukr.-U.S.S.R.] 16 De 49.06N 24.43 E
Galicea Mare 15 Ge 44.06N 23.18 E
Galicia 5 Fg 43.00N 8.00W
Galicia 13 Eb 43.00N 8.00W
Galicia (EN) = Galicija 5 If 49.50N 21.00 E
Galicia (EN) = Galicija [Eur.] 10 Qg 49.50N 21.00 E
Galicia (EN) = Galicja 10 Qg 49.50N 21.00 E
Galicia (EN) = Galicja 5 If 49.50N 21.00 E
Galicija [Eur.] = Galicia (EN) 10 Qg 49.50N 21.00 E
Galicija [Ukr.-U.S.S.R.] 10 Jg 49.00N 24.00 E
Galicija = Galicia (EN) 5 If 49.50N 21.00 E
Galicja = Galicia (EN) 5 If 49.50N 21.00 E
Galicja = Galicia (EN) 10 Qg 49.50N 21.00 E
Galilee, Lake- 59 Jd 22.20S 145.55 E
Galimy 20 Kd 62.19N 156.00 E
Galina Point 49 Id 18.24N 76.53W
Galion 44 Fe 40.44N 82.46W
Galion, Baie du- 51h Bb 14.44N 60.57W
Galiton 14 Cm 37.30N 8.52 E
Galiuro Mountains 46 Jj 32.40N 110.20W
Gâlka'yo 31 Lh 6.49N 47.23 E
Galkino 17 Ki 55.40N 62.55 E
Gallarate 14 Ce 45.40N 8.47 E
Gallatin 44 Dg 36.24N 86.27W
Gallatin Range 46 Jd 45.15N 111.05W
Gallatin River 46 Jd 45.56N 111.29W
Galle 22 Ki 6.02N 80.13 E
Gállego 13 Lc 41.39N 0.51W
Gallegos, Rio- 52 Jk 51.36S 68.59W
Gallinas, Punta- 52 Id 12.25N 71.40W
Gallinas Peak 45 Di 34.15N 105.45W
Gallipoli 14 Lj 40.03N 17.58 E
Gallipoli Peninsula (EN) = Gelibolu Yarimadası 15 Ji 40.20N 26.30 E
Gallipolis 44 Ff 38.49N 82.14W
Gällivare 6 Ib 67.08N 20.42 E
Galljaaral 18 Fd 40.02N 67.35 E
Gallo 13 Jd 40.48N 2.09W
Gällö 7 De 62.55N 15.14 E
Gallo, Capo- 14 Hl 38.15N 13.19 E
Gallo Mountains 45 Bi 34.00N 108.15W
Galloway 9 If 55.00N 4.25W
Galloway, Mull of- 9 Ig 54.38N 4.50W
Gallup 39 If 35.32N 108.44W
Gallur 13 Kc 41.52N 1.19W
Gallura 14 Dj 41.00N 9.15 E
Galmaarden/Gammerages 12 Fd 50.45N 3.58 E
Galole 36 Hc 1.30S 40.02 E
Galt 44 Gd 43.22N 80.19W
Gal Tardo 35 He 3.37N 45.58 E
Galtasen 8 Eg 57.48N 13.30 E
Galty Mountains/Na Gaibhlte 9 Ei 52.23N 8.11W
Galut 27 Hb 46.43N 100.08 E
Galveston 39 Jg 29.18N 94.48W
Galveston Bay 38 Jg 29.36N 94.57W
Galveston Island 45 Il 29.13N 94.55W
Gálvez 56 Hd 32.02S 61.13W
Galway/Gaillimh 9 Eh 53.20N 9.00W
Galway/Gaillimh 6 Fe 53.16N 9.03W
Galway Bay/Cuan na Gaillimhe 5 Fe 53.10N 9.15W
Gamaches 12 De 49.59N 1.33 E
Gamagōri 29 Ed 34.49N 137.13 E
Gamarra 54 Db 8.19N 73.44W
Gamba [China] 27 Ef 28.17N 88.31 E
Gamba [Gabon] 36 Ac 2.37S 10.00 E
Gambaga 34 Ec 10.32N 0.26W
Gambela 31 Kh 8.15N 34.36 E
Gambell 40 Ed 63.46N 171.46W
Gambia 30 Fg 13.28N 16.34W
Gambia 31 Fg 13.25N 16.00W
Gambie 34 Bc 13.28N 16.34W
Gambier, Iles- = Gambier Islands (EN) 57 Ng 23.09S 134.58W
Gambier Islands (EN) = Gambier, Iles- 57 Ng 23.09S 134.58W
Gambo 35 Ce 4.39N 22.16 E
Gamboma 36 Cc 1.53S 15.51 E
Gambos 36 Be 14.45S 14.05 E
Gamboula 35 Be 4.08N 15.09 E
Gamda → Zamtang 27 He 32.23N 101.05 E
Gamelão 55 Db 15.29S 57.50W
Gamkonora, Gunung- 26 If 1.21N 127.31 E
Gamlakarleby/Kokkola 6 Ic 63.50N 23.07 E
Gamla Uppsala 8 Ge 59.54N 17.38 E
Gamleby 7 Dh 57.54N 16.24 E
Gamo Gofa 35 Fd 5.45N 37.20 E
Gamua 64h Bb 13.15S 176.08W
Gamud 35 Fe 4.05N 38.06 E
Gamvik 7 Ga 71.03N 28.14 E
Ganāne, Webi- = Juba (EN) 30 Lh 0.15S 42.38 E
Gananoque 44 Ic 44.20N 76.10W
Ganāveh 24 Nh 29.32N 50.31 E
Gancedo 55 Bh 27.30S 61.42W
Ganceviči 16 Ec 52.45N 26.29 E
Gand/Gent = Ghent (EN) 11 Jc 51.03N 3.43 E
Ganda 36 Be 12.59S 14.40 E
Gandadiwata, Bulu- 26 Gg 2.42S 119.27 E
Gandajika 36 Dd 6.45S 23.57 E
Gandak 25 Hc 25.39N 85.13 E
Gander 39 Ne 48.57N 54.34W
Ganderkesee 12 Ka 53.04N 8.33 E
Gandesa 13 Mc 41.03N 0.26 E
Gandhinagar 22 Jg 23.21N 72.40 E
Gāndhi Sāgar 25 Fd 24.30N 75.30 E
Gandía 13 Lf 38.58N 0.11W
Gandía-Grao de Gandía 13 Lf 38.59N 0.09W
Gandisê Shan 21 Kf 31.00N 83.00 E
Gandu 54 Kf 13.45S 39.30W
Ganetti 35 Eb 17.58N 31.13 E
Ganga = Ganges (EN) 21 Lg 23.20N 90.30 E
Gangaw 25 Id 22.10N 94.08 E
Gangca (Shaliuhe) 27 Hd 37.30N 100.14 E
Ganges 11 Jk 43.56N 3.42 E
Ganges (EN) = Ganga 21 Lg 23.20N 90.30 E
Ganges, Mouths of the- (EN) 21 Lg 23.20N 90.30 E
Gangi 14 Im 37.48N 14.12 E
Gango 36 Cd 9.48S 15.40 E
Gangtok 22 Kg 27.20N 88.37 E
Gangu 27 Ie 34.45N 105.12 E
Gangziyao 28 Cf 36.17N 114.06 E
Gan He 27 Mb 49.12N 125.14 E
Ganhe 27 La 50.43N 123.00 E
Gani 26 Ig 0.47S 128.13 E
Ganjgah 24 Md 37.42N 48.16 E
Gan Jiang 21 Ng 29.12N 116.00 E
Ganjig → Horqin Zuoyi Houqi 27 Lc 42.57N 122.14 E
Gannan 27 Lb 47.53N 123.26 E
Gannat 11 Jh 46.06N 3.12 E
Gannett Peak 38 Ie 43.10N 109.40W
Gansbaai 37 Bf 34.35S 19.22 E
Gansu Sheng (Kan-su Sheng) = Kansu (EN) 27 Hd 38.00N 102.00 E
Ganta 34 Dd 7.14N 8.59W
Gantang → Taiping 28 Ei 30.18N 118.07 E
Ganyu (Qingkou) 28 Eg 34.50N 119.07 E
Ganzhou 22 Ng 25.49N 114.56 E
Gao 34 Eb 18.15N 1.00W
Gao [Mali] 31 Hg 16.15N 0.01 E
Gao [Niger] 34 Gb 15.25N 5.45 E
Gao'an 27 Kf 28.27N 115.24 E
Gaobeidian → Xincheng 28 Ce 39.20N 115.50 E
Gaocheng 28 Ce 38.02N 114.50 E
Gaolan (Shidongsi) 27 Hd 36.23N 103.55 E
Gaoliangjian → Hongze 27 Ke 33.10N 119.58 E
Gaoligong Shan 27 Gf 25.45N 98.45 E
Gaolou Ling 27 Ig 24.47N 106.48 E
Gaomi 28 Ef 36.23N 119.45 E
Gaoping 27 Jd 35.46N 112.55 E
Gaoqing (Tianzhen) 28 Df 37.10N 117.50 E
Gaotai 27 Gd 39.20N 99.58 E
Gaotingzhen → Daishan 28 Gi 30.15N 122.13 E
Gaoua 34 Ec 10.20N 3.11W
Gaoual 34 Cc 11.45N 13.12W
Gaoyang 28 Ce 38.42N 115.47 E
Gaoyi 28 Cf 37.37N 114.37 E
Gaoyou 28 Eh 32.46N 119.27 E
Gaoyou Hu 27 Ke 32.50N 119.15 E
Gaozhou 27 Jg 21.56N 110.47 E
Gap 11 Mj 44.34N 6.05 E
Gar 27 Ce 32.12N 79.57 E
Gara, Lough-/Loch Ui Ghadra 9 Eh 53.55N 8.30W
Gara'ad 35 Hd 6.54N 49.20 E
Garabato 55 Bi 28.56S 60.09W
Garachiné 49 Hi 8.04N 78.22W
Garachiné, Punta- 49 Hi 8.06N 78.25W
Gara Dragoman 15 Fg 42.55N 22.56 E
Ga'raet el Oubeïra 14 Cn 36.50N 8.23 E
Gara Kostenec 15 Gg 42.18N 23.52 E
Garalo 34 Dc 11.00N 7.26W
Gara Muleta 35 Gd 9.05N 41.43 E
Garanhuns 53 Mf 8.54S 36.29W
Garapan 64b Ba 15.12N 145.43 E
Garapuava 55 Ic 16.06S 46.33W
Garavuti 18 Gf 37.36N 68.29 E
Garba 35 Cd 9.12N 20.30 E
Garbahārrey 35 Ge 3.20N 42.17 E
Garberville 46 Df 40.06N 123.48W
Gārbosh, Kūh-e- 24 Nf 32.36N 50.04 E
Garça 55 Hf 22.14S 49.37W
Garças, Rio das- 55 Fb 15.54S 52.16W
Garcias 55 Fe 20.34S 52.13W
Gard 11 Jj 44.00N 4.00 E
Gard 11 Kk 43.51N 4.37 E
Garda 14 Ee 45.34N 10.42 E
Garda, Lago di- = Garda, Lake- (EN) 5 Hf 45.35N 10.35 E
Garda, Lake- (EN) = Garda, Lago di- 5 Hf 45.35N 10.35 E
Gardabani 16 Ni 41.29N 45.05 E
Garde, Cap de- 14 Bn 36.58N 7.47 E
Gardelegen 10 Hd 52.32N 11.22 E
Garden City [Ga.-U.S.] 44 Gi 32.06N 81.09W
Garden City [Ks.-U.S.] 43 Gd 37.58N 100.53W
Garden Grove 46 Gj 33.46N 117.57W
Garden Peninsula 44 Dc 45.40N 86.35W
Gardermoen 8 Dd 60.13N 11.06 E
Gardey 55 Cm 37.17S 59.21W
Gardēz 23 Kc 33.37N 69.07 E
Gardiner 46 Jd 45.02N 110.42W
Gardiner Range 59 Fc 19.15S 128.50 E
Gardner → Nikumaroro Atoll 57 Je 4.40S 174.32W
Gardner Pinnacles 57 Kb 25.00N 167.55W
Gardno, Jezioro- 10 Nb 54.43N 17.05 E
Gardone Riviera 14 Ee 45.37N 10.34 E
Gardždai/Gargždaj 7 Ei 55.43N 21.24 E
Gareloi 40a Cb 51.47N 178.48W
Garessio 14 Cf 44.12N 8.02 E
Garfagnana 14 Ef 44.05N 10.30 E
Gargaliánoi 15 El 37.04N 21.38 E
Gargano 5 Hg 41.50N 16.00 E
Gargano, Testa del- 14 Ki 41.35N 16.12 E
Gargantua, Cape- 44 Eb 47.36N 85.02W
Gargždaj/Gargždai 7 Ei 55.43N 21.24 E
Gari 19 Gd 59.28N 62.25 E
Garibaldi 55 Gi 29.15S 51.32W
Garibaldi, Mount- 46 Db 49.51N 123.01W
Garies 37 Bf 30.30S 18.00 E
Garigliano 14 Hi 41.13N 13.45 E
Garimpo 55 Ed 18.41S 54.50W
Garissa 31 Ki 0.28S 39.38 E

Index Symbols

1 Independent Nation
2 State, Region
3 District, County
4 Municipality
5 Colony, Dependency
Continent
Physical Region
Historical or Cultural Region
Mount, Mountain
Volcano
Hill
Mountains, Mountain Range
Hills, Escarpment
Plateau, Upland
Pass, Gap
Plain, Lowland
Delta
Salt Flat
Valley, Canyon
Crater, Cave
Karst Features
Depression
Polder
Desert, Dunes
Forest, Woods
Heath, Steppe
Oasis
Cape, Point
Coast, Beach
Cliff
Peninsula
Isthmus
Sandbank
Island
Atoll
Rock, Reef
Islands, Archipelago
Rocks, Reefs
Coral Reef
Well, Spring
Geyser
River, Stream
Waterfall Rapids
River Mouth, Estuary
Lake
Salt Lake
Intermittent Lake
Reservoir
Swamp, Pond
Canal
Glacier
Ice Shelf, Pack Ice
Ocean
Sea
Gulf, Bay
Strait, Fjord
Lagoon
Bank
Seamount
Tablemount
Ridge
Shelf
Basin
Escarpment, Sea Scarp
Fracture
Trench, Abyss
National Park, Reserve
Point of Interest
Recreation Site
Cave, Cavern
Historic Site
Ruins
Wall, Walls
Church, Abbey
Temple
Scientific Station
Airport
Port
Lighthouse
Mine
Tunnel
Dam, Bridge

Name	Map	Grid	Lat.	Long.
Garkida	34	Hc	10.25N	12.34 E
Garland	45	Hj	32.54N	96.39W
Garlasco	14	Ce	45.12N	8.55 E
Garliava/Garljava	8	Jj	54.46N	23.55 E
Garljava/Garliava	8	Jj	54.46N	23.55 E
Garm	18	He	39.02N	70.18 E
Garmisch-Partenkirchen	10	Hi	47.30N	11.06 E
Garmsar	24	Oe	35.20N	52.13 E
Garnet Bank (EN)	55	Hk	33.05S	49.25W
Garnet Range	46	Ic	46.45N	113.15W
Garnett	45	Ig	38.17N	95.14W
Garonne	5	Ff	45.02N	0.36W
Garonne, Canal latéral à la-	11	Fj	44.34N	0.09W
Garopába	55	Hi	28.04S	48.40W
Garoua	31	Ih	9.18N	13.24 E
Garoua Boulaï	35	Ad	5.53N	14.33 E
Garoubi	34	Fc	13.07N	2.18 E
Garôwe	31	Lh	8.25N	48.33 E
Garpenberg	8	Gd	60.19N	16.12 E
Garphyttan	8	Fe	59.19N	14.56 E
Garrel	12	Kb	52.57N	8.01 E
Garreru	64a	Bc	7.20N	134.33 E
Garri, Küh-e-	24	Mf	33.59N	48.25 E
Garrigues	11	Kj	44.10N	4.30 E
Garrison	45	Fc	47.40N	101.25W
Garron Point/An Gearran	9	Hf	55.05N	5.58W
Garrovillas	13	Fe	39.43N	6.33W
Garruchos	55	Ei	28.11S	55.39W
Garry	9	Je	56.45N	3.45W
Garry Bay	42	Ic	69.00N	85.10W
Garry Lake	38	Jc	66.00N	100.00W
Garsen	36	Hc	2.16S	40.07 E
Gartar/Qianning	27	He	30.27N	101.29 E
Gartempe	11	Gh	46.47N	0.50 E
Gartog → Markam	27	Gf	29.32N	98.33 E
Garut	26	Eh	7.13S	107.54 E
Garuva	55	Hh	26.01S	48.51W
Garvie Mountains	62	Cf	45.30S	168.50 E
Garwa	25	Gd	24.11N	83.49 E
Garwolin	10	Ke	51.54N	21.37 E
Gary	43	Jc	41.36N	87.20W
Garyarsa	27	De	31.40N	80.26 E
Garzê	27	Ge	31.42N	99.58 E
Garzón [Col.]	54	Cc	2.13N	75.38W
Garzón [Ur.]	56	Jd	34.36S	54.33W
Gasan-Kuli	19	Fh	37.29N	53.59 E
Gascogne = Gascony (EN)	11	Gk	43.30N	0.10 E
Gasconade River	45	Kg	38.40N	91.33W
Gascony (EN) = Gascogne	11	Gk	43.30N	0.10 E
Gascoyne Junction	59	De	25.03S	115.12 E
Gascoyne River	57	Ca	24.52S	113.37 E
Gasefjord	41	Je	70.00N	27.30W
Gaseland	41	Jd	70.20N	29.00W
Gash	30	Kg	16.48N	35.51 E
Gas Hu	27	Fd	38.08N	90.45 E
Gashua	31	Ig	12.52N	11.03 E
Gaspar Strait (EN)=Kelasa, Selat-	26	Eg	2.40S	107.15 E
Gaspé	39	Me	48.50N	64.29W
Gaspé, Cap de -	42	Lg	48.45N	64.10W
Gaspé, Péninsule de-= Gaspe Peninsula (EN)	38	Me	48.30N	65.00W
Gaspe Peninsula (EN)= Gaspé, Péninsule de-	38	Me	48.30N	65.00W
Gassan	29	Gb	38.34N	140.01 E
Gassol	34	Hd	8.32N	10.28 E
Gaston, Lake-	44	Ig	36.78N	78.00W
Gastonia	43	Kd	35.16N	81.11W
Gastoúni	15	El	37.51N	21.15 E
Gastre	56	Gf	42.17S	69.14W
Gästrikland	8	Gd	60.30N	16.30 E
Gata, Akrotérion-	24	Ea	34.34N	33.02 E
Gata, Cabo de -	5	Fh	36.43N	2.12W
Gata, Sierra de-	13	Fd	40.15N	6.45W
Gātaia	15	Ed	45.26N	21.26 E
Gatčina	19	Dd	59.34N	30.09 E
Gate	45	Fh	36.51N	100.01W
Gate City	44	Fg	36.38N	82.37W
Gateshade	9	Lg	54.58N	1.37W
Gateshead	42	Hb	70.35N	100.15W
Gathemo	12	Bf	48.46N	0.58W
Gâtinais	11	If	48.00N	2.20 E
Gâtine, Hauteurs de-	11	Fh	46.38N	0.50 E
Gatineau, Rivière-	42	Jg	45.27N	75.42W
Gatlinburg	44	Fh	35.43N	83.31W
Gato, Cumbres del-	48	Fd	27.00N	106.35W
Gatooma	37	Jj	18.21S	29.55 E
Gattinara	14	Cc	45.37N	8.22 E
Gatún, Lago-=Gatun Lake (EN)	47	Ig	9.12N	79.55W
Gatun Lake (EN)=Gatún, Lago-	47	Ig	9.12N	79.55W
Gatvand	24	Mf	32.15N	48.50 E
Gatwick Airport	12	Bc	51.08N	0.12W
Gaucín	13	Gh	36.31N	5.19W
Gauhati	22	Lg	26.11N	91.44 E
Gauiena/Gaujiena	8	Lg	57.25N	26.28 E
Gauja	7	Fh	57.10N	24.16 E
Gaujiena/Gauiena	8	Lg	57.25N	26.28 E
Gaula [Nor.]	8	Da	63.21N	10.14 E
Gaula [Nor.]	8	Ac	61.22N	5.41 E
Gauldalen	8	Db	63.00N	11.00 E
Gauley River	44	Gf	38.10N	81.12W
Gau-Odernheim	12	Ke	49.46N	8.12 E
Gausdal	8	Cc	61.20N	9.55 E
Gausta	7	Bg	59.50N	8.39 E
Gävbandi	24	Oi	27.11N	53.04 E
Gävbüs, Küh-e-	24	Oi	27.10N	54.00 E
Gavdhopoúla	15	Go	34.56N	24.00 E
Gávdhos	5	Ii	34.50N	24.05 E
Gáveh	24	Le	35.00N	46.58 E
Gavere	12	Fd	50.56N	3.40 E
Gavkhūnī, Bātlāq-e-	24	Of	32.06N	52.52 E
Gäv Kosh	24	Le	34.00N	48.00 E
Gävle	6	Hc	60.40N	17.10 E
Gävleborg	7	Df	61.30N	16.15 E
Gävlebukten	8	Gd	60.40N	17.20 E
Gavorrano	14	Eh	42.55N	10.54 E
Gavri	8	Lh	56.49N	27.58 E
Gavrilov-Jam	7	Jh	57.19N	39.51 E
Gäw Koshi	23	Id	28.38N	57.12 E
Gawler	59	Hf	34.37S	138.44 E
Gawler Ranges	57	Be	32.30S	136.00 E
Gaxun Nur	21	Me	42.25N	101.00 E
Gaya [India]	22	Kg	24.47N	85.00 E
Gaya [Niger]	34	Fc	11.53N	3.27 E
Gaya He	28	Jc	42.58N	129.52 E
Gaylord	44	Ec	45.02N	84.40W
Gayndah	59	Ke	25.37S	151.36 E
Gaz	27	Nf	32.48N	51.37 E
Gaza	37	Kj	23.30S	33.00 E
Gaz-Ačak	19	Gj	41.11N	61.27 E
Gazalkent	18	Id	41.33N	69.46 E
Gazaoua	34	Gc	13.32N	7.55 E
Gazelle, Récif de la-	63b	Be	20.11S	165.27 E
Gaziantep	22	Ff	37.05N	37.22 E
Gaziemir	15	Kk	38.19N	27.10 E
Gazimūr	20	Hf	52.57N	120.22 E
Gazipaşa	24	Ee	36.17N	32.20 E
Gazli	19	Gj	40.09N	63.23 E
Gbarnga	31	Hh	7.00N	9.29W
Gboko	34	Gd	7.21N	8.58 E
Gbon	34	Dd	9.50N	6.27W
Gdańsk	10	Ob	54.25N	18.40 E
Gdansk=Danzig (EN)	6	He	54.23N	18.40 E
Gdansk, Gulf of- (EN)= Gdanska, Zatoka-	5	He	54.40N	19.15 E
Gdánska, Zatoka=Gdansk, Gulf of- (EN)	5	He	54.40N	19.15 E
Gdov	7	Gg	58.47N	27.54 E
Gdynia	6	He	54.32N	18.33 E
Gearhart Mountain	46	Ee	42.30N	120.53W
Gêba	34	Bc	11.58N	15.00W
Gebe, Pulau-	26	Ig	0.05S	129.20 E
Gebze	24	Cb	40.48N	29.25 E
Gecha	35	Fd	7.29N	35.25 E
Gedi	36	Hc	3.18S	40.01 E
Gedinne	12	Ge	49.59N	4.56 E
Gediz	24	Cc	39.02N	29.25 E
Gedo	35	Ge	2.20N	41.20 E
Gedo	35	Ge	3.00N	42.00 E
Gedo	35	Ff	9.00N	37.29 E
Gedser	7	Ci	54.35N	11.57 E
Gedser Odde	8	Dj	54.34N	11.59 E
Geel	11	Kc	51.10N	5.00 E
Geelong	58	Fh	38.08S	144.21 E
Geelvink Channel	59	Ce	28.30S	114.10 E
Geer	12	Hd	50.51N	5.42 E
Geeste	12	Jb	52.36N	7.16 E
Geesthacht	10	Gc	53.26N	10.22 E
Gê'gyai	27	De	32.29N	80.52 E
Ge Hu	28	Ei	31.36N	119.51 E
Geidam	34	Hc	12.53N	11.56 E
Geigar	35	Ec	11.59N	32.46 E
Geihoku	29	Cd	34.44N	132.17 E
Geikie	42	He	57.48N	103.46W
Geilo	7	Bf	60.31N	8.12 E
Geiranger	8	Bb	62.06N	7.12 E
Geisenheim	12	Je	49.59N	7.58 E
Geislingen an der Steige	10	Fh	48.37N	9.51 E
Geita	36	Fc	2.52S	32.10 E
Geithus	7	Bg	59.57N	9.59 E
Gejiu	21	Mg	23.22N	103.14 E
Gel [Sud.]	30	Jh	7.46N	29.36 E
Gel [Sud.]	35	Ed	6.08N	31.17 E
Gela	14	Im	37.04N	14.15 E
Gela, Golfo di-	14	Im	37.04N	14.10 E
Geladi	35	Hd	6.57N	46.25 E
Geldenaken/Jodoigne	12	Gd	50.43N	4.52 E
Gelderland	12	Hb	52.10N	5.50 E
Geldermalsen	12	Hc	51.53N	5.19 E
Geldern	10	Ce	51.31N	6.20 E
Geldrop	12	Hc	51.25N	5.33 E
Geleen	11	Ld	50.58N	5.52 E
Gelembé	15	Kj	39.10N	27.50 E
Gelemso	35	Gd	8.48N	40.32 E
Gelendžik	19	Dg	44.33N	38.06 E
Gelengdeng	34	Hd	10.56N	15.32 E
Gelibolu	55	Bb	40.24N	26.40 E
Gelibolu Yarimadası = Gallipoli Peninsula (EN)	15	Ja	40.20N	26.30 E
Gélise	11	Gj	44.11N	0.17 E
Gellinsör	35	Hd	6.24N	46.46 E
Gelnhausen	10	Ff	50.12N	9.11 E
Gelsenkirchen	10	De	51.31N	7.06 E
Gemena	31	Ih	3.15N	19.46 E
Gemerek	24	Ge	39.11N	36.05 E
Gemert	12	Hc	51.33N	5.41 E
Gemi, Jabal-	35	Ed	9.01N	34.09 E
Gemlik	24	Cb	40.26N	29.09 E
Gemlik Körfezi	15	Ki	40.25N	28.45 E
Gemona del Friuli	14	Hd	46.16N	13.09 E
Gemünden (Felda)	12	Ld	50.42N	9.03 E
Gemünden (Wohra)	12	Kd	50.58N	8.58 E
Gemünden am Main	10	Ff	50.03N	9.42 E
Genale	30	Lh	0.15S	42.30 E
Genç	24	Ic	38.46N	40.35 E
Gendringen-Ulft	12	Ib	51.52N	6.23 E
Genemuiden	12	Ib	52.37N	6.02 E
General Acha	56	He	37.23S	64.36W
General Alvear [Arg.]	56	Gd	34.58S	67.42W
General Alvear [Arg.]	56	He	36.03S	60.01W
General Arenales	56	Bl	34.18S	61.18W
General Artigas	55	Dh	26.53S	56.17W
General Belgrano	56	Ie	35.46S	58.30W
General Belgrano Station	66	Af	77.50S	38.00W
General Bernardo O'Higgins	66	Ro	63.19S	57.54W
General Bravo	48	Je	25.48N	99.10W
General Cabrera	56	Hd	32.48S	63.52W
General Capdevila	55	Bh	27.26S	61.28W
General Carneiro	55	Gh	26.28S	51.25W
General Carrera, Lago-	52	Ij	46.30S	72.00W
General Cepeda	48	Je	25.23N	101.27W
General Conesa [Arg.]	55	Dm	36.30S	57.20W
General Conesa [Arg.]	56	Hf	40.06S	64.26W
General Enrique Martínez	55	Fj	33.12S	53.50W
General Galarza	55	Ck	32.43S	59.24W
General Güemes	56	Hb	24.40S	65.00W
General Guide	56	Id	36.40S	57.46W
General José de San Martín	55	Bh	26.33S	59.21W
General Juan Madariaga	56	Ie	37.00S	57.09W
General La Madrid	56	Hf	37.16S	61.17W
General Lavalle	56	Ie	36.24S	56.58W
General Manuel Belgrano, Cerro-	52	Jh	29.01S	67.49W
General O'Brien	55	Bl	34.54S	60.45W
General Pico	56	He	35.40S	63.44W
General Pinedo	56	Hc	27.19S	61.17W
General Pinto	55	Bl	34.46S	61.53W
General Pirán	55	Dm	37.16S	57.45W
General Roca	56	Ge	39.02S	67.35W
General Salgado	55	Ge	20.39S	50.22W
General Santos	22	Oi	6.05N	125.10 E
General Sarmiento	55	Cl	34.33S	58.43W
General Terán	48	Je	25.16N	99.41W
General-Toševo	15	Lf	43.42N	28.02 E
General Treviño	48	Je	26.14N	99.29W
General Trías	48	Fe	28.21N	106.22W
General Vargas	55	Ei	29.42S	54.40W
General Viamonte	55	Bl	35.01S	61.01W
General Villegas	56	He	35.02S	63.01W
Genesee River	44	Id	43.16N	77.36W
Geneseo	44	Id	42.46N	77.49W
Geneva [Al.-U.S.]	44	Ej	31.02N	85.52W
Geneva [Nb.-U.S.]	45	Hf	40.32N	97.36W
Geneva [N.Y.-U.S.]	44	Id	42.53N	76.59W
Geneva (EN) = Genève	6	Gf	46.10N	6.10 E
Geneva, Lake- (EN) = Léman, Lac-	5	Gf	46.25N	6.30 E
Genève	6	Gf	46.10N	6.10 E
Genève = Geneva (EN)	6	Gf	46.10N	6.10 E
Genevois	11	Mh	46.00N	6.10 E
Genhe → Ergun Zuoqi	22	Od	50.47N	121.32 E
Geni	35	Ed	8.31N	33.10 E
Geničesk	19	Df	46.14N	34.48 E
Genil	13	Gg	37.42N	5.19W
Genk	11	Ld	50.58N	5.30 E
Genkai-Nada	29	Ae	33.45N	130.00 E
Gennargentu	5	Gg	40.00N	9.20 E
Gennep	12	Hc	51.42N	5.59 E
Genoa (EN) = Genova	6	Gg	44.25N	8.57 E
Genoa = Genova (EN)	6	Gg	44.25N	8.57 E
Genoa, Gulf of- (EN) = Genova, Golfo di-	5	Gg	44.10N	8.55 E
Genova	6	Gg	44.25N	8.57 E
Genova = Genoa (EN)	6	Gg	44.25N	8.57 E
Genova, Golfo di- = Genoa, Gulf of- (EN)	5	Gg	44.10N	8.55 E
Genova-Nervi	14	Df	44.23N	9.02 E
Genova-Voltri	14	Cf	44.26N	8.45 E
Genovesa, Isla-	54a	Ba	0.20N	89.58W
Gent/Gand = Ghent (EN)	11	Jc	51.03N	3.43 E
Gentbrugge, Gent-	12	Fc	51.03N	3.45 E
Gent-Gentbrugge	12	Fc	51.03N	3.45 E
Genthin	10	Id	52.24N	12.10 E
Gent-Sint-Amandsberg	12	Fc	51.04N	3.45 E
Genú, Kühhä-ye-	23	Id	27.25N	56.09 E
Genyem	26	Lg	2.46S	140.12 E
Genzano di Lucania	14	Kj	40.51N	16.02 E
Genzano di Roma	14	Fi	41.42N	11.41 E
Geographe Bay	57	Cg	33.35S	115.15 E
Geographe Channel	59	Cd	24.40S	113.20 E
Geographical Society Øer	41	Jd	72.40N	22.20W
Geokčaj	16	Ki	40.40N	47.42 E
Geok-Tepe	19	Fh	38.10N	57.58 E
Geomagnetic Pole (1975) (EN)	66	Hf	78.40S	109.33 E
Georga, Zemlja-	21	Ga	80.30N	49.00 E
George	38	Mf	58.30N	66.00W
George	37	Cf	33.58S	22.24 E
George, Lake- [Austl.]	59	Jg	35.05S	149.25 E
George, Lake- [Fl.-U.S.]	44	Gk	29.17N	81.36W
George, Lake- [Ug.]	36	Fc	0.00	30.12 E
George, Lake- [U.S.]	44	Kd	43.35N	73.35W
George Gill Range	59	Gd	24.15S	131.35 E
Georges Bank (EN)	43	Nc	41.15N	67.30W
George Sound	62	Be	44.50S	167.20 E
George Town	58	Hi	41.06S	146.50 E
George Town	22	Mi	5.25N	100.20 E
Georgetown [Austl.]	58	Ff	18.18S	143.33 E
Georgetown [Bah.]	49	Jb	23.30N	75.46W
Georgetown [Cay.Is.]	49	He	19.18N	81.23W
Georgetown [De.-U.S.]	44	Jf	38.42N	75.23W
Georgetown [Gam.]	31	Fg	13.32N	14.46W
Georgetown [Guy.]	53	Ke	6.48N	58.10W
Georgetown [Ky.-U.S.]	44	Ef	38.13N	84.33W
Georgetown [Oh.-U.S.]	44	Ff	38.50N	83.54W
Georgetown [S.C.-U.S.]	43	Le	33.23N	79.18W
Georgetown [St.Hel.]	31	Fi	7.56S	14.25W
Georgetown [St.Vin.]	51	Ti	13.16N	61.08W
George V Coast	66	Je	68.30S	147.30 E
George VI Sound	66	Qf	71.00S	68.00W
George West	45	Hk	28.20N	98.07W
Georgia (EN)	5	Kg	42.00N	44.00 E
Georgia, Strait of -	46	Fa	49.20N	123.20W
Georgia del Sur, Islas-/ South Georgia	52	Ng	54.15S	36.45W
Georgian Bay	38	Kg	45.15N	80.50W
Georgian SSR (EN) = Gruzinskaja SSR	19	Eg	42.00N	43.00 E
Georgijevka [Kaz.-U.S.S.R.]	19	Hg	43.02N	74.43 E
Georgijevka [Kaz.-U.S.S.R.]	19	If	49.19N	81.35 E
Georgijevsk	16	Mg	44.09N	43.28 E
Georgina River	57	Eg	23.30S	139.47 E
Georgsmarienhütte	12	Ed	52.16N	8.02 E
Gera	10	Gf	51.08N	10.56 E
Gera	12	Nd	50.52N	12.05 E
Gera	10	Hf	50.45N	11.55 E
Geraardsbergen/Grammont	12	Fd	50.46N	3.52 E
Gerais, Chapadão dos-	55	Jc	17.40S	45.35W
Geral, Serra- [Braz.]	55	Gi	29.10S	50.15W
Geral, Serra- [Braz.]	52	Kh	26.30S	50.30W
Geral, Serra- [Braz.]	55	Gf	23.54S	50.46W
Geral da Serra, Coxilha-	55	Ej	30.20S	55.15W
Geral de Goiás, Serra-	52	Lg	13.00S	46.15W
Geraldine	62	Cf	44.05S	171.15 E
Geral do Paraná, Serra-	55	Ib	14.45S	47.30W
Geraldton [Austl.]	58	Cg	28.46S	114.36 E
Geraldton [Ont.-Can.]	42	Ig	49.44N	86.57W
Gérardmer	11	Mf	48.04N	6.53 E
Gerāsh	24	Fi	27.34N	54.06 E
Gerbičì, Gora-	20	Fc	66.39N	105.02 E
Gerca	15	Ja	48.10N	26.17 E
Gerçüş	24	Id	37.34N	41.23 E
Gerecse	10	Oi	47.41N	18.29 E
Gerede	24	Eb	40.52N	32.39 E
Gerede	24	Eb	40.48N	32.12 E
Gerês, Serra do-	13	Ec	41.48N	8.00W
Gereshk	23	Jc	31.48N	64.34 E
Gérgal	13	Jg	37.07N	2.33W
Gering	45	Ef	41.50N	103.40W
Gerlachovský štít	10	Qg	49.12N	20.09 E
Gerlogubi	35	Hd	6.56N	45.03 E
Gerlos	14	Gc	47.14N	12.02 E
Gerlovo	15	Kf	43.03N	27.35 E
German Democratic Republic (EN) = Deutsche Demokratische Republik	6	He	52.00N	12.30 E
Germania	55	Al	34.34S	62.03W
Germania Land	41	Kc	76.50N	20.00W
Germany, Federal Republic of- (EN) = Bundesrepublik Deutschland	6	Ge	51.00N	9.00 E
Germencik	15	Kl	37.51N	27.37 E
Germersheim	12	Je	49.13N	8.22 E
Germì	24	Mc	39.01N	48.03 E
Germiston	37	De	26.15S	28.05 E
Gernsbach	12	Kf	48.46N	8.19 E
Gernsheim	12	Ke	49.45N	8.29 E
Gero	28	Wg	35.48N	137.14 E
Gerolstein	12	Id	50.13N	6.40 E
Gerona	13	Ob	42.10N	2.40 E
Gerona/Girona	13	Oc	41.59N	2.49 E
Gerpinnes	12	Gd	50.20N	4.31 E
Gers	11	Gj	44.09N	0.39 E
Gers	11	Gk	43.40N	0.30 E
Gersprenz	12	Le	49.59N	9.04 E
Gêrzê	27	De	32.20N	84.04 E
Gerze	24	Fb	41.48N	35.12 E
Gescher	12	Jc	51.57N	7.00 E
Geseke	12	Kc	51.39N	8.31 E
Geser	26	Jg	3.53S	130.54 E
Gesunda	8	Fd	60.54N	14.32 E
Gesunden	8	Fa	63.10N	15.55 E
Geta	7	Ef	60.23N	19.50 E
Getafe	13	Id	40.18N	3.43W
Gete	11	Ld	50.55N	5.08 E
Getinge	7	Ch	56.49N	12.44 E
Gettysburg	45	Gd	45.01N	99.57W
Getúlio Vargas	55	Fh	27.50S	52.16W
Getz Ice Shelf	66	Nf	74.15S	125.00W
Geul	12	Hd	50.40N	5.43 E
Gevelsberg	12	Jc	51.19N	7.20 E
Gévora	13	Ff	38.53N	6.57W
Gevgelija	15	Hi	41.08N	22.31 E
Gevsjön	8	Ea	63.25N	12.40 E
Gewane	35	Gc	10.10N	40.39 E
Gex	11	Mh	46.20N	6.04 E
Gexianzhuang → Qinghe	28	Cf	37.03N	115.39 E
Geyersberg	10	Fg	49.50N	9.30 E
Geyik Dağı	24	Ee	36.54N	32.10 E
Geyikli	15	Jj	39.48N	26.12 E
Geyser, Banc du-	37	Mg	12.25S	46.25 E
Geysir	5	Dc	64.19N	20.18W
Geyve	24	Db	40.30N	30.18 E
Ghabāri, Darb al-	24	Qj	25.10N	29.50 E
Ghadāmis	31	Ic	30.08N	9.30 E
Ghadduwah	33	Bd	26.26N	14.18 E
Ghaghara	21	Kg	26.50N	84.50 E
Ghaghe	63a	Db	7.23S	158.12 E
Ghallah, Wādī al-	30	Jg	10.25N	27.32 E
Ghamrah, Wādī al-	24	Hj	25.47N	38.45 E
Ghana	31	Hh	8.00N	2.00W
Ghanzi	31	Jk	21.42S	21.38 E
Ghanzi	37	Cd	22.00S	23.00 E
Ghâr ad Dimā'	14	Cn	36.27N	8.26 E
Gharaqābād	24	Ne	35.06N	49.50 E
Gharbī, Al Hajar al-	24	Qj	24.10N	56.15 E
Gharbīyah, Aş Şahrā' al-= Western Desert (EN)	30	Jf	27.30N	27.30 E
Ghardaïa	31	Hc	32.29N	3.40 E
Ghārib, Jabal-	33	Fd	28.07N	32.54 E
Gharrāf, Shatt al-	24	Le	32.00N	46.48 E
Gharsah, Shatt al-	32	Jc	34.06N	7.50 E
Gharyān	33	Bc	32.10N	13.01 E
Gharyān	33	Bc	30.35N	12.00 E
Ghāt	31	Id	24.58N	10.11 E
Ghatere	63a	Db	7.58S	159.01 E
Ghatti	32	Jj	31.16N	37.31 E
Ghazāl, Bahr el-	30	Gg	13.01N	15.28 E
Ghazāl, Bahr el-	35	Bc	14.09N	16.30 E
Ghazaouet	32	Gb	35.06N	1.51W
Ghazipur	25	Gc	25.35N	83.34 E
Ghaznī	22	If	33.33N	68.26 E
Ghaznī	23	Kc	33.00N	68.00 E
Ghent (EN) = Gand/Gent	11	Jc	51.03N	3.43 E
Ghent (EN) = Gent/Gand	11	Jc	51.03N	3.43 E
Gheorghe Gheorghiu-Dej	15	Jc	46.12N	26.46 E
Gheorghieni	15	Ic	46.43N	25.37 E
Gheorghiu-Dej	19	De	51.00N	39.31 E
Gherla	15	Gb	47.02N	23.55 E
Ghidigeni	15	Kc	46.03N	27.30 E
Ghidole (EN) = Gidole	35	Fd	5.37N	37.29 E
Ghilarza	14	Cj	40.07N	8.50 E
Ghimeş, Pasul-	15	Jc	46.33N	26.07 E
Ghisonaccia	11a	Ba	42.00N	9.24 E
Ghizunabeana Islands	63a	Db	7.33S	158.45 E
Ghowr	23	Jc	34.00N	65.00 E
Ghriss	13	Mi	35.15N	0.10 E
Ghubbat al Qamar	21	Hh	16.00N	52.30 E
Ghudāf, Wādī al-	24	Je	32.56N	43.30 E
Ghurāb, Jabal al-	24	Hf	34.00N	38.42 E
Ghurayrah	33	Hf	18.37N	42.41 E
Ghūriān	23	Jc	34.21N	61.30 E
Ghurrab, Jabal al-	14	Cn	36.36N	8.23 E
Ghuzayyil, Sabkhat-	33	Dd	29.50N	19.45 E
Giaginskaja	16	Lg	44.47N	40.05 E
Giala, Jabal-	24	Ei	27.20N	32.57 E
Gialo Oasis (EN) = Jālū, Wāhāt-	30	Jf	29.00N	21.20 E
Gialoúsa	24	Fe	35.35N	34.15 E
Gia Nghia	25	Lf	11.59N	107.42 E
Giannutri	14	Hg	42.15N	11.05 E
Giant's Causeway/Clochán an Aifir	9	Gf	55.15N	6.35W
Giarre	14	Jm	37.43N	15.11 E
Giave	14	Ia	21.07N	76.08W
Gibbon Point	51b	Bb	18.14N	63.00W
Gibb River	59	Fc	16.25S	126.25 E
Gibbs Islands	66	Re	61.30S	55.31W
Gibeon	37	Bc	25.09S	17.43 E
Gibostad	7	Db	69.21N	18.00 E
Gibraleón	13	Fg	37.23N	6.58W
Gibraltar	5	Fh	36.11N	5.22W
Gibraltar	5	Fh	36.11N	5.22W
Gibraltar, Estrecho de-= Gibraltar, Strait of- (EN)	5	Fh	35.57N	5.36W
Djebel Ṭāriq, El Bôghāz-	5	Fh	35.57N	5.36W
Gibraltar, Strait of- (EN) = Gibraltar, Estrecho de-	5	Fh	35.57N	5.36W
Gibson Desert	57	Dg	24.30S	126.00 E
Gidami	35	Ed	8.58N	34.40 E
Giddings	45	Hk	30.11N	96.56W
GidigIc	15	Lb	47.04N	28.38 E
Gidole=Ghidole (EN)	35	Fd	5.37N	37.29 E
Gien	11	Ig	47.42N	2.38 E
Giens, Presqu'île de-	11	Mk	43.02N	6.08 E
Gier	11	Ki	45.35N	4.46 E
Gießen	10	Ef	50.35N	8.39 E
Gieten	12	Ia	53.01N	6.48 E
Giethoorn	12	Ib	52.43N	6.07 E
Gifford	42	Jb	70.21N	83.05W
Gifford Seamount (EN)	52	Hi	39.00S	82.00W
Gifhorn	10	Gd	52.29N	10.33 E
Gift Lake	42	Fe	55.49N	115.57W
Gifu	22	Pf	35.25N	136.45 E
Gifu Ken	36	Mh	35.50N	137.00 E
Gigant	16	Lf	46.29N	41.20 E
Giganta, Sierra de la-	36	Bc	26.07N	111.36W
Giganta, Sierra de la-	36	Bc	26.18N	111.39W
Gigen	15	Hf	43.42N	24.29 E
Gigha	9	Hf	55.41N	5.44W
Giglio	14	Eh	42.20N	10.55 E
Gignod	14	Bd	45.45N	7.20 E
Gijón	6	Fg	43.32N	5.40W
Gikongoro	36	Ec	2.30S	29.35 E
Gila Bend	46	Ij	32.57N	112.43W
Gila Bend Mountains	46	Ij	33.10N	113.10W
Gīlān	23	Gb	37.00N	49.50 E
Gilan-e-Gharb	24	Le	34.08N	45.55 E
Gila River	43	Ge	32.43N	114.33W
Gilbert	58	Gf	16.35S	141.15 E
Gilbert River	57	Ff	17.11S	142.25 E
Gilbert Islands	57	Lc	0.01S	174.00 E
Gilbert Seamount (EN)	40	If	52.50N	150.10W
Gilbués	54	Ie	9.50S	45.21W
Gilé	37	Lc	16.09S	38.19 E
Giles Meteorological Station	59	Fe	25.02S	128.18 E
Gilford Island	46	Ea	50.46N	126.25W
Gilgandra	59	Jf	31.42S	148.39 E
Gilgáu	42	Gb	47.17N	23.43 E
Gilgil	36	Gc	0.30S	36.19 E
Gilgit	25	Ea	35.44N	74.38 E
Gilgit	25	Ja	35.55N	74.18 E
Giljuj	20	Hf	54.17N	127.05 E
Gillam	42	Hd	56.21N	94.43W
Gilleleje	8	Eh	56.12N	12.19 E
Gillen, Lake-	59	Ee	26.10S	124.40 E
Gillenfeld	12	Id	50.07N	6.54 E
Gillette	43	Fc	44.18N	105.30W
Gillian, Lake -	42	Kc	69.30N	75.30W
Gillingham	9	Nj	51.24N	0.33 E
Gilort	15	Ge	44.36N	23.27 E
Gilroy	46	Eh	37.00N	121.34W
Giluwe, Mount-	60	Ci	6.43S	143.53 E
Gīlvän	24	Md	36.47N	49.04 E
Gimbi	35	Fd	9.10N	35.51 E
Gimie, Mount-	50	Ff	13.52N	61.01 E
Gimli	42	Hf	50.39N	97.00W
Gimo	8	Hd	60.11N	18.11 E
Gimone	11	Hk	43.30N	1.06 E
Ginda	35	Fb	15.27N	39.06 E
Ginetu	63a	Ac	9.30S	152.43 E

Index Symbols

[1] Independent Nation	Historical or Cultural Region	Pass, Gap
[2] State, Region	Mount, Mountain	Plain, Lowland
[3] District, County	Volcano	Delta
[4] Municipality	Hill	Salt Flat
[5] Colony, Dependency	Mountains, Mountain Range	Valley, Canyon
Continent	Hills, Escarpment	Crater, Cave
Physical Region	Plateau, Upland	Karst Features

Depression	Coast, Beach	Rock, Reef
Polder	Cliff	Islands, Archipelago
Desert, Dunes	Peninsula	Rocks, Reefs
Forest, Woods	Isthmus	Coral Reef
Heath, Steppe	Sandbank	Well, Spring
Oasis	Island	Geyser
Cape, Point	Atoll	River, Stream

Waterfall Rapids	Canal	Lagoon
River Mouth, Estuary	Glacier	Bank
Lake	Ice Shelf, Pack Ice	Seamount
Salt Lake	Ocean	Tablemount
Intermittent Lake	Sea	Ridge
Reservoir	Gulf, Bay	Shelf
Swamp, Pond	Strait, Fjord	Basin

Escarpment, Sea Scarp	Historic Site	Port
Fracture	Ruins	Lighthouse
Trench, Abyss	Wall, Walls	Mine
National Park, Reserve	Church, Abbey	Tunnel
Point of Interest	Temple	Dam, Bridge
Recreation Site	Scientific Station	
Cave, Cavern	Airport	

Ŝin Gin	59	Kd	25.00 S	151.58 E
Ŝingin	59	Df	31.21 S	115.42 E
Ŝingoog	26	le	8.50N	125.07 E
Ŝinir	35	Gd	7.08N	40.43 E
Ŝinosa	14	Kj	40.35N	16.45 E
Ŝinowan	29b	Ab	26.17N	127.45 E
Ŝinzo de Limia	13	Eb	42.03N	7.43W
Ŝiofra Oasis (EN) = Jufrah, Wāḩāt al- ◫	30	If	29.10N	16.00 E
Ŝioia, Golfo di- ◪	14	Jl	38.30N	15.45 E
Ŝioia del Colle	14	Kj	40.48N	16.55 E
Ŝioia Tauro	14	Jl	38.25N	15.54 E
Ŝion	35	Fd	8.24N	37.55 E
Ŝióna Öros	15	Fk	38.35N	22.15 E
Ŝiovi, Passo dei- ◳	14	Cf	44.33N	8.57 E
Ŝiraltovce	10	Rg	49.07N	21.31 E
Ŝirardot ▱	54	Dc	4.18N	74.49W
Ŝirdle Ness ▱	9	Kd	57.08N	2.02W
Ŝiresun	23	Ea	40.55N	38.24 E
Ŝiresun Dağları ▱	24	Hb	40.40N	38.10 E
Ŝiri ◳	36	Cb	0.28N	17.59 E
Ŝiridih	25	Hd	24.11N	86.18 E
Ŝiriftu	36	Gb	2.00N	39.45 E
Ŝirne/Kyrenia	24	Ee	35.20N	33.19 E
Ŝirón	54	Cd	3.10S	79.09W
Ŝirona/Gerona	13	Oc	41.59N	2.49 E
Ŝironde [3]	11	Fj	44.55N	0.30W
Ŝironde ◳	5	Ff	45.35N	1.03W
Ŝironella	13	Nb	42.02N	1.53 E
Ŝirou ▱	11	Hk	43.46N	1.23 E
Ŝirvan	9	If	55.15N	4.51W
Ŝirvas	7	He	62.31N	33.44 E
Ŝisborne	58	Ih	38.39S	178.01 E
Ŝisenyi	36	Ec	1.42S	29.15 E
Ŝislaved	8	Eg	57.18N	13.32 E
Ŝisors	11	He	49.17N	1.47 E
Ŝissar	18	Ge	38.31N	68.36 E
Ŝissarski Hrebet ▱	18	Ge	39.00N	68.40 E
Ŝistad	8	Ff	58.27N	15.55 E
Ŝistel	12	Ec	51.10N	2.57 E
Ŝistral ▱	13	Ea	43.28N	7.35W
Ŝitarama	36	Ec	2.05S	29.16 E
Ŝitega	36	Ec	3.26S	29.56 E
Ŝitu	24	Me	35.20N	48.05 E
Ŝiudicarie, Valli- ◳	14	Ld	46.00N	10.40 E
Ŝiulianova	14	Hh	42.45N	13.57 E
Ŝiumalău, Vîrful- ▱	15	If	47.25N	25.29 E
Ŝiurgeni	15	Ke	44.35N	27.48 E
Ŝiurgiu	15	If	43.53N	25.57 E
Ŝive	8	Ci	55.51N	9.15 E
Ŝivors	11	Ki	45.35N	4.46 E
Ŝivry-en-Argonne	12	Gf	48.57N	4.53 E
Ŝivry Island ◳	64d	Bb	7.07N	151.53 E
Ŝiwa	34	Gc	11.18N	7.27 E
Ŝiza (EN) = Al Jīzah	31	Ke	30.01N	31.13 E
Ŝiżduvan	19	Gg	40.06N	64.40 E
Ŝiżiga	20	Ld	62.03N	160.30 E
Ŝiżiginskaja Guba ◪	20	Kd	61.10N	158.30 E
Ŝizo ◳	63a	Cc	8.07S	156.50 E
Ŝizo	60	Fi	8.06S	156.51 E
Ŝizycko	10	Rb	54.03N	21.47 E
Ŝjalicĕs, Mali i- ▱	15	Dg	42.01N	20.28 E
Ŝjamyš, Gora- ▱	16	Oi	40.20N	46.25 E
Ŝjende	8	Cc	61.30N	8.35 E
Ŝjerstad	8	Cf	58.52N	9.00 E
Ŝjervatn ◳	8	Cb	62.40N	9.25 E
Ŝjirokastra	15	Di	40.05N	20.10 E
Ŝjoa Haven	39	Jc	68.38N	95.57W
Ŝjevik	6	Hc	60.48N	10.42 E
Ŝjuhĕs, Kep i- ▱	15	Ci	40.25N	19.18 E
Ŝlace Bay	42	Lg	46.12N	59.57W
Ŝlacier Bay ◳	40	Le	58.40N	136.00W
Ŝlacier Peak ▱	43	Cb	48.07N	121.07W
Ŝlacier Strait ◳	42	Ja	76.15N	79.00W
Ŝladbeck	12	Ic	51.34N	6.59 E
Ŝladenbach	12	Kd	50.46N	8.34 E
Ŝladewater	45	Ij	32.33N	94.56W
Ŝladstone [Austl.]	58	Gg	23.51 S	151.16 E
Ŝladstone [Man.-Can.]	45	Ga	50.15N	98.50W
Ŝladstone [Mi.-U.S.]	44	Ib	45.51N	87.03W
Ŝladstone [Mo.-U.S.]	45	Ig	39.13N	94.34W
Ŝlafsfjorden ◳	8	Ee	59.35N	12.35 E
Ŝláma ▱	5	Hd	59.12N	10.57 E
Ŝláma ▱	7a	Ab	65.48N	23.00W
Ŝlamis Castle	9	Ke	56.37N	3.00W
Ŝlamoč	23	Ff	44.03N	16.51 E
Ŝlan [Aus.] ▱	7	Dg	58.35N	15.55 E
Ŝlan [Aus.]	14	Id	46.36N	14.25 E
Ŝlan [F.R.G.]	10	Dg	49.47N	7.43 E
Ŝlan-Münchweiler	12	Je	49.28N	7.26 E
Ŝlarner Alpen ▱	14	Cd	47.00N	9.00 E
Ŝlärnisch ▱	14	Cd	47.00N	9.00 E
Ŝlarus [3]	14	Dd	46.55N	9.05 E
Ŝlarus	14	Cd	47.03N	9.04 E
Ŝlasgow [Ky.-U.S.]	44	Eg	37.00N	85.55W
Ŝlasgow [Mt.-U.S.]	43	Fb	48.12N	106.38W
Ŝlasgow [Scot.-U.K.]	6	Fd	55.53N	4.15W
Ŝlashütte	10	Jf	50.51N	13.47 E
Ŝlass ▱	9	Id	57.25N	4.00W
Ŝlassboro	44	Jf	39.42N	75.07W
Ŝlass Mountains ▱	45	Kk	30.25N	103.15W
Ŝlastonbury	9	Kj	51.09N	2.43W
Ŝlauchau	10	Jf	50.49N	12.32 E
Ŝlava	8	Ee	59.33N	12.34 E
Ŝlazov	6	Ld	58.09N	52.40 E
Ŝleann Dá Loch/ Glendalough	9	Gh	53.00N	6.20W
Ŝledićske Planine ▱	15	Df	43.49N	20.55 E
Ŝleinalpe ▱	14	Jc	47.10N	15.05 E
Ŝleisdorf	14	Kc	46.55N	15.43 E
Ŝlen ◳	12	Bb	52.50N	0.07W
Ŝlénan, Iles de- ◳	11	Cg	47.43N	4.00W
Ŝlen Arbor	44	Ee	44.53N	85.58W
Ŝlen Canyon	62	Df	44.55 S	171.06 E
Ŝlen Canyon	46	Jh	37.05N	111.41W
Ŝlencoe [Mn.-U.S.]	45	Id	44.46N	94.09W
Ŝlencoe [S.Afr.]	37	Ee	28.12 S	30.07 E

Glendale [Az.-U.S.]	43	Ee	33.32N	112.11W
Glendale [Ca.-U.S.]	43	De	34.10N	118.17W
Glendalough/Gleann Dá Loch	9	Gh	53.00N	6.20W
Glendive	43	Gb	47.06N	104.43W
Glendo Reservoir ◳	46	Me	42.31N	104.58W
Glen Innes	61	Dh	41.39S	172.39 E
Glennallen	58	Gg	29.44 S	151.44 E
Glenner ▱	40	Jd	62.07N	145.33W
Glenns Ferry	14	Dd	46.46N	9.12 E
Glenorchy	46	He	42.57N	115.18W
Glenrock	62	Cf	44.52 S	168.24 E
Glen Rose	46	Me	42.52N	105.52W
Glenrothes	45	Hj	32.14N	97.45W
Glens Falls	9	Je	56.12N	3.05W
Glenville	44	Id	43.17N	73.41W
Glenwood [Ia.-U.S.]	44	Gf	38.57N	80.51W
Glenwood [Mn.-U.S.]	45	If	41.03N	95.45W
Glenwood Springs	45	Id	45.39N	95.23W
Glibokaja	43	Fd	39.32N	107.19W
Glina	15	Ja	48.05N	26.00 E
Glinjany	14	Ke	45.20N	16.06 E
Glittertind ▱	10	Ug	49.46N	24.33 E
Gliwice	5	Gc	61.39N	8.33 E
Globe	10	Of	50.17N	18.40 E
Globino	43	Ee	33.24N	110.47 W
Głogów	16	He	49.24N	33.18 E
Glomfjord	10	Me	51.40N	16.05 E
Glommersträsk	7	Cc	66.49N	13.58 E
Glonn ▱	7	Ed	65.16N	19.38 E
Glorieuses, Iles- ◳	10	Hh	48.11N	11.45 E
Glottof, Mount- ▱	30	Lj	11.30S	47.20 E
Gloucester ▱	40	le	57.30N	153.30W
Gloucester [Eng.-U.K.]	9	Kj	51.55N	2.15W
Gloucester [Ma.-U.S.]	9	Kj	51.53N	2.14W
Gloucester, Cape- ◳	44	Ld	42.41N	70.39W
Gloucestershire [3]	60	Di	5.27 S	148.25 E
Glover Island ◳	9	Lj	51.50N	1.55W
Glover's Reef ◳	51p	Bb	11.59N	61.47W
Gloversville	49	De	16.49N	87.48W
Głowno	44	Jd	43.03N	74.21W
Głubczyce	10	Pe	51.58N	19.44 E
Glubokoje [Bye.-U.S.S.R.]	19	Cd	55.08N	27.41 E
Glubokoje [Kaz.-U.S.S.R.]	18	Ie	50.06N	82.19 E
Glubokoje, Ozero- ◳	10	Md	60.30N	29.25 E
Głuchołazy	10	Nf	50.20N	17.22 E
Glücksburg	10	Fb	54.50N	9.33 E
Glückstadt	10	Fc	53.47N	9.25 E
Gluhov	19	De	51.43N	33.57 E
Gluša	16	Fc	53.06N	28.52 E
Glyngøre	8	Ch	56.46N	8.52 E
Gmünd [Aus.]	14	Hd	46.54N	13.32 E
Gmünd [Aus.]	14	Ib	48.46N	14.59 E
Gmunden	14	Hc	47.55N	13.48 E
Gnarp	7	De	62.03N	17.16 E
Gnesta	7	Dg	59.03N	17.18 E
Gniben ◳	8	Dh	56.01N	11.18 E
Gniew	10	Oc	53.51N	18.49 E
Gniewkowo	10	Od	52.54N	18.25 E
Gniezno	10	Nd	52.31N	17.37 E
Gnjilane	15	Eg	42.28N	21.29 E
Gnosjö	7	Ch	57.22N	13.44 E
Gnowangerup	59	Df	33.56 S	117.50 E
Goa, Damän and Diu [3]	13	Sb	15.35N	74.00 E
Goageb	37	Be	26.44 S	17.15 E
Goälpära	25	Ic	26.10N	90.37 E
Goat ▱	37	Bd	24.55 S	18.55 E
Goat Island ◳	10	Qg	49.53N	18.50 E
Goat Point ◳	24	Pb	45.41N	17.33W
Goba	31	Kh	7.01N	39.59 E
Gobabis	31	Kc	22.30 S	18.58 E
Gobabis [3]	37	Bd	22.05 S	19.00 E
Göbel	15	Lj	40.00N	28.09 E
Gober	34	Gc	13.48N	6.51 E
Gobernador Gregores	56	Fg	48.45 S	70.15W
Gobernador Ingeniero Valentín Virasoro	56	Ic	28.03 S	56.02W
Gobernador Mansilla	55	Ck	32.33 S	59.22W
Gobi, Pustynja = Gobi Desert (EN) ◳	21	Me	43.00N	106.00 E
Gobi Altai (EN) = Gobijski Altaj ▱	21	Me	44.00N	102.00 E
Gobi Desert (EN) = Gobi, Pustynja ◳	21	Me	43.00N	106.00 E
Gobijski Altaj = Gobi Altai (EN) ▱	21	Me	44.00N	102.00 E
Gobö	28	Mh	33.53N	135.10 E
Göçbeyli	15	Kj	39.13N	27.25 E
Goceano	14	Dj	40.30N	9.15 E
Goceano, Catena del- ▱	15	Gh	41.33N	23.42 E
Goce Delčev	10	Ce	51.40N	6.10 E
Gochas	37	Bd	24.55 S	18.55 E
Goczałkowickie, Jezioro- ◳	10	Pg	49.53N	18.50 E
Göd	10	Pi	65.41N	17.33W
Godalming	12	Bc	51.11N	0.36W
Godär ▱	39	Qh	29.45N	57.30 E
Godär-e Shah ◳	24	Me	34.45N	48.10 E
Godävari ▱	21	Kh	17.00N	81.45 E
Godbout, Riviére- ▱	44	Na	49.21N	67.42W
Gode	35	Gd	5.55N	43.40 E
Godeč	15	Gf	43.01N	23.03 E
Godelbukta Breidvika ◳	66	Df	70.15S	24.15 E
Goderich	44	Ee	43.45N	81.43W
Goderville	12	Ce	49.39N	0.22 E
Godhavn/Qeqertarssuaq	41	Nc	69.20N	53.35W
Godhra	25	Gd	22.45N	73.38 E
Godinlabe	35	Hd	5.54N	46.42 E
Gödöllő	10	Pi	47.36N	19.22 E
Godoy Cruz	56	Gd	32.55 S	68.50W
Gods Lake	42	Db	54.40N	94.20W
Gods Mercy, Bay of - ◳	42	If	54.40N	94.24W
Gods River ▱	42	le	56.22N	92.52W
Godthåb/Nûk	67	Nc	64.15N	51.40W

Godthåbfjord ◳	41	Gf	64.20N	51.30W
Godwin Austen (EN) = K2 ▱	21	Jf	35.53N	76.30 E
Godwin Austen (EN) = Qogir Feng ▱	21	Jf	35.53N	76.30 E
Goedereede	12	Fc	51.49N	3.58 E
Goéland, Lac au- ◳	42	Jg	49.45N	76.50W
Goélands, Lac aux- ◳	42	Le	55.30N	64.30W
Goële ◳	12	Ee	49.10N	2.40 E
Goelette Island ◳	37b	Bc	10.13 S	51.08 E
Goeree ◳	11	Jc	51.50N	3.55 E
Goes	12	Fc	51.30N	3.54 E
Gogama	42	Jg	47.40N	81.43W
Gô-Gawa ▱	28	Je	35.01N	132.13 E
Gogebic Range ▱	44	Cb	46.45N	89.25W
Gogland, Ostrov- ◳	7	Gf	60.05N	27.00 E
Gog Magog Hills ▱	12	Cb	52.09N	0.11 E
Gogounou	34	Fc	10.50N	2.50 E
Gogrial	35	Dd	8.32N	28.07 E
Gogu, Vîrful- ▱	15	Fd	45.12N	22.30 E
Goğu Karadeniz Dağları ▱	24	Db	15.39N	9.21W
Gohelle ◳	16	Gb	40.40N	40.00 E
Goiandira	12	Ed	50.28N	2.45 E
Goianésia	54	Ig	18.08 S	48.06W
Goiânia	54	Ig	15.19 S	49.04W
Goianinha	53	La	16.40 S	49.16W
Goiás [2]	54	Ke	6.16 S	35.12W
Goiás	54	If	12.00 S	48.00W
Goiatuba	54	Ih	15.56 S	50.08W
Goikul	64a	Bc	7.22 S	134.36 E
Göinge ◳	8	Eh	56.20N	13.50 E
Goio-Erê	56	Jb	24.12 S	53.02W
Goioxim	55	Gg	25.14 S	52.01W
Goirle	12	Hc	51.34N	5.05 E
Góis	13	Dd	40.09N	8.07W
Goito	14	Ee	45.15N	10.40 E
Gojam [3]	35	Fc	10.33N	37.35 E
Gojôme	29	Gb	39.56N	140.07 E
Gojra	25	Eb	31.09N	72.41 E
Gojthski, Pereval- ◳	16	Kg	44.15N	39.18 E
Gokase-Gawa ▱	28	Be	32.35N	131.42 E
Gokasho-Wan ◳	29	Ed	34.20N	136.40 E
Gökbel Dağı ▱	15	Kl	37.28N	28.00 E
Gökçay ▱	24	Ed	36.36N	33.23 E
Gökçeada ◳	24	Ac	40.10N	25.50 E
Gökçeören	15	Lk	38.35N	28.32 E
Gökçeyazi	15	Kj	39.38N	27.39 E
Gökdere ◳	24	Ed	36.39N	33.03 E
Gökırmak ▱	24	Fb	41.24N	35.08 E
Göksu [Tur.] ▱	16	Fc	53.06N	28.52 E
Göksu [Tur.] ▱	24	Fd	37.37N	35.35 E
Göksun	15	Mi	40.23N	29.58 E
Gök Tepe ▱	15	Mm	36.53N	29.17 E
Göktepe	15	Ll	37.16N	28.36 E
Gokwe	37	Dc	18.13 S	28.55 E
Gol	7	Bf	60.42N	8.57 E
Goläghät	25	Ic	26.31N	93.58 E
Golaja Pristan	16	Hf	46.29N	32.31 E
Golańcz	10	Nd	52.57N	17.18 E
Golconda [Il.-U.S.]	45	Lh	37.22N	88.29W
Golconda [Nv.-U.S.]	46	Gf	40.57N	117.30W
Gölcük	24	Cb	40.44N	29.44 E
Golčův Jeníkov	10	Lg	49.49N	15.28 E
Gołdap	10	Sb	54.19N	22.19 E
Gold Beach	46	Ce	42.25N	124.25W
Gold Coast	58	Gg	27.58 S	153.25 E
Gold Coast	30	Gh	5.20N	0.45W
Gold Coast ◳	34	Ef	5.10N	0.59 E
Golden [B.C.-Can.]	43	Dg	39.46N	105.13W
Golden [Co.-U.S.]	62	Ed	40.50 S	172.52 E
Goldendale	46	Dd	45.49N	120.50W
Golden Gate ◳	46	Dh	37.49N	122.29W
Golden Hinde ▱	42	Kl	29.23N	90.16W
Golden Meadow	46	Kg	49.39N	125.45W
Golden Vale/Machaire na Mumhan ◳	9	Fi	52.30N	8.00W
Goldfield	46	Gh	37.42N	117.14W
Gold River	46	Bb	49.41N	126.08W
Goldsboro	43	Ld	35.23N	77.59W
Goldsworthy	59	Dd	20.20 S	119.30 E
Gôle	24	Jb	40.48N	42.36 E
Golegã	13	De	39.24N	8.29W
Goleniów	10	Kc	53.36N	14.50 E
Goleta, Cerro- ▱	15	Eh	41.42N	21.33 E
Golfito	48	Ih	18.38N	100.04W
Golfo Aranci	47	Ng	8.38N	83.11W
Gölgeli Dağları ▱	14	Dj	41.00N	9.37 E
Gölhisar	15	Ml	37.15N	29.00 E
Goliad	15	Ll	37.08N	29.30 E
Golija [Yugo.] ▱	45	Hl	28.40N	97.23W
Golija [Yugo.] ▱	15	Df	43.19N	20.18 E
Goljak ▱	15	Ef	43.02N	18.47 E
Goljama Kamčija ▱	15	Eg	42.44N	21.31 E
Goljama Sjutkja ▱	15	Kf	43.03N	27.29 E
Goljam Perelik ▱	15	Hh	41.54N	24.01 E
Goljam Persenk ▱	15	Hg	42.16N	24.33 E
Gölköy	15	Hh	41.49N	24.34 E
Gölköl ◳	24	Gb	40.15N	37.26 E
Göllheim	15	Kj	39.19N	27.59 E
Gölmarmara	12	Ke	49.35N	8.03 E
Golmud He ▱	15	Kk	38.42N	27.56 E
Golo ▱	36	Bd	36.54N	95.11 E
Gologory ◳	11a	Ba	42.31N	9.32 E
Gologory ▱	10	Ug	49.35N	24.30 E
Golovin	40	Bd	64.33N	163.02W
Golovnin Seamount (EN) ▱	20	Kg	46.50N	157.00 E
Golpäyegän	23	Db	40.17N	30.19 E
Gölpazari	24	Cb	40.17N	30.19 E
Golspie	42	le	56.22N	92.52W
Gol Tappeh	24	Kd	36.35N	45.45 E

Golubac	15	Ee	44.39N	21.38 E
Golub-Dobrzyń	10	Pc	53.08N	19.02 E
Golungo Alto	36	Bd	9.08 S	14.47 E
Golyšmanovo	19	Gd	56.23N	68.23 E
Goma	31	Ji	1.37 S	29.12 E
Gómara	13	Jc	41.37N	2.13W
Gombe	31	Ig	10.17N	11.10 E
Gomel	34	Hc	10.10N	12.44 E
Gomelskaja Oblast [3]	5	Jz	22.25N	31.00 E
Gómez Farias	19	Ce	52.20N	29.40 E
Gómez Palacio	30	Ff	28.06N	17.08W
Gomo Co ◳	48	le	24.57N	101.02W
Goms ◪	27	Zc	33.45N	85.35 E
Gonäbäd	14	Cd	46.25N	8.10 E
Gonaïves	23	Ic	34.20N	58.42 E
Gonam ▱	47	Je	19.27N	72.43W
Gonäve, Golfe de la- ◳	20	le	57.18N	131.20 E
Gonäve, Ile de la- ◳	47	Je	19.00N	73.30W
Gonbad-e Qäbüs	47	Ib	37.15N	55.09 E
Gonda	25	Gc	27.08N	81.56 E
Gonder [3]	35	Fc	12.00N	37.30 E
Gonder	25	Gd	21.27N	80.12 E
Gondia	30	Gg	14.20N	3.10W
Gondo ◳	13	Dc	41.09N	8.32W
Gondomar	21	Kg	23.00N	81.00 E
Gondwana ◳	27	Gc	41.50N	97.00 E
Gönen	24	Bb	40.06N	27.39 E
Gönen ▱	15	Kj	40.08N	27.31 E
Gonfreville-l'Orcher	12	Ce	49.30N	0.14 E
Gong'an (Doushi)	27	Je	30.05N	112.12 E
Gongbo'gyamda	27	Ff	29.59N	93.25 E
Gonggar	27	Ff	29.17N	90.50 E
Gongga Shan ▱	21	Mg	29.34N	101.53 E
Gonghe	27	Hd	36.21N	100.47 E
Gongliu/Tokkuztara	27	Dc	43.30N	82.15 E
Gongola ▱	31	Ih	9.30N	.12.04 E
Gongpoquan	27	Gc	41.50N	97.00 E
Gongshan	27	Gf	27.39N	98.35 E
Gongxian ▱	27	Kf	26.05N	119.32 E
Gongxian (Xiaoyi)	28	Bg	34.46N	112.57 E
Gongzhuling → Huaide	27	Lc	43.30N	124.52 E
Goni	55	Dk	33.31 S	56.24W
Goniądz	10	Sc	53.30N	22.45 E
Gonishän	24	Pd	37.04N	54.06 E
Gonjo	27	Ge	30.52N	98.20 E
Gonohe	29	Ae	40.31N	141.19 E
Go-no-ura	29	Ae	33.45N	129.41 E
Gônuk ◳	24	Fd	37.37N	35.35 E
Gonzales	45	Hl	29.30N	97.27W
Gonzáles, Riacho- ▱	55	Df	22.48 S	57.54W
González	48	Jf	22.50N	98.27W
Goodenough, Cape- ◳	66	le	66.16 S	126.10 E
Goodenough Bay ◳	60	Ej	9.55 S	150.00 E
Goodenough Island ◳	60	Ei	9.22 S	150.16 E
Good Hope, Cape of-/Groeie Hoop, Kaap die- ◳	30	Il	34.21 S	18.28 E
Goodhouse	37	Be	28.57 S	18.13 E
Gooding	42	Gd	42.56N	114.43W
Goodland	43	Gd	39.21N	101.43W
Goodnews Bay	40	Cd	59.07N	161.35W
Goodsir, Mount- ▱	46	Ga	51.12N	116.20W
Good Spirit Lake	42	Na	51.34N	102.40W
Goodwin Sands ◳	12	Dc	51.15N	1.35 E
Goodyear	46	Ij	33.26N	112.21W
Goole	9	Md	53.42N	0.52W
Goomalling	59	Df	31.19 S	116.49 E
Goondiwindi	58	Fg	28.33 S	150.19 E
Goonyella	59	Jd	21.43 S	147.58 E
Goor	12	Ib	52.14N	6.37 E
Goose Bay	39	Md	53.19N	60.24W
Goose Lake	43	Cc	41.57N	120.25W
Goose River ▱	45	Hc	47.25N	96.52W
Goplo, Jezioro- ◳	10	Od	52.35N	18.20 E
Göppingen	10	Fg	48.42N	9.40 E
Góra	10	Me	51.40N	16.33 E
Góra Kalwaria	10	Re	51.59N	21.12 E
Gorakhpur	22	Kg	26.45N	83.22 E
Goransko	15	Bf	43.07N	18.50 E
Gorata ▱	15	Ih	41.45N	25.55 E
Goražde	23	Jb	40.48N	42.36 E
Gorda, Cayo ◳	48	Ei	35.55N	121.27W
Gorda, Punta- [Ca.-U.S.] ◳	49	Fl	15.58N	82.15W
Gorda, Punta- [Cuba] ◳	46	Cf	40.16N	124.20W
Gorda, Punta- [Nic.] ◳	49	Fb	22.24N	82.10W
Gördes	49	Fl	14.21N	83.12W
Gördes ▱	15	Lk	38.38N	28.18 E
Gordil	15	Lj	38.46N	27.58 E
Gordion ◳	35	Cd	9.44N	21.35 E
Gordon [Nb.-U.S.]	24	Ec	39.37N	32.00 E
Gordon [Wi.-U.S.]	45	Ec	42.48N	102.12W
Gordon Horne Peak ▱	45	Kc	46.15N	91.47W
Gordonvale	43	Rb	51.46N	118.50W
Goré [Eth.]	59	Jc	17.05 S	145.47 E
Goré [N.Z.]	35	Fd	8.09N	35.34 E
Gorele	62	Cg	46.06 S	168.56 E
Görele	35	Bd	7.55N	16.38 E
Göreniska	24	Hb	41.02N	39.00 E
Gorey/Guaire	14	Id	46.20N	14.10 E
Gorgän	9	Gi	52.40N	6.18W
Gorgän, Khalij-e- ◳	24	Jf	33.21N	43.40 E
Gorgany ▱	24	Pc	36.59N	54.05 E
Gorgol [3]	10	Uf	49.35N	24.30 E
Gorgol el Abiod ▱	32	Ef	16.14N	12.58W
Gorgona, Isla- ◳	54	Cc	2.59N	78.12W
Gorham	32	Df	15.45N	13.00W
Gori	19	Eg	42.00N	44.02 E

Gorinchem	11	Kc	51.50N	5.00 E
Goring	12	Ac	51.31N	1.08W
Goris	16	Oj	39.31N	46.22 E
Gorizia	14	He	45.57N	13.38 E
Gorj [2]	15	Gd	45.00N	23.20 E
Gorjačegorsk	20	De	55.24N	88.55 E
Gorjačij Ključ	16	Kg	44.36N	39.07 E
Gorjanci	14	Je	45.45N	15.20 E
Gorki [Bye.-U.S.S.R.]	16	Gb	54.17N	31.00 E
Gorki [R.S.F.S.R.]	5	Kf	57.38N	40.05 E
Gorki [R.S.F.S.R.]	20	Bc	65.05N	65.15 E
Gorko-Solenoje, Ozero- ◳	16	Oe	49.20N	46.05 E
Gorkovskaja Oblast [3]	19	Ed	56.15N	44.45 E
Gorkovskoje Vodohranilišče = Gorky Reservoir (EN) ◳	5	Kd	57.00N	43.10 E
Gorkum ◳	10	Hf	50.10N	11.08 E
Gorky Reservoir (EN) = Gorkovskoje Vodohr. ◳				
Gørlev	8	Di	55.32N	11.14 E
Gorlice	10	Rg	49.40N	21.10 E
Görlitz	10	Ke	51.10N	15.00 E
Gorlovka	5	Jf	48.18N	38.03 E
Gornalunga ▱	14	Jm	37.24N	15.03 E
Gorna Orjahovica	15	If	43.07N	25.41 E
Gornjak [R.S.F.S.R.]	20	Df	51.00N	81.29 E
Gornjak [Ukr.-U.S.S.R.]	50	Uf	50.16N	24.13 E
Gornji Milanovac	15	De	44.02N	20.27 E
Gornji Vakuf	23	Kd	43.56N	17.36 E
Gorno-Altajsk	22	Kd	51.58N	85.58 E
Gorno-Altajskaja Avtonomnaja Oblast [3]	20	Df	51.00N	87.00 E
Gorno-Badahšanskaja Avtonomnaja Oblast [3]	19	Hh	38.15N	73.00 E
Gorno-Čujski	20	Ge	57.40N	111.40 E
Gornozavodsk [R.S.F.S.R.]	20	Jg	46.30N	141.55 E
Gornozavodsk [R.S.F.S.R.]	17	Ig	58.25N	58.20 E
Gorny [R.S.F.S.R.]	16	Pd	51.45N	48.34 E
Gorny [R.S.F.S.R.]	17	If	50.48N	136.26 E
Gornyje Ključi	28	Lb	45.15N	133.30 E
Gorochan ▱	35	Fd	9.26N	37.05 E
Gorodec [Bye.-U.S.S.R.]	19	Ed	56.40N	43.30 E
Gorodec [R.S.F.S.R.]	8	Mf	58.30N	29.55 E
Gorodenka	16	De	48.42N	25.32 E
Gorodišče [Bye.-U.S.S.R.]	16	Vc	53.16N	26.03 E
Gorodišče [R.S.F.S.R.]	16	Nc	53.16N	45.42 E
Gorodišče [Ukr.-U.S.S.R.]	16	He	49.17N	31.27 E
Gorodnica	16	Ed	50.49N	27.22 E
Gorodok [Bye.-U.S.S.R.]	19	Cd	55.26N	29.59 E
Gorodok [Ukr.-U.S.S.R.]	16	Ce	49.10N	23.39 E
Gorodok [Ukr.-U.S.S.R.]	16	Ce	49.47N	23.39 E
Gorodovikovsk	19	Ef	46.05N	41.59 E
Gorohovec	10	Uf	50.28N	24.47 E
Gorohovec	7	Kh	56.12N	42.42 E
Goroka	58	Fe	6.02 S	145.22 E
Gorom-Gorom	34	Ec	14.26N	0.14W
Gorong, Kepulauan- ◳	26	Jg	4.05 S	131.20 E
Gorongosa, Serra da- ▱	37	Ee	18.24 S	34.06 E
Gorontalo	22	Oi	0.33N	123.03 E
Goroual ▱	34	Ec	14.42N	0.53 E
Górowo Iławeckie	10	Qb	54.17N	20.30 E
Gorron	11	Ff	48.25N	0.49W
Goršečnoje	16	Kd	51.33N	38.09 E
Gorski Kotar ◪	14	le	45.26N	14.40 E
Gorssel	12	Ib	52.12N	6.13 E
Gort	9	Eh	53.04N	8.50W
Goru, Vîrful- ▱	15	Jd	45.48N	26.25 E
Görükle	15	Li	40.14N	28.50 E
Gorzów [2]	10	Ld	52.45N	15.15 E
Gorzów Wielkopolski	10	Ld	52.44N	15.15 E
Górzów Wielkopolski	10	Ld	52.44N	15.15 E
Goschen Strait ◳	60	Ej	10.09 S	150.56 E
Gosen	28	Of	37.44N	139.11 E
Goseong	28	Kf	33.26 S	151.21 E
Goshen	44	Ee	41.35N	85.50W
Goshogawara	29	Pd	40.48N	140.27 E
Gosier	51e	Bb	16.12N	61.30W
Gospić	14	Je	51.54N	10.28 E
Gosport	9	Lk	50.48N	1.08W
Gossen ◳	8	Bb	62.50N	6.55 E
Gossi	34	Eb	15.47N	1.15W
Gossinga	35	Dd	8.39N	25.59 E
Gostivar	15	Eh	41.48N	20.54 E
Gostynin	10	Ne	51.53N	17.00 E
Gostynin	10	Pd	52.26N	19.29 E
Gota älv ▱	5	Hd	57.42N	11.52 E
Göta Kanal ◳	7	Dg	58.50N	13.58 E
Götaland ◳	5	Hd	57.30N	14.30 E
Götaland ◳	7	Dg	57.30N	14.30 E
Göteborg	5	Hd	57.43N	11.58 E
Göteborg och Bohus [2]	7	Cg	58.30N	11.50 E
Gotel Mountains ▱	30	Ih	7.00N	11.40 E
Gotemba	29	Fd	35.18N	138.56 E
Götene	7	Cg	58.32N	13.29 E
Gotha	10	Gf	50.57N	10.43 E
Gothenburg	45	Ff	40.56N	100.09W
Gothèye	34	Ec	13.52N	1.34 E
Gotland ◳	5	Id	57.30N	18.30 E
Gotland [2]	7	Eh	57.30N	18.30 E
Goto-Nada ◳	29	Ae	32.45N	129.30 E
Goto-Retto ◳	29	Me	32.50N	129.00 E
Gotowasi	26	If	0.38N	128.26 E
Gotska Sandön ◳	7	Eg	58.25N	19.15 E
Götsu	28	Lg	35.00N	132.14 E
Göttingen	10	Fe	51.32N	9.56 E
Gottwaldov	10	Ng	49.13N	17.39 E
Goubangzi	28	Kc	41.23N	121.48 E
Goudiri	34	Cc	14.11N	12.43W
Gouet ◳	11	Df	48.32N	2.45W
Gough Island ◳	3	Gm	40.20 S	10.00W
Gough Lake	46	la	52.02N	112.28W
Goulais River- ▱	42	Kg	48.35N	74.50W
Goulbin Kaba ▱	34	Fc	13.42N	6.10 E
Goulburn	58	Fh	34.45 S	149.43 E

Index Symbols

[1] Independent Nation	⬗ Historical or Cultural Region	◳ Pass, Gap	◳ Depression	◳ Coast, Beach	◳ Rock, Reef	▱ Waterfall Rapids	◳ Canal	◳ Lagoon	▱ Escarpment, Sea Scarp	▱ Historic Site	◳ Port
[2] State, Region	▱ Mount, Mountain	◳ Plain, Lowland	◳ Polder	◳ Cliff	◫ Islands, Archipelago	◳ River Mouth, Estuary	◳ Bank	◳ Bank	▱ Fracture	▱ Ruins	◳ Lighthouse
[3] District, County	▱ Volcano	◳ Delta	◳ Desert, Dunes	◳ Peninsula	◳ Rocks, Reefs	◳ Lake	◳ Ice Shelf, Pack Ice	▱ Seamount	▱ Trench, Abyss	▱ Wall, Walls	◳ Mine
[4] Municipality	▱ Hill	◳ Salt Flat	◳ Forest, Woods	◳ Isthmus	◳ Coral Reef	▱ Salt Lake	◳ Ocean	◳ Tableland	▱ National Park, Reserve	▱ Church, Abbey	◳ Tunnel
[5] Colony, Dependency	▱ Mountains, Mountain Range	◳ Valley, Canyon	◳ Heath, Steppe	◳ Sandbank	◳ Well, Spring	◳ Intermittent Lake	◳ Sea	◳ Ridge	▱ Point of Interest	▱ Temple	◳ Dam, Bridge
◳ Continent	▱ Hills, Escarpment	◳ Crater, Cave	◳ Oasis	◳ Island	◳ Geyser	◳ Reservoir	◳ Gulf, Bay	◳ Shelf	▱ Recreation Site	▱ Scientific Station	
◳ Physical Region	◳ Plateau, Upland	◳ Karst Features	◳ Cape, Point	◳ Atoll	◳ River, Stream	◳ Swamp, Pond	◳ Strait, Fjord	◳ Basin	◳ Cave, Cavern	▱ Airport	

Index Symbols

[1] Independent Nation	Historical or Cultural Region	Pass, Gap	Depression	Coast, Beach	Rock, Reef
[2] State, Region	Mount, Mountain	Plain, Lowland	Polder	Cliff	Islands, Archipelago
[3] District, County	Volcano	Delta	Desert, Dunes	Peninsula	River Mouth, Estuary
Municipality	Hill	Salt Flat	Forest, Woods	Rocks, Reefs	Lake
Colony, Dependency	Mountains, Mountain Range	Valley, Canyon	Heath, Steppe	Coral Reef	Salt Lake
Continent	Hills, Escarpment	Crater, Cave	Oasis	Well, Spring	Intermittent Lake
Physical Region	Plateau, Upland	Karst Features	Cape, Point	Island	Geyser
				Atoll	River, Stream

Waterfall Rapids	Canal	Lagoon	Escarpment, Sea Scarp	Historic Site	Port
River Mouth, Estuary	Glacier	Bank	Fracture	Ruins	Lighthouse
Lake	Ice Shelf, Pack Ice	Seamount	Trench, Abyss	Church, Abbey	Mine
Salt Lake	Ocean	Tablemount	National Park, Reserve	Temple	Wall, Walls
Intermittent Lake	Sea	Ridge	Point of Interest	Scientific Station	Tunnel
Geyser	Reservoir	Shelf	Recreation Site	Airport	Dam, Bridge
River, Stream	Swamp, Pond	Gulf, Bay	Cave, Cavern		
		Strait, Fjord			
		Basin			

Index Symbols

- [1] Independent Nation
- [2] State, Region
- [3] District, County
- [4] Municipality
- [5] Colony, Dependency
- Continent
- Physical Region

- ▲ Historical or Cultural Region
- ▲ Mount, Mountain
- ▲ Volcano
- ▲ Hill
- ▲ Mountains, Mountain Range
- ▲ Hills, Escarpment
- ▲ Plateau, Upland

- Pass, Gap
- Plain, Lowland
- Delta
- Salt Flat
- Valley, Canyon
- Crater, Cave
- Karst Features

- Depression
- Polder
- Desert, Dunes
- Forest, Woods
- Heath, Steppe
- Oasis
- Cape, Point

- Coast, Beach
- Cliff
- Peninsula
- Isthmus
- Sandbank
- Island
- Atoll

- Rock, Reef
- Islands, Archipelago
- Rocks, Reefs
- Coral Reef
- Well, Spring
- Geyser
- River, Stream

- Waterfall Rapids
- River Mouth, Estuary
- Lake
- Salt Lake
- Intermittent Lake
- Reservoir
- Swamp, Pond

- Canal
- Glacier
- Ice Shelf, Pack Ice
- Tablemount
- Ocean
- Sea
- Gulf, Bay

- Lagoon
- Bank
- Seamount
- National Park, Reserve
- Ridge
- Shelf
- Basin

- Escarpment, Sea Scarp
- Fracture
- Trench, Abyss
- Point of Interest
- Recreation Site
- Cave, Cavern

- Historic Site
- Ruins
- Wall, Walls
- Church, Abbey
- Temple
- Scientific Station
- Airport

- Port
- Lighthouse
- Mine
- Tunnel
- Dam, Bridge

Name	Page	Grid	Lat.	Long.
Gustavs/Kustavi	8	Id	60.30N	21.25 E
Gustavs/Kustavi	8	Id	60.33N	21.21 E
Gustavsfors	8	Ee	59.12N	12.06 E
Gustavus	40	Le	58.25N	135.44W
Güstrow	10	Ic	53.48N	12.10 E
Gusum	8	Gf	58.16N	16.29 E
Gütersloh	10	Ee	51.54N	8.23 E
Guthrie [Ok.-U.S.]	45	Hi	35.53N	97.25W
Guthrie [Tx.-U.S.]	45	Fj	33.37N	100.19W
Gutian	27	Kf	26.40N	118.42 E
Gutiérrez Zamora	48	Kg	20.27N	97.05W
Gutii, Virful-	15	Gb	47.42N	23.52 E
Guting → Yutai	28	Dg	35.00N	116.40 E
Gutland	11	Me	49.40N	6.10 E
Gutu	37	Ec	19.39S	31.10 E
Guyana	53	Ke	5.00N	59.00W
Guyane Française = French Guiana (EN)	53	Ke	4.00N	53.00W
Guyang	27	Jc	41.02N	110.04 E
Guyenne	11	Gj	44.35N	1.00 E
Guymon	43	Gd	36.41N	101.29W
Guyonneau, Anse-	51e	Ab	16.14N	61.47W
Guyuan	27	Id	36.01N	106.17 E
Guyuan (Pingdingbu)	28	Cd	41.40N	115.41 E
Guzar	18	Fe	38.37N	66.18 E
Güzelyurt/Mórphou	24	Ee	35.12N	32.59 E
Güzhān	24	Le	34.20N	46.57 E
Guzhen	28	Dh	33.20N	117.19 E
Guzhou → Rongjiang	27	If	25.58N	108.30 E
Guzmán, Laguna de-	48	Fb	31.20N	107.30W
Gvardejsk	7	Ei	54.40N	21.03 E
Gvardejskoje	16	Hg	45.06N	33.59 E
Gvary	8	Ce	59.23N	9.09 E
Gwa	25	Ie	17.36N	94.35 E
Gwadabawa	34	Gc	13.22N	5.14 E
Gwādar	22	Ig	25.07N	62.19 E
Gwai	30	Jj	17.59S	26.52 E
Gwai	37	Dc	19.17S	27.39 E
Gwalior	22	Jg	26.13N	78.10 E
Gwanda	37	Dd	20.56S	29.00 E
Gwane	36	Eb	4.43N	25.50 E
Gwda	10	Mc	53.04N	16.44 E
Gweebarra Bay/Béal an Bheara	9	Eg	54.52N	8.20W
Gwelo	31	Jj	19.27S	29.49 E
Gwent	9	Kj	51.45N	2.55W
Gweta	37	Dd	20.13S	25.14 E
Gwydir River	59	Je	29.27S	149.48 E
Gwynedd	9	Ji	52.50N	3.50W
Gyaca	27	Ff	29.09N	92.38 E
Gya'gya → Saga	27	Ef	29.22N	85.15 E
Gyai Qu	27	Fe	31.30N	94.40 E
Gyaisi/Jiulong	27	Hf	28.58N	101.33 E
Gya La	27	Gf	29.05N	98.41 E
Gyala Shankou	27	Gf	29.05N	98.41 E
Gyangzê	27	Ef	29.00N	89.38 E
Gyaring Co	27	Ee	31.10N	88.15 E
Gyaring Hu	27	Ge	34.55N	98.00 E
Gyda	20	Cb	70.52N	78.30 E
Gydanskaja Guba	20	Cb	71.20N	76.30 E
Gydanski Poluostrov = Gyda Peninsula (EN)	21	Jb	70.50N	79.00 E
Gyda Peninsula (EN) = Gydanski Poluostrov	21	Jb	70.50N	79.00 E
Gyigang → Zayü	27	Gf	28.43N	97.25 E
Gyirong (Zongga)	27	Ef	28.57N	85.12 E
Gyldenløves Fjord	41	Hf	64.10N	40.30W
Gyldenløves Høj	8	Di	55.33N	11.52 E
Gympie	58	Gg	26.11S	152.40 E
Gyoma	10	Qj	46.56N	20.50 E
Gyöngyös	10	Pi	47.47N	19.56 E
Györ	6	Hf	47.41N	17.38 E
Györ	10	Ni	47.40N	17.39 E
Györ-Sopron	10	Ni	47.40N	17.15 E
Gypsumville	42	Hf	51.45N	98.35W
Gysinge	8	Gd	60.17N	16.53 E
Gyttorp	8	Fe	59.31N	14.58 E
Gyula	10	Rj	46.39N	21.17 E

H

Name	Page	Grid	Lat.	Long.
Haacht	12	Gd	50.59N	4.38 E
Häädemeeste/Hjademeste	8	Uf	58.00N	24.28 E
Ha'afeva	65b	Ba	19.57S	174.43W
Haafusia	64h	Bb	13.18S	176.09W
Haag, Mount-	66	Qf	77.40S	79.00W
Haaksbergen	12	Ib	52.09N	6.45 E
Haamstede, Westerschouwen-	12	Fc	51.42N	3.45 E
Haanja Kõrgustik	8	Lg	57.30N	27.30 E
Ha'ano	65b	Ba	19.40S	174.17W
Ha'apai Group	57	Jf	19.47S	174.27W
Haapajärvi	7	Fe	63.45N	25.20 E
Haapamäki	8	Kb	62.15N	24.28 E
Haapasaari	8	Ld	60.15N	27.10 E
Haapaselkä [Fin.]	8	Mc	61.35N	28.15 E
Haapaselkä [Fin.]	8	Mb	62.10N	28.10 E
Haapiti	65e	Fc	17.34S	149.52W
Haapsalu	19	Cd	58.57N	23.32 E
Ha'arava	24	Fg	30.58N	32.24 E
Haardt	10	Dg	49.15N	8.00 E
Haardtkopf	12	Je	49.51N	7.04 E
Haaren, Wünnenberg-	12	Kc	51.34N	8.44 E
Haarlem	11	Kb	52.23N	4.38 E
Haarlemmermeer	12	Gb	52.20N	4.41 E
Haarlerberg	12	Ib	52.20N	6.25 E
Haarstrang	12	Kc	51.30N	8.20 E
Haast	58	Hi	43.52S	169.01 E
Haast Pass	62	Cf	44.06S	169.21 E
Habahe/Kaba	27	Eb	47.53N	86.12 E
Habarovsk	22	Pe	48.27N	135.06 E
Habarovski Kraj	20	If	53.00N	137.00 E
Ḩabarūt	23	Hf	17.22N	52.42 E
Ḩabashīyah, Jabal-	35	Ib	16.55N	50.05 E
Habaswein	36	Gb	1.01N	39.29 E
Habay [Alta.-Can.]	42	Fe	58.52N	118.45W
Habay [Bel.]	12	He	49.45N	5.38 E
Habay [Som.]	35	Ge	1.08N	43.46 E
Ḩabbān	35	Hc	14.21N	47.05 E
Ḩabbānīyah, Hawr al-	24	Jf	33.17N	43.29 E
Habibas, Iles-	13	Ki	35.44N	1.08W
Habichtswald	10	Fe	51.20N	9.25 E
Habo	8	Fg	57.55N	14.04 E
Haboro	27	Pc	44.22N	141.42 E
Ḩabshān	24	Ok	23.50N	53.37 E
Hache	10	Ec	53.05N	8.50 E
Hachenburg	12	Jd	50.39N	7.50 E
Hachijō	29	Fe	35.15N	139.45 E
Hachijō-Fuji	29	Fe	33.08N	139.46 E
Hachijō-Jima	27	Oe	33.05N	139.50 E
Hachiman	29	Ed	35.46N	136.57 E
Hachimori	29	Fa	40.22N	140.00 E
Hachinohe	22	Qe	40.30N	141.29 E
Hachiōji	29	Fd	35.39N	139.18 E
Hachiro-Gata	29	Fa	40.00N	140.00 E
Hacibey De	24	Kd	36.58N	44.18 E
Hackar Dağı	24	Ib	40.50N	41.10 E
Hackås	7	De	62.55N	14.31 E
Håckren	8	Ea	63.10N	13.35 E
Hačmas	19	Eg	41.25N	48.52 E
Hadagang	28	Kb	45.24N	131.12 E
Hadamar	12	Kd	50.27N	8.03 E
Ḩadan, Ḩarrat-	33	He	21.30N	41.23 E
Hadano	29	Fd	35.22N	139.14 E
Ḩadāribah, Ra's al-	35	Fa	22.04N	36.54 E
Hadd, Ra's al-	21	Hg	22.32N	59.59 E
Haddad	30	Ig	14.40N	18.46 E
Ḩadded	35	Hc	10.10N	48.28 E
Haddington	9	Kf	55.58N	2.47W
Haddummati Atoll	25a	Bb	1.45N	73.30 E
Hadejia	34	Hc	12.27N	10.03 E
Hadejia	34	Hc	12.50N	10.51 E
Hadeland	8	Dd	60.25N	10.35 E
Hadeln	10	Ec	53.45N	8.45 E
Hadera	24	Ff	32.26N	34.55 E
Haderslev	8	Bi	55.15N	9.30 E
Hadībah	23	Hg	12.39N	54.02 E
Hadım	24	Ed	36.59N	32.28 E
Hadimköy	24	Cb	41.09N	28.37 E
Hadīyah	23	Ed	25.34N	38.41 E
Hadjer el Hamis	35	Bc	12.51N	14.50 E
Hadjout	13	Oh	36.31N	2.25 E
Hadleigh	12	Cb	52.03N	0.56 E
Hadley Bay	42	Gb	72.30N	108.30W
Ha Dong	25	Ld	20.58N	105.46 E
Ḩadramawt	21	Gh	15.00N	50.00 E
Hadrian's Wall	9	Kg	54.59N	2.26W
Hadsten	8	Dh	56.20N	10.03 E
Hadsund	8	Dh	56.43N	10.07 E
Hadytajaha	17	Nc	66.57N	69.12 E
Hadyžensk	16	Kg	44.25N	39.31 E
Hadzibeiski Liman	15	Nc	46.40N	30.30 E
Haedo, Cuchilla de-	55	Dj	31.40S	56.18W
Haeju	28	He	38.02N	125.42 E
Haena	60	Oc	22.13N	159.34W
Ḩafar al 'Atk	24	Lj	25.56N	46.47 E
Ḩafar al Bātin	23	Gd	28.27N	46.00 E
Haffner Bjerg	41	Fc	76.30N	63.00W
Ḩaffūz	14	Do	35.38N	9.40 E
Hafik	24	Gc	39.52N	37.24 E
Ḩafīrat al 'Aydā	23	Ed	26.26N	39.12 E
Ḩafit	24	Pk	23.59N	55.49 E
Ḩafit, Jabal-	24	Pj	24.03N	55.46 E
Hafnarfjördur	7a	Bb	64.04N	21.57W
Haft Gel	24	Mg	31.27N	49.27 E
Hāfūn	35	Ic	10.10N	51.05 E
Hāfūn, Rās- = Hafun, Ras- (EN)	30	Mg	10.27N	51.24 E
Hafun, Ras- (EN) = Hāfūn, Rās-	30	Mg	10.27N	51.24 E
Hāfūn Bay North	35	Ic	10.37N	51.15 E
Hāfūn Bay South	35	Ic	10.15N	51.05 E
Hagadera	36	Hb	0.02N	40.17 E
Hagby	8	Gh	56.33N	16.10 E
Hageland	12	Gd	50.55N	4.45 E
Hagemeister	40	Ge	58.40N	161.00W
Hagen	10	De	51.21N	7.28 E
Hagenow	10	Hc	53.26N	11.12 E
Hagere Hiywet	35	Fd	8.58N	37.53 E
Hagerman	46	He	42.49N	114.54W
Hagerstown	43	Ld	39.39N	77.43W
Hagetmau	11	Fk	43.40N	0.35W
Hagfors	7	Cf	60.02N	13.42 E
Häggenås	8	Fa	63.24N	14.55 E
Hagi	28	Kg	34.24N	131.25 E
Ha Giang	25	Kd	22.50N	104.59 E
Hágios Theódóros	24	Fe	35.20N	34.01 E
Hagman, Puntan-	64b	Ba	15.09N	145.48 E
Hagondange	11	Me	49.15N	6.10 E
Hags Head/Ceanna Cailliche	9	Di	52.57N	9.28W
Hague, Cap de la-	5	Ff	49.43N	1.57W
Haguenau	11	Nf	48.49N	7.47 E
Hagunia	32	Ed	27.26N	12.24W
Hahajima-Rettō	60	Cb	26.37N	142.10 E
Hahns Peak	45	Cf	40.56N	107.01W
Hahót	10	Mj	46.38N	16.56 E
Hai'an	28	Fh	32.33N	120.26 E
Haicheng	27	Lc	40.51N	122.43 E
Haidenaab	10	Ig	49.35N	12.08 E
Hai Duong	25	Ld	20.56N	106.19 E
Haifa (EN) = Hefa	22	Ff	32.50N	35.00 E
Haifeng	27	Kg	22.58N	115.21 E
Haiger	12	Kd	50.45N	8.13 E
Hai He	28	De	38.57N	117.43 E
Haikakan Sovetakan Socialistakan Respublika/Armjanskaja SSR	19	Eg	40.00N	45.00 E
Haikang (Leizhou)	27	Jg	20.56N	110.06 E
Haikou	22	Ng	20.05N	110.20 E
Hā'il	22	Gg	27.33N	41.42 E
Hailang He	28	Jb	44.33N	129.33 E
Hailar	22	Ne	49.14N	119.42 E
Hailar He	21	Ne	49.30N	117.50 E
Hailin	27	Mc	44.35N	129.22 E
Hailong (Meihekou)	27	Mc	42.32N	125.37 E
Hailsham	12	Cd	50.52N	0.16 E
Hailun	27	Mb	47.29N	126.55 E
Hailuoto/Karlö	5	Ib	65.02N	24.42 E
Haima Tan	27	Kd	10.52N	116.53 E
Haimen [China]	28	Fi	31.53N	121.10 E
Haimen [China]	28	Fj	28.40N	121.27 E
Haina	12	Kc	51.03N	8.56 E
Hainan Dao	21	Mh	19.00N	109.00 E
Hainaut	11	Jd	50.20N	3.50 E
Hainaut	12	Fd	50.30N	4.00 E
Hainburg an der Donau	14	Kb	48.09N	16.56 E
Haines	39	Fd	59.14N	135.27W
Haines Junction	42	Dd	60.45N	137.30W
Hainich	10	Ge	51.05N	10.27 E
Hainleite	10	Ge	51.20N	10.48 E
Hai Phong	22	Mg	20.52N	106.41 E
Haiti = Haïti (EN)	39	Lh	19.00N	72.25W
Haïti (EN) = Haiti	39	Lh	19.00N	72.25W
Haixing (Suji)	28	De	38.10N	117.29 E
Haixin Shan	27	Hd	37.00N	100.03 E
Haiyan (Sanjiaocheng)	27	Hd	36.58N	100.50 E
Haiyan (Wuyuanzhen)	28	Fi	30.31N	120.56 E
Haiyang (Dongcun)	28	Ff	36.46N	121.09 E
Haiyang Dao	28	Ge	39.03N	123.12 E
Haiyou → Sanmen	27	Lf	29.08N	121.22 E
Haiyuan	27	Id	36.35N	105.40 E
Haizhou	28	Eg	34.34N	119.08 E
Haizhou Wan	21	Nf	35.00N	119.30 E
Ḩajar Banga	35	Cc	11.30N	23.00 E
Hajdarken	19	Hh	39.55N	71.24 E
Hajdú-Bihar	10	Ri	47.25N	21.30 E
Hajdúböszörmény	10	Ri	47.40N	21.31 E
Hajdúhadház	10	Ri	47.41N	21.40 E
Hajdúnánás	10	Ri	47.51N	21.26 E
Hajdúság	10	Ri	47.35N	21.30 E
Hajdúszoboszló	10	Ri	47.27N	21.24 E
Hajihi-Zaki	29	Fb	38.19N	138.31 E
Ḩājjīābād [Iran]	24	Ph	28.19N	55.55 E
Ḩājjīābād [Iran]	24	Ph	28.21N	54.27 E
Ḩājjīābād-e Māsīleh	24	Ne	34.49N	51.13 E
Hajnówka	10	Td	52.45N	23.36 E
Hajós	10	Pj	46.24N	19.07 E
Hajpudyrskaja Guba	17	Ib	68.40N	59.30 E
Haka	25	Id	22.39N	93.37 E
Hakase-Yama	29	Fc	37.22N	139.43 E
Hakasskaja Avtonomnaja Oblast	20	Df	53.30N	90.00 E
Hakata-Wan	29	Be	33.40N	130.20 E
Hakefjord	8	Dg	57.41N	11.44 E
Hakkâri	23	Fb	37.34N	43.45 E
Hakken-Zan	29	Dd	34.10N	135.54 E
Hakkōda San	29	Ga	40.40N	140.53 E
Hako-Dake	29a	Ca	44.40N	142.25 E
Hakodate	22	Qe	41.45N	140.43 E
Hakone-Yama	29	Fd	35.13N	139.00 E
Hakui	28	Nf	36.53N	136.47 E
Hakupu	64k	Bb	19.06S	169.50W
Haku-San	29	Ec	36.09N	136.45 E
Hal/Halle	11	Kd	50.44N	4.14 E
Halab	24	Md	36.17N	48.03 E
Ḩalab = Aleppo (EN)	22	Ff	36.12N	37.10 E
Ḩalabjah	24	Ke	35.10N	45.59 E
Halač	19	Gh	39.04N	64.53 E
Halachó	48	Ng	20.29N	90.05W
Halahei	28	Ga	46.11N	122.46 E
Ḩalā'ib	31	Kf	22.13N	36.38 E
Halalii Lake	65a	Ab	21.52N	160.11W
Halangingie Point	64k	Bb	19.03S	169.58W
Hålaveden	8	Ff	58.05N	14.45 E
Halawa	65a	Eb	21.10N	156.44W
Halawa, Cape-	65a	Eb	21.10N	156.43W
Ḩalbā	24	Ge	34.33N	36.05 E
Halberstadt	10	He	51.54N	11.03 E
Halcon, Mount-	26	Hd	13.16N	121.00 E
Haldean-Sogotyn-Daba	27	Gb	49.05N	97.55 E
Halden	7	Cg	59.09N	11.23 E
Haldensleben	10	Hd	52.18N	11.25 E
Haldia	25	Hd	22.08N	88.05 E
Haldwani	25	Fc	29.13N	79.31 E
Hale, Mount-	59	De	26.00S	117.10 E
Haleakala Crater	65a	Ec	20.43N	156.12W
Haleiwa	65a	Cb	21.36N	158.06W
Halemaumau	65a	Fd	19.24N	155.17W
Hale River	59	Hd	24.56S	135.53 E
Halesworth	12	Db	52.21N	1.30 E
Haleyville	44	Dh	34.14N	87.37W
Ḩalfā al Gadida	31	Kg	15.19N	35.34 E
Half Assini	34	Ed	5.03N	2.53W
Halfeti	24	Gd	37.15N	37.52 E
Halfway	42	Fe	56.13N	121.26W
Halh-Gol	27	Kb	48.01N	118.10 E
Haliburton	44	Hc	45.03N	78.33W
Halifax	39	Me	44.39N	63.36W
Halifax, Mount-	59	Jc	19.05S	146.20 E
Halifax Bay	59	Jc	18.50S	146.30 E
Ḩālil	23	Id	27.28N	58.44 E
Ḩalīleh, Ra's-e-	24	Nh	28.46N	50.56 E
Halilovo	16	Ud	51.27N	58.10 E
Ḩalin	35	Hd	9.08N	48.47 E
Haliut → Urad Zhonghou Lianheqi	27	Ic	41.34N	108.32 E
Haljala	8	Le	59.22N	26.09 E
Haljasavej	20	Cd	63.20N	78.30 E
Hall	40	Ed	60.40N	173.05W
Halladale	9	Jc	58.30N	3.50W
Hallam Peak	46	Fa	52.11N	118.46W
Halland	8	Eh	57.00N	12.45 E
Halland	7	Ch	56.45N	13.00 E
Hallandsås	8	Eh	56.23N	13.00 E
Halla-san	28	Ih	33.22N	126.32 E
Ḩallat 'Ammār	24	Gh	29.08N	36.02 E
Hall Beach	42	Jc	68.10N	81.56W
Halle	10	He	51.30N	12.00 E
Halle	10	He	51.30N	11.50 E
Halle/Hal	11	Kd	50.44N	4.14 E
Halle (Westfalen)	12	Kb	52.05N	8.22 E
Halleberg	8	Ef	58.23N	12.25 E
Hällefors	8	Fe	59.47N	14.30 E
Hälleforsnäs	8	Ge	59.10N	16.30 E
Hallein	14	Hc	47.41N	13.06 E
Hällekis	8	Ef	58.38N	13.25 E
Hallen	7	De	63.11N	14.05 E
Hallenberg	12	Kc	51.07N	8.38 E
Hallencourt	12	De	49.59N	1.53 E
Halle-Neustadt	10	He	51.31N	11.53 E
Hallertau	10	Hh	48.35N	11.50 E
Hällestad	8	Ff	58.44N	15.34 E
Hallettsville	45	Hl	29.27N	96.57W
Halley Bay	66	Af	75.31S	26.38W
Halli	8	Kc	61.52N	24.50 E
Hallie-Jackson Bank (EN)	63c	Ba	9.45S	166.10 E
Halligen	10	Eb	54.35N	8.35 E
Hallingdal	7	Bf	60.40N	9.15 E
Hallingdalselva	8	Cd	60.23N	9.35 E
Hallingskarvet	5	Gc	60.37N	7.45 E
Hall Islands	57	Gd	8.37N	152.00 E
Halliste Jõgi	8	Kf	58.23N	24.25 E
Hall Lake	42	Jc	68.40N	82.20W
Hall Land	41	Fb	81.12N	61.10W
Hallock	45	Hb	48.47N	96.57W
Hall Peninsula	38	Mc	63.30N	66.00W
Hallsberg	7	Dg	59.04N	15.07 E
Halls Creek	58	Df	18.13S	127.40 E
Hallstahammar	7	Dg	59.37N	16.13 E
Hallstatt	14	Hb	47.33N	13.39 E
Hallstavik	7	Ef	60.03N	18.36 E
Halluin	12	Fd	50.47N	3.08 E
Halmahera	57	Dd	1.00N	128.00 E
Halmahera, Laut- = Halmahera Sea (EN)	57	De	1.00S	129.00 E
Halmahera Sea (EN) = Halmahera, Laut-	57	De	1.00S	129.00 E
Halmer-Ju	19	Gb	67.58N	64.40 E
Halmeu	15	Gb	47.58N	23.01 E
Halmstad	6	Hd	56.39N	12.50 E
Haloze	14	Jd	46.20N	15.50 E
Ḩalq al Wādī	32	Jb	36.49N	10.18 E
Hals	7	Cg	57.00N	10.19 E
Hälsingland	8	Gc	61.30N	17.00 E
Halsön	8	Ib	62.50N	21.10 E
Halstead	12	Cc	51.57N	0.38 E
Halsteren	12	Gc	51.32N	4.16 E
Haltang He	27	Fd	39.00N	94.40 E
Halten Bank (EN)	7	Bd	64.45N	8.45 E
Haltern	12	Jc	51.44N	7.11 E
Haltiatunturi	7	Eb	69.18N	21.16 E
Haltom City	45	Hj	32.48N	97.16W
Halturin	18	Ed	58.35N	48.55 E
Hālūl	24	Oj	25.40N	52.25 E
Halver	12	Jc	51.12N	7.29 E
Ham	11	Je	49.45N	3.04 E
Ham, Roches de-	12	Ae	49.02N	1.02W
Hamada	29	Cd	34.53N	132.03 E
Hamadān	22	Gf	34.48N	48.30 E
Hamadān	23	Gb	35.00N	48.40 E
Hamadia	13	Ni	35.28N	1.52 E
Hamaguir	32	Gc	30.54N	3.02W
Hamāh	23	Eb	35.08N	36.45 E
Hamakita	29	Ed	34.49N	137.45 E
Hamamasu	29a	Bb	43.36N	141.21 E
Hamamatsu	27	Oe	34.42N	137.44 E
Hamanaka	29a	Db	43.05N	145.05 E
Hamanaka-Wan	29a	Db	43.07N	145.10 E
Hamana-Ko	29	Ed	34.45N	137.34 E
Hamanen, Oued el-	32	Hd	25.52N	1.26 E
Hamaoka	29	Fd	34.39N	138.07 E
Hamar	6	Hc	60.48N	11.06 E
Hamar-Daran, Hrebet-	20	Ff	51.10N	105.00 E
Hamasaka	29	Dd	35.38N	134.27 E
Ḩamāṭah, Jabal-	33	Ge	24.12N	35.00 E
Hamatonbetsu	28	Qb	45.07N	142.23 E
Hambantota	25	Gg	6.10N	81.07 E
Hambre, Cayos del-	49	Fb	22.15N	82.47W
Hamburg	10	Fc	53.35N	10.00 E
Hamburg [F.R.G.]	6	Ge	53.33N	10.00 E
Hamburg [S.Afr.]	37	Df	33.18S	27.28 E
Hamburg-Altona	10	Fc	53.33N	9.57 E
Hamburg-Harburg	10	Fc	53.28N	10.00 E
Hamburgsund	8	Df	58.33N	11.16 E
Ḩamḑah	33	Hf	19.02N	43.36 E
Ḩamḑh, Wādī al-	21	Fg	25.58N	36.42 E
Häme	7	Ff	61.00N	24.30 E
Häme	8	Kc	61.30N	25.30 E
Hämeenkangas	8	Jc	61.45N	22.40 E
Hämeenlinna/Tavastehus	7	Ff	61.00N	24.27 E
Hämeenselkä	8	Kb	62.30N	25.00 E
Hamelin Pool	59	Ce	26.15S	114.05 E
Hameln	10	Fd	52.06N	9.21 E
Hamero Hadad	35	Gd	7.28N	42.13 E
Hamersley Range	59	Dd	21.55S	116.45 E
Hamgyŏng-Namdo	28	Id	40.00N	127.30 E
Hamgyŏng-Pukto	28	Jd	41.45N	129.50 E
Hamgyŏng-Sanmaek	28	Jd	41.00N	128.45 E
Hamhŭng	22	Of	39.54N	127.32 E
Hami/Kumul	22	Le	42.48N	93.27 E
Ḩamīdīyeh	24	Mg	31.29N	48.26 E
Hamilton [Austl.]	59	Ig	37.45S	142.02 E
Hamilton [Ber.]	39	Mf	32.17N	64.46W
Hamilton [Mt.-U.S.]	43	Eb	46.15N	114.09W
Hamilton [N.Z.]	58	Ih	37.47S	175.17 E
Hamilton [Oh.-U.S.]	43	Kd	39.23N	84.33W
Hamilton [Ont.-Can.]	39	Le	43.15N	79.51W
Hamilton [Scot.-U.K.]	9	If	55.47N	4.03W
Hamilton [Tx.-U.S.]	45	Gk	31.42N	98.07W
Hamilton, Lake-	45	Ji	34.30N	93.05W
Hamilton, Mount-	46	Hg	39.14N	115.32W
Hamilton River	59	Hd	23.30S	139.47 E
Hamīn, Wādī al-	33	Dc	30.28N	22.00 E
Hamina/Fredrikshamn	7	Gf	60.34N	27.12 E
Hamm	10	De	51.41N	7.48 E
Ḩammām al 'Alīl	24	Jd	36.10N	43.16 E
Ḩammām al Anf	32	Jb	36.44N	10.20 E
Ḩammāmāt	32	Jb	36.24N	10.37 E
Ḩammāmāt, Khalīj-	32	Jb	36.05N	10.40 E
Hammam Bou Hadjar	13	Li	35.23N	0.58W
Hammami	30	Ff	23.03N	11.30W
Hammam Righa	13	Oh	36.23N	2.24 E
Ḩammār, Hawr al-	23	Gc	30.50N	47.10 E
Hammarstrand	8	Ga	63.06N	16.21 E
Hamme	12	Gc	51.06N	4.08 E
Hammelburg	10	Ff	50.07N	9.54 E
Hammerdal	7	De	63.36N	15.21 E
Hammeren	8	Fi	55.18N	14.47 E
Hammerfest	6	Ia	70.40N	23.45 E
Hamminkeln	12	Ic	51.44N	6.35 E
Hamminkeln-Dingden	12	Ic	51.46N	6.37 E
Hammond [In.-U.S.]	44	De	41.36N	87.30W
Hammond [La.-U.S.]	43	Ie	30.30N	90.28W
Hammonton	44	Jf	39.38N	74.48W
Hamont, Hamont-Achel-	12	Hc	51.15N	5.33 E
Hamont-Achel	12	Hc	51.15N	5.33 E
Hamont-Achel-Hamont	12	Hc	51.15N	5.33 E
Hamoyet, Jabal-	30	Kg	17.33N	38.02 E
Hampden	62	Df	45.20S	170.49 E
Hampshire	9	Lk	51.00N	1.10W
Hampshire Downs	9	Lj	51.15N	1.15W
Hampton [Ia.-U.S.]	45	Je	42.45N	93.12W
Hampton [Va.-U.S.]	44	Ig	37.02N	76.23W
Hampton Butte	46	Ee	43.46N	120.17W
Hamp'yong	28	Ig	35.04N	126.31 E
Ḩamrā'	35	Dc	10.54N	29.54 E
Hamra [R.S.F.S.R.]	20	Gd	60.17N	114.10 E
Hamra [Swe.]	8	Fc	61.39N	15.00 E
Ḩamrā', Al Ḩamādah al-	30	If	29.30N	12.00 E
Hamra, Saguia el-	30	Ff	27.24N	13.43W
Hamrān	24	Kd	36.22N	45.44 E
Ḩamrat ash Shaykh	35	Dc	14.35N	27.58 E
Ḩamrīn, Jabal-	24	Ke	34.30N	44.30 E
Hāmūn-e Hirmand, Daryācheh-ye-	23	Jc	31.30N	61.20 E
Han	34	Ec	10.41N	2.27W
Hana	60	Oc	20.45N	155.59W
Hanahan	44	Hi	32.55N	80.00W
Hanaizum	29	Gb	38.51N	141.12 E
Ḩanak	23	Ed	25.33N	36.56 E
Hanalei	65a	Ba	22.13N	159.30W
Hanamaki	28	Pe	39.23N	141.07 E
Hanang	30	Ki	4.26S	35.24 E
Hanaoka	29	Ga	40.21N	140.34 E
Hanapepe	65a	Bb	21.55N	159.35W
Hanau	10	Ef	50.08N	8.55 E
Han-Bogdo	27	Ic	43.12N	107.10 E
Hanceville	42	Ff	51.55N	123.02W
Hancheng	27	Jd	35.30N	110.25 E
Hanchuan	28	Bi	30.39N	113.46 E
Hancock	44	Cb	47.07N	88.35W
Handa	29	Ed	34.53N	136.56 E
Handan	22	Nf	36.35N	114.28 E
Handen	8	He	59.10N	18.08 E
Handeni	36	Gd	5.26S	38.01 E
Handlová	10	Oh	48.44N	18.46 E
Handöl	8	Ea	63.16N	12.26 E
Handyga	22	Pc	62.40N	135.36 E
Hanegev = Negev Desert (EN)	24	Fg	30.30N	34.55 E
Hanford	46	Fh	36.20N	119.39W
Hangaj, Hrebet- (Changajn Nuruu) = Khangai Mountains (EN)	21	Le	47.30N	100.00 E
Han-gang	27	Md	37.45N	126.11 E
Hanga Roa	65d	Ab	27.09S	109.26W
Hang'bu He	28	Di	31.33N	117.05 E
Hanggin Houqi (Xamba)	27	Ic	40.59N	107.07 E
Hanggin Qi (Xin Zhen)	27	Id	39.54N	108.55 E
Hangö/Hanko	7	Fg	59.50N	22.57 E
Hangöudde/Hankoniemi	8	Je	59.50N	23.10 E
Hangu	28	De	39.16N	117.50 E
Hangzhou	22	Of	30.18N	120.11 E
Hangzhou Wan	28	Fi	30.25N	121.00 E
Ḩanīsh	33	Hg	13.45N	42.45 E
Ḩanīsh al Kabīr, Jazīrat al-	33	Hg	13.43N	42.45 E
Hanja, Vozvyšennost-	8	Lg	57.30N	27.30 E
Ḩanjūrah, Ra's-	24	Pj	24.44N	54.39 E
Hanka, Ozero- = Khanka Lake (EN)	21	Pe	45.00N	132.24 E
Hankasalmi	8	Lb	62.23N	26.26 E
Hankensbüttel	10	Gd	52.44N	10.36 E
Hanko/Hangö	7	Fg	59.50N	22.57 E
Hankoniemi/Hangöudde	8	Je	59.50N	23.10 E
Hankou, Wuhan-	28	Ci	30.35N	114.16 E
Hanksville	46	Jg	38.25N	110.10W
Hanlar	16	Oi	40.34N	46.20 E
Hanmej, Gora-	17	Lc	67.08N	66.00 E
Hanmer Springs	62	Ee	42.31S	172.50 E
Hann, Mount-	59	Fc	15.50S	125.50 E
Hanna [Alta.-Can.]	42	Gf	51.38N	111.54W
Hanna [Wy.-U.S.]	46	Lf	41.52N	106.34W
Hannah Bay	42	Jf	51.15N	79.50W
Hannibal	43	Id	39.42N	91.22W
Hanningfield Reservoir	12	Cc	51.37N	0.28 E
Hannō	29	Fd	35.53N	139.17 E
Hannover	6	Ge	52.22N	9.43 E
Hann River	59	Fc	17.10S	126.10 E
Hannuit/Hannut	12	Hd	50.40N	5.05 E
Hannut/Hannuit	12	Hd	50.40N	5.05 E
Hano	8	Fi	56.00N	14.50 E
Hanöbukten	8	Fi	55.45N	14.30 E
Ha Noi	22	Mg	21.02N	105.51 E
Hanover [N.H.-U.S.]	44	Kd	43.42N	72.17W
Hanover [Ont.-Can.]	44	Gc	44.09N	81.02W
Hanover [Pa.-U.S.]	44	If	39.47N	76.59W
Hanover [S.Afr.]	37	Cf	31.04S	24.29 E
Hanover, Isla-	56	Fh	51.00S	74.40W
Hanpan, Cape-	59	Ka	5.01S	154.37 E
Han Pijesak	14	Mf	44.05N	18.57 E

Index Symbols

Independent Nation; State, Region; District, County; Municipality; Colony, Dependency; Continent; Physical Region

Historical or Cultural Region; Mount, Mountain; Volcano; Hill; Mountains, Mountain Range; Hills, Escarpment; Plateau, Upland

Pass, Gap; Plain, Lowland; Delta; Salt Flat; Valley, Canyon; Crater, Cave; Karst Features

Depression; Polder; Desert, Dunes; Forest, Woods; Heath, Steppe; Oasis; Cape, Point

Coast, Beach; Cliff; Peninsula; Isthmus; Sandbank; Island; Atoll

Rock, Reef; Islands, Archipelago; Rocks, Reefs; Coral Reef; Well, Spring; Geyser; River, Stream

Waterfall Rapids; River Mouth, Estuary; Lake; Salt Lake; Intermittent Lake; Reservoir; Swamp, Pond

Canal; Glacier; Ice Shelf, Pack Ice; Ocean; Sea; Gulf, Bay; Strait, Fjord

Lagoon; Bank; Seamount; Tablemount; Ridge; Shelf; Basin

Escarpment, Sea Scarp; Fracture; Trench, Abyss; National Park, Reserve; Point of Interest; Recreation Site; Cave, Cavern

Historic Site; Ruins; Wall, Walls; Church, Abbey; Temple; Scientific Station; Airport

Port; Lighthouse; Mine; Tunnel; Dam, Bridge

sen Mountains 66 Ee 68.16S 58.47 E
shan 28 Ei 31.43N 118.07 E
shou 28 Aj 28.55N 111.58 E
Shui 21 Nf 30.34N 114.17 E
stholm 8 Cg 57.07N 8.38 E
Sum 28 Eb 44.33N 119.58 E
-sur-Lesse, Rochefort- 12 Hd 50.08N 5.11 E
-sur-Nied 12 If 48.59N 6.26 E
itajskoje, Ozero- 20 Ec 68.25N 91.00 E
tau 19 Hg 44.13N 73.48 E
tengri Feng 27 Dc 42.03N 80.11 E
ts 9 Lj 51.10N 1.10W
ty-Mansijsk 22 Ic 61.00N 69.06 E
ty-Mansijski Nacionalny
rug 19 Hc 62.00N 72.30 E
tzsch 42 Kc 67.32N 72.26W
ušovice 10 Mf 50.05N 16.55 E
wang 27 He 31.25N 104.13 E
yang 28 Ci 30.34N 114.01 E
yang, Wuhan- 28 Ci 30.33N 114.16 E
yū 29 Fc 36.11N 139.32 E
yuan (Fulin) 27 Hf 29.25N 102.12 E
zhong [China] 27 Mf 32.59N 107.11 E
zhong [China] 27 Ie 33.07N 107.00 E
zhuang 28 Dg 34.38N 117.23 E
Atoll 57 Mf 18.15S 140.54W
uach 30 Ig 16.30N 19.55 E
ud el Hamra 32 Ic 31.58N 5.59 E
Xi 28 Ej 28.28N 119.56 E
xue 28 Bi 30.02N 112.25 E
aranda 7 Fd 65.50N 24.10 E
čeranga 20 Gg 49.42N 112.20 E
su 28 Jd 41.13N 128.51 E
l 24 Fh 29.18N 34.57 E
l al Barqan 24 Lh 28.55N 47.57 E
l al Manāqish 24 Lh 29.02N 47.32 E
l as Şābirīyah 24 Lh 29.48N 47.50 E
a, Zaliv-/Hara Laht 8 Ke 59.35N 25.30 E
a-Ajrag 27 Ib 45.50N 109.20 E
abali 19 Ef 47.25N 47.16 E
ad 23 Ge 24.14N 49.11 E
aiki Atoll 57 Mf 17.28S 143.27W
a Laht/Hara, Zaliv- 8 Ke 59.35N 25.30 E
amachi 28 Pf 37.38N 140.58 E
am Dāgh 23 Gb 37.35N 46.43 E
ami, Pereval- 16 Oh 42.48N 46.12 E
and 24 Of 32.34N 52.26 E
ani'ia Point 63a Ed 10.21S 161.16 E
a Nur 27 Fb 48.05N 93.12 E
ardêre 35 He 4.32N 47.53 E
are 31 Kj 17.50S 31.10 E
at 35 Fb 16.05N 39.28 E
a-Tas, Krjaž- 20 Fb 72.00N 107.00 E
atini 64n Bc 10.28S 160.58W
at Zuwayyah 31 Jf 24.14N 21.59 E
a-Us-Nur 27 Fb 48.00N 92.10 E
az 35 Bc 13.57N 19.26 E
āz 24 Od 36.40N 52.43 E
āzah, Jabal- 35 Eb 15.03N 30.27 E
aze 35 Cd 9.55N 20.48 E
bel 24 Cd 6.16N 10.21W
bin 22 Oe 45.45N 126.37 E
bor Beach 44 Fd 43.51N 82.39W
bour Breton 42 Lg 47.29N 55.50W
bour Grace 42 Mg 47.41N 53.15W
burg, Hamburg- 10 Fc 53.28N 10.00 E
court 44 Ob 46.30N 65.15W
cuvar Mountains 46 Ii 34.00N 113.30W
cyzsk 16 Kf 47.59N 38.11 E
danger 8 Bd 60.20N 6.30 E
dangerfjorden 5 Gc 60.10N 6.00 E
dangerjøkulen 8 Bd 60.35N 7.25 E
dangervidda 7 Bf 60.20N 7.30 E
delot Plage, Neufchâtel
rdelot- 12 Dd 50.38N 1.35 E
denberg 12 Ib 52.34N 6.37 E
derwijk 11 Lb 52.21N 5.36 E
din 43 Fb 45.44N 107.37W
ding 37 Df 30.34S 29.58 E
dinsburg 44 Dg 37.47N 86.28W
dler 12 Kc 51.06N 8.14 E
doi 25 Gc 27.25N 80.07 E
dy, Peninsula- 56 Gi 55.25S 68.30W
eid 8 Bb 62.22N 6.02 E
eidlandet 7 Ae 62.20N 5.55 E
e Indian 42 Ec 66.18N 128.38W
elbeke 12 Fd 50.51N 3.18 E
en 12 Ia 53.11N 6.38 E
en (Ems) 12 Jb 52.47N 7.14 E
er 31 Lh 9.18N 42.08 E
erge 35 Gd 9.00N 41.30 E
eri Mālinwarfā 35 He 4.34N 47.21 E
ewa 35 Gd 9.54N 41.58 E
fleur 12 Ce 49.30N 0.12 E
g 8 Hd 60.11N 18.24 E
geysa 31 Lh 9.30N 44.03 E
ghița 15 Ic 46.25N 25.45 E
ghita, Munții- 15 Ic 46.31N 25.33 E
ghita, Vîrful- 15 Ic 46.27N 25.35 E
gla 8 Lg 57.31N 26.25 E
horin 27 Hb 47.13N 102.50 E
38.15N 97.40 E
Hu
rib 23 Gg 14.56N 45.30 E
richa, Hamâda el- 34 Ea 22.36N 3.31W
rihari 62 De 43.09S 170.34 E
ri Kurk 8 Je 59.00N 22.50 E
rim 24 Gd 36.12N 36.31 E
rim, Jabal al- 24 Qj 25.58N 56.14 E
rima-Nada 29 Dd 34.30N 134.35 E
ringey, London- 12 Bc 51.36N 0.06W
rirūd 21 If 37.24N 60.38 E
rjångsfjället 8 Ea 63.01N 12.35 E
rjavalta 7 Ff 61.19N 22.08 E
rjedalen 8 Eb 62.20N 13.05 E
rjehågna 8 Ec 61.44N 12.08 E
rkan 8 Fa 63.20N 14.55 E
rkov 6 Je 50.00N 36.15 E

Harkovskaja Oblast 19 Df 49.40N 36.30 E
Harlan [Ia.-U.S.] 45 If 41.39N 95.19W
Harlan [Ky.-U.S.] 44 Fg 36.51N 83.19W
Harlan County Lake 45 Gf 40.04N 99.16W
Harlech Castle 9 Ii 52.52N 4.07W
Harlem 46 Kb 48.32N 108.47W
Harleston 12 Db 52.24N 1.18 E
Harlingen [Neth.] 11 La 53.10N 5.24 E
Harlingen [Tx.-U.S.] 43 Hf 26.11N 97.42W
Harlovka 7 Ib 68.47N 37.20 E
Harlovka 7 Ib 68.47N 37.15 E
Harlow 9 Nj 51.47N 0.08 E
Harlowton 46 Kc 46.26N 109.50W
Harlu 7 Hf 61.51N 30.54 E
Hårman 15 Id 45.43N 25.41 E
Harmancık 24 Cc 39.41N 29.10 E
Harmånger 7 Df 61.56N 17.13 E
Harmanli 15 Ih 41.56N 25.54 E
Harmil 35 Gb 16.30N 40.12 E
Harmony 45 Ke 43.33N 91.59W
Harnai 25 Ee 17.48N 73.06 E
Harney Basin 38 Ge 43.15N 120.40W
Harney Lake 43 Dc 43.14N 119.07W
Harney Peak 43 Gc 44.00N 103.30W
Härnön 8 Gb 62.35N 18.00 E
Härnösand 6 Hc 62.38N 17.56 E
Haro 13 Jb 42.35N 2.51W
Harovsk 19 Ed 59.59N 40.11 E
Harøya 8 Bb 62.45N 6.25 E
Harøyfjorden 8 Bb 62.45N 6.35 E
Harpenden 12 Bc 51.48N 0.21W
Harper [Ks.-U.S.] 45 Gh 37.17N 98.01W
Harper [Lbr.] 31 Gh 4.22N 7.43W
Harper, Mount- 40 Kd 64.14N 143.50W
Harper Pass 62 De 42.44S 171.53 E
Harplinge 8 Eh 56.45N 12.43 E
Harqin Qi (Jinshan) 28 Ed 41.57N 118.40 E
Harqin Zuoyi Mongolzu
Zizhixian 28 Ed 41.05N 119.40 E
Ḩarrah 23 Hg 14.57N 50.19 E
Ḩarrat al 'Uwayrid 23 Ed 27.00N 37.30 E
Harricana 42 Jf 51.10N 79.47W
Harricana, Rivière- 44 Ha 51.10N 79.45W
Harrington-Harbour 42 Lf 50.26N 59.30W
Harris 9 Gd 57.53N 6.55W
Harris 51c Bc 16.28N 62.10W
Harris, Lake- 44 Gk 28.46N 81.49W
Harris, Sound of- 9 Fd 57.45N 7.08W
Harrisburg 39 Le 40.16N 76.52W
Harrismith 37 De 28.18S 29.03 E
Harrison [Ar.-U.S.] 45 Jh 36.14N 93.07W
Harrison [Mi.-U.S.] 44 Ec 44.01N 84.48W
Harrison [Nb.-U.S.] 45 Ee 42.41N 103.53W
Harrison, Cape- 42 Lf 54.56N 57.55W
Harrison Bay 40 Ib 70.30N 151.30W
Harrisonburg 44 Hf 38.27N 78.54W
Harrison Lake 46 Eb 49.31N 121.59W
Harrison Point 51q Ab 13.18N 59.38W
Harrisonville 45 Ig 38.39N 94.21W
Harrisville [Mi.-U.S.] 44 Fc 44.39N 83.17W
Harrisville [W.V.-U.S.] 44 Gf 39.13N 81.04W
Harrodsburg 44 Eg 37.46N 84.51W
Harrogate 9 Lh 54.00N 1.33W
Harrow, London- 12 Bc 51.36N 0.20W
Harry S. Truman
Reservoir 45 Jg 38.00N 93.45W
Har Sai Shan 27 Gd 35.26N 97.41 E
Harsewinkel 12 Kc 51.58N 8.14 E
Harshō 35 Hc 11.17N 47.30 E
Harsim 24 Lf 33.48N 46.50 E
Harsīn 24 Le 34.16N 47.35 E
Harstad 7 Db 68.47N 16.30 E
Harsvik 7 Cd 64.03N 10.02 E
Hart 44 Dd 43.42N 86.22W
Hart 42 Dc 65.51N 136.22W
Hartao 28 Gc 42.30N 122.08 E
Hartbees 30 Jk 28.45S 20.33 E
Hartberg 14 Jc 47.17N 15.58 E
Hårteigen 8 Bd 60.12N 7.04 E
Hartford [Ct.-U.S.] 39 Le 41.46N 72.41W
Hartford [Ky.-U.S.] 44 Dg 37.27N 86.55W
Hartford City 44 Ee 40.29N 85.23W
Hartington 45 He 42.37N 97.16W
Hartland 44 Nb 46.18N 67.32W
Hartland Point 9 Ij 51.02N 4.31W
Hartlepool 9 Lg 54.42N 1.11W
Hartley 37 Ec 18.07S 30.08 E
Hartmannberge 37 Ac 17.30S 12.23 E
Hartola 7 Gf 61.35N 26.01 E
Harts 28.24S 24.18 E
Hartselle 44 Dh 34.27N 86.56W
Harts Range 59 Gd 23.05S 134.55 E
Hartsville 44 Gh 34.23N 80.04W
Hartwell 44 Fh 34.21N 82.56W
Hartwell Lake 44 Fh 34.30N 82.55W
Harun, Bukit- 26 Gf 4.06N 115.46 E
Haruno 29 Ce 33.30N 133.30 E
Harves Bank (EN) 51c Ac 16.52N 62.35W
Harvey [Austl.] 59 Df 33.05S 115.54 E
Harvey [N.D.-U.S.] 43 Hb 47.47N 99.56W
Harvey Bay 59 Kd 25.00S 153.00 E
Harwich 9 Oj 51.57N 1.17 E
Haryana 25 Fc 29.30N 76.30 E
Harz 5 He 51.45N 10.30 E
Hasaki 29 Gd 35.44N 140.48 E
Hasama 29 Gb 38.42N 141.13 E
Hasan 20 Ih 42.26N 130.39 E
Ḩasanābād [Iran] 24 Ph 28.47N 54.19 E
Ḩasanābād [Iran] 24 Nd 36.28N 50.17 E
Hasan Dağı 23 Db 38.08N 34.12 E
Ḩasan Langī 24 Qi 27.22N 56.52 E
Hasavjurt 16 Oh 43.16N 46.35 E
Häsbayyā 24 Ff 33.43N 35.52 E
Hasdo 25 Hd 21.44N 82.44 E
Hase 10 Dd 52.41N 7.18 E
Hasekijata 15 Kg 42.08N 27.30 E
Hasenkamp 55 Cj 31.31S 59.51W

Hashimoto 29 Dd 34.19N 135.37 E
Hashtpar 24 Md 37.48N 48.55 E
Hasi Hausert 32 Ee 22.35N 14.18W
Haskell 43 He 33.10N 99.44W
Haskerland 12 Hb 52.58N 5.47 E
Haskerland-Joure 12 Hb 52.58N 5.47 E
Haskovo 15 Ih 41.56N 25.33 E
Haskovo 15 Ih 41.50N 25.55 E
Hasle 8 Fi 55.11N 14.43 E
Haslemere 9 Mj 51.06N 0.43W
Haslev 8 Di 55.20N 11.58 E
Hășmașu Mare, Vîrful- 15 Ic 46.30N 25.50 E
Haspengouws Plateau/
Hesbaye 11 Ld 50.35N 5.10 E
Haspres 12 Fd 50.15N 3.25 E
Hassa 24 Gd 36.50N 36.29 E
Hassan 25 Ff 13.00N 76.05 E
Hassberge 10 Gf 50.12N 10.29 E
Hassela 7 De 62.07N 16.42 E
Hassel Sound 42 Ha 78.30N 99.00W
Hasselt 11 Ld 50.56N 5.20 E
Hassi Bel Guebbour 32 Id 28.30N 6.41 E
Hassi el Ghella 13 Ki 35.27N 1.03W
Hassi-Mamèche 13 Mi 35.51N 0.04 E
Hassi Messaoud 31 He 31.43N 6.03 E
Hassi R'mel 32 Hc 32.55N 3.16 E
Hassi Serouenout 32 Ie 24.00N 7.50 E
Hässleholm 7 Ch 56.09N 13.46 E
Hasslö 8 Fh 56.05N 15.25 E
Haßloch 12 Ke 49.23N 8.16 E
Hastière 12 Gd 50.13N 4.50 E
Hastière-Hastière par-delà 12 Gd 50.13N 4.50 E
Hastière-par-delà, Hastière- 12 Gd 50.13N 4.50 E
Hastings [Bar.] 51q Ab 13.04N 59.35W
Hastings [Eng.-U.K.] 9 Nk 50.51N 0.36 E
Hastings [Mi.-U.S.] 44 Ed 42.39N 85.17W
Hastings [Mn.-U.S.] 45 Jd 44.44N 92.51W
Hastings [Nb.-U.S.] 43 Hc 40.35N 98.23W
Hastings [N.Z.] 61 Eg 39.38S 176.50 E
Hästveda 8 Eh 56.16N 13.56 E
Hašuri 16 Mi 41.59N 43.33 E
Hasvik 7 Fa 70.29N 22.09 E
Ḩasy al Qaţţār 33 Ec 30.14N 27.11 E
Ḩasy Hague 33 Bd 26.17N 10.31 E
Hat'ae-Do 28 Hg 34.23N 125.17 E
Hatanga 22 Mb 71.58N 102.30 E
Hatanga 21 Mb 72.55N 106.00 E
Hatch 45 Cj 32.40N 107.09W
Hatches Creek 59 Hd 20.56S 135.12 E
Hațeg 15 Fd 45.37N 22.57 E
Hatgal 27 Ha 50.26N 100.09 E
Ḩaţibah, Ra's- 23 Ee 21.59N 38.55 E
Ha Tien 25 Kf 10.23N 104.29 E
Ha Tinh 25 Le 18.20N 105.54 E
Hato Mayor 49 Md 18.46N 69.15W
Ḩattā, Jabal- 24 Qj 24.45N 56.04 E
Hattem 12 Ib 52.28N 6.06 E
Hatten 12 Ka 53.03N 8.23 E
Hatteras, Cape- 38 Lf 35.13N 75.32W
Hatteras Inlet 44 Jh 35.00N 75.40W
Hatteras Island 43 Ld 35.25N 75.30W
Hattfjelldal 7 Cd 65.36N 14.00 E
Hattiesburg 43 Je 31.19N 89.16W
Hattingen 12 Jc 51.24N 7.10 E
Hatu Iti, Ile- 61 Ma 8.42S 140.43W
Hatutaa, Ile- 57 Me 7.30S 140.38W
Hatvan 10 Pi 47.40N 19.41 E
Hat Yai 25 Kg 7.01N 100.27 E
Hatyrka 20 Md 62.03N 175.05 E
Hau Bon 25 Lf 13.24N 108.27 E
Haubourdin 12 Ed 50.36N 2.59 E
Hauge 7 Bg 58.21N 6.17 E
Haugesund 6 Gd 59.25N 5.18 E
Hauho 8 Kc 61.10N 24.33 E
Hauhungaroa Range 62 Fc 38.40S 175.35 E
Haukeligrend 7 Bg 59.51N 7.11 E
Haukipudas 7 Fd 65.15N 25.28 E
Haukivesi 5 Ic 62.05N 28.30 E
Haukivuori 8 Lb 62.01N 27.13 E
Hauraha 63a Ed 10.49S 161.57 E
Hauraki Gulf 61 Eg 36.35S 175.00 E
Hauroko, Lake- 62 Bf 45.55S 167.20 E
Hausa 32 Ed 22.37N 11.01W
Hausruck 14 Hb 48.07N 13.35 E
Haut, Isle au- 44 Mc 44.03N 68.38W
Haut Atlas=High Atlas (EN)
30 Ge 32.00N 6.00W
Haute-Champagne 12 Ge 49.18N 4.15 E
Haute-Corse 11a Aa 42.30N 9.00 E
Haute-Garonne 11 Hk 43.25N 1.30 E
Haute-Guinée 34 Dc 11.30N 10.00W
Haute-Kotto 35 Cd 7.00N 23.00 E
Haute-Loire 11 Ji 45.05N 4.00 E
Haute-Marne 11 Lf 48.05N 5.10 E
Hauterive 44 Ma 49.11N 68.16W
Hautes-Alpes 11 Mj 44.40N 6.30 E
Haute-Sangha 35 Be 4.30N 16.00 E
Haute-Saône 11 Mg 47.40N 6.10 E
Haute-Saône,
Plateau de- 11 Lg 47.50N 6.00 E
Haute-Savoie 11 Mi 46.00N 6.20 E
Hautes Fagnes/Hoge
Venen 10 Bf 50.30N 6.00 E
Hautes-Pyrénées 11 Gk 43.00N 0.10 E
Haute-Vienne 11 Hi 45.50N 1.10 E
Haute-Volta=Upper Volta
(EN) 31 Gg 13.00N 2.00W
Haut-Mbomou 35 Dd 6.00N 26.00 E
Hautmont 11 Jd 50.15N 3.56 E
Haut-Ogooué 36 Bc 2.00S 14.00 E
Haut Rhin 11 Ng 48.00N 7.20 E
Hauts-Bassins 34 Ec 12.30N 4.30W
Hauts-de-Seine 11 If 48.50N 2.11 E
Hauts-Plateaux 30 He 34.00N 0.01 E
Haut-Zaïre 36 Eb 2.30N 25.30 E
Hauula 65a 21.36N 157.54W
Hauz-Han 18 Cf 37.16N 61.15 E

Hauz-Hanskoje Vodohr. 18 Cf 37.10N 61.20 E
Havana 45 Kf 40.18N 90.04W
Havana (EN)=La Habana 39 Kg 23.08N 82.22W
Havant 9 Mk 50.51N 0.59W
Havast 18 Gd 40.16N 68.51 E
Havasu, Lake- 46 Hi 34.30N 114.20W
Havel 10 Hd 52.53N 11.58 E
Havelange 12 Hd 50.23N 5.14 E
Havelange-Méan 12 Hd 50.22N 5.20 E
Havelberg 10 Id 52.49N 12.05 E
Havelland 10 Id 52.25N 12.45 E
Havelländisches Luch 10 Id 52.40N 12.40 E
Havelock [N.C.-U.S.] 44 Ih 34.53N 76.54W
Havelock [N.Z.] 62 Ed 41.17S 173.46 E
Havelock North 62 Gc 39.40S 176.53 E
Havelte 12 Ib 52.46N 6.16 E
Haverfordwest 9 Ij 51.49N 4.58W
Haverhill [Eng.-U.K.] 9 Ni 52.05N 0.26 E
Haverhill [Ma.-U.S.] 44 Ld 42.47N 71.05W
Havering, London- 12 Cc 51.36N 0.11 E
Havířov 10 Og 49.48N 18.27 E
Havlíčkův Brod 10 Lg 49.36N 15.34 E
Havøysund 7 Fa 71.03N 24.40 E
Havran 24 Bc 39.33N 27.06 E
Havre 39 Ie 48.33N 109.41W
Havre-Saint-Pierre 39 Md 50.15N 63.36W
Havsa 15 Jh 41.33N 26.49 E
Havza 24 Fb 41.05N 35.45 E
Hawaii 58 Kb 24.00N 167.00W
Hawaiian Islands 57 Kb 24.00N 167.00W
Hawaiian Ridge (EN) 3 Kg 24.00N 165.00W
Hawaii Island 57 Lc 19.30N 155.30W
Ḩawallī 23 Gd 29.19N 48.02 E
Ḩawār 24 Nj 25.40N 50.45 E
Hawarden 62 Ee 42.56S 172.39 E
Ḩawashīyah, Wādī- 24 Eh 28.31N 32.58 E
Ḩawaymī, Sha'īb al- 24 Kg 30.58N 44.15 E
Hawd 30 Lh 7.40N 47.43 E
Ḩawḑ Al Waqf 24 Ei 26.03N 32.22 E
Hawea, Lake- 62 Cf 44.30S 169.20 E
Hawera 61 Dg 39.35S 174.17 E
Hawi 58 Lb 20.14N 155.50W
Hawick 9 Kf 55.25N 2.47W
Ḩawīzah, Hawr al- 24 Lg 31.35N 47.38 E
Hawkdun Range 62 Cf 44.50S 170.00 E
Hawke Bay 61 Eg 39.25S 177.20 E
Hawke Harbour 42 Lf 53.01N 55.50W
Hawker 59 Hf 31.53S 138.25 E
Hawkes, Mount- 66 Rg 83.55S 56.05W
Hawke's Bay 62 Gc 39.30S 176.40 E
Hawkesbury 44 Jc 45.36N 74.37W
Hawkhurst 12 Cc 51.02N 0.30 E
Hawkinsville 44 Fi 32.17N 83.28W
Hawksbill 44 Hf 38.33N 78.23W
Hawk Springs 46 Mf 41.48N 104.09W
Ḩawmat as Sūq 32 Jc 33.53N 10.51 E
Hawng Tuk 25 Jd 20.28N 99.56 E
Ḩawrā' 35 Hb 15.43N 48.18 E
Ḩawrān, Wādī al- 23 Fc 33.58N 42.34 E
Ḩawsh 'Īsá 24 Dg 30.55N 30.17 E
Hawthorne 43 Dd 38.32N 118.38W
Hawthorne, Mount- 66 Pf 72.10S 98.39W
Haxtun 45 Ef 40.39N 102.38W
Hay 58 Fh 34.30S 144.51 E
Hay 38 Hc 60.51N 115.44W
Hayachine-San 29 Gb 39.34N 141.29 E
Hayakita 29a Bb 42.45N 141.48 E
Hayange 11 Me 49.20N 6.03 E
Hayasui-no-Seto 28 Kh 33.20N 132.00 E
Hayato 29 Bf 31.45N 130.43 E
Haybān 35 Ec 11.13N 30.31 E
Haybān, Jabal- 35 Ec 11.15N 30.31 E
Hayden 46 Jj 33.00N 110.47W
Hayes [Man.-Can.] 42 Ie 57.00N 92.15W
Hayes [N.W.T.-Can.] 42 Hc 67.20N 95.02W
Hayes, Mount- 40 Jd 63.37N 146.43W
Hayes Halvø=Hayes
Peninsula (EN) 67 Od 77.40N 64.30W
Hayes Peninsula (EN)=
Hayes Halvø 67 Od 77.40N 64.30W
Ḩayl 24 Qj 24.33N 56.06 E
Hayl, Wādī al- 24 He 34.47N 39.18 E
Hayling Island 12 Bd 50.48N 0.58W
Haymana 24 Ec 39.27N 32.30 E
Haymana Platosu 24 Ec 39.25N 32.45 E
Haynin 23 Gf 15.50N 48.18 E
Hayrabolu 24 Bb 41.12N 27.06 E
Ḩayrān 33 Hf 16.02N 42.49 E
Hay River 59 Hd 25.00S 138.00 E
Hay River 42 Fd 60.51N 115.40W
Hayrüt 35 Ib 15.59N 52.09 E
Hays 43 Hd 38.53N 99.20W
Hay Springs 45 Ee 42.41N 102.41W
Haystack Peak 46 Ig 39.50N 113.55W
Hayward [Ca.-U.S.] 46 Dh 37.40N 122.05W
Hayward [Wi.-U.S.] 45 Kc 46.01N 91.29W
Haywards Heath 12 Bc 51.00N 0.06W
Hazar, Wādī- 35 Hb 17.50N 49.07 E
Hazarasp 18 Cd 41.19N 61.08 E
Hazard 44 Fg 37.15N 83.12W
Hazar Gölü 24 Hc 38.30N 39.25 E
Hazāribāgh 25 Hd 23.59N 85.21 E
Hazebrouck 11 Id 50.43N 2.32 E
Hazelton 42 Ee 55.15N 127.40W
Hazen 45 Fc 47.18N 101.38W
Hazen Strait 42 Ga 77.15N 110.00W
Ḩazeva 24 Fg 30.48N 35.15 E
Hazlehurst [Ga.-U.S.] 44 Fj 31.52N 82.36W
Hazlehurst [Ms.-U.S.] 45 Kk 31.52N 90.24W
Hazleton 44 Je 40.58N 76.00W
Hazlett, Lake- 59 Fd 21.30S 128.50 E
Hazrah, Ra's al- 24 Nj 24.22N 51.36 E
Hazro 24 Ic 38.15N 40.47 E
Heacham 12 Cb 52.55N 0.29 E
Headley 12 Bc 51.07N 0.49W
Healdsburg 46 Dg 38.37N 122.52W
Heanor 12 Aa 53.00N 1.18W

Heard Island 30 On 53.00S 73.35 E
Hearne 45 Hk 30.53N 96.36W
Hearst 42 Jg 49.41N 83.40W
Heart River 45 Fc 46.47N 100.51W
Heathrow Airport London 12 Bc 51.28N 0.30W
Hebbronville 45 Gm 27.18N 98.41W
Hebei Sheng (Ho-pei Sheng)
=Hopeh (EN) 27 Kd 39.00N 116.00 E
Heber City 46 Jf 40.30N 111.25W
Hebi 27 Jd 35.53N 114.09 E
Hebian 27 Jd 38.35N 113.06 E
Hebiji 28 Cf 36.00N 114.08 E
Hebrides 5 Fd 57.00N 6.30W
Hebrides, Sea of the- 9 Ge 57.00N 7.00W
Hebron [N.D.-U.S.] 45 Ec 46.54N 102.03W
Hebron [Newf.-Can.] 42 Le 58.15N 62.35W
Heby 8 Ge 59.56N 16.53 E
Hecate Strait 42 Ef 53.20N 131.00W
Hecelchakán 48 Ng 20.10N 90.08W
Hechi (Jnchengjiang) 27 Ig 24.44N 108.02 E
Hechingen 10 Eh 48.21N 8.59 E
Hechuan 27 Ie 30.07N 106.15 E
Hecla 45 Gd 45.43N 98.09W
Hecla and Griper Bay 42 Ga 76.00N 111.30W
Hecla Island 45 Ha 51.08N 96.45W
Heddalsvatnet 8 Ce 59.30N 9.15 E
Hede 7 Ce 62.25N 13.30 E
Hede → Sheyang 28 Fh 33.47N 120.15 E
Hedemarken 8 Dd 60.50N 11.20 E
Hedemora 7 Df 60.17N 15.59 E
Hedensted 8 Ci 55.46N 9.42 E
Hedesunda 7 Df 60.25N 17.00 E
Hedesunda fjärdarna 8 Gd 60.20N 17.00 E
Hedmark 7 Cf 61.30N 11.45 E
Hedo-Misaki 29b Bb 26.52N 128.16 E
Heemskerk 12 Gb 52.30N 4.42 E
Heemstede 12 Gb 52.21N 4.37 E
Heerenveen 11 Lb 52.57N 5.55 E
Heerhugowaard 12 Gb 52.40N 4.50 E
Heerlen 11 Ld 50.54N 5.59 E
Hefa=Haifa (EN) 22 Ff 32.50N 35.00 E
Hefei 22 Nf 31.47N 117.15 E
Hefeng 27 Jf 29.49N 110.01 E
Hegang 22 Pe 47.20N 130.12 E
Hegau 10 Ei 47.50N 8.45 E
Hegura Jima 27 Od 37.50N 136.55 E
Heide 10 Fb 54.12N 9.06 E
Heidelberg 10 Eg 49.25N 8.42 E
Heidenheim an der Brenz 10 Gh 48.41N 10.09 E
Heidenreichstein 14 Jb 48.52N 15.07 E
Hei-Gawa 29 Gb 39.38N 141.58 E
Heigun-Tō 29 Ce 33.47N 132.15 E
Hei He 27 Hd 38.15N 100.15 E
Heihe → Aihui 22 Od 50.13N 127.26 E
Heilbron 37 De 27.21S 27.58 E
Heilbronn 10 Fg 49.08N 9.13 E
Heiligenblut 14 Gd 47.02N 12.50 E
Heiligenhafen 10 Gb 54.22N 10.59 E
Heiligenhaus 12 Ic 51.19N 6.58 E
Heiligenstadt 10 Ge 51.23N 10.08 E
Heilinzi 28 Ib 44.33N 126.41 E
Heilong Jiang 21 Qd 52.56N 141.10 E
Heilongjiang Sheng
(Hei-lung-chiang Sheng)=
Heilungkiang (EN) 27 Mb 48.00N 128.00 E
Heiloo 12 Gb 52.36N 4.43 E
Hei-lung-chiang
Sheng → Heilongjiang
Sheng=Heilungkiang (EN)
27 Mb 48.00N 128.00 E
Heilungkiang (EN)=
Heilongjiang Sheng
(Hei-lung-chiang Sheng)
27 Mb 48.00N 128.00 E
Heilungkiang (EN)=Hei-
lung-chiang
Sheng → Heilongjiang
Sheng 27 Mb 48.00N 128.00 E
Heimæy 7a c 63.26N 20.17W
Heimbach 12 Id 50.38N 6.29 E
Heimdal 7 Ce 63.21N 10.22 E
Heimsheim 12 Kf 48.48N 8.51 E
Heinävesi 7 Ge 62.26N 28.36 E
Heinola 7 Gf 61.13N 26.02 E
Heinsberg 12 Ic 51.04N 6.05 E
Heishan 28 Gd 41.42N 122.07 E
Heishan Xia 27 Hd 37.18N 104.39 E
Heishui [China] 28 Ec 42.06N 119.22 E
Heishui [China] 27 He 32.03N 103.05 E
Heist, Knokke- 12 Fc 51.21N 3.15 E
Heist-op-den-Berg 12 Gc 51.05N 4.43 E
Hei-Zaki 29 Hb 39.39N 142.00 E
Hejgijaha 17 Pd 65.27N 72.50 E
Hejian 28 De 38.27N 116.05 E
Hejing 27 Ec 42.18N 86.18 E
Hejjaha 17 Kb 68.18N 62.32 E
Hekimhan 24 Gc 38.49N 37.56 E
Hekinan 29 Ed 34.52N 136.58 E
Hekla 5 Ec 64.00N 19.40W
Hekou 28 Ci 31.20N 114.25 E
Hekou → Yanshan 28 Dj 28.18N 117.41 E
Hel 10 Ob 54.37N 18.48 E
Helagsfjället 7 Ce 62.55N 12.27 E
Helan 27 Id 38.35N 106.16 E
Helan Shan 27 Id 39.00N 106.00 E
Helden's Point 51c Ab 17.24N 62.50W
Helena [Ar.-U.S.] 43 Ie 34.32N 90.35W
Helena [Guy.] 54 Gb 6.41N 57.55W
Helena [Mt.-U.S.] 39 He 46.36N 112.01W
Helen Glacier 66 Ge 66.40S 93.55 E
Helen Reef 57 Ed 2.53N 131.47 E
Helensburgh 9 Ie 56.01N 4.44W
Helensville 62 Fb 36.40S 174.27 E
Helgaå 8 Fh 55.53N 14.08 E
Helgasjön 8 Fh 56.55N 14.45 E
Helgeland 7 Cd 66.15N 13.05 E
Helgoland 10 Db 54.12N 7.53 E

Index Symbols

Independent Nation
State, Region
District, County
Municipality
Colony, Dependency
Continent
Physical Region

Historical or Cultural Region
Mount, Mountain
Volcano
Hill
Mountains, Mountain Range
Hills, Escarpment
Plateau, Upland

Pass, Gap
Plain, Lowland
Delta
Salt Flat
Valley, Canyon
Crater, Cave
Karst Features

Depression
Polder
Desert, Dunes
Forest, Woods
Heath, Steppe
Oasis
Cape, Point

Coast, Beach
Cliff
Peninsula
Isthmus
Sandbank
Island
Atoll

Rock, Reef
Islands, Archipelago
Rocks, Reefs
Coral Reef
Well, Spring
Geyser
River, Stream

Waterfall Rapids
River Mouth, Estuary
Lake
Salt Lake
Intermittent Lake
Reservoir
Swamp, Pond

Canal
Glacier
Ice Shelf, Pack Ice
Ocean
Sea
Gulf, Bay
Strait, Fjord

Lagoon
Bank
Seamount
Tablemount
Ridge
Shelf
Basin

Escarpment, Sea Scarp
Fracture
Trench, Abyss
National Park, Reserve
Point of Interest
Recreation Site
Cave, Cavern

Historic Site
Ruins
Wall, Walls
Church, Abbey
Temple
Scientific Station
Airport

Port
Lighthouse
Mine
Tunnel
Dam, Bridge

Name	Page	Grid	Lat	Long
Helgoländer Bucht ◻	10	Eb	54.10N	8.04 E
Helikón Óros ▲	15	Fk	38.20N	22.50 E
Helixi	28	Ei	30.39N	119.01 E
Heljulja	8	Nc	61.37N	30.38 E
Hella	7a	Bc	63.50N	20.24W
Hellberge ▲	10	Hd	52.34N	11.17 E
Hélleh	24	Nh	29.10N	50.40 E
Hellendoorn	11	Mb	52.24N	6.26 E
Hellendoorn-Nijverdal	12	Ib	52.22N	6.27 E
Hellenic Trough (EN) ▨	5	li	35.00N	24.00 E
Hellental	12	Id	50.29N	6.26 E
Hellesylt	7	Be	62.05N	6.54 E
Hellin	13	Kf	38.31N	1.41W
Hells Canyon ▨	43	Db	45.20N	116.45W
Hellweg	12	Kc	51.40N	8.00 E
Helmand ⬧	21	If	31.12N	61.34 E
Helmand ⬧	23	Jc	31.00N	64.00 E
Helme ⬧	10	He	51.20N	11.20 E
Helmeringhausen	37	Be	25.54S	16.57 E
Helmond	11	Lc	51.29N	5.40 E
Helmsdale	9	Jc	58.10N	3.43W
Helmsdale	9	Jc	58.07N	3.40W
Helmstedt	10	Gd	52.14N	11.00 E
Helong	27	Mc	42.32N	129.00 E
Helpe Majeure ⬧	12	Fd	50.11N	3.47 E
Helpringham	12	Bb	52.56N	0.18W
Helpter Berge ▲	10	Jc	53.30N	13.36 E
Helsingborg	6	Hd	56.03N	12.42 E
Helsinge	8	Ee	56.01N	12.12 E
Helsingfors/Helsinki	6	Ic	60.10N	24.58 E
Helsingør	7	Ch	56.02N	12.37 E
Helsinki/Helsingfors	6	Ic	60.10N	24.58 E
Helska, Mierzeja- ⬧	10	Ob	54.45N	18.39 E
Helston	9	Hk	50.05N	5.16W
Helvecia	55	Bj	31.06S	60.05W
Helwân (EN) = Ḥulwân	33	Fd	29.51N	31.20 E
Ḥemâr ⬧	24	Qg	31.42N	57.31 E
Hemčík ⬧	20	Ef	51.40N	92.10 E
Hemel Hempstead	9	Mj	51.46N	0.28W
Hemer	12	Jc	51.23N	7.46 E
Hemnesberget	7	Cc	66.14N	13.38 E
Hemsby	12	Db	52.41N	1.42 E
Hemse	8	Hg	57.14N	18.22 E
Hemsedal ⬧	8	Cd	60.50N	8.40 E
Hemsö ⬧	7	Ee	62.45N	18.05 E
Hen	8	Dd	60.13N	10.14 E
Henan	27	He	34.33N	101.55 E
Hen and Chickens Islands ◻	62	Fa	35.55S	174.45 E
Henan Sheng (Ho-nan Sheng) = Honan (EN) ▨	27	Je	34.00N	114.00 E
Henares ⬧	13	Id	40.24N	3.30W
Henashi-Zaki ▶	29	Fa	40.37N	139.51 E
Henbury	59	Gd	24.35S	133.15 E
Hendaye	11	Ek	43.22N	1.47W
Hendek	24	Db	40.48N	30.45 E
Henderson [Arg.]	55	Bm	36.18S	61.43W
Henderson [Ky.-U.S.]	44	Dg	37.50N	87.35W
Henderson [N.C.-U.S.]	44	Hg	36.20N	78.25W
Henderson [Nv.-U.S.]	43	Dd	36.02N	115.01W
Henderson [Tx.-U.S.]	45	Jj	32.09N	94.48W
Henderson Island	57	Og	24.22S	128.19W
Henderson Seamount (EN) ▨	43	Df	25.34N	119.33W
Hendersonville [N.C.-U.S.]	44	Fh	35.19N	82.28W
Hendersonville [Tn.-U.S.]	44	Dh	36.18N	86.37W
Hendijān	24	Mg	30.14N	49.43 E
Hendorâbi, Jazireh-ye- ◻	24	Pi	26.40N	53.37 E
Hendrik Verwoerddam ◻	30	Km	46.36S	37.55 E
Hengâm, Jazireh-ye- ◻	24	Pi	26.39N	55.53 E
Hengduan Shan ▲	21	Lg	27.30N	99.00 E
Hengelo [Neth.]	11	Mb	52.15N	6.45 E
Hengelo [Neth.]	12	Ib	52.03N	6.20 E
Heng Shan [China] ▲	27	Jd	39.42N	113.45 E
Hengshan [China]	27	Jf	27.16N	112.51 E
Heng Shan [China] ▲	27	Jf	27.18N	112.41 E
Hengshan [China]	27	Id	37.51N	109.20 E
Hengshan [China]	28	Kb	45.24N	131.01 E
Hengshui	27	Kd	37.39N	115.46 E
Hengxian	27	Ig	22.46N	109.15 E
Hengyang	22	Ng	26.56N	112.35 E
Henik Lakes ⬧	42	Hd	61.05N	97.20W
Hénin-Liétard	11	Id	50.25N	2.56 E
Henley-on-Thames	12	Bc	51.32N	0.54W
Hennan	8	Fb	62.05N	15.45 E
Hennan	7	De	62.02N	15.54 E
Hennebont	11	Cg	47.48N	3.17W
Hennef (Sieg)	12	Jd	50.47N	7.17 E
Hennigsdorf bei Berlin	10	Jd	52.38N	13.12 E
Henrietta Maria, Cape - ▶	42	Je	55.09N	82.19W
Henrietty, Ostrov- ◻	20	Ka	77.00N	157.00 E
Henry, Mount- ▲	43	Mb	48.53N	115.31W
Henry Bay ◻	66	Ie	66.40S	120.40 E
Henryetta	45	Ii	35.27N	95.59W
Henry Kater Peninsula ◻	42	Kk	69.15N	67.30W
Henry Mountains ▲	46	Jh	37.55N	110.50W
Henrys Fork River ⬧	46	Je	43.45N	111.56W
Henslow, Cape- ▶	63a	Ec	9.56S	160.38 E
Hentej ▲	21	Me	48.50N	109.00 E
Hentiesbaai	37	Ad	22.08S	14.18 E
Henzada	22	Lh	17.38N	95.28 E
Heping → Yanhe	27	If	28.31N	108.28 E
Heppenheim (Bergstraße)	12	Je	49.38N	8.39 E
Heppner	46	Fd	45.21N	119.33W
Hepu (Lianzhou)	27	Ig	21.40N	109.12 E
Hequ	27	Jd	39.22N	111.15 E
Herakol Dağı ▲	24	Id	37.45N	42.35 E
Heralds Cays ◻	59	Jc	16.55S	149.10 E
Herāt ▨	23	Jc	34.30N	62.00 E
Herât	22	If	34.20N	62.12 E
Hérault ▨	11	Jk	43.40N	3.26 E
Hérault ⬧	11	Jk	43.17N	3.26 E
Herbert [N.Z.]	62	Df	45.13S	170.46 E
Herbert [Sask.-Can.]	46	La	50.26N	107.12W
Herberton	59	Jc	17.23S	145.23 E
Herbert River ⬧	59	Jc	18.32S	146.17 E
Herborn	10	Ef	50.41N	8.19 E
Herby	10	Of	50.45N	18.40 E
Hercegnovi	15	Bg	42.27N	18.32 E
Hercegovina ▨	14	Lg	43.00N	17.50 E
Hercegovina ⬧	5	Hg	43.00N	17.50 E
Herdubreid ▲	7a	Cb	65.11N	16.21W
Heredia ▨	49	Fh	10.30N	84.00W
Heredia	47	Hf	10.00N	84.07W
Hereford ◻	9	Ki	52.15N	2.50W
Hereford [Eng.-U.K.]	9	Ki	52.04N	2.43W
Hereford [Tx.-U.S.]	43	Ge	34.49N	102.24W
Hereford and Worcester ▨	9	Ki	52.10N	2.35W
Hereheretue Atoll ◻	57	Mf	19.54S	144.58W
Hereke	15	Mi	40.48N	29.39 E
Herekino	62	Ea	35.16S	173.13 E
Herent	12	Gd	50.54N	4.40 E
Herentals	12	Gc	51.11N	4.50 E
Herfølge	8	Ei	55.25N	12.10 E
Herford	10	Ed	52.08N	8.41 E
Héricourt	11	Mg	47.35N	6.45 E
Herington	45	Hg	38.40N	96.57W
Heriot	61	Ci	45.51S	169.16 E
Heris	24	Lc	38.14N	47.07 E
Herk	12	Hd	50.58N	5.07 E
Herk-de-Stad	12	Hd	50.56N	5.10 E
Herkimer	44	Jd	43.02N	74.59W
Herlen He ⬧	27	Kb	48.48N	117.00 E
Hermagor	14	Hd	46.37N	13.22 E
Hermanas	48	Jd	27.14N	101.14W
Herma Ness ▶	9	Ma	60.50N	0.54W
Hermano Peak ▲	45	Bh	37.17N	108.48W
Hermansverk	8	Bc	61.11N	6.51 E
Hermanus	37	Bd	34.25S	19.16 E
Hermeskeil	12	Ie	49.39N	6.57 E
Hermiston	46	Fd	45.51N	119.17W
Hermitage	45	Cd	33.44N	170.05 E
Hermit Islands ◻	57	Fe	1.32S	145.05 E
Hermosa de Santa Rosa, Sierra- ▲	48	Id	28.00N	101.45W
Hermosillo	39	Hg	29.04N	110.58W
Hermoso Campo	55	Bh	27.36S	61.21W
Hérnad ⬧	10	Qh	48.00N	20.58 E
Hernandarias	56	Jc	25.22S	54.45W
Hernández [Arg.]	55	Bk	32.21S	60.02W
Hernández [Mex.]	48	Hf	23.02N	102.02W
Hernani	13	Ka	43.16N	1.58W
Herne	10	De	51.33N	7.13 E
Herne Bay	9	Oj	51.23N	1.08 E
Herning	6	Gd	56.08N	8.59 E
Heroica Alvarado	48	Lh	18.46N	95.46W
Heroica Tlapacoyan	48	Kh	19.58N	97.13W
Heroica Zitácuaro	48	Jh	19.24N	100.22W
Herouville-Saint-Clair	12	Be	49.12N	0.19W
Herowābād	24	Md	37.37N	48.32 E
Herradura	55	Ch	26.29S	58.18W
Herre	8	Ce	59.06N	9.34 E
Herrera	55	Ck	32.26S	58.38W
Herrera ▨	49	Gj	7.54N	80.38W
Herrera del Duque	13	Ge	39.10N	5.03W
Herrera de Pisuerga	13	Hb	42.36N	4.20W
Herrera, Punta- ▶	48	Ph	19.10N	87.30W
Herrljunga	8	Ef	58.05N	13.02 E
Hers ⬧	11	Hk	43.47N	1.20 E
Herschel ◻	42	Bc	69.35S	139.05W
Herselt	12	Gc	51.03N	4.53 E
Herserange	12	He	49.31N	5.47 E
Hershey	44	Ie	40.17N	76.39W
Hersilia	55	Bj	30.00S	61.51W
Herson	6	Jf	46.38N	32.35 E
Hersonesski, Mys- ▶	16	Kg	44.33N	33.25 E
Hersonskaja Oblast ▨	16	Jf	46.30N	33.30 E
Herstal	12	Hd	50.40N	5.38 E
Herten	12	Jc	51.36N	7.08 E
Hertford ◻	9	Mj	51.50N	0.05W
Hertford	9	Mj	51.48N	0.05W
Hertfordshire ▨	9	Mj	51.45N	0.20W
Hertugen Af Orleans Land	41	Jc	78.15N	21.12W
Hervás	13	Gd	40.16N	5.51W
Herve	12	Hd	50.38N	5.48 E
Herve, Plateau van-/Herveland ⬧	12	Hd	50.40N	5.50 E
Herveland/Herve, Plateau van- ⬧	12	Hd	50.40N	5.50 E
Hervey Bay	59	Ke	25.15S	152.50 E
Herzberg	10	Je	51.41N	13.14 E
Herzberg am Harz	10	Ge	51.39N	10.20 E
Herzbrock	12	Kc	51.53N	8.15 E
Herzele	12	Fd	50.53N	3.53 E
Herzliyya	24	Ff	32.10N	34.51 E
Herzogenrath	12	Id	50.52N	6.06 E
Herzog-Ernst-Bucht (Vahsel Bay) ◻	66	Af	77.48S	34.39W
Hesämābād	24	Me	35.52N	48.25 E
Hesbaye/Haspengouws Plateau ▣	12	Hd	50.35N	5.10 E
Hesdin	11	Id	50.22N	2.02 E
Hesel	12	Ja	53.18N	7.36 E
Heshi	24	Md	37.30N	48.15 E
Heshun	27	Jd	37.18N	113.32 E
Hesse = Hessen (EN) ▨	10	Ff	50.30N	9.00 E
Hesselberg ▲	10	Gg	49.05N	10.35 E
Hessle ◻	10	Cb	50.10N	11.45 E
Hessen	12	Ke	49.47N	8.08 E
Hessen = Hesse (EN) ▨	10	Ff	50.30N	9.00 E
Hess Tablemount (EN) ▨	21	Mb	71.54N	102.00 E
Heta	20	Eb	71.35N	99.45 E
Hettange-Grande	12	Ie	49.24N	6.09 E
Hettinger	45	Ec	46.00N	102.39W
Heuberg ▲	10	En	48.06N	8.55 E
Heuchin	12	Ed	50.28N	2.16 E
Heuru	63a	Ed	10.12S	161.25 E
Hève, Cap de la- ▶	11	Fe	49.31N	0.04W
Heves ▨	10	Qi	47.50N	20.17 E
Heves	10	Qi	47.50N	20.15 E
Hexham	9	Kg	54.58N	2.06W
Hexi	27	Hf	27.44N	102.09 E
Hexian	28	Ei	31.43N	118.22 E
Hexian (Babu)	22	Ng	24.28N	111.34 E
Hexigten Qi (Jingfeng)	27	Kc	43.15N	117.31 E
Heydarābād	24	Kd	37.06N	45.27 E
Heysham	9	Kg	54.02N	2.54W
Heyuan	27	Jg	23.41N	114.43 E
Heywood	59	Ig	38.08S	141.38 E
Heze (Caozhou)	27	Kd	35.14N	115.28 E
Hezuo	27	Hd	35.02N	102.57 E
Hialeah	44	Gm	25.49N	80.17W
Hiawatha	45	Jg	39.51N	95.32W
Hibara-Ko ⬧	29	Gc	37.42N	140.03 E
Hibbing	43	Ib	47.25N	92.56W
Hibernia Reef ◻	59	Eb	12.00S	123.25 E
Hibiki-Nada ▤	29	Bd	34.15N	130.40 E
Hibiny ▲	7	Hc	67.40N	33.35 E
Hiburi-Jima ◻	29	Ce	33.10N	132.18 E
Hickory	44	Gg	35.44N	81.21W
Hick's Cay ◻	49	Ce	17.39N	88.08W
Hida-Gawa ⬧	29	Ed	35.25N	137.03 E
Hidaka [Jap.]	28	Qc	42.53N	142.28 E
Hidaka [Jap.]	29	Dd	35.28N	134.47 E
Hidaka-Gawa ⬧	29	De	33.53N	135.08 E
Hidaka Sanmyaku ▲	28	Qc	42.25N	142.50 E
Hidalgo	47	Jd	20.30N	99.00W
Hidalgo [Mex.]	47	Ef	24.15N	99.26W
Hidalgo [Mex.]	48	Jd	27.14N	101.14W
Hidalgo del Parral	39	Jg	26.56N	105.40W
Hida-Sanchi ▲	29	Ec	36.20N	137.00 E
Hida-Sanmyaku ▲	28	Nf	36.10N	137.30 E
Hiddensee ◻	10	Jb	54.33N	13.07 E
Hidra ◻	8	Bf	58.15N	6.35 E
Hidrolândia	55	Hc	16.58S	49.16W
Hidrolina	55	Hh	14.37S	49.25W
Hieflau	14	Ic	47.36N	14.44 E
Hiei-Zan ▲	29	Dd	35.05N	135.50 E
Hienghène	61	Cd	20.35S	164.56 E
Hierro ◻	30	Ff	27.45N	18.00W
Higashi	29	Cd	34.25N	132.43 E
Higashihiroshima	29	Cd	34.25N	132.43 E
Higashi-izu	29	Fd	34.48N	139.02 E
Higashi-matsuyama	29	Fc	36.02N	139.22 E
Higashimuroran	29a	Bb	42.21N	141.02 E
Higashine	28	Pe	38.26N	140.24 E
Higashiōsaka	29	Dd	34.40N	135.37 E
Higashi Rishiri	29a	Ba	45.16N	141.15 E
Higashi-Shina-Kai = East China Sea (EN) ▨	21	Og	29.00N	125.00 E
Higgins	45	Fh	36.07N	100.02W
Higham Ferrers	12	Bb	52.18N	0.35W
High Atlas (EN) = Haut Atlas ▲	30	Ge	32.00N	6.00W
Highland ▨	9	Id	57.30N	6.00W
Highland Park	45	Me	42.11N	87.48W
High Level	42	Fe	58.30N	117.05W
Highmore	45	Gd	44.31N	99.27W
High Plains ▣	38	If	38.30N	103.00W
High Point	43	Ld	35.58N	79.59W
High Prairie	42	Fe	55.27N	116.30W
High River	42	Gf	50.35N	113.52W
Highrock Lake ⬧	42	He	55.49N	100.23W
High Springs	44	Fk	29.50N	82.36W
High Tatra (EN) = Vysoké Tatry ▲	10	Pg	49.10N	20.00 E
High Willhays ▲	9	Jk	50.41N	3.59W
Highwood Mountains ▲	46	Jc	47.25N	110.30W
High Wycombe	12	Bc	51.38N	0.46W
Higuera de Zaragoza	48	Ee	25.59N	109.16W
Higüero, Punta- ▶	50	Cd	18.22N	67.16W
Higuerote	50	Cg	10.29N	66.06W
Hiidenvesi ⬧	8	Le	60.20N	24.10 E
Hii-Gawa ⬧	29	Cd	35.26N	132.52 E
Hiiraan ▨	35	He	4.00N	45.30 E
Hiitola	7	Gf	61.16N	29.42 E
Hiiumaa/Hiuma ◻	5	Id	58.50N	22.40 E
Hijar	13	Kc	41.10N	0.27W
Ḥijāz ⬧	23	Dd	23.00N	40.00 E
Ḥijāz, Jabal al- ▲	33	Hf	19.45N	41.55 E
Hiji	29	Be	33.22N	131.32 E
Hiji-Gawa ⬧	29	Ce	33.32N	132.29 E
Hikami	29	Dd	35.11N	135.02 E
Hikari	29	Be	33.58N	131.56 E
Hiketa	29	Dd	34.13N	134.24 E
Hikiā	8	Kd	60.45N	24.55 E
Hiki-Gawa ⬧	29	De	33.35N	135.26 E
Ḥikmah, Ra's al- ▶	24	Bg	31.17N	27.44 E
Hikone	29	Dd	35.15N	136.15 E
Hiko-San ▲	29	Be	33.29N	130.56 E
Hikueru Atoll ◻	57	Mf	17.36S	142.37W
Hikurangi	62	Hb	37.55S	178.04 E
Hikurangi ▲	62	Fb	35.36S	174.17 E
Hila	26	Ih	7.35S	127.24 E
Hilāl, Ra's al- ▶	33	Dc	32.55N	22.11 E
Hiland	12	Ld	50.22N	2.02 E
Hilchenbach	12	Kc	51.00N	8.06 E
Hildburghausen	10	Gf	50.25N	10.45 E
Hilden	12	Id	51.10N	6.56 E
Hildesheim	10	Fd	52.09N	9.58 E
Hillaby, Mount- ▲	50	Gf	13.12N	59.35W
Hillared	8	Eg	57.38N	13.09 E
Hillary Coast ▣	66	Kf	79.00S	161.00 E
Hill Bank	49	Ce	17.35N	88.42W
Hill City	45	Gg	39.22N	99.51W
Hillcrest Center	46	Fi	35.23N	118.57W
Hille	12	Kb	52.20N	8.45 E
Hillegom	12	Gb	52.18N	4.35 E
Hillerød	8	Dj	54.36N	11.30 E
Hillerstorp	8	Eg	57.19N	13.52 E
Hillesøen	63a	Ed	10.12S	161.25 E
Hillingdon, London-	12	Bc	51.31N	0.27W
Hillsboro [Il.-U.S.]	45	Lg	39.09N	89.29W
Hillsboro [Oh.-U.S.]	44	Ff	39.12N	83.37W
Hillsboro [Or.-U.S.]	46	Dd	45.31N	122.59W
Hillsboro [Tx.-U.S.]	45	Hj	32.01N	97.08W
Hillsborough	51p	Cb	12.29N	61.28W
Hillsdale	44	Ee	41.55N	84.38W
Hillsville	44	Gg	36.46N	80.44W
Hillswich	9	La	60.28N	1.30W
Hilo	58	Lc	19.44N	155.05W
Hilo Bay ◻	65a	Fd	19.44N	155.05W
Hilok	21	Md	51.19N	106.59 E
Hilok ⬧	20	Gf	51.22N	110.30 E
Hilton Head Island	44	Gi	32.12N	80.45W
Hiltrup, Münster-	12	Jc	51.54N	7.38 E
Hilvan	24	Hd	37.30N	38.58 E
Hilvarenbeek	12	Hc	51.29N	5.08 E
Hilversum	11	Lb	52.14N	5.10 E
Himāchal Prādesh ▨	25	Fb	31.00N	78.00 E
Himalaya = Himalayas (EN)	21	Kg	29.00N	83.00 E
Himalaya (EN) = Himalaya ▲	21	Kg	29.00N	83.00 E
Himara	15	Ci	40.07N	19.44 E
Himeji	27	Be	35.25N	137.03 E
Hime-Jima ◻	29	Be	33.43N	131.40 E
Hime-Kawa ⬧	29	Ec	37.02N	137.50 E
Hime-Shima ◻	29	Ae	32.49N	128.41 E
Hime-Zaki ▶	29	Ae	32.49N	128.41 E
Himi	28	Nf	36.51N	136.59 E
Himki	7	Ii	55.56N	37.28 E
Himmelbjerget ▲	8	Ge	56.06N	9.42 E
Himmerfjärden ◻	8	Ge	59.00N	17.43 E
Himmerland ▣	8	Ge	56.50N	9.45 E
Himo	36	Gc	3.23S	37.33 E
Ḥims = Homs (E)	23	Ff	34.44N	36.43 E
Hims, Baḥrat- ⬧	24	Ge	34.39N	36.34 E
Hinai	29	Ga	40.13N	140.35 E
Hinchinbrook ◻	46	Jd	60.22N	146.30W
Hinchinbrook Island ◻	59	Jc	18.25S	146.15 E
Hinckley	12	Ab	52.33N	1.22W
Hindås	8	Eg	57.42N	12.27 E
Hindhead	12	Bc	51.06N	0.44W
Hindi, Badwēynta = Indian Ocean (EN) ▨	3	Gl	21.00S	82.00 E
Hindmarsh, Lake- ⬧	59	Ig	36.05S	141.55 E
Hinds	62	Df	44.00S	171.34 E
Hindson ◻	8	Di	55.33N	10.40 E
Hindukush ▲	21	Jf	35.00N	71.00 E
Hindustan ▣	21	Jg	25.00N	79.00 E
Hinesville	44	Gj	31.51N	81.36W
Hinganghāt	25	Fd	20.34N	78.50 E
Hinis	24	Jc	39.22N	41.42 E
Hinis ⬧	24	Jc	39.18N	42.12 E
Hinlopenstretet ▨	41	Oc	79.15N	21.00 E
Hinneya ◻	5	Hb	68.30N	16.00 E
Hinojosa del Duque	13	Gf	38.30N	5.09W
Hinokage	29	Be	32.39N	131.24 E
Hinokami	29	Cd	35.10N	132.38 E
Hino-Misaki ▶	29	Cd	35.26N	132.38 E
Hino-Misaki ▶	29	De	33.53N	135.04 E
Hinterrhein ⬧	14	Dd	46.49N	9.25 E
Hinton	42	Fe	53.25N	117.34W
Hi-Numa ⬧	29	Gc	36.16N	140.30 E
Hinzir Burun ▶	24	Fb	36.15N	35.45 E
Hiou ◻	63b	Ca	13.08S	166.33 E
Hipólito	48	Ie	25.41N	101.26W
Hippolytushoef, Wieringen-	12	Gb	52.54N	4.59 E
Hippone	14	Bn	36.52N	7.44 E
Hirado	28	Jh	33.23N	129.33 E
Hirado-Shima ◻	28	Jh	33.19N	129.32 E
Hiraka	29	Gb	39.46N	140.29 E
Hirakata	29	Dd	34.48N	135.38 E
Hirākud ⬧	25	Gd	21.15N	84.15 E
Hiraman ⬧	36	Gc	1.07S	39.55 E
Hiranai	29	Ga	40.54N	140.57 E
Hirara	27	Pg	24.48N	125.17 E
Hira-Shima ◻	28	Jh	33.09N	129.29 E
Hirata	29	Cd	35.26N	132.49 E
Hiratsuka	29	Fd	35.19N	139.19 E
Hirfanlı baraji Gölü ⬧	24	Ec	39.10N	33.32 E
Hirgis	24	Fb	39.10N	33.32 E
Hirgis-Nur ⬧	21	Le	49.12N	93.24 E
Hirhafok	32	Je	23.53N	5.47 E
Hirlāu	15	Jb	47.26N	26.54 E
Hiromi	29	Be	33.22N	131.32 E
Hiroo	29	Pc	42.17N	143.19 E
Hirosaki	28	Df	40.35N	140.28 E
Hiroshima	29	Cd	34.24N	132.27 E
Hiroshima Ken ▨	28	Lg	34.35N	132.50 E
Hiroshima-Wan ⬧	29	Cd	34.15N	132.20 E
Hirschhorn (Neckar)	12	Ke	49.27N	8.54 E
Hirson	11	Je	49.55N	4.05 E
Hîrşova	15	Ke	44.41N	27.56 E
Hirtibaciu ⬧	15	Hc	45.44N	24.14 E
Hirtshals	7	Bh	57.35N	9.58 E
Hirvensalmi	8	Lc	61.38N	26.48 E
His	35	Hc	10.50N	46.54 E
Hisai	29	Dd	34.40N	136.28 E
Hisaka-Shima ◻	28	Jh	32.48N	128.52 E
Hisar ▲	15	Jg	42.35N	27.00 E
Hisar	25	Fb	29.10N	75.43 E
Hisarcik	15	Mj	39.39N	29.15 E
Hisarja	15	Hg	42.30N	24.42 E
Ḥişmá ▣	24	Gg	28.30N	35.50 E
Hişn al-'Abr	33	If	16.08N	47.14 E
Hişn as-Şaḥābi	33	Dc	30.01N	20.48 E
Hispaniola (EN) = La Española ◻	38	Lh	19.00N	71.00W
Histon	12	Cb	52.15N	0.06 E
Histria ⸰	15	Ke	44.30N	28.45 E
Hīt	24	Jf	33.38N	42.49 E
Hita	28	Kh	33.19N	130.56 E
Hitachi	29	Gc	36.36N	140.39 E
Hitachi-ōta	29	Gc	36.32N	140.31 E
Hitchin	12	Bc	51.57N	0.16W
Hitiaa	65c	Fc	17.36S	149.18W
Hitotsuse-Gawa ⬧	29	Be	32.03N	131.26 E
Hitoyoshi	28	Kh	32.15N	130.45 E
Hitra ◻	5	Gc	63.30N	8.45 E
Hiuchi-ga-Take ▲	29	Fc	36.57N	139.17 E
Hiuchi-Nada ▤	29	Cd	34.05N	133.15 E
Hiuma/Hiiumaa ◻	5	Id	58.50N	22.40 E
Hiv	16	Oi	41.46N	47.57 E
Hiva	19	Gg	41.25N	60.23 E
Hiva Oa, Ile- ◻	57	Ne	9.45S	139.00W
Hiw	24	Ei	26.01N	32.16 E
Hjademeste/Häädemeeste	8	Uf	58.00N	24.26 E
Hjallerup	8	Dg	57.10N	10.09 E
Hjälmare kanal ⬧	8	Fe	59.25N	15.55 E
Hjälmaren ⬧	5	Hd	59.15N	15.45 E
Hjelm ◻	8	Dh	56.10N	10.50 E
Hjelmelandsvågen	7	Bg	59.15N	6.10 E
Hjelmsøya ◻	7	Fa	71.05N	24.43 E
Hjerkinn	8	Cb	62.13N	9.32 E
Hjo	7	Dg	58.18N	14.17 E
Hjørring	7	Bh	57.28N	9.59 E
Hlatikulu	37	Ee	26.58S	31.19 E
Hlavní město Praha ▨	10	Kf	50.05N	14.25 E
Hlavní město SSR Bratislava ▨	10	Nh	48.10N	17.10 E
Hlinsko	10	Lg	49.46N	15.54 E
Hlohovec	10	Nh	48.25N	17.48 E
Hluhluwe	37	Ee	28.02S	32.17 E
Hmelnickaja Oblast ▨	19	Cf	49.30N	27.00 E
Hmelnicki	19	Cf	49.24N	26.57 E
Hmelnik	16	Ee	49.33N	27.59 E
Hnilec ⬧	10	Rh	48.53N	21.01 E
Ho	34	Fd	6.36N	0.28 E
Hoa Binh	25	Ld	20.50N	105.20 E
Hoai Nhon	25	Lf	14.26N	109.01 E
Hoanib ⬧	37	Ac	19.23S	13.06 E
Hoare Bay ◻	42	Lc	65.30N	63.10W
Hoback Peak ▲	46	Je	43.10N	110.33W
Hobart [Austl.]	58	Fi	42.53S	147.19 E
Hobart [Ok.-U.S.]	45	Gi	35.01N	99.06W
Hobbs	43	Ge	32.42N	103.08W
Hobbs Coast ▣	66	Nf	74.50S	131.00W
Hobda ⬧	8	Eg	50.55N	54.38 E
Hoboken, Antwerpen-	12	Gc	51.10N	4.21 E
Hobøksar	27	Eb	46.47N	85.43 E
Hobq Shamo ▨	27	Ic	40.30N	108.00 E
Hoburgen ▶	7	Eh	56.55N	18.07 E
Hobyä	31	Lh	5.20N	48.38 E
Hocalar	15	Mk	38.37N	29.57 E
Hochalmspitze ▲	14	Hc	47.01N	13.19 E
Hochfeiler/Gran Pilastro ▲	14	Fd	46.58N	11.44 E
Hochgolling ▲	14	Hc	47.16N	13.45 E
Ho Chi Minh (Saigon)	22	Mh	10.45N	106.40 E
Hochschwab ▲	14	Jc	47.36N	15.10 E
Höchstadt an der Aisch	10	Gg	49.42N	10.44 E
Hochstetters Forland ◻	41	Kc	75.45N	20.00 E
Höchst im Odenwald	12	Ke	49.48N	9.00 E
Hochtor ▲	14	Gc	47.05N	12.48 E
Hockenheim	12	Ke	49.19N	8.33 E
Hodaka-Dake ▲	29	Ec	36.17N	137.39 E
Hodda ▲	35	Ic	11.30N	50.45 E
Hoddesdon	12	Cc	51.45N	0.00
Hodgenville	44	Eg	37.34N	85.44W
Hodh ▣	30	Gg	16.10N	8.40W
Hodh el Chargui ▨	32	Ff	17.00N	7.15W
Hodh el Gharbi ▨	32	Ff	16.30N	10.00W
Hódmezővásárhely	10	Qi	46.25N	20.20 E
Hodna, Chott el- ⬧	32	Hb	35.25N	4.45 E
Hodna, Monts du- ▲	32	Hb	35.50N	4.50 E
Hodna, Plaine du- ▣	13	Qj	35.35N	4.00 E
Hodonín	10	Nh	48.52N	17.08 E
Hodorov	16	Ee	49.24N	24.18 E
Hodžambas	28	Ee	38.06N	65.01 E
Hodža-Pirjah, Gora- ▲	18	Fe	38.47N	67.35 E
Hodžejli	19	Fg	42.23N	59.20 E
Hœdic, Ile de- ◻	11	Dg	47.20N	2.52W
Hoegaarden	12	Gd	50.47N	4.53 E
Hoei/Huy	11	Ld	50.31N	5.14 E
Hoë Karoo ▣	30	Jl	30.00S	21.30 E
Hoek van Holland	11	Kc	51.59N	4.09 E
Hoeselt	12	Hd	50.51N	5.29 E
Hof	10	Hf	50.19N	11.55 E
Höfdakaupstadur	7a	Bb	65.50N	20.19W
Hofgeismar	10	Fe	51.29N	9.23 E
Hofheim	12	Kd	50.05N	8.27 E
Hofmeyr	37	Cd	31.39S	25.50 E
Höfn	7a	Cb	64.15N	15.13W
Hofors	8	Gc	60.33N	16.17 E
Hofsjökull ▲	5	Id	64.49N	18.48W
Höfu	28	Kg	34.03N	131.34 E
Höganäs	8	Eh	56.12N	12.33 E
Hogarth, Mount- ▲	59	Hd	21.43S	136.58 E
Hogback Mountain ▲	46	Id	44.54N	112.07W
Hog Cliffs ▩	51	Ba	17.38N	61.44W
Hoge Venen/Hautes Fagnes ▲	10	Bf	50.30N	6.00 E
Högfors/Karkkila	8	Le	60.32N	24.11 E
Hog Island ◻	51p	Bb	12.00N	61.44W
Hogne, Somme-Leuze-	12	Hd	50.17N	5.18 E
Hog Point ▶	51d	Ba	17.43N	61.48W
Högsby	7	Dg	57.10N	16.02 E
Høgste Breakulen ▲	8	Bc	61.41N	7.02 E
Høgstegia ▲	8	Db	62.23N	10.08 E
Hogsty Reef ◻	49	Kc	21.41N	73.49W
Hōhang-nyōng ▲	28	Jd	41.48N	128.20 E
Hohe Acht ▲	10	Cf	50.23N	7.00 E
Hohe Eifel ▲	12	Id	50.16N	6.50 E
Hohenems	14	Dc	47.22N	9.41 E
Hohenloher Ebene ▣	12	Lf	49.20N	9.40 E
Hohes Venn ▲	8	Bf	50.30N	6.00 E
Hohe Tauern ▲	14	Gc	47.10N	12.30 E
Hohhot	27	Jc	40.51N	111.38 E
Hōhoku	29	Bd	34.17N	130.57 E
Hoh-Grenzhausen	12	Je	50.26N	7.40 E
Höhtiäinen ⬧	8	Mb	62.55N	29.45 E
Hoh Xil Hu ⬧	27	Fd	35.35N	91.06 E
Hoh Xil Shan ▲	21	Lf	35.20N	91.00 E
Hoi An	25	Le	15.52N	108.19 E

Index Symbols

[1] Independent Nation	Historical or Cultural Region	Pass, Gap	Depression
[2] State, Region	Mount, Mountain	Plain, Lowland	Polder
[3] District, County	Volcano	Delta	Desert, Dunes
[4] Municipality	Hill	Salt Flat	Forest, Woods
[5] Colony, Dependency	Mountains, Mountain Range	Valley, Canyon	Heath, Steppe
■ Continent	Hills, Escarpment	Crater, Cave	Oasis
▣ Physical Region	Plateau, Upland	Karst Features	Cape, Point

Coast, Beach	Rock, Reef	Waterfall Rapids	Canal
Cliff	Islands, Archipelago	River Mouth, Estuary	Glacier
Peninsula	Rocks, Reefs	Lake	Ice Shelf, Pack Ice
Isthmus	Coral Reef	Salt Lake	Ocean
Sandbank	Well, Spring	Intermittent Lake	Sea
Island	Geyser	Reservoir	Gulf, Bay
Atoll	River, Stream	Swamp, Pond	Strait, Fjord

Lagoon	Escarpment, Sea Scarp	Historic Site	Port
Bank	Fracture	Ruins	Lighthouse
Seamount	Trench, Abyss	Wall, Walls	Mine
Tablemount	National Park, Reserve	Church, Abbey	Tunnel
Ridge	Point of Interest	Temple	Dam, Bridge
Shelf	Recreation Site	Scientific Station	
Basin	Cave, Cavern	Airport	

Index Symbols

Independent Nation	Historical or Cultural Region	Pass, Gap	Depression
State, Region	Mount, Mountain	Plain, Lowland	Polder
District, County	Volcano	Delta	Desert, Dunes
Municipality	Hill	Salt Flat	Forest, Woods
Colony, Dependency	Mountains, Mountain Range	Valley, Canyon	Heath, Steppe
Continent	Hills, Escarpment	Crater, Cave	Oasis
Physical Region	Plateau, Upland	Karst Features	Cape, Point

Coast, Beach	Rock, Reef	Waterfall Rapids	Canal
Cliff	Islands, Archipelago	River Mouth, Estuary	Glacier
Peninsula	Rocks, Reefs	Lake	Ice Shelf, Pack Ice
Isthmus	Coral Reef	Salt Lake	Ocean
Sandbank	Well, Spring	Intermittent Lake	Sea
Island	Geyser	Reservoir	Gulf, Bay
Atoll	River, Stream	Swamp, Pond	Strait, Fjord

Lagoon	Escarpment, Sea Scarp	Historic Site	Port
Bank	Fracture	Ruins	Lighthouse
Seamount	Trench, Abyss	Wall, Walls	Mine
Tablemount	National Park, Reserve	Church, Abbey	Tunnel
Ridge	Point of Interest	Temple	Dam, Bridge
Shelf	Recreation Site	Scientific Station	
Basin	Cave, Cavern	Airport	

Name		Coords				Name		Coords			

Hude (Oldenburg) 12 Ka 53.07N 8.28 E
Huder 27 Lb 49.59N 121.30 E
Hudiksvall 6 Hc 61.44N 17.07 E
Hudson ⌐ 38 Le 40.42N 74.02W
Hudson [Fl.-U.S.] 44 Fk 28.22N 82.42W
Hudson [N.Y.-U.S.] 44 Kd 42.15N 73.47W
Hudson, Lake- ⌐ 45 Ih 36.20N 95.05W
Hudson Bay 42 Hf 52.52N 102.23W
Hudson Bay ⌐ 38 Kd 60.00N 86.00W
Hudson Canyon (EN) ⌐ 44 Kf 39.27N 72.12W
Hudson Hope 42 Fe 56.02N 121.55W
Hudson Land ⌐ 41 Jd 73.45N 22.30W
Hudson Mountains ⌐ 66 Pf 74.32 S 99.20W
Hudson Strait ⌐ 38 Lc 62.30N 72.00W
Hudžirt 27 Hb 47.05N 102.45 E
Hue 22 Mh 16.28N 107.36 E
Huebra ⌐ 13 Fc 41.02N 6.48W
Huechucuicui, Punta- ⌐ 56 Ff 41.47 S 74.02W
Hueco Montains ⌐ 45 Dj 32.05N 105.55W
Huedin 15 Gc 46.52N 23.03 E
Huehuetenango [3] 49 Bf 15.40N 91.35W
Huehuetenango 47 Fe 15.20N 91.28W
Huejutla de Reyes 48 Jg 21.08N 98.25W
Huelgoat 11 Cf 48.22N 3.45W
Huelma 13 Ig 37.39N 3.27W
Huelva [3] 13 Fg 37.40N 7.00W
Huelva 6 Fh 37.16N 6.57W
Huelva, Ribera de- ⌐ 13 Gg 37.27N 6.00W
Huércal Overa 13 Kg 37.23N 1.57W
Huerfano Mountain ⌐ 45 Bh 36.30N 108.10W
Huertas, Cabo de- ⌐ 13 Lf 38.21N 0.24W
Huerva ⌐ 13 Lc 41.39N 0.52W
Huesca 13 Lb 42.08N 0.25W
Huesca [3] 13 Lb 42.10N 0.10W
Huéscar 13 Jg 37.49N 2.32W
Hueso, Sierra del- ⌐ 35 Cn 105.20W
Huesos, Arroyo de los- ⌐ 55 Cm 36.30 S 59.09W
Huetamo de Núñez 48 Ih 18.35N 100.53W
Huete 13 Jd 40.08N 2.41W
Ḥufrat an Naḥās 35 Cd 9.45N 24.19 E
Huftarøy ⌐ 8 Ad 60.05N 5.15 E
Hugh Butler Lake ⌐ 45 Ff 40.22N 100.42W
Hughenden 58 Fg 20.51 S 144.12 E
Hughes 40 Ic 66.03N 154.16W
Hughes Range ⌐ 46 Hb 49.55N 115.28W
Hugo 45 Ii 34.01N 95.31W
Huguan 28 Bf 36.05N 113.12 E
Huhur He ⌐ 28 Fc 43.55N 120.47 E
Hui'an 27 Kf 25.07N 118.47 E
Huiarau Range ⌐ 62 Gc 38.35 S 177.10 E
Huib-Hochplato ⌐ 37 Be 27.10 S 16.50 E
Huichang 27 Kf 25.33N 115.45 E
Huicheng → Shexian 28 Ej 29.53N 118.27 E
Huicholes, Sierra de los- ⌐ 48 Gf 22.00N 104.00W
Huich'ŏn 27 Mc 40.10N 126.17 E
Huifa He ⌐ 28 Ic 43.06N 126.53 E
Hui He [China] ⌐ 27 Kb 48.51N 119.12 E
Hui He [China] ⌐ 28 Be 39.21N 112.37 E
Huiji He ⌐ 28 Ch 33.53N 115.37 E
Huila [2] 54 Cc 2.30N 75.45W
Huila [3] 36 Ce 15.00 S 15.00 E
Huila, Nevado del- ⌐ 52 Ie 3.00N 76.00W
Huilai 27 Kg 23.05N 116.18 E
Huili 27 Hf 26.37N 102.19 E
Huimanguillo 48 Mi 17.51N 93.23W
Huimin 27 Kd 37.29N 117.30 E
Huinan (Chaoyang) 28 Ic 42.41N 126.03 E
Huisne ⌐ 11 Gg 47.59N 0.11 E
Huissen 12 Hc 51.56N 5.55 E
Huiten Nur ⌐ 27 Fd 35.30N 91.55 E
Huittinen 8 Jc 61.11N 22.42 E
Huivuilay, Isla de- ⌐ 48 Dd 27.03N 110.01W
Huixian [China] 28 Bg 35.27N 113.47 E
Huixian [China] 27 Ie 33.46N 106.06 E
Huixtla 47 Fe 15.09N 92.28W
Huize 27 Hf 26.28N 103.18 E
Huizen 12 Hb 52.18N 5.16 E
Huizhou 27 Jg 23.02N 114.28 E
Hu Kou ⌐ 28 Dj 29.44N 116.14 E
Hu Kou ⌐ 27 Jd 36.09N 110.20 E
Hŭksan-Chedo ⌐ 27 Me 34.30N 125.20 E
Hukuntsi 37 Cd 23.59 S 21.44 E
Hulan 27 Mb 46.03N 126.36 E
Hulan He ⌐ 27 Mb 45.54N 126.42 E
Ḥulayfā' 23 Fd 26.00N 40.47 E
Hulett 46 Md 44.41N 104.36W
Hulga ⌐ 17 Jd 64.15N 60.58 E
Hulin 27 Nb 45.52N 132.58 E
Hulin He ⌐ 28 Hb 45.19N 124.06 E
Hull 42 Jg 45.26N 75.43W
Hull → Kingston-upon-Hull 6 Jc 53.45N 0.20W
Hull → Orona Atoll ⌐ 57 Je 4.29 S 172.10W
Hull Bay 66 Nf 74.55 S 137.40W
Hull Glacier ⌐ 66 Nf 75.05 S 137.15W
Hull Mountain ⌐ 46 Dg 39.31N 122.59W
Hüls, Krefeld- 12 Ic 51.22N 6.31 E
Hultsfred 7 Dh 57.29N 15.50 E
Huludao 27 Lc 40.44N 120.59 E
Hulun Nur ⌐ 21 Ne 49.00N 117.30 E
Ḥulwān = Helwān (EN) 33 Fd 29.51N 31.20 E
Ḥulwāt, Qūr al- ⌐ 24 Hh 28.49N 38.50 E
Huma [China] 27 Ma 51.44N 126.36 E
Huma [Ton.] 65b Bc 21.19 S 174.56W
Humacao 49 Od 18.09N 65.50W
Huma He ⌐ 27 Ma 51.42N 126.42 E
Humaitá [Braz.] 53 Jf 7.31 S 63.02W
Humaitá [Par.] 56 Ic 27.03 S 58.33W
Humansdorp 37 Cf 34.02 S 24.46 E
Humbe 36 Bf 16.42 S 14.54 E
Humber ⌐ 5 Fe 53.40N 0.10W
Humberside [3] 6 Je 53.50N 0.30W
Humbolat River ⌐ 38 He 40.02N 118.31W
Humboldt ⌐ 61 Cd 21.53 S 166.25 E
Humboldt [Ia.-U.S.] 45 Ie 42.43N 94.13W
Humboldt [Nb.-U.S.] 45 If 40.10N 95.57W
Humboldt [Sask.-Can.] 42 Gf 52.12N 105.07W
Humboldt [Tn.-U.S.] 44 Ch 35.49N 88.55W

Humboldt Gletscher ⌐ 41 Fc 79.40N 63.45W
Humboldt Range ⌐ 46 Ff 40.15N 118.10W
Hume, Lake- ⌐ 59 Jg 36.05 S 147.05 E
Humenné 10 Rh 48.56N 21.55 E
Hummelfjall ⌐ 8 Bb 62.27N 11.17 E
Hümmling, Der- ⌐ 10 Dd 52.52N 7.31 E
Hutton, Mount- ⌐ 38 Hf 35.20N 111.40W
Humppila 7 Ff 60.56N 23.22 E
Humuya, Rio- ⌐ 49 Df 15.13N 87.57W
Hün 31 If 29.07N 15.56 E
Húnaflói ⌐ 5 Db 65.50N 20.50W
Hunan Sheng (Hu-nan Sheng) [3] 27 Jf 28.00N 112.00 E
Hu-nan Sheng → Hunan Sheng [3] 27 Jf 28.00N 112.00 E
Hunchun 28 Kc 42.52N 130.21 E
Hundested 8 Di 55.58N 11.52 E
Hunedoara [2] 15 Fd 45.45N 22.52 E
Hünfeld 10 Ff 50.40N 9.46 E
Hünfelden 12 Kd 50.19N 8.11 E
Hunga Ha'apai ⌐ 65b Ab 20.33 S 175.24W
Hungary (EN) = Magyarország [1] 6 Hf 47.00N 20.00 E
Hunga Tonga ⌐ 65b Ab 20.32 S 175.23W
Hungen 12 Kd 50.28N 8.54 E
Hüngnam 27 Md 39.50N 127.38 E
Hungry Horse Reservoir ⌐ 46 Ib 48.15N 113.50W
Hun He [China] ⌐ 28 Be 39.47N 113.15 E
Hun He [China] ⌐ 28 Gd 40.41N 122.12 E
Hunhedoara ⌐ 15 Fd 45.45N 22.54 E
Hunish, Rubha- ⌐ 9 Gd 57.43N 6.20W
Hun Jiang ⌐ 28 Hd 40.52N 125.42 E
Hunjiang 27 Mc 41.55N 126.27 E
Hunneberg ⌐ 8 Ef 58.20N 12.27 E
Hunnebostrand 8 Df 58.27N 11.18 E
Hunsrück ⌐ 10 Cg 49.50N 6.40 E
Hunstanton 9 Ni 52.57N 0.30 E
Hunte ⌐ 10 Ed 52.30N 8.19 E
Hunter, Ile- ⌐ 57 Ig 22.24 S 172.03 E
Hunter Island ⌐ 59 Ih 40.30 S 144.45 E
Hunter Ridge (EN) ⌐ 57 Ig 21.30 S 174.30 E
Hunter River ⌐ 59 Kf 32.30 S 151.42 E
Hyères 9 Mk 43.07N 6.07 E
Hyères, Iles d'- ⌐ 11 Ml 43.00N 6.20 E
Hyesan 27 Mc 41.24N 128.10 E
Hyltebruk 44 He 40.31N 78.02W
Hyndman Peak ⌐ 44 Jc 45.05N 74.08W
Hyŏgo Ken [2] 44 He 40.53N 85.30W
Hyrov 43 Kd 38.24N 82.26W
Hyrula 62 Fd 37.33 S 175.10 E
Hyrum 9 Kf 34.44N 86.35W
Hyrynsalmi 42 Jk 45.40N 79.13W
Hysham 43 He 30.43N 95.33W
Hythe [Eng.-U.K.] 48 Og 21.01N 89.52W
Hythe [Eng.-U.K.] 12 Ic 51.39N 6.47 E
Hyūga 37 Ec 15.37 S 30.39 E
Hyūga-Nada 27 Jd 39.38N 113.44 E
Hyvinge/Hyvinkää 25 Ea 36.04N 29.74.40 E
Hyvinkää/Hyvinge 11 Ma 53.13N 6.40 E

Hútti 33 Hf 16.14N 43.58 E
Hutou 27 Nb 46.00N 133.36 E
Hutte Sauvage, Lac de la- 42 Ke 55.57N 65.45W
Hutubi 27 Ec 44.07N 86.57 E
Hutuiti, Caleta- ⌐ 65d Bb 27.07 S 109.17W
Hutuo He ⌐ 28 Be 38.14N 116.05 E
Huvhojtun, Gora- ⌐ 20 Le 57.44N 160.45 E
Huxley, Mount- ⌐ 62 Cf 44.04 S 169.41 E
Huy ⌐ 10 Ge 51.55N 10.55 E
Huy/Hoei 11 Ld 50.31N 5.14 E
Huzhou → Wuxing 27 Le 30.47N 120.07 E
Hvaler ⌐ 8 De 59.05N 11.00 E
Hvalynsk 19 Ee 52.30N 48.07 E
Hvammstangi 7a Bb 65.24N 20.57W
Hvannadalshnúkur ⌐ 5 Ec 64.01N 16.41W
Hvar 14 Kg 43.07N 16.45 E
Hvar ⌐ 14 Kg 43.11N 16.27 E
Hvarski kanal ⌐ 14 Kg 43.15N 16.37 E
Hvatovka 16 Oc 52.21N 46.36 E
Hveragerdi 7a Bb 64.00N 21.12W
Hveravellir 7a Bb 64.54N 19.35W
Hvide Sande 8 Ci 55.59N 8.08 E
Hvitá [Ice.] ⌐ 7a Bb 64.35N 21.46W
Hvitá [Ice.] ⌐ 7a Bb 64.00N 20.58W
Hvittingfoss 8 De 59.29N 10.01 E
Hvojnaja 7 Ig 58.56N 34.31 E
Hwach'on-ni 28 Ie 38.58N 126.02 E
Hwang-Hae = Yellow Sea (EN) ⌐ 21 Of 36.00N 124.00 E
Hwanghae-Namdo [2] 28 He 38.15N 125.30 E
Hwanghae-Pukto [2] 28 He 38.30N 126.25 E
Hwangju 28 He 38.40N 125.45 E
Hyannis [Ma.-U.S.] 44 Le 41.39N 70.17W
Hyannis [Nb.-U.S.] 45 Ff 42.00N 101.44W
Hybo 8 Gc 61.48N 16.12 E
Hyde Park 50 Gi 6.30N 58.16W
Hyderābād [India] 22 Jh 17.23N 78.28 E
Hyderābād [Pak.] 22 Ig 25.22N 68.22 E

Iaco, Rio- ⌐ 54 Ee 9.03 S 68.35W
Iacobeni 15 Ib 47.26N 25.19 E
Iakora 15 Ib 23.08 S 46.38 E
Ialomiţa [2] 15 Ke 44.30N 27.30 E
Ialomiţa ⌐ 15 Ke 44.42N 27.51 E
Ialomiţei, Balta- ⌐ 15 Ke 44.30N 28.00 E
Iapó, Rio- ⌐ 55 Ga 24.30 S 50.24W
Iaşi 6 If 47.10N 27.36 E
Iaşi [2] 15 Kb 47.07N 27.39 E
Iba 26 Gc 15.20N 119.58 E
Ibadan 31 Hh 7.23N 3.54 E
Ibague 53 Ie 4.27N 75.14W
Ibaiti 56 Jb 23.50 S 50.10W
Iballja 15 Cg 42.11N 20.00 E
Ibans, Laguna de- ⌐ 49 Ef 15.53N 84.52W
Ibara 15 Df 43.44N 20.45 E
Ibaraki 29 Cd 34.36N 133.28 E
Ibaraki Ken [2] 29 Pf 36.25N 140.30 E
Ibaré 55 Ej 30.49 S 54.16W
Ibarra 53 Ie 0.21N 78.07W
Ibarreta 56 Ic 24.44N 121.44 E
Ibb 22 Gh 13.58N 44.12 E
Ibba 35 Be 4.48N 29.06 E
Ibba ⌐ 35 Dd 7.09N 28.41 E
Ibbenbüren 12 Jb 52.16N 7.44 E
Ibdekkene ⌐ 34 Fb 18.28N 0.38 E
Ibembo 36 Cb 2.38N 23.37 E
Ibenga ⌐ 36 Cb 2.30N 18.08 E
Iberá, Esteros del- ⌐ 55 Di 28.05 S 57.05W
Iberá, Laguna- ⌐ 55 Di 28.30 S 57.09W
Iberian Basin (EN) ⌐ 3 De 40.00N 16.00W
Iberian Mountains (EN) = Sistema Ibérico ⌐ 5 Fg 41.30N 2.30W
Iberian Peninsula (EN) = Península Ibérica ⌐ 5 Fg 40.00N 4.00W
Iberville, Lac d' - ⌐ 42 Ke 56.00N 73.10W
Ibestad 7 Db 68.48N 17.08 E
Ibi [Nig.] 34 Gd 8.11N 9.45 E
Ibi [Sp.] 13 Ld 38.38N 0.34W
Ibiá 54 Ig 19.29 S 46.32W
Ibiagui 53 Ja 13.03 S 44.12W
Ibiai 55 Jc 16.51 S 44.55W
Ibibobo 54 Fh 21.35 S 62.58W
Ibicaraí 54 Ih 14.51 S 39.36W
Ibicuí, Rio- ⌐ 52 Kh 29.25 S 56.47W
Ibicuí da Armada, Rio- ⌐ 55 Dj 29.50 S 55.12W
Ibicuy ⌐ 55 Ck 33.44 S 59.10W
Ibicuy, Rio- ⌐ 55 Ck 33.48 S 59.10W
Ibigawa 29 Cd 35.50N 136.35 E
Ibipetuba 54 Jf 11.00 S 44.32W
Ibiraiaras 55 Gi 28.22 S 51.39W
Ibirama 55 Hh 27.04 S 49.31W

Ibirapuitã, Rio- ⌐ 55 Ei 29.22 S 55.57W
Ibirocai, Arroio- ⌐ 55 Di 29.26 S 56.43W
Ibiruba 55 Fi 28.38 S 53.06W
Ibitinga 55 He 21.45 S 48.49W
Ibitinga, Represa- ⌐ 55 He 21.41 S 49.00W
Ibity ⌐ 37 Hd 20.10 S 46.58 E
Ibiza 13 Nf 38.54N 1.26 E
Ibiza/Eivissa = Iviza (EN) ⌐ 5 Gh 39.00N 1.25 E
Iblei, Monti- ⌐ 14 Im 37.10N 14.55 E
Ibn Ḥāni', Ra's- ⌐ 24 Fe 35.35N 35.43 E
Ibn Qawrah 35 Ib 15.43N 50.32 E
Ibo 36 Gf 12.22 S 40.36 E
Ibo-Gawa ⌐ 29 Dd 34.46N 134.35 E
Iboundji, Mont- ⌐ 36 Bc 1.08 S 11.48 E
Ibrā' 23 Ie 22.38N 58.40 E
Ibrah ⌐ 35 Dc 10.36N 25.20 E
Ibrāhīm, Jabal- ⌐ 21 Gg 20.25N 41.09 E
Ibresi 7 Li 55.18N 47.05 E
'Ibrī 23 Ie 23.16N 56.32 E
Ibrīm ⌐ 33 Fe 22.39N 31.59 E
Ibshawāy 24 Dh 29.22N 30.41 E
Ibuki-Sanchi ⌐ 29 Ed 35.35N 136.25 E
Ibuki-Yama ⌐ 29 Ed 35.25N 136.24 E
Ibusuki 28 Ki 31.16N 130.39 E
Iça 20 Ke 55.28N 155.58 E
Ica [2] 54 Cf 14.20 S 75.30W
Ica 53 Ig 14.04 S 75.42W
Iça, Rio- ⌐ 52 Jf 3.07 S 67.58W
Icaiché 48 Oh 18.05N 89.10W
Icamaquã, Rio- ⌐ 55 Ei 28.34 S 56.00W
Icana, Rio- ⌐ 52 Je 0.15N 67.19W
Icara 55 Hi 28.42 S 49.18W
Icaraima 55 Ff 23.23 S 53.41W
Iceland (EN) = Island [1] 6 Eb 65.00N 18.00W
Iceland (EN) = Island ⌐ 5 Eb 65.00N 18.00W
Iceland Basin (EN) ⌐ 3 Eb 60.00N 20.00W
Ichalkaranji 25 Ee 16.42N 74.28 E
Ichibusa-Yama ⌐ 29 Be 32.19N 131.06 E
Ichihara 29 Pg 35.31N 140.05 E
Ichi-Kawa ⌐ 29 Dd 34.46N 134.43 E
Ichikawa 29 Oe 35.44N 139.55 E
Ichinohe 28 Pd 40.13N 141.17 E
Ichinomiya 29 Ed 35.18N 136.48 E
Ichinoseki 28 Pe 38.55N 141.08 E
Ich'ŏn [N. Kor.] 28 Ie 38.29N 126.53 E
Ich'ŏn [S. Kor.] 28 If 37.17N 127.27 E
Ichtegem 12 Fc 51.06N 3.00 E
Ičigemski Hrebet ⌐ 20 Ld 59.30N 164.00 E
Ičinskaja Sopka, Vulkan- ⌐ 21 Rd 55.39N 157.40 E
Ičnja 16 De 50.52N 32.25 E
Icó 54 Ke 6.24 S 38.51W
Icy Cape ⌐ 40 Gb 70.20N 161.52W
Idaarderadeel 12 Ha 53.06N 5.50 E
Idaarderadeel-Grow 12 Ha 53.06N 5.50 E
Idabel 45 Jj 33.54N 94.50W
Idaho [2] 43 Ec 45.00N 115.00W
Idaho Falls 39 Ed 43.43N 112.02W
Idalia 45 Eg 39.43N 102.14W
Idān 35 Hd 6.03N 49.01 E
Idanha-a-Nova 13 Je 39.55N 7.14W
Idar-Oberstein 10 Dg 49.43N 7.19 E
Idarwald ⌐ 12 Je 49.50N 7.13 E
Idel 7 Id 64.08N 34.12 E
Ideles 32 Ie 23.48N 5.55 E
Ider ⌐ 27 Hb 49.16N 100.41 E
Idfu 33 Fe 24.58N 32.52 E
Idhi Óros ⌐ 5 Ih 35.15N 24.45 E
Idhra 15 Gl 37.20N 23.30 E
Idhra ⌐ 15 Gl 37.21N 23.28 E
Idhras, Kólpos- ⌐ 15 Gl 37.21N 23.28 E
Idice ⌐ 14 Ff 44.35N 11.49 E
Idil 24 Id 37.21N 41.54 E
Idíni 36 Ab 17.58N 15.40W
Idiofa 36 Cc 4.59 S 19.36 E
Idjevan 16 Ni 40.52N 45.04 E
Idjwil, Kédia d'- ⌐ 34 Ba 22.38N 12.33W
Idkerberget 8 Fd 60.23N 15.14 E
Idle ⌐ 9 Mh 53.27N 0.48W
Idlib 23 Eb 35.56N 36.38 E
Idokogo 36 Ab 0.35N 9.19 E
Idolo, Isla del- ⌐ 48 Ec 21.52N 97.27W
Idre 8 Ec 61.52N 12.43 E
Idrica 7 Hh 56.18N 28.55 E
Idrija 14 Ff 46.00N 14.02 E
Idro, Lago d'- ⌐ 14 Ee 45.47N 10.30 E
Idstein 10 Ef 50.14N 8.16 E
Idževan 16 Ni 40.52N 45.04 E
Iecava 7 Fh 56.36N 24.11 E
Iecava ⌐ 8 Kh 56.33N 24.11 E
Iepê 55 Gf 22.40 S 51.05W
Ieper/Ypres 11 Id 50.51N 2.53 E
Ierápetra 15 Ii 35.01N 25.45 E
Ierisós 15 Gi 40.24N 23.53 E
Ierisoú, Kólpos- ⌐ 15 Gi 40.26N 23.55 E
Iernut 15 Hc 46.27N 24.15 E
Ie-Shima ⌐ 29b Ab 26.43N 127.47 E
Ieshima-Shotō ⌐ 29 Dd 34.40N 134.30 E
Iesolo 14 Ge 45.32N 12.38 E
Iezeru, Vîrful- ⌐ 15 Hd 45.28N 24.57 E
Ifakara 36 Ed 8.08 S 36.41 E
Ifaki 34 Gd 7.48N 5.14 E
'Ifāl, Wādī al- ⌐ 24 Hh 28.07N 35.12 E
Ifalik Atoll ⌐ 57 Fd 7.15N 144.27 E
Ifanadiana 37 Hd 21.17 S 47.15 E
Ife 34 Fd 7.28N 4.34 E
Iferouâne 31 Hg 19.04N 8.24 E
Ifetesene ⌐ 32 Ie 26.20N 6.58 E
Ifni ⌐ 32 Dd 29.15N 10.08W
Ifon 34 Fd 6.58N 5.52 E
Iforas, Adrar des- ⌐ 30 Ge 19.00N 2.00 E
Iga ⌐ 29 Ed 34.49N 136.12 E
Igal 14 Ec 46.32N 17.57 E
Iganga 36 Eb 0.37N 33.29 E
Igara Paraná, Rio- ⌐ 54 Dd 2.09N 71.47W
Igarapava 55 Ie 20.03 S 47.47W
Igarapé-Açu 54 Id 1.07 S 47.37W
Igarapé-Miri 54 Id 1.59 S 48.58W

Igarka 22 Kc 67.28N 86.39 E
Igatimí 56 Ib 24.05 S 55.31W
Igatimi 55 Di 29.26 S 56.43W
Igawa 36 Fd 8.46 S 34.29 E
Igbetti 34 Fd 8.45N 4.02 E
Igdır 24 Ke 39.56N 44.03 E
Iggesund 7 Df 61.38N 17.09 E
Iglesias 14 Ck 39.19N 8.32 E
Iglesiente ⌐ 5 Gh 39.30N 8.40 E
Igli 32 Gc 30.27N 2.19W
Iglim al Janūbīyah = Southern Region (EN) [2] 35 Dd 6.00N 30.00 E
Iglino 17 Hi 54.50N 56.25 E
Igloolik 39 Kc 69.24N 81.49W
Ignace 42 Ig 49.26N 91.41W
Ignalina 7 Gi 55.22N 26.11 E
Ignatovo 7 If 60.49N 37.58 E
Igneada 21 Ee 41.50N 27.58 E
Igneada Burun ⌐ 15 Lh 41.54N 28.02 E
Igombe ⌐ 36 Fc 4.25 S 31.56 E
Igoumenitsa 15 Fj 39.30N 20.16 E
Igra 19 Fc 57.33N 53.11 E
Igreja, Morro da- ⌐ 55 Hi 28.08 S 49.30W
Igren 16 Ie 48.29N 35.12 E
Igrim 19 Gc 63.12N 64.29 E
Iguaçu, Rio- ⌐ 52 Kh 25.36 S 54.33W
Igualada 13 Nc 41.35N 1.38 E
Iguala de la Independencia 47 Ee 18.21N 99.32W
Iguana, Sierra de la- ⌐ 48 Id 26.30N 100.15W
Iguape 55 Ig 24.43 S 47.33W
Iguariaça, Serra do- ⌐ 55 Ei 29.03 S 55.10W
Iguassu = Iguassu Falls (EN) = Iguazú, Cataratas del- ⌐ 52 Kh 25.41 S 54.26W
Iguatemi 54 If 14.35 S 49.02W
Iguatemi, Rio- ⌐ 55 Ff 23.55 S 54.10W
Iguatu 55 Mf 6.22 S 39.18W
Iguazú, Cataratas del- = Iguassu Falls (EN) 52 Kh 25.41 S 54.26W
Iguéla 36 Ac 1.55 S 9.19 E
Iguidi, 'Erg- ⌐ 30 Gf 27.00N 6.05W
Ihavandiffulu Atoll ⌐ 25a Ba 7.00N 72.55 E
Iheya-Jima ⌐ 29b Ab 27.03N 127.57 E
Ih-Hajrhan 27 Ib 46.56N 105.56 E
Ihiala 34 Gd 5.51N 6.55 E
Ihirene ⌐ 32 He 20.28N 4.35 E
Ihnāsiyat al Madīnah 24 Dh 29.05N 30.56 E
Ih-Obo-Ula ⌐ 27 Ac 44.55N 95.20 E
Ihosy 37 Hd 22.25 S 46.07 E
Ihotry, Lac- ⌐ 37 Gd 21.56 S 43.44 E
Ihrhoeve, Westoverledingen- 12 Ja 53.10N 7.22 E
Ihsaniye 24 Dc 36.55N 34.46 E
Ihtiman 15 Gg 42.26N 23.49 E
Ih-Ula 27 Mb 49.27N 101.23 E
Ii 7 Fd 65.19N 25.22 E
Iida 29 Ng 35.31N 137.50 E
Iide-San ⌐ 29 Fc 37.52N 139.42 E
Iijoki ⌐ 7 Fd 65.20N 25.12 E
Iisaku/Isaku 8 Le 59.14N 27.40 E
Iisalmi 7 Ge 63.34N 27.11 E
Iisvesi ⌐ 8 Kc 61.04N 24.10 E
Iittala 8 Kc 61.04N 24.10 E
Iivaara ⌐ 7 Gc 65.47N 29.40 E
Iiyama 29 Fc 36.52N 138.22 E
Iizuka 29 Be 33.38N 130.41 E
Ijara 36 Fb 1.35 S 40.32 E
Ijebu Ode 34 Fd 6.49N 3.56 E
IJmuiden, Velsen- 12 Gb 52.28N 4.35 E
Ijoubbâne, 'Erg- ⌐ 34 Da 22.30N 6.00W
IJssel ⌐ 11 Lb 52.30N 6.00 E
IJsselmeer ⌐ 11 Lb 52.45N 5.25 E
IJsselmuiden 12 Hb 52.34N 5.56 E
IJsselstein 12 Hb 52.01N 5.02 E
Ijui 56 Jc 28.23 S 53.55W
Ijui, Rio- ⌐ 55 Fh 27.58 S 55.20W
Ijüin 29 Bf 31.37N 130.24 E
Ijuizinho, Rio- ⌐ 55 Ei 28.54 S 54.28W
Ijuw 64e Bb 0.31 S 166.57 E
Ijzendijke 12 Fc 51.20N 3.37 E
IJzer ⌐ 11 Ic 51.09N 2.43 E
Ik [R.S.F.S.R.] ⌐ 5 Ld 55.55N 52.36 E
Ik [R.S.F.S.R.] ⌐ 7 Ff 61.05N 23.03 E
Ikaalinen 37 Hd 21.10 S 46.32 E
Ikalamavony 62 Ae 42.17 S 171.42 E
Ikamatua 29 Fc 37.52N 139.42 E
Ikaría ⌐ 15 Jl 37.35N 26.10 E
Ikarian Pélagos ⌐ 15 Jl 37.30N 26.15 E
Ikast 8 Ch 56.08N 9.10 E
Ikatski Hrebet ⌐ 20 Gf 54.00N 111.15 E
Ikawa 29 Fd 35.13N 138.14 E
Ikeda [Jap.] 29 Cd 34.01N 133.48 E
Ikeda [Jap.] 28 Pd 42.55N 143.27 E
Ikeda-Ko ⌐ 29 Bf 31.14N 130.34 E
Ikej 20 Ff 54.12N 100.04 E
Ikeja 34 Fd 6.36N 3.21 E
Ikela 31 Ji 1.11 S 23.16 E
Ikelemba ⌐ 36 Cb 0.07N 18.17 E
Ikerre 34 Gd 7.30N 5.14 E
Ikerrsuaq ⌐ 41 Ie 65.00N 39.45W
Iki ⌐ 29 Ae 33.45N 129.45 E
Iki-Kaikyō ⌐ 28 Jh 33.40N 129.50 E
Ikitsuki-Shima ⌐ 29 Ae 33.22N 129.25 E
Ikizdere 24 Ib 40.47N 40.33 E
Ikom 34 Gd 5.58N 8.42 E
Ikongo 36 Gd 9.04 S 36.51 E
Ikopa ⌐ 37 Hc 16.50 S 46.50 E
Ikot Ekpene 34 Gd 5.10N 7.43 E
Ikuno 29 Dd 35.10N 134.48 E
Ikurangi, Mount- ⌐ 64p Bb 21.12 S 159.45W
Ila 34 Fd 7.40N 4.40 E
Ilaferh ⌐ 32 Hf 22.30N 2.30 E
Ilagan 26 Gb 17.10N 121.54 E
Ilām 25 Hc 26.54N 87.56 E
Ilām va Poshtkūh [3] 23 Gc 33.00N 47.00 E
Ilanski 20 Ee 56.10N 96.03 E
Ilaro 34 Fd 6.53N 3.01 E
İława 10 Pc 53.37N 19.33 E

Index Symbols

[1]	Independent Nation	⌐	Historical or Cultural Region	⌐	Pass, Gap	⌐	Depression	⌐	Coast, Beach	⌐	Rock, Reef	⌐	Waterfall Rapids	⌐	Canal	⌐	Lagoon	⌐	Escarpment, Sea Scarp	⌐	Historic Site	⌐	Port
[2]	State, Region	⌐	Mount, Mountain	⌐	Plain, Lowland	⌐	Polder	⌐	Cliff	⌐	Islands, Archipelago	⌐	River Mouth, Estuary	⌐	Glacier	⌐	Bank	⌐	Fracture	⌐	Ruins	⌐	Lighthouse
[3]	District, County	⌐	Volcano	⌐	Delta	⌐	Desert, Dunes	⌐	Peninsula	⌐	Rocks, Reefs	⌐	Lake	⌐	Ice Shelf, Pack Ice	⌐	Seamount	⌐	Trench, Abyss	⌐	Wall, Walls	⌐	Mine
[4]	Municipality	⌐	Hill	⌐	Salt Flat	⌐	Forest, Woods	⌐	Isthmus	⌐	Coral Reef	⌐	Salt Lake	⌐	Ocean	⌐	Tablemount	⌐	National Park, Reserve	⌐	Church, Abbey	⌐	Tunnel
[5]	Colony, Dependency	⌐	Mountains, Mountain Range	⌐	Valley, Canyon	⌐	Heath, Steppe	⌐	Sandbank	⌐	Well, Spring	⌐	Intermittent Lake	⌐	Sea	⌐	Ridge	⌐	Point of Interest	⌐	Temple	⌐	Dam, Bridge
■	Continent	⌐	Hills, Escarpment	⌐	Crater, Cave	⌐	Oasis	⌐	Island	⌐	Geyser	⌐	Reservoir	⌐	Gulf, Bay	⌐	Shelf	⌐	Recreation Site	⌐	Scientific Station		
⌐	Physical Region	⌐	Plateau, Upland	⌐	Karst Features	⌐	Cape, Point	⌐	Atoll	⌐	River, Stream	⌐	Swamp, Pond	⌐	Strait, Fjord	⌐	Basin	⌐	Cave, Cavern	⌐	Airport		

Index Symbols

[1] Independent Nation
[2] State, Region
[3] District, County
[4] Municipality
[5] Colony, Dependency
Continent
Physical Region

Historical or Cultural Region
Mount, Mountain
Volcano
Hill
Mountains, Mountain Range
Hills, Escarpment
Plateau, Upland

Pass, Gap
Plain, Lowland
Delta
Salt Flat
Valley, Canyon
Crater, Cave
Karst Features

Depression
Polder
Desert, Dunes
Forest, Woods
Heath, Steppe
Oasis
Cape, Point

Coast, Beach
Cliff
Peninsula
Isthmus
Sandbank
Island
Atoll

Rock, Reef
Islands, Archipelago
Rocks, Reefs
Coral Reef
Well, Spring
Geyser
River, Stream

Waterfall Rapids
River Mouth, Estuary
Lake
Salt Lake
Intermittent Lake
Sea
Gulf, Bay
Swamp, Pond
Strait, Fjord

Canal
Glacier
Ice Shelf, Pack Ice
Ocean
Sea
Ridge
Shelf
Basin

Lagoon
Bank
Seamount
Tablemount
Trench, Abyss
Fracture
National Park, Reserve
Point of Interest
Recreation Site
Cave, Cavern

Escarpment, Sea Scarp
Ruins
Wall, Walls
Church, Abbey
Temple
Scientific Station
Airport

Historic Site
Port
Lighthouse
Mine
Tunnel
Dam, Bridge

Irpen 19 De 50.31N 30.16 E
Irpinia 14 Ij 40.55N 15.00 E
Irrawaddy 25 Ie 17.00N 95.00 E
Irrawaddy 21 Lh 15.50N 95.06 E
Irrawaddy, Mouths of the- (EN) 21 Lh 16.30N 95.00 E
Irrel 12 Ie 49.51N 6.28 E
Irsåva 10 Th 48.15N 23.05 E
Irsina 14 Kj 40.45N 16.14 E
Irtek 16 Rd 51.29N 52.42 E
Irthlingborough 12 Bb 52.19N 0.36W
Irtyš 21 Ic 61.04N 68.52 E
Irtyšsk 19 He 53.21N 75.27 E
Irumu 36 Eb 1.27N 29.52 E
Irún 13 Ka 43.21N 1.47W
Irurzun 13 Kb 42.55N 1.50W
Irves Šaurums 8 Ig 57.48N 22.05 E
Irvine 9 If 55.37N 4.40W
Irving 45 Hj 32.49N 96.56W
Is, Jabal- 35 Fa 21.49N 35.39 E
Isa, Ra's- 33 Hf 15.11N 42.39 E
Isabel 45 Fd 45.24N 101.26W
Isabel, Bahía- 54a Ab 0.38S 91.25W
Isabela 51a Ab 18.31N 67.07W
Isabela → Basilan City 26 He 6.42N 121.58 E
Isabela, Cabo- 49 Ld 19.56N 71.01W
Isabela, Isla- [Ec.] 52 Gf 0.30S 91.06W
Isabela, Isla- [Mex.] 48 Gg 21.51N 105.55W
Isabella, Cordillera- 47 Gf 13.30N 85.30W
Isabel Segunda 49 Od 18.09N 65.27W
Isabey 15 Ml 38.00N 29.24 E
Isaccea 15 Ld 45.16N 28.28 E
Isachsen 39 Ib 78.50N 103.30W
Isafjörour 6 Db 66.03N 23.09W
Isahaya 28 Jh 32.50N 130.03 E
Isakov, Seamount (EN) 57 Ga 31.35N 151.07 E
Isaku/Iisaku 8 Le 59.14N 27.41 E
Isana, Rio- 54 Ec 0.26N 67.19W
Isandja 36 Dc 2.59S 22.00 E
Isanga 36 Dc 1.26S 22.18 E
Isangi 36 Db 0.46N 24.15 E
Isanlu Makutu 34 Gd 8.16N 5.48 E
Isaouane-n-Irarraren 32 Id 27.15N 8.00 E
Isaouane-n-Tifernine 32 Id 27.00N 7.30 E
Isar 10 Ih 48.49N 12.58 E
Isarco/Eisack 14 Fd 46.27N 11.18 E
Isarco, Valle-/Eisacktal 14 Fd 46.45N 11.35 E
Isbergues 12 Ed 50.37N 2.27 E
Iscayachi 54 Eh 21.31S 65.03W
Ischgl 14 Ec 47.01N 10.17 E
Ischia 14 Hj 40.45N 13.55 E
Ischia 14 Hj 40.44N 13.57 E
Ise 27 Oe 34.29N 136.42 E
Isefjord 8 Di 55.50N 11.50 E
Išejevka 7 Li 54.28N 48.17 E
Isen 10 Ih 48.20N 12.45 E
Isenach 12 Ke 49.38N 8.28 E
Isen-Zaki 29b Bb 27.39N 128.55 E
Iseo, Lago d'- 14 Ee 45.45N 10.05 E
Iseran, Col de l'- 11 Ni 45.25N 7.02 E
Isère 11 Kj 44.59N 4.51 E
Isère 11 Li 45.10N 5.50 E
Išerit, Gora- 17 If 61.08N 59.10 E
Iserlohn 10 De 51.22N 7.42 E
Isernia 14 Ii 41.36N 14.14 E
Isesaki 29 Fc 36.19N 139.12 E
Iset 21 Id 56.36N 66.24 E
Isetskoje 17 Lh 56.29N 65.21 E
Ise-Wan 28 Ng 34.40N 136.42 E
Iseyin 34 Fd 7.58N 3.36 E
Isfahan (EN)=Eşfahān 22 Hf 32.40N 51.38 E
Isfana 18 Ge 39.51N 69.32 E
Isfara 18 Hd 40.07N 70.38 E
Isfendiyar Dağları 23 Da 41.45N 34.10 E
Isfjorden 41 Nc 78.15N 15.00 E
Isha Baydabo 31 Lh 3.04N 43.48 E
Ishasha River 36 Ec 0.50S 29.40 E
Ishavet=Arctic Ocean (EN) 67 Be 85.00N 170.00 E
Isherton 54 Gc 2.19N 59.22W
Ishigaki 27 Lg 24.20N 124.09 E
Ishikari 29a Bb 43.13N 141.18 E
Ishikari-Dake 29a Cb 43.33N 143.00 E
Ishikari-Gawa 29a Bb 43.15N 141.20 E
Ishikari-Heiya 29a Bb 43.00N 141.40 E
Ishikari-Wan 27 Pc 43.25N 141.00 E
Ishikawa [Jap.] 27 Mf 26.27N 127.50 E
Ishikawa [Jap.] 29 Gc 37.09N 140.27 E
Ishikawa Ken 28 Nf 36.35N 136.40 E
Ishim Steppe (EN)= Išimskaja Step 21 Id 55.00N 67.30 E
Ishinomaki 27 Pd 38.25N 141.18 E
Ishinomaki-Wan 29 Gb 38.20N 141.15 E
Ishioka 28 Pf 36.11N 140.16 E
Ishitate-San 29 De 33.44N 134.03 E
Ishizuchi-Yama 29 Ce 33.45N 133.05 E
Ishodnaja, Gora- 20 Nd 64.50N 173.26W
Ishpeming 44 Db 46.30N 87.40W
Isidro Alves 55 Ee 20.09S 55.12W
Isigny-sur-Mer 11 Ee 49.19N 1.06W
Isii 29 Dd 34.04N 134.26 E
Işıklar Dağı 24 Bb 40.50N 27.05 E
Işikli 15 Mk 38.19N 29.51 E
Isikli Göl 15 Mk 38.14N 29.55 E
Isili 14 Dk 39.44N 9.06 E
Isilkul 19 He 54.55N 71.16 E
Išim 22 Id 56.09N 69.27 E
Išim 21 Jd 57.45N 71.12 E
Išimbaj 19 Fe 53.28N 56.02 E
Išimskaja Step=Ishim Steppe (EN) 21 Id 55.00N 67.30 E
Isinga 20 Gf 52.55N 112.00 E
Isiolo 36 Gb 0.21N 37.35 E
Isiro 31 Jh 2.48N 27.41 E
Isisford 59 Id 24.16S 144.26 E
Isjangulovo 17 Hj 52.12N 56.36 E
Iskandar 18 Gd 41.35N 69.43 E
Iskăr 15 Hf 43.44N 24.27 E
Iskăr, Jazovir- 15 Gg 42.25N 23.35 E
Iškašim 19 Hh 36.44N 71.39 E
İskenderun=Alexandretta (EN) 22 Ff 36.37N 36.07 E
İskenderun Körfezi= Alexandretta, Gulf of- (EN) 23 Eb 36.30N 35.40 E
İskilip 24 Fb 40.45N 34.29 E
Iski-Naukat 18 Id 40.14N 72.41 E
Iskininski 16 Rf 47.13N 52.36 E
Iskitim 20 Df 54.38N 83.18 E
Iskushuban 35 Ic 10.13N 50.14 E
Iskut 42 Ee 56.45N 131.48W
Isla-Cristina 13 Eg 37.12N 7.19W
İslâhiye 24 Gd 37.26N 36.41 E
Islāmābād 22 Jf 33.42N 73.10 E
Islāmābād → Anantnāg 25 Fb 33.44N 75.09 E
Isla Mujeres 48 Pg 21.12N 86.43W
Island=Iceland (EN) 6 Eb 65.00N 18.00W
Island=Iceland (EN) 5 Eb 65.00N 18.00W
Island Harbour 51b Ab 18.16N 63.02W
Island Lagoon 59 Hf 31.30S 136.40 E
Island Lake 42 If 53.45N 94.30W
Island Lake 42 If 53.58N 94.46W
Island Pond 44 Lc 44.50N 71.53W
Islands, Bay of - [Can.] 42 Lg 49.10N 58.15W
Islands, Bay of- [N.Z.] 62 Fa 35.10S 174.10 E
Islao, Massif de l'- 30 Lk 22.30S 45.20 E
Islas de la Bahia 49 De 16.20N 86.30W
Islay 5 Fd 55.46N 6.10W
Islaz 15 Hf 43.44N 24.45 E
Isle 11 Fj 44.55N 0.15W
Isle of Man 9 Ig 54.15N 4.30W
Isle of Wight 9 Lk 50.40N 1.15W
Isleta 45 Ci 34.55N 106.42W
Isle-Verte 44 Ma 48.01N 69.22W
Ismael Cortinas 55 Dk 33.56S 57.08W
Ismailia (EN)=Al Ismā'īlīyah 33 Fc 30.35N 32.16 E
Ismailly 16 Pi 40.47N 48.13 E
Ismantorps Borg 8 Gh 56.45N 16.40 E
Isnā 31 Kf 25.18N 32.33 E
Isny im Allgäu 10 Gi 47.42N 10.02 E
Isojärvi 8 Ic 61.45N 21.45 E
Isojoki 7 Ee 62.07N 21.58 E
Isojoki/Storå 7 Ee 62.07N 21.58 E
Isoka 36 Fe 10.08S 32.38 E
Isola del Liri 14 Hi 41.41N 13.34 E
Isola di Capo Rizzuto 14 Ll 38.58N 17.05 E
Isonzo 14 He 45.43N 13.33 E
Isonzo (EN)=Soča 14 He 45.43N 13.33 E
Isosyöte 7 Gd 65.37N 27.35 E
Isparta 23 Db 37.46N 30.33 E
Isperih 15 Jf 43.43N 26.50 E
Ispica 14 In 36.47N 14.55 E
İspir 24 Ib 40.29N 41.00 E
Ispiriz Dağı 24 Jc 38.03N 43.55 E
Israel (EN)=Yisra'el 22 Ff 31.30N 35.00 E
Isratu 35 Fb 16.20N 39.55 E
Issa 8 Mh 56.55N 28.50 E
Issano 54 Gb 5.49N 59.25W
Issaran, Ra's- 24 Eh 28.50N 32.56 E
Issel 10 Cd 52.00N 6.10 E
Isser 13 Ph 36.51N 3.40 E
Issia 34 Dd 6.30N 6.35W
Issia 34 Dd 6.29N 6.35W
Issoire 11 Ji 45.33N 3.15 E
Issoudun 11 Hh 46.57N 2.00 E
Issyk 18 Kc 43.20N 77.28 E
Issyk-Kul, Ozero- 21 Je 42.25N 77.15 E
Issyk-Kulskaja Oblast 19 Hg 42.10N 78.00 E
Ist 14 If 44.17N 14.47 E
İstanbul 22 Ee 41.01N 28.58 E
İstanbul-Bakırköy 15 Li 40.59N 28.52 E
İstanbul-Beyoğlu 15 Lh 41.02N 28.59 E
İstanbul Boğazi=Bosporus (EN) 5 Ig 41.00N 29.00 E
İstanbul-Kadıköy 15 Mi 40.59N 29.01 E
Isteren 8 Db 62.00N 11.50 E
Istgāh-e Eqbālīyeh 24 Ne 35.50N 50.45 E
Isthilart 55 Dj 31.11S 57.58W
Istiaia 15 Gk 38.57N 23.09 E
Istisu 16 Nj 39.57N 46.00 E
Istmina 54 Cb 5.09N 76.42W
Isto, Mount- 38 Ec 69.12N 143.48W
Istok 15 Dg 42.47N 20.29 E
Istokpoga, Lake- 44 Gl 27.22N 81.17W
Istra = Istria (EN) 5 Hf 45.00N 14.00 E
Istres 11 Kk 43.31N 4.59 E
Istria 15 Le 44.34N 28.43 E
Istria (EN) = Istra 5 Hf 45.00N 14.00 E
Isulan 26 He 7.02N 124.29 E
Itabaiana 54 Kf 10.41S 37.26W
Itabaianinha 54 Kf 11.16S 37.47W
Itaberá 55 Hf 23.51S 49.09W
Itaberaba 54 Jf 12.32S 40.18W
Itaberai 54 Ig 16.02S 49.48W
Itabira 54 Jg 19.37S 43.13W
Itabirito 55 Ke 20.15S 43.48W
Itabuna 53 Mg 14.48S 39.16W
Itacaiúna, Rio- 54 Ie 5.21S 49.08W
Itacarambi 55 Jb 15.01S 44.03W
Itacoatiara 53 Kf 3.08S 58.25W
Itacolomi, Pico do- 55 Ke 20.26S 43.29W
Itacuai, Rio- 54 Dd 4.20S 70.12W
Itacumbi 55 Ei 28.44S 55.08W
Itacurubi del Rosario 55 Dg 24.29S 56.41W
Itaguari, Rio- 55 Jb 14.11S 44.40W
Itaguaru 55 Hb 15.44S 49.37W
Itaguí 54 Cb 6.12N 75.40W
Itaimbézinho 55 Gi 28.38S 50.34W
Itaituba 53 Kf 4.17S 55.59W
Itajaí 53 Lh 26.53S 48.39W
Itajai Açu, Rio- 55 Hh 26.54S 48.33W
Itajubá 54 Ih 22.26S 45.27W
Itajuipe 54 Kf 14.41S 39.22W
Itaka 20 Gf 53.54N 118.42 E
Italia = Italy (EN) 6 Hg 42.50N 12.50 E
Itálica 13 Fg 37.25N 6.05W
Italy (EN) = Italia 6 Hg 42.50N 12.50 E
Itambacuri 54 Jg 18.01S 41.42W
Itambé, Pico de- 52 Lg 18.23S 43.21W
Itämeri=Baltic, Sea (EN) 5 Hd 57.00N 19.00 E
Itampolo 37 Gd 24.41S 43.57 E
Itanagar 25 Ic 26.57N 93.15 E
Itanará, Rio- 55 Eg 24.00S 55.53W
Itanhaém 56 Kb 24.11S 46.47W
Itano 29 Dd 34.09N 134.28 E
Itapaci 55 Hb 14.57S 49.34W
Itapagé 54 Kd 3.41S 39.34W
Itapajipe 55 Hd 19.54S 49.22W
Itaparaná, Rio- 54 Fe 5.47S 63.03W
Itapebi 54 Kg 15.56S 39.32W
Itapecerica 55 Je 20.28S 45.07W
Itapecuru-Mirim 54 Jd 3.24S 44.20W
Itapemirim 54 Jh 21.01S 40.50W
Itaperina, Pointe- 30 Lk 24.59S 47.06 E
Itaperuna 54 Jh 21.12S 41.54W
Itapetinga 54 Jg 15.15S 40.15W
Itapetininga 56 Kb 23.36S 48.03W
Itapetininga, Rio- 55 Hf 23.35S 48.27W
Itapeva 55 Hf 23.58S 48.52W
Itapeva, Lagoa- 55 Hi 29.30S 49.55W
Itapicuru, Rio- [Braz.] 54 Kf 11.47S 37.32W
Itapicuru, Rio- [Braz.] 52 Lf 2.52S 44.12W
Itapipoca 54 Kd 3.31S 39.33W
Itapiranga [Braz.] 54 Gd 2.45S 58.01W
Itapiranga [Braz.] 55 Fh 27.08S 53.43W
Itapirapuã, Pico- 55 Hg 24.17S 49.12W
Itápolis 55 He 21.35S 48.46W
Itaporã 55 Ef 22.01S 54.54W
Itaporanga [Braz.] 55 Hf 23.42S 49.29W
Itaporanga [Braz.] 54 Ke 7.18S 38.10W
Itapúa 55 Eh 26.50S 55.50W
Itapuã 55 Gj 30.16S 51.01W
Itapuranga 54 Ig 15.35S 49.59W
Itaqui 56 Ic 29.08S 56.33W
Itaquyry 55 Eg 24.56S 55.13W
Itararé 55 Hg 24.07S 49.20W
Itararé, Rio- 55 Hf 23.10S 49.42W
Itārsi 25 Fd 22.37N 77.45 E
Itarumã 55 Gd 18.42S 51.25W
Itati 55 Ch 27.16S 58.15W
Itatinga 55 Hf 23.07S 48.36W
Itatski 20 De 56.07N 89.20 E
Itaum 55 Ef 22.00S 55.20W
Itaúna 54 Jh 20.04S 44.34W
Itaya-Tōge 29 Gc 37.50N 140.13 E
Itbāy 30 Kf 22.00N 35.30 E
Itbayat 26 Hb 20.46N 121.50 E
Itchen 12 Ad 50.57N 1.22W
Ite 54 Dg 17.50S 70.58W
Itéa 15 Fk 38.26N 22.25 E
Ithaca 43 Lc 42.26N 76.30W
Ithaca (EN)=Itháki 15 Dk 38.24N 20.40 E
Itháki 15 Dk 38.22N 20.43 E
Itháki = Ithaca (EN) 15 Dk 38.24N 20.40 E
Ith Hils 10 Fd 52.05N 9.35 E
Ithnayn, Harrat- 24 Ii 26.40N 40.10 E
Itigi 36 Fd 5.42S 34.29 E
Itimbiri 30 Jh 2.02N 22.44 E
Itiopya=Ethiopia (EN) 31 Kh 9.00N 39.00 E
Itiquira 54 Hg 17.05S 54.56W
Itiquira, Rio- 52 Kg 17.18S 56.44W
Itirapina 55 If 22.15S 47.49W
Itiúba 54 Kf 10.43S 39.51W
Itivdleq 41 Ge 66.38N 53.51W
Itō 28 Og 34.58N 139.05 E
Itoigawa 28 Nf 37.02N 137.51 E
Itoko 36 Dc 1.00S 21.45 E
Itoman 29b Ab 26.07N 127.40 E
Iton 11 Hf 49.09N 1.12 E
Itremo, Massif de l'- 37 Hd 20.45S 46.30 E
Itsā 24 Dh 29.15N 30.48 E
Itsukaichi 29 Cd 34.22N 132.22 E
Itsuki 29 Be 32.24N 130.50 E
Ittiri 14 Cj 40.36N 8.34 E
Itu [Braz.] 55 If 23.16S 47.19W
Itu [Nig.] 34 Gd 5.12N 7.59 E
Itu, Rio- 55 Ei 29.25S 55.51W
Itui, Rio- 54 Dd 4.38S 70.19W
Ituiutaba 54 Ig 18.58S 49.28W
Itula 36 Ec 3.29S 27.52 E
Itumbiara 54 Ig 18.25S 49.13W
Itumkale 16 Nh 42.43N 45.35 E
Ituna 46 Na 51.10N 103.30W
Itungi Port 36 Fd 9.35S 33.56 E
Itupiranga 54 Ie 5.09S 49.20W
Iturama 55 Gd 19.44S 50.11W
Iturbide 48 Oh 19.40N 89.37W
Ituri 30 Jh 1.40N 27.01 E
Iturregui 55 Bm 36.50S 61.08W
Iturup, Ostrov- 21 Qe 44.54N 147.30 E
Iturup, Ostrov-/Etorofu Tō 21 Qe 44.54N 147.30 E
Itutinga 55 Je 21.18S 44.40W
Ituverava 56 Kb 20.20S 47.47W
Ituxi, Rio- 52 Jf 7.18S 64.51W
Ituzaingó 55 Dh 27.36S 56.41W
Itz 10 Gg 49.58N 10.52 E
Itzehoe 10 Fc 53.55N 9.31 E
Ivacevići 16 Dc 52.43N 25.21 E
Ivai 55 Gg 25.01S 50.52W
Ivai, Rio- [Braz.] 55 Fi 29.08S 53.16W
Ivai, Rio- [Braz.] 52 Kh 23.18S 53.42W
Ivaiporã 55 Gg 24.15S 51.45W
Ivajlovgrad 15 Jh 41.32N 26.08 E
Ivakoany, Massif de l'- 37 Hd 23.50S 46.25 E
Ivalojoki 7 Gc 68.43N 27.36 E
Ivančice 10 Mg 49.06N 16.22 E
Ivangorod 7 Gg 59.23N 28.20 E
Ivangrad 15 Cg 42.51N 19.52 E
Ivanhoe 58 Fh 32.54S 144.18 E
Ivanić-Grad 14 Ke 45.42N 16.24 E
Ivaniči 10 Uf 50.38N 24.24 E
Ivanjica 15 Df 43.35N 20.14 E
Ivanjska 14 Lf 44.55N 17.04 E
Ivankov 16 Fd 50.57N 29.58 E
Ivano-Frankovo 10 Tg 49.52N 23.48 E
Ivano-Frankovsk 6 If 48.55N 24.43 E
Ivano-Frankovskaja Oblast 19 Cf 48.40N 24.40 E
Ivanovka [R.S.F.S.R.] 20 Hf 50.18N 127.59 E
Ivanovka [Ukr.-U.S.S.R.] 16 Gf 46.57N 30.28 E
Ivanovo [Bye.-U.S.S.R.] 16 Dc 52.10N 25.32 E
Ivanovo [R.S.F.S.R.] 6 Kd 57.00N 40.59 E
Ivanovskaja Oblast 19 Ed 57.00N 41.50 E
Ivanovskoje 8 Me 59.12N 28.59 E
Ivanščica 14 Kd 46.11N 16.10 E
Ivdel 19 Gc 60.42N 60.28 E
Ivenec 8 Lk 53.55N 26.49 E
Ivigtut 41 Hf 61.15N 48.00W
Ivindo 30 Ii 0.09S 12.09 E
Ivinheima 55 Ff 22.10S 53.37W
Ivinheima, Rio- 54 Hh 23.14S 53.42W
Ivinski razliv 7 If 61.10N 35.00 E
Iviza (EN)=Eivissa/Ibiza 5 Gh 39.00N 1.25 E
Iviza (EN)=Ibiza/Eivissa 5 Gh 39.00N 1.25 E
Ivje 10 Vc 53.55N 25.51 E
Ivohibe 37 Hd 22.29S 46.52 E
Ivoire, Côte d'-=Ivory Coast (EN) 30 Gh 5.00N 5.00W
Ivolândia 55 Gc 16.34S 50.51W
Ivory Coast (EN)=Côte d'Ivoire 31 Gh 8.00N 5.00W
Ivory Coast (EN)=Ivoire, Côte d'- 30 Gh 5.00N 5.00W
Ivösjön 8 Fh 56.05N 14.25 E
Ivrea 14 Be 45.28N 7.52 E
Ivrindi 15 Kj 39.34N 27.29 E
Ivry-la-Bataille 12 Df 48.53N 1.28 E
Ivry-sur-Seine 12 Ef 48.49N 2.23 E
Ivujivik 39 Lc 62.25N 77.54W
Iwai-Shima 29 Be 33.47N 131.58 E
Iwaizumi 28 Pe 39.50N 141.48 E
Iwaki 22 Qf 36.55N 140.48 E
Iwaki-Gawa 29 Ga 41.01N 140.22 E
Iwaki-Hisanohama 29 Gc 37.09N 140.59 E
Iwaki-Jōban 29 Gc 37.02N 140.50 E
Iwaki-Kawamae 29 Gc 37.12N 140.45 E
Iwaki-Miwa 29 Gc 37.09N 140.42 E
Iwaki-Nakoso 29 Gc 36.56N 140.48 E
Iwaki-Onahama 29 Gc 36.57N 140.53 E
Iwaki-San 29 Ga 40.40N 140.20 E
Iwaki-Taira 29 Gc 37.05N 140.55 E
Iwaki-Uchigō 29 Gc 37.04N 140.50 E
Iwaki-Yoshima 29 Gc 37.05N 140.50 E
Iwaki-Yotsukura 29 Gc 37.07N 140.58 E
Iwakuni 27 Ne 34.09N 132.11 E
Iwami 29 Dd 35.35N 134.20 E
Iwami-Kōgen 29 Cd 35.00N 132.30 E
Iwamizawa 27 Pc 43.12N 141.46 E
Iwanai 28 Pc 42.58N 140.30 E
Iwanuma 29 Gb 38.07N 140.52 E
Iwase 29 Gc 36.21N 140.06 E
Iwasuge-Yama 29 Fc 36.44N 138.32 E
Iwata 29 Ed 34.42N 137.48 E
Iwate 28 Pe 39.30N 141.30 E
Iwate Ken 28 Pe 39.30N 141.15 E
Iwate San 28 Pe 39.49N 141.26 E
Iwo 34 Fd 7.38N 4.11 E
Iwŏn 27 Mc 40.19N 128.37 E
Iwuy 12 Fd 50.14N 3.19 E
Ixiamas 54 Ef 13.45S 68.09W
Ixmiquilpan 48 Jg 20.29N 99.14W
Ixopo 37 Ef 30.08S 30.00 E
Ixtapa, Punta- 48 Ii 17.39N 101.40W
Ixtepec 47 Ee 16.34N 95.06W
Ixtlahuacán del Rio 48 Hg 20.52N 103.15W
Ixtlán del Rio 47 Dd 21.02N 104.22W
Iyah 35 Hd 9.00N 49.38 E
Iyo 28 Lh 33.46N 132.42 E
Iyo-mishima 29 Ce 33.58N 133.33 E
Iyo-Nada 29 Ce 33.40N 132.15 E
Iž 7 Mh 56.00N 52.41 E
Iž 14 Jf 44.03N 15.06 E
Izabal 49 Cf 15.30N 89.00W
Izabal, Lago de- 47 Ge 15.30N 89.10W
Izad Khvāst 24 Og 31.31N 52.07 E
Izamal 47 Gd 20.56N 89.01W
Izamal 48 Og 20.56N 89.01W
Izapa 47 Ff 14.55N 92.10W
'Izbat al Jājah 24 Dj 24.48N 30.35 E
'Izbat Dush 24 Dj 24.34N 30.42 E
Izberbaš 19 Eg 42.33N 47.52 E
Izbiceni 15 Hf 43.50N 24.39 E
Izborsk 8 Mg 57.39N 28.01 E
Izegem 12 Fd 50.55N 3.12 E
Izeh 24 Mg 31.50N 49.52 E
Izena-Shima 29b Ab 26.56N 127.56 E
Iževsk 6 Ld 56.51N 53.14 E
Izjaslav 16 Ed 50.09N 26.51 E
Izjum 19 Df 49.12N 37.17 E
Izki 23 Ie 22.57N 57.49 E
Ižma 5 Lb 65.19N 52.54 E
Ižma 17 Fd 65.02N 53.55 E
Izmail 6 If 45.21N 28.50 E
İzmir=Smyrna (EN) 22 Ef 38.25N 27.09 E
İzmir, Gulf of- (EN)=İzmir Körfezi 24 Bc 38.30N 26.50 E
İzmir-Bornova 24 Bc 38.27N 27.14 E
İzmir Körfezi=İzmir, Gulf of- (EN) 24 Bc 38.30N 26.50 E
İzmit 22 Ee 40.46N 29.55 E
İzmit Körfezi 24 Cb 40.45N 29.35 E
İzmor 24 Ab 40.11N 25.55 E
Iznajar, Embalse de- 13 Hg 37.15N 4.30W
Iznalloz 13 Ig 37.23N 3.31W
İznik 24 Cb 40.26N 29.43 E
İznik Gölü 23 Ca 40.26N 29.30 E
Izobilny 16 Lg 45.19N 41.42 E
Izola 14 He 45.32N 13.40 E
Izōrskaja Vozvyšennost 8 Me 59.35N 29.30 E
Izozog, Bañados del- 54 Fg 18.50S 62.10W
Izra' 24 Gf 32.51N 36.15 E
Izsák 10 Pj 46.48N 19.22 E
Iztočni Rodopi 15 Ih 41.44N 25.31 E
Izúcar de Matamoros 48 Jh 18.36N 98.28W
Izu-Hantō 28 Og 34.55N 138.55 E
Izuhara 28 Jg 34.12N 129.17 E
Izu Islands (EN)=Izu-shotō 21 Pf 32.00N 140.00 E
Izumi [Jap.] 28 Kh 32.05N 130.22 E
Izumi [Jap.] 29 Dd 34.29N 135.26 E
Izumi [Jap.] 29 Gb 38.19N 140.51 E
Izumi-sano 29 Dd 34.24N 135.18 E
Izumo 28 Lg 35.22N 132.46 E
Izu-Shotō=Izu Islands (EN) 21 Pf 32.00N 140.00 E
Izvesti CIK, Ostrova-= Izvestiya Tsik Islands (EN) 20 Da 75.55N 82.30 E
Izvestiya Tsik Islands (EN)= Izvesti CIK, Ostrova- 20 Da 75.55N 82.30 E

J

Jaala 8 Lc 61.03N 26.29 E
Jaama/Jama 8 Lf 58.59N 27.45 E
Jääsjärvi 8 Lc 61.35N 26.05 E
Jaba 24 Qe 35.55N 56.35 E
Jabal, Baḩr al-=Mountain Nile (EN) 30 Kh 9.30N 30.30 E
Jabal Abū Rujmayn 24 Ge 34.50N 37.56 E
Jabal al Awliyā' 35 Eb 15.14N 32.30 E
Jabal az Zannah 24 Oj 24.11N 52.38 E
Jabalón 13 Hf 38.53N 4.05W
Jabalpur 22 Jg 23.10N 79.57 E
Jabal Şabāyā 33 Hf 18.35N 41.03 E
Jabālyah 24 Fg 31.32N 34.29 E
Jabal Zuqar, Jazīrat- 33 Hg 14.00N 42.45 E
Jabbārah 33 Hf 19.27N 40.03 E
Jabbeke 12 Fc 51.11N 3.05 E
Jabjabah, Wādī- 35 Ea 22.37N 33.17 E
Jablah 24 Fe 35.21N 35.55 E
Jablanac 14 If 44.43N 14.53 E
Jablanica 15 Dh 41.15N 20.30 E
Jablanica [Bul.] 15 Hf 43.01N 24.06 E
Jablanica [Yugo.] 14 Lg 43.39N 17.45 E
Jabločny 20 Jg 47.09N 142.03 E
Jablonec nad Nisou 10 Lf 50.44N 15.10 E
Jablonicki, Pereval- 5 If 48.18N 24.28 E
Jablonovo 20 Gf 51.51N 112.50 E
Jablonovy Hrebet= Yablonovy Range (EN) 21 Nd 53.30N 115.00 E
Jablunkovský průsmyk 10 Og 49.31N 18.45 E
Jaboatão 54 Ke 8.07S 35.01W
Jaboti 55 De 20.48S 56.23W
Jabrīn 24 Ni 27.51N 51.26 E
Jabuka 14 Jg 43.05N 15.28 E
Jabung, Tanjung- 26 Dg 1.01S 104.22 E
Jabuticabal 56 Kb 21.16S 48.19W
Jabuticatubas 55 Kd 19.30S 43.45W
Jaca 13 Lb 42.34N 0.33W
Jacaltenango 49 Bf 15.40N 91.44W
Jacaré, Rio- 55 Je 4.11S 45.16W
Jacarei 55 Jf 23.19S 45.58W
Jacarezinho 56 Kb 23.09S 49.59W
Jáchal, Rio- 52 Ji 30.44S 68.08W
Jaciara [Braz.] 55 Ib 14.12S 46.41W
Jaciara [Braz.] 55 Eb 15.59S 54.57W
Jackman 44 Lc 45.38N 70.16W
Jack Mountain 46 Eb 48.47N 120.57W
Jackpot 46 Hf 41.59N 114.09W
Jacksboro 45 Gj 33.13N 98.10W
Jacks Mountain 44 Ie 40.45N 77.30W
Jackson [Al.-U.S.] 44 Dj 31.31N 87.53W
Jackson [Bar.] 51q Ab 13.10N 59.43W
Jackson [Ky.-U.S.] 44 Fg 37.33N 83.23W
Jackson [Mi.-U.S.] 43 Kc 42.15N 84.24W
Jackson [Mn.-U.S.] 45 Ie 43.37N 94.59W
Jackson [Mo.-U.S.] 45 Lh 37.23N 89.40W
Jackson [Ms.-U.S.] 39 Jf 32.18N 90.12W
Jackson [Oh.-U.S.] 44 Ff 39.03N 82.40W
Jackson [Tn.-U.S.] 43 Jd 35.37N 88.49W
Jackson [Wy.-U.S.] 46 Je 43.29N 110.38W
Jackson, Cape- 62 Fd 40.59S 174.19 E
Jackson, Mount- [Ant.] 66 Qf 71.23S 63.22W
Jackson, Mount- [Austl.] 59 Df 30.15S 119.16 E
Jackson Bay 62 Ce 43.55S 168.40 E
Jackson Head 62 Ce 43.58S 168.37 E
Jackson Lake 46 Je 43.55N 110.40W
Jacksonville [Ar.-U.S.] 45 Ji 34.52N 92.07W
Jacksonville [Fl.-U.S.] 39 Kf 30.20N 81.40W
Jacksonville [Il.-U.S.] 45 Kg 39.44N 90.14W
Jacksonville [N.C.-U.S.] 43 Le 34.45N 77.26W
Jacksonville [Tx.-U.S.] 43 He 31.58N 95.17W
Jacksonville Beach 43 Ke 30.18N 81.24W
Jacmel 47 Je 18.14N 72.32W
Jacobābad 25 Dc 28.17N 68.26 E
Jacobina 54 Jf 11.11S 40.31W
Jacob Lake 46 Ih 36.45N 112.13W
Jacobs 45 La 50.15N 89.46W
Jacona de Plancarte 48 Hh 19.57N 102.16W
Jacques-Cartier, Détroit de - 42 Lg 50.00N 63.30W
Jacques Cartier, Mont - 42 Kg 48.58N 65.57W
Jacuba, Rio- 55 Fd 18.25S 52.28W
Jacui, Rio- 52 Ki 30.02S 51.15W
Jacui-Mirim, Rio- 55 Fi 28.51S 53.07W
Jacundá 54 Id 4.33S 49.28W
Jacundá, Rio- 54 Hd 1.57S 50.26W
Jacupiranga 56 Kb 24.42S 48.00W
Jada 34 Hd 8.46N 12.09 E
Jadal 34 Fb 18.37N 5.00 E

Index Symbols

Independent Nation; State, Region; District, County; Municipality; Colony, Dependency; Continent; Physical Region; Historical or Cultural Region; Mount, Mountain; Volcano; Hill; Mountains, Mountain Range; Hills, Escarpment; Plateau, Upland; Pass, Gap; Plain, Lowland; Delta; Salt Flat; Valley, Canyon; Crater, Cave; Karst Features; Depression; Polder; Desert, Dunes; Forest, Woods; Heath, Steppe; Oasis; Cape, Point; Coast, Beach; Cliff; Peninsula; Isthmus; Sandbank; Island; Atoll; Rock, Reef; Islands, Archipelago; Rocks, Reefs; Coral Reef; Well, Spring; Geyser; River, Stream; Waterfall Rapids; River Mouth, Estuary; Lake; Salt Lake; Intermittent Lake; Reservoir; Swamp, Pond; Canal; Glacier; Ice Shelf, Pack Ice; Ocean; Sea; Gulf, Bay; Strait, Fjord; Lagoon; Bank; Seamount; Tablemount; Ridge; Shelf; Basin; Escarpment, Sea Scarp; Fracture; Trench, Abyss; National Park, Reserve; Point of Interest; Recreation Site; Cave, Cavern; Historic Site; Ruins; Wall, Walls; Church, Abbey; Temple; Scientific Station; Airport; Port; Lighthouse; Mine; Tunnel; Dam, Bridge

Name	Page	Grid	Lat.	Long.
Jadar [Yugo.]	15	Ce	44.38N	19.16 E
Jaddi, Rās-	25	Cc	25.14N	63.31 E
Jade	10	Ec	53.25N	8.05 E
Jadebusen	10	Ec	53.30N	8.10 E
Jadīd Ra's al Fil	35	Dc	12.40N	25.43 E
Jadito Wash	46	Ji	35.22N	110.50W
J.A.D. Jensens Nunatakker	41	Hf	62.45N	48.20W
Jädraås	8	Gd	60.51N	16.28 E
Jadransko More=Adriatic Sea (EN)	5	Hg	43.00N	16.00 E
Jadrin	7	Li	55.57N	46.11 E
Jādū	33	Bc	31.57N	12.01 E
Ja'ēl	35	Ic	10.56N	51.09 E
Jaén [3]	13	If	38.00N	3.30W
Jaén	13	Ig	37.46N	3.47W
Jæren	8	Af	58.45N	5.45 E
Jærens rev	8	Af	58.45N	5.29 E
Jaffa, Cape-	59	Hg	36.58S	139.40 E
Jaffna	22	Ji	9.40N	80.00 E
Jafr, Qā' al-	24	Gg	30.17N	36.20 E
Jägala Jõgi	8	Ke	59.28N	25.04 E
Jagdalpur	22	Kh	19.04N	82.02 E
Jagdaqi	27	La	50.26N	124.02 E
Jaghbūb, Wāḥāt al-=Jarabub Oasis (EN)	30	Jf	29.41N	24.43 E
Jagotin	16	Gd	50.17N	31.47 E
Jagst	10	Fg	49.14N	9.11 E
Jaguapitã	55	Gf	23.07S	51.33W
Jaguaquara	54	Kf	13.32S	39.58W
Jaguarão	56	Jd	32.34S	53.23W
Jaguarão, Rio-	55	Fk	32.39S	53.12W
Jaguarari	54	Jf	10.16S	40.12W
Jaguari	55	Ei	29.30S	54.41W
Jaguari, Rio- [Braz.]	55	Ei	29.42S	55.07W
Jaguari, Rio- [Braz.]	55	If	22.41S	47.17W
Jaguariaíva	56	Kb	24.15S	49.42W
Jaguaribe	54	Ke	5.53S	38.37W
Jaguaribe, Rio	52	Mf	4.25S	37.45W
Jaguaruana	54	Kd	4.50S	37.47W
Jagüey Grande	49	Gb	22.32N	81.08W
Jahadyjaha	17	Pc	67.03N	72.01 E
Jahām, 'Irq-	24	Li	26.12N	47.00 E
Jahorina	14	Mg	43.42N	18.35 E
Jahrom	23	Hd	28.31N	53.33 E
Jahroma	7	Ih	56.20N	37.29 E
Jaice	23	Ff	44.21N	17.17 E
Jaicoa, Cordillera-	51a	Ab	18.25N	67.05W
Jaicós	54	Je	7.21S	41.08W
Jailolo	26	If	1.05N	127.30 E
Jailolo, Selat-	26	If	0.05N	129.05 E
Jaina, Isla de-	48	Ng	20.14N	90.40W
Jainca	27	Hd	35.57N	102.00 E
Jaipur	22	Jg	26.55N	75.49 E
Jaisalmer	25	Ec	26.55N	70.54 E
Jaja	20	De	56.12N	86.26 E
Jājarm	24	Qd	36.58N	56.27 E
Jajdúdorog	10	Ri	47.49N	21.30 E
Jajere	34	Hc	11.59N	11.26 E
Jajpan	18	Hd	40.23N	70.50 E
Jajsan	16	Td	50.51N	56.14 E
Jajva	19	Fd	59.20N	57.16 E
Jajva	17	Hg	59.16N	56.42 E
Jakarta	22	Mj	6.10S	106.46 E
Jakobshavn/Ilulissat	67	Nc	69.20N	50.50W
Jakobstad/Pietarsaari	7	Fe	63.40N	22.42 E
Jakoruda	15	Gg	42.02N	23.40 E
Jakupica	15	Eh	41.43N	21.26 E
Jakutsk	22	Oc	62.13N	129.49 E
Jakutskaja ASSR [3]	20	Hc	67.00N	130.00 E
Jal	45	Ej	32.07N	103.12W
Jalaid Qi (Inder)	27	Lb	46.41N	122.52 E
Jalājil	24	Kj	25.41N	45.28 E
Jalālābād	23	Lc	34.26N	70.28 E
Jalālah al Baḥrīyah, Jabal al-	24	Eh	29.20N	32.20 E
Jalālah al Qiblīyah, Jabal al-	24	Eh	28.42N	32.22 E
Jalán, Rio-	49	Df	15.43N	86.34W
Jalapa [3]	49	Cf	14.35N	89.55W
Jalapa [Guat.]	47	Gf	14.38N	89.59W
Jalapa [Mex.]	48	Mi	17.43N	92.49W
Jalapa [Nic.]	47	Gf	13.55N	86.08W
Jalapa Enríquez	39	Jh	19.32N	96.55W
Jalasjarvi	7	Fe	62.30N	22.45 E
Jales	55	Ge	20.16S	50.33W
Jālgaon	25	Fd	21.01N	75.34 E
Jalhay	12	Hd	50.34N	5.58 E
Jalībah	24	Lg	30.35N	46.32 E
Jalib Shahab	24	Lg	30.23N	46.09 E
Jalingo	34	Hd	8.53N	11.22 E
Jalisco [2]	47	Dd	20.20N	103.40W
Jāliṭah=La Galite (EN)	30	He	37.32N	8.56 E
Jāliṭah, Canal de-	14	Cm	37.20N	9.00 E
Jallas	13	Cb	42.54N	9.08W
Jālna	25	Fe	19.50N	75.53 E
Jalón	13	Kc	41.47N	1.04W
Jalostotitlán	48	Hg	21.12N	102.28W
Jalpa	48	Hg	21.38N	102.58W
Jalpaiguri	25	Hc	26.31N	88.44 E
Jalpan	48	Jg	21.14N	99.29W
Jalpug, Ozero-	16	Fg	45.25N	28.40 E
Jalta	19	Dg	44.30N	34.10 E
Jaltepec, Rio-	48	Li	17.26N	94.59W
Jālū	33	Dd	28.30N	21.05 E
Jālū, Wāḥāt-=Gialo Oasis (EN)	30	Jf	29.00N	21.20 E
Jaluit Atoll	57	Hd	6.00N	169.35 E
Jalūlā'	24	Ke	34.16N	45.10 E
Jalutorovsk	19	Gd	56.40N	66.18 E
Jam [Iran]	24	Pe	35.45N	55.02 E
Jam [Iran]	24	Oi	27.50N	52.22 E
Jama/Jaama	8	Lf	58.59N	27.45 E
Jamaari	34	Gc	12.06N	10.14 E
Jamaica	49	Jc	20.12N	75.09W
Jamaica	38	Lh	18.15N	77.30W
Jamaica [1]	39	Lh	18.15N	77.30W
Jamaica Channel	47	Ie	18.00N	75.30W
Jamaica Channel (EN)=Jamaïque, Canal de-	49	Jd	18.00N	75.30W
Jamaïque, Canal de-=Jamaica Channel (EN)	49	Jd	18.00N	75.30W
Jamal, Poluostrov-=Yamal Peninsula (EN)	21	Ib	70.00N	70.00 E
Jamalo-Nenecki Nacionalny okrug [3]	20	Cc	67.00N	75.00 E
Jamālpur	25	Hd	24.55N	89.56 E
Jamāme	31	Lh	0.04N	42.46 E
Jamantau, Gora-	5	Le	54.15N	58.06 E
Jamanxim, Rio-	52	Kf	4.43S	56.18W
Jamari, Rio-	54	Fe	8.27S	63.30W
Jamarovka	20	Gf	50.38N	110.16 E
Jambi	22	Oj	1.38S	123.42 E
Jambi [3]	26	Dg	1.36S	103.37 E
Jambol [2]	15	Jg	42.15N	26.35 E
Jambol	15	Jg	42.29N	26.30 E
Jambongan, Pulau-	26	Ge	6.41N	117.25 E
Jambuair, Tanjung-	26	Ce	5.16N	97.30 E
Jambusar	25	Ed	22.03N	72.48 E
James Bay	38	Kd	51.00N	80.30W
Jameson Land	41	Jd	70.45N	23.45W
James River [U.S.]	38	Je	42.52N	97.18W
James River [U.S.]	44	Ig	36.56N	76.27W
James Ross	66	Re	64.15S	57.45W
James Ross Strait	42	Hc	69.50N	96.30W
Jamestown [Austl.]	59	Hf	33.12S	138.36 E
Jamestown [N.D.-U.S.]	43	Hb	46.54N	98.42W
Jamestown [N.Y.-U.S.]	43	Lc	42.05N	79.15W
Jamestown [St.Hel.]	31	Gj	15.56S	5.43W
Jamestown Reservoir	45	Gc	47.15N	98.40W
Jamm	8	Mf	58.24N	28.15 E
Jammer Bugt	7	Bh	57.20N	9.30 E
Jammu	22	Jf	32.44N	74.52 E
Jammu and Kashmir [3]	25	Fb	34.00N	76.00 E
Jāmnagar	22	Jg	22.28N	70.04 E
Jamno, Jezioro-	10	Mb	54.15N	16.10 E
Jampol	16	Fe	48.16N	28.17 E
Jämsä	7	Ff	61.52N	25.12 E
Jamsah	24	Ei	27.38N	33.35 E
Jämsänkoski	8	Kc	61.55N	25.11 E
Jamshedpur	22	Kg	22.48N	86.11 E
Jamsk	20	Ke	59.37N	154.10 E
Jämtland [2]	7	De	63.00N	14.40 E
Jämtland	8	Fa	63.25N	14.05 E
Janā	24	Mi	27.22N	49.54 E
Jana	21	Pb	71.31N	136.32 E
Janakpur	25	Hc	26.42N	85.55 E
Janaucu, Ilha-	54	Hc	0.30N	50.10W
Janaul	17	Gh	56.16N	54.59 E
Janda, Laguna de la-	13	Gh	36.15N	5.51W
Jandaia	55	Gc	17.06S	50.07W
Jandaq	24	Pe	34.02N	54.26 E
Jandiatuba, Rio-	54	Ed	3.28S	68.42W
Jandowae	59	Ke	26.47S	151.06 E
Jandula	13	Hf	38.03N	4.06W
Jane Peak	62	Cf	45.20S	168.19 E
Janesville	43	Jc	42.41N	89.01W
Jangada	55	Db	15.14S	56.29W
Jangada, Rio-	55	Db	15.12S	56.24W
Jangao Shan	27	Gf	25.31N	98.08 E
Jange	27	Ie	31.59N	105.28 E
Jangijer	18	Gd	40.18N	68.50 E
Jangijul	19	Gg	41.07N	69.03 E
Jangirabad	18	Ed	40.03N	65.59 E
Jango	55	Ee	20.27S	55.29W
Jangxi Sheng (Chiang-hsi Sheng)=Kiangsi (EN) [2]	27	Kf	28.00N	116.00 E
Jangy-Bazar	18	Hd	41.40N	70.52 E
Janikowo	10	Od	52.45N	18.07 E
Janīn	24	Ff	32.28N	35.18 E
Janisjarvi, Ozero-	7	He	62.00N	31.00 E
Janja	14	Nf	44.40N	19.19 E
Jan Mayen	5	Fa	71.00N	8.30W
Jan Mayen Ridge (EN)	5	Fb	69.00N	8.00W
Jano-Indigirskaja Nizmennost	20	Ib	71.00N	139.30 E
Janos	47	Cb	30.56N	108.08W
Jánoshalma	10	Pj	46.18N	19.20 E
Jánosháza	10	Ni	47.07N	17.10 E
Janów Lubelski	10	Sf	50.43N	22.24 E
Janów Podlaski	10	Td	52.11N	23.11 E
Jansenville	37	Cf	32.56S	24.40 E
Jansha Jang	21	Mg	28.46N	104.38 E
Janski Zaliv	21	Pb	72.00N	136.00 E
Jantarny	8	Hj	54.53N	19.55 E
Jantra	15	If	43.38N	25.34 E
Januária	54	Jg	15.29S	44.22W
Janūbīyah, Aş Şaḥrā' al-=Southern Desert (EN)	30	Jf	24.00N	30.00 E
Janykurgan	19	Gg	43.55N	67.14 E
Janzhang Ansha	27	Ke	9.30N	116.59 E
Japan (EN)=Nippon	21	Pf	35.00N	135.00 E
Japan (EN)=Nippon [1]	22	Pf	38.00N	137.00 E
Japan, Sea of- (EN)=Japonskoje More	21	Pf	40.00N	134.00 E
Japan, Sea of- (EN)=Nippon Kai	21	Pf	40.00N	134.00 E
Japan, Sea of- (EN)=Tong-Hae	21	Pf	40.00N	134.00 E
Japan Basin (EN)	27	Nc	40.00N	135.00 E
Japan Trench (EN)	3	If	37.00N	143.00 E
Japiim	54	De	7.37S	72.54W
Japonskoje More=Japan, Sea of- (EN)	21	Pf	40.00N	134.00 E
Jäppilä	8	Lb	62.23N	27.26 E
Japtiksale	17	Pb	69.25N	72.29 E
Japurá	54	Ed	1.24S	69.25W
Japurá, Rio-	52	Jf	3.08S	64.46W
Jaqué	49	Hj	7.31N	78.10W
Jaquet, Point-	51g	Ba	15.38N	61.26W
Jaquirana	55	Gi	28.54S	50.23W
Jar	7	Mg	58.17N	52.06 E
Jarabub Oasis (EN)=Jaghbūb, Wāḥāt al-	30	Jf	29.41N	24.43 E
Jarābulus	24	Hd	36.49N	38.01 E
Jaraguá [Braz.]	55	Hb	15.45S	49.20W
Jaraguá [Braz.]	55	Hh	26.29S	49.04W
Jaraguá, Serra do-	55	Hh	26.40S	49.15W
Jaraguari	55	Ee	20.09S	54.25W
Jaraiz de la Vera	13	Gd	40.04N	5.45W
Jarama	13	Id	40.02N	3.39W
Jaramillo	56	Gg	47.11S	67.09W
Jarandilla	13	Gd	40.08N	5.39W
Jaransk	19	Ed	57.18N	47.55 E
Jarānwāla	25	Eb	31.20N	73.26 E
Jarash	24	Ff	32.17N	35.54 E
Jarau, Cêrro do-	55	Dj	30.18S	56.32W
Jarbah	30	Ie	33.48N	10.54 E
Järbo	7	Df	60.43N	16.36 E
Jarcevo [R.S.F.S.R.]	16	Hb	55.05N	32.45 E
Jarcevo [R.S.F.S.R.]	20	Ed	60.15N	90.10 E
Jardāwīyah	24	Jj	25.24N	42.42 E
Jardim	54	Gh	21.28S	56.09W
Jardine River	59	Ib	11.10S	142.30 E
Jardines de la Reina, Archipiélago de los-	47	Id	20.50N	78.55W
Jardinópolis	55	Ie	21.02S	47.46W
Jarega	17	Fe	63.27N	53.31 E
Jaremča	16	De	48.31N	24.33 E
Jarenga	7	Le	62.08N	49.03 E
Jarez de Garcías Salinas	47	Dd	22.39N	103.00W
Järfälla	8	Ge	59.24N	17.50 E
Jargava	15	Lc	46.27N	28.27 E
Jari, Rio-	52	Kf	1.09S	51.54W
Jarīd, Shaṭṭ al-	30	He	33.42N	8.26 E
Jarīr, Wādī-	24	Jj	25.38N	42.30 E
Jarjis	32	Jc	33.30N	11.07 E
Jarkovo	17	Mh	57.26N	67.05 E
Jarmah	33	Bd	26.32N	13.04 E
Järna	8	Ge	59.06N	17.34 E
Jarnac	11	Fi	45.41N	0.10W
Järnlunden	8	Ff	58.10N	15.40 E
Jarny	11	Le	49.09N	5.53 E
Jarocin	10	Ne	51.59N	17.31 E
Jaroměř	10	Lf	50.21N	15.55 E
Jaroměřice nad Rokytnou	10	Lg	49.06N	15.54 E
Jaroslavl	6	Jd	57.37N	39.52 E
Jaroslavskaja Oblast [3]	19	Dd	57.45N	39.15 E
Jaroslavski	28	Lb	44.10N	132.13 E
Jarosław	10	Sf	50.02N	22.42 E
Järpen	8	Ea	63.21N	13.29 E
Jarrāḥī	24	Mg	30.44N	48.46 E
Jarroto, Ozero-	17	Oc	67.55N	71.40 E
Jar-Sale	20	Cc	66.50N	70.50 E
Jartai	27	Id	39.45N	105.46 E
Jartai Yanchi	27	Id	39.45N	105.40 E
Jarudej	17	Od	65.50N	71.50 E
Jarud Qi (Lubei)	27	Lc	44.30N	120.55 E
Järva-Jaani/Jarva-Jaani	8	Ke	59.00N	25.49 E
Jarva-Jani/Järva-Jaani	8	Ke	59.00N	25.49 E
Järvakandi/Jarvakandi	8	Kf	58.45N	24.44 E
Jarvakandi/Järvakandi	8	Kf	58.45N	24.44 E
Järvenpää	7	Ff	60.28N	25.06 E
Jarvis Island	57	Ke	0.23S	160.01W
Järvsö	7	Df	61.43N	16.10 E
Jaščera	8	Ne	59.05N	30.00 E
Jaselda	16	Ec	52.07N	26.29 E
Jasień	10	Le	51.46N	15.01 E
Jasikan	34	Fd	7.24N	0.28 E
Jasinja	10	Uh	48.14N	24.31 E
Jasinovataja	16	Je	48.05N	37.57 E
Jasiołka	10	Rg	49.47N	21.30 E
Jasira	35	He	1.57N	45.16 E
Jasired Mayd	35	He	11.12N	47.13 E
Jāsk	23	Id	25.38N	57.46 E
Jaškul	16	Nf	46.17N	45.10 E
Jaškul	16	Nf	46.11N	45.17 E
Jasło	10	Rg	49.45N	21.29 E
Jasmund	10	Jb	54.32N	13.35 E
Jasnogorsk	16	Jb	54.29N	37.42 E
Jasny [R.S.F.S.R.]	19	Fe	51.01N	59.59 E
Jasny [R.S.F.S.R.]	20	Hf	53.18N	128.03 E
Jason Islands	56	Hh	51.00S	61.00W
Jasper [Alta.-Can.]	39	Hd	52.53N	118.05W
Jasper [Al.-U.S.]	43	Je	33.50N	87.17W
Jasper [Fl.-U.S.]	44	Fj	30.31N	82.57W
Jasper [In.-U.S.]	44	Df	38.24N	86.56W
Jasper [Tn.-U.S.]	44	Eh	35.04N	85.38W
Jasper [Tx.-U.S.]	45	Jk	30.55N	93.59W
Jasper Seamount (EN)	38	Gf	30.32N	122.42W
Jaşşān	24	Kf	32.58N	45.53 E
Jastrebarsko	14	Je	45.40N	15.39 E
Jastrowie	10	Mc	53.26N	16.49 E
Jastrzebie Zdrój	10	Og	49.58N	18.34 E
Jászapáti	10	Qi	47.31N	20.09 E
Jászárokszállás	10	Pi	47.38N	19.59 E
Jászberény	10	Pi	47.30N	19.55 E
Jászság	10	Pi	47.25N	20.00 E
Jat, Uad el-	30	Ff	26.47N	13.03W
Jatai	53	Kg	17.53S	51.43W
Jatapu, Rio-	54	Gd	2.30S	58.17W
Játiva/Xátiva	13	Lf	38.59N	0.31W
Jatobá, Rio-	55	Ea	12.23S	54.07W
Jaú	56	Kb	22.18S	48.33W
Jaú, Rio-	54	Fd	1.55S	61.25W
Jaua, Cerro-	54	Fc	4.48N	64.26W
Jauaperi, Rio-	54	Fc	1.26S	61.35W
Jauja	54	Cf	11.48S	75.30W
Jaumave	48	Jf	23.25N	99.23W
Jaunanna	8	Lg	57.13N	27.10 E
Jaunelgava/Jaunjelgava	7	Fh	56.37N	25.06 E
Jaunfeld	14	Id	46.35N	14.45 E
Jaungulbene	8	Lh	57.00N	26.42 E
Jaunjelgava/Jaunelgava	7	Fh	56.37N	25.06 E
Jaunpiebalga	8	Lg	57.05N	26.03 E
Jaunpur	25	Gc	25.44N	82.41 E
Jauru	55	Ed	18.35S	54.17W
Jauru, Rio- [Braz.]	54	Hg	18.40S	54.36W
Jauru, Rio- [Braz.]	55	Dc	16.22S	57.46W
Java (EN)=Jawa	21	Mj	7.20S	110.00 E
Javalambre	13	Ld	40.06N	1.00W
Javalambre, Sierra de-	13	Ld	40.05N	1.00W
Javan	18	Ge	38.19N	69.01 E
Javānrūd	24	Le	34.48N	46.30 E
Javari, Rio-	52	If	4.21S	70.02W
Java Sea (EN)=Jawa, Laut-	21	Mj	5.00S	110.00 E
Java Trench (EN)	3	Hk	10.30S	110.00 E
Jávea	13	Mf	38.47N	0.10 E
Javier	13	Kb	42.36N	1.13W
Javor	14	Mf	44.07N	18.59 E
Javorie	10	Ph	48.27N	19.18 E
Javornik	10	Jh	48.10N	13.35 E
Javorníky	10	Og	49.20N	18.20 E
Javorov	16	Cd	50.00N	23.27 E
Javorová skála	10	Kg	49.31N	14.30 E
Jävre	7	Ed	65.09N	21.29 E
Jawa=Java (EN)	21	Mj	7.20S	110.00 E
Jawa, Laut-=Java Sea (EN)	21	Mj	5.00S	110.00 E
Jawa Barat [3]	26	Eh	7.00S	107.00 E
Jawa Tengah [3]	26	Eh	7.30S	110.00 E
Jawa Timur [3]	26	Fh	8.00S	113.00 E
Jawf, Wādī-	33	If	15.50N	45.30 E
Jawor	10	Me	51.03N	16.11 E
Jaworzno	10	Pf	50.13N	19.15 E
Jaya, Puncak-	57	Ee	4.10S	137.00 E
Jayapura	58	Fe	2.32S	140.42 E
Jayawijaya, Pegunungan-	26	Kg	4.30S	139.30 E
Jāyezān	24	Mg	30.50N	49.52 E
Jazāyer va Banāder-e Khalīj-e Fārs va Daryā-ye 'Omān [3]	23	Id	27.30N	56.00 E
Jaz Mūrīān, Hāmūn-e-	23	Id	27.20N	58.55 E
Jazva	17	Hf	60.23N	56.50 E
Jazvān	24	Md	36.58N	48.40 E
Jazykovo	7	Li	54.20N	47.22 E
Jazzīn	24	Ff	33.32N	35.34 E
Jdiouia	13	Mi	35.56N	0.50 E
Jeannetty, Ostrov-	20	Ka	76.45N	158.25 E
Jean-Rabel	49	Kd	19.52N	73.11W
Jebala	13	Gi	35.25N	5.30W
Jebal Bārez, Kūh-e-	23	Id	28.30N	58.20 E
Jebba	34	Fd	9.08N	4.50 E
Jebel	15	Ed	45.33N	21.14 E
Jebha	13	Hi	35.13N	4.40W
Jedincy	16	Ee	48.06N	27.19 E
Jedisa	16	Nh	42.32N	44.14 E
Jędrzejów	10	Qf	50.39N	20.18 E
Jeetze	10	Hc	53.09N	11.04 E
Jefferson	45	Ie	42.01N	94.23W
Jefferson, Mount- [Nv.-U.S.]	43	Dd	38.46N	116.55W
Jefferson, Mount- [Or.-U.S.]	46	Ed	44.40N	121.47W
Jefferson City	39	Jf	38.34N	92.10W
Jefferson River	46	Jd	45.56N	111.30W
Jeffersonville	44	Ef	38.17N	85.44W
Jef-Jef el Kebir	35	Ca	20.30N	21.25 E
Jefremov	19	De	53.11N	38.07 E
Jega	34	Fc	12.13N	4.23 E
Jegersfontein	37	De	29.44S	25.29 E
Jegorjevsk	7	Ji	55.25N	39.07 E
Jegorlyk	16	Lf	46.32N	41.52 E
Jegorlykskaja	16	Lf	46.34N	40.44 E
Jehegnadzor	16	Nj	39.47N	45.18 E
Jeja	16	Kf	46.39N	38.36 E
Jejsk	19	Df	46.40N	38.15 E
Jejuí Guazú, Río-	55	Dg	24.13S	57.09W
Jēkabpils/Jekabpils	19	Cd	56.30N	25.59 E
Jekabpils/Jēkabpils	19	Cd	56.30N	25.59 E
Jekaterinovka	16	Nc	52.04N	44.30 E
Jekkevarre	7	Eb	69.28N	20.00 E
Jelabuga	19	Fd	55.48N	52.05 E
Jelai	26	Fg	2.59S	110.45 E
Jelan	16	Md	50.57N	43.43 E
Jelancy	20	Ff	52.44N	106.27 E
Jelanec	16	Gf	47.42N	31.50 E
Jelcz	10	Ne	51.01N	17.18 E
Jelec	6	Je	52.37N	38.30 E
Jeleckj	17	Lc	67.03N	64.15 E
Jelenia Góra	10	Lf	50.55N	15.46 E
Jelenia Góra [2]	10	Lf	50.55N	15.45 E
Jelgava	19	Cd	56.39N	23.41 E
Jelica	15	Df	43.47N	20.20 E
Jelin vrh	15	Cf	43.02N	19.27 E
Jelizavety, Mys-	5	Qd	54.30N	142.40 E
Jelizovo [Bye.-U.S.S.R.]	16	Fc	53.24N	29.00 E
Jelizovo [R.S.F.S.R.]	20	Kf	53.06N	158.20 E
Jelling	8	Ci	55.45N	9.26 E
Jelnja	16	Hb	54.35N	33.12 E
Jeloguj	20	Dd	63.10N	87.45 E
Jelow Gīr	24	Lf	32.58N	47.48 E
Jeløy	8	De	58.30N	10.40 E
Jelsk	16	Fd	51.49N	29.13 E
Jelva	17	Ee	63.05N	50.50 E
Jemaja, Pulau-	26	Ef	2.55N	105.45 E
Jemanželinsk	19	Ge	54.45N	61.20 E
Jember	26	Fh	8.10S	113.42 E
Jemca	7	Je	63.32N	41.56 E
Jemca	7	Je	63.04N	40.18 E
Jemeppe-sur-Sambre	12	Gd	50.28N	4.40 E
Jeminay	27	Eb	47.28N	85.48 E
Jemnice	10	Lg	49.01N	15.35 E
Jena	10	Hf	50.56N	11.35 E
Jenakijevo	16	Ke	48.12N	38.18 E
Jenašimski Polkan, Gora-	20	Ee	59.50N	92.45 E
Jendyr	17	Mf	61.38N	67.20 E
Jeneponto	26	Gh	5.41S	119.42 E
Jenisej=Yenisey (EN)	21	Kb	71.50N	82.40 E
Jenisejsk	20	Ee	58.27N	92.10 E
Jenisejski Krjaž=Yenisey Ridge (EN)	21	Ld	59.00N	92.30 E
Jenisejski Zaliv=Yenisey Bay (EN)	20	Db	72.00N	81.00 E
Jennersdorf	14	Kd	46.56N	16.08 E
Jennings	45	Jk	30.13N	92.39W
Jenny Lind	42	Hc	68.50N	101.30W
Jenny Point	51g	Bb	15.28N	61.15W
Jensen	46	Kf	40.22N	109.17W
Jens Munk	42	Jc	69.40N	79.40W
Jequié	53	Lg	13.51S	40.05W
Jequitaí	55	Jc	17.15S	44.28W
Jequitaí, Rio	55	Jc	17.04S	44.50W
Jequitinhonha, Rio-	52	Mg	15.51S	38.53W
Jerada	32	Gc	34.19N	2.09W
Jeralijev	19	Fg	43.12N	51.43 E
Jerbogačën	20	Fd	61.15N	107.57 E
Jérémie	47	Je	18.39N	74.08W
Jeremoabo	54	Kf	10.04S	38.21W
Jerer	35	Gd	7.40N	43.48 E
Jerevan	6	Kg	40.11N	44.30 E
Jerez, Punta-	48	Kf	22.54N	97.46W
Jerez de la Frontera	13	Fh	36.41N	6.08W
Jerez de los Caballeros	13	Ff	38.19N	6.46W
Jergeni	5	Kf	47.00N	44.00 E
Jericho	59	Jd	23.36S	146.08 E
Jermak	19	He	52.02N	76.55 E
Jermakovskoje	20	Ef	53.16N	92.24 E
Jermentau	19	He	51.38N	73.10 E
Jermolajevo	17	Gj	52.43N	55.48 E
Jeroaquara	55	Gb	15.23S	50.25W
Jerofej Pavlovič	20	Hf	53.58N	121.57 E
Jerome	46	He	42.43N	114.31W
Jersa	17	Fc	66.19N	52.32 E
Jersey	9	Kl	49.15N	2.10W
Jersey City	43	Mc	40.44N	74.04W
Jerseyville	45	Kg	39.07N	90.20W
Jeršov	19	Ee	51.20N	48.17 E
Jertarski	17	Lh	56.47N	64.25 E
Jerte	13	Fe	39.58N	6.17W
Jerusalem (EN)=Yerushalayim	22	Ff	31.46N	35.14 E
Jeruslan	16	Od	50.20N	46.25 E
Jervis Bay	59	Kg	35.05S	150.44 E
Jerzu	14	Dk	39.47N	9.31 E
Jesberg	12	Lc	51.00N	9.09 E
Jesenice [Yugo.]	14	Jf	44.14N	15.34 E
Jesenice [Yugo.]	14	Id	46.27N	14.04 E
Jesenik	10	Nf	50.14N	17.12 E
Jesi	14	Hg	43.31N	13.14 E
Jesil	19	Ge	51.58N	66.24 E
Jeskianhor, Kanal-	18	Fe	39.15N	66.00 E
Jessej	20	Fc	68.29N	102.10 E
Jessentuki	16	Mg	44.03N	42.51 E
Jessheim	7	Cf	60.09N	11.11 E
Jessore	25	Hd	23.10N	89.13 E
Ještěd	10	Kf	50.42N	14.59 E
Jestro, Wabe-	30	Lh	4.11N	42.09 E
Jesup	43	Ke	31.36N	81.53W
Jesús Carranza	48	Li	17.26N	95.02W
Jesús María	56	Hd	30.59S	64.06W
Jesús María, Boca de-	48	Ke	24.29N	97.40W
Jesús María, Río-	48	Gg	21.55N	104.30W
Jetmore	45	Gg	38.03N	99.54W
Jever	10	Dc	53.35N	7.54 E
Jevgenjevka	18	Kc	43.27N	77.40 E
Jevišovka	10	Mh	48.52N	16.36 E
Jevlah	19	Eg	40.35N	47.10 E
Jevnaker	7	Cf	60.15N	10.28 E
Jevpatorija	19	Df	45.12N	33.18 E
Jevrejskaja Avtonomnaja Oblast [3]	20	Ig	48.30N	132.00 E
Jeyḩūn	24	Pi	27.16N	55.12 E
Jeypore	25	He	18.51N	82.35 E
Jezercës	5	Hg	42.26N	19.49 E
Jezero	14	Lf	44.21N	17.10 E
Jeziorak, Jezioro-	10	Pc	53.50N	19.35 E
Jeziorany	10	Qc	53.58N	20.46 E
Jeziorka	10	Rd	52.10N	21.06 E
Jhang Sadar	25	Eb	31.16N	72.19 E
Jhānsi	22	Jg	25.26N	78.35 E
Jhelum	25	Eb	32.56N	73.44 E
Jhelum	21	Jf	31.12N	72.08 E
Jiaji → Qionghai	27	Jh	19.25N	110.28 E
Jialing Jiang	21	Mg	29.34N	106.35 E
Jiamusi	22	Pe	46.49N	130.21 E
Ji'an [China]	27	Mc	41.08N	126.10 E
Ji'an [China]	22	Ng	27.12N	114.59 E
Jianchang	28	Ed	40.49N	119.46 E
Jianchuan	27	Gf	26.32N	99.53 E
Jiande (Baisha)	27	Kf	29.31N	119.17 E
Jiang'an	27	If	28.40N	105.07 E
Jiangao Shan	27	Gf	25.31N	98.08 E
Jiangbiancun	27	Kf	27.13N	115.57 E
Jiangcheng	27	Hg	22.37N	101.48 E
Jiangdu (Xiannümiao)	28	Eh	32.30N	119.33 E
Jianghua (Shuikou)	27	Jg	24.58N	111.56 E
Jiangjin	27	If	29.15N	106.18 E
Jiangle	27	Kf	26.48N	117.29 E
Jiangling (Jingzhou)	27	Je	30.21N	112.10 E
Jiangmen	27	Jg	22.35N	113.02 E
Jiangpu	28	Eh	32.03N	118.37 E
Jiangshan	28	Ej	28.45N	118.37 E
Jiangsu Sheng (Chiang-su Sheng)=Kiangsu (EN) [2]	27	Ke	33.00N	120.00 E
Jiangyou (Zhongba)	27	He	31.48N	104.39 E
Jianhu	28	Eh	33.28N	119.47 E
Jianli	27	Jf	29.50N	112.55 E
Jian'ou	27	Kf	27.08N	118.20 E
Jianping (Yebaishou)	27	Kc	41.55N	119.37 E
Jianshi	27	Ie	30.32N	109.43 E
Jianshui	27	Hg	23.39N	102.46 E
Jianyang	27	Kf	27.23N	118.03 E
Jiaocheng	27	Jd	37.32N	112.09 E
Jiaoding Shan	27	Lc	41.11N	120.01 E
Jiaohe [China]	27	Mc	43.43N	127.20 E
Jiaohe [China]	28	De	38.01N	116.17 E
Jiaolai He [China]	28	Ef	37.07N	119.35 E
Jiaolai He [China]	28	Fc	43.02N	120.48 E
Jiaoliu He	28	Gb	45.21N	122.48 E
Jiaonan (Wanggezhuang)	28	Eg	35.53N	119.58 E

Index Symbols

- [1] Independent Nation
- [2] State, Region
- [3] District, County
- [4] Municipality
- [5] Colony, Dependency
- Continent
- Physical Region
- Historical or Cultural Region
- Mount, Mountain
- Volcano
- Hill
- Mountains, Mountain Range
- Hills, Escarpment
- Plateau, Upland
- Pass, Gap
- Plain, Lowland
- Delta
- Salt Flat
- Valley, Canyon
- Crater, Cave
- Karst Features
- Depression
- Polder
- Desert, Dunes
- Forest, Woods
- Heath, Steppe
- Oasis
- Cape, Point
- Coast, Beach
- Cliff
- Peninsula
- Isthmus
- Sandbank
- Island
- Atoll
- Rock, Reef
- Islands, Archipelago
- Rocks, Reefs
- Coral Reef
- Well, Spring
- Geyser
- River, Stream
- Waterfall Rapids
- River Mouth, Estuary
- Lake
- Salt Lake
- Intermittent Lake
- Reservoir
- Swamp, Pond
- Canal
- Glacier
- Ice Shelf, Pack Ice
- Ocean
- Sea
- Gulf, Bay
- Strait, Fjord
- Lagoon
- Bank
- Seamount
- Tablemount
- Ridge
- Shelf
- Basin
- Escarpment, Sea Scarp
- Fracture
- Trench, Abyss
- National Park, Reserve
- Point of Interest
- Recreation Site
- Cave, Cavern
- Historic Site
- Ruins
- Wall, Walls
- Church, Abbey
- Temple
- Scientific Station
- Airport
- Port
- Lighthouse
- Mine
- Tunnel
- Dam, Bridge

International Map Index

Name	Map	Grid	Lat	Long
Jiaoxian	27	Kd	36.20N	120.00 E
Jiaozhou-Wan ◪	28	Ff	36.10N	120.15 E
Jiaozuo	22	Nf	35.15N	113.18 E
Jiashan	28	Fi	30.51N	120.54 E
Jiashan (Mingguang)	28	Dh	32.47N	118.00 E
Jiashi/Payzawat	27	Cd	39.29N	76.39 E
Jiawang	28	Dg	34.27N	117.26 E
Jiaxian	28	Bh	33.58N	113.13 E
Jiaxing	27	Le	30.44N	120.46 E
Jiayin (Chaoyang)	27	Nb	48.52N	130.21 E
Jiayu	27	Jf	30.00N	113.57 E
Jiayuguan	27	Gd	39.49N	98.18 E
Jibalei	35	Ic	10.07N	50.47 E
Jibão, Serra do- ▲	55	Jb	14.48S	45.15W
Jibiya	34	Gc	13.06N	7.14 E
Jibou	15	Gb	47.16N	23.15 E
Jicarón, Isla- ⬥	49	Gj	7.16N	81.47W
Jičín	10	Lf	50.26N	15.22 E
Jiddah	22	Fg	21.29N	39.12 E
Jiddat al Ḩarāsīs ⬚	23	Ie	20.05N	56.00 E
Jiehu → Yinan	28	Eg	35.33N	118.27 E
Jieshou	28	Ch	33.17N	115.22 E
Jiesjjavrre ▭	7	Fb	69.40N	24.12 E
Jieyang	27	Kg	23.32N	116.25 E
Jieznas/Eznas	8	Kj	54.34N	24.17 E
Jifn, Wādī al- ▶	24	Jj	25.48N	42.15 E
Jiftûn, Jazā'ir- ⬥	24	Ei	27.13N	33.56 E
Jīgley	35	He	4.25N	45.22 E
Jiguaní	49	Ic	20.22N	76.26W
Jigüey, Bahia de- ◪	49	Hb	22.08N	78.05W
Jigzhi	27	He	33.28N	101.29 E
Jihlava ▭	10	Mh	48.55N	16.37 E
Jihlava	10	Lg	49.24N	15.34 E
Jihlavské vrchy ▲	10	Lg	49.15N	15.20 E
Jihočeský kraj ▭	10	Kg	49.05N	14.30 E
Jihomoravský kraj ▭	10	Mg	49.10N	16.40 E
Jijel	32	Ib	36.48N	5.46 E
Jijel ▭	32	Ib	36.45N	5.45 E
Jijia ▭	15	Lc	46.54N	28.05 E
Jijiga	35	Gd	9.21N	42.48 E
Jijona	13	Lf	38.32N	0.30W
Jikharrah	33	Dd	29.17N	21.38 E
Jilava	15	Je	44.20N	26.05 E
Jilf al Kabir, Ḩaḑabat al- ▲	33	Ee	23.30N	26.00 E
Jilib	31	Lh	0.29N	42.47 E
Jilin	27	Mc	43.51N	126.33 E
Jilin Sheng (Chi-lin Sheng) = Kirin (EN) ▭	27	Mc	43.00N	126.00 E
Jiliu He ▭	27	La	52.02N	120.41 E
Jiloca ▭	13	Kc	41.21N	1.39W
Jima = Jimma (EN)	31	Kh	7.39N	36.49 E
Jimāl, Wādī- ▶	24	Fj	24.40N	35.06 E
Jimani	49	Ld	18.28N	71.51W
Jimbe	36	De	11.05S	24.00 E
Jimbolia	15	Dd	45.48N	20.43 E
Jimena	13	Ig	37.50N	3.28W
Jimena de la Frontera	13	Gh	36.26N	5.27W
Jiménez	47	Dc	27.08N	104.55W
Jiménez del Teul	48	Gf	23.10N	104.05W
Jimma (EN) = Jima	31	Kh	7.39N	36.49 E
Jimo	28	Ff	36.24N	120.27 E
Jimsar	27	Ec	43.59N	89.04 E
Jimulco ▲	48	He	25.20N	103.10W
Jinâh	24	Dj	25.30N	30.31 E
Jinan = Tsinan (EN)	22	Nf	36.35N	117.00 E
Jincheng [China]	27	Jd	35.32N	112.53 E
Jincheng [China]	28	Fd	41.12N	121.25 E
Jinchuan /Quqên	27	He	31.02N	102.02 E
Jind	25	Fc	29.19N	76.19 E
Jindřichův Hradec	10	Kg	49.09N	15.00 E
Jinfo Shan ▲	27	If	29.01N	107.14 E
Jing'an	27	Dc	44.39N	82.30 E
Jingbian (Zhangxiapan)	28	Cj	28.51N	115.21 E
Jingde	27	Id	37.32N	108.45 E
Jingdezhen	28	Ei	30.18N	118.30 E
Jingfeng → Hexigten Qi	22	Ng	29.18N	117.18 E
Jinggang Shan ▲	27	Kc	43.15N	117.31 E
Jinggu	27	Jf	26.42N	114.07 E
Jinghai	27	Hg	23.28N	100.39 E
Jinghe/Jing	28	De	38.57N	116.56 E
Jinghong (Yunjinghong)	27	Ga	44.39N	82.50 E
Jinghong Dao ⬥	27	Hg	21.59N	100.48 E
Jingjiang	27	Je	9.45N	114.28 E
Jingle	28	Fh	32.01N	120.15 E
Jingmen	28	Ae	38.22N	111.56 E
Jingning	27	Id	31.00N	112.11 E
Jingping → Pinglu	27	Id	35.30N	105.45 E
Jingpo Hu ▭	28	Be	39.32N	112.14 E
Jingshan	28	Jc	43.50N	128.53 E
Jingtai	28	Bi	31.04N	113.08 E
Jingxian [China]	27	Hd	37.10N	104.08 E
Jingxian [China]	27	If	26.40N	109.37 E
Jingxing (Weishui)	27	Ke	30.41N	118.29 E
Jingyu	28	Ce	38.03N	114.09 E
Jingyuan	28	Ic	42.25N	126.48 E
Jingzhi	28	Ef	36.35N	104.40 E
Jingzhou → Jiangling	28	Ef	36.18N	119.22 E
Jinhu	27	Je	30.21N	112.10 E
Jinhua	28	Eh	33.01N	119.01 E
Jining [China]	27	Kf	29.09N	119.38 E
Jining [China]	22	Nf	37.26N	116.36 E
Jining [China]	22	Ne	41.02N	113.07 E
Jinja	31	Kh	0.26N	33.13 E
Jin Jiang ▭	27	Jf	28.23N	115.48 E
Jinkou	28	Ci	30.20N	114.07 E
Jinotega ▭	49	Eg	14.00N	85.25W
Jinotega	47	Gf	13.06N	86.00W
Jinotepe	47	Gf	11.51N	86.12W
Jinping	15	Hg	22.45N	103.15 E
Jinsha	27	If	27.18N	106.16 E
Jinsha → Nantong	28	Fh	32.06N	120.52 E
Jinshan	28	Fi	30.54N	121.09 E
Jinshan → Harqin Qi	28	Ed	41.57N	118.40 E
Jinshi	28	Aj	29.03N	111.52 E
Jinta	27	Gc	40.00N	99.00 E
Jintan	28	Ei	31.45N	119.34 E

Name	Map	Grid	Lat	Long
Jinxi	27	Lc	40.46N	120.50 E
Jinxian [China]	27	Ld	39.06N	121.44 E
Jinxian [China]	28	Dj	28.21N	116.16 E
Jinxiang	28	Dg	35.04N	116.19 E
Jinyang	27	Hf	27.39N	103.12 E
Jinyun	28	Fj	28.39N	120.05 E
Jinzhai (Meishan)	28	Ci	31.40N	115.52 E
Jinzhou	22	Oe	41.09N	121.08 E
Jinzû-Gawa ▭	29	Ec	36.45N	137.13 E
Jiparaná, Rio- ▭	52	Jf	8.03S	62.52W
Jipijapa	54	Bd	1.22S	80.34W
Jiquilisco	49	Cg	13.19N	88.35W
Jiquilisco, Bahia de- ◪	49	Cg	13.10N	88.28W
Jirjā	33	Fd	26.20N	31.53 E
Jishou	27	If	28.18N	109.43 E
Jishu	28	Ib	44.16N	126.50 E
Jisr ash Shughur	24	Ge	35.48N	36.19 E
Jiu ▭	15	Gd	43.47N	23.48 E
Jiucai Ling ▲	27	Jf	25.33N	111.18 E
Jiucheng → Wucheng	28	Df	37.12N	116.04 E
Jiujiang	22	Ng	29.39N	116.00 E
Jiuling Shan ▲	27	Jf	28.55N	114.50 E
Jiulong/Gyaisi	27	Hf	28.58N	101.33 E
Jiuquan (Suzhou)	22	Lf	39.46N	98.34 E
Jiurongcheng	28	Gf	37.22N	122.33 E
Jiutai	27	Mc	44.10N	125.50 E
Jiwani, Rās- ▶	25	Cc	25.01N	61.44 E
Jixi [China]	28	Ei	30.04N	118.36 E
Jixi [China]	22	Pe	45.15N	130.55 E
Jixian [China]	28	Cg	35.23N	114.04 E
Jixian [China]	28	Cf	37.34N	115.34 E
Jixian [China]	28	Dd	40.03N	117.24 E
Jiyang	28	Df	36.59N	117.11 E
Jiyuan	28	Bg	35.06N	112.35 E
Jiz, Wādī al- ▭	28	Dg	39.05N	117.45 E
Jīzān	35	Ib	16.12N	52.14 E
Jize	22	Gb	16.54N	42.32 E
Jizera ▭	28	Cf	36.54N	114.52 E
Jizerské Hory ▲	10	Kf	50.10N	14.43 E
Jizl, Wādī al- ▭	10	Lf	50.50N	15.13 E
Jizô-Zaki ▶	24	Hj	25.39N	38.25 E
Jmbe	28	Ls	35.33N	133.18 E
Jnchengjiang → Hechi	36	De	10.20S	16.40 E
Joaçaba	27	Ig	24.44N	108.02 E
Joal-Fadiout	55	Ld	27.10S	51.30W
João Câmara	34	Bc	14.10N	16.51W
João Monlevade	54	Ke	5.32S	35.48W
João Pessoa	55	Kd	19.50S	43.08W
João Pinheiro	53	Mf	7.07S	34.52W
Joaquín V. González	54	Ig	17.45S	46.10W
Jobado	56	Hb	25.00S	64.11W
Jódar	49	Ic	20.54N	77.17W
Jodhpur	13	Jg	37.50N	3.21W
Jodoigne/Geldenaken	22	Jg	26.17N	73.02 E
Joensuu	12	Gd	50.43N	4.52 E
Joerg Plateau ▲	6	Ic	62.36N	29.46 E
Joes Hill ▲	66	Qf	75.00S	69.30W
Jõetsu	12	Hb	52.58N	5.47 E
Joeuf	27	Dd	37.06N	138.15 E
Jõf di Montasio ▲	12	Ie	49.14N	6.01 E
Joffre, Mount- ▲	14	Hd	46.26N	13.26 E
Jogbani	46	Ha	50.32N	115.13W
Jõgeva/Jygeva	25	Hc	26.25N	87.15 E
Joghatây	7	Gg	58.46N	26.26 E
Joghatây, Küh-e- ▲	24	Qd	36.36N	57.01 E
Jõhana	24	Qd	36.30N	57.00 E
Johannesburg	29	Ec	36.31N	136.54 E
John Day	31	Jk	26.15S	28.00 E
John Day River ▭	29	Ce	32.57N	132.35 E
John H. Kerr Reservoir ◪	46	Fd	44.25N	118.57W
John Martin Reservoir ◪	43	Cb	45.44N	120.39W
John o' Groat's	44	Hg	36.31N	78.18W
Johnson	45	Bg	38.05N	103.02W
Johnson, Pico de- ▲	9	Lc	58.38N	3.05W
Johnson City [Tn.-U.S.]	45	Fh	37.34N	101.45W
Johnson City [Tx.-U.S.]	48	Cc	29.13N	112.07W
Johnsons Crossing	43	Kd	36.19N	82.21W
Johnsons Point	45	Kk	30.17N	98.25W
Johnstone, Lake-	42	Ed	60.29N	133.17W
Johnstone Strait	51d	Bb	17.02N	61.53W
Johnston Island	59	Ef	32.20S	120.40 E
Johnston Island ⬥	42	Ca	50.25N	126.00W
Johnstown [N.Y.-U.S.]	57	Kc	17.00N	168.30W
Johnstown [Pa.-U.S.]	58	Kc	17.00N	168.30W
Johor Baharu	44	Jd	43.01N	74.22W
Joia	43	Lc	40.20N	78.56W
Joigny	22	Mi	1.28N	103.45 E
Joinville	55	Ei	28.39S	54.08W
Joinville Island ⬥	11	Aj	47.59N	3.24 E
Jokau	53	Lh	26.18S	48.50W
Jokela	11	Lf	48.27N	5.08 E
Jokelbugten ◪	66	Re	63.15S	55.45W
Jokioinen	35	Ed	8.24N	33.49 E
Jokkmokk	8	Kd	60.33N	24.59 E
Jøkulleggi ▲	41	Kc	78.25N	19.00W
Jolfā	8	Jd	60.49N	23.28 E
Joliet	7	Ec	66.36N	19.51 E
Joliette	8	Cc	61.03N	8.12 E
Jolo	24	Kc	38.57N	45.38 E
Jolo Group ▭	43	Jc	41.32N	88.05W
Jølstravatnet ▭	42	Kg	46.01N	73.26W
Jomala	26	He	6.00N	121.00 E
Jombang	20	Oi	6.00N	121.09 E
Jomda	8	Bc	61.30N	6.15 E
Jönåker	8	Hd	60.09N	19.58 E
Jonava/Ionava	26	Fh	7.33S	112.14 E
Joné	8	Gf	58.44N	16.40 E
Jones Bank	7	Fi	55.05N	24.17 E
Jonesboro [Ar.-U.S.]	9	Fl	49.50N	8.00W
Jonesboro [La.-U.S.]	43	Id	35.50N	90.42W
Jones Mountains ▲	45	Jj	32.15N	92.43W
Jones Sound	66	Pf	73.32S	94.00W
Jonesville	58	Kb	76.00N	85.00W
Jonglei	36	Nc	36.41N	83.06W
Jonglei ▭	35	Ed	7.20N	32.00 E

Name	Map	Grid	Lat	Long
Jonglei	35	Ed	6.50N	31.18 E
Jonglei, Tur'ah- = Jonglei Canal (EN) ▭	35	Ed	9.22N	31.30 E
Jonglei Canal (EN) = Jonglei, Tur'ah-	35	Ed	9.22N	31.30 E
Joniškėlis/Ioniškelis	8	Ki	56.00N	24.14 E
Joniškis/Ioniškis	7	Fh	56.16N	23.37 E
Jönköping	6	Hd	57.47N	14.11 E
Jönköping ▭	7	Dh	57.30N	14.30 E
Jonquière	42	Kg	48.25N	71.15W
Jonuta	48	Mh	18.05N	92.08W
Jonzac	11	Fi	45.27N	0.26W
Joplin	39	Jf	37.06N	94.31W
Jordan	43	Fb	47.19N	106.55W
Jordan ▭	23	Ec	31.46N	35.33 E
Jordan (EN) = Al Urdun ▭	23	Ec	31.00N	36.00 E
Jordan Valley	46	Ge	42.58N	117.03W
Jordão, Rio- ▭	55	Fg	25.46S	52.07W
Jorhāt	22	Lg	26.45N	94.13 E
Jörn	7	Ed	65.04N	20.02 E
Joroinen	7	Ge	62.11N	27.50 E
Jørpeland	7	Bg	59.01N	6.03 E
Jos	31	Hh	9.55N	8.54 E
José A. Guisasola	55	Bn	38.40S	61.05W
José Battle y Ordóñez	56	Ek	33.28S	55.07W
José Bonifácio	55	He	21.03S	49.41W
José de San Martin	54	Fh	44.02S	70.29W
Joselandia	55	Dc	16.32S	56.12W
José Otávio	55	Ej	31.17S	54.07W
José Pedro Varela	56	Ek	33.27S	54.32W
Joseph, Lake-	44	Hc	45.14N	79.45W
Joseph Bonaparte Gulf ◪	57	Df	14.55S	128.15 E
Josephine Seamount (EN)	5	Kh	36.52N	14.20W
Joseph Lake	25	Kf	52.48N	65.17W
Joshimath	25	Fb	30.34N	79.34 E
Joškar-Ola	6	Kd	56.40N	47.55 E
Jos Plateau ▲	30	Hh	10.00N	9.30 E
Josselin	11	Dg	47.57N	2.33W
Jostedalen ▭	8	Bc	61.35N	7.20 E
Jostedalsbreen ▭	7	Bd	61.40N	7.00 E
Jostefonn ▲	8	Bc	61.26N	6.43 E
Jost Van Dyke ⬥	51a	Db	18.28N	64.45W
Jotunheimen ▲	5	Gc	61.40N	8.20 E
Joubertberge ▲	37	Ac	18.45S	13.55 E
Joué-lès-Tours	11	Gg	47.21N	0.40 E
Jouquara, Rio- ▭	55	Db	15.06S	57.06W
Joure, Haskerland-	12	Hb	52.58N	5.47 E
Joutsa	7	Gf	61.44N	26.07 E
Joutseno	7	Gf	61.06N	28.30 E
Jovan, Deli- ▲	15	Fe	44.15N	22.13 E
Jovellanos	49	Gb	22.48N	81.12W
Joviânia	55	Hc	17.49S	49.30W
Jowhar	31	Lh	2.46N	45.32 E
Jow Kär	24	Me	34.26N	48.42 E
Jowzjān ▭	23	Kb	36.30N	66.00 E
Joya, Laguna de la- ▭	48	Mj	15.55N	93.40W
Jreida	32	Df	18.19N	16.03W
Jrian Jaya ▭	26	Kg	3.55S	138.00 E
Juan Aldama	47	Dd	24.19N	103.21W
Juana Ramírez, Isla- ⬥	48	Kg	21.50N	97.40W
Juan Blanquier	55	Cl	35.46S	59.18W
Juancheng	28	Cg	35.33N	115.30 E
Juan de Fuca, Strait of-	38	Gk	48.20N	124.00W
Juan de Nova, Ile- ⬥	30	Lj	17.03S	42.45 E
Juan E. Barra	55	Bm	37.48S	60.29W
Juan Fernández, Archipelago- = Juan Fernández, Islands (EN) ▭	52	Ii	33.00S	80.00W
Juan Fernández Islands (EN) = Juan Fernández, Archipelago- ▭	52	Ii	33.00S	80.00W
Juan G. Bazán	55	Bg	24.33S	60.50W
Juanguinejo	50	Fg	11.05N	63.57W
Juanjuy	54	Ce	7.11S	76.45W
Juan L. Lacaze	55	Dl	34.26S	57.27W
Juárez [Arg.]	56	Ie	37.40S	59.48W
Juárez [Mex.]	48	Id	27.37N	100.44W
Juárez, Sierra de- ▲	48	Bb	32.00N	115.60W
Juarzohn	34	Dd	5.20N	8.58W
Juàzeirinho	54	Fc	7.04S	36.35W
Juàzeiro	53	Lf	9.25S	40.30W
Juàzeiro do Norte	54	Mf	7.12S	39.20W
Jūbā	31	Kh	4.51N	31.37 E
Juba (EN) = Ganāne, Webi- ▭	30	Lh	0.15S	42.38 E
Jūbāl, Maḍīq- ▭	24	Ei	27.40N	33.55 E
Jubaland (EN) ▭	30	Lh	1.00N	42.00 E
Jubayl [Eg.]	24	Ee	28.12N	33.38 E
Jubayl [Leb.]	24	Fe	34.07N	35.39 E
Jubayt [Sud.]	35	Fb	18.57N	36.50 E
Jubayt [Sud.]	35	Fa	20.59N	36.18 E
Jubbada Dhexe ▭	35	Ge	1.15N	42.30 E
Jubbada Hoose ▭	35	Gf	0.30S	42.00 E
Jubbah	24	Ih	28.02N	40.56 E
Jubilee Lake ▭	59	Fe	29.10S	126.40 E
Juby, Cap- ▶	30	Ff	27.57N	12.55W
Júcar/Xúquer ▭	13	Lf	39.09N	0.14W
Juçara	55	Gb	15.53S	50.51W
Jucaro	49	Hc	21.37N	78.51W
Jüchen	12	Ic	51.06N	6.30 E
Juchipila	48	Hg	21.25N	103.07W
Juchipila, Rio- ▭	48	Hf	21.20N	103.25W
Juchitán de Zaragoza	39	Jh	16.26N	95.01W
Jučugej	20	Jd	63.20N	142.15 E
Juàzeiro do Norte	20	Jd	63.20N	142.15 E
Jucurutu	54	Me	5.33S	37.02W
Judayyidat 'Ar'ar	23	Fc	31.22N	41.26 E
Judenburg	14	Ic	47.10N	14.40 E
Juding Shan ▲	27	Hf	31.30N	104.00 E
Judith Mountains ▲	43	Kc	47.12N	109.15W
Judith River ▭	46	Kc	47.44N	109.38W
Judoma ▭	20	Ie	59.08N	135.03 E
Judomski Hrebet ▲	20	Jd	61.05N	141.30 E
Juegang → Rudong	28	Fh	32.19N	121.11 E
Juelsminde	8	Dj	55.43N	10.01 E

Name	Map	Grid	Lat	Long
Jufrah, Wāḩāt al- = Giofra Oasis (EN) ▭	30	If	29.10N	16.00 E
Jug ▭	5	Kc	60.45N	46.20 E
Jug	17	Hh	57.43N	56.12 E
Jugo-Osetinskaja Avtonomnaja Oblast ▭	19	Ig	42.20N	44.05 E
Jugorski Poluostrov ▲	17	Kb	69.30N	62.30 E
Jugorski Šar, Proliv- ▭	19	Gb	69.45N	60.35 E
Jugoslavija → Yugoslavia (EN) ▭	6	Hg	44.00N	19.00 E
Jugo-Tala	20	Kc	66.03N	151.05 E
Jugydjan	17	Gf	61.42N	54.58 E
Juhaym	24	Kh	29.36N	45.24 E
Juhnov	16	Ib	54.43N	35.12 E
Juhor ▲	15	Ef	43.50N	21.15 E
Juhua Dao ⬥	28	Fd	40.32N	120.48 E
Juigalpa	49	Eg	12.05N	85.24W
Juina, Rio- ▭	55	Ca	12.36S	58.57W
Juine ▭	11	If	48.32N	2.23 E
Juininha, Rio- ▭	55	Ca	12.55S	59.13W
Juist ⬥	10	Cc	53.40N	7.00 E
Juiz de Fora	53	Ng	21.45S	43.20W
Jujuy ▭	56	Gb	23.00S	66.00W
Jukagirskoje Ploskogorje ▲	20	Kc	66.00N	155.30 E
Jukonda ▭	17	Mg	59.38N	67.20 E
Juksejevo	17	Jg	59.52N	54.16 E
Jula ▭	7	Ke	63.48N	44.44 E
Juldybajevo	17	Jj	52.20N	57.52 E
Julesburg	45	Ef	40.59N	102.16W
Juli	54	Fg	16.13S	69.27W
Juliaca	52	Hg	15.30S	70.08W
Julia Creek	59	Id	20.39S	141.45 E
Julian Alps (EN) = Julijske Alpe ▲	14	Hd	46.20N	13.45 E
Juliana Top ▲	54	Gc	3.41N	56.32W
Julianehâb/Qaqortoq	67	Nc	60.50N	46.10W
Jülich	10	Cf	50.56N	6.22 E
Jülicher Börde ▭	12	Id	50.50N	6.30 E
Julijske Alpe = Julian Alps (EN) ▲	14	Hd	46.20N	13.45 E
Julimes	48	Gc	28.25N	105.27W
Júlio de Castilhos	55	Fi	29.14S	53.41W
Jullundur	22	Jf	31.19N	75.34 E
Julong/New Kowloon	22	Ng	22.20N	114.09 E
Julu	28	Cf	37.13N	115.02 E
Juma	7	Hd	65.05N	33.13 E
Juma He ▭	28	De	39.31N	116.08 E
Jumaynah, Ra's al- ▲	24	Eh	29.01N	33.58 E
Jumbe	48	De	24.50N	111.47W
Jumento Cays (EN) = Jumentos Cays ⬥	49	Ic	22.30N	75.45W
Jumet, Charleroi-	11	Kd	50.27N	4.26 E
Jumièges	12	Ce	49.26N	0.49 E
Jumilla	13	Kf	38.29N	1.17W
Jümme ▭	12	Ja	53.13N	7.31 E
Junagādh	25	Ed	21.31N	70.28 E
Junan (Shizilu)	28	Eg	35.10N	118.50 E
Junaynah, Ra's al- ▲	24	Eh	29.01N	33.58 E
Juncal	48	De	24.50N	111.47W
Juncos	51a	Cb	18.13N	65.55W
Junction [Tx.-U.S.]	45	Gk	30.29N	99.46W
Junction [Ut.-U.S.]	46	Ig	38.14N	112.13W
Junction City	43	Hd	39.02N	96.50W
Jundiaí	56	Kb	23.11S	46.52W
Jundiai do Sul	55	Gg	23.27S	50.17W
Jundúbah	32	Ia	36.30N	8.45 E
Jundúbah ▭	32	Ib	36.28N	8.41 E
Juneau	39	Fd	57.20N	134.27W
Junee	59	Jf	34.52S	147.35 E
Jungar Qi (Shagedu)	27	Jd	39.37N	110.58 E
Jungfrau ▲	14	Bd	46.32N	7.58 E
Junggar Pendi = Dzungarian Basin ▭	21	Ke	45.00N	88.00 E
Junín ▭	54	Df	11.30S	75.00W
Junín [Arg.]	53	Ji	34.35S	60.57W
Junín [Peru]	54	Cf	11.10S	76.00W
Junín, Lago de- ▭	54	Cf	11.02S	76.05W
Junín de los Andes	56	Fe	39.56S	71.05W
Juniville	12	Ge	49.24N	4.23 E
Jūniyah	24	Ff	33.59N	35.38 E
Junjaha ▭	17	Jc	66.25N	62.00 E
Junlian	27	Hf	28.12N	104.34 E
Junsele	7	De	63.41N	16.54 E
Juntura	46	Fe	43.45N	118.05W
Junxian (Danjiang)	27	Ja	32.31N	111.32 E
Juodupè	8	Kh	56.03N	25.44 E
Juojärvi ▭	8	Mb	62.45N	28.35 E
Juoksengi	7	Fe	66.34N	23.51 E
Jupiá, Represa de- ▭	55	Hf	20.47S	51.39W
Juquiá	55	Ig	24.19S	47.38W
Juquiá, Rio- ▭	55	Ig	24.22S	47.49W
Jur ▭	20	Ie	59.48N	137.29 E
Jur ▭	30	Jh	8.39N	29.18 E
Jura ▭	14	Ac	47.25N	6.15 E
Jura ▭	5	Gf	46.45N	6.30 E
Jura ⬥	11	Jh	46.50N	5.50W
Jūra ▭	9	Hf	56.00N	5.50W
Jūra/Jūra ▭	7	Fi	55.03N	22.10 E
Jūra, Sound of- ▭	9	Hf	55.55S	5.22W
Juradó	54	Cb	7.07N	77.46W
Juratiški	8	Kj	54.02N	26.00 E
Jurayb ▭	24	Jh	29.09N	46.03 E
Jurayby'āt	24	Jk	29.08N	45.30 E
Jurbarkas	7	Fi	55.05N	22.46 E
Jurdī, Wādī- ▭	24	Ec	28.20N	32.44 E
Jurga	20	De	55.42N	84.55 E
Jurgamyš	17	Nb	55.32N	64.55 E
Jurjaha ▭	17	Jc	66.42N	56.00 E
Jurjev-Polski	16	Ja	56.31N	39.44 E
Jurjuzan ▭	17	Hj	54.56N	56.57 E
Jurjuzan	17	Ij	54.52N	58.28 E
Jurla	17	Hg	59.20N	54.16 E

Name	Map	Grid	Lat	Long
Jurmala/Jūrmala	19	Cd	56.59N	23.38 E
Jūrmala/Jurmala	19	Cd	56.59N	23.38 E
Jurmo ⬥	8	Ie	59.50N	21.35 E
Jurong	28	Ei	31.56N	119.10 E
Juruá	54	Be	3.27S	66.03W
Juruá, Rio- ▭	52	Jf	2.37S	65.44W
Juruena, Rio- ▭	52	Kf	7.20S	58.03W
Jurumirim, Represa de- ▭	56	Kb	23.20S	49.00W
Juruti	54	Gd	2.09S	56.04W
Jurva	8	Ib	62.41N	21.59 E
Jusan-Kō ▭	29a	Bc	41.00N	140.20 E
Jusayrah	24	Nj	25.53N	50.36 E
Jusheng	27	Mb	48.44N	126.37 E
Ju Shui ▭	28	Ci	31.09N	114.52 E
Juškozero	19	Dc	64.45N	32.08 E
Jussarö ⬥	8	Je	59.50N	23.35 E
Justo Daract	56	Gd	33.52S	65.11W
Jusva	17	Gg	58.59N	54.57 E
Jutai	54	Ee	5.11S	68.54W
Jutai, Rio- ▭	52	Jf	2.43S	66.57W
Jüterbg	10	Je	51.59N	13.05 E
Juti	55	Ef	22.52S	54.37W
Jutiapa ▭	49	Bf	14.10N	89.54W
Jutiapa [Guat.]	47	Gf	14.17N	89.54W
Jutiapa [Hond.]	49	Df	15.46N	86.34W
Juticalpa	47	Gf	14.42N	86.15W
Jutland (EN) = Jylland ▭	5	Gd	56.00N	9.15 E
Juuka	7	Ge	63.14N	29.15 E
Juva	7	Gf	61.54N	27.51 E
Juventud, Isla de la- = Pines, Isle of- (EN) ⬥	38	Kg	21.40N	82.50W
Juxian	27	Kd	35.33N	118.45 E
Jüybār	24	Od	36.38N	52.53 E
Juye	28	Dg	35.23N	116.05 E
Jüyom	24	Oh	28.10N	54.02 E
Juža	7	Kh	56.36N	42.01 E
Južnaja Keltma ▭	17	Gf	60.30N	55.40 E
Južna Morava ▭	15	Ef	43.41N	21.24 E
Južni Rodopi ▲	15	Ji	41.15N	25.30 E
Južnoje	20	Jg	46.13N	143.27 E
Južno-Jenisejski	20	Ee	58.48N	94.45 E
Južno-Kurilsk	20	Jh	44.05N	145.52 E
Južno-Sahalinsk	22	Qe	46.58N	142.42 E
Južno-Uralsk	20	Ke	52.46N	61.15 E
Južnyj, Mys- ▶	20	Ke	57.42N	156.55 E
Južny Bug ▭	5	Jf	46.59N	31.58 E
Južny Ural = Southern Urals (EN) ▲	5	Le	54.00N	58.30 E
Jygeva/Jõgeva	7	Gg	58.46N	26.26 E
Jylland = Jutland (EN) ▭	5	Gd	56.00N	9.15 E
Jylland Bank	8	Bh	56.55N	7.20 E
Jyske Ås	8	Dg	57.15N	10.14 E
Jyväskylä	6	Ic	62.14N	25.44 E

K

Name	Map	Grid	Lat	Long
K2 = Godwin Austen (EN) ▲	21	Jf	35.53N	76.30 E
Ka ▭	34	Fc	11.39N	4.11 E
Kaabong	36	Fb	3.31N	34.09 E
Kaahka	19	Fh	37.21N	59.38 E
Kaala ▲	65a	Cb	21.31N	158.09W
Kaala-Gomén	63b	Be	20.40S	164.24 E
Kaalualu Bay ◪	65a	Fe	18.58N	155.37W
Kaamanen	7	Gb	69.06N	27.12 E
Kaap Kruis	37	Ad	21.46S	13.58 E
Kaap Plateau (EN) = Kaapplato ▲	30	Jk	27.30S	23.45 E
Kaapplato = Kaap Plateau (EN) ▲	30	Jk	27.30S	23.45 E
Kaapprovinsie/Cape Province ▭	37	Cf	32.00S	22.00 E
Kaapstad / Cape Town	31	Il	33.55S	18.22 E
Kaarst	12	Ic	51.15N	6.37 E
Kaarta ▭	34	Cc	14.35N	10.00W
Kaba/Habahe	27	Bb	43.57N	86.12 E
Kabaena, Pulau- ⬥	26	Hh	5.15S	121.55 E
Kabah ⬙	48	Og	20.07N	89.29W
Kabala	34	Cd	9.35N	11.33W
Kabale	36	Ec	1.15S	29.59 E
Kabalega Falls ⬙	36	Fb	2.17N	31.41 E
Kabalo	31	Ji	6.03S	26.55 E
Kabamare	36	Eb	1.34N	27.07 E
Kabamet	36	Gb	0.30N	35.45 E
Kabanjahe	26	Cf	3.06N	98.30 E
Kabardino-Balkarskaja ASSR ▭	19	Gg	43.30N	43.30 E
Kabare	36	Ec	2.29S	28.48 E
Kabasalan	26	He	7.48N	122.45 E
Kaba-Shima [Jap.] ⬥	29	Ae	32.34N	129.47 E
Kaba-Shima [Jap.] ⬥	29	Ae	32.34N	129.47 E
Kabba	34	Gd	7.50N	6.04 E
Kâbdalis	7	Ec	66.09N	20.00 E
Kaberamaido	36	Fb	1.45N	33.10 E
Kabetogama Lake ▭	45	Jb	48.28N	92.59W
Kabhegy ▲	10	Ni	47.03N	17.39 E
Kabinda	31	Ji	6.08S	24.29 E
Kabir, Wādī al- ▭	14	Dn	36.33N	9.52 E
Kabīr Kūh ▲	24	Lf	33.25N	46.45 E
Kabkābīyah	35	Cc	13.39N	24.05 E
Kableškovo	15	Kg	42.39N	27.34 E
Kabna	35	Eb	19.10N	32.41 E
Kabo	35	Bd	7.35N	18.38 E
Kabompo	36	De	13.36S	24.12 E
Kabompo ▭	36	Ed	8.53S	25.40 E
Kabongo	36	Ed	7.19S	25.35 E
Kabou	34	Fd	9.27N	0.49 E
Kabūdīyah, Ra's- ▶	32	Jb	35.14N	11.10 E
Kabūd Rāhang	24	Me	35.13N	48.44 E
Kābul	22	If	34.31N	69.12 E
Kābul ▭	23	Kc	34.50N	69.00 E
Kābul ▭	21	Jf	33.55N	72.14 E
Kabunda	36	Ee	12.13S	29.23 E

Index Symbols

① Independent Nation	⬒ Historical or Cultural Region	⬓ Pass, Gap
② State, Region	▲ Mount, Mountain	⬓ Plain, Lowland
③ District, County	▲ Volcano	⬓ Delta
④ Municipality	▲ Hill	⬓ Salt Flat
⑤ Colony, Dependency	▲ Mountains, Mountain Range	⬓ Valley, Canyon
⬒ Continent	▲ Hills, Escarpment	⬓ Crater, Cave
⬓ Physical Region	▲ Plateau, Upland	⬓ Karst Features

⬓ Depression	⬓ Coast, Beach	⬓ Rock, Reef
⬓ Polder	⬓ Cliff	⬓ Islands, Archipelago
⬓ Desert, Dunes	⬓ Peninsula	⬓ Rocks, Reefs
⬓ Forest, Woods	⬓ Isthmus	⬓ Coral Reef
⬓ Heath, Steppe	⬓ Sandbank	⬓ Well, Spring
⬓ Oasis	⬓ Island	⬓ Geyser
⬓ Cape, Point	⬓ Atoll	⬓ River, Stream

⬓ Waterfall Rapids	⬓ Canal	⬓ Lagoon
⬓ River Mouth, Estuary	⬓ Glacier	⬓ Bank
⬓ Lake	⬓ Ice Shelf, Pack Ice	⬓ Seamount
⬓ Salt Lake	⬓ Ocean	⬓ Tablemount
⬓ Intermittent Lake	⬓ Sea	⬓ Ridge
⬓ Reservoir	⬓ Shelf	⬓ Shelf
⬓ Swamp, Pond	⬓ Strait, Fjord	⬓ Basin

⬓ Escarpment, Sea Scarp	⬓ Historic Site	⬓ Port
⬓ Fracture	⬓ Ruins	⬓ Lighthouse
⬓ Trench, Abyss	⬓ Wall, Walls	⬓ Mine
⬓ National Park, Reserve	⬓ Church, Abbey	⬓ Tunnel
⬓ Point of Interest	⬓ Temple	⬓ Dam, Bridge
⬓ Recreation Site	⬓ Scientific Station	
⬓ Cave, Cavern	⬓ Airport	

Kabunga 36 Ec 1.42S 28.08 E
Kaburuang, Pulau- 26 If 3.48N 126.48 E
Kabushi-ga-Take 29 Fd 35.54N 138.44 E
Kabwe 31 Jj 14.27S 28.27 E
Kabylie 32 Ib 36.15N 5.25 E
Kača 16 Hg 44.44N 33.32 E
Kačanik 15 Eg 42.14N 21.15 E
Kačanovo 8 Lg 57.24N 27.53 E
Kačergine 8 Jj 54.53N 23.49 E
Kachia 34 Gd 9.52N 7.57 E
Kachikau 37 Cc 18.09S 24.29 E
Kachin 25 Jc 26.00N 97.30 E
Kačiry 19 He 53.04N 76.07 E
Kačkanar 19 Fd 58.42N 59.35 E
Kačug 20 Ff 54.00N 105.52 E
Kaczawa 10 Me 51.18N 16.27 E
Kadada 16 Oc 53.09N 46.01 E
Kadań 10 Jf 50.23N 13.16 E
Kadan Kyun 25 Jf 12.30N 98.22 E
Kadeï 30 Ih 3.31N 16.03 E
Kadijevka 19 Df 48.32N 38.40 E
Kadiköy 24 Bb 40.51N 26.50 E
Kadıköy, İstanbul 15 Mi 40.59N 29.01 E
Kadina 59 Hf 33.58S 137.43 E
Kadınhanı 24 Ec 38.15N 32.14 E
Kadiolo 34 Dc 10.34N 5.45W
Kadiri 25 Ff 14.07N 78.10 E
Kadirli 23 Eb 37.23N 36.05 E
Kadja 35 Cc 12.02N 22.28 E
Kadmat Island 25 Ef 11.14N 72.47 E
Kadnikov 7 Jg 59.30N 40.24 E
Kadoka 45 Fe 43.50N 101.31W
Kaduj 7 Ig 59.14N 37.09 E
Kaduna 34 Gc 11.00N 7.30 E
Kaduna 30 Hh 8.45N 5.48 E
Kaduna 31 Hg 10.31N 7.26 E
Kāduqlī 31 Jg 11.01N 29.43 E
Kadykčan 20 Jd 63.05N 146.58 E
Kadžaran 16 Oj 39.11N 46.10 E
Kadžerom 17 Gd 64.41N 55.54 E
Kadži-Saj 18 Kc 42.08N 77.10 E
Kaech'ŏn 28 He 39.42N 125.53 E
Kaédi 31 Fg 16.08N 13.31W
Kaélé 34 Hc 10.07N 14.27 E
Kaena Point 65a Cb 21.35N 158.17W
Kaeo 62 Ea 35.06S 173.47 E
Kaesŏng 22 Of 37.58N 126.33 E
Kaesŏng Si 28 Ie 38.05N 126.30 E
Kāf 24 Gg 31.24N 37.29 E
Kafakumba 36 Dd 9.41S 23.44 E
Kafan 19 Eh 39.12N 46.28 E
Kafanchan 34 Gd 9.35N 8.18 E
Kaffrine 34 Bc 14.06N 15.33W
Kafia Kingi 35 Cd 9.16N 24.25 E
Kafiréos, Dhiékplous- 15 Hl 38.00N 24.40 E
Kafirévs, Ákra- 15 Hk 38.10N 24.35 E
Kafr ad Dawwār 24 Dg 31.08N 30.07 E
Kafr ash Shaykh 33 Fc 31.07N 30.56 E
Kafta 35 Fc 13.54N 37.11 E
Kafu 36 Fb 1.39N 32.05 E
Kafue 30 Ef 15.56S 28.55 E
Kafue 31 Jj 15.47S 28.11 E
Kafue Dam 36 Ef 15.45S 28.28 E
Kafue Flats 36 Ef 15.40S 26.25 E
Kafufu 36 Fd 7.12S 31.31 E
Kaga 28 Nf 36.18N 136.18 E
Kaga Bandoro 35 Bd 7.02N 19.13 E
Kagalaska 40a Cb 51.47N 176.23W
Kagalnik 16 Kf 47.04N 39.18 E
Kagami 29 Be 32.34N 130.40 E
Kagan 19 Gh 39.43N 64.32 E
Kagarlyk 16 Ge 49.53N 30.56 E
Kagawa Ken 28 Mg 34.15N 134.15 E
Kagera 30 Ki 0.57S 31.47 E
Kağızman 24 Jb 40.09N 43.07 E
Kagoshima 22 Pf 31.36N 130.33 E
Kagoshima Bay (EN) = Kagoshima-Wan 28 Ki 31.27N 130.40 E
Kagoshima Ken 28 Ki 31.45N 130.40 E
Kagoshima-Taniyama 29 Bf 31.31N 130.31 E
Kagoshima-Wan = Kagoshima Bay (EN) 28 Ki 31.27N 130.40 E
Kagul 15 Ld 45.32N 28.27 E
Kagul 19 Cf 45.53N 28.14 E
Kahal Tabelbala 32 Gd 28.45N 2.15W
Kahama 36 Fc 3.50S 32.36 E
Kahemba 31 Ii 7.17S 19.00 E
Kahi 16 Oi 41.23N 46.59 E
Kahiu Point 65a Eb 21.13N 156.58W
Kahler Asten 10 Ee 51.11N 8.29 E
Kahnūj 24 Qi 27.58N 57.47 E
Kahoku 29 Gb 38.30N 141.20 E
Kahoku-Gata 29 Ec 36.40N 136.40 E
Kahoolawe Island 57 Lb 20.33N 156.35W
Kahouanne, Ilet à- 51e Ab 16.22N 61.47W
Kahovka 19 Df 46.47N 33.32 E
Kahovskoje Vodohranilišče = Kakhovka Reservoir (EN) 5 Jf 47.25N 34.10 E
Kahramanmaraş 23 Eb 37.36N 36.55 E
Kahrūyeh 24 Ng 31.43N 51.48 E
Kāhta 24 Hd 37.46N 38.36 E
Kahuku 65a Db 21.41N 157.57W
Kahuku Point 65a Db 21.43N 157.59W
Kahului 65a Ec 20.53N 156.27W
Kahului Bay 65a Ec 20.55N 156.30W
Kahurangi Point 62 Ed 40.46S 172.13 E
Kai, Kepulauan- 57 Ee 5.35S 132.45 E
Kaiama 34 Fd 9.36N 3.57 E
Kaiapoi 62 Ee 43.23S 172.39 E
Kaibab Plateau 46 Ih 36.30N 112.15W
Kai Besar 26 Jh 5.35S 133.00 E
Kaidu He/Karaxabar He 27 Ec 41.55N 86.38 E
Kaieteur Falls 54 Gc 5.10N 59.28W
Kaifeng 22 Nf 34.45N 114.25 E
Kaihua 28 Ej 29.10N 118.24 E
Kai Kecil 26 Jh 5.45S 132.40 E
Kaikohe 62 Ea 35.24S 173.48 E
Kaikoura 61 Dh 42.25S 173.41 E
Kaili 27 If 26.35N 107.59 E
Kailu 27 Lc 43.37N 121.19 E
Kailua [Hi.-U.S.] 65a Fd 19.39N 155.59W
Kailua [Hi.-U.S.] 65a Db 21.23N 157.44W
Kaimana 26 Jg 3.39S 133.45 E
Kaimanawa Mountains 62 Fc 39.15S 176.00 E
Kaimon-Dake 29 Bf 31.10N 130.32 E
Kain, Tournai- 12 Fd 50.38N 3.22 E
Kainach 14 Jd 46.54N 15.31 E
Kainan [Jap.] 29 Dd 34.09N 135.12 E
Kainan [Jap.] 29 De 33.36N 134.22 E
Kainantu 60 Di 6.15S 145.53 E
Kainji Dam 34 Fd 9.55N 4.40 E
Kainji Reservoir 34 Fc 10.30N 4.35 E
Kaipara Harbour 62 Fb 36.25S 174.15 E
Kaiparowits Plateau 46 Jh 37.20N 111.15W
Kaiser Franz Josephs Fjord 41 Jd 73.30N 24.00W
Kaisersesch 12 Jd 50.14N 7.09 E
Kaiserslautern 10 Dg 49.27N 7.45 E
Kaiserstuhl 10 Dh 48.06N 7.40 E
Kaishantun 27 Mc 42.43N 129.37 E
Kaišiadorys/Kajšjadoris 7 Fi 54.53N 24.31 E
Kaita 29 Cd 34.20N 132.32 E
Kaitaia 62 Ea 35.07S 173.14 E
Kaitangata 62 Cg 46.17S 169.51 E
Kaithal 25 Fc 29.48N 76.23 E
Kaitong → Tongyu 27 Lc 44.47N 123.05 E
Kaituma River 50 Gh 8.11N 59.41W
Kaiwaka 61 Dg 36.10S 174.26 E
Kaiwi Channel 60 Oc 21.13N 157.30W
Kaixian 27 Ie 31.10N 108.25 E
Kaiyuan [China] 27 Lc 42.33N 124.04 E
Kaiyuan [China] 27 Hg 23.47N 103.15 E
Kaiyuh Mountains 40 Hd 64.00N 158.00W
Kaja 30 Jg 12.02N 22.28 E
Kajaani 6 Ic 64.14N 27.41 E
Kajaapu 26 Dh 5.26S 102.24 E
Kajabbi 58 Fg 20.02S 140.02 E
Kajak 20 Fb 71.30N 103.15 E
Kajang 26 Df 2.59N 101.47 E
Kajdak, Sor- 16 Rg 44.40N 53.30 E
Kajerkan 20 Dc 69.25N 87.30 E
Kajiado 36 Gc 1.51S 36.47 E
Kajiki 29 Bf 31.44N 130.40 E
Kajmakčalan 15 Ei 40.58N 21.48 E
Kajnar 15 Lb 47.50N 28.06 E
Kajo Kaji 35 Ee 3.53N 31.40 E
Kajrakkumskoje Vodohranilišče 18 Hd 40.20N 70.05 E
Kajrakty 19 Hf 48.31N 73.14 E
Kajšjadoris/Kaišiadorys 7 Fi 54.53N 24.31 E
Kajuru 34 Gc 10.19N 7.41 E
Kaka 35 Fd 7.28N 39.06 E
Kākā 35 Ec 10.36N 32.11 E
Kakagi Lake 45 Jb 49.13N 93.52W
Kakamas 37 Ce 28.45S 20.33 E
Kakamega 36 Fb 0.17N 34.45 E
Kakamigahara 29 Ed 35.25N 136.50 E
Kakanj 14 Mf 44.08N 18.05 E
Kaka Point 65a Ec 20.32N 156.33W
Kakata 34 Cd 6.32N 10.21W
Kake 29 Cd 34.36N 132.19 E
Kakegawa 29 Ed 34.46N 138.00 E
Kakenge 36 Dc 4.51S 21.55 E
Kakeroma-Jima 29b Ba 28.08N 129.15 E
Kakhovka Reservoir (EN) = Kahovskoje Vodohranilišče 5 Jf 47.25N 34.10 E
Kākī 24 Nh 28.19N 51.34 E
Kākināda 22 Kh 16.56N 82.13 E
Kakisa Lake 42 Fd 60.55N 117.40W
Kakizaki 29 Fc 37.16N 138.22 E
Kaklkan 24 Cd 36.15N 29.24 E
Kakogawa 29 Dd 34.46N 134.51 E
Kakpin 34 Ed 8.39N 3.48W
Kaktovik 40 Kb 70.08N 143.37W
Kakuda 29 Gc 37.58N 140.47 E
Kakuma 36 Fb 3.43N 34.52 E
Kakunodate 28 Pe 39.40N 140.32 E
Kakva 17 Jg 59.37N 60.50 E
Kakya 36 Gc 1.36S 39.02 E
Kalaa 13 Mi 35.35N 0.20 E
Kalaa Khasba 14 Co 35.38N 8.36 E
Kalaallit Nunaat/Grønland = Greenland (EN) 39 Pb 70.00N 40.00W
Kalaallit Nunaat/Grønland = Greenland (EN) 38 Pb 70.00N 40.00W
Kalabahi 26 Hh 8.13S 124.31 E
Kalabáka 15 Ej 39.42N 21.38 E
Kalabera 64b Ba 15.14N 145.48 E
Kalabo 36 De 14.58S 22.41 E
Kalābsha 33 Fe 23.33N 32.50 E
Kalač 19 Ee 50.23N 41.01 E
Kalačinsk 19 Hd 55.03N 74.34 E
Kalač-na-Donu 19 Ef 48.43N 43.32 E
Kaladan 25 Id 20.09N 92.57 E
Ka Lae 60 Od 18.55N 155.41W
Kalahari Desert 30 Jk 23.00S 22.00 E
Kalaheo 65a Bb 21.56N 159.32W
Kalai-Mor 19 Gh 35.37N 62.31 E
Kalaj Humo 18 He 38.25N 70.47 E
Kalajoki 7 Fd 64.15N 23.57 E
Kalakan 20 Ge 55.10N 116.45 E
Kalaldi 34 Hd 6.30N 14.04 E
Kalāleh 24 Pd 37.25N 55.40 E
Kalámai 6 Ih 37.02N 22.07 E
Kalamákion 15 Gl 37.55N 23.43 E
Kalamazoo 43 Jc 42.17N 85.32W
Kalambo Falls 36 Fd 8.36S 31.14 E
Kalamitski Zaliv 16 Hg 45.00N 33.25 E
Kálamos 15 Dk 38.37N 20.55 E
Kalamunda, Perth- 59 Df 31.57S 116.03 E
Kalan 23 Eb 39.07N 39.32 E
Kalandula 31 Ii 9.06S 15.58 E
Kalanshiyū, Sarīr- 30 Jf 27.00N 21.30 E
Kalao, Pulau- 26 Hh 7.18S 120.58 E
Kalaotoa, Pulau- 26 Hh 7.22S 121.47 E
Kalapana 65a Gd 19.21N 154.59W
Kalaraš 16 Ff 47.16N 28.16 E
Kälarne 8 Gb 62.59N 16.05 E
Kalarski Hrebet 20 Ge 56.30N 118.50 E
Kalasin [Indon.] 26 Ff 0.12N 114.16 E
Kalasin [Thai.] 25 Ke 16.29N 103.31 E
Kalāt 25 Dc 29.02N 66.35 E
Kalāteh 24 Pd 36.29N 54.10 E
Kalau 65b Bc 21.28S 174.57W
Kalaupapa 65a Eb 21.12N 156.59W
Kalaus 16 Ng 45.43N 44.07 E
Kalavárdha 15 Km 36.20N 27.57 E
Kálavrita 15 Fk 38.02N 22.07 E
Kalbā' 24 Qj 25.03N 56.21 E
Kalbīyah, Sabkhat al- 14 Eo 35.51N 10.17 E
Kaldbakur 7a Ab 65.49N 23.39W
Kaldygajty 16 Re 49.20N 52.38 E
Kale [Tur.] 24 Cd 37.26N 28.51 E
Kale [Tur.] 24 Cd 36.14N 29.59 E
Kalecik 24 Eb 40.06N 33.25 E
Kalehe 36 Ec 2.06S 28.55 E
Kalemie 31 Ji 5.56S 29.12 E
Kāl-e Shur 23 Jb 35.05N 60.59 E
Kalevala 19 Db 65.12N 31.10 E
Kalewa 25 Id 23.12N 94.18 E
Kaleybar 24 Lc 38.47N 47.02 E
Kalgoorlie 58 Dh 30.45S 121.28 E
Kaliakoúdha 15 Ek 38.48N 21.46 E
Kaliakra, Nos- 15 Lf 43.18N 28.30 E
Kalibo 26 Hd 11.43N 122.22 E
Kali Limni 15 Kn 35.35N 27.08 E
Kalima 31 Ji 2.34S 26.37 E
Kalimantan/Borneo 21 Ni 1.00N 114.00 E
Kalimantan Barat 26 Ff 0.01N 110.30 E
Kalimantan Selatan 26 Gg 2.30S 115.30 E
Kalimantan Tengah 26 Fg 2.00S 113.30 E
Kalimantan Timur 26 Gf 1.30N 116.30 E
Kálimnos 15 Jm 36.57N 26.59 E
Kálimnos 15 Jl 37.00N 27.00 E
Kalinin [R.S.F.S.R.] 6 Jd 56.52N 35.55 E
Kalinin [Tur.-U.S.S.R.] 19 Fg 42.07N 59.40 E
Kalininabad 18 Gf 37.53N 68.57 E
Kaliningrad [R.S.F.S.R.] 6 Ie 54.43N 20.30 E
Kaliningrad [R.S.F.S.R.] 7 Ii 55.55N 37.57 E
Kaliningradskaja Oblast 19 Ce 54.45N 21.20 E
Kalinino [Arm.-U.S.S.R.] 16 Ni 41.08N 44.14 E
Kalinino [R.S.F.S.R.] 16 Kg 45.05N 38.59 E
Kalininsk [Mold.-U.S.S.R.] 15 Ka 48.07N 27.16 E
Kalininsk [R.S.F.S.R.] 16 Nd 51.30N 44.30 E
Kalininskaja Oblast 19 Dd 57.20N 34.40 E
Kalinkoviči 19 Ce 52.07N 29.23 E
Kalino 17 Hg 58.15N 57.35 E
Kalinovik 14 Mg 43.31N 18.26 E
Kalinovka 16 Fe 49.29N 28.32 E
Kaliro 36 Fb 0.54N 33.30 E
Kalispell 39 He 48.12N 114.19W
Kalisz 10 Of 51.45N 18.05 E
Kalisz 10 Oe 51.46N 18.06 E
Kalisz Pomorski 10 Lc 53.19N 15.54 E
Kalitva 16 Le 48.10N 40.46 E
Kaliua 36 Fd 5.04S 31.48 E
Kalix 7 Fd 65.51N 23.08 E
Kalixälven 7 Fd 65.47N 23.13 E
Kalja 17 Jf 60.20N 60.01 E
Kaljazin 19 Dd 57.15N 37.55 E
Kalkandere 24 Ib 40.55N 40.28 E
Kalkar 12 Ic 51.44N 6.18 E
Kalkaska 44 Ec 44.44N 85.11W
Kalkfeld 37 Bd 20.53S 16.11 E
Kalkfontein 37 Cd 22.07S 20.54 E
Kalkim 15 Kj 39.48N 27.13 E
Kalkrand 37 Bd 24.03S 17.33 E
Kall 7 Ce 63.28N 13.15 E
Kållands Halvö 8 Ef 58.35N 13.05 E
Kållandsö 8 Ef 58.40N 13.10 E
Kallaste 7 Gg 58.41N 27.08 E
Kallavesi 5 Ic 62.50N 27.45 E
Kalletal 12 Kb 52.08N 8.57 E
Kallhäll 8 Ge 59.27N 17.48 E
Kallidhromon Óros 15 Fk 38.44N 22.34 E
Kallinge 7 Dh 56.14N 15.17 E
Kallonis, Kolpos- 15 Jj 39.07N 26.08 E
Kallsjön 7 Ce 63.35N 13.00 E
Kalmar 6 Hd 56.40N 16.22 E
Kalmar 7 Dh 57.20N 16.00 E
Kalmarsund 7 Dh 56.40N 16.25 E
Kalmit 12 Ke 49.19N 8.05 E
Kalmius 16 Jf 47.03N 37.34 E
Kalmthout 12 Gc 51.23N 4.28 E
Kalmyckaja ASSR 19 Ef 46.30N 45.30 E
Kalmykovo 16 Qe 49.05N 51.47 E
Kalnciems 8 Jh 56.48N 23.34 E
Kalnik 14 Kd 46.10N 16.30 E
Kalocsa 10 Oj 46.32N 19.00 E
Kalofer 15 Hg 42.37N 24.59 E
Kalohi Channel 65a Ec 21.00N 156.56W
Kaloko 36 Ed 6.47S 25.47 E
Kalole 36 Ec 3.42S 27.22 E
Kaloli Point 65a Gd 19.37N 154.57W
Kalomo 36 Ef 17.02S 26.30 E
Kalpa 25 Fb 31.37N 78.10 E
Kalpákion 15 Dj 39.53N 20.35 E
Kalpeni Island 25 Ef 10.05N 73.38 E
Kalpin 27 Cc 40.31N 79.03 E
Kalsūbai 21 Jh 19.36N 73.43 E
Kaltern/Caldaro 14 Fd 46.25N 11.14 E
Kaltungo 34 Hd 9.49N 11.19 E
Kaluga 6 Je 54.31N 36.16 E
Kalulushi 36 Ee 12.50S 28.05 E
Kalumburu Mission 59 Fb 14.18S 126.39 E
Kalundborg 7 Ci 55.41N 11.06 E
Kaluš 19 Cf 49.03N 24.23 E
Kałuszyn 10 Rd 52.13N 21.49 E
Kalužskaja Oblast 19 De 54.20N 35.30 E
Kalvåg 8 Ac 61.46N 4.53 E
Kalvarija 7 Fi 54.27N 23.14 E
Kalya 36 Fd 6.28S 30.03 E
Kalyān 25 Ee 19.15N 73.09 E
Kám 10 Mi 47.06N 16.53 E
Kama 36 Ec 3.32S 27.07 E
Kama [R.S.F.S.R.] 17 Nf 60.27N 69.00 E
Kama [U.S.S.R.] 5 Ld 55.45N 52.00 E
Kamae 29 Be 32.48N 131.56 E
Kamaï 35 Ba 21.12N 17.30 E
Kamaing 25 Jc 25.31N 96.44 E
Kamaishi 28 Pe 39.16N 141.53 E
Kamakou 65a Eb 21.07N 156.52W
Kamakura 29 Fd 35.19N 139.32 E
Kamālia 25 Eb 30.44N 72.39 E
Kamalo 65a Eb 21.03N 156.53W
Kaman 24 Ec 39.25N 33.45 E
Kamand, Āb-e- 24 Mf 33.28N 49.04 E
Kamanjab 37 Ac 19.35S 14.51 E
Kamanyola 36 Ec 2.46S 29.00 E
Kamaran 23 Ff 15.12N 42.35 E
Kamarang 54 Fb 5.53N 60.35W
Kama Reservoir (EN) = Kamskoje Vodohranilišče 5 Ld 58.50N 56.15 E
Kamaši 19 Gh 38.48N 66.29 E
Kamativi 37 Dc 18.19S 27.03 E
Kambalda 59 Ef 31.10S 121.37 E
Kambalnaja Sopka, Vulkan- 20 Kf 51.17N 156.57 E
Kambara 29 Fd 35.07N 138.36 E
Kambara 63d Cc 18.57S 178.57W
Kambarka 7 Nh 56.18N 54.14 E
Kambia 34 Cd 9.07N 12.55W
Kambja 8 Lf 58.11N 26.43 E
Kambove 36 Ee 10.52S 26.35 E
Kamčatka 20 Le 56.10N 162.30 E
Kamčatka, Poluostrov- = Kamchatka Peninsula (EN) 21 Rd 56.00N 160.00 E
Kamčatskaja Oblast 20 Kf 54.50N 159.00 E
Kamčatski Zaliv 20 Le 55.30N 163.00 E
Kamchatka Peninsula (EN) = Kamčatka, Poluostrov- 21 Rd 56.00N 160.00 E
Kamčija 15 Kf 43.02N 27.53 E
Kamčijska Plato 15 Kg 42.56N 27.32 E
Kameda [Jap.] 29 Fc 37.52N 139.06 E
Kameda [Jap.] 29a Bc 41.49N 140.46 E
Kameda-Hantō 29a Bc 41.45N 141.00 E
Kámeiros 15 Km 36.18N 27.56 E
Kamelik 16 Pc 52.06N 49.30 E
Kamen 12 Jc 51.36N 7.40 E
Kaménai 15 Im 36.25N 25.25 E
Kamende 36 Dd 6.28S 24.33 E
Kamenec 10 Td 52.23N 23.49 E
Kamenec-Podolski 19 Cf 48.39N 26.33 E
Kamenjak, Rt- 14 Hf 44.46N 13.56 E
Kamenka [Kaz.-U.S.S.R.] 16 Qd 51.07N 50.20 E
Kamenka [Mold.-U.S.S.R.] 16 Fe 48.03N 28.45 E
Kamenka [R.S.F.S.R.] 16 Kd 50.43N 39.25 E
Kamenka [R.S.F.S.R.] 19 Ee 53.13N 44.03 E
Kamenka [R.S.F.S.R.] 7 Kd 65.54N 44.04 E
Kamenka [R.S.F.S.R.] 28 Nb 44.28N 136.01 E
Kamenka [Ukr.-U.S.S.R.] 19 Df 49.03N 32.06 E
Kamenka-Bugskaja 10 Uf 50.01N 24.25 E
Kamenka-Dneprovskaja 16 If 47.29N 34.29 E
Kamen-Kaširski 16 Dd 51.36N 24.59 E
Kamen-na-Obi 20 Df 53.47N 81.20 E
Kamennogorsk 7 Gf 60.59N 29.12 E
Kamennoje, Ozero- 7 Hd 64.30N 30.15 E
Kamennomostski 16 Lg 44.17N 40.12 E
Kamen-Rybolov 28 Kb 44.45N 132.04 E
Kamenskoje 20 Ld 62.30N 166.12 E
Kamensk-Šahtinski 16 Le 48.18N 40.16 E
Kamensk-Uralski 22 Id 56.28N 61.54 E
Kamenz/Kamjenc 10 Ke 51.16N 14.06 E
Kameoka 29 Dd 35.00N 135.35 E
Kameškovo 7 Jh 56.22N 41.01 E
Kamet 25 Fd 30.55N 79.35 E
Kameyama 29 Ed 34.51N 136.27 E
Kami-Agata 29 Ad 34.38N 129.25 E
Kamiah 46 Gc 46.14N 116.02W
Kamicharo 29a Cb 43.11N 143.52 E
Kamienna 10 Re 51.06N 21.47 E
Kamienna Góra 10 Mf 50.47N 16.01 E
Kamień Pomorski 10 Kc 53.58N 14.46 E
Kamieńsk 10 Pe 51.12N 19.30 E
Kamieskroon 37 Bf 30.09S 17.56 E
Kami-furano 29a Cb 43.29N 142.27 E
Kamiiso 28 Pd 41.49N 140.39 E
Kamiita 29 Dd 34.08N 134.24 E
Kamiji 36 Dd 6.39S 23.17 E
Kamikawa 29a Cb 43.50N 142.47 E
Kami-Koshiki-Jima 29 Af 31.50N 129.55 E
Kamina 31 Ji 8.44S 24.59 E
Kaminak Lake 42 Id 62.13N 95.00W
Kaminokuni 29a Bc 41.48N 140.05 E
Kamino-Shima 29 Ad 34.30N 129.25 E
Kaminoyama 28 Pe 38.09N 140.17 E
Kaminuriak Lake 42 Hd 63.00N 95.45W
Kamioka 28 Nf 36.16N 137.18 E
Kami-shihoro 29a Cb 43.13N 143.16 E
Kamisunagawa 29a Bb 43.28N 141.58 E
Kamitsushima 29 Ad 34.39N 129.28 E
Kamituga 36 Ec 3.04S 28.11 E
Kamiyama 29 De 33.58N 134.21 E
Kami-yūbetsu 29a Ca 44.11N 143.34 E
Kamjenc/Kamenz 10 Ke 51.16N 14.06 E
Kamloops 39 Gd 50.40N 120.20W
Kamloops Plateau 46 Ea 50.10N 120.35W
Kamnik 14 Id 46.14N 14.37 E
Kamo [Arm.-U.S.S.R.] 16 Ni 40.22N 45.05 E
Kamo [Jap.] 29 Fc 37.39N 139.03 E
Kamo [N.Z.] 62 Fa 35.41S 174.17 E
Kamōda-Misaki 29 De 33.50N 134.45 E
Kamogawa 29 Gd 35.06N 140.05 E
Kamp 14 Jb 48.23N 15.48 E
Kampala 31 Kh 0.19N 32.35 E
Kampar 26 Df 4.18N 101.09 E
Kampar 26 Mi 0.32N 103.08 E
Kampen 11 Lb 52.33N 5.54 E
Kampene 36 Ec 3.36S 26.40 E
Kamphaeng Phet 25 Je 16.26N 99.33 E
Kamp-Lintfort 12 Ic 51.30N 6.32 E
Kamp'o 28 Jg 35.48N 129.30 E
Kâmpóng Cham 22 Mh 12.00N 105.27 E
Kâmpóng Chhnăng 25 Kf 12.15N 104.40 E
Kâmpóng Saôm 22 Mh 10.38N 103.30 E
Kâmpóng Saôm, Chhâk- 25 Kf 10.50N 103.32 E
Kâmpóng Thum 25 Kf 12.42N 104.54 E
Kâmpôt 25 Kf 10.37N 104.11 E
Kampti 34 Ec 10.08N 3.27W
Kampuchea (Cambodia) 22 Mh 13.00N 105.00 E
Kamrau, Teluk- 26 Jg 3.32S 133.37 E
Kamsack 42 Hf 51.34N 101.54W
Kamsar 34 Cc 10.40N 14.36W
Kamskoje Ustje 7 Li 55.14N 49.16 E
Kamskoje Vodohranilišče = Kama Reservoir (EN) 5 Ld 58.50N 56.15 E
Kam Summa 35 Ge 0.21N 42.44 E
Kamuenai 29a Bb 43.08N 140.26 E
Kamui-Dake 29a Cb 42.25N 142.52 E
Kamui-Misaki 27 Pc 43.20N 140.20 E
Kámuk, Cerro- 49 Fi 9.17N 83.04W
Kamvoúnia Óri 15 Ei 40.00N 21.52 E
Kāmyārān 24 Le 34.47N 46.56 E
Kamyšin 6 Ke 50.06N 45.24 E
Kamyšlov 19 Gd 56.52N 62.43 E
Kamyšovaja Buhta 16 Hg 44.31N 33.33 E
Kamysty-Ajat 17 Jj 53.01N 61.35 E
Kamyzjak 19 Ef 46.06N 48.05 E
Kan 24 Ne 35.45N 51.16 E
Kan 20 Ee 56.31N 93.47 E
Kana 37 Dc 18.32S 27.24 E
Kanaaupscow 42 Jf 54.01N 76.32W
Kanaaupscow 42 Jf 53.40N 77.08W
Kanab 43 Ed 37.03N 112.32W
Kanab Creek 46 Ih 36.24N 112.38W
Kanaga 40a Cb 51.45N 177.10W
Kanagawa Ken 28 Og 35.30N 139.10 E
Kanaliasem 26 Dg 1.44S 103.35 E
Kanami-Zaki 29b Bb 27.53N 128.58 E
Kananga 31 Ji 5.54S 22.25 E
Kanariktok 42 Le 55.03N 60.10W
Kanaš 7 Li 55.31N 47.31 E
Kanathea 63d Cb 17.16S 179.09W
Kanaya 29 Fd 34.48N 138.07 E
Kanayama 29 Ed 35.39N 137.09 E
Kanazawa 22 Pf 36.34N 136.39 E
Kanbalu 25 Jd 23.12N 95.31 E
Kanbe 25 Je 16.42N 96.01 E
Kanchanaburi 25 Jf 14.02N 99.33 E
Kānchenjunga 21 Kg 27.42N 88.08 E
Kānchipuram 25 Ff 12.50N 79.43 E
Kandalakša 6 Jb 67.09N 32.21 E
Kandalaksha, Gulf of- (EN) = Kandalakšski Zaliv 5 Jb 66.35N 32.45 E
Kandalakšski Zaliv = Kandalaksha, Gulf of- (EN) 5 Jb 66.35N 32.45 E
Kandangan 26 Gg 2.47S 115.16 E
Kándanos 15 Gn 35.20N 23.44 E
Kandava 7 Fh 57.03N 22.46 E
Kandavu Island 57 If 19.00S 178.13 E
Kandavu Passage 63d Ac 18.45S 178.00 E
Kandel 12 Ke 49.05N 8.12 E
Kandel 10 Eh 48.04N 8.01 E
Kandheliousa 15 Jm 36.30N 26.58 E
Kandi 31 Hg 11.08N 2.56 E
Kandıra 24 Db 41.04N 30.09 E
Kandla 25 Ed 23.02N 70.14 E
Kando-Gawa 29 Cd 35.22N 132.40 E
Kandovān, Gardaneh-ye- 24 Nd 36.09N 51.18 E
Kandrian 60 Di 6.13S 149.33 E
Kandry 17 Gi 54.34N 54.10 E
Kandy 22 Ki 7.18N 80.38 E
Kane 44 He 41.40N 78.48W
Kane Bassin 67 Od 79.35N 67.00W
Kaneh 24 Pi 27.04N 54.18 E
Kanem 35 Bc 15.00N 16.00 E
Kanem 30 Ig 14.45N 15.30 E
Kaneohe 60 Oc 21.25N 157.48W
Kaneohe Bay 65a Db 21.28N 157.48W
Kanestron, Ákra- 15 Gj 39.56N 23.45 E
Kanev 16 Ge 49.42N 31.29 E
Kanevskaja 19 Df 46.06N 38.58 E
Kaneyama 29 Fc 37.27N 139.30 E
Kang 37 Cd 23.44S 22.50 E
Kangaba 34 Dc 11.56N 8.25W
Kangal 24 Gc 39.15N 37.24 E
Kangalassy 20 Hd 62.17N 129.58 E
Kangâmiut 41 Ge 65.39N 53.55W
Kangān [Iran] 24 Oi 27.50N 52.03 E
Kangān [Iran] 24 Qj 25.48N 57.28 E
Kangar 26 De 6.26N 100.12 E
Kangaré 34 Dc 11.37N 8.08W
Kangaroo Island 57 Eh 35.50S 137.05 E
Kangasala 8 Kc 61.28N 24.05 E
Kangasniemi 7 Gf 61.59N 26.38 E
Kangâtsiaq 41 Ge 68.20N 53.18W
Kangāvar 24 Le 34.30N 47.58 E
Kangbao 28 Cd 41.51N 114.37 E
Kangding/Dardo 27 He 30.01N 101.58 E
Kangean, Kepulauan- = Kangean Islands (EN) 26 Gh 6.55S 115.30 E
Kangean, Pulau- 26 Gh 6.54S 115.20 E
Kangean Islands (EN) = Kangean, Kepulauan- 26 Gh 6.55S 115.30 E
Kangeeak Point 42 Lc 68.01N 64.45W
Kangen 30 Kh 6.47N 33.09 E
Kangerdlugssuaq 41 Ie 68.20N 31.40W
Kangetet 36 Gb 1.58N 36.06 E

Index Symbols

Independent Nation
State, Region
District, County
Municipality
Colony, Dependency
Continent
Physical Region
Historical or Cultural Region
Mount, Mountain
Volcano
Hill
Mountains, Mountain Range
Hills, Escarpment
Plateau, Upland
Pass, Gap
Plain, Lowland
Delta
Salt Flat
Valley, Canyon
Crater, Cave
Karst Features
Depression
Polder
Desert, Dunes
Forest, Woods
Heath, Steppe
Oasis
Cape, Point
Coast, Beach
Cliff
Peninsula
Isthmus
Sandbank
Island
Atoll
Rock, Reef
Islands, Archipelago
Rocks, Reefs
Coral Reef
Well, Spring
Geyser
River, Stream
Waterfall Rapids
River Mouth, Estuary
Lake
Salt Lake
Intermittent Lake
Reservoir
Swamp, Pond
Canal
Glacier
Ice Shelf, Pack Ice
Ocean
Sea
Gulf, Bay
Strait, Fjord
Lagoon
Bank
Seamount
Tablemount
Ridge
Shelf
Basin
Escarpment, Sea Scarp
Fracture
Trench, Abyss
National Park, Reserve
Point of Interest
Recreation Site
Cave, Cavern
Historic Site
Ruins
Wall, Walls
Church, Abbey
Temple
Scientific Station
Airport
Port
Lighthouse
Mine
Tunnel
Dam, Bridge

Name	Page	Grid	Lat	Long
Kanggup'o	28	Id	41.07N	127.31 E
Kanggye	27	Mc	40.58N	126.36 E
Kangi	35	Dd	8.10N	27.39 E
Kangjin	28	Ig	34.38N	126.46 E
Kangmar	27	Ef	28.32N	89.43 E
Kangnŭng	27	Md	37.44N	128.54 E
Kango	36	Bb	0.09N	10.08 E
Kangondu	36	Gc	1.06S	37.42 E
Kangping	28	Gc	42.45N	123.20 E
Kangrinboqê Feng	27	De	31.04N	81.30 E
Kangto	25	Ic	27.52N	92.30 E
Kangwŏn-Do [N.Kor.] [2]	28	Ie	38.45N	127.35 E
Kangwŏn-Do [S.Kor.] [2]	28	Jf	37.45N	128.15 E
Kani	34	Dd	8.29N	6.36W
Kaniama	36	Dd	7.31S	24.11 E
Kanibadam	18	Hd	40.17N	70.25 E
Kaniet Islands	57	Fe	0.53S	145.30 E
Kanija	15	Lc	46.16N	28.13 E
Kanimeh	18	Ed	40.18N	65.09 E
Kanina	15	Ci	40.26N	19.31 E
Kanin Kamen	17	Bb	68.15N	45.15 E
Kanin Nos	19	Eb	68.39N	43.14 E
Kanin Nos, Mys-	5	Kb	68.39N	43.16 E
Kanin Peninsula (EN)= Kanin Poluostrov	5	Kb	68.00N	45.00 E
Kanin Poluostrov=Kanin Peninsula (EN)	5	Kb	68.00N	45.00 E
Kanioumé	34	Eb	15.46N	3.09W
Kanita	29a	Bc	41.02N	140.38 E
Kanjiža	15	Dc	46.04N	20.03 E
Kankaanpää	7	Ff	61.48N	22.25 E
Kankakee	43	Jc	41.07N	87.52W
Kankakee River	45	Lf	41.23N	88.16W
Kankalabé	34	Cc	11.00N	12.00W
Kankan	31	Gg	10.23N	9.18W
Kanker	25	Gd	20.17N	81.29 E
Kankesanturai	25	Gg	9.49N	80.02 E
Kankossa	32	Ef	15.55N	11.31W
Kankunski	20	He	57.39N	126.25 E
Kanla	10	Hf	50.48N	11.35 E
Kanmav Kyun	25	Jf	11.40N	98.28 E
Kanmon-Kaikyō	29	Bd	33.56N	130.57 E
Kanmuri-Yama	29	Cd	34.28N	132.05 E
Kannapolis	43	Kd	35.30N	80.37W
Kannone-Jima	29	Jj	28.51N	128.58 E
Kannonkoski	8	Kb	62.58N	25.15 E
Kannus	7	Fe	63.54N	23.54 E
Kano [2]	34	Gc	12.00N	9.00 E
Kano	31	Hg	12.00N	8.31 E
Kanona	36	Fe	13.04S	30.38 E
Kan'onji	28	Lg	34.07N	133.39 E
Kanoya	28	Ki	31.23N	130.51 E
Kanozero, Ozero-	7	Ic	67.00N	34.05 E
Kānpur	22	Kg	26.28N	80.21 E
Kansas	38	Jf	39.07N	94.36W
Kansas [2]	43	Hd	38.45N	98.15W
Kansas City [Ks.-U.S.]	39	Jf	39.07N	94.39W
Kansas City [Mo.-U.S.]	39	Jf	39.05N	94.35W
Kanshi	27	Kg	24.57N	116.52 E
Kansk	22	Ld	56.13N	95.41 E
Kansŏng	28	Je	38.22N	128.28 E
Kansu (EN)=Gansu Sheng (Kan-su Sheng) [2]	27	Hd	38.00N	102.00 E
Kansu (EN)=Kan-su Sheng→Gansu Sheng [2]	27	Hd	38.00N	102.00 E
Kan-su Sheng→Gansu Sheng=Kansu (EN) [2]	27	Hd	38.00N	102.00 E
Kansyat	26	Kg	2.15S	138.51 E
Kant	18	Jc	42.52N	74.50 E
Kantang	25	Jg	7.23N	99.32 E
Kantchari	34	Fc	12.29N	1.31 E
Kanté	34	Fd	9.57N	1.03 E
Kantemirovka	19	Df	49.45N	39.53 E
Kantō-Heiya	29	Fc	36.00N	139.30 E
Kanton Atoll	57	Je	2.50S	171.41W
Kantō-Sanchi	29	Fc	36.00N	138.45 E
Kantubek	18	Bb	45.06N	59.16 E
Kanturk/Ceann Toirc	9	Ei	52.10N	8.55W
Kanuma	29	Fc	36.34N	139.45 E
Kanye	31	Jk	24.58S	25.21 E
Kanyu	37	Cd	20.04S	24.36 E
Kanzenze	36	Ee	10.31S	25.12 E
Kao	65b	Aa	19.40S	175.01W
Kaohsiung	22	Og	22.38N	120.17 E
Kaŏk Nhêk	25	Lf	13.05N	107.04 E
Kaoko Otavi	37	Ac	18.15S	13.37 E
Kaokoveld [3]	37	Ac	18.00S	13.00 E
Kaokoveld	30	Ij	19.30S	13.30 E
Kaolack	31	Fg	14.09N	16.04W
Kao Neua, Col de-	25	Le	18.23N	105.10 E
Kaouadja	35	Cd	8.00N	23.14 E
Kaouar	34	Hb	19.05N	12.52 E
Kapaa	65a	Ba	22.05N	159.19W
Kapanga	31	Ji	8.21S	22.35 E
Kapar	24	Ld	36.32N	47.30 E
Kapčagaj	19	Hg	43.52N	77.03 E
Kapčagajskoje Vodohranilišče	19	Hg	43.45N	78.00 E
Kapchorwa	36	Fb	1.24N	34.27 E
Kap Dan	41	Ie	65.32N	37.30W
Kapelle	12	Fc	51.39N	3.57 E
Kapellskär	8	He	59.43N	19.04 E
Kapena	36	Ee	10.47S	28.20 E
Kapenguria	36	Gb	1.14N	35.07 E
Kapfenberg	14	Jc	47.26N	15.18 E
Kapidaği Yarimadası	15	Ki	40.28N	27.50 E
Kapingamarangi Atoll	57	Gd	1.04N	154.46 E
Kapingamarangi Rise (EN)	57	Gd	1.00N	157.00 E
Kapiri Mposhi	36	Ee	13.58S	28.41 E
Kāpīsā [3]	23	Kc	34.45N	69.30 E
Kapit	26	Ff	2.01N	112.56 E
Kapiti Island	62	Fd	40.50S	174.55 E
Kapka, Massif du-	35	Cb	15.07N	21.45 E
Kapoeta	31	Kh	4.47N	33.35 E
Kapona	36	Ed	7.11S	29.09 E
Kapos	10	Oj	46.44N	18.29 E

Name	Page	Grid	Lat	Long
Kaposvár	10	Nj	46.22N	17.48 E
Kapp	8	Dd	60.42N	10.52 E
Kappeln	10	Fb	54.40N	9.56 E
Kapša	7	Hg	59.52N	33.45 E
Kapsan	28	Jd	41.05N	128.18 E
Kapsukas	7	Fi	54.33N	23.23 E
Kapuas [Indon.]	26	Mj	0.25S	109.40 E
Kapuas [Indon.]	26	Fg	3.01S	114.20 E
Kapuas Hulu, Pegunungan-=Kapuas Mountains (EN)	26	Ff	1.25N	113.15 E
Kapuas Mountains (EN)= Kapuas Hulu, Pegunungan	26	Ff	1.25N	113.15 E
Kapugargin	15	Lm	36.40N	28.50 E
Kapušany	10	Rg	49.03N	21.21 E
Kapuskasing	39	Ke	49.25N	82.26W
Kapustin Jar	16	Ne	48.35N	45.45 E
Kapustoje	7	Ic	67.17N	34.12 E
Kaputdžuh, Gora-	16	Oj	39.12N	46.01 E
Kapuvár	10	Ni	47.36N	17.02 E
Kara	17	Lb	69.10N	64.45 E
Kara	34	Fd	9.33N	1.12 E
Kara [3]	34	Fd	9.35N	1.05 E
Kara Ada [Tur.]	15	Km	36.58N	27.28 E
Kara Ada [Tur.]	15	Jk	38.25N	26.20 E
Kara-Balta	19	Hg	42.49N	73.57 E
Karabas	19	Hf	49.30N	73.00 E
Karabaš	17	Ji	55.29N	60.13 E
Karabekaul	19	Gh	38.28N	64.10 E
Karabiga	15	Ki	40.24N	27.18 E
Karabil, Vozvyšennost-	18	Df	36.20N	63.30 E
Kara-Bogaz-Gol	19	Fg	41.01N	52.59 E
Kara-Bogaz-Gol, proliv-	16	Ri	41.04N	52.59 E
Kara-Bogaz-Gol, Zaliv-	5	Lg	41.00N	53.15 E
Karabuk	23	Da	41.12N	32.37 E
Karabulak [Kaz.-U.S.S.R.]	18	Lb	44.54N	78.29 E
Karabulak [Kaz.-U.S.S.R.]	19	Gg	42.31N	69.47 E
Kara Burun	15	Km	36.32N	27.58 E
Karaburun [Tur.]	24	Cb	41.21N	28.40 E
Karaburun [Tur.]	24	Bc	38.37N	26.31 E
Karabutak	19	Gf	49.57N	60.08 E
Karacabey	24	Cb	40.13N	28.21 E
Karaca Dağ	24	Hd	37.40N	39.50 E
Karačajevo-Čerkesskaja Avtonomnaja Oblast [3]	19	Eg	43.45N	41.45 E
Karačajevsk	16	Lh	43.44N	41.58 E
Karacaköy	24	Cb	41.22N	28.30 E
Karacaoğlan	15	Kh	41.32N	27.04 E
Karacasu	24	Cd	37.43N	28.37 E
Karačev	19	De	53.04N	34.59 E
Karāchi	22	Ig	24.52N	67.03 E
Kara Dağ [Tur.]	24	Jd	37.40N	43.42 E
Kara Dağ [Tur.]	24	Ed	37.23N	33.10 E
Karadah	16	Oh	42.29N	46.54 E
Karadeniz=Black Sea (EN)	5	Jg	43.00N	35.00 E
Kara Dong	27	Dd	38.26N	81.50 E
Karagajly	19	Hf	49.20N	75.48 E
Karaganda	22	Je	49.50N	73.10 E
Karagandinskaja Oblast [3]	19	Hf	50.00N	74.00 E
Karaginski, Ostrov-	21	Sd	58.48N	164.05 E
Karaginski Zaliv	21	Sd	58.50N	164.00 E
Karagöl	15	Mm	36.42N	29.50 E
Karagoš, Gora-	20	Df	51.44N	89.24 E
Karahalli	15	Mk	38.20N	29.32 E
Karaidelski	17	Hi	55.49N	57.05 E
Kara-Irtyš	21	Ke	47.52N	84.16 E
Karaisali	24	Fd	37.16N	35.03 E
Karaj	24	Ne	35.48N	50.59 E
Karaj	24	Ne	35.07N	51.35 E
Karak, Gora-	19	Gq	44.59N	63.05 F
Kara-Kala	19	Fh	38.28N	56.18 E
Karakalpak ASSR (EN)= Karakalpakskaja ASSR [3]	19	Fg	43.30N	59.00 E
Karakalpakskaja ASSR= Karakalpak ASSR (EN) [3]	19	Fg	43.30N	59.00 E
Karakax/Moyu	27	Cd	37.17N	79.42 E
Karakax He	27	Dd	38.06N	80.24 E
Karakeçi	24	Hd	37.26N	39.26 E
Karakelong, Pulau-	26	If	4.15N	126.48 E
Karakoçan	24	Ic	38.02N	40.07 E
Karakoin, Ozero-	18	Ga	46.10N	68.40 E
Karakojsu	16	Oh	42.30N	47.05 E
Karakolka	18	Kd	41.29N	77.24 E
Karakoram	21	Jf	34.00N	78.00 E
Karakoram Pass	21	Jf	35.30N	77.50 E
Karakore	35	Gc	10.25N	40.01 E
Karakoro	34	Cc	14.43N	12.03 E
Karakorum Shan	27	Cd	36.00N	76.00 E
Karakorum Shankou	27	Cd	35.30N	77.50 E
Karaköse	23	Fb	39.44N	43.03 E
Karaköy	24	Ic	39.04N	41.42 E
Kara-Kul	18	Id	41.34N	72.47 E
Karakul, Ozero-	19	Hh	39.05N	73.25 E
Karakumski kanal imeni V.I. Lenina	19	Gh	37.42N	64.20 E
Karakumy	21	Hf	39.00N	60.00 E
Karakuwisa	37	Bc	18.56S	19.40 E
Karam	20	Fe	55.09N	107.37 E
Karama	26	Gg	2.18S	119.06 E
Karaman	23	Db	37.11N	33.14 E
Karamanli	15	Ml	37.22N	29.49 E
Karamay	22	Ke	45.30N	84.55 E
Karamea	61	Dh	41.15S	172.06 E
Karamea Bight	62	Dd	41.25S	171.50 E
Karamet-Nijaz	19	Gh	37.43N	64.31 E
Karamiran He	27	Dd	37.50N	84.35 E
Karamiran Shankou	27	Ed	36.15N	87.05 E
Karamiševo	8	Mg	57.44N	28.50 E
Karamoja [3]	36	Fb	2.45N	34.15 E
Karamürsel	15	Mi	40.42N	29.36 E
Kara-myk	19	Hh	39.30N	71.51 E
Karamyš	16	Nd	51.18N	45.00 E
Karān	24	Mi	27.43N	49.49 E
Karaova	15	Kl	37.05N	27.40 E

Name	Page	Grid	Lat	Long
Karapınar	24	Ed	37.43N	33.33 E
Kara-Saki	29	Ad	34.40N	129.29 E
Kara-Sal	16	Mf	47.18N	43.36 E
Karasay	27	Dd	36.48N	83.48 E
Karasburg	31	Ik	28.00S	18.43 E
Kara Sea (EN)=Karskoje More	67	Hd	76.00N	80.00 E
Karašica	14	Me	45.36N	18.36 E
Karasjok	7	Fb	69.27N	25.30 E
Kara Strait (EN)=Karskije Vorota, Proliv-	21	Hb	70.30N	58.00 E
Karasu	24	Db	41.04N	30.47 E
Karasu [Tur.]	21	Ff	38.52N	38.48 E
Karasu [Tur.]	24	Ic	38.49N	41.28 E
Karasu [Tur.]	24	Jc	38.32N	43.10 E
Karasu Dağları	24	Ic	39.30N	40.45 E
Karasuk	20	Cf	53.44N	78.08 E
Karasuk	20	Cf	53.35N	77.30 E
Karasuyama	29	Gc	36.39N	140.08 E
Karatá, Laguna-	49	Fg	13.56N	83.30W
Karatal	19	Hf	46.26N	77.10 E
Karataş [Tur.]	24	Fd	36.36N	35.21 E
Karataş [Tur.]	15	Lk	38.34N	28.17 E
Karataş Burun	24	Fb	36.35N	35.22 E
Karatau	19	Hg	43.10N	70.29 E
Karatau, Hrebet-	21	Ie	43.40N	69.00 E
Karatj	7	Ec	66.43N	18.33 E
Karatobe	16	Re	49.42N	53.33 E
Karaton	19	Ff	46.25N	53.34 E
Karatsu	28	Jh	33.26N	130.00 E
Karatsu-Wan	29	Be	33.30N	130.00 E
Kara-Turgaj	21	Ie	48.01N	62.45 E
Karaul [Kaz.-U.S.S.R.]	19	Hf	49.00N	79.20 E
Karaul [R.S.F.S.R.]	20	Db	70.10N	83.08 E
Karaulbazar	18	Ee	39.29N	64.47 E
Karaulkala	18	Bc	42.18N	58.41 E
Karáva	15	Ej	39.19N	21.36 E
Karavanke	14	Id	46.25N	14.25 E
Karavastase, Gjiri i-	15	Ci	40.55N	19.30 E
Karavastase, Laguna e-	15	Ci	40.55N	19.30 E
Karávi	15	Gm	36.45N	23.35 E
Karavonisia	15	Jn	35.59N	26.26 E
Karawa	36	Db	3.20N	20.18 E
Karaxabar He/Kaidu He	27	Ec	41.55N	86.38 E
Karažal	19	Hf	47.59N	70.53 E
Karbalā'	22	Gf	32.36N	44.02 E
Karbalā' [3]	24	Jf	32.30N	43.45 E
Kårbole	7	Df	61.59N	15.19 E
Karcag	10	Qi	47.19N	20.56 E
Kardhámaina	15	Km	36.47N	27.09 E
Kardhámila	15	Jk	38.31N	26.06 E
Kardhiotissa	15	Im	36.38N	25.01 E
Kardhitsa	15	Ej	39.22N	21.55 E
Kärdla/Kjardla	7	Fg	59.01N	22.42 E
Kărdžali	15	Ih	41.39N	25.22 E
Kărdžali [2]	15	Ih	41.30N	25.30 E
Kareha, Jbel-	13	Gi	35.15N	5.30W
Karelia (EN)	5	Jc	64.00N	32.00 E
Karelskaja ASSR [3]	19	Dc	63.30N	33.30 E
Karema	36	Fd	6.49S	30.26 E
Karen [2]	25	Je	17.30N	97.45 E
Karen	25	If	12.51N	92.53 E
Karesuando	7	Fb	68.27N	22.29 E
Karēt	30	Gf	24.00N	7.30W
Kärevere/Kjarevere	8	Lf	58.23N	26.30 E
Kargala	16	Sd	51.59N	55.10 E
Kargapazarı Dağı	24	Ib	40.07N	41.35 E
Kargapolje	17	Li	55.57N	64.27 E
Kargasok	20	De	59.07N	81.01 E
Kargat	20	De	55.10N	80.17 E
Kargı	24	Fb	41.08N	34.30 E
Kargil	25	Fb	34.34N	76.06 E
Kargilik/Yecheng	22	Jf	37.54N	77.26 E
Kargopol	19	Dc	61.32N	38.58 E
Karhula	7	Gf	60.31N	26.57 E
Kari	34	Hc	11.14N	10.34 E
Kariai	6	Ig	40.15N	24.15 E
Kariba	31	Jj	16.30S	28.45 E
Kariba, Lake-	30	Jj	17.00S	28.00 E
Kariba-Dake	29a	Ab	42.37N	139.56 E
Kariba Dam	37	Dc	16.30S	28.50 E
Karibib	31	Ik	21.58S	15.51 E
Karibib [3]	37	Bd	22.00S	16.00 E
Kariet-Arkmane	13	Ji	35.06N	2.45W
Karigasniemi	7	Fb	69.24N	25.50 E
Karijärvi	8	Jc	61.35N	22.30 E
Karikachi Tōge	29a	Cb	43.10N	142.40 E
Kārikāl	25	Ff	10.55N	79.50 E
Karikari, Cape-	62	Ea	34.47S	173.24 E
Karima (EN)=Kuraymah	31	Kg	18.33N	31.51 E
Karimama	34	Fc	12.04N	3.11 E
Karimata, Kepulauan-=Karimata Islands (EN)	26	Eg	1.25S	109.05 E
Karimata, Pulau-	26	Eg	1.36S	108.55 E
Karimata, Selat-=Karimata Strait (EN)	21	Mj	2.05S	108.40 E
Karimata Islands (EN)= Karimata, Kepulauan-	26	Eg	1.25S	109.05 E
Karimata Strait (EN)= Karimata, Selat-	21	Mj	2.05S	108.40 E
Karīmganj	25	Id	24.42N	92.33 E
Karīmnagar	25	Fe	18.26N	79.09 E
Karimunjawa, Kepulauan-=Karimunjawa Islands (EN)	26	Fh	5.50S	110.25 E
Karimunjawa Islands (EN)= Karimunjawa, Kepulauan-	26	Fh	5.50S	110.25 E
Karin [Som.]	35	Hc	10.59N	49.13 E
Karin [Som.]	35	Hc	10.51N	45.45 E
Karis/Karjaa	7	Ff	60.05N	23.40 E
Karisimbi	30	Ji	1.30S	29.27 E
Káristos	15	Hk	38.01N	24.25 E
Karjaa/Karis	7	Ff	60.05N	23.40 E
Karkār	35	Hd	9.57N	49.20 E
Karkaralinsk	19	Hf	49.23N	75.31 E
Karkar Island	57	Fe	4.40S	146.00 E
Karkas, Kūh-e	24	Nf	33.27N	51.48 E
Karkheh	23	Gc	31.31N	47.55 E

Name	Page	Grid	Lat	Long
Karkinitski zaliv	5	Jf	45.55N	33.00 E
Karkkila/Högfors	7	Ff	60.32N	24.11 E
Karkku	8	Jc	61.25N	23.01 E
Kärkölä	8	Kd	60.55N	25.15 E
Kärla/Kjarla	8	Jf	58.16N	22.05 E
Karlholm	8	Gd	60.31N	17.37 E
Karlik Shan	21	Le	43.00N	94.30 E
Karlino	10	Lb	54.03N	15.51 E
Karliova	24	Ic	39.18N	41.01 E
Karl Marx, Pik-	19	Hh	37.08N	72.29 E
Karl-Marx-Stadt	6	He	50.50N	12.55 E
Karl-Marx-Stadt [2]	10	If	50.45N	12.50 E
Karlö/Hailuoto	5	Ib	65.02N	24.42 E
Karlobag	14	Jf	44.32N	15.05 E
Karlovac	14	Je	45.29N	15.33 E
Karlovka	16	Ie	49.28N	35.08 E
Karlovo	15	Hg	42.38N	24.48 E
Karlovy Vary	10	If	50.14N	12.52 E
Karlsbad	12	Kf	48.55N	8.35 E
Karlsborg	7	Df	58.32N	14.31 E
Karlshamn	7	Dh	56.10N	14.51 E
Karlskoga	7	Dg	59.20N	14.31 E
Karlskrona	6	Hd	56.10N	15.35 E
Karlsöarna	8	Gg	57.15N	18.00 E
Karlsruhe	10	Eg	49.01N	8.24 E
Karlstad [Mn.-U.S.]	45	Hb	48.35N	96.31W
Karlstad [Swe.]	6	Hd	59.22N	13.30 E
Karluk	40	Ie	57.34N	154.28W
Karmah=Kerma (EN)	35	Eb	19.38N	30.25 E
Karmana	18	Ed	40.09N	65.15 E
Karmøy	7	Ag	59.15N	5.15 E
Karnāli	25	Gc	28.45N	81.16 E
Karnataka (Mysore) [3]	25	Ff	13.30N	76.00 E
Karnobat	15	Jg	42.39N	26.59 E
Kärnten = Carinthia (EN) [2]	14	Hd	46.45N	14.00 E
Kärnten = Carinthia (EN)	14	Hd	46.45N	14.00 E
Karoi	37	Dc	16.50S	29.40 E
Karonga	31	Ki	9.56S	33.56 E
Karora	35	Fb	17.39N	38.22 E
Káros	15	Im	36.53N	25.39 E
Kárpathos	15	Kn	35.30N	27.14 E
Kárpathos=Karpathos (EN)	5	Ih	35.40N	27.10 E
Karpathos (EN)= Kárpathos	5	Ih	35.40N	27.10 E
Karpáthou, Stenón-	15	Kn	35.50N	27.30 E
Karpenision	15	Ek	38.55N	21.47 E
Karpinsk	17	Jg	59.45N	60.01 E
Karpuzlu	15	Kl	37.33N	27.50 E
Kars	23	Fa	40.37N	43.05 E
Karsakpaj	19	Gf	47.48N	66.45 E
Kärsämäki	7	Fe	64.00N	25.46 E
Karsava/Kārsava	7	Gh	56.47N	27.42 E
Kārsava/Karsava	7	Gh	56.47N	27.42 E
Karši	22	If	38.53N	65.48 E
Karşiyaka	15	Ki	40.26N	28.00 E
Karsiyaka	15	Kk	38.27N	27.07 E
Karskije Vorota, Proliv-= Kara Strait (EN)	21	Hb	70.30N	58.00 E
Karskoje More=Kara Sea (EN)	67	Hd	76.00N	80.00 E
Kars Platosu	24	Jb	40.40N	43.07 E
Karst (EN)=Kras	5	Hf	45.48N	14.00 E
Kårsta	8	He	59.39N	18.14 E
Karstula	7	Fe	62.52N	24.47 E
Kartal	24	Cb	40.53N	29.10 E
Kartaly	19	Ge	53.03N	60.40 E
Kartaly-Ajat	17	Jj	53.01N	61.50 E
Karttula	8	Lb	62.53N	26.58 E
Kartuzy	10	Ob	54.20N	18.12 E
Karumai	29	Ga	40.20N	141.28 E
Karumba	59	Ic	17.29S	140.50 E
Karūn	21	Gf	30.25N	48.12 E
Karungi	7	Fc	66.03N	23.57 E
Karungu	36	Fc	0.51S	34.09 E
Karunki	7	Fc	66.02N	24.01 E
Karūr	25	Ff	10.57N	78.05 E
Karvia	7	Fe	62.08N	22.34 E
Karviná	10	Og	49.51N	18.32 E
Kārwār	25	Ef	14.48N	74.08 E
Karwendel Gebirge	14	Fc	47.28N	11.20 E
Karymskoje	20	Gf	51.37N	114.21 E
Kas	35	Cc	12.34N	24.14 E
Kaş	24	Cd	36.12N	29.38 E
Kasaba [Tur.]	15	Mm	36.18N	29.44 E
Kasaba [Zam.]	36	Ee	10.44S	29.43 E
Kasado-Shima	29	Be	33.57N	131.50 E
Kasah	16	Mi	40.03N	43.52 E
Kasai	29	Dd	34.56N	134.49 E
Kasai	30	Ii	3.02S	16.57 E
Kasai Occidental [2]	36	Dc	5.00S	21.30 E
Kasai Oriental [2]	36	Dc	3.00S	23.00 E
Kasaji	36	De	10.22S	23.27 E
Kasaku	36	Ec	1.55S	25.50 E
Kasama [Jap.]	29	Gc	36.22N	140.16 E
Kasama [Zam.]	31	Kj	10.13S	31.12 E
Kasan	18	Ee	39.01N	65.35 E
Kasane	31	Jj	17.48S	25.09 E
Kasanga	36	Fd	8.28S	31.09 E
Kasangulu	36	Bc	4.36S	15.10 E
Kasansaj	18	Hd	41.10N	71.32 E
Kasaoka	29	Cd	34.30N	133.29 E
Kāsaragod	25	Ef	12.30N	75.00 E
Kasari	29b	Ba	28.27N	129.41 E
Kašary	16	Le	49.02N	41.03 E
Kasatori-Yama	29	Ce	33.33N	132.55 E
Kasba Lake	42	Hd	60.20N	102.10W
Kasba Tatla	32	Fc	32.36N	6.16W
Kaseda	28	Ki	31.25N	130.19 E
Kasempa	36	Ee	13.27S	25.50 E
Kasenga	31	Jj	10.22S	28.37 E
Kasenye	36	Fb	1.24N	30.26 E
Kasese [Ug.]	36	Fb	0.10N	30.05 E
Kasese [Zaire]	36	Ec	1.38S	27.07 E
Kashaf	23	Jb	35.58N	61.07 E

Name	Page	Grid	Lat	Long
Kāshān	22	Hf	33.59N	51.29 E
Kashi	22	Jf	39.29N	75.58 E
Kashihara	29	Dd	34.31N	135.47 E
Kashima [Jap.]	29	Cd	35.31N	132.59 E
Kashima [Jap.]	29	Gd	35.58N	140.38 E
Kashima [Jap.]	29	Be	33.07N	130.07 E
Kashima-Nada	29	Gc	36.30N	140.45 E
Kashiobwe	36	Ed	9.39S	28.37 E
Kashiwazaki	28	Of	37.25N	138.30 E
Kashkū'īyeh	24	Qh	28.58N	56.37 E
Kāshmar	23	Ib	35.12N	58.27 E
Kashmir	21	Jf	34.00N	76.00 E
Kashmor	25	Dc	28.26N	69.35 E
Kasimov	19	Ee	54.59N	41.28 E
Kašin	19	Dd	57.23N	37.37 E
Kasindi	36	Eb	0.02N	29.43 E
Kašira	7	Ji	54.52N	38.11 E
Kasiruta, Pulau-	26	Ig	0.25S	127.12 E
Kasisty	20	Fb	73.40N	109.45 E
Kaškadarinskaja Oblast [3]	19	Gh	38.50N	66.10 E
Kaškadarja	18	Ee	39.35N	64.38 E
Kaskaskia River	45	Lh	37.59N	89.56W
Kaskelen	19	Hg	43.09N	76.37 E
Kaskinen/Kaskö	7	Ee	62.23N	21.13 E
Kaskö/Kaskinen	7	Ee	62.23N	21.13 E
Kasli	17	Ji	55.53N	60.48 E
Kaslo	46	Gb	49.55N	116.55W
Kasongo	31	Ji	4.27S	26.40 E
Kasongo-Lunda	36	Cd	6.28S	16.49 E
Kásos	15	Jn	35.25N	26.55 E
Kásou, Stenón-	15	Jn	35.25N	26.35 E
Kaspi	16	Ni	41.58N	44.25 E
Kaspičan	15	Kf	43.18N	27.11 E
Kaspijsk	19	Eg	42.57N	47.35 E
Kaspijski	19	Ef	45.25N	47.22 E
Kaspijskoje More=Caspian Sea (EN)	5	Lg	42.00N	50.30 E
Kasplja	16	Gb	55.24N	30.43 E
Kasr, Ra's-	35	Fb	18.04N	38.33 E
Kassaar/Kassar	8	Jf	58.47N	22.40 E
Kassalā	31	Kg	15.28N	36.24 E
Kassalā [3]	35	Fc	14.50N	35.30 E
Kassándra	15	Gi	40.00N	23.30 E
Kassandra, Gulf of- (EN) = Kassándras, Kólpos-	15	Gi	40.05N	23.30 E
Kassándras, Ákra-	15	Gj	39.57N	23.21 E
Kassándras, Kólpos- = Kassandra, Gulf of- (EN)	15	Gi	40.05N	23.30 E
Kassar/Kassaar	8	Jf	58.47N	22.40 E
Kassel	10	Fe	51.19N	9.30 E
Kassinga	36	Cf	15.06S	16.06 E
Kassiópi	15	Cj	39.47N	19.55 E
Kastamonu	23	Da	41.22N	33.47 E
Kastanéai	15	Jh	41.39N	26.28 E
Kastellaun	12	Jd	50.04N	7.27 E
Kastéllion [Grc.]	15	In	35.12N	25.20 E
Kastéllion [Grc.]	15	Gn	35.30N	23.39 E
Kastéllos, Ákra-	15	Kn	35.23N	27.09 E
Kasterlee	12	Gc	51.15N	4.57 E
Kastlösa	8	Gh	56.28N	16.25 E
Kastoria	15	Ei	40.31N	21.16 E
Kastorias, Límni-	15	Ei	40.31N	21.18 E
Kastornoje	16	Kd	51.51N	38.07 E
Kastós	15	Dk	38.35N	20.55 E
Kasuga	29	Be	33.32N	130.27 E
Kasugai	29	Ed	35.14N	136.58 E
Kasulu	36	Fc	4.34S	30.06 E
Kasumbalesa	36	Ee	12.13S	27.48 E
Kasumi	29	Dd	35.38N	134.38 E
Kasumi-ga-Ura	28	Pf	36.00N	140.25 E
Kasumkent	16	Pi	41.42N	48.10 E
Kasungan	26	Fg	1.58S	113.24 E
Kasungu	36	Fe	13.02S	33.29 E
Kasupe	36	Gf	15.10S	35.18 E
Kasūr	25	Eb	31.07N	74.27 E
Kaszuby	10	Ob	54.10N	18.15 E
Kataba	31	Jj	16.05S	25.10 E
Katahdin, Mount-	43	Nb	45.55N	68.55W
Katajsk	17	Kh	56.18N	62.35 E
Katako-Kombe	36	Dc	3.24S	24.25 E
Katanga	36	Ed	10.00S	25.30 E
Katanga	20	Fd	60.10N	102.10 E
Katangli	20	Jf	51.43N	143.16 E
Katanning	59	Df	33.42S	117.33 E
Katav-Ivanovsk	17	Ii	54.47N	58.15 E
Katchall	25	Ig	7.57N	93.22 E
Katchi	32	Ef	17.00N	13.55W
Katende, Chutes de-	36	Dd	6.30S	22.10 E
Katerini	15	Fi	40.16N	22.30 E
Katesh	36	Gc	4.31S	35.23 E
Katete	36	Fe	14.06S	32.05 E
Katha	25	Jd	24.11N	96.21 E
Katherine	58	Ef	14.28S	132.16 E
Katherine River	59	Gb	14.39S	131.42 E
Kāthīāwār	21	Jg	21.58N	70.30 E
Kathmandu	22	Kg	27.43N	85.19 E
Kathua	36	Gc	1.17S	39.03 E
Kati	34	Dc	12.43N	8.05W
Katihār	25	Hc	25.32N	87.35 E
Katiki, Volcán-	65d	Bb	27.06S	109.16W
Katima Mulilo	36	Df	17.28S	24.14 E
Katiola	34	Dd	8.08N	5.06W
Katiola [3]	34	Dd	8.13N	5.02W
Katiu Atoll	61	Mc	16.26S	144.22W
Katla	7a	Bc	63.36N	18.58W
Katlabuh, Ozero-	15	Ld	45.25N	29.00 E
Katlanovo	15	Eh	41.54N	21.41 E
Katmai, Mount-	40	Ie	58.17N	154.56W
Káto Akhaia	15	Ek	38.09N	21.33 E
Katofio	36	Ee	11.02S	28.01 E
Katompi	36	Ed	6.11S	26.20 E
Katonga	36	Fb	0.10N	30.40 E
Katon-Karagaj	19	If	49.11N	85.37 E
Káto Ólimbos	15	Fj	39.55N	22.28 E
Katoomba	59	Kf	33.42S	150.18 E
Katopasa, Gunung-	26	Hg	1.14S	121.25 E

Index Symbols

- [1] Independent Nation
- [2] State, Region
- [3] District, County
- [4] Municipality
- [5] Colony, Dependency
- Continent
- Physical Region
- Historical or Cultural Region
- Mount, Mountain
- Volcano
- Hill
- Mountains, Mountain Range
- Hills, Escarpment
- Plateau, Upland
- Pass, Gap
- Plain, Lowland
- Delta
- Salt Flat
- Valley, Canyon
- Crater, Cave
- Karst Features
- Depression
- Polder
- Desert, Dunes
- Forest, Woods
- Heath, Steppe
- Oasis
- Cape, Point
- Coast, Beach
- Cliff
- Peninsula
- Isthmus
- Sandbank
- Island
- Atoll
- Rock, Reef
- Islands, Archipelago
- Rocks, Reefs
- Coral Reef
- Well, Spring
- Geyser
- River, Stream
- Waterfall Rapids
- River Mouth, Estuary
- Lake
- Salt Lake
- Intermittent Lake
- Reservoir
- Swamp, Pond
- Canal
- Glacier
- Ice Shelf, Pack Ice
- Ocean
- Sea
- Gulf, Bay
- Strait, Fjord
- Lagoon
- Bank
- Seamount
- Tablemount
- Ridge
- Shelf
- Basin
- Escarpment, Sea Scarp
- Fracture
- Trench, Abyss
- National Park, Reserve
- Point of Interest
- Recreation Site
- Cave, Cavern
- Historic Site
- Ruins
- Wall, Walls
- Church, Abbey
- Temple
- Scientific Station
- Airport
- Port
- Lighthouse
- Mine
- Tunnel
- Dam, Bridge

Index Symbols

[1] Independent Nation	Historical or Cultural Region	Pass, Gap
[2] State, Province	Mount, Mountain	Plain, Lowland
[3] District, County	Volcano	Delta
[4] Municipality	Hill	Salt Flat
[5] Colony, Dependency	Mountains, Mountain Range	Valley, Canyon
Continent	Hills, Escarpment	Crater, Cave
Physical Region	Plateau, Upland	Karst Features

Depression	Coast, Beach	Rock, Reef
Polder	Cliff	Islands, Archipelago
Desert, Dunes	Peninsula	Rocks, Reefs
Forest, Woods	Isthmus	Coral Reef
Heath, Steppe	Sandbank	Well, Spring
Oasis	Island	Geyser
Cape, Point	Atoll	River, Stream

Waterfall Rapids	Canal	Lagoon
River Mouth, Estuary	Glacier	Bank
Lake	Ice Shelf, Pack Ice	Seamount
Salt Lake	Ocean	Tablemount
Intermittent Lake	Sea	Ridge
Reservoir	Gulf, Bay	Shelf
Swamp, Pond	Strait, Fjord	Basin

Escarpment, Sea Scarp	Historic Site	Port
Fracture	Ruins	Lighthouse
Trench, Abyss	Wall, Walls	Mine
National Park, Reserve	Church, Abbey	Tunnel
Point of Interest	Temple	Dam, Bridge
Recreation Site	Scientific Station	
Cave, Cavern	Airport	

Index Symbols

[1] Independent Nation	Pass, Gap	Depression	Coast, Beach	Rock, Reef
[2] State, Region	Plain, Lowland	Polder	Cliff	Islands, Archipelago
[3] District, County	Delta	Desert, Dunes	Peninsula	Rocks, Reefs
[4] Municipality	Salt Flat	Forest, Woods	Isthmus	Coral Reef
[5] Colony, Dependency	Valley, Canyon	Heath, Steppe	Sandbank	Well, Spring
■ Continent	Crater, Cave	Oasis	Island	Geyser
◻ Physical Region	Karst Features	Cape, Point	Atoll	River, Stream
Historical or Cultural Region				
Mount, Mountain				
Volcano				
Hill				
Mountains, Mountain Range				
Hills, Escarpment				
Plateau, Upland				

Waterfall Rapids	Canal	Lagoon	Escarpment, Sea Scarp	Historic Site	Port
River Mouth, Estuary	Glacier	Bank	Fracture	Ruins	Lighthouse
Lake	Ice Shelf, Pack Ice	Seamount	Trench, Abyss	Wall, Walls	Mine
Salt Lake	Ocean	Tablemount	National Park, Reserve	Church, Abbey	Tunnel
Intermittent Lake	Sea	Ridge	Point of Interest	Temple	Dam, Bridge
Reservoir	Gulf, Bay	Shelf	Recreation Site	Scientific Station	
Swamp, Pond	Strait, Fjord	Basin	Cave, Cavern	Airport	

Kisújszállás 10 Qi 47.13N 20.46 E
Kisuki 29 Cd 35.17N 132.54 E
Kisumu 31 Ki 0.06S 34.45 E
Kisvárda 10 Sh 48.13N 22.05 E
Kita 31 Gg 13.03N 9.30W
Kitab 19 Gh 39.08N 66.54 E
Kita-Daitō-Jima 27 Nf 25.55N 131.20 E
Kitaibaraki 28 Pf 36.48N 140.45 E
Kita-Iō-Jima 60 Cb 25.26N 141.17 E
Kitaj, Ozero- 15 Md 45.35N 29.15 E
Kitakami 27 Pd 39.30N 141.10 E
Kitakami-Gawa 29 Gb 38.25N 141.19 E
Kitakami-Sanchi 29 Gb 39.30N 141.30 E
Kitakata 28 Of 37.39N 139.52 E
Kitakyushū 22 Pf 33.53N 130.50 E
Kitale 31 Kh 1.01N 35.00 E
Kitamaiaioi 29a Cb 43.33N 143.57 E
Kitami 27 Pc 43.48N 143.54 E
Kitami-Fuji 29a Cb 43.42N 143.14 E
Kitami-Sanchi 28 Qb 44.30N 142.30 E
Kitami Tōge 29a Cb 43.55N 142.55 E
Kitan-Kaikyō 29 Dd 34.15N 135.00 E
Kita-Taiheyō = Pacific Ocean (EN) 60 Ch 22.00N 167.00 E
Kita-Ura 29 Gc 36.00N 140.34 E
Kit Carson 45 Eg 38.46N 102.48W
Kitchener 42 Jh 43.27N 80.29W
Kitee 7 He 62.06N 30.09 E
Kitessa 35 Dd 5.22N 25.22 E
Kitgum 36 Fb 3.19N 32.53 E
Kithira = Cythera (EN) 15 Fm 36.09N 23.00 E
Kithira = Kythera (EN) 5 Ih 36.15N 23.00 E
Kithira Channel (EN) = Kithiron Dhiékplous 15 Fm 36.00N 23.00 E
Kithiron, Dhiékplous- = Kithira Channel (EN) 15 Fm 36.00N 23.00 E
Kithnos 15 Hl 37.25N 24.26 E
Kithnos 15 Hl 37.23N 24.25 E
Kithnou, Stenón- 15 Hl 37.25N 24.30 E
Kitimat 39 Gd 54.05N 128.38W
Kitimat Ranges 42 Ef 53.58N 128.39W
Kitoushi-Yama 29a Cb 43.27N 143.25 E
Kitriani 15 Hm 36.54N 24.44 E
Kitridge Point 51q Bb 13.09N 59.25W
Kitros 15 Fi 40.22N 22.35 E
Kitsuki 29 Be 33.25N 131.37 E
Kittanning 44 He 40.49N 79.31W
Kittery 44 Ld 43.05N 70.45W
Kittilä 7 Fc 67.40N 24.54 E
Kitui 31 Ki 1.22S 38.01 E
Kitunda 36 Fd 6.48S 33.13 E
Kitutu 36 Ec 3.17S 28.05 E
Kitwe-Nkana 31 Jj 12.49S 28.13 E
Kitzbühel 14 Gc 47.27N 12.23 E
Kitzbüheler Alpen 14 Gc 47.20N 12.20 E
Kitzingen 10 Gg 49.44N 10.10 E
Kiunga [Kenya] 36 Hc 1.45S 41.29 E
Kiunga [Pap.N.Gui.] 60 Ci 6.07S 141.18 E
Kiuruvesi 7 Ge 63.39N 26.37 E
Kivalina 40 Gc 67.59N 164.33W
Kivercy 16 Dd 50.50N 25.31 E
Kivijärvi [Fin.] 8 Ld 60.55N 27.40 E
Kivijärvi [Fin.] 7 Fe 63.10N 25.09 E
Kivik 7 Di 55.41N 14.15 E
Kiviõli/Kiviyli 7 Gg 59.23N 26.59 E
Kiviyli/Kiviõli 7 Gg 59.23N 26.59 E
Kivu 36 Ec 2.30S 27.30 E
Kivu, Lac- = Kivu, Lake- (EN) 30 Ii 2.00S 29.10 E
Kivu, Lake- (EN) = Kivu, Lac- 30 Ii 2.00S 29.10 E
Kiwai Island 60 Ci 8.30S 143.25 E
Kiyāmaki Dāgh 24 Kc 38.47N 45.51 E
Kiyiköy 24 Cb 41.25N 28.01 E
Kiyosato 29a Db 43.51N 144.35 E
Kizel 19 Fd 59.03N 57.40 E
Kizema 7 Kf 61.09N 44.46 E
Kizilcabölük 15 Ml 37.37N 29.01 E
Kizilca Daği 24 Cd 36.55N 29.52 E
Kizilcahaman 24 Eb 40.28N 32.39 E
Kizil Dağ 24 Ed 36.25N 32.42 E
Kizilhisar 15 Ml 37.33N 29.18 E
Kizilirmak 21 Fe 41.45N 35.59 E
Kizilirmak 24 Eb 40.22N 33.59 E
Kiziljurt 16 Oh 43.13N 46.55 E
Kizilskoje 17 Ij 52.44N 58.54 E
Kiziltepe 24 Id 37.12N 40.36 E
Kizimen, Vulkan- 20 Le 55.03N 160.27 E
Kižinga 20 Ff 51.51N 109.55 E
Kizir 20 Ef 54.10N 93.30 E
Kizljar 19 Eg 43.50N 46.42 E
Kizljarski Zaliv 16 Og 44.35N 46.55 E
Kizukuri 29a Bc 40.48N 140.22 E
Kizyl-Arvat 19 Fh 39.01N 56.20 E
Kizyl-Atrek 19 Fh 37.38N 54.47 E
Kizyl-Su 19 Fh 39.46N 53.01 E
Kjahta 20 Ff 50.26N 106.25 E
Kjalvaz 16 Pj 38.38N 48.20 E
Kjardla/Kärdla 7 Fg 59.01N 22.42 E
Kjarevere/Kärevere 8 Lf 58.23N 26.30 E
Kjarla/Kärla 8 Jf 58.16N 22.05 E
Kjellerup 8 Ch 56.17N 9.26 E
Kjøllefjord 7 Ga 70.56N 27.27 E
Kjölur 7a Bb 64.50N 19.25W
Kjøpsvik 7 Db 68.06N 16.21 E
Kjubjume 20 Jd 63.28N 140.30 E
Kjurdamir 19 Eg 40.20N 48.07 E
Kjusjur 20 Hb 70.35N 127.45 E
Kjustendil 15 Fg 42.17N 22.41 E
Kjustendil 15 Fg 42.17N 22.41 E
Kjyosumi-Yama 29 Gd 35.10N 140.09 E
Klabat, Gunung- 26 If 1.28N 125.02 E
Kladanj 23 Gf 44.14N 18.42 E
Kladno 10 Kf 50.09N 14.07 E
Kladovo 15 Fe 44.37N 22.37 E
Klagenfurt 6 Hf 46.38N 14.18 E
Klaipėda/Klajpeda 6 Id 55.43N 21.07 E
Klajpeda/Klaipėda 6 Id 55.43N 21.07 E
Klamath 46 Cf 41.32N 124.02W
Klamath Falls 39 Ge 42.13N 121.46W
Klamath Mountains 43 Cc 41.40N 123.20W
Klamath River 46 Cf 41.33N 124.04W
Klamono 26 Jg 1.08S 131.30 E
Klarälven 5 Hd 59.23N 13.32 E
Klaten 26 Fh 7.42S 110.35 E
Klatovy 10 Jg 49.24N 13.19 E
Klavreström 8 Fg 57.08N 15.08 E
Klawer 37 Bf 31.44S 18.36 E
Klazienaveen, Emmen- 12 Jb 52.44N 7.01 E
Kleck 16 Ec 53.03N 26.40 E
Klecko 10 Nd 52.38N 17.26 E
Kleinblittersdorf 12 Je 49.09N 7.02 E
Kleine Nete 12 Gc 51.08N 4.34 E
Kleine Sluis, Anna Paulowna- 12 Gb 52.52N 4.52 E
Klein-Karoo = Little Karroo (EN) 37 Cf 33.42S 21.20 E
Kleinsee 37 Be 29.40S 17.05 E
Klekovača 14 Kf 44.26N 16.31 E
Kléla 34 Dc 11.40N 5.40W
Kleppe 8 Af 58.46N 5.40 E
Klerksdorp 37 De 26.58S 26.39 E
Kletnja 19 De 53.27N 33.17 E
Kletski 16 Me 49.19N 43.04 E
Kleve 10 Ce 51.47N 6.09 E
Klibreck, Ben- 9 Ic 58.19N 4.30W
Klička 20 Gf 50.24N 118.01 E
Klimoviči 19 De 53.37N 32.01 E
Klimovo 16 Hc 52.23N 32.16 E
Klin 19 Dd 56.20N 36.42 E
Klina 15 Dg 42.37N 20.35 E
Klincy 19 De 52.46N 32.17 E
Klingbach 12 Ke 49.11N 8.24 E
Klingenthal 10 If 50.22N 12.28 E
Klinovec 10 If 50.24N 12.58 E
Klintehamn 7 Eh 57.24N 18.12 E
Klippan 8 Eh 56.08N 13.06 E
Klipplaat 37 Cf 33.02S 24.21 E
Kliškovcy 15 Ja 48.23N 26.13 E
Klisura 15 Hg 42.42N 24.27 E
Klitmøller 8 Cg 57.02N 8.31 E
Kljazma 5 Kd 56.10N 42.58 E
Ključevskaja Sopka, Vulkan- 21 Sd 56.04N 160.38 E
Kljuci 20 Le 56.14N 160.58 E
Kłobuck 10 Of 50.55N 18.57 E
Kłodawa 10 Od 52.16N 18.55 E
Kłodzka, Kotlina- 10 Mf 50.30N 16.35 E
Kłodzko 10 Mf 50.28N 16.40 E
Kløfta 8 Dd 60.04N 11.09 E
Kloga/Klooga 8 Ke 59.24N 24.10 E
Kłomnice 10 Pf 50.56N 19.21 E
Klondike Plateau 42 Dd 63.10N 139.55W
Klondike River 42 Dd 64.03N 139.26W
Klooga/Kloga 8 Ke 59.24N 24.10 E
Kloosteezande, Hontenisse- 12 Gc 51.23N 4.00 E
Klosi 15 Dh 41.29N 20.06 E
Klosterneuburg 14 Kb 48.18N 16.19 E
Klosters/Claustra 14 Dd 46.52N 9.52 E
Kloten 14 Cc 47.27N 8.35 E
Klotz, Lac - 42 Kd 60.40N 73.00W
Kluane Lake 42 Dd 61.15N 138.40W
Kluczbork 10 Of 50.59N 18.13 E
Knaben 8 Bf 58.39N 7.04 E
Knäred 8 Eh 56.32N 13.19 E
Kneža 15 Hf 43.30N 24.05 E
Knife River 45 Fc 47.20N 101.23W
Knin 14 Kf 44.02N 16.12 E
Knislinge 8 Fh 56.11N 14.05 E
Knittelfeld 14 Ic 47.13N 14.49 E
Knivsta 8 Ge 59.43N 17.48 E
Knjaževac 15 Ff 43.34N 22.15 E
Knobly Mountain 44 Hf 39.15N 79.05W
Knockmealdown Mountains/Cnoc Mhaoldonn 9 Fi 52.15N 8.00W
Knokke-Heist [Bel.] 12 Fc 51.21N 3.15 E
Knokke-Heist [Bel.] 11 Jc 51.21N 3.17 E
Knokke-Westkapelle 12 Fc 51.19N 3.18 E
Knolls grund 8 Gg 57.30N 17.30 E
Knøsen 8 Dg 57.12N 10.18 E
Knosós = Cnossus (EN) 15 In 35.18N 25.10 E
Knox, Cape- 42 Ef 54.11N 133.05W
Knox Coast 66 He 66.30S 105.00 E
Knoxville [Ia.-U.S.] 45 Jf 41.19N 93.06W
Knoxville [Tn.-U.S.] 39 Kf 35.58N 83.56W
Knud Rasmussen Land 67 Nd 80.00N 55.00W
Knüllgebirge 10 Ff 50.50N 9.30 E
Knutsholstind 8 Cc 61.26N 8.34 E
Knysna 31 Jl 34.02S 23.02 E
Ko, Kut 25 Kf 11.40N 102.35 E
Koartac 42 Kd 60.50N 69.30W
Koba 26 Eg 2.29S 106.24 E
Koba, Pulau- 26 Jh 6.25S 134.28 E
Kobar Sink 35 Gc 14.00N 40.30 E
Kobayashi 28 Ki 31.59N 130.59 E
Kobdo 22 Le 48.01N 91.38 E
Kobdo (Chovd) 27 Fb 48.06N 92.11 E
Kōbe 27 Pf 34.41N 135.10 E
Kobeljaki 16 Ie 49.08N 34.12 E
København 8 Ei 55.40N 12.10 E
København = Copenhagen (EN) 6 Hi 55.40N 12.35 E
Kobenni 32 Ff 15.55N 9.05W
Kobern-Gondorf 12 Jd 50.19N 7.28 E
Kobjaj 20 Hd 63.30N 126.26 E
Koblenz 10 Df 50.21N 7.36 E
Kobo 35 Fc 12.09N 39.39 E
Koboldo 20 If 52.58N 132.42 E
Kobra 7 Mg 59.19N 50.54 E
Kobrin 19 Ce 52.13N 24.23 E
Kobrinskoje 8 Ne 59.22N 30.14 E
Kobroor, Pulau- 26 Jh 6.12S 134.32 E
Kobuk 38 Cc 66.45N 161.00W
Kobuleti 16 Li 41.47N 41.45 E
Koca 24 Eb 41.41N 32.15 E
Kocabaş 24 Bb 40.22N 27.19 E
Koca Çay 15 Lj 38.43N 28.30 E
Koca Çay [Tur.] 24 Bb 40.08N 27.57 E
Koca Çay [Tur.] 24 Cd 36.17N 29.16 E
Koca Çay/Orhaneli 15 Lj 39.56N 28.32 E
Kočani 15 Fh 41.55N 22.25 E
Kocasu 15 Mj 39.42N 29.31 E
Kočečum 20 Fd 64.17N 100.10 E
Kočetovka 16 Lc 53.01N 40.31 E
Kočevje 14 Ie 45.39N 14.51 E
Kočevski rog 14 Ie 45.41N 15.00 E
Koch 42 Jc 69.35N 78.20W
Kŏch'ang 28 Ig 35.41N 127.55 E
Ko Chang 25 Kf 12.00N 102.23 E
Kōchi 27 Ne 33.33N 133.33 E
Kōchi Ken 28 Lh 33.20N 133.30 E
Kochisar Ovasi 24 Ec 38.50N 33.30 E
Kock 10 Se 51.39N 22.27 E
Kočkorka 18 Jc 42.11N 75.45 E
Kočmar 15 Kf 43.41N 27.28 E
Kočubej 19 Eg 44.23N 46.31 E
Kočubejevskoje 16 Lg 44.41N 41.50 E
Kodiak 39 Dd 57.48N 152.23W
Kodiak 38 Dd 57.30N 153.30W
Kodino 7 Je 63.44N 39.40 E
Kodok 35 Ed 9.53N 32.07 E
Kodomari 29a Bc 41.08N 140.18 E
Kodori 16 Lh 42.49N 41.10 E
Kodry 15 Lb 47.15N 28.15 E
Kodyma 16 Ge 48.01N 30.48 E
Kodža Balkan 15 Jg 42.50N 27.00 E
Koekenaap 37 Bf 31.29S 18.19 E
Koes 37 Be 25.59S 19.08 E
Kofa Mountains 46 Ij 33.20N 114.00W
Kofarli 15 Kl 37.45N 27.42 E
Kofaz 24 Bb 41.58N 27.12 E
Koffiefontein 37 Ce 29.30S 25.00 E
Kofiau, Pulau- 26 Ig 1.11S 129.50 E
Köflach 14 Jc 47.04N 15.05 E
Koforidua 31 Gh 6.05N 0.15W
Kōfu [Jap.] 29 Cd 35.18N 133.29 E
Kōfu [Jap.] 27 Od 35.39N 138.35 E
Koga 29 Fc 36.12N 139.42 E
Kogaluc 42 Je 59.38N 77.30W
Kōge 29 Dd 35.24N 134.15 E
Køge 7 Ci 55.27N 12.11 E
Køge Bugt 8 Ei 55.30N 12.20 E
Kogel 17 He 62.38N 57.07 E
Kogilnik 15 Md 45.51N 29.38 E
Kogilnik (Kunduk) 15 Md 45.51N 29.38 E
Kogon 34 Cc 11.09N 14.42W
Kogota 29 Gb 38.32N 141.01 E
Kohala Mountains 65a Fc 20.05N 155.43W
Kohāt 25 Eb 33.35N 71.26 E
Kohila 8 Ke 59.11N 24.40 E
Kohima 25 Ic 25.40N 94.07 E
Koh-i Mārān 25 Dc 29.05N 66.50 E
Kohinggo 63a Cc 8.13S 157.10 E
Kohma 7 Jh 56.57N 41.07 E
Kohtla-Jarve/Kohtla-Järve 19 Cd 59.25N 27.14 E
Kohtla-Järve/Kohtla-Jarve 19 Cd 59.25N 27.14 E
Kohu Daği 15 Mm 36.30N 29.50 E
Kohunlich 48 Oh 18.30N 88.55W
Koide 29 Fc 37.14N 138.57 E
Koigi/Kojgi 8 Kf 58.49N 25.40 E
Koin 17 Ee 63.10N 51.15 E
Koindu 34 Cd 8.28N 10.20W
Koitere 7 He 62.58N 30.45 E
Kojā 23 Jd 25.34N 61.13 E
Kojandytau 18 Lb 44.20N 78.45 E
Kojda 7 Kc 66.23N 42.31 E
Koje-Do 28 Jg 34.52N 128.37 E
Kojetin 10 Ng 49.21N 17.20 E
Kojgi/Koigi 8 Kf 58.49N 25.40 E
Ko-Jima [Jap.] 29 Fe 33.07N 139.40 E
Ko-Jima [Jap.] 28 Od 41.22N 139.47 E
Kojō 27 Md 38.57N 127.52 E
Kojonup 59 Df 33.50S 117.09 E
Kojtaš 18 Fd 40.14N 67.22 E
Kojtezek, Pereval- 18 If 37.29N 72.45 E
Kojur 24 Nd 36.23N 51.43 E
Kojva 17 Ig 58.15N 58.14 E
Kokab 35 Cc 10.03N 22.04 E
Kokai-Gawa 29 Gd 35.52N 140.08 E
Kokand 22 Je 40.33N 70.57 E
Kökar 7 Eg 59.55N 20.55 E
Kökarsfjärden 8 Ie 59.55N 20.45 E
Kokas 26 Jg 2.42S 132.26 E
Kokava nad Rimavicou 10 Ph 48.34N 19.50 E
Kokawa 29 Dd 34.17N 135.26 E
Kokčetav 22 Id 53.17N 69.25 E
Kokčetavskaja Oblast 19 Ge 53.30N 70.00 E
Kokemäenjoki 8 Ic 61.33N 21.42 E
Kokemäki/Kumo 7 Ff 61.15N 22.21 E
Kok-Jangak 19 Hg 40.59N 73.15 E
Kokkina 24 Ee 35.10N 32.36 E
Kokkola/Gamlakarleby 6 Ic 63.50N 23.07 E
Koko [Eth.] 35 Fc 10.20N 36.04 E
Koko [Nig.] 34 Fc 11.26N 4.30 E
Kokomo 43 Jc 40.29N 86.08W
Kokonau 26 Kg 4.43S 136.26 E
Kokong 37 Cd 24.27S 23.03 E
Koko Nor (EN) = Qinghai Hu 21 Mf 37.00N 100.20 E
Kokpekty 19 If 48.45N 82.24 E
Kokšaal-Tau, Hrebet- 19 Hg 41.00N 78.00 E
Kokšenga 7 Kf 61.27N 42.38 E
Koksijde 12 Ec 51.06N 2.39 E
Koksoak 42 Ke 58.31N 68.11W
Kokstad 31 Jl 30.32S 29.29 E
Koktal 18 Lb 44.05N 79.44 E
Koktokay/Fuyun 27 Ke 47.13N 89.39 E
Kokubu 28 Ki 31.44N 130.46 E
Kola 19 Db 68.53N 33.01 E
Kola, Pulau- 26 Jh 5.30S 134.35 E
Kolahun 34 Cd 8.17N 10.05W
Kolaka 26 Hg 4.03S 121.36 E
Kolamadulu Atoll 25a Bb 2.25N 73.10 E
Kola Peninsula (EN) = Kolski Poluostrov 5 Jb 67.30N 37.00 E
Kolār Gold Fields 25 Ff 12.55N 78.17 E
Kolari 7 Fc 67.20N 23.48 E
Kolárovo 10 Ni 47.55N 18.00 E
Kolašin 15 Cg 42.49N 19.32 E
Kolbäck 8 Ge 59.34N 16.15 E
Kolbäcksån 8 Ge 59.32N 16.16 E
Kolbio 36 Hc 1.09S 41.12 E
Kolbuszowa 10 Rf 50.15N 21.47 E
Kolby 8 Di 55.48N 10.33 E
Kolčugino 7 Jh 56.16N 39.23 E
Kolda 34 Cc 12.53N 14.57W
Kolding 6 Gd 55.31N 9.29 E
Kole [Zaire] 36 Dc 3.31S 22.27 E
Kole [Zaire] 36 Eb 2.07N 25.26 E
Koléa 13 Oh 36.38N 2.46 E
Kolendo 20 Jf 53.43N 142.57 E
Kolente 34 Cd 8.55N 13.08W
Kolesnoje 15 Mc 46.04N 29.45 E
Kolga 8 Ke 59.28N 25.29 E
Kolga, Zaliv-/Kolga Laht 8 Ke 59.30N 25.15 E
Kolga Laht/Kolga, Zaliv- 8 Ke 59.30N 25.15 E
Kolgompja, Mys- 8 Me 59.44N 28.35 E
Kolgujev, Ostrov- 5 Kb 69.05N 49.15 E
Kolhāpur 22 Jh 16.42N 74.13 E
Kolhozabad 18 Gf 37.35N 68.39 E
Kolhozbentskoje, Vodohranilišče- 18 Df 37.10N 62.30 E
Koli 7 Ge 63.06N 29.53 E
Kolimbiné 34 Cc 14.45N 11.00 E
Kolin 10 Lf 50.02N 15.13 E
Kolito 35 Fd 7.25N 38.07 E
Koljučinskaja Guba 20 Nc 66.50N 174.30W
Kolka 8 Jg 57.44N 22.27 E
Kolkasrags 7 Fh 57.46N 22.37 E
Kolki 16 Dd 51.07N 25.42 E
Kollinai 15 Fl 37.17N 22.22 E
Kollumúli 7a Cb 65.47N 14.21W
Kolmården 8 Gf 58.41N 16.35 E
Köln = Cologne (EN) 6 Ge 50.56N 6.57 E
Köln-Lövenich 12 Id 50.57N 6.50 E
Kolno 10 Rc 53.25N 21.56 E
Köln-Porz 10 Df 50.53N 7.03 E
Koło 10 Od 52.12N 18.38 E
Koloa 65a Bb 21.54N 159.28W
Kołobrzeg 10 Lb 54.12N 15.33 E
Kolodnja 16 Hb 54.49N 32.11 E
Kologriv 7 Kg 58.51N 44.17 E
Kolokani 34 Dc 13.34N 8.03W
Koloko 34 Dc 11.05N 5.19W
Kolokolkova Guba 17 Fb 68.30N 52.30 E
Kololo 35 Gd 7.27N 41.59 E
Kolombangara Island 60 Fi 8.00S 157.05 E
Kolomna 6 Jd 55.05N 38.49 E
Kolomyja 19 Cf 48.32N 25.01 E
Kolondiéba 34 Dc 11.06N 6.53W
Kolonga 65b Ac 21.08S 175.04W
Kolonodale 26 Hg 2.00S 121.19 E
Kolosovka 19 Hd 56.28N 73.36 E
Kolossa 34 Dc 13.52N 7.35W
Kolovai 65b Ac 21.06S 175.20W
Kolozero, Ozero- 7 Hb 68.15N 33.15 E
Kolp 7 Ig 59.20N 36.50 E
Kolpaševo 22 Kd 58.20N 82.50 E
Kolpino 7 Hg 59.45N 30.33 E
Kolpny 16 Jc 52.16N 37.00 E
Kolski Poluostrov = Kola Peninsula (EN) 5 Jb 67.30N 37.00 E
Kolťubanovski 16 Rc 52.57N 52.02 E
Kolubara 15 De 44.40N 20.15 E
Koluszki 10 Pe 51.44N 19.49 E
Koluton 19 Ge 51.42N 69.25 E
Kolva [R.S.F.S.R.] 19 Fb 65.55N 57.20 E
Kolva [R.S.F.S.R.] 17 Hf 60.22N 56.33 E
Kolvickoje, Ozero- 7 Hc 67.05N 33.30 E
Kolvrå 8 Ch 56.18N 9.08 E
Kolwezi 31 Jj 10.43S 25.28 E
Kolyma 21 Sc 69.30N 161.00 E
Kolyma Plain (EN) = Kolymskaja Nizmennost 21 Rc 68.30N 154.00 E
Kolyma Range (EN) = Kolymskoje Nagorje 21 Rc 62.30N 155.00 E
Kolymskaja Nizmennost = Kolyma Plain (EN) 21 Rc 68.30N 154.00 E
Kolymskoje Nagorje = Kolyma Range (EN) 21 Rc 62.30N 155.00 E
Kolyšlej 16 Nc 52.40N 44.31 E
Kolžat 19 Ig 43.29N 80.37 E
Kom 15 Gf 43.10N 23.03 E
Kom 36 Gb 1.05N 38.02 E
Komádi 10 Rj 47.00N 21.30 E
Komadugu Gana 34 Hc 13.05N 12.24 E
Komadugu Yobe 30 Ig 13.42N 13.24 E
Komagane 29 Ed 35.43N 137.54 E
Koma-ga-Take [Jap.] 29 Fd 35.45N 138.13 E
Koma-ga-Take [Jap.] 29 Gb 39.47N 140.50 E
Koma-ga-Take [Jap.] 29a Bb 42.04N 140.40 E
Komandorski Islands (EN) = Komandorskije Ostrova 21 Sd 55.00N 167.00 E
Komandorskije Ostrova = Komandorski Islands (EN) 21 Sd 55.00N 167.00 E
Komandorskiye Basin (EN) 20 Le 57.00N 168.00 E
Komarin 16 Gd 51.27N 30.32 E
Komarno 10 Tg 49.34N 23.43 E
Komárno 10 Oi 47.46N 18.09 E
Komárom 10 Oi 47.40N 18.15 E
Komárom 10 Oi 47.44N 18.07 E
Komatipoort 37 Ee 25.25S 31.55 E
Komatsu 27 Od 36.24N 136.37 E
Komatsujima 29 Dd 34.01N 134.35 E
Komba, Pulau- 26 Hh 7.47S 123.35 E
Kombissiri 34 Ec 12.04N 1.20W
Kombolcha 35 Fc 11.05N 39.45 E
Komebail Lagoon 64a Ac 7.24N 134.27 E
Komen/Comines 12 Ed 50.46N 2.59 E
Komi ASSR 19 Fc 64.00N 55.00 E
Komi-Permjacki Nacionalny Okrug 19 Fd 60.00N 54.30 E
Komló 10 Oj 46.12N 18.16 E
Kommunarsk 16 Ke 48.27N 38.52 E
Kommunary 8 Nd 60.55N 30.10 E
Kommunizma, Pik- = Communism Peak (EN) 21 Jf 38.57N 72.08 E
Komodo, Pulau- 26 Gh 8.36S 119.30 E
Komoé 30 Gh 5.12N 3.44W
Komoé 34 Ec 10.25N 4.20W
Komono 36 Bc 3.15S 13.14 E
Komoran, Pulau- 26 Kh 8.18S 138.45 E
Komoro 29 Fc 36.19N 138.24 E
Komotini 15 Ih 41.07N 25.24 E
Komovi 15 Cg 42.41N 19.39 E
Kompasberg 30 Jl 31.46S 24.32 E
Komrat 16 Ff 46.17N 28.38 E
Komsa 20 Dd 61.40N 89.25 E
Komsomolec 17 Kj 53.45N 62.02 E
Komsomolec, Ostrov- 21 La 80.30N 95.00 E
Komsomolec, Zaliv- 16 Rg 45.30N 52.45 E
Komsomolsk [R.S.F.S.R.] 7 Jh 57.02N 40.22 E
Komsomolsk [R.S.F.S.R.] 20 De 57.25N 86.02 E
Komsomolsk [Tur.-U.S.S.R.] 19 Gh 39.02N 63.36 E
Komsomolski [Kaz.-U.S.S.R.] 19 Ff 47.20N 53.44 E
Komsomolski [R.S.F.S.R.] 16 Og 45.22N 46.01 E
Komsomolski [R.S.F.S.R.] 7 Ki 54.27N 45.45 E
Komsomolski [R.S.F.S.R.] 19 Gb 67.35N 63.47 E
Komsomolski [R.S.F.S.R.] 17 Kf 61.20N 63.15 E
Komsomolski [R.S.F.S.R.] 20 Mc 69.12N 172.55 E
Komsomolsk-na-Amure 22 Pd 50.36N 137.02 E
Komsomolsk-na-Ustjurte 19 Fg 44.07N 58.17 E
Komsomolskoje [Ukr.-U.S.S.R.] 16 Je 49.36N 36.33 E
Komsomolskoje [Ukr.-U.S.S.R.] 16 Jf 47.37N 38.05 E
Komsomolskoj Pravdy, Ostrova- 20 Fa 77.15N 107.30 E
Kōmun-Do 28 Ig 34.02N 127.19 E
Kömür Burun 15 Jk 38.39N 26.25 E
Komusan 27 Mc 42.07N 129.42 E
Kona 34 Ec 14.57N 3.53W
Kona Coast 65a Fd 19.35N 155.56W
Konakovo 19 Dd 56.42N 36.46 E
Konar 23 Lc 34.25N 70.32 E
Konārak 25 Hh 19.54N 86.07 E
Konarha 23 Lb 35.15N 71.00 E
Konda 19 Gc 60.40N 69.46 E
Kondagaon 25 Ge 19.36N 81.40 E
Kondinin 59 Df 32.30S 118.16 E
Kondinskoje 17 Mg 59.40N 67.25 E
Kondoa 31 Ki 4.54S 35.47 E
Kondopoga 6 Jc 62.13N 34.17 E
Kondratjevo 8 Md 60.36N 28.02 E
Kondrovo 19 De 54.49N 35.55 E
Kondurča 7 Mj 53.31N 50.24 E
Koné 61 Bd 21.04S 164.52 E
Konečnaja 19 He 50.45N 78.27 E
Konevic, Ostrov- 8 Nd 60.50N 30.45 E
Kong 34 Ed 9.09N 4.37W
Kŏng 25 Lf 13.32N 105.58 E
Kŏng, Kaôh- 25 Kf 11.20N 103.00 E
Konga/Koonga 8 Jf 58.34N 24.00 E
Kongauru 64a Ac 7.04N 134.17 E
Kong Christian IX Land = King Christian IX Land (EN) 67 Mc 68.00N 36.30W
Kong Christian X Land = King Christian X Land (EN) 67 Md 72.20N 32.30W
Kongeå 8 Ci 55.23N 8.39 E
Kong Frederik VIII Land = King Frederik VIII Land (EN) 67 Md 78.30N 28.00W
Kong Frederik VI Kyst = King Frederik VI Coast (EN) 67 Nc 63.00N 43.30W
Konginkangas 8 Kb 62.46N 25.48 E
Kongju 28 If 36.27N 127.08 E
Kong Karls Land 41 Oc 78.50N 28.00 E
Kong Kong 35 Ed 7.26N 33.14 E
Kongolo 31 Ji 5.23S 27.00 E
Kongor 35 Ed 7.10N 31.21 E
Kong Oscars Fjord 67 Md 72.20N 23.00W
Kongoussi 34 Ec 13.19N 1.32W
Kongsberg 7 Bg 59.39N 9.39 E
Kongsøya 41 Oc 78.55N 28.40 E
Kongsvinger 7 Cf 60.12N 12.00 E
Kongur Shan 21 Jf 38.40N 75.21 E
Kongwa 36 Gd 6.12S 36.25 E
Kong Wilhelms Land 41 Jc 75.48N 23.15W
Koniecpol 10 Pf 50.48N 19.41 E
Königslutter am Elm 10 Gd 52.15N 10.49 E
Königswinter 12 Jd 50.41N 7.11 E
Königs Wusterhausen 10 Jd 52.17N 13.37 E
Konin 10 Od 52.13N 18.16 E
Konin 10 Od 52.15N 18.15 E
Konispoli 15 Dj 39.39N 20.10 E
Kónitsa 15 Di 40.03N 20.45 E
Konj 14 Kg 43.43N 16.55 E
Konjed Jān 24 Nf 33.30N 50.27 E
Konjic 14 Lg 43.39N 17.58 E
Konjuh 14 Mf 44.18N 18.33 E
Konkan 25 Ee 18.05N 73.25 E
Konkiep 37 Be 28.00S 17.23 E
Konko 36 Ed 10.12S 27.27 E
Konkouré 34 Cd 9.58N 13.42W
Konnevesi 8 Lb 62.40N 26.35 E
Konnevesi 8 Lb 62.37N 26.19 E
Konnivesi 8 Lc 61.10N 26.10 E
Konoša 6 Kc 60.58N 40.15 E

Index Symbols

Independent Nation
State, Region
District, County
Municipality
Colony, Dependency
Continent
Physical Region
Historical or Cultural Region
Mount, Mountain
Volcano
Hill
Mountains, Mountain Range
Hills, Escarpment
Plateau, Upland
Pass, Gap
Plain, Lowland
Delta
Salt Flat
Valley, Canyon
Crater, Cave
Karst Features
Depression
Polder
Desert, Dunes
Forest, Woods
Heath, Steppe
Oasis
Cape, Point
Coast, Beach
Cliff
Peninsula
Isthmus
Sandbank
Island
Atoll
Rock, Reef
Islands, Archipelago
Rocks, Reefs
Coral Reef
Well, Spring
Geyser
River, Stream
Waterfall Rapids
River Mouth, Estuary
Lake
Salt Lake
Intermittent Lake
Reservoir
Swamp, Pond
Canal
Glacier
Ice Shelf, Pack Ice
Ocean
Sea
Gulf, Bay
Strait, Fjord
Lagoon
Bank
Seamount
Tablemount
Ridge
Shelf
Basin
Escarpment, Sea Scarp
Fracture
Trench, Abyss
National Park, Reserve
Point of Interest
Recreation Site
Cave, Cavern
Historic Site
Ruins
Wall, Walls
Church, Abbey
Temple
Scientific Station
Airport
Port
Lighthouse
Mine
Tunnel
Dam, Bridge

Kōnosu 29 Fc 36.04N 139.30 E
Konotop 6 Je 51.14N 33.12 E
Konqi He 21 Ke 41.48N 86.47 E
Konrei 64a Bb 7.43N 134.37 E
Konsei-Tōge 29 Fc 36.52N 139.22 E
Konsen-Daichi 29a Db 43.20N 144.50 E
Końskie 10 Qe 51.12N 20.26 E
Konstantinovka 16 Je 48.29N 37.43 E
Konstantinovsk 16 Lf 47.35N 41.05 E
Konstanz 10 Fi 47.40N 9.11 E
Kontagora 31 Hg 10.24N 5.29 E
Kontcha 34 Hd 7.58N 12.14 E
Kontich 12 Gc 51.08N 4.27 E
Kontiolahti 7 Ge 62.46N 29.51 E
Kontiomäki 7 Gd 64.21N 28.09 E
Kontum 25 Lf 14.21N 108.00 E
Kontum, Plateau de- 25 Lf 13.55N 108.05 E
Konusin, Mys- 7 Kc 67.10N 43.50 E
Konya 22 Ff 37.52N 32.31 E
Konya Ovası 24 Ed 37.30N 33.20 E
Konz 12 Ie 49.42N 6.35 E
Konza 36 Gc 1.45 S 37.07 E
Konžakovski Kamen, Gora- 5 Ld 59.38N 59.08 E
Koocanusa, Lake- 46 Hb 48.45N 115.15W
Kook, Punta- 65d Ab 27.08 S 109.26W
Koolau Range 65a Db 21.21N 157.47W
Koonga/Konga 8 Jf 58.34N 24.00 E
Koorda 59 Df 30.50 S 117.29 E
Koosa 8 Lf 58.33N 27.07 E
Kootenay Lake 46 Gb 49.35N 116.50W
Kootenay River 38 He 49.15N 117.39W
Kopa 18 Jc 43.31N 75.48 E
Kopaonik 15 Df 43.15N 20.50 E
Kópasker 7a Ca 66.18N 16.27W
Kópavogur 7a Bb 64.06N 21.55W
Kopejsk 19 Gd 55.08N 61.39 E
Koper 14 He 45.33N 13.44 E
Kopervik 7 Ag 59.17N 5.18 E
Kopetdag, Hrebet- 21 Hf 37.45N 58.15 E
Kop Geçidi 24 Ib 40.01N 40.28 E
Ko Phangan 25 Jg 9.45N 100.00 E
Köping 7 Dg 59.31N 16.00 E
Köpingsvik 8 Gh 56.53N 16.43 E
Kopjevo 20 Df 54.59N 89.55 E
Kopliku 15 Cg 42.13N 19.26 E
Köpmanholmen 7 Ee 63.10N 18.34 E
Koporje 8 Me 59.40N 29.08 E
Koporski Zaliv 8 Me 59.45N 28.45 E
Koppal 25 Fe 15.21N 76.09 E
Koppang 7 Cf 61.34N 11.04 E
Koppány 10 Oj 46.35N 18.26 E
Kopparberg 8 Fe 59.52N 14.59 E
Kopparberg [2] 7 Df 61.00N 14.30 E
Kopparstenarna 8 Hf 58.32N 19.20 E
Koppom 8 Ee 59.43N 12.09 E
Koprivnica 14 Kd 46.10N 16.50 E
Kopru 24 Dd 36.49N 31.10 E
Köprüören 15 Mj 39.30N 29.47 E
Korab 5 Ig 41.44N 20.32 E
Korablino 7 Jj 53.57N 40.00 E
Korahe 35 Gd 6.36N 44.16 E
Korak 64a Bc 7.21N 134.34 E
Koralpe 14 Id 46.45N 15.00 E
Koramlik 27 Ed 37.32N 85.42 E
Korana 14 Je 45.30N 15.35 E
Korangi 25 Dd 24.47N 67.08 E
Koraput 25 Ge 18.49N 82.43 E
Korba 25 Gd 22.21N 82.41 E
Korbach 10 Ee 51.17N 8.52 E
Körby 8 Ei 55.51N 13.39 E
Korça 15 Di 40.37N 20.46 E
Korčula 14 Kh 42.57N 16.55 E
Korčula 14 Lh 42.58N 17.08 E
Korčulanski Kanal 14 Kg 43.03N 16.40 E
Kordān 24 Ne 35.56N 50.50 E
Kordel 12 Ie 49.50N 6.38 E
Kordestān [3] 23 Gb 35.30N 47.00 E
Kord Küy 23 Hb 36.48N 54.07 E
Kordun 14 Je 45.10N 15.35 E
Korea Bay (EN)=Sōjosŏn-man 21 Of 39.15N 125.00 E
Korean Peninsula (EN) 21 Of 35.30N 125.30 E
Korea Strait (EN)=Taehan-Haehyŏp 21 Of 34.40N 129.00 E
Korea Strait (EN)=Tsushima-Kaikyō 21 Of 34.40N 129.00 E
Korec 16 Ed 50.37N 27.10 E
Korem 35 Fc 12.30N 39.32 E
Korenovsk 19 Df 45.28N 39.28 E
Korf 20 Ld 60.18N 166.01 E
Korfovski 20 Ig 48.11N 135.04 E
Korgen 7 Cc 66.05N 13.50 E
Kõrgesaare/Kyrgesare 8 Je 59.00N 22.25 E
Korhogo 31 Gh 9.27N 5.38W
Korhogo [3] 34 Dd 9.35N 5.55W
Koribundu 34 Cd 7.43N 11.42W
Korienzé 34 Eb 15.24N 3.47W
Korinthiakós Kólpos=Corinth, Gulf of- (EN) 5 Ih 38.12N 22.30 E
Kórinthos 15 Fl 37.55N 22.53 E
Kórinthos = Corinth (EN) 15 Fl 37.55N 22.53 E
Korinthou, Dhiórix- = Corinth Canal (EN) 15 Fl 37.57N 22.58 E
Koriolei 31 Lh 1.48N 44.30 E
Kőrishegy 10 Ni 47.12N 17.49 E
Koritnik 15 Dg 42.05N 20.34 E
Kōriyama 27 Pd 37.24N 140.23 E
Korjakskaja Sopka, Vulkan- 21 Rd 53.20N 158.47 E
Korjakski Nacionalny okrug [3] 20 Le 60.00N 163.00 E
Korjakskoje Nagorje=Koryak Range (EN) 21 Tc 62.30N 172.00 E
Korjažma 19 Ec 61.18N 47.07 E
Korjukovka 16 Hd 51.47N 32.17 E
Korkino 17 Ji 54.54N 61.25 E
Korkodon 20 Kd 64.43N 154.05 E
Korkuteli 24 Dd 37.04N 30.13 E
Korla 22 Ke 41.44N 86.09 E
Kormakiti Burun 24 Ee 35.24N 32.56 E
Körmend 10 Mi 47.01N 16.36 E
Kormy, Gora- 20 Fd 62.15N 106.08 E
Kornati 14 Jg 43.49N 15.20 E
Kornejevka 17 Ni 54.01N 68.27 E
Kornešty 15 Kb 47.23N 28.00 E
Korneuburg 14 Kb 48.21N 16.20 E
Kórnik 10 Nd 52.17N 17.04 E
Kornsjø 7 Cg 58.57N 11.39 E
Koro 34 Ec 14.05N 3.04W
Koroba 59 Ia 5.40 S 142.45 E
Koroča 16 Jd 50.50N 37.13 E
Köroğlu Dağları 23 Da 40.40N 32.35 E
Köroğlu Tepe 24 Db 40.31N 31.53 E
Korogwe 36 Gd 5.09 S 38.29 E
Koro Island 57 If 17.32 S 179.42 E
Koroit 59 Ig 38.17 S 142.22 E
Korolevo 10 Th 48.08N 23.07 E
Korolevu 63d Ac 18.12 S 177.53 E
Korom, Bahr 35 Bc 10.35N 19.45 E
Koromiri 64p Cc 21.15 S 159.43W
Koronadal 26 He 6.12N 125.01 E
Korónia, Límni- 15 Gi 40.40N 23.10 E
Koronowo 10 Nc 53.19N 17.57 E
Koronowski e, Jezioro- 10 Nc 53.22N 17.55 E
Koror 57 Ed 7.20N 134.30 E
Koror 58 Ed 7.20N 134.29 E
Körös 10 Qj 46.43N 20.12 E
Koro Sea 61 Ec 18.00 S 180.00
Korosten 6 Ie 50.57N 28.39 E
Korostyšev 16 Fd 50.18N 29.05 E
Korotaiha 17 Jb 68.55N 60.55 E
Koro Toro 31 Ig 16.05N 18.30 E
Korovin Volcano 40a Db 52.22N 174.10W
Korpijärvi 8 Lc 61.15N 27.10 E
Korpilahti 7 Fe 62.01N 25.33 E
Korpo/Korppoo 8 Id 60.10N 21.35 E
Korppoo/Korpo 8 Id 60.10N 21.35 E
Korsakov 20 Jg 46.37N 142.51 E
Korshäs 7 Ee 62.47N 21.12 E
Korsholm/Mustasaari 8 Ia 63.05N 21.43 E
Korso 8 Kd 60.21N 25.06 E
Korsør 7 Ci 55.20N 11.09 E
Korsun-Ševčenkovski 16 Ge 49.26N 31.18 E
Korsze 10 Rb 54.10N 21.09 E
Kortemark 12 Fc 51.02N 3.02 E
Kortrijk/Courtrai 11 Jd 50.50N 3.16 E
Korucu 15 Kj 39.28N 27.22 E
Koru Dağ 15 Ji 40.42N 26.45 E
Koryak Range (EN)=Korjakskoje Nagorje 21 Tc 62.30N 172.00 E
Korzybie 10 Mb 54.18N 16.50 E
Kos 15 Km 36.53N 27.18 E
Kos 15 Km 36.50N 27.10 E
Kosa 17 Gg 59.56N 55.01 E
Kosa 17 Gf 60.11N 55.10 E
Kosai 29 Ed 34.43N 137.30 E
Kosaja Gora 16 Jb 54.09N 37.31 E
Kosaka 29 Ga 40.20N 140.44 E
Kō-Saki 29 Ad 34.05N 129.13 E
Ko Samui 25 Jg 9.30N 99.58 E
Kosan-ŭp 27 Md 38.51N 127.25 E
Kosčagyl 16 Rf 46.52N 53.47 E
Kościan 10 Md 52.06N 16.38 E
Kościerzyna 10 Nb 54.08N 18.00 E
Kosciusko 45 Lj 32.58N 89.35W
Kosciusko, Mount- 57 Fg 36.27 S 148.16 E
Kose/Koze 8 Ke 59.11N 25.05 E
Köse Dağ 24 Gb 40.06N 37.58 E
Kosha 35 Ea 20.49N 30.32 E
Koshigaya 29 Fd 35.55N 139.45 E
Koshiji 29 Fc 37.24N 138.45 E
Koshiki-Kaikyō 29 Bf 31.45N 130.05 E
Koshiki Rettō 27 Me 31.45N 129.45 E
Koshimizu 29a Db 43.51N 144.25 E
Kōshoku 28 Of 36.38N 138.06 E
Kōshyū Seamount (EN) 29 Df 31.35N 135.50 E
Košice 6 If 48.43N 21.15 E
Kosjerić 15 Cf 44.00N 19.55 E
Kosju 17 Ic 66.18N 59.53 E
Kosju 17 Id 65.38N 58.59 E
Kōsk 15 Ll 37.51N 28.03 E
Koski 8 Jd 60.39N 23.09 E
Koskolovo 8 Me 59.34N 28.30 E
Koslan 19 Ec 63.29N 48.52 E
Kosma 17 Dd 65.43N 49.50 E
Kosmaj 15 De 44.28N 20.33 E
Kosŏng 27 Md 38.40N 128.19 E
Kosov 15 Ia 48.15N 25.08 E
Kosovo 15 Eg 42.40N 21.05 E
Kosovo [3] 15 Dg 42.35N 21.00 E
Kosovska Mitrovica 15 Dg 42.53N 20.52 E
Kosrae (Kusaie) 57 Hd 5.19N 162.59 E
Kossol Passage 64a Bb 7.52N 134.36 E
Kossol Reef 64a Bb 7.57N 134.41 E
Kossou, Barrage de- 34 Dd 7.01N 5.29W
Kossovo 16 Dc 52.47N 25.10 E
Kostajnica 14 Ke 45.13N 16.33 E
Kostenec 15 Gg 42.16N 23.49 E
Koster 37 De 25.57 S 26.42 E
Kosteröarna 8 Df 58.55N 11.05 E
Kostjukoviči 16 Hc 53.23N 32.06 E
Kostjukovka 16 Gc 52.32N 30.58 E
Kostolac 15 Ee 44.44N 21.12 E
Kostopol 16 Ed 50.53N 26.29 E
Kostriževka 15 Ia 48.31N 25.45 E
Kostroma 6 Kd 57.47N 40.59 E
Kostromskaja Oblast [3] 19 Ed 58.30N 44.00 E
Kostrzyń 10 Nd 52.25N 17.14 E
Kostrzyn 10 Kd 52.37N 14.39 E
Kosva 17 Hg 58.50N 56.45 E
Koszalin 10 Mb 54.12N 16.09 E
Koszalin [2] 10 Mb 54.10N 16.10 E
Kőszeg 10 Mi 47.23N 16.33 E
Kota 22 Jg 25.16N 75.55 E
Kotaagung 26 Dh 5.30 S 104.38 E
Kota Baharu 22 Mi 6.08N 102.15 E
Kotabaru 26 Gg 3.14 S 116.13 E
Kotabumi 22 Mj 4.50 S 104.54 E
Kotadabok 26 Dg 0.30 S 104.33 E
Kota Kinabalu 22 Ni 5.59N 116.04 E
Kotamobagu 26 Hf 0.46N 124.19 E
Ko Tao 25 Jf 10.05N 99.52 E
Kotari 14 Jf 44.05N 15.30 E
Ko Tarutau 25 Jg 6.35N 99.40 E
Kota Tinggi 26 Df 1.44N 103.54 E
Kotel 15 Jg 42.53N 26.27 E
Kotelnič 19 Ed 58.20N 48.20 E
Kotelnikovo 16 Mf 47.38N 43.09 E
Kotelny, Ostrov- 21 Pb 75.45N 138.44 E
Kotelva 16 Id 50.03N 34.45 E
Köthen 10 He 51.45N 11.58 E
Kotido 36 Fb 3.00N 34.09 E
Kotjužany 29 Gb 47.50N 28.27 E
Kotka 7 Gf 60.28N 26.55 E
Kot Kapūra 25 Eb 30.35N 74.54 E
Kotlas 6 Kc 61.16N 46.35 E
Kotlenik 15 Df 43.51N 20.42 E
Kotlenski prohod 15 Jg 42.53N 26.27 E
Kotlik 40 Gd 63.02N 163.33W
Kotlin, Ostrov- 8 Md 60.00N 29.45 E
Kotly 8 Me 59.30N 28.48 E
Kotobi 34 Ed 6.42N 4.08W
Kotohira 29 Cd 34.11N 133.48 E
Koton Karifi 34 Gd 8.06N 6.48 E
Kotor 15 Bg 42.25N 18.46 E
Kotorosl 7 Jh 57.38N 39.57 E
Kotorska, Boka- 15 Bg 42.25N 18.40 E
Kotor Varoš 14 Lf 44.37N 17.22 E
Kotouba 34 Ed 8.41N 3.12W
Kotovo 19 Ee 50.18N 44.48 E
Kotovsk [Mold.-U.S.S.R.] 16 Ff 46.49N 28.33 E
Kotovsk [R.S.F.S.R.] 19 Ee 52.35N 41.32 E
Kotovsk [Ukr.-U.S.S.R.] 19 Cf 47.43N 29.33 E
Kotra 10 Uc 53.32N 24.17 E
Kotri 25 Dc 25.22N 68.18 E
Kötschach 14 Gd 46.40N 13.00 E
Kottayam 25 Fg 9.35N 76.31 E
Kotte 25 Gg 6.54N 80.02 E
Kotto 30 Jh 4.14N 22.02 E
Kotton 35 Id 9.37N 50.32 E
Kotu 65b Ba 19.57 S 174.48W
Kotu Group 57 Jg 20.00 S 174.45W
Kotuj 21 Mb 71.55N 102.05 E
Kotujkan 20 Fb 70.40N 103.25 E
Koturdepe 16 Rj 39.26N 53.40 E
Kotzebue 39 Cc 66.53N 162.39W
Kotzebue Sound 38 Cc 66.20N 163.00W
Kouandé 34 Fc 10.20N 1.42 E
Kouango 35 Be 4.58N 19.59 E
Kouba Modounga 35 Bb 15.40N 18.15 E
Koudougou 31 Gg 11.44N 4.31W
Kouéré 34 Ec 10.27N 3.59W
Koufália 15 Fi 40.47N 22.35 E
Koufonísion [Grc.] 15 Jo 34.56N 26.10 E
Koufonísion [Grc.] 15 Im 36.55N 25.35 E
Koufonísiou, Stenón- 15 Jo 35.00N 26.10 E
Kouilou [3] 36 Bc 4.00 S 12.00 E
Kouilou 30 Ii 4.28 S 11.41 E
Koukdjuak 42 Kc 66.47N 73.10W
Kouki 35 Bd 7.10N 17.18 E
Koukourou 35 Cd 7.12N 20.02 E
Koulamoutou 36 Bc 1.08 S 12.29 E
Koulikoro 34 Dc 12.51N 7.34W
Koulountou 34 Cc 13.15N 13.37W
Koumac 58 Hg 20.30 S 164.12 E
Koumac, Grand Récif de- 63b Be 20.32 S 164.04 E
Koumbi-Saleh 32 Ff 15.47N 7.58W
Koumi 29 Fc 36.05N 138.28 E
Koumpentoum 34 Cc 13.59N 14.34W
Koumra 35 Bd 8.55N 17.33 E
Koundara 31 Fg 12.29N 13.18W
Koundian 34 Cc 13.08N 10.42W
Kounoúpoi 15 Jm 36.32N 26.27 E
Kounradski 19 Hf 46.57N 75.01 E
Kounta 34 Eb 17.30N 0.40W
Koupéla 34 Ec 12.11N 0.21W
Kouqian → Yongji 28 Ic 43.40N 126.30 E
Kourou 54 Hb 5.09N 52.39W
Kouroussa 34 Dc 10.39N 9.53W
Koury 34 Ec 12.10N 4.48W
Koussané 34 Cc 14.52N 11.15W
Kousséri 34 Ic 12.05N 15.02 E
Koussi, Emi- 30 Ig 19.55N 18.30 E
Koutiala 31 Gg 12.23N 5.27W
Koutoumo 63b Cf 22.40 S 167.32 E
Koutous 34 Hc 14.30N 10.00 E
Kouvola 7 Gf 60.52N 26.42 E
Kouyou 36 Cc 0.45 S 16.38 E
Kova 20 Fe 58.20N 100.20 E
Kovač 15 Cf 43.31N 19.07 E
Kovačica 15 Dd 45.06N 20.38 E
Koval 10 Pd 52.31N 19.10 E
Kovalevka 15 Nc 46.42N 30.31 E
Kovarskas/Kavarskas 8 Ki 55.24N 25.03 E
Kovdor 19 Db 67.33N 30.25 E
Kovdozero, Ozero- 7 Hc 66.47N 32.00 E
Kovel 19 Ce 51.13N 24.43 E
Kovenskaja 17 Mf 61.24N 67.39 E
Kovin 15 De 44.45N 20.59 E
Kovinskaja Grjada 20 Fe 57.15N 101.00 E
Kovrov 19 Ed 56.24N 41.20 E
Kovylkino 7 Ki 54.02N 43.58 E
Kowŏn 27 Md 39.26N 127.15 E
Kowtal-e Do Rāh 23 Lb 36.07N 71.15 E
Kowt-e 'Ashrow 23 Kc 34.27N 68.48 E
Kōyama 29 Bf 31.19N 130.57 E
Köyceğiz 24 Cd 36.55N 28.43 E
Köycegiz Gölü 15 Lm 36.55N 28.40 E
Koyoshi-Gawa 29 Gb 39.24N 140.01 E
Koyuk 40 Gd 64.56N 161.08W
Koyukuk 38 Dc 64.56N 157.30W
Kozaklı 24 Fc 39.13N 34.49 E
Kozan 24 Fd 37.27N 35.49 E
Kozáni 15 Ei 40.18N 21.47 E
Kozara 14 Ke 45.00N 16.55 E
Kozawa 29a Bb 42.58N 140.40 E
Koze/Kose 8 Ke 59.11N 25.05 E
Kozelsk 19 De 54.01N 35.46 E
Koževnikovo 20 De 56.18N 84.00 E
Kozhikode → Calicut 22 Jh 11.19N 75.46 E
Kozienice 10 Re 51.35N 21.33 E
Kožim 17 Id 65.43N 59.31 E
Kožim 17 Id 65.45N 59.15 E
Kozima 14 He 45.37N 13.56 E
Kozjak 15 Eh 41.06N 21.54 E
Kozloduj 15 Gf 43.47N 23.44 E
Kozlovka 7 Li 55.52N 48.13 E
Kozlovščina 10 Vc 53.14N 25.20 E
Kozlu 24 Db 41.25N 31.46 E
Kozluk 24 Ic 38.11N 41.29 E
Koźmin 10 Ne 51.50N 17.28 E
Kozmodemjansk 7 Lh 56.20N 46.36 E
Kožozero, Ozero- 7 Je 63.05N 38.05 E
Kożuchów 10 Le 51.45N 15.35 E
Kožuf 15 Fh 41.09N 22.10 E
Kōzu-Shima 27 Oe 34.15N 139.10 E
Kožva 17 Hd 65.07N 56.57 E
Kožva 17 Hd 65.10N 57.00 E
Kozyrevsk 20 Ke 55.59N 159.59 E
Kpalimé 34 Fd 6.54N 0.38 E
Kpandu 34 Fd 7.00N 0.18 E
Kpessi 34 Fd 8.04N 1.16 E
Kra, Isthmus of- (EN)=Kra, Khokhok- 21 Lh 10.20N 99.00 E
Kra, Khokhok-=Kra, Isthmus of- (EN) 21 Lh 10.20N 99.00 E
Kraba 15 Ch 41.12N 19.59 E
Krabbfjärden 8 Gf 58.45N 17.40 E
Krabi 25 Jg 8.05N 98.53 E
Krabit, Mali i- 15 Cg 42.07N 19.59 E
Kra Buri 25 Jf 10.24N 98.47 E
Krâchéh 22 Mh 12.29N 106.01 E
Kragerø 7 Bg 58.52N 9.25 E
Kragujevac 15 De 44.01N 20.55 E
Kraichbach 12 Ke 49.22N 8.31 E
Kraichgau 10 Eg 49.10N 8.50 E
Kraichtal 12 Ke 49.07N 8.46 E
Krajina 14 Kf 44.45N 16.35 E
Krajina 15 Fe 44.10N 22.30 E
Krajište 15 Fg 42.35N 22.25 E
Krajnovka 16 Oh 43.57N 47.24 E
Kråka 8 Ca 63.28N 9.00 E
Krakatau, Gunung- 21 Mj 6.07 S 105.24 E
Krak des Chevaliers 24 Ge 34.46N 36.19 E
Krakovec 10 Tg 49.56N 23.13 E
Kraków [2] 10 Pf 50.05N 20.00 E
Kraków 6 He 50.03N 19.58 E
Kraków-Nowa Huta 10 Qf 50.04N 20.05 E
Krakowsko-Częstochowska, Wyżyna- 10 Pf 50.50N 19.15 E
Kralendijk 50 Bf 12.10N 68.16W
Kraljevica 14 Ie 45.16N 14.34 E
Kraljevo 15 Df 43.44N 20.43 E
Kralupy nad Vltavou 10 Kf 50.14N 14.19 E
Kramatorsk 16 Je 48.43N 37.32 E
Kramfors 7 De 62.56N 17.47 E
Krammer 12 Gc 51.38N 4.15 E
Kranenburg 12 Ic 51.47N 6.01 E
Kranidhion 15 Gl 37.23N 23.09 E
Kranj 14 Id 46.14N 14.22 E
Krapina 14 Jd 46.10N 15.53 E
Krapkowice 10 Nf 50.29N 17.56 E
Kras=Karst (EN) 5 Hf 45.48N 14.00 E
Krasavino 19 Ec 60.59N 46.28 E
Krasiczyn 10 Sg 49.48N 22.39 E
Krasilov 16 Ee 49.37N 26.59 E
Kraskino 28 Kc 42.44N 130.48 E
Krāslava/Kraslava 7 Gi 55.54N 27.10 E
Kraslava/Krāslava 7 Gi 55.54N 27.10 E
Krasnaja Poljana 16 Lh 43.40N 40.12 E
Kraśnik 10 Sf 50.56N 22.13 E
Kraśnik Fabryczny, Kraśnik- 10 Sf 50.58N 22.12 E
Kraśnik-Kraśnik Fabryczny 10 Sf 50.58N 22.12 E
Krasnoarmejsk [Kaz.-U.S.S.R.] 19 Ge 53.57N 69.43 E
Krasnoarmejsk [R.S.F.S.R.] 19 Ee 51.02N 45.42 E
Krasnoarmejsk [Ukr.-U.S.S.R.] 16 Je 48.11N 37.12 E
Krasnoarmejski 20 Mc 69.37N 172.02 E
Krasnodar 6 Jf 45.02N 39.00 E
Krasnodarski Kraj [3] 19 Df 45.20N 39.30 E
Krasnodon 16 Ke 48.17N 39.44 E
Krasnogorodskoje 8 Mh 56.47N 28.18 E
Krasnogorsk [R.S.F.S.R.] 20 Jg 48.26N 142.10 E
Krasnogorsk [R.S.F.S.R.] 7 Ii 55.51N 37.20 E
Krasnogorski 17 Ji 54.36N 61.15 E
Krasnograd 19 Df 49.22N 35.27 E
Krasnogvardejsk 18 Fe 39.45N 67.16 E
Krasnogvardejskoje 16 Lg 45.49N 41.31 E
Krasnoholmski 17 Gh 56.02N 55.05 E
Krasnoilsk 15 Ia 48.02N 25.48 E
Krasnojarsk 22 Ld 56.01N 92.50 E
Krasnojarski 17 Ij 51.58N 59.57 E
Krasnojarski Kraj [3] 20 Ee 57.30N 95.00 E
Krasnojarskoje Vodohranilišče 20 Ee 55.05N 91.30 E
Krasnoje 10 Ug 49.49N 24.39 E
Krasnoje Selo 7 Hg 59.43N 30.03 E
Krasnoje Znamja 18 Df 36.50N 62.29 E
Krasnokamensk 20 Gf 50.00N 118.05 E
Krasnokamsk 19 Fd 58.04N 55.45 E
Krasnokutsk 19 He 52.59N 75.59 E
Krasnolesje 8 Jj 54.23N 22.25 E
Krasnolesny 16 Kd 51.52N 39.35 E
Krasnooktjabrski [Kirg.-U.S.S.R.] 18 Jc 42.45N 74.20 E
Krasnooktjabrski [R.S.F.S.R.] 7 Lh 56.43N 47.37
Krasnooskolskoje Vodohranilišče 16 Je 49.25N 37.35
Krasnoostrovski 8 Md 60.12N 28.39
Krasnoperekopsk 19 Df 45.57N 33.47
Krasnorečenski 28 Mb 44.38N 135.15
Krasnoščelje 7 Ic 67.23N 37.02
Krasnoselki 10 Uc 53.14N 24.30
Krasnoselkup 20 Dc 65.41N 82.28
Krasnoslobodsk [R.S.F.S.R.] 16 Ne 48.40N 44.31
Krasnoslobodsk [R.S.F.S.R.] 7 Ki 54.27N 43.47
Krasnoturinsk 19 Gd 59.46N 60.18
Krasnoufimsk 19 Fd 56.37N 57.46
Krasnouralsk 19 Gd 58.24N 60.03
Krasnousolski 19 Fe 53.54N 56.29
Krasnovišersk 19 Fc 60.23N 57.03
Krasnovodsk 22 He 40.00N 53.00
Krasnovodskaja Oblast [3] 19 Fh 39.50N 55.00
Krasnovodski Poluostrov 16 Rc 40.30N 53.15
Krasnovodski Zaliv 16 Rj 39.50N 53.15
Krasnozatonski 19 Fc 61.41N 51.01
Krasnozavodsk 7 Jh 56.29N 38.13
Krasnoznamensk [Kaz.-U.S.S.R.] 19 Ge 51.03N 69.30
Krasnoznamensk [R.S.F.S.R.] 8 Jj 54.52N 22.27
Krasny Čikoj 20 Ff 50.25N 108.45
Krasny Holm 7 Ig 58.04N 37.09
Krasny Jar [R.S.F.S.R.] 20 De 57.07N 84.40
Krasny Jar [R.S.F.S.R.] 19 Hd 55.14N 72.56
Krasnyje Barrikady 16 Of 46.13N 47.50
Krasnyje Okny 15 Mb 47.34N 29.23
Krasny Kut 19 Ee 50.58N 46.58
Krasny Liman 16 Je 48.59N 37.47
Krasny Luč 16 Ke 48.09N 38.57
Krasny Oktjabr 19 Gd 55.37N 64.48
Krasny Profintern 7 Jh 57.47N 40.29
Krasnystaw 10 Tf 50.59N 23.10
Krasny Sulin 16 Lf 47.53N 40.09
Kratovo 15 Fg 42.05N 22.12
Kraulshavn 41 Gd 74.10N 57.00W
Krăvanh, Chuŏr Phnum- 21 Mh 12.00N 103.15
Krawang 26 Eh 6.19 S 107.17
Krefeld 10 Ce 51.20N 6.34
Krefeld-Hüls 12 Ic 51.22N 6.31
Kremastá, Límni- 15 Ek 38.50N 21.30
Kremenchug Reservoir (EN)=Kremenčugskoje Vodohranilišče 5 Jf 49.20N 32.30
Kremenčug 6 Jf 49.04N 33.25
Kremenčugskoje Vodohranilišče=Kremenchug Reservoir (EN) 5 Jf 49.20N 32.30
Kremenec 16 Dd 50.06N 25.43
Kremennaja 16 Ke 49.03N 38.14
Kremmling 45 Cf 40.03N 106.24W
Krems 14 Jb 48.25N 15.36
Krems an der Donau 14 Jb 48.25N 15.36
Kremsmünster 14 Ib 48.03N 14.08
Krenitzin Islands 40a Eb 54.08N 166.00W
Kresta, Zaliv- 20 Nc 65.30N 179.00W
Krestcy 7 Hg 58.15N 32.31
Krestovy, Pereval- 16 Nh 42.32N 44.30
Kretek 26 Fh 7.59 S 110.19
Kretinga 7 Ei 55.55N 21.17
Kreuzau 12 Id 50.45N 6.29
Kreuzberg 10 Ff 50.22N 9.58
Kreuzlingen 14 Dc 47.39N 9.10
Kreuztal 10 Df 50.58N 7.59
Kria Vrisi 15 Fi 40.41N 22.18
Kribi 31 Hh 2.57N 9.55
Kričev 16 Ge 53.43N 31.43
Kričim 15 Hg 42.08N 24.31
Krim 14 Ie 45.56N 14.28
Krimml 14 Gc 47.13N 12.11
Krimpen aan den IJssel 12 Gc 51.55N 4.35
Kriós, Ákra- 5 Ih 35.14N 23.35
Krishna 21 Kh 15.57N 80.59
Krishnanagar 25 Hd 23.24N 88.30
Kristdala 8 Gg 57.24N 16.11
Kristiansand 6 Gd 58.10N 8.00
Kristianstad 7 Dh 56.02N 14.08
Kristianstad [2] 7 Ch 56.15N 14.00
Kristiansund 6 Gc 63.07N 7.45
Kristiinankaupunki/Kristinestad 7 Ee 62.17N 21.23
Kristineberg 7 Ed 65.04N 18.35
Kristinehamn 7 Dg 59.20N 14.07
Kristinestad/Kristiinankaupunki 7 Ee 62.17N 21.23
Kriti = Crete (EN) 5 Ih 35.15N 24.45
Kriti = Crete (EN) [2] 15 Hn 35.35N 25.00
Kritikón Pélagos = Crete, Sea of- (EN) 15 Hn 36.00N 25.00
Krivaja 14 Mf 44.27N 18.10
Kriva Palanka 15 Fg 42.12N 22.21
Krivići 8 Lj 54.44N 27.20
Krivodol 15 Gf 43.23N 23.29
Krivoje Ozero 16 Gf 47.57N 30.21
Krivoj Rog 6 Jf 47.54N 33.21
Križevci 14 Kd 46.02N 16.32
Krk 14 Ie 45.05N 14.35
Krk 14 Ie 45.02N 14.35
Krka [Yugo.] 14 Jg 43.43N 15.51
Krka [Yugo.] 14 Je 45.53N 15.36
Krkonoše 10 Lf 50.46N 15.35
Krn 14 Hd 46.16N 13.40
Krndija 14 Le 45.27N 17.55
Krnjača, Beograd- 15 De 44.52N 20.28
Krnov 10 Nf 50.05N 17.41
Krobia 10 Me 51.47N 16.58
Krøderen 8 Cd 60.15N 9.40
Krokeai 15 Fm 36.53N 22.33
Krokek 8 Gf 58.40N 16.24
Kroken 7 Dd 65.22N 14.16

Index Symbols

[1] Independent Nation
[2] State, Region
[3] District, County
[4] Municipality
[5] Colony, Dependency
Continent
Physical Region
Historical or Cultural Region
Mount, Mountain
Volcano
Hill
Mountains, Mountain Range
Hills, Escarpment
Plateau, Upland
Pass, Gap
Plain, Lowland
Delta
Salt Flat
Valley, Canyon
Crater, Cave
Karst Features
Depression
Polder
Desert, Dunes
Forest, Woods
Heath, Steppe
Oasis
Cape, Point
Coast, Beach
Cliff
Peninsula
Isthmus
Sandbank
Island
Atoll
Rock, Reef
Islands, Archipelago
Rocks, Reefs
Coral Reef
Well, Spring
Geyser
River, Stream
Waterfall Rapids
River Mouth, Estuary
Lake
Salt Lake
Intermittent Lake
Reservoir
Swamp, Pond
Canal
Glacier
Ice Shelf, Pack Ice
Ocean
Sea
Gulf, Bay
Strait, Fjord
Lagoon
Bank
Seamount
Tablemount
Ridge
Shelf
Basin
Escarpment, Sea Scarp
Fracture
Trench, Abyss
National Park, Reserve
Point of Interest
Recreation Site
Cave, Cavern
Historic Site
Ruins
Wall, Walls
Church, Abbey
Temple
Scientific Station
Airport
Port
Lighthouse
Mine
Tunnel
Dam, Bridge

Index Symbols

[1] Independent Nation	Historical or Cultural Region	Pass, Gap
[2] State, Region	Mount, Mountain	Plain, Lowland
[3] District, County	Volcano	Delta
[4] Municipality	Hill	Salt Flat
[5] Colony, Dependency	Mountains, Mountain Range	Valley, Canyon
Continent	Hills, Escarpment	Crater, Cave
Physical Region	Plateau, Upland	Karst Features

Depression	Coast, Beach	Rock, Reef
Polder	Cliff	Islands, Archipelago
Desert, Dunes	Peninsula	Rocks, Reefs
Forest, Heath, Steppe	Isthmus	Coral Reef
Oasis	Sandbank	Well, Spring
Cape, Point	Island	Geyser
		River, Stream

Waterfall Rapids	Canal	Lagoon
River Mouth, Estuary	Glacier	Bank
Lake	Ice Shelf, Pack Ice	Seamount
Salt Lake	Ocean	National Park, Reserve
Intermittent Lake	Sea	Point of Interest
Reservoir	Ridge	Recreation Site
Swamp, Pond	Gulf, Bay	Basin
	Strait, Fjord	Shelf

Escarpment, Sea Scarp	Historic Site
Fracture	Ruins
Trench, Abyss	Wall, Walls
Church, Abbey	Mine
Temple	Tunnel
Scientific Station	Dam, Bridge
Airport	Port
	Lighthouse

Name	Page	Grid	Lat.	Long.
Kwangsi Chuang (EN)= Guangxi Zhuangzu Zizhiqu (Kuang-hsi-chuang-tsu Tzu-chih-ch'ü) [2]	27	Ig	24.00N	109.00 E
Kwangsi Chuang (EN)= Kuang-hsi-chuang-tsu Tzu-chih-ch'ü → Guangxi Zhuangzu Zizhiqu [2]	27	Ig	24.00N	109.00 E
Kwangtung (EN)= Guangdong Sheng (Kuang-tung Sheng) [2]	27	Jg	23.00N	113.00 E
Kwangtung (EN)=Kuang-tun Sheng → Guangdong Sheng [2]	27	Jg	23.00N	113.00 E
Kwanmo-bong	28	Jd	41.42N	129.13 E
Kwara [2]	34	Fd	8.30N	5.00 E
Kweichow (EN)=Guizhou Sheng (Kuei-chou Sheng) [2]	27	If	27.00N	107.00 E
Kweichow (EN)=Kuei-chou Sheng → Guizhou Sheng [2]	27	If	27.00N	107.00 E
Kweneng [3]	37	Cd	24.00S	24.00 E
Kwenge	30	Ii	4.50S	18.44 E
Kwethluk	40	Gd	60.49N	161.27W
Kwidzyn	10	Oc	53.45N	18.56 E
Kwigillingok	40	Ge	59.51N	163.08W
Kwilu	30	Ii	3.22S	17.22 E
Kwisa	10	Le	51.35N	15.25 E
Kwoka, Gunung-	26	Jg	0.31S	132.27 E
Kyabé	31	Ih	9.27N	18.57 E
Kyabram	59	Jg	36.19S	145.03 E
Kyaikkami	25	Je	16.04N	97.34 E
Kyaikto	25	Je	17.18N	97.01 E
Kyaka	36	Fc	1.16S	31.25 E
Kyancutta	58	Eh	33.08S	135.34 E
Kyan-Zaki	29b	Ab	26.05N	127.40 E
Kyaukpyu	25	Id	20.51N	92.58 E
Kyaukse	25	Jd	21.36N	96.08 E
Kybartai/Kibartaj	8	Jj	54.38N	22.44 E
Kyeintali	25	Ie	18.00N	94.29 E
Kyelang	25	Fb	32.35N	77.02 E
Kyfhauser	10	He	51.25N	11.10 E
Kyjov	10	Ng	49.01N	17.08 E
Kyle, Lake-	37	Ed	20.12S	31.00 E
Kyle of Lochalsh	9	Hd	57.17N	5.43W
Kyll	10	Cg	49.48N	6.42 E
Kyllburg	12	Id	50.02N	6.35 E
Kyma	7	Ld	64.48N	47.31 E
Kymi [2]	7	Gf	61.00N	28.00 E
Kymijoki	8	Ld	60.30N	26.52 E
Kyn	17	Ih	57.52N	58.32 E
Kynnefjäll	8	Df	58.42N	11.41 E
Kynsivesi	8	Lb	62.25N	26.10 E
Kyoga, Lake-	30	Kh	1.30N	33.00 E
Kyōga-Dake	29	Be	33.00N	130.05 E
Kyōga-Misaki	28	Mg	35.45N	135.11 E
Kyonan	29	Fd	35.07N	139.49 E
Kyŏnggi-Do [2]	28	If	37.30N	127.15 E
Kyŏnggi-man	28	Hf	37.25N	126.00 E
Kyŏngju	27	Md	35.50N	129.13 E
Kyŏngsang-Namdo [2]	28	Jg	35.15N	128.30 E
Kyŏngsang-Pukto [2]	28	Jf	36.20N	128.40 E
Kyŏngsŏng	28	Jd	41.40N	129.40 E
Kyōto	22	Pf	35.00N	135.45 E
Kyōto Fu [2]	28	Mg	35.25N	135.15 E
Kypros/Kıbrıs=Cyprus (EN) [1]	22	Ff	35.00N	33.00 E
Kypros/Kıbrıs=Cyprus (EN)	21	Ff	35.00N	33.00 E
Kyra	20	Gg	49.36N	111.58 E
Kyren	20	Ff	51.41N	102.10 E
Kyrenia/Girne	24	Ee	35.20N	33.19 E
Kyrgesare/Körgesaare	8	Je	59.00N	22.25 E
Kyrgyz Sovetik Socialistik Respublikasy/Kirgizskaja SSR [2]	19	Hg	41.30N	75.00 E
Kyritz	10	Id	52.57N	12.24 E
Kyrkheden	8	Ed	60.10N	13.29 E
Kyrksæterora	7	Be	63.17N	9.06 E
Kyrkslätt/Kirkkonummi	8	Kd	60.07N	24.26 E
Kyrö	8	Jd	60.42N	22.45 E
Kyrönjoki	8	Ia	63.14N	21.45 E
Kyrösjärvi	8	Jc	61.45N	23.10 E
Kyröskoski	8	Jc	61.40N	23.11 E
Kyštym	19	Gd	55.42N	60.34 E
Kysucké Nové Mesto	10	Og	49.18N	18.48 E
Kythera (EN)=Kíthira	5	Ih	36.15N	23.00 E
Kythraia	24	Ee	35.15N	33.29 E
Kyuquot Sound	46	Bb	49.55N	127.25W
Kyūshū	21	Pf	32.50N	131.00 E
Kyushu-Palau Ridge (EN)	3	Ih	20.00N	136.00 E
Kyushū-Sanchi	29	Be	32.40N	131.10 E
Kyyjärvi	7	Fe	63.02N	24.34 E
Kyyvesi	8	Lc	61.55N	27.05 E
Kyzikos	24	Bb	40.28N	27.47 E
Kyzyl	22	Ld	51.42N	94.27 E
Kyzylart, Pereval-	19	Hh	39.22N	73.20 E
Kyzyl-Kija	19	Hg	40.14N	72.12 E
Kyzylkum	21	Ie	42.00N	64.00 E
Kyzylrabot	19	Hh	37.28N	74.45 E
Kyzylsu [U.S.S.R.]	18	Gf	37.22N	69.22 E
Kyzylsu [U.S.S.R.]	18	He	39.17N	71.25 E
Kyzylžar	19	Gf	48.17N	69.49 E
Kzyl-Orda	22	Ie	44.48N	65.28 E
Kzyl-Ordinskaja Oblast [3]	19	Gf	45.00N	65.00 E
Kzyltu	19	He	53.41N	72.15 E
L				
Laa an der Thaya	14	Kb	48.43N	16.23 E
Laakdal	12	Gc	51.05N	4.59 E
La Alberca	13	Fd	40.29N	6.06W
La Alcarria	13	Jd	40.31N	2.45W
La Almunia de Doña Godina	13	Kc	41.29N	1.22W
La Ametlla de Mar	13	Md	40.54N	0.48 E
La Ardilla, Cerro-	48	Hf	22.15N	102.40W
La Armuña	13	Gc	41.05N	5.35W
Laasphe	12	Kd	50.56N	8.24 E
La Asunción	54	Fa	11.02N	63.53W
Laau Point	65a	Db	21.06N	157.16W
Laayoune	13	Ni	35.42N	2.00 E
Lab	15	Eg	42.45N	21.01 E
Laba	16	Kg	45.10N	39.40 E
La Babia	48	Hc	28.34N	102.04W
Laba Daği	15	Kl	37.22N	27.33 E
Labaddey	35	Ge	0.32N	42.45 E
Labadie Bank	9	Ek	50.30N	8.15W
La Banda	56	Hc	27.44S	64.15W
La Bañeza	13	Gb	42.18N	5.54W
La Barca	48	Hg	20.17N	102.34W
Labardén	55	Cm	36.57S	58.06W
La Barge	46	Je	42.16N	110.12W
La Barra, Punta-	49	Lh	11.30N	70.10W
La-Barre-en-Ouche	12	Cf	48.57N	0.40 E
La Baule-Escoublac	11	Dg	47.17N	2.24W
Labbezanga	34	Fc	14.59N	0.43 E
Labé	31	Fg	11.19N	12.17W
Labe=Elbe (EN)	5	Ge	53.50N	9.00 E
La Belle	44	Gl	26.46N	81.26W
Labelle	44	Jb	46.17N	74.45W
La Berzosa	13	Fd	40.35N	6.40W
Labin	14	Ie	45.05N	14.08 E
Labinsk	19	Eg	44.35N	40.44 E
Labis	26	Df	2.23N	103.02 E
La Bisbal/La Bisbal d'Empordà	13	Pc	41.57N	3.03 E
La Bisbal d'Empordà/La Bisbal	13	Pc	41.57N	3.03 E
La Blanca, Laguna-	55	Bj	30.14S	60.38W
Laboe	10	Gb	54.24N	10.13 E
Laborec	10	Rh	48.31N	21.54 E
Laborie	51k	Bb	13.45N	61.00W
Labota	26	Hg	2.52S	122.10 E
Labouheyre	11	Fj	44.13N	0.55W
Laboulaye	56	Hd	34.07S	63.24W
Labra, Peña-	13	Ha	43.03N	4.26W
Labrador	38	Md	55.00N	70.00W
Labrador, Coast of-	38	Me	56.00N	60.35W
Labrador Basin (EN)	3	Dd	53.00N	48.00W
Labrador City	39	Md	52.57N	66.54W
Labrador Sea	38	Nd	57.00N	53.00W
Labrang → Xiahe	27	Hd	35.18N	102.30 E
Lábrea	53	Jf	7.16S	64.46W
Labrieville	44	Ma	49.19N	69.34W
Labrit	11	Fj	44.06N	0.33W
Labuan, Pulau-	26	Ge	5.19N	115.13 E
Labudalin → Ergun Youqi	27	La	50.16N	120.09 E
Labuha	26	Ig	0.37S	127.29 E
Labuhan	26	Eh	6.22S	105.50 E
Labuhanbajo	26	Gh	8.29S	119.54 E
Labuhanbilik	26	Df	2.31N	100.10 E
Labuk, Teluk-	26	Ge	6.10N	117.50 E
La Bureba	13	Ib	42.36N	3.24W
Labutta	25	Ie	16.09N	94.46 E
Labytnangi	22	Ic	66.39N	66.21 E
Lac [3]	35	Ac	13.30N	14.20 E
Lača, Ozero-	7	Jf	61.20N	38.50 E
La Cadena	48	Ge	25.53N	104.12W
La Calamine/Kelmis	12	Hd	50.43N	6.00 E
La Calandria	55	Cj	30.48S	58.39W
Lac Allard	42	Lf	50.30N	63.30W
La Campiña	13	Hg	37.45N	4.45W
Lacanau	11	Ej	44.59N	1.05W
Lacanau, Étang de-	11	Ej	44.58N	1.07W
Lacanau-Océan	11	Ei	45.00N	1.12W
Lacantún, Río-	48	Ni	16.36N	90.39W
La-Capelle	11	Je	49.58N	3.55 E
Laćarak	15	Ce	45.00N	19.34 E
La Carlota [Arg.]	56	Hd	33.26S	63.18W
La Carlota [Phil.]	26	Hd	10.25N	122.55 E
La Carlota [Sp.]	13	Hg	37.40N	4.56W
La Carolina	13	If	38.15N	3.37W
Lacaune	11	Ik	43.43N	2.42 E
Lacaune, Monts de-	11	Ik	43.40N	2.36 E
Laccadive Islands	21	Jh	11.00N	72.00 E
Lac du Bonnet	45	Ha	50.35N	96.05W
La Ceiba [Hond.]	39	Kh	15.47N	86.50W
La Ceiba [Ven.]	49	Li	9.28N	71.04W
Lacepede Bay	59	Hg	36.45S	139.45 E
Lacepede Islands	59	Ec	16.50S	122.10 E
La Cerdaña/La Cerdanya	13	Nb	42.24N	1.40 E
La Cerdanya/La Cerdaña	13	Nb	42.24N	1.40 E
Lacey	46	Dc	47.07N	122.49W
Lac Giao	25	Lf	12.40N	108.03 E
La Chaise-Dieu	11	Ji	45.19N	3.42 E
La Charité-sur-Loire	11	Jg	47.11N	3.01 E
La Châtre	11	Hh	46.35N	1.59 E
La Chaux-de-Fonds	14	Ac	47.06N	6.50 E
Lachay, Punta-	54	Cf	11.18S	77.39W
La China, Sierra-	55	Bm	36.47S	60.34W
Lachine	44	Kc	45.26N	73.40W
Lachlan River	57	Fh	34.21S	143.57 E
La Chorrera [Col.]	54	Dd	0.45S	73.00W
La Chorrera [Pan.]	47	Ig	8.53N	79.47W
Laçi	15	Ch	41.38N	19.43 E
Lačin	16	Oj	39.39N	46.33 E
La Ciotat	11	Lk	43.10N	5.36 E
Łąck	10	Pd	52.28N	19.40 E
Lackawanna	44	Hd	42.49N	78.49W
Lac La Biche	42	Gf	54.46N	111.58W
Lac la Martre	42	Fd	63.21N	117.00W
Lac Mégantic	42	Kg	45.35N	70.53W
La Colina	55	Bm	37.20S	61.32W
La Coloma	49	Fb	22.15N	83.34W
La Colorada	48	Dc	28.41N	110.25W
Lacombe	42	Gf	52.28N	113.44W
Lacon	45	Lf	41.02N	89.24W
La Concepción [Pan.]	49	Fi	8.31N	82.37W
La Concepción [Ven.]	49	Lh	10.48N	71.46W
La Concha	48	Gg	21.46N	105.29W
Laconi	14	Dk	39.51N	9.03 E
Laconia	43	Mc	43.32N	71.29W
Laconia, Gulf of- (EN) = Lakonikós Kólpos	15	Fm	36.35N	22.40 E
La Coronilla	55	Fk	33.44S	53.31W
La Coruña	6	Fg	43.22N	8.23W
La Coruña [3]	13	Da	43.10N	8.25W
La Côte-Saint-André	11	Li	45.23N	5.15 E
La Couronne	11	Gi	45.37N	0.06 E
La Courtine-le-Trucq	11	Ii	45.42N	2.16 E
Lacq	11	Fk	43.25N	0.38W
Lacroix-sur-Meuse	12	Hf	48.58N	5.31 E
La Crosse [Ks.-U.S.]	45	Gg	38.32N	99.18W
La Crosse [Wi.-U.S.]	39	Je	43.49N	91.15W
La Cruz [Arg.]	56	Ic	29.10S	56.38W
La Cruz [C.R.]	49	Eh	11.04N	85.39W
La Cruz [Mex.]	47	Cd	23.55N	106.54W
La Cruz [Ur.]	56	Id	33.56S	56.15W
La Cruz de Río Grande	49	Eg	13.06N	84.10W
La Cruz de Taratara	49	Mh	11.03N	69.44W
La Cuesta	48	Hc	28.45N	102.25W
La Cumbre	56	Hd	30.58S	64.30W
Lac Yora	35	Cb	19.08N	20.35 E
Ladário	55	Dd	19.01S	57.35W
Ladbergen	12	Jb	52.08N	7.45 E
Lądek-Zdrój	10	Mf	50.21N	16.50 E
Ladenburg	12	Ke	49.28N	8.37 E
La Désirade	50	Fd	16.19N	61.03W
La Digue Island	37b	Ca	4.21S	55.50 E
Lādik	24	Fb	40.36N	36.45 E
Ladismith	37	Cf	33.30S	21.16 E
Ladispoli	14	Gi	41.56N	12.05 E
Lado, Jabal-	35	Ed	5.06N	31.35 E
Ladoga, Lake- (EN)= Ladožkoje Ozero	5	Jc	61.00N	31.00 E
Ladong	27	Ig	24.49N	109.34 E
La Dorada	54	Db	5.22N	74.42W
Ladožkoje Ozero=Ladoga, Lake (EN)	5	Jc	61.00N	31.00 E
Ladrones, Islas-	49	Fj	7.52N	82.26W
Laduškin	8	Ij	54.35N	20.10 E
Ladva-Vetka	7	If	61.20N	34.29 E
Lady Ann Strait	42	Ja	75.45N	80.00W
Ladybrand	37	De	29.19S	27.25 E
Lady Evelyn Lake	44	Gb	47.20N	80.10W
Lady Newnes Ice Shelf	66	Kf	73.40S	167.30 E
Ladysmith [B.C.-Can.]	46	Db	48.58N	123.49W
Ladysmith [S.Afr.]	31	Jk	28.33S	29.45 E
Ladysmith [Wi.-U.S.]	43	Ib	45.28N	91.07W
Ladyžin	16	Fe	48.40N	29.13 E
Lae	58	Fe	6.43S	147.01 E
Lae Atoll	57	Hd	8.56N	166.14 E
La Eduvigis	55	Ch	26.50S	59.05W
Laem, Khao-	25	Kf	14.19N	101.11 E
Laer [F.R.G.]	12	Kb	52.06N	8.05 E
Laer [F.R.G.]	12	Jb	52.04N	7.21 E
Lærdalsøyri	8	Bd	61.06N	7.29 E
La Escala/L'Escala	13	Pb	42.07N	3.08 E
La Esmeralda	54	Ec	3.10N	65.33W
Læsø	7	Bh	57.15N	10.00 E
Læsø Rende	8	Dg	57.15N	10.45 E
La Española=Hispaniola (EN)	38	Lh	19.00N	71.00W
La Esperanza [Bol.]	54	Ff	14.34S	62.10W
La Esperanza [Hond.]	49	Cf	14.20N	88.10W
La Estrada	13	Db	42.41N	8.29W
Lafayette [Al.-U.S.]	44	Ei	32.54N	85.24W
Lafayette [In.-U.S.]	43	Jc	40.25N	86.53W
Lafayette [La.-U.S.]	39	Jf	30.14N	92.01W
La Fère	12	Fe	49.40N	3.22 E
La Ferrière-sur-Risle	12	Cf	48.59N	0.48 E
La Ferté-Bernard	11	Gf	48.11N	0.40 E
La Ferté-Frênel	12	Cf	48.50N	0.30 E
La Ferté-Macé	11	Ff	48.36N	0.22W
La Ferté-Milon	12	Fe	49.10N	3.07 E
La Ferté-Saint-Aubin	11	Hg	47.43N	1.56 E
La Ferté-sous-Jouarre	11	Jf	48.57N	3.08 E
Laffān, Ra's-	24	Nj	25.54N	51.35 E
Lafia	34	Gd	8.29N	8.31 E
Lafiagi	34	Gd	8.52N	5.15 E
La Flèche	11	Fg	47.42N	0.05W
Lafnitz	14	Kd	46.57N	16.16 E
La Foa	63b	Be	21.43S	165.49 E
La Follette	44	Eg	36.23N	84.07W
La Fria	49	Ki	8.13N	72.15W
Laft	24	Pi	26.54N	55.46 E
La Fuente de San Esteban	13	Fd	40.48N	6.15W
Laga, Monti della-	14	Hh	42.45N	13.35 E
La Galite (EN)=Jāliṭah	30	He	37.32N	8.56 E
La Gallareta	55	Bi	29.34S	60.23W
Lagamar	55	Id	18.13S	46.48W
Lagan	8	Eh	56.33N	12.56 E
Lagan	8	Eh	56.55N	13.59 E
Lagan/Abhainn an Lagáin	9	Hg	54.37N	5.53W
Lagarina, Val-	14	Fe	45.50N	11.10 E
La Garita Mountains	45	Ch	38.00N	106.40W
Lagarto	54	Kf	10.54S	37.41W
Lagash	24	Lg	31.27N	46.13 E
Lagawe	26	Hc	16.49N	121.06 E
Lage	12	Kc	51.59N	8.48 E
Lågen	7	Cf	61.08N	10.25 E
Lagh Bogal	36	Gb	0.42N	40.55 E
Laghmān [3]	23	Lb	35.00N	70.15 E
Laghouat	31	He	33.48N	2.53 E
Laghouat [3]	32	Hc	33.30N	3.15 E
La Gloria	49	Ki	8.38N	73.48W
Lagny	11	If	48.52N	2.43 E
Lagoa	13	Dg	37.08N	8.27W
Lagôa	55	Eb	14.08S	55.20W
Lagoa da Prata	55	Je	20.01S	45.33W
Lagoa Vermelha	56	Jc	28.13S	51.32W
Lagodehi	16	Oi	41.50N	46.14 E
La Gomera	49	Bf	14.05N	91.03W
Lagonegro	14	Jj	40.07N	15.46 E
Lagonoy Gulf	26	Hd	13.35N	123.45 E
Lagoon	64n	Ab	10.23S	161.05W
Lagos	13	Dg	37.06N	8.40W
Lagos	31	Hh	6.27N	3.23 E
Lágos	15	Ih	41.01N	25.07 E
Lagos [2]	34	Fd	6.30N	3.30 E
Lagos, Baía de-	13	Dg	37.06N	8.39W
Lagosa	36	Ed	5.57S	29.53 E
Lagos de Moreno	47	Dd	21.21N	101.55W
La Grand-Combe	11	Kj	44.13N	4.02 E
La Grande	43	Db	45.20N	118.05W
La Grande Fosse	9	Kl	49.40N	3.00W
La Grande-Motte	11	Kk	43.34N	4.07 E
La Grande Rivière	38	Ld	53.50N	79.00W
La Grande Trench (EN)= Hurd Deep	9	Kl	49.40N	3.00W
La Grange	44	Ef	38.24N	85.23W
Lagrange	44	Ee	41.39N	85.25W
La Grange [Ga.-U.S.]	43	Je	33.02N	85.02W
La Grange [Tx.-U.S.]	45	Hl	29.54N	96.52W
La Gran Sabana	54	Fb	5.30N	61.30W
La Grita	54	Db	8.08N	71.59W
Lagskär	8	He	59.50N	20.00 E
La Guaira	53	Jd	10.36N	66.56W
La Guajira [2]	54	Da	11.30N	72.30W
Lagua Lichan, Puntan-	64b	Ba	15.16N	145.50 E
Laguardia	13	Jb	42.33N	2.35W
La Guardia [Sp.]	13	Dc	41.54N	8.53W
La Guardia [Sp.]	13	Ie	39.47N	3.29W
La Guasima	48	Kg	21.06N	97.49W
La Guerche-sur-l'Aubois	11	Ih	46.57N	2.57 E
Laguiole	11	Ij	44.41N	2.51 E
Laguna	56	Kc	28.29S	48.47W
Laguna Alsina	55	Am	36.49S	62.13W
Laguna Beach	46	Gj	33.33N	117.51W
Laguna Blanca	55	Cg	25.08S	58.15W
Laguna de Bay	26	Hd	14.23N	121.15 E
Laguna Limpia	55	Ch	26.29S	59.41W
Laguna Mountains	46	Gj	32.55N	116.25W
Laguna Paiva	56	Hd	31.19S	60.39W
Laguna Superior	47	Fe	16.20N	94.25W
Laguna Veneta	14	Ge	45.25N	12.20 E
Laguna Yema	55	Bg	24.15S	61.15W
Lagunillas [Bol.]	54	Fg	19.38S	63.43W
Lagunillas [Mex.]	48	Ii	17.50N	101.44W
Lagunillas [Ven.]	49	Lh	10.08N	71.16W
Lagunillas [Ven.]	49	Li	8.31N	71.24W
Laha	27	Lb	48.13N	124.36 E
La Habana [3]	49	Fb	22.45N	82.10W
La Habana=Havana (EN)	39	Kg	23.08N	82.22W
Lahad Datu	26	Ge	5.02N	118.19 E
Laham	34	Fc	14.54N	4.25 E
Lahat	26	Dg	3.48S	103.32 E
Lahdenpohja	7	Hf	61.33N	30.13 E
Lahewa	26	Cf	1.24N	97.11 E
Lahij	23	Fg	13.04N	44.53 E
Lāhījān	23	Hb	37.12N	50.01 E
Lahn	10	Df	50.18N	7.37 E
Lahnstein	12	Jd	50.20N	7.29 E
Laholm	7	Ch	56.31N	13.02 E
Laholmsbukten	8	Eh	56.35N	12.50 E
Lahore	22	Jf	31.35N	74.18 E
Lahr	10	Dh	48.20N	7.52 E
Lahti	6	Ic	60.58N	25.40 E
Laï	31	Ih	9.24N	16.18 E
Laiagam	60	Ci	5.31S	143.39 E
Lai'an	28	Eh	32.28N	118.26 E
Lai Chau	25	Kd	22.02N	103.10 E
Laich o'Moray	9	Jd	57.40N	3.30W
Laie	65a	Db	21.39N	157.56W
Laifeng	27	If	29.31N	109.23 E
Laighean/Leinster	9	Gh	53.00N	7.00W
L'Aigle	11	Gf	48.45N	0.38 E
Laignes	11	Kg	47.50N	4.22 E
Laihia	7	Fe	62.58N	22.01 E
Lainioälven	7	Fc	67.22N	22.39 E
Lairg	9	Ic	58.01N	4.25W
Lairi	35	Bc	10.49N	17.06 E
Laïri, Batha de-	35	Bc	12.28N	16.45 E
Lais	26	Dg	3.32S	102.03 E
La Isabela	49	Gb	22.57N	80.01W
Laisamis	36	Gb	1.36N	37.48 E
Laiševo	7	Li	55.26N	49.32 E
Laishui	28	Ce	39.23N	115.42 E
Laisvall	7	Dc	66.08N	17.10 E
Laitila	7	Ef	60.53N	21.41 E
Laiwu	28	Df	36.12N	117.40 E
Laiwui	26	Ig	1.22S	127.40 E
Laixi (Shuiji)	28	Ff	36.52N	120.31 E
Laiyang	27	Ld	36.59N	120.39 E
Laiyuan	27	Jd	39.19N	114.43 E
Laizhou Wan	28	Ef	37.30N	119.30 E
Laja	56	Fe	37.16S	72.42W
Laja	17	Hc	66.20N	56.16 E
La Jara	13	He	39.40N	4.55W
Lajeado	55	Gi	29.27S	51.58W
Lajeado, Serra do-	55	Hd	19.08S	49.56W
Lajerd	24	Oe	35.24N	53.04 E
Lajes [Braz.]	54	Ke	5.41S	36.14W
Lajes [Braz.]	53	Kh	27.48S	50.19W
Lajes do Pico	32	Bb	38.23N	28.16W
Lajosmizse	10	Pi	47.01N	19.33 E
La Junta [Co.-U.S.]	43	Gd	37.59N	103.33W
La Junta [Mex.]	48	Fc	28.28N	107.20W
Lak Bor	36	Hb	1.18N	40.40 E
Lake Cargelligo	59	Jf	33.18S	146.23 E
Lake Charles	39	Jf	30.12N	93.12W
Lake City	43	Ke	30.12N	82.38W
Lake District	9	Jg	54.30N	3.10W
Lake Fork Creek	46	Jf	40.13N	110.07W
Lake Geneva	45	Le	42.36N	88.26W
Lake George	44	Kd	43.25N	73.45W
Lake Grace	59	Df	33.06S	118.28 E
Lake Harbour	42	Kd	62.51N	69.53W
Lake Havasu City	46	Hi	34.27N	114.22W
Lake Itasca	45	Ic	46.51N	95.13W
Lake Jackson	45	Il	29.02N	95.27W
Lake King	59	Df	33.05S	119.40 E
Lakeland	43	Kf	28.03N	81.57W
Lake Louise	46	Ga	51.26N	116.11W
Lakemba	63d	Cc	18.13S	178.47W
Lakemba Passage	63d	Cb	17.53S	178.32W
Lake Mills	45	Je	43.25N	93.32W
Lake Minchumina	40	Ia	63.53N	152.19W
Lake Murray	60	Ci	6.54S	141.28 E
Lake Oswego	46	Dd	45.26N	122.39W
Lake Placid	44	Kc	44.18N	73.59W
Lake Providence	45	Kj	32.48N	91.11W
Lake Pukaki	62	Df	44.11S	170.08 E
Lake Range	46	Ff	40.15N	119.25W
Lake River	42	Jf	54.28N	82.30W
Lakes Entrance	59	Jg	37.53S	147.59 E
Lakeside	46	If	41.13N	112.57W
Lake Tekapo	62	Df	44.00S	170.29 E
Lakeview	43	Cc	42.11N	120.21W
Lakeville	45	Jd	44.39N	93.14W
Lake Wales	44	Gl	27.55N	81.35W
Lakewood [Co.-U.S.]	45	Dg	39.44N	105.06W
Lakewood [Oh.-U.S.]	44	Ge	41.29N	81.50W
Lake Worth	44	Gl	26.37N	80.03W
Lakhdar, Chergui Kef-	13	Pi	35.57N	3.16 E
Lakhdaria	13	Ph	36.34N	3.35 E
Lāki	15	Hh	41.50N	24.50 E
Lakin	45	Fh	37.58N	101.15W
Lakinsk	7	Jh	56.04N	39.58 E
Lákmos Óros	15	Ej	39.40N	21.07 E
Lakon, Ile-	57	Hf	14.17S	167.30 E
Lakonikós Kólpos = Laconia, Gulf of- (EN)	15	Fm	36.35N	22.40 E
Lakota	34	Dd	5.53N	5.42W
Lakota [I.C.]	34	Dd	5.51N	5.41W
Lakota [N.D.-U.S.]	45	Gb	48.02N	98.21W
Laksefjorden	7	Ga	70.58N	27.00 E
Lakselv	7	Fa	70.03N	25.01 E
Lakshadweep [3]	25	Ef	11.00N	72.00 E
La Laguna	55	Bb	14.30S	61.06W
Lalanna	37	Hd	23.28S	45.05 E
Lalapaşa	15	Jh	41.50N	26.44 E
Lāleh Zār, Kūh-e-	21	Hg	29.24N	56.46 E
La Leonesa	55	Ch	27.03S	58.43W
Lālī	24	Mf	32.21N	49.06 E
Lalibela	35	Fc	12.00N	39.04 E
La Libertad [2]	54	Ce	8.00S	78.30W
La Libertad [ElSal.]	47	Gf	13.29N	89.16W
La Libertad [Guat.]	49	Be	16.47N	90.07W
La Libertad [Guat.]	49	Bf	15.30N	91.50W
La Libertad [Hond.]	49	Df	14.43N	87.36W
La Ligua	56	Fd	32.27S	71.14W
Lalín	13	Db	42.39N	8.07W
La Línea	13	Gh	36.10N	5.19W
Lalin He	28	Hb	45.28N	125.43 E
Lalitpur	25	Fd	24.41N	78.25 E
Lalla Khedidja	13	Qh	36.27N	4.14 E
Lālmanir Hāt	25	Hc	25.54N	89.27 E
La Loche	42	Ge	56.29N	109.27W
La Loupe	11	Hf	48.28N	1.01 E
La Louvière	11	Kd	50.29N	4.11 E
L'Alpe-d'Huez	11	Mi	45.06N	6.04 E
La Lucila	55	Bj	30.25S	61.01W
Lalzit, Gjiri i-	15	Ch	41.31N	19.29 E
La Machine	11	Jh	46.53N	3.28 E
La Maddalena	14	Di	41.13N	9.24 E
La Maiella	5	Hg	42.05N	14.07 E
La Maladeta/Malditos, Montes-	13	Mb	42.40N	0.50 E
La Malbaie	42	Kg	47.39N	70.10W
La Mancha	5	Fh	39.05N	3.00W
La Manche	5	Fe	50.20N	1.00W
Lamap	61	Cc	16.26S	167.43 E
Lamar	43	Gd	38.05N	102.37W
La Maragatería	13	Fb	42.25N	6.10W
La Marina	13	Lf	38.35N	0.05W
La Marmora	14	Dk	39.59N	9.20 E
La Marque	45	Il	29.22N	94.58W
Lamas	54	Ce	6.25S	76.35W
Lamastre	11	Kj	44.59N	4.35 E
Lamawan	28	Ad	40.05N	111.25 E
Lambach	14	Hb	48.05N	13.53 E
Lamballe	11	Df	48.28N	2.31W
Lambar, Río-	55	Jd	19.30S	45.00W
Lambaréné	31	Ii	0.42S	10.13 E
Lambari	55	Je	21.58S	45.21W
Lambasa	61	Ec	16.26S	179.24 E
Lambay/Reachrainn	9	Gh	53.29N	6.01W
Lambayeque [2]	54	Ce	6.20S	80.00W
Lambayeque	54	Ce	6.42S	79.55W
Lambert Glacier	66	Ff	71.00S	70.00 E
Lambert Land	41	Jc	79.10N	21.00W
Lamberts Bay	31	Il	32.05S	18.17 E
Lambro	14	De	45.08N	9.32 E
Lambsheim	12	Ke	49.31N	8.17 E
Lambton, Cape-	42	Fb	71.04N	123.08W
Lamé	35	Ad	9.15N	14.32 E
Lame Deer	46	Ld	45.37N	106.40W
Lamego	13	Ec	41.06N	7.49W
Lamentin	51e	Ab	16.16N	61.38W
La Mesa	46	Gj	32.46N	117.01W
Lamesa	43	Ge	32.44N	101.57W
La Meta	14	Hj	41.41N	13.56 E
Lamezia Terme	14	Kl	38.59N	16.17 E
Lamia	15	Fk	38.54N	22.26 E
Lamina	55	De	20.34S	56.14W
Lamlam, Mount-	64c	Bb	13.20N	144.40 E
Lammermuir Hills	9	Kf	55.52N	2.40W
Lammhult	8	Fg	57.10N	14.35 E
Lammi	7	Ff	61.05N	25.01 E
Lamoil	64d	Ba	7.39N	151.41 E
Lamon Bay	21	Oh	14.25N	122.00 E
Lamone	14	Gf	44.29N	12.08 E
Lamoni	45	Jf	40.37N	93.56W
Lamont	44	Fj	30.21N	83.50W
La Montaña	52	If	10.00S	72.50W
La Moraña	13	Hd	40.45N	4.55W
La Mosquitia	49	Ef	15.00N	84.20W
La Mothe-Achard	11	Eh	46.37N	1.40W
Lamotrek Atoll	57	Fd	7.30N	146.20 E

Index Symbols

[1] Independent Nation
[2] State, Region
[3] District, County
[4] Municipality
[5] Colony, Dependency
Continent
Physical Region
Historical or Cultural Region
Mount, Mountain
Volcano
Hill
Mountains, Mountain Range
Hills, Escarpment
Plateau, Upland
Pass, Gap
Plain, Lowland
Delta
Salt Flat
Valley, Canyon
Crater, Cave
Karst Features
Depression
Polder
Desert, Dunes
Forest, Woods
Heath, Steppe
Oasis
Cape, Point
Coast, Beach
Cliff
Peninsula
Isthmus
Sandbank
Island
Atoll
Rock, Reef
Islands, Archipelago
Rocks, Reefs
Coral Reef
Well, Spring
Geyser
River, Stream
Waterfall Rapids
River Mouth, Estuary
Lake
Salt Lake
Intermittent Lake
Reservoir
Swamp, Pond
Canal
Glacier
Ice Shelf, Pack Ice
Ocean
Sea
Gulf, Bay
Strait, Fjord
Lagoon
Bank
Seamount
Tablemount
Ridge
Shelf
Basin
Escarpment, Sea Scarp
Fracture
Trench, Abyss
National Park, Reserve
Point of Interest
Recreation Site
Cave, Cavern
Historic Site
Ruins
Wall, Walls
Church, Abbey
Temple
Scientific Station
Airport
Port
Lighthouse
Mine
Tunnel
Dam, Bridge

Name	Map	Grid	Lat.	Long.
motte-Beuvron	11	Ig	47.36N	2.01 E
Moure	45	Gc	46.21N	98.18W
mpang	25	Je	18.16N	99.34 E
mpasas	45	Gk	31.03N	98.12W
mpazos de Naranjo	48	Id	27.01N	100.31W
mpedusa	14	Go	35.30N	12.35 E
mpertheim	10	Eg	49.36N	8.28 E
mpeter	9	Ii	52.07N	4.05W
mphun	25	Je	18.35N	99.00 E
mpione	14	Go	35.35N	12.20 E
mpung	26	Dg	5.00S	105.00 E
mu	31	Li	2.16S	40.54 E
mud	54	Ce	6.09S	77.55W
Mure	11	Lj	44.54N	5.47 E
n	16	Ec	52.09N	27.18 E
na	14	Fd	46.37N	11.09 E
na, Rio de la-	48	Li	17.49N	95.09W
nai City	65a	Ec	20.50N	156.55W
naihale	65a	Ec	20.49N	156.52W
nai Island	57	Lb	20.50N	156.55W
naken	12	Hd	50.53N	5.39 E
nark	9	Jf	55.41N	3.48W
nbi Kyun	25	Jf	10.50N	98.15 E
ncang (Menglangba)	27	Gg	22.37N	99.57 E
ncang Jiang=Mekong EN)	21	Mh	10.15N	105.55 E
ncashire	9	Kh	53.55N	2.40W
ncashire Plain	9	Kh	53.40N	2.45W
ncaster	9	Kh	53.45N	2.50W
ncaster [Ca.-U.S.]	43	De	34.42N	118.08W
ncaster [Eng.-U.K.]	9	Kg	54.03N	2.48W
ncaster [Mo.-U.S.]	45	Jf	40.31N	92.32W
ncaster [N.H.-U.S.]	44	Lc	44.29N	71.34W
ncaster [Oh.-U.S.]	44	Ff	39.43N	82.37W
ncaster [Ont.-Can.]	44	Jc	45.12N	74.30W
ncaster [Pa.-U.S.]	43	Lc	40.01N	76.19W
ncaster [S.C.-U.S.]	44	Gh	34.43N	80.47W
ncaster Sound	38	Kb	74.13N	84.00W
nçeiro	55	Fe	20.59S	53.43W
ncelin	59	Df	31.01S	115.19 E
nciano	14	Ih	42.14N	14.23 E
nčin	15	Ha	48.31N	24.49 E
ncun	28	Ff	36.25N	120.11 E
ncut	10	Sf	50.05N	22.13 E
nd	8	Cd	60.45N	10.00 E
ndana	36	Bd	5.15S	12.10 E
ndau an der Isar	10	Ih	48.41N	12.41 E
ndau in der Pfalz	10	Eg	49.12N	8.07 E
nd Bay	66	Mf	75.25S	141.45W
ndeck	14	Ec	47.08N	10.34 E
nden	12	Hd	50.45N	5.05 E
nder	43	Fc	42.50N	108.44W
nderneau	11	Bf	48.27N	4.15W
nder River	59	Gd	20.25S	132.00 E
nderyd	8	Eg	57.05N	13.16 E
ndes	11	Fj	44.15N	1.00W
ndes	11	Fj	44.00N	0.50W
ndesbergen	12	Lb	52.34N	9.08 E
ndeta	55	Ak	32.01S	62.04W
ndete	13	Ke	39.54N	1.22W
ndfallis	25	If	13.40N	93.02 E
nd Glacier	66	Mf	75.40S	141.45W
ndi Kotal	25	Eb	34.06N	71.09 E
ndless Corner	36	Ee	14.53S	28.04 E
ndrecies	12	Fd	50.08N	3.42 E
ndsberg am Lech	10	Gh	48.03N	10.52 E
ndsbro	8	Fg	57.22N	14.54 E
nd's End	5	Fe	50.03N	5.44W
nds End	42	Fa	76.25N	122.45W
ndshut	10	Ih	48.32N	12.09 E
ndskrona	8	Ei	55.52N	12.50 E
ndsort	8	Gf	58.45N	17.50 E
ndsortsdjupet	8	Hf	58.40N	18.30 E
ndstuhl	12	Je	49.25N	7.34 E
ndusky	46	Kc	47.54N	108.37W
Neuve-Lyre	12	Cf	48.54N	0.45 E
nfeng → Lankao	28	Cg	34.49N	114.48 E
ng	46	Mb	49.56N	104.23W
n'nga Co	27	De	30.41N	81.17 E
angadhás	15	Gi	40.45N	23.04 E
angádhia	15	Fl	37.39N	22.03 E
angan	7	De	63.19N	14.44 E
angano, Lake-	35	Fd	7.36N	38.43 E
angao	27	Ie	32.20N	108.53 E
angara	26	Hg	4.02S	123.00 E
angarfoss	7a	Cb	65.35N	14.15W
angasian	26	Ie	8.16N	125.39 E
angdon	45	Gb	48.46N	98.22W
angeac	11	Ji	45.06N	3.29 E
angeais	11	Gg	47.20N	0.24 E
angeb	35	Fb	17.46N	36.41 E
angebaan	37	Bf	33.06S	18.02 E
angeberg	37	Cf	33.56S	20.45 E
angedijk	12	Gb	52.42N	4.48 E
angeland	7	Ci	55.00N	10.50 E
angelands Bælt	8	Dj	54.50N	10.55 E
angelmävesi	8	Kc	61.30N	24.20 E
angen	12	Ke	49.59N	8.40 E
angenberg	12	Kc	51.17N	8.34 E
angenburg	45	Fa	50.50N	101.43W
angenfeld (Rheinland)	12	Ic	51.06N	6.57 E
angenhagen	10	Fd	52.27N	9.45 E
angenselbold	12	Ld	50.11N	9.02 E
angenthal	14	Bc	47.13N	7.49 E
angeoog	10	Dc	53.46N	7.32 E
angeri	20	Jf	50.08N	143.20 E
angesund	8	Ce	59.00N	9.45 E
angesundsfjorden	8	Cf	59.00N	9.48 E
angevåg	8	Bb	62.27N	6.12 E
angfang → Anci	27	Kd	39.29N	116.40 E
ångfjället	8	Eb	62.10N	12.20 E
angfjorden	8	Bb	62.45N	7.30 E
anghe	14	Bf	44.30N	8.00 E
angholm	9	Kf	55.09N	3.00W
angjökull	5	Ec	64.39N	20.00W
angkawi, Pulau-	26	Ce	6.22N	99.48 E
angkon	26	Ge	6.32N	116.42 E
Langlade	44	Ja	48.12N	75.57W
Langnau im Emmental	14	Bd	46.56N	7.46 E
Langogne	11	Jj	44.43N	3.51 E
Langon	11	Fj	44.33N	0.15W
Langorūd	24	Md	37.11N	50.10 E
Langøya	7	Db	68.44N	14.50 E
Langreo	13	Ga	43.18N	5.41W
Langres	11	Lg	47.52N	5.20 E
Langres, Plateau de-	5	Gf	47.41N	5.03 E
Langrune-sur-Mer	12	Be	49.19N	0.22W
Langsa	22	Li	4.28N	97.58 E
Långsele	8	Ga	63.11N	17.04 E
Långshyttan	8	Gd	60.27N	16.01 E
Lang Son	25	Ld	21.50N	106.44 E
Lang Suan	25	Jg	9.55N	99.07 E
Languedoc	5	Gg	44.00N	4.00 E
Languedoc	11	Jj	44.00N	4.00 E
Langueyú, Arroyo-	55	Cm	36.39S	58.27W
Langwedel	12	Lb	52.58N	9.13 E
Langxi	28	Ei	31.08N	119.11 E
Langzhong	27	Ie	31.40N	106.04 E
Lan Hsu	27	Lg	22.00N	121.30 E
Laniel	44	Hb	47.06N	79.15W
Lanin, Volcán-	52	Ii	39.38S	71.30W
Lankao	27	Cd	35.12N	79.50 E
Lankao (Lanfeng)	27	Kg	21.00N	116.00 E
Lankao (Lanfeng)	28	Cg	34.49N	114.48 E
Länkipohja	8	Kc	61.44N	24.48 E
Lannemezan	11	Gk	43.08N	0.23 E
Lannemezan, Plateau de-	11	Gk	43.09N	0.27 E
Lannion	11	Cf	48.44N	3.28W
Lannion, Baie de-	11	Cf	48.43N	3.34W
La Noria	56	Gb	20.23S	69.53W
Lansdowne House	42	If	52.13N	87.53W
L'Anse	44	Cb	46.45N	88.27W
Lansing [Ia.-U.S.]	45	Ke	43.22N	91.13W
Lansing [Mi.-U.S.]	39	Ke	42.43N	84.34W
Lansjärv	7	Fc	66.39N	22.12 E
Łańskie, Jezioro-	10	Qc	53.33N	20.30 E
Lantar	20	Ie	56.05N	137.35 E
Lanta Yai, Ko-	25	Jg	7.35N	99.03 E
Lanteri	55	Ci	28.50S	59.39W
Lanterne	11	Mg	47.44N	6.03 E
Lanús	55	Cl	34.43S	58.24W
Lanusei	14	Dk	39.53N	9.32 E
Lanvaux, Landes de-	11	Dg	47.47N	2.36W
Lanxi [China]	28	Ej	29.13N	119.28 E
Lanxi [China]	28	Ha	46.15N	126.16 E
Lanxian (Dongcun)	28	Ae	38.17N	111.38 E
Lanyi He	28	Ae	38.40N	110.53 E
Lanzarote	30	Ff	29.00N	13.40W
Lanzhou	22	Mf	36.03N	103.41 E
Lanzo Torinese	14	Be	45.16N	7.28 E
Lao	14	Jk	39.47N	15.48 E
Laoag	22	Oh	18.12N	120.36 E
Laoang	26	Id	12.34N	125.00 E
Lao Cai	22	Mg	22.30N	103.57 E
Laocheng	28	Hc	42.37N	124.04 E
Laoha He	27	Lc	43.24N	120.39 E
Lao He	28	Cj	29.02N	115.47 E
Laohuanghe Kou	28	Ef	37.39N	119.02 E
Laois	9	Fi	53.00N	7.30W
Laojunmiao → Yumen	22	Lf	39.50N	97.44 E
Laojun Shan	27	Je	33.45N	111.38 E
Lao Ling	28	Id	41.24N	126.10 E
Laon	11	Je	49.34N	3.37 E
Laona	45	Ld	45.34N	88.40W
Laonnois	12	Fe	49.35N	3.40 E
La Orchila, Isla-	54	Ea	11.48N	66.10W
La Oroya	53	Ig	11.32S	75.57W
Laos	22	Mh	18.00N	105.00 E
Laoshan (Licun)	28	Ff	36.10N	120.25 E
Laotougou	28	Jc	42.54N	129.09 E
Laou	13	Gi	35.26N	5.05W
Laoye Ling	28	Kb	44.50N	130.10 E
Lapa	56	Kc	25.45S	49.42W
Lapai	34	Gd	9.03N	6.43 E
Lapalisse	11	Jh	46.15N	3.38 E
La Palma	30	Ff	28.40N	17.52W
La Palma [ElSal.]	49	Cf	14.19N	89.11W
La Palma [Pan.]	47	Ig	8.25N	78.09W
La Palma del Condado	13	Fg	37.23N	6.33W
La Paloma	55	El	34.40S	54.10W
La Pampa	56	Ge	37.00S	66.00W
La Panne/De Panne	12	Ec	51.06N	2.35 E
La Paragua	54	Fb	6.50N	63.20W
La Partida, Isla-	48	De	24.30N	110.25W
La Paz	49	Df	14.15N	87.50W
La Paz	54	Eg	15.00S	68.00W
La Paz [Arg.]	56	Id	30.45S	59.39W
La Paz [Arg.]	56	Gd	33.28S	67.33W
La Paz [Bol.]	53	Jg	16.30S	68.09W
La Paz [Col.]	49	Kh	10.23N	73.10W
La Paz [Hond.]	47	Gf	14.16N	87.40W
La Paz [Mex.]	39	Hg	24.10N	110.18W
La Paz [Ur.]	55	Dl	34.46S	56.13W
La Paz [Ven.]	49	Lh	10.41N	72.00W
La Paz, Bahía de-	47	Bd	24.09N	110.25W
La Paz, Llano de-	48	De	24.00N	110.30W
La Paz Centro	49	Dg	12.20N	86.41W
La Pedrera	54	Ed	1.18S	69.40W
Lapeer	44	Fd	43.03N	83.19W
La Pelada	55	Bj	30.52S	60.59W
La Pérouse, Bahia-	65d	Bb	27.04S	109.18W
La Perouse Strait (EN)= Laperuza, Proliv-	21	Qe	45.30N	142.00 E
La Perouse Strait (EN)= Sōya-Kaikyō	21	Qe	45.30N	142.00 E
Laperuza, Proliv-=La Perouse Strait (EN)	21	Qe	45.30N	142.00 E
La Pesca	47	Ed	23.47N	97.47W
Lápethos	24	Ee	35.20N	33.10 E
La Petite Pierre	12	Jf	48.52N	7.19 E
La Picasa, Laguna-	55	Al	34.20S	62.14W
La Piedad Cavadas	48	Hg	20.21N	102.00W
La Pine	46	Ee	43.40N	121.30W
Lapinjärvi/Lappträsk	8	Ld	60.36N	26.09 E
Lapinlahti	7	Ge	63.22N	27.30 E
La Plaine	51g	Bb	15.20N	61.15W
La Plana	13	Ld	40.00N	0.05W
Lapland (EN)=Lappi	5	Ib	66.50N	22.00 E
Lapland (EN)=Lappland	5	Ib	66.50N	22.00 E
La Plant	45	Fd	45.10N	100.38W
La Plata	53	Ki	34.55S	57.57W
La Pobla de Lillet	13	Nb	42.15N	1.59 E
La Pobla de Segur/Pobla de Segur	13	Mb	42.15N	0.58 E
La Pocatièr	44	Lb	47.21N	70.02W
La Porte	44	De	41.36N	86.43W
Lapovo	15	Ee	44.11N	21.06 E
Lappajärvi	7	Fe	63.08N	23.40 E
Lappeenranta/Villmanstrand	6	Ic	61.04N	28.11 E
Lappfjärd/Lapväärtti	8	Ib	62.15N	21.32 E
Lappi	7	Gc	67.40N	26.30 E
Lappi	8	Ic	61.06N	21.50 E
Lappi=Lapland (EN)	5	Ib	66.50N	22.00 E
Lappland=Lapland (EN)	5	Ib	66.50N	22.00 E
Lappo/Lapua	7	Fe	62.57N	23.00 E
Lappträsk/Lapinjärvi	8	Ld	60.36N	26.09 E
Lapri	20	He	55.45N	124.59 E
Laprida	56	He	37.33S	60.49W
Lâpseki	24	Bb	40.20N	26.41 E
Laptev Sea (EN)=Laptevyh, More-	67	Fd	76.00N	126.00 E
Laptevyh, More-=Laptev Sea (EN)	67	Fd	76.00N	126.00 E
Lapua/Lappo	7	Fe	62.57N	23.00 E
La Puebla	13	Pe	39.46N	3.01 E
La Puebla de Cazalla	13	Gg	37.14N	5.19W
Lapuna	55	Ba	13.19S	60.28W
La Puntilla	52	Hf	2.11S	81.01W
La Purisima	48	Cd	26.10N	112.04W
Lăpuş	15	Hb	47.30N	24.01 E
Lăpuş	15	Gb	47.39N	23.24 E
La Push	46	Cc	47.55N	124.38W
Lapväärtti/Lappfjärd	8	Ib	62.15N	21.32 E
Łapy	10	Sd	53.00N	22.53 E
Laqīyat al Arba'in	35	Da	20.03N	28.02 E
La Quemada	48	Hf	22.27N	102.45W
La Quiaca	56	Gb	22.06S	65.37W
L'Aquila	6	Hg	42.22N	13.22 E
Lar	23	Hd	27.41N	54.17 E
Lara	54	Ea	10.10N	69.50W
Larache	32	Fb	35.12N	6.09W
Laragne-Montéglin	11	Lj	44.19N	5.49 E
Lārak	23	Id	26.52N	56.22 E
La Rambla	13	Hg	37.36N	4.44W
Laramie	39	Ie	41.19N	105.35W
Laramie Mountains	43	Fc	42.00N	105.40W
Laramie Peak	46	Me	42.17N	105.27W
Laramie River	46	Me	42.12N	104.32W
Laranjal, Rio-	55	Ff	23.12S	53.45W
Laranjeiras do Sul	56	Jc	25.25S	52.25W
Larantuka	26	Hh	8.21S	122.59 E
Larat	26	Jh	7.09S	131.45 E
Larat, Pulau-	26	Jh	7.10S	131.50 E
La Raya	49	Ji	8.20N	74.34W
L'Arba	13	Ph	36.34N	3.09 E
L'Arbaa-Naït-Irathen	13	Qh	36.38N	4.12 E
L'Arbresle	11	Ki	45.50N	4.37 E
Lärbro	7	Eh	57.47N	18.47 E
Larche, Col de-	11	Mj	44.25N	6.53 E
Larde	37	Fc	16.28S	39.43 E
Larderello	14	Eg	43.14N	10.53 E
La Réale	11	Fj	44.35N	0.02W
Laredo [Sp.]	13	Ia	43.24N	3.25W
Laredo [Tx.-U.S.]	39	Jg	27.31N	99.30W
Laren	12	Hb	52.16N	5.16 E
Lārestān	21	Hg	27.00N	55.30 E
Larestan	24	Pi	27.00N	55.30 E
Large Island	51p	Cb	12.24N	61.30W
Largentière	11	Kj	44.32N	4.18 E
L'Argentière-la-Bessée	11	Mj	44.47N	6.33 E
Largo, Cayo-	49	Gc	21.38N	81.28W
Largs	9	If	55.48N	4.52W
La Ribagorça/Ribagorza	13	Mb	42.15N	0.30 E
La Ribera	13	Kb	42.30N	2.00W
Larimore	45	Hc	47.54N	97.38W
Larino	14	Ii	41.48N	14.54 E
La Rioja	56	Gc	30.00S	67.30W
La Rioja	13	Jb	42.20N	2.20W
La Rioja	53	Jh	29.25S	66.50W
Lárisa	6	Ih	39.38N	22.25 E
La Rivière-Thibouville, Nassandres-	12	Ce	49.07N	0.44 E
Lārkāna	25	Dc	27.33N	68.13 E
Larmor-Plage	11	Cg	47.42N	3.23W
Larnaka/Lárnax	23	Dc	34.55N	33.38 E
Lárnax/Larnaka	23	Dc	34.55N	33.38 E
Larne/Latharna	9	Hg	54.51N	5.49W
Larned	45	Gg	38.11N	99.06W
La Robla	13	Gb	42.48N	5.37W
La Roche	63b	De	21.28S	168.02 E
La Roche-en-Ardenne	11	Ld	50.11N	5.35 E
La Rochefoucauld	11	Gi	45.44N	0.23 E
La Roche-Guyon	12	De	49.05N	1.38 E
La Rochelle	6	Ff	46.10N	1.09W
La Roche-sur-Yon	11	Eh	46.40N	1.26W
La Roda	13	Je	39.13N	2.09W
La Romana	47	Ke	18.25N	68.58W
La Ronge	42	Ge	55.06N	105.17W
La Ronge, Lac-	38	Id	55.05N	104.59W
Larose	45	Kl	29.35N	90.23W
La Rosita	48	Ic	28.24N	101.43W
Larouco	13	Ec	41.56N	7.40W
Larreynaga	49	Dg	12.40N	86.34W
Larrey Point	59	Dc	20.00S	119.10 E
Larrimah	58	Ef	15.35S	133.12 E
Larsa	24	Kg	31.16N	45.49 E
Lars Christensen Kyst	66	Fe	69.30S	68.00 E
Larsen, Mount-	66	Kf	74.51S	162.12 E
Larsen Ice Shelf	66	Qe	68.30S	62.30W
Lartijas Padomju Socialistiska Respublika/ Latvijskaja SSR	19	Cd	57.00N	25.00 E
La Rumorosa	48	Aa	32.34N	116.06W
Laruns	11	Fk	43.00N	0.25W
Larvik	7	Bg	59.04N	10.00 E
La Sabana [Arg.]	55	Ch	27.52S	59.57W
La Sabana [Col.]	54	Ec	2.20N	68.32W
Las Adjuntas, Presa de-	48	Jf	23.55N	98.45W
La Sagra	13	Id	40.05N	4.00W
La Sagra	13	Jg	37.57N	2.34W
La Salle	45	Lf	41.20N	89.06W
La Salle, Pic-	47	Je	18.22N	71.59W
La Sal Mountains	46	Kg	38.30N	109.10W
Las Alpujarras	13	Ih	36.50N	3.25W
La Sanabria	13	Fb	42.08N	6.30W
Las Animas	45	Eg	38.04N	103.13W
Lās 'ānōd	35	Hd	8.26N	47.24 E
La Sarre	42	Jg	48.48N	79.12W
Las Aves, Islas-	54	Ea	11.58N	67.33W
Las Avispas	55	Bi	29.53S	61.18W
Las Bardenas	13	Kb	42.10N	1.25W
Las Bonitas	50	Di	7.52N	65.40W
Las Breñas	56	Hc	27.05S	61.05W
Las Cabezas de San Juan	13	Gh	36.59N	5.56W
Lascahobas	49	Ld	18.50N	71.56W
Lascano	55	Ek	33.40S	54.12W
Las Casitas, Cerro-	47	Cd	23.31N	109.53W
Lascaux, Grotte de-	11	Hi	45.03N	1.11 E
Las Cejas	56	Hc	26.53S	64.44W
Las Chilcas, Arroyo-	55	Cm	37.16S	58.26W
Las Choapas	47	Fe	17.55N	94.05W
Las Cinco Villas	13	Kb	42.05N	1.07W
Las Cruces	43	Fe	32.23N	106.29W
Läsdāred	35	Hc	10.10N	46.01 E
Lās Dawa'o	35	Hc	10.22N	49.03 E
La Segarra	13	Nc	41.30N	1.10 E
La Selva	13	Oc	41.40N	2.50 E
La Serena	13	Gf	38.45N	5.30W
La Serena	53	Ih	29.54S	71.16W
La Seu d'Urgell/Seo de Urgel	13	Nb	42.21N	1.28 E
La-Seyne-sur-Mer	11	Lk	43.06N	5.53 E
Las Flores	56	Ie	36.03S	59.07W
Lāsh-e Joveyn	23	Jc	31.43N	61.37 E
Las Heras	56	Gd	32.51S	68.49W
Lashkar Gāh	22	If	31.35N	64.21 E
Las Hurdes	13	Fd	40.20N	6.20W
La Sila	5	Hh	39.15N	16.30 E
Łasin	10	Pc	53.32N	19.05 E
Łask	10	Pe	51.36N	19.07 E
Las Lajas	56	Fe	38.31S	70.22W
Las Lomitas	56	Hb	24.42S	60.36W
Las Margaritas	48	Ni	16.19N	91.59W
Las Mariñas	13	Da	43.20N	8.15W
Las Marismas	13	Fg	37.00N	6.15W
Las Mercedes	54	Eb	9.07N	66.24W
Las Mestenas	48	Gc	28.13N	104.35W
Las Minas, Cerro-	47	Gf	14.33N	88.39W
Las Minas, Sierra de-	47	Ge	15.05N	90.00W
Las Mixtecas, Sierra del-	48	Ki	17.45N	97.15W
La Sola, Isla-	54	Fa	11.20N	63.34W
La Solana	13	If	38.56N	3.14W
Lasolo	26	Hg	3.29S	122.04 E
La Sorcière	51k	Bb	13.59N	60.56W
La Souterraine	11	Hh	46.14N	1.29 E
Las Palmas	32	Ed	28.20N	14.20W
Las Palmas de Gran Canaria	31	Ff	28.06N	15.24W
Las Petas	55	Cc	16.23S	59.11W
La Spezia	6	Gg	44.07N	9.50 E
Las Piedras	56	Id	34.45S	56.13W
Las Plumas	53	Jj	43.40S	67.15W
Lās Qoray	35	Hc	11.15N	48.22 E
Las Rosas	55	Bk	32.28S	61.34W
Lassen Peak	43	Cc	40.29N	121.31W
Lassigny	12	Ee	49.35N	2.51 E
Laßnitz	14	Jd	46.46N	15.32 E
Lasso	64b	Ba	15.02N	145.38 E
Las Tablas	49	Gj	7.46N	80.17W
Last Mountain Lake	42	Gf	51.10N	105.15W
Las Toscas	55	Ci	28.21S	59.17W
Lastoursville	36	Bc	0.49S	12.42 E
Lastovo	14	Kh	42.46N	16.55 E
Lastovo	14	Kh	42.45N	16.50 E
Lastovski kanal	14	Kh	42.50N	16.59 E
Las Tres Virgenes, Volcán-	47	Bc	27.27N	112.34W
Las Tunas	49	Ic	21.00N	77.00W
Las Tunas, Punta-	51a	Bb	18.30N	66.37W
Las Varillas	56	Hd	31.52S	62.43W
Las Vegas [N.M.-U.S.]	43	Fd	35.36N	105.13W
Las Vegas [Nv.-U.S.]	39	Hf	36.11N	115.08W
Las Villuercas	13	Ge	39.33N	5.27W
Łaszczów	10	Tf	50.32N	23.40 E
Lata	65c	Db	14.14S	169.29W
Latacunga	54	Cd	0.55S	78.37W
La Tagua	54	Dd	0.03S	74.40W
Latakia (EN)=Al Lādhiqīyah	22	Ff	35.31N	35.07 E
Latarc, Causse du-	11	Jk	43.57N	3.11 E
Late Island	61	Gc	18.48S	174.39W
Laterza	14	Kj	40.37N	16.48 E
La Teste	11	Ej	44.38N	1.09W
Latgale	8	Lh	56.45N	27.30 E
Latgales Augstiene/ Latgalskaja Vozvyšennost	8	Lh	56.10N	27.30 E
Latgalskaja Vozvyšennost/ Latgales Augstiene	8	Lh	56.10N	27.30 E
Latharna/Larne	9	Hg	54.51N	5.49W
Lathen	12	Jb	52.52N	7.19 E
La Tigra	55	Bh	27.06S	60.34W
Latina	14	Gi	41.28N	12.52 E
Latisana	14	Ge	45.47N	13.00 E
Latium (EN) = Lazio	14	Gh	42.02N	12.23 E
La Toja	13	Db	42.27N	8.50W
La Toma	56	Gd	33.03S	65.37W
La Tontouta	63b	Ce	22.00S	166.15 E
Latorica	10	Rh	48.28N	21.50 E
La Tortuga, Isla-	54	Ea	10.56N	65.20W
La-Tour-du-Pin	11	Li	45.34N	5.27 E
La Trimouille	11	Hh	46.28N	1.03 E
La Trinidad	49	Dg	12.58N	86.14W
La Trinidad de Orichuna	50	Bi	7.07N	69.45W
La Trinité	50	Fe	14.44N	60.58W
Latronico	14	Kj	40.05N	16.01 E
Lattari, Monti-	14	Ij	40.40N	14.30 E
La Tuque	42	Kg	47.27N	72.47W
Lātūr	25	Fe	18.24N	76.35 E
Latvian SSR (EN)=Latvijas PSR	19	Cd	57.00N	25.00 E
Latvijas PSR=Latvian SSR (EN)	19	Cd	57.00N	25.00 E
Latvijskaja Sovetskaja Socialističeskaja Respublika	19	Cd	57.00N	25.00 E
Latvijskaja SSR/Latvijas Padomju Socialistiska Respublika	19	Cd	57.00N	25.00 E
Lau	30	Kh	6.56N	30.16 E
Laubach	12	Kd	50.33N	8.59 E
Lauchert	10	Fh	48.05N	9.15 E
Lauchhammer	10	Je	51.30N	13.48 E
Lauenburg	10	Gc	53.22N	10.34 E
Lauf an der Pegnitz	10	Hg	49.31N	11.17 E
Laughlan Islands	63a	Ac	9.15S	153.40 E
Laughlin Peak	45	Dh	36.38N	104.12W
Lau Group	57	Jf	18.20S	178.30W
Lauhanvuori	8	Jb	62.10N	22.10 E
Laujar de Andarax	13	Jh	36.59N	2.51W
Laukaa	7	Fe	62.25N	25.57 E
Laukuva	8	Ji	55.35N	22.08 E
Laulau, Bahia-	64b	Ba	15.08N	145.46 E
Launceston [Austl.]	58	Fi	41.26S	147.08 E
Launceston [Eng.-U.K.]	9	Ik	50.38N	4.21W
La Unión [Bol.]	55	Bb	15.18S	61.05W
La Unión [Chile]	56	Ff	40.17S	73.05W
La Unión [Col.]	54	Cc	1.37N	77.08W
La Unión [ElSal.]	47	Gf	13.20N	87.51W
La Unión [Mex.]	48	Ii	17.58N	101.49W
La Unión [Peru]	54	Ce	9.46S	76.48W
La Unión [Sp.]	13	Lg	37.37N	0.52W
La Unión [Ven.]	49	Ni	8.13N	67.46W
Laura	59	Ic	15.34S	144.28 E
La Urbana	50	Ci	7.08N	66.56W
Laurel [Ms.-U.S.]	43	Je	31.42N	89.08W
Laurel [Mt.-U.S.]	43	Fb	45.40N	108.46W
Laureles	55	Ej	31.23S	55.52W
Laurel Hill	44	He	40.02N	79.17W
Laurel Mountain	44	Hf	39.20N	79.50W
Laurens	44	Fh	34.30N	82.01W
Laurentian Plateau (EN)= Laurentien, Plateau-	38	Md	50.00N	70.00W
Laurentian Scarp	44	Ic	45.50N	76.15W
Laurentide Scarp	44	Kb	46.38N	73.00W
Laurentien, Plateau-= Laurentian Plateau (EN)	38	Md	50.00N	70.00W
Lauria	14	Jj	40.02N	15.50 E
Lau Ridge (EN)	3	Kl	25.00S	179.00 E
Laurie River	42	He	56.00N	100.58W
Laurinburg	44	Hh	34.47N	79.27W
Laurium	44	Cb	47.14N	88.26W
Lauro Muller	55	Hi	28.24S	49.23W
Lausanne	6	Gf	46.30N	6.40 E
Lausitzer Gebirge	10	Kf	50.48N	14.40 E
Lausitzer Neiße	10	Kd	52.04N	14.46 E
Laut, Pulau-	26	Ef	4.43N	107.59 E
Laut, Pulau-	21	Nj	3.40S	116.10 E
Lautaret, Col du-	11	Mi	45.02N	6.24 E
Lautaro	56	Fe	38.31S	72.27W
Lautém	26	Ih	8.22S	126.54 E
Lauter	10	Eg	48.58N	8.11 E
Lauterbach	10	Ff	50.38N	9.24 E
Lauterbourg	12	Kf	48.59N	8.11 E
Lauterecken	12	Je	49.39N	7.36 E
Lauthala	63d	Cb	16.45S	179.41W
Laut Kecil, Kepulauan-	26	Gg	4.50S	115.45 E
Lautoka	61	Ec	17.37S	177.27 E
Lauvergne Island	64d	Cb	7.00N	152.00 E
Lauwersmeer	12	Ia	53.25N	6.15 E
Lauzerte	11	Hj	44.15N	1.08 E
Lauzon	44	Lb	46.50N	71.10W
Lauzoue	11	Gj	44.03N	0.15 E
Lava	10	Rb	54.37N	21.14 E
Lava, Nosy- [Mad.]	37	Hb	12.49S	48.41 E
Lava, Nosy- [Mad.]	37	Hb	14.33S	47.36 E
Lavaca River	45	Hl	28.50N	96.36W
Lava Flow	45	Bi	34.45N	108.20W
Laval	11	Ff	48.01N	0.46W
Lavalle	55	Ci	29.01S	59.11W
Lavalleja	55	El	34.00S	55.00W
Lāvān, Jazīreh-ye-	23	Hd	26.48N	53.00 E
Lavanggu	63a	Ed	11.37S	160.15 E
Lavant	14	Id	46.38N	14.56 E
Lavapié, Punta-	52	Ii	37.09S	73.35W
Lāvar Meydān	24	Pg	30.20N	54.30 E
Lavassaare	8	Kf	58.29N	24.16 E
Lavaur	11	Hk	43.42N	1.49 E
La Vecilla	13	Gb	42.51N	5.24W
La Vega	47	Je	19.13N	70.31W
La Vela de Coro	49	Mh	11.27N	69.34W
Lavelanet	11	Hl	42.56N	1.51 E
Lavello	14	Ji	41.03N	15.48 E
La Venta	47	Fe	18.08N	94.03W
Laventie	12	Ed	50.38N	2.46 E
La Ventura	48	Ie	24.37N	100.54W
La Vera	13	Gd	40.05N	5.30W
L'Averdy, Cape-	63a	Ba	5.33S	155.04 E
Laverton	59	Ee	28.38S	122.25 E
Lavia	7	Ff	61.36N	22.36 E
La Victoria	54	Ea	10.14N	67.20W
La Vila Jojosa/Villajoyosa	13	Lf	38.30N	0.14W
La Villita, Presa-	48	Hh	18.05N	102.05W
La Viña	54	Ce	6.54S	79.28W

Index Symbols

- Independent Nation
- State, Region
- District, County
- Municipality
- Colony, Dependency
- Continent
- Physical Region
- Historical or Cultural Region
- Mount, Mountain
- Volcano
- Hill
- Mountains, Mountain Range
- Hills, Escarpment
- Plateau, Upland
- Pass, Gap
- Plain, Lowland
- Delta
- Salt Flat
- Valley, Canyon
- Crater, Cave
- Karst Features
- Depression
- Polder
- Desert, Dunes
- Forest, Woods
- Heath, Steppe
- Oasis
- Cape, Point
- Coast, Beach
- Cliff
- Peninsula
- Isthmus
- Sandbank
- Island
- Atoll
- Rock, Reef
- Islands, Archipelago
- Rocks, Reefs
- Coral Reef
- Well, Spring
- Geyser
- River, Stream
- Waterfall Rapids
- River Mouth, Estuary
- Lake
- Salt Lake
- Intermittent Lake
- Reservoir
- Swamp, Pond
- Canal
- Glacier
- Ice Shelf, Pack Ice
- Ocean
- Sea
- Gulf, Bay
- Strait, Fjord
- Lagoon
- Bank
- Seamount
- Tablemount
- Ridge
- Shelf
- Basin
- Escarpment, Sea Scarp
- Fracture
- Trench, Abyss
- National Park, Reserve
- Point of Interest
- Recreation Site
- Cave, Cavern
- Historic Site
- Ruins
- Wall, Walls
- Church, Abbey
- Temple
- Scientific Station
- Airport
- Port
- Lighthouse
- Mine
- Tunnel
- Dam, Bridge

La Vôge 11 Mf 48.05N 6.05 E
Lavoisier Island 66 Qe 66.12S 66.44W
Lavougba 35 Cd 5.37N 23.19 E
La Voulte-sur-Rhône 11 Kj 44.48N 4.47 E
Lavouras 55 Db 14.59S 56.47W
Lavras 54 Jh 21.14S 45.00W
Lavras do Sul 55 Fj 30.49S 53.55W
Lavrentija 20 Nc 65.33N 171.02W
Lávrion 15 Hl 37.43N 24.03 E
Lavumisa 37 Ee 27.15S 31.55 E
Lawas 26 Gf 4.51N 115.24 E
Lawdar 23 Gg 13.53N 45.52 E
Lawe 12 Ed 50.38N 2.42 E
Lawers, Ben- 9 Ie 56.33N 4.15W
Lawit, Gunong- 26 Ff 1.23N 112.55 E
Lawqah 24 Jh 29.49N 42.45 E
Lawra 34 Ec 10.39N 2.52W
Lawrence [Ks.-U.S.] 43 Hd 38.58N 95.14W
Lawrence [Ma.-U.S.] 43 Mc 42.42N 71.09W
Lawrence [N.Z.] 62 Cf 45.55S 169.42 E
Lawrenceburg [Ky.-U.S.] 44 Ef 38.02N 84.54W
Lawrenceburg [Tn.-U.S.] 44 Dh 35.15N 87.20W
Lawson, Mount- 59 Ja 7.44S 146.37 E
Lawton 39 Jf 34.37N 98.25W
Lawu, Gunung- 21 Nj 7.38S 111.11 E
Lawz, Jabal al- 24 Fh 28.41N 35.18 E
Laxå 7 Dg 58.59N 14.37 E
Lay 11 Eh 46.18N 1.17W
Laylá 23 Ge 22.17N 46.45 E
Layon 11 Fg 47.20N 0.45W
Layou 51g Bb 15.23N 61.26W
Layou 51n Ba 13.12N 61.17W
Laysan Island 57 Jb 25.50N 171.50W
Layton 46 Jf 41.04N 111.58W
La Zarca 48 Ge 25.50N 104.44W
Lazarev 20 Jf 52.13N 141.35 E
Lazarevac 15 De 44.23N 20.16 E
Lázaro Cárdenas, Presa- 48 Ge 25.35N 105.05W
Lazdijai/Lazdijaj 7 Fi 54.13N 23.33 E
Lazdijaj/Lazdijai 7 Fi 54.13N 23.33 E
Lāzeh 24 Oi 26.48N 53.22 E
Lazio = Latium (EN) 14 Gh 42.02N 12.23 E
Lazo 28 Mc 43.25N 134.01 E
Lazovsk 16 Ff 47.38N 28.12 E
Łazy 10 Pf 50.27N 19.26 E
Lea 9 Nj 51.30N 0.01 E
Lead 43 Gc 44.21N 103.46W
Leader 46 Ka 50.53N 109.31W
Lead Hill 45 Jh 37.06N 92.38W
Leadville 45 Cg 39.15N 106.20W
Leaf River 45 Lk 31.00N 88.45W
League City 45 Il 29.31N 95.05W
Leamington 44 Fd 42.03N 82.36W
Leandro N. Alem 55 Bl 34.30S 61.24W
Leane, Lough-/Loch Léin 9 Di 52.05N 9.35W
Le'an Jiang 28 Dj 28.58N 116.41 E
Learmonth 59 Cd 22.13S 114.04 E
Leavenworth [Ks.-U.S.] 45 Ig 39.19N 94.55W
Leavenworth [Wa.-U.S.] 46 Ec 47.36N 120.40W
Łeba 10 Nb 54.47N 17.33 E
Łeba 10 Nb 54.43N 17.25 E
Lebach 12 Ie 49.24N 6.55 E
Lébamba 36 Bc 2.12S 11.30 E
Lebanon [In.-U.S.] 44 De 40.03N 86.28W
Lebanon [Ky.-U.S.] 44 Eg 37.34N 85.15W
Lebanon [Mo.-U.S.] 45 Jh 37.41N 92.40W
Lebanon [N.H.-U.S.] 44 Kd 43.38N 72.15W
Lebanon [Or.-U.S.] 46 Dd 44.32N 122.54W
Lebanon [Pa.-U.S.] 44 Ie 40.21N 76.25W
Lebanon [Tn.-U.S.] 44 Dg 36.12N 86.18W
Lebanon (EN) = Lubnān 22 Ff 33.50N 35.50 E
Lebanon Mountains (EN) = Lubnān, Jabal- 23 Ec 34.00N 36.30 E
Lebap 18 Cd 41.02N 61.54 E
Le Bec-Hellouin 12 Ce 49.14N 0.43 E
Lebedin 19 De 50.36N 34.30 E
Lebediny 20 He 58.25N 125.58 E
Lebedjan 19 De 53.02N 39.07 E
Le Bény-Bocage 12 Bf 48.56N 0.50W
Lebjažje [Kaz.-U.S.S.R.] 19 He 51.28N 77.46 E
Lebjažje [R.S.F.S.R.] 17 Mi 55.16N 66.29 E
Le Blanc 11 Hh 46.38N 1.04 E
Lebo 36 Db 4.29N 23.57 E
Lebomboberge 30 Kk 26.15S 32.00 E
Lebombo Mountains 30 Kk 26.15S 32.00 E
Lębork 10 Nb 54.33N 17.44 E
Le Bourget 12 Ef 48.56N 2.25 E
Lebrija 13 Fh 36.55N 6.04W
Łebsko, Jezioro- 10 Nb 54.44N 17.24 E
Lebu 56 Fe 37.37S 73.39W
Le Carbet 51h Ab 14.43N 61.11W
Le Cateau 12 Fd 50.06N 3.33 E
Le Catelet 12 Fd 50.01N 3.15 E
Lecce 6 Hg 40.23N 18.11 E
Lecco 14 De 45.51N 9.23 E
Lech 10 Gh 48.44N 10.56 E
Lech 14 Ec 47.12N 10.09 E
Le Champ du Feu 11 Nf 48.24N 7.15 E
Lechang 27 Jf 25.15N 113.25 E
Le Château-d'Oléron 11 Ei 45.54N 1.12W
Le Chesne 11 Ke 49.31N 4.46 E
Le Cheylard 11 Kj 44.54N 4.25 E
Lechfeld 10 Gh 48.10N 10.50 E
Lechiguiri, Cerro- 48 Li 16.43N 95.30W
Lechtaler Alpen 14 Ec 47.15N 10.30 E
Léconi 36 Bc 1.11S 13.16 E
Léconi 36 Bc 1.35S 14.14 E
Le Cornate 14 Eg 43.10N 10.58 E
Le Coudray-Saint-Germer 12 De 49.25N 1.50 E
Le Creusot 11 Kh 46.48N 4.26 E
Le Croisic 11 Dg 47.18N 2.30W
Le Crotoy 12 Dd 50.13N 1.37 E
Łęczna 10 Se 51.19N 22.52 E
Łęczyca 10 Pd 52.04N 19.13 E
Led 7 Ke 62.20N 43.00 E
Lede 12 Fd 50.57N 3.59 E
Ledesma 13 Gc 41.05N 6.00W
Le Diamant 51h Ac 14.29N 61.02W
Ledjanaja, Gora- [R.S.F.S.R.] 21 Tc 61.45N 171.15 E
Ledjanaja, Gora- [R.S.F.S.R.] 21 Qe 49.28N 142.45 E
Lednik Entuziastov 66 Cf 70.30S 16.00 E
Lednik Mušketova 66 Cf 72.00S 14.00 E
Ledo, Cabo- 36 Bd 9.41S 13.12 E
Ledolom Tajmyrski 66 Ge 66.00S 83.00 E
Le Donjon 11 Jh 46.21N 3.48 E
Le Dorat 11 Hh 46.13N 1.05 E
Lędyczek 10 Mc 53.33N 16.58 E
Lee/An Laoi 9 Ej 51.55N 8.30W
Leech Lake 43 Ib 47.09N 94.23W
Leeds [Al.-U.S.] 44 Di 33.33N 86.33W
Leeds [Eng.-U.K.] 6 Fe 53.50N 1.35W
Leeds [N.D.-U.S.] 45 Gb 48.17N 99.27W
Leek 12 Ia 53.10N 6.24 E
Leer 10 Dc 53.14N 7.26 E
Leer (Ostfriesland) 10 Dc 53.14N 7.26 E
Leerdam 12 Hc 51.53N 5.06 E
Lées 11 Fk 43.38N 0.14W
Leesburg 43 Kf 29.49N 81.53W
Leeste, Weyhe- 12 Kb 52.59N 8.50 E
Leesville 45 Jk 31.08N 93.16W
Leeuwarden 11 La 53.12N 5.46 E
Leeuwarderadeel 12 Ha 53.16N 5.46 E
Leeuwarderadeel-Stiens 12 Ha 53.16N 5.46 E
Leeuwin, Cape- 59 Cf 34.25S 115.00 E
Leeward Islands 47 Le 17.00N 63.00W
Leeward Islands (EN) = Sous le Vent, Iles- 57 Lf 16.38S 151.30W
Léfini 36 Cc 2.57S 16.10 E
Lefka 15 Jh 41.52N 26.16 E
Lefke/Levka 24 Ee 35.07N 32.51 E
Lefkosa/Levkôsia = Nicosia (EN) 22 Ff 35.10N 33.22 E
Le François 51h Bb 14.37N 60.54W
Lefroy, Lake- 59 Ef 31.15S 121.40 E
Łęg 10 Rf 50.38N 21.49 E
Leganés 13 Id 40.19N 3.45W
Legazpi 22 Oh 13.09N 123.44 E
Legden 12 Jb 52.02N 7.06 E
Legges Tor 59 Jh 41.32S 147.40 E
Leggett 46 Dg 39.52N 123.43W
Leghorn (EN) = Livorno 6 Hg 43.33N 10.19 E
Legionowo 10 Qd 52.25N 20.56 E
Léglise 12 He 49.48N 5.32 E
Legnago 14 Fe 45.11N 11.18 E
Legnano 14 Ce 45.36N 8.54 E
Legnica 10 Me 51.15N 16.10 E
Legnica 10 Me 51.13N 16.09 E
Le Grand-Quevilly 12 De 49.25N 1.02 E
Le Grand Veymont 11 Lj 44.52N 5.32 E
Le Grau-du-Roi 11 Kk 43.32N 4.08 E
Léguer 11 Cf 48.44N 3.32W
Leh 25 Fb 34.10N 77.35 E
Le Havre 6 Gf 49.30N 0.08 E
Lehi 46 Jf 40.24N 111.51W
Lehmann 55 Bj 31.08S 61.27W
Le Hohneck 11 Nf 48.02N 7.01 E
Le Houlme 12 De 49.31N 1.02 E
Lehrte 10 Fd 52.23N 9.58 E
Lehtimäki 8 Jb 62.47N 23.55 E
Lehua Island 65a Aa 22.01N 160.06W
Lehututu 37 Cd 23.53S 21.49 E
Leibnitz 14 Jd 46.46N 15.32 E
Leibo 27 Hf 28.13N 103.34 E
Leicester 6 Fe 52.38N 1.05W
Leicester 9 Mi 52.40N 1.00W
Leicestershire 9 Mi 52.38N 1.00W
Leichhardt Range 59 Jd 20.40S 147.05 E
Leichhardt River 59 Hc 17.35S 139.48 E
Leiden 11 Kc 52.09N 4.30 E
Leidschendam 12 Gb 52.05N 4.26 E
Leie 11 Jc 51.03N 3.43 E
Leifear/Lifford 9 Fg 54.50N 7.29W
Leigh Creek 58 Eh 30.28S 138.25 E
Leighton Buzzard 12 Bc 51.55N 0.39W
Leigong Shan 27 If 26.23N 108.15 E
Leikanger 7 Ae 62.07N 5.20 E
Léim an Mhadaidh/Limavady 9 Gf 55.03N 6.57W
Leimen 12 Ke 49.21N 8.41 E
Leimus 49 Ef 14.44N 84.07W
Leine 10 Fd 52.40N 9.40 E
Leinster/Laighean 9 Gh 53.00N 7.00W
Leipzig 6 He 51.18N 12.20 E
Leipzig 10 Ie 51.20N 12.20 E
Leira 8 Cd 60.58N 9.18 E
Leiria 13 De 39.40N 8.50W
Leiria 13 De 39.45N 8.48W
Leirvik 7 Ag 59.47N 5.30 E
Leisi/Lejsi 8 Jf 58.33N 22.30 E
Leisler, Mount- 59 Fd 23.30S 129.20 E
Leiston 12 Db 52.12N 1.34 E
Leitariegos, Puerto de- 13 Fa 43.00N 6.25W
Leitha 14 Lc 47.52N 17.18 E
Leithagebirge 14 Kc 47.58N 16.40 E
Leitir Ceanainn/Letterkenny 9 Fg 54.57N 7.44W
Leitrim/Liatroim 9 Eg 54.20N 8.20W
Leiva, Cerro- 54 Dc 2.54N 74.48W
Leiyang 27 Jf 26.30N 112.57 E
Leizhou → Haikang 27 Jg 20.56N 110.06 E
Leizhou Bandao 21 Ng 20.40N 110.05 E
Lejasciems 8 Lg 57.08N 26.36 E
Lejsi/Leisi 8 Jf 58.33N 22.30 E
Lek 11 Lc 52.00N 6.00 E
Leka 7 Cd 65.05N 11.37 E
Lékana 36 Cc 2.19S 14.36 E
Leketi, Monts de la- 30 Ii 2.34S 14.17 E
Lekhainá 15 El 37.56N 21.16 E
Lekhal 13 Ph 36.20N 3.51 E
Lekitobi 26 Hg 1.58S 124.33 E
Lekki Lagoon 34 Fd 6.30N 4.07 E
Leknes 7 Cb 68.10N 13.42 E
Łęknica 10 Ke 51.32N 14.48 E
Lékoumou 36 Bc 3.00S 13.50 E
Leksand 7 Df 60.44N 15.01 E
Leksozero, Ozero- 7 He 63.45N 31.00 E
Leksula 26 Ig 3.46S 126.31 E
Leksvik 7 Ce 63.40N 10.37 E
Le Lamentin 50 Fe 14.37N 61.01W
Leland 45 Kj 33.24N 90.54W
Lelång 8 Ee 59.10N 12.10 E
Le Lavandou 11 Mk 43.08N 6.22 E
Lelčicy 16 Fd 51.49N 28.21 E
Leleiwi Point 65a Gd 19.44N 155.00W
Lelepa 63b Dc 17.36S 168.13 E
Leleque 56 Ff 42.23S 71.03W
Leli 63a Ec 8.45S 161.02 E
Leli → Tianlin 27 Ig 24.22N 106.11 E
Lelija 14 Mg 43.26N 18.29 E
Leling 28 Df 37.44N 117.13 E
Léliogat 63b Ce 21.18S 167.35 E
Lelle 7 Fg 58.53N 25.00 E
Le Locle 14 Ac 47.05N 6.45 E
Le Lorrain 51h Ab 14.50N 61.04W
Lelystad 11 Lb 52.31N 5.27 E
Le Madonie 14 Hm 37.50N 14.00 E
Le Maire, Estrecho de- 56 Hh 54.50S 65.00W
Léman, Lac- = Geneva, Lake- (EN) 5 Gf 46.25N 6.30 E
Leman Bank 9 Oh 53.10N 1.58 E
Lemankoa 63a Ba 5.03S 154.34 E
Le Mans 6 Gf 48.00N 0.12 E
Le Marin 51h Bc 14.28N 60.52W
Le Mars 45 He 42.47N 96.10W
Le Mas-d'Azil 11 Hk 43.05N 1.22 E
Lembach 12 Je 49.00N 7.48 E
Lembeck 12 Ic 51.44N 6.59 E
Lemberg 12 Je 49.00N 7.23 E
Lembolovskaja Vozvyšennost 8 Md 60.50N 30.15 E
Lembruch 12 Kb 52.32N 8.21 E
Leme 55 If 22.12S 47.24W
Lemelerberg 12 Ib 52.29N 6.23 E
Lemesós/Limassol 23 Dc 34.40N 33.02 E
Lemgo 10 Ed 52.02N 8.54 E
Lemhi Range 46 Id 44.30N 113.25W
Lemieux Islands 42 Ld 64.00N 64.20W
Lemju 17 He 63.50N 56.57 E
Lemland 8 Id 60.05N 20.10 E
Lemmer, Lemsterland- 12 Hb 52.51N 5.42 E
Lemmon 43 Gb 45.56N 102.10W
Lemmon, Mount- 46 Jj 32.26N 110.47W
Lemnos (EN) = Límnos 5 Ih 39.55N 25.15 E
Le-Molay-Littry 12 Be 49.15N 0.53W
Le-Mont-Saint-Michel 11 Ef 48.38N 1.30W
Le Morne Rouge 51h Ab 14.46N 61.08W
Lemotol Bay 64d Bb 7.21N 151.35 E
Le Moyne, Lac- 42 Ke 57.00N 68.00W
Lempa, Río- 47 Gf 13.14N 88.49W
Lempäälä 8 Jc 61.19N 23.45 E
Lempira 49 Cf 14.20N 88.40W
L'Empordà/Ampurdán 13 Ob 42.12N 2.45 E
Lemro 25 Id 20.25N 93.20 E
Lemsid 32 Ed 26.33N 13.51W
Lemsterland 12 Hb 52.51N 5.42 E
Lemsterland-Lemmer 12 Hb 52.51N 5.42 E
Le Murge 5 Hg 40.50N 16.40 E
Le Muy 11 Mk 43.28N 6.33 E
Lemvig 8 Ch 56.32N 8.18 E
Lemya 17 Jc 66.30N 62.00 E
Lena 21 Ob 72.25N 126.40 E
Lena, Mount- 46 Kf 40.50N 109.27W
Lénakel 63b Dd 19.32S 169.16 E
Lena Mountains (EN) = Prilenskoje Plato 21 Oc 60.45N 125.00 E
Lena Tablemount (EN) 30 Ln 53.00S 45.00 E
Lençóis Paulista 55 Hf 22.36S 48.47W
Lendava 14 Kd 46.34N 16.27 E
Lendery 7 He 63.26N 31.12 E
Lendinara 14 Fe 45.05N 11.36 E
Le Neubourg 12 Ce 49.09N 0.55 E
Lenger 19 Gg 42.10N 69.55 E
Lengerich 10 Dd 52.11N 7.52 E
Lengoué 36 Cb 0.49N 15.47 E
Lengshuijiang 27 Jf 27.41N 111.28 E
Lengua de Vaca, Punta- 56 Fd 30.14S 71.38W
Lengulu 36 Eb 3.15N 26.30 E
Lenhovda 7 Dh 57.00N 15.17 E
Lenina, Pik- = Lenin Peak (EN) 21 Jf 39.19N 73.01 E
Leninabad 22 Ie 40.17N 69.37 E
Leninabadskaja Oblast 19 Gh 40.00N 69.10 E
Leninakan 6 Kg 40.47N 43.50 E
Lenin Canal (EN) = Volgo-Donskoj sudohodny kanal imeni V. I. Lenina 5 Kf 48.40N 43.37 E
Leningrad 6 Jc 59.55N 30.15 E
Leningradskaja 66 Je 69.30S 159.23 E
Leningradskaja 16 Kf 46.17N 39.25 E
Leningradskaja Oblast 19 Dd 60.00N 31.40 E
Leningradski [R.S.F.S.R.] 20 Mc 69.17N 178.10 E
Leningradski [Tad.-U.S.S.R.] 19 Hh 38.09N 70.01 E
Lenino 16 Ig 45.17N 35.44 E
Leninogorsk [Kaz.-U.S.S.R.] 22 Kd 50.27N 83.32 E
Leninogorsk [R.S.F.S.R.] 19 Fe 54.38N 52.30 E
Lenin Peak (EN) = Lenina, Pik- 21 Jf 39.19N 73.01 E
Leninsk [R.S.F.S.R.] 16 Ne 48.42N 45.11 E
Leninsk [Tur.-U.S.S.R.] 18 Bc 42.04N 59.24 E
Leninsk [Uzb.-U.S.S.R.] 18 Id 40.40N 72.20 E
Leninski [Kaz.-U.S.S.R.] 19 He 52.13N 76.50 E
Leninski [Mold.-U.S.S.R.] 15 Lb 47.50N 28.16 E
Leninski [R.S.F.S.R.] 20 He 58.32N 125.58 E
Leninsk-Kuzneckí 22 Kd 54.38N 86.10 E
Leninskoje [Kaz.-U.S.S.R.] 19 Ge 54.05N 65.23 E
Leninskoje [R.S.F.S.R.] 7 Lg 58.21N 47.07 E
Leninskoje [R.S.F.S.R.] 20 Ig 47.59N 132.38 E
Leninváros 10 Ri 47.56N 21.05 E
Lenkoran 6 Kh 38.44N 48.50 E
Lenne 10 De 51.25N 7.30 E
Lenne 12 Jc 51.15N 7.50 E
Lennestadt 12 Kc 51.08N 8.01 E
Lennestadt-Grevenbrück 12 Kc 51.08N 8.01 E
Lennox Hills 9 Ie 56.05N 4.10W
Leno-Angarskoje Plato 20 Fe 55.00N 104.30 E
Lenoir 44 Gh 35.55N 81.32W
Le Nouvion-en-Thiérache 12 Fd 50.01N 3.47 E
Lens 11 Id 50.26N 2.50 E
Lensk 22 Nc 61.00N 114.50 E
Lenti 10 Mi 46.37N 16.33 E
Lentiira 7 Gd 64.21N 29.50 E
Lentini 14 Jm 37.17N 15.01 E
Lentua 7 Gd 64.14N 29.36 E
Lentvaris 8 Kj 54.38N 25.13 E
Léo 34 Ec 11.06N 2.06W
Leoben 14 Jc 47.23N 15.06 E
Léogâne 49 Kd 18.31N 72.38W
Leok 26 Hf 1.11N 121.26 E
Leola 45 Gd 45.43N 98.56W
Leominster 9 Ki 52.14N 2.45W
León 13 Gc 42.00N 6.00W
León 11 Ek 43.53N 1.18W
León [Mex.] 39 Ig 21.10N 101.42W
León [Nic.] 49 Dg 12.35N 86.35W
León [Nic.] 39 Kh 12.26N 86.54W
León [Sp.] 6 Fg 42.36N 5.34W
León [Sp.] 13 Gb 42.40N 6.00W
León, Montes de- 13 Fb 42.30N 6.20W
León, Puerto del- 13 Hh 36.50N 4.21W
Leonardville 37 Bd 23.29S 18.49 E
Leonberg 12 Kf 48.48N 9.01 E
Leone, Monte- 14 Cd 46.15N 8.10 E
Leones 55 Ak 32.39S 62.18W
Leonessa 14 Gh 42.34N 12.58 E
Leonforte 14 Im 37.38N 14.23 E
Leōnidhion 15 Fl 37.10N 22.52 E
Leonora 58 Dg 28.53S 121.20 E
Leon River 45 Hk 30.59N 97.24W
Leopold and Astrid Coast 66 Ge 67.10S 84.10 E
Leopoldina 54 Jh 21.32S 42.38W
Leopold McClintock, Cape- 42 Fa 77.38N 116.20W
Leopoldo de Bulhões 55 Hc 16.37S 48.46W
Leopoldsburg 12 Hc 51.07N 5.15 E
Leopoldville → Kinshasa 31 Ii 4.18S 15.18 E
Leovo 16 Ff 46.29N 28.15 E
Lepa 65c Bb 14.01S 171.28W
Le Palais 11 Cg 47.21N 3.09W
Lepar, Pulau- 26 Eg 2.57S 106.50 E
Le Parcq 12 Ed 50.23N 2.06 E
Lepaterique 49 Df 14.02N 87.27W
Lepe 13 Eg 37.15N 7.12W
Lepel 19 Ce 54.53N 28.46 E
Lepenica 15 Ee 44.10N 21.08 E
Le Petit Caux 12 De 49.55N 1.20 E
Le Petit-Couronne 12 De 49.23N 1.01 E
Le Petit-Quevilly 12 De 49.26N 1.02 E
Lephepe 37 Dd 23.22S 25.52 E
Leping 27 Kf 28.59N 117.07 E
Lepini, Monti- 14 Gi 41.35N 13.00 E
Le Plessis-Belleville 12 Ee 49.06N 2.46 E
Le Pont-de-Claix 11 Li 45.07N 5.42 E
Le Portel 12 Dd 50.42N 1.34 E
Leppävesi 8 Kb 62.15N 25.55 E
Leppävirta 8 Lb 62.29N 27.47 E
Le Prêcheur 51h Ab 14.48N 61.14W
Lepsøya 8 Bb 62.35N 6.10 E
Lepsy 18 La 46.18N 78.20 E
Lepsy 19 Hf 46.12N 78.55 E
Leptis Magna 33 Bc 32.38N 14.18 E
Le Puy 11 Ji 45.02N 3.53 E
Leqemt (EN) = Nekemt 31 Kh 9.05N 36.33 E
Le Quesnoy 12 Fd 50.15N 3.38 E
Lercara Friddi 14 Hm 37.45N 13.36 E
Lerchenfeld Glacier 66 Af 77.50S 34.50W
Lere 34 Gc 10.23N 8.35 E
Léré 35 Ad 9.39N 14.13 E
Lérida 54 Dc 0.06N 70.43W
Lérida 13 Nc 42.00N 1.10 E
Lérida/Lleida 13 Mc 41.37N 0.37 E
Lérins, Iles de- 11 Nk 43.31N 7.03 E
Lerma 13 Ib 42.02N 3.45W
Lerma, Río- 48 Hg 20.13N 102.46W
Lermontov 16 Mg 44.06N 42.45 E
Le Robert 51h Bb 14.41N 60.57W
Léros 15 Jl 37.08N 26.50 E
Lerum 7 Ch 57.46N 12.16 E
Lerwick 9 La 60.09N 1.09W
Léry 12 De 49.17N 1.13 E
Les Abrets 11 Li 45.32N 5.35 E
Le Saint-Esprit 51h Bb 14.34N 60.57W
Les Albères/Albères, Montes- 11 In 42.28N 2.56 E
Les Allobroges 63b Dc 16.47S 168.09 E
Les Andelys 11 He 49.15N 1.25 E
Les Anses-d'Arlets 51h Ac 14.29N 61.05W
Les-Baux-de-Provence 11 Kk 43.45N 4.48 E
Les Borges Blanques/Borjas Blancas 13 Mc 41.31N 0.52 E
Lesbos (EN) = Lésvos 5 Ih 39.10N 26.32 E
L'Escala/La Escala 13 Pb 42.07N 3.08 E
Les Cayes 47 Je 18.12N 73.45W
Les Coëvrons 11 Ff 48.12N 0.10W
Le Serre 14 Kl 38.30N 16.30 E
Les Escoumins 44 Ma 48.25N 69.29W
Les Eyzies-de-Tayac 11 Hj 44.56N 1.01 E
Les Falaises 12 Ce 49.44N 0.21 E
Leshan 27 Hf 29.34N 103.45 E
Les Herbiers 11 Eh 46.52N 1.01W
Lesina, Lago di- 14 Ji 41.55N 15.25 E
Lesja 8 Cb 62.07N 8.52 E
Lesjöfors 7 Dg 59.59N 14.11 E
Leskino 20 Cb 72.25N 79.40 E
Lesko 10 Sg 49.29N 22.21 E
Leskov 66 Ad 56.40S 28.10W
Leskovac 15 Eg 42.59N 21.57 E
Leskoviku 15 Di 40.09N 20.35
Les Mangles 51e Ab 16.23N 61.27
Les Mauges 11 Fg 47.10N 1.00
Les Minquiers 9 Km 48.58N 2.08
Les Monédières 11 Hi 45.30N 1.52
Les Mureaux 12 Df 49.00N 1.55
Lesnaja 10 Vd 52.55N 25.52
Lesnaja 16 Cc 52.11N 23.30
Lesneven 11 Bf 48.34N 4.19
Lešnica 15 Ce 44.39N 19.19
Lesnoj [R.S.F.S.R.] 19 Gd 57.01N 67.50
Lesnoj [R.S.F.S.R.] 19 Fd 59.49N 52.10
Lesnoj, Ostrov- 8 Md 60.02N 28.20
Lesný 10 If 50.02N 12.37
Lesogorski 8 Mc 61.01N 28.51
Lesosibirsk 22 Ld 58.15N 92.30
Lesotho 31 Jk 29.30S 28.30
Lesozavodsk 20 Ig 45.26N 133.25
Lesozavodski 7 Hc 66.45N 32.50
Lesparre-Médoc 11 Fi 45.18N 0.56
L'Espérance Rock 57 Jh 31.26S 178.54
Les Ponts-de-Cé 11 Fg 47.25N 0.31
Les Posets 13 Mb 42.39N 0.25
Les Sables-d'Olonne 11 Eh 46.30N 1.47
Lessay 11 Ee 49.13N 1.32
Lesse 11 Kd 50.14N 4.54
Lessebo 7 Dh 56.45N 15.16
Lessen/Lessines 12 Fd 50.43N 3.50
Les Sept Iles 11 Cf 48.53N 3.28
Lesser Antilles (EN) = Antillas Menores 38 Mh 15.00N 61.00
Lesser Caucasus (EN) = Maly Kavkaz 5 Kg 41.00N 44.35
Lesser Khingan Range (EN) = Xiao Hinggan Ling 21 Oe 48.45N 127.00
Lesser Slave Lake 38 Hd 55.25N 115.30
Lesser Sunda Islands (EN) 21 Oj 9.13S 121.12
Lessines/Lessen 12 Fd 50.43N 3.50
Lessini 14 Fe 45.41N 11.13
Les Tantes 51p Bb 12.19N 61.33
Les Thilliers-en-Vexin 12 De 49.14N 1.36
Les Triagoz 11 Cf 48.53N 3.40
Les Trois-Ilets 51h Ab 14.33N 61.03
Lešukonskoje 7 Kd 64.52N 45.40
Lésvos = Lesbos (EN) 5 Ih 39.10N 26.32
Leszno 10 Me 51.50N 16.35
Leszno 10 Me 51.51N 16.35
Letälven 8 Fe 59.05N 14.20
Le Tanargue 11 Kj 44.37N 4.09
Letchworth 12 Bc 51.58N 0.13
Letea, Ostrovul- 15 Md 45.20N 29.20
Le Teil 11 Kj 44.33N 4.41
Letenye 10 Mj 46.26N 16.44
Lethbridge 39 He 49.42N 110.50
Lethem 53 Ke 3.20N 59.50
Le Thillot 11 Mg 47.53N 6.46
Leti, Kepulauan- = Leti Islands (EN) 26 Ih 8.13S 127.50
Letiahau 30 Jk 21.04S 24.25
Leticia 53 Jf 4.09S 69.57
Leti Islands (EN) = Leti, Kepulauan- 26 Ih 8.13S 127.50
Leting 28 Ee 39.25N 118.55
Letka 7 Mg 58.59N 50.14
Letlhakane 37 Dd 21.25S 25.36
Letnerečenski 7 Id 64.19N 34.25
Letni Bereg 7 Jd 64.50N 38.20
Letohrad 10 Mf 50.03N 16.31
Le Touquet-Paris-Plage 11 Hd 50.31N 1.35
Letovice 10 Mg 49.33N 16.36
Letpadan 25 Je 17.47N 95.45
Le Translay 12 De 49.58N 1.41
Le Tréport 11 Hd 50.04N 1.22
Letsôk-aw Kyun 25 Jf 11.37N 98.15
Letterkenny/Leitir Ceanainn 9 Fg 54.57N 7.44
Leu 15 Ge 44.11N 24.00
Leuca 14 Mk 39.48N 18.21
Leucas (EN) = Levkás 15 Dk 38.43N 20.38
Leucate 11 Jl 42.55N 3.02
Leucate, Étang de- 11 Il 42.51N 3.00
Leuk 14 Bd 46.20N 7.38
Leukónoikon 24 Ee 35.15N 33.42
Leulumoega 65c Ba 13.49S 171.55
Leuna 10 Ie 51.19N 12.01
Leušeny 15 Lc 46.51N 28.11
Leuser, Gunung- 21 Li 3.45N 97.11
Leutkirch im Allgäu 10 Gi 47.50N 10.02
Leuven/Louvain 11 Kd 50.53N 4.42
Leuze-en-Hainaut 12 Fd 50.36N 3.36
Levádhia 15 Fk 38.26N 22.53
Levaja Hetta 20 Cc 65.15N 73.20
Levanger 7 Ce 63.45N 11.18
Levante, Riviera di- 14 Df 44.15N 9.30
Levanzo 14 Gm 38.00N 12.20
Levaši 16 Oh 42.27N 47.20
Le Vauclin 51h Bb 14.33N 60.51W
Levelland 43 Ge 33.35N 102.23W
Lévêque, Cape- 59 Ec 16.25S 122.55
Le Verdon-sur-Mer 11 Ei 45.33N 1.04W
Leverkusen 10 Ce 51.01N 6.59
Leverkusen-Opladen 10 De 51.04N 7.01
Lévézou 11 Ij 44.09N 2.53
Levice 10 Oh 48.13N 18.37
Levico Terme 14 Fd 46.01N 11.18
Le Vigan 11 Jk 43.59N 3.36
Levin 61 Eh 40.37S 175.17
Lévis 42 Kg 46.48N 71.10W
Levisa Fork 44 Ff 38.06N 82.37W
Levitha 15 Jm 37.00N 26.28
Levittown 44 Je 40.09N 74.50W
Levka/Lefke 24 Ee 35.07N 32.51
Levká Óri 15 Gn 35.20N 24.00
Levkás 15 Dk 38.50N 20.42
Levkás = Leucas (EN) 15 Dk 38.43N 20.38

Index Symbols

Independent Nation
State, Region
District, County
Municipality
Colony, Dependency
Continent
Physical Region
Historical or Cultural Region
Mount, Mountain
Volcano
Hill
Mountains, Mountain Range
Hills, Escarpment
Plateau, Upland
Pass, Gap
Plain, Lowland
Delta
Salt Flat
Valley, Canyon
Crater, Cave
Karst Features
Depression
Polder
Desert, Dunes
Forest, Woods
Heath, Steppe
Oasis
Cape, Point
Coast, Beach
Cliff
Peninsula
Isthmus
Sandbank
Island
Atoll
Rock, Reef
Islands, Archipelago
Rocks, Reefs
Coral Reef
Well, Spring
Geyser
River, Stream
Waterfall Rapids
River Mouth, Estuary
Lake
Salt Lake
Intermittent Lake
Reservoir
Swamp, Pond
Canal
Glacier
Ice Shelf, Pack Ice
Ocean
Sea
Gulf, Bay
Strait, Fjord
Lagoon
Bank
Seamount
Tablemount
Ridge
Shelf
Basin
Escarpment, Sea Scarp
Fracture
Trench, Abyss
National Park, Reserve
Point of Interest
Recreation Site
Cave, Cavern
Historic Site
Ruins
Wall, Walls
Church, Abbey
Temple
Scientific Station
Airport
Port
Lighthouse
Mine
Tunnel
Dam, Bridge

evkōsia/Lefkosa=Nicosia (EN)	22	Ff	35.10N	33.22 E
evoča	10	Qg	49.02N	20.35 E
evroux	11	Hh	46.59N	1.37 E
evski	15	If	43.22N	25.08 E
v Tolstoj	16	Kc	53.12N	39.28 E
vuka	63d	Bb	17.41S	178.50 E
vuo/Lévuo	8	Kh	56.02N	24.28 E
vuo/Levuo	8	Kh	56.02N	24.28 E
wes [De.-U.S.]	44	Jf	38.47N	75.08W
wes [Eng.-U.K.]	9	Nk	50.52N	0.01 E
win Brzeski	10	Nf	50.46N	17.37 E
wis, Butt of-	9	Gc	58.31N	6.15W
wis, Isle of-	5	Fd	58.10N	6.40W
wis and Clark Lake	45	He	42.50N	97.45W
wisburg	44	Gg	37.49N	80.28W
wis Pass	62	Ee	42.24S	172.24 E
wis Range	38	He	48.30N	113.15W
wis River	46	Dd	45.51N	122.48W
wis Smith Lake	44	Dh	34.00N	87.07W
wiston [Id.-U.S.]	39	He	46.25N	117.01W
wiston [Me.-U.S.]	43	Mc	44.06N	70.13W
wistown [Mt.-U.S.]	43	Fb	47.04N	109.26W
wistown [Pa.-U.S.]	44	Ie	40.37N	77.36W
wisville	45	Jj	33.22N	93.35W
xington [Ky.-U.S.]	39	Kf	38.03N	84.30W
xington [Nb.-U.S.]	43	Hc	40.47N	99.45W
xington [N.C.-U.S.]	44	Gh	35.49N	80.15W
xington [Ok.-U.S.]	45	Hi	35.01N	97.20W
xington [Va.-U.S.]	44	Hg	37.47N	79.27W
ygues, Iles-	30	Nm	48.45S	69.30 E
yre	11	Ej	44.39N	1.01W
ysdown-on-Sea	12	Cc	51.23N	0.55 E
yte	21	Oh	10.50N	124.50 E
z	11	Kj	44.13N	4.43 E
żajsk	10	Sf	50.16N	22.24 E
zard, Pointe à-	51e	Ab	16.08N	61.47W
zarde, Rivière-	51h	Ab	14.36N	61.01W
zha	15	Ch	41.47N	19.39 E
zignan-Corbières	11	Ik	43.12N	2.46 E
gov	19	De	51.41N	35.17 E
ari	27	Fe	30.48N	93.25 E
asa	22	Lg	29.42N	91.07 E
azê	27	Ef	29.13N	87.44 E
azhong	27	Ee	31.28N	86.36 E
okseumawe	26	Ce	5.10N	97.08 E
oksukon	26	Ce	5.03N	97.19 E
Hôpital	12	Ie	49.10N	6.44 E
orong	27	Ge	30.45N	95.48 E
Hospitalet de l'Infant/Hospitalet del Infante	13	Md	40.59N	0.56 E
ozhag	27	Ff	28.18N	90.51 E
ünzhub (Poindo)	27	Fe	30.17N	91.20 E
ádhi	15	Jm	36.55N	26.10 E
ákoura	15	Fk	38.32N	22.37 E
amone	11a	Aa	42.04N	8.43 E
ancheng	27	Kf	25.48N	116.48 E
ancourt	12	Ee	49.20N	2.28 E
ane	12	Dd	50.43N	1.36 E
angcheng	28	Bd	40.32N	112.28 E
angpran, Gunung-	26	Ff	1.04N	114.23 E
angshan (Houji)	28	Dg	35.48N	116.07 E
angzhou → Wuwei	22	Mf	37.58N	102.48 E
angzi Hu	27	Je	30.15N	114.32 E
anjiang	27	Jg	21.42N	110.14 E
anshui	28	Eh	33.47N	119.16 E
anxian	27	Jg	24.48N	112.26 E
anyin	27	La	53.26N	123.50 E
anyungang	27	Ke	34.38N	119.27 E
anyungang (Xinpu)	22	Nf	34.34N	119.15 E
anzhou → Hepu	27	Ig	21.40N	109.12 E
anzhushan	28	Kb	45.28N	131.45 E
aocheng	27	Kd	36.27N	115.58 E
iaodong Bandao=Liaotung Peninsula (EN)	21	Of	40.00N	122.20 E
iaodong Wan=Liaotung, Gulf of- (EN)	27	Lc	40.00N	121.30 E
iao He	21	Oe	40.39N	122.12 E
iaoning Sheng (Liao-ning Sheng) [2]	27	Lc	41.00N	123.00 E
iao-ning Sheng → Liaoning Sheng [2]	27	Lc	41.00N	123.00 E
iaotung, Gulf of- (EN)= Liaodong Wan	27	Lc	40.00N	121.30 E
iaotung Peninsula (EN)= Liaodong Bandao	21	Of	40.00N	122.20 E
iaoyang	27	Lc	41.16N	123.10 E
iaoyuan	22	Oe	42.55N	125.09 E
iaozhong	28	Gd	41.30N	122.42 E
iard	38	Gc	61.52N	121.18W
iard River	42	Ee	59.15N	126.09W
iat, Pulau-	26	Eg	2.53S	107.05 E
iatorp	8	Fh	56.40N	14.16 E
iatroim/Leitrim [2]	9	Eg	54.20N	8.20W
iban	30	Lh	5.05N	40.05 E
ibano	55	Bm	37.32S	61.18W
ibby	46	Hb	48.23N	115.33W
ibenge	31	Ih	3.39N	18.38 E
ibengé	36	Cb	3.39N	18.38 E
iberal	43	Gd	37.02N	100.55W
iberec	10	Lf	50.46N	15.03 E
iberia	47	Gf	10.38N	85.27W
iberia [1]	31	Fh	6.00N	10.00W
Libertad [Ur.]	55	Dl	34.38S	56.39W
Libertad [Ven.]	49	Li	8.08N	71.28W
Libertad [Ven.]	54	Eb	8.20N	69.37W
Libertade, Rio-	54	He	9.35S	52.17W
Libertador General Bernardo O'Higgins [2]	56	Fd	33.35S	70.45W
Libertador Gen. San Martín	56	Hb	23.48S	64.48W
Libertador General San Martín, Cumbre del-	52	Jh	24.55S	66.40W
Liberty [Mo.-U.S.]	45	Ig	39.15N	94.25W
Liberty [Tx.-U.S.]	45	Ik	30.03N	94.47W
Lībiyā=Libya (EN) [1]	31	If	27.00N	17.00 E
Lībīyah, Aş Şaḩrā' al-= Libyan Desert (EN)	30	Jf	24.00N	25.00 E
Libo	27	If	25.28N	107.52 E
Libobo, Tanjung-	26	Ig	0.54S	128.28 E
Liboi	36	Hb	0.24N	40.57 E
Libourne	11	Fj	44.55N	0.14W
Libramont-Chevigny	12	He	49.55N	5.23 E
Librazhdi	15	Dh	41.11N	20.19 E
Libreville	31	Hh	0.23N	9.27 E
Libro Point	26	Gd	11.26N	119.29 E
Libya (EN)=Lībiyā [1]	31	If	27.00N	17.00 E
Libyan Desert (EN)≐ Lībīyah, Aş Şaḩrā' al-	30	Jf	24.00N	25.00 E
Licantén	56	Fe	34.59S	72.00W
Licata	14	Hm	37.06N	13.56 E
Lice	24	Ic	38.28N	40.39 E
Licenciado Matienzo	55	Cm	37.55S	58.54W
Lich	12	Kd	50.31N	8.50 E
Licheng → Jinhu	28	Eh	33.01N	119.01 E
Lichfield	9	Li	52.42N	1.48W
Lichinga	31	Kj	13.20S	35.20 E
Lichtenau	12	Kc	51.37N	8.54 E
Lichtenburg	37	De	26.08S	26.08 E
Lichtenfels	10	Hf	50.09N	11.04 E
Lichtenvoorde	12	Ic	51.59N	6.34 E
Licking River	44	Ef	39.06N	84.30W
Licosa, Punta-	14	Ij	40.15N	14.54 E
Licuare	37	Fc	17.54S	36.49 E
Licun → Laoshan	28	Ff	36.10N	120.25 E
Licungo	37	Fc	17.40S	37.22 E
Lida	19	Ce	53.56N	25.18 E
Lidan	8	Ef	58.31N	13.09 E
Liddel	9	Kf	55.04N	2.57W
Liddon Gulf	42	Gb	75.00N	113.30W
Liden	7	De	62.42N	16.48 E
Lidhorikion	15	Fk	38.32N	22.12 E
Lidhult	8	Eh	56.50N	13.26 E
Lidingö	7	Eg	59.22N	18.08 E
Lidköping	7	Cg	58.30N	13.10 E
Lido	34	Fc	12.54N	3.44 E
Lido, Venezia-	14	Ge	45.25N	12.22 E
Lido di Ostia	14	Gi	41.44N	12.16 E
Lidzbark	10	Pc	53.17N	19.49 E
Lidzbark Warmiński	10	Qb	54.09N	20.35 E
Lié	11	Df	48.00N	2.40W
Liebenau	12	Lb	52.36N	9.06 E
Liebig, Mount-	59	Gd	23.15S	131.20 E
Liechtenstein [1]	6	Gf	47.10N	9.30 E
Liège [3]	12	Hd	50.30N	5.40 E
Liège/Luik	6	Ge	50.38N	5.34 E
Lieksa	7	He	63.19N	30.01 E
Lielupė	7	Fh	57.03N	23.56 E
Lielvarde/Lielvārde	8	Kh	56.40N	24.49 E
Lielvārde/Lielvarde	8	Kh	56.40N	24.49 E
Lienen	12	Jb	52.09N	7.59 E
Lienz	14	Gd	46.50N	12.47 E
Liepaja/Liepāja	6	Id	56.35N	21.01 E
Liepāja/Liepaja	6	Id	56.35N	21.01 E
Liepajas, Ozero-/Liepājas Ezers	8	Ih	56.35N	20.35 E
Liepājas ezers/Liepaja, Ozero-	8	Ih	56.35N	20.35 E
Liepna	8	Lg	57.16N	27.35 E
Liepupe	8	Kg	57.22N	24.22 E
Lier/Lierre	11	Kc	51.08N	4.34 E
Lierbyen	8	De	59.47N	10.14 E
Lierneux	12	Hd	50.17N	5.48 E
Lierre/Lier	11	Kc	51.08N	4.34 E
Liesborn, Wadersloh-	12	Kc	51.43N	8.16 E
Lieser	10	Dg	49.55N	7.01 E
Liesing	14	Jc	47.20N	15.02 E
Liestal	14	Bc	47.29N	7.44 E
Lieşti	15	Kd	45.37N	27.31 E
Lieto	8	Jd	60.30N	22.27 E
Lietuvos Tarybu Socialistine Respublika/Litovskaja SSR [2]	19	Cd	56.00N	24.00 E
Lietuvos TSR=Lithuanian SSR (EN) [2]	19	Cd	56.00N	24.00 E
Lietvesi	8	Lc	61.30N	28.00 E
Lieurey	12	Ce	49.14N	0.29 E
Lieuvin	11	Ge	49.10N	0.30 E
Lievestuoreenjärvi	8	Lb	62.20N	26.10 E
Liévin	11	Id	50.25N	2.46 E
Lievre, Rivière du-	44	Jc	45.35N	75.25W
Liezen	14	Ic	47.34N	14.14 E
Lifford/Leifear	9	Fg	54.50N	7.29W
Li Fiord	42	Ia	80.17N	94.35W
Lifjell	8	Ce	59.30N	8.52 E
Lifou, Ile-	57	Hg	20.53S	167.13 E
Lifuka	65b	Ba	19.48S	174.21W
Līgatne/Ligatne	8	Kg	57.07N	25.00 E
Ligatne/Līgatne	8	Kg	57.07N	25.00 E
Lighthouse Reef	49	De	17.20N	87.32W
Lignano Sabbiadoro	14	He	45.52N	13.09 E
Lignières	11	Ih	46.45N	2.10 E
Lignon	11	Ki	45.44N	4.08 E
Ligny-en-Barrois	11	Lf	48.41N	5.20 E
Ligonha	37	Fc	16.51S	39.09 E
Ligure, Mar-=Ligurian Sea (EN)	5	Gg	43.30N	9.00 E
Liguria [2]	14	Cf	44.30N	8.50 E
Ligurian Sea (EN)=Ligure, Mar-	5	Gg	43.30N	9.00 E
Lihir Group	57	Ge	3.05S	152.40 E
Lihme	8	Ch	56.36N	8.44 E
Lihoslavl	7	Ih	57.09N	35.29 E
Lihou Reefs and Cays	57	Gf	17.25S	151.40 E
Lihue	60	Oc	21.59N	159.22W
Lihula	7	Fg	58.44N	23.49 E
Liinahamari	7	Hb	69.40N	31.22 E
Lijiang (Dayan)	22	Mg	26.56N	100.15 E
Lijin	28	Ef	37.29N	118.15 E
Lika	14	Jf	44.46N	15.10 E
Lika	14	Jf	44.30N	15.30 E
Likasi	31	Jj	10.59S	26.43 E
Likati	36	Db	2.53N	24.03 E
Likati	36	Db	3.21N	23.53 E
Likėnai/Likenaj	8	Kh	56.11N	24.42 E
Likenaj/Likėnai	8	Kh	56.11N	24.42 E
Likenäs	8	Ed	60.37N	13.02 E
Likhapani	25	Jc	27.19N	95.54 E
Likiep Atoll	57	Hc	9.53N	169.09 E
Likolo	36	Cc	0.43S	19.40 E
Likoma Island	36	Fe	12.04S	34.44 E
Likoto	36	Dc	1.10S	24.45 E
Likouala [3]	36	Cb	2.00N	17.30 E
Likouala	36	Cc	1.13S	16.48 E
Likouala aux Herbes	36	Cc	0.50S	17.11 E
Liku	64k	Bb	19.02S	169.47W
L'Ile Rousse	11a	Aa	42.38N	8.56 E
Lilibeo, Capo- → Boeo, Capo-	14	Gm	37.34N	12.41 E
Lilienfeld	14	Jb	48.01N	15.38 E
Lilienthal	12	Ka	53.08N	8.55 E
Lilla Edet	7	Cg	58.08N	12.08 E
Lille [Bel.]	12	Gc	51.14N	4.50 E
Lille [Fr.]	6	Ge	50.38N	3.04 E
Lille Bælt=Little Belt (EN)	5	Gd	55.20N	9.45 E
Lillebonne	11	Ge	49.31N	0.33 E
Lille Fiskebanke	8	Bh	56.56N	6.20 E
Lillehammer	7	Cf	61.08N	10.30 E
Lille Hellefiske Bank (EN)	41	Ge	65.05N	54.00W
Lillers	11	Id	50.34N	2.29 E
Lillesand	7	Bg	58.15N	8.24 E
Lillestrøm	8	De	59.57N	11.05 E
Lillhärdal	7	Df	61.51N	14.04 E
Lillie Glacier	66	Kf	70.45S	163.55 E
Lillo	13	Ie	39.43N	3.18W
Lillooet	42	Ff	50.42N	121.56W
Lillooet Range	46	Eb	50.00N	121.45W
Lillooet River	42	Fg	49.45N	122.10W
Lilongwe	31	Kj	13.59S	33.47 E
Liloy	26	He	8.08N	122.40 E
Lim [Afr.]	35	Bd	7.54N	15.46 E
Lim [Yugo.]	14	Ng	43.45N	19.13 E
Lima	13	Dc	41.41N	8.50W
Lima [2]	54	Cf	12.00S	76.35W
Lima [Mt.-U.S.]	46	Id	44.38N	112.36W
Lima [Oh.-U.S.]	43	Kc	40.43N	84.06W
Lima [Par.]	55	Df	23.54S	56.20W
Lima [Peru]	53	Ig	12.03S	77.03W
Lima [Swe.]	8	Ed	60.56N	13.21 E
Lima, Pulau-Pulau-	26	Gg	3.03S	107.24 E
Limagne	11	Jh	46.00N	3.20 E
Līmah	24	Qj	25.56N	56.25 E
Liman [R.S.F.S.R.]	16	Og	45.45N	47.14 E
Liman [Ukr.-U.S.S.R.]	15	Md	45.42N	29.46 E
Limanskoje	15	Mc	46.38N	29.54 E
Limari, Río-	56	Fd	30.44S	71.43W
Limassol/Lemesós	23	Dc	34.40N	33.02 E
Limavady/Léim an Mhadaidh	9	Gf	55.03N	6.57W
Limay	12	Df	48.59N	1.44 E
Limay, Río-	52	Ji	38.59S	68.00W
Limbara	14	Dj	40.51N	9.10 E
Limbaži	7	Fh	57.31N	24.47 E
Limbé	49	Kd	19.42N	72.24W
Limbe, Blantyre-	36	Gf	15.49S	35.03 E
Limbot	63b	Cb	14.12S	167.34 E
Limboto	26	Hf	0.37N	122.57 E
Limbourg	12	Hd	50.37N	5.56 E
Limbourg/Limburg	11	Lc	51.05N	5.40 E
Limburg [Bel.] [3]	12	Hc	51.00N	5.30 E
Limburg [Neth.] [3]	12	Hc	51.14N	5.50 E
Limburg/Limbourg	11	Lc	51.05N	5.40 E
Limburg an der Lahn	10	Ef	50.23N	8.03 E
Limedsforsen	8	Ed	60.54N	13.23 E
Limeira	56	Kb	22.34S	47.24W
Limerick/Luimneach [2]	9	Ei	52.30N	9.00W
Limerick/Luimneach	6	Fe	52.40N	8.38W
Limestone, Hadabat-	33	Fe	24.50N	32.00 E
Limfjorden	5	Gd	56.55N	9.10 E
Limia	13	Dc	41.41N	8.50W
Limingen	7	Cd	64.47N	13.36 E
Liminka	7	Fd	64.49N	25.29 E
Limmat	14	Cc	47.30N	8.15 E
Limmen Bight	59	Hb	14.45S	135.40 E
Limmen Bight River	59	Hc	15.15S	135.30 E
Límni	15	Gk	38.46N	23.19 E
Límnos=Lemnos (EN)	5	Ih	39.55N	25.15 E
Limoeiro	54	Ke	7.52S	35.27W
Limoges	6	Gf	45.51N	1.15 E
Limogne, Causse de-	11	Hj	44.20N	1.55 E
Limon	43	Gd	39.16N	103.41W
Limón [3]	49	Fi	10.00N	83.15W
Limón [C.R.]	39	Kh	10.00N	83.02W
Limón [Hond.]	49	Ef	15.52N	85.33W
Limone Piemonte	14	Bf	44.12N	7.34 E
Limousin	11	Hi	45.30N	1.50 E
Limousin, Plateau du-	11	Hi	45.50N	1.10 E
Limoux	11	Ik	43.04N	2.14 E
Limpopo	30	Jk	25.12S	33.32 E
Limu Ling	27	Ie	19.02N	109.43 E
Limuru	36	Gc	1.06S	36.39 E
Līnah	24	Jh	28.42N	43.48 E
Lin'an	27	Ke	30.14N	119.39 E
Linapacan	26	Gd	11.27N	119.49 E
Linares [Chile]	53	Ii	35.51S	71.36W
Linares [Mex.]	47	Ed	24.52N	99.34W
Linares [Sp.]	13	If	38.05N	3.38W
Linares Viejo	55	Bf	23.09S	61.46W
Linaro, Capo-	14	Fh	42.02N	11.50 E
Lincang	22	Mg	23.48N	100.04 E
Lincheng	28	Cf	37.26N	114.34 E
Lincheng → Xuecheng	28	Dg	34.48N	117.14 E
Lincoln	9	Mh	53.20N	0.30W
Lincoln [Arg.]	56	Hd	34.52S	61.32W
Lincoln [Eng.-U.K.]	9	Mh	53.14N	0.33W
Lincoln [Il.-U.S.]	45	Lf	40.09N	89.22W
Lincoln [Nb.-U.S.]	39	Je	40.48N	96.42W
Lincoln [N.Z.]	62	Ee	43.38S	172.29 E
Lincoln, Mount-	45	Cg	39.21N	106.07W
Lincoln City	46	Cd	44.59N	124.01W
Lincoln Sea	67	Ne	83.00N	56.00W
Lincolnshire [3]	9	Mh	53.00N	0.10W
Lindashalvøya	8	Ad	60.40N	5.15 E
Lindau	10	Fi	47.33N	9.41 E
Linde [Neth.]	12	Hb	52.49N	5.52 E
Linde [R.S.F.S.R.]	20	Hd	64.59N	124.36 E
Linden [Guy.]	54	Gb	6.00N	58.18W
Linden [Tn.-U.S.]	44	Dh	35.37N	87.50W
Lindenows Fjord	41	Hf	60.25N	43.00W
Linderödssåsen	8	Ei	55.53N	13.56 E
Lindesberg	7	Dg	59.35N	15.15 E
Lindesnes	5	Gd	58.00N	7.02 E
Lindhorst	12	Lb	52.22N	9.17 E
Líndhos	15	Lm	36.06N	28.04 E
Lindi [3]	36	Gd	9.30S	38.20 E
Lindi	31	Ki	10.00S	39.43 E
Lindi	30	Jh	0.33N	25.05 E
Lindis Pass	62	Cf	44.35S	169.39 E
Lindlar	12	Jc	51.01N	7.23 E
Lindome	8	Eg	57.34N	12.05 E
Lindong → Bairin Zuoqi	27	Kc	43.59N	119.22 E
Lindsay [Ca.-U.S.]	46	Fh	36.12N	119.05W
Lindsay [Ont.-Can.]	44	Hc	44.21N	78.44W
Lindsdal	8	Gh	56.44N	16.18 E
Line Islands	57	Le	0.01S	157.00W
Linfen	27	Jd	36.03N	111.32 E
Lingayen	22	Oh	16.01N	120.14 E
Lingayen Gulf	26	Hc	16.15N	120.14 E
Lingbi	28	Dh	33.33N	117.33 E
Lingbo	7	Df	61.03N	16.41 E
Lingchuan	28	Bg	35.46N	113.16 E
Lingen (Ems)	10	Dd	52.31N	7.19 E
Lingfield	12	Bc	51.10N	0.01W
Lingga, Kepulauan-=Lingga Archipelago (EN)	21	Mj	0.02S	104.35 E
Lingga, Pulau-	26	Dg	0.12S	104.35 E
Lingga Archipelago (EN)= Lingga, Kepulauan-	21	Mj	0.02S	104.35 E
Linghed	8	Fd	60.47N	15.51 E
Lingling	27	Jf	26.24N	111.41 E
Lingomo	36	Db	0.38N	21.59 E
Lingqiu	28	Ce	39.26N	114.14 E
Lingshan	27	Ig	22.30N	109.17 E
Lingshan Dao	28	Fg	35.45N	120.10 E
Lingshi	28	Af	36.50N	111.46 E
Lingshou	28	Ce	38.18N	114.22 E
Linguère	31	Fg	15.24N	15.07W
Lingwu	27	Id	38.05N	106.20 E
Lingxian	28	Df	37.20N	116.35 E
Lingyuan	28	Ed	41.15N	119.23 E
Linh, Ngoc-	21	Mh	15.04N	107.59 E
Linhai	27	La	51.36N	124.22 E
Linhai (Taizhou)	27	Lf	28.52N	121.08 E
Linhares	54	Jg	19.25S	40.04W
Linhe	27	Ic	40.49N	107.28 E
Linhuaiguan	28	Dh	32.54N	117.39 E
Linjiang	28	Id	41.49N	126.55 E
Linköping	6	Hd	58.25N	15.37 E
Linkou	27	Nb	45.18N	130.18 E
Linkuva	8	Jh	56.02N	23.58 E
Linlü Shan	28	Bf	36.02N	113.42 E
Linn, Mount-	46	Df	40.03N	122.48W
Linneryd	8	Fh	56.40N	15.07 E
Linnhe, Loch-	9	He	56.37N	5.25W
Linnich	12	Id	50.59N	6.16 E
Linosa	14	Go	35.50N	12.50 E
Linovo	10	Ud	52.28N	24.35 E
Linqing	27	Kd	36.48N	115.49 E
Linqu	28	Ef	36.31N	118.32 E
Linquan	28	Ch	33.04N	115.16 E
Linru	28	Bg	34.10N	112.51 E
Lins	56	Kb	21.40S	49.45W
Linsell	8	Eb	62.09N	13.53 E
Linshu (Xiazhuang)	28	Eg	34.56N	118.38 E
Linslade	12	Bc	51.55N	0.40W
Linta	37	Ge	25.02S	44.05 E
Lintao	27	Hd	35.20N	104.00 E
Linthal	14	Cd	46.55N	9.00 E
Linton [Eng.-U.K.]	12	Cb	52.06N	0.16 E
Linton [N.D.-U.S.]	45	Fc	46.16N	100.14W
Linxi [China]	22	Ne	43.36N	118.02 E
Linxi [China]	28	Ee	39.42N	118.26 E
Linxia	22	Mf	35.28N	102.59 E
Linxian	27	Jd	37.57N	111.00 E
Linxiang	28	Bj	29.29N	113.28 E
Linyi [China]	28	Df	37.11N	116.51 E
Linyi [China]'	27	Kd	35.09N	118.15 E
Linz	6	Hf	48.18N	14.18 E
Linze (Shahezhen)	27	Hd	39.10N	100.21 E
Lion, Golfe du-=Lion, Gulf of- (EN)	5	Gg	43.00N	4.00 E
Lion, Gulf of- (EN)=Lion, Golfe du-	5	Gg	43.00N	4.00 E
Lions Den	37	Ec	17.16S	30.02 E
Lion-sur-Mer	12	Be	49.18N	0.19W
Lioppa	26	Ih	7.40S	126.00 E
Lios Mór/Lismore	9	Fi	52.08N	7.55W
Lios na gCearrbhach/ Lisburn	9	Gg	54.31N	6.03W
Lios Tuathail/Listovel	9	Di	52.27N	9.29W
Liouesso	36	Cb	1.02N	15.43 E
Lipa	26	Hd	13.57N	121.10 E
Lipany	10	Qg	49.10N	20.58 E
Lipari	14	Il	38.30N	14.55 E
Lipari	14	Il	38.28N	14.57 E
Lipari Islands (EN)=Eolie o Lipari, Isole-	5	Hh	38.35N	14.55 E
Lipeck	6	Je	52.37N	39.35 E
Lipeckaja Oblast [3]	19	De	52.45N	39.10 E
Lipenská přehradni nádrž	10	Kh	48.45N	14.05 E
Liperi	7	Ge	62.32N	29.22 E
Lipez, Cordillera de-	54	Eh	22.00S	66.45W
Liphook	12	Bc	51.04N	0.48W
Lipkani	15	Ja	48.13N	26.48 E
Lipljan	15	Eg	42.32N	21.08 E
Lipno	10	Pd	52.51N	19.10 E
Lipova	15	Ec	46.05N	21.42 E
Lipovcy	20	Ih	44.15N	131.45 E
Lippborg, Lippetal-	12	Kc	51.40N	8.02 E
Lippe	10	Ce	51.39N	6.38 E
Lipper Bergland	12	Kb	52.05N	8.57 E
Lippetal	12	Kc	51.40N	8.13 E
Lippetal-Eickelborn	12	Kc	51.39N	8.13 E
Lippetal-Lippborg	12	Kc	51.40N	8.02 E
Lippischer Wald	12	Kc	51.56N	8.45 E
Lippstadt	10	Ee	51.40N	8.21 E
Lipsko	10	Re	51.09N	21.39 E
Lipsoí	15	Jl	37.20N	26.45 E
Liptako	30	Hg	14.15N	0.02 E
Liptovský Mikuláš	10	Pg	49.05N	19.38 E
Lira	36	Fb	2.15N	32.54 E
Liranga	36	Cc	0.40S	17.36 E
Liri	14	Hi	41.25N	13.52 E
Liria	13	Le	39.38N	0.36W
Lís	13	De	39.53N	8.58W
Lisa	15	Cf	43.08N	19.42 E
Lisac	15	Eg	42.45N	21.56 E
Lisakovsk	19	Ge	52.33N	62.28 E
Lisala	31	Jh	2.09N	21.31 E
Lisboa [2]	13	Ce	39.00N	9.08W
Lisboa=Lisbon (EN)	6	Fh	38.43N	9.08W
Lisbon	45	Hc	46.27N	97.41W
Lisbon (EN)=Lisboa	6	Fh	38.43N	9.08W
Lisbon Canyon (EN)	13	Cf	38.20N	9.20W
Lisburn/Lios na gCearrbhach	9	Gg	54.31N	6.03W
Lisburne, Cape-	40	Fc	68.52N	166.14W
Liscannor Bay/Bá Thuath Reanna	9	Di	52.55N	9.25W
Lisec	10	Uh	48.48N	24.45 E
Li Shan	28	Ag	35.25N	111.58 E
Lishi	27	Jd	37.29N	111.08 E
Lishu	28	Hc	43.19N	124.20 E
Lishui	27	Kf	28.30N	119.55 E
Lisianski Island	57	Jb	26.02N	174.00W
Lisičansk	19	Df	48.53N	38.28 E
Lisieux	11	Ge	49.09N	0.14 E
Liska	15	Dh	41.19N	20.58 E
L'Isle-Adam	12	Ee	49.07N	2.14 E
L'Isle-Jourdain	11	Hk	43.37N	1.05 E
L'Isle sur-la-Sorgue	11	Lk	43.55N	5.03 E
Lismore	58	Gg	28.48S	153.17 E
Lismore/Lios Mór	9	Fi	52.08N	7.55W
Liss	24	Hg	31.14N	38.31 E
Liss	12	Bc	51.02N	0.54W
List	10	Ea	55.01N	8.26 E
Lista	8	Bf	58.10N	6.40 E
Listafjorden	8	Bf	58.10N	6.35 E
Lister, Mount-	66	Kf	78.04S	162.41 E
Lištica	14	Lg	43.23N	17.39 E
Listovel/Lios Tuathail	9	Di	52.27N	9.29W
Listowel	44	Gd	43.44N	80.57W
Liswarta	10	Pe	51.06N	19.01 E
Lit	8	Fa	63.19N	14.49 E
Litang [China]	27	Ig	23.12N	109.05 E
Litang [China]	27	He	30.02N	100.18 E
Litani Rivier	54	Hc	3.18N	54.06W
Litchfield	45	Id	45.08N	94.31W
Lithgow	58	Gh	33.29S	150.09 E
Líthinon, Ákra-	15	Ho	34.55N	24.44 E
Lithuania (EN)	5	Id	56.00N	24.00 E
Lithuanian SSR (EN)= Lietuvos TSR [2]	19	Cd	56.00N	24.00 E
Litókhoron	15	Fi	40.06N	22.30 E
Litoměřice	10	Kf	50.32N	14.08 E
Litovel	10	Ng	49.43N	17.05 E
Litovko	20	Ig	49.17N	135.10 E
Litovskaja Sovetskaja Socialističeskaja Respublika [2]	19	Cd	56.00N	24.00 E
Litovskaja SSR/Lietuvos Tarybu Socialistine Respublika [2]	19	Cd	56.00N	24.00 E
Little Abaco Island	47	Ic	26.53N	77.43W
Little Abitibi River	44	Ha	49.29N	79.32W
Little Aden	23	Fg	12.45N	44.52 E
Little America	46	Kf	41.32N	109.47W
Little Andaman	21	Lh	10.45N	92.30 E
Little Bahama Bank (EN)	47	Ic	26.30N	78.00W
Little Barrier Island	62	Fb	36.10S	175.05 E
Little Beaver Creek	45	Ec	46.17N	103.56W
Little Belt (EN)=Lille Bælt	5	Gd	55.20N	9.45 E
Little Belt Mountains	46	Jc	46.45N	110.35W
Little Blue River	45	Hg	39.41N	96.40W
Little Bow River	46	Ib	49.53N	112.29W
Little Carpathians (EN) = Malé Karpaty	10	Nh	48.30N	17.20 E
Little Cayman	47	He	19.41N	80.03W
Little Colorado River	38	Hc	36.11N	111.48W
Little Current	42	Jg	45.58N	81.56W
Little Current	42	Jf	50.57N	84.36W
Little Dry Creek	46	Lc	47.21N	106.22W
Little Exuma Island	49	Jb	23.27N	75.37W
Little Falls	43	Ib	45.59N	94.21W
Littlefield	45	Ej	33.55N	102.20W
Little Fort	46	Ea	51.25N	120.12W
Little Grand Rapids	42	Hf	52.02N	95.25W
Little Halibut Bank	9	Lc	58.20N	1.15W
Littlehampton	12	Bd	50.48N	0.32W
Little Inagua Island	47	Jd	21.30N	73.00W
Little Karroo (EN)=Klein-Karoo	37	Cf	33.42S	21.20 E
Little Missouri	38	Ie	47.30N	102.25W
Little Namaland (EN)= Namakwaland	37	Be	29.00S	17.00 E
Little Nicobar	25	Ig	7.20N	93.40 E
Little Ouse	9	Ni	52.30N	0.22 E
Littleport	12	Cb	52.27N	0.18 E
Little Powder River	46	Md	45.28N	105.20W
Little Quill Lake	46	Ma	51.55N	104.05W
Little River	62	Ee	43.46S	172.47 E
Little Rock	39	Jf	34.44N	92.15W
Little Rocky Mountains	46	Kb	48.00N	108.45W

Index Symbols

[1] Independent Nation
[2] State, Region
[3] District, County
Municipality
Colony, Dependency
Continent
Physical Region
Historical or Cultural Region
Mount, Mountain
Volcano
Hill
Mountains, Mountain Range
Hills, Escarpment
Plateau, Upland
Pass, Gap
Plain, Lowland
Delta
Salt Flat
Valley, Canyon
Crater, Cave
Karst Features
Depression
Polder
Desert, Dunes
Forest, Woods
Heath, Steppe
Oasis
Cape, Point
Coast, Beach
Cliff
Peninsula
Isthmus
Sandbank
Island
Atoll
Rock, Reef
Islands, Archipelago
Rocks, Reefs
Coral Reef
Well, Spring
Geyser
River, Stream
Waterfall Rapids
River Mouth, Estuary
Lake
Salt Lake
Intermittent Lake
Reservoir
Swamp, Pond
Canal
Glacier
Ice Shelf, Pack Ice
Ocean
Sea
Gulf, Bay
Strait, Fjord
Lagoon
Bank
Seamount
Tablemount
Ridge
Shelf
Basin
Escarpment, Sea Scarp
Fracture
Trench, Abyss
National Park, Reserve
Point of Interest
Recreation Site
Cave, Cavern
Historic Site
Ruins
Wall, Walls
Church, Abbey
Temple
Scientific Station
Airport
Port
Lighthouse
Mine
Tunnel
Dam, Bridge

Little Scarcies 34 Cd 8.51N 13.09W
Little Sioux River 45 Hf 41.49N 96.04W
Little Sitkin 40a Cb 51.55N 178.30 E
Little Smoky 42 Fe 55.39N 117.37W
Little Snake River 45 Bf 40.27N 108.26W
Littleton [Co.-U.S.] 45 Dg 39.37N 105.01W
Littleton [N.H.-U.S.] 44 Lc 44.18N 71.46W
Little White River [Ont.-Can.] 44 Fb 46.15N 83.00W
Little White River [S.D.-U.S.] 45 Fe 43.44N 100.40W
Littoral [3] 34 He 4.30N 10.00 E
Litvínov 10 Jf 50.36N 13.36 E
Liuba 27 Ie 33.39N 106.53 E
Liuhe 27 Mc 42.16N 125.45 E
Liu He [China] 28 Gd 41.48N 122.43 E
Liu He [China] 28 Ic 42.46N 126.13 E
Liuheng Dao 28 Gj 29.43N 122.08 E
Liujia Xia 27 Hd 35.50N 103.00 E
Liukang Tenggaja, Kepulauan- 26 Gh 6.45 S 118.50 E
Liupai → Tian'e 27 If 25.05N 107.12 E
Liupan Shan 27 Id 35.40N 106.15 E
Liuqu He 28 Fd 40.10N 120.15 E
Liuwa Plain 36 De 14.27 S 22.25 E
Liuyang 28 Bj 28.09N 113.38 E
Liuzhangzhen → Yuanqu 27 Jd 35.19N 111.44 E
Liuzhou 22 Mg 24.22N 109.20 E
Livāni/Livány 7 Gh 56.22N 26.12 E
Livanjsko Polje 14 Kg 43.51N 16.50 E
Livany/Livāni 7 Gh 56.22N 26.12 E
Livarot 12 Ce 49.01N 0.09 E
Livengood 40 Jc 65.32N 148.33W
Livenza 14 Ge 45.35N 12.51 E
Livenzi 15 Ge 44.14N 23.47 E
Live Oak 44 Fj 30.18N 82.59W
Livermore 46 Eh 37.41N 121.46W
Livermore, Mount- 45 Dk 30.37N 104.08W
Liverpool [Eng.-U.K.] 6 Fe 53.25N 2.55W
Liverpool [N.S.-Can.] 42 Lh 44.02N 64.43W
Liverpool, Cape- 42 Jb 73.38N 78.05W
Liverpool Bay [Can.] 42 Ec 70.00N 129.00W
Liverpool Bay [Eng.-U.K.] 9 Jh 53.30N 3.16W
Liverpool Range 59 Kf 31.40 S 150.30 E
Liverpool River 59 Gb 12.00 S 134.00 E
Livigno 14 Ed 46.32N 10.04 E
Livingston [Guat.] 49 Cf 15.50N 88.45W
Livingston [Mt.-U.S.] 43 Eb 45.40N 110.34W
Livingston [Newf.-Can.] 42 Kf 53.40N 66.10W
Livingston [Tn.-U.S.] 44 Eg 36.23N 85.19W
Livingston [Tx.-U.S.] 45 Ik 30.43N 94.56W
Livingston, Lake- 45 Ik 30.45N 95.15W
Livingstone, Chutes de- = Livingstone Falls (EN) 30 Ii 4.50 S 14.30 E
Livingstone Falls (EN) = Livingstone, Chutes de- 30 Ii 4.50 S 14.30 E
Livingstone Memorial 36 Fe 12.19 S 30.18 E
Livingstone Mountains 36 Fd 9.45 S 34.20 E
Livingstonia 36 Fe 10.36 S 34.07 E
Livingston Island 66 Qe 62.36 S 60.30W
Livno 14 Lg 43.50N 17.01 E
Livny 19 De 52.28N 37.37 E
Livonia 44 Fd 42.25N 83.23W
Livonia (EN)=Livonija 5 Id 58.50N 27.30 E
Livonija=Livonia (EN) 5 Id 58.50N 27.30 E
Livorno=Leghorn (EN) 6 Hg 43.33N 10.19 E
Livradois, Monts du- 11 Ji 45.30N 3.33 E
Livramento do Brumado 54 Jf 13.39 S 41.50W
Livron-sur-Drôme 11 Kj 44.46N 4.51 E
Liwale 36 Gd 9.46 S 37.56 E
Liwiec 10 Rd 52.35N 21.33 E
Liwonde 36 Gf 15.01 S 35.13 E
Lixi 27 Hf 26.21N 102.03 E
Lixian [China] 27 Ie 34.11N 105.02 E
Lixian [China] 27 Jf 29.40N 111.45 E
Lixian [China] 28 Ce 38.29N 115.34 E
Lixin 28 Dh 33.09N 116.12 E
Lixoúrion 15 Dk 38.12N 20.26 E
Liyang 28 Ei 31.26N 119.29 E
Lizard 9 Hl 49.57N 5.13W
Lizard Point 5 Ff 49.56N 5.13W
Lizhu 28 Fj 29.58N 120.26 E
Lizy sur Ourcq 12 Fe 49.01N 3.02 E
Ljady 8 Mf 58.35N 28.55 E
Ljahoviči 16 Ec 53.04N 26.15 E
Ljahovskije Ostrova = Lyakhov Islands (EN) 21 Qb 73.30N 141.00 E
Ljalja 17 Jg 59.10N 61.30 E
Ljamin 17 Of 61.18N 71.45 E
Ljangar 18 Ed 40.23N 65.59 E
Ljangasovo 7 Lg 58.33N 49.29 E
Ljapin 17 Je 63.38N 61.58 E
Ljaskelja 8 Nc 61.39N 31.03 E
Ljaskovec 15 If 43.06N 25.43 E
Ljig 15 De 44.14N 20.15 E
Ljuban [Bye.-U.S.S.R.] 16 Ec 52.48N 27.59 E
Ljuban [R.S.F.S.R.] 7 Hg 59.22N 31.13 E
Ljubar 16 Ee 49.55N 27.44 E
Ljubaševka 15 Nb 47.50N 30.07 E
Ljubelj 14 Id 46.26N 14.16 E
Ljubercy 19 Dd 55.40N 37.55 E
Ljubešov 10 Ve 51.45N 25.37 E
Ljubim 7 Jg 58.22N 40.41 E
Ljubimec 15 Jh 41.50N 26.05 E
Ljubinje 14 Mh 42.57N 18.06 E
Ljubišnja 15 Cf 43.20N 19.07 E
Ljubljana 6 Hf 46.02N 14.30 E
Ljuboml 16 Cd 51.15N 23.59 E
Ljubotin 16 Ie 49.59N 35.55 E
Ljubovija 15 Ce 44.12N 19.22 E
Ljubuški 14 Lg 43.12N 17.33 E
Ljubytino 7 Hg 58.50N 33.25 E
Ljudinovo 19 De 53.51N 34.28 E
Ljugarn 7 Eh 57.19N 18.42 E
Ljungan 5 Hc 62.19N 17.23 E
Ljungaverk 8 Gb 62.29N 16.03 E
Ljungby 7 Ch 56.50N 13.56 E
Ljungbyholm 8 Gh 56.38N 16.10 E
Ljungdalen 7 Ce 62.51N 12.47 E
Ljungsbro 8 Ff 58.31N 15.30 E
Ljungskile 8 Df 58.14N 11.55 E
Ljusdal 7 Df 61.50N 16.05 E
Ljusnan 5 Hc 61.12N 17.08 E
Ljusne 7 Df 61.13N 17.08 E
Ljusterö 8 He 59.30N 18.35 E
Ljuta 8 Mf 58.33N 28.45 E
Llandilo 9 Jj 51.53N 3.59W
Llandovery 9 Jj 51.59N 3.48W
Llandrindod Wells 9 Ji 52.15N 3.23W
Llandudno 9 Jh 53.19N 3.49W
Llanelli 9 Ij 51.42N 4.10W
Llanes 13 Ha 43.25N 4.45W
Llangefni 9 Ih 53.16N 4.18W
Llangollen 9 Ji 52.58N 3.10W
Llano 45 Gk 30.45N 98.41W
Llano Estacado 38 If 33.30N 102.40W
Llano River 45 Gk 30.35N 98.25W
Llanos 52 Je 5.00N 70.00W
Llanos de Sonora 47 Bc 28.20N 111.00W
Llanquihue, Lago- 56 Ff 41.08 S 72.48W
Llata 54 Ce 9.25 S 76.47W
Lleida/Lérida 13 Mc 41.37N 0.37 E
Llerena 13 Ff 38.14N 6.01W
Lleyn 9 Ii 52.54N 4.30W
Llica 54 Eg 19.52 S 68.16W
Llívia 13 Nb 42.28N 1.59 E
Llobregat 13 Oc 41.19N 2.09 E
Lloret de Mar 13 Oc 41.42N 2.51 E
Llorona, Punta- 49 Fi 8.37N 83.44W
Llorri/Orri, Pic d'- 13 Nb 42.23N 1.12 E
Lloydminster 42 Gf 53.17N 110.00W
Lluchmayor 13 Oe 39.29N 2.54 E
Llullaillaco, Volcán- 52 Jh 24.43 S 68.33W
Lo 63b Ca 13.21 S 166.38 E
Loa 46 Jg 38.24N 111.38W
Loa, Río- 56 Fb 21.26 S 70.04W
Loanatit, Pointe- 63b Dd 19.21 S 169.14 E
Loange 30 Ji 4.17 S 20.02 E
Loango 36 Bc 4.39 S 11.48 E
Loano 14 Cf 44.08N 8.15 E
Loban 7 Mh 56.59N 51.12 E
Lobatse 31 Jk 25.13 S 25.41 E
Löbau/Lubij 10 Ke 51.06N 14.40 E
Lobaye 30 Ih 3.41N 18.35 E
Lobaye [3] 35 Be 4.00N 17.40 E
Lobenstein 10 Hf 50.27N 11.39 E
Loberia 56 Ie 38.09 S 58.47W
Łobez 10 Lc 53.39N 15.36 E
Lobito 31 Ij 12.22 S 13.34 E
Lobo 34 Dd 6.02N 6.47W
Lobos 56 Ie 35.11 S 59.06W
Lobos 32 Ed 28.45N 13.49W
Lobos, Cabo- 48 Cc 29.55N 112.45W
Lobos, Cay- 49 Ib 22.24N 77.32W
Lobos, Cayo- 48 Ph 18.22N 87.24W
Lobos, Isla- 48 Dd 27.20N 110.36W
Lobos, Islas de- 48 Kg 21.27N 97.15W
Lobos de Afuera, Islas- 54 Be 6.57 S 80.42W
Lobos de Tierra, Isla- 54 Be 6.27 S 80.52W
Lobva 19 Gd 59.12N 60.30 E
Łobżonka 10 Nc 53.07N 17.18 E
Locana 14 Be 45.25N 7.27 E
Locarno 14 Cd 46.10N 8.48 E
Loch Aillionn/Allen, Lough- 9 Eg 54.08N 8.08W
Loch Arabhach/Arrow, Lough- 9 Eg 54.05N 8.20W
Lochboisdale 9 Fd 57.09N 7.19W
Loch Cairlinn/Carlingford Lough 9 Gg 54.05N 6.14W
Loch Ce/Key, Lough- 9 Eg 54.00N 8.15W
Loch Coirib/Corrib, Lought- 9 Dh 53.05N 9.10W
Loch Con/Conn, Lough- 9 Dg 54.04N 9.20W
Loch Cuan/Strangford Lough 9 Hg 54.26N 5.36W
Loch Deirgeirt/Derg, Lough- 9 Ei 53.00N 8.20W
Lochearnhead 9 Ie 56.23N 4.18W
Loch Éirne Iochtair/Lower Lough Erne 9 Fg 54.30N 7.50W
Loch Éirne Uachtair/Upper Lough Erne 9 Fg 54.20N 7.30W
Lochem 12 Ib 52.10N 6.25 E
Loches 11 Gg 47.08N 1.00 E
Loch Feabhail/Foyle, Lough- 9 Ff 55.05N 7.10W
Loch Garman/Wexford 6 Fe 52.20N 6.27W
Loch Garman/Wexford [2] 9 Gi 52.20N 6.40W
Lochgilphead 9 He 56.03N 5.26W
Loch Hinninn/Ennell, Lough- 9 Fh 53.28N 7.24W
Lochinver 9 Hc 58.09N 5.15W
Loch Lao/Belfast Lough 9 Hg 54.40N 5.50W
Loch Léin/Leane, Lough- 9 Di 52.05N 9.35W
Loch Leven 9 Je 56.13N 3.10W
Loch Long 9 Ie 56.04N 4.50W
Lochmaddy 9 Fd 57.36N 7.10W
Loch Measca/Mask, Lough- 9 Dh 53.35N 9.20W
Lochnagar 9 Je 56.55N 3.10W
Loch nEathach/Neagh, Lough- 5 Fe 54.38N 6.24W
Loch Ness 9 Id 57.15N 4.30W
Łochów 10 Rd 52.32N 21.48 E
Loch Pholl an Phúca/Poulaphuca Reservoir 9 Gh 53.10N 6.30W
Loch Rí/Ree, Lough- 9 Fh 53.35N 8.00W
Lochsa River 46 Hc 46.08N 115.36W
Loch Sileann/Sheelin, Lough- 9 Fh 53.48N 7.20W
Loch Suili/Swilly, Lough- 9 Ff 55.10N 7.38W
Loch Uí Ghadra/Gara, Lough- 9 Eh 53.55N 8.30W
Lochy 9 He 56.49N 5.06W
Lochy, Loch- 9 Ie 56.55N 4.55W
Lockerbie 9 Jf 55.07N 3.22W
Lockhart 45 Hl 29.53N 97.41W
Lock Haven 44 Ie 41.09N 77.28W
Löcknitz 10 Hc 53.07N 11.16 E
Lockport 44 Hd 43.11N 78.39W
Locminé 11 Dg 47.53N 2.50W
Locri 14 Kl 38.14N 16.16 E
Lod 24 Fg 31.58N 34.54 E
Lodalskåpa 7 Bf 61.47N 7.12 E
Loddon 12 Db 52.32N 1.29 E
Loddon River 59 Ig 36.41 S 143.55 E
Lodejnoje Pole 19 Dc 60.44N 33.33 E
Lodève 11 Jk 43.43N 3.19 E
Lodi [Ca.-U.S.] 46 Eg 38.08N 121.16W
Lodi [It.] 14 De 45.19N 9.30 E
Lødingen 7 Db 68.25N 16.00 E
Lodja 31 Ji 3.29 S 23.26 E
Lodosa 13 Jb 42.25N 2.05W
Lödöse 8 Ef 58.02N 12.08 E
Lodwar 31 Kh 3.07N 35.36 E
Łódź 6 He 51.46N 19.30 E
Łódź [2] 10 Pe 51.45N 19.30 E
Loei 25 Ke 17.32N 101.34 E
Loeriesfontein 37 Bf 30.56 S 19.26 E
Lofanga 65b Ba 19.50 S 174.33W
Loffa 30 Fh 6.36N 11.05W
Loffa [3] 34 Dd 7.45N 10.00W
Lofoten 5 Hb 68.30N 15.00 E
Lofoten Basin (EN) 5 Ga 70.00N 4.00 E
Lofsdalen 8 Eb 62.07N 13.16 E
Loftahammar 8 Gg 57.52N 16.40 E
Loga 34 Fc 13.37N 3.14 E
Logan [N.M.-U.S.] 45 Ei 35.22N 103.25W
Logan [Oh.-U.S.] 44 Ff 39.32N 82.24W
Logan [Ut.-U.S.] 43 Ec 41.44N 111.50W
Logan [W.V.-U.S.] 44 Gg 37.52N 81.58W
Logan, Mount- [Can.] 38 Ec 60.34N 140.24W
Logan, Mount- [Wa.-U.S.] 46 Eb 48.32N 120.57W
Logan Martin Lake 44 Di 33.40N 86.15W
Logan Mountains 42 Ed 61.00N 128.00W
Logansport 44 De 40.45N 86.21W
Loge 30 Ii 7.49 S 13.06 E
Logojsk 8 Lj 54.12N 27.57 E
Logone 30 Ig 12.06N 15.02 E
Logone Birni 34 Ic 11.47N 15.06 E
Logone Occidental [3] 35 Bd 8.40N 16.00 E
Logone Occidental 35 Bd 9.07N 16.26 E
Logone Oriental [3] 35 Bd 8.20N 16.30 E
Logone Oriental 35 Bd 9.07N 16.26 E
Logroño [3] 13 Jb 42.15N 2.30W
Logroño [Arg.] 55 Bi 29.30 S 61.42W
Logroño [Sp.] 13 Jb 42.28N 2.27W
Logrosán 13 Ge 39.20N 5.29W
Løgstør 7 Bh 56.58N 9.15 E
Logudoro 14 Cj 40.35N 8.40 E
Løgumkloster 8 Ci 55.03N 8.57 E
Lögurinn 7a Cb 65.15N 14.30W
Lohja/Lojo 7 Ff 60.15N 24.05 E
Lohjanjärvi 8 Jd 60.15N 23.55 E
Lohjanselkä/Lojo åsen 8 Kd 60.15N 24.10 E
Löhme 12 Kc 51.41N 8.42 E
Löhne 10 Ed 52.11N 8.41 E
Lohne 12 Kb 52.40N 8.14 E
Lohra 12 Kd 50.44N 8.38 E
Lohr am Main 10 Ff 49.59N 9.35 E
Lohusuu/Lokusu 8 Lf 58.53N 27.01 E
Lohvica 16 Hd 50.22N 33.15 E
Loi, Phou- 25 Kd 20.16N 103.12 E
Loi-Kaw 25 Je 19.41N 97.13 E
Loile 36 Dc 0.52 S 20.12 E
Loimaa 7 Ff 60.51N 23.03 E
Loimijoki 8 Jc 61.13N 22.38 E
Loing 11 If 48.23N 2.48 E
Loir 11 Fg 47.33N 0.32W
Loir, Vaux du- 11 Gg 47.45N 0.25 E
Loire [3] 11 Ji 45.30N 4.00 E
Loire 5 Ff 47.16N 2.11W
Loire, Canal latéral à la- 11 Jh 46.29N 3.59 E
Loire, Val de- 11 Hg 47.40N 1.35 E
Loire-Atlantique [3] 11 Eg 47.15N 1.50W
Loiret [3] 11 Ig 47.55N 2.20 E
Loir-et-Cher [3] 11 Hg 47.30N 1.30 E
Loisach 10 Hi 47.56N 11.27 E
Loison 12 He 49.30N 5.17 E
Loja [Ec.] 53 If 4.00 S 79.13W
Loja [Sp.] 13 Hg 37.10N 4.09W
Lojo/Lohja 7 Ff 60.15N 24.05 E
Lojo åsen/Lohjanselkä 8 Kd 60.15N 24.10 E
Loka 35 Ee 4.16N 31.01 E
Lokači 10 Uf 50.43N 24.44 E
Lokalahti 8 Id 60.41N 21.28 E
Lokandu 36 Ec 2.31 S 25.47 E
Lokantekojärvi 7 Gc 68.55N 27.40 E
Lokbatan 16 Pi 40.21N 49.42 E
Lokčim 17 Ef 61.48N 51.45 E
Løken 8 De 59.48N 11.29 E
Lokeren 11 Jc 51.06N 4.00 E
Lokichar 36 Gb 2.23N 35.39 E
Lokichokio 36 Fb 4.12N 34.21 E
Lokitaung 36 Gb 4.16N 35.45 E
Løkken [Den.] 8 Cg 57.22N 9.43 E
Løkken [Nor.] 7 Be 63.05N 9.36 E
Loknja 7 Hh 56.49N 30.09 E
Loko 34 Gd 8.00N 7.50 E
Lokoja 34 Gd 7.48N 6.44 E
Lokomo 34 Ie 2.41N 15.19 E
Lokoro 36 Cc 1.43 S 18.23 E
Lokossa 34 Fd 6.38N 1.43 E
Lokot 16 Ic 52.33N 34.31 E
Lokoti 34 Hd 6.22N 14.20 E
Loksa 7 Fg 59.34N 25.44 E
Loks Land 42 Ld 62.27N 64.30W
Lokuru 63a Cc 8.35 S 157.20 E
Lokusu/Lohusuu 8 Lf 58.53N 27.01 E
Lokwa Kangole 36 Gb 3.32N 35.54 E
Lol 30 Jh 9.13N 28.59 E
Lola 34 Dd 7.48N 8.32W
Lolimi 35 Ee 4.35N 33.59 E
Loliondo 36 Gc 2.03 S 35.37 E
Lolland 5 He 54.45N 11.30 E
Lollar 12 Kd 50.38N 8.42 E
Lolo 36 Db 2.13N 23.00 E
Lolo 36 Bc 0.40 S 12.28 E
Lolodorf 34 He 3.14N 10.44 E
Lolo Pass 46 Hc 46.40N 114.33W
Loloway 63b Cb 15.17 S 167.58 E
Lom 15 Gf 43.49N 23.14 E
Lom [Afr.] 34 Hd 5.20N 13.24 E
Lom [Bul.] 15 Gf 43.50N 23.15 E
Loma Bonita 48 Lh 18.07N 95.53W
Lomaloma 63d Cb 17.17 S 178.59W
Lomami 30 Jh 0.46N 24.16 E
Loma Mountains 30 Fh 9.10N 11.07W
Lomas de Vallejos 55 Dh 27.44 S 57.56W
Loma Verde 55 Cl 35.16 S 58.24W
Lomba 36 Df 15.36 S 21.32 E
Lombarda, Serra- 54 Hc 2.50N 51.50W
Lombarde, Prealpi- 14 De 46.00N 9.30 E
Lombardia = Lombardy (EN) 14 De 45.40N 9.30 E
Lombardy (EN) = Lombardia 14 De 45.40N 9.30 E
Lomblen, Pulau- 21 Oj 8.25 S 123.30 E
Lombok, Pulau- 21 Nj 8.45 S 116.30 E
Lombok, Selat- 26 Gh 8.30 S 115.50 E
Lomé 31 Hh 6.08N 1.13 E
Lomela 31 Ji 2.18 S 23.17 E
Lomela 30 Ji 0.14 S 20.42 E
Lomellina 14 Ce 45.15N 8.45 E
Loméméti 63b Dd 19.30 S 169.27 E
Lomié 34 He 3.10N 13.37 E
Lomlom 63c Bb 10.19 S 166.16 E
Lomma 8 Ei 55.41N 13.05 E
Lomme 12 Hd 50.08N 5.10 E
Lommel 11 Lc 51.14N 5.18 E
Lomnica 10 Ug 49.02N 24.47 E
Lomond, Loch- 9 Ie 56.08N 4.38W
Lomonosov 19 Cd 59.55N 29.40 E
Lomonosovki 19 Ge 52.50N 66.28 E
Lomonosov Ridge (EN) 67 De 88.00N 140.00 E
Lomont 11 Mg 47.21N 6.36 E
Lompobatang, Gunung- 26 Gh 5.20 S 119.55 E
Lompoc 43 Ce 34.38N 120.27W
Lomsegga 8 Cc 61.49N 8.22 E
Łomża 10 Sc 53.11N 22.05 E
Łomża [2] 10 Sc 53.10N 22.05 E
Lønahorg 8 Bd 60.42N 6.25 E
Loncoche 56 Fe 39.22 S 72.38W
Londa 25 Ee 15.28N 74.31 E
Londerzeel 12 Gc 51.01N 4.18 E
Londiani 36 Gc 0.10 S 35.36 E
Londinières 12 De 49.50N 1.24 E
London [Eng.-U.K.] 6 Fe 51.30N 0.10W
London [Kir.] 64g Bb 1.58N 157.29W
London [Ky.-U.S.] 44 Eg 37.08N 84.05W
London [Ont.-Can.] 39 Ke 42.59N 81.14W
London-Barnet 12 Bc 51.39N 0.12W
London-Bexley 12 Cc 51.26N 0.09 E
London Bridge 51p Bb 12.17N 61.35W
London-Bromley 12 Cc 51.25N 0.01 E
London-Croydon 9 Mj 51.23N 0.07W
Londonderry/Doire 6 Fd 55.00N 7.19W
Londonderry, Cape- 59 Fb 13.45 S 126.55 E
London-Ealing 12 Bc 51.30N 0.19W
London-Enfield 12 Bc 51.40N 0.04W
London-Greenwich 9 Mj 51.28N 0.00
London-Haringey 12 Bc 51.36N 0.06W
London-Harrow 12 Bc 51.36N 0.20W
London-Havering 12 Cc 51.36N 0.11 E
London-Hillingdon 12 Bc 51.31N 0.27W
London-Kingston-upon-Thames 9 Mj 51.28N 0.19W
London-Redbridge 12 Cc 51.35N 0.08 E
London-Sutton 12 Bc 51.21N 0.12W
London-Wandsworth 12 Bc 51.27N 0.12W
London-Westminster 12 Bc 51.30N 0.07W
Londrina 53 Kh 23.18 S 51.09W
Lone Pine 46 Fh 36.36N 118.04W
Longa 36 Ce 14.41 S 18.29 E
Longa [Ang.] 36 Cf 16.25 S 19.04 E
Longa [Ang.] 36 Be 10.15 S 13.30 E
Longa, Proliv- = De Long Strait (EN) 21 Tb 70.20N 178.00 E
Longá, Rio- 54 Jd 3.09 S 41.56W
Long Akah 26 Ff 3.19N 114.47 E
Longarone 14 Gd 46.16N 12.18 E
Longbangun 26 Gf 0.36N 115.11 E
Long Bay [Bar.] 51q Bb 13.04N 59.29W
Long Bay [S.C.-U.S.] 43 Le 33.35N 78.45W
Long Beach [Ca.-U.S.] 39 Hf 33.46N 118.11W
Long Beach [N.Y.-U.S.] 44 Ke 40.35N 73.40W
Long Beach [Wa.-U.S.] 46 Cc 46.21N 124.03W
Long Branch 43 Mc 40.17N 73.59W
Long Buckby 12 Ab 52.18N 1.04W
Long Cay 49 Jb 22.37N 74.20W
Longchuan 27 Kg 24.10N 115.17 E
Long Creek 46 Nb 49.07N 103.00W
Long Eaton 12 Ab 52.54N 1.16W
Longfeng 28 Ha 46.31N 125.02 E
Longford/An Longfort [2] 9 Fh 53.40N 7.40W
Longford/An Longfort 9 Fh 53.44N 7.47W
Long Forties 9 Nd 57.10N 0.05 E
Long Hu 28 Dj 29.37N 116.12 E
Longhua 28 Dd 41.18N 117.44 E
Longido 36 Gc 2.44 S 36.41 E
Long Island [Atg.] 51d Bb 17.08N 61.45W
Long Island [Bah.] 38 Lg 23.10N 75.10W
Long Island [Can.] 42 Jf 54.50N 79.20W
Long Island [Can.] 44 Nc 44.20N 66.15W
Long Island [Pap.N.Gui.] 57 Fe 5.36 S 148.00 E
Long Island [U.S.] 38 Le 40.50N 73.00W
Long Island Sound 44 Ke 41.05N 72.58W
Longjiang 27 Lb 47.20N 123.09 E
Longjuzhai → Danfeng 27 Je 33.44N 110.22 E
Longkou 27 Ld 37.39N 120.20 E
Longlac 42 Ig 49.50N 86.32W
Long Lake [N.D.-U.S.] 45 Fc 46.43N 100.07W
Long Lake [Ont.-Can.] 45 Mb 49.32N 86.45W
Longmalinau 26 Gf 3.30N 116.31 E
Long Men 27 Je 34.40N 110.30 E
Longmont 45 Df 40.10N 105.06W
Longnan 27 Jg 24.54N 114.48 E
Longobucco 14 Kk 39.27N 16.37 E
Longoz 15 Kf 43.02N 27.41 E
Longping → Luodian 27 If 25.26N 106.47 E
Long Point 44 Gd 42.34N 80.15W
Long Point Bay 44 Gd 42.40N 80.14W
Longpujungan 26 Gf 2.34N 115.40 E
Longquan 27 Kf 28.06N 119.05 E
Long Range Mountains 42 Lg 48.00N 58.30W
Longreach 58 Fg 23.26 S 144.15 E
Long Sand 12 Dc 51.37N 1.10 E
Longs Peak 38 Ie 40.15N 105.37W
Long Sutton 12 Cb 52.47N 0.08 E
Longtan 28 Eh 32.10N 119.03 E
Longtown 9 Kf 55.01N 2.58W
Longué 11 Fg 47.23N 0.07W
Longueau 12 Ee 49.52N 2.21 E
Longueville-sur-Scie 12 De 49.48N 1.06 E
Longuyon 11 Le 49.26N 5.36 E
Long Valley 46 Ji 34.37N 111.16W
Longview [Tx.-U.S.] 43 Ie 32.30N 94.44W
Longview [Wa.-U.S.] 43 Cb 46.08N 122.57W
Longwu 27 Hg 24.07N 102.18 E
Longwy 11 Le 49.31N 5.46 E
Longxi 27 Hd 35.01N 104.38 E
Longxian 27 Id 35.00N 106.53 E
Longxian → Wengyuan 27 Jg 24.21N 114.13 E
Longxi Shan 27 Kf 26.35N 117.17 E
Long Xuyen 25 Lf 10.23N 105.25 E
Longyan 27 Kf 25.06N 117.01 E
Longyao 28 Cf 37.21N 114.46 E
Longyearbyen 67 Kd 78.13N 15.38 E
Longyou 28 Ej 29.01N 119.10 E
Longzhou 27 Ig 22.23N 106.49 E
Lonigo 14 Fe 45.23N 11.23 E
Löningen 10 Dd 52.44N 7.46 E
Lonja 14 Ke 45.27N 16.41 E
Lonjsko Polje 14 Ke 45.24N 16.42 E
Lönsboda 8 Fh 56.24N 14.19 E
Lons-le-Saunier 11 Lh 46.40N 5.33 E
Lontra, Ribeirão- 55 Fe 21.28 S 53.37W
Lookout, Cape- [N.C.-U.S.] 43 Le 34.35N 76.32W
Lookout, Cape- [Or.-U.S.] 46 Dd 45.20N 124.00W
Lookout Mountain 44 Eh 34.40N 85.20W
Lookout Pass 43 Db 47.27N 115.42W
Loolmalasin 36 Gc 3.03 S 35.49 E
Loop Head/Ceann Léime 9 Di 52.34N 9.56W
Loosdrechtse Plassen 12 Hb 52.11N 5.08 E
Lop 27 Dd 37.01N 80.16 E
Lopatina, Gora- 21 Qd 50.52N 143.10 E
Lopatino 16 Nc 52.37N 45.47 E
Lopatka, Mys- 21 Rd 50.52N 156.40 E
Lop Buri 25 Kf 14.48N 100.37 E
Lopča 20 He 55.44N 122.45 E
Lopévi 63b Dc 16.30 S 168.21 E
Lopez, Cap- = Lopez, Cape- (EN) 30 Hi 0.37 S 8.43 E
Lopez, Cape- (EN) = Lopez, Cap- 30 Hi 0.37 S 8.43 E
Lop Nur 21 Le 40.30N 90.30 E
Lopnur/Yuli 27 Ec 41.22N 86.09 E
Lopori 30 Ih 1.14N 19.49 E
Loppersum 12 Ia 53.19N 6.45 E
Lopphavet 7 Ea 70.25N 22.00 E
Loppi 8 Kd 60.43N 24.27 E
Lopud 14 Lh 42.41N 17.57 E
Łopuszno 10 Qf 50.57N 20.15 E
Lora del Río 13 Gg 37.39N 5.32W
Lorain 43 Kc 41.28N 82.11W
Lorán, Boca- 54 Fb 9.00N 60.45W
Lorca 13 Kg 37.40N 1.42W
Lorch 12 Jd 50.03N 7.49 E
Lord Howe Island 57 Gh 31.35 S 159.05 E
Lord Howe Rise (EN) 3 Jm 32.00 S 162.00 E
Lord Mayor Bay 42 Ic 69.45N 92.00W
Lordsburg 45 Bj 32.21N 108.43W
Loreley 12 Jd 50.08N 7.43 E
Lorena 55 Jf 22.44 S 45.08W
Lorengau 60 Dh 2.01 S 147.17 E
Lorestān [3] 23 Gc 33.30N 48.40 E
Loreto [2] 54 Dd 5.00 S 75.00W
Loreto [Arg.] 55 Dh 27.46 S 57.17W
Loreto [Bol.] 54 Fg 15.13 S 64.40W
Loreto [Braz.] 54 Ie 7.05 S 45.09W
Loreto [It.] 14 Hg 43.26N 13.36 E
Loreto [Mex.] 48 If 22.16N 101.58W
Loreto [Mex.] 47 Bc 26.01N 111.21W
Loreto [Par.] 56 Ib 23.16 S 57.11W
Loreto Aprutino 14 Hh 42.26N 13.59 E
Lorica 54 Cb 9.14N 75.49W
Lorient 6 Ff 47.45N 3.22W
Lőrinci 10 Pi 47.44N 19.41 E
Lorn, Firth of- 9 He 56.20N 5.40W
Lorne 59 Ig 38.33 S 143.59 E
Lörrach 10 Di 47.37N 7.40 E
Lorrain, Plateau- 11 Me 49.00N 6.30 E
Lorrain, Rivière du- 51h Ab 14.50N 61.03W
Lorraine 11 Lf 49.00N 6.00 E
Lorraine, Plaine- 11 Lf 48.10N 5.50 E
Lorsch 12 Ke 49.39N 8.34 E
Los 7 Df 61.44N 15.10 E
Los, Iles de- = Los Islands (EN) 34 Cd 9.30N 13.48W

Index Symbols

[1] Independent Nation
[2] State, Region
[3] District, County
[4] Municipality
[5] Colony, Dependency
Continent
Physical Region
Historical or Cultural Region
Mount, Mountain
Volcano
Hill
Mountains, Mountain Range
Hills, Escarpment
Plateau, Upland
Pass, Gap
Plain, Lowland
Delta
Salt Flat
Valley, Canyon
Crater, Cave
Karst Features
Depression
Polder
Desert, Dunes
Forest, Woods
Heath, Steppe
Oasis
Cape, Point
Coast, Beach
Cliff
Peninsula
Isthmus
Sandbank
Island
Atoll
Rock, Reef
Islands, Archipelago
Rocks, Reefs
Coral Reef
Well, Spring
Geyser
River, Stream
Waterfall Rapids
River Mouth, Estuary
Lake
Salt Lake
Intermittent Lake
Reservoir
Swamp, Pond
Canal
Glacier
Ice Shelf, Pack Ice
Ocean
Sea
Gulf, Bay
Strait, Fjord
Lagoon
Bank
Seamount
Tablemount
Ridge
Shelf
Basin
Escarpment, Sea Scarp
Fracture
Trench, Abyss
National Park, Reserve
Point of Interest
Recreation Site
Cave, Cavern
Historic Site
Ruins
Wall, Walls
Church, Abbey
Temple
Scientific Station
Airport
Port
Lighthouse
Mine
Tunnel
Dam, Bridge

Name	Map	Grid	Lat	Long
Los Alamos	39	If	35.53N	106.19W
Los Amates	49	Cf	15.16N	89.06W
Los Amores	55	Ci	28.06S	59.59W
Los Angeles	39	Hf	34.03N	118.15W
Los Angeles	53	Ii	37.28S	72.21W
Los Angeles Aqueduct	46	Fi	35.22N	118.05W
Losap Atoll	57	Gd	6.54N	152.44 E
Los Banos	46	Eh	37.04N	120.51W
Los Blancos	56	Hb	23.36 S	62.36W
Los Charrúas	55	Cj	31.10S	58.11W
Los Chiles	49	Eh	11.02N	84.43W
Los Conquistadores	55	Cj	30.36S	58.28W
Los Frailes, Islas-	50	Fg	11.12N	63.45W
Los Frentones	55	Bh	26.25S	61.25W
Los Gatos	46	Eh	37.14N	121.59W
Losheim	12	Ie	49.31N	6.45 E
Los Hermanos, Islas-	54	Fa	11.45N	64.25W
Losice	10	Sd	52.14N	22.43 E
Lošinj	14	If	44.35N	14.28 E
Los Islands (EN)=Los, Iles de-	34	Cd	9.30N	13.48W
Los Juries	55	Ai	28.28S	62.06W
Los Lagos	56	Fe	39.51S	72.50W
Los Lagos	57	Ff	41.20S	73.00W
Los Llanos de Aridane	32	Dd	28.39N	17.54W
Los Médanos, Istmo de-	49	Mh	11.35N	69.45W
Los Mochis	56	Ig	25.45N	108.53W
Los Monegros	13	Lc	41.29N	0.03W
Los Monjes, Islas-	49	Kg	12.24N	70.55W
Los Navalmorales	13	He	39.43N	4.38W
Loso	36	Ec	1.10S	27.10 E
Los Palacios	49	Fb	22.35N	83.12W
Los Palacios y Villafranca	13	Gg	37.10N	5.56W
Los Pedroches	13	Hf	38.27N	4.45W
Los Pirpintos	55	Ah	26.08S	62.05W
Los Remedios, Rio de-	48	Fe	24.41N	106.28W
Los Reyes de Salgado	48	Hh	19.35N	102.29W
Los Roques, Islas-	54	Ea	11.50N	66.45W
Los Roques Basin (EN)	50	Cf	12.20N	67.40W
Los Santos	49	Gj	7.45N	80.30W
Los Santos	49	Gj	7.56N	80.25W
Losser	12	Jb	52.16N	7.01 E
Lossiemouth	9	Jd	57.43N	3.18W
Lössnen	8	Eb	62.30N	12.50 E
Los Taques	49	Lh	11.50N	70.16W
Los Telares	56	Hc	28.59S	63.26W
Los Teques	54	Ea	10.21N	67.02W
Los Testigos, Islas-	54	Fa	11.23N	63.06W
Lost River	46	Ef	41.56N	121.30W
Lost River Range	46	Id	44.10N	113.35W
Lost Trail Pass	46	Eh	45.41N	113.57W
Los Vilos	56	Fd	31.55S	71.31W
Lot	5	Gg	44.18N	0.20 E
Lot	11	Hj	44.30N	1.30 E
Lota	56	Fe	37.05S	73.10W
Lotagipi Swamp	35	Ee	4.36N	34.55 E
Løten	8	Dd	60.49N	11.19 E
Lot-et-Garonne	11	Gj	44.20N	0.30 E
Lothair	37	Ee	26.26S	30.27 E
Lothian	9	Jf	55.55N	3.30W
Lothian	9	Jf	55.55N	3.05W
Loto	36	Dc	2.47S	22.30 E
Lotofaga	65c	Ba	13.59S	171.50W
Lotoi	36	Cc	1.38S	18.30 E
Lotru	15	Hd	45.20N	24.16 E
Lotrului, Munţii-	15	Gd	45.30N	23.52 E
Lotta	7	Hb	68.39N	30.20 E
Lottefors	8	Gc	61.25N	16.24 E
Löttorp	8	Gg	57.10N	16.59 E
Lotuke, Jabal-	35	Ee	4.07N	33.48 E
Louang Namtha	25	Kd	20.57N	101.25 E
Louangphrabang	22	Mh	19.52N	102.08 E
Loubomo	31	Ii	4.12S	12.41 E
Loučná	10	Lf	50.06N	15.48 E
Loudéac	11	Df	48.10N	2.45W
Loudima	36	Bc	4.07S	13.04 E
Loudon	44	Eh	35.44N	84.20W
Loudun	11	Gh	47.00N	0.04 E
Loué	11	Fg	48.00N	0.09W
Loue	11	Lg	47.01N	5.27 E
Loufan	28	Ae	38.04N	111.47 E
Louga	34	Bb	15.37N	16.13W
Louga	34	Bb	15.00N	15.30W
Louge	11	Hk	43.27N	1.20 E
Loughborough	9	Li	52.47N	1.11W
Lougheed	42	Ha	77.30N	105.00W
Loughrea/Baile Locha Riach	9	Eh	53.12N	8.34W
Louhans	11	Lh	46.38N	5.13 E
Louhi	19	Db	66.04N	33.01 E
Louisa	44	Ff	38.07N	82.36W
Louiseville	44	Kb	46.16N	72.57W
Louisiade Archipelago	57	Gf	11.00S	153.00 E
Louisiana	45	Kg	39.27N	91.03W
Louisiana	43	Ie	31.15N	92.15W
Louis Trichardt	37	Dd	23.01S	29.43 E
Louisville (Ky.-U.S.)	39	Kf	38.16N	85.45W
Louisville (Ms.-U.S.)	45	Lj	33.07N	89.03W
Louis-XIV, Pointe -	42	Jf	54.50N	79.30W
Loukoléla	36	Cc	1.02S	17.07 E
Louian Yiji	27	Ec	40.32N	89.50 E
Loulé	13	Dg	37.08N	8.02W
Loum	34	Ge	4.43N	9.44 E
Lount Lake	45	Ia	50.10N	94.20W
Louny	10	Jf	50.22N	13.49 E
Loup City	45	Gf	41.17N	98.58W
Loup River	43	Hc	41.24N	97.19W
Loups Marins, Lacs des -	42	Ke	56.40N	74.00W
Lourdes	11	Fk	43.06N	0.03W
Lourenço Marques → Maputo				
Lousã, Serra da-	13	Dd	40.04N	8.13W
Loushan Guan	27	Jf	28.02N	106.51 E
Loûstîn	10	Jf	50.12N	13.48 E
Louth [Austl.]	59	Jf	30.32S	145.07 E
Louth [Eng.-U.K.]	9	Mh	53.22N	0.01W
Louth/Lú	9	Gh	53.55N	6.30W
Loutrá Aidhipsoú	15	Gk	38.51N	23.03 E
Loutrá Killinis	15	El	37.52N	21.07 E
Loutrákion	15	Fl	37.59N	23.00 E
Louvain/Leuven	11	Kd	50.53N	4.42 E
Louvet Point	51k	Bb	13.58N	60.53W
Louviers	11	He	49.13N	1.10 E
Lövånger	7	Ed	64.22N	21.18 E
Lovászi	10	Mj	46.33N	16.34 E
Lovat	5	Jd	58.14N	31.28 E
Loveč	15	Bg	42.24N	18.49 E
Loveč	15	Hf	43.08N	24.43 E
Loveč	15	Hf	43.08N	24.43 E
Loveland	45	Df	40.24N	105.05W
Lovell	43	Fc	44.50N	108.24W
Lovelock	43	Dc	40.11N	118.28W
Loves	12	Id	50.57N	6.50 E
Lovisa	14	Ad	46.40N	16.00 E
Lovere	14	Ee	45.49N	10.04 E
Loving	7	Gf	60.27N	26.14 E
Lovington	43	Ge	33.27N	103.21W
Loviisa/Lovisa	7	Gf	60.27N	26.14 E
Lovisa/Loviisa	7	Gf	60.27N	26.14 E
Lovoi	36	Ed	8.05S	26.40 E
Lovosice	10	Kf	50.31N	14.03 E
Lovozero	7	Ib	68.01N	35.01 E
Lovozero, Ozero-	7	Ic	67.50N	35.10 E
Lövstabruk	8	Gd	60.24N	17.53 E
Lövstabukten	8	Gd	60.35N	17.45 E
Lovua	36	Dd	6.07S	20.35 E
Lovua	36	De	11.31S	23.35 E
Low, Cape -	42	Id	63.06N	85.18W
Lowa	30	Ji	1.24S	25.52 E
Lowell	43	Mc	42.39N	71.18W
Löwenberg in der Mark	10	Jd	52.53N	13.09 E
Lower Arrow Lake	46	Fb	49.40N	118.08W
Lower Austria (EN)=Niederösterreich	14	Jb	48.30N	15.45 E
Lower California (EN)=Baja California	38	Mg	28.00N	112.00W
Lower Hutt	62	Fd	41.13S	174.55 E
Lower Lake	46	Ef	41.15N	120.02W
Lower Lake	46	Dg	38.55N	122.36W
Lower Lough Erne/Loch Éirne Íochtair	9	Fg	54.30N	7.50W
Lower Post	42	Ee	59.55N	128.30W
Lower Red Lake	45	Ic	48.00N	94.50W
Lower Rhine (EN) = Neder-Rijn	11	Mc	51.59N	6.20 E
Lower Saxony (EN)=Niedersachsen	10	Fd	52.00N	10.00 E
Lower Trajan's Wall (EN)=Nižni Trajanov Val	15	Ld	45.45N	28.30 E
Lower Tunguska (EN)=Nižnjaja Tunguska	21	Kc	65.48N	88.04 E
Lowestoft	9	Oi	52.29N	1.45 E
Lowestoft Ness	9	Oi	52.28N	1.44 E
Lowgar	23	Kc	33.50N	69.00 E
Łowicz	10	Pd	52.07N	19.56 E
Lowlands	51l	Jf	56.00N	4.00W
Lowrah	21	If	31.33N	66.33 E
Lowshān	24	Md	36.39N	49.32 E
Low Tatra (EN) = Nizke Tatry	10	Ph	48.54N	19.40 E
Lowther	42	Hb	74.35N	97.40W
Lowville	44	Jd	43.47N	75.30W
Loxton [Austl.]	59	If	34.27S	140.35 E
Loxton [S.Afr.]	37	Cf	31.30S	22.22 E
Loyalty Islands (EN)=Loyauté, Îles-	57	Hg	21.00S	167.00 E
Loyauté, Îles-=Loyalty Islands (EN)	57	Hg	21.00S	167.00 E
Loyoro	36	Fb	3.21N	34.17 E
Lozère	11	Jj	44.30N	3.30 E
Lozère, Mont-	11	Jj	44.25N	3.46 E
Loznica	15	Ce	44.32N	19.13 E
Lozovaja	19	Df	48.53N	36.15 E
Lú/Louth	9	Gd	59.36N	62.20 E
Lua	9	Gh	53.55N	6.30W
Luacano	36	Cb	2.46N	18.26 E
Luachimo	36	De	11.16S	21.38 E
Luachimo	36	Dd	6.33S	20.59 E
Luaha-Sibuha	31	Ji	7.22S	20.49 E
Luahoko	36	Cg	0.31S	98.28 E
Luala	65b	Ba	19.40S	174.24W
Lualaba	37	Fc	67.57S	36.30 E
Luama	29	Jh	0.26N	25.20 E
Luama	36	Ec	4.46S	26.53 E
Lua Makika	65a	Ec	20.35N	156.34W
Luampa	36	De	14.32S	24.10 E
Lu'an	27	Ji	31.44N	116.30 E
Luanda	31	Ii	8.50S	13.15 E
Luanda	36	Bd	8.30S	13.20 E
Luang, Khao-	30	Ij	10.19S	16.40 E
Luang, Thale-	25	Kg	7.30N	100.15 E
Luang Chiang Dao, Doi-	25	Je	19.23N	98.54 E
Luanginga	30	Jl	15.11S	22.55 E
Luang Prabang Range	25	Ke	18.30N	101.15 E
Luangue	36	Cd	4.17N	20.01 E
Luangwa	30	Kj	15.36S	30.25 E
Luan He	27	Jf	39.20N	119.10 E
Luaniva	65b	Bb	13.18S	176.07W
Luannan (Bencheng)	28	Ee	39.30N	118.42 E
Luanping (Anijangying)	28	Dd	40.55N	117.19 E
Luanshya	30	Kj	13.08S	28.25 E
Luanxian	27	Kd	39.45N	118.44 E
Luanza	36	Ee	8.40S	28.40 E
Luao	36	De	10.42S	22.12 E
Luapula	36	De	12.36S	28.33 E
Luapula	36	Ee	10.40S	29.15 E
Luarca	13	Fa	43.32N	6.32W
Luashi	36	De	10.56S	23.37 E
Luba	34	Ge	3.28N	8.40 E
Lubaantum	49	Ce	16.17N	88.58W
Lubaczów	10	Tf	50.10N	23.07 E
Lubaczówka	10	Sf	50.08N	22.35 E
Lubalo	36	Cd	7.22S	19.20 E
Lubalo	36	Cd	9.07S	19.15 E
Lubamba	36	Ed	5.14S	26.02 E
Lubań	10	Le	51.08N	15.18 E
Lubăna/Lubana	8	Lh	56.49N	26.49 E
Lubāna/Lubana	8	Lh	56.49N	26.49 E
Lubanas, Ozero-/Lubānas Ezers	8	Lh	56.40N	27.00 E
Lubānas Ezers/Lubanas, Ozero-	8	Lh	56.40N	27.00 E
Lubang Islands	26	Hd	13.45N	120.15 E
Lubango	31	Ij	14.55S	13.28 E
Lubao	31	Ji	5.22S	25.45 E
Lubartów	10	Se	51.28N	22.46 E
Lubawa	10	Pc	53.30N	19.45 E
Lübbecke	12	Ed	52.18N	8.37 E
Lubbeek	12	Ld	50.53N	4.50 E
Lübben/Lubin	10	Je	51.57N	13.54 E
Lübbenau/Lubnjaw	10	Je	51.52N	13.58 E
Lübeck	10	He	53.52N	10.42 E
Lübecker Bucht	10	Gb	54.00N	10.55 E
Lübeck-Travemünde	10	Gc	53.57N	10.52 E
Lubefu	36	Dc	4.10S	23.00 E
Lubefu	36	Dc	4.43S	24.25 E
Lubei→ Jarud Qi	27	Lc	44.30N	120.55 E
Lubelska, Wyżyna-	10	Sf	51.00N	23.00 E
Lubenec	10	Jf	50.08N	13.20 E
Lubenka	16	Sd	50.28N	54.06 E
Lubero	36	Ec	0.06S	29.06 E
Lubéron, Montagne du-	11	Lk	43.48N	5.22 E
Lubie, Jezioro-	10	Lc	53.30N	15.50 E
Lubień Kujawski	10	Pd	52.25N	19.10 E
Lubij/Löbau	10	Ke	51.06N	14.40 E
Lubilash	36	De	9.02S	23.45 E
Lubin	10	Me	51.24N	16.13 E
Lubin/Lübben	10	Je	51.57N	13.54 E
Lublin	6	Ie	51.15N	22.35 E
Lublin	10	Se	51.15N	22.35 E
Lubliniec	10	Of	50.40N	18.41 E
Lubnān=Lebanon (EN)	22	Ff	33.50N	35.50 E
Lubnān, Jabal-=Lebanon Mountains (EN)	23	Ec	34.00N	36.30 E
Lubnjow/Lübbenau	10	Je	51.52N	13.58 E
Lubny	19	De	50.01N	33.00 E
Luboń	10	Md	52.23N	16.54 E
Lubraniec	10	Od	52.33N	18.50 E
Lubsza	10	Ke	51.46N	14.59 E
Lubudi	29	Ji	9.13S	25.38 E
Lubudi	36	Ed	9.57S	25.58 E
Lubu Kamčija	36	Cc	4.10S	19.53 E
Lubuklinggau	26	Dg	3.10S	102.52 E
Lubuksikaping	26	Df	0.08N	100.10 E
Lubumba	36	Ec	3.58S	29.06 E
Lubumbashi	31	Jj	11.40S	27.30 E
Lubuskie, Pojezierze-	10	Ld	52.18N	15.20 E
Lubutu	31	Ji	0.44S	26.35 E
Lucala	36	Bd	6.38S	12.34 E
Lucala	36	Cd	9.16S	15.16 E
Lucania, Mount-	42	Dd	61.01N	140.29W
Lucas	55	Ea	13.05S	55.56W
Lucca	14	Eg	43.50N	10.29 E
Luce Bay	9	Ig	54.47N	4.50W
Lucedale	45	Lk	30.55N	88.35W
Lučegorsk	20	Ig	46.25N	134.20 E
Lucélia	55	Ge	21.44S	51.01W
Lucena [Phil.]	26	Hd	13.56N	121.37 E
Lucena [Sp.]	13	Hg	37.24N	4.29W
Lucena del Cid	13	Ld	40.08N	0.17W
Luc-en-Diois	11	Lj	44.37N	5.27 E
Lučenec	10	Ph	48.20N	19.41 E
Lucera	14	Ji	41.30N	15.20 E
Lucerne (EN) = Luzern	14	Cc	47.05N	8.20 E
Lucerne, Lake- (EN) = Vierwaldstätter-See	14	Cc	47.00N	8.30 E
Lucero	48	Fb	30.49N	106.30W
Lucheng	28	Bf	36.18N	113.15 E
Lucheringo	37	Fb	11.43S	36.15 E
Lucheux	12	Fd	50.12N	2.25 E
Luchico	30	Lj	12.15S	44.25 E
Luchico	36	Cd	6.13S	19.42 E
Lüchow	10	Hd	52.58N	11.09 E
Lucipara, Kepulauan-	26	Ih	5.30S	127.33 E
Lucira	36	Be	13.52S	12.32 E
Luck	19	Ce	50.47N	25.20 E
Luckau	10	Je	51.51N	13.43 E
Luckenwalde	10	Jd	52.05N	13.10 E
Lucknow	22	Kg	26.51N	80.55 E
Luçon	11	Eh	46.27N	1.10W
Lucrecia, Cabo-	49	Jc	21.04N	75.37W
Luc-sur-Mer	12	Be	49.18N	0.21W
Lucunga	36	Bd	6.49S	14.35 E
Lucusse	36	De	12.33S	20.51 E
Lüda→Dalian=Dairan (EN)	27	Lf	38.55N	121.39 E
Luda Kamčija	15	Kg	43.03N	27.29 E
Ludbreg	14	Kd	46.15N	16.37 E
Lüdenscheid	10	Se	51.13N	7.37 E
Lüderitz	31	Ik	26.38S	15.10 E
Lüderitz	37	Be	26.35S	15.10 E
Lüderitz Bay	22	Jf	30.54N	75.51 E
Ludhiāna	10	Se	51.46N	7.28 E
Ludington	43	Kc	43.57N	86.27W
Ludlow	9	Ki	52.22N	2.43W
Ludogorie	15	Jf	43.46N	26.56 E
Ludogorsko Plato	15	Kf	43.35N	27.00 E
Luduş	15	Hc	46.29N	24.06 E
Ludvika	7	Cf	60.09N	15.11 E
Ludwigsburg	10	Fh	48.54N	9.11 E
Ludwigshafen am Rhein	10	Eg	49.29N	8.26 E
Ludwigslust	10	Hc	53.19N	11.30 E
Ludza	8	Lh	56.32N	27.45 E
Luebo	36	Dd	5.21S	21.25 E
Lueki	36	Ec	3.24S	25.57 E
Lueki	36	Ec	3.22S	25.51 E
Luele	36	Dd	7.55S	20.00 E
Luembé	36	Dd	6.43S	24.11 E
Luembe	36	Dd	6.37S	21.06 E
Luena [Ang.]	31	Ij	11.48S	19.55 E
Luena [Ang.]	36	Ed	9.27S	25.47 E
Luena [Zam.]	36	Df	15.20S	23.30 E
Luena [Zaire]	36	Ed	16.54S	21.52 E
Luenha	37	Ec	16.24S	33.48 E
Luera Peak	45	Cj	33.47N	107.49W
Lueta	36	Dd	7.04S	21.40 E
Lueyang	27	Ie	33.25N	106.14 E
Lufeng	27	Kg	22.57N	115.41 E
Lufico	36	Bd	6.22S	13.30 E
Lufira	29	Ji	8.16S	26.27 E
Lufira, Chutes de la-	36	Ee	9.50S	27.30 E
Lufkin	43	Ie	31.20N	94.44W
Lug	15	Ce	45.23N	20.45 E
Luga	19	Cd	59.43N	28.18 E
Luga	19	Cd	58.44N	29.50 E
Lugano	14	Cd	46.00N	8.57 E
Lugano, Lago di-	14	Cd	46.00N	9.00 E
Lugards Falls	30	Ki	3.03S	38.42 E
Lügde	12	Lc	51.57N	9.15 E
Lugela	37	Fc	16.26S	36.39 E
Lugenda	30	Kj	11.26S	38.33 E
Lugnaquillia	5	Fe	52.58N	6.27W
Lugo [It.]	14	Ff	44.25N	11.54 E
Lugo [Sp.]	13	Ea	43.00N	7.34W
Lugoj	15	Ed	45.41N	21.55 E
Lugovoj [Kaz.-U.S.S.R.]	19	Ig	42.55N	72.47 E
Lugovoj [R.S.F.S.R.]	19	Gd	59.44N	65.55 E
Lugovski	20	Ge	58.05N	112.55 E
Luh	36	Ec	2.17S	26.32 E
Luh	7	Kh	56.14N	42.28 E
Luhe	10	Gc	53.18N	10.11 E
Luhe	28	Eh	32.21N	118.50 E
Luhin Sum	27	Kb	46.41N	118.38 E
Luhit	25	Jc	27.48N	95.28 E
Luhovicy	7	Ic	54.59N	39.02 E
Luhuo	36	Dd	8.41S	17.56 E
Lui	36	Dd	8.26S	21.45 E
Luia	36	Df	17.22S	22.59 E
Luiana	36	Dj	17.27S	23.14 E
Luie	36	Cc	4.33S	17.41 E
Luik/Liège	6	Ge	50.38N	5.34 E
Luilaka	30	Ji	0.52S	20.12 E
Luilu	36	Ec	6.22S	23.50 E
Luimbale	36	Ce	12.15S	15.19 E
Luimneach/Limerick	6	Fe	52.40N	8.38W
Luimneach/Limerick	5	Ei	52.30N	9.00W
Luing	9	He	56.13N	5.39W
Luino	14	Cd	46.00N	8.44 E
Luio	36	De	13.15S	21.39 E
Lui Pātru, Vîrful-	15	Gd	45.30N	23.08 E
Luis Correia	54	Jd	2.53S	41.40W
Luishia	36	Eh	11.35S	27.07 E
Luitpold Coast	66	Af	78.30S	32.00W
Luiza	36	Dd	7.12S	22.25 E
Luján [Arg.]	56	Id	34.34S	59.07W
Luján [Arg.]	56	Jd	33.06S	68.56W
Lujiang	28	Dh	31.15N	117.17 E
Lukafu	36	Ee	10.30S	27.33 E
Lukala	36	Bd	5.30S	14.25 E
Lukanga Swamp	30	Jj	14.25S	27.45 E
Lukavac	14	Mf	44.33N	18.32 E
Lukenie	36	Cc	5.46S	29.06 E
Lukenie	30	Ih	2.44S	18.09 E
Lukeville	46	Ik	31.57N	112.50W
Lukojanov	19	Ed	55.02N	44.30 E
Lukolela	36	Cc	1.03S	17.12 E
Lukonzolwa	36	Eh	8.47S	28.39 E
Lukov	10	Ue	51.14N	24.25 E
Lukovit	15	Hf	43.12N	24.10 E
Łuków	10	Se	51.56N	22.23 E
Lukuga	36	Ec	5.40S	26.55 E
Lukula	36	Bd	5.23S	12.57 E
Lukulu	36	De	14.23S	23.15 E
Lukusashi	36	Ec	14.38S	30.00 E
Luleå	5	Ib	65.34N	22.10 E
Luleälven	5	Ib	65.35N	22.03 E
Lüleburgaz	24	Ca	41.24N	27.21 E
Lüliang Shan	21	Nf	37.45N	111.25 E
Lulimba	36	Ec	4.46S	28.38 E
Luling	45	Hl	29.41N	97.39W
Lulong	28	Ee	39.53N	118.52 E
Lulonga	30	Ih	0.37N	18.23 E
Lulonga	30	Ih	0.43N	18.23 E
Lulua	36	Dd	5.02S	21.07 E
Lulu Fakahega, Mount-	64h	Bb	13.16S	176.10W
Luma	65c	Db	14.14S	169.32W
Lumajang	26	Fh	8.08S	113.13 E
Lumajangdong Co	22	Lf	34.00N	81.37 E
Lumbala [Ang.]	31	Jj	14.06S	21.25 E
Lumbala [Ang.]	36	Df	12.39S	22.32 E
Lumberton	44	Gg	34.37N	79.00W
Lumbo	37	Gc	15.00S	40.44 E
Lumbrales	13	Fd	46.66N	6.43W
Lumbres	12	Fd	50.42N	2.08 E
Lumby	46	Fa	50.15N	118.58W
Lumding	22	Nf	25.45N	93.10 E
Lumeje	36	De	11.34S	20.48 E
Lumesule	30	Kj	11.14S	38.06 E
Lumi	60	Ch	3.29S	142.03 E
Lummen	12	Ld	51.00N	5.30 E
Lumparland	8	Id	60.10N	20.15 E
Lumphät	25	Lf	13.30N	106.59 E
Lumsden [N.Z.]	62	Cf	45.44S	168.26 E
Lumsden [Sask.-Can.]	46	Ma	50.34N	104.53W
Lumut	26	Df	4.14N	100.38 E
Luna	13	Gb	42.40N	5.49W
Luna, Laguna de-	55	Bi	28.06S	56.46W
Lunan Shan	27	Hf	27.00N	102.30 E
Lunayyr, Harrat-	24	Gj	25.10N	37.50 E
Lunca Ilvei	15	Hb	47.22N	24.59 E
Lund	7	Ci	55.42N	13.11 E
Lundazi	31	Kj	12.19S	33.13 E
Lunde	8	Gb	62.53N	17.51 E
Lundevatn	8	Bf	58.20N	6.35 E
Lundi	30	Kx	21.19S	32.24 E
Lundu	26	Ef	1.40N	109.51 E
Lundy Island	9	Ij	51.10N	4.40W
Lüneburg	10	Gc	53.15N	10.24 E
Lüneburger Heide	10	Gc	53.10N	10.20 E
Lunel	11	Kk	43.41N	4.08 E
Lünen	10	De	51.37N	7.31 E
Lunéville	11	Mf	48.36N	6.30 E
Lunga	19	Jr	14.34S	26.26 E
Lungué-Bungo	37	Jg	28.38S	16.27 E
Lungwebungu	36	De	14.19S	23.14 E
Lüni	25	Id	24.41N	71.14 E
Lūni	25	Ic	26.00N	73.00 E
Lunigiana	14	Df	44.20N	9.55 E
Luninec	19	Ce	52.16N	26.50 E
Lunino	16	Nc	53.35N	45.14 E
Lunsemfwa	36	Fe	14.54S	30.12 E
Luntai/Bügür	27	Dc	41.46N	84.10 E
Luobei (Fengxiang)	27	Nb	47.36N	130.58 E
Luobuzhuang	27	Ec	39.30N	88.15 E
Luocheng	27	Ig	24.51N	108.53 E
Luodian (Longping)	27	If	25.26N	106.47 E
Luoding	22	Pg	22.43N	111.33 E
Luo He	27	Id	33.30N	114.08 E
Luo He	27	Id	32.18N	109.12 E
Luoma Hu	28	Fg	34.10N	118.12 E
Luonteri	19	Gd	59.44N	65.55 E
Luoping	27	Hg	24.58N	104.19 E
Luopioinen	8	Kc	61.22N	24.40 E
Luoshan	28	Ch	32.13N	114.32 E
Luotian	28	Ci	30.48N	115.23 E
Luoxiao Shan	27	Jf	26.35N	114.00 E
Luoyang	22	Nf	34.41N	112.25 E
Luoyuan	27	Kf	26.31N	119.32 E
Luozi	36	Bc	4.57S	14.08 E
Lupa	36	Fd	8.39S	33.12 E
Lupane	37	Dc	18.56S	27.48 E
Żupawa	10	Nb	54.42N	17.07 E
Lupeni	15	Gd	45.21N	23.14 E
Luperón	49	Ld	19.54N	70.57W
Łupków	10	Sg	49.12N	22.06 E
Luputa	36	Dd	7.10S	23.42 E
Lūq	31	Lh	3.56N	42.32 E
Luqiao	28	Fj	28.39N	120.05 E
Luqu	27	He	34.36N	102.30 E
Luque	56	Ic	25.16S	57.34W
Luquillo	51a	Cb	18.22N	65.43W
Luray	44	Hf	38.40N	78.28W
Lure	11	Mg	47.41N	6.30 E
Lure, Montagne de-	11	Lj	44.07N	5.47 E
Luremo	36	Cd	8.30S	17.51 E
Lurgan/An Lorgain	9	Gg	54.28N	6.20W
Lurín	54	Cf	12.17S	76.52W
Lúrio	37	Fb	13.32S	40.30 E
Lúrio	30	Kj	13.31S	40.42 E
Lusaka	31	Jj	15.25S	28.17 E
Lusambo	31	Ji	4.58S	23.27 E
Lusanga	36	Cc	4.44S	18.58 E
Lusangi	36	Ec	4.37S	27.08 E
Lu Shan	27	Kf	29.30N	115.55 E
Lushan [China]	28	Bh	33.44N	112.54 E
Lushan [China]	27	Je	34.04N	111.02 E
Lushi	28	Bg	34.03N	111.02 E
Lushnja	15	Ci	40.56N	19.42 E
Lushoto	30	Ki	4.47S	38.17 E
Lu Shui	28	Bj	29.54N	113.39 E
Lushui (Luzhangji)	27	Gf	26.00N	98.50 E
Lüshun→Port Arthur (EN)	27	Ld	38.50N	121.13 E
Lusignan	11	Gh	46.26N	0.07 E
Lusk	43	Gc	42.46N	104.27W
Lussac-les-Châteaux	11	Gh	46.24N	0.43 E
Lustrafjorden	8	Cc	61.20N	7.20 E
Lūt, Dasht-e-=Lut, Dasht-i- (EN)	21	Hf	33.00N	57.00 E
Lut, Dasht-i- (EN)=Lūt, Dasht-e-	21	Hf	33.00N	57.00 E
Lu Tao	27	Lg	22.35N	121.30 E
Lutembo	36	De	13.28S	21.22 E
Luti	63a	Cb	7.14S	157.00 E
Lütjenburg	10	Gb	54.17N	10.35 E
Luton	9	Mj	51.53N	0.25W
Luton Airport	12	Bc	51.50N	0.22W
Lutong	26	Ff	4.28N	114.00 E
Lutshima	36	Cd	5.22S	18.59 E
Lutshima	36	Cd	5.22S	18.59 E
Lutterworth	12	Ab	52.27N	1.12W
Lutui	36	De	12.40S	20.12 E
Lutugino	26	Ie	48.23N	39.13 E
Lützow-Holmbukta	66	Be	69.10S	37.30 E
Lutzputs	37	Ce	28.22S	20.37 E
Luuk	26	Hf	5.58N	121.18 E
Luverne	45	Hd	43.39N	96.13W
Luvidjo	36	Dd	5.26S	22.59 E
Luvua	36	Ji	6.46S	26.58 E
Luvuei	36	De	13.06S	21.12 E
Luwegu	36	Ki	8.31S	37.23 E
Luwingu	30	Jj	10.16S	29.54 E
Luwuk	26	Hg	0.56S	122.47 E
Luxembourg	6	Ge	50.00N	5.30 E
Luxembourg/Luxemburg	11	Lf	49.45N	6.05 E
Luxembourg/Luxemburg	11	Lf	49.45N	6.05 E
Luxembourg/Luxemburg	11	Lf	49.45N	6.05 E
Luxeuil-les-Bains	11	Mg	47.49N	6.23 E
Luxi	22	Nm	24.34N	103.44 E
Luxi (Mangshi)	27	Gg	24.29N	98.40 E
Luxor (EN)=Al Uqşur	33	Ek	43.39N	1.08W
Luy	5			
Luy de Béarn	11	Fk	43.38N	0.47W

Index Symbols

- ☐ Independent Nation
- ☐ State, Region
- ☐ District, County
- ☐ Municipality
- ☐ Colony, Dependency
- ■ Continent
- ☐ Physical Region
- ▲ Historical or Cultural Region
- ▲ Mount, Mountain
- ▲ Volcano
- ▲ Hill
- ▲ Mountains, Mountain Range
- ▲ Hills, Escarpment
- ▲ Plateau, Upland
- ☐ Pass, Gap
- ☐ Plain, Lowland
- ☐ Delta
- ☐ Salt Flat
- ☐ Valley, Canyon
- ☐ Crater, Cave
- ☐ Karst Features
- ☐ Depression
- ☐ Polder
- ☐ Desert, Dunes
- ☐ Forest, Woods
- ☐ Heath, Steppe
- ☐ Oasis
- ☐ Cape, Point
- ☐ Coast, Beach
- ☐ Cliff
- ☐ Peninsula
- ☐ Isthmus
- ☐ Sandbank
- ☐ Island
- ☐ Atoll
- ☐ Rock, Reef
- ☐ Islands, Archipelago
- ☐ Rocks, Reefs
- ☐ Coral Reef
- ☐ Well, Spring
- ☐ Geyser
- ☐ Reservoir
- ☐ River, Stream
- ☐ Waterfall Rapids
- ☐ River Mouth, Estuary
- ☐ Lake
- ☐ Salt Lake
- ☐ Intermittent Lake
- ☐ Sea
- ☐ Gulf, Bay
- ☐ Strait, Fjord
- ☐ Canal
- ☐ Bank
- ☐ Seamount
- ☐ Tableland
- ☐ Ridge
- ☐ Shelf
- ☐ Basin
- ☐ Lagoon
- ☐ Glacier
- ☐ Ice Shelf, Pack Ice
- ☐ Ocean
- ☐ Escarpment, Sea Scarp
- ☐ Fracture
- ☐ Trench, Abyss
- ☐ National Park, Reserve
- ☐ Point of Interest
- ☐ Recreation Site
- ☐ Cave, Cavern
- ☐ Historic Site
- ☐ Ruins
- ☐ Wall, Walls
- ☐ Church, Abbey
- ☐ Temple
- ☐ Scientific Station
- ☐ Airport
- ☐ Port
- ☐ Lighthouse
- ☐ Mine
- ☐ Tunnel
- ☐ Dam, Bridge

Luy de France 11 Fk 43.38N 0.47W
Luyi 28 Ch 33.51N 115.28 E
Luz 55 Jd 19.48S 45.41W
Luz, Costa de la- 13 Fh 36.40N 6.20W
Luza 19 Ec 60.39N 47.15 E
Luza 5 Kc 60.40N 46.25 E
Luzarches 12 Ee 49.07N 2.25 E
Luzern 14 Cc 47.05N 8.10 E
Luzern = Lucerne (EN) 14 Cc 47.05N 8.20 E
Luzhai 27 Ig 24.31N 109.46 E
Luzhangjie→Lushui 27 Gf 26.00N 98.50 E
Luzhou 22 Mg 28.55N 105.20 E
Luziânia 54 Ig 16.15S 47.56W
Luzická Nisa 10 Kd 52.04N 14.46 E
Luzilândia 54 Jd 3.28S 42.22W
Lužnice 10 Kg 49.16N 14.25 E
Luzon 21 Oh 16.00N 121.00 E
Luzon Sea 26 Gd 12.30N 119.00 E
Luzon Strait (EN) 21 Og 21.00N 122.00 E
Luz-Saint-Sauveur 11 Gl 42.52N 0.01 E
Lužskaja Guba 8 Me 59.35N 28.25 E
Lužskaja Vozvyšennost 8 Mf 58.15N 28.45 E
Luzy 11 Jh 46.47N 3.58 E
Łużyca 10 Oe 51.33N 18.15 E
Lvov 6 If 49.50N 24.00 E
Lvovskaja Oblast 19 Cf 49.45N 24.00 E
Lwowa 60 Hj 10.44S 165.45 E
Lwówek 10 Md 52.28N 16.10 E
Lwówek Śląski 10 Le 51.07N 15.35 E
Lyakhov Islands (EN)= Ljahovskije Ostrova 21 Qb 73.30N 141.00 E
Lyall, Mount- 62 Bf 45.17S 167.33 E
Lyallpur 22 Jf 31.25N 73.05 E
Lychsele 7 Ed 64.36N 18.40 E
Lycia 15 Mm 36.30N 29.30 E
Lyckeby 8 Fh 56.12N 15.39 E
Lyckebyån 8 Fh 56.11N 15.40 E
Lyčkovo 7 Hh 57.57N 32.24 E
Lydd 9 Nk 50.57N 0.55 E
Lydd Airport 12 Cd 50.58N 0.56 E
Lydenburg 37 Ee 25.10S 30.29 E
Lydia 15 Lk 38.35N 28.30 E
Lygna 8 Bf 58.10N 7.02 E
Lygnern 8 Eg 57.29N 12.20 E
Lyme Bay 9 Kk 50.38N 3.00W
Lyminge 12 Dc 51.07N 1.05 E
Lymington 9 Lk 50.46N 1.33W
Łyna 10 Rb 54.37N 21.14 E
Lynchburg 43 Ld 37.24N 79.09W
Lynd 58 Ff 18.56S 144.30 E
Lynden 46 Db 48.57N 122.27W
Lyndon River 59 Cd 23.29S 114.06 E
Lyngdal 7 Bg 58.08N 7.05 E
Lyngen 7 Eb 69.58N 20.30 E
Lyngør 8 Cf 58.38N 9.10 E
Lyngseidet 7 Eb 69.35N 20.13 E
Lynn 44 Ld 42.28N 70.57W
Lynnaj, Gora- 20 Ld 62.55N 163.58 E
Lynn Canal 40 Le 58.50N 135.15W
Lynn Deeps 12 Cb 52.58N 0.20 E
Lynn Lake 39 Id 56.51N 101.03W
Lyntupy 8 Li 55.02N 26.27 E
Lynx Lake 42 Gd 62.25N 106.20W
Lyon 6 Gf 45.45N 4.51 E
Lyon Inlet 42 Jc 66.20N 83.40W
Lyonnais, Monts du- 11 Ki 45.40N 4.30 E
Lyon River 59 De 25.00S 115.20 E
Lyons [Ga.-U.S.] 44 Fi 32.12N 82.19W
Lyons [Ks.-U.S.] 45 Gg 38.21N 98.12W
Lyons, Forêt de- 12 De 49.25N 1.30 E
Lyons-la-Forêt 12 De 49.24N 1.28 E
Lyra Reef 60 Eh 1.50S 153.35 E
Lys 11 Jc 51.03N 3.43 E
Łysa Góra 10 Nd 52.07N 17.33 E
Lysaja, Gora- 8 Lj 54.12N 27.40 E
Lysá nad Labem 10 Kf 50.12N 14.50 E
Lysefjorden 8 Be 59.00N 6.14 E
Lysekil 7 Cf 58.16N 11.26 E
Lyskovo 19 Ed 56.03N 45.03 E
Lyss 14 Bc 47.04N 7.37 E
Lysva 19 Fd 58.07N 57.47 E
Lytham Saint Anne's 9 Jh 53.45N 3.01W
Lyttelton 62 Ee 43.36S 172.43 E
Lytton 46 Ea 50.14N 121.34W
Lyža 17 Hd 65.42N 56.40 E

M

Ma, Oued el- 32 Fe 24.03N 9.10W
Ma, Song 25 Le 19.45N 105.55 E
Maâdis, Djebel- 13 Qi 35.52N 4.44 E
Maalaea Bay 65a Ec 20.47N 156.29W
Ma'āmīr 24 Mg 30.04N 48.20 E
Ma'ān 23 Ec 30.12N 35.44 E
Ma'āniyah 24 Jg 30.44N 43.00 E
Maanselkä 5 Ib 68.07N 28.29 E
Maanselka 7 Ge 63.54N 28.30 E
Ma'anshan 27 Ke 31.38N 118.30 E
Maardu 8 Ke 59.28N 24.56 E
Maarianhamina/Mariehamn 7 Ef 60.06N 19.57 E
Ma 'arrat an Nu 'mān 24 Ge 35.38N 36.40 E
Maarssen 12 Hb 52.08N 5.03 E
Maas = Meuse (EN) 5 Ge 51.49N 5.01 E
Maaseik 11 Lc 51.06N 5.48 E
Maaseik-Neeroeteren 12 Hc 51.05N 5.42 E
Maasin 26 Hd 10.08N 124.50 E
Maasmechelen/Mechelen 12 Hd 50.57N 5.40 E
Maassluis 12 Gc 51.55N 4.17 E
Maastricht 11 Ld 50.52N 5.43 E
Maasupa 63a Ec 9.18S 161.15 E
Ma'āzah, Al Haḑabat al- 24 Ei 27.44N 31.44 E
Mabalane 37 Ed 23.38S 32.31 E
Mabaruma 50 Gh 8.12N 59.47W
Mabechi-Gawa 29 Ga 40.31N 141.31 E
Mabella 45 Lb 48.37N 89.58W
Mabel Lake 46 Fa 50.35N 118.44W
Mablethorpe 9 Nh 53.21N 0.15 E
Mabote 37 Ed 22.03S 34.08 E
Ma'būs Yūsuf 31 Jf 25.45N 21.00 E
Maçaão 13 Ee 39.33N 8.00W
McAdam 42 Kg 45.36N 67.20W
Macajaí, Rio- 54 Fc 2.25N 60.50W
McAllen 43 Hf 26.12N 98.15W
Macaloge 37 Fb 12.25S 35.25 E
Mac Alpine Lake 42 Hc 66.40N 102.50W
Macambará 55 Di 29.08S 56.03W
Macamic 44 Ha 48.48N 79.01W
Macamic, Lac- 44 Ha 48.46N 79.00W
Macao (EN)=Aomen/ Macau 22 Ng 22.10N 113.33 E
Macao (EN)=Aomen/Macau 27 Jg 22.12N 113.33 E
Macao (EN)=Macau/ Aomen 22 Ng 22.10N 113.33 E
Macao (EN)=Macau/Aomen 27 Jg 22.12N 113.33 E
Macapá 53 Ke 0.02N 51.03W
Macará 54 Cd 4.21S 79.56W
Macaracas 49 Gj 7.44N 80.33W
Macareo, Caño- 54 Fb 9.47N 61.36W
McArthur 44 Ff 39.14N 82.29W
Mc Arthur River 59 Hc 15.54S 136.40 E
Maçãs 13 Fc 41.29N 6.39W
Macas 54 Cd 2.18S 78.06W
Macatete, Sierra de- 48 Dd 28.00N 110.05W
Macau 53 Mf 5.07S 36.38W
Macau/Aomen=Macao (EN) 27 Jg 22.12N 113.33 E
Macau/Aomen=Macao (EN) 22 Ng 22.10N 113.33 E
Macaúbas 54 Jf 13.02S 42.42W
Macauley Island 57 Ih 30.13S 178.33W
Macaya, Pic de- 47 Je 18.23N 74.02W
McBeth Fiord 42 Kc 69.43N 69.20W
McCamey 45 Ek 31.08N 102.13W
McCammon 46 Ie 42.39N 112.12W
Mc Carthy 40 Kd 61.26N 142.55W
McClellanville 44 Hi 33.06N 79.28W
MacClenny 44 Fj 30.18N 82.07W
Macclesfield 9 Kh 53.16N 2.07W
Macclesfield Bank (EN) 26 Fc 15.50N 114.20 E
McClintock 42 Ie 57.48N 94.12W
McClintock, Mount- 66 Jg 80.13S 157.26 E
Mc Clintock Channel 38 Ib 71.00N 101.00W
McCluer Gulf (EN)=Berau, Teluk- 26 Jg 2.30S 132.30 E
Mc Clure Strait 38 Hb 74.30N 116.00W
McClusky 45 Fc 47.29N 100.27W
McComb 45 Ie 31.14N 90.27W
McConaughy, Lake- 45 Ff 41.18N 101.46W
McConnelsville 44 Gf 39.39N 81.51W
McCook 43 Gc 40.12N 100.38W
McCormick 44 Fi 33.55N 82.19W
McDame 42 Ee 59.13N 129.14W
McDermitt 46 Gf 41.59N 117.36W
Macdhui, Ben- 9 Jd 57.04N 3.40W
Macdonald, Lake- 59 Fd 23.30S 129.00 E
Mc Donald Islands 30 On 52.59S 72.50 E
McDonald Peak [Ca.-U.S.] 46 Ef 40.58N 120.26W
McDonald Peak [Mt.-U.S.] 46 Ic 47.29N 113.46W
Macdonald Range 46 Hb 49.12N 114.46W
Macdonnell Ranges 57 Eg 23.45S 132.20 E
McDouglas Sound 42 Hd 75.15N 97.30W
Macduff 9 Kd 57.40N 2.29W
Macedo de Cavaleiros 13 Fc 41.32N 6.58W
Macedonia (EN)= Makedhonia 5 Ig 41.00N 23.00 E
Macedonia (EN)= Makedhonia 15 Fh 41.00N 23.00 E
Macedonia (EN) = Makedonija 15 Eh 41.50N 22.00 E
Macedonia (EN)= Makedonija 5 Ig 41.00N 23.00 E
Macedonia (EN)= Makedonija 15 Fh 41.00N 23.00 E
Maceió 53 Mf 9.40S 35.43W
Macenta 34 Dd 8.33N 9.28W
Macerata 14 Hg 43.18N 13.27 E
McGehee 45 Kj 33.38N 91.24W
McGill 46 Hg 39.23N 114.47W
Macgillycuddy's Reeks/Na Cruacha Dubha 9 Di 52.00N 9.50W
McGrath 40 Hd 62.58N 155.38W
MacGregor 45 Gb 49.57N 98.49W
McGregor 45 Jc 46.36N 93.19W
McGregor Lake 46 Ia 50.31N 112.53W
Mc Gregor Range 59 Ie 26.40S 142.45 E
McGuire, Mount- 46 Hd 45.10N 114.36W
Machachi 54 Cd 0.30S 78.34W
Machado 55 Je 21.41S 45.56W
Machagai 56 Hc 26.56S 60.03W
Machaila 37 Ed 22.15S 32.58 E
Machaire na Mumhan/ Golden Vale 9 Fi 52.30N 8.00W
Machaire Rátha/Maghera 9 Gg 54.51N 6.40W
Machakos 36 Gc 1.31S 37.16 E
Machala 54 Cd 3.16S 79.58W
Machaneng 37 Dd 23.12S 27.30 E
Machareti 54 Fh 20.49S 63.24W
Machar Marshes 35 Ed 9.20N 33.10 E
Machattie, Lake- 59 Hd 24.50S 139.48 E
Machault 12 Ge 49.21N 4.30 E
Macheke 37 Ec 18.05S 31.51 E
Macheng 27 Je 31.10N 115.00 E
Machias 44 Nc 44.43N 67.28W
Machida 29 Fd 35.32N 139.27 E
Machilipatnam (Bandar) 25 Ge 16.10N 81.08 E
Machiques 54 Da 10.04N 72.34W
Machona, Laguna- 48 Mh 18.20N 93.40W
Machów 10 Rf 50.34N 21.40 E
Machupicchu 53 Ig 13.07S 72.34W
Macia 37 Ef 25.02S 33.06 E
Mc Ilwraith Range 59 Ib 13.45S 143.20 E
Măcin 15 Ld 45.15N 28.09 E
Macina 30 Gg 14.30N 5.00W
McIntosh 45 Fd 45.55N 101.21W
Macintyre River 59 Je 29.25S 148.45 E
Maçka 24 Hb 40.50N 39.38 E
Mackay [Austl.] 58 Fg 21.09S 149.11 E
Mackay [Id.-U.S.] 46 Ie 43.55N 113.37W
Mackay, Lake- 57 Dg 22.30S 129.00 E
McKay Lake 45 Mb 49.35N 86.22W
McKean Atoll 57 Je 3.36S 174.08W
McKeand 42 Kd 63.00N 65.05W
McKeesport 44 He 40.21N 79.52W
Mackenzie 38 Fc 69.15N 134.08W
McKenzie 44 Cg 36.08N 88.31W
Mackenzie, District of- 42 Gd 65.00N 115.00W
Mackenzie Bay [Ant.] 66 Fe 68.20S 71.15 E
Mackenzie Bay [Can.] 38 Fc 69.00N 136.30W
McKenzie Island 42 If 51.05N 93.48W
Mackenzie King 38 Hb 77.45N 111.00W
Mackenzie Mountains 38 Gc 64.00N 130.00W
McKenzie River 46 Dd 44.07N 123.06W
Mackenzie River 59 Jd 24.00S 149.55 E
McKerrow, Lake- 62 Cf 44.30S 168.05 E
Mackinac, Straits of- 43 Kb 45.49N 82.45W
Mackinaw City 44 Ec 45.47N 84.44W
McKinley, Mount- 38 Dc 63.30N 151.00W
McKinley Park 40 Jd 63.44N 148.54W
McKinney 45 Hj 33.12N 96.37W
Mackinnon Road 36 Gc 3.44S 39.03 E
McLaughlin 45 Fd 45.49N 100.49W
McLean 45 Fi 35.14N 100.36W
McLeans Town 44 Il 26.39N 77.59W
Maclean Strait 42 Ha 77.30N 103.10W
Maclear 37 Df 31.02S 28.23 E
Macleay River 59 Kf 30.52S 153.01 E
Mc Leod, Lake- 57 Cg 24.10S 113.35 E
McLeod Bay 42 Gd 62.53N 110.15W
McLeod Lake 42 Ff 54.59N 123.02W
McLoughlin, Mount- 46 De 42.27N 122.19W
McLure 46 Ea 51.03N 120.14W
Macmillan 42 Dd 62.52N 135.55W
McMillan, Lake- 45 Dj 32.40N 104.20W
McMillan Pass 42 Ed 63.00N 130.00W
McMinnville [Or.-U.S.] 46 Dd 45.13N 123.12W
McMinnville [Tn.-U.S.] 44 Eh 35.41N 85.46W
McMurdo 66 Kf 77.51S 166.37 E
McNaughton Lake 42 Ff 52.40N 117.50W
Macomb 45 Kf 40.27N 90.40W
Macomer 14 Cj 40.16N 8.47 E
Macomia 37 Gb 12.15S 40.08 E
Mâcon 11 Kh 46.18N 4.50 E
Macon [Ga.-U.S.] 39 Kf 32.50N 83.38W
Macon [Mo.-U.S.] 45 Jg 39.44N 92.28W
Macon [Ms.-U.S.] 45 Lj 33.07N 88.34W
Macondo 36 De 12.36S 23.43 E
Mâconnais, Monts du- 11 Kh 46.18N 4.45 E
Macoris, Cabo- 49 Ld 19.47N 70.28W
Macouba 51h Ab 14.52N 61.09W
McPherson 43 Hd 38.22N 97.40W
Mc Pherson Range 59 Ke 28.20S 153.00 E
Macquarie 66 Jd 54.30S 158.30 E
Macquarie Harbour 59 Jh 42.20S 145.25 E
Macquarie Ridge (EN) 3 Jo 57.00S 159.00 E
Macquarie River 57 Fh 30.07S 147.24 E
Mac Robertson Land 66 Fe 70.00S 65.00 E
Macroom/Maigh Chromtha 9 Ej 51.54N 8.57W
Macugnaga 14 Be 45.58N 7.58 E
Macujer 54 Dc 0.24N 73.07W
Macuro 50 Fg 10.39N 61.56W
Macusani 54 Df 14.05S 70.26W
Macuspana 48 Mi 17.48N 92.36W
Mačva 15 Ce 44.49N 19.30 E
McVicar Arm 42 Fc 65.10N 120.30W
Ma'dabā 24 Fg 31.43N 35.48 E
Madagali 34 Hc 10.53N 13.38 E
Madagascar 30 Lj 20.00S 47.00 E
Madagascar (EN)= Madagasikara 31 Lj 19.00S 46.00 E
Madagascar Basin (EN) 3 Fl 27.00S 53.00 E
Madagascar Plateau (EN) 3 Fm 30.00S 45.00 E
Madagasikara=Madagascar (EN) 31 Lj 19.00S 46.00 E
Madā'in Şāliḩ 24 Gi 26.48N 37.53 E
Madalai 64a Ac 7.20N 134.28 E
Madama 34 Ha 21.58N 13.39 E
Madan 15 Hh 41.30N 24.57 E
Madang 58 Fe 5.13S 145.48 E
Madanīyīn 31 Ie 33.21N 10.30 E
Madanīyīn 32 Jc 33.00N 10.45 E
Madaoua 34 Gc 14.05N 5.58 E
Madara 15 Kf 43.17N 27.06 E
Madara-Shima 29 Ae 33.35N 129.45 E
Madaroumfa 34 Gc 13.18N 7.09 E
Madau 63a Ac 9.00S 152.26 E
Madawaska Highlands 44 Hc 45.20N 78.15W
Maddalena 14 Di 41.15N 9.25 E
Maddalena, Colle della- 11 Mj 44.25N 6.53 E
Maddaloni 14 Ii 41.02N 14.23 E
Made, Made en Drimmelen- 12 Gc 51.41N 4.48 E
Made en Drimmelen- 12 Gc 51.41N 4.48 E
Made en Drimmelen-Made 12 Gc 51.41N 4.48 E
Madeir 35 Dd 7.50N 29.12 E
Madeira 31 Fe 32.40N 16.45W
Madeira 30 Fe 32.44N 17.00W
Madeira, Arquipélago da-= Madeira Islands (EN) 30 Fe 32.40N 16.45W
Madeira, Rio- 52 Kf 3.22S 58.45W
Madeira Islands (EN)= Madeira, Arquipélago da- 30 Fe 32.40N 16.45W
Madeleine, Ile de la - 42 Lg 47.26N 61.44W
Madeleine, Monts de la- 11 Jh 46.03N 3.50 E
Maden 24 Hc 38.23N 39.40 E
Madenassa Veld 30 Jj 19.00N 25.30 E
Madera [Ca.-U.S.] 46 Eh 36.57N 120.03W
Madera [Mex.] 47 Cc 29.12N 108.07W
Mader-Chih 13 Ri 35.26N 5.07 E
Madero, Puerto del- 13 Jc 41.48N 2.05W
Madesimo 14 Dd 46.26N 9.21 E
Madgaon 25 Ee 15.22N 73.49 E
Madhya Pradesh 25 Fd 22.00N 79.00 E
Madimba 36 Cc 4.58S 15.08 E
Madina do Boé 34 Cc 11.45N 14.13W
Madinani 34 Dd 9.37N 6.57W
Madīnat al Abyār 33 Dc 32.11N 20.36 E
Madīnat ash Sha'b 22 Gh 12.50N 44.56 E
Madingo-Kayes 36 Bc 4.10S 12.18 E
Madingou 36 Bc 4.09S 13.34 E
Madirovalo 37 Hc 16.29S 46.30 E
Madison [Fl.-U.S.] 44 Fj 30.28N 83.25W
Madison [In.-U.S.] 44 Ef 38.44N 85.23W
Madison [Mn.-U.S.] 45 Hd 45.01N 96.11W
Madison [S.D.-U.S.] 45 He 44.00N 97.07W
Madison [Wi.-U.S.] 39 Ke 43.05N 89.22W
Madison [W.V.-U.S.] 44 Gf 38.03N 81.50W
Madison Range 46 Jd 45.15N 111.20W
Madison River 46 Jd 45.56N 111.30W
Madisonville 43 Jd 37.20N 87.30W
Madiun 26 Fh 7.37S 111.31 E
Mado Gashi 36 Gb 0.44N 39.10 E
Madoi (Huangheyan) 22 Lf 35.00N 98.56 E
Madon 11 Mf 48.36N 6.06 E
Madona 7 Gh 56.53N 26.22 E
Madra Dağı 15 Kj 39.23N 27.12 E
Madrakah, Ra's al- 23 If 18.59N 57.45 E
Madranbaba Dağı 15 Ll 37.38N 28.12 E
Madras [India] 22 Kh 13.05N 80.17 E
Madras [Or.-U.S.] 46 Ed 44.38N 121.08W
Madre, Laguna- [Mex.] 47 Ed 25.00N 97.40W
Madre, Laguna- [Tx.-U.S.] 43 Hf 27.00N 97.35W
Madre, Sierra- 38 Jh 15.20N 92.20W
Madre de Dios 54 Df 12.00S 70.15W
Madre de Dios 54 Df 12.36S 69.59W
Madre de Dios, Isla- 52 Ik 50.15S 75.05W
Madre de Dios, Rio- 52 Jg 10.59S 66.08W
Madre del Sur, Sierra-= Southern Sierra Madre (EN) 38 Jj 17.00N 100.00W
Madre Occidental, Sierra-= Western Sierra Madre (EN) 38 Ig 25.00N 105.00W
Madre Oriental, Sierra-= Eastern Sierra Madre (EN) 38 Jg 22.00N 99.30W
Madrid 13 Id 40.30N 3.40W
Madrid 6 Fg 40.24N 3.41W
Madrid-Aravaca 13 Id 40.27N 3.47W
Madridejos 13 Ie 39.28N 3.32W
Madrid-El Pardo 13 Id 40.32N 3.46W
Madrid-Vallecas 13 Id 40.23N 3.37W
Madrid-Villaverde 13 Id 40.21N 3.42W
Madrigal de las Altas Torres 13 Hc 41.05N 5.00W
Mad River 46 Cf 40.57N 124.07W
Madriz 49 Dg 13.30N 86.30W
Madrona, Sierra- 13 Hf 38.25N 4.10W
Madula 36 Eb 0.28N 25.23 E
Madura, Palau- 21 Nj 7.00S 113.20 E
Madurai 22 Ji 9.56N 78.07 E
Madvār, Kūh-e- 23 Hc 30.36N 54.52 E
Madwin 33 Cd 28.42N 17.31 E
Madyan 21 Fg 27.40N 35.35 E
Madžalis 16 Oh 42.08N 47.50 E
Maebara 28 Be 33.34N 130.13 E
Maebashi 27 Od 36.23N 139.04 E
Mae Hong Son 25 Je 19.16N 97.56 E
Mæl 8 Ce 59.56N 8.48 E
Mae Nam Khong=Mekong (EN) 21 Mh 10.15N 105.55 E
Maesawa 29 Gb 39.03N 141.07 E
Mae Sot 25 Je 16.40N 98.35 E
Maestra, Sierra- 38 Lh 20.00N 76.45W
Maevatanana 37 Hc 16.56S 46.49 E
Maéwo, Ile- 57 Hf 15.10S 168.10 E
Mafeteng 37 De 29.45S 27.18 E
Mafia Channel 36 Gd 7.50S 39.35 E
Mafia Island 30 Ki 7.50S 39.50 E
Mafikeng 31 Jk 25.53S 25.39 E
Mafra [Braz.] 56 Kc 26.07S 49.49W
Mafra [Port.] 13 Cf 38.56N 9.20W
Magadan 22 Rd 59.34N 150.48 E
Magadanskaja Oblast 20 Kd 62.30N 154.00 E
Magadi 36 Gc 1.54S 36.17 E
Magallanes, Estrecho de- = Magellan, Strait of- (EN) 52 Ik 54.00S 71.00W
Magallanes y Antártica Chilena 56 Fh 51.30S 73.30W
Magangué 54 Db 9.14N 74.46W
Maganik 15 Cg 42.44N 19.16 E
Maganoy 26 He 6.51N 124.31 E
Magaria 34 Gc 12.59N 8.50 E
Magazine Mountain 45 Ji 35.10N 93.38W
Magdagači 20 Hf 53.29N 125.55 E
Magdala 55 Bm 36.06S 61.42W
Magdalena 54 Db 10.00N 74.15W
Magdalena [Arg.] 55 Dl 35.04S 57.32W
Magdalena [Bol.] 54 Ff 13.20S 64.08W
Magdalena [Mex.] 47 Bb 30.38N 110.57W
Magdalena [N.M.-U.S.] 45 Ci 34.07N 107.14W
Magdalena, Bahía- 48 Ce 24.35N 112.00W
Magdalena, Isla- 47 Bd 24.55N 112.15W
Magdalena, Llano de la- 47 Bd 24.30N 111.40W
Magdalena, Rio- [Col.] 52 Id 11.06N 74.51W
Magdalena, Rio- [Mex.] 48 Cb 30.48N 112.32W
Magda Plateau 42 Jb 72.18N 82.55W
Magdeburg 6 He 52.10N 11.40 E
Magdeburg 10 Hd 52.15N 11.35 E
Magdeburger Börde 10 Hd 52.00N 11.30 E
Magdelaine Cays 57 Gf 16.35S 150.15 E
Magee 45 Lk 31.52N 89.44W
Magee, Island-/Oileán Mhic Aodha 9 Hg 54.50N 5.50W
Magelang 26 Fh 7.28S 110.13 E
Magellan, Strait of- (EN) = Magallanes, Estrecho de- 52 Ik 54.00S 71.00W
Magellan Seamounts (EN) 57 Gc 17.30N 152.00 E
Magenta 14 Ce 45.28N 8.53 E
Magerøya 7 Fa 71.03N 25.45 E
Magetan 26 Fh 7.39S 111.20 E
Maggiorasca 14 Df 44.33N 9.29 E
Maggiore, Lago- 14 Ce 45.55N 8.40 E
Maghāghah 33 Fd 28.39N 30.50 E
Maghama 32 Ef 15.31N 12.50W
Maghera/Machaire Rátha 9 Gg 54.51N 6.40W
Maghnia 32 Gc 34.51N 1.44W
Magic Reservoir 46 He 43.20N 114.18W
Măgina, Sierra- 13 Ig 37.45N 3.30W
Magistralny 20 Fe 56.03N 107.35 E
Maglaj 14 Mf 44.33N 18.06 E
Măglenik 15 Ih 41.20N 25.45 E
Maglie 14 Mj 40.07N 18.18 E
Mägliž 15 Ig 42.36N 25.33 E
Magnetawan River 44 Gc 45.46N 80.37W
Magnetic Island 59 Jc 19.10S 146.50 E
Magnitka 17 Ii 55.21N 59.43 E
Magnitnaja, Gora- 17 Ij 53.10N 59.10 E
Magnitogorsk 6 Le 53.27N 59.04 E
Magnolia 45 Jj 33.16N 93.14W
Magnor 7 Cg 59.57N 12.12 E
Magny-en-Vexin 11 He 49.09N 1.47 E
Mago 20 Jf 53.18N 140.20 E
Magoé 37 Ec 15.48S 31.43 E
Magoebaskloof 37 Ed 23.51S 30.02 E
Magog 44 Kc 45.16N 72.09W
Magosa=Famagusta (EN) 23 Dc 35.07N 33.57 E
Magra [Alg.] 13 Qi 35.29N 4.58 E
Magra [It.] 14 Df 44.03N 9.58 E
Magtā Lahjar 32 Ef 17.50N 13.20W
Maguarinho, Cabo- 54 Id 0.20S 48.20W
Magude 37 Ee 25.02S 32.40 E
Magumeri 34 Hc 12.07N 12.49 E
Magura, Gora- 10 Th 48.50N 23.44 E
Magwe 25 Jd 20.00N 95.00 E
Magwe 22 Lg 20.09N 94.55 E
Magyarország=Hungary (EN) 6 Hf 47.00N 20.00 E
Mahābād 23 Gb 36.45N 45.53 E
Mahabalipuram 25 Gf 12.37N 80.12 E
Mahabe 37 Hc 17.05S 45.20 E
Mahabo 37 Gd 20.21S 44.39 E
Mahačkala 6 Kg 42.58N 47.30 E
Mahadday Wěyne 35 He 3.00N 45.32 E
Mahādeo Range 25 Ee 17.50N 74.15 E
Mahafaly, Plateau- 37 Gd 24.30S 44.00 E
Mahagi 36 Fb 2.18N 30.59 E
Mahajamba 37 Hc 15.33S 47.08 E
Mahājan 25 Ec 28.47N 73.50 E
Mahajanga 31 Lj 15.17S 46.43 E
Mahajanga 37 Hc 16.30S 47.00 E
Mahajilo 37 Hc 19.42S 45.22 E
Mahakam 21 Nj 0.35S 117.17 E
Mahalapye 37 Dd 23.07S 26.46 E
Mahalevona 37 Hc 15.26S 49.55 E
Mahallāt 24 Nf 33.55N 50.27 E
Mahamid 35 Cb 15.09N 20.25 E
Māhān 24 Qg 30.05N 57.19 E
Mahānadi 25 Kg 20.19N 86.45 E
Mahanoro 37 Hc 19.53S 48.49 E
Maharadze 19 Eg 41.53N 42.01 E
Mahārāshtra 25 Ee 18.00N 75.00 E
Mahārlū, Daryācheh-ye- 24 Oh 29.25N 52.50 E
Mahās 35 He 4.24N 46.07 E
Maha Sarakham 25 Ke 16.12N 103.16 E
Mahavavy 30 Lj 15.57S 45.54 E
Mahbés 32 Dd 27.10N 9.50W
Mahḑah 24 Pj 24.24N 55.59 E
Mahdia 54 Gb 5.16N 59.09W
Mahe 25 Ff 11.42N 75.32 E
Mahébourg 37a Bb 20.24S 57.42 E
Mahé Island 30 Mi 4.40S 55.28 E
Mahendra Giri 25 Ge 18.58N 84.21 E
Mahenge 31 Ki 8.41S 36.43 E
Maheno 62 Df 45.10S 170.50 E
Mahi 25 Ed 22.16N 72.58 E
Mahia Peninsula 61 Eg 39.10S 177.55 E
Mahmūdābād 24 Lc 39.25N 47.15 E
Mahmūdābād 24 Od 36.38N 52.15 E
Mahmūd-e 'Erāqī 23 Kb 35.01N 69.20 E
Mahmudiye 24 Dc 39.30N 31.00 E
Mahmutşevketpaşa 15 Mh 41.09N 29.11 E
Mahneshān 24 Ld 36.45N 47.38 E
Mahnevo 17 Jg 58.27N 61.42 E
Mahnomen 45 Ic 47.19N 95.59W
Mahón/Mao 13 Qe 39.53N 4.15 E
Mahoré/Mayotte 30 Lj 12.50S 45.10 E
Mahrāt, Jabal- 35 Ib 17.00N 52.00 E
Mahsana 25 Ed 23.36N 72.24 E
Mahuan Dao 27 Kd 10.50N 115.47 E
Mahua Point 63a Fd 10.28S 162.05 E
Maiana Atoll 57 Id 0.55N 173.00 E
Maiao, Ile- (Tubai-Manu) 57 Lf 17.34S 150.35W
Maicao 54 Da 11.23N 72.15W
Maicasagi, Lac- 44 Ia 49.52N 76.48W
Maîche 11 Mg 47.15N 6.48 E
Maicuru, Rio- 54 Hd 2.10S 54.17W
Maidenhead 12 Bc 51.31N 0.42W
Maidstone 9 Nj 51.17N 0.32 E
Maiduguri 31 Ig 11.51N 13.09 E
Maigh Chromtha/Macroom 9 Ej 51.54N 8.57W
Maigudo 35 Fd 7.26N 37.10 E
Maihara 29 Ed 35.20N 136.18 E
Maikala Range 25 Gd 22.30N 81.30 E
Maiko 36 Eb 0.14N 25.33 E
Maikona 36 Gb 2.56N 37.38 E
Maikoor, Pulau- 26 Jh 6.15S 134.15 E
Main 10 Ef 50.00N 8.18 E
Mainalon Óros 15 Fl 37.40N 22.15 E

Index Symbols

1 Independent Nation
2 State, Region
3 District, County
4 Municipality
5 Colony, Dependency
Continent
Physical Region
Historical or Cultural Region
Mount, Mountain
Volcano
Hill
Mountains, Mountain Range
Hills, Escarpment
Plateau, Upland
Pass, Gap
Plain, Lowland
Delta
Salt Flat
Valley, Canyon
Crater, Cave
Karst Features
Depression
Polder
Desert, Dunes
Forest, Woods
Heath, Steppe
Oasis
Cape, Point
Coast, Beach
Cliff
Peninsula
Isthmus
Sandbank
Island
Atoll
Rock, Reef
Islands, Archipelago
Rocks, Reefs
Coral Reef
Well, Spring
Geyser
River, Stream
Waterfall Rapids
River Mouth, Estuary
Lake
Salt Lake
Intermittent Lake
Reservoir
Swamp, Pond
Canal
Glacier
Ice Shelf, Pack Ice
Ocean
Sea
Gulf, Bay
Strait, Fjord
Lagoon
Bank
Seamount
Tablemount
Ridge
Shelf
Basin
Escarpment, Sea Scarp
Fracture
Trench, Abyss
National Park, Reserve
Point of Interest
Recreation Site
Cave, Cavern
Historic Site
Ruins
Wall, Walls
Church, Abbey
Temple
Scientific Station
Airport
Port
Lighthouse
Mine
Tunnel
Dam, Bridge

ain Barrier Range 59 If 31.25S 141.25 E
ainburg 10 Hh 48.39N 11.47 E
ain Camp 64g Ba 2.01N 157.25W
ain Channel 44 Gc 45.22N 81.50W
ai-Ndombe, Lac- 30 Ii 2.10S 18.15 E
ain-Donau-Kanal 10 Gg 49.55N 10.50 E
aindong → Coqên 27 Ee 31.15N 85.13 E
aine 11 Ff 48.15N 0.10W
aine 43 Nb 45.15N 69.15W
aine [Fr.] 11 Fg 47.25N 0.37W
aine [Fr.] 11 Eg 47.09N 1.27W
aine, Gulf of- 38 Me 43.00N 68.00W
aine-et-Loire 11 Fg 47.30N 0.20W
ainé-Soroa 34 Hc 13.18N 12.02 E
ainistir Fhear Mai/Fermoy 9 Ei 52.08N 8.16W
ainistir na Búille/Boyle 9 Eh 53.58N 8.18W
ainistir na Corann/Midleton 9 Ej 51.55N 8.10W
ainistir na Féile/Abbeyfeale 9 Di 52.24N 9.18W
ainit, Lake- 26 Ie 9.26N 125.32 E
ainland [Scot.-U.K.] 5 Fc 60.20N 1.22W
ainland [Scot.-U.K.] 5 Fd 59.00N 3.10W
aintal 12 Kd 50.08N 8.51 E
aintenon 11 Hf 48.35N 1.35 E
aintirano 31 Lj 18.03S 44.03 E
ainz 10 Eg 50.00N 8.15 E
aio 32 Cf 23.10N 15.10W
aio 30 Eg 15.15N 23.10W
aipo, Volcán- 52 Ji 34.10S 69.50W
aipú 56 Ie 36.52S 57.52W
aiquetia 54 Ea 10.36N 66.57W
aira 14 Bf 44.49N 7.38 E
airi 54 Jf 11.43S 40.08W
airipotaba 55 Hc 17.21S 49.31W
aisān 24 Lg 32.00N 47.00 E
aisi, Punta- 47 Jd 20.15N 74.09W
aišiagala/Maišiagala 8 Kj 54.51N 25.14 E
aišjagala/Maišiagala 8 Kj 54.51N 25.14 E
aiter 13 Qi 35.23N 4.17 E
aitland [Austl.] 59 Hf 34.22S 137.40 E
aitland [Austl.] 58 Gh 32.44S 151.33 E
aiz, Isla Grande del- 49 Fg 12.10N 83.03W
aiz, Isla Pequeña del- 49 Fg 12.18N 82.59W
aiz, Islas del- 47 Hf 12.15N 83.00W
aizhokunggar 27 Ff 29.50N 91.40 E
aizières-lès-Metz 12 Ie 49.13N 6.09 E
aizuru 28 Mg 35.27N 135.20 E
aizuru-Nishimaizuru 29 Dd 35.28N 135.19 E
aizuru-Wan 29 Dd 35.30N 135.20 E
aja 21 Pd 60.17N 134.41 E
ajagual 49 Ji 8.35N 74.37W
ajakovski 16 Mh 42.02N 42.47 E
ajangat 27 Fb 48.20N 91.58 E
ajardah, Wādī- 14 Em 37.07N 10.13 E
ajāz al Bāb 14 Dn 36.39N 9.37 E
ajdanpek 15 Ee 44.25N 21.56 E
ajene 22 Nj 3.33S 118.57 E
ajērtēn = Mijirtein (EN) 30 Lh 9.00N 50.00 E
ajevica 14 Mf 44.40N 18.40 E
aji 35 Fd 6.10N 35.35 E
ajia He 27 Kd 38.09N 117.53 E
ajja 20 Id 61.38N 130.25 E
ajkain 19 He 51.27N 75.52 E
ajkamys 18 Ka 46.34N 77.37 E
ajkop 6 Kg 44.35N 40.07 E
ajli-Saj 18 Id 41.15N 72.30 E
ajma'ah 24 Kj 25.54N 45.20 E
ajmak 19 Hg 42.40N 71.14 E
ajmakan 20 Ie 57.30N 135.23 E
ajmeča 20 Fb 71.20N 104.15 E
ajn 20 Mc 65.03N 172.10 E
ajna [R.S.F.S.R.] 20 Ef 53.00N 91.28 E
ajna [R.S.F.S.R.] 7 Li 54.09N 47.37 E
ajor, Puig- 13 Oe 39.48N 2.48 E
ajor, Puig-/Mayor, Puig- 13 Oe 39.48N 2.48 E
ajorca (EN) = Mallorca 5 Gh 39.30N 3.00 E
ajrur 35 Db 16.40N 26.53 E
ajski [R.S.F.S.R.] 16 Nh 43.36N 44.03 E
ajski [R.S.F.S.R.] 20 Hf 52.18N 129.38 E
aju, Pulau 26 If 1.20N 126.25 E
ajuro Atoll 57 Id 7.09N 171.12 E
akabana 31 Ii 3.28S 12.36 E
akaha 65a Cb 21.29N 158.13W
akahuena Point 65a Bb 21.52N 159.27W
akalamabedi 37 Cd 20.20S 23.53 E
akale 26 Gg 3.06S 119.51 E
akallé 56 Ic 27.13S 59.17W
akalondi 34 Fc 12.50N 1.41 E
akamby, Nosy- 37 Hc 15.42S 45.54 E
akanči 19 If 46.51N 81.57 E
akanza 36 Cb 1.36N 19.07 E
akapala 65a Fc 20.13N 155.45W
akapu Point 64k Ba 18.59S 169.55W
akapuu Head 65a Db 21.18N 157.39W
akara, Prohod- 15 Ih 41.16N 25.26 E
ákares 15 Il 37.05N 25.42 E
akarfi 34 Gc 11.23N 7.53 E
akari 34 Hc 12.35N 14.28 E
akari Mountains 36 Ed 6.05S 29.50 E
akarjev 7 Kh 57.57N 43.49 E
akarov 20 Jg 48.39N 142.51 E
akarov Basin (EN) 67 Ce 87.00N 170.00 E
akarov Seamount (EN) 57 Gb 29.30N 153.30 E
akarska 14 Lg 43.18N 17.02 E
akā Rūd 24 Nd 36.21N 51.16 E
Makasar → Ujung Pandang 22 Nj 5.07S 119.24 E
akasar, Selat- = Makassar Strait (EN) 21 Nj 2.00S 117.30 E
Makassar Strait (EN) = Makasar, Selat- 21 Nj 2.00S 117.30 E
Makat 6 Lf 47.40N 53.28 E
Makatea, Ile- 57 Mf 15.50S 148.15W
Makaw 25 Jc 26.27N 96.42 E
Makawao 65a Ec 20.51N 156.19W
Makay, Massif du- 37 Hd 21.15S 45.15 E
Makedhonia 15 Fi 40.40N 22.30 E
Makedhonia = Macedonia (EN) 15 Fh 41.00N 23.00 E
Makedhonia = Macedonia (EN) 5 Ig 41.00N 23.00 E
Makedonija = Macedonia (EN) 5 Ig 41.00N 23.00 E
Makedonija = Macedonia (EN) 15 Eh 41.50N 22.00 E
Makedonija = Macedonia (EN) 15 Fh 41.00N 23.00 E
Makejevka 16 Jf 48.00N 37.58 E
Makelulu, Mount- 64a Bb 7.34N 134.35 E
Makemo Atoll 57 Mf 16.35S 143.40W
Makeni 31 Fh 8.53N 12.03W
Makgadikgadi Pans 30 Jk 20.50S 25.30 E
Makhfar al Buşayyah 24 Lg 30.08N 46.07 E
Makhfar al Hammām 24 He 35.51N 38.45 E
Makhmūr 24 Je 35.46N 43.35 E
Makhyah, Wādī- 23 Gf 17.40N 49.01 E
Maki 29 Fc 37.45N 138.52 E
Makian, Pulau- 26 If 0.20N 127.25 E
Makikihi 62 Df 44.38S 171.09 E
Makinsk 19 He 52.40N 70.26 E
Makkah = Mecca (EN) 22 Fg 21.27N 39.49 E
Makkovik 42 Le 55.05N 59.11W
Maknassy 32 Ic 34.37N 9.36 E
Makó 10 Qj 46.13N 20.29 E
Makokou 31 Ih 0.34N 12.52 E
Makongai 63d Bb 17.27S 178.58 E
Makongolosi 36 Fd 8.24S 33.09 E
Makorako 62 Gc 39.09S 176.03 E
Makoua 31 Ih 0.01N 15.39 E
Makoura 63b Dc 17.08S 168.26 E
Makov 10 Og 49.22N 18.29 E
Maków Mazowiecki 10 Rd 52.52N 21.06 E
Makrá 15 Im 36.16N 25.53 E
Makrān 21 Hg 26.00N 60.00 E
Makrónisos 15 Hl 37.42N 24.07 E
Maksatiha 7 Ih 57.48N 35.55 E
Makteir 30 Ff 21.50N 11.40W
Makthar 14 Do 35.50N 9.13 E
Makthar 32 Ib 35.51N 9.12 E
Makū 23 Hd 27.52N 52.26 E
Mākū 24 Kc 39.17N 44.31 E
Makubetsu 29a Cb 42.54N 143.19 E
Makumbato 36 Fd 8.51S 34.50 E
Makumbi 36 Dd 5.51S 20.41 E
Makunduchi 36 Gd 6.25S 39.33 E
Makung 27 Kg 23.35N 119.35 E
Makurazaki 28 Ki 31.16N 139.19 E
Makurdi 31 Hh 7.44N 8.32 E
Makushin Volcano 40a Eb 53.53N 166.50W
Makušino 19 Gd 55.13N 67.13 E
Makuyuni 36 Gc 3.33S 36.06 E
Malå 7 Ed 65.11N 18.44 E
Mala/Mallow 9 Ei 52.08N 8.39W
Mala, Punta- 47 Ig 7.28N 80.00W
Malabang 26 He 7.38N 124.03 E
Malabar Coast 21 Jh 10.00N 76.15 E
Malabo 31 Hh 3.45N 8.47 E
Malabrigo 55 Ci 29.20S 59.58W
Malacca, Strait of- (EN) = Melaka, Selat- 21 Mi 2.30N 101.20 E
Malacky 10 Nh 48.27N 17.01 E
Malad City 46 Ie 42.12N 112.15W
Malá Fatra 10 Og 49.08N 18.50 E
Málaga 13 Hh 36.48N 4.45W
Málaga [Col.] 54 Db 6.42N 72.44W
Málaga [Sp.] 6 Fh 36.43N 4.25W
Malagarasi 30 Ji 5.12S 29.47 E
Malagón 13 Ie 39.10N 3.51W
Malaimbandi 37 Hd 20.20S 45.36 E
Malaita Island 57 He 9.00S 161.00 E
Malaja Kuonamka 20 Gb 70.50N 113.20 E
Malaja Ob 20 Bc 66.08N 65.50 E
Malaja Sosva 19 Gc 63.10N 64.22 E
Malaja Višera 19 Dd 58.52N 32.14 E
Malaja Viska 16 Ge 48.39N 31.38 E
Malakāl 31 Kh 9.31N 31.39 E
Malakal Harbor 64a Ac 7.20N 134.26 E
Malakal Pass 64a Ac 7.17N 134.28 E
Mala Kapela 14 Jf 44.55N 15.28 E
Malakobi 63a Db 7.19S 158.07 E
Mallamalla Range 25 Fe 16.17N 79.29 E
Malang 22 Nj 7.59S 112.37 E
Malange 36 Cd 9.30S 16.30 E
Malange 31 Ii 9.33S 16.22 E
Malangen 7 Eb 69.30N 18.20 E
Malanville 34 Fc 11.52N 3.23 E
Malao 63b Cb 15.10S 166.51 E
Mała Panew 10 Nf 50.44N 17.52 E
Mälaren 5 Hd 59.30N 17.15 E
Malargüe 56 Ge 35.28S 69.35W
Malartic, Lac- 44 Ha 48.15N 78.05W
Malaspina Glacier 40 Ke 59.50N 140.30W
Malatya 22 Ff 38.21N 38.19 E
Malāvi 24 Lf 33.10N 47.50 E
Malawi 31 Kj 13.30S 34.00 E
Malawi, Lake- 30 Kj 12.00S 34.30 E
Malaya 26 Df 4.00N 102.00 E
Malaybalay 26 Ie 8.09N 125.05 E
Malāyer 24 Me 34.16N 48.12 E
Malāyer 23 Gc 34.17N 48.50 E
Malay Peninsula (EN) 21 Mi 6.00N 102.00 E
Malaysia 22 Mi 4.00N 102.00 E
Malaysia, Semenanjung- 26 Df 4.00N 102.00 E
Malazgirt 24 Jc 39.09N 42.31 E
Malberg 12 Id 50.03N 6.35 E
Mälbor 24 Og 30.45N 52.05 E
Malbork 10 Pb 54.02N 19.01 E
Malbrán 56 Hc 29.21S 62.27W
Malchin 10 Ic 53.44N 12.47 E
Maldegem 12 Fc 51.13N 3.27 E
Malden 45 Lh 36.34N 89.57W
Malden Island 57 Le 4.03S 154.59W
Malditos, Montes-/La Maladeta 13 Mb 42.40N 0.50 E
Maldive Islands 21 Ji 3.15N 73.00 E
Mal di Ventre 14 Ck 40.00N 8.20 E
Maldives 22 Ji 3.15N 73.00 E
Maldon 9 Nj 51.45N 0.40 E
Maldonado 55 El 34.40S 54.55W
Maldonado 56 Jd 34.54S 54.57W
Maldonado, Punta- 48 Ji 16.20N 98.35W
Male 22 Ji 4.10N 73.30 E
Malé 14 Ed 46.21N 10.55 E
Mâle, Lac du- 44 Ja 48.30N 75.30W
Malea, Cape- (EN) = Maléas, Ákra- 15 Gm 36.26N 23.12 E
Maléas, Ákra- = Malea, Cape- (EN) 15 Gm 36.26N 23.12 E
Male Atoll 21 Ji 4.29N 73.30 E
Malebo, Pool- 30 Ii 4.17S 15.20 E
Mālegaon 25 Ed 20.33N 74.32 E
Maléha 34 Dc 11.48N 9.43W
Malek 35 Ed 6.04N 31.36 E
Malé Karpaty = Little Carpathians (EN) 10 Nh 48.30N 17.20 E
Malek Kandī 24 Ld 37.09N 46.06 E
Malékoula, Ile 57 Hf 16.15S 167.30 E
Malema 37 Fb 14.57S 37.25 E
Malemba Nkulu 36 Ed 8.02S 26.48 E
Malenga 7 Ie 63.50N 36.25 E
Măleruş 15 Id 45.54N 25.32 E
Malesherbes 11 If 48.18N 2.25 E
Malgobek 16 Nh 43.32N 44.34 E
Malgomaj 7 Dd 64.47N 16.12 E
Malhada 55 Kb 14.21S 43.47W
Malhanski Hrebet 20 Ff 50.30N 109.00 E
Malhão da Estrêla 13 Ed 40.19N 7.37W
Malha Wells 35 Db 15.08N 26.12 E
Malheur Lake 43 Dc 43.20N 118.45W
Malheur River 46 Gd 44.03N 116.59W
Mali 31 Gg 17.00N 4.00W
Mali 34 Cc 12.05N 12.18W
Mali 25 Jc 25.42N 97.30 E
Mali 63d Bb 16.20S 179.21 E
Mália 15 In 35.17N 25.28 E
Maliakós Kólpos 15 Fk 38.52N 22.38 E
Malik, Wādī al- 30 Kg 18.02N 30.58 E
Mali kanal 15 Cd 45.42N 19.19 E
Malik Siah, Kūh-i- 23 Jd 29.51N 60.52 E
Målilla 8 Fg 57.23N 15.48 E
Mali Lošinj 14 If 44.32N 14.28 E
Malimba, Monts- 36 Ed 7.32S 29.30 E
Malin 16 Fd 50.46N 29.14 E
Malinalco 48 Jh 18.57N 99.30W
Malinaltepec 48 Ji 17.03N 98.40W
Malindi 31 Li 3.13S 40.07 E
Malines/Mechelen 11 Kc 51.02N 4.29 E
Malin Head/Cionn Mhálanna 5 Fd 55.23N 7.24W
Malino, Bukit- 26 Hf 0.45N 120.47 E
Malinovoje Ozero 20 Cf 51.40N 79.55 E
Malinyi 36 Gd 8.56S 36.08 E
Malipo 27 Hg 23.07N 104.42 E
Maliqi 15 Di 40.43N 20.41 E
Malita 26 Ie 6.25N 125.36 E
Maljen 15 Dd 44.07N 20.03 E
Maljovica 15 Gg 42.11N 23.22 E
Malka 16 Nh 43.44N 44.15 E
Malkara 24 Bb 40.53N 26.54 E
Malki Lom 15 Jf 43.39N 26.04 E
Malko Tărnovo 15 Kh 41.59N 27.32 E
Mallacoota 59 Jg 37.30S 149.50 E
Mallaig 9 Hd 57.00N 5.50W
Mallāq, Wādī- 14 Cn 36.32N 8.51 E
Mallawī 33 Fd 27.44N 30.50 E
Mallery Lake 42 Hd 64.00N 98.00W
Malles Venosta / Mals 14 Ed 46.41N 10.32 E
Mallet 55 Gg 25.55S 50.50W
Mallorca = Majorca (EN) 5 Gh 39.30N 3.00 E
Mallow/Mala 9 Ei 52.08N 8.39W
Malm 7 Cd 64.04N 11.13 E
Malmbäck 8 Fg 57.35N 14.28 E
Malmberget 7 Ec 67.10N 20.40 E
Malmédy 11 Md 50.26N 6.02 E
Malmesbury 37 Bf 33.28S 18.44 E
Malmö 6 Hd 55.36N 13.00 E
Malmöhus 7 Ci 55.45N 13.30 E
Malmön 8 Df 58.21N 11.20 E
Malmslätt 8 Ff 58.25N 15.30 E
Malmyž 19 Fd 56.31N 50.41 E
Malo 63b Cb 15.41S 167.10 E
Maloarhangelsk 16 Jc 52.26N 36.29 E
Maloelap 57 Id 8.45N 171.03 E
Maloggia/Malojapaß 14 Dd 46.24N 9.41 E
Malojapaß/Maloggia 14 Dd 46.24N 9.41 E
Malojaroslavec 16 Jb 55.02N 36.28 E
Maloje Polesje 10 Jf 50.10N 24.30 E
Malolo 63d Ab 17.45S 177.10 E
Malolos 26 Hd 14.51N 120.49 E
Malombe, Lake- 36 Ge 14.38S 35.12 E
Malone 44 Jc 44.52N 74.19W
Malonga 36 De 10.24S 23.10 E
Małopolska 10 Pf 50.45N 20.00 E
Malorita 16 Dd 51.48N 24.05 E
Malošujka 7 Ie 63.47N 37.22 E
Måløy 7 Af 61.56N 5.07 E
Malozemelskaja Tundra 17 Ec 68.00N 52.00 E
Malpaso 48 Mi 17.20N 93.30W
Malpelo, Isla de- 52 He 3.59N 81.35W
Malprabha 25 Fe 16.12N 76.03 E
Mals / Malles Venosta 14 Ed 46.41N 10.32 E
Malsch 12 Kf 48.53N 8.20 E
Malše 10 Kh 48.59N 14.29 E
Malta 5 Hh 35.54N 14.31 E
Malta 6 Hh 35.50N 14.30 E
Malta [Lat.-U.S.S.R.] 8 Lh 56.18N 27.15 E
Malta [Mt.-U.S.] 43 Fb 48.21N 107.52W
Malta, Canale di- [Eur.] = Malta Channel (EN) 14 In 36.30N 14.30 E
Malta Channel (EN) = Malta, Canale di- [Eur.] 14 In 36.30N 14.30 E
Maltahöhe 37 Bd 25.00S 16.30 E
Maltahöhe 31 Ik 24.50S 17.00 E
Maltepe 15 Mi 40.55N 29.08 E
Malton 9 Mg 54.08N 0.48W
Maluku 26 Ig 4.00S 128.00 E
Maluku, Kepulauan- = Moluccas (EN) 57 De 2.00S 128.00 E
Maluku, Laut- = Molucca Sea (EN) 21 Oj 0.05S 125.00 E
Malumfashi 34 Gc 11.48N 7.37 E
Malunda 26 Gg 3.00S 118.50 E
Malung 7 Cf 60.40N 13.44 E
Malungsfors 8 Ed 60.44N 13.33 E
Malūţ 35 Ec 10.26N 32.12 E
Maluu 63a Ec 8.21S 160.38 E
Malvern [Ar.-U.S.] 45 Ji 34.22N 92.49W
Malvern [Eng.-U.K.] 9 Ki 52.07N 2.19W
Malvinas 55 Ci 29.37S 58.59W
Malvinas, Islas-/Falkland Islands 53 Kk 51.45S 59.00W
Malvinas, Islas-/Falkland Islands 52 Kk 51.45S 59.00W
Maly, Ostrov- 8 Ld 60.02N 27.58 E
Malya 36 Fc 2.59S 33.31 E
Maly Anjuj 20 Lc 68.35N 161.03 E
Maly Čeremšan 7 Mi 54.20N 50.01 E
Malý Dunaj 10 Nh 48.08N 17.09 E
Malygina, Proliv- 20 Cb 73.00N 70.30 E
Maly Jenisej 20 Ef 51.40N 94.26 E
Maly Kavkaz = Lesser Caucasus (EN) 5 Kg 41.00N 44.35 E
Maly Ljahovski, Ostrov- 20 Jb 74.07N 140.36 E
Maly Tajmyr, Ostrov- 20 Fa 78.08N 107.08 E
Maly Uzen 5 Kf 48.50N 49.38 E
Mama 20 Ge 58.20N 112.54 E
Mamadyš 7 Mi 55.45N 51.24 E
Mamagota 63a Bb 6.46S 155.24 E
Mamaia 15 Le 44.17N 28.37 E
Mamakan 20 Ge 57.48N 114.05 E
Mamantel 48 Nh 18.33N 91.05W
Mamanutha Group 63d Ab 17.34S 177.04 E
Mamaqān 24 Kd 37.51N 45.59 E
Mambaj 55 Ib 14.28S 46.07W
Mambajao 26 He 9.15N 124.43 E
Mambasa 36 Eb 1.21N 29.03 E
Mambéré 35 Be 3.31N 16.03 E
Mambili 36 Cb 0.07N 16.08 E
Mamborê 55 Fg 24.18S 52.32W
Mambova 36 Ef 17.44S 25.11 E
Mambrui 36 Hc 3.07S 40.09 E
Mamburao 26 Hd 13.14N 120.35 E
Mamedkala 16 Ph 42.12N 48.06 E
Mamer 12 Ie 49.38N 6.02 E
Mamers 11 Gf 48.21N 0.23 E
Mamfe 34 Gd 5.46N 9.17 E
Mamiá, Lago- 54 Fd 4.15S 63.05W
Mamisonski, Pereval- 16 Mh 42.43N 43.45 E
Mamljutka 19 Ge 54.57N 68.35 E
Mammoth Cave 44 Dg 37.10N 86.08W
Mammoth Hot Springs 46 Jd 44.59N 110.43W
Mamoré, Rio- 52 Jg 10.23S 65.53W
Mamou 31 Fg 10.23N 12.05W
Mampikony 37 Hc 16.05S 47.37 E
Mampodre, Picos de- 13 Ga 43.02N 5.12W
Mampong 34 Ed 7.04N 1.24W
Mamry, Jezioro- 10 Rb 54.08N 21.42 E
Mamuju 26 Gg 2.41S 118.54 E
Mamuno 37 Cd 22.17S 20.02 E
Ma'mūrah, Ra's al- 14 En 36.27N 10.49 E
Mamurokawa 29 Gb 38.54N 140.15 E
Mamutzu 37 Hb 12.47S 45.14 E
Man 31 Gh 7.24N 7.33W
Man 34 Dd 7.13N 7.41W
Man, Calf of- 9 Ig 54.03N 4.48W
Man, Isle of- 5 Fe 54.15N 4.30W
Mana 60 Oc 22.02N 159.46W
Mana 20 Ee 55.57N 92.28 E
Manacapuru 54 Fd 3.18S 60.37W
Manacor 13 Pe 39.34N 3.12 E
Manado 22 Oi 1.29N 124.51 E
Managua 39 Kh 12.09N 86.17W
Managua 49 Dg 12.05N 86.20W
Managua, Lago de- 47 Gf 12.20N 86.20W
Manakara 31 Lk 22.07S 48.00 E
Manama (EN) = Al Manāmah 22 Hg 26.13N 50.35 E
Manambolo 37 Gc 19.19S 44.17 E
Manam Island 57 Fe 4.05S 145.03 E
Manamo, Caño- 54 Fb 9.55N 62.16W
Mananara 37 Hc 16.10S 49.45 E
Mananara 37 Hd 23.21S 47.42 E
Mananjary 31 Lk 21.14S 48.17 E
Manankoro 34 Dc 10.28N 7.25W
Manantenina 37 Hd 24.17S 47.18 E
Manaoba 63a Ec 8.19S 160.47 E
Manapire, Río- 50 Ci 7.42N 66.07W
Manapouri 58 Hi 45.34S 167.36 E
Manapouri, Lake- 62 Bf 45.30S 167.30 E
Manār, Jabal- 33 Hg 14.10N 44.17 E
Manas 22 Ke 44.18N 86.13 E
Manas, Gora- 18 Hc 42.18N 71.06 E
Manas He 27 Eb 45.38N 85.12 E
Manas Hu 27 Eb 45.45N 85.55 E
Manasija, Manastir- 15 Ee 44.06N 21.28 E
Manati 49 Ic 21.19N 76.56W
Manati 49 Nd 18.26N 66.29W
Manatuto 26 Ih 8.30S 126.01 E
Manaure 49 Kh 11.46N 72.28W
Manaus 53 Jf 3.08S 60.01W
Manavgat 24 Dd 36.47N 31.26 E
Manbij 24 Gd 36.31N 37.57 E
Manbūbnagar 25 Fe 16.44N 77.59 E
Mancelona 44 Ec 44.54N 85.04W
Mancha Real 13 Ig 37.47N 3.37W
Manche 11 Ee 49.00N 1.10W
Mancheng 28 Ce 38.57N 115.19 E
Manchester [Ct.-U.S.] 44 Ke 41.47N 72.31W
Manchester [Eng.-U.K.] 6 Fe 53.30N 2.15W
Manchester [Ia.-U.S.] 45 Ke 42.29N 91.27W
Manchester [Ky.-U.S.] 44 Fg 37.09N 83.46W
Manchester [N.H.-U.S.] 43 Mc 42.59N 71.28W
Manchester [Tn.-U.S.] 44 Dh 35.29N 86.05W
Manchok 34 Gd 9.40N 8.31 E
Manchuria (EN) 22 Oe 47.00N 125.00 E
Manciano 14 Fh 42.35N 11.31 E
Mand 23 Hd 28.11N 51.17 E
Manda [Chad] 35 Bd 9.11N 18.13 E
Manda [Tan.] 36 Fe 10.28S 34.35 E
Manda, Jabal- 35 Cd 8.39N 24.27 E
Mandabe 37 Gd 21.02S 44.56 E
Mandaguari 56 Jb 23.32S 51.42W
Manda Island 36 Hc 2.17S 40.57 E
Mandal 7 Bg 58.02N 7.27 E
Mandalay 25 Jd 21.00N 96.00 E
Mandalay 22 Lg 22.00N 96.05 E
Mandal-Gobi 27 Ib 45.45N 106.12 E
Mandalī 24 Kf 33.45N 45.32 E
Mandalselva 8 Bf 58.02N 7.28 E
Mandalt → Sonid Zuoqi 27 Kc 43.50N 116.45 E
Mandalya körfezi 24 Bd 37.12N 27.20 E
Mandan 43 Gb 46.50N 100.54W
Mandaon 26 Hd 12.13N 123.17 E
Mandara, Monts- = Mandara Mountains (EN) 34 Hc 10.45N 13.40 E
Mandara Mountains (EN) = Mandara, Monts- 34 Hc 10.45N 13.40 E
Mandas 14 Dk 39.38N 9.07 E
Mandasor 25 Fd 24.04N 75.04 E
Mandera 31 Lh 3.56N 41.52 E
Manderscheid 12 Id 50.06N 6.49 E
Mandeville 49 Id 18.02N 77.30W
Mandi 25 Fb 31.43N 76.55 E
Mandiana 34 Dc 10.38N 8.41W
Mandimba 37 Fb 14.21S 35.39 E
Mandingues, Monts- 34 Cc 13.00N 11.00W
Mandioli, Pulau- 26 Ig 0.44S 127.14 E
Mandioré, Laguna- 55 Dd 18.08S 57.33W
Mandirituba 55 Hg 25.46S 49.19W
Mandji 36 Bc 1.42S 10.24 E
Mandla 25 Gd 22.36N 80.23 E
Mandø 8 Ci 55.15N 8.35 E
Mandoúdhion 15 Gk 38.48N 23.29 E
Mandrákion 15 Km 36.36N 27.08 E
Mandritsara 37 Hc 15.49S 48.48 E
Mandurah 59 Df 32.32S 115.43 E
Manduria 14 Lj 40.24N 17.38 E
Māndvi 25 Dd 22.50N 69.22 E
Mandya 25 Ff 12.33N 76.54 E
Måne 8 Ce 59.56N 8.48 E
Măneciu Ungureni 15 Id 45.19N 25.59 E
Manendragarh 25 Gd 23.10N 82.35 E
Maneromango 36 Gd 7.16S 38.46 E
Manevići 16 Dd 51.19N 25.33 E
Manfalūţ 33 Fd 27.19N 30.58 E
Manfredonia 14 Ji 41.38N 15.55 E
Manfredonia, Golfo di- 14 Ki 41.35N 16.05 E
Manga [Afr.] 30 Ig 15.00N 14.00 E
Manga [Braz.] 54 Jf 14.46S 43.56W
Mangabeiras, Chapada das- 52 Lg 10.00S 46.30W
Mangai 36 Cc 4.03S 19.35 E
Mangaia Island 57 Lg 21.55S 157.55W
Mangakino 62 Fc 38.22S 175.46 E
Mangalia 15 Lf 43.48N 28.35 E
Mangalmé 35 Bc 12.21N 19.37 E
Mangalore 22 Jh 12.52N 74.53 E
Mangareva, Ile- 57 Ng 23.07S 134.57W
Mangfall 10 Ii 47.51N 12.08 E
Manggar 26 Eg 2.53S 108.16 E
Manggautu 63a Dd 11.30S 159.59 E
Mangin Yoma 25 Jd 24.20N 95.42 E
Mangistau 16 Qg 44.03N 51.57 E
Mangit 19 Gg 42.07N 60.01 E
Mangkalihat, Tanjung- 26 Gf 1.02N 118.59 E
Manglares, Cabo- 54 Cc 1.36N 79.02W
Mangnai 27 Fd 37.48N 91.55 E
Mangniu He 28 Ib 45.10N 126.58 E
Mango [Fiji] 63d Cb 17.27S 179.09W
Mango [Ton.] 65b Bb 20.20S 174.43W
Mangoche 36 Ge 14.28S 35.16 E
Mangoky [Mad.] 37 Hd 23.27S 45.13 E
Mangoky [Mad.] 30 Lk 21.29S 43.41 E
Mangole, Pulau- 26 Ig 1.53S 125.50 E
Mangonui 62 Ea 34.59S 173.32 E
Mangrove Cay 49 Ia 24.51N 76.14W
Mangrullo, Cuchilla- 55 Fk 32.27S 53.50W
Mangshi → Luxi 27 Gg 24.29N 98.40 E
Mangualde 13 Ed 40.36N 7.46W
Mangueira, Lagoa- 56 Jd 33.06S 52.48W
Mangueni, Plateau de- 30 If 22.35N 12.40 E
Mangui 27 La 52.03N 122.09 E
Mangula 37 Ec 16.52S 30.08 E
Mangum 45 Gi 34.53N 99.30W
Manguredjipa 36 Eb 0.21N 28.44 E
Mangyšlak 19 Fg 43.40N 51.15 E
Mangyšlak, Plato- 19 Fg 43.25N 53.00 E
Mangyšlakskaja Oblast 19 Fg 44.00N 53.30 E
Mangyšlakski Zaliv 16 Qg 44.45N 51.00 E
Manhattan 43 Hd 39.11N 96.35W
Manhica 37 Ee 25.24S 32.48 E
Mani 36 Ed 6.27S 25.20 E
Mani 54 Dc 4.49N 72.17W
Mānī', Wādī al- 24 Ie 34.16N 41.02 E
Mania 37 Hc 19.42S 45.22 E
Maniago 14 Gd 46.10N 12.43 E
Manica 37 Ec 19.00S 33.20 E
Manica 37 Ec 18.56S 32.53 E
Manicaland 37 Ec 19.00S 32.30 E
Manicoré 53 Jf 5.49S 61.17W

ndex Symbols

Independent Nation; State, Region; District, County; Municipality; Colony, Dependency; Continent; Physical Region
Historical or Cultural Region; Mount, Mountain; Volcano; Hill; Mountains, Mountain Range; Hills, Escarpment; Plateau, Upland
Pass, Gap; Plain, Lowland; Delta; Salt Flat; Valley, Canyon; Crater, Cave; Karst Features
Depression; Polder; Desert, Dunes; Forest, Woods; Heath, Steppe; Oasis; Cape, Point
Coast, Beach; Cliff; Peninsula; Isthmus; Sandbank; Island; Atoll
Rock, Reef; Islands, Archipelago; Rocks, Reefs; Coral Reef; Well, Spring; Geyser; River, Stream
Waterfall Rapids; River Mouth, Estuary; Lake; Salt Lake; Intermittent Lake; Reservoir; Swamp, Pond
Canal; Glacier; Ice Shelf, Pack Ice; Ocean; Sea; Gulf, Bay; Strait, Fjord
Lagoon; Bank; Seamount; Tablemount; Ridge; Shelf; Basin
Escarpment, Sea Scarp; Fracture; Trench, Abyss; National Park, Reserve; Point of Interest; Recreation Site; Cave, Cavern
Historic Site; Ruins; Wall, Walls; Church, Abbey; Temple; Scientific Station; Airport
Port; Lighthouse; Mine; Tunnel; Dam, Bridge

Manicoré, Rio- 54 Fe 5.51 S 61.19 W
Manicouagan 42 Kg 49.10 N 68.15 W
Manicouagan 42 Kf 51.00 N 68.20 W
Manicouagan, Réservoir- 38 Md 51.30 N 68.19 W
Manigotagan 45 Ha 51.06 N 96.18 W
Manihi Atoll 57 Mf 14.24 S 145.56 W
Manihiki Anchorage 64n Ab 10.23 S 161.03 W
Manihiki Atoll 57 Kf 10.24 S 161.01 W
Manika, Plateau de la- 36 Ed 10.00 S 26.00 E
Manila [Phil.] 22 Oh 14.35 N 121.00 E
Manila [Ut.-U.S.] 46 Kf 40.59 N 109.43 W
Manila Bay 21 Oh 14.30 N 120.45 E
Manilaid/Manilajd 8 Kf 58.08 N 24.03 E
Manilajd/Manilaid 8 Kf 58.08 N 24.03 E
Manily 20 Ld 62.30 N 165.20 E
Maningrida Settlement 59 Gb 12.05 S 134.10 E
Maniouro, Pointe- 63b Dc 17.41 S 168.35 E
Manipa, Selat- 26 Ig 3.20 S 127.23 E
Manipur [3] 25 Id 25.00 N 94.00 E
Manipur 25 Id 22.52 N 94.05 E
Manisa 23 Cb 38.36 N 27.26 E
Manisa Dağı 15 Kk 38.33 N 27.28 E
Manises 13 Le 39.29 N 0.27 W
Manissau a-Missu, Rio- 54 Hf 10.58 S 53.20 W
Manistee 44 Dc 44.15 N 86.18 W
Manistee River 44 Dc 44.15 N 86.21 W
Manistique 43 Jb 45.57 N 86.15 W
Manitique Lake 44 Eb 46.15 N 85.45 W
Manitoba [3] 42 Hf 55.00 N 97.00 W
Manitoba, Lake- 38 Jd 51.00 N 98.45 W
Manitou Islands 44 Ec 45.10 N 86.00 W
Manitou Lake 44 Gc 45.48 N 82.00 W
Manitoulin Island 42 Jg 45.45 N 82.30 W
Manitou Springs 45 Dg 38.52 N 104.55 W
Manitouwadge 45 Nb 49.08 N 85.47 W
Manitowoc 43 Jc 44.06 N 87.40 W
Manitsoq/Sukkertoppen 41 Ge 65.25 N 53.00 W
Maniwaki 42 Jg 46.23 N 75.58 W
Manizales 53 Ie 5.05 N 75.32 W
Manja 17 Jd 64.23 N 60.50 E
Manja 37 Gd 21.23 S 44.20 E
Manjača 14 Lf 44.35 N 17.05 E
Manjacaze 37 Ed 24.42 S 33.33 E
Manjakandriana 37 Hc 18.55 S 47.47 E
Manji 29a Bb 43.09 N 141.59 E
Manjimup 59 Df 34.14 S 116.09 E
Mānjra 25 Fe 18.49 N 77.52 E
Män Kät 25 Jd 22.05 N 98.01 E
Mankato [Ks.-U.S.] 45 Gg 39.47 N 98.12 W
Mankato [Mn.-U.S.] 43 Ic 44.10 N 94.01 W
Mankono 34 Dd 8.04 N 6.12 W
Mankono [3] 34 Dd 7.58 N 6.02 W
Mankoya 31 Jj 14.50 S 25.00 E
Manley Hot Springs 40 Ic 65.00 N 150.37 W
Manlleu 13 Ob 42.00 N 2.17 E
Manmād 25 Ed 20.15 N 74.27 E
Manmanoc, Mount- 26 Hc 17.40 N 121.06 E
Manna 26 Dh 4.27 S 102.55 E
Mannahill 59 Hf 32.26 S 139.59 E
Mannar 25 Fg 8.59 N 79.54 E
Mannar, Gulf of- 21 Ji 8.30 N 79.00 E
Mannheim 6 Gf 49.29 N 8.28 E
Manning [Alta.-Can.] 42 Fe 56.55 N 117.33 W
Manning [S.C.-U.S.] 44 Gi 33.42 N 80.12 W
Manning, Cape- 64g Ba 2.02 N 157.26 W
Manning Strait 63a Db 7.24 S 158.04 E
Manningtree 12 Dc 51.57 N 1.04 E
Mann Ranges 59 Fe 26.00 S 129.30 E
Mann River 59 Gb 12.20 S 134.07 E
Mannu, Capo- 14 Cj 40.02 N 8.22 E
Mannu, Rio- [It.] 14 Cj 40.50 N 8.23 E
Mannu, Rio- [It.] 14 Cj 40.41 N 8.59 E
Mano 34 Cd 6.56 N 11.31 W
Mano [Jap.] 29 Fc 37.58 N 138.20 E
Mano [S.L.] 34 Cd 7.55 N 12.00 W
Manoa 54 Ee 9.40 S 65.27 W
Man of War, Cayos- 49 Fg 13.02 N 83.22 W
Manokwari 58 Ee 2.30 S 134.36 E
Manombo 37 Gd 22.55 S 43.28 E
Manompana 37 Hc 16.41 S 49.45 E
Manonga 36 Fc 4.08 S 34.12 E
Manono 31 Ji 7.18 S 27.25 E
Manono 65c Aa 13.50 S 172.05 W
Manosque 11 Lk 43.50 N 5.47 E
Manouane, Lac- 42 Kf 50.40 N 70.45 W
Mano-Wan 29 Fc 37.55 N 138.15 E
Manp'ojin 28 Id 41.09 N 126.17 E
Manra Atoll (Sydney) 57 Je 4.27 S 171.15 W
Manresa 13 Nc 41.44 N 1.50 E
Mansa 31 Jj 11.12 S 28.53 E
Mansa Konko 34 Bc 13.28 N 15.33 W
Mansel 38 Lc 62.00 N 79.50 W
Mansfield [Austl.] 59 Jg 37.03 S 146.05 E
Mansfield [Eng.-U.K.] 9 Lh 53.09 N 1.11 W
Mansfield [La.-U.S.] 45 Jj 32.02 N 93.43 W
Mansfield [Oh.-U.S.] 43 Kc 40.46 N 82.31 W
Mansfield [Pa.-U.S.] 44 Ie 41.47 N 77.05 W
Mansfield, Mount- 44 Kc 44.33 N 72.49 W
Mansle 11 Gi 45.52 N 0.11 E
Manso, Rio- 55 Db 14.42 S 56.16 W
Manso, Rio- ou Mortes, Rio das- 52 Kg 11.45 S 50.44 W
Mansôa 34 Bc 12.04 N 15.19 W
Mansourah 13 Qh 36.04 N 4.28 E
Mansourah, Djebel- 13 Qh 36.02 N 4.28 E
Manta 54 Bd 0.57 S 80.42 W
Manta, Bahia de- 54 Bd 0.50 S 80.40 W
Mantalingajan, Mount- 26 Ge 8.48 N 117.40 E
Manteca 46 Eh 37.48 N 121.13 W
Mantecal [Ven.] 50 Di 6.52 N 65.38 W
Mantecal [Ven.] 50 Bi 7.33 N 69.09 W
Manteigas 13 Ed 40.24 N 7.32 W
Manteo 44 Jh 35.55 N 75.40 W
Mantes-la-Jolie 11 Hf 48.59 N 1.43 E
Manti 46 Jg 39.16 N 111.38 W
Mantiqueira, Serra da- 52 Lh 22.00 S 44.45 W
Manto 49 Df 14.55 N 86.23 W
Manton 44 Ec 44.24 N 85.24 W
Mantova 14 Ee 45.09 N 10.48 E
Mäntsälä 8 Kd 60.38 N 25.20 E
Mänttä 7 Fe 62.02 N 24.38 E
Mantua 49 Eb 22.17 N 84.17 W
Manturovo 19 Ed 58.22 N 44.44 E
Mäntyharju 7 Gf 61.25 N 26.53 E
Mäntyluoto 8 Ic 61.35 N 21.29 E
Manu 54 Df 12.15 S 70.50 W
Manuae Atoll 57 Lf 19.21 S 158.56 W
Manua Islands 57 Kf 14.13 S 169.35 W
Manuangi Atoll 57 Mf 19.12 S 141.16 W
Manūbah 14 En 36.48 N 10.06 E
Manuel 48 Jf 22.44 N 98.19 W
Manuel Alves, Rio- 54 If 11.19 S 48.28 W
Manuel Bonavides 48 Hc 29.05 N 103.55 W
Manuel Derqui 55 Ch 27.50 S 58.48 W
Manuel J. Cobo 55 Dl 35.49 S 57.54 W
Manuel Ocampo 55 Bk 33.46 S 60.39 W
Manuga Reefs 63a Ad 11.00 S 153.21 E
Manui, Pulau- 26 Hg 3.35 S 123.08 E
Manujān 24 Qi 27.24 N 57.32 E
Mānūk, Tell- 24 Hf 33.10 N 38.50 E
Manukau 58 Ih 36.56 S 174.56 E
Manulu Lagoon 64g Bb 1.56 N 157.20 W
Manus Island 57 Fe 2.05 S 147.00 E
Many 45 Jk 31.34 N 93.29 W
Manyara, Lake- 36 Gc 3.35 S 35.50 E
Manyas 24 Bb 40.02 N 27.58 E
Manyč 5 Kf 47.15 N 40.00 E
Manyč-Gudilo, Ozero- 5 Kf 46.25 N 42.35 E
Manyoni 36 Fd 5.45 S 34.50 E
Manzanal, Puerto del- 13 Fb 42.32 N 6.10 W
Manzanares 13 Ie 39.00 N 3.22 W
Manzaneda, Cabeza de- 13 Eb 42.20 N 7.15 W
Manzanilla 13 Fg 37.23 N 6.25 W
Manzanillo [Cuba] 39 Lg 20.21 N 77.07 W
Manzanillo [Mex.] 39 Ih 19.03 N 104.20 W
Manzanillo, Bahia de- [Dom.Rep.] 49 Ld 19.45 N 71.46 W
Manzanillo, Bahia de- [Mex.] 48 Gh 19.04 N 104.25 W
Manzanillo, Punta- 49 Hi 9.38 N 79.32 W
Manzano Mountains 45 Ci 34.45 N 106.20 W
Manzhouli 22 Ne 49.33 N 117.28 E
Manzilah, Buḩayrat al- 24 Eg 31.15 N 32.00 E
Manzil Bū Ruqaybah 32 Ib 37.10 N 9.48 E
Manzil bū Zalafah 14 En 36.41 N 10.35 E
Manzil Tamīn 14 En 36.47 N 10.59 E
Manzini 37 Ee 26.29 S 31.22 E
Mao 63b Dc 17.29 S 168.29 E
Mao [Chad] 31 Ig 14.07 N 15.19 E
Mao [Dom.Rep.] 47 Je 19.34 N 71.05 W
Mao/Mahón 13 Qe 39.53 N 4.15 E
Maoke, Pegunungan- 57 Ee 4.00 S 138.00 E
Maomao Shan 27 Hd 37.12 N 103.10 E
Maoming 22 Ng 21.41 N 110.52 E
Maoniu Shan 27 He 32.50 N 104.12 E
Maotou Shan 27 Hg 24.31 N 100.38 E
Maouri, Dallol- 34 Fc 12.05 N 3.32 E
Mapai 37 Ed 22.51 S 31.58 E
Mapanda 36 Gd 9.32 S 24.16 E
Mapati 36 Bc 3.38 S 13.21 E
Mapi 58 Ee 7.05 S 139.23 E
Mapi 26 Kh 7.00 S 139.16 E
Mapia, Kepulauan- 26 Jf 0.50 N 134.20 E
Mapimi, Bolsón de- 38 Ig 27.30 N 103.15 W
Mapinhane 37 Fd 22.15 S 35.07 E
Mapire 50 Di 7.45 N 64.42 W
Mapiri 54 Eg 15.15 S 68.10 W
Maple Creek 42 Gg 49.55 N 109.27 W
Maprik 60 Ch 3.38 S 143.03 E
Mapuera, Rio- 54 Gd 1.05 S 57.02 W
Maputo [3] 37 Ee 26.00 S 32.30 E
Maputo (Lourenço Marques) 31 Kk 25.58 S 32.34 E
Maputo, Baia de- 30 Kk 26.05 S 33.00 E
Maqên (Dawu) 27 He 34.29 N 100.01 E
Maqran, Wādī al- 23 Ie 20.55 N 47.12 E
Maqu 27 He 34.05 N 101.45 E
Maquan He/Damqog Kanbab 27 Df 29.36 N 84.09 E
Maquela do Zombo 31 Ii 6.03 S 15.08 E
Maquinchao 56 Gf 41.15 S 68.44 W
Maquoketa 45 Ke 42.04 N 90.40 W
Mar, Serra do- 55 Lh 25.00 S 48.00 W
Mara 36 Fc 1.31 S 33.56 E
Mara [3] 36 Fc 2.30 S 34.00 E
Maraã 54 Ed 1.50 S 65.22 W
Marab 35 Fc 14.54 N 37.55 E
Marabá 54 Ie 5.21 S 49.07 W
Marabahan 26 Fg 3.00 S 114.45 E
Marabá Paulista 55 Gf 22.06 S 51.56 W
Maraca, Ilha de- 54 Hc 2.05 N 50.25 W
Maracaibo 53 Id 10.40 N 71.37 W
Maracaibo, Lago de- = Maracaibo, Lake- (EN) 52 Ie 9.50 N 71.30 W
Maracaibo, Lake- (EN) = Maracaibo, Lago de- 52 Ie 9.50 N 71.30 W
Maracaju 54 Gh 21.38 S 55.09 W
Maracaju, Serra de- [Braz.] 52 Kh 21.00 S 55.00 W
Maracaju, Serra de- [S.Amer.] 55 Ef 23.57 S 55.01 W
Maracanã 54 Id 0.46 S 47.27 W
Maracás 54 Jf 13.26 S 40.27 W
Maracay 53 Jd 10.15 N 67.36 W
Marādah 33 Cd 29.14 N 19.13 E
Maradi 31 Hg 13.29 N 7.06 E
Maradi [2] 34 Gc 14.15 N 7.15 E
Marāgheh 23 Gb 37.23 N 46.40 E
Marāh 23 Gd 25.04 N 45.28 E
Maraho 35 Bb 18.21 N 17.28 E
Marahuaca, Cerro- 54 Ec 3.34 N 65.27 W
Marajó, Baia de- 52 Lf 1.00 S 48.30 W
Marajó, Ilha de- 52 Lf 1.00 S 49.30 W
Marakei Atoll 57 Id 1.58 N 173.25 E
Maralal 36 Gb 1.06 N 36.42 E
Maralinga 59 Gf 30.13 S 131.35 E
Maralwexi/Bachu 27 Cd 39.46 N 78.15 E
Maramag 26 He 7.46 N 125.00 E
Maramasike Island 60 Gi 9.30 S 161.25 E
Maramba 31 Jj 17.51 S 25.52 E
Marampa 34 Cd 8.41 N 12.28 W
Maramureş [2] 15 Gb 47.40 N 24.00 E
Maranchón 13 Jc 41.03 N 2.12 W
Marand 23 Gb 38.26 N 45.46 E
Marandellas 37 Ec 18.10 S 31.36 E
Marang 26 De 5.12 N 103.13 E
Maranhão [2] 54 Je 5.00 S 45.00 W
Maranhão, Rio- 54 If 14.34 S 49.02 W
Marano, Laguna di- 14 He 45.44 N 13.10 E
Maranoa River 59 Je 27.50 S 148.37 E
Marañón, Rio- 52 If 4.30 S 73.35 W
Marans 11 Fh 46.18 N 1.00 W
Marão 37 Ed 24.18 S 34.07 E
Marão, Serra do- 13 Ec 41.15 N 7.55 W
Maraoué 34 Dd 6.54 N 5.31 W
Marapanim 54 Id 0.42 S 47.42 W
Marapi, Gunung- 26 Dg 0.23 S 100.28 E
Marargiu, Capo- 14 Cj 40.20 N 8.23 E
Marari, Serra do- 55 Gh 27.30 S 51.00 W
Mara Rosa 55 Ha 13.58 S 49.09 W
Mărăşeşti 15 Kd 45.53 N 27.14 E
Maratea 14 Jk 39.59 N 15.43 E
Marathón 15 Gk 38.09 N 23.58 E
Marathon 45 Ek 30.12 N 103.15 W
Marathon 42 Ig 48.46 N 86.26 W
Maratua, Pulau- 26 Gf 2.15 N 118.36 E
Marau 55 Fi 28.27 S 52.12 W
Maravari 63a Cb 7.54 S 156.44 E
Marāveh Tappeh 24 Pd 37.55 N 55.57 E
Maravilha 55 Fh 26.47 S 53.09 W
Maravillas Creek 45 El 29.34 N 102.47 W
Maravovo 63a Dc 9.17 S 159.38 E
Marāwah 33 Dc 32.29 N 21.25 E
Marawi 26 He 8.13 N 124.15 E
Marawī 35 Eb 18.29 N 31.49 E
Marāwiḩ 24 Oj 24.18 N 53.18 E
Marayes 56 Gd 31.29 S 67.20 W
Marbella 13 Hh 36.31 N 4.53 W
Marble Bar 59 Dd 21.11 S 119.44 E
Marble Canyon 46 Jh 36.30 N 111.50 W
Marble Falls 45 Gk 30.34 N 98.17 W
Marble Hall 37 Dd 24.57 S 29.13 E
Marburg an der Lahn 10 Ef 50.49 N 8.46 E
Marca, Ponta da- 30 Ij 16.31 S 11.42 E
Marcal 10 Ni 47.38 N 17.32 E
Marcala 49 Df 14.07 N 88.00 W
Marçal Dağlari 15 Kl 37.09 N 28.00 E
Marcali 10 Nj 46.35 N 17.25 E
March 10 Mh 48.10 N 16.59 E
March 9 Ni 52.33 N 0.06 E
Marche 11 Hh 46.10 N 1.30 E
Marche = Marches (EN) [2] 14 Hh 43.30 N 13.15 E
Marche, Plateau de la- 11 Hh 46.16 N 1.30 E
Marche-en-Famenne 11 Ld 50.14 N 5.20 E
Marchena 13 Gg 37.20 N 5.24 W
Marchena, Isla- 54a Aa 0.20 N 90.30 W
Marches (EN) = Marche [2] 14 Hh 43.30 N 13.15 E
Marchesato 14 Kk 39.05 N 17.00 E
Marchfeld 14 Kb 48.15 N 16.40 E
Mar Chiquita, Laguna- 55 Dm 37.37 S 57.24 W
Mar Chiquita, Laguna- 52 Ji 30.42 S 62.36 W
Marciana Marina 14 Eh 42.48 N 10.12 E
Marcigny 11 Kh 46.16 N 4.02 E
Marcilly-sur-Eure 12 Df 48.49 N 1.21 E
Marcinelle, Charleroi- 12 Gd 50.25 N 4.28 E
Marck 12 Dd 50.57 N 1.57 E
Marcoing 12 Fd 50.07 N 3.11 E
Marcos Juaréz 56 Hd 32.42 S 62.06 W
Marcus Baker, Mount- 40 Jd 61.26 N 147.45 W
Marcus Island (EN) = Minami-Tori-Shima 57 Gb 26.32 N 142.09 E
Marcy, Mount- 43 Mc 44.07 N 73.56 W
Mardakert 16 Oi 40.12 N 46.52 E
Mardakjan 16 Qi 40.29 N 50.12 E
Mardān 25 Eb 34.09 N 71.52 E
Mardarovka 15 Mb 47.30 N 29.40 E
Mar del Plata 53 Ki 38.01 S 57.35 W
Marden 12 Cc 51.10 N 0.30 E
Mardin 23 Fb 37.18 N 40.44 E
Mardın Dağları 24 Id 37.20 N 41.00 E
Maré, Ile- 57 Hg 21.30 S 168.00 E
Mare, Muntele- 15 Gc 46.29 N 23.14 E
Marechal Cândido Rondon 55 Eg 24.34 S 54.04 W
Maree, Loch- 9 Hd 57.40 N 5.30 W
Mareeba 59 Jc 17.00 S 145.26 E
Marēg 35 He 3.47 N 47.18 E
Maremma 14 Fh 42.30 N 11.30 E
Marennes 11 Ei 45.49 N 1.07 W
Marettimo 14 Gm 37.56 N 12.05 E
Mareuil-en-Brie 12 Ff 48.57 N 3.45 E
Marfa 43 Ge 30.18 N 104.01 W
Marfil, Laguna- 55 Bb 15.30 S 60.20 W
Margai Caka 27 Ed 35.10 N 86.55 E
Marganec 19 Df 47.38 N 34.40 E
Margaret River 59 Df 33.57 S 115.04 E
Margarida 55 De 21.41 S 56.44 W
Margarita, Isla de- 54 Fa 11.00 N 64.00 W
Margarita Belén 55 Ch 27.16 S 58.58 W
Margaritovo 15 Dj 39.21 N 20.26 E
Margate [Eng.-U.K.] 9 Oj 51.24 N 1.24 E
Margate [S.Afr.] 37 Ef 30.55 S 30.15 E
Margeride, Monts de la- 11 Jj 44.50 N 3.25 E
Marghera, Venezia- 14 Ge 45.28 N 12.44 E
Margherita di Savoia 14 Ki 41.22 N 16.09 E
Marghine, Catena del- 14 Cj 40.20 N 8.50 E
Marghita 15 Fb 47.21 N 22.20 E
Marghūb, Kūh-e- 24 Qf 33.06 N 57.30 E
Margilan 19 Hg 40.28 N 71.46 E
Margina 15 Fd 45.51 N 22.16 E
Marguerite Bay 66 Qe 68.30 S 68.30 W
Margut 12 He 49.35 N 5.16 E
Marha 20 Hd 60.35 N 123.10 E
Marha 21 Nc 63.20 N 118.50 E
Mari 24 Ie 34.39 N 40.53 E
Mari 24 Ee 34.44 N 33.18 E
Maria Atoll [W.F.] 57 Ng 22.00 S 136.10 W
Maria Atoll [W.F.] 57 Lg 21.48 S 154.41 W
Maria Cleofas, Isla- 48 Fg 21.16 N 106.14 W
Maria Elena 56 Gb 22.21 S 69.40 W
Mariager 8 Ch 56.39 N 10.00 E
Mariager Fjord 8 Dh 56.40 N 10.20 E
Maria Grande, Arroyo- 55 Ci 29.21 S 58.45 W
Maria Ignacia 55 Cm 37.24 S 59.30 W
Maria Island [Austl.] 59 Jh 42.40 S 148.05 E
Maria Island [Austl.] 59 Hb 14.55 S 135.40 E
Maria Island [St.Luc.] 51k Bb 13.44 N 60.56 W
Mariakani 36 Gc 3.52 S 39.28 E
Maria Laach 12 Jd 50.25 N 7.15 E
Maria Madre, Isla- 48 Fg 21.35 N 106.33 W
Maria Magdalena, Isla- 48 Fg 21.25 N 106.25 W
Mariana Islands 57 Fc 16.00 N 145.30 E
Marianao 47 Hd 23.05 N 82.26 W
Mariana Trench (EN) 3 Ih 14.00 N 147.30 E
Marianna [Ar.-U.S.] 45 Ki 34.46 N 90.46 W
Marianna [Fl.-U.S.] 44 Ej 30.47 N 85.14 W
Mariannelund 8 Fg 57.37 N 15.34 E
Mariano I. Loza 55 Ci 29.22 S 58.12 W
Mariánské Lázně 10 Ig 49.58 N 12.43 E
Marias, Islas- 38 Ig 21.25 N 106.28 W
Marias Pass 46 Ib 48.19 N 113.21 W
Marias River 43 Eb 47.56 N 110.30 W
Maria Theresa Reef 57 Lh 36.58 S 151.23 W
Mariato, Punta- 47 Hg 7.13 N 80.53 W
Maria van Diemen, Cape- 62 Ea 34.29 S 172.39 E
Mariazell 14 Jc 47.46 N 15.19 E
Ma'rib 23 Gf 15.30 N 45.21 E
Maribo 8 Dj 54.46 N 11.31 E
Maribor 14 Jd 46.33 N 15.39 E
Marica 5 Ig 40.52 N 26.12 E
Marica 15 Ig 42.02 N 25.50 E
Maricao 51a Bb 18.10 N 66.58 W
Maricopa 46 Ij 33.04 N 112.03 W
Maricourt 42 Kd 61.36 N 71.57 W
Marīdī 35 Dd 6.05 N 29.24 E
Marīdī 35 De 4.55 N 29.28 E
Marié, Rio- 54 Ed 0.25 S 66.26 W
Marie Byrd Land (EN) 66 Nf 80.00 S 120.00 W
Mariec 7 Lh 56.31 N 49.51 E
Marie Galante 47 Le 15.56 N 61.16 W
Marie-Galante, Canal de- 51e Bc 15.55 N 61.25 W
Mariehamn/Maarianhamina 7 Ef 60.06 N 19.57 E
Marie Louise Island 37b Bb 6.11 S 53.09 E
Mariembourg, Couvin- 12 Gd 50.06 N 4.31 E
Marienburg 12 Jd 50.04 N 7.08 E
Marienmünster 12 Lc 51.50 N 9.13 E
Marienstatt 12 Jd 50.40 N 7.49 E
Mariental 31 Ik 24.36 S 17.59 E
Mariestad 7 Cg 58.43 N 13.51 E
Marietta [Ga.-U.S.] 43 Ke 33.57 N 84.33 W
Marietta [Oh.-U.S.] 44 Gf 39.26 N 81.27 W
Mariga 34 Gd 9.36 N 5.57 E
Marignac 11 Gl 42.55 N 0.39 E
Marignane 11 Lk 43.25 N 5.13 E
Marigot [Dom.] 50 Fe 15.32 N 61.18 W
Marigot [Guad.] 50 Ec 18.04 N 63.06 W
Marigot [Haiti] 49 Kd 18.14 N 72.19 W
Marigot [Mart.] 51h Ab 14.49 N 61.02 W
Marigot [St.Luc.] 51k Ab 13.58 N 61.02 W
Mariinsk 20 De 56.13 N 87.45 E
Mariinski Posad 7 Lh 56.08 N 47.48 E
Mariinskoje 20 Jf 51.43 N 140.19 E
Marijovo 15 Eh 41.04 N 21.45 E
Marijskaja ASSR [3] 19 Ed 56.40 N 48.00 E
Marilia 56 Jb 22.13 S 50.01 W
Mariluz 55 Fg 24.02 S 53.13 W
Marimba 36 Cd 8.22 S 17.02 E
Marimbondo, Cachoeira do- 55 He 20.18 S 49.10 W
Marin 13 Db 42.23 N 8.42 W
Marin, Cul-de-Sac du- 51h Bc 14.27 N 60.53 W
Marina di Catanzaro 14 Kl 38.49 N 16.36 E
Marina di Gioiosa Ionica 14 Kl 38.18 N 16.20 E
Marina di Pisa 14 Eg 43.40 N 10.16 E
Marina di Ravenna 14 Gf 44.29 N 12.17 E
Marina Gorka 19 Ce 53.31 N 28.12 E
Marinduque 26 Hd 13.24 N 121.58 E
Marineland 44 Gk 29.43 N 81.12 W
Marines 12 De 49.09 N 1.59 E
Marinette 43 Jb 45.06 N 87.38 W
Maringá 53 Kh 23.25 S 51.55 W
Maringa 30 Ih 1.14 N 19.48 E
Marinha Grande 13 De 39.45 N 8.56 W
Marino [It.] 14 Gi 41.46 N 12.39 E
Marino [Van.] 63b Db 14.59 S 168.03 E
Marins, Pico dos- 55 Jf 22.27 S 45.10 W
Marinsko 8 Mf 58.46 N 28.39 E
Marion 30 Km 46.36 S 37.55 E
Marion [Al.-U.S.] 44 Di 32.38 N 87.26 W
Marion [Ia.-U.S.] 45 Ke 42.02 N 91.36 W
Marion [Il.-U.S.] 45 Lh 37.44 N 88.56 W
Marion [In.-U.S.] 44 Ee 40.33 N 85.40 W
Marion [Oh.-U.S.] 43 Kc 40.35 N 83.08 W
Marion [S.C.-U.S.] 44 Hh 34.11 N 79.23 W
Marion [Va.-U.S.] 44 Gg 36.51 N 81.30 W
Marion, Lake- 44 Gi 33.30 N 80.25 W
Marion Reefs 57 Gf 19.10 S 152.20 E
Maripa 54 Ea 7.26 N 65.09 W
Mariposa 46 Fh 37.29 N 119.58 W
Mariquita, Cerro- 48 Jf 23.13 N 98.22 W
Marisa 26 Hf 0.28 N 121.56 E
Mariscala 55 El 34.03 S 54.47 W
Mariscal Estigarribia 56 Hb 22.02 S 60.38 W
Maritime [3] 34 Fd 6.30 N 1.20 E
Mariusa, Caño 50 Fh 9.43 N 61.26 W
Mariusa, Isla- 50 Fh 9.39 N 61.19 W
Marīvan 24 Le 35.31 N 46.10 E
Märjamaa/Marjamaa 8 Kf 58.54 N 24.21 E
Marjamaa/Märjamaa 8 Kf 58.54 N 24.21 E
Marjanovka [R.S.F.S.R.] 19 He 54.58 N 72.38 E
Marjanovka [Ukr.-U.S.S.R.] 10 Uf 50.23 N 24.55
Mark 12 Gc 51.39 N 4.39
Mark [F.R.G.] 12 Jc 51.13 N 7.36
Mark [Swe.] 8 Eg 57.35 N 12.35
Marka 31 Lh 1.43 N 44.46
Markako, Ozero- 19 If 48.45 N 85.50
Markala 34 Dc 13.39 N 6.05
Markam (Gartog) 27 Gf 29.32 N 98.33
Markaryd 7 Ch 56.26 N 13.36
Marken 12 Hb 52.27 N 5.05
Markerwaard 12 Hb 52.31 N 5.15
Market Deeping 12 Bb 52.40 N 0.18
Market Harborough 9 Mi 52.29 N 0.55
Markham, Mount- 66 Kg 82.51 S 161.21
Markham Bay 42 Kd 63.30 N 71.40
Markham River 59 Ja 6.35 S 146.25
Marki 10 Rd 52.20 N 21.07
Märkische Schweiz 10 Jd 52.35 N 14.00
Markit 27 Cd 38.53 N 77.35
Markounda 35 Bd 7.37 N 16.59
Markovac 15 Ee 44.14 N 21.06
Markovka 16 Ke 49.31 N 39.32
Markovo 22 Tc 64.40 N 170.25
Markoye 34 Fc 14.39 N 0.02
Marksburg 12 Jd 50.16 N 7.40
Marksville 45 Jk 31.08 N 92.04
Marktoberdorf 10 Gi 47.47 N 10.37
Marktredwitz 10 If 50.00 N 12.05
Markuleśty 15 Lb 47.51 N 28.07
Marl 10 De 51.39 N 7.05
Marlagne 12 Gd 50.25 N 4.40
Marlborough [2] 62 Ed 41.50 S 173.40
Marlborough [Austl.] 59 Jd 22.49 S 149.53
Marlborough [Guy.] 50 Gi 7.29 N 58.38
Marle 11 Je 49.44 N 3.46
Marlin 45 Hk 31.18 N 96.53
Marlinton 44 Gf 38.14 N 80.06
Marlow [Eng.-U.K.] 12 Bc 51.34 N 0.46
Marlow [Ok.-U.S.] 45 Hi 34.39 N 97.57
Marmande 11 Gj 44.30 N 0.10
Marmara 24 Bb 40.35 N 27.33
Marmara, Sea of- (EN) = Marmara Denizi 5 Ig 40.40 N 28.15
Marmara Adasi 24 Bb 40.38 N 27.37
Marmara Denizi = Marmara, Sea of- (EN) 5 Ig 40.40 N 28.15
Marmara Ereğlisi 15 Ki 40.58 N 27.57
Marmara Gölü 15 Lk 38.37 N 28.02
Marmarica (EN) = Barqah al Bahrīyah 30 Je 31.40 N 24.30
Marmaris 23 Cb 36.51 N 28.16
Marmelos, Rio- 54 Fe 6.08 S 61.47
Marmion Lake 45 Kb 48.54 N 91.30
Marmolada 14 Fd 46.26 N 11.51
Marmora 44 Ic 44.29 N 77.41
Marmore, Cascata delle- 14 Gh 42.35 N 12.45
Marne 10 Ec 53.57 N 9.00
Marne 5 Gf 48.49 N 2.24
Marne [3] 11 Kf 48.55 N 4.10
Marne à la Saône, Canal de la- 11 Kf 48.44 N 4.36
Marne au Rhin, Canal de la- 11 Nf 48.35 N 7.47
Mārnes 7 Dc 67.09 N 14.06
Marneuli 16 Ni 41.29 N 44.45
Maro 35 Bd 8.25 N 18.46
Maro 35 Bb 19.23 N 16.38
Maroa 54 Ec 2.43 N 67.33
Maroantsetra 31 Lj 15.27 S 49.44
Marokau Atoll 61 Mc 18.02 S 142.17
Marolambo 37 Hd 20.04 S 48.08
Maromandia 37 Hb 14.11 S 48.06
Maromme 11 He 49.28 N 1.02
Maromokotro 37 Hb 14.01 S 48.58
Maroni, Fleuve- 52 Ke 5.45 N 53.58
Marónia 15 Ii 40.55 N 25.31
Maronne 11 Hi 45.04 N 1.56
Maroochydore 59 Ke 26.39 S 153.06
Maro Reef 57 Jb 25.25 N 170.35
Maros 26 Dc 46.15 N 20.12
Maros 26 Gg 5.00 S 119.34
Maroua 31 Ig 10.36 N 14.20
Marovoay 37 Hc 16.06 S 46.37
Marowijne Rivier 54 Hb 5.45 N 53.58
Marqādah 24 Ie 35.44 N 40.46
Mar Qu 27 He 31.58 N 101.54
Marquard 37 De 28.54 S 27.28
Marquenterre 12 Dd 50.20 N 1.41
Marquesas Islands (EN) = Marquises, Iles- 57 Ne 9.00 S 139.30
Marquette 43 Jb 46.33 N 87.24
Marquion 12 Fd 50.13 N 3.05
Marquis [Gren.] 51p Bb 12.06 N 61.37
Marquis [St.Luc.] 51k Ba 14.02 N 60.55
Marquis, Cape- 51k Ba 14.03 N 60.54
Marquise 12 Dd 50.49 N 1.42
Marquises, Iles- = Marquesas Islands (EN) 57 Ne 9.00 S 139.30
Marracuene 37 Ee 25.44 S 32.41
Marradi 14 Ff 44.04 N 11.37
Marrah, Jabal- 30 Jg 13.04 N 24.21
Marrak 33 Hf 16.26 N 41.54
Marrakech 31 Ge 31.38 N 8.00
Marrakech [3] 32 Fc 32.00 N 8.00
Marrawah 59 Ih 40.56 S 144.41
Marree 58 Eg 29.39 S 138.04
Marreh, Kūh-e- 24 Oh 29.15 N 52.20
Marrero 45 Kl 29.54 N 90.07
Marresalja 17 Mb 69.44 N 66.59
Marresalskije Koški, Ostrova- 17 Mb 69.30 N 67.10
Marromeu 37 Fc 18.17 S 35.56
Marrti 7 Gc 67.28 N 28.22
Marrupa 37 Fb 13.12 S 37.30
Marsá al 'Alam 33 Fd 25.05 N 34.54
Marsá al Burayqah 33 Cc 30.25 N 19.35

Index Symbols

[1] Independent Nation
[2] State, Region
[3] District, County
[4] Municipality
[5] Colony, Dependency
Continent
Physical Region
Historical or Cultural Region
Mount, Mountain
Volcano
Hill
Mountains, Mountain Range
Hills, Escarpment
Plateau, Upland
Pass, Gap
Plain, Lowland
Delta
Salt Flat
Valley, Canyon
Crater, Cave
Karst Features
Depression
Polder
Desert, Dunes
Forest, Woods
Heath, Steppe
Oasis
Cape, Point
Coast, Beach
Cliff
Peninsula
Isthmus
Sandbank
Island
Atoll
Rock, Reef
Islands, Archipelago
Rocks, Reefs
Coral Reef
Well, Spring
Geyser
River, Stream
Waterfall Rapids
River Mouth, Estuary
Lake
Salt Lake
Intermittent Lake
Reservoir
Swamp, Pond
Canal
Glacier
Ice Shelf, Pack Ice
Ocean
Sea
Gulf, Bay
Strait, Fjord
Lagoon
Bank
Seamount
Tablemount
Ridge
Shelf
Basin
Escarpment, Sea Scarp
Fracture
Trench, Abyss
National Park, Reserve
Point of Interest
Recreation Site
Cave, Cavern
Historic Site
Ruins
Wall, Walls
Church, Abbey
Temple
Scientific Station
Airport
Port
Lighthouse
Mine
Tunnel
Dam, Bridge

Name	Map	Grid	Lat	Long
arsá al Uwayjah	33	Cc	30.55N	17.52 E
arsa Ben Mehidi	13	Ji	35.05N	2.11W
arsabit	31	Kh	2.20N	37.59 E
arsala	14	Gm	37.48N	12.26 E
arsá Shaʿb	35	Fa	22.52N	35.47 E
arsá Umm Ghayj	24	Fj	25.38N	34.30 E
arsberg	10	Ee	51.27N	8.51 E
arsciano	14	Gd	42.54N	12.20 E
arsdiep	12	Gb	52.58N	4.45 E
arseille = Marseilles (EN)	6	Gg	43.18N	5.24 E
arseille-en-Beauvaisis	11	Je	49.35N	1.57 E
arseilles (EN) = Marseille	6	Gg	43.18N	5.24 E
arshall [Ak.-U.S.]	40	Gd	61.52N	162.04W
arshall [Ar.-U.S.]	45	Ji	35.55N	92.38W
arshall [Il.-U.S.]	45	Mg	39.23N	87.42W
arshall [Lbr.]	34	Cd	6.09N	10.23W
arshall [Mn.-U.S.]	43	Hc	44.27N	95.47W
arshall [Mo.-U.S.]	45	Jg	39.07N	93.12W
arshall [Tx.-U.S.]	43	Ie	32.33N	94.23W
arshall Islands	58	Hd	9.00N	168.00 E
arshall Islands	57	Hd	9.00N	168.00 E
arshall River	59	Hd	22.59S	136.59 E
arshalltown	43	Ic	42.03N	92.54W
arshfield	45	Kd	44.40N	90.10W
arsh Harbour	47	Ic	26.33N	77.03W
arshinān, Kūh-e-	24	Of	32.53N	52.24 E
arsh Island	45	Kl	29.35N	91.53W
arsica	14	Hi	41.55N	13.35 E
arsico Nuovo	14	Jj	40.25N	15.44 E
arsjaty	17	Jf	60.05N	60.29 E
arsland	45	Ee	42.29N	103.16W
arsla-Tour	12	He	49.06N	5.54 E
arson	12	Gf	48.55N	4.32 E
arsta	8	Ge	59.37N	17.51 E
arstal	8	Dj	54.51N	10.31 E
arstrand	8	Dg	57.53N	11.35 E
arta	14	Fh	42.14N	11.42 E
artaban, Gulf of- (EN)	25	Je	16.32N	97.37 E
artap	34	Hd	6.54N	13.03 E
artapura [Indon.]	26	Dg	4.19S	104.22 E
artapura [Indon.]	26	Fg	3.25S	114.51 E
artelange/Martelingen	12	He	49.50N	5.44 E
artelingen/Martelange	12	He	49.50N	5.44 E
artes, Sierra de-	13	Le	39.20N	0.57W
artha's Vineyard	43	Md	41.25N	70.40W
artigny	14	Bd	46.06N	7.05 E
artigues	11	Lk	43.24N	5.03 E
artil	13	Gi	35.37N	5.17W
artim Vaz, Ilhas-	52	Nh	20.30S	28.51W
artin	13	Lc	41.18N	0.19W
artin [Czech.]	10	Og	49.04N	18.55 E
artin [S.D.-U.S.]	43	Gc	43.10N	101.44W
artin [Tn.-U.S.]	44	Cg	36.21N	88.51W
artina Franca	14	Lj	40.42N	17.20 E
artinez de Hoz	55	Bl	35.19S	61.37W
artinez de la Torre	48	Kg	20.04N	97.03W
artin García, Isla-	55	Cl	34.11S	58.15W
artin Hills	66	Pg	82.04S	88.01W
artinho Campos	55	Jd	19.20S	45.13W
artinique	3	Mh	14.40N	61.00W
artinique	39	Mh	14.40N	61.00W
artinique, Canal de la- = Martinique Passage (EN)				
Martinique Passage	50	Fe	15.10N	61.20W
Martinique Passage (EN) = Martinique, Canal de la-	47	Le	15.10N	61.20W
Martin Lake	44	Ei	32.50N	85.55W
Martin Peninsula	66	Of	74.25S	114.10W
Martinsburg	44	If	39.28N	77.59W
Martins Ferry	44	Ge	40.07N	80.45W
Martinsville [In.-U.S.]	44	Bf	39.26N	86.25W
Martinsville [Va.-U.S.]	43	Ld	36.43N	79.53W
Marton	62	Fd	40.05S	175.23 E
Martos	13	Ig	37.43N	3.58W
Martre, Lac la-	42	Fd	63.20N	118.00W
Martuk	19	Fe	50.47N	56.31 E
Martuni	16	Ni	40.06N	45.18 E
Maru	34	Gc	12.21N	6.24 E
Marud	25	Ee	18.19N	72.58 E
Marudi	26	Ff	4.11N	114.19 E
Marudu, Teluk-	26	Ge	6.45N	116.55 E
Marugame	29	Cd	34.18N	133.47 E
Maruko	29	Fc	36.19N	138.15 E
Mārūn	24	Mg	31.02N	49.36 E
Marungu, Monts-	30	Jf	7.42S	30.00 E
Maruoka	29	Ec	36.09N	136.16 E
Maruseppu	29a	Ca	44.01N	143.19 E
Marutea Atoll [W.F.]	57	Ng	21.30S	135.34W
Marutea Atoll [W.F.]	57	Mf	17.00S	143.10W
Maruyama-Gawa	29	Dd	35.40N	134.50 E
Marvão	13	Ge	39.24N	7.23W
Marvast	29	Pg	30.30N	54.15 E
Marvast, Kavir-e-	24	Pg	30.20N	54.25 E
Mårvatn	8	Cg	60.10N	8.15 E
Marv-Dasht	23	Hd	29.50N	52.40 E
Marvejols	11	Jj	44.33N	3.17 E
Marvine, Mount-	46	Jg	38.40N	111.39W
Marx	16	Od	51.42N	46.46 E
Mary	22	If	37.36N	61.50 E
Maryborough [Austl.]	58	Gg	25.32S	152.42 E
Maryborough [Austl.]	59	Ig	37.03S	143.45 E
Marydale	23	Ce	29.23S	22.05 E
Maryjskaja Oblast	19	Gh	37.15N	62.30 E
Maryland [2]	43	Ld	39.00N	76.45W
Maryland	34	De	4.45N	8.00W
Maryport	9	Jd	54.43N	3.30W
Mary River	59	Gb	12.53S	131.38 E
Marysville [Ca.-U.S.]	46	Eg	39.09N	121.35W
Marysville [Ks.-U.S.]	45	Hf	39.50N	96.38W
Marysville [N.B.-Can.]	44	Nc	45.59N	66.35W
Marysville [Wa.-U.S.]	46	Fd	48.03N	122.11W
Maryville [Mo.-U.S.]	45	Ic	40.21N	94.52W
Maryville [Tn.-U.S.]	44	Fh	35.46N	83.58W
Marzūq	31	If	25.55N	13.55 E

Name	Map	Grid	Lat	Long
Marzūq, Ḥamādat-	33	Bd	26.00N	12.30 E
Marzūq, Ṣaḥrā-	30	If	24.30N	13.00 E
Masachapa	49	Dh	11.47N	86.31W
Masai Steppe	30	Ki	4.45S	37.00 E
Masaka	36	Fc	0.20S	31.44 E
Masalembo, Kepulauan-	26	Fh	5.30S	114.26 E
Masalog, Puntan-	64b	Ba	15.01N	145.41 E
Masally	19	Eh	39.01N	48.40 E
Masan	27	Md	35.11N	128.24 E
Masasi	31	Kj	10.43S	38.48 E
Masaya	49	Dh	12.00N	86.10W
Masaya [3]	47	Gf	11.58N	86.06W
Masbate	21	Oh	12.15N	123.30 E
Masbate [3]	26	Hd	12.10N	123.35 E
Mascara	32	Hb	35.24N	0.08 E
Mascara [3]	32	Hb	35.30N	0.15 E
Mascarene Islands	30	Mk	21.00S	57.00 E
Mascarene Basin (EN)	3	Fk	15.00S	56.00 E
Mascarene Islands-/ Mascareignes, Iles-	30	Mk	21.00S	57.00 E
Mascarene Plateau (EN)	3	Gk	10.00S	60.00 E
Mascota	48	Gg	20.32N	104.49W
Masela, Pulau-	26	Ih	8.09S	129.50 E
Maseru	31	Jk	29.28S	27.29 E
Masfūt	24	Qk	24.48N	56.06 E
Mashaba	37	Ed	20.02S	30.29 E
Mashābih	24	Gj	25.37N	36.32 E
Mashan	28	Kb	45.12N	130.32 E
Mashhad	22	Hf	36.18N	59.36 E
Mashike	28	Pc	43.51N	141.31 E
Mashiki	29	Be	32.47N	130.50 E
Mashīz	24	Qh	29.56N	56.37 E
Mashkel	21	Ig	28.02N	63.25 E
Mashonaland North [3]	37	Ec	17.00N	31.00 E
Mashonaland South [3]	37	Ec	18.00S	31.00 E
Mashra' ar Raqq	35	Bd	8.25N	29.16 E
Mashū-Ko	29a	Db	43.35N	144.30 E
Masiaca	48	Ec	26.45N	109.18W
Masīlah, Wādī al-	21	Hh	15.10N	51.08 E
Masi-Manimba	36	Cc	4.46S	17.55 E
Masindi	36	Fb	1.42N	31.43 E
Maṣīrah, Jazīrat-	21	Hg	20.29N	58.33 E
Maṣīrah, Khalīj-	21	Hg	20.15N	57.40 E
Masisi	36	Ec	1.24S	28.49 E
Masjed-Soleymān	23	Gc	31.58N	49.18 E
Mask, Lough-/Loch	9	Dh	53.35N	9.20W
Maskanah	24	Hd	36.01N	38.05 E
Maskelynes, Iles-	63b	Cc	16.32S	167.49 E
Maslovare	14	Lf	44.34N	17.33 E
Masoala, Cap-	30	Mj	15.59S	50.13 E
Masoala, Presqu'île de-	37	Ic	15.40S	50.12 E
Mason	45	Gk	30.45N	99.14W
Mason Bay	62	Bg	46.55S	167.45 E
Mason City	39	Je	43.09N	93.12W

Name	Map	Grid	Lat	Long
Masovia (EN) = Mazowsze				
Masparro, Rio-	5	Ie	52.40N	20.20 E
Masqaṭ = Muscat (EN)	49	Mi	8.04N	69.26W
Massa	22	Hg	23.29N	58.33 E
Massachusetts [2]	14	Ef	44.01N	10.09 E
Massachusetts Bay	43	Mc	42.15N	71.50W
Massaciuccoli, Lago di-	44	Ld	42.20N	70.50W
Massafra	14	Eg	43.50N	10.20 E
Massaguet	14	Lj	40.35N	17.07 E
Massakori	35	Bc	12.28N	15.26 E
Massa Marittima	35	Bc	13.00N	15.44 E
Massangano	14	Fd	43.03N	10.53 E
Massangena	36	Bd	9.37S	14.17 E
Massape	37	Ed	21.32S	32.57 E
Massawa (EN) = Mitsiwa	54	Jd	3.31S	40.19W
Massénya	31	Kg	15.37N	39.39 E
Masset	43	Mc	44.56N	74.57W
Masseube	35	Bc	11.24N	16.10 E
Massey Sound	42	Ef	54.02N	132.09W
Massiac	11	Gk	43.26N	0.35 E
Massiaru	12	Ia	78.00N	94.00W
Massinga	11	Ji	45.15N	3.13 E
Masson Island	8	Kg	57.52N	24.27 E
Massuma	44	Gd	40.48N	81.32W
Mastābah	37	Fd	23.20S	35.22 E
Māstaga	66	Ge	66.08S	96.34 E
Masterton	36	De	14.05S	22.00 E
Mastūrah	33	Ge	20.49N	39.26 E
Masuda	10	Pi	40.32N	49.59 E
Masuria (EN)	61	Eh	40.57S	175.39 E
Masurian Lakes (EN)	33	Ge	23.06N	38.48 E
Maşyāf	27	Ne	34.40N	131.51 E
Maşzewo	26	Dg	2.30S	101.51 E
Mataabé, Cap-	5	Ie	53.50N	21.30 E
Matabeleland North [3]	5	Ie	53.45N	21.45 E
Matabeleland South [3]	24	Ge	35.03N	36.21 E
Matachel	10	Lc	53.29N	15.02 E
Matachewan	63b	Cb	15.38S	166.46 E
Matacu	37	Dc	19.00S	27.30 E
Matadi	37	Dd	21.00S	29.30 E
Matador	13	Ff	38.50N	6.17W
Matagalpa [3]	42	Jg	47.56N	80.39W
Matagalpa	55	Bc	17.21S	61.28W
Matagami	31	Ii	5.49S	13.27 E
Matagami, Lac-	45	Fi	34.01N	100.49W
Mata Gassile	49	Eg	13.00N	85.30W
Matagorda Bay	49	Kh	12.53N	85.57W
Matagorda Peninsula	42	Ig	49.45N	77.35W
Mataiea	42	Jf	50.11N	78.42W
Mataiva Atoll	34	Ge	9.38N	16.23 E
Mataj	45	Hl	28.35N	96.20W
Matak, Pulau-	45	Hl	28.15N	96.30W
Matakana Island	45	Hl	28.32N	96.07W

Name	Map	Grid	Lat	Long
Matala	65e	Fc	17.46S	148.40W
Matalaa, Pointe-	19	Hf	45.51N	78.43 E
Matale	26	Ff	3.18N	106.16 E
Mataliele	62	Gb	37.35S	176.05 E
Matam	30	Ki	4.45S	37.00 E
Matamey	36	Fc	0.20S	31.44 E
Matamoros [Mex.]	32	Jb	35.44N	10.35 E
Matamoros [Mex.]	26	Fh	5.30S	114.26 E
Matana, Danau-	19	Eh	39.01N	48.40 E
Maʿtan as Sarra	27	Md	35.11N	128.24 E
Matancita	31	Kj	10.43S	38.48 E
Matane	49	Dh	12.00N	86.10W
Matankari	47	Gf	11.58N	86.06W
Matanza	21	Oh	12.15N	123.30 E
Matanzas	26	Hd	12.10N	123.35 E
Matanzas [3]	32	Hb	35.24N	0.08 E
Matão	32	Hb	35.30N	0.15 E
Matapalo, Cabo-				
Matapan, Cape- (EN) = Taínaron, Ákra-				
Matape, Río-				
Mata Point				
Matara	30	Mk	21.00S	57.00 E
Mataram	48	Gg	20.32N	104.49W
Mataranka	26	Ih	8.09S	129.50 E
Mataró	13	Nc	41.32N	2.27 E
Matarraña/Matarranya	13	Mc	41.14N	0.22 E
Matarranya/Matarraña	13	Mc	41.14N	0.22 E
Mataso	63b	Cc	17.15S	168.25 E
Matatula, Cape-	65c	Cb	14.15S	170.34W
Mataura	62	Cg	46.34S	168.44 E
Mataura	62	Cg	46.12S	168.52 E
Mata-Utu	58	Jf	13.17S	176.08W
Mata-Utu, Baie de-	64b	Bb	13.19S	176.07W
Matavai	61	Gb	13.28S	172.35W
Matavera	64p	Cb	21.13S	159.44W
Mataverj	65d	Ab	27.10S	109.27W
Matawai	62	Gc	38.21S	177.32 E
Matawin, Réservoir-	44	Kb	46.45N	73.50W
Matawin, Rivière-	44	Kb	46.55N	72.55W
Maṭāy	24	Dh	28.25N	30.46 E
Maṭbakhayn	33	Hf	17.29N	41.48 E
Matca	15	Kd	45.51N	27.32 E
Matemo, Ilha-	37	Gb	12.13S	40.36 E
Matera	14	Kj	40.40N	16.36 E
Matese	14	Ii	41.25N	14.20 E
Mátészalka	10	Si	47.57N	22.20 E
Matfors	7	De	62.21N	17.02 E
Matha	11	Fi	45.52N	0.19W
Mathematicians Seamounts (EN)	47	Be	15.30N	111.00W
Matheson	44	Ga	48.32N	80.28W
Mathis	45	Hl	28.06N	97.50W
Mathrákion	15	Cj	39.46N	19.31 E
Mathura	25	Fc	27.30N	77.41 E
Mati	15	Cd	41.39N	19.34 E
Matias Cardoso	1	Be	6.57N	126.13 E
Matias Romero	55	Kb	14.52S	43.56W
Maticora, Rio-	47	Ee	16.53N	95.02W

Name	Map	Grid	Lat	Long
Mattoon	36	Ce	14.43S	15.02 E
Matua, Ostrov-	64h	Bc	13.20S	176.08W
Matucana	25	Gg	7.28N	80.37 E
Matundu Island	37	Df	30.24S	28.43 E
Matundu	34	Cb	15.40N	13.15W
Maturín	34	Gc	13.26N	8.28 E
Matvejev Kurgan	47	Dc	25.32N	103.15W
Maüa	39	Jg	25.53N	87.32W
Maubeuge	26	Hg	2.28S	121.20 E
Ma-ubin	33	De	21.41N	21.52 E
Matina	38	De	25.09N	111.59W
Matinha	42	Kg	48.51N	67.32W
Mâțir	34	Cl	11.51S	76.24W
Matiyure, Río-	61	Ec	19.10S	179.46 E
Matkaselkja	36	Db	4.21N	23.40 E
Mâtmâṭah	36	Gd	8.50S	39.01 E
Matnog	53	Je	9.45N	63.11W
Mato, Cerro-	16	Kf	47.34N	38.55 E
Mato, Río-	37	Fb	13.52S	37.09 E
Matočkin Šar, Proliv-	11	Jd	50.17N	3.58 E
Mato Grosso [Braz.]	25	Je	16.44N	95.39 E
Mato Grosso [Braz.]	42	Kg	48.51N	67.32W
Mato Grosso, Planalto do- = Mato Grosso, Plateau of- (EN)	34	Cf	11.51S	76.24W
Mato Grosso, Plateau of- (EN) = Mato Grosso, Planalto do-				
Mato Grosso do Sul [2]	52	Kg	15.30S	56.00W
Matos Costa	54	Hg	20.00S	55.00W
Matosinhos	55	Gh	26.27S	51.09W
Matou → Qiuxian	13	Dc	41.11N	8.42W
Mátra	28	Cf	36.47N	114.30 E
Maṭraḥ	5	Hf	47.53N	19.57 E
Matrei in Osttirol	23	Ie	23.29N	58.31 E
Maṭrūḥ	14	Gc	47.00N	12.34 E
Matsiatra	24	Je	31.21N	27.14 E
Matsudo	37	Md	21.25S	45.33 E
Matsue	28	Og	35.48N	139.55 E
Matsukawa [Jap.]	27	Nd	35.28N	130.04 E
Matsukawa [Jap.]	29	Ec	37.40N	140.28 E
Matsu Liehtao	29	Ed	35.36N	137.53 E
Matsumae	27	Kf	26.05N	119.56 E
Matsumae-Hantō	28	Bf	41.26N	140.07 E
Matsumoto	28	Bf	41.40N	140.15 E
Matsuo	27	Od	36.14N	137.58 E
Matsu-Ōminato	29	Gb	39.58N	141.02 E
Matsusaka	29a	Bc	41.16N	141.09 E
Matsushima	29	Ne	34.34N	136.32 E
Matsutō	28	Gb	38.22N	141.04 E
Matsuura	29	Ae	36.31N	136.33 E
Matsuyama	23	Ae	33.22N	129.42 E
Matsuzaki	29	Fd	34.44N	138.45 E
Mattagami Lake	14	Je	49.54N	77.32W
Mattagami River	42	Jf	50.43N	81.30W
Mattawa	19	Hg	44.19N	78.42W
Matterhorn [Eur.]	14	Be	45.58N	7.39 E
Matterhorn [Nv.-U.S.]	46	Hf	41.49N	115.23W
Matthew, Ile-	57	Ig	22.20S	171.20 E
Matthews Ridge	54	Fb	7.30N	60.10W
Matthew Town	47	Hf	45.51N	73.40W
Maṭṭī, Sabhat-	24	Sj	23.30N	52.00 E
Mattighofen	14	Hb	48.06N	13.09 E

Name	Map	Grid	Lat	Long
Mattoon	45	Lg	39.29N	88.22W
Matucana	20	Kg	48.00N	153.10 E
Matundu Island	54	Cl	11.51S	76.24W
Matundu	61	Ec	19.10S	179.46 E
Maturín	36	Db	4.21N	23.40 E
Maua	36	Gd	8.50S	39.01 E
Maubeuge	53	Je	9.45N	63.11W
Ma-ubin	16	Kf	47.34N	38.55 E
Mayyit, Al Baḥr al- = Dead Sea (EN)	37	Fb	13.52S	37.09 E
Mazabuka	11	Jd	50.17N	3.58 E
Mazagão	25	Je	16.44N	95.39 E
Mazamet	54	Hd	0.07S	51.17W
Mazandarān [3]	66	Bf	74.00S	8.00W
Mazandarān, Daryā-ye- = Caspian Sea (EN)	66	Ce	65.00S	2.35 E
Mazar	54	Gd	3.24S	57.42W
Mazar del Vallo	54	Gd	3.22S	57.44W
Mazara del Vallo	36	Gc	0.40S	36.02 E
Mazar-e Sharif	57	Fb	20.01N	145.13 E
Mazar-é Sharif	57	Lg	20.45N	156.20W
Mazarrón, Golfo de-	57	Lg	20.09S	157.23W
Mazatenango	25	Jf	12.45N	98.20 E
Mazatlán	12	Df	48.59N	1.49 E
Mažeikiai/Mažejkiaj	56	Fe	35.45S	72.15W
Mažejkiaj/Mažeikiai	11	Fh	46.55N	0.45W
Mazḥafah, Jabal-	11	Fk	43.14N	0.53W
Maẓḥūr, ʿIrq al-	56	Ff	41.38S	73.37W
Mazinga	44	Fe	41.34N	83.39W
Mazirbe	26	Hh	8.37S	122.14 E
Mazoe	31	Jj	19.58S	23.26 E
Mazoe	14	If	44.26N	14.55 E
Mazomeno	57	Lc	19.50N	155.28W
Mazong Shan	65a	Db	21.08N	157.13W
Mazonwze	65a	Fd	19.38S	155.36W
Mazowsze = Masovia (EN)	25	Gc	25.40N	82.38 E
Mazsalaca	65a	Db	21.21N	157.47W
Mazunga	64p	Bb	21.13S	159.48W
Mazurskie, Pojezierze-	25	Id	20.49N	92.22 E
Mazzarino	42	Cc	67.30N	125.00W
Mba	5	Lf	16.50S	153.55W
Mbabane	46	Ed	45.11N	121.05W
Mbabo, Tchabal-	57	Lf	16.27S	152.55W
Mbacké	45	Kk	30.15N	90.30W
Mbaéré	11	Mk	43.16N	6.23 E
Mbaïki	11	Mk	45.13N	2.20 E
Mbakaou	11	Mi	45.13N	6.30 E
Mbakaou, Barrage de-	31	Fg	20.00N	12.00W

Name	Map	Grid	Lat	Long
Mayreau Island	51n	Bb	12.39N	61.23W
May-sur-Orne	12	Be	49.06N	0.22W
Maysville	44	Ff	38.39N	83.46W
Mayumba [Gabon]	31	Ii	3.25S	10.39 E
Mayumba [Zaire]	36	Ed	7.16S	27.03 E
Mayuma La	27	De	30.35N	82.27 E
Mayville	44	Hd	42.15N	79.32W
Mazabuka	21	Ff	31.30N	35.30 E
Mazagão	36	Ef	15.51S	27.46 E
Mazamet	54	Hd	0.07S	51.17W
Mazandarān [3]	11	Ik	43.30N	2.24 E
Mazandarān [3]	23	Hb	36.00N	54.00 E
Mazar	5	Lg	42.00N	50.30 E
Mazar del Vallo	14	Gm	37.39N	12.35 E
Mazara del Vallo	22	If	36.42N	67.06 E
Mazar-e Sharif	13	Kg	37.30N	1.18W
Mazarrón, Golfo de-	27	Dd	39.00N	80.50 E
Mazatenango	49	Ch	14.32N	91.30W
Mazatlán	39	Ig	23.13N	106.25W
Mažeikiai/Mažejkiaj	7	Fh	56.20N	22.22 E
Mažejkiaj/Mažeikiai	7	Fh	56.20N	22.22 E
Mazḥafah, Jabal-	24	Fh	28.48N	34.57 E
Maẓḥūr, ʿIrq al-	21	Gf	27.25N	43.55 E
Mazinga	51c	Ab	17.29N	62.58W
Mazirbe	8	Jg	57.40N	22.10 E
Mazoe	37	Ec	17.30S	30.58 E
Mazoe	30	Kj	16.32S	33.25 E
Mazomeno	36	Ec	4.55S	27.13 E
Mazong Shan	27	Gc	41.33N	97.10 E
Mazonwze	10	Qd	52.40N	20.20 E
Mazowsze = Masovia (EN)				
Mazsalaca	8	Kg	57.45N	24.59 E
Mazunga	37	Dd	21.44S	29.52 E
Mazurskie, Pojezierze-	10	Qc	53.40N	21.00 E
Mazzarino	14	Im	37.18N	14.13 E
Mba	63d	Ab	17.32S	177.42 E
Mbabane	31	Kk	26.18S	31.07 E
Mbabo, Tchabal-	34	Hd	7.16N	12.09 E
Mbacké	34	Bc	14.48N	15.55W
Mbaéré	35	Bc	3.47N	17.31 E
Mbaïki	31	Ih	3.53N	18.00 E
Mbakaou	34	Hd	6.19N	12.49 E
Mbakaou, Barrage de-	34	Hd	6.25N	13.00 E
Mbala	31	Ki	8.50S	31.22 E
Mbalam	34	He	2.13N	13.49 E
Mbale	31	Kh	1.05N	34.10 E
Mbali	35	Bc	4.27N	18.20 E
Mbalmayo	34	He	3.31N	11.30 E
Mbam	34	Hd	4.24N	11.17 E
Mbamba Bay	36	Fc	11.17S	34.46 E
Mbandaka	31	Ih	0.04N	18.16 E
Mbanga	34	Ge	4.30N	9.34 E
Mbanika	63a	Dc	9.05S	159.12 E
Mbanza Congo	36	Bd	6.16S	14.15 E
Mbanza-Ngungu	31	Ii	5.35S	14.47 E
Mbarangandu	36	Gd	8.57S	37.24 E
Mbarara	36	Fc	0.36S	30.38 E
Mbari	35	Cc	4.34N	22.43 E
Mbatiki	63d	Bb	17.46S	179.08 E
Mbava	63a	Cb	7.49S	156.37 E
Mbé	34	Hd	7.51N	13.36 E
Mbengga	63d	Bc	18.23S	178.08 E
Mbengwi	34	Hd	6.01N	10.00 E
Mbéré	35	Bd	9.00N	16.26 E
Mbeya	31	Ki	8.54S	33.27 E
Mbeya [3]	36	Ff	8.00S	33.30 E
Mbi	35	Be	4.28N	18.07 E
Mbigou	36	Bc	1.53S	11.56 E
Mbinda	31	Ii	2.07S	12.52 E
Mbinga	36	Ge	10.56S	35.01 E
Mbingué	34	Dc	10.00N	5.54W
Mbini	34	Ge	1.34N	9.37 E
Mbini [3]	34	He	1.30N	10.00 E
Mbini [3]	30	Ih	1.30N	10.30 E
Mboki	35	De	5.19N	25.58 E
Mbokonimbeti	63a	Ec	8.57S	160.05 E
Mbomo	36	Bb	0.24N	14.44 E
Mbomou = Bomu (EN) [3]	35	Cd	5.30N	23.30 E
Mbomou = Bomu (EN)	30	Jh	4.08N	22.26 E
Mborokua	63a	Dc	9.02S	158.44 E
Mbour	34	Bc	14.24N	16.58W
Mbozi	32	Ef	16.01N	12.35W
Mbrés	35	Bd	6.40N	19.48 E
Mbuba	34	Bd	7.14S	12.52 E
M'Bridge	63d	Bb	16.48S	178.37 E
Mbuji-Mayi	31	Ji	6.09S	23.33 E
Mbulo	63a	Dc	8.46S	158.21 E
Mbulu	36	Fc	3.51S	35.32 E
Mburucuyá	55	Ci	28.03S	58.14W
Mbutha	63d	Bb	16.39S	179.51 E
Mbuyuni	36	Gd	7.23S	36.32 E
Mbwemburu	36	Gd	9.02S	38.39 E
Mcalester	43	He	34.56N	95.46W
Mcensk	19	Se	53.17N	36.32 E
M'Chedallah	13	Qh	36.22N	4.16 E
Mcherrah	32	Gd	27.00N	4.30W
Mchinga	36	Gd	9.44S	39.42 E
Mchinji	36	Fe	13.48S	32.54 E
Mdandou	34	Bn	36.05N	7.49 E
M'Daourouch	13	Gl	35.41N	5.19W
Mdennah	32	Fd	24.37N	4.50W
Mdiq	13	Gi	35.41N	5.19W
Mead	44	He	49.29N	83.50W
Mead, Lake-	40	Hb	70.50N	156.25W
Meade	62	Gb	37.15S	176.15 E
Meade	40	Hb	71.37N	100.20W
Meade Peak	46	Je	42.30N	111.15W
Meadow Lake	42	Gf	54.07N	108.26W
Meadville	44	He	41.38N	80.10W
Me-akan-Dake	29a	Cb	43.23N	143.59 E
Mealhada	13	Dd	40.22N	8.27W

Mealy Mountains 42 Lf 53.20N 59.30W
Meama 65b Ba 19.45S 174.34W
Méan, Havelange- 12 Hd 50.22N 5.20 E
Meander Reef 26 Ge 8.09N 119.14 E
Meander River 42 Fe 59.02N 117.42W
Meanguera, Isla- 49 Dg 13.12N 87.43W
Mearim, Rio- 52 Lf 3.04S 44.35W
Meath/An Mhí 9 Gh 53.35N 6.40W
Meaux 11 If 48.57N 2.52 E
Mecca (EN)=Makkah 22 Fg 21.27N 39.49 E
Mechara 35 Gd 8.34N 40.28 E
Mechelen/Maasmechelen 12 Hd 50.57N 5.40 E
Mechelen/Malines 11 Kc 51.02N 4.29 E
Mecheraa-Asfa 13 Ni 35.24N 1.03 E
Mecheria 32 Gc 33.33N 0.17W
Mechernich 12 Id 50.36N 6.39 E
Mechongué 55 Cn 38.09S 58.13W
Mecidiye 15 Ji 40.38N 26.32 E
Mecitözü 24 Fb 40.31N 35.19 E
Mecklemburgischer Höhenrücken 10 Ic 53.40N 12.10 E
Mecklenburg 10 Hc 53.30N 12.00 E
Mecklenburger Bucht 10 Hb 54.20N 11.40 E
Mecklenburger Schweiz 10 Ic 53.45N 12.35 E
Mecoacán, Laguna- 48 Mh 18.20N 93.10W
Meconta 37 Fb 14.59S 39.50 E
Mecsek 10 Oj 46.10N 18.18 E
Mecubúri 37 Gb 14.10S 40.31 E
Mecúfi 37 Gb 13.17S 40.33 E
Mecula 37 Fb 12.05S 37.39 E
Médala 32 Ff 15.30N 5.37W
Medan 22 Li 3.35N 98.40 E
Médanos [Arg.] 56 He 38.50S 62.41W
Médanos [Arg.] 55 Ck 33.24S 59.05W
Medanosa, Punta- 56 Gg 48.06S 65.55W
Mede 14 Ce 45.06N 8.44 E
Médéa 32 Hb 36.16N 2.45 E
Médéa 32 Hb 36.20N 3.25 E
Medebach 12 Kc 51.12N 8.43 E
Medellín 26 Hd 11.08N 123.58 E
Medellín 53 Ie 6.15N 75.35W
Medelpad 8 Gb 62.35N 16.15 E
Medemblik 12 Hb 52.46N 5.06 E
Medenica 10 Tg 49.21N 23.45 E
Mederdra 32 Df 16.54N 15.40W
Medetziz 24 Fd 37.25N 34.40 E
Medford [Or.-U.S.] 39 Ge 42.19N 122.52W
Medford [Wi.-U.S.] 45 Kd 45.09N 90.20W
Medgidia 15 Le 44.15N 28.17 E
Medi 35 Ed 5.06N 30.44 E
Media Luna, Arrecife de la- 49 Ff 15.13N 82.36W
Medianeira 55 Eg 25.17S 54.05W
Mediaş 15 Hc 46.10N 24.21 E
Medical Lake 46 Gc 47.34N 117.41W
Medicine Bow 46 Lf 41.54N 106.12W
Medicine Bow Mountains 46 Lf 41.10N 106.25W
Medicine Butte 46 Jf 41.29N 110.48W
Medicine Hat 39 Hd 50.03N 110.40W
Medicine Lake 46 Mb 48.28N 104.24W
Medicine Lodge 45 Gh 37.17N 98.35W
Međimurje 14 Kd 46.25N 16.30 E
Medina (EN)=Al Madīnah [Sau.Ar.] 22 Fg 24.28N 39.36 E
Medina Az-Zahra 13 Hg 37.52N 4.50W
Medinaceli 13 Jc 41.10N 2.26W
Medina del Campo 13 Hc 41.18N 4.55W
Medina de Rioseco 13 Gc 41.53N 5.02W
Medina-Sidonia 13 Gh 36.27N 5.55W
Medininkai/Medininkai 8 Kj 54.32N 25.46 E
Medininkaj/Medininkai 8 Kj 54.32N 25.46 E
Medio, Arroyo del- 55 Bk 33.16S 60.15W
Mediterranean Sea (EN)= Akdeniz 5 Hh 35.00N 20.00 E
Mediterranean Sea (EN)= Khatikhon, Yam- 5 Hh 35.00N 20.00 E
Mediterranean Sea (EN)= Méditerranée, Mer- 5 Hh 35.00N 20.00 E
Mediterranean Sea (EN)= Mediterraneo, Mar- 5 Hh 35.00N 20.00 E
Mediterranean Sea (EN)= Mediterràneo, Mar- 5 Hh 35.00N 20.00 E
Mediterranean Sea (EN)= Mesoyéios Thálassa 5 Hh 35.00N 20.00 E
Mediterranean Sea (EN)= Mutawassiţ, Al Baḩr al- 5 Hh 35.00N 20.00 E
Méditerranée, Mer-= Mediterranean Sea (EN) 5 Hh 35.00N 20.00 E
Mediterràneo, Mar-= Mediterranean Sea (EN) 5 Hh 35.00N 20.00 E
Mediterraneo, Mar-= Mediterranean Sea (EN) 5 Hh 35.00N 20.00 E
Medje 36 Eb 2.25N 27.18 E
Medjerda, Monts de la- 32 Ib 36.35N 8.15 E
Mednogorsk 19 Fe 51.26N 57.40 E
Medny, Ostrov- 20 Lf 54.40N 167.50 E
Médoc 11 Fi 45.00N 1.00W
Mêdog 27 Gf 29.18N 95.27 E
Médouneu 36 Bb 1.01N 10.48 E
Medveđa 15 Eg 42.51N 21.36 E
Medvedica [R.S.F.S.R.] 5 Kf 49.35N 42.41 E
Medvedica [R.S.F.S.R.] 7 Ih 57.05N 37.31 E
Medvednica 14 Je 45.55N 15.58 E
Medvedok 7 Mh 57.24N 50.06 E
Medvenka 16 Jd 51.27N 36.08 E
Medveži, Ostrova-=Bear Islands (EN) 21 Sb 70.52N 161.26 E
Medvežjegorsk 19 Dc 62.56N 34.29 E
Medway 12 Cc 51.23N 0.31 E
Medzilaborce 10 Rg 49.16N 21.55 E
Meekatharra 58 Cg 26.36S 118.29 E
Meeker 45 Cf 40.02N 107.55W
Meerane 10 If 50.51N 12.28 E
Meerbusch 12 Ic 51.16N 6.40 E
Meerut 25 Fc 28.59N 77.42 E
Meeteetse 46 Kd 44.09N 108.52W
Mefarlane, Lake- 59 Hf 32.00S 136.40 E
Mega [Eth.] 31 Kh 4.03N 38.20 E
Mega [Indon.] 26 Jg 0.41S 131.53 E
Mega, Pulau- 26 Dg 4.00S 101.02 E
Megalo 35 Gd 6.52N 40.47 E
Megálon Khorion 15 Km 36.27N 27.21 E
Megalópolis 15 Fl 37.24N 22.08 E
Megálo Sofráno 15 Jm 36.04N 26.25 E
Meganision 15 Dk 38.38N 20.43 E
Meganom, Mys- 16 Ig 44.48N 35.05 E
Mégara 15 Gk 38.00N 23.21 E
Megève 11 Mi 45.52N 6.37 E
Meghalaya 25 Ic 26.00N 91.00 E
Megid 33 Dd 28.35N 22.10 E
Megion 19 Hc 61.00N 76.15 E
Megiscane, Lac- 44 Ia 48.30N 76.04W
Megri 16 Oj 38.55N 46.15 E
Mehadia 15 Fe 44.54N 22.22 E
Mehaigne 12 Hd 50.32N 5.13 E
Meharry, Mount- 59 Dd 23.00S 118.35 E
Mehdia 13 Ni 35.25N 1.45 E
Mehdīshahr 24 Oe 35.44N 53.22 E
Mehedinţi 15 Fe 44.30N 23.00 E
Mehetia, Ile- 61 Lc 17.52S 148.03W
Mehrabān 24 Lc 38.05N 47.08 E
Mehrān 24 Pi 26.52N 55.24 E
Mehrān 24 Lf 33.07N 46.10 E
Mehrenga 7 Je 63.17N 41.20 E
Mehrīz 24 Pg 31.35N 54.28 E
Mehtar Lām 23 Lc 34.39N 70.10 E
Mehun-sur-Yèvre 11 Ig 47.09N 2.13 E
Meia Meia 36 Gd 5.49S 35.48 E
Meia Ponte, Rio- 54 Ig 18.32S 49.36W
Meiganga 34 Hd 6.31N 14.18 E
Meighen 42 Ha 79.55N 99.00W
Meihekou→Hailong 27 Mc 42.32N 125.37 E
Meiktila 25 Jd 20.52N 95.52 E
Meilü→Wuchuan 27 Jg 21.28N 110.44 E
Meinerzhagen 12 Jc 51.07N 7.39 E
Meiningen 10 Gf 50.33N 10.25 E
Meio, Rio do- 55 Ja 13.20S 44.34W
Meisenheim 12 Je 49.43N 7.40 E
Meishan [China] 27 He 30.05N 103.48 E
Meishan [China] 28 Ei 31.06N 119.43 E
Meishan → Jinzhai 28 Ci 31.40N 115.52 E
Meißen 10 Je 51.09N 13.29 E
Meißner 10 Fe 51.12N 9.50 E
Meitan (Yiquan) 27 If 27.48N 107.32 E
Meixian 27 Kg 24.21N 116.07 E
Meiyukou 28 Bd 40.01N 113.08 E
Méjean, Causse- 11 Jj 44.16N 3.22 E
Mejillones 56 Fb 23.06S 70.27W
Mékambo 36 Bb 1.01N 13.56 E
Mekdela 35 Fc 11.28N 39.20 E
Mekele=Meqele (EN) 31 Kg 13.30N 39.28 E
Mékhé 34 Bb 15.07N 16.38W
Mekherrhane, Sebkha- 30 Hf 26.22N 1.20 E
Meknès 32 Fc 33.00N 5.30W
Meknès 31 Ge 33.54N 5.32W
Mekong (EN)=Lancang Jiang 21 Mh 10.15N 105.55 E
Mekong (EN)=Mae Nam Khong 21 Mh 10.15N 105.55 E
Mekong (EN)=Mékôngk 21 Mh 10.15N 105.55 E
Mekong (EN)=Mènam Khong 21 Mh 10.15N 105.55 E
Mekong Delta (EN) 21 Mi 10.20N 106.40 E
Mekongga, Gunung- 26 Hg 3.35S 121.15 E
Mékôngk=Mekong (EN) 21 Mh 10.15N 105.55 E
Mekoryuk 40 Fd 60.23N 166.12W
Mékrou 34 Fc 12.24N 2.49 E
Mel, Ilha do- 55 Hg 25.31S 48.20W
Melaab 13 Ni 35.43N 1.20 E
Mêlağēn 35 Hc 10.25N 49.52 E
Melaka 22 Mi 2.12N 102.15 E
Melaka, Selat-=Malacca, Strait of- (EN) 21 Mi 2.30N 101.20 E
Melamo, Cabo- 30 Lj 14.24S 40.49 E
Melanesia 57 Hf 13.00S 164.00 E
Melanesian Basin (EN) 3 Jj 0.05S 160.35 E
Melawi 26 Ff 0.05N 111.29 E
Melbourne [Ar.-U.S.] 45 Kh 36.04N 91.54W
Melbourne [Austl.] 58 Fh 37.49S 144.58 E
Melbourne [Eng.-U.K.] 12 Ab 52.49N 1.26W
Melbourne [Fl.-U.S.] 43 Kf 28.05N 80.37W
Melbourne-Dandenong 59 Jg 37.59S 145.12 E
Melchor Múzquiz 47 Dc 27.53N 101.31W
Melchor Ocampo 48 Hi 17.59N 102.11W
Meldorf 10 Fb 54.05N 9.05 E
Mele, Capo- 14 Cg 43.57N 8.10 E
Melekeiok 64a Bc 7.29N 134.38 E
Melela 57 Fc 17.04S 38.36 E
Melenci 15 Dd 45.31N 20.19 E
Melenki 7 Ed 55.23N 41.42 E
Meleto Dağı 24 Ic 38.35N 41.32 E
Meleuz 19 Fe 52.58N 55.59 E
Mélèzes, Rivière aux- 42 Ke 57.00N 69.00W
Melfa 14 Hi 41.30N 13.35 E
Melfi [Chad] 35 Bc 11.04N 17.56 E
Melfi [It.] 14 Jj 41.00N 15.39 E
Melfort 42 Hf 52.52N 104.36W
Melgaço 54 Hd 1.47S 50.44W
Melibocus 10 Eg 49.42N 8.40 E
Melilla 32 Ge 35.19N 2.58W
Melincué, Laguna- 55 Bk 33.42S 61.28W
Melipilla 56 Fd 33.42S 71.13W
Melita 45 Fb 49.16N 101.00W
Melíti 15 Ei 40.50N 21.35 E
Melito di Porto Salvo 14 Jm 37.55N 15.47 E
Melito di Porto Salvo, Punta di- 14 Jm 37.57N 15.45 E
Melitopol 6 Jf 46.50N 35.22 E
Melk 14 Jb 48.13N 15.19 E
Mella 14 Ee 45.13N 10.13 E
Mellakou 13 Ni 35.15N 1.14 E
Mellanfryken 8 Ee 59.40N 13.15 E
Melle [Fr.] 11 Fh 46.13N 0.08W
Melle [F.R.G.] 12 Kb 52.12N 8.21 E
Mellen 45 Kc 46.20N 90.40W
Mellerud 7 Cg 58.42N 12.28 E
Mellish Reef 59 Lc 17.25S 155.50 E
Mellish Seamount (EN) 57 Ia 34.00N 178.15 E
Mellit 35 Dc 14.08N 25.33 E
Mělník 10 Kf 50.21N 14.30 E
Melnik 15 Gh 41.31N 23.24 E
Melo 53 Ki 32.22S 54.11W
Melo, Rio- 55 De 21.25S 57.55W
Melrhir, Chott- 30 He 34.20N 6.20 E
Melrose 46 Id 45.38N 112.40W
Melsetter 37 Ec 19.48S 32.50 E
Melsungen 10 Fe 51.08N 9.33 E
Meltaus 7 Fc 66.54N 25.22 E
Melton Constable 12 Db 52.51N 1.02 E
Melton Mowbray 9 Mi 52.46N 0.53W
Meluco 37 Fb 12.33S 39.37 E
Meluli 37 Fc 16.28S 39.44 E
Melun 11 If 48.32N 2.40 E
Melville 38 Ib 75.15N 110.00W
Melville 46 Na 50.55N 102.48W
Melville, Cape- 59 Ib 14.10S 144.30 E
Melville, Lake- 42 Lf 53.42N 59.30W
Melville Bay 59 Hb 12.05S 136.45 E
Melville Bay (EN)=Melville Bugt 67 Od 75.35N 62.30W
Melville Bugt=Melville Bay (EN) 67 Od 75.35N 62.30W
Melville Hills 42 Fc 69.20N 123.00W
Melville Island 57 Ef 11.40S 131.00 E
Melville Peninsula 38 Kc 68.00N 84.00W
Melville Sound 42 Gc 68.05N 107.30W
Melvin, Lough- 9 Eg 54.25N 8.10W
Mélykút 10 Pj 46.13N 19.23 E
Memaliaj 15 Ci 40.20N 19.58 E
Memambetsu 29a Db 43.55N 144.11 E
Memba, Baia de- 37 Gb 14.11S 40.35 E
Memberamo 26 Kg 1.28S 137.52 E
Memboro 26 Gh 9.22S 119.32 E
Mēmele 8 Kh 56.24N 24.10 E
Memmert 10 Cc 53.39N 6.53 E
Memmingen 10 Gi 47.59N 10.10 E
Mempawan 26 Ef 0.22N 108.58 E
Memphis 33 Fd 29.52N 31.15 E
Memphis [Mo.-U.S.] 45 Jf 40.28N 92.10W
Memphis [Tn.-U.S.] 39 Jf 35.08N 90.03W
Memphis [Tx.-U.S.] 45 Fi 34.44N 100.32W
Memrut Dağı 24 Jc 38.40N 42.12 E
Memuro 28 Qc 42.55N 143.03 E
Memuro-Dake 29a Cb 42.52N 142.45 E
Mena 35 Gd 5.30N 41.06 E
Mena [Ar.-U.S.] 45 Ii 34.35N 94.15W
Mena [Ukr.-U.S.S.R.] 19 De 51.33N 32.14 E
Menabe 30 Lk 20.00S 44.40 E
Menai Strait 9 Ih 53.12N 4.12W
Ménaka 31 Hg 15.55N 2.26 E
Mènam Khong=Mekong (EN) 21 Mh 10.15N 105.55 E
Menangalaku 26 Gh 9.36S 119.01 E
Menard 45 Gk 30.55N 99.47W
Menawashei 35 Dc 12.40N 25.01 E
Menčul, Gora- 10 Th 48.16N 23.49 E
Mendala, Puncak- 26 Lg 4.44S 140.20 E
Mendanau, Pulau- 26 Eg 2.51S 107.26 E
Mendanha 55 Kd 18.06S 43.30W
Mende 11 Jj 44.31N 3.30 E
Mendebo 30 Kh 6.50N 39.40 E
Mendelejevsk 7 Mi 55.57N 52.22 E
Menden (Sauerland) 10 De 51.26N 7.48 E
Mendes 13 Mi 35.39N 0.52 E
Méndez 48 Je 25.07N 98.34W
Mendi [Eth.] 35 Fd 9.48N 35.05 E
Mendi [Pap.N.Gui.] 60 Ci 6.10S 143.40 E
Mendig 12 Jd 50.22N 7.16 E
Mendip Hills 9 Kj 51.15N 2.40W
Mendocino 46 Dg 39.19N 123.48W
Mendocino, Cape- 38 Ge 40.25N 124.25W
Mendocino Fracture Zone (EN) 3 Lf 40.00N 145.00W
Mendota [Ca.-U.S.] 46 Eh 36.45N 120.23W
Mendota [Il.-U.S.] 45 Lf 41.33N 89.07W
Mendoza 53 Ji 32.54S 68.50W
Mendoza 56 Gd 34.30S 68.30W
Mené, Landes du- 11 Df 48.15N 2.32W
Mene de Mauroa 49 Lh 10.43N 71.01W
Mene Grande 54 Db 9.49S 70.56W
Menemen 24 Bc 38.36N 27.04 E
Menen/Menin 11 Jd 50.48N 3.07 E
Meneng Point 64e Bb 0.33S 166.57 E
Meneses 55 Dj 30.53S 56.30W
Ménez Hom 11 Bf 48.13N 4.16W
Menfi 14 Gm 37.36N 12.58 E
Mengcheng 27 Ke 33.11N 116.30 E
Mengdingjie 27 Gg 23.31N 99.07 E
Menggala 26 Eg 4.28S 105.17 E
Mengíbar 13 Ig 37.58N 3.48W
Mengjin 28 Bg 34.50N 112.26 E
Mengla 27 Hg 21.30N 101.35 E
Menglangba→Lancang 27 Gg 22.37N 99.57 E
Menglian 27 Gg 22.20N 99.27 E
Mengoun Huizu Zizhixian 28 De 38.04N 117.06 E
Mengyin 28 Dg 35.42N 117.56 E
Mengzi 22 Mg 23.23N 103.34 E
Menihek Lakes 42 Kf 54.00N 66.30W
Menin/Menen 11 Jd 50.48N 3.07 E
Menindee 59 If 32.24S 142.26 E
Menindee Lake 59 If 22.00S 142.23 E
Meningie 59 Hg 35.42S 139.20 E
Menjapa, Gunung- 26 Gf 1.05N 116.05 E
Menno 45 Hg 43.14N 97.34W
Menoikion Óros 15 Gh 41.11N 23.48 E
Menominee 44 Dc 45.07N 87.39W
Menongue 31 Ij 14.40S 17.39 E
Menor, Mar- 13 Lg 37.43N 0.48W
Menorca=Minorca (EN) 5 Gg 40.00N 4.00 E
Menor do Araguaia, Braço-ou Javaes 54 He 9.50S 50.12W
Mentana 14 Gh 42.02N 12.38 E
Mentasta Lake 40 Kd 62.55N 143.45W
Mentawai, Kepulauan-=Mentawai Islands (EN) 21 Lj 2.00S 99.30 E
Mentawai, Selat- 21 Lj 2.00S 99.30 E
Mentawai Islands (EN)=Mentawai, Kepulauan- 21 Lj 2.00S 99.30 E
Menton 11 Nk 43.47N 7.30 E
Mentougou 28 De 39.56N 116.02 E
Menyuan 27 Hd 37.30N 101.35 E
Menzelinsk 7 Mi 55.45N 53.09 E
Menzies 59 Ee 29.41S 121.02 E
Menzies, Mount- 66 Ff 73.30S 61.50 E
Meon 12 Ad 50.49N 1.15W
Meoqui 47 Cc 28.17N 105.29W
Meponda 37 Eb 13.25S 34.52 E
Meppel 11 Mb 52.42N 6.11 E
Meppen 10 Dd 52.41N 7.19 E
Meqele(EN)=Mekele 31 Kg 13.30N 39.28 E
Mê Qu 27 He 33.58N 102.10 E
Mequinensa, Pantà de-/ Mequinenza, Embalse de- 13 Lc 41.15N 0.02W
Mequinenza, Embalse de-/ Mequinensa, Pantà de- 13 Lc 41.15N 0.02W
Mera 14 Dd 46.11N 9.25 E
Merabello, Gulf of- (EN) = Merabéllou, Kólpos- 15 In 35.14N 25.47 E
Merabéllou, Kólpos- = Merabello, Gulf of- (EN) 15 In 35.14N 25.47 E
Merak 26 Eh 5.56S 106.00 E
Meråker 7 Ce 63.26N 11.45 E
Méralab 63b Db 14.27S 168.03 E
Meramangye, Lake- 59 Ge 28.25S 132.15 E
Meran / Merano 14 Fd 46.40N 11.09 E
Merano / Meran 14 Fd 46.40N 11.09 E
Meratus, Pegunungan- 26 Gg 2.45S 115.40 E
Merauke 58 Fe 8.28S 140.20 E
Mercadal 13 Qe 39.59N 4.05 E
Mercato Saraceno 14 Gg 43.57N 12.12 E
Merced 43 Cd 37.18N 120.29W
Mercedario, Cerro- 52 Ii 31.59S 70.14W
Mercedes [Arg.] 56 Id 34.39S 59.27W
Mercedes [Arg.] 56 Ic 29.12S 58.05W
Mercedes [Arg.] 53 Ji 33.40S 65.30W
Mercedes [Ur.] 53 Ki 33.16S 58.01W
Merchants Bay 42 Lc 67.10N 62.50W
Merchtem 12 Gd 50.58N 4.14 E
Mercury Islands 62 Fb 36.35S 175.50 E
Mercy, Cape- 42 Ld 64.56N 63.40W
Mercy Bay 42 Fb 74.15N 118.10W
Meredith, Cape- 56 Hh 52.12S 60.38W
Meredith, Lake- 45 Fi 35.36N 101.42W
Meredoua 32 Hd 25.20N 2.05 E
Merefa 19 Df 49.51N 36.00 E
Merelbeke 12 Fd 51.00N 3.45 E
Merenga 20 Kd 61.43N 156.05 E
Mergui 22 Lh 12.26N 98.36 E
Mergui Archipelago 21 Lh 12.00N 98.00 E
Méri 34 Hc 10.47N 14.06 E
Meriç 15 Jh 41.11N 26.25 E
Meriç 24 Bb 40.52N 26.12 E
Mérida 54 Db 8.30N 71.10W
Mérida [Mex.] 39 Kg 20.58N 89.37W
Mérida [Sp.] 13 Ff 38.55N 6.20W
Mérida [Ven.] 53 Ie 8.36N 71.08W
Merida, Cordillera de- 52 Ie 8.40N 71.00W
Meridian 39 Kf 32.22N 88.42W
Mérig 63b Cb 14.19S 167.48 E
Mérignac 11 Fj 44.50N 0.38W
Merikarvia 7 Ef 61.51N 21.30 E
Merín, Laguna- 56 Jd 32.45S 52.50W
Meringur 59 If 34.24S 141.29 E
Merir Island 57 Ed 4.19N 132.19 E
Merizo 64c Bb 13.16N 144.40 E
Merke 18 Ic 42.52N 73.12 E
Merkem, Houthulst- 12 Ed 50.57N 2.51 E
Merkine/Merkiné 8 Kj 54.07N 24.20 E
Merkiné/Merkine 8 Kj 54.07N 24.20 E
Merkis/Merkys 7 Fi 54.10N 24.11 E
Merksem, Antwerpen- 12 Gc 51.15N 4.27 E
Merksplas 12 Gc 51.22N 4.52 E
Merkys/Merkis 7 Fi 54.10N 24.11 E
Meroe 35 Eb 16.56N 33.59 E
Meroe 35 Eb 16.05N 33.55 E
Merouane, Chott- 32 Ic 34.00N 6.02 E
Merredin 59 Df 31.29S 118.16 E
Merrick 9 If 55.08N 4.29W
Merrill 43 Jb 45.11N 89.41W
Merriman 45 Fe 42.55N 101.42W
Merritt 42 Ff 50.07N 120.47W
Merritt Island 43 Kf 28.21N 80.42W
Merritt Reservoir 45 Fe 42.35N 100.55W
Mersa Fatma 35 Gc 14.53N 40.19 E
Mersa Teklay 35 Fb 17.25N 38.45 E
Mersea Island 12 Cc 51.47N 0.57 E
Merseburg 10 He 51.22N 12.00 E
Mers el Kebir 13 Li 35.44N 0.43W
Mersey 9 Kh 53.25N 3.00W
Merseyside 9 Kh 53.30N 3.00W
Mersin 23 Db 36.48N 34.38 E
Mersing 26 Df 2.26N 103.50 E
Mers-les-Bains 12 Dd 50.04N 1.23 E
Mērsrags/Mersrags 8 Jg 57.19N 23.01 E
Mersrags/Mērsrags 8 Jg 57.19N 23.01 E
Merta 25 Ec 26.39N 74.02 E
Merta Road 25 Ec 26.43N 73.55 E
Mertert 12 Ie 49.42N 6.29 E
Merthyr Tydfil 9 Jj 51.46N 3.23W
Merti 36 Gb 1.04N 38.40 E
Mértola 13 Eg 37.38N 7.40W
Mertule Maryam 35 Fc 10.50N 38.15 E
Mertvy Kultuk, Sor- 16 Rg 45.30N 53.40 E
Mertz Glacier 66 Je 67.40S 144.45 E
Meru 36 Gb 0.03N 37.39 E
Méru 11 Ie 49.14N 2.08 E
Meru, Mount- 36 Gc 3.14S 36.45 E
Merure 55 Fb 15.33S 53.05W
Merville 12 Ed 50.38N 2.38 E
Merzifon 23 Ea 40.53N 35.29 E
Merzig 10 Cg 49.27N 6.38 E
Meša 7 Li 55.34N 49.24 E
Mesa [Az.-U.S.] 39 Hf 33.25N 111.50W
Mesa [Co.-U.S.] 45 Bg 39.14N 108.08W
Mesabi Range 43 Ib 47.30N 92.50W
Mesagne 14 Lj 40.34N 17.48 E
Mescalero 45 Dj 33.09N 105.46W
Meščera=Moscow Basin 5 Kd 55.00N 40.30 E
Meschede 10 Ee 51.21N 8.17 E
Mescit Dağı 24 Ib 40.22N 41.11 E
Meščovsk 16 Ib 54.19N 35.18 E
Mesegon 64d Bb 7.09N 151.55 E
Mesfinto 35 Fc 13.28N 37.23 E
Me-Shima 28 Jh 32.01N 128.25 E
Meshkīnshahr 24 Lc 38.24N 47.40 E
Mesima 14 Jl 38.30N 15.55 E
Mesjagutovo 17 Ii 55.35N 58.20 E
Meskiana 14 Bo 35.38N 7.40 E
Meskiana, Oued- 14 Bo 35.48N 7.53 E
Meslo 35 Fd 6.22N 39.50 E
Mesnil-Val, Criel-sur-Mer- 12 Dd 50.03N 1.20 E
Mesola 14 Gf 44.55N 12.14 E
Mesolóngion 15 Ek 38.22N 21.26 E
Mesopotamia 52 Kh 30.00S 58.00W
Mesopotamia (EN) 23 Fc 34.00N 44.00 E
Mesoyéios Thálassa= Mediterranean Sea (EN) 5 Hh 35.00N 20.00 E
Mesquite [Nv.-U.S.] 46 Hh 36.48N 114.04W
Mesquite [Tx.-U.S.] 45 Hj 32.46N 96.36W
Mesra 13 Mi 35.50N 0.10 E
Messaad 32 Hc 34.10N 3.30 E
Messalo 30 Lj 11.40S 40.46 E
Messará, Órmos- 15 Ho 35.00N 24.40 E
Messina [It.] 6 Hh 38.11N 15.34 E
Messina [S.Afr.] 31 Kk 22.23S 30.00 E
Messina, Strait of- (EN) = Messina, Stretto di- 5 Hh 38.15N 15.35 E
Messina, Stretto di- = Messina, Strait of- (EN) 5 Hh 38.15N 15.35 E
Messini 15 El 37.15N 21.50 E
Messini 15 Fl 37.03N 22.01 E
Messiniakós Kólpos 15 Fm 36.45N 22.10 E
Messojaha 20 Cc 67.52N 77.27 E
Mesta 15 Hi 40.51N 24.44 E
Mestecăniş, Pasul- 15 Ib 47.28N 25.20 E
Mesters Vig 41 Jd 72.15N 24.20W
Mestia 16 Mh 43.03N 42.43 E
Mestre, Espigão- 54 If 12.30S 46.00W
Mestre, Venezia- 14 Ge 45.29N 12.14 E
Mesuji 26 Eg 4.08S 105.52 E
Meta 54 Dc 3.30N 73.00W
Meta, Rio- 52 Je 6.12N 67.28W
Meta Incognita Peninsula 38 Mc 62.40N 68.00W
Metairie 45 Kl 29.59N 90.09W
Metaliferi, Munţii- 15 Fc 46.10N 22.50 E
Metallifere, Colline- 14 Eg 43.10N 10.55 E
Metán 56 Hc 25.29S 64.57W
Metangula 37 Eb 12.43S 34.49 E
Metaponto 14 Kj 40.20N 16.50 E
Metauro 14 Hg 43.50N 13.03 E
Metautu 65c Ba 13.57S 171.54W
Meteghan 44 Nc 44.11N 66.10W
Metelen 12 Jb 52.09N 7.12 E
Metéora 15 Ej 39.43N 21.40 E
Meteor Seamount (EN) 30 Hm 48.00S 8.30 E
Meteor Trench (EN) 3 Do 55.00S 27.00 E
Methana 15 Gl 37.35N 23.23 E
Methánon, Khersónisos- 15 Gl 37.36N 23.22 E
Methven 62 De 43.38S 171.38 E
Methwold 12 Cb 52.31N 0.33 E
Metković 14 Lg 43.03N 17.39 E
Metlakatla 40 Me 55.08N 131.35W
Metlika 14 Je 45.39N 15.19 E
Metlili Chaamba 32 Hc 32.16N 3.38 E
Metmårfag 32 Ed 26.26N 13.26W
Metohija 15 Dg 42.40N 20.27 E
Metro 26 Eh 5.05S 105.20 E
Metropolis 45 Lh 37.09N 88.44W
Metsovon 15 Ej 39.46N 21.11 E
Métsovon, Zigós- = Métsovon Pass (EN) 15 Ej 39.47N 21.15 E
Métsovon Pass (EN) = Métsovon, Zigós- 15 Ej 39.47N 21.15 E
Mettet 12 Gd 50.19N 4.40 E
Mettingen 12 Jb 52.19N 7.47 E
Mettlach 12 Ie 49.30N 6.36 E
Mettmann 12 Ic 51.15N 6.58 E
Metu 31 Kh 8.20N 35.38 E
Metuje 10 Lf 50.20N 15.55 E
Metz 6 Gf 49.08N 6.10 E
Metzervisse 12 Ie 49.19N 6.17 E
Meu 11 Ef 48.02N 1.47W
Meulaboh 26 Cf 4.09N 96.08 E
Meulan 12 De 49.01N 1.54 E
Meulebeke 12 Fd 50.57N 3.17 E
Meureudu 26 Ce 5.16N 96.16 E
Meurthe 11 Mf 48.47N 6.09 E
Meurthe-et-Moselle 11 Mf 48.35N 6.10 E
Meuse 11 Lf 49.00N 5.30 E
Meuse 5 Ge 51.49N 5.01 E
Meuse (EN)=Maas 5 Ge 51.49N 5.01 E
Meuse, Côtes de- 11 Le 49.10N 5.30 E
Meuzenti 35 Bb 18.14N 17.06 E
Mexia 45 Hk 31.41N 96.29W
Mexiana, Ilha 54 Ic 0.00 49.35W
Mexicali 39 Hf 32.40N 115.29W
Mexicana, Altiplanicie-= Mexico, Plateau of- (EN) 38 Ig 25.30N 104.00W
Mexican Hat 46 Kh 37.09N 109.52W
Mexicanos, Laguna de los- 48 Fc 28.09N 106.57W
Mexico 45 Kg 39.10N 91.53W
México 39 Ig 23.00N 102.00W

Index Symbols

Independent Nation
State, Region
District, County
Municipality
Colony, Dependency
Continent
Physical Region
Historical or Cultural Region
Mount, Mountain
Volcano
Hill
Mountains, Mountain Range
Hills, Escarpment
Plateau, Upland
Pass, Gap
Plain, Lowland
Delta
Salt Flat
Valley, Canyon
Crater, Cave
Karst Features
Depression
Polder
Desert, Dunes
Forest, Woods
Heath, Steppe
Oasis
Cape, Point
Coast, Beach
Cliff
Peninsula
Isthmus
Sandbank
Island
Atoll
Rock, Reef
Islands, Archipelago
Rocks, Reefs
Coral Reef
Well, Spring
Geyser
River, Stream
Waterfall Rapids
River Mouth, Estuary
Lake
Salt Lake
Intermittent Lake
Reservoir
Swamp, Pond
Canal
Glacier
Ice Shelf, Pack Ice
Ocean
Sea
Gulf, Bay
Strait, Fjord
Lagoon
Bank
Seamount
Tablemount
Ridge
Shelf
Basin
Escarpment, Sea Scarp
Fracture
Trench, Abyss
National Park, Reserve
Point of Interest
Recreation Site
Cave, Cavern
Historic Site
Ruins
Wall, Walls
Church, Abbey
Temple
Scientific Station
Airport
Port
Lighthouse
Mine
Tunnel
Dam, Bridge

éxico [2] 47 Ee 19.20N 99.30W
éxico, Golfo de- = Mexico, Gulf of- (EN) 38 Kg 25.00N 90.00W
exico, Gulf of- (EN) = México, Golfo de- 38 Kg 25.00N 90.00W
exico, Plateau of- (EN) = Mexicana, Altiplanicie- 38 Ig 25.30N 104.00W
exico Basin (EN) 3 Bg 25.00N 92.00W
exico City (EN) = Ciudad de México 39 Jh 19.24N 99.09W
eybod 24 Of 32.16N 53.59 E
eydān-e Gel 24 Ph 29.04N 54.50 E
eyisti 15 Mm 36.08N 29.34 E
eyisti 15 Mm 36.09N 29.40 E
eymaneh 22 If 35.55N 64.47 E
eymeh 24 Nf 33.27N 51.10 E
eymeh 24 Lf 32.05N 47.16 E
eža 7 Hi 55.43N 31.30 E
ezcala 48 Ji 17.56N 99.37W
ezcalapa, Rio- 48 Mh 18.36N 92.39W
ezdra 15 Gf 43.09N 23.42 E
eždurečenski 19 Gd 59.36N 65.53 E
eždušarski, Ostrov- 19 Fa 71.20N 53.00 E
èze 11 Jk 43.25N 3.36 E
ezen 5 Kb 66.00N 43.59 E
ezen 6 Kb 65.50N 44.13 E
ézenc, Mont- 11 Kj 44.55N 4.11 E
ęženin 10 Sc 53.07N 22.29 E
ezenskaja Guba 5 Kb 66.40N 43.45 E
ezenskaja Pižma 7 Ld 64.30N 48.32 E
ežgorje 10 Th 48.30N 23.37 E
ežica 14 Id 46.31N 14.52 E
ézidon-Canon 12 Be 49.05N 0.04W
ézin 11 Gj 44.03N 0.16 E
ezőberény 10 Rj 46.49N 21.02 E
ezőcsát 10 Qi 47.49N 20.55 E
ezőföld 10 Oj 46.55N 18.35 E
ezőkovácsháza 10 Qj 46.24N 20.55 E
ezőkövesd 10 Qi 47.49N 20.35 E
ezőtúr 10 Qi 47.00N 20.38 E
ežozerny 17 Ii 54.10N 59.25 E
ežpjanje 7 Ki 55.25N 45.00 E
ezquital 48 Gf 23.29N 104.23W
ezquital, Rio- 48 Gf 22.55N 104.54W
ezquitic 48 Hf 22.23N 103.41W
gači 20 Jf 51.02N 142.18 E
glin 16 Hc 53.04N 32.53 E
how 25 Fd 22.33N 75.46 E
iahuatlán de Porfirio Díaz 48 Ki 16.20N 96.36W
iajadas 13 Ge 39.09N 5.54W
iaméré 35 Bd 9.02N 19.55 E
iami [Az.-U.S.] 46 Jj 33.24N 110.52W
iami [Fl.-U.S.] 39 Kg 25.46N 80.12W
iami [Ok.-U.S.] 43 Id 36.53N 94.53W
iami Beach 43 Kf 25.47N 80.08W
iānābād 24 Qd 37.02N 57.27 E
iāndowāb 23 Gb 36.58N 46.06 E
iandrivazo 37 Hc 19.30S 45.28 E
ianduhe 27 Lb 49.12N 121.09 E
iāneh 23 Gb 37.26N 47.42 E
iang, Khao- 25 Ke 17.42N 101.01 E
iangas, Pulau- 26 Ie 5.35N 126.35 E
ianning 27 Hf 28.31N 102.10 E
iānwāli 25 Eb 32.35N 71.33 E
ianyang 27 He 31.23N 104.49 E
ianyang (Xiantaozhen) 28 Bi 30.22N 113.27 E
iaodao Qundao 27 Ld 38.10N 120.45 E
iao'er Shan 27 Jf 25.50N 110.22 E
iao Ling 27 If 26.05N 108.00 E
iarinarivo 37 Hc 18.56S 46.54 E
iass 19 Gd 55.01N 60.06 E
iass 19 Gd 56.06N 64.30 E
iasskoje 17 Ji 55.15N 61.55 E
iasteczko Krajeńskie 10 Nc 53.06N 17.01 E
iastko 10 Mb 54.01N 17.00 E
Michael, Mount- 59 Ja 6.25S 145.20 E
Michajlova Island 66 Ge 66.30S 85.00 E
Michalovce 10 Rh 48.46N 21.55 E
Michelstadt 12 Le 49.41N 9.01 E
Miches 49 Md 18.59N 69.03W
Michigan [2] 43 Jc 44.00N 85.00W
Michigan, Lake- 38 Ke 44.00N 87.00W
Michigan City 43 Jc 41.43N 86.54W
Michipicoten Bay 44 Eb 47.55N 84.56W
Michipicoten Island 42 Ig 47.45N 85.45W
Michoacán [2] 47 De 19.10N 101.50W
Michów 10 Se 51.32N 22.19 E
Mico, Rio- 49 Eg 12.11N 84.16W
Micoud 51k Bb 13.50N 60.54W
Micronesia 57 Gc 11.00N 159.00 E
Micronesia, Federated States of- [5] 58 Gd 6.30N 152.00 E
Mičurin 15 Kg 42.10N 27.51 E
Mičurinsk 6 Ke 52.54N 40.31 E
Midai, Pulau- 26 Ef 3.00N 107.47 E
Midar 32 Gc 34.57N 3.32W
Mid-Atlantic Ridge (EN) 3 Di 0.00 20.00W
Middelburg [Neth.] 11 Jc 51.30N 3.37 E
Middelburg [S.Afr.] 37 Cf 31.30S 25.00 E
Middelburg [S.Afr.] 37 De 25.47S 29.28 E
Middelfart 7 Bi 55.30N 9.45 E
Middelharnis 12 Gc 51.45N 4.12 E
Middelkerke 12 Ec 51.11N 2.49 E
Middelkerke-Westende 12 Ec 51.10N 2.46 E
Middle Alkali Lake 46 Ef 41.28N 120.04W
Middle America Trench (EN) 3 Mh 15.00N 95.00W
Middle Andaman 25 If 12.30N 92.50 E
Middle Atlas (EN) = Moyen Atlas 30 Ge 33.30N 4.30W
Middlebury 44 Kc 44.01N 73.10W
Middle Caicos 49 Lc 21.47N 71.43W
Middle Fork Feather River 46 Eg 38.47N 121.36W
Middle Island 37b Ab 9.22S 46.21 E
Middle Loup River 45 Gf 41.17N 98.23W
Middlemarch 62 Df 45.30S 170.07 E
Middle Reef 63a Ee 12.35S 160.30 E
Middlesboro 43 Kd 36.36N 83.43W
Middlesbrough 9 Lg 54.35N 1.14W
Middlesex 49 Ce 17.02N 88.31W
Middlesex 12 Bc 51.35N 0.10W
Middlesex 9 Mj 51.30N 0.05W
Middleton 40 Je 59.25N 146.25W
Middleton Reef 57 Gg 29.30S 159.10 E
Middletown [Ct.-U.S.] 44 Ke 41.33N 72.39W
Middletown [N.Y.-U.S.] 44 Je 41.26N 74.26W
Middletown [Oh.-U.S.] 44 Ef 39.31N 84.25W
Midelt 32 Gc 32.41N 4.45W
Mid Glamorgan [3] 9 Jj 51.35N 3.35W
Midhordland 8 Ad 60.15N 5.55 E
Midhurst 12 Bd 50.59N 0.44W
Midi, Canal du- 5 Gg 43.36N 1.25 E
Midi de Bigorre, Pic du- 11 Gl 42.56N 0.08 E
Midi d'Ossau, Pic du- 11 Fl 42.51N 0.26W
Mid-Indian Basin (EN) 3 Gj 10.00S 80.00 E
Mid-Indian Ridge (EN) 3 Gj 3.00S 75.00 E
Midland [Mi.-U.S.] 44 Ed 43.37N 84.14W
Midland [Ont.-Can.] 42 Jh 44.45N 79.53W
Midland [S.D.-U.S.] 45 Fd 44.04N 101.10W
Midland [Tx.-U.S.] 43 Ge 32.00N 102.05W
Midlands [3] 37 Dc 19.00S 30.00 E
Midlands 9 Li 52.40N 1.50W
Midleton/Mainistir na Corann 9 Ej 51.55N 8.10W
Midnapore 25 Hd 22.26N 87.20 E
Midongy du Sud 37 Hd 23.34S 47.01 E
Midou 11 Fk 43.54N 0.30W
Midouze 11 Fk 43.48N 0.51W
Mid-Pacific Mountains (EN) 3 Jg 20.00N 170.00 E
Midway Islands [5] 58 Jb 28.13N 177.22W
Midway Islands 57 Jb 28.13N 177.22W
Midwest 46 Le 43.25N 106.16W
Midwest City 45 Hi 35.27N 97.24W
Midyat 24 Id 37.25N 41.23 E
Midžor 5 Ig 43.24N 22.40 E
Miechów 10 Qf 50.23N 20.01 E
Miedwie, Jezioro- 10 Kc 53.15N 14.55 E
Międzychód 10 Ld 52.36N 15.53 E
Międzylesie 10 Mf 50.10N 16.40 E
Międzyrzec Podlaski 10 Se 52.00N 22.47 E
Międzyrzecz 10 Ld 52.27N 15.34 E
Międzyrzecze Łomżyńskie 10 Rd 52.45N 21.45 E
Miehikkälä 8 Ld 60.40N 27.42 E
Mie Ken [2] 28 Ng 34.35N 136.25 E
Miekojärvi 7 Fc 66.36N 24.23 E
Mielan 11 Gk 43.26N 0.19 E
Mielec 10 Rf 50.18N 21.25 E
Mielno 10 Mb 54.16N 16.01 E
Mien 8 Fh 56.25N 14.50 E
Mier 48 Jd 26.26N 99.09W
Miercurea Ciuc 15 Ic 46.21N 25.48 E
Mieres 13 Ga 43.15N 5.46W
Miersig 15 Ec 46.53N 21.51 E
Mier y Noriega 48 If 23.25N 100.07W
Miesbach 10 Hi 47.47N 11.50 E
Mieso 35 Gd 9.15N 40.45 E
Mifune 29 Be 32.43N 130.48 E
Migang Shan 27 Id 35.32N 106.13 E
Miguel Alemán, Presa- 48 Kh 18.13N 96.32W
Miguel Auza 48 He 24.18N 103.25W
Miguel Hidalgo, Presa- 48 Ed 26.40N 108.45W
Miha Chakaja 19 Eg 42.17N 42.02 E
Mihăilesti 15 Ie 44.20N 25.54 E
Mihail Kogălniceanu 15 Le 44.22N 28.27 E
Mihajlov 19 De 54.16N 39.03 E
Mihajlovgrad 15 Gf 43.25N 23.13 E
Mihajlovgrad [2] 15 Gf 43.25N 23.13 E
Mihajlovka [Kaz.-U.S.S.R.] 18 Hc 43.01N 71.31 E
Mihajlovka [R.S.F.S.R.] 19 Ee 50.05N 43.15 E
Mihajlovsk 17 Ih 56.29N 59.07 E
Mihalıççık 24 Dc 39.52N 31.30 E
Mihara 29 Cd 34.24N 133.05 E
Mihara-Yama 29 Fd 34.43N 139.23 E
Mi He 28 Ef 37.12N 119.10 E
Mihonoseki 29 Cd 35.34N 133.18 E
Miho-Wan 29 Cd 35.30N 133.20 E
Miiraku 29 Ae 32.45N 128.40 E
Mijaly 16 Re 48.54N 53.50 E
Mijares/Millars 13 Le 39.55N 0.01W
Mijdaḥah 35 Hc 14.00N 48.26 E
Mijdrecht 12 Gb 52.12N 4.52 E
Mijirtein (EN) = Majërtën 30 Lh 9.00N 50.00 E
Mikasa 28 Pc 43.20N 141.40 E
Mikata 29 Dd 35.34N 135.54 E
Miki 29 Dd 34.17N 134.07 E
Mikinai = Mycenae (EN) 15 Fl 37.43N 22.45 E
Mikindani 36 Ge 10.17S 40.07 E
Mikkeli [2] 7 Ge 62.00N 27.30 E
Mikkeli/Sankt Michel 6 Ic 61.41N 27.15 E
Mikomoto-Jima 29 Fd 34.34N 138.56 E
Mikonos 15 Il 37.27N 25.23 E
Mikonos 15 Il 37.27N 25.20 E
Mikonou, Stenón- 15 Il 37.30N 25.20 E
Mikrá Préspa, Limni- 15 Ei 40.45N 21.06 E
Mikre 15 Hf 43.02N 24.31 E
Mikró Sofráno 15 Jm 36.05N 26.24 E
Mikulov 10 Mh 48.49N 16.39 E
Mikumi 36 Gd 7.24S 36.59 E
Mikun 19 Fc 62.21N 50.05 E
Mikuni 29 Ec 36.13N 136.09 E
Mikuni-Sanmyaku 28 Of 36.15N 138.40 E
Mikuni-Tōge 29 Fc 36.46N 138.50 E
Mikuni-Yama 29 Dd 35.21N 134.01 E
Mikura-Jima 27 Oe 33.50N 139.35 E
Milaca 45 Jd 45.45N 93.39W
Miladummadulu Atoll 25a Ba 6.15N 73.15 E
Milagro 54 Cd 2.07S 79.36W
Milājerd 24 Me 34.37N 49.12 E
Milan [Mo.-U.S.] 45 Jf 40.12N 93.07W
Milan [Tn.-U.S.] 44 Ch 35.55N 88.46W
Milan (EN) = Milano 6 Gf 45.28N 9.12 E
Milange 37 Fc 16.05S 35.47 E
Milano = Milan (EN) 6 Gf 45.28N 9.12 E
Milâs 24 Bd 37.19N 27.47 E
Milazzo 14 Jl 38.13N 15.14 E
Milazzo, Capo di- 14 Jl 38.16N 15.14 E
Milazzo, Golfo di- 14 Jl 38.15N 15.20 E
Milbank 43 Hb 45.13N 96.38W
Mildenhall 12 Cb 52.21N 0.31 E
Mildura 58 Fh 34.12S 142.09 E
Mile 27 Hg 24.28N 103.26 E
Mile 35 Gc 11.08N 40.55 E
Miléai 15 Gj 39.20N 23.09 E
Miles 58 Gg 26.40S 150.11 E
Miles City 43 Fb 46.25N 105.51W
Milet = Miletus (EN) 15 Kl 37.30N 27.16 E
Miletus (EN) = Milet 15 Kl 37.30N 27.16 E
Milevec 15 Fg 42.34N 22.27 E
Milevsko 10 Kg 49.27N 14.22 E
Milford 46 Ig 38.24N 113.01W
Milford Haven 9 Hj 51.44N 5.02W
Milford Lake 45 Hg 39.15N 97.00W
Milford Sound 61 Ch 44.40S 167.55 E
Milford Sound 62 Bf 44.35S 167.50 E
Milgis 36 Gb 1.48N 38.06 E
Milḩ, Baḩr al- 23 Fc 32.40N 43.35 E
Milḩ, Ra's al- 33 Ec 31.55N 25.02 E
Miliana 13 Oh 36.17N 2.14 E
Mili Atoll 57 Id 6.08N 171.55 E
Milicz 10 Ne 51.32N 17.17 E
Milkovo 20 Kf 54.43N 158.43 E
Milk River 43 Eb 49.09N 112.05W
Milk River 46 Ib 49.09N 112.05W
Milkūh 23 Jc 32.45N 61.55 E
Mill 42 Jd 63.57N 78.00W
Millars/Mijares 13 Le 39.55N 0.01W
Millau 11 Jj 44.06N 3.05 E
Milledgeville 44 Fi 33.04N 83.14W
Mille Lacs, Lac des - 42 Ig 48.50N 90.30W
Mille Lacs Lake 43 Ib 46.15N 93.40W
Millen 44 Gi 32.48N 81.57W
Miller [Nb.-U.S.] 45 Gf 40.57N 99.26W
Miller [S.D.-U.S.] 45 Gd 44.31N 98.59W
Millerovo 19 Ef 48.52N 40.25 E
Miller Seamount (EN) 40 Kf 53.30N 144.20W
Millerton 62 Dd 41.38S 171.52 E
Millevaches, Plateau de- 11 Ii 45.45N 2.11 E
Millicent 59 Ig 37.36S 140.22 E
Millington 44 Ch 35.20N 89.54W
Millinocket 44 Mc 45.39N 68.43W
Mill Island 66 He 65.30S 100.40 E
Millmerran 59 Ke 27.52S 151.16 E
Mills Lake 42 Fd 61.28N 118.15W
Millstatt 14 Hd 46.48N 13.35 E
Millville 44 Jf 39.24N 75.02W
Millwood Lake 45 Jj 33.45N 94.00W
Milne Land 41 Jd 71.20N 27.30W
Milo 30 Gg 11.04N 9.14W
Milolii 65a Fd 19.11N 155.55W
Milos 15 Hm 36.45N 24.26 E
Milos = Milos (EN) 15 Hm 36.41N 24.25 E
Milos (EN) = Milos 15 Hm 36.41N 24.25 E
Milparinka 59 Ie 29.44S 141.53 E
Miltenberg 10 Fg 49.42N 9.15 E
Milton [Fl.-U.S.] 44 Dj 30.38N 87.03W
Milton [N.Z.] 62 Cg 46.07S 169.58 E
Milton-Freewater 46 Fd 45.56N 118.23W
Milton Keynes 9 Mi 52.03N 0.42W
Miltou 35 Bc 10.14N 17.26 E
Milumbe, Monts- 36 Ed 8.00S 27.30 E
Miluo 28 Bj 28.51N 113.05 E
Miluo Jiang 27 Jf 28.51N 112.59 E
Milwaukee 39 Ke 43.02N 87.55W
Milwaukee Depth (EN) 3 Do 55.10S 26.00W
Milwaukee Seamounts (EN) 57 Ia 32.28N 171.55 E
Milwaukie 46 Dd 45.27N 122.38W
Mimi-Gawa 29 Be 32.20N 131.37 E
Mimizan 11 Ej 44.12N 1.14W
Mimoň 10 Kf 50.40N 14.44 E
Mimongo 36 Bc 1.38S 11.39 E
Mimoso 55 Hb 15.10S 48.05W
Mîna 13 Mi 35.58N 0.31 E
Mina [Mex.] 48 Id 26.01N 100.32W
Mina [Nv.-U.S.] 46 Fg 38.24N 118.07W
Mina, Cerro- 49 Ki 8.21N 73.10W
Mīnā' Abd Allāh 24 Mh 29.01N 48.10 E
Mīnā' al Aḩmadī 24 Mh 29.04N 48.09 E
Mīnāb 24 Qi 27.09N 57.05 E
Mīnāb 24 Qi 27.01N 56.53 E
Mīnā' Barānīs 33 Ge 23.55N 35.28 E
Minahassa = Minahassa Peninsula (EN) 21 Oi 1.00N 124.35 E
Minahassa Peninsula (EN) = Minahassa 21 Oi 1.00N 124.35 E
Minakuchi 29 Ed 34.59N 136.11 E
Minamata 28 Kh 32.13N 130.24 E
Minami-Daitō-Jima 27 Nf 25.50N 131.15 E
Minami-furano 29a Cb 43.10N 142.32 E
Minami-Iō-Jima 60 Cc 24.14N 141.28 E
Minami-kayabe 29a Bc 41.53N 141.01 E
Minami-Tori-Shima = Marcus Island (EN) 57 Gb 26.32N 142.09 E
Minas [Cuba] 49 Ic 21.29N 77.37W
Minas [Indon.] 26 Df 0.50N 101.29 E
Minas [Ur.] 53 Ki 34.23S 55.14W
Minas de Ríotinto 13 Fg 37.42N 6.35W
Minas Gerais [2] 54 Jg 18.00S 44.30W
Mīnā' Su'ūd 24 Mh 28.44N 48.24 E
Minatitlán [Mex.] 47 Fe 17.59N 94.31W
Minatitlán [Mex.] 48 Gh 19.22N 104.04W
Minaya 13 Je 39.17N 2.19W
Minbu 25 Id 20.11N 94.53 E
Minbya 25 Id 20.22N 93.16 E
Minchinmávida, Volcán- 56 Ff 42.49S 72.28W
Mincio 14 Ee 45.04N 10.59 E
Mindanao 21 Oi 8.00N 125.00 E
Mindanao Sea 21 Oi 9.15N 123.40 E
Mindel 10 Gh 48.31N 10.23 E
Mindelheim 10 Gh 48.03N 10.29 E
Mindelo 31 Eg 16.53N 25.00W
Minden [F.R.G.] 10 Ed 52.17N 8.55 E
Minden [La.-U.S.] 45 Jj 32.37N 93.17W
Minden [Nb.-U.S.] 45 Gf 40.30N 98.57W
Mindif 34 Hc 10.24N 14.26 E
Mindoro 21 Oh 12.50N 121.05 E
Mindoro Strait 26 Hd 12.20N 120.40 E
Mindouli 36 Bc 4.17S 14.21 E
Mindszent 10 Qj 46.32N 20.12 E
Mine 29 Bd 34.12N 131.11 E
Minehead 9 Jj 51.13N 3.29W
Mine Head 9 Fj 52.00N 7.35W
Mineiros 54 Hg 17.34S 52.34W
Mineral del Monte 48 Jg 20.08N 98.40W
Mineralnyje Vody 19 Eg 44.12N 43.08 E
Mineral Wells 43 He 32.48N 98.07W
Minerva Reefs 57 Jg 23.50S 179.00W
Minervino Murge 14 Ki 41.05N 16.05 E
Minervois 11 Ik 43.25N 2.45 E
Minfeng/Niya 27 Dd 37.04N 82.46 E
Minga 36 Ee 11.08S 27.56 E
Mingala 35 Cd 5.06N 21.49 E
Mingan 42 Lf 50.18N 64.01W
Mingečaur 16 Oi 40.46N 47.02 E
Mingečaurskoje Vodohranilišče 16 Oi 40.55N 46.45 E
Mingenew 59 De 29.11S 115.26 E
Minggang 28 Ci 32.27N 114.02 E
Mingguang → Jiashan 28 Dh 32.47N 118.00 E
Ming He 28 Cf 37.14N 114.47 E
Minglanilla 13 Ke 39.32N 1.36W
Mingoyo 36 Ge 10.06S 39.38 E
Mingshui 27 Mb 47.15N 125.53 E
Mingshui → Zhangqiu 28 Df 36.44N 117.33 E
Mingteke 27 Bd 37.09N 74.58 E
Mingteke Daban 27 Bd 37.00N 74.50 E
Minguez, Puerto- 13 Ld 40.50N 0.59W
Mingulay 9 Fe 56.50N 7.40W
Mingyuegou 28 Jc 43.08N 128.55 E
Minhe 27 Hd 36.20N 102.50 E
Minho 13 Dc 41.52N 8.51W
Minho 13 Dc 41.40N 8.30W
Minicoy Island 21 Ji 8.17N 73.02 E
Minigwal, Lake- 59 Ee 29.35S 123.10 E
Minija 8 Ii 55.20N 21.12 E
Minilya 59 Cd 23.51S 113.58 E
Minilya River 59 Cd 23.56S 113.51 E
Minipi Lake 42 Lf 52.28N 60.50W
Ministra, Sierra- 13 Jc 41.07N 2.30W
Minjar 17 Hi 55.04N 57.33 E
Min Jiang 21 Mg 28.46N 104.38 E
Minmaya 28 Pd 41.10N 140.28 E
Minna 31 Hh 9.37N 6.33 E
Minna Bluff 66 Kf 78.32S 166.30 E
Minneapolis [Ks.-U.S.] 45 Hg 39.08N 97.42W
Minneapolis [Mn.-U.S.] 39 Je 44.59N 93.13W
Minnedosa 42 Hf 50.14N 99.51W
Minnedosa River 45 Fb 49.53N 100.08W
Minnesota [2] 43 Ib 46.00N 94.15W
Minnesota River 43 Ic 44.54N 93.10W
Miño 5 Fg 41.52N 8.51W
Mino 29 Ed 35.32N 136.54 E
Minobu 29 Fd 35.22N 138.24 E
Minobu-Sanchi 29 Fd 35.15N 138.20 E
Minokamo 29 Ed 35.26N 137.00 E
Mino-Mikawa-Kōgen 29 Ed 35.10N 137.25 E
Minorca (EN) = Menorca 5 Gg 40.00N 4.00 E
Minot 39 Ie 48.14N 101.18W
Minqin 27 Hd 38.42N 103.11 E
Minqing 27 Kf 26.15N 118.52 E
Minquan 28 Cg 34.39N 115.08 E
Min Shan 27 He 33.35N 103.00 E
Minsk 6 Ie 53.54N 27.34 E
Minskaja Oblast [3] 19 Ce 53.50N 27.40 E
Minskaja Vozvyšennost 8 Lj 54.00N 27.10 E
Mińsk Mazowiecki 10 Rd 52.11N 21.34 E
Minta 34 He 4.35N 12.48 E
Minto, Lac- 42 Ke 57.15N 74.50W
Minto, Mount- 66 Kf 71.47S 168.45 E
Minto Inlet 42 Fb 71.19N 117.00W
Minto Reef 57 Gd 8.08N 154.17 E
Minturn 45 Cg 39.35N 106.26W
Minūdasht 24 Pd 37.10N 55.25 E
Minuf 24 Dg 30.28N 30.56 E
Minusinsk 20 Ef 53.43N 91.48 E
Minvoul 36 Bb 2.09N 12.08 E
Minwakh 35 Hb 16.48N 48.06 E
Minxian 27 He 34.26N 104.02 E
Miory 7 Gi 55.39N 27.41 E
Mios Num 26 Kg 1.30S 135.10 E
Miquan 27 Ec 44.05N 87.33 E
Miquelon 42 Jg 49.00N 76.00W
Mira 13 Dg 37.43N 8.47W
Mira [It.] 14 Ge 45.26N 12.08 E
Mira [Port.] 13 Dd 40.26N 8.44W
Mira, Peña- 13 Fc 41.55N 6.28W
Mīrābād 23 Jc 30.25N 61.50 E
Mirabela 55 Jc 16.15S 44.11W
Miracatu 55 Ig 24.17S 47.28W
Miracema 54 Jh 21.25S 42.11W
Mirador, Serra do- 55 Hh 26.45S 49.50W
Miraflores [Col.] 54 Db 5.12N 73.12W
Miraflores [Col.] 54 Dc 1.30N 72.16W
Mirah, Wādī al- 24 If 32.26N 41.42 E
Miraj 25 Ee 16.50N 74.38 E
Miramar 56 Ie 38.16S 57.51W
Miramar, Laguna- 48 Ni 16.20N 91.20W
Miramas 11 Kk 43.35N 5.00 E
Mirambeau 11 Fi 45.22N 0.34W
Miramichi Bay 42 Kg 47.07N 65.10W
Miramont-de-Guyenne 11 Gj 44.36N 0.22 E
Miran 27 Ed 39.15N 88.50 E
Miranda [2] 54 Ea 10.15N 66.25W
Miranda [Arg.] 55 Cm 36.32S 59.09W
Miranda [Braz.] 54 Gh 20.14S 56.22W
Miranda de Corvo 13 Dd 40.06N 8.20W
Miranda de Ebro 13 Jb 42.41N 2.57W
Miranda do Douro 13 Fc 41.30N 6.16W
Mirande 11 Gk 43.31N 0.25 E
Mirandela 13 Ec 41.29N 7.11W
Mirandola 14 Ff 44.53N 11.04 E
Mirandópolis 55 Ge 21.09S 51.06W
Mirante do Paranapanema 55 Gf 22.17S 51.54W
Mira Por Vos 49 Jb 22.04N 74.38W
Mirapuxi, Rio- 55 Ga 13.06S 51.10W
Mirassol 55 He 20.46S 49.28W
Miravalles 13 Fb 42.45N 6.53W
Miravalles, Volcán- 38 Kh 10.45N 85.10W
Miravete, Puerto de- 13 Ge 39.43N 5.43W
Mir-Bašir 16 Oi 40.19N 46.58 E
Mirbāţ 23 Hf 16.58N 54.50 E
Mirdita 15 Ch 41.49N 19.56 E
Mirebalais 49 Kd 18.50N 72.06W
Mirebeau 11 Gh 46.47N 0.11 E
Mirecourt 11 Mf 48.18N 6.08 E
Mirepoix 11 Hk 43.05N 1.53 E
Mirgorod 19 Df 50.00N 33.40 E
Miri 22 Ni 4.23N 113.59 E
Miria 34 Gc 13.43N 9.07 E
Mirim, Lagoa- 52 Ki 32.45S 52.50W
Mirina 15 Ij 39.52N 25.04 E
Miriñay, Esteros del- 55 Di 28.49S 57.10W
Miriñay, Rio- 55 Dj 30.10S 57.39W
Mirny 66 Ge 66.33S 93.01 E
Mirny 22 Nc 62.33N 113.53 E
Mironovka 16 Ge 49.40N 31.01 E
Mirosławiec 10 Mc 53.21N 16.05 E
Mirpur 25 Eb 33.11N 73.46 E
Mirpur Khās 22 Ig 25.32N 69.00 E
Mirqah Sūr 24 Kd 36.50N 44.19 E
Mirsāle 35 Hd 5.58N 47.54 E
Mirşani 15 He 44.01N 24.01 E
Mirtóön Pélagos 15 Gm 37.00N 24.00 E
Miryang 28 Jg 35.29N 128.45 E
Mirzāpur 25 Gc 25.09N 82.35 E
Misaki 29 Ce 33.23N 132.07 E
Misawa 28 Pd 40.41N 141.24 E
Misery, Mount- 51c Ab 17.22N 62.48W
Mishan 27 Nb 45.34N 131.50 E
Mishawaka 44 De 41.40N 86.11W
Mi-Shima 28 Kg 34.47N 131.10 E
Mishima 29 Fd 35.07N 138.54 E
Mishraq, Khashm- 24 Lj 24.13N 46.18 E
Misilmeri 14 Hl 38.02N 13.27 E
Misima Island 60 Ej 10.40S 152.45 E
Misiones [3] 55 Dh 27.00S 57.00W
Misiones [2] 56 Jc 27.00S 55.00W
Misiones, Sierra de- 55 Eh 26.45S 54.20W
Miski, Enneri- 35 Bb 18.10N 17.45 E
Miškino 17 Ki 55.20N 63.55 E
Miskitos, Cayos- 47 Hf 14.23N 82.46W
Miskolc [2] 10 Qh 48.06N 20.43 E
Miskolc 6 If 48.06N 20.47 E
Mismār 35 Fb 18.13N 35.38 E
Misool, Pulau- 26 Jg 1.52S 130.10 E
Misquah Hills 43 Ib 47.17N 92.00W
Mişr = Egypt (EN) [1] 31 Jf 27.00N 30.00 E
Mişr al Jadīdah, Al Qāhirah- 33 Fc 30.06N 31.20 E
Mişrātah 31 Ie 32.23N 15.06 E
Mişrātah [3] 33 Cd 29.00N 16.00 E
Mişrātah, Ra's- 30 Ie 32.25N 15.05 E
Misserghin 13 Li 35.37N 0.44W
Missinaibi 42 Jf 50.44N 81.30W
Missinaibi Lake 44 Fa 48.23N 83.40W
Missinipe 42 He 55.36N 104.45W
Mission [S.D.-U.S.] 45 Fe 43.18N 100.40W
Mission [Tx.-U.S.] 45 Gm 26.13N 98.20W
Mission City 46 Db 49.08N 122.18W
Mission Range 46 Ic 47.30N 113.55W
Mississippi 38 Kg 29.00N 89.15W
Mississippi [2] 43 Je 32.50N 89.30W
Mississippi Delta 38 Kg 29.10N 89.15W
Mississippi Fan (EN) 43 Jf 26.45N 88.30W
Mississippi River 44 Ic 45.26N 76.16W
Mississippi Sound 45 Lk 30.15N 89.00W
Misso 8 Lg 57.33N 27.23 E
Missoula 39 He 46.52N 114.01W
Missour 32 Gc 33.03N 3.59W
Missouri 38 Jf 38.50N 90.08W
Missouri [2] 43 Id 38.30N 93.30W
Missouri, Coteau du- 45 Gc 46.00N 99.30W
Missouri Valley 45 If 41.33N 95.53W
Mistassibi 42 Kg 48.53N 72.13W
Mistassini 44 Ka 48.58N 72.40W
Mistassini, Lac- 38 Ld 51.00N 75.00W
Mistassini, Rivière- 42 Kg 48.42N 72.20W
Mistelbach an der Zaya 14 Kb 48.34N 16.34 E
Misterhult 8 Gg 57.28N 16.33 E
Mistrás 15 Fl 37.04N 22.22 E
Mistretta 14 Im 37.56N 14.22 E
Misugi 29 Ed 34.33N 136.15 E
Misumi [Jap.] 29 Bd 34.46N 131.58 E
Misumi [Jap.] 29 Be 32.37N 130.29 E
Mita, Punta- 48 Gg 32.04N 105.33W
Mitare, Río- 49 Mh 11.28N 69.56W
Mitchell [Austl.] 59 Je 26.29S 147.58 E
Mitchell [Or.-U.S.] 46 Ed 44.34N 120.09W
Mitchell [S.D.-U.S.] 43 Hc 43.40N 98.01W
Mitchell, Mount- 38 Kf 35.46N 82.16W
Mitchell Range 59 Hb 12.50S 135.35 E
Mitchell River 57 Ff 15.12S 141.35 E
Mitchell River Mission 59 Ic 15.28S 141.44 E
Mitchelstown/Baile Mhistéala 9 Ei 52.16N 8.16W
Mithimna 15 Jj 39.22N 26.10 E
Mitiaro Island 57 Lf 19.49S 157.43W
Mitidja, Plaine de la- 13 Oh 36.36N 3.00 E
Mitilini 15 Jj 39.06N 26.33 E
Mitilinis, Stenón- 15 Jj 39.10N 26.35 E
Mitla 47 Ee 16.55N 96.17W
Mitla, Laguna- 48 Ii 17.03N 100.25W
Mito 27 Pd 36.22N 140.28 E
Mitomoni 36 Ge 11.32S 35.19 E

Index Symbols

[1] Independent Nation
[2] State, Region
[3] District, County
[4] Municipality
[5] Colony, Dependency
Continent
Physical Region
Historical or Cultural Region
Mount, Mountain
Volcano
Hill
Mountains, Mountain Range
Hills, Escarpment
Plateau, Upland
Pass, Gap
Plain, Lowland
Delta
Salt Flat
Valley, Canyon
Crater, Cave
Karst Features
Depression
Polder
Desert, Dunes
Forest, Woods
Heath, Steppe
Oasis
Cape, Point
Coast, Beach
Cliff
Peninsula
Isthmus
Sandbank
Island
Atoll
Rock, Reef
Islands, Archipelago
Rocks, Reefs
Coral Reef
Well, Spring
Geyser
River, Stream
Waterfall Rapids
River Mouth, Estuary
Lake
Salt Lake
Intermittent Lake
Reservoir
Swamp, Pond
Canal
Glacier
Ice Shelf, Pack Ice
Ocean
Sea
Gulf, Bay
Strait, Fjord
Lagoon
Bank
Seamount
Tablemount
Ridge
Shelf
Basin
Escarpment, Sea Scarp
Fracture
Trench, Abyss
National Park, Reserve
Point of Interest
Recreation Site
Cave, Cavern
Historic Site
Ruins
Wall, Walls
Church, Abbey
Temple
Scientific Station
Airport
Port
Lighthouse
Mine
Tunnel
Dam, Bridge

Index Symbols

⬚ Independent Nation	▲ Historical or Cultural Region	⊏ Pass, Gap	⬚ Depression	⬚ Coast, Beach	⬚ Rock, Reef
⊡ State, Region	▲ Mount, Mountain	⬚ Plain, Lowland	⬚ Polder	⬚ Cliff	⬚ Islands, Archipelago
⊡ District, County	▲ Volcano	⬚ Delta	⬚ Desert, Dunes	⬚ Peninsula	⬚ Rocks, Reefs
⊡ Municipality	▲ Hill	⬚ Salt Flat	⬚ Forest, Woods	⬚ Isthmus	⬚ Coral Reef
⊡ Colony, Dependency	▲ Mountains, Mountain Range	⬚ Valley, Canyon	⬚ Heath, Steppe	⬚ Sandbank	⬚ Well, Spring
■ Continent	▲ Hills, Escarpment	⬚ Crater, Cave	⬚ Oasis	⬚ Island	⬚ Geyser
⊡ Physical Region	▱ Plateau, Upland	⬚ Karst Features	⬚ Cape, Point	⊙ Atoll	⬚ River, Stream

⬚ Waterfall Rapids	⬚ Canal	⬚ Lagoon	⬚ Escarpment, Sea Scarp
⬚ River Mouth, Estuary	⬚ Glacier	⬚ Bank	⬚ Trench, Abyss
⬚ Lake	⬚ Ice Shelf, Pack Ice	⬚ Seamount	⬚ Fracture
⬚ Salt Lake	⬚ Ocean	⬚ Tablemount	⬚ National Park, Reserve
⬚ Intermittent Lake	⬚ Sea	⬚ Ridge	⬚ Point of Interest
⬚ Reservoir	⬚ Gulf, Bay	⬚ Shelf	⬚ Recreation Site
⬚ Swamp, Pond	⬚ Strait, Fjord	⬚ Basin	⬚ Cave, Cavern

⬚ Historic Site	⬚ Port
⬚ Ruins	⬚ Lighthouse
⬚ Wall, Walls	⬚ Mine
⬚ Church, Abbey	⬚ Tunnel
⬚ Temple	⬚ Dam, Bridge
⬚ Scientific Station	
⬚ Airport	

Monte Lindo Grande, Riacho- 55 Cg 25.45S 58.06W
Montello [Nv.-U.S.] 46 Hf 41.16N 114.12W
Montello [Wi.-U.S.] 45 Le 43.48N 89.20W
Montemorelos 47 Ec 25.12N 99.49W
Montemor-o-Novo 13 Df 38.39N 8.13W
Montemor-o-Velho 13 Dd 40.10N 8.41W
Montemuro, Serra de- 13 Dc 40.58N 8.01W
Montenegro 56 Jc 29.42S 51.28W
Montenegro (EN) = Crna Gora [2] 15 Cg 42.30N 19.18 E
Montenegro (EN)=Crna Gora 15 Cg 42.30N 19.18 E
Monte Plata 49 Md 18.48N 69.47W
Montepuez 37 Gb 12.32S 40.27 E
Montepuez 37 Fb 13.07S 39.00 E
Montepulciano 14 Fg 43.05N 11.47 E
Monte Quemado 56 Hc 25.48S 62.52W
Monte Real 13 De 39.51N 8.52W
Montereale, Passo di- 14 Hh 42.31N 13.13 E
Montereau-Faut-Yonne 11 If 48.23N 2.57 E
Monterey 43 Cd 36.37N 121.55W
Monterey Bay 43 Cd 36.45N 121.55W
Monteria 53 Ie 8.46N 75.53W
Montero 54 Fg 17.20S 63.15W
Monteros 56 Gc 27.10S 65.30W
Monterotondo 14 Gh 42.03N 12.37 E
Monterrey 39 Ig 25.40N 100.19W
Montesano 46 Dc 46.59N 123.36W
Monte San Savino 14 Fg 43.20N 11.43 E
Monte Sant'Angelo 14 Ji 41.42N 15.57 E
Monte Santu, Capo di- 14 Dj 45.05N 9.44 E
Montes Claros 53 Lg 16.43S 43.52W
Montes Claros de Goiás 55 Gb 15.54S 51.13W
Montesilvano 14 Ih 42.31N 14.09 E
Montevarchi 14 Fg 43.31N 11.34 E
Montevideo [2] 55 Dl 34.50S 56.10W
Montevideo [Mn.-U.S.] 45 Id 44.57N 95.43W
Montevideo [Ur.] 53 Ki 34.53S 56.11W
Monte Vista 45 Ch 37.35N 106.09W
Montfaucon 12 He 49.17N 5.08 E
Montfort-l'Amaury 12 Df 48.47N 1.49 E
Montfort-sur-Risle 12 Ce 49.18N 0.40 E
Montgenèvre, Col de- 11 Mj 44.56N 6.44 E
Montgomery 39 Kf 32.23N 86.18W
Montgomery Pass 46 Fh 38.00N 118.20W
Montguyon 11 Fi 45.13N 0.11W
Monthermé 12 Ge 49.53N 4.44 E
Monthey 14 Ad 46.15N 6.56 E
Monthois 12 Ge 49.19N 4.43 E
Monticello [Ar.-U.S.] 45 Kj 33.38N 91.47W
Monticello [Fl.-U.S.] 44 Fj 30.33N 83.52W
Monticello [Ia.-U.S.] 45 Ke 42.15N 91.12W
Monticello [In.-U.S.] 44 De 40.45N 86.46W
Monticello [Ky.-U.S.] 44 Eg 36.50N 84.51W
Monticello [N.Y.-U.S.] 44 Je 41.39N 74.41W
Monticello [Ut.-U.S.] 43 Fd 37.52N 109.21W
Montiel 13 Jf 38.42N 2.52W
Montiel, Campo de- 13 Jf 38.46N 2.44W
Montiel, Cuchilla de- 55 Cj 31.05S 59.10W
Montignac 11 Hi 45.04N 1.10 E
Montigny-le-Roi 11 Lf 48.00N 5.30 E
Montigny-les-Metz 11 Me 49.06N 6.09 E
Montigny-le-Tilleul 12 Gd 50.23N 4.22 E
Montijo [Pan.] 49 Gj 7.59N 81.03W
Montijo [Port.] 13 Df 38.42N 8.58W
Montijo [Sp.] 13 Ff 38.55N 6.37W
Montijo, Golfo de- 49 Gj 7.40N 81.07W
Montilla 13 Hg 37.35N 4.38W
Montividiu 55 Gc 17.24S 51.14W
Montivilliers 11 Ge 49.33N 0.12 E
Mont Joli 42 Kg 48.35N 68.11W
Mont-Laurier 42 Jg 46.33N 75.30W
Mont Louis 44 Oa 49.15N 65.43W
Mont-Louis 11 Il 42.31N 2.07 E
Montluçon 11 Ih 46.20N 2.36 E
Montmagny 42 Kg 46.59N 70.33W
Montmarault 11 Ih 46.19N 2.57 E
Montmédy 11 Le 49.31N 5.22 E
Montmirail 11 Jf 48.52N 3.32 E
Montmorency 12 Ef 49.00N 2.20 E
Montmorillon 11 Gh 46.26N 0.52 E
Montmort-Lucy 12 Ff 48.55N 3.49 E
Monto 59 Kd 24.52S 151.07 E
Montoire-sur-le-Loir 11 Gg 47.45N 0.52 E
Montone 14 Gf 44.24N 12.14 E
Montoro 13 Hf 38.01N 4.23W
Montpelier [Id.-U.S.] 43 Ec 42.19N 111.18W
Montpelier [Vt.-U.S.] 39 Le 44.16N 72.35W
Montpellier 6 Gg 43.36N 3.53 E
Montpon-Ménestérol 11 Gi 45.01N 0.10 E
Montréal 39 Le 45.31N 73.34W
Montreal Lake 42 Gf 54.20N 105.40W
Montreal River 44 Hb 47.08N 79.27W
Montréjeau 11 Gk 43.05N 0.35 E
Montreuil [Fr.] 11 Hd 50.28N 1.46 E
Montreuil [Fr.] 12 Ef 48.52N 2.26 E
Montreuil-l'Argillé 12 Cf 48.56N 0.29 E
Montreux 14 Ad 46.26N 6.55 E
Montrose [Co.-U.S.] 43 Fd 38.29N 107.53W
Montrose [Scot.-U.K.] 9 Ke 56.43N 2.29W
Monts, Pointe des- 44 Na 49.19N 67.23W
Mont-Saint-Aignan 12 De 49.28N 1.05 E
Mont-Saint-Michel, Baie du- 11 Ef 48.40N 1.40W
Montsalvy 11 Ij 44.42N 2.30 E
Montsant, Serra del-/Montsant, Sierra de- 13 Mc 41.17N 0.50 E
Montsant, Sierra de-/Montsant, Serra del- 13 Mc 41.17N 0.50 E
Montsec, Serra del-/Montsech, Sierra del- 13 Mb 42.02N 0.50 E
Montsech, Sierra del-/Montsec, Serra del- 13 Mb 42.02N 0.50 E
Montseny/Pallars, Montsent de- 13 Nb 42.29N 1.02 E
Montseny, Sierra de- 13 Oc 41.48N 2.24 E
Montserrado [3] 34 Cd 6.35N 10.35W
Montserrat [5] 39 Mh 16.45N 62.12W
Montserrat, Monasterio de- 13 Nc 41.35N 1.49 E
Montserrat, Monasterio de-/Montserrat, Monèstir de- 13 Nc 41.35N 1.49 E
Montserrat, Monèstir de- 13 Nc 41.35N 1.49 E
Montserrat, Monèstir de-/Montserrat, Monasterio de- 13 Nc 41.35N 1.49 E
Montuosa, Isla- 49 Fj 7.28N 82.14W
Montville 12 De 49.33N 1.07 E
Monument Peak 46 He 42.07N 114.14W
Monument Valley 46 Jh 36.50N 110.20W
Monveda 36 Db 2.57N 21.27 E
Monviso 5 Gg 44.40N 7.07 E
Monywa 25 Jd 22.07N 95.08 E
Monza 14 De 45.35N 9.16 E
Monze 36 Ef 16.16S 27.29 E
Monzen 29 Ec 37.17N 136.46 E
Monzón 13 Mc 41.55N 0.12 E
Mo'oka 29 Fc 36.27N 139.59 E
Moonbeam 44 Fa 49.25N 82.11W
Moonie 59 Ke 27.40S 150.19 E
Moonie River 59 Je 29.19S 148.43 E
Moonta 59 Hf 34.04S 137.35 E
Moora 58 Ch 30.39S 116.00 E
Moorcroft 46 Md 44.16N 104.57W
Moore 45 Hi 35.20N 97.29W
Moore, Lake- 57 Cg 29.50S 117.35 E
Moorea, Ile- 57 Mf 17.32S 149.50W
Moore's Island 44 Il 26.18N 77.33W
Moorhead 43 Hb 46.53N 96.45W
Moormerland 12 Ja 53.18N 7.26 E
Moormerland-Neermoor 12 Ja 53.18N 7.26 E
Moorreesburg 37 Bf 33.09S 18.40 E
Moosburg an der Isar 10 Hh 48.28N 11.56 E
Moose 38 Kd 50.48N 81.18W
Moosehead Lake 43 Nb 45.40N 69.40W
Moose Jaw 39 Id 50.23N 105.32W
Moose Jaw River 46 Ma 50.34N 105.17W
Moose Lake 45 Jc 46.25N 92.45W
Mooselookmeguntic Lake 44 Lc 44.53N 70.48W
Moose Mountain 45 Eb 49.45N 102.37W
Moose Mountain Creek 45 Eb 49.12N 102.10W
Moosomin 42 Hf 50.09N 101.40W
Moosonee 39 Kd 51.17N 80.39W
Mopeia 37 Fc 17.59S 35.43 E
Mopelia, Atoll- → Maupihaa Atoll 57 Lf 16.50S 153.55W
Mopti 31 Gg 14.30N 4.12W
Mopti [3] 34 Ec 14.40N 4.15W
Moqokorei 35 He 4.04N 46.08 E
Moquegua [2] 54 Dg 16.50S 70.55W
Moquegua 54 Dg 17.12S 70.56W
Mór 10 Oi 47.23N 18.12 E
Mor, Glen- 9 Id 57.10N 4.40W
Mora [Cam.] 34 Hc 11.03N 14.09 E
Mora [Port.] 13 Df 38.56N 8.10W
Mora [Sp.] 13 Ie 39.41N 3.46W
Mora [Swe.] 7 Df 61.00N 14.33 E
Morača 15 Cg 42.16N 19.09 E
Morača, Manastir- 15 Cg 42.46N 19.24 E
Morādābād 22 Jg 28.50N 78.47 E
Morada Nova de Minas 55 Jd 18.25S 45.22W
Mora d'Ebre/Mora de Ebro 13 Mc 41.05N 0.38 E
Mora de Ebro/Móra d'Ebre 13 Mc 41.05N 0.38 E
Mora de Rubielos 13 Ld 40.15N 0.45W
Morafenobe 37 Gc 17.49S 44.55 E
Morağ 10 Pc 53.56N 19.56 E
Mórahalom 10 Pj 46.13N 19.53 E
Moraleda, Canal- 56 Ff 44.30S 73.30W
Moraleja 13 Fd 40.04N 6.39W
Morales [Col.] 49 Ki 8.17N 73.52W
Morales [Guat.] 49 Cf 15.29N 88.49W
Morales, Laguna- 48 Kf 23.35N 97.45W
Moramanga 37 Hc 18.57S 48.11 E
Moran 46 Je 43.50N 110.28W
Morane Atoll 57 Ng 23.10S 137.07W
Morangas, Ribeirão- 55 Fd 19.39S 52.19W
Morant Bay 49 Ie 17.53N 76.25W
Morant Cays 47 Ie 17.24N 75.59W
Morant Point 49 Ie 17.55N 76.10W
Morar, Loch- 9 He 56.58N 5.45W
Morarano 37 Hc 17.46S 48.10 E
Mora River 45 Di 35.44N 104.23W
Moraska, Góra- 10 Md 52.30N 16.52 E
Morat/Murten 14 Bd 46.56N 7.08 E
Morata, Puerto de- 13 Kc 41.29N 1.31W
Moratalla 13 Kf 38.12N 1.53W
Moratuwa 25 Fg 6.46N 79.53 E
Morava 5 Hf 48.10N 16.59 E
Morava=Moravia (EN) 5 Hf 49.30N 17.00 E
Morava=Moravia (EN) 10 Mg 49.30N 17.00 E
Moravia (EN)=Morava 5 Hf 49.30N 17.00 E
Moravia (EN)=Morava 10 Mg 49.30N 17.00 E
Moravian Gate (EN)= Moravská Brána 5 Hf 49.33N 17.42 E
Moravian Upland (EN)= Českomoravská Vrchovina 5 Hf 49.20N 15.30 E
Moravica 15 Df 43.51N 20.05 E
Moravská Brána=Moravian Gate(EN) 5 Hf 49.33N 17.42 E
Moravské Budějovice 10 Lg 49.03N 15.49 E
Morawa 59 De 29.13S 116.00 E
Morawhanna 54 Gb 8.16N 59.45W
Moray Firth 5 Fd 57.50N 3.30W
Morbach 12 Je 49.49N 7.07 E
Morbihan [3] 11 Dg 47.55N 2.50W
Morbihan 11 Dg 47.35N 2.48W
Morbylånga 7 Dh 56.31N 16.23 E
Morcenx 11 Fj 44.02N 0.55W
Mordāb 24 Md 37.26N 49.25 E
Mordaga 27 La 51.14N 120.43 E
Morden 42 Hg 49.11N 98.05W
Mordovo 16 Lc 52.05N 40.46 E
Mordovskaja ASSR [3] 19 Ee 54.20N 44.30 E
Möre 8 Fh 56.25N 15.55 E
More, Ben- 9 Ie 56.23N 4.31W
Morea 37 Bd 22.41S 15.54 E
More Assynt, Ben- 9 Ic 58.07N 4.51W
Moreau River 43 Gb 45.18N 100.43W
Morecambe 9 Kg 54.04N 2.53W
Morecambe Bay 9 Kg 54.07N 3.00W
Moree 58 Fg 29.28S 149.51 E
Morehead [Ky.-U.S.] 44 Ff 38.11N 83.25W
Morehead [Pap.N.Gui.] 60 Ci 8.50S 141.57 E
Morehead City 39 Lf 34.43N 76.43W
Moreiz, Gora- 19 Gb 69.30N 62.05 E
Moreju 17 Ib 68.20N 59.45 E
Morelia 39 Ih 19.42N 101.07W
Morella 13 Ld 40.37N 0.06W
Morelos 48 Ic 28.25N 100.53W
Morelos [2] 47 Ee 18.45N 99.00W
Morena, Sierra- 5 Fh 38.00N 5.00W
Moreni 15 Ie 44.59N 25.39 E
Møre og Romsdal [2] 7 Be 62.40N 7.50 E
Moresby 42 Ef 52.45N 131.50W
Moreton Bay 59 Ke 27.20S 153.15 E
Moreton Island 59 Ke 27.10S 153.25 E
Moret-sur-Loing 11 If 48.22N 2.49 E
Moreuil 12 Ee 49.46N 2.29 E
Morez 11 Mh 46.31N 6.02 E
Morezu 15 Hd 45.09N 24.01 E
Mörfelden 12 Ke 49.59N 8.34 E
Morgan City 45 Kl 29.42N 91.12W
Morganfield 44 Dg 37.41N 87.55W
Morganton 44 Gh 35.45N 81.41W
Morgantown [Ky.-U.S.] 44 Dg 37.14N 86.41W
Morgantown [W.V.-U.S.] 44 Hf 39.38N 79.57W
Morges 14 Ad 46.31N 6.30 E
Morghāb 23 Jb 38.18N 61.12 E
Morhange 11 Mf 48.55N 6.38 E
Mori [China] 27 Fc 43.49N 90.11 E
Mori [Jap.] 28 Pc 42.06N 140.35 E
Moriarty 45 Ci 34.59N 106.03W
Morichal Largo, Rio- 50 Eh 9.27N 62.25W
Moriguchi 29 Dd 34.44N 135.34 E
Morin Dawa (Nirji) 27 Lb 48.30N 124.28 E
Morioka 22 Qf 39.42N 141.09 E
Moriyoshi 29 Ga 40.07N 140.22 E
Moriyoshi-Yama 29 Gb 39.59N 140.33 E
Morjärv 7 Fc 66.04N 22.43 E
Morki 7 Lh 56.28N 49.00 E
Morko 8 Gf 59.00N 17.40 E
Morkoka 20 Gc 65.03N 115.40 E
Mørkøv 8 Di 55.40N 11.32 E
Morlaix 11 Cf 48.35N 3.50W
Morlanwelz 12 Gd 50.27N 4.14 E
Mörlunda 8 Fg 57.19N 15.51 E
Mormanno 14 Jk 39.53N 15.59 E
Morne-à-l'Eau 50 Fd 16.21N 61.31W
Morne Diablotin 47 Le 15.30N 61.24W
Mornington, Isla- 56 Eg 49.45S 75.23W
Mornington Island 59 Hc 16.35S 139.24 E
Moro 46 Ed 45.29N 120.44W
Morobe 58 Fe 7.45S 147.37 E
Morocco (EN)=Al Maghrib [1] 31 Ge 32.00N 5.50W
Morogoro 31 Ki 6.49S 37.40 E
Morogoro [3] 36 Gd 8.20S 37.00 E
Moro Gulf 26 He 6.51N 123.00 E
Moroleón 48 Ig 20.08N 101.12W
Morombe 31 Lk 21.44S 43.23 E
Morón [Arg.] 55 Cl 34.39S 58.37W
Morón [Cuba] 47 Id 22.06N 78.38W
Morón [Ven.] 54 Ea 10.29N 68.11W
Morona, Rio- 54 Cd 4.45S 77.04W
Morondava 31 Lk 20.15S 44.17 E
Morón de la Frontera 13 Gg 37.08N 5.27W
Morones, Sierra- 48 Hg 21.55N 103.05W
Moroni 31 Lj 11.41S 43.16 E
Moron Us He 21 Lf 34.42N 94.50 E
Morotai, Pulau- 57 Dd 2.20N 128.25 E
Moroto 31 Kh 2.32N 34.39 E
Morovița 15 Ed 45.16N 21.16 E
Morozov 15 Ig 42.30N 25.10 E
Morozovsk 19 Ef 48.20N 41.50 E
Morpeth 9 Lf 55.10N 1.41W
Morphou/Güzelyurt 24 Ee 35.12N 32.59 E
Morrilton 45 Ji 35.09N 92.45W
Morrinhos 54 Ig 17.44S 49.07W
Morrinsville 62 Fb 37.39S 175.32 E
Morris [Il.-U.S.] 45 Lf 41.22N 88.26W
Morris [Man.-Can.] 42 Hg 49.21N 97.22W
Morris [Mn.-U.S.] 45 Id 45.35N 95.55W
Morris, Mount- 59 Ge 26.09S 131.04 E
Morrisburg 44 Jc 44.54N 75.11W
Morris Jesup, Kap- 67 Me 83.45N 35.50W
Morrison Dennis Cays 49 Ff 14.28N 82.53W
Morristown 44 Fg 36.13N 83.18W
Morrito 49 Eh 11.37N 85.05W
Morro, Punta del- 48 Kh 19.51N 96.27W
Morro Bay 43 Cd 35.22N 120.51W
Morro do Chapéu 54 Jf 11.33S 41.09W
Morrosquillo, Golfo de- 49 Ji 9.35N 75.40W
Morro Vermelho, Serra do- 55 Jc 17.45S 45.20W
Mörrum 8 Fh 56.11N 14.45 E
Morrumbala 37 Fc 17.20S 35.35 E
Morrumbene 37 Fd 23.39S 35.20 E
Mörrumsån 8 Fh 56.09N 14.44 E
Mors 8 Ch 56.50N 8.45 E
Moršansk 19 Ee 53.26N 41.49 E
Morsbach 12 Jd 50.52N 7.45 E
Morsberg 12 Ke 49.43N 8.54 E
Mörsil 7 Ce 63.19N 13.38 E
Mörskom/Myrskylä 8 Kd 60.40N 25.51 E
Morsott 14 Co 35.40N 8.01 E
Mortagne 11 Mf 48.33N 6.27 E
Mortagne-au-Perche 11 Gf 48.31N 0.33 E
Mortagne-sur-Sèvre 11 Fg 47.00N 0.57W
Mortain 11 Ff 48.39N 0.56W
Mortara 14 Ce 45.15N 8.44 E
Mortcha 30 Jg 16.00N 21.10 E
Morteau 11 Mg 47.04N 6.37 E
Morteaux-Couliboeuf 12 Bf 48.56N 0.04W
Morteros 56 Hd 30.42S 62.00W
Mortes, Rio das- 55 Je 21.09S 44.53W
Mortesoro 35 Ec 10.12N 34.09 E
Mortlock Islands 57 Gd 5.27N 153.40 E
Morton 46 Dc 46.33N 122.17W
Mortsel 12 Gc 51.10N 4.28 E
Morumbi 55 Ef 23.46S 54.06W
Morvan 11 Jg 47.05N 4.00 E
Morven 59 Je 26.25S 147.07 E
Morvern 9 He 56.35N 5.50W
Morvi 25 Ed 22.49N 70.50 E
Morwell 58 Fh 38.14S 146.24 E
Morzine 11 Mh 46.11N 6.43 E
Moržovec, Ostrov- 7 Kc 66.45N 42.35 E
Moša 7 Je 62.25N 39.48 E
Mosbach 10 Fg 49.21N 9.09 E
Mosby 8 Bf 58.14N 7.54 E
Mošćny, Ostrov- 7 Gg 60.00N 27.50 E
Mosconi 55 Bl 35.44S 60.34W
Moscos Islands 25 Jf 14.00N 97.45 E
Moscow [Id.-U.S.] 43 Db 46.44N 116.59W
Moscow (EN)=Moskva 5 Jd 55.08N 38.50 E
Moscow (EN)=Moskva [R.S.F.S.R.] 6 Jd 55.45N 37.35 E
Moscow Basin (EN)= Meščera 5 Kd 55.00N 40.30 E
Moscow Canal (EN)= Moskvy, kanal imeni- 5 Jd 56.43N 37.08 E
Moscow Upland (EN)= Moskovskaja Vozvyšennost 5 Jd 56.30N 37.30 E
Mosel=Moselle (EN) 5 Ge 50.22N 7.36 E
Moselberge 12 Ie 49.57N 6.56 E
Moselle [3] 11 Me 49.00N 6.30 E
Moselle 5 Ge 50.22N 7.36 E
Moselle (EN)=Mosel 5 Ge 50.22N 7.36 E
Moses Lake 43 Db 47.08N 119.17W
Mosgiel 61 Di 45.53S 170.22 E
Moshi 31 Ki 3.21S 37.20 E
Mosina 10 Md 52.16N 16.51 E
Mosjøen 7 Cd 65.50N 13.12 E
Moskalvo 20 Jf 53.39N 142.37 E
Moskenesøy 7 Cc 67.59N 13.00 E
Moskovskaja Oblast [3] 19 Dd 55.45N 37.45 E
Moskovskaja Vozvyšennost =Moscow Upland (EN) 5 Jd 56.30N 37.30 E
Moskovski 18 Gf 37.40N 69.39 E
Moskva [R.S.F.S.R.] = Moscow (EN) 6 Jd 55.45N 37.35 E
Moskva [Tur.-U.S.S.R.] 18 Ee 38.27N 64.24 E
Moskva=Moscow (EN) 5 Jd 55.08N 38.50 E
Moskva, Pik- 18 He 38.55N 71.52 E
Moskvy, kanal imeni-= Moscow Canal (EN) 5 Jd 56.43N 37.08 E
Moslavačka Gora 14 Ke 45.38N 16.42 E
Moso 63b Dc 17.32S 168.15 E
Mosomane 37 Dd 24.01S 26.19 E
Mosoni-Duna 10 Ni 47.44N 17.47 E
Mosonmagyaróvár 10 Ni 47.52N 17.17 E
Mosor 14 Kg 43.30N 16.40 E
Mosquero 45 Ei 35.47N 103.58W
Mosquito, Baie - 42 Jd 60.40N 78.00W
Mosquito Coast (EN)= Mosquitos, Costa de- 38 Kh 13.00N 83.45W
Mosquito, Riacho- 55 Cf 22.12S 57.57W
Mosquitos, Costa de-= Mosquito Coast (EN) 38 Kh 13.00N 83.45W
Mosquitos, Golfo de los- 38 Ki 9.00N 81.20W
Moss 6 Hd 59.26N 10.42 E
Mossaka 36 Cc 1.13S 16.48 E
Mossâmedes 55 Gc 16.07S 50.11W
Mossbank 46 Mb 49.55N 105.59W
Mossburn 61 Ci 45.41S 168.15 E
Mosselbaai 31 Jl 34.11S 22.08 E
Mossendjo 36 Bc 2.57S 12.44 E
Mossman 58 Ff 16.28S 145.22 E
Mossø 8 Ch 56.05N 9.50 E
Mossoró 53 Mf 5.11S 37.20W
Moss Point 45 Lk 30.25N 88.29W
Mossuril 37 Gb 14.58S 40.40 E
Most 10 Jf 50.32N 13.39 E
Mostaganem [3] 32 Hb 35.40N 0.30 E
Mostaganem 31 He 35.56N 0.05 E
Mostar 14 Lg 43.21N 17.49 E
Mostardas 55 Gj 31.06S 50.57W
Møsting, Kap- 41 Hf 63.45N 41.00W
Mostiska 16 Ce 49.48N 23.09 E
Mostiștea 15 Je 44.15N 26.54 E
Most na Soci 14 Hd 46.09N 13.45 E
Mostovskoj 16 Lg 44.22N 40.48 E
Mosty 19 Ce 53.27N 24.33 E
Mosul (EN)=Al Mawşil 22 Gf 36.20N 43.08 E
Møsvatn 7 Bg 59.50N 8.05 E
Mota 63b Ca 13.40S 167.42 E
Mota 35 Fc 11.05N 37.53 E
Motaba 36 Cb 2.03N 18.03 E
Motacusito 55 Bd 17.35S 61.31W
Mota del Marques 13 Gc 41.38N 5.10W
Motagua 38 Kh 15.44N 88.14W
Motajica 14 Le 45.04N 17.40 E
Motala 7 Dg 58.33N 15.03 E
Motala ström 8 Gf 58.38N 16.10 E
Motatán 49 Li 9.24N 70.36W
Motatán, Rio- 49 Li 9.32N 71.02W
Motegi 29 Gc 36.32N 140.10 E
Motehuala 47 Dd 23.39N 100.39W
Mothe 63d Cc 18.40S 178.30W
Motherwell 9 Jf 55.48N 4.00W
Motīhāri 25 Gc 26.39N 84.55 E
Motilla del Palancar 13 Ke 39.34N 1.53W
Motiti Island 62 Gb 37.40S 176.25 E
Motlav 63b Ca 13.40S 167.40 E
Motobu 29b Ab 26.40N 127.55 E
Motol 10 Vd 52.17N 25.40 E
Motovski Zaliv 7 Hb 69.30N 32.30 E
Motoyoshi 29 Gb 38.48N 141.31 E
Motozintla de Mendoza 48 Mj 15.22N 92.14W
Motril 13 Ih 36.45N 3.31W
Motru 15 Ge 44.33N 23.27 E
Motru 15 Fe 44.48N 23.00 E
Motsuta-Misaki 29a Ab 42.36N 139.49 E
Mott 45 Ec 46.22N 102.20W
Motteville 12 Ce 49.38N 0.51 E
Motu 62 Gb 37.51S 177.35 E
Motueka 62 Ed 41.07S 173.01 E
Motuhora Island 62 Gb 37.50S 177.00 E
Motu-Iti 65d Ac 27.11S 109.27W
Motu-Iti → Tupai Atoll 61 Kc 16.17S 151.50W
Motul 47 Gd 21.06N 89.17W
Motu-Nui 65d Ac 27.12S 109.28W
Motu One Atoll 57 Lf 15.48S 154.33W
Motupae 64n Ac 10.27S 161.02W
Motupena Point 63a Bb 6.32S 155.09 E
Moturiki 63d Bb 17.46S 178.45 E
Motutapu 64p Cb 21.14S 159.43W
Motu Tautara 65d Ab 27.05S 109.26W
Motutunga Atoll 57 Mf 17.06S 144.22W
Moubray Bay 66 Kf 72.11S 170.15 E
Mouchard 11 Lh 46.58N 5.48 E
Mouchoir Bank (EN) 47 Jd 20.57N 70.42W
Mouchoir Passage 49 Lc 21.10N 71.00W
Moudjéria 32 Ef 17.52N 12.20W
Mouila 31 Ii 1.52S 11.01 E
Mouka 35 Cd 7.16N 21.52 E
Moul 34 Hb 15.03N 13.18 E
Mould Bay 39 Hb 76.15N 119.30W
Moule 50 Fd 16.20N 61.21W
Moule à Chique, Cap- 51k Bb 13.43N 60.57W
Moulins 11 Jh 46.34N 3.20 E
Moulmein 22 Le 16.30N 97.38 E
Moulouya 30 Ge 35.06N 2.20W
Moult 12 Be 49.07N 0.10W
Moultrie 44 Fj 31.11N 83.47W
Moultrie, Lake- 44 Gi 33.20N 80.05W
Mouly, Pointe de- 63b Ce 20.43S 166.23 E
Moúnda, Ákra- 15 Dk 38.03N 20.47 E
Moundou 31 Ih 8.34N 16.05 E
Moundsville 44 Gf 39.54N 80.44W
Mo'unga'one 65b Ba 19.38S 174.29W
Moungoudou 36 Bc 2.40S 12.41 E
Mountainair 45 Ci 34.31N 106.15W
Mountain Grove 45 Jh 37.08N 92.16W
Mountain Home [Ar.-U.S.] 45 Jh 36.21N 92.23W
Mountain Home [Id.-U.S.] 43 Dc 43.08N 115.41W
Mountain Nile (EN)=Jabal, Baḩr al- 30 Kh 9.30N 30.30 E
Mountain Village 40 Gd 62.05N 163.44W
Mount Airy 44 Gg 36.31N 80.37W
Mount Barker 59 Df 34.38S 117.40 E
Mount Carmel 45 Mf 38.25N 87.46W
Mount Desert Island 44 Mc 44.20N 68.20W
Mount Douglas 58 Fg 21.30S 146.50 E
Mount Eba 59 Hf 30.12S 135.40 E
Mount Forest 44 Gd 43.59N 80.44W
Mount Frere 37 Df 31.00S 28.58 E
Mount Gambier 58 Fh 37.50S 140.46 E
Mount Hagen 60 Ci 5.52S 144.13 E
Mount Hope 59 Hf 34.07S 135.23 E
Mount Isa 58 Eg 20.44S 139.30 E
Mountlake Terrace 46 Dc 47.47N 122.18W
Mount Lavinia 25 Fg 6.50N 79.52 E
Mount Lebanon 44 Ge 40.23N 80.03W
Mount Lofty Ranges 59 Hg 35.15S 138.50 E
Mount Magnet 58 Cg 28.04S 117.49 E
Mount Maunganui 61 Eg 37.38S 176.12 E
Mount Morgan 59 Kd 23.39S 150.23 E
Mountnorris Bay 59 Gb 11.20S 132.45 E
Mount Peck 46 Ha 50.10N 115.02W
Mount Pleasant [Ia.-U.S.] 45 Kf 40.58N 91.33W
Mount Pleasant [Mi.-U.S.] 44 Ed 43.35N 84.47W
Mount Pleasant [S.C.-U.S.] 44 Hi 32.47N 79.52W
Mount Pleasant [Tx.-U.S.] 45 Ij 33.09N 94.58W
Mount Pleasant [Ut.-U.S.] 46 Jg 39.33N 111.27W
Mount's Bay 9 Hk 50.03N 5.25W
Mount Somers 62 De 43.42S 171.25 E
Mount Sterling [Il.-U.S.] 45 Kg 39.59N 90.45W
Mount Sterling [Ky.-U.S.] 44 Ff 38.04N 83.56W
Mount Vancouver 42 Dd 60.20N 139.41W
Mount Vernon [Al.-U.S.] 44 Cj 31.05N 88.01W
Mount Vernon [Austl.] 59 Dd 24.13S 118.14 E
Mount Vernon [Il.-U.S.] 43 Jd 38.19N 88.55W
Mount Vernon [In.-U.S.] 44 Dg 37.56N 87.54W
Mount Vernon [Ky.-U.S.] 44 Eg 37.21N 84.20W
Mount Vernon [Oh.-U.S.] 44 Fe 40.23N 82.30W
Mount Vernon [Wa.-U.S.] 43 Cb 48.25N 122.20W
Moura [Austl.] 59 Jd 24.35S 150.00 E
Moura [Port.] 13 Ef 38.08N 7.27W
Mourão 13 Ef 38.23N 7.21W
Mourdi 35 Cb 17.50N 22.25 E
Mourdi, Dépression du-= Mourdi Depression (EN) 30 Jg 18.10N 23.00 E
Mourdiah 34 Dc 14.26N 7.31W
Mourdi Depression (EN)= Mourdi, Dépression du- 30 Jg 18.10N 23.00 E
Mourmelon-le-Grand 12 Ge 49.08N 4.22 E
Mourne Mountains/Beanna Boirche 9 Gg 54.10N 6.04W
Mouscron/Moeskroen 11 Jd 50.44N 3.13 E
Moussoro 31 Ig 13.39N 16.29 E
Moustiers-Sainte-Marie 11 Mk 43.51N 6.13 E
Moutier/Münster 14 Bc 47.16N 7.22 E
Moutiers 11 Mi 45.29N 6.32 E
Moutong 26 Hf 0.28N 121.13 E
Mouy 12 Ee 49.19N 2.19 E
Mouydir 30 Hf 25.00N 4.10 E
Mouyondzi 36 Bc 3.58S 13.57 E
Mouzaia 13 Oh 36.28N 2.41 E
Mouzon 12 He 49.36N 5.05 E
Movas 48 Ec 28.10N 109.25W

Index Symbols

[1] Independent Nation
[2] State, Region
[3] District, County
[4] Municipality
[5] Colony, Dependency
Continent
Physical Region
Historical or Cultural Region
Mount, Mountain
Volcano
Hill
Mountains, Mountain Range
Hills, Escarpment
Plateau, Upland
Pass, Gap
Plain, Lowland
Delta
Salt Flat
Valley, Canyon
Crater, Cave
Karst Features
Depression
Polder
Desert, Dunes
Forest, Woods
Heath, Steppe
Oasis
Cape, Point
Coast, Beach
Cliff
Peninsula
Isthmus
Sandbank
Island
Atoll
Rock, Reef
Islands, Archipelago
Rocks, Reefs
Coral Reef
Well, Spring
Geyser
River, Stream
Waterfall Rapids
River Mouth, Estuary
Lake
Salt Lake
Intermittent Lake
Reservoir
Swamp, Pond
Canal
Glacier
Ice Shelf, Pack Ice
Ocean
Sea
Gulf, Bay
Strait, Fjord
Lagoon
Bank
Seamount
Tablemount
Ridge
Shelf
Basin
Escarpment, Sea Scarp
Fracture
Trench, Abyss
National Park, Reserve
Point of Interest
Recreation Site
Cave, Cavern
Historic Site
Ruins
Wall, Walls
Church, Abbey
Temple
Scientific Station
Airport
Port
Lighthouse
Mine
Tunnel
Dam, Bridge

Index Symbols

[1] Independent Nation — [2] State, Region — [3] District, County — [4] Municipality — [5] Colony, Dependency — Continent — Physical Region

Historical or Cultural Region — Mount, Mountain — Volcano — Hill — Mountains, Mountain Range — Hills, Escarpment — Plateau, Upland

Pass, Gap — Plain, Lowland — Delta — Salt Flat — Valley, Canyon — Crater, Cave — Karst Features

Depression — Polder — Desert, Dunes — Forest, Woods — Heath, Steppe — Oasis — Cape, Point

Coast, Beach — Cliff — Peninsula — Isthmus — Sandbank — Island — Atoll

Rock, Reef — Islands, Archipelago — Rocks, Reefs — Coral Reef — Well, Spring — Geyser — River, Stream

Waterfall Rapids — River Mouth, Estuary — Lake — Salt Lake — Intermittent Lake — Reservoir — Swamp, Pond

Canal — Glacier — Ice Shelf, Pack Ice — Ocean — Sea — Gulf, Bay — Strait, Fjord

Lagoon — Bank — Seamount — Tablemount — Shelf — Ridge — Basin

Escarpment, Sea Scarp — Fracture — Trench, Abyss — National Park, Reserve — Point of Interest — Recreation Site — Cave, Cavern

Historic Site — Ruins — Wall, Walls — Church, Abbey — Temple — Scientific Station — Airport

Port — Lighthouse — Mine — Tunnel — Dam, Bridge

rzeqeja 15 Ci 41.01N 19.36 E
Zab 32 Hc 32.35N 3.20 E
e 10 Jg 49.46N 13.24 E
iha 36 Gd 5.54S 37.47 E
imba 36 Fe 11.54S 33.36 E
uzu 31 Kj 11.27S 33.55 E
ab 10 Ig 49.01N 12.02 E
aldwijk 12 Gc 51.59N 4.12 E
alehu 65a Fd 19.04N 155.35W
antali/Nådendal 7 Ff 60.27N 22.02 E
arden 12 Hb 52.18N 5.10 E
as/An Nás 9 Gh 53.13N 6.39W
badid 35 Gd 9.38N 43.29 E
bão 13 De 39.31N 8.21W
bari 29 Ed 34.37N 136.05 E
berera 36 Gc 4.12S 36.56 E
bereżnyje Čelny 6 Ld 55.42N 52.19 E
bha 25 Fb 30.22N 76.09 E
bileque, Rio- 55 De 20.55S 57.49W
bire 58 Ee 3.22S 135.29 E
bī Shu'ayb, Jabal an- 21 Gh 15.17N 43.59 E
bq 24 Fh 28.04N 34.25 E
bul 31 Ie 36.27N 10.44 E
bul [3] 32 Ib 36.45N 10.45 E
bulus 24 Ff 32.13N 35.16 E
busanke 36 Fb 0.01N 32.03 E
cala 37 Gb 14.33S 40.40 E
cala-a-Velha 31 Lj 14.33S 40.36 E
caome 49 Dg 13.31N 87.30W
caroa 37 Fb 14.23S 39.55 E
ceredine 13 Ph 36.08N 3.26 E
chikatsuura 29 De 33.39N 135.55 E
chingwea 36 Ge 10.23S 38.46 E
chi-San 29 De 33.42N 135.51 E
chod 10 Mf 50.26N 16.10 E
chuge 25 If 10.35N 92.28 E
chvak Fiord 42 Le 59.03N 63.45W
cka 7 Ee 59.18N 18.10 E
Clocha Liatha/
Greystones 9 Gh 53.09N 6.04W
cogdoches 45 Ik 31.36N 94.39W
a Comaraigh/Comeragh
Mountains 9 Fi 52.13N 7.35W
acori, Sierra- 48 Ec 29.50N 108.50W
acozari, Rio- 48 Ec 29.48N 109.42W
acozari de Garcia 47 Cb 30.24N 109.39W
a Cruacha/Blue Stack 9 Eg 54.45N 8.06W
a Cruacha Dubha/
Macgillycuddy's Reeks 9 Di 52.00N 9.50W
acunday, Rio- 55 Eh 26.03S 54.45W
ada → Danxian 27 Ih 19.38N 109.32 E
ådendal/Naantali 7 Ff 60.27N 22.02 E
adiād 25 Ed 22.42N 72.52 E
ādlac 15 Dc 46.10N 20.45 E
ador [3] 32 Gb 35.00N 3.00W
ador 32 Gb 35.11N 2.56W
ádusa 15 Fi 40.38N 22.04 E
advoicy 19 Dc 63.52N 34.20 E
advornaja 16 De 48.38N 24.34 E
adym 22 Jc 65.35N 72.42 E
aeba-San 29 Fc 36.51N 138.41 E
ærbø 8 Af 58.40N 5.39 E
æstved 7 Ci 55.14N 11.46 E
afada 34 Hc 11.06N 11.20 E
äfels 14 Dc 47.06N 9.04 E
aftah 14 Dn 36.57N 9.04 E
aftan Rock 64b Bb 14.50N 145.32 E
aft-e-Safid 24 Mg 31.40N 49.17 E
aft-e-Shāh 24 Kf 33.59N 45.30 E
aft Khāneh 24 Ke 34.02N 45.28 E
afūsah, Jabal- 30 Ie 31.50N 12.00 E
āg 25 Dc 27.24N 65.08 E
aga 22 Oh 13.28N 123.39 E
āga, Kreb en- 22 Fe 24.00N 6.00W
agagami Lake 44 Ea 49.28N 85.02W
agagami River 45 Na 50.25N 84.20W
agahama [Jap.] 29 Ed 35.23N 136.16 E
agahama [Jap.] 29 Ce 33.36N 132.29 E
agai 29 Gb 38.06N 140.02 E
agai 40 Ge 55.11N 159.55W
Na Gaibhlte/Galty
Mountains 9 Ei 52.23N 8.11W
Nāgāland [3] 25 Ic 26.30N 94.00 E
Nagano 22 Pf 36.39N 138.11 E
Nagano Ken [2] 28 Nf 36.10N 138.00 E
Nagano-Matsushiro 29 Fc 36.34N 138.10 E
Nagano-Shinonoi 29 Fc 36.35N 138.06 E
Nagaoka 27 Od 37.27N 138.51 E
Nāgappattinam 25 Ff 10.46N 79.50 E
Nagara-Gawa 29 Ed 35.02N 136.43 E
Nagarote 49 Dg 12.16N 86.34W
Nagarzê 27 Ff 28.59N 90.28 E
Nagasaki 22 Of 32.47N 129.56 E
Nagasaki-Hantō 29 Ae 32.40N 129.45 E
Nagasaki Ken [2] 28 Jh 33.00N 129.50 E
Naga-Shima 29 Ce 33.50N 132.05 E
Nagashima 29 Ed 34.12N 136.19 E
Nagashima 29 Be 32.10N 130.10 E
Naga-Shima-Kaikyō 29 Be 32.15N 130.10 E
Nagato 28 Kg 34.21N 131.10 E
Nagayo 29 Ae 32.50N 129.52 E
Nāgda 25 Fd 23.27N 75.25 E
Nāgercoil 25 Fg 8.10N 77.26 E
Naghora Point 60 Gj 10.50S 162.24 E
Nagichot 35 Ee 4.16N 33.34 E
Nagi-San 29 Dd 35.10N 134.10 E
Nagiso 29 Ed 35.36N 137.36 E
Nago 27 Mf 26.35N 128.01 E
Nagold 10 Eh 48.52N 8.42 E
Nagorno-Karabahskaja
Avtonomnaja Oblast [3] 19 Eh 39.55N 46.45 E
Nagorny [R.S.F.S.R.] 20 He 55.45N 124.58 E
Nagorny [R.S.F.S.R.] 20 Md 63.10N 179.05 E
Nagorsk 7 Mg 59.21N 50.48 E
Nago-Wan 29b Ab 26.35N 127.55 E
Nagoya 22 Pf 35.10N 136.55 E
Nāgpur 22 Jg 21.09N 79.06 E
Nagqu 22 Lf 31.30N 92.00 E
Nag's Head 51c Ab 17.13N 62.38W
Nagua 49 Md 19.23N 69.50W
Naguabo 51a Cb 18.13N 65.44W
Nagyatád 10 Nj 46.13N 17.22 E
Nagybajom 10 Mj 46.23N 16.31 E
Nagyecsed 10 Si 47.52N 22.24 E
Nagyhalász 10 Rh 48.08N 21.46 E
Nagykálló 10 Ri 47.53N 21.51 E
Nagykanizsa 10 Mj 46.27N 16.59 E
Nagykáta 10 Pi 47.25N 19.45 E
Nagykőrös 10 Pi 47.02N 19.47 E
Nagykunság 10 Qj 46.55N 20.15 E
Nagy-Milic 10 Rh 48.35N 21.28 E
Naha 22 Og 26.13N 127.40 E
Nahanni Butte 42 Fd 61.04N 123.24W
Nahari 29 De 33.25N 134.01 E
Naharyya 24 Ff 33.00N 35.05 E
Nahāvand 23 Gc 34.12N 48.22 E
Nahe 10 Dg 49.58N 7.57 E
Nahičevan 6 Kh 39.13N 45.27 E
Nahičevanskaja ASSR [3] 19 Eh 39.15N 45.35 E
Na'himābād 24 Qg 30.51N 56.31 E
Nahodka 22 Pe 42.48N 132.52 E
Nahr al 'Āsī=Orontes (EN) 23 Eb 36.02N 35.58 E
Nahr Quassel 13 Oi 35.45N 2.46 E
Nahuala, Laguna- 48 Ji 16.50N 99.40W
Nahuel Huapi, Lago- 56 Ff 40.58S 71.30W
Nahunta 44 Gj 31.12N 81.59W
Naie 29a Bb 43.24N 141.52 E
Naiguatá, Pico- 54 Ea 10.33N 66.46W
Naila 10 Hf 50.19N 11.42 E
Naiman Qi (Daqin Tal) 27 Lc 42.49N 120.38 E
Nain 39 Md 57.00N 61.40W
Nā'in 24 Of 32.52N 53.05 E
Na'īnābād 24 Pd 36.14N 54.39 E
Nairai 63d Bb 17.49S 179.24 E
Nairn 9 Jd 57.35N 3.53W
Nairobi 31 Ki 1.17S 36.49 E
Nairobi [3] 36 Gc 1.17S 36.50 E
Naissaar/Najssar 8 Ke 59.35N 24.25 E
Naitamba 63d Cb 17.01S 179.17W
Naizishan 28 Ic 43.41N 127.27 E
Najafābād 23 Hc 32.37N 51.21 E
Najd 23 Fe 25.00N 44.30 E
Najd 21 Gg 25.00N 44.30 E
Nájera 13 Jb 42.25N 2.44W
Najerilla 13 Jb 42.31N 2.42W
Naj' Ḥammādī 33 Fd 26.03N 32.15 E
Najibābād 25 Fc 29.58N 78.10 E
Najin 27 Nc 42.15N 130.18 E
Najō 29 Ec 35.47N 136.12 E
Najrān 33 Hf 17.30N 44.10 E
Najrān 33 Hf 17.30N 44.10 E
Najssar/Naissaar 8 Ke 59.35N 24.25 E
Najstenjarvi 7 He 62.18N 32.42 E
Naju 28 Ig 35.02N 126.43 E
Najzataš, Pereval- 18 If 37.52N 73.46 E
Nakadōri-Jima 28 Jh 32.58N 129.05 E
Nakagawa 29a Ca 44.47N 142.05 E
Naka-Gawa [Jap.] 29 Gc 36.20N 140.36 E
Naka-Gawa [Jap.] 29 De 33.56N 134.42 E
Nakagusuku-Wan 29b Ab 26.15N 127.50 E
Nakahechi 29 De 33.47N 135.29 E
Naka-lō-Jima 60 Cc 24.47N 141.20 E
Naka-Jima 29 Ce 33.58N 132.37 E
Nakajō 28 Oe 38.03N 139.24 E
Naka-Koshiki-Jima 29 Af 31.48N 129.50 E
Nakalele Point 65a Eb 21.02N 156.35W
Nakama 29 Be 33.50N 130.43 E
Nakaminato 29 Gc 36.22N 140.36 E
Nakamura 28 Lh 32.59N 132.56 E
Nakanai Mountains 59 Ka 5.35S 151.10 E
Nakano 29 Fc 36.45N 138.22 E
Naka-no-Dake 29 Fc 37.04N 139.06 E
Nakanojō 29 Fc 36.35N 138.51 E
Naka-no-Shima 28 Lf 36.05N 133.04 E
Naka-no-Shima 27 Mf 29.50N 129.50 E
Nakasato 29a Bc 40.58N 140.26 E
Naka-satsunai 29a Cb 42.42N 143.08 E
Nakashibetsu 28 Rc 43.36N 145.00 E
Nakasongola 36 Fb 1.19N 32.28 E
Nakatonbetsu 29a Ca 44.58N 142.17 E
Nakatsu 28 Kh 33.34N 131.13 E
Nakatsugawa 28 Ng 35.29N 137.30 E
Nakfa 35 Fb 16.40N 38.30 E
Nakhon Pathom 25 Kf 13.49N 100.06 E
Nakhon Phanom 25 Mh 17.22N 104.46 E
Nakhon Ratchasima 22 Mh 14.57N 102.09 E
Nakhon Sawan 22 Mh 15.42N 100.06 E
Nakhon Si Thammarat 22 Li 8.26N 99.58 E
Nakijin 29b Ab 26.42N 127.59 E
Nakina 39 Kd 50.10N 86.42W
Nakkila 8 Ic 61.22N 22.00 E
Naklo nad Notecia 10 Nc 53.08N 17.35 E
Naknek 40 He 58.44N 157.02W
Nakonde 36 Fd 9.19S 32.46 E
Nakskov 7 Ci 54.50N 11.09 E
Näkten 8 Fb 62.50N 14.40 E
Naktong-gang 28 Jg 35.07N 128.57 E
Nakuru 31 Ki 0.20S 35.56 E
Nakusp 46 Ga 50.15N 117.48W
Näl 25 Dc 26.02N 65.29 E
Nalajch → Nalajha 27 Ib 47.45N 107.16 E
Nalajha (Nalajch) 27 Ib 47.45N 107.16 E
Nalčik 6 Kg 43.29N 43.37 E
Nallıhan 24 Db 40.11N 31.21 E
Nalón 13 Fa 43.32N 6.04W
Nālūt 31 Ie 31.52N 10.59 E
Nalwasha 36 Gc 0.43S 36.26 E
Na Machairí/Brandon
Head 9 Ci 52.16N 10.15W
Namacurra 37 Fc 17.29S 37.01 E
Namai Bay 64a Bb 7.32N 134.39 E
Namak, Daryācheh-ye-=
Namak Lake (EN) 21 Hf 34.45N 51.36 E
Namak Lake (EN)=
Namak, Daryācheh-ye- 21 Hf 34.45N 51.36 E
Namakan Lake 45 Jb 48.27N 92.35W
Namak-e Mighān, Kavīr-e- 24 Me 34.13N 49.49 E
Namakia 37 Hc 15.56S 45.48 E
Namakwaland=Little
Namamland (EN) 37 Be 29.00S 17.00 E
Namanga 36 Gc 2.33S 36.47 E
Namangan 22 Je 41.00N 71.40 E
Namanganskaja Oblast [3] 19 Hg 41.00N 71.20 E
Namanyere 36 Fd 7.31S 31.03 E
Namapa 37 Fb 13.43S 39.50 E
Namaqua Seamount (EN) 37 Af 31.30S 11.20 E
Namarrói 37 Fc 15.57S 36.51 E
Namasagali 36 Fb 1.01N 32.57 E
Namasale 36 Fb 1.30N 32.37 E
Namatanai 60 Eh 3.40S 152.27 E
Namathu 63d Bb 17.21S 179.26 E
Nambavatu 63d Bb 16.36S 178.55 E
Namber 26 Jg 1.04S 134.49 E
Nambour 59 Ke 26.38S 152.58 E
Nambouwalu 61 Ec 16.59S 178.42 E
Nam Can 25 Kg 8.46N 104.59 E
Namche Bazar 25 Hc 27.49N 86.43 E
Nam Co 21 Lf 30.45N 90.35 E
Namčy 20 Hd 62.35N 129.40 E
Namdalen 7 Cd 64.38N 12.35 E
Nam Dinh 22 Mg 20.25N 106.10 E
Nämdö 8 He 59.10N 18.40 E
Nam Du, Quan Dao- 25 Kg 9.42N 104.22 E
Namêche, Andenne- 12 Hd 50.28N 5.00 E
Namelakl Passage 64a Bc 7.24N 134.38 E
Namen/Namur 11 Kd 50.28N 4.52 E
Namerikawa 29 Ec 36.45N 137.20 E
Náměšt nad Oslavou 10 Mg 49.12N 16.09 E
Nametil 37 Fc 15.43S 39.21 E
Namib Desert/
Namibwoestyn 30 Ik 23.00S 15.00 E
Namibia (South West
Africa) [1] 31 Ik 22.00S 17.00 E
Namibwoestyn/Namib
Desert 30 Ik 23.00S 15.00 E
Namie 28 Pf 37.29N 140.59 E
Namīn 24 Mc 38.25N 48.30 E
Namioka 29 Ga 40.42N 140.35 E
Namiquipa 48 Fc 29.15N 107.40W
Namiranga 37 Gb 10.33S 40.30 E
Namjagbarwa Feng 21 Lg 29.38N 95.04 E
Namja La 27 Df 29.58N 82.34 E
Namkham 25 Jd 23.50N 97.41 E
Namlea 26 Ig 3.18S 127.06 E
Namling 27 Ef 29.44N 89.05 E
Namnoi, Khao- 25 Jf 10.36N 98.38 E
Namoi River 59 Je 30.00S 148.07 E
Namoluk Island 57 Gd 5.55N 153.08 E
Namonuito Atoll 57 Gd 8.46N 150.02 E
Namorik Atoll 57 Hd 5.36N 168.07 E
Namous 32 Gc 30.28N 0.14W
Nampa 43 Dc 43.34N 116.34W
Nampala 34 Db 15.17N 5.33W
Nam Phan=Cochin China
(EN) 21 Mg 11.00N 107.00 E
Nam Phong 25 Ke 16.45N 102.52 E
Nampi 28 De 38.02N 116.42 E
Namp'o 27 Md 38.44N 125.25 E
Nampula [3] 37 Fb 15.00S 39.30 E
Nampula 31 Kj 15.07S 39.15 E
Namsê Shankou 27 Df 29.58N 82.34 E
Namsos 6 Hc 64.30N 11.30 E
Namtu 25 Jd 23.05N 97.24 E
Namu 46 Ba 51.49N 127.52W
Namu Atoll 57 Hd 8.00N 168.10 E
Namuka-I-Lau 63d Cc 18.51S 178.38W
Namúli, Serra- 30 Kj 15.21S 37.00 E
Namuno 37 Fb 13.37S 38.48 E
Namur [3] 12 Gd 50.20N 4.50 E
Namur/Namen 11 Kd 50.28N 4.52 E
Namur-Saint Servais 12 Gd 50.28N 4.50 E
Namuruputh 36 Gb 4.34N 35.57 E
Namur-Wépion 12 Gd 50.25N 4.52 E
Namutoni 37 Bc 18.30S 17.55 E
Namwala 36 Ef 15.45S 26.26 E
Namwŏn 28 Ig 35.24N 127.23 E
Namysłów 10 Ne 51.05N 17.42 E
Nan 21 Mh 15.42N 100.09 E
Nan 25 Ke 18.48N 100.46 E
Nana 35 Bd 5.00N 15.50 E
Nana Barya 35 Bd 7.59N 17.43 E
Nanae 29a Bc 41.53N 140.41 E
Nanaimo 42 Fg 49.10N 123.56W
Nanakuli 65a Cb 21.23N 158.08W
Nana-Mambéré [3] 35 Bd 6.00N 16.00 E
Nanango 59 Ke 26.40S 152.00 E
Nanao 27 Od 37.03N 136.58 E
Nanao-Wan 29 Ec 37.10N 137.00 E
Nanatsu-Shima 29 Ec 37.35N 136.50 E
Nancha 27 Mb 47.08N 129.09 E
Nanchang 22 Ng 28.40N 115.58 E
Nancheng 27 Kf 27.32N 116.36 E
Nanchong 22 Mf 30.47N 106.03 E
Nancowry 25 Ig 7.59N 93.32 E
Nancy 6 Gf 48.41N 6.12 E
Nanda Devi 21 Jf 30.23N 79.59 E
Nandaime 49 Dh 11.46N 86.03W
Nandan [China] 27 Ig 24.59N 107.31 E
Nandan [Jap.] 28 Mg 34.15N 134.43 E
Nandarran → Qingyuan 28 Ce 38.46N 115.29 E
Nander 22 Jh 19.09N 77.20 E
Nandewar Range 59 Kf 30.40S 151.10 E
Nandi 61 Ec 17.48S 177.25 E
Nandu Jiang 27 Jg 20.04N 110.22 E
Nanduri 63d Bb 16.27S 179.09 E
Nandyāl 25 Fe 15.29N 78.29 E
Nanfen 28 Gd 41.06N 123.45 E
Nanfeng 27 Kf 27.15N 116.30 E
Nanga-Eboko 34 He 4.41N 12.22 E
Nanga Parbat 21 Jf 35.15N 74.36 E
Nangapinoh 26 Fg 0.20S 111.44 E
Nangarhār [3] 23 Lc 34.15N 70.30 E
Nangatayap 26 Fg 1.32S 110.34 E
Nangis 11 If 48.33N 3.00 E
Nangnim-san 28 Id 40.21N 126.55 E
Nangnim-Sanmaek 28 Id 40.30N 127.00 E
Nangong 27 Kd 37.22N 115.23 E
Nangqên 27 Ge 32.15N 96.13 E
Nanguan 28 Af 36.42N 111.41 E
Nanguantao → Guantao 28 Cf 36.33N 115.18 E
Nangweshi 36 Df 16.26S 23.20 E
Nan Hai=South China Sea
(EN) 21 Ni 10.00N 113.00 E
Nanhaoqian → Shangyi 28 Bd 41.06N 113.58 E
Nanhe 28 Cf 36.58N 114.41 E
Nanhua 27 Hf 25.16N 101.18 E
Nanhui 28 Fi 31.03N 121.46 E
Nan Hulsan Hu 27 Gd 36.45N 95.45 E
Nanjian 27 Hf 25.05N 100.32 E
Nanjiang 27 Ie 32.22N 106.45 E
Nanjing=Nanking (EN) 22 Nf 31.59N 118.51 E
Nankai Trough (EN) 27 Ne 32.00N 135.00 E
Nanking (EN)=Nanjing 22 Nf 31.59N 118.51 E
Nankoku 29 Ce 33.39N 133.44 E
Nanle 28 Cf 36.06N 115.12 E
Nanling 28 Ei 30.55N 118.19 E
Nan Ling 21 Ng 25.00N 112.00 E
Nanlou Shan 28 Ic 43.24N 126.40 E
Nanma → Yiyuan 28 Ef 36.11N 118.10 E
Nanning 22 Mg 22.50N 108.18 E
Nannup 59 Df 33.59S 115.45 E
Nanortalik 41 Hf 60.32N 45.45W
Nanpan Jiang 27 Ig 24.56N 106.12 E
Nānpāra 25 Gc 27.52N 81.30 E
Nanping [China] 22 Ng 26.42N 118.09 E
Nanping [China] 27 He 33.15N 104.13 E
Nanpu 28 Ee 39.16N 118.12 E
Nanqiao → Fengxian 28 Fi 30.55N 121.27 E
Nansei-Shotō=Ryukyu
Islands (EN) 21 Og 26.30N 128.00 E
Nansen Cordillera (EN) 67 Ge 87.00N 90.00 E
Nansen Land 41 Hb 83.20N 46.00W
Nanshan Islands (EN)=
Nansha Qundao 21 Ni 9.40N 113.30 E
Nansha Qundao=
Nanshan Islands (EN) 21 Ni 9.40N 113.30 E
Nansio 36 Fc 2.08S 33.03 E
Nant 11 Jj 44.01N 3.18 E
Nantais, Lac- 42 Kd 61.00N 73.50W
Nanterre 11 If 48.54N 2.12 E
Nantes 6 Ff 47.13N 1.33W
Nantes à Brest, Can. de- 11 Bf 48.12N 4.06W
Nanteuil-le-Haudouin 12 Ee 49.08N 2.48 E
Nanticoke 44 Je 41.13N 76.00W
Nantō 29 Ed 34.17N 136.29 E
Nantong 27 Le 32.00N 120.52 E
Nantong (Jinsha) 28 Fh 32.06N 120.52 E
Nantou 27 Lg 23.54N 120.51 E
Nantua 11 Lh 46.09N 5.37 E
Nantucket 44 Le 41.17N 70.06W
Nantucket Island 43 Mc 41.16N 70.03W
Nantucket Sound 44 Le 41.30N 70.15W
Nanuku Passage 63d Cb 16.45S 179.15W
Nanuku Reef 63d Cb 16.40S 179.26W
Nanumanga Island 57 Ie 6.18S 176.20 E
Nanumea Atoll 57 Ie 5.43S 176.00 E
Nanuque 54 Jg 17.50S 40.21W
Nanusa, Pulau-Pulau- 26 If 4.42N 127.06 E
Nanwan Shuiku 28 Bh 32.02N 113.57 E
Nanwei Dao 27 Je 8.42N 111.40 E
Nanweng He 27 Ma 51.10N 125.59 E
Nanxian 28 Bj 29.22N 112.25 E
Nanxiang 28 Fi 31.18N 121.17 E
Nanxiong 27 Jf 25.13N 114.18 E
Nanxun 28 Fi 30.53N 120.26 E
Nanyandang Shan 27 Lf 27.37N 120.06 E
Nanyang 22 Nf 32.56N 112.32 E
Nanyang Hu 28 Dg 35.15N 116.39 E
Nanyō 28 Pe 38.03N 140.10 E
Nanyuki 31 Kh 0.01N 37.04 E
Nanzhang 27 Je 31.45N 111.53 E
Nanzhao 27 Je 33.28N 112.29 E
Nao, Cabo de la- 5 Gh 38.44N 0.14 E
Naococane, Lac- 42 Kf 52.50N 70.40W
Naoero/Nauru [1] 58 He 0.31S 166.56 E
Naoetsu 29 Fc 37.11N 138.14 E
Não-me-Toque 55 Fi 28.28S 52.49W
Naours, Souterrains de- 12 Ed 50.05N 2.17 E
Napa 46 Dg 38.18N 122.17W
Napanee 44 Ic 44.15N 76.57W
Napassoq 41 Ge 65.45N 52.38W
Napata 35 Eb 18.29N 31.51 E
Na-Peng 25 Lg 23.10N 98.26 E
Napf 14 Bc 47.01N 7.56 E
Napier 58 Ih 39.30S 176.54 E
Napier, Mount- 59 Fc 17.32S 129.10 E
Napier Mountains 66 Ee 66.30S 53.40 E
Naples [Fl.-U.S.] 43 Kf 26.08N 81.48W
Naples [Id.-U.S.] 46 Gb 48.34N 116.24W
Naples (EN) = Napoli 6 Hg 40.50N 14.15 E
Naples, Gulf of- (EN) =
Napoli, Golfo di- 14 Ij 40.45N 14.10 E
Napo 27 Ig 23.25N 105.49 E
Napo, Rio- 52 If 3.20S 72.40W
Napoleon 45 Ge 46.30N 99.46W
Napoli = Naples (EN) 6 Hg 40.50N 14.15 E
Napoli, Golfo di- = Naples,
Gulf of- (EN) 14 Ij 40.45N 14.10 E
Napostá 55 An 38.26S 62.15W
Napuka, Ile- 57 Mf 14.12S 141.15W
Naqa 35 Eb 16.16N 33.17 E
Naqadeh 23 Gb 36.57N 45.23 E
Naqsh-e-Rostam 24 Og 30.01N 52.50 E
Nar 9 Ni 52.45N 0.24 E
Nāra 25 Dc 24.07N 69.07 E
Nara [Jap.] 27 Oe 34.41N 135.50 E
Nara [Mali] 34 Db 15.11N 7.15W
Naračenskibani 15 Hh 41.54N 24.45 E
Naracoorte 59 Ig 36.58S 140.44 E
Nara-Ken [2] 28 Mg 34.20N 135.55 E
Naranjo 48 Ee 25.48N 108.31W
Naranjos [Bol.] 55 Cd 18.38S 59.09W
Naranjos [Mex.] 48 Kg 21.21N 97.41W
Narao 29 Ae 32.52N 129.04 E
Narathiwat 25 Kg 6.25N 101.48 E
Nārāyanganj 25 Id 23.37N 90.30 E
Narbonne 11 Ik 43.11N 3.00 E
Narca, Ponta da- 36 Bd 6.07S 12.16 E
Narcea 13 Fa 43.28N 6.06W
Narcondam 25 If 13.15N 94.30 E
Nardò 14 Mj 40.11N 18.02 E
Naré 55 Bj 30.58S 60.28W
Nares Land 41 Hb 82.25N 47.30W
Nares Strait 38 Lb 78.50N 73.00W
Narew 10 Td 52.55N 23.29 E
Narew 10 Qd 52.26N 20.42 E
Narian, Pointe- 63b Be 20.05S 164.00 E
Narin Gol 27 Fd 36.54N 92.51 E
Nariño [2] 54 Cc 1.30N 78.00W
Narita 29 Gd 35.47N 140.18 E
Narjan-Mar 6 Lb 67.39N 53.00 E
Närke 8 Ff 59.05N 15.05 E
Narlı 24 Gd 37.27N 37.09 E
Narmada 21 Jg 21.38N 72.36 E
Narman 24 Ib 40.21N 41.52 E
Nārnaul 25 Fc 28.03N 76.06 E
Narni 14 Gh 42.31N 12.31 E
Naroč 8 Lj 54.27N 26.45 E
Naroč 8 Lj 54.57N 26.49 E
Naroč, Ozero- 16 Eb 54.50N 26.45 E
Naroda 17 Jd 64.15N 61.00 E
Narodnaja, Gora- 5 Mb 65.04N 60.09 E
Naro-Fominsk 19 Dd 55.24N 36.43 E
Narok 36 Gc 1.05S 35.52 E
Narovlja 16 Fd 51.48N 29.31 E
Närpes/Närpio 8 Ib 62.28N 21.20 E
Närpio/Närpes 8 Ib 62.28N 21.20 E
Narrabri 59 Jf 30.19S 149.47 E
Narrandera 59 Jf 34.45S 146.33 E
Narrogin 59 Df 32.56S 117.10 E
Narromine 59 Jf 32.14S 148.15 E
Narrows, The- 51c Ab 17.12N 62.38W
Narryer, Mount- 59 De 26.30S 116.25 E
Narsimhapur 25 Fd 22.57N 79.12 E
Narssalik 41 Hf 61.42N 49.11W
Narssaq [Grld.] 41 Hf 61.00N 46.00W
Narssaq [Grld.] 41 Gf 64.00N 51.33W
Narssarssuaq 41 Hf 61.10N 45.15W
Narthákion 15 Fj 39.14N 22.22 E
Nartkala 16 Mh 43.32N 43.47 E
Narubis 37 Be 26.55S 18.35 E
Narugo 29 Gb 38.44N 140.43 E
Năruja 15 Jd 45.50N 26.47 E
Naru-Shima 29 Ae 32.50N 128.56 E
Naruto 28 Mg 34.11N 134.37 E
Naruto-Kaikyō 29 Dd 34.15N 134.40 E
Narva 7 Gg 59.29N 28.02 E
Narva 6 Id 59.23N 28.11 E
Narva Jõesuu/Narva-Jyesuu 8 Me 59.21N 28.04 E
Narva-Jyesuu/Narva Jõesuu 8 Me 59.21N 28.04 E
Narva laht 7 Gg 59.30N 27.40 E
Narvik 6 Hb 68.26N 17.25 E
Narvski Zaliv 7 Gg 59.30N 27.40 E
Narvskoje Vodohranilišče 8 Me 59.10N 28.30 E
Narym 20 De 58.58N 81.40 E
Naryn 21 Je 40.54N 71.45 E
Naryn 22 Je 41.26N 75.59 E
Naryncol 19 Ig 42.43N 80.08 E
Narynskaja Oblast [3] 19 Hg 41.20N 75.40 E
Nås 7 Df 60.27N 14.29 E
Na Sailti/Saltee Islands 9 Gi 52.07N 6.36W
Näsåker 7 De 63.23N 16.54 E
Nasarawa 34 Gd 8.32N 7.43 E
Năsăud 15 Hb 47.17N 24.24 E
Nasawa 63b Db 15.12S 168.06 E
Na Sceiri/Skerries 9 Gh 53.35N 6.07W
Nash Point 9 Jj 51.24N 3.27W
Nashtārud 24 Nd 36.45N 51.02 E
Nashua 44 Ld 42.44N 71.28W
Nashville [Ar.-U.S.] 45 Jj 33.57N 93.51W
Nashville [Ga.-U.S.] 44 Fj 31.12N 83.15W
Nashville [Il.-U.S.] 45 Lg 38.21N 89.23W
Nashville [In.-U.S.] 44 Df 39.12N 86.15W
Nashville [Tn.-U.S.] 39 Kf 36.09N 86.48W
Nashville Seamount (EN) 38 Nf 35.00N 57.20W
Našice 14 Me 45.30N 18.06 E
Nasielsk 10 Qd 52.36N 20.48 E
Näsijärvi 5 Ic 61.35N 23.40 E
Nāsik 22 Jg 20.05N 73.48 E
Nāşir 35 Ed 8.36N 33.04 E
Naskaupi 42 Lf 53.47N 60.51W
Nasorolevu 63d Bb 16.38S 179.24 E
Naşr [Eg.] 24 Dg 30.36N 30.23 E
Naşr [Lib.] 33 Dd 28.59N 21.13 E
Naşrābād 24 Of 32.09N 52.08 E
Nass 42 Ee 55.00N 129.50W
Nassandres 12 Ce 49.07N 0.44 E
Nassandres-La Rivière
Thibouville 12 Ce 49.07N 0.44 E
Nassau [Bah.] 39 Lg 25.05N 77.21W
Nassau [F.R.G.] 12 Jd 50.19N 7.48 E
Nassau, Bahia- 56 Gi 55.25S 67.40W
Nassau Island 57 Kf 11.33S 165.25W
Nassau River 59 Ic 15.58S 141.30 E
Nasser, Birkat-=Nasser,
Lake-(EN) 30 Kf 22.40N 32.00 E

Index Symbols

[1] Independent Nation
[2] State, Region
[3] District, County
[4] Municipality
[5] Colony, Dependency
Continent
Physical Region
Historical or Cultural Region
Mount, Mountain
Volcano
Hill
Mountains, Mountain Range
Hills, Escarpment
Plateau, Upland
Pass, Gap
Plain, Lowland
Delta
Salt Flat
Valley, Canyon
Crater, Cave
Karst Features
Depression
Polder
Desert, Dunes
Forest, Woods
Heath, Steppe
Oasis
Cape, Point
Coast, Beach
Cliff
Peninsula
Isthmus
Sandbank
Island
Atoll
Rock, Reef
Islands, Archipelago
Rocks, Reefs
Coral Reef
Well, Spring
Geyser
River, Stream
Waterfall Rapids
River Mouth, Estuary
Lake
Salt Lake
Intermittent Lake
Reservoir
Swamp, Pond
Canal
Glacier
Ice Shelf, Pack Ice
Ocean
Sea
Gulf, Bay
Strait, Fjord
Lagoon
Bank
Seamount
Tablemount
Ridge
Shelf
Basin
Escarpment, Sea Scarp
Fracture
Trench, Abyss
National Park, Reserve
Point of Interest
Recreation Site
Cave, Cavern
Historic Site
Ruins
Wall, Walls
Church, Abbey
Temple
Scientific Station
Airport
Port
Lighthouse
Mine
Tunnel
Dam, Bridge

Name	Map	Grid	Lat.	Long.
Nasser, Lake-(EN)=Nasser, Birkat-	30	Kf	22.40N	32.00 E
Nassian	34	Ed	9.24N	4.29W
Nässjö	7	Dh	57.39N	14.41 E
Nassogne	12	Hd	50.08N	5.21 E
Na Staighrí Dubha/ Blackstairs Mountains	9	Gi	52.33N	6.49W
Nastapoka Islands	42	Je	56.50N	76.50W
Nastätten	12	Jd	50.12N	7.52 E
Nastola	8	Kd	60.57N	25.56 E
Nasu	29	Gc	37.02N	140.06 E
Nasu-Dake	29	Fc	37.07N	139.58 E
Näsviken	8	Gc	61.45N	16.52 E
Natá	49	Gi	8.20N	80.31W
Nata	30	Jk	20.14S	26.10 E
Nata	37	Dd	20.13S	26.11 E
Natal [2]	37	Ee	29.00S	30.00 E
Natal [B.C.-Can.]	46	Hb	49.44N	114.50W
Natal [Braz.]	53	Mf	5.47S	35.13W
Natal [Indon.]	26	Cf	0.33N	99.07 E
Natal Basin (EN)	3	Fm	30.00S	40.00 E
Natanz	24	Nf	33.31N	51.54 E
Natashquan	42	Lf	50.09N	61.37W
Natashquan	42	Lf	50.11N	61.49W
Natchez	43	Ie	31.34N	91.23W
Natchitoches	43	Ie	31.46N	93.05W
Natewa Bay	63d	Bb	16.35S	179.40 E
Nathorsts Land	41	Jd	72.20N	27.00W
Nathula	63d	Ab	16.53S	177.25 E
Natitingou	31	Hg	10.19N	1.22 E
Natityāy, Jabal-	33	Fe	23.01N	34.22 E
Natividad, Isla-	48	Bd	27.55N	115.10W
Natividade	54	If	11.43S	47.47W
Natori	28	Pe	38.11N	140.58 E
Natron, Lake-	30	Ki	2.25S	36.00 E
Naṭrūn, Wādī an-	24	Dg	30.25N	30.13 E
Natsudomari-Zaki	29a	Bc	41.00N	140.53 E
Nåttarö	8	Hf	58.50N	18.10 E
Nättraby	8	Fh	56.12N	15.31 E
Natuna Besar, Pulau-	26	Ef	4.00N	108.15 E
Natuna Islands (EN)= Bunguran, Kepulauan-	21	Mi	2.45N	109.00 E
Naturaliste, Cape-	57	Ch	33.32S	115.01 E
Naturaliste Channel	59	Ce	25.25S	113.00 E
Naturita	45	Bg	38.14N	108.34W
Naturno / Naturns	14	Ed	46.39N	11.00 E
Naturns / Naturno	14	Ed	46.39N	11.00 E
Nau	18	Gd	40.09N	69.22 E
Nau, Cap de la-/Nao, Cabo de la-	5	Gh	38.44N	0.14 E
Naucelle	11	Ij	44.12N	2.21 E
Nauëji-Akmjane/Naujoji-Akmenė	7	Fh	56.21N	22.50 E
Naugo/Nauvo	8	Id	60.10N	21.50 E
Nauhcampatépetl → Cofre de Perote, Cerro-	48	Kh	19.29N	97.08W
Nauja Bay	42	Kc	68.58N	75.00W
Naujamestis/Naujamiestis	8	Ki	55.41N	24.09 E
Naujamiestis/Naujamestis	8	Ki	55.41N	24.09 E
Naujoji-Akmenė/Nauëji-Akmjane	7	Fh	56.21N	22.50 E
Naukluft	37	Bd	24.10S	16.10 E
Naumburg [F.R.G.]	12	Lc	51.15N	9.10 E
Naumburg [G.D.R.]	10	He	51.09N	11.49 E
Nā'ūr	24	Fg	31.53N	35.50 E
Nauru	57	He	0.31S	166.56 E
Nauru/Naoero [1]	58	He	0.31S	166.56 E
Nauški	20	Ff	50.28N	106.07 E
Nausori	61	Ec	18.02S	178.32 E
Nauta	54	Dd	4.32S	73.33W
Nautanwa	25	Gc	27.26N	83.25 E
Nautla	48	Kg	20.13N	96.47W
Nauvo/Naugo	8	Id	60.10N	21.50 E
Nava	48	Ic	28.25N	100.45W
Navacerrada, Puerto de-	13	Id	40.47N	4.00W
Nava del Rey	13	Gc	41.20N	5.05W
Navahermosa	13	He	39.38N	4.28W
Navajo Mountain	46	Jh	37.02N	110.52W
Navajo Reservoir	45	Ch	36.55N	107.30W
Navalmoral de la Mata	13	Ge	39.54N	5.32W
Navan/An Uaimh	9	Gh	53.39N	6.41W
Navarin, Mys-	21	Tc	62.16N	179.10 E
Navarino, Isla-	52	Jk	55.05S	67.40W
Navarra [3]	13	Kb	42.45N	1.40W
Navarra=Navarre (EN)	13	Kb	43.00N	1.30W
Navarre (EN)=Navarra	13	Kb	43.00N	1.30W
Navarro	55	Cl	35.01S	59.16W
Navarro Mills Lake	45	Hk	31.56N	96.45W
Navašino	7	Ki	55.33N	42.12 E
Navasota	45	Hk	30.23N	96.05W
Navasota River	45	Hk	30.20N	96.09W
Navassa	47	Ie	18.24N	75.01W
Navaste Jõgi/Navesti	8	Kf	58.56N	24.58 E
Nävekvarn	8	Gf	58.38N	16.49 E
Naver	9	Ic	58.30N	4.15W
Navesti/Navaste Jõgi	8	Kf	58.56N	24.58 E
Navia	13	Fa	43.32N	6.43W
Navia	13	Fa	43.33N	6.44W
Navidad, Bahía de-	48	Gh	19.10N	104.45W
Navidad Bank (EN)	49	Mc	20.00N	68.50W
Naviti	63d	Ab	17.07S	177.15 E
Navlja	16	Ic	52.42N	34.03 E
Navlja	19	De	52.50N	34.31 E
Năvodari	15	Le	44.19N	28.36 E
Navoi	19	Gg	40.10N	65.15 E
Navoja	47	Cc	27.06N	109.26W
Navolato	48	Fe	24.47N	107.42W
Navoloki	7	Jh	57.28N	41.59 E
Návpaktoș	15	Ek	38.24N	21.50 E
Návplion	15	Fl	37.34N	22.48 E
Navrongo	34	Ec	10.54N	1.06W
Navsāri	25	Ed	20.55N	72.55 E
Navtílos	15	Gn	35.57N	23.13 E
Navua	63d	Bc	18.13S	178.10 E
Navy Board Inlet	42	Jb	73.30N	81.00W
Nawa	24	Gf	32.53N	36.03 E
Nawābshāh	25	Dc	26.15N	68.25 E
Nawāṣīf, Ḥarrat-	33	He	21.20N	42.10 E
Ņaws, Ra's-	23	If	17.18N	55.16 E
Náxos	15	Il	37.06N	25.23 E
Naxos	14	Jm	37.49N	15.15 E
Náxos=Naxos (EN)	5	Ih	37.02N	25.35 E
Naxos (EN)=Náxos	5	Ih	37.02N	25.35 E
Nayarit [2]	47	Cd	22.00N	105.00W
Nayarit, Sierra-	47	Dd	22.00N	103.50W
Nayau	63d	Cb	17.58S	179.03W
Nāy Band [Iran]	24	Oi	27.23N	52.38 E
Nāy Band [Iran]	24	Qf	32.20N	57.34 E
Nāy Band, Ra's-e-	24	Oi	27.23N	52.34 E
Nayoro	27	Pc	44.21N	142.28 E
Nazaré [Braz.]	54	Kf	13.02S	39.00W
Nazaré [Port.]	13	Ce	39.36N	9.04W
Nazareth (EN)=Naẕerat	24	Ff	32.42N	35.18 E
Nazarovo	20	Ee	56.01N	90.36 E
Nazas	48	Ge	25.14N	104.08W
Nazas, Río-	38	Ig	25.35N	105.00W
Nazca	53	Ig	14.50S	74.55W
Nazca Ridge (EN)	3	Nl	22.00S	82.00W
Naze	27	Mf	28.23N	129.30 E
Naẕerat=Nazareth (EN)	24	Ff	32.42N	35.18 E
Nazilli	23	Cb	37.55N	28.21 E
Nazimiye	24	Hc	39.11N	39.50 E
Nazimovo	20	Ee	59.30N	90.58 E
Nazino	20	Cd	60.15N	78.58 E
Nazlū	24	Kd	37.42N	45.16 E
Nazran	16	Nh	43.15N	44.46 E
Nazret	35	Fd	8.34N	39.18 E
Nazw'a	23	Ie	22.54N	57.31 E
Nazym	17	Nf	61.12N	68.57 E
Nazyvajevsk	19	Hd	55.34N	71.21 E
Nbâk	32	Ef	17.15N	14.59W
Nchanga	36	Ee	12.31S	27.52 E
Ncheu	36	Fe	14.49S	34.38 E
Ndala	36	Fc	4.46S	33.16 E
Ndalatando	36	Bd	9.18S	14.54 E
Ndali	34	Fd	9.51N	2.43 E
Ndélé	31	Jh	8.24N	20.39 E
Ndélélé	34	He	4.02N	14.56 E
Ndendé	36	Bc	2.23S	11.23 E
Ndindi	36	Bc	3.46S	11.09 E
N'djamena (Fort-Lamy)	31	Ig	12.07N	15.03 E
Ndola	31	Jj	12.58S	28.38 E
Ndouana, Pointe-	63b	Dc	16.35S	168.09 E
Ndrhamcha, Sebkha de-	32	Df	18.45N	15.48W
Nduindui	60	Fi	9.48S	159.58 E
Ndui Ndui	63b	Cb	15.24S	167.46 E
Né	11	Fi	45.40N	0.23W
Nea	63c	Ab	10.51S	165.47 E
Nea	7	Ce	63.13N	11.02 E
Néa Alikarnassós	15	In	35.20N	25.09 E
Néa Artáki	15	Gk	38.31N	23.38 E
Neagari	29	Ec	36.26N	136.26 E
Neagh, Lough-/Loch nEathach	5	Fe	54.38N	6.24W
Neagră, Marea-=Black Sea (EN)	5	Jg	43.00N	35.00 E
Neah Bay	46	Cb	48.22N	124.37W
Néa Ionía	15	Fj	39.23N	22.56 E
Neajlov	15	Je	44.11N	26.12 E
Neale, Lake-	59	Fd	24.20S	130.00 E
Neamț [2]	15	Jb	47.00N	26.20 E
Neápolis [Grc.]	15	In	35.15N	25.37 E
Neápolis [Grc.]	15	Ei	40.19N	21.23 E
Neápolis [Grc.]	15	Gm	36.31N	23.04 E
Near Islands	38	Bd	52.40N	173.30W
Neath	9	Jj	51.37N	3.50W
Neath	9	Jj	51.40N	3.48W
Néa Zíkhni	15	Gh	41.02N	23.50 E
Néba	63b	Ae	20.09S	163.55 E
Nebaj	49	Bf	15.24N	91.08W
Nebbou	34	Ec	11.18N	1.53W
Nebit-Dag	22	Hf	39.30N	54.22 E
Neblina, Pico da-	52	Je	1.08N	66.10W
Nebo	59	Jd	21.40S	148.39 E
Nebo, Mount-	46	Jg	39.49N	111.46W
Nebolči	7	Hg	59.08N	33.21 E
Nebraska [2]	43	Gc	41.30N	100.00W
Nebraska City	43	Hc	40.41N	95.52W
Nebrodi (Caronie)	14	Im	37.55N	14.35 E
Necedah	45	Kd	44.02N	90.03W
Nechako	42	Ff	53.55N	122.44W
Nechako Reservoir	42	Ef	53.00N	126.10W
Nechar, Djebel-	13	Qi	35.52N	4.59 E
Neches River	45	Jl	29.55N	93.52W
Nechí	49	Ji	8.07N	74.46W
Nechí, Río-	49	Ji	8.08N	74.46W
Neckako Plateau	42	Ff	53.25N	124.40W
Neckar	10	Eg	49.31N	8.26 E
Neckarsulm	10	Fg	49.11N	9.14 E
Necker Island	57	Kb	23.35N	164.42W
Necochea	53	Ki	38.34S	58.45W
Necy	12	Bf	48.50N	0.07W
Nedeley	35	Bb	15.34N	18.10 E
Nederland	45	Jl	29.58N	93.59W
Nederland=Netherlands (EN) [1]	6	Ge	52.15N	5.30 E
Nederlandse Antillen [5]	50	Ec	18.06N	63.10W
Nederlandse Antillen = Netherlands Antilles (EN) [5]	53	Jd	12.15N	69.00W
Neder-Rijn = Lower Rhine (EN)	11	Mc	51.59N	6.20 E
Nêdong	22	Lg	29.14N	91.46 E
Nedstrand	8	Ae	59.21N	5.51 E
Nedstrandefjorden	8	Ae	59.20N	5.50 E
Neede	12	Ib	52.08N	6.37 E
Needham Market	12	Db	52.09N	1.02 E
Needham's Point	51q	Ab	13.05N	59.36W
Needles	43	Ee	34.51N	114.37W
Neembucú [3]	55	Dh	27.00S	58.00W
Neenah	45	Ld	44.11N	88.28W
Neepawa	45	Ga	50.13N	99.29W
Neermoor, Moormerland-	12	Ja	53.18N	7.26 E
Neeroeteren, Maaseik-	12	Hc	51.05N	5.42 E
Neerpelt	12	Hc	51.13N	5.25 E
Nefasit	35	Fb	15.18N	39.04 E
Nefedova	19	Hd	58.48N	72.34 E
Né Finn/Nephin	9	Dg	54.01N	9.22W
Neftah	32	Ic	33.52N	7.53 E
Neftečala	16	Pj	39.19N	49.13 E
Neftegorsk [R.S.F.S.R.]	16	Kg	44.22N	39.42 E
Neftegorsk [R.S.F.S.R.]	20	Jf	53.00N	143.00 E
Neftegorsk [R.S.F.S.R.]	19	Fe	52.45N	51.13 E
Neftejugansk	19	Hc	61.05N	72.45 E
Neftekamsk	19	Fd	56.06N	54.17 E
Neftekumsk	19	Eg	44.43N	44.59 E
Neftjanyje Kamin	16	Qi	40.15N	50.49 E
Negage	36	Cd	7.46S	15.18 E
Negara	26	Fh	8.22S	114.37 E
Negele=Neghelle (EN)	31	Kh	5.20N	39.37 E
Negev Desert (EN)= Hānegev	24	Fg	30.30N	34.55 E
Neghelle (EN)=Negele	31	Kh	5.20N	39.37 E
Negla, Arroyo-	55	Df	22.52S	56.41W
Negola	36	Be	14.10S	14.30 E
Negomano	37	Fb	11.26S	38.33 E
Negombo	25	Fg	7.13N	79.50 E
Negonego Atoll	57	Mf	18.47S	141.48W
Negotin	15	Fe	44.13N	22.32 E
Negotino	15	Fh	41.29N	22.06 E
Negra, Cordillera-	54	Ce	9.25S	77.40W
Negra, Coxilha-	55	Ej	31.02S	55.45W
Negra, Peña-	13	Fb	42.11N	6.30W
Negra, Ponta-	55	Jf	23.21S	44.36W
Negra, Punta-	52	Hf	6.06S	81.10W
Negra, Serra-	55	Fc	16.30S	52.10W
Negra o de los Difuntos, Laguna-	55	Fl	34.03S	53.40W
Negreira	13	Db	42.54N	8.44W
Negreni	15	He	44.34N	24.36 E
Negreşti	15	Gb	47.52N	23.26 E
Negrine	32	Ic	34.29N	7.31 E
Negrinho, Rio-	55	Ed	19.20S	55.05W
Negro, Cabo-	13	Gi	35.41N	5.17W
Negro, Río- [Arg.]	55	Ch	27.27S	58.54W
Negro, Río- [Arg.]	52	Jj	41.02S	62.47W
Negro, Río- [Bol.]	54	Ff	14.11S	63.07W
Negro, Rio- [Braz.]	54	Gg	19.13S	57.17W
Negro, Rio- [Braz.]	56	Jc	26.01S	50.30W
Negro, Río- [Par.]	56	Ib	24.23S	57.11W
Negro, Río- [S.Amer.]	52	Kf	3.08S	59.55W
Negro, Río- [S.Amer.]	55	Ce	20.11S	58.10W
Negro, Río- [Ur.]	52	Ki	33.24S	58.22W
Negros	21	Oi	10.00N	123.00 E
Negru, Rîu-	15	Id	45.45N	25.46 E
Negru Vodă	15	Lf	43.49N	28.12 E
Nehajevski	16	Ld	50.27N	41.46 E
Nehalem River	46	Dd	45.40N	123.56W
Nehāvand	24	Me	35.56N	49.31 E
Nehe	27	Lb	48.28N	124.53 E
Nehoiu	15	Jd	45.26N	26.17 E
Néhoué, Baie de-	63b	Be	20.21S	164.09 E
Neiba	49	Ld	18.28N	71.25W
Neiba, Bahía de-	49	Ld	18.15N	71.02W
Neidín/Kenmare	9	Dj	51.53N	9.35W
Neige, Crêt de la-	11	Lh	46.16N	5.56 E
Neiges, Piton des-	30	Mk	21.05S	55.29 E
Neijiang	22	Mg	29.38N	104.58 E
Neilton	46	Dc	47.25N	123.52W
Nei-meng-ku Tzu-chih-ch'ü → Nei Monggol Zizhiqu [2]	27	Jc	44.00N	112.00 E
Nei Monggol Gaoyuan	21	Ne	42.00N	111.00 E
Nei Monggol Zizhiqu (Nei-meng-ku Tzu-chih-ch'ü)=Inner Mongolia (EN) [2]	27	Jc	44.00N	112.00 E
Neiqiu	28	Cf	37.17N	114.30 E
Neiva	53	Ie	2.56N	75.18W
Neja	19	Ed	58.19N	43.52 E
Nejanilini Lake	42	He	59.30N	97.50W
Nejdek	10	If	50.19N	12.44 E
Nejo	35	Fd	9.30N	35.32 E
Nejva	17	Kh	57.54N	62.18 E
Nekemt=Leqemt (EN)	31	Kh	9.05N	36.33 E
Neksø	8	Fi	55.04N	15.09 E
Nelemnoje	20	Kc	65.23N	151.08 E
Nelgese	20	Ic	66.40N	136.30 E
Nelichu	35	Ed	6.08N	34.25 E
Nelidovo	19	Dd	56.13N	32.50 E
Neligh	45	Ge	42.08N	98.02W
Neljaty	20	Ge	56.29N	115.50 E
Nelkan	20	Jd	64.15N	143.03 E
Nellore	22	Jh	12.56N	79.08 E
Nelma	20	Ig	47.40N	139.08 E
Nelson [2]	62	Ed	41.45S	172.30 E
Nelson	38	Jd	57.04N	92.30W
Nelson [B.C.-Can.]	42	Fg	49.29N	117.17W
Nelson [N.Z.]	58	Ii	41.16S	173.15 E
Nelson, Cape- [Austl.]	57	Fh	38.26S	141.33 E
Nelson, Cape- [Pap.N.Gui.]	59	Ja	9.00S	149.15 E
Nelson Island	40	Gd	60.35N	164.45W
Nelson's Dockyard	51d	Bb	17.00N	61.46W
Nelspruit	31	Kk	25.30S	30.58 E
Néma	31	Gg	16.36N	7.15W
Néma, Dahr-	32	Ff	16.14N	7.30W
Neman	5	Id	55.18N	21.23 E
Neman	7	Fi	55.03N	22.01 E
Nembrala	26	Hi	10.53S	122.50 E
Nemda	7	Kh	57.31N	43.15 E
Neméa	15	Fl	37.49N	22.39 E
Neméa	15	Fl	37.49N	22.40 E
Nëmëçkes, Mali i-	15	Di	40.08N	20.24 E
Nemenčinė	8	Kj	54.50N	25.39 E
Nëmërçkes, Mali i-	15	Di	40.08N	20.24 E
Nemira, Vîrful-	15	Jc	46.15N	26.19 E
Nemirov [Ukr.-U.S.S.R.]	10	Tf	50.08N	23.28 E
Nemirov [Ukr.-U.S.S.R.]	16	Fe	48.59N	28.50 E
Némiscau	42	Jf	51.30N	77.00W
Nemjuga	7	Kd	65.29N	43.40 E
Nemours	11	If	48.16N	2.42 E
Nemunas	5	Id	55.18N	21.23 E
Nemunėlis	8	Kh	56.24N	24.10 E
Nemuro	27	Qc	43.20N	145.35 E
Nemuro-Hantō	29a	Db	43.20N	145.35 E
Nemuro-Kaikyō=Nemuro Strait (EN)	20	Jh	43.50N	145.30 E
Nemuro Strait (EN)= Kunaširski Proliv	20	Jh	43.50N	145.30 E
Nemuro Strait (EN)= Nemuro-Kaikyō	20	Jh	43.50N	145.30 E
Nemuro-Wan	29a	Db	43.25N	145.25 E
Nenagh/An tAonach	9	Ei	52.52N	8.12W
Nenana	40	Jd	64.30N	149.00W
Nenana	40	Jd	64.34N	149.07W
Nendo Island	57	Hf	10.40S	165.54 E
Nene	9	Ni	52.48N	0.13 E
Nenecki Nacionalny Okrug [3]	19	Fb	67.30N	54.00 E
Nenjiang	22	Oe	49.10N	125.12 E
Nen Jiang	21	Oe	45.26N	124.39 E
Neo	29	Ed	35.38N	136.37 E
Neodesha	45	Ih	37.25N	95.41W
Néon Karlovásion	15	Jl	37.47N	26.42 E
Neosho	45	Ih	36.52N	94.22W
Neosho River	45	Ih	35.48N	95.18W
Néouvielle, Massif de-	11	Gl	42.51N	0.07 E
Nepal [1]	22	Kg	28.00N	84.00 E
Nepalganj	25	Gc	28.03N	81.37 E
Nephi	43	Ed	39.43N	111.50W
Nephin/Né Finn	9	Dg	54.01N	9.22W
Nepisiguit River	44	Ob	47.37N	65.38W
Nepoko	30	Jh	1.40N	27.01 E
Nepomuk	10	Jg	49.29N	13.34 E
Ner	10	Od	52.10N	18.40 E
Nera [It.]	14	Gh	42.26N	12.24 E
Nera [Rom.]	15	Ee	44.49N	21.22 E
Nérac	11	Gj	44.08N	0.21 E
Neratovice	10	Kf	50.16N	14.31 E
Nerău	15	Dd	45.58N	20.34 E
Nerča	20	Gf	51.54N	116.30 E
Nerčinsk	20	Gf	51.58N	116.35 E
Nerčinski Zavod	20	Gf	51.17N	119.30 E
Nerehta	19	Ed	57.28N	40.34 E
Nereju	15	Jd	45.42N	26.43 E
Nereta	8	Kh	56.12N	25.24 E
Neretva	14	Lg	43.02N	17.27 E
Neretvanski kanal	14	Lg	43.03N	17.11 E
Nerica	17	Fd	65.20N	52.45 E
Neringa	7	Ei	55.24N	21.05 E
Neringa	7	Ei	55.18N	21.00 E
Neringa-Joudkrante/ Neringa-Juodkranté	8	Ii	55.35N	21.01 E
Neringa-Juodkranté/ Neringa-Juodkrante	8	Ii	55.35N	21.01 E
Neringa-Nida	8	Ii	55.18N	20.53 E
Neringa-Preila/Neringa-Prejla	8	Ii	55.20N	20.59 E
Neringa-Prejla/Neringa-Preila	8	Ii	55.20N	20.59 E
Neriquinha	36	Df	15.45S	21.33 E
Neris/Njaris	8	Kj	54.55N	25.45 E
Nerja	13	Ih	36.44N	3.52W
Nerjungri	20	He	56.40N	124.47 E
Nerl [R.S.F.S.R.]	7	Jh	56.11N	40.34 E
Nerl [R.S.F.S.R.]	7	Ih	57.07N	37.39 E
Nerpio	13	Jf	38.09N	2.18W
Nerussa	16	Hc	52.33N	33.47 E
Nerva	13	Fg	37.42N	6.32W
Nervi, Genova-	14	Df	44.23N	9.02 E
Nervión	13	Ja	43.14N	2.53W
Nes	8	Cd	60.34N	9.59 E
Nes, Ameland-	12	Ha	53.26N	5.48 E
Nesbyen	7	Bf	60.34N	9.06 E
Nesebăr	15	Kg	42.39N	27.44 E
Nesjøen	8	Db	63.00N	12.00 E
Neskaupstaður	7a	Db	65.09N	13.42W
Nesle	12	Ee	49.46N	2.45 E
Nesna	7	Cc	66.12N	13.02 E
Ness City	45	Gg	38.27N	99.54W
Nesterov [R.S.F.S.R.]	7	Fi	54.42N	22.34 E
Nesterov [Ukr.-U.S.S.R.]	16	Cd	50.03N	24.00 E
Néstos	15	Hi	40.51N	24.44 E
Nesttun	8	Ad	60.19N	5.20 E
Nesviž	16	Ec	53.13N	26.39 E
Netanya	24	Ff	32.20N	34.51 E
Netcong	44	Je	40.54N	74.43W
Nete	11	Kc	51.10N	4.15 E
Nethe	12	Lc	51.44N	9.23 E
Netherdale	59	Jd	21.08S	148.32 E
Netherlands (EN)= Nederland [1]	6	Ge	52.15N	5.30 E
Netherlands Antilles (EN) = Nederlandse Antillen [5]	53	Jd	12.15N	69.00W
Neto	14	Lk	39.12N	17.09 E
Netphen	12	Kd	50.55N	8.06 E
Nettebach	12	Jd	50.26N	7.28 E
Nettersheim	12	Id	50.30N	6.38 E
Nettetal	12	Ic	51.18N	6.12 E
Nettiling Lake	38	Lc	66.30N	70.40W
Nettuno	14	Gi	41.27N	12.39 E
Netzahualcóyotl, Presa-	48	Mi	17.00N	93.30W
Neubourg, Campagne du-	11	Ge	49.08N	1.00 E
Neubrandenburg	10	Jc	53.34N	13.16 E
Neubrandenburg [2]	10	Jc	53.35N	13.15 E
Neuburg an der Donau	10	Hh	48.44N	11.11 E
Neuchâtel [2]	14	Ac	47.05N	6.50 E
Neuchâtel/Neuenburg	14	Ad	46.59N	6.56 E
Neuchâtel, Lac de- / Neuenburger See	14	Ad	46.55N	6.55 E
Neuenbürg	12	Kf	48.50N	8.35 E
Neuenburg/Neuchâtel	14	Ad	46.59N	6.56 E
Neuenburger See/ Neuchâtel, Lac de-	14	Ad	46.55N	6.55 E
Neuenhaus	12	Ib	52.30N	6.58 E
Neuenkirchen	12	Jb	52.15N	7.22 E
Neuerburg	12	Id	50.01N	6.18 E
Neufchâteau [Bel.]	11	Le	49.51N	5.26 E
Neufchâteau [Fr.]	11	Lf	48.21N	5.42 E
Neufchâtel-en-Bray	11	He	49.44N	1.27 E
Neufchâtel-Hardelot	12	Dd	50.37N	1.38 E
Neufchâtel Hardelot-Hardelot Plage	12	Dd	50.38N	1.35 E
Neufchâtel-sur-Aisne	12	Ge	49.26N	4.02 E
Neuffossé, Canal de-	12	Ed	50.45N	2.15 E
Neuhaus am Rennweg	10	Hf	50.31N	11.09 E
Neuilly-en-Thelle	12	Ee	49.13N	2.17 E
Neuilly-Saint-Front	12	Fe	49.10N	3.16 E
Neu-Isenburg	12	Kd	50.03N	8.42 E
Neukirchen-Vluyn	12	Ic	51.27N	6.35 E
Neum	14	Lh	42.55N	17.38 E
Neumagen Dhron	12	Ie	49.51N	6.54 E
Neumarkter Sattel	14	Id	47.06N	14.22 E
Neumarkt in der Oberpfalz	10	Hg	49.17N	11.28 E
Neumünster	10	Fb	54.04N	9.59 E
Neunkirchen [Aus.]	14	Kc	47.43N	16.05 E
Neunkirchen [F.R.G.]	10	Dg	49.21N	7.11 E
Neunkirchen [F.R.G.]	12	Jd	50.51N	7.20 E
Neunkirchen [F.R.G.]	12	Kd	50.48N	8.00 E
Neuquén	53	Ji	39.00S	68.05W
Neuquén [2]	56	Ge	39.00S	70.00W
Neuquén, Río-	52	Ji	38.59S	68.00W
Neurupping	10	Id	52.56N	12.48 E
Neuse River	44	Ih	35.06N	76.30W
Neusiedl am See	14	Kc	47.56N	16.50 E
Neusiedler See (Fertö)	10	Mi	47.50N	16.45 E
Neuß	10	Ce	51.12N	6.42 E
Neustadt (Hessen)	12	Ld	50.51N	9.07 E
Neustadt am Rübenberge	10	Fd	52.30N	9.28 E
Neustadt an der Aisch	10	Gg	49.35N	10.36 E
Neustadt an der Orla	10	Hf	50.44N	11.45 E
Neustadt an der Weinstraße	10	Eg	49.21N	8.09 E
Neustadt bei Couburg	10	Hf	50.19N	11.07 E
Neustadt in Holstein	10	Gb	54.06N	10.49 E
Neustrelitz	10	Jc	53.22N	13.05 E
Neu-Ulm	10	Gh	48.24N	10.01 E
Neuville-les-Dieppe	12	De	49.55N	1.06 E
Neuville-sur-Saône	11	Ki	45.52N	4.51 E
Neuwerk	10	Ec	53.55N	8.30 E
Neuwied	10	Df	50.26N	7.28 E
Neva	5	Jd	59.55N	30.15 E
Nevada [2]	43	Dd	39.00N	117.00W
Nevada [Ia.-U.S.]	45	Je	42.01N	93.27W
Nevada [Mo.-U.S.]	43	Id	37.51N	94.22W
Nevada, Sierra- [Sp.]	5	Fh	37.05N	3.10W
Nevada, Sierra- [U.S.]	38	Hf	38.00N	119.15W
Nevada del Cocuy, Sierra-	52	Ie	6.10N	72.15W
Nevada de Santa Marta, Sierra-	52	Id	10.50N	73.40W
Nevado, Cerro-	52	Ie	3.59N	74.04W
Nevado de Ampato	52	Ig	15.50S	71.52W
Neve, Serra da-	30	Ij	13.52S	13.26 E
Nevel	19	Cd	56.02N	29.55 E
Nevele	12	Fc	51.02N	3.33 E
Nevelsk	20	Jg	46.37N	141.57 E
Neverkino	16	Oc	52.47N	46.48 E
Nevers	11	Jg	46.59N	3.10 E
Nevesinje	14	Mg	43.16N	18.07 E
Nevinnomyssk	19	Eg	44.38N	41.58 E
Nevis	47	Le	17.10N	62.34W
Nevis, Ben-	5	Fd	56.48N	5.01W
Nevis Peak	51c	Ab	17.10N	62.34W
Nevjansk	19	Gd	57.32N	60.13 E
Nevşehir	23	Db	38.38N	34.43 E
Nevskoje	28	Lb	45.42N	133.40 E
Newala	36	Ge	10.56S	39.18 E
New Albany [In.-U.S.]	43	Jd	38.18N	85.49W
New Albany [Ms.-U.S.]	45	Li	34.29N	89.00W
New Alresford	12	Ac	51.05N	1.10W
New Amsterdam	53	Ke	6.17N	57.36W
Newark [De.-U.S.]	44	Jf	39.41N	75.45W
Newark [N.J.-U.S.]	43	Mc	40.44N	74.11W
Newark [N.Y.-U.S.]	44	Id	43.03N	77.06W
Newark [Oh.-U.S.]	43	Kc	40.03N	82.25W
Newark-on-Trent	9	Mh	53.05N	0.49W
New Bedford	43	Mc	41.38N	70.56W
New Bern	43	Ld	35.07N	77.03W
Newberry [Mi.-U.S.]	44	Eb	46.21N	85.30W
Newberry [S.C.-U.S.]	44	Gh	34.17N	81.37W
New Braunfels	43	Hf	29.42N	98.08W
New Britain	44	Ke	41.40N	72.47W
New Britain Island	57	Ge	5.40S	151.00 E
New Britain Trench (EN)	60	Ei	6.00S	153.00 E
New Brunswick	44	Je	40.29N	74.27W
New Brunswick [3]	42	Kg	46.30N	66.45W
New Buckenham	12	Db	52.28N	1.05 E
New Buffalo	44	De	41.47N	86.45W
Newburgh	43	Mc	41.30N	74.00W
Newbury	9	Lj	51.25N	1.20W
New Caledonia (EN) = Nouvelle-Calédonie [5]	58	Hg	21.30S	165.30 E
New Caledonia (EN)= Nouvelle-Calédonie	57	Hg	21.30S	165.30 E
New Caledonia Basin (EN)	3	Jm	30.00S	165.00 E
New Carlisle	44	Oa	48.01N	65.20W
New Castile (EN)=Castilla la Nueva	13	Id	40.00N	3.45W
New Castle [In.-U.S.]	44	Ef	39.55N	85.22W
New Castle [Pa.-U.S.]	43	Kc	41.00N	80.22W
Newcastle [Austl.]	58	Gh	32.56S	151.46 E
Newcastle [N.B.-Can.]	42	Kg	47.00N	65.34W
Newcastle [N.Ire.-U.K.]	9	Hg	54.12N	5.54W
Newcastle [S.Afr.]	37	De	27.49S	29.55 E
Newcastle [St.C.N.]	51c	Ab	17.13N	62.34W
Newcastle/An Caisleán Nua	9	Hg	54.12N	5.54W
Newcastle Creek	59	Gc	17.20S	133.23 E
Newcastle-under-Lyme	9	Kh	53.00N	2.14W

Index Symbols

- [1] Independent Nation
- [2] State, Region
- [3] District, County
- [4] Municipality
- [5] Colony, Dependency
- Continent
- Physical Region
- Historical or Cultural Region
- Mount, Mountain
- Volcano
- Hill
- Mountains, Mountain Range
- Hills, Escarpment
- Plateau, Upland
- Pass, Gap
- Plain, Lowland
- Delta
- Salt Flat
- Valley, Canyon
- Crater, Cave
- Karst Features
- Depression
- Polder
- Desert, Dunes
- Forest, Woods
- Heath, Steppe
- Oasis
- Cape, Point
- Coast, Beach
- Cliff
- Peninsula
- Isthmus
- Sandbank
- Island
- Atoll
- Rock, Reef
- Islands, Archipelago
- Rocks, Reefs
- Coral Reef
- Well, Spring
- Geyser
- River, Stream
- Waterfall Rapids
- River Mouth, Estuary
- Lake
- Salt Lake
- Intermittent Lake
- Reservoir
- Swamp, Pond
- Canal
- Glacier
- Ice Shelf, Pack Ice
- Ocean
- Sea
- Gulf, Bay
- Strait, Fjord
- Lagoon
- Bank
- Seamount
- Tablemount
- Ridge
- Shelf
- Basin
- Escarpment, Sea Scarp
- Fracture
- Trench, Abyss
- National Park, Reserve
- Point of Interest
- Recreation Site
- Cave, Cavern
- Historic Site
- Ruins
- Wall, Walls
- Church, Abbey
- Temple
- Scientific Station
- Airport
- Port
- Lighthouse
- Mine
- Tunnel
- Dam, Bridge

wcastle-upon-Tyne 6 Fd 54.59N 1.35W
wcastle Waters 58 Ef 17.24S 133.24 E
wcastle West/An
aisleán Nua 9 Di 52.27N 9.03W
w Delhi 22 Jg 28.36N 77.12 E
w Denver 46 Ga 50.00N 117.22W
well 45 Ed 44.43N 103.25W
well, Lake- 46 Ja 50.25N 111.56W
w England 38 Le 44.00N 71.20W
w England Range 57 Gh 30.00S 151.50 E
w England Seamounts
N) 38 Mf 38.00N 61.00W
wenham, Cape- 40 Ge 58.37N 162.12W
w Forest 9 Lk 50.55N 1.35W
wfoundland [3] 42 Lf 52.00N 56.00W
wfoundland, Island of- 38 Ne 48.30N 56.00W
wfoundland Basin (EN)
3 De 45.00N 40.00W
w Galloway 9 If 55.05N 4.10W
w Georgia 57 Ge 8.30S 157.20 E
w Georgia Island 60 Fi 8.15S 157.30 E
w Georgia Sound (The
lot) 60 Fi 8.00S 158.10 E
w Glasgow 42 Lg 45.35N 62.39W
w Guinea/Pulau Irian 57 Fe 5.00S 140.00 E
w Guinea Trench (EN) 60 Bg 0.05N 135.50 E
w Hampshire [2] 43 Mc 43.35N 71.40W
w Hampton 45 Je 43.03N 92.19W
w Hanover Island 57 Ge 2.30S 150.15 E
w Harmony 44 Df 38.08N 87.56W
w Haven 39 Le 41.18N 72.56W
whaven 9 Nk 50.47N 0.03 E
w Hebrides/Nouvelles
ébrides 57 Hf 16.01S 167.01 E
w Hebrides Trench (EN)
3 Jl 20.00S 168.00 E
w Iberia 43 If 30.00N 91.49W
w Ireland Island 57 Ge 3.20S 152.00 E
w Jersey [2] 43 Mc 40.15N 74.30W
ew Kowloon/Julong 22 Ng 22.20N 114.09 E
ew Liskeard 42 Jg 47.30N 79.40W
ew London 43 Mc 41.21N 72.07W
ew Madrid 45 Lh 36.36N 89.32W
ewman 59 Dd 23.15S 119.35 E
ewmarket [Eng.-U.K.] 9 Ni 52.15N 0.25 E
ewmarket [Ont.-Can.] 44 Hc 44.03N 79.28W
ew Martinsville 44 Gf 39.39N 80.52W
ew Meadows 46 Gd 44.58N 116.32W
ew Mexico [2] 43 Fe 34.30N 106.00W
ewnan 44 Ei 33.23N 84.48W
ew Norfolk 59 Jh 42.47S 147.03 E
ew Orleans 39 Jg 29.58N 90.07W
ew Philadelphia 44 Ge 40.30N 81.27W
ew Pine Creek 46 Ee 42.01N 120.18W
ew-Plymouth 58 Ih 39.04S 174.04 E
ewport [Ar.-U.S.] 45 Ki 35.37N 91.17W
ewport [Eng.-U.K.] 12 Cc 51.59N 0.15 E
ewport [Eng.-U.K.] 9 Lk 50.42N 1.18W
ewport [Fl.-U.S.] 44 Ej 30.14N 84.12W
ewport [Or.-U.S.] 43 Cc 44.38N 124.03W
ewport [R.I.-U.S.] 44 Le 41.30N 71.19W
ewport [Tn.-U.S.] 44 Fh 35.58N 83.11W
ewport [Vt.-U.S.] 44 Kc 44.56N 72.13W
ewport [Wales-U.K.] 9 Kj 51.35N 3.00W
ewport [Wa.-U.S.] 46 Gb 48.11N 117.03W
ewport Beach 43 De 33.37N 117.54W
ewport News 39 Lf 37.04N 76.28W
ewport Pagnell 12 Bb 52.05N 0.43W
ew Providence Island 47 Ic 25.02N 77.24W
ewquay 9 Hk 50.25N 5.05W
ew Quebec Crater (EN) =
Nouveau-Québec, Cratère
du- 42 Kd 61.30N 73.55W
ew Richmond [Oh.-U.S.] 44 Ef 38.57N 84.16W
ew Richmond [Que.-Can.] 44 Oa 48.10N 65.52W
ew River [Blz.] 49 Cd 18.22N 88.24W
ew River [Guy.] 54 Gc 3.23N 57.36W
ew River [U.S.] 44 Ff 38.50N 82.06W
ew Rockford 45 Gc 47.41N 99.15W
ew Romney 12 Cd 50.59N 0.56 E
ew Ross/Ros Mhic Thriúin 9 Gi 52.24N 6.56W
ewry/an t-Iúr 9 Gg 54.11N 6.20W
ew Salem 45 Fc 46.51N 101.25W
ew Sandy Bay 51n Ba 13.20N 61.08W
ew Schwabenland (EN) 66 Cf 72.30S 1.00 E
New Siberia (EN) = Novaja
Sibir, Ostrov- 21 Qb 75.00N 149.00 E
New Siberian Islands (EN)
= Novosibirskije
Ostrova 21 Qb 75.00N 142.00 E
New Smyrna Beach 44 Gk 29.02N 80.56W
New South Wales 59 Jf 33.00S 146.00 E
Newton [Ia.-U.S.] 45 Jf 41.42N 93.03W
Newton [Il.-U.S.] 45 Lg 38.59N 88.10W
Newton [Ks.-U.S.] 43 Hd 38.03N 97.21W
Newton [Ma.-U.S.] 44 Ld 42.21N 71.13W
Newton [Ms.-U.S.] 45 Lj 32.19N 89.10W
Newton [N.J.-U.S.] 44 Je 41.03N 74.45W
Newton Abbot 9 Jk 50.32N 3.36W
Newton Stewart 9 Ig 54.57N 4.29W
Newtontoppen 67 Kd 72.02N 17.30 E
New Town 45 Ec 47.59N 102.30W
Newtown 9 Ji 52.32N 3.19W
Newtownabbey/Baile na
Mainistreach 9 Hg 54.42N 5.54W
Newtownards/Baile Nua na
hArda 9 Hg 54.36N 5.41W
New Ulm 43 Ic 44.19N 94.28W
New Westminster 42 Fg 49.12N 122.55W
New York 39 Le 40.43N 74.01W
New York [2] 43 Lc 43.00N 75.00W
New York State Barge
Canal 44 Hd 43.05N 78.43W
New Zealand [1] 58 Ii 41.00S 174.00 E
New Zealand 57 Ii 41.00S 174.00 E
Nexpa, Río- 48 Hh 18.05N 102.46W
Neyagawa 29 Dd 34.46N 135.36 E
Neyrīz 24 Ph 29.12N 54.19 E
Neyshābūr 23 Ib 36.12N 58.50 E
Nežárka 10 Kg 49.11N 14.43 E
Nežin 19 De 51.02N 31.57 E
Ngabé 36 Cc 3.12S 16.11 E
Ngahere 62 De 42.24S 171.26 E
Ngajangel 64a Ba 8.05N 134.43 E
Ngala 34 Hc 12.20N 14.11 E
Ngaliema, Chutes- = Stanley
Falls (EN) 30 Jh 0.30N 25.30 E
Ngamegei Passage 64a Bb 7.44N 134.34 E
Ngami, Lake- 37 Cd 20.37S 22.40 E
Ngamiland [3] 37 Cc 19.09S 22.47 E
Ngamring 27 Ef 29.14N 87.12 E
Ngangala 35 Ee 4.42N 31.55 E
Ngangerabeli Plain 36 Hc 1.30S 40.15 E
Ngangla Ringco 27 De 31.40N 83.00 E
Nganglong Kangri 27 De 32.45N 81.12 E
Nganglong Kangri 21 Kf 32.00N 83.00 E
Ngangzê Co 27 Ee 31.00N 86.55 E
Ngao 25 Je 18.45N 99.59 E
Ngaoundéré 31 Ih 7.19N 13.35 E
Ngapara 62 Df 44.57S 170.45 E
Ngara 36 Fc 2.28S 30.39 E
Ngardmau 64a Bb 7.37N 134.35 E
Ngardmau Bay 64a Bb 7.39N 134.35 E
Ngardololok 64a Ac 7.00N 134.16 E
Ngaregur 64a Bb 7.45N 134.38 E
Ngarekeukl 64a Ac 7.00N 134.14 E
Ngariungs 64a Ba 8.03N 134.43 E
Ngaruangl 64a Ba 8.10N 134.39 E
Ngaruangl Passage 64a Ba 8.07N 134.40 E
Ngaruawahia 62 Fb 37.40S 175.09 E
Ngaruroro 62 Gc 39.34S 176.55 E
Ngatangiia 64p Cb 21.14S 159.43W
Ngatangiia Harbour 64p Cb 21.14S 159.43W
Ngateguil, Point- 64a Bc 7.26N 134.37 E
Ngatik Atoll 57 Gd 5.51N 157.16 E
Ngatpang 64a Bc 7.28N 134.32 E
Ngau Island 63d Bc 18.02S 179.18 E
Ngauruhoe 62 Fc 39.09S 175.38 E
Ngawa/Aba 27 He 32.55N 101.45 E
Ngayu 36 Eb 1.35N 27.13 E
Ngemelis Islands 64a Ac 7.07N 134.15 E
Ngeregong 64a Ac 7.07N 134.22 E
Ngergoi 64a Ac 7.05N 134.17 E
Ngesebus 64a Ac 7.03N 134.16 E
Nggamea 63d Cb 16.46S 179.46W
Nggatokae 63a Dc 8.46S 158.11 E
Nggela Pile 63a Ec 9.08S 160.20 E
Nggela Sule 63a Ec 9.03S 160.12 E
Nggelelevu 63d Cb 16.05S 179.09W
Ngidinga 36 Cd 5.37S 15.17 E
Ngiro, Ewaso- 36 Gb 0.28N 39.55 E
Ngiva 31 Ij 17.03S 15.47 E
Ngo 36 Cc 2.29S 15.45 E
Ngoangoa 35 Dd 5.58N 25.10 E
Ngobasangel 64a Ac 7.16N 134.20 E
Ngoko 36 Cb 1.40N 16.03 E
Ngola Shankou 27 Gd 35.30N 99.36 E
Ngoma 36 Ef 15.58S 25.56 E
Ngoring Hu 27 Gd 35.00N 97.30 E
Ngorongoro Crater 30 Ki 3.10S 35.35 E
Ngoui 34 Cb 16.09N 13.55W
Ngouna 63b Dc 17.26S 168.21 E
Ngounié [3] 36 Bc 2.00S 11.00 E
Ngounié 36 Bc 0.37S 10.18 E
Ngoura 35 Bc 12.52N 16.27 E
Ngouri 35 Bc 13.38N 15.22 E
Ngourti 34 Hb 15.19N 13.12 E
Ngousouboot, Pointe- 63b Ca 13.58S 167.27 E
Ngudu 36 Fc 2.58S 33.20 E
Nguigmi 31 Ig 14.15N 13.07 E
Ngulu Atoll 57 Ed 8.18N 137.29 E
Nguni 36 Gc 0.50S 38.20 E
Ngunza 31 Ij 11.12S 13.51 E
Nguru 31 Ig 12.53N 10.28 E
Nhachengue 37 Fd 22.51S 35.11 E
Nhamundá 54 Gd 2.14S 56.43W
Nhamundá, Rio- 54 Gd 2.12S 56.41W
Nhandeara 55 Ge 20.40S 50.02W
Nhandutiba 55 Jb 14.37S 44.12W
Nharea 36 Ce 11.28S 16.53 E
Nha Trang 22 Mh 12.15N 109.11 E
Nhecolândia 55 Dd 19.16S 57.04W
Nhia 36 Be 10.15S 14.12 E
Nhulunbuy 58 Ef 12.00S 35.58 E
Niafounké 34 Eb 15.56N 4.00W
Niagara Escarpment 44 Gc 44.30N 80.35W
Niagara Falls 38 Le 43.05N 79.04W
Niagara Falls [N.Y.-U.S.] 43 Lc 43.06N 79.02W
Niagara Falls [Ont.-Can.] 42 Jh 43.06N 79.04W
Niagara River 44 Hd 43.15N 79.04W
Niagassola 34 Dc 12.19N 9.07W
Niah 26 Ff 3.52N 113.44 E
Niakaramandougou 34 Dd 8.40N 5.17W
Niamey 31 Hg 13.31N 2.07 E
Niamey [2] 34 Fc 14.00N 2.00 E
Niandan 34 Dc 10.35N 9.45W
Niangara 31 Jh 3.42N 27.52 E
Niangay, Lac- 34 Eb 15.50N 3.00W
Niangoloko 34 Ec 10.17N 4.55W
Nia-Nia 36 Eb 1.24N 27.36 E
Nianzishan 27 Lb 47.31N 122.50 E
Niao Dao 27 Gd 37.20N 99.50 E
Niaoshu Shan 27 He 34.54N 104.04 E
Niari [3] 36 Bc 4.30S 13.00 E
Niari 36 Bc 3.56S 12.12 E
Nias, Palau- 21 Li 1.05N 97.35 E
Niassa [3] 37 Fb 13.00S 36.00 E
Niassa, Lago- = Nyasa,
Lake- (EN) 30 Kj 12.00S 34.30 E
Niau, Ile- 57 Mf 16.09S 146.21W
Nibāk 24 Nj 24.24N 50.50 E
Nibe 8 Ch 56.59N 9.38 E
Nica 17 Lh 57.29N 64.33 E
Nica/Nīca 8 Ih 56.25N 20.56 E
Nica/Nīca 8 Ih 56.25N 20.56 E
Nicanor Olivera 55 Cn 38.17S 59.12W
Nicaragua [1] 39 Kh 13.00N 85.00W
Nicaragua, Lago de- =
Nicaragua, Lake- (EN) 38 Kh 11.35N 85.25W
Nicaragua, Lake- (EN) =
Nicaragua, Lago de- 38 Kh 11.35N 85.25W
Nicastro 14 Kl 38.59N 16.19 E
Nice 6 Gg 43.42N 7.15 E
Niceville 44 Dj 30.31N 86.29W
Nichicum, Lac- 42 Kf 53.08N 70.55W
Nichinan [Jap.] 29 Cd 35.10N 133.16 E
Nichinan [Jap.] 28 Ki 31.36N 131.23 E
Nicholas Channel 49 Gb 23.25N 80.05W
Nicholas Channel (EN) =
Nicolás, Canal- 47 Hd 23.25N 80.05W
Nicholasville 44 Eg 37.53N 84.34W
Nicholls Town 49 Ia 25.08N 78.00W
Nicholson Range 59 De 27.15S 116.45 E
Nicholson River 57 Ef 17.31S 139.36 E
Nickerson Ice Shelf 66 Mf 75.45S 145.00W
Nickol Bay 59 Dd 20.40S 116.50 E
Nicobar Islands 21 Li 8.00N 93.30 E
Nicocli 49 Ii 8.26N 76.48W
Nicolajevka 15 Nb 47.33N 30.41 E
Nicola River 46 Ea 50.25N 121.18W
Nicolás, Canal- = Nicholas
Channel (EN) 47 Hd 23.25N 80.05W
Nicolet 44 Kb 46.14N 72.37W
Nicopolis (EN) =
Nikópolis 15 Dj 39.00N 20.45 E
Nicosia 14 Im 37.45N 14.24 E
Nicosia (EN) = Lefkosa/
Levkôsia 22 Ff 35.10N 33.22 E
Nicosia (EN) = Levkôsia/
Lefkosa 22 Ff 35.10N 33.22 E
Nicotera 14 Jl 38.33N 15.56 E
Nicoya 47 Gf 10.09N 85.27W
Nicoya, Golfo de- 47 Hg 9.47N 84.48W
Nicoya, Peninsula de- =
Nicoya Peninsula (EN) 38 Ki 10.00N 85.25W
Nicoya Peninsula (EN) =
Nicoya, Peninsula de- 38 Ki 10.00N 85.25W
Nicuadala 37 Fc 17.37S 36.50 E
Niculitel 15 Ld 45.11N 28.29 E
Nida 10 Qf 50.18N 20.52 E
Nidda 12 Ld 50.25N 9.00 E
Nidda 10 Ef 50.06N 8.34 E
Nidder 12 Kd 50.12N 8.47 E
Nideggen 12 Id 50.42N 6.29 E
Nidelva [Nor.] 8 Cf 58.24N 8.48 E
Nidelva [Nor.] 8 Da 63.26N 10.25 E
Nido, Sierra del- 48 Fc 29.30N 106.45W
Nidže 15 Ei 41.00N 21.50 E
Nidzica 10 Qf 50.12N 20.04 E
Nidzica 10 Qc 53.22N 20.26 E
Nidzkie, Jezioro- 10 Rc 53.37N 21.30 E
Niebüll 10 Eb 54.48N 8.50 E
Nied 12 Ie 49.23N 6.40 E
Nieddu 14 Dj 40.44N 9.34 E
Niederbayern 10 Ih 48.35N 12.30 E
Niederbronn-les-Bains 11 Nf 48.58N 7.38 E
Niedere Tauern 14 Hc 47.20N 14.00 E
Niederlausitz 10 Ke 51.40N 14.15 E
Nieder-Olm 12 Ke 49.54N 8.13 E
Niederösterreich = Lower
Austria (EN) [2] 14 Jb 48.30N 15.45 E
Niedersachsen = Lower
Saxony (EN) [2] 10 Fd 52.00N 10.00 E
Niederwald 10 Df 50.10N 8.00 E
Niederzier 12 Id 50.53N 6.28 E
Niefang 34 He 1.50N 10.14 E
Niegocin, Jezioro- 10 Rb 54.00N 21.50 E
Niel 12 Gc 51.07N 4.20 E
Nielfa, Puerto de- 13 Hf 38.32N 4.23W
Niéllé 34 Dc 10.12N 5.38W
Niellim 35 Bd 9.42N 17.49 E
Niemba 36 Ed 5.57S 28.26 E
Niemba 36 Ed 5.57S 28.26 E
Niemodlin 10 Nf 50.39N 17.37 E
Niéna 34 Dc 11.25N 6.20W
Nienburg (Weser) 10 Fd 52.38N 9.13 E
Niepołomice 10 Qf 50.03N 20.13 E
Niermalak, Pointe- 63b Cb 14.21S 167.24 E
Niers 12 Be 51.43N 5.57 E
Nierstein 12 Ke 49.53N 8.20 E
Niesky/Niska 10 Ke 51.18N 14.49 E
Nieszawa 10 Od 52.50N 18.55 E
Nieuport/Nieuwpoort 11 Ic 51.08N 2.45 E
Nieuw Amsterdam 54 Gb 5.53N 55.05W
Nieuwe-Pekela 12 Ia 53.04N 6.59 E
Nieuweschans 12 Ja 53.11N 7.15 E
Nieuw Milligen, Apeldoorn- 12 Hb 52.14N 5.45 E
Nieuw Nickerie 53 Ke 5.57N 56.59W
Nieuwolda 12 Ia 53.14N 6.59 E
Nieuwoudtville 37 Bf 31.22S 19.06 E
Nieuwpoort/Nieuport 11 Ic 51.08N 2.45 E
Nieuw Weerdinge,
Emmen- 12 Jb 52.52N 7.01 E
Nieves 48 He 24.00N 103.01W
Nièvre [3] 11 Jg 47.05N 3.30 E
Nièvre 11 Jh 46.59N 3.10 E
Nigata 28 Lg 34.13N 132.29 E
Niğde 23 Db 37.59N 34.42 E
Nigenān 24 Qe 34.13N 57.19 E
Niger [1] 31 Hg 16.00N 8.00 E
Niger 30 Hh 5.33N 6.33 E
Niger [2] 34 Gd 9.40N 6.00 E
Niger Basin (EN) 30 Gg 15.00N 2.00 E
Niger Delta 30 Hh 4.50N 6.00 E
Nigeria [1] 31 Hh 10.00N 8.00 E
Night Hawk Lake 44 Ga 48.28N 81.00W
Nightingale Island 30 Fi 37.24S 12.28W
Nigrita 15 Gi 40.54N 23.30 E
Nihiru Atoll 57 Mf 16.42S 142.50W
Nihoa Island 57 Kb 23.06N 161.58W
Nihonmatsu 28 Pf 37.35N 140.26 E
Nihuil, Embalse del- 56 Ge 35.05S 68.45W
Niigata 22 Pf 37.55N 139.03 E
Niigata Ken [2] 28 Of 37.30N 138.50 E
Niihama 28 Lh 33.58N 133.16 E
Niihau Island 57 Kb 21.55N 160.10W
Nii-Jima 27 Oe 34.20N 139.15 E
Niikappu-Gawa 29a Cb 42.22N 142.16 E
Niimi 28 Lg 34.59N 133.28 E
Niisato 29 Gb 39.36N 141.49 E
Niitsu 28 Of 37.48N 139.07 E
Nijar 13 Jh 36.58N 2.12W
Nijkerk 12 Hb 52.14N 5.29 E
Nijlen 12 Gc 51.10N 4.39 E
Nijmegen 11 Lc 51.50N 5.50 E
Nijvel/Nivelles 11 Kd 50.36N 4.20 E
Nijverdal, Hellendoorn- 12 Ib 52.22N 6.27 E
Nikel 19 Db 69.24N 30.13 E
Niki 15 Ei 40.55N 21.25 E
Nikitin Seamount (EN) 21 Kj 3.00S 83.00 E
Nikki 34 Fd 9.56N 3.12 E
Nikkō 29 Fc 36.44N 139.35 E
Nikolajev [Ukr.-U.S.S.R.] 16 Ce 49.32N 23.58 E
Nikolajev [Ukr.-U.S.S.R.] 6 Jf 46.58N 32.00 E
Nikolajevka 18 Kc 43.37N 77.01 E
Nikolajevo 8 Mf 58.14N 29.32 E
Nikolajevsk 19 Ee 50.02N 45.31 E
Nikolajevskaja Oblast [3] 19 Df 47.20N 32.00 E
Nikolajevski 20 Hf 54.50N 129.25 E
Nikolajevsk-na-Amure 22 Qd 53.08N 140.44 E
Nikolsk [R.S.F.S.R.] 19 Ee 53.42N 46.03 E
Nikolsk [R.S.F.S.R.] 19 Ed 59.33N 45.31 E
Nikolski [Ak.-U.S.] 40a Eb 53.15N 168.22W
Nikolski [Kaz.-U.S.S.R.] 19 Gf 47.55N 67.33 E
Nikonga 36 Fc 4.40S 31.28 E
Nikopol [Bul.] 15 Hf 43.42N 24.54 E
Nikopol [Ukr.-U.S.S.R.] 19 Df 47.35N 34.25 E
Nikópolis = Nicopolis (EN)
15 Dj 39.00N 20.45 E
Nikpey 24 Md 36.50N 48.10 E
Niksar 24 Gb 40.36N 36.58 E
Nikšić 15 Bg 42.46N 18.58 E
Nikumaroro Atoll (Gardner)
57 Je 4.40S 174.32W
Nikunau Island 57 Ie 1.23S 176.26 E
Nil, Kūh-e- 24 Ng 30.52N 50.49 E
Nil, Nahr an- = Nile (EN) 30 Ke 30.10N 31.06 E
Nila, Pulau- 26 Ih 6.44S 129.31 E
Nilakka 7 Ge 63.07N 26.33 E
Niland 46 Hj 33.14N 115.31W
Nilandu Atoll 25a Bb 3.00N 72.55 E
Nile [3] 36 Fb 3.00N 31.30 E
Nile (EN) = Nil, Nahr an- 30 Ke 30.10N 31.06 E
Nile Delta (EN) 30 Ke 31.20N 31.00 E
Nileh, Kūh-e- 24 Nf 32.59N 50.32 E
Niles 44 De 41.50N 86.15W
Nilka 27 Dc 43.47N 82.20 E
Nīl Kowtal 23 Kc 34.48N 67.22 E
Nilsiä 7 Ge 63.12N 28.05 E
Nilüfer 15 Li 40.18N 28.27 E
Nimba [3] 34 Dd 6.45N 8.45W
Nimba, Monts- = Nimba
Mountains (EN) 30 Gh 7.35N 8.28W
Nimba Mountains (EN) =
Nimba, Monts- 30 Gh 7.35N 8.28W
Nîmes 6 Gg 43.50N 4.21 E
Nimjad 27 Dd 17.25N 15.41W
Nimmitabel 59 Jg 36.31S 149.16 E
Nimpkish River 46 Ba 50.32N 126.59W
Nimrode Glacier 66 Kg 82.27S 161.00 E
Nimrud 24 Jd 36.06N 43.20 E
Nimrūz [3] 23 Jc 30.30N 62.00 E
Nims 12 Ie 49.51N 6.28 E
Nimule 31 Kh 3.36N 32.03 E
Nimún, Punta- 48 Ng 20.46N 90.25W
Nin 14 Jf 44.14N 15.11 E
Nina 37 Bd 22.57S 18.14 E
Nīnawá [3] 24 Je 35.45N 42.45 E
Nīnawá = Nineveh (EN) 23 Fb 36.22N 43.09 E
Nine Degree Channel 21 Ji 9.00N 73.00 E
Ninetyeast Ridge (EN) 3 Gj 10.00S 90.00 E
Ninety Mile Beach [Austl.]
59 Jg 38.15S 147.25 E
Ninety Mile Beach [N.Z.] 62 Ea 34.45S 173.00 E
Nineveh (EN) = Nīnawá 23 Fb 36.22N 43.09 E
Ning'an 27 Mc 44.22N 129.23 E
Ningbo 22 Og 29.55N 121.28 E
Ningcheng (Tianyi) 27 Kc 41.34N 119.25 E
Ningde 27 Kf 26.44N 119.29 E
Ningdu 27 Kf 26.31N 115.59 E
Ningguo 28 Ei 30.39N 119.00 E
Ninghai 28 Fj 29.19N 121.26 E
Ning-hsia-hui-tsu Tzu-chih-
ch'ü → Ningxia Huizu
Zizhiqu = Ningsia Hui (EN)
[2] 27 Id 37.00N 106.00 E
Ningjin [China] 28 Df 37.39N 116.48 E
Ningjin [China] 28 Cf 37.37N 114.55 E
Ningjing Shan 27 Ge 31.45N 97.15 E
Ninglang 27 Hf 27.17N 100.52 E
Ningling 28 Cg 34.27N 115.18 E
Ningnan 27 Hf 27.05N 102.44 E
Ningqiang 27 Ie 32.48N 106.15 E
Ningsia Hui (EN) = Ning-
hsia-hui-tsu Tzu-chih-
ch'ü → Ningxia Huizu
Zizhiqu [2] 27 Id 37.00N 106.00 E
Ningsia Hui (EN) = Ningxia
Huizu Zizhiqu
(Ning-hsia-hui-tsu Tzu-
chih-ch'ü) [2] 27 Id 37.00N 106.00 E
Ningwu 27 Jd 38.59N 112.14 E
Ningxia Huizu Zizhiqu
(Ning-hsia-hui-tsu Tzu-
chih-ch'ü) = Ningsia Hui
(EN) [2] 27 Id 37.00N 106.00 E
Ningxian 27 Id 35.27N 107.50 E
Ningxiang 28 Bj 28.16N 112.33 E
Ningyang 28 Dg 35.45N 116.48 E
Ningyō-Tōge 29 Cd 35.19N 133.56 E
Ninh Binh 25 Ld 20.15N 105.59 E
Ninh Hoa 25 Lf 12.29N 109.08 E
Ninigo Group 57 Fe 1.15S 144.15 E
Niniva 65b Ba 19.46S 174.38W
Ninnis Glacier 66 Je 68.12S 147.12 E
Ninohe 27 Pc 40.16N 141.18 E
Ninove 12 Fd 50.50N 4.00 E
Nioaque 54 Gh 21.08S 55.48W
Niobrara 38 Je 42.45N 98.00W
Niobrara 45 He 42.25N 98.00W
Niogħalvfjerdsfjorden 41 Kc 79.30N 18.45W
Nioki 36 Cc 2.43S 17.41 E
Niono 34 Dc 14.15N 6.00W
Nioro du Rip 34 Bc 13.45N 15.48W
Nioro du Sahel 31 Gg 15.14N 9.37W
Niort 11 Fh 46.19N 0.28W
Nipawin 42 Hf 53.22N 104.00W
Nipe, Bahía de- 49 Jc 20.47N 75.42W
Nipesotsu-Yama 29a Cb 43.27N 143.02 E
Nipigon 39 Ke 49.01N 88.16W
Nipigon, Lake- 38 Ke 49.50N 88.30W
Nipigon Bay 45 Mb 48.53N 87.50W
Nipissing, Lake- 38 Le 46.17N 80.00W
Nippon = Japan (EN) [1] 22 Pf 38.00N 137.00 E
Nippon-Kai = Japan, Sea of-
(EN) 21 Pf 40.00N 134.00 E
Nippur 24 Kf 32.10N 45.10 E
Niquelândia 54 If 14.27S 48.27W
Niquero 49 Ic 20.03N 77.35W
Niquitao, Teta de- 49 Li 9.07N 70.30W
Niquivil 56 Gd 30.25S 68.42W
Nir 24 Lc 38.02N 47.59 E
Nirasaki 29 Fd 35.43N 138.27 E
Nirji → Morin Dawa 27 Lb 48.30N 124.28 E
Nirmal 25 Fe 19.06N 78.21 E
Niš 6 Ig 43.19N 21.54 E
Nisa 13 Ee 39.31N 7.39W
Nişāb 23 Gg 14.24N 46.38 E
Nisāh, Sha'īb- 24 Lj 24.11N 47.11 E
Nišava 15 Ef 43.22N 21.46 E
Niscemi 14 Im 37.09N 14.23 E
Nishibetsu-Gawa 29a Db 43.23N 145.17 E
Nishikawa 29 Gb 38.26N 140.08 E
Nishiki 29 Bd 34.16N 131.57 E
Nishinomiya 29 Dd 34.43N 135.20 E
Nishino'omote 27 Ne 30.44N 131.00 E
Nishino-Shima 60 Cb 27.30N 140.53 E
Nishi-No-Shima 28 Lf 36.06N 133.00 E
Nishiokoppe 29a Cb 44.20N 142.57 E
Nishi-Sonogi-Hantō 29 Ae 32.55N 129.45 E
Nishiwaki 29 Dd 34.59N 134.58 E
Nisiros 15 Km 36.35N 27.10 E
Niska/Niesky 10 Ke 51.18N 14.49 E
Niška Banja 15 Ff 43.18N 22.01 E
Nisko 10 Sf 50.31N 22.09 E
Nismes, Viroinval- 12 Gd 50.05N 4.33 E
Nisoi Aiyaiou [2] 15 Il 37.40N 25.40 E
Nisporeny 16 Ff 47.06N 28.10 E
Nissan 8 Eh 56.40N 12.51 E
Nissan 63a Ba 4.30S 154.14 E
Nisser 8 Ce 59.10N 8.30 E
Nissum Bredning 8 Ch 56.40N 8.20 E
Nissum Fjord 8 Ch 56.20N 8.15 E
Nita 29 Cd 35.12N 133.00 E
Nitchequon 42 Kf 53.15N 70.44W
Niterói 53 Lh 22.53S 43.07W
Nith 9 Jf 55.00N 3.35W
Nitra 10 Oi 47.46N 18.10 E
Nitra 10 Oh 48.19N 18.05 E
Niuafo'ou Island 57 Jf 15.35S 175.38W
Niuatoputapu Island 57 Jf 15.57S 173.45W
Niue [5] 58 Kf 19.02S 169.55W
Niue Island 57 Kf 19.02S 169.55W
Niu'erhe 27 La 51.30N 121.40 E
Niufu 29a Ca 44.35N 142.35 E
Niulakita Island 57 If 10.45S 179.30 E
Niutaca, Corrente- 55 De 20.42S 57.37W
Niutao Island 57 Ie 6.06S 177.16 E
Niutg, Gunung- 26 Ef 1.00N 109.55 E
Niutoushan 27 Ke 31.00N 119.35 E
Niuzhuang 28 Gd 40.57N 122.30 E
Nivala 7 Fe 63.58N 25.01 E
Nive 11 Ek 43.30N 1.29W
Nivelles/Nijvel 11 Kd 50.36N 4.20 E
Nivernais 11 Jg 47.00N 3.30 E
Nivernais, Canal du- 11 Jg 47.40N 3.40 E
Nivernais, Côtes du- 11 Jg 47.10N 3.30 E
Nivillers 12 Ee 49.28N 2.10 E
Nixon 45 Hl 29.16N 97.46W
Niya/Minfeng 27 Dd 37.04N 82.46 E
Nīyābād 24 Le 35.12N 46.20 E
Niyodo-Gawa 29 Ce 33.28N 133.29 E
Niza 24 Ph 28.25N 55.55 E
Nizāmābād 25 Fe 18.40N 78.07 E
Nizankoviči 10 Sg 49.40N 22.48 E
Nizip 23 Eb 37.01N 37.46 E
Nízke Tatry = Low Tatra
(EN) 10 Ph 48.54N 19.40 E
Nízký-Jeseník 10 Ng 49.50N 17.30 E
Nižná 10 Pg 49.19N 19.32 E
Nižneangarsk 22 Md 55.47N 109.33 E
Nižnegorski 16 Ig 45.27N 34.44 E
Nižnejansk 20 Ib 71.24N 136.00 E
Nižnekamsk 19 Fd 55.38N 51.49 E
Nižnekolymsk 20 Lc 68.38N 160.56 E
Nižnetroicki 17 Fi 54.20N 53.41 E
Nižneudinsk 20 Ef 54.54N 99.03 E
Niżnevartovsk 22 Jc 61.00N 77.00 E
Nižni Baskunčak 19 Ef 48.13N 46.50 E
Nižni Bestjah 20 Hd 61.48N 129.55 E
Nižni Casučej 20 Gf 50.27N 115.08 E
Nižnije Serogozy 16 If 46.49N 34.24 E
Nižni Kuranah 20 He 58.40N 125.48 E
Nižni Lomov 19 Ee 53.32N 43.41 E
Nižni Odes 17 Ge 63.40N 54.52 E

Index Symbols

[1] Independent Nation
[2] State, Region
[3] District, County
[5] Municipality
[5] Colony, Dependency
Continent
Physical Region
Historic or Cultural Region
Mount, Mountain
Volcano
Hill
Mountains, Mountain Range
Hills, Escarpment
Plateau, Upland
Pass, Gap
Plain, Lowland
Delta
Salt Flat
Valley, Canyon
Crater, Cave
Karst Features
Depression
Polder
Desert, Dunes
Forest, Woods
Heath, Steppe
Oasis
Cape, Point
Coast, Beach
Cliff
Peninsula
Isthmus
Sandbank
Island
Atoll
Rock, Reef
Islands, Archipelago
Rocks, Reefs
Coral Reef
Well, Spring
Geyser
River, Stream
Waterfall Rapids
River Mouth, Estuary
Lake
Salt Lake
Intermittent Lake
Reservoir
Swamp, Pond
Canal
Glacier
Ice Shelf, Pack Ice
Ocean
Sea
Gulf, Bay
Strait, Fjord
Lagoon
Bank
Seamount
Tablemount
Ridge
Shelf
Basin
Escarpment, Sea Scarp
Fracture
Trench, Abyss
National Park, Reserve
Point of Interest
Recreation Site
Cave, Cavern
Historic Site
Ruins
Wall, Walls
Church, Abbey
Temple
Scientific Station
Airport
Port
Lighthouse
Mine
Tunnel
Dam, Bridge

Nižni Oseredok, Ostrov-⊞ 16 Pg 45.45N 48.35 E
Nižni Tagil 6 Ld 57.55N 59.57 E
Nižni Trajanov Val=Lower Trajan's Wall (EN) 15 Ld 45.45N 28.30 E
Nižnjaja Omra 17 Ge 62.46N 55.46 E
Nižnjaja Peša 19 Eb 66.43N 47.36 E
Nižnjaja Pojma 20 Ee 56.08N 97.18 E
Nižnjaja Salda 1 Jg 58.05N 60.48 E
Nižnjaja Tavda 19 Gd 57.40N 66.12 E
Nižnjaja Tojma 7 Ke 62.22N 44.15 E
Nižnjaja Tunguska=Lower Tunguska (EN) 21 Kc 65.48N 88.04 E
Nižnjaja Tura 17 Ig 58.37N 59.49 E
Nižnjaja Zolotica 7 Jd 65.41N 40.13 E
Nižny Pjandž 18 Gf 37.14N 68.35 E
Nizza Monferrato 14 Cf 44.46N 8.21 E
Najas 17 Je 62.25N 60.47 E
Njamunas 5 Id 55.18N 21.23 E
Njandoma 19 Ec 61.43N 40.12 E
Njaris/Neris 8 Kj 54.55N 25.45 E
Njazepetrovsk 17 Ih 56.03N 59.38 E
Njazidja/Grande Comore 30 Lj 11.35S 43.20 E
Njegoš 15 Bg 42.53N 18.45 E
Njinjo 36 Gd 8.48S 38.54 E
Njombe 30 Ki 6.56S 35.06 E
Njombe 31 Ki 9.20S 34.46 E
Njudung 8 Fg 57.25N 14.50 E
Njuja 20 Gd 60.32N 116.25 E
Njuk, Ozero- 7 Hd 64.25N 31.45 E
Njuksenica 7 Kf 60.28N 44.15 E
Njukža 20 He 56.30N 121.40 E
Njunes 7 Eb 68.45N 19.30 E
Njurba 22 Nc 63.17N 118.20 E
Njurundabommen 7 De 62.16N 17.22 E
Njutånger 8 Gc 61.37N 17.03 E
Njuvčim 17 Ef 61.22N 50.42 E
Nkai 37 Dc 19.00S 28.54 E
Nkambe 34 Hd 6.38N 10.40 E
Nkawkaw 34 Ed 6.33N 0.46W
Nkayi 31 Ii 4.05S 13.18 E
Nkhata Bay 36 Fe 11.36S 34.18 E
Nkongsamba 31 Hh 4.57N 9.56 E
Nkota Kota 31 Kj 12.55S 34.18 E
Nkululu 36 Ki 6.26S 32.49 E
Nkusi 36 Fh 1.07N 30.40 E
Nkwalini 37 Ee 28.45S 31.30 E
'Nmai 25 Jc 25.42N 97.30 E
Nmaki 24 Pg 31.16N 55.29 E
Nnewi 34 Gd 6.01N 6.55 E
Nö 29 Ec 37.05N 137.59 E
Noailles 12 Ee 49.20N 2.12 E
Noäkhāli 25 Id 22.49N 91.06 E
Noatak 40 Gc 67.34N 162.59W
Nobel 44 Gc 45.25N 80.06W
Nobeoka 27 Ne 32.35N 131.40 E
Noblesville 44 Gc 40.03N 86.00W
Noboribetsu 28 Pc 42.25N 141.11 E
Noce 14 Fd 46.09N 11.04 E
Nocra 35 Fc 15.40N 39.55 E
Nodaway River 45 Ig 39.54N 94.58W
Noën 27 Hc 43.15N 102.20 E
Noeuf, Ile des- 37b Bb 6.14S 53.03 E
Noeux-les-Mines 12 Ed 50.29N 2.40 E
Nogajskaja Step 16 Mg 44.15N 46.00 E
Nogales [Az.-U.S.] 43 Ee 31.21N 110.55W
Nogales [Mex.] 39 Hf 31.20N 110.56W
Nogaro 11 Fk 43.46N 0.02W
Nogat 10 Pb 54.11N 19.15 E
Nõgata 29 Be 33.44N 130.44 E
Nogent-le-Rotrou 11 Gf 48.19N 0.50 E
Nogent-sur-Marne 12 Ef 48.50N 2.29 E
Nogent-sur-Oise 12 Ee 49.16N 2.28 E
Nogent-sur-Seine 11 Jf 48.29N 3.30 E
Noginsk [R.S.F.S.R.] 20 Ed 64.25N 91.10 E
Noginsk [R.S.F.S.R.] 19 Dd 55.54N 38.28 E
Nogliki 20 Jf 51.45N 143.15 E
Nõgo-Hakusan 29 Ec 35.46N 136.31 E
Nogoyá 16 Id 32.24S 59.48W
Nogoya, Arroyo- 55 Ck 32.55S 59.59W
Nógrád 10 Ph 48.00N 19.35 E
Nogueira, Serra da- 13 Fc 41.42N 6.52W
Noguera Pallaresa 13 Mb 42.15N 0.54 E
Noguera Ribagorçana/Noguera Ribagorzana 13 Mc 41.40N 0.43 E
Noguera Ribagorzana/Noguera Ribagorçana 13 Mc 41.40N 0.43 E
Noh, Laguna- 48 Nh 18.40N 90.20W
Nohain 11 If 47.24N 3.15 E
Noheji 28 Pd 40.52N 141.08 E
Nohfelden 12 Je 49.35N 7.09 E
Noidore, Rio- 55 Fb 14.50S 52.34W
Noir, Causse- 11 Jj 44.09N 3.15 E
Noire, Montagne- 11 Ik 43.28N 2.18 E
Noires, Montagnes- 11 Cf 48.09N 3.40W
Noirétable 11 Jj 45.49N 3.46 E
Noirmoutier, Ile de- 11 Dh 46.58N 2.12W
Noirmoutier-en-l'Ile 11 Dg 47.00N 2.15W
Nojima-Zaki 29 Gd 34.54N 139.50 E
Nojiri-Ko 29 Fc 36.49N 138.13 E
Noka 63c Bb 10.40S 166.03 E
Nokaneng 37 Cc 19.40S 22.12 E
Nokia 9 Ff 61.28N 23.30 E
Nok Kundi 25 Cc 28.48N 62.46 E
Nokomis 46 Ma 51.30N 105.00W
Nokou 35 Ac 14.35N 14.47 E
Nokra 35 Fb 15.42N 39.56 E
Nol 8 Eg 57.55N 12.03 E
Nola [C.A.R.] 35 Be 3.32N 16.04 E
Nola [It.] 14 Ij 40.55N 14.33 E
Nolin Lake 44 Dg 37.20N 86.10W
Nolinsk 17 Fc 57.33N 49.57 E
Nomad 58 Fe 6.21S 142.12 E
Noma Omuramba 19 Nc 19.10S 22.16 E
Noma-Zaki 29 Bf 31.25N 130.06 E
Nombre de Dios 48 Gf 23.51N 104.14W
Nome 39 Cc 64.30N 165.24W
Nomeny 12 If 48.54N 6.14 E

Nomo-Saki 29 Ae 32.35N 129.45 E
Nomozaki 29 Ae 32.35N 129.45 E
Nomuka 65b Bb 20.15S 174.48W
Nomuka Group 57 Jg 20.20S 174.45W
Nomuka Iki 65b Bb 20.17S 174.49W
Nomwin Atoll 57 Gd 8.32N 151.47 E
Nonacho Lake 42 Gd 62.40N 109.30W
Nonancourt 12 Df 48.46N 1.12 E
Nonette 12 Ee 49.12N 2.24 E
Nong'an 27 Mc 44.24N 125.08 E
Nong Han 25 Ke 17.21N 103.06 E
Nong Khai 22 Mh 17.52N 102.45 E
Nongoma 37 Ee 27.53S 31.38 E
Nonoava 48 Fd 27.28N 106.44W
Nonouti Atoll 57 Ie 0.40S 174.21 E
Nonsan 28 If 36.12N 127.05 E
Nonsuch Bay 51d Bb 17.03N 61.42W
Norman, Lake- 44 Gh 35.35N 81.00W
Noord-Beveland 12 Fc 51.35N 3.45 E
Noord-Brabant 12 Gc 51.30N 5.00 E
Noord-Holland 12 Gb 52.40N 4.50 E
Noordhollandskanaal 11 Kb 52.55N 4.50 E
Noordoewer 37 Be 28.45S 17.37 E
Noordoostpolder 11 Lb 52.42N 5.45 E
Noordoostpolder 12 Hb 52.42N 5.44 E
Noordoostpolder-Emmeloord 12 Hb 52.42N 5.44 E
Noordwijk aan Zee 11 Kb 52.14N 4.26 E
Noordwijk aan Zee, Noordwijk- 12 Gb 52.14N 4.26 E
Noordwijk-Noordwijk aan Zee 12 Gb 52.14N 4.26 E
Noordzee=North Sea (EN) 5 Gd 55.20N 3.00 E
Noordzeekanaal 11 Kb 52.30N 4.35 E
Noormarkku/Norrmark 8 Ic 61.35N 21.52 E
Noorvik 40 Gc 66.50N 161.12W
Nootka Island 46 Bb 49.32N 126.42W
Nootka Sound 46 Bb 49.33N 126.38W
Nóqui 36 Bd 5.50S 13.27 E
Nora [It.] 14 Dk 39.00N 9.02 E
Nora [Swe.] 7 Dg 59.31N 15.02 E
Noranda 42 Jg 48.15N 79.01W
Noraskog 8 Fe 59.40N 14.50 E
Norberg 8 Fd 60.04N 15.56 E
Norcia 14 Hd 42.48N 13.05 E
Nord 41 Kb 81.45N 17.30W
Nord [Cam.] 34 Hd 9.00N 13.50 E
Nord [Fr.] 11 Jd 50.20N 3.40 E
Nord [U.V.] 34 Cc 13.40N 2.50W
Nord, Canal du- 11 Id 49.57N 2.55 E
Nord, Mer du-=North Sea (EN) 5 Gd 55.20N 3.00 E
Nordausques 12 Ed 50.49N 2.05 E
Nordaustlandet 67 Jd 79.48N 22.24 E
Nordborg 8 Ci 55.03N 9.45 E
Nordby 8 Ci 55.27N 8.25 E
Norddeutsches Tiefland=North German Plain (EN) 5 He 53.00N 11.00 E
Norden 10 Dc 53.36N 7.12 E
Nordenham 10 Ec 53.39N 8.29 E
Nordenskjöld, Ostrova-=Nordenskjöld, Archipelago (EN) 20 Ea 76.50N 96.00 E
Nordenskjöld Archipelago (EN)=Nordenskjölda, Ostrova- 20 Ea 76.50N 96.00 E
Norderney 10 Dc 53.42N 7.10 E
Norderstedt 10 Fc 53.41N 9.58 E
Nordfjord 8 Bc 61.50N 6.15 E
Nordfjord 7 Af 61.55N 5.10 E
Nordfjordeid 7 Af 61.54N 6.00 E
Nordfold 7 Dc 67.46N 15.12 E
Nordfriesische Inseln=North Frisian Islands (EN) 10 Ea 54.50N 8.30 E
Nordfriesland 10 Eb 54.40N 8.55 E
Nordgau 10 Hg 49.15N 11.50 E
Nordgrønland=North Greenland (EN) 41 Gc 79.30N 50.00W
Nordhausen 10 Ge 51.31N 10.48 E
Nordhordland 7 Ad 60.50N 5.50 E
Nordhorn 10 Dd 52.26N 7.05 E
Nord-Jylland 8 Ce 57.15N 10.00 E
Nordkapp [Nor.]=North Cape (EN) 5 Ia 71.11N 25.48 E
Nordkapp [Sval.] 41 Nb 80.31N 20.00 E
Nordkinn 7 Ia 71.08N 27.39 E
Nordkinnhalvøya 7 Ga 70.55N 27.45 E
Nord-Kvaløy 7 Ea 70.10N 19.11 E
Nordland 7 Cc 67.06N 13.20 E
Nördlingen 10 Gh 48.51N 10.30 E
Nordloher Tief 12 Ja 53.10N 7.45 E
Nordmark 8 Fe 59.50N 14.06 E
Nordmøre 8 Ca 63.00N 8.30 E
Nordostrundingen 67 Le 81.30N 11.00W
Nord-Ostsee Kanal=Kiel Canal (EN) 5 Ge 53.53N 9.08 E
Nord-Ouest 34 Hd 9.00N 10.30 E
Nordøyane 8 Bb 62.40N 6.15 E
Nordreisa 7 Eb 69.46N 21.03 E
Nordre Rønner 8 Dg 57.22N 10.56 E
Nordrhein-Westfalen=North Rhine-Westphalia (EN) 10 De 51.30N 7.30 E
Nordsee=North Sea (EN) 5 Gd 55.20N 3.00 E
Nord Strand 10 Ea 54.30N 8.55 E
Nordtiroler Kalkalpen 10 Hi 47.30N 11.30 E
Nord-Trøndelag 7 Cd 64.25N 12.00 E
Nordvestfjord 41 Jd 71.30N 26.30W
Nore/An Fheoir 9 Gi 52.25N 6.58W
Norefjell 7 Cd 60.16N 9.29 E

Norefjorden 8 Cd 60.10N 9.00 E
Norfolk 9 Oi 52.40N 1.05 E
Norfolk 9 Mi 52.45N 0.40W
Norfolk [Nb.-U.S.] 43 Hc 42.02N 97.25W
Norfolk [Va.-U.S.] 39 Lf 38.40N 76.14W
Norfolk Island 58 Hg 29.05S 167.59 E
Norfolk Island 57 Hg 29.05S 167.59 E
Norfolk Ridge (EN) 57 Hg 29.05S 168.00 E
Norfork Lake 45 Jh 36.25N 92.10W
Norg 12 Ia 53.04N 6.32 E
Norge=Norway (EN) 6 Gc 62.00N 10.00 E
Norheimsund 7 Bf 60.22N 6.08 E
Norikura-Dake 29 Ec 36.06N 137.33 E
Norilsk 22 Kc 69.20N 88.06 E
Normal 45 Lf 40.31N 88.59W
Norman 43 Hd 35.15N 97.26W
Norman, Lake- 44 Gh 35.35N 81.00W
Normanby Island 60 Ej 10.00S 151.00 E
Normanby River 59 Ib 14.25S 144.08 E
Normand, Bocage- 11 Ef 49.00N 1.10W
Normandie=Normandy (EN) 11 Gf 49.00N 0.10 E
Normandie=Normandy (EN) 5 Gf 49.00N 0.10 E
Normandie, Collines de-=Normandy Hills (EN) 5 Ff 48.50N 0.40W
Normandin 44 Ka 48.52N 72.30W
Normandie= 11 Gf 49.00N 0.10 E
Normandy (EN)= 5 Gf 49.00N 0.10 E
Normandy, Collines de- 5 Ff 48.50N 0.40W
Normandy Hills (EN)=Normandie, Collines de- 5 Ff 48.50N 0.40W
Norman Island 51a Db 18.20N 64.37W
Norman River 59 Ic 17.28S 140.39 E
Normanton 58 Ff 17.40S 141.05 E
Norman Wells 39 Gc 65.17N 126.51W
Norquinco 56 Ff 41.51S 70.54W
Norra Dellen 8 Gc 61.55N 16.40 E
Norrahammar 8 Fg 57.42N 14.06 E
Norrala 8 Gc 61.22N 16.59 E
Norra Midsjöbanken 8 Gh 56.10N 17.30 E
Norra Ny 7 Df 60.24N 13.15 E
Norra Storfjället 7 Dd 65.53N 15.14 E
Norrbotten 7 Ef 67.26N 19.35 E
Nørre Åby 8 Ci 55.27N 9.54 E
Nørre Alslev 8 Dj 54.54N 11.54 E
Nørre-Nebel 8 Ci 55.47N 8.18 E
Norrent-Fontes 12 Ed 50.35N 2.24 E
Nørresundby 7 Bh 57.04N 9.55 E
Norrhult 7 Dh 57.08N 15.10 E
Norris Lake 44 Pg 36.20N 83.55W
Norristown 44 Je 40.07N 75.20W
Norrköping 6 Hd 58.36N 16.11 E
Norrland 7 Hc 64.27N 17.20 E
Norrland 7 Dd 65.00N 18.00 E
Norrmark/Noormarkku 8 Ic 61.35N 21.52 E
Norrsundet 8 Gd 60.56N 17.08 E
Norrtälje 7 Fg 59.46N 18.42 E
Norseman 58 Dh 32.12S 121.46 E
Norsewood 62 Gd 40.04S 176.13 E
Norsjö 7 Ed 64.55N 19.29 E
Norsjø 8 Ce 59.20N 9.20 E
Norsk 20 Hf 52.20N 129.59 E
Norske Havet=Norwegian, Sea (EN) 5 Gc 70.00N 2.00 E
Norske Øer 41 Kc 79.00N 18.00W
Norsoup 63b Cc 16.04S 167.23 E
Norte, Baía- 55 Hh 27.30S 48.35W
Norte, Cabo- [Braz.] 54 Ic 1.40N 50.00W
Norte, Cabo- [Pas.] 65d Ab 27.03S 109.24W
Norte, Canal do- 54 Hc 0.30N 50.30W
Norte, Punta- 56 Hf 42.04S 63.45W
Norte, Serra do- 54 Gf 11.00S 59.00W
Norte del Cabo San Antonio, Punta- 56 Ie 36.17S 56.47W
Norte de Santander 54 Db 8.00N 73.00W
Nortelândia 54 Gf 14.25S 56.48W
North, Cape - 42 Lg 47.02N 60.25W
North Adams 44 Kd 42.42N 73.02W
Northallerton 9 Lg 54.20N 1.26W
Northam [Austl.] 58 Ch 31.39S 116.40 E
Northam [S.Afr.] 37 Dd 24.58S 27.11 E
North America 38 Jf 40.00N 100.00W
North American Basin (EN) 3 Cf 30.00N 60.00W
Northampton [Austl.] 59 Hd 28.21S 114.37 E
Northampton [Eng.-U.K.] 9 Mi 52.14N 0.54W
Northampton [Ma.-U.S.] 44 Kd 42.19N 72.38W
Northampton Seamounts (EN) 57 Jb 25.20N 172.04W
Northamptonshire 9 Mi 52.25N 0.55W
North Andaman 25 If 13.15N 92.55 E
North Arm 42 Gd 62.00N 114.30W
North Astrolabe Reef 63b Bc 18.39S 178.32 E
North Augusta 44 Gi 33.30N 81.58W
North Aulatsivik 42 Le 59.45N 64.04W
North Australian Basin 3 Hk 14.30S 116.30 E
North Battleford 39 Id 52.47N 108.17W
North Bay 42 Je 46.19N 79.28W
North Belcher Islands 42 Je 56.45S 79.45W
North Berwick 9 Ke 56.04N 2.44W
North Buganda 36 Fh 0.50N 32.10 E
North Caicos 21 Ic 21.56N 71.59W
North Canadian River 43 Hd 35.17N 95.31W
North Cape 57 Mk 34.25S 173.03 E
North Cape (EN)=Nordkapp [Nor.] 5 Ia 71.11N 25.48 E
North Caribou Lake 42 If 52.48N 90.45W
North Carolina 43 Jd 35.30N 80.00W
North Channel 42 Jg 46.02N 82.50W
North Channel/Sruth na Maoile 5 Fd 55.10N 5.40W
Northchapel 12 Bc 51.03N 0.38W
North Charleston 44 Hi 32.53N 80.00W
North Chicago 45 Me 42.20N 87.51W

North Cove 46 Cc 46.47N 124.06W
North Dakota 43 Gb 47.30N 100.15W
North Downs 9 Nj 51.20N 0.10 E
North East 44 Hd 42.13N 79.51W
North-East 37 Dd 21.00S 27.30 E
Northeast Cape 40 Fd 63.18N 168.42W
North-Eastern 36 Hb 1.00N 40.15 E
Northeast Islands 64d Ba 7.36N 151.57 E
Northeast Pacific Basin (EN) 3 Lg 20.00N 140.00W
Northeast Pass 64d Ba 7.30N 151.59 E
North East Point 64g Bb 1.57N 157.16W
Northeast Point [Bah.] 49 Kc 21.18N 72.54W
Northeast Point [Bah.] 49 Kb 22.43N 73.50W
Northeast Providence Channel 47 Ic 25.40N 77.09W
Northeim 10 Fe 51.42N 10.00 E
North Entrance 64a Bb 7.59N 134.37 E
Northern [Ghana] 34 Ed 9.30N 1.00W
Northern [Mwi.] 36 Fe 11.00S 34.00 E
Northern [S.L.] 34 Cd 9.15N 11.45W
Northern [Ug.] 36 Fb 2.45N 32.45 E
Northern [Zam.] 36 Fb 11.00S 30.00 E
Northern Cay 49 Ce 17.27N 87.28W
Northern Cook Islands 57 Kf 10.00S 161.00W
Northern Dvina (EN)=Severnaja Dvina 5 Kc 64.32N 40.30 E
Northern Guinea 30 Gh 8.30N 1.00W
Northern Indian Lake 42 He 57.20N 97.17W
Northern Ireland 9 Gg 54.40N 6.45W
Northern Mariana Islands 58 Fc 16.00N 145.30 E
Northern Sporades (EN)=Vórioi Sporádhes, Nísoi-
Northern Territory 59 Ec 20.00S 134.00 E
Northern Urals (EN)=Severny Ural 5 Lc 62.00N 59.00 E
Northern Uvals (EN)=Severnyje Uvaly 5 Kd 59.30N 49.00 E
North Esk 5 Ke 56.45N 2.30W
Northfield 45 Jd 44.27N 93.09W
North Fiji Basin (EN) 3 Jk 16.00S 174.00 E
North Foreland 9 Oj 51.23N 1.27 E
North Fork Grand River 45 Ed 45.47N 102.16W
North Fork John Day River 46 Fd 44.45N 119.38W
North Fork Moreau River 45 Ed 45.09N 102.50W
North Fork Pass 42 Gd 64.00N 138.00W
North Fork Powder River 46 La 43.40N 106.30W
North Fork Red 45 Gd 34.25N 99.14W
North Fort Myers 44 Gl 26.40N 81.54W
North Frisian Islands (EN)=Nordfriesische Inseln 10 Ea 54.50N 8.30 E
North German Plain (EN)=Norddeutsches Tiefland 5 He 53.00N 11.00 E
North Greenland (EN)=Nordgrønland 41 Gc 79.30N 50.00W
North Highlands 46 Eg 38.40N 121.23W
North Horr 36 Gb 3.19N 37.04 E
North Island [N.Z.] 57 Ih 39.00S 176.00 E
North Island [Sey.] 37b Bc 10.07S 51.11 E
North Kent 42 Ia 76.40N 90.15W
North Korea (EN)=Chosŏn M.I.K. 22 Oe 40.00N 127.30 E
North Lakhimpur 25 Ic 27.14N 94.07 E
Northland 62 Ea 35.30S 173.40 E
North Las Vegas 46 Hh 36.12N 115.07W
North Lincoln Land 42 Ja 76.15N 80.00W
North Little Rock 43 Ie 34.46N 92.14W
North Loup River 45 Ge 41.03N 98.24W
North Magnetic Pole (1980) 67 Qd 77.03N 101.08W
North Malosmadulu Atoll 25a Ba 5.35N 72.55 E
North Mamm Peak 46 Cg 39.23N 107.52W
North Mayreau Channel 51b Bb 12.41N 61.20W
North Miami 44 Gm 25.56N 80.09W
North Minch 5 Fd 58.05N 5.55W
North Palisade 46 Fh 37.10N 118.38W
North Pass [F.S.M.] 64d Ba 7.41N 151.48 E
North Pass [U.S.] 45 Ll 29.10N 89.15W
North Platte 43 Gc 41.08N 100.46W
North Platte 38 le 41.15N 100.45W
North Point 46 Gd 45.03N 117.55W
North Point [Bar.] 64n Ab 10.22S 161.02 E
North Pole 67 Ge 90.00N 0.00
Northport 46 Di 33.14N 87.35W
North Powder 46 Gd 45.03N 117.55W
North Raccoon River 45 Jf 41.53N 93.31W
North Reef 63a Ee 12.13S 160.04 E
North Rhine-Westphalia (EN)=Nordrhein-Westfalen 10 De 51.30N 7.30 E
North Rim 46 Ih 36.12N 112.03W
North River 42 Ie 58.53N 94.42W
North Rona 5 Fd 59.10N 5.49W
North Ronaldsay 9 Kb 59.25N 2.30W
North Saskatchewan 38 Id 53.15N 105.06W
North Sea 5 Gd 55.20N 3.00 E
North Sea (EN)=Nord, Mer du- 5 Gd 55.20N 3.00 E
North Sea (EN)=Noordzee 5 Gd 55.20N 3.00 E
North Sea (EN)=Nordsee 5 Gd 55.20N 3.00 E
North Sentinel 25 If 11.33N 92.15 E
North Shoshone Peak 46 Gg 39.10N 117.29W
Severo-Sibirskaja Niz.= 21 Mb 72.00N 104.00 E
North Sound 51d Bb 17.07N 61.45W
North Sound 49 Bb 19.25N 81.26W
North Stradbroke Island 59 Ke 27.35S 153.30 E
North Taranaki Bight 62 Fc 38.50S 174.25 E
North Thompson 42 Ff 50.41N 120.11W

North Tokelau Trough (EN) 3 Kj 3.00S 165.00W
North Tonawanda 44 Hd 43.02N 78.54W
North Trap 62 Bb 47.20S 167.55 E
North Tyne 9 Kg 54.59N 2.08W
North Uist 9 Fd 57.37N 7.22W
Northumberland 9 Kf 55.15N 2.10W
Northumberland Islands 57 Gg 21.40S 150.00 E
Northumberland Strait 42 Lg 46.00N 63.30W
North Umpqua River 46 Db 43.16N 123.27W
North Vancouver 46 Db 49.19N 123.04W
North Walsham 12 Db 52.49N 1.23 E
Northway 40 Kd 62.59N 141.43W
North West Bluff 51c Bc 16.49N 62.12W
North West Cape 57 Cg 21.45S 114.10 E
North-Western 36 Le 13.00S 25.00 E
Northwest Frontier 25 Bb 33.00N 70.30 E
Northwest Highlands 5 Fd 57.30N 5.00W
Northwest Pacific Basin (EN) 3 Je 40.00N 155.00 E
North West Point 64g Ab 2.02N 157.30W
Northwest Providence Channel 44 Hi 26.10N 78.20W
Northwest Reef 64a Bb 7.59N 134.33 E
North West River 42 Lf 53.32N 60.09W
Northwest Territories 42 Hc 60.00N 102.00W
Northwich 9 Kh 53.16N 2.32W
North York Moors 9 Mg 54.25N 0.50W
North Yorkshire 9 Lg 54.15N 1.40W
Norton [Ks.-U.S.] 43 Gd 39.50N 100.01W
Norton [Va.-U.S.] 44 Fg 36.56N 82.37W
Norton [Zimb.] 37 Ec 17.53S 30.41 E
Norton Bay 40 Gd 64.45N 161.15W
Norton Sound 38 Fc 64.45N 161.15W
Norvegia, Kapp- 66 Bf 71.25S 12.18W
Norwalk [Ct.-U.S.] 44 Kf 41.07N 73.27W
Norwalk [Oh.-U.S.] 44 Fe 41.14N 82.37W
Norway 44 Gc 45.47N 87.55W
Norway (EN)=Norge 6 Gc 62.00N 10.00 E
Norway House 42 Hf 53.58N 97.50W
Norwegian Basin (EN) 3 Bc 68.00N 2.00W
Norwegian Sea (EN)=Norske Havet 5 Gc 70.00N 2.00 E
Norwegian Trench (EN) 5 Gc 59.00N 4.30 E
Norwich [Eng.-U.K.] 6 Ge 52.38N 1.18 E
Norwich [Ct.-U.S.] 44 Kf 41.32N 72.05W
Norwich [N.Y.-U.S.] 44 Jd 42.33N 75.33W
Norwich Airport 12 Da 52.40N 1.18 E
Norwood 44 Ef 39.10N 84.28W
Nosappu-Misaki 29a Db 43.23N 145.47 E
Noshappu-Misaki 29a Ba 45.27N 141.39 E
Noshiro 27 Pc 41.02N 140.02 E
Nosovaja 19 Ec 68.15N 54.31 E
Nosovka 19 De 50.54N 31.37 E
Nosratābād 23 Jd 29.54N 59.59 E
Nossa Senhora das Candeias 54 Kf 12.40S 38.33W
Nossa Senhora do Livramento 55 Db 15.48S 56.22W
Noss Head 9 Jc 58.30N 3.05W
Nossob 30 Jk 26.55S 20.40 E
Nossob 37 Ic 26.55S 20.40 E
Nosy-Be 30 Lj 13.20S 48.15 E
Nosy-Be 31 Lj 13.22S 48.16 E
Nosy-Varika 37 Md 20.35S 48.30 E
Nota 7 Hb 68.07N 30.10 E
Notch Peak 46 Ig 39.08N 113.24W
Noțec 10 Ld 52.44N 15.26 E
Notecka, Puszcza- 10 Ld 52.45N 16.00 E
Note Kemopla 63c b 10.55S 165.51 E
Notengo, Laguna de- 48 Ig 16.15N 98.10W
Notia Pindhos 15 Jg 39.30N 21.20 E
Nótioi Sporádhes=Dodecanese (EN) 1 h 36.00N 27.00 E
Nótios Evvoïkós Kólpos 15 Gk 38.20N 23.50 E
Nótö 8 le 60.00N 21.45 E
Noto [It.] 14 Jn 36.55N 15.04 E
Noto [Jap.] 28 Nf 37.18N 137.09 E
Noto, Golfo di- 14 Jn 36.50N 15.10 E
Notodden 7 Bg 59.34N 9.17 E
Noto-Hantö 27 Od 37.20N 137.00 E
Noto-Jima 29 Ec 37.07N 137.00 E
Notoro-Ko 29a Ca 44.05N 144.10 E
Notoro-Misaki 29a Ba 44.07N 144.15 E
Notranjsko 14 le 45.46N 14.26 E
Notre-Dame, Monts- 38 Me 48.00N 69.49W
Notre Dame Bay 42 Ff 49.50N 55.00W
Notre-Dame-de-Courson 12 Cf 48.59N 0.16 E
Notre-Dame-de-Gravenchon 54 Ge 49.29N 0.35 E
Notre-Dame-du-Lac 44 Mb 47.38N 68.49W
Notre-Dame-du-Nord 44 Hd 47.36N 79.29W
Notsé 11 Fd 6.59N 1.12 E
Notsuke-Zaki 8 Ee 58.54N 9.16 E
Nottawasaga Bay 44 Gc 44.40N 80.30W
Nottaway 38 Ld 51.25N 79.50W
Nottaway River 38 Ld 51.25N 79.50W
Nøtterøy 8 Fe 52.58N 1.10W
Nottingham 42 Jd 63.20N 78.00W
Nottingham 9 Mh 53.05N 1.00W
Nottinghamshire 9 Mh 53.10N 1.05W
Nottoway 44 Ie 36.33N 76.55W
Nottoway River 12 Jc 51.56N 7.21 E
Nottuln 46 Lb 49.55N 106.30W
Notukeu Creek 30 Df 21.00N 16.50W
Nouâdhibou 31 Fg 18.07N 15.59W
Nouâdhibou, Dahklet- 32 Df 18.06N 15.57W
Nouâdhibou, Râs-=Blanc, Cape- 30 Df 21.00N 16.50W
Nouakchott 27 Pf 20.54N 17.01W
Nouakchott, District de- 31 Fg 18.07N 15.59W
Nouamrhar 32 Df 18.06N 15.57W
Nouméa 58 Hg 22.16S 166.26 E
Nouna 34 Ec 12.44N 3.52W
Noupoort 37 Cf 31.10S 24.57 E

Index Symbols

[1] Independent Nation	Historical or Cultural Region	Pass, Gap	Depression
[2] State, Region	Mount, Mountain	Plain, Lowland	Polder
[3] District, County	Volcano	Delta	Desert, Dunes
[4] Municipality	Hill	Salt Flat	Forest, Woods
[5] Colony, Dependency	Mountains, Mountain Range	Valley, Canyon	Heath, Steppe
Continent	Hills, Escarpment	Crater, Cave	Oasis
Physical Region	Plateau, Upland	Karst Features	Cape, Point

Coast, Beach	Rock, Reef	Waterfall Rapids	Canal
Cliff	Islands, Archipelago	River Mouth, Estuary	Glacier
Peninsula	Rocks, Reefs	Lake	Ice Shelf, Pack Ice
Isthmus	Coral Reef	Salt Lake	Ocean
Sandbank	Well, Spring	Intermittent Lake	Ridge
Island	Geyser	Sea	Shelf
Atoll	River, Stream	Gulf, Bay	Basin
		Strait, Fjord	

Lagoon	Escarpment, Sea Scarp	Historic Site	Port
Bank	Fracture	Ruins	Lighthouse
Seamount	National Park, Reserve	Wall, Walls	Mine
Tablemount	Point of Interest	Church, Abbey	Tunnel
Trench, Abyss	Recreation Area	Temple	Dam, Bridge
Recreation Area	Shelf	Scientific Station	
Cave, Cavern	Airport		

Nouveau-Comptoir 42 Jf 52.35N 78.40W
Nouveau-Québec, Cratère du- = New Quebec Crater (EN) 42 Kd 61.30N 73.55W
Nouvelle-Calédonie = New Caledonia (EN) 58 Hg 21.30S 165.30 E
Nouvelle-Calédonie=New Caledonia 57 Hg 21.30S 165.30 E
Nouvelle-France, Cap de - 42 Kd 62.33N 73.35W
Nouvelles Hébrides/New Hebrides 57 Hf 16.01S 167.01 E
Nouvion 12 Dd 50.12N 1.47 E
Nouzonville 11 Ke 49.49N 4.45 E
Novabad 18 He 39.01N 70.09 E
Nová Baňa 10 Oh 48.26N 18.39 E
Nová Bystřice 10 Lg 49.02N 15.06 E
Nova Cruz 54 Ke 6.28S 35.26W
Nova Esperança 55 Ff 23.08S 52.13W
Nova Friburgo 54 Jh 22.16S 42.32W
Nova Gaia 36 Ce 10.05S 17.32 E
Nova Gorica 14 He 45.57N 13.39 E
Nova Gradiška 14 Le 45.16N 17.23 E
Nova Granada 55 He 20.29S 49.19W
Nova Iguaçu 53 Lh 22.45S 43.27W
Novaja Igirma 20 Fe 57.10N 103.55 E
Novaja-Ivanovka 15 Md 45.59N 29.04 E
Novaja Kahovka 16 Hf 46.43N 33.23 E
Novaja Kazanka 16 Pe 48.58N 49.37 E
Novaja Ladoga 7 Hf 60.05N 32.16 E
Novaja Ljalja 19 Gd 59.03N 60.36 E
Novaja Odessa 16 Gf 47.18N 31.47 E
Novaja Sibir, Ostrov- = New Siberia (EN) 21 Qb 75.00N 149.00 E
Novaja Vodolaga 16 Ie 49.45N 35.52 E
Novaja Zemlja=Novaya Zemlya (EN) 21 Hb 74.00N 57.00 E
Nova Lamego 34 Cc 12.17N 14.13W
Nova Lima 54 Jh 19.59S 43.51W
Nova Londrina 55 Ff 22.45S 53.00W
Nova Mambone 37 Fd 20.58S 35.00 E
Nova Olinda do Norte 54 Gd 3.45S 59.03W
Nová Paka 10 Lf 50.29N 15.31 E
Nova Prata 55 Gi 28.47S 51.36W
Novara 14 Ce 45.28N 8.38 E
Nova Roma 55 Ia 13.51S 46.57W
Nova Russas 54 Jd 4.42S 40.34W
Nova Scotia [3] 42 Lh 45.00N 63.00W
Nova Scotia 38 Me 45.00N 63.00W
Nova Sintra 32 Cf 14.54N 24.40W
Nova Sofala 37 Ed 20.10S 34.44 E
Novato 46 Dg 38.06N 122.34W
Nova Varoš 15 Cf 43.28N 19.49 E
Nova Venécia 54 Jg 18.43S 40.24W
Novaya Zemlya (EN) = Novaja Zemlja 21 Hb 74.00N 57.00 E
Nova Zagora 15 Jg 42.29N 26.01 E
Novelda 13 Lf 38.23N 0.46W
Novellara 14 Ef 44.51N 10.44 E
Nové Mesto nad Váhom 10 Nh 48.46N 17.50 E
Nové Zámky 10 Oi 47.59N 18.11 E
Novgorod 6 Jd 58.31N 31.17 E
Novgorodka 8 Mg 57.00N 28.37 E
Novgorod-Severski 19 De 52.01N 33.16 E
Novgorodskaja Oblast [3] 19 Dd 58.20N 32.40 E
Novi Bečej 15 Dd 45.36N 20.08 E
Novigrad [Yugo.] 14 He 45.19N 13.34 E
Novigrad [Yugo.] 14 Jf 44.11N 15.33 E
Novi Kričim 15 Hg 42.03N 24.28 E
Novi Ligure 14 Cf 44.46N 8.47 E
Novillero 48 Gf 22.21N 105.39W
Novion-Porcien 12 Ge 49.36N 4.25 E
Novi Pazar [Bul.] 15 Kf 43.21N 27.12 E
Novi Pazar [Yugo.] 15 Df 43.08N 20.31 E
Novi Sad 6 Hf 45.15N 19.50 E
Novi Travnik 14 Lf 44.10N 17.39 E
Novi Vinodolski 14 Ie 45.08N 14.47 E
Novoaleksandrovsk 16 Lg 45.24N 41.14 E
Novoaleksejevka [Kaz.-U.S.S.R.] 16 Sd 50.08N 55.42 E
Novoaleksejevka [Ukr.-U.S.S.R.] 16 If 46.16N 34.39 E
Novoaltajsk 20 Df 53.24N 83.58 E
Novoanninski 16 Ee 50.31N 42.45 E
Novoarhangelsk 16 Ge 48.39N 30.50 E
Novo Aripuanã 54 Fe 5.08S 60.22W
Novoazovsk 16 Kf 47.05N 38.05 E
Novobirjusinski 20 Ee 56.58N 97.55 E
Novobogdanovka 16 If 47.05N 35.18 E
Novočeboksarsk 7 Lh 56.08N 47.29 E
Novočeremšansk 7 Mi 54.23N 50.10 E
Novočerkassk 19 Ef 47.25N 40.03 E
Novodevičje 7 Lj 53.35N 48.51 E
Novograd-Volynski 19 Ce 50.36N 27.36 E
Novogrudok 16 Dc 53.37N 25.50 E
Nôvo Hamburgo 56 Jc 29.41S 51.08W
Novohopërsk 16 Ld 51.06N 41.37 E
Novo Horizonte 55 He 21.28S 49.13W
Novoizborsk 8 Mg 57.43N 28.05 E
Novojenisejsk 20 Ee 58.19N 92.27 E
Novojerudinski 20 Ee 59.47N 93.30 E
Novokačalinsk 20 Ig 45.05N 131.59 E
Novokazalinsk 22 Ie 45.50N 62.10 E
Novokubansk 16 Lg 45.06N 41.01 E
Novokujbyševsk 19 Ee 53.08N 49.58 E
Novokuzneck 22 Kd 53.45N 87.06 E
Novolazarevskaja 66 Cf 70.46S 11.50 E
Novolukoml 7 Gi 54.38N 29.07 E
Novo Mesto 14 Je 45.48N 15.10 E
Novomičurinsk 7 Ji 54.02N 39.48 E
Novomihajlovka 20 Ih 44.17N 133.50 E
Novo Miloševo 15 Dd 45.43N 20.18 E
Novomirgorod 16 Ge 48.45N 31.39 E
Novomoskovsk [R.S.F.S.R.] 6 Je 54.05N 38.13 E
Novomoskovsk [Ukr.-U.S.S.R.] 19 Df 48.37N 35.16 E
Novonikolajevski 16 Md 50.55N 42.24 E
Novoorsk 19 Fe 51.24N 58.59 E
Novopokrovskaja 16 Lg 45.56N 40.42 E
Novopolock 19 Cd 55.31N 28.40 E
Novorossijsk 6 Jg 44.45N 37.45 E
Novorybnaja 20 Fb 72.50N 105.45 E
Novoržev 19 Cd 57.02N 29.20 E
Novo-Šahtinsk 19 Df 47.47N 39.54 E
Novoselica 15 Ja 48.13N 26.17 E
Novoselje 8 Mf 58.05N 29.00 E
Novoselki 10 Ud 52.04N 24.25 E
Novoselovo 20 Ef 54.55N 91.00 E
Novosergijevka 19 Fe 52.03N 53.39 E
Novosibirsk 22 Kd 55.02N 82.55 E
Novosibirskaja Oblast [3] 20 Ce 55.30N 80.00 E
Novosibirskije Ostrova = New Siberian Islands (EN) 21 Qb 75.00N 142.00 E
Novosibirskoje Vodohranilišče 20 Df 54.40N 82.35 E
Novosil 16 Jc 52.59N 37.01 E
Novosineglazovski 17 Ji 55.05N 61.25 E
Novosokolniki 19 Dd 56.19N 30.12 E
Novospasskoje 7 Lj 53.09N 47.44 E
Novotroick 19 Fe 51.12N 58.35 E
Novotroickoje 19 Hg 43.39N 73.45 E
Novoukrainka 16 Ge 48.19N 31.32 E
Novouljanovsk 7 Li 54.10N 48.23 E
Novouzensk 19 Ee 50.29N 48.08 E
Novovjatsk 7 Lg 58.31N 49.43 E
Novovolynsk 19 Ce 50.46N 24.09 E
Novovoronežski 16 Kd 51.17N 39.16 E
Novozybkov 19 De 52.32N 32.00 E
Novska 14 Ke 45.20N 16.59 E
Novy Bug 16 Hf 47.43N 32.29 E
Nový Bydžov 10 Lf 50.15N 15.29 E
Novy Jaričev 10 Ug 49.50N 24.21 E
Novyje Aneny 15 Mc 46.53N 29.13 E
Novyje Burasy 16 Oc 52.06N 46.06 E
Nový Jičín 10 Og 49.36N 18.01 E
Novy Oskol 19 De 50.43N 37.54 E
Novy Pogost 8 Li 55.30N 27.32 E
Novy Port 22 Jc 67.40N 72.52 E
Novy Tap 17 Mh 56.55N 67.15 E
Novy Terek 16 Oh 43.37N 47.25 E
Novy Uzen 19 Fg 43.19N 52.55 E
Novy Vasjugan 20 Ce 58.34N 76.29 E
Novy Zaj 7 Mi 55.17N 52.02 E
Nowa Dęba 10 Rf 50.26N 21.46 E
Nowa Huta, Kraków- 10 Qf 50.04N 20.05 E
Nowa Ruda 10 Mf 50.35N 16.31 E
Nowa Sarzyna 10 Sf 50.23N 22.22 E
Nowa Sól 10 Le 51.48N 15.44 E
Now Bandegān 24 Oh 28.52N 53.53 E
Nowbarān 24 Me 35.08N 49.42 E
Nowdesheh 24 Le 35.11N 46.15 E
Nowe 10 Oc 53.40N 18.43 E
Nowe Miasto Lubawskie 10 Pc 53.27N 19.35 E
Nowe Miasto-nad-Pilicą 10 Qe 51.38N 20.35 E
Nowe Warpno 10 Kc 53.44N 14.20 E
Nowfel low Shātow 24 Ne 34.27N 50.55 E
Nowgong 25 Ic 26.21N 92.40 E
Nowogard 10 Lc 53.40N 15.08 E
Nowogród 10 Rc 53.15N 21.53 E
Nowood River 46 Ld 44.17N 107.58W
Nowra 59 Kf 34.53S 150.36 E
Nowshahr 24 Nd 36.39N 51.31 E
Nowy Dwór Gdański 10 Pb 54.13N 19.06 E
Nowy Dwór Mazowiecki 10 Qd 52.26N 20.43 E
Nowy Korczyn 10 Qf 50.20N 20.50 E
Nowy Sącz [2] 10 Qg 49.40N 20.40 E
Nowy Sącz 10 Qg 49.38N 20.42 E
Nowy Targ 10 Qg 49.29N 20.02 E
Nowy Tomyśl 10 Md 52.20N 16.07 E
Noya 13 Db 42.47N 8.53W
Noya/Anoia 13 Nc 41.28N 1.56 E
Noyant 11 Gg 47.31N 0.08 E
Noyon 11 Ie 49.35N 3.00 E
Nozaki-Jima 29 Ae 33.11N 129.08 E
Nozay 11 Eg 47.34N 1.38W
Nsanje 36 Gf 16.55S 35.16 E
Nsawan 34 Ed 5.48N 0.21W
Nschodnia 10 Rf 50.30N 21.18 E
Nsefu 36 Fe 13.03S 32.07 E
Nsukka 34 Gd 6.52N 7.23 E
Ntadembele 36 Cc 2.11S 17.08 E
Ntchisi 36 Fe 13.22S 34.00 E
Ntem 30 Hh 2.10N 9.57 E
Ntoum 36 Ab 0.22N 9.47 E
Ntui 34 He 4.27N 11.38 E
Ntusi 36 Fb 0.03N 31.13 E
Nuageuses, Iles- 30 Nm 48.40S 68.58 E
Nuanetsi 37 Ed 21.22S 30.45 E
Nuanetsi 30 Kk 22.40S 31.49 E
Nūbah, Jibāl an- 30 Kg 12.00N 30.45 E
Nubian Desert (EN) = Nūbiyah, Aş Şahrā' an- 30 Kf 20.30N 33.00 E
Nūbiyah, Aş Şahrā' an- = Nubian Desert (EN) 30 Kf 20.30N 33.00 E
Nudha 63a Ec 9.32S 160.48 E
Nueces Plain 43 Hf 28.30N 99.15W
Nueces River 43 Hf 27.50N 97.30W
Nueltin Lake 38 Jc 60.50N 99.30W
Nü'er He 28 Fd 41.06N 121.09 E
Nueva Asunción [3] 55 Be 21.00S 60.20W
Nueva Ciudad Guerrero 48 Jd 26.35N 99.15W
Nueva Esparta [2] 54 Fa 11.00N 64.00W
Nueva Germania 55 Df 23.54S 56.34W
Nueva Gerona 47 Hd 21.53N 82.48W
Nueva Imperial 56 Fe 38.44S 72.57W
Nueva Italia de Ruiz 48 Hh 19.01N 102.06W
Nueva Ocotepeque 49 Cf 14.24N 89.13W
Nueva Palmira 55 Ck 33.53S 58.25W
Nueva Rosita 39 Ig 27.57N 101.13W
Nueva San Salvador 47 Gf 13.41N 89.17W
Nueva Segovia [3] 49 Dg 13.40N 86.10W
Nueve de Julio 56 He 35.27S 60.52W
Nuevitas 47 Id 21.33N 77.16W
Nuevitas, Bahía de- 49 Ic 21.30N 77.12W
Nuevo, Cayo- 48 Mg 21.51N 92.05W
Nuevo, Golfo- 52 Jj 42.42S 64.36W
Nuevo Berlín 55 Ck 32.59S 58.03W
Nuevo Casas Grandes 39 If 30.25N 107.55W
Nuevo Laredo 39 Jg 27.30N 99.31W
Nuevo León [2] 47 Ec 25.40N 100.00W
Nuevo Mundo, Cerro- 54 Eh 21.55S 66.53W
Nuevo Rocafuerte 54 Cd 0.56S 75.25W
Nugaal [3] 35 Hd 8.30N 48.00 E
Nugālēd, Dēh- 30 Lh 7.58N 49.51 E
Nugālēd, Dōho- 35 Hd 8.35N 48.35 E
Nûgâtsiaq 41 Gd 71.39N 53.45W
Nugget Point 62 Cg 46.27S 169.49 E
Nûgssuaq 41 Gd 70.30N 51.30W
Nuguria Islands 57 Ge 3.20S 154.45 E
Nuguš 17 Gj 53.05N 56.00 E
Nuhaka 62 Gc 39.02S 177.45 E
Nui Atoll 57 Ie 7.15S 177.10 E
Nuijama 8 Md 60.58N 28.32 E
Nuiqsut 40 Ib 70.20N 151.00W
Nu Jiang 21 Lh 16.31N 97.37 E
Nûk/Godthåb 67 Nc 64.15N 51.40W
Nukapu 63c Ab 10.07S 165.59 E
Nukey Bluff 59 Hf 32.35S 135.40 E
Nukhayb 23 Fc 32.02N 42.15 E
Nukhaylak 31 Jg 19.08N 26.20 E
Nukiki 63a Cb 6.45S 156.29 E
Nukuaeta 64h Ac 13.22S 176.11W
Nuku'alofa 58 Jg 21.08S 175.12W
Nukufetau Atoll 57 Ie 8.00S 178.22 E
Nukufotu 64h Bb 13.11S 176.10W
Nukuhifala 64h Bb 13.17S 176.05W
Nukuhione 64h Bb 13.16S 176.06W
Nuku Hiva, Ile- 57 Me 8.54S 140.06W
Nukulaelae Atoll 57 Ie 9.23S 179.52 E
Nukuloa 64h Bb 13.11S 176.09W
Nukumanu Islands 57 Ge 4.30S 159.30 E
Nukumbasanga 63d Cb 16.18S 179.15W
Nukunonu Atoll 57 Je 9.10S 171.53W
Nukuoro Atoll 57 Gd 3.51N 154.58 E
Nukus 22 He 42.50N 59.29 E
Nukutapu 64h Bb 13.13S 176.08W
Nukuteatea 64h Bb 13.12S 176.08W
Nulato 40 Hd 64.43N 158.06W
Nules 13 Le 39.51N 0.09W
Nullagine 58 Dg 21.53S 120.06 E
Nullagine River 59 Ed 20.43S 120.33 E
Nullarbor 59 Gf 31.26S 130.55 E
Nullarbor Plain 57 Dh 31.00S 129.00 E
Nulu'erhu Shan 27 Kc 41.40N 119.50 E
Numakawa 29a Ba 45.15N 141.51 E
Numan 34 Hd 9.28N 12.02 E
Numancia [Phil.] 26 Ie 9.52N 125.58 E
Numancia [Sp.] 13 Jc 41.47N 2.30W
Numanohata 29a Bb 42.40N 141.41 E
Numata [Jap.] 29a Bb 43.49N 141.55 E
Numata [Jap.] 28 Of 36.38N 139.03 E
Numatinna 35 Dd 7.14N 27.37 E
Numazu 28 Og 35.06N 138.52 E
Nümbrecht 12 Jd 50.54N 7.33 E
Numedal 7 Bf 60.05N 9.05 E
Numena 36 Ee 11.46S 26.31 E
Número Cinco, Canal- 55 Cm 37.14S 58.06W
Número Doce, Canal- 55 Cm 36.30S 59.08W
Número Dos, Canal- 55 Cm 36.51S 58.03W
Número Nueve, Canal- 55 Cm 36.08S 58.36W
Número Once, Canal- 55 Bm 36.28S 60.01W
Número Quince, Canal- 55 Dl 35.55S 57.45W
Número Uno, Canal- 55 Cm 36.40S 58.35W
Numfoor, Pulau- 26 Jg 1.03S 134.54 E
Nuneaton 9 Li 52.32N 1.28W
Nungarin 59 Df 31.11S 118.06 E
Nungnain Sum 27 Kb 45.45N 118.56 E
Nungo 37 Fb 13.25S 37.46 E
Nunivak 38 Cd 60.00N 166.30W
Nunkirchen, Wadern- 12 Ie 49.32N 6.53 E
Nunn 45 Df 40.45N 104.46W
Nunspeet 12 Hb 52.22N 5.46 E
Nunukan Timur, Pulau- 26 Gf 4.05N 117.40 E
Nuomin He 27 Lb 48.21N 124.32 E
Nuorgam 7 Ga 70.05N 27.51 E
Nuoro 6 Gg 40.19N 9.20 E
Nupani 63c Ab 10.04S 165.40 E
Nūq 24 Pg 30.55N 55.35 E
Nuqayr 24 Mi 27.48N 48.21 E
Nuqrah 24 Ij 25.34N 41.24 E
Nuqruş, Jabal- 33 Fe 24.49N 34.36 E
Nuquí 54 Cb 5.43N 77.16W
Nūr 24 Od 36.15N 52.20 E
Nūr 24 Pg 31.25N 54.20 E
Nura 19 Gf 48.57N 62.20 E
Nura 21 Id 50.30N 69.59 E
Nūrābād 24 Ng 30.48N 51.27 E
Nuraghe Santu Antine 14 Cj 40.29N 8.45 E
Nurata 19 Gg 40.34N 65.35 E
Nur Dağları 24 Gd 36.45N 36.20 E
Nure 14 De 45.03N 9.49 E
Nurek 19 Gh 38.25N 69.20 E
Nurhak Dağı 23 Eb 38.04N 37.29 E
Nūri 35 Eb 18.30N 32.02 E
Nurki 20 Ie 56.42N 138.28 E
Nurlat 19 Fe 54.28N 50.48 E
Nurlati 7 Li 55.38N 48.17 E
Nurmes 7 Ge 63.33N 29.07 E
Nurmijärvi 8 Kd 60.28N 24.48 E
Nurmo 8 Jb 62.50N 22.54 E
Nürnberg 6 Hf 49.27N 11.05 E
Nurra 14 Cj 40.45N 8.15 E
Nurri, Mount- 59 Jf 31.42S 146.02 E
Nurugas 37 Bc 19.11S 18.54 E
Nurzec 10 Sd 52.33N 22.28 E
Nusa Tenggara Barat [3] 26 Gh 8.50S 117.30 E
Nusa Tenggara Timur [3] 26 Hh 9.30S 122.00 E
Nusaybin 24 Id 37.03N 41.13 E
Nushagak 40 He 58.57N 158.29W
Nushan 27 Gf 25.00N 99.00 E
Nu-Shima 29 Dd 34.10N 134.50 E
Nutak 42 Le 57.31N 62.00W
Nuttal 25 Dc 28.45N 68.08 E
Nuutele 65c Bb 14.02S 171.22W
Nuwākot 25 Gc 28.08N 83.53 E
Nuwara 25 Gg 6.58N 80.46 E
Nuwaybi 'al Muzayyinah 33 Fd 28.58N 34.39 E
Nyabing 59 Df 33.32S 118.09 E
Nyagquka/Yajiang 27 He 30.07N 100.58 E
Nyagrong/Xinlong 27 He 30.57N 100.12 E
Nyahanga 36 Fc 2.23S 33.33 E
Nyahua 36 Fc 4.58S 33.34 E
Nyainqêntanglha Feng 27 Fe 30.12N 90.33 E
Nyainqêntanglha Shan 21 Kf 30.10N 90.00 E
Nyakanazi 36 Fc 3.00S 31.15 E
Nyala 31 Jg 12.03N 24.53 E
Nyalam 27 Ef 28.15N 85.55 E
Ny-Ålesund 41 Nc 78.56N 11.57 E
Nyalikungu 36 Fc 3.11S 33.47 E
Nyamandhlovu 37 Dc 19.51S 28.16 E
Nyamapanda 37 Ec 16.55S 32.52 E
Nyamlell 35 Dd 9.07N 26.58 E
Nyamtumbo 36 Ge 10.30S 36.06 E
Nyanding 35 Ed 8.40N 32.41 E
Nyanga 30 Ii 2.58S 10.15 E
Nyanga [3] 36 Bc 3.00S 11.00 E
Nyanza [3] 36 Fc 0.30S 34.30 E
Nyanza-Lac 36 Ec 4.21S 29.36 E
Nyasa, Lake- (EN) = Niassa, Lago- 30 Kj 12.00S 34.30 E
Nyaunglebin 25 Je 17.57N 96.44 E
Nyborg 7 Ci 55.19N 10.48 E
Nybro 7 Dh 56.45N 15.54 E
Nyda 17 Pc 66.40N 72.50 E
Nyda 20 Cc 66.36N 72.54 E
Nyeboe Land 41 Gb 81.45N 56.40W
Nyêmo 27 Ff 29.30N 90.07 E
Nyeri 36 Gc 0.25S 36.57 E
Nyerol 35 Ed 8.41N 32.02 E
Ny Friesland 41 Nc 79.30N 17.00 E
Nyhammar 8 Fd 60.17N 14.58 E
Nyhem 8 Fb 62.54N 15.40 E
Nyika 30 Ki 2.37S 38.44 E
Nyika Plateau 30 Kj 10.40S 33.50 E
Nyikog Qu 27 He 30.24N 100.40 E
Nyimba 36 Fe 14.33S 30.48 E
Nyingchi 27 Ff 29.38N 94.23 E
Nyirbátor 10 Si 47.50N 22.08 E
Nyiregyháza 10 Ri 47.57N 21.43 E
Nyiri Desert 36 Gc 2.20S 37.20 E
Nyiro, Mount- 36 Gb 2.08N 36.51 E
Nyírség 10 Ri 47.50N 21.55 E
Nykøbing [Den.] 7 Ci 54.46N 11.53 E
Nykøbing [Den.] 7 Ci 55.55N 11.41 E
Nykøbing [Den.] 8 Ch 56.48N 8.52 E
Nyköping 7 Dg 58.45N 17.00 E
Nyköpingsån 8 Gf 58.45N 17.01 E
Nykroppa 8 Fe 59.38N 14.18 E
Nyland 8 Ga 63.00N 17.46 E
Nylstroom 37 Dd 24.42S 28.20 E
Nymburk 10 Lf 50.11N 15.03 E
Nymphe Bank (EN) 9 Fj 51.30N 7.05W
Nynäshamn 7 Dg 58.54N 17.57 E
Nyngan 58 Fh 31.34S 147.11 E
Nyon 14 Ad 46.23N 6.15 E
Nyong 30 Hh 3.17N 9.54 E
Nyonga 36 Fd 6.43S 32.04 E
Nyons 11 Lj 44.22N 5.08 E
Nýřany 10 Jg 49.43N 13.13 E
Nyrob 17 Hf 60.42N 56.45 E
Nyš 20 Jf 51.30N 142.48 E
Nysa 10 Nf 50.29N 17.20 E
Nysa Kłodzka 10 Nf 50.49N 17.50 E
Nysa Łużycka 10 Kd 52.04N 14.46 E
Nyslott/Savonlinna 7 Gf 61.52N 28.53 E
Nyssa 46 Ge 43.53N 117.00W
Nystad/Uusikaupunki 7 Ef 60.48N 21.25 E
Nysted 8 Dj 54.40N 11.45 E
Nytva 17 Fg 57.56N 55.20 E
Nyūdō-Zaki 28 Od 40.00N 139.35 E
Nyunzu 36 Ed 5.57S 28.01 E
Nyüzen 29 Ec 36.56N 137.30 E
Nzambi 36 Bc 3.58S 11.16 E
Nzara 35 De 4.40N 28.14 E
Nzega 36 Fc 4.13S 33.11 E
Nzérékoré 31 Gh 7.45N 8.49W
Nzeto 36 Bd 7.05S 12.50 E
Nzi 30 Gh 5.57N 4.50W
Nzilo, Barrage de- 36 Ee 10.35S 25.30 E
Nzo 34 Dd 6.16N 7.03W
Nzoro 36 Eb 3.18N 29.26 E
Nzwani/Anjouan 30 Lj 12.15S 44.25 E

O

Oa, Mull of- 9 Gf 55.35N 6.20W
Oahe, Lake- 38 Ie 45.30N 100.25W
Oahu Island 57 Lb 21.30N 158.00W
O-akan-Dake 29a Db 43.27N 144.10 E
Oakdale [Ca.-U.S.] 46 Eh 37.46N 120.51W
Oakdale [La.-U.S.] 45 Jk 30.49N 92.40W
Oakham 9 Mi 52.40N 0.44W
Oak Harbor 46 Db 48.18N 122.39W
Oak Lake 45 Fb 49.40N 100.45W
Oakland [Ca.-U.S.] 39 Gf 37.47N 122.13W
Oakland [Md.-U.S.] 44 Hf 39.25N 79.24W
Oakley [Id.-U.S.] 46 Ie 42.15N 113.53W
Oakley [Ks.-U.S.] 43 Gd 39.08N 100.51W
Oak Park 45 Mf 41.53N 87.48W
Oak Ridge 43 Kd 36.01N 84.16W
Oakridge 46 De 43.45N 122.28W
Oakville 44 Hd 43.27N 79.41W
Oamaru 61 Di 45.05S 170.59 E
Oancea 15 Ld 45.55N 28.06 E
Oani-Gawa 29 Ga 40.12N 140.16 E
Ōarai 29 Gc 36.18N 140.33 E
Oaro 62 Ee 42.31S 173.30 E
Oasis 46 Hf 41.01N 114.37W
Oasis 32 Hd 26.00N 5.00 E
Oates Coast 66 Jf 70.00S 160.00 E
Oaxaca [2] 47 Ee 17.00N 96.30W
Oaxaca, Sierra Madre de- 48 Ki 17.30N 96.30W
Oaxaca de Juárez 39 Jh 17.03N 96.43W
Ob 21 Ic 66.45N 69.30 E
Oba 42 Jg 48.55N 84.17W
Obala 34 He 4.10N 11.32 E
Obama [Jap.] 28 Mg 35.30N 135.45 E
Obama [Jap.] 29 Be 32.43N 130.13 E
Obama-Wan 29 Dd 35.30N 135.40 E
Oban [N.Z.] 61 Ci 46.52S 168.10 E
Oban [Scot.-U.K.] 9 He 56.25N 5.29W
Obanazawa 28 Pe 38.36N 140.24 E
Obando 53 Je 4.07N 67.45W
Oban Hills 34 Gd 5.30N 8.35 E
Obeliai/Obeljaj 8 Ki 55.58N 25.59 E
Obeljaj/Obeliai 8 Ki 55.58N 25.59 E
Oberá 56 Ic 27.29S 55.08W
Oberbayern 10 Hi 47.50N 11.50 E
Oberderdingen 12 Ke 49.04N 8.48 E
Oberfranken 10 Hf 50.10N 11.30 E
Oberhausen 10 Ce 51.28N 6.51 E
Oberkirchen, Schmallenberg- 12 Kc 51.09N 8.18 E
Oberland [Switz.] 14 Bd 46.35N 7.30 E
Oberland [Switz.] 14 Dd 46.45N 9.05 E
Oberlausitz 10 Ke 51.15N 14.30 E
Oberlin 45 Fg 39.49N 100.32W
Obermoschel 12 Je 49.44N 7.46 E
Obernkirchen 12 Lb 52.16N 9.08 E
Oberösterreich = Upper Austria (EN) [2] 14 Hb 48.15N 14.00 E
Oberpfalz 10 Ig 49.30N 12.10 E
Oberpfälzer Wald = Bohemian Forest (EN) 10 Ig 49.50N 12.30 E
Oberpullendorf 14 Kc 47.30N 16.31 E
Ober-Ramstadt 12 Ke 49.50N 8.45 E
Oberstdorf 10 Gi 47.24N 10.16 E
Oberursel (Taunus) 12 Kd 50.12N 8.35 E
Obervellach 14 Hd 46.56N 13.12 E
Oberwesel 12 Jd 50.06N 7.44 E
Ob Gulf (EN) = Obskaja Guba 21 Jc 69.00N 73.00 E
Obi, Kepulauan- 26 Ig 1.30S 127.45 E
Obi, Pulau- 57 De 1.30S 127.45 E
Obi, Selat- 26 Ig 0.52S 127.33 E
Óbidos [Braz.] 53 Kf 1.55S 55.31W
Óbidos [Port.] 13 Ce 39.22N 9.09W
Obihiro 27 Pc 42.55N 143.12 E
Obilić 15 Eg 42.41N 21.05 E
Obira 29a Ba 44.01N 141.38 E
Obispos 49 Li 8.36N 70.05W
Obispo Trejo 56 Hd 30.46S 63.25W
Obitočnaja Kosa 16 Jf 46.35N 36.15 E
Oblučje 20 Ig 48.59N 131.05 E
Obninsk 19 Dd 55.05N 36.37 E
Obo 31 Jh 5.24N 26.30 E
Obock 35 Gc 11.57N 43.17 E
Obojan 19 De 51.13N 36.16 E
Obokote 36 Ec 0.52S 26.19 E
Obol 7 Gi 55.24N 29.01 E
Oborniki 10 Md 52.39N 16.51 E
Obouya 36 Cc 0.56S 15.43 E
Obozerski 19 Ec 63.28N 40.20 E
Obra 10 Ld 52.36N 15.28 E
Obrenovac 15 De 44.39N 20.12 E
Obrovac 14 Jf 44.12N 15.41 E
Obrovo 10 Vd 52.27N 25.43 E
Obruchev Rise (EN) 20 Lf 52.30N 166.00 E
Obruk Platosu 24 Ec 38.02N 33.30 E
Obšči Syrt 5 Le 51.50N 51.00 E
Obskaja Guba = Ob Gulf (EN) 21 Jc 69.00N 73.00 E
Ob' Tablemount (EN) 30 Ln 52.30S 42.00 E
Ōbu 29 Ed 35.01N 136.58 E
Obuasi 34 Ed 6.12N 1.40W
Obudu 34 Gd 6.40N 9.10 E
Obuhov 16 Gd 50.07N 30.37 E
Obva 17 Gg 58.35N 55.25 E
Obzor 15 Kg 42.49N 27.53 E
Oca 13 Ib 42.46N 3.26W
Oca, Montes de- 13 Ib 42.20N 3.15W
Očakov 19 Df 46.38N 31.33 E
Ocala 43 Kf 29.11N 82.07W
Očamcira 16 Lh 42.46N 41.27 E
Ocampo [Mex.] 48 Hd 27.20N 102.21W
Ocampo [Mex.] 48 Ec 28.11N 108.23W
Ocaña [Col.] 54 Db 8.15N 73.20W
Ocaña [Sp.] 13 Ie 39.56N 3.31W
Occhito, Lago di- 14 Ii 41.35N 14.55 E
Ocean Bight 49 Kc 21.15N 73.15W
Ocean City [Md.-U.S.] 43 Ld 38.20N 75.05W
Ocean City [N.J.-U.S.] 44 Jf 39.16N 74.35W
Ocean Falls 42 Ef 52.21N 127.40W
Oceania 57 Ie 5.00S 175.00 E
Ocean Point 44 Il 26.16N 77.03W
Oceanside 43 De 33.12N 117.23W
Ocean Springs 45 Lk 30.25N 88.50W
Ocejón, Pico- 13 Ic 41.07N 3.15W
Očenyrd, Gora- 17 Mb 68.05N 66.20 E
Očer 19 Fd 57.53N 54.45 E
Ochagavia 13 Kb 42.55N 1.05W
Ochiai 29 Cd 35.02N 133.45 E
Ochi-Gata 29 Ec 36.55N 136.48 E
Ochiishi-Misaki 29a Db 43.10N 145.28 E
Ochil Hills 9 Je 56.23N 3.35W
Och'ŏnjang 28 Jd 40.55N 128.50 E
Ocho Rios 49 Id 18.25N 77.07W
Ochsenfurt 10 Gg 49.39N 10.05 E
Ochtrup 12 Jb 52.13N 7.11 E
Öckelbo 7 Dd 60.53N 16.43 E
Öckerö 8 Dg 57.43N 11.39 E
Ocmulgee River 44 Fj 31.58N 82.32W
Ocna Mureş 15 Gc 46.23N 23.51 E

Index Symbols

- [1] Independent Nation
- [2] State, Region
- [3] District, County
- [4] Municipality
- [5] Colony, Dependency
- Continent
- Physical Region
- Historical or Cultural Region
- Mount, Mountain
- Volcano
- Hill
- Mountains, Mountain Range
- Hills, Escarpment
- Plateau, Upland
- Pass, Gap
- Plain, Lowland
- Delta
- Salt Flat
- Valley, Canyon
- Crater, Cave
- Karst Features
- Depression
- Polder
- Desert, Dunes
- Forest, Woods
- Heath, Steppe
- Oasis
- Cape, Point
- Coast, Beach
- Cliff
- Peninsula
- Isthmus
- Sandbank
- Island
- Atoll
- Rock, Reef
- Islands, Archipelago
- Rocks, Reefs
- Coral Reef
- Well, Spring
- Geyser
- River, Stream
- Waterfall Rapids
- River Mouth, Estuary
- Lake
- Salt Lake
- Intermittent Lake
- Reservoir
- Swamp, Pond
- Canal
- Glacier
- Ice Shelf, Pack Ice
- Ocean
- Sea
- Gulf, Bay
- Strait, Fjord
- Lagoon
- Bank
- Seamount
- Tablemount
- Ridge
- Shelf
- Basin
- Escarpment, Sea Scarp
- Fracture
- Trench, Abyss
- National Park, Reserve
- Point of Interest
- Recreation Site
- Cave, Cavern
- Historic Site
- Ruins
- Wall, Walls
- Church, Abbey
- Temple
- Scientific Station
- Airport
- Port
- Lighthouse
- Mine
- Tunnel
- Dam, Bridge

Ocna Sibiului 15 Hc 45.53N 24.03 E
Ocoa, Bahia de- 49 Ld 18.22N 70.39W
Oconee River 44 Fj 31.58N 82.32W
Oconto 45 Md 44.55N 87.52W
Ocosingo 48 Mi 17.04N 92.15W
Ocotal 49 Dg 13.38N 86.29W
Ocotepeque [3] 49 Cf 14.30N 89.00W
Ocotlán 47 Dd 20.21N 102.46W
Ocotlán de Morelos 48 Ki 16.48N 96.43W
Ocracoke Inlet 44 Ih 35.10N 76.05W
Ocracoke Island 44 Jh 35.09N 75.53W
Ocreza 13 Ee 39.32N 7.50W
Octeville-sur-Mer 12 Ce 49.33N 0.07 E
October Revolution Island (EN)=Oktjabrskoj Revoljuci, Ostrov- 21 Lb 79.30N 97.00 E
Ocú 49 Gj 7.57N 80.47W
Ocumare del Tuy 50 Cg 10.07N 66.46W
Oda [Ghana] 34 Ed 5.55N 0.59W
Oda [Jap.] 29 Ce 33.34N 132.48 E
Ōda 28 Lg 35.11N 132.30 E
Oda, Jabal- 35 Fa 20.21N 36.39 E
Ódáðahraun 7a Cb 65.09N 17.00W
Ōdai 29 Ed 34.24N 136.24 E
Odaigahara-San 29 Ed 34.11N 136.06 E
Odalen 8 Dd 60.15N 11.40 E
Ōdate 28 Pd 40.16N 140.34 E
Odawara 28 Og 35.15N 139.10 E
Odda 7 Bf 60.04N 6.33 E
Odder 8 Di 55.58N 10.10 E
Odeleite 13 Eg 37.21N 7.27W
Odemira 13 Dg 37.36N 8.38W
Ödemiş 24 Bc 38.13N 27.59 E
Odendaalsrus 37 De 27.48S 26.45 E
Odense 6 Hd 55.24N 10.23 E
Odenthal 12 Jc 51.02N 7.07 E
Odenwald 10 Eg 49.40N 9.00 E
Oder [Eur.] 5 He 53.40N 14.33 E
Oder [F.R.G.] 10 Ge 51.40N 10.02 E
Oderbruch 10 Kd 52.40N 14.15 E
Oderské vrchy 10 Ng 49.40N 17.45 E
Oderzo 14 Ge 45.47N 12.29 E
Ödeshög 7 Dg 58.14N 14.39 E
Odessa [Tx.-U.S.] 39 If 31.51N 102.22W
Odessa [Ukr.-U.S.S.R.] 6 Jf 46.28N 30.44 E
Odessa [Wa.-U.S.] 46 Fc 47.20N 118.41W
Odesskaja Oblast [3] 19 Df 46.45N 30.30 E
Odet 11 Bg 47.52N 4.06W
Odiel 13 Fg 37.10N 6.54W
Odienné 31 Gh 9.30N 7.34W
Odienné [3] 34 Dd 9.45N 7.45W
Odivelas 13 Df 38.12N 8.18W
Ödmården 8 Gc 61.05N 16.40 E
Odobeşti 15 Kd 45.46N 27.03 E
Ŏdŏngk 25 Kf 11.48N 104.45 E
Odoorn 12 Ib 52.51N 6.50 E
Odorheiu Secuiesc 15 Ic 46.18N 25.18 E
Ōdose-Zaki 29a Bc 40.46N 140.03 E
Odra 5 He 53.40N 14.33 E
Ödweyne 35 Hd 9.23N 45.04 E
Odžaci 15 Cd 45.31N 19.16 E
Odžak 14 Me 45.01N 18.18 E
Odzi 37 Ec 19.47S 32.24 E
Oeiras 13 Eg 37.38N 7.40W
Oeiras [Braz.] 54 Je 7.01S 42.08W
Oeiras [Port.] 13 Cf 38.41N 9.19W
Oelde 12 Kc 51.49N 8.09 E
Oelerbeek 12 Ib 52.21N 6.38 E
Oelrichs 45 Ee 43.15N 103.10W
Oelsnitz 10 If 50.25N 12.10 E
Oelwein 45 Ke 42.41N 91.55W
Oeno Island 57 Ng 23.56S 130.44W
Oer-Erkenschwick 12 Jc 51.38N 7.15 E
Oeste, Punta- 51a Ab 18.05N 67.57W
Oeventrop, Arnsberg- 12 Kc 51.24N 8.08 E
Ōe-Yama 29 Dd 35.27N 135.06 E
Of 24 Ib 40.57N 40.16 E
O'Fallon Creek 46 Mc 46.50N 105.09W
Ofanto 14 Ki 41.21N 16.13 E
Ofaqim 24 Fg 31.17N 34.37 E
Offa 34 Fd 8.09N 4.43 E
Offaly/Uíbh Fhailí [2] 9 Fh 53.20N 7.30W
Offenbach am Main 10 Ef 50.06N 8.46 E
Offenbach-Hundheim 12 Je 49.37N 7.33 E
Offenburg 10 Dh 48.29N 7.56 E
Offida 14 Hh 42.56N 13.41 E
Offoué 36 Bc 0.04S 11.44 E
Offranville 12 De 49.52N 1.03 E
Ofidhoúsa 15 Jm 36.33N 26.09 E
Ofolanga 65b Ba 19.36S 174.27W
Ofu 65c Db 14.11S 169.42W
Ōfunato 28 Pe 39.04N 141.43 E
Oga 28 Oe 40.43N 141.18 E
Ogachi 29 Gb 39.05N 140.28 E
Ogaden 30 Lh 7.30N 45.00 E
Oga-Hantō 28 Oe 39.55N 139.50 E
Ōgaki 28 Ng 35.21N 136.37 E
Ogallala 43 Gc 41.08N 101.43W
Ogasawara-Shotō=Bonin Islands (EN) 21 Qg 27.00N 142.10 E
Ogawara-Ko 29a Bc 40.45N 141.20 E
Ogbomosho 31 Hh 8.08N 4.16 E
Ogden 39 He 41.14N 111.58W
Ogdensburg 44 Jc 44.42N 75.31W
Ogeechee River 44 Gj 31.51N 81.06W
Oghāsh 24 Lc 39.10N 46.55 E
Ogi 29 Fc 37.50N 138.16 E
Ogilvie Mountains 42 Dc 65.00N 140.00W
Ogi-no-Sen 29 Dd 35.26N 134.26 E
Oginski Kanal 16 Dc 52.20N 25.55 E
Oglanly 16 Sj 39.50N 54.33 E
Oglethorpe 44 Ei 31.28N 84.04W
Ogliastra 14 Dk 39.55N 9.35 E
Oglio 14 Ee 45.02N 10.39 E
Ognon 11 Lg 47.20N 5.29 E
Ogo 35 Hd 9.48N 45.35 E
Ogoamas, Bulu- 26 Hf 0.40N 120.12 E
Ogodža 20 If 52.48N 132.40 E
Ogoja 34 Gd 6.40N 8.48 E
Ogoki 42 If 51.38N 85.56W
Ogoki 42 If 51.38N 85.55W
Ogoki Reservoir 42 If 51.35N 86.00W
Ogonëk 20 Ie 59.40N 138.01 E
Ogooué 30 Hi 0.49S 9.00 E
Ogooué-Ivindo [3] 36 Bb 0.30N 13.00 E
Ogooué-Lolo [3] 36 Bc 1.00S 13.00 E
Ogooué-Maritime [3] 36 Ac 2.00S 9.30 E
Ogōri [Jap.] 29 Bd 34.06N 131.25 E
Ogōri [Jap.] 29 Be 33.24N 130.34 E
Ogosta 15 Gf 43.45N 23.51 E
Ogražden 15 Fh 41.30N 22.55 E
Ogre 8 Kh 56.42N 24.33 E
Ogre 7 Fh 56.50N 24.39 E
Ogulin 14 Je 45.16N 15.14 E
Ogun [2] 34 Fd 7.00N 3.40 E
Oguni [Jap.] 29 Fb 38.04N 139.45 E
Oguni [Jap.] 29 Be 33.07N 131.04 E
Ogurčinski, Ostrov- 16 Rj 38.55N 53.05 E
Oğuzeli 24 Gd 37.00N 37.30 E
Oha 22 Qd 53.34N 142.56 E
Ohai 62 Bf 45.56S 167.57 E
Ohakune 62 Fc 39.25S 175.25 E
Ohanet 32 Id 28.40N 8.50 E
Ohansk 17 Gh 57.42N 55.25 E
Ōhara 29 Gd 35.15N 140.23 E
Ōhasama 29 Gb 39.28N 141.17 E
Ohata 20 Je 59.20N 143.05 E
Ōhata 28 Pd 41.24N 141.10 E
Ohau, Lake- 62 Cf 44.15S 169.50 E
Ohey 12 Hd 50.26N 5.08 E
O'Higgins, Cabo- 65d Bb 27.05S 109.15W
Ohio 38 Kf 36.59N 89.08W
Ohio [2] 43 Kc 40.15N 82.45W
Ohm 10 Ef 50.51N 8.48 E
Ohmberge 10 Ge 51.30N 10.28 E
'Ohonua 65b Bc 21.20S 174.57W
Ohopoho 31 Ij 18.03S 13.45 E
Ohotsk 22 Qd 59.23N 143.18 E
Ohotskoje More=Okhotsk, Sea of- (EN) 21 Qd 53.00N 150.00 E
Ohre 10 Hd 52.18N 11.47 E
Ohře 10 Kf 50.32N 14.08 E
Ohrid 15 Dh 41.07N 20.48 E
Ohrid, Lake- (EN) = Ohridsko Jezero 5 Ig 41.00N 20.45 E
Ohrid, Lake- (EN) = Ohrit, Liqen i- 5 Ig 41.00N 20.45 E
Ohridsko Jezero=Ohrid, Lake- (EN) 5 Ig 41.00N 20.45 E
Öhringen 10 Fg 49.12N 9.30 E
Ohrit, Liqen i- = Ohrid, Lake- (EN) 5 Ig 41.00N 20.45 E
Ohura 62 Fc 38.51S 174.59 E
Oiapoque 54 Hc 3.50N 51.50W
Oich 9 Id 57.10N 4.45W
Oi-Gawa 29 Fd 34.46N 138.17 E
Oil City 44 He 41.26N 79.44W
Oildale 46 Fi 35.25N 119.01W
Oileán Baoi/Dursey 9 Cj 51.36N 10.12W
Oileán Ciarraí/Castleisland 9 Di 52.14N 9.27W
Oileán Coarach/Mutton 9 Di 52.49N 9.31W
Oileán Mhic Aodha/Magee, Island- 9 Hg 54.50N 5.50W
Oinoúsai 15 Jk 38.32N 26.13 E
Oinoúsai, Nisoi- 15 Jk 38.31N 26.14 E
Oirschot 12 Hc 51.30N 5.18 E
Oisans 11 Mi 45.02N 6.02 E
Oise [3] 11 Ie 49.30N 2.30 E
Oise 11 Ie 49.00N 2.04 E
Oise à l'Aisne, Canal de l'- 11 Je 49.36N 3.11 E
Oisemont 12 De 49.57N 1.46 E
Oissel 12 De 49.20N 1.06 E
Oisterwijk 12 Hc 51.35N 5.11 E
Oistins 51q Ab 13.04N 59.33W
Oistins Bay 51q Ab 13.03N 59.33W
Ōita 27 Ne 33.14N 131.36 E
Ōita Ken [2] 28 Kh 33.15N 131.20 E
Oiti Óros 15 Fk 38.49N 22.17 E
Oituz, Pasul- 15 Jc 46.03N 26.23 E
Oiwake 29a Bb 42.52N 141.48 E
Ojat 7 Hf 60.31N 33.05 E
Öje 8 Ed 60.49N 13.51 E
Ojestos de Jalisco 48 Ig 21.50N 101.35W
Ojika-Jima 29 Ae 33.13N 129.03 E
O-Jima 29 Be 34.00N 130.45 E
Ojinaga 47 Dc 29.34N 104.25W
Ojiya 28 Of 37.18N 138.48 E
Ojmjakon 20 Jd 63.28N 142.49 E
Ojocaliente 48 Hf 22.34N 102.15W
Ojo Caliente 48 Fb 30.25N 106.33W
Ojos del Salado, Nevado- 52 Jh 27.06S 68.32W
Ojos Negros 13 Kd 40.44N 1.30W
Ojtal 19 Hg 42.54N 73.21 E
Oka [R.S.F.S.R.] 21 Md 55.00N 102.03 E
Oka [U.S.S.R.] 5 Kd 56.20N 43.59 E
Okaba 26 Kh 8.06S 139.42 E
Okahandja [3] 37 Bd 21.30S 17.30 E
Okahandja 31 Ik 21.59S 16.58 E
Okahukura 62 Fc 38.47S 175.14 E
Okaihau 62 Ea 35.19S 173.46 E
Okak Islands 42 Le 57.28N 61.48W
Okanagan Lake 42 Fg 49.55N 119.30W
Okano 36 Bc 0.05S 10.57 E
Okanogan River 43 Db 48.06N 119.43W
Okapa 59 Ja 6.31S 145.32 E
Okāra 25 Eb 30.49N 73.27 E
Okarem 19 Fh 38.07N 54.05 E
Okato 62 Ec 39.12S 173.53 E
Okaukuejo 37 Bc 19.10S 15.54 E
Okavango 30 Jj 18.53N 22.24 E
Okavango [3] 37 Cc 18.00S 21.00 E
Okavango Swamp 30 Jj 19.30S 23.00 E
Ōkawa 29 Be 33.12N 130.23 E
Okaya 28 Of 36.03N 138.03 E
Okayama 22 Pf 34.39N 133.55 E
Okayama Ken [2] 28 Lg 34.50N 133.45 E
Okazaki 28 Ng 34.57N 137.10 E
Okeechobee 44 Gl 27.15N 80.50W
Okeechobee, Lake- 38 Kg 26.55N 80.45W
Okefenokee Swamp 44 Fj 30.42N 82.20W
Okehampton 9 Jk 50.44N 4.00W
Okene 34 Gd 7.33N 6.14 E
Oker 10 Gd 52.30N 10.22 E
Oketo 29a Cb 43.41N 143.32 E
Okha 25 Dd 22.27N 69.04 E
Ókhi Óros 15 Hk 38.04N 24.28 E
Okhotsk, Sea of- (EN)= Hok-Kai 21 Qd 53.00N 150.00 E
Okhotsk, Sea of- (EN)= Ohotskoje More 21 Qd 53.00N 150.00 E
Okhthonia, Ákra- 15 Hk 38.32N 24.14 E
Oki-Daitō-Jima 27 Ng 24.30N 131.00 E
Okiep 37 Be 29.39S 17.53 E
Okinawa 29b Ab 26.20N 127.47 E
Okinawa Islands (EN)= Okinawa-Shotō 21 Og 26.40N 128.00 E
Okinawa-Jima 27 Mf 26.40N 128.20 E
Okinawa Ken [2] 29b Ab 26.31N 127.59 E
Okinawa-Shotō=Okinawa Islands (EN) 21 Og 26.40N 128.00 E
Okinoerabu-Jima 27 Mf 27.20N 128.35 E
Okino-Shima [Jap.] 27 Ne 32.44N 132.33 E
Okino-Shima [Jap.] 29 Bd 34.15N 130.08 E
Okino-Tori-Shima 21 Pg 20.25N 136.00 E
Oki Ridge (EN) 28 Mf 37.00N 135.00 E
Oki-Shotō 27 Nd 36.00N 132.50 E
Okitipupa 34 Fd 6.30N 4.48 E
Oki Trench (EN) 29 Dc 37.00N 135.30 E
Oklahoma [2] 43 Hd 35.30N 98.00W
Oklahoma City 39 Jf 35.28N 97.32W
Okmulgee 45 Ii 35.37N 95.58W
Oknica 15 Ka 48.22N 27.24 E
Oko 35 Fa 22.20N 35.56 E
Okoko 36 Fb 2.06N 33.53 E
Okolo 36 Fb 2.40N 31.09 E
Okolona 44 Ef 38.08N 85.41W
Okondja 36 Bc 0.41S 13.47 E
Okonek 10 Mc 53.33N 16.50 E
Okoppe 28 Qb 44.28N 143.08 E
Okotoks 46 Ia 50.44N 113.59W
Okoyo 36 Cc 1.28S 15.04 E
Okrzeika 10 Re 51.40N 21.30 E
Øksfjord 7 Fa 70.14N 22.22 E
Oksino 17 Fc 67.33N 52.10 E
Okstindane 5 Hb 66.02N 14.10 E
Oktemberjan 16 Ni 40.09N 44.03 E
Oktjabrsk [Kaz.-U.S.S.R.] 6 Lf 48.40N 57.11 E
Oktjabrsk [R.S.F.S.R.] 7 Lj 53.13N 48.40 E
Oktjabrski [Bye.-U.S.S.R.] 16 Fc 52.38N 28.54 E
Oktjabrski [Kaz.-U.S.S.R.] 17 Kj 52.37N 62.43 E
Oktjabrski [R.S.F.S.R.] 20 Ee 56.05N 99.25 E
Oktjabrski [R.S.F.S.R.] 19 Fe 54.31N 53.28 E
Oktjabrski [R.S.F.S.R.] 17 Hh 56.31N 57.12 E
Oktjabrski [R.S.F.S.R.] 7 Kf 61.05N 43.08 E
Oktjabrski [R.S.F.S.R.] 20 Hf 53.00N 128.42 E
Oktjabrski [R.S.F.S.R.] 20 Kf 52.38N 156.15 E
Oktjabrski [R.S.F.S.R.] 16 Mf 47.56N 43.38 E
Oktjabrskoje 19 Gc 62.28N 66.01 E
Oktjabrskoj Revoljuci, Ostrov-=October Revolution Island (EN) 21 Lb 79.30N 97.00 E
Oku 29b Bb 26.50N 128.17 E
Ōkuchi 28 Kh 32.04N 130.37 E
Okulovka 7 Hg 58.24N 33.18 E
Okushiri 28 Oc 42.09N 139.29 E
Okushiri-Kaikyō 29a Ab 42.15N 139.40 E
Okushiri-Tō 27 Oc 42.10N 139.25 E
Okuta 34 Fd 9.13N 3.11 E
Oku Tango-Hantō 29 Dd 35.40N 135.10 E
Okwa 30 Jk 22.26S 22.58 E
Ola 20 Ke 59.37N 151.20 E
Ólafsfjördur 7a Ba 66.04N 18.39W
Ólafsvik 7a Ab 64.53N 23.43W
Ola Grande, Punta- 51a Bc 17.55N 66.08W
Olaine/Olajne 7 Fh 56.49N 23.59 E
Olajne/Olaine 7 Fh 56.49N 23.59 E
Olancha 46 Gh 36.17N 117.59W
Olanchito 49 Df 15.30N 86.35W
Olancho [3] 49 Ef 14.45N 86.00W
Öland 5 Hd 56.45N 16.40 E
Ölands norra udde 8 Gg 57.22N 17.05 E
Ölands södra grund 8 Gh 55.40N 17.25 E
Ölands södra udde 8 Gh 56.11N 16.24 E
Olanga 7 Hc 66.08N 30.38 E
Olathe 45 Ig 38.53N 94.49W
Olavarria 53 Ji 36.53S 60.20W
Oława 10 Nf 50.57N 17.17 E
Oława 10 Nf 50.57N 17.17 E
Olbernhau 10 Jf 50.40N 13.20 E
Olbia 6 Gg 40.55N 9.31 E
Olbia, Golfo di- 14 Dj 40.55N 9.40 E
Old Bahama Channel 49 Ib 22.30N 78.05W
Old Bahama Channel (EN)= Bahamas, Canal Viejo de- 49 Ib 22.30N 78.05W
Old Castile (EN)=Castilla la Vieja 13 Ic 41.30N 4.00W
Old Crow 39 Fc 67.35N 139.50W
Oldeani 36 Gc 3.21S 35.33 E
Oldebroek 12 Hb 52.26N 5.53 E
Oldenburg 10 Ec 53.10N 8.12 E
Oldenburg in Holstein 10 Gb 54.18N 10.53 E
Oldenzaal 11 Mb 52.19N 6.56 E
Old Faithful Geyser 46 Jd 44.30N 110.45W
Old Fletton 12 Bb 52.34N 0.15W
Oldham 9 Kh 53.33N 2.07W
Old Hickory Lake 44 Dg 36.18N 86.30W
Oldman River 46 Jb 49.56N 111.42W
Old Marsh Bed 59 Gd 20.55S 130.30 E
Old Mkuski 36 Ee 14.22S 29.22 E
Old Road 51d Bb 17.01N 61.50W
Old Road Town 51c Ab 17.19N 62.48W
Olds 42 Gf 51.47N 114.06W
Old Town 44 Mc 44.56N 68.39W
Old Wives Lake 46 Ma 50.06N 106.00W
Olean 44 Hd 42.05N 78.26W
Olecko 10 Sb 54.03N 22.30 E
Oleiros 13 Ee 39.55N 7.55W
Olëkma 21 Oc 60.22N 120.42 E
Olëkminsk 22 Oc 60.30N 120.15 E
Olëkminski Stanovik 20 Gf 54.00N 119.00 E
Ølen 7 Ag 59.36N 5.48 E
Olenegorsk 19 Db 68.10N 33.13 E
Olenëk 21 Nb 73.00N 119.55 E
Olenëkski Zaliv 20 Hb 73.10N 121.00 E
Olenica 7 Ic 66.29N 35.19 E
Olenj, Ostrov- 20 Cb 72.25N 77.45 E
Olenty 16 Re 49.45N 52.10 E
Oléron, Ile d'- 5 Ff 45.56N 1.18W
Olesko 10 Ug 49.53N 24.58 E
Oleśnica 10 Ne 51.13N 17.23 E
Olesno 10 Of 50.53N 18.25 E
Olevsk 16 Ed 51.13N 27.41 E
Olga 20 Ih 43.46N 135.21 E
Olga, Mount- 59 Ge 25.19S 130.46 E
Olgastretet 41 Oc 78.30N 24.00 E
Ølgod 8 Ci 55.49N 8.37 E
Olhão 13 Eg 37.02N 7.50W
Olhovatka 16 Kd 50.17N 39.17 E
Oli 34 Fd 9.40N 4.29 E
Oliana 13 Nb 42.04N 1.19 E
Olib 14 If 44.23N 14.47 E
Oliena 14 Dj 40.16N 9.24 E
Olifants [Afr.] 30 Kk 24.03S 32.40 E
Olifants [Nam.] 37 Be 25.30S 19.30 E
Olifantshoek 37 Ce 27.57S 22.42 E
Olimarao Atoll 57 Fd 7.42N 145.53 E
Olimbia 15 El 37.39N 21.38 E
Ólimbos 15 Kn 35.44N 27.13 E
Ólimbos, Óros-=Olympus, Mount- (EN) 5 Ig 40.05N 22.21 E
Ólimbos Óros 15 Jj 39.05N 26.20 E
Olimpia 55 He 20.44S 48.54W
Olinda 54 Le 8.01S 34.51W
Olite 13 Kb 42.29N 1.39W
Oliva [Arg.] 56 Hd 32.03S 63.34W
Oliva [Sp.] 13 Lf 38.55N 0.07W
Oliva, Monasterio de la- 13 Kb 42.20N 1.25W
Oliva de la Frontera 13 Ff 38.16N 6.55W
Oliveira 55 Je 20.41S 44.49W
Oliveira dos Brejinhos 54 Jf 12.19S 42.54W
Olivença 37 Fb 11.46S 35.13 E
Olivenza 13 Ef 38.41N 7.06W
Oliver 46 Fb 49.11N 119.33W
Olivet 11 Hg 47.52N 1.54 E
Olivia 45 Id 44.46N 94.59W
Olja 16 Og 45.47N 47.35 E
Olji Moron He 28 Fb 44.16N 121.42 E
Oljutorski, Mys- 21 Td 59.55N 170.25 E
Oljutorski Zaliv 20 Ld 60.00N 168.00 E
Olkusz 10 Pf 50.17N 19.35 E
Ollan 64d Bb 7.14N 151.38 E
Ollerton 12 Aa 53.13N 1.01W
Olmedo 13 Hc 41.17N 4.41W
Olmos 54 Ce 5.59S 79.46W
Olney [Eng.-U.K.] 12 Bb 52.09N 0.42W
Olney [Il.-U.S.] 45 Lg 38.44N 88.05W
Olney [Tx.-U.S.] 45 Gj 33.22N 98.45W
Oloči 20 Gf 51.20N 119.53 E
Olofström 7 Dh 56.16N 14.30 E
Oloitokitok 36 Gc 2.56S 37.30 E
Oloj 20 Kc 66.20N 159.29 E
Olojski Hrebet 20 Lc 65.50N 162.30 E
Olombo 36 Cc 1.18S 15.53 E
Olomburi 63a Ec 8.59S 161.09 E
Olomouc 6 Hf 49.36N 17.16 E
Olona 14 De 45.06N 9.21 E
Olonec 19 Dc 61.01N 32.58 E
Olonešty 15 Mc 46.29N 29.52 E
Olongapo 22 Oh 14.50N 120.16 E
Oloron, Gave d'- 11 Ek 43.33N 1.05W
Oloron-Sainte-Marie 11 Fk 43.12N 0.36W
Olosega 65c Db 14.11S 169.39W
Olot 13 Ob 42.11N 2.29 E
Olovjannaja 20 Gf 50.56N 115.35 E
Olovo 14 Mf 44.07N 18.35 E
Olpe 10 De 51.02N 7.51 E
Olpoy 63b Cb 14.52S 166.33 E
Olroyd River 59 Ib 14.10S 141.50 E
Olsberg 12 Kc 51.21N 8.30 E
Olshammar 8 Ff 58.45N 14.48 E
Olst 12 Ib 52.20N 6.08 E
Olsztyn 6 Ie 53.48N 20.29 E
Olsztyn [2] 10 Qc 53.50N 20.30 E
Olsztynek 10 Qc 53.36N 20.17 E
Olt [2] 15 He 44.25N 24.30 E
Olt 5 If 43.43N 24.51 E
Oltedal 8 Bf 58.50N 6.02 E
Olten 14 Bc 47.22N 7.55 E
Olteni 15 Ie 44.11N 25.17 E
Oltenia 15 Ge 44.30N 23.30 E
Oltenița 15 Je 44.05N 26.38 E
Olteț 15 He 44.14N 24.27 E
Oltu 24 Ib 40.33N 41.59 E
Oluanpi 21 Og 21.54N 120.51 E
Olutanga 26 He 7.22N 122.52 E
Olvera 13 Gh 36.56N 5.16W
Olym 16 Kc 52.27N 38.05 E
Olympia 39 Ge 47.03N 122.53W
Olympic Mountains 46 Dc 47.50N 123.45W
Olympus, Mount- 38 Ge 47.48N 123.43W
Olympus, Mount- (EN)= Ólimbos, Óros- 5 Ig 40.05N 22.21 E
Om 20 Cf 54.59N 73.22 E
Ōma 29a Bc 41.30N 140.55 E
Oma 17 Cc 66.45N 46.20 E
Ōmachi 28 Nf 36.30N 137.52 E
Omae-Zaki 29 Fd 34.36N 138.14 E
Ōmagari 28 Pe 39.27N 140.29 E
Omagh/An Ómaigh 9 Fg 54.36N 7.18W
Omaha 39 Je 41.16N 95.57W
Omak 46 Fb 48.24N 119.31W
Omakau 62 Cf 45.06S 169.36 E
Omak Lake 46 Fb 48.16N 119.23W
Oman (EN)='Umān [1] 22 Hg 21.00N 57.00 E
Oman, Gulf of- (EN)= 'Umān, Khalīj- 21 Hg 25.00N 58.00 E
Omarama 61 Ch 44.29S 169.58 E
Omar Gambon 35 He 3.10N 45.47 E
Omaru-Gawa 29 Be 32.07N 131.34 E
Omaruru 37 Bd 21.28S 15.56 E
Omaruru [3] 37 Bd 21.30S 15.00 E
Omatako 37 Bd 21.07S 16.43 E
Omatako, Omuramba- 30 Jj 17.57S 20.25 E
Omate 54 Dg 16.41S 70.59W
Ōma-Zaki 29a Bc 41.32N 140.55 E
Ombai, Selat- 26 Hh 8.30S 125.00 E
Ombella-Mpoko [3] 35 Bd 5.00N 18.00 E
Omberg 8 Ff 58.20N 14.39 E
Ombo 8 Ae 59.15N 6.00 E
Omboué 36 Ac 1.34S 9.15 E
Ombrone 14 Fh 42.39N 11.01 E
Ombu 27 Ee 31.18N 86.33 E
Omčak 20 Jd 61.38N 147.55 E
Omdurman (EN)=Umm Durmān 31 Kg 15.38N 32.30 E
Ōme 29 Fd 35.47N 139.15 E
Omegna 14 Ce 45.53N 8.24 E
Omeo 59 Jg 37.06S 147.36 E
Ömerköy 15 Lj 39.50N 28.04 E
Ometepe, Isla de- 47 Gf 11.30N 85.35W
Ometepec 47 Ee 16.41N 98.25W
Omhajer 35 Fc 14.19N 36.40 E
Ōmihachiman 29 Ed 35.08N 136.05 E
Omihi 62 Ee 43.01S 172.51 E
Omineca 42 Fe 56.05N 124.05W
Omineca Mountains 42 Ee 56.35N 125.55W
Omiš 14 Kg 43.27N 16.42 E
Ōmi-Shima [Jap.] 29 Bd 34.25N 131.15 E
Ōmi-Shima [Jap.] 29 Cd 34.15N 133.00 E
Omitara 37 Bd 22.18S 18.01 E
Ōmiya 27 Od 35.54N 139.38 E
Ommanney Bay 42 Hb 73.00N 101.00W
Omme Å 8 Ci 55.55N 8.25 E
Ommen 12 Ib 52.31N 6.25 E
Omo 30 Kh 4.32N 36.04 E
Omø 8 Di 55.10N 11.10 E
Omoa, Bahía de- 49 Cf 15.50N 88.10W
Omodeo, Lago- 14 Cj 40.10N 8.55 E
Omoloj 20 Ib 71.08N 132.01 E
Omolon 21 Rc 68.42N 158.36 E
Omolon 20 Lc 65.12N 160.27 E
Omono-Gawa 29 Gb 39.44N 140.04 E
Omont 12 Ge 49.36N 4.44 E
Omoto-Gawa 29 Gb 39.51N 141.58 E
Omsk 22 Jd 55.00N 73.24 E
Omskaja Oblast [3] 19 Hd 56.00N 72.30 E
Omsukčan 20 Kd 62.27N 155.50 E
Omsukčanski Hrebet 20 Kd 63.00N 155.10 E
Ōmu 28 Qb 44.34N 142.58 E
Omu, Vîrful- 15 Id 45.26N 25.25 E
Omulew 10 Rc 53.05N 21.32 E
Ōmura 28 Jh 32.54N 129.57 E
Ōmura-Wan 29 Ae 33.00N 129.50 E
Omurtag 15 Jf 43.06N 26.25 E
Ōmuta 28 Kh 33.02N 130.27 E
Omutinski 19 Gd 56.31N 67.45 E
Omutninsk 19 Fd 58.43N 52.12 E
Oña 13 Ib 42.44N 3.24W
Onagawa 29 Gb 38.26N 141.27 E
Onakayale 37 Bc 17.30S 15.01 E
Onaman Lake 45 Ma 50.00N 87.29W
Onamia 45 Jc 46.04N 93.40W
Onamue 64d Bb 7.21N 151.31 E
Onaping Lake 44 Gb 46.57N 81.30W
Onatchiway, Lac- 44 La 49.03N 71.03W
Onawa 45 He 42.02N 96.06W
Onch'ŏn 28 He 38.49N 125.13 E
Oncócua 36 Bf 16.40S 13.24 E
Onda 13 Le 39.58N 0.15W
Ondangua 31 Ij 17.55S 16.00 E
Ondărroa 13 Ja 43.19N 2.25W
Ondava 10 Rh 48.27N 21.48 E
Ondo [2] 34 Gd 7.00N 5.00 E
Ondo [Jap.] 29 Cd 34.12N 132.32 E
Ondo [Nig.] 34 Fd 7.06N 4.50 E
Ondor Sum 28 Bc 42.30N 113.00 E
Ondozero, Ozero- 7 He 63.40N 33.15 E
One and Half Degree Channel 21 Ji 1.30N 73.10 E
Oneata 63d Cc 18.27S 178.29W
Oneata Passage 63d Cc 18.32S 178.28W
Onega 6 Jc 63.57N 38.05 E
Onega 5 Jc 63.58N 37.55 E
Onega, Lake- (EN)= Onežskoje Ozero 5 Jc 61.30N 35.45 E
Onega Peninsula (EN)= Onežski Poluostrov 5 Jc 64.35N 38.00 E
One Hundred Mile House 42 Ff 51.38N 121.16W
Oneida 44 Jd 43.04N 75.40W
Oneida Lake 44 Jd 43.13N 76.00W
O'Neill 43 Hc 42.27N 98.39W
Onejime 29 Bf 31.14N 130.47 E
Onekotan, Ostrov- 21 Re 49.25N 154.45 E
Oneonta [Al.-U.S.] 44 Di 33.57N 86.29W
Oneonta [N.Y.-U.S.] 44 Jd 42.28N 75.04W
Oneroa 64p Cb 21.15S 159.43W
Onežskaja Guba 5 Jc 64.20N 36.30 E
Onežski Poluostrov=Onega Peninsula (EN) 5 Jc 64.35N 38.00 E
Onežskoje Ozero=Onega, Lake- (EN) 5 Jc 61.30N 35.45 E
Ongea Levu 63d Cc 19.08S 178.24W

Index Symbols

[1] Independent Nation
[2] State, Region
[3] District, County
[4] Municipality
[5] Colony, Dependency
Continent
Physical Region
Historical or Cultural Region
Mount, Mountain
Volcano
Hill
Mountains, Mountain Range
Hills, Escarpment
Plateau, Upland
Pass, Gap
Plain, Lowland
Delta
Salt Flat
Valley, Canyon
Crater, Cave
Karst Features
Depression
Polder
Desert, Dunes
Forest, Woods
Heath, Steppe
Oasis
Cape, Point
Coast, Beach
Cliff
Peninsula
Isthmus
Sandbank
Island
Atoll
Rock, Reef
Islands, Archipelago
Rocks, Reefs
Coral Reef
Well, Spring
Geyser
River, Stream
Waterfall Rapids
River Mouth, Estuary
Lake
Salt Lake
Intermittent Lake
Reservoir
Swamp, Pond
Canal
Glacier
Ice Shelf, Pack Ice
Ocean
Sea
Gulf, Bay
Strait, Fjord
Lagoon
Bank
Seamount
Tablemount
Ridge
Shelf
Basin
Escarpment, Sea Scarp
Fracture
Trench, Abyss
National Park, Reserve
Point of Interest
Recreation Site
Cave, Cavern
Historic Site
Ruins
Wall, Walls
Church, Abbey
Temple
Scientific Station
Airport
Port
Lighthouse
Mine
Tunnel
Dam, Bridge

Ongijn-Gol 27 Hc 44.30N 103.40 E
Ongjin 27 Md 37.56N 125.22 E
Ongniud Qi (Wudan) 27 Kc 42.58N 119.01 E
Ongole 25 Ge 15.30N 80.03 E
Ongon 27 Jb 45.49N 113.08 E
Onhaye 12 Gd 50.15N 4.50 E
Oni 16 Mh 42.35N 43.27 E
Onigajō-Yama 29 Ce 33.07N 132.41 E
Onilany 30 Lk 23.34S 43.45 E
Onishibetsu 29a Ca 45.21N 142.06 E
Onitsha 31 Hh 6.10N 6.47 E
Ono 29 Dd 34.51N 134.57 E
Ono 63d Bc 18.54S 178.29 E
Ōno [Jap.] 28 Ng 35.59N 136.29 E
Ōno [Jap.] 29 Cd 34.18N 132.17 E
Onoda 29 Be 33.59N 131.11 E
Ōno-Gawa 29 Be 33.15N 131.43 E
Ōnohara-Jima 29 Fd 34.02N 139.23 E
Onohoj 20 Ff 51.55N 108.01 E
Ono-i-Lau Islands 57 Jg 20.39S 178.42W
Onojō 29 Be 33.34N 130.29 E
Onomichi 28 Lg 34.25N 133.12 E
Onon 21 Nd 51.42N 115.50 E
Onoto 50 Dh 9.36N 65.12W
Onotoa Atoll 57 Ie 1.52S 175.34 E
Ons, Isla de- 13 Db 42.23N 8.56W
Onsala 7 Ch 57.25N 12.01 E
Onseepkans 37 Be 28.45S 19.17 E
Onslow 58 Cg 21.39S 115.06 E
Onslow Bay 43 Le 34.20N 77.20W
On-Take 29 Bf 31.35N 130.39 E
Ontake-San 29 Ed 35.53N 137.29 E
Ontario [3] 42 If 50.00N 86.00W
Ontario [Ca.-U.S.] 46 Gi 34.04N 117.39W
Ontario [Or.-U.S.] 43 Dc 44.02N 116.58W
Ontario, Lake- 38 Le 43.40N 78.00W
Ontario Peninsula 38 Ke 43.50N 81.00W
Onteniente/Ontinyent 13 Lf 38.49N 0.37W
Ontinyent/Onteniente 13 Lf 38.49N 0.37W
Ontojärvi 7 Gd 64.08N 29.09 E
Ontonagon 44 Cb 46.52N 89.19W
Ontong Java Atoll 57 Ge 5.20S 159.30 E
Ō-Numa 29a Bc 41.59N 140.41 E
Oodnadatta 58 Eg 27.33S 135.28 E
Ooidonk 12 Fc 51.01N 3.35 E
Ookala 65a Fc 20.01N 155.17W
Ooldea 58 Eh 30.27S 131.50 E
Oologah Lake 45 Ih 36.39N 95.36W
Ooltgensplaat, Oostflakkee- 12 Gc 51.41N 4.21 E
Oostburg 12 Fc 51.20N 3.30 E
Oostelijk Flevoland 12 Hb 52.30N 5.40 E
Oostende/Ostende 11 Ic 51.14N 2.55 E
Oosterhout 11 Kc 51.38N 4.51 E
Oosterschelde=East Schelde (EN) 11 Jc 51.30N 4.00 E
Oosterwolde, Ooststellingwerf- 12 Ha 53.00N 6.18 E
Oosterzele 12 Fd 50.57N 3.48 E
Oostflakkee 12 Gc 51.41N 4.21 E
Oostflakkee-Ooltgensplaat 12 Gc 51.41N 4.21 E
Oostkamp 12 Fc 51.09N 3.14 E
Oost-Souburg, Vlissingen- 12 Fc 51.28N 3.36 E
Ooststellingwerf 12 Ib 53.00N 6.18 E
Ooststellingwerf-Oosterwolde 12 Ha 53.00N 6.18 E
Oost Vieland, Vieland- 12 Ha 53.17N 5.06 E
Oost-Vlaanderen [3] 12 Fc 51.00N 3.40 E
Ootmarsum 12 Ib 52.25N 6.54 E
Opala 36 Dc 0.37S 24.21 E
Opalenica 10 Md 52.19N 16.23 E
Opanake 25 Gg 6.36N 80.37 E
Opari 35 Ee 3.56N 32.03 E
Oparino 7 Lg 59.53N 48.25 E
Opasatika 44 Fa 49.31N 82.58W
Opasatika Lake 44 Fa 49.06N 83.08W
Opasatika River 44 Fa 50.15N 82.25W
Opatija 14 Ie 45.20N 14.19 E
Opatów 10 Rf 50.49N 21.26 E
Opatówka 10 Rf 50.42N 21.50 E
Opava 10 Ng 49.57N 17.54 E
Opava 10 Og 49.51N 18.17 E
Opelika 43 Je 32.39N 85.23W
Opelousas 45 Jk 30.32N 92.05W
Opémisca, Lac- 44 Ja 49.58N 74.57W
Opheim 46 Lb 48.51N 106.24W
Ophir 40 Hd 63.10N 156.31W
Ophthalmia Range 59 Dd 23.15S 119.30 E
Opienge 36 Eb 0.12N 27.30 E
Opihikao 65a Gd 19.26N 154.53W
Opinaca 42 Jf 52.14N 78.02W
Opiscotéo, Lac- 42 Kf 53.09N 68.10W
Opladen, Leverkusen- 10 De 51.04N 7.01 E
Opobo 34 Ge 4.34N 7.27 E
Opočka 19 Cd 56.42N 28.41 E
Opoczno 10 Qe 51.23N 20.17 E
Opole [2] 10 Nf 50.40N 17.55 E
Opole 10 Nf 50.41N 17.55 E
Opole Lubelskie 10 Re 51.09N 21.58 E
Oporny 19 Ff 46.13N 54.29 E
Opotiki 62 Gc 38.01S 177.17 E
Opp 44 Dj 31.17N 86.22W
Oppa-Wan 29 Gb 38.35N 141.30 E
Oppdal 7 Be 62.36N 9.40 E
Oppenheim 10 Eg 49.51N 8.21 E
Oppland [2] 7 Bf 61.10N 9.40 E
Opportunity 46 Gc 47.39N 117.15W
Opsa 8 Li 55.31N 26.54 E
Opsterland 12 Ia 53.03N 6.04 E
Opsterland-Beetsterzwaag 12 Ia 53.03N 6.04 E
Opua 61 Dg 35.18S 174.07 E
Opunake 62 Ec 39.27S 173.51 E
Oputo 48 Eb 30.03N 109.20W
Oquossoc 44 Lc 45.04N 70.44W
Or 16 Ud 51.12N 58.33 E
Ōra 33 Cd 28.20N 19.35 E
Oradea 6 If 47.04N 21.56 E
Orahovac 15 Dg 42.24N 20.40 E
Orahovica 14 Le 45.32N 17.53 E
Orai 25 Fc 25.59N 79.28 E
Oraibi Wash 46 Ji 35.26N 110.49W
Oran 31 Ge 35.42N 0.38W
Oran [3] 32 Gb 36.00N 0.35W
Orange [Austl.] 58 Fh 33.17S 149.06 E
Orange [Fr.] 11 Kj 44.08N 4.48 E
Orange [Tx.-U.S.] 43 Ie 30.01N 93.44W
Orange [Va.-U.S.] 44 Hf 38.14N 78.07W
Orange/Oranje 30 Ik 28.38N 16.27 E
Orange, Cabo- 52 Ke 4.24N 51.33W
Orangeburg 43 Ke 33.30N 80.52W
Orange Free State/Oranje Vrystaat [2] 37 De 29.00S 26.00 E
Orange Lake 44 Fk 29.25N 82.13W
Orange Park 44 Gj 30.10N 81.42W
Orangeville 44 Gd 43.55N 80.06W
Orange Walk 47 Ge 18.06N 88.33W
Orango 30 Fg 11.05N 16.08W
Oranienburg 10 Jd 52.45N 13.14 E
Oranje/Orange 30 Ik 28.38N 16.27 E
Oranje Gebergte 54 Hc 3.00N 55.00W
Oranjemund 37 Be 28.38S 16.24 E
Oranjestad 54 Da 12.33N 70.06W
Oranje Vrystaat/Orange Free State [2] 37 De 29.00S 26.00 E
Oranžerei 16 Og 45.50N 47.36 E
Orapa 37 Dd 21.16S 25.22 E
Orăştie 15 Gd 45.50N 23.12 E
Orava 10 Pg 49.08N 19.10 E
Oravița 15 Ed 45.02N 21.42 E
Oravská Priehradni Nádrž 10 Pg 49.20N 19.35 E
Orb 11 Jk 43.15N 3.18 E
Orba 14 Cf 44.53N 8.37 E
Orba Co 27 De 34.33N 81.06 E
Ørbæk 8 Di 55.16N 10.41 E
Orbec 12 Ce 49.01N 0.25 E
Orbetello 14 Fh 42.27N 11.13 E
Orbetello, Laguna di- 14 Fh 42.25N 11.15 E
Orbigo 13 Gc 41.58N 5.40W
Orbiquet 12 Ce 49.09N 0.14 E
Orbost 59 Jg 37.42S 148.27 E
Örbyhus 8 Gd 60.14N 17.42 E
Orcadas 66 Re 60.40S 44.30W
Orcas Island 46 Db 48.39N 122.55W
Orchies 12 Fd 50.28N 3.14 E
Orchon→Orhon 21 Md 50.21N 106.05 E
Orcia 14 Fh 42.58N 11.21 E
Orco 14 Be 45.10N 7.52 E
Ord, Mount- 59 Fc 17.20S 125.35 E
Ordenes 13 Da 43.04N 8.24W
Ordos Desert (EN)=Mu Us Shamo 21 Mf 38.45N 109.10 E
Ord River 57 Df 15.30S 128.21 E
Ordu 23 Ea 41.00N 37.53 E
Ordubad 16 Oj 38.55N 46.01 E
Ordynskoje 20 Df 54.22N 81.58 E
Ordžonikidze [Ukr.-U.R.S.S.] 16 If 47.40N 34.04 E
Ordžonikidze [Kaz.-U.S.S.R.] 17 Jj 52.25N 61.45 E
Ordžonikidze [R.S.F.S.R.] 6 Kg 43.03N 44.40 E
Ordžonikidzeabad 19 Gh 38.34N 69.02 E
Ore älv 8 Fc 61.08N 14.35 E
Orebić 14 Lh 42.58N 17.11 E
Örebro 6 Hd 59.17N 15.13 E
Örebro [2] 7 Dg 59.30N 15.00 E
Oredež 8 Nf 58.50N 30.13 E
Oregon 44 Fe 41.38N 83.28W
Oregon [2] 43 Cc 44.00N 121.00W
Oregon City 43 Cb 45.21N 122.36W
Oregon Inlet 44 Jh 35.50N 75.35W
Öregrund 8 Hd 60.20N 18.26 E
Orehov 16 If 47.34N 35.47 E
Orehovo-Zujevo 6 Jd 55.49N 38.59 E
Orel 6 Je 52.59N 36.05 E
Orel 16 Ie 48.31N 34.55 E
Orel, Gora- 20 Jf 53.55N 140.01 E
Orellana [Peru] 54 Ce 6.54S 75.04W
Orellana [Peru] 54 Cd 4.40S 78.10W
Orem 43 Ec 40.19N 111.42W
Ore Mountains (EN)= Erzgebirge 5 He 50.30N 13.15 E
Ore Mountains (EN)= Krušné Hory 5 He 50.30N 13.15 E
Ören 24 Bd 37.18N 29.17 E
Orenbel 24 Hb 40.00N 39.10 E
Orenburg 6 Le 51.54N 55.06 E
Orenburgskaja Oblast [3] 19 Fe 52.00N 55.00 E
Örencik 24 Cc 39.16N 29.34 E
Orense [3] 13 Eb 42.10N 7.30W
Orense [Arg.] 56 Ie 38.40S 59.47W
Orense [Sp.] 13 Eb 42.20N 7.51W
Oreón, Dhiavlos- 15 Fk 38.54N 22.55 E
Orepuki 62 Bg 46.17S 167.44 E
Orestiás 15 Jh 41.30N 26.31 E
Øresund 5 Hd 55.50N 12.40 E
Oreti 62 Cg 46.28S 168.17 E
Orewa 62 Fb 36.35S 174.42 E
Orford 12 Db 52.05N 1.32 E
Orford Ness 12 Oi 52.05N 1.34 E
Orgañá/Organyà 13 Nb 42.13N 1.20 E
Organ Needle 45 Cj 32.21N 106.33W
Organyà/Orgañá 13 Nb 42.13N 1.20 E
Orgaz 13 Ie 39.39N 3.54W
Orgejev 19 Cf 47.23N 28.50 E
Orgelet 11 Lh 46.31N 5.37 E
Orgon Tal 28 Bc 43.20N 112.40 E
Orgosolo 14 Dj 40.12N 9.21 E
Orgūn 23 Kc 32.57N 69.11 E
Orhaneli 15 Lj 39.54N 29.00 E
Orhaneli/Koca Çay 15 Lj 39.56N 28.32 E
Orhangazi 15 Mi 40.30N 29.18 E
Orhomenós 15 Fk 38.35N 22.54 E
Orhon (Orchon) 21 Md 50.21N 106.05 E
Orhy, Pico de- 13 La 42.59N 1.00W
Oria 13 Ja 43.17N 2.08W
Orichuna, Río- 50 Bi 7.30N 68.13W
Orick 46 Cf 41.17N 124.04W
Oriental 48 Kh 19.22N 97.37W
Oriental, Cordillera- 49 Md 18.55N 69.15W
Oriente 56 He 38.44S 60.37W
Orihuela 13 Lf 38.05N 0.57W
Oriku 15 Ci 40.17N 19.25 E
Ori Lekánis 15 Hh 41.08N 24.33 E
Orillia 42 Jh 44.37N 79.25W
Orimattila 7 Ff 60.48N 25.45 E
Orinoco, Río- 52 Je 8.37N 62.15W
Oripää 8 Jd 60.51N 22.41 E
Orissa [3] 25 Gd 21.00N 84.00 E
Orissaare/Orissare 7 Fg 58.34N 23.05 E
Orissare/Orissaare 7 Fg 58.34N 23.05 E
Oristano 14 Ck 39.54N 8.36 E
Oristano, Golfo di- 14 Ck 39.50N 8.30 E
Orituco, Río- 50 Ch 8.45N 67.27W
Orivesi 5 Ic 62.15N 29.25 E
Orivesi 7 Ff 61.41N 24.21 E
Oriximiná 54 Gd 1.45S 55.52W
Orizaba 39 Jh 18.51N 97.06W
Orizaba, Pico de- (Citlaltépetl, Volcán-) 38 Jh 19.01N 97.16W
Orizona 55 Hc 17.03S 48.18W
Orjahovo 15 Gf 43.44N 23.58 E
Ørje 8 De 59.29N 11.39 E
Orjen 15 Bg 42.34N 18.33 E
Orjiva 13 Ih 36.54N 3.25W
Orkanger 7 Be 63.19N 9.52 E
Orkdalen 8 Ca 63.15N 9.50 E
Örkelljunga 8 Eh 56.17N 13.17 E
Orkla 8 Ca 63.18N 9.50 E
Orkney 37 De 27.00S 26.39 E
Orkney [3] 9 Kb 59.00N 3.00W
Orkney Islands 5 Fd 59.00N 3.00W
Orlândia 55 Ie 20.43S 47.53W
Orlando 39 Kg 28.32N 81.23W
Orlando, Capo d'- 14 Il 38.10N 14.45 E
Orlanka 10 Td 52.52N 23.12 E
Orléanais 11 Hf 48.40N 1.20 E
Orléans 6 Gf 47.55N 1.54 E
Orlice 10 Lf 50.12N 15.49 E
Orlické Hory 10 Mf 50.10N 16.30 E
Orlik 20 Ef 52.30N 99.55 E
Orlovskaja Oblast [3] 19 De 52.45N 36.30 E
Orlovski 16 Mf 46.52N 42.06 E
Orlovski, mys- 7 Jc 67.16N 41.18 E
Orly 11 If 48.45N 2.24 E
Ormāra 25 Cc 25.12N 64.38 E
Ormes 12 Ce 49.03N 0.59 E
Ormoc 26 Hd 11.00N 124.37 E
Ormond 62 Gc 38.33S 177.55 E
Ormond Beach 44 Gk 29.17N 81.02W
Ornain 11 Kf 48.46N 4.47 E
Ornans 11 Mg 47.06N 6.09 E
Ornäs 8 Fd 60.31N 15.32 E
Orne [3] 11 Gf 48.40N 0.05 E
Orne [Fr.] 11 Ie 49.17N 6.11 E
Orne [Fr.] 11 Be 49.19N 0.14W
Orne Seamount (EN) 61 Je 27.30S 157.30W
Orneta 10 Qb 54.08N 20.08 E
Ornö 7 Eg 59.05N 18.25 E
Örnsköldsvik 7 Ee 63.18N 18.43 E
Oro 28 Id 40.01N 127.27 E
Oro, Río de- 55 Ch 27.04S 58.34W
Oro, Río del- 48 Ge 25.35N 105.03W
Orocué 54 Dc 4.48N 71.20W
Orodara 34 Ec 10.59N 4.55W
Orofino 46 Gc 46.29N 116.15W
Orogrande 45 Cj 32.23N 106.08W
Orohena, Mont- 65e Fc 17.31S 149.28W
Oroluk Atoll 57 Gd 7.32N 155.18 E
Orom 36 Fb 3.20N 33.40 E
Oromocto 42 Kg 45.51N 66.29W
Oron 34 Ge 4.50N 8.14 E
Orona Atoll (Hull) 57 Je 4.29S 172.10W
Orongo 65d Ac 27.10S 109.26W
Oronsay 9 Ge 56.01N 6.14W
Orontes (EN)=Nahr al 'Āṣī 23 Eb 36.02N 35.58 E
Oropesa [Sp.] 13 Ge 39.55N 5.10W
Oropesa [Sp.] 13 Ld 40.06N 0.09W
Oroqen Zizhiqi (Alihe) 27 La 50.35N 123.42 E
Oroquieta 26 He 8.29N 123.48 E
Orós 54 Ke 6.15S 38.55W
Orós, Açude- 54 Ke 6.15S 39.05W
Orosei 14 Dj 40.23N 9.42 E
Orosei, Golfo di- 14 Dj 40.15N 9.45 E
Orosháza 10 Qj 46.34N 20.40 E
Oro-Shima 29 Be 33.52N 130.02 E
Oroszlány 10 Oi 47.29N 18.19 E
Orote Peninsula 64c Bb 13.26N 144.38 E
Orote Point 64c Bb 13.27N 144.37 E
Orotukan 20 Kd 62.17N 151.50 E
Oroville [Ca.-U.S.] 46 Eg 39.31N 121.33W
Oroville [Wa.-U.S.] 46 Fb 48.56N 119.26W
Orp-Jauche 12 Gd 50.40N 4.57 E
Orqohan 27 Lb 49.36N 121.23 E
Orr 45 Jb 48.03N 92.50W
Orrefors 8 Fh 56.50N 15.45 E
Orri, Pic d'-/Llorri 13 Nb 42.23N 1.12 E
Orša 6 Je 54.30N 30.24 E
Orsa 7 Df 61.07N 14.37 E
Orsasjön 8 Fc 61.05N 14.35 E
Orsay 12 Ef 48.42N 2.11 E
Orsjön 8 Gc 61.35N 16.20 E
Orsk 6 Le 51.12N 58.34 E
Orşova 15 Fe 44.42N 22.25 E
Ørsta 7 Be 62.12N 6.09 E
Örsundsbro 8 Ge 59.44N 17.18 E
Orta, Lago d'- 14 Ce 45.50N 8.25 E
Ortaca 24 Cd 36.49N 28.47 E
Ortakent 15 Kl 37.02N 27.21 E
Ortaklar 15 Kl 37.53N 27.30 E
Orta Nova 14 Ji 41.19N 15.42 E
Orte 14 Gh 42.27N 12.23 E
Ortegal, Cabo- 13 Ea 43.45N 7.53W
Ortenberg 12 Ld 50.21N 9.03 E
Orthez 11 Fk 43.29N 0.46W
Orthon, Río- 54 Ef 10.50S 66.04W
Ortigueira [Braz.] 56 Jb 24.12S 50.55W
Ortigueira [Sp.] 13 Fa 43.34N 6.44W
Ortisei / Sankt Ulrich 14 Fd 46.34N 11.40 E
Ortiz [Mex.] 48 Dc 28.15N 110.43W
Ortiz [Ven.] 50 Ch 9.37N 67.17W
Ortlergruppe/Ortles 14 Ed 46.30N 10.40 E
Ortles/Ortlergruppe 14 Ed 46.30N 10.40 E
Ortolo 11a Ab 41.30N 8.55 E
Ortona 14 Ih 42.21N 14.24 E
Ortonville 45 Hd 45.19N 96.27W
Orto-Tokoj 18 Kc 42.20N 76.02 E
Örtze 10 Fd 52.40N 9.57 E
Orukuizu 64a Ac 7.10N 134.17 E
Orūmīyeh 22 Gf 37.33N 45.04 E
Orūmīyeh, Daryācheh-ye-= Urmia, Lake- (EN) 21 Gf 37.40N 45.30 E
Oruro [2] 54 Eg 18.40S 67.30W
Oruro 53 Jg 17.59S 67.09W
Orust 8 Df 58.10N 11.38 E
Orūzgān [3] 23 Kc 33.15N 66.00 E
Orūzgān 23 Kc 32.56N 66.38 E
Orval, Abbaye d'- 12 He 49.38N 5.22 E
Orvault 11 Eg 47.16N 1.37W
Orvieto 14 Gh 42.43N 12.07 E
Orville Escarpment 66 Qf 75.45S 65.30W
Örvilos, Óros- 15 Gh 41.23N 23.36 E
Orwell 12 Dc 51.58N 1.18 E
Orxois 12 Fe 49.08N 3.12 E
Orz 10 Rd 52.50N 21.30 E
Orzinuovi 14 De 45.24N 9.55 E
Orzyc 10 Rd 52.47N 21.13 E
Orzysz 10 Rc 53.49N 21.56 E
Oš 19 Hg 40.32N 72.50 E
Os 7 Ce 62.30N 11.12 E
Osa 19 Fd 57.17N 55.26 E
Osa 8 Lh 56.21N 26.29 E
Osa 10 Oc 53.33N 18.45 E
Osa, Península de- 47 Hg 8.35N 83.33W
Osage 45 Je 43.17N 92.49W
Osage River 43 Id 38.35N 91.57W
Osaka 29 Ed 35.57N 137.14 E
Ōsaka 22 Pf 34.40N 135.30 E
Ōsaka Bay (EN)=Ōsaka-Wan 28 Mg 34.36N 135.27 E
Ōsaka-Fu [2] 28 Mg 34.45N 135.35 E
Osakarovka 19 He 50.32N 72.39 E
Ōsaka-Wan=Osaka Bay (EN) 28 Mg 34.36N 135.27 E
Osām 15 Hf 43.42N 24.51 E
Osan 28 If 37.09N 127.04 E
Osasco 55 If 23.32S 46.46W
Osat 14 Nf 44.02N 19.20 E
Osawatomie 45 Ig 38.31N 94.57W
Osborne 45 Gg 39.26N 98.42W
Osburger Hochwald 12 Ie 49.40N 6.50 E
Osby 7 Ch 56.22N 13.59 E
Osceola [Ar.-U.S.] 45 Li 35.42N 89.58W
Osceola [Ia.-U.S.] 43 Ic 41.02N 93.46W
Osceola [Mo.-U.S.] 45 Jh 38.03N 93.42W
Oschatz 10 Je 51.18N 13.07 E
Oschersleben 10 Hd 52.02N 11.15 E
Oschiri 14 Dj 40.43N 9.06 E
Osen 7 Cd 64.18N 10.31 E
Osered 16 Ld 50.01N 40.48 E
Osetr 16 Kb 55.00N 38.45 E
Ōse-Zaki 28 Jh 32.38N 128.42 E
Oshamanbe 28 Pc 42.30N 140.22 E
Oshawa 42 Jh 43.54N 78.51W
Oshekehia Lake 37 Bc 18.08S 15.45 E
Oshika 29 Gb 38.17N 141.31 E
Oshika-Hantō 28 Pe 38.22N 141.27 E
Oshikango 37 Bc 17.22S 15.55 E
Oshima 29 Ce 33.55N 132.11 E
Ō-Shima [Jap.] 29 De 33.28N 135.50 E
Ō-Shima [Jap.] 29 Ae 33.30N 129.33 E
Ō-Shima [Jap.] 29 Ae 32.34N 128.54 E
Ō-Shima [Jap.] 29 Be 33.54N 130.27 E
Ō-Shima [Jap.] 27 Oe 34.45N 139.30 E
Ōshima [Jap.] 29 Fd 34.44N 139.20 E
Ō-Shima [Jap.] 29 Bf 31.32N 131.25 E
Ō-Shima [Jap.] 29 De 33.38N 134.30 E
Ō-Shima [Jap.] 29 Cd 34.10N 133.05 E
Ōshima [Jap.] 29 Ae 33.04N 129.36 E
Ō-Shima [Jap.] 28 Od 41.30N 139.15 E
Ō-Shima [Jap.] 28 Jh 32.04N 128.26 E
Ōshima-Hantō 28 Pd 41.40N 140.30 E
Ōshima-Kaikyō 29b Ba 28.10N 129.15 E
Oshkosh [Nb.-U.S.] 45 Ef 41.24N 102.21W
Oshkosh [Wi.-U.S.] 43 Jc 44.01N 88.33W
Oshnavīyeh 24 Kd 37.02N 45.06 E
Oshogbo 31 Hh 7.46N 4.34 E
Oshtorān Kūh 23 Gc 33.20N 49.16 E
Oshtorīnān 24 Me 34.01N 48.38 E
Oshwe 36 Cc 3.24S 19.30 E
Osich'ŏn-ni 28 Jd 41.25N 128.16 E
Osijek 6 Hf 45.33N 18.42 E
Osilo 14 Cj 40.45N 8.40 E
Osimo 14 Hg 43.28N 13.29 E
Osinki 7 Lj 52.52N 49.31 E
Osinniki 20 Df 53.37N 87.31 E
Osipaonica 15 Ee 44.33N 21.04 E
Osipoviči 16 Fc 53.19N 28.40 E
Osječenica 14 Kf 44.29N 16.17 E
Oskaloosa 45 Jf 41.18N 92.39W
Oskarshamn 7 Dh 57.16N 16.26 E
Oskarström 8 Eh 56.48N 12.58 E
Oskélanéo 44 Ja 48.08N 75.05W
Oskino 20 Fd 60.48N 107.58 E
Öskjuvatn 7a Cb 65.02N 16.45W
Oskol 16 Je 49.06N 37.25 E
Oskū 24 Ld 37.55N 46.06 E
Oslava 10 Mg 49.05N 16.22 E
Ösling 11 Le 49.55N 6.00 E
Osljanka, Gora- 17 Ig 59.10N 58.33 E
Oslo [2] 7 Cg 59.55N 10.45 E
Oslo 6 Hd 59.55N 10.45 E
Oslofjorden 5 Hd 59.20N 10.35 E
Osmānābād 25 Fe 18.10N 76.03 E
Osmancık 24 Fb 40.59N 34.49 E
Osmaneli 15 Ni 40.22N 30.01 E
Osmaniye 23 Eb 37.05N 36.14 E
Osmino 8 Mf 58.54N 29.15 E
Osmjanskaja Vozvyšennost 8 Kj 54.30N 26.00 E
Ošmjany 16 Db 54.27N 25.57 E
Osmo 8 Gf 58.59N 17.54 E
Osmussaar/Osmussar 8 Je 59.20N 23.15 E
Osmussar/Osmussaar 8 Je 59.20N 23.15 E
Osnabrück 6 Ge 52.16N 8.03 E
Osning 12 Kb 52.10N 8.05 E
Oso, Sierra del- 48 Gd 26.00N 105.25W
Osoblaga 10 Nf 50.27N 17.58 E
Osogovske Planine 15 Fg 42.10N 22.30 E
Osor 14 If 44.42N 14.24 E
Osório 56 Jc 29.54S 50.16W
Osorno 53 Ij 40.34S 73.09W
Osoyoos 42 Fg 49.02N 119.28W
Osøyra 7 Af 60.11N 5.28 E
Ospino 50 Bh 9.18N 69.27W
Osprey Reef 57 Ff 13.55S 146.40 E
Oss 11 Lc 51.46N 5.31 E
Ossa, Mount- 57 Fi 41.54S 146.01 E
Óssa, Óros- 15 Fj 39.49N 22.40 E
Ossabaw Island 44 Gj 31.47N 81.06W
Ossa de Montiel 13 Jf 38.58N 2.45W
Osse 11 Gj 44.07N 0.17 E
Ossining 44 Ke 41.10N 73.52W
Ossjøen 8 Dc 61.15N 11.55 E
Osškaja Oblast [3] 19 Hg 40.45N 73.20 E
Ossora 20 Le 59.15N 163.02 E
Östanvik 8 Fc 61.10N 15.13 E
Ostaškov 19 Dd 57.09N 33.07 E
Ostbevern 12 Jb 52.03N 7.51 E
Oste 10 Fc 53.33N 9.10 E
Ostende/Oostende 11 Ic 51.14N 2.55 E
Oster 16 Gd 50.55N 30.57 E
Oster [Ukr.-U.S.S.R.] 16 Gd 50.53N 30.55 E
Oster [U.S.S.R.] 16 Gc 53.47N 31.45 E
Osterburg in der Altmark 10 Hd 52.47N 11.44 E
Österbybruk 8 Gd 60.12N 17.54 E
Österdalälven 7 Df 60.33N 15.08 E
Østerdalen 7 Cf 62.00N 10.40 E
Österfjorden 8 Ad 60.30N 5.20 E
Österforse 8 Ga 63.09N 17.01 E
Östergarnsholm 8 Hg 57.25N 19.00 E
Östergötland 8 Ff 58.25N 15.35 E
Östergötland [2] 7 Dg 58.25N 15.45 E
Osterholz Scharmbeck 10 Ec 53.14N 8.48 E
Österlen 8 Fi 55.30N 14.10 E
Östermark/Teuva 7 Ee 62.29N 21.44 E
Osterode am Harz 10 Ge 51.44N 10.11 E
Osterøya 7 Af 60.35N 5.35 E
Österreich = Austria (EN) [1] 6 Hf 47.30N 14.00 E
Östersjön=Baltic Sea (EN) 5 Hd 57.00N 19.00 E
Østersøen=Baltic Sea (EN) 5 Hd 57.00N 19.00 E
Östersund 6 Hc 63.11N 14.39 E
Osterwick, Rosendahl- 12 Jb 52.01N 7.12 E
Østfold [2] 7 Cg 59.20N 11.30 E
Ostfriesische Inseln=East Frisian Islands (EN) 10 Dc 53.45N 7.25 E
Ostfriesland=East Friesland (EN) 10 Dc 53.20N 7.40 E
Østgrønland=East Greenland (EN) [2] 41 Id 72.00N 35.00W
Östhammar 7 Ed 60.16N 18.22 E
Osthofen 12 Ke 49.42N 8.20 E
Östmark 8 Ed 60.17N 12.45 E
Ostrach 10 Fh 48.05N 9.25 E
Östra Silen 8 Ee 59.15N 12.20 E
Ostrava 6 Hf 49.50N 18.17 E
Ostrhauderfehn 12 Ja 53.08N 7.37 E
Ostróda 10 Pc 53.43N 19.59 E
Ostrog 16 Ed 50.19N 26.32 E
Ostrogožsk 19 De 50.52N 39.05 E
Ostrołęka [2] 10 Rc 53.05N 21.35 E
Ostrołęka 10 Rc 53.06N 21.34 E
Ostrošicki Gorodok 8 Lj 54.03N 27.46 E
Ostrov [Bye.-U.S.S.R.] 10 Vd 52.48N 26.01 E
Ostrov [Czech.] 10 If 50.18N 12.57 E
Ostrov [Rom.] 15 Ke 44.07N 27.22 E
Ostrov [R.S.F.S.R.] 16 Cd 57.23N 28.22 E
Ostrov [R.S.F.S.R.] 8 Mf 58.28N 28.44 E
Ostrovec 8 Lj 54.38N 26.06 E
Ostrovicës, Mali i- 15 Di 40.34N 20.27 E
Ostrovskoje 7 Kh 57.50N 42.13 E
Ostrov Zmeiny 16 Gg 45.15N 30.12 E
Ostrowiec Świętokrzyski 10 Rf 50.57N 21.23 E
Ostrów Lubelski 10 Se 51.30N 22.52 E
Ostrów Mazowiecka 10 Rd 52.49N 21.54 E
Ostrów Wielkopolski 10 Ne 51.39N 17.49 E
Ostryna 10 Uc 53.41N 24.37 E
Ostrzeszów 10 Ne 51.25N 17.57 E
Ostsee=Baltic Sea (EN) 5 Hd 57.00N 19.00 E
Oststeirisches Hügelland 14 Jd 47.00N 15.45 E
Osttirol [2] 14 Gd 46.55N 12.30 E
Ostuni 14 Lj 40.44N 17.35 E
Osumi 15 Ci 40.48N 19.52 E
Ōsumi 29 Bf 31.36N 130.59 E
Ōsumi-Hantō 29 Bf 31.15N 130.50 E
Ōsumi Islands (EN)=Ōsumi-Shotō 21 Pf 30.35N 130.59 E
Ōsumi-Shotō=Ōsumi Islands (EN) 21 Pf 30.35N 130.59 E
Osuna 13 Gg 37.14N 5.07W
Osveja 8 Mi 55.59N 28.10 E
Osvejskoje, Ozero- 8 Mh 56.00N 28.15 E
Oswego 43 Lc 43.27N 76.31W
Oswestry 9 Ji 52.52N 3.04W

Index Symbols

[1] Independent Nation
[2] State, Region
[3] District, County
[4] Municipality
[5] Colony, Dependency
Continent
Physical Region
Historical or Cultural Region
Mount, Mountain
Volcano
Hill
Mountains, Mountain Range
Hills, Escarpment
Plateau, Upland
Pass, Gap
Plain, Lowland
Delta
Salt Flat
Valley, Canyon
Crater, Cave
Karst Features
Depression
Polder
Desert, Dunes
Forest, Woods
Heath, Steppe
Oasis
Cape, Point
Coast, Beach
Cliff
Peninsula
Isthmus
Sandbank
Island
Atoll
Rock, Reef
Islands, Archipelago
Rocks, Reefs
Coral Reef
Well, Spring
Geyser
River, Stream
Waterfall Rapids
River Mouth, Estuary
Lake
Salt Lake
Intermittent Lake
Reservoir
Swamp, Pond
Canal
Glacier
Ice Shelf, Pack Ice
Ocean
Sea
Gulf, Bay
Strait, Fjord
Lagoon
Bank
Seamount
Tablemount
Ridge
Shelf
Basin
Escarpment, Sea Scarp
Fracture
Trench, Abyss
National Park, Reserve
Point of Interest
Recreation Site
Cave, Cavern
Historic Site
Ruins
Wall, Walls
Church, Abbey
Temple
Scientific Station
Airport
Port
Lighthouse
Mine
Tunnel
Dam, Bridge

Oświęcim 10 Pf 50.03N 19.12 E
Osyka 45 Kk 31.00N 90.28W
Ōta 29 Fc 36.18N 139.22 E
Ota 29 Ec 35.56N 136.03 E
Otago [2] 62 Cf 45.00S 169.10 E
Otago Peninsula 62 Df 45.50S 170.45 E
Ōtake 28 Lg 34.12N 132.13 E
Otakeho 62 Fc 39.33S 174.03 E
Otaki 62 Fd 40.45S 175.08 E
Ōtakime-Yama 29 Gc 37.22N 140.42 E
Otanoshike 29a Db 43.01N 144.16 E
Otar 19 Hg 43.31N 75.12 E
Otaru 27 Pc 43.13N 141.00 E
Otautau 62 Bg 46.09S 168.00 E
Otava 10 Kg 49.26N 14.12 E
Otava 8 Lc 61.39N 27.04 E
Otavi 37 Bc 19.39S 17.20 E
Ōtawara 28 Pf 36.52N 140.02 E
Otelu Roşu 15 Fd 45.32N 22.22 E
Otematata 62 Df 44.37S 170.11 E
Otepää/Otepja 7 Gg 58.03N 26.30 E
Otepää, Vozvyšennost-/
Otepää Kõrgustik 8 Lf 58.00N 26.40 E
Otepää Kõrgustik/Otepää,
Vozvyšennost- 8 Lf 58.00N 26.40 E
Otepja/Otepää 7 Gg 58.03N 26.30 E
Oteros 47 Cc 26.55N 108.30W
Othain 12 He 49.31N 5.23 E
Othello 46 Fc 46.50N 119.10W
Othonoi 15 Cj 39.50N 19.25 E
Óthris Óros 15 Fj 39.02N 22.37 E
Oti 30 Hh 7.48N 0.08 E
Otira 62 De 42.51S 171.33 E
Otish, Monts- 38 Md 52.45N 69.15W
Otjikondo 37 Bc 19.50S 15.23 E
Otjimbingwe 37 Bd 22.21S 16.08 E
Otjiwarongo 31 Ik 20.29S 16.36 E
Otjiwarongo [3] 37 Bd 20.30S 17.30 E
Otjosondjou, Omuramba- 30 Ij 19.55S 20.00 E
Otjosondu 37 Bd 21.12S 17.58 E
Otmuchowskie, Jezioro- 10 Nf 50.27N 17.15 E
Otnes 7 Cf 61.46N 11.12 E
Otobe 29a Bc 41.57N 140.08 E
Otočac 14 Jf 44.52N 15.14 E
Otofuke 29a Cb 42.59N 143.10 E
Otofuke-Gawa 29a Cb 42.56N 143.12 E
Otog Qi (Ulan) 27 Id 39.07N 108.00 E
Otoineppu 29a Ca 44.43N 142.16 E
Otok 14 Me 45.09N 18.53 E
Otopeni 15 Je 44.33N 26.04 E
Otorohanga 62 Fc 38.11S 175.12 E
Otorten, Gora- 17 If 61.50N 59.13 E
Ōtoyo 29 Ce 33.46N 133.40 E
Otra 5 Gd 58.09N 8.00 E
Otradnaja 16 Lg 44.23N 41.31 E
Otradnoje, Ozero- 8 Nd 60.50N 30.25 E
Otradny 7 Mj 53.23N 51.24 E
Otranto 14 Mj 40.09N 18.30 E
Otranto, Canale d'-=
Otranto, Strait of- (EN) 5 Hg 40.00N 19.00 E
Otranto, Capo d'- 14 Mj 40.06N 18.31 E
Otranto, Strait of- (EN)=
Otranto, Canale d'- 5 Hg 40.00N 19.00 E
Otranto, Strait of- (EN)=
Otrantos, Kanali i- 15 Bi 40.00N 19.00 E
Otranto, Terra d'- 14 Mj 40.20N 18.15 E
Otrantos, Kanali i-=Otranto,
Strait of- (EN) 15 Bi 40.00N 19.00 E
Ötscher 14 Jc 47.51N 15.12 E
Ōtsu 28 Mg 35.00N 135.52 E
Ōtsuchi 28 Pe 39.21N 141.54 E
Ōtsuki [Jap.] 29 Fd 35.36N 138.54 E
Ōtsuki [Jap.] 29 Ce 32.50N 132.41 E
Otta 8 Cc 61.46N 9.31 E
Otta 7 Bf 61.46N 9.32 E
Otta 64d Bb 7.09N 151.54 E
Ottadalen 8 Bc 61.55N 8.00 E
Ottana 14 Dj 40.15N 9.05 E
Otta Pass 64d Bb 7.09N 151.53 E
Ottawa [Il.-U.S.] 45 Lf 41.21N 88.51W
Ottawa [Ks.-U.S.] 43 Hd 38.37N 95.16W
Ottawa [Oh.-U.S.] 44 Ee 41.02N 84.03W
Ottawa [Ont.-Can.] 39 Le 45.25N 75.42W
Ottawa Islands 38 Kd 59.30N 80.10W
Ottawa River 38 Le 45.20N 73.58W
Ottemby 7 Dh 56.16N 16.24 E
Otterberg 12 Je 49.30N 7.46 E
Otter Creek 44 Fk 29.19N 82.48W
Otterndorf 10 Ec 53.48N 8.54 E
Otteroy 8 Bb 62.40N 6.50 E
Otter Rapids 44 Ga 50.15N 81.45W
Otterup 8 Di 55.31N 10.24 E
Ottumwa 43 Ic 41.01N 92.25W
Ottweiler 12 Je 49.23N 7.10 E
Otukpa 34 Gd 7.05N 7.40 E
Otumpa 55 Ah 27.19S 62.13W
Otuquis, Bañados de- 54 Gg 19.20S 58.30W
Otuquis, Río- 55 Cd 19.41S 58.20W
Oturkpo 34 Gd 7.13N 8.09 E
Otu Tolu Group 65b Bb 20.21S 174.32W
Otuzco 54 Ce 7.54S 78.35W
Otway, Cape- 59 Ig 38.52S 143.31 E
Otwock 10 Rd 52.07N 21.16 E
Otynja 10 Uh 48.40N 24.57 E
Ötz 14 Ec 47.12N 10.54 E
Ötztaler Ache 14 Ec 47.14N 10.50 E
Ötztaler Alpen 10 Gi 46.45N 10.55 E
Ou 25 Kd 20.04N 102.13 E
'O'ua 65b Bb 20.02S 174.41W
Oua 63b Ce 21.14S 167.05 E
Ouachita, Lake- 45 Ji 34.40N 93.25W
Ouachita Mountains 38 Jf 34.40N 94.25W
Ouachita River 43 Ie 31.38N 91.49W
Ouadane 31 Ff 20.57N 11.35W
Ouaddaï [3] 35 Cc 13.00N 21.00 E
Ouaddaï [3] 30 Jg 13.00N 21.00 E
Ouagadougou 31 Gg 12.22N 1.31W
Ouahigouya 31 Gg 13.35N 2.25W
Ouaka [3] 35 Cd 6.00N 21.00 E
Ouaka 30 Ih 4.59N 19.56 E
Oualata 32 Ff 17.18N 7.00W
Oualata, Dahr- 32 Ff 17.48N 7.24W
Oualidia 32 Fc 32.44N 9.02W
Ouallam 34 Fc 14.19N 2.05 E
Ouallene 32 He 24.35N 1.17 E
Ouanda-Djallé 35 Cd 8.54N 22.48 E
Ouandjia 35 Cd 8.35N 23.12 E
Ouandjia 35 Cd 9.35N 21.43 E
Ouango 35 Ce 4.19N 22.33 E
Ouangolodougou 34 Dd 9.58N 5.09W
Ouanne 11 Ig 47.57N 2.47 E
Ouarane 30 Ff 21.00N 10.00W
Ouargaye 34 Fc 11.32N 0.01 E
Ouargla 31 He 31.57N 5.20 E
Ouargla [3] 32 Id 30.00N 6.30 E
Ouarkziz, Jbel- 30 Gf 28.00N 8.20W
Ouarra 30 Jh 5.05N 24.26 E
Ouarsenis, Djebel- 13 Ni 35.53N 1.38 E
Ouarsenis, Massif de l'- 32 Hb 35.50N 2.05 E
Ouarzazate 32 Fc 31.00N 6.30W
Ouarzazate 32 Fc 30.55N 6.55W
Oubangui 30 Ii 0.30S 17.42 E
Ouborré, Pointe- 63b Dd 18.47S 169.16 E
Ouche, Pays d'- 11 Gf 48.55N 0.45 E
Ōuchi 29 Gb 39.27N 140.06 E
Oud Beijerland 12 Gc 51.50N 4.26 E
Oude IJssel 12 Ic 52.00N 6.10 E
Oudenaarde/Audenarde 11 Jd 50.51N 3.36 E
Oudenbosch 12 Gc 51.35N 4.34 E
Oude Rijn 11 Kb 52.05N 4.20 E
Oudon 11 Fg 47.37N 0.42W
Oudtshoorn 31 Jl 33.35S 22.14 E
Oued Ben Tili 32 Fd 25.48N 9.32W
Oued el Abtal 13 Mi 35.27N 0.41 E
Oued Fodda 13 Nh 36.11N 1.32 E
Oued Lili 13 Ni 35.31N 1.16 E
Oued Rhiou 32 Hb 35.58N 0.55 E
Oued-Taria 13 Mi 35.07N 0.05 E
Oued Tlelat 13 Li 35.33N 0.27W
Oued Zem 31 Ge 32.52N 6.34W
Ouégoa 63b Be 20.21S 164.26 E
Ouéllé 34 Ed 7.18N 4.01W
Ouémé 30 Hh 6.29N 2.32 E
Ouémé [3] 34 Fd 7.00N 2.35 E
Ouen 63b Cf 22.26S 166.48 E
Ouenza 32 Ib 35.57N 8.07 E
Ouenza, Djebel- 14 Co 35.57N 8.05 E
Ouessa 34 Ec 11.03N 2.47W
Ouessant, Ile d'- 11 Af 48.28N 5.05W
Ouesso 31 Ih 1.37N 16.04 E
Ouest [3] 34 Hd 5.20N 10.30 E
Ouest, Baie de l'- 64h Ab 13.15S 176.13W
Ouezzane 32 Fc 34.48N 5.36W
Oughter, Lough- 9 Fg 54.00N 7.29W
Ouham [3] 35 Bd 7.00N 18.00 E
Ouham 30 Ih 9.18N 18.14 E
Ouham-Pendé [3] 35 Bd 7.00N 16.00 E
Ouidah 34 Fd 6.22N 2.05 E
Ouistreham 11 Fe 49.17N 0.15W
Ouistreham-Riva Bella 12 Be 49.17N 0.16W
Oujda [3] 32 Gc 33.00N 2.00W
Oujda 31 Ge 34.40N 1.54W
Oujeft 32 Ee 20.02N 13.03W
Oulainen 7 Fd 64.16N 24.57 E
Oulchy-le-Château 12 Fe 49.12N 3.21 E
Ouled Djellal 32 Ic 34.25N 5.04 E
Ouled Naïl, Monts des-
32 Hc 34.40N 3.25 E
Oulou, Bahr- 35 Cd 9.48N 21.32 E
Oulu [2] 7 Gd 65.00N 27.00 E
Oulu/Uleåborg 6 Ib 65.01N 25.30 E
Oulu, Lake- (EN)=
Oulujärvi 5 Ic 64.20N 27.15 E
Oulujärvi=Oulu, Lake- (EN)
5 Ic 64.20N 27.15 E
Oulujoki 5 Ib 65.01N 25.25 E
Oum Chalouba 31 Jg 15.48N 20.46 E
Oumé 34 Dd 6.25N 5.30W
Oumé 34 Dd 6.23N 5.25W
Oum el Bouaghi [3] 32 Ib 35.30N 7.10 E
Oum el Bouaghi 32 Ib 35.53N 7.07 E
Oum er Rbia 30 Ge 33.19N 8.20W
Oum Hadjer 35 Bc 13.18N 19.41 E
Oumm ed Droûs Guebli,
Sebkhet- 32 Ee 24.03N 11.45W
Oumm ed Droûs Telli,
Sebkhet- 32 Ee 24.20N 11.30W
Ounasjoki 5 Ib 66.30N 25.45 E
Oundle 12 Bb 52.29N 0.28W
Ounianga 35 Cb 19.10N 20.30 E
Ounianga Kébir 31 Jg 19.04N 20.29 E
Ountivou 34 Fd 7.21N 1.34 E
Ouolossébougou 34 Dc 12.00N 7.55W
Oupeye 12 Hd 50.42N 5.39 E
Oupu 27 Ma 52.45N 126.00 E
Our 12 Ie 49.53N 6.18 E
Ouray 45 Cg 38.01N 107.40W
Ouray, Mount- 45 Cg 38.25N 106.14W
Ource 11 Kf 48.06N 4.23 E
Ourcq 11 Je 49.01N 3.01 E
Ourcq, Canal de l'- 12 If 48.51N 2.22 E
Ourém 54 Id 1.33S 47.06W
Ouricuri 54 Je 7.35S 40.05W
Ourinhos 53 Lh 22.59S 49.52W
Ouro, Rio do- 55 Ha 13.20S 48.59W
Ouro Fino 55 If 22.17S 46.22W
Ouro Prêto 54 Jh 20.23S 43.30W
Ourthe [Bel.] 11 Ld 50.38N 5.35 E
Ourville-en-Caux 12 Ce 49.44N 0.36 E
Ous 19 Gc 60.55N 61.31 E
Ōu-Sanmyaku 28 Pe 39.00N 141.00 E
Ouse [Eng.-U.K.] 9 Nk 50.47N 0.03 E
Ouse [Eng.-U.K.] 9 Mh 53.42N 0.41W
Oust 11 Dg 47.35N 2.06W
Outagouna 34 Fb 15.11N 0.43 E
Outaouais, Rivière- 38 Le 45.20N 73.58W
Outardes, Rivière aux-
42 Kg 49.05N 68.23W
Outat Oulad El Hajj 32 Gc 33.21N 3.42W
Outer Dowsing 9 Oh 53.25N 1.05 E
Outer Hebrides 9 Fd 57.50N 7.32W
Outer Santa Barbara
Passage 46 Fj 33.10N 118.30W
Outer Silver Pit 9 Og 54.05N 2.00 E
Outjo 31 Ik 20.08S 16.08 E
Outjo [3] 37 Ac 19.30S 14.30 E
Outlook 46 La 51.30N 107.03W
Outokumpu 7 Ge 62.44N 29.01 E
Outram Mountain 46 Eb 49.19N 121.05W
Outreau 12 Dd 50.42N 1.35 E
Out Skerries 9 Ma 60.30N 0.50W
Outwell 12 Cb 52.37N 0.14 E
Ouvéa, Ile- 57 Hg 20.35S 166.35 E
Ouvèze 11 Kk 43.59N 4.51 E
Ouxian 28 Ej 28.58N 118.53 E
Ouyen 59 Ig 35.04S 142.20 E
Ouyou Bézédinga 34 Hb 16.32N 13.15 E
Ouzera 13 Oh 36.15N 2.51 E
Ovacık [Tur.] 24 Ed 36.11N 33.40 E
Ovacık [Tur.] 24 Hc 39.22N 39.13 E
Ovada 14 Cf 44.38N 8.38 E
Ova Gölü 15 Mm 36.16N 29.22 E
Ovakent 15 Lk 38.06N 28.02 E
Ovalau Island 63d Bb 17.40S 178.48 E
Ovalle 53 Ii 30.36S 71.12W
Oval Peak 46 Eb 48.15N 120.25W
Ovamboland 37 Bc 18.30S 16.00 E
Ovamboland [3] 37 Bc 18.00S 16.00 E
Ovan 36 Bb 0.30N 12.10 E
Ovanåker 7 Df 61.21N 15.54 E
Ovar 13 Dd 40.52N 8.38W
Ovau 63a Cb 6.48S 156.02 E
Ovejas 49 Ji 9.32N 75.14W
Overath 12 Jd 50.57N 7.18 E
Øverbygd 7 Eb 69.01N 19.18 E
Overflakkee 11 Kc 51.45N 4.10 E
Overhalla 7 Cd 64.30N 12.00 E
Overije 12 Gd 50.46N 4.32 E
Overijssel [3] 12 Ib 52.25N 6.30 E
Överkalix 7 Fc 66.19N 22.50 E
Overland Park 45 Ig 38.59N 94.40W
Övermark/Ylimarkku 8 Ib 62.37N 21.28 E
Overpelt 12 Hc 51.12N 5.25 E
Overri 34 Gd 5.29N 7.02 E
Overton 46 Hh 36.33N 114.27W
Övertorneå 7 Fc 66.23N 23.40 E
Överum 8 Gg 57.59N 16.19 E
Ovidiu 15 Le 44.16N 28.34 E
Oviedo 13 Ga 43.20N 6.00W
Oviedo [Dom.Rep.] 49 Le 17.47N 71.22W
Oviedo [Sp.] 6 Fg 43.22N 5.50W
Oviši 8 Ig 57.34N 21.35 E
Ovo, Capo dell'- 14 Lj 40.18N 17.30 E
Øvre Årdal 7 Bf 61.19N 7.48 E
Övre Fryken 8 Ed 60.00N 13.05 E
Övre Soppero 7 Eb 68.05N 21.41 E
Ovruč 19 Ce 51.19N 28.50 E
Ovsjanka 20 Hf 53.32N 126.58 E
Owaka 62 Cg 46.27S 169.40 E
Owando 31 Ii 0.29S 15.55 E
Owani 28 Pd 40.31N 140.35 E
Owase 28 Ng 34.04N 136.12 E
Owatonna 43 Ic 44.05N 93.14W
Owego 44 Id 42.06N 76.16W
Owen, Mount- 62 Ed 41.33S 172.32 E
Owendo 36 Ab 0.17N 9.30 E
Owen Falls Dam 36 Fb 0.24N 33.11 E
Owensboro 43 Jd 37.46N 87.07W
Owens Lake 46 Gh 36.25N 117.56W
Owen Sound 42 Jh 44.34N 80.56W
Owens River 46 Gh 36.31N 117.57W
Owen Stanley Range 57 Fe 9.20S 148.00 E
Owl Creek Mountains
46 Ke 43.30N 108.35W
Owney, Kowlal-e- 23 Kc 34.27N 68.22 E
Owo 34 Gd 7.11N 5.35 E
Owosso 44 Ed 43.00N 84.10W
Owyhee 46 Gf 41.57N 116.06W
Owyhee, Lake- 46 Ge 43.28N 117.20W
Owyhee Mountains 46 Ge 43.00N 116.45W
Owyhee River [U.S.] 46 Ge 43.40N 117.16W
Owyhee River [U.S.] 43 Dc 43.46N 117.02W
Oxberg 8 Fc 61.07N 14.10 E
Oxbow 45 Eb 49.14N 102.11W
Oxelösund 7 Dg 58.40N 17.06 E
Oxford 9 Lj 51.50N 1.30W
Oxford [Eng.-U.K.] 6 Fe 51.46N 1.15W
Oxford [Ms.-U.S.] 45 Li 34.22N 89.32W
Oxford [N.C.-U.S.] 44 Hg 36.19N 78.35W
Oxford [N.Z.] 62 Ee 43.17S 172.11 E
Oxford Lake 42 Hf 54.50N 95.35W
Oxfordshire [3] 9 Lj 51.50N 1.20W
Oxia 15 Ek 38.18N 21.06 E
Oxkutzcab 48 Og 20.18N 89.25W
Oxnard 43 De 34.12N 119.11W
Ox or Slieve Gamph
Mountains/Sliabh
Gamh 9 Eg 54.10N 8.50W
Oxted 12 Bc 51.14N 0.01W
Oyabe 29 Ec 36.40N 136.52 E
Oyahue 53 Jh 21.08S 68.45W
O-Yama 29 Fd 34.04N 139.31 E
Ōyama 28 Of 36.21N 139.50 E
Ōyama 29 Ec 36.35N 137.18 E
Ōyano 29 Be 32.35N 130.27 E
Oyapock, Fleuve- 52 Ke 4.08N 51.40W
Oyem 31 Ih 1.37N 11.35 E
Oyen 46 Ja 51.22N 110.28W
Øyeren 8 De 59.50N 11.14 E
Oykel 9 Id 57.50N 4.25W
Oyo [2] 34 Fd 8.00N 3.50 E
Oyo [Nig.] 34 Fd 7.51N 3.56 E
Oyo [Sud.] 35 Fa 21.55N 36.06 E
Ōyodo-Gawa 29 Bf 31.55N 131.28 E
Oyonnax 11 Lh 46.15N 5.40 E
Oyster Bay 59 Jh 42.10S 148.10 E
Øystese 8 Bd 60.23N 6.13 E
Özalp 24 Jc 38.39N 43.59 E
Ozamiz 26 He 8.08N 123.50 E
Ozark 44 Ej 31.28N 85.38W
Ozark Plateau 38 Jf 37.00N 93.00W
Ozark Reservoir 45 Ii 35.25N 94.05W
Ozarks, Lake of the- 43 Id 37.39N 92.50W
Ózd 10 Qh 48.13N 20.18 E
Ozeblin 14 Jf 44.35N 15.53 E
Ozernoj, Zaliv- 20 Le 57.00N 163.20 E
Ozernovski 20 Kf 51.21N 156.32 E
Ozerny 16 Vd 51.08N 60.55 E
Ozersk 8 Ij 54.24N 21.59 E
Ozery [Bye.-U.S.S.R.] 10 Uc 53.38N 24.18 E
Ozery [R.S.F.S.R.] 7 Ji 54.54N 38.32 E
Ozëzdy 19 Gf 48.03N 67.09 E
Ozieri 14 Cj 40.35N 9.00 E
Ozinki 19 Ee 51.12N 49.47 E
Ozogina 20 Kc 66.12N 151.05 E
Ozona 43 Ge 30.43N 101.12W
Ozorków 10 Pe 51.58N 19.19 E
Ozouri 36 Ac 0.55S 8.55 E
Ozren [Yugo.] 14 Mf 44.37N 18.15 E
Ozren [Yugo.] 14 Mg 43.59N 18.30 E
Ozren [Yugo.] 15 Ef 43.36N 21.54 E
Ōzu [Jap.] 29 Be 32.52N 130.52 E
Ōzu [Jap.] 28 Lh 33.30N 132.23 E

P

Pääjärvi 8 Kb 62.50N 24.45 E
Paama 63b Dc 16.28S 168.13 E
Pa-an 25 Je 16.53N 97.38 E
Paar 10 Hh 48.45N 11.35 E
Paarl 31 Il 33.45S 18.56 E
Paauilo 65a Fc 20.03N 155.22W
Paavola 7 Fd 64.36N 25.12 E
Pabbay 9 Fd 57.47N 7.20W
Pabellón, Ensenada del-
48 Fe 24.27N 107.36W
Pabianice 10 Pe 51.40N 19.22 E
Pābna 25 Hd 24.00N 89.15 E
Pabradė/Pabrade 7 Fi 54.59N 25.50 E
Pabrade/Pabradė 7 Fi 54.59N 25.50 E
Pacaás Novos, Serra dos-
54 Ff 10.50S 64.00W
Pacajá, Rio- 54 Hd 1.56S 50.55W
Pacajus 54 Kd 4.10S 38.28W
Pacaraima, Serra-
52 Je 4.30N 60.40W
Pacasmayo 54 Ce 7.24S 79.34W
Paceco 14 Gm 37.59N 12.33 E
Pachala 35 Ed 7.10N 34.06 E
Pacheco 48 Eb 30.06N 108.21W
Pachino 14 Jn 36.43N 15.05 E
Pachitea, Rio- 54 De 8.46S 74.32W
Pachuca de Soto 47 Ed 20.07N 98.44W
Pacific-Antarctic Ridge (EN)
3 Kp 62.00S 157.00W
Pacific City 46 Dd 45.12N 123.57W
Pacific Grove 46 Eh 36.38N 121.56W
Pacific Islands, Trust
Territory of the- 58 Gc 10.00N 155.00 E
Pacífico, Océano-=Pacific
Ocean (EN) 3 Ki 5.00N 155.00W
Pacific Ocean 3 Ki 5.00N 155.00W
Pacific Ocean (EN)=Kita-
Taiheiyō 60 Ch 22.00N 167.00 E
Pacific Ocean (EN)=
Pacífico, Océano- 3 Ki 5.00N 155.00W
Pacific Ocean (EN)=
Pacifique, Océan- 3 Ki 5.00N 155.00W
Pacific Ocean (EN)=
Taiheiyō 3 Ki 5.00N 155.00W
Pacific Ocean (EN)=Tihi
Okean 3 Ki 5.00N 155.00W
Pacific Ranges 42 Ef 50.55N 125.10W
Pacifique, Océan-=Pacific
Ocean (EN) 3 Ki 5.00N 155.00W
Packsattel 14 Id 46.58N 14.58 E
Pacuí, Rio- 55 Jc 16.46S 45.01W
Pacuneiro, Rio- 55 Fa 13.02S 53.25W
Pacy-sur-Eure 12 De 49.01N 1.23 E
Paczków 10 Mf 50.27N 17.00 E
Padana, Pianura-=Po
Valley (EN) 5 Gf 45.20N 10.00 E
Padang 22 Mj 0.57S 100.21 E
Padangsidempuan 26 Cf 1.22N 99.16 E
Padangtikar, Pulau- 26 Eg 0.50S 109.30 E
Padany 7 He 63.19N 33.25 E
Padasjoki 8 Kc 61.21N 25.17 E
Padauiri, Rio- 54 Fd 0.15S 64.05W
Paddle Prairie 42 Fe 58.02N 117.50W
Paderborn 10 Ee 51.43N 8.46 E
Paderborn-Elsen 12 Kc 51.44N 8.41 E
Paderborn-Schloß Neuhaus 12 Kc 51.44N 8.42 E
Padeş, Vîrful- 15 Fd 45.40N 22.20 E
Padilla 54 Fg 19.19S 64.20W
Padina 15 Ke 44.50N 27.07 E
Padornelo, Portillo del-
13 Fb 42.03N 6.50W
Padova = Padua (EN) 14 Fe 45.25N 11.53 E
Padre, Morro do- 55 Ic 16.48S 47.35W
Padre Bernardo 55 Hb 15.21S 48.30W
Padre Island 43 Hf 27.00N 97.15W
Padrón 13 Db 42.44N 8.40W
Padua (EN) = Padova 14 Fe 45.25N 11.53 E
Paducah [Ky.-U.S.] 39 Kf 37.05N 88.36W
Paducah [Tx.-U.S.] 45 Fi 34.01N 100.18W
Padula 14 Jj 40.20N 15.39 E
Paea 65e Fc 17.41S 149.35W
Paegam-san 28 Id 40.35N 126.15 E
Paengnyong-Do 27 Ld 38.00N 124.40 E
Paeroa 61 Eg 37.23S 175.41 E
Paestum 14 Jj 40.25N 15.01 E
Paeu 63c Bb 11.22S 166.50 E
Pafuri 37 Ed 22.26S 31.20 E
Pag 14 Jf 44.27N 15.03 E
Pag 14 If 44.30N 15.00 E
Pagadian 26 He 7.49N 123.25 E
Pagai, Kepulauan-=Pagi
Islands (EN) 21 Lj 2.45S 100.00 E
Pagai Selatan 26 Dg 3.00S 100.20 E
Pagai Utara 26 Cg 2.42S 100.07 E
Pagan Island 57 Fc 18.07N 145.46 E
Pagasitikós Kólpos 15 Fj 39.15N 23.00 E
Pagatan 26 Gg 3.36S 115.56 E
Pagat Point 64c Bb 13.30N 144.53 E
Page 46 Jh 36.57N 111.27W
Pagėgiai 8 Ii 55.09N 21.54 E
Paget, Mount- 66 Ad 54.26S 36.33W
Pagi Islands (EN)=Pagai,
Kepulauan- 21 Lj 2.45S 100.00 E
Paglia 14 Gh 42.42N 12.11 E
Pago Bay 64c Bb 13.25N 144.48 E
Pagoda Point 21 Lh 15.57N 94.15 E
Pāgodār 24 Qh 28.10N 57.22 E
Pago Pago 58 Jf 14.16S 170.42W
Pago Pago Harbor 65c Cb 14.17S 170.40W
Pago Redondo 55 Ci 29.35S 59.13W
Pagosa Springs 45 Ch 37.16N 107.01W
Pagoua Bay 51g Ba 15.32N 61.17W
Pagwa River 45 Na 50.01N 85.10W
Pahačí 20 Ld 60.30N 169.00 E
Pahala 65a Fd 19.12N 155.29W
Pâhara, Laguna- 49 Ff 14.18N 83.15W
Pahiatua 62 Fd 40.27S 175.50 E
Pahkāing Bum 21 Lg 26.00N 95.30 E
Pahoa 65a Gd 19.30N 154.57W
Pahokee 44 Gl 26.49N 80.40W
Pahtakor 18 Fd 40.16N 67.55 E
Pahute Mesa 46 Gh 37.20N 116.40W
Paia 63b Dc 16.35S 168.12 E
Paide/Pajde 7 Fg 58.57N 25.35 E
Paignton 9 Jk 50.28N 3.30W
Päijänne 5 Ic 61.35N 23.30 E
Páikon Óros 15 Fh 40.56N 22.21 E
Paila 48 He 25.39N 102.07W
Pailín 25 Kf 12.51N 102.36 E
Pailitas 49 Ki 8.58N 73.38W
Pailolo Channel 65a Eb 21.05N 156.42W
Paimio/Pemar 8 Jd 60.27N 22.42 E
Paimionjoki 8 Jd 60.25N 22.40 E
Paimpol 11 Cf 48.46N 3.03W
Painan 26 Dg 1.21S 100.34 E
Paine, Mount- 66 Mg 86.46S 147.32W
Painel 55 Gh 27.55S 50.06W
Painesville 44 Ge 41.43N 81.15W
Painted Desert 43 Ed 36.00N 111.20W
Paintsville 44 Fg 37.49N 82.48W
País do Vinho 13 Ec 41.15N 7.55W
Paisley 9 If 55.50N 4.26W
Paita 8 Be 5.06S 81.07W
Païta 63b Cf 22.08S 166.22 E
Paiva 13 Dc 41.04N 8.16W
Paj 7 If 61.43N 34.28 E
Pajala 7 Fc 67.12N 23.22 E
Pajares, Puerto de- 13 Ga 43.00N 5.46W
Pajaros, Punta- 48 Ph 19.36N 87.25W
Pajaros Point 51a Db 18.31N 64.18W
Pajatén 54 Ce 7.29S 77.22W
Pajde/Paide 7 Fg 58.57N 25.35 E
Pajęczno 10 Oe 51.09N 19.00 E
Pajer, Gora- 19 Gb 66.40N 64.20 E
Paj-Hoj 5 Mb 69.00N 62.30 E
Pajule 36 Fb 2.58N 32.56 E
Pakanbaru 22 Mi 0.32N 101.27 E
Pakaraima Mountains 54 Fb 4.05N 61.30W
Pakch'on 28 He 39.44N 125.35 E
Pakhiá 15 Im 36.16N 25.50 E
Pakhna 24 Ee 34.46N 32.48 E
Pákhnes 15 Gn 35.18N 23.58 E
Paki 34 Gc 11.30N 8.09 E
Pakima 36 Dc 3.21S 24.06 E
Pakin Atoll 57 Gd 7.04N 157.48 E
Pakistan [1] 22 Ig 30.00N 70.00 E
Pakleni Otoci 14 Kg 43.10N 16.23 E
Pakokku 25 Jd 21.17N 95.06 E
Pakowki Lake 46 Jb 49.22N 110.57W
Pak Phanang 25 Kg 8.21N 100.12 E
Pakrac 14 Le 45.26N 17.12 E
Pakruojis/Pakruojis 7 Fi 55.57N 23.50 E
Pakruojis/Pakruojis 7 Fi 55.57N 23.50 E
Paks 10 Oj 46.38N 18.52 E
Paktīā [3] 23 Kc 33.30N 69.30 E
Pakwach 36 Fb 2.28N 31.30 E
Pakxé 22 Mh 15.07N 105.47 E
Pakxèng 25 Kd 20.10N 102.40 E
Pala 35 Ad 9.22N 14.54 E
Palacca Point 49 Kc 21.15N 73.26W
Palacios [Arg.] 55 Bj 30.43S 61.37W
Palacios [Tx.-U.S.] 45 Hl 28.42N 96.13W
Palafrugell 13 Pc 41.55N 3.10 E
Palagruža 14 Kh 42.24N 16.15 E
Palaiokastritsa 15 Cj 39.40N 19.41 E
Palaiokhóra 15 Gn 35.14N 23.41 E
Palaiseau 12 Ef 48.43N 2.15 E
Palamás 15 Fj 39.28N 22.05 E
Palamós 13 Pc 41.51N 3.08 E
Palamuse/Palamuze 8 Lf 58.39N 26.35 E
Palamut 15 Kk 38.59N 27.41 E
Palamuze/Palamuse 8 Lf 58.39N 26.35 E
Palana 22 Rd 59.07N 159.58 E
Palancia 13 Le 39.40N 0.12W
Palanga 19 Cd 55.57N 21.05 E
Palangkaraya 26 Fg 2.16S 113.56 E
Pālanpur 25 Ed 24.10N 72.26 E

Index Symbols

[1] Independent Nation
[2] State, Region
[3] District, County
[4] Municipality
[5] Colony, Dependency
Continent
Physical Region
Historical or Cultural Region
Mount, Mountain
Volcano
Hill
Mountains, Mountain Range
Hills, Escarpment
Plateau, Upland
Pass, Gap
Plain, Lowland
Delta
Salt Flat
Valley, Canyon
Crater, Cave
Karst Features
Depression
Polder
Desert, Dunes
Forest, Woods
Heath, Steppe
Oasis
Cape, Point
Coast, Beach
Cliff
Peninsula
Isthmus
Sandbank
Island
Atoll
Rock, Reef
Islands, Archipelago
Rocks, Reefs
Coral Reef
Well, Spring
Geyser
River, Stream
Waterfall Rapids
River Mouth, Estuary
Lake
Salt Lake
Intermittent Lake
Reservoir
Swamp, Pond
Canal
Glacier
Ice Shelf, Pack Ice
Ocean
Sea
Gulf, Bay
Strait, Fjord
Lagoon
Bank
Seamount
Tablemount
Ridge
Shelf
Basin
Escarpment, Sea Scarp
Fracture
Trench, Abyss
National Park, Reserve
Point of Interest
Recreation Site
Cave, Cavern
Historic Site
Ruins
Wall, Walls
Church, Abbey
Temple
Scientific Station
Airport
Port
Lighthouse
Mine
Tunnel
Dam, Bridge

Palaoa Point 65a Ec 20.44N 156.58W
Palapye 31 Jk 22.33S 27.08 E
Palasa 26 Hf 0.29N 120.24 E
Palatka [Fl.-U.S.] 43 Kf 29.39N 81.38W
Palatka [R.S.F.S.R.] 20 Kd 60.05N 151.00 E
Palau 14 Di 41.11N 9.23 E
Palau [5] 58 Ed 7.30N 134.30 E
Palau Islands 57 Ed 7.30N 134.30 E
Palauli 65c Aa 13.44S 172.14W
Palauli Bay 65c Aa 13.47S 172.14W
Palau Trench (EN) 60 Af 6.30N 134.30 E
Palavas-les-Flots 11 Jk 43.32N 3.56 E
Palaw 25 Jf 12.58N 98.39 E
Palawan 21 Ni 9.30N 118.30 E
Palawan Passage 26 Gd 10.00N 118.00 E
Palayan 26 Hc 15.33N 121.06 E
Pālayankottai 25 Fg 8.43N 77.44 E
Palazzo, Punta- 11a Aa 42.22N 8.33 E
Palazzolo Acreide 14 Im 37.04N 14.54 E
Palazzolo sull'Oglio 14 De 45.36N 9.53 E
Paldiski 19 Cd 59.20N 24.06 E
Pale di San Martino 14 Fd 46.14N 11.53 E
Paleleh 26 Hf 1.04N 121.57 E
Palembang 22 Mj 2.55S 104.45 E
Palena 14 Ii 41.59N 14.08 E
Palencia [3] 13 Hb 42.25N 4.30W
Palencia 13 Hb 42.01N 4.32W
Palen Lake 46 Hj 33.46N 115.12W
Palenque 39 Jh 17.30N 92.00W
Palenque [Mex.] 48 Ni 17.31N 91.58W
Palenque [Pan.] 49 Hi 9.13N 79.41W
Palenque, Punta- 49 Ld 18.14N 70.09W
Palermo 6 Hh 38.07N 13.22 E
Palermo, Golfo di- 14 Hl 38.10N 13.25 E
Palestine 43 He 31.46N 95.38W
Palestine (EN) 23 Dc 32.15N 34.47 E
Palestrina 14 Gi 41.50N 12.53 E
Pālghāt 25 Ff 10.47N 76.39 E
Palgrave Point 37 Ad 20.28S 13.16 E
Palhoça 55 Hh 27.38S 48.40W
Pāli 25 Ec 25.46N 73.20 E
Palinuro 14 Jj 40.02N 15.17 E
Palinuro, Capo- 14 Jj 40.02N 15.16 E
Palisades Reservoir 46 Je 43.04N 111.26W
Paliseul 12 He 49.54N 5.08 E
Palivere 8 Jf 59.00N 23.45 E
Palizada 48 Mh 18.15N 92.05W
Paljakka 7 Gd 64.45N 28.07 E
Paljavaam 20 Mc 68.50N 170.50 E
Paljenik 5 Hg 44.15N 17.36 E
Pälkäne 8 Kc 61.20N 24.16 E
Palkino 8 Mg 57.29N 28.10 E
Palk Strait 21 Ji 10.00N 79.45 E
Palla Bianca/Weißkugel 14 Ed 46.48N 10.44 E
Pallars 13 Mb 42.25N 0.55 E
Pallars, Montsent de-/Montseny 13 Nb 42.29N 1.02 E
Pallasovka 19 Ee 50.03N 46.55 E
Pallastunturi 7 Fb 68.06N 24.02 E
Palliser, Cape- 61 Eh 41.37S 175.16 E
Palliser, Iles- 57 Mf 15.30S 146.30W
Palma [Moz.] 37 Gb 10.46S 40.28 E
Palma [Sp.] 6 Gh 39.34N 2.39 E
Palma, Badia de-/Palma, Bahia de- 13 Oe 39.27N 2.35 E
Palma, Bahia de-/Palma, Badia de- 13 Oe 39.27N 2.35 E
Palma, Rio- 54 If 12.33S 47.52W
Palma, Sierra de la- 48 Id 26.00N 101.35W
Palma del Rio 13 Gg 37.42N 5.17W
Palma di Montechiaro 14 Hm 37.11N 13.46 E
Palmar, Laguna del- 55 Bi 29.35S 60.42W
Palmar, Rio- 49 Lh 10.11N 71.52W
Palmar, Salto- 55 Cg 24.18S 59.18W
Palmares 54 Ke 8.41S 35.36W
Palmares do Sul 55 Gj 30.16S 50.31W
Palmarito 54 Db 7.37N 70.10W
Palmarola 14 Gj 40.55N 12.50 E
Palmar Sur 47 Hg 8.58N 83.29W
Palmas 56 Jc 26.30S 52.00W
Palmas, Cape- 30 Gh 4.22N 7.44W
Palmas, Golfo di- 14 Cl 39.00N 8.30 E
Palmas Bellas 49 Gi 9.14N 80.05W
Palma Soriano 47 Id 20.13N 76.00W
Palm Bay 44 Gk 28.01N 80.35W
Palm Beach 43 Kf 26.42N 80.02W
Palmdale 46 Fi 34.35N 118.07W
Palmeira 55 Gg 25.25S 50.00W
Palmeira das Missões 56 Jc 27.55S 53.17W
Palmeira dos Indios 54 Ke 9.25S 36.37W
Palmeirais 54 Je 5.58S 43.04W
Palmeiras, Rio- 55 Gb 15.25S 51.10W
Palmeiras de Goiás 55 Hc 16.47S 49.53W
Palmeirinhas, Ponta das- 30 Ii 9.05S 13.00 E
Palmela 13 Df 38.34N 8.54W
Palmer 40 Jd 61.36N 149.07W
Palmer Archipelago 66 Qe 64.10S 62.00W
Palmer Land (EN) 66 Qf 71.30S 65.00W
Palmer Station 66 Qe 64.46S 64.05W
Palmerston 62 Df 45.29S 170.43 E
Palmerston Atoll 57 Kf 18.04S 163.10W
Palmerston North 58 Ii 40.28S 175.17 E
Palmetto Point 51d Ba 17.35N 61.52W
Palmi 14 Jl 38.21N 15.51 E
Palmira [Col.] 53 Ie 3.32N 76.16W
Palmira [Cuba] 49 Gb 22.14N 80.23W
Palm Islands 59 Jc 18.40S 146.30 E
Palmital 55 Fg 24.39S 52.16W
Palmitas 55 Dk 33.27S 57.48W
Palmito 55 Cd 18.53S 58.22W
Palmitos 55 Fh 27.05S 53.08W
Palm Springs 43 De 33.50N 116.33W
Palmyra 23 Ec 34.33N 38.17 E
Palmyra Atoll 57 Kd 5.52N 162.06W
Palo Alto 43 Cd 37.27N 122.09W
Paloh 26 Ef 1.43N 109.18 E
Paloich 35 Ec 10.28N 32.32 E
Palomani, Nevado- 52 Jg 14.38S 69.14W
Palomar Mountain 43 De 33.22N 116.50W
Palomera, Sierra- 13 Kd 40.40N 1.12W
Palopo 22 Oj 3.00S 120.12 E
Palos, Cabo de- 5 Fh 37.38N 0.41W
Palo Santo 55 Cg 25.34S 59.21W
Palotina 55 Fg 24.17S 53.50W
Palouse River 46 Fc 46.35N 118.13W
Palpa 54 Cf 14.32S 75.11W
Palsa 8 Lg 57.23N 26.24 E
Pålsboda 8 Fe 59.04N 15.20 E
Paltamo 7 Gd 64.25N 27.50 E
Palu [Indon.] 22 Nj 0.53S 119.53 E
Palu [Tur.] 24 Hc 38.42N 39.57 E
Palu, Pulau- 26 Hh 8.20S 121.43 E
Pam 63b Be 20.15S 164.17 E
Pama 34 Fc 11.15N 0.42 E
Pāmark/Pomarkku 8 Ic 61.42N 22.00 E
Pambarra 37 Fd 21.56S 35.06 E
Pambeguwa 34 Gc 10.40N 8.17 E
Pamekasan 26 Fh 7.10S 113.28 E
Pamiers 11 Hk 43.07N 1.36 E
Pamir 21 Jf 38.00N 73.00 E
Pamir 19 Hh 37.01N 72.41 E
Pāmiut/Frederikshåb 41 Hf 62.00N 49.45W
Pamlico Sound 43 Ld 35.20N 75.55W
Pampa 43 Gd 35.32N 100.58W
Pampa del Indio 55 Ch 26.02S 59.55W
Pampa del Infierno 55 Bh 26.31S 61.10W
Pampa de los Guanacos 56 Hc 26.14S 61.51W
Pampas 54 Df 12.24S 74.54W
Pampas 52 Ji 35.00S 63.00W
Pampeiro 55 Ej 30.38S 55.16W
Pamplona [Col.] 54 Db 7.23N 72.38W
Pamplona [Sp.] 6 Fg 42.49N 1.38W
Pamukkale 15 Ml 37.47N 29.04 E
Pamukova 15 Ni 40.31N 30.09 E
Pamunkey River 44 Ig 37.32N 76.48W
Pan, Tierra del- 13 Gc 41.50N 6.00W
Pana 36 Bc 1.41S 12.39 E
Panagjurište 15 Hg 42.30N 24.11 E
Panaitan, Pulau- 26 Eh 6.36S 105.12 E
Panaitolikón Óros 15 Ek 38.43N 21.39 E
Panaji (Panjim) 22 Jh 15.29N 73.50 E
Panakhaïkón Óros 15 Ek 38.12N 21.54 E
Panamá [1] 39 Li 9.00N 80.00W
Panamá = Panama (EN) [3] 49 Hi 9.00N 79.00W
Panamá=Panama City (EN) 39 Li 8.58N 79.31W
Panama (EN) = Panamá [3] 49 Hi 9.00N 79.00W
Panamá, Bahia de- 49 Hi 8.50N 79.15W
Panamá, Canal de-= Panama Canal (EN) 47 Ig 9.20N 79.55W
Panamá, Golfo de-= Panama, Gulf of- (EN) 38 Li 8.00N 79.10W
Panama, Gulf of- (EN)= Panamá, Golfo de- 38 Li 8.00N 79.10W
Panama, Isthmus of- (EN)= Panamá, Istmo de- 38 Li 9.20N 79.30W
Panamá, Istmo de-= Panama, Isthmus of- (EN) 38 Li 9.20N 79.30W
Panama Canal (EN)= Panamá, Canal de- 47 Ig 9.20N 79.55W
Panama City [La.-U.S.] 39 Kf 30.10N 85.41W
Panama City (EN)=Panamá 39 Li 8.58N 79.31W
Panamá La Vieja 49 Hi 9.00N 79.29W
Panambi 55 Fi 28.18S 53.30W
Panamint Range 46 Gh 36.30N 117.20W
Panao 54 Ce 9.49S 76.00W
Panarea 14 Jl 38.40N 15.05 E
Panaro 14 Ff 44.55N 11.25 E
Pana Tinai 63a Ad 11.14S 153.10 E
Pana-Wina 63a Ad 11.11S 153.01 E
Panay 21 Oh 11.15N 122.30 E
Pancake Range 46 Hg 39.00N 115.45W
Pančevo 15 De 44.52N 20.39 E
Pančićev vrh 15 Df 43.15N 20.45 E
Panciu 15 Kd 45.54N 27.05 E
Pancros 63b Db 15.58S 168.12 E
Panda 37 Ed 24.03S 34.43 E
Panda ma Tenga 37 Dc 18.32S 25.38 E
Pandan 26 Hd 11.43N 122.06 E
Pan de Azúcar 55 El 34.48S 55.14W
Pandeiros, Ribeirão- 55 Jb 15.42S 44.36W
Pandelis/Pandėlys 8 Kh 56.01N 25.21 E
Pandėlys/Pandelis 8 Kh 56.01N 25.21 E
Pandharpur 25 Fe 17.40N 75.20 E
Pándheon 15 Fi 40.05N 22.20 E
Pāndhurna 25 Fd 21.36N 78.31 E
Pandivere Kõrgustik/Pandivere Vozvyšennost 8 Le 59.00N 26.15 E
Pandivere Vozvyšennost/Pandivere Kõrgustik 8 Le 59.00N 26.15 E
Pando 56 Id 34.43S 55.57W
Pando [2] 54 Ef 11.20S 67.40W
Pandokrátor 15 Cj 39.45N 19.52 E
Pandora 49 Fi 9.45N 82.57W
Pandrup 8 Cg 57.14N 9.41 E
Pandu 36 Cb 4.59N 19.16 E
Panevežis/Panevėžys 19 Cd 55.44N 24.22 E
Panevėžys/Panevežis 19 Cd 55.44N 24.22 E
Panfilov 19 Ig 44.08N 80.01 E
Panga 36 Eb 1.51N 26.25 E
Pangai 65b Ba 19.48S 174.21W
Pangaion Óros 15 Hi 40.50N 24.05 E
Pangalanes, Canal de- 30 Lk 22.48S 47.50 E
Pangani 36 Gd 5.26S 38.58 E
Pangani or Ruvu 36 Gc 5.26S 38.58 E
Pange 12 Ie 49.05N 6.22 E
Panggoe 58 Ge 7.01S 157.05 E
Pangi 36 Ec 3.11S 26.38 E
Pangkajene 26 Gg 4.50S 119.32 E
Pangkalanberandan 26 Cf 4.01N 98.17 E
Pangkalanbuun 26 Fg 2.41S 111.37 E
Pangkalaseang, Tanjung- 26 Hg 0.42S 123.26 E
Pangkalpinang 26 Eg 2.08S 106.08 E
Pangnirtung 39 Mc 66.08N 65.44W
Pang-Pang 63b Dc 17.41S 168.32 E
Panguitch 43 Ed 37.49N 112.26W
Panguma 34 Cd 8.24N 11.13W
Pangutaran Group 26 He 6.15N 120.30 E
Panhandle 45 Fi 35.21N 101.23W
Pania Mutombo 36 Dd 5.11S 23.51 E
Paniau 65a Ab 21.57N 160.05W
Panié, Mont- 61 Bd 20.36S 164.46 E
Pānīpat 25 Fc 29.23N 76.58 E
Paniza, Puerto de- 13 Kc 41.15N 1.20W
Panjang 26 Eh 5.29S 105.18 E
Panjang, Pulau- 26 Ef 2.44N 108.55 E
Panjgūr 25 Cc 26.58N 64.06 E
Panjim → Panaji 22 Jh 15.29N 73.50 E
Panjwīn 24 Ke 35.36N 45.58 E
Pankow, Berlin- 10 Jd 52.34N 13.24 E
Pankshin 34 Gd 9.20N 9.27 E
P'anmunjŏm 28 If 37.57N 126.40 E
Panopah 26 Fg 1.56S 111.11 E
Panorama 56 Jb 21.21S 51.51W
Panshan 28 Gd 41.12N 122.03 E
Panshi 27 Mc 42.56N 126.02 E
Pant 12 Cc 51.53N 0.39 E
Pantanal 52 Kg 18.00S 56.00W
Pantar, Pulau- 26 Hh 8.25S 124.07 E
Pantego 44 Ih 35.34N 76.36W
Pantelleria 14 Fn 36.50N 11.57 E
Pantelleria 5 Hh 36.45N 12.00 E
Pantelleria, Canale di- 14 Fn 36.40N 11.45 E
Pante Makassar 26 Hh 9.12S 124.23 E
Pantoja 54 Cd 0.58S 75.10W
Pánuco 48 Jf 22.03N 98.10W
Pánuco 39 Jg 22.16N 97.47W
Panxian 27 Hf 25.45N 104.39 E
Panyam 34 Gd 9.25N 9.13 E
Panzi 36 Cd 7.13S 17.58 E
Panzós 49 Cf 15.24N 89.40W
Pao, Rio- [Ven.] 50 Bh 8.33N 68.01W
Pao, Rio- [Ven.] 50 Dh 8.06N 64.17W
Paola [It.] 14 Kk 39.21N 16.03 E
Paola [Ks.-U.S.] 45 Ig 38.35N 94.53W
Paoli 44 Df 38.33N 86.28W
Paopao 65e Fc 17.30S 149.49W
Paoua 35 Bd 7.15N 16.26 E
Pápa 10 Ni 47.20N 17.28 E
Papa 65a Fd 19.13N 155.52W
Papaaloa 65a Fd 19.59N 155.13W
Papagaios 55 Jd 19.32S 44.45W
Papagayo, Golfo del- 47 Gf 10.45N 85.45W
Papaikou 65a Fd 19.47N 155.06W
Papakura 62 Fb 37.03S 174.57 E
Papaloapan, Rio- 48 Lh 18.42N 95.38W
Papanduva 55 Gh 26.25S 50.09W
Papangpanjang 26 Dg 0.27S 100.25 E
Papantla de Olarte 47 Ed 20.27N 97.19W
Papar 26 Ge 5.44N 115.56 E
Paparoa Range 62 De 42.05S 171.35 E
Papa Stour 9 La 60.30N 1.40W
Papa Westray 9 Kb 59.22N 2.54W
Papeete 58 Mf 17.32S 149.34W
Papenburg 10 Dc 53.04N 7.24 E
Papenburg-Aschendorf (Ems) 12 Ja 53.04N 7.22 E
Papenoo 65e Fc 17.30S 149.25W
Papes Ezers/Papes Ozero 8 Ih 56.15N 20.55 E
Papes Ozero/Papes Ezers 8 Ih 56.15N 20.55 E
Papetoai 65e Fc 17.30S 149.52W
Papey 7a Cb 64.36N 14.11W
Paphos/Baf 24 Ee 34.50N 32.35 E
Papija 15 Kg 42.07N 27.51 E
Papikion Óros 15 Ih 41.15N 25.18 E
Papilė/Papile 8 Jh 56.09N 22.45 E
Papile/Papilė 8 Jh 56.09N 22.45 E
Papillion 45 Hf 41.09N 96.03W
Papua, Gulf of- 57 Fe 8.32S 145.00 E
Papua New Guinea [1] 58 Fe 6.00S 150.00 E
Papua Passage 64p Bc 21.15S 159.47W
Papuk 14 Le 45.31N 17.39 E
Papun 25 Je 18.04N 97.27 E
Para 7 Ji 54.23N 40.53 E
Pará [2] 54 Hd 4.00S 53.00W
Pará, Rio- 55 Jd 19.13S 45.07W
Para, Rio- 52 Lf 1.30S 48.55W
Parabel 20 De 58.40N 81.30 E
Parabel 20 De 58.43N 81.31 E
Paraburdoo 59 Dd 23.15S 117.45 E
Paracas 54 Cf 13.49S 76.16W
Paracatu 54 Ig 17.13S 46.52W
Paracatu, Rio- [Braz.] 55 Ic 17.30S 46.32W
Paracatu, Rio- [Braz.] 55 Jc 16.30S 45.04W
Paracel Islands (EN)=Xisha Qundao 21 Nh 16.30N 112.15 E
Pārachinār 25 Eb 33.54N 70.06 E
Paraćin 15 Ef 43.52N 21.25 E
Paracuru 54 Kd 3.24S 39.04W
Parada Km 329 55 Ek 32.30S 55.25W
Paradip 25 Hd 20.19N 86.42 E
Paradise [Ca.-U.S.] 46 Eg 39.46N 121.37W
Paradise [Mi.-U.S.] 44 Eb 46.38N 85.03W
Paragould 45 Kh 36.03N 90.29W
Paragua, Rio- 54 Fb 6.55N 62.55W
Paraguá, Rio- 54 Ff 13.34S 61.53W
Paraguaçu, Rio- 52 Mg 12.45S 38.54W
Paraguaçu Paulista 55 Gf 22.25S 50.34W
Paraguai, Rio- 52 Kh 27.18S 58.38W
Paraguaipoa 49 Lh 11.21N 71.57W
Paraguaná, Peninsula de- 52 Jd 11.55N 70.00W
Paraguari [3] 55 Dg 26.00S 57.10W
Paraguari 56 Ic 25.38S 57.09W
Paraguay [1] 53 Kh 23.00S 58.00W
Paraguay, Rio- 52 Kh 27.18S 58.38W
Paraiba [2] 54 Ke 7.10S 36.30W
Paraiba do Sul, Rio- 52 Lh 21.37S 41.03W
Paraibuna, Represa do- 55 Jf 23.25S 45.35W
Paraibuna, Rio- 55 Jf 23.22S 45.40W
Parainen/Pargas 7 Ff 60.18N 22.18 E
Paraíso [Braz.] 55 Fd 19.03S 52.59W
Paraíso [Mex.] 48 Mh 18.24N 93.14W
Paraiso, Rio- 55 Bb 15.08S 61.52W
Parakou 31 Hh 9.21N 2.37 E
Param 64d Bb 7.22N 151.48 E
Paramaribo 53 Ke 5.50N 55.10W
Paramera, Sierra de la- 13 Hd 40.30N 4.46W
Paramithiá 15 Dj 39.28N 20.31 E
Paramušir, Ostrov- 21 Rd 50.25N 155.50 E
Paraná 53 Ji 31.45S 60.30W
Paraná [2] 56 Jb 24.00S 51.00W
Paranã, Pico- 55 Hg 25.14S 48.48W
Paraná, Rio- 52 Ki 33.43S 59.15W
Paranã, Rio- 52 Lg 12.30S 48.14W
Paraná de las Palmas, Rio- 55 Cl 34.18S 58.33W
Paranaguá 53 Lh 25.31S 48.30W
Paraná-Guazú, Rio- 55 Ck 34.00S 58.25W
Paranaíba 54 Hg 19.40S 51.11W
Paranaíba, Rio- 52 Kh 20.07S 51.05W
Paranaiguara 55 Gd 18.53S 50.28W
Paranapanema, Rio- 52 Kh 22.40S 53.09W
Paranapiacaba, Serra do- 52 Lh 24.20S 49.00W
Paranapuã-Guaçu, Ponta do- 55 Ig 24.24S 47.00W
Paranavai 56 Jb 23.04S 52.28W
Parandak 24 Ne 35.21N 50.42 E
Paranéstion 15 Hh 41.16N 24.30 E
Paranhos 55 Ef 23.55S 55.25W
Paraoa Atoll 57 Mf 19.09S 140.43W
Paraopeba 55 Jd 19.18S 44.25W
Paraopeba, Rio- 55 Jd 18.50S 45.11W
Parapara 63b Ca 13.32S 167.20 E
Paraparaumu 62 Fd 40.55S 175.00 E
Paraspóri 15 Kn 35.54N 27.14 E
Parati 55 Jf 23.13S 44.43W
Paratodos, Serra- 55 Jb 14.40S 44.50W
Paratunka 20 Kf 52.52N 158.12 E
Pārāu, Kūh-e- 24 Le 34.37N 47.05 E
Paraúna 55 Gc 17.02S 50.26W
Paravae 64n Bc 10.27S 160.58W
Paray-le-Monial 11 Kh 46.27N 4.07 E
Parbati 25 Fc 25.51N 76.36 E
Parbhani 25 Fe 19.16N 76.47 E
Parchim 10 Hc 53.26N 11.51 E
Parczew 10 Se 51.39N 22.54 E
Pardo 55 Cm 36.15S 59.22W
Pardo, Rio- [Braz.] 55 Fi 29.59S 52.23W
Pardo, Rio- [Braz.] 54 Hh 21.46S 52.09W
Pardo, Rio- [Braz.] 55 He 20.10S 48.38W
Pardo, Rio- [Braz.] 55 Hf 22.55S 49.58W
Pardo, Rio- [Braz.] 55 Jb 15.48S 44.48W
Pardo, Rio- [Braz.] 54 Kg 15.39S 38.57W
Pardubice 10 Lf 50.02N 15.45 E
Parea 65e Eb 16.49S 150.58W
Parecis, Chapada dos- 52 Kg 13.00S 60.00W
Parecis, Rio- 55 Da 12.56S 56.43W
Paredes de Nava 13 Hb 42.09N 4.41W
Parelhas 54 Ke 6.41S 36.39W
Paren 20 Ld 62.28N 163.05 E
Parent 42 Kg 47.55N 74.37W
Parentis-en-Born 11 Ej 44.21N 1.04W
Pareora 62 Df 44.29S 171.13 E
Parepare 22 Nj 4.01S 119.38 E
Párga 15 Dj 39.17N 20.24 E
Pargas/Parainen 7 Ff 60.18N 22.18 E
Pargolovo 8 Nd 60.03N 30.30 E
Parham 51d Bb 17.05N 61.46W
Parhar 19 Gh 37.31N 69.23 E
Pari, Rio- 55 Db 15.36S 56.08W
Paria, Golfo de-/Paria, Gulf of- 54 Fa 10.20N 62.00W
Paria, Gulf of-/Paria, Golfo de- 54 Fa 10.20N 62.00W
Paria, Peninsula de- 50 Eg 10.40N 62.30W
Pariaguán 54 Fb 8.51N 64.43W
Pariaman 26 Dg 0.38S 100.08 E
Paria River 46 Jh 36.52N 111.36W
Paricutin, Volcán- 48 Hh 19.28N 102.15W
Parida, Isla- 49 Fi 8.07N 82.20W
Pari das Pedras 55 Ja 12.45S 44.47W
Parigi 26 Hg 0.48S 120.10 E
Parika 54 Gb 6.52N 58.25W
Parikkala 7 Gf 61.33N 29.30 E
Parima, Serra- 52 Je 3.00N 64.20W
Parinacota 56 Ga 18.12S 69.16W
Pariñas, Punta- 52 Hf 4.40S 81.20W
Paringul Mare, Virful- 15 Gd 45.20N 23.30 E
Parintins 53 Kf 2.36S 56.44W
Paris [Fr.] 6 Gf 48.52N 2.20 E
Paris [Il.-U.S.] 45 Mg 39.36N 87.42W
Paris [Kir.] 64g Ab 1.56N 157.31W
Paris [Ky.-U.S.] 44 Ef 38.13N 84.14W
Paris [Tn.-U.S.] 44 Cg 36.19N 88.20W
Paris [Tx.-U.S.] 43 He 33.40N 95.33W
Paris Basin (EN)=Parisien, Bassin- 5 Gf 49.00N 2.00 E
Parisien, Bassin-=Paris Basin (EN) 5 Gf 49.00N 2.00 E
Parita 49 Gi 8.00N 80.31W
Parita, Bahia de- 49 Gi 8.08N 80.24W
Parit Buntar 26 De 5.07N 100.30 E
Parkano 7 Fe 62.01N 23.01 E
Parkent 18 Gd 41.18N 69.40 E
Parker 46 Hi 34.09N 114.17W
Parker, Mount- 59 Fc 17.10S 128.20 E
Parkersburg 43 Kd 39.17N 81.33W
Parker Seamount (EN) 40 If 52.35N 151.15W
Parkes 58 Fh 33.08S 148.11 E
Park Falls 45 Kd 45.56N 90.32W
Parkland 46 Dc 47.09N 122.26W
Park Range 43 Fc 40.00N 106.30W
Park Rapids 45 Ic 46.55N 95.04W
Park River 45 Hb 48.24N 97.45W
Park Valley 46 If 41.50N 113.21W
Parma 14 Ef 44.56N 10.26 E
Parma [It.] 6 Hg 44.48N 10.20 E
Parma [Oh.-U.S.] 44 Ge 41.24N 81.44W
Parnaguá 54 Jf 10.13S 44.38W
Parnaíba 53 Lf 2.54S 41.47W
Parnaíba, Rio- 52 Lf 3.00S 41.50W
Parnamirim [Braz.] 54 Ke 8.05S 39.34W
Parnamirim [Braz.] 54 Ke 5.55S 35.15W
Parnarama 54 Je 5.41S 43.06W
Parnassós Óros=Parnassus (EN) 5 Ih 38.30N 22.37 E
Parnassus 62 Ee 42.43S 173.17 E
Parnassus (EN)=Parnassós Óros 5 Ih 38.30N 22.37 E
Párnis Óros 15 Gk 38.10N 23.40 E
Párnon Óros 15 Fl 37.12N 22.38 E
Pärnu/Pjarnu 6 Id 58.24N 24.32 E
Pärnu-Jaagupi/Pjarnu-Jagupi 8 Kf 58.36N 24.25 E
Pärnu Jõgi/Pjarnu 7 Fg 58.23N 24.34 E
Pärnu Laht/Pjarnu, Zaliv- 7 Fg 58.15N 24.25 E
Parola 8 Kc 61.03N 24.22 E
Paroo River 57 Fh 31.28S 143.32 E
Paropamisus/Salseleh-ye Safīd Kūh 21 If 34.30N 63.30 E
Páros 15 Il 37.05N 25.09 E
Páros 15 Il 37.06N 25.12 E
Parowan 46 Ih 37.51N 112.57W
Parpaillon 11 Mj 44.35N 6.40 E
Parque Industrial 55 Jd 19.57S 44.01W
Parral 56 Fe 36.09S 71.50W
Parral, Rio- 48 Gd 27.35N 105.25W
Parras, Sierra de- 48 He 25.25N 102.00W
Parras de la Fuente 47 Dc 25.25N 102.11W
Parravicini 55 Dm 36.27S 57.46W
Parrett 9 Jj 51.13N 3.01W
Parrita 49 Ei 9.30N 84.19W
Parry, Cape - 42 Fb 70.12N 124.35W
Parry, Kap- [Grld.] 41 Jd 72.28N 22.00W
Parry, Kap- [Grld.] 41 Ec 77.00N 71.00W
Parry Bay 42 Jc 68.00N 82.00W
Parry Islands 38 Ib 76.00N 110.00W
Parry Peninsula 42 Fc 69.45N 124.35W
Parry Sound 42 Jg 45.21N 80.02W
Parsęta 10 Lb 54.12N 15.33 E
Parsons [Ks.-U.S.] 43 Hd 37.20N 95.16W
Parsons [W.V.-U.S.] 44 Hf 39.06N 79.43W
Parsons Range 59 Hb 13.30S 135.15 E
Partanna 14 Gm 37.43N 12.53 E
Parthenay 11 Fh 46.39N 0.15W
Partille 8 Eg 57.44N 12.07 E
Partinico 14 Hl 38.03N 13.07 E
Partizansk 20 Ih 43.13N 133.05 E
Partizánske 10 Oh 48.38N 18.23 E
Partizanskoje 20 Ee 55.30N 94.30 E
Paru, Rio- 52 Kf 1.33S 52.38W
Paru de Este, Rio- 54 Hc 1.10N 54.40W
Paru de Oeste, Rio- 52 Kf 1.30S 56.00W
Paruru 63a Ec 9.51S 160.49 E
Parvān [3] 23 Kb 35.15N 69.30 E
Pārvomaj 15 Ig 42.06N 25.13 E
Parys 37 De 27.04S 27.16 E
Paša 7 Hf 60.28N 32.55 E
Pasadena [Ca.-U.S.] 39 Hf 34.09N 118.09W
Pasadena [Tx.-U.S.] 45 Il 29.42N 95.13W
Paşaeli Yarimadası 15 Lh 41.20N 28.25 E
Paşalimani Adasi 15 Ki 40.28N 27.37 E
Pasangkaju 26 Gg 1.10S 119.20 E
Pāsārgād 24 Og 30.17N 52.55 E
Pasarwajo 26 Hh 5.29S 122.50 E
Pascagoula 43 Je 30.23N 88.31W
Paşcani 15 Jb 47.15N 26.44 E
Pasco 43 Db 46.14N 119.06W
Pasco [2] 54 Cf 10.30S 75.15W
Pascoal 55 Ba 13.38S 61.06W
Pascoal, Monte- 54 Kg 16.54S 39.24W
Pascua, Isla de-/Rapa Nui= Easter Island (EN) 57 Qg 27.07S 109.22W
Pas-de-Calais [3] 11 Id 50.30N 2.20 E
Pas-en-Artois 12 Ed 50.09N 2.30 E
Pasewalk 10 Jc 53.31N 13.59 E
Pasinler 24 Ib 40.00N 41.41 E
Pašino 20 De 55.11N 83.02 E
Pasión, Rio de la- 49 Be 16.28N 90.33W
Pasir Mas 26 De 6.02N 102.08 E
Pasirpengarayan 26 Df 0.51N 100.16 E
Pasir Puteh 26 De 5.50N 102.24 E
Påskallavik 8 Gg 57.10N 16.27 E
Paškovski 16 Kg 45.01N 39.05 E
Pasłęk 10 Pb 54.05N 19.39 E
Pasłęka 10 Pb 54.25N 19.50 E
Pasman 14 Jg 43.57N 15.21 E
Pasni 22 Ig 25.16N 63.28 E
Paso de Indios 56 Gf 43.52S 69.06W
Paso del Cerro 55 Ej 31.31S 55.46W
Paso de los Libres 56 Ic 29.43S 57.05W
Paso de los Toros 56 Id 32.49S 56.31W
Paso Tranqueras 55 Ej 31.12S 55.45W
Passamaquoddy Bay 44 Nc 45.06N 66.59W
Passa Três, Serra- 55 Hb 14.40S 49.30W
Passau 10 Jh 48.35N 13.29 E
Passero, Capo- 14 Jn 36.40N 15.10 E
Passo Fundo 56 Jc 28.15S 52.24W
Passo Fundo, Rio- 55 Fh 27.16S 52.42W
Passos 54 Ig 20.43S 46.37W
Pastaza, Rio- 52 If 4.50S 76.25W
Pasteur 56 He 35.08S 62.14W
Pasto 53 Ie 1.13N 77.17W
Pastora Peak 46 Kh 36.47N 109.10W
Pastoria, Laguna de- 48 Ki 16.00N 97.40W
Pastos Bons 54 Je 6.36S 44.05W
Pastrana 13 Jd 40.25N 2.55W
Paštrik 15 Dg 42.14N 20.32 E
Pasubio 14 Fe 45.47N 11.10 E
Pasvalis/Pasvalys 7 Fh 56.02N 24.28 E
Pasvalys/Pasvalis 7 Fh 56.02N 24.28 E
Pásztó 10 Pi 47.55N 19.42 E

Index Symbols

[1] Independent Nation
[2] State, Region
[3] District, County
[4] Municipality
[5] Colony, Dependency
Continent
Physical Region
Historical or Cultural Region
Mount, Mountain
Volcano
Hill
Mountains, Mountain Range
Hills, Escarpment
Plateau, Upland
Pass, Gap
Plain, Lowland
Delta
Salt Flat
Valley, Canyon
Crater, Cave
Karst Features
Depression
Polder
Desert, Dunes
Forest, Woods
Heath, Steppe
Oasis
Cape, Point
Coast, Beach
Cliff
Peninsula
Isthmus
Sandbank
Island
Atoll
Rock, Reef
Islands, Archipelago
Rocks, Reefs
Coral Reef
Well, Spring
Geyser
River, Stream
Waterfall Rapids
River Mouth, Estuary
Lake
Salt Lake
Intermittent Lake
Reservoir
Swamp, Pond
Canal
Glacier
Ice Shelf, Pack Ice
Ocean
Sea
Gulf, Bay
Strait, Fjord
Lagoon
Bank
Seamount
Tablemount
Ridge
Shelf
Basin
Escarpment, Sea Scarp
Fracture
Trench, Abyss
National Park, Reserve
Point of Interest
Recreation Site
Cave, Cavern
Historic Site
Ruins
Wall, Walls
Church, Abbey
Temple
Scientific Station
Airport
Port
Lighthouse
Mine
Tunnel
Dam, Bridge

Patagonia 52 Jj 44.00S 68.00W
Patagonica, Cordillera- 52 Ij 46.00S 71.30W
Patan 25 Hc 27.40N 85.20 E
Pātan 25 Ed 23.50N 72.07 E
Patani 26 If 0.18N 128.48 E
Pata Peninsula 64d Bb 7.23N 151.35 E
Patchogue 44 Ke 40.46N 73.01W
Pate 36 Hc 2.08S 41.00 E
Patea 62 Fc 39.46S 174.29 E
Patea 62 Fc 39.46S 174.30 E
Pategi 34 Gd 8.44N 5.45 E
Patensie 37 Cf 33.46S 24.49 E
Paternò 14 Jm 37.34N 15.54 E
Paterson 43 Mc 40.55N 74.10W
Paterson Inlet 62 Bg 46.55S 168.00 E
Paterson Range 59 Ed 21.45S 122.05 E
Pathānkot 25 Fb 32.17N 75.39 E
Pathfinder Reservoir 46 Le 42.30N 106.50W
Pathfinder Seamount (EN) 40 Kf 50.55N 143.15W
Pathiu 25 Jf 10.41N 99.20 E
Patia, Río- 54 Cc 2.13N 78.40W
Patiāla 25 Fb 30.19N 76.24 E
Patiño, Estero- 55 Cg 24.05S 59.55W
Patio 65e Db 16.35S 151.29W
Pati Point 64c Ba 13.36N 144.57 E
Pătîrlagele 15 Jd 45.19N 26.21 E
Pativilca 54 Cf 10.42S 77.47W
Pátmos 15 Jl 37.19N 26.34 E
Pátmos 15 Jl 37.20N 26.33 E
Patna 22 Kg 25.36N 85.07 E
Patnos 24 Jc 39.14N 42.52 E
Pato Branco 56 Jc 26.13S 52.40W
Patom Plateau (EN)= Patomskoje Nagorje 20 Ge 59.00N 115.30 E
Patomskoje Nagorje=Patom Plateau (EN) 20 Ge 59.00N 115.30 E
Patos 53 Mf 7.01S 37.16W
Patos, Isla de- 50 Fg 10.38N 61.52W
Patos, Lagoa dos- 52 Ki 31.06S 51.15W
Patos, Laguna de los- 55 Aj 30.25S 62.15W
Patos, Ribeirão dos- 55 Gd 18.58S 50.30W
Patos, Rio dos- [Braz.] 55 Da 13.33S 56.29W
Patos, Rio dos- [Braz.] 55 Hb 14.59S 48.46W
Patos de Minas 53 Lg 18.35S 46.32W
Patosi 15 Ci 40.38N 19.39 E
Patquia 56 Gd 30.03S 66.53W
Pátrai 6 Ih 38.15N 21.44 E
Patrai, Gulf of- (EN) = Patraïkós Kólpos 15 Ek 38.15N 21.30 E
Patraïkós Kólpos = Patrai, Gulf of- (EN) 15 Ek 38.15N 21.30 E
Patricio Lynch, Isla- 56 Eg 48.36S 75.26W
Patricios 55 Bl 35.27S 60.42W
Patrocínio 54 Ig 18.57S 46.59W
Patta Island 30 Li 2.07S 41.03 E
Pattani 25 Kg 6.51N 101.16 E
Patteson, Passage- 63b Db 15.26S 168.09 E
Patti 14 Il 38.08N 14.58 E
Patti, Golfo di- 14 Jl 38.10N 15.05 E
Patton Seamount (EN) 38 Dd 54.40N 150.30W
Pattullo, Mount- 42 Ee 56.14N 129.39W
Patu 54 Ke 6.06S 37.38W
Patuākhāli 25 Id 22.16N 90.18 E
Patuca, Punta- 49 Ef 15.51N 84.18W
Patuca, Río- 47 He 15.50N 84.18W
Pătulele 15 Fe 44.21N 22.47 E
Patutahi 62 Gc 38.37S 177.53 E
Patuxent Range 66 Qg 84.43S 64.30W
Pátzcuaro 48 Ih 19.31N 101.36W
Pau 11 Fk 43.18N 0.22W
Pau, Gave de- 11 Ek 43.33N 1.12W
Paucartambo 54 Df 13.18S 71.40W
Paucerne, Rio- 55 Ba 13.34S 61.14W
Pau dos Ferros 54 Ke 6.07S 38.10W
Pauillac 11 Fi 45.12N 0.45W
Pauini 54 Ee 7.40S 66.58W
Pauini, Rio- 54 Ee 7.47S 67.15W
Pauksa Taung 25 Ie 19.55N 94.18 E
Paulatuk 39 Gc 69.23N 124.00W
Paulaya, Río- 49 Ef 15.51N 85.06W
Paulding Bay 66 Ie 66.35S 123.00 E
Paulina Peak 46 Ee 43.41N 121.15W
Păuliş 15 Ec 46.07N 21.35 E
Paulistana 54 Je 8.09S 41.09W
Paulo Afonso 53 Mf 9.21S 38.14W
Paulo Afonso, Cachoeira de- 52 Mf 9.24S 38.12W
Pauls Valley 45 Hi 34.44N 97.13W
Paungde 25 Je 18.29N 95.30 E
Pavant Range 46 Ig 39.00N 112.15W
Pāveh 24 Le 35.03N 46.22 E
Pavia 14 De 45.10N 9.10 E
Pavilly 12 Ce 49.34N 0.58 E
Pāvilosta/Pavilosta 7 Eh 56.55N 21.13 E
Pavilosta/Pāvilosta 7 Eh 56.55N 21.13 E
Pavlikeni 15 If 43.14N 25.18 E
Pavlodar 22 Jd 52.18N 76.57 E
Pavlodarskaja Oblast [3] 19 He 52.00N 76.30 E
Pavlof Islands 40 Ge 55.15N 161.20W
Pavlof Volcano 40 Ge 55.24N 161.55W
Pavlograd 16 Ie 48.32N 35.53 E
Pavlovka 17 Hi 55.25N 56.33 E
Pavlovo 19 Ed 55.58N 43.04 E
Pavlov Seamount (EN) 20 Lf 50.40N 162.00 E
Pavlovsk 16 Ld 50.27N 40.08 E
Pavlovskaja 19 Df 46.06N 39.48 E
Pavullo nel Frignano 14 Ef 44.20N 10.50 E
Pavuvu 63a Dc 9.04S 159.08 E
Pawa 63a Ed 10.15S 161.44 E
Pawhuska 45 Hh 36.40N 96.20W
Pawnee 45 Hh 36.20N 96.48W
Pawnee River 45 Gg 38.10N 99.06W
Pawtucket 44 Le 41.53N 71.23W
Paximádhia, Nisídhes- 15 Ho 35.00N 24.35 E
Paxoí 15 Dj 39.12N 20.10 E
Paxson 40 Jd 63.02N 145.30W
Payakumbuk 26 Dg 0.14S 100.38 E
Payas, Cerro- 49 Ef 15.50N 85.00W
Payerne 14 Ad 46.49N 6.58 E
Payette 46 Gd 44.05N 116.57W
Payette 43 Dc 44.05N 116.56W
Payne, Baie- 42 Ke 59.55N 69.35W
Payne, Lac- 42 Ke 59.30N 74.00W
Paysandú [2] 55 Dk 32.00S 57.15W
Paysandú 53 Ki 32.19S 58.05W
Pays de Léon 11 Bf 48.28N 4.30W
Pays d'Othe 11 Jf 48.06N 3.37 E
Payson [Az.-U.S.] 46 Ji 34.14N 111.20W
Payson [Ut.-U.S.] 46 Jf 40.03N 111.44W
Payzawat/Jiashi 27 Cd 39.29N 76.39 E
Pāzanān 24 Mg 30.35N 49.59 E
Pazar 24 Ib 41.11N 40.53 E
Pazarbası Burun 24 Db 41.13N 30.17 E
Pazarcık 24 Gd 37.31N 37.19 E
Pazardžik 15 Hg 42.12N 24.20 E
Pazardžik [2] 15 Hg 42.12N 24.20 E
Pazarköy 15 Kj 39.51N 27.24 E
Pazaryeri 24 Cc 40.00N 29.54 E
Pazin 14 He 45.14N 13.56 E
Pčinja 15 Eh 41.49N 21.40 E
Pea 65b Ac 21.11S 175.14W
Peabirú 55 Ff 23.54S 52.20W
Peace Point 42 Ge 59.12N 112.33W
Peace River 39 Hd 56.14N 117.17W
Peace River [Can.] 38 Hd 56.14N 117.17W
Peace River [Fl.-U.S.] 44 Fl 26.55N 82.05W
Peachland 46 Fb 49.46N 119.44W
Peach Springs 46 Ii 35.32N 113.25W
Peacock Hills 42 Gc 66.05N 110.00W
Peak District 9 Lh 53.17N 1.45W
Peake Creek 59 He 28.05S 136.07 E
Peaked Mountain 44 Mb 46.34N 68.49W
Peale, Mount- 43 Fd 38.26N 109.14W
Pearl 45 Lb 48.42N 88.44W
Pearland 45 Il 29.34N 95.17W
Pearl and Hermes Reef 57 Jb 27.55N 175.45W
Pearl City 65a Db 21.23N 157.58W
Pearl Harbor 65a Cb 21.20N 158.00W
Pearl River 43 Je 30.11N 89.32W
Pearsall 45 Gl 28.53N 99.06W
Pearsoll Peak 46 De 42.18N 123.50W
Peary Channel 42 Ha 79.25N 101.00W
Peary Land 67 Me 82.40N 30.00W
Pease River 45 Gi 34.12N 99.07W
Pebane 37 Fc 17.14S 38.10 E
Pebas 54 Dd 3.20S 71.49W
Peć 15 Dg 42.39N 20.18 E
Peca 14 Id 46.29N 14.48 E
Peças, Ilha das- 55 Hg 25.26S 48.19W
Pecatonica River 45 Le 42.29N 89.03W
Pečeneževskoje Vodohranilišče 16 Jd 50.05N 36.50 E
Pečenga 6 Jb 69.33N 31.07 E
Pečenga 7 Hb 69.39N 31.27 E
Pechea 15 Kd 45.38N 27.48 E
Pechora (EN)=Pečora 5 Lb 68.13N 54.10 E
Pechora (EN)=Pečora 6 Lb 65.10N 57.11 E
Pechora Bay (EN)= Pečorskaja Guba 19 Fb 68.40N 54.45 E
Pechora Sea (EN)= Pečorskoje More 19 Fb 69.45N 54.30 E
Pecica 15 Ec 46.10N 21.04 E
Peçin 15 Kl 37.19N 27.45 E
Peckelsheim, Willebadessen- 12 Lc 51.36N 9.08 E
Pečora=Pechora (EN) 6 Lb 65.10N 57.11 E
Pečora=Pechora (EN) 5 Lb 68.13N 54.10 E
Pecora, Capo- 14 Ck 39.27N 8.23 E
Pečorskaja Guba=Pechora Bay (EN) 19 Fb 68.40N 54.45 E
Pečorskoje More=Pechora Sea (EN) 19 Fb 69.45N 54.30 E
Pečory 7 Gh 57.49N 27.38 E
Pecos 43 Ge 31.25N 103.30W
Pecos 38 Ig 29.42N 101.22W
Pecos Plain 43 Ge 33.20N 104.30W
Pécs 6 Hf 46.05N 18.14 E
Pécs [2] 10 Oj 46.06N 18.15 E
Pedasí 49 Gj 7.32N 80.02W
Pedder, Lake- 59 Jh 43.00S 146.15 E
Peddie 37 Df 33.14S 27.07 E
Pededze 8 Lh 56.53N 27.01 E
Pedernales [Dom.Rep.] 49 Ld 18.02N 71.45W
Pedernales [Ven.] 50 Eh 9.58N 62.16W
Pedernales, Salar de- 56 Gc 26.15S 69.10W
Pedja Jõgi 8 Lf 58.20N 26.10 E
Pêdo Shankou 27 Df 29.12N 83.26 E
Pedra Azul 54 Jg 16.01S 41.16W
Pedra Branca 54 Ke 5.27S 39.43W
Pedra do Sino 55 Kf 22.27S 43.03W
Pedra Lume 32 Cf 16.46N 22.54W
Pedras, Rio das- 55 Ia 13.30S 47.09W
Pedras Altas, Coxilha- 55 Fj 31.45S 53.35W
Pedregal 54 Da 11.01N 70.08W
Pedreiras 54 Jd 4.34S 44.39W
Pedriceña 48 He 25.06N 103.47W
Pedrizas, Puerto de las- 13 Hh 36.55N 4.30W
Pedro Afonso 54 Ie 8.59S 48.11W
Pedro Bank (EN) 49 He 17.00N 78.30W
Pedro Betancourt 49 Gb 22.44N 81.17W
Pedro Cays 47 Ie 17.00N 77.50W
Pedro de Valdivia 56 Gb 22.37S 69.38W
Pedro Gomes 55 Ed 18.04S 54.32W
Pedro Gonzáles, Isla- 49 Hi 8.24N 79.06W
Pedro II 54 Jd 4.25S 41.28W
Pedro II, Ilha- 54 Ec 1.10N 66.44W
Pedro Juan Caballero 56 Ib 22.34S 55.37W
Pedro Leopoldo 55 Jd 19.38S 44.03W
Pedro Luro 56 He 39.29S 62.41W
Pedro Lustoza 55 Gg 25.49S 51.51W
Pedro Montoya 48 Jg 21.38N 99.49W
Pedro Osorio 56 Jd 31.51S 52.45W
Pedro R. Fernández 55 Ci 28.45S 58.39W
Pedro Severo 55 Ec 17.40S 54.02W
Pedroso, Sierra del- 13 Gf 38.35N 5.35W
Peebles 9 Jf 55.39N 3.12W
Pee Dee River 38 Lf 33.21N 79.16W
Peekskill 44 Ke 41.18N 73.56W
Peel 38 Fc 67.37N 134.40W
Peel 11 Lc 51.25N 5.50 E
Peel 9 Ig 54.13N 4.40W
Peel Sound 42 Hb 73.00N 96.00W
Peene 10 Jb 54.09N 13.46 E
Peer 12 Hc 51.08N 5.28 E
Peera Peera Poolanna Lake 59 He 26.30S 138.00 E
Peetz 45 Ef 40.58N 103.07W
Pegasus, Port- 62 Bg 47.10S 167.40 E
Pegasus Bay 61 Dh 43.20S 172.50 E
Pegnitz 10 Gg 49.29N 11.00 E
Pegnitz 10 Hg 49.45N 11.33 E
Pego 13 Lf 38.51N 0.07W
Pegtymel 20 Mc 69.47N 174.00 E
Pegu 22 Lh 17.30N 96.30 E
Pegu [3] 25 Je 17.52N 95.40 E
Pegu Yoma 21 Lh 19.00N 95.50 E
Pegwell Bay 12 Dc 51.18N 1.23 E
Pehčevo 15 Fh 41.46N 22.54 E
Pehlivanköy 15 Jh 41.21N 26.55 E
Pehuajó 56 He 35.48S 61.53W
Pei-ching Shih→Beijing Shi [4] 27 Kc 40.15N 116.30 E
Peine 10 Gd 52.19N 10.14 E
Peipsi järv=Peipus, Lake- (EN) 5 Id 58.45N 27.30 E
Peipus, Lake- (EN)= Čudskoje Ozero 5 Id 58.45N 27.30 E
Peipus, Lake- (EN)=Peipsi järv 5 Id 58.45N 27.30 E
Peixe 54 If 12.03S 48.32W
Peixe, Lagoa do- 55 Gj 31.18S 51.00W
Peixe, Rio do- [Braz.] 55 Ge 21.31S 51.58W
Peixe, Rio do- [Braz.] 55 Gb 14.06S 50.51W
Peixe, Rio do- [Braz.] 55 Hc 17.37S 48.29W
Peixe, Rio do- [Braz.] 55 Fc 16.32S 52.38W
Peixe, Rio do- [Braz.] 55 Gh 27.27S 51.54W
Peixe de Couro, Rio- 55 Ec 17.21S 55.29W
Peixes, Rio dos- 55 Hb 15.10S 49.30W
Peixian (Yunhe) 28 Dg 34.44N 116.56 E
Peixoto, Represa de- 54 Ih 20.30S 46.30W
Pejantan, Pulau- 26 Ef 0.07N 107.14 E
Pejde/Pöide 8 Jf 58.30N 22.50 E
Pek 15 Ee 44.46N 21.33 E
Pekalongan 26 Eh 6.53S 109.40 E
Pekan 26 Df 3.30N 103.25 E
Pekin 43 Jc 40.35N 89.40W
Peking (EN)=Beijing 22 Nf 39.55N 116.23 E
Pekulnei, Hrebet- 20 Mc 66.30N 176.00 E
Pelabuhanratu 26 Eh 6.59S 106.33 E
Pelagie, Isole- 5 Hh 35.40N 12.40 E
Pelagonija 15 Eh 41.05N 21.30 E
Pélagos 15 Hj 39.20N 24.05 E
Pelaihari 26 Fg 3.48S 114.45 E
Pelat, Mont- 11 Mj 44.16N 6.42 E
Pelawanbesar 26 Gf 1.10N 117.54 E
Pélé 63b Dc 17.30S 168.24 E
Peleaga, Vîrful- 15 Fd 45.22N 22.53 E
Peleduj 20 Ge 59.40N 112.38 E
Pelée, Montagne- 47 Le 14.48N 61.10W
Pelee, Point- 44 Fe 41.54N 82.30W
Pelee Island 44 Fe 41.46N 82.39W
Peleliu Island 57 Ed 7.01N 134.15 E
Peleng, Pulau- 26 Hg 1.20S 123.10 E
Pelhřimov 10 Lg 49.26N 15.13 E
Pelican Lake 45 Gb 49.20N 99.35W
Pelicanpunt 37 Ad 22.54S 14.26 E
Peligre, Lac de- 49 Ld 18.52N 71.56W
Pelinaion Óros 15 Ik 38.32N 26.00 E
Pelješac 14 Lh 42.55N 17.25 E
Pelkosenniemi 7 Gc 67.07N 27.30 E
Pella 45 Jf 41.25N 92.55W
Pélla 15 Fi 40.46N 22.34 E
Pellegrini 56 He 36.16S 63.09W
Pellice 14 Bf 44.50N 7.38 E
Pellinge/Pellinki 8 Kd 60.15N 25.50 E
Pellinki/Pellinge 8 Kd 60.15N 25.50 E
Pello 7 Fc 66.47N 24.01 E
Pellworm 10 Eb 54.30N 8.40 E
Pelly 38 Fc 62.47N 137.19W
Pelly Bay 42 Ic 68.50N 90.10W
Pelly Bay 39 Kc 68.52N 89.55W
Pelly Crossing 42 Dd 62.50N 136.35W
Pelly Mountains 42 Ed 61.30N 132.00W
Peloncillo Mountains 46 Kj 32.15N 109.10W
Pelón de Nado, Cerro- 48 Jg 20.05N 99.55W
Peloponnesus (EN)= Pelopónnisos 5 Ih 37.40N 22.00 E
Peloponnesus (EN) = Pelopónnisos 15 El 37.40N 22.00 E
Pelopónnisos [2] 15 El 37.40N 22.00 E
Pelopónnisos = Peloponnesus (EN) 15 El 37.40N 22.00 E
Pelopónnisos= Peloponnesus (EN) 5 Ih 37.40N 22.00 E
Peloritani 14 Jl 38.05N 15.20 E
Peloro, Capo- o Faro, Punta del- 14 Jl 38.16N 15.39 E
Pelotas 53 Ki 31.46S 52.20W
Pelotas, Rio- 56 Jc 27.28S 51.55W
Pelplin 10 Oc 53.56N 18.42 E
Pelvoux, Massif du- 5 Gg 44.55N 6.20 E
Pelym 19 Gd 59.40N 63.05 E
Pelymskí Tuman, Ozero- 17 Kf 60.05N 63.05 E
Pemalang 26 Eh 6.54S 109.22 E
Pemar/Paimio 8 Jd 60.27N 22.42 E
Pematangsiantar 22 Li 2.57N 99.03 E
Pemba [3] 36 Hd 5.02S 40.00 E
Pemba [Moz.] 31 Lj 12.57S 40.30 E
Pemba [Zam.] 36 Ef 16.31S 27.22 E
Pemba Channel 36 Gd 5.10S 39.20 E
Pemba Island 30 Ki 5.10S 39.48 E
Pemberton [Austl.] 59 Df 34.28S 116.01 E
Pemberton [B.C.-Can.] 46 Da 50.20N 122.48W
Pembina 42 Gf 54.45N 114.17W
Pembina 43 Hb 48.58N 97.15W
Pembina River 43 Hb 48.56N 97.15W
Pembroke [Ont.-Can.] 42 Jg 45.49N 77.07W
Pembroke [Wales-U.K.] 9 Ij 51.41N 4.55W
Pembuang 26 Fg 3.24S 112.33 E
Peña, Sierra de la- 13 Lb 42.31N 0.38W
Peñafiel 13 Dc 41.12N 8.17W
Peñafiel 13 Hc 41.36N 4.07W
Peñagolosa/Penyagolosa 13 Ld 40.13N 0.21W
Peña Gorda, Cerro- 48 Gg 20.40N 104.55W
Peñalara 13 Id 40.51N 3.57W
Penalva 54 Id 3.18S 45.10W
Penamacor 13 Ed 40.10N 7.10W
Peña Nevada, Cerro- 38 Jg 23.46N 99.52W
Penápolis 55 Ge 21.24S 50.04W
Peñaranda de Bracamonte 13 Gd 40.54N 5.12W
Peñarroya 13 Ld 40.28N 0.43W
Peñarroya-Pueblonuevo 13 Gf 38.18N 5.16W
Peñas, Cabo de- 5 Fg 43.39N 5.51W
Penas, Golfo de- 52 Ij 47.22S 74.50W
Peñas, Punta- 54 Fa 10.44N 61.51W
Peñasco, Río- 45 Dj 32.45N 104.19W
Pendé 35 Ad 9.07N 16.26 E
Pendembu [S.L.] 34 Cd 9.06N 12.12W
Pendembu [S.L.] 34 Cd 8.06N 10.42W
Pendik 15 Mi 40.53N 29.13 E
Pendjari 34 Fc 10.54N 0.51 E
Pendle Hill 9 Kh 53.52N 2.17W
Pendleton 39 He 45.40N 118.47W
Pendolo 26 Hg 2.05S 120.42 E
Pend Oreille Lake 43 Db 48.10N 116.11W
Pend Oreille River 43 Db 49.04N 117.37W
Pendžikent 19 Gh 39.29N 67.38 E
Peneda 13 Dc 41.58N 8.15W
Penedo 54 Kf 10.17S 36.36W
Penetanguishene 44 Hc 44.47N 79.55W
Penganga 25 Fe 19.53N 79.09 E
Pengcheng 27 Jd 36.25N 114.08 E
Penge 36 Dd 5.31S 24.37 E
Pengho Jiao 27 Jc 16.03N 112.35 E
Penghu Liehtao= Pescadores (EN) 27 Kg 23.30N 119.30 E
Penglai (Dengzhou) 27 Ld 37.44N 120.45 E
Pengshui 27 If 29.17N 108.13 E
Pengze 27 Kf 29.52N 116.34 E
Penha 55 Hh 26.46S 48.39W
Penhalonga 37 Ec 18.54S 32.40 E
Penibético, Sistema- 13 Ig 37.00N 3.30W
Peniche 13 Ce 39.21N 9.23W
Penicuik 9 Jf 55.50N 3.14W
Penida, Nusa- 26 Gh 8.44S 115.32 E
Peninsula Ibérica=Iberian Peninsula (EN) 5 Fg 40.00N 4.00W
Peñíscola 13 Md 40.21N 0.25 E
Penisola Salentina= Salentine Peninsula (EN) 5 Hg 40.30N 18.00 E
Penitente, Serra do- 54 Ie 8.45S 46.20W
Pénjamo 48 Ig 20.26N 101.44W
Penju, Kepulauan- 26 Ih 5.22S 127.46 E
Penmarch, Pointe de- 11 Bg 47.48N 4.22W
Penne 14 Hh 42.27N 13.55 E
Penne, Punta- 14 Lj 40.41N 17.56 E
Pennell Coast 66 Kf 71.00S 167.00 E
Penner 21 Kh 14.35N 80.10 E
Penn Hills 44 He 40.28N 79.53W
Pennines 5 Fe 54.10N 2.05W
Pennsylvania [2] 43 Lc 40.45N 77.30W
Penn Yan 44 Id 42.41N 77.03W
Penny Ice Cap 42 Kc 67.00N 65.10W
Penny Strait 42 Ha 76.35N 97.10W
Peno 7 Hh 56.57N 32.45 E
Penobscot Bay 44 Mc 44.15N 68.52W
Penobscot River 43 Nc 44.30N 68.50W
Penola 59 Ig 37.23S 140.50 E
Peñón del Rosario, Cerro- 48 Jh 19.40N 98.12W
Penong 58 Eh 31.55S 133.01 E
Penonomé 47 Hg 8.31N 80.22W
Pénot, Mont- 63b Cc 16.20S 167.31 E
Penrhyn Atoll 57 Le 9.00S 158.00W
Penrith 9 Kg 54.40N 2.44W
Penrith, Sydney- 59 Kf 33.45S 150.42 E
Pensacola 39 Kf 30.25N 87.13W
Pensacola Mountains 66 Rg 83.45S 55.00W
Pensacola Seamount (EN) 57 Lc 18.17N 157.20W
Pensamiento 55 Bb 14.44S 61.35W
Pensiangan 26 Gf 4.33N 116.19 E
Pentecôte, Ile- 57 Hf 15.45S 168.10 E
Penticton 42 Fg 49.30N 119.35W
Pentland 59 Jd 20.32S 145.24 E
Pentland Firth 9 Jc 58.44N 3.13W
Pentland Hills 9 Jf 55.48N 3.23W
Penwith 9 Hk 50.13N 5.40W
Penyagolosa/Peñagolosa 13 Ld 40.13N 0.21W
Penza 6 Ke 53.13N 45.00 E
Penzance 6 Ff 50.07N 5.33W
Penzenskaja Oblast [3] 19 Ee 53.15N 44.40 E
Penzhina Bay (EN)= Penžinskaja Guba 20 Ld 61.00N 163.00 E
Penžina 21 Sc 62.28N 165.18 E
Penžinskaja Guba= Penzhina Bay (EN) 20 Ld 61.00N 163.00 E
Penžinski Hrebet 20 Ld 62.15N 166.35 E
Peoples Creek 46 Kb 48.24N 108.19W
Peoria 39 Ke 40.42N 89.36W
Peoúia 24 Ee 34.53N 32.23 E
Pepa 36 Ed 7.42S 29.47 E
Pepel 34 Cd 8.35N 13.03W
Peperiguaçu, Rio- 55 Fh 27.10S 53.50W
Peqini 15 Ch 41.03N 19.45 E
Pequena, Lagoa- 55 Fj 31.36S 52.04W
Pequiri, Rio- 54 Gg 17.23S 55.38W
Perabumulih 26 Dg 3.27S 104.15 E
Perälä 8 Ib 62.28N 21.36 E
Perales, Puerto de- 13 Fd 40.15N 6.41W
Pérama 15 Hn 35.22N 24.42 E
Peräseinäjoki 8 Jb 62.34N 23.04 E
Perche, Col de la- 11 Il 42.30N 2.06 E
Perche, Collines du- 11 Gf 48.25N 0.40 E
Percival Lakes 59 Ed 21.25S 125.00 E
Percy Islands 59 Kd 21.40S 150.15 E
Perdasdefogu 14 Dk 39.41N 9.26 E
Perdida, Sierra- 48 Hd 27.30N 103.30W
Perdido, Monte- 5 Gg 42.40N 0.05 E
Perdido, Rio- 55 Df 22.10S 57.33W
Perdizes 55 Id 19.21S 47.17W
Perečin 10 Sh 48.44N 22.29 E
Pereginskoje 16 De 48.49N 24.12 E
Pereira 54 Cc 4.48N 75.42W
Pereira Barreto 56 Jb 20.38S 51.07W
Perejaslav-Hmelnicki 16 Gd 50.04N 31.27 E
Perejil, Isla de- 13 Ig 35.55N 5.26W
Pereljub 16 Qd 51.52N 50.20 E
Peremennyj, Cape- 66 He 66.08S 105.30 E
Peremyšliany 10 Ug 49.38N 24.35 E
Perenjori 59 De 29.26S 116.17 E
Pereščepino 16 Ie 48.59N 35.22 E
Pereslavl-Zalesski 7 Jh 56.45N 38.55 E
Peretu 15 Ie 44.03N 25.05 E
Peretyčiha 20 Ig 47.10N 138.15 E
Perevolocki 16 Sd 51.51N 54.15 E
Pergamino 56 Hd 33.53S 60.35W
Pergamon 15 Kj 39.08N 27.13 E
Perge 24 Dd 37.00N 30.10 E
Pergine Valsugana 14 Fd 46.04N 11.14 E
Pergola 14 Gg 43.34N 12.50 E
Perham 45 Ic 46.36N 95.34W
Perho 7 Fe 63.13N 24.25 E
Periam 15 Dc 46.03N 20.52 E
Péribonca, Rivière- 42 Kg 48.44N 72.06W
Perico 56 Hb 24.23S 65.00W
Pericos 48 Fe 25.03N 107.42W
Périgord 11 Gi 45.00N 0.30 E
Perigoso, Canal- 54 Ic 0.05N 49.40W
Périgueux 11 Gi 45.11N 0.43 E
Perijá, Sierra de- 52 Ie 10.00N 73.00W
Peristerá 15 Gj 39.12N 23.59 E
Perito Moreno 53 Ij 46.36S 70.56W
Perkam, Tanjung-=Urville, Cape d'- (EN) 26 Kg 1.28S 137.54 E
Perković 14 Kg 43.41N 16.06 E
Perlas, Archipiélago de las- 47 Ig 8.25N 79.00W
Perlas, Cayos de- 49 Fg 12.28N 83.28W
Perlas, Laguna de- 49 Fg 12.30N 83.40W
Perlas, Punta de- 49 Fg 12.23N 83.30W
Perleberg 10 Hc 53.04N 11.52 E
Perlez 15 Dd 45.12N 20.23 E
Perm 6 Ld 58.00N 56.15 E
Përmeti 15 Di 40.14N 20.21 E
Permskaja Oblast [3] 19 Fd 59.00N 57.00 E
Pernambuco [2] 54 Ke 8.30S 37.30W
Pernik 15 Gg 42.36N 23.02 E
Pernik [2] 15 Fg 42.35N 22.50 E
Perniö/Bjärna 7 Ff 60.12N 23.08 E
Péronne 11 Ie 49.56N 2.56 E
Perote 48 Kh 19.34N 97.14W
Perpignan 6 Gg 42.41N 2.53 E
Perro, Laguna del- 45 Di 34.40N 105.57W
Perros-Guirec 11 Cf 48.49N 3.27W
Perry [Fl.-U.S.] 44 Fj 30.07N 83.35W
Perry [Ga.-U.S.] 44 Fi 32.27N 83.44W
Perry [Ia.-U.S.] 45 If 41.50N 94.06W
Perry [Ok.-U.S.] 45 Hh 36.17N 97.17W
Perry Lake 45 Ig 39.20N 95.30W
Perryton 45 Fh 36.24N 100.48W
Perryville 40 He 55.54N 159.10W
Persan 12 Ee 49.09N 2.16 E
Perşani, Munţii- 15 Id 45.40N 25.15 E
Persberg 8 Fe 59.45N 14.15 E
Persembe 24 Gb 41.04N 37.46 E
Persepolis 24 Oh 29.57N 52.52 E
Perseverancia 54 Ff 14.44S 62.48W
Persian Gulf (EN)=Al-Khalīj al-'Arabī 21 Hg 27.00N 51.00 E
Persian Gulf (EN)=Khalīj-e Fārs 21 Hg 27.00N 51.00 E
Perstorp 8 Eh 56.08N 13.23 E
Pertek 24 Hc 38.50N 39.22 E
Perth [Austl.] 58 Ch 31.56S 115.50 E
Perth [Ont.-Can.] 44 Ic 44.54N 76.15W
Perth [Scot.-U.K.] 9 Je 56.24N 3.28W
Perth Amboy 44 Je 40.32N 74.17W
Perth-Andover 44 Nb 46.44N 67.42W
Perth-Armadale 59 Df 32.09S 116.00 E
Perth-Fremantle 59 Df 32.03S 115.45 E
Perth-Kalamunda 59 Df 31.57S 116.03 E
Perth-Mundaring 59 Df 31.54S 116.10 E
Perthus, Col de-/Portús, Coll del- 13 Ob 42.28N 2.51 E
Perthus, Col du- 13 Ob 42.28N 2.51 E
Pertuis 11 Lk 43.41N 5.30 E
Pertusato, Capo- 11a Bb 41.21N 9.11 E
Perú [1] 53 Ig 10.00S 76.00W
Peru [Il.-U.S.] 45 Lf 41.20N 89.08W
Peru [In.-U.S.] 44 De 40.45N 86.04W
Perú, Altiplano del- 54 Df 15.00S 72.00W
Peruaçu, Rio- 55 Jb 15.11S 44.07W
Peru Basin (EN) 3 Mk 17.00S 90.00W
Peru-Chile Trench (EN) 3 Nl 20.00S 73.00W
Perugia 6 Hg 43.08N 12.22 E
Perugorria 55 Ci 29.20S 58.37W
Peruibe 55 Ig 24.19S 47.00W
Perušić 14 Jf 44.39N 15.22 E
Péruwelz 12 Fd 50.31N 3.35 E

Index Symbols

[1] Independent Nation
[2] State, Region
[3] District, County
[4] Municipality
[5] Colony, Dependency
Continent
Physical Region
Historical or Cultural Region
Mount, Mountain
Volcano
Hill
Mountains, Mountain Range
Hills, Escarpment
Plateau, Upland
Pass, Gap
Plain, Lowland
Delta
Salt Flat
Valley, Canyon
Crater, Cave
Karst Features
Depression
Polder
Desert, Dunes
Forest, Woods
Heath, Steppe
Oasis
Cape, Point
Coast, Beach
Cliff
Peninsula
Isthmus
Sandbank
Island
Atoll
Rock, Reef
Islands, Archipelago
Rocks, Reefs
Coral Reef
Well, Spring
Geyser
River, Stream
Waterfall Rapids
River Mouth, Estuary
Lake
Salt Lake
Intermittent Lake
Reservoir
Swamp, Pond
Canal
Glacier
Ice Shelf, Pack Ice
Ocean
Sea
Gulf, Bay
Strait, Fjord
Lagoon
Bank
Seamount
Tablemount
Ridge
Shelf
Basin
Escarpment, Sea Scarp
Fracture
Trench, Abyss
National Park, Reserve
Point of Interest
Recreation Site
Cave, Cavern
Historic Site
Ruins
Wall, Walls
Church, Abbey
Temple
Scientific Station
Airport
Port
Lighthouse
Mine
Tunnel
Dam, Bridge

Name	Page	Grid	Lat.	Long.
Pervari	24	Jd	37.54N	42.36 E
Pervomajsk [R.S.F.S.R.]	19	Ee	54.52N	43.48 E
Pervomajsk [Ukr.-U.S.S.R.]	16	Ke	48.36N	38.32 E
Pervomajsk [Ukr.-U.S.S.R.]	19	Df	48.03N	30.52 E
Pervomajsk [Bye.-U.S.S.R.]	10	Vc	53.52N	25.33 E
Pervomajskij [Kaz.-U.S.S.R.]	19	Ie	50.15N	81.59 E
Pervomajskij [R.S.F.S.R.]	16	Lc	53.18N	40.15 E
Pervomajskij [R.S.F.S.R.]	19	Ec	64.26N	40.48 E
Pervomajskij [R.S.F.S.R.]	17	Ji	54.52N	61.08 E
Pervomajskij [R.S.F.S.R.]	16	Sd	51.34N	54.59 E
Pervomajskij [Ukr.-U.S.S.R.]	16	Je	49.24N	36.15 E
Pervouralsk	19	Fd	57.00N	60.00 E
Pervy Kurilski Proliv	20	Kf	50.50N	156.50 E
Perwez/Perwijs	12	Gd	50.37N	4.49 E
Perwijs/Perwez	12	Gd	50.37N	4.49 E
Pes	7	Ig	59.10N	35.18 E
Peša	17	Cc	66.50N	47.32 E
Pesaro	14	Gg	43.54N	12.55 E
Pescadores (EN)=Penghu Liehtao	27	Kg	23.30N	119.30 E
Pescadores, Punta-	48	Ef	23.45N	109.45W
Pesčany, Mys-	16	Qh	43.10N	51.18 E
Pesčany, Ostrov	20	Gb	74.20N	115.55 E
Pescara	14	Ih	42.28N	14.13 E
Pescara	6	Hg	42.28N	14.13 E
Pescasseroli	14	Hi	41.48N	13.47 E
Peschici	14	Ki	41.57N	16.01 E
Pescia	14	Eg	43.54N	10.41 E
Pescocostanzo	14	Ii	41.53N	14.04 E
Peshāwar	22	Jf	34.01N	71.33 E
Peshkopia	15	Dh	41.41N	20.26 E
Pesio	14	Bf	44.28N	7.53 E
Peskovka	7	Mg	59.03N	52.22 E
Pesmes	11	Lg	47.17N	5.34 E
Pesočny	8	Nd	60.05N	30.20 E
Peso da Régua	13	Ec	41.10N	7.47W
Pesqueira	54	Ke	8.22S	36.42W
Pesqueria, Río-	48	Je	25.54N	99.11W
Pessac	11	Fj	44.48N	0.37W
Pest [2]	10	Pi	47.25N	19.20 E
Pešter	15	Df	43.05N	20.02 E
Peštera	15	Hg	42.02N	24.18 E
Pestovo	19	Dd	58.36N	35.47 E
Petacalco, Bahía de-	47	De	17.57N	102.05W
Petah Tiqwa	24	Ff	32.05N	34.53 E
Petäjävesi	8	Kb	62.15N	25.12 E
Petal	45	Lk	31.21N	89.17W
Petalioi	15	Hl	38.01N	24.17 E
Petalioi, Gulf of- (EN) = Petalión, Kólpos-	15	Hk	38.00N	24.05 E
Petalión, Kólpos- = Petalioi, Gulf of- (EN)	15	Hk	38.00N	24.05 E
Petaluma	46	Dg	38.14N	122.39W
Pétange/Petingen	12	He	49.33N	5.53 E
Petare	54	Ea	10.29N	66.49W
Petatlán	48	Ii	17.31N	101.16W
Petatlán, Río-	48	Fd	26.09N	107.45W
Petauke	36	Fe	14.15S	31.20 E
Petén	47	Fe	16.15N	89.50W
Petén [3]	49	Be	16.50N	90.00W
Petén Itzá, Lago-	49	Ce	16.59N	89.50W
Petenwell Lake	45	Ld	44.05N	89.45W
Peterborough [Austl.]	59	Hf	32.58S	138.50 E
Peterborough [Eng.-U.K.]	9	Mi	52.35N	0.15W
Peterborough [Ont.-Can.]	42	Jh	44.18N	78.19W
Peterhead	9	Ld	57.30N	1.46W
Peter I, Oy-	66	Pe	68.47S	90.35W
Peter Island	51a	Db	18.22N	64.35W
Peterlee	9	Lg	54.46N	1.19W
Petermann Gletscher	41	Fb	80.45N	61.00W
Petermann Ranges	59	Fd	25.00S	129.45 E
Petermanns Bjerg	67	Md	73.10N	28.00W
Peter Pond Lake	42	Ge	55.55N	108.40W
Petersberg	10	He	51.35N	11.57 E
Petersburg [Ak.-U.S.]	40	Me	56.49N	132.57W
Petersburg [In.-U.S.]	44	Df	38.30N	87.16W
Petersburg [Va.-U.S.]	43	Ld	37.14N	77.24W
Petersburg [W.V.-U.S.]	44	Hf	39.01N	79.09W
Petersfield	9	Mk	51.00N	0.56W
Petershagen	12	Kb	52.23N	8.58 E
Peter the Great Bay (EN)= Petra Velikogo, Zaliv-	21	Pe	42.40N	132.00 E
Petilia Policastro	14	Kk	39.07N	16.47 E
Petingen/Pétange	12	He	49.33N	5.53 E
Petit-Bourg	51e	Ab	16.12N	61.36W
Petit-Canal	51e	Bb	16.23N	61.29W
Petit Canouan	51n	Bb	12.47N	61.17W
Petit Cul-de-Sac Marin	51e	Ab	16.12N	61.33W
Petit Kabylie	13	Rh	36.35N	5.25 E
Petite Rivière de l'Artibonite	49	Kd	19.08N	72.29W
Petites Pyrénées	11	Hk	43.05N	1.10 E
Petite-Terre, Iles de la-	51e	Bb	16.10N	61.07W
Petit-Goâve	49	Kd	18.26N	72.52W
Petit Martinique Island	51p	Ca	12.32N	61.22W
Petit-Mécatina, Rivière du-	42	Lf	50.39N	59.25W
Petit Morin	11	Jf	48.56N	3.07 E
Petit Mustique Island	51n	Bb	12.51N	61.13W
Petit Nevis Island	51n	Bb	12.58N	61.15W
Petitot	42	Fd	60.14N	123.29W
Petit Saint-Bernard, Col du-	14	Ae	45.40N	6.55 E
Petit Saint Vincent Island	51n	Bb	12.33N	61.23W
Petit Savanne	51g	Bb	15.15N	61.17W
Petitsikapau Lake	42	Kf	54.40N	66.25W
Petkula	7	Gc	67.40N	26.41 E
Petlalcingo	48	Kh	18.05N	97.54W
Peto	47	Gd	20.08N	88.55W
Petorca	56	Fd	32.15S	71.00W
Petoskey	44	Ec	45.22N	84.57W
Petra	24	Fg	30.19N	35.29 E
Petralia Soprana	14	Im	37.47N	14.06 E
Petra Pervogo, Hrebet-	18	He	39.00N	71.10 E
Petra Velikogo, Zaliv- = Peter the Great Bay (EN)	21	Pe	42.40N	132.00 E
Petre, Point-	44	Id	43.50N	77.09W
Petre Bay	62	Je	43.55S	176.40W
Petrel	66	Re	63.28S	56.17W
Petrela	15	Ch	41.15N	19.51 E
Petrella Tifernina	14	Ii	41.41N	14.42 E
Petrič	15	Gh	41.24N	23.13 E
Pétrie, Récif-	61	Bc	18.30S	164.20 E
Petrikov	16	Fc	52.08N	28.31 E
Petrila	15	Gd	45.27N	23.25 E
Petrinja	14	Ke	45.27N	16.17 E
Petrodvorec	7	Gg	59.53N	29.50 E
Petrólea	54	Db	8.30N	72.35W
Petrolia	44	Fd	42.52N	82.09W
Petrolina	54	Je	9.24S	40.30W
Petrolina de Goiás	55	Hc	16.06S	49.20W
Petronanski prohod	15	Gf	43.08N	23.08 E
Petronell	14	Kb	48.07N	16.51 E
Petropavlovka	20	Ff	50.38N	105.19 E
Petropavlovsk	22	Id	54.54N	69.06 E
Petropavlovsk-Kamčatski	22	Rd	53.01N	158.39 E
Petrópolis	53	Lh	22.31S	43.10W
Petroşani	15	Gd	45.25N	23.22 E
Petrovac [Yugo.]	15	Bg	42.12N	18.57 E
Petrovac [Yugo.]	15	Ee	44.22N	21.25 E
Petrova Gora	14	Je	45.17N	15.47 E
Petrovaradin	15	Cd	45.15N	19.53 E
Petrovka	15	Nc	46.55N	30.40 E
Petrovsk	19	Ee	52.18N	45.23 E
Petrovski Jam	7	Ie	63.18N	35.15 E
Petrovsk-Zabajkalski	22	Md	51.17N	108.50 E
Petrov Val	16	Nd	50.10N	45.12 E
Petrozavodsk	6	Jc	61.47N	34.20 E
Petuhovo	19	Gd	55.06N	67.58 E
Petuški	7	Ji	55.59N	39.28 E
Petworth	12	Bd	50.59N	0.36W
Peuetsagoe, Gunung-	26	Cf	4.55N	96.20 E
Peumo	56	Fd	34.24S	71.10W
Peureulak	26	Cf	4.48N	97.53 E
Pevek	22	Tc	69.42N	170.17 E
Pevensey	12	Cd	50.48N	0.21 E
Pevensey Bay	12	Cd	50.48N	0.22 E
Peza	7	Kd	65.34N	44.33 E
Pézenas	11	Jk	43.27N	3.25 E
Pezinok	10	Nh	48.18N	17.16 E
Pfaffenhofen an der Ilm	10	Hh	48.32N	11.31 E
Pfaffenhoffen	12	Jf	48.51N	7.37 E
Pfalz	12	Je	49.20N	7.57 E
Pfalzel, Trier-	12	Ie	49.46N	6.41 E
Pfälzer Bergland	10	Dg	49.35N	7.30 E
Pfälzer Wald	10	Dg	49.15N	7.50 E
Pfarrkirchen	10	Ih	48.26N	12.52 E
Pfinz	12	Ke	49.11N	8.25 E
Pfinztal	12	Ke	49.02N	8.30 E
Pforzheim an der Enz	10	Eh	48.53N	8.42 E
Pfrimm	12	Ke	49.39N	8.22 E
Pfullendorf	10	Fi	47.55N	9.15 E
Pfunds	12	Ed	46.58N	10.33 E
Pfungstadt	12	Ke	49.48N	8.36 E
Phalaborwa	37	Ed	23.55S	31.13 E
Phalodi	25	Ec	27.08N	72.22 E
Phangan, Ko-	25	Jg	9.45N	100.00 E
Phangnga	25	Jg	8.28N	98.32 E
Phan Ly Cham	25	Lf	11.13N	108.31 E
Phanom	25	Jg	8.49N	98.50 E
Phan Rang	25	Lf	11.34N	108.59 E
Phan Thiet	25	Lf	10.56N	108.06 E
Pharr	45	Gm	26.12N	98.11W
Phatthalung	25	Kg	7.38N	100.04 E
Phayao	25	Ke	18.07N	100.11 E
Phenix City	43	Je	32.29N	85.01W
Phet Buri	25	Jf	13.06N	99.56 E
Phetchabun, Thiu Khao-	25	Ke	16.20N	100.55 E
Phichit	25	Ke	16.24N	100.21 E
Philadelphia [Ms.-U.S.]	45	Lj	32.46N	89.07W
Philadelphia [Pa.-U.S.]	39	Lf	39.57N	75.07W
Philae	33	Fe	23.35N	32.52 E
Philip	45	Fd	44.02N	101.40W
Philippeville	11	Kd	50.12N	4.33 E
Philippi	44	Gf	39.08N	80.03W
Philippi (EN) = Filippoi	15	Hh	41.02N	24.18 E
Philippi, Lake-	59	Hd	24.20S	139.00 E
Philippi Glacier	66	Ge	66.45S	88.20 E
Philippine Basin (EN)	3	Ih	17.00N	132.00 E
Philippine Islands (EN)= Pilipinas	21	Oh	13.00N	122.00 E
Philippines (EN)=Pilipinas [1]	22	Oh	13.00N	122.00 E
Philippine Sea (EN)	21	Oh	20.00N	130.00 E
Philippine Trench (EN)	3	Ii	9.00N	127.00 E
Philippsburg	12	Ke	49.14N	8.27 E
Philipsburg [Mt.-U.S.]	46	Ic	46.20N	113.08W
Philipsburg [Neth.Ant.]	50	Ed	18.01N	63.04W
Philip Smith Mountains	40	Jc	68.30N	148.00W
Philipstown	37	Cf	30.26S	24.29 E
Phillipsburg	45	Gg	39.45N	99.19W
Philpots	42	Jb	74.55N	80.00W
Phitsanulok	22	Mh	16.49N	100.15 E
Phnom Penh (EN)=Phnum Pénh	22	Mh	11.33N	104.55 E
Phnum Pénh=Phnom Penh (EN)	22	Mh	11.33N	104.55 E
Phoenix	39	Hf	33.27N	112.05W
Phoenix→Rawaki Atoll	57	Je	3.43S	170.43W
Phoenix Islands	57	Je	4.00S	172.00W
Phôngsali	25	Kd	21.41N	102.06 E
Phrae	25	Ke	18.07N	100.11 E
Phra Nakhom Si Ayutthaya	22	Mh	14.21N	100.33 E
Phrygia	15	Mk	38.30N	29.50 E
Phu Cuong	25	Lf	10.58N	106.39 E
Phuket	22	Li	7.54N	98.24 E
Phuket, Ko-	21	Li	8.00N	98.20 E
Phulbani	25	Gd	20.28N	84.14 E
Phumĭ Mlu Prey	25	Lf	13.48N	105.16 E
Phumĭ Sâmraông	25	Kf	14.11N	103.31 E
Phu My	25	Lf	14.10N	109.03 E
Phuoc Binh	25	Lf	11.50N	106.58 E
Phu Quoc, Dao-	25	Kf	10.12N	104.00 E
Phu Tho	25	Ld	21.24N	105.13 E
Phu Vinh	25	Lg	9.56N	106.20 E
Piaanu Pass	64d	Ab	7.20N	151.26 E
Piacenza	14	De	45.01N	9.40 E
Piana degli Albanesi	14	Hm	37.59N	13.17 E
Piana Mwanga	36	Ed	7.40S	28.10 E
Piancó	54	Ke	7.12S	37.57W
Pianguan	27	Jd	39.28N	111.32 E
Pianosa [It.]	14	Jh	42.15N	15.45 E
Pianosa [It.]	14	Eh	42.35N	10.05 E
Piaseczno	10	Rd	52.05N	21.01 E
Piaski	10	Se	51.08N	22.51 E
Piątek	10	Pd	52.05N	19.28 E
Piatra	15	If	43.49N	25.10 E
Piatra Neamţ	15	Jc	46.55N	26.20 E
Piatra Olt	15	He	44.22N	24.16 E
Piauí [2]	54	Je	7.00S	43.00W
Piauí, Rio-	52	Lf	6.38S	42.42W
Piave	5	Hf	45.32N	12.44 E
Piaxtla, Punta-	48	Ff	23.38N	106.50W
Piaxtla, Rio-	48	Ff	23.42N	106.49W
Piazza Armerina	14	Im	37.23N	14.22 E
Pibor	35	Ed	8.26N	33.13 E
Pibor Post	35	Ed	6.48N	33.08 E
Pica	56	Gb	20.30S	69.21W
Picachos, Cerro dos-	48	Bc	29.25N	114.10W
Picardie = Picardy (EN)	11	Je	50.00N	3.30 E
Picardy (EN) = Picardie	11	Je	50.00N	3.30 E
Picayune	45	Lk	30.26N	89.41W
Picentini, Monti-	14	Jj	40.45N	15.10 E
Pichanal	53	Jh	23.20S	64.15W
Pichilemu	56	Fd	34.23S	72.00W
Pichilingue	48	De	24.20N	110.20W
Pichna	10	Oe	51.50N	18.40 E
Pichones, Cayos-	49	Ff	15.45N	82.55W
Pichucalco	48	Mi	17.31N	93.04W
Pickering	9	Mg	54.14N	0.46W
Pickering, Vale of-	9	Mg	54.10N	0.45W
Pickle Lake	42	If	51.29N	90.10W
Pickwick Lake	44	Ch	34.55N	88.10W
Pico	30	Ee	38.28N	28.20W
Picos	53	Lf	7.05S	41.28W
Pico Truncado	56	Gg	46.48S	67.58W
Picquigny	11	Ie	49.57N	2.09 E
Picton	61	Dh	41.18S	174.00 E
Pictou	42	Lg	45.41N	62.43W
Picunda	16	Lh	43.12N	40.21 E
Pidurutalagala	21	Ki	7.00N	80.46 E
Piedecuesta	54	Db	6.59N	73.03W
Piedimonte Matese	14	Ii	41.20N	14.22 E
Piedmont [Al.-U.S.]	44	Ei	33.55N	85.37W
Piedmont [Mo.-U.S.]	45	Kh	37.09N	90.42W
Piedmont (EN) = Piemonte [2]	14	Be	45.00N	8.00 E
Piedmont Plateau	38	Kf	35.00N	81.00W
Piedra	13	Kc	41.19N	1.48W
Piedra, Monasterio de-	13	Kc	41.10N	1.50W
Piedrabuena	13	He	39.02N	4.10W
Piedrafita, Puerto de-	13	Fb	42.36N	6.57W
Piedrahita	13	Gd	40.28N	5.19W
Piedras	54	Cd	3.38S	79.54W
Piedras, Punta-	56	Ie	35.25S	57.08W
Piedras, Río de las-	54	Ef	12.30S	69.14W
Piedras Negras	39	Ig	28.42N	100.31W
Piedras Negras	49	Be	17.12N	91.15W
Piedra Sola	56	Id	32.04S	56.21W
Piekary Śląskie	10	Of	50.24N	18.58 E
Pieksämäki	7	Ge	62.18N	27.08 E
Pielach	14	Jb	48.15N	15.22 E
Pielavesi	7	Ge	63.14N	26.45 E
Pielinen	5	Ic	63.15N	29.40 E
Piemonte = Piedmont (EN) [2]	14	Be	45.00N	8.00 E
Pieniężno	10	Qb	54.15N	20.08 E
Pieni Salpausselkä	8	Lc	61.10N	27.20 E
Piennes	12	He	49.19N	5.47 E
Pienza	14	Fg	43.04N	11.41 E
Pierce	46	Hc	46.29N	115.48W
Piéria Óri	15	Fi	40.12N	22.07 E
Pierre	39	Ie	44.22N	100.21W
Pierrefitte-sur-Aire	12	Hf	48.54N	5.20 E
Pierrefonds	12	Ee	49.21N	2.59 E
Pierrelatte	11	Kj	44.23N	4.42 E
Pieskehaure	7	Dc	66.57N	16.30 E
Piešťany	10	Nh	48.36N	17.50 E
Pietarsaari/Jakobstad	7	Fe	63.40N	22.42 E
Pietermaritzburg	31	Kk	29.37S	30.16 E
Pietersburg	31	Jk	23.54S	29.25 E
Pietraperzia	14	Im	37.25N	14.08 E
Pietrasanta	14	Eg	43.57N	10.14 E
Piet Retief	37	Ee	27.01S	30.50 E
Pietrii, Vîrful-	15	Fd	45.23N	22.40 E
Pietroşani	15	If	43.43N	25.38 E
Pietrosu, Vîrful- [Rom.]	15	Ib	47.08N	25.11 E
Pietrosu, Vîrful- [Rom.]	5	If	47.23N	25.33 E
Pieve di Cadore	14	Gd	46.26N	12.22 E
Pigeon Island	51k	Ba	14.06N	60.58W
Pigeon River	45	Lb	48.02N	89.41W
Piggott	45	Kh	36.23N	90.11W
Pigg's Peak	37	Ee	25.58S	31.15 E
Pigs, Bay of- (EN)= Cochinos, Bahía de-	49	Gb	22.07N	81.10W
Pigüé	55	Am	37.37S	62.25W
Pi He	28	Dh	32.26N	116.34 E
Pihkva järv=Pskov, Lake- (EN)	7	Gg	58.00N	28.00 E
Pihlajavesi	7	Gf	61.45N	28.45 E
Pihlava	8	Ic	61.33N	21.36 E
Pihtipudas	7	Fe	63.23N	25.34 E
Piikkiö	8	Jd	60.26N	22.31 E
Piirisaar/Pirissar	8	Lf	58.23N	27.40 E
Pijijiapan	48	Mj	15.42N	93.14W
Pijol, Pico-	49	Df	15.06N	87.35W
Pikalevo	7	Ig	59.32N	34.03 E
Pikangikum	42	If	51.49N	94.00W
Pikelot Island	57	Fd	8.05N	147.38 E
Pikes Peak	43	Fd	38.51N	105.03W
Piketberg	37	Bf	32.54S	18.46 E
Pikiutdleq	41	Hf	64.45N	40.10W
Pikou	28	Ge	39.24N	122.21 E
Pikounda	36	Cb	0.33N	16.42 E
Piła	10	Mc	53.10N	16.44 E
Piła [2]	10	Mc	53.10N	16.45 E
Pila	55	Cm	36.01S	58.08W
Pila, Sierra de la-	13	Kf	38.16N	1.11W
Pilar [Arg.]	55	Bj	31.27S	61.15W
Pilar [Braz.]	54	Ke	9.36S	35.56W
Pilar [Par.]	56	Ic	26.52S	58.23W
Pilas Group	26	He	6.45N	121.35 E
Pilat, Mont-	11	Ki	45.23N	4.35 E
Pilatus	14	Cd	46.59N	8.20 E
Pilaya, Río-	54	Fh	20.55S	64.04W
Pilcaniyeu	56	Ff	41.08S	70.40W
Pilcomayo, Río-	52	Kh	25.21S	57.42W
Pile, Jezioro-	10	Mc	53.35N	16.30 E
Pili	15	Ej	39.28N	21.37 E
Pilibhit	25	Fc	28.38N	79.48 E
Pilica	10	Re	51.52N	21.17 E
Pilion Óros	15	Gj	39.24N	23.05 E
Pilipinas=Philippine Islands (EN)	21	Oh	13.00N	122.00 E
Pilipinas=Philippines (EN) [1]	22	Oh	13.00N	122.00 E
Pilis	10	Oi	47.41N	18.53 E
Pillahuincó, Sierra de-	55	Bn	38.18S	60.45W
Pillar, Cape-	59	Jh	43.15S	148.00 E
Pilna	7	Ki	55.33N	45.55 E
Pilões, Rio-	55	Gc	16.14S	50.54W
Pilões, Serra dos-	55	Ic	17.50S	47.13W
Pilón, Río-	48	Je	25.32N	99.32W
Pilos	15	Em	36.55N	21.42 E
Pilos = Pylos (EN)	15	Em	36.56N	21.40 E
Pilot Peak	46	Hf	41.02N	114.06W
Pilot Rock	46	Fd	45.29N	118.50W
Pilsen (EN)=Plzeň	6	Hf	49.45N	13.24 E
Piltene	7	Eh	57.15N	21.42 E
Pilzno	10	Rg	49.59N	21.17 E
Pim	19	Hc	61.18N	71.57 E
Pimba	59	Hf	31.15S	136.47 E
Pimenteiras	54	Je	6.14S	41.25W
Pimža Jõgi	8	Lg	57.57N	27.59 E
Pina	13	Lc	41.29N	0.32W
Pinacate, Cerro-	48	Cb	31.45N	113.31W
Pinaki Atoll	57	Nf	19.22S	138.44W
Pinamar	55	Dm	37.07S	56.50W
Piñami, Arroyo-	48	Cd	27.44N	113.47W
Pinar	13	Gh	36.46N	5.26W
Pinarbaşi	24	Gc	38.50N	36.30 E
Pinar del Rio	39	Kg	22.25N	83.42W
Pinar del Rio [3]	49	Eb	22.35N	83.40W
Pinarello	11a	Bb	41.41N	9.22 E
Pinarhisar	15	Kh	41.37N	27.30 E
Pinchbeck	12	Bb	52.48N	0.09W
Pincher Creek	42	Gg	49.30N	113.48W
Pinçon, Mont-	11	Ff	48.58N	0.37W
Pîncota	15	Ec	46.20N	21.42 E
Pindaíba, Ribeirão	55	Gb	14.48S	52.00W
Pindaré, Rio-	54	Jd	3.17S	45.28W
Pindaré-Mirim	54	Id	3.37S	45.21W
Pindaval	55	Dc	17.08S	56.09W
Pindhos Óros=Pindus Mountains (EN)	5	Ih	39.45N	21.30 E
Pindus Mountains (EN)= Pindhos Óros	5	Ih	39.45N	21.30 E
Pine Bluff	43	Ie	34.13N	92.01W
Pine Bluffs	46	Mf	41.11N	104.04W
Pine Creek	59	Gb	13.49S	131.49 E
Pine Falls	42	Hf	50.35N	96.15W
Pinega	19	Ec	64.42N	43.22 E
Pinega	5	Kc	64.08N	41.54 E
Pine Island Glacier	66	Of	75.00S	101.00W
Pineland	45	Jk	31.15N	93.58W
Pine Mountain [Ga.-U.S.]	44	Ei	32.51N	84.47W
Pine Mountain [U.S.]	44	Fg	36.55N	83.20W
Pine Pass	42	Fe	55.50N	122.30W
Pine Point	39	Hc	61.01N	114.15W
Pine Ridge	45	Ee	43.02N	102.33W
Pinerolo	14	Bf	44.53N	7.21 E
Pines, Isle of- (EN)= Juventud, Isla de la-	38	Kg	21.40N	82.50W
Pines, Isle of- (EN)=Pins, Ile des-	57	Hg	22.37S	167.30 E
Pines, Lake O' The-	45	Ij	32.46N	94.35W
Pinetown	37	Ee	29.52S	30.46 E
Ping	21	Mh	15.42N	100.09 E
Pingbian	27	Hg	22.56N	103.46 E
Pingchang	27	Ie	31.38N	107.06 E
Pingding	28	Bf	37.48N	113.37 E
Pingdingbu → Guyuan	28	Cd	41.40N	115.41 E
Pingding Shan	27	Mb	46.39N	128.30 E
Pingdingshan	27	Je	33.41N	113.27 E
Pingdu	28	Ef	36.47N	119.57 E
Pingelap Atoll	57	Hd	6.13N	160.42 E
Pingelly	59	Df	32.32S	117.05 E
Pinggu	28	Dd	40.08N	117.07 E
Pingguo	27	Ig	23.21N	107.34 E
Pinghu	28	Fi	30.42N	121.02 E
Pingjiang	28	Bj	28.45N	113.37 E
Pingle	27	Jg	24.43N	110.42 E
Pingli	27	Ie	32.27N	109.21 E
Pingliang	22	Mf	35.32N	106.41 E
Pinglu (Jingping)	28	Be	39.32N	112.14 E
Pingluo	22	Mf	38.56N	106.34 E
Pingma → Tiandong	27	Ig	23.40N	107.09 E
Pingnan	27	Jg	23.38N	110.23 E
Pingouins, Ile des-	30	Mm	46.25S	50.19 E
Pingquan	27	Kc	41.00N	118.36 E
Pingshan	28	Ce	38.21N	114.01 E
Pingshun	28	Bf	36.12N	113.26 E
Pingtan	27	Kf	25.31N	119.48 E
Pingtung	27	Lg	22.40N	120.29 E
Pingüicas, Cerro-	48	Jg	21.10N	99.42W
Pingvallavatn	7a	Bb	64.15N	21.09W
Pingvellir	7a	Bb	64.17N	21.03W
Pingwu	27	He	32.27N	104.35 E
Pingxiang [China]	27	Ig	22.11N	106.46 E
Pingxiang [China]	27	Jf	27.43N	113.48 E
Pingyang	27	Lf	27.40N	120.30 E
Pingyao	27	Jd	37.12N	112.13 E
Pingyi	28	Dg	35.30N	117.38 E
Pingyin	28	Df	36.17N	116.26 E
Pingyu	28	Ci	32.58N	114.36 E
Pingyuan	28	Df	37.10N	116.25 E
Pinhal	55	If	22.12S	46.45W
Pinhão	55	Gg	25.43S	51.38W
Pinheir Machado	55	Fj	31.34S	53.23W
Pinhel	13	Ed	40.46N	7.04W
Pini, Pulau-	26	Cf	0.08N	98.40 E
Piniós [Grc.]	15	Fj	39.53N	22.44 E
Piniós [Grc.]	15	El	37.48N	21.14 E
Pinipel	63a	Ba	4.24S	154.08 E
Pinjug	7	Lf	60.16N	47.54 E
Pinka	10	Mi	47.00N	16.35 E
Pink Mountain	42	Fe	56.06N	122.35W
Pinnaroo	59	Ig	35.16S	140.55 E
Pinneberg	10	Fc	53.39N	9.48 E
Pinnes, Ákra-	15	Hi	40.07N	24.18 E
Pinolosean	26	Hf	0.23N	124.07 E
Pinos	48	If	22.18N	101.34W
Pinos, Mount-	38	Hf	34.50N	119.09W
Pinos-Puente	13	Ig	37.15N	3.45W
Pinrang	26	Gg	3.48S	119.38 E
Pins, Cap des-	63b	Ce	21.04S	167.28 E
Pins, Ile des-=Pines, Isle of- (EN)	57	Hg	22.37S	167.30 E
Pins, Pointe aux-	44	Gd	42.15N	81.51W
Pinsk	19	Ce	52.08N	26.06 E
Pinta, Isla-	54a	Aa	0.35N	90.44W
Pintas, Sierra de las-	48	Bb	31.40N	115.10W
Pinto [Arg.]	56	Hc	29.09S	62.39W
Pinto [Sp.]	13	Id	40.14N	3.41W
Pintwater Range	46	Hh	36.55N	115.30W
Pio	63a	Ed	10.12S	161.42 E
Pioche	46	Hh	37.56N	114.27W
Piombino	14	Eh	42.55N	10.32 E
Piombino, Canale di-	14	Eh	42.55N	10.30 E
Pioneer Mountains	46	Id	45.40N	113.00W
Pioner, Ostrov-	21	Lb	79.50N	92.30 E
Pionerski [R.S.F.S.R.]	19	Gc	61.12N	62.57 E
Pionerski [R.S.F.S.R.]	7	Ei	54.57N	20.13 E
Pionki	10	Re	51.30N	21.27 E
Piorini, Lago-	54	Fd	3.35S	63.15W
Piorini, Rio-	54	Fd	3.23S	63.30W
Piotrków [2]	10	Pe	51.25N	19.40 E
Piotrków Trybunalski	10	Pe	51.25N	19.42 E
Piove di Sacco	14	Ge	45.18N	12.02 E
Pipa Dingzi	27	Mc	43.57N	128.14 E
Pipéri	15	Hj	39.19N	24.21 E
Pipestone	45	Hd	44.01N	96.19W
Pipestone Creek	45	Fb	49.42N	100.45W
Pipi	35	Cd	7.27N	22.48 E
Pipinas	55	Dl	35.32S	57.20W
Pipmouacan, Réservoir -	42	Kg	49.40N	70.20W
Piqan→Shanshan	27	Fc	42.52N	90.10 E
Piqua	44	Ee	40.08N	84.14W
Piqueras, Puerto de-	13	Jb	42.03N	2.32W
Piquiri, Rio-	56	Jb	24.03S	54.14W
Piquiri, Serra do-	55	Fg	24.53S	52.25W
Piracanjuba	55	Hc	17.18S	49.01W
Piracanjuba, Rio- [Braz.]	55	Hd	18.14S	48.48W
Piracanjuba, Rio- [Braz.]	55	Hc	17.18S	48.13W
Piracema	55	Je	20.31S	44.29W
Piracicaba	56	Kb	22.43S	47.38W
Piracicaba, Rio-	55	Hf	22.36S	48.19W
Piraçununga	55	Ie	21.59S	47.25W
Piracuruca	54	Jd	3.56S	41.42W
Piraeus (EN) = Piraiévs	6	Ih	37.57N	23.38 E
Pirai do Sul	55	Hg	24.31S	49.56W
Piraiévs = Piraeus (EN)	6	Ih	37.57N	23.38 E
Piraju	55	Hf	23.12S	49.23W
Pirajuí	55	He	21.59S	49.29W
Piramide, Cerro-	52	Ij	49.01S	73.32W
Piran	14	He	45.32N	13.34 E
Pirané	56	Ic	25.43S	59.06W
Piranhas	55	Gc	16.31S	51.51W
Piranhas, Rio-	55	Gc	16.01S	51.52W
Pirān Shahr	24	Kd	36.40N	45.05 E
Pirapora	53	Lg	17.21S	44.56W
Piraraja	56	Jd	33.44S	54.45W
Pirate Well	49	Kb	22.26N	73.04W
Piratini	55	Fj	31.27S	53.06W
Piratini, Rio-	55	Fk	32.01S	52.25W
Piratinim, Rio-	55	Ei	28.06S	55.27W
Pirdop	15	Hg	42.42N	24.11 E
Pirenópolis	55	Hb	15.51S	48.57W
Pires do Rio	54	Ig	17.18S	48.17W
Pirgos	15	El	37.41N	21.27 E
Pirgós	15	Fi	40.38N	22.44 E
Piriápolis	55	El	34.54S	55.17W
Pirin	15	Gh	41.40N	23.30 E
Pirineos=Pyrenees (EN)	5	Gg	42.40N	1.00 E
Pirineus, Serra dos-	55	Hc	16.15S	49.10W
Piripiri	54	Jd	4.16S	41.47W
Pirissar/Piirisaar	8	Lf	58.23N	27.40 E
Piritu	50	Bh	9.23N	69.12W
Piritu, Islas-	50	Dg	10.10N	64.56W
Pirizal	55	Dc	16.16S	56.23W
Pirjatin	16	Hd	50.14N	32.30 E
Pirmasens	10	Dg	49.12N	7.36 E
Pirna	10	Jf	50.58N	13.56 E
Piron	63a	Ad	11.20S	153.27 E
Pirón	13	Hc	41.23N	4.31W
Pirot	15	Ff	43.09N	22.36 E
Pirre, Cerro-	49	Ij	7.49N	77.43W
Pirrit Hills	66	Pg	81.17S	85.21W
Pirsagat	16	Pj	39.53N	49.19 E
Pīr Tāj	24	Me	35.45N	48.07 E
Pirttikyla/Pörtom	8	Ib	62.42N	21.37 E
Piru	26	Ig	3.04S	128.12 E
Pis	64d	Ba	7.41N	151.46 E
Pisa	14	Eg	43.43N	10.23 E
Pisa	10	Rc	53.15N	21.52 E
Pisagua	56	Fa	19.36S	70.13W

Index Symbols

[1] Independent Nation
[2] State, Region
[3] District, County
[4] Municipality
[5] Colony, Dependency
Continent
Physical Region
Historical or Cultural Region
Mount, Mountain
Volcano
Hill
Mountains, Mountain Range
Hills, Escarpment
Plateau, Upland
Pass, Gap
Plain, Lowland
Delta
Salt Flat
Valley, Canyon
Crater, Cave
Karst Features
Depression
Polder
Desert, Dunes
Forest, Woods
Heath, Steppe
Oasis
Cape, Point
Coast, Beach
Cliff
Peninsula
Isthmus
Sandbank
Island
Atoll
Rock, Reef
Islands, Archipelago
Rocks, Reefs
Coral Reef
Well, Spring
Geyser
River, Stream
Waterfall Rapids
River Mouth, Estuary
Lake
Salt Lake
Intermittent Lake
Reservoir
Swamp, Pond
Canal
Glacier
Ice Shelf, Pack Ice
Ocean
Sea
Gulf, Bay
Strait, Fjord
Lagoon
Bank
Seamount
Tablemount
Ridge
Shelf
Basin
Escarpment, Sea Scarp
Fracture
Trench, Abyss
National Park, Reserve
Point of Interest
Recreation Site
Cave, Cavern
Historic Site
Ruins
Wall, Walls
Church, Abbey
Temple
Scientific Station
Airport
Port
Lighthouse
Mine
Tunnel
Dam, Bridge

Index Symbols

[1] Independent Nation	Historical or Cultural Region	Pass, Gap	Depression	Coast, Beach
[2] State, Region	Mount, Mountain	Plain, Lowland	Polder	Cliff
[3] District, County	Volcano	Delta	Desert, Dunes	Peninsula
[4] Municipality	Hill	Salt Flat	Forest, Woods	Isthmus
[5] Colony, Dependency	Mountains, Mountain Range	Valley, Canyon	Heath, Steppe	Sandbank
Continent	Hills, Escarpment	Crater, Cave	Oasis	Island
Physical Region	Plateau, Upland	Karst Features	Cape, Point	Atoll

Rock, Reef	Waterfall Rapids	Canal	Lagoon
Islands, Archipelago	River Mouth, Estuary	Glacier	Bank
Rocks, Reefs	Lake	Ice Shelf, Pack Ice	Seamount
Coral Reef	Salt Lake	Ocean	Tablemount
Well, Spring	Intermittent Lake	Sea	Ridge
Geyser	Reservoir	Gulf, Bay	Shelf
River, Stream	Swamp, Pond	Strait, Fjord	Basin

Escarpment, Sea Scarp	Historic Site	Port
Fracture	Ruins	Lighthouse
Trench, Abyss	Wall, Walls	Mine
National Park, Reserve	Church, Abbey	Tunnel
Point of Interest	Temple	Dam, Bridge
Recreation Site	Scientific Station	
Cave, Cavern	Airport	

Index Symbols

Symbol	Meaning		Symbol	Meaning
[1]	Independent Nation			Historical or Cultural Region
[2]	State, Region			Mount, Mountain
[3]	District, County			Volcano
[4]	Municipality			Hill
[5]	Colony, Dependency			Mountains, Mountain Range
	Continent			Hills, Escarpment
	Physical Region			Plateau, Upland

Pass, Gap	Depression	Coast, Beach	Rock, Reef	Waterfall Rapids
Plain, Lowland	Polder	Cliff	Islands, Archipelago	River Mouth, Estuary
Delta	Desert, Dunes	Peninsula	Rocks, Reefs	Lake
Salt Flat	Forest, Woods	Isthmus	Coral Reef	Salt Lake
Valley, Canyon	Heath, Steppe	Sandbank	Well, Spring	Intermittent Lake
Crater, Cave	Oasis	Island	Geyser	Reservoir
Karst Features	Cape, Point		Atoll	River, Stream

Canal	Lagoon	Escarpment, Sea Scarp	Historic Site	Port
Glacier	Bank	Fracture	Ruins	Lighthouse
Ice Shelf, Pack Ice	Seamount	Trench, Abyss	Wall, Walls	Mine
Ocean	Tablemount	National Park, Reserve	Church, Abbey	Tunnel
Sea	Ridge	Point of Interest	Temple	Dam, Bridge
Shelf	Basin	Recreation Site	Scientific Station	
Swamp, Pond	Gulf, Bay	Cave, Cavern	Airport	
	Strait, Fjord			

Princess Margaret Range 42 Ia 79.00N 88.30W
Princess Royal 42 Ef 52.55N 128.50W
Princeton [B.C.-Can.] 42 Fg 49.27N 120.31W
Princeton [Il.-U.S.] 45 Lf 41.23N 89.28W
Princeton [In.-U.S.] 44 Df 38.21N 87.34W
Princeton [Ky.-U.S.] 44 Dg 37.07N 87.53W
Princeton [Mo.-U.S.] 45 Jf 40.24N 93.35W
Prince William Sound 38 Ec 60.40N 147.00W
Príncipe 30 Hh 1.37N 7.25 E
Prineville 46 Ed 44.18N 120.51W
Prineville Reservoir 46 Ed 44.08N 120.42W
Prins Christians Sund 41 Hf 60.00N 43.10W
Prinsesse Astrid Kyst 66 Cf 70.45S 12.30 E
Prinsesse Ragnhild Kyst 66 Df 70.15S 27.30 E
Prins Harald Kyst 66 De 69.30S 36.00 E
Prins Karls Forland 41 Nc 78.32N 11.10 E
Prinzapolka 47 Hf 13.24N 83.34W
Prinzapolka, Rio- 49 Fg 13.24N 83.34W
Priora, Mount- 59 Ja 6.51S 145.58 E
Priozersk 19 Dc 61.04N 30.07 E
Pripet Marshes (EN) 5 Ie 52.00N 27.00 E
Pripjat 5 Je 51.21N 30.09 E
Pripoljarny Ural=Subpolar Urals (EN) 5 Lb 65.00N 60.00 E
Prirečny 19 Db 69.02N 30.15 E
Prišib 16 Pj 39.06N 48.38 E
Prislop, Pasul- 15 Hb 47.37N 24.55 E
Pristan-Prževalsk 18 Lc 42.33N 78.18 E
Pristen 16 Jd 51.15N 36.42 E
Priština 15 Eg 42.40N 21.10 E
Pritzwalk 10 Ic 53.09N 12.11 E
Privas 11 Kj 44.44N 4.36 E
Priverno 14 Hi 41.28N 13.11 E
Privolžkaja Vozvyšennost=Volga Hills (EN) 5 Ke 52.00N 46.00 E
Privolžsk 7 Jh 57.27N 41.16 E
Privolžski 16 Od 51.23N 46.02 E
Prizren 15 Dg 42.13N 20.45 E
Prizzi 14 Hm 37.43N 13.26 E
Prjaža 7 Hf 61.43N 33.37 E
Prnjavor 14 Lf 44.52N 17.40 E
Probolinggo 26 Fh 7.45S 113.13 E
Prochowice 10 Me 51.17N 16.22 E
Procida 14 Hj 40.45N 14.00 E
Proctor Reservoir 45 Gj 32.02N 98.32W
Proddatur 25 Ff 14.44N 78.33 E
Profitis Ilias [Grc.] 15 Fm 36.53N 22.22 E
Profitis Ilias [Grc.] 15 Fj 39.50N 22.38 E
Profondeville 12 Gd 50.23N 4.52 E
Progonati 15 Ci 40.13N 19.56 E
Prograničnik 18 Dg 35.43N 63.12 E
Progreso [Mex.] 39 Kg 21.17N 89.40W
Progreso [Mex.] 48 Id 27.28N 101.04W
Progress 20 Hg 49.41N 129.40 E
Prohladny 16 Nh 43.45N 44.01 E
Prohorovka 16 Jd 51.02N 36.42 E
Prokopjevsk 22 Kd 53.53N 86.45 E
Prokuplje 15 Ef 43.15N 21.36 E
Proletari 7 Hg 58.26N 31.43 E
Proletarsk [R.S.F.S.R.] 19 Ef 46.41N 41.44 E
Proletarsk [Tad.-U.S.S.R.] 18 Gd 40.10N 69.31 E
Proletarski 16 Id 50.51N 35.46 E
Proletarskoje Vodohranilišče 16 Mf 46.30N 42.10 E
Proliv Soela/Soela Väin 8 Jf 58.40N 22.30 E
Prome 22 Lh 18.49N 95.13 E
Promissão, Represa- 56 Kb 21.32S 49.52W
Promissão 55 He 21.32S 49.52W
Promyšlenny 17 Kc 67.35N 63.55 E
Pronja [Bye.-U.S.S.R.] 16 Gc 53.27N 31.03 E
Pronja [U.S.S.R.] 16 Lb 54.21N 40.24 E
Pronsfeld 12 Id 50.10N 6.20 E
Prophet 42 Fe 58.46N 122.45W
Propriá 54 Kf 10.13S 36.51W
Propriano 11a Ab 41.40N 8.54 E
Prorva 16 Rg 45.57N 53.13 E
Proserpine 59 Jd 20.24S 148.34 E
Prosna 10 Nd 52.10N 17.39 E
Prosotsáni 15 Gh 41.11N 23.59 E
Prosperidad 26 Ie 8.34N 125.52 E
Prospihino 20 Ee 58.37N 99.20 E
Prosser 46 Fc 46.12N 119.46W
Prostějov 10 Ng 49.29N 17.07 E
Proszowice 10 Qf 50.12N 20.18 E
Próti 15 El 37.03N 21.33 E
Protoka 16 Jg 45.43N 37.46 E
Protva 7 Ii 54.51N 37.16 E
Provadija 15 Kf 43.11N 27.26 E
Prøven 41 Gd 72.15N 55.40W
Provence 11 Lk 44.00N 6.00 E
Provence 5 Gg 44.00N 6.00 E
Providence [Ky.-U.S.] 44 Dg 37.24N 87.39W
Providence [R.I.-U.S.] 39 Le 41.50N 71.25W
Providence, Cape- 62 Bg 46.01S 166.28 E
Providence Bay 44 Fc 45.44N 82.18W
Providence Island 30 Mi 9.14S 51.02 E
Providencia, Isla de- 47 Hf 13.21N 81.22W
Providenciales 49 Kc 21.49N 72.15W
Providenija 22 Uc 64.23N 173.18W
Provincetown 44 Ld 42.03N 70.11W
Provins 11 Jf 48.33N 3.18 E
Provo 39 He 40.14N 111.39W
Prozor 14 Lg 43.49N 17.37 E
Prudentópolis 55 Gg 25.12S 50.57W
Prudhoe Bay 39 Eb 70.20N 148.25W
Prudnik 10 Nf 50.19N 17.34 E
Prüm 12 Ie 49.49N 6.28 E
Prüm 10 Cf 50.13N 6.25 E
Prune Island 51n Bb 12.35N 61.24W
Prussia (EN) 10 Pc 53.45N 20.00 E
Pruszcz Gdański 10 Ob 54.16N 18.36 E
Pruszków 10 Qd 52.11N 20.48 E
Prut 5 If 45.28N 28.14 E
Pružany 19 Ce 52.36N 24.28 E
Prvić 14 If 44.54N 14.48 E
Prydz Bay 66 Fe 69.00S 76.00 E
Pryor 45 Ih 36.19N 95.19W
Przasnysz 10 Qc 53.01N 20.55 E
Przedbórz 10 Pe 51.06N 19.53 E
Przemyśl [2] 10 Sg 49.45N 22.45 E
Przemyśl 10 Sg 49.47N 22.47 E
Prževalsk 22 Je 42.29N 78.24 E
Przeworsk 10 Sf 50.05N 22.29 E
Przysucha 10 Qe 51.22N 20.38 E
Psakhná 15 Gk 38.35N 23.38 E
Psará 15 Ik 38.35N 25.37 E
Psathoúra 15 Hj 39.30N 24.11 E
Pščišč 16 Kg 45.03N 39.25 E
Psebaj 16 Lg 44.07N 40.47 E
Psël 5 Jf 49.05N 33.30 E
Psérimos 15 Km 36.56N 27.09 E
Psina 10 Of 50.02N 18.16 E
Pšiš, Gora- 16 Lh 43.24N 41.14 E
Pskem 18 Hd 41.38N 70.01 E
Pskent 18 Gd 40.54N 69.23 E
Pskov 6 Id 57.50N 28.20 E
Pskov, Lake- (EN)=Pihkva järv 7 Gg 58.00N 28.00 E
Pskov, Lake- (EN)=Pskovskoje Ozero 5 Id 58.00N 28.00 E
Pskova 8 Mg 57.47N 28.30 E
Pskovskaja Oblast [3] 19 Cd 57.20N 29.20 E
Pskovskoje Ozero=Pskov, Lake- (EN) 5 Id 58.00N 28.00 E
Psunj 14 Le 45.24N 17.20 E
Ptič 16 Fc 52.09N 28.52 E
Ptolemaïs 15 Ei 40.31N 21.41 E
Ptuj 14 Jd 46.25N 15.52 E
Pua-a, Cape- 65c Aa 13.26S 172.43W
Puah, Pulau- 26 Hg 0.30S 122.34 E
Puapua 65c Aa 13.34S 172.09W
Pucallpa 53 If 8.20S 74.30W
Pučež 7 Kh 56.59N 43.11 E
Pucheng [China] 27 Kf 27.55N 118.30 E
Pucheng [China] 27 Id 35.00N 109.38 E
Pucho 36 Cf 17.35S 16.30 E
Pucioasa 15 Id 45.05N 25.25 E
Pučišća 14 Kg 43.21N 16.44 E
Puck 10 Ob 54.44N 18.27 E
Pucka, Zatoka- 10 Ob 54.40N 18.35 E
Pudasjärvi 7 Gd 65.23N 27.00 E
Pudož 19 Dc 61.50N 36.32 E
Pudukkottai 25 Ff 10.23N 78.49 E
Puebla [2] 47 Ee 18.50N 98.00W
Puebla, Sierra de- 48 Kh 19.50N 97.00W
Puebla de Alcocer 13 Gf 38.59N 5.15W
Puebla de Don Fabrique 13 Jg 37.58N 2.26W
Puebla de Guzmán 13 Eg 37.37N 7.15W
Puebla de Sanabria 13 Fb 42.03N 6.38W
Puebla de Trives 13 Eb 42.20N 7.15W
Puebla de Zaragoza 39 Jh 19.03N 98.12W
Pueblo 39 If 38.16N 104.37W
Pueblo Libertador 55 Cj 30.13S 59.23W
Pueblo Nuevo [Mex.] 48 Gf 23.23N 105.23W
Pueblo Nuevo [Ven.] 49 Mh 11.58N 69.55W
Pueblo Nuevo Tiquisate 49 Bf 14.17N 91.22W
Pueblo Viejo, Laguna de- 48 Kf 22.10N 97.55W
Puelches 56 Ge 38.09S 65.55W
Puenteáreas 13 Db 42.11N 8.30W
Puente de la Reina 13 Kb 42.40N 1.49W
Puentedeume 13 Da 43.24N 8.10W
Puente-Genil 13 Hg 37.23N 4.47W
Puentelarrá 13 Ib 42.45N 3.03W
Pueo Point 65a Ab 21.54N 160.04W
Pu'er 27 Hg 23.00N 101.00 E
Puerca, Punta- 51a Cb 18.15N 65.35W
Puerco, Rio- 45 Ci 34.22N 107.50W
Puerco River 46 Ji 34.52N 110.05W
Puerto Abente 55 Df 22.55S 57.43W
Puerto Acosta 54 Eg 15.32S 69.15W
Puerto Adela 55 Eg 24.33S 54.22W
Puerto Aisén 53 Ij 45.24S 72.42W
Puerto Alegre 54 Ff 13.53S 61.36W
Puerto Ángel 47 Ee 15.40N 96.29W
Puerto Arista 48 Mj 15.56N 93.48W
Puerto Armuelles 47 Hg 8.17N 82.52W
Puerto Asís 54 Cc 0.29N 76.32W
Puerto Ayacucho 53 Je 5.40N 67.35W
Puerto Ayora 54a Ab 0.45S 90.23W
Puerto Barrios 39 Kh 15.43N 88.36W
Puerto Bermejo 55 Ch 26.56S 58.30W
Puerto Berrio 54 Db 6.30N 74.25W
Puerto Boyacá 54 Db 5.45N 74.29W
Puerto Caballo 55 Ce 20.12S 58.12W
Puerto Cabello 53 Jd 10.28N 68.01W
Puerto Cabezas 47 Hf 14.02N 83.23W
Puerto Carreño 53 Je 6.12N 67.22W
Puerto Casado 56 Ib 20.20S 57.55W
Puerto Colombia 49 Jh 10.59N 74.57W
Puerto Colón 55 Df 23.11S 57.33W
Puerto Constanza 55 Ck 33.50S 59.03W
Puerto Cooper 56 Ib 23.03S 57.43W
Puerto Cortés [C.R.] 49 Fi 8.58N 83.32W
Puerto Cortés [Hond.] 39 Kh 15.48N 87.56W
Puerto Cumarebo 54 Ea 11.29N 69.21W
Puerto de Eten 54 Ce 6.56S 79.52W
Puerto de la Cruz 32 Dd 28.23N 16.33W
Puerto de Lajas, Cerro- 47 Cc 28.59N 107.02W
Puerto del Rosario 32 Ed 28.30N 13.52W
Puerto de Mazarrón 13 Kg 37.34N 1.15W
Puerto de San José 47 Ff 13.55N 90.49W
Puerto Deseado 53 Jj 47.45S 65.55W
Puerto de Sóller 13 Oe 39.48N 2.41 E
Puerto Escondido [Mex.] 47 Ee 15.48N 96.57W
Puerto Escondido [Mex.] 48 De 25.48N 111.20W
Puerto Esperanza [Arg.] 55 Eh 26.01S 54.39W
Puerto Esperanza [Par.] 55 Ce 20.26S 58.06W
Puerto Estrella 49 Lg 12.14N 71.13W
Puerto Fonciere 55 Df 22.29S 57.48W
Puerto Francisco de Orellana 54 Cd 0.27S 76.57W
Puerto Frey 55 Bb 14.42S 61.10W
Puerto Gaitán 54 Dc 4.20N 72.10W
Puerto General Diaz 55 Eg 25.12S 54.32W
Puerto Goya 55 Ci 29.09S 59.20W
Puerto Grether 54 Fg 17.12S 64.21W
Puerto Guarani 55 De 21.18S 57.55W
Puerto Heath 54 Ef 12.30S 68.40W
Puerto Huasco 56 Fc 28.28S 71.14W
Puerto Huitoto 54 Dc 0.18N 74.03W
Puerto Iguazú 56 Jc 25.34S 54.34W
Puerto Indio 55 Eg 24.52S 54.29W
Puerto Ingeniero Ibañez 56 Fg 46.18S 71.56W
Puerto Isabel 55 Dd 18.11S 57.37W
Puerto Jesús 49 Eh 10.07N 85.16W
Puerto Juárez 39 Kg 21.11N 86.49W
Puerto la Concordia 54 Dc 2.38N 72.47W
Puerto la Cruz 53 Jd 10.13N 64.38W
Puerto Leguízamo 53 If 0.12S 74.46W
Puerto Lempira 49 Ff 15.15N 83.46W
Puerto Libertad 47 Bc 29.55N 112.43W
Puerto Limón [Col.] 54 Cc 1.02N 76.32W
Puerto Limón [Col.] 54 Dc 3.23N 73.30W
Puertollano 13 Hf 38.41N 4.07W
Puerto Lopez 54 Dc 4.06N 72.58W
Puerto López 49 Lh 11.56N 71.17W
Puerto Lumbreras 13 Kg 37.34N 1.49W
Puerto Madero 48 Mj 14.44N 92.25W
Puerto Madryn 56 Gf 42.46S 65.03W
Puerto Magdalena 48 Ce 24.35N 112.05W
Puerto Maldonado 53 Jg 12.36S 69.11W
Puerto Marangatú 55 Eg 24.39S 54.21W
Puerto Mayor Otaño 55 Eh 26.19S 54.44W
Puerto Mihanovich 55 De 20.52S 57.59W
Puerto Monte Lindo 55 Df 23.57S 57.12W
Puerto Montt 53 Ij 41.28S 72.57W
Puerto Morelos 48 Pg 20.50N 86.52W
Puerto Mutis 54 Cb 6.14N 77.25W
Puerto Naranjito 55 Eh 26.57S 55.18W
Puerto Nariño 54 Ec 4.56N 67.48W
Puerto Natales 53 Ik 51.44S 72.31W
Puerto Nuevo 55 Ce 20.33S 58.03W
Puerto Nuevo, Punta- 51a Bb 18.30N 66.21W
Puerto Ordaz 54 Fb 8.22N 62.41W
Puerto Padre 49 Ic 21.12N 76.36W
Puerto Páez 54 Eb 6.13N 67.28W
Puerto Peñasco 47 Bb 31.20N 113.33W
Puerto Piña 49 Hj 7.35N 78.10W
Puerto Pinasco 56 Ib 22.43S 57.50W
Puerto Píritu 50 Dg 10.04N 65.03W
Puerto Plata 47 Je 19.48N 70.41W
Puerto Presidente Stroessner 55 Eg 25.33S 54.39W
Puerto Princesa 22 Ni 9.44N 118.44 E
Puerto Quijarro 55 Dc 17.47S 57.46W
Puerto Real 13 Fh 36.32N 6.11W
Puerto Rico [5] 39 Mh 18.15N 66.30W
Puerto Rico 38 Mh 18.15N 66.30W
Puerto Rico [Arg.] 56 Jc 26.48S 54.59W
Puerto Rico [Bol.] 54 Ef 11.05S 67.38W
Puerto Rico [Col.] 54 Cc 1.54N 75.10W
Puerto Rico Trench (EN) 3 Bg 20.00N 66.00W
Puerto Rondón 54 Db 6.18N 71.06W
Puerto San José 55 Eg 26.32S 54.50W
Puerto Santa Cruz 53 Jk 50.09S 68.30W
Puerto Sastre 56 Ib 22.06S 57.59W
Puerto Siles 54 Ef 12.48S 65.05W
Puerto Suárez 53 Kg 18.57S 57.51W
Puerto Tacurú Pytá 55 Df 23.49S 57.09W
Puerto Tirol 55 Ch 27.23S 59.05W
Puerto Tres Palmas 55 Df 21.43S 57.58W
Puerto Triunfo 55 Eg 26.45S 55.06W
Puerto Vallarta 47 Cd 20.37N 105.15W
Puerto Varas 56 Ff 41.19S 72.59W
Puerto Victoria 55 Eh 26.20S 54.39W
Puerto Viejo 49 Eh 10.26N 83.59W
Puerto Villamizar 49 Ki 8.19N 72.26W
Puerto Villazón 55 Ba 13.32S 61.57W
Puerto Wilches 54 Db 7.20N 73.54W
Puerto Ybapobó 55 Df 23.42S 57.12W
Pueu 65e Fc 17.44S 149.13W
Pugačev 19 Ee 52.03N 48.48 E
Puget Sound 46 Dc 48.00N 122.30W
Puglia = Apulia (EN) [2] 14 Ki 41.15N 16.15 E
Pu He 28 Gd 41.21N 122.47 E
Puhja 8 Lf 58.13N 26.17 E
Puigcerdá 13 Nb 42.26N 1.56 E
Puigmal 13 Ob 42.23N 2.07 E
Puir 20 Jf 53.10N 141.25 E
Puisaye, Collines de la- 11 Jg 47.35N 3.18 E
Puisieux 12 Ed 50.07N 2.42 E
Pujehun 34 Cd 7.21N 11.42W
Pujeşti 15 Kc 46.25N 27.29 E
Puji → Wugong 27 Ie 34.15N 108.14 E
Pujiang 28 Ei 29.28N 119.53 E
Pujili 54 Cd 0.57S 78.42W
Puka 15 Cg 42.03N 19.54 E
Pukaki, Lake- 62 Df 44.05S 170.10 E
Pukalani 65a Ec 20.50N 156.21W
Pukapuka Atoll 57 Kf 10.53S 165.49W
Pukapuka Atoll [W.F.] 57 Nf 14.49S 138.48W
Pukaruha Atoll 57 Nf 18.20S 137.02W
Pukatawagan 42 He 55.44N 101.19W
Pukchin 28 Hd 40.12N 125.45 E
Pukch'ŏng 27 Mc 40.14N 128.19 E
Pukega, Pointe- 64h Ab 13.17S 176.13W
Pukekohe 62 Fb 37.12S 174.54 E
Pukemiro 62 Fb 37.37S 175.01 E
Pukeuri Junction 62 Df 45.02S 171.02 E
Pukšenga 7 Je 63.36N 41.55 E
Puksoozero 19 Ec 62.38N 40.32 E
Puksubaek-san 28 Id 40.42N 127.15 E
Pula [It.] 14 Ck 39.01N 9.00 E
Pula [Yugo.] 14 Hf 44.52N 13.50 E
Pula, Capo di- 14 Dl 38.59N 9.01 E
Pulandian → Xinjin 27 Ld 39.24N 121.59 E
Pulap Atoll 57 Fd 7.39N 149.25 E
Pulaski [Tn.-U.S.] 44 Dh 35.12N 87.02W
Pulaski [Va.-U.S.] 44 Gg 37.03N 80.47W
Pulau 26 Kh 5.50S 138.15 E
Pulau Halura 26 Hi 10.19S 120.11 E
Pulau Irian/New Guinea 57 Fe 5.00S 140.00 E
Pulau Sapudi 26 Fh 7.06S 114.20 E
Puławy 10 Re 51.25N 21.57 E
Pulborough 12 Bd 50.57N 0.31W
Pulheim 12 Ic 51.00N 6.48 E
Pulkau 14 Kb 48.43N 16.21 E
Pulkkila 7 Fd 64.16N 25.52 E
Pullman 43 Db 46.44N 117.10W
Pulo Anna Island 57 Ed 4.40N 131.58 E
Pulog, Mount- 21 Oh 16.36N 120.54 E
Pulpito, Punta- 48 Dd 26.30N 111.30W
Pulsano 14 Lj 40.23N 17.21 E
Pultusk 10 Rd 52.43N 21.05 E
Pülümür 24 Hc 39.30N 39.54 E
Pulusuk Island 57 Fd 6.42N 149.19 E
Puluwat Atoll 57 Fd 7.22N 149.11 E
Puma Yumco 27 Ff 28.35N 90.20 E
Pumpénai/Pumpenaj 8 Ki 55.53N 24.25 E
Pumpenaj/Pumpénai 8 Ki 55.53N 24.25 E
Pumpkin Creek 46 Mc 46.15N 105.45W
Puná, Isla- 54 Bd 2.50S 80.10W
Punākha 25 Hc 27.37N 89.52 E
Punaluu 65a Fd 19.08N 155.30W
Punch 25 Eb 33.46N 74.06 E
Punda Milia 37 Ed 22.40S 31.05 E
Pune (Poona) 22 Jh 18.32N 73.52 E
Pünel 24 Md 37.33N 49.07 E
Pungan 18 Hd 40.45N 70.50 E
P'unggi 28 Jf 36.52N 128.32 E
Púngoè 37 Ec 19.50S 34.48 E
P'ungsan 28 Jd 40.40N 128.05 E
Punia 36 Ec 1.28S 26.27 E
Punitaqui 56 Fd 30.50S 71.16W
Punjab [3] 25 Fb 31.00N 76.00 E
Punjab 21 Jf 30.00N 74.00 E
Punjad [3] 25 Eb 30.00N 74.00 E
Punkaharju 8 Mc 61.48N 29.24 E
Punkalaidun 8 Jc 61.07N 23.06 E
Puno 53 Ig 15.50S 70.02W
Puno [2] 54 Ef 15.00S 70.00W
Punta, Cerro de- 47 Ke 18.10N 66.36W
Punta Alta 53 Ji 38.53S 62.04W
Punta Arenas 53 Ik 53.09S 70.55W
Punta Cardón 54 Da 11.38N 70.14W
Punta de Mata 50 Eh 9.43N 63.38W
Punta Gorda [Blz.] 47 Ge 16.07N 88.48W
Punta Gorda [Fl.-U.S.] 44 Fl 26.56N 82.03W
Punta Gorda [Nic.] 49 Fh 11.31N 83.47W
Punta Gorda, Bahía de- 49 Fh 11.15N 83.45W
Punta Gorda, Río- 49 Fh 11.30N 83.47W
Punta Indio 55 Dl 35.16S 57.14W
Punta Prieta 47 Bc 28.58N 114.17W
Puntarenas [3] 49 Ei 9.00N 83.15W
Puntarenas 39 Ki 9.58N 84.50W
Punta Róbalo 49 Fi 9.02N 82.15W
Punto Fijo 54 Da 11.42N 70.13W
Puolanka 7 Gd 64.52N 27.40 E
Puolo Point 65a Bb 21.54N 159.36W
Puqi 27 Jf 29.43N 113.52 E
Puquio 54 Df 14.42S 74.08W
Purace, Volcán- 54 Cc 2.21N 76.23W
Purari 60 Ci 7.52S 145.10 E
Purcell Mountains 42 Fg 49.55N 116.15W
Purdy Islands 57 Fe 2.53S 146.20 E
Purgatoire River 45 Eg 38.04N 103.10W
Puri 25 He 19.48N 85.51 E
Purificación 47 Ed 23.58N 98.42W
Purikari Neem/Purikarinem 8 Ke 59.36N 25.35 E
Purikarinem/Purikari Neem 8 Ke 59.36N 25.35 E
Purmani/Puurmani 8 Lf 58.30N 26.14 E
Purmerend 11 Kb 52.31N 4.57 E
Purna [India] 25 Fe 19.07N 77.02 E
Purna [India] 25 Fd 21.05N 76.00 E
Purnač 7 Jc 67.00N 40.15 E
Purnea 25 Hc 25.47N 87.28 E
Purukcahu 26 Fg 0.35S 114.35 E
Purūlia 25 Hd 23.20N 86.22 E
Puruni River 50 Gi 6.00N 59.12W
Purus, Rio- 52 Jf 3.42S 61.28W
Puruvesi 7 Gf 61.50N 29.25 E
Purwakarta 26 Eh 6.34S 107.26 E
Purwokerto 26 Eh 7.25S 109.14 E
Pusala Dağı 24 Ed 37.12N 32.54 E
Pusan 22 Of 35.06N 129.03 E
Pusan Si [2] 28 Jg 35.10N 129.05 E
Pushi He 28 Hd 40.17N 124.43 E
Puškin 19 Dd 59.43N 30.24 E
Puškino [Abz.-U.S.S.R.] 16 Pj 39.28N 48.33 E
Puškino [R.S.F.S.R.] 16 Od 51.14N 46.59 E
Puškino [R.S.F.S.R.] 7 Ih 56.02N 37.53 E
Puškinskije Gory 8 Mh 56.59N 28.59 E
Pušlahta 7 Id 64.48N 36.33 E
Püspökladány 10 Ri 47.19N 21.07 E
Püssi/Pjussi 8 Le 59.17N 26.57 E
Pusteci 15 Di 40.47N 20.54 E
Pusteria, Val-/Pustertal 14 Gd 46.45N 12.20 E
Pustertal/Pusteria, Val- 14 Gd 46.45N 12.20 E
Pustomyty 10 Tg 49.37N 23.59 E
Pustoška 7 Gh 56.20N 29.22 E
Putao 25 Jc 27.21N 97.24 E
Putaruru 62 Fc 38.03S 175.47 E
Putian 27 Kf 25.32N 119.01 E
Putignano 14 Lj 40.51N 17.07 E
Putila 15 Ib 48.00N 25.07 E
Putivl 16 Hd 51.22N 33.55 E
Putjatin 28 Lc 42.52N 132.25 E
Putla de Guerrero 48 Ki 17.02N 97.56W
Putna 15 Kd 45.34N 27.30 E
Putna 15 Ib 47.52N 25.37 E
Putnok 10 Qh 48.18N 20.26 E
Puto 63a Ba 5.41S 154.43 E
Putorana, Plato-=Putoran Mountains (EN) 21 Lc 69.00N 95.00 E
Putoran Mountains (EN)=Putorana, Plato- 21 Lc 69.00N 95.00 E
Puttalam 25 Fg 8.02N 79.49 E
Putte 12 Gc 51.04N 4.38 E
Puttelange-aux-Lacs 12 Ie 49.03N 6.56 E
Putten 12 Hb 52.16N 5.35 E
Putten 12 Gc 51.50N 4.15 E
Puttgarden, Burg auf Fehmarn- 10 Hb 54.30N 11.13 E
Püttlingen 12 Ie 49.17N 6.53 E
Putumayo [2] 54 Cc 0.30N 76.00W
Putumayo, Rio- 52 Jf 3.07S 67.58W
Putuo (Shenjiamen) 28 Gj 29.57N 122.18 E
Putussibau 26 Ff 0.50N 112.56 E
Puu Kukui 65a Ec 20.54N 156.35W
Puulavesi 5 Ic 61.50N 26.40 E
Puumala 7 Gf 61.32N 28.11 E
Puu o Umi 65a Fc 20.05N 155.42W
Puurmani/Purmani 8 Lf 58.30N 26.14 E
Puurs 12 Gc 51.05N 4.17 E
Puuwai 65a Ab 21.54N 160.12W
Puyallup 46 Dc 47.11N 122.18W
Puyang 27 Jd 35.41N 115.00 E
Puy-de-Dôme [3] 11 Ii 45.40N 3.00 E
Puy-l'Evêque 11 Hj 44.30N 1.08 E
Puymorens, Col de- 11 Hl 42.34N 1.49 E
Puyo 54 Cd 1.29S 77.58W
Puysegur Point 62 Bg 46.10S 166.37 E
Pwani [3] 36 Gd 7.30S 39.00 E
Pweto 31 Ji 8.28S 28.54 E
Pwllheli 9 Ii 52.53N 4.25W
Pyapon 25 Je 16.17N 95.41 E
Pyhäjärvi 7 Fe 63.40N 25.59 E
Pyhäjärvi [Fin.] 7 Ff 61.00N 22.20 E
Pyhäjärvi [Fin.] 7 Fe 63.35N 25.57 E
Pyhäjärvi [Fin.] 8 Kc 62.45N 25.25 E
Pyhäjärvi [Fin.] 8 Jc 61.30N 23.35 E
Pyhäjoki 7 Fd 64.28N 24.13 E
Pyhäjoki 7 Fd 64.28N 24.14 E
Pyhäntä 7 Gd 64.06N 26.19 E
Pyhäranta 8 Id 60.57N 21.27 E
Pyhäselkä 7 Ge 62.30N 29.40 E
Pyhäselkä 8 Mb 62.26N 29.58 E
Pyhätunturi 7 Gc 67.01N 27.09 E
Pyhävesi 8 Lc 61.25N 26.35 E
Pyhävuori 8 Ib 62.17N 21.38 E
Pyhrnpaß 14 Ic 47.38N 14.18 E
Pyhtää/Pyttis 7 Gf 60.29N 26.32 E
Pyinmana 22 Lh 19.44N 96.13 E
Pylos (EN) = Pilos 15 Em 36.56N 21.40 E
Pyltsamaa/Põltsamaa 8 Lf 58.23N 26.08 E
Pyltsamaa/Põltsamaa 7 Fg 58.39N 25.59 E
Pylva/Põlva 7 Gg 58.04N 27.06 E
Pymatuning Reservoir 44 Ge 41.37N 80.30W
P'yŏngan-Namdo [2] 28 Ie 39.20N 126.00 E
P'yŏngan-Pukto [2] 28 Hd 40.00N 125.15 E
P'yŏnggang 27 Md 38.25N 127.17 E
P'yŏngsan 27 Md 38.20N 126.24 E
P'yongt'aek 28 If 36.59N 127.05 E
P'yŏngyang 22 Of 39.01N 125.45 E
P'yŏngyang Si [2] 28 He 39.04N 125.50 E
Pyramiden 41 Nc 77.54N 16.41 E
Pyramid Lake 43 Dc 40.00N 119.35W
Pyramid Mountains 45 Bj 32.00N 108.30W
Pyrénées=Pyrenees (EN) 5 Gg 42.40N 1.00 E
Pyrenees (EN)=Pirineos 5 Gg 42.40N 1.00 E
Pyrenees (EN)=Pyrénées 5 Gg 42.40N 1.00 E
Pyrenees (EN)=Serralada Pirinenca 5 Gg 42.40N 1.00 E
Pyrénées-Atlantiques [3] 11 Fk 43.15N 0.50W
Pyrénées-Orientales [3] 11 Il 42.30N 2.20 E
Pyrzyce 10 Kc 53.10N 14.55 E
Pyšma 19 Gd 57.08N 66.18 E
Pytalovo 7 Gh 57.06N 27.59 E
Pyttegga 8 Bd 62.13N 7.42 E
Pyttis/Pyhtää 7 Gf 60.29N 26.32 E
Pyu 25 Je 18.29N 96.26 E
Pyzaspea/Põõsaspea Neem 8 Je 59.15N 23.25 E
Pyzdry 10 Nd 52.11N 17.41 E

Q

Qā', Wādī al- 24 Hi 27.04N 38.34 E
Qābis [3] 32 Ic 33.00N 9.30 E
Qābis 31 Ie 33.53N 10.07 E
Qābis, Khalīj-=Gabès, Gulf of-(EN) 30 Ie 34.00N 10.25 E
Qabr Hūd 35 Hb 16.09N 49.34 E
Qāderābād 24 Og 30.17N 53.16 E
Qādir Karam 24 Ke 35.12N 44.53 E
Qaḑub 23 Hg 12.38N 53.57 E
Qā'emshahr 24 Od 36.30N 52.55 E
Qafṣah 31 He 34.25N 8.48 E
Qafṣah [3] 32 Ic 34.30N 9.00 E
Qa'fūr 14 Dn 36.20N 9.19 E
Qagan 27 Kb 49.16N 118.04 E
Qagan Moron He 28 Ec 43.13N 119.02 E
Qagan Nur 27 Jc 43.20N 112.58 E
Qagan Nur [China] 28 Bd 41.33N 113.48 E
Qagan Nur [China] 27 Jc 43.25N 114.50 E
Qagan Nur [China] 28 Hb 45.14N 124.17 E
Qagan Nur→Zhengxiangbai Qi 27 Jc 42.16N 114.59 E
Qagan Us→Dulan 22 Lf 36.29N 98.29 E
Qagchêng/Xiangcheng 27 Gf 28.56N 99.46 E
Qahar Youyi Houqi (Bayan Qagan) 28 Bd 41.28N 113.10 E
Qahar Youyi Qianqi (Togrog Ul) 28 Bd 40.46N 113.13 E
Qahar Youyi Zhongqi 28 Bd 41.15N 112.36 E
Qahd, Wādī- 24 Ii 26.13N 40.49 E
Qaidam He 27 Gd 36.48N 95.50 E
Qaidam Pendi=Tsaidam Basin (EN) 27 Fd 37.00N 95.00 E

Index Symbols

[1] Independent Nation
[2] State, Region
[3] District, County
[4] Municipality
[5] Colony, Dependency
Continent
Physical Region
Historical or Cultural Region
Mount, Mountain
Volcano
Hill
Mountains, Mountain Range
Hills, Escarpment
Plateau, Upland
Pass, Gap
Plain, Lowland
Delta
Salt Flat
Valley, Canyon
Crater, Cave
Karst Features
Depression
Polder
Desert, Dunes
Forest, Woods
Heath, Steppe
Oasis
Cape, Point
Coast, Beach
Cliff
Peninsula
Isthmus
Sandbank
Island
Atoll
Rock, Reef
Islands, Archipelago
Rocks, Reefs
Coral Reef
Well, Spring
Geyser
River, Stream
Waterfall Rapids
River Mouth, Estuary
Lake
Salt Lake
Intermittent Lake
Reservoir
Swamp, Pond
Canal
Glacier
Ice Shelf, Pack Ice
Ocean
Sea
Gulf, Bay
Strait, Fjord
Lagoon
Bank
Seamount
Tablemount
Ridge
Shelf
Basin
Escarpment, Sea Scarp
Fracture
Trench, Abyss
National Park, Reserve
Point of Interest
Recreation Site
Cave, Cavern
Historic Site
Ruins
Wall, Walls
Church, Abbey
Temple
Scientific Station
Airport
Port
Lighthouse
Mine
Tunnel
Dam, Bridge

'an Nahl 35 Ec 13.38N 34.57 E
t 23 Kc 32.07N 66.54 E
at Abū Ghār 24 Lg 30.25N 46.09 E
at al Akhdar 23 Ed 28.06N 37.05 E
at al Marqab 24 Fe 35.09N 35.57 E
at al Mu'azzam 24 Gi 27.45N 37.31 E
at aş Şanam 14 Co 35.46N 8.21 E
at Bīshah 22 Gh 20.00N 42.36 E
at Dīzah 24 Kd 36.11N 45.07 E
at Şāliḥ 24 Lg 31.31N 47.16 E
at Sukkar 24 Lg 31.53N 46.56 E
eh Asgar 24 Qh 29.30N 56.35 E
eh Kūh 24 Mf 33.00N 49.10 E
eh Mūreh 24 Pe 35.35N 55.58 E
eh-ye Now 23 Jc 34.59N 63.08 E
eh-ye Sahar 24 Mg 31.40N 48.33 E
ash Shuyūkh 23 Gd 29.12N 47.55 E
ibāt 35 Fc 12.58N 36.09 E
narz, Godār-e- 24 Qf 33.26N 56.14 E
ūb 24 Dg 30.11N 31.13 E
ata 37 Df 31.58S 27.24 E
ado 22 Lf 31.15N 97.12 E
inis 33 Dc 31.40N 20.01 E
isar 24 Nf 33.45N 51.26 E
ūdah 32 Ic 35.00N 9.21 E
ūdah [3] 32 Ic 34.50N 9.20 E
āq/Thule 67 Od 77.35N 69.40W
dahār [3] 23 Kc 31.00N 65.45 E
dahār 22 If 31.35N 65.45 E
dala 35 Hc 11.23N 49.53 E
gdin Gol 28 Cc 43.27N 115.03 E
ţarat al Faḥş 14 Dn 36.23N 9.54 E
qal 27 Dc 43.48N 80.47 E
ortoq/Julianehåb 67 Nc 60.50N 46.10W
ā Dāgh 24 Lc 38.48N 47.13 E
ah 33 Ed 29.37N 26.30 E
ah Būlāq 24 Ke 34.32N 45.12 E
ah Dagh 24 Jd 37.00N 43.30 E
ah Tappah 24 Ke 34.25N 44.56 E
ānqū 24 Ld 37.23N 47.43 E
do 31 Lh 9.30N 49.03 E
eh Āghāj 24 Ld 36.46N 48.46 E
eh Sū [Iran] 23 Ib 37.00N 56.50 E
eh Sū [Iran] 23 Hc 34.52N 51.25 E
eh Ẕiā'Od Dīn 24 Kc 38.53N 45.02 E
kilik/Ruoqiang 22 Kf 39.02N 88.00 E
nayn, Jazīrat al- 24 Oj 24.56N 52.52 E
nayt, Jabal- 23 Fe 21.02N 40.22 E
qan/Qiemo 22 Kf 38.08N 85.32 E
qan He 21 Kf 39.30N 88.15 E
rqannah, Juzur-=
rkennah Islands (EN) 30 Ie 34.44N 11.12 E
tājannah 14 En 36.51N 10.20 E
ūn, Birkat- 23 Fd 29.28N 30.40 E
yat Abū Nujaym 33 Cc 30.35N 15.24 E
yat al Gharab 24 Kg 31.27N 44.48 E
yat al Qaddāḥiyah 33 Cc 31.22N 15.14 E
yat al 'Ulyā 23 Gd 27.33N 47.42 E
yat az Zarrūq 33 Cc 32.22N 15.09 E
yat az Zuwaytīnah 33 Dc 30.58N 20.07 E
şabah, Ra's al- 24 Fh 28.02N 34.38 E
şabāt, Hanshīr al- 14 Dn 36.24N 9.54 E
sigiánguit/Christianshåb 41 Ge 68.45N 51.30W
şr al Azraq 24 Gg 31.53N 36.49 E
sr Al Hayr 24 Ge 34.23N 37.36 E
şr al Qarahbullī 33 Bc 32.45N 13.43 E
şr 'Amij 24 If 33.30N 41.45 E
şr Bū Hādi 33 Cc 31.03N 16.40 E
şr Burqu' 24 Gf 32.37N 37.58 E
sr-e Shīrīn 23 Gc 34.31N 45.35 E
şr Farāfirah 31 Jf 27.15N 28.10 E
sr Ḥamān 23 Ge 20.50N 45.50 E
şr Qārūn 24 Dh 29.25N 30.25 E
şş Abū Sa'īd 24 Bi 27.00N 27.35 E
tana 24 Gf 33.26N 36.05 E
tar 21 Hg 25.30N 51.15 E
tar [1] 22 Hg 25.30N 51.15 E
tlīsh 24 Qd 37.50N 57.19 E
ţrānī, Jabal- 24 Dh 29.41N 30.35 E
trūyeh 24 Ph 29.09N 54.43 E
attara Depression (EN)=
aţţārah, Munkhafaḍ al- 30 Je 30.00N 27.30 E
ţţārah, Munkhafaḍ al-=
)attara Depression (EN) 30 Je 30.00N 27.30 E
awām al Hamzah 24 Kg 31.43N 44.58 E
awz Abu Dulū' 35 Eb 16.55N 32.30 E
awz Rajab 35 Fb 16.04N 35.34 E
aysān 35 Ec 10.45N 34.48 E
ayyārah 24 Je 35.48N 43.17 E
azvīn [Iran] 22 Gf 36.16N 50.00 E
azvīn [Iraq] 24 Je 34.21N 42.05 E
eqertarssuaq/Godhavn 67 Nc 69.20N 53.35W
eshm 24 Qi 26.58N 56.16 E
eshm 23 Id 26.45N 55.45 E
eydār 24 Md 36.07N 48.35 E
eys, Jazīreh-ye- 23 Hd 26.32N 53.58 E
ezel Owzan 23 Gb 36.45N 49.22 E
ian'an [China] 28 Ed 40.01N 118.42 E
ian'an [China] 28 Hb 44.58N 124.01 E
ianfangzi 28 Ad 40.01N 111.23 E
ian Gorlos (Qianguozhen) 27 Lb 45.05N 124.52 E
ian He 28 Dh 32.55N 117.10 E
ianjiang [China] 27 Ig 23.37N 108.58 E
ianjiang [China] 28 Bi 30.25N 112.54 E
ianjiang [China] 27 If 29.30N 108.45 E
ianning/Gartar 27 He 30.27N 101.29 E
ian Shan 27 Lc 40.35N 123.00 E
iansuo 27 Hf 25.27N 100.41 E
ianwei 27 Hf 29.08N 103.56 E
ianxi [China] 27 If 27.03N 106.04 E
ianxi [China] 28 Ed 40.08N 118.19 E
ianyang (Anjiang) 27 Jf 27.19N 110.13 E
iaojia 27 Hf 27.00N 103.00 E
iaowan 27 Gc 40.36N 96.42 E
ibilī 32 Ic 33.42N 8.58 E
Qichun (Caojiahe) 28 Ci 30.15N 115.26 E
Qidaogou 28 Id 41.31N 126.18 E
Qidong 28 Fi 31.48N 121.39 E
Qiemo/Qarqan 22 Kf 38.08N 85.32 E
Qift 24 Ei 26.00N 32.49 E
Qijiang 27 If 29.00N 106.39 E
Qijiaojing 27 Fc 43.28N 91.36 E
Qike → Xunke 27 Mb 49.34N 128.28 E
Qili → Shitai 28 Di 30.12N 117.28 E
Qilian (Babao) 27 Hd 38.14N 100.15 E
Qilian Shan 27 Gd 39.12N 98.35 E
Qilian Shan 21 Lf 38.30N 100.00 E
Qimantag 27 Fd 37.00N 91.00 E
Qimen 27 Kf 29.57N 117.39 E
Qinā 31 Kf 26.10N 32.43 E
Qinā, Wādī- 24 Ei 26.12N 32.44 E
Qin'an 27 Ie 34.50N 105.35 E
Qingchengzi 28 Gd 40.44N 123.36 E
Qingchuan 27 Ie 32.32N 105.11 E
Qingdao=Tsingtao (EN) 22 Of 36.05N 120.21 E
Qingduizi 28 Fd 41.27N 121.52 E
Qingfeng 28 Cg 35.54N 115.07 E
Qinggang 27 Mb 46.41N 126.03 E
Qinggil/Qinghe 27 Fb 46.43N 90.24 E
Qinghai Hu=Koko Nor (EN) 21 Mf 37.00N 100.20 E
Qinghai Sheng (Ch'ing-hai Sheng)=Tsinghai (EN) [2] 27 Gd 36.00N 96.00 E
Qing He 28 Hc 42.16N 124.10 E
Qinghe/Qinggil 27 Fb 46.43N 90.24 E
Qinghe (Gexianzhuang) 28 Cf 37.03N 115.39 E
Qinghemen 28 Fd 41.45N 121.25 E
Qingjian 27 Jd 37.10N 110.09 E
Qingjiang 22 Nf 33.31N 119.03 E
Qing Jiang 27 Je 30.24N 111.30 E
Qingjiang (Zhangshuzhen) 27 Kf 28.02N 115.31 E
Qingkou → Ganyu 28 Eg 34.50N 119.07 E
Qinglong 28 Ed 40.26N 118.58 E
Qinglong He 28 Ee 39.51N 118.51 E
Qingshan 28 Ci 30.39N 114.27 E
Qingshuihe 27 Jd 39.56N 111.41 E
Qingshui Jiang 27 If 27.11N 109.48 E
Qingtian 27 Lf 28.12N 120.17 E
Qingxian 28 De 38.35N 116.48 E
Qingxu 28 Bf 37.36N 112.21 E
Qingyang [China] 27 Id 36.01N 107.48 E
Qingyang [China] 28 Di 30.38N 117.50 E
Qingyuan 27 Lc 42.06N 124.56 E
Qingyuan (Nandaran) 28 Ce 38.46N 115.29 E
Qingyun (Xiejiaji) 28 Df 37.46N 117.22 E
Qing Zang Gaoyuan=Tibet, Plateau of- (EN) 21 Kf 32.30N 87.00 E
Qin He 28 Bg 35.01N 113.25 E
Qinhuangdao 27 Kg 40.00N 119.32 E
Qin Ling 21 Mf 34.00N 108.00 E
Qinshui 28 Bg 35.41N 112.10 E
Qintong 28 Fh 32.39N 120.06 E
Qinxian 28 Bf 36.46N 112.42 E
Qinyang 28 Bg 35.05N 112.56 E
Qinyuan 28 Bf 36.29N 112.20 E
Qinzhou 27 Ig 22.02N 108.30 E
Qionghai (Jiaji) 27 Jh 19.25N 110.28 E
Qionglai 27 He 30.24N 103.28 E
Qiongzhou Haixia 21 Ng 20.10N 110.15 E
Qipan Guan 27 Ie 32.45N 106.11 E
Qiqihar 22 Oe 47.21N 123.58 E
Qir 24 Oh 28.29N 53.04 E
Qira 27 Dd 37.02N 80.53 E
Qiryat Gat 24 Fg 31.36N 34.46 E
Qiryat Shemona 24 Ff 33.13N 35.34 E
Qiryat Yam 24 Ff 32.51N 35.04 E
Qishn 23 Hf 15.26N 51.40 E
Qi Shui 28 Ci 30.09N 115.22 E
Qishuyan 28 Fi 31.41N 120.04 E
Qitai 22 Ke 44.01N 89.28 E
Qitaihe 27 Nb 45.49N 130.51 E
Qiuxian (Matou) 28 Cf 36.50N 115.10 E
Qixia 27 Ff 37.18N 120.50 E
Qixian [China] 28 Bf 37.23N 112.21 E
Qixian [China] 28 Cg 34.33N 114.46 E
Qixian (Zhaoge) 28 Cg 35.35N 114.12 E
Qiyang 27 Jf 26.44N 111.50 E
Qizhou 28 Ci 30.04N 115.20 E
Qogir Feng=Godwin Austen (EN) 21 Jf 35.53N 76.30 E
Qog Qi 27 Ic 41.31N 107.00 E
Qog Ul 27 Kc 44.50N 116.19 E
Qohrūd, Kūhhā-ye- 21 Hf 32.40N 53.00 E
Qoltag 27 Ec 42.20N 88.45 E
Qom 22 Hf 34.39N 50.54 E
Qom 24 Ne 34.48N 51.02 E
Qomolangma Feng=Everest, Mount- (EN) 21 Kg 27.59N 86.56 E
Qomrud 24 Ne 34.43N 51.04 E
Qomsheh 23 Hc 32.00N 51.50 E
Qondūz [3] 23 Kb 36.45N 68.30 E
Qondūz 22 If 36.45N 68.51 E
Qondūz 23 Kb 37.00N 68.16 E
Qoqek/Tacheng 22 Ke 46.45N 82.57 E
Qōrnoq 41 Gf 64.30N 51.19W
Qorveh 24 Le 35.10N 47.48 E
Qoşbeh-ye Naşşār 23 Gc 30.02N 48.27 E
Qoţbābād [Iran] 24 Oh 28.39N 53.37 E
Qoţbābād [Iran] 24 Qi 27.46N 56.06 E
Qotūr 24 Kc 38.28N 44.25 E
Qotūr 24 Kc 38.46N 45.16 E
Quadda 31 Jh 8.04N 22.24 E
Quadros, Lagoa dos- 55 Gi 29.42S 50.05W
Quairading 59 Df 32.01S 117.25 E
Quakenbrück 10 Dd 52.41N 7.57 E
Quanah 45 Gi 34.18N 99.44W
Quanbao Shan 27 Je 34.08N 111.26 E
Quang Ngai 25 Le 15.07N 108.48 E
Quang Tri 25 Le 16.45N 107.11 E
Quan He 28 Ch 32.55N 115.52 E
Quanjiao 28 Eh 32.09N 118.16 E
Quan Long 25 Lg 9.11N 105.08 E
Quanzhou [China] 22 Ng 24.57N 118.35 E
Quanzhou [China] 27 Jf 26.01N 111.04 E
Qu'Appelle River 42 Hf 50.27N 101.19W
Quarai 56 Id 30.23S 56.27W
Quarai, Rio- 55 Dj 30.12S 57.36W
Quaregnon 12 Fd 50.26N 3.51 E
Quartu Sant'Elena 14 Dk 39.14N 9.11 E
Quartz Lake 42 Jb 70.57N 80.40W
Quartz Mountain 46 De 43.10N 122.40W
Quartzsite 46 Hj 33.40N 114.13W
Quatre, Isle- 51n Bb 12.57N 61.15W
Quatsino Sound 46 Aa 50.25N 128.10W
Qūchān 22 Hf 37.06N 58.30 E
Qué 36 Ce 14.43S 15.06 E
Queanbeyan 59 Jg 35.21S 149.14 E
Québec 39 Le 46.49N 71.13W
Québec [3] 42 Kf 54.00N 72.00W
Quebó 55 Db 14.36S 56.04W
Quebra Anzol, Rio- 55 Id 19.09S 47.38W
Quebracho 55 Dj 31.57S 57.57W
Quebradillas 51a Bb 18.28N 66.56W
Quedas do Iguaçu 55 Fg 25.31S 52.54W
Quedlinburg 10 He 51.47N 11.09 E
Queen, Cape- 42 Jd 64.43N 78.18W
Queen Alexandra Range 66 Jg 84.00S 168.00 E
Queen Bess, Mount- 42 Ff 51.18N 124.33W
Queenborough 12 Cc 51.25N 0.46 E
Queen Charlotte Islands 38 Gd 51.30N 129.00W
Queen Charlotte Sound 42 Ef 51.30N 129.30W
Queen Charlotte Strait 38 Gd 50.40N 127.25W
Queen Elizabeth Islands 38 Ib 79.00N 105.00W
Queen Elizabeth Range 66 Kg 83.20S 162.00 E
Queen Mary Land 66 Ge 69.00S 96.00 E
Queen Maud Gulf 38 Ic 68.25N 102.30W
Queen Maud Land (EN) 66 Cf 72.30S 12.00 E
Queen Maud Range 66 Lg 86.00S 160.00W
Queens Channel [Austl.] 59 Fb 14.45S 129.25 E
Queens Channel [N.W.T.-Can.] 42 Ha 76.11N 96.00W
Queensland 59 Id 22.00S 145.00 E
Queenstown [Austl.] 59 Jh 42.05S 145.33 E
Queenstown [Guy.] 50 Gi 7.12N 58.29W
Queenstown [N.Z.] 62 Cf 45.02S 168.40 E
Queenstown [S.Afr.] 31 Jl 31.52S 26.52 E
Queguay, Cuchilla del- 55 Dj 31.50S 57.30W
Queguay Grande, Río- 55 Ck 32.09S 58.09W
Queich 12 Ke 49.14N 8.23 E
Queimadas 54 Kf 10.58S 39.38W
Queiros 55 Ge 21.49S 50.13W
Quela 36 Cd 9.15S 17.05 E
Quelimane 31 Kj 17.51S 36.52 E
Quemado 45 Bi 34.20N 108.30W
Quemado de Güines 49 Gb 22.48N 80.15W
Quembo 36 De 14.57S 20.22 E
Quemú-Quemú 56 He 36.03S 63.33W
Quepos 49 Ei 9.25N 84.09W
Que Que 31 Jj 18.55S 29.49 E
Quequén 56 Ie 38.32S 58.42W
Quequén Grande, Río- 55 Cn 38.34S 58.43W
Quequén Salado, Río- 55 Bn 38.56S 60.31W
Quercy 11 Hj 44.15N 1.15 E
Querétaro [2] 47 Ed 21.00N 99.55W
Querétaro 39 Ig 20.36N 100.23W
Querobabi 48 Db 30.03N 111.01W
Quesada [C.R.] 49 Eh 10.19N 84.26W
Quesada [Sp.] 13 Ig 37.51N 3.04W
Queshan 27 Je 32.42N 114.04 E
Quesnel 42 Ff 52.59N 122.30W
Quesnel Lake 42 Ff 52.32N 121.05W
Questa 45 Dh 36.42N 105.36W
Quetena 54 Eh 22.10S 67.25W
Quetico Lake 45 Kb 48.37N 91.52W
Quetta 22 If 30.12N 67.00 E
Quevas, Cerro- 48 Dc 29.15N 111.20W
Quevedo 54 Cd 1.02S 79.27W
Queyras 11 Mj 44.44N 6.49 E
Quezaltenango 39 Jh 14.50N 91.31W
Quezaltenango [3] 49 Bf 14.45N 91.40W
Quezon 26 Ge 9.14N 117.56 E
Quezon City 22 Oh 14.38N 121.00 E
Qufu 28 Dg 35.35N 116.59 E
Quianguoshen → Qian Gorlos 27 Lb 45.05N 124.52 E
Quianshan 28 Di 30.38N 116.35 E
Quibala 36 Be 10.44S 14.59 E
Quibaxe 36 Bd 8.30S 14.36 E
Quibdó 54 Cb 5.42N 76.39W
Quiberon, Baie de- 11 Dg 47.32N 3.00W
Quiberon, Presqu'île de- 11 Cg 47.30N 3.08W
Quibor 49 Mi 9.56N 69.37W
Quiché [3] 49 Bf 15.30N 90.55W
Quierschied 12 Je 49.19N 7.03 E
Quiha 35 Fc 13.28N 39.33 E
Quiindy 55 Dh 25.58S 57.16W
Quijarro 55 Cd 19.26S 58.08W
Quilá 48 Fe 24.23N 107.13W
Quilán, Cabo- 56 Ff 43.16S 74.23W
Quillabamba 54 Df 12.49S 72.43W
Quillacollo 54 Eg 17.26S 66.17W
Quillagua 56 Gb 21.39S 69.33W
Quillan 11 Il 42.52N 2.11 E
Quillebeuf-sur-Seine 12 Ce 49.28N 0.31 E
Quillota 56 Fd 32.53S 71.16W
Quilmes 56 Id 34.44S 58.16W
Quilon 25 Fg 8.53N 76.36 E
Quilpie 59 Ie 26.37S 144.15 E
Quilqué 56 Fd 33.03S 71.27W
Quimari, Alto de- 49 Ii 8.07N 76.23W
Quimbele 36 Cd 6.30S 16.14 E
Quimili 56 He 27.38S 62.25W
Quimome 55 Bc 17.42S 61.16W
Quimome, Rio- 55 Bc 17.36S 61.09W
Quimper 11 Bf 48.00N 4.06W
Quimperlé 11 Cg 47.52N 3.33W
Quinault River 46 Cc 47.23N 124.18W
Quincy [Ca.-U.S.] 46 Eg 39.56N 120.57W
Quincy [Fl.-U.S.] 44 Ej 30.37N 84.32W
Quincy [Il.-U.S.] 43 Id 39.56N 91.23W
Quincy [Ma.-U.S.] 44 Ld 42.15N 71.01W
Quincy [Wa.-U.S.] 46 Fc 47.14N 119.51W
Quindío [2] 54 Cc 4.30N 75.40W
Quingey 11 Lg 47.06N 5.53 E
Quinhagak 40 Ge 59.45N 161.43W
Qui Nhon 22 Mh 13.46N 109.14 E
Quiñihual 55 Bm 37.47S 61.36W
Quiniluban Group 26 Hd 11.27N 120.48 E
Quinn River 46 Ff 40.25N 119.00W
Quiñones 48 De 24.22N 111.25W
Quintanar de la Orden 13 Ie 39.34N 3.03W
Quintana Roo [2] 47 Ge 19.40N 88.30W
Quinze, Lac des- 44 Hb 47.30N 79.00W
Quionga 37 Gb 10.35S 40.33 E
Quirigua 49 Cf 15.18N 89.07W
Quirihue 56 Fe 36.17S 72.32W
Quirima 36 Ce 10.48S 18.09 E
Quirinópolis 54 Hg 18.32S 50.30W
Quiroga 13 Eb 42.29N 7.16W
Quiros, Cap- 63b Cb 14.56S 167.01 E
Quisiro 49 Lh 10.53N 71.17W
Quissanga 37 Gb 12.25S 40.29 E
Quissico 37 Ed 24.43S 34.45 E
Quita Sueno Bank 47 Hf 14.20N 81.15W
Quitengues 36 Be 14.06S 14.05 E
Quiterage 37 Gb 11.45S 40.27 E
Quitéria, Rio- 55 Ge 20.16S 51.08W
Quitexe 36 Cd 7.56S 15.03 E
Quitilipi 55 Bh 26.52S 60.13W
Quitman [Ga.-U.S.] 44 Fj 30.47N 83.33W
Quitman [Ms.-U.S.] 45 Lj 32.03N 88.43W
Quito 53 If 0.13S 78.30W
Quitovac 48 Cb 31.32N 112.42W
Quixadá 54 Kd 4.58S 39.01W
Quixeramobim 54 Ke 5.12S 39.17W
Qujiang 28 Cj 28.14N 115.46 E
Qu Jiang [China] 27 Kf 29.32N 119.31 E
Qu Jiang [China] 27 Ie 30.01N 106.24 E
Qujing 27 Hf 25.31N 103.45 E
Qul'ān, Jazā'ir- 24 Fj 24.22N 35.23 E
Qulansiyah 23 Hg 12.41N 53.29 E
Qulaybiah 32 Jb 36.51N 11.06 E
Qulbān al 'Isāwīyah 24 Gg 30.38N 37.53 E
Qulbān an Nabk al Gharbī 24 Gg 31.15N 37.26 E
Qumar He 21 Lf 34.42N 94.50 E
Qumarlêb 27 Ge 34.35N 95.18 E
Qunayfidhah, Nafūd- 24 Kj 24.45N 45.30 E
Quoi 64d Ba 7.32N 151.59 E
Quoich 42 Id 63.56N 93.25W
Quorn 59 Hf 32.21S 138.03 E
Quqên/Jinchuan 27 He 31.02N 102.02 E
Quraitu 24 Ke 34.36N 45.30 E
Qurayyāt, Juzur- 32 Jb 35.48N 11.02 E
Qurbah 14 En 36.35N 10.52 E
Qurdūd 35 Dc 10.17N 29.56 E
Qūr Laban 24 Cg 30.23N 28.59 E
Qurunbāliyah 14 En 36.36N 10.30 E
Qūş 33 Fd 25.55N 32.45 E
Quşay'ir 35 Ic 14.55N 50.20 E
Qutdligssat 41 Gd 70.12N 53.00W
Quthing 37 Df 30.24S 27.42 E
Quţū 33 Hf 18.30N 41.04 E
Quwaiz 33 He 20.27N 44.53 E
Quxian 27 Kf 28.54N 118.53 E
Qüxü 27 Ff 29.23N 90.45 E
Quyang 28 Ce 38.37N 114.41 E
Quy Chau 25 Le 19.33N 105.06 E
Quzhou 28 Cf 36.47N 114.56 E
Qyteti Stalin 15 Ci 40.48N 19.54 E

R

Raab 10 Ni 47.41N 17.38 E
Raahe/Brahestad 7 Fd 64.41N 24.29 E
Rääkkylä 8 Mb 62.19N 29.37 E
Raalte 12 Ib 52.23N 6.17 E
Raamsdonk 12 Gc 51.41N 4.54 E
Raanes Peninsula 42 Ia 78.20N 86.20W
Raasay, Island of- 9 Gd 57.25N 6.04W
Raasay, Sound of- 9 Gd 57.25N 6.05W
Raasiku/Raziku 8 Ke 59.22N 25.11 E
Rab 14 If 44.46N 14.46 E
Rab 14 If 44.45N 14.46 E
Rába 10 Ni 47.41N 17.38 E
Raba 10 Qf 50.09N 20.30 E
Raba 22 Nj 8.27S 118.46 E
Rabāble 35 Hd 8.14N 48.18 E
Rabaçal 13 Ec 41.30N 7.12W
Rabat [Malta] 14 Io 35.50N 14.29 E
Rabat [Mor.] 31 Ge 34.02N 6.50W
Rabat-Salé [2] 32 Fc 34.02N 6.50W
Rabaul 58 Ge 4.12S 152.11 E
Rábca 10 Ni 47.41N 17.37 E
Rabenau 12 Kd 50.40N 8.52 E
Rabī', Ash Shallāl ar-= Fourth Cataract (EN) 30 Kg 18.47N 32.03 E
Rabiah 24 Jd 36.47N 42.07 E
Rábida, Monasterio de- 13 Fg 37.12N 6.55W
Rābigh 23 Ee 22.48N 39.02 E
Rabinal 49 Bf 15.06N 90.27W
Rabka 10 Pg 49.36N 19.56 E
Rabočeostrovsk 7 Id 64.59N 34.44 E
Rabyānah, Şaḥrā'- 30 Jf 24.30N 21.00 E
Rabyānah, Wāḥāt al-= Rebiana Oasis (EN) 33 De 24.14N 21.59 E
Răcăciuni 15 Jc 46.20N 26.59 E
Racalmuto 14 Hm 37.24N 13.44 E
Răcășdia 15 Ee 44.59N 21.38 E
Racconigi 14 Bf 44.46N 7.46 E
Race, Cape- 38 Ne 46.40N 53.10W
Race Point 44 Ld 42.04N 70.14W
Rach Gia 22 Mh 10.01N 105.05 E
Rachid 32 Ef 18.48N 11.41W
Raciąż 10 Qd 52.47N 20.06 E
Racibórz 10 Of 50.06N 18.13 E
Racine 43 Jc 42.43N 87.48W
Ráckeve 10 Oi 47.10N 18.57 E
Racos 15 Ic 46.03N 25.30 E
Råda 8 Ed 60.00N 13.36 E
Radama, Iles- 37 Hb 14.00S 47.47 E
Radan 15 Ef 43.02N 21.30 E
Rădăuţi 15 Ib 47.51N 25.55 E
Radbuza 10 Jg 49.46N 13.24 E
Radeberg 10 Je 51.07N 13.55 E
Radebeul 10 Je 51.06N 13.39 E
Radeče 14 Jd 46.04N 15.11 E
Radehov 10 Uf 50.13N 24.43 E
Radenthein 14 Hd 46.48N 13.43 E
Radevormwald 12 Jc 51.12N 7.22 E
Radew 10 Lb 54.07N 15.50 E
Radford 44 Gg 37.07N 80.34W
Radnevo 15 Ig 42.18N 25.56 E
Radolfzell 10 Ei 47.44N 8.58 E
Radom [2] 10 Re 51.25N 21.10 E
Radom 6 Ie 51.25N 21.10 E
Radomir 15 Fg 42.33N 22.58 E
Radomka 10 Re 51.43N 21.26 E
Radomsko 10 Pe 51.05N 19.25 E
Radomyšl 16 Fd 50.29N 29.14 E
Radomyśl Wielki 10 Rf 50.12N 21.16 E
Radoškoviči 8 Lj 54.12N 27.17 E
Radotín 10 Kg 49.59N 14.22 E
Radovanu 15 Je 44.12N 26.31 E
Radoviš 15 Fh 41.38N 22.28 E
Radøy 8 Ad 60.40N 5.00 E
Radstadt 14 Hc 47.23N 13.27 E
Radun 10 Vb 54.02N 25.07 E
Radunia 10 Ob 54.25N 18.45 E
Raduša 15 Dg 42.08N 21.25 E
Radvaniči 14 Lg 43.52N 17.29 E
Radvaniči 10 Ue 51.59N 24.09 E
Radviliškis 7 Fi 55.50N 23.33 E
Radymno 10 Sg 49.57N 22.48 E
Radziejów 10 Od 52.38N 18.32 E
Radzyń Podlaski 10 Se 51.48N 22.38 E
Rae 42 Fd 62.50N 116.00W
Rāe Bareli 25 Gc 26.13N 81.14 E
Rae Isthmus 42 Ic 66.55N 86.10W
Raesfeld 12 Ic 51.46N 6.51 E
Raeside, Lake- 59 Ee 29.30S 121.50 E
Raetihi 62 Fc 39.26S 175.17 E
Raevavae, Ile- 57 Mg 23.52S 147.40W
Raevski, Groupe- 61 Mc 16.45S 144.14W
Rāf, Jabal- 24 Hh 29.12N 39.48 E
Rafaela 53 Ji 31.17S 61.30W
Rafai 35 Ce 4.58N 23.56 E
Rafḥā' 23 Fd 29.42N 43.30 E
Rafi 34 Fc 13.28N 4.10 E
Rāfkā 24 Qe 35.55N 57.36 E
Rafsanjān 23 Ic 30.24N 56.01 E
Råfsö/Reposaari 8 Ic 61.37N 21.27 E
Raga 31 Jh 8.28N 25.41 E
Ragay Gulf 26 Hd 13.30N 122.45 E
Ragged Island 49 Jb 22.12N 75.44W
Ragged Island Range 47 Id 22.42N 75.55W
Ragged Point 51q Bb 13.10N 59.25W
Raglan 62 Fb 37.48S 174.52 E
Raguenau 44 Ma 49.04N 68.32W
Ragusa 14 In 36.55N 14.44 E
Raguva 8 Ki 55.30N 24.45 E
Raha 26 Hg 4.51S 122.43 E
Raḥā, Ḥarrat ar- 24 Gi 27.40N 36.40 E
Rahad al Bardī 35 Cc 11.18N 23.53 E
Rahama 34 Gc 10.25N 8.41 E
Rahat, Ḥarrat- 23 Fe 23.00N 40.05 E
Rahat Dağı 15 Ml 37.08N 29.49 E
Rahden 12 Kb 52.26N 8.37 E
Rāhgāmāti 25 Id 22.38N 92.12 E
Rahīmyār Khan 25 Ec 28.25N 70.18 E
Rahmanovskije Ključi 19 If 49.35N 86.35 E
Rahmet 19 Gf 49.19N 65.16 E
Råholt 8 Dd 60.16N 11.11 E
Rahouia 13 Ni 35.32N 1.01 E
Rahov 16 De 48.02N 24.18 E
Rahrbach, Kirchhundem- 12 Jc 51.02N 7.59 E
Raia 13 Df 39.00N 8.17W
Raiatea, Ile- 57 Lf 16.50S 151.25W
Raices 55 Cj 31.54S 59.16W
Rāichūr 22 Jh 16.12N 77.22 E
Raiganj 25 Hc 25.37N 88.07 E
Raigarh 25 Gd 21.54N 83.24 E
Raijua, Pulau- 26 Hi 10.37S 121.36 E
Rainbow Peak 46 Hd 44.55N 115.17W
Rainier, Mount- 38 Ge 46.52N 121.46W
Rainy Lake 43 Ib 48.42N 93.10W
Rainy River 45 Ib 48.43N 94.29W
Rainy River 45 Ib 48.50N 94.41W
Raipur 22 Kg 21.14N 81.38 E
Raisi, Punta- 14 Hl 38.11N 13.06 E
Raisio/Reso 7 Ff 60.29N 22.11 E
Raita Bank (EN) 60 Mb 25.25N 169.30W
Raja Ampat, Kepulauan- 26 Jg 0.50S 130.25 E
Rājahmundry 22 Kh 16.59N 81.47 E
Rajakoski 7 Gb 68.59N 29.07 E
Rajang 21 Ni 2.07N 111.12 E
Rājapālaiyam 25 Fg 9.27N 77.34 E
Rājasthān [3] 25 Ec 26.00N 74.00 E
Rājasthān Canal 25 Eb 31.10N 75.00 E
Rajbiraj 25 Hc 26.30N 86.50 E
Rajčihinsk 20 Hg 49.43N 129.27 E
Rajevski 17 Gi 54.04N 54.56 E
Rājgarh 25 Fc 28.38N 75.23 E
Rajgródzkie, Jezioro- 10 Sc 53.45N 22.38 E
Rajka 10 Ni 48.00N 17.12 E
Rajkot 22 Jg 22.18N 70.47 E
Raj-Nāndgaon 25 Gd 21.06N 81.02 E
Rajony Respublikanskogo Podčinenija [Kirg.-U.S.S.R.] [3] 19 Hg 42.30N 73.50 E
Rajony Respublikanskogo Podčinenija [Tad.-U.S.S.R.] [3] 19 Gh 38.50N 69.30 E

Index Symbols

[1] Independent Nation
[2] State, Region
[3] District, County
[4] Municipality
[5] Colony, Dependency
Continent
Physical Region
Historical or Cultural Region
Mount, Mountain
Volcano
Hill
Mountains, Mountain Range
Hills, Escarpment
Plateau, Upland
Pass, Gap
Plain, Lowland
Delta
Salt Flat
Valley, Canyon
Crater, Cave
Karst Features
Depression
Polder
Desert, Dunes
Forest, Woods
Heath, Steppe
Oasis
Cape, Point
Coast, Beach
Cliff
Peninsula
Isthmus
Sandbank
Island
Atoll
Rock, Reef
Islands, Archipelago
Rocks, Reefs
Coral Reef
Well, Spring
Geyser
River, Stream
Waterfall Rapids
River Mouth, Estuary
Lake
Salt Lake
Intermittent Lake
Reservoir
Swamp, Pond
Canal
Glacier
Ice Shelf, Pack Ice
Ocean
Sea
Gulf, Bay
Strait, Fjord
Lagoon
Bank
Seamount
Tablemount
Ridge
Shelf
Basin
Escarpment, Sea Scarp
Fracture
Trench, Abyss
National Park, Reserve
Point of Interest
Recreation Site
Cave, Cavern
Historic Site
Ruins
Wall, Walls
Church, Abbey
Temple
Scientific Station
Airport
Port
Lighthouse
Mine
Tunnel
Dam, Bridge

Name	Page	Grid	Lat.	Long.
Rājshāhi	25	Hd	24.22N	88.36 E
Rakahanga Atoll	57	Kl	10.02S	161.05W
Rakaia	62	Ee	43.54S	172.13 E
Rakaia	62	Ee	43.45S	172.01 E
Rakan, Ra's-	24	Ni	26.10N	51.13 E
Rakata, Pulau-	26	Eh	6.10S	105.26 E
Raka Zangbo	27	Ef	29.24N	87.58 E
Rakhawt, Wādī-	35	Ib	18.16N	51.50 E
Rakht-e Shāh	24	Mf	33.17N	49.23 E
Rakitnoje	28	Mb	45.36N	134.17 E
Rakitovo	15	Hh	41.59N	24.05 E
Rakkestad	8	De	59.26N	11.21 E
Rakoniewice	10	Md	52.10N	16.16 E
Rakops	37	Cd	21.01S	24.20 E
Rakovnicka panev	10	Jf	50.10N	13.30 E
Rakovník	10	Jf	50.06N	13.43 E
Rakovski	15	Hg	42.18N	24.58 E
Raków	10	Rf	50.42N	21.03 E
Rakušečny, Mys-	16	Qh	42.52N	51.55 E
Råkvåg	7	Ce	63.46N	10.05 E
Rakvere	7	Gg	59.22N	26.22 E
Raleigh [N.C.-U.S.]	39	Lf	35.47N	78.39W
Raleigh [Ont.-Can.]	45	Kb	49.31N	91.56W
Raleigh Bay	44	Ih	35.00N	76.20W
Ralik Chain	57	Hd	8.00N	167.00 E
Rama	47	Hf	12.09N	84.15W
Rama, Río-	49	Eg	12.08N	84.13W
Ramādah	32	Jc	32.19N	10.24 E
Ramadīn, Wādī-	24	Ej	24.57N	32.34 E
Ramales de la Victoria	13	Ia	43.15N	3.27W
Ramalho, Serra do-	55	Ja	13.45S	44.00W
Ramapo Bank (EN)	57	Fb	27.15N	145.10 E
Ramatlabama	37	De	25.37S	25.30 E
Ramberg	10	He	51.45N	11.05 E
Rambervillers	11	Mf	48.21N	6.38 E
Rambi	63d	Cb	16.30S	179.59W
Rambouillet	11	Hf	48.39N	1.50 E
Rambutyo Island	57	Fe	2.18S	147.48 E
Rāmhormoz	24	Mg	31.16N	49.36 E
Ramigala/Ramygala	8	Ki	55.28N	24.23 E
Ramis	35	Gd	8.02N	41.36 E
Ramla	24	Fg	31.55N	34.52 E
Ramlīyah, 'Aqabat ar-	24	Di	26.01N	30.42 E
Ramlu	35	Gc	13.20N	41.45 E
Ramm, Jabal-	24	Fh	29.35N	35.24 E
Rammāk, Ghurd ar-	24	Ch	29.40N	29.20 E
Rāmnagar	25	Fc	29.24N	79.07 E
Ramnäs	8	Ge	59.46N	16.12 E
Ramón Santamarina	55	Cn	38.26S	59.20W
Ramos	63a	Ec	8.16S	160.11 E
Ramos, Río-	48	Ge	25.35N	105.03W
Ramotswa	37	Dd	24.52S	25.50 E
Rāmpur	25	Fc	28.49N	79.02 E
Ramree	25	Ie	19.06N	93.48 E
Rams	24	Qj	25.53N	56.02 E
Rāmsar	24	Nd	36.53N	50.41 E
Ramsele	7	De	63.33N	16.29 E
Ramsey [Eng.-U.K.]	12	Bb	52.27N	0.07W
Ramsey [Ont.-Can.]	44	Fb	47.29N	82.24W
Ramsey [U.K.]	9	Ig	54.20N	4.21W
Ramsey Lake	42	Jg	47.20N	83.00W
Ramsgate	9	Oj	51.20N	1.25 E
Rāmshīr	24	Mg	30.50N	49.30 E
Ramsjö	7	De	62.11N	15.39 E
Ramstein-Miesenbach	12	Je	49.27N	7.32 E
Ramsund	7	Db	68.29N	16.32 E
Ramu	60	Di	4.02S	144.41 E
Ramu	36	Hb	3.56N	41.13 E
Ramvik	7	De	62.49N	17.51 E
Ramville, Ilet-	51h	Bb	14.42N	60.53W
Ramygala/Ramigala	8	Ki	55.28N	24.23 E
Rana	7	Dc	66.20N	14.08 E
Rañadoiro, Sierra del-	13	Fa	43.20N	6.45W
Ranai	26	Ef	3.55N	108.23 E
Ranakah, Potjo-	26	Hh	8.38S	120.31 E
Rana Kao, Volcán-	65d	Ac	27.11S	109.27W
Rana Roi, Volcán-	65d	Ab	27.05S	109.23W
Rana Roraka, Volcán-	65d	Bb	27.07S	109.18W
Ranau	26	Ge	5.58N	116.41 E
Ranča	14	Lf	44.24N	17.22 E
Rancagua	53	Ii	34.10S	70.45W
Rance	11	Ef	48.31N	1.59W
Rance, Sivry-Rance-	12	Gd	50.09N	4.16 E
Rancharia	55	Gf	22.15S	50.55W
Rancheria, Río-	49	Kh	11.34N	72.54W
Rānchī	22	Kg	23.21N	85.20 E
Ranchos	55	Cl	35.32S	58.22W
Ranco, Lago-	56	Ff	40.14S	72.24W
Randa	35	Gc	11.51N	42.40 E
Randaberg	8	Ae	59.00N	5.36 E
Randazzo	14	Im	37.53N	14.57 E
Randers	7	Ch	56.28N	10.03 E
Randers Fjord	8	Dh	56.35N	10.20 E
Randijaure	7	Ec	66.42N	19.18 E
Randow	10	Kc	53.41N	14.04 E
Randsfjorden	7	Cf	60.25N	10.25 E
Ranérou	34	Cb	15.18N	13.58W
Ranfurly	62	Df	45.08S	170.06 E
Rangasa, Tanjung-	26	Gg	3.33S	118.56 E
Ranger	45	Gj	32.28N	98.41W
Rangiora	62	Ee	43.18S	172.36 E
Rangiroa Atoll	57	Mf	15.10S	147.35W
Rangitaiki	62	Gb	37.55S	176.53 E
Rangitata	62	Df	44.10S	171.30 E
Rangitikei	62	Fd	40.17S	175.13 E
Rangkasbitung	26	Eh	6.21S	106.15 E
Rangoon	22	Lh	16.47N	96.10 E
Rangoon [3]	25	Je	16.40N	95.20 E
Rangpur	25	Hc	25.44N	89.16 E
Rāniyah	24	Kd	36.15N	44.53 E
Rankin Inlet	39	Jc	62.45N	92.10W
Rankoshi	29a	Bb	42.47N	140.31 E
Rannoch, Loch-	9	Ie	56.41N	4.20W
Ranobe	37	Gc	17.10S	44.08 E
Ranon	63b	Dc	16.09S	168.07 E
Ranong	25	Jg	9.59N	98.40 E
Ranongga Island	60	Fi	8.05S	156.34 E
Ranova	16	Lb	54.07N	40.14 E
Ransaren	7	Dd	65.14N	14.59 E
Rantabe	37	Hc	15.42S	49.39 E
Rantasalmi	8	Mb	62.04N	28.18 E
Rantaupanjang	26	Fg	1.23S	112.04 E
Rantauprapat	26	Cf	2.06N	99.50 E
Rantekombola, Bulu-	21	Oj	3.21S	120.01 E
Rantoul	45	Lf	40.19N	88.09W
Ranua	7	Gd	65.55N	26.32 E
Ranyah, Wādī-	33	He	21.18N	43.20 E
Raohe	27	Nb	46.48N	133.58 E
Raon-l'Étape	11	Mf	48.24N	6.51 E
Raoui, Erg er-	32	Gd	29.15N	2.45W
Raoul Island	57	Jg	29.15S	177.52W
Raoyang	28	Ce	38.14N	115.44 E
Raoyang He	28	Gd	41.13N	122.12 E
Rapa, Ile-	57	Mg	27.36S	144.20W
Rapallo	14	Df	44.21N	9.14 E
Rapang	26	Gg	3.50S	119.48 E
Rapa Nui/Pascua, Isla de-= Easter Island (EN)	57	Qg	27.07S	109.22W
Raper, Cape -	42	Kc	69.41N	67.24W
Rapid City	39	Ie	44.05N	103.14W
Rapid Creek	45	Ee	43.54N	102.37W
Rapid River	44	Dc	45.58N	86.59W
Räpina/Rjapina	8	Lf	58.03N	27.35 E
Rapla	7	Fg	59.02N	24.47 E
Rappahannock River	44	Ig	37.34N	76.18W
Rápulo, Río-	52	Jg	13.43S	65.32W
Rāqūbah	31	If	28.58N	19.02 E
Raraka Atoll	57	Mf	16.10S	144.54W
Raroia Atoll	57	Mf	16.05S	142.26W
Rarotonga Island	57	Lg	21.14S	159.46W
Rasa, Punta-	52	Jj	40.51S	62.19W
Ra's Abū Daraj	24	Eh	29.23N	32.33 E
Ra's Abū Rudays	24	Eh	28.53N	33.11 E
Ra's Abū Shajarah	35	Fa	21.04N	37.14 E
Ra's Ajdīr	33	Bc	33.09N	11.34 E
Ra's al 'Ayn	24	Id	36.51N	40.04 E
Ra's al-Barr	24	Dg	31.31N	31.50 E
Ra's al Ḥikmah	24	Bg	31.08N	27.50 E
Ra's al Jabal	14	Em	37.13N	10.08 E
Ra's al Khafjī	24	Mh	28.25N	48.30 E
Ra's al Khaymah	23	Id	25.47N	55.57 E
Ra's al Mish'āb	24	Mh	28.12N	48.37 E
Ra's al Unūf	33	Cc	30.31N	18.34 E
Ra's an Naqb	24	Fh	30.00N	35.29 E
Ra's as Sidr	24	Eh	29.36N	32.40 E
Ra's at Tannūrah	24	Ni	26.42N	50.10 E
Ras Beddouza	30	Ge	32.22N	9.18W
Ras Dashan	30	Kg	13.19N	38.20 E
Raseiniai/Rasejnjaj	7	Fi	55.23N	23.07 E
Rasejnjaj/Raseiniai	7	Fi	55.23N	23.07 E
Râs el Mâ	34	Eb	16.37N	4.27W
Ras-el-Ma	13	Ji	35.08N	2.29W
Ras el Oued	13	Ri	35.57N	5.02 E
Ra's Ghārib	33	Fd	28.21N	33.06 E
Rashād	35	Ec	11.51N	31.04 E
Rāshayyā	24	Ff	33.30N	35.51 E
Rashīd=Rosetta (EN)	33	Fc	31.24N	30.25 E
Rashīd, Maşabb-	24	Dg	31.30N	30.20 E
Rasht	22	Gf	37.16N	49.36 E
Rāsiga 'Alūla	35	Ic	11.59N	50.50 E
Rās Jumbo	35	Gf	1.37S	41.31 E
Raška	15	Df	43.18N	20.38 E
Ra's Madhar, Jabal-	24	Gj	25.46N	37.32 E
Ra's Matārimah	24	Eh	29.27N	32.43 E
Rasmussen Basin	42	Hc	67.56N	95.15W
Rason Lake	59	Ee	28.45S	124.20 E
Rasskazovo	19	Ee	52.39N	41.57 E
Rassua, Ostrov-	20	Kg	47.40N	153.00 E
Rassvet	20	Ee	57.00N	91.32 E
Ras-Tarf, Cap-	13	Ii	35.17N	3.41W
Rastatt	10	Eh	48.51N	8.12 E
Rastede	12	Ka	53.15N	8.12 E
Rastigaissa	7	Ga	70.03N	26.18 E
Råstojaure	7	Eb	68.45N	20.30 E
Ra's Ţurunbī	24	Fj	25.40N	34.35 E
Rasūl	24	Pi	27.10N	55.30 E
Ra's Zayt	33	Fd	27.56N	33.31 E
Rat	40a	Bb	51.55N	178.20 E
Ratak Chain	57	Id	9.00N	171.00 E
Ratangarh	25	Ec	28.05N	74.36 E
Rätansbyn	7	De	62.29N	14.32 E
Rat Buri	25	Jf	13.32N	99.49 E
Rathbun Lake	45	Jf	40.54N	93.05W
Ráth Droma/Rathdrum	9	Gi	52.56N	6.13W
Rathdrum/Ráth Droma	9	Gi	52.56N	6.13W
Rathenow	10	Id	52.36N	12.20 E
Rathlin Island/Reachlainn	9	Gf	55.18N	6.13W
Ráth Luirc/An Ráth	9	Ei	52.21N	8.41W
Rathor, Pik-	18	If	37.55N	72.14 E
Rätikon	14	Dc	47.03N	9.40 E
Ratingen	12	Ic	51.18N	6.51 E
Rätische Alpen=Rhaetian Alps (EN)	14	Dd	46.30N	10.00 E
Rat Islands	38	Ad	52.00N	178.00 E
Ratlām	25	Fd	23.19N	75.04 E
Ratmanova, Ostrov-	20	Lc	65.45N	169.00W
Ratnāgiri	25	Ee	16.59N	73.18 E
Ratnapura	25	Gg	6.41N	80.24 E
Ratno	16	Dd	51.42N	24.31 E
Raton	43	Gd	36.54N	104.24W
Ratqh, Wādī ar-	24	Ie	34.25N	40.55 E
Rätta	20	Dd	63.35N	84.05 E
Rattlesnake Hills	46	Le	42.45N	107.10W
Rattray Head	9	Ld	57.38N	1.46W
Rättvik	7	Df	60.53N	15.06 E
Ratz, Mount-	38	Fd	57.23N	132.19W
Ratzeburg	10	Gc	53.42N	10.46 E
Raub	26	Df	3.48N	101.52 E
Rauch	56	Ie	36.46S	59.06W
Raucourt-et-Flaba	12	Ge	49.36N	4.57 E
Raudeberg	8	Ab	61.59N	5.09 E
Rauer Islands	66	Fe	68.51S	77.50 E
Raufarhöfn	7a	Ca	66.27N	15.57W
Raufjellet	8	Dc	61.15N	11.00 E
Raufoss	7	Cf	60.43N	10.37 E
Raukotaha	64n	Ac	10.28S	161.01W
Raukumara Range	62	Gc	38.00S	178.00 E
Rauland	8	Be	59.44N	8.00 E
Raúl Leoni, Represa- (Guri)	54	Fb	7.30N	63.00W
Rauma	7	Be	62.33N	7.43 E
Rauma/Raumo	7	Ef	61.08N	21.30 E
Raumo/Rauma	7	Ef	61.08N	21.30 E
Rauna	8	Kg	57.14N	25.39 E
Raunds	12	Bb	52.20N	0.32W
Raurimu	62	Fc	39.07S	175.24 E
Raurkela	22	Kg	22.13N	84.53 E
Rausu	28	Rb	44.01N	145.12 E
Rausu-Dake	29a	Da	44.06N	145.07 E
Rautalampi	8	Lb	62.38N	26.50 E
Ravahere Atoll	57	Mf	18.14S	142.09W
Ravan	14	Mf	44.15N	18.16 E
Ravanica, Manastir-	15	Ef	43.58N	21.30 E
Ravānsar	24	Le	34.43N	46.40 E
Ravanusa	14	Hm	37.16N	13.58 E
Rāvar	24	Qg	31.12N	56.53 E
Rava-Russkaja	16	Cd	50.13N	23.37 E
Ravels	12	Gc	51.22N	4.59 E
Ravelsbach	14	Jb	48.30N	15.50 E
Ravels-Poppel	12	Hc	51.27N	5.02 E
Ravenna [It.]	14	Gf	44.25N	12.12 E
Ravenna [Nb.-U.S.]	45	Gf	41.02N	98.55W
Ravensburg	10	Fi	47.47N	9.37 E
Ravenshoe	58	Ff	17.37S	145.29 E
Ravensthorpe	59	Ef	33.35S	120.02 E
Ravi	21	Jf	30.35N	71.49 E
Ravnina	19	Gh	37.57N	62.42 E
Rawaki Atoll (Phoenix)	57	Je	3.43S	170.43W
Rāwalpindi	22	Jf	33.35N	73.03 E
Rawa Mazowiecka	10	Qe	51.46N	20.16 E
Rawāndūz	24	Kd	36.37N	44.31 E
Rawdah	24	Ie	35.15N	41.05 E
Rawene	62	Ea	35.24S	173.30 E
Rawicz	10	Me	51.37N	16.52 E
Rawka	10	Qd	52.07N	20.08 E
Rawlinna	58	Dh	31.01S	125.20 E
Rawlins	43	Fc	41.47N	107.14W
Rawlinson Range	59	Fd	24.50S	128.00 E
Rawson [Arg.]	55	Bl	34.36S	60.04W
Rawson [Arg.]	53	Jj	43.18S	65.06W
Rawura, Ras-	36	He	10.20S	40.30 E
Raxaul	25	Gc	26.59N	84.51 E
Ray, Cape -	42	Lg	47.37N	59.19W
Raya, Bukit-	21	Nj	1.32S	111.05 E
Rayadrug	25	Ff	14.42N	76.52 E
Rayāt	24	Kd	36.40N	44.58 E
Rayleigh	12	Cc	51.35N	0.37 E
Raymond [Alta.-Can.]	46	Ib	49.27N	112.39W
Raymond [Wa.-U.S.]	46	Dc	46.41N	123.44W
Raymondville	43	Hf	26.29N	97.47W
Rayne	45	Jk	30.14N	92.16W
Rayón [Mex.]	48	Jg	21.51N	99.40W
Rayón [Mex.]	48	Dc	29.43N	110.35W
Rayones	48	Ie	25.01N	100.05W
Rayong	25	Kf	12.40N	101.17 E
Raysūt	23	Hf	16.54N	54.02 E
Raytown	45	Ig	39.00N	94.28W
Raz, Pointe du-	11	Bf	48.02N	4.44W
Razan	24	Me	35.23N	49.02 E
Razdan	16	Ni	40.28N	44.43 E
Razdelnaja	16	Gf	46.50N	30.05 E
Razdolinsk	20	Ee	58.25N	94.44 E
Razdolnaja	28	Kc	43.20N	131.49 E
Razdolnoje [R.S.F.S.R.]	28	Kc	43.33N	131.55 E
Razdolnoje [Ukr.-U.S.S.R.]	16	Hg	45.47N	33.30 E
Razgrad	15	Jf	43.32N	26.31 E
Razgrad [2]	15	Jf	43.32N	26.31 E
Razī	24	Mc	38.32N	48.08 E
Raziku/Raasiku	8	Ke	59.22N	25.11 E
Razlog	15	Gh	41.53N	23.28 E
Razo	32	Cf	16.37N	24.36W
Ré, Ile de-	5	Ff	46.12N	1.25W
Reachlainn	9	Gf	55.18N	6.13W
Reachlainn/Rathlin Island	9	Gf	55.18N	6.13W
Reachrainn/Lambay	9	Gh	53.29N	6.01W
Read	42	Gc	69.12N	114.30W
Reading [Eng.-U.K.]	9	Mj	51.28N	0.59W
Reading [Pa.-U.S.]	43	Lc	40.20N	75.55W
Real, Cordillera- [Bol.]	54	Eg	16.30S	68.30W
Real, Cordillera- [Ec.]	52	If	3.00S	78.00W
Real Audiencia	55	Cm	36.11S	58.35W
Real del Castillo	48	Aa	31.58N	116.19W
Realicó	56	He	35.02S	64.15W
Réalmont	11	Ik	43.47N	2.12 E
Reao Atoll	57	Nf	18.31S	136.23W
Reatini, Monti-	14	Gh	42.35N	12.50 E
Rebais	12	Ff	48.51N	3.14 E
Rebecca, Lake-	59	Ee	29.55S	122.10 E
Rebiana Oasis (EN)= Rabyānah, Wāḥāt al-	33	De	24.14N	21.59 E
Rebollera	13	Hf	38.25N	4.02W
Reboly	7	He	63.52N	30.47 E
Rebord Manamblen	37	Hd	24.05S	46.30 E
Rebun	28	Pb	45.23N	141.02 E
Rebun-Dake	29a	Ba	45.22N	141.01 E
Rebun-Suidō	29a	Ba	45.15N	141.05 E
Rebun-Tō	27	Pb	45.23N	141.10 E
Recalde	55	Bm	36.39S	61.05W
Recanati	14	Hg	43.24N	13.32 E
Recaş	15	Ed	45.48N	21.30 E
Recherche, Archipelago of the-	57	Dh	34.06S	122.45 E
Rečica	19	De	52.22N	30.25 E
Recife	53	Mf	8.03S	34.54W
Recife, Cape-	30	Jl	34.02S	25.45 E
Recke	12	Jb	52.23N	7.43 E
Recklinghausen	10	De	51.37N	7.12 E
Recknitz	10	Ib	54.14N	12.28 E
Recoaro Terme	14	Fe	45.42N	11.13 E
Reconquista	56	Ic	29.09S	59.39W
Recovery Glacier	66	Ag	81.10S	28.00W
Recreo	56	Gc	29.16S	65.04W
Recz	10	Lc	53.16N	15.33 E
Reda	10	Ob	54.38N	18.30 E
Redange	12	He	49.46N	5.54 E
Red Bank	44	Eh	35.07N	85.17W
Red Bay	42	Lf	51.44N	56.25W
Red Bluff	43	Cc	40.11N	122.15W
Red Bluff Reservoir	45	Ek	31.57N	103.56W
Redbridge, London-	12	Cc	51.35N	0.08 E
Red Butte	46	Ii	35.55N	112.03W
Redcar	9	Lg	54.37N	1.04W
Red Cliff	51c	Ab	17.05N	62.32W
Redcliff	37	Dc	19.02S	29.50 E
Redcliffe, Mount-	59	Ee	28.25S	121.32 E
Red Cloud	45	Gf	40.05N	98.32W
Red Deer	39	Hd	52.16N	113.48W
Red Deer [Can.]	42	Hf	52.55N	101.27W
Red Deer [Can.]	38	Id	50.56N	109.54W
Redding	39	Ge	40.35N	122.24W
Redditch	9	Li	52.19N	1.56W
Rede	9	Kf	55.08N	2.13W
Redenção	54	Kd	4.13S	38.43W
Redfield	43	Hc	44.53N	98.31W
Red Hill	65a	Ec	20.43N	156.15W
Red Hills	45	Gh	37.25N	99.25W
Redkino	7	Ih	56.40N	36.19 E
Red Lake	42	If	51.05N	93.55W
Red Lake	42	If	51.03N	93.49W
Red Lake River	45	Hc	47.55N	97.01W
Red Lakes	43	Ib	48.05N	94.45W
Redlands	46	Gi	34.03N	117.11W
Red Lodge	46	Kd	45.11N	109.15W
Redmond	43	Cc	44.17N	121.11W
Red Mountain [Ca.-U.S.]	46	Df	41.35N	123.06W
Red Mountain [Mt.-U.S.]	46	Ic	47.07N	112.44W
Red Oak	45	If	41.01N	95.14W
Redon	11	Dg	47.39N	2.05W
Redonda	50	Ed	16.55N	62.19W
Redondela	13	Db	42.17N	8.36W
Redondo	13	Ef	38.39N	7.33W
Redondo Beach	46	Fj	33.51N	118.23W
Redoubt Volcano	38	Dc	60.29N	152.45W
Red River [N.Amer.]	38	Jd	50.24N	96.48W
Red River [U.S.]	38	Jf	31.00N	91.40W
Red River (EN)=Hông, Sông-	21	Mg	20.17N	106.34 E
Red River (EN)=Yuan Jiang [Asia]	21	Mg	20.17N	106.34 E
Red Rock, Lake-	45	Jf	41.30N	93.20W
Red Rock River	46	Id	44.59N	112.52W
Redruth	9	Hk	50.13N	5.14W
Red Sea (EN)=Aḥmar, Al Baḥr al-	30	Kf	25.00N	38.00 E
Redstone	42	Fd	64.17N	124.33W
Redstone	46	Da	52.08N	123.42W
Red Volta (EN)=Volta Rouge	30	Gh	10.34N	0.30W
Redwater Creek	46	Mb	48.03N	105.13W
Red Wing	43	Ic	44.34N	92.31W
Redwood City	46	Dh	37.29N	122.13W
Redwood Falls	45	Id	44.32N	95.07W
Ree, Lough-/Loch Rí	9	Fh	53.35N	8.00W
Reed City	44	Ed	43.53N	85.31W
Reedley	46	Fh	36.24N	119.37W
Reeds Peak	45	Cj	33.09N	107.51W
Reedsport	43	Cc	43.42N	124.06W
Reedy Glacier	66	Ng	85.30S	134.00W
Reef Islands	57	Hf	10.15S	166.10 E
Reefton	62	De	42.07S	171.52 E
Reepham	12	Db	52.45N	1.07 E
Rees	12	Ic	51.46N	6.24 E
Reese River	46	Gf	40.39N	116.54W
Refahiye	24	Hc	39.54N	38.46 E
Reforma, Río-	48	Ed	26.56N	108.12W
Reftele	8	Eg	57.11N	13.35 E
Reftinski	17	Jh	57.10N	61.43 E
Refugio	45	Hl	28.18N	97.17W
Refugio, Punta-	48	Cc	29.30N	113.30W
Rega	10	Lb	54.10N	15.18 E
Regar	19	Gh	38.34N	68.13 E
Regen	10	Jh	48.58N	13.08 E
Regen	10	Ig	49.01N	12.06 E
Regensburg	6	Hf	49.01N	12.06 E
Reggane	31	Hf	26.42N	0.10 E
Regge	12	Ib	52.26N	6.29 E
Reggio di Calabria	6	Hh	38.06N	15.39 E
Reggio nell'Emilia	14	Ef	44.43N	10.36 E
Reghin	15	Hc	46.46N	24.42 E
Regina [Fr.Gui.]	54	Hc	4.19N	52.08W
Regina [Sask.-Can.]	39	Id	50.25N	104.39W
Registan (EN)=Rīgestān	21	If	31.00N	65.00 E
Registro	55	Ig	24.30S	47.50W
Registro do Araguaia	55	Gb	15.44S	51.50W
Regnitz	10	Gg	49.54N	10.49 E
Regocijo	48	Gf	23.35N	105.11W
Reguengos de Monsaraz	13	Ef	38.25N	7.32W
Rehburg-Loccum	12	Lb	52.28N	9.14 E
Rehoboth [3]	37	Bd	23.50S	17.00 E
Rehoboth	37	Bd	23.18S	17.03 E
Reḥovot	24	Fg	31.54N	34.49 E
Reichelsheim (Odenwald)	12	Ke	49.43N	8.51 E
Reichenbach	10	If	50.37N	12.18 E
Reichshoffen	12	Jf	48.56N	7.40 E
Reichshoft	12	Jd	50.55N	7.39 E
Reichshoft-Denklingen	12	Jd	50.55N	7.39 E
Reidsville	44	Hg	36.21N	79.40W
Reigate	9	Mj	51.14N	0.13W
Reims	6	Gf	49.15N	4.02 E
Rein=Rhine (EN)	5	Ge	51.52N	6.02 E
Reina Adelaida, Archipiélago-	52	Ik	52.10S	74.25W
Reindeer	42	He	55.34N	103.10W
Reindeer Bank (EN)	51p	Ac	11.50N	62.05W
Reindeer Lake	38	Id	57.15N	102.40W
Reineskarvet	8	Cd	60.47N	8.13
Reinga, Cape-	62	Ea	34.25S	172.41
Reinhardswald	10	Fe	51.30N	9.30
Reinheim	12	Je	49.08N	7.11
Reinosa	13	Ha	43.00N	4.08W
Reisa	7	Eb	69.48N	21.00
Reitoru Atoll	57	Mf	17.52S	143.05W
Reitz	37	De	27.53S	28.31
Rejmyra	8	Ff	58.50N	15.55
Rejowiec Fabryczny	10	Te	51.08N	23.13
Reka Devnja	15	Kf	43.13N	27.36
Rekarne	8	Ge	59.20N	16.25
Reken	12	Jc	51.48N	7.03
Reliance	39	Ic	62.42N	109.08W
Relizane	32	Hb	35.45N	0.33
Remagen	12	Jd	50.34N	7.14
Remarkable, Mount-	59	Hf	32.48S	138.10
Rembang	26	Fh	6.42S	111.20
Remedios	49	Gi	8.14N	81.51W
Remedios, Punta-	49	Cg	13.31N	89.49W
Remedios, Río-	49	Mh	11.01N	69.15W
Remich	12	Ie	49.32N	6.22
Rémire	54	Hc	4.53N	52.17W
Remiremont	11	Mf	48.01N	6.35
Remire Reef	37b	Bb	5.05S	53.22
Remontnoje	16	Mf	46.33N	43.40
Remoulins	11	Kk	43.56N	4.34
Remscheid	10	De	51.11N	7.12
Rena	7	Cf	61.08N	11.22
Rena	8	Dc	61.08N	11.23
Renaix/Ronse	11	Jd	50.45N	3.36
Renana, Fossa-	5	Gf	48.40N	7.50
Renard Islands	63a	Ad	10.50S	153.00
Renaud Island	66	Qe	65.40S	66.00W
Rende	14	Kk	39.20N	16.11 E
Rendezvous Bay	51b	Ab	18.10N	63.07W
Rend Lake	45	Lg	38.05N	88.58W
Rendova Island	60	Fi	8.32S	157.20 E
Rendsburg	10	Fb	54.18N	9.40 E
Renfrew	42	Jg	45.28N	76.41W
Rengat	26	Dg	0.24S	102.33 E
Rengo	56	Fd	34.25S	70.52W
Reni	16	Fg	45.29N	28.18 E
Renko	8	Kd	60.54N	24.17 E
Renkum	12	Hc	51.58N	5.45 E
Renland	41	Jd	71.15N	27.20W
Renmark	58	Fh	34.11S	140.45 E
Rennell, Islas-	56	Fh	52.00S	74.00W
Rennell Island	57	Hf	11.40S	160.10 E
Rennes	6	Ff	48.05N	1.41W
Rennes, Bassin de-	11	Ef	48.05N	1.40W
Rennesøy	8	Ae	59.05N	5.40 E
Rennick Glacier	66	Kf	70.30S	161.45 E
Rennie Lake	42	Gd	61.10N	105.30W
Reno	39	Hf	39.31N	119.48W
Reno	14	Gf	44.38N	12.16 E
Renqiu	28	De	38.42N	116.06 E
Rensselaer [In.-U.S.]	44	De	40.57N	87.09W
Rensselaer [N.Y.-U.S.]	44	Kd	42.37N	73.44W
Renterria	13	Ka	43.19N	1.54W
Renton	46	Dc	47.30N	122.11W
Renwez	12	Ge	49.50N	4.36 E
Renxian	28	Cf	37.07N	114.41 E
Reo	26	Hh	8.19S	120.30 E
Repartimento, Serra do-	55	Jc	17.40S	44.50W
Répce	10	Ni	47.41N	17.02 E
Repino	8	Md	60.10N	29.58 E
Repong, Pulau-	26	Ef	2.22N	105.53 E
Reposaari/Räfsö	8	Ic	61.37N	21.27 E
Republic	46	Fb	48.39N	118.44W
Republican	38	Jf	39.03N	96.48W
Repulse Bay	39	Kc	66.32N	86.15W
Repulse Bay [Austl.]	59	Jd	20.35S	148.45 E
Repulse Bay [Can.]	42	Ic	66.20N	86.00W
Repvåg	7	Fa	70.45N	25.41 E
Requena [Peru]	54	Dd	5.00S	73.50W
Requena [Sp.]	13	Ke	39.29N	1.06W
Requin Bay	51p	Bb	12.02N	61.38W
Réquista	11	Ij	44.02N	2.32 E
Reşadiye Yarimadası	15	Km	36.40N	27.45 E
Reschenpass/Resia, Passo di-	14	Ed	46.50N	10.30 E
Resen	15	Eh	41.05N	21.01 E
Reserva	55	Gg	24.38S	50.52W
Reserve	45	Bj	33.43N	108.45W
Rešetilovka	16	Ie	49.33N	34.05 E
Reshui	27	Hd	37.38N	100.30 E
Resia, Passo di-/Reschenpass	14	Ed	46.50N	10.30 E
Resistencia	53	Kh	27.30S	58.59W
Reşiţa	15	Ed	45.18N	21.55 E
Resko	10	Lc	53.47N	15.25 E
Reso/Raisio	7	Ff	60.29N	22.11 E
Resolute	39	Jb	74.41N	94.54W
Resolution	38	Mc	61.30N	65.00W
Resolution Island	42	Ld	61.35N	64.39W
Resolution Island	62	Bf	45.40S	166.35 E
Respublikai Soveth Socialisti Todžikiston/ Tadžikskaja SSR [2]	19	Hh	39.00N	71.00 E
Respublika Sovetike Sočialiste Moldovenjaske/ Moldavskaja SSR [2]	19	Cf	47.00N	29.00 E
Ressa	16	Ib	54.45N	35.10 E
Ressons-sur-Matz	12	Ee	49.33N	2.45 E
Restigouche River	44	Na	48.04N	66.20W
Restinga de Sefton, Isla-	52	Hi	37.00S	83.50W
Restinga Sêca	55	Fi	29.49S	53.23W
Reszel	10	Rb	54.04N	21.09 E
Retalhuleu [3]	49	Bf	14.20N	91.50W
Retalhuleu	47	Ff	14.32N	91.41W
Retavas/Rietavas	8	Ii	55.43N	21.49 E
Retezatului, Munţii-	15	Fd	45.25N	23.00 E
Rethel	11	Ke	49.31N	4.22 E
Rethem (Aller)	12	Lb	52.47N	9.23 E
Réthinnon	15	Hn	35.22N	24.28 E
Retie	12	Hc	51.17N	5.05 E

Index Symbols

- [1] Independent Nation
- [2] State, Region
- [3] District, County
- [4] Municipality
- [5] Colony, Dependency
- Continent
- Physical Region
- Historical or Cultural Region
- Mount, Mountain
- Volcano
- Hill
- Mountains, Mountain Range
- Hills, Escarpment
- Plateau, Upland
- Pass, Gap
- Plain, Lowland
- Delta
- Salt Flat
- Valley, Canyon
- Crater, Cave
- Karst Features
- Depression
- Polder
- Desert, Dunes
- Forest, Woods
- Heath, Steppe
- Oasis
- Cape, Point
- Coast, Beach
- Cliff
- Peninsula
- Isthmus
- Sandbank
- Island
- Atoll
- Rock, Reef
- Islands, Archipelago
- Rocks, Reefs
- Coral Reef
- Well, Spring
- Geyser
- River, Stream
- Waterfall Rapids
- River Mouth, Estuary
- Lake
- Salt Lake
- Intermittent Lake
- Reservoir
- Swamp, Pond
- Canal
- Glacier
- Ice Shelf, Pack Ice
- Ocean
- Sea
- Gulf, Bay
- Strait, Fjord
- Lagoon
- Bank
- Seamount
- Tablemount
- Ridge
- Shelf
- Basin
- Escarpment, Sea Scarp
- Fracture
- Trench, Abyss
- National Park, Reserve
- Point of Interest
- Recreation Site
- Cave, Cavern
- Historic Site
- Ruins
- Wall, Walls
- Church, Abbey
- Temple
- Scientific Station
- Airport
- Port
- Lighthouse
- Mine
- Tunnel
- Dam, Bridge

ourne 12 Ge 49.26N 4.02 E
tság 10 Pi 47.56N 19.08 E
tihovka 28 Lb 44.10N 132.45 E
z 14 Jc 48.45N 15.57 E
z, Pays de- 11 Eg 47.07N 1.58W
union=Reunion (EN) 30 Mk 21.06S 55.36 E
union=Reunion (EN) [5] 31 Mk 21.06S 55.36 E
union (EN)=Réunion 30 Mk 21.06S 55.36 E
union (EN)=Réunion [5] 31 Mk 21.06S 55.36 E
us 13 Nc 41.09N 1.07 E
usel 12 Hc 51.22N 5.10 E
uss 14 Cc 47.28N 8.14 E
ut 16 Ff 47.15N 29.09 E
utlingen 10 Fh 48.29N 9.13 E
utte 14 Ec 47.29N 10.43 E
vda [R.S.F.S.R.] 17 Ih 56.48N 59.57 E
vda [R.S.F.S.R.] 7 Ic 67.57N 34.32 E
vel 11 Hk 43.28N 2.00 E
velstoke 42 Ff 50.59N 118.12W
vermont 11 Lh 46.27N 5.25 E
villagigedo 40 Me 55.35N 131.23W
villagigedo, Islas- 38 Hh 19.00N 111.30W
vin 11 Ke 49.56N 4.38 E
voljucii, Pik- 18 Ie 38.33N 72.28 E
vsundssjön 8 Fb 62.50N 15.15 E
wa 63d Bc 18.08S 178.33 E
wa 25 Gd 24.32N 81.18 E
wāri 25 Fc 28.11N 76.37 E
x, Mount- 66 Qf 74.54S 75.57W
xburg 46 Je 43.49N 111.47W
xpoède 12 Ed 50.56N 2.32 E
y 23 Hb 35.35N 51.25 E
y, Arroyo del- 55 Ci 29.12S 59.36W
y, Isla del- 47 Ig 8.22N 78.55W
y, Laguna del- 48 Hd 27.00N 103.25W
y Bouba 34 Hd 8.40N 14.11 E
yes, Point- 46 Dg 38.00N 123.01W
yhanli 24 Gd 36.18N 36.32 E
ykjalid 7a Cb 65.39N 16.55W
ykjanes 5 Dc 63.49N 22.43W
ykjanes Ridge (EN) 3 Dc 62.00N 27.00W
ykjavik 6 Dc 64.09N 21.57W
ynolds Range 59 Gd 22.20S 132.50 E
ynosa 39 Jg 26.07N 98.18W
yssouze 11 Kh 46.27N 4.54 E
ž 17 Kh 57.54N 62.20 E
ž 17 Jh 57.23N 61.24 E
zé 11 Eg 47.12N 1.34W
zekne/Rēzekne 6 Id 56.30N 27.19 E
ēzekne/Rezekne 6 Id 56.30N 27.19 E
zelm, Lacul- 15 Le 44.54N 28.57 E
zina 16 Ff 47.43N 28.58 E
ēznas, Ozero-/Rēznas
Ezers 8 Lh 56.20N 27.30 E
ēznas Ezers/Reznas,
Ozero- 8 Lh 56.20N 27.30 E
ezovo 15 Lh 41.59N 28.02 E
ezvān 24 Qi 27.34N 56.06 E
ezve 15 Lh 41.59N 28.01 E
gotina 15 Fe 44.01N 22.17 E
haetian Alps (EN)=Alpi
Retiche 14 Dd 46.30N 10.00 E
haetian Alps (EN)=
Rätische Alpen 14 Dd 46.30N 10.00 E
hallamane 30 Ff 23.15N 10.00W
hauderfehn 12 Ja 53.08N 7.34 E
haunen 12 Je 49.51N 7.21 E
heda-Wiedenbrück 10 Ee 51.51N 8.18 E
heden 12 Ib 52.01N 6.01 E
heden-Dieren 12 Ib 52.03N 6.08 E
heider Land 12 Ja 53.13N 7.18 E
hein 12 Ke 49.52N 8.07 E
hein=Rhine (EN) 5 Ge 51.52N 6.02 E
heinberg 12 Ic 51.33N 6.36 E
heine 10 Dd 52.17N 7.27 E
heinfall 14 Cc 47.41N 8.38 E
heinfelden 10 Di 47.34N 7.48 E
heingaugebirge 12 Jd 50.05N 8.00 E
heinisches Schiefergebirge
=Rhenish Slate Mountains
(EN) 5 Ge 50.25N 7.10 E
heinland-Pfalz=Rhineland-
Palatinate (EN) [2] 10 Cf 50.00N 7.00 E
heinsberg 10 Ic 53.06N 12.53 E
heinstetten 12 Kf 48.58N 8.18 E
henen 12 Hc 51.58N 5.35 E
henish Slate Mountains
(EN)=Rheinisches
Schiefergebirge 5 Ge 50.25N 7.10 E
Rheris 32 Gc 30.41N 4.57W
Rheydt, Mönchengladbach- 12 Ic 51.10N 6.27 E
Rhin=Rhine (EN) 5 Ge 51.52N 6.02 E
Rhine (EN)=Rein 5 Ge 51.52N 6.02 E
Rhine (EN)=Rhein 5 Ge 51.52N 6.02 E
Rhine (EN)=Rhin 5 Ge 51.52N 6.02 E
Rhine (EN)=Rijn 5 Ge 51.52N 6.02 E
Rhine Bank (EN) 56 Ji 50.30S 53.30W
Rhineland-Palatinate (EN)=
Rheinland Pfalz [2] 10 Cf 50.00N 7.00 E
Rhinelander 43 Jb 45.38N 89.25W
Rhinluch 10 Id 52.50N 12.50 E
Rhino Camp 36 Fb 2.58N 31.24 E
Rhiou 13 Mi 35.59N 0.53 E
Rhir, Cap- 32 Fc 30.38N 9.54W
Rho 14 De 45.32N 9.02 E
Rhode Island [2] 43 Mc 41.40N 71.30W
Rhode Island Sound 44 Le 41.25N 71.15W
Rhodes (EN)=Ródhos 6 Ih 36.26N 28.13 E
Rhodes (EN)=Ródhos 5 Ih 36.10N 28.00 E
Rhodesia→Zimbabwe [1] 31 Jj 20.00S 30.00 E
Rhodes Peak 46 Hc 46.41N 114.47W
Rhodope Mountains (EN)=
Rodopi 5 Ig 41.30N 24.30 E
Rhomara 13 Hi 35.10N 4.57W
Rhön 10 Gf 50.25N 10.05 E
Rhondda 9 Jj 51.40N 3.30W
Rhône 5 Gg 43.20N 4.50 E
Rhône [3] 11 Ki 46.00N 4.30 E
Rhône au Rhin, Canal du-
11 Lg 47.06N 5.19 E
Rhourd el Baguel 32 Ic 31.24N 6.57 E
Rhue 11 Ii 45.23N 2.29 E
Rhum 9 Ge 57.00N 6.20W
Rhyl 9 Jh 53.19N 3.29W
Riaba 34 Ge 3.24N 8.42 E
Riacho de Santana 54 Jf 13.37S 42.57W
Riangnom 35 Ed 9.55N 30.01 E
Riaño 13 Ga 42.58N 5.01W
Riánsares 13 Ie 39.32N 3.18W
Říåny 10 Kg 50.00N 14.39 E
Rias Altas 13 Da 43.30N 8.30W
Rias Bajas 13 Db 42.30N 9.00W
Riau [3] 26 Df 1.00N 102.00 E
Riau Archipelago (EN)=
Riau, Kepulauan- 21 Mi 1.00N 104.30 E
Riau Kepulauan-=Riau
Archipelago (EN) 21 Mi 1.00N 104.30 E
Riaza 13 Ic 41.17N 3.28W
Riaza 13 Ic 41.42N 3.55W
Ribadavia 13 Db 42.17N 8.08W
Ribadeo 13 Ea 43.32N 7.02W
Ribadesella 13 Ga 43.28N 5.04W
Ribagorza/La Ribagorça 13 Mb 42.15N 0.30 E
Ribamar 54 Jd 2.33S 44.03W
Ribas do Rio Pardo 55 Fe 20.27S 53.46W
Ribatejo 13 De 39.15N 8.30W
Ribáuè 37 Fb 14.57S 38.17 E
Ribble 9 Kh 53.44N 2.50W
Ribe 7 Bi 55.21N 8.46 E
Ribe [2] 8 Ci 55.35N 8.45 E
Ribécourt-Dreslincourt 12 Ee 49.31N 2.55 E
Ribeira [Braz.] 55 Hg 24.39S 49.00W
Ribeira [Sp.] 13 Db 42.33N 9.00W
Ribeira, Rio- 55 Ig 24.40S 47.24W
Ribeira Brava 32 Cf 16.37N 24.18W
Ribeira Grande 32 Bf 17.11N 25.04W
Ribeirão Prêto 53 Lh 21.10S 47.48W
Ribeirãozinho 55 Fc 16.22S 52.36W
Ribeiro Gonçalves 54 Ie 7.32S 45.14W
Ribemont 12 Fe 49.48N 3.28 E
Ribera 14 Hm 37.30N 13.16 E
Ribérac 11 Gi 45.15N 0.20 E
Riberalta 53 Jg 10.59S 66.06W
Ribnica 14 Ie 45.44N 14.44 E
Ribnitz-Damgarten 10 Ib 54.15N 12.28 E
Ricardo Flores Magón 48 Fc 29.58N 106.58W
Riccia 14 Ii 41.29N 14.50 E
Riccione 14 Gg 43.59N 12.39 E
Rice Lake 44 Hc 44.08N 78.13W
Rich 32 Gc 32.15N 4.30W
Richan 45 Jb 49.59N 92.49W
Richard Collinson Inlet 42 Gb 72.45N 113.00W
Richards 42 Ec 69.20N 134.35W
Richard's Bay 31 Kk 28.47S 32.06 E
Richardson 45 Hj 32.57N 96.44W
Richardson Mountains 38 Fc 66.00N 135.20W
Richard Toll 34 Bb 16.28N 15.41W
Richât, Guel er- 32 Ee 21.07N 11.24W
Richel 12 Ha 53.18N 5.10 E
Richel Griend 12 Ha 53.18N 5.15 E
Richelieu 11 Gg 47.01N 0.19 E
Richer 45 Hb 49.39N 96.28W
Richey 46 Mc 47.39N 105.04W
Richfield 43 Ed 38.46N 112.05W
Richibucto 44 Ob 46.41N 64.52W
Richland 43 Db 46.17N 119.18W
Richland Center 45 Ke 43.22N 90.21W
Richmond [Austl.] 59 Id 20.44S 143.08 E
Richmond [Ca.-U.S.] 43 Cd 37.57N 122.22W
Richmond [Eng.-U.K.] 9 Lg 54.24N 1.44W
Richmond [In.-U.S.] 43 Kd 39.50N 84.54W
Richmond [Ky.-U.S.] 43 Kd 37.45N 84.18W
Richmond [N.Z.] 62 Ed 41.21S 173.11 E
Richmond [S.Afr.] 37 Cf 31.23S 23.56 E
Richmond [Tx.-U.S.] 45 Il 29.35N 95.46W
Richmond [Va.-U.S.] 39 Lf 37.30N 77.28W
Richmond, Mount- 62 Ed 41.28S 173.24 E
Richmond Hill 44 Hd 43.52N 79.27W
Richmond Peak 51n Ba 13.17N 61.13W
Richthofen, Mount- 45 Df 40.29N 105.57W
Rickmansworth 12 Bc 51.38N 0.28W
Ricobayo, Embalse de- 13 Gc 41.35N 5.50W
Ridā' 33 Hg 14.25N 44.50 E
Ridderkerk 12 Gc 51.52N 4.36 E
Ridgecrest 46 Gi 35.38N 117.36W
Ridgway 44 He 41.25N 78.45W
Riding Mountain 45 Fa 50.55N 100.25W
Riecito, Rio- 50 Bi 6.50N 68.51W
Ried 12 Ke 49.50N 8.25 E
Ried im Innkreis 14 Hb 48.13N 13.30 E
Riedlingen 10 Fh 48.09N 9.28 E
Riemst 12 Hd 50.48N 5.36 E
Ries 10 Gh 48.55N 10.40 E
Riesa 10 Je 51.18N 13.18 E
Riesco, Isla- 56 Fh 53.00S 72.30W
Riesi 14 Im 37.17N 14.05 E
Riet 30 Jk 29.00S 23.53 E
Rietavas/Retavas 8 Ii 55.43N 21.49 E
Rietberg 12 Kc 51.48N 8.26 E
Rietbron 37 Cf 32.54S 23.09 E
Rietfontein [Nam.] 37 Cd 21.58S 20.58 E
Rietfontein [S.Afr.] 37 Ce 26.44S 20.01 E
Rieti 14 Gh 42.24N 12.51 E
Rif 30 Ge 35.00N 4.00W
Rifle 45 Cg 39.32N 107.47W
Rifstangi 5 Eb 66.32N 16.12W
Rift Valley [3] 36 Gb 0.30N 36.00 E
Rift Valley 30 Kh 0.30N 36.00 E
Riga/Rīga 6 Id 56.57N 24.06 E
Riga/Rīga 6 Id 56.57N 24.06 E
Riga, Gulf of- (EN)=Rīgas
Jūras Līcis 5 Id 57.30N 23.35 E
Riga, Gulf of- (EN)=Riia
Laht 5 Id 57.30N 23.35 E
Riga, Gulf of- (EN)=Rižski
Zaliv 5 Id 57.30N 23.35 E
Rigachikum 34 Gc 10.38N 7.28 E
Rīgas Jūras Līcis=Riga,
Gulf of- (EN) 5 Id 57.30N 23.35 E
Rigestān=Registan (EN) 21 If 31.00N 65.00 E
Riggins 46 Gd 45.25N 116.19W
Rigolet 42 Lf 54.10N 58.26W
Rig-Rig 35 Ac 14.16N 14.21 E
Rihand Sagar 25 Hd 24.05N 83.05 E
Riia Laht=Riga, Gulf of-
(EN) 5 Id 57.30N 23.35 E
Riihimäki 7 Ff 60.45N 24.46 E
Riiser-Larsen-Halvøya 66 De 68.55S 34.00 E
Riito 48 Ba 32.10N 114.45W
Riječki zaljev = Rijeka, Gulf
of- (EN) 14 Ie 45.15N 14.25 E
Rijeka 6 Hf 45.21N 14.24 E
Rijeka, Gulf of- (EN)=
Riječki zaljev 14 Ie 45.15N 14.25 E
Rijksmuseum Kröller-
Müller 12 Hb 52.06N 5.47 E
Rijn=Rhine (EN) 5 Ge 51.52N 6.02 E
Rijssen 12 Ib 52.18N 6.37 E
Rijswijk 12 Gb 52.03N 4.21 E
Rika 10 Th 48.08N 23.22 E
Rikā, Wādī ar- 33 He 22.25N 44.50 E
Rikubetsu 29a Cb 43.28N 143.43 E
Rikuzentakada 28 Pe 39.01N 141.38 E
Rila 15 Gh 42.08N 23.33 E
Rila 15 Gg 42.08N 23.08 E
Riley 46 Fe 43.32N 119.29W
Riley, Mount- 45 Ck 31.58N 107.05W
Rilski Manastir 15 Gg 42.08N 23.20 E
Rima 30 Hg 13.04N 5.10 E
Rimatara, Ile- 57 Lg 22.38S 152.51W
Rimava 10 Qh 48.15N 20.21 E
Rimavská Sobota 10 Qh 48.23N 20.01 E
Rimbo 7 Eg 59.45N 18.22 E
Rimé 35 Bc 14.02N 18.03 E
Rimforsa 8 Ff 58.08N 15.40 E
Rimini 14 Gf 44.04N 12.34 E
Rimito/Rymättylä 8 Jd 60.25N 21.55 E
Rimnic 15 Kd 45.32N 27.31 E
Rîmnicu Sărat 15 Kd 45.23N 27.03 E
Rîmnicu Vîlcea 15 Hd 45.06N 24.22 E
Rimouski 39 Me 48.27N 68.32W
Rimše/Rimšė 8 Li 55.30N 26.33 E
Rimšė/Rimše 8 Li 55.30N 26.33 E
Rinbung 27 Ef 29.15N 89.52 E
Rincon 50 Bf 12.14N 68.20W
Rincón 51a Ab 18.21N 67.16W
Rincón, Bahia de- 51a Bc 17.57N 66.19W
Rincón del Bonete, Lago
Artificial de- 56 Id 32.45S 56.00W
Rincón de Romos 48 Hf 22.14N 102.18W
Rindal 7 Be 63.03N 9.13 E
Ringe 8 Di 55.14N 10.29 E
Ringebu 8 Dc 61.31N 10.10 E
Ringerike 8 Dd 60.05N 10.15 E
Ringgold Isles 57 Jf 16.15S 179.25W
Ringim 34 Gc 12.09N 9.10 E
Ringkøbing [2] 8 Ch 56.10N 8.45 E
Ringkøbing 7 Bh 56.05N 8.15 E
Ringkøbing Fjord 7 Bi 56.00N 8.15 E
Ringlådes 15 Dj 39.25N 20.04 E
Ringsjön 8 Ei 55.50N 13.30 E
Ringsted 7 Ci 55.27N 11.49 E
Ringvassøy 7 Eb 69.55N 19.15 E
Rinia 15 Il 37.25N 25.13 E
Rinjani, Gunung- 26 Gh 8.24S 116.28 E
Rinn Chathóir/Cahore
Point 9 Gi 52.34N 6.11W
Rinn Dúain/Hook Head 9 Gi 52.07N 6.55W
Rinteln 10 Fd 52.11N 9.05 E
Rinya 10 Nk 45.57N 17.27 E
Rio Azul 55 Gg 25.43S 50.47W
Riobamba 53 If 1.40S 78.38W
Rio Branco 53 Jf 9.58S 67.48W
Rio Branco 55 Fk 32.34S 53.25W
Rio Branco do Sul 55 Hg 25.10S 49.18W
Rio Brilhante 54 Hh 21.48S 54.33W
Rio Bueno 56 Ff 40.19S 72.58W
Rio Caribe 54 Fa 10.42N 63.07W
Rio Chico 50 Dg 10.19N 65.59W
Rio Claro [Braz.] 55 If 22.24S 47.33W
Rio Claro [Trin.] 50 Fg 10.18N 61.11W
Rio Colorado 56 He 39.01S 64.05W
Rio Cuarto 53 Ji 33.08S 64.20W
Rio de Janeiro 53 Lh 22.54S 43.15W
Rio de Janeiro [2] 54 Jh 22.30S 42.30W
Rio de Jesús 49 Gj 7.59N 81.10W
Rio de Oro 32 Ee 24.00N 14.00W
Rio de Oro 49 Ki 8.57N 73.23W
Rio de Oro, Bahía de- 32 De 23.45N 15.50W
Rio do Sul 56 Kc 27.13S 49.39W
Rio Fortuna 55 Hi 28.06S 49.07W
Rio Gallegos 53 Jk 51.37S 69.10W
Rio Grande 53 Ki 32.02S 52.05W
Rio Grande [Arg.] 56 Gh 53.47S 67.42W
Rio Grande [Nic.] 49 Dg 12.59N 86.34W
Rio Grande [P.R.] 51a Cb 18.23N 65.50W
Rio Grande City 45 Gm 26.23N 98.49W
Rio Grande de Añasco 51a Ab 18.17N 67.10W
Rio Grande de Manati 51a Bb 18.29N 66.32W
Rio Grande de Matagalpa 47 Hf 12.54N 83.32W
Rio Grande do Norte [2] 54 Ke 5.40S 36.00W
Rio Grande do Sul [2] 56 Jc 30.00S 54.00W
Rio Grande Rise (EN) 3 Cm 31.00S 35.00W
Riohacha 54 Da 11.32N 72.54W
Rio Hato 49 Gi 8.23N 80.10W
Rio Lagartos 48 Og 21.36N 88.10W
Rio Largo 54 Ke 9.29S 35.51W
Riom 11 Ji 45.54N 3.07 E
Rio Maior 13 De 39.20N 8.56W
Rio Mayo 56 Fg 45.41S 70.16W
Riom-és-Montagnes 11 Ii 45.17N 2.40 E
Rio Miranda 54 Gg 19.25S 57.20W
Rio Mulatos 54 Eg 19.42S 66.47W
Rion 15 Ek 38.18N 21.47 E
Rio Negro [Chile] 56 Ff 40.47S 73.14W
Rio Negro [Arg.] [2] 56 Gf 40.00S 67.00W
Rio Negro [Braz.] 56 Kc 26.06S 49.48W
Rio Negro [Braz.] 55 Dd 19.33S 56.32W
Rio Negro [Ur.] [2] 55 Dk 32.45S 57.20W
Rio Negro, Pantanal do-
54 Gg 18.50S 56.00W
Rionero in Vulture 14 Jj 40.56N 15.40 E
Rioni 16 Lh 42.10N 41.38 E
Rio Novo 55 Dc 16.28S 56.30W
Rio Pardo 56 Jc 29.59S 52.22W
Rio Prêto, Serra do- 55 Gd 18.18S 50.42W
Rio San Juan [3] 49 Eh 11.10N 84.30W
Rio Segundo 56 Hd 31.40S 63.55W
Riosucio 54 Cb 7.27N 77.07W
Rio Tercero 56 Hd 32.11S 64.06W
Rio Tinto 54 Ke 6.48S 35.05W
Rioverde 47 Dd 21.56N 100.01W
Rio Verde 54 Hg 17.43S 50.56W
Rio Verde, Serra do- 55 Fc 17.32S 52.25W
Rio Verde de Mato Grosso 54 Hg 18.56S 54.52W
Rio Verde do Sul 55 Ef 22.54S 55.27W
Rioz 11 Mg 47.25N 6.04 E
Řip 10 Kf 50.24N 14.18 E
Ripanj 15 De 44.38N 20.32 E
Ripley [Eng.-U.K.] 12 Aa 53.02N 1.24W
Ripley [Tn.-U.S.] 44 Ch 35.44N 89.33W
Ripley [W.V.-U.S.] 44 Gf 38.49N 81.44W
Ripoll 13 Ob 42.12N 2.12 E
Ripon 9 Lg 54.08N 1.31W
Riposto 14 Jm 37.44N 15.12 E
Ripple Mountain 46 Gb 49.02N 117.05W
Risan 15 Bg 42.31N 18.42 E
Risaralda [2] 54 Cb 5.00N 75.45W
Risbäck 7 Dd 64.42N 15.32 E
Rīshah, Wādī- 24 Kj 25.33N 44.05 E
Rī Shahr 24 Nh 28.55N 50.50 E
Rishiri 28 Pb 45.11N 141.15 E
Rishiri-Suidō 29a Ba 45.10N 141.30 E
Rishiri-Tō 27 Pb 45.11N 141.15 E
Rishiri-Yama 29a Ba 45.11N 141.15 E
Rishmūk 24 Ng 31.15N 50.20 E
Rishon Leẓiyyon 24 Fg 31.58N 34.48 E
Rising Star 45 Gj 32.06N 98.58W
Risle 11 Ge 49.26N 0.23 E
Risnjak 14 Ie 45.26N 14.37 E
Rîşnov 15 Id 45.35N 25.27 E
Risør 7 Bg 58.43N 9.14 E
Risoux, Mont- 11 Mh 46.36N 6.10 E
Risøyhamn 7 Db 69.00N 15.45 E
Riß 10 Fh 48.17N 9.49 E
Risti 7 Fg 59.03N 24.01 E
Ristiina 8 Lc 61.30N 27.16 E
Ristijarvi 7 Gd 64.30N 28.13 E
Ristna, Mys-/Ristna
Neem 8 If 58.55N 21.55 E
Ristna Neem/Ristna, Mys-
8 If 58.55N 21.55 E
Risō 24 Qf 33.52N 57.28 E
Ritchie's Archipelago 25 If 12.14N 93.10 E
Ritidian Point 64c Ba 13.39N 144.51 E
Ritscher-Hochland 66 Bf 73.20S 9.30W
Ritter, Mount- 43 Dd 37.42N 119.20W
Ritterhude 12 Ka 53.11N 8.45 E
Rituerto 13 Jc 41.36N 2.22W
Ritzville 46 Fc 47.08N 118.23W
Riva-Bella, Ouistreham- 12 Be 49.17N 0.16W
Rivadavia [Arg.] 56 Hb 24.11S 62.53W
Rivadavia [Arg.] 56 Gd 33.11S 68.28W
Riva del Garda 14 Ee 45.53N 10.50 E
Rivas 39 Kh 11.26N 85.51W
Rivas [3] 49 Eh 11.25N 85.50W
Rive-de-Gier 11 Ki 45.22N 4.37 E
Rivellata, Punta di a- 11a Aa 42.35N 8.40 E
Rivera 55 Ej 31.30S 55.15W
Rivera [Arg.] 56 He 37.12S 63.14W
Rivera [Ur.] 53 Ki 30.54S 55.31W
River Cess 34 Dd 5.27N 9.35W
Riverdale 45 Fc 47.30N 101.22W
Riverina 59 Jg 35.25S 145.30 E
River Inlet 42 Ef 51.41N 127.15W
Rivers [2] 34 Ge 4.50N 6.30 E
Rivers, Lake of the- 46 Mb 49.45N 105.45W
Riversdale [N.Z.] 62 Cf 45.54S 168.44 E
Riversdale [S.Afr.] 37 Cf 34.07S 21.15 E
Riverside 43 De 33.59N 117.22W
Riverton [N.Z.] 62 Bg 46.21S 168.00 E
Riverton [Wy.-U.S.] 43 Fc 43.02N 108.23W
Rivesaltes 11 Il 42.46N 2.52 E
Riviera Beach 44 Ge 26.47N 80.04W
Rivière-à-Pierre 44 Kb 46.58N 72.11W
Rivière-du-Loup 42 Kg 47.50N 69.32W
Rivière-Pilote 51h Bc 14.29N 60.54W
Rivière-Salée 51h Bb 14.32N 60.59W
Rivoli 14 Be 45.04N 7.31 E
Rivungo 36 Df 16.15S 22.00 E
Riwaka 62 Ed 41.05S 173.00 E
Riwoqê 27 Ge 31.13N 96.29 E
Rixensart 12 Gd 50.43N 4.35 E
Riyadh (EN)=Ar Riyāḑ 22 Gg 24.38N 46.43 E
Rize 23 Fa 41.02N 40.31 E
Rize, Gora- 18 Bf 37.48N 58.13 E
Rize Dağları 24 Ib 40.30N 40.50 E
Rizhao 27 Kd 35.27N 119.28 E
Rizokarpásso/Dipkarpas 24 Fe 35.36N 34.23 E
Rižski Zaliv=Riga, Gulf of-
(EN) 5 Id 57.30N 23.35 E
Rizzuto, Capo- 14 Ll 38.53N 17.05 E
Rjabovo 8 Md 60.17N 29.01 E
Rjapina/Räpina 8 Lf 58.03N 27.35 E
Rjazan 6 Je 54.38N 39.44 E
Rjazanovski 7 Ji 55.08N 39.35 E
Rjazanskaja Oblast [3] 19 Ee 54.30N 40.40 E
Rjažsk 6 Ke 53.43N 40.04 E
Rjukan 7 Bg 59.52N 8.34 E
Rjuven 8 Be 59.13N 7.10 E
Rkiz 32 Df 16.50N 15.20W
Rldal 8 Be 59.49N 6.48 E
Roa [Nor.] 8 Dd 60.17N 10.37 E
Roa [Sp.] 13 Ic 41.42N 3.55W
Road Town 47 Le 18.27N 64.37W
Roag, Loch- 9 Gc 58.16N 6.50W
Roan Antelope 36 Ee 13.08S 28.24 E
Roannais 11 Kh 46.05N 4.10 E
Roanne 11 Kh 46.02N 4.04 E
Roanoke 38 Lf 35.56N 76.43W
Roanoke [Al.-U.S.] 44 Ei 33.09N 85.22W
Roanoke [Va.-U.S.] 39 Lf 37.16N 79.57W
Roanoke Rapids 44 Ig 36.28N 77.40W
Roan Plateau 46 Kg 39.35N 108.55W
Roaringwater Bay 9 Dj 51.25N 9.30W
Roatán 49 De 16.18N 86.35W
Roatán, Isla de- 49 De 16.23N 86.30W
Robāţ [Iran] 24 Qd 37.55N 57.42 E
Robāţ [Iran] 24 Pg 30.04N 54.49 E
Robāt-e-Khān 23 Ic 33.21N 56.02 E
Robāt-e-Kord 24 Qf 33.45N 56.37 E
Robāţ Karīm 24 Ne 35.28N 51.05 E
Robbie Bank (EN) 61 Fb 11.03S 176.53W
Robe, Mount- 59 If 31.40S 141.20 E
Röbel 10 Ic 53.23N 12.36 E
Robert Lee 45 Fk 31.54N 100.29W
Roberts 55 Bl 35.09S 61.57W
Roberts, Mount- 59 Ke 28.13S 152.28 E
Roberts Creek Mountain 46 Gg 39.52N 116.18W
Robertsfors 7 Ed 64.11N 20.51 E
Robert S. Kerr Lake 45 Ii 35.25N 95.00W
Robertson 37 Bf 33.46S 19.50 E
Robertson Bay 66 Kf 71.25S 170.00 E
Robertson Range 59 Ed 23.10S 121.00 E
Robertsport 34 Cd 6.45N 11.22W
Roberval 42 Kg 48.31N 72.13W
Robi 35 Fd 7.38N 39.52 E
Robinson Crusoe (EN) =
Robinson Crusoe, Isla- 52 Ii 33.38S 78.52W
Robinson Crusoe, Isla- =
Robinson Crusoe (EN) 52 Ii 33.38S 78.52W
Robinson Range 59 De 25.45S 119.00 E
Robinson River 59 Hc 16.03S 137.16 E
Roboré 53 Kg 18.20S 59.45W
Rob Roy 63a Cb 7.23S 157.36 E
Robson, Mount- 38 Hd 53.07N 119.09W
Robstown 45 Hm 27.27N 97.40W
Roby 45 Fj 32.45N 100.23W
Roca, Cabo da- 5 Fh 38.47N 9.30W
Rocamadour 11 Hj 44.48N 1.38 E
Roca Partida, Isla- 47 Be 19.01N 112.02W
Roca Partida, Punta- 48 Lh 18.42N 95.10W
Rocas, Atol das- 52 Mf 3.52S 33.49W
Roccaraso 14 Ii 41.51N 14.05 E
Ročegda 19 Ec 62.42N 43.23 E
Rocha [2] 55 Fk 34.00S 54.00W
Rocha 56 Jd 34.29S 54.20W
Rochdale 9 Kh 53.38N 2.09W
Rochechouart 11 Gi 45.49N 0.49 E
Rochedo 55 Ed 19.57S 54.52W
Rochefort [Bel.] 11 Ld 50.10N 5.13 E
Rochefort [Fr.] 11 Fi 45.56N 0.59W
Rochefort-Han-sur-Lesse 12 Hd 50.08N 5.11 E
Rochelle 45 Lf 41.56N 89.04W
Rocher River 42 Gd 61.23N 112.45W
Roche's Bluff 51c c 16.42N 62.09W
Rochester [Eng.-U.K.] 9 Nj 51.24N 0.30 E
Rochester [In.-U.S.] 44 De 41.04N 86.13W
Rochester [Mn.-U.S.] 43 Ic 44.02N 92.29W
Rochester [N.H.-U.S.] 44 Ld 43.18N 70.59W
Rochester [N.Y.-U.S.] 39 Le 43.10N 77.36W
Rochlitzer Berg 10 Ie 51.05N 12.48 E
Rocigalgo 13 He 39.35N 4.35W
Rockall 5 Ed 57.35N 13.48W
Rockall Rise (EN) 5 Ed 57.00N 14.00W
Rock Creek Butte 46 Fd 44.49N 118.07W
Rockefeller Plateau 66 Ng 80.00S 135.00W
Rockenhausen 12 Je 49.38N 7.50 E
Rockford 43 Jc 42.17N 89.06W
Rockglen 46 Mb 49.10N 105.57W
Rockhampton 58 Gg 23.23S 150.31 E
Rock Hill 43 Ke 34.55N 81.01W
Rockingham [Austl.] 59 Df 32.17S 115.44 E
Rockingham [N.C.-U.S.] 44 Hh 34.56N 79.46W
Rock Island 43 Ic 41.30N 90.34W
Rockland 43 Nc 44.06N 69.06W
Rocklands Reservoir 59 Ig 37.15S 142.00 E
Rockledge 44 Gk 28.20N 80.43W
Rockneby 8 Gh 56.49N 16.20 E
Rockport 45 Hl 28.01N 97.04W
Rock River 45 Kf 41.29N 90.37W
Rock Sound 44 Im 24.53N 76.09W
Rock Spring 43 Fc 41.35N 109.13W
Rocksprings 45 Fk 30.01N 100.13W
Rockville [In.-U.S.] 44 Df 39.45N 87.15W
Rockville [Md.-U.S.] 44 If 39.05N 77.09W
Rockwood 44 Eh 35.52N 84.41W
Rocky Ford 45 Eg 38.03N 103.43W
Rocky Island Lake 44 Fb 46.56N 83.04W
Rocky Mount 43 Ld 35.56N 77.48W
Rocky Mountain 43 Eb 47.49N 112.49W
Rocky Mountain House 42 Gf 52.22N 114.55W
Rocky Mountains 38 He 48.00N 116.00W
Rocky Point [Blz.] 49 Cd 18.22N 88.06W
Rocky Point [Nam.] 37 Ac 19.01S 12.29 E
Rocroi 12 Ge 49.55N 4.31 E
Rodach 10 Gf 50.08N 10.52 E
Rodalben 12 Je 49.14N 7.38 E
Roda Velha, Rio- 55 Ja 12.27S 45.33W
Rødberg 8 Cd 60.16N 8.58 E
Rødby 8 Dj 54.42N 11.24 E
Rødby Havn, Rødby- 7 Ci 54.39N 11.21 E
Rødby-Rødby Havn 7 Ci 54.39N 11.21 E
Roddickton 42 Lf 50.51N 56.07W
Rødding 8 Ci 55.22N 9.04 E

Index Symbols

- [1] Independent Nation
- [2] State, Region
- [3] District, County
- [4] Municipality
- [5] Colony, Dependency
- Continent
- Physical Region
- Historical or Cultural Region
- Mount, Mountain
- Volcano
- Hill
- Mountains, Mountain Range
- Hills, Escarpment
- Plateau, Upland
- Pass, Gap
- Plain, Lowland
- Delta
- Salt Flat
- Valley, Canyon
- Crater, Cave
- Karst Features
- Depression
- Polder
- Desert, Dunes
- Forest, Woods
- Heath, Steppe
- Oasis
- Cape, Point
- Coast, Beach
- Cliff
- Peninsula
- Isthmus
- Sandbank
- Island
- Atoll
- Rock, Reef
- Islands, Archipelago
- Rocks, Reefs
- Coral Reef
- Well, Spring
- Geyser
- River, Stream
- Waterfall Rapids
- River Mouth, Estuary
- Lake
- Salt Lake
- Intermittent Lake
- Reservoir
- Swamp, Pond
- Canal
- Glacier
- Ice Shelf, Pack Ice
- Ocean
- Sea
- Gulf, Bay
- Strait, Fjord
- Lagoon
- Bank
- Seamount
- Tablemount
- Ridge
- Shelf
- Basin
- Escarpment, Sea Scarp
- Fracture
- Trench, Abyss
- National Park, Reserve
- Point of Interest
- Recreation Site
- Cave, Cavern
- Historic Site
- Ruins
- Wall, Walls
- Church, Abbey
- Temple
- Scientific Station
- Airport
- Port
- Lighthouse
- Mine
- Tunnel
- Dam, Bridge

Index Symbols

Symbol	Meaning	Symbol	Meaning
[1]	Independent Nation		Historical or Cultural Region
[2]	State, Region		Mount, Mountain
[3]	District, County		Volcano
[4]	Municipality		Hill
[5]	Colony, Dependency		Mountains, Mountain Range
	Continent		Hills, Escarpment
	Physical Region		Plateau, Upland
	Pass, Gap		Depression
	Plain, Lowland		Polder
	Delta		Desert, Dunes
	Salt Flat		Forest, Woods
	Valley, Canyon		Heath, Steppe
	Crater, Cave		Oasis
	Karst Features		Cape, Point
	Coast, Beach		Rock, Reef
	Cliff		Islands, Archipelago
	Peninsula		Rocks, Reefs
	Isthmus		Coral Reef
	Sandbank		Well, Spring
	Island		Geyser
	Atoll		River, Stream
	Waterfall Rapids		Canal
	River Mouth, Estuary		Glacier
	Lake		Ice Shelf, Pack Ice
	Salt Lake		Ocean
	Intermittent Lake		Sea
	Reservoir		Gulf, Bay
	Swamp, Pond		Strait, Fjord
	Lagoon		Escarpment, Sea Scarp
	Bank		Fracture
	Seamount		Trench, Abyss
	Tablemount		National Park, Reserve
	Ridge		Point of Interest
	Shelf		Recreation Site
	Basin		Cave, Cavern
	Historic Site		Port
	Ruins		Lighthouse
	Wall, Walls		Mine
	Church, Abbey		Tunnel
	Temple		Dam, Bridge
	Scientific Station		
	Airport		

Index Symbols

[1] Independent Nation	Pass, Gap	Depression	Coast, Beach	Rock, Reef
[2] State, Region	Plain, Lowland	Polder	Cliff	Islands, Archipelago
[3] District, County	Delta	Desert, Dunes	Peninsula	Rocks, Reefs
[4] Municipality	Salt Flat	Forest, Woods	Isthmus	Coral Reef
[5] Colony, Dependency	Valley, Canyon	Heath, Steppe	Sandbank	Well, Spring
Continent	Crater, Cave	Oasis	Island	Geyser
Physical Region	Karst Features	Cape, Point	Atoll	River, Stream

Historical or Cultural Region	Waterfall Rapids	Canal	Lagoon
Mount, Mountain	River Mouth, Estuary	Glacier	Bank
Volcano	Lake	Ice Shelf, Pack Ice	Fracture
Hill	Salt Lake	Ocean	Seamount
Mountains, Mountain Range	Intermittent Lake	Sea	Tablemount
Hills, Escarpment	Reservoir	Gulf, Bay	Ridge
Plateau, Upland	Swamp, Pond	Strait, Fjord	Shelf / Basin

Escarpment, Sea Scarp	Historic Site	Port
Trench, Abyss	Ruins	Lighthouse
National Park, Reserve	Wall, Walls	Mine
Point of Interest	Church, Abbey	Tunnel
Recreation Site	Temple	Dam, Bridge
Cave, Cavern	Scientific Station	
	Airport	

International Map Index

Name	Map	Grid	Lat	Long
Saint Helena Sound	44	Gi	32.27N	80.25W
Saint Helens [Austl.]	59	Jh	41.20S	148.15 E
Saint Helens [Eng.-U.K.]	9	Kh	53.28N	2.44W
Saint Helens [Or.-U.S.]	46	Dd	45.52N	122.48W
Saint Helens, Mount-	46	Dd	46.12N	122.11W
Saint Helier	9	Kl	49.12N	2.07W
Saint-Hubert	12	Hd	50.03N	5.23 E
Saint-Hyacinthe	44	Kc	45.38N	72.57W
Saint Ignace Island	45	Mb	48.48N	87.55W
Saint Ignatius	46	Hc	47.19N	114.06W
Saint Ives [Eng.-U.K.]	9	Hk	50.12N	5.29W
Saint Ives [Eng.-U.K.]	12	Bb	52.18N	0.04W
Saint James	45	Ie	43.59N	94.38W
Saint James, Cape -	42	Ef	51.57N	131.01W
Saint-Jean	42	Kg	45.13N	73.15W
Saint-Jean, Baie de-	51b	Bc	17.55N	62.51W
Saint-Jean, Lac-	38	Le	48.35N	72.00W
Saint-Jean-d'Angély	11	Fi	45.57N	0.31W
Saint-Jean-de-Luz	11	Ek	43.23N	1.40W
Saint-Jean-de-Maurienne	11	Mi	45.17N	6.21 E
Saint-Jean-de-Monts	11	Dh	46.47N	2.04W
Saint-Jean-du-Gard	11	Jj	44.06N	3.53 E
Saint-Jean-Pied-de-Port	11	Ek	43.10N	1.14W
Saint-Jérôme [Que.-Can.]	42	Kg	45.46N	74.00W
Saint-Jérôme [Que.-Can.]	44	La	48.26N	71.52W
Saint Joe River	46	Gc	47.21N	116.42W
Saint John	50	Dc	18.20N	64.42W
Saint John [Can.]	38	Me	45.15N	66.04W
Saint John [Ks.-U.S.]	45	Gd	38.00N	98.46W
Saint John [Lbr.]	34	Cd	5.55N	10.05W
Saint John [N.B.-Can.]	39	Me	45.16N	66.03W
Saint John's [Atg.]	47	Le	17.06N	61.51W
Saint Johns [Az.-U.S.]	46	Ki	34.30N	109.22W
Saint John's [Mi.-U.S.]	44	Ed	43.00N	84.33W
Saint John's [Mont.]	51c	Bc	16.48N	62.11W
Saint John's [Newf.-Can.]	39	Ne	47.34N	52.43W
Saint Johnsbury	44	Kc	44.25N	72.01W
Saint Johns River	44	Gj	30.24N	81.24W
Saint Joseph [Dom.]	51g	Bb	15.24N	61.26W
Saint Joseph [La.-U.S.]	45	Kk	31.55N	91.14W
Saint Joseph [Mart.]	51h	Ab	14.40N	61.05W
Saint Joseph [Mo.-U.S.]	45	Id	39.46N	94.51W
Saint Joseph [New Caledonia]	63b	Ce	20.27S	166.36 E
Saint Joseph [Reu.]	37a	Bb	21.22S	55.37 E
Saint Joseph, Lake-	42	If	51.06N	90.36W
Saint Joseph Island	44	Fb	46.13N	83.57W
Saint Joseph River	44	Dd	42.06N	86.29W
Saint-Junien	11	Gi	45.53N	0.54 E
Saint-Jean-en-Chaussée	12	Ee	49.30N	2.26 E
Saint Kilda	9	Ed	57.49N	8.36W
Saint Kitts/Saint Christopher	38	Mh	17.21N	62.48W
Saint-Lary-Soulan	11	Gl	42.49N	0.19 E
Saint Laurent	53	Ke	5.30N	54.02W
Saint Laurent = Saint Lawrence (EN)	38	Me	49.15N	67.00W
Saint Lawrence	38	Bc	63.30N	170.30W
Saint Lawrence	38	Me	49.15N	67.00W
Saint Lawrence (EN) = Saint Laurent	38	Me	49.15N	67.00W
Saint Lawrence, Gulf of-	38	Me	48.00N	62.00W
Saint-Léger-en-Yvelines	12	Df	48.43N	1.46 E
Saint-Léonard	44	Nb	47.10N	67.56W
Saint-Léonard-de-Noblat	11	Hi	45.50N	1.29 E
Saint-Lewis	42	Lf	52.22N	55.58W
Saint-Lô	11	Ee	49.07N	1.05W
Saint Louis	39	Jf	38.38N	90.11W
Saint-Louis [Guad.]	51b	Ec	15.57N	61.20W
Saint-Louis [Sen.]	31	Fg	16.02N	16.30W
Saint-Loup-sur-Semouse	11	Mg	47.53N	6.16 E
Saint Lucia	37	Ee	28.23S	32.25 E
Saint Lucia	39	Mh	13.53N	60.58W
Saint Lucia	38	Mh	13.53N	60.58W
Saint Lucia, Cape -	30	Kk	28.32S	32.24 E
Saint Lucia, Lake-	37	Ee	28.00S	32.30 E
Saint Lucia Channel	50	Fe	14.09N	60.57W
Saint Lucia Channel (EN) = Sainte-Lucie, Canal de-	50	Fe	14.09N	60.57W
Saint Magnus Bay	9	La	60.25N	1.35W
Saint-Maixent-l'Ecole	11	Fh	46.25N	0.12W
Saint-Malo	6	Ff	48.39N	2.01W
Saint-Malo, Golfe de-	5	Ff	48.45N	2.00W
Saint-Marc	47	Je	19.06N	72.43W
Saint-Marc, Canal de-	49	Kd	18.50N	72.45W
Saint Margaret's at Cliffe	12	Dc	51.09N	1.19 E
Saint Margaret's Hope	9	Kc	58.49N	2.57W
Saint Maries	46	Gc	47.19N	116.35W
Saint Martin	47	Le	18.04N	63.04W
Saint-Martin, Cap-	51h	Ab	14.52N	61.13W
Saint-Martin-Boulogne	12	Dd	50.43N	1.40 E
Saint-Martin-de-Ré	11	Eh	46.12N	1.22W
Saint-Martin-des-Besaces	12	Be	49.01N	0.51W
Saint Martins	44	Oc	45.21N	65.32W
Saint-Martin-Vésubie	11	Nj	44.04N	7.15 E
Saint Mary, Cape-	44	Nc	44.05N	66.13W
Saint Mary Peak [Austl.]	59	Hf	31.30S	138.35 E
Saint Mary Peak [U.S.]	46	Hc	46.40N	114.20W
Saint Mary's	9	Gl	49.55N	6.20W
Saint Marys [Austl.]	59	Jh	41.35S	148.10 E
Saint Marys [Oh.-U.S.]	44	Ee	40.32N	84.22W
Saint Marys [W.V.-U.S.]	44	Gf	39.24N	81.13W
Saint Mary's, Cape -	42	Mg	46.49N	54.12W
Saint Mary's Bay [N.S.-Can.]	44	Nc	44.25N	66.10W
Saint Mary's Bay [N.W.T.-Can.]	42	Mg	46.50N	53.47W
Saint Marys River	44	Gj	30.45N	81.30W
Saint-Mathieu, Pointe de-	5	Ff	48.20N	4.46W
Saint Matthew	38	Bb	60.30N	172.45W
Saint Matthias Group	57	Fe	1.30S	149.48 E
Saint-Maur-des-Fossés	11	Hf	48.48N	2.30 E
Saint-Maurice, Rivière-	42	Kg	46.21N	72.31W
Saint Michael	40	Gd	63.29N	162.02W
Saint Michaels	46	Ki	35.46N	109.04W
Saint-Michel	12	Ge	49.55N	4.08 E

Name	Map	Grid	Lat	Long
Saint-Mihiel	11	Lf	48.54N	5.33 E
Saint-Nazaire	11	Dg	47.17N	2.12W
Saint Neots	12	Bb	52.13N	0.16W
Saint-Nicolas/Sint Niklaas	11	Kc	51.10N	4.08 E
Saint-Nicolas-d'Aliermont	12	De	49.53N	1.13 E
Saint-Nicolas-de-Port	11	Mf	48.38N	6.18 E
Saint-Omer	11	Id	50.45N	2.15 E
Saintonge	11	Fi	45.50N	0.30W
Saint Patrick's	51c	Bc	16.41N	62.12W
Saint Paul	34	Cd	6.23N	10.48W
Saint Paul	37a	Bb	21.00S	55.16 E
Saint Paul	30	Ol	38.55S	77.41 E
Saint Paul [Ak.-U.S.]	40	Ee	57.07N	170.17W
Saint Paul [Alta.-Can.]	42	Gf	53.59N	111.17W
Saint Paul [Mn.-U.S.]	39	Je	44.58N	93.07W
Saint Paul [Nb.-U.S.]	45	Gf	41.13N	98.27W
Saint Paul, Cape-	34	Fd	5.49N	0.57 E
Saint-Paul-lès-Dax	11	Ek	43.44N	1.03W
Saint Paul's	51c	Ab	17.24N	62.49W
Saint Paul's Point	64q	Ab	25.04S	130.05W
Saint-Péray	11	Kj	44.57N	4.50 E
Saint Peter	45	Jd	44.17N	93.57W
Saint Peter Port	9	Kl	49.27N	2.32W
Saint Peter's	51c	Bc	16.46N	62.12W
Saint Petersburg	39	Kg	27.46N	82.38W
Saint Petersburg Beach	44	Fl	27.45N	82.45W
Saint-Pierre [Mart.]	50	Fe	14.45N	61.11W
Saint-Pierre [May.]	31	Mk	21.19S	55.29 E
Saint-Pierre [St.P.M.]	42	Lg	46.46N	56.12W
Saint-Pierre, Lac-	44	Kb	46.10N	72.50W
Saint Pierre and Miquelon (EN) = Saint-Pierre et Miquelon	39	Ne	46.55N	56.10W
Saint-Pierre-en-Port	12	Ce	49.48N	0.29 E
Saint-Pierre et Miquelon	38	Ne	46.55N	56.10W
Saint-Pierre et Miquelon = Saint Pierre and Miquelon (EN)	39	Ne	46.55N	56.10W
Saint Pierre Island	37b	Bb	9.19S	50.43 E
Saint-Pierre-sur-Dives	12	Be	49.01N	0.02W
Saint-Pol-de-Léon	11	Cf	48.41N	3.59W
Saint-Pol-sur-Mer	12	Id	51.02N	2.21 E
Saint-Pol-sur-Ternoise	11	Id	50.23N	2.20 E
Saint-Pons	11	Ik	43.29N	2.46 E
Saint-Pourçain-sur-Sioule	11	Jh	46.18N	3.17 E
Saint-Quentin	11	Je	49.51N	3.17 E
Saint-Quentin, Canal de-	12	Fe	49.36N	3.11 E
Saint-Raphaël	11	Mk	43.25N	6.46 E
Saint-Rémy-de-Provence	11	Kk	43.47N	4.50 E
Saint-Rigaux, Mont-	11	Kh	46.12N	4.29 E
Saint-Riquier	12	Dd	50.08N	1.57 E
Saint Roch Basin	42	Ic	68.50N	95.00W
Saint Rogatien Bank (EN)	60	Mc	24.40N	167.10W
Saint-Romain-de-Colbosc	12	Ce	49.32N	0.22 E
Saint-Saëns	12	De	49.40N	1.17 E
Saint Saulfieu	12	Ee	49.47N	2.15 E
Saint-Savin	11	Gh	46.34N	0.52 E
Saint-Sébastien, Cap-	37	Hb	12.26S	48.44 E
Saint-Seine-l'Abbaye	11	Kg	47.26N	4.47 E
Saint-Servais, Namur-	12	Gd	50.28N	4.50 E
Saint Simon	12	Fe	49.45N	3.10 E
Saint Simons Island	44	Gj	31.14N	81.21W
Saint Stanislas Bay	64g	Bb	1.53N	157.30W
Saint Stephen	42	Kg	45.12N	67.17W
Saint-Sylvain	12	Be	49.03N	0.13W
Saint Teresa Beach	44	Ek	29.58N	84.28W
Saint Thomas	42	Gd	42.47N	81.12W
Saint Thomas	47	Le	18.21N	64.55W
Saint-Trond/Sint-Truiden	11	Ld	50.49N	5.12 E
Saint-Tropez	11	Mk	43.16N	6.38 E
Saint-Tropez, Golfe de-	11	Mk	43.17N	6.38 E
Saint-Valéry-en-Caux	11	Ge	49.52N	0.44 E
Saint-Valery-sur-Somme	11	Hd	50.11N	1.38 E
Saint-Vallier	11	Ki	45.10N	4.49 E
Saint-Venant	12	Ed	50.37N	2.33 E
Saint Vincent	14	Be	45.45N	7.39 E
Saint Vincent	38	Mh	13.15N	61.12W
Saint-Vincent, Baie de-	63b	Cf	22.00S	166.05 E
Saint Vincent, Cap-	30	Lk	21.57S	43.16 E
Saint Vincent and the Grenadines	59	Hf	35.00S	138.05 E
Saint-Vincent-de-Tyrosse	39	Mh	13.15N	61.12W
Saint Vincent Island	11	Ek	43.40N	1.18W
Saint Vincent Passage	44	Ek	29.40N	85.07W
Saint-Wandrille-Rançon	50	Ff	13.30N	61.00W
Saint-Yrieix-la-Perche	12	Ce	49.32N	0.46 E
Saipan	11	Hi	45.31N	1.12 E
Saipan Channel	64a	Ad	6.54N	134.08 E
Saipan Island	64b	Ba	15.05N	145.41 E
Sairecabur, Cerro-	57	Fc	15.12N	145.45 E
Saitama Ken	54	Ak	22.43S	67.54W
Sajak	28	Of	36.00N	139.50 E
Sajama, Nevado de-	19	Hf	46.55N	77.22 E
Sajan	52	Eg	18.07S	69.00W
Sajānan	28	Jg	18.06S	68.54W
Sajid	14	Dm	37.03N	9.14 E
Sajir, Ra's-	38	De	38.49N	63.51 E
Sajmenski Kanal = Saimaa Canal (EN)	35	Ib	16.45N	53.35 E
Sajn-Sand	22	Ne	44.55N	110.11 E
Sajó	10	Ri	47.56N	21.08 E
Sajószentpéter	10	Qh	48.13N	20.43 E
Sajram	18	Gc	42.18N	69.45 E
Sajzi	24	Of	32.41N	52.07 E
Saka	36	Gc	0.09S	39.20 E
Sakaide	28	Mg	34.19N	133.51 E
Sakaiminato	29	Cd	35.33N	133.15 E
Sakākah	27	Je	29.59N	40.06 E
Sakakawea, Lake-	43	Gb	47.50N	102.20W
Sakala, Vozvyšennost-/ Sakala Kõrgustik	8	Kf	58.00N	25.30 E

Name	Map	Grid	Lat	Long
Sakala Kõrgustik/Sakala, Vozvyšennost-	8	Kf	58.00N	25.30 E
Sakami	42	Jf	53.18N	76.45W
Sakami, Lac-	42	Jf	53.15N	76.45W
Sākāne, 'Erg i-n-	34	Ea	20.40N	0.51W
Sakania	36	Ee	12.43S	28.33 E
Sakao	63b	Cb	14.58S	167.07 E
Sakar	20	Jf	11.39N	78.10 E
Sakar	18	De	38.59N	63.45 E
Sakaraha	37	Gd	22.54S	44.32 E
Sakar-Čaga	18	Cf	37.39N	61.40 E
Sakārinah, Jabal as-	14	Do	35.45N	9.05 E
Sakartvelos Sabčata Socialisturi Respublica/ Gruzinskaja SSR	19	Eg	42.00N	44.00 E
Sakarya	23	Da	41.07N	30.39 E
Sakata	27	Od	38.55N	139.50 E
Sakchu	28	Hd	40.23N	125.02 E
Sakhalin (EN) = Sahalin, Ostrov-	21	Qd	51.00N	143.00 E
Saki	16	Hg	45.07N	33.37 E
Šakiai/Šakjaj	7	Fi	54.57N	23.01 E
Sakishima Islands (EN) = Sakishima-Shotō	21	Og	24.30N	125.00 E
Sakishima-Shotō = Sakishima Islands (EN)	21	Og	24.30N	125.00 E
Sakito	29	Ae	33.02N	129.34 E
Sakiz Boğazı	15	Jk	38.20N	26.12 E
Šakjaj/Šakiai	7	Fi	54.57N	23.01 E
Sakmara	5	Le	51.46N	55.01 E
Sakon Nakhon	25	Ke	17.10N	104.01 E
Sakrivier	37	Cf	30.54S	20.28 E
Šakša	17	Hi	54.47N	56.15 E
Saksaulski	19	Gf	47.05N	61.13 E
Sakskøbing	8	Dj	54.48N	11.39 E
Saku	28	Of	36.09N	138.26 E
Sakuma	29	Bf	35.05N	137.47 E
Sakura	29	Gd	35.43N	140.13 E
Sakurai	29	Bf	34.31N	135.50 E
Sakura-Jima	29	Bf	31.35N	130.40 E
Sākyla	8	Jc	61.02N	22.20 E
Sal	30	Eg	16.45N	22.55W
Sal	19	Ef	47.31N	40.45 E
Sal, Cay-	49	Gb	23.42N	80.24W
Sal, Punta-	49	Df	15.53N	87.37W
Šala	35	Cb	17.00N	20.53 E
Sala	10	Nh	48.09N	17.53 E
Sala	7	Dg	59.55N	16.36 E
Salabangka, Kepulauan-	26	Jg	3.02S	122.25 E
Salaca	8	Kg	57.39N	24.15 E
Salacgriva/Salacgrīva	7	Fh	57.46N	24.27 E
Salacgrīva/Salacgriva	7	Fh	57.46N	24.27 E
Sala Consilina	14	Jj	40.23N	15.36 E
Salada	48	Hc	28.36N	103.28W
Salada, Laguna-	48	Ba	32.20N	115.40W
Saladas	56	Ic	28.15S	58.38W
Saladillo	56	Ie	35.38S	59.46W
Saladillo, Arroyo-	55	Bj	31.22S	60.30W
Saladillo Amargo, Arroyo-	55	Ci	31.01S	60.19W
Saladillo Dulce, Arroyo-	55	Bj	31.01S	60.19W
Salado, Arroyo- [Arg.]	56	Bm	36.27S	61.06W
Salado, Arroyo- [Mex.]	48	De	24.25N	111.30W
Salado, Riacho-	55	Ch	26.30S	58.18W
Salado, Rio-	55	Ci	34.16N	106.52W
Salado, Rio-	47	Ec	26.52N	99.19W
Salado, Rio- [Arg.]	52	Ji	31.42S	60.44W
Salado, Rio- [Arg.]	56	Be	38.49S	64.57W
Salado, Rio- [Arg.]	52	Ki	35.44S	57.21W
Salado, Valle-	48	He	24.47N	102.50W
Salaga	34	Ed	8.33N	0.31W
Salagle	35	Le	1.50N	42.18 E
Salāhuddīn	24	Je	34.40N	44.00 E
Salailua	65c	Aa	13.41S	172.34W
Salairski Krjaž	20	Df	54.00N	85.00 E
Salaj	15	Fb	47.10N	23.00 E
Salal	35	Bc	14.51N	17.13 E
Salālah [Oman]	22	Hh	17.05N	54.10 E
Salālah [Sud.]	35	Ea	21.19N	36.13 E
Salama	49	Bf	15.06N	90.16W
Salamanca [Chile]	13	Gd	40.50N	6.00W
Salamanca [Mex.]	56	Fd	31.47S	70.58W
Salamanca [N.Y.-U.S.]	47	Bd	20.34N	101.12W
Salamanca [Sp.]	44	Hd	42.11N	78.43W
Salamat	9	Fg	40.58N	5.39W
Salamat, Bahr-	35	Cc	11.00N	20.30 E
Salamina	35	Bd	9.27N	18.06 E
Salamis	19	Id	10.30N	74.48W
Salamís	15	Gl	37.58N	23.29 E
Salamís	24	Ee	35.10N	33.54 E
Salamís	15	Gl	37.55N	23.30 E
Sālang, Tünel-e-	23	Kb	35.19N	69.02 E
Salani	65c	Bb	14.00S	171.34W
Salantaj/Salantai	8	Ih	56.05N	21.30 E
Salantaj/Salantai	8	Ih	56.05N	21.30 E
Salas	13	Fa	43.24N	6.16W
Salas de los Infantes	13	Ib	42.01N	3.17W
Salat	64d	Cb	7.14N	152.01 E
Salat	26	Fh	7.19S	110.30 E
Salavat	6	Le	53.25N	55.58 E
Salawati, Pulau-	26	Jg	1.07S	130.52 E
Sala y Gómez	57	Qg	26.28S	105.28W
Sala y Gómez Ridge (EN)	3	Ml	25.00S	98.00W
Salazar	55	Am	36.18S	62.12W
Salbris	11	Ij	47.26N	2.03 E
Salcantay, Nevado de-	52	Ig	13.22S	72.34W
Šalčininkai/Salčininkai	8	Kj	54.18N	25.30 E
Šalčininkai/Šalčininkai	8	Kj	54.18N	25.30 E
Salda Gölü	15	Ml	37.33N	29.42 E
Saldanha	31	Il	33.00S	17.56 E
Saldungaray	56	Bf	37.59N	40.06 E
Saldus	19	Cd	56.40N	22.31 E
Sale	59	Jg	38.06S	147.04 E
Salé	32	Fc	34.04N	6.48W

Name	Map	Grid	Lat	Long
Salebabu, Pulau-	26	If	3.55N	126.40 E
Šālehābād	24	Me	34.56N	48.20 E
Salehard	22	Ic	66.33N	66.40 E
Saleimoa	65c	Ba	13.48S	171.52W
Sal-Rei	65c	Aa	13.44S	172.10W
Salem [Fl.-U.S.]	44	Fk	29.58N	83.28W
Salem [Il.-U.S.]	45	Lg	38.38N	88.57W
Salem [India]	22	Jh	11.39N	78.10 E
Salem [In.-U.S.]	44	Df	38.36N	86.06W
Salem [Ma.-U.S.]	44	Ld	42.31N	70.55W
Salem [Mont.]	51c	Bc	16.45N	62.13W
Salem [Mo.-U.S.]	45	Kh	37.39N	91.32W
Salem [N.J.-U.S.]	44	Jf	39.35N	75.28W
Salem [Oh.-U.S.]	44	Ge	40.54N	80.52W
Salem [Or.-U.S.]	39	Ge	44.57N	123.01W
Salem [S.D.-U.S.]	45	He	43.44N	97.23W
Salem [Va.-U.S.]	44	Gg	37.17N	80.03W
Salemi	14	Gm	37.49N	12.48 E
Sälen	8	Ec	61.10N	13.16 E
Salentine Peninsula (EN) = Penisola Salentina	1	Hg	40.30N	18.00 E
Sale Pit	9	Oh	53.40N	1.30 E
Salerno	6	Hg	40.41N	14.47 E
Salerno, Golfo di-	14	Ij	40.30N	14.40 E
Salers	11	Ij	45.08N	2.30 E
Salève, Mont-	11	Mh	46.07N	6.10 E
Salgir	16	Ig	45.38N	35.01 E
Salgótarján	10	Ph	48.07N	19.49 E
Salgueiro	54	Ke	8.04S	39.06W
Salher	25	Ed	20.41N	73.52 E
Salhus	7	Af	60.30N	5.16 E
Sali	14	Ig	43.56N	15.10 E
Šali	16	Nh	43.06N	45.56 E
Salice Terme	14	Df	44.55N	9.01 E
Salida	43	Fd	38.32N	106.00W
Salies-de-Béarn	11	Fk	43.29N	0.55W
Salihli	23	Cb	38.29N	28.09 E
Salima	36	Fe	13.47S	34.26 E
Salīma, Wāḥāt- = Salimah Oasis (EN)	31	Jf	21.22N	29.19 E
Salimah Oasis (EN) = Salīma, Wāḥāt-	31	Jf	21.22N	29.19 E
Salina	14	Il	38.35N	14.50 E
Salina [Ks.-U.S.]	39	Jf	38.50N	97.37W
Salina [Ut.-U.S.]	46	Hf	38.58N	111.51W
Salina Cruz	47	Ee	16.10N	95.12W
Salinas [Ca.-U.S.]	39	Gf	36.40N	121.38W
Salinas [Ec.]	52	Bd	2.13S	80.58W
Salinas [P.R.]	51a	Bc	17.59N	66.17W
Salinas, Bahia de-	49	Eh	11.03N	85.43W
Salinas, Cabo de-/Ses Salines, Cap de-	13	Pe	39.16N	3.03 E
Salinas, Punta- [Dom.Rep.]	49	Ld	18.12N	70.34W
Salinas, Punta- [P.R.]	51a	Bb	18.29N	66.10W
Salinas, Rio-	49	Be	16.28N	90.33W
Salinas de Hidalgo	48	If	22.38N	101.43W
Salinas Peak	45	Cj	33.18N	106.31W
Saline, Point-	50	Fg	12.00N	61.48W
Saline Island	51p	Cb	12.26N	61.29W
Saline River [Ks.-U.S.]	45	Hg	38.51N	97.30W
Saline River [Ar.-U.S.]	45	Jj	33.10N	92.08W
Salines, Pointe des-	51b	Bc	14.24N	60.53W
Salinópolis	54	Id	0.37S	47.20W
Salins-les-Bains	11	Lh	46.57N	5.53 E
Salisbury [Dom.]	42	Jd	63.35N	77.00W
Salisbury [Eng.-U.K.]	51g	Bb	15.26N	61.27W
Salisbury [Md.-U.S.]	9	Lj	51.05N	1.48W
Salisbury [N.C.-U.S.]	43	Ld	38.22N	75.36W
Salisbury Plain	44	Gh	35.40N	80.29W
Säliste	9	Lj	51.15N	1.55W
Šalja	15	Gd	45.47N	23.53 E
Saljany	19	Fd	57.15N	58.43 E
Šalka-Jega-Kara, Ozero-	19	Eh	39.35N	48.59 E
Salkhad	16	Qd	50.35N	51.40 E
Salla	24	Gc	32.29N	36.43 E
Sallent de Gállego	7	Gc	66.50N	28.40 E
Salling	13	Ld	42.46N	0.20W
Salliqueló	8	Ch	56.40N	9.00 E
Sallisaw	56	He	36.45S	62.56W
Sallūm	45	Ii	35.28N	94.47W
Sallūm, Khalīj as- = Salum, Gulf of- (EN)	35	Fb	19.23N	37.06 E
Sallyana	33	Ec	31.40N	25.20 E
Salm	25	Gc	28.22N	82.10 E
Salmás	23	Fb	38.11N	44.47 E
Salmi	7	Hf	61.24N	31.54 E
Salmo	46	Gb	49.12N	117.17W
Salmon	41	Hh	45.11N	113.54W
Salmon Arm	42	Ff	50.42N	119.16W
Salmon Bank (EN)	60	Kb	26.56N	176.28W
Salmon Falls Creek Reservoir	46	Hd	42.05N	114.45W
Salmon Mountain	46	Hc	45.38N	114.50W
Salmon Mountains	46	Df	41.00N	123.00W
Salmon River	38	Hc	45.51N	116.46W
Salmon River Mountains	43	Dc	44.45N	115.30W
Salmtal	12	Ie	49.56N	6.48 E
Salmyš	16	Sc	52.09N	55.21 E
Salo [C.A.R.]	35	Cd	3.12N	16.07 E
Salo [Fin.]	7	Ff	60.23N	23.08 E
Salobra, Rio-	55	Ml	25.00S	98.00W
Salobreña	13	Ih	36.44N	3.35W
Salomon, Cap-	51h	Ab	14.30N	61.06W
Salon-de-Provence	6	Gg	43.38N	5.06 E
Salonga	30	Ii	0.10S	19.50 E
Salonika (EN) = Thessaloniki	6	Ig	40.38N	22.56 E
Salonika, Gulf of- (EN) = Thermaïkós Kólpos	1	Ig	40.20N	22.45 E
Salonta	15	Fc	46.48N	21.39 E
Salop	9	Ki	52.40N	2.50W
Salop	9	Ki	52.40N	2.50W
Salor	13	Ee	39.39N	7.03W

Name	Map	Grid	Lat	Long
Salou	13	Nc	41.04N	1.08 E
Salouël	12	Ee	49.52N	2.15 E
Saloum	34	Bc	13.50N	16.45W
Salpausselkä	5	Ic	61.00N	26.30 E
Sal-Rei	32	Cf	16.11N	22.55W
Salsbruket	7	Cd	64.48N	11.52 E
Salseleh-ye Safid Küh/ Paropamisus	21	If	34.30N	63.30 E
Salsipuedes, Canal de-	48	Cc	28.40N	113.00W
Salsipuedes, Punta-	49	Fi	8.28N	81.29 E
Salsk	19	Ef	46.28N	41.29 E
Šalski	7	If	61.48N	36.03 E
Salso [It.]	14	Hm	37.06N	13.57 E
Salso [It.]	14	Hm	37.06N	13.57 E
Salsola	14	Ji	41.37N	15.40 E
Salsomaggiore Terme	14	Df	44.49N	9.59 E
Salt	13	Oc	41.59N	2.47 E
Salta	56	Hb	25.00S	64.30W
Salta	53	Jh	24.47S	65.24W
Saltash	9	Ik	50.24N	4.12W
Salt Basin	45	Dk	31.50N	105.00W
Saltburn by the Sea	9	Mg	54.35N	0.58W
Salt Cay	49	Lc	21.20N	71.11W
Salt Creek	46	Bb	36.15N	116.49W
Salt Draw	45	Bk	31.39N	103.28W
Saltee Islands/Na Sailtí	9	Gi	52.07N	6.36W
Salten	7	Cc	67.45N	15.31 E
Salt Fork Arkansas River	45	Hh	36.36N	97.03W
Salt Fork Brazos	45	Gj	33.15N	100.00W
Salt Fork Red	45	Gi	34.30N	99.22W
Saltholm	8	Ei	55.40N	12.45 E
Saltillo	39	Ig	25.25N	101.01W
Salt Lake City	39	He	40.46N	111.53W
Salto [2]	55	Dj	31.25S	57.00W
Salto	14	Gh	42.23N	12.54 E
Salto [Arg.]	56	Hd	34.17S	60.15W
Salto [Ur.]	53	Ki	31.23S	57.58W
Salto da Divisa	54	Kg	16.00S	39.57W
Salto Grande	55	Hf	22.54S	49.59W
Salton Sea	38	Hf	33.20N	115.50W
Salt River	43	Ee	33.23N	112.18W
Saltsjöbaden	8	He	59.17N	18.18 E
Saltvik	8	Ef	60.17N	20.03 E
Saluafata Harbour	65c	Ba	13.53S	171.38W
Saluda	44	Ig	37.36N	76.36W
Salum, Gulf of-(EN) = Sallūm, Khalīj as-	33	Ec	31.40N	25.20 E
Salūm	14	Bf	44.39N	7.29 E
Saluzzo	56	Eh	50.55S	75.05W
Salvación, Bahía-	53	Mg	12.59S	38.31W
Salvador [Braz.]	34	Ja	23.14N	12.05 E
Salvador [Niger]	45	Kl	29.45N	90.15W
Salvador, Lake-	56	Hb	22.10S	63.43W
Salvaterra de Magos	13	Be	39.01N	8.48W
Salvatierra [Mex.]	48	Jg	20.13N	100.53W
Salvatierra [Sp.]	13	Jb	42.51N	2.23W
Salwa, Dawḥat as-	24	Nj	25.30N	50.40 E
Salwá Baḥrī	33	Fe	24.44N	32.56 E
Salween	21	Lh	16.31N	97.37 E
Salyersville	44	Fg	37.45N	83.04W
Salza	14	Ic	47.40N	14.43 E
Salzach	10	Ih	48.12N	12.56 E
Salzburg [2]	6	Hf	47.48N	13.02 E
Salzburg [2]	14	Gc	47.20N	13.00 E
Salzburger Kalkalpen	14	Gc	47.35N	12.55 E
Salzgitter	10	Gd	52.05N	10.20 E
Salzkammergut	14	Hc	47.45N	13.30 E
Salzkotten	12	Kc	51.40N	8.36 E
Salzwedel	10	Hd	52.51N	11.09 E
Samadlaj, Ra's-	24	Fj	25.00N	34.56 E
Samagaltaj	20	Ef	50.36N	95.03 E
Samaḥ [Lib.]	33	Cd	28.10N	19.10 E
Samaḥ [Sau.Ar.]	24	Hh	28.52N	45.30 E
Samaipata	54	Fg	18.09S	63.52W
Samalayuca	48	Hb	31.21N	106.28W
Samales Group	26	He	6.00N	121.45 E
Samalga Pass	40a	Ea	52.48N	169.25W
Samālūt	33	Fd	28.18N	30.42 E
Samambaia, Rio-	55	Ff	22.45S	53.21W
Samaná	49	Md	19.13N	69.19W
Samaná, Bahía de-	47	Ke	19.10N	69.25W
Samaná, Cabo-	49	Md	19.18N	69.09W
Samana Cay	49	Kb	23.06N	73.42W
Samandaği	24	Fd	36.07N	35.56 E
Samani	27	Pc	42.07N	142.56 E
Samanli Dağlari	15	Mi	40.32N	29.10 E
Samar	21	Oh	12.00N	125.00 E
Samara [R.S.F.S.R.]	5	Le	53.10N	50.04 E
Samara [Ukr.-U.S.S.R.]	16	Ie	48.33N	35.12 E
Samarai	58	Gf	10.36S	150.39 E
Samarinda	22	Nj	0.30S	117.09 E
Samarkandskaja Oblast [3]	19	Gg	40.10N	66.20 E
Sāmarrā'	23	Fc	34.12N	43.52 E
Samar Sea	26	Hd	11.50N	124.32 E
Samaru	34	Hc	11.10N	7.38 E
Samatan	11	Gk	43.30N	0.56 E
Samate	26	Jg	0.58S	131.04 E
Samba [Zaire]	36	Ec	4.38S	26.22 E
Samba [Zaire]	36	Db	0.14N	21.19 E
Samba Caju	36	Cd	8.45S	15.25 E
Sambalpur	25	Gd	21.27N	83.58 E
Sambar, Tanjung-	26	Fg	2.59S	110.19 E
Sambas	26	Ff	1.20N	109.15 E
Sambava	37	Ib	14.15S	50.10 E
Sâmbêr	11	Kd	50.28N	4.52 E
Sâmbêr	11	Kl	50.28N	4.52 E
Sâmbhar	25	Ec	26.55S	75.12 E
Sambiase	14	Kl	38.58N	16.17 E
Sambito, Rio-	54	Jd	6.45S	42.15W
Sambor	19	Cf	49.32N	23.11 E
Samborombón, Bahía-	56	Ie	36.00S	57.12W
Samborombón, Rio-	55	Dl	35.43S	57.20W
Sambre	11	Kd	50.28N	4.52 E
Sambre à l'Oise, Canal de la-	11	Je	49.39N	3.20 E
Samburg	20	Cc	67.00N	78.25 E

Index Symbols

mch'ŏk 27 Md 37.27N 129.10 E
mch'ŏnp'o 27 Me 34.55N 128.04 E
ndi Dağı 24 Kd 37.19N 44.15 E
ndŏng-ni 28 Ie 39.21N 126.14 E
ndŭng 28 Ie 38.59N 126.11 E
ne [Indon.] 26 Ih 8.59S 125.40 E
ne [Tan.] 36 Gc 4.04S 37.44 E
ner 12 Dd 50.38N 1.45 E
n Ford Fiord 42 Kb 70.40N 70.35W
nfya 36 Ee 11.20S 29.32 E
nhor 16 Oi 40.48N 46.01 E
ni 15 Dk 38.15N 20.39 E
ni Ghar 23 Kc 31.43N 67.01 E
nirah 24 Ji 26.18N 42.05 E
nisu-Jima 27 Oe 31.40N 140.00 E
nli 15 Kj 39.48N 27.51 E
nnah, Jabal- 24 Ei 26.26N 33.34 E
noa I Sisifo = Western
amoa (EN) [1] 58 Jf 13.40S 172.30W
moa Islands 57 Jf 14.00S 171.00W
mobor 14 Je 45.48N 15.43 E
mojlovka 16 Md 51.10N 43.43 E
mokov 15 Gg 42.20N 23.33 E
molva 8 Lf 58.16N 27.45 E
mos 15 Jl 37.45N 26.58 E
mos 5 Ih 37.45N 26.48 E
mosir, Pulau- 26 Cf 2.35N 98.50 E
mothrace (EN) =
amothráki 15 Ii 40.27N 25.35 E
mothráki 15 Ii 40.29N 25.31 E
mothráki = Samothrace
EN) 15 Ii 40.27N 25.35 E
mpacho 56 Hd 33.23S 64.43W
mpaga 26 Gg 2.19S 119.07 E
mpit 26 Fg 3.00S 113.03 E
mpit 22 Nj 2.32S 112.57 E
mpoku 29 Fb 38.30N 139.30 E
mpwe 36 Ed 9.20S 27.23 E
m Rayburn Reservoir 45 Ik 31.27N 94.37W
mro, Ozero- 8 Mf 58.55N 28.50 E
msjøen 8 Da 63.05N 10.40 E
msø 7 Ci 55.50N 10.35 E
msø Bælt 8 Di 55.50N 10.45 E
m Son 25 Ld 19.44N 105.54 E
msun 22 Fe 41.17N 36.20 E
msun Dağı 15 Kl 37.40N 27.15 E
mtredia 16 Mh 42.11N 42.17 E
muel, Mount- 59 Gc 19.41S 134.09 E
muhú 55 Bh 27.31S 60.24W
mui, Ko- 21 Li 9.30N 100.00 E
mur 16 Pi 41.53N 48.32 E
mur-Apšeronski Kanal 16 Pi 40.35N 49.35 E
mus 20 De 56.46N 84.44 E
mut Prakan 25 Kf 13.36N 100.36 E
mut Sakhon 25 Kf 13.31N 100.15 E
n 31 Gg 13.08N 4.53W
n [Asia] 25 Lf 13.32N 105.57 E
n [Pol.] 10 Rf 50.45N 21.51 E
n'ā' 22 Gh 15.23N 44.12 E
na 14 Ke 45.03N 16.23 E
naag [3] 35 Hc 10.10N 47.50 E
nabū 24 Di 27.30N 30.47 E
nae 66 Bf 70.18S 2.22W
nāfir 24 Fi 27.55N 34.42 E
năg 35 Hd 7.45N 48.00 E
naga 30 Hh 3.35N 9.38 E
n Agustin 55 Cn 38.01S 58.21W
n Agustin, Cabo- 48 Bc 28.05N 115.20W
n Agustin, Cape- 26 Ie 6.16N 126.11 E
nak Islands 40 Gf 54.25N 162.35W
nalona, Presa- 48 Fe 24.53N 107.00W
n Ambrosio, Isla- 56 Ec 26.21S 79.52W
nana 26 Ig 2.04S 125.08 E
nana, Pulau- 26 Ig 2.12S 125.55 E
nandaj 23 Gb 35.19N 47.00 E
n Andreas 46 Eg 38.12N 120.41W
n Andrés [3] 47 Hf 12.35N 81.42W
n Andres, Cerro- 48 Ih 19.48N 100.36W
n Andrés, Isla de- 52 Hd 12.32N 81.42W
n Andrés, Laguna de- 48 Kf 22.40N 97.50W
San Andrés de Giles 55 Cl 34.27S 59.27W
San Andrés del Rabanedo 13 Gb 42.37N 5.36W
San Andres Mountains 43 Fe 32.55N 106.45W
San Andrés Peak 45 Cj 32.43N 106.30W
San Andrés Tuxtla 47 Ee 18.27N 95.13W
San Andrés y
Providencia [2] 54 Ba 12.30N 81.45W
Sananduva 55 Gh 27.57S 51.48W
San Angelo 43 Ge 31.28N 100.26W
San Antonio [Blz.] 49 Ce 16.30N 89.02W
San Antonio [Chile] 56 Fd 33.35S 71.38W
San Antonio [Tx.-U.S.] 39 Jg 29.28N 98.31W
San Antonio [Ur.] 55 Dj 31.20S 57.45W
San Antonio, Cabo- [Arg.] 52 Ki 36.40S 56.42W
San Antonio, Cabo- [Cuba] 38 Kg 21.52N 84.57W
San Antonio, Cabo de-/Sant Antoni, Cap- 13 Mf 38.48N 0.12 E
San Antonio, Canal- 55 Aj 31.42S 62.15W
San Antonio, Punta- 48 Bc 29.45N 115.45W
San Antonio, Sierra de- 48 Db 30.00N 110.20W
San Antonio Abad 13 Nf 38.58N 1.18 E
San Antonio Bay 45 Hl 28.20N 96.45W
San Antonio de Caparo 49 Lj 7.35N 71.27W
San Antonio de Cortés 49 Cf 15.05N 88.04W
San Antonio de los Baños 49 Fb 22.53N 82.30W
San Antonio de los Cobres 56 Gb 24.11S 66.21W
San Antonio del Táchira 54 Db 7.50N 72.27W
San Antonio de Tamanaco 50 Ch 9.14N 66.03W
San Antonio Oeste 53 Jj 40.44S 64.57W
San Antonio River 43 Hf 28.30N 96.50W
Sanare 49 Mi 9.45N 69.39W
Sanary-sur-Mer 11 Lk 43.07N 5.48 E
San Augustin 53 Ie 1.53N 76.16W
San Augustine 45 Ik 31.32N 94.07W
Sanāw 35 Ib 17.50N 51.05 E
San Bartolomeo in Galdo 14 Ji 41.24N 15.01 E
San Baudilio de Llobregat/
Sant Boi de Llobregat 13 Oc 41.21N 2.03 E
San Benedetto del Tronto 14 Hh 42.57N 13.53 E
San Benedetto Po 14 Ee 45.02N 10.55 E
San Benedicto, Isla- 47 Be 19.18N 110.49W
San Benito [Guat.] 49 Ce 16.55N 89.54W
San Benito [Tx.-U.S.] 45 Hm 26.08N 97.38W
San Benito, Islas- 48 Bc 28.20N 115.35W
San Benito Abad 49 Ji 8.56N 75.02W
San Benito Mountain 46 Eh 36.22N 120.38W
San Bernardino 39 Hf 34.06N 117.17W
San Bernardino, Passo del-/
Sankt Bernardin Paß 14 Dd 46.30N 9.10 E
San Bernardino
Mountains 46 Gi 34.10N 117.00W
San Bernardino Strait 26 Hd 12.32N 124.10 E
San Bernardo [Arg.] 55 Bh 27.17S 60.42W
San Bernardo [Chile] 56 Fd 33.36S 70.43W
San Bernardo [Mex.] 48 De 25.32N 111.45W
San Bernardo, Islas de- 49 Ji 9.45N 75.50W
San Bernardo, Punta de- 49 Ji 9.42N 75.42W
San Bernardo del Viento 54 Cb 9.22N 75.57W
San Blas [3] 49 Hi 7.50N 81.10W
San Blas [Mex.] 47 Cd 21.31N 105.16W
San Blas [Mex.] 47 Cc 26.05N 108.46W
San Blas [Mex.] 48 Id 27.25N 101.40W
San Blas, Archipiélago de- 49 Hi 9.30N 78.30W
San Blas, Cape- 43 Jf 29.40N 85.22W
San Blas, Cordillera de- 49 Hi 9.18N 79.00W
San Blas, Golfo de- 49 Hi 9.30N 79.00W
San Blas, Punta- 49 Hi 9.34N 78.58W
San Borja 54 Ef 14.49S 66.51W
San Borjas, Sierra de- 48 Cc 28.40N 113.45W
San Buenaventura 48 Id 27.05N 101.32W
Sancai 35 Fc 10.43N 35.40 E
San Carlos [Arg.] 55 Eh 27.45S 55.54W
San Carlos [Chile] 56 Fe 36.25S 71.58W
San Carlos [Mex.] 48 Je 24.35N 98.56W
San Carlos [Mex.] 48 Ic 29.01N 100.51W
San Carlos [Nic.] 49 Eh 11.07N 84.47W
San Carlos [Pan.] 49 Hi 8.29N 79.57W
San Carlos [Par.] 55 Df 22.16S 57.18W
San Carlos [Phil.] 26 Hd 10.30N 123.25 E
San Carlos [Phil.] 26 Hc 15.55N 120.20 E
San Carlos [Ur.] 56 Jd 34.48S 54.55W
San Carlos [Ven.] 54 Eb 9.40N 68.39W
San Carlos, Bahía- 48 Cd 27.55N 112.45W
San Carlos, Mesa de- 48 Bc 29.40N 115.25W
San Carlos, Punta- 48 Cd 28.00N 112.45W
San Carlos, Riacho- 55 Df 22.49S 57.53W
San Carlos, Río- [C.R.] 49 Eh 10.47N 84.12W
San Carlos, Río- [Ven.] 50 Bh 9.07N 68.25W
San Carlos de Bariloche 53 Ij 41.08S 71.15W
San Carlos de Bolívar 56 He 36.15S 61.06W
San Carlos de la Ràpita/
Sant Carles de la Ràpita 13 Md 40.37N 0.36 E
San Carlos del Zulia 54 Db 9.01N 71.55W
San Carlos de Río Negro 54 Ec 1.55N 67.04W
San Carlos Reservoir 46 Jj 33.13N 110.24W
San Cataldo [It.] 14 Mj 40.23N 18.18 E
San Cataldo [It.] 14 Hm 37.29N 13.59 E
San Cayetano 55 Cn 38.20S 59.37W
Sancerre 11 Ig 47.20N 2.50 E
Sancerrois, Collines du- 11 Ig 47.20N 2.30 E
Sanchahe 28 Ib 44.59N 126.03 E
Sánchez 49 Md 19.14N 69.36W
Sánchez Magallanes 48 Mh 18.17N 93.59W
San Clemente [Ca.-U.S.] 43 De 33.26N 117.37W
San Clemente [Sp.] 13 Je 39.24N 2.26W
San Clemente del Tuyú 55 Dm 36.22S 56.43W
San Clemente Island 46 Fj 32.55N 118.30W
Sancois 11 Ih 46.50N 2.55 E
San Cosme 55 Ch 27.22S 58.31W
San Cristóbal [Arg.] 56 Hd 30.19S 61.14W
San Cristóbal [Bol.] 55 Ba 13.56S 61.50W
San Cristóbal [Cuba] 49 Fb 22.43N 83.03W
San Cristóbal [Dom.Rep.] 49 Ld 18.25N 70.06W
San Cristóbal [Mex.] 48 Li 17.49N 94.32W
San Cristóbal [Ven.] 53 Ie 7.46N 72.14W
San Cristobal, Baia de- 48 Bd 27.25N 114.40W
San Cristóbal, Isla- 52 Hf 0.50S 89.26W
San Cristóbal de las Casas 47 Fe 16.45N 92.38W
San Cristóbal Island 57 Hf 10.36S 161.45 E
San Cristóbal Verapaz 49 Bf 15.23N 90.24W
Sancti Spíritus 47 Id 21.56N 79.27W
Sancti Spíritus [3] 49 Hb 22.00N 79.30W
Sancy, Puy de- 11 Ii 45.32N 2.50 E
Sand 7 Bg 59.29N 6.15 E
Sand 37 Ed 22.25S 30.05 E
Sanda 24 Dd 34.53N 135.14 E
Sandai 26 Fg 1.15S 110.31 E
Sandakan 22 Ni 5.50N 118.07 E
Sandal, Baie de- 63b Ce 20.49S 167.10 E
Sandal, Ozero- 7 Ie 62.25N 34.10 E
Sandane 7 Bf 61.46N 6.13 E
Sandanski 15 Gh 41.34N 23.17 E
Sandaré 34 Cc 14.42N 10.18W
Sandared 8 Eg 57.43N 12.47 E
Sandarne 8 Gc 61.16N 17.10 E
Sanday 9 Kb 59.15N 2.30W
Sande 8 De 59.36N 10.12 E
Sandefjord 7 Cg 59.08N 10.14 E
Sandégué 34 Ed 7.59N 3.33W
Sandeid 7 Ag 59.33N 5.50 E
Sanders 46 Ki 35.13N 109.20W
Sanderson 43 Ge 30.09N 102.24W
Sandersville 44 Fi 32.59N 82.48W
Sandfontein 37 Bd 22.11S 19.58 E
Sandgate 12 Dc 51.04N 1.09 E
Sandhammaren 8 Fi 55.23N 14.12 E
Sandhamn 8 He 59.17N 18.55 E
Sand Hills 43 Gc 41.45N 102.00W
Sandia 54 Ef 14.17S 69.26W
Sandia Crest 45 Ci 35.13N 106.27W
San Diego [Bol.] 55 Bc 16.04S 60.28W
San Diego [Ca.-U.S.] 39 Hf 32.43N 117.09W
San Diego, Cabo- 52 Jk 54.38S 65.07W
Sandıklı 24 Dc 38.28N 30.17 E
San Dimitri Point 14 In 36.05N 14.05 E
Sand in Taufers / Campo
Tures 14 Fd 46.55N 11.57 E
Sand Lake 45 Ia 50.05N 94.39W
Sand Mountain 44 Dh 34.20N 86.02W
Sandnes 7 Ag 58.51N 5.44 E
Sandnessjøen 7 Cc 66.01N 12.38 E
Sandoa 31 Ji 9.41S 22.52 E
Sandö bank 8 Hf 58.10N 19.15 E
Sandomierska, Kotlina- 10 Rf 50.30N 22.00 E
Sandomierz 10 Rf 50.41N 21.45 E
San Domino 14 Jh 42.05N 15.30 E
Sandoná 54 Cc 1.18N 77.28W
San Donà di Piave 14 Ge 45.38N 12.34 E
Sandoval, Boca de- 48 Ke 24.58N 97.32W
Sandover River 59 Hd 21.43S 136.32 E
Sandoway 25 Ie 18.28N 94.22 E
Sandown 9 Lk 50.39N 1.09W
Sand Point 40 Ge 55.20N 160.30W
Sandpoint 43 Db 48.16N 116.33W
Sandras Dağı 15 Ll 37.04N 28.51 E
Sandray 9 Fe 56.54N 7.25W
Sandspit 42 Ef 53.15N 131.50W
Sand Springs [Mt.-U.S.] 46 Lc 47.09N 107.27W
Sand Springs [Ok.-U.S.] 45 Hh 36.09N 96.07W
Sandstone [Austl.] 59 De 27.59S 119.17 E
Sandstone [Mn.-U.S.] 45 Jc 46.08N 92.52W
Sandu 27 Jf 26.08N 113.16 E
Sandusky [Mi.-U.S.] 44 Fd 43.25N 82.50W
Sandusky [Oh.-U.S.] 43 Kc 41.27N 82.42W
Sandveld 37 Cd 21.20S 20.10 E
Sandvig-Allinge 7 Di 55.15N 14.49 E
Sandvika 8 De 59.54N 10.31 E
Sandviken 7 Df 60.37N 16.46 E
Sandwich 9 Oj 51.17N 1.20 E
Sandwich Bay 42 Lf 53.35N 57.15W
Sandy 12 Bb 52.07N 0.17W
Sandy Cape [Austl.] 59 Ih 41.25S 144.45 E
Sandy Cape [Austl.] 57 Gg 24.40S 153.15 E
Sandy Desert 25 Cc 28.46N 62.30 E
Sandykači 19 Gh 36.32N 62.35 E
Sandy Lake 42 If 53.02N 92.55W
Sandy Lake 42 If 53.02N 93.14W
Sandy Point 44 Il 26.01N 77.24W
Sandy Point Town 50 Ed 17.22N 62.50W
Sandžak 15 Cf 43.10N 20.00 E
Sanem 12 He 49.33N 5.56 E
San Estanislao 56 Ib 24.39S 56.26W
San Esteban 49 Ef 15.17N 85.52W
San Esteban, Bahía de- 48 Ee 25.40N 109.15W
San Esteban, Isla- 48 Cc 28.42N 112.36W
San Esteban de Gormaz 13 Ic 41.35N 3.12W
San Felice Circeo 14 Hi 41.14N 13.05 E
San Felipe [Chile] 56 Fd 32.45S 70.44W
San Felipe [Col.] 54 Ec 1.55N 67.06W
San Felipe [Mex.] 47 Bb 31.00N 114.52W
San Felipe [Mex.] 48 Ig 21.29N 101.13W
San Felipe [Ven.] 54 Ea 10.20N 68.44W
San Felipe, Cayos de- 49 Fc 21.58N 83.30W
San Felipe, Cerro de- 13 Kd 40.24N 1.51W
San Felipe Creek 46 Hj 33.09N 115.46W
San Feliu de Guíxols 13 Pc 41.47N 3.02 E
San Feliu de Llobregat/Sant
Feliu de Llobregat 13 Oc 41.23N 2.03 E
San Felix, Isla- 56 Dc 26.17S 80.05W
San Fermin, Punta- 48 Bb 30.25N 114.40W
San Fernando [Chile] 56 Fd 34.35S 71.00W
San Fernando [Mex.] 48 Bb 29.59N 115.17W
San Fernando [Mex.] 47 Ed 24.51N 98.10W
San Fernando [Phil.] 26 Hc 16.37N 120.19 E
San Fernando [Phil.] 26 Hc 15.01N 120.41 E
San Fernando [Sp.] 13 Fh 36.28N 6.12W
San Fernando [Trin.] 54 Fa 10.17N 61.28W
San Fernando, Rio- [Bol.] 55 Cc 17.13S 58.23W
San Fernando, Río- [Mex.] 48 Ke 24.55N 97.40W
San Fernando de Apure 53 Je 7.54N 67.28W
San Fernando de Atabapo 54 Ec 4.03N 67.42W
Sanford [Fl.-U.S.] 43 Kf 28.48N 81.16W
Sanford [Me.-U.S.] 44 Ld 43.26N 70.46W
Sanford [N.C.-U.S.] 44 Hh 35.29N 79.10W
Sanford, Mount- 40 Kd 62.13N 144.09W
San Francisco [Arg.] 56 Hd 31.26S 62.05W
San Francisco [Bol.] 55 Cc 17.42S 59.38W
San Francisco [Ca.-U.S.] 39 Gf 37.48N 122.24W
San Francisco [Pan.] 49 Gi 8.15N 80.58W
San Francisco, Isla- 48 De 24.50N 110.35W
San Francisco Bay 38 Gf 37.43N 122.17W
San Francisco Creek 45 El 29.53N 102.19W
San Francisco de Arriba 48 Hd 26.15N 102.50W
San Francisco de Bellocq 55 Bn 38.42S 60.01W
San Francisco de la Paz 49 Df 14.55N 86.14W
San Francisco del Laishi 55 Ch 26.14S 58.38W
San Francisco del Oro 47 Cc 26.52N 105.51W
San Francisco del Rincón 48 Ig 21.01N 101.51W
San Francisco de Macoris 47 Je 19.18N 70.15W
San Francisco Gotera 49 Cg 13.42N 88.06W
San Francisco Javier 13 Nf 38.42N 1.25 E
San Francisco Mountains 46 Kj 33.45N 109.00W
San Francisco River 46 Kj 32.59N 109.22W
San Fratello 14 Il 38.01N 14.36 E
San Gabriel 55 Di 28.58S 58.12W
San Gabriel, Punta- 48 Cc 28.25N 112.50W
San Gabriel Mountains 46 Gi 34.20N 117.45W
San Gallán, Isla- 54 Cf 13.50S 76.28W
Sangamon River 45 Kf 40.07N 90.20W
Sangar [Iran] 24 Md 37.08N 49.02 E
Sangar [R.S.F.S.R.] 22 Oc 63.55N 127.31 E
Sangatte 12 Dd 50.56N 1.45 E
San Gavino Monreale 14 Ck 39.33N 8.47 E
Sangay, Volcán- 52 If 2.00S 78.20W
Sange 36 Ed 7.02S 28.21 E
Sangeang, Pulau- 26 Gh 8.12S 119.04 E
San Gemini 14 Gh 42.37N 12.33 E
Sanger 46 Fh 36.42N 119.27W
Sangerhausen 10 He 51.28N 11.18 E
San Germán [Cuba] 49 Ic 20.36N 76.08W
San Germán [P.R.] 49 Nd 18.05N 67.03W
Sanggan He 28 Cd 40.24N 115.18 E
Sanggau 26 Ff 0.08N 110.36 E
Sangha 30 Ii 1.13S 16.49 E
Sangha [C.A.R.] [3] 35 Be 3.30N 16.00 E
Sangha [Con.] [3] 36 Cb 2.00N 15.00 E
Sangihe, Kepulauan- =
Sangihe Islands (EN) 21 Oi 3.00N 125.30 E
Sangihe, Pulau- 26 If 3.35N 125.32 E
Sangihe Islands (EN) =
Sangihe, Kepulauan- 21 Oi 3.00N 125.30 E
San Gil 54 Db 6.32N 73.08W
San Gimignano 14 Fg 43.28N 11.02 E
San Giovanni in Fiore 14 Kk 39.15N 16.42 E
San Giovanni in Persiceto 14 Ff 44.38N 11.11 E
San Giovanni Rotondo 14 Ji 41.42N 15.44 E
San Giovanni Valdarno 14 Fg 43.34N 11.32 E
Sangju 28 Jf 36.25N 128.10 E
Sāngli 22 Jh 16.52N 74.34 E
Sangmélima 34 He 2.56N 11.59 E
Sangoli 24 Pd 37.25N 54.35 E
San Gorgonio 38 Hf 34.05N 116.50W
San Gottardo/Sankt
Gotthard = Saint Gotthard
Pass (EN) 5 Gf 46.30N 8.30 E
Sangradouro Grande, Rio- 55 Dc 16.24S 57.10W
Sangre de Cristo
Mountains 38 If 37.30N 105.15W
San Gregorio 55 Al 34.19S 62.02W
Sangre Grande 50 Fg 10.35N 61.07W
Sangri 27 Ff 29.20N 92.15 E
Sangro 14 Ih 42.14N 14.32 E
Sangue, Rio- 54 Gf 11.00S 58.40W
Sangüesa 13 Kb 42.35N 1.17W
Sanguinaires, Iles- 11 Ab 41.53N 8.35 E
San Gustavo 55 Cj 30.41S 59.23W
Sangyuan → Wuqiao 28 Df 37.38N 116.23 E
Sangzhi 27 Jf 29.23N 110.11 E
Sanhe [China] 28 Dd 40.00N 117.01 E
Sanhe [China] 27 La 50.30N 120.04 E
Sanhe-San 29 Cd 35.08N 132.37 E
Sanhezhen 28 Di 31.30N 117.15 E
San Hilario [Arg.] 55 Ch 26.02S 58.39W
San Hilario [Mex.] 48 De 24.22N 110.59W
San Hipolito, Bahía- 48 Cd 26.55N 113.55W
San Ignacio [Arg.] 55 Eh 27.16S 55.32W
San Ignacio [Blz.] 47 Ge 17.10N 89.04W
San Ignacio [Bol.] 54 Ef 14.53S 65.36W
San Ignacio [Bol.] 54 Fg 16.23S 60.59W
San Ignacio [Mex.] 48 Ff 25.55N 106.25W
San Ignacio [Mex.] 47 Bc 27.27N 112.51W
San Ignacio [Par.] 56 Ic 26.52S 57.03W
San Ignacio, Isla de- 48 Ee 25.25N 108.55W
San Ignacio, Laguna- 48 Cd 26.55N 113.15W
San Ildefonso, Cape- 26 Hc 16.02N 121.59 E
San Ildefonso, Cerro- 49 Cf 15.31N 88.17W
San Ildefonso o La Granja 13 Id 40.54N 4.00W
Saniquellie 34 Dd 7.22N 8.43W
San Isidro [Arg.] 56 Id 34.27S 58.30W
San Isidro [Phil.] 26 Hd 11.24N 124.21 E
San Isidro de El General 47 Hg 9.22N 83.42W
Saniyah 24 If 33.49N 42.43 E
San Jacinto 49 Ji 9.50N 75.07W
San Jacinto Peak 46 Gj 33.49N 116.41W
San Jaime 55 Cj 30.20S 58.19W
San Javier [Arg.] 56 Id 30.35S 59.57W
San Javier [Chile] 56 Fe 35.36S 71.45W
San Javier [Sp.] 13 Lg 37.48N 0.51W
San Javier [Ur.] 55 Ck 32.41S 58.08W
San Javier, Río- 55 Bj 31.30S 60.20W
San Jerónimo Taviche 48 Ki 16.44N 96.35W
Sanjiachang 27 Hg 24.45N 101.53 E
Sanjiaocheng → Haiyan 27 Hd 36.58N 100.50 E
Sanjō 28 Of 37.37N 138.57 E
San Joaquín 54 Ff 13.04S 64.49W
San Joaquín, Río- 54 Ff 13.08S 63.41W
San Joaquín, Sierra de- 55 Eg 24.48S 56.00W
San Joaquin River 46 Eh 36.43N 121.50W
San Joaquin Valley 38 Gf 36.50N 120.10W
San Jon 45 Ei 35.06N 103.20W
San Jorge 56 Hd 31.54S 61.52W
San Jorge, Bahía de- 48 Cb 31.10N 113.15W
San Jorge, Golfe de-/Sant
Jordi, Golf de- 13 Md 40.53N 1.00 E
San Jorge, Golfo- 52 Jj 46.00S 67.00W
San Jorge, Río- 49 Ji 9.07N 74.44W
San Jorge, Serranía- 55 Be 20.21S 60.59W
San Jorge Island 63a Dc 8.27S 159.35 E
San José [2] 55 Dl 34.15S 56.45W
San José [3] 49 Ei 9.40N 84.00W
San José [Arg.] 55 Eh 27.46S 55.47W
San Jose [Ca.-U.S.] 39 Gf 37.20N 121.53W
San José [C.R.] 39 Ki 9.56N 84.05W
San José [Mex.] 48 Dd 27.32N 110.09W
San José [Par.] 55 Dg 25.33S 56.45W
San Jose [Phil.] 26 Hc 15.48N 121.00 E
San Jose [Phil.] 26 Hd 12.21N 121.04 E
San José, Isla- [Mex.] 47 Bc 25.00N 110.38W
San José, Isla- [Pan.] 49 Hi 8.15N 79.07W
San José, Salinas de- 55 Bd 19.07S 60.54W
San José, Serranía de- 55 Bc 17.52S 60.49W
San Jose de Buenavista 26 Hd 10.46N 122.30 E
San José de Chiquitos 54 Fg 17.51S 60.47W
San José de Feliciano 55 Cj 30.23S 58.45W
San José de Gracia 48 Fd 26.08N 107.58W
San José de Guanipa 54 Fb 8.54N 64.09W
San José de Jachal 56 Gd 30.14S 68.45W
San José de las Lajas 49 Fb 22.58N 82.09W
San José del Cabo 47 Cd 23.03N 109.41W
San José del Guaviare 53 Ie 2.35N 72.38W
San José del Rosario 55 Dg 24.12S 56.48W
San José de Mayo 56 Id 34.20S 56.42W
San José de Ocuné 54 Dc 4.15N 70.20W
San José de Tiznados 50 Ch 9.23N 67.33W
San Juan [2] 56 Gd 31.00S 69.00W
San Juan [Arg.] 53 Ji 31.30S 68.30W
San Juán [Bol.] 55 Cc 17.52S 59.59W
San Juán [Bol.] 55 Bd 18.08S 60.08W
San Juan [C.Amer.] 38 Kh 10.56N 83.42W
San Juan [Dom.Rep.] 47 Je 18.48N 71.14W
San Juan [P.R.] 39 Mh 18.28N 66.07W
San Juan [U.S.] 38 Hf 37.18N 110.28W
San Juan, Cabezas de- 51a Cb 18.23N 65.36W
San Juan, Cabo- 30 Hh 1.10N 9.21 E
San Juan, Muela de- 13 Kd 40.26N 1.44W
San Juan, Pico- 47 Hd 21.59N 80.09W
San Juan, Punta- 65d Ab 27.03S 109.22W
San Juan, Río- [Arg.] 56 Gd 32.17S 67.22W
San Juan, Río- [Mex.] 48 Jd 26.10N 99.00W
San Juan, Río- [Mex.] 48 Lh 18.36N 95.40W
San Juan, Río- [Ven.] 50 Eg 10.14N 62.39W
San Juan, Volcán- 48 Gg 21.30N 104.57W
San Juan Bautista [Par.] 56 Ic 26.38S 57.10W
San Juan Bautista [Sp.] 13 Ne 39.05N 1.30 E
San Juan Bautista Tuxtepec 48 Kh 18.06N 96.07W
San Juan de Colón 49 Ki 8.02N 72.16W
San Juan de Guadalupe 48 He 24.38N 102.44W
San Juan del César 49 Kh 10.46N 72.59W
San Juan de Lima, Punta- 48 Hh 18.36N 103.42W
San Juan del Norte 47 Hf 10.55N 83.42W
San Juan de los Cayos 54 Ea 11.10N 68.25W
San Juan de los Lagos 48 Hg 21.15N 102.14W
San Juan de los Morros 54 Ea 9.55N 67.21W
San Juan del Río [Mex.] 48 Jg 20.29N 100.00W
San Juan del Río [Mex.] 48 Ge 24.47N 104.27W
San Juan del Sur 47 Gf 11.15N 85.52W
San Juan de Payara 50 Ci 7.39N 67.36W
San Juanico, Isla- 48 Fg 21.55N 106.40W
San Juanico, Punta- 48 Cd 26.05N 112.15W
San Juan Island 46 Db 48.32N 123.05W
San Juan Mountains 43 Fd 37.35N 107.10W
San Juan Neembucú 55 Dh 26.39S 57.56W
San Juan Nepomuceno
[Col.] 54 Cb 9.57N 75.05W
San Juan Nepomuceno
[Par.] 55 Eh 26.06S 55.58W
San Juan y Martínez 49 Fb 22.16N 83.50W
San Julián 53 Jj 49.19S 67.40W
San Just, Sierra de- 13 Ld 40.46N 0.48W
San Justo 56 Hd 30.47S 60.35W
Sankarani 30 Gg 12.01N 8.19W
Sankt Anton am Arlberg 14 Ec 47.08N 10.16 E
Sankt Augustin 12 Jd 50.47N 7.11 E
Sankt Bernardin Paß/San
Bernardino, Passo del- 14 Dd 46.30N 9.10 E
Sankt Gallen 14 Dc 47.25N 9.25 E
Sankt Gallen [2] 14 Dc 47.20N 9.10 E
Sankt Goar 10 Df 50.09N 7.43 E
Sankt Goarshausen 12 Jd 50.09N 7.44 E
Sankt Gotthard/San
Gottardo = Saint Gotthard
Pass (EN) 5 Gf 46.30N 8.30 E
Sankt Ingbert 10 Dg 49.17N 7.07 E
Sankt Johann im Pongau 14 Hc 47.21N 13.12 E
Sankt Michael im Lungau 14 Hc 47.06N 13.38 E
Sankt Michel/Mikkeli 6 If 61.41N 27.15 E
Sankt Moritz 14 Dd 46.30N 9.52 E
Sankt Peter-Ording 10 Eb 54.18N 8.38 E
Sankt Pölten 14 Jb 48.12N 15.38 E
Sankt Ulrich / Ortisei 14 Fd 46.34N 11.40 E
Sankt Veit an der Glan 14 Id 46.46N 14.22 E
Sankt-Vith 11 Md 50.17N 6.08 E
Sankt Wendel 10 Dg 49.28N 7.10 E
Sankt Wolfang im
Salzkammergut 14 Hc 47.44N 13.27 E
Sankuru 30 Ji 4.17S 20.25 E
San Lázaro 56 Ib 22.10S 57.55W
San Lázaro, Cabo- 47 Bd 24.48N 112.19W
San Lazaro, Sierra de- 48 Df 23.25N 110.00W
San Leandro 46 Dh 37.43N 122.09W
San Lorenzo 47 Fe 17.44N 94.45W
San Lorenzo [Arg.] 55 Bk 32.45S 60.44W
San Lorenzo [Ec.] 53 Ie 1.17N 78.50W
San Lorenzo [Hond.] 49 Dg 13.25N 87.27W
San Lorenzo, Isla- [Mex.] 48 Cc 28.38N 112.51W
San Lorenzo, Isla- [Peru] 54 Cf 12.05S 77.15W
San Lorenzo, Río- [Mex.] 48 Je 25.07N 98.32W
San Lorenzo, Río- [Mex.] 48 Fe 24.15N 107.24W
San Lorenzo de El Escorial 13 Hd 40.35N 4.09W
San Louis Potosí [2] 47 Dd 22.30N 100.30W
Sanlúcar de Barrameda 13 Fh 36.47N 6.21W
Sanlúcar la Mayor 13 Fg 37.23N 6.12W
San Lucas [Mex.] 48 Gf 22.33N 104.24W
San Lucas [Mex.] 47 Cd 22.53N 109.54W
San Lucas, Cabo- 38 Ig 22.50N 109.55W
San Lucas, Serrania de- 54 Db 8.00N 74.20W
San Lucido 14 Kk 39.18N 16.03 E
San Luis [Arg.] 53 Ji 33.20S 66.20W
San Luis [2] 56 Gd 34.00S 66.00W
San Luis [Bol.] 55 Cc 17.39S 58.42W
San Luis [Cuba] 49 Jc 20.12N 75.51W
San Luis [Guat.] 49 Ce 16.14N 89.27W
San Luis [Mex.] 48 Dc 29.33N 111.05W
San Luis, Isla- 48 Bb 29.58N 114.26W
San Luis, Sierra de- 49 Mh 11.11N 69.42W
San Luis de la Paz 48 Ig 21.18N 100.31W
San Luis del Palmar 55 Ch 27.31S 58.34W
San Luis de Palenque 54 Db 5.25N 71.40W
San Luis Gonzaga, Bahía- 48 Bc 30.00N 114.25W
San Luis Obispo 39 Gf 35.17N 120.40W
San Luis Pass 45 Il 29.05N 95.08W
San Luis Peak 45 Ch 37.59N 106.56W
San Luis Potosí 39 Ig 22.09N 100.59W
San Luis Río Colorado 47 Bb 32.29N 114.48W
San Luis Valley 43 Fd 37.25N 106.00W
Sanluri 14 Ck 39.34N 8.54 E
San Manuel [Arg.] 55 Cm 37.47S 58.50W
San Manuel [Az.-U.S.] 46 Jj 32.36N 110.38W

Index Symbols

[1] Independent Nation
[2] State, Region
[3] District, County
[4] Municipality
[5] Colony, Dependency
Continent
Physical Region
Historical or Cultural Region
Mount, Mountain
Volcano
Hill
Mountains, Mountain Range
Hills, Escarpment
Plateau, Upland
Pass, Gap
Plain, Lowland
Delta
Salt Flat
Valley, Canyon
Crater, Cave
Karst Features
Depression
Polder
Desert, Dunes
Forest, Woods
Heath, Steppe
Oasis
Cape, Point
Coast, Beach
Cliff
Peninsula
Isthmus
Sandbank
Island
Atoll
Rock, Reef
Islands, Archipelago
Rocks, Reefs
Coral Reef
Well, Spring
Geyser
River, Stream
Waterfall Rapids
River Mouth, Estuary
Lake
Salt Lake
Intermittent Lake
Reservoir
Swamp, Pond
Canal
Glacier
Ice Shelf, Pack Ice
Ocean
Sea
Gulf, Bay
Strait, Fjord
Lagoon
Bank
Seamount
Tablemount
Ridge
Shelf
Basin
Escarpment, Sea Scarp
Fracture
Trench, Abyss
National Park, Reserve
Point of Interest
Recreation Site
Cave, Cavern
Historic Site
Ruins
Wall, Walls
Church, Abbey
Temple
Scientific Station
Airport
Port
Lighthouse
Mine
Tunnel
Dam, Bridge

International Map Index

Index Symbols

- ① Independent Nation
- ② State, Region
- ③ District, County
- ④ Municipality
- ⑤ Colony, Dependency
- ■ Continent
- ▤ Physical Region
- Historical or Cultural Region
- Mount, Mountain
- Volcano
- Hill
- Mountains, Mountain Range
- Hills, Escarpment
- Plateau, Upland
- Pass, Gap
- Plain, Lowland
- Delta
- Salt Flat
- Valley, Canyon
- Crater, Cave
- Karst Features
- Depression
- Polder
- Desert, Dunes
- Forest, Woods
- Heath, Steppe
- Oasis
- Cape, Point
- Coast, Beach
- Cliff
- Peninsula
- Isthmus
- Sandbank
- Island
- Atoll
- Rock, Reef
- Islands, Archipelago
- Rocks, Reefs
- Coral Reef
- Well, Spring
- Geyser
- River, Stream
- Waterfall Rapids
- River Mouth, Estuary
- Lake
- Salt Lake
- Intermittent Lake
- Reservoir
- Swamp, Pond
- Canal
- Glacier
- Ice Shelf, Pack Ice
- Ocean
- Sea
- Gulf, Bay
- Strait, Fjord
- Lagoon
- Bank
- Seamount
- Tablemount
- Ridge
- Shelf
- Basin
- Escarpment, Sea Scarp
- Fracture
- Trench, Abyss
- National Park, Reserve
- Point of Interest
- Recreation Site
- Cave, Cavern
- Historic Site
- Ruins
- Wall, Walls
- Church, Abbey
- Temple
- Scientific Station
- Airport
- Port
- Lighthouse
- Mine
- Tunnel
- Dam, Bridge

ão Mateus, Rio- 55 Ia 13.48S 46.54W
ão Miguel 30 Ee 37.47N 25.30W
ão Miguel, Rio- 55 Ic 16.03S 46.07W
ão Miguel do Araguaia 55 Ga 13.19S 50.13W
ão Miguel d'Oeste 55 Fh 26.45S 53.34W
aona, Isla- 49 Md 18.09N 68.40W
aône 5 Gf 45.44N 4.50 E
aône-et-Loire 11 Kh 46.40N 4.30 E
aonek 26 Jg 0.28S 130.47 E
ão Nicolau 30 Eg 16.35N 24.15W
ão Nicolau [Ang.] 36 Be 14.15S 12.24 E
ão Nicolau [Braz.] 55 Ei 28.11S 55.16W
ão Patricio, Rio- 55 Hb 15.02S 49.15W
ão Paulo 53 Lh 23.32S 46.37W
ão Paulo 56 Kb 22.00S 49.00W
ão Paulo de Olivença 54 Ed 3.27S 68.48W
ão Pedro, Ribeirão 55 Ic 16.54S 46.32W
ão Pedro do Sul [Braz.] 55 Ei 29.37S 54.10W
ão Pedro do Sul [Port.] 13 Dd 40.45N 8.04W
ão Pedro e São Paulo, Penedos de- 52 Ne 0.56N 29.22W
ão Raimundo Nonato 54 Je 9.01S 42.42W
ão Romão [Braz.] 55 Ed 18.33S 54.27W
ão Romão [Braz.] 54 Ig 16.22S 45.04W
ão Roque 55 De 21.43S 57.46W
ão Roque, Cabo de- 52 Mf 5.29S 35.16W
ão Roque, Serra de- 55 Ib 14.40S 46.50W
ão Sebastião 55 Jf 23.48S 45.25W
ão Sebastião, Ilha de- 52 Lh 23.50S 45.18W
ão Sebastião, Ponta- 30 Kk 22.05S 35.24 E
ão Sebastião da Boa Vista 54 Id 1.42S 49.31W
ão Sebastião do Paraiso 54 Ih 20.55S 47.00W
ão Sepé 55 Fj 30.10S 53.34W
ão Simão 54 Hg 18.56S 50.30W
ão Tiago 30 Eg 15.05N 23.40W
ão Tomé 30 Hh 0.12N 6.39 E
ão Tomé 31 Hh 0.20N 6.44 E
ão Tomé, Cabo de- 54 Jh 22.00S 40.59W
ão Tome and Principe (EN) = São Tomé e Príncipe 31 Hh 1.00N 7.00 E
ão Tomé e Príncipe=Sao Tome and Principe (EN) 31 Hh 1.00N 7.00 E
aoura 32 Gd 27.50N 2.50W
aoura 30 Gf 28.48N 0.50W
ão Vicente 30 Eg 16.50N 25.00W
ão Vicente [Braz.] 55 Ia 13.38S 46.31W
ão Vicente [Braz.] 56 Kb 23.58S 46.23W
ão Vicente, Cabo de- 5 Fh 37.01N 9.00W
ão Xavier, Serra de- 55 Ei 29.15S 54.15W
apai 15 Ih 41.02N 25.42 E
apanca 15 Ni 40.41N 30.16 E
apanca Gölü 15 Ni 40.43N 30.15 E
ape [Braz.] 54 Ke 7.06S 35.13W
ape [Indon.] 26 Gh 8.34S 118.59 E
ape, Selat- 26 Gh 8.39S 119.18 E
apele 34 Gd 5.55N 5.42 E
apelo Island 44 Gj 31.28N 81.15W
aphane 15 Mj 39.01N 29.14 E
aphane Dağı 15 Mj 39.03N 29.16 E
apiéntza 15 Em 36.45N 21.42 E
apkina 17 Fc 66.44N 52.25 E
apo, Serrania del- 49 Hi 7.50N 78.17W
aponé 34 Ec 12.03N 1.36W
apopema 55 Gf 23.55S 50.35W
aposoa 54 Ce 6.56S 76.48W
apphire Mountains 46 Ic 46.20N 113.45W
apporo 22 Qe 43.03N 141.21 E
apri 14 Jj 40.04N 15.38 E
apucai, Rio- 55 He 20.08S 48.27W
apulpa 43 Hd 36.00N 96.06W
apulut 26 Gf 4.42N 116.29 E
āqiyat Sīdī Yūsuf 14 Cn 36.13N 8.21 E
aqqez 23 Gb 36.14N 46.16 E
arāb 23 Gb 37.56N 47.32 E
araburi 25 Kf 14.30N 100.55 E
araf Doungous 35 Bc 12.33N 19.42 E
arafjagān 24 Ne 34.28N 50.28 E
Saragmatha=Everest, Mount- (EN) 21 Kg 27.59N 86.56 E
Saragossa (EN)=Zaragoza [Sp.] 6 Fg 41.38N 0.53W
Sarai 7 Jj 53.44N 41.03 E
Sarajevo 6 Hg 43.50N 18.25 E
Saraji Mine 59 Jd 22.30S 148.20 E
Sarakhs 23 Jb 36.32N 61.11 E
Sarakiná 15 Hk 38.40N 24.37 E
Sarakol 17 Kj 52.03N 62.47 E
Saraktaš 19 Fe 51.47N 56.18 E
Saraland 44 Cj 30.49N 88.02W
Saramati 25 Jc 25.44N 95.02 E
Saran 19 Hf 49.46N 72.52 E
Saran, Gunung- 26 Fg 0.25S 111.18 E
Saranac Lake 44 Jc 44.20N 74.08W
Saranci 15 Gg 42.43N 23.46 E
Saranda 15 Cj 39.52N 20.00 E
Sarandi 55 Fh 27.56S 52.55W
Sarandi, Arroyo- 55 Cj 30.13S 59.19W
Sarandi del Yí 55 Ek 33.21S 55.38W
Sarandi Grande 55 Dk 33.44S 56.20W
Saranga 7 Lh 57.12N 46.34 E
Sarangani Bay 26 Ie 5.57N 125.11 E
Sarangani Islands 26 Ie 5.25N 125.26 E
Saranley 35 Ge 2.23N 42.16 E
Saransk 6 Ke 54.11N 45.11 E
Sarapul 6 Ld 56.28N 53.48 E
Sarapulskoje 20 Ig 48.50N 135.58 E
Sarare 49 Mi 9.47N 69.10W
Sararé, Rio- 55 Cb 14.51S 59.58W
Sarasota 43 Kf 27.20N 82.34W
Sarata 16 Ff 46.01N 29.41 E
Sărăţel 15 Kb 47.03N 27.25 E
Saratoga 46 Lf 41.27N 106.48W
Saratoga Springs 43 Mc 43.04N 73.47W
Saratok 26 Ff 1.24N 111.31 E
Saratov 6 Ke 51.34N 46.02 E
Saratov Reservoir (EN)= Saratovskoje Vodohranilišče 5 Ke 52.50N 47.50 E
Saratovskaja Oblast 19 Ee 51.30N 47.00 E
Saratovskoje Vodohranilišče =Saratov Reservoir (EN) 5 Ke 52.50N 47.50 E
Saravan 25 Le 15.43N 106.25 E
Sarawak 26 Ff 2.30N 113.30 E
Saray 24 Bb 41.26N 27.55 E
Saraya 34 Cc 12.50N 11.45W
Sarāyā 24 Fe 35.47N 35.58 E
Sarayköy 24 Cd 37.55N 28.56 E
Sarbāz 23 Jd 26.39N 61.15 E
Sárbogárd 10 Oj 46.53N 18.38 E
Sarca 14 Ee 45.52N 10.52 E
Sarcelle, Passe de la- 63b Cf 22.28S 167.13 E
Sarcelles 12 Ef 49.00N 2.23 E
Sarcidano 14 Dk 39.40N 9.15 E
Sardara 14 Ck 39.37N 8.49 E
Sar Dasht [Iran] 24 Mf 32.32N 48.52 E
Sar Dasht [Iran] 24 Kd 36.09N 45.28 E
Sardegna 14 Cj 40.00N 9.00 E
Sardegna = Sardinia (EN) 5 Gh 40.00N 9.00 E
Sardegna, Mar di- 14 Bk 40.00N 7.30 E
Sardes 15 Lk 38.29N 28.03 E
Sardinal 49 Eh 10.31N 85.39W
Sardinata 54 Db 8.07N 72.48W
Sardinia (EN) = Sardegna 5 Gh 40.00N 9.00 E
Sardis Lake 45 Li 34.27N 89.43W
Sarektjåkkå 7 Dc 67.25N 17.46 E
Sarema/Saaremaa 5 Id 58.25N 22.30 E
Sar-e Pol 23 Kb 36.14N 65.55 E
Sar Eskand Khān 24 Ld 37.29N 47.04 E
Sar-e Yazd 24 Pg 31.36N 54.35 E
Sargasso Sea 38 Mg 29.00N 65.00W
Sargatskoje 19 Hd 55.37N 73.30 E
Sargodha 25 Eb 32.05N 72.40 E
Sargun 18 Fe 38.31N 67.59 E
Sarh 31 Ih 9.09N 18.23 E
Sarhe 11 Fg 47.30N 0.32W
Sarhro, Jebel- 32 Fc 31.00N 6.00W
Sārī [Iran] 22 Hf 36.34N 53.04 E
Sārī [Iraq] 24 Je 34.42N 44.42 E
Sariá 15 Kn 35.50N 27.15 E
Sariçakaya 24 Db 40.02N 30.31 E
Sarigan Island 57 Fc 16.42N 145.47 E
Sarigöl 24 Cc 38.14N 28.43 E
Sarıkamış 24 Jb 40.15N 42.35 E
Sarıkaya 24 Fc 39.48N 35.24 E
Sarikei 26 Ff 2.07N 111.31 E
Sariköy 15 Ki 40.12N 27.36 E
Sarina 59 Jd 21.26S 149.13 E
Sarine 14 Bd 46.59N 7.16 E
Sariñena 13 Lc 41.48N 0.10W
Sarıoğlan 24 Fc 39.05N 35.59 E
Sarir 33 Dd 27.30N 22.30 E
Sariwŏn 27 Md 38.30N 125.45 E
Sarıyer 24 Cb 41.10N 29.03 E
Sarj, Jabal as- 14 Do 35.56N 9.32 E
Šarja 6 Kd 58.24N 45.30 E
Sark 9 Kl 49.26N 2.21W
Sarkad 10 Rj 46.45N 21.23 E
Sarkand 19 Hf 45.25N 79.54 E
Şarkikaraağaç 24 Dc 38.04N 31.23 E
Şarkişla 24 Gc 39.21N 36.26 E
Šarkovščina 8 Li 55.22N 27.32 E
Şarköy 24 Bb 40.37N 27.06 E
Sarlat-la-Canéda 11 Hj 44.53N 1.13 E
Šarlyk 16 Sc 52.54N 54.42 E
Sarmi 58 Ee 1.51S 138.44 E
Sarmiento 53 Jj 45.35S 69.05W
Sarmizegetuza 15 Fd 45.31N 22.47 E
Särna 8 Ec 61.41N 13.08 E
Sarnen 14 Cd 46.54N 8.15 E
Sărnena Gora 15 Ig 42.35N 25.30 E
Sarnia 42 Jh 42.58N 82.23W
Sarny 19 Ce 51.21N 26.36 E
Saroako 26 Hg 2.31S 121.22 E
Sarolangun 26 Dg 2.18S 102.42 E
Saroma 29a Ca 44.02N 143.45 E
Saroma-Ko 28 Qb 44.10N 143.40 E
Šaromy 20 Kf 54.23N 158.14 E
Saronic Gulf (EN) = Saronikós Kólpos 15 Gl 37.45N 23.30 E
Saronikós Kólpos = Saronic Gulf (EN) 15 Gl 37.45N 23.30 E
Saronno 14 De 45.38N 9.02 E
Saros, Gulf of- (EN) = Saros Körfezi 24 Bb 40.30N 26.20 E
Saros Körfezi = Saros, Gulf of- (EN) 24 Bb 40.30N 26.20 E
Sárospatak 10 Rh 48.19N 21.35 E
Sar Passage 64a Ac 7.12N 134.23 E
Sarpinskije Ozera 16 Nf 47.45N 45.00 E
Sar Planina 15 Dg 42.05N 20.50 E
Sarpsborg 8 De 59.17N 11.07 E
Sarqaq 41 Gd 70.00N 51.39W
Sarrabus 14 Dk 39.20N 9.30 E
Sarralbe 11 Ne 49.00N 7.01 E
Sarrāt, Wādī- 14 Co 35.59N 8.23 E
Sarre 10 Cg 49.42N 6.34 E
Sarrebourg 11 Nf 48.44N 7.03 E
Sarreguemines 11 Ne 49.06N 7.03 E
Sarre-Union 12 Jf 48.56N 7.05 E
Sarria 13 Eb 42.47N 7.24W
Sarstún, Rio- 49 Cf 15.54N 88.54W
Sartang 20 Ic 67.30N 133.20 E
Sartène 11a Ab 41.37N 8.59 E
Sarthe 11 Gf 48.00N 0.05 E
Sartu → Anda 28 Ha 46.35N 125.00 E
Sarufutsu 29a Ca 45.18N 142.13 E
Saru-Gawa 29a Cb 42.30N 142.00 E
Saruhanlı 24 Bc 38.44N 27.34 E
Sarukaishi-Gawa 29 Gb 39.25N 141.08 E
Sārūq 24 Me 34.25N 49.30 E
Saruyama-Misaki 29 Ec 37.18N 136.43 E
Sárvár 10 Mi 47.15N 16.56 E
Sarvestān 24 Oh 29.16N 53.13 E
Sárviz 10 Oj 46.22N 18.48 E
Saryagač 18 Gd 41.28N 69.11 E
Sarybarak 18 Hc 43.24N 71.29 E
Sary-Bulak 18 Jd 41.54N 75.47 E
Saryč, Mys- 5 Jg 44.23N 33.45 E
Saryg-Sep 20 Ef 51.30N 95.40 E
Sary-Išikotrau 18 Kb 45.15N 76.25 E
Sarykamys 19 Ff 46.00N 53.41 E
Sarykamyšskoje, Ozero- 19 Fg 41.58N 57.58 E
Sarykolski Hrebet 18 Je 38.30N 74.15 E
Šaryn-Gol 27 Ib 49.20N 106.30 E
Saryozek 19 Hg 44.22N 77.54 E
Saryšagan 19 Hf 46.05N 73.38 E
Saryšiganak, Zaliv- 18 Ca 46.35N 61.25 E
Sarysu 21 Ie 45.12N 66.36 E
Sary-Taš 19 Hh 39.44N 73.16 E
Saryžaz 18 Lc 42.54N 79.31 E
Sarzana 14 Df 44.07N 9.58 E
Sasabe 48 Db 31.27N 111.31W
Sasabeneh 35 Gd 8.00N 43.44 E
Sasa-ga-Mine 29 Ce 33.49N 133.17 E
Sasago-Tōge 29 Fd 35.37N 138.45 E
Sasamungga 63a Cb 7.02S 156.47 E
Sasarām 25 Gd 24.57N 84.02 E
Sasari, Mount- 63a Dc 8.11S 159.33 E
Sascut 15 Kc 46.11N 27.04 E
Sásd 10 Oj 46.15N 18.07 E
Sasebo 27 Me 33.12N 129.44 E
Saseginaga, Lac- 44 Hb 47.05N 78.34W
Saskatchewan 42 Gf 54.00N 106.00W
Saskatchewan 38 Jd 53.12N 99.16W
Saskatoon 39 Id 52.07N 106.38W
Saskylah 20 Gb 72.00N 114.00 E
Saslaya, Cerro- 49 Eg 13.45N 85.03W
Sasovo 19 Ee 54.22N 41.54 E
Sassafras Mountain 44 Fh 35.03N 82.48W
Sassandra 30 Gh 4.58N 6.05W
Sassandra 34 Dd 5.20N 6.10W
Sassandra 31 Gh 4.57N 6.05W
Sassari 6 Gg 40.43N 8.34 E
Sassenberg 12 Kc 51.59N 8.03 E
Sassenheim 12 Gb 52.14N 4.33 E
Sassetot-le-Mauconduit 12 Ce 49.48N 0.32 E
Saßnitz 10 Jb 54.31N 13.39 E
Sasso Marconi 14 Ff 44.24N 11.15 E
Sassuolo 14 Ef 44.33N 10.47 E
Sastobe 18 Hc 42.34N 70.03 E
Sastre 55 Bj 31.45S 61.50W
Sasyk, Ozero- (Kunduk) 16 Fg 45.45N 29.40 E
Sasykkol, Ozero- 19 If 46.40N 81.00 E
Sata 29 Bf 31.04N 130.42 E
Sata, Cape- (EN)=Sata Misaki 21 Pf 30.59N 130.37 E
Satakunta 8 Jc 61.30N 23.00 E
Sata-Misaki=Sata, Cape- (EN) 21 Pf 30.59N 130.37 E
Satan, Pointe de- 63b Dd 19.00S 169.17 E
Sātāra 25 Ee 17.41N 73.59 E
Sataua 65c Aa 13.28S 172.40W
Satawal Island 57 Fd 7.21N 147.02 E
Satawan Atoll 57 Gd 5.25N 153.35 E
Satellite Bay 42 Fa 77.25N 117.15W
Säter 7 Df 60.21N 15.45 E
Satihaure 7 Ec 67.30N 18.45 E
Satipo 54 Df 11.16S 74.37W
Satit 35 Fc 14.20N 35.50 E
Satka 19 Fd 55.03N 59.01 E
Šatki 7 Ki 55.11N 44.08 E
Sätmäla Range 25 Fe 19.30N 78.45 E
Satna 25 Gd 24.35N 80.50 E
Šator 14 Kf 44.09N 16.37 E
Sátoraljaújhely 10 Rh 48.24N 21.40 E
Sātpura Range 21 Jg 21.25N 76.10 E
Satsuma-Hantō 29 Bf 31.25N 130.25 E
Satsunai-Gawa 29a Cb 42.55N 143.15 E
Satsunan-Shotō 27 Mf 29.00N 130.00 E
Sattahip 25 Kf 12.39N 100.54 E
Satulung 15 Gb 47.34N 23.26 E
Satu Mare 15 Fb 47.48N 22.53 E
Satu Mare 15 Fb 47.46N 22.56 E
Satun 25 Kg 6.39N 100.03 E
Saturniná ou Papagaio, Rio- 55 Ca 13.55S 58.18W
Saualpe 14 Id 46.50N 14.40 E
Sauce 56 Ic 30.00S 58.46W
Sauce Corto, Arroyo- 55 Bm 36.55S 61.48W
Sauceda Mountains 46 Ij 32.30N 112.30W
Sauce Grande, Rio- 55 Bn 38.59S 61.07W
Saucillo 47 Cc 28.01N 105.17W
Sauda 8 Be 59.39N 6.20 E
Saudade, Serra da- [Braz.] 55 Jd 19.20S 45.50W
Saudade, Serra da- [Braz.] 55 Fc 16.20S 53.53W
Saudarkrókur 7a Bb 65.45N 19.39W
Saudi Arabia (EN)=Al 'Arabīyah As-Su'ūdīyah 22 Gg 25.00N 45.00 E
Sauer [Eur.] 10 Cg 49.44N 6.31 E
Sauer [Fr.] 12 Kf 48.55N 8.10 E
Sauerland 10 De 51.10N 8.00 E
Sauêruiná, Rio- 54 Gf 12.00S 58.40W
Sauga Jõgi 8 Kf 58.19N 24.25 E
Saugatuck 44 Dd 42.40N 86.12W
Saugues 11 Jj 44.58N 3.33 E
Sauk Centre 45 Id 45.44N 94.57W
Sauk Rapids 45 Id 45.34N 94.09W
Saül 54 Hc 3.37N 53.12W
Šaulder 18 Gc 42.47N 68.24 E
Sauldre 11 Hg 47.16N 1.30 E
Saulieu 11 Kg 47.16N 4.14 E
Saulkrasti/Saulkrasty 7 Fh 57.17N 24.29 E
Saulkrasty/Saulkrasti 7 Fh 57.17N 24.29 E
Saulnois 12 If 48.52N 6.30 E
Sault 11 Lj 44.05N 5.25 E
Sault Sainte Marie [Mi.-U.S.] 43 Kb 46.30N 84.21W
Sault Sainte Marie [Ont.-Can.] 39 Ke 46.31N 84.20W
Saumarez Reefs 57 Gg 21.50S 153.40 E
Saumâtre, Étang- 49 Kd 18.35N 72.00W
Saumlaki 26 Jh 7.57S 131.19 E
Saumur 11 Fg 47.16N 0.05W
Saunders 66 Ad 57.47S 26.27W
Saunders Coast 66 Mf 77.45S 150.00W
Saurimo 31 Ji 9.38S 20.24 E
Sauro 14 Kj 40.18N 16.21 E
Sautar 36 Ce 11.09S 18.25 E
Sauteurs 51p Bb 12.14N 61.38W
Sauveterre, Causse de- 11 Jj 44.22N 3.17 E
Sauveterre-de-Guyenne 11 Fj 44.42N 0.05W
Sauvo/Sagu 8 Jd 60.21N 22.42 E
Sauwald 14 Hb 48.28N 13.40 E
Sava 5 Ig 44.50N 20.28 E
Savage River 59 Jh 41.33S 145.09 E
Savai'i Island 57 Jf 13.35S 172.25W
Savala 16 Ld 51.06N 41.29 E
Savalou 34 Fd 7.56N 1.58 E
Savanes 34 Fc 10.30N 0.30 E
Savan Island 51n Bb 12.48N 61.12W
Savanna 45 Ke 42.05N 90.08W
Savannah 38 Kf 32.02N 80.53W
Savannah [Ga.-U.S.] 39 Kf 32.04N 81.05W
Savannah [Tn.-U.S.] 44 Ch 35.14N 88.14W
Savannah Beach 44 Gi 32.01N 80.51W
Savannakhét 22 Mh 16.33N 104.45 E
Savanna-la-Mar 47 Ie 18.13N 78.08W
Savanne 45 Kb 48.59N 90.12W
Savannes Bay 51k Bb 13.45N 60.56W
Savant Lake 42 If 50.15N 90.42W
Savant Lake 45 Ka 50.30N 90.20W
Savaştepe 24 Bc 39.22N 27.40 E
Savdirī 35 Dc 14.25N 29.05 E
Savé 31 Hh 8.02N 2.29 E
Save [Afr.] 30 Kk 21.00S 35.02 E
Save [Fr.] 11 Hk 43.47N 1.17 E
Saveån 8 Dg 57.43N 11.59 E
Säveh 23 Hb 35.01N 50.20 E
Săveni 15 Jb 47.57N 26.52 E
Saverdun 11 Hk 43.14N 1.35 E
Saverne 11 Nf 48.44N 7.22 E
Savigliano 14 Bf 44.38N 7.40 E
Savigsivik 41 Fc 76.00N 64.45W
Săvineşti 15 Jc 46.51N 26.28 E
Savinjske Alpe 14 Id 46.20N 14.30 E
Savinski 19 Ec 62.57N 40.13 E
Savio 14 Gf 44.19N 12.20 E
Săvîrşin 15 Fc 46.01N 22.14 E
Savitaipale 7 Gf 61.12N 27.42 E
Šavnik 15 Cg 42.57N 19.06 E
Savo 63a Dc 9.08S 159.48 E
Savo 8 Lb 62.30N 27.30 E
Savoie 11 Mi 45.30N 6.25 E
Savoie = Savoy (EN) 11 Mi 45.24N 6.30 E
Savona 14 Cf 44.17N 8.30 E
Savonlinna/Nyslott 7 Gf 61.52N 28.53 E
Savonranta 7 Ge 62.11N 29.12 E
Savonselkä 8 Lb 62.05N 27.20 E
Savoonga 40 Ed 63.42N 170.27W
Savoy (EN) = Savoie 11 Mi 45.24N 6.30 E
Şavşat 24 Jb 41.15N 42.20 E
Savsjö 7 Dh 57.25N 14.40 E
Savudrija, Rt- 14 He 45.30N 13.31 E
Savukoski 7 Gc 67.17N 28.10 E
Savur 24 Id 37.33N 40.53 E
Savusavu 61 Ec 17.34S 178.15 E
Savusavu Bay 63d Bb 16.45S 179.15 E
Savu Sea (EN)=Sawu, Laut- 21 Oj 9.40S 122.00 E
Savuto 14 Kk 39.02N 16.06 E
Sawahlunto 26 Dg 0.40S 100.47 E
Sawai Mādhopur 25 Fc 25.59N 76.22 E
Sawākin 31 Kg 19.07N 37.20 E
Sawākin, Jazā'ir-=Suakin Archipelago (EN) 30 Kg 19.07N 37.20 E
Sawankhalok 25 Je 17.19N 99.54 E
Sawara 29 Gd 35.53N 140.29 E
Sawasaki-Hana 28 Of 37.47N 138.12 E
Sawatch Range 45 Cg 39.10N 106.25W
Sawbā=Sobat (EN) 30 Kh 9.45N 31.45 E
Sawbridgeworth 12 Cc 51.49N 0.09 E
Sawdā', Jabal as- 33 Cd 28.40N 15.30 E
Sawfajjin 33 Cc 31.54N 15.07 E
Sawhāj=Sohag (EN) 31 Kf 26.33N 31.42 E
Sawkanah 33 Cd 29.04N 15.47 E
Sawla 34 Ed 9.17N 2.25W
Sawqirah 23 If 18.10N 56.30 E
Şawqirah, Ghubbat- 23 If 18.35N 56.45 E
Sawtooth Mountains 46 He 44.00N 115.00W
Sawu, Kepulauan- 26 Hi 10.30S 121.50 E
Sawu, Laut-=Savu Sea (EN) 21 Oj 9.40S 122.00 E
Sawu, Pulau- 21 Ok 10.30S 121.54 E
Sawwān, Ard as- 24 Gg 31.00N 37.00 E
Sax 13 Lf 38.32N 0.49W
Saxby River 59 Ic 18.25S 140.53 E
Saxmundham 12 Db 52.13N 1.30 E
Saxony (EN)=Sachsen 10 Jf 51.00N 13.30 E
Say 34 Fc 13.07N 2.21 E
Sayabec 44 Na 48.36N 67.37W
Saya de Malha Bank (EN) 30 Nj 11.00S 61.00 E
Sayago 13 Fc 41.20N 6.10W
Sayan 54 Cf 11.08S 77.12W
Sayang, Pulau- 26 If 0.18N 129.54 E
Sayaxché 49 Be 16.31N 90.10W
Saydā 23 Ec 33.33N 35.22 E
Sayhūt 22 Hh 15.12N 51.14 E
Saylorville Lake 45 Jf 41.48N 93.46W
Säynätsalo 8 Kb 62.08N 25.46 E
Sayō 29 Dd 35.01N 134.22 E
Sayram Hu 27 Dc 44.35N 81.10 E
Sayula 48 Hh 19.52N 103.37W
Saywūn 35 Hb 15.56N 48.47 E
Sazanit, Ishull i- 15 Ci 40.30N 19.16 E
Sázava 10 Kg 49.53N 14.24 E
Sázava 10 Kg 49.52N 14.54 E
Sbaa 32 Gd 28.13N 0.10W
Sbisseb 13 Pi 35.42N 3.51 E
Sbruč 16 Ee 48.32N 26.25 E
Scaër 11 Cf 48.02N 3.42W
Scafell Pike 9 Jg 54.27N 3.12W
Scalea 14 Jk 39.49N 15.47 E
Scalone, Passo dello- 14 Jk 39.38N 15.57 E
Scammon, Laguna- 48 Bd 27.45N 114.15W
Scammon Bay 40 Fd 61.53N 165.38W
Scandinavia (EN) 5 Hc 65.00N 16.00 E
Scanno 14 Hi 41.54N 13.53 E
Scansano 14 Fh 42.41N 11.20 E
Scapa Flow 9 Jc 58.54N 3.05W
Scapegoat Mountain 46 Ic 47.19N 112.50W
Ščapino 20 Ke 55.15N 159.25 E
Ščara 16 Dc 53.27N 24.44 E
Scaramia, Capo- 14 In 36.47N 14.29 E
Scarba 9 He 56.11N 5.42W
Scarborough [Eng.-U.K.] 9 Mg 54.17N 0.24W
Scarborough [Trin.] 54 Fa 11.11N 60.44W
Scarpe 12 Jd 50.30N 3.27 E
Ščastje 16 Ke 48.44N 39.14 E
Sceaux 12 Ef 48.47N 2.17 E
Ščekino 16 Jb 54.01N 37.29 E
Ščekurja 17 Jd 64.15N 60.52 E
Ščeljajur 19 Fb 65.21N 53.25 E
Scenic 45 Ee 43.47N 102.30W
Ščerbakty 19 He 52.29N 78.14 E
Schaalsee 10 Gc 53.35N 10.57 E
Schaarbeek/Schaerbeek 12 Gd 50.51N 4.23 E
Schaerbeek/Schaarbeek 12 Gd 50.51N 4.23 E
Schaffhausen 14 Cc 47.45N 8.40 E
Schaffhausen 14 Cc 47.40N 8.40 E
Schagen 12 Gb 52.48N 4.48 E
Schärding 14 Hb 48.27N 13.26 E
Scharmützelsee 10 Kd 52.15N 14.03 E
Scharnhörn 10 Ec 53.57N 8.25 E
Scheeßel 12 La 53.10N 9.29 E
Schefferville 39 Md 54.47N 64.49W
Scheibbs 14 Jb 48.00N 15.10 E
Schela 15 Gd 45.10N 23.18 E
Schelde 11 Kc 51.22N 4.15 E
Schelde (EN)=Escaut 11 Kc 51.22N 4.15 E
Schell Creek Range 43 Ed 39.10N 114.40W
Schenectady 43 Mc 42.48N 73.57W
Scheno 35 Fd 9.35N 39.25 E
Scherfede, Warburg- 12 Lc 51.32N 9.02 E
Scherpenheuvel-Zichem 12 Gd 50.59N 4.59 E
Scheveningen, 's-Gravenhage- 11 Kb 52.06N 4.18 E
Schiedam 11 Kc 51.55N 4.24 E
Schiermonnikoog 11 Ma 53.28N 6.15 E
Schifferstadt 12 Ke 49.23N 8.22 E
Schiffgraben 10 Hd 52.02N 11.10 E
Schifflange 12 Ie 49.30N 6.01 E
Schijndel 12 Hc 51.37N 5.28 E
Schiltigheim 11 Nf 48.36N 7.45 E
Schio 14 Fe 45.43N 11.21 E
Schipbeek 12 Ib 52.15N 6.14 E
Schladming 14 Hc 47.23N 13.41 E
Schlei 10 Fb 54.35N 9.50 E
Schleiden 10 Cf 50.32N 6.28 E
Schleiz 10 Hf 50.35N 11.49 E
Schleswig 10 Fb 54.31N 9.33 E
Schleswig Holstein 10 Gb 54.00N 10.30 E
Schlitz 10 Ff 50.40N 9.34 E
Schloß Holte-Stukenbrock 12 Kc 51.55N 8.38 E
Schloß Neuhaus, Paderborn- 12 Kc 51.44N 8.42 E
Schluchsee 10 Ei 47.49N 8.10 E
Schlüchtern 10 Ff 50.21N 9.31 E
Schmallenberg 12 Kc 51.09N 8.18 E
Schmallenberg-Bödefeld-Freiheit 12 Kc 51.15N 8.24 E
Schmallenberg-Oberkirchen 12 Kc 51.09N 8.18 E
Schmelz 12 Ie 49.26N 6.51 E
Schmida 14 Kb 48.20N 16.14 E
Schneeberg 10 If 50.36N 12.38 E
Schneeberg [Aus.] 14 Jc 47.46N 15.52 E
Schneeberg [F.R.G.] 10 Hf 50.00N 11.51 E
Schneifel 12 Id 50.16N 6.23 E
Schoberpaß 14 Ic 47.27N 14.40 E
Schoberspitze 14 Ic 47.17N 14.09 E
Schœlcher 51h Ab 14.37N 61.06W
Schönebeck 10 Hd 52.01N 11.45 E
Schönecken 12 Id 50.10N 6.28 E
Schongau 10 Gi 47.49N 10.54 E
Schöningen 10 Gd 52.08N 10.57 E
Schoondijke 12 Fc 51.21N 3.33 E
Schoonebeek 12 Ib 52.40N 6.53 E
Schoonhoven 12 Gc 51.55N 4.51 E
Schorfheide 10 Jd 52.55N 13.35 E
Schoten 12 Gc 51.15N 4.30 E
Schotten 12 Ld 50.30N 9.08 E
Schouten Islands 57 Fe 3.30S 144.30 E
Schouwen 11 Jc 51.43N 3.50 E
Schramberg 10 Eh 48.14N 8.23 E
Schreiber 42 Ig 48.48N 87.15W
Schriesheim 12 Ke 49.29N 8.40 E
Schrobenhausen 10 Hh 48.33N 11.16 E
Schruns 14 Dc 47.04N 9.55 E
Schuls / Scuol 14 Ed 46.48N 10.17 E
Schultz Lake 42 Hd 64.45N 97.30W
Schurz 46 Fg 38.58N 118.46W
Schussen 10 Fi 47.37N 9.32 E
Schüttorf 12 Jb 52.19N 7.14 E
Schwabach 10 Hg 49.20N 11.02 E
Schwaben=Swabia (EN) 10 Gh 48.20N 10.30 E
Schwäbisch-Bayerisches Alpenvorland=Swabian-Bavarian Plateau (EN) 5 Hf 48.15N 10.30 E
Schwäbische Alb=Swabian Jura (EN) 5 Gf 48.25N 9.30 E

Index Symbols

1 Independent Nation
2 State, Region
3 District, County
4 Municipality
5 Colony, Dependency
Continent
Physical Region

Historical or Cultural Region
Mount, Mountain
Volcano
Hill
Mountains, Mountain Range
Hills, Escarpment
Plateau, Upland

Pass, Gap
Plain, Lowland
Delta
Salt Flat
Valley, Canyon
Crater, Cave
Karst Features

Depression
Polder
Desert, Dunes
Forest, Woods
Heath, Steppe
Oasis
Cape, Point

Coast, Beach
Cliff
Peninsula
Isthmus
Sandbank
Island
Atoll

Rock, Reef
Islands, Archipelago
Rocks, Reefs
Coral Reef
Well, Spring
Geyser
River, Stream

Waterfall Rapids
River Mouth, Estuary
Lake
Salt Lake
Intermittent Lake
Reservoir
Swamp, Pond

Canal
Glacier
Ice Shelf, Pack Ice
Ocean
Sea
Gulf, Bay
Strait, Fjord

Lagoon
Bank
Seamount
Tablemount
Ridge
Shelf
Basin

Escarpment, Sea Scarp
Fracture
Trench, Abyss
National Park, Reserve
Point of Interest
Recreation Site
Cave, Cavern

Historic Site
Ruins
Wall, Walls
Church, Abbey
Temple
Scientific Station
Airport

Port
Lighthouse
Mine
Tunnel
Dam, Bridge

Schwäbisch Gmünd 10 Fh 48.48N 9.47 E
Schwäbisch Hall 10 Fg 49.06N 9.44 E
Schwalbach (Saar) 12 Ie 49.18N 6.84 E
Schwalm 12 Lc 51.07N 9.24 E
Schwalm 10 Ff 50.45N 9.25 E
Schwalmstadt 10 Ff 50.55N 9.12 E
Schwalmtal 12 Ic 51.15N 6.15 E
Schwandorf 10 Ig 49.20N 12.07 E
Schwaner, Pegunungan- 26 Fg 0.40S 112.40 E
Schwanewede 12 Ka 53.14N 8.36 E
Schwarzach 12 Ig 49.30N 12.10 E
Schwarzbach 12 Je 49.17N 7.40 E
Schwarze Elster 10 Ie 51.49N 12.51 E
Schwarzer Mann 12 Id 50.15N 6.22 E
Schwarzrand 37 Be 26.00S 17.10 E
Schwarzwald=Black Forest (EN) 5 Gf 48.00N 8.15 E
Schwarzwalder Hochwald 12 Ie 49.39N 6.55 E
Schwatka Mountains 40 Hc 67.25N 157.00W
Schwaz 14 Fc 47.20N 11.42 E
Schwechat 14 Kb 48.08N 16.28 E
Schwechat 14 Kb 48.08N 16.28 E
Schwedt 10 Kc 53.04N 14.18 E
Schweich 12 Ie 49.49N 6.45 E
Schweinfurt 10 Gf 50.03N 10.14 E
Schweiz / Suisse / Svizra / Svizzera = Switzerland (EN) [1] 6 Gf 46.00N 8.30 E
Schweizer-Reneke 37 De 27.11S 25.18 E
Schwelm 12 Jc 51.17N 7.17 E
Schwerin [2] 10 Hc 53.35N 11.25 E
Schwerin 10 Hc 53.38N 11.23 E
Schweriner See 10 Hc 53.45N 11.28 E
Schwerte 12 Jc 51.27N 7.34 E
Schwetzingen 12 Ke 49.23N 8.34 E
Schwielochsee 10 Kd 52.03N 14.12 E
Schwyz [2] 14 Cc 47.10N 8.50 E
Schwyz 14 Cc 47.03N 8.40 E
Sciacca 14 Hm 37.31N 13.03 E
Scicli 14 In 36.47N 14.42 E
Ščigry 19 De 51.53N 36.55 E
Scilly, Isles of- 5 Ff 49.57N 6.15W
Scioto River 44 Ff 38.44N 83.01W
Ščirec 10 Tg 49.34N 23.54 E
Scobey 46 Mb 48.47N 105.25W
Scordia 14 Im 37.18N 14.51 E
Scoresby Land 41 Jd 71.45N 26.30W
Scoresbysund 67 Md 70.35N 21.40W
Scoresby Sund 67 Md 70.20N 23.30W
Scorff 11 Cg 47.46N 3.21W
Ščors 19 De 51.48N 31.59 E
Scotia Ridge (EN) 3 Co 57.00S 45.00W
Scotia Sea (EN) 52 Mk 57.00S 40.00W
Scotland [2] 9 Ie 56.30N 4.30W
Scotland 5 Fd 56.30N 4.30W
Scotlandville 45 Kk 30.31N 91.11W
Scotstown 44 Lc 45.31N 71.17W
Scott 42 Gf 52.27N 108.23W
Scott, Cape- [Austl.] 59 Fb 13.30S 129.50 E
Scott, Cape - [B.C.-Can.] 42 Ef 50.47N 128.25W
Scott, Mount- 46 De 42.56N 122.01W
Scott Base 66 Kf 77.51S 166.46 E
Scottburgh 37 Ef 30.19S 30.40 E
Scott Channel 46 Aa 50.45N 128.30W
Scott City 45 Fg 38.29N 100.54W
Scott Coast 66 Kf 76.30S 162.30 E
Scott Glacier [Ant.] 66 He 66.15S 100.05 E
Scott Glacier [Ant.] 66 Mg 85.45S 153.00W
Scott Inlet 42 Kb 71.05N 71.05W
Scott Island 66 Le 67.24S 179.55W
Scott Islands 46 Aa 50.48N 128.40W
Scott Peak 46 Id 44.21N 112.50W
Scott Reef 59 Eb 14.00S 121.50 E
Scottsbluff 39 Ie 41.52N 103.40W
Scottsboro 44 Dh 34.40N 86.01W
Scottsburg 44 Ef 38.41N 85.46W
Scottsdale [Austl.] 59 Jh 41.10S 147.31 E
Scottsdale [Az.-U.S.] 43 Ee 33.30N 111.56W
Scotts Head 51g Bb 15.13N 61.23W
Scottsville 44 Dg 36.45N 86.11W
Scottville 44 Dd 43.59N 86.17W
Scranton 39 Le 41.24N 75.40W
Scrivia 14 Ce 45.03N 8.54 E
Scrub Cays 49 Ia 24.07N 76.55W
Scrub Island 51b Bb 18.17N 62.57W
Ščučin 16 Dc 53.39N 24.48 E
Ščučinsk 19 He 53.00N 70.11 E
Ščučja 17 Nc 66.45N 68.20 E
Ščučje 19 Gd 55.15N 62.43 E
Scugog, Lake- 44 Hc 44.10N 78.51W
Ščugor 17 Hd 64.12N 57.32 E
Scunthorpe 9 Mh 53.36N 0.38W
Scuol / Schuls 14 Ed 46.48N 10.17 E
Scutari, Lake- (EN)= Shkodrës, Liqen i- 5 Hg 42.10N 19.20 E
Scutari, Lake- (EN)= Skadarsko Jezero 5 Hg 42.10N 19.20 E
Seaford 9 Nk 50.46N 0.06 E
Seahorse Point 42 Jd 63.47N 80.10W
Sea Islands 43 Ke 31.20N 81.20W
Seal 42 Ie 59.04N 94.47W
Seal Island 44 Nd 43.30N 66.01W
Sealpunt 30 Jl 34.06S 23.24 E
Searcy 45 Ki 35.15N 91.44W
Searles Lake 46 Gi 35.43N 117.20W
Seaside [Ca.-U.S.] 46 Eh 36.37N 121.50W
Seaside [Or.-U.S.] 46 Dc 46.01N 123.55W
Seattle 39 Ge 47.36N 122.20W
Seaward Kaikoura Range 62 Ee 42.15S 173.35 E
Seba 26 Hi 10.29S 121.50 E
Sébaco 49 Dg 12.51N 86.06W
Sebago Lake 44 Ld 43.50N 70.35W
Sebaiera 32 Ee 24.51N 13.02W
Sebaou 13 Ph 36.55N 3.51 E
Sebastian, Cape- 46 Ce 42.19N 124.26W
Sebastián Vizcaíno, Bahía- 38 Hg 28.00N 114.30W
Sebastopol 46 Dg 38.24N 122.49W
Sebatik, Pulau- 26 Gf 4.10N 117.45 E
Sebba 34 Fc 13.26N 0.32 E
Sebderat 35 Fb 15.27N 36.39 E
Sébé 36 Bc 1.02S 13.06 E
Šebekino 19 De 50.27N 37.00 E
Sébékoro 34 Dc 12.49N 8.50W
Seberi 55 Fh 27.29S 53.24W
Sebeş 15 Gd 45.58N 23.34 E
Sebeş 15 Gd 46.00N 23.34 E
Sebes-Körös 15 Dc 46.55N 20.59 E
Sebeşului, Munţii- 15 Gd 45.38N 23.27 E
Sebewaing 44 Fd 43.44N 83.27W
Sebež 19 Cd 56.19N 28.31 E
Sebha Oasis (EN)=Sabhā, Wāḥāt 30 If 27.00N 14.25 E
Şebınkarahisar 24 Hb 40.18N 38.26 E
Sebiş 15 Fc 46.22N 22.07 E
Sebou 30 Ge 34.16N 6.41W
Sebring 44 Gl 27.30N 81.26W
Sebugal 13 Ed 40.21N 7.05W
Sebuku, Pulau- 26 Gg 3.30S 116.22 E
Šebunino 20 Jg 46.24N 141.56 E
Secas, Islas- 49 Gi 7.58N 82.02W
Secchia 14 Ee 45.04N 11.00 E
Sechura 54 Be 5.33S 80.51W
Sechura, Bahia de- 54 Be 5.40S 81.00W
Sechura, Desierto de- 54 Be 6.00S 80.30W
Seckau 14 Ic 47.16N 14.47 E
Seclin 12 Fd 50.33N 3.02 E
Secondigny 11 Fh 46.37N 0.25W
Secos, Ilhéus- 32 Cf 14.58N 24.40W
Secretary Island 62 Bf 45.15S 166.55 E
Sécure, Rio- 54 Fg 15.10S 64.52W
Seda 8 Kg 57.38N 25.12 E
Šéda 13 Df 38.56N 8.03W
Seda [Lat.-U.S.S.R.] 8 Kg 57.32N 25.43 E
Seda [Lith.-U.S.S.R.] 8 Jh 56.10N 22.00 E
Sedalia 43 Id 38.42N 93.14W
Sedan 11 Ke 49.42N 4.57 E
Sedanka 40a Eb 53.50N 166.10W
Sedano 13 Ib 42.43N 3.45W
Sedbergh 9 Kg 54.20N 2.31W
Seddenga 35 Ea 20.33N 30.18 E
Seddon 62 Fd 41.40S 174.04 E
Seddon, Kap- 41 Gc 75.20N 58.45W
Seddonville 62 Dd 41.33S 171.59 E
Seddülbahir 15 Ji 40.03N 26.10 E
Sedelnikovo 19 Hd 56.57N 75.18 E
Séderon 11 Lj 44.12N 5.32 E
Sédhiou 34 Bc 12.44N 15.33W
Sedini 14 Ci 40.51N 8.49 E
Šedok 16 Lg 44.13N 40.52 E
Sedom 24 Fg 31.04N 35.24 E
Sedona 46 Ji 34.52N 111.46W
Sedrada 14 Bn 36.08N 7.32 E
Šédro 14 Kg 43.05N 16.42 E
Sedro Woolley 46 Db 48.30N 122.14W
Šeduva 7 Fi 55.48N 23.45 E
Sée 11 Ef 48.39N 1.26W
Seeheim [F.R.G.] 12 Ke 49.46N 8.40 E
Seeheim [Nam.] 37 Be 26.50S 17.45 E
Seeis 37 Bd 22.29S 17.39 E
Seeland 14 Bc 47.05N 7.05 E
Seeling, Mount- 66 Qg 82.28S 103.00W
Seelow 10 Kd 52.31N 14.23 E
Sées 11 Gf 48.36N 0.10 E
Seesen 10 Ge 51.54N 10.11 E
Seewarte Seamounts (EN) 30 Ee 33.00N 28.30W
Şefaatli 24 Fc 39.31N 34.46 E
Sefadu 34 Cd 8.39N 10.59W
Seferihisar 24 Bc 38.11N 26.51 E
Séféto 34 Dc 14.08N 9.51W
Sefid Dasht 24 Nf 32.09N 51.10 E
Sefrou 32 Gc 33.50N 4.50W
Sefuri-San 29 Be 33.26N 130.22 E
Segaf, Kepulauan- 26 Jg 2.10S 130.28 E
Ségalas 11 Hj 44.09N 2.30 E
Segamat 26 Df 2.30N 102.49 E
Segangane 13 Ii 35.10N 3.01W
Şegarcea 15 Ge 44.06N 23.45 E
Šegarka 20 De 57.16N 84.02 E
Segbana 34 Fc 10.56N 3.42 E
Segeg 35 Gd 7.40N 42.50 E
Segesta 14 Gm 37.55N 12.50 E
Segeža 6 Jc 63.44N 34.19 E
Seghe 63a Cc 8.25S 157.51 E
Seglinge 8 Id 60.15N 20.40 E
Segmon 8 Ee 59.17N 13.01 E
Segorbe 13 Le 39.51N 0.29W
Ségou [3] 34 Dc 14.00N 6.20W
Ségou 31 Gg 13.27N 6.15W
Segovia 13 Hd 40.57N 4.07W
Segovia [3] 13 Ic 41.10N 4.00W
Segozero, Ozero- 5 Jc 63.18N 33.45 E
Segré 11 Fg 47.41N 0.52W
Segre 13 Mc 41.40N 0.43 E
Seguam 40a Db 52.17N 172.30W
Séguédine 34 Ha 20.12N 12.59 E
Séguéla 34 Dd 7.57N 6.40W
Séguéla [3] 34 Dd 8.05N 6.32W
Seguin 43 Hf 29.34N 97.58W
Segula 40a Bb 52.01N 178.07 E
Segura 13 Lf 38.06N 0.38W
Segura, Sierra de- 13 Jf 38.00N 2.45W
Segura de la Sierra 13 Jf 38.18N 2.39W
Sehithwa 37 Cd 20.27S 22.42 E
Seia 13 Ed 40.25N 7.42W
Seibal 49 Be 16.27N 90.05W
Seiche 11 Eg 48.00N 1.46W
Seiland 7 Fa 70.25N 23.15 E
Seiling 45 Gh 36.09N 98.56W
Seille [Fr.] 11 Me 49.07N 6.11 E
Seille [Fr.] 11 Kh 46.31N 4.56 E
Sein, Ile de- 11 Bf 48.02N 4.51W
Seinäjoki 7 Fe 62.47N 22.50 E
Seine 5 Gf 49.26N 0.26 E
Seine, Baie de la-=Seine, Bay of the- (EN) 5 Ff 49.30N 0.30W
Seine, Bay of the- (EN)= Seine, Baie de la- 5 Ff 49.30N 0.30W
Seine, Val de- 11 Jf 48.30N 3.20 E
Seine-et-Marne [3] 11 If 48.30N 3.00 E
Seine-Maritime [3] 11 Ge 49.45N 1.00 E
Seine-Saint-Denis [3] 11 If 48.55N 2.30 E
Seine Seamount (EN) 5 Ei 33.45N 14.25W
Seini 15 Gb 47.45N 23.17 E
Seistan (EN)=Sīstān 21 If 30.30N 62.00 E
Seixal 13 Cf 38.38N 9.06W
Séjaha 20 Cb 70.10N 72.30 E
Sejerø 8 Di 55.55N 11.10 E
Sejerø Bugt 8 Di 55.50N 11.15 E
Sejm 5 Je 51.27N 32.34 E
Sejmčan 20 Kd 62.52N 152.27 E
Sejny 10 Tb 54.07N 23.20 E
Sekakes 37 Df 30.04S 28.21 E
Sekenke 36 Fc 4.16S 34.10 E
Šeki 19 Eg 41.10N 47.11 E
Seki [Jap.] 29 Ed 35.28N 136.54 E
Seki [Tur.] 24 Cd 36.44N 29.33 E
Sekincau, Gunung- 26 Dh 5.05S 104.18 E
Seki-Zaki 29b Be 33.16N 131.54 E
Sekoma 37 Cd 24.36S 23.58 E
Sekondi-Takoradi 31 Gh 4.53N 1.45W
Sekota 35 Fc 12.37N 39.03 E
Šeksna 19 Dd 59.13N 38.32 E
Šelagski, Mys- 20 Mb 70.10N 170.45 E
Selah 46 Ec 46.39N 120.32W
Selajar, Pulau- 26 Hh 6.05S 120.30 E
Selajar, Selat- 26 Hh 5.42S 120.28 E
Selaön 8 Ge 59.25N 17.10 E
Selaru, Pulau- 26 Jh 8.09S 131.00 E
Selatan, Cape- (EN)= Selatan, Tanjung- 21 Nj 4.10S 113.48 E
Selatan, Tanjung-=Selatan, Cape- (EN) 21 Nj 4.10S 113.48 E
Selawik 40 Gc 66.37N 160.03W
Selawik Lake 40 Hc 66.30N 160.40W
Selb 10 If 50.10N 12.08 E
Selbjørn 8 Ae 60.00N 5.10 E
Selbjørnsfjorden 8 Ae 59.55N 5.10 E
Selbu 8 Da 63.13N 11.02 E
Selbukta 66 Bf 71.40S 12.25W
Selbusjøen 8 Da 63.15N 10.55 E
Selby [Eng.-U.K.] 9 Lh 53.48N 1.04W
Selby [S.D.-U.S.] 45 Fd 45.31N 100.02W
Selco 16 Ic 53.23N 34.05 E
Selçuk 24 Bd 37.56N 27.22 E
Seldovia 40 Ie 59.27N 151.43W
Sele 14 Ij 40.29N 14.56 E
Sele, Piana del- 14 Ij 40.30N 14.55 E
Selebi-Pikwe 31 Jk 22.13S 27.58 E
Selečka Planina 15 Eh 41.05N 21.35 E
Šelehov 20 Ff 52.10N 104.01 E
Selemdža 21 Od 51.49N 128.53 E
Selencia 24 Kf 33.04N 44.33 E
Selendi 15 Lk 38.40N 28.41 E
Selendi 15 Lk 38.45N 28.53 E
Selenduma 20 Ff 50.55N 106.10 E
Selenga (Selenge) 21 Md 52.16N 106.16 E
Selenge [Mong.] 27 Hb 49.25N 103.59 E
Selenge [Zaire] 36 Cc 1.58S 18.11 E
Selenge → Selenga 21 Md 52.16N 106.16 E
Selenginsk 20 Ff 51.59N 106.57 E
Selenica 15 Ci 40.32N 19.38 E
Selennjah 20 Jc 67.55N 145.00 E
Sélestat 11 Nf 48.16N 7.27 E
Selety 19 He 53.06N 73.00 E
Seletyteniz, Ozero- 19 He 53.15N 73.15 E
Selevac 15 De 44.30N 20.53 E
Seleznevo 8 Md 60.44N 28.37 E
Selfoss 7a Bc 63.56N 21.00W
Seli 34 Cd 8.33N 12.48W
Sélibabi 32 Ef 15.10N 12.11W
Seliger, Ozero- 19 Dd 57.20N 33.05 E
Seligman 46 Ii 35.20N 112.53W
Šelihova, Zaliv-=Shelikhov Gulf (EN) 21 Rc 60.00N 158.00 E
Selimağa 15 Lj 39.35N 28.33 E
Selimiye 24 Bd 37.24N 27.40 E
Selingenstadt 12 Kd 50.03N 8.59 E
Selinunte 14 Gm 37.35N 12.48 E
Seližarovo 7 Hh 56.51N 33.29 E
Seljatin 15 Ib 47.52N 25.14 E
Selje 8 Ab 62.03N 5.22 E
Seljord 7 Bg 59.29N 8.37 E
Selkirk [Man.-Can.] 45 Ha 50.09N 96.52W
Selkirk [Scot.-U.K.] 9 Kf 55.33N 2.50W
Selkirk Mountains 42 Ff 50.00N 117.00W
Sella 13 Ga 43.28N 5.04W
Sellasia 15 Fl 37.10N 22.25 E
Selle 12 Fd 50.19N 3.23 E
Selles-sur-Cher 11 Hg 47.16N 1.33 E
Sells 46 Jk 31.55N 111.53W
Selm 12 Jc 51.42N 7.28 E
Selma [Al.-U.S.] 43 Je 32.25N 87.01W
Selma [Ca.-U.S.] 46 Fh 36.34N 119.37W
Selmer 44 Ch 35.11N 88.36W
Selmęt Wielki, Jezioro- 10 Sc 53.50N 22.30 E
Šelon 7 Hg 58.14N 30.50 E
Selong 26 Gh 8.39S 116.32 E
Selsey 12 Bd 50.44N 0.47W
Selsey Bill 9 Mk 50.43N 0.48W
Seltz 12 Kf 48.53N 8.06 E
Selu, Pulau- 26 Jh 7.32S 130.54 E
Selukwe 37 Dc 19.40S 30.00 E
Sélune 11 Ef 48.39N 1.26W
Selva 55 Ai 29.46S 62.03W
Selvagens, Ilhas- 30 Fe 30.05N 15.55W
Selvänä 24 Kd 37.25N 44.51 E
Selvas 52 Jf 5.00S 68.00W
Selway River 46 Hc 46.08N 115.36W
Selwyn, Détroit de- 63b Dc 16.04S 168.11 E
Selwyn Lake 42 He 60.00N 104.30W
Selwyn Mountains 38 Fc 63.10N 130.20W
Selwyn Range 57 Fg 21.35S 140.35 E
Selz 12 Ke 49.59N 8.02 E
Šemaha 16 Pi 40.39N 48.38 E
Semani 15 Ci 40.54N 19.26 E
Semara 31 Ff 26.44N 11.41W
Semarang 22 Nj 6.58S 110.25 E
Sematan 26 Ef 1.48N 109.46 E
Semau, Pulau- 26 Hi 10.13S 123.22 E
Sembakung 26 Gf 3.47N 117.30 E
Sembé 36 Bb 1.39N 14.36 E
Semberija 14 Nf 44.45N 19.10 E
Sembuan 26 Gg 0.19S 115.30 E
Semenicului, Munţii- 15 Fd 45.05N 22.05 E
Semenov 7 Kh 56.49N 44.29 E
Semenovka 16 Hc 52.11N 32.40 E
Semeru, Gunung- 21 Nj 7.58S 113.35 E
Semichi Islands 40a Db 52.42N 174.00 E
Semidi Islands 40 He 56.07N 156.44W
Semiluki 19 De 51.43N 39.02 E
Semily 10 Lf 50.36N 15.20 E
Seminoe Reservoir 46 Le 42.00N 106.50W
Seminole [Ok.-U.S.] 45 Hi 35.14N 96.14W
Seminole [Tx.-U.S.] 45 Ej 32.43N 102.39W
Seminole, Lake- 43 Ke 30.46N 84.50W
Semipalatinsk 22 Kd 50.28N 80.13 E
Semipalatinskaja Oblast [3] 19 If 48.30N 80.10 E
Semirara Islands 26 Hd 11.57N 121.27 E
Semirom 24 Ng 31.22N 51.47 E
Semisopochnoi 40a Cb 52.00N 179.35 E
Semitau 26 Ff 0.33N 111.58 E
Semiun, Pulau- 26 Ef 4.31N 107.44 E
Semizbugy 19 He 50.12N 74.48 E
Semliki 30 Kh 1.14N 30.28 E
Semmering 14 Jc 47.38N 15.49 E
Semnān [3] 23 Hb 35.00N 53.30 E
Semnān 22 Hf 35.33N 53.24 E
Semnon 11 Eg 47.54N 1.45W
Semois 11 Ke 49.53N 4.45 E
Šemonaiha 19 Ie 50.39N 81.54 E
Semporna 26 Gf 4.28N 118.36 E
Semuda 26 Fg 2.51S 112.58 E
Semur-en-Auxois 11 Kg 47.29N 4.20 E
Sên 25 Kf 12.32N 104.28 E
Senador Mourão 55 Kc 17.51S 43.22W
Senador Pompeu 54 Ke 5.35S 39.22W
Senaja 26 Ge 6.45N 117.03 E
Sena Madureira 54 Ee 9.04S 68.40W
Senanga 36 Df 16.07S 23.16 E
Senarpont 12 De 49.53N 1.43 E
Senatobia 45 Li 34.39N 89.58W
Sendai [Jap.] 28 Ki 31.49N 130.18 E
Sendai [Jap.] 22 Qf 38.15N 140.53 E
Sendai-Gawa [Jap.] 29 Bf 31.51N 130.12 E
Sendai-Gawa [Jap.] 29 Dd 35.34N 134.11 E
Sendai-Wan 28 Pe 38.10N 141.15 E
Senden 12 Jc 51.51N 7.30 E
Sendenhorst 12 Jc 51.50N 7.50 E
Senderg 24 Qi 26.52N 57.37 E
Seneca 45 Hg 39.50N 96.04W
Seneca Lake 44 Id 42.40N 76.57W
Sénégal=Senegal (EN) 30 Fg 15.48N 16.32W
Sénégal=Senegal (EN) [1] 31 Fg 14.00N 14.00W
Senegal (EN)=Sénégal [1] 31 Fg 14.00N 14.00W
Senegal (EN)=Sénégal 30 Fg 15.48N 16.32W
Sénégal Oriental [3] 34 Cc 13.30N 13.00W
Senekal 37 De 28.30S 27.32 E
Senetosa, Punta di- 11a Ab 41.33N 8.47 E
Seney 44 Eb 46.21N 85.56W
Senftenberg/Zły Komorow 10 Ke 51.31N 14.01 E
Sengata 22 Ni 0.28N 117.33 E
Sengilej 7 Lj 53.58N 48.46 E
Senguerr, Rio- 56 Gg 45.32S 68.54W
Sengwa 37 Dc 17.05S 28.03 E
Senhor do Bonfim 53 Lg 10.27S 40.11W
Senica 10 Nh 48.41N 17.23 E
Senigallia 14 Hg 43.43N 13.13 E
Senirkent 24 Dc 38.07N 30.33 E
Senj 14 If 45.00N 14.54 E
Senja 5 Hb 69.20N 17.30 E
Senjsko Bilo 14 Jf 44.55N 15.03 E
Senkaku-Shotō 27 Lf 25.45N 124.00 E
Şenkaya 24 Jb 40.35N 42.21 E
Senkevičevka 10 Vf 50.29N 25.05 E
Şenkursk 19 Ec 62.08N 42.53 E
Senlin Shan 28 Kc 43.12N 130.38 E
Senlis 11 Ie 49.12N 2.35 E
Senmonorom 25 Lf 12.27N 107.12 E
Senn, Dahr Ou- 32 Ef 17.55N 11.00W
Sennestadt, Bielefeld- 12 Kc 51.57N 8.35 E
Senneterre 42 Jg 48.24N 77.14W
Senno 7 Gi 54.47N 29.41 E
Sennoj 16 Oc 52.07N 46.59 E
Senorbì 14 Dk 39.32N 9.08 E
Senqu 37 Be 28.38S 16.27 E
Sens 11 Jf 48.12N 3.17 E
Sensée 12 Fd 50.16N 3.06 E
Sensuntepeque 49 Cg 13.52N 88.38W
Senta 15 Dd 45.56N 20.05 E
Sentinel Peak 42 Ff 54.58N 122.00W
Sentinel Range 66 Pf 78.10S 85.30W
Senyavin Islands 57 Gd 6.55N 158.00 E
Şenyurt 24 Id 37.06N 40.40 E
Senzaki-Wan 29 Bd 34.25N 131.20 E
Senžarka 17 Mi 54.45N 67.50 E
Seo de Urgel/La Seu d'Urgell 13 Nb 42.21N 1.28 E
Seoni 25 Fd 22.05N 79.32 E
Seoul (EN)=Sŏul 22 Of 37.34N 127.00 E
Séoune 11 Gj 44.10N 0.41 E
Sepanjang, Pulau- 26 Gh 7.10S 115.50 E
Separation Point 62 Ed 40.47S 173.00 E
Sepetovka 19 Ce 50.12N 27.04 E
Sepik River 57 Fe 3.51S 144.34 E
Sępólno Krajeńskie 10 Nc 53.28N 17.32 E
Sępopol 10 Qb 54.15N 21.00 E
Sępopolska, Nizina- 10 Rb 54.15N 21.10 E
Septemvri 15 Hg 42.13N 24.06 E
Septentrional, Cordillera- 49 Ld 19.35N 70.45W
Septeuil 12 Df 48.54N 1.41 E
Sept-Iles 39 Md 50.12N 66.23W
Sepúlveda 13 Ic 41.18N 3.45W
Sequeros 13 Fd 40.31N 6.01W
Sequillo 13 Gc 41.45N 5.30W
Sera 29 Cd 34.36N 133.01 E
Sera, Pulau- 26 Jh 7.40S 131.05 E
Šerabad 19 Gh 37.43N 66.59 E
Šerabad 18 Ff 37.22N 67.03 E
Serafettin Dağları 24 Ic 39.05N 41.10 E
Serafimovič 16 Me 49.36N 42.47 E
Serahs 19 Gh 36.30N 61.13 E
Seraidi 14 Bn 36.55N 7.40 E
Seraing 11 Ld 50.36N 5.31 E
Seram 57 De 3.00S 129.00 E
Seram, Laut-=Ceram Sea (EN) 57 De 2.30S 128.00 E
Serang 26 Eh 6.07S 106.09 E
Serasan, Pulau- 26 Ef 2.30N 109.03 E
Serasan, Selat- 26 Ef 2.20S 109.00 E
Serbia (EN) = Srbija [2] 15 Df 44.00N 21.00 E
Serbia (EN) = Srbija 5 Ig 43.00N 21.00 E
Serbia (EN)=Srbija 15 Df 44.00N 21.00 E
Şercaia 15 Id 45.50N 25.08 E
Serchio 14 Eg 43.47N 10.16 E
Serdo 35 Gc 11.58N 41.18 E
Serdoba 16 Nc 52.34N 44.01 E
Serdobsk 16 Ee 52.29N 44.16 E
Sereba 35 Gc 13.12N 40.32 E
Serebrjansk 19 If 49.43N 83.20 E
Serebrjanski 7 Ib 68.52N 35.32 E
Sered' 10 Nh 48.17N 17.45 E
Seredka 8 Mf 58.10N 28.25 E
Şereflikoçhisar 24 Ec 38.56N 33.33 E
Serein 11 Jg 47.55N 3.31 E
Seremban 26 Df 2.43N 101.56 E
Serengeti Plain 36 Fc 2.50S 35.00 E
Serenje 36 Fe 13.14S 30.14 E
Šereševo 10 Ud 52.31N 24.19 E
Seret 16 De 48.38N 25.52 E
Serfopoúla 15 Hl 37.15N 24.36 E
Sergač 19 Ed 55.33N 45.28 E
Sergeievka 28 Lc 43.23N 133.22 E
Sergeja Kirova, Ostrova- 20 Da 77.10N 90.00 E
Sergejevka [Kaz.-U.S.S.R.] 19 Ge 53.51N 67.28 E
Sergejevka [R.S.F.S.R.] 28 Kb 44.20N 131.40 E
Sergino 22 Ic 62.30N 65.40 E
Sergipe [2] 54 Kf 10.30S 37.10W
Sergokala 16 Oh 42.30N 47.40 E
Sergozero, Ozero- 7 Ic 66.45N 36.50 E
Seria 26 Ff 4.37N 114.19 E
Serian 26 Ff 1.10N 110.34 E
Seriana, Val- 14 De 45.50N 9.50 E
Seribu, Kepulauan- 26 Fh 5.36S 106.33 E
Sérifontaine 12 De 49.21N 1.46 E
Sérifos 15 Hl 37.09N 24.30 E
Sérifos 15 Hl 37.10N 24.30 E
Sérifou, Stenón- 15 Hl 37.15N 24.30 E
Serik 24 Dd 36.55N 31.06 E
Seringapatam Reef 59 Eb 13.40S 122.05 E
Serio 14 De 45.16N 9.45 E
Šerlovaja Gora 20 Gf 50.34N 116.18 E
Sermata, Kepulauan- 26 Ih 8.10S 128.40 E
Sermilik 41 Ie 66.00N 38.45W
Sernovodsk 7 Mj 53.54N 51.09 E
Sernur 7 Lh 56.57N 49.11 E
Sernyje Vody 7 Mj 53.53N 50.59 E
Sero 24 Kd 37.33N 44.40 E
Serock 10 Rd 52.31N 21.03 E
Serodino 55 Bk 32.37S 60.57W
Serov 22 Id 59.29N 60.31 E
Serowe 31 Jk 22.23S 26.43 E
Serpa 13 Eg 37.56N 7.36W
Serpent, Vallée du- 34 Dc 14.50N 8.00W
Serpentine Lakes 59 Fe 28.30S 129.10 E
Serpent's Mouth/Serpiente, Boca de la- 54 Fa 10.10N 61.58W
Serpiente, Boca de la-/ Serpent's Mouth 54 Fa 10.10N 61.58W
Serpis 13 Lf 38.59N 0.09W
Serpnevoje 15 Lc 46.23N 28.59 E
Serpuhov 6 Je 54.55N 37.25 E
Serra, Aparados da- 55 Hi 28.45S 49.45W
Serra Bonita 55 Ib 15.13S 46.49W
Serra das Araras 55 Jb 15.30S 45.21W
Serra do Navio 53 Ke 0.59N 52.03W
Serra do Salitre 55 Id 19.06S 46.41W
Serra Dourada 55 Ka 12.50S 43.56W
Sérrai 15 Gh 41.05N 23.33 E
Serralada Litoral Catalana/ Cadena Costero Catalana= Catalan Coastal Range (EN) 5 Gg 41.35N 1.40 E
Serralada Pirinenca= Pyrenees (EN) 5 Gg 42.40N 1.00 E
Serrana Bank 47 Hf 14.23N 80.12W
Serranilla Bank 47 Ie 15.50N 79.50W
Serranópolis 55 Fd 18.16S 52.00W
Serra San Bruno 14 Kl 38.35N 16.20 E
Serrat, Cap- 32 Ib 37.14N 9.13 E
Serra Talhada 54 Ke 7.59S 38.18W
Serre 11 Je 49.41N 3.23 E
Serre, Massif de la- 11 Lg 47.10N 5.35 E
Serre-Ponçon, Réservoir de- 11 Mj 44.27N 6.16 E
Serres 11 Lj 44.26N 5.43 E
Serrezuela 56 Gd 30.38S 65.23W
Serrinha 54 Kf 11.39S 39.00W
Serriola, Bocca- 14 Gg 43.31N 12.21 E
Serro 55 Kd 18.37S 43.23W
Serrota 13 Gd 40.30N 5.04W
Serrote, Rio- 55 Ee 21.27S 54.40W

Index Symbols

[1] Independent Nation
[2] State, Region
[3] District, County
[4] Municipality
[5] Colony, Dependency
Continent
Physical Region
Historical or Cultural Region
Mount, Mountain
Volcano
Hill
Mountains, Mountain Range
Hills, Escarpment
Plateau, Upland
Pass, Gap
Plain, Lowland
Delta
Salt Flat
Valley, Canyon
Crater, Cave
Karst Features
Depression
Polder
Desert, Dunes
Forest, Woods
Heath, Steppe
Oasis
Cape, Point
Coast, Beach
Cliff
Peninsula
Isthmus
Sandbank
Island
Atoll
Rock, Reef
Islands, Archipelago
Rocks, Reefs
Coral Reef
Well, Spring
Geyser
River, Stream
Waterfall Rapids
River Mouth, Estuary
Lake
Salt Lake
Intermittent Lake
Reservoir
Swamp, Pond
Canal
Glacier
Ice Shelf, Pack Ice
Ocean
Sea
Gulf, Bay
Strait, Fjord
Lagoon
Bank
Seamount
Tablemount
Ridge
Shelf
Basin
Escarpment, Sea Scarp
Fracture
Trench, Abyss
National Park, Reserve
Point of Interest
Recreation Site
Cave, Cavern
Historic Site
Ruins
Wall, Walls
Church, Abbey
Temple
Scientific Station
Airport
Port
Lighthouse
Mine
Tunnel
Dam, Bridge

ersou, Plateau du- 13 Ni 35.30N 2.00 E
ertã 13 De 39.48N 8.06W
ertão 52 Lg 10.00S 41.00W
ertãozinho 55 Ie 21.08S 47.59W
êrtar 27 He 32.20N 100.20 E
erti 34 Hd 7.30N 11.22 E
erua, Pulau- 26 Jh 6.18S 130.01 E
erui 26 Kg 1.53S 136.14 E
erule 37 Dd 21.55S 27.19 E
érvia 15 Ei 40.11N 22.00 E
êrxü 27 Ge 32.56N 98.02 E
eryitsi 15 Ii 40.00N 25.10 E
eryševo 20 Hf 51.02N 128.25 E
esayap 26 Gf 3.36N 117.15 E
ese 36 Eb 2.11N 25.47 E
eseganaga Lake 45 Ka 50.10N 90.15W
ese Islands 36 Fc 0.20S 32.20 E
esfontein 37 Ac 19.07S 13.39 E
esheke 36 Df 17.29S 24.18 E
esia 14 Ce 45.05N 8.37 E
esibi 35 Ea 20.05N 30.31 E
esimbra 13 Cf 38.26N 9.06W
ešma 7 Mi 55.20N 51.12 E
Sesnut 8 Be 59.42N 7.21 E
Sessa Aurunca 14 Hi 41.14N 13.56 E
Ses Salines, Cap de-/ Salinas, Cabo de- 13 Pe 39.16N 3.03 E
Sestao 13 Ja 43.18N 3.00W
Sesto Fiorentino 14 Fg 43.50N 11.12 E
Sesto San Giovanni 14 De 45.32N 9.14 E
Sestriere 14 Af 44.57N 6.53 E
Sestri Levante 14 Df 44.16N 9.24 E
Sestroreck 7 Gf 60.06N 29.59 E
Šešupė 7 Fi 55.00N 22.10 E
Šešuvis 8 Ji 55.12N 22.31 E
Sesvenna, Piz- 14 Ed 46.42N 10.25 E
Sesvete 14 Ke 45.50N 16.07 E
Šeta/Šéta 8 Ki 55.14N 24.18 E
Šéta/Šeta 8 Ki 55.14N 24.18 E
Setaka 29 Be 33.09N 130.28 E
Setana 28 Oc 42.26N 139.51 E
Sète 11 Jk 43.24N 3.41 E
Sete de Setembro, Rio- 55 Fa 12.56S 52.51W
Sete Lagoas 54 Jg 19.27S 44.14W
Setenil 13 Gh 36.51N 5.11W
Sete Quedas, Saltos das- = Guaira Falls (EN) 56 Jb 24.02S 54.16W
Setermoen 7 Eb 68.52N 18.28 E
Setesdal 7 Bg 59.05N 7.35 E
Setesdalsheiane 8 Be 59.30N 7.10 E
Seti 25 Gc 28.58N 81.06 E
Sétif [3] 32 Ib 36.05N 5.00 E
Sétif 31 He 36.12N 5.24 E
Seto 29 Ed 35.13N 137.05 E
Setonaikai = Inland Sea (EN) 21 Pf 34.10N 133.00 E
Setouchi 29b Ba 28.08N 129.20 E
Šetpe 19 Fg 44.06N 52.02 E
Settat 32 Fc 33.00N 7.37W
Settat [3] 32 Fc 33.00N 7.30W
Setté Cama 36 Ac 2.32S 9.45 E
Sette-Daban, Hrebet- 20 Id 62.00N 138.00 E
Settle 9 Kg 54.04N 2.16W
Setúbal [2] 13 Df 38.20N 8.30W
Setúbal 6 Fh 38.32N 8.54W
Setúbal, Baía de- 13 Df 38.27N 8.53W
Setúbal o de Guadalupe, Laguna- 55 Bj 31.33S 60.35W
Seudre 11 Ei 45.48N 1.09W
Seugne 11 Fi 45.42N 0.32W
Seui 14 Dk 39.50N 9.19 E
Seuil-d'Argonne 12 Hf 48.58N 5.03 E
Seul, Lac- 38 Jd 50.20N 92.30W
Seulles 12 Be 49.20N 0.27W
Seurre 11 Lg 47.00N 5.09 E
Sevan 19 Eg 40.32N 44.57 E
Sevan, Lake- (EN) = Sevan, Ozero- 5 Kg 40.20N 45.20 E
Sevan, Ozero- = Sevan, Lake- (EN) 5 Kg 40.20N 45.20 E
Sévaré 34 Ec 14.32N 4.06W
Sevastopol 6 Jg 44.36N 33.32 E
Ševčenko 22 He 43.35N 51.05 E
Ševčenko, Zaliv- 18 Ca 46.30N 60.15 E
Sevenoaks 9 Nj 51.16N 0.12 E
Sever 13 Ee 39.40N 7.32W
Sévérac-le-Château 11 Jj 44.19N 3.04 E
Severn 9 Kj 51.20N 3.10W
Severn [Can.] 38 Kd 56.02N 87.36W
Severn [U.K.] 9 Kj 51.35N 2.40W
Severnaja Dvina = Northern Dvina (EN) 5 Kc 64.32N 40.30 E
Severnaja Keltma 17 Ff 61.30N 54.00 E
Severnaja Pseašho, Gora- 16 Lh 43.47N 40.30 E
Severnaja Sosva 19 Gc 64.10N 65.28 E
Severnaja Zemlja = Severnaya Zemlya (EN) 21 Lb 79.30N 98.00 E
Severnaya Zemlya (EN) = Severnaja Zemlja 21 Lb 79.30N 98.00 E
Severn Lake 42 If 53.52N 90.58W
Severnoje [R.S.F.S.R.] 16 Rb 54.05N 52.32 E
Severnoje [R.S.F.S.R.] 20 Ce 56.21N 78.23 E
Severny 19 Gb 67.38N 64.06 E
Severnyje Uvaly = Northern Uvals (EN) 5 Kd 59.30N 49.00 E
Severny Kommunar 17 Gg 58.23N 54.02 E
Severny Ledovity Okean = Arctic Ocean (EN) 67 Be 85.00N 170.00 E
Severny Ural = Northern Urals (EN) 5 Lc 62.00N 59.00 E
Severobajkalsk 20 Fe 55.40N 109.25 E
Severočeský kraj [3] 10 Kf 50.35N 14.15 E
Severodoneck 16 Ke 48.57N 38.31 E
Severodvinsk 6 Jc 64.34N 39.50 E
Severo-Jenisejski 20 Ed 60.28N 93.01 E
Severo-Kazahstanskaja Oblast [3] 19 Ge 54.30N 68.00 E
Severo-Krymski Kanal 16 Ig 45.30N 34.35 E
Severo-Kurilsk 22 Rd 50.40N 156.08 E
Severomoravský kraj [3] 10 Ng 49.45N 17.50 E
Severomorsk 19 Db 69.04N 33.24 E
Severo-Osetinskaja ASSR [3] 19 Eg 43.00N 44.10 E
Severo-Sibirskaja Nizmennost = North Siberian Plain (EN) 21 Mb 72.00N 104.00 E
Severouralsk 19 Gc 60.09N 60.01 E
Sevier 46 Ig 38.35N 112.14W
Sevier Bridge Reservoir 46 Jg 39.21N 111.57W
Sevier Desert 46 Ig 39.25N 112.50W
Sevier Lake 43 Ed 38.55N 113.09W
Sevier River 43 Ed 39.04N 113.06W
Sevilla [3] 13 Gg 37.30N 5.30W
Sevilla [Col.] 54 Cc 4.16N 75.53W
Sevilla [Sp.] = Seville (EN) 6 Fh 37.23N 5.59W
Sevilla, Isla- 49 Fi 8.14N 82.24W
Seville (EN) = Sevilla [Sp.] 6 Fh 37.23N 5.59W
Sevlijevo 15 If 43.01N 25.06 E
Sèvre Nantaise 11 Eg 47.12N 1.33W
Sèvre Niortaise 11 Eh 46.18N 1.08W
Sevron 11 Lh 46.32N 5.16 E
Sevsk 16 Ic 52.08N 34.30 E
Sewa 34 Cd 7.18N 12.08W
Seward [Ak.-U.S.] 39 Ec 60.06N 149.26W
Seward [Nb.-U.S.] 45 Hf 40.55N 97.06W
Seward Peninsula 38 Cc 65.00N 164.00W
Sewell 56 Fd 34.05S 70.21W
Seyāhkal 24 Md 37.09N 49.52 E
Seybaplaya 48 Nh 19.39N 90.40W
Seybaplaya, Punta- 48 Nh 19.45N 90.42W
Seybouse, Oued- 14 Bn 36.53N 7.46 E
Seychelles [1] 31 Mi 8.00S 55.00 E
Seychelles Islands 30 Mi 4.35S 55.40 E
Seydān 24 Og 30.01N 53.01 E
Seydişehir 24 Dd 37.25N 31.51 E
Seyðisfjörður 6 Eb 65.16N 14.00W
Seyfe Gölü 24 Fc 39.13N 34.23 E
Seyf Țāleh 24 Le 35.57N 46.19 E
Seyhan 23 Db 36.43N 34.53 E
Seyitgazi 24 Dc 39.27N 30.43 E
Seyitömer 15 Mj 39.34N 29.52 E
Seyla' 35 Gc 11.21N 43.30 E
Seymour [Austl.] 59 Jg 37.02S 145.08 E
Seymour [In.-U.S.] 44 Ef 38.58N 85.53W
Seymour [Mo.-U.S.] 45 Jh 37.09N 92.46W
Seymour [S.Afr.] 37 Df 32.33S 26.46 E
Seymour [Tx.-U.S.] 43 He 33.35N 99.16W
Sezana 14 He 45.42N 13.52 E
Sézanne 11 Jf 48.43N 3.43 E
Sfaktiria 15 Em 36.56N 21.40 E
Sfax (EN) = Şafāqis [3] 32 Jc 34.30N 10.30 E
Sfax (EN) = Şafāqis 31 Ie 34.44N 10.46 E
Sferracavallo, Capo- 14 Dk 39.43N 9.40 E
Sfîntu Gheorghe [Rom.] 15 Me 44.53N 29.26 E
Sfîntu Gheorghe [Rom.] 15 Id 45.52N 25.47 E
Sfîntu Gheorghe, Braţul- 15 Me 44.53N 29.36 E
Sfîntu Gheorghe, Ostrovul- 15 Md 45.07N 29.22 E
Sfizef 13 Li 35.14N 0.15W
's-Gravenhage/Den Haag = The Hague (EN) 6 Ge 52.06N 4.18 E
's-Gravenhage-Scheveningen 11 Kb 52.06N 4.18 E
Shaan-hsi Sheng → Shaanxi Sheng = Shensi (EN) [2] 27 Id 36.00N 109.00 E
Shaanxi Sheng (Shaan-hsi Sheng) = Shensi (EN) [2] 27 Id 36.00N 109.00 E
Shaba [2] 36 Ed 8.30S 25.00 E
Sha'bah, Wādī ash- 24 Ij 25.59N 41.55 E
Shabani 37 Ed 20.19S 30.04 E
Shabeellaha Dhexe [3] 35 He 3.00N 46.00 E
Shabellaha Hoose [3] 35 Ge 2.00N 44.40 E
Shabēlle, Webi- = Shebeli Webi (EN) 30 Lh 0.12S 42.45 E
Shabestar 24 Kc 38.11N 45.42 E
Shabunda 36 Ec 2.42S 27.20 E
Shache/Yarkant 27 Cd 38.24N 77.15 E
Shacheng → Huailai 27 Kc 40.29N 115.30 E
Shackleton Coast 66 Kg 82.00S 162.00 E
Shackleton Glacier 66 Lg 84.35S 176.15W
Shackleton Ice Shelf 66 He 66.00S 101.00 E
Shackleton Range 66 Ag 80.40S 26.00W
Shaddādī 24 Id 36.02N 40.45 E
Shādegān 24 Mg 30.40N 48.38 E
Shadwān, Jazīrat- 33 Fd 27.30N 33.55 E
Shaftesbury 9 Kk 51.01N 2.12W
Shagedu → Jungar Qi 27 Jd 39.37N 110.58 E
Shāghir Bazar 24 Id 36.52N 40.53 E
Shag Rocks 66 Rd 54.26S 36.33W
Shāh 'Abbās 24 Oe 34.44N 52.10 E
Shah Alam 26 Df 3.05N 101.29 E
Shahdol 25 Gd 23.13N 81.18 E
Sha He [China] 28 Ch 33.39N 114.38 E
Sha He [China] 28 Cf 37.09N 114.46 E
Shahezhen → Linze 27 Hd 39.10N 100.21 E
Shah Jahān, Kūh-e- 24 Qd 37.02N 57.54 E
Shahjahānpur 25 Fc 27.53N 79.55 E
Shah Kūh 23 Hb 36.35N 54.31 E
Shahmīrzād 24 Oe 35.47N 53.20 E
Shāhpūr 24 Nh 32.50N 51.45 E
Shāhpūr 24 Nh 29.39N 51.03 E
Shahrak 24 Nd 36.14N 50.40 E
Shahr-e-Bābak 24 Pg 30.10N 55.09 E
Shahr-e Khafr 24 Oh 28.56N 53.14 E
Shahr Kord 23 Hc 32.19N 50.50 E
Shāhrūd 24 Md 37.17N 48.43 E
Shahu, Kūh-e- 24 Le 34.45N 46.30 E
Shāh Zeyd 24 Od 36.13N 52.22 E
Shā'ib al Banāt, Jabal- 30 Kf 26.59N 33.29 E
Sha'īt, Wādī- 24 Ej 24.33N 33.01 E
Shakaga-Dake 29 Be 33.11N 130.53 E
Shakawe 31 Ji 18.23S 21.51 E
Shak Bay (Denham) 59 Ce 25.55S 113.32 E
Shaker Heights 44 Ge 41.29N 81.36W
Shaki 34 Fd 8.40N 3.23 E
Shakotan-Dake 29a Bb 43.16N 140.26 E
Shakotan-Hantō 29a Bb 43.15N 140.30 E
Shakotan-Misaki 29a Bb 43.23N 140.28 E
Shaktoolik 40 Gd 64.20N 161.09W
Shāl 24 Me 35.54N 49.46 E
Shala, Lake- 35 Fd 7.29N 38.32 E
Shalamzār 24 Nf 32.02N 50.49 E
Shalānbōd 35 Ge 1.40N 44.42 E
Shaler Mountains 42 Gb 71.45N 111.00W
Shaliuhe → Gangca 27 Hd 37.30N 100.14 E
Shaluli Shan 21 Lf 30.45N 99.45 E
Shām, Bādiyat ash- = Syrian Desert (EN) 21 Ff 32.00N 40.00 E
Shām, Jabal ash- 21 Hg 23.10N 57.20 E
Shamattawa 42 Ie 55.52N 92.05W
Shambe 35 Ed 7.07N 30.46 E
Shambu 35 Fd 9.33N 37.07 E
Shamīl 24 Qi 27.30N 56.53 E
Shāmīyah 21 Ff 34.00N 39.59 E
Shammar, Jabal- 21 Gg 27.20N 41.45 E
Shamo, Lake- 35 Fd 5.50N 37.40 E
Shamokin 44 Ie 40.47N 76.34W
Shamrock 45 Fi 35.13N 100.15W
Shams 24 Pg 31.04N 55.02 E
Shamsī 35 Db 19.03N 29.54 E
Shamwa 37 Ec 17.18S 31.34 E
Shan [2] 25 Jd 22.00N 98.00 E
Shandī 31 Kg 16.42N 33.26 E
Shandian He 28 Dc 42.20N 116.20 E
Shandong Bandao = Shantung Peninsula (EN) 21 Of 37.00N 121.00 E
Shandong Sheng (Shan-tung Sheng) = Shantung (EN) [2] 27 Kd 36.00N 119.00 E
Shandūr Pass 25 Ea 36.04N 72.31 E
Shangani 37 Dc 19.42S 29.22 E
Shangani 37 Dc 18.30S 27.11 E
Shangbahe 28 Ci 30.39N 115.06 E
Shangcai 28 Ch 33.16N 114.15 E
Shangcheng 28 Ci 31.49N 115.24 E
Shangdu 27 Jc 41.31N 113.32 E
Shanggao 28 Cj 28.15N 114.55 E
Shanghai 22 Of 31.14N 121.28 E
Shanghai Shi (Shang-hai Shih) [4] 27 Le 31.14N 121.28 E
Shang-hai Shih → Shanghai Shi [4] 27 Le 31.14N 121.28 E
Shanghang 27 Kf 25.04N 116.21 E
Shanghe 28 Df 37.19N 117.09 E
Shanghekou 27 Lc 40.26N 124.51 E
Shangpaihe → Feixi 28 Di 31.42N 117.09 E
Shangqiu (Zhuji) 27 Ke 34.24N 115.37 E
Shangrao 27 Kf 28.29N 117.59 E
Shan Guan 27 Kf 27.28N 117.05 E
Shangxian 27 Ie 33.55N 109.57 E
Shangyi (Nanhaoqian) 28 Bd 41.06N 113.58 E
Shangyu (Baiguan) 28 Fi 30.01N 120.53 E
Shangzhi 27 Mb 45.13N 127.55 E
Shanhaiguan 28 Ed 40.01N 119.45 E
Shanhetun 28 Ib 44.43N 127.14 E
Shan-hsi Sheng → Shanxi Sheng = Shansi (EN) [2] 27 Jd 37.00N 112.00 E
Shanklin 12 Ad 50.37N 1.11W
Shanmatang Ding 27 Jg 24.45N 111.50 E
Shannon 41 Kc 75.20N 18.10W
Shannon 62 Fd 40.33S 175.25 E
Shannon/Aerfort na Sionainne 9 Ei 52.42N 8.57W
Shannon/An tSionainn 5 Fe 52.36N 9.41W
Shannon, Mount- 59 Ie 29.58S 141.30 E
Shannon, Mouth of the- 9 Di 52.30N 9.53W
Shanshan (Piqan) 27 Fc 42.52N 90.10 E
Shansi (EN) = Shan-hsi Sheng → Shanxi Sheng [2] 27 Jd 37.00N 112.00 E
Shansi (EN) = Shanxi Sheng (Shan-hsi Sheng) [2] 27 Jd 37.00N 112.00 E
Shansonggang 28 Ic 42.30N 126.13 E
Shanṭah, Ra's- 24 Qi 26.22N 56.26 E
Shantar Islands (EN) = Šantarskije Ostrova 21 Pd 55.00N 137.36 E
Shantou 22 Ng 23.26N 116.42 E
Shantung (EN) = Shandong Sheng (Shan-tung Sheng) [2] 27 Kd 36.00N 119.00 E
Shantung (EN) = Shan-tung Sheng → Shandong Sheng [2] 27 Kd 36.00N 119.00 E
Shantung Peninsula (EN) = Shandong Bandao 21 Of 37.00N 121.00 E
Shan-tung Sheng → Shandong Sheng = Shantung (EN) [2] 27 Kd 36.00N 119.00 E
Shanxian 28 Dg 34.47N 116.05 E
Shanxi Sheng (Shan-hsi Sheng) = Shansi (EN) [2] 27 Jd 37.00N 112.00 E
Shanyin (Daiyue) 28 Be 39.30N 112.48 E
Shanyincheng 28 Be 39.27N 112.56 E
Shaoguan 22 Ng 24.57N 113.34 E
Shaoshan 27 Jf 27.55N 112.32 E
Shaowu 27 Kf 27.21N 117.29 E
Shaoxing 22 Og 30.00N 120.30 E
Shaoyang 22 Ng 27.13N 111.31 E
Shapinsay 9 Kb 59.03N 2.51W
Shaqlāwah 24 Kd 36.23N 44.18 E
Shaqq al Ju'ayfir 35 Db 15.16N 26.00 E
Shaqrā' 23 Gg 13.21N 45.42 E
Shaqū 24 Qi 27.14N 56.22 E
Sharāf 24 Jg 30.37N 43.45 E
Sharafah 35 Dc 12.04N 27.07 E
Sharafkhāneh 24 Kc 38.11N 45.29 E
Sharāh, Jibāl ash- 24 Fg 30.10N 35.30 E
Sharā 'Iwah 24 Oj 25.02N 52.14 E
Shareh 24 Kd 37.38N 44.50 E
Shari 27 Pc 43.55N 144.40 E
Shārī, Buḩayrat- 24 Ke 34.23N 44.07 E
Shari-Dake 29a Db 43.46N 144.43 E
Sharifābād [Iran] 24 Nd 36.12N 50.08 E
Sharifābād [Iran] 24 Ne 35.25N 51.47 E
Shark Bay 57 Cg 25.30S 113.30 E
Sharm ash Shaykh 33 Fd 27.50N 34.16 E
Sharon 44 Ge 41.16N 80.30W
Sharon Springs 45 Fg 38.54N 101.45W
Sharp 9 Fc 58.05N 7.05W
Sharqīyah, Aş Şaḩrā' ash- = Arabian Desert (EN) 30 Kf 28.00N 32.00 E
Sharshar, Jabal- 24 Dk 23.52N 30.20 E
Shary 23 Fd 27.15N 43.27 E
Shashe 37 Dd 21.24S 27.27 E
Shashemene 35 Fd 7.13N 38.36 E
Shashi 22 Nf 30.22N 112.11 E
Shashi 30 Jk 22.12S 29.21 E
Shasta, Mount- 38 Ge 41.20N 122.20W
Shasta Lake 43 Cc 40.50N 122.25W
Shāţi', Wādī ash- 33 Bd 27.10N 13.25 E
Shattuck 45 Gh 36.16N 99.53W
Shaunavon 42 Gg 49.40N 108.25W
Shawan 27 Ec 44.21N 85.37 E
Shawano 45 Ld 44.47N 88.36W
Shawinigan 42 Kg 46.33N 72.45W
Shawnee 43 Hd 35.20N 96.55W
Shawneetown 45 Lh 37.42N 88.08W
Shaw River 59 Dd 20.20S 119.17 E
Shāwshāw, Jabal- 24 Ci 26.03N 28.56 E
Shayang 28 Bi 30.42N 112.34 E
Shaybārā 24 Gj 25.25N 36.51 E
Shaykh Aḩmad 24 Lf 32.53N 46.26 E
Shaykh Fāris 24 Lf 32.05N 47.36 E
Shaykh Sa'd 24 Lf 32.34N 46.17 E
Shaykh 'Uthmān 23 Fg 12.52N 44.59 E
Shebar, Kowtal-e- 23 Kc 34.54N 68.14 E
Shebele, Wabe- = Shebeli Webi (EN) 30 Lh 0.12S 42.45 E
Shebeli Webi (EN) = Shabēlle, Webi- 30 Lh 0.12S 42.45 E
Shebeli Webi (EN) = Shebele, Wabe- 30 Lh 0.12S 42.45 E
Sheberghān 22 If 36.41N 65.45 E
Sheboygan 45 Me 43.46N 87.44W
Shebshi Mountains 30 Ih 8.30N 11.45 E
Shedin Peak 42 Ee 55.50N 127.00W
Sheelin, Lough-/Loch Síleann 9 Fh 53.48N 7.20W
Sheenjek 40 Kc 66.45N 144.33W
Sheep Haven/Cuan na gCaorach 9 Ff 55.10N 7.52W
Sheep Mountain 46 Hj 32.32N 114.14W
Sheep Range 46 Hh 36.45N 115.05W
s'Heerenberg, Bergh- 12 Ic 51.53N 6.16 E
Sheerness 9 Nj 51.27N 0.45 E
Sheffield [Al.-U.S.] 44 Dh 34.46N 87.40W
Sheffield [Eng.-U.K.] 6 Fe 53.23N 1.30W
Sheffield [Tx.-U.S.] 45 Fk 30.43N 101.50W
Shefford 12 Bb 52.02N 0.20W
Shek Hasan 35 Fc 12.04N 35.53 E
Shek Husen 35 Gd 7.45N 40.42 E
Shelburne [N.S.-Can.] 42 Kh 43.46N 65.19W
Shelburne [Ont.-Can.] 44 Gc 44.04N 80.12W
Shelby [Mt.-U.S.] 43 Eb 48.30N 111.51W
Shelby [N.C.-U.S.] 44 Gh 35.17N 81.32W
Shelbyville [Il.-U.S.] 45 Lg 39.24N 88.48W
Shelbyville [In.-U.S.] 44 Ef 39.31N 85.47W
Shelbyville [Tn.-U.S.] 44 Dh 35.29N 86.27W
Shelbyville, Lake- 45 Lg 39.30N 88.40W
Sheldon 45 Ie 43.11N 95.51W
Sheldon Point 40 Gd 63.32N 164.52W
Shelikhov Gulf (EN) = Šelihova, Zaliv- 21 Rc 60.00N 158.00 E
Shelikof Strait 40 Ie 57.30N 155.00W
Shell 46 Ld 44.33N 107.44W
Shellbrook 42 Gf 53.13N 106.24W
Shellharbour 58 Gh 34.35S 150.52 E
Shelter Point 62 Cg 47.06S 168.13 E
Shelton 46 Dc 47.13N 123.06W
Shenandoah 45 If 40.46N 95.22W
Shenandoah Mountain 44 Hf 38.58N 79.00W
Shenandoah Valley 44 Hf 38.45N 78.45W
Shenchi 28 Be 39.05N 112.11 E
Shendam 34 Gd 8.53N 9.32 E
Shending Shan 27 Nb 46.34N 133.27 E
Shenge 34 Cd 7.55N 12.57W
Shëngjini 15 Ch 41.49N 19.35 E
Shengsi (Caiyuanzhen) 28 Gi 30.42N 122.29 E
Shengsi Liedao 27 Le 30.45N 122.40 E
Shengxian 27 Lf 29.35N 120.45 E
Shengze 28 Fi 30.55N 120.39 E
Shenjiamen → Putuo 28 Gj 29.57N 122.18 E
Shenmu 27 Jd 38.52N 110.35 E
Shenqiu (Huaidian) 27 Ke 33.27N 115.05 E
Shensi (EN) = Shaan-hsi Sheng → Shaanxi Sheng [2] 27 Id 36.00N 109.00 E
Shensi (EN) = Shaanxi Sheng (Shaan-hsi Sheng) [2] 27 Id 36.00N 109.00 E
Shenton, Mount- 59 Ee 28.00S 123.22 E
Shenxian 28 Ce 38.01N 115.33 E
Shenyang (Mukden) 22 Oe 41.48N 123.24 E
Shenze 28 Ce 38.11N 115.11 E
Shepherd, Iles- = Shepherd Islands (EN) 63b Dc 16.55S 168.35 E
Shepherd Islands (EN) = Shepherd, Iles- 63b Dc 16.55S 168.35 E
Shepparton 58 Fh 36.23S 145.25 E
Sheppey 9 Nj 51.24N 0.50 E
Shepshed 12 Ab 52.45N 1.17W
Sheqi 28 Bh 33.04N 112.56 E
Sherard, Cape - 42 Jb 74.36N 80.10W
Sherard Osborn Fjord 41 Gb 82.10N 51.30W
Sherborne 9 Kk 50.57N 2.31W
Sherbro Island 30 Fh 7.33N 12.42W
Sherbrooke 39 Le 45.24N 71.54W
Sherda 35 Ba 20.08N 16.45 E
Shere Hill 34 Gd 9.57N 9.03 E
Sheridan [Mt.-U.S.] 46 Id 45.27N 112.12W
Sheridan [Wy.-U.S.] 39 Ie 44.48N 106.58W
Sheridan Lake 45 Eg 38.30N 102.15W
Sheringham 9 Oi 52.57N 1.12 E
Sherman 43 He 33.38N 96.36W
Sherman Station 44 Mc 45.54N 68.26W
Sherridon 42 He 55.07N 101.05W
's-Hertogenbosch/Den Bosch 11 Lc 51.41N 5.19 E
Sherwood Forest 9 Lh 53.10N 1.10W
She Shui 28 Ci 30.52N 114.22 E
Shetland [3] 9 La 60.30N 1.30W
Shetland Islands (Zetland) 5 Fc 60.30N 1.30W
Shewa [3] 35 Fd 9.20N 38.55 E
Shewa Gimira 35 Fd 7.00N 35.50 E
Shexian 28 Bf 36.33N 113.40 E
Shexian (Huicheng) 28 Ej 29.53N 118.27 E
Sheyang (Hede) 28 Fh 33.47N 120.15 E
Sheyenne River 43 Hb 47.05N 96.50W
Shiant Islands 9 Gd 57.54N 6.30W
Shibām 35 Hb 15.56N 48.38 E
Shibamīnah, Wādī- 23 Ie 22.12N 55.30 E
Shibata [Jap.] 28 Of 37.57N 139.20 E
Shibata [Jap.] 29 Gb 38.05N 140.50 E
Shibayama-Gata 29 Ec 36.21N 136.23 E
Shibazhan 27 Ma 42.28N 125.20 E
Shibecha 28 Rc 43.17N 144.36 E
Shibetsu [Jap.] 28 Rc 43.40N 145.08 E
Shibetsu [Jap.] 27 Pc 44.10N 142.23 E
Shibetsu-Gawa 29a Db 43.40N 145.06 E
Shibīn al Kawm 33 Fc 30.33N 31.01 E
Shibiutan 29a Ca 44.47N 142.35 E
Shibi-Zan 29 Bf 31.59N 130.22 E
Shīb Kūh 23 Hd 27.20N 52.40 E
Shibukawa 28 Of 36.29N 139.00 E
Shibushi 29 Bf 31.28N 131.07 E
Shibushi-Wan 28 Ki 31.25N 131.12 E
Shichinohe 29 Ga 40.41N 141.10 E
Shichiyo Islands 64d Bb 7.23N 151.40 E
Shidao 27 Ld 36.51N 122.18 E
Shido 29 Dd 34.19N 134.10 E
Shidongsi → Gaolan 27 Hd 36.23N 103.55 E
Shiel, Loch- 9 He 56.50N 5.50W
Shiga Ken [2] 28 Ng 35.15N 136.10 E
Shigu 27 Gf 26.54N 99.44 E
Shi He 28 Ch 32.32N 115.52 E
Shihezi 27 Ec 44.18N 86.02 E
Shiiba 29 Be 32.28N 131.09 E
Shijaku 15 Ch 41.20N 19.34 E
Shijiazhuang 22 Nf 38.00N 114.30 E
Shijiusuo 28 Eg 35.24N 119.32 E
Shika 29 Ec 37.01N 136.46 E
Shikabe 29a Bb 42.02N 140.47 E
Shikārpur 25 Dc 27.57N 68.38 E
Shiki Islands 64d Bb 7.24N 151.53 E
Shikine-Jima 29 Fd 34.19N 139.13 E
Shikoku 21 Pf 33.30N 133.30 E
Shikoku Basin (EN) 27 Oe 30.00N 135.30 E
Shikoku-Sanchi 29 Ce 33.45N 133.35 E
Shikotsu-Ko 28 Pc 42.48N 141.20 E
Shilabo 35 Gd 6.05N 44.45 E
Shiliu → Changjiang 27 Ih 19.20N 109.03 E
Shilla 25 Fb 32.24N 78.12 E
Shillong 22 Lg 25.34N 91.53 E
Shimabara 28 Kh 32.47N 130.22 E
Shimabara-Hantō 29 Be 32.45N 130.15 E
Shimabara-Wan 29 Be 32.50N 130.30 E
Shimada 29 Fd 34.49N 138.09 E
Shima-Hantō 29 Ed 34.25N 136.45 E
Shimane-Hantō 29 Cd 35.30N 133.00 E
Shimane Ken [2] 28 Lg 35.00N 132.20 E
Shimanto-Gawa 29 Ce 32.56N 133.00 E
Shimaura-Tō 29 Bd 34.50N 131.50 E
Shimian 27 Hf 29.10N 102.26 E
Shimizu [Jap.] 29a Cb 43.01N 142.51 E
Shimizu [Jap.] 28 Og 35.01N 138.29 E
Shimizu-Tōge 29 Fc 36.53N 138.55 E
Shimoda 28 Og 34.40N 138.57 E
Shimodate 29 Fc 36.19N 139.58 E
Shimoga 22 Jh 13.55N 75.34 E
Shimo-Jima 29 Be 32.25N 130.05 E
Shimokawa 29a Ca 44.18N 142.38 E
Shimokita-Hantō 29a Bc 41.15N 141.05 E
Shimo-Koshiki-Jima 29 Af 31.40N 129.40 E
Shimo la Tewa 36 Gc 3.57S 39.44 E
Shimoni 36 Gc 4.39S 39.23 E
Shimonoseki 27 Ne 33.57N 130.57 E
Shimono-Shima 29 Ad 34.15N 129.15 E
Shimotsu 29 Dd 34.07N 135.08 E
Shimotsuma 29 Fc 36.11N 139.58 E
Shin, Loch- 9 Ic 58.07N 4.32W
Shinano 29 Fc 36.47N 138.10 E
Shinano-Gawa 29 Fc 37.57N 139.04 E
Shināş 24 Qj 24.43N 56.27 E
Shindand 23 Jc 33.18N 62.08 E
Shinga 36 Dc 3.16S 24.38 E
Shingbwiyang 25 Jc 26.41N 96.13 E
Shingū 27 Oe 33.44N 135.59 E
Shingwidzi 37 Ed 23.01S 30.43 E
Shinji 29 Cd 35.24N 132.54 E
Shinji-Ko 28 Lg 35.27N 133.02 E
Shinjō 27 Pd 38.46N 140.18 E
Shinkafe 34 Gc 13.05N 6.31 E
Shinminato 29 Ec 36.47N 137.04 E
Shinnanyō 29 Bd 34.05N 131.45 E
Shinshiro 29 Ed 34.53N 137.30 E
Shintoku 28 Qc 43.12N 142.55 E
Shintotsugawa 29a Bb 43.32N 141.40 E
Shinyanga 31 Ki 3.40S 33.26 E
Shinyanga [3] 36 Fc 3.30S 33.00 E
Shiogama 29 Gb 38.19N 141.01 E
Shiojiri 28 Nf 36.06N 137.58 E
Shiokubi-Misaki 29a Bc 41.43N 140.57 E
Shio-no-Misaki 27 Oe 33.25N 135.45 E
Shipai → Huaining 28 Di 30.25N 116.39 E

Index Symbols

[1] Independent Nation
[2] State, Region
[3] District, County
[4] Municipality
[5] Colony, Dependency
Continent
Physical Region
Historical or Cultural Region
Mount, Mountain
Volcano
Hill
Mountains, Mountain Range
Hills, Escarpment
Plateau, Upland
Pass, Gap
Plain, Lowland
Delta
Salt Flat
Valley, Canyon
Crater, Cave
Karst Features
Depression
Polder
Desert, Dunes
Forest, Woods
Heath, Steppe
Oasis
Cape, Point
Coast, Beach
Cliff
Peninsula
Isthmus
Sandbank
Island
Atoll
Rock, Reef
Islands, Archipelago
Rocks, Reefs
Coral Reef
Well, Spring
Geyser
River, Stream
Waterfall Rapids
River Mouth, Estuary
Lake
Salt Lake
Intermittent Lake
Reservoir
Swamp, Pond
Canal
Glacier
Ice Shelf, Pack Ice
Ocean
Sea
Gulf, Bay
Strait, Fjord
Lagoon
Bank
Seamount
Tablemount
Ridge
Shelf
Basin
Escarpment, Sea Scarp
Fracture
Trench, Abyss
National Park, Reserve
Point of Interest
Recreation Site
Cave, Cavern
Historic Site
Ruins
Wall, Walls
Church, Abbey
Temple
Scientific Station
Airport
Port
Lighthouse
Mine
Tunnel
Dam, Bridge

Shiping 27 Hg 23.44N 102.28 E
Shipki La 27 Ce 31.49N 78.45 E
Shippegan 42 Lg 47.45N 64.42W
Shiprock 45 Bh 36.47N 108.41W
Shipshaw, Rivière- 44 La 48.30N 71.15W
Shipu 28 Fj 29.17N 121.57 E
Shipugi Shankou 27 Ce 31.49N 78.45 E
Shiquan 27 Ie 33.05N 108.15 E
Shiquanhe 22 Jf 32.24N 79.52 E
Shiquan He 27 Ce 32.28N 79.44 E
Shiragami Dake 29 Ga 40.30N 140.01 E
Shiragami-Misaki 28 Pd 41.25N 140.12 E
Shirahama 29 De 33.40N 135.20 E
Shirakawa [Jap.] 29 Ed 35.36N 137.12 E
Shirakawa [Jap.] 29 Ec 36.17N 136.53 E
Shirakawa [Jap.] 28 Pf 37.07N 140.13 E
Shirane-San [Jap.] 27 Od 36.48N 139.22 E
Shirane-San [Jap.] 29 Fd 35.40N 138.13 E
Shirane-San [Jap.] 29 Fc 36.38N 138.32 E
Shiranuka 28 Rc 42.57N 144.05 E
Shiraoi 28 Pc 42.31N 141.16 E
Shirase Coast 66 Mf 78.30S 156.00W
Shirataka 29 Gb 38.11N 140.06 E
Shirataki 29a Cb 43.53N 143.09 E
Shirāz 22 Hg 29.36N 52.32 E
Shirbīn 24 Dg 31.11N 31.32 E
Shire 30 Kj 17.42S 35.19 E
Shiren 28 Id 41.54N 126.34 E
Shiretoko-Dake 29a Da 44.15N 145.14 E
Shiretoko-Hantō 29a Da 44.00N 145.00 E
Shiretoko-Misaki 27 Qc 44.21N 145.20 E
Shirgāh 24 Od 36.17N 52.54 E
Shiribetsu-Gawa 29a Bb 42.52N 140.21 E
Shiriha-Misaki 29a Db 42.56N 144.45 E
Shirikishinai 29a Bc 41.48N 141.05 E
Shīrīn 24 Qi 27.10N 56.41 E
Shīrīn sū 24 Me 35.29N 48.27 E
Shiriya-Zaki 27 Pc 41.26N 141.28 E
Shīr Kūh 21 Hf 31.37N 54.04 E
Shirley Mountains 46 Le 42.15N 106.30W
Shiroishi 28 Pe 38.00N 140.37 E
Shirone 29 Fc 37.46N 139.00 E
Shirotori 29 Ed 35.53N 136.52 E
Shirouma-Dake 29 Ec 36.45N 137.46 E
Shirshov Ridge (EN) 20 Me 57.30N 171.00 E
Shirvān 24 Lf 33.33N 46.49 E
Shirwan Mazīn 24 Kd 37.03N 44.10 E
Shishaldin Volcano 38 Cd 54.45N 163.57W
Shishi-Jima 29 Be 32.17N 130.15 E
Shishmaref 40 Fc 66.14N 166.09W
Shishou 27 Jf 29.42N 112.23 E
Shitai (Qili) 28 Di 30.12N 117.28 E
Shitara 29 Ed 35.05N 137.34 E
Shitou Shan 27 Ma 51.02N 125.12 E
Shivwits Plateau 46 Ih 36.10N 113.40W
Shiwa 28 Pe 39.33N 141.35 E
Shiwan Dashan 27 Ig 21.45N 107.35 E
Shiwa Ngandu 36 Fe 11.12S 31.43 E
Shiwpuri 25 Fc 25.26N 77.39 E
Shixian 28 Jc 43.05N 129.46 E
Shiyan 27 Je 32.34N 110.48 E
Shiyang He 27 Hd 39.00N 103.25 E
Shizilu → Junan 28 Eg 35.10N 118.50 E
Shizugawa 29 Gb 38.40N 141.28 E
Shizui 28 Ic 43.03N 126.09 E
Shizuishan (Dawukou) 27 Id 39.03N 106.24 E
Shizukuishi 29 Gb 39.42N 140.59 E
Shizunai 28 Qc 42.20N 142.22 E
Shizunai-Gawa 29a Cb 42.20N 142.22 E
Shizuoka 22 Pf 34.58N 138.23 E
Shizuoka Ken [2] 28 Og 35.00N 138.25 E
Shkodra 6 Hg 42.05N 19.30 E
Shkodrës, Liqen i-=Scutari, Lake- (EN) 5 Hg 42.10N 19.20 E
Shkumbini 15 Ch 41.01N 19.26 E
Shoal Lake 45 Fa 50.26N 100.34W
Shoal Lake 45 Ib 49.32N 95.00W
Shoal Lakes 45 Ha 50.20N 97.40W
Shōbara 28 Lg 34.51N 133.01 E
Shodo-Shima 29 Dd 34.30N 134.15 E
Shō-Gawa 29 Ec 36.47N 137.04 E
Shokanbetsu-Dake 29a Bb 43.43N 141.31 E
Shokotsu-Gawa 29a Ca 44.23N 143.17 E
Sholāpur 22 Jh 17.41N 75.55 E
Shoqān 24 Qd 37.20N 56.58 E
Shoranūr 25 Ff 10.46N 76.17 E
Shoreham-by-Sea 9 Mk 50.49N 0.16W
Shortland Islands 60 Fi 6.55S 155.53 E
Shosambetsu 29a Ba 44.32N 141.46 E
Shoshone 46 He 42.56N 114.24W
Shoshone Mountains 43 Dd 39.15N 117.25W
Shoshone Peak 46 Gh 36.56N 116.16W
Shoshone River 46 Kd 44.52N 108.11W
Shoshong 37 Dd 23.02S 26.31 E
Shoshoni 46 Ke 43.14N 108.07W
Shotor Khūn 23 Jc 34.20N 64.55 E
Shouchang 28 Ej 29.23N 119.12 E
Shouguang 28 Ef 36.53N 118.44 E
Shouxian (Shouyang) 28 Dh 32.35N 116.47 E
Shouyang → Shouxian 28 Dh 32.35N 116.47 E
Shōwa 29 Gb 39.51N 140.03 E
Show Low 46 Ji 34.15N 110.02W
Shqiperia=Albania (EN) [1] 6 Hg 41.00N 20.00 E
Shreveport 39 Jf 32.30N 93.45W
Shrewsbury 9 Ki 52.43N 2.45W
Shuangcheng 27 Mb 45.21N 126.17 E
Shuangjiang 27 Gg 23.27N 99.50 E
Shuangjiang → Tongdao 27 If 26.14N 109.45 E
Shuangliao 27 Lc 43.30N 123.30 E
Shuangyang 27 Mc 43.31N 125.28 E
Shuangyashan 22 Pe 46.37N 131.10 E
Shucheng 28 Di 31.28N 116.57 E
Shufu 27 Cd 39.27N 75.52 E
Shuguri Falls 36 Gd 8.31S 37.23 E
Shu He 28 Eg 34.07N 118.30 E
Shuicheng 27 Hf 26.34N 104.52 E
Shuiding → Huocheng 27 Dc 44.03N 80.49 E
Shuiji → Laixi 28 Ff 36.52N 120.31 E
Shuijiahu → Changfeng 28 Dh 32.29N 117.10 E
Shuikou → Jianghua 27 Jg 24.58N 111.56 E
Shuiye 28 Cf 36.08N 114.06 E
Shuizhai → Xiangcheng 28 Ch 33.27N 114.53 E
Shūl 24 Ng 30.10N 51.38 E
Shulan 27 Mc 44.26N 126.55 E
Shule 27 Cd 39.25N 76.06 E
Shule He 21 Le 40.20N 92.50 E
Shulu (Xinji) 28 Cf 37.56N 115.14 E
Shumagin Islands 40 He 55.07N 159.45W
Shumarinai-Ko 29a Ca 44.20N 142.13 E
Shunayn, Sabkhat- 33 Dc 30.10N 21.00 E
Shungnak 40 Hc 66.53N 157.02W
Shunyi 28 Dd 40.09N 116.38 E
Shuolong 27 Ig 22.51N 106.55 E
Shuoxian 27 Jd 39.18N 112.25 E
Shūr [Iran] 24 Pi 26.59N 55.47 E
Shūr [Iran] 24 Oh 28.12N 52.09 E
Shūr [Iran] 24 Ne 35.09N 51.30 E
Shūr [Iran] 24 Oh 28.33N 53.12 E
Shūr Āb 24 Pg 31.45N 55.15 E
Shurāb 23 Ic 33.07N 55.18 E
Shūsf 23 Jc 31.48N 60.01 E
Shūsh 24 Mf 32.12N 48.17 E
Shushica 15 Ci 40.34N 19.34 E
Shūshtar 23 Gc 32.03N 48.51 E
Shuswap Lake 46 Fa 50.57N 119.15W
Shūt 24 Oe 34.44N 52.53 E
Shuwak 35 Fc 14.23N 35.52 E
Shuyang 27 Ke 34.01N 118.52 E
Shuzenji 29 Fd 34.58N 138.55 E
Shwebo 25 Jd 22.34N 95.42 E
Shwell 25 Jd 23.56N 96.17 E
Shyok 25 Fa 35.13N 75.53 E
Sia 26 Jh 6.49S 134.19 E
Siagne 11 Mk 43.32N 6.57 E
Siāh Band 23 Kc 33.25N 65.21 E
Siāh-Chashmeh 24 Kc 39.04N 44.23 E
Siāh-Kūh 24 Oe 34.38N 52.16 E
Siak 26 Df 1.13N 102.09 E
Sialkot [Pak.] 25 Ea 35.15N 73.17 E
Sialkot [Pak.] 22 Jf 32.30N 74.31 E
Sianów 10 Mb 54.15N 16.16 E
Siantan, Pulau- 26 Ef 3.10N 106.15 E
Siargao 26 Ie 9.53N 126.02 E
Šiaškotan, Ostrov- 21 Re 48.49N 154.06 E
Siátista 15 Ei 40.16N 21.33 E
Siau, Pulau- 26 If 2.42N 125.24 E
Šiauliai/Šjauljaj 6 Id 55.53N 23.19 E
Siavonga 36 Ef 16.32S 28.43 E
Siazan 19 Eg 41.04N 49.06 E
Sibā'i, Jabal as- 33 Fd 25.43N 34.09 E
Sibaj 19 Fe 52.42N 58.39 E
Sibari 14 Kk 39.45N 16.27 E
Sibasa 37 Ed 22.56S 30.29 E
Šibenik 14 Jg 43.44N 15.53 E
Siberimanua 26 Cg 2.09S 99.34 E
Siberut, Pulau- 21 Lj 1.20S 98.55 E
Siberut, Selat- 26 Cg 0.42S 98.35 E
Sibi 25 Dc 29.33N 67.53 E
Sibigo 26 Cf 2.51N 95.55 E
Sibillini, Monti- 14 Hh 42.55N 13.15 E
Sibircatajaha 17 Lb 69.05N 64.43 E
Sibircevo 20 Ih 44.16N 132.20 E
Sibirjakova, Ostrov- 20 Cb 72.50N 79.00 E
Sibiti 36 Bc 3.41S 13.21 E
Sibiu [2] 15 Hd 45.46N 24.12 E
Sibiu 6 If 45.48N 24.09 E
Sibolga 22 Li 1.45N 98.48 E
Sibsāgar 25 Ic 26.59N 94.38 E
Sibu 22 Ni 2.18N 111.49 E
Sibuguey Bay 26 He 7.30N 122.40 E
Sibut 31 Ih 5.44N 19.05 E
Sibutu Islands 26 Gf 4.45N 119.20 E
Sibutu Passage 26 Gf 4.56N 119.36 E
Sibuyan 26 Hd 12.25N 122.34 E
Sibuyan Sea 26 Hd 12.50N 122.40 E
Siby 34 Dc 12.22N 8.22W
Sibyllenstein 10 Ke 51.12N 14.05 E
Sicani, Monti- 14 Hm 37.40N 13.15 E
Sicasica 54 Eg 17.22S 67.45W
Si Chon 25 Jg 9.00N 99.56 E
Sichuan Pendi 21 Mf 30.01N 105.00 E
Sichuan Sheng (Ssu-ch'uan Sheng)=Szechwan (EN) [2] 27 He 30.00N 103.00 E
Sicilia [2] 14 Im 37.45N 14.15 E
Sicilia = Sicily (EN) 5 Hh 37.30N 14.00 E
Sicilia, Canale di-=Sicily, Strait of- (EN) 5 Hh 37.20N 11.20 E
Sicilia, Mar di- 14 Gn 36.30N 13.00 E
Sicily (EN) = Sicilia 5 Hh 37.30N 14.00 E
Sicily, Strait of- (EN)= Sicilia, Canale di- 5 Hh 37.20N 11.20 E
Sicily, Strait of- (EN)= Tūnis, Canal de- 5 Hh 37.20N 11.20 E
Sico Tinto, Rio- 49 Ef 15.58N 84.58W
Sicuani 53 Ig 14.15S 71.15W
Šid 15 Cd 45.08N 19.14 E
Sidamo [3] 35 Fd 5.48N 38.50 E
Siddipet 25 Fe 18.06N 78.51 E
Side 24 Dd 36.46N 31.22 E
Sidéradougou 34 Ec 10.40N 4.15W
Siderno 14 Kl 38.16N 16.18 E
Siders/Sierre 14 Bd 46.17N 7.32 E
Siderty 19 He 52.32N 74.50 E
Šiderty 19 He 51.40N 74.50 E
Sidheros, Ákra- 15 Jn 35.19N 26.19 E
Sidhirókastron 15 Gh 41.14N 23.23 E
Sidī 'Abd ar Raḥmān 24 Cg 30.58N 28.44 E
Sidi Aïch 13 Qh 36.37N 4.41 E
Sidi-Akacha 13 Nh 36.28N 1.18 E
Sidi Ali 13 Mh 36.06N 0.25 E
Sīdī 'Alī al Makkī, Ra's- 14 Em 37.11N 10.17 E
Sīdī Barrānī 33 Ec 31.36N 25.55 E
Sidi Bel Abbes [3] 32 Gc 34.45N 0.35W
Sidi Bel Abbes 32 Gb 35.12N 0.38W
Sidi Bennour 32 Fc 32.39N 8.26W
Sidi di Daoud 13 Ph 36.51N 3.52 E
Sidi Ifni 31 Ff 29.33N 10.10W
Sidi Kacem 32 Fc 34.13N 5.42W
Sidikalang 26 Cf 2.45N 98.19 E
Sidi Lakhdar 13 Mh 36.10N 0.27 E
Sīdī Zayd, Jabal- 14 En 36.29N 10.20 E
Sidlaw Hills 9 Ke 56.30N 3.00W
Sidmouth 9 Jk 50.41N 3.15W
Sidney [B.C.-Can.] 42 Fg 48.39N 123.24W
Sidney [Mt.-U.S.] 43 Gb 47.43N 104.09W
Sidney [Nb.-U.S.] 43 Gc 41.09N 102.59W
Sidney [Oh.-U.S.] 44 Ee 40.16N 84.10W
Sidney Lanier, Lake- 44 Fh 34.15N 83.57W
Sidobre 11 Ik 43.40N 2.30 E
Sidorovsk 20 Dc 66.35N 82.30 E
Sidra 10 Tc 53.33N 23.30 E
Sidra, Gulf of-(EN)=Surt, Khalīj- 30 Ie 31.30N 18.00 E
Sidrolândia 55 Ee 20.55S 54.58W
Siedlce [2] 10 Sd 52.10N 22.15 E
Siedlce 10 Sd 52.11N 22.16 E
Siedlecka, Wysoczyzna- 10 Sd 52.10N 22.15 E
Sieg [F.R.G.] 10 Df 50.45N 7.05 E
Sieg [F.R.G.] 12 Kd 50.55N 8.01 E
Siegburg 10 Df 50.48N 7.12 E
Siegen 10 Ef 50.52N 8.02 E
Siemiatycze 10 Sd 52.26N 22.53 E
Siĕmréab 25 Kf 13.22N 103.51 E
Siena 14 Fg 43.19N 11.21 E
Sieniawa 10 Sf 50.11N 22.36 E
Sienne 11 Ee 49.00N 1.34W
Sieradz 10 Oe 51.36N 18.45 E
Sieradz [2] 10 Oe 51.35N 18.45 E
Sieradzka, Niecka- 10 Oe 51.35N 18.50 E
Sierck-les-Bains 12 Ie 49.26N 6.21 E
Sierpc 10 Pd 52.52N 19.41 E
Sierra Blanca 45 Dk 31.11N 105.21W
Sierra Blanca Peak 43 Fe 33.23N 105.48W
Sierra Colorada 56 Gf 40.35S 67.48W
Sierra Leone [1] 31 Fh 8.30N 11.30W
Sierra Leone Basin (EN) 3 Di 5.00N 17.00W
Sierra Leone Rise (EN) 3 Di 5.30N 21.00W
Sierra Madre 21 Oh 16.20N 122.00 E
Sierra Mojada 47 Dc 27.17N 103.42W
Sierre/Siders 14 Bd 46.17N 7.32 E
Siete Palmas 55 Cg 25.13S 58.20W
Siete Puntas, Rio- 55 Df 23.54S 57.20W
Şieu 15 Hb 47.11N 24.13 E
Sifié 34 Dd 7.59N 6.55W
Sífnos 15 Hm 37.00N 24.40 E
Sig 32 Gb 35.32N 0.11W
Siğacik Körfezi 15 Jk 38.12N 26.45 E
Sigean 11 Ik 43.02N 2.59 E
Sighetu Marmaţiei 15 Gb 47.56N 23.53 E
Sighişoara 15 Hc 46.13N 24.48 E
Sigli 26 Ce 5.23N 95.57 E
Siglufjördur 7a Ba 66.09N 18.55W
Sigmaringen 10 Fh 48.05N 9.13 E
Signal Peak 46 Hj 33.22N 114.03W
Signy Island 66 Re 60.43S 45.38W
Signy-l'Abbaye 12 Ge 49.42N 4.25 E
Signy-le-Petit 12 Ge 49.54N 4.17 E
Sigtuna 7 Dg 59.37N 17.43 E
Siguanea, Ensenada de la- 49 Fc 21.38N 83.05W
Siguatepeque 49 Df 14.32N 87.49W
Sigüenza 13 Jc 41.04N 2.38W
Siguiri 31 Gg 11.25N 9.10W
Sigulda 7 Fh 57.09N 24.53 E
Si He 28 Dg 35.11N 116.42 E
Sihong 28 Eh 33.28N 118.13 E
Sihote-Alin 21 Pe 48.00N 138.00 E
Sihou → Changdao 28 Ff 37.56N 120.42 E
Sihuas 54 Ce 8.34S 77.37W
Siikainen 8 Ic 61.52N 21.50 E
Siilinjärvi 7 Ge 63.02N 27.40 E
Siirt 23 Fb 37.56N 41.57 E
Sijunjung 26 Dg 0.42S 100.58 E
Sikaiana 63a Fc 8.22S 162.45 E
Sikakap 26 Dg 2.46S 100.13 E
Sikanni Chief 42 Fe 58.17N 121.46W
Sikar 25 Fc 27.37N 75.09 E
Sikasso 31 Gg 11.20N 5.40W
Sikasso [3] 34 Dc 10.55N 7.00W
Sikéa [Grc.] 15 Fm 36.46N 22.56 E
Sikéa [Grc.] 15 Gi 40.03N 23.58 E
Sikeston 43 Jd 36.53N 89.35W
Sikinos 15 Im 36.50N 25.05 E
Sikkim [3] 25 Hc 27.50N 88.30 E
Siklós 10 Ok 45.51N 18.18 E
Sikonge 36 Fd 5.38S 32.46 E
Šikotan, Ostrov/Tō, Shikotan- 20 Jh 43.47N 146.45 E
Siktjah 20 Hc 69.55N 125.10 E
Sil 13 Eb 42.27N 7.43W
Sila Grande 14 Kk 39.20N 16.30 E
Sila Greca 14 Kk 39.30N 16.30 E
Šilale/Šilalė 7 Fi 55.29N 22.12 E
Šilalė/Šilale 7 Fi 55.29N 22.12 E
Silao 48 Ig 20.56N 101.26W
Silaogou 28 Be 39.59N 113.03 E
Sila Piccola 14 Kk 39.05N 16.35 E
Silba 14 If 44.23N 14.42 E
Silchar 25 Id 24.49N 92.48 E
Silda 16 Ud 51.47N 59.50 E
Sildagapet 8 Ab 62.05N 5.10 E
Sile 14 Ge 45.28N 12.35 E
Şile 24 Cb 41.05N 29.35 E
Šilega 19 Ec 64.03N 44.02 E
Silesia (EN)=Śląsk 10 Me 51.00N 16.45 E
Silesia (EN)=Śląsk 5 He 51.00N 16.45 E
Silet 32 He 22.39N 4.35 E
Silhouette Island 37b Ca 4.29S 55.14 E
Silifke 23 Db 36.22N 33.56 E
Siligir 20 Gc 68.27N 114.50 E
Siliguri 22 Kg 26.42N 88.26 E
Siling Co 21 Kf 31.50N 89.00 E
Siling Jiao 27 Ke 8.20N 115.27 E
Silisili, Mauga- 65c Aa 13.35S 172.27W
Silistra [2] 15 Kf 44.07N 27.16 E
Silistra 15 Ke 44.07N 27.16 E
Silivri 24 Cb 41.04N 28.15 E
Siljan 7 Df 60.50N 14.45 E
Šilka 20 Gf 51.51N 116.02 E
Šilka 21 Od 53.22N 121.32 E
Silkeborg 7 Bh 56.10N 9.34 E
Sillamäe/Sillamjae 7 Gg 59.24N 27.43 E
Sillamjae/Sillamäe 7 Gg 59.24N 27.43 E
Sillaro 14 Ff 44.34N 11.51 E
Silleiro, Cabo- 13 Db 42.07N 8.54W
Sillé-le-Guillaume 11 Ff 48.12N 0.08W
Sillian 14 Gd 46.45N 12.25 E
Sillil 35 Gc 11.00N 43.26 E
Siloam Springs 45 Ih 36.11N 94.32W
Siloana Plains 36 Df 17.15S 23.10 E
Šilovo 19 Ee 54.24N 40.52 E
Silsbee 45 Ik 30.21N 94.11W
Siltou 35 Bb 16.52N 15.43 E
Šilutė/Šilute 19 Cd 55.21N 21.30 E
Šilute/Šilutė 19 Cd 55.21N 21.30 E
Silvan 24 Ic 38.08N 41.01 E
Silvassa 25 Ed 20.20N 73.05 E
Silver Bank (EN) 49 Mc 20.30N 69.45W
Silver Bay 43 Ib 47.17N 91.16W
Silver City 43 Fe 32.46N 108.17W
Silverdalen 8 Fg 57.32N 15.44 E
Silver Lake 46 Ee 43.06N 120.53W
Silver Spring 44 If 39.02N 77.03W
Silver Springs 46 Fg 39.25N 119.13W
Silverthrone Mountain 46 Ba 51.31N 126.06W
Silverton [Co.-U.S.] 45 Ch 37.49N 107.40W
Silverton [Tx.-U.S.] 45 Fi 34.28N 101.19W
Silves [Braz.] 54 Gd 2.54S 58.27W
Silves [Port.] 13 Dg 37.11N 8.26W
Silvi 14 Ih 42.34N 14.06 E
Silvia 54 Cc 2.37N 76.24W
Silviers River 46 Fe 43.22N 118.48W
Silvretta 14 Ed 46.50N 10.15 E
Silyānah [3] 32 Ib 36.00N 9.30 E
Silyānah 32 Ib 36.05N 9.22 E
Silyānah, Wādī- 14 Dn 36.33N 9.25 E
Sim 17 Hi 54.59N 57.41 E
Sim 17 Hi 54.32N 56.30 E
Sim, Cap- 32 Fc 31.23N 9.51W
Simanggang 26 Ff 1.15N 111.26 E
Šimanovsk 20 Hf 52.01N 127.36 E
Simao 27 Hg 22.40N 101.02 E
Simard, Lac- 44 Hb 47.38N 78.40W
Simareh 24 Mf 32.08N 48.03 E
Simav 23 Ca 40.23N 28.31 E
Simav 24 Cc 39.05N 28.59 E
Simav Dağ 15 Lj 39.04N 28.54 E
Simav Gölü 15 Lj 39.09N 28.55 E
Simayama-Jima 29 Ae 32.40N 128.38 E
Simba 36 Db 0.36N 22.55 E
Simbo 36 Fc 4.53S 29.44 E
Simbo 63a Cc 8.18S 156.34 E
Simbruini, Monti- 14 Hj 41.55N 13.15 E
Simcoe 44 Gd 42.50N 80.18W
Simcoe, Lake - 42 Jh 44.27N 79.20W
Simen 35 Fc 13.25N 38.00 E
Simenti 34 Cc 13.00N 13.25W
Simeria 15 Gd 45.51N 23.01 E
Simeto 14 Jm 37.24N 15.06 E
Simeulue, Pulau- 21 Li 2.35N 96.05 E
Simferopol 6 Jf 44.57N 34.06 E
Simhah, Jabal- 23 Hf 17.20N 54.50 E
Simi 15 Km 36.36N 27.50 E
Simi 15 Km 36.35N 27.50 E
Simiti 49 Kj 7.58N 73.58W
Simitli 15 Gh 41.53N 23.06 E
Simla 22 Jf 31.06N 77.10 E
Şimleu Silvaniei 15 Fb 47.14N 22.48 E
Simmental 14 Bd 46.35N 7.25 E
Simmerath 12 Id 50.36N 6.18 E
Simmerbach 12 Je 49.48N 7.31 E
Simmern 10 Dg 49.59N 7.31 E
Simmertal 12 Je 49.48N 7.33 E
Simnas 8 Jj 54.20N 23.45 E
Simo 7 Fd 65.39N 24.55 E
Simojärvi 7 Gc 66.06N 27.03 E
Simojoki 7 Fd 65.37N 25.03 E
Simojovel de Allende 48 Mi 17.12N 92.38W
Simonstown 37 Bf 34.14S 18.26 E
Simpele 7 Gf 61.26N 29.22 E
Simpelejärvi 8 Mc 61.30N 29.25 E
Simplon 14 Bd 46.15N 8.00 E
Simpson Desert 57 Eg 25.00S 137.00 E
Simpson Hill 59 Fe 26.30S 126.30 E
Simpson Peninsula 42 Ic 68.45N 89.10W
Simrishamn 7 Di 55.33N 14.20 E
Simsonbaai 51b Ab 18.02N 63.08W
Simušir, Ostrov- 21 Re 46.58N 152.02 E
Sina 25 Fe 17.22N 75.54 E
Sīnā'=Sinai Peninsula (EN) 30 Kf 29.30N 34.00 E
Sinabang 26 Cf 2.29N 96.23 E
Sinadaqo 35 Hd 5.22N 46.22 E
Sinai, Mount- (EN)=Mūsa, Jabal- 24 Eh 28.32N 33.59 E
Sinaia 15 Id 45.21N 25.33 E
Sinai Peninsula (EN)= Sīnā' 30 Kf 29.30N 34.00 E
Sinajana 64c Bb 13.28N 144.45W
Sinaloa [2] 47 Cc 25.00N 107.30W
Sinaloa, Llanos de- 47 Cc 25.00N 107.30W
Sinaloa, Rio- 48 Ee 25.18N 108.30W
Sinaloa de Leyva 48 Ee 25.50N 108.14W
Sinalunga 14 Fg 43.12N 11.44 E
Sinamaica 54 Da 11.05N 71.51W
Sinan 27 If 27.56N 108.11 E
Sinara 17 Kh 56.17N 62.23 E
Sināwin 33 Bc 31.02N 10.36 E
Sinazongwe 36 Ef 17.15S 27.28 E
Şincai 15 Hc 46.39N 24.23 E
Sincanli 24 Dc 38.45N 30.15 E
Sincé 49 Ji 9.14N 75.06W
Sincelejo 53 Ie 9.18N 75.24W
Sinch'am 28 Jc 42.07N 129.25 E
Sinch'ang 28 Jd 40.07N 128.28 E
Sinch'on 28 He 38.28N 125.27 E
Sinclair, Lake- 44 Fi 33.11N 83.16W
Sind [3] 25 Cc 25.30N 69.00 E
Sind 21 Ig 25.30N 69.00 E
Sindal 8 Dg 57.28N 10.13 E
Sindangbarang 26 Eh 7.27S 107.08 E
Sindara 36 Bc 1.02S 10.40 E
Sindelfingen-Böblingen 10 Fh 48.41N 9.01 E
Sindfeld 12 Kc 51.32N 8.48 E
Sindi 7 Fg 58.24N 24.42 E
Sındırgı 24 Cc 39.14N 28.10 E
Sindirgi Geçidi 15 Lj 39.10N 28.04 E
Sîndominic 15 Ic 46.35N 25.47 E
Sindri 25 Hd 23.42N 86.29 E
Sinegorje 20 Kd 62.03N 150.25 E
Sinegorski 16 Le 48.00N 40.53 E
Šine-Ider 27 Gb 48.56N 99.33 E
Sinekli 15 Lh 41.14N 28.12 E
Sinelnikovo 16 Ie 48.18N 35.31 E
Sines 13 Dg 37.57N 8.52W
Sines, Cabo de- 13 Dg 37.57N 8.53W
Sine-Saloum [3] 34 Bc 14.00N 15.50W
Singako 35 Bd 9.50N 19.29 E
Singapore / Singapura 22 Mi 1.17N 103.51 E
Singapore Strait (EN)= Singapura, Selat- 26 Df 1.15N 104.00 E
Singapura / Singapore 22 Mi 1.17N 103.51 E
Singapura, Selat-= Singapore Strait (EN) 26 Df 1.15N 104.00 E
Singaraja 26 Gh 8.07S 115.06 E
Singatoka 63d Ac 18.08S 177.30 E
Sing Buri 25 Kf 14.53N 100.25 E
Singen 10 Ei 47.46N 8.50 E
Sîngeroz Băi 15 Hb 47.22N 24.41 E
Singida [3] 36 Fd 5.30S 34.30 E
Singida 31 Ki 4.49S 34.45 E
Singitic Gulf (EN) = Singitikós Kólpos 15 Gi 40.10N 23.55 E
Singitikós Kólpos = Singitic Gulf (EN) 15 Gi 40.10N 23.55 E
Singkaling Hkamti 25 Jc 26.00N 95.42 E
Singkang 26 Hg 4.08S 120.01 E
Singkawang 26 Ef 0.54N 109.00 E
Singkep, Pulau- 26 Dg 0.30S 104.25 E
Singkil 26 Cf 2.17N 97.49 E
Singleton [Austl.] 59 Kf 32.34S 151.10 E
Singleton [Eng.-U.K.] 12 Bd 50.55N 0.44W
Singleton, Mount- 59 De 29.28S 117.18 E
Singö 8 Hd 60.10N 18.45 E
Siniscola 14 Dj 40.34N 9.41 E
Sini vrăh 15 Ih 41.51N 25.01 E
Sinj 14 Kg 43.42N 16.38 E
Sinjah 35 Ec 13.09N 33.56 E
Sinjai 26 Hh 5.07S 120.15 E
Sinjaja 8 Mg 57.05N 28.33 E
Sinjajevina 15 Cf 43.00N 19.18 E
Sinjār 24 Id 36.19N 41.52 E
Sinjār, Jabal- 24 Id 36.23N 41.52 E
Sinjuža 16 Ge 48.03N 30.50 E
Sinkiang (EN)= Hsin-chiang-wei-wu-erh Tzu-chih-ch'ü → Xinjiang Uygur Zizhiqu [2] 27 Ec 42.00N 86.00 E
Sinkiang (EN)= Xinjiang Uygur Zizhiqu (Hsin-chiang-wei-wu-erh Tzu-chih-ch'ü) [2] 27 Ec 42.00N 86.00 E
Sin-le-Noble 12 Fd 50.22N 3.07 E
Sinmi-Do 28 He 39.33N 124.53 E
Sinn 12 Kd 50.39N 8.20 E
Sinn al Kadhdhāb 33 Fe 23.30N 32.05 E
Sinnamary 54 Hb 5.23N 53.00W
Sinni 14 Kj 40.08N 16.41 E
Sînnicolau Mare 15 Dc 46.05N 20.38 E
Sinnūris 24 Dh 29.25N 30.52 E
Sinnyŏng 28 Jf 36.02N 128.47 E
Sinoe [3] 34 Dd 5.20N 8.40W
Sinoe, Lacul- 15 Le 44.38N 28.53 E
Sinoia 31 Kj 17.22S 30.12 E
Sinop 23 Ea 41.59N 35.09 E
Sinop Burun 24 Fa 42.02N 35.12 E
Sinp'o 28 Jd 40.02N 128.12 E
Sinsang 28 Ie 39.39N 127.25 E
Sinsheim 12 Eg 49.15N 8.53 E
Sint-Amandsberg, Gent- 12 Fc 51.04N 3.45 E
Sîntana 15 Ec 46.21N 21.30 E
Sint-Andries, Brugge- 12 Fc 51.12N 3.10 E
Sintang 26 Ff 0.04N 111.30 E
Sint Eustatius 47 Le 17.30N 62.59W
Sint-Gillis-Waas 12 Gc 51.13N 4.08 E
Sint Kruis 50 Bf 12.18N 69.08W
Sint Laureins 12 Fc 51.15N 3.31 E
Sint Maarten 50 Ec 18.04N 63.04W
Sint Nicolaas 50 Bf 12.26N 69.55W
Sint-Niklaas/Saint-Nicolas 11 Kc 51.10N 4.08 E
Sint-Oedenrode 12 Hc 51.34N 5.28 E
Sinton 45 Hl 28.02N 97.33W
Sint-Pieters-Leeuw 12 Gd 50.47N 4.14 E
Sintra 13 Cf 38.48N 9.23W
Sint-Truiden/Saint-Trond 11 Ld 50.49N 5.12 E
Sintu 35 Fd 8.12N 36.56 E
Sinú, Rio- 49 Ji 9.24N 75.49W
Sinŭiju 22 Oe 40.06N 124.24 E
Sinujiif 35 Hd 8.30N 48.59 E
Sinzig 12 Jd 50.33N 7.15 E
Sió 10 Oj 46.23N 18.40 E
Siocon 26 He 7.42N 122.08 E
Siófok 10 Oj 46.54N 18.03 E
Sioma 36 Df 16.40S 23.35 E

Index Symbols

[1] Independent Nation
[2] State, Region
[3] District, County
Municipality
Colony, Dependency
Continent
Physical Region
Historical or Cultural Region
Mount, Mountain
Volcano
Hill
Mountains, Mountain Range
Hills, Escarpment
Plateau, Upland
Pass, Gap
Plain, Lowland
Delta
Salt Flat
Valley, Canyon
Crater, Cave
Karst Features
Depression
Polder
Desert, Dunes
Forest; Woods
Heath, Steppe
Oasis
Cape, Point
Coast, Beach
Cliff
Peninsula
Isthmus
Sandbank
Island
Atoll
Rock, Reef
Islands, Archipelago
Rocks, Reefs
Coral Reef
Well, Spring
Geyser
River, Stream
Waterfall Rapids
River Mouth, Estuary
Lake
Salt Lake
Intermittent Lake
Reservoir
Swamp, Pond
Canal
Glacier
Ice Shelf, Pack Ice
Ocean
Sea
Gulf, Bay
Strait, Fjord
Lagoon
Bank
Seamount
Tablemount
Ridge
Shelf
Basin
Escarpment, Sea Scarp
Fracture
Trench, Abyss
National Park, Reserve
Point of Interest
Recreation Site
Cave, Cavern
Historic Site
Ruins
Wall, Walls
Church, Abbey
Temple
Scientific Station
Airport
Port
Lighthouse
Mine
Tunnel
Dam, Bridge

Index Symbols

[1] Independent Nation	Historical or Cultural Region	Pass, Gap	Depression	Coast, Beach	Rock, Reef	Waterfall Rapids	Canal	Lagoon	Escarpment, Sea Scarp	Historic Site	Port
[2] State, Region	Mount, Mountain	Plain, Lowland	Polder	Cliff	Islands, Archipelago	River Mouth, Estuary	Glacier	Bank	Fracture	Ruins	Lighthouse
[3] District, County	Volcano	Delta	Desert, Dunes	Peninsula	Rocks, Reefs	Lake	Ice Shelf, Pack Ice	Seamount	Trench, Abyss	Wall, Walls	Mine
[4] Municipality	Hill	Salt Flat	Forest, Woods	Isthmus	Coral Reef	Salt Lake	Ocean	Tablemount	National Park, Reserve	Church, Abbey	Tunnel
[5] Colony, Dependency	Mountains, Mountain Range	Valley, Canyon	Heath, Steppe	Sandbank	Well, Spring	Intermittent Lake	Sea	Ridge	Point of Interest	Temple	Dam, Bridge
Continent	Hills, Escarpment	Crater, Cave	Oasis	Island	Geyser	Reservoir	Gulf, Bay	Shelf	Recreation Site	Scientific Station	
Physical Region	Plateau, Upland	Karst Features	Cape, Point	Atoll	River, Stream	Swamp, Pond	Strait, Fjord	Basin	Cave, Cavern	Airport	

Index Symbols

[1] Independent Nation
[2] State, Region
[3] District, County
[4] Municipality
[5] Colony, Dependency
■ Continent
Physical Region

Historical or Cultural Region
Mount, Mountain
Volcano
Hill
Mountains, Mountain Range
Hills, Escarpment
Plateau, Upland

Pass, Gap
Plain, Lowland
Delta
Salt Flat
Valley, Canyon
Crater, Cave
Karst Features

Depression
Polder
Desert, Dunes
Forest, Woods
Heath, Steppe
Oasis
Cape, Point

Coast, Beach
Cliff
Peninsula
Isthmus
Sandbank
Island
Atoll

Rock, Reef
Islands, Archipelago
Rocks, Reefs
Coral Reef
Well, Spring
Geyser
River, Stream

Waterfall Rapids
River Mouth, Estuary
Lake
Salt Lake
Intermittent Lake
Sea
Ridge

Canal
Bank
Ice Shelf, Pack Ice
Ocean
Tablemount
Shelf
Basin

Lagoon
Glacier
Fracture
Trench, Abyss
National Park, Reserve
Point of Interest
Recreation Site

Escarpment, Sea Scarp
Ruins
Wall, Walls
Church, Abbey
Temple
Scientific Station
Airport

Historic Site
Port
Lighthouse
Mine
Tunnel
Dam, Bridge

Swamp, Pond
Strait, Fjord
Gulf, Bay
Reservoir
Cave, Cavern
Seamount
Shelf

Name	Pg	Grid	Lat	Long
South Korea (EN)=Taehan-Min'guk [1]	22	Of	38.00N	127.30 E
South Lake Tahoe	46	Eg	38.57N	120.01W
Southland [2]	62	Bf	45.45 S	168.00 E
South Loup River	45	Gf	41.04N	98.40W
South Lueti	36	Df	16.14S	23.12 E
South Magnetic Pole (1980)	66	Ie	65.08S	139.03 E
South Malosmadulu Atoll [o]	25a	Ba	5.10N	72.58 E
South Mountain	46	Ge	42.44N	116.54W
South Nahanni	42	Fd	61.03N	123.22W
South Negril Point	47	Ie	18.16N	78.22W
South Orkney Islands	66	Re	60.35S	45.30W
South Pass	38	Ie	42.22N	108.55W
South Pass [F.S.M.]	64d	Bb	7.14N	151.48 E
South Pass [U.S.]	45	Ll	28.55N	89.20W
South Platte	38	Ie	41.07N	100.42W
South Point	51q	Ab	13.02N	59.31W
South Pole	66	Bg	90.00S	0.00
South Porcupine	48	Ga	48.28N	81.13W
Southport [Eng.-U.K.]	9	Jh	53.39N	3.01W
Southport [N.C.-U.S.]	44	Hi	33.55N	78.01W
South Reef	63a	Ea	13.00S	160.32 E
South Ronaldsay	9	Kc	58.46N	2.50W
South Rukuru	36	Fe	10.44S	34.14 E
South Saint Paul	45	Jd	44.52N	93.02W
South Sandwich Islands	66	Ad	56.00S	26.30W
South Sandwich Trench (EN)	3	Do	56.30S	25.00W
South Saskatchewan River	38	Id	53.15N	105.05W
South Shetland Islands	66	Re	62.00S	58.00W
South Shields	9	Lg	55.00N	1.25W
South Sioux City	45	He	42.28N	96.24W
South Sister	46	Ed	44.12N	121.45W
South Taranaki Bight	62	Fc	39.40S	174.15 E
South Trap	62	Bg	47.30S	167.55 E
South Tyne	9	Kg	54.59N	2.08W
South Uist	9	Fd	57.15N	7.24W
South Umpqua River	46	De	43.20N	123.25W
Southwell	12	Ba	53.04N	0.57W
South Wellesley Islands	59	Hc	17.05S	139.25 E
South West Africa → Namibia [1]	31	Ik	22.00S	17.00 E
South West Cape	57	Hi	47.17S	167.27 E
South West Cape	59	Jh	43.34S	146.02 E
Southwest Cape	51a	Dc	17.42N	64.53W
Southwest Indian Ridge (EN)	3	Fm	32.00S	55.00 E
Southwest Miramichi River	44	Ob	46.50N	65.45W
Southwest Pacific Basin (EN)	3	Km	40.00S	150.00W
Southwest Pass	45	Ll	29.00N	89.20W
Southwest Point	49	Jb	22.10N	74.10W
South West Point	64g	Ab	1.52N	157.33W
South West Point	51p	Cb	12.27N	61.30W
Southwold	9	Oi	52.20N	1.40 E
South Yorkshire [3]	9	Lh	53.30N	1.25W
Soutpansberg	37	Dd	22.58S	29.50 E
Soverato	14	Kl	38.41N	16.33 E
Sovetabad	18	Gd	40.14N	69.42 E
Sovetsk [R.S.F.S.R.]	19	Ed	57.36N	48.58 E
Sovetsk [R.S.F.S.R.]	19	Cd	55.05N	21.52 E
Sovetskaja Gavan	22	Qe	48.58N	140.18 E
Sovetski [R.S.F.S.R.]	7	Lh	56.47N	48.30 E
Sovetski [R.S.F.S.R.]	8	Md	60.29N	28.40 E
Sovetski [R.S.F.S.R.]	19	Gc	61.20N	63.29 E
Sovetskoje	19	Ef	47.17N	44.30 E
Soviet Union EN) → Union of Soviet Socialist Republics(EN)	22	Jd	60.00N	80.00E
Şowghān	24	Qh	28.20N	56.54 E
Sowie, Góry-	10	Mf	50.38N	16.30 E
Sōya	29a	Ba	45.28N	141.53 E
Sōya-Kaikyō = La Perouse Strait (EN)	21	Qe	45.30N	142.00 E
Sōya-Misaki	27	Pb	45.31N	141.56 E
Soyatita	48	Fe	25.45N	107.22W
Soyo	36	Bd	6.05S	12.20 E
Sož	5	Je	51.57N	30.48 E
Sozopol	15	Kg	42.25N	27.42 E
Spa	11	Ld	50.29N	5.52 E
Spain (EN)=España [1]	5	Gf	40.00N	4.00W
Špakovskoje	16	Lg	45.06N	42.00 E
Spalding	9	Mi	52.47N	0.10W
Spanish Fork	46	Jf	40.07N	111.39W
Spanish Peak	46	Fd	44.24N	119.46W
Spanish Point	51d	Ba	17.33N	61.44W
Spanish Sahara (EN) → Western Sahara (EN) [5]	31	Ff	24.30N	13.00W
Spanish Town [B.V.I.]	51a	Db	18.27N	64.26W
Spanish Town [Jam.]	47	Ie	17.59N	76.57W
Sparbu	7	Ce	63.55N	11.28 E
Spargi, Isola-	14	Di	41.15N	9.20 E
Sparks	43	Dd	39.32N	119.45W
Sparreholm	8	Ge	59.04N	16.49 E
Sparta [Il.-U.S.]	45	Kf	38.07N	89.42W
Sparta [N.C.-U.S.]	44	Gg	36.30N	81.07W
Sparta [Tn.-U.S.]	44	Eh	35.56N	85.29W
Sparta [Wi.-U.S.]	45	Ke	43.57N	90.47W
Sparta (EN) = Spárti	15	Fl	37.05N	22.26 E
Spartanburg	44	Gg	34.57N	81.55W
Spartel, Cap-	30	Ge	35.48N	5.56W
Spárti = Sparta (EN)	15	Fl	37.05N	22.26 E
Spartivento, Capo- [It.]	14	Cl	38.53N	8.50 E
Spartivento, Capo- [It.]	5	Hh	37.55N	16.04 E
Spas-Demensk	16	Ib	54.24N	34.01 E
Spas-Klepiki	7	Ji	55.10N	40.13 E
Spassk-Rjazanski	7	Ji	54.27N	40.22 E
Spátha, Ákra- = Spatha, Cape- (EN)	15	Gn	35.42N	23.44 E
Spatha, Cape- (EN) = Spátha, Ákra-	15	Gn	35.42N	23.44 E
Spearfish	43	Gc	44.30N	103.52W
Spearman	45	Fh	36.12N	101.12W
Speedway	44	Dd	39.47N	86.15W
Speicher	12	Ie	49.56N	6.38 E
Speightstown	50	Gf	13.15N	59.39W
Speke Gulf	36	Fc	2.20S	33.15 E
Spello	14	Gh	42.59N	12.40 E
Spenard	40	Jd	61.11N	149.55W
Spence Bay	39	Jc	69.32N	93.31W
Spencer [Ia.-U.S.]	43	Hc	43.09N	95.09W
Spencer [In.-U.S.]	44	Df	39.17N	86.46W
Spencer [Nb.-U.S.]	45	Ge	42.53N	98.42W
Spencer [W.V.-U.S.]	44	Gf	38.48N	81.22W
Spencer, Cape-	59	Hg	35.18S	136.53 E
Spencer Gulf	57	Eh	34.00 S	137.00 E
Spenge	12	Kb	52.08N	8.29 E
Spenser Mountains	62	Ee	42.10S	172.35 E
Sperillen	8	Dd	60.30N	10.05 E
Sperkhiós	15	Fk	38.52N	22.34 E
Sperlonga	14	Hi	41.15N	13.26 E
Sperone, Capo-	14	Cl	38.55N	8.25 E
Sperrin Mountains/Sliabh Speirin	15	Fg	54.50N	7.05W
Spessart	10	Fg	49.55N	9.30 E
Spétsai	15	Gl	37.16N	23.09 E
Spétsai	15	Gl	37.16N	23.08 E
Spey	9	Jd	57.40N	3.06W
Spey Bay	9	Jd	57.40N	3.05W
Speyer	10	Eg	49.19N	8.26 E
Speyer-bach	12	Ke	49.19N	8.26 E
Speyside	50	Fg	11.18N	60.32W
Spezzano Albanese	14	Kk	39.40N	16.19 E
Spicer Islands	42	Jc	68.10N	79.00W
Spiekeroog	10	Dc	53.46N	7.42 E
Spiez	14	Bd	46.41N	7.42 E
Spijkenisse	12	Gc	51.51N	4.21 E
Spilimbergo	14	Gd	46.07N	12.54 E
Spilion	15	Hn	35.13N	24.32 E
Spilsby	12	Ca	53.11N	0.06 E
Spina	14	Gf	44.42N	12.08 E
Spinazzola	14	Kj	40.58N	16.05 E
Spincourt	12	He	49.20N	5.40 E
Spirit River	42	Fe	55.47N	118.50W
Spirovo	7	Ih	57.27N	35.01 E
Spiš	10	Qg	49.05N	20.30 E
Spišská Nová Ves	10	Qh	48.57N	20.34 E
Spitak	16	Ni	40.49N	44.14 E
Spitsbergen	67	Kd	78.00N	19.00 E
Spitsbergen	67	Hd	78.45N	16.00 E
Spittal an der Drau	14	Hd	46.48N	13.30 E
Spitzbergen Bank (EN)	41	Oc	76.00N	23.00 E
Split	14	If	43.31N	16.26 E
Split Lake	42	If	56.10N	96.10W
Spluga, Passo dello-	14	Dd	46.29N	9.20 E
Splügenpaß	14	Dd	46.29N	9.20 E
Spógi/Spogi	8	Lh	56.02N	26.52 E
Spógi/Spogi	8	Lh	56.02N	26.52 E
Spokane	39	He	47.40N	117.23W
Spokane, Mount-	46	Gc	47.55N	117.07W
Spokane River	46	Fc	47.44N	118.20W
Špola	19	Df	49.01N	31.24 E
Spoleto	14	Gh	42.44N	12.44 E
Spooner	45	Kd	45.50N	91.53W
Spoon River	45	Kf	40.18N	90.04W
Sporovo	10	Vd	52.25N	25.27 E
Spotsylvania	44	If	38.12N	77.35W
Sprague	46	Gc	47.18N	117.59W
Sprague River	46	Ee	42.34N	121.51W
Spray	46	Fd	44.50N	119.48W
Spreča	14	Mf	44.44N	18.06 E
Spree	10	Jd	52.32N	13.13 E
Spreewald	10	Je	51.55N	14.00 E
Spremberg/Grodk	10	Ke	51.33N	14.22 E
Sprengisandur	7a	Bb	64.48N	18.07W
Springbok	31	Ik	29.43S	17.15 E
Spring Creek	45	Fd	45.45N	100.08W
Springdale	45	Ih	36.11N	94.08W
Springe	10	Fd	52.13N	9.33 E
Springer	45	Dh	36.22N	104.36W
Springer, Mount-	44	Ja	49.48N	74.51W
Springerville	45	Ki	34.08N	109.17W
Springfield [Co.-U.S.]	45	Eh	37.24N	102.37W
Springfield [Il.-U.S.]	39	Jf	39.47N	89.40W
Springfield [Ma.-U.S.]	43	Mc	42.07N	72.36W
Springfield [Mn.-U.S.]	45	Jd	44.14N	94.59W
Springfield [Mo.-U.S.]	39	Jf	37.14N	93.17W
Springfield [N.Z.]	62	De	43.20S	171.56 E
Springfield [Oh.-U.S.]	43	Kd	39.55N	83.48W
Springfield [Or.-U.S.]	43	Cc	44.03N	123.01W
Springfield [S.D.-U.S.]	45	Ge	42.49N	97.54W
Springfield [Tn.-U.S.]	44	Dg	36.31N	86.52W
Springfontein	37	De	30.19S	25.36 E
Spring Garden	50	Gb	6.59N	58.31W
Spring Hall	51q	Ab	13.19N	59.36W
Springhill [La.-U.S.]	45	Jj	33.00N	93.28W
Springhill [N.S.-Can.]	42	Lg	45.39N	64.03W
Spring Mountains	46	Hh	36.10N	115.40W
Springsure	59	Jd	24.07S	148.05 E
Spring Valley	46	Hg	39.10N	114.30W
Spring Valley	45	Je	43.41N	92.23W
Springville	46	Je	40.10N	111.37W
Spruce Knob	44	Hf	38.42N	79.32W
Spruce Mountain [Az.-U.S.]				
Spruce Mountain [Nv.-U.S.]	46	Hf	40.33N	114.49W
Spulico, Capo-	14	Kk	39.58N	16.38 E
Spurn Head	12	Ca	53.34N	0.07 E
Squamish	46	Fg	49.42N	123.09W
Squillace	14	Kl	38.47N	16.31 E
Squillace, Golfo di-	14	Kl	38.45N	16.50 E
Squinzano	14	Mj	40.26N	18.02 E
Srbica	15	Df	42.46N	20.47 E
Srbija = Serbia (EN)	15	Df	44.00N	21.00 E
Srbija = Serbia (EN)	15	Df	44.00N	21.00 E
Srbija = Serbia (EN)	15	Ig	43.00N	21.00 E
Srbobran	15	Cd	45.33N	19.48 E
Srê Âmbêl	25	Kf	11.07N	103.46 E
Sredinny Hrebet	21	Rd	56.00N	158.00 E
Sredna Gora	15	Hg	42.30N	25.00 E
Srednekolymsk	20	Kc	67.27N	153.41 E
Srednerusskaja Vozvyšennost=Central Russian Uplands (EN)	5	Je	52.00N	38.00 E
Srednesatyginski Tuman, Ozero-	17	Lg	59.45N	65.25 E
Srednesibirskoje Ploskogorje = Central Siberian Uplands (EN)	21	Mc	65.00N	105.00 E
Sredni Kujto, Ozero-	7	Hd	65.05N	31.30 E
Sredni Ural=Central Urals (EN)	5	Ld	58.00N	59.00 E
Sredni Urgal	22	Pe	51.13N	132.58 E
Sredni Vereckij, Pereval-	16	Ce	48.49N	23.07 E
Srednjaja Ahtuba	16	Ne	48.43N	44.52 E
Srednjaja Olëkma	20	He	55.26N	120.40 E
Śrem	10	Nd	52.08N	17.01 E
Sremska Mitrovica	15	Ce	44.58N	19.37 E
Sremski Karlovci	15	Cd	45.12N	19.56 E
Sretensk	22	Nd	52.15N	117.43 E
Sri Gangānagar	25	Ec	29.55N	73.53 E
Srinagar	22	Jf	34.05N	74.49 E
Srikākulam	25	Ge	18.18N	83.54 E
Sri Lanka (Ceylon) [1]	22	Ki	7.40N	80.50 E
Srinagar	22	Jf	34.05N	74.49 E
Srivardhan	25	Ee	18.02N	73.01 E
Środa Śląska	10	Me	51.10N	16.36 E
Środa Wielkopolska	10	Nd	52.14N	17.17 E
Srpska Crnja	15	Dd	45.43N	20.42 E
Sruth na Maoile/North Channel	5	Fd	55.10N	5.40W
SSSR=Union of Soviet Socialist Republics (USSR) (EN) [1]	22	Jd	60.00N	80.00 E
SSSR → Sojuz Sovetskih Socialisticeskih Respublik [1]	22	Jd	60.00N	80.00 E
Ssu-ch'uan Sheng → Sichuan Sheng = Szechwan (EN) [2]	27	He	30.00N	103.00 E
Staaten River	59	Ic	16.24S	141.17 E
Stabroek	12	Gc	51.20N	4.22 E
Stack Skerry	9	Ib	59.02N	4.30W
Stade	12	Fc	53.36N	9.29 E
Staden	12	Fd	50.59N	3.01 E
Stadhavet	8	Ab	62.54N	5.00 E
Städjan	8	Ec	61.58N	12.52 E
Stadlandet	8	Ab	62.05N	5.20 E
Stadskanaal	11	Ma	53.00N	6.55 E
Stadthagen	12	Jb	52.56N	7.02 E
Stadskanaal-Musselkanaal	12	Lb	52.19N	9.12 E
Stadtkyll	10	Kf	50.21N	6.32 E
Stadtlohn	12	Ic	51.59N	6.56 E
Stadtoldendorf	10	Fe	51.54N	9.39 E
Staffa	9	Ge	56.25N	6.10W
Staffanstorp	8	Ei	55.38N	13.13 E
Staffelsee	10	Hi	47.42N	11.10 E
Staffora	14	De	45.04N	9.01 E
Stafford	9	Li	52.50N	2.00W
Stafford	9	Li	52.48N	2.07W
Stafford	9	Li	52.55N	2.00W
Staffordshire [3]	9	Li	52.55N	2.00W
Staicele/Stajcele	8	Lg	57.51N	24.44 E
Stainach	14	Ic	47.32N	14.06 E
Staines	12	Bc	51.26N	0.31W
Stajcele/Staicele	8	Lg	57.44N	24.39 E
Stakčin	5	Sg	49.00N	22.13 E
Stalać	15	Ef	43.40N	21.25 E
Stalham	12	Db	52.46N	1.31 E
Stalingrad → Volgograd	6	Kf	48.44N	44.25 E
Ställdalen	8	Fe	59.56N	14.56 E
Stalowa Wola	10	Sf	50.35N	22.02 E
Stamberger See	10	Ii	47.54N	11.19 E
Stamford [Ct.-U.S.]	44	Ke	41.03N	73.32W
Stamford [Eng.-U.K.]	9	Mi	52.39N	0.29W
Stamford [Tx.-U.S.]	45	Gj	32.57N	99.48W
Stamford, Lake-	45	Gj	33.05N	99.35W
Stampriet	37	Bd	24.20S	18.28 E
Stamsund	7	Cb	68.08N	13.51 E
Stanberry	45	If	40.13N	94.35W
Stancija Jakkabag	18	Fe	38.59N	66.42 E
Stancija-Karakul	19	Gh	39.30N	63.50 E
Standerton	37	De	26.58S	29.07 E
Standish	44	Fd	44.00N	83.57W
Stånga	8	Fg	57.17N	18.28 E
Stångån	8	Ff	58.27N	15.37 E
Stange	8	Dd	60.43N	11.11 E
Stanger	37	Ee	29.27S	31.14 E
Stanke Dimitrov	15	Gg	42.16N	23.07 E
Stanley [Austl.]	59	Jh	40.46S	145.18 E
Stanley [Falk. Is.]	53	Kk	51.42S	57.51W
Stanley [N.D.-U.S.]	45	Fb	48.19N	102.23W
Stanley Falls (EN) = Ngaliema, Chutes-	30	Jh	0.30N	25.30 E
Stann Creek	49	Ce	16.50N	88.30W
Stanovoj Hrebet=Stanovoy Range (EN)	21	Nd	56.00N	114.00 E
Stanovoy Range (EN) = Stanovoj Hrebet	21	Od	56.20N	126.00 E
Stanovoy Upland (EN) = Stanovoje Nagorje	21	Nd	56.00N	114.00 E
Stans	14	Cd	46.58N	8.22 E
Stansted Airport	12	Cc	51.54N	0.13 E
Stansted Mountfitchet	12	Cc	51.54N	0.12 E
Stanthorpe	59	Ke	28.39S	151.57 E
Stanton Banks	5	Fe	56.15N	7.50W
Staphorst	12	Ib	52.38N	6.14 E
Staples	45	Ic	46.21N	94.48W
Stapleton	45	Ff	41.29N	100.31W
Starachowice	10	Re	51.03N	21.04 E
Staraja Majna	19	Ue	54.34N	48.59 E
Staraja Russa	7	Hh	57.59N	31.23 E
Staraja-Vyževka	10	Ue	51.27N	24.34 E
Stará L'ubovňa	10	Qg	49.18N	20.42 E
Stara Moravica	15	Cd	45.52N	19.28 E
Stara Pazova	15	De	44.59N	20.10 E
Stara Planina = Balkan Mountains (EN)	5	Ig	43.15N	25.00 E
Stara Zagora [2]	15	Ig	42.25N	25.38 E
Stara Zagora	6	Ig	42.25N	25.38 E
Starbuck Island	57	Le	5.37 S	155.53W
Staretina	14	Kf	44.02N	16.43 E
Stargard Szczeciński	10	Lc	53.20N	15.02 E
Stari Begejski kanal	15	Dd	45.29N	20.25 E
Starica	7	Ih	56.30N	34.56 E
Starigrad	15	Df	43.23N	20.10 E
Stari Vlah	15	Df	43.23N	20.10 E
Starke	44	Fk	29.57N	82.07W
Starkville	45	Lj	33.28N	88.48W
Starnberg	10	Hh	48.00N	11.21 E
Starobelsk	19	Df	49.15N	38.58 E
Starodub	19	De	52.35N	32.46 E
Starogard Gdański	10	Oc	53.59N	18.33 E
Starokonstantinov	16	Ee	49.43N	27.13 E
Starominskaja	19	Df	46.31N	39.06 E
Staroščerbinovskaja	16	Kf	46.37N	38.42 E
Starosubhangulovo	17	Hj	53.06N	57.20 E
Starotimoškino	7	Lj	53.43N	47.32 E
Start Point	9	Jk	50.13N	3.38W
Staryje Dorogi	16	Fc	53.02N	28.17 E
Stary Krym	16	Kg	45.02N	35.05 E
Stary Oskol	19	De	51.18N	37.51 E
Stary Sambor	16	Ce	49.29N	23.01 E
Stary Terek	16	Og	44.01N	47.24 E
Staßfurt	10	He	51.52N	11.35 E
Staszów	10	Rf	50.34N	21.10 E
State College	44	Je	40.48N	77.52W
Staten Island (EN) = Estados, Isla de los-	52	Jk	54.47 S	64.15W
Statesboro	44	Gi	32.27N	81.47W
Statesville	44	Gh	35.47N	80.53W
Stathelle	8	Ce	59.03N	9.41 E
Stathmós Krioneríou	15	Ek	38.20N	21.35 E
Statland	7	Cd	64.30N	11.08 E
Staunton	44	Hf	38.10N	79.05W
Stavanger	6	Gd	58.58N	5.45 E
Stavelot	12	Hd	50.23N	5.56 E
Staveren	11	Lb	52.53N	5.22 E
Stavern	8	Df	59.00N	10.02 E
Stavnoje	10	Sh	48.59N	22.45 E
Stavropol	16	Kf	45.02N	41.59 E
Stavropolskaja Vozvyšennost	16	Mg	45.10N	43.00 E
Stavropolski Kraj [3]	19	Eg	45.00N	43.15 E
Stavrós [Grc.]	15	Fj	39.19N	22.14 E
Stavrós [Grc.]	15	Gi	40.40N	23.42 E
Stavroúpolis	15	Hh	41.12N	24.42 E
Stawell	59	Ig	37.04S	142.46 E
Stawiski	10	Sc	53.23N	22.09 E
Stawiszyn	10	Oe	51.55N	18.07 E
Stayton	46	Dd	44.48N	122.48W
Steamboat Springs	43	Fc	40.29N	106.50W
Stebnik	10	Tg	49.14N	23.34 E
Steele	45	Gc	46.51N	99.55W
Steelpoort	37	Ed	24.48S	30.12 E
Steenbergen	12	Gc	51.35N	4.19 E
Steen River	42	Fe	59.38N	117.06W
Steensby Inlet	42	Jb	70.10N	78.25W
Steenstrups Gletscher	41	Gc	75.15N	57.30W
Steenvoorde	12	Ed	50.48N	2.35 E
Steenwijk	11	Mb	52.47N	6.08 E
Ştefăneşti	15	Kb	47.48N	27.12 E
Stefanie, Lake- (EN) = Chew Bahir	30	Kh	4.38N	36.50 E
Stefansson	42	Gb	73.30N	105.30W
Ştefleşti, Virful-	15	Gd	45.32N	23.48 E
Stege	8	Ej	54.59N	12.18 E
Steiermark = Styria (EN)	14	Ic	47.15N	15.00 E
Steiermark = Styria (EN) [2]	14	Ic	47.15N	15.00 E
Steigerwald	10	Gg	49.40N	10.20 E
Steilrandberge	37	Ac	17.53S	13.20 E
Steinach	10	Hf	50.25N	11.08 E
Steinbach	42	Hg	49.32N	96.41W
Steinen, Rio-	54	Hf	12.05S	53.46W
Steinfeld (Oldenburg)	12	Kb	52.36N	8.13 E
Steinfort/Steinfurt	12	He	49.40N	5.55 E
Steinfurt/Steinfort	12	He	50.09N	7.20 E
Steinfurt-Borghorst	12	Jb	52.08N	7.25 E
Steinhagen	12	Kb	52.01N	8.24 E
Steinhausen	37	Bd	21.49S	18.20 E
Steinhuder Meer	10	Fd	52.28N	9.19 E
Steinkjer	7	Cd	64.01N	11.30 E
Steinkopf	37	Be	29.18S	17.43 E
Steinshamn	8	Bb	62.47N	6.29 E
Steinsøy	7	Ac	61.00N	4.30 E
Steirisch-Niederösterreichische Kalkalpen	14	Jc	47.45N	15.30 E
Stekene	12	Gc	51.12N	4.02 E
Stekolny	20	Ke	60.00N	150.50 E
Stella	37	Ce	26.33S	24.53 E
Stello	11a	Ba	42.47N	9.25 E
Stelvio, Passo dello-/Stilfer Joch	14	Ed	46.32N	10.27 E
Stemwede	12	Kb	52.28N	8.22 E
Stenay	12	He	49.29N	5.11 E
Stendal	10	Hd	52.36N	11.51 E
Stende	8	Ig	57.10N	22.38 E
Stende	8	Ig	57.40N	21.57 E
Stenhouse Bay	59	Hg	35.15S	136.56 E
Stenstorp	8	Ef	58.16N	13.43 E
Stenungsund	7	Cg	58.05N	11.49 E
Stepanakert	16	Ni	40.59N	46.44 E
Stepanavan	16	Ni	40.59N	44.20 E
Stephens, Cape-	62	Rg	40.42S	173.57 E
Stephens, Mount-	66	Rg	83.23S	51.27W
Stephens Passage	40	Me	57.50N	133.50W
Stephenville [Newf.-Can.]	42	Lg	48.33N	58.35W
Stephenville [Tx.-U.S.]	45	Gj	32.13N	98.12W
Steps Point	65c	Cb	14.22 S	170.45W
Sterea Ellás kai Évvoia [2]	15	Hk	38.20N	24.30 E
Sterkstroom	37	Df	31.32S	26.32 E
Sterlibaševo	17	Gj	53.05N	55.15 E
Sterling [Co.-U.S.]	43	Gc	40.37N	103.13W
Sterling [Il.-U.S.]	45	Lf	41.48N	89.42W
Sterling City	45	Fk	31.50N	100.59W
Sterlitamak	6	Lc	53.37N	55.58 E
Šternberk	10	Ng	49.45N	17.19 E
Sterzing / Vipiteno	14	Fd	46.54N	11.26 E
Stettin (EN) = Szczecin	6	He	53.24N	14.32 E
Stettiner Haff	10	Kc	53.46N	14.14 E
Stettler	42	Gf	52.19N	112.43W
Steubenville	43	Kc	40.22N	80.39W
Stevenage	9	Mj	51.54N	0.11W
Stevenson Entrance	40	Ie	57.45N	152.00W
Stevens Point	43	Jc	44.31N	89.34W
Stewart	42	Dd	63.18N	139.24W
Stewart	42	Dd	55.56N	129.59W
Stewart Crossing	42	Dd	63.19N	136.33W
Stewart Island	57	Hi	47.00S	167.50 E
Stewart Islands	57	He	8.20S	162.40 E
Steyerberg	12	Lb	52.34N	9.02 E
Steyning	12	Bd	50.53N	0.20W
Steynsburg	37	Df	31.15S	25.49 E
Steyr	14	Ib	48.03N	14.25 E
Steyr	14	Ib	48.03N	14.25 E
Ştiavnické vrchy	10	Oh	48.15N	18.50 E
Stidia	13	Li	35.50N	0.05W
Stiene	8	Kg	57.19N	24.28 E
Stiens, Leeuwarderadeel-	12	Ha	53.16N	5.46 E
Stigliano	14	Kj	40.24N	16.14 E
St. Ignace	43	Kb	45.52N	84.43W
Stigtomta	8	Gf	58.48N	16.47 E
Stikine	38	Df	56.40N	132.30W
Stikine Ranges	42	Ee	57.35N	131.00W
Stilfer Joch/Stelvio, Passo dello-	14	Ed	46.32N	10.27 E
Stilfontein	37	De	26.50S	26.50 E
Stilis	15	Fk	38.55N	22.37 E
Stillwater [Mn.-U.S.]	45	Jd	45.04N	92.49W
Stillwater [Ok.-U.S.]	43	Hd	36.07N	97.04W
Stillwater Range	46	Fg	39.50N	118.15W
Stilo	14	Kl	38.29N	16.28 E
Stilo, Punta-	14	Kl	38.27N	16.35 E
Štimlje	15	Eg	42.26N	21.03 E
Stínişoarei, Munţii-	15	If	47.20N	26.00 E
Stinnett	45	Fi	35.50N	101.27W
Štip	15	Fh	41.44N	22.12 E
Stirling	9	Je	56.07N	3.57W
Stirling Range	59	Bf	34.25S	117.50 E
Stjernøya	7	Fa	70.18N	22.45 E
Stjørdalshalsen	7	Ce	63.28N	10.44 E
Stobi	15	Eh	41.33N	21.59 E
Stobrawa	10	Nf	50.50N	17.32 E
Stockach	10	Fi	47.51N	9.01 E
Stockbridge	12	Ac	51.06N	1.29W
Stockerau	14	Kb	48.23N	16.13 E
Stockholm [2]	7	Dg	59.20N	18.00 E
Stockholm	6	Hd	59.20N	18.03 E
Stockport	9	Kh	53.25N	2.10W
Stocks Seamount (EN)	52	Mg	12.15N	37.00W
Stockton [Ca.-U.S.]	39	Gf	37.57N	121.17W
Stockton [Mo.-U.S.]	45	Jh	37.42N	93.48W
Stockton-on-Tees	9	Lg	54.34N	1.19W
Stockton Plateau	43	Gf	30.30N	102.30W
Stoczek Łukowski	10	Re	51.58N	21.58 E
Stöde	8	Fc	62.25N	16.35 E
Stoeng Trêng	25	Lf	13.31N	105.58 E
Stoer, Point of-	9	Hc	58.20N	5.25W
Stogovo	10	Ve	51.52N	25.44 E
Stoholm	8	Ch	56.29N	9.10 E
Stoj, Gora-	16	Ce	48.39N	23.15 E
Stoke-on-Trent	9	Kh	53.00N	2.10W
Stokksnes	7a	Cb	64.14N	14.58W
Stokmarknes	7	Db	68.34N	14.55 E
Stol	15	Fe	44.11N	22.09 E
Stolac	14	Lg	43.05N	17.58 E
Stolbcy	16	Ec	53.31N	26.43 E
Stolberg	10	Cf	50.46N	6.14 E
Stolbovoj, Ostrov-	20	Ib	74.05N	136.00 E
Stolin	16	Ec	51.57N	26.52 E
Stolzenau	12	Lb	52.31N	9.04 E
Ston	14	Lg	42.50N	17.42 E
Stone	9	Ki	52.54N	2.10W
Stonehaven	9	Ke	56.58N	2.13W
Stonehenge	9	Lj	51.11N	1.49W
Stonehenge	59	Id	24.22S	143.17 E
Stoner	45	Bh	37.37N	108.18W
Stonewall	45	Ic	50.09N	97.21W
Stony	40	Id	61.45N	156.35W
Stony Rapids	42	Gf	59.16N	105.50W
Stony River	40	Id	61.47N	156.41W
Stony Stratford	12	Bb	52.03N	0.51W
Stony Tunguska (EN) = Podkamennaja Tunguska	21	Lc	61.36N	90.18 E
Storå	10	Fc	53.50N	9.25 E
Storå	8	Ch	56.19N	8.18 E
Storå	7	Be	59.43N	15.08 E
Storå/Isojoki	7	Ee	62.07N	21.58 E
Stora Gla	8	Ee	59.30N	12.30 E
Stora Lulevatten	7	Db	67.08N	19.20 E
Storavan	8	Gb	65.42N	18.15 E
Storby	7	Ef	60.13N	19.34 E
Stord	6	Gd	59.55N	5.25 E
Storð	8	Ag	59.55N	5.22 E
Storð	8	Bb	62.23N	7.01 E

Index Symbols

- [1] Independent Nation
- [2] State, Region
- [3] District, County
- [4] Municipality
- [5] Colony, Dependency
- Continent
- Physical Region
- Historical or Cultural Region
- Mount, Mountain
- Volcano
- Hill
- Mountains, Mountain Range
- Hills, Escarpment
- Plateau, Upland
- Pass, Gap
- Plain, Lowland
- Delta
- Salt Flat
- Valley, Canyon
- Crater, Cave
- Karst Features
- Cape, Point
- Depression
- Polder
- Desert, Dunes
- Forest, Woods
- Heath, Steppe
- Oasis
- Coast, Beach
- Cliff
- Peninsula
- Isthmus
- Sandbank
- Island
- Atoll
- Rock, Reef
- Islands, Archipelago
- Rocks, Reefs
- Coral Reef
- Well, Spring
- Geyser
- River, Stream
- Waterfall Rapids
- River Mouth, Estuary
- Lake
- Salt Lake
- Intermittent Lake
- Reservoir
- Swamp, Pond
- Canal
- Glacier
- Ice Shelf, Pack Ice
- Ocean
- Sea
- Gulf, Bay
- Strait, Fjord
- Lagoon
- Bank
- Seamount
- Tablemount
- Ridge
- Shelf
- Basin
- Escarpment, Sea Scarp
- Fracture
- Trench, Abyss
- National Park, Reserve
- Point of Interest
- Recreation Site
- Scientific Station
- Airport
- Historic Site
- Ruins
- Wall, Walls
- Church, Abbey
- Temple
- Port
- Lighthouse
- Mine
- Tunnel
- Dam, Bridge

Store Bælt=Great Belt (EN) 5 Hd 55.30N 11.00 E
Storebro 8 Fg 57.35N 15.51 E
Storefiskbank 9 Qe 56.50N 4.00 E
Store Heddinge 8 Ei 55.19N 12.25 E
Store Hellefiske Bank (EN) 41 Ge 67.30N 55.00W
Store Koldewey 41 Kc 76.20N 18.30W
Store Kvien 8 Dc 61.34N 10.33 E
Støren 7 Ce 63.02N 10.18 E
Store Nupsfonn 8 Be 59.54N 7.08 E
Store Sølnkletten 8 Dc 61.59N 10.18 E
Storfjorden [Nor.] 8 Bb 62.25N 6.30 E
Storfjorden [Sval.] 41 Nc 77.30N 20.00 E
Storfors 8 Fe 59.32N 14.16 E
Storis Passage 42 Hc 67.40N 98.30W
Storkerson Bay 42 Fb 73.00N 124.00W
Storkerson Peninsula 42 Gb 73.00N 106.30W
Storlien 7 Ce 63.19N 12.06 E
Stormarn [3] 10 Gc 53.45N 10.20 E
Storm Bay 59 Jh 43.10S 147.30 E
Storm Lake 43 Hc 42.39N 95.13W
Stornoway 9 Gc 58.12N 6.23W
Storøya 41 Ob 80.08N 27.50 E
Storožinec 16 De 48.10N 25.46 E
Storsjøen [Nor.] 8 Dd 60.25N 11.40 E
Storsjøen [Nor.] 8 Dd 61.35N 11.15 E
Storsjön [Swe.] 8 Gd 60.35N 16.45 E
Storsjön [Swe.] 5 Hc 63.15N 14.20 E
Storsteinfjellet 7 Db 68.14N 17.52 E
Storstrøm [2] 8 Dj 55.00N 11.50 E
Storstrømmen 41 Jc 77.20N 23.00W
Storsudret 8 Hh 57.00N 18.15 E
Storuman 7 Dd 65.14N 16.54 E
Storuman 6 Hb 65.06N 17.06 E
Storvätteshågna 8 Eb 62.07N 12.27 E
Storvigelen 8 Eb 62.32N 12.04 E
Storvik 8 Gd 60.35N 16.32 E
Storvreta 8 Ge 59.58N 17.42 E
Stöttingfjället 7 Dd 64.38N 17.44 E
Stoughton 46 Nb 49.41N 103.03W
Stour [Eng.-U.K.] 9 Lk 50.43N 1.46W
Stour [Eng.-U.K.] 9 Oj 51.52N 1.16 E
Stourbridge 9 Ki 52.27N 2.09W
Støvring 8 Ch 56.53N 9.51 E
Stowmarket 12 Cb 52.11N 0.59 E
Strabane/An Srath Bán 9 Fg 54.49N 7.27W
Stradella 14 De 45.05N 9.18 E
Straelen 12 Ic 51.27N 6.16 E
Strakonice 10 Jg 49.16N 13.55 E
Straldža 15 Jg 42.36N 26.41 E
Stralsund 6 He 54.18N 13.06 E
Strand 37 Bf 34.06S 18.50 E
Stranda 7 Be 62.19N 6.54 E
Strand Bay 42 Ia 79.00N 94.00W
Strangford Lough/Loch Cuan 9 Hg 54.26N 5.36W
Strängnäs 8 Ge 59.23N 17.02 E
Stranraer 9 Hg 54.54N 5.02W
Strasbourg [Fr.] 6 Gf 48.35N 7.45 E
Strasbourg [Sask.-Can.] 46 Ma 51.04N 104.57W
Strašeny 16 Ff 47.06N 28.34 E
Straßwalchen 14 Hc 47.59N 13.15 E
Stratford [N.Z.] 62 Fc 39.21S 174.17 E
Stratford [Ont.-Can.] 44 Gd 43.22N 80.57W
Stratford [Tx.-U.S.] 45 Eh 36.20N 102.04W
Stratford-upon-Avon 9 Li 52.12N 1.41W
Strathclyde [3] 9 If 55.50N 4.50W
Strathgordon 59 Jh 42.54S 146.10 E
Strathmore 9 Je 56.40N 3.05W
Strathmore 46 Ia 51.03N 113.23W
Strathroy 44 Gd 42.57N 81.38W
Strathy Point 9 Ic 58.35N 4.01W
Straubenhardt 12 Kf 48.50N 8.34 E
Straubing 10 Ih 48.53N 12.34 E
Straumnes 7a Aa 66.26N 23.08W
Straumsjøen 7 Db 68.41N 14.30 E
Strausberg 10 Jd 52.35N 13.53 E
Strawberry Mountain 46 Fd 44.19N 118.43W
Strawberry River 46 Jf 40.10N 110.24W
Straža 15 Fg 42.15N 22.14 E
Stražica 15 If 43.14N 25.58 E
Strážiště 10 Kg 49.32N 14.58 E
Stražovské vrchy 10 Oh 48.55N 18.30 E
Streaky Bay 59 Gf 32.48S 134.13 E
Streaky Bay 59 Gf 32.35S 134.10 E
Streator 45 Lf 41.07N 88.50W
Středočeská pahorkatina 10 Kg 49.30N 14.15 E
Středočeský kraj [3] 10 Kg 49.55N 14.30 E
Středoslovenský kraj [3] 10 Ph 48.50N 19.10 E
Strehaia 15 Ge 44.37N 23.12 E
Strei 15 Gd 45.51N 23.03 E
Střela 10 Jg 49.54N 13.32 E
Strelasund 10 Jb 54.20N 13.05 E
Strelka 20 Ee 58.03N 93.05 E
Strelna 7 Jc 66.04N 38.39 E
Strenči 7 Fh 57.39N 25.38 E
Stresa 14 Ce 45.53N 8.32 E
Streževoj 20 Cd 60.42N 77.35 E
Stříbro 10 Ig 49.46N 13.00 E
Strickland River 59 Ia 6.00S 142.05 E
Strîmbeni 15 He 44.28N 24.58 E
Strimón 15 Gi 40.47N 23.51 E
Strimonikós Kólpos 15 Gi 40.40N 23.50 E
Strjama 15 Hg 42.10N 24.56 E
Strofádhes, Nisoi- 15 Dl 37.15N 21.00 E
Ströhen, Wagenfeld- 12 Kb 52.32N 8.39 E
Stromberg 12 Je 49.57N 7.46 E
Stromboli 14 Jl 38.45N 15.15 E
Strömfors/Ruotsinpyhtää 8 Ld 60.32N 26.27 E
Stromness 9 Jc 58.57N 3.18W
Strömsbro 8 Gd 60.42N 17.10 E
Strömsbruk 7 Dc 61.53N 17.19 E
Strömsnäsbruk 8 Eh 56.33N 13.43 E
Strömstad 7 Cf 58.56N 11.10 E
Strömsund 7 De 63.51N 15.35 E
Strongili 15 Hm 36.58N 24.55 E
Stròngoli 14 Lk 39.16N 17.03 E
Stronsay 9 Kb 59.08N 2.38W
Stropkov 10 Rg 49.12N 21.40 E
Stroud 9 Kj 51.45N 2.12W
Struer 7 Bh 56.29N 8.37 E
Struga 15 Dh 41.11N 20.41 E
Strugi-Krasnyje 7 Gg 58.17N 29.08 E
Strule 9 Fg 54.40N 7.20W
Struma 5 Ig 40.47N 23.51 E
Strumble Head 9 Hi 52.02N 5.04W
Strumica 15 Fh 41.26N 22.39 E
Stry 16 De 49.24N 24.13 E
Stry 19 Cf 49.14N 23.49 E
Strydenburg 37 Ce 29.58S 23.40 E
Stryn 7 Bf 61.55N 6.47 E
Strynsvatn 8 Bc 61.55N 7.05 E
Strzegom 10 Mf 50.57N 16.21 E
Strzegomka 10 Me 51.08N 16.50 E
Strzelce Krajeńskie 10 Ld 52.53N 15.32 E
Strzelce Opolskie 10 Of 50.31N 18.19 E
Strzelin 10 Nf 50.47N 17.03 E
Strzelno 10 Od 52.38N 18.11 E
Strzyżów 10 Rg 49.52N 21.47 E
Stuart 40 Gd 63.35N 162.30W
Stuart, Mount- 46 Ec 47.29N 120.54W
Stuart Bluff Range 59 Gd 22.45S 132.15 E
Stuart Lake 42 Ff 54.33N 124.35W
Stuart Range 59 Ge 29.10S 134.55 E
Stubaier Alpen 14 Fc 47.10N 11.05 E
Stubbekøbing 8 Ej 54.43N 12.03 E
Stubbenkammer 10 Jb 54.35N 13.40 E
Stubbs Bay 51n Ba 13.08N 61.10W
Štubik 15 Fe 44.18N 22.21 E
Stucka 7 Fh 56.36N 25.17 E
Studenica, Manastir- 15 Df 43.28N 20.37 E
Studholme Junction 62 Df 44.44S 171.08 E
Stugun 7 De 63.10N 15.36 E
Stuhr 12 Ka 53.02N 8.45 E
Stupino 7 Ji 54.57N 38.03 E
Stura di Demonte 14 Bf 44.40N 7.53 E
Stura di Lanzo 14 Be 45.06N 7.44 E
Sturge Island 66 Ke 67.27S 164.18 E
Sturgeon Bay 45 Md 44.50N 87.23W
Sturgeon Falls 42 Jg 46.22N 79.55W
Sturgeon Lake 45 Kb 50.00N 90.45W
Sturgis [Mi.-U.S.] 44 Ee 41.48N 85.25W
Sturgis [S.D.-U.S.] 45 Ed 44.25N 103.31W
Sturkö 8 Fh 56.05N 15.40 E
Sturt Creek 59 Fd 20.08S 127.24 E
Sturt Desert 59 Ie 28.30S 141.00 E
Stutterheim 37 Df 32.33S 27.28 E
Stuttgart [Ar.-U.S.] 45 Ki 34.30N 91.33W
Stuttgart [F.R.G.] 6 Gf 48.46N 9.11 E
Stviga 16 Ec 52.04N 27.55 E
Stykkishólmur 7a Ab 65.04N 22.44W
Styr 19 Ce 52.07N 26.35 E
Styria (EN) = Steiermark 14 Ic 47.15N 15.00 E
Styria (EN) = Steiermark [2] 14 Ic 47.15N 15.00 E
Styrsö 8 Dg 57.37N 11.46 E
Suafa Point 63a Ec 8.19S 160.41 E
Suai 26 Ih 9.21S 125.17 E
Suakin Archipelago (EN) = Sawākin, Jazā'ir- 30 Kg 19.07N 37.20 E
Suao 27 Lg 24.36N 121.51 E
Suardi 55 Bj 30.32S 61.58W
Suavanao 60 Fi 7.34S 158.44 E
Subačius/Subačjus 8 Ki 55.44N 24.53 E
Subačius/Subačius 8 Ki 55.44N 24.53 E
Subang 26 Eh 6.34S 107.45 E
Subansiri 25 Jc 26.48N 93.49 E
Subao Ding 27 Jf 27.10N 110.18 E
Šubarkuduk 19 Ff 49.09N 56.31 E
Šubarši 16 Te 48.38N 57.12 E
Subate 8 Lh 56.01N 26.04 E
Subay', 'Urūq- 33 He 22.15N 43.05 E
Subayṭilah 32 Ib 35.14N 9.08 E
Subbético, Sistema- 13 Jf 38.30N 2.30W
Subei (Dangchengwan) 27 Fd 39.36N 94.58 E
Subi, Pulau- 26 Ef 2.55N 108.50 E
Subiaco 14 Hi 41.55N 13.06 E
Sublette 45 Fh 37.29N 100.50W
Submeseta Norte 5 Fg 42.20N 4.50W
Submeseta Sur 5 Fh 39.30N 3.30W
Subotica 15 Cc 46.06N 19.40 E
Subpolar Urals (EN) = Pripoljarny Ural 5 Lb 65.00N 60.00 E
Subugo 36 Gc 1.40S 35.49 E
Suceava 15 Jb 47.32N 26.32 E
Suceava [2] 15 Ib 47.40N 25.45 E
Suceava 15 Jb 47.38N 26.15 E
Sucha Beskidzka 10 Pg 49.44N 19.36 E
Süchbaatar → Suhe-Bator 22 Md 50.15N 106.12 E
Suchedniów 10 Qe 51.03N 20.51 E
Suchiapa, Río- 48 Mi 16.36N 93.01W
Suchitepéquez [3] 49 Bf 14.25N 91.20W
Sucia, Bahía- 51a Ac 17.57N 67.10W
Sucio, Río- 49 Ij 7.27N 77.07W
Suck/An tSuca 9 Eh 53.16N 8.03W
Suckling, Mount- 59 Ja 9.45S 148.55 E
Sucre [Bol.] 53 Jg 19.02S 65.17W
Sucre [Col.] [2] 54 Db 9.00N 75.00W
Sucre [Col.] 54 Db 8.50N 74.43W
Sucre [Ven.] [2] 54 Fa 10.25N 63.30W
Suçuarana, Serra da- 55 Jb 14.25S 45.00W
Sucunduri, Rio- 54 Ge 5.30S 59.40W
Sućuraj 14 Lg 43.08N 17.12 E
Sucuriú, Rio- 54 Hh 20.47S 51.38W
Sud, Canal du- 49 Kd 18.40N 73.05W
Sud, Massif du- 49 Kd 18.25N 73.55W
Suda 7 Ig 59.11N 37.33 E
Suda 7 Ig 59.12N 37.30 E
Sudak 19 Dg 44.50N 34.59 E
Sudan 30 Ig 11.30N 15.00 E
Sudan (EN) = As Sūdān [1] 31 Jg 15.00N 30.00 E
Sudbury [Eng.-U.K.] 9 Ni 52.02N 0.44 E
Sudbury [Ont.-Can.] 39 Ke 46.30N 81.00W
Suddie 50 Gi 7.07N 58.29W
Sude 10 Gc 53.22N 10.45 E
Sudeten (EN) 5 He 50.30N 16.00 E
Sudirman, Pegunungan- 26 Kg 4.12S 137.00 E
Sudočje, Ozero- 18 Bc 43.25N 58.30 E
Sudogda 7 Ji 55.59N 40.50 E
Sudost 16 Hc 52.19N 33.24 E
Sud-Ouest [Cam.] [3] 34 Gd 5.20N 9.20 E
Sud-Ouest [U.V.] [3] 34 Ec 10.30N 3.15W
Sudovaja Višnja 10 Tg 49.43N 23.26 E
Südradde 12 Jb 52.41N 7.34 E
Südtirol / Trentino-Alto Adige [2] 14 Fd 46.30N 11.20 E
Sudža 16 Id 51.13N 35.16 E
Sue 30 Jh 7.41N 28.03 E
Sueca 13 Le 39.12N 0.19W
Suess Land 41 Jd 72.45N 26.00W
Suez (EN) = As Suways 31 Kf 29.58N 32.33 E
Suez, Gulf of-(EN) = Suways, Khalīj as- 30 Kf 28.10N 33.27 E
Suez Canal (EN) = Suways, Qanāt as- 30 Ke 29.55N 32.33 E
Suffolk 9 Ni 52.25N 1.00 E
Suffolk 43 Ld 36.44N 76.37W
Suffolk [3] 9 Li 52.10N 1.05W
Sufiān 24 Kc 38.17N 45.59 E
Sugana, Val- 14 Fd 46.00N 11.40 E
Suga-no-Sen 29 Dd 35.22N 134.31 E
Sugar Island 44 Eb 46.25N 84.12W
Sugarloaf Mountain 44 Lc 45.01N 70.22W
Suğla Gölü 24 Ed 37.20N 32.02 E
Sugoj 20 Kd 64.15N 154.29 E
Suguta 36 Gb 2.03N 36.33 E
Suha 15 Ke 44.08N 27.36 E
Suhai Hu 27 Fd 38.55N 94.05 E
Şuḩār 23 Ie 24.22N 56.45 E
Suhe-Bator (Süchbaatar) 22 Md 50.15N 106.12 E
Suhiniči 16 Ib 54.06N 35.20 E
Suhl 10 Gf 50.36N 10.42 E
Suhl [2] 10 Gf 50.35N 10.40 E
Suhodolskoje, Ozero- 8 Nd 60.35N 30.30 E
Suhoj Log 17 Kh 56.55N 62.01 E
Suhona 5 Kc 60.46N 46.24 E
Suhr 14 Cc 47.25N 8.04 E
Suhumi 6 Kg 43.01N 41.02 E
Suhurlui 15 Kd 45.25N 27.35 E
Suiá-Missu, Rio- 54 Hf 11.13S 53.15W
Suibara 29 Fc 37.50N 139.12 E
Suichang 27 Kf 28.34N 119.15 E
Suid Africa / South Africa [1] 31 Jl 30.00S 26.00 E
Suide 27 Jd 37.28N 110.15 E
Suifen He 28 Kc 43.20N 131.49 E
Suifenhe 27 Nc 44.25N 131.09 E
Sui He 28 Eh 33.29N 118.06 E
Suihua 27 Mb 46.38N 126.57 E
Suijiang 27 Hf 28.37N 104.00 E
Suileng 27 Mb 47.17N 127.08 E
Suining [China] 27 Ie 30.30N 105.34 E
Suining [China] 28 Dh 33.54N 117.56 E
Suipacha 55 Cl 34.45S 59.41W
Suiping 28 Bh 33.09N 113.59 E
Suippe 11 Je 49.25N 3.57 E
Suippes 11 Ke 49.08N 4.32 E
Suir/An tSiúir 9 Gi 52.15N 7.00W
Suisse / Svizra / Svizzera / Schweiz = Switzerland (EN) [1] 6 Gf 46.00N 8.30 E
Suisse Normande 12 Bf 48.53N 0.50W
Suita 29 Dd 34.45N 135.32 E
Suixi 28 Dh 33.55N 116.47 E
Suixian [China] 28 Cg 34.25N 115.04 E
Suixian [China] 27 Je 31.44N 113.25 E
Suiyang 28 Kb 44.26N 130.53 E
Suizhong 27 Lc 40.21N 120.20 E
Suj 27 Ic 42.12N 108.01 E
Šuja 7 If 61.54N 34.15 E
Šuja [R.S.F.S.R.] 7 If 61.59N 34.15 E
Šuja [R.S.F.S.R.] 19 Ed 56.52N 41.23 E
Sujer 17 Li 55.59N 65.47 E
Suji → Haixing 28 De 38.10N 117.29 E
Sujstamo 8 Nc 61.49N 31.05 E
Sukabumi 26 Eh 6.55S 106.56 E
Sukadana 26 Eg 1.15S 109.57 E
Sukagawa 28 Pf 37.17N 140.23 E
Sukaja 26 Fg 7.27S 108.12 E
Sukeva 7 Ge 63.54N 27.26 E
Sukhothai 25 Je 17.01N 99.49 E
Suki 35 Ec 13.23N 33.58 E
Sukkertoppen/Manitsoq 41 Ge 65.25N 53.00W
Sukkozero 19 Dc 63.09N 32.23 E
Sukkur 22 Ig 27.42N 68.52 E
Sukon 26 Hg 0.56S 123.10 E
Sukses 37 Bd 21.01S 16.52 E
Suksun 17 Hh 57.07N 57.24 E
Sukumo 27 Ne 32.56N 132.44 E
Sukumo-Wan 29 Ce 32.55N 132.40 E
Sul, Baía- 55 Hh 27.40S 48.35W
Sul, Canal do- 54 Id 0.10S 49.30W
Sula [Nor.] 7 Af 61.10N 4.55 E
Sula [Nor.] 8 Bb 62.25N 6.10 E
Sula [R.S.F.S.R.] 7 Ld 64.41N 47.46 E
Sula [R.S.F.S.R.] 17 Fc 67.16N 52.07 E
Sula [Ukr.-U.S.S.R.] 16 He 49.40N 32.43 E
Sula, Kepulauan- = Sulu Islands (EN) 57 De 1.52S 125.22 E
Sulaimāniya 23 Gb 35.33N 45.26 E
Sūlaimaniya [3] 24 Ke 35.40N 45.30 E
Sulaimān Range 21 Jf 30.30N 70.10 E
Sulak 16 Oh 43.17N 47.31 E
Sulak 19 Eg 43.17N 47.34 E
Sula Sgeir 9 Gb 59.05N 6.10W
Sulawesi/Celebes 21 Oj 2.00S 121.10 E
Sulawesi, Laut- = Celebes Sea (EN) 21 Oj 3.00N 122.00 E
Sulawesi Selatan [3] 26 Gg 4.00S 120.00 E
Sulawesi Tengah [3] 26 Hg 1.00S 121.00 E
Sulawesi Tenggara [3] 26 Hg 4.00S 122.30 E
Sulawesi Utara [3] 26 Hf 1.00N 123.00 E
Sulaymān 14 En 36.42N 10.30 E
Sulb 35 Ea 20.26N 30.20 E
Sulcis 14 Ck 39.05N 8.40 E
Suldalsvatn 8 Be 59.35N 6.45 E
Süldeh 24 Od 36.34N 52.01 E
Sulechów 10 Ld 52.06N 15.37 E
Sulęcin 10 Ld 52.26N 15.08 E
Suleja 17 Ii 55.11N 58.50 E
Sulejów 10 Pe 51.22N 19.53 E
Süleoğlu 15 Jh 41.46N 26.55 E
Sule Skerry 9 Ib 59.10N 4.10W
Sulima 34 Cd 6.58N 11.35W
Sulina 15 Md 45.09N 29.40 E
Sulina, Bratul- 15 Md 45.09N 29.41 E
Sulingen 10 Ed 52.41N 8.48 E
Sulitjelma 7 Dc 67.09N 16.03 E
Sulitjelma 7 Dc 67.08N 16.24 E
Suljukta 19 Gh 39.56N 69.37 E
Sulkava 7 Gf 61.47N 28.23 E
Sullana 53 Hf 4.53S 80.42W
Süller 15 Mk 38.09N 29.29 E
Sullivan [In.-U.S.] 44 Df 39.06N 87.24W
Sullivan [Mo.-U.S.] 45 Kg 38.13N 91.10W
Sullivan Lake 46 Ja 52.00N 112.00W
Sully-sur-Loire 11 Ig 47.46N 2.22 E
Sulmona 14 Hh 42.03N 13.55 E
Sulphur [La.-U.S.] 45 Jk 30.14N 93.23W
Sulphur [Ok.-U.S.] 45 Hi 34.31N 96.58W
Sulphur Creek 45 Ed 44.46N 102.25W
Sulphur River 45 Jj 33.07N 93.52W
Sulphur Springs 45 Ij 33.08N 95.36W
Sulphur Springs Draw 45 Fj 32.12N 101.36W
Sultandağı 24 Dc 38.32N 31.14 E
Sultan Dağları 24 Dc 38.20N 31.20 E
Sultanhanı 24 Ec 38.15N 33.33 E
Sultanhisar 15 Ll 37.53N 28.10 E
Sultānpur 25 Gc 26.16N 82.04 E
Sulu Archipelago 21 Oi 6.00N 121.00 E
Sulu Basin (EN) 26 Ge 8.00N 121.30 E
Sulu Islands (EN) = Sula, Kepulauan- 57 De 1.52S 125.22 E
Suluova 24 Fb 40.47N 35.42 E
Sulūq 33 Dc 31.40N 20.15 E
Sulu Sea 21 Ni 9.00N 120.00 E
Sulz am Neckar 10 Eh 48.21N 8.37 E
Sulzbach (Saar) 12 Je 49.18N 7.04 E
Sulzbach-Rosenberg 10 Hg 49.30N 11.45 E
Sulzberger Bay 66 Mf 77.00S 152.00W
Šumadija 15 De 44.20N 20.40 E
Sumalata 26 Hf 0.59N 122.30 E
Sumāmus 24 Nd 36.50N 50.30 E
Šumanaj 18 Bc 42.37N 58.55 E
Sumatera = Sumatra (EN) 21 Mj 0.01N 102.00 E
Sumatera Barat [3] 26 Dg 1.00S 100.30 E
Sumatera Selatan [3] 26 Dg 3.30S 104.00 E
Sumatera Utara [3] 26 Cf 2.00N 99.00 E
Sumatra (EN) = Sumatera 21 Mj 0.01N 102.00 E
Šumava = Bohemian Forest (EN) 5 Hf 49.00N 13.30 E
Sumayr 33 Hf 17.47N 41.26 E
Sumba, Pulau- 21 Nj 10.00S 120.00 E
Sumba, Selat- = Sumba Strait (EN) 26 Hh 9.05S 120.00 E
Sumbar 16 Jj 38.00N 55.15 E
Sumba Strait (EN) = Sumba, Selat- 26 Hh 9.05S 120.00 E
Sumbawa, Pulau- 21 Nj 8.40S 118.00 E
Sumbawa Besar 26 Gh 8.30S 117.26 E
Sumbawanga 36 Fd 7.58S 31.37 E
Sumber 27 Ib 46.21N 108.20 E
Sumbi Point 63a Cb 7.19S 157.04 E
Sumbu 36 Fd 8.31S 30.29 E
Sumburgh Head 9 Lb 59.51N 1.16W
Sumedang 26 Eh 6.52S 107.55 E
Šūme'eh Sarā 24 Md 37.18N 49.19 E
Sümeg 10 Nj 46.59N 17.17 E
Šumen 15 Jf 43.16N 26.55 E
Šumen [2] 15 Jf 43.20N 27.00 E
Sumenep 26 Fh 7.01S 113.52 E
Šumerlja 6 Kd 55.30N 46.26 E
Sumgait 16 Pi 40.37N 49.37 E
Sumgait 6 Kg 40.33N 49.40 E
Sumidouro, Rio- 55 Da 13.28S 56.39W
Šumiha 19 Gd 55.14N 63.19 E
Sumkino 19 Gd 58.09N 68.21 E
Summer, Lake- [N.M.-U.S.] 45 Di 34.38N 104.26W
Summer, Lake- [N.Z.] 62 Ee 42.40S 172.15 E
Summer Lake 46 Ee 42.50N 120.45W
Summerland 46 Fb 49.39N 119.33W
Summerside 42 Lg 46.24N 63.47W
Summersville 44 Gf 38.17N 80.52W
Summerville 44 Eh 34.29N 85.21W
Summit Lake 42 Fe 54.17N 122.38W
Summit Mountain 46 Gg 39.23N 116.28W
Summit Peak 45 Ch 37.21N 106.42W
Sumoto 29 Dd 34.20N 134.54 E
Šumperk 10 Mg 49.58N 16.59 E
Sumprabum 25 Jc 26.33N 97.34 E
Sumsar 18 Hd 41.13N 71.23 E
Šumskaja Oblast [3] 19 De 51.00N 34.15 E
Šumšu, Ostrov- 20 Kf 50.45N 156.20 E
Sumter 43 Ke 33.55N 80.20W
Sumuştā al Waqf 24 Dh 28.55N 30.51 E
Sumy 6 Je 50.54N 34.48 E
Suna 7 Mh 57.53N 50.07 E
Suna 7 Ie 62.08N 34.12 E
Sunagawa 28 Pc 43.29N 145.55 E
Sunak, Gora- 19 Hf 47.05N 72.35 E
Sunan 28 He 39.15N 125.40 E
Sunan (Hongwansi) 27 Gd 38.59N 99.25 E
Sunart, Loch- 9 He 56.45N 5.45W
Sunaysilah 24 Ie 35.35N 41.53 E
Sunburst 46 Jb 48.53N 111.55W
Sunbury 44 Ie 40.52N 76.47W
Sunchales 56 Hd 30.56S 61.34W
Suncho Corral 56 Hc 27.56S 63.27W
Sunch'ŏn [N. Kor.] 27 Me 34.57N 127.29 E
Sunch'ŏn [S. Kor.] 27 Md 39.25N 125.56 E
Sun City 46 Ij 33.36N 112.17W
Suncun → Xinwen 27 Kd 35.49N 117.38 E
Sunda, Selat- = Sunda Strait (EN) 21 Mj 6.00S 105.45 E
Sundance 46 Md 44.24N 104.23W
Sundarbans 25 Hd 22.00N 89.00 E
Sundargarh 25 Gd 22.07N 84.02 E
Sunda Strait (EN) = Sunda, Selat- 21 Mj 6.00S 105.45 E
Sunday Strait 59 Ec 16.20S 123.15 E
Sundborn 8 Fd 60.39N 15.46 E
Sundbron 8 Ha 63.01N 18.11 E
Sundbyberg 8 Ge 59.22N 17.58 E
Sunde 7 Ag 59.50N 5.43 E
Sunderland 9 Lg 54.55N 1.23W
Sundern (Sauerland) 12 Kc 51.20N 8.00 E
Sundgau 11 Ng 47.40N 7.15 E
Sündiken Dağları 24 Dc 39.55N 31.00 E
Sundridge 44 Hc 45.46N 79.24W
Sundsvall 6 Hc 62.23N 17.18 E
Sundsvallsbukten 8 Gb 62.20N 17.35 E
Sunflower, Mount- 45 Eg 39.04N 102.01W
Sungaidareh 26 Dg 0.58S 101.30 E
Sungaigerong 26 Dg 2.59S 104.52 E
Sungaiguntung 26 Df 0.18N 103.37 E
Sungai Kolok 25 Kg 6.02N 101.58 E
Sungai Lembing 26 Df 3.55N 103.02 E
Sungailiat 26 Eg 1.51S 106.08 E
Sungaipenuh 26 Dg 2.05S 101.23 E
Sungai Petani 26 De 5.39N 100.30 E
Sungai Siput 26 Df 4.49N 101.04 E
Sungari (EN) = Songhua Jiang 21 Pe 47.42N 132.30 E
Sungqu → Songpan 27 He 32.37N 103.34 E
Sungurlu 24 Fb 40.10N 34.23 E
Sunharon Roads 64b Bb 14.57N 145.36 E
Suning 28 Ce 38.25N 115.50 E
Sunja 14 Ke 45.21N 16.33 E
Sunjiapuzi 28 Ic 42.02N 126.34 E
Sunkar, Gora- 18 Ib 44.12N 73.55 E
Sun Kosi 25 Hc 26.55N 87.09 E
Sunnadalsøra 7 Be 62.40N 8.33 E
Sunnan 7 Cd 64.04N 11.38 E
Sunndalen 8 Cb 62.40N 8.45 E
Sunndalsfjorden 8 Cb 62.45N 8.25 E
Sunne 7 Cg 59.50N 13.09 E
Sunnerbo 8 Eh 56.45N 13.50 E
Sunnersta 8 Ge 59.48N 17.39 E
Sunnfjord 8 Ac 61.25N 5.20 E
Sunnhordland 8 Ae 59.55N 6.00 E
Sunnmøre 8 Bb 62.20N 6.40 E
Sunnyside 46 Fc 46.20N 120.00W
Sunnyvale 46 Dh 37.23N 122.01W
Su-no-Zaki 29 Fd 34.58N 139.45 E
Sun River 46 Jc 47.30N 111.25W
Sunsas, Serrania de- 55 Cc 17.57S 59.35W
Suntar 20 Gd 62.04N 117.40 E
Suntar-Hajata, Hrebet- = Suntar-Khayata Range (EN) 21 Qc 62.00N 143.00 E
Suntar-Khayata Range (EN) = Suntar-Hajata, Hrebet- 21 Qc 62.00N 143.00 E
Suntaži 8 Kh 56.49N 24.57 E
Sun Valley 43 Ec 43.42N 114.21W
Sunwu 27 Mb 49.27N 127.19 E
Sunyani 31 Gh 7.20N 2.20W
Sunža 16 Oh 43.33N 46.08 E
Suojarvi 19 Dc 62.04N 32.21 E
Suokonmäki 8 Kb 62.47N 24.30 E
Suolahti 7 Fe 62.34N 25.52 E
Suomenlahti = Finland, Gulf of- (EN) 5 Ic 60.00N 27.00 E
Suomenniemi 8 Lc 61.19N 27.27 E
Suomenselkä 5 Ic 62.50N 25.00 E
Suomi/Finland [1] 6 Ic 64.00N 26.00 E
Suomussalmi 7 Gd 64.54N 29.00 E
Suō-Nada 29 Be 33.50N 131.30 E
Suonenjoki 7 Ge 62.37N 27.08 E
Suontee 8 Lc 61.40N 26.35 E
Suordah 20 Ic 66.43N 132.04 E
Suozhen → Huantai 28 Ef 36.57N 118.05 E
Supamo, Río- 50 Fi 6.48N 61.50W
Superior [Az.-U.S.] 46 Jj 33.18N 110.06W
Superior [Mt.-U.S.] 46 Hc 47.12N 114.53W
Superior [Nb.-U.S.] 45 Gf 40.01N 98.04W
Superior [Wi.-U.S.] 39 Je 46.44N 92.05W
Superior, Lake- 38 Ke 48.00N 88.00W
Suphan Buri 25 Kf 14.29N 100.10 E
Süphan Dağı 23 Fb 38.54N 42.48 E
Supiori, Pulau- 26 Kg 0.45S 135.30 E
Supoj 16 Ge 49.38N 31.50 E
Support Force Glacier 66 Rg 83.05S 47.30W
Suprasl 10 Tc 53.13N 23.20 E
Supraśl 10 Sc 53.12N 22.55 E
Sup'ung 27 Lc 40.27N 124.57 E
Sup'ung-chosuji 28 Hd 40.30N 125.05 E
Suq ash Shuyūkh 24 Lg 30.53N 46.28 E
Suqian 27 Ke 33.55N 118.13 E
Sūq Suwayq 24 Hj 24.23N 38.27 E
Suquṭrā = Socotra (EN) 21 Hh 12.30N 54.00 E
Sūr 22 Hg 22.31N 59.30 E
Şūr 23 Ec 33.16N 35.11 E
Sur, Cabo- 65d Ac 27.12S 109.26W
Sur, Point- 46 Eh 36.18N 121.54W
Sura 16 Nc 53.52N 45.44 E
Sura 5 Kd 56.06N 46.00 E
Šurab 18 Hd 40.03N 70.33 E
Surabaya 22 Nj 7.15S 112.45 E

Index Symbols

[1] Independent Nation
[2] State, Region
[3] District, County
[4] Municipality
[5] Colony, Dependency
Continent
Physical Region
Historical or Cultural Region
Mount, Mountain
Volcano
Hill
Mountains, Mountain Range
Hills, Escarpment
Plateau, Upland
Pass, Gap
Plain, Lowland
Delta
Salt Flat
Valley, Canyon
Crater, Cave
Karst Features
Depression
Polder
Desert, Dunes
Forest, Woods
Heath, Steppe
Oasis
Cape, Point
Coast, Beach
Cliff
Peninsula
Isthmus
Sandbank
Island
Atoll
Rock, Reef
Islands, Archipelago
Rocks, Reefs
Coral Reef
Well, Spring
Geyser
River, Stream
Waterfall Rapids
River Mouth, Estuary
Lake
Salt Lake
Intermittent Lake
Reservoir
Swamp, Pond
Canal
Glacier
Ice Shelf, Pack Ice
Ocean
Sea
Gulf, Bay
Strait, Fjord
Lagoon
Bank
Seamount
Tablemount
Ridge
Shelf
Basin
Escarpment, Sea Scarp
Fracture
Trench, Abyss
National Park, Reserve
Point of Interest
Recreation Site
Cave, Cavern
Historic Site
Ruins
Wall, Walls
Church, Abbey
Temple
Scientific Station
Airport
Port
Lighthouse
Mine
Tunnel
Dam, Bridge

Šurahammar 8 Ge 59.43N 16.13 E
Šūrak 23 Id 25.43N 58.48 E
Šurakarta 22 Nj 7.35 S 110.50 E
Šūrān 24 Ge 35.17N 36.45 E
Šurany 10 Oh 48.06N 18.11 E
Šurar 35 Gd 7.29N 40.54 E
Šurat 22 Jg 21.10N 72.50 E
Šurat Thani 22 Li 9.06N 99.20 E
Šuraž [Bye.-U.S.S.R.] 7 Hi 55.26N 30.43 E
Šuraž [R.S.F.S.R.] 19 De 53.02N 32.29 E
Šurčin 15 De 44.47N 20.17 E
Šur del Cabo San Antonio,
 Punta- 56 Ie 36.52 S 56.40W
Šurduc 15 Gb 47.15N 23.21 E
Šūre 10 Cg 49.44N 6.31 E
Šurendranagar 25 Ed 22.42N 71.41 E
Šurgères 11 Fh 46.06N 0.45W
Šurgut 22 Jc 61.14N 73.20 E
Šurgutiha 20 Dd 63.47N 87.20 E
Šurhandarinskaja Oblast [3] 18 Ff 37.14N 67.20 E
Šurhob 19 Hh 38.34N 70.04 E
Šurigao 26 Ie 9.45N 125.30 E
Šurin 25 Kf 14.53N 103.30 E
Šuriname [1] 53 Ke 4.00N 56.00W
Šuripà, Rio- 49 Mj 7.47N 69.53W
Šüriyah = Syria (EN) [1] 22 Ff 35.00N 38.00 E
Šūrmaq 24 Og 31.03N 52.48 E
Šurmelin 12 Fe 49.04N 3.31 E
Šūrmene 24 Ib 40.55N 40.07 E
Šurna 8 Cb 62.59N 8.40 E
Šurnadalsøra 8 Cb 62.59N 8.39 E
Šurovikino 19 Ef 48.36N 42.54 E
Šurovo 20 Fe 55.39N 105.36 E
Šur-Pakri/Suur-Pakri 8 Je 59.50N 23.45 E
Šurprise, Ile- 63b Ad 18.32 S 163.02 E
Šurprise, Lac- 44 Ja 49.20N 74.57W
Šurrey [1] 9 Mj 51.25N 0.30W
Šurrey [1] 9 Mj 51.20N 0.05W
Šursee 14 Cc 47.10N 8.07 E
Šursk 16 Nc 53.04N 45.42 E
Šurskoje 7 Li 54.31N 46.44 E
Šurt 31 Ie 31.13N 16.35 E
Šurt, Khalīj- = Sidra,
 Gulf of-(EN) 30 Ie 31.30N 18.00 E
Šurte 8 Eg 57.49N 12.01 E
Šurtsey 7a Bc 63.20N 20.38W
Šürüç 24 Hd 36.58N 38.24 E
Šurud Ad 30 Lg 10.42N 47.09 E
Šuruga-Wan 28 Oq 34.55N 138.35 E
Šurulangun 26 Dg 2.37 S 102.45 E
Šurvey Pass 40 Ic 67.52N 154.10W
Šur-Vjajn/Suur Väin
 8 Jf 58.30N 23.20 E
Šurwold 12 Jb 52.57N 7.31 E
Šuša 8 Di 55.11N 11.46 E
Šuša 16 Oj 39.43N 46.44 E
Šusa [It.] 14 Be 45.08N 7.03 E
Šusa [Jap.] 29 Bd 34.37N 131.36 E
Šusa, Val di- 14 Be 45.10N 7.10 E
Šušac 14 Kh 42.46N 16.30 E
Šušak [Lib.] 33 Dc 32.54N 21.58 E
Šüsah [Tun.] = Sousse (EN) 31 Ie 35.49N 10.38 E
Šüsah = Sousse (EN) [3] 31 Ie 35.45N 10.30 E
Šusak 14 If 44.31N 14.18 E
Šusaki 27 Ne 33.22N 133.17 E
Šusami 29 De 33.33N 135.29 E
Šusamyr 18 Ic 42.09N 73.59 E
Šusanville 43 Cc 40.25N 120.39W
Šusehri 24 Hb 40.11N 38.06 E
Šuseja 8 Kh 56.23N 25.00 E
Šušenskoje 20 Ef 53.19N 92.01 E
Šušice 10 Jg 49.14N 13.30 E
Šusitna 40 Id 61.16N 150.30W
Šuslonger 7 Lh 56.18N 48.12 E
Šusoh 26 Cf 3.43N 96.50 E
Šusong 28 Di 30.10N 116.06 E
Šuspiro 55 Ej 30.38 S 54.22W
Šuspiro del Moro, Puerto
 del- 13 Ig 37.08N 3.40W
Šusquehanna River 43 Ld 39.33N 76.05W
Šusques 56 Gb 23.25 S 66.29W
Šussex 9 Mk 50.55N 0.30W
Šussex 44 Oc 45.43N 65.31W
Šussex, Vale of- 9 Mk 51.00N 0.10W
Šusubona 63a Dc 8.19 S 159.27 E
Šusuman 22 Qc 62.47N 148.10 E
Šusurluk 24 Cc 39.54N 28.10 E
Šusuzmüsellim 15 Kh 41.06N 27.03 E
Šusz 8 Ji 55.08N 23.53 E
Šusz 10 Pc 53.44N 19.20 E
Šutęsti 15 Kd 45.13N 27.26 E
Šutherland 37 Cf 32.24 S 20.40 E
Šutherland Falls 62 Bf 44.48 S 167.44 E
Šutherlin 46 Bc 43.25N 123.19W
Šutla 14 Je 45.51N 15.41 E
Šutlej 13 Jg 29.23N 71.02 E
Šutton 44 Gf 38.41N 80.43W
Šutton, London- 12 Bc 51.21N 0.12W
Šutton Bridge 12 Cb 52.46N 0.11 E
Šutton in Ashfield 12 Aa 53.07N 1.16W
Šutton Scotney 12 Ac 51.09N 1.20W
Šuttor River 59 Jd 21.25 S 147.45 E
Šuttsu 28 Pc 42.48N 140.14 E
Šütüler 24 Dd 37.30N 30.59 E
Šutwik 40 He 56.34N 157.05W
Šu'uholo 16 Ud 51.46N 58.46 E
Šuure-Jaani 7 Fg 58.31N 25.29 E
Šuur-Pakri/Sur-Pakri 8 Je 59.50N 23.45 E
Šuur Väin/Sur-Vjajn 8 Jf 58.30N 23.20 E
Šuva 58 If 18.08 S 178.25 E
Šuvadiva Atoll 21 Ji 0.30N 73.13 E
Šuva Gora 15 Eh 41.51N 21.03 E
Šuva Planina 15 Ff 43.08N 22.13 E
Šuvasvesi 7 Ge 62.40N 28.10 E
Šuvorov 16 Jb 54.08N 36.32 E

Suvorovo [Mold.-U.S.S.R.] 15 Mc 46.33N 29.35 E
Suvorovo [Ukr.-U.S.S.R.] 15 Ld 45.35N 29.00 E
Suvorovskaja 16 Mg 44.10N 42.38 E
Suwa 28 Of 36.02N 138.08 E
Suwa-Ko 29 Fc 36.03N 138.05 E
Suwałki 10 Sb 54.07N 22.56 E
Suwałki [2] 10 Sb 54.05N 22.55 E
Suwalskie, Pojezierze- 10 Sb 54.15N 23.00 E
Suwannee River 44 Fk 29.18N 83.09W
Suwanose-Jima 27 Mf 29.40N 129.45 E
Suwarrow Atoll 57 Kf 13.15 S 163.05W
Suwayqīyah, Hawr as- 24 Lf 32.40N 46.03 E
Suways, Khalīj as- = Suez,
 Gulf of-(EN) 30 Kf 28.10N 33.27 E
Suways, Qanāt as- = Suez
 Canal (EN) 30 Ke 29.55N 32.33 E
Suwŏn 27 Md 37.16N 127.01 E
Suxian 27 Ke 33.36N 116.58 E
Suzaka 29 Fc 36.39N 138.18 E
Suzdal 7 Jh 56.28N 40.27 E
Suzhou 22 Of 31.16N 120.37 E
Suzhou/Jiuquan 22 Lf 39.46N 98.34 E
Suzi He 28 Hd 41.56N 124.20 E
Suzu 27 Od 37.25N 137.17 E
Suzuka 29 Ed 34.51N 136.35 E
Suzuka-Sanmyaku 29 Ed 35.10N 136.20 E
Suzu-Misaki 28 Nf 37.28N 137.20 E
Suzun 20 Df 53.47N 82.19 E
Suzzara 14 Ef 45.00N 10.45 E
Svæholthalvøya 7 Ga 70.30N 26.05 E
Svågan 8 Gc 61.54N 16.33 E
Svalbard [5] 67 Kd 78.00N 20.00 E
Svaljava 16 Ce 48.32N 22.59 E
Svalov 8 Ei 55.55N 13.06 E
Svaneholm 8 Di 55.08N 15.09 E
Svaneke 8 Fh 56.16N 14.46 E
Svängsta 8 Ac 61.30N 5.05 E
Svaney 16 Id 51.44N 34.59 E
Svapa 7 Ec 67.39N 21.04 E
Svappavaara 8 Fd 60.45N 15.55 E
Svärdsjö 8 Fe 59.08N 14.31 E
Svartå 8 Fe 59.20N 14.35 E
Svartälven 8 Fe 59.17N 15.15 E
Svartán [Swe.] 8 Ff 58.28N 15.33 E
Svartán [Swe.] 8 Ge 59.37N 16.33 E
Svartán [Swe.]
 41 Gd 71.30N 55.20W
Svartenhuk Halvø =
 Svartenhuk Peninsula (EN)
 41 Gd 71.30N 55.20W
Svartenhuk Peninsula (EN)
 = Svartenhuk, Halvø 41 Gd 71.30N 55.20W
Svartisen 7 Cc 66.38N 13.58 E
Svatoj Nos, Mys- 20 Jb 72.45N 140.45 E
Svatovo 19 Df 49.24N 38.13 E
Svay Riêng 25 Lf 11.05N 105.48 E
Sveabreen 66 Cf 72.08 S 1.53 E
Sveagruva 41 Nc 78.39N 16.25 E
Svealand 7 Bd 60.30N 15.30 E
Svealand 5 Hc 60.30N 15.30 E
Svedala 8 Ei 55.30N 13.14 E
Sveg 7 De 62.02N 14.21 E
Svékšna 8 Ii 55.32N 21.30 E
Svelgen 7 Af 61.45N 5.18 E
Svelvik 8 De 59.37N 10.24 E
Švenčenėlaj/Švenčioneliai 7 Gi 55.09N 26.02 E
Švenčénis/Švenčionys 7 Gi 55.07N 26.12 E
Švenčioneliai/Švenčenėlaj 7 Gi 55.09N 26.02 E
Švenčionys/Svenčénis 7 Gi 55.07N 26.12 E
Svendborg 8 Di 55.03N 10.37 E
Svendsen Peninsula 42 Ja 77.50N 84.00W
Svenljunga 7 Ch 57.30N 13.07 E
Svenska högarna 8 He 59.35N 19.35 E
Svenskøya 41 Oc 78.43N 26.30 E
Svenstavik 7 De 62.46N 14.27 E
Sventoj/Šventoji 8 Ih 56.04N 20.59 E
Šventoji 7 Fi 55.05N 24.24 E
Šventoji/Sventoj 8 Ih 56.04N 20.59 E
Sverdlovsk 10 Sb 56.11N 60.36 E
Sverdlovskaja Oblast [3] 19 Gd 59.00N 62.00 E
Sverdrup, Ostrov- 20 Cb 74.30N 79.35 E
Sverdrup Channel 42 Ha 80.00N 96.30W
Sverdrup Islands 38 Jb 79.00N 98.00W
Sverige = Sweden (EN) [1] 6 Hc 62.00N 15.00 E
Svetac 14 Jg 43.02N 15.45 E
Svete/Svete 8 Jh 56.40N 23.38 E
Svete/Svete 8 Jh 56.40N 23.38 E
Sveti Naum 15 Di 40.55N 20.45 E
Sveti Nikola, Prohod- 15 Ff 43.27N 22.36 E
Sveti Nikole 15 Eh 41.52N 21.57 E
Sveti Stefan 15 Sg 42.16N 18.54 E
Svetlaja 20 Ig 46.31N 138.18 E
Svetli 20 Ge 58.34N 116.00 E
Svetlogorsk [Bye.-U.S.S.R.] 19 Ce 52.38N 29.42 E
Svetlogorsk [R.S.F.S.R.] 8 Ij 54.55N 20.08 E
Svetlograd 16 He 45.19N 42.40 E
Svetlovodsk 16 He 49.02N 33.15 E
Svetly [R.S.F.S.R.] 16 Sg 50.51N 60.53 E
Svetly [R.S.F.S.R.] 7 Ei 54.41N 20.08 E
Svetly Jar 16 Ne 48.29N 44.46 E
Svetogorsk 7 Gf 61.07N 28.58 E
Svetozarevo 15 Ef 43.59N 21.15 E
Sviča 10 Ug 49.04N 24.06 E
Svid 7 Jf 61.13N 38.45 E
Svidnik 10 Rg 49.18N 21.35 E
Svidnik 10 Rg 49.23N 14.58 E
Svijaga 10 Ed 55.39N 48.28 E
Svilaja 15 Kg 43.50N 16.26 E
Svilengrad 15 Jh 41.46N 26.12 E
Svincovy Rudnik 15 Fe 44.48N 22.09 E
Svinecea Mare, Virful- 15 Fe 44.48N 22.09 E
Svir 5 Jc 60.30N 32.48 E
Svir 8 Lj 54.50N 26.34 E
Svirica 7 Hf 60.30N 32.54 E
Svirsk 20 Fg 53.27N 28.59 E
Svisloč 16 Fc 53.27N 28.59 E
Svisloč 16 Dc 53.03N 24.07 E
Svištov 15 If 43.37N 25.20 E

Svit 10 Qg 49.03N 20.12 E
Svitava 10 Mg 49.11N 16.38 E
Svitavy 10 Mg 49.46N 16.27 E
Svizra / Svizzera / Schweiz
 / Suisse = Switzerland
 (EN) [1] 6 Gf 46.00N 8.30 E
Svizzera / Schweiz / Suisse
 / Svizra = Switzerland
 (EN) [1] 6 Gf 46.00N 8.30 E
Svobodny 5 Jb 68.10N 39.43 E
Svobodny 22 Od 51.24N 128.07 E
Svoge 15 Gg 42.58N 23.21 E
Svolvær 7 Db 68.14N 14.34 E
Svratka 10 Mh 48.52N 16.38 E
Svrljig 15 Ff 43.25N 22.08 E
Svulrya 8 Gd 60.25N 12.24 E
Svytaya Anna Trough (EN) 67 He 80.00N 70.00 E
Swabia (EN) = Schwaben 10 Gh 48.20N 10.30 E
Swabian-Bavarian Plateau
 (EN) = Schwäbisch-
 Bayerisches
 Alpenvorland 5 Hf 48.15N 10.30 E
Swabian Jura (EN) =
 Schwäbische Alb 5 Gf 48.25N 9.30 E
Swaffham 12 Cb 52.39N 0.41 E
Swain Reefs 57 Gg 21.40 S 152.15 E
Swains Atoll 57 Jf 11.03 S 171.05W
Swainsboro 44 Fi 32.36N 82.20W
Swakop 37 Ad 22.41 S 14.31 E
Swakopmund 37 Ad 22.30 S 15.00 E
Swakopmund 31 Ik 22.41 S 14.34 E
Swale 9 Lg 54.06N 1.20W
Swalmen 9 Lk 51.14N 6.02 E
Swanage 9 Lk 50.37N 1.58W
Swan Hill 59 Ig 35.21 S 143.34 E
Swan Range 46 Ic 47.50N 113.40W
Swan River 42 Hf 52.06N 101.16W
Swansboro 44 Ih 34.36N 77.07W
Swansea [Austl.] 59 Jh 42.08 S 148.04 E
Swansea [Wales-U.K.] 6 Fe 51.38N 3.57W
Swansea Bay 9 Jj 51.35N 3.52W
Swans Island 44 Mc 44.10N 68.25W
Swanson Lake 45 Ff 44.00N 101.06W
Swan Valley 46 Ja 43.28N 111.20W
Swartberge 30 Jl 33.23 S 21.48 E
Swarzędz 10 Nd 52.26N 17.05 E
Swastika 44 Ga 48.07N 80.12W
Swaziland [1] 31 Kk 26.30 S 31.10 E
Sweden (EN) = Sverige [1] 6 Hc 62.00N 15.00 E
Swedru 34 Ed 5.32N 0.42W
Sweet Grass Hills 46 Jb 48.55N 111.30W
Sweet Home 46 Dd 44.24N 122.44W
Sweetwater 43 Ge 32.28N 100.25W
Sweetwater River 43 Fc 42.31N 107.50W
Swellendam 37 Cf 34.02 S 20.26 E
Świder 10 Rd 52.08N 21.12 E
Świdnica 10 Mf 50.51N 16.29 E
Świdwin 10 Se 51.14N 22.41 E
Świebodzin 10 Lc 53.47N 15.47 E
Świebodzin 10 Ld 52.15N 15.32 E
Świecie 10 Oc 53.25N 18.28 E
Świętej Anny, Góra- 10 Of 50.28N 18.13 E
Świętokrzyskie, Góry- 10 Qf 50.50N 20.50 E
Swift Current 42 Gf 50.17N 107.50W
Swift Current Creek 46 La 50.40N 107.44W
Swift River 42 Ed 60.05N 131.11W
Swilly, Lough-/Loch Suili 9 Ff 55.10N 7.38W
Swinburne, Cape - 42 Hb 71.14N 98.33W
Swindon 9 Lj 51.34N 1.47W
Swinford/Béal Átha na
 Muice 9 Eh 53.57N 8.57W
Świnoujście 10 Kc 53.53N 14.14 E
Swischenahner Meer 12 Ka 53.12N 8.01 E
Swisttal 12 Id 50.44N 6.54 E
Switzerland (EN) =
 Schweiz / Suisse / Svizra
 / Svizzera [1] 6 Gf 46.00N 8.30 E
Switzerland (EN) = Suisse
 / Svizra / Svizzera /
 Schweiz [1] 6 Gf 46.00N 8.30 E
Switzerland (EN) = Svizra
 / Svizzera / Schweiz /
 Suisse [1] 6 Gf 46.00N 8.30 E
Switzerland (EN) =
 Svizzera / Schweiz /
 Suisse / Svizra [1] 6 Gf 46.00N 8.30 E
Syčevka 16 Ib 55.51N 34.15 E
Syców 10 Ne 51.19N 17.43 E
Sydfalster-Gedser 7 Ci 54.35N 11.57 E
Sydkap Ice Cap 42 Ja 76.30N 85.00W
Sydney [Austl.] 58 Gh 33.52 S 151.13 E
Sydney [N.S.-Can.] 39 Me 46.09N 60.11W
Sydney → Manra Atoll 57 Je 4.27 S 171.15W
Sydney-Campbelltown 57 Kf 34.04 S 150.49 E
Sydney Lake 45 La 50.40N 94.24W
Sydney Mines 44 Le 46.14N 60.22W
Sydney-Penrith 59 Kf 33.45 S 150.42 E
Syktyvkar 5 Lc 61.40N 50.46 E
Sylacauga 44 Di 33.10N 86.15W
Sylane 7 Ce 63.02N 12.13 E
Sylarna 7 Ce 63.02N 12.13 E
Sylhet 25 Id 24.54N 91.52 E
Sylling 8 De 59.54N 10.17 E
Sylt 10 Ea 54.55N 8.20 E
Sylva 17 Hf 57.40N 56.57 E
Sylvania 44 Gi 32.45N 81.38W
Sylvania Tablemount (EN)
 60 Ge 11.58N 165.00 E
Sylvan Pass 43 Ec 44.28N 110.08W
Sylvester 44 Fj 31.32N 83.49W
Sylvester, Lake- 59 Hc 18.50 S 135.50 E
Sym 20 Ed 60.15N 90.02 E
Syndassko 20 Fb 73.14N 108.05 E
Synja 15 Id 65.12N 64.45 E
Synnfjell 8 Cc 61.05N 9.45 E
Syowa 66 De 69.00 S 39.35 E

Syracuse [Ks.-U.S.] 45 Fh 37.59N 101.45W
Syracuse [N.Y.-U.S.] 39 Le 43.03N 76.09W
Syracuse (EN) = Siracusa 6 Hh 37.04N 15.18 E
Syrdarinskaja Oblast [3] 19 Gg 40.30N 68.40 E
Syrdarja 19 Gg 40.52N 68.38 E
Syrdarja = Syr Darya (EN)
 21 Ie 46.03N 61.00 E
Syr Darya (EN) =
 Syrdarja 21 Ie 46.03N 61.00 E
Syria (EN) 22 Ff 35.00N 38.00 E
Syria (EN) = Sūriyah [1] 22 Ff 35.00N 38.00 E
Syriam 25 Je 16.46N 96.15 E
Syrian Desert- (EN) = Shām,
 Bādiyat ash- 21 Ff 32.00N 40.00 E
Syrkovoje, Ozero- 17 Lf 60.40N 65.00 E
Syrski 16 Kc 52.36N 39.28 E
Sysert 17 Jh 56.31N 60.49 E
Sysmä 7 Ff 61.30N 25.41 E
Sysola 19 Fc 61.42N 50.58 E
Syssleback 8 Ed 60.44N 12.52 E
Sysulp, Gora- 15 Ha 48.29N 24.17 E
Syverma, Plato- 21 Lc 67.00N 99.00 E
Syzran 6 Ke 53.09N 48.27 E
Szabolcs-Szatmár [2] 10 Sh 48.00N 22.10 E
Szamocin 10 Nc 53.02N 17.08 E
Szamos 15 Fa 48.07N 22.20 E
Szamotuły 10 Md 52.37N 16.35 E
Szarvas 10 Qj 46.52N 20.33 E
Szczawnica Krościenko 10 Qg 49.26N 20.30 E
Szczebrzeszyn 10 Sf 50.42N 22.59 E
Szczecin 10 Kc 52.35N 14.30 E
Szczecin = Stettin (EN) 6 Hc 53.24N 14.32 E
Szczecinek 10 Mc 53.43N 16.42 E
Szczeciński, Zalew- 10 Kc 53.46N 14.14 E
Szczekociny 10 Pf 50.38N 19.50 E
Szczercow 10 Pe 51.18N 19.09 E
Szczucin 10 Rf 50.18N 21.04 E
Szczuczyn 10 Sc 53.34N 22.18 E
Szczytno 10 Qc 53.34N 21.00 E
Szechwan (EN) = Sichuan
 Sheng (Ssu-ch'uan Sheng)
 [2] 27 He 30.00N 103.00 E
Szechwan (EN) = Ssu-
 ch'uan Sheng = Sichuan
 Sheng [2] 27 He 30.00N 103.00 E
Szécseny 10 Ph 48.05N 19.31 E
Szeged 6 If 46.15N 20.10 E
Szeged [2] 10 Qj 46.16N 20.08 E
Szeghalom 10 Ri 47.02N 21.10 E
Székesfehérvár 6 Hf 47.12N 18.25 E
Szekszárd 10 Oj 46.21N 18.43 E
Szendrő 10 Qh 48.24N 20.44 E
Szentendre 10 Pi 47.40N 19.05 E
Szentes 10 Qj 46.39N 20.16 E
Szentgotthárd 10 Mj 46.57N 16.17 E
Szérencs 10 Rh 48.10N 21.12 E
Szeskie Wzgórza 10 Sb 54.14N 22.22 E
Szigetvár 10 Nj 46.03N 17.48 E
Szkwa 10 Rc 53.10N 21.52 E
Szlichtyngowa 10 Me 51.43N 16.15 E
Szob 10 Oi 47.49N 18.52 E
Szolnok 10 Qi 47.11N 20.12 E
Szolnok [2] 10 Qi 47.15N 20.30 E
Szombathely 10 Mi 47.14N 16.37 E
Szprotawa 10 Le 51.34N 15.33 E
Szreniawa 10 Qf 50.10N 20.35 E
Sztum 10 Pc 53.56N 19.01 E
Szubin 10 Nc 53.00N 17.44 E
Szydłów 10 Rf 50.35N 21.01 E
Szydłowiec 10 Qe 51.14N 20.51 E

T

Taakoka 64p Cc 21.15 S 159.43W
Taalintehdas/Dalsbruk 8 Jd 60.02N 22.31 E
Taavetti 8 Ld 60.55N 27.36 E
Tab 10 Oj 46.44N 18.02 E
Tabacal 56 Hb 23.15 S 64.15W
Tâbah 24 Ji 27.02N 42.08 E
Tabaqah 24 He 35.52N 38.34 E
Tabar Islands 57 Ge 2.50 S 152.00 E
Tabarqah 32 Ib 36.57N 8.45 E
Tabas 24 Qf 33.36N 56.54 E
Tabasará, Serranía de-
 49 Gi 8.33N 81.40W
Tabasco [2] 47 Fe 18.00N 92.40W
Tabasco y Campeche, Llanos
 de- 47 Fe 18.15N 91.00W
Tabāsīno 7 Lh 56.59N 47.43 E
Tābask, Kūh-e- 24 Nh 29.52N 51.49 E
Tabay 55 Ci 28.18 S 58.17W
Tabelbala 32 Gd 29.24N 3.15W
Taber 8 Fg 57.41N 14.05 E
Taberg 8 Fg 57.41N 14.05 E
Tabernacle 51c Ab 17.23N 62.46W
Tabernes de Valldigna 13 Je 39.04N 0.16W
Tabiteuea Atoll 57 Ie 1.20 S 174.50 E
Tabla 34 Fc 13.46N 3.01 E
Tablas 26 Hc 12.24N 122.02 E
Tablas Strait 26 Hc 12.40N 121.48 E
Tablat 13 Ph 36.25N 3.19 E
Tablazo, Bahía del- 49 Lh 10.52N 71.35W
Table Cape 60 Ie 39.06 S 178.00 E
Table Rock Lake 45 Jh 36.35N 93.30W
Tabocas 55 Ed 11.58N 55.58W
Taboco, Rio- 55 Ed 19.53 S 55.58W
Tábor 10 Kg 49.25N 14.41 E
Tabora 36 Bb 5.01 S 32.48 E
Tabora [2] 36 Bb 5.20 S 32.30 E
Tabory 17 Lg 58.31N 64.33 E
Tabou 31 Gh 4.25N 7.21W
Tabrīz 22 Gf 38.05N 46.18 E

Tábua 13 Dd 40.21N 8.02W
Tabuaeran Atoll (Fanning)
 57 Ld 3.52N 159.20W
Tabūk 22 Fg 28.23N 36.35 E
Tabukusuku 26 Hc 17.24N 121.25 E
Taburbah 14 Dn 36.50N 9.50 E
Tabursuq 14 Dn 36.28N 9.15 E
Tabursuq, Monts de- 14 Dn 36.28N 9.05 E
Tabusintac 44 Ob 47.24N 65.02W
Tabwemasana 63b Cb 15.22 S 166.45 E
Täby 7 Eg 59.30N 18.03 E
Tacámbaro de Codallos 48 Ih 19.14N 101.28W
Tacarcuna, Cerro- 49 Ij 8.05N 77.17W
Tacarigua, Laguna de- 50 Dg 10.15N 65.50W
Tacheng/Qoqek 22 Ke 46.45N 82.57 E
Tachibana-Wan 29 Be 32.45N 130.05 E
Tachichilte, Isla de- 48 Ee 24.59N 108.04W
Tachikawa [Jap.] 29 Fd 35.42N 139.23 E
Tachikawa [Jap.] 29 Fb 38.48N 139.58 E
Táchira [2] 54 Db 7.50N 72.05W
Tachiumet 33 Bd 26.19N 10.03 E
Tachov 10 Jg 49.48N 12.40 E
Tachungnya 64b Bb 14.58N 145.36 E
Tacinski 16 Le 48.13N 41.17 E
Tacir 15 Mi 40.32N 29.44 E
Tacloban 22 Oh 11.15N 125.00 E
Tacna 53 Ig 18.01 S 70.15W
Tacna [2] 54 Dg 17.40 S 70.20W
Tacoma 39 Ge 47.15N 122.27W
Tacotalpa, Rio- 48 Mi 17.50N 92.52W
Tacuaral 55 Cd 18.59 S 58.07W
Tacuarembó 55 Ek 32.10 S 55.30W
Tacuarembó, Rio- 55 Ek 32.25 S 55.29W
Tacuari, Rio- 55 Ek 34.33 S 53.18W
Tacuati 55 Df 23.27 S 56.35W
Tadami 29 Fc 37.21N 139.17 E
Tadami-Gawa 29 Fc 37.38N 139.45 E
Tadarimana, Rio- 55 Cc 16.43 S 54.31W
Tademaït, Plateau du- 30 Hf 28.30N 2.15 E
Tadine 63b Ce 21.33 S 167.53 E
Tadjeraout 32 He 21.17N 1.20 E
Tadjetaret 32 Ie 22.00N 7.30 E
Tadjourah 35 Gc 11.45N 42.54 E
Tadjourah, Golfe de- 35 Gc 11.45N 43.00 E
Tadoule Lake 42 He 58.35N 98.20W
Tadoussac 44 Ma 48.09N 69.43W
Tadzhik SSR (EN) =
 Tadžikskaja SSR [2] 19 Hh 39.00N 71.00 E
Tadžikskaja Sovetskaja
 Socialističeskaja
 Respublika [2] 19 Hh 39.00N 71.00 E
Tadžikskaja SSR/
 Respublikai Soveth
 Socialisti Todžikiston [2] 19 Hh 39.00N 71.00 E
Tadžikskaja SSR = Tadzhik
 SSR (EN) [2] 19 Hh 39.00N 71.00 E
T'aebaek-Sanmaek 21 Of 37.40N 128.50 E
Taechon 28 If 36.21N 126.36 E
T'aech'on 28 He 39.55N 125.30 E
Taedong-gang 28 He 38.42N 125.15 E
Taegu 22 Of 35.52N 128.36 E
Taeha-dong 28 Kf 37.31N 130.48 E
Taehan-Haehyŏp = Korea
 Strait (EN) 21 Of 34.40N 129.00 E
Taehan-Min' guk = South
 Korea (EN) [1] 22 Of 38.00N 127.30 E
Taehuksan-Do 28 Hg 34.40N 125.25 E
Taejŏn 22 Of 36.20N 127.26 E
Tafahi Island 57 Jf 15.52 S 173.55W
Tafalla 13 Kb 42.31N 1.40W
Tafassasset 30 If 21.56N 10.12 E
Tafassasset, Ténéré du- 34 Ha 21.20N 11.00 E
Taff 9 Jj 51.27N 3.09W
Tafilalt 32 Gc 31.18N 4.18W
Tafiré 34 Dd 9.04N 5.10W
Tafi Viejo 56 Gc 26.44 S 65.16W
Taflan 24 Gb 41.25N 36.09 E
Tafna 13 Ki 35.18N 1.28W
Tafraout 32 Fd 29.43N 9.00W
Tafresh 24 Ne 34.41N 50.01 E
Taft 24 Ng 31.45N 54.14 E
Taftán, Kūh-e- 21 Ig 28.36N 61.06 E
Taftanäz 24 Qf 35.58N 36.47 E
Taga 65c Aa 13.46 S 172.28W
Taga Dzong 25 Hc 27.04N 89.53 E
Tagajō 29 Gc 38.18N 140.58 E
Tagama 30 Jg 15.50N 8.12 E
Taganrog 6 Jf 47.12N 38.56 E
Taganrogski Zaliv 16 Kf 46.50N 38.25 E
Tagant [3] 34 Ba 18.30N 10.30W
Tagant 30 Fg 17.31N 12.07W
Tagarev, Gora- 18 Ae 38.59N 57.18 E
Tagawa 29 Be 33.39N 130.48 E
Tagbilaran 26 He 9.39N 123.51 E
Tageru, Jabal- 35 Db 16.25N 27.10 E
Taggia 14 Bg 43.52N 7.51 E
Tagh 22 Ge 30.55N 2.02W
Tagil 17 Kg 58.33N 62.30 E
Tagish Lake 42 Ed 60.00N 134.00W
Tagliamento 14 Gc 45.38N 13.06 E
Taglio di Po 14 Gc 45.00N 12.12 E
Tagomago, Isla de- 13 Ne 39.02N 1.39 E
Tagounit 32 Fd 29.58N 5.35W
Tagpochau, Ogso- 64b Ba 15.11N 145.45 E
Tāgrīfat 29 Db 29.12N 17.21 E
Taguaranga 54 If 12.25 S 36.28W
Taguersimet 30 Em 24.09N 15.07W
Tagula 63a Ad 11.20 S 153.00 E
Tagula Island 57 Gf 11.30 S 153.30 E
Tagum 26 Ie 7.21N 125.50 E
Tagus (EN) = Tajo 5 Fh 38.40N 9.24W
Tagus (EN) = Tejo 5 Fh 38.40N 9.24W
Tahaa, Ile- 61 Kc 16.38 S 151.30W
Tahakopa 62 Cg 46.31 S 169.23 E
Tahan, Gunong- 21 Mi 4.39N 102.14 E
Tahanea Atoll 57 Mf 16.52 S 144.45W

Index Symbols

[1] Independent Nation
[2] State, Region
[3] District, County
[4] Municipality
[5] Colony, Dependency
Continent
Physical Region

Historical or Cultural Region
Mount, Mountain
Volcano
Hill
Mountains, Mountain Range
Hills, Escarpment
Plateau, Upland

Pass, Gap
Plain, Lowland
Delta
Salt Flat
Valley, Canyon
Crater, Cave
Karst Features

Depression
Polder
Desert, Dunes
Forest, Woods
Heath, Steppe
Oasis
Cape, Point

Coast, Beach
Cliff
Peninsula
Isthmus
Sandbank
Island
Atoll

Rock, Reef
Islands, Archipelago
Rocks, Reefs
Coral Reef
Well, Spring
Geyser
River, Stream

Waterfall Rapids
River Mouth, Estuary
Lake
Salt Lake
Intermittent Lake
Reservoir
Swamp, Pond

Canal
Glacier
Ice Shelf, Pack Ice
Ocean
Sea
Gulf, Bay
Strait, Fjord

Lagoon
Bank
Seamount
Tablemount
Ridge
Shelf
Basin

Escarpment, Sea Scarp
Fracture
Trench, Abyss
National Park, Reserve
Point of Interest
Recreation Site
Cave, Cavern

Historic Site
Ruins
Wall, Walls
Church, Abbey
Temple
Scientific Station
Airport

Port
Lighthouse
Mine
Tunnel
Dam, Bridge

Tahat 30 Hf 23.18N 5.32 E
Tahe 27 La 52.22N 124.48 E
Ţāherī 24 Oi 27.42N 52.21 E
Tahgong, Puntan- 64b Ba 15.06N 145.39 E
Tahiataš 18 Bc 42.20N 59.33 E
Tahifet 32 Ie 22.56N 5.59 E
Tahir Geçidi 24 Jc 39.52N 42.20 E
Tahiti, Ile- 57 Mf 17.37S 149.27W
Tahkuna Neem/Takuna, Mys- 8 Je 59.05N 22.30 E
Tahlequah 45 Ii 35.55N 94.58W
Tahoe, Lake- 46 Fg 38.54N 120.00W
Tahoua [2] 34 Gb 16.00N 5.30 E
Tahoua 31 Hg 14.54N 5.16 E
Ţahţā 33 Fd 26.46N 31.28 E
Tahta-Bazar 18 Dg 35.55N 62.55 E
Tahtabrod 19 Ge 52.40N 67.35 E
Tahtakarača Pereval 18 Fe 39.17N 66.55 E
Tahtaköprü 15 Mj 39.57N 29.39 E
Tahtakupyr 19 Gg 43.01N 60.22 E
Tahtali Dağlari 24 Gc 38.46N 36.47 E
Tahtamygda 20 Hf 54.09N 123.38 E
Tahuata, Ile- 57 Ne 9.57S 139.05W
Tahulandang, Pulau- 26 If 2.20N 125.25 E
Tahuna 26 If 3.37N 125.29 E
Tai 34 Dd 5.52N 7.27W
Tai'an [China] 28 Gd 41.24N 122.27 E
Tai'an [China] 27 Kd 36.09N 117.05 E
Taiarapu, Presqu'île de- 65e Fc 17.47S 149.14W
Taibai Shan 27 Ie 33.57N 107.40 E
Taibilla, Canal del- 13 Kg 37.43N 1.22W
Taibilla, Sierra de- 13 Jf 38.10N 2.10W
Taibus Qi (Baochang) 27 Kc 41.55N 115.22 E
Taicang 28 Fi 31.26N 121.06 E
Taichung 22 Og 24.09N 120.41 E
Taieri 62 Dg 46.03S 170.12 E
Taiga 20 De 56.04N 85.37 E
Taigonos Peninsula (EN) = Tajgonos, Poluostrov- 20 Ld 61.35N 161.00 E
Taigu 28 Bf 37.26N 112.33 E
Taihang Shan 21 Nf 37.00N 114.00 E
Taihape 62 Fc 39.41S 175.48 E
Taihe [China] 28 Ch 33.11N 115.38 E
Taihe [China] 27 Jf 26.50N 114.52 E
Taiheiyō = Pacific Ocean (EN) 3 Ki 5.00N 155.00W
Tai Hu 21 Of 31.15N 120.10 E
Taihu 27 Ke 30.26N 116.10 E
Taikang 27 Je 34.00N 114.56 E
Taiki 29a Cb 42.30N 143.16 E
Tailai 27 Lb 46.24N 123.26 E
Tailles, Plateau des- 12 Hd 50.15N 5.45 E
Taim 55 Fk 32.30S 52.35W
Tain 9 Id 57.48N 4.04W
Tainan 22 Og 23.00N 120.11 E
Tainaron, Ákra- = Matapan, Cape- (EN) 5 Ih 36.23N 22.29 E
Taiof 63a Ba 5.31S 154.39 E
Taipei 22 Og 25.03N 121.30 E
Taiping 26 Df 4.51N 100.44 E
Taiping (Gantang) 28 Ei 30.18N 118.07 E
Taipingchuan 28 Gb 44.24N 123.11 E
Taiping Dao 27 Jd 10.15N 113.42 E
Taiping Ling 27 Lb 47.36N 120.12 E
Tairadate 29a Bc 41.09N 140.38 E
Tairadate-Kaikyō 29a Bc 41.10N 140.40 E
Taisei 29a Ab 42.14N 139.49 E
Taisetsu-Zan 21 Qe 43.40N 142.48 E
Taisha 29 Cd 35.24N 132.40 E
Taishaku-San 29 Fc 36.58N 139.28 E
Tai Shan 21 Nf 36.30N 117.20 E
Taishō 29 Ce 33.12N 132.57 E
Taitao, Peninsula de- = Taitao Peninsula (EN) 52 Ij 46.30S 74.25W
Taitao Peninsula (EN) = Taitao, Península de- 52 Ij 46.30S 74.25W
Taitung 27 Lg 22.45N 121.09 E
Taiwa 29 Gb 38.26N 140.52 E
Taiwan [1] 22 Og 23.30N 121.00 E
Taiwan Haixia = Formosa Strait (EN) 21 Ng 24.00N 119.00 E
Taixian 28 Fh 32.31N 120.08 E
Taixing 28 Fh 32.10N 120.00 E
Taiyang Shan 27 Ie 33.37N 106.26 E
Taiyetos Óros- 15 Fl 37.06N 22.18 E
Taiyuan 22 Nf 37.50N 112.37 E
Taiyue Shan 28 Bf 36.48N 112.00 E
Taizhou 28 Eh 32.29N 119.55 E
Taizhou → Linhai 27 Lf 28.52N 121.08 E
Taizhou Wan 28 Fj 28.40N 121.37 E
Taizi He 28 Gd 41.00N 122.23 E
Ta'izz 22 Gh 13.38N 44.02 E
Tājābād 24 Pg 30.02N 54.24 E
Tajarhī 33 Be 24.21N 14.28 E
Tajgonos, Mys- 20 Ld 60.35N 160.10 E
Tajgonos, Poluostrov- = Taigonos Peninsula (EN) 20 Ld 61.35N 161.00 E
Tajima 28 Of 37.12N 139.46 E
Tajimi 29 Ed 35.19N 137.08 E
Tājirwin 14 Co 35.54N 8.33 E
Tajito 48 Cb 30.58N 112.18W
Tajmba 20 Ed 60.22N 98.50 E
Tajmyr 20 Ea 76.05N 98.55 E
Tajmyr, Ozero- 21 Mb 74.30N 102.30 E
Tajmyr, Poluostrov- = Taymyr Peninsula (EN) 21 Mb 76.00N 104.00 E
Tajmyra 21 Lb 76.00N 99.40 E
Tajmyrlur 20 Hb 72.30N 121.39 E
Tajmyrski (Dolgano-Nenecki) Nacionalny okrug [3] 20 Eb 72.00N 95.00 E
Tajo = Tagus (EN) 5 Fh 38.40N 9.24W
Tajo-Segura, Canal de Trasvase- 13 Je 39.30N 2.05W
Tajrish 23 Hb 38.48N 51.25 E
Tajšet 22 Ld 55.57N 98.00 E
Tajumulco, Volcán- 38 Jh 15.02N 91.54W
Tajuña 13 Id 40.07N 3.35W
Tak 25 Je 16.52N 99.08 E
Taka Atoll 3 Ii 4.00N 146.45 E
Takāb 24 Ld 36.24N 47.07 E
Takaba 36 Hb 3.27N 40.14 E
Takahagi 28 Pf 36.42N 140.41 E
Takahama 29 Dd 35.29N 135.33 E
Takahara-Gawa 29 Ec 36.27N 137.15 E
Takaharu 29 Bf 31.55N 130.59 E
Takahashi 28 Lg 34.47N 133.37 E
Takahashi-Gawa 29 Cd 34.32N 133.42 E
Takahata 29 Gc 38.00N 140.12 E
Takahe, Mount- 66 Of 76.17S 112.05W
Takaka 62 Ed 40.51S 172.48 E
Takakuma-Yama 29 Bf 31.28N 130.49 E
Takalar 26 Gh 5.28S 119.24 E
Takalous 32 Ie 23.25N 7.02 E
Takamatsu 27 Ne 34.21N 134.03 E
Takamori 29 Be 32.48N 131.08 E
Takanabe 29 Be 32.08N 131.31 E
Takanawa-Hantō 29 Ce 34.00N 132.55 E
Takanawa-San 29 Ce 33.57N 132.50 E
Takanosu 29 Ga 40.14N 140.22 E
Takaoka [Jap.] 28 Nf 36.45N 137.01 E
Takaoka [Jap.] 29 Bf 31.57N 131.17 E
Takapoto Atoll 61 Lb 15.00S 148.10W
Takapuna 62 Fb 36.48S 174.47 E
Takara-Jima 27 Mf 29.10N 129.05 E
Takarazuka 29 Dd 34.49N 135.21 E
Takaroa Atoll 61 Mb 14.28S 144.58W
Takasaki 28 Of 36.20N 139.01 E
Taka-Shima [Jap.] 29 Be 32.40N 131.50 E
Taka-Shima [Jap.] 29 Af 31.26N 129.45 E
Takatshwane 37 Cd 22.36S 21.55 E
Takatsu-Gawa 29 Bd 34.42N 131.49 E
Takatsuki 28 Mg 34.51N 135.37 E
Takayama 28 Nf 36.08N 137.15 E
Takebe 29 Cd 34.53N 133.54 E
Takefu 28 Ng 35.54N 136.10 E
Takehara 29 Cd 34.21N 132.54 E
Takeo 29 Ae 33.12N 130.00 E
Tåkern 8 Ff 58.20N 14.50 E
Take-Shima 8 Kf 37.22N 131.58 E
Tākestān 23 Gb 36.05N 49.14 E
Taketa 29 Be 32.58N 131.24 E
Takêv 25 Kf 10.59N 104.47 E
Takhādīd 24 Kh 29.59N 44.30 E
Takhār [3] 23 Kb 36.30N 69.30 E
Takhmaret 13 Mi 35.06N 0.41 E
Takht-e Soleimān 24 Nd 36.20N 51.00 E
Taki [Jap.] 29 Cd 35.16N 132.38 E
Taki [Pap.N.Gui.] 63a Bb 6.29S 155.50 E
Takijuq Lake 42 Gc 66.05N 113.00W
Takikawa 28 Pc 43.33N 141.54 E
Takingeun 26 Cf 4.38N 96.50 E
Takinoue 29a Ca 44.13N 143.03 E
Takko 29 Ga 40.20N 141.09 E
Takla Lake 42 Ee 55.30N 126.00W
Takla Landing 42 Ee 55.29N 125.58W
Takla Makan (EN) = Taklimakan Shamo 21 Kf 39.00N 83.00 E
Taklimakan Shamo = Takla Makan (EN) 21 Kf 39.00N 83.00 E
Takob 18 Ge 38.51N 69.00 E
Tako-Bana 29 Cd 35.35N 133.05 E
Takolokouzet, Massif de- 34 Gb 18.40N 9.30 E
Taku 29 Be 33.19N 130.06 E
Takuan, Mount- 63a Bb 6.27S 155.36 E
Takua Pa 25 Jg 8.52N 98.21 E
Takum 34 Gd 7.16N 9.59 E
Takuma 29 Cd 34.14N 133.40 E
Takume Atoll 57 Mf 15.49S 142.12W
Takuna, Mys-/Tahkuna Neem 8 Je 59.05N 22.30 E
Takutea Island 57 Lf 19.49S 158.19W
Tala 48 Hg 20.40N 103.42W
Talāh 32 Ib 35.35N 8.40 E
Talaimmannar 25 Fg 9.05N 79.44 E
Talāiyeh 24 Kd 37.50N 45.00 E
Talaja 20 Kd 61.03N 152.30 E
Talak 30 Hg 18.20N 6.00 E
Talamanca, Cordillera de- 49 Fi 9.30N 83.40W
Talara 53 Hf 4.35S 81.25W
Talas 19 Hg 42.29N 72.14 E
Talas 18 Ic 44.05N 70.20 E
Talasea 59 Ka 5.20S 150.05 E
Talasski Alatau, Hrebet- 18 Hc 42.10N 72.00 E
Talata Mafara 34 Gc 12.34N 6.04 E
Talaud, Kepulauan- = Talaud Islands (EN) 21 Oi 4.20N 126.50 E
Talaud Islands (EN) = Talaud, Kepulauan- 21 Oi 4.20N 126.50 E
Talavera, Isla- 55 Dh 27.32S 56.26W
Talavera de la Reina 13 He 39.57N 4.50W
Talawdī 35 Ec 10.38N 30.23 E
Talbot Inlet 42 Ja 77.55N 77.35W
Talca 53 Ii 35.26S 71.40W
Talcahuano 53 Ii 36.43S 73.07W
Tälcher 25 Hd 20.57N 85.13 E
Taldom 7 Ih 56.45N 37.32 E
Taldy-Kurgan 22 Je 44.59N 78.23 E
Taldy-Kurganskaja Oblast [3] 19 Hf 44.00N 78.00 E
Taleh 35 Hd 9.09N 48.26 E
Tal-e Khosravī 24 Ng 30.47N 51.29 E
Talence 11 Fj 44.49N 0.36W
Ţalesh, Kūhhā-Ye- 24 Md 37.35N 48.38 E
Talgar 19 Hg 43.18N 77.13 E
Taliabu, Pulau- 26 Hg 1.48S 124.48 E
Talica 19 Gd 57.01N 63.43 E
Talimardžan 19 Gh 38.21N 65.31 E
Tali Post 35 Ed 5.54N 30.47 E
Talisajan 22 Ni 1.37N 118.11 E
Taliwang 26 Gh 8.44S 116.52 E
Talkeetna 40 Id 62.20N 150.07W
Talkeetna Mountains 40 Jd 62.10N 148.15W
Talkheh 24 Kd 37.40N 45.46 E
Talladega 44 Di 33.26N 86.06W
Tall 'Afar 23 Fb 36.22N 42.27 E
Tallah 24 Dh 28.05N 30.44 E
Tallahassee 39 Kf 30.25N 84.16W
Tallahatchie River 45 Kj 33.33N 90.10W
Tall al Abyaḑ 24 Hd 36.41N 38.57 E
Tallapoosa River 44 Di 32.30N 86.16W
Tallard 11 Mj 44.28N 6.03 E
Tällberg 8 Fd 60.49N 15.00 E
Tall Birāk at Taḩtānī 24 Id 36.38N 41.05 E
Tallinn 6 Id 59.25N 24.45 E
Tall Kayf 24 Jd 36.29N 43.08 E
Tall Kūshik 24 Jd 36.48N 42.04 E
Tallulah 45 Kj 32.25N 91.11W
Tălmaciu 15 Hd 45.39N 24.16 E
Talmenka 20 Df 53.51N 83.45 E
Talmest 32 Fc 31.09N 9.00W
Talnah 20 Dc 69.30N 88.15 E
Talnoje 16 Ge 48.53N 30.42 E
Talo 30 Kg 10.44N 37.55 E
Talofofo 64c Bb 13.20N 144.46 E
Talon 20 Je 59.48N 148.50 E
Tāloqān 23 Kb 36.44N 69.33 E
Talovaja 16 Ld 51.06N 40.48 E
Talpa de Allende 48 Gg 20.23N 104.51W
Talsi 7 Fh 57.17N 22.37 E
Taltal 53 Ih 25.24S 70.29W
Taltson 42 Gd 61.24N 112.45W
Taluk 26 Dg 0.32S 101.35 E
Talvik 7 Fa 70.03N 22.58 E
Talwār 24 Md 36.00N 48.00 E
Tama 35 Cc 14.45N 22.25 E
Tamaghzah 32 Ic 34.23N 7.57 E
Tamala 16 Mc 52.33N 43.18 E
Tamalameque 49 Ki 8.52N 73.38W
Tamale 31 Gh 9.24N 0.50W
Tamames 13 Fd 40.39N 6.06W
Tamana 29 Be 32.55N 130.33 E
Tamanaco, Rio- 50 Dh 9.25N 65.23W
Tamana Island 57 Ie 2.29S 175.59 E
Tamano 28 Lg 34.30N 133.56 E
Tamanoura 29 Ae 32.38N 128.37 E
Tamanrasset 30 Hf 22.03N 0.10 E
Tamanrasset 31 Hf 22.47N 5.31 E
Tamanrasset [3] 32 Ie 23.00N 5.30 E
Tamar 9 Ik 50.22N 4.10W
Tamara 15 Cg 42.27N 19.33 E
Támara 54 Db 5.50N 72.10W
Tamarit de Llitera/Tamarite de Litera 13 Mc 41.52N 0.26 E
Tamarite de Litera/Tamarit de Llitera 13 Mc 41.52N 0.26 E
Tamarro 14 Ii 41.09N 14.50 E
Tamarugal, Pampa del- 56 Gb 21.00S 69.25W
Tamási 10 Oj 46.38N 18.17 E
Tamassoumit 32 Ef 18.35N 12.39W
Tamaulipas [2] 47 Ed 24.00N 98.45W
Tamaulipas, Llanos de- 47 Ed 25.00N 98.25W
Tamaulipas, Sierra de- 48 Jf 23.30N 98.30W
Tamayama 29 Gb 39.50N 141.11 E
Tamazula de Gordiano 48 Hh 19.38N 103.15W
Tamazunchale 47 Ed 21.16N 98.47W
Tambach 36 Gb 0.36N 35.31 E
Tambacounda 31 Fg 13.12N 15.48W
Tambara 37 Ec 16.44S 34.15 E
Tambelan, Kepulauan- = Tambelan Islands (EN) 26 Ef 1.00N 107.30 E
Tambelan, Pulau- 26 Ef 0.58N 107.34 E
Tambelan Islands (EN) = Tambelan, Kepulauan- 26 Ef 1.00N 107.30 E
Tambo 59 Jd 24.53S 146.15 E
Tambohorano 37 Gc 17.29S 43.58 E
Tambora, Gunung- 26 Gh 8.14S 117.55 E
Tambores 55 Dj 31.52S 56.16W
Tambov 6 Ke 52.43N 41.27 E
Tambovskaja Oblast [3] 19 Ee 52.45N 41.40 E
Tambre 13 Db 42.49N 8.53W
Tambunan 26 Ge 5.40N 116.22 E
Tambura 31 Jh 5.36N 27.28 E
Tamchaket 32 Ef 17.20N 10.40W
Tame 54 Db 6.27N 71.45W
Tâmega 13 Dc 41.05N 8.21W
Tâmega 13 Dc 41.05N 8.21W
Tamel Aike 56 Fg 48.19S 70.58W
Tamesí 47 Ed 22.13N 97.52W
Tamesna 30 Hg 18.25N 3.33 E
Tamgak, Monts- 30 Hg 19.11N 8.42 E
Tamgue, Massif du- 30 Fg 12.00N 12.18W
Tamiahua 48 Kg 21.16N 97.27W
Tamiahua, Laguna de- 47 Ed 21.35N 97.35W
Tamianglajang 26 Gg 2.07S 115.10 E
Tamil Nādu [3] 25 Ff 11.00N 78.00 E
Tamiš 15 De 44.51N 20.39 E
Tamise/Temse 12 Gc 51.08N 4.13 E
Tamitatoala, Rio- 54 Hf 11.56S 53.36W
Ţāmīyah 24 Dh 29.29N 30.58 E
Tam Ky 25 Le 15.34N 108.29 E
Tammela 8 Jd 60.48N 23.46 E
Tammerfors/Tampere 6 Ic 61.30N 23.45 E
Tammisaari/Ekenäs 7 Fg 59.58N 23.26 E
Tämnaren 8 Gd 60.10N 17.20 E
Tamnava 15 De 44.25N 20.05 E
Tamou 34 Fc 12.45N 2.11 E
Tampa 39 Kg 27.57N 82.27W
Tampa Bay 43 Kf 27.45N 82.35W
Tampake-Misaki 29a Bb 43.43N 141.20 E
Tampere/Tammerfors 6 Ic 61.30N 23.45 E
Tampico 39 Jg 22.13N 97.51W
Tampin 26 Df 2.28N 102.14 E
Tamri 32 Fc 30.43N 9.50 E
Tamsag-Bulak 27 Kb 47.14N 117.21 E
Tamsalu 7 Gg 59.10N 26.07 E
Tamsweg 14 Hc 47.08N 13.48 E
Tamu 25 Id 24.13N 94.19 E
Tamuin 48 Jg 21.59N 98.45W
Tamuin 47 Ed 22.00N 98.44W
Tamuin, Rio- 48 Jg 21.47N 98.28W
Tamworth [Austl.] 58 Gh 31.05S 150.55 E
Tamworth [Eng.-U.K.] 9 Li 52.39N 1.40W
Tamyang 28 Ig 35.19N 126.59 E
Tana [Eur.] 5 Ia 70.28N 28.18 E
Tana [Kenya] 30 Li 2.32S 40.31 E
Tana, Lake- 30 Kg 12.00N 37.20 E
Tanabe 28 Mh 33.42N 135.44 E
Tana bru 7 Ga 70.16N 28.10 E
Tanacross 40 Kd 63.23N 143.21W
Tanafjorden 7 Ga 70.54N 28.40 E
Tanaga 40a Cb 51.50N 178.00W
Tanagro 14 Jj 40.38N 15.14 E
Tanagura 29 Gc 37.02N 140.23 E
Tanahbala, Pulau- 26 Cg 0.25S 98.25 E
Tanahgrogot 26 Gg 1.55S 116.12 E
Tanahjampea, Pulau- 26 Hh 7.05S 120.42 E
Tanahmasa, Pulau- 26 Cg 0.12S 98.27 E
Tanah Merah 26 De 5.48N 102.09 E
Tanahmerah 26 Lh 6.05S 140.17 E
Tanakpur 25 Gc 29.05N 80.07 E
Tanalyk 17 Ij 51.46N 58.45 E
Tanami 59 Fc 19.59S 129.43 E
Tanami Desert 57 Eg 20.00S 132.00 E
Tan An 25 Lf 10.32N 106.25 E
Tanana 40 Ic 65.10N 152.05W
Tanana 38 Dc 65.09N 151.55W
Tanapag 64b Ba 15.14N 145.45 E
Tanapag, Puetton- 64b Ba 15.14N 145.44 E
Tanāqīb, Ra's at- 24 Mi 27.50N 48.53 E
Tanaro 14 Ce 45.01N 8.47 E
Tanba-Sanchi 29 Dd 35.15N 135.35 E
Tancheng 28 Eg 34.37N 118.20 E
Tanch'ŏn 27 Mc 40.25N 128.57 E
Tancitaro, Pico de- 47 De 19.26N 102.18W
Tanda 34 Ed 7.48N 3.10W
Tanda, Lac- 34 Eb 15.45N 4.42W
Tandag 26 Ie 9.04N 126.12 E
Tandaltī 35 Ec 13.01N 31.52 E
Tăndărei 15 Ke 44.39N 27.40 E
Tandjungbalai 26 Cf 2.58N 99.48 E
Tandil 53 Ki 37.20S 59.05W
Tandil, Sierras del- 55 Cm 37.24S 59.06W
Tandjilé [3] 35 Bd 9.30N 16.30 E
Tando Ādam 25 Dc 25.46N 68.40 E
Tandsjöborg 7 Df 61.42N 14.43 E
Tanḑubāyah 35 Db 18.40N 28.37 E
Taneatua 62 Gc 38.04S 177.00 E
Tane-Ga-Shima 27 Ne 30.40N 131.00 E
Taneichi 29 Ga 40.24N 141.43 E
Tan Emellel 32 Id 27.28N 9.45 E
Tanew 10 Sf 50.27N 22.16 E
Tanezrouft 30 Gf 24.00N 0.45W
Tanezzuft 33 Bd 25.51N 10.19 E
Tanf, Jabal at- 24 Hf 33.30N 38.42 E
Tanga [3] 36 Gd 5.30S 38.00 E
Tanga 31 Ki 5.04S 39.06 E
Tangail 25 Hd 24.15N 89.55 E
Tanga Islands 57 Ge 3.30S 153.15 E
Tangalla 25 Gg 6.01N 80.48 E
Tanganyika [2] 36 Fd 6.00S 35.00 E
Tanganyika, Lac- = Tanganyika, Lake- (EN) 30 Ji 6.00S 29.30 E
Tanganyika, Lake- 30 Ji 6.00S 29.30 E
Tanganyika, Lake- (EN) = Tanganyika, Lac- 30 Ji 6.00S 29.30 E
Tangará 54 Ke 6.11S 35.49W
Tangarare 63a Dc 9.35S 159.39 E
Tangdan → Dongchuan 27 Hf 26.07N 103.05 E
Tāngehgol 24 Pd 37.25N 55.50 E
Tanger = Tangier (EN) [3] 32 Fb 35.45N 5.45W
Tanger = Tangier (EN) 31 Ge 35.48N 5.48W
Tangerang 26 Eh 6.11S 106.37 E
Tangermünde 10 Hd 52.33N 11.57 E
Tanggu 27 Kd 39.00N 117.36 E
Tanggula Shan (Dangla Shan) 21 Lf 33.00N 92.00 E
Tanggula Shankou 27 Fe 32.42N 92.27 E
Tanggulashanqu/Tuotuohe 22 Lf 34.15N 92.29 E
Tang He 28 Bh 32.10N 112.20 E
Tanghe 27 Je 32.37N 112.57 E
Tangier (EN) = Tanger 31 Ge 35.48N 5.48W
Tangier (EN) = Tanger [3] 32 Fb 35.45N 5.45W
Tang La 21 Kg 28.00N 89.15 E
Tango 29 Dd 35.44N 135.05 E
Tangra Yumco 21 Kf 31.00N 86.25 E
Tangshan 22 Nf 39.35N 118.09 E
Tanguiéta 34 Fc 10.37N 1.16 E
Tanguro, Rio- 55 Fa 12.36S 52.56W
Tangxian 28 Ce 38.46N 114.58 E
Tangyin 28 Cg 35.54N 114.21 E
Tangyuan 27 Mb 46.45N 129.53 E
Tanhoj 20 Ff 51.33N 105.07 E
Tanhuijo, Arrecife- 48 Kg 21.07N 97.17W
Taniantaweng Shan 27 Ge 30.00N 98.00 E
Tanimbar, Kepulauan- = Tanimbar Islands (EN) 57 Ee 7.30S 131.30 E
Tanimbar Islands (EN) = Tanimbar, Kepulauan- 57 Ee 7.30S 131.30 E
Tanjung [Indon.] 26 Gg 2.11S 115.23 E
Tanjung [Indon.] 26 Dg 1.23S 103.58 E
Tanjungpandan 26 Eg 2.45S 107.39 E
Tanjungpinang 26 Df 0.55N 104.27 E
Tanjungredep 26 Gf 2.09N 117.29 E
Tanjungselor 26 Gf 2.51N 117.22 E
Tankenberg 12 Ib 52.21N 6.58 E
Tanna, Ile- 57 Hf 19.30S 169.20 E
Tännäs 7 Ce 62.27N 12.40 E
Tanner, Mount- 46 Fb 49.40N 118.34W
Tannis Bugt 8 Dg 57.40N 10.15 E
Tannu-Ola 21 Ld 51.00N 94.00 E
Tano 34 Ed 5.07N 2.56W
Tanout 31 Hg 14.58N 8.53 E
Ţanţā 31 Ke 30.47N 31.00 E
Tan Tan 32 Ed 28.30N 11.02W
Tan-Tan [3] 32 Ed 28.30N 11.00W
Tan Tan Plage 32 Ed 28.26N 11.15W
Tantoyuca 48 Jg 21.21N 98.14W
Tanum 7 Cg 58.43N 11.20
Tanzania [1] 31 Ki 6.00S 35.00
Tao, Ko- 25 Jf 10.05N 99.52
Tao'an (Taonan) 27 Lb 45.20N 122.46
Tao'er He 21 Oe 45.42N 124.05
Taoghe 37 Cd 20.37S 22.35
Tao He 27 Hd 35.50N 103.20
Taojiang 28 Bj 28.33N 112.05
Taonan → Tao'an 27 Lb 45.20N 122.46
Taongi Atoll 57 Hc 14.37N 168.58
Taormina 14 Jm 37.51N 15.17
Taos 43 Fd 36.24N 105.24W
Taoudenni 31 Gf 22.42N 3.56W
Taougrite 13 Mh 36.15N 0.55
Taounate 32 Gc 34.33N 4.39W
Taounate [3] 32 Gc 34.04N 4.06W
Taoura 14 Cn 36.10N 8.02
Taourirt 32 Gc 34.25N 2.54W
Taouz 32 Gc 31.00N 4.00W
Taoyuan 27 Lg 25.00N 121.18
Tapa 19 Cd 59.15N 25.59
Tapachula 39 Jh 14.54N 92.17W
Tapaga, Cape- 65c Bb 14.01S 171.23W
Tapah 26 Df 4.11N 101.16
Tapajera 55 Fi 28.09S 52.01W
Tapajós, Rio- 52 Kf 2.24S 54.41W
Tapaktuan 26 Cf 3.16N 97.11
Tapalqué 55 Bm 36.21S 60.01W
Tapan 26 Dg 2.10S 101.04
Tapanahoni Rivier 54 Hc 4.22N 54.27W
Tapanlieh 27 Lg 21.58N 120.47
Tapanui 62 Cf 45.57S 169.16
Tapauá 54 Fe 5.45S 64.23W
Tapauá, Rio- 52 Jf 5.40S 64.21W
Tapenagá, Rio- 55 Ci 28.04S 59.10W
Taperas 55 Bc 17.54S 60.23W
Tapes 56 Jd 30.40S 51.23W
Tapes, Serra do- 55 Fj 30.25S 51.55W
Tapeta 34 Dd 6.29N 8.51W
Taphan Hin 25 Ke 16.12N 100.26
Tapili 36 Eb 3.25N 27.40
Tapini 60 Di 8.19S 146.59
Tapiola, Espoo- 8 Kd 60.11N 24.49
Tapirai 55 Id 19.52S 46.01W
Tapirapuã 55 Db 14.51S 57.45W
Tapolca 10 Nj 46.53N 17.26
Tappahannock 44 Ig 37.55N 76.54W
Tappi-Zaki 28 Pd 41.18N 140.22
Tappu 29a Ba 44.04N 141.52
Tapsuj 17 Je 62.20N 61.30
Tāpti 21 Jg 21.06N 72.41
Tapul Group 26 He 5.30N 121.00
Tapurucuara 54 Ed 0.24S 65.02W
Taputapu, Cape- 65c Ch 14.19S 170.50W
Tāqbostān 24 Le 34.30N 46.58
Ţaqţaq 24 Ke 35.53N 44.35
Taquara 56 Jc 29.39S 50.47W
Taquaral, Serra do- 55 Fb 15.42S 52.30W
Taquari 55 Fc 17.50S 53.17W
Taquari, Pantanal de- 54 Gg 18.10S 56.30W
Taquari, Rio- [Braz.] 55 Gi 29.56S 51.44W
Taquari, Rio- [Braz.] 55 Hf 23.16S 49.12W
Taquari, Rio- [Braz.] 52 Kg 19.15S 57.17W
Taquari, Serra do- 55 Fd 18.18S 53.49W
Taquaritinga 55 He 21.24S 48.30W
Taquarituba 55 Hf 23.31S 49.15W
Taquaruçu, Rio- 55 Fe 21.35S 52.08W
Tar 18 Id 40.38N 73.26
Tara 15 Cf 43.55N 19.25
Tara 9 Gh 53.34N 6.35W
Tara [Austl.] 59 Ke 27.17S 150.28
Tara [Jap.] 29 Be 33.02N 130.11
Tara [R.S.F.S.R.] 20 Ce 56.40N 74.50
Tara [R.S.F.S.R.] 19 Hd 56.54N 74.22
Tara [Yugo.] 15 Bf 43.21N 18.51
Taraba 34 Hd 8.34N 10.15
Tarabuco 54 Fg 19.10S 64.57W
Ţarābulus = Tripoli (EN) [3] 33 Bc 32.40N 13.15
Ţarābulus [Leb.] = Tripoli (EN) 23 Ec 34.26N 35.51
Ţarābulus [Lib.] = Tripoli (EN) 31 Ie 32.54N 13.11
Ţarābulus = Tripolitania (EN) 30 Ie 31.00N 14.00
Ţarābulus = Tripolitania (EN) 33 Bc 30.00N 15.00
Taradale 62 Gc 39.32S 176.51
Tarāghin 33 Bd 25.59N 14.26
Tarahumara, Sierra- 47 Cc 28.26N 106.50W
Tarakan 22 Ni 3.18N 117.38
Tarakan, Pulau- 26 Gf 3.21N 117.36
Taraklija 16 Fg 45.57N 28.41
Tarama Jima 27 Lg 24.40N 124.40
Taran, Mys- 7 Ei 54.57N 19.59
Taranaki [2] 62 Fc 39.10S 174.40
Tarancón 13 Jd 40.01N 3.00W
Taranga Island 62 Fa 36.00S 174.45
Taransay 9 Fd 57.55N 7.10W
Taranto 6 Hg 40.28N 17.14 E
Taranto, Golfo di- = Taranto, Gulf of- (EN) 5 Hg 40.10N 17.20 E
Taranto, Gulf of- (EN) = Taranto, Golfo di- 5 Hg 40.10N 17.20 E
Tarapacá [2] 56 Ga 20.00S 69.20W
Tarapacá 56 Ga 19.55S 69.31W
Tarapaina 63a Ec 9.23S 161.24 E
Tarapoto 54 Ce 6.30S 76.25W
Taraquá 54 Ec 0.06N 68.28W
Tarara 63a Bb 6.02S 155.24 E
Tarare 11 Ki 45.54N 4.26 E
Tararua Range 62 Fd 40.40S 175.25 E
Tarašča 16 Ge 49.34N 30.31 E
Tarascon 11 Kk 43.48N 4.40 E
Tarascon-sur-Ariège 11 Hl 42.51N 1.36 E
Tarat 32 Id 26.08N 9.21 E
Tarata 54 Dg 17.27S 70.02W

Index Symbols

[1] Independent Nation
[2] State, Region
[3] District, County
[4] Municipality
[5] Colony, Dependency
Continent
Physical Region
Historical or Cultural Region
Mount, Mountain
Volcano
Hill
Mountains, Mountain Range
Hills, Escarpment
Plateau, Upland
Pass, Gap
Plain, Lowland
Delta
Salt Flat
Valley, Canyon
Crater, Cave
Karst Features
Depression
Polder
Desert, Dunes
Forest, Woods
Heath, Steppe
Oasis
Cape, Point
Coast, Beach
Cliff
Peninsula
Isthmus
Sandbank
Island
Atoll
Rock, Reef
Islands, Archipelago
Rocks, Reefs
Coral Reef
Well, Spring
Geyser
River, Stream
Waterfall Rapids
River Mouth, Estuary
Lake
Salt Lake
Intermittent Lake
Reservoir
Swamp, Pond
Canal
Glacier
Ice Shelf, Pack Ice
Ocean
Sea
Gulf, Bay
Strait, Fjord
Lagoon
Bank
Seamount
Tablemount
Ridge
Shelf
Basin
Escarpment, Sea Scarp
Fracture
Trench, Abyss
National Park, Reserve
Point of Interest
Recreation Site
Cave, Cavern
Historic Site
Ruins
Wall, Walls
Church, Abbey
Temple
Scientific Station
Airport
Port
Lighthouse
Mine
Tunnel
Dam, Bridge

Tarauacá 54 De 8.10S 70.46W
Tarauacá, Rio 52 Jf 6.42S 69.48W
Taravao 65eFc 17.44S 149.19W
Taravao, Baie de- 65eFc 17.43S 149.17W
Taravo 11a Ab 41.42N 8.48 E
Tarawa Atoll 57 Id 1.25N 173.00 E
Tarawera 62 Gc 39.02S 176.35 E
Tarazi 24 Mg 31.05N 48.18 E
Tarazona 13 Kc 41.54N 1.44W
Tarazona de la Mancha 13 Ke 39.15N 1.55W
Tarbagataj, Hrebet 21 Ke 47.10N 83.00 E
Tarbagatay Shan 27 Db 47.10N 83.00 E
Tarbat Ness 9 Jd 57.50N 3.40W
Tarbert [Scot.-U.K.] 9 Gd 57.54N 6.49W
Tarbert [Scot.-U.K.] 9 Hf 55.52N 5.26W
Tarbes 11 Gk 43.14N 0.05 E
Tarboro 44 Ih 35.54N 77.32W
Tarcăului, Munţii- 15 Jc 46.45N 26.20 E
Tarcoola 59 Gf 30.41S 134.33 E
Tardenois 12 Fe 49.12N 3.40 E
Tardienta 13 Lc 41.59N 0.32W
Tardoire 11 Gi 45.52N 0.14 E
Tardoki-Jani, Gora- 20 Ig 48.50N 137.55 E
Taree 58 Gh 31.54S 152.28 E
Taremert-n-Akli 32 Id 25.53N 5.18 E
Tarentaise 11 Mi 45.30N 6.30 E
Ţarfā', Ra's aţ- 33 Hf 17.02N 42.22 E
Ţarfā', Wādī aţ- 24 Dh 28.38N 30.43 E
Ţarfah, Jazīrat aţ- 34 Mg 14.37N 42.55 E
Tarfaya 31 Ff 27.57N 12.55W
Targa 13 Gj 35.41N 4.09 E
Târgovişki prohod 15 Jf 43.12N 26.30 E
Târgovişte 15 Jf 43.15N 26.34 E
Târgovişte 15 Jf 43.15N 26.34 E
Tarhankut, Mys- 16 Hg 45.21N 32.30 E
Tarhăus, Vîrful- 15 Jc 46.38N 26.10 E
Tarhūnah 33 Bc 32.26N 13.38 E
Tarhūni, Jabal at- 33 De 22.12N 22.25 E
Táriba 49 Kj 7.49N 72.13W
Tarif 23 He 24.01N 53.45 E
Tarifa 13 Gh 36.01N 5.36W
Tarifa, Punta de- 13 Ih 36.00N 3.37W
Tarija 53 Jh 21.31S 64.45W
Tarija 54 Fh 21.30S 64.00W
Tarik 64d Bb 7.21N 151.47 E
Tariku 26 Kg 2.55S 138.26 E
Tarim [P.D.R.Y.] 23 Gf 16.03N 49.00 E
Tarim [Sau.Ar.] 24 Fi 27.54N 35.24 E
Tarim Basin (EN) = Tarim Pendi 21 Qd 50.00N 141.15 E
Tarime 36 Fc 1.21S 34.22 E
Tarim He 21 Ke 41.05N 86.40 E
Tarim Pendi = Tarim Basin (EN) 21 Ke 41.00N 84.00 E
Tarin Kowt 23 Kc 32.52N 65.38 E
Taritatu 26 Kg 2.54S 138.27 E
Tarjalan 27 Hb 49.38N 101.59 E
Tarjannevesi 8 Kb 62.10N 24.05 E
Tarjat 27 Gb 48.10N 99.40 E
Tarka, Vallée de- 34 Gc 14.30N 6.30 E
Tarkastad 37 Df 32.00S 26.16 E
Tarkio 45 If 40.27N 95.23W
Tarko-Sale 20 Cd 64.55N 78.05 E
Tarkwa 34 Ed 5.18N 1.59W
Tarlac 22 Oh 15.29N 120.35 E
Tarm 8 Ci 55.55N 8.32 E
Tarma 54 Cf 11.25S 75.42W
Tarn 11 Hj 44.06N 1.02 E
Tarn 11 Hk 43.50N 2.00 E
Tarna 10 Pi 47.31N 19.59 E
Tárnaby 7 Dd 65.43N 15.16 E
Tarn-et-Garonne 11 Hj 44.00N 1.10 E
Tarnica 32 Sg 49.06N 22.47 E
Tarnobrzeg 10 Rf 50.35N 21.41 E
Tarnobrzeg 10 Rf 50.35N 21.40 E
Tarnogród 10 Sf 50.23N 22.45 E
Tarnos 11 Ek 43.32N 1.28W
Tarnów 6 Ie 50.01N 21.00 E
Tarnów 10 Qf 50.01N 21.00 E
Tarnowskie Góry 10 Of 50.27N 18.52 E
Tärnsjö 8 Gd 60.09N 16.56 E
Taro 11 Mf 45.00N 10.15 E
Taron 63a Aa 4.28S 153.04 E
Taroom 58 Fg 25.39S 149.49 E
Taroudant 32 Fc 30.29N 8.52W
Tarpon Springs 44 Fk 28.09N 82.45W
Tarquinia 14 Fh 42.15N 11.45 E
Tarra, Rio- 49 Ki 9.04N 72.27W
Tarrafal 32 Cf 15.17N 23.46W
Tarragona 6 Gg 41.07N 1.15 E
Tarragona 13 Mc 41.10N 1.00 E
Tarraleah 59 Jk 42.10S 146.30 E
Tarrant 44 Di 33.38N 86.46W
Tarrasa 6 Gg 41.34N 2.01 E
Tárrega 13 Nc 41.39N 1.09 E
Tarsus 23 Db 36.55N 34.53 E
Tart 27 Fd 37.07N 92.57 E
Tartagal 56 Hb 22.32S 63.49W
Tartaro 14 Fe 45.02N 11.30 E
Tartas 11 Fk 43.50N 0.48W
Tartas 20 Ce 55.37N 76.44 E
Tartu 6 Id 58.23N 26.44 E
Tartūs 23 Ec 34.53N 35.53 E
Tarumae-Yama 29a Bb 42.41N 141.23 E
Tarumizu 28 Ki 31.29N 130.42 E
Tarusa 18 Jg 54.43N 37.11 E
Tārūt 24 Ni 26.34N 50.04 E
Tarutino, Ko- 25 Jg 6.39N 99.40 E
Tarutung 16 Ff 46.12N 29.09 E
Tarutyne 26 Cf 2.01N 98.58 E
Tarvisio 14 Hd 46.30N 13.35 E
Tarvo 55 Bb 15.06S 60.34W
Tarvo, Rio- 55 Bb 14.47S 61.03W
Tasajera, Sierra- 48 Gc 29.35N 105.35W
Tašanta 20 Dg 49.43N 89.11 E
Tasaral, Ostrov- 18 Ja 46.15N 74.05 E
Tašauz 19 Fg 41.52N 59.59 E

Tašauzskaja Oblast 19 Fg 41.00N 58.40 E
Tasāwah 33 Bd 26.59N 13.29 E
Tasbuget 19 Gg 44.43N 65.38 E
Tasejeva 20 Ee 58.06N 94.01 E
Tasendjanet 32 Hd 25.40N 0.59 E
Tashk, Daryācheh-ye- 23 Hd 29.45N 53.35 E
Tasikmalaya 22 Mj 7.20S 108.12 E
Tåsinge 8 Di 55.00N 10.36 E
Tasiussaq 41 Gd 73.18N 56.00W
Taskan 20 Kd 62.58N 150.20 E
Taškent 22 Ie 41.20N 69.18 E
Taškentskaja Oblast 19 Gh 41.20N 69.18 E
Taškepri 19 Gh 36.17N 62.38 E
Taškeprinskoje, Vodohranilišče- 18 Df 36.15N 62.40 E
Tasker 34 Hb 15.04N 10.42 E
Taşköprü 24 Fb 41.30N 34.14 E
Taš-Kumyr 19 Hg 41.20N 72.14 E
Taşlıçay 24 Jc 39.38N 43.23 E
Tasman, Mount- 62 De 43.34S 170.09 E
Tasman Basin (EN) 3 Jn 43.00S 158.00 E
Tasman Bay 61 Dh 41.10S 173.15 E
Tasmania 59 Jh 43.00S 147.00 E
Tasmania 57 Fi 43.00S 147.00 E
Tasman Peninsula 59 Jh 43.05S 147.50 E
Tasman Plateau (EN) 3 Im 48.00S 146.00 E
Tasman Sea 57 Hh 40.00S 163.00 E
Tāşnad 15 Fb 47.29N 22.35 E
Taşova 24 Gb 40.46N 36.20 E
Tassah, Wādī- 24 Cn 36.35N 8.54 E
Tassara 34 Gb 16.01N 5.39 E
Taštagol 20 Df 52.47N 88.00 E
Tåstrup 8 Ei 55.39N 12.19 E
Tastür 14 Dn 36.33N 9.27 E
Tasty-Taldy 19 Ge 50.47N 66.31 E
Ţaşūj 24 Kc 38.19N 45.21 E
Taşuou 24 Dd 36.19N 33.53 E
Tasuu 32 Fd 29.40N 8.00W
Tata 10 Oi 47.39N 18.19 E
Tata [Hun.] 10 Oi 47.39N 18.19 E
Tata [Mor.] 32 Fd 29.45N 7.59W
Tataba 26 Hg 1.18S 122.49 E
Tatabánya 10 Oi 47.34N 18.25 E
Takakoto Atoll 57 Nf 17.20S 138.23W
Tata Mailau 21 Ih 8.55S 125.30 E
Tatarbunary 16 Fg 45.49N 29.35 E
Tatarsk 22 Jd 55.13N 75.58 E
Tatarskaja ASSR 19 Fd 55.20N 50.52 E
Tatarski Proliv = Tatar Strait (EN) 21 Qd 50.00N 141.15 E
Tatar Strait (EN) = Tatarski Proliv 21 Qd 50.00N 141.15 E
Tatau 26 Ff 2.53N 112.51 E
Taţăwin 32 Jc 32.56N 10.27 E
Tateyama 28 Oj 34.59N 139.52 E
Tathlina Lake 42 Fd 60.30N 117.30W
Tathlith 23 Ff 19.32N 43.30 E
Tatiščevo 16 Nd 51.40N 45.35 E
Tatla Lake 46 Ca 51.58N 124.25W
Tatla Lake 46 Ca 51.55N 124.36W
Tatlow, Mount- 46 Da 51.23N 123.52W
Tatnam, Cape - 42 Ie 57.16N 91.00W
Tatra Mountains (EN) 5 Hf 49.15N 20.00 E
Tatsuno [Jap.] 29 Dc 34.52N 134.33 E
Tatsuno [Jap.] 29 Ed 35.58N 137.58 E
Tatsuruhama 29 Ec 37.04N 136.53 E
Tatta 25 Dd 24.45N 67.55 E
Tatui 55 If 23.21S 47.51W
Tatum 45 Jj 33.16N 103.19W
Tatvan 23 Fb 38.30N 42.16 E
Tau 8 Ae 59.04N 5.54 E
Tau [Am.Sam.] 65c Db 14.15S 169.30W
Tau [Ton.] 65b Bc 21.01S 175.00W
Tauá 54 Je 6.01S 40.26W
Tauberbischofsheim 10 Fg 49.37N 9.40 E
Taučik 19 Fg 44.15N 51.20 E
Tauere Atoll 57 Mf 17.22S 141.30W
Tauern 5 Hf 47.15N 13.15 E
Tauhunu 64n Ac 10.25S 161.03W
Tauhunu 64n Ac 10.25S 161.03W
Taujsk 20 Je 59.46N 149.20 E
Taujskaja Guba 20 Je 59.15N 150.00 E
Taukum 18 Ab 44.50N 75.30 E
Taumako 63c Ba 9.57S 167.13 E
Taumarunui 62 Fc 38.52S 175.15 E
Taum Sauk Mountain 45 Kh 37.34N 90.44W
Taunay 55 De 20.18S 56.05W
Taung 37 Ce 27.33S 24.47 E
Taungdwingyi 25 Jd 20.01N 95.33 E
Taunggyi 25 Jd 20.47N 97.02 E
Taungthonlon 25 Jd 24.58N 95.48 E
Taungup 25 Je 18.51N 94.14 E
Taunton [Eng.-U.K.] 9 Jj 51.01N 3.06W
Taunton [Ma.-U.S.] 44 Le 41.54N 71.06W
Taunus 10 Ef 50.10N 8.15 E
Taunusstein 12 Kd 50.08N 8.10 E
Taupo 61 Eg 38.41S 176.05 E
Taupo, Lake- 61 Eg 38.50S 175.55 E
Tauragé/Taurage 7 Fi 55.16N 22.19 E
Taurage/Tauragé 7 Fi 55.16N 22.19 E
Tauranga 58 Ff 37.42S 176.10 E
Taurianova 14 Kl 38.21N 16.01 E
Taurion 11 Hi 45.53N 1.24 E
Taurisano 14 Mk 39.57N 18.13 E
Tauroa Point 62 Ea 35.10S 173.04 E
Taurus Mountains (EN) = Toros Dağları 21 Ff 37.00N 33.00 E
Tauste 13 Lc 41.55N 1.15W
Tauu Islands 57 Ge 4.45S 157.00 E
Tavas [Tur.] 24 Dc 39.54N 30.03 E
Tavas [Tur.] 24 Cc 37.34N 29.04 E
Tavas Ovasi 15 Li 37.30N 28.55 E
Tavastehus/Hämeenlinna 7 Ff 61.00N 24.27 E

Tavau/Davos 14 Dd 46.47N 9.50 E
Tavda 19 Gd 58.03N 65.15 E
Tavda 21 Id 57.47N 67.16 E
Tavendroua 63b Cc 16.21S 167.22 E
Taveta 36 Gc 3.24S 37.41 E
Taveuni Island 61 Fc 16.51S 179.58W
Taviano 14 Mk 39.59N 18.05 E
Tavignano 11a Ba 42.06N 9.33 E
Tavira 13 Gg 37.07N 7.39W
Tavistock 9 Ik 50.33N 4.08W
Tavolara 14 Dj 40.55N 9.40 E
Tavoliere 14 Ji 41.35N 15.25 E
Tavoy 22 Lh 14.05N 98.12 E
Tavrichanka 19 Ej 39.15N 21.40 E
Tavropoú, Tekhniti Limni- 15 Jj 39.55N 26.05 E
Tavşan Adalari 24 Cc 39.35N 29.30 E
Tavşanli 61 Ec 17.27S 177.51 E
Tavua 9 Ij 51.04N 4.11W
Tawakoni, Lake- 45 Ij 32.55N 96.00W
Tawas City 43 Kc 44.16N 83.31W
Tawau 22 Ni 4.15N 117.54 E
Tawfiqiyah 35 Ed 9.26N 31.37 E
Ţawilah, Juzur- 24 Ei 27.35N 33.46 E
Tawitawi Group 26 He 5.10N 120.15 E
Ţawkar 31 Kg 18.26N 37.44 E
Ţawûq 26 Ke 35.08N 44.27 E
Tāwūrghā', Sabkhat- 33 Cc 31.10N 15.15 E
Tawzar 12 Ic 33.55N 8.08 E
Taxco de Alarcón 48 Jh 18.33N 99.36W
Taxkorgan 27 Cd 37.47N 75.14 E
Tay, Firth of- 9 Ke 56.28N 3.00W
Tay, Loch- 9 Je 56.30N 4.10W
Tayandu, Kepulauan- 26 Jh 5.30S 132.15 E
Tayėgle 35 Ge 4.02N 44.36 E
Taylor [Nb.-U.S.] 45 Gf 41.46N 99.23W
Taylor [Tx.-U.S.] 43 He 30.34N 97.25W
Taylor, Mount- 43 Fd 35.14N 107.37W
Taylorville 45 Lg 39.33N 89.18W
Taymyr Peninsula (EN) = Tajmyr, Poluostrov- 21 Mb 76.00N 104.00 E
Tay Ninh 25 Lf 11.18N 106.06 E
Tayside 9 Je 56.30N 3.40W
Taytay 26 Gd 10.49N 119.31 E
Taza 32 Gc 34.00N 4.00W
Taza [Mor.] 31 Ge 34.13N 4.01W
Taza [R.S.F.S.R.] 20 Gf 34.55N 111.05 E
Tāzah Khurmātū 24 Ke 35.18N 44.20 E
Tazawa-Ko 29 Db 39.43N 140.40 E
Tazawako 29 Db 39.42N 140.44 E
Tazenakht 32 Fc 30.35N 7.12W
Tazerbo Oasis (EN) = Tāzirbū, Wāḩāt al- 33 Jf 25.45N 21.00 E
Tazin 30 Jf 25.45N 21.00 E
Tazlāu 15 Jc 46.16N 26.47 E
Tazmalt 13 Qh 36.43N 4.08 E
Tazoukiert 34 Fb 24.46N 1.13W
Tazovskaja Guba 17 Qb 69.05N 76.00 E
Tazrouk 20 Cc 67.28N 78.42 E
Tazroukt 32 Jc 32.00N 4.00 E
Tazumal 49 Cg 14.00N 89.40W
Tazza 49 Cg 14.00N 89.40W
Tbilisi 16 Mh 41.43N 44.49 E
Tchad = Chad (EN) 31 Ig 15.00N 19.00 E
Tchad, Lac- = Chad, Lake- (EN) 30 Ig 13.20N 14.00 E
Tchamba [Cam.] 34 Hd 8.37N 12.48 E
Tchamba [Togo] 34 Fd 9.02N 1.25 E
Tchibanga 36 Bc 2.51S 11.02 E
Tchien 34 Dd 6.04N 8.08W
Tchigaï, Plateau du- 30 If 21.30N 14.50 E
Tchin Tabaraden 34 Gb 15.58N 5.50 E
Tcholliré 34 Hd 8.24N 14.10 E
Tczew 10 Ob 54.06N 18.47 E
Tea, Rio- 54 Ed 0.30S 65.09W
Teacapán 48 Gf 22.33N 105.45W
Teaiti Point 64p Bb 21.11S 159.47W
Te Anau 61 Bf 45.25S 167.43 E
Te Anau, Lake- 61 Ci 45.15S 167.45 E
Teapa 48 Mi 17.33N 92.57W
Te Araroa 61 Eg 37.38S 178.22 E
Te Aroha 62 Fb 37.32S 175.42 E
Tea Tree 59 Gd 22.11S 133.17 E
Te Atu Kura 64p Bb 21.14S 159.45W
Teawamutu 62 Fc 38.00S 175.19 E
Tébessa 16 Il 43.28N 41.43 E
Tébessa 31 Hc 35.24N 8.07 E
Tébessa, Oued- 32 Jc 35.00N 7.45 E
Tebicuary, Rio- [Par.] 55 Ch 26.36S 58.16W
Tebicuary, Rio- [Par.] 55 Dh 26.26S 56.51W
Tebingtinggi [Indon.] 26 Bf 3.36S 103.05 E
Tebingtinggi [Indon.] 26 Cf 3.20N 99.09 E
Tebulosmta, Gora- 16 Nh 42.33N 45.16 E
Teča 17 Kh 56.17N 62.59 E
Tecate 47 Ab 32.34N 116.38W
Tecer Dağlari 24 Gc 39.27N 37.11 E
Techirghiol 15 Le 44.03N 28.36 E
Tecklenburg 12 Kb 52.13N 7.49 E
Tecomán 48 Hh 18.55N 103.53W
Tecomate, Laguna- 48 Ji 16.45N 99.25W
Tecoripa 48 Ec 28.37N 109.57W
Tecpan de Galeana 48 Ih 17.15N 100.41W
Tecuala 48 Gf 22.23N 105.27W
Tecuci 15 Kd 45.52N 27.25 E
Tedegra 35 Ba 20.46N 19.34 E

Tedori-Gawa 29 Ec 36.29N 136.28 E
Tedžen 21 If 37.24N 60.38 E
Tedženstroj 19 Gh 36.54N 60.53 E
Teeli 20 Ef 50.57N 90.18 E
Teenuse Jõgi/Tenuze 7 Jf 58.44N 23.58 E
Tees 9 Lg 54.34N 1.16W
Tees Bay 9 Lg 54.35N 1.05W
Teesside 6 Fe 54.35N 1.14W
Tefé 53 Jf 3.22S 64.42W
Tefé, Rio- 54 Fd 3.35S 64.47W
Tefedest 32 Ie 24.40N 5.30 E
Tefenni 24 Cd 37.18N 29.47 E
Tegal 19 He 52.44N 77.30 E
Tegal 22 Mj 6.52S 109.08 E
Tegea (EN) = Teyéa 15 Fl 37.27N 22.25 E
Tegelen 12 Ic 51.20N 6.08 E
Tegernsee 10 Hi 47.43N 11.46 E
Tegina 34 Gc 10.04N 6.11 E
Tégoua 63b Ca 13.15S 166.37 E
Tegucigalpa 39 Kh 14.06N 87.13W
Teguelda I-n-Tessoum 34 Gb 17.26N 6.36 E
Teguldet 20 De 57.20N 88.20 E
Tehachapi 35 Fb 35.08N 118.27W
Tehachapi Mountains 46 Fi 34.56N 118.40W
Tehamiyam 35 Fb 18.20N 36.32 E
Te Hapua 61 Df 34.30S 172.55 E
Tehauoo 65eFc 17.49S 149.18W
Tehek Lake 42 Hd 64.55N 95.30W
Téhini 34 Ed 9.36N 3.40W
Tehi-n-Isser 32 Ie 24.48N 8.08 E
Tehoru 26 Ig 3.23S 129.30 E
Tehrān 22 Hb 35.40N 51.26 E
Tehrān 23 Hb 35.30N 51.30 E
Tehuacán 47 Ee 18.27N 97.23W
Tehuantepec 47 Ee 16.20N 95.14W
Tehuantepec, Golfo de- = Tehuantepec, Gulf of- (EN) 38 Jh 16.00N 94.50W
Tehuantepec, Gulf of- (EN) = Tehuantepec, Golfo de- 38 Jh 16.00N 94.50W
Tehuantepec, Isthmus of- (EN) = Tehuantepec, Istmo de- 38 Jh 17.00N 94.30W
Tehuantepec, Istmo de- = Tehuantepec, Isthmus of- (EN) 38 Jh 17.00N 94.30W
Tehuantepec Ridge (EN) 47 Ef 13.30N 98.00W
Tehuata Atoll 57 Mf 16.50S 141.55W
Teiga Plateau 35 Db 15.38N 25.40 E
Teignmouth 9 Jk 50.33N 3.30W
Teili/Delet 8 Id 60.15N 20.35 E
Teith 9 Je 56.14N 4.20W
Teiuş 15 Gc 46.12N 23.41 E
Teixeira Pinto 34 Bc 12.04N 16.02W
Teja 20 Ed 60.27N 92.38 E
Tejkovo 19 Ed 56.50N 40.34 E
Tejo = Tagus (EN) 5 Fh 38.40N 9.24W
Teju 25 Jc 27.55N 96.10 E
Te Kaha 62 Gb 37.45S 177.41 E
Te Kao 62 Ea 34.39S 172.58 E
Tekapo, Lake- 62 Gc 38.28S 177.52 E
Te Karaka 62 Gc 38.28S 177.52 E
Tekax 48 Og 20.12N 89.17W
Teke 15 Mh 41.04N 29.39 E
Teke Burun [Tur.] 15 Jh 41.21N 26.57 E
Teke Burun [Tur.] 15 Ji 40.02N 26.10 E
Tekeli 19 Ib 44.48N 78.57 E
Tekes 27 Dc 43.10N 81.43 E
Tekes He 27 Dc 43.35N 82.30 E
Tekeze 35 Fc 14.20N 37.57 E
Tekija 15 Fc 44.41N 22.25 E
Tekirdağ 23 Ca 40.59N 27.31 E
Tekman 24 Jc 39.36N 41.30 E
Te Kopuru 62 Eb 36.02S 173.55 E
Te Kou 64p Bb 21.14S 159.46W
Tekouiat 32 Id 22.30N 2.30 E
Tekro 35 Cb 19.34N 20.57 E
Te Kuiti 62 Fc 38.20S 175.10 E
Tela 49 Ge 15.44N 87.27W
Telagh 32 Gc 34.47N 0.34W
Telataí 34 Fb 16.31N 1.30 E
Telavåg 8 Af 60.16N 4.49 E
Telavi 19 Ig 41.55N 45.29 E
Tel Aviv-Yafo 22 Ff 32.04N 34.46 E
Telč 10 Lg 49.11N 15.27 E
Telchac Puerto 48 Og 21.21N 89.16W
Telciu 15 Hb 47.26N 24.24 E
Tele 36 Db 2.48N 23.54 E
Teleac 61 Eg 37.38S 178.22 E
Telečkoje Ozero 20 Df 51.30N 87.45 E
Telefomin 60 Ci 5.08S 141.31 E
Telegraph Creek 42 Ec 57.54N 131.09W
Telekitonga 65b Bb 20.24S 174.32W
Telekivavu'u 65b Bb 20.19S 174.32W
Telémaco Borba 55 Gg 24.23S 50.28W
Telemark 7 Bg 50.30N 8.45 E
Telemark 8 Bd 59.30N 8.45 E
Telén 56 Ge 36.16S 65.30W
Telén 56 Ge 36.16S 65.30W
Telengul 16 Gf 48.20N 31.16 E
Telenešty 15 Lb 47.30N 28.16 E
Teleorman 15 If 43.52N 25.26 E
Telerhteba, Djebel- 32 Ie 24.10N 6.51 E
Telescope Peak 46 Gh 36.10N 117.05W
Telescope Point 51p Bb 17.31N 61.36W
Telese 14 Ii 41.13N 14.32 E

Tellaro 14 Jn 36.50N 15.06 E
Tell Atlas (EN) = Atlas Tellien 30 He 36.00N 2.00 E
Tell City 44 Dg 37.57N 86.46W
Teller 40 Fc 65.16N 166.22W
Telok Anson 26 Df 4.02N 101.01 E
Teloloapan 48 Jh 18.21N 99.51W
Telposiz, Gora- 5 Lc 63.54N 59.10 E
Telsen 56 Gf 42.24S 66.57W
Telšiai/Telšjaj 19 Cd 55.59N 22.17 E
Telšjaj/Telšiai 19 Cd 55.59N 22.17 E
Teltow 10 Jd 52.24N 13.16 E
Tema 22 Mj 5.27S 105.16 E
Temacine 32 Ic 33.01N 6.01 E
Téma 31 Gh 5.37N 0.01W
Te Manga 64p Bb 21.13S 159.45W
Tematangi Atoll 57 Mg 21.41S 140.40W
Tembenči 20 Ed 64.36N 99.58 E
Témbi 15 Fj 39.53N 22.35 E
Tembilahan 26 Dg 0.19S 103.09 E
Temblador 50 Eh 8.59N 62.44W
Tembleque 13 Ie 39.42N 3.30W
Temblor Range 46 Fi 35.30N 119.55W
Tembo 36 Cd 7.42S 17.17 E
Tembo, Chutes- 30 Ii 8.50S 15.20 E
Tembo, Mont- 36 Bb 1.50N 12.00 E
Tembué 37 Eb 14.51S 32.50 E
Teme 9 Ki 52.09N 2.18W
Temerin 15 Cd 45.25N 19.53 E
Temerloh 26 Df 3.27N 102.25 E
Teminabuan 26 Jg 1.26S 132.01 E
Temir 19 Ff 49.08N 57.09 E
Temir 16 Te 48.31N 57.29 E
Temirlanovka 18 Gc 42.36N 69.17 E
Temirtau 22 Jd 50.05N 72.56 E
Témiscaming 44 Ka 46.44N 79.06W
Témiscouata, Lac- 44 Mb 47.40N 68.50W
Temki 35 Bc 11.29N 18.13 E
Temnikov 7 Ki 54.40N 43.13 E
Temo 14 Cj 40.17N 8.28 E
Temoe, Ile- 57 Ng 23.20S 134.29W
Temores 48 Ed 27.16N 108.15W
Tempe 46 Jj 33.25N 111.56W
Tempio Pausania 14 Dj 40.54N 9.06 E
Temple 43 He 31.06N 97.21W
Templeman, Mount- 46 Ga 50.43N 117.14W
Templemore/An Teampall Mór 9 Fi 52.48N 7.50W
Templin 10 Jc 53.07N 13.30 E
Tempoal, Rio- 48 Kg 21.47N 98.27W
Tempué 36 Ce 13.27S 18.53 E
Temrjuk 16 Gg 45.15N 37.23 E
Temse/Tamise 12 Gc 51.08N 4.13 E
Temuco 53 Ii 38.44S 72.36W
Temuka 62 Cd 0.59S 77.48W
Tenacatita, Bahía de- 48 Gh 19.10N 104.50W
Tenala/Tenhola 8 Jd 60.04N 23.18 E
Tenāli 25 Je 16.15N 80.35 E
Tenancingo de Degollado 48 Jh 18.58N 99.36W
Tenasserim 25 Jf 13.00N 99.00 E
Tenasserim 25 Jf 12.24N 98.37 E
Tenasserim 21 Lh 13.35N 97.52 E
Tenby 9 Ij 51.41N 4.43W
Tence 11 Kj 45.07N 4.17 E
Tench Island 60 Eh 1.38S 150.42 E
Tenda, Col di- 14 Bf 44.09N 7.34 E
Tende 11 Nj 44.05N 7.36 E
Tende, Col de- 14 Bf 44.09N 7.34 E
Ten Degree Channel 21 Lh 10.00N 92.30 E
Tendó 29 Gb 38.22N 140.22 E
Tendrara 32 Gc 33.03N 2.00W
Tendre, Mont- 14 Ad 46.36N 6.19 E
Tendrovskaja Kosa 16 Gf 46.15N 31.45 E
Ténenkou 34 Ec 14.28N 4.55W
Tenente Lira, Rio- 55 Db 15.56S 57.39W
Ténéré 30 Hf 17.35N 10.55 E
Ténéré, 'Erg du- 30 Ig 19.00N 10.55 E
Tenerife 30 Ff 28.19N 16.34W
Ténès 32 Hb 36.31N 1.18 E
Ténès, Cap- 13 Nh 36.33N 1.21 E
Teng 25 Je 19.52N 97.45 E
Tengah, Kepulauan- 26 Gh 7.30S 117.30 E
Tengchong 27 Gg 24.59N 98.32 E
Te Nggano, Lake- 60 Gj 11.45S 160.25 E
Tenggarong 26 Gg 0.24S 116.58 E
Tengger Shamo 21 Mf 38.00N 104.10 E
Tengiz, Ozero- 21 Id 50.25N 69.00 E
Tengréla 34 Dc 10.29N 6.24W
Tengxian [China] 27 Jg 23.18N 110.49 E
Tengxian [China] 27 Jf 35.07N 117.10 E
Tenhola/Tenala 8 Jd 60.04N 23.18 E
Teniente General Rosendo M. Fraga 55 Af 23.45S 62.09W
Tenkási 25 Fg 8.58N 77.18 E
Tenke 36 De 10.33S 26.08 E
Tenkodogo 34 Ec 11.47N 0.22W
Tenna 14 Hg 43.14N 13.47 E
Tennant Creek 58 Cc 19.40S 134.10 E
Tennessee 38 Kf 37.04N 88.33W
Tennessee 43 Jd 35.50N 85.30W
Tennessee 51p Bb 17.38N 61.36W
Tennille 44 Fi 32.56N 82.49W
Tennoji 29a Cc 36.10N 137.00 E
Tenojoki 7 Ga 70.28N 28.18 E
Tenom 26 Gc 5.08N 115.57 E
Tenosique de Pino Suárez 47 Fe 17.29N 91.26W
Tenri 29 Ed 34.36N 135.49 E
Tenryū 29 Ed 34.52N 137.47 E
Tenryū-Gawa 28 Ng 34.35N 137.48 E
Ten Sleep 46 Ld 44.02N 107.27W
Tenterden 12 Cc 51.03N 0.42 E

Index Symbols

1 Independent Nation	Historical or Cultural Region	Pass, Gap
2 State, Region	Mount, Mountain	Plain, Lowland
3 District, County	Volcano	Delta
4 Municipality	Hill	Salt Flat
5 Colony, Dependency	Mountains, Mountain Range	Valley, Canyon
Continent	Hills, Escarpment	Crater, Cave
Physical Region	Plateau, Upland	Karst Features

Depression	Coast, Beach	Rock, Reef
Polder	Cliff	Islands, Archipelago
Desert, Dunes	Peninsula	Rocks, Reefs
Forest, Woods	Isthmus	Coral Reef
Heath, Steppe	Sandbank	Well, Spring
Oasis	Island	Geyser
Cape, Point	Atoll	River, Stream

Waterfall Rapids	Canal	Lagoon
River Mouth, Estuary	Glacier	Bank
Lake	Ice Shelf, Pack Ice	Seamount
Salt Lake	Ocean	Tablemount
Intermittent Lake	Sea	Ridge
Reservoir	Gulf, Bay	Shelf
Swamp, Pond	Strait, Fjord	Basin

Escarpment, Sea Scarp	Historic Site	Port
Fracture	Ruins	Lighthouse
Trench, Abyss	Wall, Walls	Mine
National Park, Reserve	Church, Abbey	Tunnel
Point of Interest	Temple	Dam, Bridge
Recreation Site	Scientific Station	
Cave, Cavern	Airport	

Index Symbols

⊡	Independent Nation
⊡	State, Region
⊡	District, County
⊡	Municipality
⊡	Colony, Dependency
⊡	Continent
⊡	Physical Region
〰	Historical or Cultural Region
▲	Mount, Mountain
▲	Volcano
	Hill
▲	Mountains, Mountain Range
	Hills, Escarpment
	Plateau, Upland
	Pass, Gap
	Plain, Lowland
	Delta
	Salt Flat
	Valley, Canyon
	Crater, Cave
	Karst Features
	Depression
	Polder
	Desert, Dunes
	Forest, Woods
	Heath, Steppe
	Oasis
	Cape, Point
	Coast, Beach
	Cliff
	Peninsula
	Isthmus
	Sandbank
	Island
	Atoll
	Rock, Reef
	Islands, Archipelago
	Rocks, Reefs
	Coral Reef
	Well, Spring
	Geyser
	Reservoir
	River, Stream
	Waterfall Rapids
	River Mouth, Estuary
	Lake
	Salt Lake
	Intermittent Lake
	Sea
	Gulf, Bay
	Strait, Fjord
	Canal
	Glacier
	Ice Shelf, Pack Ice
	Ocean
	Ridge
	Shelf
	Basin
	Lagoon
	Bank
	Seamount
	Tableland
	Trench, Abyss
	Fracture
	National Park, Reserve
	Point of Interest
	Recreation Site
	Cave, Cavern
	Escarpment, Sea Scarp
	Ruins
	Wall, Walls
	Church, Abbey
	Temple
	Scientific Station
	Airport
	Historic Site
	Lighthouse
	Mine
	Tunnel
	Dam, Bridge
	Port

Tihāmat 'Asīr	33	Hf	17.30N	42.20 E
Tihi Okean=Pacific Ocean (EN)	3	Ki	5.00N	155.00W
Tihoreck	6	Kf	45.51N	40.09 E
Tihuța, Pasul-	15	Hb	47.15N	25.00 E
Tihvin	19	Dd	59.38N	33.31 E
Tiirismaa	8	Kc	61.01N	25.31 E
Tījī	33	Bc	32.01N	11.22 E
Tījirīt	32	Ee	20.30N	15.00W
Tijuana	39	Hf	32.32N	117.01W
Tijucas	55	Hh	27.14S	48.38W
Tijucas, Baía do-	55	Hh	27.15S	48.31W
Tijucas, Rio-	55	Hh	27.15S	48.38W
Tijucas, Serra do-	55	Hh	27.16S	49.10W
Tijucas do Sul	55	Hg	25.56S	49.10W
Tijuco, Rio-	55	Gd	18.40S	50.05W
Tikal	39	Kh	17.20N	89.39W
Tikanlik	27	Ec	40.42N	87.38 E
Tikchik Lakes	40	Hd	60.07N	158.35W
Tikehau Atoll	61	Lb	15.00S	148.10W
Tikei, Ile-	61	Mb	14.58S	144.32W
Tikitiki	62	Hb	37.47S	178.25 E
Tikkakoski	8	Kb	62.24N	25.38 E
Tikkurila	8	Kd	60.18N	25.03 E
Tiko	34	Ge	4.05N	9.22 E
Tikopia Island	57	Hf	12.19S	168.49 E
Tikrīt	23	Fc	34.36N	43.42 E
Tikšeozero, Ozero-	7	Hc	66.15N	31.45 E
Tiksi	22	Ob	71.36N	128.48 E
Tiladummati Atoll	25a	Ba	6.50N	73.05 E
Tilamuta	26	Hf	0.30N	122.20 E
Tilburg	11	Lc	51.34N	5.05 E
Tilbury, Gravesend-	9	Nj	51.28N	0.23 E
Tilcara	56	Gb	23.34S	65.22W
Til-Châtel	11	Lg	47.31N	5.10 E
Tileagd	15	Fb	47.04N	22.12 E
Tilemsès	34	Fb	15.37N	4.44 E
Tilemsi, Vallée du-	30	Hg	19.00N	0.02 E
Tilia	32	Gd	27.22N	0.02W
Tiličiki	20	Ld	60.20N	166.03 E
Tiligul	16	Gf	47.07N	30.57 E
Tiligulski Liman	16	Gf	46.50N	31.10 E
Till	9	Kf	55.41N	2.12W
Tillabéry	34	Fc	14.13N	1.27 E
Tillamook	46	Dd	45.27N	123.51W
Tillamook Bay	46	Dd	45.30N	123.53W
Tillanchong	25	Ig	8.30N	93.37 E
Tillberga	8	Ge	59.41N	16.37 E
Tille	11	Lg	47.07N	5.21 E
Tillia	34	Fb	16.08N	4.47 E
Tillières-sur-Avre	12	Df	48.46N	1.04 E
Tillingham	12	Cd	50.58N	0.44 E
Tillsonburg	44	Gd	42.51N	80.44W
Tilly-sur-Seulles	12	Be	49.11N	0.37W
Tiloa	34	Fb	15.04N	2.03 E
Tilos	15	Km	36.25N	27.25 E
Tilpa	59	If	30.57S	144.24 E
Tim	16	Jd	51.37N	37.11 E
Tim	16	Jc	52.15N	37.22 E
Ţimā	33	Fd	26.54N	31.26 E
Timagami	44	Gb	47.00N	80.05W
Timagami, Lake-	42	Jg	46.57N	80.05W
Timane, Rio-	55	Be	20.16S	60.08W
Timan Ridge (EN)= Timanski Krjaž	5	Lc	65.00N	51.00 E
Timanski Bereg	17	Eb	68.20N	51.45 E
Timanski Krjaž=Timan Ridge (EN)	5	Lc	65.00N	51.00 E
Timaru	58	Ii	44.24S	171.15 E
Timaševsk	19	Df	45.35N	38.58 E
Timbalier Bay	45	Kl	29.10N	90.20W
Timbalier Island	45	Kl	29.04N	90.28W
Timbaúba	54	Ke	7.31S	35.19W
Timbédra	32	Ff	16.14N	8.10W
Timbó	55	Hh	26.50S	49.18W
Timbuktu (EN)= Tombouctou	31	Gg	16.46N	2.59W
Timedouine, Ras-	13	Qh	36.28N	4.09 E
Timétrine	34	Eb	19.20N	0.42W
Timétrine	34	Eb	19.27N	0.26W
Timfi Óros	15	Dj	39.57N	20.50 E
Timfristós	15	Ek	38.57N	21.49 E
Timia	34	Gb	18.04N	8.40 E
Timimoun	31	Hf	29.15N	0.15 E
Timimoun, Sebkha de-	32	Hd	29.00N	0.05 E
Timiris, Cap—	32	Df	19.23N	16.32W
Timirjazevo	19	Ge	53.45N	66.33 E
Timiș	15	De	44.51N	20.39 E
Timiș [2]	15	Ed	45.38N	21.13 E
Timiskaming, Lake-	44	Hb	47.35N	79.35W
Timișoara	6	If	45.45N	21.13 E
Ti-m-Merhsoï	34	Gb	18.00N	5.40 E
Timmins	39	Ke	48.28N	81.20W
Timmoudi	32	Gd	29.19N	1.08W
Timms Hill	45	Kd	45.27N	90.11W
Timok	15	Fe	44.13N	22.40 E
Timon	54	Je	5.06S	42.49W
Timor, Laut-=Timor Sea (EN)	57	Df	11.00S	128.00 E
Timor, Pulau-	21	Oj	8.50S	126.00 E
Timor Sea (EN)=Timor, Laut-	57	Df	11.00S	128.00 E
Timor Timur [3]	26	Ih	8.35S	126.00 E
Timor Trough (EN)	3	Ij	9.50S	126.00 E
Timote	56	He	35.21S	62.14W
Timotes	54	Db	8.59N	70.44W
Timpton	20	He	58.43N	127.12 E
Timrå	7	De	62.29N	17.18 E
Tims Ford Lake	44	Dh	35.15N	86.10W
Tin, Ra's at-	33	Dc	32.37N	23.08 E
Tinaca Point	21	Oi	5.33N	125.20 E
Tinaco	50	Bh	9.42N	68.26W
Tinakula	63c	Ab	10.24S	165.47 E
Ti-n-Alkoum	32	Je	24.34N	10.11 E
Ti-n-Amzi [Alg.]	32	He	20.32N	4.37 E
Ti-n-Amzi [Niger]	34	Fb	17.54N	4.32 E
Tinaquillo	50	Bh	9.55N	68.18W
Tinchebray	12	Bf	48.46N	0.44W
Tindalo	35	Ed	5.39N	31.03 E
Tindari	14	Jl	38.10N	15.04 E
Tindila	34	Dc	10.16N	8.15W
Tindouf	31	Gf	27.42N	8.09W
Tindouf, Hamada de-	32	Fd	27.45N	8.25W
Tindouf, Sebkha de-	32	Fd	27.45N	7.35W
Tinée	11	Nk	43.55N	7.11 E
Tineo	13	Fa	43.20N	6.25W
Ti-n-Essako	34	Fb	18.27N	2.29 E
Tin Fouye	32	Id	28.15N	7.45 E
Tinghert, Ḩamādat-	30	Hf	28.50N	10.00 E
Tinglev	8	Cj	54.56N	9.15 E
Tingmiarmiut	41	Hf	62.25N	42.15W
Tingo Maria	54	Ce	9.10S	76.00W
Tingri (Xêgar)	27	Ef	28.41N	87.00 E
Tingsryd	7	Dh	56.32N	14.59 E
Tingstäde	8	Hg	57.44N	18.36 E
Tingvoll	7	Be	62.54N	8.12 E
Tinian Channel	64b	Bb	14.54N	145.37 E
Tinian Island	57	Fc	15.00N	145.38 E
Tini Wells	35	Cb	15.02N	22.48 E
Tinkisso	34	Dc	11.21N	9.10W
Tinnelva	8	Ce	59.34N	9.15 E
Tinniswood, Mount-	46	Da	50.19N	123.50W
Tinnoset	8	Ce	59.43N	9.02 E
Tinnsjo	8	Ce	59.54N	8.55 E
Tinogasta	56	Gc	28.04S	67.34W
Tinos	15	Il	37.35N	25.10 E
Tinos	15	Il	37.32N	25.10 E
Tinou, Stenón-	15	Il	37.38N	25.10 E
Tinrhert, Hamada de-	30	Hf	28.50N	10.00 E
Tinrhir	32	Fc	31.31N	5.32W
Tinsukia	25	Jc	27.30N	95.22 E
Tintagel Head	9	Ik	50.41N	4.46W
Tintamarre, Ile-	51b	Bb	18.07N	63.00W
Ti-n-Tarabine	32	Ie	21.16N	7.24 E
Tintăreni	15	Ge	44.36N	23.29 E
Tintina	56	Hc	27.02S	62.43W
Tinto	13	Fg	37.12N	6.55W
Ti-n-toumma	30	Ig	16.04N	12.40 E
Tinwald	62	De	43.55S	171.43 E
Ti-n-Zaouâtene	31	Hg	19.56N	2.55 E
Tiobraid Árann/Tipperary	9	Ei	52.29N	8.10W
Tiobraid Árann/Tipperary [2]	9	Ei	52.40N	8.20W
Tioga	45	Eb	48.24N	102.56W
Tioman, Pulau-	26	Df	2.48N	104.11 E
Tione di Trento	14	Ed	46.02N	10.43 E
Tioro, Selat-=Tioro, Strait (EN)	26	Hg	4.40S	122.20 E
Tioro Strait (EN)=Tioro, Selat-	26	Hg	4.40S	122.20 E
Tiøtta	7	Cd	65.50N	12.24 E
Tiouilit	32	Df	18.52N	16.10W
Tipasa	13	Oh	36.35N	2.27 E
Tipitapa	47	Gf	12.12N	86.06W
Tipperary/Tiobraid Árann	9	Ei	52.29N	8.10W
Tipperary/Tiobraid Árann [2]	9	Ei	52.40N	8.20W
Tipton, Mount-	46	Hi	35.32N	114.12W
Tip Top Mountain	45	Nb	48.16N	85.59W
Tiptree	12	Cc	51.49N	0.45 E
Tiracambu, Serra do-	54	Id	3.15S	46.30W
Tirahart	32	He	23.45N	2.30 E
Tirān	24	Nf	32.42N	51.09 E
Tīrān, Maḑīq-	24	Fi	27.55N	34.28 E
Tirana	6	Hg	41.20N	19.50 E
Tirania	32	Ie	23.08N	9.01 E
Tirano	14	Ed	46.13N	10.10 E
Tiraspol	19	Cf	46.50N	29.37 E
Tirat Karmel	24	Ff	32.46N	34.58 E
Tire	23	Cb	38.04N	27.45 E
Tirebolu	24	Hb	41.00N	38.50 E
Tiree	9	Ge	56.31N	6.49W
Tiree, Passage of-	9	Ge	56.30N	6.30W
Tîrgoviște	15	Ie	44.56N	25.27 E
Tîrgu Bujor	15	Kd	45.52N	27.54 E
Tîrgu Cărbunești	15	Ge	44.57N	23.31 E
Tîrgu Frumos	15	Jb	47.12N	27.00 E
Tîrgu Jiu	15	Gd	45.03N	23.17 E
Tîrgu Lăpuș	15	Gb	47.27N	23.52 E
Tîrgu Mureș	6	If	46.33N	24.34 E
Tîrgu Neamț	15	Jb	47.12N	26.22 E
Tîrgu Ocna	15	Jc	46.17N	26.37 E
Tîrgu Secuiesc	15	Jd	46.00N	26.08 E
Tîrgușor	15	Le	44.27N	28.25 E
Tirich Mir	21	Jf	36.15N	71.50 E
Tirins	15	Fl	37.36N	22.48 E
Tiririca, Serra da-	55	Ic	17.06S	47.06W
Tiris	30	Ff	23.10N	13.30W
Tiris Zemmour [3]	32	Fe	24.00N	10.00W
Tirlemont/Tienen	12	Gd	50.48N	4.57 E
Tirljanski	17	Ii	54.12N	58.33 E
Tîrnava Mare	15	Gc	46.09N	23.42 E
Tîrnava Mică	15	Gc	46.11N	23.55 E
Tîrnăveni	15	Hc	46.20N	24.17 E
Tirnavos	15	Fj	39.45N	22.17 E
Tiro	34	Cd	9.45N	10.39W
Tirol/Tirolo=Tyrol (EN)	14	Fd	47.00N	11.20 E
Tirol=Tyrol (EN) [2]	14	Fc	47.10N	11.25 E
Tirolo/Tirol=Tyrol (EN)	14	Fd	47.00N	11.20 E
Tiros	55	Jd	19.00S	45.58W
Tirreno, Mar-=Tyrrhenian Sea (EN)	5	Hh	40.00N	12.00 E
Tirschenreuth	10	Ig	49.53N	12.21 E
Tirso	14	Ck	39.53N	8.32 E
Tirstrup	8	Dh	56.18N	10.42 E
Tirua Point	62	Fc	38.23S	174.38 E
Tiruchchirappalli	22	Jh	10.49N	78.41 E
Tiruliaj/Tiruliai	8	Ji	55.44N	23.18 E
Tiruliai/Tiruliaj	8	Ji	55.44N	23.18 E
Tirunelveli	22	Ji	8.44N	77.42 E
Tirupati	25	Ff	13.39N	79.25 E
Tirza	8	Lg	57.09N	26.37 E
Tisa=Tisza (EN)	5	If	45.15N	20.17 E
Tis Abay	35	Fc	11.20N	37.40 E
Tisdale	42	Hf	52.51N	104.04W
Tisnaren	8	Ff	58.55N	15.55 E
Tisovec	10	Ph	48.42N	19.57 E
Tissemsilt	32	Hb	35.36N	1.49 E
Tissø	8	Di	55.35N	11.20 E
Tisza	5	If	45.15N	20.17 E
Tisza (EN)=Tisa	5	If	45.15N	20.17 E
Tiszaföldvár	10	Qj	46.59N	20.15 E
Tiszafüred	10	Qi	47.37N	20.46 E
Tiszakécske	10	Qj	46.56N	20.06 E
Tiszántúl	10	Qj	47.00N	21.00 E
Tiszavasvári	10	Ri	47.58N	21.21 E
Titao	34	Ec	13.46N	2.04W
Titarisios	15	Fj	39.47N	22.23 E
Titicaca, Lago-	52	Jg	15.50S	69.20W
Titikaveka	64p	Bc	21.15S	159.45W
Titlagarh	25	Gd	20.18N	83.09 E
Titlis	14	Cd	46.47N	8.26 E
Titograd	6	Hg	42.26N	19.16 E
Titova Korenica	14	Jf	44.45N	15.42 E
Titovo Užice	15	Cf	43.52N	19.51 E
Titov Veles	15	Eh	41.42N	21.48 E
Titov vrh	15	Dh	41.58N	20.50 E
Titran	7	Be	63.40N	8.18 E
Titteri	13	Pi	35.59N	3.15 E
Titule	36	Eb	3.17N	25.32 E
Titusville [Fl.-U.S.]	43	Kf	28.37N	80.49W
Titusville [Pa.-U.S.]	44	He	41.37N	79.42W
Tituvenaj/Tytuvėnai	8	Ji	55.33N	23.09 E
Tiva	36	Gc	2.20S	39.55 E
Tivaouane	34	Bc	14.57N	16.49W
Tiveden	8	Ff	58.45N	14.40 E
Tiverton	9	Jk	50.55N	3.29W
Tivoli [Gren.]	51p	Bb	12.10N	61.37W
Tivoli [It.]	14	Gi	41.58N	12.48 E
Ţiwāl	35	Cc	10.22N	22.43 E
Tiwi	36	Gc	4.14S	39.35 E
Tiyo	35	Gc	14.41N	40.57 E
Tizatlán	48	Jh	19.21N	98.15W
Tizimín	47	Gd	21.09N	88.09W
Tizi Ouzou [3]	32	Hb	36.35N	4.05 E
Tizi Ouzou	32	Hb	36.42N	4.03 E
Tiznados, Rio-	50	Ch	8.16N	67.47W
Tiznit	32	Fd	29.43N	9.43W
Tiznit [3]	32	Fd	29.07N	9.04W
Tjačev	10	Th	48.02N	23.36 E
Tjanšan	27	Dc	42.00N	80.01 E
Tjasmin	16	He	49.03N	32.50 E
Tjeggelvas	7	Dc	66.35N	17.40 E
Tjeukemeer	11	Lb	52.54N	5.50 E
Tjolotjo	37	Dc	19.46S	27.45 E
Tjøme	8	De	59.10N	10.25 E
Tjorn	8	Df	58.00N	11.38 E
Tjub-Karagan, Mys-	16	Qg	44.38N	50.20 E
Tjubuk	17	Jh	56.03N	60.58 E
Tjuhtet	20	De	56.32N	89.29 E
Tjukalinsk	19	Hd	55.52N	72.12 E
Tjuleni, Ostrov-	16	Og	44.30N	47.30 E
Tjuleni, Ostrova-	16	Qg	44.55N	50.10 E
Tjulgan	19	Fe	52.22N	56.12 E
Tjumen	22	Id	57.09N	65.32 E
Tjumenskaja Oblast [3]	19	Gd	57.00N	69.00 E
Tjung	20	Hd	63.42N	121.30 E
Tjup	18	Lc	42.44N	78.20 E
Tjuri/Türi	7	Fg	58.50N	25.27 E
Tjust	8	Gg	57.50N	16.15 E
Tjuters Maly, Ostrov-	8	Le	59.45N	26.53 E
Tjuzašu, Pereval-	18	Ic	42.19N	73.50 E
Tkibuli	16	Mh	42.19N	42.59 E
Tkvarčeli	19	Eg	42.52N	41.40 E
Tlacolula	48	Ki	16.57N	96.29W
Tlacotalpan	48	Lh	18.37N	95.40W
Tlahualilo, Sierra del-	48	Hd	26.30N	103.20W
Tlalnepantla	48	Jh	19.33N	99.12W
Tlapa de Comonfort	48	Ji	17.33N	98.33W
Tlapaneco, Rio-	48	Jh	18.00N	98.48W
Tlaquepaque	48	Hg	20.39N	103.19W
Tlaxcala [2]	47	Ee	19.25N	98.10W
Tlaxcala	47	Ee	19.19N	98.14W
Tlemcen	32	Gc	34.52N	1.19W
Tlemcen [3]	32	Gc	34.45N	1.30W
Tleń	10	Oc	53.38N	18.20 E
Tleta Rissana	13	Gi	35.14N	5.59W
Tletat ed Douair	13	Oi	35.59N	2.55 E
Tljarata	16	Oh	42.06N	46.22 E
Tlumač	10	Vh	48.46N	25.06 E
Tłuszcz	10	Rd	52.26N	21.26 E
Tmassah	33	Cd	26.22N	15.48 E
Tō, Shikotan-/Šikotan, Ostrov-	20	Jh	43.47N	146.45 E
Toaca, Vîrful-	15	Ic	46.55N	25.59 E
Toagel Mlungui	64a	Ab	7.32N	134.28 E
Toamasina	31	Lj	18.10S	49.24 E
Toamasina [3]	37	Hc	18.00S	48.40 E
Toau Atoll	61	Lc	15.55S	146.00W
Toay	56	He	36.40S	64.21W
Toba	28	Ng	34.29N	136.51 E
Toba, Danau-=Toba, Lake- (EN)	26	Li	2.35N	98.50 E
Toba, Lake- (EN)=Toba, Danau-	26	Li	2.35N	98.50 E
Tobago	52	Jd	11.15N	60.40W
Tobago Basin (EN)	50	Ff	12.30N	60.30W
Tobago Cays	51n	Bb	12.39N	61.22W
Toba Kākar Range	25	Db	31.15N	68.00 E
Tobarra	13	Kf	38.35N	1.41W
Tobe	29	Ce	33.44N	132.47 E
Tobejuba, Isla-	50	Fh	9.20N	60.52W
Tobelo	26	If	1.25N	127.31 E
Tobermory [Ont.-Can.]	44	Gc	45.15N	81.40W
Tobermory [Scot.-U.K.]	9	Ge	56.37N	6.05W
Tōbetsu	29a	Bb	43.14N	141.29 E
Tobi Island	57	Ed	3.00N	131.10 E
Tobin, Kap-	41	Jd	70.30N	21.30W
Tobin, Mount-	46	Gf	40.22N	117.32W
Tobin Lake [Austl.]	59	Fd	21.45S	125.50 E
Tobin Lake [Sask.-Can.]	42	Hf	53.40N	103.20W
Tobi-Shima	29	Fb	39.12N	139.32 E
Toblach / Dobbiaco	14	Gd	46.44N	12.14 E
Toboali	26	Eg	3.00S	106.30 E
Tobol	19	Ge	52.40N	62.39 E
Tobol	21	Id	58.10N	68.12 E
Tobolsk	22	Id	58.12N	68.16 E
Tobruk (EN)=Ţubruq	31	Je	32.05N	23.59 E
Tobseda	19	Fb	68.36N	52.20 E
Tobyš	17	Ed	65.30N	51.00 E
Tocantinópolis	53	Lf	6.20S	47.25W
Tocantins, Rio-	52	Lf	1.45S	49.10W
Tocantinzinho, Rio-	55	Ha	13.57S	48.20W
Toccoa	44	Fh	34.35N	83.19W
Toce	14	Ce	45.56N	8.29 E
Tochigi	29	Fc	36.23N	139.44 E
Tochigi Ken [2]	28	Of	36.50N	139.50 E
Tochio	29	Fc	37.29N	138.58 E
Töcksfors	8	De	59.31N	11.50 E
Toco	50	Fg	10.50N	60.57W
Tocoa	49	Df	15.41N	86.03W
Toconao	56	Gb	23.11S	68.01W
Tocopilla	53	Ih	22.05S	70.12W
Tocumen	49	Hi	9.05N	79.23W
Tocuyo, Rio-	49	Mh	11.03N	68.20W
Todd Mountain	44	Nb	46.32N	66.43W
Todi	14	Gh	42.47N	12.24 E
Tödi	14	Cd	46.49N	8.55 E
Todo-ga-Saki	27	Pd	39.33N	142.05 E
Todos os Santos, Baía de-	52	Mg	12.48S	38.38W
Todos Santos	47	Bd	23.27N	110.13W
Todos Santos, Bahía-	48	Ab	31.48N	116.42W
Tofino	42	Eg	49.09N	125.54W
Tofte	8	De	59.33N	10.34 E
Toftlund	8	Ci	55.11N	9.04 E
Tofua Island	61	Fc	19.45S	175.05W
Toga	63b	Ca	13.26S	166.41 E
Tōgane	29	Gd	35.33N	140.21 E
Tog Dārōr	35	Hc	10.25N	50.00 E
Togdere	35	Hd	9.01N	47.07 E
Tog-Dheer [3]	35	Hd	9.50N	45.50 E
Togi	29	Ec	37.08N	136.43 E
Togiak	40	Ge	59.04N	160.24W
Togian, Kepulauan-=Togian Islands (EN)	26	Hg	0.20S	122.00 E
Togian Islands (EN)= Togian, Kepulauan-	26	Hg	0.20S	122.00 E
Togliatti	6	Ke	53.31N	49.26 E
Togni	35	Fb	18.05N	35.10 E
Togo	31	Hh	8.00N	1.10 E
Togrog Ul → Qahar Youyi Qianqi	28	Bd	40.46N	113.13 E
Togtoh	27	Jc	40.17N	111.15 E
Toguĉin	20	De	55.16N	84.33 E
Toguzak	17	Kj	54.05N	62.48 E
Togwotee Pass	43	Ec	43.45N	110.04W
Tohen	35	Ic	11.44N	51.15 E
Tohma	24	Hc	38.31N	38.25 E
Tohmajärvi	7	He	62.11N	30.23 E
Tohopekaliga, Lake-	44	Gk	28.12N	81.23W
Toi	29	Fd	34.54N	138.47 E
Toijala	7	Ff	61.10N	23.52 E
Toi-Misaki	28	Ki	31.26N	131.19 E
Toisvesi	8	Jb	62.20N	23.45 E
Tōjō	29	Cd	34.53N	133.16 E
Tojtepa	18	Gd	41.03N	69.22 E
Tok	10	Jg	49.43N	13.50 E
Tok	16	Rc	52.46N	52.22 E
Tok	40	Kd	63.20N	142.59W
Tokachi-Dake	29a	Cb	43.25N	142.41 E
Tokachi-Gawa	29a	Cb	42.41N	143.37 E
Tokachi-Heiya	29a	Cb	43.00N	143.20 E
Tokachimitsumata	29a	Cb	43.31N	143.07 E
Tōkai [Jap.]	29	Gc	36.27N	140.34 E
Tōkai [Jap.]	29	Ed	35.01N	136.51 E
Tokaj	16	Ld	51.18N	41.04 E
Tokaj	10	Rh	48.07N	21.25 E
Tōkamachi	28	Of	37.08N	138.46 E
Tokanui	62	Cg	46.34S	168.57 E
Tokara Islands (EN)= Tokara-Rettō	21	Og	29.35N	129.45 E
Tokara-Kaikyō	28	Ki	30.10N	130.15 E
Tokara-Rettō=Tokara Islands (EN)	21	Og	29.35N	129.45 E
Tokashiki-Jima	29b	Ab	26.13N	127.21 E
Tokat	23	Ea	40.19N	36.34 E
Tŏkch'ŏn	28	Ie	39.45N	126.15 E
Tok-Do	28	Kf	37.22N	131.58 E
Tokelau [5]	58	Je	9.00S	171.46W
Tokelau/Union Islands	57	Je	9.00S	171.45W
Toki	29	Ed	35.22N	137.11 E
Tokke	8	Ce	59.00N	9.15 E
Tokke	8	Be	59.27N	7.58 E
Tokkuztara/Gongliu	27	Dc	43.30N	82.15 E
Tokmak [Kirg.-U.S.S.R.]	19	Hg	42.49N	75.19 E
Tokmak [Ukr.-U.S.S.R.]	19	Df	47.13N	35.43 E
Tokomaru Bay	61	Eg	38.08S	178.20 E
Tokoname	29	Ed	34.53N	136.49 E
Tokoro	29a	Da	44.08N	144.03 E
Tokoroa	61	Eg	38.13S	175.52 E
Tokoro-Gawa	29a	Da	44.08N	144.04 E
Toksovo	8	Nd	60.10N	30.32 E
Toksu/Xinhe	27	Dc	41.34N	82.38 E
Toksun	27	Ec	42.47N	88.38 E
Toktogul	19	Hg	41.50N	73.01 E
Toktogulskoje Vodohranilišče	18	Id	41.45N	73.00 E
Tokuji	29	Bd	34.11N	131.39 E
Tokulu	65b	Bb	20.06S	174.48W
Toku-no-Shima	27	Mf	27.45N	128.50 E
Tokunoshima	29b	Bb	27.45N	129.00 E
Tokur	20	If	53.09N	132.50 E
Tokushima	27	Ne	34.04N	134.34 E
Tokushima Ken [2]	28	Mh	33.50N	134.10 E
Tokuyama [Jap.]	29	Ed	35.43N	136.27 E
Tokuyama [Jap.]	28	Kg	34.03N	131.49 E
Tokwe	37	Ed	20.09S	31.54 E
Tōkyō	22	Pf	35.40N	139.46 E
Tokyo Bay (EN)=Tōkyō-Wan	28	Og	35.38N	139.57 E
Tōkyō To [2]	28	Og	35.40N	139.20 E
Tōkyō-Wan=Tokyo Bay (EN)	28	Og	35.38N	139.57 E
Tola	21	Me	48.57N	104.48 E
Tolaga Bay	62	Hc	38.22S	178.18 E
Tolbazy	17	Gi	54.02N	55.59 E
Tolbuhin [2]	15	Kf	43.34N	27.50 E
Tolbuhin	15	Kf	43.34N	27.50 E
Toledo [3]	13	Ie	39.50N	4.00W
Toledo [Blz.]	49	Ce	16.25N	88.50W
Toledo [Braz.]	56	Jb	24.44S	53.45W
Toledo [Oh.-U.S.]	39	Ke	41.39N	83.32W
Toledo [Phil.]	26	Hd	10.23N	123.38 E
Toledo [Sp.]	6	Fh	39.52N	4.01W
Toledo, Montes de-	13	He	39.35N	4.20W
Toledo Bend Reservoir	43	Ie	31.30N	93.45W
Tolentino	14	Hg	43.12N	13.17 E
Tolfa	14	Fh	42.09N	11.56 E
Tolfa, Monti della-	14	Fh	42.10N	11.55 E
Tolga	7	Ce	62.25N	11.00 E
Toli	27	Db	45.57N	83.37 E
Toliary [3]	37	Gd	22.00S	44.00 E
Toliary	31	Lk	23.21S	43.39 E
Tolima [2]	54	Cc	3.45N	75.15W
Tolima, Nevado del-	52	Ie	4.40N	75.19W
Toling→Zanda	27	Ce	31.28N	79.50 E
Tolitoli	26	Hf	1.02N	120.49 E
Toll	64d	Bb	7.22N	151.37 E
Tollarp	8	Ei	55.56N	13.59 E
Tollja, Zaliv-	20	Ea	76.40N	100.00 E
Tolmačevo	8	Nf	58.48N	30.01 E
Tolmezzo	14	Hd	46.24N	13.01 E
Tolmin	14	Hd	46.11N	13.44 E
Tolna	10	Oj	46.26N	18.47 E
Tolna [2]	10	Oj	46.30N	18.35 E
Tolo	36	Cc	2.56S	18.34 E
Tolo, Gulf of- (EN)=Tolo, Teluk-	21	Oj	2.00S	122.30 E
Tolo, Teluk-=Tolo, Gulf of- (EN)	21	Oj	2.00S	122.30 E
Toločin	7	Gi	54.25N	29.41 E
Tolosa	13	Ja	43.08N	2.04W
Tolstoj, Mys-	5	Rd	59.10N	155.05 E
Toltén	56	Fe	39.13S	73.14W
Tolú	54	Cb	9.32N	75.34W
Toluca, Nevado de-	38	Jh	19.08N	99.44W
Toluca de Lerdo	39	Jh	19.17N	99.40W
Tom	21	Kd	56.50N	84.27 E
Toma	34	Ec	12.46N	2.53W
Tomah	45	Ke	43.59N	90.30W
Tomakomai	27	Pc	42.38N	141.36 E
Tomamae	29a	Ba	44.18N	141.39 E
Tomanivi	63d	Bb	17.37S	178.01 E
Tomar	13	De	39.36N	8.25W
Tómaros	15	Dj	39.32N	20.45 E
Tomaševka	16	Cd	51.33N	23.40 E
Tomás Young	55	Ai	28.36S	62.11W
Tomaszów Lubelski	10	Tf	50.28N	23.25 E
Tomaszów Mazowiecki	10	Qe	51.32N	20.01 E
Tomatlán	48	Gh	19.56N	105.15W
Tombador, Serra dos-	54	Gf	12.00S	57.40W
Tombigbee River	43	Je	31.04N	87.58W
Tomboco	36	Bd	6.45S	13.18 E
Tombouctou=Timbuktu (EN)	31	Gg	16.46N	2.59W
Tombstone	46	Jk	31.43N	110.04W
Tomé	56	Fe	36.37S	72.57W
Tomé-Açu	54	Id	2.25S	48.09W
Tomelilla	7	Ci	55.33N	13.57 E
Tomelloso	13	Ie	39.10N	3.01W
Tomichi Creek	45	Cg	38.31N	106.58W
Tomie	29	Ae	32.37N	128.46 E
Tominé	34	Cc	10.53N	13.18W
Tomini, Gulf of- (EN)= Tomini, Teluk-	21	Oj	0.20S	121.00 E
Tomini, Teluk-=Tomini, Gulf of- (EN)	21	Oj	0.20S	121.00 E
Tominian	34	Ec	13.17N	4.35W
Tomioka [Jap.]	29	Gc	37.20N	140.59 E
Tomioka [Jap.]	29	Fc	36.15N	138.52 E
Tomkinson Ranges	59	Fe	26.10S	129.05 E
Tomma	7	Cc	66.15N	12.48 E
Tomo, Rio-	54	Eb	5.20N	67.48W
Tomochic	48	Fc	28.20N	107.51W
Tomorit, Mali i-	15	Di	40.40N	20.09 E
Tomotu Neo	63c	Ab	10.41S	165.47 E
Tomotu Noi	63c	Bb	10.50S	166.02 E
Tompa	10	Pj	46.12N	19.33 E
Tompe	26	Gg	0.12S	119.48 E
Tompo	20	Id	62.50N	134.47 E
Tompo	20	Id	64.00N	136.00 E
Tom Price	59	Dd	22.40S	117.55 E
Tomsk	22	Kd	56.30N	84.58 E
Tomskaja Oblast [3]	20	De	58.20N	81.30 E
Tomtabacken	8	Fg	57.30N	14.28 E
Tomur Feng	21	Ke	42.02N	80.05 E
Tom White, Mount-	40	Kd	60.40N	143.40W
Tonaki-Shima	29b	Ab	26.21N	127.09 E
Tonalá	47	Fe	16.04N	93.45W
Tonale, Passo del-	14	Ed	46.16N	10.35 E
Tonami	29	Ec	36.38N	136.57 E
Tonara	14	Dj	40.02N	9.10 E
Tonasket	46	Fb	48.42N	119.26W
Tonb-e Bozorg	24	Pi	26.15N	55.03 E
Tonbetsu-Gawa	29a	Ca	45.08N	142.23 E
Tonbridge	9	Nj	51.12N	0.16 E
Tondano	26	Hf	1.19N	124.54 E
Tondela	13	Dd	40.31N	8.05W
Tønder	7	Bi	54.56N	8.54 E
Tone-Gawa	29	Gd	35.44N	140.51 E
Tonekābon	23	Hb	36.53N	50.56 E
Toney	66	Of	75.48S	115.48W
Tonga [1]	58	Jf	20.00S	175.00W
Tonga	35	Ed	9.28N	31.03 E

Index Symbols

- [1] Independent Nation
- [2] State, Region
- [3] District, County
- [4] Municipality
- [5] Colony, Dependency
- Continent
- Physical Region
- Historical or Cultural Region
- Mount, Mountain
- Volcano
- Hill
- Mountains, Mountain Range
- Hills, Escarpment
- Plateau, Upland
- Pass, Gap
- Plain, Lowland
- Delta
- Salt Flat
- Valley, Canyon
- Crater, Cave
- Karst Features
- Depression
- Polder
- Desert, Dunes
- Forest, Woods
- Heath, Steppe
- Oasis
- Cape, Point
- Coast, Beach
- Cliff
- Peninsula
- Isthmus
- Sandbank
- Island
- Atoll
- Rock, Reef
- Islands, Archipelago
- Rocks, Reefs
- Coral Reef
- Well, Spring
- Geyser
- River, Stream
- Waterfall Rapids
- River Mouth, Estuary
- Lake
- Salt Lake
- Intermittent Lake
- Reservoir
- Swamp, Pond
- Canal
- Glacier
- Ice Shelf, Pack Ice
- Ocean
- Sea
- Gulf, Bay
- Strait, Fjord
- Lagoon
- Bank
- Seamount
- Tablemount
- Ridge
- Shelf
- Basin
- Escarpment, Sea Scarp
- Fracture
- Trench, Abyss
- National Park, Reserve
- Point of Interest
- Recreation Site
- Cave, Cavern
- Historic Site
- Ruins
- Wall, Walls
- Church, Abbey
- Temple
- Scientific Station
- Airport
- Port
- Lighthouse
- Mine
- Tunnel
- Dam, Bridge

Tongaat 37 Ee 29.37S 31.03 E
Tonga Islands 57 Jf 20.00S 175.00W
Tonga Ridge (EN) 57 Jg 21.00S 175.00W
Tongariki 63b Dc 17.01S 168.37 E
Tongatapu Group 57 Jg 21.10S 175.10W
Tongatapu Island 61 Fd 21.10S 175.10W
Tonga Trench (EN) 3 Kl 20.00S 173.00W
Tongbai 28 Bh 32.21N 113.24 E
Tongbai Shan 27 Je 32.20N 113.14 E
Tongcheng [China] 28 Bj 29.15N 113.49 E
Tongcheng [China] 28 Di 31.04N 116.56 E
Tongcheng → Dong'e 28 Df 36.19N 116.14 E
Tongchuan 27 Id 35.10N 109.03 E
Tongdao (Shuangjiang) 27 If 26.14N 109.45 E
Tongde 27 Hd 35.29N 100.32 E
Tongeren/Tongres 11 Ld 50.47N 5.28 E
Tonggu 28 Cj 28.33N 114.21 E
Tongguzbasti 27 Dd 38.23N 82.00 E
Tonggu Zhang 27 Kg 24.12N 116.22 E
Tong-Hae=Japan, Sea of- (EN) 21 Pf 40.00N 134.00 E
Tonghai 22 Mg 24.15N 102.45 E
Tonghe 27 Mb 46.01N 128.42 E
Tonghua 22 Oe 41.43N 125.55 E
Tongjiang 27 Nb 47.39N 132.30 E
Tongjosŏn-man 21 Of 39.30N 128.00 E
Tongliao 22 Oe 43.37N 122.15 E
Tongling 27 Ke 30.49N 117.47 E
Tonglu 28 Ej 29.48N 119.39 E
Tongmun'gŏ-ri 27 Mc 40.58N 127.08 E
Tongoa 63b Dc 16.54S 168.33 E
Tongoy 56 Fd 30.15S 71.30W
Tongren [China] 27 If 27.45N 109.09 E
Tongren [China] 27 Hd 35.40N 102.07 E
Tongres/Tongeren 11 Ld 50.47N 5.28 E
Tongsa Dzong 25 Ic 27.31N 90.30 E
Tongshan 28 Cj 29.36N 114.30 E
Tongta 25 Jd 21.20N 99.16 E
Tongtian He/Zhi Qu 21 Lf 33.26N 96.36 E
Tongue 9 Ic 58.28N 4.25W
Tongue of the Ocean 49 Ia 24.12N 77.10W
Tongue River 43 Fb 46.24N 105.52W
Tongxian 27 Kd 39.52N 116.38 E
Tongxin 27 Id 36.59N 105.50 E
Tongxu 28 Cg 34.29N 114.27 E
Tongyu (Kaitong) 27 Lc 44.47N 123.05 E
Tongyu Yunhe 28 Eg 34.46N 119.51 E
Tongzi 27 If 28.09N 106.50 E
Tonichi 48 Ec 28.35N 109.34W
Tönisvorst 12 Ic 51.19N 6.28 E
Tonj 35 Dd 7.17N 28.45 E
Tonj 30 Jh 7.31N 29.25 E
Tonk 25 Fc 26.10N 75.47 E
Tonkin (EN)=Bac-Phan 21 Mg 22.00N 105.00 E
Tonkin, Gulf of- (EN)= Beibu Wan 21 Mh 20.00N 108.00 E
Tonkin, Gulf of- (EN)=Vinh Bac Phan 21 Mh 20.00N 108.00 E
Tônlé Sab, Bœng-=Tonle Sap (EN) 21 Mh 13.00N 104.00 E
Tonle Sap (EN)=Tônlé Sab, Bœng- 21 Mh 13.00N 104.00 E
Tonnay-Charente 11 Fi 45.57N 0.54W
Tonneins 11 Gj 44.23N 0.19 E
Tönning 10 Eb 54.19N 8.57 E
Tōno 28 Pe 39.19N 141.32 E
Tonopah 43 Dd 38.04N 117.14W
Tonoshō 29 Dd 34.29N 134.11 E
Tonosí 49 Gj 7.24N 80.27W
Tønsberg 7 Cg 59.17N 10.25 E
Tonstad 7 Bg 58.40N 6.43 E
Tonumeia 65b Bb 20.28S 174.46W
Tonya 24 Hb 40.53N 39.16 E
Tooele 43 Ec 40.32N 112.18W
Toora-Hem 20 Ef 52.28N 96.22 E
Tootsi 8 Kf 58.34N 24.43 E
Toowoomba 58 Gg 27.33S 151.57 E
Topalu 15 Le 44.33N 28.03 E
Topa Taung 25 Jd 21.08N 95.12 E
Topeka 39 Jf 39.03N 95.41W
Topki 20 De 55.18N 85.40 E
Topko, Gora- 20 Ie 57.00N 137.23 E
Topl'a 10 Rh 48.45N 21.45 E
Toplet 15 Fe 44.48N 22.24 E
Toplica 15 Ef 43.13N 21.51 E
Toplița 15 Ic 46.55N 25.20 E
Topola 15 De 44.16N 20.42 E
Topol'čany 10 Oh 48.34N 18.10 E
Topolnica 15 Hg 42.11N 24.18 E
Topolobampo 47 Cc 25.36N 109.03W
Topolobampo, Bahía de- 48 Ee 25.30N 109.05W
Topolog 15 Hd 44.56N 24.16 E
Topolovgrad 15 Jg 42.05N 26.20 E
Topozero, Ozero- 5 Jb 65.40N 32.00 E
Toppenish 46 Ec 46.23N 120.19W
Toprakkale 24 Gd 37.06N 36.07 E
Top Springs 59 Gc 16.38S 131.50 E
Toquepala 54 Eg 17.38S 69.56W
Tor 35 Ed 7.51N 33.36 E
Tora 64d Ba 7.39N 151.53 E
Toraigh/Tory Island 9 Ef 55.16N 8.13W
Tora Island Pass 64d Ba 7.39N 151.53 E
Toråker 8 Gd 60.31N 16.29 E
Torbalı 24 Bc 38.10N 27.21 E
Torbat-e Heydarīyeh 22 Hf 35.16N 59.13 E
Torbat-e Jam 23 Jb 35.14N 60.36 E
Torbay 9 Jk 50.28N 3.30W
Torbert, Mount- 40 Id 61.25N 152.24W
Torch Lake 44 Ec 45.00N 85.19W
Torčin 10 Vf 50.44N 25.05 E
Tordesillas 13 Hc 41.30N 5.00W
Tordino 14 Hh 42.44N 13.59 E
Töre 7 Fd 65.54N 22.39 E
Töreboda 7 Dg 58.43N 14.08 E
Torekov 8 Eh 56.26N 12.37 E
Torenberg 11 Lb 52.15N 5.55 E
Torez 16 Kf 47.59N 38.41 E
Torgau 10 Ie 51.34N 13.00 E
Torgelow 10 Kc 53.38N 14.01 E
Torgun 16 Od 50.10N 46.20 E
Torhamn 8 Fh 56.05N 15.50 E
Torhout 11 Jc 51.04N 3.06 E
Toribulu 26 Hg 0.19S 120.01 E
Torigni-sur-Vire 12 Be 49.05N 0.59W
Torii-Tōge 29 Ed 35.59N 137.49 E
Tori-Jima 29b Ab 26.35N 126.50 E
Torino = Turin (EN) 6 Gf 45.03N 7.40 E
Toriparu 55 Fc 16.20S 53.55W
Tori-Shima [Jap.] 27 Pe 30.25N 140.15 E
Tori-Shima [Jap.] 29b Bb 27.52N 128.14 E
Torit 35 Ee 4.24N 32.34 E
Torixoreu 54 Hg 16.15S 52.26W
Torkoviči 7 Hg 58.53N 30.20 E
Törmänen 7 Gb 68.36N 27.29 E
Tormes 13 Fc 41.18N 6.29W
Tornado Mountain 46 Hb 49.58N 114.39W
Tornavacas, Puerto de- 13 Gd 40.16N 5.37W
Torneå/Tornio 7 Fd 65.51N 24.08 E
Torneälven 5 Ib 65.48N 24.08 E
Torneträsk 7 Eb 68.22N 19.06 E
Torngat Mountains 38 Md 59.00N 64.00W
Tornio/Torneå 7 Fd 65.51N 24.08 E
Tornionjoki 5 Ib 65.48N 24.08 E
Tornquist 55 An 38.06S 62.14W
Toro 13 Gc 41.31N 5.24W
Toro 8 Gf 58.50N 17.50 E
Toro, Cerro del- 52 Jh 29.08S 69.48W
Toro, Isla del- 48 Kg 21.35N 97.32W
Toro, Monte- 13 Qe 39.59N 4.07 E
Toroiaga, Vîrful- 15 Hb 47.44N 24.43 E
Torokina 63a Bb 6.14S 155.03 E
Tōro-Ko 29a Db 43.08N 144.30 E
Törökszentmiklós 10 Qi 47.11N 20.25 E
Torola, Río- 49 Cg 13.52N 88.30W
Toronto 39 Le 43.39N 79.23W
Toropec 19 Dd 56.31N 31.39 E
Tororo 36 Fb 0.41N 34.11 E
Toros Dağları=Taurus Mountains (EN) 21 Ff 37.00N 33.00 E
Torquato Severo 55 Ej 31.02S 54.11W
Torquay 9 Jk 50.29N 3.29W
Torrá, Cerro- 52 Ie 4.38N 76.15W
Torrance 46 Fj 33.50N 118.19W
Torre Annunziata 14 Ij 40.45N 14.27 E
Torreblanca 13 Md 40.13N 0.12 E
Torrecilla 13 Hh 36.41N 5.00W
Torrecilla en Cameros 13 Jb 42.16N 2.37W
Torre del Greco 14 Ij 40.47N 14.22 E
Torre del Mar 13 Hh 36.44N 4.06W
Torredembarra 13 Nc 41.09N 1.24 E
Torre de Moncorvo 13 Ec 41.10N 7.03W
Torre de' Passeri 14 Hh 42.14N 13.56 E
Torredonjimeno 13 Ig 37.46N 3.57W
Torrejón de Ardoz 13 Id 40.27N 3.29W
Torrelaguna 13 Id 40.50N 3.32W
Torrelavega 13 Ha 43.21N 4.03W
Torre Miró, Puerto de- 13 Ld 40.42N 0.05W
Torremolinos 13 Hh 36.37N 4.30W
Torrens, Lake- 57 Eh 31.00S 137.50 E
Torrens Creek 59 Jd 20.46S 145.02 E
Torrent de l'Horta/Torrente 13 Le 39.26N 0.28W
Torrente/Torrent de l'Horta 13 Le 39.26N 0.28W
Torrenueva 13 If 38.38N 3.22W
Torreón 39 Ig 25.33N 103.26W
Torre-Pacheco 13 Lg 37.44N 0.57W
Torre Pellice 14 Bf 44.49N 7.13 E
Tôrres 64d Ab 7.19N 151.27 E
Tôrres 56 Kc 29.21S 49.44W
Torrès, Iles-=Torres Islands (EN) 57 Hf 13.15S 166.37 E
Torres Islands (EN)=Torrès, Iles- 57 Hf 13.15S 166.37 E
Torres Novas 13 De 39.29N 8.32W
Torres Strait 57 Ff 10.25S 142.10 E
Torres Vedras 13 Ce 39.06N 9.16W
Torrevieja 13 Lg 37.59N 0.41W
Torridon, Loch- 9 Hd 57.35N 5.50W
Torriglia 14 Df 44.31N 9.10 E
Torrijos 13 He 39.59N 4.17W
Torrington [Ct.-U.S.] 44 Ke 41.48N 73.08W
Torrington [Wy.-U.S.] 43 Gc 42.04N 104.11W
Torroella de Montgrí 13 Pb 42.02N 3.08 E
Torröjen 7 Cf 63.55N 12.56 E
Torrox 13 Ih 36.46N 3.58W
Torsås 7 Dh 56.24N 16.00 E
Torsby 7 Cf 60.08N 13.00 E
Torshälla 8 Ge 59.25N 16.28 E
Torsken 7 Db 69.20N 17.06 E
Torsö 7 Cg 58.50N 13.50 E
Torto 14 Hm 37.58N 13.46 E
Tortola 47 Le 18.27N 64.36W
Tortoli 14 Dk 39.55N 9.39 E
Tortona 14 Cf 44.54N 8.52 E
Tortorici 14 Il 38.02N 14.49 E
Tortosa 13 Md 40.48N 0.31 E
Tortosa, Cabo de-/Tortosa, Cap de- 13 Md 40.43N 0.55 E
Tortosa, Cap de-/Tortosa, Cabo de- 13 Md 40.43N 0.55 E
Tortue, Ile de la- 47 Jd 20.04N 72.49W
Tortuga, Isla- 48 Dd 27.26N 111.55W
Tortum 24 Ib 40.19N 41.35 E
Torud 24 Pe 35.26N 55.07 E
Torugart, Pereval- 21 Je 40.32N 75.24 E
Torul 24 Hb 40.35N 39.18 E
Toruń [2] 10 Oc 53.00N 18.35 E
Toruń 10 Oc 53.02N 18.35 E
Torunos 49 Li 8.30N 70.04W
Toruńska, Kotlina- 10 Oc 53.00N 18.30 E
Torup 7 Ch 56.58N 13.05 E
Tõrva/Tyrva 7 Fg 58.01N 25.59 E
Tory Island/Toraigh 9 Ef 55.16N 8.13W
Torysa 10 Rh 48.39N 21.21 E
Toržok 19 Dd 57.03N 35.01 E
Tosa 28 Lh 33.29N 133.25 E
Tosas, Puerto de-/Toses, Port de- 13 Ob 42.20N 2.01 E
Tosashimizu 28 Lh 32.46N 132.57 E
Tosa-Wan 28 Lh 33.25N 133.35 E
Tosa-yamada 29 Ce 33.36N 133.40 E
Toscana = Tuscany (EN) [2] 14 Eg 43.25N 11.00 E
Toses, Port de-/Tosas, Puerto de- 13 Ob 42.20N 2.01 E
Toshibetsu-Gawa [Jap.] 29a Cb 42.54N 143.25 E
Toshibetsu-Gawa [Jap.] 29a Ab 42.25N 139.48 E
Tōshi-Jima 29 Ed 34.31N 136.52 E
To-Shima 29 Fd 34.31N 139.17 E
Tosno 7 Hg 59.34N 30.50 E
Toson-Cengel 27 Gb 48.47N 98.15 E
Toson Hu 27 Gd 37.08N 96.52 E
Töss 14 Cc 47.33N 8.33 E
Tossa de Mar 13 Oc 41.43N 2.56 E
Tostado 56 Hc 29.14S 61.46W
Tõstamaa/Tystama 8 Jf 58.17N 23.52 E
Tosu 29 Be 33.22N 130.30 E
Tosya 24 Fb 41.01N 34.02 E
Totak 8 Be 59.40N 7.55 E
Totana 13 Kg 37.46N 1.30W
Toten 8 Dd 60.40N 10.50 E
Toteng 37 Cd 20.23S 22.59 E
Tôtes 11 He 49.41N 1.03 E
Totes Gebirge 14 Hc 47.42N 13.55 E
Tõtias 35 Ge 3.57N 43.58 E
Totland 12 Ad 50.40N 1.32W
Totma 19 Ed 60.00N 42.45 E
Totness 54 Gb 5.53N 56.19W
Toto 36 Bd 7.10S 14.25 E
Totonicapán [3] 49 Bf 15.00N 91.20W
Totonicapán 47 Ff 14.55N 91.22W
Totora 54 Eg 17.42S 65.09W
Totoras 55 Bk 32.35S 61.11W
Totota 34 Dd 6.49N 9.56W
Totoya 63d Cc 18.57S 179.50W
Totten Glacier 66 He 66.45S 116.10 E
Totton 12 Ad 50.55N 1.29W
Tottori 27 Nd 35.30N 134.14 E
Tottori Ken [2] 28 Lg 35.25N 133.50 E
Tou, Motu- 64p Bb 21.11S 159.48W
Touâjil 32 Ee 21.45N 12.35W
Touat 30 Gf 27.40N 0.01W
Touba [3] 34 Dd 8.15N 7.45W
Touba 34 Dd 8.17N 7.41W
Toubkal, Jebel- 30 Ge 31.03N 7.55W
Touch 11 Hk 43.38N 1.24 E
Toucy 11 Jg 47.44N 3.18 E
Tougan 34 Ec 13.04N 3.04W
Touggourt 31 He 33.06N 6.04 E
Tougué 34 Cc 11.27N 11.41W
Touho 63b Be 20.47S 165.14 E
Touil 32 Hb 35.33N 2.36 E
Toûil 13 Oi 35.33N 2.36 E
Toukoto 34 Dc 13.28N 9.52W
Toul 11 Lf 48.41N 5.54 E
Touléplеu 34 Dd 6.35N 8.25W
Toulon 6 Gg 43.07N 5.56 E
Toulouse 6 Gg 43.36N 1.26 E
Toulumne River 46 Eh 37.36N 121.10W
Toumodi 34 Dd 6.33N 5.01W
Tounassine, Hamada- 32 Fd 28.36N 5.10W
Toungo 34 Hd 8.07N 12.03 E
Toungoo 22 Lh 18.56N 96.26 E
Touques 11 Ge 49.22N 0.06 E
Toura 35 Bc 10.30N 15.19 E
Touraine 11 Hg 47.12N 1.30 E
Touraine, Val de- 11 Hg 47.20N 1.30 E
Tourcoing 11 Jd 50.43N 3.09 E
Touriñan, Cabo de- 13 Ca 43.03N 9.18W
Tourine 32 Ee 22.00N 12.15W
Tournai/Doornik 11 Jd 50.36N 3.23 E
Tournai-Kain 12 Fd 50.38N 3.22 E
Tournon 11 Ki 45.04N 4.50 E
Tournus 11 Kh 46.34N 4.54 E
Touros 54 Ke 5.12S 35.28W
Tours 6 Gf 47.23N 0.41 E
Tourteron 12 Ge 49.32N 4.39 E
Toury 11 Hf 48.12N 1.56 E
Touside, Pic- 35 Ba 21.02N 16.25 E
Toussoro 35 Cd 9.02N 23.55 E
Toutouba 63b Cb 15.34S 167.16 E
Touwsrivier 37 Cf 33.20S 20.00 E
Toužim 10 If 50.04N 12.59 E
Tovar 49 Li 8.20N 71.46W
Tovarkovski 16 Kc 53.43N 38.13 E
Tovdalselva 8 Cf 58.12N 8.06 E
Tove 12 Bb 52.04N 0.50W
Tōwa 29 Gb 39.23N 141.15 E
Towada 28 Pd 40.35N 141.13 E
Towada-Kō 29 Ga 40.28N 140.55 E
Towanda 44 Ie 41.46N 76.27W
Tower 45 Jc 47.48N 92.17W
Towner 45 Fb 48.21N 100.25W
Townsend 46 Jc 46.19N 111.31W
Townshend, Cape- 59 Kd 22.15S 150.30 E
Townsville 58 Ff 19.16S 146.48 E
Towot 35 Ed 6.12N 34.25 E
Towson 44 If 39.24N 76.36W
Towuti, Danau- 26 Hg 2.45S 121.32 E
Toxkan He 27 Dc 41.08N 80.11 E
Tōya 29a Bb 42.39N 140.48 E
Toyah Creek 45 Ek 31.18N 103.27W
Tōya-Ko 28 Pc 42.33N 140.50 E
Toyama 22 Pf 36.41N 137.13 E
Toyama Ken [2] 28 Nf 30.40N 137.10 E
Toyama Trench (EN) 29 Ec 38.00N 138.00 E
Toyama-Wan 28 Nf 37.00N 137.15 E
Tōyō 28 Mh 33.22N 134.18 E
Toyohashi 27 Oe 34.46N 137.23 E
Toyokoro 29a Cb 42.48N 143.28 E
Toyonaka 29 Dd 34.47N 135.28 E
Toyo'oka 27 Od 35.33N 137.54 E
Toyosaka 29 Fc 37.55N 139.12 E
Toyota 28 Ng 35.05N 137.09 E
Toyotama 29 Ad 34.27N 129.19 E
Toyotomi 29a Ba 45.08N 141.47 E
Toyoura 29 Bd 34.10N 130.55 E
Trabancos 13 Gc 41.27N 5.11W
Traben Trabach 12 Je 49.57N 7.07 E
Trabzon 22 Fe 40.59N 39.43 E
Traer 45 Je 42.12N 92.28W
Trafalgar, Cabo- 13 Fh 36.11N 6.02W
Tragacete 13 Kd 40.21N 1.51W
Traiguén 56 Fe 38.15S 72.41W
Trail 39 He 49.06N 117.43W
Traill 41 Jd 72.45N 24.00W
Trairas, Rio- 55 Hb 14.07S 48.31W
Trairi 54 Kd 3.17S 39.15W
Traisen 14 Jb 48.22N 15.46 E
Trakai/Trakaj 7 Fi 54.38N 24.57 E
Trakaj/Trakai 7 Fi 54.38N 24.57 E
Trakt 17 Ee 62.44N 51.11 E
Trakya = Thrace (EN) 15 Jh 41.20N 26.45 E
Trakya = Thrace (EN) 5 Ig 41.20N 26.45 E
Tralee/Trá Lí 9 Di 52.16N 9.42W
Tralee Bay/Bá Thrá Lí 9 Di 52.15N 9.59W
Trá Lí/Tralee 9 Di 52.16N 9.42W
Trá Mhór/Tramore 9 Fi 52.10N 7.10W
Tramore/Trá Mhór 9 Fi 52.10N 7.10W
Tramping Lake 46 Ka 52.10N 108.48W
Trãn 15 Fg 42.50N 22.39 E
Tranås 7 Dg 58.03N 14.59 E
Trancoso 13 Ed 40.47N 7.21W
Tranebjerg 8 Di 55.50N 10.36 E
Tranemo 8 Eg 57.29N 13.21 E
Trang 22 Li 7.33N 99.36 E
Trani 14 Ki 41.17N 16.25 E
Transantarctic Mountains (EN) 66 Lg 85.00S 175.00W
Transcaucasia (EN) 5 Kg 41.00N 45.00 E
Transilvania = Transylvania (EN) 15 Hc 46.30N 25.00 E
Transilvania = Transylvania (EN) 5 If 46.30N 25.00 E
Transkei 30 Jl 31.30S 29.00 E
Transkei 37 Df 32.45S 28.30 E
Transtrand 8 Ec 61.05N 13.19 E
Transtrandsfjällen 8 Ec 61.15N 12.58 E
Transvaal [2] 37 Dd 25.00S 30.00 E
Transylvania (EN) = Transilvania 15 Hc 46.30N 25.00 E
Transylvania (EN) = Transilvania 5 If 46.30N 25.00 E
Transylvanian Alps (EN)= Carpații Meridionali 5 If 45.30N 24.15 E
Trants Bay 51c Bc 16.46N 62.09W
Trapani 6 Hh 38.01N 12.29 E
Trapper Peak 46 Hd 45.54N 114.18W
Trappes 12 Ef 48.47N 2.01 E
Traralgon 59 Jg 38.12S 146.32 E
Trarza [3] 32 Ef 18.00N 15.00W
Trarza 30 Fg 17.20N 14.40W
Trașcăului, Munții- 15 Gc 46.23N 23.33 E
Trasimeno, Lago- 14 Gg 43.10N 12.05 E
Träslövsläge 8 Eg 57.04N 12.16 E
Trás os Montes e Alto Douro 13 Ec 41.30N 7.15W
Trat 25 Kf 12.13N 102.16 E
Traun 14 Ib 48.13N 14.14 E
Traun 14 Ib 48.16N 14.22 E
Traunsee 14 Hc 47.52N 13.48 E
Traunstein 10 Ii 47.53N 12.39 E
Trave 10 Gc 53.54N 10.50 E
Travemünde, Lübeck- 10 Gc 53.57N 10.52 E
Travers, Mount- 61 Dh 42.01S 172.44 E
Traverse, Lake- 45 Hd 45.43N 96.40W
Traverse City 43 Jc 44.46N 85.37W
Traverse Islands 66 Ad 56.36S 27.43W
Travers Reservoir 46 Ia 50.14N 112.51W
Travesia 49 Df 15.20N 87.53W
Travis, Lake- 45 Hk 30.27N 98.00W
Travnik 23 Ff 44.14N 17.40 E
Travo 11a Bb 41.54N 9.24 E
Trbovlje 14 Jd 46.10N 15.03 E
Treasurers 63c Ba 9.53S 167.09 E
Treasury Islands 63a Bb 7.22S 155.37 E
Trebbia 14 De 45.04N 9.41 E
Třebíč 10 Lg 49.13N 15.53 E
Trebinje 14 Mh 42.43N 18.21 E
Trebisacce 14 Kk 39.52N 16.32 E
Trebišnjica 14 Lg 43.01N 17.47 E
Trebišov 10 Rh 48.40N 21.43 E
Treblinka 10 Sd 52.40N 22.03 E
Trebnje 14 Je 45.54N 15.01 E
Třeboň 10 Kg 49.01N 14.48 E
Třeboňská pánev 10 Kg 49.00N 14.50 E
Trégorrois 11 Cf 48.45N 3.15W
Tregrosse Islets 57 Gf 17.40S 150.45 E
Tréguier 11 Cf 48.47N 3.14W
Treherne 45 Gb 49.38N 98.41W
Treignac 11 Hi 45.32N 1.48 E
Treinta y Tres [2] 55 Ek 33.00S 54.15W
Treinta y Tres 56 Jd 33.14S 54.23W
Treis-Karden 12 Jd 50.11N 7.17 E
Trélazé 11 Fg 47.27N 0.28W
Trelew 56 Gf 43.15S 65.18W
Trelleborg 6 Hd 55.22N 13.10 E
Trélon 12 Gd 50.04N 4.06 E
Tremadoc Bay 9 Ii 52.40N 4.10W
Tremblant, Mount- 38 Le 46.15N 74.34W
Tremiti, Isole-=Tremiti Islands (EN) 5 Hg 42.10N 15.30 E
Tremiti Islands (EN)= Tremiti, Isole- 5 Hg 42.10N 15.30 E
Tremonton 46 If 41.43N 112.10W
Tremp 13 Mb 42.10N 0.54 E
Třemšín 10 Jg 49.33N 13.48 E
Trenche, Rivière- 44 Kb 47.35N 72.58W
Trenčín 10 Oh 48.54N 18.04 E
Trenque Lauquen 56 He 35.58S 62.42W
Trent 9 Mh 53.42N 0.41W
Trent, Vale of- 9 Li 52.45N 1.50W
Trentino-Alto Adige / Südtirol [2] 14 Fd 46.30N 11.20 E
Trento 14 Fd 46.04N 11.08 E
Trenton [Mo.-U.S.] 45 Jf 40.05N 93.37W
Trenton [N.J.-U.S.] 39 Le 40.13N 74.45W
Trenton [Ont.-Can.] 44 Ic 44.06N 77.35W
Tréon 12 Df 48.41N 1.20 E
Trepassey 42 Mg 46.44N 53.22W
Tres Arboles [Ur.] 56 Id 32.24S 56.43W
Tres Arroyos 53 Ji 38.22S 60.15W
Tres Bocas 55 Ck 32.44S 59.45W
Tres Carações 54 Ih 21.42S 45.16W
Tres Cruces, Cerro- 48 Mj 15.28N 92.24W
Três de Maio 55 Eh 27.47S 54.14W
Tres Esquinas 54 Cc 0.43N 75.15W
Tres Isletas 55 Bh 26.21S 60.26W
Treska 15 Eh 41.59N 21.19 E
Treskavica 14 Mg 43.35N 18.24 E
Três Lagoas 53 Kh 20.48S 51.43W
Três Marias, Represa- 54 Ig 18.15S 45.15W
Tres Montes, Peninsula- 56 Eg 46.50S 75.30W
Três Passos 56 Jc 27.27S 53.56W
Tres Picos, Cerro- [Arg.] 52 Ji 38.09S 61.57W
Tres Picos, Cerro- [Mex.] 48 Li 16.36N 94.13W
Três Pontas 55 Je 21.22S 45.31W
Tres Puntas, Cabo- [Arg.] 52 Jj 47.06S 65.53W
Tres Puntas, Cabo- [Guat.] 49 Cf 15.58N 88.37W
Três Ranchos 55 Id 18.22S 47.47W
Três Rios 55 Kf 22.07S 43.12W
Třešť 10 Lg 49.18N 15.28 E
Tres Valles 48 Kh 18.15N 96.08W
Tres Zapotes 47 Ee 18.28N 95.24W
Tretten 7 Cf 61.19N 10.19 E
Treuer Range 59 Gd 22.15S 130.50 E
Treungen 8 Ce 59.02N 8.33 E
Trêve, Lac la- 44 Ja 49.58N 75.31W
Trevi 14 Gh 42.52N 12.45 E
Trévières 12 Be 49.19N 0.54W
Treviglio 14 De 45.31N 9.35 E
Trevinca, Peña- 13 Fb 42.15N 6.46W
Treviño 13 Jb 42.44N 2.45W
Treviso 14 Ge 45.40N 12.15 E
Trevose Head 9 Hk 50.33N 5.01W
Trgovište 15 Fg 42.21N 22.06 E
Triánda 15 Lm 36.24N 28.10 E
Triangle 37 Ed 21.02S 31.28 E
Triángulos, Arrecifes- 48 Mg 20.57N 92.16W
Trianísia 15 Jm 36.18N 26.45 E
Tribeč 10 Oh 48.27N 18.15 E
Tribune 45 Fg 38.28N 101.45W
Tricarico 14 Kj 40.37N 16.09 E
Tricase 14 Mk 39.56N 18.22 E
Trichūr 25 Ff 10.31N 76.13 E
Tri City 46 De 43.02N 123.15W
Trie-Château 12 De 49.17N 1.50 E
Triel-sur-Seine 12 Ef 48.59N 2.01 E
Trier 10 Cg 49.45N 6.38 E
Trier-Ehrang 12 Ie 49.49N 6.41 E
Trier-Pfalzel 12 Ie 49.46N 6.41 E
Trieste 6 Hf 45.40N 13.46 E
Trieste, Golfo di- 14 He 45.40N 13.30 E
Trieux 11 Cf 48.50N 3.03W
Trifels 12 Je 49.11N 7.59 E
Triglav 5 Hf 46.23N 13.50 E
Trigno 14 Ih 42.04N 14.48 E
Tríkala 15 Ej 39.33N 21.46 E
Trikhonís, Límni- 15 Ek 38.34N 21.30 E
Trikomo/Trikomon 24 Ee 35.17N 33.52 E
Trikomon/Trikomo 24 Ee 35.17N 33.52 E
Trikora, Puncak- 26 Kg 4.15S 138.45 E
Trilport 12 Ef 48.57N 2.57 E
Trim/Baile Átha Troim 9 Gh 53.34N 6.47W
Trincheras 48 Gc 28.55N 104.18W
Trincomalee 22 Ki 8.34N 81.14 E
Trindade 54 Ig 16.40S 49.30W
Trindade, Ilha da- 52 Nh 20.31S 29.19W
Třinec 10 Og 49.41N 18.42 E
Tring 12 Bc 51.47N 0.39W
Tringía 15 Ej 39.38N 21.25 E
Trinidad 52 Jd 10.30N 61.15W
Trinidad [Bol.] 53 Jg 14.47S 64.47W
Trinidad [Ca.-U.S.] 46 Cf 41.07N 124.07W
Trinidad [Co.-U.S.] 39 If 37.10N 104.31W
Trinidad [Cuba] 47 Id 21.48N 79.59W
Trinidad [Mex.] 48 Ec 28.25N 109.06W
Trinidad [Ur.] 56 Id 33.32S 56.54W
Trinidad, Golfo- 56 Eg 49.55S 75.25W
Trinidad, Isla- 55 Bn 39.08S 61.58W
Trinidad, Laguna- 55 Be 20.21S 61.35W
Trinidad and Tobago [1] 53 Jd 11.00N 61.00W
Trinidade Spur (EN) 3 Cl 21.00S 35.00W
Trinitapoli 14 Ki 41.21N 16.05 E
Trinity 45 Ik 30.57N 95.22W
Trinity 38 Jg 29.47N 94.42W
Trinity Bay [Austl.] 59 Jc 16.25S 145.35 E
Trinity Bay [Can.] 42 Mg 48.15N 53.10W
Trinity Islands 40 Ie 56.33N 154.25W
Trinity Range 46 Ff 40.20N 118.45W
Trinity River 46 Df 41.11N 123.42W
Trinkitat 35 Fb 18.41N 37.43 E
Trino 14 Ce 45.12N 8.18 E
Trionto 14 Kk 39.37N 16.45 E
Trionto, Capo- 14 Kk 39.37N 16.45 E
Triora 14 Bf 43.59N 7.46 E
Tripoli (EN)=Ţarābulus [3] 33 Bc 32.40N 13.15 E
Tripoli (EN)=Ţarābulus [Leb.] 23 Ec 34.26N 35.51 E
Tripoli (EN)=Ţarābulus [Lib.] 31 Ie 32.54N 13.11 E
Trípolis 15 Fl 37.31N 22.22 E
Tripolitania (EN)= Tarabulus 30 Ie 31.00N 14.00 E
Tripolitania (EN)= Ţarābulus 33 Bc 30.00N 15.00 E

Index Symbols

- [1] Independent Nation
- [2] State, Region
- [3] District, County
- [4] Municipality
- [5] Colony, Dependency
- Continent
- Physical Region
- Historical or Cultural Region
- Mount, Mountain
- Volcano
- Hill
- Mountains, Mountain Range
- Hills, Escarpment
- Plateau, Upland
- Pass, Gap
- Plain, Lowland
- Delta
- Salt Flat
- Valley, Canyon
- Crater, Cave
- Karst Features
- Depression
- Polder
- Desert, Dunes
- Forest, Woods
- Heath, Steppe
- Oasis
- Cape, Point
- Coast, Beach
- Cliff
- Peninsula
- Isthmus
- Sandbank
- Island
- Atoll
- Rock, Reef
- Islands, Archipelago
- Rocks, Reefs
- Coral Reef
- Well, Spring
- Geyser
- River, Stream
- Waterfall Rapids
- River Mouth, Estuary
- Lake
- Salt Lake
- Intermittent Lake
- Reservoir
- Swamp, Pond
- Canal
- Glacier
- Ice Shelf, Pack Ice
- Ocean
- Sea
- Gulf, Bay
- Strait, Fjord
- Lagoon
- Bank
- Seamount
- Tablemount
- Ridge
- Shelf
- Basin
- Escarpment, Sea Scarp
- Fracture
- Trench, Abyss
- National Park, Reserve
- Point of Interest
- Recreation Site
- Cave, Cavern
- Historic Site
- Ruins
- Wall, Walls
- Church, Abbey
- Temple
- Scientific Station
- Airport
- Port
- Lighthouse
- Mine
- Tunnel
- Dam, Bridge

Tripura [3] 25 Id 24.00N 92.00 E
Trisanna 14 Ec 47.07N 10.30 E
Tristan da Cunha 30 Fi 37.05S 12.17W
Tristan da Cunha Group 30 Fi 37.15S 12.30W
Triste, Golfo- 50 Bg 10.40N 68.10W
Triunfo 55 Ee 20.46S 55.47W
Trivandrum 22 Ji 8.29N 76.55 E
Trivento 14 Ii 41.47N 14.33 E
Trjavna 15 Ig 42.52N 25.30 E
Trnava 10 Nh 48.22N 17.35 E
Troarn 12 Be 49.11N 0.11W
Trobriand Islands 57 Ge 8.30S 151.05 E
Trödje 8 Gd 60.49N 17.12 E
Trofors 7 Cd 65.34N 13.25 E
Trögd 8 Ge 59.30N 17.15 E
Trogir 14 Kg 43.32N 16.15 E
Troglav [Yugo.] 14 Kg 43.58N 16.36 E
Troglav [Yugo.] 14 Mg 43.02N 18.33 E
Trøgstad 8 De 59.38N 11.18 E
Troia 14 Ji 41.22N 15.18 E
Troick [R.S.F.S.R.] 22 Id 54.06N 61.35 E
Troick [R.S.F.S.R.] 20 Ee 57.23N 94.55 E
Troickoje [R.S.F.S.R.] 20 Df 52.58N 84.45 E
Troickoje [R.S.F.S.R.] 20 Ig 49.30N 136.32 E
Troickoje [Ukr.-U.S.S.R.] 15 Nb 47.38N 30.12 E
Troicko Pečorsk 19 Fc 62.44N 56.06 E
Troina 14 Im 37.47N 14.36 E
Troisdorf 12 Jd 50.49N 7.10 E
Trois Fourches, Cap des- 32 Gb 35.26N 2.58W
Trois-Pistoles 44 Ma 48.07N 69.10W
Trois Pitons, Morne- 51g Bb 15.22N 61.20W
Trois-Ponts 12 Hd 50.22N 5.52 E
Trois-Rivières [Guad.] 51e Ac 15.59N 61.39W
Trois-Rivières [Que.-Can.] 39 Le 46.21N 72.33W
Troissereux 12 Ee 49.29N 2.03 E
Troisvierges/Ulflingen 12 Hd 50.07N 6.00 E
Trojah 15 Hg 42.53N 24.43 E
Trojanovka 10 Ve 51.21N 25.25 E
Trojanski Manastir 15 Hg 42.53N 24.48 E
Trojanski prohod 15 Hg 42.48N 24.40 E
Trojebratski 19 Ge 54.25N 66.03 E
Trollhättan 7 Cg 58.16N 12.18 E
Trollheimen 7 Be 62.50N 9.05 E
Trollhetta 8 Cb 62.51N 9.19 E
Trolltindane 8 Bd 62.29N 7.43 E
Tromba 55 Ha 13.28S 48.45W
Trombetas, Rio- 52 Kf 1.55S 55.35W
Tromelin 30 Mj 15.52S 54.25 E
Tromøya 8 Cf 58.30N 8.50 E
Troms [3] 7 Eb 69.07N 19.15 E
Tromsø 6 Hb 69.40N 19.00 E
Tron 8 Db 62.10N 10.43 E
Tronador, Monte- 52 Ij 41.10S 71.54W
Trondheim 6 Hc 63.25N 10.25 E
Trondheimsfjorden 5 Hc 63.40N 10.50 E
Tronto 14 Hh 42.54N 13.55 E
Tropea 14 Jl 38.41N 15.54 E
Tropeiros, Serra dos- 55 Jb 14.43S 44.33W
Tropoja 15 Dg 42.24N 20.10 E
Trosa 7 Dg 58.54N 17.33 E
Troškūnai/Troškunaj 8 Ki 55.32N 24.59 E
Troškunaj/Troškūnai 8 Ki 55.32N 24.59 E
Trostberg 10 Ih 48.02N 12.33 E
Trostjanec 16 Id 50.29N 34.59 E
Trotuş 15 Kc 46.03N 27.14 E
Trou Gras Point 51k Bb 13.52N 60.53W
Troumasse 51k Bb 13.49N 60.54W
Trout Lake [Mi.-U.S.] 44 Eb 46.12N 85.01W
Trout Lake [N.W.T.-Can.] 42 Fd 60.35N 121.10W
Trout Lake [Ont.-Can.] 42 If 51.12N 93.19W
Trout Lake [Ont.-Can.] 42 If 53.54N 89.56W
Trout Peak 46 Kd 44.36N 109.32W
Trout River 42 Lg 49.29N 58.08W
Trouville-sur-Mer 11 Ge 49.22N 0.05 E
Trowbridge 9 Kj 51.20N 2.13W
Troy [Al.-U.S.] 43 Je 31.48N 85.58W
Troy [Mo.-U.S.] 45 Kg 38.59N 90.59W
Troy [Mt.-U.S.] 46 Hb 48.28N 115.53W
Troy [N.Y.-U.S.] 43 Mc 42.43N 73.40W
Troy [Oh.-U.S.] 44 Ee 40.02N 84.12W
Troy (EN)=Truva 24 Bc 39.57N 26.15 E
Troyes 6 Gf 48.18N 4.05 E
Troy Peak 43 Dd 38.19N 115.30W
Trstenik 15 Df 43.37N 21.00 E
Trubčevsk 19 De 52.36N 33.46 E
Truc Giang 25 Lf 10.14N 106.23 E
Truchas Peak 45 Di 35.58N 105.39W
Trucial Coast (EN) 21 Hg 24.00N 53.00 E
Trucial States (EN) → United Arab Emirates (EN) [1] 22 Hg 24.00N 54.00 E
Truckee 46 Eg 39.20N 120.11W
Trudfront 16 Og 45.56N 47.41 E
Trudovoje 20 Ih 43.18N 132.05 E
Trufanova 7 Kd 64.29N 44.05 E
Trujillo [2] 54 Db 9.25N 70.30W
Trujillo [Hond.] 47 Ge 15.55N 86.00W
Trujillo [Peru] 53 If 8.10S 79.02W
Trujillo [Sp.] 13 Ge 39.28N 5.53W
Trujillo [Ven.] 54 Db 9.22N 70.26W
Trujillo, Rio- 48 Hf 23.39N 103.08W
Truk Islands 57 Gd 7.25N 151.47 E
Trumann 45 Ki 35.41N 90.31W
Trumbull, Mount- 43 Ed 36.25N 113.10W
Trun 12 Gf 48.51N 0.02 E
Trung Phan=Annam (EN) 21 Me 15.00N 108.00 E
Truro [Eng.-U.K.] 9 Hk 50.16N 5.03W
Truro [N.S.-Can.] 39 Me 45.22N 63.16W
Truskavec 16 Ce 49.17N 23.34 E
Truth or Consequences (Hot Springs) 43 Fe 33.08N 107.15W
Trutnov 10 Lf 50.34N 15.54 E
Truva=Troy (EN) 24 Bc 39.57N 26.15 E
Truyère 11 Ij 44.38N 2.34 E
Trysil 8 Ec 61.25N 12.25 E
Trysil 7 Cf 61.18N 12.16 E
Trysilelva 5 Hd 59.23N 13.32 E
Trysilfjellet 8 Ec 61.18N 12.11 E
Trzcianka 10 Mc 53.03N 16.28 E
Trzcińsko Zdrój 10 Kd 52.58N 14.35 E
Trzebiatów 10 Lb 54.04N 15.14 E
Trzebież 10 Kc 53.42N 14.31 E
Trzebinia-Siersza 10 Pf 50.11N 19.25 E
Trzebnica 10 Ne 51.19N 17.03 E
Trzebnicki, Wał- 10 Me 51.30N 16.20 E
Trzebnickie, Wzgórza- 10 Me 51.15N 17.00 E
Trzemeszno 10 Nd 52.35N 17.50 E
Tsaidam Basin (EN)= Qaidam Pendi 27 Fd 37.00N 95.00 E
Tsamandá, Óri- 15 Dj 39.48N 20.21 E
Tsarap 25 Fb 33.31N 76.56 E
Tsaratanana 37 Hc 16.46S 47.38 E
Tsaratanana (EN)= Tsaratanana, Massif du- 30 Lj 14.00S 49.00 E
Tsaratanana, Massif du-= Tsaratanana (EN) 30 Lj 14.00S 49.00 E
Tsau 37 Cd 20.10S 22.27 E
Tsavo 36 Gc 2.59S 38.28 E
Tses 37 Be 25.58S 18.08 E
Tsévié 34 Fd 6.25N 1.13 E
Tshabong 31 Jk 26.02S 22.06 E
Tshane 31 Jk 24.01S 21.43 E
Tshangalele, Lac- 36 Ee 10.55S 27.03 E
Tshela 31 Ii 4.59S 12.56 E
Tshesebe 37 Dd 20.43S 27.37 E
Tshibala 36 Dd 6.56S 21.28 E
Tshibamba 36 Dd 9.06S 22.34 E
Tshikapa 31 Ji 6.25S 20.48 E
Tshilenge 36 Dd 6.15S 23.46 E
Tshimbalanga 36 Dd 9.43S 23.06 E
Tshimbulu 36 Dd 6.29S 22.51 E
Tshinsenda 36 Ee 12.16S 27.55 E
Tshofa 36 Ed 5.14S 25.15 E
Tshopo 36 Eb 0.33N 25.07 E
Tshuapa 30 Ji 0.14S 20.42 E
Tshwaane 37 Cd 22.38S 22.05 E
Tsiafajavona 37 Hc 19.21S 47.15 E
Tsihombe 37 He 25.17S 45.30 E
Tsimlyansk Reservoir (EN)= Cimljanskoje Vodohranilišče 5 Kf 48.00N 43.00 E
Tsinan (EN)=Jinan 22 Nf 36.35N 117.00 E
Tsinghai (EN)=Ch'ing-hai Sheng→Qinghai Sheng [2] 27 Gd 36.00N 96.00 E
Tsinghai (EN)=Qinghai Sheng (Ch'ing-hai Sheng) [2] 27 Gd 36.00N 96.00 E
Tsingtao (EN)=Qingdao 22 Of 36.05N 120.21 E
Tsiribihina 37 Gc 19.42S 44.31 E
Tsiroanomandidy 37 Hc 18.50S 46.00 E
Tsis 64d Bb 7.18N 151.50 E
Tsjokkarassa 7 Fb 69.59N 24.32 E
Tsodilo Hill 37 Cc 18.50S 21.45 E
Tsu 27 Oe 34.43N 136.31 E
Tsubame 29 Fc 37.39N 138.56 E
Tsubata 28 Nf 36.40N 136.44 E
Tsubetsu 29a Db 43.43N 144.01 E
Tsuchiura 28 Pf 36.05N 140.12 E
Tsugaru-Hantō 29a Bc 41.00N 140.30 E
Tsugaru-Kaikyō=Tsugaru Strait (EN) 21 Qe 41.40N 140.55 E
Tsugaru Strait (EN)= Tsugaru-Kaikyō 21 Qe 41.40N 140.55 E
Tsuken-Jima 29b Ab 26.15N 127.57 E
Tsukidate 29 Gb 38.44N 141.01 E
Tsukigata 29a Bb 43.20N 141.39 E
Tsukuba-San 29 Gc 36.13N 140.06 E
Tsukumi 29 Be 33.04N 131.52 E
Tsukura-Se 29 Af 31.18N 129.47 E
Tsukushi-Sanchi 29 Be 33.25N 130.30 E
Tsumeb 31 Ij 19.13S 17.42 E
Tsumeb [3] 37 Bc 19.00S 17.30 E
Tsumkwe 37 Cc 19.32S 20.30 E
Tsuna 29 Dd 34.26N 134.54 E
Tsuno-Shima 29 Bd 34.22N 130.52 E
Tsuru 29 Fd 35.35N 138.50 E
Tsuruga 27 Od 35.39N 136.04 E
Tsuruga-Wan 29 Ed 35.45N 136.05 E
Tsurugi 29 Ec 36.26N 136.37 E
Tsurugi-San 29 De 33.51N 134.03 E
Tsurui 29a Db 43.14N 144.21 E
Tsurumi-Dake 29 Be 33.18N 131.27 E
Tsurumi-Saki 29 Ce 32.56N 132.05 E
Tsuruoka 28 Oe 38.44N 139.50 E
Tsuruta 29 Ga 40.44N 140.26 E
Tsushima 21 Of 34.30N 129.20 E
Tsushima [Jap.] 29 Ce 33.07N 132.30 E
Tsushima [Jap.] 29 Ed 35.10N 136.43 E
Tsushima-Kaikyō=Korea, Strait (EN) 21 Of 34.40N 129.00 E
Tsuwano 29 Bd 34.28N 131.46 E
Tsuyama 28 Lg 35.03N 134.00 E
Tua 13 Ec 41.13N 7.26W
Tuai 62 Gc 38.49S 177.08 E
Tuaim/Tuam 9 Eh 53.31N 8.50W
Tuakau 62 Fb 37.15S 174.57 E
Tual 26 Jh 5.40S 132.45 E
Tuam/Tuaim 9 Eh 53.31N 8.50W
Tuamotu, Iles-=Tuamotu Archipelago (EN) 57 Mf 19.00S 142.00W
Tuamotu Archipelago (EN) =Tuamotu, Iles- 57 Mf 19.00S 142.00W
Tuamotu Ridge (EN) 3 Ll 20.00S 145.00W
Tuapa 64k Ba 18.57S 169.54W
Tuapse 6 Jg 44.07N 39.05 E
Tuaran 26 Ge 6.11N 116.14 E
Tuasivi 65c Aa 13.40S 172.07W
Tuasivi, Cape- 65c Aa 13.40S 172.07W
Tuatapere 61 Ci 46.08S 167.41 E
Tuba 20 Ef 54.00N 91.40 E
Tuba City 46 Jh 36.08N 111.14W
Tubai, Ile- 57 Mg 23.18S 149.30W
Tubai-Manu→Maiao, Ile- 57 Lf 17.34S 150.35W
Tubal, Wādī at- 24 Jf 32.19N 42.13 E
Tuban 26 Fh 6.54S 112.03 E
Tubarão 56 Kc 28.30S 49.01W
Ţubayq, Jabal at- 24 Gh 29.32N 37.30 E
Tubbataha Reefs 26 Ge 8.51N 119.56 E
Tubeke/Tubize 12 Gd 50.41N 4.12 E
Tübingen 10 Fh 48.32N 9.03 E
Tubize/Tubeke 12 Gd 50.41N 4.12 E
Ţubruq=Tobruk (EN) 31 Je 32.05N 23.59 E
Tubuaï, Iles-/Australes, Iles-=Tubuai Islands (EN) 57 Lg 23.00S 150.00W
Tubuai Islands (EN)= Australes, Iles-/Tubuaï, Iles- 57 Lg 23.00S 150.00W
Tubuai Islands (EN)= Tubuaï, Iles-/Australes, Iles- 57 Lg 23.00S 150.00W
Tubutama 48 Db 30.53N 111.29W
Tucacas 54 Ea 10.48N 68.19W
Tucacas, Punta- 49 Mh 10.52N 68.13W
Tucavaca 55 Cd 18.36S 58.55W
Tucavaca, Rio- 55 Cd 18.37S 58.59W
Tuchola 10 Nc 53.35N 17.50 E
Tucholska, Równina- 10 Oc 53.40N 18.30 E
Tuchów 10 Rg 49.54N 21.03 E
Tucker Glacier 66 Kf 72.35S 169.20 E
Tucson 39 Hf 32.13N 110.58W
Tucuarembó 56 Id 31.44S 55.59W
Tucumán [2] 56 Gc 27.00S 65.30W
Tucumcari 43 Gd 35.10N 103.44W
Tucunui 54 Id 3.42S 49.27W
Tucupido 54 Eb 9.17N 65.47W
Tucupita 54 Fb 9.04N 62.03W
Tudela 13 Kb 42.05N 1.36W
Tudia, Sierra de- 13 Ff 38.05N 6.20W
Tudmur 23 Ec 34.33N 38.17 E
Tudora 15 Jb 47.31N 26.38 E
Tuela 13 Ec 41.30N 7.12W
Tuensang 25 Ic 26.17N 94.40 E
Tuerto 13 Gb 42.18N 5.53W
Tufanbeyli 24 Gc 38.18N 36.11 E
Tufi 58 Fe 9.08S 149.20 E
Tugela 30 Kk 29.14S 31.30 E
Tug Fork 44 Ff 38.25N 82.35W
Tuguegarao 26 Hc 17.37N 121.44 E
Tugulym 17 Lh 57.04N 64.39 E
Tugur 20 If 53.51N 136.52 E
Tuhai He 28 Ee 38.05N 118.13 E
Tujiabu → Yongxiu 27 Kf 29.05N 115.49 E
Tujmazy 19 Fe 54.35N 53.42 E
Tukan 17 Hj 53.50N 57.31 E
Tukangbesi, Kepulauan-= Tukangbesi Islands (EN) 26 Hh 5.40S 123.50 E
Tukangbesi Islands (EN)= Tukangbesi, Kepulauan- 26 Hh 5.40S 123.50 E
Tukayel 35 Hd 8.05N 45.20 E
Tukayyid 24 Kh 29.47N 45.36 E
Tukituki 62 Gc 39.36S 176.56 E
Tuko Village 64n Ab 10.22S 161.02W
Tūkrah 33 Dc 32.32N 20.34 E
Tuktoyaktuk 39 Fc 69.27N 133.02W
Tukums 7 Fh 56.59N 23.10 E
Tukuringra, Hrebet- 20 Hf 54.30N 126.00 E
Tukuyu 36 Fd 9.15S 33.39 E
Tula 47 Ed 20.06N 99.19W
Tula 36 Gc 0.50S 39.51 E
Tula [Mex.] 48 Jf 23.00N 99.43W
Tula [R.S.F.S.R.] 6 Je 54.12N 37.37 E
Tula de Allende 48 Jg 20.03N 99.21W
Tula Mountains 66 Ee 66.54S 51.06 E
Tulancingo 47 Ed 20.05N 98.22W
Tulare 46 Fh 36.13N 119.21W
Tulare Lake Bed 46 Fh 36.03N 119.49W
Tularosa 45 Cj 33.04N 106.01W
Tularosa Valley 45 Cj 32.45N 106.10W
Tulcán 54 Cc 0.48N 77.43W
Tulcea [2] 15 Md 45.12N 29.10 E
Tulcea 15 Ld 45.10N 28.48 E
Tulčin 16 Fe 48.39N 28.52 E
Tulelake 46 Ef 41.57N 121.29W
Tulemalu Lake 42 Hd 62.55N 99.25W
Tulgheş 15 Ic 46.57N 25.46 E
Tuli 37 Dd 21.55S 29.12 E
Tuli 37 Dd 21.48S 29.04 E
Tulia 45 Fi 34.32N 101.46W
Tulihe 27 La 50.30N 121.51 E
Tullahoma 44 Dh 35.22N 86.11W
Tullamore/An Tulach Mhór 9 Fh 53.16N 7.30W
Tulle 11 Hi 45.16N 1.46 E
Tulln 14 Kb 48.22N 16.03 E
Tulln 14 Kb 48.20N 16.03 E
Tullner Becken 14 Jb 48.25N 15.55 E
Tullow/An Tulach 9 Gi 52.48N 6.44W
Tullus 35 Cc 11.03N 24.33 E
Tully 59 Jc 17.56S 145.56 E
Ţulmaythah 33 Dc 32.43N 20.57 E
Tuloma 5 Jb 68.52N 32.49 E
Tulos, Ozero- 7 He 63.35N 30.35 E
Tulsa 39 Jf 36.09N 95.58W
Tulskaja Oblast [3] 19 De 54.00N 37.30 E
Tuluá 54 Cc 4.05N 76.12W
Tuluksak 40 Gd 61.06N 160.58W
Tulum 47 Gd 20.15N 87.27W
Tulum 48 Pg 20.13N 87.28W
Tulun 22 Md 54.35N 100.33 E
Tulungagung 26 Fh 8.04S 111.54 E
Tuma 7 Ji 55.10N 40.36 E
Tuma, Rio- 49 Eg 13.03N 84.44W
Tumaco 53 Ie 1.49N 78.46W
Tumaco, Rada de- 54 Cc 1.50N 78.40W
Tumacuari, Pico- 54 Fc 1.15N 64.40W
Tuman-gang 28 Kc 42.18N 130.41 E
Tumba 8 Ge 59.12N 17.49 E
Tumbarumba 59 Jg 35.47S 148.01 E
Tumbes [2] 54 Bd 3.50S 80.30W
Tumbes 53 Hf 4.05S 80.35W
Tumča 7 Hc 66.35N 31.45 E
Tumd Youqi 27 Jc 40.33N 110.32 E
Tumd Zuoqi 27 Jc 40.43N 111.06 E
Tumen 22 Oe 42.58N 129.49 E
Tumen Jiang 28 Kc 42.18N 130.41 E
Tumeremo 54 Fb 7.18N 61.30W
Tumkur 25 Ff 13.21N 77.05 E
Tummel 9 Je 56.43N 3.44W
Tummo 33 Be 23.00N 14.10 E
Tumon Bay 64c Ba 13.31N 144.48 E
Tumpat 26 De 6.12N 102.10 E
Tumu 34 Ec 10.52N 1.59W
Tumucumaque, Serra- 52 Ke 2.20N 55.00W
Tumwater 46 Dc 47.01N 122.54W
Tuna, Punta- 51a Cc 18.00N 65.52W
Tunapuna 50 Fg 10.38N 61.23W
Tunas 55 Hg 24.58S 49.06W
Tunas, Sierra de las- 48 Fc 29.40N 107.15W
Tunas Chicas, Laguna- 55 Am 36.01S 62.20W
Tunaydah 24 Cj 25.31N 29.21 E
Tunçbilek 15 Mj 39.37N 29.29 E
Tunduma 36 Fd 9.18S 32.46 E
Tunduru 36 Ge 11.07S 37.21 E
Tundža 15 Jh 41.40N 26.34 E
Tunga 34 Gd 8.07N 9.12 E
Tungabhadra 25 Fe 15.57N 78.15 E
Tungaru 35 Ec 10.14N 30.42 E
Tungnaá 7a Bb 64.10N 19.34W
Tungokočen 20 Gf 53.33N 115.34 E
Tungsten 42 Ed 62.05N 127.42W
Tungua 65b Bb 20.01S 174.46W
Tuni 25 Ge 17.21N 82.33 E
Tūnis=Tunis (EN) [3] 32 Jb 36.30N 10.00 E
Tūnis=Tunis (EN) 31 Ie 36.48N 10.11 E
Tūnis=Tunisia (EN) [1] 31 He 34.00N 9.00 E
Tunis (EN)=Tūnis 31 Ie 36.48N 10.11 E
Tunis (EN)=Tūnis [3] 32 Jb 36.30N 10.00 E
Tūnis, Canal de-=Sicily, Strait of- (EN) 5 Hh 37.20N 11.20 E
Tūnis, Khalīj- 32 Jb 37.00N 10.30 E
Tunisia (EN)=Tūnis [1] 31 He 34.00N 9.00 E
Tunja 53 Ie 5.31N 73.22W
Tunkhannock 44 Je 41.32N 75.57W
Tunliu 28 Bf 36.18N 112.53 E
Tunnhovdfjorden 8 Cd 60.25N 8.55 E
Tunø 8 Di 55.55N 10.25 E
Tunumuk 42 Ec 69.00N 134.57W
Tununak 40 Fd 60.35N 165.16W
Tunungayualok 42 Le 56.05N 61.05W
Tunxi 27 Kf 29.45N 118.15 E
Tuo He 28 Dh 33.16N 117.45 E
Tuo Jiang 27 If 28.55N 105.26 E
Tuostah 20 Ic 67.50N 135.40 E
Tuotuo He 27 Fe 34.03N 92.46 E
Tuotuohe/Tanggulashanqu 22 Lf 34.15N 92.29 E
Tupã 56 Jb 21.56S 50.30W
Tupaciguara 55 Hd 18.35S 48.42W
Tupai Atoll (Motu-Iti) 61 Kc 16.17S 151.50W
Tupanciretã 56 Jc 29.05S 53.51W
Tupelo 43 Je 34.16N 88.43W
Tupik 20 Gf 54.28N 119.57 E
Tupinambarana, Ilha- 54 Gd 3.00S 58.00W
Tupiraçaba 55 Hb 14.29S 48.34W
Tupper Lake 44 Jc 44.13N 74.29W
Tupungato, Cerro- 56 Gd 33.22S 69.47W
Tuquan 27 Lb 45.22N 121.33 E
Túquerres 54 Cc 1.06N 77.37W
Tur 15 Fa 48.04N 22.33 E
Tura 19 Gd 57.12N 66.56 E
Tura [India] 25 Ic 25.31N 90.13 E
Tura [R.S.F.S.R.] 22 Mc 64.17N 100.15 E
Turabah [Sau.Ar.] 23 Fe 21.13N 41.39 E
Turabah [Sau.Ar.] 23 Fd 28.13N 42.59 E
Turagua, Serranías- 50 Di 7.20N 64.35W
Turakina 62 Fd 40.02S 175.13 E
Turān 24 Qe 35.40N 56.50 E
Turan 20 Ef 52.08N 93.55 E
Turana, Hrebet- 20 If 51.30N 132.00 E
Turangi 62 Fc 38.59S 175.48 E
Turano 14 Gh 42.26N 12.47 E
Turanskaja Nizmennost 21 Ie 43.30N 63.00 E
Turawa 10 Of 50.45N 18.05 E
Turawskie, Jezioro- 10 Of 50.43N 18.10 E
Turbaco 49 Jh J0.19N 75.25W
Turbat 25 Cc 25.59N 63.04 E
Turbo 53 Ie 8.06N 76.43W
Turcoaia 15 Ld 45.07N 28.11 E
Turda 15 Gc 46.34N 23.47 E
Tūreh 24 Me 34.02N 49.17 E
Tureia Atoll 57 Ng 20.50S 138.32W
Turek 10 Od 52.02N 18.30 E
Turenki 8 Kd 60.55N 24.38 E
Turfan Depression (EN)= Turpan Pendi 21 Ke 42.30N 89.30 E
Turgai Gates (EN)= Turgajskaja Ložbina 21 Id 51.00N 64.30 E
Turgai Upland (EN)= Turgajskoje Plato 21 Id 51.00N 64.00 E
Turgaj [Kaz.-U.S.S.R.] 19 Gf 49.38N 63.28 E
Turgaj [U.S.S.R.] 21 Ie 48.01N 62.45 E
Turgajskaja Ložbina=Turgai Gates (EN) 21 Id 51.00N 64.30 E
Turgajskaja Oblast [3] 19 Ge 50.30N 66.00 E
Turgajskoje Plato=Turgai Upland (EN) 21 Id 51.00N 64.00 E
Turgeon, Rivière- 44 Ha 50.00N 78.55W
Turgutlu 24 Bc 38.30N 27.50 E
Turhal 24 Gb 40.24N 36.06 E
Türi/Tjuri 7 Fg 58.50N 25.27 E
Turia 13 Le 39.27N 0.19W
Turiaçu, Baía de- 54 Id 1.30S 45.15W
Turiec 10 Og 49.06N 18.52 E
Turijsk 10 Ue 51.10N 24.37 E
Turimiquire, Cerro- 54 Fa 10.03N 64.00W
Turin (EN) = Torino 6 Gf 45.03N 7.40 E
Turinsk 19 Gd 58.03N 63.42 E
Turja 16 Dd 51.48N 24.52 E
Turka [R.S.F.S.R.] 20 Ff 52.57N 108.13 E
Turka [Ukr.-U.S.S.R.] 10 Tg 49.07N 23.01 E
Turkana 36 Gb 4.00N 35.30 E
Turkana, Lake-/Rudolf, Lake- 30 Kh 3.30N 36.00 E
Türkeli 24 Fb 41.57N 34.21 E
Turkenstanski Hrebet 19 Gh 39.35N 69.00 E
Turkestan 22 Ie 43.18N 68.15 E
Türkeve 10 Qi 47.06N 20.45 E
Turkey (EN)=Türkiye [1] 22 Fg 39.00N 35.00 E
Turkey Creek 59 Fc 17.02S 128.12 E
Turki 16 Mc 52.01N 43.16 E
Türkiye=Turkey (EN) [1] 22 Fg 39.00N 35.00 E
Turkmenistan Sovet Socialistik Respublikasy/ Turkmenskaja SSR [2] 19 Fh 40.00N 60.00 E
Turkmen-Kala 18 Df 37.26N 62.19 E
Turkmenskaja Sovetskaja Socialističeskaja Respublika [2] 19 Fh 40.00N 60.00 E
Turkmenskaja SSR/ Turkmenistan Sovet Socialistik Respublikasy [2] 19 Fh 40.00N 60.00 E
Turkmenskaja SSR= Turkmen SSR (EN) [2] 19 Fh 40.00N 60.00 E
Turkmenski Zaliv 16 Ff 39.00N 53.30 E
Turkmen SSR (EN)= Turkmenskaja SSR [2] 19 Fh 40.00N 60.00 E
Türkoğlu 24 Gd 37.31N 36.49 E
Turks and Caicos Islands [5] 39 Ff 21.45N 71.35W
Turks Island Passage 49 Lc 21.25N 71.19W
Turks Islands 47 Jd 21.24N 71.07W
Turku/Åbo 6 Ic 60.27N 22.17 E
Turku-Pori [2] 7 Ff 61.00N 22.30 E
Turkwel 36 Gb 3.06N 36.06 E
Turlock 46 Eh 37.30N 120.51W
Turmantas 8 Li 55.42N 26.34 E
Turnagain, Cape- 62 Gd 40.30S 176.37 E
Turneffe Islands 47 Ge 17.22N 87.51W
Turnhout 11 Kc 51.19N 4.57 E
Turnov 10 Lf 50.35N 15.09 E
Turnu Roşu, Pasul- 15 Hd 45.33N 24.16 E
Turnu Măgurele 15 Hf 43.45N 24.52 E
Turočak 20 Df 52.16N 87.05 E
Turó de L'Home 13 Oc 41.45N 2.25 E
Turopolje 14 Ke 45.38N 16.07 E
Turpan 22 Ke 42.56N 89.10 E
Turpan Pendi=Turfan Depression 21 Ke 42.30N 89.30 E
Turquino, Pico- 47 Ie 19.59N 76.51W
Turrialba 49 Fi 9.54N 83.41W
Tursuntski Tuman, Ozero- 17 Kf 60.35N 63.55 E
Turtas 17 Ng 58.57N 69.10 E
Turtas 17 Ng 59.06N 68.50 E
Turtkul 19 Gg 41.35N 61.00 E
Turtle Mountain 45 Fb 49.05N 100.15W
Turugart Shankou 21 Je 40.32N 75.24 E
Turuhan 20 Dc 65.56N 87.42 E
Turuhansk 20 Dc 65.49N 87.59 E
Turvânia 55 Gc 16.39S 50.09W
Turvo 55 Hi 28.56S 49.41W
Turvo, Rio- [Braz.] 55 Hd 19.56S 49.55W
Turvo, Rio- [Braz.] 55 Gc 17.46S 50.12W
Tusaun/Thusis 14 Dd 46.42N 9.26 E
Tuscaloosa 43 Je 33.13N 87.33W
Tuscan Archipelago (EN)= Arcipelago Toscano 5 Hg 42.45N 10.20 E
Tuscania 14 Fh 42.25N 11.52 E
Tuscany (EN) = Toscana [2] 14 Eg 43.25N 11.00 E
Tuscarora Mountain 44 Ie 40.10N 77.45W
Tuscarora Mountains 46 Gf 41.00N 116.20W
Tuščibas, Zaliv- 18 Ba 46.10N 59.45 E
Tuscola 45 Lg 39.48N 88.17W
Tusenøyane 41 Oc 77.05N 22.00 E
Tuskar 16 Jd 51.40N 36.15 E
Tuskegee 44 Ei 32.26N 85.42W
Tuşnad Băi 15 Ic 46.09N 25.51 E
Tustna 8 Ca 63.10N 8.05 E
Tuszyma 10 Rf 50.09N 21.30 E
Tuszyn 10 Pe 51.37N 19.34 E
Tutajev 19 Dd 57.52N 39.32 E
Tutak 24 Jc 39.32N 42.46 E
Tuticorin 25 Fg 8.47N 78.08 E
Tutira 62 Gc 39.12S 176.53 E
Tutóia 54 Jd 2.45S 42.16W
Tutoko Peak 62 Bf 44.36S 167.58 E
Tutončana 20 Ed 64.05N 93.50 E
Tutova 15 Kc 46.06N 27.32 E
Tutrakan 15 Je 44.03N 26.37 E
Tuttle Creek Lake 45 Hg 39.22N 96.40W
Tuttlingen 10 Ei 47.59N 8.49 E
Tutuala 26 Ih 8.24S 127.15 E
Tutuila Island 57 Jf 14.18S 170.42W
Tutupaca, Volcán- 54 Dg 17.01S 70.22W
Tuupovaara 8 Nb 62.29N 30.36 E
Tuusniemi 7 Ge 62.49N 28.30 E
Tuvalu (Ellice Islands) [1] 58 Ie 8.00S 178.00 E
Tuvalu Islands 57 Ie 8.00S 178.00 E
Tuvana-i-Ra Island 61 Fd 21.00S 178.43W
Tuvana-i-Tholo Island 57 Ig 21.02S 178.49W
Tuvinskaja ASSR [3] 20 Ef 51.30N 94.00 E
Tuvutha 63d Cb 17.40S 178.48W
Tuwayq, Jabal- 21 Gg 25.30N 46.20 E
Tuxer Alpen 14 Fc 47.10N 11.45 E
Tuxford 12 Ba 53.13N 0.53W
Tuxpan 48 Hh 19.33N 103.24W
Tuxpán 47 Cd 21.57N 105.18W
Tuxpan, Arrecife- 48 Kg 21.02N 97.13W
Tuxpan, Rio- 48 Kg 20.53N 97.18W
Tuxpan de Rodriguez Cano 47 Ed 20.57N 97.24W
Tuxtla Gutiérrez 39 Jh 16.45N 93.07W
Tùy 13 Db 42.03N 8.38W
Tuy, Rio- 50 Dg 10.24N 65.59W
Tuy An 25 Lf 13.17N 109.16 E

Index Symbols

[1] Independent Nation
[2] State, Region
[3] District, County
[4] Municipality
[5] Colony, Dependency
Continent
Physical Region
Historical or Cultural Region
Mount, Mountain
Volcano
Hill
Mountains, Mountain Range
Hills, Escarpment
Plateau, Upland
Pass, Gap
Plain, Lowland
Delta
Salt Flat
Valley, Canyon
Crater, Cave
Karst Features
Depression
Polder
Desert, Dunes
Forest, Woods
Heath, Steppe
Oasis
Cape, Point
Coast, Beach
Cliff
Peninsula
Isthmus
Sandbank
Island
Atoll
Rock, Reef
Islands, Archipelago
Rocks, Reefs
Coral Reef
Well, Spring
Geyser
River, Stream
Waterfall Rapids
River Mouth, Estuary
Lake
Salt Lake
Intermittent Lake
Reservoir
Swamp, Pond
Canal
Glacier
Ice Shelf, Pack Ice
Ocean
Sea
Gulf, Bay
Strait, Fjord
Lagoon
Bank
Seamount
Tablemount
Ridge
Shelf
Basin
Escarpment, Sea Scarp
Fracture
Trench, Abyss
National Park, Reserve
Point of Interest
Recreation Site
Cave, Cavern
Historic Site
Ruins
Wall, Walls
Church, Abbey
Temple
Scientific Station
Airport
Port
Lighthouse
Mine
Tunnel
Dam, Bridge

Name	Page	Grid	Lat.	Long.
Tuy Hoa	25	Lf	13.05N	109.18 E
Tūyserkān	24	Me	34.33N	48.27 E
Tuz, Lake- (EN)=Tuz Gölü	21	Ff	38.45N	33.25 E
Tuz Gölü=Tuz, Lake- (EN)	21	Ff	38.45N	33.25 E
Tuzkan, Ozero-	18	Fd	40.35N	67.30 E
Tūz Khurmātū	23	Fc	34.53N	44.38 E
Tuzla	14	Mf	44.33N	18.41 E
Tuzlov	16	Lf	47.23N	40.08 E
Tuzluca	24	Jb	40.03N	43.39 E
Tuzly	15	Nd	45.56N	30.05 E
Tvååker	8	Eg	57.03N	12.24 E
Tvărdica	15	Ig	42.42N	25.54 E
Tvedestrand	7	Bg	58.37N	8.55 E
Tverca	7	Ih	56.52N	35.59 E
Tweed	9	Lf	55.46N	2.00W
Tweedsmuir Hills	9	Jf	55.30N	3.22W
Tweerivier	37	Be	25.35S	19.37 E
Twello, Voorst-	12	Ib	52.14N	6.07 E
Twente	11	Mb	52.17N	6.40 E
Twentekanaal	12	Ib	52.13N	6.53 E
Twilight Cove	59	Ff	32.20S	126.00 E
Twin Buttes Reservoir	45	Fk	31.20N	100.35W
Twin Falls	39	He	42.34N	114.28W
Twin Islands	42	Jf	53.50N	80.00W
Twin Peaks	46	Hd	44.35N	114.29W
Twisp	46	Eb	48.22N	120.07W
Twiste	12	Lc	51.29N	9.09 E
Twistringen	10	Ed	52.48N	8.39 E
Two Butte Creek	45	Eg	38.02N	102.08W
Two Harbors	45	Kc	47.01N	91.40W
Two Rivers	45	Md	44.09N	87.34W
Two Thumb Range	62	De	43.45S	170.40 E
Tychy	10	Of	50.09N	18.59 E
Tyczyn	10	Sg	49.58N	22.02 E
Tydal	7	Ce	63.04N	11.34 E
Tygda	20	Hf	53.07N	126.20 E
Tyin	8	Cc	61.15N	8.15 E
Tyin	8	Cc	61.14N	8.14 E
Tyler	43	He	32.21N	95.18W
Tylertown	45	Kk	31.07N	90.09W
Tylösand	8	Eh	56.39N	12.44 E
Tylöskog	8	Ff	58.40N	15.10 E
Tym	20	De	59.30N	80.07 E
Tymovskoje	20	Jf	50.50N	142.41 E
Tympákion	15	Hn	35.06N	24.45 E
Tynda	22	Od	53.07N	126.20 E
Tyne	9	Lf	55.01N	1.26W
Tyne and Wear	9	Lg	55.00N	1.35W
Tynemouth	9	Lf	55.01N	1.24W
Týn nad Vltavou	10	Kg	49.14N	14.26 E
Tynset	7	Ce	62.17N	10.47 E
Tyra, Cayos-	49	Fg	12.50N	83.20W
Tyrifjorden	8	De	60.05N	10.10 E
Tyringe	8	Eh	56.10N	13.35 E
Tyrma	20	If	50.01N	132.10 E
Tyrnyauz	16	Mh	43.23N	42.56 E
Tyrol (EN)=Tirol	14	Fc	47.10N	11.25 E
Tyrol (EN)=Tirol/Tirolo	14	Fd	47.00N	11.20 E
Tyrol (EN)=Tirolo/Tirol	14	Fd	47.00N	11.20 E
Tyrone	44	He	40.41N	78.15W
Tyrrell, Lake-	59	Ig	35.20S	142.50 E
Tyrrel Lake	42	Gd	63.05N	105.30W
Tyrrhenian Basin (EN)	5	Hh	40.00N	13.00 E
Tyrrhenian Sea (EN)= Tirreno, Mar-	5	Hh	40.00N	12.00 E
Tyrva/Tõrva	7	Fg	58.01N	25.59 E
Tyrvää	8	Jc	61.21N	22.53 E
Tysmenica	10	Uh	48.49N	24.56 E
Tyśmienica	10	Se	51.33N	22.30 E
Tysnesøy	7	Af	60.00N	5.35 E
Tysse	8	Ad	60.22N	5.45 E
Tyssedal	8	Bd	60.07N	6.34 E
Tystama/Tõstamaa	8	Jf	58.17N	23.52 E
Tystberga	8	Gf	58.52N	17.15 E
Tyszowce	10	Tf	50.36N	23.41 E
Tytuvėnai/Tituvenaj	8	Ji	55.33N	23.09 E
Tywyn	9	Ii	52.35N	4.05W
Tzanconeja, Rio-	48	Ni	16.51N	91.47W
Tzaneen	37	Ed	23.50S	30.09 E
Tzintzuntzan	48	Ih	19.38N	101.34W
Tzucacab	48	Og	20.04N	89.05W

U

Name	Page	Grid	Lat.	Long.
Uaboe	64e	Ab	0.31S	166.54 E
Uacurizal, Ilha do-	55	Dc	16.25S	56.05W
Ua Huka, Ile-	57	Ne	8.54S	139.33W
Uanukuhahaki	65b	Ba	19.58S	174.29W
Ua Pou, Ile-	57	Me	9.23S	140.03W
Uaroo	59	Dd	23.00S	115.10 E
Uatumã, Rio-	52	Kf	2.26S	57.37W
Uaupés	53	Jf	0.08S	67.05W
Uaupés, Rio-	52	Je	0.02N	67.16W
Uaxactún	47	Ge	17.25N	89.29W
Ub	15	De	44.27N	20.05 E
Ubá	54	Jh	21.07S	42.56W
Übach-Palenberg [F.R.G.]	10	Cf	50.56N	6.05 E
Ubagan	19	Ge	54.23N	64.40 E
Ubaila	24	If	33.06N	40.15 E
Ubaitaba	54	Kf	14.18S	39.20W
Ubajay	55	Cj	31.47S	58.18W
Ubangi	30	Ii	0.30S	17.42 E
Ubatuba	55	Jf	23.26S	45.04W
Ubay	26	Hd	10.03N	124.28 E
Ubaye	11	Mj	44.28N	6.18 E
Ubayyiḍ, Wādī al-	24	Fc	32.34N	43.48 E
Ube	28	Kh	33.56N	131.15 E
Ubeda	13	If	38.01N	3.22W
Ubekendt Ejland	41	Gd	71.10N	53.45W
Uberaba	53	Lg	19.45S	47.55W
Uberaba, Lagoa-	55	Dc	17.30S	57.45W
Uberlândia	53	Lg	18.56S	48.18W
Überlingen	10	Fi	47.46N	9.10 E
Ubiaja	34	Gd	6.39N	6.23 E
Ubiña, Peña-	13	Ga	43.01N	5.57W
Ubiratã	55	Fg	24.32S	52.56W
Ubon Ratchathani	22	Mh	15.15N	104.54 E
Ubort	16	Fc	52.06N	28.30 E
Ubrique	13	Gh	36.41N	5.27W
Ubsu-Nur (Uvs nuur)	21	Ld	50.20N	92.45 E
Ubundu	31	Ji	0.21S	25.29 E
Učaly	19	Fe	54.20N	59.31 E
Učami	20	Ed	63.50N	96.39 E
Učaral	19	If	46.08N	80.52 E
Ucayali, Rio-	52	If	4.30S	73.30W
Uccle/Ukkel	12	Gd	50.48N	4.19 E
Üçdoruk Tepe	24	Ib	40.45N	41.05 E
Ucero	13	Ic	41.31N	3.04W
Uchiko	29	Ce	33.34N	132.38 E
Uchi Lake	45	Ja	51.05N	92.35W
Uchinomi	29	Dd	34.30N	134.19 E
Uchinoura	29	Bf	31.16N	131.05 E
Uchiura-Wan	28	Pc	42.18N	140.35 E
Uchte	12	Ed	52.30N	8.55 E
Učka	14	Ie	45.17N	14.12 E
Uckange	12	Ie	49.18N	6.09 E
Uckermark	10	Jc	53.10N	13.35 E
Uckfield	12	Cd	50.58N	0.06 E
Učkuduk	19	Gg	42.10N	63.30 E
Učkurgan	18	Id	41.01N	72.04 E
Ucrainskaja Sovetskaja Socialističeskaja Respublika	19	Df	49.00N	32.00 E
Ucross	46	Ld	44.33N	106.31W
Ucua	36	Bd	8.40S	14.12 E
Učur	21	Pd	58.48N	130.35 E
Uda [R.S.F.S.R.]	21	Pd	54.42N	135.14 E
Uda [R.S.F.S.R.]	21	Ff	51.45N	107.25 E
Uda [R.S.F.S.R.]	20	Ee	56.05N	99.34 E
Udačny	20	Gc	66.25N	112.20 E
Udaipur	22	Jg	24.35N	73.41 E
Udaj	16	Hd	50.05N	33.07 E
Udaquiola	55	Cm	36.34S	58.31W
Udbina	14	Jf	44.32N	15.46 E
Uddevalla	7	Cg	58.21N	11.55 E
Uddjaure	5	Hb	65.58N	17.50 E
Uden	12	Hc	51.40N	5.37 E
Udgir	25	Fe	18.23N	77.07 E
Udhampur	25	Fb	32.56N	75.08 E
Udimski	7	Kf	61.09N	45.52 E
Udine	14	Hd	46.03N	13.14 E
Udipi	25	Ef	13.21N	74.45 E
Udmurtskaja ASSR	19	Fd	57.20N	52.50 E
Udoha	8	Mg	57.58N	29.50 E
Udomlja	7	Ih	57.56N	35.02 E
Udon-Jima	29	Fd	34.28N	139.17 E
Udon Thani	25	Ke	17.25N	102.48 E
Udot	64d	Bb	7.23N	151.43 E
Udskaja Guba	21	Pd	55.00N	136.00 E
Udskoje	20	If	54.36N	134.30 E
Udy	16	Je	49.47N	36.35 E
Udžary	16	Oi	40.31N	47.40 E
Udzungwa Range	36	Gd	8.05S	35.50 E
Uebonti	26	Hg	0.55S	121.38 E
Uecker	10	Kc	53.45N	14.04 E
Ueckermünde	10	Kc	53.44N	14.03 E
Ueda	27	Od	36.24N	138.16 E
Uele	30	Jh	4.09N	22.26 E
Uelen	20	Oc	66.13N	169.48W
Uelzen	10	Gd	52.58N	10.34 E
Ueno	29	Ed	34.46N	136.06 E
Uere	30	Jh	3.42N	25.24 E
Ufa	5	Le	54.40N	56.00 E
Ufa	6	Le	54.44N	55.56 E
Uftjuga	7	Lf	61.28N	46.12 E
Ugab	30	Ik	21.12S	13.38 E
Ugale/Ugåle	8	Ig	57.19N	21.52 E
Ugåle/Ugale	8	Ig	57.19N	21.52 E
Ugalla	36	Fd	5.08S	30.42 E
Uganda	31	Kh	1.00N	32.00 E
Ugărčin	15	Hf	43.06N	24.25 E
Ugashik	40	He	57.32N	157.25W
Ughelli	34	Gd	5.30N	5.59 E
Ugijar	13	Ih	36.57N	3.03W
Uglegorsk	20	Jg	49.05N	142.06 E
Uglekamensk	20	Ih	43.18N	133.08 E
Ugleuralski	17	Hg	58.59N	57.38 E
Uglič	19	Dd	57.33N	38.23 E
Ugljan	14	Jf	44.05N	15.10 E
Uglovoje	28	Lc	43.20N	132.06 E
Ugnev	10	Tf	50.20N	23.45 E
Ugo	29	Gb	39.13N	140.23 E
Ugolnyje Kopi	20	Md	64.42N	177.50 E
Ugoma	36	Ec	4.55S	26.50 E
Ugra	16	De	54.30N	36.07 E
Ugtal-Cajdam	27	Ib	48.25N	105.30 E
Uh	10	Rh	48.33N	22.00 E
Uherské Hradiště	10	Ng	49.04N	17.27 E
Úhlava	10	Jg	49.45N	13.23 E
Uhlenhorst	37	Bd	23.45S	17.55 E
Uhta	6	Lc	63.33N	53.40 E
Uibh Fhaili/Offaly	9	Fh	53.20N	7.30W
Uig	9	Gd	57.30N	6.20W
Uige	31	Ii	7.35S	15.04 E
Uige	36	Cd	7.00S	15.30 E
'Uiha	65b	Ba	19.54S	174.25W
Uijec	64d	Bb	7.10N	151.57 E
Üijŏngbu	28	If	37.44N	127.02 E
Uiju	28	Hd	40.12N	124.32 E
Uil	19	Ff	48.36N	52.30 E
Uil	19	Ff	49.04N	54.42 E
Uilpata, Gora-	16	Mh	42.47N	43.44 E
Uinta Mountains	43	Ec	40.45N	110.05W
Uinta River	46	Kf	40.14N	109.51W
Uis	37	Ad	21.08S	14.49 E
Üisŏng	28	Jf	36.21N	128.42 E
Uitenhage	31	Jl	33.40S	25.28 E
Uithoorn	12	Gb	52.14N	4.52 E
Uithuizen	12	Ia	53.25N	6.42 E
Uithuizerwad	12	Ia	53.30N	6.40 E
Ujae Atoll	57	Hd	9.05N	165.40 E
Ūjān	24	Og	30.45N	52.05 E
Ujandina	20	Jc	68.23N	145.50 E
Ujar	20	Ee	55.48N	94.20 E
Ujarrás	49	Fi	9.50N	83.40W
Ujedinenija, Ostrov-	20	Da	77.30N	82.30 E
Ujelang Atoll	57	Hd	9.49N	160.55 E
Újfehértó	10	Ri	47.48N	21.41 E
Uji	29	Dd	34.53N	135.47 E
Uji	19	Ge	54.20N	63.58 E
Uji-Guntō	28	Ji	31.10N	129.28 E
Ujiie	29	Fc	36.41N	139.57 E
Ujiji	31	Ji	4.55S	29.41 E
Ujjain	22	Jg	23.11N	75.46 E
Ujunglamuru	26	Gg	4.40S	119.58 E
Ujung Pandang (Makasar)	22	Nj	5.07S	119.24 E
Uk	20	Ee	55.04N	98.52 E
Ukata	34	Gc	10.50N	5.50 E
Ukeng, Bukit-	26	Gf	1.45N	115.08 E
Ukerewe Island	36	Fc	2.03S	33.00 E
Uke-Shima	29b	Ba	28.02N	129.15 E
Ukhayḍir	24	Jf	32.26N	43.36 E
Ukiah [Ca.-U.S.]	43	Cd	39.09N	123.13W
Ukiah [Or.-U.S.]	46	Fd	45.08N	118.56W
Uki Ni Masi	63a	Ed	10.15S	161.44 E
Ukkel/Uccle	12	Gd	50.48N	4.19 E
Ukmergė/Ukmerge	7	Fi	55.14N	24.47 E
Ukmerge/Ukmergė	7	Fi	55.14N	24.47 E
Ukraine (EN)	5	Jf	49.00N	32.00 E
Ukrainian SSR (EN)= Ukrainskaja SSR	19	Df	49.00N	32.00 E
Ukrainskaja SSR/Ukrainska Radyanska Socialistična Respublika	19	Df	49.00N	32.00 E
Ukrainskaja SSR=Ukrainian SSR (EN)	19	Df	49.00N	32.00 E
Ukrainska Radyanska Socialistična Respublika/ Ukrainskaja SSR	19	Df	49.00N	32.00 E
Ukrina	14	Le	45.05N	17.56 E
Uku-Jima	29	Ae	33.16N	129.07 E
Ula	24	Cd	37.05N	28.26 E
Ulah Lake	45	Hh	36.58N	96.10W
Ulaidh/Ulster	9	Gg	54.30N	7.00W
Ulalu	64d	Bb	7.25N	151.40 E
Ulan (Xiligou)	27	Gd	36.55N	98.16 E
Ulan → Otog Qi	27	Id	39.07N	108.00 E
Ulanbaatar → Ulan-Bator	22	Me	47.55N	106.53 E
Ulan-Badrah	28	Ac	43.58N	110.37 E
Ulan-Bator (Ulaanbaatar)	22	Me	47.55N	106.53 E
Ulanbel	19	Hg	44.49N	71.10 E
Ulan-Burgasy, Hrebet-	20	Ff	52.30N	108.30 E
Ulangom	22	Le	49.58N	92.02 E
Ulanhad/Chifeng	27	Kc	42.16N	118.57 E
Ulan Hol	19	Ef	45.27N	46.46 E
Ulan Hot/Horqin Youyi Qianqi	22	Oe	46.04N	122.00 E
Ulan Hua → Siziwang Qi	28	Ad	41.31N	111.41 E
Ulan-Hus	27	Eb	49.02N	89.23 E
Ulanów	10	Sf	50.30N	22.16 E
Ulansuhai Nur	27	Ic	40.56N	108.49 E
Ulan-Tajga	27	Ga	50.45N	98.30 E
Ulan-Ude	22	Md	51.50N	107.37 E
Ulan Ul Hu	27	Fe	34.45N	90.25 E
Ulas	24	Gc	39.27N	37.03 E
Ulawa Island	60	Gi	9.46S	161.57 E
Ulbeja	20	Je	59.20N	144.25 E
Ulchin	28	Jf	36.59N	129.24 E
Ulcinj	15	Ch	41.56N	19.13 E
Uleåborg/Oulu	6	Ib	65.01N	25.30 E
Ulefoss	7	Bg	59.17N	9.16 E
Ulegej	22	Ke	48.56N	89.57 E
Ulety	20	Gf	51.22N	112.30 E
Uleza	15	Ch	41.40N	19.53 E
Ulfborg	8	Ch	56.16N	8.20 E
Ulflingen/Troisvierges	12	Hd	50.07N	6.00 E
Ulft, Gendringen-	12	Ic	51.54N	6.24 E
Ulgain Gol	27	Kb	45.31N	117.50 E
Ulhāsnagar	25	Ee	19.10N	73.07 E
Uliastai → Dong Ujimqin Qi	27	Kc	45.31N	116.58 E
Uliga	58	Id	7.09N	171.13 E
Ulindi	30	Ji	1.40S	25.52 E
Ulithi Atoll	57	Ed	9.58N	139.40 E
Ulja	20	Je	58.48N	141.40 E
Uljanovka [R.S.F.S.R.]	8	Ne	59.37N	30.55 E
Uljanovka [Ukr.-U.S.S.R.]	16	Ge	48.20N	30.13 E
Uljanovsk	6	Ke	54.20N	48.24 E
Uljanovskaja Oblast	19	Ee	54.00N	48.00 E
Uljanovski	19	He	50.05N	73.45 E
Uljasutaj	22	Le	47.45N	96.49 E
Ulkan	20	Fe	55.55N	107.55 E
Ulla	13	Db	42.39N	8.44W
Ullapool	9	Hd	57.54N	5.10W
Ullared	7	Ch	57.08N	12.43 E
Ulldecona	13	Md	40.36N	0.27 E
Ullsfjorden	7	Eb	69.58N	20.00 E
Ullswater	9	Kg	54.34N	2.54W
Ullŭng-Do	28	Kf	37.29N	130.52 E
Ullvettern	8	Fe	59.25N	14.15 E
Ulm	10	Fh	48.25N	10.00 E
Ulmen	12	Id	50.13N	6.59 E
Ulmeni	15	Jd	45.04N	26.39 E
Ulmu	15	Je	44.16N	26.55 E
Ulongwé	37	Eb	14.43S	34.21 E
Ulricehamn	7	Ch	57.47N	13.25 E
Ulrichstein	12	Ld	50.35N	9.12 E
Ulrum	12	Ia	53.22N	6.20 E
Ulrum-Zoutkamp	12	Ia	53.20N	6.18 E
Ulsan	27	Md	35.33N	129.19 E
Ulsteinvik	7	Ae	62.20N	5.53 E
Ulster	10	Ff	50.51N	9.59 E
Ulster/Ulaidh	9	Gg	54.30N	7.00W
Ulster Canal	9	Gg	54.27N	6.40W
Ulu	35	Ec	10.43N	33.29 E
Ulu/Uulu	8	Kf	58.13N	24.29 E
Ulúa, Rio-	47	Ge	15.56N	87.43W
Ulubat Gölü	24	Cb	40.10N	28.35 E
Ulubey	24	Cc	38.09N	29.33 E
Uludağ	23	Ca	40.04N	29.13 E
Uludere	24	Jd	37.27N	42.51 E
Ulugqat/Wuqia	27	Cd	39.40N	75.07 E
Ulukışla	24	Fd	37.33N	34.30 E
Ulungur He	21	Ke	46.58N	87.28 E
Ulungur Hu	27	Eb	47.20N	87.10 E
Ulus	24	Eb	41.35N	32.39 E
Ulus Dağ	15	Lj	39.18N	28.24 E
Ulva	9	Ge	56.28N	6.12W
Ulverston	9	Jg	54.12N	3.06W
Ulverstone	59	Jh	41.09S	146.10 E
Ulvik	8	Bd	60.34N	6.54 E
Ulvön	8	Ha	63.05N	18.40 E
Ulysses	45	Fh	37.35N	101.22W
Ulytau	19	Gf	48.35N	67.05 E
Ulytau, Gora-	19	Gf	48.45N	67.00 E
Uly-Žilanšik	19	Gf	48.51N	63.47 E
Uma	27	La	52.36N	120.38 E
Umag	14	He	45.25N	13.32 E
Umala	54	Eg	17.24S	67.58W
Umán	48	Og	20.53N	89.45W
Uman	64d	Bb	7.18N	151.53 E
Uman	19	Df	48.47N	30.09 E
'Umān	21	Hg	22.10N	58.00 E
'Umān=Oman (EN)	22	Hg	21.00N	57.00 E
'Umān, Khalīj-=Oman, Gulf of- (EN)	21	Hg	25.00N	58.00 E
Umanak	41	Gd	70.36N	52.15W
Ūmánarssuaq/Farvel, Kap-	67	Nb	59.50N	43.50W
Umatac	64c	Bb	13.18N	144.40 E
Umba	19	Db	66.41N	34.17 E
Umbelasha	35	Cd	9.51N	24.50 E
Umbertide	14	Gg	43.18N	12.20 E
Umberto de Campos	54	Jd	2.37S	43.27W
Umboi Island	57	Fe	5.36S	148.00 E
Umbozero, Ozero-	7	Ic	67.45N	34.20 E
Umbria	14	Gh	43.00N	12.30 E
Ume	37	Dc	17.15S	28.20 E
Umeå	6	Ic	63.50N	20.15 E
Umeälven	5	Ic	63.47N	20.16 E
Umm al Arānib	33	Bd	26.08N	14.45 E
Umm al Hayf, Wādī-	23	Hf	18.37N	53.59 E
Umm al Jamaājim	24	Ki	26.59N	45.19 E
Umm al Qaywayn	23	Id	25.35N	55.34 E
Ummanz	10	Jb	54.30N	13.10 E
Umm ar Rizam	33	Dc	32.32N	23.00 E
Umm as Samīm	23	Ie	21.30N	56.45 E
Umm Bāb	24	Nj	25.12N	50.48 E
Umm Bel	35	Dc	13.32N	28.04 E
Umm Buru	35	Cb	15.01N	23.36 E
Umm Dhibbān	35	Dc	14.14N	29.37 E
Umm Durmān=Omdurman (EN)	31	Kg	15.38N	32.30 E
Umm Inderaba	35	Eb	15.12N	31.54 E
Umm Kaddādah	35	Dc	13.36N	26.42 E
Umm Lajj	23	Ed	25.04N	37.13 E
Umm Naqqāt, Jabal-	24	Fj	25.30N	34.14 E
Umm Qam'ul	24	Pj	24.47N	54.42 E
Umm Ruwābah	31	Kg	12.54N	31.13 E
Umm Sayyālah	35	Ec	14.25N	31.00 E
Umm Urūmah	24	Gj	25.46N	36.33 E
Umnak	38	Cd	58.25N	168.10W
Umne-Gobi	27	Fb	49.06N	91.43 E
Umpqua River	46	Ce	43.42N	124.03W
Umpulu	36	Ce	12.42S	17.40 E
Umsini, Gunung-	26	Jg	1.35S	133.30 E
Umtali	31	Kj	18.58S	32.40 E
Umtata	31	Jl	31.35S	28.47 E
Umuarama	56	Jb	23.45S	53.20W
Umurbey	15	Ji	40.14N	26.36 E
Umvukwes	37	Ec	17.01S	30.52 E
Umvuma	37	Ec	19.19S	30.35 E
Umzingwani	37	Dd	22.12S	29.56 E
Una	14	Ke	45.16N	16.55 E
Unabetsu-Dake	29a	Db	43.52N	144.51 E
Unac	14	Kf	44.29N	16.08 E
Unai	54	Ig	16.23S	46.53W
Unalakleet	40	Gd	63.53N	160.47W
Unalaska	38	Cd	53.45N	166.45W
Unare, Rio-	50	Dg	10.06N	65.12W
Unauna, Pulau-	26	Hg	0.10S	121.35 E
'Unayzah [Jor.]	24	Fg	30.29N	35.48 E
'Unayzah [Sau. Ar.]	22	Gg	26.06N	43.56 E
Uncia	54	Eg	18.27S	66.37W
Uncompahgre Peak	43	Fd	38.04N	107.28W
Uncompahgre Plateau	45	Bg	38.30N	108.25W
Unden	8	Ff	58.45N	14.25 E
Underberg	37	De	29.50S	29.22 E
Under-Han	22	Ne	47.19N	110.39 E
Undjuljung	20	Hc	66.20N	124.40 E
Undu Point	63d	Cb	16.08S	179.57W
Undva Neem/Kiprarenukk, Mys-	8	If	58.25N	21.45 E
Uneča	16	Hc	52.50N	32.44 E
'Ung, Jabal al-	14	Dn	36.45N	9.35 E
Unga	40	Ge	55.15N	160.45W
Ungava, Péninsule d'-= Ungava Peninsula (EN)	38	Lc	60.00N	74.00W
Ungava Bay	38	Md	59.30N	67.30W
Ungava Peninsula (EN)= Ungava, Péninsule d'-	38	Lc	60.00N	74.00W
Ungeny	16	Ef	47.13N	27.50 E
Unggi	28	Kc	42.21N	130.23 E
Ungureni	15	Jb	47.53N	26.47 E
Ungwatiri	35	Fb	16.55N	36.05 E
União	54	Jd	4.35S	42.52W
União da Vitória	56	Jc	26.13S	51.05W
União dos Palmares	54	Ke	9.10S	36.02W
Uničov	10	Ng	49.49N	17.07 E
Uniejów	10	Oe	51.58N	18.49 E
Unije	14	If	44.38N	14.15 E
Unimak	38	Cd	54.50N	164.00W
Unimak Pass	40	Gf	54.35N	164.43W
Unini, Rio-	54	Fd	1.41S	61.30W
Union [Mo.-U.S.]	45	Kg	38.27N	91.00W
Union [S.C.-U.S.]	44	Gh	34.42N	81.37W
Union City	44	Cg	36.26N	89.03W
Uniondale	37	Cf	33.40S	23.08 E
Unión de Reyes	49	Gb	22.48N	81.32W
Unión de Tula	48	Gh	19.58N	104.16W
Union Island	50	Ff	12.36N	61.26W
Union Islands/Tokelau	57	Je	9.00S	171.45W
Union of Soviet Socialist Republics (USSR) (EN)= SSSR	22	Jd	60.00N	80.00 E
Union Seamount (EN)	42	Eg	49.35N	132.45W
Union Springs	44	Ei	32.09N	85.49W
Uniontown	44	Hf	39.54N	79.44W
Unionville	45	Jf	40.29N	93.01W
United Arab Emirates (EN) =Al Imārāt al 'Arabīyah al Muttaḥidah	22	Hg	24.00N	54.00 E
United Arab Republic (EN) → Egypt (EN)	31	Jf	27.00N	30.00 E
United Kingdom	6	Fe	54.00N	2.00W
United Kingdom of Great Britain and Northern Ireland	6	Fe	54.00N	2.00W
United States	39	Jf	38.00N	97.00W
United States of America	39	Jf	38.00N	97.00W
Unity [Or.-U.S.]	46	Fd	44.29N	118.13W
Unity [Sask.-Can.]	42	Gf	52.27N	109.10W
Universales, Montes-	13	Kd	40.18N	1.33W
University City	45	Kg	38.39N	90.19W
Unna	10	De	51.32N	7.41 E
Unnāb, Wādī al-	24	Gg	30.11N	36.39 E
Unnukka	8	Lb	62.25N	27.55 E
Unst	5	Fc	60.45N	0.55W
Unstrut	10	He	51.10N	11.48 E
Unterfranken	10	Fg	50.00N	10.00 E
Unterwalden-Nidwalden	14	Cd	46.55N	8.30 E
Unterwalden-Obwalden	14	Cd	46.50N	8.20 E
Unuli Horog	27	Fd	35.12N	91.58 E
Ünye	23	Ea	41.08N	37.17 E
Unža	5	Kd	57.20N	43.08 E
Unzen-Dake	29	Be	32.45N	130.17 E
Uoleva	65b	Ba	19.51S	174.24W
Uozu	28	Nf	36.48N	137.24 E
Úpa	10	Lf	50.22N	15.54 E
Upata	54	Fb	8.01N	62.24W
Upemba, Lac-	36	Ed	8.36S	26.26 E
Upernavik	41	Gd	72.20N	56.00W
Upin	26	Ig	2.56S	129.11 E
Upington	31	Jk	28.25S	21.15 E
Upland	12	Kc	51.18N	8.42 E
Upolu Island	57	Jf	13.55S	171.45W
Upolu Point	60	Oc	20.16N	155.52W
Upper	34	Ec	10.30N	1.30W
Upper Arlington	44	Fe	40.01N	83.03W
Upper Arrow Lake	46	Ga	50.30N	117.55W
Upper Austria (EN) = Oberösterreich	14	Hb	48.15N	14.00 E
Upper Hutt	62	Fd	41.07S	175.04 E
Upper Klamath Lake	43	Cc	42.23N	122.00W
Upper Lake	46	Ef	41.44N	120.08W
Upper Lough Erne/Loch Éirne Uachtair	9	Fg	54.20N	7.30W
Upper Red Lake	45	Ib	48.10N	94.40W
Upper Sandusky	44	Fe	40.48N	83.17W
Upper Sheik	35	Hd	9.57N	45.09 E
Upper Thames Valley	9	Lj	51.40N	1.40W
Upper Trajan's Wall (EN)= Verhni Traijanov Val	15	Lc	46.40N	29.00 E
Upper Volta (EN)=Haute-Volta	31	Gg	13.00N	2.00W
Uppingham	12	Bb	52.35N	0.43W
Uppland	8	Gd	60.00N	17.50 E
Upplands Väsby	8	Ge	59.31N	17.54 E
Uppsala	7	Df	60.00N	17.45 E
Uppsala	6	Hd	59.52N	17.38 E
Upsala	45	Kb	49.02N	90.29W
Upshi	25	Fb	33.50N	77.49 E
Upton	46	Md	44.06N	104.38W
Uqbān	33	Hf	15.30N	42.23 E
'Uqlat aş Şuqūr	24	Jj	25.53N	42.15 E
Uqturpan/Wuski	27	Cc	41.10N	79.16 E
Ur	23	Gc	30.58N	46.06 E
Urabá, Golfo de-	54	Cb	8.25N	77.00W
Uracoa	50	Eh	9.00N	62.21W
Uracoa, Rio-	50	Eh	9.08N	62.20W
Uradarja	18	Fe	38.51N	66.02 E
Urad Qianqi	27	Ic	40.49N	108.37 E
Urad Zhonghou Lianheqi (Haliut)	27	Ic	41.34N	108.32 E
Uraga-Suido	29	Fd	35.15N	139.45 E
Ura-Guba	7	Hb	69.18N	32.48 E
Urahoro	29a	Cb	42.48N	143.38 E
Urahoro-Gawa	29a	Cb	42.44N	143.40 E
Uraj	19	Gc	60.08N	64.40 E
Urakawa	28	Qc	42.09N	142.47 E
Ural	5	Lf	47.00N	51.48 E
Ural Mountains (EN)= Uralskije Gory	5	Ld	57.00N	60.00 E
Uralsk	6	Le	51.14N	51.22 E
Uralskaja Oblast	19	Ff	49.45N	51.00 E
Uralskije Gory=Ural Mountains (EN)	5	Ld	57.00N	60.00 E
Urambo	36	Fd	5.04S	32.03 E
Uranium City	39	Id	59.34N	108.36W
Uraricoera	54	Fc	3.27N	60.59W
Uraricoera, Rio-	52	Je	3.02N	60.30W
Ura-Tjube	19	Gh	39.53N	69.01 E
Urawa	28	Og	35.51N	139.39 E
'Uray'irah	24	Mj	25.57N	48.53 E
Urayq, Nafūd al-	24	Jj	25.17N	42.25 E
Urbana [Il.-U.S.]	45	Lf	40.07N	88.12W
Urbana [Oh.-U.S.]	44	Fe	40.06N	83.45W
Urbandale	45	Jf	41.38N	93.48W
Urbania	14	Gg	43.40N	12.31 E

Index Symbols

1 Independent Nation
2 State, Region
3 District, County
4 Municipality
5 Colony, Dependency
Continent
Physical Region
Historical or Cultural Region
Mount, Mountain
Volcano
Hill
Mountains, Mountain Range
Hills, Escarpment
Plateau, Upland
Pass, Gap
Plain, Lowland
Delta
Salt Flat
Valley, Canyon
Crater, Cave
Karst Features
Depression
Polder
Desert, Dunes
Forest, Woods
Heath, Steppe
Oasis
Cape, Point
Coast, Beach
Cliff
Peninsula
Isthmus
Sandbank
Island
Atoll
Rock, Reef
Islands, Archipelago
Rocks, Reefs
Coral Reef
Well, Spring
Geyser
River, Stream
Waterfall Rapids
River Mouth, Estuary
Lake
Salt Lake
Intermittent Lake
Reservoir
Swamp, Pond
Canal
Glacier
Ice Shelf, Pack Ice
Ocean
Sea
Gulf, Bay
Strait, Fjord
Lagoon
Bank
Seamount
Tablemount
Ridge
Shelf
Basin
Escarpment, Sea Scarp
Fracture
Trench, Abyss
National Park, Reserve
Point of Interest
Recreation Site
Cave, Cavern
Historic Site
Ruins
Wall, Walls
Church, Abbey
Temple
Scientific Station
Airport
Port
Lighthouse
Mine
Tunnel
Dam, Bridge

Urbano Santos 54 Jd 3.12S 43.23W
Urbino 14 Gg 43.43N 12.38 E
Urbino, Étang d'- 11a Ba 42.02N 9.28 E
Urbión, Picos de- 13 Jb 42.01N 2.52W
Urcel 12 Fe 49.30N 3.33 E
Urcos 54 Df 13.42S 71.38W
Urdinarrain 55 Ck 32.41S 58.53W
Urdoma 7 Lf 61.47N 48.29 E
Urdžar 19 If 47.05N 81.37 E
Ure 9 Lg 54.01N 1.12W
Uré 49 Jj 7.46N 75.31W
Uren 19 Ed 57.29N 45.48 E
Urenui 62 Fc 39.00S 174.23 E
Ures 47 Bc 29.26N 110.24W
Ureshino 29 Ab 33.06N 129.59 E
'Urf, Jabal al- 24 Ei 27.49N 32.55 E
Urfa 23 Eb 37.08N 38.46 E
Urfa Platosu 24 Hd 37.10N 38.50 E
Urgal 20 If 51.00N 132.50 E
Urgel, Llanos de- 13 Lc 41.25N 0.36W
Urgel, Llanos de-/Urgell, Pla d'- 13 Lc 41.25N 0.36W
Urgell, Pla d'- 13 Lc 41.25N 0.36W
Urgell, Pla d'-/Urgel, Llanos de- 13 Lc 41.25N 0.36W
Urgen 28 Ab 44.45N 110.40 E
Urgenč 22 Ie 41.33N 60.38 E
Ürgüp 24 Fc 38.38N 35.56 E
Urgut 19 Gh 39.23N 67.14 E
Uri 25 Eb 34.05N 74.02 E
Uri [2] 14 Cd 46.40N 8.30 E
Uribia 54 Da 11.42N 72.17W
Uricki 19 Ge 53.19N 65.34 E
Urique, Río- 48 Fd 26.29N 107.58W
Urjala 8 Jc 61.05N 23.32 E
Urjupinsk 19 Ee 50.48N 42.02 E
Urk 11 Lb 52.39N 5.36 E
Urkan 20 Hf 53.27N 126.56 E
Urla 24 Bc 38.18N 26.46 E
Urlaţi 15 Je 44.59N 26.14 E
Urluk 20 Ff 50.03N 107.55 E
Urmi 20 Ig 48.43N 134.16 E
Urmia, Lake- (EN)= Orūmīyeh, Daryācheh-ye 21 Gf 37.40N 45.30 E
Uromi 34 Gd 6.42N 6.20 E
Uroševac 15 Eg 42.22N 21.10 E
Urshult 8 Fh 56.32N 14.47 E
Ursus 10 Qd 52.12N 20.53 E
Urtazym 17 Ij 52.15N 58.50 E
Urtigueira, Serra da- 55 Gg 24.15S 51.00W
Uru, Rio- 55 Hb 15.24S 49.36W
Uruaçu 54 If 14.30S 49.10W
Uruana 55 Hb 15.30S 49.41W
Uruapan del Progreso 47 De 19.25N 101.58W
Uruará, Rio- 54 Hd 2.00S 53.38W
Urubamba, Río- 52 Ig 10.43S 73.48W
Urubici 55 Hi 28.02S 49.37W
Urubú, Cachoeira do- 55 Ha 12.52S 48.13W
Urucará 54 Gd 2.32S 57.45W
Uruçuí 54 Je 7.14S 44.33W
Urucuia, Rio- [Braz.] 55 Ib 15.38S 46.10W
Urucuia, Rio- [Braz.] 55 Jc 16.08S 45.05W
Urucum, Serra do- 55 Dd 19.13S 57.33W
Urucurituba 54 Gd 2.41S 57.40W
Uruguai, Rio- 52 Ki 34.12S 58.18W
Uruguaiana 53 Kh 29.45S 57.05W
Uruguay [1] 53 Ki 33.00S 56.00W
Uruguay, Río- 52 Ki 34.12S 58.18W
Urukthapel 64a Ac 7.15N 134.24 E
Urumbaba Dağı 15 Lj 38.25N 28.49 E
Ürümqi 22 Ke 43.48N 87.35 E
Urup 16 Lg 44.59N 41.10 E
Urup, Ostrov- 21 Qe 46.00N 150.00 E
Uruša 20 Hf 54.03N 122.55 E
Urussu 7 Mi 54.38N 53.24 E
Uruwira 36 Fd 6.27S 31.21 E
Urville, Cape D'- (EN)= Perkam, Tanjung- 26 Kg 1.28S 137.54 E
Uryū 29a Bb 43.39N 141.51 E
Uryū-Gawa 29a Bb 43.40N 141.54 E
Urziceni 15 Je 44.43N 26.38 E
Uržum 19 Fd 57.10N 50.01 E
Usa 29 Be 33.31N 131.22 E
Usa [R.S.F.S.R.] 16 Nc 53.02N 45.18 E
Usa [R.S.F.S.R.] 5 Lb 65.57N 56.55 E
Uşak 23 Cb 38.41N 29.25 E
Usakos 37 Bd 22.01S 15.32 E
Ušakovo 20 Hf 51.54N 126.35 E
Ušakovskoje 20 Nb 71.00N 178.35W
Usambara Mountains 30 Ki 4.45S 38.30 E
Usarp Mountains 66 Jf 71.10S 160.00 E
Usas Escarpment 66 Nf 76.00S 125.00W
Ušba, Gora- 16 Mh 43.06N 42.40 E
Usborne, Mount- 56 Ih 51.42S 58.50W
Ušće 15 Df 43.29N 20.38 E
Usedom 10 Jb 54.00N 14.00 E
Useldange 12 He 49.46N 5.59 E
'Ushayrah [Sau. Ar.] 33 He 21.46N 40.38 E
'Ushayrah [Sau. Ar.] 24 Kj 25.35N 45.46 E
Ushibuka 29 Be 32.13N 130.01 E
Ushikubi-Misaki 29a Bc 41.08N 140.48 E
Ushimado 29 Dd 34.37N 134.09 E
'Ushsh, Wādī al- 24 Fd 27.18N 42.15 E
Ushuaia 53 Jk 54.47S 68.20W
Usingen 12 Kd 50.20N 8.32 E
Usinsk 19 Fb 65.57N 57.29 E
Usküdar 24 Cb 41.01N 29.03 E
Üsküp 15 Kh 41.44N 27.24 E
Uslar 10 Fe 51.40N 9.39 E
Úslava 10 Jg 49.54N 13.32 E
Usman 16 Kd 51.54N 39.20 E
Usman 19 De 52.00N 39.43 E
Usmas, Ozero-/Usmas Ezers 8 Ig 57.13N 22.00 E
Usmas Ezers/Usmas, Ozero- 8 Ig 57.13N 22.00 E
Usogorsk 19 Ec 63.28N 48.35 E
Usoke 36 Fd 5.06S 32.20 E
Usolje 19 Fd 59.25N 56.41 E
Usolje-Sibirskoje 20 Ff 52.47N 103.38 E
Usora 14 Mf 44.43N 18.04 E
Ussel 11 Ii 45.33N 2.19 E
USSR (EN)=Sojuz Sovetskih Socialističeskih Respublik [1] 22 Jd 60.00N 80.00 E
Ussuri 21 Pe 48.28N 135.02 E
Ussurijsk 22 Pe 43.48N 131.59 E
Usta 7 Kh 56.53N 45.28 E
Ust-Barguzin 20 Ff 53.27N 108.59 E
Ust-Bolšereck 20 Kf 52.40N 156.18 E
Ust-Cilma 19 Fb 65.27N 52.06 E
Ust-Čorna 10 Uh 48.17N 24.02 E
Ust-Donecki 16 Lf 47.39N 40.55 E
Ust-Džeguta 16 Mg 44.05N 42.01 E
Uster 14 Cc 47.20N 8.43 E
Ustevatn 8 Bd 60.30N 8.00 E
Ust-Hajrjuzovo 20 Ke 57.04N 156.50 E
Ustica 5 Hh 38.40N 13.10 E
Ustica 14 Hl 38.42N 13.11 E
Ust-Ilimsk 22 Md 58.03N 102.43 E
Ustilug 10 Uf 50.50N 24.09 E
Ústí nad Labem 10 Kf 50.40N 14.02 E
Ústí nad Orlicí 10 Mg 49.58N 16.24 E
Ust-Išim 19 Hd 57.44N 71.10 E
Ustja 19 Ec 61.33N 42.36 E
Ust-Judoma 20 Ie 59.10N 135.02 E
Ustjurt, Plato 21 He 43.00N 56.00 E
Ustjužna 7 Ig 58.53N 36.28 E
Ustka 10 Mb 54.35N 16.50 E
Ust-Kamčatsk 22 Sd 56.15N 162.30 E
Ust-Kamenogorsk 22 Ke 49.58N 82.38 E
Ust-Kan 20 Df 50.57N 84.55 E
Ust-Kara 19 Gb 69.15N 64.59 E
Ust-Karsk 20 Gf 52.41N 118.45 E
Ust-Katav 17 Ii 54.56N 58.10 E
Ust-Kujga 22 Pc 70.00N 135.36 E
Ust-Kut 22 Md 56.46N 105.40 E
Ust-Labinsk 16 Kg 45.13N 39.40 E
Ust-Luga 7 Gg 59.39N 28.15 E
Ust-Maya 22 Pc 60.25N 134.32 E
Ust-Muja 20 Ge 56.28N 115.30 E
Ust-Nera 22 Qc 64.34N 143.12 E
Ust-Njukža 20 He 56.30N 121.48 E
Uštobe 19 Hf 45.13N 77.59 E
Ust-Olenëk 20 Gb 72.58N 119.42 E
Ust-Omčug 20 Jd 61.05N 149.30 E
Ust-Ordynski 20 Ff 52.48N 104.45 E
Ust-Ordynski Burjatski Nacionalny okrug [3] 20 Ff 53.30N 104.00 E
Ustovo 15 Hh 41.34N 24.47 E
Ust-Pinega 7 Jd 64.10N 41.58 E
Ust-Pit 20 Ee 58.59N 92.00 E
Ust-Port 20 Dc 69.45N 84.25 E
Ust-Požva 17 Hg 59.05N 56.05 E
Ustrzyki Dolne 10 Sg 49.26N 22.37 E
Ust-Sobolevka 20 Ig 46.10N 137.59 E
Ust-Šonoša 7 Jf 61.11N 41.20 E
Ust-Uda 20 Ff 54.10N 103.03 E
Ust-Ujskoje 17 Ki 54.15N 63.57 E
Ust-Umalta 20 If 51.42N 133.18 E
Ustupo 49 Ii 9.08N 77.56W
Usu 22 Ke 44.27N 84.37 E
Usui-Tōge 29 Fc 36.22N 138.38 E
Usuki 28 Kh 33.08N 131.49 E
Usuki-Wan 29 Be 33.10N 131.50 E
Usulután 49 Cg 13.21N 88.27W
Usumacinta 38 Jh 18.22N 92.40W
Usumun 20 Hf 52.46N 126.37 E
Usu-San 29a Bb 42.32N 140.49 E
Usva 17 Hg 58.40N 57.35 E
Usva 17 Hg 58.17N 57.47 E
Utah [2] 43 Ed 39.30N 111.30W
Utah Lake 43 Ec 40.13N 111.49W
Utajärvi 7 Gd 64.45N 26.23 E
Utashinai 29a Cb 43.31N 142.03 E
Utata 20 Ff 50.51N 102.45 E
Ute Creek 45 Ei 35.21N 103.50W
Utembo 30 Jj 17.06S 22.01 E
Utena 7 Fi 55.29N 25.40 E
Ute Reservoir 45 Ei 35.21N 103.31W
Utete 36 Gd 7.59S 38.47 E
Uthai Thani 25 Ke 15.20N 100.02 E
Utiariti 55 Ca 13.02S 58.17W
Utica 43 Lc 43.06N 75.15W
Utiel 13 Ke 39.34N 1.12W
Utiel, Sierra de- 13 Ke 39.36N 1.08W
Utila 49 De 16.06N 86.54W
Utila, Isla de- 49 De 16.06N 86.56W
Utique 14 Em 37.04N 10.04 E
Utirik Atoll 57 Hc 11.15N 169.48 E
Utlängan 8 Fh 56.00N 15.45 E
Utljukski Liman 16 If 46.20N 35.15 E
Uto 28 Kh 32.40N 130.41 E
Utö [Fin.] 8 Ie 59.45N 21.25 E
Utö [Swe.] 7 Eg 58.55N 18.15 E
Utoro 29a Da 44.06N 144.58 E
Utrata 10 Qd 52.13N 20.15 E
Utrecht [3] 12 Hb 52.05N 5.08 E
Utrecht [Neth.] 6 Ge 52.05N 5.08 E
Utrecht [S.Afr.] 37 Ee 27.28S 30.20 E
Utrera 13 Gg 37.11N 5.47W
Utsira 8 Ae 59.20N 4.55 E
Utsjoki 7 Gb 69.53N 27.00 E
Utsunomiya 22 Pf 36.33N 139.52 E
Uttaradit 25 Ke 17.38N 100.06 E
Uttar Pradesh [3] 25 Fc 28.00N 80.00 E
Utuado 49 Nd 18.16N 66.42W
Utukok 40 Gb 70.04N 162.18W
Utuloa 64h Ab 13.16S 176.11W
Utupua Island 57 Hf 11.20S 166.36 E
Uturoa 65eDb 16.44S 151.26W
Utva 16 Rd 51.29N 52.40 E
Uudenmaa [2] 7 Ff 60.30N 25.00 E
Uukuniemi 8 Nc 61.47N 30.01 E
Uulu/Ulu 8 Kf 58.13N 24.29 E
Uusikaupunki/Nystad 7 Ef 60.48N 21.25 E
Uusimaa 8 Kd 60.30N 25.00 E
Uva 19 Fd 56.58N 52.14 E
Uvac 15 Cf 43.36N 19.30 E
Uvalde 43 Hf 29.13N 99.47W
Uvarovo 19 Ee 52.00N 42.15 E
Uvdal 8 Cd 60.20N 8.30 E
Uvéa, Ile- 57 Jf 13.18S 176.10W
Uvelka 17 Ji 54.05N 61.35 E
Uvelski 17 Ji 54.26N 61.27 E
Uvildy, Ozero- 17 Ji 55.35N 60.30 E
Uvinza 36 Fd 5.06S 30.22 E
Uvira 31 Ji 3.24S 29.08 E
Uvs nuur→Ubsu-Nur 21 Ld 50.20N 92.45 E
Uwa 29 Ce 33.21N 132.30 E
Uwajima 27 Ne 33.13N 132.34 E
Uwajima-Wan 29 Ce 33.15N 132.30 E
Uwa-Kai 29 Ce 33.20N 132.15 E
Uwayl 35 Dd 8.46N 27.24 E
'Uwaynāt, Jabal al-= 'Uweinat, Gebel- (EN) 30 Jf 21.54N 24.58 E
'Uwaynat Wannīn 33 Bd 28.05N 12.59 E
'Uweinat, Gebel- (EN)= 'Uwaynāt, Jabal al- 30 Jf 21.54N 24.58 E
Uwekuli 26 Hg 1.25S 121.06 E
Uwi, Pulau- 26 Ef 1.05N 107.24 E
Uxin Qi (Dabqig) 27 Id 38.27N 109.08 E
Uxmal 39 Kg 20.20N 89.46W
Uyo 34 Gd 5.07N 7.57 E
Uyuni 53 Jh 20.28S 66.50W
Uyuni, Salar de- 52 Jh 20.20S 67.42W
Už [Eur.] 10 Rh 48.33N 22.00 E
Už [Ukr.-U.S.S.R.] 16 Gd 51.15N 30.12 E
Uza 8 Mg 57.47N 29.38 E
Uzbekistan Sovet Socialistik Respublikasy/Uzbekskaja SSR [2] 19 Gg 41.00N 64.00 E
Uzbekskaja Sovetskaja Socialističeskaja Respublika [2] 19 Gg 41.00N 64.00 E
Uzbekskaja SSR/Uzbekiston Sovet Socialistik Respublikasy [2] 19 Gg 41.00N 64.00 E
Uzbekskaja SSR=Uzbek SSR (EN) [2] 19 Gg 41.00N 64.00 E
Uzbek SSR (EN)= Uzbekskaja SSR [2] 19 Gg 41.00N 64.00 E
Uzbel Shankou 27 Bd 38.42N 73.48 E
Uzen 19 Fg 43.22N 52.50 E
Uzerche 11 Hi 45.25N 1.34 E
Uzès 11 Kj 44.01N 4.25 E
Uzgen 18 Id 40.44N 73.21 E
Užgorod 19 Cf 48.37N 22.22 E
Uzin 16 Ge 49.52N 30.27 E
Uzlovaja 16 Kb 54.01N 38.12 E
Uzlovoje 10 Sh 48.23N 22.27 E
Užokski, pereval- 16 Ce 49.02N 22.58 E
Uzümlü 15 Mm 36.44N 29.14 E
Uzun Ada 15 Jk 38.28N 26.42 E
Uzunagač [Kaz.-U.S.S.R.] 18 Kc 43.08N 76.20 E
Uzunagač [Kaz.-U.S.S.R.] 18 Kc 43.36N 76.19 E
Uzunköprü 24 Bb 41.16N 26.41 E
Užur 20 De 55.20N 90.00 E
Užventis 8 Ji 55.44N 22.37 E
Uzynkair, Mys- 18 Bb 45.47N 59.20 E

V

Vääksy 8 Kc 61.11N 25.33 E
Vaal 30 Jk 29.24S 23.38 E
Vaala 7 Gd 64.34N 26.50 E
Vaals 12 Id 50.46N 6.01 E
Vaalwater 37 Dd 24.20S 28.03 E
Vaasa [2] 7 Fe 63.12N 23.00 E
Vaasa/Vasa 6 Ic 63.06N 21.36 E
Vaassen, Epe- 12 Hb 52.17N 5.58 E
Vabalninkas 8 Ki 55.58N 24.49 E
Vác 10 Pi 47.47N 19.08 E
Vacacaí, Rio- 55 Fi 29.55S 53.06W
Vacaria 56 Jc 28.30S 50.56W
Vacaria, Rio- 55 Fe 21.55S 53.59W
Vacaville 46 Eg 38.21N 121.59W
Vaccarès, Étang de- 11 Kk 43.32N 4.34 E
Vache, Ile à- 49 Kd 18.04N 73.38W
Väddö 8 Hd 60.00N 18.50 E
Vadehavet 8 Ci 55.15N 8.40 E
Vădeni 15 Kd 45.22N 27.56 E
Vadheim 8 Ac 61.13N 5.49 E
Vadodara 22 Jg 22.18N 73.12 E
Vado Ligure 14 Cf 44.17N 8.27 E
Vadsø 6 Ia 70.05N 29.46 E
Vadstena 7 Dg 58.27N 14.54 E
Vaduz 6 Gf 47.08N 9.30 E
Værlandet 8 Ac 61.20N 4.45 E
Vaga 5 Kc 62.48N 42.56 E
Vagaj 17 Mh 56.28N 67.18 E
Vagaj 17 Nh 57.55N 69.01 E
Vågåmo 7 Bf 61.53N 9.06 E
Vaganjski vrh 14 Jf 44.21N 15.30 E
Vågåvatn 8 Cc 61.50N 8.50 E
Vaggeryd 7 Dh 57.30N 14.07 E
Vaghena 63a Cb 7.25S 157.43 E
Vagil 17 Kg 59.45N 62.40 E
Vagis, Gora- 20 Jf 52.20N 142.15 E
Vagnhärad 8 Gf 58.57N 17.31 E
Vågsøy 8 Ac 62.00N 5.05 E
Váh 10 Ni 47.55N 18.00 E
Vah 21 Jc 60.45N 76.45 E
Vahitahi Atoll 57 Nf 18.44S 138.52W
Vahruši 7 Mg 58.43N 50.02 E
Vahš 18 Gf 37.43N 68.49 E
Vahsel Bay→Herzog-Ernst-Bucht 66 Af 77.48S 34.39W
Vahtan 7 Lh 57.59N 46.42 E
Vaïaau 65eDb 16.52S 151.28W
Vaigat 41 Gd 70.30N 54.00W
Vaihingen an der Enz 12 Kf 48.56N 8.58 E
Vaihú 65d Ab 27.10S 109.23W
Väike-Maarja/Vjaike-Maarja 8 Le 59.04N 26.12 E
Väike-Pakri/Vjajke-Pakri 8 Je 59.50N 23.50 E
Väike Väin/Vjajke-Vjajn 8 Jf 58.30N 23.10 E
Vailala 64h Bb 13.13S 176.09W
Vailala, Pointe- 64h Ab 13.13S 176.10W
Vaileka 63d Bb 17.23S 178.09 E
Vailheu, Récif- 37 Gb 11.48S 43.04 E
Vailly-sur-Aisne 12 Fe 49.25N 3.31 E
Vainikkala 8 Md 60.52N 28.18 E
Vainode/Vajnëde 8 Ih 56.26N 21.45 E
Vairaatea Atoll 57 Nf 19.19S 139.20W
Vaison-la-Romaine 11 Lj 44.14N 5.04 E
Vaitape 65eDb 16.31S 151.45W
Vaïtoare 65eDb 16.41S 151.28W
Vaitupu Island 57 Ie 7.28S 178.41 E
Vajgač, Ostrov- 5 La 70.00N 59.30 E
Vajnëde/Vainode 8 Ih 56.26N 21.45 E
Vakaga [3] 35 Cd 10.00N 23.30 E
Vakfıkebir 24 Hb 41.03N 39.20 E
Vaksdal 8 Ad 60.29N 5.44 E
Val 20 Jf 52.19N 143.09 E
Vala 7 Mh 56.59N 51.16 E
Valaam 7 Hf 61.24N 30.59 E
Valaam, Ostrov- 8 Nc 61.20N 31.05 E
Valahia = Walachia (EN) 15 He 44.00N 25.00 E
Valahia = Walachia (EN) 5 Ig 44.00N 25.00 E
Valais [2] 14 Bd 46.15N 7.30 E
Valamares, Mali i- 15 Di 40.47N 20.28 E
Valamaz 7 Mh 57.36N 52.14 E
Valandovo 15 Fh 41.19N 22.34 E
Valašské Meziříčí 10 Ng 49.29N 17.58 E
Valáxa 15 Hk 38.49N 24.29 E
Vålberg 8 Ee 59.24N 13.12 E
Valburg 12 Hc 51.55N 5.49 E
Valcabra 13 Jg 37.30N 2.43W
Vălčedrăm 15 Gf 43.42N 23.27 E
Valcheta 56 Gf 40.42S 66.09W
Valdagno 14 Fe 45.39N 11.18 E
Valdahon 11 Mg 47.09N 6.21 E
Valdai Hills (EN)= Valdajskaja Vozvyšennost 5 Jd 57.00N 33.30 E
Valdaj 19 Dd 57.59N 33.14 E
Valdajskaja Vozvyšennost= Valdai Hills (EN) 5 Jd 57.00N 33.30 E
Valdarno 14 Fg 43.45N 11.15 E
Valdavia 13 Hb 42.24N 4.16W
Valdecañas, Embalse de- 13 Ge 39.45N 5.30W
Valdeganga 13 Ke 39.09N 1.40W
Val-de-Marne [3] 11 If 48.47N 2.29 E
Valdemārpils/Valdemarpils 7 Fh 57.24N 22.39 E
Valdemarpils/Valdemārpils 7 Fh 57.24N 22.39 E
Valdemarsvik 7 Dg 58.12N 16.32 E
Valdepeñas 13 If 38.46N 3.23W
Valderaduey 13 Gc 41.31N 5.42W
Valderas 13 Gb 42.05N 5.27W
Valderrama, Cienaga de- 49 Ki 8.56N 72.10W
Valderrobres/Vall-de-roures 13 Ld 40.53N 0.09W
Valdés, Peninsula- 52 Jj 42.30S 64.00W
Valdez 39 Ec 61.07N 146.16W
Val d'Isère 11 Mi 45.27N 6.59 E
Valdivia 53 Ii 39.48S 73.14W
Valdivia Seamount (EN) 30 Hk 25.20S 6.15 E
Valdobbiadene 14 Fe 45.54N 12.00 E
Val-d'Oise [3] 11 Ie 49.10N 2.10 E
Val-d'Or 39 Le 48.07N 77.47W
Valdosta 39 Kf 30.50N 83.17W
Valdres 8 Cc 60.55N 9.10 E
Vale [Geo.-U.S.S.R.] 16 Mi 41.36N 42.51 E
Vale [Or.-U.S.] 46 Gd 44.01N 117.15W
Valea Ierii 15 Gc 46.39N 23.21 E
Valea lui Mihai 15 Fb 47.31N 22.09 E
Valea Vişeului 15 Hb 47.51N 24.10 E
Valença [Braz.] 55 Kf 22.15S 43.43W
Valença [Braz.] 54 Kf 13.22S 39.05W
Valença do Minho 13 Db 42.02N 8.38W
Valença do Piauí 54 Je 6.24S 41.45W
Valençay 11 Hg 47.09N 1.34 E
Valence [Fr.] 11 Gj 44.06N 0.55 E
Valence [Fr.] 11 Kj 44.56N 4.54 E
Valencia 6 Fh 39.28N 0.22W
Valencia [3] 13 Le 39.20N 0.50W
Valencia 13 Le 39.30N 0.40W
València/Valencia 6 Fh 39.28N 0.22W
Valencia/València 6 Fh 39.28N 0.22W
València, Golf de-/Valencia, Golfo de- 5 Fh 39.30N 0.00
Valencia, Golfo de-/València, Golf de- 5 Fh 39.30N 0.00
Valencia, Lago de- 50 Cg 10.11N 67.45W
Valencia de Alcántara 13 Ee 39.25N 7.14W
Valencia de Don Juan 13 Gb 42.18N 5.31W
Valencia-El Grao 13 Le 39.27N 0.20W
Valenciennes 11 Jd 50.21N 3.32 E
Vălenii de Munte 15 Jd 45.11N 26.02 E
Valentia/Dairbhre 9 Cj 51.55N 10.20W
Valentin 28 Mc 43.07N 134.19 E
Valentine 43 Gc 42.52N 100.33W
Valenza 14 Ce 45.01N 8.38 E
Våler 7 Cf 60.40N 11.50 E
Valera 54 Db 9.19N 70.37W
Valerie Seamount (EN) 57 Ki 42.00S 163.30W
Valga 19 Cd 57.49N 26.05 E
Valge Jõgi 8 Ke 59.32N 25.36 E
Valhalla Mountains 46 Gb 49.45N 117.48W
Valiente, Peninsula- 49 Gi 9.05N 81.51W
Valier 46 Ib 48.18N 112.15W
Valinco, Golfe de- 11a Ab 41.40N 8.49 E
Valjevo 15 Ce 44.16N 19.53 E
Valka 7 Gh 57.47N 26.01 E
Valkeakoski 7 Ff 61.16N 24.02 E
Valkeala 8 Ld 60.57N 26.48 E
Valkenswaard 12 Hc 51.21N 5.28 E
Valkininkai/Valkininkaj 8 Kj 54.18N 25.55 E
Valkininkaj/Valkininkai 8 Kj 54.18N 25.55 E
Valko/Valkom 8 Ld 60.25N 26.15 E
Valkom/Valko 8 Ld 60.25N 26.15 E
Valkumej 20 Mc 69.41N 170.30 E
Valladolid [3] 13 Hc 41.35N 4.40W
Valladolid [Mex.] 47 Gd 20.41N 88.12W
Valladolid [Sp.] 6 Fg 41.39N 4.43W
Valldal 8 Bb 62.20N 7.21 E
Vall-de-Roures/Valderrobres 13 Ld 40.53N 0.09W
Vall de Uxó 13 Le 39.49N 0.14W
Valle [2] 54 Cc 3.40N 76.30W
Valle [3] 49 Dg 13.30N 87.35W
Valle 7 Bg 59.12N 7.32 E
Vallecas, Madrid- 13 Id 40.23N 3.37W
Valle d'Aosta / Vallée d'Aoste [2] 14 Be 45.45N 7.15 E
Valle de Cabuerniga 13 Ha 43.14N 4.18W
Valle de Guanape 50 Dh 9.54N 65.41W
Valle dei Templi 14 Hm 37.18N 13.35 E
Valle de la Pascua 54 Eb 9.13N 66.00W
Valle de Santiago 48 Ig 20.23N 101.12W
Valle de Topia 48 Fe 25.13N 106.25W
Valle de Zaragoza 48 Gd 27.28N 105.49W
Valledupar 54 Da 10.28N 73.15W
Vallée d'Aoste / Valle d'Aosta [2] 14 Be 45.45N 7.15 E
Vallée Jonction 44 Lb 46.23N 70.55W
Valle Hermoso 48 Ke 25.39N 97.52W
Vallejera, Puerto de- 13 Gd 40.30N 5.42W
Vallejo 43 Cd 38.07N 122.14W
Vallejo, Sierra de- 48 Gg 20.55N 105.20W
Valle Nacional 48 Ki 17.47N 96.19W
Vallenar 53 Ih 28.35S 70.46W
Vallentuna 8 He 59.32N 18.05 E
Valles/Vallès 13 Oc 41.35N 2.15 E
Valles de los Daidos 13 Hd 40.39N 4.09W
Valletta 6 Hh 35.54N 14.31 E
Valley City 43 Hb 46.55N 97.59W
Valley Falls 46 Ee 42.31N 120.15W
Valleyfield 42 Kg 45.15N 74.08W
Valley Station 44 Ef 38.06N 85.52W
Valleyview 42 Fe 55.02N 117.08W
Vallgrund 7 Ee 63.12N 21.14 E
Vallhagar 8 Hg 57.20N 18.10 E
Vallimanca 55 Bm 36.21S 61.02W
Vallimanca, Arroyo- 55 Bl 35.40S 60.02W
Vallo della Lucania 14 Jj 40.14N 15.16 E
Valloires, Abbaye de- 12 Dd 50.20N 1.47 E
Vallorbe 14 Ad 46.43N 6.23 E
Valls 13 Nc 41.17N 1.15 E
Valls d'Andorra→Andorra [1] 6 Gg 42.30N 1.30 E
Vallsta 8 Gc 61.32N 16.22 E
Vallvik 8 Gc 61.11N 17.11 E
Valmaseda 13 Ia 43.12N 3.12W
Valmiera 19 Cd 57.32N 25.29 E
Valmont 12 Ce 49.44N 0.31 E
Valnera 13 Ia 43.10N 3.45W
Valognes 11 Ee 49.31N 1.28W
Valois, Plaine du- 11 Ie 49.10N 2.45 E
Valoria la Buena 13 Hc 41.48N 4.32W
Valpaços 13 Ec 41.36N 7.19W
Valparaiso 44 De 41.28N 87.03W
Valparaiso [Braz.] 55 Ge 21.13S 50.51W
Valparaiso [Chile] 53 Ii 33.02S 71.38W
Valparaiso [Mex.] 48 Hf 22.46N 103.34W
Valpovo 14 Me 45.39N 18.25 E
Valréas 11 Kj 44.23N 4.59 E
Vals 30 Jk 27.23S 26.31 E
Vals, Tanjung- 26 Kh 8.26S 137.38 E
Valsjöbyn 7 Dd 64.04N 14.08 E
Valtellina 14 Dd 46.10N 9.55 E
Valtimo 7 Ge 63.40N 28.48 E
Váltou, Óri- 15 Ej 39.10N 21.20 E
Valujki 19 De 50.12N 38.08 E
Valul-Lui Traian 15 Le 44.15N 28.30 E
Valverde 32 Dd 27.48N 17.55W
Valverde de Júcar 13 Je 39.43N 2.12W
Valverde del Camino 13 Fg 37.34N 6.45W
Valverde del Fresno 13 Ff 40.13N 6.52W
Vamdrup 8 Ci 55.25N 9.17 E
Våmhus 7 Df 61.08N 14.28 E
Vamizi, Ilha- 37 Gb 11.02S 40.40 E
Vammala 7 Ff 61.20N 22.54 E
Vámos 15 Hn 35.25N 24.12 E
Van 23 Fb 38.28N 43.20 E
Van, Lake- (EN)=Van Gölü 21 Gf 38.33N 42.46 E
Vanajanselkä 7 Ff 61.09N 24.15 E
Vanak 24 Ng 31.41N 50.52 E
Vanak 24 Ng 31.32N 51.19 E
Vanån 8 Fd 60.31N 14.14 E
Vanault-les-Dames 12 Gf 48.51N 4.46 E
Vanavana Atoll 57 Ng 20.47S 139.09W
Vanavara 20 Fd 60.22N 102.16 E
Van Buren [Ar.-U.S.] 45 Ii 35.26N 94.21W
Van Buren [Me.-U.S.] 44 Nb 47.09N 67.56W
Vanč 18 He 38.23N 71.29 E
Vanceburg 44 Ff 38.36N 83.19W
Vancouver [B.C.-Can.] 39 Ge 49.16N 123.07W
Vancouver [Wa.-U.S.] 43 Cb 45.39N 122.40W
Vancouver Island 38 Ge 49.45N 126.00W
Vandalia [Il.-U.S.] 45 Lg 38.58N 89.06W
Vandalia [Oh.-U.S.] 44 Ef 39.53N 84.12W
Vanderbijl Park 37 De 26.42S 27.54 E
Vanderhoof 42 Ff 54.01N 124.01W
Vanderlin Island 59 Hc 15.45S 137.00 E
Van Diemen, Cape- 59 Gb 11.10S 130.25 E
Van Diemen Gulf 59 Gb 11.50S 132.00 E
Vandmtor, Ozero- 17 Le 62.15N 65.45 E
Vändra/Vjandra 7 Fg 58.40N 25.01 E
Vänern 5 Hd 58.55N 13.30 E
Vänersborg 7 Cg 58.22N 12.19 E

Index Symbols

[1] Independent Nation
[2] State, Region
[3] District, County
[4] Municipality
[5] Colony, Dependency
Continent
Physical Region
Historical or Cultural Region
Mount, Mountain
Volcano
Hill
Mountains, Mountain Range
Hills, Escarpment
Plateau, Upland
Pass, Gap
Plain, Lowland
Delta
Salt Flat
Valley, Canyon
Crater, Cave
Karst Features
Depression
Polder
Desert, Dunes
Forest, Woods
Heath, Steppe
Oasis
Cape, Point
Coast, Beach
Cliff
Peninsula
Isthmus
Sandbank
Island
Atoll
Rock, Reef
Islands, Archipelago
Rocks, Reefs
Coral Reef
Well, Spring
Geyser
River, Stream
Waterfall Rapids
River Mouth, Estuary
Lake
Salt Lake
Intermittent Lake
Reservoir
Swamp, Pond
Canal
Glacier
Ice Shelf, Pack Ice
Ocean
Sea
Gulf, Bay
Strait, Fjord
Lagoon
Bank
Seamount
Tablemount
Ridge
Shelf
Basin
Escarpment, Sea Scarp
Fracture
Trench, Abyss
National Park, Reserve
Point of Interest
Recreation Site
Cave, Cavern
Historic Site
Ruins
Wall, Walls
Church, Abbey
Temple
Scientific Station
Airport
Port
Lighthouse
Mine
Tunnel
Dam, Bridge

Index Symbols

☐ Independent Nation	☐ Historical or Cultural Region	☐ Pass, Gap
☐ State, Region	☐ Mount, Mountain	☐ Plain, Lowland
☐ District, County	☐ Volcano	☐ Delta
☐ Municipality	☐ Hill	☐ Salt Flat
☐ Colony, Dependency	☐ Mountains, Mountain Range	☐ Valley, Canyon
☐ Continent	☐ Hills, Escarpment	☐ Crater, Cave
☐ Physical Region	☐ Plateau, Upland	☐ Karst Features

☐ Depression	☐ Coast, Beach	☐ Rock, Reef
☐ Polder	☐ Cliff	☐ Islands, Archipelago
☐ Desert, Dunes	☐ Peninsula	☐ Rocks, Reefs
☐ Forest, Woods	☐ Isthmus	☐ Coral Reef
☐ Heath, Steppe	☐ Sandbank	☐ Well, Spring
☐ Oasis	☐ Island	☐ Geyser
☐ Cape, Point	☐ Atoll	☐ River, Stream

☐ Waterfall Rapids	☐ Canal	☐ Lagoon
☐ River Mouth, Estuary	☐ Glacier	☐ Bank
☐ Lake	☐ Ice Shelf, Pack Ice	☐ Seamount
☐ Salt Lake	☐ Ocean	☐ Tablemount
☐ Intermittent Lake	☐ Sea	☐ Ridge
☐ Reservoir	☐ Gulf, Bay	☐ Shelf
☐ Swamp, Pond	☐ Strait, Fjord	☐ Basin

☐ Escarpment, Sea Scarp	☐ Historic Site	☐ Port
☐ Fracture	☐ Ruins	☐ Lighthouse
☐ Trench, Abyss	☐ Wall, Walls	☐ Mine
☐ National Park, Reserve	☐ Church, Abbey	☐ Tunnel
☐ Point of Interest	☐ Temple	☐ Dam, Bridge
☐ Recreation Site	☐ Scientific Station	
☐ Cave, Cavern	☐ Airport	

Vetlužski [R.S.F.S.R.] 7 Kh 57.11N 45.07 E
Vetlužski [R.S.F.S.R.] 7 Kg 58.26N 45.28 E
Vetreny 20 Jd 61.43N 149.40 E
Vetreny Pojas, Kriaž- 7 Ie 63.20N 37.30 E
Vetrino 8 Mi 55.25N 28.31 E
Vetschau/Wětošow 10 Ke 51.47N 14.04 E
Vettore 14 Hh 42.49N 13.16 E
Vetzstein 10 Hf 50.25N 11.25 E
Veules-les-Roses 12 Ce 49.52N 0.48 E
Veulettes-sur-Mer 12 Ce 49.51N 0.36 E
Veurne/Furnes 11 Ic 51.04N 2.40 E
Vevey 14 Ad 46.28N 6.50 E
Vevis/Vievis 8 Kj 54.45N 24.58 E
Vexin 11 He 49.10N 1.40 E
Veynes 11 Lj 44.32N 5.49 E
Vézelay 11 Jg 47.28N 3.44 E
Vežen 15 Hg 42.45N 24.24 E
Vézère 11 Gj 44.53N 0.53 E
Vezirköprü 24 Fb 41.09N 35.28 E
Viadana 14 Ef 44.56N 10.31 E
Viale 55 Bj 31.53S 60.01W
Viana 54 Jd 3.13S 45.00W
Viana del Bollo 13 Eb 42.11N 7.06W
Viana do Alentejo 13 Df 38.20N 8.00W
Viana do Castelo 13 Dc 41.42N 8.50W
Viana do Castelo [2] 13 Dc 41.55N 8.25W
Vianden 12 Ie 49.55N 6.16 E
Viangchan (Vientiane) 22 Mh 17.58N 102.36 E
Vianópolis 55 Hc 16.45S 48.32W
Viar 13 Gg 37.36N 5.50W
Viareggio 14 Eg 43.52N 10.14 E
Viarmes 12 Ee 49.08N 2.22 E
Viaur 11 Hj 44.08N 1.58 E
Viborg [2] 8 Ch 56.30N 9.30 E
Viborg 7 Bh 56.26N 9.24 E
Vibo Valentia 14 Kl 38.40N 16.06 E
Vic 13 Oc 41.56N 2.15 E
Vicari 14 Hm 37.49N 13.34 E
Vicecomodoro Marambio 66 Re 64.16S 56.44W
Vicente Guerrero 47 Dd 23.45N 103.59W
Vicenza 14 Fe 45.33N 11.33 E
Vichada [2] 54 Ec 5.00N 69.30W
Vichada, Rio- 52 Je 4.55N 67.50W
Vichadero 55 Ej 31.48S 54.43W
Vichy 11 Jh 46.07N 3.25 E
Vicksburg 43 Ie 32.14N 90.56W
Vico, Lago di- 14 Gh 42.19N 12.10 E
Vic-sur-Aisne 12 Fe 49.24N 3.07 E
Vic-sur-Cère 11 Ij 44.59N 2.37 E
Victor Bay 66 Ie 66.20S 136.30 E
Victor Harbour 59 Hg 35.34S 138.37 E
Victoria 38 Hb 71.00N 114.00W
Victoria [3] 37 Ed 21.00S 31.00 E
Victoria [Arg.] 56 Hd 32.37S 60.10W
Victoria [Austl.] 59 Ig 38.00S 145.00 E
Victoria [B.C.-Can.] 39 Ge 48.25N 123.22W
Victoria [Cam.] 34 Ge 4.01N 9.12 E
Victoria [Chile] 56 Fe 38.13S 72.20W
Victoria [Gren.] 50 Ff 12.12N 61.42W
Victoria [Mala.] 26 Ge 5.17N 115.15 E
Victoria [Malta] 14 In 36.02N 14.14 E
Victoria [Rom.] 15 Hd 45.44N 24.41 E
Victoria [Sey.] 31 Mi 4.38S 55.27 E
Victoria [Tx.-U.S.] 39 Jg 28.48N 97.00W
Victoria/Ying zhan 22 Ng 22.17N 114.09 E
Victoria, Lake- [Afr.] 30 Ki 1.00S 33.00 E
Victoria, Lake- [Austl.] 59 If 34.00S 141.15 E
Victoria, Mount- [Bur.] 21 Lg 21.14N 93.55 E
Victoria, Mount- [Pap.N.Gui.] 57 Fe 8.53S 147.33 E
Victoria, Sierra de la- 55 Fg 25.55S 54.00W
Victoria and Albert Mountains 42 Ka 79.00N 75.00W
Victoria de Durango 39 Ig 24.02N 104.40W
Victoria de las Tunas 47 Id 20.58N 76.57W
Victoria Falls 31 Jj 17.56S 25.50 E
Victoria Falls 30 Jj 17.55S 25.21 E
Victoria Fjord 41 Hb 82.20N 48.00W
Victoria Land (EN) 66 Jf 75.00S 159.00 E
Victoria Nile 30 Kh 2.14N 31.26 E
Victoria Peak [B.C.-Can.] 46 Ba 50.03N 126.06W
Victoria Peak [Blz.] 49 Ce 16.48N 88.37W
Victoria River 57 Df 15.12S 129.43 E
Victoria River Downs 59 Gc 16.24S 131.00 E
Victoria Strait 42 Hc 69.30N 100.00W
Victoriaville 42 Kg 46.03N 71.58W
Victoria West 37 Cf 31.25S 23.04 E
Victorija 41 Pb 80.10N 36.45 E
Victorville 46 Gi 34.32N 117.18W
Victory, Mount- 59 Ja 9.10S 149.05 E
Vičuga 19 Ed 57.15N 42.00 E
Vicuña 56 Fc 29.59S 70.44W
Vicuña Mackenna 56 Hd 33.54S 64.23W
Vidå 8 Cj 54.58N 8.41 E
Vidal 46 Hi 34.11N 114.34W
Vidalia 45 Kk 31.34N 91.26W
Videbæk 8 Ch 56.05N 8.38 E
Videira 56 Jc 27.00S 51.08W
Videla 55 Bj 30.56S 60.39W
Videle 15 Ie 44.17N 25.31 E
Vidigueira 13 Ef 38.13N 7.48W
Vidin [2] 15 Ff 43.59N 22.52 E
Vidin 15 Ff 43.59N 22.52 E
Vidisha 25 Fd 23.42N 77.47 E
Vidlič 15 Ff 43.08N 22.47 E
Vidojevica 15 Ef 43.10N 21.32 E
Vidöstern 8 Fg 57.04N 14.01 E
Vidourle 11 Kk 43.32N 4.08 E
Vidra [Rom.] 15 Jd 45.55N 26.54 E
Vidra [Rom.] 15 Je 44.16N 26.09 E
Vidsel 7 Ed 65.49N 20.31 E
Viduša 14 Mh 42.54N 18.18 E
Vidzeme 8 Kg 57.10N 26.00 E
Vidzemes Augstiene/ Vidzemskaja Vozvyšennost 8 Kh 56.45N 26.00 E
Vidzemskaja Vozvyšennost/ Vidzemes Augstiene 8 Kh 56.45N 26.00 E
Vidzy 8 Li 55.23N 26.47 E
Vie 12 Be 49.09N 0.04W
Viechtach 10 Ig 49.05N 12.53 E
Viedma 53 Jj 40.50S 63.00W
Viedma, Lago- 52 Ij 49.35S 72.35W
Vieille Case 51g Ba 15.36N 61.24W
Vieja, Sierra- 45 Dk 30.30N 104.40W
Viejo, Cerro- 47 Bb 30.20N 112.15W
Viekšniai/Viekšnjai 8 Jh 56.14N 22.28 E
Viekšnjai/Viekšniai 8 Jh 56.14N 22.28 E
Viella 13 Mb 42.42N 0.48 E
Vielsalm 12 Hd 50.17N 5.55 E
Viels-Maisons 12 Ff 48.54N 3.24 E
Vienna [Mo.-U.S.] 45 Kg 38.11N 91.57W
Vienna [W.V.-U.S.] 44 Gf 39.20N 81.33W
Vienna (EN) = Wien 6 Hf 48.12N 16.22 E
Vienna Woods (EN) = Wienerwald 14 Jb 48.10N 16.00 E
Vienne 11 Ki 45.31N 4.52 E
Vienne [3] 11 Gh 46.30N 0.30 E
Vienne 5 Gf 47.13N 0.05 E
Vientiane → Viangchan 22 Mh 17.58N 102.36 E
Vientos, Paso de los- = Windward Passage (EN) 38 Lh 20.00N 73.50W
Vieques, Isla de- 47 Ke 18.08N 65.25W
Vieques, Pasaje de- 51a Cb 18.08N 65.40W
Vieques, Sonda de- 51a Cb 18.17N 65.25W
Vierge Point 51k Bb 13.49N 60.53W
Viersen 10 Ce 51.15N 6.23 E
Vierville-sur-Mer 12 Be 49.22N 0.54W
Vierwaldstätter-See = Lucerne, Lake- (EN) 14 Cc 47.00N 8.30 E
Vierzon 11 Ig 47.13N 2.05 E
Viesca 48 He 25.21N 102.48W
Viesite/Viesite 8 Kh 56.20N 25.38 E
Viesite/Viesite 8 Kh 56.20N 25.38 E
Vieste 14 Ki 41.53N 16.10 E
Viet Nam [1] 22 Mh 13.00N 108.00 E
Viet Tri 25 Ld 21.18N 105.26 E
Vieux Fort 50 Ff 13.44N 60.57W
Vieux-Fort, Pointe du- 51e Ac 15.57N 61.43W
Vieux Fort Bay 51k Bb 13.44N 60.58W
Vieux-Habitants 51e Ab 16.04N 61.46W
Vievis/Vevis 8 Kj 54.45N 24.58 E
Viga 7 Kg 59.15N 43.42 E
Vigala 8 Kf 58.43N 24.22 E
Vigan 26 Hc 17.34N 120.23 E
Vigeland 8 Bf 58.05N 7.18 E
Vigevano 14 Ce 45.19N 8.51 E
Vigia 54 Id 0.48S 48.08W
Vigía Chico 48 Ph 19.46N 87.35W
Vignacourt 12 Ed 50.01N 2.12 E
Vignemale 13 Lb 42.46N 0.08W
Vigneulles-lès-Hattonchâtel 12 Hf 48.59N 5.43 E
Vignoble 11 Lh 46.50N 5.30 E
Vignola 14 Ef 44.29N 11.00 E
Vigny 12 De 49.05N 1.56 E
Vigo 6 Fg 42.14N 8.43W
Vigo, Ría de- 13 Db 42.15N 8.45W
Vigra 8 Bb 62.30N 6.05 E
Vigrestad 8 Af 58.34N 5.42 E
Vihanti 7 Fd 64.30N 25.00 E
Vihiers 11 Fg 47.09N 0.32W
Vihorevka 20 Fe 56.12N 101.09 E
Vihorlat 10 Sh 48.55N 22.10 E
Vihren 15 Gh 41.46N 23.24 E
Vihti 7 Ff 60.25N 24.20 E
Viiala 8 Jc 61.13N 23.47 E
Viinijärvi 8 Mb 62.45N 29.15 E
Viinijärvi 8 Mb 62.39N 29.14 E
Viitasaari 7 Fe 63.04N 25.52 E
Viivikonna/Vijvikonna 8 Le 59.14N 27.41 E
Vijayawāda 22 Kh 16.31N 80.37 E
Vijvikonna/Viivikonna 8 Le 59.14N 27.41 E
Vik 7a Bc 63.25N 19.01W
Vika 8 Fd 60.57N 14.27 E
Vikarbyn 8 Fd 60.55N 15.01 E
Vikbolandet 8 Gf 58.30N 16.40 E
Viken 8 Eh 56.09N 12.34 E
Viken 8 Ff 58.40N 14.20 E
Vikenara Point 63a Dc 8.34S 159.53 E
Vikersund 8 De 59.59N 10.02 E
Vikingbanken 9 Pa 60.20N 2.30 E
Vikmanshyttan 8 Fd 60.17N 15.49 E
Vikna 7 Cd 64.53N 10.58 E
Vikna 7 Cd 64.54N 11.00 E
Viksoyri 7 Bf 61.05N 6.34 E
Vila da Bispo 13 Dg 37.05N 8.55W
Vila da Maganja 37 Fc 17.18S 37.31 E
Vila de Rei 13 De 39.40N 8.09W
Vila do Conde 13 Dc 41.21N 8.45W
Vila do Porto 32 Bb 36.56N 25.09W
Vila Flor 13 Ec 41.18N 7.09W
Vilafranca del Penedès/ Villafranca del Panadés 13 Nc 41.21N 1.42 E
Vila Franca de Xira 13 Df 38.57N 8.59W
Vila Franca do Campo 32 Bb 37.43N 25.26W
Vila Franca do Save 37 Ed 21.09S 34.32 E
Vila Gamito 37 Eb 14.10S 32.59 E
Vila Gouveia 37 Ec 18.03S 33.11 E
Vilaine 11 Dg 49.23N 2.27W
Viļaka/Viljaka 7 Gh 57.14N 27.46 E
Vila Machado 37 Ec 19.17S 34.12 E
Vilanculos 31 Kk 22.00S 35.19 E
Viļani/Viljani 7 Gh 56.33N 26.59 E
Vila Nova 36 Ce 12.38S 16.04 E
Vila Nova da Cerveira 13 Dc 41.56N 8.45W
Vila Nova de Famalicão 13 Dc 41.25N 8.32W
Vila Nova de Foz Côa 13 Ec 41.05N 7.12W
Vila Nova de Gaia 13 Dc 41.08N 8.37W
Vila Nova do Sales 36 Be 11.25S 14.18 E
Vilanova i la Geltrú/ Villanueva y Geltrú 13 Nc 41.14N 1.44 E
Vila Paiva de Andrada 37 Ec 18.41S 34.04 E
Vila Pouca de Aguiar 13 Ec 41.30N 7.39W
Vila Real [2] 13 Ec 41.35N 7.35W
Vila Real 13 Ec 41.18N 7.45W
Vila-Real de los Infantes/ Villarreal de los Infantes 13 Le 39.56N 0.06W
Vila Real de Santo António 13 Eg 37.12N 7.25W
Vilar Formoso 13 Fd 40.37N 6.50W
Vila Velha 54 Jh 20.20S 40.17W
Vila Velha de Ródão 13 Ee 39.40N 7.42W
Vila Viçosa 13 Ef 38.47N 7.25W
Vîlcea [2] 15 He 45.10N 24.10 E
Vilches 13 If 38.12N 3.30W
Vildbjerg 8 Ch 56.12N 8.46 E
Viled 7 Lf 61.22N 47.15 E
Vilejka 19 Ce 54.30N 26.53 E
Vilhelmina 7 Dd 64.37N 16.39 E
Vilhena 53 Jg 12.43S 60.07W
Vilija 16 Db 54.55N 25.40 E
Viljaka/Viļaka 7 Gh 57.14N 27.46 E
Viljandi 19 Cd 58.22N 25.35 E
Viljany/Viļani 7 Gh 56.33N 26.59 E
Viljuj 21 Oc 64.24N 126.26 E
Viljujsk 20 Hd 63.40N 121.33 E
Viljujskoje Plato = Vilyui Range (EN) 21 Mc 66.00N 108.00 E
Viljujskoje Vodohranilišče 20 Gd 62.30N 111.00 E
Vilkaviškis 7 Fi 54.43N 23.02 E
Vilkickogo, Ostrov- [R.S.F.S.R.] 20 Cb 73.30N 76.00 E
Vilkickogo, Ostrov- [R.S.F.S.R.] 20 Ka 75.40N 152.30 E
Vilkickogo, Proliv- = Vilkitski Strait (EN) 21 Mb 77.55N 103.00 E
Vilkija 7 Fi 55.03N 23.35 E
Vilkitski Strait (EN) = Vilkickogo, Proliv- 21 Mb 77.55N 103.00 E
Vilkovo 16 Fg 45.23N 29.35 E
Villa Aberastain 56 Gd 31.39S 68.35W
Villa Ahumada 47 Cb 30.37N 106.31W
Villa Altagracia 49 Ld 18.40N 70.10W
Villa Ana 55 Ci 28.29S 59.37W
Villa Angela 56 Hc 27.35S 60.43W
Villa Atuel 56 Gd 34.50S 67.54W
Villa Berthet 55 Bh 27.17S 60.25W
Villablino 13 Fb 42.56N 6.19W
Villa Bruzual 54 Eb 9.20N 69.06W
Villa Cañás 55 Bk 34.00S 61.36W
Villacañas 13 Ie 39.38N 3.20W
Villacarrillo 13 If 38.07N 3.05W
Villacastín 13 Hd 40.47N 4.25W
Villach 14 Hd 46.36N 13.50 E
Villacidro 14 Ck 39.27N 8.44 E
Villa Clara 55 Cj 31.50S 58.49W
Villaclara [3] 49 Hb 22.30N 80.00W
Villa Constitución [Arg.] 56 Hd 33.14S 60.20W
Villa Constitución [Mex.] 47 Bc 25.09N 111.43W
Villa Coronado 48 Gd 26.45N 105.10W
Villada 13 Hb 42.15N 4.58W
Villa de Arriaga 48 Ig 21.54N 101.23W
Villa de Cos 48 Hf 23.17N 102.21W
Villa de Cura 50 Cg 10.02N 67.29W
Villa de María 56 Hc 29.54S 63.43W
Villa de Reyes 48 Ig 21.48N 100.56W
Villa de San Antonio 49 Df 14.16N 87.36W
Villadiego 13 Ib 42.31N 4.00W
Villa Dolores 56 Gd 31.56S 65.12W
Villa Elisa 55 Ck 32.10S 58.24W
Villa Flores 48 Mi 16.14N 93.14W
Villa Florida 55 Dh 26.23S 57.09W
Villafranca del Bierzo 13 Fb 42.36N 6.48W
Villafranca del Cid 13 Ld 40.25N 0.15W
Villafranca de los Barros 13 Ff 38.34N 6.20W
Villafranca del Panadés/ Vilafranca del Penedès 13 Nc 41.21N 1.42 E
Villafranca di Verona 14 Ee 45.21N 10.50 E
Villa Frontera 47 Dc 26.56N 101.27W
Villagarcía de Arosa 13 Db 42.36N 8.45W
Villa General Roca 56 Gd 32.39S 66.28W
Villa Gesell 55 Dm 37.15S 56.55W
Villagrán 48 Je 24.29N 99.29W
Villaguay 56 Id 31.51S 59.01W
Villa Guillermina 55 Ci 28.14S 59.28W
Villa Hayes 56 Ic 25.06S 57.34W
Villa Hermandarias 55 Cj 31.13S 59.59W
Villahermosa 39 Jh 17.59N 92.55W
Villa Hidalgo 48 Gd 26.16N 104.54W
Villa Huidobro 56 Hd 34.50S 64.35W
Villajoyosa/La Vila Jojosa 13 Lf 38.30N 0.14W
Villalba 13 Ea 43.18N 7.41W
Villaldama 48 Id 26.30N 100.26W
Villalón de Campos 13 Gb 42.06N 5.02W
Villalpando 13 Gc 41.52N 5.24W
Villamalea 13 Ke 39.22N 1.35W
Villamanrique 13 Jf 38.33N 3.00W
Villa María 53 Ji 32.25S 63.15W
Villamartín 13 Gh 36.52N 5.38W
Villa Matamoros 48 Gd 26.50N 105.35W
Villa Media Agua 56 Gd 31.59S 68.25W
Villamil 54a Ab 0.56S 91.01W
Villa Minetti 55 Bi 28.37S 61.39W
Villa Montes 53 Jh 21.15S 63.30W
Villandraut 11 Fj 44.28N 0.22W
Villa Nueva 56 Gd 32.54S 68.47W
Villanueva 49 Kh 10.37N 72.59W
Villanueva [Mex.] 48 Hf 22.21N 102.53W
Villanueva [N.M.-U.S.] 45 Di 35.17N 105.23W
Villanueva de Córdoba 13 Hf 38.20N 4.37W
Villanueva del Arzobispo 13 Jf 38.10N 3.00W
Villanueva de la Serena 13 Gf 38.58N 5.48W
Villanueva del Fresno 13 Ef 38.23N 7.10W
Villanueva de los Infantes 13 If 38.44N 3.01W
Villanueva del Río y Minas 13 Gg 37.39N 5.42W
Villanueva y Geltrú/Vilanova i la Geltrú 13 Nc 41.14N 1.44 E
Villa Ocampo [Arg.] 56 Ic 28.28S 59.22W
Villa Ocampo [Mex.] 47 Cc 26.27N 105.31W
Villa Ojo de Agua 56 Hc 29.31S 63.42W
Villa Oliva 55 Dh 26.01S 57.53W
Villa Pesqueira 48 Ec 29.08N 109.58W
Villaputzu 14 Dk 39.26N 9.34 E
Villa Ramírez 55 Bk 32.11S 60.12W
Villarcayo 13 Ib 42.56N 3.34W
Villar del Arzobispo 13 Le 39.44N 0.49W
Villa Regina 56 Ge 39.06S 67.04W
Villarica [Chile] 56 Fe 39.16S 72.16W
Villarica [Par.] 53 Kh 25.45S 56.26W
Villa Rosario 54 Db 7.50N 72.29W
Villarreal de los Infantes/ Vila-Real de los Infantes 13 Le 39.56N 0.06W
Villarrobledo 13 Je 39.16N 2.36W
Villasalto 14 Dk 39.29N 9.23 E
Villa San Giovanni 14 Jl 38.13N 15.38 E
Villa San Martin 56 Hc 28.18S 64.12W
Villasimius 14 Dk 39.08N 9.31 E
Villatoro, Puerto de- 13 Gd 40.33N 5.10W
Villa Unión [Mex.] 47 Cd 23.12N 106.16W
Villa Unión [Mex.] 48 Ic 28.15N 100.43W
Villaverde, Madrid- 13 Id 40.21N 3.42W
Villavicencio 53 Ie 4.09N 73.37W
Villaviciosa 13 Ga 43.29N 5.26W
Villazón 54 Eh 22.06S 65.36W
Ville-de-Laval 44 Kc 45.33N 73.44W
Ville de Paris [3] 11 If 48.52N 2.20 E
Ville de Toulouse Bank (EN) 38 Hh 11.30N 117.00W
Villedieu-les-Poêles 11 Ef 48.50N 1.13W
Ville-en-Tardenois 12 Fe 49.11N 3.48 E
Villefranche-de-Lauragais 11 Hk 43.24N 1.44 E
Villefranche-de-Rouergue 11 Ij 44.21N 2.03 E
Villefranche-sur-Saône 11 Ki 45.59N 4.43 E
Ville-Marie 44 Hb 47.20N 79.26W
Villemur-sur-Tarn 11 Hk 43.52N 1.31 E
Villena 13 Lf 38.38N 0.51W
Villeneuve d'Ascq 12 Fd 50.38N 3.09 E
Villeneuve-Saint-Georges 12 Ef 48.44N 2.27 E
Villeneuve-sur-Lot 11 Gj 44.24N 0.43 E
Villeneuve-sur-Yonne 11 Jf 48.05N 3.18 E
Ville Platte 45 Jk 30.42N 92.16W
Villers-Bocage [Fr.] 12 Be 49.05N 0.39W
Villers-Bocage [Fr.] 12 Ee 50.00N 2.20 E
Villers-Bretonneux 12 Ee 49.52N 2.31 E
Villers-Carbonnel 12 Ee 49.52N 2.54 E
Villers-Cotterêts 12 Fe 49.15N 3.05 E
Villers-la-Ville 12 Gd 50.35N 4.32 E
Villers-sur-Mer 12 Ce 49.19N 0.01W
Villerupt 11 Le 49.28N 5.56 E
Villerville 12 Ce 49.24N 0.08 E
Ville-sur-Tourbe 12 Ge 49.11N 4.47 E
Villeurbanne 11 Ki 45.59N 4.43 E
Villiersdorp 37 Bf 33.59S 19.17 E
Villingen-Schwenningen 10 Eh 48.04N 8.28 E
Villmanstrand/Lappeenranta 6 Ic 61.04N 28.11 E
Villmar 12 Kd 50.23N 8.12 E
Vilnius/Vilnjus 6 Ie 54.41N 25.19 E
Vilnjus/Vilnius 6 Ie 54.41N 25.19 E
Vilok 10 Sh 48.08N 22.50 E
Vilppula 8 Kb 62.01N 24.31 E
Vils [F.R.G.] 10 Jh 48.35N 13.10 E
Vils [F.R.G.] 10 Hg 49.10N 11.59 E
Vilsandi 8 If 58.20N 21.45 E
Vilsbiburg 10 Ih 48.27N 12.21 E
Vilshofen 10 Jh 48.38N 13.11 E
Vilusi 15 Bg 42.44N 18.36 E
Vilvoorde/Vilvorde 11 Kd 50.56N 4.26 E
Vilvorde/Vilvoorde 11 Kd 50.56N 4.26 E
Vilyui Range (EN) = Viljujskoje Plato 21 Mc 66.00N 108.00 E
Vimeu 12 Dd 50.05N 1.35 E
Vimianzo 13 Ca 43.07N 9.02W
Vimmerby 7 Dh 57.40N 15.51 E
Vimoutiers 11 Gf 48.55N 0.12 E
Vimperk 10 Jg 49.03N 13.47 E
Vimy 12 Ed 50.22N 2.49 E
Vina 34 Id 7.45N 15.36 E
Viña del Mar 53 Ii 33.02S 71.34W
Vinalhaven Island 44 Mc 44.05N 68.52W
Vinalopó 13 Lf 38.11N 0.36W
Vinaros/Vinaroz 13 Md 40.28N 0.29 E
Vinaroz/Vinaros 13 Md 40.28N 0.29 E
Vinători 15 Hc 46.14N 24.56 E
Vincennes 43 Jd 38.41N 87.32W
Vincennes Bay 66 He 66.30S 109.30 E
Vincente, Puntan- 64b Bb 14.56N 145.40 E
Vinci 14 Eg 43.47N 10.55 E
Vindafjorden 8 Ae 59.20N 5.55 E
Vindelälven 7 Ee 63.54N 19.52 E
Vindeln 7 Ed 64.12N 19.44 E
Vinderup 8 Ch 56.29N 8.47 E
Vindhya Range 21 Kg 24.37N 82.00 E
Vindö 8 He 59.20N 18.40 E
Vineland 44 Jf 39.29N 75.02W
Vingåker 7 Dg 59.02N 15.52 E
Vingeanne 11 Lg 47.45N 5.18 E
Vinh 22 Mh 18.40N 105.40 E
Vinhais 13 Fc 41.50N 7.00W
Vinh Bac Phan = Tonkin, Gulf of- (EN) 21 Mh 20.00N 108.00 E
Vinh Linh 25 Le 17.04N 107.02 E
Vinica [Yugo.] 14 Jg 45.28N 77.00 E
Vinica [Yugo.] 15 Fh 41.53N 22.30 E
Vinita 45 Ih 36.39N 95.09W
Vînju Mare 15 Fe 44.25N 22.52 E
Vinkovci 14 Me 45.17N 18.49 E
Vinnica 6 If 49.14N 28.29 E
Vinnickaja Oblast [3] 19 Cf 49.00N 28.50 E
Vinniki 16 De 49.48N 24.11 E
Vino, Tierra del- 13 Gc 41.30N 5.30W
Vinogradov 16 Ce 48.09N 23.02 E
Vinslöv 8 Eh 56.06N 13.55 E
Vinson Massif 66 Pf 78.35S 85.25W
Vinstervatn 8 Cc 61.20N 9.00 E
Vinstra 7 Bf 61.36N 9.45 E
Vinstra 8 Cc 61.36N 9.45 E
Vintilă Vodă 15 Jd 45.28N 26.43 E
Vintjärn 8 Gd 60.50N 16.03 E
Vinton 45 Ke 42.10N 92.00W
Vintschgau/Venosta, Val- 14 Ed 46.40N 10.35 E
Vipiteno / Sterzing 14 Fd 46.54N 11.26 E
Vipya Plateau 36 Fe 11.09S 34.00 E
Viqueque 26 Ih 8.52S 126.22 E
Vir 14 Jf 44.18N 15.03 E
Virac 26 Hd 13.35N 124.15 E
Viramgām 25 Ed 23.07N 72.02 E
Virandozero 7 Id 64.01N 36.03 E
Viranşehir 24 Hd 37.13N 39.45 E
Virbalis 8 Jj 54.37N 22.49 E
Vircava 8 Jh 56.35N 23.43 E
Virden 42 Hg 49.51N 100.55W
Virdois/Virrat 7 Fe 62.14N 23.47 E
Vire 11 Ff 48.50N 0.53W
Vire 11 Ee 49.20N 1.07W
Virei 36 Bf 15.43S 12.54 E
Vireux-Wallerand 12 Gd 50.05N 4.44 E
Virgenes, Cabo- 52 Jk 52.19S 68.21W
Virgin Gorda 50 Dc 18.30N 64.25W
Virginia [2] 43 Ld 37.30N 78.45W
Virginia [Mn.-U.S.] 43 Ib 47.31N 92.32W
Virginia [S.Afr.] 37 De 28.12S 26.49 E
Virginia Beach 43 Ld 36.51N 75.59W
Virginia City 46 Fg 39.19N 119.39W
Virgin Islands 38 Mg 18.20N 66.45W
Virgin Islands of the United States [5] 39 Mh 18.20N 64.52W
Virgin Mountains 46 Ih 36.40N 113.50W
Virgin Passage 51a Cb 18.20N 65.10W
Virgin River 46 Hh 36.35N 114.18W
Virihaure 7 Dc 67.22N 16.33 E
Virkby/Virkkala 8 Kd 60.13N 24.01 E
Virkkala/Virkby 8 Kd 60.13N 24.01 E
Virmasvesi 8 Lb 62.50N 26.55 E
Virôchey 25 Lf 13.59N 106.49 E
Viroin 11 Kd 50.05N 4.43 E
Viroinval 12 Gd 50.05N 4.33 E
Viroinval-Nismes 12 Gd 50.05N 4.33 E
Virojoki 7 Gf 60.35N 27.42 E
Viroqua 45 Ke 43.34N 90.53W
Virovitica 14 Le 45.50N 17.23 E
Virpazar 15 Cg 42.15N 19.06 E
Virrat/Virdois 7 Fe 62.14N 23.47 E
Virserum 7 Dh 57.19N 15.35 E
Virsko More 14 If 44.20N 15.00 E
Virton 11 Le 49.34N 5.32 E
Virton-Ethe 12 He 49.35N 5.35 E
Virtsu 7 Fg 58.37N 23.31 E
Virudanagar 25 Fg 9.36N 77.58 E
Virvičja/Virvyčia 8 Jh 56.14N 22.30 E
Virvyčia/Virvičja 8 Jh 56.14N 22.30 E
Vis 14 Kg 43.02N 16.10 E
Vis 14 Kg 43.03N 16.12 E
Visalia 43 Dd 36.20N 119.18W
Visayan Sea 26 Hd 11.35N 123.51 E
Visby 7 Eh 57.38N 18.18 E
Viscount Melville Sound 38 Hb 74.10N 113.00W
Visé/Wezet 12 Hd 50.44N 5.42 E
Višegrad 15 Jh 41.59N 26.20 E
Višegrad 14 Ng 43.48N 19.17 E
Višera [R.S.F.S.R.] 19 Fc 61.57N 52.25 E
Višera [R.S.F.S.R.] 5 Ld 59.55N 56.50 E
Viseu [2] 13 Ed 40.45N 7.50W
Viseu [Braz.] 54 Id 1.12S 46.07W
Viseu [Port.] 13 Ed 40.39N 7.55W
Vişeu de Sus 15 Hb 47.43N 24.26 E
Vishākhapatnam 22 Kh 17.42N 83.18 E
Visingsö 8 Ff 58.03N 14.20 E
Viskafors 8 Eg 57.38N 12.50 E
Viskan 7 Cg 57.14N 12.12 E
Viški Kanal 14 Kg 43.07N 16.17 E
Vislanda 7 Dh 56.47N 14.27 E
Vislinski Zaliv 10 Pb 54.27N 19.40 E
Visnes 8 Ae 59.21N 5.14 E
Višnevka 15 Lc 46.22N 28.27 E
Visoki Dečani 15 Dg 42.33N 20.16 E
Visoko 14 Mg 43.59N 18.11 E
Visokoi 66 Ad 56.42S 27.12W
Visonggo 63d Bb 16.13S 179.40 E
Visp 14 Bd 46.17N 7.53 E
Vissefjärda 8 Fh 56.32N 15.35 E
Vista 46 Gj 33.12N 117.15W
Visten 8 Ee 59.40N 13.20 E
Vistonis, Órmos- 15 Ii 40.58N 25.05 E
Vistonis, Limni- 15 Ih 41.03N 25.07 E
Vistula (EN) = Wisła 5 He 54.22N 18.55 E
Vištytis 8 Jj 54.27N 22.44 E
Visuvisu Point 63a Cb 7.57S 157.31 E
Vit 15 Hf 43.41N 24.45 E
Vitebsk 6 Jd 55.12N 30.11 E
Vitebskaja Oblast [3] 19 Cd 55.20N 29.00 E
Viterbo 14 Gh 42.25N 12.06 E
Vithkuqi 15 Di 40.31N 20.35 E
Vitichi 54 Eh 20.13S 65.29W
Vitigudino 13 Fc 41.01N 6.26W
Viti Levu 57 If 18.00S 178.00 E
Vitim 20 Ge 59.33N 112.28 E
Vitim 21 Nd 59.26N 112.34 E
Vitimski 20 Ge 58.18N 113.18 E
Vitimskoje Ploskogorje 20 Gf 54.00N 114.00 E
Vitinja 15 Gg 42.47N 23.45 E
Vitjaz Strait 60 Di 5.35S 147.00 E
Vitolište 15 Eh 41.11N 21.50 E
Vitoria 13 Jb 42.51N 2.40W
Vitória 53 Lh 20.19S 40.21W
Vitória da Conquista 53 Lg 14.51S 40.51W
Vitória de Santo Antão 54 Ke 8.07S 35.18W
Vitorog 14 Lf 44.08N 17.03 E
Vitosa 15 Gg 42.33N 23.15 E
Vitré 11 Ef 48.08N 1.12W
Vitry-en-Artois 12 Ed 50.20N 2.59 E
Vitry-le-François 11 Kf 48.44N 4.35 E
Vitsi 15 Ei 40.39N 21.23 E

Index Symbols

[1] Independent Nation
[2] State, Region
[3] District, County
[4] Municipality
[5] Colony, Dependency
Continent
Physical Region
Historical or Cultural Region
Mount, Mountain
Volcano
Hill
Mountains, Mountain Range
Hills, Escarpment
Plateau, Upland
Pass, Gap
Plain, Lowland
Delta
Salt Flat
Valley, Canyon
Crater, Cave
Karst Features
Depression
Polder
Desert, Dunes
Forest, Woods
Heath, Steppe
Oasis
Cape, Point
Coast, Beach
Cliff
Peninsula
Isthmus
Sandbank
Island
Atoll
Rock, Reef
Islands, Archipelago
Rocks, Reefs
Coral Reef
Well, Spring
Geyser
River, Stream
Waterfall Rapids
River Mouth, Estuary
Lake
Salt Lake
Intermittent Lake
Reservoir
Swamp, Pond
Canal
Glacier
Ice Shelf, Pack Ice
Ocean
Sea
Gulf, Bay
Strait, Fjord
Lagoon
Bank
Seamount
Tablemount
Ridge
Shelf
Basin
Escarpment, Sea Scarp
Fracture
Trench, Abyss
National Park, Reserve
Point of Interest
Recreation Site
Cave, Cavern
Historic Site
Ruins
Wall, Walls
Church, Abbey
Temple
Scientific Station
Airport
Port
Lighthouse
Mine
Tunnel
Dam, Bridge

Vittangi 7 Ec 67.41N 21.39 E
Vitteaux 11 Kg 47.24N 4.32 E
Vittel 11 Lf 48.12N 5.57 E
Vittinge 8 Ge 59.54N 17.04 E
Vittoria 14 In 36.57N 14.32 E
Vittorio Veneto 14 Ge 45.59N 12.18 E
Vityaz Depth (EN) 3 Je 44.00N 151.00 E
Vityaz I Depth (EN) 3 Ih 11.20N 141.30 E
Vityaz II Depth (EN) 3 Kl 23.27S 175.00W
Vityaz III Depth (EN) 3 Km 32.00S 178.00W
Vityaz Seamount (EN) 57 Jc 13.30N 173.15W
Vityaz Trench (EN) 3 Jj 10.00S 170.00 E
Vivarais, Monts du- 11 Ki 44.55N 4.15 E
Vivarais, Plateaux du- 11 Kj 44.50N 4.45 E
Viver 13 Le 39.55N 0.36W
Vivero 13 Ea 43.40N 7.35W
Viverone, Lago di- 14 Ce 45.25N 8.05 E
Vivi 20 Ed 63.52N 97.50 E
Vivian 45 Jj 32.53N 93.59W
Viviers 11 Kj 44.29N 4.41 E
Vivo 37 Dd 23.03S 29.17 E
Vivorată 55 Dm 37.40S 57.39W
Vivorillo, Cayos- 49 Ff 15.50N 83.18W
Viwa 63d Ab 17.08S 176.56 E
Vizcaíno, Desierto de- 47 Bc 27.40N 114.40W
Vizcaíno, Sierra- 48 Bd 27.20N 114.00W
Vizcaya 13 Ja 43.15N 2.55W
Vizcaya, Golfo de- 5 Fg 44.00N 4.00W
Vize 15 Kh 41.34N 27.45 E
Vize, Ostrov 21 Jb 79.30N 77.00 E
Vizianagaram 25 Ge 18.07N 83.25 E
Vizille 11 Li 45.05N 5.46 E
Vizinga 19 Fc 61.05N 50.10 E
Viziru 15 Kd 45.00N 27.42 E
Vižnica 16 De 48.14N 25.12 E
Vizzini 14 Im 37.10N 14.45 E
Vjaike-Maarja/Väike-Maarja 8 Le 59.04N 26.12 E
Vjajke-Pakri/Väike-Pakri 8 Je 59.50N 23.50 E
Vjajke-Vjajn/Väik Vain 8 Jf 58.30N 23.10 E
Vjalje, Ozero- 8 Ne 59.00N 30.20 E
Vjalozero, Ozero- 7 Ic 66.50N 35.10 E
Vjandra/Vändra 7 Fg 58.40N 25.01 E
Vjartsilja 7 He 62.10N 30.48 E
Vjatka 5 Ld 55.36N 51.30 E
Vjatskije Poljany 19 Fd 56.14N 51.04 E
Vjatski Uval 7 Lg 58.00N 49.45 E
Vjazemski 20 Ig 47.31N 134.45 E
Vjazma 6 Jd 55.13N 34.18 E
Vjazniki 7 Kh 56.15N 42.12 E
Vjeio, Rio- 49 Dg 12.17N 86.54W
Vjosa 15 Ci 40.37N 19.20 E
Vlaamse Banken 12 Ec 51.15N 2.30 E
Vlaanderen/Flandres= Flanders (EN) 5 Ge 51.00N 3.20 E
Vlaanderen/Flandres= Flanders (EN) 11 Jc 51.00N 3.20 E
Vlaardingen 11 Kc 51.54N 4.21 E
Vlădeasa, Vîrful- 15 Fc 46.45N 22.48 E
Vlădeni 15 Kb 47.25N 27.20 E
Vladičin Han 15 Fg 42.43N 22.04 E
Vladimir 6 Kd 56.10N 40.25 E
Vladimirskaja Oblast 19 Ed 56.00N 40.40 E
Vladimirski Tupik 16 Hb 55.42N 33.18 E
Vladimir-Volynski 19 Ce 50.51N 24.22 E
Vladivostok 22 Pe 43.10N 131.56 E
Vlad Ţepeş 15 Ke 44.21N 27.05 E
Vlagtwedde 12 Ja 53.02N 7.08 E
Vlagtwedde-Ter Apel 12 Jb 52.52N 7.06 E
Vlahina 15 Fi 41.54N 22.52 E
Vlăhiţa 15 Ic 46.21N 25.31 E
Vlamse Vlakte=Flanders Plain (EN) 11 Id 50.40N 2.50 E
Vlasenica 14 Mf 44.11N 18.57 E
Vlašic [Yugo.] 14 Lf 44.19N 17.40 E
Vlašim 10 Kg 49.42N 14.54 E
Vlasotince 15 Fg 42.58N 22.08 E
Vlasovo 20 Ib 70.40N 134.35 E
Vlieland 11 Ka 53.15N 5.00 E
Vlieland 12 Ha 53.17N 5.06 E
Vlieland-Oost Vlieland 12 Ha 53.17N 5.06E
Vliestroom 12 Ha 53.17N 5.10 E
Vlissingen 11 Jc 51.26N 3.35 E
Vlissingen-Oost-Souburg 12 Fc 51.28N 3.36 E
Vloesberg/Flobecq 12 Fd 50.44N 3.44 E
Vlora 6 Hg 40.27N 19.30 E
Vlorës, Gjiri i- 15 Ci 40.25N 19.25 E
Vlotho 12 Kb 52.10N 8.51 E
Vltava=Moldau (EN) 5 He 50.21N 14.30 E
Vöcklabruck 14 Hb 48.01N 13.39 E
Vodice 14 Jg 43.46N 15.47 E
Vodla 7 If 61.49N 36.00 E
Vodlozero, Ozero- 7 Ie 62.20N 37.00 E
Vodňany 10 Kg 49.09N 14.11 E
Vodnjan 14 Hf 44.57N 13.51 E
Vodny 17 Fe 63.32N 53.20 E
Voerde (Niederrhein) 10 Ce 51.35N 6.41 E
Voeren/Fouron 12 Hd 50.45N 5.48 E
Vogel Peak 34 Hd 8.24N 11.47 E
Vogelsberg 10 Ff 50.30N 9.15 E
Voghera 14 Df 44.59N 9.01 E
Vogtland 10 If 50.30N 12.05 E
Voh 63b Be 20.58S 164.42 E
Võhandu Jõgi/Vyhandu 8 Lf 58.03N 27.40 E
Vohémar 37 Ib 13.22S 50.00 E
Vohipeno 37 Hd 22.20S 47.52 E
Vöhl 12 Kc 51.12N 8.56 E
Vohma 7 Lg 58.45N 46.36 E
Vohma 19 Ed 58.58N 46.45 E
Voi 31 Ki 3.23S 38.34 E
Voikoski 8 Lc 61.16N 26.48 E
Voinjama 31 Gh 8.25N 9.45W
Vóion Óros 15 Ei 40.15N 21.03 E
Voire 11 Kf 48.27N 4.25 E
Voiron 11 Li 45.22N 5.35 E
Voitsberg 14 Jc 47.02N 15.09 E
Voïvïïs, Limni- 15 Fj 39.32N 22.45 E
Vojens 8 Ci 55.15N 9.19 E
Vojkar 17 Ld 65.38N 64.40 E
Vojmsjön 7 Dd 65.00N 16.24 E
Vojnić 14 Je 45.19N 15.42 E
Vojnilov 10 Ug 49.04N 24.33 E
Vojvodina 15 Cd 45.00N 20.00 E
Voj-Vož 19 Fc 62.56N 54.59 E
Voknavolok 7 Hd 64.57N 30.31 E
Vokré, Hoséré- 30 Ih 8.21N 13.15 E
Volary 10 Jh 48.55N 13.54 E
Volcán 49 Fi 8.46N 82.38W
Volcanica, Cordillera- 38 Ih 18.00N 101.00W
Volcano 65a Fd 19.26N 155.20W
Volcano Islands (EN)=Iō/Kazan-Rettō 21 Qg 25.00N 141.00 E
Volcano Islands (EN)=Kazan-Rettō/Iō 21 Qg 25.00N 141.00 E
Volcán Rana Roi 65d Ab 27.05S 109.23W
Volčansk [R.S.F.S.R.] 17 Jg 59.59N 60.04 E
Volčansk [Ukr.-U.S.S.R.] 16 Jd 50.16N 37.01 E
Volčiha 20 Df 52.02N 80.23 E
Volda 7 Be 62.09N 6.06 E
Voldafjorden 8 Ab 62.10N 6.00 E
Volga 5 Kf 45.55N 47.52 E
Volga 7 Jh 57.57N 38.25 E
Volga-Baltic Canal (EN)= Volgo-Baltijski vodny put imeni V. I. Lenina 5 Jd 59.58N 37.10 E
Volga Delta (EN) 5 Kf 46.30N 47.00 E
Volga Hills (EN)= Privolžkaja Vozvyšennost 5 Ke 52.00N 46.00 E
Volgo-Baltijski vodny put imeni V.I. Lenina=Volga-Baltic Canal (EN) 5 Jd 59.58N 37.10 E
Volgodonsk 19 Ef 47.33N 42.08 E
Volgo-Donskoj sudohodny kanal imeni V. I. Lenina= Lenin Canal (EN) 5 Kf 48.40N 43.37 E
Volgograd (Stalingrad) 6 Kf 48.44N 44.25 E
Volgograd Reservoir (EN)= Volgogradskoje Vodohranilišče 5 Kf 49.20N 45.00 E
Volgogradskaja Oblast 19 Ef 49.30N 44.30 E
Volgogradskoje Vodohranilišče=Volgograd Reservoir (EN) 5 Kf 49.20N 45.00 E
Volhov 5 Jc 60.08N 32.20 E
Volhov 6 Jd 59.55N 32.20 E
Volhynia 5 Ie 51.00N 25.00 E
Volissós 15 Ik 38.29N 25.55 E
Volja 17 Je 63.11N 61.16 E
Volka 10 Vd 52.43N 25.43 E
Völkermarkt 14 Id 46.39N 14.38 E
Völklingen 10 Cg 49.15N 6.51 E
Volkmarsen 12 Lc 51.24N 9.07 E
Volkovysk 16 Dc 53.10N 24.31 E
Volkovysskaja Vozvyšennost 10 Kc 53.10N 24.30 E
Volksrust 37 De 27.24S 29.53 E
Vollenhove 12 Hb 52.40N 5.57 E
Vollsjö 8 Ei 55.42N 13.46 E
Volme 12 Jc 51.24N 7.27 E
Volmunster 12 Je 49.07N 7.21 E
Volna, Gora- 20 Kd 63.30N 154.57 E
Volnjansk 16 If 47.54N 35.29 E
Volnovaha 16 Jf 47.37N 37.36 E
Voločajevka 2-ja 20 Ig 48.36N 134.36 E
Voločisk 16 Ee 49.31N 26.13 E
Volodarsk 7 Kh 56.14N 43.13 E
Volodarski 16 Pf 46.26N 48.31 E
Volodarskoje 19 Ge 53.18N 68.08 E
Vologda 6 Jd 59.12N 39.55 E
Vologodskaja Oblast 19 Ed 60.00N 41.00 E
Volokolamsk 7 Ih 56.03N 35.58 E
Volokonovka 16 Jd 50.29N 37.52 E
Vólos 6 Ih 39.22N 22.57 E
Vološka 7 Jf 61.42N 39.15 E
Vološka 7 Jf 61.21N 40.03 E
Volosovo 7 Gg 59.28N 29.31 E
Volovec 10 Jh 48.42N 23.17 E
Volovo 16 Kc 53.35N 38.01 E
Voložin 16 Eb 54.06N 26.32 E
Volquart Boons Kyst 41 Jd 70.20N 24.20W
Volsini, Monti- 14 Fh 42.40N 11.55 E
Volsk 19 Ee 52.02N 47.23 E
Volta 30 Hh 5.46N 0.41 E
Volta 34 Fd 7.00N 0.30 E
Volta Blanche=White Volta (EN) 30 Gh 8.38N 0.59W
Volta Lake 30 Hh 7.30N 0.15 E
Volta Noire=Black Volta (EN) 30 Gh 8.38N 1.30W
Volta Noire=Black Volta (EN) 34 Ec 12.30N 4.00W
Volta Redonda 53 Lh 22.32S 44.07W
Volta Rouge=Red Volta (EN) 30 Gh 10.34N 0.30W
Volterra 14 Eg 43.24N 10.51 E
Voltoya 13 Hc 41.13N 4.31W
Voltri, Genova- 14 Cf 44.26N 8.45 E
Volturino 14 Jj 40.25N 15.48 E
Volturno 14 Hi 41.01N 13.55 E
Volubilis 32 Fc 34.04N 5.33W
Vólvi, Limni- 15 Gi 40.41N 23.28 E
Volynskaja Grjada 10 Ue 51.05N 25.00 E
Volynskaja Oblast 19 Ce 51.10N 25.00 E
Volynskaja Vozvyšennost 16 Dd 50.30N 25.00 E
Volžsk 19 Ed 55.55N 48.19 E
Volžski [R.S.F.S.R.] 6 Kf 48.48N 44.44 E
Volžski [R.S.F.S.R.] 7 Mj 53.28N 50.08 E
Voma 63d Bc 18.00S 178.08 E
Vomano 14 Ih 42.39N 14.02 E
Vonavona 63a Cc 8.12S 157.05 E
Vondrozo 37 Hd 22.47S 47.17 E
Von Frank Mountain 40 Id 63.33N 154.20W
Vónitsa 15 Dk 38.55N 20.53 E
Vonne 11 Gh 46.25N 0.15 E
Võnnu/Vynnu 8 Lf 58.15N 27.10 E
Voorne 12 Gc 51.52N 4.05 E
Voorschoten 12 Gb 52.08N 4.28 E
Voorst 12 Ib 52.10N 6.09 E
Voorst-Twello 12 Ib 52.14N 6.07 E
Vop 16 Hb 54.56N 32.44 E
Vopnafjördur 7a Cb 65.45N 14.50W
Vora 15 Ch 41.23N 19.40 E
Vörå/Vöyri 8 Ja 63.09N 22.15 E
Vorarlberg 14 Dc 47.15N 9.50 E
Vóras Óros 15 Ei 41.00N 21.50 E
Vorau 14 Jc 47.24N 15.53 E
Vorden 12 Ib 52.06N 6.20 E
Vorderrhein 14 Dd 46.49N 9.26 E
Vordingborg 7 Ci 55.01N 11.55 E
Voreifel 12 Jd 50.10N 7.00 E
Vorga Šor 17 Kc 67.35N 63.40 E
Voria Píndhos 15 Dj 40.20N 20.55 E
Vórioi Sporádhes, Nisoi-= Northern Sporades (EN) 5 Ih 39.15N 23.55 E
Vórios Evvoïkós Kólpos= Évvoia, Gulf of- (EN) 15 Gk 38.45N 23.10 E
Vorkuta 6 Mb 67.27N 63.58 E
Vorma 7 Cf 60.09N 11.27 E
Vormsi 8 Je 59.02N 23.05 E
Vormsi 7 Fg 59.00N 23.15 E
Vorniceni 15 Jb 47.59N 26.40 E
Vorogovo 20 Dd 60.58N 89.28 E
Vorona 16 Md 51.22N 42.03 E
Voroncovo [R.S.F.S.R.] 20 Db 71.40N 83.40 E
Voroncovo [R.S.F.S.R.] 8 Mg 57.15N 28.49 E
Voronež 6 Je 51.40N 39.10 E
Voronež 16 Kd 51.31N 39.05 E
Voronežskaja Oblast 19 Ee 51.00N 40.15 E
Voronin Trough (EN) 67 Ge 80.00N 85.00 E
Voronja 7 Ib 69.09N 35.47 E
Voronovo 8 Kj 54.09N 25.19 E
Voropajevo 8 Li 55.07N 27.19 E
Vorošilovgrad 6 Jf 48.34N 39.20 E
Vorošilovgradskaja Oblast 19 Df 49.00N 39.10 E
Vorotan 16 Oj 39.15N 46.43 E
Vorotynec 7 Kh 56.02N 45.52 E
Vorožba 16 Id 51.10N 34.11 E
Vorskla 16 Ie 48.52N 34.05 E
Vorsma 7 Ki 55.58N 43.17 E
Vörts Järv/Vyrtsjarv, Ozero- 7 Gg 58.15N 26.05 E
Võru/Vyru 19 Cd 57.52N 27.05 E
Voruh 18 He 39.52N 70.35 E
Vosges 5 Gf 48.30N 7.10 E
Vosges 11 Mf 48.10N 6.20 E
Voskresensk 7 Ji 55.22N 38.42 E
Voskresenskoje 7 Kh 56.51N 45.27 E
Voss 8 Bd 60.40N 6.30 E
Vossa 8 Ad 60.39N 5.42 E
Vossevangen 7 Bd 60.39N 6.26 E
Vostočno-Kazahstanskaja Oblast 19 If 49.00N 84.00 E
Vostočno-Kounradski 19 Hf 46.58N 75.07 E
Vostočno Sibirskoje More= East Siberian Sea (EN) 67 Cd 74.00N 166.00 E
Vostočny [R.S.F.S.R.] 20 Jg 48.19N 142.40 E
Vostočny [R.S.F.S.R.] 17 Jg 58.48N 61.52 E
Vostočny, Hrebet- 20 Lf 55.00N 160.30 E
Vostočny Sajan=Eastern Sayans (EN) 21 Ld 53.00N 97.00 E
Vostok 66 Hf 78.28S 106.48 E
Vostok Island 57 Lf 10.06S 152.23W
Vostrecovo 20 Ig 45.56N 134.59 E
Vošu/Vyzu 8 Ke 59.30N 25.50 E
Votkinsk 19 Fd 57.05N 53.59 E
Votkinskoje Vodohranilišče = Votkinsk Reservoir (EN) 5 Ld 57.30N 55.10 E
Votkinsk Reservoir (EN) = Votkinskoje Vodohranilišče 5 Ld 57.30N 55.10 E
Votuporanga 55 He 20.24S 49.59W
Vouga 36 Ce 12.14S 16.48 E
Vouga 13 Dd 40.41N 8.40W
Vouillé 11 Gh 46.38N 0.10 E
Voulgára 15 Ej 39.06N 21.54 E
Vouliagméni 15 Gl 37.49N 23.47 E
Voúrinos Óros 15 Ei 40.11N 21.40 E
Voúxa, Ákra- 15 Gn 35.38N 23.36 E
Vouziers 11 Ke 49.24N 4.42 E
Voves 11 Hf 48.16N 1.38 E
Vovodo 35 Cd 5.40N 24.21 E
Voxna 8 Fc 61.21N 15.34 E
Voxnan 8 Gc 61.17N 16.26 E
Voyeykov Ice Shelf 66 Ie 66.20S 124.38 E
Vöyri/Vörå 8 Ja 63.09N 22.15 E
Vože, Ozero- 7 Jf 60.35N 39.05 E
Vožega 7 Jf 60.33N 39.13 E
Vožega 7 Jf 60.30N 40.12 E
Voznesenje 7 If 61.01N 35.27 E
Voznesensk 19 Df 47.35N 31.20 E
Vozroždenija, Ostrov- 18 Bb 45.05N 59.15 E
Vraca 15 Gf 43.12N 23.33 E
Vraca 15 Dh 41.54N 20.45 E
Vraca 15 Gf 43.12N 23.33 E
Vradijevka 16 Gf 47.51N 30.34 E
Vrakhiónas 15 Dl 37.48N 20.45 E
Vran 14 Lg 43.39N 17.27 E
Vrancea 15 Jd 45.50N 26.42 E
Vranica 14 Lg 43.57N 17.44 E
Vranje 15 Eg 42.33N 21.54 E
Vranov nad Topl'ou 10 Rh 48.54N 21.41 E
Vrāška čuka, Prohod- 15 Ff 43.50N 22.23 E
Vratnica 15 Eg 42.08N 21.07 E
Vratnik, prohod- 15 Jg 42.49N 26.10 E
Vrbas 14 Le 45.07N 17.31 E
Vrbas 15 Cd 45.34N 19.39 E
Vrbno pod Pradědem 10 Nf 50.08N 17.23 E
Vrbovsko 14 Je 45.22N 15.05 E
Vrchlabí 10 Lf 50.38N 15.37 E
Vrede 37 De 27.30S 29.06 E
Vreden 12 Ib 52.02N 6.50 E
Vredenburg 37 Bf 32.54S 17.59 E
Vredendal 37 Bf 31.41S 18.35 E
Vresse, Vresse-sur-Semois- 12 Ge 49.52N 4.56 E
Vresse-sur-Semois 12 Ge 49.52N 4.56 E
Vresse-sur-Semois-Vresse 12 Ge 49.52N 4.56 E
Vretstorp 8 Fe 59.02N 14.52 E
Vrhnika 14 Ie 45.58N 14.18 E
Vries 12 Ia 53.05N 6.36 E
Vriezenveen 12 Ib 52.26N 6.36 E
Vrigstad 8 Fg 57.21N 14.28 E
Vron 12 Dd 50.19N 1.45 E
Vršac 15 Ed 45.07N 21.18 E
Vryburg 31 Jk 26.55S 24.45 E
Vryheid 37 Ee 27.52S 30.38 E
Vsetin 10 Ng 49.21N 18.00 E
Vsevidof, Mount- 40a Eb 53.07N 168.43W
Vsevoložsk 7 Hf 60.04N 30.41 E
Vstrečny 20 Lc 68.00N 165.58 E
Vtačnik 10 Oh 48.42N 18.37 E
Vuanggava 63d Cc 18.52S 178.54W
Vučitrn 15 Dg 42.49N 20.58 E
Vučjak 15 Fh 41.28N 22.20 E
Vuka 14 Me 45.21N 19.00 E
Vukovar 14 Me 45.21N 19.00 E
Vuktyl 19 Fc 63.50N 57.25 E
Vulavu 63a Dc 8.31S 159.48 E
Vulcan 15 Gd 45.23N 23.16 E
Vulcan, Vîrful- 15 Fc 46.14N 22.58 E
Vulcano 14 Il 38.25N 15.00 E
Vulkanešty 16 Fg 45.38N 28.27 E
Vulture 14 Jj 40.57N 15.38 E
Vung Tau 25 Lf 10.21N 107.04 E
Vunindawa 63d Bb 17.49S 178.19 E
Vunisea Station 61 Ec 19.03S 178.09 E
Vuohijarvi 8 Lc 61.10N 26.40 E
Vuoksa 8 Nd 60.35N 30.42 E
Vuoksa, Ozero- [R.S.F.S.R.] 8 Mc 61.00N 30.00 E
Vuoksa, Ozero- [R.S.F.S.R.] 8 Md 60.38N 29.55 E
Vuollerim 7 Ec 66.25N 20.36 E
Vuosjärvi 8 Ka 63.00N 25.30 E
Vuotso 7 Gb 68.06N 27.08 E
Vuranimala 63a Ec 9.05S 160.51 E
Vyborg 6 Ic 60.42N 28.45 E
Vyčegda 5 Kc 61.18N 46.36 E
Vyčegodski 7 Lf 61.17N 46.48 E
Východočeský kraj 10 Lf 50.10N 16.00 E
Východoslovenska nižina 10 Rh 48.35N 21.50 E
Východoslovenský kraj 10 Rg 49.00N 21.15 E
Vyg 7 Ie 63.17N 35.17 E
Vygoda [Ukr.-U.S.S.R.] 15 Nc 46.38N 30.24 E
Vygoda [Ukr.-U.S.S.R.] 10 Uh 48.52N 24.01 E
Vygozero, Ozero- 5 Jc 63.35N 34.45 E
Vyhandu/Võhandu Jõgi 8 Lf 58.03N 27.40 E
Vyja 7 Le 62.57N 46.42 E
Vyksa 19 Ed 55.20N 42.12 E
Vym 19 Fc 62.13N 50.25 E
Vynnu/Võnnu 8 Lf 58.15N 27.10 E
Vyrica 19 Dd 59.24N 30.19 E
Vyrnwy 9 Ki 52.45N 2.50W
Vyrtsjarv, Ozero-/Võrts Järv 7 Gg 58.15N 26.05 E
Vyru/Võru 19 Cd 57.52N 27.05 E
Vyša 16 Mb 54.03N 42.06 E
Vyšgorod 16 Gd 50.38N 30.29 E
Vyšgorodok 8 Mh 56.55N 28.05 E
Vyškov 10 Mg 49.17N 17.00 E
Vyškovsk, pereval 10 Th 48.38N 23.45 E
Vyšni Voloček 19 Dd 57.37N 34.32 E
Vysock 7 Gf 60.36N 28.36 E
Vysoké Tatry=High Tatra (EN) 10 Pg 49.10N 20.00 E
Vysokogorny 20 If 50.07N 139.10 E
Vysokogorsk 28 Mb 44.23N 135.23 E
Vysokoje 10 Td 52.22N 23.26 E
Vysokovsk 7 Ih 56.21N 36.29 E
Vyšši Brod 10 Kh 48.37N 14.18 E
Vytebet 16 Ic 53.53N 35.38 E
Vytegra 19 Dc 61.01N 36.28 E
Vyvenka 20 Ld 60.10N 165.20 E
Vyzu/Vošu 8 Ke 59.30N 25.50 E
Vzmorje 20 Jg 47.45N 142.30 E

W

Wa 34 Ec 10.03N 2.29W
Waal 11 Lc 51.55N 4.30 E
Waalre 12 Hc 51.23N 5.27 E
Waalwijk 12 Hc 51.41N 5.04 E
Waar, Meos- 26 Jg 2.05S 134.23 E
Waardgronden 12 Ha 53.15N 5.05 E
Waarschoot 12 Fc 51.09N 3.36 E
Wabana 42 Mg 47.38N 52.57W
Wabao, Cap- 63b Ce 21.36S 167.51 E
Wabasca 42 Ge 56.00N 113.53W
Wabasca 42 Fe 58.21N 115.20W
Wabash 38 Kf 37.46N 88.02W
Wabash 44 Ee 40.48N 85.49W
Wabasha 45 Jd 44.23N 92.02W
Wabash River 45 Lh 37.46N 88.02W
Wabowden 42 Hf 54.55N 98.38W
Wąbrzeźno 10 Oc 53.17N 18.57 E
Wabu Hu 27 Ke 32.20N 116.55 E
Wachau 14 Jb 48.20N 15.25 E
Wachile 35 Fe 4.33N 39.03 E
Wachusett Seamount (EN) 57 Lh 32.00S 151.20W
Waco 39 Jf 31.55N 97.08W
Waconda Lake 45 Gg 39.30N 98.30W
Wadayama 29 Dd 35.20N 134.51 E
Wad Bandah 35 Dc 13.06N 27.57 E
Waddān 33 Cd 29.10N 16.08 E
Waddān, Jabal- 33 Cd 29.20N 16.20 E
Waddeneilanden=West Frisian Islands (EN) 11 Ka 53.30N 5.00 E
Waddenzee 12 Ha 53.20N 5.30 E
Waddington, Mount- 38 Gd 51.23N 125.15W
Wadena 45 Ic 46.26N 95.08W
Wadern 12 Ie 49.32N 6.53 E
Wadern-Nunkirchen 12 Ie 49.32N 6.53 E
Wadersloh 12 Kc 51.44N 8.15 E
Wadersloh-Liesborn 12 Kc 51.43N 8.16 E
Wadesboro 44 Gh 34.58N 80.04W
Wadhams 46 Ba 51.30N 127.31W
Wādī Bīshah 23 Fe 21.24N 43.26 E
Wādī Fajr 23 Ec 30.17N 38.18 E
Wādī Ḥalfā' 31 Kf 21.56N 31.20 E
Wādī Jimāl, Jazīrat- 24 Fj 24.40N 35.10 E
Wādī Mūsá 24 Fg 30.19N 35.29 E
Wādī Shiḥan 35 Ib 18.10N 52.57 E
Wad Madanī 31 Kg 14.24N 33.32 E
Wad Nimr 35 Ec 14.32N 32.08 E
Wadowice 10 Pg 49.53N 19.30 E
Wadsworth 46 Fg 39.38N 119.17W
Wafangdian → Fuxian 27 Ld 39.38N 121.59 E
Wafrah 23 Gd 28.25N 47.56 E
Waga-Gawa 29 Gb 39.18N 141.07 E
Wagenfeld 12 Kb 52.33N 8.35 E
Wagenfeld-Ströhen 12 Kb 52.32N 8.39 E
Wageningen 12 Hc 51.57N 5.41 E
Wagēr, Qar- 35 Hc 10.01N 45.30 E
Wager Bay 38 Kc 65.26N 88.40W
Wagga Wagga 58 Fh 35.07S 147.22 E
Waghäusel 12 Ke 49.15N 8.30 E
Wagin 58 Ch 33.18S 117.21 E
Waginger See 10 Ii 47.58N 12.50 E
Wagoner 45 Ii 35.58N 95.22W
Wagon Mound 45 Dh 36.01N 104.42W
Wagontire Mountain 46 Fe 43.21N 119.53W
Wagrien 10 Gb 54.15N 10.45 E
Wągrowiec 10 Nd 52.49N 17.11 E
Wah 25 Eb 33.48N 72.42 E
Waha 31 If 28.10N 19.57 E
Wahai 26 Ig 2.48S 129.30 E
Wahiawa 60 Oc 21.30N 158.02W
Wahoo 45 Hf 41.13N 96.37W
Wahpeton 43 Hb 46.16N 96.36W
Waialeale, Mount- 65a Ba 22.04N 159.30W
Waialua 65a Cb 21.35N 158.08W
Waianae 65a Cb 21.27N 158.12W
Waiau 62 Ee 42.47S 173.22 E
Waiau 61 Dh 42.39S 173.03 E
Waiblingen 10 Fh 48.50N 9.18 E
Waibstadt 12 Ke 49.18N 8.56 E
Waidhofen an der Thaya 14 Jb 48.49N 15.17 E
Waidhofen an der Ybbs 14 Ic 47.58N 14.46 E
Waigame 26 Ig 1.50S 129.49 E
Waigeo, Pulau- 57 Ee 0.14S 130.45 E
Waihi 62 Fb 37.24S 175.50 E
Waihou 62 Fb 37.10S 175.33 E
Waikabubak 26 Gh 9.38S 119.25 E
Waikare, Lake- 62 Fb 37.25S 175.10 E
Waikaremoana, Lake- 61 Eg 38.45S 177.05 E
Waikato 62 Fb 37.23S 174.43 E
Waikawa 62 Cg 46.38S 169.08 E
Waikouaiti 62 Df 45.36S 170.41 E
Wailangilala 63d Cb 16.45S 179.06W
Wailua 65a Ba 22.03N 159.20W
Wailuku 60 Oc 20.53N 156.30W
Waimamaku 62 Ea 35.34S 173.29 E
Waimanalo Beach 65a Db 21.20N 157.42W
Waimangaroa 62 Dd 41.43S 171.46 E
Waimate 62 Df 44.45S 171.03 E
Waimea 65a Fc 20.02N 155.40W
Waimes 12 Id 50.25N 6.07 E
Wainfleet All Saints 12 Ca 53.06N 0.15 E
Wainganga 21 Jh 19.36N 79.48 E
Waingapu 26 Hh 9.39S 120.16 E
Waini Point 50 Gh 8.24N 59.49W
Waini River 50 Gh 8.24N 59.51W
Wainwright [Ak.-U.S.] 40 Gb 70.38N 160.01W
Wainwright [Alta.-Can.] 42 Gf 52.49N 110.52W
Waiouru 62 Fg 39.29S 175.40 E
Waipahu 65a Cb 21.23N 158.01W
Waipara 62 Ee 43.03S 172.45 E
Waipawa 62 Gc 39.56S 176.35 E
Waipiro 62 Hc 38.02S 178.20 E
Waipu 62 Fa 35.59S 174.26 E
Waipukurau 62 Gd 40.00S 176.33 E
Wairakei 62 Gc 38.37S 176.05 E
Wairarapa, Lake- 62 Fd 41.15S 175.15 E
Wairau 62 Fd 41.31S 174.03 E
Wairoa 61 Eg 39.03S 177.26 E
Wairoa 62 Fb 36.11S 174.02 E
Waitaki 62 Df 44.56S 171.09 E
Waitangi 61 Fh 43.56S 176.34W
Waitara 61 Dg 39.00S 174.14 E
Waitati 62 Df 45.45S 170.34 E
Waitemata 62 Fb 36.50S 174.40 E
Waitotara 62 Fc 39.48S 174.44 E
Waiuku 62 Fb 37.15S 174.44 E
Waiwerang 26 Hh 8.23S 123.09 E
Waiyevo 61 Fc 16.48S 179.59W
Wājid 35 Ge 3.50N 43.14 E
Wajima 28 Nf 37.24N 136.54 E
Wajir 31 Ih 1.42N 40.04 E
Waka [Eth.] 35 Fd 7.09N 37.19 E
Waka [Zaire] 36 Db 1.01N 20.13 E
Wakamatsu-Shima 29 Ae 32.54N 129.00 E
Wakasa-Wan 27 Od 35.45N 135.40 E
Wakatipu, Lake- 61 Ci 45.05S 168.35 E
Wakaya 63d Bb 17.37S 179.00 E
Wakayama 22 Pf 34.13N 135.11 E
Wakayama Ken 28 Mh 33.55N 135.20 E
Wake 29 Dd 34.48N 134.08 E
Wa Keeney 45 Gg 39.01N 99.53W
Wakefield [Eng.-U.K.] 9 Lh 53.42N 1.29W
Wakefield [N.Z.] 62 Ed 41.24S 173.03 E

Index Symbols

1 Independent Nation
2 State, Region
3 District, County
4 Municipality
5 Colony, Dependency
Continent
Physical Region
Historical or Cultural Region
Mount, Mountain
Volcano
Hill
Mountains, Mountain Range
Hills, Escarpment
Plateau, Upland
Pass, Gap
Plain, Lowland
Delta
Salt Flat
Valley, Canyon
Crater, Cave
Karst Features
Depression
Polder
Desert, Dunes
Forest, Woods
Heath, Steppe
Oasis
Cape, Point
Coast, Beach
Cliff
Peninsula
Isthmus
Sandbank
Island
Atoll
Rock, Reef
Islands, Archipelago
Rocks, Reefs
Coral Reef
Well, Spring
Geyser
River, Stream
Waterfall Rapids
River Mouth, Estuary
Lake
Salt Lake
Intermittent Lake
Reservoir
Swamp, Pond
Canal
Glacier
Ice Shelf, Pack Ice
Ocean
Sea
Gulf, Bay
Strait, Fjord
Lagoon
Bank
Seamount
Tablemount
Ridge
Shelf
Basin
Escarpment, Sea Scarp
Fracture
Trench, Abyss
National Park, Reserve
Point of Interest
Recreation Site
Cave, Cavern
Historic Site
Ruins
Wall, Walls
Church, Abbey
Temple
Scientific Station
Airport
Port
Lighthouse
Mine
Tunnel
Dam, Bridge

Index Symbols

- Independent Nation
- State, Region
- District, County
- Municipality
- Colony, Dependency
- Continent
- Physical Region
- Historical or Cultural Region
- Mount, Mountain
- Volcano
- Hill
- Mountains, Mountain Range
- Hills, Escarpment
- Plateau, Upland
- Pass, Gap
- Plain, Lowland
- Delta
- Salt Flat
- Valley, Canyon
- Crater, Cave
- Karst Features
- Depression
- Polder
- Desert, Dunes
- Forest, Woods
- Heath, Steppe
- Oasis
- Cape, Point
- Coast, Beach
- Cliff
- Peninsula
- Isthmus
- Sandbank
- Island
- Atoll
- Rock, Reef
- Islands, Archipelago
- Rocks, Reefs
- Coral Reef
- Well, Spring
- Geyser
- River, Stream
- Waterfall Rapids
- River Mouth, Estuary
- Lake
- Salt Lake
- Intermittent Lake
- Sea
- Swamp, Pond
- Canal
- Glacier
- Ice Shelf, Pack Ice
- Ocean
- Gulf, Bay
- Strait, Fjord
- Lagoon
- Bank
- Seamount
- Tableland
- Ridge
- Shelf
- Basin
- Escarpment, Sea Scarp
- Fracture
- Trench, Abyss
- National Park, Reserve
- Point of Interest
- Recreation Site
- Cave, Cavern
- Historic Site
- Ruins
- Wall, Walls
- Church, Abbey
- Temple
- Scientific Station
- Airport
- Port
- Lighthouse
- Mine
- Tunnel
- Dam, Bridge

Western Samoa (EN)= Samoa I Sisifo 58 Jf 13.40S 172.30W
Western Sayans (EN)= Zapadny Sajan 21 Ld 53.00N 94.00 E
Western Sierra Madre (EN) =Madre Occidental, Sierra- 38 Ig 25.00N 105.00W
Western Turkistan (EN) 21 He 41.00N 60.00 E
Westerschelde=West Schelde (EN) 11 Jc 51.25N 3.45 E
Westerschouwen 12 Fc 51.41N 3.43 E
Westerschouwen-Haamstede 12 Fc 51.42N 3.45 E
Westerstede 10 Dc 53.15N 7.56 E
Westerwald 10 Df 50.40N 7.55 E
Westerwoldse A 12 Ja 53.10N 7.10 E
West European Basin (EN) 3 De 47.00N 15.00W
West Falkland 52 Kk 51.40S 60.00W
West Falkland/Gran Malvina, Isla- 52 Kk 51.40S 60.00W
West Fayu Island 57 Fd 8.05N 146.44 E
West Fork Big Blue River 45 Hf 40.42N 96.59W
Westfriesland=West Friesland (EN) 11 Kb 52.45N 4.50 E
West Friesland (EN)= Westfriesland 11 Kb 52.45N 4.50 E
West Frisian Islands (EN)= Waddeneilanden 11 Ka 53.30N 5.00 E
Westgate-on-Sea 12 Dc 51.22N 1.21 E
West Glacier 46 Ib 48.30N 113.59W
West Glamorgan 9 Jj 51.40N 3.55W
West Grand Lake 44 Nc 45.15N 67.52W
West Greenland (EN) = Vestgrønland 41 He 69.00N 49.30W
West Helena 45 Ki 34.33N 90.39W
West Hollywood 44 Gm 25.59N 80.11W
Westhope 45 Fb 48.55N 101.01W
West Ice Shelf 66 Ge 67.00S 85.00 E
West Indies 47 Je 19.00N 70.00W
West Indies (EN)=Indias Occidentales 47 Je 19.00N 70.00W
West Island 37b Ab 9.22S 46.13 E
Westkapelle 12 Fc 51.31N 3.26 E
Westkapelle, Knokke- 12 Fc 51.19N 3.18 E
West Lafayette 44 De 40.27N 86.55W
Westland 62 De 43.10S 170.30 E
West Liberty 44 Fg 37.55N 83.16W
Westlock 42 Gf 54.09N 113.52W
West Lunga 36 De 13.06S 24.39 E
Westmalle 12 Gc 51.18N 4.41 E
West Mariana Basin (EN) 3 Ih 15.00N 137.00 E
Westmeath/An Iarmhí 9 Fh 53.30N 7.30W
West Melanesian Trench (EN) 60 Dh 1.00S 150.00 E
West Memphis 43 Id 35.08N 90.11W
West Mersea 12 Cc 51.46N 0.54 E
West Midlands 9 Li 52.30N 2.00W
Westminster 44 If 39.35N 76.59W
Westminster, London- 12 Bc 51.30N 0.07W
West Monroe 45 Jj 32.31N 92.09W
Westmorland 9 Kg 54.30N 2.40W
West Nicholson 31 Jk 21.03S 29.22 E
West Nueces River 45 Gl 29.16N 99.56W
Weston [Mala.] 26 Ge 5.13N 115.36 E
Weston [W.V.-U.S.] 44 Gf 39.03N 80.28W
Weston [Wy.-U.S.] 46 Md 44.42N 105.18W
Weston-super-Mare 9 Kj 51.21N 2.59W
Westoverledingen 12 Ja 53.10N 7.27 E
Westoverledingen - Ihrhove 12 Ja 53.10N 7.27 E
West Palm Beach 39 Kg 26.43N 80.04W
West Pensacola 44 Dj 30.27N 87.15W
West Plains 43 Id 36.44N 91.51W
West Point [Ms.-U.S.] 45 Lj 33.36N 88.39W
West Point [Nb.-U.S.] 45 Hf 41.51N 96.43W
Westport 58 Ii 41.45S 171.36 E
Westport/Cathair na Mart 9 Dh 53.48N 9.32W
Westray 9 Kb 59.20N 3.00W
Westree 44 Gb 47.27N 81.32W
Westrich 12 Je 49.20N 7.25 E
West Road 12 Cd 50.52N 0.50 E
West Schelde (EN)= Westerschelde 11 Jc 51.25N 3.45 E
West Scotia Basin (EN) 52 Kk 57.00S 53.00W
West Siberian Plain (EN)= Zapadno Sibirskaja Ravnina 21 Jc 60.00N 75.00 E
Weststellingwerf 12 Ib 52.53N 6.00 E
Weststellingwerf-Wolvega 12 Ib 52.53N 6.00 E
West Sussex 9 Mk 51.00N 0.40W
West Tavaputs Plateau 46 Jf 40.00N 110.25W
West-Terschelling, Terschelling- 12 Ha 53.21N 5.13 E
West Union [Ia.-U.S.] 45 Ke 42.57N 91.49W
West Union [Oh.-U.S.] 44 Ff 38.48N 83.33W
West Virginia 43 Kd 38.45N 80.30W
West-Vlaanderen 12 Ec 51.00N 3.00 E
Westwood 46 Ef 40.18N 121.00W
West Wyalong 59 Jf 33.55S 147.13 E
West Yellowstone 43 Eb 44.30N 111.05W
West Yorkshire 9 Lh 53.40N 1.30W
Wetar, Pulau- 57 De 7.48S 126.18 E
Wetaskiwin 42 Gf 52.58N 113.22W
Wete 36 Gd 5.04S 39.43 E
Wětošow/Vetschau 10 Ke 51.47N 14.04 E
Wetter 12 Kd 50.18N 8.49 E
Wetter (Hessen) 12 Kd 50.54N 8.43 E
Wetter (Ruhr) 12 Jc 51.23N 7.24 E
Wetterau 10 Ef 50.15N 8.50 E
Wetteren 11 Jc 51.00N 3.53 E
Wetzlar 10 Ef 50.33N 8.30 E
Wevelgem 12 Fd 50.48N 3.10 E
Wewahitchka 44 Ej 30.07N 85.12W
Wewak 58 Fe 3.34S 143.38 E
Wexford/Loch Garman 9 Gi 52.20N 6.40W
Wexford/Loch Garman 6 Fe 52.20N 6.27W
Wexford Harbour/Cuan Loch Garman 9 Gi 52.20N 6.25W
Wey 9 Mj 51.23N 0.28W
Weyburn 42 Hg 49.41N 103.52W
Weyhe 12 Kb 52.59N 8.52 E
Weyhe-Leeste 12 Kb 52.59N 8.50 E
Weymouth 9 Kk 50.36N 2.28W
Wezet/Visé 12 Hd 50.44N 5.42 E
Whakatane 61 Eg 37.58S 177.00 E
Whale Cove 42 Id 62.14N 92.10W
Whalsay 9 Ma 60.22N 0.59W
Whangarei 58 Ih 35.43S 174.19 E
Wharfe 9 Lh 53.51N 1.07W
Wharton 45 Hl 29.19N 96.06W
Wharton Basin (EN) 3 Hk 19.00S 100.00 E
Wharton Lake 42 Hd 64.00N 99.55W
Whataroa 62 De 43.16S 170.22 E
Wheatland 46 Me 42.03N 104.57W
Wheat Ridge 45 Dg 39.46N 105.07W
Wheeler 42 Ke 57.02N 67.14W
Wheeler 46 Dd 45.42N 123.52W
Wheeler Lake 44 Dh 34.40N 87.05W
Wheeler Peak [N.M.-U.S.] 43 Fd 36.34N 105.25W
Wheeler Peak [U.S.] 38 Hf 38.59N 114.19W
Wheeling 43 Kc 40.05N 80.43W
Whidbey Island 46 Db 48.15N 122.40W
Whitby 9 Mg 54.29N 0.37W
Whitchurch [Eng.-U.K.] 9 Ki 52.58N 2.41W
Whitchurch [Eng.-U.K.] 12 Bc 51.53N 0.50W
Whitchurch [Eng.-U.K.] 12 Ac 51.13N 1.20W
White 42 Jc 65.50N 85.00W
White, Lake- 59 Fd 21.05S 129.00 E
White Bay 38 Nd 50.00N 56.30W
White Bear Lake 45 Jd 45.04N 93.01W
White Butte 45 Ec 46.23N 103.19W
White Carpathians (EN) = Bilé Karpaty 10 Nh 48.55N 17.50 E
White Cliffs 59 If 30.51S 143.05 E
White Cloud 44 Ed 43.33N 85.46W
Whitecourt 42 Ff 54.09N 115.41W
Whitefish 43 Eb 48.25N 114.20W
Whitefish Bay 43 Kb 46.40N 84.50W
Whitefish Point 44 Eb 46.45N 85.00W
Whitefish Range 46 Hb 48.40N 114.26W
Whitehall [Mi.-U.S.] 44 Dd 43.24N 86.21W
Whitehall [Mt.-U.S.] 46 Id 45.52N 112.06W
Whitehall [Oh.-U.S.] 44 Ff 39.58N 82.54W
Whitehall [Wi.-U.S.] 45 Kd 44.22N 91.19W
Whitehaven 9 Jg 54.33N 3.35W
Whitehorse 39 Fc 60.43N 135.03W
White Island [Ant.] 66 Ee 66.44S 48.35 E
White Island [N.Z.] 62 Gb 37.30S 177.10 E
White Lake 45 Jl 29.45N 92.30W
White Lake (EN)=Beloje Ozero 5 Jc 60.11N 37.35 E
Whiteman Range 59 Ja 5.50S 149.55 E
Whitemark 59 Jh 40.07S 148.01 E
White Mountain 40 Db 64.35N 163.04W
White Mountain Peak 43 Dd 37.38N 118.15W
White Mountains [Ak.-U.S.] 40 Jc 65.30N 147.00W
White Mountains [U.S.] 46 Fh 37.30N 118.15W
White Mountains [U.S.] 43 Mc 44.10N 71.35W
Whitemouth Lake 45 Ib 49.14N 95.40W
Whitemouth River 45 Ha 50.07N 96.02W
White Nile (EN)=Abyaḍ, Al Baḥr al- 30 Kg 15.38N 32.31 E
White Nile (EN)=Abyaḍ, Al Baḥr al- 35 Ec 12.40N 32.30 E
White Pass [N.Amer.] 40 Le 59.37N 135.08W
White Pass [Wa.-U.S.] 46 Ec 46.38N 121.24W
Whiteriver 46 Kj 33.50N 109.58W
White River [In.-U.S.] 44 Df 38.25N 87.44W
White River [Nv.-U.S.] 46 Hh 37.18N 115.08W
White River [Ont.-Can.] 42 Ig 48.35N 85.17W
White River [S.D.-U.S.] 45 Fe 43.34N 100.45W
White River [Tx.-U.S.] 45 Fj 33.14N 100.56W
White River [U.S.] 46 Kf 40.04N 109.41W
White River [U.S.] 43 Hc 43.45N 99.30W
White River [U.S.] 38 Jf 33.53N 91.03W
White River [Yuk.-Can.] 42 Dd 63.10N 139.32W
White Salmon 46 Ed 45.44N 121.29W
Whitesand Bay 9 Ik 50.20N 4.35W
White Sea (EN)=Beloje More 5 Kb 66.00N 44.00 E
White sea-Baltic Canal (EN) =Belomorsko-Baltijski Kanal 5 Jc 63.30N 34.48 E
White Settlement 45 Hj 32.45N 97.27W
White Sulphur Springs 46 Jc 46.33N 110.54W
Whiteville 44 Hh 34.20N 78.42W
White Volta 30 Gh 8.38N 0.59W
White Volta (EN)=Volta Blanche 30 Gh 8.38N 0.59W
Whitewater 45 Bg 38.59N 108.27W
Whitewater Baldy 45 Bj 33.20N 108.39W
Whitewater Bay 44 Gm 25.16N 81.00W
Whitewater Lake 45 La 50.50N 89.10W
Whitewood 45 Ea 50.20N 102.15W
Whitianga 62 Fb 36.50S 175.42 E
Whitmore Mountains 66 Og 82.35S 104.30W
Whitney 44 Hc 45.30N 78.14W
Whitney, Lake- 45 Hk 31.55N 97.23W
Whitney, Mount- 38 Hf 36.35N 118.18W
Whitstable 12 Dc 51.21N 1.06 E
Whitsunday Island 59 Jd 20.15S 149.00 E
Whittier 40 Jd 60.46N 148.41W
Whittlesea 59 Jg 37.31S 145.07 E
Whittlesey 12 Bb 52.33N 0.08W
Wholdaia Lake 42 Hd 60.45N 104.10W
Whyalla 59 Hf 33.02S 137.35 E
Wiarton 44 Gc 44.45N 81.09W
Wiawso 34 Ed 6.12N 2.29W
Wibaux 46 Mc 46.59N 104.11W
Wichita 39 Jf 37.41N 97.20W
Wichita Falls 39 Jf 33.54N 98.30W
Wichita Mountains 45 Gi 34.45N 98.40W
Wichita River 45 Gi 34.07N 98.10W
Wick 9 Jc 58.26N 3.06W
Wick 9 Jc 58.25N 3.05W
Wickenburg 46 Ij 33.58N 112.44W
Wickepin 59 Df 32.46S 117.30 E
Wickham 12 Ad 50.54N 1.10W
Wickham Market 12 Db 52.09N 1.22 E
Wickiup Reservoir 46 Ee 43.40N 121.43W
Wickliffe 44 Cg 36.58N 89.05W
Wicklow/Cill Mhantáin 9 Gi 53.00N 6.30W
Wicklow/Cill Mhantáin 9 Gi 52.59N 6.03W
Wicklow Head/Ceann Chill Mhantáin 9 Hi 52.58N 6.00W
Wicklow Mountains/ Sléibhte Chill Mhantáin 9 Gh 53.02N 6.24W
Wicko, Jezioro- 10 Mb 54.33N 16.35 E
Wickrath, Mönchengladbach- 12 Ic 51.08N 6.25 E
Widawa 10 Me 51.13N 16.55 E
Wide Bay 59 Ka 5.05S 152.05 E
Widefield 45 Dg 38.42N 104.40W
Widgiemooltha 59 Ef 31.30S 121.34 E
Wi-Do 28 Ig 35.38N 126.17 E
Więcbork 10 Nc 53.22N 17.30 E
Wied 12 Jd 50.27N 7.28 E
Wiedenbrück 12 Kc 50.51N 8.19 E
Wiehengebirge 10 Ed 52.20N 8.40 E
Wiehl 12 Jd 50.57N 7.32 E
Wieliczka 10 Qg 49.59N 20.04 E
Wielimie, Jezioro- 10 Mc 53.47N 16.50 E
Wielki Dział 10 Tf 50.18N 23.25 E
Wielkopolska 10 Ne 51.50N 17.20 E
Wielkopolskie-Kujawskie, Pojezierze- 10 Md 52.25N 16.30 E
Wieluń 10 Oe 51.14N 18.34 E
Wien 14 Kb 48.15N 16.25 E
Wien = Vienna (EN) 6 Hf 48.12N 16.22 E
Wiener Becken 14 Kc 48.00N 16.28 E
Wiener Neustadt 14 Kc 47.48N 16.15 E
Wienerwald=Vienna Woods (EN) 14 Jb 48.10N 16.00 E
Wieprz 10 Re 51.32N 21.49 E
Wieprza 10 Mb 54.26N 16.22 E
Wieprz-Krzna, Kanał- 10 Se 51.56N 22.56 E
Wierden 12 Ib 52.22N 6.36 E
Wieringen 12 Hb 52.56N 5.02 E
Wieringen-Den Oever 12 Hb 52.56N 5.02 E
Wieringen-Hippolytushoef 12 Gb 52.54N 4.59 E
Wieringermeer 12 Hb 52.51N 5.01 E
Wieringermeer Polder 12 Gb 52.50N 5.00 E
Wieringermeer-Wieringerwerf 12 Hb 52.51N 5.01 E
Wieringerwerf, Wieringermeer- 12 Hb 52.51N 5.01 E
Wieruszów 10 Oe 51.18N 18.08 E
Wierzchowo, Jezioro- 10 Mc 53.50N 16.45 E
Wierzyca 10 Oc 53.51N 18.50 E
Wiesbaden 6 Ge 50.05N 8.15 E
Wiese 10 Di 47.35N 7.35 E
Wieslautern 12 Je 49.05N 7.49 E
Wiesloch 10 Eg 49.18N 8.42 E
Wietingsmoor 12 Kb 52.39N 8.39 E
Wietmarschen 12 Jb 52.32N 7.08 E
Wieżyca 10 Ob 54.17N 18.10 E
Wigan 9 Kh 53.32N 2.35W
Wigger 14 Bc 47.15N 7.55 E
Wiggins 45 Lk 30.51N 89.08W
Wight, Isle of- 5 Fe 50.40N 1.20W
Wigry, Jezioro- 10 Tb 54.05N 23.07 E
Wigston 12 Ab 52.35N 1.06W
Wigtown 9 Ig 54.52N 4.26W
Wigtown Bay 9 Ig 54.46N 4.15W
Wijchen 12 Hc 51.48N 5.44 E
Wijdefjorden 41 Nc 79.50N 15.30 E
Wijk bij Duurstede 12 Hc 51.59N 5.22 E
Wil 14 Dc 47.27N 9.05 E
Wilbur 46 Fc 47.46N 118.42W
Wilburton 45 Ii 34.55N 95.19W
Wilcannia 58 Fh 31.34S 143.23 E
Wild Coast 30 Jl 32.00S 29.50 E
Wilder Seamount (EN) 57 Jd 9.00N 173.00W
Wildeshausen 10 Ed 52.54N 8.26 E
Wild Horse 46 Jb 49.01N 110.12W
Wildspitze 14 Ed 46.53N 10.52 E
Wilga 10 Re 51.50N 21.20 E
Wilhelm-II-Land 66 Ge 69.00S 90.00 E
Wilhelminakanaal 12 Gc 51.43N 4.53 E
Wilhelm-Pieck-Stadt-Guben 10 Ke 51.57N 14.43 E
Wilhelmshaven 10 Ec 53.31N 8.08 E
Wilhelmstal 37 Bd 21.54S 16.20 E
Wilkes-Barre 43 Lc 41.15N 75.50W
Wilkesboro 44 Gg 36.09N 81.09W
Wilkes Land (EN) 66 Hf 71.00S 120.00 E
Wilkins Coast 66 Qe 69.40S 63.00W
Wilkins Sound 66 Qf 70.15S 73.00W
Willamette River 46 Dd 45.39N 122.46W
Willandra Billabong Creek 59 If 33.08S 144.06 E
Willapa Bay 46 Dc 46.37N 124.00W
Willard 45 Ci 34.36N 106.02W
Willards, Punta- 46 Gc 28.50N 112.35W
Willcox 46 Kj 32.15N 109.50W
Willebadessen 12 Lc 51.38N 9.02 E
Willebadessen-Peckelsheim 12 Lc 51.36N 9.08 E
Willebroek 12 Gc 51.04N 4.22 E
Willemstad [Neth.] 12 Gc 51.41N 4.26 E
Willemstad [Neth.Ant.] 53 Jd 12.06N 68.56W
Willeroo 59 Gc 15.17S 131.35 E
William Bill Dannelly Reservoir 44 Di 32.15N 86.45W
Williams 43 Ed 35.15N 112.11W
Williamsburg [Ky.-U.S.] 44 Eg 36.44N 84.10W
Williamsburg [Va.-U.S.] 44 Ig 37.17N 76.43W
Williams Lake 42 Ff 52.08N 122.09W
Williamson Glacier 66 He 66.30S 114.30 E
Williamsport 43 Lc 41.16N 77.03W
Williamston 44 Ih 35.50N 77.06W
Williamstown 44 Ef 38.38N 84.34W
Willich 12 Ic 51.16N 6.33 E
Willikie's 51d Bb 17.03N 61.42W
Willingdon, Mount- 46 Ga 51.48N 116.17W
Willis Group 57 Gf 16.20S 150.00 E
Williston [N.D.-U.S.] 43 Gb 48.09N 103.37W
Williston [S.Afr.] 37 Cf 31.20S 20.53 E
Williston Lake 38 Gd 50.57N 122.23W
Willits 46 Dg 39.25N 123.21W
Willmar 43 Hb 45.07N 95.03W
Willoughby Bay 51d Bb 17.02N 61.44W
Willow Bunch Lake 46 Mb 49.27N 105.28W
Willowlake 42 Fd 62.42N 123.08W
Willowmore 37 Cf 33.17S 23.29 E
Willows 46 Dg 39.31N 122.12W
Willow Springs 45 Kh 36.59N 91.58W
Wills, Lake- 59 Fd 21.20S 128.40 E
Wills Point 45 Ij 32.43N 95.57W
Wilma Glacier 66 Ee 67.12S 56.00 E
Wilmington [De.-U.S.] 43 Ld 39.44N 75.33W
Wilmington [N.C.-U.S.] 39 Lf 34.13N 77.55W
Wilmington [Oh.-U.S.] 44 Ff 39.28N 83.50W
Wilnsdorf 12 Kd 50.49N 8.06 E
Wilseder Berg 10 Fc 53.10N 9.56 E
Wilson 43 Ld 35.44N 77.55W
Wilson, Cape- 42 Jc 66.59N 81.27W
Wilson, Mount- 45 Ch 37.51N 107.59W
Wilson Bluff 66 Ff 74.20S 66.47 E
Wilson Lake [Al.-U.S.] 44 Dh 34.49N 87.30W
Wilson Lake [Ks.-U.S.] 45 Gg 38.57N 98.40W
Wilsons Promontory 59 Jg 38.55S 146.20 E
Wilton River 59 Gb 14.45S 134.33 E
Wilts 9 Lj 51.20N 2.00W
Wiltshire 9 Lj 51.30N 2.00W
Wiltz 11 Le 49.58N 5.55 E
Wiluna 59 Ee 26.36S 120.13 E
Wimereux 12 Dd 50.46N 1.37 E
Winamac 44 De 41.03N 86.36W
Winburg 37 De 28.37S 27.00 E
Winchelsea 12 Cd 50.55N 0.43 E
Winchester [Eng.-U.K.] 9 Lj 51.04N 1.19W
Winchester [In.-U.S.] 44 Ee 40.10N 84.59W
Winchester [Ky.-U.S.] 44 Ef 38.01N 84.11W
Winchester [Va.-U.S.] 43 Ld 39.11N 78.12W
Windeck 12 Jd 50.49N 7.34 E
Windemin, Pointe- 63b Cc 16.34S 167.27 E
Winder 44 Fi 34.00N 83.47W
Windermere 9 Kg 54.22N 2.56W
Windermere [B.C.-Can.] 46 Ha 50.30N 115.58W
Windermere [Eng.-U.K.] 9 Kg 54.23N 2.54W
Windhoek 31 Ik 22.34S 17.06 E
Windhoek 37 Bd 22.30S 17.00 E
Windischgarsten 14 Ic 47.43N 14.20 E
Wind Mountain 45 Dj 32.02N 105.34W
Windom 45 Ie 43.52N 95.07W
Windom Mountain 45 Ch 37.37N 107.35W
Windorah 59 Ie 25.26S 142.39 E
Window Rock 46 Ki 35.41N 109.03W
Wind River 46 Ke 43.08N 108.12W
Wind River Peak 46 Ke 42.42N 109.07W
Wind River Range 43 Fc 43.05N 109.25W
Windrush 9 Lj 51.42N 1.25W
Windsor [Eng.-U.K.] 9 Mj 51.29N 0.38W
Windsor [N.S.-Can.] 42 Lh 44.59N 64.09W
Windsor [Ont.-Can.] 42 Jh 42.18N 83.01W
Windsor Forest 44 Gj 31.58N 81.10W
Windward Islands 47 Lf 13.00N 61.00W
Windward Islands (EN)= Barlovento, Islas de- 38 Mh 15.00N 61.00W
Windward Islands (EN) = Sotavento, Islas de- 52 Jd 11.10N 67.00W
Windward Islands (EN)= Vent, Iles du- 57 Mf 17.30S 149.30W
Windward Passage (EN)= Vent, Canal du- 49 Lh 20.00N 73.50W
Windward Passage (EN)= Vientos, Paso de los- 38 Lh 20.00N 73.50W
Winfield [Al.-U.S.] 44 Di 33.56N 87.49W
Winfield [Ks.-U.S.] 43 Hd 37.15N 96.59W
Wingene 12 Fc 51.04N 3.16 E
Wingen-sur-Moder 12 Jf 48.55N 7.22 E
Winisk 38 Kd 55.17N 85.05W
Winisk 39 Kd 55.15N 85.12W
Winisk Lake 42 If 52.55N 87.20W
Winkler 45 Hb 49.11N 97.56W
Winklern 14 Gd 46.52N 12.52 E
Winneba 34 Ed 5.20N 0.37W
Winnebago, Lake- 43 Jc 44.00N 88.25W
Winnemucca 43 Dc 40.58N 117.44W
Winnemucca Lake 46 Ff 40.10N 119.20W
Winner 43 Hc 43.22N 99.51W
Winnett 46 Kc 47.00N 108.21W
Winnfield 45 Jk 31.55N 92.38W
Winnibigoshish, Lake- 45 Ic 47.27N 94.12W
Winnipeg 39 Je 49.53N 97.09W
Winnipeg 38 Jd 50.38N 96.19W
Winnipeg, Lake- 38 Jd 52.00N 97.00W
Winnipeg Beach 45 Ha 50.31N 96.58W
Winnipegosis 42 Hf 51.39N 99.56W
Winnipegosis, Lake- 38 Jd 52.30N 100.00W
Winnipesaukee, Lake- 44 Ld 43.35N 71.20W
Winnsboro 45 Kj 32.10N 91.43W
Winnweiler 12 Je 49.34N 7.51 E
Winona [Mn.-U.S.] 43 Ic 44.03N 91.39W
Winona [Mo.-U.S.] 45 Kh 37.06N 91.19W
Winona [Ms.-U.S.] 45 Lj 33.29N 89.44W
Winschoten 11 Na 53.08N 7.02 E
Winsen 10 Gc 53.22N 10.13 E
Winslow [Az.-U.S.] 43 Ed 35.01N 110.42W
Winslow [Eng.-U.K.] 12 Bc 51.57N 0.52W
Winslow Reef 57 Je 1.36S 174.57W
Winston-Salem 43 Kd 36.06N 80.15W
Winterberg 10 Ee 51.12N 8.32 E
Winter Harbour 42 Gb 74.46N 110.40W
Winter Haven 43 Kf 28.01N 81.44W
Winter Park [Co.-U.S.] 45 Dg 39.47N 105.45W
Winter Park [Fl.-U.S.] 44 Gk 28.36N 81.20W
Winters 45 Gk 31.57N 99.58W
Winterset 45 If 41.20N 94.01W
Winterswijk 11 Mc 51.58N 6.44 E
Winterthur 14 Cc 47.30N 8.45 E
Winton [Austl.] 58 Fg 22.23S 143.02 E
Winton [N.C.-U.S.] 44 Ig 36.24N 76.56W
Winton [N.Z.] 62 Cg 46.09S 168.20 E
Wipper [G.D.R.] 10 He 51.47N 11.42 E
Wipper [G.D.R.] 10 He 51.20N 11.10 E
Wisbech 9 Ni 52.40N 0.10 E
Wiscasset 44 Mc 44.00N 69.40W
Wisch 12 Ic 51.55N 6.22 E
Wisch-Terborg 12 Ic 51.55N 6.22 E
Wisconsin 43 Jc 44.45N 89.30W
Wisconsin 38 Je 43.00N 91.15W
Wisconsin Range 66 Ng 85.45S 125.00W
Wisconsin Rapids 43 Jc 44.23N 89.49W
Wiseman 40 Ic 67.25N 150.06W
Wisła 10 Og 49.39N 18.50 E
Wisła=Vistula (EN) 5 He 54.22N 18.55 E
Wiślana, Mierzeja- 10 Pb 54.25N 19.30 E
Wiślane, Żuławy- 10 Ob 54.10N 19.00 E
Wiślany, Zalew- 10 Pb 54.27N 19.40 E
Wisłok 10 Sf 50.13N 22.32 E
Wisłoka 10 Rf 50.27N 21.23 E
Wismar 10 Hc 53.54N 11.28 E
Wismarbucht 10 Hc 53.57N 11.25 E
Wissant 12 Dd 50.53N 1.40 E
Wissembourg 11 Ne 49.02N 7.57 E
Wissen 10 Df 50.47N 7.45 E
Wissenkerke 12 Fc 51.35N 3.45 E
Wissey 12 Cb 52.34N 0.21 E
Witbank 31 Jk 25.56S 29.07 E
Witchekar Lake 45 Fb 49.15N 100.16W
Witdraai 37 Ce 26.58S 20.41 E
Witham 12 Cc 51.47N 0.38 E
Witham 9 Ni 52.56N 0.04 E
Withernsea 9 Nh 53.44N 0.02 E
Witkowo 10 Nd 52.27N 17.47 E
Witmarsum, Wonseradeel- 12 Ha 53.06N 5.28 E
Witney 9 Lj 51.48N 1.29W
Witnica 10 Kd 52.40N 14.55 E
Witputz 37 Be 27.37S 16.42 E
Witten 10 De 51.26N 7.20 E
Wittenberg [G.D.R.] 10 Ie 51.52N 12.39 E
Wittenberg [Wi.-U.S.] 45 Ld 44.49N 89.10W
Wittenberge 10 Hc 53.00N 11.45 E
Wittenoom 59 Dd 22.17S 118.19 E
Wittingen 10 Gd 52.44N 10.43 E
Wittlich 10 Cg 49.59N 6.53 E
Wittmund 10 Dc 53.34N 7.47 E
Wittow 10 Jb 54.38N 13.19 E
Wittstock 10 Ic 53.09N 12.30 E
Witu 36 Hc 2.23S 40.26 E
Witu Islands 60 Dh 4.40S 149.18 E
Witvlei 37 Bd 22.23S 18.32 E
Witzenhausen 10 Fe 51.20N 9.52 E
Wivenhoe 12 Cc 51.51N 0.58 E
Wizard Reef 30 Mi 8.57S 51.01 E
Wizna 10 Sc 53.13N 22.26 E
Wjdawka 10 Oe 51.32N 18.52 E
W. J. Van Blommestein Meer 54 Hc 4.45N 55.00W
Wkra 10 Qd 52.27N 20.44 E
Władysławowo 10 Ob 54.49N 18.25 E
Włocławek 10 Pd 52.39N 19.02 E
Włocławek 10 Od 52.40N 19.00 E
Włodawa 10 Te 51.34N 23.32 E
Włoszczowa 10 Pf 50.25N 19.59 E
Wodonga 59 Jg 36.17S 146.54 E
Wodzisław Śląski 10 Of 50.00N 18.28 E
Woensdrecht 12 Gc 51.25N 4.18 E
Woerden 12 Gb 52.05N 4.53 E
Woerth 12 Jf 48.56N 7.45 E
Woëvre, Plaine de la- 11 Le 49.15N 5.50 E
Wohlthat-Massif 66 Cf 71.35S 12.20 E
Woippy 12 Ie 49.09N 6.09 E
Wojerecy/Hoyerswerda 10 Ke 51.26N 14.15 E
Wokam, Pulau- 26 Jh 5.37S 134.30 E
Woken He 28 Ja 46.19N 129.34 E
Woking 9 Mj 51.20N 0.34W
Wokingham 12 Bc 51.25N 0.50W
Wolbrom 10 Pf 50.24N 19.46 E
Wolcott 44 Id 43.13N 76.42W
Wołczyn 10 Oe 51.01N 18.03 E
Woldberg 12 Hb 52.25N 5.55 E
Woleai Atoll 57 Fd 7.21N 143.52 E
Woleu-Ntem 36 Bb 2.00N 12.00 E
Wolf, Isla- 54a Aa 1.23N 91.49W
Wolf, Volcán- 54a Ab 0.01S 91.20W
Wolfach 10 Eh 48.18N 8.13 E
Wolf Creek 45 Gh 36.35N 99.30W
Wolf Creek 46 Ic 47.00N 112.04W
Wolfen 10 Ie 51.40N 12.17 E
Wolfenbüttel 10 Gd 52.10N 10.33 E
Wolfhagen 10 Fe 51.19N 9.10 E
Wolf Point 43 Fb 48.05N 105.39W
Wolfratshausen 10 Hi 47.54N 11.25 E
Wolf River 45 Ld 44.11N 88.48W
Wolfsberg 14 Id 46.50N 14.50 E
Wolfsburg 10 Gd 52.26N 10.48 E
Wolfstein 12 Je 49.35N 7.36 E
Wolgast 10 Jb 54.03N 13.46 E
Wolica 10 Tf 50.54N 23.12 E
Wolin 10 Kc 53.51N 14.38 E
Wolin 10 Kc 53.50N 14.35 E
Wollaston 12 Bb 52.15N 0.40W
Wollaston, Islas- 56 Gi 55.40S 67.30W
Wollaston Forland 41 Jd 74.35N 20.15W
Wollaston Lake 38 Id 58.15N 103.20W
Wollaston Lake 42 He 58.05N 103.38W
Wollaston Peninsula 38 Hc 70.00N 115.00W
Wollongong 58 Gh 34.25S 150.54 E
Wöllstein 12 Je 49.49N 7.58 E
Wolmaransstad 37 De 27.12S 26.13 E
Wołomin 10 Rd 52.21N 21.14 E
Wołów 10 Me 51.29N 16.55 E

Index Symbols

1 Independent Nation
2 State, Region
3 District, County
4 Municipality
5 Colony, Dependency
Continent
Physical Region
Historical or Cultural Region
Mount, Mountain
Volcano
Hill
Mountains, Mountain Range
Hills, Escarpment
Plateau, Upland
Pass, Gap
Plain, Lowland
Delta
Salt Flat
Valley, Canyon
Crater, Cave
Karst Features
Depression
Polder
Desert, Dunes
Forest, Woods
Heath, Steppe
Oasis
Cape, Point
Coast, Beach
Cliff
Peninsula
Isthmus
Sandbank
Island
Atoll
Rock, Reef
Islands, Archipelago
Rocks, Reefs
Coral Reef
Well, Spring
Geyser
River, Stream
Waterfall Rapids
River Mouth, Estuary
Lake
Salt Lake
Intermittent Lake
Reservoir
Swamp, Pond
Canal
Glacier
Ice Shelf, Pack Ice
Ocean
Sea
Gulf, Bay
Strait, Fjord
Lagoon
Bank
Seamount
Tablemount
Ridge
Shelf
Basin
Escarpment, Sea Scarp
Fracture
Trench, Abyss
National Park, Reserve
Point of Interest
Recreation Site
Cave, Cavern
Historic Site
Ruins
Wall, Walls
Church, Abbey
Temple
Scientific Station
Airport
Port
Lighthouse
Mine
Tunnel
Dam, Bridge

Name	Map	Grid	Lat	Long
Wolseley	42	Hf	50.25N	103.19W
Wolstenholme, Cap- ►	42	Jd	62.34N	77.30W
Wolstenholme Fjord ►	41	Ec	76.40N	69.45W
Wolsztyn	10	Md	52.08N	16.06 E
Wolvega, Weststellingwerf-	12	Ib	52.53N	6.00 E
Wolverhampton	9	Ki	52.36N	2.08W
Wolverton	9	Mi	52.04N	0.50W
Wŏnju	27	Md	37.21N	127.58 E
Wŏnsan	22	Of	39.10N	127.26 E
Wonseradeel	12	Ha	53.06N	5.28 E
Wonseradeel-Witmarsum	12	Ha	53.06N	5.28 E
Wonthaggi	59	Jg	38.36S	145.35 E
Woodall Mountain ▲	45	Li	34.45N	88.11W
Woodbridge	9	Oi	52.06N	1.19 E
Woodbridge Bay ◪	51g	Bb	15.19N	61.25W
Woodhall Spa	12	Ba	53.09N	0.13W
Woodland [Ca.-U.S.]	46	Eg	38.41N	121.46W
Woodland [Wa.-U.S.]	46	Dd	45.54N	122.45W
Woodlark Island ►	57	Ge	9.05S	152.50 E
Woodridge	45	Mb	49.17N	96.09W
Wood River	46	Lb	50.08N	106.10W
Wood River Lakes ►	40	He	59.30N	158.45W
Woodroffe, Mount- ▲	59	Ge	26.20S	131.45 E
Woods, Lake- ►	59	Gc	17.50S	133.30 E
Woods, Lake of the- ►	38	Je	49.15N	94.45W
Woodside	46	Jg	39.21N	110.18W
Woodstock [Eng.-U.K.]	9	Lj	51.52N	1.21W
Woodstock [N.B.-Can.]	42	Kg	46.09N	67.34W
Woodstock [Ont.-Can.]	44	Gd	43.08N	80.45W
Woodstock [Vt.-U.S.]	44	Kd	43.37N	72.31W
Woodville [Ms.-U.S.]	45	Kk	31.01N	91.18W
Woodville [N.Z.]	62	Fd	40.20S	175.52 E
Woodville [Tx.-U.S.]	45	Ik	30.46N	94.25W
Woodward	43	Hd	36.26N	99.24W
Wooler	9	Kf	55.33N	2.01W
Woomera	59	Hf	31.11S	137.10 E
Wooramel River ►	59	Ce	25.47S	114.10 E
Wooster	44	Ge	40.46N	81.57W
Worcester ▣	9	Ki	52.15N	2.10W
Worcester [Eng.-U.K.]	9	Ki	52.11N	2.13W
Worcester [Ma.-U.S.]	43	Mc	42.16N	71.48W
Worcester [S.Afr.]	31	Il	33.39S	19.27 E
Worcester Range ▲	66	Jf	78.50S	161.00 E
Wörgl	14	Ge	47.29N	12.04 E
Workai, Pulau- ►	26	Jh	6.40S	134.40 E
Workington	9	Jg	54.39N	3.33W
Worksop	9	Lh	53.18N	1.07W
Workum	12	Hb	52.59N	5.27 E
Worland	43	Fc	44.01N	107.57W
Wormer	12	Gb	52.30N	4.52 E
Wormhout	12	Ed	50.53N	2.28 E
Worms	10	Eg	49.38N	8.21 E
Worms Head ►	9	Ij	51.34N	4.20W
Wörrstadt	12	Ke	49.50N	8.06 E
Wörth am Rhein	12	Ke	49.03N	8.16 E
Wörther-See ►	14	Id	46.37N	14.10 E
Worthing	9	Mk	50.48N	0.23W
Worthington	43	Hc	43.37N	95.36W
Wosi	26	Ig	0.11S	127.58 E
Wotho Atoll ◉	57	Hc	10.06N	165.59 E
Wotje Atoll ◉	57	Id	9.27N	170.02 E
Woudenberg	12	Hc	52.05N	5.25 E
Wounnioné, Pointe- ►	63b	Db	14.54S	168.02 E
Wounta, Laguna de- ▨	49	Fg	13.38N	83.34W
Wour	35	Ba	21.21N	15.57 E
Wousi	63b	Cb	15.22S	166.39 E
Wowoni, Pulau- ►	26	Hg	4.08S	123.06 E
Woy Woy	59	Kf	33.30S	151.20 E
Wrangel, Ostrov- = Wrangel Island (EN) =	21	Tb	71.00N	179.30 E
Wrangel Island (EN) = Wrangel, Ostrov-	21	Tb	71.00N	179.30 E
Wrangell	39	Fd	56.28N	132.23W
Wrangell, Cape- ►	40a	Ab	52.50N	172.26 E
Wrangell Mountains ▲	38	Ec	62.00N	143.00W
Wrath, Cape- ►	5	Fd	58.37N	5.01W
Wray	43	Gc	40.05N	102.13W
Wreake ►	12	Ab	52.41N	1.05W
Wreck Reef ⬚	57	Gg	22.15S	155.10 E
Wrecks, Bay of- ◪	64g	Bb	1.52N	157.17W
Wrexham	9	Kh	53.03N	3.00W
Wright Island ►	66	Of	74.03S	116.45W
Wright Patman Lake ▨	45	Ij	33.16N	94.14W
Wrightson, Mount- ▲	46	Jk	31.42N	110.50W
Wrigley	42	Fd	63.13N	123.38W
Wrigley Gulf ◪	66	Nf	74.00S	129.00W
Wrocław ▣	10	Me	51.05N	17.00 E
Wrocław = Breslau (EN)	6	Me	51.06N	17.00 E
Wronki	10	Md	52.43N	16.23 E
Wrotham	12	Cc	51.18N	0.19 E
Wroxham	12	Db	52.42N	1.24 E
Września	10	Nd	52.20N	17.34 E
Wschowa	10	Me	51.48N	16.19 E
Wu'an	28	Cf	36.42N	114.12 E
Wuchale	35	Fc	11.31N	39.37 E
Wuchang, Wuhan-	28	Ib	44.55N	127.11 E
Wuchang, Wuhan-	28	Ci	30.32N	114.18 E
Wucheng (Jiucheng)	28	Df	37.12N	116.04 E
Wuchiu Hsü ►	27	Kg	25.00N	119.27 E
Wuchuan	28	Ad	41.08N	111.25 E
Wuchuan (Duru)	27	If	28.28N	107.57 E
Wuchuan (Meilu)	27	Jg	21.28N	110.44 E
Wuda	27	Id	39.30N	106.33 E
Wudan → Ongniud Qi	27	Kc	42.58N	119.01 E
Wudao	27	Ld	39.28N	121.30 E
Wudaoliang	27	Fd	35.15N	93.14 E
Wudi	28	Df	37.44N	117.36 E
Wudil	34	Gc	11.49N	8.51 E
Wuding	27	Hf	25.36N	102.27 E
Wudu	27	He	33.24N	105.00 E
Wugang	27	Jf	26.48N	110.32 E
Wugong (Puji)	27	Je	34.15N	108.14 E
Wuhai	27	Id	39.32N	106.55 E
Wuhan	22	Nf	30.30N	114.20 E
Wuhan-Hankou	28	Ci	30.35N	114.16 E
Wuhan-Hanyang	28	Ci	30.33N	114.16 E
Wuhan- Wuchang	28	Ci	30.32N	114.18 E
Wuhe	27	Ke	33.08N	117.51 E
Wuhu	22	Nf	31.18N	118.27 E
Wuhu (Wanzhi)	28	Ei	31.21N	118.23 E
Wujia He ►	27	Ic	40.56N	108.52 E
Wu Jiang ►	21	Mg	29.43N	107.24 E
Wujiang	28	Fi	31.09N	120.38 E
Wukari	31	Hh	7.51N	9.47 E
Wukro	35	Fc	13.48N	39.37 E
Wular ▨	25	Eb	34.30N	74.30 E
Wulff Land ▨	41	Hb	82.19N	50.00W
Wulian (Hongning)	28	Eg	35.45N	119.13 E
Wuliangbei	27	Hg	24.00N	101.00 E
Wuliaru, Pulau- ►	26	Jh	7.27S	131.04 E
Wuling Shan ▲	21	Mg	28.20N	110.00 E
Wulongbei	28	Fd	38.41N	121.46 E
Wulongji → Huaibin	28	Ci	32.27N	115.23 E
Wulur	26	Ih	7.09S	128.39 E
Wum	34	Hd	6.23N	10.04 E
Wumei Shan ▲	28	Cj	28.47N	114.50 E
Wümme ►	12	Ka	53.10N	8.40 E
Wuning	28	Cj	29.17N	115.05 E
Wünnenberg	12	Kc	51.31N	8.42 E
Wünnenberg-Haaren	12	Kc	51.34N	8.44 E
Wunnummin Lake ▨	42	If	52.55N	89.10W
Wun Rog	35	Dd	9.00N	28.21 E
Wunstrof	10	Fd	52.26N	9.25 E
Wuntho	25	Jd	23.54N	95.41 E
Wupper ►	10	Ce	51.05N	7.00 E
Wuppertal	10	De	51.16N	7.11 E
Wuqi	27	Id	36.57N	108.15 E
Wuqiao	27	Cd	39.40N	75.07 E
Wuqiao (Sangyuan)	28	Df	37.38N	116.23 E
Wuqing (Yangcun)	28	De	39.23N	117.04 E
Würm ►	12	Kf	48.53N	8.42 E
Würselen	34	Gc	13.18N	5.26 E
Würselen	12	Id	50.49N	6.08 E
Würzburg	6	Gf	49.48N	9.56 E
Wushaoling ►	27	Hd	37.15N	102.50 E
Wuski/Uqturpan	27	Cc	41.10N	79.16 E
Wusong	28	Fi	31.23N	121.29 E
Wüst Seamount (EN) ▨	30	Gl	34.00S	3.40W
Wusuli Jiang ►	21	Ob	44.28N	135.02 E
Wutach ►	10	Ei	47.37N	8.15 E
Wu Xia ▨	27	Je	31.02N	110.10 E
Wutai [China]	28	Be	38.43N	113.14 E
Wutai [China]	27	Dc	44.38N	82.06 E
Wutai Shan ▲	21	Mf	39.04N	113.28 E
Wutonggiao	12	Gc	51.23N	4.36 E
Wuustwezel	57	Fe	1.43S	142.50 E
Wuvulu Island ►	28	Bf	36.50N	112.51 E
Wuwei	28	Bf	36.50N	112.51 E
Wuwei (Liangzhou)	22	Mf	37.58N	102.48 E
Wuxi [China]	27	Id	31.32N	120.18 E
Wuxi [China]	27	Ie	31.27N	109.34 E
Wu Xia ▨	27	Je	31.02N	110.10 E
Wuxiang (Duancun)	28	Bf	36.50N	112.51 E
Wuxing (Huzhou)	12	Le	30.47N	120.07 E
Wuxue → Guangji	27	Kf	29.58N	115.32 E
Wuyang [China]	28	Bh	33.26N	113.35 E
Wuyang [China]	28	Jd	36.29N	113.07 E
Wuyang → Zhenyuan	27	If	27.05N	108.26 E
Wuyi [China]	27	Cf	37.49N	115.54 E
Wuyi [China]	28	Ej	28.54N	119.50 E
Wuyiling	27	Mb	48.37N	129.20 E
Wuyi Shan ▲	21	Ng	27.00N	117.00 E
Wuyuan [China]	22	Me	41.08N	108.17 E
Wuyuan [China]	28	Dj	29.15N	117.52 E
Wuyuanzhen → Haiyan	28	Fi	30.31N	120.56 E
Wuzhen	28	Ae	38.54N	111.49 E
Wuzhai	28	Ai	31.42N	112.00 E
Wuzhi Shan [China] ▲	28	Ed	40.31N	118.02 E
Wuzhi Shan [China] ▲	27	Ih	18.54N	109.40 E
Wuzhong	27	Id	38.00N	106.10 E
Wuzhou	28	Ng	23.32N	111.21 E
Wyalkatchem	59	Df	31.10S	117.22 E
Wyandotte	44	Fd	42.12N	83.10W
Wyandra	59	Je	27.15S	145.59 E
Wye ►	9	Kj	51.37N	2.39W
Wye	12	Cc	51.11N	0.56 E
Wyemandoo, Mount- ▲	59	De	28.31S	118.32 E
Wylie, Lake- ▨	10	Be	54.42N	8.34 E
Wymondham	44	Gh	35.07N	81.02W
Wyndham [Austl.]	12	Db	52.34N	1.07 E
Wyndham [N.Z.]	59	Df	15.28S	128.06 E
Wyndmere	62	Cg	46.20S	168.51 E
Wynne	45	Hc	46.16N	97.08W
Wynniatt Bay ◪	45	Ik	35.14N	90.47W
Wynyard [Austl.]	42	Gb	72.50N	111.00W
Wynyard [Sask.-Can.]	59	Jh	40.59S	145.41 E
Wyoming ▣	42	Hf	51.47N	104.10W
Wyoming [2]	44	Ed	42.54N	85.42W
Wyoming Peak ▲	43	Fc	43.00N	107.30W
Wyśmierzyce	43	Fc	42.36N	110.37W
Wysoka	10	Qe	51.38N	20.49 E
Wysokie Mazowieckie	10	Nc	53.11N	17.05 E
Wyszków	10	Sd	52.56N	22.32 E
Wyszogród	10	Rd	52.36N	21.28 E
Wytheville	10	Qd	52.23N	20.11 E
Wyville Thomson Ridge (EN) ▨	44	Gg	36.57N	81.07W
Wyvis, Ben- ▲	9	Fa	60.10N	8.00W
	9	Id	57.42N	4.30W

X

Name	Map	Grid	Lat	Long
Xaintrie ▨	11	Ii	45.00N	2.10 E
Xainza	27	Ee	30.50N	88.37 E
Xaitongmoin	27	Ee	29.26N	88.08 E
Xai-Xai	31	Kk	25.04S	33.39 E
Xamba → Hanggin Houqi	27	Ic	40.59N	107.07 E
Xam Nua	25	Kd	20.25N	104.02 E
Xangongo	31	Ij	16.46S	14.59 E
Xang Qu ►	27	Jc	40.52N	113.56 E
Xanten	10	Ce	51.40N	6.27 E
Xánthi	15	Hh	41.08N	24.53 E
Xanthos ▨	24	Cd	36.20N	29.20 E
Xanxerê	56	Jc	26.53S	52.23W
Xapuri	54	Ef	10.39S	68.31W
Xar Hudag	27	Jb	45.06N	114.30 E
Xar Moron ►	28	Ac	42.37N	111.02 E
Xar Moron He ►	28	Fc	43.24N	120.39 E
Xarrama ►	13	Df	38.14N	8.20W
Xàtiva/Játiva	13	Lf	38.59N	0.31W
Xau, Lake- ▨	37	Cd	21.15S	24.44 E
Xavantes, Reprêsa de- ▨	55	Hf	23.20S	49.35W
Xavantina	55	Fe	21.15S	52.48W
Xayar	27	Dc	41.15N	82.50 E
Xebert	28	Fc	44.00N	122.00 E
Xêgar → Tingri	27	Ef	28.41N	87.00 E
Xenia	44	Ff	39.41N	83.56W
Xiabin Ansha ▨	27	Kg	9.48N	116.38 E
Xiachengzi	28	Kb	44.41N	130.26 E
Xiacun → Rushan	28	Hf	36.55N	121.30 E
Xiaguan	27	Hf	25.32N	100.12 E
Xiahe (Labrang)	27	Hd	35.18N	102.30 E
Xiajin	28	Cf	36.57N	116.00 E
Xi'an	22	Mf	34.15N	108.50 E
Xianfeng	27	If	29.41N	109.09 E
Xiangcheng	28	Bh	33.51N	113.29 E
Xiangcheng/Qagchêng	27	Gf	28.56N	99.46 E
Xiangcheng (Shuizhai)	28	Ch	33.27N	114.53 E
Xiangfan	22	Nf	32.03N	112.05 E
Xiangfeng → Laifeng	27	If	29.41N	109.24 E
Xianghua Ling ▲	27	Jf	25.26N	112.32 E
Xianghuang Qi (Xin Bulag)	27	Jc	42.12N	113.59 E
Xiang Jiang ►	21	Ng	29.26N	113.08 E
Xiangkhoang	25	Ke	19.20N	103.22 E
Xiangkhoang, Plateau de- ▨	25	Ke	19.30N	103.10 E
Xiangquan He ►	27	Ce	32.05N	79.20 E
Xiangshan (Dancheng)	28	Lf	29.29N	121.52 E
Xiangshan Gang ◪	28	Fj	29.35N	121.82 E
Xiangtan	22	Ng	27.54N	112.55 E
Xiangtang	28	Cj	28.26N	115.59 E
Xiangxian [China]	28	Bf	38.41N	112.53 E
Xiangxian [China]	28	Bf	36.32N	113.02 E
Xiangxiang	27	Lf	28.50N	120.42 E
Xiangyang	29	Je	32.05N	114.07 E
Xianning	27	Je	29.52N	114.17 E
Xiannümiao → Jiangdu	28	Eh	32.30N	119.33 E
Xiantaozhen → Mianyang	28	Bi	30.22N	113.27 E
Xianxia Ling ▲	27	Kf	28.24N	118.40 E
Xianxian	28	De	38.12N	116.07 E
Xianyang	27	Ie	34.26N	108.40 E
Xianyou	27	La	51.46N	124.09 E
Xiao'ergou	27	Lb	49.10N	123.43 E
Xiaogan	27	Je	30.57N	113.57 E
Xiao He ►	28	Bf	37.38N	112.24 E
Xiao Hinggan Ling = Lesser Khingan Range (EN) ▲	21	Oe	48.45N	127.00 E
Xiaoling He ►	28	Fd	40.55N	121.12 E
Xiaoluan He ►	28	Dd	41.36N	117.05 E
Xiaoqing He ►	28	Ef	37.19N	118.59 E
Xiaowutai Shan ▲	28	Ce	39.57N	114.59 E
Xiaoxian	28	Dg	34.11N	116.56 E
Xiaoyi	28	Af	37.07N	111.48 E
Xiaoyi → Gongxian	28	Bg	34.46N	112.57 E
Xiapu	28	Kf	26.57N	119.59 E
Xiawa	28	Fc	42.36N	120.33 E
Xiayi	28	Dg	34.14N	116.07 E
Xiazhuang → Linshu	28	Eg	34.56N	118.38 E
Xicalango, Punta- ►	48	Nh	19.41N	92.00W
Xichang	22	Mg	27.52N	102.15 E
Xichou → Yangyuan	28	Cd	40.08N	114.10 E
Xicotencatl	48	Jf	23.00N	98.56W
Xicotepec de Juárez	48	Kg	20.17N	97.57W
Xiejiaji → Qingyun	28	Df	37.46N	117.22 E
Xifei He ►	28	Dh	32.38N	116.39 E
Xifeng	28	Hc	42.45N	124.44 E
Xifengzhen	27	Id	35.40N	107.42 E
Xi He [China] ►	22	Kg	29.15N	88.52 E
Xi He [China] ►	27	Hc	42.23N	101.03 E
Xiheying	28	Dj	29.38N	116.53 E
Xihua	28	Ch	33.48N	114.31 E
Xi Jang ►	21	Ng	23.05N	114.23 E
Xiji [China]	18	Id	35.52N	105.35 E
Xiji [China]	27	Ia	46.09N	127.08 E
Xi Jiang ►	28	Ng	23.05N	114.23 E
Xijir Ulan Hu ▨	27	Fd	35.12N	90.18 E
Xikouzi	28	Df	42.58N	120.29 E
Xiligou → Ulan	27	Gd	36.55N	98.16 E
Xilin	28	Le	24.30N	105.05 E
Xilin Gol ►	27	Jb	43.58N	116.05 E
Xilin Hot → Abagnar Qi	27	Jb	51.47N	104.10W
Xilitla	48	Ed	42.54N	85.42W
Xilókastron	15	Fk	38.05N	22.38 E
Ximiao	27	Hc	41.04N	100.14 E
Xin'an	28	Bg	34.43N	112.07 E
Xin'anjiang	28	Ei	29.27N	119.15 E
Xin'anjiang Shuiku ▨	28	Kf	29.25N	119.05 E
Xin'anzhen → Guannan	27	Ke	34.04N	119.21 E
Xin'anzhen → Xinyi	27	Ke	34.17N	118.14 E
Xin Barag Youqi (Altan-Emel)	27	Kb	48.41N	116.47 E
Xin Barag Zuoqi (Amgalang)	27	Kb	48.13N	118.14 E
Xin Bulag → Xianghuang Qi	27	Jc	42.12N	113.59 E
Xincai	28	Ch	32.40N	114.57 E
Xinchang	28	Fj	29.30N	120.54 E
Xincheng [China]	28	Bf	37.57N	112.33 E
Xincheng [China]	28	De	39.53N	114.40 E
Xincheng [China]	27	Id	38.33N	106.10 E
Xincheng (Gaobeidian)	28	Ce	39.20N	115.50 E
Xindi → Honghu	28	Bj	29.50N	113.28 E
Xing'an → Ankang	28	Af	32.40N	109.03 E
Xingcheng	28	Fd	40.38N	120.43 E
Xingguo	28	Dj	26.22N	115.21 E
Xinghai	27	Gd	35.45N	99.59 E
Xinghe	27	Jc	40.52N	113.56 E
Xinghua	28	Eh	32.56N	119.49 E
Xingkai Hu = Khanka Lake (EN) ▨	21	Pe	45.00N	132.24 E
Xinglong	28	Dd	40.25N	117.31 E
Xinglongzhen	28	Ia	46.26N	127.03 E
Xingren	27	If	25.26N	105.08 E
Xingtai	27	Nf	37.00N	114.30 E
Xingtang	28	Ce	38.26N	114.33 E
Xingu, Rio- ►	52	Kf	1.30S	51.53W
Xingxingxia	27	Gc	41.47N	95.07 E
Xingyang	28	Bg	34.47N	113.21 E
Xinri	55	Hf	23.20S	49.35W
Xingzi (Huangcaoba)	55	Fe	21.15S	52.48W
Xingzi	27	Dc	41.15N	82.50 E
Xinhe	28	Cf	44.00N	122.00 E
Xinhe/Toksu	27	Dc	41.34N	82.38 E
Xin Hot → Abag Qi	44	Ff	39.41N	83.56W
Xinhuai He ►	28	Kb	44.41N	130.26 E
Xinhui → Aohan Qi	28	Hf	36.55N	121.30 E
Xining	22	Mf	36.37N	101.46 E
Xinji → Shulu	27	Hf	25.32N	100.12 E
Xinjian	27	Hd	35.18N	102.30 E
Xin Jiang ►	28	Cf	36.57N	116.00 E
Xinjiangkou → Songzi	22	Mf	34.15N	108.50 E
Xinjiang Uygur Zizhiqu (Hsin-chiang-wei-wu-erh Tzu-chih-ch'ü)=Sinkiang (EN) [2]	21	Gf	28.56N	99.46 E
Xinjin	28	Gf	36.25N	120.02 E
Xinjin	27	Nf	32.03N	112.05 E
Xinkai He ►	22	Ng	22.15N	114.10 E
Xinle	27	Jf	25.26N	112.32 E
Xinlin	21	Ng	29.26N	113.08 E
Xinlitan [China]	25	Ke	19.20N	103.22 E
Xinlitan [China]	25	Ke	19.30N	103.10 E
Xinlong/Nyagrong	27	Gf	32.05N	79.20 E
Xinmin	28	Gc	42.00N	122.50 E
Xinpu → Lianyungang	28	Nf	34.34N	119.15 E
Xinqing	27	Mb	48.15N	129.31 E
Xintai	28	Dg	35.54N	117.44 E
Xinwen (Suncun)	27	Kd	35.49N	117.38 E
Xinxian [China]	28	Bf	38.24N	112.43 E
Xinxian [China]	28	Ci	31.42N	114.50 E
Xinxiang	22	Mf	35.17N	113.50 E
Xinyang	22	Ne	32.05N	114.07 E
Xinye	28	Bh	32.30N	112.22 E
Xinyi (Xin'anzhen)	27	Kf	28.24N	117.43 E
Xinyi He ►	28	De	38.12N	116.07 E
Xinyuan/Künes	27	Dc	43.24N	83.18 E
Xinyuan → Tianjun	22	Lf	37.18N	99.15 E
Xinzhan	28	Ic	43.52N	127.20 E
Xin Zhen → Hanggin Qi	27	Id	39.54N	108.55 E
Xiongyue	28	Bg	34.25N	113.46 E
Xinzhou	28	Ci	30.51N	114.49 E
Xioashan	28	Fi	30.10N	120.16 E
Xiong Xian	28	De	38.59N	116.06 E
Xionyuecheng	28	Gd	40.12N	122.08 E
Xiping [China]	28	Ej	28.27N	119.29 E
Xiping [China]	28	Bh	33.22N	114.00 E
Xisha Qundao = Paracel Islands (EN) ▨	21	Nh	16.30N	112.15 E
Xishuangbanna	22	Mg	22.15N	100.00 E
Xishuanghe → Kenli	28	Ef	37.35N	118.30 E
Xitianmu Shan ▲	28	Ei	30.21N	119.25 E
Xiuwanzi → Chongli	28	Cd	40.57N	115.12 E
Xiong Xian (Xinli)	28	De	38.59N	116.06 E

Name	Map	Grid	Lat	Long
Ya'an	22	Mg	30.00N	102.57 E
Yabassi	34	Ge	4.28N	9.58 E
Yabe	29	Be	32.42N	130.59 E
Yabebyry	55	Bh	27.24S	57.11W
Yabelo	35	Fe	4.53N	38.07 E
Yablonovy Range (EN) = Jablonovy Hrebet ▲	21	Nd	53.30N	115.00 E
Yabrai Shan ▲	27	Hc	40.00N	103.10 E
Yabrīn ▨	35	Ha	23.15N	48.59 E
Yabucoa	51a	Cb	18.03N	65.53W
Yabuli	27	Mc	44.56N	128.37 E
Yacare Cururú, Cuchilla- ▲	59	Jc	19.00S	146.40 E
Yacaré Norte, Riacho- ►	55	Cf	22.43S	58.14W
Yacaré Sur, Riacho- ►	55	Cf	22.43S	58.14W
Yachats	46	Cd	44.20N	124.03W
Yacuma, Rio- ►	54	Ef	13.38S	65.23W
Yacyretá, Isla- ►	55	Dh	27.25S	56.30W
Yadé, Massif du- ▲	35	Bd	7.00N	15.30 E
Yádgir	25	Fe	16.46N	77.08 E
Yadong/Chomo	27	Ef	27.38N	89.03 E
Yae-Dake ▲	29b	Ab	26.38N	127.56 E
Yaeyama-Rettō ◯	21	Lg	24.20N	124.00 E
Yafran	33	Bc	32.04N	12.31 E
Yağcılar	15	Lj	39.25N	28.23 E
Yagishiri-Tō ►	29a	Ba	44.26N	141.25 E
Yagoua	34	Ic	10.20N	15.14 E
Yagradagzê Shan ▲	27	Gd	35.09N	95.39 E
Yaguajay	49	Hb	22.19N	79.14W
Yaguari	55	Dg	31.31S	54.58W
Yaguari, Arroyo- ►	55	Di	29.44S	57.37W
Yahalica de Gonzáles Gallo	48	Hg	21.08N	102.51W
Yahuma	36	Db	1.06N	23.10 E
Yaizu	29	Fc	36.50N	139.55 E
Yajiang/Nyagquka	27	He	30.07N	100.58 E
Yakacik	24	Ad	36.05N	32.45 E
Yake-Dake ▲	29	Ec	36.14N	137.35 E
Yakeishi-Dake ▲	29	Gb	39.10N	140.50 E
Yakeshi → Xuguit Qi	27	Lb	49.16N	120.41 E
Yake-Yama ▲	29	Gb	39.58N	140.48 E
Yakima	39	Ge	46.36N	120.31W
Yakima River ►	46	Fc	46.15N	119.02W
Yako	34	Ee	12.58N	2.16W
Yaku-Shima ►	27	Pc	42.15N	140.16 E
Yakutat	40	Le	59.33N	139.44W
Yakutat Bay ◪	40	Ke	59.45N	140.45W
Yala	25	Kg	6.32N	101.19 E
Yalahán, Laguna de- ▨	48	Pg	21.30N	87.15W
Yalcubul, Punta- ►	48	Og	21.35N	88.35W
Yale Point ▲	46	Kh	36.25N	109.48W
Yalewa Kalou ►	63d	Ab	16.40S	177.46 E
Yalgoo	59	De	28.20S	116.41 E
Yalikavak	15	Kl	37.06N	27.18 E
Yaliköy	15	Lh	41.29N	28.17 E
Yalinga	35	Cd	6.31N	23.13 E
Yaloké	35	Bd	5.19N	17.05 E
Yalong Jiang ►	21	Mg	26.37N	101.48 E
Yalova	24	Cb	40.39N	29.15 E
Yalu Jiang ►	21	Of	39.55N	124.20 E
Yalvaç	24	Dc	38.17N	31.11 E
Yäm, Ramlat- ▨	28	Be	33.33N	130.45 E
Yamada [Jap.]	29	Pe	39.28N	141.57 E
Yamada [Jap.]	29	Be	33.33N	130.45 E
Yamada-Wan ◪	29	Hb	39.30N	142.00 E
Yamaga	29	Be	33.01N	130.41 E
Yamagata	29	Pd	38.15N	140.15 E
Yamagata Ken [2]	29	Pe	38.30N	140.00 E
Yamagawa	29	Bf	31.12N	130.39 E
Yamaguchi	29	Bd	34.10N	131.29 E
Yamaguchi Ken [2]	28	Kh	34.10N	131.30 E
Yamakuni	29	Be	33.24N	131.02 E
Yamal Peninsula (EN) = Jamal, Poluostrov- ►	21	Ib	70.00N	70.00 E
Yamamoto	29	Ga	40.06N	140.03 E
Yamanaka	29	Be	36.15N	136.22 E
Yamanashi Ken [2]	28	Og	35.30N	138.45 E
Yamashiro	29	Be	33.57N	133.43 E
Yamato Rise (EN) ▲	28	Me	39.30N	134.30 E
Yamatsuri	29	Gc	36.53N	140.25 E
Yamazaki	29	Dd	35.00N	134.33 E
Yambi, Mesa de- ▲	54	Dc	1.30N	71.20W
Yambio	31	Jh	4.34N	28.23 E
Yambo	35	Bf	8.25N	36.00 E
Yambu Head ►	51n	Ba	13.09N	61.09W
Yambuya	36	Db	1.16N	24.33 E
Yame	29	Be	33.13N	130.34 E
Yamethin	51	Jd	20.26N	96.09 E
Yamma Yamma, Lake- ▨	59	Ie	26.17S	141.25 E
Yamoto	29	Gb	38.25N	141.13 E
Yamoussoukro	34	Dd	6.49N	5.17W
Yampa River ►	43	Fc	40.32N	108.59W
Yampi Sound	59	Ec	16.11S	123.40 E
Yamuna ►	21	Kg	25.30N	81.53 E
Yamunanagar	25	Fb	30.08N	76.59 E
Yamzho Yumco ▨	27	Ef	29.00N	90.40 E
Yanagawa	29	Be	33.10N	130.24 E
Yanahara	29	Dd	34.57N	134.05 E
Yanahuanca	54	Cf	10.30S	76.30W
Yanai	28	Ge	33.58N	132.07 E
Yan'an	25	Ge	16.51N	82.15 E
Yanaoca	54	Mf	36.36N	109.30 E
Yanbian	54	If	14.13S	71.26W
Yanbu'	27	Hf	26.51N	101.32 E
Yanceng	23	Ee	24.05N	38.03 E
Yancheng [China]	36	Bb	36.39N	110.03 E
Yancheng [China]	28	Lb	33.16N	120.10 E
Yanchi	18	If	37.47N	107.24 E
Yandina	63a	Dc	9.07S	159.13 E
Yandja	36	Cc	1.41S	17.43 E

Index Symbols

- [1] Independent Nation
- [2] State, Region
- [3] District, County
- [4] Municipality
- [5] Colony, Dependency
- Continent
- Physical Region
- Historical or Cultural Region
- Mount, Mountain
- Volcano
- Hill
- Mountains, Mountain Range
- Hills, Escarpment
- Plateau, Upland
- Pass, Gap
- Plain, Lowland
- Delta
- Salt Flat
- Valley, Canyon
- Crater, Cave
- Karst Features
- Cape, Point
- Depression
- Polder
- Desert, Dunes
- Forest, Woods
- Heath, Steppe
- Oasis
- Coast, Beach
- Cliff
- Peninsula
- Isthmus
- Sandbank
- Island
- Atoll
- Rock, Reef
- Islands, Archipelago
- Rocks, Reefs
- Coral Reef
- Well, Spring
- Geyser
- River, Stream
- Waterfall Rapids
- River Mouth, Estuary
- Lake
- Salt Lake
- Intermittent Lake
- Reservoir
- Sea
- Gulf, Bay
- Strait, Fjord
- Swamp, Pond
- Canal
- Glacier
- Ice Shelf, Pack Ice
- Ocean
- Ridge
- Shelf
- Basin
- Lagoon
- Bank
- Seamount
- Tablemount
- Point of Interest
- Recreation Site
- Cave, Cavern
- Escarpment, Sea Scarp
- Fracture
- Trench, Abyss
- National Park, Reserve
- Scientific Station
- Airport
- Historic Site
- Ruins
- Wall, Walls
- Church, Abbey
- Temple
- Port
- Lighthouse
- Mine
- Tunnel
- Dam, Bridge

Yuzawa [Jap.] 29 Fc 36.56N 138.47 E
Yuzhou → Chongqing = Chungking (EN) 22 Mg 29.34N 106.27 E
Yvel 11 Dg 47.59N 2.23W
Yvelines [3] 11 Hf 48.50N 1.50 E
Yverdon 14 Ad 46.46N 6.40 E
Yvetot 11 Ge 49.37N 0.46 E
Yvette 12 Ef 48.40N 2.20 E
Yxlan 8 He 59.40N 18.50 E
Yxningen 8 Gf 58.15N 16.20 E

Z

Zaajatskaja 17 Jj 52.53N 61.35 E
Zaalajski Hrebet 18 Ie 39.25N 72.50 E
Zaanstad 11 Kb 52.26N 4.49 E
Žabaj 17 Nj 51.42N 68.22 E
Žabajkalsk 20 Gg 49.40N 117.21 E
Zabarjad 33 Ge 23.37N 36.12 E
Zāb-e Küchek 24 Ke 36.00N 45.15 E
Zabīb, Ra's az- 14 Em 37.16N 10.04 E
Zabid 23 Fg 14.12N 43.18 E
Zabīd, Wādī- 23 Fg 14.07N 43.06 E
Žabinka 16 Dc 52.13N 24.01 E
Ząbkowice Śląskie 10 Mf 50.36N 16.53 E
Žabljak 15 Cf 43.09N 19.08 E
Zabłudów 10 Tc 53.01N 23.20 E
Zabok 14 Jd 46.02N 15.55 E
Žábol [3] 23 Kc 32.00N 67.15 E
Zabolotje [Bye.-U.S.S.R.] 8 Kk 53.56N 24.46 E
Zabolotje [Ukr.-U.S.S.R.] 10 Ue 51.37N 24.26 E
Zabolotov 15 Ia 48.25N 25.23 E
Zabré 34 Ec 11.10N 0.38W
Zábřeh 10 Mg 49.53N 16.52 E
Zabrze 10 Of 50.18N 18.46 E
Zacapa 49 Cf 15.00N 89.30W
Zacapa 47 Gf 14.58N 89.32W
Zacapu 48 Ih 19.50N 101.43W
Zacatecas 39 Ig 22.47N 102.35W
Zacatecas [2] 47 Dd 23.00N 103.00W
Zacatecoluca 49 Cg 13.30N 88.52W
Zacatepec 48 Jh 18.39N 99.12W
Zacatlán 48 Kh 19.56N 97.58W
Zaccar, Djebel- 13 Oh 36.20N 2.13 E
Zacoalco de Torres 48 Hg 20.14N 103.35W
Zacualtipán 48 Jg 20.39N 98.36W
Zaculeu 49 Bf 15.21N 91.29W
Zadar 6 Hg 44.07N 15.15 E
Zadarski Kanal 14 Jf 44.10N 15.10 E
Zadetkyi Kyun 25 Jg 9.58N 98.13 E
Zadi 36 Bc 4.46S 14.52 E
Zadoi 27 Fe 33.10N 94.58 E
Zadonsk 16 Kc 52.23N 38.58 E
Za'farānah 33 Fd 29.07N 32.33 E
Zafferano, Capo- 14 Hl 38.07N 13.32 E
Zafir 23 He 23.07N 53.46 E
Zafra 13 Ff 38.25N 6.25W
Żagań 10 Le 51.37N 15.19 E
Zagare/Žagarė 8 Jh 56.19N 23.14 E
Žagarė/Zagare 8 Jh 56.19N 23.14 E
Zágheb 24 Mf 33.30N 48.42 E
Zāgh Marz 24 Od 36.47N 53.17 E
Zaghraf, Wādī- 24 Fb 28.40N 34.20 E
Zaghwān 32 Jb 36.24N 10.09 E
Zaghwān [3] 32 Jb 36.24N 10.10 E
Zaghwān, Jabal- 14 En 36.21N 10.07 E
Zagora 31 Ge 30.19N 5.50W
Zagora 14 Kg 43.40N 16.15 E
Zagória 15 Dj 39.45N 20.50 E
Zagorje 14 Jd 46.05N 16.00 E
Zagorodje 10 Vd 52.15N 25.30 E
Zagórów 10 Nd 52.11N 17.55 E
Zagorsk 6 Jd 56.18N 38.08 E
Zagórz, Sanok- 10 Sg 49.31N 22.17 E
Zagreb 6 Hf 45.48N 16.00 E
Zāgros, Kūhhā-ye- = Zagros Mountains (EN) 21 Gf 33.40N 47.00 E
Zagros Mountains (EN) = Zāgros, Kūhhā-ye- 21 Gf 33.40N 47.00 E
Żagubica 15 Ee 44.12N 21.48 E
Za'gya Zangbo 27 Ee 31.55N 88.58 E
Zagyva 10 Qi 47.10N 20.12 E
Zähedän 22 Ig 29.30N 60.52 E
Zahlah 24 Ff 33.51N 35.53 E
Zahony 19 Gh 37.48N 62.29 E
Zahrān 33 Hf 17.40N 43.30 E
Zahrez Chergui 13 Pi 35.14N 3.32 E
Zailijski Alatau, Hrebet- 18 Kc 43.00N 77.00 E
Žailma 19 Ke 51.32N 61.40 E
Zaire 30 Ii 6.04S 12.24 E
Zaire 30 Ii 6.04S 12.24 E
Zaïre [3] 36 Bd 6.30S 13.30 E
Zaire (Congo, Dem. Rep. of the-) [1] 31 Ji 1.00S 25.00 E
Zaisan, Lake- (EN) = Zajsan, Ozero- 21 Ke 48.10N 83.50 E
Zaj 7 Mi 55.36N 51.47 E
Zajsan, Ozero- = Zaisan, Lake- (EN) 21 Ke 48.10N 83.50 E
Zak 30 Jk 29.39S 21.11 E
Zakamensk 20 Ff 50.23N 103.20 E
Zakarpatskaja Oblast [3] 19 Eg 48.20N 23.20 E
Zakataly 19 Eg 41.38N 46.37 E
Zakháro 15 El 37.29N 21.39 E
Zākhū 23 Fb 37.08N 42.41 E
Zákinthos 15 Dl 37.47N 20.54 E
Zákinthos = Zante (EN) 5 Ih 37.47N 20.47 E
Zakinthou Dhiavlos 15 Dl 37.50N 21.00 E
Zakopane 10 Pg 49.19N 19.57 E
Zákos 35 Bc 10.54N 19.49 E
Žaksy 19 Ge 51.53N 67.20 E
Zala [1] 10 Mj 46.40N 16.50 E

Zala 10 Nj 46.43N 17.16 E
Zālābīyah 24 He 35.39N 39.51 E
Zalaegerszeg 10 Mj 46.50N 16.51 E
Zaláf 24 Gf 32.55N 37.20 E
Zalalövö 10 Mj 46.51N 16.36 E
Zalamea de la Serena 13 Gf 38.39N 5.39W
Zalamea la Real 13 Fg 37.41N 6.39W
Zalantun → Butha Qi 27 Lb 48.02N 122.42 E
Zalari 20 Ff 53.36N 102.32 E
Zalaszentgrót 10 Nj 46.57N 17.05 E
Zalău 15 Gb 47.12N 23.03 E
Zalešćiki 16 De 48.39N 25.44 E
Žalim 23 Fe 22.43N 42.10 E
Zalingei 35 Cc 12.54N 23.29 E
Zalṭan 33 Cd 28.55N 19.50 E
Zaltbommel 12 Hc 51.49N 5.17 E
Žaltidjal 15 Ih 41.30N 25.05 E
Žaltyr 19 Le 51.35N 69.58 E
Žaltyr, Ozero- 16 Qf 47.25N 51.05 E
Zamakh 23 Gf 16.28N 47.35 E
Zamami-Shima 29b Ab 26.15N 127.18 E
Zamarkh 33 If 16.30N 47.18 E
Zambeze = Zambezi (EN) 30 Kj 18.50S 36.17 E
Zambezi (EN) = Zambeze 30 Kj 18.50S 36.17 E
Zambézia [3] 37 Fc 17.00S 37.00 E
Zambezi Escarpment 37 Ec 16.15S 30.10 E
Zambia [1] 31 Jj 15.00S 30.00 E
Zamboanga 26 He 6.54N 122.04 E
Zamboanga Peninsula 26 He 7.32N 122.16 E
Zambrah, Jazīrat- 32 Jb 37.08N 10.48 E
Zambrano 49 Jj 9.45N 74.49W
Zambrów 10 Sd 53.00N 22.15 E
Zamfara 34 Fc 12.02N 4.03 E
Zamkova, Gora- 16 Vc 53.34N 25.53 E
Zamkowa, Góra- 10 Qb 54.25N 20.25 E
Zammar 24 Jd 36.47N 42.40 E
Zamora [Ec.] 54 Cd 4.04S 78.52W
Zamora [Sp.] 13 Gc 41.30N 5.45W
Zamora, Rio- 54 Cd 2.59S 78.15W
Zamora de Hidalgo 47 De 19.59N 102.16W
Zamość 10 Tf 50.44N 23.15 E
Zamość 10 Tf 50.44N 23.15 E
Zampa-Misaki 29b Ab 26.26N 127.43 E
Zamtang (Gamda) 27 He 32.23N 101.05 E
Zamura, Punta- 49 Mi 11.26N 68.50W
Zamzam 33 Cc 31.24N 15.17 E
Zanaga 36 Bc 2.51S 13.50 E
Žanatas 19 Gg 43.36N 69.43 E
Zancara 13 Ie 39.18N 3.18W
Zanda (Toling) 27 Ce 31.28N 79.50 E
Zandvoort 11 Kb 52.22N 4.32 E
Zanesville 43 Kd 39.55N 82.02W
Zangelan 16 Oj 39.05N 46.38 E
Zanhuang 28 Cf 37.38N 114.26 E
Zanjan 23 Gb 36.35N 48.15 E
Zanjan [3] 23 Gb 36.40N 48.29 E
Zanjanrüd 24 Ld 37.08N 47.47 E
Zannone 14 Hj 40.55N 13.05 E
Zante (EN) = Zákinthos 5 Ih 37.47N 20.47 E
Zanthus 59 If 31.02S 123.34 E
Zanzibar 31 Ki 6.10S 39.11 E
Zanzibar [3] 36 Gd 6.00S 39.50 E
Zanzibar [2] 36 Gd 6.10S 39.20 E
Zanzibar Channel 36 Gd 6.00S 39.00 E
Zanzibar Island 30 Ki 6.10S 39.20 E
Zaolin 27 Jd 39.09N 113.03 E
Zaō-San 29 Gb 38.08N 140.28 E
Zaouatallaz 32 Je 24.52N 8.26 E
Zaousfana 32 Gc 30.30N 2.18W
Zaoyang 27 Je 32.08N 112.45 E
Zaozhuang 20 Ke 34.58N 117.34 E
Zapacos Norte, Rio- 55 Ac 17.03S 62.23W
Zapacos Sur, Rio- 55 Ac 17.03S 62.23W
Zapadnaja Dvina 7 Hh 56.17N 32.03 E
Zapadnaja Dvina = Western Dvina (EN) 5 Id 57.04N 24.03 E
Zapadna Morava 15 Ef 43.41N 21.24 E
Západné Karpaty = West Carpathians (EN) 4 Ig 49.30N 19.00 E
Zapadni Rodopi 15 Hh 41.45N 24.05 E
Zapadno-Karelskaja Vozvyšennost 7 Gc 63.40N 31.40 E
Zapadno Sibirskaja Ravnina = West Siberian Plain (EN) 21 Jc 60.00N 75.00 E
Zapadny Sajan = Western Sayans (EN) 21 Ld 53.00N 94.00 E
Západočeský kraj [3] 10 Ig 49.45N 13.00 E
Západoslovenský kraj [3] 10 Nh 48.20N 18.00 E
Zapala 53 Ii 38.55S 70.05W
Zapardiel 13 Gc 41.29N 5.02W
Zapata 45 Gm 26.52N 99.19W
Zapata, Peninsula de- 49 Gb 22.20N 81.35W
Zapatera, Isla- 49 Eh 11.45N 85.50W
Zapatosa, Cienaga de- 49 Ki 9.05N 73.50W
Zapljusje 8 Mf 58.24N 29.56 E
Zapoljarny 19 Db 69.26N 30.48 E
Zapopan 48 Hg 20.43N 103.24W
Zaporožje 6 Jf 47.50N 35.10 E
Zaporožskaja Oblast [3] 19 Df 47.15N 35.50 E
Zapotitlán, Punta- 48 Lh 18.33N 94.49W
Zapovednik Belovežskaja Pušča 10 Kd 52.45N 24.15 E
Za Qu 27 Gf 33.00N 96.55 E
Zara 24 Gc 39.55N 37.48 E
Zaráf, Bahr az- 35 Ed 9.25N 31.10 E
Zarafšan 19 Hj 41.39N 64.10 E
Zaragoza [Col.] 13 Lc 41.35N 1.00W
Zaragoza [Mex.] 54 Db 7.30N 74.52W
Zaragoza [Mex.] 48 Jf 23.58N 99.46W
Zaragoza [Mex.] 48 Ic 28.29N 100.55W
Zaragoza [Mex.] 48 If 22.02N 100.44W

Zaragoza [Sp.] = Saragossa (EN) 6 Fg 41.38N 0.53W
Zarajsk 7 Ji 54.47N 38.53 E
Zarand [Iran] 24 Og 30.48N 56.53 E
Zarand [Iran] 24 Ne 35.08N 49.00 E
Zarand-e-Kohneh 24 Ne 35.17N 50.30 E
Zărandului, Munţii- 15 Fc 46.10N 22.15 E
Zaranj 22 If 31.06N 61.53 E
Zarasai/Zarasaj 7 Gi 55.43N 26.19 E
Zarasaj/Zarasai 7 Gi 55.43N 26.19 E
Zárate 53 Ki 34.05S 59.02W
Zarauz 13 Ja 43.17N 2.10W
Zaraza 54 Fb 9.21N 65.19W
Žarcovski 7 Hi 55.53N 32.16 E
Zard Küh 21 Hf 32.22N 50.04 E
Zardob 16 Oi 40.14N 47.42 E
Zarečensk 7 Hc 66.40N 31.23 E
Zarghaṭ 24 Ii 26.32N 40.29 E
Zarghun 25 Db 30.31N 68.50 E
Zarghūn Shahr 24 Eb 33.20N 68.25 E
Zaria 31 Hg 11.04N 7.42 E
Žarkamys 19 If 48.48N 80.55 E
Žarma 19 If 48.48N 80.55 E
Žārneşti 16 Id 45.33N 25.18 E
Žarqān 24 Oh 29.46N 52.43 E
Zarrineh 24 Kd 37.05N 45.40 E
Zarrinshahr 24 Nf 32.30N 51.25 E
Zaruma 54 Cd 3.42S 79.38W
Zarumilla 54 Bd 3.30S 80.16W
Žary 10 Le 51.38N 15.09 E
Zarzaïtine 19 Hf 48.52N 72.54 E
Zarzaïtine 32 Jb 37.08N 10.48 E
Zasa 8 Ki 56.15N 26.01 E
Zåskar 25 Fb 34.10N 77.20 E
Žaškov 16 Ge 49.15N 30.09 E
Zaslavl 8 Lj 54.00N 27.22 E
Zaslavskoje Vodohranilišče 8 Lj 54.00N 27.22 E
Zastavna 15 Ia 48.25N 25.49 E
Zastron 37 Df 30.18S 27.07 E
Žatec 15 If 50.20N 13.33 E
Zatišje 17 Mb 47.47N 29.48 E
Zatobolsk 17 Kj 53.12N 63.43 E
Zatoka 15 Nc 46.07N 30.25 E
Zauche 10 Id 52.15N 12.35 E
Žavadovskogo Island 66 Ge 36.50S 86.00 E
Zavāreh 24 Of 33.30N 52.29 E
Zaventem 12 Gd 50.53N 4.28 E
Zavety Iliča 20 Jg 49.02N 140.19 E
Zavidovići 14 Mf 44.27N 18.09 E
Zavitinsk 20 Hg 50.01N 129.26 E
Zavodoukovsk 19 Gd 56.33N 66.32 E
Zavodovski 66 Ad 56.20S 27.35W
Zavolžje 7 Kh 56.38N 43.21 E
Zavolžsk 7 Kh 57.32N 42.10 E
Zawidów 10 Le 51.01N 15.02 E
Zawiercie 10 Pf 50.30N 19.25 E
Zawilah 24 Ob 26.10N 15.07 E
Zāwiyat al Mukhaylá 33 Dc 32.10N 22.17 E
Zāwiyat Masūs 33 Dc 31.35N 21.01 E
Zāwiyat Qirzah 33 Bc 31.00N 14.20 E
Zāwiyat Shammās 24 Bg 31.31N 26.24 E
Zawr, Ra's az- 24 Mi 27.26N 49.19 E
Zaya 14 Kb 48.31N 16.55 E
Zāyandeh 24 Of 32.20N 52.50 E
Zaydūn, Wādī- 24 Ej 25.53N 33.04 E
Zayü (Gyigang) 27 Gf 28.43N 97.25 E
Zaza, Rio- 49 Hc 21.37N 79.32W
Zazir 32 If 19.50N 5.13 E
Zbaraž 16 Be 49.42N 25.47 E
Zbąszyń 10 Ld 52.16N 15.55 E
Zborov 16 Be 49.37N 25.09 E
Ždánického les 10 Mg 49.05N 16.50 E
Ždanov 6 Jf 47.06N 37.33 E
Ždanovsk 16 Oj 39.45N 47.33 E
Žďár nad Sázavou 10 Mg 49.35N 16.03 E
Ždiar 20 Qg 49.16N 20.15 E
Zdolbunov 16 Ed 50.33N 26.15 E
Zduńska Wola 10 Oe 51.36N 18.57 E
Zealand (EN) = Sjælland 5 Hd 55.30N 11.45 E
Zebediela 37 Da 24.19S 29.16 E
Zebès, Mali i- 15 Dh 41.55N 20.14 E
Zebil 15 Le 44.57N 28.46 E
Zeča 14 If 44.46N 14.19 E
Zeddine 13 Nh 36.12N 1.50 E
Zedelgem 12 Fc 51.09N 3.08 E
Zeebrugge 12 Fc 51.20N 3.13 E
Zeeland 11 Jc 51.27N 3.45 E
Zeeland [3] 12 Fc 51.27N 3.45 E
Zeerust 37 Dc 25.33S 26.06 E
Zefat 24 Ff 32.58N 35.30 E
Zegrzyńskie, Jezioro- 10 Rd 52.30N 21.05 E
Zehdenick 10 Jc 52.59N 13.20 E
Zeil, Mount- 59 Gd 23.25S 132.25 E
Zeitz 10 Ie 51.03N 12.08 E
Žejmena/Žejmena 8 Jh 56.14N 23.58 E
Zeist 11 Lb 52.05N 5.15 E
Zeja 21 Od 50.13N 127.35 E
Zeja 21 Od 53.13N 127.15 E
Zejmena/Zejmena 8 Jh 56.14N 23.58 E
Zejskoje Vodohranilišče 20 Hf 54.40N 127.30 E
Žekog 20 Df 34.58N 101.35 E
Želanija, Mys- 21 Ib 76.57N 68.35 E
Zelaya [3] 49 Dg 13.00N 84.00W
Želča 8 Lf 58.18N 27.50 E
Zele 12 Gc 51.04N 4.02 E
Želechów 10 Re 51.49N 21.54 E
Zelee, Cape- 63a Ec 9.44S 161.34 E
Zelenchukskaja 16 Lh 43.51N 41.34 E
Zelengora 14 Mg 43.22N 18.35 E
Zelenoborski 19 Dc 61.29N 63.59 E
Zelenoborski 7 Db 66.50N 32.18 E
Zelenodolsk 16 Lc 55.53N 48.31 E
Zelenogorsk 19 Cc 60.12N 29.42 E

Zelenograd 7 Ih 56.01N 37.12 E
Zelenogradsk 8 Ij 54.57N 20.27 E
Zelenokumsk 19 Eg 44.23N 43.53 E
Zeletin 15 Kc 46.03N 27.23 E
Železné hory 10 Lg 49.50N 15.45 E
Železnodorožny [R.S.F.S.R.] 20 Fe 57.55N 102.50 E
Železnodorožny [R.S.F.S.R.] 7 Ei 54.23N 21.19 E
Železnodorožny [R.S.F.S.R.] 19 Fc 62.37N 50.55 E
Železnogorsk 20 Fe 56.40N 104.05 E
Železnovodsk 16 Mg 44.08N 43.00 E
Zelfana 32 Hc 32.24N 4.14 E
Želiezovce 10 Oh 48.03N 18.40 E
Želivka 10 Lg 49.43N 15.06 E
Željin 15 Df 43.29N 20.48 E
Zell am See 14 Gc 47.19N 12.47 E
Zell am Ziller 14 Fc 47.14N 11.53 E
Zelów 10 Pe 51.28N 19.13 E
Želtau Ajtau 18 Ib 44.30N 74.00 E
Želtje Vody 16 He 48.23N 33.31 E
Želudok 10 Vc 53.33N 25.07 E
Želva 8 Ki 55.13N 25.13 E
Žemaičiu Aukštuma/ Žemaičju-Naumiestis/ Žemaitskaja Vozvyšennost 8 Ji 55.45N 22.30 E
Žemaičju-Naumiestis/ Žemaičiu Aukštuma/ Žemaitskaja Vozvyšennost 8 Ii 55.21N 21.37 E
Žemaitija [3] 8 Ji 55.55N 22.30 E
Žemaičju-Naumiestis/ Žemaiciy-Naumiestis/ Žemaitskaja Vozvyšennost 8 Ii 55.21N 21.37 E
Žemaičiu Aukštuma/ Žemaičju-Naumiestis 8 Ji 55.45N 22.30 E
Zembin 8 Mj 54.24N 28.19 E
Zembretta, Ile- 14 Em 37.07N 10.53 E
Zémio 35 Ec 5.02N 25.08 E
Zemmora 13 Mi 35.43N 0.45 E
Zemmour 30 Ff 25.30N 12.00W
Zemplínska Šírava, údolná nádrž- 10 Sh 48.50N 22.02 E
Zempoala 47 Je 20.29N 98.39W
Zempoaltepec 38 Jh 17.00N 96.50W
Zemst 12 Gd 50.59N 4.28 E
Zemun, Beograd- 15 De 44.53N 20.25 E
Zengfeng Shan 28 Ic 42.25N 128.44 E
Zenica 23 Fa 44.13N 17.55 E
Zenkov 16 Id 50.13N 34.22 E
Zenne 12 Gc 51.04N 4.26 E
Zenobia Peak 45 Bf 40.40N 108.48W
Zentsūji 29 Cd 34.14N 133.47 E
Zenzach 13 Pi 35.21N 3.22 E
Zenza do Itombe 36 Bd 9.16S 14.13 E
Žepče 14 Mf 44.26N 18.03 E
Zepu/Poskam 27 Cd 38.12N 77.18 E
Žeralda 13 Oh 36.43N 2.50 E
Zeravšan 21 If 39.22N 63.45 E
Zerbst 10 Ie 51.58N 12.05 E
Žerdevka 7 Jj 51.53N 41.28 E
Zerind 15 Ec 46.37N 21.31 E
Zermatt 14 Bd 46.02N 7.44 E
Zernograd 16 Mf 46.42N 40.19 E
Zeroua 14 Ed 46.42N 10.07 E
Zernez 14 Ed 46.42N 10.07 E
Zešart 7 De 62.05N 49.31 E
Zestafoni 16 Mh 42.07N 43.02 E
Zeta 15 Cg 42.28N 19.16 E
Zetland → Shetland Islands 5 Fc 60.30N 1.30W
Zetland 19 Fg 43.34N 52.04 E
Žetykol, Ozero- 16 Vd 51.05N 60.55 E
Zeune Islands 63a Bb 6.18S 155.50 E
Zeven 10 Fc 53.18N 9.17 E
Zevenaar 12 Lc 51.55N 6.05 E
Zevenbergen 12 Gc 51.38N 4.36 E
Zeydābād 24 Ph 29.37N 55.33 E
Zeydar 24 Pd 36.20N 55.53 E
Zeytinbağı 15 Li 40.23N 28.47 E
Zeytindağ 15 Kk 38.58N 27.04 E
Zêzere 13 De 39.28N 8.20W
Žežmarjaj/Žiežmariai 8 Kj 54.47N 24.36 E
Zghartā 24 Te 34.24N 35.54 E
Zgierz 10 Pe 51.52N 19.25 E
Zgorzelec 10 Le 51.12N 15.01 E
Zhabdun → Zhongba 27 Dg 29.41N 84.10 E
Zhag'yab 27 Gf 30.40N 97.40 E
Zhangbei 27 Jc 41.13N 114.43 E
Zhangde → Anyang 28 Cf 36.06N 114.21 E
Zhangdian → Zibo 27 Kd 36.48N 118.04 E
Zhang He 28 Cf 36.27N 114.42 E
Zhangguangcai Ling 28 Jb 45.00N 129.00 E
Zhangjiakou 27 Jc 40.49N 114.57 E
Zhangjiapan → Jingbian 27 Id 37.32N 108.45 E
Zhangling 27 La 52.39N 123.31 E
Zhanglou 27 If 30.13N 111.48 E
Zhangwu 27 Lc 42.23N 122.33 E
Zhangye 28 Mf 38.57N 100.28 E
Zhangzhou 22 Ng 24.38N 117.39 E
Zhanhe 27 Mb 49.21N 128.07 E
Zhanhua (Fuguo) 28 Dg 38.13N 117.48 E
Zhanjiang 22 Mg 21.13N 110.23 E
Zhanyi 27 Hf 25.40N 103.46 E
Zhao'an 27 Kg 23.49N 117.10 E
Zhaodong 28 Cg 35.35N 114.12 E
Zhaoge → Qixian 28 Cf 35.36N 114.12 E
Zhaojue 27 Hf 28.02N 102.50 E

Zhaoqing 27 Jg 23.04N 112.28 E
Zhaosu/Monggolküre 27 Dc 43.10N 81.07 E
Zhaosutai He 28 Gc 42.42N 123.35 E
Zhaotong 22 Mg 27.20N 103.46 E
Zhaoxian 28 Cf 37.46N 114.46 E
Zhaoyang Hu 28 Ff 35.00N 116.48 E
Zhaoyuan [China] 28 Hb 45.30N 125.06 E
Zhaozhou 28 Hb 45.42N 125.15 E
Zhari Namco 27 If 31.05N 85.35 E
Zhaxi → Weixin 27 If 27.46N 105.04 E
Zhaxi Co 27 Ee 32.12N 85.10 E
Zhecheng 28 Ff 34.05N 115.17 E
Zheduo Shankou 27 He 30.06N 101.48 E
Zhejiang Sheng (Che-Chiang Sheng) [2] 27 Kf 29.00N 120.00 E
Zhen'an 27 Ie 33.27N 109.10 E
Zhenba 27 Ie 32.37N 107.50 E
Zhenghe 27 Kf 27.20N 118.58 E
Zhenghe Qunjiao 26 Fd 10.20N 114.20 E
Zhenglan Qi (Dund Hot) 28 Cc 42.14N 115.59 E
Zhengxiangbai Qi (Qagan Nur) 27 Jc 42.16N 114.59 E
Zhengyang 22 Nf 32.36N 114.23 E
Zhengzhou 22 Nf 34.42N 113.41 E
Zhenhai 28 Fj 29.57N 121.43 E
Zhenjiang 22 Nf 32.03N 119.26 E
Zhenkang (Fengweiba) 27 Gg 23.54N 99.00 E
Zhenlai 27 Lb 45.50N 123.14 E
Zhenning 27 If 26.05N 105.46 E
Zhenxiong 27 Hf 27.28N 104.52 E
Zhenyuan 22 Hg 23.52N 100.53 E
Zhenyuan (Wuyang) 27 If 27.05N 108.26 E
Zhicheng 27 Je 30.17N 111.29 E
Zhidan (Bao'an) 27 Id 36.48N 108.46 E
Zhidoi 27 Ge 34.46N 95.46 E
Zhijiang 27 If 27.32N 109.42 E
Zhi Qu/Tongtian He 21 Lf 33.26N 96.36 E
Zhiziluo → Bijiang 27 Gf 26.39N 99.02 E
Zhob 22 Kg 32.04N 69.50 E
Zhongba (Zhabdun) 27 Dg 29.41N 84.10 E
Zhongdian → Jiangyou 27 He 31.48N 104.39 E
Zhongdian 27 Gf 27.42N 99.41 E
Zhongguó 21 Mg 35.00N 105.00 E
Zhonghua Renmin Gongheguo = China (EN) [1] 22 Mf 35.00N 105.00 E
Zhongjian Dao 26 Fc 15.52N 111.13 E
Zhongmou 28 Ef 34.45N 114.01 E
Zhongning 27 Id 37.28N 105.41 E
Zhongshan 22 Jj 22.31N 113.23 E
Zhongwei 22 Mf 37.30N 105.09 E
Zhongxian 27 Ie 30.20N 108.02 E
Zhongxiang 27 Je 31.10N 112.38 E
Zhongxing → Siyang 28 Eh 33.43N 118.40 E
Zhongyaozhan 27 Ma 50.46N 125.53 E
Zhongye Qundao 27 Fd 11.20N 114.30 E
Zhoukoudianzhen 28 Ce 39.41N 115.55 E
Zhoukouzhen 27 Je 33.32N 114.40 E
Zhoushan Dao 28 Gi 30.00N 122.00 E
Zhoushan Qundao 21 Of 30.00N 122.00 E
Zhuanghe 27 Ld 39.42N 122.58 E
Zhucheng 27 Kd 35.58N 119.28 E
Zhu Dao 28 Fe 39.05N 121.10 E
Zhuggou 27 He 33.46N 104.18 E
Zhuhe 28 Bj 29.44N 113.07 E
Zhuizishan → Weichang 27 Kc 41.55N 117.39 E
Zhuji → Shangqiu 28 Fj 29.43N 120.13 E
Zhujiang 22 Jj 22.20N 113.45 E
Zhumadian 28 Ef 32.54N 114.03 E
Zhuolu 28 Cd 40.23N 115.13 E
Zhuoxian 27 Kd 39.26N 116.00 E
Zhuozhang He 28 Bf 36.36N 113.10 E
Zhuozi 28 Bd 40.52N 112.33 E
Zhuozi Shan 27 Id 39.36N 107.00 E
Zhushan 27 Je 32.16N 110.12 E
Zhuzhou 22 Ng 27.52N 113.12 E
Ziama Mansouria 32 Ib 36.40N 5.29 E
Ziar nad Hronom 10 Oh 48.36N 18.52 E
Zibā' 23 Ed 27.21N 35.40 E
Zibo (Zhangdian) 27 Kd 36.48N 118.04 E
Zicavo 11a Bb 41.54N 9.08 E
Zichang 10 Vg 49.17N 24.12 E
Zielona Góra 10 Le 51.56N 15.31 E
Zielona Góra [3] 10 Le 51.56N 15.30 E
Zierikzee 11 Jc 51.38N 3.55 E
Žiežmariai/Žežmarjaj 8 Kj 54.47N 24.36 E
Žiftá 24 Dg 30.43N 31.15 E
Žigalovo 20 Ff 54.48N 105.08 E
Zigana Geçidi 24 Hb 40.38N 39.25 E
Zigansk 19 Ib 66.45N 123.30 E
Zigey 35 Bc 14.43N 15.47 E
Zighan, Wāḥāt- 33 Dd 25.35N 22.06 E
Zigong 22 Mg 29.20N 104.48 E
Zigui 31 Of 31.01N 110.42 E
Ziguinchor 31 Fg 12.35N 16.16W
Žigulevsk 19 Ee 53.27N 49.29 E
Zijng Shan 28 Jb 47.12N 112.50 E
Zijpenberg 12 Lc 52.04N 6.00 E
Zilair 19 Je 52.14N 57.24 E
Zile 24 Gb 40.18N 35.53 E
Žilina 6 Hf 49.14N 18.45 E
Žilino 8 Ij 54.55N 21.48 E
Zillah 31 Of 28.33N 17.35 E
Ziller 14 Fc 47.24N 11.50 E
Zillertaler Alpen 14 Fc 47.00N 11.55 E
Žiloj 19 Fg 40.19N 50.33 E
Zilupe 8 Lh 56.25N 28.07 E
Zima 20 Ff 53.55N 102.04 E
Zimapán 48 Ji 20.45N 99.21W
Zimatlán de Alvarez 48 Ki 16.52N 96.47W
Zimba 36 Ef 17.02S 26.30 E
Zimbabwe [1] 30 Jj 20.16S 30.55 E
Zimbabwe (Rhodesia) [1] 31 Jj 20.00S 30.00 E

Index Symbols

[1] Independent Nation
[2] State, Region
[3] District, County
[4] Municipality
[5] Colony, Dependency
[c] Continent
[p] Physical Region

Historical or Cultural Region · Mount, Mountain · Volcano · Hill · Mountains, Mountain Range · Hills, Escarpment · Plateau, Upland · Pass, Gap · Plain, Lowland · Delta · Salt Flat · Desert, Dunes · Forest, Woods · Heath, Steppe · Oasis · Crater, Cave · Karst Features · Depression · Polder · Coast, Beach · Cape, Point · Cliff · Peninsula · Isthmus · Sandbank · Island · Atoll · Rock, Reef · Islands, Archipelago · Rocks, Reefs · Coral Reef · Well, Spring · Geyser · River, Stream · Waterfall, Rapids · River Mouth, Estuary · Lake · Salt Lake · Intermittent Lake · Reservoir · Swamp, Pond · Canal · Glacier · Ice Shelf, Pack Ice · Ocean · Sea · Ridge · Shelf · Basin · Gulf, Bay · Strait, Fjord · Lagoon · Bank · Seamount · Tablemount · Point of Interest · Recreation Site · Cave, Cavern · Escarpment, Sea Scarp · Fracture · Trench, Abyss · National Park, Reserve · Church, Abbey · Temple · Scientific Station · Airport · Historic Site · Ruins · Wall, Walls · Mine · Tunnel · Dam, Bridge · Port · Lighthouse

Name	Map	Grid	Lat.	Long.
Zimbor	15	Gc	47.00N	23.16 E
Zimi	34	Cd	7.19N	11.18W
Zimni Bereg ◫	7	Jd	66.00N	40.45 E
Zimnicea	15	If	43.40N	25.22 E
Zimovniki	16	Mf	47.08N	42.29 E
Zina	34	Hc	11.16N	14.58 E
Zincirli ◫	24	Gd	37.00N	36.41 E
Zinder	31	Hg	13.48N	8.59 E
Zinder [2]	34	Hb	15.00N	10.00 E
Zinga	35	Be	3.43N	18.35 E
Zingst ◫	10	Ib	54.25N	12.50 E
Zinjibär	33	Ig	13.08N	45.23 E
Zinnik/Soignies	11	Kd	50.35N	4.04 E
Zinsel du Nord ◫	12	Jf	48.49N	7.44 E
Zion [Ill.-U.S.]	45	Me	42.27N	87.50W
Zion [St.C.N.]	51c	Ab	17.09N	62.32W
Zipaquirá	54	Db	5.02N	74.01W
Zirc	10	Ni	47.16N	17.52 E
Žirje ◫	14	Jg	43.39N	15.40 E
Zirkel, Mount- ◫	45	Cf	40.52N	106.36W
Žirnovsk	19	Ee	51.01N	44.48 E
Ziro	25	Ic	27.32N	93.32 E
Zi Shui ◫	27	Jf	28.41N	112.43 E
Žitava ◫	10	Oi	47.53N	18.11 E
Žitkoviči	16	Fc	52.16N	28.02 E
Zitkovo	7	Gf	60.42N	29.23 E
Žitomir	6	Ie	50.16N	28.40 E
Žitomirskaja Oblast [3]	19	Ce	50.40N	28.30 E
Zittau	10	Kf	50.54N	14.50 E
Zitterwald ◫	12	Id	50.27N	6.25 E
Zitundo	37	Ee	26.44S	32.49 E
Živinice	14	Mf	44.27N	18.39 E
Ziwa Magharibi [3]	36	Fc	2.00S	31.30 E
Ziway, Lake- ◫	35	Fd	8.00N	38.48 E
Ziya He ◫	28	De	38.39N	117.33 E
Ziyang	27	Ie	32.34N	108.37 E
Ziz ◫	32	Gc	30.29N	4.26W
Žizdra	16	Ic	53.45N	34.43 E
Žizdra ◫	16	Jb	54.14N	36.12 E
Zlatar ◫	15	Cf	43.23N	19.51 E
Zlaté Moravce	10	Oh	48.23N	18.24 E
Zlatibor ◫	15	Cf	43.40N	19.43 E
Zlatica	15	Hg	42.43N	24.08 E
Zlatica ◫	15	Dd	45.49N	20.10 E
Zlatijata ◫	15	Gf	43.40N	23.36 E
Zlatiški prohod ◫	15	Hg	42.45N	24.05 E
Zlatna	15	Gc	46.07N	23.13 E
Zlatograd	15	Ih	41.23N	25.06 E
Zlatoust	6	Ld	55.10N	59.40 E
Zlatoustovsk	20	If	52.59N	133.41 E
Zletovo	15	Fh	41.59N	22.15 E
Žliţan	33	Bc	32.28N	14.34 E
Žlobin	19	De	52.59N	30.03 E
Złocieniec	10	Mc	53.33N	16.01 E
Złoczew	10	Oe	51.25N	18.36 E
Zlot	15	Ee	44.01N	21.59 E
Złotoryja	10	Le	51.08N	15.55 E
Złotów	10	Nc	53.22N	17.02 E
Zmeinogorsk	6	Gc	52.27N	31.44 E
Žmerinka	20	Df	51.10N	82.13 E
Žmigród	10	Me	51.29N	16.55 E
Zmijev	16	Je	49.41N	36.20 E
Zmijevka	16	Jc	52.40N	36.24 E
Zna ◫	7	Ih	57.33N	34.25 E
Znamenka [R.S.F.S.R.]	16	Lc	52.24N	41.28 E
Znamenka [Ukr.-U.S.S.R.]	16	He	48.41N	32.40 E
Znamensk	8	Ij	54.39N	21.15 E
Znamenskoje	19	Hd	57.08N	73.55 E
Žnin	10	Nd	52.52N	17.43 E
Znojmo	10	Mh	48.51N	16.03 E
Zobia	36	Eb	2.53N	26.02 E
Zóbuè	37	Ec	15.36S	34.26 E
Žodino	16	Fb	54.07N	28.19 E
Žodiški	8	Lj	54.40N	26.33 E
Zoetermeer	12	Gb	52.04N	4.30 E
Zogang/Wangda	27	Gf	29.37N	97.58 E
Žohova, Ostrov- ◫	20	Ka	76.10N	153.05 E
Zohreh ◫	24	Mg	30.04N	49.34 E
Zolgé	27	He	33.38N	103.00 E
Zoločev [Ukr.-U.S.S.R.]	16	Id	50.18N	35.59 E
Zoločev [Ukr.-U.S.S.R.]	19	Cf	49.49N	24.58 E
Zolotaja Gora	20	Hf	54.21N	126.41 E
Zolotoje	16	Ke	48.40N	38.30 E
Zolotonoša	16	He	49.40N	32.02 E
Zolotuhino	16	Jc	52.07N	36.25 E
Žolymbet	19	He	51.45N	71.44 E
Zomba	31	Kj	15.23S	35.20 E
Zongga → Gyirong	27	Ef	28.57N	85.12 E
Zongo	36	Cb	4.21N	18.36 E
Zonguldak	23	Da	41.27N	31.49 E
Zongyang	28	Di	30.42N	117.12 E
Zonkwa	34	Gd	9.47N	8.17 E
Zonnebeke	12	Ed	50.52N	2.59 E
Zontehuitz, Cerro- ◫	48	Mi	16.50N	92.38W
Zonúz	24	Kc	38.35N	45.50 E
Zonza	13	Ge	41.44N	9.10 E
Zorita	13	Ge	39.17N	5.42W
Zorkassa, Gora- ◫	18	Ge	38.01N	68.10 E
Zorleni	15	Kc	46.16N	27.43 E
Zorritos	54	Bd	3.40S	80.40W
Zorzor	34	Dd	7.47N	9.26W
Zottegem	12	Fd	50.52N	3.48 E
Zou [3]	34	Fd	8.00N	2.15 E
Zouar	31	If	20.27N	16.32 E
Zouïrât	31	Ff	22.46N	12.27W
Zoutkamp, Ulrum-	12	Ia	53.20N	6.18 E
Zouxian	28	Dg	35.24N	116.59 E
Žovten	15	Nb	47.14N	30.14 E
Žovtnevoje	16	Hf	46.52N	32.02 E
Zpouping	28	Df	36.53N	117.44 E
Zrenjanin	15	Dd	45.23N	20.23 E
Zrinska Gora ◫	14	Ke	45.10N	16.15 E
Zrmanja ◫	14	Jf	44.12N	15.35 E
Zruč nad Sázavou	10	Lg	49.45N	15.07 E
Zschopau ◫	10	Je	51.08N	13.03 E
Žuantobe	19	Gg	44.47N	68.52 E
Zuata, Rio- ◫	50	Di	7.52N	65.22W
Zubayr, Jazā'ir az- ◫	33	Hf	15.05N	42.08 E
Zubcov	7	Ih	56.10N	34.31 E
Zubova Poljana	7	Ki	54.05N	42.50 E
Zudañez	54	Fg	19.06S	64.44W
Zuénoula	34	Dd	7.26N	6.03W
Zuénoula [3]	34	Dd	7.22N	6.12W
Zuera	13	Lc	41.52N	0.47W
Zufäf ◫	33	Hf	16.43N	41.46 E
Zufallspitze/Cevedale ◫	14	Ed	46.27N	10.37 E
Zufär ◫	21	Hh	17.30N	54.00 E
Zug [2]	14	Cc	47.10N	8.40 E
Zug [Switz.]	14	Cc	47.10N	8.30 E
Zug [W.Sah.]	32	Ee	21.36N	14.09W
Zugdidi	19	Eg	42.29N	41.48 E
Zugersee ◫	14	Cc	47.10N	8.30 E
Zugspitze ◫	10	Gi	47.25N	10.59 E
Zuid Beveland ◫	12	Fc	51.25N	3.45 E
Zuidelijke Flevoland ◫	12	Hb	52.25N	5.20 E
Zuid-Holland [3]	12	Gc	52.00N	4.30 E
Zuid-Ijsselmeerpolders [3]	12	Hb	52.20N	5.20 E
Zuidlaren	12	Ia	53.06N	6.42 E
Zuid-Willemsvaart ◫	12	Hd	50.50N	5.41 E
Zuidwolde	12	Ib	52.40N	6.25 E
Zújar ◫	13	Ge	39.01N	5.47W
Zújar, Embalse del- ◫	13	Gf	38.50N	5.20W
Zujevka	19	Fd	58.26N	51.12 E
Žukovka	19	De	53.33N	33.47 E
Žukovski	7	Ji	55.37N	38.12 E
Zula	35	Fb	15.14N	39.40 E
Zulia [2]	54	Db	10.00N	72.10W
Zulia, Rio- ◫	49	Ki	9.04N	72.18W
Zülpich	12	Id	50.42N	6.39 E
Zumbo	37	Ec	15.36S	30.25 E
Zundert	12	Gc	51.29N	4.40 E
Zungeru	34	Gd	9.48N	6.09 E
Zunhua	28	Dd	40.12N	117.58 E
Zuni	45	Bi	35.04N	108.51W
Zuni River ◫	46	Ki	34.39N	109.40W
Zunyi	22	Mg	27.40N	106.56 E
Zuoquan	28	Bf	37.05N	113.22 E
Zuoyun	28	Be	39.58N	112.40 E
Zupanja	14	Me	45.04N	18.42 E
Zuqäq ◫	33	Hf	18.04N	40.48 E
Zurak	34	Hd	9.14N	10.34 E
Zürich	6	Gf	47.20N	8.35 E
Zurich, Lake- (EN) = Zürichsee ◫	14	Cc	47.15N	8.45 E
Zürichsee = Zurich, Lake- (EN) ◫	14	Cc	47.15N	8.45 E
Zurmi	34	Gc	12.47N	6.47 E
Žuromin	10	Pc	53.04N	19.55 E
Žur	34	Gc	11.26N	5.14 E
Zuša ◫	16	Jc	53.27N	36.25 E
Zusam ◫	10	Gh	48.42N	10.45 E
Žut ◫	14	Jg	43.52N	15.19 E
Zutiua, Rio- ◫	54	Id	3.43S	45.30W
Zutphen	11	Mb	52.08N	6.12 E
Zuwärah	33	Bc	32.56N	12.06 E
Zvenigorodka	16	Ge	49.04N	30.59 E
Zverinogolovskoje	17	Li	54.28N	64.50 E
Zvezdny	20	Fe	56.40N	106.30 E
Žvičina ◫	10	Lf	50.25N	15.41 E
Žvirca	10	Uf	50.24N	24.16 E
Zvolen	10	Ph	48.35N	19.08 E
Zvornik	14	Nf	44.23N	19.07 E
Zwardoń	10	Og	49.30N	18.59 E
Zwarte Bank = Black Bank (EN) ◫	12	Fa	53.15N	3.55 E
Zweibrücken	10	Dg	49.15N	7.22 E
Zweisimmen	14	Bd	46.34N	7.25 E
Zwesten	12	Lc	51.03N	9.11 E
Zwettl in Niederösterreich	14	Jb	48.37N	15.10 E
Zwickau	10	If	50.44N	12.30 E
Zwickauer Mulde ◫	10	Ie	51.10N	12.48 E
Zwierzyniec	10	Sf	50.37N	22.58 E
Zwijndrecht	12	Gc	51.50N	4.41 E
Zwischenahn	10	Dc	53.11N	8.00 E
Zwoleń	10	Re	51.22N	21.35 E
Zwolle	11	Mb	52.30N	6.05 E
Žychlin	10	Pd	52.15N	19.39 E
Żyrardów	10	Qd	52.04N	20.25 E
Zyrjanka	20	Kc	65.45N	105.51 E
Zyrjanovsk	19	If	49.45N	84.16 E
Žywiec	10	Pg	49.41N	19.12 E

Index Symbols

- [1] Independent Nation
- [2] State, Region
- [3] District, County
- [4] Municipality
- [5] Colony, Dependency
- Continent
- Physical Region

- Historical or Cultural Region
- Mount, Mountain
- Volcano
- Hill
- Mountains, Mountain Range
- Hills, Escarpment
- Plateau, Upland

- Pass, Gap
- Plain, Lowland
- Delta
- Salt Flat
- Valley, Canyon
- Crater, Cave
- Karst Features

- Depression
- Polder
- Desert, Dunes
- Forest, Woods
- Heath, Steppe
- Oasis
- Cape, Point

- Coast, Beach
- Cliff
- Peninsula
- Isthmus
- Sandbank
- Island
- Atoll

- Rock, Reef
- Islands, Archipelago
- Rocks, Reefs
- Coral Reef
- Well, Spring
- Geyser
- River, Stream

- Waterfall Rapids
- River Mouth, Estuary
- Lake
- Salt Lake
- Intermittent Lake
- Reservoir
- Swamp, Pond

- Canal
- Glacier
- Ice Shelf, Pack Ice
- Ocean
- Sea
- Gulf, Bay
- Strait, Fjord

- Lagoon
- Bank
- Seamount
- Tablemount
- Ridge
- Shelf
- Basin

- Escarpment, Sea Scarp
- Fracture
- Trench, Abyss
- National Park, Reserve
- Point of Interest
- Recreation Site
- Cave, Cavern

- Historic Site
- Ruins
- Wall, Walls
- Church, Abbey
- Temple
- Scientific Station
- Airport

- Port
- Lighthouse
- Mine
- Tunnel
- Dam, Bridge